SUPER
WORD
FINDER

SUPER WORD FINDER

PETER UPSALL
ELSIE JOHNSON

STRUIK

Struik Publishers (Pty) Ltd
(a member of the Struik Publishing Group (Pty) Ltd)
Cornelis Struik House
80 McKenzie Street
Cape Town
8001

Reg. No.: 54/00965/07

First published in 1993

Printed and bound by CTP Book Printers, Parow

ISBN 1 86825 516 6

CONTENTS

INTRODUCTION

Regular crossword puzzles are based on the principle of concealing a word or phrase within a cryptic clue. Nearly all magazines and newspapers carry at least one 'brain-teaser', as they have come to be called – and few brains haven't been teased by them at some time or another! Their entertainment value is unquestioned and the fun lies not so much in searching dictionaries for the right words, but in unravelling the clues.

Clue-letter puzzles are now well established all over the English-speaking world. Every week, thousands of crossword puzzlers sit down to pit their wits against the guile of the crossword compilers, who write clues in such a manner as to completely confound the entrant with the various possibilities and highly acceptable, alternative word-answers. Clue-letter crosswords now attract people by offering prizes for an all-correct solution. This facet of the game has created a need for word books set in numerical, as well as alphabetical sequence.

The *Super Word Finder* exclusively deals with clue-letter crossword puzzles. Consequently, words have been tabulated alphabetically in numbered columns, which makes locating words containing identical clue-letters far less time consuming. Alternative words that could be referred to by the clue-letters of the word contained in the crossword grid are also included.

It is all very well being able to locate words with identical clue-letters, but what do the words mean? Are they the correct alternatives, or do they have no bearing whatsoever on the given clue? This was an important factor to consider in compiling this book, as many people trying their luck at solving clue-letter crossword puzzles are not necessarily skilled in the use of the English language. For many, English isn't their home language, and even when it is, most crossword puzzlers do not feel inclined to refer to two books – one to find the word and the other to find out its meaning.

The compilers immediately saw the need for having both the

meaning and synonym(s) of a specific word in one book. With the help of the *Super Word Finder*, an accompanying dictionary is no longer necessary. In addition, this book is free of bracketed etymology and confusing addenda. (As a matter of fact, keeping it simple was something of a criterion throughout this book's compilation.) Meanings are explicit, unambiguous, concise and above all, accurate. Synonyms were also found to be better substitutes for long, wordy definitions, especially in the case of adjectives and adverbs.

A separate section of the book is devoted to a Block Word Finder, which consists of extremely helpful lists. There is a comprehensive, alphabetised list of proverbs, names of the presidents of the United States, mythological characters, commonly used foreign and Latin terms and their meanings, chemical elements and their symbols, and many more lists sourced from fascinating topics.

The *Super Word Finder* is an essential tool for any clue-letter crossword puzzler and will be invaluable to those addicted to other word games, such as blockwords, *Scrabble* and *Boggle*.

A

A	B	A	Lightweight material made from camel or goat hair.
A	B	B	Yarn for weaver's woof or warp;
A	B	C	Abbreviation for Alphabet, Railway timetable, initial steps.
A	C	E	Expert Airman, high ranking card, domino face, hole-in-one (golf), unreturnable service (tennis), unit;
A	C	T	Deed, action, decree, something done, division of dramatic work; Behave, work, operate, function, react.
A	D	D	Join one to another, combine augment, enlarge, subjoin, tot up affix, supplement, Attach; Unite, append
A	D	O	Fussy excitement, bother, hub-hub, commotion, Fuss, bustle, flurry, disturbance.
A	F	T	Rearward, astern, behind; Abaft, rear, tailend.
A	G	A	Man of authority and great wealth; Turkish military title.
A	G	E	Length or duration of a lifetime, chronological period of time, historical era, division of geologic time.
A	G	O	In the past; Since, gone, past.
A	I	D	Assistance, help, succour, serve, encourage, befriend; subsidy, support, patronage.
A	I	L	Affect with physical or emotional pain or discomfort; Oppress, afflict, trouble, distress, suffer.
A	I	M	Direct sight towards a target or objective, meaning, purport, import, significance, direction, goal; Aspire.
A	I	R	Atmosphere, element, odour, broadcast, publicity, demeanor, haughtiness, manner, style. Tune, melody.
A	L	A	In the manner of, after the fashion. Winglike, petal-like. Ancient drum.
A	L	B	Priestly vestment, clerical vestment, glaciated shelf.
A	L	E	Beer, malted beverage, brew.
A	L	K	Resin.
A	L	L	Everybody, everything, altogether, both, throughout, whole, total, entire, complete.
A	L	P	Mountain, meadowland, range, pasture.
A	M	A	Water bucket. Japanese woman diver, Hawaiian outrigger canoe.
A	M	P	Electrical unit, ampere.
A	N	A	(prefix) Up, towards, up to, again, back. Reminiscences, anecdotes, equal quantity (medical).
A	N	D	Included, as well as, combined with; Also; Conjunction.
A	N	T	Insect; Termite; suffix.
A	N	U	Tuberous herb.
A	N	Y	One, unmeasured, indiscriminate; Some, singular, unlimited, indefinite. \
A	P	E	Tailless Monkey. Uncouth person. Mimic, copy, imitate, resemble, emulate, Fool, dupe, duplicate.
A	P	T	Appropriate, apposite, quick, ready, prepared, given, inclined, prone, fitting; Pertinent, applicable.
A	R	C	Electrical contact, spotlight, lamp. Squash court quarter circle, angular measure. Arch, bow, curve.
A	R	E	Metric unit of surface area;
A	R	K	Chest, coffer, closed receptacle, Biblical boat, raft, flatboat, craft, Recess in Synagogue.
A	R	M	Limb, sleeve, chair rest, branch, estuary, cove, creek, lever, inlet. Weapon, empower, authorise, Equip.
A	R	N	Alder tree.
A	R	T	Craft, skill, aptitude, cunning, deception, sublety, sensibility, ingenuity, intellect, wiles, tricks, study.
A	S	H	Cinder, residue, waste; Forest Tree.
A	S	K	Request, invite, interrogate; Question, enquire.
A	S	P	Venemous snake, cobra, Egyptian Cobra.
A	S	S	Mule, donkey; Fool.
A	T	E	Past tense of Eat; swallowed, consumed.
A	U	K	Diving Sea-bird; Member of Auk people.
A	V	E	Hail, farewell; Salutation.
A	W	E	Dread, intimidate, veneration, reverence, wonder, cow, daunt, fright, fear, Inspire, exaltation, adoration.
A	W	L	Cobbler's tool, pointed instrument.
A	W	N	Chaff, Javelin, arrowhead, missile, barb.
A	X	E	Chopper, hatchet. Chop, cut, split sever, dismiss, discharge, curtail, impair.
A	Y	E	Yes, yeah, affirmative. Always, forever, ever, continually; Unchangingly, immutably, unendingly.
A	Z	O	Chemical Compound N = N.

B

B	A	A	Bleat.
B	A	D	Reprehensible, poor, worthless, blemished, unfavourable, inauspicious, decayed, Immoral, Mischievous.
B	A	G	Container, receptacle, pouch, trophy, collection; Sack, purse, spoils, assortment. (sl.) Unattractive woman
B	A	H	Intimation of disdain, contempt.
B	A	M	Metallic noise, fool, hoax.
B	A	N	Prohibit, forbid, outlaw, proclamation; Prohibition, disapproval, edict.
B	A	P	Breadroll, loaf.
B	A	R	Rigid pole, rod, grating, handrail, counter; Sandbank, Reef, public room, ingot, musical line. Barrier, save.
B	A	T	Stick, club, cudgel, wooden implement, racket, clayslap, jockey whip, stroke. Nocturnal flying mammal.
B	A	Y	Chestnut, dam, compartment, arch, ship's hospital, inlet, laurel, light brown. Bark of an animal.
B	E	D	Furniture, garden plot, watercourse; Berth, cot, couch, cradle, crib, channel, foundation, layer, seam, vein.

1	2	3	
B	E	E	A four-winged insect that makes honey. Honeybee. The letter "B".
B	E	G	Ask, entreat, petition, supplicate; Request, implore, beseech, adjure, importune.
B	E	N	Mountain peak, Moringa seed.
B	E	T	Wager, stake, pledge.
B	E	Y	Eastern courtesy title.
B	I	B	Protective clothing, apron, coloured feathers.
B	I	D	Offer, attempt, auction, announcement, propose, proffer, tender, summon, command.
B	I	G	Large, huge, enormous, gigantic, grownup, pregnant, imposing, important, great, bulky, massive, fruitful.
B	I	N	Container, refuse holder, tin, box, receptacle, frame, crib.
B	I	S	Again, twice, repeated.
B	I	T	Piece, part, fragment, scrap, morsel, iota, particle, p.p. of bite, snaffle, curb (bridle).
B	O	A	Snake. Feather or fur neck wrap.
B	O	B	Curtsey, hairstyle, shilling, dip, duck, sled, weight.
B	O	D	Fellow, chap, guy, body.
B	O	G	Swamp, marsh, morass, quagmire, slough, fen.
B	O	K	South African buck, Sportsman.
B	O	N	Kidney bean, broad bean.
B	O	O	Derisive sound, hoot, protest, jeer, disapprove.
B	O	P	Swot (with fist), jazz music, dance.
B	O	S	Horned mammal, ox, cow. Mistake or bungle.
B	O	T	Fly larva.
B	O	W	Obeisance, genuflect, nod, stoop, bob, curtsey, knotted ribbon, tie, weapon, archway, bend, crook.
B	O	X	Rigid lidded receptacle, container, case, chest, evergreen tree, window recess, Carton, cabinet, shrub.
B	O	Y	Lad, male youth, stripling, page, man servant.
B	R	A	Brassiere, undergarment.
B	U	B	Strong drink, brother, lad, (sl.) boy.
B	U	D	Incomplete flower or leaf, youthful, fresh; germinate, unfolding, sprout, blossom, Shoot, graft, burgeon.
B	U	G	Creeping or crawling invertebrate. Annoy, Irritate.
B	U	M	Tramp, loafer, beggar, vagrant; Hobo, layabout, Behind, backside, buttocks, posterior, Derriere, rump.
B	U	N	Coiled hair, hare's tail. Leavened bread.
B	U	S	Public transport, omnibus, passenger vehicle.
B	U	T	Yet, still, however, furthermore, moreover, nevertheless, except, otherwise, that, unless, when, before.
B	U	Y	Purchase, obtain, acquire, bribe, accept, approve, believe.
B	Y	E	Farewell. Cricket term.

C

C	A	B	Taxi, compartment, cage.
C	A	C	Bad, unpleasant, incorrect, diseased.
C	A	D	Bounder, blighter, worthless fellow, social outcast.
C	A	M	Rotating machinery, shaft within machine.
C	A	N	Tin, container, vessel, pannikin. Able to. Preserve.
C	A	P	Headpiece, layer, cover, seal, climax, surmount, exceed, transcend.
C	A	R	Motor vehicle, automobile, carriage, coach, compartment.
C	A	T	Feline, domesticated mammal, Malicious woman. (sl.) Guy, person, swinger.
C	A	W	Cry of crow, raven or rook.
C	A	Y	Monkey. Islet, shoal, reef, sandbank.
C	E	E	C shaped. Third letter of alphabet.
C	I	D	Moorish title. C.I.D.
C	I	G	Cigarette.
C	I	T	Townsman, tradesman, shopkeeper.
C	L	Y	Seize, steal, pocket.
C	O	B	Pony, hack, male swan, corncob, fish, gull, seal.
C	O	D	Spiny-finned fish, fool, hoax.
C	O	G	Gear tooth, wheel tooth. Trick, deception, false-hood, wheedle, coax.
C	O	L	Mountain pass, anticyclonic pressure.
C	O	N	Negative, opposition. Swindle, trick, fool, defraud.
C	O	O	Sound of dove or pigeon, soft sound of affection, talk fondly, sound of surprise.
C	O	P	Capture, arrest. Policeman. Top, head, crest.
C	O	R	Heart.
C	O	S	Lettuce, Aegian Island.
C	O	T	Bed, crib, stretcher, hut, fingerguard.
C	O	W	Domestic Bovine, female cattle. Daunt, awe, intimidate, scare, alarm. Unpleasant woman. Steer.
C	O	X	Coxswain, steer, direct.
C	O	Y	Shy, bashful, demure, diffident, modest, timid.
C	O	Z	Cousin.

1	2	3	
C	R	U	Graded quality (wine).
C	R	Y	Sob, bawl, lament, weep, scream, shriek, outburst, clamour. Vendor's call.
C	U	B	Young animal, young shark, whelp, young person, junior scout. Apprentice. Novice. To hunt.
C	U	D	Regurgitated food, gum, chew tobacco.
C	U	E	Word, phrase, signal, hint, intimation. Long handled instrument. Billiard rod.
C	U	P	Receptacle, bowl, drinking vessel, chalice, Socket, recess. Curve. Beaker, goblet, mug. Prize.
C	U	R	Mongrel, dog, social outcast.
C	U	T	Cleave, gash, slash, trim, pare, sever, reduce, lower, interrupt, stop, cease, slit. Chop, hew.
C	W	M	Steep valley.
C	W	T	One hundredweight.

D

1	2	3	
D	A	B	Prod, pat. Adept, skilful, expert. Flatfish.
D	A	D	Father, daddy, dadda.
D	A	G	Shred, applique, dagger, pierce, stick-in.
D	A	H	Dash (telephone code). Burmese Knife.
D	A	K	Relay. Transport.
D	A	M	Reservoir, millpond, confined water, barrier. Female parent. Obstruct, impede. Hinder.
D	A	N	Honourable title.
D	A	O	Hardwood, large tree.
D	A	P	Skip, jump, punch, notch, dip, dib.
D	A	S	Hindu servant.
D	A	W	Jackdaw.
D	A	Y	Light hours, period of time, appointed time, generation, lifetime.
D	E	B	Debutante.
D	E	E	Fourth letter of Alphabet.
D	E	N	Cave, cavern, animal's lair, haunt, retreat, resort. Playroom.
D	E	W	Condensed vapour, distilled water, droplets, sweat, perspiration.
D	E	Y	Dairymaid. Turkish title.
D	I	B	Dab, pat. To fish.
D	I	D	Past tense of DO. Performed.
D	I	E	Pass from physical life. Expire, perish, wither, decay, fade, cease, decease. Stamp.
D	I	G	Remove earth, delve, burrow, unearth, excavate, grub, exhume, disinter, prod, (sl.) like, admire, appreciate.
D	I	M	Dull, dark, obscure, indistinct, ill-defined, indefinite, shadowy, cloudy, faint, obtuse, slow of perception.
D	I	N	Uproar, pandemonium, hullabaloo, hub-bub, racket, clamour; Paper size, film, Photo sensitivity rating.
D	I	P	Immerse, souse, duck, douse, dunk, submerge; Incline casually, bend, curtsey, dive.
D	I	S	Trump Card.
D	I	T	Telegraphic code.
D	I	V	Demon, evil spirit.
D	O	D	Metal plate, die stamp, mild oath.
D	O	E	Female of buck. Female adult fallow-deer.
D	O	G	Carnivorous mammal. Canine, mongrel, cur. To hunt, to hound, to track, to follow.
D	O	L	Measurement of pain.
D	O	M	Religious title, Hindu caste.
D	O	N	Wear, dress up, put on, assume. Spanish title.
D	O	P	Dip, pot, shell, goblet, diamond holder, South African Brandy.
D	O	R	Drone, mock, trick.
D	O	S	Matrimonial property.
D	O	T	Speck, spot, particle, period, decimal point, intersperse, scatter, telegraphic code, dowry.
D	O	W	To thrive, to prosper. To recover from illness.
D	R	Y	Freedom from moisture, anhydrous, withered, sapless, juiceless, unmoistened, thirsty. Empty. Impassive.
D	U	B	Confer knighthood. Provide new sound track, re-record. Overlay.
D	U	D	Ineffective, fake, worthless, defective.
D	U	E	Owing, debt; Fated, inevitable, sufficient, adequate, payable, scheduled, directly.
D	U	G	Unearthed, exhumed, excavated, nudged. Teat, nipple, pap, udder.
D	U	N	Dull-coloured, dark, gloomy, demand persistently, fortified residence.
D	U	O	Duet, pair, two.
D	U	P	Open.
D	U	X	Academic head of class or school.
D	Y	E	Colour, hue, tint, tinge, stain, shade.

E

1	2	3	
E	A	R	Organ of hearing and equilibrium. Fruit of cereal. Lug. Cultivate, heed, regard. Attention.

1	2	3	
E	A	T	Ingest, chew, swallow, devour, consume, ravage, corrode, erode.
E	A	U	Watery solution of perfume. Liqueur.
E	B	B	Recede, decline, diminish, lessen, wane, subside.
E	C	O	Habitat.
E	C	U	Old french coin.
E	E	L	Elongated snake-like fish.
E	F	E	Pygmy language.
E	F	T	Lizard, newt.
E	G	G	Shell encased membranous material deposited by females. To incite, Urge, Goad.
E	G	O	Self, self-esteem.
E	K	E	Augment, stretch, squeeze, add, increase.
E	L	D	Period of life, age.
E	L	F	Fairy, dwarf, sprite, gnome, imp, pixie.
E	L	K	Antelope.
E	L	L	Unit of length. Extension at right angles. Conduit elbow.
E	L	M	Tree.
E	M	U	Ostrich-like bird.
E	N	D	Terminate, kill, conclude, close, extremity, tip, remnant, aim, purpose, object, goal.
E	N	G	Large tree. Symbol of pronunciation.
E	N	S	Essence.
E	O	N	Era, period of time, age, cycle.
E	R	E	Before, soon.
E	R	F	Plot of land, building lot.
E	R	G	Unit of work.
E	R	N	White-tailed sea eagle.
E	R	R	Sin, offend, roam, wander, stray.
E	R	S	Fodder of the pea family. Vetch.
E	T	C	Etceterra, and so forth.
E	V	E	Evening. Original woman. Preceding day.
E	W	E	Mature female sheep.
E	Y	E	Organ of sight. Look, glance, gaze, view, see, observe, watch. Eye of Hurricane, Needle.

F

F	A	D	Vogue, rage, craze, fashion, style, whim.
F	A	G	Drudge, toil, tire, menial. Cigarette. Homosexual (sl.).
F	A	N	Device for cooling air. Impel air. Stimulate, aircraft propellor.
F	A	R	Distant, remote, long, comprehensive.
F	A	T	Plump, corpulent, obese, abundant, over-weight, fleshy, stout, chubby, rotund, portly. Grease, oil, lard.
F	A	Y	Fairy, elf. Fasten tightly.
F	E	D	Nourished, fattened, supplied.
F	E	E	Gratuity, reward, wage, tip, remuneration, pay, toll.
F	E	N	Peatland, marsh.
F	E	U	Lease. Tenure.
F	E	W	Not many. Scant, rare, scarce, minority.
F	E	Z	Cone-shaped hat.
F	I	B	Trivial falsehood. White lie.
F	I	D	Wooden spar, wedge.
F	I	E	Exclamation of disgust. Affectation of being shocked.
F	I	G	Pear-shaped fruit. Gesture of contempt.
F	I	L	Iraqi coin.
F	I	N	Membranous propelling device of fish. (sl.) Five dollar bill.
F	I	R	Evergreen Tree.
F	I	T	Seizure, paroxysm. Suited, qualified, appropriate; Seemly, proper, meet, prudent, Apt.
F	I	X	Mend, restore, cure, fasten, attach, predicament, dilemma.
F	L	U	Influenza, bad cold.
F	L	Y	Winged insect. Take flight. Fish-hook dressed with feathers. Operate an aeroplane.
F	O	B	Pocket watch. Deceit, trick, cheat, delude.
F	O	E	Adversary, enemy, antagonist, opponent.
F	O	G	Thick mist, murky atmosphere, Pasture.
F	O	P	Foolish person, conceited pretender. Coxcomb, dandy, dude, dupe, cheat.
F	O	R	Because, in favour of, inspite of, notwithstanding, by reason of, namely, pro.
F	O	X	Carnivorous mammal related to wolf. Outwit, fool, bewilder, baffle, confuse, A crafty or sly fellow.
F	R	A	Brother.
F	R	O	Back, backward, from, away.
F	R	Y	Pan, cook. Broil. Small person. Fish or thing.

1	2	3	
F	U	D	Hare's tail, rabbit's tail. Wool waste.
F	U	G	Odorous emanation. Stuffy atmosphere. Fog.
F	U	N	Amusement, enjoyment, playfulness, jest, sport, game, play. Trick, hoax, merriment.
F	U	R	Animal pelt. A garment made from animal hair. Incrustation. Mould.

G

G	A	B	Talk rapidly, chatter, idle talk. Hook, notch. Boast. Mouth.
G	A	D	Wander about. Sharp pointed stylus. Spear, spur, rod, stick. Mild oath.
G	A	G	Silence by force. Heave with nausea. Retch. Obstruct, choke, balk. Joke.
G	A	L	(Sl.) Girl. Unit of acceleration.
G	A	M	Tooth. Mouth. (sl.) Leg.
G	A	P	Hole, chasm, cleft, notch, breach. Parting or an interruption.
G	A	R	Needlefish. Pike. To compel.
G	A	S	Vapour used for energy, lighting and heating. Anaesthetic. Empty talk. Boasting.
G	A	T	Gun, revolver.
G	A	Y	Lively, merry, light-hearted, showy. Homo-sexual. (sl).
G	E	E	Exclamation of surprise; command to a horse;
G	E	L	Glutenous substance. Jelly-like substance. Stick together Coagulate.
G	E	M	Precious stone, treasure, jewel. To blossom.
G	E	N	General information. (abbr.)
G	E	O	Yawn, chasm. Land. Of the earth.
G	E	T	Obtain, gain, earn, take possession of, achieve, catch (an illness).
G	I	B	Male castrated cat. An old woman. A removal plate of material.
G	I	D	Sheep disease.
G	I	G	Light carriage, chaise. Joke, whim. Prod, Jab. Arrangement of fish hooks.
G	I	M	Neat, trim.
G	I	N	Alcoholic drink. Mechanical contrivance or trap.
G	I	P	Clean fish.
G	N	U	African antelope. Wilderbeest.
G	O	A	Gazelle.
G	O	B	A lump or mass of indefinte shape. Mouthful. Waste matter in old Mine workings. (sl) Mouth.
G	O	D	Deity, Supreme Being. The Almighty, Creator, Jehovah. Inanimate idol of worship.
G	O	G	Stir, excitement, eagerness. Bog, quagmire.
G	O	O	Sticky substance.
G	O	T	Past tense of get.
G	O	Y	Gentile. Non-practising Jew.
G	U	E	Two stringed musical instrument.
G	U	M	Glue, fixative. To seal, to unite. Chewing gum.
G	U	N	Weapon, missile, firearm, pistol, musket, rifle, cannon. Shoot. Something which discharges.
G	U	P	Nonsense. Guppy fish.
G	U	T	Burn, cremate, incinerate. Remove inside of, cut out, excise, extract. The stomach.
G	U	Y	Tackle, cordage, rigging, stay, line, halliard. Fellow, bloke, chap. Object of ridicule. Figure of fun. Butt.
G	Y	M	Gymnasium. Stadium, forum, Academy, training school, trade school.
G	Y	P	Male college servant. Fraud, swindle. Give a hard time. To pain or annoy.

H

H	A	D	past of have.
H	A	G	Old crone, witch, harpy.
H	A	M	Cured Pork. Amateur radio operator. Amateur performer. Ineffective actor. Bungler.
H	A	S	Possesses, acquires, owns.
H	A	T	Head covering, headgear, bonnet, cap.
H	A	W	Hedge. Yard.
H	A	Y	Cut grass. Pasturage. Dry grass used as animal fodder.
H	E	M	Fold back edge and stitch down. Edge, border. Utter sound. Surround.
H	E	N	Domestic fowl. Female bird.
H	E	P	Jazzy.
H	E	R	Relating to a female. Woman, girl.
H	E	T	Heated.
H	E	W	Cut with an axe. Fell, chop, cut.
H	I	D	Past of hide. Eluded.
H	I	E	Hasten, be eager, strive.
H	I	M	Relating to a male. Man, boy.
H	I	P	Region between pelvis and upper part of femur. Haunch. Bramble, Dog Rose. Hip Hoorah!

1	2	3	
H	I	S	Belonging to him.
H	I	T	Strike, smack, censure. Success. Attack. Collision.
H	O	B	Hobgoblin, elf. Kettle rest.
H	O	D	Implement for carrying brick and mortar.
H	O	E	Agricultural implement. To weed, cultivate. Promontory, hill, cliff.
H	O	G	Domestic swine, pig, sow, boar. Take more than one's share. Uncouth individual.
H	O	P	Skip, Jump, Bounce.
H	O	T	Heated. Fiery. Ardent, vehement. Lecherous, eager. Unsafe. Peppery. Spicy.
H	O	W	Manner or method in which something is performed. That. American Indian greeting.
H	O	Y	Shout, call.
H	U	B	Centre, focal point. Axis.

I

I	C	E	Frozen water. Cover with icing. To place in reserve, Freeze. (sl) diamonds.
I	D	E	Freshwater fish. Carp.
I	D	O	Modified Esperanto. Artificial language.
I	L	K	Family, kind, sort, type, bread, species.
I	L	L	Sick, ailing, unwell, nauseated, evil. A negative prefix.
I	M	P	Urchin, wicked spirit, demon.
I	N	K	Liquid of various colours used for writing and printing. Pigmented fluid.
I	N	N	Public house, hotel, tavern.
I	O	N	Atom, free electron, charged sub-atomic particle.
I	R	E	Resentment, fury, rage, anger. Irk, annoy, irritate, disgust, bore.
I	T	S	Belonging to it. It has. It is.
I	V	Y	Ornamental climbing shrub. Evergreen vine. Academic.

J

J	A	B	Dig, job, nudge, prod, stab. Poke, prick, puncture.
J	A	D	Quarrying cut.
J	A	G	Jab, stab, puncture. Bender, booze-up, spree, drunk, tear. Convey, ferry, lug, tot. Prick, binge, carry.
J	A	M	Crush, squash, squeeze, crowd. Ram, stuff, tamp. Dilemma, fix, pickle, plight. Press, cram. Preserved fruit.
J	A	P	(Abbrev.) Japanese.
J	A	R	Container, glass bottle, vase. Conflict, discord, jangle, vibrate. Collision, jolt. Clash, shake, impact, upset.
J	A	W	Lower bone of face. Mouth. Upbraid, berate, scold. Gabble, prattle, yak. gab.
J	A	Y	Pugnacious sounding bird. Bumpkin, hill-billy, rustic.
J	E	T	Spray of water, spurt, squirt. Stream. Pitch black, inky, ebony black.
J	E	W	One whose religion is Judaism. Israelite. Person who drives a hard bargain.
J	I	B	Boggle, stumble. Gag, balk, demure. Perpendicular structure of crane.
J	I	G	Lively dance, rapid movement. Device used in fishing. Mechanical device. Gimmick, ploy, wile, trick.
J	O	B	Employment, profession, trade, vocation. Assignment, chore, work, calling, Occupation, pursuit. Duty.
J	O	G	Jab, nudge, prod, poke, shake, dig, punch. Between running or walking.
J	O	T	Iota, speck, tittle, whit, particle. Scribble, scrawl. Write hurriedly.
J	O	Y	Delight, ecstasy, rapture, pleasure, enjoyment, joyfulness.
J	U	G	Jar, pitcher, bottle, Prison, jail, imprison, confine, constrain, incarcerate, shut.
J	U	T	Protrude, stand out, stick out. Project, bulge, overhang, extend.

K

K	A	A	Rock Python.
K	A	F	Fountain conferring immortality.
K	A	Y	Key, reef, shoal.
K	E	A	New Zealand parrot.
K	E	B	Sheep louse.
K	E	F	Tranquility, languor. The material that produces Kef.
K	E	G	Barrel, cask.
K	E	N	Knowledge, comprehension, understanding, perception, grasp.
K	E	Y	Instrument which opens a lock. Password. Vent. Depressible digit, musical note, Tone, pitch.
K	I	D	Youngster, youth, juvenile, nipper, child. Hoax, hoodwink, trick, fool, dupe, rag, rib. Young goat.
K	I	F	Indian hemp.
K	I	N	Clan, folk, race, tribe, stock, family. Relative, relation.
K	I	P	(sl.) Doze, catch forty winks. Light sleep.
K	I	T	Equipment, baggage. Apparatus.

1	2	3	
K	O	B	Roan antelope, water buck.

L

L	A	B	Place devoted to experimental study. Laboratory.
L	A	C	Substance exuded by lac insect. Shellac. Hard coating yielded by animal substances.
L	A	D	Son, stripling, youngster, boy.
L	A	G	Loiter, procrastinate, delay, hang back. Hindmost, final. To wrap with insulation material.
L	A	M	Thrash, wallop, batter, beat. Get away, flight, break-out, escape.
L	A	P	Front portion of the lower trunk and thighs of a seated person. Circuit. Lapladder, Lick, Lap-up.
L	A	R	Malayan gibbon.
L	A	T	Pillar, stick, club. Monetary unit. Lativian.
L	A	W	Conduct, action, governing principle of conduct. Command, edict, decree, canon, Ordinance, regulation.
L	A	X	Slack, relaxed, loose, careless, delinquent, negligent, forgetful, unmindful.
L	A	Y	Secular, temporal. Tune, strain, air, melody. Allege. Set, spread. Aim, direct, attribute, credit, ascribe.
L	B	W	(Cricket) Leg before wicket.
L	E	A	Open space, pasture, grassland. Measure of yarn.
L	E	D	Conducted, induced, helped.
L	E	E	Shelter, lea, meadow.
L	E	G	Lower limb of a vertebrate. Supporting appendage of animals. Support of furniture etc. Branch or Section.
L	E	I	Garland, wreath, necklace of flowers.
L	E	K	Monetary unit. Sight of bird display and courtship.
L	E	O	Lion. Sign of the Zodiac.
L	E	T	Lease, rent, charter, hire, permit, allow, sanction, authorise, concede, grant. Stroke.
L	E	X	Law, legal, enactment.
L	E	Y	Lea, pasture. Pewter.
L	I	B	Women's liberation. Liberation, liberty, freedom, scope, deliverance.
L	I	D	Covering, stopper, top.
L	I	E	Untruth, falsehood, fib, misrepresentation, prevarication, falsification, perjury, Rest, recline, repose.
L	I	N	Cease. Female unicorn in Chinese mythology.
L	I	P	Labium. Section of a mouth. Fleshy folds surrounding an orifice. Part of mouth used as organ of speech.
L	I	T	Set alight, illuminated, ignited, kindled.
L	O	B	Throw overhand. Slow bowled ball. Hit ball in a high arc (tennis). Cash Till. Move slowly and heavily.
L	O	G	Length of tree trunk. Woodcut for fuel. Record, note, journalise, Logbook.
L	O	O	Lavatory, convenience, privy, water closet, toilet.
L	O	P	Cut off, amputate, dock. Bound, hop, leap, spring, vault, bounce, jump.
L	O	T	Much, many, mass. Array, cluster, crowd, group, batch, bundle. Fate, circumstance, destiny. Share.
L	O	W	Inferior, squat, short, humble, lowly. Rude, abject, mean, servile, wretched, sordid, Vile, crude, raw, rough.
L	O	Y	Tool for digging holes, spade.
L	S	D	Money. Hallucinatory drug.
L	U	G	Ear, lobe. Tug, haul, drag. Oaf, lout.
L	U	X	Unit of illumination.
L	Y	E	Alkaline liquor. Caustic.
L	Y	M	Bloodhound.

M

M	A	B	Queen of the Fairies.
M	A	C	Son of.
M	A	D	Crazy, demented, deranged, unbalanced, loony, illogical irrational indignant, Affronted, wild, furious.
M	A	G	Chatter.
M	A	M	Madam, ma'am, mum, mother, mommy.
M	A	N	Human being. Homo Sapiens. Person. Male. Mankind. Fellow, Gentleman.
M	A	P	Graph, diagram, outline, sketch, design, layout, plan, chart.
M	A	R	Blemish, damage, harm, hurt, impair, spoil, tarnish, injure, scar.
M	A	T	Floor covering, carpet, rug. Dull, lack lustre, lustreless, muted, dim, flat.
M	A	W	Craw, crop, stomach.
M	A	X	Perfect score, complete success (sl.) gin.
M	A	Y	Past of might. Have permission, have ability, have liberty. Evergreen shrub. Hawthorn.
M	E	N	Plural of Man.
M	E	T	Past of meet.
M	E	W	Cage, coop, corral, fence, hem. Immure, pen, shut in, enclose. Cat call. Sea gull.
M	H	O	Electrical unit of conductivity.
M	I	D	Centre, central, medial, centremost, halfway. Amid, among, amongst, midst, During, throughout, middle.
M	I	L	one-thousandth of an inch. Part of.

1	2	3	
M	I	M	Prim, demure, precise.
M	I	R	Russian commune.
M	I	X	Combine, blend, fuse, meld, merge, mingle, enjoin, associate. Mixture, amalgam.
M	O	A	Extinct bird from New Zealand.
M	O	B	Disorderly crowd of people. Rabble, horde, throng. Scold, rail, berate.
M	O	D	Modern. Choral contest. Eisteddfod.
M	O	E	Grimace; Mop.
M	O	G	Move away.
M	O	N	Cambodian language.
M	O	O	Cow noise. Low.
M	O	P	Floor swab. Floor cleaner at end of handle. Clobber, beat, lambaste. Whip. Dust with mop.
M	O	R	Type of Humus layer.
M	O	T	Bon Mot. Witticism.
M	O	W	Cut grass with machine or tool. Clip, crop, cut, reap, pare, trim. Bring down, drop, floor, knock down, fell.
M	R	S	Mistress. Married Miss.
M	U	D	Sludge, slime, mire, slush.
M	U	G	Countenance, features, face, dial, visage. Blockhead, dimwit, dolt, dope, idiot, dunce. Hit and run, Rob.
M	U	M	Mother, ma, mom, mater, mommy, mummy. Old woman. Silent, dumb, mute.
M	U	N	Man.
M	U	X	To spoil, a mess.
M	Y	A	Shellfish.

N

1	2	3	
N	A	B	Apprehend, detain, pick up, pull in, arrest, catch, grab, snatch, seize, cop, nick. Steal. Constable, bobby.
N	A	F	Unfashionable, unsuitable.
N	A	G	Find fault incessantly. Carp, fuss, henpeck, harrass, pester, plague, tease, bother. Heckle, goad, urge.
N	A	P	A short sleep. Forty winks. Doze, Siesta, snooze, catnap. Interlude, pause, rest. Card game. Racing Tip.
N	A	Y	No. Nix, nope. Indeed, truly. Yeah. Even.
N	C	O	Non-commissioned Officer.
N	E	B	Beak, bill, picker, nib.
N	E	E	Woman's maiden family surname. Born as.
N	E	F	Casket. Model ship.
N	E	K	Col. South African mountain pass.
N	E	O	New, Modern. Like. Akin to.
N	E	P	Knot in fibre. Catmint.
N	E	T	Meshed arrangement of thread, cord or rope. Woven material. Trap, snare. Make profit, clean up. Gain.
N	E	W	Newly come into existence. Freshly made. Unfamiliar, fresh, modern, new frangled, Novel, recent, more.
N	I	B	Writing instrument, pen. Beak, neb, pecker, bill.
N	I	L	Nothing, naught, nix, none, zero.
N	I	M	Pinch, snitch, swipe, lift, nab, nick, steal.
N	I	P	Squeeze, frustrate, thwart, arrest. Flit, fly, hasten, hustle, run, rush, hurry. Dram, drop, slug, snort, tot.
N	I	S	Not so, imp, hobgoblin.
N	I	T	Parasite, Egg of the louse.
N	I	X	Nothing, nought, nil. No, nay, nope. Negative, veto.
N	O	B	Aristocrat. Knave at Cribbage.
N	O	D	Inclination of the head. Inclination of assent. Drowse, doze, snooze.
N	O	G	Peg, noggin, ale, drink, small pot, brick.
N	O	M	de Guerre, fictitious name, pseudonym.
N	O	N	Not, reverse, absence of.
N	O	R	Or not, neither, and not, than.
N	O	T	Negation, negative, except.
N	O	W	At this time, today, nowadays, presently, at once, directly, forthwith, immediately. Instantly, right away.
N	O	X	Measurement of light unit. Personification of night.
N	O	Y	Unit of perceived noise.
N	U	B	Substance, core, crux, gist, kernel, meat, upshot.
N	U	N	Female member of Religious order, Sister. Member of sisterhood.
N	U	T	Seed, kernel. Problem, issue. Crank, lunatic. Fanatic.
N	U	X	Vomica, poisonous seed, tree, bark.
N	Y	E	Brood, flock.
N	Y	X	Goddess of Night, daughter of Chaos.

O

O	A	F	Clumsy slow-witted person, fat head, chump, dolt, dunce, lout, clod, slob, blunderer.

1	2	3	
O	A	K	Tough dark durable wood. Oak tree.
O	A	R	Wooden pole with flat blade used for propelling a boat. Paddle. Row, pull, oarsman.
O	A	T	Cereal, grain.
O	B	I	Fetish, magic. Japanese sash.
O	D	D	Without corresponding mate. Unmatched, unpaired. Accidental, incidental. By chance, Curious, erratic.
O	D	E	Poem or song.
O	E	R	Over (poetical).
O	F	F	Away, over, slim. Slack, sluggish. Removed, distant, opposite. Bad.
O	F	T	Often, frequently, repeatedly.
O	H	M	Electrical resistance. (Unit of).
O	I	L	Lubricant, grease, combustible substance, vegetable extract, mineral extract. Petroleum. Lubricate.
O	L	D	Antediluvian, antique, ancient, venerable, time worn. Of long standing, continuing, Enduring, long lived.
O	L	M	Blind lizard.
O	N	E	Singular, lone, only, solitary, unique, sole, separate, particular, single. Undivided, united, associated.
O	O	M	South African Uncle.
O	P	E	Unblock, unclose, undo, unstop, open.
O	P	T	Elect, mark, pick, prefer, select, single out, take, choose.
O	R	B	Globe, sphere, ball, eye. Lamp, circle.
O	R	C	Whale. An ogre.
O	R	D	Edge, beginning.
O	R	E	Substance from which valuable matter is extracted. Unrefined material.
O	R	T	Scrap, bit, refuse, leftover.
O	U	R	Belonging to us, inherent in us, associated with us. What we possess. Relating to us.
O	U	T	Without, outside, outdoors. Beyond. Chase, dismiss, evict, eject. Douse, quench.
O	V	A	Plural of OVUM. Eggs.
O	W	E	Due, payable, on account. Be under obligation, indebted.
O	W	L	Nocturnal birds of prey. Person of solemn appearance. Person with nocturnal mode of life. Wise person.
O	W	N	Possess, retain, hold, have, admit, concede, confess, acknowledge.
O	X	Y	Containing oxygen.
O	Z	S	Ounces (abbreviation).

P

P	A	D	Protection. Embellish, exaggerate, magnify, embroider, overcharge, overstate, Tiptoe. Protective cushion.
P	A	L	Friend, companion, comrade, crony, buddy, chum, associate.
P	A	N	Vessel, container. All, whole. General. Follow the action. Take in entire scene.
P	A	P	Sustenance. Nourishment, food. Something lacking in solid substance. Rubbish, slop.
P	A	R	Equivalent. Equality. equitability, parity, sameness, average, norm, standard. Parallel.
P	A	S	Precedence, dance pattern.
P	A	T	Tap, dab, slap, caress, soothe. Aptly, readily, promptly. Glib, firm, unyielding. Small measure or amount.
P	A	W	Foot of quadruped. Large clumsy hand. Touch clumsily.
P	A	X	Peace, Kiss of peace. Liturgical greeting.
P	A	Y	Discharge an obligation. Compensate, remunerate, recompense, satisfy. Remit, tender, settle, expend.
P	E	A	Round edible vegetable. Leguminous plant. Small piece of coal.
P	E	D	Foot. Involving the feet.
P	E	G	Tapered piece of wood, metal or other material. Support. Pin, prong, plug. To attach
P	E	N	Writing instrument. To write. enclose, cage, fence, hedge, shut in, jail. Penitentiary, prison. Female swan.
P	E	P	Energy, vigor, vitality, drive.
P	E	R	Via, by dint of, by means of, by virtue of. Through, with, by. For each.
P	E	S	Segment of hind limb of vertebrate. Foot.
P	E	T	Animal kept for pleasure. Cherished, indulged, beloved. Cosset, cuddle, caress. Favourite.
P	E	W	Seat, bench, enclosure usually in church.
P	I	A	Perennial herb, arrowroot.
P	I	E	Baked meat under dough. Pastry with filling. Cinch. Kid's stuff, simple, easy.
P	I	G	Hog, swine, pork, ham, bacon. Someone with bad habits. Guzzler. Crude casting of metal.
P	I	N	Peg, bolt, broach, clip. To secure. To fit. Enclose, confine. To fasten
P	I	P	Seed of fruit. Defeat, outdo.
P	I	T	Underground tunnel. Digging. Tomb. Abyss. Oppose, vie.
P	L	Y	Measure of thickness. Layer. Twist, bias. Inclination, bend, curvature, fold. Manipulate, manoeuvre, offer.
P	O	D	Husk, shell, skin, slough, hull. Foot, hoof. Stalk, seed pouch, bag, sac. Cocoon. Potbelly, Corporation.
P	O	E	New Zealand Bird.
P	O	I	Then, later, next. Musical term. Hawaiian pasty.
P	O	P	Cause to explode, burst open. Shoot, hit, assault. Break. Hock, pawn. Carbonated beverage, Soda, Swat.
P	O	T	Container, receptacle. Jackpot, kitty, pool, Marijuana, canabis.
P	O	X	Disease characterised by pustules.
P	R	O	In favour of. For. Adept, authority, master, professional, expert.

1	2	3	
P	R	Y	Snoop. Investigate inquisitively. To raise, pull apart, lever or separate.
P	U	B	Public house, bar, taproom, tavern.
P	U	G	Type of dog. Hobgoblin. Turned up nose. Boxer. Mortar.
P	U	N	Double entendre. Play on words.
P	U	P	Small dog, puppy, whelp, young seal. Twerp, squirt.
P	U	S	Fluid matter discharged by open sore. Suppuration.
P	U	T	Place, lay, establish, set, fix, throw with overhand pushing motion. The action of sinking a golfball.
P	U	Y	Volcanic hill.
P	Y	A	Monetary coin.
P	Y	R	Fire, heat.
P	Y	X	Tabernacle, box, chest, coffer. Test a coin.

Q

Q	U	A	European night heron. As (Latin).
Q	U	I	Who (Latin).
Q	U	O	Whither (Latin). Something given or received in exchange.

R

R	A	B	Beater for mixing hair with mortar.
R	A	D	Quick, ready, eager. Unit of radiation.
R	A	G	Waste cloth. Tatter, torn fragment, remnant. Newspaper, periodical. To tease.
R	A	H	Hurrah!
R	A	J	Ruler. Reign.
R	A	M	Male goat. Male of small antelopes. Buck. Plunge, drive, dig, stab, stick, thrust.
R	A	N	Past of run. Hank of twine.
R	A	P	Knock, hit, tap. Smart blow. The least bit. The blame.
R	A	T	Rodent, destructive pest. Renegade, defector, turncoat. Desert, renounce, repudiate. Inform, squeal.
R	A	W	Uncooked, unprocessed, unwrought. Crude, unedited, unbound, uncultivated. Sore, sensitive.
R	A	X	Elongate, stretch.
R	A	Y	Beam, shaft. Radiating light. Species of fish.
R	E	D	Ruddy, florid, warm, glowing. Communist, Bolshevist. Crimson, Scarlet.
R	E	E	Sift. Irrational, befuddled.
R	E	F	Referee.
R	E	H	Saline efflorescence.
R	E	M	Dosage of ionising radiation injurious to human tissue. Rapid bye movement.
R	E	P	Representative, Sales person. Yarn used in clothing and upholstery fabric. Repertory.
R	E	S	Sing, matter, point, subject.
R	E	T	Soak or expose. Flack, hemp. Moisten fibre.
R	E	V	Step up number of revolutions per minute. Operate at increased speed. Reverend.
R	E	X	King. Hair characteristic of domestic rabbit and various rodents.
R	I	A	Narrow inlet, creek.
R	I	B	Curved bony cartilaginous rods in lateral walls of the frame of vertebrates. Vertical ridge formed in knitting.
R	I	D	Set someone or something free. Liberate, release. Unburden, eradicate, exterminate. Remove, uproot.
R	I	G	To fit out with necessary tackle. Provide with clothes. Dress, Distinctive type of vessel, Bark, Banter, sport.
R	I	M	Brim, brink, edge, fringe, hem, margin, perimeter, periphery, verge, border. Margin, outline.
R	I	N	Japanese monetary unit.
R	I	P	Tear, cleave, rend, rive, split, Tidal current, undertow. Libertine, rake.
R	O	B	Take possessions unlawfully. Mug, plunder, ransack, rifle, loot, Swindle, pillage, ravage, sack. Deprive.
R	O	C	Legendary bird of great size. Radio controlled bomb.
R	O	D	Bar, wand, cane, stick, shaft, ingot.
R	O	E	Eggs or ovaries of an invertebrate. Eggs of fish.
R	O	O	Kangaroo.
R	O	T	Decay, decompose, putrify, spoil, taint, deteriorate, degenerate. Demoralise, deprave, pervert, warp.
R	O	W	Propel boat with oars, paddle, pull, punt, skull. Line, queue, rank, file, string, tier, Quarrel, dispute, scold.
R	U	B	Clean, polish, buff, smooth, burnish, shine, chaff, abrade, graze, Obstacle, snag, Irk, vex, annoy.
R	U	D	Red, hue, complexion.
R	U	E	Regret, deplore, repent.
R	U	G	Coarse woollen fabric, fabric with nap or pile. Floor covering, carpet, mat. Warm covering for the lap.
R	U	M	Alcoholic liquor; grog. Queer, quaint, odd, fantastic. Unlikely.
R	U	N	Go faster than a walk. Move the legs quickly. Hasten, gallop. Flee, retreat, escape. Function, operate.
R	U	T	Track worn by habitual passage. Groove, channel, furrow. Heat, sexual excitement.
R	Y	E	Cultivated grain. Rye Whiskey, Rye bread.

S

S	A	C	Pouch within animal or plant. Soft walled cavity usually containing fluid. Lachrymal sac, tearduct gland.
S	A	D	Affected by sorrow. Melancholy, mournful, unhappy, downcast, dejected, dismal. Desolate, grief stricken.
S	A	G	Fall away, drop off. Slide, Slump, droop, wilt. Basin, hollow, sink, sinkhole. Depression, dip, down slide.
S	A	M	Imaginary character representing American government. Uncle Sam.
S	A	P	Deplete, drain, undermine. Weaken, debilitate, disable. Fool, dupe, fall guy, chump. Fluid of plant juice.
S	A	T	Past of sit. Seated, perched, settled.
S	A	W	Past of see. Adage, byword, proverb. Saying. Manually operated or power driven tool used in cutting.
S	A	X	Knife-like chopping tool. Saxophone. Wind instrument.
S	A	Y	Express in words, declare, state, tell, announce, proclaim, aver, avow, articulate. Nearly, about, almost.
S	E	A	Ocean, briny, deep. Saline waters of the earth. Seashore, seaside waves.
S	E	C	Dry (flavour).
S	E	E	Perceive with the eyes. Apprehend through sight. Observe, detect, discover; Ascertain, examine, View.
S	E	G	Castrated mature adult animal. Bull, boar.
S	E	T	Place in specified position. Fix, lay, put, install, wedge, spread, arrange.
S	E	W	Stitch, unite, attach, fasten, secure with thread, work with needle and thread.
S	E	X	Male or female. By parental reproduction. Gender. Sexual intercourse, sex play.
S	H	E	Female person or animal. Feminine pronoun.
S	H	Y	Bashful, coy, demure. Diffident, modest, retiring. Hesitant, reluctant. Scant, scarce, insufficient. Avoid.
S	I	B	Kindred, related to, sibling. Friendly, receptive, well disposed.
S	I	C	Exactly reproducing an original. Intended exactly as written. As written. Urge, exort, goad.
S	I	L	Yellow ochre. Pigment.
S	I	N	Imperfection, offence, transgression, iniquity, wrong doing, crime, evil.
S	I	P	Imbibe, quaff, swallow, drink, sup.
S	I	R	Gentleman, lord, knight. Esteemed man, respectful form of address. Superior person. Salutation.
S	I	S	Expression of disgust (South African). Sister.
S	I	T	To rest on the buttocks or haunches. Be seated. Squat. Convene, meet, open. Incubate, brood.
S	I	X	Number, half a dozen. Sextet.
S	K	I	Travel over ice or water, glide over snow. Curved strip of wood used on feet. Winter sport.
S	K	Y	Expanse of space around the earth. Firmament, Heavens. Celestial sphere. The Blue.
S	L	Y	Cunning, adroit, smart, clever, artful, crafty, underhand, unscrupulous. Clandestine. Shifty, devious.
S	N	Y	Sny, Bend upward.
S	O	B	Weep, wail, cry. Blubber, snivel.
S	O	D	Turf, grass, peat, grass covered square of turf. Skunk, wretch, louse, cur, bugger. Bog, morass, marsh.
S	O	L	Sun, solar, old coin, monetary unit. Fluid colloidal system. Aerosol.
S	O	N	Male offspring. Male child. Person associated with Nation, school, race, belief. Disciple.
S	O	P	Weakling, doormat, sissy. Propitiatory gift, bribe. Wet, drench, soak. saturate.
S	O	S	International call for help.
S	O	T	Fool, idiot, drunk, tipple, guzzle. Drunkard.
S	O	U	Penny, trifle, abbreviation of South.
S	O	W	Plant, scatter, throw, drop (seed), distribute, implant. Female pig. Needlework.
S	O	X	Covering for the feet worn under shoes. Socks.
S	O	Y	Oriental condiment made from Beans.
S	P	A	Locality of mineral springs. Water cure. Baths, Hydro, Health Resort.
S	P	Y	Secret observations. Watch furtively. Secret agent, sleuth. informer. Espy, behold, detect, observe.
S	T	Y	Enclosure for swine. Pig pen. (Sl.) filthy abode. Inflamed swelling on eyelid.
S	U	B	Subordinate, dependant, subject, tributary, under. Substitute, alternate, locum tenens. Replacement.
S	U	E	Petition, appeal, prosecute, solicit, urge, entreat, plead, woo. Diminutive of Suzan.
S	U	D	Soap bubble. Foam induced by agitating soap or detergent in water.
S	U	M	Amount, aggregate, number, total, arithmetic, Epitomise, condense, inventory. Synopsis, figure, cast. tot.
S	U	N	Day star. Sol. Helios. Power, splendour. Expose to rays of sun. Place in sunshine.
S	U	P	Imbibe, quaff, sip, swallow, drink, take supper.
S	Y	N	With, by means of, together, like.

T

T	A	B	Account, invoice, bill, reckoning, score, statement. Price, cost, rate, tariff, charge. Scrutiny, surveillance.
T	A	D	Lad, shaveling, son, stripling, boy.
T	A	G	Label, ticket. Cliche, banality, commonplace, platitude. Shadow, tail, dog, trail. Banality.
T	A	N	Convert to leather by impregnation with tannin. Preserve material. Tanning agent. Expose skin to sun.
T	A	P	Faucet, hydrant, stopcock, valve. Syphon. Strike, hit, rap. Designate, nominate. A dance.
T	A	R	Bituminous viscous liquid. Coal tar. Macadam. To spread with tar. Smear, stain. Sailor, mariner, seaman.
T	A	T	To work fabric with needle and thread. Stretch fabric on frame.
T	A	U	Tee shaped mark. St. Anthony's cross. A pastoral staff.

1	2	3	
T	A	W	Letter of Hebrew alphabet. Sign, cross.
T	A	X	Assess income. Determine amount. Make subject to payment. Levy, burden, strain.
T	E	A	A shrub, cultivated mainly in the Far East. Infusion of tea leaves with boiling water. Light refreshment.
T	E	C	Detective.
T	E	D	Dry out. Spread out. Scatter.
T	E	E	Wooden peg used to raise golf ball before hitting it. Area from which golf ball is played.
T	E	G	Fleece. A two-year old Doe.
T	E	N	Quantity symbolised by the numerals 10 or X.
T	E	R	Threefold, thrice, three, tri.
T	H	E	Definite article. Word used to indicate that a noun or equivalent follows. Function word.
T	H	O	Although, though.
T	H	Y	Belonging to thou. (Biblical or poetic language). Your.
T	I	B	Courtesan. Fancy woman.
T	I	C	Convulsive muscle movement. Nervous twitch. Spasm.
T	I	D	Young girl. Seasonal.
T	I	E	Bond, knot, ligament, link. Fasten, fastening. Attachment. Draw, stalemate. Anchor, moor. Band, gird.
T	I	G	Annoy, tease, pester.
T	I	N	Metal. Tinplate. Box, can, pan. Preserve. Place in cans.
T	I	P	Point, apex. Slant, incline, lean, list, tilt. Overturn, overthrow, topple, upset. Largesse, gratuity, bonus.
T	I	S	It is. It's.
T	I	T	Breast, teat. Small long-tailed bird. Young woman. Hussy. Tit mouse.
T	O	A	Tall tree.
T	O	D	Unit of wool weight.
T	O	E	Terminal digital of vertebrate's foot. Terminal segment of invertebrate's limb. Digital extimity.
T	O	G	Dress up. Smarten, spruce up. Clothing, garment.
T	O	M	Male of various animals. Male cat. Male turkey. (sl.) Money.
T	O	N	Unit of weight. Large quantity. Lot, heap. Vogue, smartness, style, fashion. 100 m.p.h.
T	O	O	As well, additionally, likewise, moreover, extremely, also. Overmuch, unduly.
T	O	P	Summit, crown, crest, maximum, choice. Dominate, excel, surpass, outdo. Chief. Child's spinning toy.
T	O	R	High craggy hill. Rocky pinnacle. Peak.
T	O	T	Add up. Totalise. Small child. Toddler. Nip, dram, slug, snifter.
T	O	W	Haul, drag, pull. Rope or chain for pulling. Something that tows. Tugboat, Towboat.
T	O	Y	Child's plaything. Games, dolls. Bauble, curio, gew gaw, novelty, trifle, trinket. Fiddle, tease, cuddle, pet.
T	R	Y	To be tested. Put to the test. Appraise, judge, weigh, inspect, scrutinise. Distress, harrass, strain, stress.
T	U	B	Bath, barrel, bathtub, basin. Bathe, wash.
T	U	G	Drag, draw, haul, lug, tow, pull. Contend, strain, strive. Powerful boat used at sea.
T	U	N	Cask, barrel, hog's head, keg, vat.
T	U	P	Be ready. Come on heat, copulate. Ram. Cuckold.
T	U	R	Caucasian goat. Pigeon Pea. Pigeon pie.
T	U	T	Game of ball. Rounders. Expression of disapproval or annoyance.
T	W	O	One more than one. Pair.
T	Y	E	Chain, rope used in sailing. Piece of enclosed land. Large pasture. Common pasturage.
T	Y	G	Ceramic drinking cup.
T	Y	R	Cheese.

U

U	C	A	Genus of Fiddler Crabs.
U	D	I	Caucasic language. Unilateral Declaration of Independence.
U	D	O	Japanese herb. Vegetable.
U	F	O	Unidentified Flying Object. Flying Saucer.
U	G	H	Expression of disgust.
U	K	E	Ukulele.
U	L	A	Gums.
U	L	T	Ultimo.
U	M	A	American lizard.
U	M	P	Umpire. Arbitrator.
U	N	G	Unction, ointment, Oil.
U	N	I	One, single.
U	N	O	United Nations Organisation.
U	N	T	European Mole.
U	R	A	Having a tail.
U	R	E	Use, custom, practice, exercise. Raincloud, Mist, Haze.
U	R	N	Vase, vessel. Ornament.
U	S	E	Practice of using something. Employment, application, operation. Appropriate, applicable, fitness, utility.
U	S	T	Appropriate, applicable, fitness, utility, benefit, value. Custom, habit, manner.

1	2	3	
U	T	U	Maori law.
U	V	A	Pulpy fruit. Grape.

V

V	A	C	Vacation (abbreviation).
V	A	D	Voluntary Aid Detachment.
V	A	G	Vagrant, homeless.
V	A	N	Wagon, motortruck, caravan.
V	A	R	Reactive volt ampere unit.
V	A	S	Duct, channel, vessel. Pledge for another's appearance in Court.
V	A	T	Barrel, tub, bath, large vessel, tank.
V	E	T	Veterinarian. Medical care for animals. To inspect, to examine.
V	E	X	Bother, annoy, provoke, irk. Anger, infuriate.
V	I	A	A route. By way of, through, along, over. Approach. Per, with. By dint of.
V	I	E	Contend, contest, rival, complete, challenge, match. Oppose, compete.
V	I	M	Vigor, animation, dash, elan, life, verve, spirit.
V	I	P	Very important person. Big shot. Big Wheel. Leader, notable. V.I.P.
V	I	S	Force, power.
V	I	Z	Namely.
V	O	E	Fiord, estuary, firth.
V	O	L	Heraldic charge consisting of two conjoined wings.
V	O	R	High frequency system.
V	O	W	Pledge, word of honour, promise. To declare. Make convenant.
V	U	G	Small cavity.
V	U	M	Avow, swear.

W

W	A	D	Bundle of banknotes. Lump of material. Fortune, boodle, packet, role. Reams, chunk, clump, hunk.
W	A	G	Move to and fro. Twitch, wiggle, oscillate, shake, wave. Humorist. Joker, comedian, wit.
W	A	N	Ashen, pale, blanched, colourless, pallid, waxen. Impotent, weak, ineffective.
W	A	P	Strike, whop, blow, knock. Fight. Bind, wrap.
W	A	R	Armed conflict. Battle, Riot. Contend, fight, endeavour, strive, struggle, challenge.
W	A	S	Something that occurred. Past. Past of BE.
W	A	X	Rise, increase, upgrade, grow. Multiply, upsurge, heighten, expand, enlarge.
W	A	Y	Path, road, street, thoroughfare, track, boulevard, avenue, lane, byway, alley. Passage, access, entrance.
W	E	B	Entanglement. Mesh. Toils, Cobweb. Fabric fibre.
W	E	D	Marry, join, combine, conjoin, unite, connect, espouse.
W	E	E	Diminutive, miniature, minute, tiny.
W	E	M	Flaw, stain, scar.
W	E	N	Sebaceous cyst. Excrescence.
W	E	T	Humid, liquid, rainy. Preserve in liquid. Lactating. Damp, dank, saturated. Drenched, sodden, soggy.
W	E	Y	Unit of weight.
W	H	O	Pronoun. What person, which person. Involved person or persons.
W	H	Y	Wherefore. What reason. On account of what.
W	I	G	Manufactured covering for the head made of human hair. Toupee, peruke, periwig. Coiffure, hairpiece.
W	I	N	Gain victory, overcome, prevail, triumph, conquer. Accomplish, achieve, attain, Acquire, earn, get, procure.
W	I	T	Perception, acumen, astuteness, perspicacity, prudence, intelligence, brain power. Mentality, sense.
W	O	E	Anguish, grief, heartache, regret, sorrow, trouble, disaster, calamity, tragedy.
W	O	N	Past of win. Earned, obtained, persuaded, swayed, got, caught, overcame.
W	O	O	Pursue, sue, solicit, plead, make love.
W	O	P	Bold, handsome, dandy.
W	O	T	To know. Knowledge.
W	O	W	Exclamation of pleasure. Sensational hit. Excite admiration. Whine.
W	R	Y	Cynical, ironic, sardonic. Wrest, wrench, wring. Contorted, awry.
W	Y	E	Resembling the letter Y.

Y

Y	A	B	Talk, language. Pimple.
Y	A	D	Pointed finger. Guide.
Y	A	K	Tibetan Ox. Idle chatter, yammer, joke, gag, chatter.
Y	A	M	Edible tuberous root. Sweet potato.

1	2	3	
Y	A	P	Chatter, scold, yip, yelp, bark.
Y	A	W	Deviation, swerve, gape, yawn. Lurch, pitch, tilt, tack, turn.
Y	E	A	Assent, affirmation, yes, aye.
Y	E	N	Longing, urge, craving, Japanese monetary unit.
Y	E	P	Agreement, yes, okay.
Y	E	S	Expression of assent, agreement, understanding or acceptance.
Y	E	T	As well, also, even, still. At some future time, eventually, finally, some time, later. Additionally. Though.
Y	E	W	Genus of Tree. Shrub.
Y	I	P	Howl, squeal, yell, yowl.
Y	O	B	Rustic, bumpkin, clodhopper, yahoo. Hick, hill billy.
Y	O	N	Further, yonder, there, beyond.
Y	O	U	Pronoun of the second person. Person being addressed. Yourself, yourselves. Yours.

Z

Z	A	G	Sharp turn, angle, zig (zag).
Z	A	P	Vim, vigor, get up and go, Expression of elation. Slap. Swat.
Z	A	X	Roofing tool.
Z	E	A	Genus of large grass. Indian corn.
Z	E	E	The letter ZED.
Z	E	N	Buddhism. Religious meditation.
Z	I	P	Manufactured fastener. Energy, vim, snap, force, dash. Close/open with zipper. Hasten, hurry, bustle.
Z	O	H	Hybrid Yak and domestic Cow.
Z	O	O	Zoological Garden. Selection of living animals on public display (sl.) Overcrowded, topsy turvy place.
Z	Y	G	Yoke, union, fusion.
Z	Y	M	Leaven. Ferment, Enzyme.

| 1 | 2 | 3 | 4 |

A

A B B A	Title of honour, Father.
A B B E	French Abbot. Priest.
A B E D	In bed.
A B E T	Aid, incite, favour, countenance. Stir up. egg, exhort, goad, advocate, encourage. Help, assist.
A B L E	Possessed of high level of efficiency. Ability. Capable, competent, efficient, expert. Skilled, Alert.
A B L Y	Masterfully, powerfully, cleverly.
A B U T	Adjoin, join, touch. Border, butt, Terminate, lean, rest, support.
A C C A	Brocade of gold and silk.
A C E R	Genus of Tree. Box Elder, Maple.
A C H E	Hurt, misery, twinge, pain, suffer, crave, hanker, long, lust, pine, yearn.
A C I D	Tart, bitter, vitriolic, sour. Dry.
A C M E	Appogee, climax, meridian, peak, pinnacle, summit, zenith, apex.
A C N E	Skin eruption. Pimples.
A C O U	Hearing, listening.
A C R E	Arable land, pasturage. Estate. Unit of Area, broad expanse, large quantity. 4840 sq ft.
A C T A	Transactions, official acts. Recorded proceedings, narratives.
A C Y L	Carboxylic acid radical.
A D A D	Pilewort fibre.
A D A M	First Man of the Human Race (Biblical). 18th Century Furniture style. Ornamental style of architecture.
A D E N	Gland. Glandular.
A D I T	Horizontal opening to mine. Tunnel, shaft, level, gallery, incline, approach, access.
A D Z E	Cutting tool, mattock.
A E O N	Age, era, cycle, period, eon. Blue Moon. Donkey's Years.
A E R O	Relating to aircraft.
A E R Y	Dwelling place high up. Ethereral.
A F A R	Far away. Distant, remote, aloof.
A G A R	Extract of red algae used in jelly and the canning industry.
A G E D	Old, elderly, ancient, antiquated. Antediluvian, matured, ripened. Ripe.
A G E E	Askew, obliquely.
A G H A	Title of respect.
A G I O	Premium, percentage, money changing. Brokerage.
A G O G	Anxious, impatient, keen, ardent, eager, excited, roused.
A G O N	Gathering, assembly, contest.
A G U A	Large toad.
A G U E	Fever, paroxysm, shivering.
A H E M	Sound used to attract attention by clearing the throat.
A H O Y	To hail. A seafaring term.
A I D E	Nurse. Assistant. A writ at law.
A I L S	Plural of ail. Ills.
A I M S	Purposes, designs, plans.
A I N T	Are not (sl.)
A I R A	Genus of annual grasses.
A I R E	Nobleman, Chief.
A I R Y	Relating to air. Atmospheric. Vaporous. Breezy. Spacious. Blythe, ethereal.
A J A R	Slightly open. Half closed.
A J O G	Jogging.
A K E E	Tree with purportedly deadly poisonous seeds.
A K I N	Like, related, allied, similar, uniform, comparable, corresponding.
A L A R	Resembling a wing. Belonging to the axle. Axilliary.
A L A S	Alack. Exclamation of Dismay.
A L B E	Albeit. Even though.
A L C A	Genus of Auk.
A L F A	Grass. Esparto. Code word for alphabetic letter A.
A L G A	Plant of the Algae group. Fungi.
A L L O	Closely related. Isomeric. All.
A L L Y	Kinsman, relative, associate. Allied. Supporter, friend.
A L M S	Charitable donation. Offering, contribution, gift, bounty.
A L O D	Real estate. Land.
A L O E	Genus of succulent plant.
A L P S	Mountainous region in Europe.
A L S O	As well. In the same manner. Correspondingly, likewise, similarly. Additionally. Besides, furthermore.
A L T O	Male voice of the highest pitch. Falsetto. High pitched.
A L U M	Sulfates of Aluminium. Sweetish sourish astringent taste.

1	2	3	4	
A	M	A	H	Indian Nurse. Ayah. Chinese female servant. Wet nurse.
A	M	A	N	Long stemmed rice.
A	M	B	O	Pulpit, reading desk.
A	M	E	N	So be it. Solemn ratification of faith. Hearty approval. Conclusion of Prayer.
A	M	I	A	Genus of fish.
A	M	I	D	In the midst of. In the middle. Surrounded by. Among, during.
A	M	M	O	Ammunition.
A	M	O	K	In a frenzy. Amuck.
A	M	Y	L	Starch.
A	N	A	L	Relating to the Anus.
A	N	B	A	Coptic title. Father.
A	N	E	R	Male in sect. Male ant.
A	N	E	W	Afresh, again, once more, over. Lately, newly, of late, recently.
A	N	K	H	Figure like a cross with upper loop. Handled Cross. Key of Life.
A	N	N	A	Unit of monetary value.
A	N	O	A	Straight horned Buffalo. Wild Ox.
A	N	O	N	Anonymous. At one. Again.
A	N	T	E	Price, wager. Pay, produce. Before.
A	N	T	I	Against, opposed to, opposing, rival. Trans.
A	N	U	S	Opening of alimentary canal. Ring.
A	P	E	D	Copied, imitated, mimiced.
A	P	E	R	Impersonator, one who copies.
A	P	E	X	Acme, zenith, pinnacle, crest, crown, summit, roof. Appogee, climax peak. Point, tip, spire.
A	P	I	S	Honey Bee.
A	P	S	E	Projecting part of building. Vault, Arch.
A	Q	U	A	Water, liquid.
A	R	A	B	Member of Arabian people. Member of Arabic speaking people. Type of Horse. Relating to arabs.
A	R	A	C	Oriental palm spirit, sap.
A	R	C	A	Chest, box, receptacle for money. Sacred Receptacle. Genus of Bivalve Mollusc.
A	R	C	H	Part of a curve. Curved structure. Span of a Bridge. Principal, Chief. Roguish, saucy.
A	R	E	A	Extent of surface. Earth's surface. Belt, region, territory, tract, zone, district. Lot, plot, section, terrain.
A	R	I	A	Air, tune, melody. Song recital.
A	R	I	D	Dry, parched, barren, sterile, dull, dusty. Insipid, tedious. Drab, lack lustre.
A	R	I	L	Raisin. Grape seed.
A	R	M	S	Guns, ammunition, weapons of War. Firearms. Human upper limbs.
A	R	M	Y	Large organised fighting force. Defenders, troops, military organisation.
A	R	N	A	Wild water Buffalo.
A	R	S	E	Ass. Bottom. Backside.
A	R	T	S	Plural of Art. Decorative designs. handicraft, skills, crafts.
A	R	T	Y	Free thinking. Having showy characteristics. Pretentious.
A	R	U	M	Genus of Lily.
A	R	Y	L	Alkyl radical. Benzyl.
A	S	H	Y	Covered in ash. Wan, pallid.
A	S	I	A	Largest continent in the World.
A	T	O	M	Marine life.
A	T	O	M	Minute particle. Molecule, mite, particle.
A	T	O	P	Positioned at the top.
A	U	L	D	Old.
A	U	N	E	Unit of measurement.
A	U	N	T	Sister of one's father or mother. Wife of one's uncle. Term of endearment.
A	U	R	A	Mood, feeling, semblancé, atmosphere, air, appearance, halo, radiance, aspect.
A	U	T	O	Motor car, automobile. Car. Self-propelling.
A	V	A	L	Endorsement on a Bill, Security.
A	V	E	R	Affirm, declare, profess, protest, assert, vouch, verify.
A	V	E	S	All classes of Birds.
A	V	I	D	Eager, greedy, ardent, breathless, impatient, keen, desirous, craving, covetous.
A	V	O	W	Assert, declare, claim, acknowledge.
A	W	A	Y	Onward, hence, thence, departed, distant. Opponent's venue.
A	W	E	D	Reverent, inspired, frightened, terrified, cowed.
A	W	N	Y	Hairy. Covered in Beard.
A	W	O	L	Absent without Leave. A.W.O.L.
A	W	R	Y	Deviating from a straight line, Askew, crooked, astray, unfavourably. Wrong, faulty.
A	X	E	D	Chopped, felled. Discharged, dismissed, curtailed, impaired, Curtailed.
A	X	E	L	Spindle, shaft, axis.
A	X	I	S	Straight line about which a body, figure or system rotates. Second vertebra of neck.
A	X	O	N	Nerve cell. Nerve fibre.
A	Y	A	H	Amah, Wet Nurse, Female Servant.

1	2	3	4	
A	Y	E	S	Supporting votes in favour of.
A	Z	O	N	Radio controlled aerial bomb.

B

B	A	A	L	Idol, false god, deity.
B	A	A	S	Boss (South African), Master.
B	A	B	A	Baby, child. Fruit cake soaked in rum.
B	A	B	E	Infant, baby. (Sl.) Girl, woman, doll.
B	A	B	U	Indian Clerk.
B	A	B	Y	Infant, suckling. Small, diminutive. Humour, indulge, (sl.) Girl sweetheart.
B	A	C	K	Opposite to front. Spinal column, backbone, spine. Backward, reversed, hind. Hindmost, rear, posterior.
B	A	D	E	Past of Bid. Commanded.
B	A	F	F	Blow, strike, thud. Biff.
B	A	F	T	Astern, abaft. Behind, aft.
B	A	G	S	Plural of Bag.
B	A	H	R	Body of water, lake, river, sea.
B	A	I	L	Security, obligation for release of prisoner, custody. To deliver. Hoop, handle. Dip and throw. Escape.
B	A	I	T	Persecute, hound, tease, badger. Lure for fish or animals. Hook, trap.
B	A	K	E	Cook, dry or harden subject to heat. Prepare food in oven. Broil, roast.
B	A	L	D	Hairless, smooth, shaven, cropped, clipped. Sparse plain, meagre. Undisguised, outright.
B	A	L	E	Harm, disaster. Torment, woe, sorrow. Bundle bound with cord, wire, or hoops.
B	A	L	K	Timber, baffle. Bilk, disappoint, thwart, frustrate, jib, shy, stumble, demur, flinch.
B	A	L	L	Spherical body or mass. Globe, orb, round sphere. Form into rounds. (sl.) Party, rout, carouse, revelry.
B	A	L	M	Cream, salve, unction, ointment. Incence, perfume, scent, fragrance. Lull, quiet. Compose, calm.
B	A	N	D	Bando, ribbon, strip, stripe, border, edge, girdle, belt. Combine, conjoin, unite. Group, detachment.
B	A	N	E	Venom, virus, poison, destruction, ruin, ruination, undoing, downfall.
B	A	N	G	Loud noise, explosive sound. Blast, burst, clap, crash, boom, report, explosion. Vigor, drive, vim, pep.
B	A	N	K	Place where money is kept safely. To place in bank. Deposit. Coast, beach, shore. Mound, hill, heap.
B	A	N	T	Reduce, diet.
B	A	R	B	Shaft, dart, hook.
B	A	R	D	Poet, singer, minstrel, troubador. Muse.
B	A	R	E	Naked, nude, bald. Stripped, uncovered, hairless, unclad, unclothed. Arid, bleak. Desolate, void.
B	A	R	F	Disgorge, heave, spew, puke, vomit.
B	A	R	K	Snarl, yap, snap, yelp. Boat, sailing ship. Outer layer of tree stem.
B	A	R	M	Yeast, fermentation.
B	A	R	N	Farm building, storage place. Store room, stable. Granary, outbuilding.
B	A	R	T	Baronet.
B	A	S	E	Basis, foundation, infrastructure, bedrock, grounds. Prop, stand, stay, support. Humble, low, mean.
B	A	S	H	Bat, slam, smack, wallop, wack, blow. Shindig, shindy.
B	A	S	K	Luxuriate, revel, frolic, wallow, sun, insulate.
B	A	S	S	Deep tone, low pitched sound. Freshwater fish, perch, trout.
B	A	T	E	Ease off, fall away, abate, die down, subside, wane, decrease diminish, exclude debar.
B	A	T	H	Wash, soak in water, bathe. Receptacle in which to bath. Vessel, swimming pool. Hydro, spring.
B	A	U	D	Telegraphic transmission speed unit.
B	A	W	D	Bold, madam, prostitute.
B	A	W	L	Bellow, clamour, bluster, roar, shout, shriek, cry, weep, sob, blubber.
B	A	W	N	Fortified castle, farm house, cattle pen.
B	A	Y	A	Weaver bird.
B	E	A	D	Round pierced stone, shell, wood, metal or other material threaded on cord. Pearl, drop, knob.
B	E	A	K	Pecker, nib, bill, proboscis, snout, promontory, headland, point, Magistrate, Judge.
B	E	A	M	Baulk, timber, shaft, ray. Gleam, radiate, shine. Behind, bottom, buttocks.
B	E	A	N	Lentil, vegetable, seed.
B	E	A	R	Large shaggy mammal. Behave, conduct, deport, manage, wield, exercise, cherish. Lead, desport.
B	E	A	T	Strike repeatedly. Batter, buffet, pound, whip, thrash. Surpass, better, exceed, excel. Outdo, outstrip.
B	E	A	U	Boyfriend, young man, beloved, flame, lover, sweetheart, suitor.
B	E	C	K	Small stream, gesture, signal, bow, curtsy, nod.
B	E	E	F	Flesh of the steer, cow or other adult bovine animal. Ox, cow, bull. Brawl, dispute, quarrel, gripe, bitch.
B	E	E	N	Past of BE.
B	E	E	P	Sound from a horn. High pitched note. Signal.
B	E	E	R	Alcoholic beverage. Ale, lager, porter.
B	E	E	T	Biennial plant with bulbous root. Beetroot. Sugarbeet.
B	E	G	S	Seeks alms, entreats, requests.
B	E	I	N	Comfortable, well off, well found.
B	E	L	L	Metallic device giving out a ringing sound. Chime, signal.
B	E	L	T	Girdle, sash, waistband. Region, territory, area. Encircle, ring, surround. Thrash, clobber, wallop.

1	2	3	4	
B	E	N	D	Curve, crook, bow, curl, double over, hook, arch, incline, Dispose, deviation, turn. Angle, turning.
B	E	N	T	Curved, changed shape, angled. Bound, determined, inclination, disposition, capacity.
B	E	R	G	Mountain, Iceberg.
B	E	R	M	Narrow shelf. edge, slope.
B	E	S	T	Choicest, prime, elite, prize, top. Beat, better, exceed, excel, surpass. Greater, largest, most.
B	E	T	A	Second letter of Greek Alphabet.
B	E	V	Y	Assembly, bunch, group, party, covey.
B	I	A	S	Disposition, inclination, leaning, partiality, prejudice. Slant, diagonal. Oblique.
B	I	D	E	Linger, remain, tarry, stay. Dwell, live.
B	I	E	R	Coffin, sepulchre, grave.
B	I	F	F	Wack, blow, sock.
B	I	K	E	Bicycle, cycle. To ride a bicycle.
B	I	L	E	Alkaline fluid secreted by liver. Ill-humour, irascibility, spleen.
B	I	L	K	Frustrate. Depart without making due payment.
B	I	L	L	Beak, nib. mouthpart of a bird. Statement, account, written advertisement. Announcement.
B	I	N	D	Tie, fasten, restrain, secure.
B	I	N	G	Storage bin.
B	I	N	T	(Sl.) Girl, woman, dame.
B	I	O	S	Mixture of vitamins.
B	I	R	D	Member of the Class Aves. Feathered vertebrate. Domestic poultry. Fowl. Boo off-stage.
B	I	R	K	Birch.
B	I	R	R	Impetus, rush.
B	I	S	E	Cold wind, gust.
B	I	T	E	Seize with teeth, champ, chomp, gnaw, nibble, chew, masticate, munch. Wear away, eat, corrode.
B	L	A	B	Disclose, divulge, tell tales, betray, gossip, chatter, jabber.
B	L	E	B	Serum-containing cuticle. Blister, bubble.
B	L	E	D	Past of bleed.
B	L	E	E	Hue, colour, complexion. Colouring.
B	L	E	W	Past of BLOW. Sounded, puffed, panted.
B	L	I	P	Short crisp sound. Image on Radar Screen.
B	L	O	B	Spot of colour. Lump of something, globule, drop. Blister, bubble, splotch, blot.
B	L	O	C	Coalition, combine, faction, party. Ring, combination.
B	L	O	T	Stain, smut, slur, flaw, defeat, stigma. Mar, blur, tarnish. Erase.
B	L	O	W	Produce current of air. Wind, fan, ruffle, gasp, huff, pant. Punch, slap, buffet. Impact, assault. Bloom.
B	L	U	B	Sob, wail, weep, cry, blue.
B	L	U	E	Colour, depressed, downhearted. Off colour, racy, spicy, shady, risque. Ocean, brine, briny. Pornographic.
B	L	U	R	Blemish, blot, smear, sully, stain, taint. Confuse, cloud, fog.
B	O	A	R	Uncastrated male swine. Hog.
B	O	A	T	Water craft. Vessel, ship, canoe. Gravy boat.
B	O	D	E	Fortell, portend, Messenger, herald.
B	O	D	Y	Physical organism, person. Human being. Man, mortal. Essential part. Core, mass, essence. Whole.
B	O	E	R	South African descendant of the Early Dutch Settlers.
B	O	I	L	Generate heat. Bring to boiling point. Cook in boiling water. Churn, erupt. Abscess, carbuncle, ulcer.
B	O	K	E	Vomit, wretch, belch, burp.
B	O	L	D	Intrepid, venturesome, forward, rude, impudent. Free, daring, Eye catching, arresting.
B	O	L	E	Tree Trunk, cylindrically shaped object.
B	O	L	L	Pod, capsule.
B	O	L	O	Machette, cut, hack.
B	O	L	T	Nut, rivet, screw. Shackle, fetter. Dash, escape. Perpendicularly, straight. Length of cloth. Gobble.
B	O	M	B	Projectile, explosive. To attack with bombs. Bombard.
B	O	N	D	Chain, fetter, shackle. Agreement, pact, transaction, contract, binding element. Knot, link, connection.
B	O	N	E	Hard tissue, rigid matter, part of the skeleton, framework, Bodily support for flesh.
B	O	N	Y	Full of bones, skeletal, thin, skinny, scrawny, lean, spare. Bone-like.
B	O	O	B	Make a mistake. Goof, dupe. Dunce, chump, dolt, goon.
B	O	O	K	Written document, collection of written sheets. Indict, charge.
B	O	O	M	Prosperity. Blast, burst, bang.
B	O	O	N	Benevolence, favour, present, gift, benefit, advantage, blessing. Jolly, jovial, merry.
B	O	O	R	Uncouth fellow. Churl, clodhopper, vulgarian, rustic.
B	O	O	T	Leather foot covering varying in height between ankle and hip. Trunk. Throw out, kick out, evict.
B	O	R	E	Drill, perforate. Gape, gaze, gawk. Ennui, pall, tire. Pierce, penetrate. Interior tube of gun, chamber.
B	O	R	N	Brought into existence, given life. Natural, innate.
B	O	S	H	Nonsense, balderdash, claptrap, bunkum.
B	O	S	S	Chief, headman, master, Head, foreman, leader. Famous, fine, first rate. Supervise, chaperone.
B	O	T	H	One and the other. Two.
B	O	U	T	Turn, time, occasion. Outburst, attack. Session, contest. Steep, soak.
B	O	W	L	Throw or toss a ball. Sphere, globe. Basin, hollow vessel, container. Beaker, goblet.
B	O	W	S	Fore-end of a ship. Plural of Bow.

1	2	3	4	
B	O	Y	G	Ogre, bugbear, obstacle, problem.
B	R	A	D	Boy, lad. Wire nail. Nail with countersunk head.
B	O	Y	S	Plural of boy.
B	R	A	G	Boast, swagger, strut, pretend.
B	R	A	N	Separated Wheat, Rye or other Cereal. Food by-product.
B	R	A	T	Child, offspring. Upstart, urchin.
B	R	A	Y	Donkey's cry. Discordant noise. Clamour, blare.
B	R	E	D	Reared, raised, nurtured.
B	R	E	E	Eyebrow. Liquor.
B	R	E	R	Brother.
B	R	E	T	Turbot.
B	R	E	W	Concoction, beverage, mixture. Prepare beer, tea. Bring about trouble. Gather. Impend.
B	R	I	E	Soft cheese.
B	R	I	G	Square rigged ship. Place of confinement, guardhouse, prison. Brigantine.
B	R	I	M	Overflow, brink, edge, margin, rim, depression, brim of a hat.
B	R	I	O	Vivacity, spirit, fire.
B	R	I	T	Minute marine animal. Crustacean. Whale feed.
B	R	O	B	Spike, wedge.
B	R	O	W	Forehead, eyebrow. Mien, intellectual capacity. Hilltop, steep place, slope.
B	U	A	L	Madeira wine.
B	U	B	O	Swollen lymph gland in groin. Genus of horned owl.
B	U	C	K	Male deer or antelope. He-goat. Male of four-footed mammals. Human male, man. Male Negro. Dollar.
B	U	F	F	Polish, shine. Colour orange yellow. Nude, naked, bare skin. Fan, enthusiast.
B	U	L	B	Bulbous plant. Fleshy root. Tuber. Turnip. Lamp, light bulb. Camera shutter.
B	U	L	K	Mass, volume, magnitude.
B	U	L	L	Sexually mature uncastrated male animal. Large clumsy person. (sl.) Policeman. Talk bull, talk rubbish.
B	U	M	P	To meet forcibly. Clash, collide, crash. Impact, jar, jolt. Swollen tissue. Lump. Knot, protuberance.
B	U	N	D	Federation, league, association.
B	U	N	T	Butt, jolt, push, shove. Furled sail. Buoy, beacon, float. Support, sustain, raise.
B	U	R	G	City, town. Unimportant village.
B	U	R	L	Woody growth in tree trunks. Mottled grain. Tie in loose ends.
B	U	R	N	Set on fire, give off light. Injury produced by burning. Beam, gleam, radiate. Scorch, toast, char, singe.
B	U	R	R	Speak with trilled uvular 'r'. Uncouth pronunciation. Rough prickly husk. Plant debris in raw wool.
B	U	R	Y	Deposit in earth. Entomb, inter, Cover from view. Put out of sight. Conceal. Submerge, engross.
B	U	S	H	Shrub, forest, Woods, jungle, wilderness, uncultivated area, backcountry. Unkempt beard.
B	U	S	K	Entertain by singing or reciting in public place. Act in the street.
B	U	S	S	Kiss. Herring boat.
B	U	S	T	Breast, chest. Part of woman's garment. Fracture, break. Punch, sock. Bender, binge, spree. Bankrupt.
B	U	S	Y	Occupied, engaged, active, bustling, industrious, assiduous, diligent, meddling.
B	U	T	T	Blow with head or horns, thrust, target, range, Laughing stock, victim. Cigarette end, stub. Rifle stock.
B	U	Z	Z	Drone of insect. Confused noise. Act ineffectually. Signal with buzzer. Dart, whizz. Flutter, stir, rumour.
B	Y	R	E	Cottage, dwelling, stable.

C

1	2	3	4	
C	A	D	E	Barrel, cask, keg. Pet animal. Procession, spectacle.
C	A	F	E	Tea Room, Coffee House, Restaurant, cafeteria. Lunch Room, Corner Shop.
C	A	G	E	Enclosure, barred cell, fenced area, framework, confine, coop, envelope, hem, pen. Incarcerate.
C	A	I	D	Alcaide. Muslim Judge. Tax Collector.
C	A	I	N	Eldest son of Adam. The first murderer. Trouble, disturbance, uproar.
C	A	K	E	Varieties of sweet breads. Fancy baked dough. Block. Encrust, besmear, coat, spread. Daub, congeal.
C	A	L	F	Fleshy hind part of leg. Young of various large animals. Awkward boy. Leather.
C	A	L	L	Shout, yell, holler, challenge, demand, summon, convene, assemble, phone, buzz, Ring up, telephone.
C	A	L	M	Still, serene, placid, tranquil, peaceful, self assured. Unmoved, stillness, quietude.
C	A	L	X	Chalk or lime.
C	A	M	E	Past of come. Arrived, reached, attained.
C	A	M	P	Encampment, outdoor dwelling, temporary shelter, group of tents, large field. Division within a group.
C	A	N	E	Rattan, wicker, bamboo. Sugar cane. Sorghum. Walking stick, rod; Punish with rod.
C	A	N	T	Bevel, tilt, incline, lean; Sing, chant. Cannot.
C	A	P	E	Sleeveless garment, cloak. Promontory, headland, point.
C	A	R	D	Playing card, compass card, programme, score card, menu, calendar, docket. Time table, schedule.
C	A	R	E	Heartache, sorrow, grief, strain, tension, stress, anxiety, worry. Safe keeping, nurse, tend. Vex, worry.
C	A	R	L	Churl, snarl.
C	A	R	P	Nag, fuss, wrangle, criticise.
C	A	R	R	Marsh, fen, alder grove.
C	A	R	T	Vehicle, wagon, carry, convey, lift, transport.

1	2	3	4	
C	A	S	E	Receptacle, box, suitcase, Case history, example, illustration, instance, event. Husk, hull, pod.
C	A	S	H	Money, legal tender. Dough, bread, tom. Exchange Promisory Notes for money.
C	A	S	K	Keg, barrel, butt, Hogshead.
C	A	S	T	Hurl, heave, pitch, toss, throw. Scatter, Jettison, discard. Relinquish, yield. Form, figure, mould.
C	A	T	E	Dainty food.
C	A	U	F	Live fish box.
C	A	U	L	Membrane, net covering, foetal membrane.
C	A	V	E	Underground chamber, grotto, cavern. Buckle, capitulate, succumb, yield, collapse.
C	A	V	Y	Rodent, guinea pig.
C	A	W	K	Chalk, limestone. Barite. Mate.
C	E	D	E	Abandon, hand over, resign, relinquish, surrender, transfer, assign, sign.
C	E	I	L	Roof, ceiling.
C	E	L	L	Dungeon, cavity, nucleus, unit.
C	E	L	T	Descendant of Early Europeans.
C	E	N	T	Unit of Money. Coin.
C	E	R	E	To wax. Wrape in cere cloth.
C	E	R	T	Certainty, sure thing.
C	E	S	S	Tax, levy, assessment, luck.
C	E	S	T	Cestus, belt, band, bridal girdle.
C	H	A	D	Sea Bream.
C	H	A	P	Boy, fellow, gentleman, lad, guy. Split, crack, blanch.
C	H	A	R	Burn, sizzle, toast, broil, braai. Cleaning woman, charwoman. Tea.
C	H	A	T	Gossip, prattle, chatter, yak. Conversation, dialogue.
C	H	A	Y	Chaise, open carriage. Dye yielding root.
C	H	E	F	Man skilled at food preparation. Cook.
C	H	E	W	Masticate, munch, crunch, gnaw, devour, eat. Ball out, scold.
C	H	I	C	Stylish, modish, charm, vogue, fashion.
C	H	I	N	Lower portion of face. Jaw. Chinwag, chat.
C	H	I	P	Fragment, flake, coin, unit, countermoney. Flaw, crack, chap, chop, hack. Potato flake, potato crisp.
C	H	I	T	Note, Memo, Voucher, memorandum. Notation. Youngster, kid, juvenile, child.
C	H	O	P	Cut, swipe, trade, swap, exchange, barter. Mouth, jowl, cut of meat, slice.
C	H	O	W	Food, victuals, eat; Type of dog of Chinese origin.
C	H	U	B	Fresh water fish. Black bass. Lake Herring.
C	H	U	G	Puff, pull, jerk, chuff.
C	H	U	M	Companion, comrade, crony, pal, associate.
C	I	N	E	Motion picture, film, bioscope.
C	I	R	E	Glazed fabric.
C	I	T	E	Name, specify, adduce, advance, allege, enumerate, number, tell, remind, remember.
C	I	T	Y	Populous place, Place larger than village or town. Important Centre. Radio City.
C	L	A	D	Clothed, decked, sheathed, covered. Sheathe, face.
C	L	A	M	Edible marine mollusc. To harvest clams. Adhere, stick to. Clamp, constrict.
C	L	A	N	Family, clique, set. Tribe, Race, lineage.
C	L	A	P	Strike together, applaud. Cheer, Slam, crash. Gonorrhoea. Bovine mastitis.
C	L	A	W	Tear, scratch, clutch, scrabble. Pincer like organs. Sharp nails on toe. Talon. Organs needed to grasp.
C	L	A	Y	Malleable material, wet earth. Nature, ability.
C	L	E	F	Musical key.
C	L	E	G	Horse fly. Gad fly.
C	L	E	M	Starve, hunger.
C	L	I	P	Cut, trim, curtail, prune, pare. Mow, crop. Reduce, lower.
C	L	O	D	Sod, turf, lump, yokel, rustic.
C	L	O	G	Hamper, trammel, obstruct, block.
C	L	O	T	Coagulate, thicken, curdle. Lout, numbskull.
C	L	O	Y	Glut, satiate, surfeit, pall. Sticky.
C	L	U	B	Cudgel, baton, bludgeon, knobkerrie, truncheon. Brotherhood, fellowship, fraternity. Guild, Society.
C	L	U	E	Indication, inkling, intimation, suggestion, hint. Acquaint, advise, inform.
C	O	A	K	Dowel pin, metal bush.
C	O	A	L	Combustible material, cinder, charcoal, anthracite, coke.
C	O	A	T	Outer garment, warm clothing. Spread, finish, protect, enclose. Cover.
C	O	A	X	Cajole, wheedle, persuade. coerce, sweet-talk.
C	O	C	A	Shrub from whose leaves cocaine is obtained.
C	O	C	K	Male domestic fowl. Male bird. Faucet, tap, valve. Winner, victor. Turn, tip, tilt. Rooster, cockerel.
C	O	C	O	Coconut palm.
C	O	D	A	Finale.
C	O	D	E	Digest of rules and laws. Cipher, key, symbol.
C	O	E	D	Co-educational, mixed school for boys and girls.
C	O	I	L	Wind, encircle, roll, twist, spiral.
C	O	I	N	Money, exchange, currency. To make money. Metal money as opposed to paper money.

1	2	3	4	
C	O	I	R	Cordage, coconut fibre.
C	O	I	X	Grass. Job's tears.
C	O	K	E	(Sl.) Cocaine. Cola drink. Fuel derived from coal.
C	O	L	D	Lacking warmth. Not hot. Chilly, Icy, Cool. Unfriendly, aloof, distant.
C	O	L	E	Kale, Cabbage.
C	O	L	L	Embrace, hug.
C	O	L	T	Young horse. Young of certain other animals. Novice, beginner, fledgling, newcomer.
C	O	M	A	Unconsciousness, stupor, torpor, languor.
C	O	M	B	Toothed instrument for separating hair or other fibre. Arrange, scrape, rake. Crest, ridge. Search.
C	O	M	E	Arrive, ensue, attain, reach.
C	O	N	E	Three-cornered sphere. Ice-cream Cone. Fir Cone.
C	O	N	K	Large nose, neb. Strike.
C	O	N	S	Arguments against the pros.
C	O	O	K	Prepare food with heat. Chef. Improvise, concoct. Falsify.
C	O	O	L	Cold, frosty, chilly, tepid. Calm, placid, serene, tranquil. Imperturbable, nonchalant. Sensational.
C	O	O	M	Coal-dust, dust of various kinds. The wooden centering on which a bridge is built. Anything arched or vaulted.
C	O	O	N	Raccoon. Filch, snitch, steal. Chinese.
C	O	O	P	Envelope, fence, enclose. Hen-house, enclosure, hock, fowl run. Imprison, jail.
C	O	O	T	Water fowl, duck.
C	O	P	E	Succeed, combat, maintain, handle, contend. Brick structure.
C	O	P	T	Christian Egyptian.
C	O	P	Y	Reproduce, duplicate, fake, mock; Reproduction, facsimile, replica. Impression, Imprint, image.
C	O	R	D	String, braid, rope, line. Nerve, tendon.
C	O	R	E	Centre, heart, kernel. Basis, foundation, substance. Origin, upshot.
C	O	R	K	Bottle top, stopper, seal, bung.
C	O	R	M	Underground stem, tuber. Crocus.
C	O	R	N	Grain, wheat, oats, cereal. To preserve, to salt. Horny epidermal outcrop. Trite, unoriginal.
C	O	S	H	Weighted weapon, black jack, knobkerrie, shillelagh, Slug, strike.
C	O	S	T	Price, outlay, charge, rate, tariff, expense, expenditure.
C	O	T	E	House, hut, shed, coop.
C	O	U	P	Exploit, successful action, plan or stratagem. Clever device, coup d'etat.
C	O	V	E	Cavern, inlet, bay, shelter, basin. (sl.) Chap, fellow, bloke.
C	O	W	L	Monk's hood. Cape. Head covering. Draped neckline. Engine covering. Revolving chimney top.
C	O	X	A	Hip joint. Hip.
C	O	X	Y	Cocksure, bumptious.
C	O	Z	E	Make cosy, chat, intimate talk.
C	O	Z	Y	Snug, comfortable, warm.
C	R	A	B	Crustacean, shy creature. Winch, scuttle, scurry. Nag, petulant, peevish. Grouse.
C	R	A	G	Rocky outcrop. Rugged mountain.
C	R	A	M	Overfeed, stuff. Jam, pack, crush.
C	R	A	N	Measurement of Herrings.
C	R	A	W	Stomach, crop, maw.
C	R	E	E	Soften grain by boiling.
C	R	E	W	Ship's company, sailors, seamen, airmen. Gang, mob, retinue.
C	R	E	X	Genus of bird.
C	R	I	B	Cradle, cot, bed, manger. Copy, plagiarize. Cage, cramp, restrain.
C	R	O	P	Harvest, in-gathering. Reap, cultivate, collection. Trim, excise. Graze, browse. Craw.
C	R	O	W	Black bird, Brag, exult. Corvine. Cry of Rooster.
C	R	O	Y	Barrier, bank, fish shelter.
C	R	U	X	Core, kernel, nub, pitch, substance, gist, matter, purport.
C	U	B	E	Six-sided square, block. Measure, cut into cubes. To the power of three.
C	U	F	F	Wrist band, sleeve band, hem. Handcuff, bracelet. Buffet, slap. Scruff.
C	U	L	L	Choose, pluck. Select, gather. To diminish the number of.
C	U	L	M	Grass stalk, corn stalk. Fodder.
C	U	L	T	Sect, unorthodox religion, ritual, system, programme.
C	U	R	B	Restrain, check, control. Pavement, sidewalk. Chain, strap, halter, guide, mnanage.
C	U	R	D	Coagulated milk.
C	U	R	E	Medicate, restore, improve, ameliorate, heal; Remedy, medication, medicine. Antidote, corrective.
C	U	R	L	Twist, wind, spiral, entwine. Coil, tendril, ringlet. Ripple, wave.
C	U	R	R	Purr, murmur.
C	U	S	K	Edible Marine Fish, burbot, cod.
C	U	S	P	Point, apex. Kink, inset.
C	U	S	S	Curse, swear. Oath, swearword. Obstinate fellow.
C	U	T	E	Ingenious, clever, sharp. Pretty, attractive. Self-conscious. Shrewd, adroit.
C	W	Y	M	Valley, steep basin, glacial erosion.
C	Y	M	E	Cluster, bunch, inflorescence.
C	Y	S	T	Sac, bladder, pouch, capsule, sheath. Growth.

1	2	3	4
C	Z	A	R

CZAR — Emperor, dictator, mogul, prince, tycoon, boss.

D

DABS — Plural of Dab.
DACE — Freshwater Fish.
DADA — Father, Dad, Daddy. Artistic Anarchy.
DADO — Lead, support.
DADO — Pedestal, base. Skirting.
DAFT — Idiotic, absurd, ridiculous.
DAGO — (Sl.) Italian, Spaniard.
DAIS — Platform, terrace, rostrum.
DALE — Valley, vale, glen. Combe.
DAME — Dowager, grande dame.
DAMN — Condemn, doom, penalise. Punish, expel, sentence. Curse, vituperate, swear.
DAMP — Dank, humid, moist, soggy. Clammy.
DANE — Native of Denmark, Great Dane (dog-).
DANG — (Sl.) Damn, blasted, confounded, Darn.
DANK — Damp, clammy, humid, moist.
DARE — Challenge, defy, defiance. Brave, venture, outface, face.
DARK — Gloomy, sombre, unlit, murky. Hidden, cryptic, enigmatic, mystifying. Swarthy, dusky, brunette.
DARN — Mend, sew, stitch. Damned, blasted, infernal.
DART — Barb, shaft. Skim, skud, shoot. Hurry, speed, scamper, scurry.
DASH — Chase, bolt, rush, scamper, spring, Baffle, disappoint, thwart, frustrate. Animation, elan, spirit, vim.
DATA — Facts, case history, reasons, evidence, documentation, references, testimony.
DATE — Specified time, point in time. Period, epoch, age. Appointment, assignation, Rendevous, engagement.
DAUB — Smear, plaster, paint.
DAUW — Burchell's Zebra.
DAVY — Affidavit.
DAWN — First light, sunrise, cock crow, daybreak. Opening, beginning. Understanding, realization.
DAZE — Stun, astound, confuse, amaze.
DDAY — Second World War Invasion date.
DEAD — Deceased, defunct, departed, lifeless, inert, anaesthised, numb, senseless, Obsolete, outmoded, dull.
DEAF — Unable or unwilling to hear.
DEAL — Dispense, divide, distribute, administer, inflict, impart, share out, dole out. Agreement, Pinewood.
DEAN — Guide, leader, chaplain, doyen, office bearer, Head of Faculty.
DEAR — Beloved, darling, Loving, affectionate, fond. Valuable, important, earnest. Expensive, costly.
DEBT — Liability, obligation, indebtedness.
DECK — Platform, floor surface of ships. Adorn, embellish, dress up. Array, clothe.
DEED — Charter, contract, convenant, pact. Transaction, legal document, Achievement, feat. Exploit, action.
DEEM — Consider, hope, expect, believe, suppose.
DEEP — Bottomless, profound, abysmal, secret, sly, astute, arch, cunning. Absorbed, engrossed, intent. rapt.
DEER — Four-footed ruminant mammal. Antelope, elk, moose, reindeer, caribou.
DEFT — Skilful, dextrous, adroit, handy.
DELF — Ditch, drain, pond. Quarry, mine.
DELL — Dale, valley, vale, Ring.
DEMI — Half, semi.
DEMY — Measurement of paper.
DENE — Valley, vale, sandhill.
DENT — Indentation, indent, niche, Headway, progress.
DENY — Repudiate, disclaim, refute, refuse, withhold, restrain, forego, abstain, constrain. Inhibit, avoid, shun.
DERM — Skin, dermis.
DESK — Lectern, table, writing desk, secretaire, escritoire.
DEWY — Moist, fresh, pure, cool, bedewed, innocent, trusting, tearful. Misty.
DHAI — Wet nurse, midwife (Indian nurse).
DHAK — East Indian Tree.
DHAL — Pigeon Pea.
DHOW — Sailing ship, outrigger.
DIAL — Clockface, numbered disc. (Sl. Human face. Manipulate a dial, tune in, control.
DICE — Numbered cube, hexagonal box, hexahedron. Gamble.
DICK — Detective, Sworn declaration.
DIED — Perished, expired, passed away, departed. Passed from life. Deceased.
DIES — Cutting tools, shaping tools, stamps, Matrix, Punches, Printing Plates.
DIET — Rules for eating, regulated food intake, eat sparingly. Fast, sustenance.
DIGS — Lodging, dwelling.
DIKA — Wild mango. Nut.

1	2	3	4	
D	I	L	L	Pickle, herb.
D	I	M	E	Ten cents. Petty sum of money.
D	I	N	E	Take dinner, consume food, feast.
D	I	N	G	Strike, beat, fling, clang, ring.
D	I	N	K	Small boat. Tennis shot. Adorn, trim, neaten.
D	I	N	T	Blow, stroke. Force, power. Impression, imprint.
D	I	O	L	Chemical compound.
D	I	R	E	Awful, disastrous, calamitous. Undesirable.
D	I	R	K	Dagger. short sword.
D	I	R	T	Dust, waste, filth, ground, soil, terra firma, earth. Dishonesty, double dealing.
D	I	S	A	Tropical orchid.
D	I	S	C	Dial, flat round plate, gramophone record.
D	I	S	H	Plate, concave vessel, platter. Distribute. Prepared food. Frustrate, cheat. Meal.
D	I	V	A	Prima donna.
D	I	V	E	Plunge, lunge, leap, spring, bound, pitch. Cheap bar, pub, saloon.
D	O	C	K	Harbour, mooring, wharf, hangar. Abridge, lessen, reduce. Tie up in port. Witness stand, witness box.
D	O	D	A	Four horned antelope.
D	O	D	O	Extinct flightless bird. Simple minded person. Dullard.
D	O	E	R	Performer, agent, executive.
D	O	E	S	Present of do. Plural of DOE.
D	O	F	F	Remove, undress. divest.
D	O	K	E	Dimple, depression.
D	O	L	E	Apportion, deal out, dispense, administer, distribute. Anguish, grief, sorrow. Unemployment money.
D	O	L	L	Puppet, plaything, toy (sl.) woman, girl, sweetheart. Dress up.
D	O	L	T	Dunce, dullard, booby.
D	O	M	E	Vaulted ceiling, roof. Overhead arch, cupola.
D	O	N	E	Transacted, finished, ended. Past of DO.
D	O	N	T	Do not. Command, entreaty, prohibition. Don't.
D	O	O	M	Condemn, sentence, relegate. Destiny, fate, calamity. Judgment.
D	O	O	R	Entrance, portal, way in.
D	O	R	P	Town, village, burg.
D	O	R	Y	Small eyed pike. Flat bottomed boat.
D	O	S	E	Measure of medicine, portion, administer medicine.
D	O	S	S	Sleep, slumber, shake down.
D	O	T	E	Idolize, worship, adore. Like, enjoy.
D	O	U	C	Highly coloured monkey.
D	O	U	P	Weaving heddle. Rounded end of the egg.
D	O	U	R	Stern, relentless, grim. Austere, harsh, stringent, strict. Sullen, gloomy.
D	O	U	T	Extinguish, quench.
D	O	V	E	Pigeon, turtle dove. Term of endearment, emblem of peace.
D	O	W	D	Dowdy person.
D	O	W	L	Filament.
D	O	W	N	Earthward direction, towards the ground, opposite of up. Lower, swallow. Downcast, unhappy. Defeat.
D	O	X	Y	Loose woman, trollop, prostitute. Opinion, doctrine.
D	O	Z	E	Nap, drowse, slumber, snooze, sleep.
D	O	Z	Y	Drowsy, sleepy, dreamy.
D	R	A	B	Dull, colourless, lifeless. Wench, slattern, harlot.
D	R	A	G	Haul, pull, lug, tow. Droop, hang, sag. Bore. Heavy, laborious, slow, tedious. Entertainer.
D	R	A	M	Tot, mite, tipple, issue of alcohol. Peg, dash, jigger, iota.
D	R	A	T	Damn. Mild oath.
D	R	A	W	Sketch, reproduce, trace, Extract, elicit, pull, drag, haul, tug. Drain, siphon. Attract, captivate, charm.
D	R	A	Y	Cart, wagon. Draught horse. Drudge.
D	R	E	W	Past of Draw.
D	R	E	Y	Squirrel's Nest.
D	R	I	B	Fragment, drop, dregs.
D	R	I	P	Droplet, drop, dribble, drib. Trickle, Clod, dope, moron, simpleton, dunce.
D	R	O	P	Droplet, dribble, globule. Particle, iota, molecule, speck. Dram, nip, tot. Fall, descent, dip, sag, Quit.
D	R	U	B	Batter, buffet, paste, wallop, beat. Castigate, trounce.
D	R	U	G	Medication, medicine, remedy. Narcotic, dope. opiate.
D	R	U	M	Solicit, canvass. Vibrate. Musical instrument, percussion instrument. Expel, dismiss.
D	U	A	D	Union of two. Pair.
D	U	A	L	Double, twofold. Plural, alternative.
D	U	A	N	Poem, song.
D	U	C	E	Dictator, leader, autocrat.
D	U	C	K	Pet, darling. Avoid, evade, dodge. Nod, bob, bow. Waterbird.
D	U	C	T	Tube, vessel, passage, canal, pipe, conductor.
D	U	D	E	Dandy, tenderfoot.

1	2	3	4	
D	U	D	S	Clothing, rags. Plural of dud.
D	U	E	L	Trial by battle. Conflict between persons, ideas, forces.
D	U	E	T	Composition for two singers. Performance by two.
D	U	F	F	Over reach, defraud, diddle, bilk, cheat. Buttocks, butt.
D	U	K	E	Nobleman. (Sl.) Fist. Cultivated cherries.
D	U	L	L	Dense, dumb, thick, stupid. Drab, lack lustre, lifeless, colourless. Blunt, obtuse. Cloudy, hazy, dreary.
D	U	L	Y	Properly, regularly, exactly.
D	U	M	B	Mute, stupid, unintelligent.
D	U	M	P	Refuse tip, garbage dump, Jettison, drop, unload, offload.
D	U	N	E	Sandy ridge, sandy hill.
D	U	N	G	Manure, compost, animal excrement.
D	U	N	K	Dip, submerge, soak.
D	U	N	T	Bruise, wound, throb.
D	U	P	E	Delude, bamboozle, chicane, con, hoodwink. Sap. sucker, fall guy. Fool.
D	U	R	N	(sl.) Darn, damn.
D	U	S	K	Evening, eventide, gloaming, nightfall, twilight. Obscure, dusky.
D	U	S	T	Dirt, trash, rubbish, debris. Pulverised particles, atoms, ashes. Fracas, hassle. Clobber, lambaste.
D	U	T	Y	Commitment, need, obligation, function, office, role, burden, task, Tax, assessment, levy, tariff. Chore.
D	Y	E	D	Stained, tinged, tinted, coloured.
D	Y	E	R	One who works with dyes.
D	Y	K	E	Ditch, drain, fence, trench, moat, water-course, canal, aqueduct, weir, lock.
D	Y	N	E	Measurement of power, unit of force.

E

1	2	3	4	
E	A	C	H	All, every, any, several, various, particular, respective, specific, per capita. A piece.
E	A	R	L	Nobleman, warrior, prince, count.
E	A	R	N	Payment for effort; Merit, rate, nett, reap, harvest, score. Get.
E	A	S	E	Rest, repose, idleness, inactivity. Unrestraint, naturalness. Relief, mitigation. Facility, readiness.
E	A	S	T	Eastward, compass point. Sunrise. Orient, regions of the East.
E	A	S	Y	Effortless, simple, smooth, untroublesome. Distinct, obvious. Plain, Forbearing, charitable. Amiable.
E	B	O	N	Black. Ebony.
E	C	A	D	Organism modified by environment. non-inheritable, acquired.
E	C	C	E	Behold.
E	C	H	O	Resound, repeat, imitate. Repercussion, result.
E	C	R	U	Beige.
E	D	A	M	Dutch pressed cheese.
E	D	D	O	Root of Taro.
E	D	D	Y	Ripple, swirl.
E	D	E	N	Garden of Eden.
E	D	G	E	Brink, fringe, hem, margin, border, periphery, verge. Advantage, insinuate.
E	D	G	Y	Tense, nervy, uneasy, up tight, restless. Skittish, excitable.
E	D	I	T	Amend, revise, prepare, adapt, alter, refine. Omit, delete, eliminate.
E	G	A	D	Refined expletive. Ye Gods.
E	G	A	L	Equal.
E	I	R	E	Republic of Ireland.
E	J	O	O	Sago Palm.
E	K	E	D	Stretched, lengthened, increased.
E	K	K	A	Two-wheeled one horse passenger carriage.
E	K	K	I	Hardwood Tree.
E	L	A	N	Ardour, vigor, vivacity.
E	L	M	Y	Characterised by, abounding in Elms.
E	L	S	E	Otherwise, besides, another, further, other, additional.
E	L	U	L	Month of the Jewish Calendar.
E	M	I	R	Nobleman, Chieftain, Ruler, Eastern Title.
E	M	I	T	Discharge, pour, release, issue, give off, exhude.
E	M	U	S	Most eminent.
E	M	Y	S	Freshwater turtle, tortoise.
E	N	V	Y	Jealousy, resentment, covetousness, invidiousness, want, yearning.
E	O	A	N	Dawning, Eastern.
E	P	E	E	Foil, rapier.
E	P	I	C	Heroic, lengthy, imposing, impressive, narrative.
E	R	G	O	Accordingly consequently, so, then, thus, hence, therefore, thereupon.
E	R	I	C	Blood money, fine, honour, price.
E	R	O	S	God of Love. Cupid.
E	R	S	T	Soonest, earliest, formerly, previously.
E	R	U	B	Jewish Sabbath Law.

1	2	3	4	
E	R	U	C	Palm fibre, cord.
E	S	P	Y	Behold, discern, note, see. Encounter, spot, perceive.
E	S	S	E	Existence, essence.
E	T	C	H	Engrave, draw, define, delineate, imprint, inscribe.
E	T	N	A	Small spirit stove.
E	T	O	N	Public School in England.
E	T	U	I	Toilet case, Scissors Case, Needle Case.
E	U	G	E	Bravo.
E	U	R	O	Kangaroo, Wallaroo.
E	U	R	Y	Broad, wide.
E	V	E	N	Flat, flush, smooth, level. Equable, stable, uniform, steady, balanced, Exactly, precisely, just, yet, still.
E	V	E	R	Constantly, always, eternally, forever, perpetually.
E	V	I	L	Wrong, bad, immoral, iniquitous, sinful, vicious, wicked. Offensive, foul, hideous. Malicious, harmful.
E	W	E	R	Pitcher, jug.
E	X	A	M	Examination, test, question time.
E	X	I	T	Way out, outlet, departure point. Departure, exodus, withdrawal. Quit, retire.
E	X	O	N	Superior officers, Yeomen of the Guard.
E	Y	A	S	Fledgling, young falcon, nestling hawk.
E	Y	E	D	Fixed with the eyes. Gazed, observed, regarded, looked, stared, gaped, ogled.
E	Y	E	S	Plural of Eye. Organs of Sight, Orbs, eyeballs. Photo receptors. Vision.
E	Y	O	T	A small Island usually in a river. Ait.
E	Y	R	A	Red brown Wildcat.
E	Y	R	E	Travelling, Journey. Circuit Court. Record.

F

F	A	B	A	Broad bean.
F	A	B	E	Gooseberry.
F	A	C	E	Countenance, appearance, semblance, visage, dial, features, pan. Facade, front. Effrontery, cheek.
F	A	C	T	Actuality, reality.
F	A	D	E	Deteriorate, decline, flag, fail, wane, moderate, lessen, ebb.
F	A	I	L	Decline, deteriorate, languish, waste, weaken. Flummox, crash, fold, bust.
F	A	I	N	Inclined, prone, ready, willing.
F	A	I	R	Attractive, bonny, handsome, beautiful. Chaste, pure. Clear, fine, cloudless. Blond, average, medium.
F	A	K	E	Act, bluff, counterfeit. Fraud, hoax, phony, impostor. Bogus, false, pseudo, forged.
F	A	L	A	Ballad.
F	A	L	L	Slip, slide, slump, Descend, drop, decline, decrease, plunge, pitch, topple. Submit, succumb. Abate.
F	A	L	X	Separating membrane.
F	A	M	E	Acclaim, renown, reputation, name, prominence, distinction, eminence, glory, honour.
F	A	N	E	Temple, Church. Pennant, Banner. Weathercock.
F	A	N	G	Tooth, claw, talon.
F	A	N	S	Admirers, followers, audience.
F	A	R	D	Cosmetics, face paint.
F	A	R	E	Price of Transport, cost of travel. Travel, proceed, journey, pass, go. Passenger, wayfarer, traveller.
F	A	R	M	Land under cultivation. Land used for agricultural purposes. Raise animals. Ranch. Till, cultivate.
F	A	R	O	Card game. Sour Beer.
F	A	R	T	Passing of wind. Expel intestinal wind from anus. Break wind. A despised person.
F	A	S	H	Bother, trouble, annoy.
F	A	S	T	Firm, secure, sure, steadfast, resolute. Hasty, quick, rapid. Wild, sporty. Abstain from food. Licentious.
F	A	T	E	Destiny, outcome, result. Unavoidability, inevitability.
F	A	U	N	Woodland Deity, Pan.
F	A	U	X	Pas. Breach of Etiquette. Gaffe. Mistake.
F	A	W	N	Grovel, cringe, cower.
F	A	Z	E	Disconcert, worry.
F	E	A	L	Faithful, constant, loyal.
F	E	A	R	Dismay, alarm, consternation, dread, horror, Reverence, awe, esteem.
F	E	A	T	Adventure, enterprise, exploit, Stunt, trick.
F	E	C	K	Efficacy, strength.
F	E	E	B	Halfwit, idiot, foot, imbecile.
F	E	E	D	Dispense food, furnish, provide, supply, consume, ingest, eat.
F	E	E	L	Handle, palpate, touch.
F	E	E	T	Plural of foot. Paws, Hooves. 3 feet = 1 yard.
F	E	L	L	Flatten, floor, drop, prostrate. Cut, hew, level. Ferocious, fierce, grim, grave. Hide, skin.
F	E	L	T	Past of FEEL. Fabric. Sensed, handled, touched.
F	E	N	D	Repel, repulse, rebuff. Defend, shield, protect. Safeguard, parry.
F	E	R	N	Non-flowering vascular plant.
F	E	S	S	Acknowledge, confess, admit, concede.

1	2	3	4	
F	E	T	E	Gala, festival, carnival, holiday, fair.
F	E	U	D	Enmity, hostility, strife, quarrel, battle.
F	I	A	R	Price, standard.
F	I	A	T	Sanction, endorsement, decree.
F	I	B	S	Prevarications, tall stories. Lies.
F	I	E	F	A feudal estate.
F	I	F	E	Flute. Musical instrument.
F	I	K	E	Sad, whim, fidget.
F	I	L	E	Steel tool, emery board. Sharpen, refine. Place on record. Register, roll, list. March, queue, row, line.
F	I	L	L	Fulfil, satisfy, satiate. Plug, close, block.
F	I	L	M	Haze, mist, scum. Motion Picture, Movie. Photographic emulsion. Reel of negatives.
F	I	N	D	Discover, meet, identify, ascertain.
F	I	N	E	Penalise, tax, forfeit. Delicate, refined, subtle. Superior, splendid, excellent. Cloudless, sunny, fair.
F	I	N	N	Native of Finland.
F	I	R	E	Inferno, holocaust, conflagration. Flame, blaze, Ardour, fervour, zeal, zest. Light, ignite, Discharge.
F	I	R	M	Solid, secure, stable, Fixed, tight. Stipulated, stated. Steady, unfaltering. Enterprise, business.
F	I	S	C	State Treasury, revenue, purse.
F	I	S	H	Aquatic vertebrate. Hint, dupe. To catch fish.
F	I	S	T	Clenched hand. Clutch, grasp.
F	I	T	Z	Son of.
F	I	V	E	One more than four.
F	I	Z	Z	Fizzle, switch, sibilate, hiss.
F	L	A	G	Banner, ensign, pendant, pennant, standard. Signal, gesture. Fail, decline, fade.
F	L	A	K	Anti-aircraft fire. Bursting Shells. Verbal battering. Telling off.
F	L	A	M	Hoax, humbug, spoof. Trick, cheat.
F	L	A	N	Open Pie. Tart.
F	L	A	P	Commotion, confusion, tumult. Hinged fold. Book jacket fold. Wave, vibrate, flutter.
F	L	A	T	Prostrate, recumbent. Colourless, dull, insipid, inane. Unpalatable, Broke, needy, poor. Apartment.
F	L	A	W	Blemish, defect.
F	L	A	X	Textile, fibre.
F	L	A	Y	Excoriate. Criticise. To skin or strip. To whip. Thrash.
F	L	E	A	Wingless biting insect.
F	L	E	D	Escaped, decamped, evaded, ran, bolted, ran away from.
F	L	E	E	Escape, abscond, decamp. Skip.
F	L	E	W	Past of FLY. Fled. Decamped.
F	L	E	X	Bend, exercise. Electric cord.
F	L	I	P	Throw, toss. Browse, leaf, riffle, scan, skim.
F	L	I	T	Fly, dart, flicker, migrate, depart.
F	L	I	X	Beaver down. Fur.
F	L	O	E	Icebergs, Icefield.
F	L	O	G	Scourge, whip, thrash, lash.
F	L	O	P	Failure, dud, loser. Fall, collapse.
F	L	O	W	Gush, stream, cascade, spout. Emit, spate, tide. Continuity, series.
F	L	U	B	Bungle, fluff, goof, luff, botch.
F	L	U	E	Down, floss, fluff, lint, pile. Pipe, outlet, chimney.
F	L	U	X	Variable, unstable. Liquify, dissolve, melt. Drift, stream, tide, outflow. Dysentery, Diarrhoea. Fluid.
F	O	A	L	Young horse. Colt. Filly.
F	O	A	M	Spume, spray, froth, Suds. Lather.
F	O	G	Y	Fuddy Duddy, Victorian, Fossil, Square.
F	O	I	E	Goose Liver.
F	O	I	L	Balk, bilk, disappoint, frustrate.
F	O	L	D	Wrinkle, crease, ridge, furrow, ruck. Collapse, ruin, bankrupt, pauperize.
F	O	L	K	Family. clan, kindred, race, tribe.
F	O	N	D	Loving, dear, devoted, doting, tender, indulgent.
F	O	N	T	Fount, source, spring.
F	O	O	D	Nourishment, victuals, edibles, grub.
F	O	O	L	Ass, idiot, imbecile, dimwit. Buffoon, clown, comic. Trifle. dally, Philander.
F	O	O	T	Terminal part of leg. Walk, ambulate, traipse. Base, nadir, bottom.
F	O	R	D	Cross over, passage, bridge.
F	O	R	E	Before, ahead, forward, in advance. Previous. Warning cry at Golf.
F	O	R	K	Device consisting of handle, shank and prongs. Confluent. Junction.
F	O	R	M	Outward appearance, figure, shape, contour, anatomy, structure, Mode, style. Procedure, regulation.
F	O	R	T	Citadel, fortress, stronghold.
F	O	S	S	Canal, ditch, trench.
F	O	U	D	Magistrate, sheriff, bailiff.
F	O	U	L	Offensive, disgusting, repellent, repugnant, vile. Squalid, indecent, obscene. Begrime, soil, smudge.
F	O	U	R	One more than three. Quarter, foursome.

1	2	3	4	
F	O	W	L	Chicken, cock, hen, Poultry. Bird.
F	O	X	Y	Sly, wily, artful, crafty, tricky, deceitful.
F	O	Z	Y	Spongy, wanting in freshness, fat, dull-witted.
F	R	A	P	Bind, secure.
F	R	A	U	German woman.
F	R	A	Y	Fracas, melee, row, brawl, scrimmage, skirmish.
F	R	E	E	Independent, sovereign, liberated, released, unregimented, detach.
F	R	E	T	Worry, fuss, chafe, fume, annoy, bother. Ripple, dimple, riffle.
F	R	I	G	Waste time, fool around.
F	R	I	T	Glass material. Fuse by heat.
F	R	O	E	Cleaving tool.
F	R	O	G	Web footed amphibian. Part of Hoof. Depression in brick.
F	R	O	M	Whence, in the face of, after, against, source.
F	R	O	W	Loose woman, slut.
F	U	E	L	Combustible, coal, coke, gas, oil, peat, wood. Fissionable material.
F	U	F	F	A puff, the spitting of a cat, a burst of anger.
F	U	S	S	Temper, rage, fugue.
F	U	L	L	Brimming, crowded, jammed, crammed, loaded, packed. Whole, complete. Satiated, gorged.
F	U	M	E	Vaporous, smoky, fumous, Rage, rave.
F	U	N	D	Supply, capital, reserve, store. Stock.
F	U	N	K	Terror, fear, Coward, quitter. Flinch, panic, dread.
F	U	R	L	Roll, fold, wrap, stow.
F	U	R	Y	Frenzy, rage, turbulence.
F	U	S	E	Timing device. Detonating device. Dissolve, melt, blend, integrate, mix.
F	U	S	S	Fret, fume, worry, gripe, bitch, carp, nag.
F	U	S	T	Mustiness, moldy, shaft of column.
F	U	Z	Z	Floss, fluff, flint, pile, down. Cop, policeman. Heat.
F	Y	K	E	Dragnet for fish.
F	Y	R	D	Norman National Militia.

G

1	2	3	4	
G	A	B	Y	Simpleton, nitwit.
G	A	D	E	Gadloid fish.
G	A	E	L	Scottish Highlander. Irishman. Scotsman.
G	A	F	F	Spar, spear, trick, gimmick.
G	A	G	A	Crazy, doting.
G	A	G	E	Pledge, mortgage. Stake, risk.
G	A	I	N	Earnings, proceeds, profit. Cut. Accomplish, achieve, attain.
G	A	I	T	Pace, speed, rapidity.
G	A	L	A	Festival, festivity, gaiety.
G	A	L	E	High wind. Rental, royalty.
G	A	L	L	Presumption, effrontery, conceit. Pomposity. Fret, annoy, irritate. Bile, gallbladder. Rancour.
G	A	L	T	Hog, Barrow.
G	A	L	V	Galvanize, galvanized.
G	A	M	E	Wild animals. Quarry, prey. Joke, sport, fun. Wager, gamble, Brave, bold.
G	A	M	Y	Malodorous, fetid, rank, smelly, diseased, lame.
G	A	N	G	Horde, coterie, band, crew.
G	A	O	L	Prison. Jail.
G	A	P	E	Stare, goggle, gaze, peer.
G	A	R	B	Dress, apparel, attire, clothing.
G	A	S	H	Slash, cut, notch, furrow, slit.
G	A	S	P	Pant, heave, huff.
G	A	T	E	Door, opening on movable frame, barrier, means of entrance. Tap, valve, faucet.
G	A	U	D	Adorn, paint, colour.
G	A	U	L	Country that is now France. Frenchman.
G	A	U	M	Understanding, perception.
G	A	U	P	To gape in astonishment.
G	A	U	R	Species of ox inhabiting some of the mountain jungles of India.
G	A	V	E	Granted, yielded. Donated.
G	A	Z	E	View, contemplate, regard.
G	E	A	L	Relating to Earth.
G	E	A	N	Sweet wild cherry.
G	E	A	R	Aparatus, machinery, equipment. Appendage. Belongings, effects. Outfit, furnish.
G	E	L	D	Neuter, castrate, sterilize.
G	E	N	A	Animals cheek.

1	2	3	4	
G	E	N	E	Hereditary factor.
G	E	N	T	Gentleman.
G	E	N	U	Knee.
G	E	R	M	Micro organism, microbe. Bud, seed, beginning, rudiment. Nucleus. Embryo.
G	E	S	T	Enterprise, exploit, feat, adventure.
G	E	U	M	Perennial herbs.
G	H	A	T	Mountain range, mountain pass. Platform, landing place.
G	H	E	E	Vegetable fat. Indian Butter.
G	I	B	E	Sneer, deride, taunt, scoff, rag.
G	I	F	T	Favour, donation, contribution, legacy, reward. Flair, faculty, genius, talent.
G	I	L	D	Overlay with gold, tinge with gold, embellish, adorn, brighten.
G	I	L	L	Unit of capacity, half a pint (Brit.) Breathing organ of Fish.
G	I	L	T	Gilded, golden, covered with gold. Immature female swine.
G	I	M	P	Decorative cord for upholstery and clothing.
G	I	N	K	Person, guy, fellow.
G	I	R	D	Encircle, bind. Brace, prepare, strenghten.
G	I	R	L	Maiden, maid, miss, lass, female. Housemaid, Girlfriend.
G	I	R	O	Autogiro.
G	I	R	T	Prepared, ready, geared.
G	I	S	T	Substance, matter, upshot, sense, scene, drift, topic.
G	I	V	E	Contribute, donate, bestow, award, provide, offer, allot, Elasticity, pliability. Give in. Give out.
G	L	A	D	Happy, joyful, joyous, light hearted.
G	L	E	E	Hilarity, merriment, mirth.
G	L	E	N	Valley, combe, dale, vale.
G	L	I	B	Fluent, talkative, eloquent, vocal.
G	L	O	W	Bloom, blossom, blush, flush. Flare, flame, blaze, Radiate, shine.
G	L	U	E	Adhesive, gum, mucilage, paste, cement. Stick, fix, adhere.
G	L	U	M	Gloomy, morose, saturnine, sulky, surly, dour.
G	L	U	T	Feast, surfeit, abundance, plenty.
G	N	A	R	To snarl or growl, to grind the teeth, creak.
G	N	A	T	Tiny biting fly. Midge, black fly, sandfly.
G	N	A	W	Bite, chew. Erode, corrode.
G	O	A	D	Exhort, prompt, urge. Stimulus, catalyst, spur. Impetus.
G	O	A	L	Aim, objective, ambition, target, purpose.
G	O	A	T	Hollow horned ruminant mammal. Ibex. Scapegoat, patsy, fall guy.
G	O	B	Y	Fish, mud sucker, mud skipper.
G	O	D	S	Plural of god.
G	O	E	L	Redeemer, reclaimant.
G	O	E	R	Speedy, attendant.
G	O	E	S	Plural of go.
G	O	G	A	Insect, spider (South African).
G	O	G	O	Rhythm dancing. Energetic dancer.
G	O	L	A	Warehouse, storeroom, granary.
G	O	L	D	Malleable metallic element. Precious metal. Riches. Golden.
G	O	L	F	Ballgame.
G	O	N	E	Departed, vanished, defunct, dead, extinct. Absent, missing, lost, Expecting, enciente, pregnant.
G	O	N	G	A metal disk usually rimmed that sounds when struck or rubbed with a drumstick.
G	O	O	D	Beneficial, favourable, helpful, right, pleasant, clever, considerable, charitable, proper, skilful, able.
G	O	O	F	Botch, bungle. Loaf, loll. Dunce, oaf.
G	O	O	K	Nonsense, drivel, junk.
G	O	O	N	Chump, dolt, thug.
G	O	O	P	Gook, gunk.
G	O	R	E	Blood, guts, viscera, gory, bloody, bloodstained, sanguine.
G	O	S	H	Ejaculation of surprise.
G	O	U	T	Metabolic disease. Clot, blob, splash, spurt.
G	O	W	K	Cuckoo, fool.
G	O	W	N	Garment, robe, fashionable outfit. Dress.
G	R	A	B	Seize, catch, nab, snatch.
G	R	A	M	Small weight, metric unit. Grain, seed, chick-pea.
G	R	A	N	Grandparent, grandmother, grandfather.
G	R	A	Y	Grey, ash coloured.
G	R	E	W	Past of grow. Thrived, raised, progressed.
G	R	E	Y	Gray, Neutral tint.
G	R	I	D	Grating, gridiron, network, girddle.
G	R	I	G	Dwarf. Cricket, grasshopper.
G	R	I	M	Cruel, inhuman, ominous, bleak, austere, severe, harsh.
G	R	I	N	Smile, beam.

1	2	3	4	
G	R	I	P	Clasp, grasp. Fascinate, mesmerize. Holdall, suitcase. Clench, clutch.
G	R	I	T	Fortitude, courage. Dust, speck, gravel.
G	R	O	G	Alcohol, drink, liquor, rum.
G	R	O	S	Durable fabric, silk fabric.
G	R	O	T	Grotto, Grotty.
G	R	O	W	Thrive, develop, expand, gain. Cultivate, produce.
G	R	U	B	Beetle larva. Scramble, scrape. Drudge, Food, victuals, scrabble, dirt.
G	R	U	E	Shiver, shudder.
G	R	U	M	Morose, glum, surly, sour.
G	U	A	N	Gamebird.
G	U	F	F	Humbug, balderdash.
G	U	H	R	Earthy deposit.
G	U	I	B	Harnessed antelope.
G	U	L	F	Harbour, inlet, crevasse, chasm, ravine.
G	U	L	L	Seabird. Cheat, deceive.
G	U	L	P	Swallow, gobble, guzzle.
G	U	N	K	Cook, thick lacquer.
G	U	R	U	Hindu teacher.
G	U	S	H	Rush, spout, stream, pour.
G	U	S	T	Squall, breeze, wind.
G	U	T	S	Courage, pluck.
G	Y	L	E	Fermentation. Brew.
G	Y	N	E	Female. Queen Ant.
G	Y	P	O	Egyptian.
G	Y	R	E	Revolve, whirl, spin, vortex.
G	Y	R	O	Gyroscope, gyrocompass, gyrohorizon, Balance wheel.
G	Y	T	E	Deranged, mad.
G	Y	V	E	Fetter, bond, chain, shackle.

H

H	A	A	B	365 Day year.
H	A	A	K	Umbrella Thorn (South African).
H	A	A	R	Cold wet sea fog.
H	A	C	K	Notch, gash, kick. chop, Cab, taxi. Common, mean, Inferior. Riding Horse. Unoriginal writer.
H	A	D	E	Unploughed field, rock fault. Lagoon, sandbar.
H	A	F	T	Hilt of sword, dagger. Handle of tool.
H	A	H	A	Expression of derision, amusement, Sunk fence.
H	A	I	K	Outer garment, wrap.
H	A	I	L	Salvo, volley, barrage. Accost, greet, address. Frozen raindrops. Bombardment.
H	A	I	R	Threadlike outgrowth of epidermis. Pigmented filaments on body. Bristle, spine. Beard, fur, whisker.
H	A	J	I	Pilgrimage to Mecca.
H	A	K	A	Maori dance.
H	A	K	E	Fish of the cod family. Stockfish. Whiting.
H	A	L	A	Hawaiian Pine.
H	A	L	E	Sound, healthy, robust.
H	A	L	F	Medial, mid, centre, middle.
H	A	L	L	Public Building. Meeting Place. Large residence, Manor House. Passage, corridor.
H	A	L	O	Nimbus, aura, prestige.
H	A	L	T	Limp, lame. Stop, pull up. Stoppage, terminate, end. suspend.
H	A	M	E	Bar for trace. attchment.
H	A	M	S	Plural of Ham.
H	A	N	D	Forelimb. Grasping organ or device. Give, deliver. Angle, aspect, Aid, assistance, support, help.
H	A	N	G	Hover, poise. Knack, art, skill. Put to death, execute. Suspend.
H	A	N	K	Skein, coil, hoop, ring.
H	A	R	D	Firm, solid, compact, intensive, arduous, difficult. Serious, severe, actual, grim. Cruel, relentless. Tight.
H	A	R	E	Rabbit-like animal.
H	A	R	K	Listen, attend, heed.
H	A	R	L	Snarl, entangle.
H	A	R	M	Injury, damage, abuse, maltreat, undermine.
H	A	R	P	Musical instrument. Lyre. Nag. Refer repeatedly.
H	A	R	T	Stag, hatch. Chop, miscellany, assortment.
H	A	S	H	Chop, mince, miscellany, assortment. Stew, mishmash, mess, mush.
H	A	S	P	Clasp, fastening.
H	A	S	T	Has.
H	A	T	E	Abomination, abhorrence, repugnance, enmity, disdain, dislike, contempt, despise.

1	2	3	4	
H	A	U	L	Pull, tug, drag, draw, heave.
H	A	V	E	Own, possess, hold, contain.
H	A	W	K	Rapacious bird, person, Peddle, sell. Retching vomit or phlegm.
H	A	Z	E	Fog, mist, pall, miasma. Obscure. Overcast, vapor.
H	A	Z	Y	Misty, vague. Dazed. Foggy, vaporous.
H	E	A	D	Seat of Intellect. Mind. Principal, Chief, director. Crisis, climax.
H	E	A	L	Cure, remedy, assuage, patch-up.
H	E	A	P	Pile, mound, stack. Much, lots, mass. Wreck, jalopy.
H	E	A	R	Listen, attend. Heed.
H	E	A	T	Rage, passion, excitement. Warm, warmth, hotness. Law, policeman.
H	E	C	K	(Sl.) Hell.
H	E	E	D	Mind, mark, obey, regard, attend.
H	E	E	L	Villain, bastard, miscreant, rascal. Slant, cant, incline. Remainder, balance. Back portion of foot.
H	E	F	T	Bulk, mass, weight. Hoist, lift, raise.
H	E	I	L	Salutation.
H	E	I	R	Inheritor, successor, beneficiary.
H	E	L	D	Grasped, kept, detained, retained.
H	E	L	L	Hades, Netherworld, Inferno, Havoc, ruin, Tomfoolery, Pandemonium, perdition.
H	E	L	M	Pillar, steering geer. Steer, guide, direct.
H	E	L	P	Aid, abet, ameliorate, improve, assist, relieve. Hired help, servant.
H	E	M	P	Rope fibre, Cannabis.
H	E	R	B	Grass, aromatic plant, Medicinal plant.
H	E	R	D	Drive, run, flock, drove, collection of.
H	E	R	E	Present, now, at this place.
H	E	R	O	Central figure in an event, action or period. Illustrious warrior. Admired man. Man of courage.
H	E	R	R	Lord, master, the German term of address equivalent to Sir.
H	E	R	S	Belonging to her.
H	E	W	N	Cut, felled, chiselled, sculpted.
H	I	C	K	Rustic, clodhopper, yokel.
H	I	D	E	Conceal, screen, obscure, seclude. Animal fur, skin, pelt.
H	I	E	D	Set off.
H	I	F	I	Hi Fidelity.
H	I	G	H	Lofty, eminent, arrogant, shrill. Dear, expensive. Drugged, doped. Malodorous, fetid.
H	I	K	E	To carry, hoist, tramp, march.
H	I	L	L	Elevation of land. Koppie, Ridge. Pile, Bank, Drift, Mound. Mountain.
H	I	L	T	Haft, handle, fully, completely.
H	I	N	D	Posterior, back, hindmost, rear, behind. Retrospect.
H	I	N	K	Reaping Hook.
H	I	N	T	Indication, inkling, intimation, clue, cue, Innuendo, insinuation. Soupcon, dash.
H	I	R	E	Engage, charter, lease, rent, let.
H	I	S	S	Sibilant sound, whisper, wheeze, catcall, hoot, razz.
H	I	S	T	Demanding silence and attention, hush, silence, to urge or summon, as by making the sound.
H	I	V	E	Beehive, apiary. Storehouse. Stockpile, store, accumulate. Eruption on the skin.
H	O	A	R	Frost, dusty coating, rime, hoary.
H	O	A	X	Dupe, delude, mislead, victimise, bamboozle, fake, fraud.
H	O	B	O	Tramp, vagrant, vagabond, drifter, bum.
H	O	C	K	Pawn, mortgage, pledge. Hamstring. Rhine wine.
H	O	E	D	Weeded.
H	O	L	D	Retain, possess, have, grasp. Delay, constrain, restrict, limit, reserve. Halt, stop, pause.
H	O	L	E	Aperture, opening, orifice, vent, gap, hiatus, fissure. Predicament, dilemma.
H	O	L	M	Low flat land near a river. Bottoms. Small island.
H	O	L	T	Burrowing animal's den. Lair. Otter's home.
H	O	L	Y	Sanctified, consecrated, hallowed, unprofane, saintly, angelic, devout, pious.
H	O	M	E	Habitat, locality, seat, domicile, residence, dwelling. Country, Fatherland, Homeland.
H	O	M	Y	Homelike.
H	O	N	E	Whet, sharpen, enlarge.
H	O	N	G	Chinese warehouse. Foreign mercantile house in China.
H	O	N	K	Hoot.
H	O	O	D	Thug, ruffian, hooligan. Headdress, headgear. Bonnet of car.
H	O	O	F	Foot, kick, trample. Eject, boot. Walk, step, dance, prance. Bovine's foot.
H	O	O	K	Crook, latch, billhook. Pin, snare. Sickle. Steal, crookery. Fish hook.
H	O	O	P	Large circle, ring, circlet. Clasp, surround, enclose.
H	O	O	T	Honk, boo, decry. Execrate. Cat call. Hiss. Toot, warn. Owl's call.
H	O	P	E	Confidence, dependence, faith, trust. Expect, await, anticipate.
H	O	P	S	Hop Plant. Flavouring of Malt Liquor.
H	O	R	N	Bony projection attached to head of animals. Musical wind instrument.
H	O	R	S	De-Combat. Out of action.

1	2	3	4	
H	O	S	E	Stockings, hosiery, socks. Garden sprinkler, watering pipe.
H	O	S	T	Householder, inn keeper, master of ceremonies. Multitude, gathering. Eucharist.
H	O	U	R	Time of day. 24th Part of Solar day. Fixed period of time.
H	O	V	E	Past of heave. Raised.
H	O	W	L	Doleful sound. Outcry, bay, ululate, wail. Weep, yowl.
H	O	Y	A	Genus of honey plant.
H	U	C	K	Hip, haunch.
H	U	E	D	Coloured, tinted.
H	U	F	F	Blow, pant, bluster, rant, puff. Flounce. Annoyance, Irritation.
H	U	G	E	Vast, enormous, mammoth, gigantic, immense, colossal, titanic.
H	U	L	K	Clumsily constructed ship. Bulk, unwieldy. Abandoned wreck.
H	U	L	L	Frame or body of ship; Main structure. Covering, casing. Cartridge.
H	U	M	P	Hunch, rounded protuberance, crooked back. Mound, hulk, convey, carry, bear.
H	U	N	K	Lump, chunk, wad, hunch.
H	U	N	T	Pursue, chase, run, track, snare, shoot. Quest, rummage.
H	U	R	L	Cast, pitch, fling, throw.
H	U	R	T	Pain, distress, injury, wound. Harm, impair, ache, outrage.
H	U	S	H	Quiet, calm, still, silence.
H	U	S	K	Pod, shell, skin, hull, case. Shell.
H	Y	L	A	Tree toad.
H	Y	L	E	Matter, material.
H	U	M	A	A fabulous restless bird.
H	Y	M	N	Song of praise. Carol.
H	Y	P	E	Hypedermic, narcotics addict.
H	Y	P	O	Hypodermic Syringe, Hypodermic injection, stimulus. Sodium thiosulfate. Fixing agent.

I

1	2	3	4	
I	A	M	B	Disyllabic rousing cadence.
I	B	E	X	Mountain goat, mountain sheep. Wild goat.
I	B	I	D	In the same place.
I	B	I	S	Wading bird.
I	C	E	D	Cold, chilled, frozen. Glacial. Covered in sugar frosting.
I	C	O	N	Image, venerated reproduction. Ikon.
I	D	E	A	Conception, impression, notion, opinion, thought.
I	D	E	M	Same, repetition, previously mentioned.
I	D	E	S	Roman date.
I	D	L	E	Inactive, inert, passive, empty, hollow, Vacant, unused.
I	D	L	Y	Lazily, indolently.
I	D	O	L	False god. Hero, pet, image. Icon.
I	D	Y	L	Descriptive poem, narrative poem. Light hearted episode.
I	F	F	Y	Uncertain, whimsical, eractic.
I	M	A	M	Prayer leader, Caliph, Reader.
I	M	P	I	Zulu warriors.
I	N	C	A	Ruler of Incaic Empire. Member of Inca people.
I	N	C	H	Unit of length. Distance or degree. Narrow margin. Advance by degrees.
I	N	K	Y	Pitch dark, black, blotted.
I	N	L	Y	Inwardly, within, intimately, thoroughly.
I	N	T	O	Function word denoting motion, direction.
I	O	R	A	Asiatic song birds. Bulbuls.
I	R	I	S	Lens of eye. Prismatic crystal. Rainbow, Quartz. Perennial herbaceous plant.
I	O	T	A	Letter of Greek alphabet. Infinitesimal amount, small degree. Jot. Tittle.
I	R	O	N	Flatten, smooth. Stirrup, soldering iron, golf club. Malleable metallic element. Pig iron, Steel.
I	S	L	E	Small island.
I	T	C	H	Irritation, prickle, sting, pruritus. Restlessness.
I	T	E	M	Likewise, also, in addition. Detail, particular. Compute, reckon. Topic, subject, matter.
I	T	M	O	Betel.
I	V	A	N	Russian.
I	W	A	N	Large Hall, Audience Chamber.
I	W	I	S	Certainly, indeed, truly.
I	X	I	A	Genus of bulbous plant. Tropical plant.
I	Y	A	R	Months of the Jewish calendar.
I	Z	A	R	Voluminous outer garment worn by Muslim women.

J

J				
J	A	C	A	Jack fruit.
J	A	C	K	Impertinent fellow. Pal, buddy. Jackstone. Smaller edition of.
J	A	D	E	Fatigue, fagged. Green, Worthless horse. Shrewish woman, wench, minx.
J	A	I	L	Gaol, prison, imprison.
J	A	M	B	The uprights of a doorframe. Doorpost.
J	A	K	E	Hick, fellow.
J	A	N	E	(sl.) Girl, woman.
J	A	P	E	Gibe, taunt, jeer. Joke.
J	A	P	S	Japanese.
J	A	R	S	Grates, rattles, bickers. Plural of Jar.
J	A	S	M	Drive, energy.
J	A	V	A	Coffee, breed of bird.
J	A	W	S	Plural of Jaw.
J	A	Z	Z	Dixieland music. Bop, swing. Enliven, popularise. Accelerate.
J	E	A	N	Twilled cloth. Drill, denim.
J	E	E	P	Multi-purpose motor vehicle.
J	E	E	R	Deride, mock, ridicule, scoff, taunt.
J	E	E	Z	Mild oath.
J	E	F	E	Chief, leader.
J	E	H	U	Reckless driver.
J	E	L	L	Congeal, set, crystallize. Solidify.
J	E	R	K	Stroke, lash, jolt, bounce, twitch. (sl.) Ass, fool.
J	E	S	S	Leather used in falconry.
J	E	S	T	Banter, joke. Quip.
J	E	T	E	Ballet term.
J	E	T	S	Plural of Jet. Spurts.
J	E	W	S	Plural of Jew.
J	E	W	Y	Jewish.
J	I	B	E	Change course. Tack, Gibe.
J	I	B	S	Plural of Jib.
J	I	F	F	Jiffy, moment.
J	I	G	S	Plural of Jig.
J	I	L	L	Female Ferret, wench.
J	I	L	T	Reject, deceive, cheat. Run out on.
J	I	N	K	Change direction, dodge, dance. Twist, turn, weave.
J	I	N	N	Supernatural spirit.
J	I	N	X	Bad luck, down.
J	I	V	E	Jazz, jitterbug; Rock 'n roll.
J	O	A	N	Country girl.
J	O	B	S	Plural of Job.
J	O	C	K	Lad, jockey, disc jockey. Jock strap.
J	O	E	Y	Baby Kangaroo. Baby animal. Young child.
J	O	G	S	Plural of Jog.
J	O	H	N	Fellow, guy, chap. Toilet. Loo.
J	O	I	N	Link, attach, unite, couple. Relate, associate, combine.
J	O	K	E	Jest, quip, witticism, wisecrack, gag, crack. Raillery. Kidding.
J	O	L	T	Bump, jerk, jounce, Setback, reversal. Impact.
J	O	S	H	Joke, tease, jest.
J	O	S	S	Chinese idol. Cut image. Foreman.
J	O	T	A	Spanish folk dance.
J	O	U	R	A day, a feast day, especially a saint's day.
J	O	V	E	Roman deity. Exclamation of Jupiter.
J	O	W	L	Mandible, jaw, cheek.
J	O	Y	S	Plural of Joy.
J	U	B	A	Negro breakdown or rustic dance, in which the spectators clap hands, slap their thighs and sing verses.
J	U	G	S	Plural of Jug.
J	U	J	U	Fetish, charm, amulet, magic.
J	U	K	E	Music box, record holder.
J	U	L	Y	7th Month.
J	U	M	P	Leap, hop, vault. Attack, mug, ambush.
J	U	N	E	6th Month.
J	U	N	K	Trash, scrap, cheap jewellery. Narcotics. Chinese sail boat.
J	U	R	Y	Selected Panel. Grand Jury. Trial Jury.

1	2	3	4	
J	U	S	T	Reasonable, justified. Right, accurate. Appropriate, suitable. Constant, uniform. Proper, fitting. Equal.
J	U	T	E	Sacking, burlap, twine, plant.
J	Y	N	X	Genus of Woodpecker. Wryneck. Jink. Devil.

K

K	A	D	Y	Straw hat. Derby.
K	A	G	U	Crested bird.
K	A	H	A	Monkey.
K	A	I	D	Tribal chief.
K	A	K	A	New Zealand Parrot.
K	A	L	E	Cabbage, cole. Fodder.
K	A	M	A	Pleasure, enjoyment. Laws of kama.
K	A	M	E	Ridge, hill, drift.
K	A	M	I	Shinto deity. Spirit.
K	A	N	G	Sleeping platform (China).
K	A	N	S	Indian grass.
K	A	T	A	Exercise practice in karate, kung-fu, judo.
K	A	V	A	A species of pepper, a narcotic drink prepared from its root and stem.
K	A	Y	A	Japanese Tree.
K	A	Y	O	K.O. Knockout.
K	E	C	K	Retch. Vomit.
K	E	E	L	Flatbottomed ship. Barge. Ship's TImbers. Ridge. Overturn, capsize. Swoon.
K	E	E	N	Sharp, eager, enthusiastic. Astute. Cry softly, lament. Biting.
K	E	E	P	Retain, Detain, withhold, reserve, hold. Celebrate, solemnize. Commemorate, Heed, notice. Observatory.
K	E	G	S	Plural of Keg.
K	E	L	P	Seaweed.
K	E	L	T	Sea Trout, Salmon.
K	E	M	P	Coarse fibre.
K	E	N	T	A leaping or punting pole.
K	E	P	I	Military cap.
K	E	P	T	Past of Keep.
K	E	R	F	Slit, notch, groove.
K	E	R	N	Part of printed letter.
K	E	T	A	Dog salmon.
K	E	Y	S	Plural of Key.
K	H	A	N	Ruler, chieftain. Asian resthouse.
K	I	B	E	Chilblain.
K	I	C	K	Strike with feet. Boot, punt. Resist, rebel. Spurn, Thrust, drive. Pleasure, fun, thrills.
K	I	E	R	Bleach vat. Dye vat.
K	I	K	U	Chrysanthemum (Japanese).
K	I	L	L	Put to death. Deprive of Life. Destroy, eliminate, slay, murder, assasinate. Dispatch, execute.
K	I	L	N	Furnace, oven.
K	I	L	O	Thousandth. Metric unit. Kilogram.
K	I	L	T	Wrap around skirt. Tartan.
K	I	N	D	Species, lineage, style. Aspect, manner. Essence, category. Type, sort, brand. Gentle. Generous.
K	I	N	E	Cows. Cine.
K	I	N	G	Monarch, Ruler, Sovereign.
K	I	N	K	Fold, indentation, loop. Eccentricity, quirk, whim. Twist.
K	I	N	O	Dried juice. Extract.
K	I	P	P	A form of generator for hydrogen sulphide or other gas.
K	I	P	S	Plural of Kip.
K	I	R	I	Wood.
K	I	R	K	Church.
K	I	S	H	Wicker basket, graphite. Style.
K	I	S	I	Snake basket.
K	I	S	S	Touch with the lips. Reverence, salute, caress.
K	I	S	T	Chest, Trunk.
K	I	T	E	Flying contrivance. Airplane. Species of falcon.
K	I	T	H	Kindred, kin, relations.
K	I	W	I	New Zealand flightless bird. New Zealander.
K	I	Y	A	Yelp, dog.
K	L	A	N	Ku Klux Klan. Secret society.
K	N	A	P	Summit. Wrap, knock.
K	N	E	E	Joint of the leg.

1	2	3	4	
K	N	E	W	Past of know.
K	N	E	Z	Slavic Prince, Duke.
K	N	O	P	Protuberance on chalice.
K	N	O	T	Intertwine, loop, bend, tangle, interlace, bunch, clump. Wading bird.
K	N	O	W	Be aware of. Discern, distinguish, understand.
K	N	U	R	Excrescence on tree trunk.
K	N	U	T	Fob.
K	O	E	L	Cuckoo.
K	O	H	L	Preparation for darkening the eyelids.
K	O	K	O	Edible roots.
K	O	L	M	Shale containing uranium oxide.
K	O	L	O	Folk dance.
K	O	N	A	Storm, wind.
K	O	O	K	Nut, freak.
K	O	R	A	Watercock.
K	O	R	O	Jar, porcelain jar.
K	O	T	O	Japanese Zither.
K	R	A	N	Silver coin.
K	U	A	N	Chinese pottery.
K	U	B	A	Caucasian carpet.
K	U	D	U	African Antelope.
K	U	K	U	New Zealand Dove.
K	U	S	U	African Mice.
K	Y	L	E	Channel, strait.
K	Y	T	E	Stomach, belly.

L

1	2	3	4	
L	A	B	S	Plural of Lab. Laboratories.
L	A	C	E	Cord, string, braid. Openwork fabric. Mesh. Net. Tie, thread, intertwine. Embroider. Add to.
L	A	C	K	Wanting, missing. Requirement, want, need. Deficiency.
L	A	C	Y	Lacelike. Fine, weblike.
L	A	D	E	Load, burden, encumber, weigh, saddle, tax, clog, Dip, bail, ladle, scoop.
L	A	D	S	Plural of Lad.
L	A	D	Y	Woman, mistress, gentlewoman, noblewoman, female.
L	A	G	S	Falls behind, lingers, delays, dawdles. Slows. Plural of Lag.
L	A	I	N	Past of Lie.
L	A	I	R	Hideaway, den, burrow, hideout, lodge.
L	A	K	E	Mere, lagoon. Stretch of water. Red pigment.
L	A	L	O	Sugar Cane shoot.
L	A	M	A	Genus of mammal. Llama, Alpaca, Buddhist Leader.
L	A	M	B	Young sheep. Lambkin. Young of others. Eucharistic Host.
L	A	M	E	Limping, disabled, weak; inarticulate. Cripple, impotent. Feeble.
L	A	M	P	Lantern. Globe. Light giving device. Heat yielding apparatus.
L	A	M	S	Strikes, thrashes. Plural of Lam.
L	A	N	D	Earth's surface. Country, estate, farm, tract. Realm, domain. Real Estate. Disembark, set down, alight.
L	A	N	E	Avenue, channel, passage, roadway, path.
L	A	N	K	Slender, thin, lean, gaunt, rawboned, scraggy, skinny, spare. Drooping, meagre.
L	A	P	P	Laplander. The language.
L	A	P	S	Plural of Lap.
L	A	R	B	Bearberry.
L	A	R	D	Pork Fat.
L	A	R	K	Singing bird. Skylark. Singer. Frolic, tease, prank, spree, romp.
L	A	S	H	Whip, flog, scourge, pour, teem, wag, scold, upbraid, Lambaste, flay.
L	A	S	S	Girl, sweetheart, maid, maidservant, wench, miss, gal.
L	A	S	T	Survive, endure. Continue, sustain, persist, latest, final, conclusive. Shoemaker's form. Anvil.
L	A	T	E	Overdue, past, recent, deceased. Tardy, eventual, latter, extinct.
L	A	T	H	Narrow strip of wood.
L	A	U	D	Extol, praise, acclaim, celebrate, flatter, admire. Glorify.
L	A	V	A	Molten rock.
L	A	V	E	Wash, bathe, lap, lip. Pour.
L	A	W	N	Cotton or Linen fabric. Glade, grass, garden, park.
L	A	W	S	Plural of Law. Customs, statutes, decrees.
L	A	Y	S	Plural of Lay.
L	A	Z	E	Lie around, relax, idle, dawdle, loll, lounge, loaf. Slouch.
L	A	Z	Y	Indolent, slothful, workshy, passive, supine, lethargic, sluggish.

1	2	3	4	
L	E	A	D	Guide, precede, surpass, conduct, escort, steer, direct, preface, usher. A metal.
L	E	A	F	Foliage, blade, page, scan, browse, lamina, thin plate.
L	E	A	K	Ooze, drip, percolate.
L	E	A	L	Faithful, loyal, true.
L	E	A	N	Slant, bend, incline, tilt. Rest, depend. Lank. Poor, scanty. Slender, spare, skinny. Meat without fat.
L	E	A	P	Jump, hop, bounce, bound, hurdle, clear, vault.
L	E	C	H	Practise lewdness, lasciviousness.
L	E	E	R	Ogle, sneer, smirk.
L	E	E	S	Sediment, deposit, dregs, grounds. Precipitate, precipitation, settlings.
L	E	F	T	Departed, abandoned, went away. Opposite to Right. Political bent. Bequeathed.
L	E	G	S	Plural of Leg.
L	E	H	R	Annealing oven for glass.
L	E	I	S	Plural of Lei.
L	E	N	D	Advance, loan. Furnish, grant. Accommodate, oblige. Assist, provide, supply.
L	E	N	O	Openweave.
L	E	N	S	Optical glass.
L	E	N	T	Past of Lend. Period of Penitence. Loaned. Inclined.
L	E	S	S	Smaller, inferior, minor, below average, fewer. Minus, excluding, without.
L	E	S	T	For fear that, unless.
L	E	T	S	Let us. Plural of Let.
L	E	V	Y	Tribute, tax, assessment, fine. Collect, exact.
L	E	W	D	Licentious, vulgar, base, libertine, lustful, salacious, lecherous.
L	I	A	R	One who utters falsehoods, prevaricator, one who juggles the truth. Perjurer.
L	I	A	S	Blue limestone.
L	I	C	E	Plural of Louse. Nits.
L	I	C	K	Taste, lap. Defeat, overcome. Tinge, trace. Touch with flame. Thrash, smite.
L	I	D	O	Luxurious Beach Resort.
L	I	E	D	Past of LIE. Song, descant, ditty, hymn.
L	I	E	S	Plural of LIE.
L	I	E	F	Beloved, precious. Willing, gladly.
L	I	E	N	Right of retention.
L	I	E	U	Instead of, in place of.
L	I	F	E	Animation, existence, Physical and mental experience. Vitality, verve, zing. Memoir, biography.
L	I	F	T	Elevate, raise, uphold, uplift, hoist, exalt, swipe, snitch, steal. Rise, aspire. Elevator, ski lift.
L	I	K	E	Favour, enjoy, relish, fancy, love, dote. Equivalent, identical, allied, same.
L	I	L	T	Cheerful song, air, ditty.
L	I	L	Y	Leafy stemmed bulbous herb with showy flowers. Fair, pure, fragile.
L	I	M	A	Bivalve Mollusc, Type of Bean.
L	I	M	B	Leg, arm, bough, branch, sprig, twig. appendage.
L	I	M	E	Citrus fruit. Limestone, calcium oxide.
L	I	M	P	Hobble, falter, stumble. Flabby, flaccid, floppy, languid, exhausted.
L	I	M	Y	Viscous.
L	I	N	E	Thread, string, cord, Align, arrange, Ancestry, Wrinkle, Boundary.
L	I	N	K	Bond, connection, coupling, liaison, tie, join, combine, ligature, nexus.
L	I	N	N	Pool, waterfall.
L	I	N	O	Linoleum.
L	I	N	T	Down, floss, fluff, fuzz, pile.
L	I	N	Y	Streaked, wrinkled.
L	I	O	N	Carnivorous mammal of the cat family. Leo.
L	I	P	S	Plural of LIP.
L	I	R	A	Italian unit of money, coin. Hurdy Gurdy.
L	I	R	K	A fold, a wrinkle.
L	I	S	P	Speech defect.
L	I	S	T	Roll, roster, register, schedule, enumerate, numerate, itemize, specify. Slant, lean.
L	I	V	E	Exist, survive, active, reside, abide, subsist, breathe, be. Alive.
L	O	A	D	Cargo, burden, freight, payload, mass, cram, convey, transport.
L	O	A	F	Lounge, dawdle, loiter, loll, laze, breadloaf.
L	O	A	M	Rich mould, topsoil.
L	O	A	N	Lend, advance, something lent, grant, transaction.
L	O	B	E	Earlobe, fissure, division, projection, flap.
L	O	B	S	Plural of LOB.
L	O	C	H	Lake, bay, inlet, cove, firth, creek, gulf, harbour, lough.
L	O	C	K	Fasten, secure, confine, shut, seal, bolt, interlock, padlock.
L	O	C	O	Locomotive. frenzied, lunatic, nuts.
L	O	D	E	Vein (ore), drain, ditch.
L	O	F	T	Upper room, attic. Gallery, hayloft.
L	O	G	E	Theatre box.

1	2	3	4	
L	O	G	O	Logotype, trademark, brand mark or insigna.
L	O	G	S	Plural of LOG.
L	O	I	N	Part of human body, cut of meat.
L	O	I	R	Dormouse.
L	O	L	L	Droop, dangle, sprawl, idle, slump, loiter, lounge.
L	O	M	A	Hilltop.
L	O	N	E	Isolated, solitary, unfrequented, uninhabited, unmarried or widowed.
L	O	N	G	Extended, lengthy, elongated, tall, large, yearn, hanker, pine.
L	O	N	K	Sheep.
L	O	O	K	Examine, observe, perceive, stare. Consider, regard, view. See.
L	O	O	M	Appear, emerge, approach, brew, impend. Aparatus for weaving.
L	O	O	N	Lunatic, diving bird.
L	O	O	P	Eye, ring, hoop, circle, surround, beset, gird, encompass.
L	O	O	S	Plural of LOO.
L	O	O	T	Booty, spoils, plunder, ransack, sack.
L	O	P	E	Canter, romp, jog.
L	O	P	H	Crest, cusp, comb.
L	O	R	D	Governor, prince, sovereign, landlord, master, pontificate, swagger, overbear.
L	O	R	E	Wisdom, doctrine, instruction, lesson, knowledge.
L	O	R	N	Derelict, alone, lonely, abandoned, forsaken, solitary.
L	O	R	Y	Papillose tongued Parrot.
L	O	S	E	Forfeit, sacrifice, destroy, mislay, squander, waste, fail.
L	O	S	S	Deprivation, lack, dispossession, forfeit, sacrifice, devastation, confusion.
L	O	S	T	Wasted, forfeited, bewildered, helpless, mislaid, denied. Doomed.
L	O	T	S	Plenty, much.
L	O	U	D	Clamorous, insistent, noisy, vehement, emphatic. Flashy, obnoxious, strident.
L	O	U	T	Oaf, yokel, boor, clod, palooka, rustic.
L	O	V	E	Desire, tenderness, benevolence, attraction, attachment, cherish, value, treasure. Passion, worship.
L	U	C	E	Heraldic representation of Pike.
L	U	C	K	Fate, fortune, chance, fortuity, accident, fluke, windfall.
L	U	D	O	Game.
L	U	F	F	Turn into the wind, sail near the wind. Windward.
L	U	G	E	Sled, toboggan.
L	U	G	S	Plural of LUG.
L	U	K	E	Lukewarm, tepid.
L	U	L	L	Soothe, calm, temporary cessation, lessening, hush.
L	U	L	U	Dandy, humdigger, corker. Super.
L	U	M	P	Clump, hunk, wad, chunk, bunch, batch, heap, mass.
L	U	N	A	Moon.
L	U	N	E	Half-moon shaped.
L	U	N	G	Respiratory organ.
L	U	N	K	Blockhead, chump, goon, numbskull.
L	U	N	T	Kindle, light, smoke, fire.
L	U	P	E	Polynesian fruit pigeon.
L	U	R	E	Entice, incentive, appeal, attraction, decoy, trap, snare. Tempt, seduce.
L	U	R	K	Skulk, prowl, sneak, steal, linger, remain, slink.
L	U	S	H	Succulent, luxuriant, green, fertile, lusty, thriving, generous, plentiful. Drunkard.
L	U	S	K	Sluggard, lazy.
L	U	S	T	Lechery, lasciviousness, craving, desire, wish, whim, vigor, fertility.
L	U	T	E	Musical stringed instrument. Seal.
L	U	X	E	Luxury, elegant.
L	Y	A	M	Bond.
L	Y	M	E	Grass.
L	Y	N	X	Wild cat, sharpsighted cat.
L	Y	R	E	Stringed musical instrument. Harp.

M

1	2	3	4	
M	A	A	M	Madam, mistress. Ma'am.
M	A	A	R	Volcanic crater.
M	A	B	A	Tropical Tree resembling ebony.
M	A	B	E	Cultured Pearl.
M	A	B	I	Bark, beverage.
M	A	C	E	Knobkerrie, shillelagh. Spice, nutmeg. Ceremonial staff.
M	A	D	E	Created, manufactured, invented, produced, fashioned, compelled.
M	A	G	I	Plural of MAGUS. Magician, magical. Sorcerer, necromancer. Wizard.

1	2	3	4	
M	A	I	D	Virgin, unmarried girl, woman, maiden, charwoman.
M	A	I	L	Post, letter, postal matter. Plate armour.
M	A	I	M	Mutilate, disable, disfigure, cripple, mangle, dismember.
M	A	I	N	Principal, chief, major, predominant, preeminent, foremost, leading, fundamental. Mainland, high seas.
M	A	K	E	Effect, cause, produce, initiate, originate, begin, start, create, father. Generate, prepare, compel. reach.
M	A	K	I	Lemur.
M	A	K	O	Bonito Shark.
M	A	L	E	Masculine, manly, mannish, virile. Man, boy.
M	A	L	L	Fashionable promenade, public avenue, pedestrian walk.
M	A	L	M	Limestone.
M	A	L	T	Grain nutrient, beer, whiskey.
M	A	M	A	Mother, mommy, mom, Mam.
M	A	M	S	Plural of MAM.
M	A	N	A	Supernatural force, power.
M	A	N	E	Heavy hair, neck hair, thick hair.
M	A	N	I	Peanut.
M	A	N	O	Grinding tool, Maneater shark.
M	A	N	X	Tail-less domestic cat said to originate on the Isle of Man.
M	A	N	Y	Lots, numbers, masses, multitude, hosts.
M	A	P	S	Plural of MAP.
M	A	R	C	Residue, substance.
M	A	R	E	Female equine, dark area of the Moon. Sea. Mud.
M	A	R	G	Margarine, butter substitute.
M	A	R	K	Stain, blemish, discolour, aim, objective, ambition, target, purpose. Token, emblem, trait, tag, logo.
M	A	R	L	Clay earth, brick.
M	A	R	S	Planet, God of War. Spoils, mutilates, blemishes, hampers, injures, impedes.
M	A	R	T	Market, Fair.
M	A	R	U	Japanese Merchant ship.
M	A	R	X	Karl Marx, father of Communism.
M	A	S	A	Corn Mash.
M	A	S	H	Hash, mixture, crush, squash.
M	A	S	K	Camouflage, disguise, blur, shield, protect, veil, vizor.
M	A	S	S	Bulk, volume, body, stack, stockpile, lump, swelling, aggregate, whole, assembly. Religious Service.
M	A	S	T	Pole, spar, mainmast.
M	A	T	E	Associate, companion, friend, buddy, pal. Peer, helper. Couple, copulate, consort.
M	A	T	H	Mathematic, calculation, absolute, definite.
M	A	T	S	Plural of MAT.
M	A	U	D	Fabric, Plaid.
M	A	U	L	Mangle, injure. Mace, mallet, fashion.
M	A	Y	A	Weaver bird. Magic, illusion.
M	A	Z	E	Intricate pattern of passages, Hedge bordered paths. Complication, bewilderment.
M	A	Z	Y	Winding, intricate.
M	E	A	D	Fermented drink, meadow.
M	E	A	K	Scythe.
M	E	A	L	Repast, food, cereal.
M	E	A	N	Stingy, penurious, low, petty, contemptible, inferior, humble. Denote, signify, express.
M	E	A	T	Food, nourishment, animal flesh, edible matter.
M	E	E	D	Amount, portion. Reward.
M	E	E	K	Mild, moderate, gentle, humble.
M	E	E	T	Gather, assemble. Suitable, fitting, proper, appropriate.
M	E	G	A	Great, large, major.
M	E	L	L	To mix, mingle, to have to do, to join in fight, to be concerned, to meddle.
M	E	L	T	Dissolve, disintegrate, soften, weaken, blend.
M	E	M	O	Memorandum, communication.
M	E	N	D	Reform, correct, rectify, repair, readjust, cure, ameliorate, heal, patch, remedy.
M	E	N	O	Less, musical direction. Remaining, persisting.
M	E	N	U	Bill of Fare, Card, Carte du jour.
M	E	R	E	Simply, alone, only, undiluted. Lake. Marsh.
M	E	R	O	Large Fish.
M	E	S	A	Isolated plateau, broad terrace, bench.
M	E	S	H	Network, snare, toils, engage, interlock, accord, harmonize, co-ordinate.
M	E	S	S	Disarrange, botch, bungle, muddle, spoil, damage, dabble, tinker, trifle, play. Eating quarters.
M	E	T	A	Behind, posterior, transformation.
M	E	T	E	Measure, appraise, allot, apportion.
M	E	T	H	Methol.
M	I	A	S	Orangutan.
M	I	C	A	Minerals.

1	2	3	4	
M	I	C	E	Plural of MOUSE.
M	I	C	K	Irishman.
M	I	C	O	Marmoset.
M	I	D	I	Dress length, fashion. Middle.
M	I	G	S	Plural of MIG.
M	I	K	E	Microphone.
M	I	L	D	Kind, gracious, considerate, bland, benign, tame, temperate, soft. Gentle.
M	I	L	E	Measurement of distance. 1760 yards.
M	I	L	K	Nourishment, fluid secreted by mammary glands, white substance. Suckle, elicit. Drain off.
M	I	L	L	Factory, machine house, plant, works, crushing plant.
M	I	L	T	Reproductive secretion of fish.
M	I	M	E	Act, perform, imitate, portray.
M	I	N	D	Memory, recollection, brain, seat of consciousness. Desire, wish, inclination. Intelligence, intellect.
M	I	N	E	Belonging to me. Quarry, diggings, excavations. Dig for ore. Colliery.
M	I	N	G	Type of Porcelain. China. Chinese Dynasty.
M	I	N	I	Curtailed, shortened, fashion length.
M	I	N	K	Four-footed carnivorous animal. Fur, pelt, of the Mink.
M	I	N	T	Coin, money. Unused, fresh, original. Aromatic plant.
M	I	N	X	Hussy, saucy jade, naughty girl.
M	I	N	Y	Like a mine, cavern.
M	I	R	Y	Boggy, muddy.
M	I	S	E	Writ.
M	I	S	S	Fail, escape, avoid, omit. Spinster, mistress. Long for. Pine for.
M	I	S	T	Fog, haze, cloud, murk, overcast.
M	I	T	E	Particle, iota, jot, molecule. Small arachnid.
M	I	T	T	Glove, hand. One mittern.
M	I	T	Y	Infested with mites.
M	O	A	N	Bewail, lament, deplore, berate. Complain, nag.
M	O	A	T	Protective ditch, trench, channel surrounding castle.
M	O	C	K	Flaunt, ridicule, deride, taunt. Parody, caricature, mimic, false.
M	O	D	E	Method, fashion, manner, technique, condition, situation, status. Position.
M	O	D	S	Modern young people.
M	O	I	L	Drudge, grind, labour. Plug, slog, toil. Hub bub, bustle.
M	O	K	E	Donkey, ass, burro.
M	O	K	O	Maori tattoo.
M	O	L	D	Type, stamp, pattern, template, matrix, shape, mildew, fungus, mould.
M	O	L	E	Congenital spot, mark on human body. Pigmented nevus. Burrowing mammal. Neutral colour. Pier.
M	O	L	L	Wanton, girlfriend, doll.
M	O	L	Y	Wild garlic.
M	O	M	E	A buffoon, a carper.
M	O	N	A	West African monkey.
M	O	N	K	Member of Monastic order. Priest, friar.
M	O	N	O	Single, containing one, radicle, particular.
M	O	O	D	Feeling, temper, disposition, aura, humour, vein.
M	O	O	N	Earth's satellite, heavenly body. Romantic symbol. Dawdle, gape.
M	O	O	R	Heath, fenn, wasteland, grassland, common. Make fast, tie up, anchor.
M	O	O	T	Argue, discuss, debate, broach, suggest. Hypothetical, debatable, unsettled.
M	O	P	E	Dawdle, gloom, brood.
M	O	P	S	Plural of MOP.
M	O	P	Y	State of moping, depressed, droopy.
M	O	R	A	Obligation, culpable delay, quantitive measure, game. Footstool, forest tree.
M	O	R	E	Additional, further, extended, protract.
M	O	R	N	Morning, dawn, forenoon, sunrise, daybreak, daylight, sun up.
M	O	R	T	Sound of hunting horn. Abundance, quantity. Death corpse.
M	O	S	S	Type of Lichen. Ericaceae.
M	O	S	T	Greatest, highest, best, largest.
M	O	T	E	Flyspeck, dot, mite, particle, speck.
M	O	T	H	Large winged insect.
M	O	U	E	Pout, grimace.
M	O	V	E	Go, depart, exit, leave, withdraw, march, proceed, progress, activate, actuate.
M	O	W	S	Cuts, reaps, crops.
M	O	Z	E	To gig, raise a nap on.
M	O	Z	O	Hired domestic male servant, handyman.
M	U	C	H	Quantity, amount, frequently, often, long, approximately, nearly.
M	U	C	K	Refuse, debris, garbage, junk, waste. Snarl, tangle.
M	U	F	F	Warm tubular hand covering, clumsy failure, duffer, bungle, bluff.
M	U	G	S	Plural of MUG.

1	2	3	4	
M	U	L	E	Hybrid horse/ass, hinny. Stubborn person. Locomotive, tractor.
M	U	L	L	Meditate, ponder, think, bemuse, befuddle, spiced wine, humus, fabric.
M	U	R	E	Immure, thrust, squeeze.
M	U	R	K	Gloomy, darken, dim.
M	U	S	A	Plantain, banana.
M	U	S	E	Meditate, ponder, contemplate, ruminate, study, trance, reverie.
M	U	S	H	Pulp, squash, crush, drivel. Command to husky sled team.
M	U	S	K	Perfume fixative, strong smelling substance. Scent.
M	U	S	S	Wrinkle, disarrange, rumple, dishevel.
M	U	S	T	Required to, requirement, Musk, mould. Necessitated, obliged to.
M	U	T	E	Inarticulate, silent, subduèd. Dumb, still.
M	U	T	T	Stupid person, mongrel dog, cur.
M	U	X	Y	Gloomy, disordered, messy.
M	Y	N	A	Mynah.
M	Y	T	H	Fable, folk tale, story, parable, legend, saga.
M	Y	X	A	Slime.
M	Y	Z	O	Sucking, sucker.

N

1	2	3	4	
N	A	B	E	Neighbourhood theatre.
N	A	B	S	Plural of NAB.
N	A	D	A	Nothingness.
N	A	I	D	Freshwater Annelid.
N	A	I	K	Indian Corporal.
N	A	I	L	Claw, talon, spike, tack, pin. Close, secure. Catch, trap.
N	A	I	O	Sandalwood tree substitute.
N	A	I	R	Indian Otter.
N	A	M	A	Hottentot.
N	A	M	E	Identification, race, family, clan. Entitle, denominate, stipulate.
N	A	N	A	Child's nurse. Nursemaid.
N	A	P	E	Back of the neck.
N	A	P	S	Plural of NAP.
N	A	R	K	Informer, spy, stool pigeon. Irritate, annoy. Killjoy, wet blanket.
N	A	S	I	Patriarch.
N	A	V	E	Hall, hub, Entrance.
N	A	V	Y	Fleet of ships. Navy blue.
N	A	Y	S	Plural of NAY.
N	A	Z	I	National Socialist Movement. Ideological German. Member of Nazi Party.
N	E	A	P	Tide. Low Tide.
N	E	A	R	Almost, nearly, closely, adjacent, nigh. Neo.
N	E	A	T	Tidy, snug, ship shape, spick and span. Trim, simple, adroit. Clever, admirable.
N	E	C	K	Head support. Cervical region. Strait. Spoon, cuddle, fondle.
N	E	E	D	Want, require, lack, obligation, poverty, penury, privation. Requirement.
N	E	E	M	Margosa oil.
N	E	E	P	Turnip.
N	E	E	R	Kidney.
N	E	S	S	Cape: Headland, promontory.
N	E	S	T	Resting place, bed, retreat, home, shelter, den, hangout. Group, assembly.
N	E	T	S	Plural of NET.
N	E	T	T	Basic, fundamental, essence, yield, profit.
N	E	W	S	Information, tidings, events, reports.
N	E	W	T	Eft, triton. Amphibian.
N	E	X	T	Adjoining, nearest, preceding, following, approaching. Intimate, close, adjacent.
N	I	B	S	Plural of NIB.
N	I	C	E	Tasty, dainty, enjoyable, pleasing, mild, virtuous.
N	I	C	K	Notch, snick, cut, groove, shape. Steal, cheat. Arrest, charge. Prison.
N	I	D	E	A brood of pheasants.
N	I	G	H	Near, impending, almost.
N	I	L	E	River, colour, green.
N	I	N	E	One more than eight.
N	I	P	A	Alcoholic beverage. Creeping palms. Thatch.
N	I	P	S	Plural of NIP.
N	I	S	I	Not final, not absolute, pending. (Legal term).
N	I	T	O	Climbing fern.
N	I	T	S	Plural of NIT.

1	2	3	4	
N	O	C	K	Tip, summit. Notch, slip, furnish.
N	O	D	E	Predicament, entanglement. Knob, protuberance, swelling.
N	O	D	S	Plural of NOD.
N	O	G	S	Plural of NOG.
N	O	I	R	Black numbers.
N	O	L	L	Knoll, crowd.
N	O	M	A	Disease.
N	O	M	E	Musical composition.
N	O	M	O	Usage, law.
N	O	N	E	Not any, neither, no one, nobody, nothing.
N	O	O	K	Cranny, corner, recess, arbour.
N	O	O	N	Midday, twelve o'clock, culmination, climax, apogee, apex, meridian.
N	O	P	E	No, negative.
N	O	R	M	Model, type, pattern. Average, standard, normal.
N	O	R	N	Fate.
N	O	S	E	Proboscis, snout, muzzle, olfaction. Aroma, scent. Meddle, pry, nuzzle.
N	O	T	E	Memo, annotation, notice, record. Perceive, observe, remark. Denote. Sound, tone. Distinction.
N	O	U	N	Subject, proper name, person, place, thing, animal, substance, quality, idea.
N	O	U	S	Mind, reason, alertness, commonsense.
N	O	V	A	Star.
N	U	B	S	Plural of NUB.
N	U	D	E	Naked, unclothed, undraped, unsupported, bare.
N	U	L	L	Invalid, void, non-existent, insignificant, empty. Zero.
N	U	M	B	Devoid of sensation, desensitized, be numbed, indifferent, listless, anaesthetized.
N	U	N	G	Bale of cloves.
N	U	R	L	To indent. Mill.
N	U	T	S	Plural of NUT.

O

1	2	3	4	
O	A	F	S	Plural of OAF.
O	A	K	S	Plural of OAK.
O	A	R	S	Plural of OAR.
O	A	T	H	Solemn declaration, profanity, irreverence, pledge, vow, curse, expletive.
O	A	T	S	Plural of OAT.
O	B	A	N	Japanese coin.
O	B	E	X	Obstacle.
O	B	E	Y	Conform, comply, mind.
O	B	I	T	Notice, record, obituary.
O	B	O	E	Wind instrument.
O	C	T	A	OCTO, containing eight.
O	C	U	L	Eye.
O	D	A	X	Large fish.
O	D	D	S	Disparities, profit, benefit, percentage, chances, variance, partiality.
O	D	E	S	Plural of ODE.
O	G	L	E	Leer, gape, gawp, rubberneck, goggle, gawk.
O	G	R	E	Monster, giant.
O	I	L	Y	Greasy, unctuously, plausible, smooth, suave.
O	K	A	Y	Alright, OK, yes. Authorise, sanction, approve.
O	K	I	E	Farmhand. Rustic.
O	K	R	A	Plant, vegetable.
O	L	E	O	Oleograph, background, backdrop.
O	L	I	D	Evil-smelling.
O	L	I	O	Medley, mixture.
O	M	E	N	Augury, toke, presage, forboding, sign, portent.
O	M	E	R	Hebrew measure.
O	M	I	T	Leave out, delete, exclude, neglect.
O	N	C	E	Only, nearly, just, ever. Formerly, someday, definitely.
O	N	E	S	Plural of ONE.
O	N	L	Y	Alone, peerless, matchless, unique, unparalleled, lone, sole, singular. Unrivalled.
O	N	T	O	On top of, upon.
O	N	U	S	Burden, load, responsibility, charge, duty, task, blame, culpability, fault.
O	N	Z	A	Spanish gold doubloon.
O	O	F	Y	Rich, wealthy.
O	O	I	D	Egg shaped.
O	O	P	S	Mild apology, surprise.

1	2	3	4	
O	O	Z	E	Mud, marsh, bog, juice, sap, emit, exude.
O	O	Z	Y	Muddy, miry, slimy.
O	P	A	H	Eliptical fish.
O	P	A	L	Irridescent stone. Semi precious stone.
O	P	E	N	Uncovered, accessible, uninterrupted, unfolded, unrolled, extended, expanded.
O	P	P	O	Friend, companion.
O	P	T	S	Plural of OPT. Chooses, decides.
O	P	U	S	Opera, musical work, composition.
O	R	A	L	Spoken, articulated, by mouth.
O	R	C	A	Killer Whale.
O	R	E	S	Plural of ORE.
O	R	F	E	Freshwater fish. Ide.
O	R	G	Y	Ritual, revelry, carousal, indulgence, display.
O	R	L	E	Heraldry.
O	R	T	H	Straight, upright, vertical, exact, parallel.
O	R	Y	X	African antelope.
O	T	I	C	Auricular, auditory.
O	T	U	S	Small-eared owl.
O	U	C	H	Ornament, expression of pain.
O	U	P	H	Elf.
O	U	R	S	Belonging to us.
O	U	S	T	Evict, eject, dislodge.
O	U	Z	O	Aniseed flavoured drink (Greek).
O	V	A	L	Eliptical, egg shaped. Cricket ground.
O	V	E	R	Across, beyond, excessively, extremely, unduly, too. Ended. Finished.
O	V	U	M	Egg cell. Macrogamete. Female gamete.
O	W	E	S	Indebted to, obligated.
O	W	L	S	Plural of OWL.
O	W	N	S	Plural of OWN. Possesses, acknowledges, admits, recognises, confesses.
O	X	E	N	Plural of OX. Cattle.
O	X	E	R	Guardrail.
O	Y	E	R	Petition hearing.
O	Y	E	Z	Cry for silence.

P

P	A	C	A	Rodent.
P	A	C	E	Rate of locomotion, speed, timing, tempo, step, walk. Fluency.
P	A	C	K	Cram, ram, tramp, stuff, crowd. Knapsack, Backpack, Rucksack. Icepack, mudpack, facepack. Troop of.
P	A	C	T	Contract, compact, treaty.
P	A	G	E	Leaf in book, newspaper, magazine. Messenger, guide. attendant.
P	A	H	I	Canoe.
P	A	H	O	Plumed prayer stick.
P	A	I	D	Made payment, made retribution, contributed, cashed, defrayed, settled.
P	A	I	K	Pummel.
P	A	I	L	Bucket.
P	A	I	N	Sensation, ache, pang, twinge, stress, suffering, agony, torment.
P	A	I	R	Two, brace, couple, twain. Combine, partner, match, join, mate.
P	A	L	E	Wan, sallow, faint, colourless, ashen, feeble, weak, dull, lack lustre.
P	A	L	I	Precipice, steep slope.
P	A	L	L	Mantle, cloak, counterpane, drape. Satiate, surfeit.
P	A	L	M	Palmae plant, leaf, branch, symbol. Hand. Stroke. Conceal.
P	A	L	P	Touch, feel, handle.
P	A	L	S	Plural of PAL.
P	A	L	Y	Wan, pallid, ashen.
P	A	N	E	Section of glass, panel.
P	A	N	G	Twinge, pain, torment.
P	A	N	S	Plural of PAN.
P	A	N	T	Gasp, puff, blow. Pulsate, throb.
P	A	P	A	Father, Dad, daddy. Pope. Pontiff.
P	A	P	S	Plural of PAP.
P	A	R	D	Leopard, sl. Partner, chum.
P	A	R	E	Trim, shave, skin.
P	A	R	K	Lawns, woodland, pasture, place of public recreation, reserve. Temporary stop or position. Carpark.
P	A	R	R	Young salmon.

1	2	3	4	
P	A	R	T	Fragment, fraction, constituent, share, portion, piece, detail, division. Sector, district, quarter.
P	A	S	S	Proceed, depart, leave, overtake, adjudicate, sanction. Achieve. Gap. Proposition.
P	A	S	T	Bygone, former, done, over, opposite of Present.
P	A	T	E	Crown of head. Paste, spread, mashed ingredients.
P	A	T	H	Track, way, route, course.
P	A	T	S	Dabs, daubs, taps.
P	A	V	E	Cover with stone, brick, asphalt or concrete. Prepare roadway, footpath.
P	A	V	O	Family of Peacocks.
P	A	W	N	Pledge, hostage, hock.
P	A	Y	E	Pay as you Earn.
P	E	A	K	Top, acme, apex, zenith.
P	E	A	L	Clang, ring, chime, knell, toll, resound, echo.
P	E	A	R	Fruit.
P	E	A	T	Turf used for fuel.
P	E	C	K	Strike with beak, pierce, kiss. Nag, carp. Measurement. Barrel.
P	E	E	K	Peep, glance, glimpse, gander.
P	E	E	L	Skin, scale, strip, exfoliate, decorticate. Pare, denude, expose.
P	E	E	N	Hammer. Flatten.
P	E	E	P	Chirp, cheep, twitter. Peek, glance, glimpse, peer, snoop.
P	E	E	R	Gaze, gape, gawk, stare. Contemporary, nobleman.
P	E	G	S	Plural of PEG.
P	E	L	L	Hasten, hurry.
P	E	L	T	Hide, fur, skin. Whack, beat, hurry, speed, drub.
P	E	N	D	Suspend, hand, impend, incline, lean.
P	E	N	T	Enclosed, confined, enclosed, reservoir, penthouse.
P	E	O	N	Foot soldier, constable, unwilling labourer, captive labourer.
P	E	P	O	Hard skinned fruit, pumpkin, cucumber.
P	E	R	I	Elf, fairy, graceful girl.
P	E	R	K	Smarten, trim, spruce. Gratuity, largesse, tip.
P	E	R	M	Permanent wave. Hairdo.
P	E	R	N	Honey buzzard.
P	E	S	O	Monetary unit.
P	E	S	T	Plague, nuisance, annoyance, pestilence, scourge.
P	H	I	Z	Face, visage, physiognomy.
P	H	O	N	Decibel, Unit of loudness.
P	H	O	T	Unit of illumination.
P	I	A	L	Relating to the Piamater, connective tissue of brain and spinal cord.
P	I	A	N	Yaws.
P	I	A	T	Weapon, anti tank gun.
P	I	C	A	Size of type on typewriter.
P	I	C	E	Monetary unit.
P	I	C	K	Cull, select, choose, pluck, harvest. Nag, pester. Choice. Spike, tool, pickaxe.
P	I	C	T	Early Scottish race.
P	I	E	D	Piebald, variegated, parti-coloured. Black and White.
P	I	E	R	Breakwater, groin, mole. Doorpost, gatepost, buttress.
P	I	E	S	Plural of PIE.
P	I	E	T	Magpie.
P	I	K	A	Small rodent.
P	I	K	E	Turnpike, toll gate, weapon, fish, snoek.
P	I	L	A	Communal fountain.
P	I	L	E	Heap, lot, amass, increase, haemorrhoid. Down, hair, carpet fabric.
P	I	L	L	Tablet, medicine, pellet, golf ball, baseball.
P	I	M	P	Solicitor, manfriend, scoundrel. Procuror.
P	I	N	E	Pine Tree, Pineapple. Lament, long for, languish. Grief, sorrow.
P	I	N	G	Noise of a bullet, metallic sound.
P	I	N	K	Flower, colour, pierce, cut. In the pink, feeling good.
P	I	N	T	Measure of capacity. 8 pints = 1 gallon.
P	I	N	Y	Full of Pines.
P	I	P	E	Musical instrument, bagpipe, vent, bosun's whistle, smoker's comfort.
P	I	P	I	Bi-valve mollusc, edible wedge shell.
P	I	P	Y	Hollow tube.
P	I	R	N	Quill.
P	I	S	E	Rammed clay.
P	I	T	H	Essence, core, marrow, sap, extract.
P	I	T	Y	Compassion, commiseration, sympathy, mercy.
P	I	X	Y	Small fairy.
P	L	A	N	Plot, scheme, design, sketch, map, blueprint.

1	2	3	4	
P	L	A	Y	Sport, dalliance, frolic, jest, fun. Gamble. Perform, act, play the piano.
P	L	E	A	Petition, appeal, pretext.
P	L	E	D	Past of PLEAD.
P	L	I	M	Inflate, swell.
P	L	O	D	Toil, drudge, jog, tramp, trudge.
P	L	O	P	Splash. Drop wearily, explosive sound, plump.
P	L	O	T	Area of ground, portion of land. Conspiracy, intrigue. Map, plan.
P	L	O	Y	Pursuit, activity, escapade, tactic.
P	L	U	G	Stopper, fill, secure, tighten, punch, publicise. Small lump. Shoot with gun.
P	L	U	M	Fruit, windfall. Colour. Beaut.
P	L	U	S	In addition, surplus, increase, add.
P	O	C	K	Pustule, spot, hole, pit.
P	O	E	M	Ode, lyric, elegy.
P	O	E	T	Writer of Poems, bard, balladeer, lyricist.
P	O	K	E	Nudge, prod, thrust, dig, jab, punch, box, clout.
P	O	K	Y	Small, confined, cramped, dull, confined, stupid, monotonous.
P	O	L	E	Mast, rod, flagpole, stick, rod. Native of Poland.
P	O	L	L	Election. Head. Parrot. Dome, nape, crown.
P	O	L	O	Ball game.
P	O	M	E	Apple, metal ball, globe, sphere.
P	O	M	P	Pageantry, ceremony, display, array, fanfare, parade.
P	O	N	D	Pool, mere.
P	O	O	H	Raspberry, catcall. Winnie the pooh.
P	O	O	L	Puddle, mere, pond, tarn, merge, combine, syndicate, cartel.
P	O	O	P	Ship's stern. Idiot. Exhaust, fag, frazzle.
P	O	O	R	Scant, meagre, destitute, broke, pitiful, cheap, inferior, bad, unwell.
P	O	P	E	Bishop of Rome, Head of Roman Catholic Church. St. Peter's Successor.
P	O	R	E	Minute orifice in skin, ponder, study.
P	O	R	K	Pig hog flesh.
P	O	R	T	Harbour, anchorage, shelter, asylum, haven, refuge, bearing, mien, Wine.
P	O	R	Y	Porous, pervious.
P	O	S	E	Posture, feign, extend, offer, propose, puzzle, confuse, confound.
P	O	S	H	Stylish, chic, exclusive, fashionable, smart, swank, trendy.
P	O	S	T	Mail, letters, record, station, despatch, notify, warn, after.
P	O	S	Y	Flower, blossom, bouquet, nosegay, garland.
P	O	U	F	Pouffe, large cushion, comforter.
P	O	U	R	Flow, discharge, emit, gush, stream, rush, surge, cascade, deluge, inundate.
P	O	U	T	Sulk, grump, project, protrude, jut, bulge, overhang.
P	R	A	M	Perambulator, baby carriage, baby buggy, bassinet.
P	R	A	Y	Entreat, implore, appeal, beseech, plead, importune, supplicate, beg.
P	R	E	P	Preparation, preparatory, homework.
P	R	E	Y	Game, quarry, victim, underdog, chase, casualty, pillage.
P	R	I	G	Fop, prude, goody-goody, prim, prissy, prudish.
P	R	I	M	Neat, orderly, formal, precise, priggish, genteel, proper, prudish, stuffy.
P	R	O	A	Malay sailing canoe.
P	R	O	D	Poke, jab, nudge, dig, urge, exhort, goad, prick, spur.
P	R	O	M	Promenade, concert, Dance.
P	R	O	P	Support, bolster, buttress, sustain, uphold, buoy, shore up, brace, stay.
P	R	O	S	Arguments in favour.
P	R	O	W	Ship's bow, projecting front. Stem.
P	R	O	X	Proximo, immediate.
P	U	C	E	Purple red, flea red, Victoria red. Eureka red, flea coloured.
P	U	C	K	Imp, devil, demon. Disc used in ice hockey.
P	U	F	F	Pant, gasp, huff, boast. Boost, praise. Sleeve pattern. Powderpuff. Puff of smoke.
P	U	K	E	Vomit, heave, purge, retch, spit.
P	U	L	E	Whine, whimper, cry, mewl.
P	U	L	L	Extract, draw, drag, haul, lug. Attraction, appeal, lure.
P	U	L	P	Mush, mash, crush, squash, bruise, mess.
P	U	M	A	Mountain lion, Cougar.
P	U	M	P	Drain, draft, draw, siphon, tap. Interrogate.
P	U	N	K	Nonsense, baloney, bunkum, beginner, fledgling, tough, ruffian, bad, wrong.
P	U	N	T	Kick, gamble, flat-bottomed boat. Bet.
P	U	N	Y	Tiny, petty, measly, paltry, piddling, trivial, weak, feeble.
P	U	P	A	Chrysalis, developing insect.
P	U	P	S	Plural of PUP.
P	U	R	E	Chaste, unadulterated, undiluted, perfect, absolute, blameless, guiltless.
P	U	R	L	Swirl, eddy, gyrate, spin, twirl, whirl, ripple. Knit.

1	2	3	4	
P	U	R	R	Murmur with content, cat noise.
P	U	S	H	Propel, shove, thrust, increase, promote, press, stimulus, ambition.
P	U	S	S	Feline, child, juvenile, moppet, face, countenance, pan, mug.
P	U	T	T	Flick, stroke, strike (at golf).
P	U	X	Y	Swamp, bog, fen, marsh, mire, moss, swampland.
P	Y	R	E	Combustible heap, funeral rite, pile.
P	Y	R	O	Pyrotechnics, fire, of fireworks.

Q

Q	U	A	D	Quadrangle, quadruplet, type block, quadruped. Courtyard, enclosure.
Q	U	A	G	Quagmire, morass, swamp, mire. Bog, fen, vlei.
Q	U	A	T	Upstart, whippersnapper, twerp, nonentity. Squat, hunker down.
Q	U	A	Y	Bank, wharf, landing place. Jetty, dock, berth, pier, slipway.
Q	U	E	Y	Heifer, young cow.
Q	U	I	D	Pound Sterling, cud, wad, chew tobacco.
Q	U	I	N	Quintuplet, fivefold, quintuplicate.
Q	U	I	P	Sally, retort, joke, crack, gag, jest, wisecrack, witticism.
Q	U	I	T	Leave, desert, retire, clear off, abandon, forsake, resign.
Q	U	I	Z	Puzzle, enquire, examine, question. Game. Scout.
Q	U	O	D	Prison, jail, bastille, confine, constrain, incarcerate, intern, jug.

R

R	A	A	D	Volksraad, Legislative Assembly (South Africa).
R	A	C	E	Nation, tribe, folk, stock, culture, run, rush, chase, dash. Creek.
R	A	C	K	Framework, grating, stand. Afflict, torment, torture.
R	A	C	Y	Pungent, spicy, zesty, snappy. Off-colour, suggestive. Sexy.
R	A	F	F	Rabble, riffraff, ragtag, proletariat, mob, masses.
R	A	F	T	Floating platform, makeshift craft, rescue boat, inflatable dinghy.
R	A	G	E	Anger, fume, fury, frenzy, agitation. Craze, chic, vogue, style.
R	A	G	S	Pural of RAGS.
R	A	I	D	Incursion, foray, invasion, foray, onslaught, assault, plunder, rifle, loot.
R	A	I	L	Railing, balustrade, banister. Scold, berate, revile.
R	A	I	N	Drizzle, downpour, drop, fall down upon. Shower.
R	A	K	E	Sport, Scour, forage, grub, implement, stir up, loosen. Rascal.
R	A	L	E	Hawk, rumble, wheeze.
R	A	M	P	Slope, parapet, curved platform. Rampart.
R	A	M	S	Plural of RAM.
R	A	N	A	Genus of Frog.
R	A	N	D	Monetary Unit, Ridge, border, Rim.
R	A	N	G	Past of Ring. Chimed, clanged.
R	A	N	I	Wife of a Rajah.
R	A	N	K	Rampant, overgrown, obscene. Flagrant, absolute, malodorous. Line, status, class.
R	A	N	T	Rave, orate, harangue, rage, storm, scold, berate, bombast.
R	A	P	E	Defile, debauch, dishonour, seduce, violate, ravish, outrage. Rape seed oil.
R	A	P	S	Plural of RAP.
R	A	P	T	Enthralled, absorbed, fascinated, intent, immersed, preoccupied, engrossed.
R	A	R	E	Unusual, precious, infrequent, exceptional, scarce, choice. Undercooked.
R	A	S	H	Urticaria, skin irritation. Hasty, ill-advised, impetuous, foolhardy, impulsive.
R	A	S	P	File, scrape, grate, scratch.
R	A	T	A	New Zealand Ironwood Tree.
R	A	T	E	Price, estimate, charge, cost, tariff, appraise, assess, earn, merit.
R	A	V	E	Rant, fume, storm, orate, harangue, enthuse, rhapsodize, drool.
R	A	Z	E	Level, Expunge, gut, demolish, overthrow, decimate, ruin, wreck.
R	A	Z	Z	Raspberry, hoot, hiss, catcall. Banter, jest, joke, Ridicule, deride.
R	E	A	D	Peruse, study, decipher, decode, register, indicate, record. Past of READ. Interpret.
R	E	A	L	True, genuine, authentic, bona fide, existing, necessary, sound, valid.
R	E	A	M	Measurement of paper, quantity. Enlarge, cheat.
R	E	A	P	Harvest, gather, crop, garner, glean, ingather, collect, benefit.
R	E	A	R	Breed; raise. Back, behind, posterior.
R	E	C	K	Consider, deem.
R	E	D	D	Disentangle, smarten, neaten, unravel, arrange.
R	E	D	E	Counsel, advice, Predict, guess, explain.
R	E	E	D	Tall grass, rattan, pipe, stalk, sedge.

1	2	3	4	
R	E	E	K	Smell, stink, stench, smoke, vapour, fume.
R	E	E	L	Sway, totter, spin, lurch, weave, stumble, teeter. Bobbin, spool.
R	E	F	T	Past of REAVE. Cleft, fissure, bereft. Left.
R	E	I	N	Curb, check, control, restrain, repress, smother, suppress. Leather harness.
R	E	I	S	Unit of money.
R	E	L	Y	Depend, lean, confide, trust, bank on, count on.
R	E	N	D	Rip, sever, rupture, split, cleave, tear, separate, divide, account.
R	E	N	T	Hire, lease, charter, let. Fracture, breach, split, torn.
R	E	P	P	Fabric.
R	E	S	P	Sheep disease.
R	E	S	T	Recline, repose, relax. Base, foundation. Remainder, balance, residue.
R	E	T	E	Network, plexus, net.
R	E	U	S	Defendant.
R	H	E	A	Flightless bird. China Grass.
R	I	C	E	Cereal, cultivated grass. Food staple.
R	I	C	H	Opulent, affluent, moneyed, well-off, wealthy, flush. Fertile, luscious. Abundant in, rife with.
R	I	C	K	Pile, bank, drift, heap, hill, stack. Sprain, twist, wrench.
R	I	D	E	Motor, drive, spin, travel. Chivy, hound. Overlap.
R	I	D	S	Plural of RID.
R	I	E	M	Rawhide, leather thong.
R	I	F	E	Prevalent, abundant, current, prevailing, ruling, alive, abounding, teeming.
R	I	F	F	Browse, flip, glance, leaf, riffle, scan, skim, thumb.
R	I	F	T	Split, gap, chink, fissure, crack, cleft, breach, rupture.
R	I	L	E	Vex, anger, provoke, irritate, inflame, muddle, nettle, grate.
R	I	L	L	Rivulet, stream, brook, cascade.
R	I	M	A	Cleft, fissure, rift, chink, crack, rime, split.
R	I	M	E	Crack, cleft, fissure, rift, rima, split, crust.
R	I	N	G	Chime, tinkle. Eye, loop, circle, round. Telephone call, peal. Dial or phone a number.
R	I	N	K	Icedrome, skating rink.
R	I	O	T	Anarchy, disorder, uprising, tumult, uproar, frolic, roister, spree.
R	I	P	E	Mature, ready, mellow, full-grown, developed, aged, ripened.
R	I	P	S	Plural of RIP.
R	I	S	E	Stand, mount, soar, ascend, boost, originate, spring, transpire, happen. Increase.
R	I	S	K	Chance, danger, hazard, jeopardy, peril, gamble, venture.
R	I	T	E	Ceremonial, ritual, liturgy, sacrament, service, occasion.
R	I	V	E	Tear, cleave, rend, rip, split, divide, separate, chop, shatter, burst, splinter.
R	O	A	D	Thoroughfare, highway, route, avenue, boulevard, street, track, passage.
R	O	A	M	Ramble, meander, saunter, drift, gallivant, range, rove.
R	O	A	N	Antelope. Bookbinding. Horse colour.
R	O	A	R	Bellow, bawl, bluster, clamour, yell, shout.
R	O	B	E	Drape, dress, vestment, clothe.
R	O	C	K	Stone. Shake, swing, undulate, quake. Diamond. Confectionary.
R	O	D	E	Travelled, cantered, galloped, motored, cycled, Past of RIDE.
R	O	E	R	Blunderbuss, shotgun.
R	O	I	L	Irritate, rile, stir up, vex. Muddy, pollute.
R	O	K	E	Smoke, steam, mist, fog.
R	O	K	Y	Foggy, misty.
R	O	L	E	Function, duty, office, guise, semblance, show, aspect. Stage act, part or character.
R	O	L	L	Register, catalogue, roster, muster, pile, wad, wrap, swathe, drape, envelop.
R	O	M	E	Vatican Capital.
R	O	M	P	Frisk, caper, gambol, cavort. Walkover, runaway.
R	O	N	E	Brushwood, thicket.
R	O	O	D	Crucifix. Unit of measure.
R	O	O	F	Top. Apex, crest, peak, summit. Canopy, cover.
R	O	O	K	Fleece, bleed, milk, cheat, defraud. Chessman. Crowlike bird.
R	O	O	M	Chamber, apartment, flat, lodgings, suite, tenement. Elbowroom, leeway, sufficient space.
R	O	O	T	Source, derivation, origin, basis, centre, essence. Applaud, cheer. Implant, fix. Root out, destroy.
R	O	P	E	Flax, fibre, string, secure, bind, tether, tie.
R	O	P	Y	Stringy, fibrous, sinewy, wiry. Dishevelled, untidy, of no consequence.
R	O	S	E	Past of RISE. Bloom, blossom.
R	O	S	Y	Hopeful, encouraging, likely, promising, rose-coloured.
R	O	T	A	Roster, Roman Catholic Curia.
R	O	T	E	Routine, grind, groove, pace, rut, treadmill, repetition.
R	O	U	É	Libertine, sport, rake, debauchee.
R	O	U	P	Fowl Pox, Infectious sinusitis.
R	O	U	T	Vanquish, defeat, debacle. Rummage, hunt. Bellow, bluster, bawl. Social function, soiree.
R	O	U	X	Base for White Sauce. Butter and flour.

1	2	3	4	
R	O	V	E	Ramble, roam, stray, range, wander, drift, meander, traipse.
R	U	B	Y	Colour red, red wine. Precious stone.
R	U	C	K	Wrinkle, crease. Main body of competitors.
R	U	D	D	Freshwater fish.
R	U	D	E	Crude, raw, rough, coarse, crass, gross, vulgar.
R	U	E	D	Regret, repented, deplored, pitied, sorrowed.
R	U	F	F	Collar, fringe, ruffle, tousle. Trump. Species of bird.
R	U	G	A	Fold, wrinkle.
R	U	I	N	Deterioration, decline, destroy, decimate, wreck, frustrate, corrupt.
R	U	L	E	Control, govern, reign, sway, maxim, law, canon, ordinance, regulation. Ordinarily.
R	U	M	P	Buttocks, rear, haunch, beam, backside, derriere, posterior.
R	U	N	E	A letter of the futhork or ancient Germanic alphabet, a secret, a mystic symbol, sentence, spell or song.
R	U	N	G	Degree, notch, stage, step, grade, degree. Past of ring.
R	U	N	T	Dwarf, stunted, contemptible.
R	U	S	E	Trick, artifice, stratagem, gambit, gimmick, ploy. Manoeuvre.
R	U	S	H	Bolt, charge, chase, dash, race, plunge, speed, dart, hurry, fly.
R	U	S	K	Dried baked bread, cake. Biscuit.
R	U	S	T	Corrode, tarnish, oxidized. Oxide.
R	U	T	A	Herb, Rue.
R	U	T	H	Pity, mercy, sympathy, penitence.
R	Y	A	L	Gold coin. Silver Coin.
R	Y	O	T	Peasant, tenant farmer.
R	Y	P	E	Ptarmigan. Grouse.

S

S	A	C	K	Bag, pocket, pouch, Dismiss, fire. Ravage, desecrate, spoil.
S	A	F	E	Secure, unharmed, unscathed. Careful, guarded. Strongbox, vault.
S	A	G	A	Legend, biography, story, history, narrative, myth.
S	A	G	E	Wise, discerning, knowing, perceptive, scholar, expert, master, wiseman. Herb.
S	A	G	O	Palm starch. Granulated Palm Pith. Pudding.
S	A	G	Y	Tasting of sage. Seasoned with sage.
S	A	I	C	Ketch.
S	A	I	D	Stated, mentioned, declared, alleged. Past of say.
S	A	I	L	Cruise, skim, scud, float, fly, dart, flit, sweep, wing.
S	A	K	E	Good, enhancement, advantage, cause, regard, reason. Benefit, welfare, safety.
S	A	K	I	Japanese Rice Wine. American Monkeys.
S	A	L	E	Auction, market, contract, transfer. For sale.
S	A	L	T	Sodium chloride, condiment, seasoning. Mariner.
S	A	M	E	Similar, comparable, like, identical, exact, consistent, invariable, uniform.
S	A	M	P	Stamped mealies. Dried Corn.
S	A	N	D	Grit, unstable grains of grit, seasand, soil.
S	A	N	E	Rational, normal, lucid, balanced, level headed, sensible, cogent.
S	A	N	G	Past of SING. Chanted, voiced, vocalised.
S	A	N	K	Foundered, subsided, dropped, disappeared from sight. Past of sink.
S	A	N	S	Without. Not having.
S	A	P	O	Toadfish.
S	A	R	D	Precious stone, agate. Sardine.
S	A	R	I	Indian garment, swathed material. Scarf.
S	A	R	K	Body garment for either sex. Shirt, chemise.
S	A	S	H	Belt, girdle, waistband, cumberbund, ribbon, rope. Sashcord/Chord.
S	A	S	S	Insolence, cheek, impertinence, lip, sauce, backchat.
S	A	T	E	Gratify, satiate, satisfy, fill, glut, gorge, pall, stuff.
S	A	V	E	Rescue, deliver, preserve, sustain, cache, collect, stockpile, store. Except. But.
S	A	W	N	Cut, hewn. Past of saw.
S	A	X	E	Light blue.
S	C	A	B	Scale, scurf, crust. Sore. Blackleg.
S	C	A	D	Heap, quantity, much, multitude, lot, abundance.
S	C	A	N	Browse, flip, glance, riff, skim, examine, audit, check, inspect, peruse.
S	C	A	R	Blemish, mark, cicatrize, scarify, blemish, disfigure, flaw, deface.
S	C	A	T	Leave hurriedly, drive away, scatter, scare off.
S	C	O	T	Scotsman. Native of Scotland, Gaelic. Assessment.
S	C	O	W	Flatbottomed boat, sailboat.
S	C	U	D	Rush, hurry, scuttle, fly, hasten, bustle, shoot, skim.
S	C	U	M	Dross, froth, refuse, rabble, dregs, trash, proletariat.
S	C	U	T	Short tail, hare's tail, rabbit's tail.

1	2	3	4	
S	E	A	L	Stamp, Adhere, join, stick, symbol. Cement. Stamp of assent or approval.
S	E	A	M	Joint, connection, coupling, junction, union, bond, fastener. Hem, sew.
S	E	A	R	Scorch, shrivel, parch, burn, dry, dehydrate, desiccate.
S	E	A	T	Chair, bench, focus, Heart, hub, base, basis, foundation. Buttocks, behind.
S	E	C	T	Group, party, faction, schism, section, sectional.
S	E	E	D	Bud, embryo, kernel, nucleus, germ, rudiment. Offspring. Plant seed.
S	E	E	K	Search, hunt, ferret, quest. Attempt, endeavour, strive. Assay, undertake.
S	E	E	M	Appear, look, sound, resemble, pretend, imply, hint.
S	E	E	N	Observed, regarded, perceived. Past of SAW.
S	E	E	P	Ooze, trickle, exude, flow, drip.
S	E	E	R	Prophet, soothsayer, forecaster.
S	E	L	F	Identity, ego, personality, individual. Oneself. Yourself.
S	E	L	L	Vend, hawk, barter, deal, market, retail. Betray, Sell out.
S	E	M	I	Half, demi, partial, incomplete, quasi, partly, hemi. (Prefix).
S	E	N	D	Transmit, consign, forward, remit, allocate, assign.
S	E	N	T	Forwarded, transmitted, despatched. Past of SEND.
S	E	P	S	Reptile, lizards.
S	E	P	T	Seven. September.
S	E	R	B	Serbian, Slavic.
S	E	R	E	Dry, parch, sear, wither, arid, waterless, thirsty.
S	E	R	F	Slave, bondsman, peon, pleasant labourer.
S	E	T	A	Hairs, bristles, spikes, spines.
S	E	W	N	Stitched, mended, hemmed, embroidered, planted.
S	E	X	T	Musical interval. Pipe organ stop.
S	H	A	D	Fish of the Herring type.
S	H	A	G	Tangled, matted, thicket.
S	H	A	H	Monarch.
S	H	A	M	Fake, hoax, hypocrisy, fictitious, mock, simulated, pretence, counterfeit, bogus.
S	H	A	Y	Vehicle. Hauler.
S	H	E	D	Discharge, discard, jettison, slough, reject. Shack, stable, hut.
S	H	I	M	A slip of metal, wood used to fill in space or to adjust parts.
S	H	I	N	Lower leg, run, dash, scamper, scurry, scamper, sprint, climb.
S	H	I	P	Vessel, craft, boat, send, consign, freight, move, disturb, transfer.
S	H	O	D	Provided with shoes, shoed.
S	H	O	E	Footwear, borgue, boot, etc. Horseshoe. Act of shoeing.
S	H	O	G	Hustle, jostle, press, shove, push.
S	H	O	P	Store, outlet, showroom, boutique, Supermarket. Sell out, betray.
S	H	O	T	Past of SHOOT. Chance, small measure, hurried.
S	H	O	W	Display, demonstrate, Stage play. Guide, appear. Exhibition.
S	H	U	N	Avoid, evade, elude, eschew, snub.
S	H	U	T	Close, seal, lock, bar, secure.
S	I	C	K	Ailing, unwell, debilitated, unhealthy, morbid, faulty.
S	I	D	E	Place, space, direction, division, flank, sector, phase, angle, viewpoint. Verge. Perimeter. Elevation.
S	I	D	I	Muslim Title.
S	I	D	Y	Aloof, pretentious, snobbishness.
S	I	F	T	Sieve, sort, separate, winnow, explore, delve, probe.
S	I	G	H	Exhale noisily.
S	I	G	N	Portent. Endorse, signature. Signal, gesture. Emblem, symbol.
S	I	L	E	Strain.
S	I	L	K	Insect larvae thread, fine fibre, spun filaments, cloth, Q.C.'s garment, jockey colours.
S	I	L	L	Framework, support, window ledge.
S	I	L	O	Silage Store, Grain elevator, underground depot.
S	I	L	T	Sediment, scum, dregs.
S	I	M	P	Dunce, dimwit, nitwit, simpleton, pinhead, wantwit.
S	I	N	G	Chant, vocalise, serenade, croon, intone, carol, squeal, inform, nark, snitch.
S	I	N	K	Founder, submerge, submerse, dive, scuttle, shipwreck, set, decline, descend.
S	I	N	N	Fein - Irish Nationalism.
S	I	N	S	Plural of SIN.
S	I	P	S	Plural of SIP.
S	I	R	E	Father, creator, founder, maker, beget, breed, spawn, hatch. Lord.
S	I	S	S	Expression of disgust (South African).
S	I	T	E	Location, place, position, spot, scene, habitat, plot, excavation, locality.
S	I	T	S	Plural of SIT.
S	I	Z	E	Magnitude, measurement, dimension, proportion, bulk, mass, expanse, width.
S	I	Z	Z	Hiss, buzz, fizz, sibilate, swish, whisper, swish.
S	K	A	G	Cigarette, butt, cig, fag, gasper, smoke.
S	K	E	D	(American) Schedule, timetable, agenda, calendar, programme.

1	2	3	4	
S	K	E	P	Farm basket. Coarse basket. Beehive.
S	K	E	W	Crooked, oblique, awry, aslant, angled, biased, slew, veer.
S	K	I	D	Slide, slur, veer, slew, sheer, side-slip.
S	K	I	M	Graze, skirt, brush, touch, top, glance, dart. Coating, film, layer.
S	K	I	N	Surface, covering, hide, case, shell, sheath. Peel, scale, strip, fleece, condemn.
S	K	I	P	Hop, caper, jump, omit, run, bolt, scamper. Bucket, mine car, hopper.
S	K	I	T	Lampoon, burlesque, take-off, comedy.
S	K	U	A	Large Gull.
S	K	Y	E	Terrier. Isle of skye.
S	L	A	B	Block, chunk, lump, ingot, bar, pavement, muck, mud. Marble slab.
S	L	A	G	Dross, debris, mine waste, lava. Hag, slattern.
S	L	A	M	Bang, strike, slug, swat, drub, bash, smash, slur, crack, slap.
S	L	A	P	Smack, spank, cuff, sock, bash, score.
S	L	A	T	Strip, panel, bar, slit, lath, louvre.
S	L	A	V	Slavonic. Slavic of Jugoslavia.
S	L	A	W	Cabbage.
S	L	A	Y	Kill, destroy, murder, despatch, finish, assasinate, liquidate, butcher, slaughter.
S	L	E	D	Sledge, sleigh.
S	L	E	W	Twist, swerve, curve, skid, Past of SLAY.
S	L	E	Y	Weaver's reed, guide.
S	L	I	D	Past of SLIDE. Glided, skidded.
S	L	I	M	Slight, slender, thin, sleek, skinny. Slenderise, reduce. Remote, unlikely.
S	L	I	P	Slide, slither, skid, topple. Escape. Error. Slump, sag. Cutting. Wharf.
S	L	I	T	Rip, rend, tear, slash, sever, gash, slice, cut.
S	L	O	B	Clot, vulgarian, layabout, heel, loafer.
S	L	O	E	Plum, blackthorn, Berry.
S	L	O	G	Strike, plod, footslog, trudge, drudge, grind, grub, slave, toil.
S	L	O	P	Pap, rubbish, spill, splash. Mess. Flow out. Let fall.
S	L	O	T	Groove, opening, passage, space, pigeon hole, niche. Sequence. Time-slot.
S	L	O	W	Tardy, inactive, retarded, limited, sluggish, halting, straggling, delay.
S	L	U	B	Fabric, material, yarn.
S	L	U	E	Slide, skid, slew, swerve, sheer, veer.
S	L	U	G	Sluggard, bum, slouch. Dram, drop, tot. Belt, clobber, slam. Garden pest.
S	L	U	M	Ghetto, warren, skid row, squalid neighbourhood. Tramp, bum, hobo. Ill-mannered person.
S	L	U	R	Stigma, stain, sully, aspersion, a blot, malign, befoul. Slide.
S	L	U	T	Slattern, drab, wanton, hussy, jade, tramp, trollop, wench, strumpet, prostitute.
S	M	E	W	Migratory sea duck.
S	M	I	T	Infect, stain, tarnish.
S	M	O	G	Industrial fog, haze, mist. Polluted air.
S	M	U	G	Complacent, priggish, self-satisfied.
S	M	U	T	Blot, stain, soil, stain, smudge, smear, defile, dirt, unclean. Pornography. Undesirable material.
S	N	A	G	Obstacle, hamper, hurdle, impediment, drag, stumbling block.
S	N	A	P	Bark, snarl, growl. Grab, jerk, cinch, snip. Vigor, vitality. Photograph.
S	N	E	B	Snib, snub, check, reprimand.
S	N	E	E	Large Knife.
S	N	I	P	Clip, cut, Bargain. Minx. Snap. Pushover, cinch.
S	N	I	T	Irritation, agitation, huff, pique, sweat, stew, tizzy, fume.
S	N	O	B	High hat, snoot, snot, name-dropper, toffee-nosed, conceited person.
S	N	O	T	Contemptible person, Louse, sod, stinker, villain, mucous.
S	N	O	W	Snowfall, T.V. Spots, Cocaine. Frozen rain.
S	N	U	B	Cold shoulder, ostracise, slight.
S	N	U	G	Cosy, compact, sheltered, neat, tidy, uncluttered, comfortable, easy, soft.
S	O	A	K	Drench, permeate, impregnate, steep, souse, wet, immerse, saturate. Drunkard, boozer.
S	O	A	P	Cleansing agent, toilet soap, soft soap, detergent, suds.
S	O	A	R	Rise, ascend, aspire, lift, mount, climb, skyrocket, shoot.
S	O	B	S	Plural of SOB.
S	O	C	K	Strike, biff, clout, slog, bash, cuff, buffet, sigh, footwear.
S	O	D	A	Sodium carbonate. Sodium Bicarbonate. Sodium Hydroxide. Soda water, Icecream Soda.
S	O	F	A	Couch, divan, ottoman.
S	O	F	T	Gentle, subdued, comfortable, simple, mild, sober, delicate, silky, flaccid.
S	O	H	O	Mecca of London's West End.
S	O	I	L	Earth, ground, land, country, homeland. Contaminate, dirty, foul, stain, despoil.
S	O	L	D	Retailed, marketed, merchandised. Past of SELL.
S	O	L	E	Single, lone, one, only, particular, exclusive, unmarried, solo, unique.
S	O	L	O	Alone, lone, single, solitary.
S	O	M	E	Certain, various, diverse, sundry, several.
S	O	N	G	Ballad, hymn, ditty, lay, aria, descant, lyric, melody. Cry, call (birdsong) Chorus.

1	2	3	4	
S	O	O	N	Presently, anon, directly, shortly, forthwith, pronto, quickly, early.
S	O	O	T	Carbon powder. Ash, black, smudge.
S	O	R	E	Painful, raw, tender, grievous, abrasion.
S	O	R	T	Kind, class, group, type, assort, species, variety, order, ilk.
S	O	S	O	Medium, average, fair, indifferent, moderate, middling, mediocre.
S	O	T	S	Plural of SOT. Sediment, coffee grounds, yeast.
S	O	U	L	Essence, spirit, heart, psyche, animus, vitality, life, conscience, quintessence. Blues.
S	O	U	P	Broth, consomme. In the soup, in trouble.
S	O	U	R	Tart, acid, dry, tangy, disagreeable, vinegary. Unpleasant.
S	O	W	F	Buzz, hum, bumble, drone, strum, thrum.
S	O	W	N	Past of SEW. Planted, strewn. Scattered.
S	O	W	S	Plural of SOW.
S	O	Y	A	Bean. Extract. Condiment, flavouring, seasoning.
S	P	A	M	Spiced Ham. Canned Pork.
S	P	A	N	Term, duration, time, interval, space. Yoke, bridge.
S	P	A	R	Rafter, beam, mast, boom, fight, box, wrangle. Chalk, gypsum.
S	P	A	T	Past of SPIT. Altercation, quarrel, tiff. Gaiter.
S	P	A	Y	Geld, render infertile.
S	P	E	C	Speculation, investment.
S	P	E	D	Past of Speed. fled, hurried, hastened.
S	P	E	W	Vomit, puke, heave, spit, disgorge, erupt, flood, gush.
S	P	I	N	Turn, Revolve, twirl, swirl, gyrate. Ride, drive. Twisting threads.
S	P	I	T	Spittle, saliva, water, Image, ringer. Sputter, roasting iron.
S	P	I	V	Gigolo, dandy.
S	P	O	T	Blot, stain, patch, mark, site, stigma, slur. Location. Identify, find, makeout, see.
S	P	R	Y	Brisk, active, alert, lively, nimble, sprightly.
S	P	U	D	Potato, Implement, spade.
S	P	U	N	Past of SPIN. Woven, Twirled.
S	P	U	R	Urge, exhort, goad, horseman's equipment, Strut, crossbeam, Horny points on cock's leg.
S	T	A	B	Prick, jab, puncture, thrust, ram, stick, poke, dig.
S	T	A	G	Adult male deer, men only, unaccompanied.
S	T	A	R	Heavenly body, asterisk, chief, principal, outstanding, main.
S	T	A	Y	Stop, curb, tarry, abide, check. Support. Remain, Brace. Arrest, halt.
S	T	E	M	Stalk, stock, dam, resist, staunch, stop, spring, arise, flow, control.
S	T	E	N	Gun.
S	T	E	P	Footstep, track, ambulate, pace, tread, degree, grade, rung, stage.
S	T	E	T	Let is stand, do not remove. Remains.
S	T	E	W	Casserole, ragout, miscellany, hash, potpourri, commotion, worry. Brothel.
S	T	I	R	Rouse, wake, challenge, rally.
S	T	O	P	Cease, desist, block, impede, stem, staunch, disrupt, halt, visit, block.
S	T	O	W	Pack, place, store, bestow.
S	T	U	B	Stump, butt, Bump, kick. Counterfoil, ticket.
S	T	U	D	Knob, nail, button, sprinkle, dot, speckle, implant festoon. Breeding establishment.
S	T	U	N	Bewilder, daze, stupefy, amaze, astound, petrify, nonplus, strike.
S	T	Y	E	Inflamed eyelid, sebaceous gland.
S	T	Y	X	River in Hades. Mythical river.
S	U	B	S	Plural of SUB. Subscriptions.
S	U	C	H	So, similar, like, analogous, comparable, characterized.
S	U	C	K	Draw in liquid, lap, suckle, nurse, today, imbibe, absorb, engulf.
S	U	D	S	Soap bubbles, foam, froth, lather, spume.
S	U	E	D	Prosecuted, entreated, petitioned, appealed, pursued.
S	U	E	R	Suitor, Plaintiff.
S	U	E	T	Hard Fat, Tallow.
S	U	E	Z	Canal in Egypt.
S	U	I	T	Please, satisfy, fit, agree, accord. Matching clothes.
S	U	L	K	Grump, pout, scowl, brood, mope, glower, lower, glumness.
S	U	L	L	Sulk, grump, pout, glum, gloom.
S	U	M	P	Pit, reservoir, tank.
S	U	M	S	Plural of SUM. Additions.
S	U	N	G	Past of SING.
S	U	N	K	Past of SINK.
S	U	R	D	Irrational, voiceless, insensate.
S	U	R	E	Established, firm, secure, stable, enduring, firm, assured, infallible, certain.
S	U	R	F	Waves, foam, swell, tide. Ride the waves. Skim, skud.
S	W	A	B	Swob, mop, clean, brush, wipe. Navy man.
S	W	A	G	Spoils, loot, plunder, booty. Bundle of personal belongings. Ornamental festoon.
S	W	A	M	Past of SWIM.

1	2	3	4	
S	W	A	N	Large bird. Bard, dally, sashay, sway, sail.
S	W	A	P	Swop, exchange, change, substitute, switch, trade, bargain.
S	W	A	T	Strike, clout, hit, sock, wallop, cram, study, learn assiduously.
S	W	A	Y	Swing, oscillate, lurch, stagger. Command, control.
S	W	I	G	Gulp, swill, drink, guzzle, tipple.
S	W	I	M	Propel through water, Waver, swim with moisture, soak.
S	W	U	M	Past of SWIM, SWAM.
S	Y	C	E	Groom, attendant.

T

T	A	A	L	Afrikaans language (South African).
T	A	C	K	Nail, peg, pin. Turn, bend, yaw, swerve, zig zag. Direction.
T	A	C	T	Diplomacy, finesse, grace, poise, savoir faire, sensitivity, discretion.
T	A	E	L	Monetary unit.
T	A	G	S	Tickets, labels.
T	A	H	R	Wild goat.
T	A	I	L	Follow, tag, dog, trail. Extremity, posterior, rear.
T	A	K	E	Grasp, seize, appropriate, annex, catch, attract, adopt, consume, ingest.
T	A	L	C	Talcum Powder, Magnesium tetrasilicate, perfumed toilet powder.
T	A	L	E	Story, narration, anecdote, yarn, myth, saga, fiction, falsehood.
T	A	L	K	Speak, converse, vocalise, voice. Divulge, reveal. Conference, Dialogue. Speech. Lecture.
T	A	L	L	Elevated, high, towering, lofty. Improbable.
T	A	M	E	Docile, domesticated, tractable, subdued, submissive, gentle, obedient, pliable.
T	A	M	P	Pack, jam, plug, cram, fill, ram, stuff, concentrate.
T	A	N	G	Taste, flavour, savour, smack, bite, piquancy, aroma, pungency, relish.
T	A	N	K	Cistern, reservoir, container, compartment, enclosure, prison. Armoured vehicle.
T	A	P	A	Snack, bite, morsel, bait.
T	A	P	E	Ribbon, band, belt, strip, Measure, record.
T	A	R	E	Allowed weight, percentage weight.
T	A	R	N	Mountain pool, lake.
T	A	R	T	Bitter, pungent, sharp, sour, acid, doxy, party girl, roundheel, chippy. Pie, flan.
T	A	S	K	Labour, toil, work, chore, job, burden, load, duty.
T	A	T	S	Teeth, dice, dominoes, bones, cubes, ivory.
T	A	U	T	Tense, tight, close, firm, stretched, trim.
T	A	X	I	Cab, taxicab, hack, hired vehicle.
T	E	A	K	Hardwood. Tree.
T	E	A	L	Waterfowl, duck.
T	E	A	M	Side, group, unit.
T	E	A	R	Rend, rip, split, cleave. Teardrop, Rush, chase.
T	E	A	T	Nipple, pap, Mamilla.
T	E	E	D	Set off (golf) Struck, delivered.
T	E	E	M	Swarm, abound, flow, pour, drench, crowd, overflow.
T	E	E	N	Teenager, teenage.
T	E	F	F	Cereal grass, forage, hay.
T	E	I	L	Tree, Linden.
T	E	L	A	Connective tissue.
T	E	L	L	Say, state, deliver, reveal, betray, inform, advise, instruct.
T	E	N	D	Attend, nurse, cultivate, till, supervise, cherish, protect. Incline, likely.
T	E	N	T	Canvas, shelter, hut, shack, lint.
T	E	N	S	Plural of TEN.
T	E	R	M	Limit, limitation, word, expression, name, call, period, phase.
T	E	R	N	Ternate, triplet, trio, seabird, gull.
T	E	S	T	Experiment, trial, inspection, check, verify, confirmation, proof, ordeal.
T	E	T	E	Headdress, wig.
T	E	X	T	Subject, theme, topic, fundamentals, issue, idea, argument, point. Written words.
T	H	A	N	Function word to denote comparison. Rather, even, when.
T	H	A	T	Demonstrative pronoun. Another, such.
T	H	A	W	Melt, liquify, dissolve, flux, fuse, liquesce, run.
T	H	E	E	Objective of THOU.
T	H	E	M	Demonstrative pronoun. They. Those.
T	H	E	N	Demonstrative pronoun. That, following.
T	H	E	W	Muscle, sinew. Beef, brawn.
T	H	E	Y	Demonstrative personal pronoun. Those ones.
T	H	I	N	Lean, lank, spare, gaunt, meagre, puny, small, slender, slight. Piping, sharp, shrill, flimsy, improbable.
T	H	I	S	Pronoun and adjective - The, these, those, person, thing, place, time, idea.

1	2	3	4	
T	H	O	U	The one that is addressed. You.
T	H	U	D	Dull sound, thump, clunk, clonk, strike, pound.
T	H	U	G	Hired hoodlum, tough, ruffian, strong arm, hood, bully, cuthroat.
T	H	U	S	So, thusly, this, that, therefore, accordingly, consequently, ergo, so, then.
T	I	C	K	Instant, minute, moment, second, trice, Mite, bloodsucker, Tick-Tock.
T	I	D	E	Flow, current, drift, flood, flux, rush, stream, course.
T	I	D	Y	Neat, spruce, chipper, orderly, shipshape, trim, sleek, uncluttered.
T	I	E	D	United, fastened, connected, joined, linked, anchored, moored, attached.
T	I	E	R	File, row, string, echelon, rank, layer, class, category, grade, league. Storey. Level.
T	I	F	F	Quarrel, altercation, dispute, miff, spat, squabble, bicker, fallout.
T	I	G	E	Shaft of a column.
T	I	K	I	Maori charm. Amulet.
T	I	L	E	Roofing material, shale, covering, ceramic plate. Slate.
T	I	L	L	Until, prior to, up till, Cultivate, dress, hoe, harrow, plant. Cash register.
T	I	L	T	Slant, incline, list, slope, tip, yaw, gradient.
T	I	M	E	Epoch, era, spell, term, date, plan, program. Often, much, repeated.
T	I	N	E	Point of fork, prong, point, spike, enclose.
T	I	N	G	Ring, tinkle, tingle, ping.
T	I	N	T	Colour, hue, stain, tinge, shade, tone, pigmentation, colouration.
T	I	N	Y	Diminutive, small, miniature, minute, pintsize, wee, miniscule, microscopic.
T	I	R	E	Fatigue, weary, exhaust, enervate, sap, bore, jade.
T	O	A	D	Leaping amphibian, frog. Sycophant.
T	O	B	Y	China jug, globefish.
T	O	D	O	Ado, bustle, excitement, commotion, tumult, pother, uproar.
T	O	E	D	Trod, pointed, oblique nailing, diagonally secured. Having toes.
T	O	F	F	Fop, dandy, swell.
T	O	G	A	Raiment, garment, wrap. Roman dress.
T	O	G	S	Clothes, garments, apparel, attire, duds.
T	O	I	L	Labour, work, sweat, slog, drudge. Web, entanglement, mesh.
T	O	L	D	Narrated, recounted, related, explained, said.
T	O	L	L	Ring, chime, peal, cost, price, expense, allure, decoy, tribute.
T	O	M	B	Grave, sepulchre, mausoleum, coffin.
T	O	M	E	Book, volume, work.
T	O	N	E	Inflection, accent, cadence, intonation, colour, hue, mood, timbre.
T	O	N	K	Honky-tonk, Swipe, carousel, Binge.
T	O	N	S	Plural of TON.
T	O	N	Y	Stylish, chic, fashionable, swish, tonish.
T	O	O	K	Grabbed, gained, captured. Past of TAKE.
T	O	O	L	Implement, instrument, utensil, mechanism, Pawn, puppet, stooge, Fashion, sculp.
T	O	O	T	Sound, honk, hoot, Advertise.
T	O	P	S	Plural of TOP. Best.
T	O	R	E	Past of TEAR. Rent, split, ripped, hurried.
T	O	R	N	Past of TORE.
T	O	R	T	Evil, crime, iniquity, sin, wrongdoing.
T	O	R	Y	English Conservative.
T	O	S	H	Nonsense, baloney, bilge, bosh, bunkum, eyewash.
T	O	S	S	Pitch, lob, throw, cast, fling, heave, hurl, sling, writhe, squirm.
T	O	T	E	Totalisator. Carry, add, total, gross.
T	O	U	R	Journey, circuit, drive, progress, expedition, travel, trek.
T	O	U	T	Tipster, publicise, herald, trumpet, plug, laud, praise, advertise.
T	O	W	N	Municipality, territory, area, burgh, dorp.
T	O	W	S	Plural of TOW.
T	R	A	M	Tramcar.
T	R	A	P	Snare, ambush, lure, ploy, ruse, bait, decoy, catch. Device for trapping.
T	R	A	Y	Board, plate.
T	R	E	E	Woody growth, resembling a tree, Shoe Form.
T	R	E	K	Travel, journey (South Africa).
T	R	E	Y	Gaming term for dice or card showing three pips.
T	R	I	M	Neat, tidy, spruce, adorn, deck, garnish, Cut, clip, pare, Shapely.
T	R	I	O	Triad, threesome, trinity, triple, triumvirate, triune, troika.
T	R	I	P	Skip, hop, skitter, spring, journey, tour, drive, expedition, trek, slip, fluff.
T	R	O	D	Past of TREAD. Tramped, walked, trudged.
T	R	O	T	Jog, move briskly, hurry, horse's gait, dance step.
T	R	O	Y	Weight. Measurement.
T	R	U	E	Loyal, exact, straight, faithful, ardent, upright, real, legitimate, trustworthy.
T	R	U	G	Fruit conveyance. Basket.
T	U	B	A	Musical instrument, bass trumpet. Transmitter for jamming radar.

1	2	3	4	
T	U	B	E	Hollow cylinder, slender channel, pipe. Underground. Railway.
T	U	B	S	Plural of TUB.
T	U	C	K	Food, grub, snuggle, coze. Fold under. Tuck in.
T	U	F	A	Porous rock.
T	U	F	F	Volcanic debris.
T	U	F	T	Bunch, clump, cluster.
T	U	M	P	Mound, molehill, anthill.
T	U	N	A	Tunny fish.
T	U	N	E	Air, harmony, melody, descant, harmony, chant, vocalize, adjust, regulate.
T	U	N	K	Tap, knock, rap, bob.
T	U	R	D	Excrement, filth, dung.
T	U	R	F	Terrace, peat, Horse Racing, bury, eject, kick, throw out. Sod. Lawn, grass.
T	U	R	N	Spin, gyrate, revolve, rotate, twirl, spin, eddy, rick, reverse, Upset. Appearance, revolution, reversal.
T	U	S	K	Enlarged tooth, protruding tooth, projection.
T	U	T	U	Ballet skirt.
T	W	A	S	It was.
T	W	E	E	Piping note, shrill note.
T	W	I	G	Shoot, branch. Discern, perceive, comprehend.
T	W	I	N	Two of a kind, matched, paired, dual, mate, double, match, reciprocal.
T	W	I	T	Ridicule, deride, lout, ass, donkey, reproach, chide, blame.
T	Y	K	E	Dog, canine, hound, pooch, cur.
T	Y	P	E	Kind, class, breed, ilk, nature. Keyface, operate typewriter, type face.
T	Y	P	O	Printer, compositor.
T	Y	R	E	Vulcanized rubber wheel.
T	Y	R	O	Amateur, novice, apprentice, rookie.

U

U	G	L	Y	Unattractive, repulsive, unsightly, base, troublesome, sullen.
U	L	N	A	Arm bone. Forearm.
U	M	B	O	Boss of a Shield. Any round or conical projection.
U	N	D	E	Waving, wavy.
U	N	D	O	Untie, unbind, disengage, unfasten, Outwit.
U	N	I	O	Genus of Freshwater mussel.
U	N	I	T	Number, item, one, fraction, individual.
U	N	T	O	Towards, at, besides, to.
U	P	A	S	Deadly poisonous Tree.
U	P	G	O	Ascend, climb, escalate, mount, scale.
U	P	O	N	On, on top of.
U	P	T	O	Until, prior, till, before.
U	R	D	U	Language, Persian script.
U	R	E	A	Soluble compound. Present in urine.
U	R	G	E	Encourage. Impel, exhort, goad, prod, prompt, desire, craving, itch, lust.
U	R	I	C	Substance in urine.
U	R	I	D	Acid found in urine.
U	R	U	S	Long-horned wild Ox.
U	S	E	D	Spent, wornout, exhausted. Accustomed. Applied, adapted, handled.
U	S	E	R	Consumer, Operator, manipulator, functionary, employer. Exploiter.
U	S	U	S	Act of making use without benefit. User.

V

V	A	I	L	Gratuity, tip.
V	A	I	N	Empty, hollow, futile, paltry, trifling, Conceited, arrogant, proud.
V	A	I	R	Squirrel skin. Heraldic Fur.
V	A	L	E	Valley, combe, dale, glen.
V	A	M	P	Contrive, concoct, improvise, flirt, Mend, recondition, reconstruct, repair.
V	A	N	E	Weathercock, flag. Windsock, Barb, sight on a compass.
V	A	N	G	Steadying brace.
V	A	R	E	Weasel.
V	A	R	Y	Alter, change, alternate, differ, deviate, digress.
V	A	S	E	Urn, container, receptacle.
V	A	S	T	Huge, enormous, giant, immense, titanic, expansive, astronomical.
V	E	A	L	Calf flesh.
V	E	E	R	Turn, shift, swerve, deflect, divert, skew, slue, pivot.

1	2	3	4	
V	E	G	A	Plain, marshy, meadow.
V	E	I	L	Mask, cloak, wrap, enclose, enshroud, screen, hide, disguise.
V	E	I	N	Blood vessel, fashion, mode, style, tone, manner, mood, disposition, nature. Seam.
V	E	L	D	South African countryside, open country.
V	E	L	O	Velocipede, tricycles.
V	E	N	A	Vein.
V	E	N	D	Sell, hawk, peddle, monger.
V	E	N	T	Aperture, orifice, outlet, expression, utterance, emit, issue, release. Ventilator.
V	E	R	B	Speech Of Grammar.
V	E	R	T	Green, Foliage.
V	E	R	Y	Exceptionally, highly, hugely, remarkably, strikingly, too, thoroughly, precisely.
V	E	S	T	Garment, clothing, undershirt, Invest, authorise, empower, pertain, belong.
V	E	T	O	Ban, forbid, embargo, taboo. Negate, disallow, prohibit, refuse, defeat.
V	I	A	L	Plastic bottle, vessel, receptacle, container, Test tube.
V	I	C	E	Wickedness, depravity, degradation, immorality, wrongdoing, indecency, perversion. Press, screw.
V	I	D	E	See.
V	I	E	D	Competed, contended, contested, rivalled, challenged, opposed.
V	I	E	W	Look, sight, examine, scrutinise, survey, vet, contemplate, gaze. Panorama, scene. Intention.
V	I	L	E	Base, despicable, low, servile, sordid, squalid, wretched, offensive.
V	I	N	E	Climbing plant. grapes.
V	I	N	T	Make wine.
V	I	N	Y	Producing vines, grapes.
V	I	O	L	Stringed instrument, viola.
V	I	R	E	Crossbow bolt, heraldic amulet.
V	I	S	A	Permit, authorization, entrance certificate, stamp. Passport document.
V	I	S	E	Jawed screw, holding tool. Clamp, vice.
V	I	V	A	Expression of approval. Viva voce. "Long live!"
V	I	V	O	Musical direction.
V	L	E	I	Lake, dam, stream. Pan.
V	O	C	E	Voice.
V	O	I	D	Null, invalid, vacant, empty, hole, cavity, destitute, annul, dissolve.
V	O	L	E	Rodent.
V	O	L	T	Electrical unit, electrical potential.
V	O	T	E	Elect, decide, choose, ballot, franchise, suffrage.
V	O	W	S	Promises, covenants, pledges. Plural of VOW.

W

W	A	D	E	Ford. Act of wading.
W	A	D	I	Dry river bed.
W	A	D	S	Plural of WAD. Plugs, pads, small bundles.
W	A	F	F	Wandering, stray, worthless, a waving or a slight, hasty movement, a signal, a piff or a blast.
W	A	F	T	Buoyant movement, scent, tune, gust, puff, gust.
W	A	G	E	Pay, hire, stipend, salary. Compensation, reward. Operate. Carry on war, etc.
W	A	G	S	Plural of WAG.
W	A	I	F	Stray, vagabond.
W	A	I	L	Cry, howl, bawl, ululate, bay, yowl, whine, weep, sob.
W	A	I	N	Wagon, Cart.
W	A	I	T	Bide, linger, remain, stay, tarry, Serve, nurse, minister to.
W	A	K	E	Awaken, rouse, stir, arouse, bestir, Funeral vigil. Wash of boat.
W	A	L	E	Wheal, weal, welt, whelk, whelp.
W	A	L	K	Step, ambulate, advance, traipse, ramble. Domain, environment, lifestyle.
W	A	L	L	Barricade, barrier, fence, divider, Enclose, cage, corral, fence, hedge, hem.
W	A	L	T	Cranky. Unsteady, listing.
W	A	N	D	Rod, stick, tube, staff, pointer, goad, whip, baton, twig.
W	A	N	E	Abate, moderate, relent, slacken, ebb, subside, droop.
W	A	N	T	Need, lack, requirement, desire, dearth, privation, poverty, penury.
W	A	R	D	Repel, fend, guard, deflect, prevent, avert, repulse. Minor. Custody. Hospital Dormitory, room.
W	A	R	E	Merchandise, goods, Aware, apprehensive. Beware.
W	A	R	M	Enthusiastic, zealous, tender, compassionate, ardent, fervent, affable, cordial. Neither hot nor cold.
W	A	R	N	Caution, forewarn, alert, inform, notify.
W	A	R	P	Twist, debase, corrupt, debauch, deprave, pervert, misrepresent.
W	A	R	T	Verruca, excrescence, horny growth.
W	A	R	Y	Cautious, vigilant, canny, careful, circumspect, distrustful, thrifty.
W	A	S	H	Rinse, cleanse, bathe, Float. Wake. Lap of water on shore. To wash up on shore.
W	A	S	P	Stinging insect. Vespa.

1	2	3	4	
W	A	T	T	Unit of Electrical power.
W	A	V	E	Ridge, trough, oscillation, advancing as waves. Flutter, signify, relinquish.
W	A	V	Y	Curly, billowy, sinuous, fluctuating.
W	A	X	Y	Indignant, angry, heated, irate, wrathful, vexed. Pliant, yielding as wax.
W	E	A	K	Feeble, fragile, frail, infirm, decrepit, puny, rickety, implausible, diluted, thin, insipid, watery.
W	E	A	L	Wale, welt, wheal, stripe.
W	E	A	N	Estrange, alienate, detach, disaffect, disunite.
W	E	A	R	Don, dress, attire. Graze, rub, drain, weary, corrode, gnaw, erode.
W	E	E	D	Eradicate, root out. Marijuana, insignificant, inconsequantial person. Plant or thing.
W	E	E	K	Seven days.
W	E	E	P	Cry, sob, wail, drip, drop, trickle, seep.
W	E	F	T	Threads crossing warp.
W	E	I	R	Dam, bank, levee, breakwater.
W	E	L	D	Join, unite, consolidate, fuse metal, seal.
W	E	L	K	Fade, wilt, wither.
W	E	L	L	Proper, fitting, going good. In good health. Spa, baths, spring. Subterranean store.
W	E	L	T	Stripe, edge, weal, shoe upper.
W	E	N	D	Meander, wander, journey, travel. Wend one's way.
W	E	N	T	Past of GO. Departed, left, absconded, decamped.
W	E	P	T	Cried, lamented, sobbed, complained, howled.
W	E	R	E	Past of To Be. Was.
W	E	S	T	Left facing North. Direction of Sun set. Compass point. Wild West.
W	H	A	P	Whop, whip, defeat.
W	H	A	T	Pronoun expressing inquiry.
W	H	E	N	Adverb of time. Then, again, albeit, although, whereas, though, while.
W	H	E	T	Incite, arouse, sharpen, heighten, Hone.
W	H	E	Y	Separated milk.
W	H	I	G	Tory, Conservative.
W	H	I	M	Caprice, vagary, fancy, humour, inclination, dream, fantasy, vision.
W	H	I	N	Hard rock.
W	H	I	P	Flog, flagellate, lash, defeat, conquer, overcome, thong, strap, arouse, incite.
W	H	I	T	Tittle, iota, jot, particle.
W	H	I	Z	Hiss, buss,fizz, hurry, dash, whirl, whisk, zip. Expert, virtuso, wizard.
W	H	O	M	Objective of WHO.
W	H	O	P	Whap, defeat, whip.
W	I	C	K	Twisted fibre, woven cotton, twisted thread.
W	I	D	E	Spacious, ample, roomy, extensive, broad, expansive.
W	I	F	E	Spouse, partner, consort, bride, missus, Mrs.
W	I	L	D	Untamed, savage, disorderly, rash, unruly, angry, boisterous, extravagant.
W	I	L	E	Stratagem, dodge, ruse, artifice, device, cunning, allure, captivate.
W	I	L	L	Wish, volition, bequeath, intention.
W	I	L	T	Droop, flop, wither, collapse, drop, welter, flag, sag.
W	I	L	Y	Sly, artful, astute, crafty, cunning, shrewd.
W	I	N	D	Coil, twist, deform, contort, curl, spiral, Gust, velocity of air, force.
W	I	N	E	Fermented grape juice.
W	I	N	G	Fly, sweep, arm, annex, projection, prolongation, Organ of flight.
W	I	N	K	Blink, nictate, twinkle, Instant, moment.
W	I	N	Y	Drunkard, drunken, vinous.
W	I	P	E	Clean, erase, expunge, efface, annihilate.
W	I	R	E	Flexible metal thread, Telegram, Connect. Instal wires.
W	I	R	Y	Muscular, fibrous, ropy, sinewy, stringy, flexible, strong.
W	I	S	E	Discerning, knowing, knowledgeable, perceptive, sagacious, expedient.
W	I	S	H	Desire, choice, hope, like, please, imposition, foist.
W	I	S	P	Strip, fragment, filament, trail, twist, wreath.
W	I	T	H	About, on, upon, over, together, pro, in favour, via, per, through, by dint.
W	O	K	E	Past of WAKE.
W	O	L	F	Destructive dog-like mammal, gulp, gobble, philander, womanizer, lecher, Roue.
W	O	M	B	Uterus, cavity.
W	O	N	T	Will not. Habit, custom, practice, manner, practice.
W	O	O	D	Forest, Golf club, bowl, cask, keg. Timber.
W	O	O	F	Filling thread, yarn.
W	O	O	L	Textile fibre, Fleece, hair of sheep, goats, spun yarn, Threads or metal.
W	O	R	D	Term, vocable, idiom, locution, command, news, report, saying, promise.
W	O	R	E	Sported, donned, dressed in, bore, Past of WEAR.
W	O	R	K	Toil, activity, employment, Pursuit, Operate, function, cultivate, prepare.
W	O	R	M	Insinuate, infiltrate, wriggle, squirm, Earthworm, Maggot.
W	O	R	N	Tired, jaded, wearied, haggard, pinched, drawn, Past of WEAR.

1	2	3	4	
W	O	R	T	Fermented Malt. Plant, Herb.
W	O	V	E	Past of WEAVE.
W	R	A	P	Cloak, drape, enclose, enshroud, veil, swathe, roll, envelop.
W	R	I	T	Formal document, Legal Summons.

X

X	E	M	A	Black headed gull.
X	E	N	O	Foreign, strange, intrusive.
X	I	N	G	Marking with X'es.
X	I	P	H	Swordlike, sword shaped.
X	M	A	S	Christmas, Yuletide.
X	R	A	Y	Electromagnetic Radiation.
X	Y	L	O	Wood, wooden.
X	Y	S	T	Open Portico, Avenue.

Y

Y	A	N	K	Jerk, lug, twitch, snatch, grap, extract, pull, tear. American. New Englander.
Y	A	P	P	Book binding.
Y	A	R	D	Courtyard, enclosure, quadrangle, garden. Three feet. 36 inches.
Y	A	R	E	Agile, active, brisk, lively, nimble spry.
Y	A	R	N	Tale, story, narration, anecdote, chat, converse, Spun thread, filament.
Y	A	W	L	Rigged sail boat.
Y	A	W	N	Gape cavernously, Inhale deeply. Opened wide.
Y	A	W	P	Bawl, howl, Squawk, yelp.
Y	A	W	S	Contagious disease.
Y	E	A	H	Yea, Yes.
Y	E	A	N	Lamb.
Y	E	A	R	Twelve calendar months.
Y	E	E	N	To lamb, to produce, Yean.
Y	E	L	L	Shout, whoop, cry, yip, call, holler, hail, wail.
Y	E	L	P	Howl, yell, yap, screech, bark.
Y	E	R	K	To bind or tie with a jerk, to throw or thrust with a sudden quick motion, to lash out, to draw tight, bind.
Y	E	T	I	Abominable Snowman. Mythical Creature. Big-foot.
Y	I	P	E	Cry out in pain, Yip.
Y	L	E	M	Primordial substance.
Y	I	G	A	Self-discipline, Hindu philosophy. Exercise.
Y	O	G	A	Person who practises Yoga.
Y	O	H	O	Effort to attract attention.
Y	O	K	E	Frame, clamp, beam, Attachment, Relationship, Tie, Link, Hitch, Harness.
Y	O	L	K	Inner portion of Egg, Nucleated Mass, Nutrient, Egg Yellow.
Y	O	N	D	Yonder, beyond.
Y	O	R	E	Before, olden times. Yesterday. Yesteryear.
Y	O	U	R	Belonging to YOU.
Y	O	W	L	Howl, yap, bawl.
Y	O	Y	O	Double disc with string attached.
Y	U	A	N	The monetary unit of China.
Y	U	B	A	Messman (Australian).
Y	U	L	E	Christmas, Christmas time. Yulelog.
Y	U	R	T	Circular domed tent.

Z

Z	A	N	Y	Clown, buffoon, harlequin, comic, Odd, uncommon, silly.
Z	E	A	L	Passion, ardour, enthusiasm, fire, energy, gusto, urgency, sincerity.
Z	E	B	U	Asiatic Ox.
Z	E	I	N	Corn protein.
Z	E	M	I	Fetish, Idol. Charm, Juju, mascot, talisman.
Z	E	R	O	Naught, nill, emptiness. Cipher, direct, cast, level.
Z	E	S	T	Taste, gusto, palate, relish, heart, delight, pleasure, lemon rind.
Z	E	T	A	Letter of Greek Alphabet.
Z	E	U	S	Genus of Fish. Mythical God.

1	2	3	4	
Z	I	M	B	Species of fly.
Z	I	N	C	Metallic element.
Z	I	N	G	Eagerness, enthusiasm, animation, dash, elan, verve, oomph, vim.
Z	I	O	N	Site of Solomon's Temple, Nirvana, Israel, Elysium. Mount Zion. Jew.
Z	I	P	S	Plural of ZIP.
Z	O	E	A	Crustaceans in larval stage.
Z	O	I	C	Pertaining to animal life.
Z	O	L	L	Cigarette. Cannibas, Marijuana.
Z	O	N	E	Belt, girdle, district, area, territory, region, sector, tract.
Z	O	O	M	Skim, fly, skitter, aerobatic manoeuvre, zero in.
Z	O	O	N	Product of fertilized ovum. individual.
Z	O	O	S	Plural of ZOO.
Z	O	O	T	Flashy, fashionable, gaudy.
Z	U	L	U	Native of Zululand. Language of the Zulus.

1	2	3	4	5

A

ABACA	Manila Hemp.
ABACK	Surprised, unawares, unexpected, unaware, suddenly, without warning. Backwards.
ABAFT	Behind, aft, after. astern, back of.
ABASE	Disgrace, humble, bemean, cheapen, ruin, corrupt, reduce, demote.
ABASH	Disconcert, humiliate, embarrass, confuse, discountenance.
ABASK	Basking, sunning, tanning.
ABATE	Decrease, diminish, reduce, lessen, abolish, weaken, taper, recede.
ABBEY	Monastery.
ABBOT	Superior. Chief Monk. Father.
ABEAM	Across, abreast, behind, following. Opposite.
ABELE	White Poplar.
ABHOR	Hate, abominate, detest, despise, disdain, scorn, loathe.
ABIDE	Bide, linger, remain, bear, endure, adhere, reside, live.
ABLER	More able, competent, expert, better able.
ABODE	Living quarters, habitation, house, residence, domicile home, dwelling.
ABOHM	Electro-magnetic unit.
ABOIL	On the boil, boiling, boiling point.
ABOMB	Atom Bomb, Nuclear Weapon, Destructive Force.
ABORT	Cast out, throw off, miscarry, cease abruptly.
ABOUT	Almost, nearly, around, practically, apropos, concerning, over, upon.
ABOVE	Overhead, aloft, beyond, over, past, on high.
ABUSE	Mishandle, debase, pervert, batter, exploit, harm, insult, berate, profanity.
ABUZZ	Buzzing, humming, busy, industrious.
ABYSS	Chasm, pit, gorge, gulf, depths, perdition, profundity.
ACERB	Bitter, sour, acid, dry, tart, sarcastic, caustic.
ACHAR	Sour pickles. Pickle Relish.
ACHED	Pained, hurt, racked, yearned, longed, pitied.
ACOCK	Tilted, cocked, ready.
ACOLD	Cold, chilly.
ACONE	Insects' Eyes.
ACORN	Oak Seed, sash knob.
ACRID	Harsh, bitter, pungent, cloying, caustic, cutting, austere, vinegary.
ACRON	Unsegmented head of insect.
ACTED	Portrayed, performed, masqueraded, characterized, represented, played.
ACTIN	Muscle protein.
ACTON	Steel Jacket.
ACTOR	Player, impersonator, performer, thespian, trouper, participant.
ACUTE	Sharp, peaked, pointed, barbed, perceptive, penetrating, piercing, incisive. Sudden.
ADAGE	Proverb, saw, byword, saying, dictum, maxim.
ADAPT	Adjust, acclimatize, qualify, accommodate, conform, reconcile.
ADAYS	Nowadays. In these times.
ADDAX	Large Antelope.
ADDED	Annexed, increased, appended, augmented additional, another, more, further.
ADDER	Snake, viper. One who adds.
ADDLE	Muddle, confuse, jumble, tumble.
ADEEM	Revoke a legacy.
ADEPS	Animal Fat, Hog's Fat.
ADEPT	Proficient, adroit, Dexterous, skilled, masterful, clever.
ADIEU	Leave taking, farewell.
ADIOS	Farewell. Goodbye.
ADLIB	Improvise, impromptu performance, extemporise.
ADMAN	Compositor, compilor of advertisements.
ADMIT	Acknowledge, concede, acquiesce, introduce, initiate, interpose, subscribe.
ADMIX	Comingle, mix, intermingle, merge, mingle, intermix.
ADOBE	Sun-baked dwelling. Hut.
ADOPT	Assume, embrace, accept, appropriate, include, espouse, naturalize.
ADORE	Revere, worship, venerate, extol, idolize, praise, esteem, love.
ADORN	Decorate, bedeck, garnish, furbish, enrich, embellish, ornament, trim.
ADOWN	Down.
ADSUM	Acknowledge one's presence at roll call.
ADULT	Full-grown, mature, ripe, grown, full-grown, grown-up, past puberty.
ADUST	Parched, burned, incinerated.
ADYTA	Sanctuaries.

1	2	3	4	5	
A	E	G	I	S	Defense, protection.
A	E	R	I	E	Eyrie, eagle's nest, High situated dwelling place. Castle.
A	E	S	O	P	Writer of Fables.
A	F	E	A	R	For fear. Afraid.
A	F	F	I	X	Attach, fasten, annex, append, subjoin, add, fix, stick, gum.
A	F	I	R	E	Burning, ablaze, alight, aglow, fiery, flaming, ignited, on fire.
A	F	O	A	M	Foaming.
A	F	O	O	T	On foot. Happening, astir, on the cards, occurring.
A	F	O	R	E	Before, previously, fore.
A	F	O	U	L	Tangled, fouled, jammed.
A	F	R	I	C	African.
A	F	T	E	R	Afterward, next, latterly, subsequently. Abaft, aft, later, behind, beyond, ensuing.
A	G	A	I	N	Afresh, anew, once more, over, also, in addition, however, conversely.
A	G	A	P	E	Shocked, dismayed, aghast, overwhelmed, thunderstruck, wide eyed, dumbfounded, open mouthed.
A	G	A	T	E	Semi-precious stone, Opal-like.
A	G	A	T	Y	Resembling an agate.
A	G	A	V	E	Cactus Plant, Aloe. Century plant.
A	G	A	Z	E	Gazing. Bewitched, amazed.
A	G	E	N	T	Deputy, proxy, commissioner. Representative. Medium or instrument responsible for.
A	G	G	E	R	Prominence, mound, rampart.
A	G	I	L	E	Nimble, spry, sprightly, dexterous, fleet, speedy.
A	G	I	S	T	Pasturage Levy.
A	G	L	O	W	Alight, ablaze, aflame, gleaming, shining, luminous, radiant, glowing, Rosy.
A	G	N	E	L	French gold coin depicting a lamb.
A	G	N	U	S	Die. Lamb of God.
A	G	O	G	E	Musical term. Tempo.
A	G	O	N	E	Since, ago, past.
A	G	O	N	Y	Distress, misery, suffering pangs, anguish, torment.
A	G	O	O	D	Heartily.
A	G	O	R	A	Ancient Greek Market place.
A	G	R	E	E	Admit, acknowledge, concede, assent, acquiesce, consent.
A	G	R	I	N	Grinning.
A	G	U	E	D	Shivering, feverish, malarial.
A	H	E	A	D	Before, forward, in advance, leading, onward. In front.
A	H	E	A	P	In fear, trembling.
A	H	I	G	H	On high, above.
A	H	I	N	D	Behind.
A	H	O	L	D	Near the wind.
A	H	U	L	L	Sails furled, hove to.
A	I	D	E	D	Helped, assisted, comforted, relieved, supported, alleviated, befriended.
A	I	D	E	R	Aiding, helper, assistant.
A	I	E	R	Y	Airy.
A	I	L	E	D	Past of AIL.
A	I	M	E	D	Past of AIM.
A	I	M	E	R	Person with aim, purpose. Taking aim.
A	I	R	E	D	Past of AIR. Ventilated, expressed, divulged, revealed, broadcast, shown.
A	I	R	E	R	Ventilator, Clothes dryer.
A	I	S	L	E	Passage, walkway, alley.
A	I	T	C	H	Eighth letter of Alphabet.
A	J	U	G	A	Genus of bugle plant.
A	K	E	L	A	Scout Cub leader.
A	L	A	C	K	Alas, expression of sorrow. (Archiac).
A	L	A	N	T	Sneezeweed.
A	L	A	R	M	Fright, fear, panic, trepidation, strain, awe, scare, astonishment, surprise, startle.
A	L	A	R	Y	Wing-shaped.
A	L	A	T	E	Winged.
A	L	B	U	M	Loose-leafed Book.
A	L	C	E	S	Genus of mammal, elk.
A	L	D	E	R	Tree. Elder.
A	L	E	R	T	Watchful, vigilant, heedful, careful, attentive, intelligent, quick, prompt, lively. Warning, signal.
A	L	G	A	E	Seaweed, fungus, duckweed.
A	L	G	I	D	Cold, chilly.
A	L	G	I	N	Kelp extracts.
A	L	G	U	M	Red Sandalwood.
A	L	I	A	S	Assumed name, otherwise called, otherwise known as.
A	L	I	B	I	Excuse, plea, pretext.
A	L	I	E	N	Foreigner, stranger, hostile, opposed, different, repugnant. Not in keeping with. Not complimentary to.

1	2	3	4	5	
A	L	I	G	N	Line up, range, adjust, regulate, fix, line, rectify, arrange. Calibrate.
A	L	I	K	E	Like, akin, similar, corresponding, uniform, parallel.
A	L	I	S	T	Listed.
A	L	I	T	E	Calcium silicate.
A	L	I	V	E	Living, vital, animated, existing, active, aware, knowing, Swarming, teeming.
A	L	K	Y	D	Synthetic Resin.
A	L	K	Y	L	Aliphatic radicals.
A	L	L	A	H	Deity. Muslim God.
A	L	L	A	Y	Relieve, alleviate, assuage, ease, calm lull, quieten, still, suppress, subdue.
A	L	L	E	Y	Grassed enclosure, passage, side road, lane. Bowling alley.
A	L	L	I	N	Inclusive, over all, comprehensive. Exhausted, Collapsed.
A	L	L	I	S	Allice Shad.
A	L	L	O	T	Allocate, apportion, assign, share, give, furnish, prescribe, distribute.
A	L	L	O	W	Allot, allocate, apportion, assign, bestow, grant, accede. Permit, let, countenance.
A	L	L	O	Y	Admixture, mixture, amalgam, composite, compound, interfusion, adulterant.
A	L	O	E	S	Plural of ALOE. Bitter Purgative.
A	L	O	F	T	Above, overhead, over, on high, upward.
A	L	O	I	N	Bitter aloe extract.
A	L	O	N	E	Separated, singular, detached, isolated, unaccompanied, lonely, solitary. Only, but, entirely, solely. Solo.
A	L	O	N	G	Onward, forward, ahead, as well, besides, furthermore, towards.
A	L	O	O	F	Distant, detached, disinterested, remote, indifferent. Haughty, proud.
A	L	O	S	E	Genus of Shad.
A	L	O	U	D	Audibly, loudly, vocally.
A	L	P	H	A	Commencement, dawn, genesis, outset, beginning, start.
A	L	T	A	R	Shrine, Communion Table, Sanctuary.
A	L	T	E	R	Change, modify, vary, transform, adapt.
A	L	U	L	A	Bastard wing (fly).
A	L	U	T	A	Soft Leather.
A	M	A	I	N	Greatly, exceedingly.
A	M	A	S	S	Accumulate, collect, hoard, gather, pile, accrue.
A	M	A	T	I	Cremona Violin.
A	M	A	Z	E	Surprise, astonish, dumbfound, flabbergast, astound.
A	M	B	E	R	Fossil resin. Ambergris, Shade, hue, of orange colour.
A	M	B	I	T	Circuit, perimeter, periphery, circumference, range, orbit, radius, scope.
A	M	B	L	E	Saunter, drift, mope, stroll, loiter, dawdle, Dally.
A	M	B	R	Y	Sacristy, Pantry, Storeroom.
A	M	E	E	R	Emir.
A	M	E	N	D	Rectify, right, correct, better, improve, raise, help. Idiot. imbecile, moron.
A	M	E	N	T	One who is mentally defective by failure to develop, a sufferer from amentia.
A	M	I	C	E	Liturgical Vestment, collar.
A	M	I	D	E	Ammonia compound.
A	M	I	G	O	Friend, mate, intimate, confidant, acquaintance, pal.
A	M	I	S	S	Faulty, unsatisfactory, wrong, imperfect.
A	M	I	T	Y	Benevolence, friendliness, goodwill, kindliness, neighbourliness, harmony.
A	M	O	L	E	Soap plant.
A	M	O	N	G	Amidst, amongst, with, between.
A	M	O	U	R	Love affair, romance, intrigue, liaison, affair, passion, love.
A	M	O	V	E	Dismiss, remove.
A	M	P	H	I	Around, on both sides, both kinds.
A	M	P	L	E	Sufficient, spacious, commodious, roomy, enough, capacious, copious.
A	M	P	L	Y	Adequately, plentifully, bountifully, acceptably, appropriately, satisfactorily.
A	M	P	U	L	Bulbous glass vessel, vial.
A	M	U	C	K	Frenzied, uncontrollable, fury, berserk.
A	M	U	S	E	Entertain, divert, engross, beguile, enchant, distract, charm, absorb.
A	N	C	O	N	Elbow, bracket.
A	N	E	A	L	ANELE. Annoint. Improve metals, toughen.
A	N	E	A	R	Close, nearby.
A	N	E	L	E	ANEAL, Extreme Unction, Annoint. Treat steel with heat or compounds.
A	N	E	N	T	Concerning, about.
A	N	G	E	L	Divine messenger. Sponsor, backer, guarantor, patron. Angel fish.
A	N	G	E	R	Fury, indignation, rage, wrath, aggravate, annoy, vex, provoke, outrage.
A	N	G	L	E	Side, direction, slant, hint, viewpoint, facet, bias, corner, degree.
A	N	G	L	O	English.
A	N	G	O	R	Acute pain, anxiety, anguish.
A	N	G	R	Y	Indignant, irate, acrimonious, wrathful, aggravated, enraged, incensed.
A	N	I	G	H	Near by. Close.
A	N	I	L	E	Old womanish.

1	2	3	4	5	
A	N	I	M	A	Active ingredient. Essence, Salt.
A	N	I	M	E	Resin, Copal.
A	N	I	O	N	Electro-negative ion.
A	N	I	S	E	Plant furnishing aniseed.
A	N	K	E	R	European liquid measure.
A	N	K	L	E	Fetlock joint, lower leg.
A	N	K	U	S	Elephant goad.
A	N	N	A	L	Compilation, yearly record. Chronical, history.
A	N	N	E	X	Add, append, join, connect, link, unite, appropriate, prompt, seize, sequester. Subsidiary structure.
A	N	N	O	Y	Upset, irritate, aggravate, bother, bug, worry, plague, tease, badger.
A	N	N	U	L	Erase, cancel, expunge, neutralise, obliterate, negate, invalidate, quash.
A	N	O	D	E	Positive electrical pole.
A	N	O	M	Y	Miracle, Unexplained.
A	N	T	I	C	Prank, caper, frolic, lark, trick, Grotesque posture.
A	N	T	R	E	Cave, cavern.
A	N	V	I	L	Iron block, machine part, musical percussion instrument. Shoemakers last.
A	O	R	T	A	Chief arterial blood vessel.
A	P	A	C	E	Quickly, swiftly, fast, expeditiously, hastily, Abreast, alongside, at same speed
A	P	A	R	T	Detached, unaccompanied, removed, isolated, alone, except, besides.
A	P	E	A	K	Vertically.
A	P	E	R	Y	Mimicry, aping, plagarism.
A	P	H	I	D	Sap sucking insect, plant louse.
A	P	I	A	N	Relating to Bees.
A	P	I	N	G	Copying, simulating, imitating, mimicking, emulating, duplicating.
A	P	I	S	H	Slavish, imitative, apelike.
A	P	O	O	P	Astern.
A	P	O	R	T	Apoop, astern.
A	P	P	L	E	Pome, fruit. Adam's apple.
A	P	P	L	Y	Direct, devote, undertake, Entreat, petition, appeal, administer.
A	P	R	I	L	Fourth Month of a Calendar Year.
A	P	R	O	N	Protective garment, cassock, Parking area.
A	P	S	I	S	Circumference.
A	P	T	L	Y	Appropriately, fittingly, befitting, convincingly, exactly, precisely, nicely.
A	R	A	K	E	Raked.
A	R	B	O	R	Bower, spindle, axis, Tree Genus.
A	R	C	E	D	Curved, bent, arched, bowed, round, rounded.
A	R	E	A	D	Solve, divine, explain, interpret.
A	R	E	A	L	Area, linguistic.
A	R	E	C	A	Betal Palm.
A	R	E	N	A	Gymnasium, ring, stadium, area.
A	R	E	T	E	Excellence, virtue, valor. Mountain ridge.
A	R	G	A	L	Therefore.
A	R	G	I	L	Potter's clay, alumna.
A	R	G	O	L	Residue, crust.
A	R	G	O	N	Inert gas.
A	R	G	O	T	Jargon, slang.
A	R	G	U	E	Debate, dispute, review, protest, remonstrate, assert, contend, persuade.
A	R	G	U	S	Guardian, watchman.
A	R	I	A	N	Aryan.
A	R	I	E	S	Goat, Sign of the Zodiac.
A	R	I	E	L	Gazelle, sprite.
A	R	I	O	T	Running riot.
A	R	I	S	E	Rise, ascend, aspire, mount, soar, begin, emanate, spring.
A	R	M	E	D	Equipped, prepared, fortified, defended, secured, strengthened. Blazoned.
A	R	M	E	T	Medieval helmet.
A	R	M	I	L	Astronomical instrument.
A	R	O	A	R	Roaring.
A	R	O	M	A	Fragrance, scent, smell, fumes, odour, bouquet, redolence, perfume.
A	R	O	S	E	Rose up, began, revolted, sprang.
A	R	R	A	S	Wall hangings, tapestry.
A	R	R	A	Y	Display, parade, clothe, attire, arrange, order, organize.
A	R	R	E	T	Decision, arrest, decree.
A	R	R	I	S	Sharp edges.
A	R	R	O	W	Shaft, dart, bolt, pointer, indication, indicator.
A	R	S	I	S	Upbeat, vocal inflection.
A	R	S	O	N	Afire, ignite, fire-raising, pyromania.
A	R	Y	A	N	Indo-European, Nordic, Gentile.

1	2	3	4	5	
A	S	C	O	T	English Race Course.
A	S	D	I	C	Anti-submarine Detection Investigation Committee. SONAR Detection.
A	S	H	E	N	Pale, blanched, pallid, wan, waxen, ghostly, white-faced, waxy.
A	S	H	E	S	Residue, cinders, clinkers. Cricket prize.
A	S	I	A	N	Asiatic, Indian, Brown.
A	S	I	D	E	Apart, confidentially, sideways, a slant, a piece, per, near, parenthesis.
A	S	K	E	D	Questioned, interrogated, requested, invited, queried, beseeched, demanded.
A	S	K	E	R	Interrogator, examiner, Petitioner, suitor, suppliant, beggar.
A	S	K	E	W	Crooked, awry, cockeyed, sideways, obliquely.
A	S	O	A	K	Soaking, sodden.
A	S	P	E	N	Quivering, quaking, shaking, Poplar tree.
A	S	P	I	C	Gelatine, savoury jelly.
A	S	S	A	Y	Attempt, endeavour, essay, estimate, appraise, assess, evaluate, survey.
A	S	S	E	S	Donkeys, mules, burros.
A	S	S	E	T	Possession, resource, capital, wealth, credit, distinction.
A	S	T	A	Y	Cable direction.
A	S	T	E	R	Genus Aster, herbaceous plant, Daisy.
A	S	T	I	R	Alert, awake, aroused, awakened, galvanized, activated.
A	S	W	A	Y	Oscillating, swinging, swaying.
A	S	W	I	M	Swimming.
A	T	I	L	T	Lance in hand, tilting.
A	T	L	A	S	Mainstay, support, Cervical vertebra. Bound Maps.
A	T	O	L	L	Coral Reef.
A	T	O	M	S	Plural of ATOM.
A	T	O	M	Y	Tiny Creature, atom, skeleton.
A	T	O	N	E	Expiate, compensate, appease, propitiate, counteract, redeem, offset, pay back.
A	T	O	N	Y	Lack of Senses.
A	T	O	P	Y	Hypersensitivity.
A	T	R	I	P	Hove to, aweigh.
A	T	T	A	R	Fragrance, perfume.
A	T	T	I	C	Upper Room, Boxroom, garret, loft.
A	U	D	I	T	Balance, examine, compute.
A	U	G	E	R	Spiral Bit, drill. Device for digging holes.
A	U	G	H	T	Naught, zero, nothing.
A	U	G	U	R	Fortell, prophesy, indicate, predict, presage, prognosticate, forecast.
A	U	L	I	C	Courtly.
A	U	L	O	S	Musical Instrument.
A	U	N	T	Y	Relative, auntie.
A	U	R	A	L	Appertaining to Ears, hearing.
A	U	R	I	C	Like Gold.
A	U	R	I	N	Poisonous red dye.
A	U	R	U	M	Gold Colour.
A	U	X	I	N	Growth promoting substance.
A	V	A	I	L	Benefit, profit, advantage, suitability, fitness, satisfy, serve, fulfill. Make available.
A	V	A	S	T	Stop, Hold Fast, nautical command.
A	V	E	R	T	Deflect, prevent, forestall, deter, obviate, preclude, thwart, frustrate.
A	V	I	A	N	Bird-like.
A	V	I	O	N	By aeroplane.
A	V	O	I	D	Shun, escape, avert, obviate, prevent, evade, elude, duck, shun, eschew.
A	W	A	I	T	Expect, look for, hope for, count on, abide, stay, wait.
A	W	A	K	E	Vigilant, wakeful, alert, ready, aware, alive, conscious, sensible, watchful.
A	W	A	R	D	Accolade, decoration, distinction, honour, Prize, accord, grant, endow.
A	W	A	R	E	Mindful, sensible, conscious, Perceptive, alert, receptive.
A	W	A	S	H	Full, brimming chockfull, brimful, submerged.
A	W	A	V	E	Fluttering, wavey.
A	W	E	E	K	Per week, weekly.
A	W	F	U	L	Fearful, dreadful, formidable, shocking, terrible, impressive, imposing, superb.
A	W	H	I	R	Whirring, spinning.
A	W	I	N	G	Flying.
A	W	N	E	D	Bearded.
A	W	N	E	R	Grain separator.
A	W	O	K	E	Past of AWAKENED.
A	W	O	R	K	Active, working.
A	X	I	A	L	AXILE, relating to Axis.
A	X	I	O	M	Rule, maxim, principle.
A	X	I	T	E	Terminal branch.
A	X	L	E	D	Having a spindle or axle.

1	2	3	4	5	
A	X	O	I	D	Relating to Axis Vertebra.
A	Z	I	D	E	Hydrozoate.
A	Z	O	I	C	Before Life.
A	Z	O	T	E	Nitrogen.
A	Z	O	T	H	Universal Remedy.
A	Z	T	E	C	Early Mexican Indian.
A	Z	U	R	E	Blue, sky-blue.
A	Z	U	R	Y	AZURY - Blue tinted.
A	Z	Y	M	E	Unleavened bread.

B

B	A	B	E	L	Scene of Noise. Confusion of Sounds, Tower, din, clamour.
B	A	C	C	Y	Tobacco. Plug of chew tobacco.
B	A	C	K	S	Plural of BACK.
B	A	C	O	N	Cured Pork. Breakfast Food. Salt Pig.
B	A	D	G	E	Emblem, insignia, decoration, award, membership disc, Token, sign, mark.
B	A	D	L	Y	Wrongly, harshly, unfavourably, corruptly, wickedly, imperfectly, hardly, wrong.
B	A	G	E	L	Glazed hard-baked doughnut, horseshoe shaped breadroll.
B	A	G	G	Y	Loose, shabby, shapeless, ill-fitting.
B	A	I	R	N	Child.
B	A	I	Z	E	Table cover, felt cloth, material.
B	A	K	E	D	Hardened, Dried, Cooked, parched, scorched, fired, sizzled.
B	A	K	E	R	Bread maker, Pastry Chef.
B	A	L	E	D	Bound, bundled, pressed, wrapped, measured.
B	A	L	E	R	Scoop, ladle, dipper, shovel, lifter. Baling machine operator.
B	A	L	E	S	Plural of BALE.
B	A	L	K	Y	Contrary, perverse, wayward, reluctant, unmanageable, hesitant, disinclined.
B	A	L	L	S	Plural of BALL.
B	A	L	M	Y	Perfumed, fragrant, aromatic, gentle, bland, mild, soothing, potty, wacky, silly.
B	A	L	S	A	Light wood, float, life raft.
B	A	M	B	I	Disney animal, meek, gentle, faun.
B	A	N	A	L	Insipid, flat, vapid, bland, fatuous, pedestrian, asinine, simple, platitudinous.
B	A	N	D	Y	Bowlegged, bowed, bandy-legged, crooked. Dispute, argue.
B	A	N	G	S	Plural of BANG.
B	A	N	J	O	Stringed musical instrument.
B	A	N	K	S	Plural of BANK.
B	A	N	N	S	Public Note of Proposed Marriage, Proclamation.
B	A	N	T	U	African.
B	A	R	B	E	Scarf, mantilla, neckerchief.
B	A	R	E	D	Stripped, divested, denuded, exposed, peeled, uncovered, voided, exhibited.
B	A	R	G	E	Flat-bottomed boat, water craft, bumble, stumble, push, shove, lumber.
B	A	R	I	C	Relating to Barium.
B	A	R	K	Y	Barklike, woody.
B	A	R	M	Y	Fermented.
B	A	R	O	N	Nobleman, tycoon, mogul, magnate, merchant prince. Superior cut of Beef.
B	A	R	R	Y	Blocked, barricaded, limited.
B	A	S	A	L	Fundamental, basic, primary, radical, elementary, rudimentary.
B	A	S	E	D	Founded, structured, underwritten, built, constructed, established.
B	A	S	I	C	Elemental, fundamental, essential, rudiment, underlying, main, principal.
B	A	S	I	L	Aromatic plant, Sweet Basil, Mountain Mint.
B	A	S	I	N	Bowl, container, hollow, sink, depression, dock, reservoir, pond.
B	A	S	I	S	Foundation, infrastructure, grounds, reason, principle, base, premise.
B	A	S	S	O	Operatic Bass singer.
B	A	S	T	E	Moisten with fat, cover at intervals. Sew.
B	A	T	C	H	Number, group, quantity, lot, amount, bundle, cluster.
B	A	T	E	D	Moderated, restrained, repressed, reduced.
B	A	T	H	E	Bath, wash, douse, soak, tub, immerse, cover, dip.
B	A	T	I	K	Hand printing, waxed material.
B	A	T	T	Y	Loony, cracked, crazed, deranged, nuts, screwy, dotty, wacky.
B	A	U	L	K	Quibble, demure, thwart, beam, rafter.
B	A	V	I	N	Brushwood, kindling.
B	A	W	D	Y	Indecent, obscene, smutty, lewd.
B	A	Y	E	D	Barked, howled, yelped.
B	A	Y	O	U	Creek, watercourse, channel.
B	E	A	C	H	Shore, seashore, stretch of sand, coast, ground, set ashore, land, moor.

1	2	3	4	5	
B	E	A	D	S	Baubles, necklace, trinkets, gadgets. Rosary.
B	E	A	D	Y	Small, bright, shiny, pebble-like.
B	E	A	L	L	Beginning and end, altogether, essence, root, substance, aggregate, entirety, gross.
B	E	A	M	Y	Shiny, radiant, grinning, happy, Broad, wide.
B	E	A	N	O	Beanfeast, good time, jamboree, spree.
B	E	A	R	D	Face hairs, growth, whiskers, fuzz, bristles. Brave, challenge, dare, oppose openly.
B	E	A	S	T	Animal, creature, quadruped, brute, bully, ruffian.
B	E	A	U	X	Boyfriends, suitors, escorts.
B	E	B	O	P	Jazz, Bop, Pop.
B	E	D	E	W	Sprinkle, splash, moisten.
B	E	D	I	M	Cloud, darken, obscure, blur.
B	E	E	C	H	Tree, Wood. Nut.
B	E	E	F	Y	Husky, burly, powerful, stolid, hefty. Rich in beef or beef taste.
B	E	E	R	Y	Befuddled, dissolute, maudlin.
B	E	F	I	T	Fitting, suitable, become, suit. Conform.
B	E	F	O	G	Obscure, becloud, cloud, dim, darken, confuse, blur, bewilder, perplex.
B	E	F	U	R	Wrap, envelop.
B	E	G	A	N	Past of BEGIN.
B	E	G	A	T	Sired, bred, fathered. Past of BEGET.
B	E	G	E	M	Adorn, bejewel.
B	E	G	E	T	Father, sire, breed, reproduce, propagate, generate.
B	E	G	I	N	Commence, start, launch, initiate, institute, introduce, open, inaugurate.
B	E	G	O	T	BEGAT.
B	E	G	U	M	Muslim Queen, Princess, Heiress.
B	E	G	U	N	Past of BEGIN.
B	E	I	G	E	Variable colour, pale, yellow, grey, fawn.
B	E	I	N	G	Existence, entity, essence, personality, soul, character, life. Because, seeing.
B	E	I	S	A	Antelope.
B	E	L	A	Y	Cancel, stop, hold. Laid low.
B	E	L	C	H	Explode, erupt, expel, emit, gush, discharge.
B	E	L	I	E	Distort, falsify, misrepresent, pervert, twist, warp, conceal, disguise.
B	E	L	L	E	Beauty, charming girl, popular woman.
B	E	L	L	Y	Stomach, abdomen, womb, interior, middle section, under section.
B	E	L	O	W	Down, under, beneath, nether, underneath.
B	E	N	C	H	Wooden seat, Chair of Justice, tribunal, Court. Worktable.
B	E	N	D	Y	Marked by bends, curves.
B	E	N	N	E	Sesame.
B	E	R	A	T	Formal authorisation.
B	E	R	C	Y	Veloute Sauce.
B	E	R	E	T	Soft brimless cap, tamoshanta.
B	E	R	O	K	Pigtailed Ape.
B	E	R	R	Y	Fruit. Lobster or Fish Egg.
B	E	R	T	H	Wharf, dock, jetty, levee, quay, slip, Billet. Appointment, situation. Bunk, bed.
B	E	R	Y	L	Semi-precious stone.
B	E	S	E	T	Attack, besiege, blockade, assail, assault, surround, infest, encircle.
B	E	S	O	M	Bundle of twigs, broom.
B	E	S	O	T	Infatuate, stupify.
B	E	T	E	L	Masticatory stimulant.
B	E	T	T	Y	Sweet pastry, Dessert.
B	E	V	E	L	Slant, angle, printer's type, bull nose.
B	E	W	I	G	Furnish with a wig.
B	E	W	I	T	Leather strip in falconry.
B	H	A	N	G	Hashish, cannabis, narcotic.
B	I	B	B	S	Timber brace.
B	I	B	L	E	Scriptures, Divine writing, Book of Rules.
B	I	D	D	Y	Gossipy woman, housemaid.
B	I	D	E	T	Ablution vessel. Small horse.
B	I	E	L	D	Shelter, Refuge.
B	I	F	F	Y	Toilet, Privy.
B	I	F	I	D	Lobed.
B	I	G	H	T	Bay, curve, bend, arm, bayou, firth, slough, gulf.
B	I	G	L	Y	Largely, pompously.
B	I	G	O	T	Zealot, dogmatist, Enthusiast, fanatic, hypocrite.
B	I	J	O	U	Trinket, jewel, theatre.
B	I	L	B	O	Fine sword. Shackles.
B	I	L	G	E	Bulging portion of cask, barrel. Ship's Hull. Lowest point. Nonsense.
B	I	L	L	Y	Container, Pot. Male Goat. Club, baton.

1	2	3	4	5	
B	I	M	B	O	Wanton, hussy, slut, trollop, tramp.
B	I	N	G	E	Spree, bender, carousal, tear, toot, drunk, orgy, splurge.
B	I	N	G	O	Dice game, social gathering, game, housey-housey.
B	I	N	N	Y	Nile Fish.
B	I	O	M	E	Geological formation.
B	I	O	T	A	Region's flora and fauna.
B	I	P	E	D	Two footed.
B	I	P	O	D	Two-legged mount.
B	I	R	C	H	Flog, Tree.
B	I	R	D	S	Plural of BIRD. Fowls.
B	I	R	T	H	Emergence, physical appearance, emanate, flow, bring forth, deliver.
B	I	S	O	N	American Buffalo.
B	I	T	C	H	Term of abuse, Gripe, beef, fuss. Female dog.
B	I	T	E	R	Nibbler, muncher, stinger, eater. One who bites.
B	I	T	S	Y	Minute, teeny, wee, small, tiny. Inconsistent.
B	I	T	T	S	Cable attachment, Bollard.
B	I	T	T	Y	Fragmentary, incomplete, scrappy, disjointed.
B	L	A	C	K	Sombre, Dark, Inky, jet, pitch, filthy, funereal, evil, Negro.
B	L	A	D	E	Dashing fellow. Broad flattened surface. Knife edge. Oar. Grass.
B	L	A	I	N	Pustule, blister, chilblain.
B	L	A	M	E	Responsibility, liability. Criticise, censure, condemn, charge. Rap, knock.
B	L	A	N	D	Insipid, vapid, gentle, suave, smooth, urbane, flat, mild, benign.
B	L	A	N	K	Expressionless, vacant, empty, void, incomplete, unexpressive, deadpan.
B	L	A	R	E	Blazon, honk, shriek, glow, flame, glare, hoot, honk.
B	L	A	S	E	Sophisticated, disenchanted, mundane, wordly, surfeited, satiated, haughty.
B	L	A	S	T	Burst, Boom, bang, wreck, blight, slam, belt, clug, smash.
B	L	A	U	D	A fragment, a broken-off slab, a screed or selection of verse. To strike. To disfigure.
B	L	A	Z	E	Conflagration, fire, flame, flare, illuminate, publicise, blazon, promulgate. Mark trees.
B	L	E	A	K	Austere, harsh, grim, gloomy, depressing, dismal, dreary, stringent.
B	L	E	A	R	Blur, blot, dim, weary, dull, tired, faint, unclear, shadowy, vague.
B	L	E	A	T	Cry, squawk, squeal, gripe, felp, fuss, beef, yelp.
B	L	E	E	D	Secrete, exude, ooze, seep, weep, bloodlet, Fleece, milk.
B	L	E	E	P	Blip, Peep, Toot, Tweet. Radio signal.
B	L	E	N	D	Mix, mingle, meld, fuse, harmonize, integrate, Mixture, alloy, compound.
B	L	E	S	S	Hallow, laud, exalt, praise, extol, consecrate, glorify, magnify.
B	L	E	S	T	Blessed, Endowed.
B	L	I	M	P	Dumpling, fatso, butterball, reactionary, diehard, Colonel Blimp, fuddy duddy.
B	L	I	N	D	Unseeing, eyeless, sightless, dazzle, decoy, daze, intoxicated, inebriated, canned.
B	L	I	N	K	Wink, bat, nictate, flicker, twinkle, flash, glimmer, shimmer.
B	L	I	S	S	Joy, happiness, ecstasy, rapture, heaven, nirvana, paradise.
B	L	I	T	Z	Bombard, shell, blast, berate, overthrow, bomb.
B	L	O	A	T	Inflate, swell, stuff, guzzle, sponge.
B	L	O	C	K	Obstruct, barricade, hinder, impede, clog, building, annex, Wing, log, chunk.
B	L	O	K	E	Fellow, man, boy, chap, gentleman, guy, gent, buck.
B	L	O	N	D	Pale yellow, flaxen. golden, fair, titian, platinum, light.
B	L	O	O	D	Circulating life fluid, serum, liquid plasma, gore, Ancestry, pedigree, Fop, Dandy.
B	L	O	O	M	Flower, blossom, blush, glow, burgeon, prime, bud, flush, grow.
B	L	O	O	P	Blimp, sound-track joint bump.
B	L	O	T	S	Plural of BLOT. Smudges, blotches.
B	L	O	W	N	Bloomed, winded, botched, bungled, broke, Past of BLOW.
B	L	O	W	Y	Windy, breezy, gusty, airy, breathless.
B	L	U	E	D	Wasted, squandered, spent.
B	L	U	E	R	More blue, disconsolate, gloomier, dispirited.
B	L	U	E	S	Miseries, despondency, depression, dumps, gloom, melancholy, unhappiness.
B	L	U	E	Y	Bluish, blue blanket, lizard, swagman's bundle.
B	L	U	F	F	Deceive, kid, delude, mislead, pretend, fake, sham, hearty, gruff, brusque. Headland.
B	L	U	N	T	Dull, obtuse, insensitive, numbed, undermine, abrupt, brusque, curt.
B	L	U	R	B	Spiel, description, plug, write-up, puff, recommendation, description.
B	L	U	R	T	Blap, blat, exclaim, ejaculate, divulge, utter impulsively. Raspberry. Razz.
B	L	U	S	H	Flush, colour, glow, redden, Rouge, rose, crimson, bloom.
B	O	A	R	D	Plank, table, Lodging, domicile. Theatre, footlights. Embark, emplane, get on.
B	O	A	S	T	Brag, crow, swagger, flaunt, parade, show off, swashbuckle, bluster, exalt.
B	O	B	B	Y	Policeman, bluebottle, bull, constable, flatfoot, gendarme, officer, copper.
B	O	C	H	E	Hun, German.
B	O	D	E	D	Portended, augured, presaged, betokened, promised, foreshadowed.
B	O	D	G	E	Botch, mess up, befuddle, muddle.
B	O	G	E	Y	Spectre, spook, wraith, apparition, ghost, phantom, hobgoblin.

1	2	3	4	5	
B	O	G	G	Y	Swampy, marshy, slushy, muddy, mucky.
B	O	G	I	E	4-wheeled swivelling truck, locomotive, mounted car, track car.
B	O	G	U	S	Counterfeit, fake, phony, pseudo, sham, spurious, forged, false.
B	O	H	E	A	Black inferior grade Tea.
B	O	I	L	S	Plural of BOIL.
B	O	I	T	E	Disco, nightclub.
B	O	L	A	R	Like clay, bole-like.
B	O	L	T	S	Plural of BOLT. Flashes, Lengths.
B	O	L	U	S	Large Pill.
B	O	M	B	S	Plural of BOMB.
B	O	N	C	E	Marble. Head, pate.
B	O	N	D	S	Contracts, pacts, ties, links, yokes, guarantees, sureties. Ropes, fasteners.
B	O	N	E	D	Studied, crammed, blundered, bungled. Deboned.
B	O	N	E	S	Ivories, Dice, dominoes, tats, smackers. Of anatomy, skeleton
B	O	N	G	O	Antelope, drums, Tree.
B	O	N	N	E	Nursemaid.
B	O	N	N	Y	Bouncing, charming, lively, handsome, lovely.
B	O	N	U	S	Windfall, reward, premium, award, dividend, in addition, added on.
B	O	O	B	Y	Dunce, chump, simpleton, dolt, fathead, goof, goon, blockhead.
B	O	O	E	D	Hooted, heckled, clamoured, razzed, catcalled, interrupted, voiced objection.
B	O	O	E	R	Perpetrator of heckling, interrupter, objector.
B	O	O	K	S	Plural of BOOK.
B	O	O	M	S	Plural of BOOM.
B	O	O	S	T	Raise, increase, augment, expand, extend, magnify, promote. Rise, upgrade, breakthrough, boom.
B	O	O	T	H	Stall, enclosure, roofed structure, kiosk.
B	O	O	T	S	Plural of BOOT.
B	O	O	T	Y	Spoils, plunder, loot, boodle, prize, swag.
B	O	O	Z	E	Drink, liquor, hooch, grog, binge, bender, tipple, swill, swig.
B	O	R	A	X	Sodium Borate.
B	O	R	E	D	Drilled, perforated, punctured, goggled, gaped. Wearied, tired, palled, fatigued, fed-up.
B	O	R	E	R	One who bores. Boring insects.
B	O	R	I	C	Related to Boron.
B	O	R	N	E	Narrow minded, limited, hidebound.
B	O	R	O	N	Non-metallic element.
B	O	S	A	L	Noseband.
B	O	S	K	Y	Thickly wooded, Shrubby, Tipsy, Drunk.
B	O	S	O	M	Heart, confidentiality, breast, soul, bust, chest.
B	O	S	S	Y	Masterful, high-handed, overbearing, imperious, domineering, imperial.
B	O	T	C	H	Bungle, fluff, goof, muff, fumble, hash, muss, muddle, mismanage, wreck.
B	O	U	G	H	Branch, limb, offshoot, arm.
B	O	U	N	D	Leap, spring, hop, hurdle, vault, jump, charge. Demarcated, confined, heel. Obliged, definitely will.
B	O	U	R	N	Brook, Rivulet, stream.
B	O	W	E	D	Bent, buckled, curved, arched, angled, bowlegged, bandy, subdued.
B	O	W	E	L	Intestine, gut, interior, inside. Eviscerate, embowel.
B	O	W	E	R	Arbour, shelter, Pergola.
B	O	W	I	E	Large curved knife.
B	O	W	L	S	Ball game, Plural of BOWL.
B	O	X	E	D	Crated, wrapped, Cuffed, clouted, slapped. Enclosed, jammed, boxed in.
B	O	X	E	R	Pugilist, fighter.
B	O	X	E	S	Plural of BOX.
B	O	X	I	N	Stymy, surround, enclose.
B	O	X	U	P	Tax up, mistake, error.
B	O	Y	E	R	Sailing Boat.
B	R	A	C	E	Pair, couple. Support, truss, suspender, bracket, strengthen, Surround, encircle.
B	R	A	C	H	Bitch-hound, Brak.
B	R	A	C	T	Modified Leaf.
B	R	A	G	S	Boasts.
B	R	A	I	D	Cord, twine, string, ribbon, interweave, trimming, binding, intermingle.
B	R	A	I	L	Rope, thong, pipe, dip net.
B	R	A	I	N	Centre of intellect, intelligence, centre of nervous system, mind.
B	R	A	K	E	Thicket, wagonette, harrow, hinder, impede, obstruct, stop, slow.
B	R	A	K	Y	Abounding in ferns.
B	R	A	N	D	Trade mark, logo, type, Slur, blot, stain, mark.
B	R	A	N	K	Bridle of scolds, halter.
B	R	A	N	T	Wild Goose.
B	R	A	S	H	Rash, effervescent, exuberant, tactless, impolite, undiplomatic, presumptious.
B	R	A	S	S	Money, impudence, effrontery, brashness, cheek, confidence, nerve, gall. Metal.

1	2	3	4	5	
B	R	A	V	E	Gallant, game, audacious, bold, stelwart, daring, unflinching, fearless, intrepid.
B	R	A	V	O	Exclamation of Approval. Cheer. Well done. Assasin, cut throat, hitman.
B	R	A	W	L	Quarrel, squabble, free-for-all, scrimmage, scuffle, wrangle, uproar, fight, scrap.
B	R	A	W	N	Muscle, might, sinew, beef, strength.
B	R	A	X	Y	Sheep malignancy.
B	R	A	Z	E	Solder.
B	R	E	A	D	Staple diet, food, provisions, viands, living, money, dough, maintenance.
B	R	E	A	K	Interval, breather. Violate. Escape. Ruin, degrade, breach, split, fracture. Score in billiards.
B	R	E	A	M	Fish. Scrape ship's bottom.
B	R	E	E	D	Procreate, beget, generate, father, engender, propogate, type, class, ilk, species, mate.
B	R	E	N	T	Steep, smooth, precipitous.
B	R	E	V	E	Royal mandate, paper brief, Writ, Note.
B	R	I	A	R	Tobacco Pipe, Wild Rose.
B	R	I	B	E	Inducement, influence, suborn, sweeten, palmoil, square, buy, corrupt.
B	R	I	C	K	Building block, building material, baked clay, stalwart, pal, solid chap.
B	R	I	D	E	Newly married woman, wife, novitiate in religious order.
B	R	I	E	F	Official mandate, limited, short, curt, abrupt, concise, coach, discuss, inform, instruct.
B	R	I	E	R	Briar, wild rose, pipe. Brush, heath.
B	R	I	N	E	Salt water, sea water, tears.
B	R	I	N	G	Fetch, carry, conduct, convey, escort, bear, effect, induce, raise.
B	R	I	N	K	Border, edge, fringe, brim, perimeter, periphery, verge, margin.
B	R	I	N	Y	Salty, the sea. Ocean, blue, deep. Drink.
B	R	I	S	K	Quick, lively, active, fast, zippy, agile, alert, nimble, abrupt.
B	R	O	A	D	Wide, extensive, extended, copious, liberal, tolerant, racy. Woman, girl.
B	R	O	C	K	Badger.
B	R	O	I	L	Brawl, fracas, fray, ruction. Bake, cook, roast, fry, burn. Embroil.
B	R	O	K	E	Poor, destitute, needy, beggared. Penniless, ruined. Broken, fractured, smashed.
B	R	O	N	X	Cocktail. Area of New York.
B	R	O	O	D	Set, cover, sit, Mope, gloom. Incubate. Meditate. Progeny, offspring.
B	R	O	O	K	Creek, gill, rivulet, stream, runnel, beck. Tolerate, allow, bear, abide.
B	R	O	O	L	Low roar, deep murmur.
B	R	O	O	M	Brush, besom, floor sweeper. Bundle of twigs.
B	R	O	T	H	Stock, soup, bouillon, concoction, gruel.
B	R	O	W	N	Colour, dark, dusky, tanned.
B	R	U	I	N	Bear.
B	R	U	I	T	Noise abroad, publicise, tout, report, declare, announce, blazon advertise.
B	R	U	J	A	Hex, hag, witch, sorceress.
B	R	U	L	E	Custard.
B	R	U	M	E	Fog, mist, vapour, film, haze.
B	R	U	N	E	Brunet, dark, swarthy.
B	R	U	N	T	Shock, stress, impact.
B	R	U	S	H	Skirmish, scrap. Sweep, touch, skim, shave. Broom. Fox's tail.
B	R	U	T	E	Animal, beast, creature, savage, bestial, beastly, bestial, feral.
B	U	C	H	U	Dried plant used for medicinal purposes.
B	U	D	D	Y	Associate, pal, chum, mate, companion, crony, comrade.
B	U	D	G	E	Stir, shift, move, deviate, yield. Intoxicating liquor. Pompous, Solemn.
B	U	F	F	O	Clown, buffoon, Comic singer.
B	U	F	F	S	Professors. Group of clever persons.
B	U	F	F	Y	Buff Coloured, beige.
B	U	G	G	Y	Carriage, automobile, vehicle.
B	U	G	L	E	Brass musical instrument, horn, trumpet.
B	U	I	L	D	Erect, raise, construct, augment, Physique, constitution.
B	U	I	L	T	Past of BUILD.
B	U	L	B	Y	Bulbous, Bulb-like.
B	U	L	G	E	Projection, protrusion, protuberance, swelling, lump, bump, outcrop.
B	U	L	G	Y	Projecting, jutting, outthrust, overhanging, full, crammed, packed.
B	U	L	K	Y	Voluminous, unwieldy, massive, stout, corpulent, weighty, portly.
B	U	L	L	A	Seal, ornament.
B	U	L	L	Y	Ruffian, hector, intimidator, tough, tormentor, Excellent, first rate. Intimidate.
B	U	L	S	E	Container for valuables, purse.
B	U	M	P	S	Plural of BUMP.
B	U	M	P	Y	Uneven, rickety, rocking.
B	U	N	C	E	Luck, bonus, windfall.
B	U	N	C	H	Batch, lot, collection, gathering, knot, parcel, group, cluster. Crowd.
B	U	N	N	Y	Rabbit, pet.
B	U	N	T	Y	Short, stocky.
B	U	R	G	H	Dorp, town, borough, remote town, hick town.

1	2	3	4	5	
B	U	R	I	N	Engraver's tool.
B	U	R	K	E	Suppress.
B	U	R	L	Y	Husky, hefty, muscular, beefy, lusty, stout.
B	U	R	N	T	Consumed by fire. Charred, roasted.
B	U	R	R	O	Donkey, mule, ass, neddy, jackass, moke.
B	U	R	R	Y	Having burrs, prickly.
B	U	R	S	A	Pouch, sac.
B	U	R	S	T	Explode, erupt, detonate, shatter, fragment, splinter, barrage, salvo, blast.
B	U	S	B	Y	Bearskin headdress.
B	U	S	E	S	Omnibuses, bus transport, vehicles.
B	U	S	H	Y	Overgrown, uncultivated, bush covered, woody, shady.
B	U	T	T	E	Flat-topped hill, ridge.
B	U	T	T	S	Targets, laughing stocks, fall guys, suckers, victims.
B	U	T	T	Y	Chum, partner, middleman. Sandwich.
B	U	X	O	M	Jolly, full bosomed, comely, lively chesty.
B	U	Y	E	R	Purchaser, customer, shopper.
B	U	Z	Z	Y	Gossipy, talkative, dazed, muzzy, intoxicated.
B	Y	D	A	Y	Off day.
B	Y	E	N	D	Fragment, snatch.
B	Y	L	A	W	Local Law.
B	Y	O	U	S	Extremely, extraordinarily.
B	Y	W	A	Y	By-Path, Country lane, off the beaten track.

C

1	2	3	4	5	
C	A	B	A	L	Clique, circle, coterie, mob, ring, camp, set. Coven, plot, intrigue, machination.
C	A	B	B	Y	Taxi driver.
C	A	B	E	R	Rafter, tree trunk, pole.
C	A	B	I	N	Hut, shack, shanty, cottage, rondavel, lodge. Ship quarters.
C	A	B	L	E	Wire rope, maritime unit of length, telegraph.
C	A	C	A	O	Dried Seed base for chocolate, cocoa.
C	A	C	H	E	Store, hideaway, place of concealment, hiding place. Bury, conceal, secrete, stash.
C	A	D	D	Y	Container, tea caddy, golf caddy.
C	A	D	E	T	Pupil, student, trainee, learner, junior, young soldier.
C	A	D	G	E	Beg habitually, sponge, borrow.
C	A	D	G	Y	Amorous, wanton, frolicsome, frisky, sporty.
C	A	D	R	E	Framework, scheme, revolutionary group, terrorist.
C	A	G	E	D	Held captive, penned, fenced in, copped, cooped up, locked up, confined.
C	A	G	E	Y	Astute, shrewd, cunning, artful, secretive, cautious. Sagacious, Perspicacious.
C	A	I	R	N	Pyramid, heap of stones. Terrier.
C	A	K	E	D	Encrusted, besmeared, coated, smeared, daubed, congealed, covered, smothered.
C	A	L	I	N	Chinese alloy.
C	A	L	I	X	Chalice, Cup, whorl. Calyx.
C	A	M	E	L	Desert saddle animal, Light fawn colour.
C	A	M	E	O	Carved Gem, medallion, brief literary piece, synopsis.
C	A	N	A	L	Aqueduct, watercourse, channel, duct, conduit.
C	A	N	D	Y	Confectionery, sweet, crystallised sugar, cook in sugar, coat with sugar.
C	A	N	E	D	Whipped, chastised, thrashed, beaten, punished.
C	A	N	E	R	Weaver of cane.
C	A	N	E	S	Plural of CANE.
C	A	N	N	A	Genus of plant.
C	A	N	N	Y	Shrewd, clever, astute, aware, cunning, wise, smart, sharp witted, quick.
C	A	N	O	E	Dugout, boat. To travel by canoe.
C	A	N	O	N	Decree, regulation, code, rule, law, statute, assize, doctrine, dogma, tenet, text, full text.
C	A	N	T	O	Division of Poem.
C	A	N	T	Y	Cheerful, lively, sprightly.
C	A	N	U	N	Zither.
C	A	P	E	R	Gambol frisk, romp, cavort, Prank, escapade, mischief, devilment, trick.
C	A	P	O	N	Castrated fowl, castrated rabbit (male).
C	A	P	R	I	Grotto Blue. Colour.
C	A	R	A	T	Unit of weight, gemstone worth.
C	A	R	E	D	Interested, concerned, troubled, worried, attended, nursed, guarded, ministered.
C	A	R	E	T	The Mark "insert".
C	A	R	E	X	Genus of Herb, Sedge.
C	A	R	G	O	Load, freight, payload, burden, haul, lading.
C	A	R	L	E	Worker, Farmhand, craftsman.

1	2	3	4	5	
C	A	R	O	B	Jacaranda.
C	A	R	O	L	Choral song, hymn, Christmas song, Joyful singing, song of praise, ballad, chorus.
C	A	R	O	M	Glance, bounce, rebound, ricochet, skim, skip.
C	A	R	R	Y	Convey, transport, bear, ferry, tote, lug, influence, conduct, acquit, support.
C	A	R	S	E	Low-lying land.
C	A	R	T	E	Card, map, chart.
C	A	R	T	Y	Resembling a cart horse.
C	A	R	U	M	Aromatic Herb.
C	A	R	V	E	Cut, slice, dissect, sever, sunder, cleave, sculpture, hack, engrave.
C	A	S	E	D	Boxed, enveloped, wrapped, packed. Investigated, examined.
C	A	S	E	S	Plural of CASE.
C	A	S	S	E	Disorder in Wines.
C	A	S	T	E	Class, breed, stock, race.
C	A	T	C	H	Capture, seize, ensnare, Dupe, hoodwink, trick. Fasten.
C	A	T	E	R	Provide food, arrange household, buy provisions, service, supervise.
C	A	T	E	S	Delicacies, dainties.
C	A	T	T	Y	Spiteful, malicious, bitchy, feline. Catapult.
C	A	U	L	K	Chalk, cork, plug, make watertight, stop up, seal, flash.
C	A	U	S	E	Effect, reason, goad, motivate, generate, engender, induce, Motive, Occasion.
C	A	V	E	D	Collapsed, dropped, wilted, succombed, bent, bowed, buckled, knuckled down.
C	A	V	E	L	A piece of wood used in casting lots, A lot.
C	A	V	I	L	Quibble, criticize, frivolous, objection, trivial criticism, carp.
C	A	W	E	D	Crowed, called raucously, squawked, squalled.
C	A	W	K	Y	Like Cawk.
C	A	X	O	N	Wig.
C	E	A	S	E	Stop, end, desist, close, conclude, halt, quit, finish, conclusion, termination.
C	E	D	A	R	Tree.
C	E	D	E	D	Granted, allowed, yielded, allotted, relinquished, transferred, assigned.
C	E	L	L	A	Inner building.
C	E	L	L	O	Violincello, musical stringed instrument.
C	E	N	S	E	Burn incense.
C	E	N	S	O	Ground rent, levy.
C	E	N	T	O	Patchwork, medley.
C	E	N	T	S	Plural of CENT.
C	E	R	E	D	Waxed.
C	E	R	E	S	Colour orange.
C	E	R	I	N	Cerotic acid.
C	H	A	F	E	Graze, rub, wear, ruffle, fret, gall, excoriate, abrade, scrape, scratch.
C	H	A	F	F	Banter, joke, jest, fun, kid. Animal food, corn husks. Anything worthless.
C	H	A	I	N	Shackle, bond, fetter, accumulative, syndicate, combine, row, succession. Measurement.
C	H	A	I	R	Preside, professorship. Seat, chariot.
C	H	A	L	K	Limestone, whitening, material for writing, drawing. Mark, delineate, draft.
C	H	A	M	A	Rock Oyster.
C	H	A	M	P	Champion. Chew, chomp, munch.
C	H	A	N	T	Warble, intone, sing, cant. Vocal song, sing song.
C	H	A	O	S	Confusion, disorder, muddle, anarchy, unruliness, lawlesness.
C	H	A	P	E	Sheath. Buckle catch.
C	H	A	P	S	Plural of CHAP. Leggings.
C	H	A	R	D	Spinach-like vegetable.
C	H	A	R	E	Narrow alley, lane.
C	H	A	R	K	To burn to charcoal, charcoal, coke.
C	H	A	R	M	Allure, appeal, charisma. Enchant, Amulet, fetish, mascot.
C	H	A	R	T	Map, plan, blueprint, graph, scheme, devise, project, design.
C	H	A	R	Y	Cautious, careful, discreet, guarded, hesitant, frugal, sparing, thrifty.
C	H	A	S	E	Pursuit, hunt, follow, trail. Run, career, rush, course, speed.
C	H	A	S	M	Abyss, cleft, crevice, ravine, gulch, gorge, schism, cleavage, split.
C	H	A	T	S	Plural of CHAT.
C	H	E	A	P	Inexpensive, reasonable, low-priced. Inferior, low, base, paltry.
C	H	E	A	T	Swindler, bilk, dupe, Deception, fraud, hoax, dishonesty, fool, double-cross.
C	H	E	C	K	Examine, test, conform, dovetail, restrain, interrupt, arrest, constrain, curb. Little squares. Check in.
C	H	E	E	K	Fleshy part of face, buttock. Temerity, insolence, tease, effrontery, nerve, gall.
C	H	E	E	P	Chirp, peep, chirrup, tweet, twitter, chipper, pipe, chitter.
C	H	E	E	R	Applause, acclamation. Comfort, console, encourage, hearten, applaud.
C	H	E	L	A	Lobster pincer, cult follower.
C	H	E	R	T	Flintstone.
C	H	E	S	S	Game of ancient origin.
C	H	E	S	T	Treasury, coffer, box container, Lung area. Breast.

1	2	3	4	5	
C	H	I	C	K	Sprout, child, chicken.
C	H	I	C	O	Bamboo screen.
C	H	I	D	E	Reprove, admonish, rebuke, reprimand, tick off, scold, berate.
C	H	I	E	F	Leader, head, boss, principal. First, foremost, principal. Primary, prominent.
C	H	I	L	D	Minor, adolescent, teenager, innocent, youngster, nipper, kid, youth, offspring.
C	H	I	L	I	Hot pepper, pepper sauce, curry.
C	H	I	L	L	Cool, ice, depress, discourage. Cold, emotionless, frigid, reserved, withdrawn.
C	H	I	M	E	Clang, gong, knell, peal, toll, ring, interrupt, declare, state, utter. Bell.
C	H	I	N	A	Country in Asia. Porcelain, crockery. Pal. companion. (Sl.)
C	H	I	N	E	Crest, cleft, ravine, ridge, hogback.
C	H	I	N	K	(Sl.) Chinese. Gap, clink, cranny, crack, fissure, Jingle, clink.
C	H	I	P	S	Fried Potato. Potato Flakes. Fragment, flake, token, flaws.
C	H	I	R	K	Cheep, chirp, cheerful cry.
C	H	I	R	M	Noise, din, clamour.
C	H	I	R	P	Chirrup, trill, chirl, bird call, cheep, peep.
C	H	I	R	R	Insect noise, shrill.
C	H	I	R	U	Tibetan antelope.
C	H	I	V	E	Perennial plant, form of onion, seasoning.
C	H	I	V	Y	Chase, badger, heckle, hound, pursue, follow, encourage, trail.
C	H	O	C	K	Wedge, block, log.
C	H	O	I	R	Company of singers, Church chorus body.
C	H	O	K	E	Suffocate, asphyxiate, smother, clog, plug, stop, silence, quieten, still.
C	H	O	K	Y	A prison, A toll-station, A watchman.
C	H	O	P	S	Mouth, jaw, jowls, trade, swaps. Cutlet, cut of meat.
C	H	O	R	D	Tone sound. Harmonize. Cord, Span.
C	H	O	R	E	Task, duty, assignment, toil, job, task.
C	H	O	S	E	Selected, picked, culled.
C	H	U	B	B	Safe, Lock.
C	H	U	C	K	Cast, throw, lob, quit, renounce, harbour, haven, abandon, eject, discard. Rotating workpiece or tool.
C	H	U	F	F	Proud, elated. Chug, Boor, clown, miser, skinflint, sullen, morose, sulky.
C	H	U	M	P	Dunce, fool, dimwit, chew, chomp.
C	H	U	N	K	Thick slice, lump, clump, hunk, wad, clod, nugget.
C	H	U	R	L	Boor, chuff, clodhopper, clown.
C	H	U	R	N	Seethe, ferment, simmer, bubble, foam. Agitate, jostle.
C	H	U	T	E	Cascade, cataract, falls, spout, waterfall. Parachute.
C	H	Y	L	E	Milky fluid. Lymph.
C	H	Y	M	E	Partially digested food.
C	I	B	O	L	Shallot. Variety of Onion.
C	I	C	A	D	Cicada. Christmas beetle. Harvest fly. Sapsucking bug.
C	I	C	E	R	Chick pea.
C	I	D	E	R	Fermented Apple Juice. Drink.
C	I	G	A	R	Roll of Tobacco for smoking. Rolled Tobacco Leaves.
C	I	L	I	A	Hairlike processes, filaments. Eyelashes.
C	I	M	E	X	Bed bug.
C	I	N	C	H	Certainty, child's play, breeze, pushover, kid stuff. Ensure, secure.
C	I	R	C	A	Approximately, about, around, near.
C	I	R	C	E	Siren.
C	I	R	R	I	Plural of CIRRUS.
C	I	S	C	O	Lake Fish.
C	I	S	S	Y	Sissy, cissie.
C	I	T	E	D	Specified, mentioned, alleged, quoted, named, adduced, enumerated.
C	I	V	E	T	Civet cat, musky perfume, spotty fur.
C	I	V	I	C	Public, national, municipal, corporate, civil.
C	I	V	I	L	Courteous, obliging, courtly, polite, genteel. Public, national, civic.
C	I	V	V	Y	Civilian.
C	L	A	C	K	Chatter, clatter, click, clink, chat, babble, yak, gabble.
C	L	A	I	M	Right, share, stake, demand, maintain, pretense, privilege, assert, contend.
C	L	A	M	P	Clutch, grapple, grasp, clench, grip, tenure, pinch, hold. Vice, Pincer.
C	L	A	M	S	Bivalve mollusc.
C	L	A	N	G	Resounding noise, echoing ring, Gong, Bang, Clash.
C	L	A	N	K	Clatter, clangour, clang, clash.
C	L	A	N	S	Plural of CLAN.
C	L	A	R	Y	Pot Herb, Beverage.
C	L	A	S	H	Impact, collide, collision, prang, discord, jolt, affray, scrimmage, fracas.
C	L	A	S	P	Hasp, catch, grip, hold, clench, embrace, clip, squeeze, clutch.
C	L	A	S	S	Category, group, league, grade, quality, variety, assort, classify, type, race.
C	L	E	A	N	Unsullied, unsoiled, immaculate, spotless, innocent, blameless, purify, cleanse.

1	2	3	4	5	
C	L	E	A	R	Transparent, translucent, lucid, pellucid, understandable, recognizable. Clarify. Rid. Getaway.
C	L	E	A	T	Strip, wedge, projection, groove, channel, slat.
C	L	E	E	K	Hook, crook, Golf club.
C	L	E	F	T	Fissure, ravine, chasm, gap, schism, split, gulch, crack, chink.
C	L	E	R	K	Cleric, recorder. Secretary, clergyman, scholar.
C	L	E	V	E	Cliff, valley.
C	L	I	C	K	Succeed, pan out, prove, sharp sound, latch, articulation, musical sound.
C	L	I	F	F	Overhanging rock. Cleve. Precipice, steep slope, rockface.
C	L	I	M	B	Ascend, scale, mount. Ascent. Surmount. Shin-up. Soar.
C	L	I	M	E	Climate. Region. Zone.
C	L	I	N	E	Grade, series. Assessment.
C	L	I	N	G	Hold together, adhere tenaciously, grip firmly. Embrace, cleave, stick, cohere.
C	L	I	N	K	Jail, cooler, jug, chokey, stir, prison. Chink, jingle.
C	L	I	N	T	Flintstone rock.
C	L	O	A	K	Mask, cover, disguise, camouflage. Screen, veil, cape, shroud, blanket.
C	L	O	C	K	Timepiece, register of time, distance, rate, velocity, number. Measure time. Callibrate.
C	L	O	N	S	Asexually produced progeny. Repeated Fission. Vegetative cuttings.
C	L	O	S	E	Shut, block, screen, obstruct, fill, plug, stop, lessen, end, cease, abate. Silent, reticent, narrow.
C	L	O	T	H	Fabric, material, natural or synthetic fibres woven or spun. Piece of fabric. Dress of the Clergy.
C	L	O	T	S	Plural of CLOT. Gouts, clumps, lumps.
C	L	O	U	D	Vapour, haze, overcast, overcloud, gloom, fog, muddle, confuse, taint, blur.
C	L	O	U	T	Cuff, box, buffet, strike, biff, sock.
C	L	O	V	E	Spice. Clove-hitch. Cloven. Clove of garlic.
C	L	O	W	N	Buffoon, comedian, jester, circus performer.
C	L	U	C	K	Noise of a hen.
C	L	U	M	P	Group, array, bunch, cluster, clutter, jumble, lumber, stump.
C	L	U	N	G	Past of Cling.
C	L	U	N	K	Thump, clonk, thud. Gurgle, Dull person.
C	L	U	N	Y	Lace.
C	O	A	C	H	Teach, train. Instruct, prompt. Vehicle, carriage,trailer, Teacher, trainer.
C	O	A	C	T	Force, compel, control, drive.
C	O	A	L	Y	Impregnated with coal. Resembling coal. Coal Heaver.
C	O	A	R	B	Religious successor.
C	O	A	S	T	Shore, Beach, strand, seaside, bank. Slide, drift, glide. Coastal region.
C	O	B	B	Y	Stocky, sturdy.
C	O	B	I	A	Large fish.
C	O	B	O	L	Computer Language.
C	O	B	R	A	Venemous Elapid Snake.
C	O	C	K	Y	Pert, insolent, cheeky, jaunty.
C	O	C	O	A	Chocolate, beverage.
C	O	D	E	D	Compiled, systemised, wrote cryptically, ciphered, symbolised, tabulated.
C	O	D	E	N	Library system.
C	O	D	E	R	Coding device, code operator, electronic circuit switch, radar unit.
C	O	D	E	X	Ancient, unbound manuscript. Drug formulas.
C	O	I	G	N	Projecting corner, intersection. Quoin.
C	O	K	E	D	Converted into coke.
C	O	L	I	C	Stomach pains, flatulence, gripes. bellyache. Biliary.
C	O	L	I	N	Gamebird.
C	O	L	L	Y	Blacken. Coal smut.
C	O	L	O	N	Part of the large intestine. Punctuation mark. Monetary unit.
C	O	L	O	R	Colour. Hue, tint, pigment. Embroider, embellish. Misrepresent. Blush, flush.
C	O	M	B	E	Hollow vessel, basin, valley, vale.
C	O	M	B	O	Combination, small band, modern orchestra. Combination of musical instruments.
C	O	M	E	R	Arrival. Newly arrived. Showing promise. Latecomer. Newcomer.
C	O	M	E	T	Nebulous celestial body.
C	O	M	F	Y	Comfortable, snug, cozy, soft, well adjusted.
C	O	M	I	C	Comedian, jester, wag, wit. Laughable, farcical, funny, droll, comical. Picture story.
C	O	M	M	A	Punctuation mark, pause, interval.
C	O	M	M	E	IL FAUT Decorous, becoming, decent, proper, seemly, conforming.
C	O	M	P	O	Mortar, Mold mixture. Composition.
C	O	N	C	H	Spiral shelled mollusc. Collector's Shell. Conchology.
C	O	N	E	D	Conic, cone-shaped, encircled, trapped by searchlight.
C	O	N	E	R	Machine operator, winder.
C	O	N	E	S	Plural of CONE.
C	O	N	E	Y	CONY. Rabbit skin, Fur, Hare.
C	O	N	G	A	Cuban Dance. Drum.
C	O	N	G	E	Leave taking, Farewell.

(70)

1	2	3	4	5	
C	O	N	G	O	Zaire, the country or the river.
C	O	N	I	C	Cone-shaped, tapering, relating to Cone.
C	O	N	T	O	Monetary unit.
C	O	O	E	D	Murmured, muttered, buzzed.
C	O	O	K	Y	Female Cook, cupcake, Dilly, off-beam.
C	O	O	L	Y	An Indian or Chinese labourer who has emigrated under contract to a foreign land.
C	O	O	M	B	Valley.
C	O	O	N	Y	Cagey, canny, clever, cunning, sly, dexterous, adroit.
C	O	O	P	T	Pre-empt, appoint, commandeer, elect. Co-opt.
C	O	P	A	L	Resin, varnish, printing ink.
C	O	P	E	D	Managed, handled, contended, faced.
C	O	P	E	R	Dealer, bargainer. One who copes.
C	O	P	R	A	Dried coconut meat.
C	O	P	S	E	Coppice, spinney, small wooded area.
C	O	P	S	Y	Covered in copse. Overgrown. Wooded.
C	O	R	A	L	Marine deposit, Lobster ovary. Lobster roe, colour.
C	O	R	E	D	Centre removed, centered.
C	O	R	E	R	Instrument for removing cores. Sample cutting device.
C	O	R	G	I	Breed of small welsh dog.
C	O	R	K	Y	Dry, withered, lively, skittish.
C	O	R	N	O	French horn.
C	O	R	N	U	Resembling a horn.
C	O	R	N	Y	Hackneyed, cliched, trite, stale, stereotyped, tired, commonplace.
C	O	R	P	S	Company, outfit, party, troop, band, troupe, contingent, staff.
C	O	S	T	A	A rib, midrib of a leaf.
C	O	S	T	S	Expenses, charges, prices, tariffs, expenditure, disbursement.
C	O	T	C	H	Seize, snatch, catch, clutch, grapple, overtake, overhaul.
C	O	T	T	A	Fort.
C	O	U	C	H	Word, express, phrase. Sofa, divan, bed. Grass, stoop. Liar. Den. Lodge.
C	O	U	G	H	Expel air from lungs, single short burst, clear air passages explosively.
C	O	U	L	D	Past of CAN.
C	O	U	N	T	Enumerate, number, tally, ascertain number, import, weigh, relay, expect. Nobleman.
C	O	U	P	E	Compartment for two. Dessert. Serving dish.
C	O	U	R	T	Quadrangle, courtyard, judge, lawcourt. Pursue, attract, charm, woo.
C	O	U	T	H	Polished sophisticated, agreeable, smooth, groomed.
C	O	V	E	D	Concave.
C	O	V	E	N	Assembly of Witches. Congregation.
C	O	V	E	R	Shelter, haven, cloak, disguise, track, travel, blanket, hide, defend, screen, wrap.
C	O	V	E	T	Desire, crave, want, hanker for.
C	O	V	E	Y	Group, band, bevy, cluster, party, brood of partridges.
C	O	V	I	N	Conspiracy, plot, intrigue, machination, scheme, cabal.
C	O	W	E	D	Abashed, intimidated, browbeaten, bulldozed, overawed, daunted.
C	O	W	E	R	Fawn, cringe, shrink, quail, kowtow, toady, grovel.
C	O	W	L	E	Safe-conduct, amnesty.
C	O	W	R	Y	Cowrie, Shell, Gastropod. Collectors' shell. Mollusc.
C	O	Y	L	Y	Bashfully, demurely, timidly, properly, archly, mischievously. Nicely.
C	O	Y	P	U	Aquatic rodent.
C	O	Z	E	N	Cheat, bilk, defraud, diddle, swindle, deceive, gyp, sponge. Beguile, betray.
C	R	A	C	K	Crevice, gap, rift, joke, gag, blow, bash, fling, whirl. proficient, adept.
C	R	A	F	T	Vessel, Art, skill, expertise, Cunning, slyness. Make, create.
C	R	A	I	G	Crag, neck.
C	R	A	K	E	Corncrake.
C	R	A	M	P	Compress, restrain, confine, clamp, hinder, impede. Spasm, sharp pain.
C	R	A	N	E	Hoisting machine. Lift. Stretch. Wading bird.
C	R	A	N	K	Crackpot, screwball, grouch, crosspatch. Rotate handle, turn over engine.
C	R	A	P	E	Crepe, transparent gauze, curl.
C	R	A	P	S	Dice game.
C	R	A	P	Y	Resembling crape, draped.
C	R	A	S	H	Impact, bump, collision, concussion, fail, fold, crack-up, collapse, wreck.
C	R	A	S	S	Coarse, raw, uncouth, rude, vulgar, rough, senseless, stupid, dense, gross.
C	R	A	T	E	Box, Packing Case, hamper. Jalopy, heap. Pack, stow, encase.
C	R	A	V	E	Desire, covet, want, plead, supplicate, demand.
C	R	A	W	L	Creep, slide, sneak, grovel, worm. Teem, abound, swarm.
C	R	A	Z	E	Fad, fashion, rage, style, vogue. Madden, unhinge, derange. Produce small cracks.
C	R	A	Z	Y	Mad, idiotic, crazed, lunatic, foolish, senseless, preposterous, potty, silly.
C	R	E	A	K	Squeak, rasping noise, grating noise, groan, grate, rasp.
C	R	E	A	M	Ointment, balm, salve. Whip, beat, drub. Fatty substance, foam. Prime, choice, prize.

1	2	3	4	5	
C	R	E	D	O	Creed, doctrinal formula.
C	R	E	E	D	Belief, confidence, liturgy, tenet, dogma, ideology, religion, cult, faith.
C	R	E	E	K	Bay, cove, inlet, arm, bayou, gulf, firth, harbour, branch, brook, stream.
C	R	E	E	L	Fish-basket, fish trap.
C	R	E	E	P	Glide, crawl, slide, sneak, steal, tiptoe, slink.
C	R	E	M	E	Sweet liquor, cream, elite.
C	R	E	N	A	Notch, cleft, indentation.
C	R	E	P	E	Crape, fabric, transparent gauze, rubber substance. Pancake.
C	R	E	P	T	Crawled, glided, slid, stole, slunk, inched, edged, sneaked.
C	R	E	S	S	Vegetation, green fodder, garden cress, watercress, salad.
C	R	E	S	T	Apex, peak, top, summit, ridge, climax, culmination, surmount, cap, crown.
C	R	I	C	K	Cramp, spasm, sharp pain, convulsion.
C	R	I	E	D	Past of CRY.
C	R	I	E	R	Proclaimer, howler, bawler, weeper.
C	R	I	E	S	Plural of CRY. Shouts, yells, howls, shrieks.
C	R	I	M	E	Offence, misdeed, wrongdoing, felony, transgression, violation, sin.
C	R	I	M	P	Crumple, crinkle, ruck, scrunch, restrain, hamper. Artificially wave, curl.
C	R	I	S	P	Brittle, incisive, biting, cutting, crumbly, crunchy. Chilly, snappy.
C	R	O	A	K	Grunt, grouch, murmur, mutter, hoarse cry.
C	R	O	A	T	Croatian.
C	R	O	C	K	Jar, pitcher, earthenware. Smut, soot, smudge. Disabled, impaired.
C	R	O	F	T	Small farm, enclosed field, crypt, vault, cavern.
C	R	O	M	E	Crook, hook.
C	R	O	N	E	Withered old woman, hag, witch, womanish old man.
C	R	O	N	Y	Friend, mate, associate, buddy, companion.
C	R	O	O	K	Bend, curve, bow, Cheat, swindle, fraud. Villain, criminal, felon. Poorly, Ill.
C	R	O	O	L	Murmur.
C	R	O	O	N	Sing softly, lull, lament, wait, low moan.
C	R	O	S	S	Upright with transverse beam, emblem of Christianity, monument, Intersecting lines. Vexed, annoyed.
C	R	O	U	P	Hoarse cough, infant laryngitis, difficult breathing, Buttocks, rump.
C	R	O	W	D	Mob, throng, assembly, gathering, multitude, Press, crush, cram.
C	R	O	W	N	Garland, wreath. Apex, top, crest, climax. Endow.
C	R	O	Z	E	Groove, cavity, cooper's tool.
C	R	U	C	K	In crude building, a curved timber supporting a roof.
C	R	U	D	E	Unrefined, raw, coarse, crass, rude, immature, obscene, unskilled, unpolished.
C	R	U	E	L	Fierce, ferocious, inhuman, savage, monstrous, heartless, brutish, relentless.
C	R	U	E	T	Condiment containers, wine or vinegar vessels, altar vessels.
C	R	U	M	B	Particle, iota, scrap, smidgen, jot, breadcrumb.
C	R	U	M	P	Crisp, brittle, crunchy, thump, loud report, bang.
C	R	U	S	E	Jar, pot, vessel.
C	R	U	S	H	Press, express, bruise, squash, smash, pulverize, extinguish, quash, suppress. Crowd, drove, horde.
C	R	U	S	T	Cake, encrust, rime, coating. Effrontery, gall, nerve, presumption.
C	R	Y	P	T	Vault, catacomb, underground chamber, compartment, cavern, grotto, cell.
C	U	B	A	N	Of Cuba.
C	U	B	E	D	Diced, cut into cubes.
C	U	B	I	C	Cubical, isometric, three-dimensional.
C	U	B	I	T	Measurement of length about 17 inches.
C	U	D	D	Y	Closet, pantry, galley, small cabin.
C	U	L	E	T	Facet of diamond.
C	U	L	E	X	Tropical Mosquito.
C	U	L	L	Y	Silly, dupe, trick, deceive. Associate, buddy, companion, comrade, crony.
C	U	P	E	L	Assaying vessel. Hearth.
C	U	P	I	D	Cherub. Roman God of Love.
C	U	R	D	Y	Resembling curds, coagulated.
C	U	R	E	D	Healed, restored, remedied, preserved, subjected to preserving process. Salted.
C	U	R	E	R	Someone who effects curing.
C	U	R	I	A	Assemble. Court. Subdivision of Roman tribes.
C	U	R	I	E	Unit of Radioactivity.
C	U	R	I	O	Knicknack, bauble, gewgaw, trinket, objet d'art, trifle, toy, bric-a-brac.
C	U	R	L	Y	Wavy, winding, entwined, spirally, twisted, ringed, rolled, kinked.
C	U	R	R	Y	Hot spice. Ingratiate oneself.
C	U	R	S	E	Denounce, anathema, malediction, execrate, damn, doom. Expletive, oath, swear.
C	U	R	V	E	Bend, turn, screw, swerve, wind, deflect, divert, spiral, twist, veer, coil.
C	U	R	V	Y	Curvaceous, curved, sinuous, rounded, well-developed.
C	U	S	E	C	Volumetric unit of flow.
C	U	S	H	Y	Easy, relaxed, soft, cozy, comfortable, pleasant.
C	U	T	E	R	More cute, sharper, cunning.

1	2	3	4	5	
C	U	T	I	S	Dermis, true skin.
C	U	T	T	Y	Short, stubby, shortened, frivolous.
C	U	V	E	E	Blend of Wine.
C	Y	C	A	D	Cycadaceae, ancient tropical plant.
C	Y	C	L	E	Period, age, era, succession, circle, Bicycle, bike. Cycle.
C	Y	D	E	R	Cider. Apple Juice.
C	Y	N	I	C	Misanthrope, pessimist, misogynist. Morose, ironical.
C	Z	E	C	H	Czechoslovakian.

D

1	2	3	4	5	
D	A	C	H	A	Russian villa, country house, summer house.
D	A	D	D	Y	Father.
D	A	I	L	Y	Each day, quotidian, diurnal, by day.
D	A	I	R	Y	Creamery, milk vendor, Establishment where milk, butter, cheese is produced. Farm.
D	A	I	S	Y	Flower, perennial herb. Michaelmas Daisy, Shasta Daisy. Tall drink. Dilly, corker.
D	A	K	E	R	Dicker.
D	A	L	A	I	Lama. Tibetan High Priest.
D	A	L	E	R	Monetary Unit.
D	A	L	L	E	A slab or tile, especially decorative. A rapid where a river runs in a gorge between steep rocks.
D	A	L	L	Y	Linger, dawdle, trifle, tarry, procrastinate.
D	A	M	P	Y	Dampish, moist, humid.
D	A	N	C	E	Jig, prance, caper, pirouette, hop, flit, flutter, flicker, quiver, hover.
D	A	N	D	Y	Fop, popinjay, swell, coxcomb. Cool, excellent, prime, five-star. Marvellous.
D	A	R	B	Y	Plasterer's float, trowel used for this purpose.
D	A	R	C	Y	Permeability, velocity of flow.
D	A	R	E	D	Ventured, braved, bearded, challenged, outfaced, defied, risked.
D	A	R	K	Y	Dusky, coloured, negro, swart, swarthy, mulatto.
D	A	S	H	Y	Ostentatious, gaudy, showy, trendy, fashionable.
D	A	T	E	D	Antiquated, archaic, outdated, passed, old. Engaged, escorted, accompanied.
D	A	T	U	M	Fact, principle, experience, inference, construction.
D	A	U	B	Y	Adhesive, sticky, viscous, glutinous.
D	A	U	L	T	A foster-child.
D	A	U	N	T	Appal, scare, intimidate, dismay.
D	A	V	I	T	Hoist, boat hoist, ship's crane.
D	A	Z	E	D	Dazzled, bewildered, distracted, fuddled, bemused, hazy, muddled.
D	E	A	L	T	Traded, trafficked, handled, dispensed, presented, participated, handed out.
D	E	A	R	Y	Diminutive of Dear, little dear, term of affection.
D	E	A	T	H	Demise, end of life, defunction, passing away, extinction, fatality, cessation.
D	E	B	A	G	Forcibly remove trousers, humiliate, tease.
D	E	B	A	R	Bar, ban, deny, prevent, stop, exclude, eliminate, rule out, suspend, forbid.
D	E	B	E	L	Subdue, conquer.
D	E	B	I	T	Liability, debt, arrears, enter, owe, demurrage, outstanding, due.
D	E	B	U	G	Detect errors, detect insects.
D	E	B	U	S	Alight from a bus.
D	E	B	U	T	Initial appearance, first sight, formal entrance into society, introduce, introduction.
D	E	C	A	Y	Rot, crumble, decompose, disintegrate, putrefy, spoil, taint, go to seed.
D	E	C	O	R	Scheme of decoration, set, furnishing.
D	E	C	O	Y	Lure, inveigle, ensnare, seduce, entice, trickery, bait, deception, trap.
D	E	C	R	Y	Disparage, underrate, belittle, abuse.
D	E	E	D	Y	Active, ernest, industrious.
D	E	F	E	R	Adjourn, postpone, delay, hold over, suspend, waive.
D	E	I	F	Y	Apothesize, idolize.
D	E	I	G	N	Condescend, stoop.
D	E	I	S	M	Belief in one God.
D	E	I	S	T	Adherent of Deism.
D	E	I	T	Y	Divinity, god, idol. Godhead, Supreme Being.
D	E	K	K	O	Gaze, look, scrutinise, scout, probe.
D	E	L	A	Y	Detain, hinder, impede, defer, postpone, suspend, decelerate, slacken, dawdle.
D	E	L	F	T	Glazed pottery.
D	E	L	P	H	Delft, glazed pottery.
D	E	L	T	A	Greek alphabet symbol. Anything resembling this symbol. Alluvial deposit. Tributary.
D	E	L	V	E	Investigate, snoop, dig, excavate, explore, probe, prospect.
D	E	M	I	T	Resign, withdraw.
D	E	M	O	B	Demobilize.
D	E	M	O	N	Imp, devil, goblin, troll, fiend.

1	2	3	4	5	
D	E	M	O	S	Demonstrators, rioters, proletariat, rabble. Demonstration.
D	E	M	U	R	Object, hesitate, vacillate, resist, protest, balk, qualm.
D	E	N	I	M	Twilled cotton fabric.
D	E	N	S	E	Compact, thick, packed, crammed. Stupid, dull, phlegmatic. Stolid.
D	E	P	O	T	Deposition, store house, store room, warehouse, workshop, Yard. Department.
D	E	P	T	H	Measurement from surface, deepness, drop, draft, wisdom, intellect, keenness.
D	E	R	A	Y	Disturbance, confusion, disarray.
D	E	R	B	Y	Hat, Race, Cheese, County town in England.
D	E	R	M	A	Skin, Dermis, Tissue.
D	E	T	E	R	Prevent, dissuade, restrain, discourage, divert, hinder, inhibit, forestall.
D	E	U	C	E	Playing Card, twospot, tie in tennis, mild oath, Devil! Dickens! Hell!
D	E	V	I	L	Imp, demon, fiend, satan. Lucifer. Scamp, rogue, villain. Seasoned broiled dish.
D	E	W	E	D	Moistened, misted, glistening, bedewed.
D	H	O	B	I	Indian washerman. Laundryman.
D	H	O	T	I	Loin cloth.
D	I	A	R	Y	Chronicle, journal, record, daily observation.
D	I	A	Z	O	Relating to diazotype, containing diazonium, compound used commercially.
D	I	C	E	D	Cubed, cut into pieces. Played dangerously, lived dangerously, gambled.
D	I	C	E	R	Player, thrower.
D	I	C	T	A	Plural of DICTUM.
D	I	D	O	T	Typographical point system.
D	I	G	H	T	Dictate, compose.
D	I	G	I	T	Number, cipher, figure, numeral, whole number, bony phalange, finger.
D	I	G	U	E	Seawall, Dike.
D	I	K	E	D	Banked, ditched.
D	I	L	L	Y	Silly, stupid. Remarkable. Dally, delay, lag. loiter, dither.
D	I	M	L	Y	Vaguely, darkly, obscurely, hazily, tarnished, clouded, blurred, blearily.
D	I	N	A	R	Monetary unit.
D	I	N	E	D	Past of DINE.
D	I	N	E	R	Partaker of Dinner, Dining car, Eating House.
D	I	N	G	O	Australian dog. Wolf-like dog.
D	I	N	G	Y	Squalid, dull, sullied, dirty, dark, soiled, murky.
D	I	N	K	Y	Smart, cute, pretty, neat, tiny, small.
D	I	P	P	Y	Dilly, silly, slightly mad.
D	I	P	U	S	Jerboas, three-toed.
D	I	R	G	E	Lament, elegy, requiem, chant.
D	I	R	T	Y	Begrimed, soiled, filthy, grubby, sordid, polluted, obscene, coarse, Soil, stain.
D	I	S	C	O	Discotheque, recorded music, dancehall, night club.
D	I	S	M	E	Ten cents. Dime.
D	I	T	A	L	Guitar tuning key.
D	I	T	C	H	Moat, trench, gutter, drain. Discard, scrap, jettison, reject.
D	I	T	T	O	Reproduction, duplicate, repeat, replica, facsimile, copy.
D	I	T	T	Y	Song, descant, lay, verse, aria, jingle.
D	I	V	A	N	Couch, sofa, day bed, settee, davenport. Smoking Room, Council. Luxurious coach.
D	I	V	E	D	Plunged, leapt, jumped, dropped, sprang.
D	I	V	E	R	Bird. Fancy diver, underwater swimmer. (Sl.) Pickpocket.
D	I	V	E	S	Plural of DIVE.
D	I	V	O	T	Piece of turf, sod.
D	I	V	V	Y	Divide, share, equalise.
D	I	X	I	E	Mess tin, pot. American Southern States.
D	I	Z	E	N	Dress gaudily.
D	I	Z	Z	Y	Giddy, silly, foolish, confused.
D	O	A	L	L	Factotum.
D	O	B	B	Y	Dotard, sprite, brownie.
D	O	D	G	E	Evade, avoid, parry, fence, shirk, sidestep, elude, skirt, duck, short-circuit.
D	O	D	G	Y	Tricky, artful, elusive, evasive, shy, hesitant.
D	O	G	G	O	Concealed, out of sight, without movement, hidden.
D	O	G	G	Y	Dog-like, specialising in dogs, straight wool, dashing, stylish. Small dog.
D	O	G	M	A	Doctrine, maxim, tenet, canon.
D	O	I	L	Y	Placemat, decorative piece of linen, lace, cloth, napkin.
D	O	I	N	G	Action, performance, plan, accomplishment, act.
D	O	L	C	E	Sweet, soft, smooth.
D	O	L	E	D	Ladled, handed out, bestowed sparingly, administered, apportioned, shared out.
D	O	L	L	Y	Contrivance, narrow gauge construction locomotive, small cart, wheeled platform. Offering. Doll.
D	O	L	O	R	Dolour, pain, sorrow, grief, distress, misery, suffering.
D	O	M	A	L	Dome-shaped.
D	O	M	E	D	Vaulted, arched, rounded, roofed with a dome.

1	2	3	4	5	
D	O	N	A	H	(Sl.) Woman, girlfriend.
D	O	N	G	A	Ravine, gully, rut.
D	O	N	N	A	Title of respect for a woman.
D	O	N	O	R	Bestower, conferer, giver, presenter.
D	O	P	E	D	Drugged, stoned, zonked, high, hopped-up, spaced out, turned on.
D	O	P	E	R	One who takes dope.
D	O	P	E	Y	Fuddled, bemused, dull, slow-witted.
D	O	R	I	C	Dorian-like, uncouth, unrefined, bold. Simple architecture.
D	O	S	E	D	Gave medicine, treated, physicked.
D	O	T	A	L	Referring to dowry. Pertaining to marriage portion.
D	O	T	E	D	Idolized, worshipped, loved, liked, fancied, enjoyed. Doting.
D	O	T	T	Y	Potty, silly, dilly, barmy, slightly mad.
D	O	U	B	T	Question, dispute, distrust, suspect, uncertainty, suspicion.
D	O	U	C	E	Modest, neat, tidy.
D	O	U	G	H	Flour mix for bread making. (Sl.) Money, bread, cash, currency.
D	O	U	S	E	Dowse, extinguish, drench, put out. Divine. Find, locate.
D	O	V	E	R	(Sl.) Doze, lose consciousness. Nap, catnap, forty winks, snooze.
D	O	W	D	Y	Slovenly, drab, frowsy, tacky, frumpy, outmoded, stodgy, unstylish, slatternly.
D	O	W	E	L	Wooden pin. Peg, Fastener.
D	O	W	E	R	Portion of Estate allocated to widow. Endowment, Talent. Bequest.
D	O	W	L	E	Filament, fluff, down fibre.
D	O	W	N	Y	Soft, feathery. Sly, crafty, cunning, tricky.
D	O	W	R	Y	Dot, marriage portion, endowment.
D	O	W	S	E	DOUSE.
D	O	Y	E	N	Senior member, old hand, leader, authority, virtuoso, expert.
D	O	Z	E	D	Slumbered, snoozed, drowsed, napped. dropped off. slept.
D	O	Z	E	N	Twelve.
D	O	Z	E	R	Snoozer, napper. Bulldozer, Hopperdozer.
D	R	A	C	O	Standard, Flag.
D	R	A	F	F	Remains, residue, dregs.
D	R	A	F	T	Outline, sketch, formulate, frame. Call up, conscription. Induct, Drink, swig.
D	R	A	I	L	Hook, troll.
D	R	A	I	N	Siphon, tap, draw off, milk, deplete, decrease, drink, draft, Gutter, Pipe.
D	R	A	K	E	Male Duck.
D	R	A	M	A	Dramatic art, literature, heavy theatre, histrionic, theatrical, diatribe. Play.
D	R	A	N	K	Past of DRINK.
D	R	A	N	T	Drawl, drone.
D	R	A	P	E	Swathe, envelop, wrap, swaddle, hang, sprawl, spreadeagle. Curtain, Hanging.
D	R	A	W	L	Drone, buzz, speak slowly.
D	R	A	W	N	Sketched, pencilled. Haggard, careworn, worn out. Taken. Attracted. Extracted. Hauled. Disemboweled.
D	R	E	A	D	Fear, dismay, trepidation, consternation, fright, horror, terror.
D	R	E	A	M	Fantasy, nightmare, vision, daydream, fancy, long, lust, pine, aspire.
D	R	E	A	R	Gloomy, bleak, depressing, dismal, joyless, sombre.
D	R	E	C	K	Refuse. Garbage, litter, rubbish, swill, junk.
D	R	E	G	S	Sediment, grounds, deposit, residue.
D	R	E	S	S	Garment, attire, clothes, don clothing, clad, preen, doll up, primp. Guise.
D	R	I	E	D	Desiccated, parched, bleached. Past of DRY. Arid.
D	R	I	E	R	Comparitive of DRY. Extracter of Moisture.
D	R	I	F	T	Flow, spate, current, tide, stream. Tenor, trend, tendency. Leaning. Meaning. Saunter, amble, roam.
D	R	I	L	L	Exercise, rehearse, practice. Perforate, prick, puncture. Drilling device.
D	R	I	L	Y	Dryly.
D	R	I	N	K	Imbibe, swallow, quaff, toast, pledge, liquor, booze. Brew. Liquid (Sl.) Sea. River, water.
D	R	I	P	S	Plural of DRIP.
D	R	I	V	E	Actuate, impel, mobilize, propel. Thrust, ram. Pathway. Avenue. Joyride. Vigor, enthusiasm.
D	R	O	I	T	Unit of weight.
D	R	O	L	L	Laughable, comical, funny, farcical, humorist, comedian, jester, wag.
D	R	O	M	E	Aerodrome, icedrome. Airport. Large prepared space. Racecourse.
D	R	O	N	E	Hum, bumble, buzz, thrum, idle, dawdle, loll, lounge, loaf. Bee. Idler, parasite, Drowse, Bagpipe.
D	R	O	O	L	Secrete saliva, water. dribble, salivate, slobber, slaver. Enthuse, Rave.
D	R	O	O	P	Sag, slouch, slump, flag, wilt, sink. fall, loll, languish, weaken.
D	R	O	P	S	Plural of DROP. Small doses of medicine.
D	R	O	S	S	Dregs, scum, residue, leavings, waste, impurity. Base, commonplace, unworthy.
D	R	O	U	K	Wet, soak.
D	R	O	V	E	Past of DRIVE. Crowd, multitude, horde, flock, herd, school, pack.
D	R	O	W	N	Submerge, swamp, engulf, douse, soak, overhwelm, overcome.
D	R	U	I	D	Prophet, bard.
D	R	U	N	K	Drunken, intoxicated, inebriated, tight, tipsy. Under the influence of alcohol. Past of drink.

1	2	3	4	5	
D	R	U	P	E	Seeded fruit. Peach, Apricot.
D	R	U	S	E	Mineral surface. Globose cluster of crystals.
D	R	U	X	Y	Partly decayed wood.
D	R	Y	A	D	Wood nymph.
D	R	Y	L	Y	Without moisture. Drily. Sarcastically, coldly, indifferently. Dull.
D	U	C	A	L	Belonging to a Duke. Befitting a Duke. Royal.
D	U	C	A	T	Unit of Value. Gold. Silver.
D	U	C	H	Y	Dukedom.
D	U	C	K	Y	Just lovely, darling, sweet.
D	U	L	C	E	Candy. Spanish Wine.
D	U	L	I	A	Veneration.
D	U	L	L	Y	Stupidly, languidly, inertly, colourlessly, drably, prosaiclly, cloudy, hazily.
D	U	L	S	E	Seaweed, Condiment.
D	U	M	B	A	Fat-tailed sheep.
D	U	M	M	Y	Mute, dunce, dullard, idiot, moron, stupid. Artifical, false, substitute. Child's Comforter.
D	U	M	P	S	Plural of DUMP. Low spirits. Dejection.
D	U	M	P	Y	Short, squat, stocky, thick.
D	U	N	C	E	Dullard, ass, stupid, booby, idiot. Ignoramus, simpleton, blockhead.
D	U	N	C	H	Jolt, Bump, nudge.
D	U	N	N	Y	Dull.
D	U	O	M	O	Cathedral.
D	U	P	E	D	Deluded, hoaxed, hoodwinked, betrayed, deluded, baffled, double-crossed.
D	U	P	E	R	Trickster, cheat, deceiver, sharp, dodger, double-crosser.
D	U	P	L	A	Prize for correctly forecasting first and second.
D	U	P	L	E	Twofold, bifold, double, dual, duplex.
D	U	R	R	A	Corn, sorghum, millet.
D	U	R	U	M	Wheat for Pasta, semolina, macaroni, spaghetti.
D	U	S	K	Y	Swarthy, dark, dim, shady, obscure, murky.
D	U	S	T	Y	Powdery, sprinkled, mucky, drab, uninviting. Arid, dry, dull, uninteresting.
D	U	T	C	H	Trouble, hot water. Equal shares. Of Holland. Dutch courage. Dutchman. Wife.
D	U	V	E	T	Down feathers, Eiderdown.
D	W	A	L	E	Belladonna.
D	W	A	R	F	Small person, midget, pygmy, Tom Thumb, imp. Stunted, suppress, overshadow. Jack.
D	W	E	L	L	Live, reside, abide, exist, inhabit, hang out, occupy.
D	W	E	L	T	Past of DWELL. Resided, inhabited.
D	Y	I	N	G	Expiring, unable to support life, fatally ill, relating to death. No hope of recovery. Present of dye.

E

E	A	G	E	R	Ardent, avid, zealous, keen anxious, enthusiastic, ambitious, restive.
E	A	G	L	E	Diurnal Bird of Prey. Lectern. Standard. Insignia. Golf Score. Coin.
E	A	R	E	D	Lugged, noticed, heeded.
E	A	R	L	Y	Timely, soon, timeously, betimes, beforehand, original, premature, previous.
E	A	R	T	H	Entire area, planet, world, globe, sphere, cosmos, creation. Ground, soil.
E	A	S	E	D	Soothed, assuaged, allayed, dulled, ameliorated, loosened, relaxed, slackened.
E	A	S	E	L	Frame, support, artist's equipment.
E	A	T	E	N	Past of EAT.
E	A	T	E	R	One who eats.
E	A	V	E	S	Overhang. Border of Roof.
E	B	B	E	D	Abated, moderated, receded, retreated, waned, declined subsided.
E	B	O	N	Y	Black wood. Black, inky, jet, pitch black.
E	C	L	A	T	Fame, notoriety, renown, repute, brilliance, lustre, distinction, splendour.
E	C	T	A	L	Outer, external.
E	D	G	E	D	Bordered, fringed, hemmed, skirted, sidled.
E	D	I	C	T	Decree, directive, order, manifesto, proclamation, law, regulation.
E	D	I	F	Y	Illuminate, enlighten, uplift, improve, enhance, better, instruct.
E	D	U	C	E	Elicit, evince, extract, wrest, wring, derive, evolve, evoke.
E	E	R	I	E	Gloomy, weird, spooky, uncanny, bizarre, unearthly.
E	G	E	S	T	Cast out. Reject. (food).
E	G	G	A	R	Moth. Egger.
E	G	G	E	D	Urged, incited, encouraged, exhorted, goaded, prompted, rallied, prodded.
E	G	R	E	T	Heron like bird.
E	I	D	E	R	Large sea duck.
E	I	G	H	T	One more than seven.
E	I	G	N	E	Eldest, first born.
E	J	E	C	T	Force out, dismiss, evict, extrude, rout, fire, reject, disgorge, spew.
E	K	I	N	G	Stretching, prolonging.

1	2	3	4	5	
E	L	A	N	D	African antelope.
E	L	A	P	S	Genus of venomous snake.
E	L	A	T	E	Exult, animate, excite, uplift, inspire, stimulate, cheer, buoy, encourage.
E	L	B	O	W	Arm joint, curve, bend. Shove, push, hustle, jostle, shoulder.
E	L	D	E	R	Older, Senior, ancient, old-timer, senior citizen, superior.
E	L	E	C	T	Choose, select, opt, designate, appoint, nominate.
E	L	E	G	Y	Song of mourning, lamentation, sorrowful composition, reflective poem. Dirge.
E	L	E	M	I	Fragrant oleoresin.
E	L	F	I	N	Pixyish, elf like, small, puckish, fairylike.
E	L	I	D	E	Ignore, omit, reduce.
E	L	I	T	E	Select, choice, cream, prime, prize, elect. Cream of society, upper class.
E	L	O	G	E	Funeral oration.
E	L	O	G	Y	Inscription on tombstone, biographic sketch.
E	L	O	P	E	Abscond, decamp, run away, marry secretly.
E	L	U	D	E	Evade, escape, avoid, circumvent, eschew, bilk, shun, baffle.
E	L	U	T	E	Extract, purify by washing.
E	L	V	E	R	Young eel.
E	M	B	A	R	Hinder, check.
E	M	B	A	Y	Encircle, surround.
E	M	B	E	D	Set firmly, prepare for sectioning, implant, entrench, fix, ingrain, lodge, root.
E	M	B	E	R	Glowing fragment, lighted coal, coke, smouldering fire, hot ash.
E	M	B	O	G	Bog down, delay.
E	M	B	O	W	Form an arch, vault.
E	M	B	O	X	Box, enclose, pack, encase.
E	M	B	U	S	Board a bus.
E	M	C	E	E	Master of Ceremonies.
E	M	E	E	R	Ameer, Emir.
E	M	E	N	D	Amend.
E	M	E	R	Y	Natural abrasive, corundum.
E	M	M	E	R	Bucket, pail. Tetrapoid wheat.
E	M	M	E	T	Ant.
E	M	O	T	E	Register Emotion, express feelings, dramatise.
E	M	P	T	Y	Void, vacant, vacuous, meaningless, inane, discharge, drain, throw out.
E	N	A	C	T	Authorize, proclaim, institute, effect, execute, legislate, ratify, perform, play.
E	N	A	T	E	Growing out, related.
E	N	D	E	D	Finished, completed, concluded, terminated, ceased, closed, wound up.
E	N	D	O	N	Abutting, touching.
E	N	D	O	W	Bequeath, bestow, confer, award, enrich, furnish, finance, subsidize.
E	N	D	U	E	Invest, provide, supply, don clothing.
E	N	E	M	A	Injection of liquid through the anus. Rectal spray.
E	N	E	M	Y	Foe, antagonist, opponent, adversary, rival, attacker, assailant.
E	N	J	O	Y	Take pleasure, receive satisfaction, relish, like, delight, love, fancy, savour.
E	N	N	U	I	Tedium, boredom, weariness.
E	N	S	U	E	Result, follow, succeed, supervene, proceed, derive, emanate, stem from.
E	N	T	A	L	Inner.
E	N	T	E	R	Come in, go in, ingress, penetrate, probe, insert, interpolate, record, register. Begin, commence.
E	N	T	R	Y	Entrance, ingression, doorway, portal, access, opening, threshold, admission.
E	N	V	O	I	Parting word, concluding remarks.
E	N	V	O	Y	Messenger, agent, representative.
E	O	S	I	N	Pigment, red dye.
E	P	A	C	T	Lunar time difference.
E	P	H	O	D	Vestment, surplice.
E	P	O	C	H	Era, cycle, period, age, day, time, interval, term.
E	P	O	D	E	Ode, verse form.
E	P	O	X	Y	Oxygen fixed to two different atoms. Resin manufactured used as structural plastics.
E	P	S	O	M	Salts, Downs.
E	P	U	R	E	Full scale plan. Map, Drawing, Cartoon.
E	Q	U	A	L	Counterpart, equivalent, peer, parallel, matching, even, like, match.
E	Q	U	E	S	Roman Knight, Order.
E	Q	U	I	P	Furnish, accouter, arm, fit out, outfit, rig, provide, prepare, qualify.
E	Q	U	U	S	Genus comprising Horse and related animals.
E	R	A	S	E	Delete, eliminate, neutralize, annul, blot out, obliterate, expunge, remove.
E	R	E	C	T	Straight, raised, upright, upstanding, erectile. Construct, make, produce, build.
E	R	G	O	T	Parasitical fungi.
E	R	I	C	A	Evergreen shrub, heath.
E	R	O	D	E	Eat away, corrode, scour, wear away, crumble, abrade.
E	R	R	E	D	Strayed, deviated, wandered, lapsed, transgressed, sinned, made error.

1	2	3	4	5	
E	R	R	O	R	Deviation, inaccuracy, miscalculation, oversight, slip up, faux pas. Fallacy. Fault.
E	R	U	C	A	Caterpillar. Herb.
E	R	U	C	T	Belch, burp, eructate. expel. spew, erupt.
E	R	U	P	T	Burst forth, belch, expel, spew, eject, disgorge, hurl, discharge, spout, spurt.
E	S	K	E	R	Esker. Glacial gravel ridge.
E	S	S	A	Y	Assay, try, attempt, strive. Article, composition, thesis, theme. Venture, go.
E	S	T	E	R	Acid yielding compound.
E	S	T	O	C	Thrusting sword.
E	S	T	O	P	Prohibit, preclude, bar.
E	T	H	E	R	Clear sky, air, heaven, atmosphere. (C2 H5 OC2 H5) Anaesthetic gas. Volatile liquid.
E	T	H	I	C	Moral obligation, principle, morality, values, morals, code of conduct.
E	T	H	O	S	Belief, ideal, standard, value, character, ethic, disposition, personality.
E	T	H	Y	L	Hydrocarbon radical.
E	T	W	E	E	Ornamental case, glasses case, needle case, etui.
E	V	A	D	E	Escape, eschew, avoid, dodge, bypass, circumvent, elude, foil, outwit.
E	V	E	N	S	Half and half, fifty fifty, quits, Odds of one to one.
E	V	E	N	T	Happening, incident, occurrence, episode, circumstance, competition, contest.
E	V	E	R	T	Upset, overthrow, confuse, rebut, refute.
E	V	E	R	Y	All, each, sundry, commonplace, usual.
E	V	I	C	T	Cast out, eject, dislodge, turn out, dispossess, dismiss.
E	V	O	K	E	Elicit, evince, extort, educe, stimulate, arouse, rouse, stir, call forth.
E	X	A	C	T	Correct, accurate, precise, right, identical, careful, extract, call forth, extort.
E	X	A	L	T	Enhance, aggrandize, boost, elevate, promote, praise, laud, acclaim, magnify.
E	X	C	E	L	Surpass, transcend, outdo, outshine, outstrip, beat, best, exceed.
E	X	E	A	T	Pass, letter of authority, temporary permit.
E	X	E	R	T	Bear down, bring pressure, use energy, exercise, ply, wield, use, make effort.
E	X	I	L	E	Outcast, expatriate, expellee, banish, deport, displace, expel.
E	X	I	S	T	Be, live, subsist, breathe, reside, dwell, endure, persist.
E	X	I	T	S	Plural of EXIT.
E	X	L	E	X	Without legal authority.
E	X	O	D	E	Farce, travesty.
E	X	P	E	L	Eject, cast out, banish, deport, exile, erupt, eruct, belch, disgorge.
E	X	T	O	L	Praise, bless, eulogize, glorify, magnify, laud, exalt.
E	X	T	R	A	Additional, superfluous, surplus, supernumerary, especially, particularly.
E	X	U	D	E	Ooze, seep, emanate, percolate, transude, emit, trickle, bleed.
E	X	U	L	T	Rejoice, celebrate, boast, crow, gloat, triumph, jubilate, glory.
E	Y	I	N	G	Watching, glancing, appraising, contemplating, viewing, considering.
E	Y	R	I	E	Aerie. Eagle's Nest. Lofty dwelling.
E	Y	R	I	R	Unit of money.

F

1	2	3	4	5	
F	A	B	L	E	Legend, myth, parable, allegory, fiction, tale, fairy tale.
F	A	C	E	D	Confronted, braved, challenged, defied, resisted, opposed. FACE.
F	A	C	E	R	Blow to the face. Garment worker. Worker who polishes jewellery.
F	A	C	E	S	Plural of FACE.
F	A	C	E	T	Phase, angle, aspect, side, polished surface. Title.
F	A	C	I	A	Facial.
F	A	C	O	N	Belt Knife.
F	A	C	T	O	By the fact.
F	A	D	D	Y	Capricious, whimsical, particular, stylish. Faddish.
F	A	D	E	D	Dimmed, paled, tarnished, flagged, declined, weakened, languished, dulled.
F	A	D	E	R	One who fades. Device for varying reproduction or intensity of light.
F	A	D	E	S	Plural of FADE.
F	A	D	G	E	Thick loaf, bundle.
F	A	E	N	A	Final pass by matador.
F	A	E	R	Y	Enchantment. Fairy.
F	A	G	I	N	One who instructs children in crime.
F	A	G	U	S	Genus of Tree.
F	A	I	N	T	Loose consciousness, blackout, swoon. Gentle, bland, soft, mild, not bold.
F	A	I	R	Y	Faery, elf, pixie, sprite, gremlin, imp, brownie.
F	A	I	T	H	Belief, credence, trust, confidence, hope reliance, religion, creed, denomination.
F	A	K	E	D	Spurious, counterfeit, falsified, feigned, simulated, phony.
F	A	K	E	R	Cheat, impostor, fraud, phony, pretender, swindler, defrauder, humbug.
F	A	K	I	R	Muslim mendicant, wonder worker. Guru.

1	2	3	4	5	
F	A	L	S	E	Inaccurate, incorrect, untrue, wrong, fallacious, misleading, dishonest, artificial, sham.
F	A	M	E	D	Illustrious, famous, celebrated, eminent, distinguished, great, renowned.
F	A	N	A	L	Beacon, lighthouse.
F	A	N	C	Y	Elaborate, intricate. Think, conceive. Liking, inclination. Ornate, decorated.
F	A	N	G	O	Medicinal Clay.
F	A	N	O	N	Religious accouterments. Regalia.
F	A	R	A	D	Unit of electrical capacity.
F	A	R	C	E	Mockery, burlesque, sham, travesty, parody, caricature.
F	A	R	C	I	Farsi, forcemeat, stuffed (with oysters usually).
F	A	R	C	Y	Cattle disease.
F	A	R	E	D	Shifted, managed, prospered, travelled, journeyed, repaired.
F	A	R	S	E	Liturgical interpolation.
F	A	T	A	L	Lethal, deadly, mortal, pestilential, ill-fated, unlucky, pernicious, malignant. Causing death.
F	A	T	E	D	Doomed, predestined, determined, preordained.
F	A	T	L	Y	Grossly, excessively.
F	A	T	T	Y	Greasy, lardy, suety, blubbery, oily. Dumpling, roly-poly.
F	A	U	L	T	Imperfection, deficiency, sin, failing, vice, weakness, defect, blame, guilt.
F	A	U	N	A	Animal life.
F	A	V	U	S	Fungal scalp.
F	E	A	S	T	Banquet, festivity, carousel, dinner, spread, entertainment, repast.
F	E	A	Z	E	Fray.
F	E	C	I	T	Artist's name.
F	E	D	U	P	Out of patience, disgusted, disgruntled, browned off, weary, bored, dissatisfied.
F	E	E	Z	E	Alarm, excitement.
F	E	I	G	N	Act, assume, counterfeit, pretend, sham, simulate, put on, affect.
F	E	I	N	T	Trick, manoeuver, ploy, stratagem, wile, dodge, fake, counterfeit, artifice.
F	E	L	I	D	Felidae. A Cat.
F	E	L	I	S	Typical cat genus.
F	E	L	O	N	Criminal, malefactor, offender, lawbreaker, miscreant, outlaw, crook.
F	E	M	U	R	Thigh bone.
F	E	N	C	E	Barricade, barrier, blockade, wall, hedge. Dodge, parry. Receiver of stolen goods.
F	E	N	D	Y	Economical, thrifty.
F	E	N	N	Y	Boggy, marshy.
F	E	R	A	E	Subdivision of mammilia.
F	E	R	A	L	Wild, brutal. Bestial, beastly, swinish, barbaric, ferocious, fierce, savage.
F	E	R	N	Y	Fernlike, abounding in ferns.
F	E	R	R	Y	Conveyance, riverboat service, carry, convey, transport.
F	E	S	T	A	Patron saint's day. Celebration.
F	E	T	A	L	FOETAL. Relating to Foetus.
F	E	T	C	H	Bring, carry, haul, draw.
F	E	T	E	D	Honoured, entertained, extolled, lionized.
F	E	T	I	D	Rank, stiking, smelly.
F	E	T	O	R	Offensive odour, stench.
F	E	T	U	S	Foetus. Embryo, unborn.
F	E	V	E	R	Illness, infection, ailment, agitation, urgency.
F	E	W	E	R	Less in number, not many.
F	I	B	R	E	Thread, filament, nerve end, vegetable matter, inner being. Fortitude, guts, courage.
F	I	C	H	U	Triangular scarf.
F	I	C	U	S	Genus of tropical tree, shrub. Rubber plant.
F	I	E	L	D	Open area, expanse, scene, sportsground, space, common, domain, sphere. Territory.
F	I	E	N	D	Imp, devil, demon, monster, wretch, bigot, fanatic. Enthusiast.
F	I	E	R	Y	Ablaze, burning, alight, hot ardent, heated, redhot, torrid, impassioned.
F	I	F	E	D	Played a Fife.
F	I	F	E	R	Fife player.
F	I	F	T	H	Number five in countability.
F	I	F	T	Y	Half of one hundred.
F	I	G	H	T	Altercation, brawl, quarrel, row, scrap, scuffle, attack, combat, contest.
F	I	L	A	R	Relating to lines or threads.
F	I	L	C	H	Steal, lift, pilfer, pinch, purloin, swipe, snitch.
F	I	L	E	D	Smoothed, burnished, listed, registered, place records in order.
F	I	L	E	R	File clerk. File worker.
F	I	L	L	Y	Young female horse. Girl.
F	I	L	M	Y	Hazy, misty, transparent, light, fluffy, gauzy, flimsy, sheer.
F	I	L	T	H	Dirt, impurity, muck. Slut, scoundrel. Unwanted vegetation.
F	I	N	A	L	Last, terminal, ultimate, concluding decisive. Irrefutable, eventual, hindmost.
F	I	N	C	H	Small bird. Weaver bird.
F	I	N	E	D	Penalized, amerced, mulcted. Punished. Extracted reparation.

1	2	3	4	5	
F	I	N	E	R	Better, keener, pleasanter, smaller, prettier, fairer, nicer, comparative of FINE.
F	I	N	I	S	Conclusion, end, close, termination, cessation, finale, climax.
F	I	O	R	D	Fjord. Narrow inlet of sea between cliffs.
F	I	R	E	D	Sacked, discharged, dismissed, roused, kindled, inspired, inflamed, ignited.
F	I	R	E	R	Lighter. One who works with enamel jewellery.
F	I	R	R	Y	Pine-clad.
F	I	R	S	T	Foremost, inaugural, initial, leading, earliest, maiden, chief, significant.
F	I	R	T	H	River mouth, arm of sea, inlet, frith.
F	I	S	H	Y	Questionable, suspicious, questionable, doubtful, dubious, suspect, ambiguous.
F	I	T	C	H	Polecat, small brush, vetch.
F	I	T	L	Y	Befitting, correctly, well, nicely, properly, rightly, justly.
F	I	V	E	R	Five-spot, five pound note, five of anything.
F	I	V	E	S	Handball game.
F	I	X	E	D	Secured, stipulated, settled. Fast, firm, immovable, definite, steady.
F	L	A	C	K	Blow, strike, flap. Tongue-lashing, telling-off.
F	L	A	F	F	Flutter.
F	L	A	I	L	Threshing implement. Strike, beat. Swing, progress erratically.
F	L	A	I	R	Faculty, talent, knack, gift, aptness, bent.
F	L	A	K	E	Scale, peel, exfoliate, desquamate. Faint. Fleck.
F	L	A	K	Y	Friable, layered. Peeling.
F	L	A	M	E	Blaze, glow, kindle, light, sweetheart, girl friend, boyfriend, beau.
F	L	A	M	Y	Blazing, glowing.
F	L	A	N	G	Miner's pick.
F	L	A	N	K	Side, border, fleshy part of quadruped.
F	L	A	R	E	Outburst, flare-up, flash, eruption, blaze, flame, torch. Device for signalling.
F	L	A	R	Y	Gaudy, bright.
F	L	A	S	H	Glint, sparkle, glisten, gleam. Instant, momentary, split second. Bolt. Expose.
F	L	A	S	K	Vessel, container.
F	L	A	W	N	Manilla grass.
F	L	A	W	Y	Defective, gusty.
F	L	A	X	Y	Flaxen.
F	L	E	A	M	Lancet, surgical knife.
F	L	E	C	K	Dapple, speckle, blemish, spot, flake, particle.
F	L	E	E	R	Mock, sneer, leer, scoff, gibe, smirk.
F	L	E	E	T	Collection of ships, Navy. Fast, hasty, rapid, speedy, nimble, swift.
F	L	E	S	H	Mankind, humanity, mortality. Man. Composition of creatures. Meat.
F	L	I	C	K	Flip, snap, click, tap. Movie, bioscope, film.
F	L	I	E	R	Aerialist, airman, aircraft. Swift mechanical device, accurate shot.
F	L	I	E	S	Plural of FLY.
F	L	I	N	G	Hurl, cast, throw, heave, launch. Shot, stab, try, attempt. Tear, booze-up.
F	L	I	N	T	Hard silica stone.
F	L	I	R	T	Flip, flick, mock, evince superficial interest, trifle, coquet, court, play.
F	L	O	A	T	Drift, hover, poise, sail, scud, skim, waft.
F	L	O	C	K	Multitude, crowd, army, scores, legion. Gather, drove, throng.
F	L	O	N	G	Layers of paper. Stereotype matrix.
F	L	O	O	D	Spate, downpour, overwhelm, deluge, inundate, swamp, submerge.
F	L	O	O	R	Lower ground surface. Pavement, building height. Fell, bowl over, knock down. Level, ground.
F	L	O	R	A	Collection of flowers. Floral. Plant-life of a region.
F	L	O	S	S	Down, fluff, fuzz, lint, pile, flue.
F	L	O	U	R	Meal, maize, grain, staple.
F	L	O	U	T	Repudiate, spurn, defy, disregard, scoff, jeer, taunt.
F	L	O	W	N	Past of FLY.
F	L	U	F	F	Nap, lint, down, floss, fuzz. Botch, muff, bungle, goof, louse up.
F	L	U	I	D	Liquid, unstable, variable, changeable, mobile, unsteady.
F	L	U	K	E	Fortunate chance, lucky shot. By chance. Barbed head of anchor.
F	L	U	K	Y	Lucky, fortuitous, contingent, by chance, capricious, accidental.
F	L	U	M	E	Water channel, gorge stream. Chute, spout.
F	L	U	M	P	Plump down.
F	L	U	N	G	Thrown, tossed, cast, hurled, pitched.
F	L	U	O	R	Mineral containing fluorine.
F	L	U	S	H	Blush, glow, colour, redden. Flat, smooth. Rich, affluent. Wash, gush. Succession. Awakening.
F	L	U	T	E	Wind instrument, musical instrument.
F	L	Y	E	R	Flier, aviator, pilot, aerialist.
F	O	A	M	Y	Soapy, frothy, spumy bubbly, sudsy, lathered.
F	O	C	A	L	Centre, focus, heart, seat, main, pin pointed.
F	O	C	U	S	Convergence, concenter, concentration, fix, rivet, fasten. Bring into focus.
F	O	G	E	Y	Fossil, fuddy-duddy, square, conservative.

1	2	3	4	5	
F	O	G	G	Y	Hazy, obscured, indistinct, unclear, murky.
F	O	I	S	T	Impose, insinuate, infiltrate, worm, trick, inflict, palm off, fob.
F	O	L	I	C	Acid.
F	O	L	I	O	Identifying number, page, reference.
F	O	L	L	Y	Foolishness, insanity, stupidity, absurdity, craziness, fatuity.
F	O	M	E	S	Fungi.
F	O	N	D	U	Ballet movement. Blended, melted.
F	O	R	A	Y	Raid, harass, maraud, invasion, incursion, sally, overrun.
F	O	R	B	Y	Adjacent.
F	O	R	C	E	Power, might, potency, strength, tension, pressure, vigor. Military might. Coercion.
F	O	R	D	O	Terminate, overcome.
F	O	R	E	L	Case, slipcase, sheath.
F	O	R	G	E	Falsify, fabricate. Fuse, mould. Blacksmith's establishment. Fashion, make. Go with vigor.
F	O	R	G	O	Renounce, forsake, abandon, quit, defect. Forfeit.
F	O	R	K	Y	Forged.
F	O	R	M	E	Shoemaker's pattern.
F	O	R	T	E	Outstanding skill, strongest point. Loudly, strongly, powerfully.
F	O	R	T	H	Onward, forward, ahead. Go forth, come forth, bring forth.
F	O	R	T	Y	Twice twenty.
F	O	R	U	M	Public meeting place. Assembly, medium of open discussion, Court.
F	O	S	S	A	Malagasy, civet cat.
F	O	S	S	E	Canal, pit cavity, trench.
F	O	U	N	D	Discovered, establish. Organize, inaugurate. Base, bottom, foundation.
F	O	U	N	T	Spring, source, fountain, font, origin, well.
F	O	X	E	D	Baffled, outwitted, outsmarted, puzzled, deluded.
F	O	Y	E	R	Lobby, entrance, hall, vestibule.
F	R	A	I	L	Weak, decrepit, flimsy, fragile, feeble, slight, puny, delicate.
F	R	A	M	E	Surround. Structure. System. Falsify. Intimidate. Contrive, concoct, draft, make. Skeletal structure.
F	R	A	N	C	Monetary unit.
F	R	A	N	K	Candid, truthful, open, forthright, direct, plain, straighforward. Frankfurter.
F	R	A	U	D	Deception, cheat, trickery, sham, swindle, sharp practice. Hoax.
F	R	E	A	K	Miscreation, mutation, abnormality. Anomaly.
F	R	E	E	D	Liberated, unfettered, loosened, emancipated, released, discharged.
F	R	E	E	R	One that frees.
F	R	E	S	H	New, Additional. Inexperienced. Bold. Recent. Youthful. Nippy, chilly. Moderately strong (wind).
F	R	I	A	R	Monk, Brother, Member of Religious order.
F	R	I	E	D	Cooked, sizzled, pan cooked; Punished, Electrocuted.
F	R	I	L	L	Ruffle, ornamental trimming, fold, border. Luxury, extravagance, brim, edge.
F	R	I	S	K	Romp, gambol, caper, cavort, frolic. Search.
F	R	I	T	H	Brushwood, hurdle, hedge.
F	R	I	T	Z	German.
F	R	O	C	K	Dress, garment, costume, smock.
F	R	O	N	D	Leaf.
F	R	O	N	S	Forehead, brow, front.
F	R	O	N	T	Face, facade. Put on, cosmetic disguise for sake of appearances.
F	R	O	T	H	Spume, suds, foam, effervescence.
F	R	O	W	N	Glower, scowl, grimace, glare, disapprove, deprecate.
F	R	O	W	Y	Rank, rancid, stale. Slatternly, blowsy, slack, fusty, stale.
F	R	O	Z	E	Became Ice. Past of FREEZE.
F	R	U	I	T	Edible product of plant growth. Reward, payment, seed.
F	R	U	M	P	Slovenly woman, dowdy dame, staid, drab, old-fashioned person.
F	R	U	S	H	Lacking strength. Decayed, mellow.
F	R	Y	E	R	Frying pan, one who prepares food by frying.
F	U	B	B	Y	Squat, chubby.
F	U	C	U	S	Facade, cosmetic. Algae.
F	U	D	G	E	Nonsense. Sweetmeat like soft toffee. Deceit, fake, cook-up.
F	U	G	A	L	Relating to musical fugue.
F	U	G	U	E	Musical composition.
F	U	L	L	Y	Entirely, amply, altogether, completely, thoroughly, wholly.
F	U	M	E	T	Spicy flavouring.
F	U	M	I	D	Smoky, vaporous.
F	U	N	D	I	Holy man, wise man. African grass.
F	U	N	D	S	Plural of FUND.
F	U	N	G	I	Mushrooms, toadstools, Plural of FUNGUS.
F	U	N	I	C	Relating to umbilical cord.
F	U	N	I	S	Umbilical cord.
F	U	N	K	Y	Afraid, cowardly, timid, nervous.

1	2	3	4	5	
F	U	N	N	Y	Comical, humorous, laughable, droll, strange, bizarre, fantastic, grotesque.
F	U	R	C	A	Forked process.
F	U	R	O	R	Furore, rage, frenzy.
F	U	R	R	Y	Encrusted. Covered in fur.
F	U	R	Z	E	Evergreen shrub.
F	U	R	Z	Y	Overgrown.
F	U	S	E	D	Cut out, merged, blended, mingled, molten.
F	U	S	I	L	Flintlock, musket.
F	U	S	S	Y	Bustling, humming, lively, fastidious, pernickety, squeamish, fidgety.
F	U	S	T	Y	Musty, rank, mouldy, malodourous, fetid, smelly, outdated, passè.
F	U	Z	Z	Y	Woolly, shaggy, blurred, hazy, indistinct, obscure, vague.

G

G	A	B	B	Y	Talkative, chatty, garrulous, loquacious, loose-lipped.
G	A	B	L	E	End wall of building, triangular shape. Roof construction.
G	A	F	F	E	Social blunder, faux pas.
G	A	G	E	R	Security for Pledge.
G	A	I	L	Y	Blithely, happily, merrily, mirthfully, radiantly, cheerfully.
G	A	L	A	S	Plural of GALA.
G	A	L	B	A	Freshwater snail.
G	A	L	E	A	Calyx, caul.
G	A	L	E	S	Plural of GALE.
G	A	L	O	P	Lively dance. Poll.
G	A	M	B	A	Musical instrument.
G	A	M	E	D	Gambled, wagered, hazarded, bet.
G	A	M	I	C	Sexual.
G	A	M	I	N	Urchin, maverick. Roguishly impudent. Monkey, imp.
G	A	M	M	A	Unit of magnetic intensity, photographic term, relating to three.
G	A	M	U	T	Range, spectrum, scope.
G	A	N	J	A	Cannabis.
G	A	N	Z	A	Wild goose.
G	A	O	L	S	Plural of GAOL.
G	A	P	E	D	Yawned, chasmed, gazed, gauped, gawked, stared.
G	A	P	P	Y	Unconnected, broken.
G	A	R	N	I	Garnish, decoration, embellishment.
G	A	R	T	H	Yard, enclosure, cloister.
G	A	S	S	Y	Gaseous, inflated, aerated, bubbly.
G	A	T	E	D	Confined, restricted, banned.
G	A	U	D	Y	Flashy, cheap, showy, brazen, garish, tawdry, vulgar, tasteless.
G	A	U	G	E	Estimate, guess, measure, scale. Standard, criterion, yardstick.
G	A	U	L	T	Clay soil.
G	A	U	M	Y	Sticky, untidy, slovenly, smeared.
G	A	U	N	T	Lean, Angular, lank, scraggy, scrawny, skinny, emaciated.
G	A	U	S	S	Magnetic flux, intensity.
G	A	U	Z	E	Transparent fabric, filmy material, Diaphanous cloth.
G	A	U	Z	Y	Filmy, transparent, flimsy, gossamer, sheer.
G	A	V	E	L	Mallet. Bundle of grain.
G	A	W	K	Y	Awkward, clumsy, ungainly.
G	A	Y	E	R	Brighter, jollier, livelier, sportier, merrier.
G	A	Z	E	D	Looked intently, stared, peered, watched, surveyed, admired, eyed.
G	A	Z	E	R	One who gazes. Narcotics Agent.
G	E	C	K	O	Tropical nocturnal lizard.
G	E	E	S	E	Plural of GOOSE.
G	E	E	S	T	Alluvial matter, loose earth.
G	E	L	I	D	Extremely cold. Icy. Chilly, freezing, frosty, glacial.
G	E	M	E	L	Paired, twin.
G	E	M	M	A	Bud.
G	E	M	M	Y	Bright, glittering.
G	E	N	E	T	Carnivorous mammal.
G	E	N	I	E	Jinn, spirit, demon.
G	E	N	I	I	Plural of GENUS. Plural of GENIE.
G	E	N	O	A	Style prevalent in Genoa, Italy. Cake.
G	E	N	R	E	Style, sort, kind, species, category, class.
G	E	N	U	S	Kind, type, marked by certain characteristic, classification.
G	E	O	D	E	Stone nodule, crystalline cavity.

1	2	3	4	5	
G	E	O	I	D	Normal earth revolutions. Patterns of earth's movement.
G	E	S	S	O	Painting preparation.
G	E	T	U	P	Outfit, costume, dress.
G	H	O	S	T	Spirit, spectre, phantom, apparition, spook. Image. Compose in the name of another.
G	H	O	U	L	Legendary evil, flesh-eating phantom. Vampire.
G	I	A	N	T	Mammoth, monster, of monstrous size, huge, colossal, gargantuan, gigantic.
G	I	B	E	D	Past of GIBE.
G	I	B	E	R	One who gibes.
G	I	B	U	S	Opera Hat.
G	I	D	D	Y	Dizzy, flighty, lightheaded, capricious, fickle, bemused, frivolous.
G	I	G	O	T	Cooked leg of Mutton. Sleeve fashion.
G	I	G	U	E	Jig. Lively dance.
G	I	R	T	H	Part of Harness. Strap, Girdle, circumference, size, dimensions. Encircle.
G	I	V	E	N	Past of GAVE.
G	I	V	E	R	One who Gives.
G	I	V	E	S	The act of giving.
G	L	A	C	E	Smooth, glossy, glazed, candied.
G	L	A	D	E	Open space, clearing, woodland, grove, marshy area, grassy patch.
G	L	A	I	K	A flash, dazzling mocking deception, a trick, a puzzle-game.
G	L	A	I	R	Viscid, slimy substance.
G	L	A	N	D	Swelling, cell group. Secreting organ.
G	L	A	N	S	Bodily extremity.
G	L	A	R	E	Scowl, glower, gaze, gaup, peer, blaze, flare, glow, dazzle, glitter.
G	L	A	R	Y	Dazzling, gleaming, flagrant, gross, gaudy, garish.
G	L	A	S	S	Drinking vessel, tumbler. Mirror, looking glass.
G	L	A	Z	E	To cover with. Cause to shine. Coating substance. Sheen, Sugar, Glow. Burnish.
G	L	A	Z	Y	Shiny, lustrous.
G	L	E	A	M	Beam, glint, glow, shine, ray, glimmer.
G	L	E	A	N	Gather, cull, extract, garner, winnow, conclude, deduce, learn.
G	L	E	B	E	Parsonage, Church property.
G	L	E	B	Y	Rich, fertile.
G	L	E	E	D	Squint, crooked, askew.
G	L	I	D	E	Slide, slip, glissade, slick, slither, creep, sneak, skulk.
G	L	I	N	T	Flash, gleam, glimmer, glisten, glitter, sparkle, lustre, polish, sheen.
G	L	O	A	T	Exult, crow, revel, act triumphantly, indicate pleasure.
G	L	O	B	E	Ball, orb, sphere, planet, world, earth.
G	L	O	B	Y	Spherical. Round.
G	L	O	O	M	Depression, sadness, melancholy, dejection, unhappiness, dumps.
G	L	O	R	Y	Jubilation, triumph, delight, exult, beauty, magnificence, honour, renown.
G	L	O	S	S	Shine, shimmer, polish, lustre, sheen. Buff, burnish. Palliate, extenuate, gloss over.
G	L	O	U	T	Sulk, scowl.
G	L	O	V	E	Hand covering. Gauntlet, mittens.
G	L	O	Z	E	Palliate, blanch, varnish, whiten, adulation, flattery.
G	L	U	E	D	Stuck together, adhered, gummed.
G	L	U	E	R	One who glues.
G	L	U	E	Y	Sticky, gummy, adhesive, cloggy, stodgy, glutinous.
G	L	U	M	E	Spiky husks.
G	L	Y	P	H	Carved figure.
G	N	A	R	L	Twist, contort. Knot in wood. Protuberance.
G	N	A	S	H	Grind teeth, bite, clash, Grind together.
G	N	O	M	E	Dwarf, wizened old man, creature of folklore. Maxim, axiom, dictum, rule.
G	N	O	M	Y	Interpreter, discerner. Ickey.
G	O	A	L	S	Plural of GOAL.
G	O	A	T	S	Plural of GOAT.
G	O	D	E	T	Patch, triangular inset, stretching device.
G	O	D	L	Y	Pious, holy, devout, religious. Divine, saintly, angelic.
G	O	I	N	G	Act of leaving. Departure, moving, wending, progressing, condition of ground. (Racecourse).
G	O	L	E	M	Robot, machine, automaton.
G	O	L	L	Y	Child's soft toy. Golliwog. Exclamation of amazement.
G	O	N	A	D	Ovary, testis.
G	O	N	E	R	Beyond retrieving. Lost, one whose fate is sealed.
G	O	O	D	S	Possessions, belongings, effects, chattels. Wares, items.
G	O	O	D	Y	Exclamation of joy. Dainty, delicacy, morsel, treat, tidbit.
G	O	O	L	Y	Stone.
G	O	O	S	E	Duck-like bird, poultry, Christmas fare. Simpleton, dilly, jerk.
G	O	R	E	D	Past of GORE.
G	O	R	G	E	Throat, stomach, groove, passage. Glut, cram, devour, overeat.

1	2	3	4	5	
G	O	R	S	E	Furze, brushwood.
G	O	R	S	Y	Abounding in gorse.
G	O	U	D	A	Cheese.
G	O	U	G	E	Force out, scoop. Carve, overcharge, swindle, Extort, wrest, cheat.
G	O	U	R	D	Type of fruit, cucumber, pumpkin. Bottle-shaped container, vessel.
G	O	U	T	Y	Swollen, bulging, overlarge, grumpy.
G	O	W	N	S	Plural of GOWN.
G	R	A	B	S	Grasps, captures, restrains, clutches, seizes. (Sl.) For the taking.
G	R	A	C	E	Prayer, blessing, benediction, invocation, thanksgiving, elegance, dignity. Adorn.
G	R	A	D	E	Standard, quality, level, degree. Qualify. Sort. Classify.
G	R	A	F	T	Trench, ditch.
G	R	A	F	T	Unite, form a variation, implant tissue, new growth. Exchange. Lawlessness. Toil. Work.
G	R	A	I	L	Desirable object, Sacred vessel.
G	R	A	I	N	Corn, wheat, particle, crumb, iota, speck, molecule.
G	R	A	N	D	Impressive, august, lordly, imposing, majestic, noble, royal, monumental.
G	R	A	N	T	Allowance, subsidy, award. Concede, acknowledge, Gift, largesse.
G	R	A	P	E	Fruit of the Vine.
G	R	A	P	H	Chart, map, diagram, sketch, outline, picture.
G	R	A	P	Y	Tasting of wine, affected with grapes.
G	R	A	S	P	Clutch, seize, clench, grip, apprehend, comprehension.
G	R	A	S	S	Green herbage, grazing, lawn, pasture, graze, lay turf. Inform on, Informer, Squealer.
G	R	A	T	E	Frame for fuel, fireplace, fret, offend, irritate, grind, rasp, perturb, annoy.
G	R	A	V	E	Tomb, Sepulchre, final resting place. Serious, earnest, sober, solemn.
G	R	A	Z	E	Skim, brush, glance, shave, abrade, chafe, rub, wear. (Sl.) Food. Eat.
G	R	E	A	T	Big, large, huge, famous, distinguished, famed, notable, prominent.
G	R	E	B	E	Diving bird.
G	R	E	E	D	Avariciousness, rapacity, gluttony, avarice, cupidity.
G	R	E	E	K	Gibberish, drivel, jabber. Native of Greece.
G	R	E	E	N	Colour. Raw, inexperienced, young, callow, untried. Common, pitch, grassed area.
G	R	E	E	T	Acknowledge, hail, address, accost, call, salute.
G	R	E	Y	S	Cavalry Regiment.
G	R	I	C	E	Young pig.
G	R	I	D	E	Scrape, graze.
G	R	I	D	S	Plural of GRID.
G	R	I	E	F	Sorrow, woe, anguish, care, heartache, affliction, heartbreak, regret.
G	R	I	L	L	Braai, broil, char. Cross examine, interrogate.
G	R	I	M	E	Dirt, filth, sully, soil, begrime, besmear. Tarnish.
G	R	I	M	Y	Smutty, dirty, filthy, soiled, begrimed, tarnished.
G	R	I	N	D	Graze, abrade, pulverize, sharpen. Drudge, toil, work, slog, slave.
G	R	I	P	E	Grumble, complain, bitch, fuss, grasp, hold, clench. Stomach ache.
G	R	I	S	T	Grain for grinding, Matter of interest, analysis. Lot, number.
G	R	I	T	S	Oatmeal, Porridge, grain particles.
G	R	O	A	N	Mutter, mumble, grumble, moan.
G	R	O	A	T	Hulled grain, grain fragments, larger than grits.
G	R	O	I	N	Lower part of the abdomen, projection, rigid structure, seawall.
G	R	O	O	M	Stable hand, bridegroom. Tend horses. Polish, tidy, smarten.
G	R	O	P	E	Reach out blindly, feel, fumble, poke, root, grapple, explore, search.
G	R	O	S	S	Coarse, crass. Obscene. Absolute, complete. Material, corpulent, overweight.
G	R	O	U	P	Gathering crowd, cluster, assembly, company, syndicate, class. Gather, assort.
G	R	O	U	T	Coarse meal, Grounds. Porridge. Mortar fluid. Coarse plaster, concrete.
G	R	O	V	E	Wood, thicket, spinney, glen.
G	R	O	W	L	Snarl, gutteral sound, rumble, grumble, enraged utterance.
G	R	O	W	N	Matured, ripened, raised, extended, developed.
G	R	U	E	L	Porridge.
G	R	U	F	F	Bluff, blunt, brusque, surly, hoarse, husky, coarse, sullen, fierce.
G	R	U	M	P	Sulk, pout, grouch, cripe, grumble, growl. Sorehead, sourpuss, crank.
G	R	U	N	T	Grumble, grouch, murmur, mutter, scold, croak, snort.
G	U	A	N	A	Iguana. American tropical Lizard.
G	U	A	N	O	Decomposed sea-fowl excrement. Bird droppings. Fertilizer.
G	U	A	R	D	Lookout, sentinel, sentry, defence, safeguard, shield, defend, protect, secure.
G	U	A	V	A	Fruit.
G	U	E	S	S	Surmise, suppose, conjecture, presumption, estimate, predict, reckon.
G	U	E	S	T	Visitor, caller, lodger, company.
G	U	I	D	E	Pilot, leader, conductor, director. Handbook, compendium, manual.
G	U	I	L	D	Fraternity, company, association, brotherhood, fellowship, league, club, union.
G	U	I	L	E	Deceit, duplicity, cunning, craftiness, persuasion.
G	U	I	L	T	Blame, culpability, responsibility, fault, sense of wrong, sin, onus.

1	2	3	4	5	
G	U	I	R	O	Percussion instrument.
G	U	I	S	E	Dress, getup, outfit, rig, costume, appearance, semblance, turnout, Mask, facade.
G	U	L	C	H	Gully, ravine, chasm, gap, gorge.
G	U	L	E	S	Colour red. Heraldic colour.
G	U	L	F	Y	Full of holes, whirlpools.
G	U	L	L	Y	Small valley, small ravine, depression. Drain. Wooded hollow. Cricket placing.
G	U	M	B	O	Thick soup. mixed stew. Sticky mud substance. Mixture, Melange.
G	U	M	M	Y	Sticky, viscous, mucky, adhesive, gluey, stodgy, cloggy, gooey.
G	U	N	N	Y	Loosely woven material, sacking, jute, burlap.
G	U	S	T	O	Zest, relish, zeal, ardour, enthusiasm, fervour, passion, enjoyment.
G	U	S	T	Y	Squally, windy, stormy, blowy, airy, breezy.
G	U	T	T	A	Doric Ornament.
G	U	T	T	Y	Full of guts. Vital, bold, courageous, stirring, challenging.
G	U	T	S	Y	Brave, intrepid, manly, plucky, spunky, valiant, bold.
G	U	Y	E	D	Ridiculed, mocked, derided, fooled.
G	Y	G	I	S	Genus of Tern. Water bird.
G	Y	P	S	Y	Wanderer, Romany, Fortune teller. Swarthy.
G	Y	R	A	L	Gyratory. Convolution.
G	Y	R	U	S	Convoluted ridge. Ridge.
G	Y	V	E	S	Plural of GYVE. Fetter, chain, bond,shackle.

H

1	2	3	4	5	
H	A	B	I	T	Custom, characteristic, practice, usage. Apparel, dress, outfit. Conduct.
H	A	C	K	S	Plural of HACK.
H	A	D	E	S	Underworld, abode of the dead. Hell.
H	A	I	L	Y	Accompanied by Hail.
H	A	I	R	S	Plural of HAIR.
H	A	I	R	Y	Covered with hair. Fleecy, whiskered, woolly, rough, shaggy, unshorn. Chancy.
H	A	L	E	S	Plough handles. Wheelbarrow handles.
H	A	L	L	O	Greeting. Hello. Holler. Shout. Attract attention.
H	A	L	M	A	Game.
H	A	L	O	S	Plural of HALO.
H	A	L	V	A	Confectionery.
H	A	L	V	E	Divide in half.
H	A	N	A	P	Drinking vessel, goblet.
H	A	N	C	E	Arc, arch.
H	A	N	C	H	Snap greedily.
H	A	N	D	S	Plural of HAND.
H	A	N	D	Y	Dexterous, practical, functional, convenient, adjacent, nearby. Adroit, deft.
H	A	N	K	S	Plural of HANK.
H	A	N	K	Y	Handkerchief.
H	A	N	S	A	League, associaton.
H	A	P	L	Y	By chance, by accident.
H	A	P	P	Y	Fortunate, lucky, glad, joyful, contended, lighthearted, apt, suitable, proper.
H	A	R	D	Y	Tough, rugged, robust.
H	A	R	E	D	Ran, bolted, sped, sprinted.
H	A	R	E	M	House alloted to women. Group of women associated with one man. Seraglio.
H	A	R	P	S	Plural of HARP.
H	A	R	P	Y	Mythical predatory monster. Leech, swindler. Depraved woman. Bat.
H	A	R	R	Y	Raid, loot, assault, ravage, devastate, attack.
H	A	R	S	H	Rough, scraggy, uneven, austere, grim, bleak, discordant, grating, jarring.
H	A	S	T	E	Hurry, expedition, hustle, speed, velocity, dash, rash action, precipitation.
H	A	S	T	Y	Hurried, fast, quick, rapid, swift, speedy, headlong, reckless.
H	A	T	C	H	Generate, engender, provoke, create, contrive, concoct. Doorway, opening, Hold.
H	A	T	E	D	Abhorred, abominated, detested, loathed, resented, despised, repudiated.
H	A	T	E	R	One who hates.
H	A	T	E	S	Plural of HATE.
H	A	U	L	M	Vegetable tops, stubble, leavings.
H	A	U	N	T	Visit, trouble, molest, frequent, linger. Stamping ground, home, habitat.
H	A	V	E	N	Shelter, asylum, refuge, sanctuary, harbour, anchorage, port.
H	A	V	E	R	Wild oat. Oat. Stall, delay.
H	A	V	O	C	Destruction, devastation, ruination, confusion, ruin, catastrophe, Desolate.
H	A	W	K	S	Plural of HAWK.
H	A	W	K	Y	Hawklike.
H	A	W	S	E	Arrangement of anchor cables.

1	2	3	4	5	
H	A	Z	E	D	Harassed, embarrassed.
H	A	Z	E	L	Colour. Edible nut.
H	E	A	D	S	Plural of HEAD.
H	E	A	D	Y	Exhilarating, intoxicating. Shrewd, clever. Wilful, headstrong.
H	E	A	P	S	Lots, many, much, extremely. Plural of HEAP.
H	E	A	R	D	Past of HEAR.
H	E	A	R	T	Hollow muscular organ. Centre, seat, soul. Courage, guts. Focal point, hub.
H	E	A	T	H	Field, common, wasteland.
H	E	A	T	S	Plural of HEAT.
H	E	A	V	E	Cast, fling, hurl, throw, pitch, toss, rock, roll. Pant, gasp. Retch, gag, vomit.
H	E	A	V	Y	Weighty, hefty, ponderous, serious, lethargic, arduous, corpulent, overcast.
H	E	D	G	E	Fence, boundary, row of shrubs. Restrict. Hesitate, delay, parry.
H	E	E	L	S	Plural of HEEL.
H	E	F	T	Y	Heavy, weighty, ponderous, beefy, burly, considerably, sizeable.
H	E	I	G	H	Exclamation to gain attention. Exultation, interrogation.
H	E	I	R	S	Plural of HEIR.
H	E	L	I	O	Heliotrope, heliograph.
H	E	L	I	X	Spiral. Type of Snails.
H	E	L	L	O	Salutation, greeting.
H	E	L	O	T	Serf, deprived person.
H	E	L	P	S	Plural of HELP.
H	E	L	V	E	Tool handle.
H	E	M	A	N	Strong man, tough, red-blooded. Virile type.
H	E	M	P	Y	Mischievous, roguish.
H	E	N	C	E	Henceforth. Therefore, thence, accordingly, thereupon, thus, consequently.
H	E	N	N	A	Small tree. Tint, dye.
H	E	N	R	Y	Unit of inductance.
H	E	P	A	R	Liver.
H	E	R	B	S	Plural of HERB.
H	E	R	B	Y	Like herbs. Abounding in herbaceous growth.
H	E	R	D	S	Plural of HERD.
H	E	R	O	N	Wading bird.
H	E	T	U	P	Aroused, excited, incited.
H	E	V	E	A	Rubber plant.
H	E	W	E	D	Cut, chopped, axed, felled.
H	E	W	E	R	One who hews.
H	E	X	E	D	Bewitched, charmed, enchanted, spellbound.
H	I	D	E	R	One who hides.
H	I	D	E	S	Plural of HIDE.
H	I	K	E	D	Walked, tramped, trudged, strode, travelled on foot. Boosted, upgraded, raised.
H	I	K	E	R	Rambler, harrier, pedestrian.
H	I	L	L	S	Plural of HILL.
H	I	L	L	Y	Undulating, mountainous, up and down. Steep. Like a hill.
H	I	L	U	M	The scar on a seed where it joined its stalk. The depression where ducts, vessels, etc, enter an organ.
H	I	N	D	I	Indian dialect.
H	I	N	D	U	Native of India.
H	I	N	G	E	Mount, fasten, flexible joint, gummed corner. Turning point. Depend.
H	I	N	N	Y	Type of mule. Hybrid horse.
H	I	N	T	S	Plural of HINT.
H	I	P	P	O	Hippopotamus.
H	I	P	P	Y	Revolutionary youth. Rebel. Flower child. Anti-establishment tendencies.
H	I	R	E	D	Rented, leased, chartered, let, employed, engaged.
H	I	R	E	R	One who hires.
H	I	R	E	S	Act of Hiring.
H	I	T	C	H	Harness, couple, yoke, become married. Thumb a lift. Uplift, Pull up. Delay.
H	I	V	E	D	Swarmed, collected, accumulated.
H	I	V	E	S	Plural of HIVE. Urticaria, skin eruption.
H	O	A	R	D	Accumulation, collection, conglomeration, stockpile, amass. Reserve, stash.
H	O	A	R	Y	Ancient, antediluvian, antique, old, venerable. Aged. Grey haired.
H	O	A	S	T	Cough.
H	O	B	B	Y	Pastime, diversion, recreation, favourite pursuit.
H	O	C	K	S	Plural of HOCK.
H	O	C	U	S	Deceive, cheat, adulterate.
H	O	D	G	E	Rustic, bumpkin, peasant, yokel, hick, clodhopper.
H	O	I	S	T	Elevate, lift, raise, uplift, heave.
H	O	K	U	M	Induced audience reaction. Nonsense, malarkey, bunkum.
H	O	L	E	R	Specified number of holes (golf).

1	2	3	4	5	
H	O	L	E	S	Plural of HOLE.
H	O	L	E	Y	Full of holes. Riddled.
H	O	L	L	Y	Pretty shrub. Christmas decoration.
H	O	M	E	R	Homing pigeon. Home run.
H	O	M	E	Y	Like home. Comfortable, snug.
H	O	N	E	D	Sharpened, stropped, smoothed, polished, keened.
H	O	N	E	R	One that hones.
H	O	N	E	Y	Sweet liquid, nectar, Sweetheart, Dear. Sweeten.
H	O	O	C	H	Liquor, alcohol, booze, grog, spirits, drink, firewater, Moonshine.
H	O	O	E	Y	Balderdash, nonsense, rubbish.
H	O	O	K	A	Hookah. Pipe for smoking through water.
H	O	O	K	Y	Full of Hooks. Resembling a hook. Truant.
H	O	O	P	S	Plural of HOOP.
H	O	O	S	H	Thick Soup.
H	O	O	T	S	Plural of HOOT.
H	O	P	E	D	Anticipated, expected, awaited, trusted, desired.
H	O	P	E	S	Plural of HOPE.
H	O	P	P	Y	Drug addict. Characterised by hopping movements. Like Hops.
H	O	R	D	E	Crowd, drove, multitude, throng, clan, crew, gang.
H	O	R	N	Y	Hard, callous. Sexually excited, lascivious, passionate, lustful.
H	O	R	S	E	Solid-hooved herbivorous mammal.
H	O	R	S	Y	Like a horse. Tweedy, flashy, belonging to the 'Dung and Paddock' Set.
H	O	S	E	D	Watered, drenched, sprayed, wet.
H	O	T	E	L	Inn, Licensed lodging house, public house, Tavern, Hospice, Hostel.
H	O	T	L	Y	Eagerly, fervidly, ardently, lasciviously, forcefully, definitely.
H	O	U	N	D	Dog, canine. Addict, devotee. Chivy, hector, ride, badger.
H	O	U	R	S	Plural of HOUR.
H	O	U	S	E	Abode, domicile, dwelling, residence, household, home. Enterprise, business. Harbour, shelter.
H	O	V	E	L	Hut, lowly abode, shelter, shed, cabin, shack, hutch.
H	O	V	E	R	Hang, poise, vacillate, float, flicker, flutter, flit, dance.
H	O	W	D	Y	Greeting. Salutation.
H	O	W	E	L	Cooper's plane.
H	U	B	B	Y	Husband.
H	U	F	F	Y	Irritated, petulant, bad tempered, nettled, peeved, proud, haughty, insolent.
H	U	L	A	S	Plural of HULA.
H	U	L	K	Y	Large, clumsy, unwieldy, bulky.
H	U	L	L	O	Salutation, greeting.
H	U	M	A	N	Man, being a man, consisting of men. Mankind. Homo Sapiens.
H	U	M	I	C	Derived from Humus.
H	U	M	I	D	Moist, damp, vaporous, wet, containing moisture.
H	U	M	I	T	Unit of humiture.
H	U	M	U	S	Organic soil. Rich deposits. Leaf mould or fertile manure. Sewer sludge.
H	U	N	C	H	Huddle, squat, bend, push, shove, hump, lump. Presentiment, foreboding.
H	U	N	K	S	Chunks, lumps, gobs, wads, clods.
H	U	N	K	Y	Industrial worker. Person of working class.
H	U	R	D	S	Hards. Coarse fibre, flax.
H	U	R	L	Y	Uproar, tumult, confusion.
H	U	R	R	Y	Hasten, accelerate, speed, run, rush, haste, swiftness, hustle.
H	U	S	K	Y	Empty, hoarse, burly, robust, Eskimo dog. Working dog.
H	U	S	S	Y	Minx, housewife, jade, saucy girl, brazen woman.
H	U	T	C	H	Pen, coop, cage, shanty, shack.
H	Y	D	R	A	Water creature.
H	Y	D	R	O	Spa, Hotel providing healing natural waters.
H	Y	E	N	A	Nocturnal carnivore.
H	Y	L	E	G	Relating to planets.
H	Y	L	I	C	Relating to matter. Material, corporeal.
H	Y	M	E	N	Vaginal membrane. God of marriage.
H	Y	M	N	S	Plural of HYMN.
H	Y	O	I	D	Bone in mouth.
H	Y	P	E	R	Super, extra.
H	Y	P	H	A	Fungal filament.
H	Y	R	A	X	Small mammal.
H	Y	T	H	E	Port, haven, shelter.

| I | C | E | N | I | Ancient British Tribe under Boadicea. |

1	2	3	4	5	Definition
I	C	H	O	R	Blood of the Gods. Blood-tinged discharge.
I	C	I	E	R	More Icy. Colder. Frozen.
I	C	I	L	Y	Frostily, frigidly, coldly.
I	C	I	N	G	Sugar coating. Frosting.
I	C	K	E	R	Gnomy.
I	C	T	I	C	Relating to ICTUS.
I	C	T	U	S	Beat, rhythm, accent.
I	D	E	A	L	Perfect, model, typical, classic. Abstract, conceptual, notional. Pattern.
I	D	I	O	M	Language, dialect, tongue, vernacular, speech, phraseology.
I	D	I	O	T	Fool, imbecile, dunce, simpleton. Jester, jerk, ass.
I	D	L	E	D	Slackened, slowed, ambled, lingered, marked time, waited.
I	D	L	E	R	Slouch, sluggard, loafer, sloth, dawdler, loiterer, lounger.
I	D	O	L	S	Plural of IDOL.
I	D	Y	L	L	Narrative poem, descriptive poem. romantic interlude. Pleasant time.
I	G	L	O	O	Eskimo, snow-hut.
I	L	E	A	L	Relating to the ileum.
I	L	E	U	M	Last part of the small intestine.
I	L	E	U	S	Pain affecting the abdomen. Colic.
I	L	I	A	C	Located in the region of the ilium.
I	L	I	A	U	Sugar cane disease.
I	L	I	U	M	A bone of the pelvis.
I	M	A	G	E	Picture, likeness, similarity. Ikon, idol. Depict, represent, envisage.
I	M	A	G	O	Mature insect. Mental image.
I	M	B	A	T	Cooling elesian wind.
I	M	B	U	E	Impregnate, permeate, stain, dye, infuse, steep, suffuse, ingrain.
I	M	I	D	E	Chemical compound.
I	M	M	I	E	Glass streaked Marble.
I	M	M	I	T	Introduce, inject.
I	M	M	I	X	Comingle.
I	M	P	E	L	Actuate, urge, move, propel, force, incite, spur, goad, motivate, inspire.
I	M	P	L	Y	Suggest, indicate, hint, insinuate, intimate, point.
I	N	A	N	E	Insubstntial, empty, vapid, innocuous, insipid, fatuous, void.
I	N	A	P	T	Inappropriate, unfit, ill-suited, unfitting, clumsy, unsuitable, improper, inept.
I	N	B	Y	E	Close, near, within.
I	N	C	O	G	Incognito.
I	N	C	U	R	Bring down on oneself, contract, induce, bring on, acquire, get, gain.
I	N	C	U	S	A bone of the ear. Anvil-shaped thundercloud.
I	N	D	E	X	Reference, indication, token, sign, mark, pointer, exponent. Forefinger.
I	N	D	R	I	Lemur.
I	N	E	P	T	Inapt, improper, inappropriate, unsuitable, graceless, awkward, unskillful.
I	N	E	R	T	Passive, quiet, inactive, idle, asleep, still, lifeless, stolid, phlegmatic.
I	N	F	E	R	Conclude, deduce, judge, speculate, ascertain, construe, interpret. Suggest.
I	N	F	I	X	Instill, impress, word derivation.
I	N	F	R	A	Below, after, behind, later, subsequently, next.
I	N	G	L	E	Fireside.
I	N	G	O	T	Mass of metal. Bar, lump, slab, stick, rod, strip.
I	N	I	O	N	Protuberance of the head.
I	N	K	E	D	Covered in Ink. Filled with ink.
I	N	K	E	R	Worker who applies ink. One who touches up.
I	N	K	L	E	Thread used for trimming.
I	N	L	A	W	Relative by marriage.
I	N	L	A	Y	Inset, decoration, adornment, insert, set-in.
I	N	L	E	T	Bay, cove, creek, gulf, harbour, arm, loch.
I	N	N	E	R	Inside, within, central, interior, internal, inward.
I	N	P	U	T	Contribution, energy, enthusiasm, vitality.
I	N	S	E	T	Panel, insert, implant, insertion.
I	N	T	E	R	Between, among. Bury, entomb.
I	N	U	R	E	Familiarize, accustom, habituate, use, harden, toughen.
I	N	U	R	N	Enclose, entomb.
I	N	V	A	R	Nickel alloy.
I	N	W	I	T	Inward knowledge, understanding, conscience, intuition.
I	O	N	I	C	Type of Architecture. Characterised by lons.
I	R	A	T	E	Angry, wrathful, irritated, indignant, enraged, incensed, choleric.
I	R	E	N	E	Liquid hydrocarbon.
I	R	I	S	H	Belonging to Ireland. Paddy, temper.
I	R	K	E	D	Annoyed, aggravated, irritated, bothered, bugged, provoked, vexed.
I	R	O	N	S	Plural of IRON.

1	2	3	4	5	
I	R	O	N	Y	Resembling iron. Sarcasm, satire, humour, ridicule, reversed results. Mockery.
I	S	L	A	M	Religious faith of Muslims.
I	S	L	E	T	Small island, isle, small isolated mass.
I	S	S	U	E	Offspring, progeny. Effect, consequence. Arise, emit. Publish. Publication. Spring.
I	T	C	H	Y	Irritated, uneasy, scratchy. Desirous, covetous, acquisitive, grasping.
I	T	E	M	S	Plural of ITEM.
I	V	I	E	D	Covered in Ivy.
I	V	O	R	Y	Creamy white colour. Elephant tusks. Made of Ivory. Suggesting Ivory.
I	Z	A	R	D	Chamois.
I	Z	T	L	E	Coarse, hard fibre. Yucca plant. Spanish bayonet.
I	Z	Z	A	T	Personal dignity, prestige.

J

J	A	C	K	S	Plural of JACK. Jackstones.
J	A	D	E	D	Tired, fatigued, weary, worn out, glutted, satiated.
J	A	G	G	Y	Jaggard, uneven, notched, rough.
J	A	I	L	S	Plural of JAIL.
J	A	L	A	P	Purgative.
J	A	M	B	E	Projecting wall. Doorway, window. Leg armour.
J	A	M	M	Y	Easy, delightful. Covered in Jam.
J	A	M	U	P	Very good, first rate.
J	A	P	A	N	Lacquerwork. Varnish.
J	A	U	N	T	Excursion, outing, junket, picnic, joyride, trip.
J	A	W	E	D	Lectured, berated, scolded. Type of Jaw.
J	E	A	N	S	Denims. Blue Jeans. Leisure wear. Unisex trousers.
J	E	E	P	S	Plural of JEEP.
J	E	L	L	Y	Gelatin, sweet, dessert, aspic, gel, coagulate, clot.
J	E	M	M	Y	Stealthy footsteps. Overcoat. Spruce, neat.
J	E	N	N	Y	Spinning jenny, travelling crane. Ass. Wren.
J	E	R	K	Y	Spasmodic, twitching, uneven, irregular, convulsive. American Biltong.
J	E	R	R	Y	German. Slipshod, makeshift.
J	E	S	T	S	Plural of JEST.
J	E	T	T	Y	Wharf, dock, levee, pier, quay, slip, berth. Projection. Jut.
J	E	W	E	L	Gem. trinket, bauble, precious stone. Paragon, phoenix. Bejewel.
J	E	W	R	Y	Nation of Jews. Jewish People.
J	I	B	E	D	Swung, tacked, sneered, teased, taunted.
J	I	B	E	S	Plural of JIBE.
J	I	F	F	Y	Moment, second, instantly.
J	I	M	M	Y	Jemmy, lever, handle.
J	I	N	N	Y	Jenny, Crane on wheels.
J	I	N	G	O	Exclamation. Arrogant nationalist.
J	I	N	K	S	Pranks, merry-making.
J	O	I	N	T	Meeting place, connection, coupling, junction, seam. Dive, hangout. Mutual, shared.
J	O	I	S	T	Timber support, stud, beam.
J	O	K	E	D	Jested, mocked, bantered. PAST OF JOKE.
J	O	K	E	R	One who JOKES.
J	O	K	E	S	Plural of JOKE.
J	O	L	L	Y	Merry, glad, happy, good natured, blithe, festive, gay, jovial, lighthearted.
J	O	L	T	S	Plural of JOLT.
J	O	N	A	H	Jinx, bad luck. Bringer of ill-luck.
J	O	U	L	E	Unit of energy.
J	O	U	S	T	Tilt, encounter, tourney.
J	U	D	A	S	Betrayer, traitor, spy-hole.
J	U	D	G	E	Decide, adjudicate, arbitrate, umpire, infer, conclude, deduce. Estimate.
J	U	I	C	E	Fluid, sap, goodness. Fuel. Alcohol, grog, spirits. Booze.
J	U	I	C	Y	Luscious, succulent, sappy, moist.
J	U	L	E	P	Tall, cold, alcoholic drink.
J	U	M	B	O	Enormous, large, gigantic, elephantine, colossal, mammoth, mighty.
J	U	M	P	S	Jitters, jimjams, shivers, willies.
J	U	M	P	Y	Nervous, edgy, fidgety, high-strung, jittery, nervy, scared.
J	U	N	C	O	The reed bunting. A North American snow bird.
J	U	N	K	Y	Hophead, addict, drug taker, write-off.
J	U	N	T	A	Revolutionary government, political committee, take-over group.
J	U	R	A	L	Relating to rights. juristic. Relating to Law.
J	U	R	A	T	Magistrate.

1	2	3	4	5	
J	U	R	O	R	Member of Jury.
J	U	T	E	S	Jute plants.
J	U	T	T	Y	Projecting, protruding.
J	U	V	I	A	Brazil Nut.
J	U	X	T	A	Near, nearby.

K

K	A	P	O	K	Soft fibres, mattress and pillow filler.
K	A	P	U	T	Finished, donefor, ruined.
K	A	R	M	A	Generated force, destiny based incarnations, Fate.
K	A	Y	A	K	Canoe.
K	E	B	A	B	Cubed marinated meat. Skewered meat.
K	E	D	G	E	Small anchor. Brisk, lively.
K	E	E	L	S	Plural of KEEL.
K	E	E	P	S	Permanent possession. Always.
K	E	E	V	E	Tub, basin.
K	E	F	I	R	Sour milk beverage.
K	E	L	L	Y	Removed topsoil.
K	E	L	P	Y	Abounding in Kelp.
K	E	M	P	T	Trim, beat.
K	E	R	Y	L	Alkyl radicals.
K	E	T	C	H	Tow-masted sailing ship.
K	E	V	E	L	Bollard, cleat. Cudgel, staff.
K	E	Y	E	D	Set, braced, wedged, stretched, nervous with anticipation. Having keys.
K	E	Y	E	R	Electric circuit switch.
K	H	A	K	I	Drab olive colour. Colour of army uniforms.
K	I	B	B	E	Lebanese dish of minced mutton and wheat.
K	I	D	D	Y	Youngster, child.
K	I	L	I	M	Woven carpet, tapestry.
K	I	N	D	S	Plural of KIND.
K	I	N	G	S	Plural of KING.
K	I	N	K	Y	Curly, twisted. Crooked. Lively, spirited. Eccentric, peculiar.
K	I	O	S	K	Roofed stall. Summerhouse, booth.
K	I	T	T	Y	Small cat, kitten, Pool, pot, fund, collection. Target ball in bowls.
K	L	O	O	F	Gorge, ravine.
K	N	A	C	K	Skill, ability, adroitness, deftness, dexterity, faculty.
K	N	A	R	L	Knot of wood. Gnarl.
K	N	A	V	E	Rascal, villain, blackguard, micreant, rogue, scoundrel.
K	N	E	A	D	Mix, blend, press, manipulate.
K	N	E	E	D	Having knees, knobby, angled, bent.
K	N	E	E	L	Bend the knee, genuflect, stoop, grovel, submit.
K	N	E	L	L	Chime, peal, toll, ring, sound.
K	N	I	F	E	Eating utensil, sharp edged instrument, stab, stick, lance.
K	N	O	C	K	Tap, rap, hit, swat. Censure. Criticise.
K	N	O	L	L	Hillock, mound, elevation. Ring, toll.
K	N	O	T	S	Plural of KNOT.
K	N	O	U	T	Flogging whip. To flog.
K	N	O	W	N	Perceived, comprehended. Something familiar.
K	N	O	W	S	Of KNOW.
K	N	U	B	S	Knob, nubs.
K	N	U	R	L	Protuberance, excrescence, knob, ridge, snarl.
K	N	U	T	S	Fops.
K	O	A	L	A	Australian furry tree-climbing animal.
K	O	B	U	S	Genus of antelope.
K	O	G	I	A	Pygmy sperm whale.
K	O	R	A	N	Muslim Book of Revelations.
K	R	A	A	L	African village. Enclosure.
K	R	A	F	T	Strong paper.
K	R	A	I	T	Venomous snake.
K	R	E	E	F	Cape Crawfish.
K	R	I	L	L	Whale food.
K	R	O	N	E	Danish, Norwegian coin. Monetary unit.
K	U	D	O	S	Credit, fame, prestige, eminence, distinction. (SI).
K	U	L	A	H	Turkish Prayer Rug.

1	2	3	4	5	
K	V	A	S	S	Russian beverage.
K	Y	L	I	E	Boomerang.
K	Y	L	I	N	Chinese design for pottery.
K	Y	L	I	X	Drinking cup, chalice.
K	Y	R	I	E	Mass.

L

L	A	B	E	L	Ticket, adhesive marker, sticker, tag. Name, description, designation.
L	A	B	O	R	Labour.
L	A	C	E	D	Tied, threaded, bound, fastened. Diluted. Trimmed, decorated, edged.
L	A	C	E	R	One that laces.
L	A	C	E	S	Plural of LACE.
L	A	C	I	S	Network, net, meshed lace.
L	A	C	K	S	Absence, dearth, want, privation. Failure, deficiency, shortage, scantiness.
L	A	D	E	N	Loaded, burdened, charged, freighted.
L	A	D	E	R	One who loads.
L	A	D	L	E	Deep-bowled spoon, scoop. Dip, bale, dole, bail.
L	A	G	E	R	Beer.
L	A	I	R	D	Scottish landowner.
L	A	I	R	S	Plural of LAIR.
L	A	I	T	Y	Laymen, lay people.
L	A	K	E	S	Plural of LAKE.
L	A	K	E	I	Retrograde movement of tide.
L	A	K	I	N	Toy, plaything.
L	A	M	E	D	Crippled, hurt.
L	A	M	E	R	Comparative of LAME.
L	A	M	E	S	Plural of LAME.
L	A	M	I	A	Vampire, witch, enchantress, hag, hex, sorceress.
L	A	M	I	N	Astrologer's charm.
L	A	M	P	S	Plural of LAMP.
L	A	N	C	E	Spear, lancet, weapon. Pierce, cut. Fling, hurl, launch.
L	A	N	D	S	Plural of LAND.
L	A	N	K	Y	Tall, thin, lean, angular, rawboned, spare, gaunt.
L	A	N	E	S	Plural of LANE.
L	A	P	E	L	Coat collar, tapered facing.
L	A	P	I	N	Castrated male rabbit.
L	A	P	S	E	Slip, blunder, mistake, error, Relapse, revert, decline.
L	A	R	C	H	Genus of Tree.
L	A	R	D	Y	Covered in Lard.
L	A	R	G	E	Big, great, fat, enormous, extensive, sizable, tremendous, extreme.
L	A	R	G	O	Slowly.
L	A	R	K	Y	Frolicsome, playful, zany, sporty, frisky, impish.
L	A	R	R	Y	Grout, sloppy mortar. Excitement, noise.
L	A	R	V	A	Caterpillar, grub, maggot, nymph.
L	A	S	E	R	Light amplification.
L	A	S	S	O	Rope with running nose. To rope with a lasso, lariat.
L	A	T	C	H	Holding device, catch, snib, fastener. Hold, grab, seize, grasp.
L	A	T	E	D	Tardy, belated, late, overdue.
L	A	T	E	R	In the future, subsequent, ensuing, subsequently, next, latterly.
L	A	T	E	X	Resinous fluid, elastic emulsion.
L	A	T	H	E	Cutting machine.
L	A	T	H	S	Plural of LATH.
L	A	T	H	Y	Thin, lath-like.
L	A	T	I	N	Official language of Romans. Member of Latin people.
L	A	T	K	E	Jewish Griddle cake.
L	A	U	G	H	Give vent to mirth. Express happy emotion. Sound of joy.
L	A	U	R	A	Early Monastery.
L	A	V	E	D	Washed, rinsed, poured, bailed, bathed.
L	A	V	E	R	Vesse, trough, cistern. Seaweed.
L	A	W	N	S	Plural of LAWN.
L	A	X	L	Y	Loosely, remissly, slackly, negligently, carelessly.
L	A	Y	B	Y	Lay aside, save, put by, salt away. Side road.
L	A	Y	E	R	Stratum, bed, thickness. Hen. Form roots.
L	A	Z	A	R	Affected by offensive disease. Leper.
L	A	Z	E	D	Idled, dawdled, dozed, slouched, loitered.

1	2	3	4	5	
L	E	A	C	H	Perforated vessel. Extract, remove.
L	E	A	D	S	Plural of LEAD. Reins. Blacklead rods.
L	E	A	D	Y	Resembling lead.
L	E	A	F	Y	Abounding with leaves. Resembling a leaf. Laminate.
L	E	A	K	S	Plural of LEAK.
L	E	A	K	Y	Exuding moisture, dripping, not watertight.
L	E	A	N	T	Canted, inclined, listed, tipped, tilted, sloped.
L	E	A	P	S	Plural of LEAP.
L	E	A	P	T	Jumped, bounded, hurdled, sprang, vaulted, cleared, negotiated.
L	E	A	R	N	Acquire knowledge, Memorize, discover, ascertain, master, unearth.
L	E	A	S	E	Hire, charter, rent, let. Tenure.
L	E	A	S	H	Shackle, tie, hobble, fetter, curb, Hamper, trammel, bind, thong. Restrict.
L	E	A	S	T	Smallest, minutest, slightest. Less.
L	E	A	V	E	Depart, go. Will, bequeath. Allow, permit, permission. Vacation, holiday.
L	E	D	G	E	Shelf, ridge, rock mass, reef, lode, vein.
L	E	D	G	Y	Abounding in ridges. Consisting of Reefs.
L	E	E	C	H	Bloodsucking worm. Hanger-on, parasite. Bleed, Milk, Sap. Tap a supply.
L	E	E	K	S	Plural of LEEK.
L	E	E	R	Y	Alert, knowing, wide-awake. Wary. Leering.
L	E	G	A	L	Lawful, legitimate, innocent, proper.
L	E	G	G	Y	Long-legged, lanky.
L	E	M	M	A	Heading, title, theme, comment.
L	E	M	O	N	Citrus fruit. Failure, flop, loser, dud.
L	E	M	U	R	Nocturnal spirit, ghost.
L	E	N	I	S	Soft, smooth breathing.
L	E	P	E	R	Someone with leprosy. Shunned person.
L	E	P	I	D	Witty, jokey.
L	E	P	I	S	Scale, flake.
L	E	T	C	H	Craving, desire. Bog, swamp.
L	E	T	H	E	Forgetfulness, oblivion.
L	E	T	I	N	Admission, added note.
L	E	T	U	P	Alleviation, abatement, ease off, fall, moderate, respite.
L	E	V	E	E	Wharf, berth, jetty, quay, slipway, dock, embankment.
L	E	V	E	L	Even, flatten, smooth, flush, parallel. Aim, direct. Builder's equipment.
L	E	V	E	R	Prise, jemmy, ease. Handle.
L	E	W	I	S	Hoist grip.
L	I	A	N	A	Climbing plant.
L	I	A	R	S	Plural of LIAR.
L	I	B	E	L	Malign, defame, denigrate, slander, vilify.
L	I	B	R	A	Sign of the Zodiac. Scale.
L	I	C	I	T	Lawful, legal, legitimate, sanctioned, licensed.
L	I	C	K	S	Plural of LICK.
L	I	E	G	E	Obligated, right, faithful, loyal. Under oath.
L	I	F	E	R	Life imprisonment.
L	I	F	T	S	Plural of LIFT.
L	I	G	H	T	Small. Flimsy, Easy, Little, Fair, Dawn, morning. Kindle, Casual. Giddy. A light. Set alight. Less.
L	I	K	E	D	Enjoyed, relished, pleased, appreciated, respected, approved.
L	I	K	E	N	Compare, become like.
L	I	L	A	C	Shrub. Colour. Flower.
L	I	M	B	O	Region in another world between the devil and the deep blue sea. Netherworld.
L	I	M	B	S	Plural of LIMB. Branches.
L	I	M	B	Y	Having limbs or branches.
L	I	M	E	N	Threshold.
L	I	M	E	R	Bird snarer. Tannery worker.
L	I	M	I	T	Boundary, edge, limitation, confine, restrict. Border, brink, margin. Put restrictions on.
L	I	M	P	S	Walks lamely.
L	I	N	E	D	Aligned, ranged, arranged, ordered. Bordered. Aged, wrinkled. Inner material.
L	I	N	E	N	Cloth, woven material, flax, underwear, household sheets, pillow cases etc. Washing.
L	I	N	E	R	Layer, inner part, facing, removable insert, Ship, Aircraft.
L	I	N	E	S	Plural of LINE.
L	I	N	G	O	Language, speech, dialect, jargon, patois, patter, vernacular.
L	I	N	K	S	Plural of LINK. Joins, associates, unites. Chains. Golf Course.
L	I	O	N	S	Plural of LION.
L	I	S	L	E	Twisted thread.
L	I	S	P	S	Plural of LISP.
L	I	S	S	E	Silk gauze, dress material.
L	I	S	T	S	Plural of LIST.

1	2	3	4	5	
L	I	T	H	E	Supple, lissome, limber, slender.
L	I	T	H	O	Lithograph.
L	I	T	H	Y	Pliable, supple.
L	I	T	R	E	Unit of measure, volume. LITER.
L	I	V	E	D	Existed, was, resided, dwelt, Past of LIVE.
L	I	V	E	N	Animate, excite, quicken, vivify.
L	I	V	E	R	Inhabitant, dweller, occupant, resident. Internal organ of vertebrates.
L	I	V	E	S	Plural of LIVE.
L	I	V	I	D	Pale, blanched, colourless, pallid. Sensational, lurid. (Sl.) Angry.
L	L	A	M	A	Animal related to Camels. Cloth made from Llama's hair.
L	O	A	C	H	Freshwater fish.
L	O	A	D	S	Plural of LOAD.
L	O	A	M	Y	Like loam. Like clay soil.
L	O	A	N	S	Plural of LOAN.
L	O	A	T	H	Unwilling, averse, disinclined, indisposed, reluctant, hesitant.
L	O	B	A	L	Lobed.
L	O	B	A	R	Relating to lobe. Lobate.
L	O	B	B	Y	Vestibule, foyer, entrance, hall. To seek votes or support.
L	O	B	E	D	Having lobes.
L	O	C	A	L	Insular, parochial, provincial, sectarian, regional. Topical. Hotel, pub.
L	O	C	U	M	Tenems. Substitute, alternate, replacement, stand-in.
L	O	C	U	S	Locality, place, position, site, situation.
L	O	D	G	E	Shack, cabin, hospice, public house. Bestow, board, entrench, deposit.
L	O	F	T	Y	Towering, high, stately, proud, arrogant, ambitious, generous, eloquent, airy.
L	O	G	A	N	Berry.
L	O	G	I	C	Reasoning, rationality, intelligence, analysis, sensibility.
L	O	L	L	Y	Ice sucker. (Sl.) Money, Bread, dough.
L	O	O	B	Y	Oaf, lout, palooka, lump.
L	O	O	F	A	Loofah.
L	O	O	N	Y	Mad, insane, dilly, silly, wacky, balmy, crazy, potty.
L	O	O	P	S	Plural of LOOP.
L	O	O	P	Y	Foolish, absurd, crazy, kinky, dotty.
L	O	O	S	E	Not tight, relaxed, slack, detached, limp, free, unattached, incoherent, fast. Release, take out.
L	O	P	E	D	Lobbed, Bounded, leapt, sprang, vaulted, romped, hopped, sprinted.
L	O	R	D	S	Plural of LORD. House of Parliament. Cricket Ground. Swaggers, swanks.
L	O	R	I	S	Lemur.
L	O	R	R	Y	Motor truck, vehicle, railway flatcar.
L	O	S	E	R	Failure, dud, flop, lemon, also-ran, underdog. Bridge card.
L	O	S	S	Y	Pertaining to Lose.
L	O	T	T	O	Game. Housy housy.
L	O	T	U	S	Legendary fruit. Shrub.
L	O	U	C	H	Slouch.
L	O	U	G	H	Inlet, bay, cove, arm, lock, creek, gulf, harbour.
L	O	U	I	S	Obsolete French gold coin.
L	O	U	S	E	Parasitic insect, headlouse, sucking anthropod. (Sl.) Cur, wretch, skunk.
L	O	U	S	Y	Louse infested, mean, contemptible, filthy, vile, abominable.
L	O	U	T	S	Plural of LOUT.
L	O	V	E	D	Esteemed, adored, cherished, prized, valued, caressed, cuddled, fondled.
L	O	V	E	R	Sexual partner, paramour, boyfriend, beloved, steady, mistress, girlfriend.
L	O	V	E	S	Plural of LOVE. Relating to LOVE.
L	O	W	E	R	Cheapen, moderate. Frown, glower. Inferior. Fall, descend. Depress. Reduce.
L	O	W	L	Y	Humble, meek, modest, retiring, withdrawing, base, prosaic, commonplace.
L	O	Y	A	L	True, devoted, faithful, staunch, steadfast, constant, resolute.
L	U	C	I	D	Coherent, sane, bright, clear, intelligible, understandable, intelligible. Articulate.
L	U	C	K	Y	Fortunate, successful, providential, opportune, happy, auspicious.
L	U	C	R	E	Wealth, money, profit, earnings, proceeds, returns, dough, bread.
L	U	G	E	R	Automatic pistol. Gun of German origin.
L	U	M	P	S	Plural of LUMP.
L	U	M	P	Y	Full of lumps. Coagulated, chunky, bulgy, rude, rough, unfinished, unpolished.
L	U	N	A	R	Relating to the Moon.
L	U	N	C	H	Midday meal. Packed sandwiches. Picnic meal. Luncheon.
L	U	N	G	E	Plunge, thrust, dive, pitch, drive, burst.
L	U	P	I	N	Flower.
L	U	R	C	H	Pitch, career, stagger, falter, totter, stumble, jerk.
L	U	R	E	D	Enticed, attracted, trapped, pulled, seduced, decoyed, suckered.
L	U	R	E	S	Plural of LURE. Decoys enticements.
L	U	R	I	D	Bright, glowing, Livid, hideous, gruesome, gaudy, sensational.

1	2	3	4	5	
L	U	R	K	S	Sneaks, creeps, pussyfoots, skulks, slinks.
L	U	S	H	Y	Tipsy, intoxicated, inebriated.
L	U	S	T	Y	Vigorous, energetic, strenuous, vital, healthy, red-blooded, full-bodied.
L	U	S	U	S	Freak, miscreation, monster, monstrosity.
L	U	T	E	R	One who plays a lute.
L	Y	I	N	G	Recumbent, prone. Dishonest, deceitful, untruthful, deceptive, delusive.
L	Y	M	P	H	Body fluid, pale coagulate fluid.
L	Y	N	C	H	Tar and feather. Execute by mob law. Subject to scorn ridicule.
L	Y	R	E	S	Plural of LYRE.
L	Y	R	I	C	Song verse, poem, tuneful words. Melodic.
L	Y	S	I	C	Relating to Lysis.
L	Y	S	I	S	Defervescence, dissolution.
L	Y	S	S	A	Rabies, hydrophobia.
L	Y	T	T	A	Blister Beetle. Cartilagenous rod of tongue.

M

M	A	C	A	W	Parrot.
M	A	C	E	R	Mace-bearer.
M	A	C	E	S	Plural of MACE.
M	A	C	H	E	Papier-Mache.
M	A	C	O	N	Variety of French Wine.
M	A	D	A	M	Polite form of address for woman. Courtesy title. Prostitute.
M	A	D	G	E	Barn Owl. Magpie.
M	A	D	I	D	Wet, drenched, dripping, soaking sodden, soppy, soused.
M	A	D	I	D	Wet, moist.
M	A	D	L	Y	In a mad manner, vigorously, energetically, to an excessive degree.
M	A	F	I	A	Political secret society. Criminal secret organisation worldwide.
M	A	F	I	C	Relating to a group of dark coloured minerals.
M	A	G	I	C	Supernatural power, incantation, enchantment, witchcraft, illusion, mysticism.
M	A	G	N	A	College or university degree. Someone receiving the degree.
M	A	G	O	T	Magot, Barbary Ape, grotesque figurine.
M	A	G	U	S	Magician, charmer, enchanter, sorcerer, wizard, conjurer.
M	A	H	D	I	Muslim leader, messianic guide.
M	A	I	D	S	Plural of MAID.
M	A	I	Z	E	Corn. Mealies.
M	A	J	O	R	Principal, chief, superior, considerable, extensive, grave. Army title.
M	A	K	E	R	Creator, manufacturer. Card shuffler. Poet.
M	A	L	A	Y	Characteristic of Malaya.
M	A	L	T	Y	Malt-flavoured, thick with malt.
M	A	M	B	A	Snake. Swahili for mouth. Black Mamba = Black mouth.
M	A	M	B	O	Lively Dance.
M	A	M	M	A	Mother, mom, ma, mammy.
M	A	M	M	Y	Mother, mom, ma, mamma, mommy. Negro nurse.
M	A	N	E	D	Having a mane. Having neck hair.
M	A	N	E	S	Plural of MANE.
M	A	N	E	T	Stage director.
M	A	N	G	E	Skin disease, contagious excema.
M	A	N	G	O	Succulent fruit.
M	A	N	G	Y	Seedy, shabby, decrepit, scruffy, sleazy, squalid.
M	A	N	I	A	Madness, fixation, obsession, fetish, compulsion, hangup, delirium, hysteria.
M	A	N	I	C	Affected with mania. Relating to mania.
M	A	N	L	Y	Virile, masculine, brave, courageous, fearless, valiant, hardy, bold.
M	A	N	N	A	Biblical sustenance, windfall, manna lichen, manna grass.
M	A	N	O	R	Mansion, castle, chateau, villa, estate, residence of a Lord.
M	A	N	S	E	Clergyman's residence, presbytery.
M	A	N	T	A	Blanket, cloak, saddle cloth. Ray.
M	A	N	U	S	Forelimb, hand, ownership, power.
M	A	O	R	I	Native of New Zealand, Polynesian.
M	A	P	L	E	Tree, type of syrup.
M	A	R	C	H	Advance, proceed, progress, frontier, border, agree, stride, Month of the year.
M	A	R	E	S	Plural of MARE.
M	A	R	G	E	Margerine, shortening. Border, margin, verge.
M	A	R	R	Y	Unite, take a spouse, wed, join, combine, link, conjugate, couple.
M	A	R	S	H	Swamp, bog, mire, quagmire, swampland, morass.

1	2	3	4	5	
M	A	S	A	I	Pastoral people of Kenya.
M	A	S	H	Y	Pulpy, crushed, bruised, squashed.
M	A	S	O	N	Stone worker, monumental mason.
M	A	S	S	A	Negro dialect, master, sugar planter.
M	A	S	S	É	A shot in billards.
M	A	S	S	Y	Huge, colossal, enormous, immense, mammoth, massive.
M	A	T	C	H	Mate, companion, equal, counterpart, equate. Bout, game, contest, opponent.
M	A	T	E	D	Married, matched, paired, partnered, accompanied. Bred, covered.
M	A	T	E	R	Mother, Mom, mommy, ma, mama, mammy, mummy.
M	A	T	E	Y	Pally, friendly, chummy.
M	A	T	I	N	Prayers.
M	A	U	V	E	Violet colour.
M	A	V	I	N	Expert, authority, professional, master, virtuoso.
M	A	V	I	S	Thrush.
M	A	X	I	M	Adage, axiom, truism, rule, moral, truth, dictum, saw.
M	A	Y	B	E	Perhaps, possibly, perchance.
M	A	Y	O	R	Chief executive officer of a municipal corporation. Elected first citizen of a town.
M	A	Z	E	R	Wooden drinking vessel.
M	E	A	L	Y	Flected, spotty, farinose, pallid, blanched.
M	E	A	N	S	Financial support, mode, method.
M	E	A	T	S	Plural of MEAT.
M	E	A	T	Y	Full of meat. Fleshy, full of substance, ipigrammatic, compact, pithy.
M	E	B	O	S	Dried sugared apricots. Confection.
M	E	C	C	A	Holy city of Islam, centre of activity, goal, objective.
M	E	D	A	L	Metal disc, emblem, image, reward for competition, decoration.
M	E	D	I	A	Medium, means, agency, voice, instrument, channel, organ, vehicle.
M	E	D	I	C	One engaged in medical work. Physician, surgeon.
M	E	D	O	C	French red wine.
M	E	E	C	H	Sneak, skulk, creep, glide, lurk, glide, slink, steal.
M	E	L	E	E	Fray, scrimmage, skirmish, scuffle, brawl, fracas, miscellany.
M	E	L	O	N	Fleshy fruit. Musk melon. Sweet melon.
M	E	N	U	S	Plural of MENU.
M	E	R	C	Y	Pity, leniency, clemency, charity, grace.
M	E	R	G	E	Mingle, coalesce, submerge, mix, blend, meld, fuse, amalgamate.
M	E	R	I	T	Earn, deserve, quality calibre, value, due, deserts, excellence, quality.
M	E	R	L	E	Blackbird. Cattle dog (Aust.)
M	E	R	R	Y	Lively, blithe, jovial, joyful, hilarious, festive, gay, lighthearted.
M	E	S	H	Y	Composed of meshes. Netted, reticulated.
M	E	S	N	E	Intermediate, intervening, middle.
M	E	S	O	N	Unstable nuclear particle.
M	E	S	S	Y	Disordered, untidy, confused, dirty, unpleasant, slovenly, dishevelled.
M	E	S	T	O	Musical term for sad.
M	E	T	A	L	Mined substance, bronze, steel, gold. Mettle. Ore.
M	E	T	E	D	Measured, allotted, administered, apportioned, dealt, dispensed.
M	E	T	E	R	Metric unit of length. Measuring instrument.
M	E	T	I	S	Halfbreed. Crossbreed.
M	E	T	R	O	French underground.
M	E	U	S	E	Escape hatch for animals. Loophole.
M	E	W	E	D	Caged, confined, cooped. Meowed. Past of MEW.
M	E	Z	Z	O	Moderate, middle.
M	I	A	O	W	Mew, meow, cat noise.
M	I	A	S	M	Pollution, vapour.
M	I	C	R	O	Small, minute, microscopic.
M	I	D	A	S	Legendary king. Golden touch, lucky.
M	I	D	D	Y	Midshipman. Loose overblouse with sailor collar.
M	I	D	G	E	Tiny fly. Diminutive person, dwarf, midget. Gnat.
M	I	D	O	N	Cricket jargon.
M	I	D	S	T	Middle, Centre, core, midpoint, among, amid.
M	I	G	H	T	Power, authority, mastery, jurisdiction, energy, force, muscle, strength.
M	I	L	C	H	Flowing, milk producing, weeping.
M	I	L	E	R	One who runs a mile.
M	I	L	E	S	Plural of MILE.
M	I	L	K	Y	Like milk, lactic, opague.
M	I	L	L	S	Plural of MILL.
M	I	M	E	D	Acted, mimicked, aped, copied, demonstrated, imitated.
M	I	M	I	C	Impersonator, player, trouper, performer, Ape, imitate, mock, parody.
M	I	N	C	E	Chop, grind, hash, prance, sashay, flounce.

1	2	3	4	5	
M	I	N	C	Y	Nice, delicate, finicky, fussy, squeamish, dainty.
M	I	N	D	S	Plural of MIND.
M	I	N	E	D	Excavated, dug, extracted, burrowed, drilled. Planted with mines.
M	I	N	E	R	Someone who works in a Mine. Soldier who lays mines. Underground worker.
M	I	N	E	S	Plural of MINE.
M	I	N	G	Y	Miserly, mean, paltry, inadequate.
M	I	N	I	M	Half note, half rest (Music). Smallest, shortest. Worker ant.
M	I	N	O	R	Lesser, secondary, casual, insignificant, inferior, average. Infant, Younger.
M	I	N	U	S	Less, subtracted, without, lacking, wanting. Sans.
M	I	R	E	D	Bogged, stuck, swamped. Delayed, involved, entangled.
M	I	R	T	H	Joy, glee, happiness, hilarity, joviality, merriment, cheerfulness.
M	I	S	E	R	Mean person, scrooge, skinflint, hoarder, tightwad, cheapskate.
M	I	S	S	Y	Young girl, young miss.
M	I	S	T	Y	Dim, obscure, foggy, hazy, cloudy, overcast, murky, filmy.
M	I	T	E	R	Mitre. Headgear, Bishop's hat, Liturgical Headdress. Bevel, Join.
M	I	T	T	S	(Sl.) Hand, paws. Mittens, gloves.
M	I	X	E	D	Blended, mingled, hashed, mulled, fused, disarranged, disordered.
M	I	X	E	R	Something or someone who mixes.
M	I	X	U	P	Confuse, addle, befuddle, bamboozle, fluster, confusion, mistake, disruption.
M	O	A	N	S	Plural of MOAN.
M	O	A	T	S	Plural of MOAT.
M	O	C	H	A	Strong coffee infusion. Leather glove.
M	O	D	A	L	Typically.
M	O	D	E	L	Copy, image, example, pattern, epitome, ideal, standard, mirror. Perfect.
M	O	D	U	S	Manner, mode of procedure.
M	O	G	U	L	Dominant person, Conquering Muslim. Magnate, merchant prince, tycoon.
M	O	I	R	A	Fate, destiny, circumstance, doom, kismet, portion.
M	O	I	R	E	Watered fabric, wavy pattern.
M	O	I	S	T	Damp, dank, slushy, clammy, humid.
M	O	L	D	Y	Antiquated, archiac, out-dated, bygone.
M	O	L	A	R	Grinding, pulverizing. Ridged tooth. Molecular.
M	O	L	E	S	Plural of MOLE.
M	O	L	L	Y	(Sl.) Moll, mollycoddle, short-tailed bird.
M	O	L	T	O	Much, very.
M	O	N	D	O	Question and answer.
M	O	M	M	Y	Mother, mama, mater.
M	O	M	U	S	Critic, carper, faultfinder, critic.
M	O	N	E	Y	Legal tender, cash, currency, wealth, capital, coinage, finances, funds.
M	O	N	T	E	Card game.
M	O	N	T	H	Moon cycle. Twelfth portion of a year. Period of time. Specific number of days.
M	O	O	C	H	Wander, drift, meander, rove, ramble, straggle, range.
M	O	O	D	S	Plural of MOOD.
M	O	O	D	Y	Subject to eratic behaviour, capricious, inconstant, broody, sulky.
M	O	O	E	D	Lowed, Cow's mating call. Past of MOO.
M	O	O	N	Y	Dreamy, droopy, disinterested.
M	O	O	R	Y	Relating to moors. Marshy.
M	O	O	S	E	Large ruminant mammal. Elk.
M	O	P	E	D	Pined, sulked, brooded. Motorised bicycle.
M	O	P	U	P	Clean up.
M	O	P	U	S	Ready money, cash.
M	O	R	A	L	Ethical, virtuous, noble, meaningful, righteous. Maxim, lesson, experience.
M	O	R	A	Y	Eel.
M	O	R	E	L	Genus of fungus. Nightshade.
M	O	R	I	N	Pale yellow pigment.
M	O	R	N	E	Heraldic Lion.
M	O	R	O	N	Fool, imbecile, pervert.
M	O	R	S	E	Signalling code.
M	O	S	E	S	Biblical leader of the Jews.
M	O	S	E	Y	Saunter, amble, mooch, drift, stroll.
M	O	S	S	Y	Covered in moss. Overgrown, green.
M	O	T	E	D	Filled with motes.
M	O	T	E	L	Drive-in Hotel. Cabins. Roadside Inn.
M	O	T	E	T	Early musical composition.
M	O	T	H	S	Plural of MOTH.
M	O	T	H	Y	Moth-eaten, full of moths. Ragged, holey.
M	O	T	I	F	Theme, topic, subject, text, feature, argument. Pattern.
M	O	T	O	R	Automobile, motorcar, Car, auto, vehicle. Drive, engine.

1	2	3	4	5	
M	O	T	T	O	Catchphrase byword, rallying call, slogan.
M	O	U	E	S	Plural of MOUE.
M	O	U	L	D	Cast, character, description, stamp. Make, construct, fashion, forge.
M	O	U	L	T	Loose feathers.
M	O	U	N	D	Knoll, hillock, heap, drift, pile, bank, heap, hill, stack.
M	O	U	N	T	Ascend, climb, scale. Mountain, augment, intensify. Testify, stage. Stick.
M	O	U	R	N	Lament, sorrow, deplore, grieve, regret, bewail, bemoan.
M	O	U	S	E	Small rodent. Pest. Snoop, nose, pry, creep. Girlfriend, best girl.
M	O	U	S	Y	Nondescript, grey, quiet.
M	O	U	T	H	Orifice, opening in face. Utter, orate, reveal. Moue. Gulf, estuary.
M	O	V	E	D	Shifted, budged. Advanced, breathed, proposed, excited, roused, impressed.
M	O	V	E	R	One who MOVES. Instigator, inciter, agitator, proposer.
M	O	W	E	D	Cut, trimmed, scythed, felled, Floored. Grimaced.
M	O	W	E	R	One who MOWS. Machine that Mows.
M	O	X	I	E	Energy, hardihoop, pep, courage, guts, pluck, fortitude.
M	O	Y	E	N	Intercession, influence.
M	U	C	I	N	Mucoprotein.
M	U	C	K	Y	Soiled, grimy, murky, junky, sticky, littered, botched, filthy.
M	U	C	U	S	Slippery secretion, viscid secretion, emanation from mucus membrane.
M	U	D	D	Y	Cloying, oozy, turbid, dull, cloudy, blurred, sticky.
M	U	F	F	Y	Resembling a muff.
M	U	F	T	I	Professional jurist, arbitrator, mode of dress.
M	U	G	G	Y	Humid, overcast, damp, mucky, sultry, sticky.
M	U	G	U	P	Snack, morsel, piece, bite.
M	U	L	C	H	Dig in, manure, turn over ground, fertilize.
M	U	L	C	T	Forfeit, fine, penalty. Bleed, milk, swindle.
M	U	L	E	Y	Hornless, bald. Mulish, stubborn.
M	U	L	L	S	Plural of MULL.
M	U	L	T	I	Many, various, multiple, much, varigated.
M	U	M	B	O	Jumbo. Gibberish, hocus-pocus.
M	U	M	M	Y	Ancient remains. Mother, mom, mommy, mammy, ma. Wither, wizen.
M	U	M	P	S	Childhood disease. Sulks, grumps, pouts, mutters.
M	U	N	C	H	Masticate, chew, chrunch, champ, chomp, ruminate, scrunch.
M	U	R	A	L	Wall decoration, painted wall surface.
M	U	R	K	Y	Dim, obscure, foggy, dark, cloudy, gloomy, dim, sombre, dull.
M	U	S	E	D	Deliberated, pondered, meditated, ruminated, mulled.
M	U	S	E	R	One who muses.
M	U	S	E	S	Plural of MUSE.
M	U	S	H	Y	Pulpy, soft, squashy, spongy, squishy, squelchy, pulpous, Sentimental, maudlin.
M	U	S	I	C	Melodious sound. Harmony. Vocal or instrumental expression. Uproar, reprisal.
M	U	S	K	Y	Animal scent, fragrance, perfume.
M	U	S	T	Y	Malodourous, rank, smelly, stale, trite, stereotyped, fusty.
M	U	T	E	D	Muffled, quiet, smothered, deadened, stifled, dimmed, flattened.
M	U	Z	Z	Y	Hazy, dazed, confused, fuzzy, faint, depressed.
M	Y	N	A	H	Asiatic starling, noisy, aggresive bird.
M	Y	R	R	H	Aromatic gum resin. Ingredient of incense.
M	Y	T	H	S	Plural of MYTH.

N

1	2	3	4	5	
N	A	B	A	L	Scrooge, skinflint, tightwad, miser,
N	A	B	A	M	Crystaline fungicide.
N	A	B	L	A	Ancient stringed instrument.
N	A	B	O	B	Man of prominence, wealthy man, Generalised derisive term. Notable, Fat cat.
N	A	C	R	E	Mother of Pearl.
N	A	D	I	R	Lowest point, point opposite zenith. Bottom, base.
N	A	E	V	E	Blemish, birthmark, spot, flaw.
N	A	G	G	Y	Quarrelsome, carping, fussy.
N	A	I	L	S	Plural of NAIL.
N	A	I	V	E	Ingenuous, artless, simple, unaffected, natural, unsophisticated, gullible.
N	A	K	E	D	Unclothed, bare, nude, buff, stripped, unclad, undressed, exposed, starkers.
N	A	K	E	R	Kettledrum.
N	A	M	E	D	Designated, baptized, denominated, mentioned, cited, specified, termed. Notable.
N	A	M	E	R	Name bestower.
N	A	N	C	Y	Queer, fag, homosexual.
N	A	N	N	Y	Nurse, child minder, trusted servant, female domestic goat.

1	2	3	4	5	
N	A	P	O	O	Finished, incapacitated, over and gone, dead, nonexistent, no.
N	A	P	P	E	Fold, overlay, sheet.
N	A	P	P	Y	Napkin, diaper. Downy, kinky, heady, stubborn. Ale, drinking vessel.
N	A	R	E	S	Plural of NARE.
N	A	R	I	S	Nasal cavity, nostril.
N	A	R	K	S	Plural of NARK.
N	A	R	K	Y	Ill-tempered, irritable.
N	A	R	R	A	Hardwood.
N	A	S	A	L	Relating to nose. Resonant, twangy.
N	A	S	T	Y	Horrid, loathsome, foul, malicious, offensive, obscene, dirty, filthy.
N	A	T	A	L	Relating to birth. Native, dating from birth. Relating to BUTTOCKS.
N	A	T	C	H	(Sl.) Naturally! Notch.
N	A	T	T	E	Woven fabric.
N	A	T	T	Y	Neat, trim, tidy, spruce, dapper, well-groomed.
N	A	V	A	L	Marine, nautical, maritime.
N	A	V	E	L	Middle of abdomen, spot marking attachment of umbilicus. Central. Belly button.
N	A	V	V	Y	Unskilled worker, dockside worker. Steam shovel. Excavate.
N	A	W	O	B	Nabob. Muslin Prince, notable, big chief.
N	E	B	B	Y	Inquisitive, meddlesome, impertinent, intrusive, officious.
N	E	C	K	S	Plural of NECK.
N	E	D	D	Y	Donkey, ass, buro, moke, jackass.
N	E	E	D	S	Requirements, obligations, demands, wants, claims, necessities.
N	E	E	D	Y	Poor, needful, destitute, poverty-stricken, unprosperous, penurious.
N	E	G	R	O	Member of Black race. Belonging to Africa, negroid-featured person.
N	E	G	U	S	King. Hot wine drink.
N	E	I	G	H	Whinny, typical calling cry of horse.
N	E	R	V	E	Filamentous band, tissue, sinew, tendon. Fortitude, grit, audacity, effrontery.
N	E	R	V	Y	Nervous, fearful, jittery, tense, edgy, uneasy, uptight. Bold, intrepid.
N	E	S	T	S	Plural of NEST.
N	E	T	T	Y	Netlike.
N	E	U	M	E	Symbol in music notation.
N	E	V	E	R	Not again, not at any time, at no time, not in any degree.
N	E	V	U	S	Pigmented area, birthmark, mole.
N	E	W	E	L	Newell post, cylindrical pillar, stairway post.
N	E	W	L	Y	Recently, afresh, anew, lately.
N	E	W	S	Y	Full of news. Given to gossip, given to news, interesting.
N	E	X	U	S	Link, tie, connection, bond, knot, ligature, yoke.
N	I	C	E	R	Comparative of NICE.
N	I	C	H	E	Cranny, nook, corner, recess.
N	I	D	A	L	Relating to NIDUS.
N	I	D	U	S	Insect nest, breeding place for germs, place of development, lodging, location.
N	I	E	C	E	Brother or sister's daughter. Relation, descendant.
N	I	F	F	Y	Smelly, odorous.
N	I	F	T	Y	Stylish, groovy, classy.
N	I	G	H	T	Dark part of solar day, Darkness, nightfall, evening, between dusk and dawn.
N	I	H	I	L	Nothing, none, nil, zero.
N	I	N	N	Y	Jerk, fool, gaumless, nitwit.
N	I	N	O	N	Sheer fabric, fabric for women's underclothing, curtaining.
N	I	N	T	H	One of nine equal parts. Following eight.
N	I	P	P	Y	Cold, chill, cool, frosty, icy, shivery, chilly, fast, zippy, alert.
N	I	S	S	E	Elf, fairy, sprite, pixie, goblin, brownie.
N	I	S	U	S	Striving, inclination, effort, endeavour.
N	I	T	R	E	NITER. Saltpeter, sodium nitrate, ethyl nitrate.
N	I	T	T	Y	Covered in nits, lousy, lice infested.
N	I	Z	A	M	Eastern ruler.
N	O	B	B	Y	Smart, stylish.
N	O	B	E	L	Inventor of dynamite. Originator of Prize.
N	O	B	L	E	Grand, august, majestic, stately, imposing, elevated, honourable, Moral.
N	O	B	L	Y	Magnificently, splendidly, self-effacingly.
N	O	D	A	L	Relating to NODES.
N	O	D	D	Y	Dunce, fool, dope, lame-brain, stupid, knucklehead, chump.
N	O	D	U	S	Complication, node, difficulty.
N	O	H	O	W	(Sl.) In no way, never.
N	O	I	L	S	Spun Fibres.
N	O	I	S	E	Din, uproar, pandemonium, racket, clamour. Gossip, blab. talk.
N	O	I	S	Y	Riotous, clangorous, rackety, uproarious, boisterous, tumultuous.
N	O	M	A	D	Wanderer, rover, wayfaring, vagrant. Desert wandering race.

1	2	3	4	5	
N	O	M	E	N	Name, appellation, denomination, designation, title, moniker.
N	O	M	I	C	Customary, conventional, ordinary.
N	O	N	C	E	Once only.
N	O	N	E	T	Combination of nine musical instruments or voices.
N	O	O	S	E	Loop, lariat, lasso, knotted rope. Scrag, string up, hang.
N	O	P	A	L	Prickly Pear.
N	O	R	M	A	Norm, rule, standard, model.
N	O	R	S	E	From Scandinavia. Norwegian.
N	O	R	T	H	Compass Point opposite South. On the left. Left of the meridian. Countries North.
N	O	S	E	D	Sniffed out, snooped, pried, scented, smelled.
N	O	S	E	Y	Inquisitive, curious, nosy, snoopy, prying.
N	O	T	A	L	Dorsal.
N	O	T	A	M	Pilot's information.
N	O	T	C	H	Nick, indentation, indenture, V-shaped depression. Rung.
N	O	T	E	D	Famous, notable, well-known, leading, prominent, popular, notorious.
N	O	T	E	S	Plural of NOTE.
N	O	V	E	L	New, recent, fresh, modern, fewfangled, singular. Book, fiction, record.
N	O	W	A	Y	In no event, never, nohow.
N	O	W	E	L	Foundary mould, mould for casting.
N	U	D	G	E	Jog, poke, dig, jab, prod.
N	U	R	S	E	Tender of the sick, nursemaid, nanny. Nourish, suckle, cherish, minister to.
N	U	T	T	Y	Having nuts, nut flavoured. Batty, dilly, zealous, enthusiastic, cracked.
N	Y	L	O	N	Synthetic material.
N	Y	M	P	H	Mythical minor divinity, Woman of loose morals, tart, floozy.
N	Y	X	I	S	Stabbing, pricking, puncture.

O

1	2	3	4	5	
O	A	K	E	N	Made of Oak. Stout, stalwart.
O	A	K	U	M	Twisted fibre for caulking and packing.
O	A	R	E	D	Rowed. Having oars.
O	A	S	I	S	Isolated fertile area in a desert. Place of refuge.
O	A	T	E	N	Made of oats, made of oatmeal.
O	A	T	H	S	Plural of OATH.
O	B	E	A	H	Use of sorcery, witchcraft. Charm, voodoo.
O	B	E	S	E	Corpulent, overweight, fat, bloated, fleshy, gross, heavy, portly, stout.
O	B	I	T	S	Plural of OBIT. Obituaries.
O	C	C	U	R	Happen, come to pass, take place. Appear, present itself. Come to mind.
O	C	E	A	N	Sea, body of salt water. Seaside. The deep, the main.
O	C	H	R	E	Yellow pigment.
O	C	T	A	D	Arrangement of eight.
O	C	T	E	T	Group of Eight.
O	D	D	L	Y	Peculiarly, strangely, curiously, erratically, unusually, quaintly.
O	D	E	U	M	Small theatre.
O	D	I	S	T	Write of Odes.
O	D	I	U	M	Hatred, enmity, subjected to widespread condomnation, disgrace, disrepute.
O	D	O	U	R	Smell, scent, perfume, fragrance, aroma.
O	F	F	A	L	Entrails, garbage, refuse, junk, trash, junk.
O	F	F	E	R	Proffer, tender, present, advance, attempt, display, extend, give.
O	F	L	A	G	German Officers' prison camp.
O	F	T	E	N	Frequently, repeatedly, many times.
O	G	L	E	D	Leered, eyed, goggled, stared, flirted.
O	G	L	E	R	One that OGLES.
O	G	L	E	S	Act of OGLING.
O	I	L	E	D	Lubricated, greased, intoxicated, inebriated.
O	I	L	E	R	Greaser, leather oiler, oilcan, oil well, oil tanker.
O	K	A	P	I	Giraffe-type animal.
O	L	D	E	N	Of old times, ancient, aged, antediluvian, elderly, old, venerable.
O	L	D	E	R	More elderly, not as young, senior.
O	L	E	U	M	Oily corrosive liquid.
O	L	E	Y	L	Derived from Oleyl alcohol.
O	L	I	V	E	Genus of Tree. Fruit from this tree. Drab green colour. Sallow.
O	L	O	G	Y	Science.
O	M	A	H	A	Nebraskan Indian.
O	M	B	R	E	Card game and player, self-shaded material, fabric design.
O	M	E	G	A	The last in order, ending, last letter of Greek Alphabet.

1	2	3	4	5	
O	M	E	N	S	Plural of OMEN.
O	N	C	E	R	Single performance.
O	N	I	O	N	Strong flavoured sharp-tasting edible bulb. Fleshy vegetable. Corn, shallot. Leek.
O	N	S	E	T	Beginning, commencement, dawning, start. Attack, assault, onslaught.
O	O	M	P	H	Dash, verve, life, vim, spirit, animation, sex appeal, zeal.
O	O	Z	E	D	Seeped, leaked, percolated, permeated bled, exuded.
O	P	E	R	A	Musical drama, theatrical production to music.
O	P	I	N	E	Opinion, opinionate, surmise, express choice, state an opinion.
O	P	I	U	M	Milky juice of the opium poppy plant. Durg, narcotic.
O	P	S	I	N	Colourless protein.
O	P	T	E	D	Chose, elected, decided.
O	P	T	I	C	Visual, optical, ocular, of the eye.
O	R	A	N	G	Orangutan, Ape.
O	R	A	T	E	Harangue, declaim, rant, sermonize, speechify, Spout.
O	R	B	E	D	Globular, round, spherical, eyed.
O	R	B	I	T	Range, radius, scope, sweep, extent, purview, ambit, circuit.
O	R	D	E	R	Command, decree. Association, type, disposition, sequence, type, breed. Succession, correctness.
O	R	E	A	D	Mountain nymph.
O	R	G	A	N	Musical instrument. Medium, means. Agency, channel. Journal, vehicle.
O	R	I	B	I	South African Antelope.
O	R	I	E	L	Bay Window.
O	R	I	O	N	Heavenly constellation. Cluster of stars.
O	R	L	O	N	Acrylic material, fabric.
O	R	L	O	P	Ship's low deck.
O	R	M	E	R	Abelone, shell.
O	R	R	I	S	Root of the Florentine Iris. Fragrant root. Gold or silver lace, braid.
O	R	T	E	T	Original plant from which clone is developed.
O	R	T	H	O	Derived from an acid, relating to diatomic molecule.
O	S	C	A	R	Award for artistic achievement in film making.
O	S	I	E	R	Willow, twigs for weaving.
O	T	H	E	R	Different, disparate, dissimilar, additional, fresh, new, more, further.
O	T	T	E	R	Fish-eating mammal, furry beaver type animal, fishing tackle.
O	U	G	H	T	Need, want, should, must, have. Obligation, commitment, duty.
O	U	I	J	A	Planchette, game played with the alphabet.
O	U	N	C	E	Unit of weight, portion, quantity, Snow leopard. Particle, dram, drop, smidgen.
O	U	T	D	O	Surpass, excel, overcome, exceed, defeat, eclipse.
O	U	T	E	R	External, outside, exterior, outward.
O	U	T	G	O	Outstrip, outlet, departure.
O	U	T	R	E	Bizarre, extravagant, unconventional.
O	U	Z	E	L	European blackbird. Other related birds. Thrush.
O	V	A	R	Y	Paired female reproductive organ.
O	V	A	T	E	Ovoid, ooid, oviform, oval, egg-shaped.
O	V	E	N	S	Plural of OVEN.
O	V	E	R	T	Open to view, manifest, apparent.
O	V	I	N	E	Relating to sheep.
O	V	I	S	M	Theory of embryos.
O	V	I	S	T	Believer in Ovism.
O	V	O	I	D	Ovate, egg-shaped.
O	V	U	L	A	Genus of marine snails.
O	V	U	L	E	Seed, small egg.
O	W	I	N	G	Outstanding, due, due to be rendered, attributable.
O	W	L	E	T	Young owl.
O	W	N	E	D	Belonged, possessed, held. Acceded, acknowledged.
O	W	N	E	R	Possessor, proprietor, holder.
O	X	B	O	W	Part of a harness. Yoke.
O	X	E	Y	E	Daisy, black-eyed Susan, field chamomile, sandpiper, plover.
O	X	I	D	E	Compound of oxygen with metallic elements. Rust.
O	X	L	I	P	Hybrid primrose.
O	Z	E	N	A	Disease of the nose. Unpleasant nasal passages.
O	Z	O	N	E	Pure and refreshing air. Sea air.

P

1	2	3	4	5	
P	A	C	E	D	Walked, stepped, trooped, tramped, timed, hurried.
P	A	C	E	R	Trotter, timer, pacemaker.
P	A	C	E	S	Plural of PACE.

1	2	3	4	5	
P	A	C	K	S	Plural of PACK.
P	A	D	D	Y	Temper, irritation, Irishman. Rice field.
P	A	D	R	E	Chaplain, priest, minister.
P	A	E	A	N	Exultant song, hymn of thanksgiving.
P	A	E	O	N	Poetic meter.
P	A	G	A	N	Heathen, unbeliever, idolator, infidel, profane, godless.
P	A	G	E	D	Leafed, skimmed, Summoned, located, tracked down, traced. Called.
P	A	G	E	S	Plural of PAGE.
P	A	I	N	S	Aches, suffering, distress, efforts, exertion, diligence, industry.
P	A	I	N	T	Pigmented concoction, coloured material, covering. Decorate, beautify, create art.
P	A	L	E	A	Husk. Chaffy scale.
P	A	L	E	D	Whitened, blanched, waned, sickened, became faint, weakened.
P	A	L	L	A	Women's dress of Ancient Rome.
P	A	L	L	S	Plural of PALL.
P	A	L	L	Y	Friendly, chummy, intimate, cosy.
P	A	L	M	Y	Bearing palms. Flourishing, prosperous, thriving.
P	A	L	P	I	Plural of PALPUS.
P	A	L	S	Y	Paralysis, condition of tremor, quivering. Nerve condition.
P	A	M	P	A	Grass covered plain.
P	A	N	D	A	Large mammal.
P	A	N	E	D	Made with panes of cloth. Panelled. Glazed, Glassed.
P	A	N	E	L	Group of persons grouped for discussion. Jury. Insert, flat box-face. Wall area.
P	A	N	G	S	Plural of PANG.
P	A	N	I	C	Fear, alarm, fright, terror, trepidation, consternation, hysteria.
P	A	N	K	S	Plural of PANK.
P	A	N	S	Y	Homosexual, effiminate youth. Garden flower, hybrid violet.
P	A	N	T	S	Trousers, shorts. Puffs, gasps.
P	A	P	A	L	Of Rome, popish, pontifical.
P	A	P	E	R	Compressed pulp containing rags, straw, wood, used for writing on, wrapping, etc. Newspaper.
P	A	P	P	Y	Soft, pulpy, yielding, mushy, squelchy, spongy, squashy, squishy.
P	A	R	C	H	Dry, dehydrate, sear, desiccate, shrivel, scorch.
P	A	R	E	D	Cut, clipped, shaved, pruned, skinned, stripped, reduced, cut back.
P	A	R	E	R	Trimmer, mechanical device for paring. Shaver.
P	A	R	G	E	Coat with plaster, provide with ornamental surface. Whitewash.
P	A	R	K	A	Hooded thigh-length pull-on garment. Windproof.
P	A	R	R	Y	Ward off, evade, turn aside, avert, prevent.
P	A	R	S	E	Analyse grammatically. Examine parts of speech. Dissect, anatomize.
P	A	R	T	S	Plural of PART.
P	A	R	T	Y	Gathering, funtime, combination, participant, person, company, orgy, debauchery.
P	A	S	H	A	Turkish ruler.
P	A	S	S	E	Out of date, faded, outworn, obsolete, superseded, belated, disused.
P	A	S	T	E	Sticky substance, pastry crust, dough. Stick, spread, adhere, beat, cuff, wack.
P	A	S	T	Y	Tasty pie, meatpie with crust, waxen, pale, unwell. Glutinous.
P	A	T	C	H	Mend, fix, repair, revamp, reconstruct. Square of material. Brach, link.
P	A	T	E	D	Type of head. Leather pated, addle pated.
P	A	T	E	R	Father, pop, pa, papa, sire, dad, daddy, governor, old man.
P	A	T	H	S	Plural of PATH.
P	A	T	I	O	Paved recreation area, paved yard, courtyard.
P	A	T	L	Y	Fluently, aptly, fitly, without hesitation.
P	A	T	T	E	A narrow band keeping a belt or sash in its place.
P	A	T	T	Y	Small pie, pasty.
P	A	T	S	Y	Scapegoat, whipping boy, chump, dupe, fall guy, sucker, victim.
P	A	U	S	E	Halt, temporary cessation, interval, gap, comma, lull, delay, hesitation.
P	A	V	E	D	Past of PAVE.
P	A	V	E	R	Paving stone layer. Concrete mixing machine.
P	A	V	E	S	Act of Paving.
P	A	V	I	D	Timid.
P	A	W	E	D	Touched, mauled, fingered, handled, palpated.
P	A	W	K	Y	Shrewd, crafty, sly, underhand.
P	A	W	N	S	Chessman. Plural of PAWN.
P	A	Y	E	E	The Receiver of what is offered or given. One who is paid.
P	A	Y	E	R	The one who PAYS.
P	E	A	C	E	Repose, freedom from clamour, harmony, quietude, accord.
P	E	A	C	H	Fruit. Inform, squeal, dandy, humdinger, beauty, lovely, sweetie.
P	E	A	K	S	Plural of PEAK.
P	E	A	K	Y	Seedy, pale, off-colour, sick. Acute, pointed, sharp.
P	E	A	L	S	Plural of PEAL.

1	2	3	4	5	
P	E	A	R	L	Lustrous secretion in molluscs. Round precious gem. Like a pearl. Bead.
P	E	A	R	T	Lively, Saucy, in good health and spirits.
P	E	A	S	E	A pudding.
P	E	A	T	Y	Like peat. Mossy, slimey.
P	E	C	A	N	Hard-shelled nut.
P	E	C	K	S	Plural of PECK.
P	E	D	A	L	Foot lever, treadle, brake, relating to foot movement. Rotate with feet. Cycle.
P	E	E	K	S	Plural of PEEK.
P	E	E	L	S	Plural of PEEL.
P	E	E	P	S	Plural of PEEP.
P	E	E	R	S	Plural of PEER.
P	E	E	R	Y	Curious, inquisitive, nosy, snoopy, prying.
P	E	E	V	E	Irritate, annoy. Grudge. Aggravate, provoke, rile.
P	E	G	G	Y	Small bird. Willow wren. Diminutive of Margaret.
P	E	K	O	E	Tea tips.
P	E	L	L	S	Rolls of parchment.
P	E	L	T	S	Plural of PELT.
P	E	N	A	L	Lawful, Punitive, penalty, disciplinary.
P	E	N	C	E	Coppers, pennies, money.
P	E	N	I	S	Male reproductive organ.
P	E	N	N	A	Quill feather.
P	E	N	N	Y	Coin of small denomination. Dimutive of Penelope.
P	E	O	N	Y	Herbaceous plant. Shrub.
P	E	R	C	H	Measurement of length. Pole. Bird rest. Land, alight, roost, sit down. Breed of fish.
P	E	R	D	U	Out of sight, concealed, hidden.
P	E	R	I	L	Danger, risk, jeopardy, menace, hazard.
P	E	R	K	Y	Brisk, zippy, lively, smart, bright.
P	E	R	R	Y	Expressed fermented juice of Pears.
P	E	S	K	Y	Vexatious, annoying, irritating, troublesome.
P	E	S	T	S	Plural of PEST.
P	E	T	A	L	Flower leaf, coloured unit of a corolla. To cover with petals.
P	E	T	E	R	Peter out, subside, dwindle, decrease, abate, lessen, fade. Whist signal.
P	E	T	I	T	Small, compact, insignificant, trifling, secondary.
P	E	T	R	E	Saltpetre.
P	E	T	T	Y	Trivial, small minded, trifling, little, minor, insignificant, puny, paltry.
P	E	W	I	T	Lapwing, peewit, laughing gull.
P	H	A	S	E	Aspect, facet, angle, appearance, look, posture, view, viewpoint.
P	H	E	N	E	Benzene derivatives.
P	H	I	A	L	Small glass bottle, vial, container for liquids.
P	H	L	O	X	Genus of Herb with variegated flowers.
P	H	O	N	E	Sound and voice transmitting device. Telephone, Earphone. To contact by phone.
P	H	O	T	O	Negative or positive imagery produced on sensitive surface by light.
P	H	R	E	N	Diaphragm, mind, phrenic nerve.
P	H	Y	L	A	Plural of PHYLUM.
P	H	Y	M	A	Nodule, external swelling, tumor.
P	H	Y	S	A	Air-breathing freshwater snails.
P	I	A	N	O	Pianoforte, musical keyboard, performed softly, quietly.
P	I	C	K	S	Plural of PICK.
P	I	C	K	Y	Choosy, pernickety, finnicky, fussy, particular, dainty, fastidious.
P	I	C	O	T	Loops forming an edging, hemstitching.
P	I	C	U	S	Genus of Woodpecker.
P	I	E	C	E	Division, part, portion, section, segment.
P	I	E	T	A	Representation of the Holy Mother.
P	I	E	T	Y	Devotion, faithfulness, fidelity, sanctity, fervor, holiness, zeal.
P	I	G	M	Y	See Pygmy.
P	I	K	E	D	Pointed, acute, peaked, sharp, peaky, spiked.
P	I	K	E	R	Vagabond, tramp, miser, drifter, bum, skinflint, tightwad.
P	I	K	L	E	Barnyard.
P	I	L	A	F	Pilau, concoction of meat and vegetables with rice.
P	I	L	E	D	Heaped, stacked, amassed, lumped, climbed, flopped, covered in fur.
P	I	L	E	S	One who piles. Stacker. Haemorrhoids.
P	I	L	O	T	Airman, flier, aviator, conductor, leader. Guide, conduct, escort, lead.
P	I	M	P	S	Plural of PIMP.
P	I	N	C	H	Squeeze, scrimp, extort, steal, contingency, theft. Arrest.
P	I	N	E	D	Longed for, yearned, craved, hankered, hungered, languished.
P	I	N	E	S	Plural of PINE.
P	I	N	K	S	Plural of PINK.

1	2	3	4	5	
P	I	N	K	Y	Tinged with pink. Little finger.
P	I	N	N	Y	Apron, pinafore.
P	I	N	T	A	Skin disease.
P	I	N	T	O	Piebald horse.
P	I	N	U	P	Glamourous cut-out.
P	I	O	U	S	Devout, holy, religious, godly.
P	I	P	E	D	Seam finished with binding. Sent by pipe. Decorated. Called in high-pitched tone.
P	I	P	E	R	Player of Bagpipes. One who pipes.
P	I	P	E	S	Plural of PIPE.
P	I	P	I	T	Small song bird.
P	I	Q	U	E	Annoyance, vexation, offense, huff, umbrage, exasperation. Provoke, irritate.
P	I	T	C	H	Throw, toss, cast. Fall, plunge, lurch. Colour black. Spiel, line. Wade in, begin.
P	I	T	H	Y	To the point, terse, concise, brief, meaty, effective, forceful, meaningful.
P	I	T	O	N	Iron spike, wedge, peg.
P	I	V	O	T	Hinge, axis. Turn, wheel, whirl, swing, sway. Heart, centre.
P	I	X	I	E	Fairy, elf, sprite, scamp, rascal.
P	I	Z	Z	A	Italian savoury.
P	L	A	C	E	Site, location, spot, position, locality, area, region, identify. Status, estimate.
P	L	A	I	D	Tartan.
P	L	A	I	N	Not fancy, homely, modest, simple, unadorned. Straight, clear, frank. Ordinary.
P	L	A	I	T	Braid, pigtail, pleat, weave, intertwine.
P	L	A	N	E	Aeroplane. Level, even, flat, smooth. Flatten, smooth. Tree. Tool.
P	L	A	N	K	Timber strip, flat wood. Plonk.
P	L	A	N	T	Sew, prepare for growth. Factory, bury, inter. Machinery, Seedling.
P	L	A	S	H	Slop, spatter, splash, douse, splatter. Surface agitation, puddle.
P	L	A	T	E	Dish, container. Silverware. Flat metal, Plaque. Armour, Baseball square. Overlay with metal. Cover.
P	L	A	T	O	Ancient Greek. Wise man. Sage.
P	L	A	Y	S	Plural of PLAY.
P	L	A	Z	A	Paved open area, public square, market place.
P	L	E	A	D	Beg, entreat, supplicate, appeal, implore.
P	L	E	A	S	Plural of PLEA.
P	L	E	A	T	Fold. tuck. Plait, crease.
P	L	E	B	S	Plural of PLEB.
P	L	I	C	A	Fold, crease, wrinkle, furrow, ruck.
P	L	I	E	D	Traded, Exercised, exerted. Layered, folded.
P	L	I	N	K	Tinkle, tingle, ting, clink.
P	L	O	T	S	Plural of PLOT.
P	L	O	Y	S	Plural of PLOY.
P	L	U	C	K	Courage, guts, heart, spirit, spunk. Animal innards. Offal. Pick, uplift.
P	L	U	G	S	Plural of PLUG.
P	L	U	M	B	Exactly, directly, sound, weigh, measure depth, ascertain quality, downright.
P	L	U	M	E	Feather, deck, array, crest, plumage, ornamentation. Pride, preen.
P	L	U	M	P	Chubby, fat, corpulent, rotund, pudgy, tubby, portly.
P	L	U	M	Y	Adorned with feathers, plumed, feathery.
P	L	U	M	S	Plural of PLUM.
P	L	U	S	H	Rich, luxurious, opulent, palatial, deluxe.
P	O	A	C	H	Cook in liquid, take game illegally. Intrude, encroach.
P	O	C	K	Y	Pitted, blemished.
P	O	D	E	X	Anal region. Rump. Buttocks, backside, rearend.
P	O	D	G	E	Pudge. Fatty.
P	O	D	G	Y	Pudgy, roly-poly, overweight.
P	O	E	M	S	Plural of POEM.
P	O	E	S	Y	Poetry, poems, poetic composition.
P	O	E	T	S	Plural of POET.
P	O	I	L	U	French soldier.
P	O	I	N	T	Detail, item. Characteristic, force, validity, subject, argument. Brink, verge, edge, cusp, tip,
P	O	I	S	E	Balance, equilibrium, aplomb, self-confidence, dignity, serenity.
P	O	K	E	D	Past of POKE.
P	O	K	E	R	Straight metal rod, Game of cards.
P	O	K	E	S	Plural of POKE.
P	O	K	E	Y	Prison, jail, lockup, cooler, stir, can.
P	O	L	A	R	Opposite, antipodal, contradictory, reverse, diametric, counter.
P	O	L	I	O	Disease. Infantile paralysis. Poliomyelitis.
P	O	L	K	A	Lively dance, jig.
P	O	L	L	Y	Parrot.
P	O	L	Y	P	Swollen mucous membrane.
P	O	N	D	S	Plural of POND.

1	2	3	4	5	
P	O	N	D	Y	Full of ponds, marshy.
P	O	N	G	O	Genus of Anthropoid apes. Orangutan. Englishman living in Africa.
P	O	O	C	H	Dog.
P	O	O	L	S	Plural of POOL.
P	O	P	P	Y	Herb, Flower. Medicine producing plant. Opium producer.
P	O	R	C	H	Verandah, portico, stoep, balcony, enclosure.
P	O	R	E	D	Examined in detail, studied. Full of pores.
P	O	R	G	Y	Fish.
P	O	R	K	Y	Obese, overweight, pudgy. Oily, greasy, unctuous. Piglike.
P	O	R	T	S	Plural of PORT.
P	O	S	E	D	Postured, offered, proposed, questioned. Masqueraded.
P	O	S	E	R	One who poses. Query, question.
P	O	S	E	S	Plural of POSE.
P	O	S	I	T	Position, fix, postulate. Presuppose, premise.
P	O	S	S	E	Body of police, detachment of lawmen, throng, crowd.
P	O	S	T	S	Plural of POST.
P	O	T	T	O	African Lemur.
P	O	T	T	Y	Little, minor, petty, small. Dilly, dotty. Chamber.
P	O	U	C	H	Receptacle, wallet, pocket, sac. Bulge, overhang, protrude, project.
P	O	U	L	E	Call girl, hooker, hustler, prostitute.
P	O	U	L	T	Young fowl.
P	O	U	N	D	Unit of money. Unit of weight. Enclosure, pen. Hammer, beat, buffet, impress.
P	O	U	T	S	Plural of POUT.
P	O	U	T	Y	Sulky. Protruding.
P	O	W	E	R	Might, control, domination, energy, force, muscle, strength. Government.
P	R	A	N	G	Crash, forced landing, pile-up. Collide, wreck, bump.
P	R	A	N	K	Joke, antic, frolic, trick, escapade, caper. Decorate, prink, embellish.
P	R	A	T	E	Jabber, chatter, gabble, blabber, waffle, boast, brag, yak.
P	R	A	W	N	Decapod crustacean. Culinary delicacy.
P	R	A	Y	S	Intercedes, begs, requests, appeals, beseeches, importunes, supplicates.
P	R	E	E	N	Dress, trim, primp. Smooth feathers, clean plumage. Pride, plume.
P	R	E	S	S	Hold tightly. Squeeze, crush, depress, push, embrace, cram, tamp, News media.
P	R	I	C	E	Cost, rate, tariff, rate, value, charge, Tag, Tab.
P	R	I	C	K	Puncture, stab, pierce, stand erect, thrust, urge, primp.
P	R	I	C	Y	Expensive, costly, valuable.
P	R	I	D	E	Collection of Lions. Conceit, egoism, arrogance, dignity, proudness, preen.
P	R	I	E	D	Spied, snooped, meddled, peeped, examined slyly.
P	R	I	E	R	One who PRIES.
P	R	I	E	S	Act of PRYING.
P	R	I	G	S	Proud, full of pride, arrogant, disdainful, insolent, overbearing, superior.
P	R	I	G	S	Plural of PRIG.
P	R	I	M	A	First, leading, first word in galley proof, Resuming word.
P	R	I	M	E	Primary, first, excellent, best, choice, youth, daybreak, motivate, stimulate.
P	R	I	M	O	Leading part (in duet).
P	R	I	M	P	Prink, preen, plume, dress up, spruce up, smarten up.
P	R	I	N	K	Primp, preen, prance, strut, sashay, flounce, dress up, spruce up.
P	R	I	N	T	Stamp, impress, impression, indentation, brand, publish, photographic copy. Floral fabric.
P	R	I	O	R	Before, previous, ahead, preceding, anterior, former, foregoing.
P	R	I	S	E	Ease off, lift, lever, prize, jemmy.
P	R	I	S	M	Tri-faced crystal form, transparent body, light reflector.
P	R	I	V	Y	Personal, private, hidden, concealed. Outside toilet, closet, convenience, latrine.
P	R	I	Z	E	Reward, booty, spoil, dividend, choice, best, appreciate, cherish, esteem.
P	R	O	B	E	Investigate, delve, explore, inquire, Inquisition, quest, research. Instrument.
P	R	O	D	S	Plural of PROD.
P	R	O	E	M	Introduction, preface, prelude, prologue, preamble.
P	R	O	N	E	Likely, liable to, apt to. Flat, face-down. Willing, inclined, predisposed, ready.
P	R	O	N	G	Fork, pointed part, antler point, branch, spur. Stab, pierce.
P	R	O	O	F	Galley, testimony, attestation, testament, reason, grounds, argument.
P	R	O	P	S	Plural of PROP. Theatrical properties.
P	R	O	S	E	Non-verse writing, prosaic, ordinary language, matter-of-fact, literary medium.
P	R	O	S	Y	Common place, prosaic, tedious, boring. Colourless, drab, lifeless.
P	R	O	U	D	Prideful, vain, stately, arrogant, pompous, splendid, glorious, superb.
P	R	O	V	E	Attest, verify, demonstrate, test, try. Raise dough, test alcohol.
P	R	O	W	L	Roam, wander, pace restlessly, stalk, rove, prey.
P	R	O	X	Y	Substitute, stand-in, deputy, power of attorney, procurator.
P	R	U	D	E	Inhibited person, priggish person, puritan, fuddy-duddy, fusspot, stuffed shirt.
P	R	U	N	E	Dried plum. Unattractive or dull person, dunce, blockhead, Trim, crop, pare.

1	2	3	4	5	
P	S	A	L	M	Hymn of praise, sacred song, Eulogy, glorification, magnification.
P	S	H	A	W	Exclamation.
P	U	B	E	S	Public region. Lower hypogastric region. Hair appearing at puberty.
P	U	B	I	C	Relating to the pubes or pubis. In that region. Loin, genital area.
P	U	B	I	S	Pelvic area.
P	U	D	G	Y	Fleshy, fat, podgy, stout, chubby, plump, tubby, stumpy.
P	U	F	F	Y	Swollen, pudgy, pompous, breathless, short-winded, gusty.
P	U	K	E	D	Vomited, threw up, shicked, heaved, spat.
P	U	K	K	A	Real, genuine, authentic, complete, indubitable, true.
P	U	L	E	D	Muled, whined, whimpered.
P	U	L	E	R	Squealer, whimperer.
P	U	L	E	X	Common flea.
P	U	L	P	Y	Soft, spongy, mushy, squashy, succulent.
P	U	L	S	E	Beat, throb, palpitate, pulsate. Distention in arteries. Leguminous seeds. Peas.
P	U	M	P	S	Plural of PUMP. Dancing shoes,delicate footwear.
P	U	N	C	H	Box, swat, clout, cuff. Vigor, drive, pep. Effectiveness, validity, cogency.
P	U	N	I	C	Treacherous, faithless, doub-crossing.
P	U	P	A	L	Characteristic of a PUPA.
P	U	P	I	L	Scholar, student, school child, learner. Aperture in iris of the eye.
P	U	P	P	Y	Small dog, whelp.
P	U	R	E	E	Thick paste. Liquidized vegetables.
P	U	R	E	R	Cleaner, more pure, chaster, holier.
P	U	R	G	E	Cleanse, purify, expurgate, eliminate, eject, expel, absolve.
P	U	R	S	E	Receptacle, bag, pocket book, wallet, pouch. Resource, funds. Scrotum.
P	U	R	S	Y	Corpulent, fleshy, gross, fat, overweight, weighty, obese.
P	U	S	H	Y	Aggressive, pushing, self-assertive, presumptuous, forward, presuming.
P	U	S	S	Y	Kitty, small cat. Catkin of pussy willow. Full of pus.
P	U	T	T	Y	Cement with linseed oil. Builder's adhesive.
P	U	T	U	P	Preserve, Rouse, Offer, Pin hair, stake, accommodate, build, exhibit, give.
P	Y	G	M	Y	Miniature, small person, dwarf, gnome, pixie. Midget.
P	Y	L	O	N	Post, tower, rigid structure, gateway.
P	Y	R	I	C	Relating to burning.
P	Y	R	U	S	Clustered flower stalks. Pear genus.
P	Y	X	I	S	Ornately decorated container.

Q

1	2	3	4	5	
Q	U	A	C	K	Charlatan, counterfeiter, pretender, humbug. Boaster. Duck's cry.
Q	U	A	D	S	Quadruplets.
Q	U	A	F	F	Imbibe, sip, swallow, drink, gulp.
Q	U	A	I	L	Cower, recoil, flinch, shrink, wince, cringe. Bird. Girl, gal, lass.
Q	U	A	K	E	Shiver, shake, tremble, vibrate, Tremor, Earthquake, shock.
Q	U	A	K	Y	Shaky, trembling, tremulous, quivering, shivering.
Q	U	A	L	E	Independent quality.
Q	U	A	L	M	Misgiving, fear, scruple, pang, scruple, suspicion, foreboding, insecurity.
Q	U	A	N	T	Punting pole. Quantum.
Q	U	A	R	T	Measurement of quantity.
Q	U	A	S	H	Annul, dissolve, vacate, abolish, abrogate, negate, nullify, vitiate, crush.
Q	U	A	S	I	Seemingly, almost, resembling, seeming, virtual.
Q	U	E	A	N	Disreputable woman. Prostitute. Bawd, hooker, hustler. Whore.
Q	U	E	E	N	Married to a king. Female ruler, woman monarch. Beauty contest winner. Privileged piece in Chess.
Q	U	E	E	R	Odd, off-beat, strange, bizzare, questionable, funny. Homosexual.
Q	U	E	L	L	Suppress, quash, extinguish, crush, put down.
Q	U	E	R	Y	Question, inquire, ask. Doubt, uncertainty, suspicion, dispute.
Q	U	E	S	T	Search, pursuit, pursuance, seeking.
Q	U	E	U	E	Line up, Wait in orderly fashion, File, Rank, row, line.
Q	U	I	C	K	Speedy, fast, rapid, swift, brisk. Nimble. Alive, sharp, alert.
Q	U	I	E	T	Peace, calm, lull, stillness, silence, quietude, hushed, placid, inactive, subdued.
Q	U	I	F	F	Puff of smoke, forelock of hair (sl.) girl, woman.
Q	U	I	L	L	Bird's feather. Pen, spindle, hollow shaft, stem, plectrum, Wind.
Q	U	I	L	T	Bedspread, bedcover, padded blanket, patchword bedcover.
Q	U	I	N	S	Quintuplets.
Q	U	I	N	T	An organ-stop a fifth above the foundation stops: the E string of a violin.
Q	U	I	R	E	Quantity of paper.
Q	U	I	R	K	Peculiarity, mannerism, turn, twist, curve, bend, quip, subterfuge.
Q	U	I	R	T	Riding whip. To strike, coerce, drive with a quirt.

1	2	3	4	5	
Q	U	I	T	E	Absolutely, totally, rather, completely, fully, exactly, pretty much.
Q	U	I	T	S	Leaves, departs, relieves, releases, conducts, acquits.
Q	U	O	I	N	Angle, wedge, corner.
Q	U	O	I	T	Flattened rope ring. Used in deck game.
Q	U	O	T	A	Allowance, share, allotment, cut, portion, slice, ration, number.
Q	U	O	T	E	Make reference, repetition, repeat, adduce, cite, mention. Current Price.

R

1	2	3	4	5	
R	A	B	B	I	Master, Jewish Teacher.
R	A	B	I	C	Relating to Rabies.
R	A	B	I	D	Having Rabies. Raging, virulent, furious, violent.
R	A	C	E	S	Plural of RACE.
R	A	C	E	D	Past of RACE.
R	A	C	E	R	One who RACES.
R	A	C	K	S	Plural of RACK.
R	A	C	O	N	Radar beacon.
R	A	D	A	R	Radio detecting device.
R	A	D	I	I	Plural of Radius.
R	A	D	I	O	Transmission and reception of electric impulses. Signals. Broadcasting instrument.
R	A	D	I	X	Radicle, root.
R	A	F	T	S	Plural of RAFT.
R	A	G	E	D	Past of RAGE. Stormed, fumed, raved, seethed.
R	A	G	E	S	Plural of RAGE.
R	A	I	D	S	Plural of RAID.
R	A	I	L	S	Plural of RAIL.
R	A	I	N	Y	Wet, showery, stormy.
R	A	I	S	E	Lift, elevate, erect, build, uplift, exalt, breed, incite, grow, increase.
R	A	J	A	H	Silk clothing fabric.
R	A	K	E	D	Past of RAKE.
R	A	K	E	R	One who rakes.
R	A	K	E	S	Plural of RAKE.
R	A	L	L	Y	Gathering, get together. Rouse, muster, stir, recover, perkup, deride, mock.
R	A	M	A	L	Relating to RAMUS.
R	A	M	A	N	Relating to RAMA.
R	A	M	O	N	Breadnut.
R	A	M	P	S	Plural of RAMP.
R	A	M	U	S	Ramification, part of Jaw. Feather barb.
R	A	N	C	H	Farm, Animal grazing establishment. Range. Work on a farm.
R	A	N	D	S	Plural of RAND. S.A. Currency.
R	A	N	D	Y	Lecherous, lustful, sexually excited. Licentious, lewd, libertine.
R	A	N	E	E	Rani. Indian Princess.
R	A	N	G	E	Wander, drift, ramble, align, line up, classify, incline, predispose, Scope.
R	A	N	G	Y	Tall, thin, long, slender, loose-limbed, gangling.
R	A	N	K	S	Plural of RANK.
R	A	N	T	Y	Ill-tempered, loud, boisterous, vociferous, bombastic.
R	A	P	E	D	Outraged, overpowered, sexually assaulted, violated.
R	A	P	I	D	Fast, quick, hasty, swift, nimble, speedy, expeditiously. Fast flowing river.
R	A	R	E	R	More rare, thinner, fewer, scarcer, exceptional, less frequent.
R	A	S	P	Y	Grating, scratchy, harsh, scraping, rough, abrasive.
R	A	T	E	D	Priced, quoted, estimated, assessed, evaluated, earned, taxed.
R	A	T	E	L	Badger-like mammal.
R	A	T	E	R	Estimator, assessor, evaluator.
R	A	T	E	S	Plural of RATE.
R	A	T	I	O	Proportion, quota, number, scale, degree, rate.
R	A	T	T	Y	Ill-tempered, irritable, vexed, irascible, cranky, cross, touchy, testy.
R	A	V	E	D	Ranted, raged, argued, enthused, harangued, declaimed.
R	A	V	E	L	Entangle, twist, complicate, muddle, snarl, perplex.
R	A	V	E	N	Black, dark, inky, Large Black Crow-like bird.
R	A	V	E	R	Maniac, ranter, enthusiast.
R	A	W	L	Y	Coarsely, uncouthly, green, unskilfully, immaturely, unfinished, unpolished.
R	A	Y	O	N	Artificial silk fabric.
R	A	Z	O	R	Cutting device used for shaving. Sharp edged.
R	E	A	C	H	Arrive, come, accomplish, achieve, contact, ken, horizon, range, purview.
R	E	A	C	T	Recoil, function, behave, resist, return, recur, operate.
R	E	A	D	Y	Fit, prepared, set, qualified, willing, prompt, dynamic, fortify, gird.

1	2	3	4	5	
R	E	A	L	M	Domain, territory, range, dimension, extent, radius, scope.
R	E	A	R	M	Fit out again, re-equip, regain armaments.
R	E	B	E	L	Aanarchist, insurgent, malcontent, radical, revolt, mutiny, insurrect.
R	E	B	I	D	Bid again.
R	E	B	U	S	Picture symbols, riddles.
R	E	B	U	T	Rebuff, repulse, confound, refute, repel.
R	E	C	A	P	Describe again briefly, rename.
R	E	C	C	E	Reconnaisance, search.
R	E	C	T	O	Writ of right, right-hand page, front cover.
R	E	C	U	R	Occur again, revert, repeat.
R	E	D	A	N	Fortification.
R	E	D	L	Y	Suffused, glowingly, ardently, fervidly, hotly, blushingly.
R	E	D	Y	E	Recolour. Dye again.
R	E	E	D	S	Plural of REED.
R	E	E	D	Y	Thin, high-pitched, squeaky, slight, slender, tenuous, stalky.
R	E	E	F	Y	Rocky, full of reefs.
R	E	E	K	S	Smells, stinks.
R	E	E	K	Y	Malodourous, rancid, reeking, stinking, rank, fetid.
R	E	E	L	S	Plural of REEL.
R	E	E	V	E	Thread, handle rope. Female Ruff (bird).
R	E	F	E	R	Assign, ascribe, submit, allude, point, specify, name. Resort.
R	E	F	I	T	Fit out again. Re-equip, repair.
R	E	F	I	X	Fix again.
R	E	G	A	L	Royal, majestic, sovereign, august, imposing, stately, splendid.
R	E	I	C	H	German government.
R	E	I	G	N	Rule, govern, control.
R	E	I	N	S	Plural of RHEIN.
R	E	L	A	X	Rest, unbend, loosen, ease, unwind, feel at home, cool off, slacken, loosen.
R	E	L	A	Y	Carry, pass on, circuit, race, pass signal, stage, lay again.
R	E	L	E	T	Re-hire, offer again.
R	E	L	I	C	Remains, momento, souvenir, keepsake. Rememberance, token.
R	E	L	I	T	Re-kindled. Lit again. Relighted.
R	E	M	I	T	Consign, transmit, pay, defer, replace, resign, remand, surrender.
R	E	N	A	L	Of the kidneys.
R	E	N	D	S	Plural of REND.
R	E	N	E	W	Refurbish, restore, renovate, refresh, modernize, update, revise, revive.
R	E	N	T	E	French annual income from rents. Annuity. Government interest.
R	E	P	A	Y	Pay back, compensate, indemnify, reimburse, refund, recompense.
R	E	P	E	L	Fend off, rebuff, repulse, resist, dispute, disgust, revolt, sicken.
R	E	P	L	Y	Answer, respond, rejoin, retort, return, Rejoinder, response, antiphon.
R	E	P	O	T	Transplant, rearrange, transpose.
R	E	S	E	T	Reprint, readjust, renew.
R	E	S	I	N	Plant secretion, extract, solvent, plastic substance, rosin, polymer, cellulose.
R	E	S	O	W	Replant, rescatter, reseed.
R	E	S	T	S	Plural of REST.
R	E	S	T	Y	Restive, sluggish, indolent.
R	E	T	C	H	Vomit, throw up, heave.
R	E	T	R	O	Backward, back, situated behind, retrograde.
R	E	V	E	L	Frolic, roister, carouse, bask, luxuriate. Festivity, Merrymaking, revelry.
R	E	V	U	E	Song and dance, theatrical entertainment. Medleys, Variety.
R	H	E	U	M	Mucous, watery discharge.
R	H	I	N	E	Ditch, runnel.
R	H	I	N	O	Cash, money. Rhinoceros. Motorised pontoon.
R	H	O	M	B	Spinning top, magical wheel.
R	H	Y	M	E	Poem, verse, song, rhythm, agree, correspond, dovetail. Poetry.
R	I	A	N	T	Pleasing, mirthful, gay, laughing, merry, jovial.
R	I	B	B	Y	Show ribs.
R	I	B	E	S	Genus of Shrubs, small coloured flowers.
R	I	D	E	R	Horseman, appendix, codicil, supplement, addendum.
R	I	D	G	E	Ledge, furrow, ruck, fold, wrinkle, corrugation, crease, rivel, crest.
R	I	D	G	Y	Furrowy, crested, corrugated.
R	I	F	L	E	Fire arm. Ransack, rob, loot, plunder, strip.
R	I	F	T	S	Plural of RIFT.
R	I	G	H	T	True, faithful, correct, precise, authentic, sane, healthy, decent, direct.
R	I	G	I	D	Strict, stiff, unbending, inflexible, adamant, stern, rigorous, austere.
R	I	G	O	R	Rigidity, rigour, asperity, hardship, austerity, difficulty, asperity, trial. Chill.
R	I	L	E	D	Angered, annoyed, upset, provoked, nettled, peeved, piqued.

1	2	3	4	5	
R	I	M	E	D	Frosted, cracked, caked, encrusted.
R	I	N	D	S	Plural of RIND.
R	I	N	D	Y	With skin or peel.
R	I	N	G	S	Plural of RING.
R	I	N	K	S	Plural of RINK.
R	I	N	S	E	Apply water, cleanse, douche, douse, wash, drench.
R	I	O	T	S	Plural of RIOT.
R	I	P	E	N	Mature, develop, age, mellow, grow, perfect, maturate, improve.
R	I	P	E	R	Comparative of RIPE. More ripe.
R	I	S	E	N	Ascended, mounted, boosted, increased, upgraded, augmented, raised.
R	I	S	E	R	Insurgent, rebel, stair slope, printing block, parachute strap.
R	I	S	K	S	Plural of RISK.
R	I	S	K	Y	Dangerous, hazardous, perilous, treacherous, precarious, unsound.
R	I	T	Z	Y	Plush, luxurious, showy, ostentatious.
R	I	V	A	L	Competitor, contestant, adversary, opponent, antagonist. Compete, vie, contend.
R	I	V	E	L	Wrinkle, crease, fold, ridge, ruck, furrow.
R	I	V	E	R	Natural surface, body of water, tributary, watercourse, straight.
R	I	V	E	T	Pin, bolt, fastener. Affix, attachment, focus.
R	O	A	C	H	Freshwater fish, hair roll, horse's mane, cockroach.
R	O	A	D	S	Plural of ROAD.
R	O	A	M	S	Plural of ROAM.
R	O	A	R	S	Plural of ROAR.
R	O	A	S	T	Broil, bake, cook, burn, scorch, swelter, Excoriate, flay, lash, lambaste with flay or tongue.
R	O	B	E	D	Dressed, garbed, arrayed, attired.
R	O	B	I	N	Songbird, Roundelay. Redbreast.
R	O	B	O	T	Automaton, android, machine.
R	O	C	K	S	Plural of ROCK.
R	O	C	K	Y	Full of rocks, stony, uneven, shaky, unsteady, unstable.
R	O	D	E	O	Roundup. Horse breaking performance, roping contest.
R	O	G	E	R	Message acknowledgement, Jolly Roger.
R	O	G	U	E	Villain, miscreant, rascal, scoundrel, swindler, cheat, scamp.
R	O	L	E	S	Plural of ROLE.
R	O	L	L	S	Plural of ROLL. Abbreviation of Rolls Royce.
R	O	L	L	Y	Turbulent, muddy, turbid.
R	O	K	E	R	Thornback Ray.
R	O	M	A	N	Native of Rome. Christian of Ancient Rome. Catholic. Upright lettering.
R	O	M	E	O	Gallant, casanova, paramour, lover.
R	O	N	D	E	Round script.
R	O	N	D	O	Verse form, instrumental composition, dance composition, gambling game.
R	O	O	K	S	Plural of ROOK.
R	O	O	M	S	Plural of ROOM.
R	O	O	M	Y	Spacious, large, capacious, wide, ample, commodious.
R	O	O	S	T	Hen house, perch. Lodging, Rookery, Alight, settle, domicile, house.
R	O	O	T	S	Plural of ROOT.
R	O	O	T	Y	Full of Roots, similar to Roots.
R	O	P	E	D	Tied, lashed, bound, confined, fastened, connected.
R	O	S	I	N	Resin.
R	O	S	E	S	Plural of ROSE.
R	O	T	O	R	Revolving part, rotating member.
R	O	U	G	E	Cosmetic, red, pink blush, colour, crimson, glow, redden.
R	O	U	G	H	Uneven, coarse, harsh, rude, tight, tough, wild, stormy, crude, uncouth.
R	O	U	N	D	Circular, rotund, globular, spherical, Rotund, nearly, almost, about, near.
R	O	U	S	E	Waken, disturb, stir, animate, intensify, provoke, challenge, kindle.
R	O	U	T	E	Path, way, road, course, itinerary, passage, Consign, transmit, despatch.
R	O	V	E	D	Wandered, roamed, rambled, drifted, meandered, ranged, strayed.
R	O	V	E	R	Wanderer, ranger, drifter, nomad, tramp. A boy scout 18 years or older.
R	O	W	A	N	Tree.
R	O	W	D	Y	Noisy, unruly, vulgar, boisterous, turbulent. Tough, punk, ruffian.
R	O	W	E	D	Propelled, paddled, skulled, scolded, berated, jawed, quarrelled.
R	O	W	E	L	Spur, goad.
R	O	W	E	R	Oarsman, boatman.
R	O	Y	A	L	Regal, kingly, majestic, sovereign, grand, august, excellent, prime.
R	U	A	D	E	Bucking, ski turn.
R	U	B	O	R	Redness of skin. Inflammation.
R	U	C	H	E	Trim, gather.
R	U	C	K	S	Plural of RUCK.
R	U	D	D	Y	Red, glowing, healthy, flushed, blowsy.

1	2	3	4	5	
R	U	D	E	R	Comparative of RUDE. More rude.
R	U	G	B	Y	Football game. Town in England. Famous School.
R	U	I	N	G	Regretting, lamenting, repenting, commiserating, sympathising.
R	U	L	E	D	Lined, guided, governed, reigned, dominated, determined, judged.
R	U	L	E	R	Monarch, King, government, regent, dictator. Drawing device.
R	U	M	B	A	Lively dance.
R	U	M	M	Y	Card game, queer, peculiar, strange, odd, bizzarre, curious, eccentric.
R	U	M	O	R	American form of rumour.
R	U	N	G	S	Plural of RUNG.
R	U	N	I	C	Secret, magical, ancient mythology.
R	U	N	I	N	Confrontation. Finish. Encounter, skirmish, quarrel, dispute.
R	U	N	N	Y	Liquid, watery.
R	U	N	O	N	Babble, chatter, gabble.
R	U	N	T	Y	Stunted, runted, scrawny, lesser.
R	U	P	E	E	Monetary unit.
R	U	R	A	L	Pastoral, countrified, bucolic, provincial rustic, idyllic, simple, modest.
R	U	S	H	Y	Covered in rushes.
R	U	S	T	Y	Corroded, blemished. Harsh, hoarse, dyspeptic. Out of practice.
R	U	T	T	Y	Uneven, grooved, furrowed, lustful, concupiscent, lascivious, horny.
R	Y	D	E	R	Old gold coin.

S

S	A	B	L	E	Antelope, Pine Martin, Heraldic Black, dusky, sombre.
S	A	B	O	T	Wooden work shoe.
S	A	B	R	E	Military sword.
S	A	D	L	Y	Mournfully, gloomily, dismally, melancholic, dolefully, drearily, sorrowfully.
S	A	F	E	R	More safe, surer, securely.
S	A	G	A	N	Jewish Priest.
S	A	G	A	S	Plural of SAGA. Adventures.
S	A	G	E	R	Wiser, cleverer, saner, more scholarly.
S	A	H	I	B	Master, Sir.
S	A	I	L	Y	Full of sail.
S	A	I	N	T	Holy person, canonised person. Good man.
S	A	I	T	H	Says.
S	A	L	A	D	Miscellany, mixture, melange, cold collation.
S	A	L	E	P	Starchy food, tapioca.
S	A	L	E	S	Plural of SALE.
S	A	L	I	C	Pertaining to Salian (salic law).
S	A	L	I	X	Type of Tree, WIlllow, Populus.
S	A	L	L	E	Sorting room, hall, salon.
S	A	L	L	Y	Leap out, rush, issue suddenly. Outburst, Spring, bound.
S	A	L	M	I	Game stew.
S	A	L	O	N	Reception Rooms, luxurious apartment, Annual exhibition, Taproom, Bar.
S	A	L	S	E	Mud volcano.
S	A	L	T	S	Plural of SALT. Laxative. Essence.
S	A	L	T	Y	Saline, piquant. Witty, humorous.
S	A	L	V	E	Ointment, cream, balm, unction, unguent, lubricant, remedy. Salvage.
S	A	L	V	O	Barrage, volley, spray, broadside, burst, shower, bombardment.
S	A	M	B	A	Lively South American dance.
S	A	M	M	Y	Wet leather. Clammy, sodden. Simpleton.
S	A	N	D	Y	Gritty, full of sand, shaky, unsound, dry, stale. Scotsman.
S	A	N	E	R	Healthier, wiser, sager, more rational, sounder.
S	A	P	I	D	Tasty, savory, savoury, palatable, appetizing, relishing, saporous.
S	A	P	O	R	Taste, flavour, savour, relish, tang.
S	A	P	P	Y	Succulent, juicy, sentimental, soppy, loony, silly.
S	A	R	D	A	Genus of marine fish. Bonito.
S	A	R	U	M	Extinct borough.
S	A	S	S	I	N	Black buck.
S	A	S	S	E	Lock, sluice, flood gates, weir.
S	A	T	A	N	Lucifer, Evil Spirit, Devil. Original liar. Manslayer.
S	A	T	E	D	Replete, satiated, surfeited, gorged, stuffed, full.
S	A	T	I	N	Heavy glossy fabric.
S	A	T	Y	R	Libertine, Hairy demon, Orangutan, Greek sylvan deity, Goatish.
S	A	U	C	E	Condiment, relish, gravy, syrup. Flavouring. Cheek, sass, back chat, lip.

1	2	3	4	5	
S	A	U	C	Y	Pert, flippant, bold, impertinent, impudent, insolent.
S	A	U	L	T	Waterfall, cascade, chute, spout, rapid.
S	A	U	N	A	Health aid, steam or humidity hot bath.
S	A	U	T	E	Fry in fat.
S	A	V	E	D	Rescued, delivered, redeemed, freed. Preserved, collected, stored, economized.
S	A	V	E	R	Economist, hoarder, rescuer, deliverer.
S	A	V	O	R	Savour. Taste, relish, tang, quality, feature, feel, experience.
S	A	V	O	Y	Type of cabbage.
S	A	V	V	Y	Understanding, commonsense, astuteness, sagaciousness.
S	A	W	E	D	Cut through, severed.
S	A	X	O	N	Relating to Anglo Saxon, From Saxony, Germany. Germanic influence.
S	A	Y	E	R	Speaker, pronouncer, commentator. Assayer.
S	A	Y	S	O	Authority, dictum, voice, say.
S	C	A	L	D	Burn, scorch, blanch, parboil, boil.
S	C	A	L	E	Flattened plate, horny outer covering in nature, chip, armour overlap, flake. Peel, husk, loosen, layer.
S	C	A	L	P	Part of human head covered with hair. Trophy, prize, triumphant score.
S	C	A	L	Y	Encrusted with scales. Mean, shabby. Reptilian.
S	C	A	M	P	Rogue, knave, rascal, joker, prankster, mischievous person.
S	C	A	N	T	Scarcity, insufficience, paucity, poverty, scanty, spare, skimpy, just enough.
S	C	A	P	E	Shaft, stem, insect antenna, feather shaft, scenic view, snipe's cry.
S	C	A	R	E	Frighten, alarm, startle.
S	C	A	R	F	Square or triangle of cloth, knitting. Neckwrap, collar, tippet. Joint.
S	C	A	R	P	Side of ditch, line of cliffs, erosion, steep slope. Rampart.
S	C	A	R	Y	Frightened, windy, afraid, timid, anxious. Frightening.
S	C	E	N	A	Opera scene, dramatic recital.
S	C	E	N	D	Upward movement, pitch, wave lift.
S	C	E	N	E	Subdivision of Play, episode, stage set, scena, view, vista, sight, exhibition.
S	C	E	N	T	Perfume, odour, smell, aroma, fragrance, bouquet, redolence.
S	C	H	M	O	Fool, idiot, jerk, jackass.
S	C	I	O	N	Descendant, branch, offshoot, lineage.
S	C	O	F	F	Mock, deride, sneer, ridicule, taunt, disdain, scorn.
S	C	O	L	D	Berate, chide, upbraid, reproach, admonish, splash in or with boiling liquid.
S	C	O	N	E	Quick bread, baked dough, cake, cookie, biscuit. Confection.
S	C	O	O	P	Bail, ladle, dip, dig, excavate, shovel, spade. News Story. Lift up.
S	C	O	O	T	Decamp, bolt, run, hurry, scamper, scurry, sprint, skip.
S	C	O	P	E	Space, room, latitude, leeway, range, ambit, breadth, sweep, radius.
S	C	O	R	E	Multitude, crowd, legion, tally, line, mark, notch, groove, Twenty. Record. Musical composition.
S	C	O	R	N	Despise, disdain, gibe, jeer, Contempt, ridicule, taunt.
S	C	O	T	S	Scottish.
S	C	O	U	R	Scrub, scrape, comb, ransack, rummage, corrode, erode. Hurry, flit.
S	C	O	U	T	Explore, probe, reconnoitre, seek out. Survey. Watchman. Boy Scout.
S	C	O	V	E	Plaster.
S	C	O	V	Y	Smeared, covered.
S	C	O	W	L	Frown, glower, gloom, lower.
S	C	R	A	B	Scratch.
S	C	R	A	G	Manhandle, throttle, choke. Scrawny person.
S	C	R	A	M	Get out, order out, begone, decamp, take off, vamoose.
S	C	R	A	P	Bit, small piece, atom, particle, fragment. Discard. Brawl, quarrel, bicker.
S	C	R	A	T	Small amount, insignificant thing.
S	C	R	A	Y	Simple container.
S	C	R	E	E	Rocky debris, stone, pebble.
S	C	R	E	W	Twist, shaft, extort, exact, pinch, cheat, scrimp, botch, confuse.
S	C	R	I	M	Reinforcing panel, durable fabric, screen, light diffuser.
S	C	R	I	P	Prescription, manuscript, Share certificate. knapsack, wallet.
S	C	R	O	G	Scrub.
S	C	R	U	B	Undergrowth. Clean, scour, rub, buff, polish. Cancel. Inferior. Underling. Undergrowth.
S	C	R	U	M	Football movement.
S	C	U	B	A	Underwater breathing apparatus.
S	C	U	F	F	Shuffle, scratch, roughen, graze, slipper, slip-on, Shamble.
S	C	U	L	L	Propel a boat, row. Oar.
S	C	U	L	P	Sculpture. Carve, engrave.
S	C	U	R	F	Scum, trash, rabble, mob. proletariat, riffraff. Dandruff.
S	C	U	T	E	Large scale, belly scale, horny plate.
S	E	A	L	S	Plural of SEAL.
S	E	A	M	S	Plural of SEAM.
S	E	A	M	Y	Sordid, off-beat, nasty, unsavoury, dark, rough, unpleasant.
S	E	A	T	S	Plural of SEAT.

1	2	3	4	5	
S	E	B	U	M	Secretion of sebacious gland, oily substance.
S	E	D	A	N	Carrying chair, portable conveyance. Hard-top. Motor car.
S	E	D	G	E	Plant, yellow iris, chestnut colour, trout fly. Grass.
S	E	D	G	Y	Grassy, gorsy, overgrown.
S	E	E	D	Y	Relating to seeds. Shabby, run-down, squalid, debilitated, spiritless.
S	E	I	N	E	Large fishing net. To fish by netting.
S	E	I	S	M	Earthquake.
S	E	I	T	Y	Individuality, selfhood, identity, personality, singularity.
S	E	I	Z	E	Take possession, grab, grasp, clutch, appropriate, capture, afflict.
S	E	M	E	N	Body fluid, seed, sperm conveyor.
S	E	N	N	A	Plant with medical properties, purgative. Persian rug.
S	E	N	O	R	Title of respect, spanish-speaking man. Mister.
S	E	N	S	E	Meaning, import, message, significance. Substance, intelligence, feel, think.
S	E	P	A	L	Modified leaf of calyx.
S	E	P	I	A	Cuttlefish, secretion, brown pigment, photograph executed in brown colour.
S	E	P	O	Y	Indian Horseman.
S	E	R	A	C	Jagged pinnacle, sharp ridge, icefall.
S	E	R	A	I	Caravanserai, seraglio, brothel, bordello.
S	E	R	G	E	Twilled fabric, suit material.
S	E	R	I	F	Typography style.
S	E	R	I	N	Small finch.
S	E	R	U	M	Substance containing antibodies. Vaccine. Fluid. Whey. Watery liquid.
S	E	R	V	E	Benefit, function, officiate, minister to, nurse, encourage, treat, play.
S	E	R	V	O	Servomechanism.
S	E	T	O	N	Suture.
S	E	T	T	O	Brawl, affray, fight, row, scrap, scuffle, altercation, encounter.
S	E	T	U	P	Build, construct, establish, introduce, treat, plot, scheme. Calculated deceit. Established environment.
S	E	V	E	N	One more than SIX.
S	E	V	E	R	Detach, separate, dissect, cut, sunder, snap, carve, split.
S	E	W	E	D	Past of SEW.
S	E	W	E	N	Sea trout.
S	E	W	E	R	One who sews. Subterranean sewage ditch, underground waste drains.
S	E	X	E	D	Sexual instincts, having sex appeal. Having its sex identified.
S	E	X	E	R	Animal sex identifier.
S	E	X	E	S	Plural of SEX.
S	H	A	C	K	Hut, shed, rondavel, lean-to, shanty, shelter. Lodge, live, dwell.
S	H	A	D	E	Hue, tint, colour, veil, screen, cover. Shadow.
S	H	A	D	Y	Screened, protected, underhand, sneaky, uncertain, unreliable, disreputable, risque.
S	H	A	F	T	Ray, beam, barb, dart, thrust, arrow, missile. Handle. Pit. Passage.
S	H	A	K	E	Jar, quiver, tremble, shudder, jog, rattle, Dismay, appal, daunt. Rid, tremor.
S	H	A	K	Y	Dithery, doddery, tremulous, weak, doubtful, insecure, unstable.
S	H	A	L	E	Rock deposit, mineral deposit.
S	H	A	L	L	Past of SHOULD. Expression of determination, must, can, will.
S	H	A	M	E	Disgrace, discredit, dishonour, infamy. Embarrassment, mortification.
S	H	A	N	K	Lower part of leg, tibia. Stem, stalk, bar.
S	H	A	P	E	Form, figure, conformation, order, condition, make, build, construct, frame.
S	H	A	R	D	Fragment, residue, piece, remains, glass fragment.
S	H	A	R	E	Part, quota, allotment, proportion, ration, stake, parcel, partake. Apportion.
S	H	A	R	K	Voracious fish, Man-eater. Trickster.
S	H	A	R	P	Honed, keen, whetted, pointed, acute, intelligent, shrewd, short, acrid, stylish.
S	H	A	V	E	Shred, sliver. Cut, pare, shear, trim, reduce, graze, skim. Shingle.
S	H	A	W	L	Wrapper, garment, scarf, collar, wrap.
S	H	E	A	F	Bundle, collection, quantity, cluster, crest.
S	H	E	A	R	Clip, cut, tonsure, prune, strip, divest. Achieve by cutting.
S	H	E	E	N	Lustre, gloss, polish, shine, glaze, glint, finish.
S	H	E	E	P	Ruminant mammal, wholly animal. Stupid, docile person.
S	H	E	E	R	Utter, absolute, filmy, diaphanous, steep, precipitate, turn, deflect, swerve.
S	H	E	E	T	Bed linen, sail, wrapping paper, expanse, plate, metal portion, layer, rope, anchor.
S	H	E	I	K	Arab Chief.
S	H	E	L	F	Thin, flat, suspended ledge. Sandbank, Reef. Bookcase, ornament display beam.
S	H	E	L	L	Hulk, case, pod, skin, pod, husk. Bombard, blitz, bomb. Spend.
S	H	E	T	H	Row, furrow, bar. Sheath.
S	H	I	C	K	Drunk, intoxicated, boozy.
S	H	I	E	D	Past of SHY. Flinched.
S	H	I	F	T	Move, change, disturb. Consume, apportion, Conversion, alteration, bend. Vary. Period of work.
S	H	I	N	E	Radiate, glow, beam, gleam, polish, burnish, display, lustre.

1	2	3	4	5	
S	H	I	N	S	Plural of SHIN.
S	H	I	N	Y	Lustrous, burnished, polished, shining, glossy, gleaming, glistening.
S	H	I	P	S	Plural of SHIP.
S	H	I	R	E	County, district, subdivision. Draught horse.
S	H	I	R	K	Evade, dodge, duck, parry, sidestep, bypass, shun, avoid, malinger.
S	H	I	R	R	Bake eggs. Gather, pucker, smock.
S	H	I	R	T	Blouse, cloth garment, undergarment, nightshirt.
S	H	I	V	E	Bung, stopper, plant fragment, splinter.
S	H	O	A	L	Shallow, barrier, reef, sandbank, bar. Throng, a school of fish.
S	H	O	C	K	Scandalize, trauma, tremor, earthquake, impact, concussion, jar, jolt. Sheaf.
S	H	O	E	R	Blacksmith, farrier.
S	H	O	N	E	Past of SHINE.
S	H	O	O	K	Past of SHAKE.
S	H	O	O	T	Discharge, weapon, launch, trigger, blast, destroy, rush, bolt.
S	H	O	R	E	Brace, prop. Seashore, beach, strand, coast, waterfront, foreshore.
S	H	O	R	T	Brief, abbreviated, abridged, low, small, dumpy, deficient.
S	H	O	U	T	Holler, whoop, yell, call, shriek, bawl, bellow, cheer.
S	H	O	V	E	Jostle, jolt, push, elbow, hustle, press, shoulder.
S	H	O	W	N	Past of SHOW.
S	H	O	W	Y	Ostentatious, garish, gaudy, loud, flamboyant, pretentious, flashy.
S	H	R	E	D	Scrap, tatter, piece, particle, bit, pare, slice, slither.
S	H	R	E	W	Virago, fishwife, harpy, spitfire. Small rodent.
S	H	R	U	B	Low, woody plant. Bush, plant, herb. Beverage.
S	H	R	U	G	Raise shoulders, expression of indifference.
S	H	U	C	K	Discard, cast aside, ditch, reject, shed, slough, jettison.
S	H	U	N	T	Push aside, switch, shift, deflect, divert, transfer, sidetrack, move.
S	H	Y	L	Y	Bashfully, coyly, demurely, diffidently, modestly, timidly, sheepishly.
S	I	B	Y	L	Fortune-teller, prophetess, sorceress.
S	I	D	E	D	Took sides, supported. Sized, circumference. Biased.
S	I	D	E	R	Adherent, partisan, supporter.
S	I	D	E	S	Plural of SIDE.
S	I	D	L	E	Crawl, creep, edge, ease, slip, move furtively.
S	I	E	G	E	Blockade beleaguer, surround, hold up. Throne, seat, privy, Quantity. Beseige.
S	I	E	V	E	Sift, screen, strain, Meshed device, Sifter. Gossip.
S	I	G	H	T	Eyesight, eye, seeing, vision, view, outlook. Eyesore, mess. Much, lot.
S	I	G	M	A	Letter symbol. Measurement of time. The sum of.
S	I	L	K	Y	Silken, soft, satiny. Ingratiating disarming, insinuating, deferential.
S	I	L	L	Y	Idiotic, simple, foolish.
S	I	L	V	A	The assemblage of trees in a region of woods. A Wood-God. A forest-dweller.
S	I	N	C	E	Subsequently, because, following, next, as, seeing, whereas for considering.
S	I	N	E	W	Tendon, fibre, brawn, power, energy, force, strength.
S	I	N	G	E	Burn, sear, scorch.
S	I	N	U	S	Nasal duct, tract, channel, recess, depression.
S	I	O	U	X	Red Indian tribe.
S	I	R	E	D	Fathered, bred, begot, generated, procreated, hatched, parented, spawned.
S	I	R	E	N	Hooter, warning klaxon, Attractive, seductive woman. Decoy, temptation.
S	I	S	A	L	Hemp, cordage, fibre, Plant.
S	I	S	S	Y	Weakling, spoilsport, milksop, prissy, pansy, effeminate.
S	I	T	E	D	Placed, situated, located, positioned.
S	I	T	D	N	Demonstration by occupation.
S	I	X	T	H	Next to Fifth.
S	I	X	T	Y	Six times ten.
S	I	Z	E	D	Graded, measured, proportioned. Sealed.
S	I	Z	E	R	Size checker. One who determines size. One who applies size.
S	K	A	T	E	Roller-skate, glide on ice. Device for ice gliding. Slip, glide, Breed of fish.
S	K	E	A	N	Dagger, dirk. Skean Dhu.
S	K	E	E	T	Clay pigeon. Poker hand.
S	K	E	I	N	Coil, Length of yarn. Hank. Flight of wild fowl, gaggle, formation.
S	K	E	L	P	Strike, slap, beat. Hustle, Metal tube.
S	K	I	E	D	Past of SKI.
S	K	I	E	R	One who SKIS.
S	K	I	E	S	Plural of SKI. Plural of SKY.
S	K	I	F	F	Light sailing boat, rowboat, small powerboat.
S	K	I	L	L	Deftness, ability, expertise, know-how, dexterity, prowess, sleight.
S	K	I	M	P	Scrimp, scrape, pinch. Poor, scanty, spare, sparse, meagre.
S	K	I	N	K	Draw out, pour, ladle.
S	K	I	N	S	Plural of SKIN.

1	2	3	4	5	
S	K	I	R	L	Shrill tone, shriek, sound of bagpipes, scream.
S	K	I	R	R	Bolt, scamper, run, skud, dart, skip, flee.
S	K	I	R	T	Woman's half dress. Edge, fringe, rim, surround, avoid, bypass, dodge, hedge.
S	K	I	T	E	Prank, caper, frolic, lark, tomfoolery. Boast, brag, boaster, braggart.
S	K	I	V	E	Pare, shave, strip. To avoid work.
S	K	O	A	L	Drinking Toast.
S	K	U	L	K	Lurk, cower, sneak, slink, pussyfoot.
S	K	U	L	L	Skeletal head, bony brain case, cranium, mind, Death's Head.
S	K	U	N	K	Black and white mammal emitting maladourous secretion. Stinker, smellbag.
S	L	A	C	K	Negligent, careless, lax, loose, relaxed, feeble, supine, sluggish.
S	L	A	D	E	Glen, glade, valley. Peat spade.
S	L	A	I	N	Past of SLAY.
S	L	A	K	E	Quench, allay, extinguish. Add water.
S	L	A	N	G	Dialect, jargon, lingo, patois, vernacular, patter.
S	L	A	N	T	Tilt, cant, incline, lean, slope. Aslant, sidewise, slope, grade, viewpoint, angle.
S	L	A	P	S	Plural of SLAP.
S	L	A	S	H	Gash, cut, swipe, incise, slit, pierce, reduce, shorten, abridge.
S	L	A	T	E	Lambaste, castigate, scathe, scourge, blister.
S	L	A	T	Y	Like slate.
S	L	A	V	E	Serf, servant, drudge, menial. Worker, grind, grum, slog, toil.
S	L	E	E	K	Glossy, smooth, lustrous, polished, glistening. Perfect, refine.
S	L	E	E	P	Doze, drowse, nap, slumber, rest, relax, repose, lethargy, languor. Death.
S	L	E	E	R	Sneer, jeer.
S	L	E	E	T	Fine snow and freezing rain mixed and driven by strong wind.
S	L	E	P	T	Past of SLEEP.
S	L	I	C	E	Portion, segment, share, quota, allotment, piece. Cut, carve, cleave, split.
S	L	I	C	K	Sleek, smooth, perfect. Smarten, spruce, slide, glissade. Greasy surface, oily.
S	L	I	D	E	Glide, slip, skid. Creep. Steal, sneak, decline. Downswing.
S	L	I	M	E	Mud, sludge, ooze, mire.
S	L	I	M	Y	Sludgy, muddy, slippy, viscous.
S	L	I	N	G	Hurl, cast, fling, heave. Hang, dangle. Cocktail.
S	L	I	N	K	Slide, skulk, glide, lurk, weasel.
S	L	I	P	S	Plural of SLIP.
S	L	O	O	M	Doze, drowse, slumber, snooze.
S	L	O	O	P	Man of War, Longboat, cutter. Log sled.
S	L	O	P	E	Hillside, slant, gradiant, ramp, shelf. Drift downward.
S	L	O	P	S	Waste material, Garbage. Gruel.
S	L	O	S	H	Splash, wash, spatter, lap, douse, Gulp. Strike.
S	L	O	T	H	Idleness, indolence, laziness, Slouch, shiftlessness, inattention. Arboreal animal.
S	L	U	E	D	Swerved, turned, dipped, sheered, veered.
S	L	U	G	S	Plural of SLUG.
S	L	U	M	P	Fall, plunge, tumble, flag, droop, topple, slouch, collapse.
S	L	U	M	S	Plural of SLUM.
S	L	U	N	G	Past of SLING.
S	L	U	N	K	Past of SLINK.
S	L	U	R	P	Lap, swill, smack, suck, slosh, guzzle, wolf.
S	L	U	S	H	Watery snow, soft mud, mire, slosh, sludge.
S	L	Y	L	Y	Craftily, astutely, crookedly, dishonesty, calculatingly, artfully, cunningly.
S	M	A	C	K	Taste, relish. Hint, smell, kiss, peck, slap, punch, belt. Boat. Completely.
S	M	A	L	L	Tiny, little, minute, trivial, petty, remote, puny, paltry, piddling.
S	M	A	R	T	Intelligent, alert, bright, wise, clever, stylish, chic, hurt, sting, bite.
S	M	A	S	H	Shatter, splinter, destroy, blow, bang, impact, crash, collapse, collision.
S	M	E	A	R	Daub, paint, besmirch, sully, begrime, taint, malign, whip, slur.
S	M	E	L	L	Aroma, odour, scent, sniff, perceive, savour, reek, stink, redolence.
S	M	E	L	T	Small fish. Whitebait. Melt, fuse. Reduce, flux, scorify, refine.
S	M	I	L	E	Pleasant facial expression. Show pleasure, grin, beam, smirk, simper.
S	M	I	R	K	Simper, grin, smile, leer, sneer.
S	M	I	T	E	Hit, smack, slap, strike, clout, whack, clobber. Afflict, torment.
S	M	I	T	H	Metalworker, blacksmith.
S	M	O	C	K	Garment, chemise. Gather, shirr, embroider.
S	M	O	K	E	Vapour, fume, steam, reek. Cigarette, Cook by smoking. Run, zip, rush.
S	M	O	L	T	Salmon, sea trout.
S	M	O	T	E	Past of SMITE.
S	M	U	T	S	Plural of SMUT.
S	N	A	C	K	In-between meal. Bite, refreshment, morsel. Savoury.
S	N	A	F	U	Confusion, muddle, Awry.
S	N	A	I	L	Gastropod mollusc. Sluggish person. Slowcoach.

1	2	3	4	5	
S	N	A	K	E	Scaly limbless reptile. Sneak, cringing person, contemptible or deceitful person.
S	N	A	K	Y	Sly, cunning, sneaky. Winding, meandering, convoluted, sinuous.
S	N	A	R	E	Trap, lure, net. Catch, ensnare, inveigle. Seduce, tempt. Decoy.
S	N	A	R	L	Growl, snap, bark. Confuse, jumble, entangle, complicate, tangle, web.
S	N	A	R	Y	Confused, entangled, complicated.
S	N	A	T	H	Scythe handle.
S	N	E	A	D	Handle, snath.
S	N	E	A	K	Liar, tale bearer, gossip, furtive person, scoundrel. Slink, weasel.
S	N	E	A	P	Rebuke, reprove, chide, reprimand, check, reproach.
S	N	E	E	R	Jeer, scoff, gibe, belittle, disparage, mock, scorn.
S	N	I	C	K	Nick, cut, snip, tap, strike, sharply.
S	N	I	D	E	Dishonest, counterfeit, bogus, phony, pseudo, false, fake. Crooked.
S	N	I	F	F	Inhale, smell.
S	N	I	F	T	Snort, sniff, snuffle.
S	N	I	P	E	Ambush, shoot at. Game bird.
S	N	I	R	T	Suppressed laughter, snort. Snigger.
S	N	O	E	K	Barracuda, Barracouta, Gamefish.
S	N	O	O	D	Hairnet.
S	N	O	O	K	Marine fish, Pike, snoek, needlefish. Gesture of derision.
S	N	O	O	P	Pry, meddle, rubberneck. Busybody, nosey parker. Peek, peer, intrude.
S	N	O	R	E	Loud breathing when asleep. Snark, snort, snuffle. Saw wood.
S	N	O	R	T	Force air violently through nose. Expel air noisily. Tot, slug, shot, nip. Guffaw.
S	N	O	U	T	Nose, beak, proboscis, snitch, conk, schnozzle, pecker.
S	N	O	W	Y	White, pure, unblemished. Snow-filled.
S	N	U	F	F	Sniffing tobacco. Tobacco medicant. Smell, sniff, Die, peg-out.
S	O	A	P	Y	Frothy, bubbly, unctuous, slick, smarmy, oily, fulsome.
S	O	A	R	E	Sorrel, Reddish-brown, of hawks. A hawk of the first year.
S	O	B	B	Y	Tearful, sentimental, soppy.
S	O	B	E	R	Abstemious, temperate, moderate. Controlled, serious, rational, subdued.
S	O	C	K	S	Footwear. Sox.
S	O	D	D	Y	Covered with turf.
S	O	F	A	R	Hitherto, as yet, thus far.
S	O	G	G	Y	Marshy, wet, saturated, soaked, awash.
S	O	L	A	R	Action of sun's light, utilizing sun's rays. Solarium, chamber. Symbol of sun.
S	O	L	D	O	Italian coin.
S	O	L	E	D	Having leather soles. Booted. Shod. Undersided.
S	O	L	E	S	Plural of SOLE.
S	O	L	F	A	Syllables, Singing exercise. Scale. Gamut.
S	O	L	I	D	Unbroken, hard, firm, stable, valid, convincing, telling. Substantial.
S	O	L	U	S	In solitude. Alone.
S	O	L	V	E	Work out, determine, find solution, explain, illuminate, decipher, unravel.
S	O	N	G	S	Plural of SONG.
S	O	N	I	C	Speed of sound, audible.
S	O	N	N	Y	Boy, lad, fond name.
S	O	O	T	Y	Black, covered in soot, dirty.
S	O	P	O	R	Deep sleep, stupor.
S	O	P	P	Y	Moist, sodden, tearful, silly. Sentimental.
S	O	R	E	S	Plural of SORE.
S	O	R	E	L	Male fallow deer.
S	O	R	E	X	Shrew.
S	O	R	G	E	Concern, anxiety, care.
S	O	R	R	Y	Sad, unhappy, saddened, regretful, remorseful, miserable, apologetic, penitent.
S	O	R	T	S	Plural of SORT.
S	O	R	U	S	Spore cluster, fern sporangia. Parasitic fungus, lichen gemmae.
S	O	U	G	H	Moan, murmur, sigh. Noisy breathing. Chant. Drone.
S	O	U	L	S	Plural of SOUL.
S	O	U	N	D	Noise, stable, valid, whole, healthy, channel, rational, fathom, vibration, seem.
S	O	U	P	Y	Thick, like soup.
S	O	U	S	E	Douse, pickle, soak, drench, saturate. Binge, bender.
S	O	U	T	H	Opposite to North. Compass point. Antarctic. Polar region.
S	O	W	A	R	Lancer, mounted orderly.
S	O	W	E	D	Past of SOW.
S	O	W	E	R	Planter, propagator, distributor of seed.
S	P	A	C	E	Expanse, distance, expansion, stretch, while, interval, term, duration, spell.
S	P	A	D	E	Garden implement, digging device. Playing card. Excavate, scoop. Shovel.
S	P	A	D	O	Impotent person. Castrated person or animal.
S	P	A	H	I	Cavalryman.

1	2	3	4	5	Definition
S	P	A	L	L	Chip, fragment, flake. Reduce, exfoliate.
S	P	A	N	G	Completely, exactly, directly. Jump, jerk, throw. Crack. Bang.
S	P	A	N	K	Hit, beat, whack, slap. Smack. Punish.
S	P	A	N	S	Plural of SPAN.
S	P	A	R	E	Extra, additional. Absolve, discharge, exempt. Save, scrimp. Lean, bony, lank.
S	P	A	R	K	Flash, glow. Suitor. Seed, embryo.
S	P	A	S	M	Paroxysm, twitch, contraction, fit, involuntary muscle movement.
S	P	A	T	E	Food, cataclysm, deluge, inundation, series, progression, current, flow.
S	P	A	W	N	Hatch, generate, create. Offspring, sperm, ova.
S	P	E	A	K	Articulate, talk, express, sound, address, lecture, converse.
S	P	E	A	R	Dagger, lance, spike, panga. Impale, transfix, penetrate, skewer. Descendant.
S	P	E	C	K	Dot, blemish, stain, atom, particle, mote. Freckle, speckle. Fat, lard.
S	P	E	C	S	Glasses, spectacles.
S	P	E	E	D	Haste, alacrity, pace, rapidity, tempo. Advance, course, velocity. Dagga (sl.).
S	P	E	L	L	Period, space, Magic, charm, enunciate, signify, denote. Relieve, take over.
S	P	E	L	T	Type of Wheat.
S	P	E	N	D	Disburse, lavish, distribute, pay, squander. Expend. While away, pass.
S	P	E	N	T	Past of SPEND.
S	P	E	R	M	Semen, spermatazoa. Spawn.
S	P	E	W	Y	Soggy, wet, boggy, marshy.
S	P	I	C	A	Type of bandage.
S	P	I	C	E	Seasoning, flavour, herbify, aroma. Fragrance. Bouquet. Hint, trace, tinge. Taste.
S	P	I	C	K	Fresh, new, spanking, neat, tidy.
S	P	I	C	Y	Aromatic, pungent, piquant, zesty, fiery, risque, racy, suggestive.
S	P	I	E	D	Saw, spotted, beheld, observed, espied.
S	P	I	E	L	Song and dance, story, tall tale, pitch, line, dramatics.
S	P	I	E	S	Plural of SPY.
S	P	I	F	F	Dress up, doll out, slick, smarten spruce.
S	P	I	K	E	Lance, sharp end, nail, spoke, impale. Mix, dilute. Impale, skewer.
S	P	I	K	Y	Pointed, sharp, spiny.
S	P	I	L	L	Waterway. Upset, slop, spatter, spray, overflow. Reveal, disclose.
S	P	I	L	T	Past of SPILL.
S	P	I	N	E	Backbone, back, vertebrae, vertebral column, spinal column.
S	P	I	N	K	Chaffinch.
S	P	I	N	Y	Thorny, sharp, spiky, difficult, irritable. Nettlesome, prickly.
S	P	I	R	E	Steeple, conical pile, sprout, pinnacle. Germinate, sprout.
S	P	I	R	Y	Tall, slender, spirally.
S	P	I	T	E	Grudge, dislike, thwarting, malicious feelings. Pique, malice.
S	P	I	T	Z	Breed of dog.
S	P	L	A	T	Splotch, splatter, sully, besmirch.
S	P	L	A	Y	Extend apart, expand, slope, slant. Awkward action. Clumsy, ungainly.
S	P	L	I	T	Slit, rent, cleave, cut, dissect, slice. Tear, Betray, separate. Cleft, fissure, schism, cleft, breach, rift.
S	P	O	D	E	Ceramic ware. China.
S	P	O	I	L	Damage, harm. Ravage, rape. Booty, loot. Decay, taint. Coddle, cosset, baby.
S	P	O	K	E	Past of SPEAK. Wheel rod, radiating bar. Chock. Block, impede.
S	P	O	O	F	Fool, delude, bluff, kid, joke. Parody, humbug.
S	P	O	O	K	Ghost, spectre, phantom, apparition. Haunt, Frighten, scare.
S	P	O	O	L	Cylinder, bobbin, film holder, fishing reel. Wind.
S	P	O	O	N	Ladle, tableware. Spoonful. Simpleton. Neck, cuddle, woo. Fishing device.
S	P	O	O	R	Animal track, footprint.
S	P	O	R	E	Minute reproductive organ. Seed. Cell. Microscopic egg.
S	P	O	R	T	Game, athletics, play, recreation, fun, jest, joke. Butt. Fun loving person.
S	P	O	T	S	Plural of SPOT.
S	P	O	U	T	Nozzle, waterspout. Utter, declaim. Stream, spurt. Gush.
S	P	R	A	T	Small fish. Twerp, squirt, pup.
S	P	R	A	Y	Shower, spread, spout, jet.
S	P	R	E	E	Revel, carouse, frolic, riot, roister, wassail. Orgy, splurge, binge.
S	P	R	I	G	Twig, shoot. Scion, heir. Dowel, brad.
S	P	R	I	T	Sprout, germinate, shoot, bud.
S	P	R	U	E	Chronic digestive disturbance.
S	P	U	M	E	Foam, spray, froth, scum, lather. Yeast.
S	P	U	M	Y	Frothy, foamy, splashy.
S	P	U	N	K	Courage, fortitude, grit, guts, grit, resolution. Semen.
S	P	U	R	N	Scorn, slight, disdain, decline, repudiate, reject.
S	P	U	R	T	Spout, squirt, jet, squitter, sprint, speed, rush, dash.
S	Q	U	A	B	Stocky, dumpy, thickset. Spill, slop. Clumsy, curt, coy.
S	Q	U	A	D	Military group, group with common purpose. Crew, band, gang.

1	2	3	4	5	
S	Q	U	A	T	Crouch, hunker, stoop. Thick, stubby, heavyset. Unlawful residence.
S	Q	U	A	W	Red Indian female.
S	Q	U	I	B	Firework, fire cracker, explosive.
S	Q	U	I	D	Cephalapod, type of cuttlefish, fish bait.
S	T	A	C	K	Pile, heap, bank, mound, drift, hill. Pyramid, steeple. Chimney.
S	T	A	F	F	Workers, personnel. Long stick, rod, pole. Group of aides.
S	T	A	G	E	Perform, act. Platform, ledge. Scene. Degree, notch, rung, step.
S	T	A	G	Y	Theatrical, dramatic. Histrionic.
S	T	A	I	D	Steady, serious, grave, solemn, decorous, formal, stuffy, smug.
S	T	A	I	N	Discolour, blotch, smear, taint, sully, debase, corrupt. Stigma, blot, dye.
S	T	A	I	R	Step, upward passage, upper access. Stairway.
S	T	A	K	E	Wager, bet, risk. Interest, share. Gamble. Pole, post, picket.
S	T	A	L	E	Rancid, off, fetid, fusty. Trite, commonplace, hackneyed. Bait, decoy.
S	T	A	L	K	Hunt, chase, pursue, flush. March, stride.
S	T	A	L	L	Stable, booth. Halt, brake, check, interrupt. Gorge, surfeit. Arrest, suspend.
S	T	A	M	P	Postage levy. Impression, brand, mark, Trample, stomp. Character, ilk. Seal.
S	T	A	N	D	Upright stance. Rostrum, Seating. Treat. Depend, bear, endure, position.
S	T	A	N	K	Past of STINK.
S	T	A	R	E	Gape, gawp, gaze, look, gander, goggle, peer.
S	T	A	R	K	Utter, complete, bare, empty, clear, vacant, void. Rigid, still, sheer.
S	T	A	R	T	Commence, begin. Commencement, beginning. Fright. Advantage, embark, create.
S	T	A	T	E	Country. Condition, status, attitude, relate, describe, express, enunciate.
S	T	A	V	E	Stick, cudgel, staff. Strip, piece, slat. Verse, music notation, bar. Fend, avert.
S	T	E	A	D	Help, aid, help, abet. Use. Bedstead. Farmhouse. Alternative, substitute. In place of.
S	T	E	A	K	Superior cut of Meat. Meat for grilling. Slice of Meat, fish.
S	T	E	A	L	Pilfer, purloin, nick, filch, annex, appropriate, fleece, plunder, sneak, lurk, rob.
S	T	E	A	M	Vapour, fumes, force, power, energy, sinew, strength.
S	T	E	E	D	Horse, mount, warhorse, nag, charger.
S	T	E	E	L	Commercial iron, refined pig iron. Weapon, instrument, knife. colour. Harden.
S	T	E	E	P	Soak, dip, imbue, impregnate, infuse. Sloping, abrupt, sheer.
S	T	E	E	R	Guide, point, tip, conduct, escort, pilot, shepherd. Ox, bullock.
S	T	E	I	N	Earthenware beer mug. Large glass.
S	T	E	L	A	Stone pillar. Monument. Inscribed wall area.
S	T	E	L	E	Shaft, handle. Cylinder.
S	T	E	M	S	Plural of STEM.
S	T	E	N	D	Leap, jump, bound.
S	T	E	P	S	Plural of STEP.
S	T	E	R	N	Grim, dour, severe, austere, implacable, inflexible. Buttocks, back, rump. Back section.
S	T	E	W	S	Plural of STEW.
S	T	I	C	H	Verse, line. Last card trick.
S	T	I	C	K	Rod, strip, bar. Adhere, stab, cleave, set. Fleece, overcharge. Abide, endure.
S	T	I	E	D	Penned. enclosed. Put in a sty.
S	T	I	F	F	Rigid, unbending, inflexible, hard, resistant. Intoxicated. Corpse, cadaver.
S	T	I	L	E	Turnstile, obstacle, barrier, gateway.
S	T	I	L	L	Motionless, placid, hush. Yet, however, nevertheless, too. Distillery. Home brewery.
S	T	I	L	T	Pole, post, pile. Architectural vertical. Long legs.
S	T	I	N	G	Sharp pain, irritation, insect attack. Goad, incite, stir. Overcharge. Cheat.
S	T	I	N	K	Smell, reek, stench, odour.
S	T	I	N	T	Task, chore, duty, job, scrimp, skimp. Cramp, limitation. Genus of wading birds.
S	T	I	P	A	Genus of grass.
S	T	I	P	E	Stalk plant stem of fungi, type of stalk. Stipendiary.
S	T	I	R	P	Lineage, stock, line of descent.
S	T	I	V	E	Stifle, pack, crowd, suffocate.
S	T	I	V	Y	Stuffy, breathless, airless, stifling, sultry.
S	T	O	A	T	Black-tip tailed weasel. Ermine.
S	T	O	C	K	Family tree, lineage, clan. Estimate. Inventory. Equipment. Equip. Farm animals. Type of Soup.
S	T	O	E	P	Verandah, balcony.
S	T	O	I	C	Spartan, Long suffering person. Unfeeling, impassive, patient, resigned.
S	T	O	K	E	Tend fire, poke, stir up. Supply fuel. Gorge.
S	T	O	L	E	Shoulder shawl. Pinched, nicked. Past of STEAL.
S	T	O	M	A	Opening, inlet, mouth, stomach, pore.
S	T	O	M	P	Tramp, stamp, stomp, stump. Tread.
S	T	O	N	E	Pebble, boulder. Rock. Seed. Pelt with stones. Pip of fruit.
S	T	O	N	Y	Hard, unfeeling, callous, cold. Poor, broke, destitute. Flinty. Rocky.
S	T	O	O	D	Past of STAND.
S	T	O	O	K	Shock. Sheaves. Place cornsheaves to dry before stacking.
S	T	O	O	L	Bench, chair, seat. Defacation. Informer, squealer. Three legged seat for milking. Fallguy.

1	2	3	4	5	
S	T	O	O	P	Bend, condescend, deign, concede. Dip, duck. Kneel. Pounce.
S	T	O	P	E	Underground excavation. Ledge.
S	T	O	R	E	Shop. Hoard. Gather, stock. Accumulate, amass. Supply. Depot. Market.
S	T	O	R	K	Large wading bird.
S	T	O	R	M	Clamour, commotion, barrage, attack, assault. Bluster, Rage, turmoil.
S	T	O	R	Y	Narrative, account, chronicle, version, report. Lie, falsehood.
S	T	O	U	P	Bucket, pail, tankard.
S	T	O	U	T	Brave, bold, stalwart. Strong. Fat, obese, portly. Beverage.
S	T	O	V	E	Cooking device. Oven. Kiln. Furnace. Range.
S	T	R	A	D	Stradivarius, Violin.
S	T	R	A	P	Leather thong, binding. Band. Belt. Strop.
S	T	R	A	W	Stalks of grain, animal bedding. Woven fibre. Valueless. Flaxen. Scatter.
S	T	R	A	Y	Wander, gallivant, err, deviate, digress. Erratic. Homeless.
S	T	R	E	W	Scatter, spread, sprinkle, disperse, disseminate. Radiate.
S	T	R	I	A	Minute channel, groove, band, line, imperfection, stripe.
S	T	R	I	P	Shred, segment. Ravage, desolate. Disrobe, undress, peel. Denude, deprive.
S	T	R	I	X	Fluting. Genus of Owl.
S	T	R	O	P	Strap, strip. Sharpen. Lather.
S	T	R	U	M	Thrum, hum, buzz, bumble. Practice music.
S	T	R	U	T	Support, brace. Swagger, sashay, flounce, mince, parade, flaunt.
S	T	U	C	K	Past of STICK.
S	T	U	D	Y	Learn, assimilate, reflect, scan. Reverie. Consider, scrutinize. Book Room.
S	T	U	F	F	Material, goods, odds and ends. Cram, pack, jam. Essence, entity.
S	T	U	M	P	Log, block. Lumber, block. Nonplus, defy, dare, beat, challenge.
S	T	U	N	G	Past of STING.
S	T	U	N	K	Past of STANK.
S	T	U	N	T	Exploit, stint, turn, trick, feat. Dwarf, suppress. Stunted, runty.
S	T	U	P	A	Buddhist shrine.
S	T	U	P	E	Hot cloth. Stupid, fool. Foment. Fomentation.
S	T	Y	L	E	Fashion, mode, manner, vein. Name, behaviour, characteristic. Trait.
S	T	Y	L	O	Stylograph. Australian plant, pasture.
S	U	A	V	E	Bland, smooth, urbane, diplomatic, politic.
S	U	D	S	Y	Frothy, bubbly, foamy.
S	U	E	D	E	Type of material. Buffed leather.
S	U	E	N	T	Smooth, placid, equable, agreeable.
S	U	E	T	Y	Fatty, like suet.
S	U	G	A	R	Sweet substance. Commodity refined from sugar cane. Term of endearment.
S	U	I	N	G	Legal prosecution.
S	U	I	T	E	Apartment, Chambers, rooms, flat. Entourage, group, batch. parcel.
S	U	I	T	S	Plural of SUIT.
S	U	L	K	S	Grumps, mumps, pouts, sourness, glumness, grouchiness.
S	U	L	K	Y	Sullen, crabby, glum, morose, surly, cranky, touchy, irritable.
S	U	L	L	Y	Soil, besmirch, taint, defile, stain, tarnish, disgrace, shame.
S	U	N	N	Y	Bright, happy, cheerful, blithe, clear, cloudless, fine, shiny.
S	U	N	U	P	Crack of Dawn, sunlight, sunrise, cockcrow, morning.
S	U	P	E	R	Exceedingly, extremely, hugely, marvellous, sensational, terrific, groovy.
S	U	P	R	A	Above.
S	U	R	E	R	More sure, certain.
S	U	R	F	Y	At the seaside. Seashore. Wavy.
S	U	R	G	E	Thrust, gush, flow, pour, stream, heave. Billow.
S	U	R	G	Y	Swirling, surfy, gushing.
S	U	R	L	Y	Churlish, sullen, crabby, rude, ungracious, fractious, waspish.
S	W	A	G	E	Metal workers tool. Bullet forming tool. Stretch, taper, cast.
S	W	A	I	N	Suitor, lover, clod, rustic, peasant.
S	W	A	L	E	Shade, coolness, hollow. Board, planking.
S	W	A	M	I	Hindu teacher, master.
S	W	A	M	P	Bog, marsh, fen, morass, deluge, engulf, flood. Overwhelm.
S	W	A	N	G	Swamp, bog, fen, marsh, vlei.
S	W	A	N	K	Show-off, swagger, pontificate. Flamboyant, ostentatious. Stylish.
S	W	A	R	D	Grassy surface, turf, sod, growth.
S	W	A	R	F	Phonograph groove waxing, cutting tool grindings. Pass out, swoon.
S	W	A	R	M	Teem, gather, abound, throng, cluster, flow.
S	W	A	R	T	Dark, dusky, swarthy.
S	W	A	S	H	Slosh, burble, gurgle, splash, slosh, splatter, splurge.
S	W	A	Z	I	Native of Swaziland.
S	W	E	A	R	Vow, vouch, affirm, blaspheme, curse, expletive. Pledge, testify.
S	W	E	A	T	Exude, ooze, seep. Perspire. Perspiration. Work, toil.

1	2	3	4	5	
S	W	E	D	E	Native of Sweden. Vegetable.
S	W	E	E	P	Lottery. Range, radius, ambit, scope. Brush, clean. Chimney cleaner.
S	W	E	E	T	Sugary, honeyed, luscious, dulcet, pleasant, fresh, melodious. Sweetheart. Comfit.
S	W	E	L	L	Dilate, expand, amplify, bulge. Marvellous, Very good.
S	W	E	P	T	Past of SWEEP.
S	W	I	F	T	Fast, quick, prompt, sudden, rapid, snappy, speedy. Genus of bird.
S	W	I	L	L	Refuse, garbage, litter, offal. Drink, guzzle, consume, shift.
S	W	I	N	E	Pig. Of pigs.
S	W	I	N	G	Sway, revolve, rotate, undulate, wiggle. Turn, deflect. Lurch. Rhythm, beat.
S	W	I	P	E	Smite, slog, hit, rap, wipe. Steal, heist, pinch.
S	W	I	R	L	Eddy, whirl, boil, surge, swoosh, whorl.
S	W	I	S	H	Hiss, sibilate, sizzle, wheeze, whiz. Stylish, modish, fashionable.
S	W	I	S	S	Of Switzerland.
S	W	O	O	N	Faint, blackout.
S	W	O	O	P	Stoop, descend, pounce, sweep, grab, seize.
S	W	O	R	D	Sabre, cutlass, rapier. Bayonet, knife, foil.
S	W	O	R	E	Declared, testified, affirmed, vouched, cursed, pledged.
S	W	O	R	N	Inveterate, entrenched, settled, confirmed.
S	W	U	N	G	Past of SWING.
S	Y	L	P	H	Imaginary being, slender girl. Fly away.
S	Y	N	O	D	Ecclesiastical Council, Church gathering. Church advisory body.
S	Y	R	U	P	Thick sweet liquid, Concentrated sugar.

T

T	A	B	B	Y	Cat. Gossip. Table bearer. Woven, Mottled.
T	A	B	E	S	Wasting disease.
T	A	B	I	D	Wasting, Thawing.
T	A	B	L	E	Bench, rostrum, eating slab, index, list, schedule. Counter, buffet. Plateau.
T	A	B	O	O	Forbidden, banned. Prohibition. Restrain, regulate. Forbid, inhibit, outlaw.
T	A	B	O	R	Small Drum.
T	A	C	H	E	Stain, blemish. Buckle, clasp.
T	A	C	I	T	Unspoken, wordless. Inferred. Implicit, understood.
T	A	C	K	S	Plural of TACK.
T	A	C	K	Y	Sticky, gummy. Frumpy, shabby, faded. Unkempt, messy, blowsy.
T	A	F	F	Y	Welshman. Toffee. Flattery.
T	A	F	I	A	A cheap rum distilled from molasses.
T	A	G	M	A	Compound body segment.
T	A	G	U	A	Ivory Palm, Ivory Nut.
T	A	I	L	S	Evening Dress for men. Plural of TAIL.
T	A	I	N	T	Contaminate, damage, decay, decompose. Defile, pollute. Besmirch.
T	A	K	E	N	Past of TAKE.
T	A	K	E	R	One who TAKES.
T	A	K	E	S	Act of TAKING.
T	A	L	E	S	Plural of TALE.
T	A	L	K	S	Plural of TALK.
T	A	L	L	Y	Number, count, Score, inventory, enumerate. Agreement. Conform, correspond.
T	A	L	M	A	Cloak, Cape.
T	A	L	O	N	Claw, moulding, bolt. Stock. Coupon.
T	A	L	P	A	Old world mole.
T	A	L	U	S	Rock debris. Slope. Ankle joint. Ankle.
T	A	M	E	D	Domesticated, curbed, trained, housebroken.
T	A	M	E	R	One who TAMES.
T	A	M	E	S	Act of TAMING.
T	A	M	I	L	Language of India.
T	A	M	I	S	Cloth strainer.
T	A	M	M	Y	Glazed cloth. Strainer. Tam-o-shanter. Beret.
T	A	N	G	O	Rythmic dance.
T	A	N	G	Y	Piquant, sharp, tasty, aromatic, spicy.
T	A	N	I	A	Edible root.
T	A	N	K	S	Plural of TANK.
T	A	N	S	Y	Aromatic Herb. Silverweed.
T	A	P	E	D	Past of TAPE.
T	A	P	E	R	Decrease dwindle, lessen, reduce. Diminish, fade.
T	A	P	I	R	Large Perissodactyl ungulate. Hoofed mammal. Filament of paper, spill.
T	A	P	I	S	Carpeting table cloth tapestry. Under consideration (Obs.)

1	2	3	4	5	
T	A	R	D	O	Musical direction - slow.
T	A	R	D	Y	Late overdue belated overdue. Detained, dilatory, laggard.
T	A	R	E	D	Weighted, counterweighted. Weight classified.
T	A	R	G	E	Archer's shield.
T	A	R	N	S	Small mountains.
T	A	R	R	Y	Procrastinate, dawdle, linger, sojourn, loiter. Covered with Tar.
T	A	R	T	S	Plural of TART.
T	A	S	K	S	Plural of TASK.
T	A	S	T	E	Appetite, flavour. Relish. Savour. Gusto, Experience, feeling, knowledge, liking.
T	A	S	T	Y	Palatable, savoury, appetizing. Quiety, restrained, subdued, unobtrusive.
T	A	T	T	Y	Cheap, paltry, shoddy, sleazy, common, base. Tattered.
T	A	U	N	T	Revile, deride, ridicule, mock. Banter, chaff, scorn.
T	A	W	N	Y	Brownish, brown-skinned, tanned.
T	A	X	E	D	Levied, burdened, charged, assessed, accused.
T	A	X	E	R	One that taxes.
T	A	X	E	S	Plural of TAX.
T	A	X	I	S	Plural of TAXI.
T	A	X	U	S	Genus of Yew Trees.
T	A	Z	Z	A	Ornamental receptacle.
T	E	A	C	H	Impart knowledge. Instruct. Edify, uplift, coach.
T	E	A	L	S	Plural of TEAL.
T	E	A	M	S	Plural of TEAM.
T	E	A	R	S	Plural of TEAR.
T	E	A	R	Y	Tearful, lachrymose, weepy, pathetic.
T	E	A	S	E	Annoy, pester, importune, plague, harry, worry, harass, bedevil. Stretch.
T	E	C	H	Y	Testy, petulant, sulky.
T	E	D	D	Y	Teddy bear. Teddy boy.
T	E	E	N	S	Adolescence. Teen years.
T	E	E	N	Y	Tiny, wee, small, minute.
T	E	E	T	H	Plural of TOOTH.
T	E	H	E	E	Titter, snigger, guffaw.
T	E	I	N	T	Tinge, tint, colour, hue.
T	E	L	E	X	Teleprinter.
T	E	L	L	Y	Television.
T	E	M	P	O	Rate, pace, speed, momentum time.
T	E	M	P	T	Lure, allure, bait, inveigle, entice, decoy, seduce, provoke, solicit.
T	E	N	C	H	Freshwater fish.
T	E	N	E	T	Doctrine, dogma, belief, persuasion, conviction, canon.
T	E	N	N	E	Tawny, heraldic orange colour.
T	E	N	O	N	Mortise projection.
T	E	N	O	R	Drift, substance, meaning, Purport, intent, tendency. Procedure. Pitch of singer.
T	E	N	S	E	Taut, tight, edgy, nervy, uptight, uneasy, strained.
T	E	N	T	H	One of ten equal parts. Tithe.
T	E	N	T	S	Plural of TENT.
T	E	N	U	E	Bearing, deportment, carraige.
T	E	P	A	L	Modified leaf forming perianth.
T	E	P	E	E	Wigwam, Indian conical tent.
T	E	P	I	D	Lukewarm, moderately warm. Warmish. Temperate mild. Not enthused.
T	E	R	E	S	Elongated cylinder, long muscle.
T	E	R	R	A	Earth.
T	E	R	R	Y	Loop in pile, towelling. Cotton fabric.
T	E	R	S	E	Abrupt, brief, concise. Compact, lean, clear-cut, crisp, taut.
T	E	S	T	A	Hard seed coating.
T	E	S	T	S	Plural of TEST.
T	E	S	T	Y	Irritable, techy, touch, fretful, irascible, cranky, cross, ratty.
T	E	T	R	A	Four, having four parts.
T	E	W	E	L	Rectum, anus. Flue.
T	H	A	N	E	Land-owner. Anglo Saxon title. Servant retainer.
T	H	A	N	K	Express gratitude. Appreciate. Acknowledge.
T	H	A	W	Y	Inclined to thaw. Sloshy, wet.
T	H	E	C	A	Sac, case, capsule. Sheath.
T	H	E	F	T	Larceny, Purloining, pinching, thieving, filching, pilferage, swiping, robbery.
T	H	E	I	R	Belonging to them.
T	H	E	M	A	Thesis, theme.
T	H	E	M	E	Motive, topic, point, subject matter.
T	H	E	R	E	In that place. In a described position or place.
T	H	E	R	M	Heat unit, calorie.

1	2	3	4	5	
T	H	E	S	E	Plural of THIS.
T	H	E	T	A	8th Letter of Greek Alphabet.
T	H	I	C	K	Stocky, chunky, squat, thickset, broad, bulky, stupid, dense. Familiar.
T	H	I	E	F	Filcher, larcenist, pilferer, purloiner, robber, burglar, pick-pocket, Hi-jacker.
T	H	I	G	H	Upper part of leg.
T	H	I	N	E	Belonging to YOU. Of THY.
T	H	I	N	G	Article, entity, being, object, substance, item, occurrence, affair, action, act.
T	H	I	N	K	Cogitate, conceive, project, realise, consider, understand, feel, estimate, imagine.
T	H	I	R	D	One after SECOND. In third place.
T	H	O	L	E	Suffer, bear, tolerate. Peg, Pin.
T	H	O	N	G	Strap, lash, leather whip, strip.
T	H	O	R	N	Prong, spine, prickle.
T	H	O	S	E	Plural of THAT.
T	H	R	E	E	One more than TWO.
T	H	R	E	W	Past of THROW.
T	H	R	O	B	Pulsate, palpitate, pulse, beat, thrump.
T	H	R	O	E	Pang, agony, attack, seizure, spell, turn, convulsion, pain, pang, ache, stitch.
T	H	R	O	W	Cast, pitch, toss, hurl, fling. Risk, venture, stroke. Overcome, exert, apply.
T	H	R	U	M	Hum, bumble, buzz, drone, strum.
T	H	U	G	S	Plural of THUG.
T	H	U	M	B	First digit, pollex. Browse, leaf through, riffle. Hitchhike.
T	H	U	M	P	Thud, clunk, clonk, knock, hammer. Pommel, whack.
T	H	Y	M	E	Common garden Herb.
T	H	Y	M	Y	Fragrant, flavoured with thyme.
T	I	A	R	A	Royal headdress, diamond headband, Crown, Semi-circular head ornamentation.
T	I	B	B	Y	Cat, female feline.
T	I	B	E	Y	Poisonous foliage.
T	I	B	I	A	Shinbone.
T	I	C	K	S	Plural of TICK.
T	I	D	A	L	Actuated by tides. Depending on tides.
T	I	D	E	D	Affected by tides.
T	I	E	U	P	Fasten, restrain, link, preoccupy, dock, amalgamate. Connection.
T	I	G	E	R	Carnivorous mammal. Tawny coated. Large feline.
T	I	G	H	T	Fast, firm, close, compact, taut, tense, difficult, stingy, intoxicated. Hard.
T	I	K	K	A	Fungus disease of plants.
T	I	L	D	E	Mark used for biconditional connective. Mark to denote nasal sound.
T	I	L	E	D	Blocked, covered, plated. Checked, mottled, Roofed, imbricated.
T	I	L	E	R	Layer of mosiac or tiles.
T	I	L	T	H	Cultivation, tilling. Plowland.
T	I	M	E	D	Clocked, measured, scheduled, programmed.
T	I	M	E	R	Timing device. One who times.
T	I	M	E	S	Famous Newspaper. Numbers. Multiplication. Ages.
T	I	M	I	D	Shy, bashful, demure, modest, diffident, coy. Vacillating, halting, funky, cowardly.
T	I	N	C	T	Tinged, tinted. Tincture.
T	I	N	E	A	Fungal skin disease.
T	I	N	E	D	Pronged, forked.
T	I	N	E	S	Plural of TINE.
T	I	N	G	E	Colour, hue, tint, stain, complexion, shade, tone. Hint, trace, touch.
T	I	N	N	Y	Like tin, made of tin. Cheap. Metallic, harsh. Empty, wordy, insignificant.
T	I	N	T	Y	Hued, coloured.
T	I	P	P	Y	Unsteady, untrustworthy. Smart, stylish.
T	I	P	S	Y	Intoxicated, inebriated, drunk. Boozy, tiddly, tight.
T	I	R	E	D	Fatigued, wearied, drained, run-down. Pooped, exhausted, worn-out.
T	I	T	A	N	Huge, colossal, gigantic. Herculean, monstrous, might, titanic.
T	I	T	H	E	One tenth. Tax. Church Levy.
T	I	T	L	E	Claim, pretension. Name, appellation, denomination. Dub.
T	I	Z	Z	Y	State of excitement. Distracted.
T	O	A	D	Y	Sycophant, fawn, cringe, grovel, kowtow.
T	O	A	S	T	Sliced bread browned by heat. Celebratory proposal.
T	O	D	A	Y	Now, this day, the present time.
T	O	D	D	Y	Spiced alcoholic drink. Remedial drink.
T	O	G	U	E	Lake trout.
T	O	I	L	E	Muslin.
T	O	I	L	S	Coils, web, entanglements, meshes. Snares.
T	O	K	A	Y	Grape grown in Hungary, wine made from this variety of grape.
T	O	K	E	N	Sign, indication, omen, badge, mark. Remembrance, expression, gesture, pledge.
T	O	M	B	S	Plural of TOMB.

1	2	3	4	5	
T	O	M	E	S	Plural of TOME.
T	O	M	M	Y	British foot soldier.
T	O	N	A	L	Harmonious, timbered, tempered, accented. Sounding. Melodic.
T	O	N	E	D	Modulated, tinted, shaded, blended, coloured. Matched.
T	O	N	G	A	Variety of Bean.
T	O	N	G	S	Plural of TONG.
T	O	N	I	C	Restorative, astringent, animated, bracing, invigorating.
T	O	N	U	S	Muscle tone. Contraction.
T	O	O	L	S	Plural of TOOL.
T	O	O	T	H	Bony appendage of the Jaw. Fang. Incisor. Molar. Tusk. Sharp jagged projection.
T	O	P	A	Z	Yellow Quartz. Gem.
T	O	P	E	E	Helmet. Men's Sun hat.
T	O	P	E	R	Drunkard, boozer, soak, lush, tippler, inebriate.
T	O	P	I	C	Subject, theme, matter, motive, point, text.
T	O	P	S	Y	Turvy. Upside down. Disarranged.
T	O	Q	U	E	Soft narrow-brimmed hat. Bonnet.
T	O	R	A	H	Jewish scriptures. Old Testament.
T	O	R	C	H	Light, burning resin-stipped stick. Portable electric light.
T	O	R	I	L	Bull-pen.
T	O	R	S	K	Codfish.
T	O	R	S	O	Trunk. Upper body. Garment.
T	O	R	U	S	Skull protuberance. Bony ridge. Architectural moulding.
T	O	S	T	O	Musical direction.
T	O	T	A	L	Whole, sum, entirety, gross, aggregate, amount, bulk, quantity, quantum. Add.
T	O	T	E	D	Carried, lifted, transported. Bore.
T	O	T	E	M	Symbollic pole, pillar.
T	O	U	C	H	Contact, stroke, pat. Feel, handle, palpate, caress, fondle. Adjoin, verge. Arouse, stir. stimulate.
T	O	U	G	H	Tenacious, stalwart, strong, hard, flinty, unyielding, resistant, obstinate. Onerous.
T	O	U	R	S	Plural of TOUR.
T	O	U	S	E	Disturbance. Ado, fuss. Dishevel, worry, rack. Tussle.
T	O	U	S	Y	Dishevelled. Tousled. Makeshift.
T	O	W	E	D	Past of TOW.
T	O	W	E	L	Absorbent cloth. Napkin. Vesperal. Altar cloth.
T	O	W	E	R	Turret, Tall structure, steeple, citadel, fortress. Soar, dominate, overlook.
T	O	W	N	Y	Townish. Townsman.
T	O	X	I	C	Relating to Poison. Poisonous.
T	O	X	I	N	Poisonous substance. Venom.
T	O	Y	E	D	Played, fiddled, dallied, trifled, sported.
T	O	Y	E	R	One who TOYS.
T	R	A	C	E	Vestige, relic, token, evidence. Track, tread. Intimation. Trail.
T	R	A	C	K	Spoor, trail, path, way, thoroughfare, footprint, scent. Imprint, impression.
T	R	A	C	T	Homily, portion, section, pamphlet. Area, path, region, stretch, lot, plot.
T	R	A	D	E	Barter, traffic, buy and sell. Vocation, calling, business, swap, argue.
T	R	A	I	L	Follow, track, drag, traipse, trace, pursue. Tag, path, track, footpath.
T	R	A	I	N	Entourage, retinue. Alternation, chain. Teach, educate, instruct. Direct, aim. Succession, sequence.
T	R	A	I	T	Characteristic, quality, attribute, feature, demonimator, point.
T	R	A	M	P	Walk, tread, step, plod, march, footslog, trudge. Hobo, wanderer, loafer.
T	R	A	M	S	Plural of TRAM.
T	R	A	N	K	Glove body.
T	R	A	N	T	Peddle. Tout. Hawk.
T	R	A	P	A	Type of Waterchestnut.
T	R	A	P	S	Plural of TRAP. Possessions, packages, luggage.
T	R	A	S	H	Garbage, litter, debris, refuse, junk. Nonsense, bosh, claptrap.
T	R	A	S	S	Volcanic debris.
T	R	A	V	E	Crossbeam.
T	R	A	W	L	Fish by netting, troll, net, drag.
T	R	E	A	D	Trample, step, stride, ambulate, walk, traipse, march, pace, Stairway. Of a tyre.
T	R	E	A	T	Confer, consult, handle, serve, stand, stake. Delicacy, special function.
T	R	E	E	D	Cornered, collared, at bay.
T	R	E	E	N	Relating to trees. Wooden.
T	R	E	N	D	Tendency, drift, tenor, movement, direction, fashion, craze, style, vogue.
T	R	E	S	S	Lock of hair, ringlet, braid, plait, frond.
T	R	E	W	S	Trousers, pants, longs.
T	R	I	A	D	Union of three, trinity, trio, triumvirate, threesome, triple.
T	R	I	A	L	Test, ordeal, affliction, trouble, experiment, attempt, distress, misfortune. Court proceedings.
T	R	I	A	S	Triassic, division of Ages, Period.
T	R	I	B	E	Clan, Nation, class, race, family, kindred, stock, house.

1	2	3	4	5	
T	R	I	C	E	Short space of time.
T	R	I	C	K	Device, feint, gambit, gimmick, artifice, ploy. Prank, caper, spell, dupe, fool.
T	R	I	E	D	Past of TRY. Endeavoured.
T	R	I	E	R	One who TRIES.
T	R	I	E	S	Plural of TRY. Rugby Score.
T	R	I	L	L	Quaver, squeak, warble, drip, dribble, trickle, weep.
T	R	I	M	S	Plural of TRIM.
T	R	I	N	E	Threefold, triple. Favourable astrological aspect.
T	R	I	O	S	Plural of TRIO.
T	R	I	P	E	Stomach, innards, entrails, guts, insides. Nonsense.
T	R	I	P	S	Plural of TRIP, Stumble.
T	R	I	T	E	Hackneyed, timeworn, banal, vapid, exhausted, platitudinous, prosaic.
T	R	O	L	L	Seine fish, net, dredge. Trollop. Demon, monster.
T	R	O	M	P	Tramp, hike, slog, trample, trudge, stomp. Belabour, pummel, pound.
T	R	O	O	P	Company, corps, band, party, crowd, throng. Walk, traipse, tread, ambulate.
T	R	O	P	E	Misused word. Additional verse.
T	R	O	T	H	Engagement, pledge, betrothal, espousal, promise.
T	R	O	U	T	Fish of the Salmonidae family. Game fish, brown trout, rainbow trout. Bass.
T	R	O	V	E	Accumulation, amassment, collection, hoard, conglomeration.
T	R	U	C	E	Armistice, cease-fire, respite, lull. Pause, de-escalation, peace. Reconciliation.
T	R	U	C	K	Wheeled cartage vehicle. Barter, trade. Traffic. Commerce, dealings.
T	R	U	E	R	Comparative of TRUE. Grinding device.
T	R	U	F	F	Bull Trout.
T	R	U	L	L	Prostitute, strumpet. Boor, lout. Wanton, jade, slattern, tramp.
T	R	U	L	Y	Sincerely, realistically, truthfully, accurately. Indeed, genuinely. Rightly.
T	R	U	M	P	Trump card, clincher. Surpass, beat, excell, outstrip, pass.
T	R	U	N	K	Torso, main tree stem, central part. Chest, suitcase. Elephant proboscis. Boot, compartment for luggage.
T	R	U	S	S	Bind, tie, bundle, pack, bracket. Tripod, beam. Hernia support. Fruit cluster.
T	R	U	S	T	Assurance, confidence, faith, reliance. Certitude, conviction, custody.
T	R	U	T	H	Probity, veracity, truism, verity, candour, authenticity, genuinesness.
T	R	Y	O	N	Bluff, put on.
T	R	Y	S	T	Rendezvous. Meeting. Engagement, appointment, assignation, date.
T	U	A	T	H	People, An ancient territorial division.
T	U	B	A	L	Involving a tube.
T	U	B	B	Y	Fat, obese, rotund, chubby, plump, podgy.
T	U	B	E	D	Tracheotomized. Fitted with tube.
T	U	B	E	R	Thickened fleshy stem. Rhizome. Potato. One who works with tubes. Musical instrument.
T	U	C	K	S	Plural of TUCK.
T	U	D	O	R	Royal House.
T	U	F	T	Y	Full of Tufts. Fluffy, knotty.
T	U	I	S	M	Use of second person. Avoidance of first person.
T	U	L	I	P	Coloured flower.
T	U	L	L	E	Sheer fabric. Mesh.
T	U	M	I	D	Bulging, protuberant, bombastic, turgid.
T	U	M	M	Y	Stomach, abdomen, belly.
T	U	N	E	D	Melodious, melodic, musical, euphonic. Harmonized, adapted, calibrated.
T	U	N	E	R	Specialist in musical instrument tuning. Device for tuning. Pitch pipe. Tuning Fork.
T	U	N	E	S	Plural of TUNE.
T	U	N	I	C	Slip-on garment. Soldier's jacket. Mantle, surcoat, tunicle. Loose garment.
T	U	N	N	Y	Game-fish. Tunny-fish. Tuna, Blue Fin.
T	U	R	F	Y	Having lush green grass. Pertaining to horse-racing.
T	U	R	N	S	Plural of Turn.
T	U	R	P	S	Turpentine.
T	U	S	C	H	Fanfare flourish.
T	U	S	K	S	Plural of TUSK.
T	U	S	K	Y	With long teeth. Toothy.
T	U	T	O	R	Coach, teacher, instructor. Instruct, advise. Mentor. Teach.
T	U	T	T	I	Musical direction.
T	U	T	T	Y	Flower, nosegay. Crude Zinc Oxide.
T	W	A	I	N	Couple, pair, two.
T	W	A	N	G	Nasal sound. Vibrate. Pluck a string. Discharge arrow. Flavour, tang. Trace.
T	W	A	N	K	Abrupt twang sound. Nasal note.
T	W	E	A	K	Twitch, jerk, jog, snatch, pinch. Twist.
T	W	E	E	D	Suiting fabric. Tweed cloth. Twill.
T	W	E	E	G	Hellbender, jag.
T	W	E	E	L	Clay furnace covering. Furnace Door.
T	W	E	E	N	In between.

1	2	3	4	5	
T	W	E	E	T	Whistle, chirp.
T	W	E	R	P	Contemptible fellow.
T	W	I	C	E	One more than once. Double. Twofold. Two times.
T	W	I	G	S	Plural of TWIG.
T	W	I	L	L	Woven fabric, tweed. Dialectic form of "it will".
T	W	I	N	E	String, cord, entwine, wind. Coil, corkscrew, curl, twist, wreath.
T	W	I	N	K	Twinkle, blink, flash, flicker.
T	W	I	N	S	Plural of TWIN.
T	W	I	R	L	Spin, gyrate, pirouette, whirl.
T	W	I	S	T	Turn, wrench, rick, sprain. Misrepresent, distort, falsify. Coil, curl, spiral.
T	W	I	T	S	Plural of TWIT.
T	W	I	X	T	Between, betwixt, mixed up, in the middle.
T	W	O	U	P	Doubled, gambling game.
T	Y	I	N	G	Fastening, Completing an agreement.
T	Y	P	A	L	Relating to types.
T	Y	P	E	D	Past of TYPE.
T	Y	P	E	S	Plural of TYPE.
T	Y	R	E	D	Having tyres, wheeled, pneumatic.
T	Y	R	O	S	Plural of TYRO.

U

U	B	O	A	T	Submarine.
U	D	D	E	R	Mammary gland, breast, nipples, teats. Milk bar.
U	H	U	R	U	Black Freedom. (Kenya)
U	K	A	S	E	Edict, directive, ruling, decree.
U	L	C	E	R	Skin lesion, abscess, sore, wound.
U	L	N	A	D	Toward the Ulna.
U	L	N	A	R	Relating to the ulna.
U	L	T	R	A	Extreme, fanatical, superlative, uncompromising, radical.
U	M	B	E	L	Inflorescence.
U	M	B	E	R	Brown pigment. Like umber.
U	M	B	R	A	Darkness, shadow. Sunspot. Freshwater fish genus. Apparition, phantom.
U	M	B	R	E	Hammerkop.
U	N	A	P	T	Inappropriate, unsuitable, backward, slow, dull. Irrelevant. Improper.
U	N	A	R	M	Disarm. Win over. Persuade.
U	N	A	R	Y	Containing one component.
U	N	B	A	R	Unlock, open, unbolt, free.
U	N	B	E	D	Remove from bed. Stir. Bestir.
U	N	B	I	D	Unbidden, uninvited. Sudden. Spontaneous.
U	N	B	O	W	Unbend. Loosen.
U	N	B	O	X	Unpack, expose.
U	N	C	A	P	Uncover. Open.
U	N	C	L	E	Relative. Father or mother's brother. Kind man.
U	N	C	U	S	Claw, hook.
U	N	C	U	T	Whole, untrimmed, unshaped, not reduced, unabridged, not curtailed, Unabbreviated.
U	N	D	E	R	Underneath, below, subject to, lower, inferior, subordinate, dependent.
U	N	D	I	D	Past of UNDO.
U	N	D	U	E	Improper, ill-timed, unapt, unsuitable, untimely, inappropriate, excessive.
U	N	F	E	D	Hungry, unnourished, neglected, impoverished.
U	N	F	I	T	Unqualified, incapable, incompetent, maladjusted, unsuitable, inapt, improper.
U	N	F	I	X	Detach, loosen, undo, disengage, unfasten, unbind.
U	N	I	F	Y	Unite, combine, organize, tie, harmonize, integrate, blend, synthesize.
U	N	I	O	N	Coalition, joining, amalgamation, consolidation, oneness, combination. Guild.
U	N	I	T	E	Join, associate, marry, relate, link, couple, band, conjoin, bind, affiliate.
U	N	I	T	Y	Singularity, identity, harmony, rapport, individuality, accord, concord, solidarity.
U	N	L	A	P	Unwrap, uncover.
U	N	L	A	W	Annul. Illegality, lawlesness.
U	N	L	A	X	Relax, rest, unbend. Unwind, loosen up, ease off.
U	N	L	A	Y	Untwist, unravel.
U	N	L	E	D	Footloose, misguided.
U	N	L	E	T	Vacant, unoccupied, tenantless, unrented.
U	N	M	A	N	Unnerve, dishearten, degrade, exhaust, abase, disqualify, prostrate. Emasculate.
U	N	P	E	G	Cease currency pegging transactions. Unfasten.
U	N	P	E	N	Release, unconfine.
U	N	R	I	G	Undress, unclothe, disassemble.

1	2	3	4	5	
U	N	R	I	P	Reveal, show, disclose.
U	N	S	A	Y	Retract, recall, recant, disavow.
U	N	S	E	T	Displace, unsettle, runny, liquid. Unmounted.
U	N	S	E	X	Remove sexual power. Geld, spay, sterilize, castrate, neuter, fix, alter.
U	N	S	O	N	Dispossess, disinherit.
U	N	T	A	X	Remove taxation.
U	N	T	I	E	Loosen, unbind, undo, unknot, extricate, disentangle, untangle, untwine.
U	N	T	I	L	Till.
U	N	W	E	D	Single, unmarried, spouseless, free, sole.
U	N	Z	I	P	Undo, open, loosen.
U	P	E	N	D	Tilt, turn upside down, expose.
U	P	F	L	Y	Fly up, ascend.
U	P	P	E	D	Past of UP.
U	P	P	E	R	One above, higher, outer, innermost, Shoe above the sole. Top. Topmost.
U	P	S	E	T	Disconcert, agitate, bother, overturn, topple disorder, unsettle, distress, worry.
U	R	B	A	N	City bound, civic, metropolitan, municipal, characteristic of the city.
U	R	E	I	C	Relating to Urea.
U	R	E	N	A	Tropical herb family.
U	R	G	E	D	Prompted, encouraged, pressured, pushed, hustled, goaded, prompted, drove.
U	R	G	E	R	One who URGES.
U	R	G	E	S	Act of URGING. Desires, appetites, passions, incentives, spurs.
U	R	I	A	L	Wild Asian sheep.
U	R	I	N	E	Liquid matter discharged by kidneys.
U	R	I	T	E	Arthropod segment.
U	R	N	A	L	Like an Urn.
U	R	N	E	D	Enclosed in an Urn.
U	R	S	U	S	Genus of Bears.
U	R	U	B	U	American Vulture.
U	R	U	T	U	American pit viper.
U	S	A	G	E	Custom, habit, practice, procedure, process, form, convention, formality.
U	S	H	E	R	Leader, conductor, harbinger, male attendant. Precede, introduce, lead, preface.
U	S	I	N	G	Act of making USE.
U	S	U	A	L	Habitual, accustomed, normal, ordinary, accepted, routine, regular, prevalent.
U	S	U	R	P	Supplant, take over, arrogate, preempt, displace. Commander.
U	S	U	R	Y	Interest, premium, legal rate of interest. Exorbitant charge.
U	T	I	L	E	Useful, practical, functional, serviceable.
U	T	T	E	R	Absolutely, completely, downright, outright. Speak, vocalize, say, state.
U	V	U	L	A	Fleshy lobe of palate. Part of bladder. Lobe of cerebellum.

V

V	A	G	A	L	Relating to the Vagus nerve.
V	A	G	U	E	Ambiguous, obscure, indeterminate, hazy, vaporous, ill-defined, unintelligible.
V	A	G	U	S	Cranial nerve.
V	A	L	E	S	Plural of VALE.
V	A	L	E	T	Domestic maleservant, page, manservant, gentleman's gentleman.
V	A	L	I	D	Cogent, convincing, lawful, legal, substantial, corroborated.
V	A	L	S	E	Waltz, three-step. Dance.
V	A	L	U	E	Worth, quality, calibre, estimate, assay, assess, survey, appreciate, cherish. Cost.
V	A	L	V	E	Cock, hydrant, spigot, faucet, tap, stopcock, gate.
V	A	M	P	S	Plural of VAMP.
V	A	N	E	S	Plural of VANE.
V	A	N	G	S	Plural of VANG.
V	A	P	I	D	Insipid, empty, inane, jejune, weak, dull, mild, unimaginative.
V	A	P	O	R	Diffused matter, steam, smoke, fumes, fog, mist. Phantasm, foolish notion.
V	A	R	E	C	Seaweed. Kelp.
V	A	R	I	A	Miscellany.
V	A	R	I	X	Abnormal dilation of veins.
V	A	R	U	S	Abnormally positioned. Pigeon-toed.
V	A	S	A	L	Relating to an anatomical vessel.
V	A	S	T	Y	Immense, great.
V	A	T	I	C	Prophetic, oracular. sibylline, apocalyptic, prophetical.
V	A	U	L	T	Crypt, tomb, catacomb, cellar. Jump, hurdle, leap, spring, soar, negotiate.
V	A	U	N	T	Swagger, boast, brag, brandish, exhibit, flaunt, parade.
V	E	A	L	Y	Like veal.
V	E	E	R	Y	The tawny thrush of North America.

1	2	3	4	5	
V	E	I	L	S	Plural of VEIL.
V	E	I	N	S	Plural of VEIN.
V	E	I	N	Y	Veined, veinous.
V	E	L	A	R	Relating to the soft palate.
V	E	L	U	M	Soft palate. Delicate membrane. Universal veil.
V	E	N	A	L	Mercenary, saleable, corrupt. Crooked, infamous, nefarious, unethical.
V	E	N	O	M	Poison, contagion, virulence, malignity, toxin.
V	E	N	T	S	Plural of VENT.
V	E	N	U	E	Meeting place, location, position, ground, line of argument. Locality of execution.
V	E	N	U	S	Beautiful woman. Roman Goddess of Love. Planet. Bivalve Mollusc.
V	E	R	G	E	Edge, border, boundary, fringe, rim, surround, margin. Abut, Adjoin. Approach.
V	E	R	S	E	Poem, poetry, stanza, rhyming words. Study, familiarize.
V	E	R	S	O	Unevenly numbered page. Back cover.
V	E	R	S	T	Russian unit of distance.
V	E	R	V	E	Energy, spirit, animation, elan, vim, life, vivacity, buoyancy, gusto, zest.
V	E	S	P	A	Genus of Hornet.
V	E	S	T	A	Wooden Match. Lucifer, taper.
V	E	S	T	S	Plural of VEST.
V	E	T	C	H	Twining plant, herbaceous legume, Ers.
V	E	X	E	D	Annoyed, cross, upset, bothered, provoked, irked, irritated, aggravated, perplexed.
V	E	X	E	R	One who VEXES.
V	I	A	N	D	Food, provender, provision, victual, edible, victuals, grub.
V	I	B	E	S	Vibrations, sensations, reactions, feelings. Vibrophones.
V	I	B	E	X	Blood clot, weal.
V	I	C	A	R	Parson, Minister, Priest.
V	I	C	E	S	Plural of VICE.
V	I	D	E	O	Television. Relating to transmission or reception of television image. Recorder.
V	I	E	W	S	Plural of VIEW.
V	I	G	I	L	Watch, nightwatch, nocturnal devotions. Act of watching, sojourn, stay.
V	I	G	O	R	Power, energy, force, potency, drive, pep, enterprise, spirit, zip, vim, zing.
V	I	L	E	R	Comparative of VILE.
V	I	L	L	A	Mansion, chateau, country house, manor.
V	I	N	E	D	Covered in vines.
V	I	N	E	S	Plural of VINE.
V	I	N	T	A	Dugout canoe.
V	I	N	T	S	Plural of VINT.
V	I	N	Y	L	Polymer compound. Vinyl Resin, Plastic.
V	I	O	L	A	Musical instrument.
V	I	P	E	R	Venomous snake. Treacherous person.
V	I	R	A	L	Pertaining to a virus.
V	I	R	G	O	Sixth sign of the Zodiac.
V	I	R	I	D	Green, verdant.
V	I	R	T	U	Study of the arts. Objects D'Art, Antique art.
V	I	R	U	S	Contagion, ineffective agent, disease, germ, poison.
V	I	S	I	T	Visitation, sojourn, stopover, call. Converse, talk, drop in, tarriance.
V	I	S	O	R	Vizor. Mask, face piece, eyeshade, windshield, face guard. Peak.
V	I	S	T	A	Extensive view. Outlook, perspective, panorama, scope, scene, range.
V	I	T	A	L	Vigorous, dynamic, lusty, essential, fundamental, animated, alive. Important.
V	I	T	E	X	Genus of tropical shrub.
V	I	T	I	S	Woody vine.
V	I	T	T	A	Streak, stripe. Plait.
V	I	V	A	T	Vive.
V	I	V	I	D	Bright, colourful, graphic, picturesque, sharp, dramatic, expressive, lively.
V	I	X	E	N	Female fox. Shrewish woman, virago, fishwife, shrew, scold.
V	I	Z	O	R	Visor. Face guard, eyeshade, mask.
V	O	C	A	L	Relating to voice. Voiced, intonated, Articulate, fluent, eloquent, voluble. Glib.
V	O	D	E	R	Speech simulator.
V	O	D	K	A	Alcoholic odourless drink.
V	O	G	U	E	Fashion, style, popularity. Trend, character, temper. Mode, practice.
V	O	I	C	E	Utterance, speech, expression, utter, talk, speak. Enunciate, pronounce.
V	O	I	D	S	Plural of VOID.
V	O	I	L	E	Sheer fabric, see-thru material.
V	O	L	A	R	Relating to the palm of the hand or the sole of the foot.
V	O	L	E	S	Plural of VOLE.
V	O	L	T	A	Turn, lavolta. Active Dance.
V	O	L	T	E	Plural of VOLTA.
V	O	L	T	S	Plural of VOLT.

1	2	3	4	5	
V	O	L	V	A	Membranous bulbous sac.
V	O	M	E	R	Bone of the skull.
V	O	M	I	T	Nausea, spew, disgorge. Bring up, regurgitate. Retch, spout.
V	O	T	E	D	Past of VOTE.
V	O	T	E	R	One who casts a VOTE.
V	O	U	C	H	Gurantee, certify, attest, confirm, witness, prove, assure, verify.
V	O	W	E	D	Past of VOW.
V	O	W	E	L	A, E, I, O, U and sometimes Y.
V	O	W	E	R	One who VOWS.
V	R	O	U	W	A woman, goodwife, housewife.
V	U	L	V	A	External female genital organ.
V	Y	I	N	G	Contending, competing, challenging.

W

W	A	C	K	Y	Foolish, crazy, harebrained, deranged, potty, mad, nuts.
W	A	D	D	Y	Walking stick, club, cudgel, peg. Rustler, cowboy.
W	A	D	E	D	Past of WADE.
W	A	D	E	R	One who WADES. Wading boot, Waterproof garment. Wading Bird such as heron, stork, etc.
W	A	D	E	S	Act of WADING.
W	A	F	E	R	Crisp, bread, cracker, Altar Bread. Seal, fasten, adhesive.
W	A	G	E	D	Past of WAGE.
W	A	G	E	L	Gull.
W	A	G	E	R	Bet, stake, gamble, guess, risk, venture, hazard. Pot, ante.
W	A	G	E	S	Remuneration, salary, reward, return, earnings, deserts.
W	A	G	G	Y	With tendency to WAG. Waggily.
W	A	G	O	N	Four-wheeled conveyance, cart, van.
W	A	I	L	S	Plural of WAIL.
W	A	I	S	T	Midriff, middle, bodice line, part of human body between thorax and hips.
W	A	I	T	S	Plural of WAIT.
W	A	I	V	E	Set aside, relinquish, cede, resign, surrender, abandon, defer, suspend.
W	A	K	E	N	Awaken, stir, arouse, bestir, rouse, whet, kindle.
W	A	K	E	S	Plural of WAKE.
W	A	L	E	D	Striped, Ridged, having wales.
W	A	L	E	R	Large saddle horse.
W	A	L	E	S	Plural of WALE.
W	A	L	K	S	Plural of WALK.
W	A	L	L	S	Plural of WALL.
W	A	L	T	Z	Three-step, dance, walk aimlessly, wander. Lug, carry, lead.
W	A	N	D	Y	Slender, slim, like a wand. Flexible.
W	A	N	E	D	Past of WANE.
W	A	N	E	S	Act of WANING.
W	A	N	L	Y	Languidly, thinly, sickly, weakly, ineffectively, insipidly.
W	A	R	D	S	Plural of WARD.
W	A	R	E	S	Goods, merchandise, trade material, commodities.
W	A	R	P	S	Plural of WARP.
W	A	R	T	S	Plural of WART.
W	A	R	T	Y	Having Warts. Verrucose, Wartlike.
W	A	S	H	Y	Feeble, watery, thin, weak, diluted.
W	A	S	P	Y	Irritable, fractious, fretful, petulant, cantankerous, crotchety, querulous.
W	A	S	T	E	Debris, garbage, litter. Extravagance, Desert, ravage, fail, weaken, shrink.
W	A	T	C	H	Timepiece. Lookout, guard, see, scrutinize, attend, look, mind, vigil.
W	A	T	E	R	Rain, liquid, irrigate, moisten, spray, tears, saliva, drool. Dilute.
W	A	V	E	D	Past of WAVE. Curled, crimped.
W	A	V	E	R	Hesitate, falter, vacillate, teeter, sway, waffle, stagger.
W	A	V	E	S	Plural of WAVE.
W	A	X	E	D	Past of WAX.
W	A	X	E	N	Like wax, pallid, pale, lacking animation. Listless.
W	A	X	E	R	Furniture waxer, One who operates waxing machine. Wax applicator.
W	E	A	L	D	Wooded area, wold, woodland. Forest.
W	E	A	R	Y	Tired, exhausted, uninterested, fatigued, fed up, disgusted, sick.
W	E	A	V	E	Plait, entwine, intertwine. Lurch, stagger, sway.
W	E	B	B	Y	Like WEB.
W	E	D	G	E	Wood taper, log, stopper, three-cornered. Fit tightly, crowd, cram, squeeze.
W	E	E	D	S	Plural of WEED.
W	E	E	D	Y	Lanky, thin, weak, insipid, unimpressive, unimportant.

1	2	3	4	5	
W	E	E	N	Y	Tiny, minute, dainty, diminutive, miniature, wee.
W	E	E	P	Y	Tearful, lachrymose, oozing, weeping.
W	E	I	G	H	Balance, measure, consider, study, contemplate, encumber, militate, count.
W	E	I	R	D	Strange, bizarre, curious, uncanny, unnatural, mysterious, queer. Fate, destiny.
W	E	I	R	S	Plural of WEIR.
W	E	L	L	S	Plural of WELL.
W	E	L	S	H	Coming from Wales. Renege, revoke, abscond, back out, cry off.
W	E	L	T	S	Plural of WELT.
W	E	N	C	H	Girl, damsel, maiden, lass, gal, miss. Wanton, hussy, slut, trollop.
W	H	A	C	K	Strike, smack, bash, wallop. Fling, whirl. Defeat, beat.
W	H	A	L	E	Giant marine mammal. Mammoth, monster. Whip, flog, attack. Thrash. Defeat.
W	H	A	N	G	Resonant sound, vibration. Beat, strike.
W	H	A	R	F	Dock, berth, jetty, pier, slipway, quay.
W	H	E	A	L	Raised skin, scar, welt, whale, streak, stripe.
W	H	E	A	T	Cereal grain, staple, breadstuff.
W	H	E	E	L	Circle, round, circular frame. Reel, turn, cycle, rotation, pivot, veer, whirl.
W	H	E	L	K	Snail, marine, mollusc. Gather whelks. Welt, weal, wale. Whelp.
W	H	E	L	M	Deluge, engulf, overwhelm, submerge. Overcome, prostrate.
W	H	E	L	P	Litter. Pup, cub. Weal, welt, whelk.
W	H	E	R	E	Wherever, whereabouts, place, location, wherever, point, situation, spot.
W	H	I	C	H	What, whichever, interrogative pronoun, function word.
W	H	I	F	F	Scent, smell, sniff, hint, breath, trace, tinge, trifle. Odour.
W	H	I	L	E	Indefinite period, space, spell, occasion, moment, bit, pass the time.
W	H	I	M	S	Plural of WHIM.
W	H	I	N	E	Whimper, complain, murmur, wail, fuss, snivel.
W	H	I	R	L	Spin, Twirl, gyrate, eddy, revolution, commotion, fling, stir, bustle. Deflect.
W	H	I	S	H	Hiss, whiz, swish, fizz, buzz, hurry, speed, whirl, wiz, whisk.
W	H	I	S	K	Beater, whip. Hasten, hurry, zip, flit, whish.
W	H	I	S	T	Card game, Bridge. Hush, silent, noiseless, still.
W	H	I	T	E	Colourless, pale, chalky, pallid, favourable, reactionary, whiten, palliate, blanched.
W	H	I	Z	Z	Whiz, swish, buzz, hurry, whirl, whisk.
W	H	O	L	E	Entire, intact, perfect, unbroken, healthy, total, cohesion, integral, entity.
W	H	O	O	P	Yell, shout, exclaim, cheer. Hoot, whit, jot, iota.
W	H	O	R	E	Prostitute, harlot, bawd, call girl, streetwalker, hooker, hetera, courtesan.
W	H	O	R	L	Swirl, eddy, whirl, whirlpool, convolution, swoosh, spiral.
W	H	O	S	E	Interrogative pronoun, belonging to whom. Possessor.
W	H	O	S	O	Whoever.
W	I	C	K	S	Plural of WICK.
W	I	D	D	Y	Hangman's Noose.
W	I	D	E	N	Enlarge, extend, lengthen, broaden.
W	I	D	E	R	More extensive, larger, broader, lengthier.
W	I	D	O	W	Woman on husband's death before remarriage. Relict. Bereaved woman. Genus of spiders.
W	I	D	T	H	Span, range, ambit, extension, length, radius, scope, panorama.
W	I	E	L	D	Manipulate, dispense, exercise, throw, control, exert, manoeuvre.
W	I	F	E	Y	Little wife.
W	I	G	A	N	Cotton fabric.
W	I	G	G	Y	Pompous, bewigged, formal, arrogant, self-important.
W	I	G	H	T	Personage, creature, mortal, human, man.
W	I	L	E	D	Attracted, beguiled, tricked, bewitched, captivated, charmed. Past of WILE.
W	I	L	E	S	Plural of WILE.
W	I	L	L	S	Plural of WILL.
W	I	L	L	Y	Wicker basket, fish trap.
W	I	N	C	E	Groan, flinch, shrink, recoil, dodge, swerve, cower, moan.
W	I	N	C	H	Hoist, reel, roll. Windlass, Hoisting machine.
W	I	N	D	S	Plural of WIND.
W	I	N	D	Y	Blowy, gusty, drafty. Wordy, inflated, flatulent, timid, verbose, scared.
W	I	N	E	D	Drank wine, imbibed. Dined.
W	I	N	E	S	Plural of WINE.
W	I	N	G	S	Plural of WING.
W	I	N	G	Y	Flying, hurrying, scurrying. Fleet.
W	I	N	K	S	Plural of WINK.
W	I	P	E	D	Erased, effaced, expunged, Plural of WIPE.
W	I	P	E	R	Someone who WIPES. Automatic wiping device.
W	I	R	E	D	Connected with wires (electricity), strengthened, bound, fenced, telegraphed.
W	I	R	E	S	Plural of WIRE.
W	I	S	E	R	Comparative of WISE.
W	I	S	P	Y	Frail, delicate, nebulous, sketchy, thin.

1	2	3	4	5	
W	I	T	C	H	Hex, sorceress, hag. Crone, Bag. Enchantress.
W	I	T	H	E	Wand, twig, band.
W	I	T	H	Y	Willow, oisier, wand, looped twig.
W	I	T	T	Y	Facetious, jocular, scintillating, funny, amusing, humorous.
W	I	V	E	S	Plural of WIFE.
W	I	Z	E	N	Wither, shrivel.
W	O	D	G	E	Lump, mass, cluster.
W	O	M	A	N	Female human.
W	O	M	B	S	Plural of WOMB.
W	O	M	E	N	Plural of WOMAN.
W	O	O	D	S	Plural of WOOD. Golf Clubs. Bowls.
W	O	O	D	Y	Made of wood. Sylvan. Overgrown.
W	O	O	E	D	Past of WOO.
W	O	O	E	R	Lover, Suitor, boyfriend, swain.
W	O	O	F	Y	Woven, textured.
W	O	O	L	D	Wind, wrap, twist.
W	O	O	Z	Y	Dizzy, vague, woolly, bleary, weak, faint.
W	O	R	D	S	Plural of WORD.
W	O	R	D	Y	Long-winded, verbose, garrulous, voluble, talkative.
W	O	R	K	S	Plural of WORK.
W	O	R	L	D	Universe, Earth, Planet, Globe. Creation, environment.
W	O	R	M	S	Plural of WORM.
W	O	R	M	Y	Infested with worms.
W	O	R	R	Y	Anxiety, concern, uneasiness, disquiet. Trouble, needle, pester, bother, goad.
W	O	R	S	E	Comparative of BAD.
W	O	R	S	T	Comparative of WORSE.
W	O	R	T	H	Value, quality, wealth, resources, valuation, class, virtue, usefulness, weight.
W	O	U	L	D	Past of WILL. Conditional verb.
W	O	U	N	D	Wrapped, tied. Injury, hurt, sore. Damage, lacerate. Lesion, trauma, contusion.
W	O	V	E	N	Past of WEAVE.
W	O	W	E	D	Impressed, overcame, overawed, entertained.
W	R	A	C	K	Ruin, destroy. Uncertainty, raze. Pain, Rack.
W	R	A	P	T	Past of WRAP.
W	R	A	T	H	Anger, rage, fury, ire, indignation, acrimony, resentment, passion.
W	R	E	A	K	Inflict, force, visit, impose, avenge.
W	R	E	C	K	Crash, smash, vandalize, destroy, decimate, sabotage, shipwreck, Pile-up. Irreparable broken.
W	R	E	S	T	Wrench, wring, extract, extort. Wring, twist, misrepresent, distort. Grapple, wrestle.
W	R	I	C	K	Sprain, strain, twist, hurt.
W	R	I	E	R	Comparative of WRY.
W	R	I	N	G	Squeeze, wrench, press, wrest, screw. Afflict, torment, agonize.
W	R	I	S	T	Lower joint of the arm. Carpus. cuff, ruffle, band.
W	R	I	T	E	Pen, scribe, draft, scribble, scrawl, record, compose.
W	R	O	N	G	Incorrect, erroneous, false. Injure, aggrieve, oppress. Evil, immoral, false, unfit, mistaken.
W	R	O	T	E	Past of WRITE.
W	R	O	T	H	Wrathful, Intense anger, incensed, commotion, turbulence.
W	R	U	N	G	Past of WRING.
W	R	Y	L	Y	Dryly, caustically.
W	U	M	P	S	Sounds of falling objects.
W	U	R	S	T	German sausage.

X	E	B	E	C	Three-masted rigged sailing ship.
X	E	R	I	C	Environment of insufficient plant moisture. Xerophytic.
X	E	R	U	S	Long-tailed ground squirrel.
X	H	O	S	A	Transkeian. The language.
X	R	A	Y	S	Plural of X-RAY.
X	Y	L	E	M	Complex plant tissue system.
X	Y	L	I	S	Genus of marsh plant.
X	Y	L	O	L	Commercial use of XYLENE. Type of Benzene.
X	Y	L	Y	L	Benzyl.

Y	A	C	H	T	Sailing ship, racing vessel, pleasure boat.
Y	A	H	O	O	Lout, ruffian, punk, tough, roughneck, hillbilly, rustic.

1	2	3	4	5	
Y	A	N	K	S	Pulls, tugs, drags, jerks, extracts, tears, grabs. Americans (Sl.)
Y	A	R	D	S	Plural of YARD.
Y	A	R	N	S	Plural of YARN.
Y	A	W	E	D	Veered off course. Swerved, Drifted, Deflected.
Y	A	W	L	S	Plural of YAWL.
Y	A	W	N	S	Plural of YAWN.
Y	A	W	N	Y	Soporific, tired, bored.
Y	A	W	P	S	Plural of YAWP.
Y	E	A	R	A	Poison oak.
Y	E	A	R	N	Long for, desire, craving. Emotional longing, express craving.
Y	E	A	R	S	Plural of YEAR. Period of time, age, cycle, class.
Y	E	A	S	T	Raising agent, leaven, fermentation. Foam, lather, spume.
Y	E	G	G	Y	Horrid, abhorent, despicable, unsavoury.
Y	E	L	L	S	Plural of YELL.
Y	E	U	K	Y	Itchy.
Y	I	E	L	D	Give over, relinquish, cede, discharge, collapse, output, production.
Y	O	D	E	L	Swiss mountaineers' call. Ululate. Howl. Yell.
Y	O	G	I	C	Relating to the practice of YOGA.
Y	O	G	I	S	Plural of YOGI.
Y	O	K	E	D	Linked, paired, wedded, coupled, bonded, knotted, hitched, joined, associated.
Y	O	K	E	L	Country bumpkin, rustic, lout, clodhopper, hick, hillbilly.
Y	O	K	E	S	Plural of YOKE.
Y	O	L	K	Y	Like egg-yoke.
Y	O	U	N	G	Juvenile, childish, infantile, youthful, inexperienced, callow. New, Fresh, tender. The offspring of.
Y	O	U	T	H	Adolescence, immaturity. Lad, stripling, youngster.
Y	O	W	L	S	Plural of YOWL.
Y	U	C	C	A	Genus of spiky flowers. Lily.
Y	U	L	E	S	Plural of YULE.
Y	U	M	M	Y	Tasty, nice, delightful, delicious, delectable, scrumptious.

Z

Z	A	B	R	A	Ancient sailing vessel.
Z	A	M	I	A	Genus of American Cycads.
Z	A	P	P	Y	Zesty, full of vim, vigorous.
Z	E	A	L	Y	Full of Zeal. Enthusiastic.
Z	E	B	R	A	Striped equine mammal.
Z	E	R	O	S	Plural of ZERO.
Z	E	S	T	Y	Pungent, piquant, spicy. Snappy, Poignant, racy.
Z	I	N	C	S	Plural of ZINC.
Z	I	N	K	E	Cornet, pointed.
Z	I	N	K	Y	Like Zinc.
Z	I	P	P	Y	Fast, quick, fleet, nimble. Brisk, snappy.
Z	O	I	S	M	Belief in animal life. Doctrine of elan vital.
Z	O	I	S	T	Adherent to ZOISM.
Z	O	N	A	L	Pertaining to ZONE
Z	O	N	E	D	Divided into zones. Partitioned.
Z	O	N	E	S	Plural of ZONE.
Z	O	O	M	S	Plural of ZOOM.
Z	O	O	T	Y	Flashy fashion, zoot style.
Z	O	P	P	A	Syncopated.
Z	O	R	R	A	Type of coarse grass.
Z	Y	M	I	N	Zyme. Enzyme.

1	2	3	4	5	6	
A	B	A	C	U	S	Calculating device.
A	B	A	S	E	D	Lowered, humbled, debased, demeaned, degraded.
A	B	A	S	I	A	Halt, Limp. Unco-ordinated muscle control.
A	B	A	T	E	D	Eased, diminished, dwindled, lessened, moderated, subsided, lulled. Precipitate entry.
A	B	A	T	E	S	Act of ABATING.
A	B	A	T	I	S	Tree-formed obstacle. Defensive barrier.
A	B	A	T	O	R	One who abates.
A	B	B	A	C	Y	Tenure of an Abbot.
A	B	B	E	S	S	Mother Superior, Mother Prioress. Head of Convent.
A	B	B	O	T	S	Plural of ABBOT.
A	B	D	U	C	E	Abduct.
A	B	D	U	C	T	Carry off, kidnap, separate.
A	B	E	L	I	A	Genus of Shrub.
A	B	I	D	E	D	Past of ABIDE.
A	B	I	E	N	T	Avoidance, withdrawal syndrome.
A	B	J	E	C	T	Downhearted, beaten, servile, helpless. Outcast.
A	B	J	U	R	E	Renounce, retract, withdraw, repudiate, forswear, forsake, relinquish.
A	B	L	A	Z	E	Alight, burning, aflame, blazing, ignited, flaming, fiery, aglow.
A	B	L	E	S	T	Most able, cleverest, comparative of ABLE.
A	B	L	O	O	M	Blooming, flowering.
A	B	L	U	S	H	Blushing, confused, flushed.
A	B	O	A	R	D	On board.
A	B	O	D	E	S	Plural of ABODE.
A	B	O	R	A	L	Aborad, opposite the mouth.
A	B	O	U	N	D	Present, available, full, overflow, teem, swarm. Abundant.
A	B	R	A	D	E	Chafe, excoriate, rub, grate, scrape, fret, corrode, ruffle, annoy, irk, bug.
A	B	R	O	A	D	Overseas, afar, away.
A	B	R	U	P	T	Precipitate, impetuous, sudden, Curt, gruff, sharp. Steep, sheer.
A	B	S	E	N	T	Away, gone, not present, left. Preoccupied, abstracted, far away, absentminded.
A	B	S	O	R	B	Assimilate, soak up, imbibe, monopolise, consume, engross, preoccupy.
A	B	S	U	R	D	Foolish, asinine, preposterous, silly, funny, fatuous, unreasonable, comic.
A	B	U	S	E	D	Violated, exploited, perverted, harmed, impaired, oppressed, manhandled.
A	B	U	S	E	R	One who ABUSES.
A	B	U	S	E	S	Plural of ABUSE.
A	C	A	C	I	A	Genus of Shrub.
A	C	A	R	U	S	Genus of Arachnids. Mites, Ticks.
A	C	C	E	D	E	Assent, consent, subscribe, concur, allow, permit, acquiese, agree.
A	C	C	E	N	T	Inflection, cadence, intonation, tone, vernacular, dialect. Emphasis, stress.
A	C	C	E	P	T	Receive, take, sustain, endure, approve, believe, comprehend, swallow.
A	C	C	E	S	S	Entry, door, admittance, entrance, Onset, attack, outburst, passage, approach.
A	C	C	O	R	D	Harmony, agreement, sympathy, empathy. Agree, conform, grant, award.
A	C	C	O	S	T	Challenge, confront, outrage, offend, address, salute, approach, pester.
A	C	C	R	U	E	Accumulate, gather, result in, collect, add.
A	C	C	U	S	E	Charge, blame, arraign, impeach, incriminate, censure, denounce, indict.
A	C	E	D	I	A	Sloth, torpor.
A	C	E	T	I	C	Acid, Vinegar.
A	C	H	I	N	G	Hurting, sore, painful, afflicted, sorrowing, hurtful, distressed.
A	C	I	D	I	C	Acid forming.
A	C	K	A	C	K	Type of gun fire. Anti-aircraft gun.
A	C	Q	U	I	T	Exonerate, vindicate liberate, justify, discharge, exculpate. Behave, deport.
A	C	R	A	W	L	Crawling.
A	C	R	O	S	S	Crosswise, transversely, over, intersecting. Angled direction.
A	C	T	I	F	Y	Activate, vitalize, energize.
A	C	T	I	N	G	Performing, pretending. Temporary, pro tem, interim, Locum.
A	C	T	I	O	N	Deed, accomplishment, act, doing, feat. Battle, combat. Service, cause, lawsuit.
A	C	T	I	V	E	Functioning, operative, working, agile, brisk, lively, energetic, industrious.
A	C	T	O	R	S	Plural of ACTOR.
A	C	T	U	A	L	Real, existing, factual, genuine, true, indisputable, bona fide, commonplace.
A	C	U	A	T	E	Sharpened, pointed.
A	C	U	I	T	Y	Sharpness, keenness, acuteness.
A	C	U	M	E	N	Keenness, perceptive, shrewdness, ability, discernment, comprehension.
A	D	A	G	I	O	Musical term, slow tempo, slowly.
A	D	D	I	C	T	Habituate, incline, predispose, devotee, enthusiast, fanatic, zealot, habitue, fan.
A	D	D	I	N	G	Calculating, totalling, toting, summing up. Connecting, including.
A	D	D	L	E	D	Confused, befuddled, flustered, dumbfounded, distracted, rotten, off.
A	D	D	U	C	E	Allege, advance, cite, assign, present.
A	D	H	E	R	E	Cleave, stick, sling, combine, unite, cohere. Hold.

1	2	3	4	5	6	
A	D	I	E	N	T	Characterised by.
A	D	I	E	U	X	Farewells.
A	D	J	O	I	N	Join, touch, border, butt, communicate, verge, annex, unite.
A	D	J	U	R	E	Urge, exhort, beg, entreat.
A	D	J	U	S	T	Adapt, conform, suit, regulate, correct, steady, rectify.
A	D	M	I	R	E	Appreciate, relish, cherish, esteem, like, reverence, respect.
A	D	O	N	I	C	Handsome, rhythymic verse.
A	D	O	N	I	S	Handsome young man.
A	D	O	R	E	D	Worshipped, beloved, idolised, revered, loved, pampered, indulged.
A	D	O	R	E	R	One who ADORES.
A	D	R	I	F	T	Drifting, unrestrained, loose, untied. Unfettered.
A	D	R	O	I	T	Clever, deft, dexterous, skillful, astute, intelligent, canny, nimble.
A	D	V	E	N	T	Arrival, approach, coming, nearing.
A	D	V	E	R	B	Verb modifier. Part of Speech.
A	D	V	E	R	T	Advertisement. Refer, allude, remark, point out.
A	D	V	I	C	E	Counsel, guidance, recommendation, intelligence, information, tidings.
A	D	V	I	S	E	Recommend, counsel, tell, inform, acquaint, warn, confer, caution.
A	E	R	A	T	E	Aerify, ventilate, make effervescent, render sparkling. Supply with oxygen.
A	E	R	I	A	L	Airy, lofty, soaring, atmospheric, towering, vapoury.
A	E	R	I	F	Y	Aerate.
A	F	F	A	I	R	Incident, proceeding, responsibility, concern. Business. Love, romance, intrigue.
A	F	F	E	C	T	Influence, inspire, impress, assume, feign, move, sway, impel. simulate, sham.
A	F	F	I	R	M	Assert, guarantee, vouch, declare, aver, avow, protest, ratify, endorse, allege.
A	F	F	O	R	D	Give, furnish, bear cost, embrace, incur, produce, impart, spare.
A	F	F	R	A	Y	Brawl, fracas, melee, fray, clash, scrimmage, skirmish, affair.
A	F	G	H	A	N	Native of Afghanistan. Coloured shawl. Wine Red coloured carpet. Chippendale.
A	F	I	E	L	D	Afar, away, out, beyond. Astray, unbounded.
A	F	L	A	M	E	Afire, burning, flaming, blazing. Flaring, ignited, alight.
A	F	L	O	A	T	Floating, drifting, untied, at sea, on water, adrift.
A	F	R	A	I	D	Frightened, anxious, scared, fearful, terrified, apprehensive. Disinclined, averse.
A	F	R	E	S	H	Anew, again, over, once more, newly, of late, recently.
A	F	T	E	R	S	(Sl.) Pudding, sweets.
A	G	A	M	I	C	Asexual.
A	G	A	R	I	C	Fungal. Mushroom medication.
A	G	E	I	N	G	Maturing, developing, growing, doddering, mellowing, ripening.
A	G	E	N	C	Y	Channel, operation, instrumentality, establishment, administration, medium.
A	G	E	N	D	A	Programme, schedule, timetable, calendar, list.
A	G	E	N	T	S	Plural of AGENT.
A	G	E	O	L	D	Ancient, antique, hoary, old, venerable, aged.
A	G	H	A	S	T	Astonished, astounded, shocked, afraid, anxious, flabbergasted, awed, dismayed.
A	G	N	A	T	E	Related, skin, allied, like, analogous, corresponding, similar, uniform.
A	G	O	N	I	C	Unangled.
A	G	O	U	T	I	Guinea pig, rodent.
A	G	R	E	E	D	Acquiesced, complied, accepted, tallied, reconciled.
A	I	D	I	N	G	Rendering aid, Assisting, helping.
A	I	L	I	N	G	Indisposed, ill, sick, unwell, poorly, debilitated, weak, sickly.
A	I	M	I	N	G	Directing, pointing, attempting, endeavouring, intending, striving, contemplating.
A	I	R	A	C	E	Skilled Pilot.
A	I	R	B	E	D	Inflated mattress.
A	I	R	G	U	N	Air pistol, air rifle.
A	I	R	I	L	Y	Gaily, jauntily, lightly, thinly, buoyantly.
A	I	R	I	N	G	Exhibiting, showing, ventilating. Strolling, outing.
A	I	R	M	A	N	Pilot, flier, aviator.
A	I	R	S	A	C	Space, cavity, exposed part, air passage.
A	I	R	W	A	Y	Air route, Air lane, air channel, breathing passageway.
A	I	S	L	E	D	Having Aisles.
A	K	I	M	B	O	Crossed, bent, crossways. Bowed.
A	L	A	R	U	M	Alarm clock, alarm bell. Alert.
A	L	B	E	I	T	Even though, although, nevertheless, even so, nonetheless. Whereas.
A	L	B	E	R	T	Watch chain.
A	L	B	I	A	N	Geologic time. Age. Period.
A	L	B	I	N	O	Defective pigmentation of skin. Translucent skin. Colourless. Impression.
A	L	B	U	M	S	Plural of ALBUM.
A	L	C	L	A	D	Rust proofing.
A	L	C	O	V	E	Niche, recess, nook. Summerhouse. Arbour.
A	L	E	R	T	S	Plural of ALERT.
A	L	E	X	I	A	Loss of ability to read.

1	2	3	4	5	6	
A	L	I	E	N	S	Plural of ALIEN. Foreigners.
A	L	I	G	H	T	Dismount, descend, land, lodge. Fall. Lighted, burning, lit, aglow.
A	L	K	A	L	I	Substance consisting largely of potassium carbonate. Soil content.
A	L	L	E	G	E	Assert, adduce, cite, state, declare, avow, profess, advance.
A	L	L	I	E	D	Related, linked, affiliated, akin, connected to, consanguine.
A	L	L	I	E	S	Plural of ALLY. Friends.
A	L	L	I	U	M	Genus of bulbous herb, wild garlic.
A	L	L	O	U	T	Total, full scale, unlimited, fully.
A	L	L	O	Y	S	Plural of ALLOY.
A	L	L	U	D	E	Refer, insinuate, imply, intimate, suggest.
A	L	L	U	R	E	Attraction, charm, appeal, charisma. Fascinate, lure seductiveness.
A	L	M	O	N	D	Nutlike stone or kernel.
A	L	M	O	S	T	Nearly, approximately, practically, well-nigh, virtually, about.
A	L	P	A	C	A	Llama-like mammal. Cloth made from alpaca wool. Garment.
A	L	P	I	N	E	Relating to lofty Mountain Range. One of physical types.
A	L	P	I	N	O	Italian mountain army.
A	L	U	M	N	A	Female graduate.
A	L	U	M	N	I	College graduates.
A	L	W	A	Y	S	For ever, evermore, eternally, in perpetum, every time. Constantly, often.
A	M	A	Z	E	D	Surprised, taken aback, astonished, dumbfounded, impressed.
A	M	A	Z	O	N	Female warrior. Termagant, virago, fishwife, battleaxe.
A	M	B	L	E	D	Strolled, walked, idled, paced, sauntered.
A	M	B	L	E	R	One who AMBLES.
A	M	B	U	S	H	Hold up, waylay, surprise, attack, assault, assail.
A	M	I	C	A	L	Friendly.
A	M	O	E	B	A	Genus of rhizopod protozoan.
A	M	O	R	A	L	Without moral sensibility. Non moral. Objective.
A	M	O	R	P	H	Gene without determinable effect. Without form.
A	M	O	U	N	T	Total, number, aggregate. Bulk, quantity, substance, purport. Comprise, embody.
A	M	P	E	R	E	Unit of electrical current.
A	M	P	L	E	R	Fuller, richer, more copious, more plentiful, profuser.
A	M	U	L	E	T	Charm, talisman, fetish, mascot, lucky piece.
A	M	U	S	E	D	Entertained, diverted, distracted, beguiled, charmed, fascinated, enchanted.
A	N	A	D	E	M	Garland, chaplet.
A	N	C	H	O	R	Ship's holding device. Source of support. Moor, fix, fasten, secure, stop, fix.
A	N	C	O	N	A	Leghorn type fowl.
A	N	E	L	E	D	Given Extreme Unction. Annointed.
A	N	G	A	R	Y	Take-over rights.
A	N	G	E	L	S	Plural of ANGEL.
A	N	G	I	N	A	Spasmodic suffocation, emotional distress. Heart condition.
A	N	G	L	E	D	Biased, slanted, aimed, bent, bowed. Schemed.
A	N	G	L	E	R	Fisherman.
A	N	G	L	E	S	Plural of ANGLE.
A	N	G	O	R	A	Mohair. Hair of Angora Goat. Breed of domestic animal.
A	N	I	M	A	L	Beast, creature, brute. Carnal, bestial, brutish, sensual.
A	N	I	M	U	S	Animosity, purpose, intention, meaning, purpose, bias.
A	N	K	L	E	D	With ankles.
A	N	K	L	E	T	Ankle ornament. Fetter. Ankle support.
A	N	L	A	C	E	Tapered dagger.
A	N	N	A	L	S	Historic record. Chronicle.
A	N	N	E	A	L	Strengthen, temper, toughen.
A	N	N	E	X	E	Annex, addition, subjoin, append, connect.
A	N	N	O	N	A	Genus of Shrub with edible fruit. Custard apple.
A	N	N	U	A	L	Taking place yearly. Yearbook.
A	N	O	I	N	T	Annoint. Oil, rub, consecrate.
A	N	O	N	Y	M	Used to remain anonymous, unidentified. Pseudonym.
A	N	O	R	A	K	Windcheater, windbreaker, parka.
A	N	O	X	I	A	Oxygen deficiency.
A	N	S	W	E	R	Response, reply, rejoinder. Comment, defence. Solution. Acknowledge, refute.
A	N	T	H	E	M	Hymn, song of praise. Psalm. Patriotic song. National Anthem.
A	N	T	H	E	R	Pollen-bearing part of stamen.
A	N	T	I	C	S	Plural of ANTIC.
A	N	T	L	E	R	Horn, Branched horn.
A	N	T	R	U	M	Cavity, sinus.
A	N	Y	H	O	W	Any which way, anyway, at random, haphazard, random, helter skelter.
A	N	Y	W	A	Y	Anyhow, in which event, in any event, anywise.
A	P	A	C	H	E	Red Indian Tribe.

1	2	3	4	5	6	
A	P	A	T	H	Y	Dull, brooding, impassivity, stoicism, indifference, lethargy, stupor, lassitude.
A	P	E	R	C	U	Insight, intuition. Sketch, outline.
A	P	I	A	R	Y	Bee Colony, Bee Hives.
A	P	I	C	A	L	Relating to the apex, speech sound. Loftiest, highest, uppermost.
A	P	I	C	E	S	Plural of APEX.
A	P	I	E	C	E	Each, per, per capita, individually, one by one, successively, singly.
A	P	L	O	M	B	Assurance, self-confidence, poise, savoir faire, composure, sangfroid, coolness.
A	P	O	G	E	E	Apex, pinnacle, summit, zenith, meridian, culmination.
A	P	P	A	L	L	Dismay, daunt, horrify, awe, overawe.
A	P	P	E	A	L	Implore, invoke, beg, beseech, supplicate. Petition, Fascination, Intrigue.
A	P	P	E	A	R	Show up, emerge, become visible, emanate, materialize. Seem, look, sound.
A	P	P	E	N	D	Add, annex, take on, subjoin, connect, fasten.
A	P	P	L	E	S	Plural of APPLE.
A	P	P	O	R	T	Materialise.
A	P	P	O	S	E	Place opposite or before.
A	Q	U	A	K	E	Quivering, quaking, shaky, trembling.
A	Q	U	A	T	E	Dilute.
A	R	A	B	I	C	Of Arabia. Language, writing.
A	R	A	B	I	S	Genus of Herb. Sickle pod, Tower Mustard.
A	R	A	B	L	E	Suitable for tiling. Tillable, fertile, productive, cultivable.
A	R	B	O	U	R	Covered walk, bower, recess, retreat. Shaft, spindle, axle. Arbor. Gazebo.
A	R	C	A	D	E	Arched passageway, rows of shops. Decorative archway.
A	R	C	A	N	E	Mysterious, secret.
A	R	C	H	E	D	Curved, concave, bent, bowed, rounded.
A	R	C	H	E	R	One skilled with bow and arrow. Bowman.
A	R	C	H	L	Y	Coyly, rouguishly, playfully, slyly, shrewdly.
A	R	C	I	N	G	Curving, arching, glowing, sparking.
A	R	C	T	I	C	Region of the North Pole. Cold, icy.
A	R	D	E	N	T	Impassioned, fervent, fiery, passionate, enthusiastic, avid, eager, faithful, staunch.
A	R	D	O	U	R	Passion, enthusiasm, fervour, eagerness, fidelity, devotion, adoration.
A	R	E	N	A	S	Plural of ARENA.
A	R	G	A	L	I	Sheep with outsize horns.
A	R	G	E	N	T	Silvery, made of silver, shining like silver.
A	R	G	O	S	Y	Richly laden merchant ship. Fleet of Ships. Storehouse.
A	R	G	U	E	D	Discussed, disputed, quarrelled, disagreed, dissented, asserted, prevailed.
A	R	G	U	E	R	One who ARGUES.
A	R	G	U	F	Y	Argue, bicker, wrangle, hassle, squabble, quibble.
A	R	G	U	T	E	Shrewd, cagey, perspicacious, astute, sharp, shrill.
A	R	I	G	H	T	Rightly, correctly, decently, well, fittingly, properly, nicely, justly.
A	R	I	S	E	N	Past of AROSE.
A	R	I	S	T	O	Aristocrat, patrician, gentleman.
A	R	M	A	D	A	Fleet of Warships.
A	R	M	I	E	S	Plural of ARMY.
A	R	M	I	N	G	Preparation, equipping, fitting out.
A	R	M	L	E	T	Armband.
A	R	M	O	R	Y	Armoury, arsenal, magazine, arms dump, depot.
A	R	M	O	U	R	Armor, defensive weaponry, armaments.
A	R	M	P	I	T	Underarm.
A	R	M	U	R	E	Fabric pattern.
A	R	N	I	C	A	Large genus of Herbs. Embrocation.
A	R	O	M	A	S	Plural of AROMA.
A	R	O	U	N	D	About, encircling, enclosing, encompassing. Extant, existing, alive, living.
A	R	O	U	S	E	Stir, excite, challenge, kindle, waken, whet, rally. Alert, thrill, inflame, provoke.
A	R	R	A	C	K	Alcoholic beverage.
A	R	R	A	N	T	Itinerant, confirmed, shameless, extreme, vagrant, unmitigated.
A	R	R	E	A	R	Liability, debts, due, indebtedness. Owing.
A	R	R	E	C	T	Erect, upstanding, upright, attentive, heedful, observant.
A	R	R	E	S	T	Interrupt, check, thwart, halt. Take into custody, detain, catch, capture, seizure.
A	R	R	I	D	E	Please delight, pleasure, gratify, beguile, entertain, divert.
A	R	R	I	V	E	Come, show up, reach, turn up. Succeed, prosper, thrive.
A	R	R	O	W	S	Plural of ARROW.
A	R	R	O	Y	O	Ravine, gap, gorge, gulch, chasm.
A	R	T	E	R	Y	Blood vessel. Highway, road, thoroughfare, track, boulevard, avenue.
A	R	T	F	U	L	Coy, shrewd, sly, subtle, astute, crafty, foxy, insidious, tricky.
A	R	T	I	S	T	Painter. One practising the Arts. Performer, entertainer. Adept at deception.
A	S	C	E	N	D	Climb, escalate, scale, clamber, shin, rise, mount, surmount, crest.
A	S	C	E	N	T	Ascension, elevation, Upward movement, rise. Eminence, Gradient, inclination.

1	2	3	4	5	6	
A	S	E	I	T	Y	Autonomy of God. Self-sufficiency.
A	S	H	A	K	E	Aquiver, shaking, trembling, shivering. Tremulous.
A	S	H	A	M	E	Being ashamed.
A	S	H	C	A	N	City Life, seamy side of city life. Refuse receptacle, trashcan.
A	S	H	I	N	E	In a shining state.
A	S	H	L	A	R	Hewn stone, masonry.
A	S	H	O	R	E	Landed, on land, on shore, aground.
A	S	H	P	A	N	Dust pan, refuse holder, litter container.
A	S	H	P	I	T	Firegrate. Tip.
A	S	K	A	N	T	Askance, indirectly, awry, askew.
A	S	K	I	N	G	Making a request. Inviting, supplicating, petitioning, beseeching, soliciting.
A	S	L	A	N	T	Askew, obliquely, slantways, sideways, sloping, awry, cockeyed.
A	S	L	E	E	P	Sleeping, inactive, inert, insensible, senseless, lifeless, inanimate, numb.
A	S	L	O	P	E	Aslant, askew, atilt, obliquely, sloping, downwards.
A	S	P	E	C	T	View, appearance, bearing, mien, look, presence, phase, angle, standpoint.
A	S	P	I	R	E	Aim, yearn, want, wish, crave, struggle for, try, set out.
A	S	S	A	I	L	Attack, assault, beset, buffet, pummel, fall upon, storm, strike.
A	S	S	E	N	T	Agree, consent, accede, subscribe, submit, yield, accept.
A	S	S	E	R	T	State firmly, declare, profess, proclaim, publish, maintain, contend, voice.
A	S	S	E	S	S	Compute, tally, evaluate, consider, reckon, weigh, levy, impose.
A	S	S	E	T	S	Possessions, effects, belongings, equity, money, wealth, capital, resources.
A	S	S	I	G	N	Allot, transfer, allocate, apportion, ascribe, prescribe, determine, entrust.
A	S	S	I	S	T	Aid, help, render assistance, comfort, succour, support, uplift, relieve.
A	S	S	I	Z	E	Edict, regulation, ordinance, hearing, trial, Superior Court Session. Stone layer.
A	S	S	O	R	T	Separate, distribute, classify, mix, match, associate.
A	S	S	U	M	E	Accept, receive, don, take over, simulate, feign, sham, pretend, suppose.
A	S	S	U	R	E	Aver, convince, persuade, secure, guarantee, promise, warrant.
A	S	T	E	R	N	Aft, abaft, behind, rearward.
A	S	T	H	M	A	Laboured breathing, coughing attack, air constriction, wheezing.
A	S	T	R	A	L	Stellar, starry, other-worldly, of space, remote, visionary, exalted.
A	S	T	R	A	Y	Wandering, adrift, missing, afield, wrong, unfavourable.
A	S	T	U	T	E	On the ball, clever, shrewd, wideawake, cunning, sagacious, cagey.
A	S	W	A	R	M	Swarming.
A	S	W	I	N	G	Swinging.
A	S	Y	L	U	M	Sanctuary, refuge, safe harbour, Institution, place for the insane. Shelter. Retreat.
A	T	A	X	I	A	Confusion, muddle, disorder, disarray.
A	T	H	O	M	E	Reception.
A	T	H	R	O	B	Throbbing.
A	T	K	I	N	S	Tommy, British foot soldier.
A	T	O	M	I	C	Relating to Atoms, minute, tiny, nuclear energy. Relating to The Bomb.
A	T	O	N	E	D	Reconciled, propitiated, expiated, made up. Made amends.
A	T	O	N	E	R	One who ATONES.
A	T	O	N	I	C	Unaccented.
A	T	O	P	I	C	Misplaced.
A	T	T	A	C	H	Adhere, fasten, affix, rivet, annex, pin, append, bind, tie, cement.
A	T	T	A	C	K	Assault, beset, harrass, raid, charge. Aggression, offensive, action, battle.
A	T	T	A	I	N	Reach, achieve, acquire, gain, accomplish, win, realise.
A	T	T	E	N	D	Accompany, conduct, escort, listen, heed. Tend, mind, supervise, handle.
A	T	T	E	S	T	Certify, witness, ratify, confirm, endorse, indicate, testify, substantiate.
A	T	T	I	R	E	Wearing apparel, clothing, raiment, togs, dress, garb, accoutre, outfit.
A	T	T	U	N	E	Harmonize, accord, accommodate, conform, reconcile, compensate, agree.
A	T	W	E	E	N	Between, betwixt, in between.
A	T	W	I	X	T	Betwixt, between, twixt, tween.
A	U	B	U	R	N	Red colour. Carroty. Titian. Redhead.
A	U	D	I	L	E	Auditory, aural, accoustic, by ear.
A	U	G	U	R	Y	Omen, interpretation, portent, indication, prophecy. Presentiment, premonition.
A	U	G	U	S	T	Majestic, grand, grandiose, imposing, magnificent, noble, stately, princely.
A	U	N	T	I	E	Aunty, wife of one's uncle. Sister of one's mother or father. Term of endearment.
A	U	R	I	F	Y	Turn into gold.
A	U	R	O	R	A	Red sky. Dawn red. Orange colour.
A	U	R	O	R	E	Hydrangea Pink.
A	U	R	O	U	S	Relating to gold.
A	U	S	S	I	E	Native of Australia.
A	U	T	H	O	R	Writer, creator, composer, originator. Founder, inventor, patriarch, maker.
A	U	T	I	S	M	Wish-fulfilling fantasy. Self-absorption.
A	U	T	U	M	N	Season between summer and winter. Fall. Maturity. Mid-years.
A	V	A	T	A	R	Incarnation, manifestation.

1	2	3	4	5	6	
A	V	E	N	G	E	Punish, revenge, vindicate, chastise, retaliate, pay back.
A	V	E	N	U	E	Lane of Trees, road, approach, pathway, alley, boulevard, thoroughfare. Drive.
A	V	E	R	S	E	Loath, disinclined, hesitant, indisposed, reluctant, unwilling, perverse.
A	V	I	A	R	Y	Birdcage, birdhouse, dovecote, enclosure.
A	V	I	A	T	E	Fly.
A	V	I	D	L	Y	Eagerly, anxiously impatiently keenly, insistently, urgently, greedily.
A	V	O	C	E	T	Long-legged wading bird.
A	V	O	W	A	L	Promise, confession, acknowledgment, declaration.
A	V	O	W	E	D	Declared, admitted, owned. Asserted, conceded.
A	W	A	K	E	N	Wake, stir, rouse, bestir, inflame, rally, whet.
A	W	A	R	D	S	Plural of AWARD.
A	W	E	I	G	H	Heave to, atrip.
A	W	H	E	E	L	Riding, cycling, on wheels.
A	W	H	I	L	E	Some while, briefly, soon, for a time.
A	W	N	I	N	G	Canopy, canvas, cotton duck. Sunshade, shelter.
A	W	O	K	E	N	Past of AWAKEN.
A	X	I	A	T	E	Axial, resembling on axis.
A	X	I	L	L	A	Armpit.
A	Z	A	L	E	A	Genus of Shrub.
A	Z	O	L	L	A	Water fern.
A	Z	U	R	E	D	Like azure, blue.
A	Z	Y	G	O	S	Azygous, single, odd.

B

B	A	A	I	N	G	Bleating.
B	A	B	B	L	E	Gibber, jabber, blabber, drivel, gabble, chatter, prattle. Yak, chat.
B	A	B	I	E	S	Plural of BABY.
B	A	B	I	S	H	Babyish, infantile.
B	A	B	O	O	N	Ape, primate. Uncouth person.
B	A	C	K	E	D	Advocated supported; Receded, retreated. Wagered, gambled. Stuck together.
B	A	C	K	E	R	Sponsor, supporter, guarantor, patron, promoter. Punter, gambler.
B	A	D	G	E	R	Pester, annoy, irritate, bait, heckle, chivy, bully, tease.
B	A	D	M	A	N	Outlaw, bandit, hoodlum, criminal, rascal, scoundrel, villain, rogue.
B	A	F	F	L	E	Counfound, frustrate, balk, flummox, mystify, puzzly, confuse, thwart.
B	A	G	F	U	L	Container full, contents, total capacity. Indeterminate quantity.
B	A	G	G	E	D	Captured, shot, hunted. Inebriated, sozzled. Enclosed, encased.
B	A	G	G	E	R	One who bags. Bag filler.
B	A	G	M	A	N	Travelling salesman, commercial traveller. (sl.) Tramp.
B	A	G	N	E	T	Fish net.
B	A	I	L	E	D	Released on surety guaranteed. Emptied, ladled, scooped, dipped.
B	A	I	L	E	E	Trustee.
B	A	I	L	E	R	Device for bailing, one who bails. Cricket toss. Guarantor.
B	A	I	L	E	Y	Castle wall. Keep.
B	A	I	L	I	E	Scottish magistrate. Sheriff.
B	A	I	L	O	R	Delivering trustee.
B	A	I	T	E	D	Teased, badgered, lured, enticed, heckled, molested, tormented.
B	A	K	E	R	S	Plural of BAKER.
B	A	K	E	R	Y	Bakehouse.
B	A	K	I	N	G	Broiling, cooking, sizzling, scalding, burning, red-hot, white-hot. Processing Bread.
B	A	L	A	A	M	Worthless copy, rejected material. Fillers.
B	A	L	A	T	A	The gum of the bullet or bully tree of South America, used as a substitute for rubber.
B	A	L	D	E	R	Comparative of BALD.
B	A	L	D	L	Y	Plainly, severly, unadorned, austerely.
B	A	L	E	E	N	Whalebone.
B	A	L	I	N	G	Wrapping, packaging, bundling.
B	A	L	K	A	N	Relating to Balkan peninsula.
B	A	L	K	E	D	Demured, stumbled, shied, refused, thwarted, disappointed, frustrated.
B	A	L	K	E	R	One that BALKS.
B	A	L	L	A	D	Narrative song, story lyrics.
B	A	L	L	E	D	Past of BALL.
B	A	L	L	E	R	A ball maker.
B	A	L	L	E	T	Artistic Dance, Theatrical performance, Costumed movement set to music.
B	A	L	L	O	T	Vote, to elect, election, count.
B	A	L	S	A	M	Oleoresin, aromatic plant substance. Balm.
B	A	L	T	I	C	Relating to the Baltic States.

1	2	3	4	5	6	
B	A	M	B	O	O	Large woody plant. Tropical growth. Furniture made from Bamboo stems.
B	A	N	A	N	A	Succulent fruit.
B	A	N	D	E	D	Wrapped, bound, tied. United.
B	A	N	D	I	T	Outlaw, villain, robber, badman, brigand, gangster, mobster, racketeer.
B	A	N	G	E	D	Past of BANG.
B	A	N	G	E	R	(Sl.) Sausage.
B	A	N	G	L	E	Bracelet, armulet, armband. Decorative jewellery.
B	A	N	G	U	P	Stylish, slap-up, satisfying.
B	A	N	I	S	H	Exile, expel, excommunicate, evict, cashier, dismiss, fire, blacklist, boycott.
B	A	N	K	E	D	Heaped, piled, stacked. Deposited money, invested, hoarded, stashed.
B	A	N	K	E	R	One who is connected with BANKING.
B	A	N	N	E	D	Barred, excluded, prohibited, forbidden, vetoed.
B	A	N	N	E	R	Flag, standard, ensign, pennant, streamer. Front-rank, excellent, first rate.
B	A	N	T	A	M	Small, petite, little, pert, saucy. Breed of fowl.
B	A	N	T	E	R	Devilry, fun, jesting, chaff, tomfoolery. Face, coax, backchat, repartee.
B	A	N	Y	A	N	Tree. Indian garment.
B	A	N	Z	A	I	Japanese cheer. Enthusiasm.
B	A	O	B	A	B	Cream of Tartar Tree.
B	A	R	B	E	D	Equipped with Barbs. Pronged, emblazoned. Bearded. Pointed.
B	A	R	B	E	L	Freshwater fish. Turtle neck.
B	A	R	B	E	R	Tonsorial artist. Hairdresser.
B	A	R	B	E	T	Tropical Bird.
B	A	R	B	O	Y	Bartender's helper.
B	A	R	D	I	C	Relating to a Bard and his poetry.
B	A	R	E	L	Y	Hardly, scarcely, almost. Meagrely, plainly, scarcely, just.
B	A	R	E	S	T	Plainest, emptiest, starkest, bleakest. Comparative of BARELY.
B	A	R	F	L	Y	Habitue of Barrooms.
B	A	R	G	E	D	Stumbled, bumped, charged, knocked, lumbered.
B	A	R	G	E	E	Bargeman.
B	A	R	I	N	G	Make bare, revealing, showing, uncovering.
B	A	R	I	S	H	Somewhat bare. Degree of bareness.
B	A	R	I	U	M	Element of alkaline earth group.
B	A	R	K	E	D	Snarled, snapped, alerted. Grazed, bumped, hurt.
B	A	R	K	E	R	Carnival Employee. Sideshow Guide.
B	A	R	L	E	Y	Cereal.
B	A	R	M	A	N	Bar tender.
B	A	R	N	E	Y	Argument, altercation, fight, row. Boisterous time. Small mine car.
B	A	R	O	N	Y	Baron's domain. Private landholding.
B	A	R	Q	U	E	Bark, three-masted vessel.
B	A	R	R	E	D	Banned, forbidden entry, exclused, ostracized, expelled.
B	A	R	R	E	L	Hooped container. Measurement. Gun core. Cylindrical housing. Spool, bobbin.
B	A	R	R	E	N	Bare, infertile, unproductive, sterile. Impotent, childless. Wasteland, wilderness.
B	A	R	R	O	W	Shallow cart, wheelbarrow, handbarrow. Mountain, hill, mound.
B	A	R	S	A	C	Semi-sweet Bordeaux Wine.
B	A	R	T	E	R	Trade, exchange, bargain, swap, traffic, truck.
B	A	R	T	O	N	Large farm. Hen coop, poultry yard.
B	A	S	A	L	T	Dark fine-grained igneous rock.
B	A	S	E	L	Y	Shamefully, corruptly, dishonourably, spuriously.
B	A	S	H	E	D	Banged, knocked, hit, socked, belted, slammed, walloped, whacked.
B	A	S	I	C	S	Plural of BASIC.
B	A	S	I	N	G	Establishing, founding, fixing, constructing, setting up.
B	A	S	K	E	D	Sported, wallowed, luxuriated, indulged, soaked up sun.
B	A	S	K	E	T	Woven receptacle, carrier, cane container.
B	A	S	S	E	T	Hound. Breed of hunting dog.
B	A	S	T	E	D	Past of BASTE.
B	A	T	E	A	U	Flat bottomed boat. Small craft.
B	A	T	H	E	D	Washed, submerged, immersed, laved. Past of BATH.
B	A	T	H	E	R	Swimmer. One who bathes.
B	A	T	H	O	S	Bottom, nadir, lowest. Anti-climax, flatness, comedown.
B	A	T	I	N	G	Excepting, aside from, saving, barring, but, excluding.
B	A	T	M	A	N	Military gentleman's gentleman.
B	A	T	T	E	D	Past of BAT.
B	A	T	T	E	N	Strip of light wood, reinforce, strengthen, fasten, clamp down.
B	A	T	T	E	R	Egg and flower mixture. Damage, maul, bruise, clobber, pommel. Beat, baste.
B	A	T	T	L	E	Military action, hostility, scrimmage, encounter, attack, onslaught, conflict.
B	A	U	B	L	E	Trinket, beads, bangles, knickknack, gewgaw, trifle, novelty.
B	A	W	L	E	D	Hollered, called, shouted, yelled, clamoured, roared, cried, sobbed, wept.

1	2	3	4	5	6	
B	A	W	L	E	R	One who BAWLS.
B	A	X	T	E	R	Baker.
B	A	Y	R	U	M	Fragrant cosmetic liquid used in hairdressing.
B	A	Z	A	A	R	Oriental market place. Department Store. Shop.
B	E	A	C	H	Y	Sandy, shore-like. Shingled.
B	E	A	C	O	N	Signal fire, Lighthouse, Warning light, bonfire.
B	E	A	D	E	D	Covered in beads, sewn with beads. Decorated.
B	E	A	D	E	R	Threader, bead worker.
B	E	A	D	L	E	Court messenger, herald, Church Usher, Officer of religion.
B	E	A	G	L	E	Breed of dog. Hound. Constable. Law Enforcer.
B	E	A	K	E	D	Pointed, Gaunt, grizzled, Rostrate.
B	E	A	K	E	R	Vessel, cup, glass, mug, receptacle.
B	E	A	M	E	D	Grinned, smiled, glowed. Looked radiant. Having beams.
B	E	A	M	E	R	Yarn winding machine. Leather worker.
B	E	A	R	E	R	Carrier, Messenger, envoy, porter, courier, emissary, holder.
B	E	A	T	E	N	Defeated, Past of BEAT.
B	E	A	T	E	R	One who BEATS.
B	E	A	U	N	E	French Red table wine.
B	E	A	U	T	Y	Physical attraction, grace, charm, perfection, excellence. Adornment. Lovely.
B	E	A	V	E	R	Semi-aquatic Rodent. Helmet vizor. Beaver-fur hat. Beard.
B	E	C	A	L	M	Allay, compose, lull, quieten, calm, soothe, tranquilise, pacify.
B	E	C	A	M	E	Past of BECOME.
B	E	C	K	E	T	Hook, bracket, loop.
B	E	C	K	O	N	Attract attention, signal, call, wave, summon, lure, gesture.
B	E	C	O	M	E	Come, arrive, emerge, grow, adopt new role, grace, adorn, suit.
B	E	D	A	M	N	Damn, curse, swear, imprecate.
B	E	D	A	U	B	Smear, smudge, dab, daub, plaster, befoul.
B	E	D	A	Z	E	Daze, paralyze, stun, bemuse, stupify.
B	E	D	B	U	G	Vermin, wingless bloodsucking bug.
B	E	D	D	E	D	Deposited, planted. Laid.
B	E	D	E	C	K	Decorate, adorn, embellish, trim, beautify, deck.
B	E	D	L	A	M	Chaotic atmosphere, scene of uproar. Mad, insane, lunatic.
B	E	D	P	A	N	Shallow vessel for convenience of the bedridden. Portable Urinal.
B	E	D	U	I	N	Bedouin. Arab Nomad. Desert wanderer.
B	E	E	P	E	R	Aircraft signalling device.
B	E	E	T	L	E	Insect. To scuttle. Pop Star. Volkswagen. Wooden Pestle. Beater.
B	E	E	V	E	S	Cattle, oxen.
B	E	E	W	A	Y	Bee space.
B	E	E	Z	E	R	(Sl.) Nose.
B	E	F	A	L	L	To take place, happen, occur. Pertain.
B	E	F	O	O	L	Lead astray, deceive, hoodwink, hoax, dupe.
B	E	F	O	R	E	Prior to, preceeding, at first, previously, confronting, awaiting, Superior.
B	E	F	O	U	L	Besmirch, defile, smear, sully, contaminate, malign, defame, slur, spatter.
B	E	G	G	A	R	One who begs. Dependant, impoverished person. Impoverish, ruin, pauper.
B	E	G	G	E	D	Past of BEG.
B	E	G	I	R	D	Belt, encircle, surround, band.
B	E	G	O	N	E	Injunction to depart. Leave, scram, clear out, decamp.
B	E	H	A	L	F	For the benefit of. Support, benefit, interest, advantage.
B	E	H	A	V	E	Act, comport, conduct, disport, carry on, acquit.
B	E	H	E	A	D	Execute, decapitate, guillotine.
B	E	H	E	L	D	Past of BEHOLD.
B	E	H	E	S	T	Command, injunction, bidding, order, request, demand, solicitation.
B	E	H	I	N	D	Aft, abaft, after, following, subsequent. Buttocks, backside, posterior, derriere.
B	E	H	O	L	D	Regard, look, see, observe, discern, distinguish, espy, note, notice.
B	E	L	A	U	D	Praise excessively.
B	E	L	D	A	M	Virago, Hag.
B	E	L	F	R	Y	Bell Tower, Campanile, turret.
B	E	L	I	A	L	Worthlessness, wickedness.
B	E	L	I	E	D	Misrepresented, falsified, perverted, twisted, contradicted, negated.
B	E	L	I	E	F	Intellectual assent. Commitment, faith, credence. Conviction, trust.
B	E	L	L	O	W	Bawl, roar, low, moo, wail, clamour.
B	E	L	O	N	G	To fit in. Suit, agree, match, tally, appertain, inhere, correspond, qualify.
B	E	L	T	E	D	Begirded, banded, encircled, surrounded. Strapped, whacked, walloped.
B	E	M	E	A	N	Debase, lower, humble, humiliate, demean, sink.
B	E	M	I	R	E	Cover with mud, smear with dirt.
B	E	M	O	A	N	Groan, complain, deplore, bewail, lament, regret, grieve, mourn.
B	E	M	U	S	E	Daze, stun, stupefy, perplex, puzzle, bewilder.

1	2	3	4	5	6	
B	E	N	D	E	R	Spree, binge, jag, tear, booze up.
B	E	N	G	A	L	Silk striped fabric.
B	E	N	I	G	N	Non-malignant, benignant, kindly, kind, gracious, amiable.
B	E	N	N	E	T	Hemlock, Daisy, garden Heliotrope.
B	E	N	U	M	B	Deaden, blunt, daze, desensitize, dull, stun, stupefy.
B	E	N	Z	O	L	Benzene.
B	E	R	A	T	E	Scold, upbraid, vituperate, revile, reprove, lash out, chide.
B	E	R	E	F	T	Bereaved, grief stricken, sorrowful, sorrowing, left alone, deprived.
B	E	R	L	I	N	Four-wheeled enclosed carriage, enclosed automobile. Wool. Capital City.
B	E	R	T	H	A	Shoulder cape, collar.
B	E	R	T	H	S	Plural of BERTH.
B	E	S	I	D	E	Next to, near, alongside, close, nearby, opposite.
B	E	S	O	I	L	Begrime, defile, besmirch, untidy.
B	E	S	P	O	T	Dot, mark, spot, soil, bespatter, spatter.
B	E	S	T	E	D	Overcame, won, defeated, worsted, overwhelmed, conquered.
B	E	S	T	I	R	Rouse, stir, waken, challenge, kindle, labour, rally.
B	E	S	T	O	W	Confer, exploit, devote, donate, present, give, furnish, award.
B	E	T	A	K	E	Go, repair to, depart.
B	E	T	I	D	E	Happen, befall, occur, develop, chance.
B	E	T	O	I	L	Exhaust, oppress with work.
B	E	T	O	N	Y	Genus of woundwort.
B	E	T	R	A	Y	Reveal, disclose, divulge, deceive, delude, renegade, inform on, give up.
B	E	T	T	E	D	Wagered, gambled, staked, played, laid. Past of BET.
B	E	T	T	E	R	More excellent, superior, more than, improved health, higher, ameliorate, excel.
B	E	T	T	O	R	One who BETS.
B	E	V	I	E	S	Plural of BEVY.
B	E	W	A	I	L	Moan, groan, lament, deplore, weep, bemoan.
B	E	W	A	R	E	Take heed, watch out, be aware, pay regard, be cautious, take care.
B	E	Y	O	N	D	Past, further, outside, without, above, additional, besides. Hereafter.
B	I	A	S	E	D	Disposed to, partial to, predilection for, prejudice, inclination, slanted, favouring.
B	I	B	B	E	R	Drunk, boozer, tippler, toper, inebriate.
B	I	B	L	E	S	Plural of BIBLE.
B	I	C	E	P	S	Flexor muscle of the upper arms.
B	I	C	K	E	R	Row, quarrel, argue, dispute, hassle, wrangle, scrap.
B	I	D	D	E	N	Past of BID.
B	I	D	D	E	R	One who BIDS.
B	I	D	E	N	T	Two-pronged instrument.
B	I	D	I	N	G	Waiting, pausing, staying, lingering, residing, living, dwelling, remaining.
B	I	F	F	E	D	Struck, clouted, hit, sloshed, socked, coshed.
B	I	F	O	L	D	Twofold, duplex, dualistic, double, dual.
B	I	G	A	M	Y	Offense of plural marriage.
B	I	G	E	N	D	Crankpin of connecting rod.
B	I	G	G	E	R	Comparative of BIG.
B	I	G	G	I	E	Big boy, big guy, bigwig, big shot. V.I.P., V.B.T.
B	I	G	G	I	N	Outhouse. Hood, cape, nightcap.
B	I	G	O	T	S	Plural of BIGOT.
B	I	G	W	I	G	Big boy, big guy, biggie, V.I.P.
B	I	K	I	N	G	Cycling, bicycling.
B	I	K	I	N	I	Skimpy swim wear. Atol in the Pacific Ocean. Atomic test ground. Brief.
B	I	L	G	E	D	Leaking, damaged below the water line.
B	I	L	K	E	D	Defrauded, cheated, avoided, eluded, frustrated, foiled, left without paying.
B	I	L	K	E	R	Absconder. Defrauder.
B	I	L	L	E	D	Invoiced, charged, tabbed. Advertised. Having a beak.
B	I	L	L	E	T	Lodging, boarding house, domicile. Lodge, quarters, canton.
B	I	L	L	I	E	Billy can. Billy goat.
B	I	L	L	O	W	Surge, swell, bulge, undulate.
B	I	N	A	R	Y	Twofold, duplex, dual, double-barreled. Bifold.
B	I	N	A	T	E	Double, twofold.
B	I	N	D	E	R	Wrapper, bandage, dressing. File cover.
B	I	N	D	L	E	Bundle of clothing and cooking pot.
B	I	N	G	E	S	Plural of BINGE.
B	I	O	P	S	Y	Removal of tissue from living body for observation.
B	I	O	T	I	C	Caused by living beings.
B	I	O	T	I	N	Vitamin B complex.
B	I	P	A	C	K	Pair of colour films.
B	I	P	E	D	S	Plural of BIPED.
B	I	P	O	D	S	Plural of BIPOD.

1	2	3	4	5	6	
B	I	R	D	E	R	Identifier of wild birds. Ornithologist.
B	I	R	D	I	E	Golf score. Small bird.
B	I	R	T	H	S	Plural of BIRTH.
B	I	S	E	C	T	Divide in two, separate, interesect, cross-section examination. Halve.
B	I	S	H	O	P	Church dignatary. Chessman.
B	I	S	L	E	Y	Marksmanship competition.
B	I	S	Q	U	E	Thick cream shellfish soup. Unglazed ceramic ware.
B	I	S	T	R	O	Cafe, night spot, nightclub, cabaret.
B	I	T	I	N	G	Sarcastic, cutting, penetrating, incisive, crisp.
B	I	T	T	E	N	Past of BIT.
B	I	T	T	E	R	Acrimonious, harsh, distasteful, severe, brutal, irreconcilable, estranged. Sour.
B	L	A	D	E	D	Having a blade or blades.
B	L	A	M	E	D	Past of BLAME.
B	L	A	N	C	H	Whiten, bleach, decolorize. Palliate, extenuate. Recoil, flinch, quail, wince. To pale.
B	L	A	R	E	D	Past of BLARE.
B	L	A	S	T	S	Plural of BLAST.
B	L	A	Z	E	D	Fired, flared, flamed, burnt glowed. Proclaimed. Emblazoned.
B	L	A	Z	E	R	Jacket, garment. Striped short coat.
B	L	A	Z	O	N	Publish afar, proclaim, emblazon.
B	L	E	A	C	H	Blanch, whiten, discolour. Make white.
B	L	E	A	K	Y	Somewhat bleak.
B	L	E	A	R	Y	Ill-defined, indistinct, unclear, vague. Washed out, worn out, spent. Exhausted.
B	L	E	N	C	H	Blanch, bleach, whiten. Pale.
B	L	E	N	D	S	Plural of BLEND.
B	L	E	N	N	Y	Scaleless fish.
B	L	I	G	H	T	Plant disease. Organism causing blight. Ruin frustrate, deterioration. Mildew.
B	L	I	N	D	S	Plural of BLIND. Curtains, Venetian blinds.
B	L	I	N	K	Y	Blink-eyed, blinking.
B	L	I	T	H	E	Happy, merry, vivacious, gay, joyous, high-spirited.
B	L	O	N	D	E	Fair-haired, fair-skinned, Blond. Light coloured. Yellow towheaded.
B	L	O	O	D	Y	Covered in blood. Expletive.
B	L	O	O	M	S	Plural of BLOOM. Flowers. Blossoms.
B	L	O	O	M	Y	Covered in blooms.
B	L	O	T	C	H	Splotch, stain, blemish, mottle.
B	L	O	T	T	O	Befuddled, intoxicated, inebriated, boozy, canned, drunk, plastered.
B	L	O	U	S	E	Shirt, outer garment, loose coat.
B	L	O	W	E	R	Puffer, braggart, Device for blowing. Whale. (Sl.) Telephone.
B	L	O	W	Z	Y	Slatternly, unkempt, dowdy, overblown, frowsy.
B	L	U	E	S	T	Comparative of BLUE.
B	L	U	I	N	G	Tinting blue. Laundry whitening.
B	L	U	I	S	H	Somewhat blue.
B	O	A	R	D	S	Plural of BOARD. Placards.
B	O	A	T	E	R	Straw basher, Straw hat.
B	O	B	B	E	D	Past tense of BOB. Surfaced. Bob up and down.
B	O	B	B	I	N	Spool, reel, spindle, flanged cylinder.
B	O	B	B	L	E	Bob, wobble. Small ball.
B	O	D	E	G	A	Wine cellar. storehouse.
B	O	D	G	E	R	Wood carver, turner.
B	O	D	I	C	E	Woman's upper garment. Vest.
B	O	D	I	E	D	Incarnate, having a body.
B	O	D	I	E	S	Plural of BODY. Structures.
B	O	D	I	L	Y	In person, altogether, entirely corporally.
B	O	D	I	N	G	Foreboding, warning, prediction, omen.
B	O	D	K	I	N	Blunt needle, Hairpin, stiletto, dagger.
B	O	F	F	I	N	Scientific expert. Backroom boy. Professor.
B	O	G	E	Y	S	Plural of BOGEY. Ghosts. Unpleasant occurrences.
B	O	G	G	L	E	Start, shy, jerk, hesitate, haggle, demure, perplex.
B	O	G	O	A	K	Fossilized Oak.
B	O	I	L	E	D	Cooked in water. Bubbled, seethed, churned, foamed, Fumed, raged.
B	O	I	L	E	R	Hot water tank. Generator, vessel, tank, kettle. Breaker.
B	O	L	D	E	R	Comparative of BOLD.
B	O	L	D	L	Y	Bravely, fearlessly, courageously, audaciously. Insolently, brazenly.
B	O	L	E	R	O	Lively Spanish dance. Spanish Jacket.
B	O	L	L	I	X	Botch, bungle, throw into disorder.
B	O	L	T	E	D	Fastened, Gulped, devoured. Dashed, ran, sprang, charged.
B	O	M	B	E	D	Bombarded, blitzed, shelled. Ruined, damaged.
B	O	N	B	O	N	Christmas cracker, sweetmeat, sweet (confectionery).

1	2	3	4	5	6	
B	O	N	D	E	D	Stuck together, adhered. Contracted, guaranteed. Put into bond warehouse.
B	O	N	G	O	S	Tom-tom type drums. Kettle drums.
B	O	N	I	N	G	Removing bones. Study hard. Chafing, Rubbing.
B	O	N	I	T	O	Type of Fish. Tunny.
B	O	N	M	O	T	Witticism.
B	O	N	N	E	T	Headgear. Women's hat. Hood. Pixie.
B	O	N	N	I	E	Lovely, fair, attractive, beautiful, pretty, comely, pulchritudinous.
B	O	O	D	L	E	Money, fortune, bundle, mint, pile, wad, roll, packet. Spoils, plunder.
B	O	O	H	O	O	Cry, wail, blubber, weep loudly.
B	O	O	I	N	G	Noisy crowd disapproval, loud indication of distaste. Hooting.
B	O	O	K	E	D	Reserved, advance warning. Recorded. Scheduled, listed. Arrested. Indicted.
B	O	O	K	I	E	Bookmaker.
B	O	O	M	E	D	Roared, blasted, blared, crashed, exploded.
B	O	O	T	E	D	Equipped with Boots. Sacked, dismissed, kicked.
B	O	O	T	E	E	Child's knitted sock. Short boot.
B	O	O	Z	E	D	Drank to excess. Intoxicated. Muddled, plastered, canned.
B	O	O	Z	E	R	Inebriate, drinker, drunkard, Bar, barroom, tavern, pub.
B	O	P	E	E	P	Peekaboo. Hide and seek. Character in fairy tale.
B	O	R	A	G	E	Salad herb.
B	O	R	D	A	R	Fuedal cottage.
B	O	R	D	E	R	Surround, margin, boundary, edge, fringe, verge, Adjoin, join. Approach, nearing.
B	O	R	E	A	L	Located in the North. Northern. Cold, icy, wintry, frosty, glacial.
B	O	R	E	A	S	Northwind.
B	O	R	I	N	G	Tedious, tiring, uninteresting, irksome, tiresome, trite.
B	O	R	R	O	W	Receive temporarily, derive benefit from another, appropriate, receive, take on loan.
B	O	R	Z	O	I	Breed of dog.
B	O	S	C	H	E	Hun, German, boche.
B	O	S	O	M	Y	Buxom, chesty, full-chested, busty.
B	O	S	S	E	D	Dominated, chivied, encouraged, mastered, commanded. Shaped.
B	O	S	T	O	N	Type of dance, Beans, Bread, terrier, card game.
B	O	T	A	N	Y	Science of plants, biology.
B	O	T	C	H	Y	Slipshod, untidy, careless, messy, slovenly, slapdash, slatternly.
B	O	T	F	L	Y	Large fly, horsefly.
B	O	T	H	E	R	Annoyance, exasperation, nuisance. Agitate, fluster, perturb, disturb, upset.
B	O	T	T	L	E	Glass container, receptacle. Preserve. Check, restrain, corner.
B	O	T	T	O	M	End, foot, underneath, underside, base, foot, ground. Buttocks, behind, backside, bum.
B	O	U	C	L	E	Textile fabric, looped yarn.
B	O	U	G	H	S	Plural of BOUGH.
B	O	U	G	H	T	Acquired for money, purchased, bribed.
B	O	U	N	C	E	Rebound, backfire, kick back, bound, spring. Dismiss, intimidate. Return.
B	O	U	N	C	Y	Buoyant, elastic, resilient, volatile, effervescent, airy, zestful.
B	O	U	N	D	S	Plural of BOUND. Boundaries, surrounds.
B	O	U	N	T	Y	Virtue, goodness, kindness, reward, liberality. Abundance, plenty.
B	O	U	R	N	E	Bourn, stream, rivulet, creek, brook.
B	O	U	R	S	E	Marketplace, exchange, business places.
B	O	U	T	O	N	An enlargement of the end of a nerve fibre in contact with part of another nerve fibre.
B	O	V	I	N	E	Relating to oxen or cows. Dull, sluggish, stupid.
B	O	W	E	L	S	Plural of BOWEL. Innards.
B	O	W	E	R	S	Plural of BOWER.
B	O	W	E	R	Y	City district, full of bowers.
B	O	W	I	N	G	Bending, submitting, curving, arcing.
B	O	W	L	E	D	Past of BOWL. Thrown, Tossed.
B	O	W	L	E	G	Curved leg, bent leg.
B	O	W	L	E	R	One who BOWLS.
B	O	W	M	A	N	Archer.
B	O	W	S	E	R	Petrol Pump, bulk liquid dispenser.
B	O	W	T	I	E	Necktie, dickie.
B	O	W	W	O	W	Doggie.
B	O	X	C	A	R	Freight car, railway truck.
B	O	X	E	R	S	Plural of BOXER.
B	O	X	I	N	G	Pugilism, defensive fisticuffs. Enclosing, surrounding.
B	O	Y	I	S	H	Young, youthful, buoyant, frisky, cheeky.
B	R	A	C	E	D	Past of BRACE. Strutted, reinforced.
B	R	A	C	E	R	Stimulant, tonic drink, freshener. Carpenter, timberman.
B	R	A	G	G	Y	Boastful, pretentious.
B	R	A	H	M	A	Bird.
B	R	A	I	N	S	Plural of BRAIN.

1	2	3	4	5	6	
B	R	A	I	N	Y	Clever, intellectual, alert, knowing, bright, quick-witted, smart.
B	R	A	I	S	E	To stew, wet cooking.
B	R	A	K	E	D	Past of BRAKE. Stopped. Apply brakes.
B	R	A	K	E	S	Plural of BRAKE.
B	R	A	N	C	H	Bough, off-shoot, limb, arm, fork, department, corps.
B	R	A	N	D	S	Plural of BRAND.
B	R	A	N	D	Y	Alcoholic liquor distilled from wine. Slivovitz, cognac, kirsch.
B	R	A	S	S	Y	Strident, shrill, brazen, harden, overblown. Shameless, blatant.
B	R	A	V	E	D	Challenged, faced, confronted, endured.
B	R	A	V	E	R	Comparative of BRAVE.
B	R	A	W	L	S	Plural of BRAWL.
B	R	A	W	N	Y	Robust, strong, lusty, sturdy, hefty, muscular, sinewy.
B	R	A	Z	E	D	Soldered.
B	R	A	Z	E	N	Impudent, brassy, unabashed, shameless, presumptious, pushy, flashy, gaudy.
B	R	E	A	C	H	Contravention, transgression, violation. Gap, rupture.
B	R	E	A	D	S	Plural of BREAD.
B	R	E	A	S	T	Bosom, chest, mammary gland. Heart. Face, confront, ascend, reach objective.
B	R	E	A	T	H	Air inhaled and exhaled.
B	R	E	E	C	H	Short trousers, pants. Gun part, cannon part. Type of birth. Buttocks, bottom.
B	R	E	E	D	S	Plural of BREED. Species.
B	R	E	E	K	S	Britches, trousers.
B	R	E	E	Z	E	Light wind, soft blowing wind, gust. Skim, slide, zip, slip.
B	R	E	E	Z	Y	Windy, gusty, blowy, airy, easygoing, casual, relaxed, informal.
B	R	E	T	O	N	Women's brimmed hat. Relating to Brittany.
B	R	E	V	E	T	Written message, official document.
B	R	E	W	E	D	Past of BREW. Stewed.
B	R	E	W	E	R	Malster, manufacturer of brewed beverages. Beer maker.
B	R	I	B	E	D	Corrupted, perverted, seduced, suborned, sweetened, fixed, bought.
B	R	I	B	E	R	One who BRIBES.
B	R	I	C	K	Y	Bricklayer. Made of brick.
B	R	I	D	A	L	Nuptial, marriage, ceremony, festive.
B	R	I	D	G	E	Connecting structure. Span. Support. Platform. Bony part of Nose. Musical arch. Framework.
B	R	I	D	L	E	Restrain, constrain, curb, inhibit, repress, govern, rule, steer. Silence, prevent, stop.
B	R	I	E	F	S	Panties, knickers. Briefs at Law. Commissions.
B	R	I	G	H	T	Vivid, shining, brilliant, beaming, radiant, colourful, intelligent, lively. Alert.
B	R	I	L	L	S	Plural of BRILL.
B	R	I	T	O	N	Inhabitant of Britain.
B	R	O	A	C	H	Approach, introduce, mention, suggest, propose, hint, begin, commence.
B	R	O	A	D	S	Waterways. (Sl.) Girls, women.
B	R	O	C	H	E	Bobbin, shuttle.
B	R	O	G	U	E	Walking shoe. Dialectal accent.
B	R	O	K	E	N	Shattered, fractured, ruptured, interrupted, disconnected, incomplete, bankrupt.
B	R	O	K	E	R	Intermediary, negotiator, dealer,processor, stockbroker.
B	R	O	L	L	Y	Umbrella, sunshade.
B	R	O	N	Z	E	Alloy copper and tin. Sculpture, to colour bronze. Made of bronze. Paint with bronze.
B	R	O	N	Z	Y	Like Bronze.
B	R	O	O	C	H	Ornament. Metal-set gems, jewelled clasp.
B	R	O	O	D	S	Plural of BROOD.
B	R	O	O	D	Y	Set for breeding, prolific, moody, contemplative, pensive, depressed.
B	R	O	O	K	S	Plural of BROOK.
B	R	O	O	K	Y	Full of Streams. Containing streams.
B	R	O	O	M	S	Plural of BROOM.
B	R	O	O	M	Y	Abounding in Broom.
B	R	O	W	N	S	Shades of Brown.
B	R	O	W	N	Y	Somewhat brown.
B	R	O	W	S	E	Graze, consume, look over, skim, examine, read at random.
B	R	U	I	S	E	Injure, rupture, contuse, batter, crush, abrasion, discoloration. Contusion.
B	R	U	I	T	S	Noise abroad, publicise, report, tout. Advertise, announce, blazon, broadcast.
B	R	U	J	A	S	Plural of BRUJA. Witches, sorceresses, enchantresses.
B	R	U	N	C	H	Combined breakfast and lunch. Late Breakfast. Early Lunch.
B	R	U	S	H	Y	Shaggy, rough, unshaven, bushy.
B	R	U	T	A	L	Bestial, brutish, inhuman, savage, severe, rigorous, vicious.
B	R	U	T	E	S	Plural of BRUTE. Beasts.
B	R	Y	O	N	Y	Genus of Bryonia. Herbaceous vine.
B	U	B	B	L	E	Globule, transparent floating sphere. Foam gurgle. Trapped air, gas. Boil.
B	U	B	B	L	Y	Foamy, gassy, effervescent. Champagne.
B	U	C	K	E	D	Past of BUCK.

1	2	3	4	5	6	
B	U	C	K	E	T	Pail, vessel, container. Barrel, can.
B	U	C	K	L	E	Clasp, brooch. Yield, submit, knuckle under. Bend, apply, direct. Fastener for belt or shoe.
B	U	D	D	E	D	Commenced growing, sprang, developed, reproduced. Grafted.
B	U	D	D	H	A	Indian Philosopher. Founder of Buddhism.
B	U	D	G	E	R	Shifter, mover, stirrer.
B	U	D	G	E	T	Monetary plan, spending power.
B	U	D	L	E	T	Little Bud.
B	U	F	F	E	D	Polished, smoothed, burnished.
B	U	F	F	E	R	Shock absorbant, modifier, cushion, Burnisher.
B	U	F	F	E	T	Pommel, strike, batter, shake, vibrate. Strive, struggle, contend, try. Snack.
B	U	G	E	Y	E	Flatbottom boat.
B	U	G	G	E	D	Irritated, annoyed, vexed, bothered. Wired up, planted with listening device.
B	U	G	G	E	R	Heretic, sodomite, worthless person, perpetrator of buggery. (Sl.) Rogue, rascal.
B	U	G	L	E	R	Bugle player, horn blower.
B	U	L	B	A	R	Relating to a BULB.
B	U	L	B	E	D	Bulb-shaped, bulbous.
B	U	L	B	I	L	Secondary plant bulb.
B	U	L	B	U	L	Songbird.
B	U	L	G	E	S	Plural of BULGE.
B	U	L	K	E	D	Having bulk. Bundled.
B	U	L	K	E	R	Pickpocket's assistant.
B	U	L	L	E	T	Projectile, shell. fast-moving, fleet.
B	U	M	B	L	E	Blunder, bungle, mumble, stumble, botch.
B	U	M	P	E	R	Generous, hearty. Buffet, shock absorbing attachment. Bouncy.
B	U	N	C	H	Y	Bunched, clustered, lumpy, tufty, irregular.
B	U	N	D	L	E	Package, parcel, batch, bunch, array, group. Pile. Move hurriedly, hustle.
B	U	N	G	E	D	Closed, plugged, filled. Threw, tossed, cast.
B	U	N	G	L	E	Mess up, botch, fluff, louse up, blunder, error, mistake, slip-up.
B	U	N	I	O	N	Swelling of first joint of foot. Outcrop.
B	U	N	K	E	D	Decamped, escaped, absconded, fled, ran off. Slept, resided.
B	U	N	K	E	R	Bin, storage box, container, receptacle for coal. Sand trap. Embankment, obstacle.
B	U	N	S	E	N	Type of stove. Burner.
B	U	N	T	E	D	Shoved, pushed, kicked.
B	U	N	T	E	R	Speckled Sandstone.
B	U	O	Y	E	D	Supported, bolstered, sustained, upheld, propped.
B	U	R	B	L	E	Chatter, prattle, gurgle, bubble, nonsense, Gush.
B	U	R	D	E	N	Load, amount, substance. CLog, encumber, lumber, weigh, overload, handicap.
B	U	R	E	A	U	Desk, sideboard, cupboard. Office, section, department.
B	U	R	G	E	E	Flag, pennant, ensign, banner, standard, streamer.
B	U	R	G	L	E	Break into, commit burglary, rob.
B	U	R	I	A	L	Interment, funeral ceremony, deposition, act of burying. Tomb, grave.
B	U	R	I	E	D	Inhumed, entombed, interred, abandoned, dismissed.
B	U	R	L	A	P	Coarse woven fabric. Jute, hemp.
B	U	R	L	E	D	Burl-like, lumpy, hard.
B	U	R	L	E	R	Imperfections remover in weaving. Dresser.
B	U	R	M	A	N	Burmese. From Burma.
B	U	R	N	E	D	Past of BURN.
B	U	R	N	E	R	Fire tender. Device for burning. Incinerator. Stove, furnace, boiler, engine.
B	U	R	N	E	T	Moth, fabric, Salad plant.
B	U	R	N	U	P	Rocket fuel consumption. Go speedily.
B	U	R	R	E	D	Rough, prickly.
B	U	R	R	O	W	Lair, den, tunnel. Excavate, dig. Snuggle, cuddle nestle. Hole, hovel.
B	U	R	S	A	R	Administrative Officer, treasurer, purser, agent. Student in receipt of scholarship.
B	U	R	S	T	S	Plural of BURST.
B	U	R	T	O	N	Stowage. Hoisting tackle. Ale.
B	U	S	B	A	R	Connecting rod. Metallic link.
B	U	S	B	O	Y	Cleaner, waiter's assistant.
B	U	S	H	E	D	Tired, exhausted, done in. Lost in the bush.
B	U	S	H	E	L	Measurement of capacity.
B	U	S	I	E	D	Actively engaged, worked, occupied.
B	U	S	I	E	S	Policemen, detectives, fuzz. Of busy.
B	U	S	I	L	Y	Actively, diligently, industriously, briskly, intently, assiduously.
B	U	S	K	E	D	Past of BUSK.
B	U	S	K	E	R	One who BUSKS. Street performer, entertainer, singing waiter.
B	U	S	K	I	N	Type of shoe.
B	U	S	M	E	N	Bus operators.
B	U	S	S	E	D	Rode in a bus. Kissed, pecked, smooched, osculated.

1	2	3	4	5	6	
B	U	S	T	E	D	(Sl.) Bankrupted. Broken, damaged.
B	U	S	T	E	R	Familiar form of address. Horse breaker. Strong wind.
B	U	S	T	L	E	Hustle, tumult, stir, flurry, furore, whirlwind, commotion, hubbub, fuss.
B	U	S	T	U	P	Violent quarrel, parting of the ways.
B	U	T	A	N	E	Inflammable material, natural gas from petroleum.
B	U	T	L	E	R	Manservant, steward. Food and drinks receptacle.
B	U	T	T	E	D	Rammed, punted, pushed, bunted, knocked. Adjoined to stuck to.
B	U	T	T	E	R	Ingratiate. Edible animal fat. Bread spread.
B	U	T	T	O	N	Fastener, disc for securing. Decorative trimming. Fasten, close.
B	U	Y	I	N	G	Purchasing, acquiring, obtaining, procuring, redeeming, bribing, accepting.
B	U	Z	Z	E	D	Droned, hummed. Telephoned. Reported, gossiped. Low flight intimidation.
B	U	Z	Z	E	R	Doorbell. Gossip, tale-bearer. Alarm.
B	Y	E	B	Y	E	Farewell, goodbye.
B	Y	E	L	A	W	Secondary law. Subsidiary law. Pass by.
B	Y	G	O	N	E	In the past, of a past age. Old, previous, before.
B	Y	L	I	N	E	Reporter's name. Heading.
B	Y	P	A	S	S	Secondary road, roundabout way. Pass by.
B	Y	P	L	A	Y	Off-centre acting. Significant gestures.
B	Y	P	L	O	T	Secondary plot. Subsidiary story.
B	Y	R	O	A	D	Secondary road. Side road. By-way.
B	Y	W	O	R	D	Maxim, adage, saying, proverb, catchword, catchphrase, slogan. Nickname.
B	Y	Z	A	N	T	Bezant, heraldic ornament.

C

C	A	B	A	L	A	Occult theosophy, mystical doctrinal interpretation.
C	A	B	A	N	A	Canopy, shelter, cabin, shack, beach cottage.
C	A	B	I	N	S	Plural of CABIN.
C	A	B	L	E	D	Telegraphed, wired, sent urgent message.
C	A	B	L	E	S	Plural of CABLE.
C	A	B	M	A	N	Taxi driver, cab driver, cabby.
C	A	C	H	E	D	Concealed, buried, hidden, stored away.
C	A	C	H	E	T	Seal of approval, stamp, philatelic embossing, postmark. Motto, slogan.
C	A	C	H	O	U	Aromatic pastille, strong smelling sweet.
C	A	C	K	L	E	Snigger, chatter, clack, prattle, gab, burble, gas. Giggle.
C	A	C	T	U	S	Genus of spiny plant.
C	A	D	D	I	E	Caddy, carrier, golfing assistant. Tea leaf container.
C	A	D	D	I	S	Worsted ribbon, tape. Type of worm.
C	A	D	E	N	T	Rhythmic, tonal.
C	A	D	E	T	S	Plural of CADET.
C	A	D	G	E	D	Begged, sponged, importuned, asked favour.
C	A	D	G	E	R	Importuner, beggar, sponger.
C	A	E	S	A	R	Autocrat, dictator.
C	A	F	T	A	N	Ankle length loose garment.
C	A	G	I	N	G	Confining, enclosing, enveloping, imprisoning, incarcerating.
C	A	H	O	O	T	Association, partnering, affiliate, hookup, collusion.
C	A	I	M	A	N	Cayman, Crocodile.
C	A	I	Q	U	E	Skiff, light boat.
C	A	J	O	L	E	Coax, wheedle, soft-soap, beguile, persuade.
C	A	K	I	N	G	Coagulating, encrusting, congealing, compacting.
C	A	L	A	S	H	Folding carriage top, light carriage, Women's headgear, hood.
C	A	L	C	A	R	Glassmaking oven. Bird spur, part of bat wing.
C	A	L	C	E	D	Shod as relating to religious.
C	A	L	C	I	C	Rich in calcium.
C	A	L	I	C	O	Plain white cotton fabric. Plant disease. Blotched, piebald.
C	A	L	I	G	O	Genus of Butterfly.
C	A	L	I	P	H	Muslim leader.
C	A	L	K	E	D	Caulked, seamed, waterproofed.
C	A	L	L	E	D	Visited, attracted attention, shouted, summoned, convened.
C	A	L	L	E	R	Visitor, sideshow barker, card player. Announcer.
C	A	L	L	O	W	Immature, green, lacking sophistication, inexperienced.
C	A	L	L	U	P	Marching orders.
C	A	L	L	U	S	Horny skin, thickened area of skin.
C	A	L	M	E	D	Soothed, allayed, relieved, composed, lulled, quietened, assuaged, appeased, pacified.
C	A	L	M	E	R	Comparative of CALM.
C	A	L	M	L	Y	In calm manner. Serenely, placidly, quietly, composedly, tranquilly.

1	2	3	4	5	6	
C	A	L	V	E	D	Given birth to a calf. Produced young calf.
C	A	L	V	E	S	Plural of CALF.
C	A	M	B	E	R	Arch toward the middle, convexity. Form a concave curve. Slight bow. Slightly arched.
C	A	M	E	L	S	Plural of CAMEL. Ships of the Desert.
C	A	M	E	O	S	Plural of CAMEO. Scenes. Views.
C	A	M	E	R	A	Image recorder, picture producing apparatus. Small hall. Judge's chamber. Not public.
C	A	M	I	O	N	Motor truck, wagon, bus.
C	A	M	I	S	A	Embroidered shirt.
C	A	M	L	E	T	Camel's hair fabric. Angora wool.
C	A	M	P	E	D	Lived outdoors, outspanned, lived under canvas, entented. Waited on doorstep.
C	A	M	P	E	R	One who lives in tents. Outdoorsman. Woodsman.
C	A	M	P	U	S	Grounds of a centre of learing. Playground, University grounds.
C	A	N	A	L	S	Plural of CANAL.
C	A	N	A	P	E	Snack, appetizer, savour, hors d'oeuvre.
C	A	N	A	R	D	Hoax, Lie, rumour, misrepresentation, untruth, prevarication, spoof, trick.
C	A	N	A	R	Y	Song bird. Yellow songster. Singer, informer, squealer (sl.)
C	A	N	C	A	N	Leggy cabaret dance.
C	A	N	C	E	L	Call off, annul, negate, neutralize. Obliterate, erase, delete, expunge. Rescind.
C	A	N	C	E	R	Malignant cell. Disease. Growth. Sign of the Zodiac.
C	A	N	D	I	D	Outspoken, truthful, straightforward, honest, scrupulous. Frank, open.
C	A	N	D	L	E	Wax taper, light, unit of luminous intensity, artificial illumination.
C	A	N	I	N	E	Dog, hound, of the dog family, doglike.
C	A	N	I	N	G	Thrashing, beating, chastising, punishment.
C	A	N	K	E	R	Malignancy, corruption, debasement, chronic inflammation, skin disease.
C	A	N	N	E	D	Preserved, condensed, potted, tinned. Drunk, intoxicated, inebriated.
C	A	N	N	E	R	One engaged in the business of canning.
C	A	N	N	O	N	Heavy calibre mounted weapon. Gun.
C	A	N	N	O	T	Opposite to CAN. Unable to, not willing to. Can't, averse to.
C	A	N	O	P	Y	Awning, verandah, shelter, covering, marquee.
C	A	N	T	A	B	Cantabrigian abridged. Relating to Cambridge.
C	A	N	T	A	L	French Cheese.
C	A	N	T	E	D	Slanted, slid, inclined, turn upside down. Leaned, tilted, sloped.
C	A	N	T	E	R	Lope, pace, 3-beat gait. One who cants. Chanter. Beggar, vagabond, hobo.
C	A	N	T	L	E	Part, portion, segment.
C	A	N	T	O	N	Territorial division, district, local governing unit, region. Billet, quarters.
C	A	N	T	O	R	Prayer leader, choir leader, synagogue official who chants. Precentor.
C	A	N	T	U	S	Principal melody, main voice.
C	A	N	U	C	K	Canadian.
C	A	N	V	A	S	Duck, drill, awning, sail cloth. Tent material. Circus. Oil painting.
C	A	N	Y	O	N	Valley, gorge, cutting, trench, trough, ravine.
C	A	P	E	R	S	Plural of CAPER.
C	A	P	F	U	L	Enough to fill a cap.
C	A	P	O	T	E	Long hooded cloak.
C	A	P	P	E	D	Horse ailment. Topped, overridden. Received University Degree. Orthidontics. Eclipsed.
C	A	P	R	I	C	Relating to a goat.
C	A	P	R	I	D	Capridae. Goat.
C	A	P	T	O	R	Capturer, one who captures.
C	A	R	A	F	E	Narrow-necked bottle. Glass water container.
C	A	R	A	P	A	Genus of tropical trees.
C	A	R	B	O	N	Non-metallic element. Artificial black, lamp black charcoal. Reproducing paper.
C	A	R	B	O	Y	Cylindrical liquid container, protected pouring vessel. Jar.
C	A	R	B	R	O	Photographic carbon process.
C	A	R	D	E	D	Programmed, mounted. Wool winding.
C	A	R	D	E	R	Carding machine operator. Threader.
C	A	R	E	E	N	Lurch, sway, wobble, weave, stagger.
C	A	R	E	E	R	Occupation, profession, pursuit. Speed, charge, rush, race.
C	A	R	E	S	S	Express affection, love, cuddle, fondle, pet, nuzzle, stroke.
C	A	R	F	A	X	Four-cornered cross roads.
C	A	R	H	O	P	Service-station attendant.
C	A	R	I	E	S	Tooth decay. Localised tooth tissue deterioration.
C	A	R	I	N	A	Keel-shaped anatomical structure. Ridge. Keel.
C	A	R	I	N	G	Concerned, loving, minding, ministering, nursing, serving, waiting on.
C	A	R	K	E	D	Worried, fretted, distressed, upset, troubled.
C	A	R	M	A	N	Railroad worker.
C	A	R	M	E	N	Chant, Incantation, poem, song.
C	A	R	N	A	L	Fleshly, animal, sensual, of the body, sexuality, sexual. Earthly, corporal, physical.
C	A	R	N	E	T	International automobile free pass.

1	2	3	4	5	6	
C	A	R	O	L	S	Joyous song, Song of Praise. Warble. Christmas hymns.
C	A	R	O	O	M	Cart licence.
C	A	R	P	A	L	Relating to the wrist.
C	A	R	P	E	D	Harped, grumbled, groused, nagged.
C	A	R	P	E	L	Seed box. Inner whorl of a flower.
C	A	R	P	E	R	One who CARPS. Critic, faultfinder, censor.
C	A	R	P	E	T	Floor rug, floor covering. Scold, berate.
C	A	R	P	U	S	Wrist.
C	A	R	R	O	T	Tapering orange root vegetable. Rolled tobacco leaves. Red Head. Enticement.
C	A	R	T	E	D	Carried, removed, wheeled, trundled.
C	A	R	T	E	L	Agreement between groups for common action. Written Agreement. Exchange of Trade Ideas.
C	A	R	T	E	R	Truck driver. Teamster.
C	A	R	T	O	N	Cardboard container. Box.
C	A	R	V	E	D	Cut, cleaved, severed, sliced, chiselled, split asunder, sculpted, divided.
C	A	R	V	E	R	Knife, meat cleaver, chopper, carving knife. Sculptor.
C	A	S	A	B	A	Winter melon.
C	A	S	E	I	N	Protein of cheese. Base of Casein plastics.
C	A	S	E	R	N	Military duty room. Barracks.
C	A	S	H	E	D	Converted into money. Changed, redeemed, transformed into currency.
C	A	S	H	E	W	Nut yielding tree. Nut.
C	A	S	I	N	G	Outer covering, packaging, wrapping. Frame.
C	A	S	I	N	O	Area utilised for public amusement. Gaming house. Salon. Gambling Den.
C	A	S	K	E	T	Ornamental chest, box, Jewel case. Coffin.
C	A	S	Q	U	E	Military headdress. Helmet. Face shield.
C	A	S	S	I	A	Genus of Herb. Senna. Cinnamon bark.
C	A	S	T	E	R	Foundary finisher. Moulder.
C	A	S	T	L	E	Mansion, Royal abode, Fortress, Stronghold, palisaded enclosure. Chess move.
C	A	S	T	O	R	Swivel wheel. Engine part. Chestnut, castor-oil plant.
C	A	S	U	A	L	Indifferent, detached, aloof, easygoing, relaxed, accidental, incidental, contingent.
C	A	S	U	L	A	Chasuble. Outer ecclesiastical vestment.
C	A	T	C	H	Y	Infectious, melodic, fitful, desultory, sporadic.
C	A	T	E	N	A	Connected, series, chain.
C	A	T	G	U	T	Tough cord made from animal intestines. Heavy linen.
C	A	T	K	I	N	Prolific flower cluster.
C	A	T	L	A	P	Weak beverage.
C	A	T	N	A	P	Forty-winks, doze, drift off. Siesta, snooze.
C	A	T	N	I	P	Strong scented herb. Cat mint.
C	A	T	S	U	P	Ketchup, relish. Tomato Sauce.
C	A	T	T	L	E	Domesticated bovine animals.
C	A	U	C	U	S	Party leaders, decision makers, political nucleus.
C	A	U	D	A	L	Relating to the tail. Posterior.
C	A	U	D	E	X	Woody base of tree or plant.
C	A	U	D	L	E	Spiced warm ale or wine.
C	A	U	G	H	T	Found, discovered, trapped, snared.
C	A	U	S	A	L	Constituting the cause, causative, arising from.
C	A	U	S	E	D	Effected, necessitated, determined, generated, produced, engendered.
C	A	U	S	E	R	Instigator, creater, one that causes.
C	A	U	S	E	S	Plural of CAUSE.
C	A	V	E	A	T	Warning, notice of caution, legal notice.
C	A	V	E	R	N	Cave, subterranean area, grotto, den.
C	A	V	I	A	R	Sturgeon's row. Delicacy, appetizer.
C	A	V	I	E	S	Guinea Pigs, Rodents.
C	A	V	I	N	G	Falling in giving way, collapsing.
C	A	V	I	T	Y	Vacuum, hole, void, opening, hollow.
C	A	V	O	R	T	Prance, caper, frolic, frisk, romp, gambol.
C	A	Y	M	A	N	Caiman, crocodile.
C	A	Y	U	S	E	Bronco, Pony, Mustang.
C	E	A	S	E	D	Stopped, desisted, concluded, terminated, ended.
C	E	D	I	N	G	Relinquishing, abandoning, leaving, waiving, yielding, transferring.
C	E	L	E	R	Y	Green stalk vegetable.
C	E	L	L	A	R	Underground room. Storeroom, wine store.
C	E	L	L	E	D	Having cells, honeycombed.
C	E	M	E	N	T	Join, unite, cohere. Cohesive, binding material. Bond. Bonding agent.
C	E	N	S	E	D	Estimated, assessed, rated, ranked.
C	E	N	S	E	R	Incense container, incense burner swung on chains.
C	E	N	S	O	R	Supervisor of morals, publications inspector. Official scrutinizer.
C	E	N	S	U	S	Official enumeration. Count of population, numbering, tally.

1	2	3	4	5	6	
C	E	N	T	R	E	Core, middle, equidistant, midway. Focus, heart. Hub. Complex. Seat.
C	E	R	E	A	L	Grain, maize, wheat, rice. Breakfast food. Oatmeal.
C	E	R	E	U	S	Genus of Cactus.
C	E	R	I	S	E	Archbishop Pink.
C	E	R	I	T	E	Mineral. Allanite.
C	E	R	I	U	M	Element of Flint.
C	E	R	M	E	T	Heat-resistant compound, titanium carbide.
C	E	R	O	I	D	Cirrhosis yellow pigment.
C	E	R	V	I	D	Deer, Moose.
C	E	R	V	I	X	Neck, lower end of uterus.
C	E	R	V	U	S	Genus of Cervidae. Elk, Deer.
C	E	S	S	E	D	Assessed, taxed, levied.
C	E	S	S	E	R	Tenant defaulter.
C	E	S	S	I	O	Ceding, cession.
C	E	S	T	U	I	Beneficiary.
C	E	S	T	U	S	Belt, girdle. Ancient knuckleduster.
C	H	A	F	E	D	Annoyed, bothered, provoked, vexed, corroded, grazed, rubbed, fretted.
C	H	A	F	E	R	Beetle. June Beetle, rose chafer, cockchafer.
C	H	A	F	F	Y	Worthless, lighthearted, jovial, bantering.
C	H	A	I	N	S	Plural of CHAIN.
C	H	A	I	R	S	Plural of CHAIR.
C	H	A	I	S	E	Pleasure carriage, 2-wheeled carriage. Post-Chaise. Chaise Longue.
C	H	A	L	E	T	Swiss dwelling place. Swiss type cottage. House.
C	H	A	L	K	S	Plural of CHALK.
C	H	A	L	K	Y	Powdery, like chalk.
C	H	A	N	C	E	Luck, uncertainty, fortune, hazard. Venture, gamble, opportunity, casual, fluke.
C	H	A	N	C	Y	Uncertain, risky, tricky, dangerous, treacherous, casual.
C	H	A	N	G	E	Alter, vary, modify, refashion, transform, convert, divergence, switch.
C	H	A	N	T	Y	Song of the Sea. Seaman's refrain. Shanty.
C	H	A	P	E	L	Subordinate place of worship. Small church. Private place of worship. Church recess.
C	H	A	P	P	Y	Little fellow, small chap. Roughened, flaky, cracked.
C	H	A	R	G	E	Command, instruct. Accuse, impeach. Ascribe, accredit, rush, burden, price, cost.
C	H	A	R	M	S	Plural of CHARM.
C	H	A	R	O	N	Ferryman in Hades.
C	H	A	R	R	Y	Like charcoal.
C	H	A	R	T	S	Plural of CHART.
C	H	A	S	E	D	Followed, hunted, rushed, preyed, dismissed, sacked, chivied. Sped, raced.
C	H	A	S	E	R	Pursuer, hunter, philanderer, casanova, womanizer. Alcoholic drink.
C	H	A	S	M	S	Plural of CHASM.
C	H	A	S	M	Y	Chasmic, like a chasm.
C	H	A	S	S	E	Saint's shrine. Dance step, sashay, sliding movement. Liqueur.
C	H	A	S	T	E	Pure, virtuous, clean, stainless, good, unsullied, modest, decent, virginal.
C	H	A	T	T	Y	Talkative, garrulous, inclined to discourse.
C	H	E	A	T	S	Plural of CHEAT.
C	H	E	C	K	S	Plural of CHECK.
C	H	E	C	K	Y	Checkered, like checks, covered in checks.
C	H	E	E	K	S	Plural of CHEEK.
C	H	E	E	K	Y	Insolent, bold, forward, outspoken, smart, impudent, pert, fresh.
C	H	E	E	R	S	Plural of CHEER.
C	H	E	E	R	Y	Jolly, happy, joyous, merry, flippant, glad, cheerful, carefree, bright.
C	H	E	E	S	E	Curd separated from whey, moulded and ripened. Dairy product.
C	H	E	E	S	Y	Suggestive of cheese. Cheese flavoured. (Sl.) Stylish, modish. Shabby.
C	H	E	Q	U	E	Bank Exchange Form, Draft, Bill.
C	H	E	R	R	Y	Succulent fruit. Pink Colour. Bowls term. (Sl.) Virginity.
C	H	E	R	T	Y	Flinty.
C	H	E	R	U	B	Angel, good child, term of endearment. Cupid. Heavenly body.
C	H	E	S	T	Y	Deep sounding. Busty. Croupy, phlegmy, weak chested.
C	H	E	V	A	L	Framed Mirror.
C	H	E	W	E	D	Masticated, ground, crushed, upbraided, reprimanded.
C	H	I	C	H	I	Frilly, ornamented, affected, showy, arty.
C	H	I	C	L	Y	Fashionably, stylishly, smartly, trendily.
C	H	I	L	L	I	Capsicum pod, hot pepper, chilli powder. Curry derivative.
C	H	I	L	L	S	Plural of CHILL.
C	H	I	L	L	Y	Cold, miserable, bleak, unwelcoming.
C	H	I	M	E	D	Past of CHIME.
C	H	I	M	E	S	Plural of CHIME.
C	H	I	N	K	S	Plural of CHINK.

1	2	3	4	5	6	
C	H	I	N	K	Y	Having chinks.
C	H	I	N	T	Z	Printed calico. Glazed cotton fabric. Floral upholstery material.
C	H	I	P	P	Y	(Sl.) Promiscuous woman. Prostitute. Hungover.
C	H	I	R	P	Y	Cheerful, happy, lively.
C	H	I	S	E	L	Metal tool, goldsmith's tool, chipping tool. Cheat, employ sharp practice.
C	H	I	T	O	N	Genus of Mollusc. Ancient Greek garment.
C	H	I	T	T	Y	Slip, account, bill. Infantile, childish.
C	H	I	V	E	S	Perennial plant related to the Onion. Tasty seasoning. (Sl.) Knife.
C	H	I	V	V	Y	Chase, hasten, pursue, harry, pester.
C	H	O	C	K	S	Plural of CHOCK.
C	H	O	I	C	E	Selection, preference, option, delicate. Selected, fine, fastidious, exquisite.
C	H	O	K	E	D	Strangulated, stifled, throttled, suppressed.
C	H	O	K	E	R	Beads, neck decoration, jewelled collar, noose.
C	H	O	K	E	Y	Jail, prison, lockup.
C	H	O	L	E	R	Irritation, irascibility. Biliousness. Rage, spleen.
C	H	O	O	S	E	Select, pick, elect, discriminate, single out, cull. Desire, want, wish.
C	H	O	O	S	Y	Pernickety, fastidious, finicky, particular, fussy.
C	H	O	P	I	N	English unit of liquid measurement.
C	H	O	P	P	Y	Variable, changeable, irregular, rough, undulating.
C	H	O	R	A	L	Belonging to a choir. Song of praise. Psalm, hymn, chorus singing.
C	H	O	R	D	S	Plural of CHORD.
C	H	O	R	E	A	Organic nervous disorder of man and dogs.
C	H	O	R	E	S	Plural of CHORE.
C	H	O	R	U	S	Concert, harmony, accord, in tune, grouped singers.
C	H	O	S	E	N	Selected, picked, elected, singled out, superior.
C	H	O	U	S	E	Trick, defraud, cheat; Gimmick, ploy, ruse.
C	H	R	I	S	M	Consecrated Oil. Holy Oil.
C	H	R	O	M	A	Colour dimension. Saturation.
C	H	R	O	M	E	Chromium.
C	H	U	B	B	Y	Tubby, plump, rotund, pudgy, roly-poly.
C	H	U	F	F	Y	Sullen, sulky, glum, surly, crabby, gloomy.
C	H	U	K	K	A	Short leather boot. Polo round.
C	H	U	M	M	Y	Friendly, intimate, familiar, pally, buddy-buddy.
C	H	U	M	P	S	Plural of CHUMP.
C	H	U	N	K	S	Plural of CHUNK.
C	H	U	R	C	H	Place of Worship, temple, House of God, religion.
C	H	U	R	L	Y	Surly, sullen, glum, rude, churlish.
C	H	U	T	E	S	Plural of CHUTE.
C	H	Y	L	E	S	Emulsified fats. Lacteals.
C	H	Y	P	R	E	Non-alcoholic perfume. Perfume containing oils and resins.
C	I	C	A	D	A	Christmas Beetle, Harvest Fly.
C	I	C	E	L	Y	Genus of Herbs. Myrrh.
C	I	C	U	T	A	Genus of perennial Herb. Hemlock.
C	I	G	A	R	S	Plural of CIGAR.
C	I	L	I	C	E	Haircloth. Hair Shirt. Undergarment.
C	I	L	I	U	M	Eyelash.
C	I	N	D	E	R	Dross, ashes, ember. Lava fragments.
C	I	N	E	M	A	Bioscope. Movies. Motion Picture House.
C	I	N	Q	U	E	The number Five.
C	I	P	H	E	R	Code. Symbolic character, monogram. Nonentity, Naught, zero. Compute, estimate.
C	I	R	C	L	E	Ring, circumference, Rotary, round, Cycle. Clique, elite group. Revolve. Wheel.
C	I	R	C	U	S	Spectacle presented in amphitheatre. Wild animal Acts. Travelling entertainment.
C	I	R	R	U	S	White Cloud. Tendril. Copulatory organ of certain male worms.
C	I	S	S	U	S	Ivy Plant.
C	I	S	T	U	S	Rock Rose.
C	I	T	I	E	S	Plural of CITY.
C	I	T	I	N	G	Mentioning, naming, specifying, reminding, summoning.
C	I	T	R	I	C	Occuring in Limes or Lemons.
C	I	T	R	O	N	Type of Lemon Tree. Shrubby Citrus Tree.
C	I	T	R	U	S	Type of fruit. Orange, Lemon, Lime, Related fruits.
C	I	V	I	C	S	Study of local government. Training for citizenship.
C	I	V	I	E	S	Civilian clothes.
C	I	V	I	S	M	Good citizenship.
C	L	A	G	G	Y	Adhesive, gooey, gummy, sticky.
C	L	A	I	M	S	Plural of CLAIM.
C	L	A	M	M	Y	Damp, moist, wet, cold and wet, lacking warmth.
C	L	A	M	P	S	Plural of CLAMP.

1	2	3	4	5	6	
C	L	A	Q	U	E	Self-seeking group of adherents.
C	L	A	R	E	T	Dry red table wine. Colour of Red.
C	L	A	R	T	Y	Sticky, dirty, muddy, gooey.
C	L	A	S	S	Y	Stylish, slick, ostentatious, elegant, high class.
C	L	A	U	S	E	Distinct section in writing. Special meaning. Proviso, condition, phrase.
C	L	A	W	E	D	Scratched, pulled, tore, clutched, dragged, scraped.
C	L	A	Y	E	Y	Like clay, tacky, malleable, pliable, resembling clay.
C	L	E	A	N	S	Plural of CLEAN.
C	L	E	A	T	S	Plural of CLEAT.
C	L	E	A	V	E	Divide into two, apportion, cut, split, separate, penetrate. Cling, adhere, stick to.
C	L	E	N	C	H	Clamp, clutch, grasp, grip, clasp, hold, fasten, tighten.
C	L	E	R	G	Y	The Priesthood, Holy Orders, Ministers, Parsons, Preachers, Men of God.
C	L	E	R	I	C	Clergyman, Clerk, Minister, Reverend, Curate, pastor, vicar, Priest.
C	L	E	R	K	S	Plural of CLERK.
C	L	E	V	E	R	Able, gifted, skillful, dexterous, intelligent, brainy, quick-witted, canny, cunning.
C	L	E	V	I	S	Connection. Bridge building hanger.
C	L	I	C	H	E	Trite phrase, hackneyed theme, Banality, platitude, rubber stamp, stale, truism.
C	L	I	C	K	S	Plural of CLICK.
C	L	I	E	N	T	Customer, patron, dependant, social case.
C	L	I	M	A	X	High point, outcome, highlight, stage, end product, culmination, intensity. Ultimate.
C	L	I	M	B	S	Plural of CLIMB.
C	L	I	N	C	H	Embrace, hold, clamp, clench, press, squeeze. Bring to fruition.
C	L	I	N	G	Y	Adhering, sticky, clutchy, dependant.
C	L	I	N	I	C	Outpatients Hospital, Medical Institution, Examining Group.
C	L	I	N	K	S	Plural of CLINK.
C	L	I	Q	U	E	Secret Group, exclusive club, Set, circle, cabal, mob, ring, camp, clan.
C	L	O	C	H	E	Woman's tight fitting hat. Helmet-like fitting for plants. Growing device.
C	L	O	C	K	S	Plural of CLOCK.
C	L	O	G	G	Y	Clogging, sticky, lumpy.
C	L	O	N	E	S	Plural of CLONE.
C	L	O	N	I	C	Relating to convulsive spasms.
C	L	O	N	U	S	Muscle spasms.
C	L	O	S	E	D	Shut, unattainable, unopened, restricted, secluded, stuffy, confined. Self-sufficient.
C	L	O	S	E	R	Comparative of CLOSE.
C	L	O	S	E	T	Cupboard, wardrobe, ante-room, Privy, Bathroom.
C	L	O	T	H	E	Dress, array, attire, drape, wrap, cover, envelop, express, enhance, portray.
C	L	O	U	D	Y	Overcast, dull, gloomy, dim, lowering, hazy, foggy, vague, murky.
C	L	O	U	G	H	Ravine, chasm, gap, gorge, gulch.
C	L	O	U	T	S	Plural of CLOUT.
C	L	O	V	E	N	Cleft, divided, rent asunder.
C	L	O	V	E	R	Genus of three-leaved herb, densely distributed plant. Well off, favoured.
C	L	O	Y	E	D	Past of CLOY.
C	L	U	M	P	S	Plural of CLUMP.
C	L	U	M	P	Y	Growing in Clumps, abounding in bunches.
C	L	U	M	S	Y	Awkward, lacking dexterity, unskilled, graceless, inelegant, unwieldy.
C	L	U	T	C	H	Grab, grasp, clench, hold; Engaging device in motoring, setting of hen's eggs.
C	O	A	L	E	R	Supplier of Coal.
C	O	A	R	S	E	Rough, rude, unmannerly, crude, vulgar, obscene, ribald, gross.
C	O	A	T	E	D	Covered, spread, painted, impregnated, overlaid.
C	O	A	T	E	E	Short coat, half length coat.
C	O	A	X	E	D	Persuaded, encouraged, wheedled, urged, pressed, importuned, inveigled, lured.
C	O	A	X	E	R	Cajoler, wheedler, flatterer.
C	O	B	A	L	T	Blue, hard, silver-white metallic element. Artist's colour.
C	O	B	B	E	R	(Sl.) Friend companion.
C	O	B	B	L	E	Patch, mend, repair. Paving stone.
C	O	B	N	U	T	Hazel nut.
C	O	B	R	A	S	Plural of COBRA.
C	O	B	W	E	B	Spider's spun flytrap, entanglement, spun thread.
C	O	C	C	U	S	Spherical bacterium, genus of scale insect. Cochineal.
C	O	C	C	Y	X	End of vertebral column, vestigial tail.
C	O	C	K	E	D	At the ready. Unevenly thrown dice. Up-ended, Three-brimmed hat.
C	O	C	K	E	R	Type of Spaniel. One who handles fighting cocks. Indulge pamper.
C	O	C	K	L	E	Bi-valve mollusc, pucker, bulge, wringle. Weed.
C	O	C	O	O	N	Pupal enclosure. Snuggery. Egg case.
C	O	D	D	E	D	Teased, bantered, kidded, hoaxed.
C	O	D	D	L	E	Cook eggs softly. Pamper, spoil. Baby, cosset. Mollycoddle.
C	O	D	G	E	R	Derogatory appellation, fellow, chap.

1	2	3	4	5	6	
C	O	D	I	F	Y	Classify, systematize. Encode.
C	O	D	I	N	G	Translating into cipher.
C	O	E	R	C	E	Impel, force, urge, constrain, oblige, compel, browbeat, intimidate.
C	O	E	V	A	L	Coexistent, concurrent, contemporaneous, simultaneous, contemporary.
C	O	F	F	E	E	Aromatic beverage.
C	O	F	F	E	R	Treasury, storehouse, chest, moneybag.
C	O	F	F	I	N	Casket, chest, box. Wooden overcoat.
C	O	G	E	N	T	Valid, satisfactory, well-founded, justified, influential, significant. Persuasive.
C	O	G	G	E	D	Provided with cogs, operated by means of teeth.
C	O	G	N	A	C	Brandy distilled from white wine. Pale liquor.
C	O	H	E	I	R	Joint Heir.
C	O	H	E	R	E	Stick, join, unite, adhere, fit together, abutt.
C	O	H	O	R	T	Band, group. One of ten divisions of warriors. Comrade.
C	O	H	U	N	E	Palm.
C	O	I	L	E	D	Past of COIL. Spiralled.
C	O	I	N	E	D	Past of COIN.
C	O	I	N	E	R	Counterfeiter, fabricator. Coin maker.
C	O	I	T	U	S	Intercourse, male ejaculation into female vagina.
C	O	L	D	E	R	Comparative of COLD.
C	O	L	D	L	Y	In a cold manner. Off-hand. Unsmilingly.
C	O	L	L	A	R	Neckband, strip, control, check, guide, adornment. Collect, capture, tackle, nab.
C	O	L	L	E	T	Metal band, flange, ferrule, collar.
C	O	L	L	I	E	Scottish Sheep Dog.
C	O	L	L	O	P	Slice of meat, rasher of bacon, portion, measure of quantity.
C	O	L	O	N	S	Plural of COLON.
C	O	L	O	N	Y	Settlement, occupation, localized population, group of organisms, cluster.
C	O	L	O	U	R	Phenomenon of Light. Hue, tint, aspect, appearance, tone, complexion, variegation.
C	O	L	U	M	N	Vertical section, stack, pillar, pole, structure, formation, bodily part. Row, file.
C	O	M	A	R	T	Covenant, Agreement.
C	O	M	A	T	E	Companion. Hairy, shaggy.
C	O	M	B	A	T	Fight, contest, encounter, conflict, struggle, battle. Action.
C	O	M	B	E	D	Past of COMB.
C	O	M	B	E	R	Large curling wave. Wool combing machine.
C	O	M	E	D	Y	Light hearted amusement. Comic Drama. Farce, Funny event. Comic Play.
C	O	M	E	L	Y	Attractive, pleasing, seemly, pleasant, proportionate. Beautiful, handsome.
C	O	M	E	T	S	Plural of COMET.
C	O	M	F	I	T	Preserve, confection, sweet.
C	O	M	I	C	S	Plural of COMIC.
C	O	M	I	N	G	Advent, manifestation, arrival, approaching.
C	O	M	I	T	Y	Civility, consideration, kindliness, courteous behaviour. Code of Nations. Goodwill.
C	O	M	M	A	S	Plural of COMMA.
C	O	M	M	I	E	(Sl.) Communist. Red.
C	O	M	M	I	T	Perpetrate, commend, entrust, accomplish, achieve, enact. Consign, relegate.
C	O	M	M	I	X	Mingle, blend, mix.
C	O	M	M	O	N	General, prevalent, ordinary, unspecial, informal, popular, vulgar, familiar.
C	O	M	O	I	D	Tress-like.
C	O	M	O	S	E	Hairy, downy.
C	O	M	P	E	L	Force, constrain, coerce, make, oblige.
C	O	M	P	L	Y	Conform, observe, obey, follow, submit, yield.
C	O	M	P	O	T	Compote. Dried Fruits cooked in Syrup. Small Dish, sweet dish.
C	O	N	C	U	R	Agree, accede, acquiesce, consent. Coincide, co-operate.
C	O	N	D	O	R	American Vulture. Largest bird.
C	O	N	F	A	B	Discussion, confabulation, huddle, parley, confer.
C	O	N	F	E	R	Bestow, give, yield, grant.
C	O	N	G	E	E	Dismiss. Leave ceremoniously. Bow in servile fashion. Ricewater.
C	O	N	G	E	R	Eel. Genus of Eels.
C	O	N	K	E	D	Stalled, failed, gave out, blacked out, passed out.
C	O	N	K	E	R	Horse chestnut.
C	O	N	M	A	N	Swindler, fast talker, deceiver, trickster, shrewdy.
C	O	N	N	E	D	Past of CON.
C	O	N	S	U	L	Official representative resident in foreign country.
C	O	N	T	R	A	Opposite, against, contrary, offset. Facing, reverse, fronting.
C	O	N	V	E	X	Arched up, bulging out, opposite to concave.
C	O	N	V	E	Y	Carry, ferry, transport, tote, lug, communicate, impart, transmit, transfer.
C	O	N	V	O	Y	Escort, consort, accompany, defend, guard, shield, protect. Group.
C	O	O	E	E	D	Called, attracted attention, yelled.
C	O	O	I	N	G	Tender talking, speaking softly, whispering soft nothings, murmuring, dove calling.

1	2	3	4	5	6	
C	O	O	K	E	D	Prepared for eating with heat. Past of COOK.
C	O	O	K	E	R	A stove, oven, range. Producer of heat.
C	O	O	K	I	E	Small cake, tart, biscuit. Term of endearment. Female Cook.
C	O	O	L	E	D	Past of COOL.
C	O	O	L	E	R	Comparative of COOL. Jail, prison, refrigerator, cool box. Cold drink.
C	O	O	L	I	E	Indian or Chinese labourer. pp Porter.
C	O	O	L	L	Y	In a cool manner.
C	O	O	P	E	D	Confined, enclosed, enveloped, hemmed in, shut in, fenced in.
C	O	O	P	E	R	Cask maker, cask repairer. Barrel maker.
C	O	P	I	E	D	Past of COPY.
C	O	P	I	E	R	One who copies. Copiest, transcriber, imitator, plagiarist.
C	O	P	I	E	S	Plural of COPY.
C	O	P	I	N	G	Slanting wall. Weather proofing course of bricks or tiles.
C	O	P	P	E	D	Found, apprehended, caught redhanded.
C	O	P	P	E	R	Metallic element. (SI.) Policeman. Old fashioned Penny. Red headed.
C	O	P	T	I	C	Relating to COPTS. Egyptian Christian Church. Art of this period.
C	O	Q	U	E	T	Flirt, charmer, bold dalliance. Wanton, Trifler.
C	O	R	B	E	L	Architectural projection.
C	O	R	B	I	E	Ghost Moth. Destructive Pest.
C	O	R	D	E	D	Provided with Cords. Ridged. Bound, twilled, ribbed.
C	O	R	D	O	N	Circle, ribbon, shield of troops. Police barrier.
C	O	R	I	N	G	Removing the core, drilling, boring.
C	O	R	K	E	D	Wine having unpleasant taste and odour due to inept corking.
C	O	R	K	E	R	Person or thing of excellent quality. Beauty, Stunner, Exquisite.
C	O	R	N	E	A	Transparent cover of eyeball which admits the light.
C	O	R	N	E	D	Preserved, salted.
C	O	R	N	E	R	Angle of convergence. Intersection. Predicament, dilemma. Trap, block, prevent escape.
C	O	R	N	E	T	Musical wind instrument. Cone-shaped piece of paper. Ice-Cream Cone.
C	O	R	O	N	A	Crown of colour, halo, sun's atmosphre. Radial zone.
C	O	R	O	Z	O	Genus of Palm.
C	O	R	P	S	E	Cadaver, dead body, carcass, remains.
C	O	R	P	U	S	The whole body, the main substance.
C	O	R	R	A	L	Pen, enclosure, roped off area. Fenced in field. Paddock.
C	O	R	S	E	T	Woman's undergarment, bodice, stays, step-in.
C	O	R	T	E	S	Spanish Parliament.
C	O	R	T	E	X	Outer layer. Bark, primary tissue. Part of brain.
C	O	S	H	E	D	Beaten with a cosh.
C	O	S	I	E	R	Comparative of COSY.
C	O	S	I	L	Y	Snugly, warmly, safely.
C	O	S	I	N	E	Complement to angle.
C	O	S	M	I	C	Relating to the Cosmos. Extraterrestrial vastness. Of the universe.
C	O	S	M	O	S	Order, Harmony. The Universe.
C	O	S	S	E	T	Spoil, coddle, pet, fondle, pamper.
C	O	S	T	A	R	Act with, star together with, co-feature with.
C	O	S	T	E	R	Costermonger. Street vendor.
C	O	S	T	L	Y	Expensive, dear, valuable, priceless, precious.
C	O	T	T	A	R	Cotter, peasant tenant, squatter.
C	O	T	T	E	R	Fastener, wedge, pin, shaft.
C	O	T	T	O	N	Plant yielding white fibrous substance. Material. Fabric. Comprehend, grasp.
C	O	U	G	A	R	Jaguar-type large cat. Mountain lion.
C	O	U	G	H	S	Plural of COUGH.
C	O	U	N	T	S	Plural of COUNT.
C	O	U	N	T	Y	District, neighbouring Cities, Local Government.
C	O	U	P	L	E	Pair, brace. Join, link, connect. Unite in sexual union. Breed. Copulate.
C	O	U	P	O	N	Ticket, Certificate of Authority to Purchase. Trading Stamp. Travel Ticket. Voucher.
C	O	U	R	S	E	Track, way, path, Channel, progress, succession, sequence, dash, rush, chase. Area.
C	O	U	R	T	S	Plural of COURT.
C	O	U	S	I	N	Child of one's uncle or aunt. Blood relative. Kin.
C	O	V	E	R	S	Plural of COVER. Blankets.
C	O	V	E	R	T	Shelter, hiding place, refuge.
C	O	W	A	R	D	One who has ignoble fear. Easily frightened, timid, irresolute in face of danger.
C	O	W	B	O	Y	Cattle herder on horseback.
C	O	W	I	N	G	Act of intimidating.
C	O	W	I	S	H	Bovine, like a cow.
C	O	W	L	E	D	Shaped like a Hood. Hooded. Equipped with a Cowl.
C	O	W	M	A	N	Cowboy, cow herd.
C	O	W	P	E	A	Black-eyed Pea, Meadow Pea.

1	2	3	4	5	6	
C	O	W	P	O	X	Cattle disease.
C	O	W	R	I	E	Seashell.
C	O	W	S	O	N	Generalised term of abuse.
C	O	Y	O	T	E	Prairie Wolf. (Sl.) Chiseler.
C	R	A	B	B	Y	Sullen, bad-tempered, sulky, dour, chuffy, surly, glum, gloomy. Crablike.
C	R	A	C	K	S	Plural of CRACK.
C	R	A	D	L	E	Baby's cot. Crib. Resting place. Beginning, infancy.
C	R	A	F	T	Y	Sly, artful, cunning, wily.
C	R	A	G	G	Y	Rugged, jagged, rough, uneven, scraggy.
C	R	A	M	B	O	Rhyming Game.
C	R	A	M	P	Y	Affected by a cramp. Strangulated.
C	R	A	N	E	D	Stretched the neck, peered, gazed intently.
C	R	A	N	E	S	Plural of CRANE.
C	R	A	N	I	A	Plural of CRANIUM.
C	R	A	N	K	Y	Grumpy, crotchety, bad-tempered. Cantankerous, cross, irascible.
C	R	A	N	N	Y	Crevice, niche, recess, byplace.
C	R	A	P	E	D	Shrouded.
C	R	A	P	P	Y	Unsatisfactory, wrong, poor, rotten.
C	R	A	T	E	D	Boxed, packed, encased, containerised.
C	R	A	T	E	R	Depression around an orifice. Depression formed by impact. Cup-shaped cavity.
C	R	A	V	A	T	Scarf of fine fabric. Necktie.
C	R	A	V	E	D	Desired, longed for, asked earnestly, demanded.
C	R	A	V	E	N	Cowardly, of little courage, disinclined, faint hearted.
C	R	A	V	E	R	One who craves.
C	R	A	Y	O	N	Wax stick, coloured drawing material.
C	R	A	Z	E	D	Mad, deranged, unbalanced, insane, demented. Full of cracks.
C	R	A	Z	E	S	Plural of CRAZE.
C	R	E	A	K	S	Plural of CREAK. Make creaking sounds.
C	R	E	A	K	Y	Apt to Creak. Squeaky, dilapidated, decrepit.
C	R	E	A	M	S	Plural of CREAM.
C	R	E	A	M	Y	Like cream, with the consistency of Cream. Coloured Cream.
C	R	E	A	S	E	Groove, line, ridge, edge, pleat. Wrinkle. Graze. Specially marked area in Cricket.
C	R	E	A	S	Y	Forming Creases. Rumpled, crumpled, wrinkled.
C	R	E	A	T	E	Cause to be, invent, bring into existence. Make, generate, procreate, produce.
C	R	E	C	H	E	Day Nursery, child minding centre.
C	R	E	D	I	T	Recognition, acknowledgment, belief, credence, influence, ascribe, attribute. Hire Purchase.
C	R	E	E	K	S	Plural of CREEK.
C	R	E	E	L	S	Plural of CREEL.
C	R	E	E	P	Y	Scary, eerie, unnatural. Creepy Crawly. (Insect).
C	R	E	O	L	E	Half Breed, of French or Spanish decent, of mixed Spanish Negro blood.
C	R	E	S	S	Y	Like Cress green, abounding in Cress.
C	R	E	T	I	N	Deformed idiot, creature with thyroid deficiency. Of Crete.
C	R	E	W	E	L	Worsted embroidery.
C	R	I	K	E	Y	Exclamation of Surprise.
C	R	I	M	E	S	Plural of CRIME. Sins, Misadventures.
C	R	I	M	P	Y	Wavy, frizzy, crimped.
C	R	I	N	G	E	Shrink, crouch, huddle, contort, wince, cower. Fawn, toady.
C	R	I	S	E	S	Plural of CRISIS. Calamaties, catastrophes, emergencies.
C	R	I	S	I	S	Contingency, emergency, exigency, Crossroads. Zero hour, turning point.
C	R	I	S	P	Y	Brittle, crisp, crumbly, crunchy, friable.
C	R	I	T	I	C	Art appraiser, reviewer, arbiter, Judge. Fault finder, censor, muckraker.
C	R	O	A	K	Y	Throaty, croupy, guttural, harsh, hoarse.
C	R	O	C	K	S	Plural of CROCK.
C	R	O	C	U	S	Genus of Perennial Herb. Saffron.
C	R	O	N	E	S	Plural of CRONE.
C	R	O	O	K	S	Plural of CROOK.
C	R	O	T	C	H	Prop, two-armed stanchion, body angle from Trunk, section of garment.
C	R	O	T	O	N	Genus of plant producing oil.
C	R	O	U	C	H	Stoop low, bend, hunch, squat, duck. Fawn, cringe.
C	R	O	U	P	Y	Chest ailment, hoarse coughing, throaty.
C	R	O	W	D	S	Plural of CROWD.
C	R	O	W	E	D	Past of CROW.
C	R	O	W	N	S	Plural of CROWN.
C	R	U	D	E	R	Comparative of CRUDE.
C	R	U	I	S	E	Sea travel. Voyage. Sail, wend, journey, proceed, amble, canter. In no hurry.
C	R	U	M	B	Y	CRUMMY, Crumbled, crumbly. (Sl.) Miserable, worthless, cheap, unsavoury.
C	R	U	N	C	H	Munch, chew, chomp, scrunch, masticate, ruminate. Boom!

1	2	3	4	5	6	Definition
C	R	U	S	T	Y	Having a crust. Crisp outer layer. Old and irritable.
C	R	U	T	C	H	Aid for the disabled. Support. Prop, forked stanchion. Human crutch. Pommel.
C	R	Y	I	N	G	Weeping, sobbing, acute, notorious, heinous. Clamouring.
C	R	Y	P	T	S	Plural of CRYPT.
C	U	B	A	G	E	Displacement, cubic content, volume.
C	U	B	I	S	M	Expression by means of simplified forms and lines. Art movement.
C	U	B	I	S	T	Adherent of Cubism. Characteristic of Cubism.
C	U	B	I	T	S	Plural of CUBIT. 1 Cubit measures about 17 inches.
C	U	B	O	I	D	Cubic in outer shape.
C	U	C	K	O	O	European bird. Vapid person. Silly, stupid, simple.
C	U	D	D	L	E	Embrace, hug, snuggle, pet, fondle, caress, love, hold, nestle.
C	U	D	G	E	L	Solid stick, baton, club, bludgeon, knobkerrie, truncheon, blackjack.
C	U	E	B	I	D	Bridge bidding formula.
C	U	L	L	E	D	Past of CULL. Depleted, lessened.
C	U	L	L	E	R	Examiner, Inspector. Selector.
C	U	L	L	E	T	Re-cycled glass.
C	U	L	L	I	S	Groove, gully, ridge, channel. Invalid Broth.
C	U	M	B	E	R	Hinder, weigh down, burden, clutter up.
C	U	M	M	E	R	Godmother, witch, midwife.
C	U	M	M	I	N	CUMIN, Aromatic Seed. Food flavouring.
C	U	N	E	A	L	Shaped like a wedge.
C	U	P	F	U	L	Measurement. Quantity.
C	U	P	O	L	A	Decorative Dome. Roof vault. Lookout. Observation Post.
C	U	P	P	E	D	Cup-shaped, concave. Holed golf ball.
C	U	P	T	I	E	Deciding contest. Competition for a Cup.
C	U	P	U	L	E	Cup-shaped, hive-like, convex. Like an acorn.
C	U	R	A	C	Y	Office of a Curate.
C	U	R	A	R	E	Indian arrow poison.
C	U	R	A	T	E	Clergyman, Vicar, Churchman.
C	U	R	B	E	D	Restrained, bridled, constrained, inhibited, denied, hampered, fettered.
C	U	R	D	L	E	Coagulate, thicken, sour, condense, ferment, spoil, congeal.
C	U	R	F	E	W	Time to be off the streets. Homecoming time. Regulation, Order. Curfew Bell.
C	U	R	I	N	G	Healing, restorative, remedying, remedial, curative, mending.
C	U	R	I	O	S	Plural of CURIO. Antiques.
C	U	R	L	E	D	Past of CURL.
C	U	R	L	E	R	Pin used in hair to cause curls. Brim turner.
C	U	R	L	E	W	Wide-ranging migratory wading bird.
C	U	R	S	E	D	Past of CURSE. Sworn at.
C	U	R	S	E	S	Plural of CURSE. Oaths.
C	U	R	S	O	R	Mathematical instrument part.
C	U	R	T	L	Y	In a curt manner. Brusquely, briefly, abruptly.
C	U	R	T	S	Y	Curtsey. Act of respect. Civility, Bended knee. Reverence. Obeisance.
C	U	R	V	E	D	Bent, arched, crooked, twisted, bowed, rounded.
C	U	S	C	U	S	Brightly coloured arboreal marsupial.
C	U	S	P	I	D	Canine Tooth.
C	U	S	S	E	D	(Sl.) Cursed.
C	U	S	T	O	M	Habit, rule, law, precept, ritual, manner, usage, wont. Patronage, trade, clientele.
C	U	S	T	O	S	Keeper, warden, custodian, guardian, watchdog.
C	U	T	E	S	T	Comparative of CUTE. Prettiest.
C	U	T	L	E	R	Dealer in cutlery. Knife sharpener.
C	U	T	L	E	T	Small chop. Cut of meat. Choice cut.
C	U	T	O	F	F	Cessation, Shutdown, Bypass, shortcut, valve, shutter.
C	U	T	O	U	T	Design, shape, picture. Cull, switch, circuit breaker. Stop.
C	U	T	T	E	R	Tailor, dressmaker. Sailing boat. Editor of film. Incisor. Tool for cutting.
C	U	T	T	L	E	Cuttlefish. (Sl.) Bully, ruffian.
C	Y	C	L	E	D	Recurred, rounded, succeeded, coursed, ran, looped. Rode.
C	Y	C	L	I	C	Relating to cycles. Recurrent, periodic.
C	Y	C	L	U	S	Cycle.
C	Y	E	S	I	S	Pregnancy.
C	Y	G	N	E	T	Young swan.
C	Y	G	N	U	S	Genus of typical swans.
C	Y	M	B	A	L	Clashing instrument, percussion instrument.
C	Y	M	O	I	D	Curving.
C	Y	M	O	S	E	Clustering.
C	Y	N	A	R	A	Having spiny leaves. Artichoke.
C	Y	N	I	C	S	Plural of CYNIC.
C	Y	N	I	P	S	Genus of Wasps.

1	2	3	4	5	6	
C	Y	N	I	S	M	Cynicism.
C	Y	P	R	E	S	Law of Charities.
C	Y	P	R	I	S	Small ostracod crustacean.
C	Y	P	R	U	S	Cedar.
C	Y	S	T	I	C	Relating to the bladder. Involving cysts.
C	Y	T	O	D	E	Protoplasmic mass.

D

1	2	3	4	5	6	
D	A	B	B	E	D	Patted, daubed, touched lightly, wiped, smeared, plastered, smudged.
D	A	B	B	E	R	Pad used by etchers. Ink-ball.
D	A	B	B	L	E	Splash, sprinkle, spatter. Show superficial interest. Meddle. Tamper.
D	A	C	O	I	T	Roving Indian Robber.
D	A	C	R	O	N	Polyester fabric.
D	A	C	T	Y	L	Trisyllable. Finger, Toe.
D	A	F	T	E	R	Comparative of DAFT. Sillier.
D	A	F	T	L	Y	Madly, crazily, stupidly, idiotically.
D	A	G	G	E	R	Stiletto, dirk, poniard.
D	A	G	G	L	E	To wet or grow wet by dragging or sprinkling. A draggle-tail.
D	A	H	L	I	A	Genus of tuberous rooted Herb. Flower.
D	A	I	N	T	Y	Choice, delicate, delectable. Delicacy, tidbit. Pernickety, particular. Flimsy.
D	A	M	A	G	E	Harm, hurt, injury, impair, misfortune, disadvantage.
D	A	M	A	S	K	Firm lustrous fabric. Table linen.
D	A	M	M	E	D	Pent up, confined, blocked, impeded, obstructed.
D	A	M	N	E	D	Condemned, doomed, cursed, sentenced, execrated, banished, punished.
D	A	M	P	E	D	Moistened, misted, fogged, stifled, extinguished, checked.
D	A	M	P	E	N	Moisten, muffle, stifle, saturate, soak, wet.
D	A	M	P	E	R	Movable plate in stove or furnace. Heat Regulator. Moistener. More damp.
D	A	M	P	L	Y	Wetly, in a damp manner. Moistened. Limply, disinterestedly.
D	A	M	S	E	L	Young girl, maiden, lass.
D	A	M	S	O	N	Sweet Plum.
D	A	N	C	E	D	Past of DANCE.
D	A	N	C	E	R	One who dances. One who moves lightly to music. Ballerina. Performer. Hoofer.
D	A	N	D	L	E	Cuddle, fondle, pet, cosset, caress.
D	A	N	G	E	R	Threat, hazard, Risk, peril, jeopardy, menace, emergency, precariousness.
D	A	N	G	L	E	Swing, hang loosely, suspend, sway.
D	A	N	I	E	L	Wise judge.
D	A	N	I	S	H	From Denmark. A type of cheese.
D	A	N	I	T	E	Violent Mormon association.
D	A	P	H	N	E	Fragrant flower.
D	A	P	P	E	D	Past of DAP.
D	A	P	P	E	R	Spruce, smart, stylish. Alert, lively, brisk, jaunty.
D	A	P	P	L	E	Horse marking. Varicoloured, mottled, flecked, checkered sunlight.
D	A	R	I	N	G	Adventurous, audacious, foolhardy, venturesome, rash, reckless, daredevil.
D	A	R	K	E	N	Make dark, cloud, blacken, tarnish, cast gloom, shade darkly.
D	A	R	K	E	R	Comparative of DARK.
D	A	R	K	L	Y	In a dark manner, darkened, mysteriously, obscurely, loweringly, gloweringly.
D	A	R	N	E	D	Mended, repaired, sewed, patched, replenished. Damned, counfounded.
D	A	R	N	E	L	Genus of grass.
D	A	R	N	E	R	Mender, repairer, one who darns.
D	A	R	T	E	D	Furnished with a dart. Jumped, sped, sprang. Barbed, shafted. Bolted, Sprinted.
D	A	R	T	E	R	Freshwater fish, Perch. Bird.
D	A	S	H	E	D	Rushed, scampered, scooted. Throw violently. Scotched.
D	A	S	H	E	R	Type of Churn. Quick-witted, smart person.
D	A	S	H	E	S	Plural of DASH.
D	A	S	S	I	E	Rodent.
D	A	T	I	N	G	Ageing. Escorting, trysting.
D	A	T	I	O	N	Legal act of conferring.
D	A	T	I	V	E	Case of a language or dative form. Movable.
D	A	U	B	E	D	Dabbed, painted, plastered, smeared.
D	A	U	B	E	R	Painter, plasterer. Bungler.
D	A	U	C	U	S	Carrot.
D	A	W	D	L	E	Lag, dally, idle, loiter, stroll, trifle, procrastinate, fritter, trail.
D	A	W	N	E	D	Appeared, materialised. Began, commenced.
D	A	Y	B	E	D	Sofa.
D	O	C	K	E	D	Berthed, tied up. Cut short, Nicked. Taken off.

1	2	3	4	5	6	
D	A	Y	B	O	Y	Day scholar.
D	A	Z	I	N	G	Stunning, dazzling, overwhelming.
D	A	Z	Z	L	E	Outshine, daze, confuse, bewilder, blind, bedazzle.
D	E	A	C	O	N	Cleric, candidate for ordination, assistant minister.
D	E	A	D	E	N	Numb, anaesthetize, render senseless, rob of feeling.
D	E	A	D	L	Y	Fatal, lethal, mortal, destructive, pernicious, toxic, poisonous, virulent.
D	E	A	F	E	N	Deprive of hearing, impair hearing. Confuse, stun, render deaf.
D	E	A	F	L	Y	As though deaf. Uncaring, confused, stunned, unhearing.
D	E	A	L	E	R	Trader, agent, trafficker, vendor, Card issuer, monger, merchant.
D	E	A	R	E	R	Comparative of DEAR. More expensive.
D	E	A	R	I	E	Little dear, darling, term of endearment.
D	E	A	R	L	Y	Lovingly, caringly. Expensively, costly. Richly. Heartily, keenly.
D	E	A	R	T	H	Shortage, scarcity, absence, defect, lack, want, privation.
D	E	B	A	S	E	Demoralize, deprave, pervert, debauch, brutalize, injure, harm, humble, humiliate.
D	E	B	A	T	E	Discussion, argument, dispute, wrangle, deliberate, contest, contend.
D	E	B	O	N	E	Remove bones.
D	E	B	R	I	S	Litter, rubble, refuse, remnants, fragments, waste, ruins.
D	E	B	T	O	R	Buyer, borrower, customer, loanee, account operator. One who is indebted. Sinner.
D	E	B	U	N	K	Expose, reveal, unmask, criticise, show up, uncloak.
D	E	B	U	T	S	Plural of DEBUT. First appearances.
D	E	C	A	D	E	Group of Ten. Ten year period. Division of a Rosary.
D	E	C	A	M	P	Escape, abscond, take off, withdraw, flee, leave, quit.
D	E	C	A	N	T	Pour liquor from one container to another. Draw off. Transfer Liquid.
D	E	C	E	I	T	Dishonesty, wiles, stratagem, guile, duplicity, cunning, stealth.
D	E	C	E	N	T	Socially acceptable, proper, decorous, conforming, correct, respectable, chaste. Acceptable.
D	E	C	I	D	E	Determine, resolve, conclude, settle, establish, fix, adjudicate.
D	E	C	K	E	D	Adorned, decorated, embellished, garnished, clothed, togged out.
D	E	C	K	E	R	Constructed with decks. Number of levels.
D	E	C	K	L	E	Frame of paper-maker's mould. Paper edge limit.
D	E	C	O	C	T	Boil down. Steep in Hot Water.
D	E	C	O	D	E	Decrypt, transcribe, translate into ordinary language. Decipher, reveal.
D	E	C	O	Y	S	Plural of DECOY.
D	E	C	R	E	E	Law, Edict, Judicial Decision, Ruling, directive, pronouncement. Dictate, make law, deem.
D	E	D	U	C	E	Infer, conclude, judge, deem, presume.
D	E	D	U	C	T	Take away, withdraw, subtract, discount, diminish, lessen, reduce.
D	E	E	D	E	D	Transferred, ceded, made over, assigned, conveyed, signed away.
D	E	E	M	E	D	Considered, reckoned, regarded, conjectured, assumed, felt, believed.
D	E	E	P	E	N	Intensify, darken, magnify, heighten, redouble, increase depth.
D	E	E	P	E	R	Comparative of DEEP.
D	E	E	P	L	Y	In a deep manner. Intensely, profoundly, intently.
D	E	F	A	C	E	Disfigure, mar, damage, impair, deform, mutilate.
D	E	F	A	M	E	Malign, slander, denigrate, scandalize misrepresent, libel.
D	E	F	E	A	T	Conquer, overwhelm, frustrate, obstruct, overpower, beat. Check. Failure, Rout.
D	E	F	E	C	T	Desert, repudiate, renege, renounce. Blemish, flaw, infirmity, fault. Default.
D	E	F	I	E	D	Challenged, dared, braved, ignored, disregarded, scorned, spurned, ridiculed.
D	E	F	I	E	R	Challenger, ridiculer, mocker, rebel.
D	E	F	I	L	E	Violate, sully, pollute, ravish, dishonour, tarnish, contaminate.
D	E	F	I	N	E	Specify, determine, conclude, decide, distinguish, characterize, explain, analyse.
D	E	F	O	R	M	Disfigure, distort, warp, mar, twist, spoil, gnarl.
D	E	F	R	A	Y	Pay, liquidate, disburse, settle, meet.
D	E	F	T	L	Y	Cleverly, adroitly, skilfully, carefully, dexterously.
D	E	G	R	E	E	Relative size, classification, grade, proportion, ratio, scale, dimension, extent.
D	E	H	O	R	N	Prevent horn growth. Remove horn.
D	E	I	C	E	R	Anti-freeze.
D	E	I	F	I	C	Divine, godly, godlike.
D	E	J	E	C	T	Depress, dishearten, discourage, weaken, dispirit, humble.
D	E	L	A	Y	S	Plural of DELAY.
D	E	L	E	T	E	Erase, blot out, cancel, efface, annul, exclude, omit.
D	E	L	U	D	E	Deceive, mislead, beguile, take in, dupe, double cross, trick.
D	E	L	U	G	E	Downpour, flood, swamp, overwhelm, inundate, drench. Torrent, spate, cataclysm.
D	E	L	U	X	E	Elaborate, sumptuous, elegant, luxurious.
D	E	L	V	E	D	Dug, excavated, grubbed, burrowed, ferreted, investigated, probed.
D	E	L	V	E	R	Digger, excavator, investigator, grubber. Ferret.
D	E	M	A	N	D	Requisition, requirement, claim, exact, summon, compel. Command, enjoiner.
D	E	M	E	A	N	Degrade, debase, lower, humble, abase, denigrate, humiliate, behave.
D	E	M	E	N	T	Lunatic, maniac, nut, loony. Madden.

1	2	3	4	5	6	
D	E	M	I	S	E	Death, cessation, discontinuance. Transmit, convey. Die, decease.
D	E	M	O	D	E	Out of fashion, old-fashioned, outdated.
D	E	M	O	T	E	Downgrade, demerit, lower, reduce, demean, suspend, exclude.
D	E	M	U	R	E	Timid, modest, retiring, reserved, proper, decorous, bashful, coy, prim.
D	E	N	I	A	L	Refusal to satisfy, rejection, nonacceptance, contradiction, negation, renunciation.
D	E	N	I	E	D	Past of DENY.
D	E	N	I	E	R	Value, unit of fineness of yarn, nylon, silk, rayon.
D	E	N	N	E	T	2-Wheeled light carriage.
D	E	N	O	T	E	Betoken, signify, indicate, mean, express, signify, insinuate, prove.
D	E	N	S	E	R	Comparative of DENSE.
D	E	N	T	A	L	Relating to Teeth.
D	E	N	T	E	D	Past of DENT.
D	E	N	T	I	N	Tooth surface material.
D	E	N	U	D	E	Bare, strip, disrobe, unclothe, undress, deprive, divest, uncover.
D	E	O	D	A	R	East Indian Cedar.
D	E	P	A	R	T	Leave, quit, retire, withdraw, digress, ramble, stray, decease, die.
D	E	P	E	N	D	Rely, bank on, count on, Hang, suspend, dangle, hinge on.
D	E	P	I	C	T	Portray, show, represent, describe, picture, render, interpret.
D	E	P	L	O	Y	Place, arrange, unfold, set in place, make use of.
D	E	P	O	N	E	Testify, swear, mount, depose. Say under oath.
D	E	P	O	R	T	Send away, exile, banish, expel. Behave, acquit, conduct, comport.
D	E	P	O	S	E	Deprive of office, divest of authority, remove, dispossess, overthrow. Testify.
D	E	P	O	T	S	Plural of DEPOT.
D	E	P	T	H	S	Plural of DEPTH.
D	E	P	U	T	E	Appoint, delegate, authorise, deputize, commission.
D	E	P	U	T	Y	Agent, proxy, substitute, delegate, representative, surrogate.
D	E	R	A	I	L	Throw off course. Interrupt, divert, jump the track, upset.
D	E	R	A	T	E	Lower the rates. Justify, vindicate.
D	E	R	I	D	E	Ridicule, mock, taunt, rag, rib, kid, chaff, quiz, razz, scorn, lampoon.
D	E	R	I	V	E	Obtain, collect, conclude, infer, take, draw. Emanate, originate, stem, spring.
D	E	R	M	A	L	Relating to the skin. Epidermal, cutaneous.
D	E	R	M	I	S	Inner skin layer. Connective tissue.
D	E	R	N	E	D	(Sl.) Damned, darned, dashed.
D	E	S	C	R	Y	Spy out, Discover, attain realisation, detect.
D	E	S	E	R	T	Sandy waste. Abandon, forsake, quit. Defect, Renounce.
D	E	S	I	G	N	Plan, blueprint, scheme, diagram, outline, project, composition, pattern.
D	E	S	I	R	E	Wish, want, need, passion, hunger, longing. Covet, aspire, crave, long for.
D	E	S	I	S	T	Stop, forbear, cease, discontinue, quit, abandon, relinquish, abstain.
D	E	S	P	O	T	Dictator, autocrat, tyrant, oppressor.
D	E	T	A	C	H	Sever, disengage, dissociate, separate, take apart, disconnect, dismember.
D	E	T	A	I	L	Particularize, specify, stipulate. Article, item, point, element, Recount. List. Group.
D	E	T	A	I	N	Retain, confine, arrest, apprehend, delay, hold, inhibit, restrain.
D	E	T	E	C	T	Find out, espy, encounter, spot, discover, catch, reveal, unmask, turn up.
D	E	T	E	S	T	Abhor, hate, loathe, repudiate, abominate, spurn.
D	E	T	O	U	R	Deviation, skirt, circumvent, bypass, circumnavigation, indirect route.
D	E	T	U	N	E	Put out of tune.
D	E	U	C	E	D	Confounded, utter, devilish, infernal, unmitigated, outright.
D	E	V	A	S	T	Devastate.
D	E	V	E	I	N	Remove dark vein.
D	E	V	I	C	E	Gadget, artifice, Ruse, stratagem. Instrument, tool, utensil. Expedient.
D	E	V	I	L	S	Plural of DEVIL.
D	E	V	I	S	E	Plan, contrive, invent, plot, scheme, concoct, bequeath., legacy, bequest.
D	E	V	O	I	D	Lacking, without, innocent, void, wanting, bare, barren.., Sans.
D	E	V	O	I	R	Duty, need, commitment, obligation, job, assignment, task, stint.
D	E	V	O	T	E	Delegate, consecrate, apply, direct, bestow, entrust, confide, commit.
D	E	V	O	U	R	Consume, ingest, eat up, feast, polish off, ravage, desolate, pillage, demolish.
D	E	V	O	U	T	Holy, pious, religious, worshipping, prayerful, zealous, adoring.
D	E	W	L	A	P	Flaccid fold of flesh. Overhanging skin. Fold of fat. Fleshy part of neck.
D	E	X	T	E	R	On the right. A good omen. Auspicious, fortunate. Breed of cattle.
D	I	A	B	L	O	Devil, fiend, Satan, demon.
D	I	A	D	E	M	Coronet, tiara, crown.
D	I	A	P	E	R	Infant's basic garment. Napkin.
D	I	A	T	O	M	Plankton, Algae.
D	I	B	B	E	R	One who dibs or dibbles.
D	I	B	B	L	E	Hand implement for planting, Pointed tool. Plant with a dibble.
D	I	C	I	N	G	Casting a dice. Playing with. In competition with.
D	I	C	K	E	R	Haggle, bargain, barter. Argue.

1	2	3	4	5	6	
D	I	C	K	E	Y	Starched shirt front. Fabric insert. Rumble seat, back seat.
D	I	C	T	U	M	Maxim, moral, truism, axiom, rule, aphorism.
D	I	D	D	E	R	Quiver, tremble, shake.
D	I	D	D	L	E	Cheat, delude, hoax. Copulate, loaf, dawdle. Dandle.
D	I	E	S	E	L	German Inventor, vehicle driven by diesel fuel. Driven by diesel engine.
D	I	E	S	I	S	Double dagger sign
D	I	E	T	E	D	Past of DIET. Fasted.
D	I	E	T	E	R	One who DIETS.
D	I	F	F	E	R	Disagree, deviate, vary, dissent, conflict, dispute, oppose, protest.
D	I	G	A	M	Y	Legal second marriage. Remarriage of Divorcee, widow, or widower.
D	I	G	E	S	T	Tolerate, swallow, stomach, compress. Literacy condensationm, abridgement. Comprehend
D	I	G	G	E	R	Miner, trench maker, furrow slice.
D	I	G	I	T	S	Plural of DIGIT. Numbers.
D	I	G	R	A	M	Group of two.
D	I	K	A	G	E	Digging of Dykes.
D	I	K	D	I	K	African Antelope.
D	I	K	T	A	T	Unilaterial treaty imposed on vanquished.
D	I	L	A	T	E	Expand, amplify, distend, swell, increase, extend, protract, widen.
D	I	L	D	O	E	Device used as penis substitute.
D	I	L	U	T	E	Water down, weaken, moderate, adulterate, think, liquefy, lessen.
D	I	M	I	T	Y	Sheer cotton fabric.
D	I	M	M	E	D	Past of DIM.
D	I	M	M	E	R	Comparative of DIM.
D	I	M	O	U	T	Limiting of light, partial darkness.
D	I	M	P	L	E	Connical depression. Crater. Smile crease.
D	I	M	P	L	Y	Having dimples.
D	I	M	W	I	T	Fool, dilly, dummy, loon, dunce, nitwit, pinhead.
D	I	N	G	E	D	Past of DING. Thrown, cast, flung. Dented.
D	I	N	G	H	Y	Rubber boat, small boat, lifeboat.
D	I	N	G	L	E	Vale, glen, narrow passage, valley, wooded ravine.
D	I	N	G	U	S	Contraption, something, gadget (Sl.)
D	I	N	K	U	M	Flair and square, genuinely, honestly. Really.
D	I	N	N	E	D	Past of DIN.
D	I	N	N	E	R	Evening meal. Main meal of the day. Official function. Formal entertainment.
D	I	O	T	I	C	Relating to two ears.
D	I	P	L	E	X	Simultaneous communication transmission.
D	I	P	O	L	E	Electrical charges.
D	I	P	P	E	D	Past of DIP.
D	I	P	P	E	R	One who dips snuff. (Sl.) Pickpocket. Palette attachment, Water scoop. Ladle. Water bird.
D	I	R	E	C	T	Straight, frank, candid, primary, verbatim, literal, word for word.
D	I	R	E	L	Y	In DIRE fashion.
D	I	R	E	S	T	Superlative of DIRE.
D	I	R	K	E	D	Stabbed with a Dirk.
D	I	S	A	R	M	Unarm, immobilize, win over, attract, bewitch, captivate. Disable, incapacitate.
D	I	S	B	A	R	Deprive attorney of legal status. Exclude, eject.
D	I	S	B	U	D	Dehorn, deflower.
D	I	S	C	A	L	Relating to a DISC.
D	I	S	C	U	S	Field event. Athletic contest, disc throwing.
D	I	S	H	E	D	Centre depression. Concave. Given out, served.
D	I	S	M	A	L	Gloomy, bleak, dreary, oppressive, sombre, funereal, depressing. Pathetic.
D	I	S	M	A	Y	Alarm, consternation, fright, trepidation, unnerve, discompose, agitate, disturb.
D	I	S	O	W	N	Deny, reject, repudiate, deny, disavow, disacknowledge.
D	I	S	P	E	L	Disperse, dissipate, banish, dismiss, scatter, expel, oust, disintegrate.
D	I	S	T	A	L	Located away from. Remote.
D	I	S	T	I	L	Infuse, concentrate, purify, dissolve, vaporize, Trickle, condense liquor from droplets.
D	I	S	U	S	E	Cessation, obsolecence, discontinuance, dilapidation, decay.
D	I	T	H	E	R	Quake, shake, tremble, twitter, hesitate, falter, vacillate. Agitation, confusion, flap.
D	I	V	E	R	S	Several, sundry, various, some, many, different, diverse. Plural of diver.
D	I	V	E	R	T	Avert, deflect, turn, veer, swerve, change, dissuade, amuse, entertain.
D	I	V	E	S	T	Undress, denude, strip, disrobe, deprive, bereave, dispossess, disinherit.
D	I	V	I	D	E	Separate, disjoint, dissect, divorce, sunder, part, share, distribute, apportion.
D	I	V	I	N	E	Holy, Godly, Godlike, deific, Predict, foresee, anticipate. Clergyman, cleric.
D	I	V	I	N	G	Swooping, penetrating, plunging, delving, swanning into water.
D	O	A	B	L	E	Practicable, possible, viable, workable, feasible.
D	O	B	B	I	N	Farm horse, docile hack.
D	O	C	C	N	T	Teaching, instructive.
D	O	C	I	L	E	Tame, amenable, quiet, manageable, pliant, obedient, biddable.

1	2	3	4	5	6	
D	O	C	K	E	R	Dockworker. Stevedore.
D	O	C	K	E	T	Summary, statement, ticket, invoice, label, card, schedule, programme.
D	O	C	T	O	R	Physician, medico, healer. Falsify, treat, patch, repair. Adulterate.
D	O	D	D	E	R	Tremble, shake, quake, falter, vacilate.
D	O	D	D	L	E	Toddle. Go slow.
D	O	D	G	E	D	Evaded, avoided, sidestepped, ducked. Eluded.
D	O	D	G	E	M	Fairground bumper car.
D	O	D	G	E	R	Haggler, trickster.
D	O	G	B	O	X	Hen-pecked husband's punishment.
D	O	G	E	A	R	Tear, smudge, abuse a book. Damaged, worn.
D	O	G	G	E	D	Determined, obstinate, single-minded, monomanic. Followed closely, spied on.
D	O	I	N	G	S	Happenings, activities.
D	O	L	I	N	G	Distributing, giving out, sharing out, administering, apportioning, dispensing, dishing out.
D	O	L	L	A	R	Unit of money.
D	O	L	L	E	D	Primped, dressed to kill, overdressed.
D	O	L	L	O	P	Share, portion, blob, splash.
D	O	L	M	A	N	Type of sleeve. Distinctive jacket.
D	O	L	M	E	N	Monument.
D	O	L	O	S	E	Deceitful, characterised by sharp practise.
D	O	L	O	U	R	Distress, misery, suffering, passion, pain, anguish, sorrow.
D	O	M	A	I	N	Dominion, desmesne, possession, distinct region, field, province, territory.
D	O	M	I	N	O	Canon's hood. Hooded cape. Half mask. Rectangular block. Game.
D	O	N	A	T	E	Give, bestow, present, give away, devote, supply.
D	O	N	K	E	Y	Ass, jenny, jackass, neddy, fool, idiot, imbecile, jerk.
D	O	O	D	A	D	Dingus, triviality, gadget, thingamajig.
D	O	O	D	L	E	Scribble, draw absentmindedly. Cheat, chisel. Fiddle, potter, tinker.
D	O	O	M	E	D	Past of DOOM.
D	O	P	I	N	G	Drugging, tripping out, doctoring, adulterating.
D	O	R	M	I	E	Golf score. Club.
D	O	R	S	A	L	Thoracic, aboral, back. On the back.
D	O	S	A	G	E	Amount of medicine, administration of treatment. Strength factor.
D	O	S	I	N	G	Administering medicine.
D	O	T	A	G	E	Feebleness, senility, advanced age, infirmity, decrepitude.
D	O	T	A	R	D	Imbecile.
D	O	T	I	N	G	Loving, affectionate, devoted, fatuous, dear, idolizing, adoring.
D	O	T	T	E	D	Spotted, speckled, stippled, covered with dots.
D	O	T	T	L	E	Pipe tobacco, scrapings from bowl of the pipe.
D	O	U	A	N	E	Customs House.
D	O	U	B	L	E	Twofold, duplicity, dual, duplicate, repeat, twin. Understudy. Pair, augment.
D	O	U	B	T	S	Plural of DOUBT. Misgivings.
D	O	U	C	H	E	Direct jet of water into body cavity. Device for administering a douche.
D	O	U	G	H	Y	Like dough, pliable, soft and colourless, pale, waxen.
D	O	U	R	L	Y	Sternly, sourly, forbiddingly, harshly, sullenly, glumly, morosely.
D	O	U	S	E	D	Soaked, ducked, sunked, deluged, drenched, soused, splattered.
D	O	W	N	E	D	Floored, laid low, levelled, dispatched, killed, overcame, conquered.
D	O	W	S	E	R	Divining rod.
D	O	Y	E	N	S	Plural of DOYEN.
D	O	Y	L	E	Y	Lace mat, doily.
D	O	Z	I	N	G	Slumbering, drowsing, snoozing, napping.
D	R	A	C	H	M	Drachma, dram.
D	R	A	F	T	S	Plural of DRAFT.
D	R	A	F	T	Y	Resembling a DRAFT. Gusty.
D	R	A	G	E	E	Sugar-coated nut, chocolate covered pill. Berry, fruit.
D	R	A	G	O	N	Monster, Scaly Serpent. Mythical Creature.
D	R	A	M	A	S	Plural of DRAMA.
D	R	A	P	E	D	Clothed, robed, wound around, swathed, enveloped, wrapped, sprawled.
D	R	A	P	E	R	Dealer, Shopkeeper, soft goods vendor, haberdasher.
D	R	A	P	E	S	Hangings, curtains.
D	R	A	W	E	E	Person on whom a bill or cheque is drawn. Recipient.
D	R	A	W	E	R	One who draws, draughtsman; Sliding receptacle in a cabinet. Undergarment.
D	R	E	A	M	T	Past of DREAM.
D	R	E	A	M	Y	Visionary, fanciful, whimsical, idealistic, otherworldly, impractical.
D	R	E	A	R	Y	Miserable, sad, dull, gloomy, dismal, dispirited, monotonous, bleak.
D	R	E	D	G	E	Sprinkle, coat, dust. Scrape river bottom, search memory, dig deeply.
D	R	E	G	G	Y	Having dregs. Muddy, cloudy, foul.
D	R	E	I	C	H	Protracted, tiresome, tedious, dreary, long. Prolonged, lengthy.
D	R	E	N	C	H	Soak, douse, deluge, wet, impregnate, saturate, steep. Drink, drain.

1	2	3	4	5	6	
D	R	E	S	S	Y	Smart, slick, spruce, spiffy, decked out, dolled up.
D	R	I	E	S	T	Superlative of DRY.
D	R	I	F	T	Y	Forming drifts, having snowdrifts.
D	R	I	V	E	L	Nonsense, balderdash, bosh, gibberish. Drool, salivate. Fritter, trifle.
D	R	I	V	E	N	Past of DRIVE. Herded, chased.
D	R	I	V	E	R	One who drives, vehicle operator, overseer, Mallet. Golf club.
D	R	O	G	U	E	Harpoon line, sea anchor, aerodynamic drag service, in-flight fueling funnel.
D	R	O	L	L	Y	In droll manner, humourously, comically, wittily.
D	R	O	M	I	C	Like a Race course. In the shape of a Race Course.
D	R	O	N	E	D	Past of DRONE.
D	R	O	O	P	Y	Sagging, lack daisical, dangling, depressed, flagging, downcast, dispirited.
D	R	O	P	S	Y	Collection of fluid in tissues. Swelling, oedema.
D	R	O	S	S	Y	Worthless, no-good, unworthy.
D	R	O	V	E	R	Driver, cattle or sheep minder.
D	R	O	V	E	S	Crowds, hordes, multitudes, throngs, flocks, herds, packs.
D	R	O	W	S	E	Doze, slumber, snooze, sleep, nod, nap.
D	R	O	W	S	Y	Sleepy, snoozy, sporofic, dreamy, nodding, lethargic.
D	R	U	D	G	E	Menial, servant, slave, scullion, peon, workhorse, donkeywork, toil.
D	R	U	I	D	S	Prophets, bards, members of a Secret Order.
D	R	U	N	K	S	Plural of DRUNK.
D	R	Y	F	L	Y	Method of fresh-water fishing. Trout fishing fly. Artificial floating fly.
D	R	Y	I	N	G	Desiccating, parching, dehydrating, draining, depleting; Bleaching. Preserving.
D	R	Y	I	S	H	In a dry manner. Like Dry.
D	R	Y	R	O	T	Decayed timber, mummified, fungal disease.
D	U	B	B	E	D	Named, called, christened, styled; substitute dialogue, translated, re-recorded.
D	U	B	B	E	R	Sound-track re-recorder.
D	U	B	B	I	N	A preparation of grease for softening leather.
D	U	C	K	E	D	Past of DUCK. Dodged.
D	U	C	K	E	R	Slaughterhouse worker.
D	U	C	T	U	S	Handwriting, caligraphy, penmanship, script, hand.
D	U	D	E	E	N	Short tobacco pipe.
D	U	D	I	N	E	Female Dude.
D	U	D	I	S	H	Like a Dude.
D	U	D	I	S	M	State of being a Dude.
D	U	E	N	N	A	Chaperone, companion, governess.
D	U	F	F	E	D	Faked, cheated.
D	U	F	F	E	L	Heavy woollen fabric.
D	U	F	F	E	R	Hawker, Pedlar, Elderly (ineffectual person), incompetent.
D	U	G	O	N	G	Sea-cow.
D	U	G	O	U	T	Canoe, hollowed out log for sailing. Primitive boat. Shelter, excavation.
D	U	I	K	E	R	Small short-horned antelope.
D	U	L	C	E	T	Melodious, sweet-sounding, pleasant, agreeable, soothing.
D	U	L	L	E	D	Blunted, deadened, desensitized, numbed, impaired, darkened, dimmed, retarded.
D	U	L	L	E	R	Comparative of DULL.
D	U	M	B	L	Y	Mutely, silently, stupidly, incoherently, densely, vaguely, in dumb manner.
D	U	M	D	U	M	Soft-nosed bullet.
D	U	M	P	E	D	Unloaded, heaped, deposited, discarded, scrapped.
D	U	N	C	E	S	Plural of DUNCE.
D	U	N	L	I	N	Sandpiper. A bird of the shoreline.
D	U	N	L	O	P	Rich white Scottish Cheese.
D	U	N	N	E	D	Past of DUN.
D	U	N	N	E	R	Debt Collector.
D	U	P	E	R	Y	Deception, chicanery, dishonesty, double-dealing, fraud, sharp practice.
D	U	P	I	N	G	Fooling, deluding, hoodwinking, spoofing, tricking, deceiving.
D	U	P	L	E	X	Twofold, double, dual. Up-and-downstairs.
D	U	R	A	I	N	Type of coal debris.
D	U	R	B	A	R	Indian festival, reception.
D	U	R	E	S	S	Stress, strain, force, coercion, constraint, compulsion, distress.
D	U	R	H	A	M	Breed of Cattle, Shorthorn.
D	U	R	I	N	G	In the course of. While, throughout, pending, amid, midst, over.
D	U	R	I	T	Y	Hardness, durability.
D	U	S	T	E	R	Dust remover, brush, housecoat, sprinkler, one who removes dust.
D	U	S	T	U	P	Quarrel, altercation, fall-out, dispute, fracas, hassle.
D	U	T	I	E	D	Taxed, levied.
D	U	T	I	E	S	Plural of DUTY.
D	W	E	L	L	S	Lives, inhabits, resides.
D	Y	A	D	I	C	Of two parts, double elements.

1	2	3	4	5	6	
D	Y	E	I	N	G	Changing colour, altering pigment, staining.
D	Y	N	A	M	O	Generator.
D	Y	N	A	S	T	Ruler, founder, one in a line of Kings.
D	Y	V	O	U	R	Bankrupt.

E

E	A	G	L	E	S	Plural of EAGLE.
E	A	G	L	E	T	Young Eagle.
E	A	R	A	G	E	Length of Ears.
E	A	R	B	O	B	Earring.
E	A	R	C	A	P	Ear muff.
E	A	R	F	U	L	Reprimand, diatribe, outpouring.
E	A	R	N	E	D	Past of EARN.
E	A	R	N	E	R	Money maker, recipient of reward. Wage earner.
E	A	R	T	H	Y	Resembling earth. Terrestrial, worldly, material, mundane, sensual, realistic.
E	A	R	W	A	X	Cerumen.
E	A	R	W	I	G	Many-jointed insect. Toady, eavesdropper, flatterer.
E	A	S	I	E	R	Comparative of EASY.
E	A	S	I	L	Y	Effortlessly, readily, freely, well, dexterously, definitely, clearly, truly.
E	A	S	I	N	G	Sliding, effortless movements, gliding. Soothing, comforting, unburdening.
E	A	S	T	E	R	Pagan festival. Annual commemoration of Resurrection.
E	A	T	A	G	E	Eatable growth of Grass. Fodder.
E	A	T	E	R	Y	Tea Room, Restaurant, Lunchroom.
E	A	T	I	N	G	Devouring, gnawing, consuming, corrosive, eroding, fretting.
E	B	B	I	N	G	Declining, sinking, disappearing, deteriorating, waning, failing, abating.
E	C	A	R	T	E	Two-handed card game.
E	C	H	A	R	D	Water content of soil. Unavailable soil water.
E	C	H	O	E	D	Past of ECHO.
E	C	H	O	E	S	Plural of ECHO.
E	C	L	A	I	R	Choux Pastry Cream Puff.
E	C	Z	E	M	A	Acute skin eruption. Pimples. Oozing skin lesions.
E	D	D	I	E	D	Past of EDDY.
E	D	I	B	L	E	Suitable as food. Digestible, nutritious, palatable, comestible, eatable, food.
E	D	I	C	T	S	Plural of EDICT.
E	D	I	T	E	D	Past of EDIT.
E	D	I	T	O	R	One who corrects. Reviser, Arranger, Publications Supervisor.
E	D	U	C	E	D	Past of EDUCE.
E	E	R	I	L	Y	Scarily, uncannily, grotesquely, weirdly.
E	F	F	A	C	E	Obliterate, erase, annul, wipe out, expunge, delete, eradicate, eliminate, exclude.
E	F	F	E	C	T	Put into practice, generate, induce, cause. Condition, result, sequel, end product.
E	F	F	E	T	E	Unfruitful, enervated, spent, worn out, degenerate, decadent, outmoded. Weak.
E	F	F	I	G	Y	Image, figure, likeness, portrait, dummy, representation, sculptured likeness.
E	F	F	L	U	X	Emanation, flow, lapse of time, effusion.
E	F	F	O	R	T	Endeavour, exertion, work, trouble, pains, striving.
E	F	F	U	S	E	Emanate, pour forth, spill, issue out, gush.
E	G	G	C	U	P	Cup made to hold an egg in the shell. Egg holder.
E	G	G	E	R	S	Egg collectors. Wild bird egg enthusiasts.
E	G	G	I	N	G	Encouraging, urging, persuading, cheering on, inciting, exhorting. Collecting eggs.
E	G	G	N	O	G	Alcoholic concoction using Eggs.
E	G	O	I	S	M	Self-importance, conceit, self-pride, swollen-headedness, vainglory.
E	G	O	I	S	T	Egotist, Egocentric, egomaniac, self-centered person. One who is self-interested.
E	G	R	E	S	S	Emergence, outlet, departure, exit, withdrawal.
E	G	R	E	T	S	Plural of EGRET.
E	I	D	E	R	S	Plural of EIDER.
E	I	G	H	T	H	One of eight equal parts. Octave.
E	I	G	H	T	S	Plural of EIGHT.
E	I	G	H	T	Y	Ten times Eight.
E	I	T	H	E	R	One of two. One or other. More than one alternative.
E	K	E	I	N	G	Stretching, increasing, lenghtening, squeezing, augmenting. Making something last.
E	L	A	N	D	S	Common African Antelopes.
E	L	A	P	S	E	Time lapse, interval, pass, expire, run on, slip by, intervene, pass.
E	L	A	T	E	D	Joyous, intoxicated, excited, exhilarated, jubilant, overjoyed, ecstatic.
E	L	A	T	E	R	Click beetle, spore capsule, filamentous appendage.
E	L	B	O	W	S	Plural of ELBOW.
E	L	D	E	R	S	Plural of ELDER. Parents, superiors.

1	2	3	4	5	6	Definition
E	L	D	E	S	T	Oldest, mature, senior. Earliest.
E	L	E	V	E	N	One more than TEN. Tea-time. Cricket team. One less than a dozen.
E	L	F	I	S	H	Like an elf, playful, tiny, petite, impish, mischievous, fay, elfin.
E	L	I	C	I	T	Evoke, educe, extract, provoke, cause.
E	L	I	D	E	D	Reduced, abridged, shortened.
E	L	I	X	I	R	Panacea, balm, therapy, cure-all, water of life. Quintessence, Alcoholic concoction.
E	L	O	P	E	D	Ran away together, fled, escaped, married secretly.
E	L	O	P	E	R	One who elopes.
E	L	U	D	E	D	Evaded, avoided, ducked, frustrated, outwitted, thwarted, escaped, eschewed.
E	L	V	I	S	H	Elfish, mischievous, puckish, spiteful, irritating.
E	M	B	A	L	M	Preserve from decay, prepare for burial, perfume, fix, protect, mummify.
E	M	B	A	N	K	Confine within embankments.
E	M	B	A	R	K	Board, begin, commence, enter, start, set out, take off.
E	M	B	E	R	S	Plural of EMBER.
E	M	B	L	E	M	Badge, symbol, insignia, crest, monogram, token.
E	M	B	O	D	Y	Incorporate, include, manifest, realize, typify, exhibit, embrace, personify.
E	M	B	O	S	S	Raise in relief, ornament, adorn, mark, stamp an impression, imprint.
E	M	B	R	Y	O	Nucleus, early stages of growth, foetus, rudiment, seed, germ.
E	M	E	R	G	E	Come forth, appear, loom, stem, materialize, emanate,issue, proceed.
E	M	E	T	I	C	Inducement to vomit.
E	M	I	G	R	E	Emigrant, political refugee, expatriate, exile, evacuee.
E	M	O	T	E	R	One who emotes. Actor, actress.
E	M	P	I	R	E	Dominion, territory, realm, land, province.
E	M	P	L	O	Y	Use, involve, engage, occupy, activate, provide work for. Exploit.
E	N	A	B	L	E	Allow, permit, sanction, authorize, commission, empower, license, let.
E	N	A	M	E	L	Durable surface coating. Hard Calcareous substance. Facing material.
E	N	C	A	G	E	Coop up, imprison, pen, cage.
E	N	C	A	M	P	Erect a camp, bivouac, settle, laager, form temporary camp.
E	N	C	A	S	E	Pack, confine, contain, enclose, envelop.
E	N	C	A	S	H	Cash in. Cash up.
E	N	C	A	V	E	Hide in a cave.
E	N	C	O	D	E	Convert a message into cipher.
E	N	C	O	R	E	Applause, Call for repetition. Request for a second appearance.
E	N	D	A	L	L	Ultimate conclusion. Goal.
E	N	D	E	A	R	Captivate, impress, embroil, cause admiration, create esteem.
E	N	D	I	N	G	Finale, cessation, closing, conclusion, finish, termination.
E	N	D	I	V	E	Salad Plant, Chicory.
E	N	D	U	R	E	Tolerate, countenance. Last, retain standing, remain in existence, suffer.
E	N	E	M	A	S	Plural of ENEMA.
E	N	E	R	G	Y	Force, power, strength, potency, might, vitality, vigour, effort, physical effect.
E	N	F	O	L	D	Embrace, enclose, envelop, wrap, shroud, swathe, clasp, surround, encircle.
E	N	G	A	G	E	Employ, participate. Promise, pledge. Intermesh, interlock. Encounter, endear, allure.
E	N	G	I	N	E	Mechanical contrivance, machinery, apparatus, locomotive, driving force.
E	N	G	U	L	F	Overwhelm, submerge, inundate, swamp, surround.
E	N	I	G	M	A	Inexplicable circumstance, mystery, unsolved problem, person of many parts.
E	N	J	O	I	N	Command, request, charge, direct, instruct, dictate, prescribe, admonish.
E	N	L	A	C	E	Encircle, enfold, entangle, entwine, interlace.
E	N	L	I	S	T	Join up, engage, enrol, enter, sign on. Attract.
E	N	M	E	S	H	Entrap, entangle, ensnarl, trammel, tangle, implicate.
E	N	M	I	T	Y	Aversion, hatred, animosity, dislike, antagonism, antipathy, hostility, bitterness.
E	N	O	U	G	H	Sufficient, satisfactory, adequate, ample, commensurate, abundance, sufficiency.
E	N	R	A	G	E	Anger, upset, antagonise, infuriate, madden, incense, offend, exacerbate.
E	N	R	A	I	L	Truck, entrain.
E	N	R	A	N	K	Place in order of rank.
E	N	R	A	P	T	Enraptured, absorbed, ecstatic, captivated.
E	N	R	I	C	H	Adorn, expand, fertilize, beautify, add to, ornament.
E	N	R	O	B	E	Invest with a robe, adorn, attire, coat, array.
E	N	R	O	L	L	Enlist, register, enter, join, sign up.
E	N	S	I	G	N	Flag, badge of office, emblem, symbol, Naval officer, junior infantry officer.
E	N	S	U	E	D	Followed, resulted, succeeded, proceeded, resulted, issued, emanated, derived.
E	N	S	U	R	E	Assure, guarantee, certify, establish, make certain, warrant.
E	N	T	A	I	L	Involve, confer, assign, legacy, inheritance, logical consequence.
E	N	T	I	C	E	Lure, inveigle, seduce, tempt, decoy, cajole, bait, beguile, invite.
E	N	T	I	R	E	Whole, complete, perfect, integral, intact, unimpaired, outright, total.
E	N	T	I	T	Y	Independent, being, individual, thing, object, system, whole.
E	N	T	O	M	B	Inter, bury, incarcerate, inhume, enshrine, deposit, ensepulchre.
E	N	T	R	A	P	Ensnare, catch, entangle, snare, lure, inveigle, entice.

1	2	3	4	5	6	
E	N	T	R	É	E	Access, admission, admittance, entrance, way in. First Dish, Starters.
E	N	V	I	E	D	Past of ENVY.
E	N	W	R	A	P	Encircle, envelope, engross, drape, swathe, enfold, sheathe, shroud.
E	N	Z	Y	M	E	Large class of proteinaceous substances. Pepsin. Life essential.
E	O	C	E	N	E	Subdivision of the Tertiary. Age, Epoch. Rock strata.
E	O	L	I	T	H	Earliest period of the stone age.
E	O	Z	O	I	C	Pre-Cambrian Era.
E	P	O	N	Y	M	A person whose name is used as the source of another name.
E	Q	U	A	L	S	Plural of EQUAL. 1 + 1 = 2.
E	Q	U	A	T	E	Equalize, represent, treat as equal, similize, associate, liken, match.
E	Q	U	I	N	E	Resembling a Horse. Belonging to the Equidae. Of the Horse.
E	Q	U	I	T	Y	Impartiality, standard conformity, without prejudice, Money value in excess of claims.
E	R	A	S	E	D	Past of ERASE. Rubbed out.
E	R	A	S	E	R	Rubber, mark remover, eradicator, obligerator, exponger.
E	R	E	M	I	C	Relating to sandy or desert places.
E	R	E	N	O	W	Before this time.
E	R	M	I	N	E	Black-tipped stoat tails. Winter pelage. Ceremonial robe. Trimming. Fur.
E	R	O	D	E	D	Corroded, rusted, eaten away, worn away, chafed, grazed, rubbed.
E	R	O	T	I	C	Sexually arousing. Amatory, Amorous, Aphrodisiac. Impassioned, lecherous, sexy.
E	R	R	A	N	D	Message, charge, mission, trip, service, favour.
E	R	R	A	N	T	Mission of chivalry, quixotically adventurous, roving, straying; Fallible.
E	R	R	A	T	A	Mistakes, errors, omissions.
E	R	R	I	N	G	Straying, adulterous, deviating.
E	R	R	O	R	S	Plural of ERROR. Mistakes.
E	R	S	A	T	Z	Synthetic, substitute, counterfeit.
E	S	C	A	P	E	Flee, abscond, decamp. Elude, evade, avoid. Flight, eschewal, getaway, breakout.
E	S	C	H	E	W	Escape, flee, avoid, bilk, duck, evade, forbear, sacrifice, shirk.
E	S	C	O	R	T	Accompany, date, conduct, convey, chaperone. Attendant, companion, boyfriend.
E	S	C	U	D	O	Monetary unit.
E	S	K	I	M	O	Native of cold northern climes.
E	S	P	I	A	L	Detection, discovery, notice.
E	S	P	I	E	D	Past of ESPY. Seen saw.
E	S	P	I	E	R	One that espies.
E	S	P	R	I	T	Sprightly wit. Vivacity, comprehension, inherent vigor.
E	S	S	E	N	E	Company of monastic Palestian Jews.
E	S	T	A	T	E	Condition, situation in life. Social or political class. Property, possessions, fortune.
E	S	T	E	E	M	Regard, admiration, respect. Appreciate, cherish, prize, admire, value.
E	T	C	H	E	D	Past of ETCH.
E	T	C	H	E	R	Engraver, hand-etching artist.
E	T	H	I	C	S	Morals, morality, principles, criteria, standards, ideals, beliefs.
E	T	H	N	I	C	Relating to a community, cultural characteristics, Racial and linguistic ties.
E	T	O	I	L	E	Principal ballet dancer.
E	U	C	H	R	E	Card game. Trick, outwit, deceive.
E	U	C	L	I	D	Euclidean geometry.
E	U	C	O	N	E	Compound eyes of insects.
E	U	L	O	G	Y	Composition of praise, oration of commendation, encomium, citation, tribute.
E	U	N	O	M	Y	Civil order.
E	U	N	U	C	H	One who is impotent. Lacking manhood. Castrated man. Chamberlain.
E	U	O	N	Y	M	Aptly named.
E	U	R	E	K	A	Triumph of discovery!
E	U	R	O	P	E	Continent.
E	U	T	A	X	Y	Good management.
E	V	A	D	E	D	Past of EVADE.
E	V	A	D	E	R	One who evades. Tax dodger.
E	V	E	N	E	R	Leveller, stabiliser, balancer, equalizer.
E	V	E	N	L	Y	Uniformly, smoothly, fairly, proportionately, equally,squarely, impartially.
E	V	E	N	T	S	Plural of EVENT.
E	V	I	L	L	Y	Wickedly, maliciously, badly, harmfully, offensively, viciously, foully.
E	V	I	N	C	E	Demonstrate, exhibit, show, proclaim, indicate.
E	V	O	K	E	D	Past of EVOKE.
E	V	O	L	V	E	Develop, unfold, educe, elaborate, derive, advance, obtain, excogitate.
E	V	U	L	S	E	Remove forcibly, extract, root out, pluck out.
E	X	A	M	E	N	Study critically, investigation, inquiry.
E	X	A	R	C	H	Head of independent church. Patriarch's deputy.
E	X	C	E	E	D	Overstep, surpass, overreach, presume, surpass, excel, outstrip, transcend.
E	X	C	E	P	T	Apart from, barring, besides, except for, excluding, exclude, object, eliminate.
E	X	C	E	S	S	Glut, surplus, surfeit, plethora, superfluous, oversupply, glut.

1	2	3	4	5	6	
E	X	C	I	S	E	Remove, cut out, extirpate, amputate, eradicate, delete, expurgate, exscind.
E	X	C	I	T	E	Stimulate, provoke, impassion, elate, exhilarate, inspire, fascinate, quicken.
E	X	C	U	S	E	Alibi, pretext, explanation, justification, apologize, condone, pardon, forgive.
E	X	E	D	R	A	Portico furnished with Seats. Large semi-circular Bench.
E	X	E	M	P	T	Free from liability, absolve, dispense, relieve, excuse, spare.
E	X	E	Q	U	Y	Funeral procession.
E	X	E	U	N	T	Stage direction. Exit all characters.
E	X	H	A	L	E	Breathe out, expire, emit, blow.
E	X	H	O	R	T	Urge, prod, prompt, spur, request earnestly, advise, warn.
E	X	H	U	M	E	Unearth, resurrect, disinter, dig up, disentomb, exhume.
E	X	I	L	E	D	Past of EXILE.
E	X	I	L	I	C	Refers to banishment per Old Testament.
E	X	O	D	U	S	Emigration, departure, egression, exit, withdrawl, flight, migration.
E	X	O	T	I	C	Foreign, imported, alien, strange, extrinsic. Romantic, unusual, alluring.
E	X	P	A	N	D	Extend, dilate, swell, spread, grow, increase, escalate, augment, heighten.
E	X	P	E	C	T	Anticipate, await, hope, foresee, assume, imagine, suppose, look forward.
E	X	P	E	N	D	Disburse, spend, distribute, pay out, use up, exhaust, dispense.
E	X	P	E	R	T	Authority, master, past master, virtuoso, skilled, proficient, masterly.
E	X	P	I	R	E	Die, decease, demise, pass away. Elapse.
E	X	P	I	R	Y	Expiration, termination, end, death, exhalation.
E	X	P	O	R	T	Trade with a foreign country. Transmit, transport, convey a commodity abroad.
E	X	P	O	S	E	Reveal, uncover, open, display, flaunt.Debunk, uncloak, disclose.
E	X	S	E	C	T	Excise, extirpate, cut out.
E	X	T	A	N	T	Existing, living, alive, existent, in existence, actual, present, contemporary.
E	X	T	E	N	D	Offer, proffer, present, allot, increase, augment, stretch. Range, reach.
E	X	T	E	N	T	Scope, range, amount, ambit, radius, field, size, dimension, proportion, magnitude.
E	X	T	O	R	T	Demand, force, exact, extract, elicit, wrest, coerce, demand, fleece.
E	X	T	R	A	S	Plural of EXTRA. Additions.
E	X	U	D	E	D	Past of EXUDE. Emitted.
E	X	V	O	T	O	According to one's prayer, by reasons of a vow; votice; a votive offering.
E	Y	E	C	U	P	Eye bath.
E	Y	E	F	U	L	Good look, satisfying view; a Beauty, good looker, stunner.
E	Y	E	I	N	G	Watching, gazing at, making eyes, flirting.
E	Y	E	L	E	T	Small reinforced ring. Loop.
E	Y	E	L	I	D	Lid of skin covering the eye. Nictating skin.
E	Y	E	P	I	T	Eyehole.

F

1	2	3	4	5	6	
F	A	B	I	A	N	Socialistic Society, policy of slow political change.
F	A	B	L	E	D	Fabulous accounts, fictional, pretended, speculated, fabricated, mythical.
F	A	B	L	E	S	Plural of FABLE.
F	A	B	R	I	C	Cloth, material, textile. Something built. Framework, construction, device, contrivance.
F	A	C	A	D	E	Pretense, veneer, face, front, guise, put-on, show. Countenance, challenge, defy.
F	A	C	E	T	S	Plural of FACET.
F	A	C	E	U	P	Facing upwards. Lying on one's back.
F	A	C	I	A	L	Relating to an outer surface, of the face, superficial. Massage of the face.
F	A	C	I	L	E	Effortless, easy, simple, smooth, dexterous, fluent, voluble, superficial, glib.
F	A	C	I	N	G	Opposing, confronting, fronting, bordering, accosting, engaging, challenging. Looking at.
F	A	C	T	O	R	Element, constituent, ingredient. Cause, agent, attorney, proxy.
F	A	C	T	U	M	Memorial, event, fact. Execution of a Will. Under seal.
F	A	C	U	L	A	Region of Sunspots.
F	A	D	D	L	E	Foolishness, nonsense.
F	A	D	I	N	G	Dwindling, declining, failing, dimming, tarnishing, disappearing, flagging.
F	A	E	C	E	S	Excrement, excreta, stool, defecation.
F	A	E	R	I	E	Fairy, mythical being, sprite, pixie.
F	A	G	E	N	D	Cigarette butt.
F	A	G	G	E	D	Tired, exhausted, pooped, worn out.
F	A	G	G	O	T	Homosexual, fag, invert, queer, pansy, nancy, fruit. Twig, stick. Meat dish.
F	A	I	L	E	D	Past of FAIL. Unsuccessful.
F	A	I	L	L	E	Woven fabric, drapery.
F	A	I	R	E	R	Comparative of FAIR.
F	A	I	R	L	Y	Moderately, modestly, averagely, passably, so-so, rather, sort of.
F	A	I	T	H	S	Plural of FAITH. Religions.
F	A	K	I	N	G	Feigning, pretending, simulating, counterfeiting, bluffing, hoaxing, shamming.
F	A	L	C	O	N	Hawk, Peregrine.

1	2	3	4	5	6	
F	A	L	L	A	L	Decoration, ornament, finery.
F	A	L	L	E	N	Past of FALL.
F	A	L	L	O	W	Uncultivated, unused potential value, recuperative idleness. Dormant, idle.
F	A	L	S	E	R	Comparative of FALSE.
F	A	L	T	E	R	Teeter, stagger, stumble, hesitate, recoil, tremble, waver, vacillate.
F	A	M	I	L	Y	Ancestral relations. Kindred, clan, race, brood, offspring. Home, household.
F	A	M	I	N	E	Scarcity of food, extreme hunger, starvation.
F	A	M	I	S	H	Hunger, starving, lack of nourishment.
F	A	M	O	U	S	Prominent, notable, well-known, distinguished, eminent, celebrated, excellent.
F	A	N	G	E	D	Toothed. Pronged. Resembling fangs.
F	A	N	G	L	E	Foppish, contrivance, gewgaw, device.
F	A	N	N	E	D	Past of FAN.
F	A	N	N	E	R	Blower, ventilator, winnower.
F	A	N	T	A	N	Chinese gambling game. Card game.
F	A	R	C	E	R	Farceur, conjurer, joker, wag.
F	A	R	I	N	A	Starch, pollen, cereal grains.
F	A	R	I	N	G	Progressing, proceeding, getting on, advancing.
F	A	R	M	E	D	Past of FARM.
F	A	R	M	E	R	One who FARMS. Cultivator, animal husband, tiller, agronomist.
F	A	R	R	O	W	Bring forth young. Litter, give birth. Litter of piglets.
F	A	S	C	I	A	Flat band, moulding, shopfront, sheet of connecting tissue.
F	A	S	H	E	D	Troubled, disgusted, inconvenienced.
F	A	S	T	E	D	Abstained from nourishment.
F	A	S	T	E	N	Fix, attach, connect, adhere, secure, join, focus, concentrate, hitch, hook. Ratify.
F	A	S	T	E	R	Comparative of FAST.
F	A	T	C	A	T	Wealthy person, political campaigner. Big Shot.
F	A	T	H	E	N	Genus of plump plant. Mugwort, buckwheat, ground ivy.
F	A	T	H	E	R	Male parent. Sire, creator, originator. Beget, procreate, generate, spawn.
F	A	T	H	O	M	Plumb, sound, know, apprehend, comprehend, penetrate. Sea depth. 6 feet = 1 fathom.
F	A	T	T	E	D	Fattened, well-fed, prepared for eating.
F	A	T	T	E	N	Make plump, enlarge, substantialise.
F	A	T	T	E	R	Comparative of FAT.
F	A	U	C	A	L	Pharyngeal, throaty.
F	A	U	C	E	S	Mouthpart.
F	A	U	C	E	T	Tap, cock, vent hole, hydrant, spigot, valve. Stopcock.
F	A	U	L	T	Y	Wrong, incorrect, mistaken, inaccurate, defective, imperfect, deficient, damaged.
F	A	U	N	A	L	Relating to FAUNA.
F	A	V	O	U	R	Benevolence, largesse, gift. Approve, accept, oblige, encourage. Resemble.
F	A	W	N	E	D	Grovelled, sucked up, kowtowed, toadied, wheedled, coaxed, deferred.
F	A	W	N	E	R	Groveller, toady, wheedler, boot licker, panderer.
F	E	A	L	T	Y	Fidelity, allegiance, devotion, ardour, support, trustworthiness, reliability.
F	E	A	R	E	D	Past of FEAR.
F	E	A	S	T	S	Plural of FEAST.
F	E	C	U	L	A	Dung pellet.
F	E	C	U	N	D	Productive, fertile, spawning, proliferant, proflific, breeding, reproducing.
F	E	D	O	R	A	Soft, low-crowned felt hat.
F	E	E	B	L	E	Weak, infirm, debilitated, frail, flimsy, fragile, ailing, aged, doddering.
F	E	E	B	L	Y	In feeble manner.
F	E	E	D	E	R	Provider of nourishment. Replenisher. Supplier. Conductor. Transmitter. Bib.
F	E	E	L	E	R	Antenna, sensory tentacle. Reaction gauge, query, probe, question.
F	E	L	I	N	E	Suggestive of a cat. Catty, cattish, sly, treacherous.
F	E	L	L	A	H	Peasant, labourer.
F	E	L	L	E	D	Cut down, chopped out. Pole-axed.
F	E	L	L	E	R	Tree cutter, wood chopper. Seam binder. Machine attachment.
F	E	L	L	O	W	Man, guy, boy, bloke. Partner, associate, mate, companion, consort.
F	E	L	O	N	Y	Misdemeanour, crime.
F	E	L	T	E	D	Matted, felt-covered.
F	E	L	T	E	R	Intertwiner.
F	E	M	A	L	E	Feminine, girl, woman, young bearing animal, womanly, womanlike, ladylike.
F	E	N	C	E	D	Barricaded, barred, penned, caged, enclosed, hedged, walled, blockaded.
F	E	N	C	E	R	Swordsman, one who fences, show jumper, fence repairer.
F	E	N	D	E	R	Buffer, piles, bumper, chafing device, impact protector.
F	E	N	I	A	N	Irish defender. Irish Secret Society.
F	E	N	N	E	L	Perennial Herb, the seed, aromatic flavour of fennel.
F	E	R	R	E	T	Type of Polecat. Informer, Spy Plane.
F	E	R	R	E	T	Hunt for, seek out, uncover, search, pry. Weasel-like animal.
F	E	R	R	I	C	Containing Iron.

1	2	3	4	5	6	
F	E	R	V	I	D	Zealous, ardent, burning. Vehement, ebullient.
F	E	S	T	A	L	Saint's day. Festive.
F	E	S	T	E	R	Rankle, inflame, corrupt, ulcerate. Pustule, Sore, Abscess.
F	E	T	I	A	L	Responsible, diplomatic, fecial.
F	E	T	I	S	H	Charm, superstition, prepossession, rite, incantation, fixation.
F	E	T	T	E	R	Shackle, manacle, confine, bind, bond, chain, hinder, restrain.
F	E	T	T	L	E	Spirits, condition, mettle, state of mind, fitness, good order.
F	E	U	D	A	L	Marked by divided domains, social system of landowners. Inter-dependent.
F	I	A	C	R	E	Hackney coach.
F	I	A	N	C	É	Betrothed, Engaged boy or girl. Future spouse.
F	I	A	S	C	O	Debacle, collapse ridiculous failure. Rout. Breakdown. Retreat.
F	I	B	B	E	D	Lied, prevaricated, told untruths, evaded, falsified, fabricated, trumped up.
F	I	B	B	E	R	Liar, falsifier, perjurer, prevaricator, storyteller.
F	I	B	R	E	S	Plural of FIBRE.
F	I	B	R	I	L	Threadlike, filamentous outgrowth make up of muscle, fibre structure.
F	I	B	R	I	N	Action of blood clotting through protein.
F	I	B	U	L	A	Bone formation. Ancient safety pin.
F	I	C	K	L	E	Inconstant, capricious, temperamental, unstable, volatile, variable.
F	I	D	D	L	E	Meddle, feel, handle, fidget, trifle, touch, dabble, potter, tinker, putter.
F	I	D	G	E	T	Trifle, play, fiddle, twiddle, worry, fret, twitter, chafe.
F	I	E	L	D	S	Plural of FIELD.
F	I	E	N	D	S	Plural of FIEND.
F	I	E	R	C	E	Savage, violent, furious, ferocious, menacing, aggressive, vicious, intense.
F	I	E	S	T	A	Carnival, feast, festival, celebration.
F	I	G	G	E	D	Insulted by the sign of the fig. Dressed, adorned. Stimulated a horse for racing.
F	I	G	H	T	S	Plural of FIGHT.
F	I	G	U	R	E	Number, cipher, digit, symbol, form. Calculate, compute, estimate, reckon.
F	I	L	I	A	L	Relationship of a child.
F	I	L	I	N	G	Rubbing, fragment. Documentation, methodical paper arrangement. Using a file.
F	I	L	L	E	D	Past of FILL.
F	I	L	L	E	R	Added substance. Filling composition. Cover. Plant, newspaper copy. Device.
F	I	L	L	E	T	Strip, stripe, band. Beef tenderloin. Boneless meat or fish. Cut into fillets.
F	I	L	L	I	P	Smart blow, buffet, arousal, stimulator. Trivial addition.
F	I	L	M	E	D	Past of FILM.
F	I	L	O	S	E	Filamentous.
F	I	L	T	E	R	Strain, percolate, infiltrate, Porous mass. Separator, Conical funnel.
F	I	L	T	H	Y	Dirty, foul, corrupt, unsavoury, unclean, impure, squalid, offensive, obscene.
F	I	N	A	L	E	End, finish, conclusion, close, climax, culmination, cessation, termination.
F	I	N	D	E	R	Discoverer, backer, astronomical telescope, camera reflector.
F	I	N	E	L	Y	Delicately, splendidly, excellently, discriminatingly, detailed, particularly.
F	I	N	E	R	Y	Ornamentation, decoration, luxury, best clothing, trappings.
F	I	N	E	S	T	Superlative of FINE.
F	I	N	G	E	R	Digit, terminating member of the hand. Touch, handle. Measurement, Steal, pilfer. Accuse.
F	I	N	I	A	L	Pinnacle, gable, canopy. Capping ornament.
F	I	N	I	N	G	Act making fine. Imposing a fine.
F	I	N	I	S	H	End, termination, conclusion. Consume, kill, assassinate, cease, accomplishment.
F	I	N	I	T	E	Within definable limits, bounded, limited, confined, defined, precise, specified.
F	I	N	N	A	N	Smoked Haddock.
F	I	N	N	E	D	Past of FIN.
F	I	N	N	E	R	Finback.
F	I	R	I	N	G	Setting alight, triggering, maturing in a kiln. Operating a firearm.
F	I	R	K	I	N	Small wooden vessel. Cask.
F	I	R	M	E	D	Hardened, solidified, fixed, tightened, stabilised, steadied, established.
F	I	R	M	L	Y	In a firm manner. Steadily, solidly, fixedly, tightly, steadfastly.
F	I	S	C	A	L	Relating to financial matters. Taxation, public revenue. Law enforcement officer.
F	I	S	H	E	D	Past of FISH.
F	I	S	H	E	R	One who FISHES. Something employed in fishing.
F	I	S	H	E	S	Plural of FISH.
F	I	S	T	E	D	Clenched. Punched.
F	I	S	T	I	C	Pugilistic.
F	I	T	F	U	L	Irregular, unsteady, intermittent, periodic, recurrent, inconstant, capricious.
F	I	T	T	E	D	Adapted, matched, suited, comfortable, assorted.
F	I	T	T	E	R	Worker with machine and hand tools. Someone who alters clothes. Shopfitter. More fit.
F	I	X	A	T	E	Rivet, focus, concentrate, fix, arrest, direct, immobilize.
F	I	X	I	N	G	Mending, adjusting, settling, solving, repairing, preparing, attaching.
F	I	X	I	T	Y	State of being fixed, something fixed. Permanent.
F	I	Z	Z	E	D	Hissed, buzzed, whooshed, whizzed, swished, bubbled up.

1	2	3	4	5	6	
F	I	Z	Z	E	R	Something that fizzes.
F	I	Z	Z	L	E	Wheeze, fizz, sibilate, swish, whoosh. Peter out, abortive effort, failure, fiasco.
F	L	A	B	B	Y	Flaccid, tubby, fat, obese, sagging, feeble, weak.
F	L	A	G	O	N	Flask, short-necked bottle, pottery vessel. Measure of quantity.
F	L	A	K	E	D	Peeled, exfoliated, layered. Sprinkled with.
F	L	A	M	B	E	Dish covered with liquor and set alight. Glazed Pottery.
F	L	A	M	E	D	Lit, excited, ignited, set ablaze.
F	L	A	N	G	E	Wheel guide on vehicle or locomotive. Tuck, insert, projecting edge. Rim, edge.
F	L	A	N	K	S	Plural of FLANK.
F	L	A	R	E	D	Blazed, erupted, exploded, ignited, flamed, raged, glittered.
F	L	A	S	H	Y	Gaudy, loud, garish, ornate, brazen, tawdry, flamboyant.
F	L	A	T	L	Y	Uniformly, evenly, smoothly, drably, blandly, bluntly, categorically.
F	L	A	T	U	S	Gas, wind, breath, puff.
F	L	A	U	N	T	Display, brandish, flash, expose, exhibit, flourish, vaunt, broadcast.
F	L	A	V	I	D	Yellow colour.
F	L	A	V	I	N	Yellow dye, pigment, riboflavin.
F	L	A	W	E	D	Past of FLAW. Damaged, faulty, imperfect.
F	L	A	X	E	N	Straw-coloured, golden, blonde, yellow.
F	L	A	Y	E	D	Past of FLAY.
F	L	A	Y	E	R	Skinner, one that flays.
F	L	E	C	H	E	Slender church spire. Movement in fencing.
F	L	E	C	K	S	Plural of FLECK.
F	L	E	D	G	E	Acquire flight wings. Attain adult winged stage. Tend featherless fledgling.
F	L	E	D	G	Y	Feathery, downy.
F	L	E	E	C	E	Coat of Wool. Shorn wool. Head hair. Pile. Buffalo meat. Rob, plunder, strip.
F	L	E	E	C	Y	Woolly, covered with wool. Downy, hairy.
F	L	E	E	T	S	Plural of FLEET.
F	L	E	N	S	H	Strip a whale or seal of skin and blubber. Flay.
F	L	E	S	H	Y	Having excess flesh. Plump, corpulent, fat, pulpy, succulent.
F	L	E	T	C	H	To feather. To hold a grudge.
F	L	E	X	E	D	Stretched muscles, bent, folded, clasped.
F	L	E	X	O	R	Bending muscle.
F	L	I	C	K	S	Motion Pictures. Movies. Plural of FLICK.
F	L	I	E	R	S	Plural of FLIER.
F	L	I	G	H	T	Ability to fly with wings. Rapid Movement. Escape, getaway. Floor, storey.
F	L	I	M	S	Y	Weak, superficial, frivolous, diaphanous, transparent, implausible, incredible.
F	L	I	N	C	H	Blanch, quail, shrink, recoil, wince, start, squinch, blench.
F	L	I	N	G	S	Plural of FLING.
F	L	I	N	T	Y	Harsh, unyielding, brittle, stern, resembling flint.
F	L	I	T	C	H	Side of cured Pork. Smoked steak or fish. Cut timber. Section of timber.
F	L	O	A	T	S	Plural of FLOAT.
F	L	O	A	T	Y	Tending to FLOAT. Buoyant.
F	L	O	C	C	I	Plural of FLOCCUS.
F	L	O	C	K	S	Plural of FLOCK.
F	L	O	C	K	Y	Resembling FLOCK.
F	L	O	O	D	S	Plural of FLOOD.
F	L	O	O	R	S	Plural of FLOOR.
F	L	O	O	Z	Y	Strumpet, tart, doxy, slut.
F	L	O	P	P	Y	Drooping, flaccid, collapsible, clumsy, tending to FLOP, limp, flimsy.
F	L	O	R	A	L	Covered in flowers, printed with flowers, flowery. Patterned with flowers.
F	L	O	R	E	T	Individual flower, small flower, dainty flower. Spun silk yarn.
F	L	O	R	I	D	Flowery, embellished with flowers. Ruddy complexioned. Ornate.
F	L	O	R	I	N	Old gold piece. Two shilling piece.
F	L	O	S	S	Y	Flashy, ornate.
F	L	O	U	R	Y	Like Flour. Covered in flour. Resembling flour. Fine, powdery.
F	L	O	W	E	D	Past of FLOW.
F	L	O	W	E	R	Coloured, reproductive section of a Plant. Blossom, bloom. Develop, bear flowers.
F	L	U	E	N	T	Flowing, easy, abundant, voluble, fluid, smooth, free of speech.
F	L	U	F	F	Y	Woolly, downy, light, feathery.
F	L	U	I	D	S	Plural of FLUID.
F	L	U	K	E	D	Past of FLUKE.
F	L	U	N	K	Y	Lackey, slave, servant, pageboy, footman, subordinate person.
F	L	U	R	R	Y	Flutter, gust, sudden commotion, outburst, spasm, stir, excitement, whirlwind.
F	L	U	T	E	D	Grooved, channelled, flutelike.
F	L	U	T	E	R	Tin can seamer.
F	L	Y	B	O	Y	Printshop worker.
F	L	Y	I	N	G	Locomotion by air. Moving in air. Moving rapidly. Fleeting brief, transitory.

1	2	3	4	5	6	
F	L	Y	M	A	N	Theatre curtain manipulator.
F	O	A	L	E	D	Gave birth to a FOAL.
F	O	A	M	E	D	Bubbled, frothed, lathered, spumed, Creamed, sprayed.
F	O	B	B	E	D	Palmed off, substituted, fended off, foisted.
F	O	C	S	L	E	Forecastle, forward section of a ship. Bows.
F	O	D	D	E	R	Animal food, hay, corn, consumable, raw material, ammunition.
F	O	E	M	A	N	Foe, enemy, antagonist.
F	O	E	T	U	S	Embryonic life. Unborn. Unhatched. Developing human.
F	O	G	E	Y	S	Plural of FOGEY.
F	O	G	G	E	D	Misted, overcast, blurred, cloudy, muddled, dazed, dim.
F	O	G	R	A	M	Fogey, fossil, antediluvian, square, fuddy-duddy.
F	O	I	B	L	E	Fault, imperfection, shortcoming, frailty, failing, vice, weakness, defect.
F	O	I	L	E	D	Frustrated, baffled, thwarted, disappointed, balked, beaten. Ornamented with Foils.
F	O	I	L	E	R	One who FOILS.
F	O	L	D	E	D	Past of FOLD.
F	O	L	D	E	R	Paper cover, file, jacket, large envelope. A machine used for folding.
F	O	L	I	A	R	Relating to Leaves.
F	O	L	I	O	S	Plural of FOLIO.
F	O	L	K	S	Y	Friendly, neighbourly, sociable, casual, rustic, excessively country.
F	O	L	L	O	W	Succeed, pursue, chase, ensue, supervene, track, trail, apprehend, comprehend.
F	O	M	E	N	T	Incite, instigate, provoke, stir up, goad, foster, nurture, agitate.
F	O	N	D	E	R	Comparative of FOND.
F	O	N	D	L	E	Pet, caress, cuddle, love, dandle, embrace, nestle, embrace, clasp.
F	O	N	D	L	Y	Affectionately, romantically, warmly, tenderly, indulgently. Optimistically.
F	O	N	D	U	E	Swiss melted cheese dish, flavoured with wine or brandy.
F	O	N	T	A	L	Original, primary. Baptismal.
F	O	O	L	E	D	Past of FOOL. Tricked, deceived.
F	O	O	T	E	D	Having feet, foot ability, sure-footed, fleet-footed. Paid, totalled.
F	O	O	T	E	R	Having specified number of feet. Pedestrian. (Sl.) Soccer.
F	O	O	T	L	E	Fiddle, trifle, potter, fool.
F	O	O	Z	L	E	Manage awkwardly. Bungle, botch, louse up, fumble.
F	O	R	A	G	E	Fodder, food for domestic animals. Search for sustenance. Raid, rummage. Scour.
F	O	R	A	Y	S	Plural of FORAY.
F	O	R	B	I	D	Ban, veto, inhibit, prohibit, outlaw, exclude, debar, obviate, check, restrain.
F	O	R	B	Y	E	Near, besides, over and above, except, unusual, remarkable. Forby.
F	O	R	C	E	D	Produced with effort, laboured, strained, artificial, inflexible, coerced, compelled.
F	O	R	C	E	R	One who FORCES.
F	O	R	C	E	S	Plural of FORCE.
F	O	R	D	E	D	Crossed, waded across, passed over, bridged.
F	O	R	E	G	O	Forfeit, yield, resign, relinquish, sacrifice, eschew.
F	O	R	E	S	T	Woods, woodlands, thicket, grove, thicket, coppice, plantation.
F	O	R	G	E	D	Past of FORGE.
F	O	R	G	E	R	Falsifier, counterfeiter, forge-worker.
F	O	R	G	E	S	Plural of FORGE.
F	O	R	G	E	T	Lose the memory, misrecollect, unlearn, neglect, overlook, disregard, ignore.
F	O	R	G	O	T	Past of FORGET.
F	O	R	K	E	D	Branched, bifurcated. Pronged, speared. Spent, disbursed.
F	O	R	M	A	L	Ceremonial, conventional, solemn, stately, precise, unbending, regular, distant.
F	O	R	M	A	T	Style, form, shape and size of publication, layout, size, proportion.
F	O	R	M	E	D	Moulded, arranged, shaped, organized, settled, matured.
F	O	R	M	E	R	Previous, prior, bygone, foregoing, precedent, succeeding, old, past, late.
F	O	R	M	I	C	Relating to Ants. Of formic acid. Pismire.
F	O	S	S	I	L	Traces of past geological ages. Preserved from the past. Petrified. Old dodderer.
F	O	S	T	E	R	Gather, nourish, cultivate, nurture, shelter, champion, lodge, house, encourage.
F	O	U	G	H	T	Past of FIGHT.
F	O	U	L	E	D	Polluted, soiled, dirtied, blackened, besmirched, smutted.
F	O	U	L	L	Y	In a foul manner.
F	O	U	N	T	S	Plural of FOUNT.
F	O	U	R	T	H	One following third. The number four. Quarter.
F	O	W	L	E	R	Bird hunter.
F	O	X	I	L	Y	In a sly manner, shrewdly, cannily, craftily. Cunning.
F	O	X	I	N	G	Fooling, deceiving, outwitting, deluding.
F	O	X	I	S	H	Like a fox, fox-like.
F	O	Y	E	R	S	Plural of FOYER.
F	R	A	C	A	S	Fight, altercation, noisy, quarrel, brawl, squabble, affray, hassle, dispute.
F	R	A	M	E	D	Formulated, drafted, contrived, concocted, devised. Outlined. Surrounded in beams.
F	R	A	M	E	R	Frame-maker, contriver, deviser.

1	2	3	4	5	6	
F	R	A	M	E	S	Plural of FRAME.
F	R	A	P	P	E	Chilled and served on cracked ice. Peppermint Frappe.
F	R	A	U	D	S	Plural of FRAUD.
F	R	A	Y	E	D	Frazzled, tattered, shredded, ragged, fretted.
F	R	E	A	K	S	Plural of FREAK.
F	R	E	E	L	Y	In a free manner. Unfettered, willingly, readily, unimpeded. Easily, smoothly.
F	R	E	E	Z	E	Chill, harden into ice. Stand still, anaesthetize, make inflexible, immovable.
F	R	E	N	C	H	From France. Civilization of France. Vermouth.
F	R	E	N	Z	Y	Fury, madness, furore, delirium. Madden, derange, distract, unhinge.
F	R	E	S	C	O	Wall painting. Mural.
F	R	E	T	T	Y	Fretful, irritable, carping, peevish.
F	R	E	T	U	M	Arm of the sea. Strait.
F	R	I	A	R	Y	Monk's home. Monastery.
F	R	I	D	A	Y	Day of the week. Commencement of a weekend.
F	R	I	D	G	E	Refrigerator, coolbox, ice-box. Cold Room.
F	R	I	E	N	D	Confidant, intimate, mate, chum, ally, colleague, acquaintance, associate.
F	R	I	E	Z	E	Sculptured band on building, building adornment. Embroidery. Upholstery fabric.
F	R	I	G	H	T	Fear, alarm, consternation, trepidation, dismay, panic, terror. Eyesore.
F	R	I	G	I	D	Cold, arctic, glacial, frosty, cold, inhibited, passionless, unresponsive.
F	R	I	L	L	Y	Fluted, trifling, frivolous, ornamental.
F	R	I	N	G	E	Border, edge, margin, verge, surround, skirt, hem. Hair style.
F	R	I	S	K	Y	Playful, kittenish, sportive, frolicsome, waggish.
F	R	I	V	O	L	Waste, fritter, squander, trifle.
F	R	O	G	G	Y	Abounding in frogs. Relating to frogs. Gruff, gravelly.
F	R	O	L	I	C	Gambol, romp, lark, play around, carouse, riot, roister, Prank, lark, caper.
F	R	O	N	D	S	Plural of FROND.
F	R	O	N	T	S	Plural of FRONT.
F	R	O	S	T	Y	Icy, cold, chilly, freezing, glacial, icy, nippy, shivery.
F	R	O	T	H	Y	Bubbly, foamy, unsubstantial, empty, frivolous, shallow, meagre.
F	R	O	W	Z	Y	Slovenly, unkempt, slatternly, stale, musty. Blowsy, dowdy, slack.
F	R	O	Z	E	N	Past of FREEZE.
F	R	U	G	A	L	Careful, thrifty, parsimonious, canny, wary, stinting, economical.
F	R	U	I	T	Y	Resembling fruit. Juicy, luscious. Rich in tone. Mellow sounding.
F	R	U	M	P	Y	Dowdy, untidy, unkempt, tacky, outmoded, stodgy, out-of-date.
F	R	Y	I	N	G	Cooking in oil, pan cooking. Heating, Sizzling.
F	U	D	D	L	E	Confuse, bewilder, fluster, muddle, addle.
F	U	D	G	E	D	Exaggerated, overstated, magnified, embellished, embroidered.
F	U	F	F	E	D	Puffed, smoked.
F	U	G	A	T	O	Musical composition.
F	U	G	U	E	S	Plural of FUGUE.
F	U	H	R	E	R	Tyrant, dictator, Leader.
F	U	L	F	I	L	Accomplish, effect, implement, perform, complete, satisfy, meet, answer.
F	U	L	H	A	M	Gambling.
F	U	L	L	E	R	Blacksmith's hammer. Groove. Portion of forging die.
F	U	L	V	I	D	Fulvous, dull browny colour, tawny.
F	U	M	B	L	E	Grope, feel, grapple, bungle, goof, botch, muff, mumble, mutter, stammer.
F	U	M	I	L	Y	In a fuming manner.
F	U	M	I	N	G	Angry, boiling, bristling, seething, raging, burning.
F	U	M	O	U	S	Consisting of FUMES. Vaporous. Smoky.
F	U	N	D	E	D	Paid for, subsidised, contributed to, endowed, patronised.
F	U	N	D	U	S	Piece of landed property. Bottom, back portion.
F	U	N	G	A	L	Consisting of FUNGI. Fungus-like.
F	U	N	G	U	S	Spongy growth. Parasitic plant. Mould, mildew, rust, mushroom, toadstool.
F	U	N	K	E	D	Backed out, panicked, flinched, shrank, dreaded, showed cowardly tendencies.
F	U	N	N	E	D	Past of FUN.
F	U	N	N	E	L	Cone-shaped utensil. Constricted channel, flue, stack. Distribute, siphon, pipe.
F	U	R	I	E	S	Plural of FURY.
F	U	R	L	E	D	Folded, Rolled up, Curled, Wrapped.
F	U	R	O	R	E	Upheaval, stir, flurry, fuss, bother, commotion, rumpus, shindig, uproar.
F	U	R	R	E	D	Covered in FUR. Relating to FUR.
F	U	R	R	O	W	Corrugation, wrinkle, crease, ridge, ruck, groove, rut, channel.
F	U	S	I	N	G	Merging, melding, mingling, liquefying, dissolving, melting. Cutting out.
F	U	S	I	O	N	Mixture, alloy, amalgam, blend, compound, amalgamation.
F	U	S	S	E	D	Past of FUSS.
F	U	S	S	E	R	One who FUSSES. Fuddy-duddy, fusspot, old maid, busy-body.
F	U	T	I	L	E	Abortive, ineffective, unavailing, vain, useless. Inadequate, unproductive.
F	U	T	U	R	E	Time to come. Hereafter, offing, afterward, by and by, prospective, delayed.

1	2	3	4	5	6
F	U	Z	Z	E	D

Covered in fluff, hazy, blurred, fluffed, woolly, frizzy.

G

G	A	B	B	A	I	Collector of subscriptions. Jewish Treasurer. Administrator.
G	A	B	B	E	D	Past of GAB.
G	A	B	B	L	E	Chatter, prattle, chatterer, rapid talker. Incoherent speech.
G	A	B	L	E	D	Constructed with a Gable. Building design.
G	A	B	L	E	T	Arch over Tabernacle.
G	A	B	O	O	N	Type of Ebony. Viper, Spittoon, Cuspidor.
G	A	D	D	E	D	Past of GAD.
G	A	D	D	E	R	One who GADS about. Rover, wanderer, aimless visitor.
G	A	D	F	L	Y	Botfly. Annoying person.
G	A	D	G	E	T	Contraption, clever device, mechanical aid. Baby care centre. Doodad, dingus.
G	A	E	L	I	C	Relating to Celts in Ireland and the Highlands.
G	A	F	F	E	D	Hooked, spurred, clobbered, secured, captured.
G	A	F	F	E	R	Employer, foreman, motion-picture electrician.
G	A	G	G	E	D	Past of GAG. Made fun, joked, cracked a witticism, quipped, choked.
G	A	G	G	E	R	One who GAGS. Joker, gagman. Foundry worker.
G	A	G	G	L	E	Group, bunch, gang.
G	A	G	M	A	N	Joke writer, comic.
G	A	I	E	T	Y	Jollity, merrymaking, revelry, hilarity, animation, happiness, vivacity.
G	A	I	N	E	D	Past of GAIN.
G	A	I	N	E	R	One who GAINS.
G	A	I	T	E	D	Horse having particular GAIT. Past of GAIT. Speed of Activities.
G	A	I	T	E	R	Legging, ankle-high shoe, overshoe. Protective covering.
G	A	L	A	X	Y	System of Stars, Milky Way, an assemblage of brilliant persons.
G	A	L	L	E	D	Abraded, chafed, annoyed, bothered, provoked, irritated, needled.
G	A	L	L	E	T	Galet, chip of stone.
G	A	L	L	E	Y	Oar-propelled ship. Ship's kitchen. Set type holder. Cooking area in 'plane or caravan.
G	A	L	L	I	C	Relating to Gaul.
G	A	L	L	O	N	Measurement of liquid.
G	A	L	L	O	P	Speed of movement. Rapid pace, run. Training distances for horses.
G	A	L	L	U	P	POLL. Sample of public opinion. Questioning on representative issue.
G	A	L	O	O	T	Person, odd person, foolish fellow, lout, rustic. Oaf.
G	A	L	O	R	E	Abundant, plentiful, profuse.
G	A	L	O	S	H	Overshoe, protective shoe.
G	A	M	B	E	T	Redshank. Bird.
G	A	M	B	I	T	Ploy, trick, gimmick, ruse, manoeuvre, plot, plan, artifice.
G	A	M	B	L	E	Game of chance, wager, speculate, venture, lay odds, bet, stake.
G	A	M	B	O	L	Leap, tumble, caper, frisk, rollick, romp, cavort, roister, revel.
G	A	M	E	L	Y	Courageously, pluckily, bravely, fearlessly, valiantly.
G	A	M	E	T	E	Mature germ cell, sperm, egg.
G	A	M	I	N	E	Tomboy, hoyden, saucy girl.
G	A	M	I	N	G	Playing, gambling, betting, staking, wagering.
G	A	M	I	N	S	Plural of GAMIN.
G	A	M	M	O	N	Lower portion of side of bacon or ham. Humbug.
G	A	N	D	E	R	Glance, glimpse, peek, look, peep. Male goose.
G	A	N	G	E	R	Foreman, gang worker.
G	A	N	G	L	Y	Gangling, spindly, rangy, lanky.
G	A	N	N	E	T	Web-footed sea bird. Voracious eater.
G	A	N	T	R	Y	Travelling crane, rolling winch. Signals support.
G	A	O	L	E	D	Past of GAOL. Imprisoned, incarcerated.
G	A	O	L	E	R	Jailer. Warder.
G	A	P	I	N	G	Yawning, gazing, staring, cavernous, gawping.
G	A	R	A	G	E	Building for housing automobiles. Repair shop for motor cars. Fuel Dispenser.
G	A	R	B	E	D	Dressed, clothed, adorned, arrayed, attired, clad.
G	A	R	B	L	E	Misquote, misrepresent, distort, falsify, pervert, twist, belie.
G	A	R	C	O	N	Menial, boy, waiter.
G	A	R	D	E	N	Cultivated land, growth of flowers and vegetables. Happy place.
G	A	R	G	L	E	Cleanse the throat with liquid mixture. Gurgle.
G	A	R	I	S	H	Flashy, tawdry, gaudy, blatant, brazen, overdone, loud, overdressed.
G	A	R	L	I	C	Onion-like condiment, plant, seasoning, aromatic bulb.
G	A	R	N	E	R	Gather, collect, hoard, store, accumulate, amass, harvest, glean, reap.
G	A	R	N	E	T	Lustrous semi-precious stone. Ruby-like jewel.
G	A	R	R	E	T	Loft, attic, small room at the top of a house.

1	2	3	4	5	6	
G	A	R	R	O	T	Cruel means of execution. Strangulation.
G	A	R	T	E	R	Circular elastic band. Girdle hanging, suspender. Noble decoration.
G	A	S	B	A	G	Chatterbox, braggart, boaster, bragger, blowhard, vaunter.
G	A	S	H	E	D	Cut, wounded. Past of GASH.
G	A	S	H	L	Y	Carefully, gingerly, softly.
G	A	S	I	F	Y	Convert solid into gas.
G	A	S	K	E	T	Device for rendering pistons or pipe joints fluid-tight. Lashing.
G	A	S	L	I	T	Lit by gas lamps.
G	A	S	P	E	D	Past of GASP.
G	A	S	P	E	R	Cigarette, fag, butt.
G	A	S	S	E	D	Affected by Gas. Asphyxiated. Chatted, nattered. Past of GAS.
G	A	S	S	E	R	One who GASSES. An oil well. Something outstanding.
G	A	S	S	E	S	Plural of GAS.
G	A	T	E	A	U	Fancy well-decorated Cake.
G	A	T	H	E	R	Collect, muster, assemble, pick, cluster. Reap, glean, infer, understand. Loom.
G	A	T	I	N	G	Lock tumbler part. Part of electromagnetic wave. Banning, barring.
G	A	U	C	H	E	Awkward, clumsy, inept, wooden, unpolished, bumbling.
G	A	U	C	H	O	Herdsman, cowboy.
G	A	U	G	E	D	Estimated, measured, scaled.
G	A	U	G	E	R	Machine shop checker. Customs Officer. Oil Pipeline control.
G	A	W	K	E	R	Gazer, Gawper, Nosey-parker, inquisitive on-looker.
G	A	Y	E	S	T	Comparative of GAY.
G	A	Z	E	B	O	Summerhouse, pagoda, pergola, alcove.
G	A	Z	I	N	G	Looking, viewing, regarding, seeing, gaping, considering, eyeing.
G	E	A	R	E	D	Past of GEAR.
G	E	E	Z	E	R	Eccentric, odd fellow. Queer person. Old man.
G	E	I	G	E	R	Electronic equipment.
G	E	I	S	H	A	Japanese girl trained in the art of entertainment. Courtesan.
G	E	L	D	E	D	Castrated (horse). Altered, neutered, desexualised, sterlized.
G	E	M	I	N	I	Sign of the Zodiac. The Twins.
G	E	M	M	E	D	Bejewelled, begemmed.
G	E	N	D	E	R	Sex, character. Grammatical part of language.
G	E	N	E	R	A	Plural of GENUS.
G	E	N	E	T	S	Plural of GENET.
G	E	N	E	V	A	Juniper flavoured alcoholic beverage. Gin.
G	E	N	I	A	L	Gracious, cordial, congenial affable, hearty, kindly, amicable, affable.
G	E	N	I	U	S	Clever person. Embodiment of quality. Talent, gift, knack, flair, brains, intellect.
G	E	N	T	L	E	Devoid of roughness. Bland, mild, soft, balmy, delicate, placid, serene, pleasant.
G	E	N	T	L	Y	In a gentle manner.
G	E	N	T	R	Y	Aristocracy, society, upper class, upper crust, quality, elite.
G	E	O	R	G	E	Automatic Pilot. Jewelled British Order of Merit. Half-crown.
G	E	R	M	A	N	Hun, Teutonic. Native of GERMANY.
G	E	R	U	N	D	Latin verbal noun.
G	E	T	T	E	R	Live wire, dynamic person, self-starter.
G	E	W	G	A	W	Bauble, trinket, knick knack, curio, novelty, trifle, whatnot.
G	E	Y	S	E	R	Gusher, active underground spring. Spurter.
G	H	A	R	R	Y	(Sl.) Motorcar, vehicle.
G	H	E	T	T	O	Poor quarter of a City. Jewish Quarter. Minority racial quarter.
G	H	O	S	T	S	Plural of GHOST.
G	I	A	N	T	S	Plural of GIANT.
G	I	B	B	E	R	Gabble, jibber, jabber, babble, chatter.
G	I	B	B	E	T	Gallows, hanging tree. Hanging Post.
G	I	B	B	O	N	Arboreal anthropoid ape.
G	I	B	I	N	G	Jibing, scoffing, scorning, jesting, flouting, jeering, sneering.
G	I	B	L	E	T	Fowl Innard. Edible fowl viscera.
G	I	F	T	E	D	Clever, intellectual, talented.
G	I	G	G	L	E	Snigger, cackle, titter, chortle, chuckle, laugh unrestrainedly.
G	I	G	O	L	O	Paid escort. Professional dancing partner.
G	I	L	D	E	D	Past of GILD. GILT.
G	I	L	D	E	R	One who gilds. Gold overlayer.
G	I	L	L	I	E	Male attendant, gamekeeper, fishing guide. Lace-up shoe.
G	I	M	B	A	L	Ship's compass or barometer support.
G	I	M	L	E	T	Woodworking tool for boring holes. A driving personality trait. Alcoholic concoction.
G	I	N	G	E	R	Pungent and aromatic spice. Red colour. Coppery.
G	I	R	D	E	D	Braced, bolstered, readied, banded, encircled, ringed, girdled, hemmed.
G	I	R	D	E	R	Beam, rafter, truss, reinforced concrete support, rolled metal unit.
G	I	R	D	L	E	Belt, band, sash, waistband. Step-in, pull-on. Surround, encircle, ring.

1	2	3	4	5	6	
G	I	T	A	N	A	Spanish Gypsy woman.
G	I	V	I	N	G	Yielding, donating, handing over, contributing, awarding, confering, granting.
G	L	A	D	L	Y	Happily, joyously, pleasurably, delightedly, gleefully, jovially, cheerfully.
G	L	A	N	C	E	Look, gaze, glimpse, gander, brush, graze, browse, buff, glimmer, glint.
G	L	A	R	E	D	Past of GLARE.
G	L	A	R	E	S	Plural of GLARE.
G	L	A	S	S	Y	Sleek, glossy, polished, glazed, staring.
G	L	A	Z	E	D	Coated, glossy, smooth, fixed expression, immobile.
G	L	A	Z	E	R	Polisher, smoother, burnisher, Panman, machine used for glazing.
G	L	E	A	M	S	Plural of GLEAM.
G	L	E	A	M	Y	Shining, beaming, flashing, glimmering, glinting, glistening.
G	L	I	B	L	Y	Fluently, volubly, eloquently, vocally, articulately.
G	L	I	D	E	D	Past of GLIDE.
G	L	I	D	E	R	Engineless aeroplane. Flat powerboat. Porch seat. An aid to gliding.
G	L	I	D	E	S	Plural of GLIDE.
G	L	I	N	T	S	Plural of GLINT.
G	L	O	B	A	L	Universal, cosmic, planetary, worldwide. Sweeping, inclusive, ecumenical.
G	L	O	O	M	Y	Sad, dark, dim, dusky, dismal, dreary, sullen, surly, oppressed, cheerless.
G	L	O	R	I	A	Sun Liturgy. Dazzling heavenly light. Lightweight woven fabric. Aureole.
G	L	O	S	S	Y	Smooth, shining, sheeny, glassy, bright, polished.
G	L	O	V	E	D	Wearing gloves.
G	L	O	V	E	R	Glove-maker. Seller of gloves.
G	L	O	W	E	D	Past of GLOW.
G	L	O	W	E	R	Scowl, glare, frown, lower, gloom, look daggers, stare.
G	L	U	I	N	G	Sticking, uniting, cementing, attaching, adding.
G	L	U	M	L	Y	Sullenly, gloomily, down-heartedly, disinterestedly, unhappily, hopelessly.
G	L	U	T	E	N	Sticky substance; Adhesive. Albuminous element. Corn gluten.
G	N	A	R	L	Y	Knotted, gnarled, grabby.
G	N	A	W	E	D	Past of GNAW.
G	N	A	W	E	R	One who GNAWS. Rodent, masticator, worrier, irritant.
G	N	O	M	I	C	Universally true.
G	N	O	M	O	N	Type of Sundial.
G	N	O	S	I	S	Act of Knowing. Knowledge of spiritual truths.
G	O	A	D	E	D	Urged, prompted, spurred, impelled, exhorted, stimulated, prodded, pricked.
G	O	A	L	I	E	Goalkeeper.
G	O	A	T	E	E	Trim beard, tufted chin hair.
G	O	B	B	E	T	Morsel, droplet, drop, piece, portion, lump.
G	O	B	B	L	E	Bolt, gulp, guzzle, wolf, slop, cram. Turkey noise.
G	O	B	L	E	T	Drinking vessel, wine cup, drinking glass, stemmed chalice.
G	O	B	L	I	N	Gnome, sprite, hobgoblin.
G	O	C	A	R	T	Handcart, stroller, perambulator. Child's six-wheeled racing transport.
G	O	D	O	W	N	Storehouse, Warehouse.
G	O	D	S	O	N	Baptisimal Sponsor.
G	O	D	W	I	T	Long-billed wading bird.
G	O	F	F	E	R	Plait, decorate, emboss book edges. Crimp.
G	O	G	G	L	E	Stare, squint, gape, gaze in astonishment. Gawk, peer.
G	O	I	T	E	R	Goitre, enlarged thyroid gland.
G	O	L	D	E	N	Gilt, gilded, gold. Shining, aureate. Tanned, rich, mellow.
G	O	L	F	E	R	Golf Player.
G	O	N	G	E	D	Decorated for bravery (Sl.) Past of GONG.
G	O	O	D	L	Y	Fair amount, seemly. Comely. Handsome, large, considerable.
G	O	O	G	L	Y	Bulging. Wide-eyed. Off-break cricket delivery.
G	O	P	H	E	R	Burrowing rodent. Ground squirrel.
G	O	R	G	E	D	Past of GORGE.
G	O	R	G	E	T	Throat covering, throat armour. Neck ornament. Insignia on a chain.
G	O	R	G	I	O	Non-gypsy.
G	O	R	G	O	N	One of three-sisters in Greek Mythology.
G	O	R	I	N	G	Act of GORING. Piercing, penetrating.
G	O	S	P	E	L	Truth. Veracity, truism. Word of God. New Testament.
G	O	S	S	I	P	Idle chatter, rumour. One who gossips. Talk, prattle, insinuate, intimate.
G	O	T	H	I	C	Teutonic. Medieval. Precocious, savage, barbaric.
G	O	U	G	E	D	Exacted, extorted, squeezed, prised, scooped.
G	O	V	E	R	N	Rule, control, exert authority, administer, regulate, determine, command, sway.
G	O	W	N	E	D	Robed, dressed, arrayed, bedecked, clothed, outfitted.
G	R	A	C	E	D	Attended, favoured, adorned, embellished.
G	R	A	C	E	S	Plural of GRACE.
G	R	A	D	E	D	Classified, arranged, categorised, grouped, qualified, sorted, evaluated.

1	2	3	4	5	6	
G	R	A	I	N	S	Plural of GRAIN.
G	R	A	I	N	Y	Granulated, Coarse.
G	R	A	M	M	E	GRAM, metric unit of mass. Weight measure.
G	R	A	N	G	E	Farmhouse, country estate. Lodge.
G	R	A	N	N	Y	Grandmother. Fusspot, fuddy-duddy.
G	R	A	N	T	S	Plural of GRANT.
G	R	A	P	E	S	Plural of GRAPE.
G	R	A	P	H	S	Plural of GRAPH.
G	R	A	P	P	A	Dry brandy made from wine.
G	R	A	S	S	Y	Covered in Grass. Green lawn. Overgrown.
G	R	A	T	E	R	Kitchen implement, cheese grater. Scraper. Shredder.
G	R	A	T	E	S	Plural of GRATE.
G	R	A	T	I	N	Made with cheese sauce. Crusted fish.
G	R	A	T	I	S	Free, without payment, without recompense. Favour. Complimentary, gratuitous.
G	R	A	V	E	L	Fine stone, dust, loose stone, fragmented rock.
G	R	A	V	E	N	Engraved. Carved.
G	R	A	V	E	R	Engraver, sculptor.
G	R	A	V	E	S	Plural of GRAVE.
G	R	A	V	I	D	Portentious. Distended, filled. Pregnant. Enciente.
G	R	A	Z	E	D	Brushed, abraded, glanced, shaved, skimmed, ricocheted. Injured, wounded.
G	R	A	Z	E	R	Animal that feeds by grazing.
G	R	A	Z	E	S	Plural of GRAZE.
G	R	E	A	S	E	Oily matter, Fat, lubricant. Smear, daub. Expedite, facilitate.
G	R	E	A	S	Y	Oily, fatty, unctuous, slick, slippery, slippy, slithery. Sebaceous.
G	R	E	A	T	S	Plural of GREAT.
G	R	E	E	D	Y	Voracious, covetous, grasping, acquisitive.
G	R	E	E	N	S	Green vegetables.
G	R	E	T	N	A	Green. English Village where eloping couples marry.
G	R	I	E	V	E	Mourn, sorrow. Suffer grief.
G	R	I	L	L	E	Grating, crossbars. Barrier, Metal screen.
G	R	I	L	S	E	Young mature salmon.
G	R	I	M	E	D	Soiled, dirtied, smudged, tarnished, fouled, besmirched.
G	R	I	M	L	Y	Fiercely, dourly, cruelly, truculently, austerely, bleakly, rigidly, sternly.
G	R	I	N	G	O	White foreigner in South American or Spain. Disparaging term.
G	R	I	P	E	D	Complained, bitched, crabbed, grouched, groused, grumbled, yammered.
G	R	I	P	E	R	One who GRIPES.
G	R	I	P	E	S	Plural of GRIPE.
G	R	I	P	P	E	Contagious virus disease. Influenza.
G	R	I	S	L	Y	Ghastly, grim, Horribly, terribly, awfully, dreadfully.
G	R	I	T	T	Y	Sandy, gravelly, Resolute, brave, plucky.
G	R	O	A	T	S	Hulled grain larger than grits.
G	R	O	C	E	R	Merchant, provisioner, grocery dealer.
G	R	O	G	G	Y	Dizzy, dazed, weak, exhausted. Intoxicated, inebriated.
G	R	O	O	M	S	Plural of GROOM.
G	R	O	O	V	E	Furrow, rut, cutting, treadmill, routine, grind.
G	R	O	O	V	Y	Cool, marvellous, keen, neat, with it. (Sl.)
G	R	O	P	E	D	Past of GROPE.
G	R	O	T	T	O	Cave, cavern, underground chamber.
G	R	O	U	C	H	Grumbler, complainer, grouser, malcontent, sorehead, grump. Grumble, mutter.
G	R	O	U	N	D	Soil, earth, foundation, base, bedrock, reason, proof, evidence, cause. Domain.
G	R	O	U	P	S	Plural of GROUP.
G	R	O	U	S	E	Grouch, complain, grumble, mutter. Sorehead, Grump, complainer.
G	R	O	U	T	Y	Sullen, surly, sulky. Thick, muddy.
G	R	O	V	E	L	Crawl, creep, fawn, cringe, cower, kowtow, toady, bootlick.
G	R	O	W	E	R	Cultivator, producer, propagater, breeder, husbandman.
G	R	O	W	L	S	Plural of GROWL.
G	R	O	W	T	H	Progress, increased status, size, stature, height, quantitative increase. Expansion.
G	R	O	Y	N	E	Sea wall. Pier. Groin, Projecting edge. Fold at lower part of abdomen.
G	R	U	B	B	Y	Dirty, soiled, grimy, filthy, unclean, squalid, nasty, foul.
G	R	U	D	G	E	Envy, malice, spite, grievance, injustice, enmity, dislike.
G	R	U	M	P	Y	Surly, churlish, sulky, complaining, dissatisfied. Grouchy, crabby.
G	R	U	N	D	Y	Mother - Prudy, prig, goody-goody.
G	R	U	N	T	S	Plural of GRUNT.
G	U	A	R	D	S	Plural of GUARD.
G	U	E	S	T	S	Plural of GUEST.
G	U	F	F	A	W	Boisterous laughter, uproarious hilarity. Noisy, coarse laughter. Chortle.
G	U	I	D	E	D	Showed the way, pointed out, led, conducted, directed, escorted, piloted.

1	2	3	4	5	6	
G	U	I	D	E	R	One who guides.
G	U	I	D	E	S	Plural of GUIDE.
G	U	I	D	O	N	Small emblem-bearing Flag. Bunting. Swallow tailed flag.
G	U	I	L	D	S	Plural of GUILD.
G	U	I	L	T	S	Plural of GUILT.
G	U	I	L	T	Y	Blameworthy, censurable, culpable, reprehensible, accountable, responsible.
G	U	I	N	E	A	Unit of currency.
G	U	I	S	E	S	Plural of GUISE.
G	U	I	T	A	R	Musical instrument. Stringed instrument.
G	U	L	L	E	D	Duped, fooled, hoodwinked, hoaxed, bamboozled, befuddled.
G	U	L	L	E	R	Cheat, imposter, comman.
G	U	L	L	E	T	Throat.
G	U	L	L	E	Y	Gully, miniature valley, gorge, wooded hollow, small ravine, grassy depression.
G	U	L	P	E	D	Past of GULP.
G	U	M	M	E	D	Past of GUM.
G	U	N	M	A	N	G-man, armed man, criminal with a gun. Hit man, gun slinger, assassin.
G	U	N	M	E	N	Plural of GUNMAN.
G	U	N	N	E	L	Gunwale. Blenny.
G	U	N	N	E	R	Artilleryman, someone in charge of artillery, guns supervisor.
G	U	N	S	E	L	Assassin, gunman, gunslinger, triggerman, hit man, hatchet man.
G	U	N	S	H	Y	Afraid of guns. Afraid of the noise of guns. Figuratively afraid of commotion.
G	U	R	G	L	E	Swirl, swoosh, eddy, slosh, burble, swash, lap, gargle, coo.
G	U	R	H	K	A	Knife-wielding Indian from Nepal.
G	U	R	N	E	Y	Stretcher on wheels, wheeled cot.
G	U	S	H	E	D	Past tense of GUSH.
G	U	S	H	E	R	Oil well, uncontrolled flow in nature, spout, geyser.
G	U	S	S	E	T	Diamond-shaped insert, pleat, gore, bracket.
G	U	T	T	E	D	Past of GUT.
G	U	T	T	E	R	Drain, gully, sewer, rainwater trough, furrow, channel. Place of dishonour.
G	U	T	T	L	E	Eat or drink noisily. Vulgar eating. Greedy, guzzler.
G	U	Z	Z	L	E	Swill, greedy eating, gulp, bolt, gobble, slosh, wolf.
G	Y	P	P	E	R	Swindler, con man, defrauder, trickster.
G	Y	P	S	U	M	Calcium sulphate mineral.
G	Y	R	A	T	E	Coil, wind, revolve, swing around rapidly.
G	Y	R	O	S	E	Undulating, sinuating.

H

H	A	B	E	A	S	Corpus. You should have the body. A writ in common law. Produce the body.
H	A	B	I	T	S	Plural of HABIT.
H	A	C	K	E	D	Past of HACK.
H	A	C	K	E	R	Implement for hacking. Chipper. Inexperience in sport. Chopper.
H	A	C	K	L	E	Bird's plumage. Animal's natural covering. Neck feathers.
H	A	C	K	L	Y	Hacked looking. Rough, broken, jagged, fractured.
H	A	G	G	I	S	Pluck Pudding from Scotland.
H	A	G	G	L	E	Argue terms, bargain, barter, trade, quibble, wrangle, dispute.
H	A	I	L	E	D	Past of HAIL.
H	A	I	R	D	O	Hairstyle, hairdressing, tonsorial achievement, coiffure.
H	A	I	R	E	D	Having hair. Description.
H	A	L	L	O	A	Hallo! Greeting. Call out. Attract attention. Halloo. Vociferate. Yell.
H	A	L	L	O	W	Bless, sanctify, consecrate, dedicate, reverence, venerate.
H	A	L	O	E	D	Marked by an aura. Surrounded by a light.
H	A	L	T	E	D	Past of HALT.
H	A	L	T	E	R	Strap for leading a horse. Rope headstall. Noose. Style in women's clothing.
H	A	L	V	E	D	Cut in half. Divided fifty-fifty.
H	A	L	V	E	S	Two pieces of equal dimensions.
H	A	M	L	E	T	Small village. Group of dwellings.
H	A	M	M	E	D	Past of Ham.
H	A	M	M	E	R	Solid-headed hand tool. Sturdy device for pounding. Knock. Strike repeatedly.
H	A	M	P	E	R	Impede, curb, fetter, hinder, trammel, shackle, encumber, foil, retard. Basket.
H	A	N	D	E	D	Past of HAND. Having hands. Favouring the left or right side. Description.
H	A	N	D	E	R	Descriptive of hand action. Back-hander. Left-hander.
H	A	N	D	L	E	Part that is grasped. Name (sl.) Moniker. Touch, manipulate, wield, operate. Treat, use, conduct.
H	A	N	G	A	R	Aircraft shelter, shed, housing.
H	A	N	G	E	D	Past of HANG.
H	A	N	G	E	R	Coathanger, hangman, overhang, decoration, anything that HANGS.

1	2	3	4	5	6	
H	A	N	K	E	D	Skeined, coiled, looped.
H	A	N	K	E	R	Crave, hunger, pine, long, yearn, thirst, ache, covet, desire.
H	A	N	K	I	E	Handkerchief.
H	A	N	S	E	L	Handsel, gesture of luck, handout.
H	A	N	S	O	M	Two-wheeled covered horse-drawn carriage.
H	A	P	P	E	N	Take place, come about, befall, occur, transpire, betide, develop.
H	A	R	A	S	S	Harry, maraud, raid, foray, worry, pester, tease, badger, bait, heckle.
H	A	R	D	E	N	Make hard, stiffen, solidify, firm, temper, calcify, petrify, congeal, set.
H	A	R	D	E	R	Comparative of HARD. Fish. Type of Mullet.
H	A	R	D	L	Y	Scarcely, barely, narrowly, harshly. Hard, fiercely, bitterly, arduously, firmly.
H	A	R	D	U	P	Poor, broke, indigent, impecunious, penniless.
H	A	R	I	N	G	Rushing, speeding, running, pelting, scrambling.
H	A	R	K	E	D	Listened, paid close attention.
H	A	R	K	E	N	Listen, attend, hear, regard.
H	A	R	L	O	T	Whore, prostitute, bawd, call girl, wanton, hustler, hooker.
H	A	R	M	E	D	Past of HARM.
H	A	R	P	E	D	Nagged, dwelt upon, repeated tiresomely, recited frequently.
H	A	R	R	I	S	Tweed, Scottish wool fabric.
H	A	R	R	O	W	Cultivating implement. Plough, cultivate. Agonize, distress, afflict, Torment.
H	A	S	H	E	D	Chopped, mashed, mixed, combined, amalgamated, messed, cluttered, minced.
H	A	S	S	L	E	Quarrel, dispute, bicker, squabble. Commotion, turmoil, uproar. Trail, struggle.
H	A	S	T	E	N	Speed, quicken, accelerate, hurry, hustle, rush, urge, run, rocket.
H	A	T	B	O	X	Container for hats.
H	A	T	I	N	G	Disliking, abhorring, loathing, detesting, abominating, deprecating, resenting.
H	A	T	P	I	N	Hat ornament. Pin for securing a hat in place.
H	A	T	R	E	D	Dislike, abhorrence, loathing, detestation, abomination, repugnance, enmity.
H	A	T	T	E	D	Bearing a headgear. Wearing a hat.
H	A	T	T	E	R	Hat dealer. Lone prospector. Eccentric.
H	A	U	L	E	D	Past of HAUL.
H	A	U	L	E	R	Haulier, cartage contractor, long distance driver. Transporter.
H	A	U	N	C	H	Buttock, beamend, hunker, rump, tail, hindquarter, fleshy portion of buttock.
H	A	U	N	T	S	Plural of HAUNT. Frequent venue, habitat, lairs, stamping grounds, Resorts.
H	A	V	A	N	A	Cuban Cigar.
H	A	V	E	N	S	Plural of HAVEN.
H	A	V	I	N	G	Keeping, controlling, experiencing, possessing, including, allowing, knowing.
H	A	W	H	A	W	Guffaw, habit of speech, Ha-ha. Affected mirth.
H	A	W	K	E	D	Peddled, sold, vended, merchandised.
H	A	W	K	E	R	Pedlar, seller, merchandiser, vendor, retailer, travelling salesman.
H	A	W	S	E	R	Heavy tow rope. Docking rope. Mooring cable.
H	A	Y	B	O	X	Fireless cooking container. Device for slow cooking.
H	A	Y	M	O	W	Hay storage place. Barn area.
H	A	Z	A	R	D	Danger, peril, risk. Chance, luck. Venture, gamble, compromise, imperil.
H	A	Z	I	L	Y	Mistily, foggily, obscurely, vaguely, dreamily.
H	A	Z	Z	I	N	G	Harassing, disconcerting, ridiculing. Persistently, embarrass.
H	E	A	D	E	D	Directed, pointed, heading towards. Having a head. Led, guided, steered.
H	E	A	D	E	R	Head first dive. Head punt at Soccer. One who heads. Foremost, leader.
H	E	A	D	O	N	Directly, unswervingly, straight, collision, course.
H	E	A	L	E	D	Past of HEAL.
H	E	A	L	E	R	Doctor, mender, restorer, one who engages in healing mind and body.
H	E	A	L	T	H	Soundness in body and mind. Vitality, well-being, stamina, wholeness, haleness.
H	E	A	P	E	D	Past of HEAP. Heaped measure-full.
H	E	A	R	E	R	One who hears. Listener, discoverer, eavesdropper. Audience, attendant.
H	E	A	R	S	E	Coffin framework, coffin carrier. Conveyance for coffins.
H	E	A	R	T	H	Fireplace, fireside, place of comfort, home, cement floor area, creative centre. Cultural area.
H	E	A	R	T	S	Plural of HEART.
H	E	A	R	T	Y	Cordial, sincere, unfeigned, warm, profound, exuberant, robust.
H	E	A	T	E	D	Excited, ardent, fervid, indignant. Hot, scalding, sizzling, boiling, feverish.
H	E	A	T	E	R	Warmer, heat imparting contrivance. Furnace, radiator, stove, burner.
H	E	A	T	H	S	Plural of HEATH.
H	E	A	T	H	Y	Abounding with heath. Resembling Heath.
H	E	A	V	E	D	Past of HEAVE.
H	E	A	V	E	N	Sky, firmament, spiritual abode, happy place, nirvana, eternity, hereafter.
H	E	A	V	E	R	One who Heaves. Labourer. Type of Lever.
H	E	A	V	E	S	Plural of HEAVE.
H	E	B	O	N	A	Something with a poisonous juice.
H	E	B	R	E	W	Israelite, characteristic of the Hebrews. Semitic language.
H	E	C	A	T	E	Witch, Hag. Greek Goddess of Witchcraft.

1	2	3	4	5	6	
H	E	C	K	L	E	Bait, badger, hound, plague, embarrass, tease, torment, molest.
H	E	C	T	I	C	Heated, fevered, feverish, fervid, burning, hot, rushed, hurried.
H	E	C	T	O	R	Bully, browbeat, domineer, apply pressure, swagger, bluster.
H	E	D	E	R	A	Shrub, Ivy vine.
H	E	D	G	E	D	Dodged, evaded, equivocated, sidestepped. Enclosed, fenced, penned, immured.
H	E	D	G	E	R	Hedge planter. Hedge trimmer.
H	E	E	D	E	D	Noticed, attended, observed, regarded, studied, interested, cared.
H	E	E	H	A	W	Loud laughter, derisive laughter. Bray, guffaw.
H	E	E	L	E	D	Tilted, listed, canted. Controlled, mastered. Equipped, armed, provided with.
H	E	I	F	E	R	Young cow.
H	E	I	G	H	T	Measurement, distance, altitude, elevation, tallness, stature, loftiness.
H	E	L	I	U	M	Inert gaseous element.
H	E	L	M	E	T	Protective head covering. Crash Helmet, Welder's Helmet. Soldier's Helmet.
H	E	L	P	E	D	Assisted, aided, comforted, supported, facilitated, promoted, improved, bettered.
H	E	L	P	E	R	Assistant, ally, helpmate, aid, attendant, employee, servant, associate, deputy.
H	E	M	M	E	D	Bordered, enclosed, edged, fringed, skirted, bound, enclosed, caged, ringed.
H	E	M	M	E	R	Hem-stitcher. Sewing machine. Stutterer. Hesitant speaker.
H	E	M	P	E	N	Made like hemp.
H	E	R	A	L	D	Harbinger, announcer, forerunner, precursor, messenger, courier.
H	E	R	B	A	L	Made of Herbs. Incorporating Herbs.
H	E	R	D	E	D	Assembled, ran together, associated. Herdsman. Leader, Driver.
H	E	R	E	A	T	At this. Because of this.
H	E	R	E	B	Y	By this. By this means.
H	E	R	E	I	N	In this. Contained in this fact.
H	E	R	E	O	F	Of this.
H	E	R	E	O	N	On this basis. On this document. On top of this.
H	E	R	E	S	Y	Deliberate denial of revealed truth. Dissent of opinion. Contrary doctrine.
H	E	R	E	T	O	Attached. Added to.
H	E	R	M	E	S	Square stone pillar statue. Messenger of the gods.
H	E	R	M	I	T	Someone who has opted out. One who exists alone. Loner. Drop-out. Recluse.
H	E	R	N	I	A	Rupture.
H	E	R	O	E	S	Plural of HERO.
H	E	R	O	I	C	Brave, courageous, unafraid, valiant, bold. Extravagant, Extreme, Powerful.
H	E	R	O	I	N	Bitter crystalline narcotic. Hard Drug.
H	E	R	O	N	S	Wading Birds.
H	E	R	P	E	S	Virus skin disease characterised by blisters.
H	E	W	I	N	G	Cutting down, Chopping, hacking, felling.
H	E	Y	D	A	Y	Time of youth and vigour. Age of successful living.
H	I	A	T	U	S	Gap, aperture. Anatomical Breach. Lapse, interruption. Vowel relationship.
H	I	C	C	U	P	Hiccough. Burp.
H	I	D	D	E	N	Concealed, obscured, buried, shrouded, guarded. Ulterior, privy, covert.
H	I	D	I	N	G	Beating, Whipping. Concealing, putting out of sight. Screening, masking, covering.
H	I	E	I	N	G	Going quickly. Hastening. Leaving.
H	I	G	H	E	R	Comparative of HIGH.
H	I	G	H	L	Y	Largely, eminently, exceedingly, very, hugely, notably, surpassingly, exceedingly.
H	I	J	A	C	K	Hold up, rob, kidnap, acquire by force, coerce, hold to ransom.
H	I	K	I	N	G	Travelling on foot, tramping, walking, rambling, wandering. Boosting, raising.
H	I	N	D	E	R	Hold back, impede, obstruct, hamper, check, inhibit, restrain, handicap, deter.
H	I	N	G	E	D	Turned upon, focused on, revolved about. Depended on, hung on. Jointed. Flexible.
H	I	N	T	E	D	Implied, suggested, intimated, foreshadowed, insinuated, clued-up, cued.
H	I	N	T	E	R	One who HINTS.
H	I	P	P	E	D	Downcast, blue, dispirited, low, depressed, melancholic, dejected.
H	I	R	I	N	G	Contracting, chartering, renting, engaging, employing, leasing.
H	I	S	S	E	D	Sibilated, buzzed, whispered, wheezed, razzed, pooh-poohed, fizzed, fizzled.
H	I	S	S	E	R	One who HISSES.
H	I	T	H	E	R	To this place. Here.
H	I	T	T	E	R	Striker, buffeter, pounder. Slogger. One who delivers a stroke.
H	O	A	R	D	S	Plural of HOARD.
H	O	A	R	S	E	Husky, raucous, gruff, croaky, strident, harsh, dry, grating, jarring, rasping.
H	O	A	X	E	D	Past of HOAX.
H	O	A	X	E	R	Duper, hoodwinder, trickster, spoofer, faker, defrauder, joker.
H	O	B	B	L	E	Limp, move unsteadily, halting progress. Hamper, curb, restrain, shackle.
H	O	B	N	O	B	Visit, associate with, chat, talk informally, socialize.
H	O	C	K	E	Y	Outdoor ballgame. Ball and stick game.
H	O	E	I	N	G	Cultivating, weeding, raking, preparing the ground.
H	O	G	G	E	D	Past of HOG.
H	O	G	G	E	T	Young HOG.

1	2	3	4	5	6	
H	O	G	G	I	N	Soil planting mixture.
H	O	G	M	A	N	Hog farmer, swineheard, hog raiser.
H	O	I	S	T	S	Plural of HOIST.
H	O	L	D	E	R	Possessor, owner, proprietor. Licence holder, container.
H	O	L	D	U	P	Robbery, armed attack, hi-jack. Delay, postponement. suspension.
H	O	L	I	E	R	Comparative of HOLY.
H	O	L	I	L	Y	In a holy way. Piously. Soberly.
H	O	L	L	E	R	Shout, call, attract attention, cry out. vociferate, yell.
H	O	L	L	O	W	Cavernous, reverberant, resounding, resonant, echoing, reverberating. Empty.
H	O	M	A	G	E	Veneration, obeisance, deference, honour, loyalty, fealty, devotion.
H	O	M	E	L	Y	Plain, unadorned, simple, domestic, modest, unalluring, commonplace.
H	O	M	I	L	Y	Sermon, discourse, address, dissertation, exhortation, admonition.
H	O	M	I	N	G	Directing homewards, travelling home. Navigating to base. On target.
H	O	N	E	S	T	Truthful, straight, genuine, upright, honourable, candid, forthright, frank, open.
H	O	N	I	N	G	Sharpening, whetting, smoothing, enlarging. Grumbling.
H	O	N	K	E	D	Past of HONK.
H	O	N	O	U	R	Esteem, respect, homage, deference. Dignify, glorify, magnify. Decorate.
H	O	O	D	E	D	Furnished with a HOOD. Cowled. Distinctive head colour. Crested. Expanding neck.
H	O	O	D	I	E	Hoody. Carrion. Hooded Crow.
H	O	O	D	O	O	Jinx witchcraft, voodoo. Ill Luck. Hex.
H	O	O	F	E	D	Having Hooves. Ungulate.
H	O	O	F	E	R	Dancer, dancing girl, ballerina, danseuse. Tap Dancer. Professional Dancer.
H	O	O	K	A	H	Water pipe for smoking certain drugs.
H	O	O	K	E	D	Nabbed, copped, nailed, nicked, pinched. Addicted. Prone to.
H	O	O	K	E	R	Prostitute, call girl, harlot, hustler, streetwalker, whore.
H	O	O	K	U	P	Connection, communication link-up.
H	O	O	P	E	D	Encircled, girdled, surrounded. Looped, banded, ringed.
H	O	O	P	E	R	Hoop maker. Skin processor.
H	O	O	P	L	A	Fairground entertainment.
H	O	O	P	O	E	Hoopoo. Cinnamon coloured crested bird.
H	O	O	T	C	H	Strong drink. Alcoholic beverage. Spirits.
H	O	O	T	E	D	Honked, Tooted. Guffawed, catcalled, razzed.
H	O	O	T	E	R	Horn, siren, whistle. Calling device.
H	O	O	V	E	R	Vacuum cleaner trade name. To vacuum. Spring clean.
H	O	O	V	E	S	Plural of HOOF.
H	O	P	I	N	G	Wishing, expecting, awaiting, depending on, anticipating.
H	O	P	P	E	D	Past of HOP.
H	O	P	P	E	R	One that HOPS. Winged insect. Tripper. Flitabout. Chute. Feeder reservoir.
H	O	R	N	E	D	Having HORNS. Peaked. Horn-shaped. Meddled, interfered, intruded.
H	O	R	N	E	R	Horn-blower.
H	O	R	N	E	T	Stinging insect. Type of Wasp.
H	O	R	R	I	D	Horrible, terrible, hateful, abhorrent, detestable, offensive, disgusting, hideous.
H	O	R	R	O	R	Fear, alarm, terror, dismay, dread, panic, trepidation, abomination, repulsion.
H	O	R	S	E	D	Mounted.
H	O	S	I	E	R	Dealer in Hosiery.
H	O	S	T	E	L	Lodge, Inn, Boarding House. Wayside nightstop.
H	O	T	B	E	D	Rapid growth area. Fermenting environment. Breeding ground.
H	O	T	D	O	G	Sausage in a Breadroll. American staple.
H	O	T	E	L	S	Plural of HOTEL.
H	O	T	P	O	T	Meat and vegetable Stew.
H	O	T	R	O	D	Supercharged vehicle.
H	O	T	T	E	R	Comparative of HOT.
H	O	U	N	D	S	Plural of HOUND.
H	O	U	R	L	Y	Every Hour. On the Hour. At intervals of one Hour.
H	O	U	S	E	D	Sheltered, accommodated, harboured, quartered. Lodged.
H	O	V	E	L	S	Plural of HOVEL.
H	O	V	E	R	S	Hangs, floats, flutters, flickers, flits, dances, poises.
H	O	W	D	A	H	Covered pavilion on the back, of a camel or elephant. Seat, Saddle.
H	O	W	L	E	D	Past of HOWL.
H	O	W	L	E	R	One who HOWLS. Stupid blunder. Ridiculous mistake.
H	O	Y	D	E	N	Tomboy, boisterous girl. Clownish youth. Ill-bred person.
H	U	B	B	U	B	Hub-bub, uproar, commotion.
H	U	B	B	L	Y	Rowdy, boisterous.
H	U	B	B	U	B	Din, clamour, hullabaloo, racket, tumult, uproar, pandemonium, hassle.
H	U	D	D	L	E	Crouch, confer, consult, advise, assume, don, draw on, confusion, chaos.
H	U	F	F	E	D	Blustered, panted, gasped, heaved. Irritated, nettled, peeved, provoked, piqued.
H	U	G	E	L	Y	Enormously, vastly, largely, immensely, exceedingly, remarkably, strikingly.

1	2	3	4	5	6	
H	U	L	L	E	D	Dehusked. Separated.
H	U	L	L	E	R	Machine used for separating hulls.
H	U	M	A	N	E	Altruistic, charitable, good, humanitarian, benevolent, compassionate. Kind.
H	U	M	B	L	E	Meek, modest, unassuming, simple, unpretentious, subdued. Low, Debase, abash.
H	U	M	B	L	Y	In HUMBLE manner. Unobtrusively, submissively, quietly.
H	U	M	M	E	D	Past of HUM.
H	U	M	M	E	R	One who HUMS. Humdinger, hummingbird.
H	U	M	O	U	R	Sense of fun. Temper. Caprice. Comedy. Wit. Indulge, grafity, coddle, pamper.
H	U	M	O	U	S	Composition of fermented plant material. Relating to HUMUS. Mould.
H	U	M	P	E	D	Carried, conveyed, toted, transported. Hump-backed, Hunched.
H	U	N	G	E	R	Craving, desire, need, lack of food. Hanker, lust, pine, yearn.
H	U	N	G	R	Y	Lack of nourishment. Famished, starved, rapacious, starving, peckish.
H	U	N	K	E	R	Squat down, rest on haunches.
H	U	N	T	E	D	Past of HUNT.
H	U	N	T	E	R	One who HUNTS. Hunstsman, systematic searcher. Horse trained for jumping.
H	U	R	D	L	E	Fence, obstacle, impediment, obstruction. Clear, leap, surmount, vault. Overcome.
H	U	R	L	E	D	Past of HURL.
H	U	R	L	E	R	One who HURLS. Thrower, pitcher.
H	U	R	R	A	H	Expression of approval. Shout of triumph. Applause. Hurray.
H	U	R	T	L	E	Progress with speed. Move violently. Run, race, rush, headlong.
H	U	S	H	E	D	Quiet, subdued, suppressed, silenced; Placid, private, confidential.
H	U	S	K	E	D	Hulled, separated. Stripped.
H	U	S	K	E	R	Remover of husks. Separating machinery.
H	U	S	S	A	R	Hungarian cavalryman. Horseman.
H	U	S	S	I	F	Housewife. Housekeeper. Needle 'n Thread Container.
H	U	S	T	L	E	Hurry, bustle, jostle, rush, push, press, shove.
H	U	T	T	E	D	Housed in huts.
H	Y	B	R	I	D	Cross-breed. Offspring of two differing species. Composite. Variety. Bastard.
H	Y	M	E	N	S	Plural of HYMEN.
H	Y	M	N	A	L	Hymn book. Collection of bound Hymns.
H	Y	P	H	A	E	Fungus threads. Filaments.
H	Y	P	H	E	N	Punctuation mark. Line used to indicate division.
H	Y	S	S	O	P	Bunch of plants used in purification rites. Aromatic Mint. Sprinkling Device.

I

1	2	3	4	5	6	
I	A	M	B	I	C	Lampoon in verse. Satiric verse in Iambs.
I	A	M	B	U	S	Iambs. Metrical foot consisting of stressed and unstressed syllables.
I	B	E	R	I	S	Fleshy leaves. Candytuft.
I	B	I	D	E	M	Avoidance of repetition. Ibid.
I	C	A	R	U	S	Mythical Winged Greek.
I	C	E	A	G	E	Pleistocene Glacial epoch.
I	C	E	A	X	E	Mountain climbing tool. Ice-cutting device.
I	C	E	B	O	X	Refrigerator. Insulated cabinet.
I	C	E	C	A	P	Polar area of ice and snow.
I	C	E	M	A	N	Ice dealer. Ice-rink Superintendent.
I	C	E	S	A	W	Ice cutting machine.
I	C	I	C	L	E	Drop of frozen water. Emotionless person.
I	C	I	E	S	T	Superlative of ICY.
I	C	O	N	I	C	Like an ICON.
I	D	E	A	L	S	Plural of IDEAL.
I	D	I	O	C	Y	Incomplete brain development. Notably stupid. Foolishness, stupidity.
I	D	I	O	T	S	Plural of IDIOT.
I	D	I	O	M	S	Plura of IDIOM.
I	D	L	E	R	S	Plural of IDLER.
I	D	L	I	N	G	Wasting time, loafing, slouching, an engine running.
I	D	Y	L	L	S	Narrative Poems. Romantic interludes.
I	G	N	I	T	E	Set alight, enkindle, inflame, light, fire.
I	G	N	O	R	E	Disregard, overlook, neglect, omit, avoid, evade, discount.
I	G	U	A	N	A	Herbivorous Lizard.
I	L	E	U	M	S	Plural of ILEUM.
I	L	L	U	S	E	Maltreat, abuse.
I	M	A	G	E	D	Reflected, mirrored.
I	M	B	I	B	E	Absorb, assimilate, drink, swallow, quaff, consume.
I	M	B	R	E	X	Pantile, curved roof tile.
I	M	B	R	U	E	Drench, soak.

1	2	3	4	5	6	
I	M	B	U	E	D	Impregnated, dyed, permeated, tinged, infused.
I	M	M	I	E	S	Streaked glass marbles.
I	M	M	U	N	E	Protected, guarded, resistant, inoculated. Free, exempt.
I	M	M	U	R	E	Imprison, shut up, incarcerate. Cage, fence, pen, hedge. Confine, constrain.
I	M	P	A	C	T	Impinge upon. Collision, clash, shock, bump, jolt, jar, brunt, percussion.
I	M	P	A	I	R	Injure, damage, spoil, vitiate. Undermine, weaken, prejudice, mar.
I	M	P	A	L	A	South African antelope.
I	M	P	A	L	E	Transfix, pierce, spike, skewer, stab, puncture, perforate, prick.
I	M	P	A	R	T	Communicate, convey, transmit, bestow, pass on, confer, teach, divulge.
I	M	P	E	D	E	Hinder, halt, block, obstruct, thwart, brake, embarrass, discomfort.
I	M	P	E	N	D	Loom, gather, brew, threaten, approach, hover, menace, promise.
I	M	P	I	N	G	Mending in Falconry.
I	M	P	I	S	H	Roguish, devilish, frolicsome, naughty, troublesome, playful, coltish, puckish.
I	M	P	O	R	T	Meaning, gist, drift, implication. Moment, significance. Importation.
I	M	P	O	S	E	Inflict, ordain, prescribe, levy, foist, burden, saddle, infringe, intrude.
I	M	P	O	S	T	Tax, levy, duty, tariff, assessment, cess.
I	M	P	U	G	N	Contradict, deny, negate, cast doubt, traverse, question, gainsay, assail.
I	M	P	U	R	E	Unclean, sullied, immoral, carnal, indecent, sensual, foul, dirty, unholy.
I	M	P	U	T	E	Charge, ascribe, imply, hint, insinuate, intimate, refer, attribute.
I	N	B	O	N	D	Laid across. Bricks laid as headers.
I	N	B	O	R	N	Innate, indigenous, inherited, natural, inherent, ingrained.
I	N	B	R	E	D	Natural, inborn, intrinsic, constitutional, congenital.
I	N	C	E	S	T	Closely related interbreeding. Statutory crime of cohabitation between related persons.
I	N	C	H	E	D	Crept forward, eased, advanced slowly. Measured in inches.
I	N	C	H	E	S	Specified dimension in inches. Gun bore size.
I	N	C	I	S	E	Cut, gash, pierce, slice, slit, engrave, etch.
I	N	C	I	T	E	Motivate, foment, instigate, provoke, trigger, agitate, excite, goad, inflame.
I	N	C	O	M	E	Revenue, recurrent benefit, earnings, profit, wages, salary.
I	N	C	U	L	T	Coarse, crude, gross, rude, uncouth, rough, inelegant.
I	N	C	U	R	S	Entails, brings, renders, liable, accrues.
I	N	C	U	S	E	Stamp in. Punch.
I	N	D	A	B	A	Parley, talk, discussion, conference.
I	N	D	E	E	D	Truly, really, actually, honestly, in reality, undeniably, admittedly.
I	N	D	E	N	T	Order by importation. Cut into, curve inward, space up, form an indentation.
I	N	D	I	A	N	Native of India. Indigenous American. Characteristic of the Indies.
I	N	D	I	C	T	Formally accuse. Summon for trial. Charge with a crime. Decree, proclaim, accuse.
I	N	D	I	G	O	Blue Dye. Coloured Blue.
I	N	D	I	T	E	Inscribe, write, compose, verbalise.
I	N	D	O	O	R	Inside, within, in a building.
I	N	D	U	C	E	Encourage, incite, urge, engender, generate, cause, prompt, prevail.
I	N	D	U	C	T	Inaugurate, initiate, install, invest, introduce.
I	N	D	U	N	A	Bossboy, chief, overseer.
I	N	F	A	M	Y	Disgrace, dishonour, disrepute, ignominy, shame, discredit, obloquy.
I	N	F	A	N	T	Baby, newborn, young, juvenile, suckling, bantling.
I	N	F	E	C	T	Cause infection, transmit disease, taint, vitiate, corrupt, communicate, germs.
I	N	F	E	S	T	Spread, beset, swarm over, overrun, teem, annoy, plague, pester.
I	N	F	I	R	M	Weak, decrepit, unsubstantial, feeble, flimsy, unsound, fragile, ill, old.
I	N	F	L	O	W	Influx, inrush, gush, spout. Influence.
I	N	F	L	U	X	Inflow, inpouring, increase, inrush, augmentation, accession.
I	N	F	O	R	M	Advise, tell, inspire, warn, educate, instruct, enlighten. Rat, snitch, squeal. (Sl.).
I	N	F	U	S	E	Imbue, ingrain, steep, inform, inspire, implant, indoctrinate, intersperse.
I	N	G	E	S	T	Eat, devour, consume, absorb, swallow, partake of, feed on, digest.
I	N	H	A	L	E	Breathe in, draw breath, breathe deeply, inspire, draw in air.
I	N	H	E	R	E	Belong, fixed attribute. Consist, exist, reside, dwell.
I	N	H	U	M	E	Bury, inter, entomb.
I	N	J	E	C	T	Insert, force in, introduce by injection, intrude.
I	N	J	U	R	E	Harm, damage, hurt, impair, mar, wound, blemish, weaken, deface, distress.
I	N	J	U	R	Y	Inflicted pain, harm, outrage, ruin, discomfort, misery, suffering, grievance. Wound.
I	N	K	I	E	R	Comparative of INKY.
I	N	K	I	N	G	Marking with INK.
I	N	K	P	O	T	Ink container.
I	N	K	S	A	C	Ink containing organ of cephalapods.
I	N	L	A	I	D	Set into the surface. Decorative.
I	N	L	A	N	D	Interior, away from the Coast. Internal, domestic.
I	N	L	A	W	S	Plural of INLAW.
I	N	L	E	T	S	Plural of INLET.
I	N	M	A	T	E	Resident, guest, confined person, lodger, tenant, occupier, institutionalised person.

1	2	3	4	5	6	
I	N	M	O	S	T	Innermost, deepest, furthest in.
I	N	N	A	R	D	Internal organ. Interior. Viscera. Internal mechanism. Inner part.
I	N	N	A	T	E	Belonging inherently, inborn, hereditary, inherited, congenital, inbred, native.
I	N	N	E	R	S	Insides, interiors, essentials, secrets.
I	N	N	I	N	G	Gathering, enclosing, division of cricket match. Turn, chance.
I	N	R	O	A	D	Incursion, foray, invasion, raid, influx.
I	N	R	U	S	H	Influx, inpouring, inflow, gush.
I	N	S	A	N	E	Of unsound mind. Mad, deranged, distraught, mental, nutty, irrational, crazy.
I	N	S	E	C	T	Segmented invertebrate animal.
I	N	S	E	R	T	Inset, insertion, injection, attachment. Introduce, interpolate, inject.
I	N	S	I	D	E	Interior, inwards, within. Inner, internal, Indoors, within.
I	N	S	I	S	T	Urge, demand, maintain, persist, persevere, press, clamour, importune.
I	N	S	O	L	E	Inner sole. Foot comfort.
I	N	S	P	A	N	Yoke, harness, hitch up.
I	N	S	T	E	P	Middle portion of human foot. Behind the hock of horse's hind leg.
I	N	S	U	L	T	Affront, abuse, ridicule, offend, humiliate. Jeer, scoff, scorn. Contempt, disdain.
I	N	S	U	R	E	Assure against loss. Procure insurance. Ensure, underwrite, guarantee, protect.
I	N	T	A	C	T	Whole, perfect, unblemished, unimpaired, virgin, maiden, flawless.
I	N	T	A	K	E	Aperture, enclosure, opening; act of taking in. Absorption, Inlet.
I	N	T	E	N	D	Signify, mean, denote, import. Design, plan, purpose. Endeavour, strive, try.
I	N	T	E	N	T	Intention, design, purpose, volition, will. Meaning, significance, sense, bent.
I	N	T	E	R	N	Confine, segregate, lock up, imprison, constrain, immure, jail, incarcerate.
I	N	T	O	N	E	Chant, utter prolonged musical tones, sing, cant, recite, utter, say.
I	N	U	N	C	T	Annoint.
I	N	U	R	E	D	Accustomed, familiarized, used, trained, disciplined.
I	N	V	A	D	E	Encroach, infringe, intrude, trespass, assault, penetrate, engulf, violate, raid.
I	N	V	E	N	T	Concoct, formulate, frame, contrive, devise, conceive, create, produce, initiate.
I	N	V	E	R	T	Reverse, transpose, turn, flip; upset, overturn. Homosexual, queer, fag.
I	N	V	E	S	T	Commit money. Speculate, initiate. Authorise, vest, infuse, imbue, beset, Array.
I	N	V	I	T	E	Ask, bid, request, solicit, summon, woo, tempt, lure, inveigle, entice.
I	N	V	O	K	E	Beg, beseech, plead, supplicate, implement, importune, implore, entreat.
I	N	W	A	R	D	Inner, internal, inside, interior, innermost, within. Homeward. Essence, spirit.
I	O	D	I	N	E	Violet coloured antiseptic. Marine plant extract. Thyroid essential element.
I	O	D	I	Z	E	Treat with Iodine. Preventive treatment.
I	O	N	I	A	N	Member of Greek philosophers' school.
I	O	N	I	Z	E	Convert into Ions.
I	R	E	F	U	L	Angry, irate, wrathful, irascible, cranky, ratty, touchy, incensed, cross.
I	R	K	I	N	G	Bothering, harrassing, annoying, provoking, vexing, boring, tiring.
I	R	O	N	E	D	Past of IRON.
I	R	O	N	E	R	One who IRONS. Laundry machine operator.
I	R	O	N	I	C	Sardonic, cynical, cutting, wry, caustic, scathing, expressing irony.
I	R	R	U	P	T	Erupt, disgorge, eject, expel, spew, belch.
I	S	L	A	N	D	Isle, land surrounded by water. Insulate, isolate, cut off, separate.
I	S	N	E	S	S	Factual existence, things as they are. State of being.
I	S	O	B	A	R	Imaginary line on a Map. Atom with different chemical proportions.
I	S	R	A	E	L	The Promised Land. Jewish Homeland.
I	S	S	U	E	D	Distributed, effected, sprang, proceeded, gave off, released, vented, published.
I	S	S	U	E	R	Distributor, operator, publisher.
I	S	S	U	E	S	Plural of ISSUE.
I	T	A	L	I	C	Underscored letters, underlined type. Emphasized meaning.
I	T	C	H	E	D	Past of ITCH.
I	T	S	E	L	F	Pronoun. The identical one.

J

1	2	3	4	5	6	
J	A	B	B	E	D	Stabbed, poked, prodded, punched.
J	A	B	B	E	R	Talk rapidly, chatter, utter nonsense, gibber, babble.
J	A	C	E	N	T	Recumbent, prone.
J	A	C	K	A	L	Wild dog that hunts in a pack. Servant, Drudge.
J	A	C	K	E	D	Hoisted, supported, lifted, hitched.
J	A	C	K	E	T	Coat, garment, casing, covering, book cover, protective wrapper, paper envelope.
J	A	D	I	S	H	Like a JADE. Overworked, worthless. Minx-like. Impish.
J	A	E	G	E	R	Armed German HUNTER.
J	A	G	G	E	D	Serrated, ragged, rough, craggy, uneven, rugged, irregular.
J	A	G	G	E	R	Pedlar, packhorse. Thorn, bramble. Frayed cable wire.
J	A	G	U	A	R	Luxury Motorcar. Powerful animal of the cat family.

(178)

1	2	3	4	5	6	
J	A	I	L	E	D	Imprisoned, confined, constrained, interned, incarcerated.
J	A	I	L	E	R	Warder, turnkey, guard.
J	A	M	M	E	D	Squeezed, squashed, pressed, rammed, crushed, pushed.
J	A	N	G	L	E	Discordant sound, clash. Discord, conflict, jar, disharmony. Din, clamour.
J	A	R	G	O	N	Terminology, language, dialect, lingo, patois, patter, slang, vernacular.
J	A	R	R	E	D	Wrangled, grated, bumped, clashed, jangled.
J	A	S	P	E	R	Opaque quartz. Dark Green.
J	A	U	N	T	S	Plural of JAUNT.
J	A	U	N	T	Y	Sprightly, airy, stylish, fashionable. Perky, debonair.
J	A	W	I	N	G	Scolding, telling-off, lecture, tongue-lashing.
J	E	E	R	E	D	Past of JEER.
J	E	E	R	E	R	One who JEERS. Scoffer, sneerer, jester.
J	E	N	N	E	T	Female donkey, Spanish horse, hinny, jenny.
J	E	R	B	O	A	Jumping rodent.
J	E	R	K	E	D	Past of JERK.
J	E	R	K	E	R	One who JERKS.
J	E	R	K	I	N	Jacket, hip-length belted coat.
J	E	R	S	E	Y	Pullover, cardigan, knitted garment. Woollen tubular closefitting garment. Breed of Cattle.
J	E	S	T	E	D	Joked, wisecracked, chaffed, bantered, scoffed, ribbed, razzed, joshed.
J	E	S	T	E	E	Laughingstock, pilgarlic, sport.
J	E	S	T	E	R	Fool, humorist, comedian, comic, wit, wag, joker, motley.
J	E	S	U	I	T	Member of a religious society. Crafty person. One given to intrigue.
J	E	T	S	A	M	Equipment cast overboard. Distinguished from FLOTSAM.
J	E	T	S	E	T	Beautiful people. Swingers. Fast and Fun.
J	E	T	T	E	D	Flew by JET. Sprayed, spewed.
J	E	T	T	E	R	One who JETS. Jet plane flyer.
J	E	W	E	L	S	Plural of JEWEL.
J	E	W	E	S	S	Female Jew.
J	E	W	I	S	H	Yiddish.
J	I	B	B	E	D	Balked, gagged, shied, stumbled, demurred.
J	I	B	B	E	R	Balky horse.
J	I	B	I	N	G	Tacking, changing course. Objecting.
J	I	G	G	E	D	Past of JIG.
J	I	G	G	E	R	Jig Operator. Measurement of liquid. Gadget. Golf Iron. Fish Trap.
J	I	G	G	L	E	Jerk, jog, shake, wriggle, jolt, oscillating movement.
J	I	G	S	A	W	Puzzle. Machine saw.
J	I	L	T	E	D	Rejected, discarded, cast off. Set aside.
J	I	N	G	L	E	Metallic sound. Clinking. Tinkle. Musical verses. Catchy advertising.
J	I	T	T	E	R	Jig continuously. Nervous movement. Jerk. Random movement.
J	O	B	B	E	R	Dealer. Stockbroker. Retailer.
J	O	B	L	O	T	Odd lot. Less than one hundred. Miscellany.
J	O	C	K	E	Y	Horse rider. Driver, Operator. Manoeuvre, manipulate, outwit.
J	O	C	O	S	E	Witty, humorous, jocular, playful, whimsical, jovial, blithe, jocund.
J	O	C	U	N	D	Merry, jocose, festive, gay, jolly, playful, sportive, mischievous.
J	O	G	G	E	D	Plodded, cantered, trudged; Jolted, nudged, pushed. Jostled.
J	O	G	G	E	R	One who JOGS. Runner, exercise, road runner, jog-trotter.
J	O	G	G	L	E	Shake, jiggle, jog, jerk, bump.
J	O	H	N	N	Y	Short jacket with back opening worn by hospital patients. Toilet (Sl.)
J	O	I	N	E	D	Connected, coupled, united, associated, married, articulated. Entered, enlisted.
J	O	I	N	E	R	Woodworker, carpenter. Jointer. One who joins organisations.
J	O	K	E	R	S	Plural of JOKER.
J	O	K	I	N	G	Jesting, playing, ragging, ribbing, wisecracking, quipping, bantering.
J	O	L	T	E	D	Jogged, jounced, jarred, bumped, jerked, jogged.
J	O	L	T	E	R	One who JOLTS.
J	O	R	D	A	N	River. Machine for Refining paper.
J	O	S	E	P	H	Cloak. Women's riding habit.
J	O	S	H	E	R	Joker, kidder, practical joker, jester.
J	O	S	T	L	E	Jog, hustle, elbow, joggle, bump, push, press, shoulder, shove.
J	O	T	T	E	D	Noted, recorded, wrote down rapidly.
J	O	T	T	E	R	Note taker. Memorandum. Notebook. Scribbler.
J	O	U	N	C	E	Jolt, bounce, bump, jar, shake, jig.
J	O	V	I	A	L	Genial, convivial, happy, merry, jocular, affable, sociable, good-natured.
J	O	Y	F	U	L	Happy, joyous, buoyant, lighthearted, glad, blithe, expansive.
J	O	Y	O	U	S	Joyful, happy, cheerful, rapturous, glad.
J	U	D	A	I	C	Characteristic of Jews. Jewish.
J	U	D	D	E	R	Jar, vibrate, shudder violently.
J	U	D	G	E	D	Past of JUDGE.

1	2	3	4	5	6	
J	U	D	G	E	S	Plural of JUDGE.
J	U	G	F	U	L	Full measure, filled jug. Good deal.
J	U	G	G	E	D	Past of JUG.
J	U	G	G	L	E	Manual dexterity, manipulate, trick, cheat, deceive. Conjure, shuffle, toss.
J	U	I	C	E	R	Juicing machine, juice extractor.
J	U	J	U	B	E	Succulent fruit drop. Gumdrop, fruity lozenges.
J	U	L	I	A	N	Roman calendar.
J	U	L	I	E	T	High-fronted slipper. Skullcap.
J	U	M	B	L	E	Miscellany, clutter, litter, medley, pot-pourri; Scramble, rummage, tumble.
J	U	M	P	E	D	Past of JUMP.
J	U	M	P	E	R	One who JUMPS. Jersey, pullover. Saddle Horse. Circuit breaker. Ploughshare.
J	U	N	G	L	E	Tangled thicket. Impenetrable vegetation. Confused mass. Clutter, muddle, maze.
J	U	N	I	O	R	Young person. Youthful. Son, offspring, adolescent. The younger.
J	U	N	K	E	R	Young German noble. Prussian aristocrat.
J	U	N	K	E	T	Banquet, Feast, Excursion. Jaunt. Confection, sweet dish. Flavoured curds. Dessert.
J	U	R	I	S	T	Scholar, Lawyer, Judge, Philosopher.
J	U	S	T	E	R	Comparative of JUST.
J	U	S	T	L	Y	Fairly, rightly, impartially, precisely, constantly.
J	U	T	T	E	D	Protruded, projected, stuck out, bulged, poked, extended, pouted.

K

1	2	3	4	5	6	
K	A	F	F	I	R	Obsolete name for indigenous South African.
K	A	F	T	A	N	Ankle-length wide-sleeved full garment. Eastern dress.
K	A	I	S	E	R	Ruler, Emperor, Sovereign. Head of German States.
K	A	N	O	N	E	Expert Skier.
K	A	N	O	O	N	Zither.
K	A	O	L	I	N	Medicinal clay. Aluminous mineral.
K	A	R	A	K	A	Musical percussion instrument. Seeded Gourd.
K	A	R	A	T	E	Japanese system of weaponless self defence.
K	A	R	O	S	S	Animal skin coverlet.
K	A	R	R	O	O	Dry scrubland in South Africa.
K	A	S	B	A	H	Casbah, Fortress. North African native section. Nightlife area.
K	E	D	G	E	D	Towed by rope.
K	E	E	L	E	D	Keel-shaped, carinated, Ridged.
K	E	E	L	E	R	Shallow washing tub.
K	E	E	N	E	R	Professional female mourner. Comparative of KEEN.
K	E	E	N	L	Y	Sharply, intelligently, acutely, perceptively, sensitively, astutely, fiercely.
K	E	E	P	E	R	Guard, warden, custodian, guardian, claviger, animal-trainer.
K	E	N	N	E	L	Dog shelter, animal lodge, Gutter.
K	E	R	N	E	L	Core, nub, meat, substance, crux, gist, upshot.
K	E	T	T	L	E	Water boiling vessel. Cooking utensil. Boiling Pot.
K	E	W	P	I	E	Cupid doll. Chubby fairy doll.
K	E	Y	M	A	N	Vitally important worker. Indispensable personnel.
K	E	Y	P	I	N	Pivot, central character, V.I.P.
K	I	B	I	T	Z	Interfere, Unwelcome observation, unwelcome comment.
K	I	B	O	S	H	Halt, check, stop, rein, resistance.
K	I	C	K	E	D	Past of KICK.
K	I	C	K	E	R	One who KICKS.
K	I	D	D	E	D	Fooled, duped, hoaxed, bamboozled. Told tall stories.
K	I	D	D	E	R	Hoaxer, tall story teller, joker, jester.
K	I	D	N	A	P	Abduct, carry off, shanghai, snatch, spirit away.
K	I	D	N	E	Y	One of pair of internal organs of vertebrates.
K	I	L	L	E	D	Past of KILL.
K	I	L	L	E	R	One who KILLS. Murderer, slayer. Lady's man.
K	I	L	T	E	D	Wearing a KILT.
K	I	L	T	E	R	Condition, fitness, fettle, shape, trim, repair.
K	I	M	O	N	O	Japanese Wrap. Body Robe. Wrapper.
K	I	N	D	E	R	Comparative of KIND.
K	I	N	D	L	E	Light, ignite. inflame, excite, stimulate. Stir, arouse, challenge. Rouse, waken.
K	I	N	D	L	Y	Benevolent, convenial, considerate. Thoughtfully, generously, well. Benign.
K	I	N	E	M	A	Cinema, bioscope, movies.
K	I	N	G	L	Y	Regal, Royal, imperial, august, majestic, sovereign. Imperious, powerful.
K	I	N	K	E	D	Curled, crimped, twisted, plaited, snarled, crooked.
K	I	P	P	E	R	Smoked fish. Breakfast dish. Smoked herring.
K	I	R	S	C	H	Colourless cherry brandy.

1	2	3	4	5	6	
K	I	R	T	L	E	Tunic-like garment. Long gown.
K	I	S	M	E	T	Fate, destiny, circumstance, lot, portion.
K	I	S	S	E	D	Past of KISS.
K	I	S	S	E	R	(Sl.) Face, features, countenance, visage, mug, pan.
K	I	T	B	A	G	Army holdall.
K	I	T	T	E	N	Small cat. Young feline.
K	L	A	X	O	N	Siren, warning signal, horn, loud honking device.
K	N	A	G	G	Y	Cragged, rough, rugged. Knotty.
K	N	A	R	R	Y	Gnarled, knotty.
K	N	A	V	E	S	Plural of KNAVE.
K	N	I	F	E	D	Stabbed, cut, slashed, wounded.
K	N	I	G	H	T	Member of special order of Knighthood. Chivalrous man. Chess piece. Champion.
K	N	I	V	E	S	Plural of KNIFE.
K	N	O	B	B	Y	Knotty, hilly, bumpy. Obstinate, hard, intricate, perplexing.
K	N	O	T	T	Y	Problematical, difficult, intricate, thought-provoking, complex. Bumpy, knobby.
K	N	O	W	E	R	One that knows.
K	O	O	D	O	O	Kudu, South African Antelope.
K	O	S	H	E	R	Ritually clean, fit to eat in Jewish Law. Proper. Legitimate, genuine.
K	O	W	T	O	W	Bow down, acquiesce, fawn, grovel, toady, cower, cringe.
K	R	A	N	T	Z	Rocky promontory. Precipice, cliff.
K	U	L	T	U	R	German culture.
K	U	M	K	U	M	Red mark on Indian's forehead. Red tumeric powder.
K	U	M	M	E	L	Caraway flavoured liqueur.

L

1	2	3	4	5	6	
L	A	A	G	E	R	Encampment, outspan, defensive position. Wagon circle, bivouac.
L	A	B	E	L	S	Plural of LABEL.
L	A	B	I	A	L	Relating to lips. Liplike. Flue pipe. Lip scale in snakes. Consonant.
L	A	B	I	L	E	Changeable, unstable, uncertain, unsteady.
L	A	B	I	U	M	Fold on margin of the Vulva. Liplike margin.
L	A	B	O	U	R	Work, toil, industry, drudge, earning power, Industry. Chilbearing. Struggle.
L	A	C	I	N	G	Threading, fastening. Adding alcohol. Trouncing. Beating. Lashing. Intertwining.
L	A	C	K	E	D	Needed, wanted, required, in short supply.
L	A	C	K	E	Y	Flunkey, attendant, footman, servant, follower, hanger-on, toady.
L	A	C	T	I	C	Relating to Milk.
L	A	D	D	E	R	Clambering aid, climbing steps. Builder's equipment. Stocking rent.
L	A	D	D	I	E	Lad, boy, shaveling, stripling, son.
L	A	D	I	D	A	Precious, affected, refined, genteel, mincing, stilted, pretentious.
L	A	D	I	E	S	Plural of LADY.
L	A	D	I	N	G	Load, cargo, freight, burden, haul, payload.
L	A	D	L	E	D	Spooned, dispensed, provided, gave, dished out.
L	A	G	G	E	D	Delayed, retarded, dwelt, loitered, dallied.
L	A	G	G	E	R	Laggard, loiterer, idler, loafer.
L	A	G	O	O	N	Lake, channel, shallow, sound, pond.
L	A	I	R	D	S	Plural of LAIRD.
L	A	M	B	E	D	Brought forth a lamb. Gave birth to a lamb.
L	A	M	B	E	R	Ewe that is lambing.
L	A	M	E	L	Y	In a lame manner. Haltingly, inarticulately, limply.
L	A	M	E	N	T	Bewail, grieve, moan, weep, deplore, cry, bemoan.
L	A	M	I	N	A	Thin plate, layer, flake.
L	A	M	I	N	G	Wounding, crippling, disabling.
L	A	M	I	S	H	Somewhat LAME. Lamely.
L	A	M	M	A	S	First day of August. Day of the consecration of Loaves.
L	A	M	M	E	D	Battered, hammered, pelted, pummelled, thrashed. Escaped, broke out. ran away.
L	A	M	P	A	S	Upholstery brocade.
L	A	N	C	E	D	Past of LANCE.
L	A	N	C	E	R	Armed cavalry soldier.
L	A	N	C	E	T	Dart, Lance, Javelin.
L	A	N	D	A	U	Four-wheeled covered carriage.
L	A	N	D	E	D	Disembarked, alighted, perched, settled, touched down. Acquired, gained. Owning land.
L	A	N	T	U	M	Large Hurdy-gurdy.
L	A	P	D	O	G	Small pet dog.
L	A	P	F	U	L	A full lap. Cuddly bundle.
L	A	P	P	E	D	Past of LAP.
L	A	P	P	E	R	Textile worker.

1	2	3	4	5	6	
L	A	P	P	E	T	Hat Streamer. Flap.
L	A	P	S	E	D	Nullified, surrendered, vanished, dropped out.
L	A	R	D	E	D	Inserted strips of fat. Prepared meat for cooking.
L	A	R	D	E	R	Pantry, storehouse, storeroom for food.
L	A	R	G	E	R	Comparative of LARGE.
L	A	R	I	A	T	Lassoo, rope noose, strip of hide with running noose.
L	A	R	R	U	P	Beat, flog, whip, thrash, whale, wallop, lather, lash, flagellate.
L	A	R	V	A	E	Wingless insects in feeding form. Grubs, maggots, pupas, Nymphs.
L	A	R	V	A	L	Relating to Larva.
L	A	R	Y	N	X	Upper part of breathing passage. Respiratory tract. Vocal cords.
L	A	S	C	A	R	East Indian seaman.
L	A	S	H	E	D	Bolted, tied. Whipped. Drenched, teemed. Lambasted, flayed.
L	A	S	H	E	R	Whipper. Weir, Pool.
L	A	S	H	E	S	Plural of LASH.
L	A	S	S	I	E	Girl, maid, damsel, gal, wench, miss.
L	A	S	T	E	D	Endured, continued, remained, abided, persisted.
L	A	S	T	E	R	Leather stretching tool. Tool operator.
L	A	S	T	L	Y	Finally, ultimately, eventually, latterly, utmost.
L	A	T	E	E	N	Type of rigging. Sail.
L	A	T	E	L	Y	Recently, latterly, of late, anew, afresh.
L	A	T	E	N	T	Dormant, lurking, potential, quiescent. Concealed, inert, immature, unripe.
L	A	T	E	S	T	Last, final, concluding, eventual, terminal, hindmost, closing.
L	A	T	H	E	R	Foam, soapy froth, suds; excitement, agitation. Whip, thrash. Spume. Hassle.
L	A	T	I	S	H	Somewhat late. Rather late.
L	A	T	T	E	R	Last, concluding, final, latest, terminal, eventual, modern, recent.
L	A	U	D	E	D	Extolled, praised, eulogised, glorified, venerated, admired, flattered.
L	A	U	D	E	R	Eulogist, supporter.
L	A	U	G	H	S	Plural of LAUGH.
L	A	U	N	C	H	Begin, commence, initiate, kick off, inaugurate. Boat. Small craft.
L	A	U	R	E	L	Shrub. Bay leaves. Aromatic leaves. Reputation. Decoration.
L	A	V	I	N	G	Lapping, bathing, washing.
L	A	V	I	S	H	Dissipate, dispense luxury, squander. Profuse, lush, opulent, grand, sumptuous.
L	A	W	F	U	L	Within the Law. Legitimate, legal, correct, right, bonafide, justifiable.
L	A	W	Y	E	R	Specialist in the practice of the Law. Counsellor, solicitor, attorney.
L	A	X	I	S	T	Believer in laxism.
L	A	X	I	T	Y	Slackness, forgetfulness, carelessness, oblivion, looseness.
L	A	Y	I	N	G	Placing, imputing, betting, producing, setting.
L	A	Y	M	A	N	Member of laity. Non-clergy. Non-professional.
L	A	Y	O	F	F	Suspend, dismiss, halt, stop work, cease activities. Unproductive period.
L	A	Y	O	U	T	Plan, design, arrangement, map, set out. Spend, expend, outlay, pay, disburse.
L	A	Z	I	E	R	Comparative of LAZY.
L	A	Z	I	L	Y	Slothfully, Idly, sluggishly, supinely, inertly, languidly, listlessly negligently.
L	A	Z	I	N	G	Drowsing, idling, dawdling, loitering, lolling, loafing, lounging.
L	E	A	D	E	D	Set in Lead.
L	E	A	D	E	N	Heavy, dun, grey, sluggish, expressionless, inert, dull, oppressive, dragging.
L	E	A	D	E	R	Chief, guide, pacesetter, conductor, commander, boss, notable, dignitary.
L	E	A	D	I	N	Antenna, guide, arrow, electrical conductor.
L	E	A	F	E	D	Browsed, flipped through, riffled, scanned, skimmed, thumbed. Having leaves.
L	E	A	G	U	E	Alliance, union, association, confederation, society, class, division. Combine.
L	E	A	K	E	D	Oozed, dripped, percolated, transpired, gossiped, divulged.
L	E	A	N	E	D	Leant, inclined, relied, slanted, listed, sloped, tilted, tipped, reclined.
L	E	A	N	E	R	Comparative of LEAN. Thinner, skimpier, less fat, skinnier, slimmer.
L	E	A	N	L	Y	In lean manner. Thinly, gauntly, scantily, haggardly.
L	E	A	N	T	O	Shed, shelter, barn section.
L	E	A	P	E	D	Sprang, skipped, leapt, jumped, bounded, hurdled, mounted, soared.
L	E	A	P	E	R	One who LEAPS. Jumper, springer, bounder.
L	E	A	S	E	D	Hired, let, rented, chartered.
L	E	A	S	E	R	One who LEASES.
L	E	A	V	E	D	Having characteristic leaves.
L	E	A	V	E	N	Infuse, imbue, inoculate, steep, suffuse, temper, quicken, ingrain, invest. Ferment.
L	E	A	V	E	R	One who LEAVES. Deserter, quitter, school-leaver.
L	E	C	T	I	N	Anti-body.
L	E	C	T	O	R	Public lecturer. Lesson reader.
L	E	D	G	E	R	Accounts book of business transactions. Memorial Stone. Horizontal timber.
L	E	E	R	E	D	Past of LEER.
L	E	E	W	A	Y	Latitude, scope, margin, elbow room, play.
L	E	G	A	C	Y	Bequest, inheritance, birthright, patrimony, gift, heritage.

1	2	3	4	5	6	
L	E	G	A	T	E	Ecclesiastical representative, Nuncio, Delegate.
L	E	G	A	T	O	Smooth musical passage.
L	E	G	B	Y	E	Cricket ball bounced of the batman's person.
L	E	G	E	N	D	Myth, fairy tale, fiction, fable. Lore, tradition. Caption, description.
L	E	G	G	E	D	Walked, marched, hiked. Type of Legs.
L	E	G	I	O	N	Horde, multitude, army, host, many, numerous, several, various, scores.
L	E	G	I	S	T	Specialist in Law. law student.
L	E	G	L	E	T	Ornament worn on the Leg.
L	E	G	M	A	N	Newspaperman, Reporter.
L	E	G	U	M	E	Seed of leguminous plant. Pea. Bean.
L	E	M	O	N	S	Plural of LEMON.
L	E	N	D	E	R	One who LENDS. Money lender.
L	E	N	G	T	H	Yardage, extent, duration, time, distance, stretch, range, orbit, reach, scope.
L	E	N	I	T	Y	Leniency, gentleness, mildness.
L	E	N	T	E	N	Relating to Lent. Meagre, spare, sparse.
L	E	N	T	I	L	Seed bearing plant, pea-like vegetable. Pulse.
L	E	P	E	R	S	Plural of LEPER.
L	E	P	P	E	R	Skilled jumping horse.
L	E	S	I	O	N	Injury, scar, flaw, impairment.
L	E	S	S	E	E	Tenant, one who leases, occupier.
L	E	S	S	E	N	Curtail, diminish, decrease, reduce, abridge, dwindle, dilute, weaken, drain.
L	E	S	S	E	R	Inferior, minor, secondary, small, insignificant, lower, under, subjacent.
L	E	S	S	O	N	Exercise, study, course. Reprimand, reproach, rebuke, admonishment.
L	E	S	S	O	R	Lease holder, landlord, rentor, property owner.
L	E	T	H	A	L	Fatal, deadly, mortal, pestilential, deathly, poisonous, venemous.
L	E	T	O	F	F	Reprieve, forgiveness. Release gadget.
L	E	T	O	U	T	Release, loosen, free.
L	E	T	T	E	R	Epistle, communication, missive, note. Memorandum, message, despatch. Alphabet.
L	E	V	A	N	T	Eastern, Levantine.
L	E	V	E	E	S	Plural of LEVEE.
L	E	V	E	L	S	Plural of LEVEL.
L	E	V	E	R	S	Plural of LEVER.
L	E	V	I	E	D	Past of LEVY.
L	E	V	I	T	E	Descendant of Levi. Jewish priestly assistant. Deason.
L	E	V	I	T	Y	Frivolity, lightness, flightiness, flippancy, inconstancy, absurdity.
L	E	W	D	L	Y	Coarsely, lustfully, licentiously, indecently, obscenely.
L	I	A	B	L	E	Responsible, answerable, likely, subject,exposed, susceptible, inclined to.
L	I	A	I	S	E	Establish liaison, form relationship, meet, become acquainted.
L	I	B	A	T	E	Pour out, drink alcohol, make an offering.
L	I	B	E	L	S	Plural of LIBEL.
L	I	B	I	D	O	Psychic energy, biological urges, sexual desire, lustful striving.
L	I	C	H	E	N	Parasitic tree growth. Moss.
L	I	C	K	E	D	Past of LICK.
L	I	C	K	E	R	One that LICKS.
L	I	D	D	E	D	Having LIDS. Covered, topped, stoppered, capped.
L	I	E	D	E	R	German Songs.
L	I	F	T	E	D	Elevated, assisted, carried, raised, reared, hoisted, heaved, boosted.
L	I	F	T	E	R	Lifting device, hoisting apparatus. Elevator. Kitchen utensil. Thief.
L	I	G	A	T	E	Tie with a ligature.
L	I	G	H	T	S	Plural of LIGHT. Offal.
L	I	G	N	U	M	Type of Tree. Woody tissue.
L	I	K	E	L	Y	Probable, conceivable, doubtless. Agreeable, hopeful, encouraging, promising.
L	I	K	I	N	G	Fondness, love, regard, inclination, fancy, weakness, taste, partially.
L	I	L	T	E	D	Sung cheerfully, gaily, tunefully, rythmically.
L	I	M	B	E	D	Having LIMBS.
L	I	M	B	E	R	Make supple, pliant, flexible, lithe.
L	I	M	I	N	G	Snaring with birdlime, entangle, catch. Whitewashing. Coating.
L	I	M	I	T	S	Plural of LIMIT.
L	I	M	M	E	R	Scoundrel, idler. Prostitute.
L	I	M	N	E	D	Painted, illuminated, embellished.
L	I	M	N	E	R	Illuminator, itinerant artist.
L	I	M	O	U	S	Slimy, muddy, sticky, tacky.
L	I	M	P	E	D	Past of LIMP.
L	I	M	P	E	R	One who LIMPS. Injured, wounded, lame.
L	I	M	P	E	T	Gastropod mollusc. Clinging person. Bore.
L	I	M	P	I	D	Clear, colourless, untroubled, serene. Transparent, translucent. Lucid.
L	I	N	A	G	E	Estimated number of lines for printing. Space. Payment by line.

1	2	3	4	5	6	
L	I	N	D	E	N	Tall Forest Tree. Decorative Tree.
L	I	N	E	A	L	Direct, linear, heriditary, relating to direct descent. Line of succession.
L	I	N	E	A	R	Straight direction. Horizontal, proportionate relationship. Ectomorphic.
L	I	N	E	R	S	Plural of LINER.
L	I	N	E	U	P	Align, line, range, correct positioning, alignment.
L	I	N	G	E	R	Remain, tarry, wait, stay, abide, delay, procrastinate, amble, lag, dawdle.
L	I	N	I	N	G	Layer of fabric, material insert, alignment. Inner piece.
L	I	N	K	E	D	Connected, conjoined, united, jointed, bonded, tied, joined, knotted.
L	I	N	N	E	T	Small Finch.
L	I	N	T	E	L	Horizontal architectural span.
L	I	O	N	E	T	Small Lion.
L	I	P	P	E	D	Having a raised edge, having a lip.
L	I	P	P	E	R	Glass lip shaper.
L	I	Q	U	I	D	Fluid, liquor, running, flowing, melting, soft. Mellow, honeyed.
L	I	Q	U	O	R	Spirits, beverage, strong drink, alcohol, intoxicant. (Sl.) Grog, booze.
L	I	S	P	E	D	Past of LISP.
L	I	S	P	E	R	Someone who LISPS.
L	I	S	S	O	M	Agile, pliant, supple, lithe, limber.
L	I	S	T	E	D	Written down, noted, registered, catalogued, scheduled. Inclined, canted, leaned.
L	I	S	T	E	N	Hear, harken, attend, eavesdrop, heed.
L	I	S	T	E	R	Recorder, Note-taker, Itemizer, assessor.
L	I	T	A	N	Y	Prayerful supplication. Ritualistic repetition. Chant, Recital.
L	I	T	C	H	I	Tropical succulent fruit.
L	I	T	H	E	R	Comparative of LITHE.
L	I	T	M	U	S	Acid and Alkaline sensitive material.
L	I	T	T	E	R	Rubbish, trash, garbage, disorder, confusion. Strew, scatter, upset.
L	I	T	T	L	E	Small, diminutive, tiny, trivial, inconsiderable, mean, paltry, slight.
L	I	V	E	L	Y	Animated, alert, eager, vigorous, keen, joyful, spirited, energetic, nimble.
L	I	V	E	R	S	Plural of LIVER.
L	I	V	E	R	Y	Costume, Uniform, dress. Retainer's outfit. Liverish. Horse stabling.
L	I	V	I	N	G	Livelihood, sustenance, support, maintenance. Alive, breathing, quick, active.
L	I	Z	A	R	D	Long-bodied reptile.
L	O	A	D	E	D	Laden, burdened, encumbered, filled, charged. (Sl.) Intoxicated.
L	O	A	D	E	R	Transport worker. Container filler. Scoop, bucket conveyer, belt attendant.
L	O	A	F	E	D	Past of LOAF.
L	O	A	F	E	R	Idler, vagabond, lounger, vagrant, bum, slouch, sluggard.
L	O	A	N	E	D	Lent, advanced, property borrowed.
L	O	A	T	H	E	Hate, abhor, detest, abominate, dislike. Disinclined, unwilling.
L	O	A	V	E	S	Plural of LOAF.
L	O	B	A	T	E	Having LOBES.
L	O	B	B	E	D	Pitched, tossed, bowl slowly, throw softly, hit high ball.
L	O	B	O	L	A	Bride price.
L	O	C	A	L	E	Scene, site, area, neighbourhood, vicinity, district.
L	O	C	A	T	E	Fix, establish, place, situate, position, site. Discover, find, uncover.
L	O	C	K	E	D	Past of LOCK.
L	O	C	K	E	R	Compartment, cupboard, lock-up, storage space, chest.
L	O	C	K	E	T	Pendant, necklace, ornament.
L	O	C	K	U	P	Prison, Jail, Gaol, penitentiary. Locking area, Safe place.
L	O	C	U	S	T	Grasshopper. Tall tree.
L	O	D	G	E	D	Housed, harboured, dwelt. Quartered. Resided. Stuck, blocked. Deposited.
L	O	D	G	E	R	Resident, inhabitant, occupant, paying guest.
L	O	D	G	E	S	Plural of LODGE.
L	O	F	T	E	D	Lobbed, clubbed, bowled high, caused to rise.
L	O	F	T	E	R	Golf club.
L	O	G	G	E	D	Recorded, registered, reported.
L	O	G	G	E	R	Lumberman. Atmospheric recorder.
L	O	G	G	I	A	Gallery, Balcony.
L	O	G	H	U	T	Log Cabin.
L	O	G	M	A	N	Logger, Lumberman, Woodsman.
L	O	I	T	E	R	Linger, dawdle, idle, lag, delay, saunter, loaf, trail, lounge.
L	O	L	L	E	D	Past of LOLL.
L	O	L	L	E	R	Lounger, loiterer, sloucher, idler, recliner.
L	O	L	L	O	P	Lounge, loll, slouch. Bobbing motion, bounding gait.
L	O	N	E	L	Y	Alone, isolated, solitary, forlorn, lonesome, desolate, cheerless, dismal.
L	O	N	G	E	D	Craved, yearned, desired, hankered, hungered, lusted, pined.
L	O	N	G	E	R	Comparative of LONG.
L	O	O	F	A	H	Sponge, Gourd, luffa skeleton. Bath sponge.

1	2	3	4	5	6	
L	O	O	K	E	D	Past of LOOK.
L	O	O	K	E	R	Spectator, onlooker, gazer, searcher.
L	O	O	K	I	N	Chance of success, participation, active sharing.
L	O	O	M	E	D	Rose up, appeared, threatened, overshadowed.
L	O	O	P	E	D	Encircled, wound around, formed loops.
L	O	O	P	E	R	Smooth hairless caterpillar.
L	O	O	S	E	D	Set free, disconnected, undid, unlocked, detached, unfastened.
L	O	O	S	E	N	Slacken, release, untie, liberate, relax, detach.
L	O	O	T	E	D	Pillaged, robbed, rifled, plundered, ransacked.
L	O	O	T	E	R	One who LOOTS.
L	O	P	I	N	G	Moving at an easy gait.
L	O	P	P	E	D	Truncated, shortened, docked, severed, curtailed, pruned, amputated.
L	O	P	P	E	R	Clot, curdle, coagulate. Cutter, pruner.
L	O	Q	U	A	T	Tree fruit.
L	O	R	D	E	D	Pontificated, swaggered, bossed, tyrannized, overawed.
L	O	R	D	L	Y	August, grand, noble, majestic, arrogant, proud, gradiose, imposing.
L	O	S	I	N	G	Surrendering, yielding. Relinquishing. Mislaying, misplacement. Depriving.
L	O	S	S	E	S	Forfeitures, deprivations, ruin, damages, injuries, reversals, defeats.
L	O	T	I	O	N	Liquid cosmetic preparation. Astringent, unction. Washing medium.
L	O	U	D	E	R	Comparative of LOUD.
L	O	U	D	L	Y	Clamorously, uproarously, stridently, hoarsely, stertorously, raucously.
L	O	U	N	G	E	Sitting room. Recline, loll, loaf, idle, rest, Cocktail lounge. Public Room.
L	O	U	S	E	D	Botched, goofed, gummed up, mucked, messed, bungled.
L	O	U	V	E	R	Window, ventilator. Light deflector.
L	O	V	E	L	Y	Beautiful, graceful, delectable, pleasant, pleasing, charming, delightful.
L	O	V	E	R	S	Plural of LOVER.
L	O	V	I	N	G	Affectionate, devoted, adoring, tender, considerate, caring, infatuated, ardent.
L	O	W	E	S	T	Superlative of LOW.
L	O	W	I	N	G	Bellowing, mooing.
L	O	W	K	E	Y	Restrained, low profile, low intensity.
L	U	B	B	E	R	Awkward fellow, clumsy clot, boor, clown. Unskilled seaman.
L	U	C	E	N	T	Luminous, radiant, clear, bright.
L	U	G	G	E	D	Hauled, dragged, heaved, pulled, tugged, dragged.
L	U	G	G	E	R	Small fishing coaster.
L	U	L	L	E	D	Soothed, hushed, rocked, calmed, pacified, composed, appeased, assuaged.
L	U	M	B	A	R	Lower part of the back.
L	U	M	B	E	R	Refuse, trash, rubbish, junk. Move awkwardly, advance clumsily.
L	U	M	P	E	D	Grouped, massed, heaped.
L	U	N	A	C	Y	Madness, insanity, mania, dementia, derangement, folly, foolishness.
L	U	N	A	R	Y	Honesty, Moonwort.
L	U	N	A	T	E	Crescent shaped.
L	U	N	G	E	D	Lurched, thrust. Burst, plunged, pitched, drove.
L	U	P	I	N	E	Lupin, Flower, colour Blue. Wolfish.
L	U	R	I	N	G	Enticing, decoying, tempting, attracting, seducing, deceiving.
L	U	R	K	E	D	Lay in wait, hid, skulked, slunk.
L	U	R	K	E	R	Skulker, bandit, burglar, sneak.
L	U	S	T	E	D	Desired, coveted, yearned, longed, leched.
L	U	S	T	R	E	Splendour, gloss, glory, radiance, brightness, resplendence, brilliance.
L	U	T	I	S	T	Lute player. Lute maker.
L	U	X	A	T	E	Throw out, dislodge, dislocate, disjoint.
L	U	X	U	R	Y	Extravagance, superfluity, embellishment, sensuality, pleasure, indulgence.
L	Y	C	E	U	M	Lecture Hall. Public Lecture Room. Lycee.
L	Y	M	P	H	S	Plural of LYMPH.
L	Y	R	I	C	S	Plural of LYRIC.
L	Y	R	I	S	T	Lyre Player.

M

1	2	3	4	5	6	
M	A	C	R	O	N	Mark to indicate stressed or long sound.
M	A	C	U	L	A	Stain, spot, blotch.
M	A	C	U	L	E	Altered skin colouration.
M	A	D	A	M	S	Plural of MADAM.
M	A	D	A	M	E	Milady, noblewoman, female address.
M	A	D	C	A	P	Harebrained, frolicsome, lively, reckless person, impulsive person.
M	A	D	D	E	N	Infuriate, anger, provoke, exasperate, inflame, incense, enrage, distract.
M	A	D	D	E	R	Comparative of MAD.

1	2	3	4	5	6	
M	A	D	M	A	N	Maniac, lunatic, fool, imbecile, idiot, loony, nut.
M	A	D	R	A	S	Dress fabric, skirting, bright coloured cloth. Handkerchief. Curry.
M	A	E	N	A	D	Distraught woman, frenzied female dancer, unnaturally excited woman.
M	A	F	F	I	A	Mafia, Secret society, secret italian organisation, Racket operators.
M	A	G	G	O	T	Grub, larva, worm. Whim, eccentric idea, obsession.
M	A	G	N	E	T	Magnetic Iron Ore. Lodestone. Irrestible force, magnetic field. Lure.
M	A	G	N	U	M	Large wine bottle. Great, high-powered.
M	A	G	P	I	E	Bird. Type of crow. Foolish chatterer. Indiscriminate collector.
M	A	G	Y	A	R	Dominant Hungarian group.
M	A	H	O	U	T	Elephant keeper. Elephant driver.
M	A	I	D	E	N	Young girl, lass, damsel, virgin, miss, female.
M	A	I	L	E	D	Past of MAIL.
M	A	I	M	E	D	Crippled, injured, disabled, hurt, harmed, mutilated, marred.
M	A	I	N	L	Y	Principally, chiefly, largely, particularly, entirely, absolutely, generally.
M	A	J	O	R	S	Plural of MAJOR.
M	A	K	E	U	P	Cosmetics, facial enhancement, Composition, fiction, compensation.
M	A	K	I	N	G	Compelling, forcing, constraining, causing, constituting, forming, shaping.
M	A	L	A	D	Y	Ailment, complaint, disorder, illness, indisposition, disease.
M	A	L	A	G	A	From Malaga. Spanish.
M	A	L	I	C	E	Spite, rancour, resentment, revenge, enmity, malevolence, ill will.
M	A	L	I	G	N	Defame, traduce, revile, abuse, vilify, disparage, slander, revile.
M	A	L	L	E	T	Wooden-headed Hammer. Striking Tool. Croquet stick. Percussion Instrument.
M	A	L	L	O	W	Perennial herb. Colour red. Sweetmeat.
M	A	L	T	E	D	Made with Malt extract. Malted Milk.
M	A	M	M	A	L	Mammalia, Man and other higher young-suckling animals.
M	A	M	M	O	N	Debasing opulence. Riches, wealth, property, possessions.
M	A	N	A	G	E	Contrive, manouevre, administer, direct, control, conduct, supervise, operate.
M	A	N	A	N	A	Tomorrow in Spanish. Procrastination.
M	A	N	D	O	M	Mankind. Humanity.
M	A	N	E	G	E	Horse training centre. School for horseriders.
M	A	N	F	U	L	Brave, manly, noble, daring, dauntless, hardy, courageous, intrepid.
M	A	N	G	E	R	Feeding trough, Feed box.
M	A	N	G	L	E	Cut, bruise, wound spoil, mutilate. Laundry wringing machine.
M	A	N	I	A	C	Lunatic, madman. Insane, deranged, mad, unsound.
M	A	N	I	O	C	Cassava.
M	A	N	N	E	D	Operated by man, performed by man. Occupied by man.
M	A	N	N	E	R	Behaviour, conduct, bearing, aspect, mien. Habit, custom, extent, degree.
M	A	N	T	E	L	Lintel arch, Beam. Fireplace surround.
M	A	N	T	I	S	Insect that adopts a praying attitude.
M	A	N	T	L	E	Cloak, covering, shell, hood.
M	A	N	T	U	A	Robe, close-fitting gown.
M	A	N	U	A	L	Handbook, concise record, book, primer, textbook, compendium. Not automatic.
M	A	N	U	R	E	Dung, fertiliser, compost, dressing.
M	A	O	I	S	M	Maoist, follower of Chinese Mao.
M	A	P	P	E	D	Charted, delineated, planned, drawn.
M	A	Q	U	I	S	French guerilla fighter. Underbrush.
M	A	R	A	U	D	Raid, harass, pillage, plunder, roam.
M	A	R	B	L	E	Chrystallised Limestone. Little round ball. Pieces of Sculpture.
M	A	R	B	L	Y	Like Marble. Hard and Smooth.
M	A	R	C	E	L	Coiffure. Type of artificial hair wave. Permanent wave. Perm.
M	A	R	G	I	N	Border, outline, boundary, verge, edge, limit, latitude, scope. Minimum.
M	A	R	I	A	N	Veneration to the Blessed Virgin.
M	A	R	I	N	A	Boat dock mooring.
M	A	R	I	N	E	Oceanic, maritime, nautical, naval, sea, navigational, thalassic, aquatic.
M	A	R	I	S	T	In the service of the Virgin Mary.
M	A	R	K	E	D	Branded, differentiated, smudged, prominent, eminent, remarkable. Noticeable.
M	A	R	K	E	R	Person or thing that MARKS. Positioner, guide, bookmark, small transmitter.
M	A	R	K	E	T	Emporium, saleroom, shop, mart, store, outlet. Sell, merchandise, retail, vend.
M	A	R	L	I	N	Oceanic game fish.
M	A	R	M	O	T	Prairie Dog. Burrowing rodent.
M	A	R	O	O	N	Claret colour, deep blue red. Set ashore, desert, isolate.
M	A	R	R	E	D	Disfigured, spoiled, damaged, injured, impaired, blemished, tarnished.
M	A	R	R	E	R	One who mars through imperfection. Botcher, bungler, spoiler.
M	A	R	R	O	N	Chestnut.
M	A	R	R	O	W	Vascular modified connective tissue. Pith, essence, gist, kernel, substance.
M	A	R	S	H	Y	Wet, spongy, like marsh, boggy, muddy.
M	A	R	T	E	N	Furry weasel type carnivorous mammal.

1	2	3	4	5	6	
M	A	R	T	I	N	Small Swallow-like bird.
M	A	R	T	Y	R	Victim, sufferer for a cause. Torment, torture, sacrifice, afflict, agonize.
M	A	R	V	E	L	Wonder, miracle, phenomenon. Surprise, amazement. Admire.
M	A	S	C	O	T	Charm, amulet, luck, talisman, phylactery, juju, fetish, pet.
M	A	S	H	E	D	Pulped, kneaded, minced, crushed. Bruised, squashed, pressed, jammed.
M	A	S	H	E	R	Fop, wolf, philanderer, dandy, lady-killer, womanizer.
M	A	S	H	I	E	Wide-bladed iron golf club.
M	A	S	K	E	D	Disguised, screened, veiled, cloaked, covered, shrouded, camouflaged.
M	A	S	K	E	R	One in disguise, mask wearer, cause of confusion. Mummer, masquerader.
M	A	S	Q	U	E	Mask, masquerade, masker, performer.
M	A	S	S	E	D	Collected, gathered, heaped, lumped, piled.
M	A	S	S	E	S	Heaps, piles, mounds, stacks. Rabble. Riffraff, proletariat, mob, trash.
M	A	S	S	I	F	Block of mountain mass. Mountain topography.
M	A	S	T	E	D	Having MASTS. Having a MAST combination.
M	A	S	T	E	R	Tutor, teacher. Possessor of mastery. Overlord. Employer, Administrative Officer. Conquer
M	A	S	T	I	C	Aromatic resinous exudation.
M	A	T	I	N	G	Pairing, matching, marrying, association, copulating.
M	A	T	I	N	S	Morning prayers.
M	A	T	R	I	X	Mould, matrice, cradle. Cavity, Die. Mixture.
M	A	T	R	O	N	Matriarch, grande dame, dowager, married woman, Head Nurse, Woman, wife.
M	A	T	T	E	D	Entangled, mixed up, interlaced, intertwined.
M	A	T	T	E	R	Subject, affair, substance, thing, order. Import, theme, topic, material.
M	A	T	U	R	E	Adult, full-fledged, grown, ripened. Payable, unpaid. Aged, developed, old.
M	A	U	L	E	D	Past of MAUL.
M	A	U	N	D	Y	Feet Washing Ceremony. Alms. Free handout.
M	A	U	S	E	R	Rifle.
M	A	X	I	M	A	Most effective, highest, greatest.
M	A	Y	B	U	G	Cockchafer.
M	A	Y	D	A	Y	Spring Festival. International distress signal.
M	A	Y	F	L	Y	Winged insect, artificial angling fly.
M	A	Y	H	A	P	Perhaps, maybe.
M	A	Y	H	E	M	Act of malice, deliberate permanent crippling, willful, damage. Felonous mutilation.
M	A	Y	I	N	G	Gathering May Blossom.
M	A	Z	I	L	Y	Confused, distracted, obscure. Hazily.
M	E	A	D	O	W	Grassland, pastureland, grassy upland area, field, veld.
M	E	A	G	E	R	Gaunt, lean, scrawny, angular, poor, scant, sparse, minimum, deficient.
M	E	A	L	I	E	Maize, corn on the cob.
M	E	A	N	L	Y	In mean manner. Niggardly, cheaply, commonly, stingily, narrowly, humbly.
M	E	A	S	L	Y	Paltry, petty, niggling, trifling, trivial, puny.
M	E	D	A	L	S	Plural of MEDAL.
M	E	D	D	L	E	Interfere, intrude, tamper, intervene, obtrude, intercede, interpose.
M	E	D	I	A	N	Mean, average, mediocre, Middle, medium, central, fair, indifferent.
M	E	D	I	A	L	Average, norm, par, mean, centre, middle.
M	E	D	I	C	O	Doctor, physician, medical practitioner, (Sl.) sawbones.
M	E	D	I	U	M	Average, middling, moderate, mediocre, moderate, Psychic, vehicle, agent.
M	E	D	I	U	S	Middle finger.
M	E	D	L	A	R	Loquat. Small deciduous tree.
M	E	D	L	E	Y	Combination, jumble, mingling, melange, hodgepodge, miscellany, mixture.
M	E	D	U	S	A	Jellyfish. Edible hedgehog, mushroom. Gorgon's head.
M	E	E	K	L	Y	Submissively, weakly, tamely, modestly, mildly, softly.
M	E	E	T	L	Y	Fitly, suitably, properly, appropriately, becomingly.
M	E	G	I	L	P	Artists oil and varnish medium.
M	E	G	O	H	M	One million OHMS.
M	E	G	R	I	M	Migraine, dizziness, whim, fancy.
M	E	L	L	O	W	Mature, aged, ripe, rich, developed. Ripen, enrich, soften.
M	E	L	O	D	Y	Tune, descant air, theme, music, harmony, song, strain, measure, strain.
M	E	L	O	N	S	Plural of MELON.
M	E	L	T	E	D	Past of MELT.
M	E	L	T	E	R	Something that is used in MELTING. Silver moulder. Refiner.
M	E	L	T	O	N	Woven fabric. Twill weave.
M	E	M	B	E	R	Portion, part, limb. Element, component, constituent, Segment, club member.
M	E	M	O	I	R	Written record, biography, journal, life history, recollection.
M	E	M	O	R	Y	Recollection, remembrance, reminiscence, process of recalling, reflection.
M	E	N	A	C	E	Threat, hazard, danger, peril, risk. Alarm, scare, endanger, compromise.
M	E	N	A	G	E	Household, quarters, habitation, establishment.
M	E	N	D	E	D	Restored, fixed, rectified, improved, repaired, patched, remedied, adjusted.
M	E	N	D	E	R	Restorer, repairer, fixer.

1	2	3	4	5	6	
M	E	N	H	I	R	Prehistoric monolith.
M	E	N	I	A	L	Servant, lackey, slave, flunkey. Subservient, obsequious, servile.
M	E	N	S	A	L	Used at the Table.
M	E	N	S	E	S	Menstruation.
M	E	N	T	A	L	Relating to the mind. Intellectual, thinking, reasoning, thinking. Insane, mindless.
M	E	N	T	O	R	Guide, counsellor, adviser, instructor, master, monitor.
M	E	R	C	E	R	Textile dealer.
M	E	R	E	L	Y	Simply, only, solely, purely, barely, utterly, just, but.
M	E	R	G	E	D	Amalgamated, joined, absorbed. Immersed, involved, consolidated, combined.
M	E	R	G	E	R	Amalgamation, consolidation, take-over, unification, union.
M	E	R	I	N	O	Fine-woold white sheep.
M	E	R	I	S	M	Expression of two contrasting parts. Thick and thin.
M	E	R	I	T	S	Plural of MERIT.
M	E	R	L	I	N	Falcon. Wizard, magician.
M	E	R	L	O	N	Intervening part of a battlement.
M	E	R	M	A	N	Fabled marine male creature.
M	E	S	H	E	D	Entantled, webbed, intermeshed, interlaced, knotted, snartled, tangled, reticulated.
M	E	S	S	E	D	Past of MESS.
M	E	T	A	L	S	Plural of METAL.
M	E	T	E	O	R	Matter in the solar system. Atmospheric phenomenon.
M	E	T	H	O	D	Manner, fashion, means, mode, system, technique, way, pattern, procedure.
M	E	T	H	Y	L	Compound.
M	E	T	I	E	R	Vocation, business, trade, calling, role, area of activity. Forte.
M	E	T	I	N	G	Alloting, apportioning, measuring, assigning.
M	E	T	R	I	C	Standard of measurement, based on a meter.
M	E	T	T	L	E	Courage, resolution, spirit, spunk, pluck, dauntlessness, guts, arbour, nerve.
M	E	W	I	N	G	Caterwauling, meowing. Confining, caging, cooping.
M	E	W	L	E	D	Cried, squalled, yowled, whimpered, whined.
M	E	W	L	E	R	A whimpering baby.
M	I	A	S	M	A	Vaporous exhalation, heavy atmosphere, pervasive influence. Pollution.
M	I	C	K	L	E	Much, great.
M	I	C	R	O	N	Unit of Length.
M	I	D	A	I	R	Flying, in the air, aloft.
M	I	D	D	A	Y	Noon, meridian, middle of the day.
M	I	D	D	E	N	Dunghill, organic debris, earthworm, organic soil deposit.
M	I	D	D	L	E	Centre, midst, medium, medial, mean, equidistant, median, mid, core.
M	I	D	G	E	T	Dwarf, manikin, pygmy, runt, homunculus.
M	I	D	O	F	F	Cricket position.
M	I	D	R	I	B	Central vein of a leaf. Dividing line.
M	I	D	W	A	Y	Middle, halfway, equidistant.
M	I	F	F	E	D	Ruffled, annoyed, cross, offended.
M	I	G	H	T	Y	Powerful, strong, huge, forceful, gigantic, tremendous, monumental.
M	I	G	N	O	N	Dainty, petite, small.
M	I	K	A	D	O	Emperor of Japan.
M	I	L	A	D	Y	Woman of gentle birth. Form of address.
M	I	L	D	E	N	To render milder.
M	I	L	D	E	R	Comparative of MILD.
M	I	L	D	E	W	Superficial fungal growth caused by damp. Mould, rust, must, blight.
M	I	L	D	L	Y	In mild manner. Gently, tenderly, blandly, calmly, placidly.
M	I	L	I	E	U	Environment, atmosphere, surroundings, ambience.
M	I	L	K	E	D	Exploited, extorted, drained, emptied, fleeced, extorted, extracted, pumped.
M	I	L	K	E	N	Milky.
M	I	L	K	E	R	Someone or something that MILKS.
M	I	L	L	E	D	Ground, manufactured, pulverized, triturated, powdered.
M	I	L	L	E	R	Corn grinder.
M	I	L	L	E	T	Small seeded annual cereal. Grain. Grasses.
M	I	L	O	R	D	Gentleman. Form of polite address.
M	I	M	I	N	G	Mimicking, acting, aping, simulating, demonstrating, imitating.
M	I	M	O	S	A	Aromatic plant.
M	I	N	C	E	D	Past of MINCE.
M	I	N	C	E	R	Grinding machine, mincing machine.
M	I	N	D	E	D	Past of MIND.
M	I	N	D	E	R	Baby-sitter, caretaker, watcher, tender.
M	I	N	E	R	S	Plural of MINER.
M	I	N	G	L	E	Blend, mix, unite, amalgamate, associate, combine, merge, socialize.
M	I	N	I	F	Y	Diminish, depreciate, minimise, abridge, curtail, lessen, dwarf.
M	I	N	I	M	S	Plural of MINIM.

1	2	3	4	5	6	
M	I	N	I	N	G	Quarrying, delving, digging, uncovering, excavating, burrowing, drilling.
M	I	N	I	O	N	Follower, sycophant, dependant, subordinate.
M	I	N	N	I	E	Weak bridge hand.
M	I	N	N	O	W	Small fish. Fishing Lure.
M	I	N	O	A	N	Relating to the Bronze Age. Of the Island of Crete.
M	I	N	O	R	S	Plural of MINOR.
M	I	N	T	E	D	Coined, stamped, produced, fabricated, moulded, forged.
M	I	N	T	E	R	Inventor, creator, forger.
M	I	N	U	E	T	Slow graceful dance.
M	I	N	U	T	E	60 Seconds. Period of time. Small, tiny, little. diminutive. Detailed, exact. Record.
M	I	R	A	G	E	Hallucination, delusion, optical illusion.
M	I	R	R	O	R	Reflector, looking glass, image representation, Model, pattern, Exemplify, Show.
M	I	S	C	U	E	Billards mistake. Incorrect stage cue. Misplay at games.
M	I	S	E	R	E	Declaration of misery.
M	I	S	E	R	S	Plural of MISER.
M	I	S	E	R	Y	Grief, anguish, distress, wretchedness, torment, suffering, tribulation.
M	I	S	F	I	T	Maladjusted person, out of place, badly fitting.
M	I	S	H	A	P	Accident, misfortune, disaster, calamity, misadventure, contretemps, tragedy.
M	I	S	L	A	Y	Misplace, lose, place incorrectly.
M	I	S	L	E	D	Deceived, deluded, misdirected, misguided, beguiled, double-crossed, lured.
M	I	S	S	A	L	Sunday Prayer-book. Book of Devotions.
M	I	S	S	E	D	Past of MISS.
M	I	S	S	E	L	Mistle thrush.
M	I	S	S	E	S	Plural of MISS.
M	I	S	S	E	T	Misplace, displease.
M	I	S	S	U	S	Madam, woman, employer. Wife.
M	I	S	T	E	R	Man's title. Designation, appelation.
M	I	S	U	S	E	Abuse, mishandle, perfect, ill-treat, outrage, maltreat.
M	I	T	R	A	L	Resembling Mitre.
M	I	T	R	E	D	Raise in Rank. Join together. Bring together at an angle.
M	I	T	R	E	S	Plural of MITRE.
M	I	T	T	E	N	Hand covering. Fingerless glove.
M	I	X	I	N	G	Mingling, blending, combining, joining, associating, intermixing, amalgamating.
M	I	Z	Z	E	N	Aftermast and sail.
M	I	Z	Z	L	E	Fine drizzle. Fog. Mist.
M	I	Z	Z	L	Y	Misty.
M	O	A	N	E	D	Past of MOAN.
M	O	A	T	E	D	Widely trenched. Surrounded by a channel.
M	O	B	B	E	D	Annoyed, attacked, crowded, surrounded.
M	O	B	C	A	P	Woman's fancy hat.
M	O	B	I	L	E	Movable, volatile, mercurial, moving. Variable, inconstant, fluid, mutable, migrant.
M	O	B	L	A	W	Law of the Rabble. Lynch Law. Rule by the masses.
M	O	C	K	E	D	Past of MOCK.
M	O	C	K	E	R	Scoffer, taunter, scorner, deceiver.
M	O	C	K	U	P	Detailed structural model.
M	O	D	E	L	S	Plural of MODEL.
M	O	D	E	N	A	Varicoloured plumage.
M	O	D	E	R	N	Contemporary, present-day, up-to-date, current, latter.
M	O	D	E	S	T	Retiring, diffident, unassuming, self-effacing. Shy, humble. Limited.
M	O	D	I	F	Y	Mutate, change, alter, refashion, vary, qualify, temper, restrain.
M	O	D	I	S	H	Stylish, fashionable, up-to-date, chic.
M	O	D	I	S	T	Follower of fashion.
M	O	D	U	L	E	Unit size. Volume measure. Image, model. Multi-stage rocket unit.
M	O	H	A	I	R	Angora Goat Hair.
M	O	H	A	W	K	Red Indian. Skating figure.
M	O	I	E	T	Y	Half, component, fraction, part.
M	O	I	L	E	D	Drudged, laboured, toiled, slogged, Clamoured, bustled.
M	O	L	A	R	S	Plural of MOLAR.
M	O	L	E	S	T	Pester, torment, annoy, bother, harass, vex, badger, heckle.
M	O	L	T	E	N	Melted, fused, liquefied, glowing, heated.
M	O	M	E	N	T	Instant, second, trice, flash, jiffy. Point, Importance, consequence, significance.
M	O	N	D	A	Y	Day of the week.
M	O	N	E	Y	S	Plural of MONEY.
M	O	N	G	E	R	Petty trader, small businessman. Purveyor of oddments. Pedlar. Dealer.
M	O	N	G	O	L	Mongoloid.
M	O	N	I	E	D	Rich, wealthy, comfortable, opulent, affluent.
M	O	N	I	E	S	Plural of MONEY. Coins, proceeds, riches, wealth.

1	2	3	4	5	6	
M	O	N	K	E	Y	Small long-tailed Primate. (Sl.) 500 pounds. Anger, temper, burden, drug addiction.
M	O	N	K	L	Y	Monastic.
M	O	N	O	D	Y	Funeral song, eulogy, dirge, lament, ode.
M	O	N	T	H	S	Plural of MONTH.
M	O	O	I	N	G	Lowing.
M	O	O	N	E	D	Past of MOON.
M	O	O	N	E	R	Loiterer, lounger.
M	O	O	R	E	D	Tied up, attached, made fast docked, secured, berthed.
M	O	O	T	E	D	Broached, introduced, discussed, debated, proposed, disputed, argued.
M	O	P	I	N	G	Brooding, sulking, grumping, sauntering, drifting, ambling, strolling.
M	O	P	I	S	H	Gloomy, sad, dejected, downcast, melancholy, glum.
M	O	P	P	E	D	Swabbed, dabbed, cleaned, wiped. Guzzled, gobbled.
M	O	P	P	E	T	Term of endearment, little doll, child, kid, youngster.
M	O	R	A	L	E	Esprit de corps, confidence, drive, self-assurance, endurance, courage.
M	O	R	A	S	S	Bog, swamp, marsh, quagmire, slough, maze, labyrinth.
M	O	R	B	I	D	Abnormally gloomy, morose, melancholy, psychotic, sickly, sullen.
M	O	R	G	E	N	Measurement of land area.
M	O	R	G	U	E	Superiority, haughtiness. Disdain. Mortuary. Filing Cabinet.
M	O	R	M	O	N	Member of the Church of the Latter Day Saints.
M	O	R	O	N	S	Plural of MORON.
M	O	R	O	S	E	Sullen, morbid, surly, churlish, sour, irascible, saturnine, cranky, testy.
M	O	R	R	I	S	Lively dance movement. Easy chair.
M	O	R	R	O	W	Tomorrow, the following day, the next day.
M	O	R	S	E	L	Tidbit, taste, bite, piece, bit, slice, scrap, delicacy, dainty, treat.
M	O	R	T	A	L	Human, temporal, Man, Person. Deadly, fatal, merciless, relentless, ruthless.
M	O	R	T	A	R	Small bowl-shaped vessel. Academic Cap. Binding material. Plaster.
M	O	S	A	I	C	Law. Writings attributed to Moses. Surface decoration. Composite. Ornamentation.
M	O	S	L	E	M	Muslim.
M	O	S	Q	U	E	Islamic place of religious worship.
M	O	S	T	L	Y	Chiefly, mainly, first, principally, generally, largely, predominantly, primarily.
M	O	T	H	E	R	Female parent, dam, origin, source. Care for, nurse, cosset. Mum, mammy.
M	O	T	I	F	S	Plural of MOTIF.
M	O	T	I	L	E	Capable of movement. Tactile.
M	O	T	I	O	N	Movement, stirring, agitation, locomotion, Proposal, action. Impulse, suggestion.
M	O	T	I	V	E	Incentive, reason, stimulus, purpose, aim, design, determinant, intent, subject.
M	O	T	L	E	Y	Medley. Parti-coloured, Heterogeneous, diverse. Miscellany, assorted. Mixed.
M	O	T	O	R	S	Plural of MOTOR.
M	O	T	T	L	E	Speckle, dapple, spot. Blotch, splodge, stain.
M	O	U	L	D	Y	Mildewed, fusty, musty, rusty.
M	O	U	L	I	N	Glacial Shaft.
M	O	U	L	T	S	Plural of MOULT.
M	O	U	N	D	S	Plural of MOUND.
M	O	U	N	T	S	Plural of MOUNT.
M	O	U	S	E	R	Rat-catching animal. Cat.
M	O	U	S	S	E	Frothy Desert. Pureed meat or vegetable dish stabilised with gelatin.
M	O	U	T	H	Y	Loud, bombastic, ranting, vociferous.
M	O	V	I	E	S	Films, cinema, moving pictures, bioscope, motion pictures, source of entertainment.
M	O	V	I	N	G	Stirring, proceeding, going, walking, marching, touching, agitating, exciting.
M	O	W	I	N	G	Cutting grass. Lawn cutting. Felling, flooring, levelling, bringing down.
M	U	C	H	L	Y	Rather a lot, much. Plentifully.
M	U	C	K	E	D	Soiled, littered, botched, bungled. Drudged. Sauntered, drifted. Complicated.
M	U	C	K	E	R	Tough, bully, wretch, blighter, churl, buffoon, failure, clodhopper. Botch, bungle.
M	U	C	O	I	D	Resembling Mucus.
M	U	C	O	U	S	Covered with Mucus. Slimy, viscous.
M	U	D	D	L	E	Confuse, derange, befuddle, bewilder, disorder, mess, foul up, complicate.
M	U	D	P	I	E	Cake of wet earth. Sand confectionery.
M	U	F	F	E	D	Fumbled, botched, bungled, blew, loused up, fluffed, goofed.
M	U	F	F	I	N	Small baked cake.
M	U	F	F	L	E	Wrap, envelop, enfold, cover, dull, disguise, stifle, suppress, deaden.
M	U	G	G	E	D	Beaten up and robbed.
M	U	G	G	E	R	Perpetrator of a hit and run robbery.
M	U	L	I	S	H	Stubborn, obstinate, pig-headed, headstrong, unruly.
M	U	L	L	E	D	Pondered, deliberated, ruminated. Heated alcoholic beverage.
M	U	L	L	E	T	Type of fish.
M	U	M	B	L	E	Mutter, grumble, murmur, utter in an undertone. Muddle, shuffle.
M	U	M	M	E	R	Masked performer. Disguised actor. Player.
M	U	M	P	E	D	Sulked, grimaced, mumbled, muddled, muttered, pouted, Cheated, diddled.

1	2	3	4	5	6	
M	U	M	P	E	R	Beggar. Pest.
M	U	R	D	E	R	Killing, assassination, extermination. Annihilate, kill, slay, butcher, slaughter.
M	U	R	M	U	R	Whisper, mutter, mumble, grumble, complain, repine.
M	U	R	P	H	Y	Potato. Staple food of Ireland.
M	U	S	C	A	T	Cultivated grape. Raisin.
M	U	S	C	L	E	Sinew, strength, energy, thew, brawn, power, contracting tissue. Overcome.
M	U	S	E	U	M	Repository, exhibition hall, gallery. Storehouse of Historic material.
M	U	S	H	E	D	Urged, travelled by sled. Squashed, pulverized, crumbled, (sl) gushed.
M	U	S	I	N	G	Ruminating, reflecting, cogitating, thinking, remembering.
M	U	S	K	E	T	Shoulder gun. Smooth bore high calibre firearm.
M	U	S	L	I	M	Moslem.
M	U	S	L	I	N	Plain woven cotton fabric.
M	U	S	S	E	D	Messed, disarranged, jumbled, muddled, disorganized, rumpled, wrinkled.
M	U	S	S	E	L	Small Mollusc. Edible marine delicacy.
M	U	S	T	E	R	Convene, collect, congregate, marshal, assemble, enlist, rally, generate.
M	U	T	A	T	E	Change, transform, commute, transfigure, transmute, alter, modify, vary.
M	U	T	E	L	Y	Dumbly, speechlessly, appealingly, silently, taciturnly.
M	U	T	I	N	G	Act of making MUTE.
M	U	T	I	N	Y	Riot, revolt at sea, rebellion, sedition, uprising, Rebel, Rise up.
M	U	T	I	S	M	Inability to speak. Dumbness, speechlessness.
M	U	T	T	E	R	Murmur, grumble, mumble, grouse. Whisper.
M	U	T	T	O	N	Flesh of mature ovine animal. Dressed Sheep meat. Central issue under debate.
M	U	T	U	A	L	Reciprocal, interchangeable, joint, respective, correlative.
M	U	Z	Z	L	E	Snout, Animal's jaws. Mouth covering, restrainer. Open end of a gun. Mouth.
M	Y	O	P	I	A	Short-sightedness, near-sightedness.
M	Y	O	P	I	C	Near-sighted, short-sighted. Purblind, Astigmatic.
M	Y	R	I	A	D	Countless, innumerable, manifold, many.
M	Y	R	T	L	E	Genus of Shrub. Periwinkle, moneywort.
M	Y	R	T	U	S	American shrub resembling the Myrtle.
M	Y	S	E	L	F	Reflexive pronoun. Me.
M	Y	S	T	I	C	Occult, obscure, veiled, incomprehensible. Mysterious. Magic. Mystical.
M	Y	T	H	O	S	Myth, legend. Folklore, tradition, lore.
M	Y	T	H	U	S	Myth, legend, mythos.

N

N	A	B	B	E	D	Apprehended, arrested, pinched, detained, seized, collared, grabbed, nicked.
N	A	B	A	L	S	Misers, skinflints, niggardly fellows.
N	A	B	O	B	S	Dignitaries, bigwigs, notables (sl.) fat cats.
N	A	E	V	U	S	Nevus, congenital pigmented skin area. Birth mark. Mole.
N	A	G	G	E	D	Harried, tormented, hectored, pestered, hepecked, plagued, chivied, goaded.
N	A	G	G	E	R	One who NAGS. Fault finder. Shrew. Nag.
N	A	I	L	E	D	Caught, found out, discovered, collared, bagged, captured. Secured.
N	A	I	L	E	R	Nailer driver. Wooden box lidder.
N	A	M	E	L	Y	That is to say, videlicet, expressly, specifically, particularly.
N	A	M	I	N	G	Christening, baptizing, calling, designating, dubbing, terming, appointing.
N	A	N	I	S	M	Being abnormally small, dwarfishness.
N	A	N	O	I	D	Dwarfish. Having a small body.
N	A	P	A	L	M	Jellied fuel added to incendiary bombs and flamethrowers.
N	A	P	E	R	Y	Table linen.
N	A	P	K	I	N	Serviette, square of cloth. Small towel. Diaper.
N	A	P	P	E	D	Dozed, snoozed, slept, rested, relaxed.
N	A	R	K	E	D	Past of NARK.
N	A	R	R	O	W	Restricted, limited, small-minded, inflexible, stingy, cramped, slender.
N	A	S	I	O	N	Division of nasal and forehead bone.
N	A	T	I	O	N	People, Race, Country, Land, State, realm.
N	A	T	I	V	E	Indigenous, natural, belonging by birth. Endemic, local, domestic.
N	A	T	R	I	X	Widely distributed genus of water snakes.
N	A	T	T	E	R	Chatter, talk, discuss idly, babble, prattle, yak.
N	A	T	U	R	E	Creation, vitality, quality, essence, disposition. Universe, species. character.
N	A	U	G	H	T	O, zero, nothing, nil, aught, nought, zilch, cipher, nix.
N	A	U	S	E	A	Queasiness, squeamishness, biliousness, disgust, sickness, qualmishness.
N	E	A	P	E	D	Left high and dry. Grounded, stranded.
N	E	A	R	B	Y	Near, nigh, close at hand, adjacent, adjoining, neighbouring, proximate.
N	E	A	R	E	D	Approached, approximated, came close, drew near.
N	E	A	R	E	R	Closer, more adjacent, more immediate.

1	2	3	4	5	6	
N	E	A	R	L	Y	Almost, about, approximately, roughly, say, virtually, comparatively.
N	E	A	T	L	Y	Smartly, cleanly, orderly, trimly, tidily, sprucely, dexterously, expertly.
N	E	B	U	L	A	Haze, cloud, mist, heavenly body in the galaxy.
N	E	B	U	L	E	Nebuly, projecting edge forming a curve, short curves. Waviness.
N	E	C	K	E	D	Restricted part, shafted. Beheaded. Kissed, hugged, embraced, petted.
N	E	C	T	A	R	Delicious drink, drink of the gods, ambrosia. Plant Juice.
N	E	E	D	B	E	Necessity, requirement, requisite.
N	E	E	D	E	D	Wanted, needful, required, requisite, lacked, hankered, pined, yearned, coveted.
N	E	E	D	L	E	Anger, frustrate, heckle, annoy, harass, plague, tease.
N	E	G	A	T	E	Deny, reverse, disclaim, nullify, neutralize, contradict, cancel.
N	E	I	G	H	S	Vocal sounds made by a horse.
N	E	K	T	O	N	Population of swimming aquatic mammals in a specific area.
N	E	P	H	E	W	Sibling's male child, kinsman, close relative.
N	E	R	E	I	D	Sea Nymph. Malevolent Nymph found in the woods.
N	E	R	O	L	I	Oil distilled from orange flowers.
N	E	R	V	A	L	Neural.
N	E	R	V	E	D	Braced, steeled, fortified, strengthened, prepared for. Courageous, plucky.
N	E	R	V	E	S	Plural of NERVE.
N	E	S	T	E	D	Roosted, rested, settled down.
N	E	S	T	L	E	Snuggle, burrow, cuddle, nuzzle, rest, shelter.
N	E	S	T	O	R	Genus of large Parrot.
N	E	T	H	E	R	Below, lower, under, beneath, bottom, inferior, low, undermost.
N	E	T	T	E	D	Gained, earned, made, yielded, profited. Caught in a net.
N	E	T	T	L	E	Irritate, provoke, rile, agitate, upset, vex exasperate. Prickle. Stinging plant.
N	E	U	R	A	L	Nervy, relating to the nervous system.
N	E	U	R	O	N	Nerve cell.
N	E	U	T	E	R	Neutral, imperfectly developed sex. Castrate, Neuter Gender.
N	E	W	I	S	H	Recently acquired, novel, rather new, not showing signs of wear.
N	I	B	B	E	D	Having a NIB.
N	I	B	B	L	E	Take gentle bites, chew prettily. Nuzzle.
N	I	C	E	L	Y	Well, correctly, befittingly, properly, decently, decorously, fastidiously.
N	I	C	E	N	E	Creed. Decree of Christian Faith formed at Nicaea in A.D. 325.
N	I	C	E	S	T	Superlative of NICE.
N	I	C	E	T	Y	Precision, Finances, discrimination, fastidiousness, exactitude.
N	I	C	H	E	D	In a Niche. Recessed. Built-in.
N	I	C	K	E	D	Notched, carved, dented, cut. Stolen, pinched.
N	I	C	K	E	L	Coin. Unit of money. Silver-white metallic element.
N	I	C	K	E	R	Sprite. Water Monster. One who NICKS. Snipper.
N	I	D	I	F	Y	To make a nest.
N	I	G	G	L	E	Nag, harass, pester, worry, carp, gnaw.
N	I	G	H	T	S	Plural of NIGHT.
N	I	M	B	L	E	Agile, quick, lively, brisk, swift, sprightly, spry, nippy.
N	I	M	B	L	Y	Quickly, briskly, swiftly, alertly.
N	I	M	B	U	S	Luminous vapour, halo, radiant light, rayed structure, rain cloud.
N	I	M	R	O	D	Tyrant, mighty hunter.
N	I	N	E	T	Y	Nine times ten.
N	I	P	P	E	D	Pinched, gripped, clamped, squeezed, crushed.
N	I	P	P	E	R	Child, kid, youngster, moppet, juvenile, Pincer.
N	I	P	P	L	E	Teat, pap, dug, papilla. Pipe coupling.
N	I	T	R	I	C	Derived from Nitrogen.
N	I	T	W	I	T	Numbskull, dimwit, pinhead, featherbrain, dumb-bell, wantwit.
N	O	B	B	L	E	Dope, doctor, swindle, cheat.
N	O	B	L	E	R	Comparative of NOBLE.
N	O	B	O	D	Y	Nonentity, zero, zilch, insignificant, nullity, unimportant person.
N	O	C	E	N	T	Damaging, hurtful, harmful, injurious, mischievous, nocuous.
N	O	D	D	E	D	Past of NOD.
N	O	D	O	S	E	Knotty, knobbed.
N	O	D	U	L	E	Lump, irregular shape, tumorous growth, small knot.
N	O	E	S	I	S	Intellectual apprehension, pure knowledge.
N	O	E	T	I	C	Abstract reasoning.
N	O	G	G	I	N	Small mug, tot, alcoholic measurement. Head, noodle, conk, bean. (sl.)
N	O	I	S	E	D	Rumoured, reported, talked about.
N	O	I	S	E	S	Plural of NOISE.
N	O	M	A	D	S	Plural of NOMAD.
N	O	M	I	S	M	Legalism, custom, ethical basis of conduct.
N	O	N	A	G	E	Period of youth, childhood, under 21, immaturity. Infancy, minority.
N	O	O	D	L	E	Simpleton, Ninny. Pasta, edible flour/water mixture.

1	2	3	4	5	6	
N	O	O	S	E	D	Strung up, lassooed, snared, roped. Bound, tied, captured.
N	O	R	D	I	C	Native of Northern Europe, Scandanavian, Teutonic.
N	O	R	M	A	L	Regular, general, common, typical, usual. Sane, lucid, right.
N	O	R	M	A	N	Native of Normandy, William the Conquerer's man.
N	O	R	R	O	Y	King at arms.
N	O	S	I	N	G	Inquiring, examining, snooping, prying, scenting, sniffing.
N	O	T	A	R	Y	Deed registering official. Public Officer. Secretary, Clerk.
N	O	T	I	C	E	Cognizance, attention, consideration, understanding. Interest, See, discern.
N	O	T	I	F	Y	Advise, apprise, warn, inform, acquaint, announce, disclose, reveal, divulge.
N	O	T	I	N	G	Distinguishing, perceiving, remarking, observing. Commenting, recording.
N	O	T	I	O	N	Idea. theory, concept, belief, thought, conception, impression, image.
N	O	U	G	A	T	Confectionery, sweetmeat.
N	O	U	G	H	T	Nothing, naught, zero.
N	O	U	N	A	L	Relating to the function of a noun.
N	O	V	E	L	S	Plural of NOVEL.
N	O	V	E	N	A	Nine-day Prayer. Special devotion.
N	O	V	I	C	E	Probationer, beginner, postulant, tyro, apprentice, novitiate.
N	O	W	A	Y	S	In no way. Never.
N	O	W	I	S	E	Noways, never, in no way, nohow.
N	O	Z	Z	L	E	Socket, projecting vent, tapering duct, channel nose (sl.)
N	U	A	N	C	E	Subtle distinction, shade of difference, expressive variation, suggestion, tinge.
N	U	B	B	I	N	Stubby, stunted, stumpy, undeveloped, imperfect. Nub, upshot, core.
N	U	B	B	L	E	Small hill, knob, lump.
N	U	B	B	L	Y	Knotty, knobby.
N	U	B	I	A	N	Member of Nubian people. One of a Negroid tribe.
N	U	B	I	L	E	Sexually suitable, marriageable.
N	U	C	L	E	I	Plural of NUCLEUS.
N	U	D	E	L	Y	Nakedly, in unclothed manner, undressed, bare.
N	U	D	G	E	D	Bumped significantly, jogged, pushed, poked.
N	U	D	G	E	S	Plural of NUDGE.
N	U	D	I	S	M	Cult of nude living. Living unclothed for health reasons.
N	U	D	I	S	T	One who practices NUDISM.
N	U	D	I	T	Y	Nakedness, unclothed condition. Bareness.
N	U	G	G	E	T	Lump of Gold, chunk, clump, wad.
N	U	M	B	E	D	Dazed, torpid, devoid of sensation, desensitized, deadened.
N	U	M	B	E	R	Arithmetical value, count, digit, cipher, numeral. Tally, amount, aggregate.
N	U	M	B	L	Y	In a NUMB manner.
N	U	N	C	I	O	Papal representative. Apostolic Delegate.
N	U	R	S	E	D	Past of NURSE.
N	U	R	S	E	R	Tender, Minder, cherisher. Nursing Bottle.
N	U	T	A	N	T	Nodding, drooping.
N	U	T	M	E	G	Aromatic kernel. Food flavouring.
N	U	T	R	I	A	Coypu fur. Pale olive grey.
N	U	Z	Z	L	E	Nudge, thrust, push, cuddle, fondle, touch tenderly, nestle.
N	Y	M	P	H	A	Labia Minora. Nymph.
N	Y	T	R	I	L	Synthetic fibre.

1	2	3	4	5	6	
O	A	F	I	S	H	Loutish, doltish, dull, idiotic, ruffianlike, stupid.
O	A	R	I	N	G	Sculling, rowing, propelling with oars, boating.
O	B	D	U	C	E	Cover, draw over, envelop in.
O	B	E	L	U	S	Mark of reference, ancient manuscript mark, marginal symbol indicating spurious word. Obelisk.
O	B	E	R	E	A	Genus of boring beetle.
O	B	E	R	E	K	Polish folk dance.
O	B	E	R	O	N	King of the Fairies!
O	B	E	Y	E	D	Submitted to, acted in accordance with instructions. Behaved as directed.
O	B	E	Y	E	R	One who OBEYS.
O	B	I	T	E	R	Incidental comment, incidentally, upon reflection.
O	B	J	E	C	T	Article, thing, gadget, individual, mass, bulk, body. View, Duty, goal, target. Oppose, argue.
O	B	L	A	T	E	Offer. Roman Catholic Religious. Flattened at both poles.
O	B	L	I	G	E	Place under an obligation. Constrain, coerce. Accommodate, gratify, assist.
O	B	L	O	N	G	Of greater length than breadth. Elongated as opposed to square or circular.
O	B	O	I	S	T	Oboe-player.
O	B	S	E	S	S	Obsess.
O	B	S	E	S	S	Occupy disproportionately, trouble continuously, besiege mentally. Preoccupy.
O	B	T	A	I	N	Acquire, get, gain, procure, secure, win, attain possession.

1	2	3	4	5	6	
O	B	T	E	C	T	Enclosed in, encased.
O	B	T	E	S	T	Beseech, beg, supplicate. Invoke as witness.
O	B	T	U	N	D	Blunt, dull. Deaden.
O	B	T	U	S	E	Lacking alert awareness; dull, dense; Mild. Blunt.
O	B	V	E	R	T	Change appearance. Present a different surface.
O	C	C	U	L	T	Eclipse, conceal, hide. Secret, undisclosed. Mysterious. Supernatural.
O	C	C	U	P	Y	Tenant, inhabit, populate, people. Seize, possess, engross, engage, immerse.
O	C	E	A	N	S	Plural of OCEAN.
O	C	E	L	O	T	American wildcat.
O	C	L	O	C	K	Time according to the dock. On the clock.
O	C	T	A	N	E	Rating of motor fuel.
O	C	T	A	N	T	Measuring device. Any of Eight parts dividing space by 3 co-ordinate planes.
O	C	T	A	V	E	Eight line stanza. Musical interval. Unit of the modern scale. Group of Eight.
O	C	T	A	V	O	Paper or page size.
O	C	T	O	S	E	Synthetic monosaccharides group with 8 carbon atoms in a molecule.
O	C	T	R	O	I	Trade privilege, monopoly. Concession.
O	C	U	L	A	R	Perceived by the eye. Seen. Visual. Relating to the eye.
O	D	D	E	S	T	Superlative of ODD.
O	D	D	I	S	H	Rather ODD.
O	D	D	I	T	Y	Peculiarity, strangeness, eccentricity, curiosity, queer person, whimsicality.
O	D	D	J	O	B	Piece work. Unskilled occupation.
O	D	D	L	O	T	Less than 100 Shares. Unusual transactional unit.
O	D	D	S	O	N	Favourable odds. Likely to win. With a better than even chance.
O	D	I	O	U	S	Repulsive, hateful, obnoxious, detestable, abominable, loathsome, disgusting.
O	E	D	E	M	A	Swelling, Tumour, Collection of fluid, Plant disease.
O	E	U	V	R	E	Life work of writer, composer or artist.
O	F	F	D	A	Y	Free day.
O	F	F	E	N	D	Insult, Affront, Provoke, Transgress, Violate, Aggrieve. Outrage, Infringe.
O	F	F	I	C	E	Bureau, Function, Post, Berth, Position, Situation, Connection.
O	F	F	I	N	G	Future, Afterward, By-and-by, Hereafter, to-be, near at hand.
O	F	F	I	S	H	Withdrawn, Aloof, Unsociable, Distant, Reserved. Unapproachable, unbending, Solitary.
O	F	F	S	E	T	Counter balance, Compensate, Make-up, Redeem, Atone (for), Outweigh.
O	G	I	V	A	L	Arched.
O	G	L	I	N	G	Looking, Gaping, Goggling, Staring, Gazing (amorously).
O	G	R	E	S	S	Virago, Shrew, Fishwife, Harpy, Scold, Vixen.
O	G	R	I	S	H	Representing a hideous monster.
O	I	D	I	U	M	Fungus, Grape mildew.
O	I	L	C	A	N	Oil receptacle for lubricating.
O	I	L	I	N	G	Lubricating.
O	I	L	M	A	N	Oil dealer, Leader in petroleum industry.
O	I	L	R	I	G	Derrick for boring and pumping oil.
O	L	D	I	S	H	Somewhat elderly.
O	L	E	I	N	E	Liquid fat.
O	L	E	O	S	E	Oily, Greasy, Fatty.
O	L	I	V	E	T	Imitation pearl.
O	L	I	V	I	L	Gum from the olive tree.
O	M	E	L	E	T	Omelette. Dish made with beaten eggs.
O	M	E	N	E	D	Divined, Presaged, Predicted, Augured, Had Premonitions.
O	M	N	I	F	Y	Enlarge, Make universal.
O	M	N	I	U	M	Gathering, Hodge-podge, Patchwork, Total of stocks.
O	N	D	I	N	E	Water spirit.
O	N	D	I	N	G	Heavy fall of rain or snow.
O	N	E	M	A	N	Relating to one individual (Play-art-music).
O	N	E	W	A	Y	Move in one direction, Function in only one possible way.
O	N	F	A	L	L	Attack, Assault, Offense, Onset, Onslaught.
O	N	F	L	O	W	Action of flowing.
O	N	I	O	N	Y	Tasting or smelling of onions.
O	N	R	U	S	H	Impetuous, Forward-rush, Onslaught of sudden grief.
O	N	W	A	R	D	Ahead, Forth, Forward, Along.
O	O	D	L	E	S	Heap, Loads, Quantities, Thousands, Trillion.
O	O	G	E	N	Y	Formation of egg.
O	O	I	D	A	L	Egg shaped.
O	O	L	I	T	E	Limestone.
O	O	L	O	G	Y	Branch of zoology appertaining to bird's eggs.
O	O	Z	I	N	G	Weeping, Seeping, Sweating, Bleeding, Exuding.
O	P	A	Q	U	E	Obscure, Ambiguous, Uncertain, Unclear, Unintelligible, Vague.
O	P	E	N	E	D	Unimpeded, Unclosed, Unobstructed, Unlocked, Wide, Yawning, Clear, Unsealed.

1	2	3	4	5	6	
O	P	E	N	E	R	Commence card game, First item on bill or series.
O	P	E	N	L	Y	Freely, Not concealed, Above suspicion.
O	P	I	A	T	E	Narcotic, Sleepy, Somnific, Sedative, Soporific.
O	P	I	N	E	D	Considered, Judged, Regarded, Speculated, Supposed, Accepted, Believed.
O	P	P	O	S	E	Counter, Match, Pit, Play(off), Resist, Contest, Dispute, Duel.
O	P	P	U	G	N	Contend, Battle, Fight, Tug, War, Resist, Oppose.
O	P	T	A	N	T	One who volunteers, Elects, Opts.
O	P	T	I	C	S	Science of light and vision.
O	P	T	I	M	E	Argued well, almost a wrangler.
O	P	T	I	N	G	Electing, Choosing.
O	P	T	I	O	N	Choice, Alternative, Election, Preference, Selection, Privilege, Right.
O	R	A	C	L	E	Revelation, Prophecy, Vision.
O	R	A	L	L	Y	Vocally, Articulate, Narrated, Unwritten, Verbal.
O	R	A	N	G	E	Citrus, Globose, sub-tropical fruit.
O	R	A	T	E	D	Declaimed, Ranted, Bombasted, Sermonized, Harangued.
O	R	A	T	O	R	Declaimer, Speaker, Petitioner.
O	R	C	H	I	D	Showy Tropical Plant.
O	R	D	A	I	N	Conduct, Direct, Keep, Manage, Appoint, Run, Dictate, Prescribe.
O	R	D	E	A	L	Trial, Affliction. Cross. Crucible, Tribulation, Visitation, Calvary, Test.
O	R	D	U	R	E	Filth, Excrement, Morally degrading.
O	R	E	X	I	S	Strive, Desire, Appetite.
O	R	G	A	S	M	Sexual Climax, Emotional excitement.
O	R	G	I	E	S	Carousals, Binges, Tear-aways, Parties, Rampages, Splurges.
O	R	I	E	N	T	East, Eastern, Direct toward, Place in relation to.
O	R	I	G	I	N	Ancestry, Blood Descent, Extraction, Lineage, Pedigree, Source, Root.
O	R	I	O	L	E	Species of bird, Golden.
O	R	I	S	O	N	Speech, Oration, Prayer, Supplication.
O	R	M	O	L	U	Ground Gold, Gilded metal, Brass decoration.
O	R	N	A	T	E	Flamboyant, Embellished, Luscious, Rococo, Florid, Elaborate, Opulent, Rich.
O	R	N	E	R	Y	Mean, Lazy, Touchy, Cantankerous, Short-tempered.
O	R	P	H	A	N	Parentless, Alone, Solitary, Abandoned, Forsaken, Lost, Neglected.
O	R	P	H	I	C	Recondite, Deep, Esoteric, Heavy, Occult, Profound, Secret, Hermetic.
O	S	C	U	L	E	Relating to kissing, Small mouth.
O	S	I	E	R	Y	Area where osiers grown, Made of willow.
O	S	M	O	S	E	Flow and dilution of fluids. Interchange.
O	S	P	R	E	Y	Sea hawk, Feather trimming.
O	S	S	I	F	Y	Transform into bone, Make rigid, Mold firmly in conventional pattern.
O	S	T	E	A	L	Relating to bone.
O	S	T	E	N	T	Manifestation, Portent, Significant sign, Excessive display.
O	S	T	I	U	M	Entrance, Opening, Mouth of river.
O	S	T	L	E	R	Groom, Stableman, Care of horses at an inn.
O	T	I	O	S	E	Vain, Empty, Hollow, Idle.
O	T	I	T	I	S	Trouble with the ear.
O	T	T	A	V	A	Octave.
O	U	S	T	E	D	Deprived, Ejected, Disinherited, Dispossessed, Divested, Robbed.
O	U	S	T	E	R	Evictor, Ejector.
O	U	T	A	G	E	Failure in use. Interruption in power supply, Lost in transportation.
O	U	T	B	I	D	Offer more.
O	U	T	C	R	Y	Commotion, Clamour, Convulsion, Ferment, Tumult, Upheaval, Hue-and-cry.
O	U	T	D	I	D	Surpassed, Outshone, Outstripped, Best, Bested, Exceeded.
O	U	T	F	I	T	Equipment, Apparatus, Gear, Material, Paraphernalia, Tackle, Clothing, Costume, Company.
O	U	T	I	N	G	Excursion, Jaunt, Junket, Roundabout, Sally, Trip, Holiday,, Expedition.
O	U	T	L	A	W	Bandit, Desperado, Brigand. Forbid, Ban, Enjoin, Prohibit.
O	U	T	L	A	Y	Expense, Cost, Disbursement, Expenditure, Payment.
O	U	T	L	E	T	Aperture, Hole, Opening, Orifice, Vent, Egress, Exit, Loophole.
O	U	T	P	U	T	Product, Production, Turnout, Yield.
O	U	T	R	U	N	Outstrip, Distance, Outspeed, Beat, Surpass.
O	U	T	S	E	T	Beginning, Commencement, Dawn, Opening, Setout, Start.
O	U	T	V	I	E	Eclipse, Out-rival, Surpass.
O	U	T	W	I	T	Defeat, Outreach, Outsmart, Undo, Outfox, Outjockey.
O	V	A	L	L	Y	State of being oval, Degree of departure from true circularity.
O	V	E	R	D	O	Overplay, Overuse, Overwork, Excessive use.
O	V	U	L	A	R	Relating to embryo.
O	W	L	E	R	Y	Abode of owls.
O	W	L	I	N	G	Smuggling wood or sheep.
O	W	L	I	S	H	Suggestive of an owl.
O	W	N	I	N	G	Possessing, Having, Holding, Retaining.

1	2	3	4	5	6	
O	X	E	Y	E	D	Having eyes like an ox (large).
O	X	F	O	R	D	Colour (dark blue), Special style of shoe.
O	X	L	I	K	E	Resembling an ox (Heavy build).
O	X	T	A	I	L	Skinned tail especially for making soups and stews.
O	X	Y	G	E	N	Non-Metallic element usually colourless and odourless.
O	X	Y	M	E	L	Honey and vinegar (remedy for cough).
O	Y	S	T	E	R	Marine bivalve, Mollusk, Forte, Strong suit, Eminency, Métier.
O	Z	O	N	I	C	Relating to ozone/pure fresh air.

P

P	A	C	I	F	Y	Appease, Assuage, Conciliate, Mollify, Placate, Propitiate, Sweeten, Calm.
P	A	C	I	N	G	Walking, Ambulating, Hoofing, Stepping, Traipsing, Treading, Trooping.
P	A	C	K	E	D	Brimful, Chock-full, Crammed, Crowded, Jammed, Stuffed, Compressed.
P	A	C	K	E	T	Parcel, Bale, Bundle, Fortune, Pile, Roll, Wad, Boodle.
P	A	D	D	E	D	Walked softly and slowly, Magnified, Overcharged, Exaggerated.
P	A	D	D	L	E	Oar, Row slowly, Swim gently, Walk through shallow water.
P	A	E	L	L	A	Shellfish and rice dish (Spanish).
P	A	G	I	N	G	Turning pages slowly, Attending on patrons of hotels, Carrying messages.
P	A	G	O	D	A	Temple, Gazebo, Summerhouse, Alcove, Garden House.
P	A	I	D	U	P	Completed financial obligation.
P	A	I	N	E	D	Distressed, Agonised, Tortured, Tormented, Aggrieved, Afflicted.
P	A	I	R	E	D	Twin, Double, Dual, Coupled, Mated, Yoked.
P	A	L	A	C	E	Palatial, Opulent, Plush, Plushy, Sumptious, Luxuriant.
P	A	L	A	T	E	Taste, Gusto, Relish, Zeal, Roof of mouth.
P	A	L	E	L	Y	Ashy, Dimly, Wanly, Faintly, Sickly, Pasty.
P	A	L	I	N	G	Becoming pale, Fading, Picket for fence.
P	A	L	L	E	D	Bored, Tired, Wearied, Jaded.
P	A	L	L	E	T	Head, Bean, Noggin, Sconce, Primitive bed, Wooden platform.
P	A	L	L	I	D	Pale, Ashen, Blanched, Wan, Waxen, Anaemic.
P	A	L	L	O	R	Sallow, Waxen, Paleness.
P	A	L	M	A	R	Relating to the palm of the hand.
P	A	L	M	E	D	Held or hidden in palm of hand.
P	A	L	T	E	R	Lie, Falsify, Evade, Equivocate, Fence, Dodge, Shuffle.
P	A	L	T	R	Y	Cheap, Base, Common, Shoddy, Limited, Petty, Puny, Trivial.
P	A	M	P	A	S	Flat plains (South America).
P	A	M	P	E	R	Cater, Cosset, Coddle, Humour, Indulge, Spoil, Regale.
P	A	N	A	M	A	Hat.
P	A	N	A	R	Y	Relating to bread.
P	A	N	D	E	R	Indulge, Humour, Cater, Procurer, Pimp.
P	A	N	D	I	T	Learned man, Teacher, peculiar to India.
P	A	N	F	R	Y	Saute, In shallow fat.
P	A	N	F	U	L	Fill a pan.
P	A	N	G	E	D	Tormented, Mental anguish, Remorse.
P	A	N	N	E	D	Criticized, Rotate motion with camera, Seeking gold.
P	A	N	N	E	L	Lining for saddle.
P	A	N	N	E	R	One who pans for gold, Worker in a bakery.
P	A	N	N	U	S	Membrane, Tissue.
P	A	N	T	E	D	Gasped, Blew, Huffed, Heaved, Puffed, Wheezed.
P	A	N	T	E	R	Trap, Snare.
P	A	N	T	R	Y	Storeroom for food and/or preparation of same.
P	A	P	A	C	Y	Office of the Pope.
P	A	P	A	Y	A	Pawpaw, Sub-tropical fruit.
P	A	P	E	R	Y	Consistency of paper.
P	A	P	I	S	H	Relating to the Pope.
P	A	P	U	L	A	Pimple, Pustule.
P	A	R	A	D	E	Show, Brandish, Display, Disport, Exhibit, Expose, Flaunt, Flash.
P	A	R	A	P	H	Flourish to signature to guard against forgery.
P	A	R	C	E	L	Bundle, Lot, Packet, Portion, Section, Divide, Segment, Group.
P	A	R	D	O	N	Absolution, Amnesty, Mercy, Acquittal, Forgiveness, Remission, Vindication, Indemnity.
P	A	R	E	N	T	Generate, Create, Author, Father, Originate, Procreate, Sire, Spawn.
P	A	R	I	A	H	Outcast, Derelict, Leper, Untouchable, Castaway.
P	A	R	I	N	G	Shaving, Reducing, Rind.
P	A	R	I	S	H	Area committed to one pastor, Diocese.
P	A	R	I	T	Y	Equality, Equivalence, Adequation, Par, Sameness, Nearness.
P	A	R	K	E	D	Enclosed, Assembled, Leave car/plane in designated area.

1	2	3	4	5	6	
P	A	R	K	E	R	Keeper/Caretaker of park.
P	A	R	K	I	N	Ginger cake.
P	A	R	L	A	Y	Betting.
P	A	R	L	E	Y	Conference, Talk, Converse, Confer, Advise, Consult, Huddle, Dialogue.
P	A	R	O	D	Y	Caricature, Burlesque, Travesty, Spoof, Rib, Ridicule.
P	A	R	O	L	E	Period of freedom, Word of honour.
P	A	R	O	U	S	Giving birth.
P	A	R	R	O	T	Bird, Repeat mechanically.
P	A	R	S	E	D	Describe grammatically.
P	A	R	S	O	N	Clergyman, Churchman, Cleric, Ecclesiastic, Minister, Preacher, Reverend.
P	A	R	T	E	D	Divided, Broke, Parcelled, Apportioned, Sectioned, Fragmented.
P	A	R	T	E	R	One who distributes or shares out.
P	A	R	T	L	Y	To a part not a whole.
P	A	R	U	R	E	Matched set of jewels.
P	A	S	S	E	D	Gone, Proceeded, Wended, Ignored, Terminated, Expired. Elapsed, Succeeded.
P	A	S	T	E	D	Gummed, Basted, Thrashed, Cuffed, Buffeted, Busted, Punched, Clouted.
P	A	S	T	E	L	Pale, Light, Delicate, Crayon, Bloodless.
P	A	S	T	O	R	Clergyman, Starling, Herdsman.
P	A	S	T	R	Y	Cakes, Pies, Tarts.
P	A	T	C	H	Y	Irregular, Uneven, Unequal.
P	A	T	E	N	T	Open, Straightforward, Clear, Apparent, Distinct, Evident, Obvious, Plain.
P	A	T	H	O	S	Quality that moves one to pity or sorrow.
P	A	T	I	N	A	Film formed on copper and bronze by long exposure to air.
P	A	T	O	I	S	Vernacular, Colloquial, Dialect, Argot, Jargon, Lingo, Patter.
P	A	T	R	O	L	Mission, Guard, Cover beat of military guard.
P	A	T	R	O	N	Saint, Sponsor, Angel, Backer, Guarantor, Customer, Client.
P	A	T	T	E	D	Tapped, Smoothed, Caressed, Flattened, Shaped.
P	A	T	T	E	N	Clog, Sandal, Wooden Shoe.
P	A	T	T	E	R	Chat, Babble, Chatter, Gabble, Prate, Yak, Clack.
P	A	U	N	C	H	Abdomen, Belly, Stomach, Tummy, Potbelly, Corporation.
P	A	U	P	E	R	Beggar, Down-and-out, Have-not, Indigent, Almsman, Ruin, Bankrupt, Impoverish.
P	A	U	S	E	D	Halted, Hesitated, Waited, Interrupted, Ceased.
P	A	U	S	E	R	One who holds back.
P	A	V	I	N	G	Covering with bricks, Easing a smooth way.
P	A	V	I	S	E	Large Shield.
P	A	W	I	N	G	Handling, Scraping with Hoof (Horse).
P	A	W	N	E	D	Pledged, Hocked, Mortgaged.
P	A	W	N	E	E	Indian tribe of North America.
P	A	W	P	A	W	Sub-tropical fruit.
P	A	Y	D	A	Y	Day when wages are paid.
P	A	Y	I	N	G	Advantageous, Gainful, Lucrative, Profitable, Remunerative. Money-making, Settling the account.
P	A	Y	N	I	M	Pagon, Heathen, Infidel.
P	A	Y	O	F	F	Paying bribe, Profit, Reward, Conclusion, Denouement, Booty.
P	A	Y	O	L	A	Undercover payment, Bribe for commercial favour.
P	E	A	C	H	Y	Marvellous, Cool, Dandy, Divine, Glorious, Groovy, Neat.
P	E	A	H	E	N	Female peafowl.
P	E	A	K	E	D	Pointed, Acute, Spiked, Sharp, Sickly.
P	E	A	L	E	D	Reverberated, Chimed, Tolled, Rang.
P	E	A	N	U	T	Ground-nut, Measly, Puny, Paltry, Trifling.
P	E	A	P	O	D	Envelope covering seed of the pea plant.
P	E	A	R	L	Y	Translucent lustre.
P	E	B	B	L	E	Stone, Rock crystal, Quartz, Agate.
P	E	B	B	L	Y	Resembling pebbles, Shingle.
P	E	C	K	E	D	Picked, Struck, Kissed, Nagged, Fussed.
P	E	C	K	E	R	Woodpecker, Courage.
P	E	C	T	I	C	Coagulating.
P	E	C	T	I	N	Powder or syrup from fruit extract.
P	E	D	A	N	T	Tutor, Precise person who parades book learning.
P	E	D	A	T	E	Related to foot.
P	E	D	D	L	E	Push, Shove, Hawk, Huckster, Vend.
P	E	D	I	O	N	Flat surfaced crystal.
P	E	D	L	A	R	Vendor, Hawker, Peddler.
P	E	E	L	E	D	Open, Bare, Denuded, Stripped, Exposed, Naked, Skinned.
P	E	E	L	E	R	Stripper, Hustler, Live-wire, Policeman, Officer, Bobby.
P	E	E	P	E	D	Peered, Snooped, Chirped, Twittered, Glimpsed, Glanced.
P	E	E	P	E	R	Voyeur, Eye, Lamp, Ocular, Orb, Ogler.
P	E	E	V	E	D	Irritated, Piqued, Annoyed, Fretful, Exasperated, Nettled, Provoked, Riled.

1	2	3	4	5	6	
P	E	G	G	E	D	Attached, Plugged, Fixed, Plodded.
P	E	G	L	E	G	Wooden leg.
P	E	G	T	O	P	Spinning top.
P	E	L	L	E	T	Small shot, Chunk of compressed animal food. Firm mass of dung.
P	E	L	M	E	T	Cornice concealing curtain fixtures.
P	E	L	O	T	A	Ball game played with a wickerwork racket.
P	E	L	T	E	R	To shower with missiles.
P	E	L	T	R	Y	Small furry skin.
P	E	L	V	I	C	Relating to the pelvis.
P	E	L	V	I	S	Basin-shaped bony cavity protecting internal organs.
P	E	N	C	I	L	Small brush, Stick of marking substance usually graphite.
P	E	N	D	E	D	Delayed, balanced, depended.
P	E	N	I	A	L	Pertaining to the penis.
P	E	N	M	A	N	Clerk, Author, Calligrapher.
P	E	N	N	E	D	Written, Enclosed, Jailed, Cooped, Hemmed (in).
P	E	N	S	U	M	Duty, Charge, Estimate, Examination.
P	E	N	T	A	D	Pertaining to five.
P	E	N	U	L	T	Next to last.
P	E	N	U	R	Y	Poverty, Destitution, Impoverishment, Indigence, Need, Privation, Want.
P	E	O	P	L	E	Society, Community, Public, Populace, Plebeians, Inhabit, Tenant, Occupy, Populate.
P	E	P	L	U	M	Short skirtlike section attached to waistline.
P	E	P	P	E	R	Pungent product, Speckle, Freckle, Sprinkle, Stipple, Pelt with shot.
P	E	P	S	I	N	Gastric juice.
P	E	P	T	I	C	Digestive.
P	E	R	D	U	E	Hidden, Obscured, Unnoticed, Watch, Forlorn hope.
P	E	R	I	O	D	End, Cessation, Time, Closing, Conclusion, Age, Epoch, Era.
P	E	R	I	S	H	Die, Decay, Decease, Demise, Expire, Succumb, Decompose, Putrefy.
P	E	R	K	E	D	Improved, Recuperated.
P	E	R	M	I	T	Let, Allow, Have, Leave, Suffer, Consent, Allowing, Sanction.
P	E	R	O	N	E	Fibula.
P	E	R	R	O	N	Outdoor Stairway, Platform.
P	E	R	S	O	N	Human, Body, Creature, Life, Individual, Man, Mortal, Soul.
P	E	R	T	L	Y	Saucily, Archly, Boldly, Aucaciously, Brazenly.
P	E	R	U	K	E	Periwig.
P	E	R	U	S	E	Scrutinise, Examine, Read, Observe, Survey, Study.
P	E	S	T	E	R	Worry, Annoy, Bedevil, Harass, Plague, Tantalise, Exasperation, Nuisance.
P	E	S	T	L	E	Beat, Pound, Pulveriser.
P	E	T	A	R	D	Bomb, Case containing explosive.
P	E	T	A	R	Y	Peat.
P	E	T	I	T	E	Small, Bantam, Little monkey, Smallish, Lilliputian.
P	E	T	R	E	L	Sea-bird.
P	E	T	R	O	L	Gasoline, Kerosene.
P	E	T	T	E	D	Caressed, Cosseted, Cuddled, Dandled, Fondled, Embraced.
P	E	W	T	E	R	Alloy of tin and lead/copper.
P	H	A	R	O	S	Beacon, Lighthouse.
P	H	A	S	M	A	Genus of stick and leaf insects.
P	H	E	N	O	L	Carbolic acid.
P	H	L	E	G	M	Apathy, Impassivity, Indifference, Insensibility, Stoicism, Composure, Stolidity.
P	H	O	B	I	A	Disabling fear, Morbid aversion, Flight.
P	H	O	N	E	D	Telephoned, Called, Buzzed.
P	H	O	N	E	Y	Counterfeit, Bogus, False, Fake, Sham, Cheat, Fraud, Hoax.
P	H	O	N	I	C	Relating to sound.
P	H	O	T	O	N	Quantum of radial energy.
P	H	R	A	S	E	Wording, Diction, Expression, Locution, Slogan, Parlance, Verbiage, Express.
P	H	Y	L	O	N	Race, Tribe.
P	H	Y	S	I	C	Remedy, Cure, Drug, Medicant, Medicine, Dose, Pharmacon.
P	H	Y	T	O	N	Potential cutting of plant.
P	I	A	C	L	E	Sacrificial offering, Crime, Sin.
P	I	A	Z	Z	A	Open square, Market place.
P	I	C	K	E	D	Selected, Chosen, Elected, Exclusive, Preferred, Singled (out).
P	I	C	K	E	R	Worker in fruit orchard, Selector, Tool for clearing small openings.
P	I	C	K	E	T	Stake, Peg, Post, Guard, Sentinel, Look-out (during strike).
P	I	C	K	L	E	Preserve, Jam, Predicament, Dilemma, Fix, Scrape, Spot.
P	I	C	K	U	P	Lift, Elevate, Hoist, Raise, Uplift, Acquire, Gain, Arrest.
P	I	C	N	I	C	Outdoor meal, Snap, Breeze, Child's play, Cinch, Pushover.
P	I	D	G	I	N	Limited use of language and grammar.
P	I	E	C	E	D	Joined, Mended, Sectioned, Cut.

1	2	3	4	5	6	Clue
P	I	E	D	O	G	Half-wild dog.
P	I	E	R	C	E	Perforate, Gash, Slice, Slit, Penetrate.
P	I	E	R	I	D	Genus of butterfly.
P	I	F	F	L	E	Nonsense, Balderdash, Bosh, Bunkum, Malarkey, Twaddle.
P	I	G	E	O	N	Gull, Fool, Chump, Dupe, Fall-guy, Hoodwink, Victimise.
P	I	G	N	U	T	Earthnut.
P	I	G	S	T	Y	Pigpen, Dump, Filthy dwelling.
P	I	L	A	F	F	Rice and meat dish (Turkey).
P	I	L	A	R	Y	Hairy, Hirsute.
P	I	L	E	U	P	Wreck, Crash, Prang.
P	I	L	F	E	R	Steal, Filch, Lift, Pinch, Purloin, Swipe, Thieve, Snitch.
P	I	L	I	N	G	Staking, Heaping, Banking, Lumping, Packing, Amassing, For foundations of structure.
P	I	L	L	A	R	Column, Pier, Pilaster, Mainstay, Backbone, Post, Support.
P	I	L	L	O	W	Cushion, Pad to support head of sleeping person, Block.
P	I	M	P	L	E	Spot, Pustule, Speckle, Sprinkle.
P	I	M	P	L	Y	Relating to pimples.
P	I	N	E	A	L	Resembling a pine cone.
P	I	N	E	R	Y	Where pineapples are grown.
P	I	N	G	E	D	Sound of bullet or mosquito.
P	I	N	I	N	G	Longing, Aching, Craving, Dreaming, Hungering, Yearning, Thirsting, Sighing.
P	I	N	I	O	N	Flight feather, Confine, Restrain, Shackle, Comb, Gear.
P	I	N	K	E	D	Pricked, Changed colour, Engine noise.
P	I	N	N	E	D	Fastened, Joined, Secured, Transfixed, Immobilised.
P	I	N	N	E	R	One who works with pins.
P	I	N	O	L	E	Corn or substitute flour.
P	I	N	T	L	E	Upright pivot pin, Hook attached for gun carriage.
P	I	P	A	G	E	Transportation of gas or petroleum or water by pipes.
P	I	P	I	N	G	Acute, Shrill, Feeble piercing treble, relating to bagpipes.
P	I	P	K	I	N	Small pot.
P	I	P	P	E	D	Intoxicated, Defeated, Muddled, Drunk, Fed-up, Plastered, Just beaten.
P	I	P	P	I	N	Apple, Corker, Dandy, Humdinger, Super.
P	I	Q	U	E	D	Irritated, Offended, Nettled, Provoked, Motivated, Stimulated, Pride, Preen.
P	I	Q	U	E	T	Two handed card game.
P	I	R	A	C	Y	Stealing on the high seas, Illegal production (copyright).
P	I	R	A	T	E	Corsair, Buccaneer, Picaroon, Sea robber, Raider, Marauder, Infringer of the law of copyright.
P	I	S	C	E	S	Zodiac sign (fishes).
P	I	S	T	I	L	Ovule-bearing organ of a seed plant.
P	I	S	T	O	L	Short fire-arm.
P	I	S	T	O	N	Sliding piece in engine block.
P	I	T	C	H	Y	Tarry, Resinous, Dark.
P	I	T	I	E	D	Commiserated, Sympathised. Past tense of pity.
P	I	T	M	A	N	One who works in a mine.
P	I	T	T	E	D	Competed, Opposed, Matched, Indented.
P	L	A	C	E	D	Located, Positioned, Sited, Stationed, Appointed, established, estimated, identified.
P	L	A	C	E	R	Extract minerals by washing gravel.
P	L	A	C	I	D	Calm, Hushed, Quiet, Untroubled, Collected, Composed, Serene, Tranquil.
P	L	A	G	U	E	Pestilence, Scourge, Invasion, Disease, Epidemic, Annoyance, Worry, Harry Tease.
P	L	A	G	U	Y	Troublesome, Harassing.
P	L	A	I	C	E	Flat fish.
P	L	A	I	N	T	Lamentation, Complaint, Protestation.
P	L	A	N	C	H	Plank floor, Flat plate.
P	L	A	N	E	D	Smoothed, Evened, Levelled, Glided down.
P	L	A	N	E	R	Machine tool for planing.
P	L	A	N	E	T	Earth, Globe, World, Heavenly world, Celestial body.
P	L	A	Q	U	E	Ornamental plate, Localised patch of skin disease, Film of destructive bacteria on teeth.
P	L	A	S	M	A	Fluid part of blood, Quartz.
P	L	A	T	E	D	Armoured, Overlaid, Covered by thin layer of metal.
P	L	A	T	E	N	Flat bed used in printing, Roller of typewriter.
P	L	A	T	E	R	Inferior race-horse.
P	L	A	Y	E	D	Acted, Sported, Manipulated, Used, Tricked, Operated, Gambled, Applied.
P	L	A	Y	E	R	Actor, Professional sportsman, Performer, Trouper, Mimic, Impersonator, Thespian.
P	L	E	A	C	H	Interwined, weaving, Braided, Plaited.
P	L	E	A	S	E	Choose, Elect, Like, Delight, Gladden, Satisfy, Content.
P	L	E	D	G	E	Security, Guarantee, Promise, Warrant, Undertake, Vow, Swear, Assurance.
P	L	E	I	A	D	Group or cluster of seven illustrious people or things.
P	L	E	N	T	Y	Bounteous, Much, Copious, Generous, Liberal, Great deal, Pile, Ample.
P	L	E	N	U	M	Space full of matter, Entire membership.

1	2	3	4	5	6	
P	L	E	U	R	A	Relating to the lungs.
P	L	I	A	N	T	Supple, Lithe, Flexible, Malleable, Plastic, Moldable, Pliable.
P	L	I	E	R	S	Pincers with roughened jaws.
P	L	I	G	H	T	Vow, Dilemma, Fix, Hole, Engagement, Covenant, Pickle, Scrape.
P	L	I	N	T	H	Brick perch, Dias, Pedestal, Squared base.
P	L	O	U	G	H	Break, Turn, Turn over, Cultivate.
P	L	O	V	E	R	Shore-inhabiting bird.
P	L	U	C	K	Y	Brave, Bold, Courageous, Dauntless, Fearless, Gutsy, Doughty.
P	L	U	M	E	D	Adorned with feathers.
P	L	U	M	P	Y	Chubby, Podgy, Roly-poly, Tubby, Rotund.
P	L	U	N	G	E	Thrust, Drive, Burst, Pitch, Fall, Drop, Plummet, Tumble.
P	L	U	R	A	L	More than one. Opposite of singular.
P	L	U	S	H	Y	Luxurious, Opulent, Palatial, Sumptuous, Upholstered, Deluxe.
P	L	Y	I	N	G	Touting, Urging, Exercising, Employing, Steering.
P	O	A	C	H	Y	Sodden, Swampy.
P	O	C	K	E	D	Indented, Pitted.
P	O	C	K	E	T	Pouch, Cavity, Impasse. Steal, Filch, Capsule, Diminutive.
P	O	D	I	U	M	Pedestal, Balcony, Dwarf wall, Footlike part.
P	O	E	T	I	C	Lyrical, Metrical.
P	O	E	T	R	Y	Rhyme, Song, Verse.
P	O	G	R	O	M	Devastation, Massacre, Looting.
P	O	I	S	E	D	Calm, Collected, Composed, Balanced, Placid, Possessed, Serene, Tranquil.
P	O	I	S	E	R	One who poises.
P	O	I	S	O	N	Venom, Virus, Contagion, Debase, Corrupt, Pervert, Stain, Bane.
P	O	K	I	N	G	Jabbing, Nudging, Punching, Snooping, Nosing, Prying, Thrusting, Protruding.
P	O	L	I	C	E	Officer, Peace Officer, Bull, Cop, Fuzz, Constable, Copper, Gendarme.
P	O	L	I	C	Y	Course, Line, Procedure, Programme, Strategy, Plan.
P	O	L	I	N	G	Propelling a punt (boat).
P	O	L	I	S	H	Burnish, Buff, Shine, Lustre, Sleek, Smooth, Refine, Glaze.
P	O	L	I	T	E	Civil, Courteous, Genteel, Well-mannered, Urbane, Courtly, Elegant.
P	O	L	I	T	Y	Administration of government.
P	O	L	L	E	D	Voted, Canvassed, Cropped, Lopped.
P	O	L	L	E	N	Reproductive dust of plants, Fine grain or cereal, Pruinous bloom on an insect's body.
P	O	L	L	E	R	One involved in voting, One who crops or trims trees and shrubs.
P	O	L	O	N	Y	Type of sausage.
P	O	M	A	C	E	Fruit pulp.
P	O	M	A	D	E	Fragrant cosmetic ointment for the hair.
P	O	M	M	E	L	Knob on hilt of sword, Ornamental part of saddle, Plunger, Pummel, Belabour.
P	O	M	P	O	M	Decorative tuft of wool. Quick firing gun, Chrysanthemum.
P	O	N	C	H	O	Blanket with slit worn as cloak (S. America).
P	O	N	D	E	R	Consider, Contemplate, Study, Think, Deliberate, Meditate, Ruminate, Evaluate.
P	O	N	E	N	T	Occidental, Western.
P	O	O	D	L	E	Dog with curly coat.
P	O	O	L	E	D	Combined, Shared, Contributed, Common interest.
P	O	O	P	E	D	Exhausted, Breathless, Prostrated, Worn-out, Swamped by wave.
P	O	O	R	E	R	Beggared, Broke, Impoverished, Indigent, Needy, Destitute, Stony, Inferior, Lacking.
P	O	O	R	L	Y	Unwell, Indisposed, Ailing, Sickly, Off-colour.
P	O	P	E	R	Y	Roman Catholicism.
P	O	P	G	U	N	Toy gun which shoots corks by means of compressed air.
P	O	P	I	S	H	Pertaining to Catholic religion.
P	O	P	L	A	R	Tree, Wood pulp used for manufacture of paper.
P	O	P	L	I	N	Strong woven cotton-like fabric.
P	O	P	P	E	D	Burst, Cracked, Exploded, Pawned.
P	O	P	P	E	R	Pan for popping corn.
P	O	P	P	E	T	Marionette, Part of lathe, Support for oarlocks on rowboat.
P	O	R	I	N	G	Studying, Gazing, Meditating, Reflecting, Brooding.
P	O	R	K	E	R	Young pig bred for table use.
P	O	R	O	U	S	Pervious, Permeable, Penetrable, Porose.
P	O	R	R	E	T	Small onion, Leek.
P	O	R	T	A	L	Door, Entrance, Gate, Doorway, Fissure leading to liver.
P	O	R	T	E	D	Carried, Conveyed.
P	O	R	T	E	R	Carrier, Bearer, Door-man, Luggage handler.
P	O	R	T	L	Y	Corpulent, Stout, Fat, Fleshy, Heavy, Obese, Overweight.
P	O	S	A	D	A	Roadside Inn (Spanish).
P	O	S	I	N	G	Posturing, Affecting, Sitting, Pretending, Puzzling. Perplexing, Extending, Suggesting.
P	O	S	S	E	T	Hot spiced milk with ale or wine sometimes thickened with bread.
P	O	S	T	A	L	Relating to mail.

1	2	3	4	5	6	
P	O	S	T	E	A	Judge's record after verdict reached.
P	O	S	T	E	D	Informed, Notified, Appointed, Placed, Positioned, Situated, Stationed.
P	O	S	T	E	R	Placard, Bill, Advertisement, Handbill.
P	O	T	A	S	H	Potassium Carbonate used in agriculture.
P	O	T	A	T	O	Edible starchy tuber.
P	O	T	E	E	N	Illicit whisky.
P	O	T	E	N	T	Powerful, Forceful, Mighty, Strong, Lusty, Robust, Concentrated, Cogent.
P	O	T	H	E	R	Commotion, Clamour, Hassle, Tumult, Uproar, Stir, Bustle, Turmoil.
P	O	T	I	O	N	Draught, Dose, Drug, Liquid mixture.
P	O	T	M	A	N	Barman, Worker in hotel usually kitchen hand.
P	O	T	T	E	D	Condensed, Canned, Capsule, Epitomised, Pocket, Pickles, Intoxicated, Plastered.
P	O	T	T	E	R	Worker of clay, Doodle, Dissipate, Fritter, Squander, Fiddle.
P	O	T	T	L	E	Measure for half gallon.
P	O	U	F	F	E	Circular hassock. Something inflated.
P	O	U	N	C	E	Seize, Assault, Swoop, Spring, Snatch, Attack, Intervene.
P	O	U	R	E	D	Emitted, Flowed, Discharged, Gushed, Surged, Flooded, Deluged, Overflowed.
P	O	U	T	E	D	Sulked, Jutted, Projected, Protruded, Sign of displeasure.
P	O	W	D	E	R	Dust, Sprinkle, Pulverize, Crush.
P	R	A	I	S	E	Commend, Acclaim, Applaud, Compliment, Extol, Bless, Glorify, Laud.
P	R	A	N	C	E	Dance, Flounce, Mince, Strut, Prink, Tread daintily.
P	R	A	T	E	D	Chatted, Babbled, Clacked, Boasted, Bragged, Blabbed, Crowed, Vaunted.
P	R	A	X	I	S	Habit, Custom, Use, Practice, Won't, Manner.
P	R	A	Y	E	D	Appealed, Begged, Craved, Supplicated, Petitioned, Sought, Implored.
P	R	A	Y	E	R	Application, Entreaty, Petition, Imploration, Suitor, Supplicant.
P	R	E	A	C	H	Sermonize, Exhort, Declare, Moralize, Homilize, Teach.
P	R	E	C	I	S	Digest, Survey, Sketch, Summary, Syllabus.
P	R	E	C	U	T	Cut to exact requirements.
P	R	E	F	A	B	Constructed in factory for assembling on site.
P	R	E	F	E	R	Select, Choose, Mark, Propose, Propound, Suggest, Advance, Promote.
P	R	E	F	I	X	Establish place in front.
P	R	E	P	A	Y	Settled in advance.
P	R	E	S	T	O	Quickly.
P	R	E	T	T	Y	Beautiful, Attractive, Bonny, Comely, Clever, Handsome, Fairly, Somewhat.
P	R	E	W	A	R	Existing before a war.
P	R	E	Y	E	D	Chased, Despoiled, Ravaged.
P	R	I	C	E	D	Valued, Rated, Appraised.
P	R	I	E	S	T	An ordained Minister.
P	R	I	M	A	L	Original, First, Primitive.
P	R	I	M	E	R	Textbook, Detonator for explosive, Paint undercoat.
P	R	I	N	C	E	Royal male heir, Nobleman, Distinguished man.
P	R	I	S	O	N	Place for forced confinement, Usually convicted felons.
P	R	I	S	S	Y	Fussy, Prim, Excessively modest.
P	R	I	V	E	T	Genus of shrubs used as hedging.
P	R	O	F	I	T	Benefit, Gain, Advantage, Avail, Serve, Return, Proceeds.
P	R	O	M	P	T	Induce, Argue, Draw, Persuade, Urge, Quick, Apt, Ready.
P	R	O	N	T	O	Fast, Posthaste, Promptly, Rapidly, Speedily, Hastily.
P	R	O	P	E	L	Throw, Impel, Push, Drive, Thrust, Move, Exhort.
P	R	O	P	E	R	Accurate, Fit, Applicable, Correct, True, Decorous, Able, Good.
P	R	O	T	E	A	Flowering shrub (S. Africa & Australia).
P	R	O	T	O	N	Elementary particle identical with nucleus of hydrogen atom.
P	R	O	V	E	D	Verified, Demonstrated, Tried, Tested, Checked, Examined, Established, Determined.
P	R	O	V	E	N	Justified.
P	R	U	N	E	D	Trimmed, Cut, Clipped, Shaved, Sheared, Pared.
P	R	Y	I	N	G	Snooping, Peeping, Nosing, Raising(up), Levering, Prizing, Inquisitive, Curious.
P	S	E	U	D	O	False, Spurious, Counterfeit, Bogus, Fake, Phony, Snide.
P	S	O	R	I	C	Relating to chronic skin disease.
P	S	Y	C	H	E	Soul, Spirit, Personality, Mind conscious & unconscious.
P	T	E	R	O	N	Wing, Feather, Side of Greek temple.
P	U	B	L	I	C	Civic, Society, Common, Accessible, Open, Popular, General, Audience.
P	U	C	K	E	R	Grease, Contract, Furrow, Wrinkle, Constrict.
P	U	D	D	L	E	Pool, Saturate.
P	U	F	F	E	D	Bloated, Swollen, Inflated, Arrogant.
P	U	F	F	E	R	Fish.
P	U	F	F	I	N	Sea-bird.
P	U	G	D	O	G	Lap dog.
P	U	L	I	N	G	Whining, Whimpering, Moaning.
P	U	L	L	E	D	Hauled, Extracted, Torn, Strained, Committed, Gained, Influence, Drawn.

1	2	3	4	5	6	
P	U	L	L	E	T	Young chicken, Young fowl.
P	U	L	L	E	Y	Wheel with grooved rim, Tackle for use with block.
P	U	L	P	E	D	Mashed, Squashed, Crushed.
P	U	L	P	I	T	Elevated Platform, high reading desk.
P	U	L	S	A	R	Star relating to radio energy.
P	U	L	S	E	D	Vibrated, Throbbed.
P	U	M	I	C	E	Cooled lava.
P	U	M	M	E	L	Batter, Beat, Hammer, Hit, Pelt, Pound, Thrash.
P	U	M	P	E	D	Drained, Drawn(off), Interrogated, Questioned, Breathless.
P	U	N	C	H	Y	Stocky, Forceful.
P	U	N	D	I	T	Teacher, Wise man, Authority.
P	U	N	I	E	R	Comparative of puny, Weaker, Feebler.
P	U	N	I	S	H	Chasten, Chastise, Discipline, Correct, Consume, Polish off, Shift, Castigate.
P	U	N	N	E	R	One who rams, Consolidates.
P	U	N	N	E	T	Basket for berry fruit.
P	U	N	T	E	D	Kicked in football.
P	U	N	T	E	R	Gambler, Better.
P	U	P	A	T	E	Become a chrysalis.
P	U	P	O	I	D	Shaped like a pupa.
P	U	P	P	E	D	Given birth to litter, Whelped.
P	U	P	P	E	T	Marionette, Doll, Tool, Pawn, Stooge.
P	U	R	D	A	H	Seclusion, Concealed by clothing (women).
P	U	R	E	L	Y	Exactly, Just, Totally, Utterly, Wholly, Clearly, Really.
P	U	R	E	S	T	Blemish free, Stainless, Immaculate.
P	U	R	F	L	E	Decorated border.
P	U	R	G	E	D	Purified, Cleared, Cleansed, Eliminated, Removed, Liquidated.
P	U	R	G	E	R	Relating to purge.
P	U	R	I	F	Y	Cleanse, Clarify, Depurate, Expurgate, Purge, Absolve.
P	U	R	I	N	E	Uric acid.
P	U	R	I	S	M	Rigid adherence, Nicety, Exactness.
P	U	R	I	S	T	Traditionalist.
P	U	R	I	T	Y	Chastity, Simplicity, Fineness.
P	U	R	L	E	D	Swirled, Curled, Gyrated, Whirled.
P	U	R	L	E	R	Spill, Fall, Cropper.
P	U	R	L	I	N	Roof timber.
P	U	R	P	L	E	Risqué, Blue, Broad, Off-colour, Shady, Spicy, Flowery, Florid.
P	U	R	R	E	D	Past tense of purr (low vibratory murmur of a cat).
P	U	R	S	E	D	Puckered, Wrinkled, Contracted, Knitted.
P	U	R	S	E	R	Treasurer, Paymaster in the Navy, Official on ship & airliner responsible for finances.
P	U	R	S	U	E	Follow, Chase, Trail, Chivy, Address, Court, Practice, Sue.
P	U	S	H	E	D	Propelled, Shoved, Thrust, Elbowed, Hustled, Pressed, Enlarged, Promoted.
P	U	S	H	E	R	One who thrusts, Type of plane with propeller behind wing, Plunger.
P	U	T	R	I	D	Bad, Decayed, Rotten, Spoiled, Fetid, Rancid, Corrupt, Depraved.
P	U	T	T	E	D	Stroke made on putting green.
P	U	T	T	E	E	Legging of cloth or leather.
P	U	T	T	E	R	Move aimlessly, Dawdle, Golf club.
P	U	Z	Z	L	E	Bewilder, Confound, Confuse, Perplex, Mystery, Conundrum, Enigma, Riddle.
P	Y	E	M	I	A	Blood-poisoning.
P	Y	R	E	N	E	Stone of a fruit.
P	Y	R	O	L	A	Genus of type of herb.
P	Y	R	O	P	E	Red gem.
P	Y	T	H	O	N	Large constricting snake.
P	Y	U	R	I	A	Pus in the urine.

Q

Q	U	A	D	R	A	Plinth, Podium, Square frame or border.
Q	U	A	G	G	Y	Boggy, Marshy.
Q	U	A	I	N	T	Strange, Curious, Eccentric, Droll, Peculiar, Queer, Fantastic, Unusual.
Q	U	A	K	E	D	Quivered, Shook, Trembled, Vibrated, Shuddered, Twittered, Rocked.
Q	U	A	K	E	R	Member of the Society of Friends.
Q	U	A	R	R	Y	Mine, Pit, Prey, Chase, Delve.
Q	U	A	R	T	O	Size of page (cut four from a sheet).
Q	U	A	R	T	Z	Silicon dioxide.
Q	U	A	S	A	R	Radio energy star far out in the galaxy.
Q	U	A	V	E	R	Eighth note, Quiver, Vibrate, Tremble, Trill.
Q	U	E	A	S	Y	Squeamish, Queer, Doubtful, Dubious, Indecisive, Shady, Unsettled.

1	2	3	4	5	6	
Q	U	E	L	C	H	Squelch, Crush, Suppress, Repress, Muffle.
Q	U	E	N	C	H	Extinguish, Douse, Crush, Suppress, Destroy, Demolish, Quell, Slake.
Q	U	E	U	E	D	Filed, Lined(up).
Q	U	E	Z	A	L	Bird (Central America).
Q	U	I	C	H	E	Flan with Cheese, Bacon and Egg.
Q	U	I	L	L	S	Parts of a feather, Spines of hedgehog and porcupine, Feather pens for writing.
Q	U	I	N	C	E	Fruit resembling apple with hard flesh.
Q	U	I	N	O	L	Resembling quinine.
Q	U	I	N	S	Y	Sore throat.
Q	U	I	R	E	D	Separated and parcelled into quires.
Q	U	I	R	K	Y	Tricky, illusive, evasive, artful.
Q	U	I	T	C	H	Couch grass.
Q	U	I	V	E	R	Shake, vibrate, Carrying case for arrows.
Q	U	O	R	U	M	Number of members necessary for making a decision.
Q	U	O	T	E	D	Cited, Repeated, Referred.
Q	U	O	T	U	M	Proportion, Part.

R

R	A	B	A	T	O	Turned-down collar, Support for ruff.
R	A	B	B	E	T	Carpenter's joint.
R	A	B	B	I	N	Master, Rabbi.
R	A	B	B	I	T	Small brown mammal, Weak batsman, Beginner at a sport.
R	A	B	B	L	E	Mob, Rout, Scum, Bourgeousie, Many, Populace, Public, Riffraff.
R	A	B	I	E	S	Virus disease transmitted by animals usually of the canine species.
R	A	C	I	A	L	Ethnic, Evolution, Segregation.
R	A	C	I	L	Y	Lively, Spiritedly, Piquantly, Pungently, Spicily.
R	A	C	I	N	G	Running, Rushing, Bolting, Charging, Chasing, Tearing, Competing, Contesting.
R	A	C	I	S	M	Racialism pertaining to racial differences.
R	A	C	K	E	D	Stretched, Strained.
R	A	C	K	E	R	One who works with racks.
R	A	C	K	E	T	For tennis, Din, Babble, Clamour, Tumult, Uproar, Work, Business occupation often illegal.
R	A	C	K	L	E	Rattle, Headstrong, Impetuous.
R	A	D	D	L	E	Interweaving, Twist, Red ochre.
R	A	D	I	A	L	Ray-like.
R	A	D	I	A	N	Angle of 57.29 degrees.
R	A	D	I	S	H	Pungent fleshy edible root.
R	A	D	I	U	M	Radioactive white metallic element.
R	A	D	I	U	S	Forearm bone, Ray, Rod, Spoke, Range, Compass, Orbit, Scope.
R	A	F	A	L	E	Gust of wind, Fire from battery gun.
R	A	F	F	E	D	Snatched, Swept, Jumbled.
R	A	F	F	I	A	Fibre of Madagascar palm.
R	A	F	F	L	E	Lottery, Draw, Sweepstake, Serrate.
R	A	F	T	E	R	Roof-timber, Timber worker with floating logs.
R	A	G	B	A	G	Collection of scraps of material.
R	A	G	D	A	Y	Carnival organised by university students for charity funds.
R	A	G	G	E	D	Tattered, Jagged, Frayed, Uneven, Torn, Frazzled, Shaggy.
R	A	G	G	L	E	Groove cut in masonry.
R	A	G	I	N	G	Furious, Wild, Blustering, Rabid, Rough, Stormy, Turbulent, Tempestuous.
R	A	G	L	A	N	Cut of sleeve extending to neckline having slanted seams.
R	A	G	L	E	T	As Raggle.
R	A	G	M	A	N	One who collects and deals in refuse and rags.
R	A	G	O	U	T	Well-seasoned thick stew.
R	A	G	T	A	G	Rabble, Riffraff, Mob, Unwashed, Dregs, Masses.
R	A	I	D	E	R	Invader, Marauder, Forager, Looter, Pillager, Sacker, Ravisher, Plunderer.
R	A	I	L	E	D	Scolded, Berated, Reviled, Upbraided, Scoffed, Fenced, Conveyed by train.
R	A	I	S	E	D	Elevated, Lifted, Uplifted, Erect, Upright, Upstanding.
R	A	I	S	I	N	Dried grape.
R	A	K	E	R	Y	Lewdness, Debauchery.
R	A	K	I	S	H	Wild, Devil-may-care, Fast, Gay, Raffish, Sporty, Dissolute, Licentious.
R	A	M	A	G	E	Tree branches.
R	A	M	B	L	E	Wander, Meander, Range, Roam, Rove, Digress, Stray, Sprawl.
R	A	M	I	F	Y	Branch, Divide, Extend by division.
R	A	M	I	S	M	Doctrine advocating logic amalgamated with rhetoric.
R	A	M	M	E	D	Butted, Pounded, Crashed, Forced, Crammed.
R	A	M	M	E	L	Underbrush, Trash.

1	2	3	4	5	6	Definition
R	A	M	P	E	D	Bounded.
R	A	M	R	O	D	Rod for ramming charge in muzzle-loading firearm, Strict disciplinarian.
R	A	M	S	O	N	Wild garlic.
R	A	N	C	I	D	Malodorous, Fetid, High, Noisome, Putrid, Reeking, Sour, Musty.
R	A	N	D	O	M	Aimless, Desultory, Haphazard, Indiscriminate, Irregular, Purposeless, Slapdash, Hit-or-miss.
R	A	N	G	E	D	Arranged in line or ranks.
R	A	N	G	E	R	Keeper of park or reserve.
R	A	N	I	N	E	Relating to frogs.
R	A	N	K	E	R	Officer commissioned from the ranks.
R	A	N	K	L	E	Fester, Burn, Inflame, Vexation.
R	A	N	K	L	Y	Boldly, Ostentatiously, Overbearing, Strongly, Bravely.
R	A	N	S	O	M	Buy, Redeem, Payment for release of captive.
R	A	N	T	A	N	Knocking, Banging, Pounding.
R	A	N	T	E	R	Noisy bombastic speaker.
R	A	P	I	E	R	Light two-edged sword.
R	A	P	I	N	E	Seize, Rob, Kidnap, Ravage, Plunder.
R	A	P	I	N	G	Despoiling, Ravishing, Violating, Sexual aggression.
R	A	P	P	E	D	Struck, Tapped, Knocked, Hit, Rebuked, Blamed, Criticized, Reproached.
R	A	P	P	E	R	Knocker on door.
R	A	R	E	F	Y	Attenuate, Make thin, Dilute, Refine.
R	A	R	E	L	Y	Seldom, Infrequently, Extra, Extremely, Uncommonly, Not often.
R	A	R	E	S	T	Distinctive, Scarcest, Sparsest, Thinnest, Unusual, Uncommon.
R	A	R	I	T	Y	Scarcity, Fewness.
R	A	S	C	A	L	Villain, Scamp, Bastard, Knave, Miscreant, Rogue, Scoundrel, Rapscallion.
R	A	S	H	E	R	Thin slice of bacon or ham.
R	A	S	H	L	Y	Brashly, Hastily, Incautiously, Inconsiderately, Thoughtlessly, Foolhardy, Daringly.
R	A	S	P	E	D	Grated, Scraped, Abraded, Unpleasant tone of voice.
R	A	S	P	E	R	Scraper, Fence.
R	A	S	T	E	R	Area where cathode ray is projected.
R	A	T	H	E	R	Instead, Alternatively, Fairly, Tolerably, Somewhat, Moderately, Significantly.
R	A	T	I	F	Y	Confirm, Approve, Endorse, Authorize, Accredit, Validate.
R	A	T	I	N	G	Classification, Sailor, Standing, Estimation of individual's traits and qualities.
R	A	T	I	O	N	Allowance, Share, Portion, Quota, Apportion.
R	A	T	I	T	E	Flat-breasted.
R	A	T	T	A	N	Drum-beat, Tough, Strong fibre from palm.
R	A	T	T	E	R	One who collects rats for financial gain.
R	A	T	T	L	E	Clatter, Clack, Shatter, Chatter, Vibrate, Abash, Confound, Discomfit.
R	A	U	C	L	E	Raucous, Jarring, Strident.
R	A	V	A	G	E	Desecrate, Desolate, Despoil, Harry, Scourge, Spoil, Pillage.
R	A	V	I	N	E	Chasm, Cleft, Gorge, Gap, Gulch, Gully.
R	A	V	I	N	G	Frenzied, Raging, Delirious.
R	A	V	I	S	H	Violate, Delight, Rape, Deflorate, Force, Outrage, Spoil.
R	A	W	I	S	H	Relating to something uncooked.
R	A	Z	I	N	G	Destroying, Demolishing, Ruining, Wrecking, Overthrowing.
R	E	A	D	E	R	One who applies himself to reading, Corrector of proofs.
R	E	A	L	L	Y	Very, Actually, Genuinely, Truly, Veritably, Well, Doubtlessly, Easily.
R	E	A	L	T	Y	Real estate, Property.
R	E	A	M	E	D	Skimmed cream, Enlarged, Cheated, Victimized, Lashed.
R	E	A	P	E	D	Garnered, Harvested, Gathered, Cropped, Obtained.
R	E	A	R	E	D	Constructed, Erected, Raised, Lifted, Elevated, Hoisted, Upheld, Brought up (child).
R	E	A	S	O	N	Explanation, Account, Justification, Motive, Cause, Consideration, Argument, Intellect.
R	E	A	S	T	Y	Rancid.
R	E	A	V	E	D	Robbed, Deprived, Plundered, Pillaged.
R	E	A	V	E	R	Brigand, Bandit, Freebooter.
R	E	B	A	C	K	Reinforce spine of book.
R	E	B	A	T	E	Decrease, Diminish, Dwindle, Lessen, Reduce, Taper, Discount, Reduction.
R	E	B	A	T	O	Lace collar or stiffened ruff.
R	E	B	I	N	D	Refasten, Renew supporting material.
R	E	B	O	I	L	Boil again for distilled water.
R	E	B	O	R	E	Mechanical treatment for worn cylinder in engine block.
R	E	B	O	R	N	Regenerated, Resurrected, Revived, Re-incarnated.
R	E	B	U	F	F	Repulse, Snub, Stave(off), Fend(off), Keep(off), Hold(off). Repel.
R	E	B	U	K	E	Admonition, Reprove, Reproach, Chiding, Rap, Reprimand, Upbraid.
R	E	B	U	R	Y	Inter again.
R	E	C	A	L	L	Remember, Cite, Recollect, Remind, Revive, Recant, Revoke, Rescind.
R	E	C	A	N	T	Abjure, Forswear, Deny, Retract, Renounce, Deny, Withdraw.
R	E	C	A	S	T	Throw again (fishing line), Refashion, Recalculate, Replace performers (play).

1	2	3	4	5	6	
R	E	C	E	D	E	Withdraw, Retire, Retreat, Retrograde, Decrease, Diminish, Reduce, Lessen.
R	E	C	E	N	T	New, Fresh, Modern, Novel, Late, Newfangled, Modernistic.
R	E	C	E	P	T	Brain washed.
R	E	C	E	S	S	Alcove, Niche, Recede, Adjourn, Dissolve, Prorogue, Terminate, Rise (court).
R	E	C	I	P	E	Formula, Prescription, Procedure.
R	E	C	I	T	E	Relate, Describe, Narrate, Recount, Repeat, State, Tell, Rehearse.
R	E	C	K	E	D	Considered, Heeded, Concerned.
R	E	C	K	O	N	Calculate, Compute, Estimate, Figure, Consider, Regard, Judge, Assume.
R	E	C	O	C	T	To cook or boil again.
R	E	C	O	I	L	Rebound, Kick (gun), Blanch, Flinch, Quail, Shrink, Wince.
R	E	C	O	R	D	Show, Note, Achievement, Indicate, Register, Document, Archive(s). Gramophone disc.
R	E	C	O	U	P	Recover, Get back, Recruit, Regain, Repossess, Retrieve, Indemnify.
R	E	C	T	A	L	Pertaining to the rectum.
R	E	C	T	O	R	Vicar, Academic, Leader.
R	E	C	T	U	M	Lower part of intestine.
R	E	C	T	U	S	Straight muscle.
R	E	C	U	M	B	Recline.
R	E	C	U	R	E	Make whole, Repair.
R	E	C	U	S	E	Disqualify, Reject.
R	E	D	D	E	N	Blush, Ruddle, Ruddy.
R	E	D	D	L	E	Mark with red chalk, Flush.
R	E	D	E	E	M	Ransom, Buy, Free, Retrieve, Emancipate, Release, Atone, Compensate.
R	E	D	H	O	T	Hot, Blistering, Boiling, Scalding, Impassioned, Blazing, Glowing, Contemporary.
R	E	D	R	A	W	Redraft, Copy, Select, Revise, Rewrite.
R	E	D	U	C	E	Decrease, Abate, Diminish, Cut back, Lower, Crush, Degrade, Slim.
R	E	D	U	C	T	Deduct.
R	E	E	C	H	Y	Rancid, Odorous.
R	E	E	D	E	D	Thatched, Woven, Corrugations (edge of coin).
R	E	E	F	E	R	Short double-breasted coat, Drugged cigarette, Refrigerated ship/car/truck/trailer.
R	E	E	K	E	D	Smelled, Stunk, Putrid.
R	E	E	L	E	D	Staggered, Swayed, Whirled, Recoiled.
R	E	F	I	L	L	Replenish, Replacement.
R	E	F	I	N	D	Recover, Retrieve.
R	E	F	I	N	E	Polish, Perfect, Round, Sleek, Slick, Clarify, Purify, Cleanse.
R	E	F	L	E	T	Metallic lustre on ceramic.
R	E	F	L	E	X	Bent, Reactive, Introspective resistance, Reversed.
R	E	F	L	O	W	Flow back, Flood.
R	E	F	L	U	X	Ebb, Recede.
R	E	F	O	R	M	Amend, Improve, Change.
R	E	F	U	E	L	Replenish fuel supply.
R	E	F	U	G	E	Asylum, Sanctuary, Shelter, Harbour, Haven, Resource, Resort, Substitute.
R	E	F	U	N	D	Reimburse, Repay, Return, Restitution.
R	E	F	U	S	E	Decline, Disapprove, Dismiss, Spurn, Reject, Deny, Disallow, Withold. Debris, Garbage, Junk.
R	E	F	U	T	E	Disprove, Break, Confound Controvert, Confute, Rebut.
R	E	G	A	I	N	Recapture, Recover, Recoup, Retrieve, Recruit, Repossess.
R	E	G	A	L	E	Dinner, Banquet, Spread (of food and wine).
R	E	G	A	R	D	Notice, Attention, Consideration, Concern, Interest, Care, Respect.
R	E	G	E	N	T	Ruling in minority, absence or disability of sovereign, Governor.
R	E	G	G	A	E	West Indian music with a heavy rhythmic beat.
R	E	G	I	M	E	Diet, Government, Administration, System, Rule.
R	E	G	I	N	A	A queen.
R	E	G	I	O	N	Area, Belt, Province, Territory, Tract, Zone, Vicinity, Domain.
R	E	G	L	E	T	Fillet, Batten, Flat Moulding.
R	E	G	L	O	W	Rekindle.
R	E	G	N	A	L	Relating to king, region or kingdom.
R	E	G	R	E	T	Deplore, Repent, Rue, Remorse, Sorrow, Anguish, Grief, Heartbreak.
R	E	G	U	L	A	Rules.
R	E	H	A	S	H	Rearrange.
R	E	I	N	E	D	Checked, Fastened, Curbed.
R	E	J	E	C	T	Decline, Dismiss, Refuse, Spurn, Discard, Repudiate, Shed, Jettison.
R	E	J	O	I	N	Reunite, Answer, Reply, Respond, Retort, Return.
R	E	L	A	I	D	Past tense of Relay.
R	E	L	A	T	E	Describe, Narrate, Recite, Report, State, Join, Associate, Combine.
R	E	L	E	N	T	Abate, Ebb, Fall, Relax, Yield, Moderate, Slacken, Wane.
R	E	L	I	E	D	Banked(on), Depended(on), Counted(on), Rallied, Trusted, Confided.
R	E	L	I	E	F	Redress, Ease, Aid, Mitigate, Help, Assist, Comfort, Lift.
R	E	L	I	S	H	Zest, Gusto, Pickle, Enjoy, Like, Admire, Cherish, Appreciate.

1	2	3	4	5	6	
R	E	L	O	A	D	Refill, Recharge a gun.
R	E	L	U	C	T	Struggle.
R	E	L	U	M	E	Rekindle.
R	E	M	A	D	E	Do over, refashioned.
R	E	M	A	I	N	Stay, Bid, Linger, Tarry, Wait, Persist, Survive.
R	E	M	A	K	E	Transform.
R	E	M	A	N	D	Return a person to custody or continued detention.
R	E	M	A	R	K	See, Behold, Discern, Comment, Observe, Observation, Commentary, Perceive.
R	E	M	E	D	Y	Cure, Medicament, Antidote, Medicine, Physic, Corrective, Countermeasure, Heal.
R	E	M	I	N	D	Remember, Recall, Recollect, Retain, Revive, Cite, Retrospect, Prompt.
R	E	M	I	S	E	Transfer, Alienate, Assign, Cede, Convey, Deed, Make over, Sign(over).
R	E	M	I	S	S	Negligent, Behindhand, Careless, Delinquent, Lax, Neglectful, Regardless, Dilatory.
R	E	M	O	T	E	Distant, Outlying, Frontier, Obscure, Retired, Negligible, Indifferent, Aloof.
R	E	M	O	V	E	Move, Dislocate, Disturb, Shift, Slip, Withdraw, Eliminate, Purge.
R	E	N	D	E	R	Return, Represent, Describe, Portray, Translate, Administer, Execute, Interpret.
R	E	N	E	G	E	Back down, Back out, Backpedal, Cry off, Welsh, Backwater.
R	E	N	N	E	T	Something used to curdle milk.
R	E	N	N	I	N	Enzyme that coagulates milk.
R	E	N	O	W	N	Fame, Celebrity, Notoriety, Reputation, Repute, Eminence, Prestige, Distinction.
R	E	N	T	A	L	Apartment, Chambers, Flat, Lodgings, Rooms, Suite, Schedule, Rent-roll.
R	E	N	T	E	D	Hired, Leased.
R	E	N	T	E	R	One who rents, leases or hires.
R	E	O	P	E	N	Resume, Continue, Recommence, Renew, Restart.
R	E	P	A	I	D	Rewarded, Compensated, Reimbursed, Indemnified.
R	E	P	A	I	R	Mend, Fix, Overhaul, Recondition, Order, Condition, Go, Journey.
R	E	P	A	N	D	Bent backward.
R	E	P	A	S	T	Meal, Food, Victuals, Feed.
R	E	P	E	A	L	Revoke, Dismantle, Rescind, Annul, Nullify, Recall, Reverse.
R	E	P	E	A	T	Reiterate, Renew, Reprise, Echo.
R	E	P	E	N	T	Regret, Deplore, Rue.
R	E	P	I	N	E	Complain, Fret, Kick, Murmur, Wail, Whine.
R	E	P	L	A	Y	To play again.
R	E	P	O	R	T	Account, Chronicle, Narrative, Gossip, Rumour, Reputation, Character, Fame.
R	E	P	O	S	E	Rest, Ease, Recline, Lie, Stretch(out), Respite.
R	E	P	U	G	N	Oppose, Refute, Reject, Repel.
R	E	P	U	T	E	Fame, Celebrity, Notoriety, Renown, Reputation, Character, Name, Regard.
R	E	S	A	I	L	To sail again.
R	E	S	A	L	E	A second hand sale.
R	E	S	C	U	E	Save, Deliver, Redeem, Release.
R	E	S	E	A	T	Fit chair with a new seat, Set valves (car engine).
R	E	S	E	L	L	To sell again.
R	E	S	E	N	T	Resist, Repel, Dislike.
R	E	S	I	D	E	Abide, Dwell, Live, Lodge, Bide, Sojourn.
R	E	S	I	G	N	Relinquish, Leave, Surrender, Yield, Abdicate, Renounce, Quit, Terminate.
R	E	S	I	L	E	Retract, Retreat.
R	E	S	I	N	Y	Resinous.
R	E	S	I	S	T	Combat, Contest, Dispute, Oppose, Duel, Fight, Traverse, Withstand.
R	E	S	O	R	B	To swallow or suck in.
R	E	S	O	R	T	Resource, Expediency, Refuge, Hang-out, Haunt, Spa, Rendezvous, Watering place.
R	E	S	T	E	D	Quieted, Reposed, Desisted.
R	E	S	U	L	T	Effect, Eventuality, Issue, Outcome, Sequel, Answer, Solution, End.
R	E	S	U	M	E	Reoccupy, Repossess, Retake, Continue, Renew, Reopen, Restart, Recommence.
R	E	T	A	I	L	Sell, Market, Merchandise, Hawk, Peddle.
R	E	T	A	I	N	Enjoy, Hold, Possess, Detain, Reserve, Withold, Remember, Remind.
R	E	T	A	K	E	Resume, Reoccupy, Repossess.
R	E	T	A	R	D	Delay, Detain, Clog, Hinder, Impede, Check, Slacken.
R	E	T	E	N	T	Something that is retained, esp.- in the mind.
R	E	T	E	S	T	A repeated test.
R	E	T	I	N	A	Optic nerve terminus.
R	E	T	I	R	E	Retreat, Withdraw, Go, Depart, Leave, Bed, Quit, Pension(off).
R	E	T	O	L	D	Past of RETELL.
R	E	T	O	O	K	Past of RETAKE.
R	E	T	O	R	T	Answer, Rejoinder, Reply, Respond, Return, Comeback, Repartee, Riposte.
R	E	T	O	S	S	To toss again.
R	E	T	R	A	L	Posterior, After, Back, Backward, Retrograde, Hindmost.
R	E	T	R	E	E	Paper damaged or imperfect.
R	E	T	R	I	M	To trim again, To smarten.

1	2	3	4	5	6	
R	E	T	U	N	D	Blunt, Refute.
R	E	T	U	R	N	Revert, Recur, React, Answer, Rejoin, Restore, Yield, Reciprocate. Recurrence, Reappearance.
R	E	T	U	S	E	Blunted or rounded apex.
R	E	V	A	M	P	Renovate, Remake, Mend, Overhaul, Recondition, Reconstruct, Repair.
R	E	V	E	A	L	Disclose, Betray, Divulge, Tell, Discover, Open, Expose, Uncover.
R	E	V	E	R	B	Reverberate, Resound, Reflect.
R	E	V	E	R	E	Adore, Venerate, Worship, Honour, Reverence, Treasure, Exalt, Admire.
R	E	V	E	R	S	Turned back front facing or lapel on a jacket.
R	E	V	E	R	T	Return, React, Recur, Regress, Reverse, Change, Inverse, Transpose.
R	E	V	E	S	T	Resume, Return to former owner, To clothe again (clerical vestments).
R	E	V	I	E	W	Revision, Examination, Audit, Criticism, Notice, Journal, Periodical, Reconsider.
R	E	V	I	L	E	Scold, Berate, Rail, Rate, Upbraid, Vituperate, Malign, Calumniate.
R	E	V	I	S	E	Redraft, Redraw, Rewrite, Review, Restyle, Correct, Revamp.
R	E	V	I	V	E	Restore, Resuscitate, Recall, Renew, Rekindle, Remember, Remind, Rouse.
R	E	V	O	K	E	Repeal, Recall, Rescind, Reverse, Recollect, Dismantle.
R	E	V	O	L	T	Insurrect, Mutiny, Rebel, Disgust, Nauseate, Repel, Repulse, Sicken.
R	E	V	V	E	D	Past of REV. (Revolutions per minute).
R	E	W	A	R	D	Dividend, Prize, Repay, Carrot, Plum, Premium, Recompense.
R	E	W	O	O	D	To reforest.
R	H	A	G	O	N	Type of sponge.
R	H	E	S	U	S	Indian monkey.
R	H	E	U	M	Y	Tending to catarrh and/or rheumatism.
R	H	I	N	A	L	Relating to the nose.
R	H	I	Z	I	C	Root.
R	H	Y	M	E	D	Terminal words have corresponding sounds.
R	H	Y	M	E	R	Mediocre poet.
R	H	Y	T	H	M	Metre, Symmetrical grouping of tones or beats.
R	I	A	L	T	O	Bridge in Venice.
R	I	B	A	L	D	Rude, Lewd, Coarse, Indecent, Scamp, Rogue, Mischief, Devil.
R	I	B	A	N	D	A ribbon used for a decoration.
R	I	B	B	E	D	Ridged or raised band.
R	I	B	B	O	N	Flat or tubed narrow fabric (usually silk or rayon).
R	I	B	L	E	T	Rib ends (lamb or veal).
R	I	B	O	S	E	Crystalline aldose sugar.
R	I	C	H	E	R	Wealthier, More affluent.
R	I	C	H	E	S	Wealth, Fortune, Property, Resources, Substance, Worth.
R	I	C	H	L	Y	Sumptously, Opulently, Abundantly, Thoroughly.
R	I	C	K	E	D	Wrenched, Sprained.
R	I	C	K	E	R	Pole, Spar.
R	I	C	T	A	L	Relating to grin or grimace.
R	I	C	T	U	S	Gaping mouth.
R	I	D	D	L	E	Conundrum, Enigma, Sieve, Strainer.
R	I	D	G	E	D	Furrowed, Ribbed.
R	I	D	I	N	G	Action of one that rides, Harassment of someone. County, Province, Sub-division.
R	I	E	V	E	R	Brigand, Freebooter, Pirate.
R	I	F	E	L	Y	Plentiful, Numerous, Replete.
R	I	F	F	L	E	Shuffle(playing cards), Small wave, Ruffle(water).
R	I	F	L	E	D	Robbed, Looted, Plundered, Pillaged, Grooved.
R	I	F	T	E	D	Broken, Fractured, Split.
R	I	G	G	E	D	Furnished, Appointed, Duped, Hoaxed, Tricked, Hoodwinked.
R	I	G	G	E	R	Mechanic on plane, Worker on oil rig.
R	I	G	L	E	T	Flat wooden moulding.
R	I	G	O	U	R	Hardship, Hardness, Asperity, Difficulty, Inflexibility, Rigidity.
R	I	G	O	U	T	Outfit, Suit of clothes, Uniform.
R	I	L	I	N	G	Irritating, Inflaming, Provoking, Grating, Nettling, Peeving.
R	I	L	L	E	D	Flowed in narrow furrow.
R	I	L	L	E	T	A small stream.
R	I	M	M	E	D	Bordered, Edged, Fringed, Hemmed.
R	I	M	M	E	R	Implement for cutting, trimming or ornamenting the edge.
R	I	M	O	S	E	Slit, Crack, Fissure, Gnarled, Tree Bark.
R	I	M	P	L	E	Wrinkle, Corrugation, Crease, Fold, Ruck, Crumple, Rumple, Scrunch.
R	I	M	S	A	W	Disc saw having teeth on a separate ring.
R	I	N	D	E	D	Having a rind.
R	I	N	D	L	E	Creek, Branch, Brook, Gutter, Runnel, Rivulet, Stream, Burn.
R	I	N	G	E	D	Looped, Combined, Surrounded, Circled, Encompassed, Girdled, Rounded(up).
R	I	N	K	E	D	To skate at a rink.
R	I	N	S	E	D	Cleansed, Cleared.

1	2	3	4	5	6	
R	I	N	S	E	R	One who rinses, A utensil holding water for rinsing.
R	I	O	T	E	D	Brawled, Misruled, Roistered, Rebelled.
R	I	O	T	E	R	Rebel, Reveller, Roisterer.
R	I	P	E	L	Y	Amply, With developed or mature appearance.
R	I	P	E	S	T	The most ripe.
R	I	P	P	E	D	Rent, Torn, Split, Cleaved, Rushed.
R	I	P	P	E	R	Corker, Dandy, Humdinger, Lulu, Nifty, Murderer who mutilates.
R	I	P	P	L	E	Ruffle, Undulated, Run irregularly, Small waves.
R	I	P	R	A	P	Foundation or sustaining wall of stones thrown together.
R	I	P	S	A	W	A saw to slit wood in the direction of the grain.
R	I	S	I	N	G	Ascent, Ascension, Towering, Insurrection, Exceeding, Improving, Lifting, Revolt.
R	I	S	K	E	D	Endangered, Compromised, Chanced, Ventured, Gambled, Jeopardized, Menaced, Dared.
R	I	S	K	E	R	Gambler.
R	I	S	Q	U	E	Suggestive, Wicked, Shady, Spicy, Blue, Off-colour, Racy, Sexy.
R	I	T	U	A	L	Rite, Ceremonial, Formality, Liturgy, Observance, Service.
R	I	V	I	N	A	Genus of tropical American herb.
R	I	V	I	N	G	Pulling, Tugging, Splitting.
R	O	A	M	E	D	Rambled, Wandered, Drifted, Meandered, Ranged, Gallivanted.
R	O	A	R	E	D	Bellowed, Guffawed, Blustered, Bawled.
R	O	A	R	E	R	Gusher (oil well).
R	O	B	B	E	D	Stole, Purloined, Looted, Plundered, Ransacked, Rifled.
R	O	B	B	E	R	Burglar, Bandit, Brigand, Housebreaker, Highwayman, Crook, Swindler.
R	O	B	I	N	G	Dressing, Invest with a robe, clerical or ceremonial.
R	O	B	U	S	T	Strong, Concentrated, Lusty, Potent, Flourishing, Booming, Prosperous, Thriving.
R	O	C	C	U	S	Genus of fishes.
R	O	C	H	E	A	Genus of flowering plant.
R	O	C	H	E	T	Ecclesiastical vestment.
R	O	C	K	E	D	Shaken, Agitated, Reeled, Tossed, Tottered, Rolled, Hustled, Rushed, Astounded.
R	O	C	K	E	R	Cradle, Chair with rockers.
R	O	C	K	E	T	Skyrocket, Shoot-up, Soar, Firework, Hurry, Haste, Whish, Jet transport.
R	O	C	O	C	O	Old fashioned, Antiquated, Dated, Ornate, Baroque, Flamboyant, Florid, Richly decorated.
R	O	D	E	N	T	Gnawing, Biting, Corroding.
R	O	D	I	N	G	Anchor line of small fishing boat.
R	O	I	L	E	D	Irritated, Aggravated, Riled, Muddied, Muddled.
R	O	L	L	E	D	Rotated, Turned, Gyrated, Revolved, Tossed, Heaved, Pitched, Wallowed.
R	O	L	L	E	R	Revolving cylinder.
R	O	L	L	U	P	Accumulate, Amass, Garner, Stockpile.
R	O	M	A	I	C	Modern Greek vernacular.
R	O	M	A	N	Y	Gipsy.
R	O	M	E	R	O	Pilgrim headed for Rome, Pilot fish.
R	O	M	I	S	T	Roman Catholic.
R	O	M	P	E	D	Gambolled, Capered, Cavorted, Frisked, Frolicked, Sported.
R	O	M	P	E	R	One piece garment usually worn by babies.
R	O	N	D	E	L	Something that forms a circle, Short poem.
R	O	O	F	E	D	Sheltered, Covered.
R	O	O	F	E	R	A worker on a roof.
R	O	O	K	E	D	Fleeced, Cheated, Swindled, Milked, Bled (dry of money).
R	O	O	K	E	R	Raker for a baker's oven.
R	O	O	K	I	E	Novice, Apprentice, Recruit, Beginner, Newcomer, Tyro, Novitiate, Freshman.
R	O	O	M	E	D	Billeted, Boarded, Lodged, Put up, Harboured.
R	O	O	M	E	R	Lodger.
R	O	O	T	E	D	Entrenched, Embedded, Fixed, Lodged, Planted, Applauded, Cheered, Supported.
R	O	O	T	E	R	Device for tearing up road surfaces, Enthusiastic supporter.
R	O	O	T	L	E	Grub around, Poke about.
R	O	P	I	N	G	Catch with a lasso.
R	O	S	A	R	Y	String of beads for counting prayers.
R	O	S	I	N	Y	Resembling rosin.
R	O	S	S	E	R	One who peels bark, Peeler, Policeman(slang).
R	O	S	T	E	R	Muster, Roll, Duty list, Roll call.
R	O	T	A	R	Y	Resembling a wheel or circle turning on its axis.
R	O	T	A	T	E	Turn, Circle, Gyrate, Revolve, Alternate, Roll.
R	O	T	G	U	T	Bad liquor.
R	O	T	T	E	D	Decayed, Decomposed, Disintegrated, Putrified, Spoiled, Tainted.
R	O	T	T	E	N	Bad, Decayed, Putrid, Spoiled, Vicious, Corrupt, Disagreeable, Unsatisfactory.
R	O	T	T	E	R	Cad, Bounder, Cur, Unprincipled, Cheat, Swindler.
R	O	T	U	L	A	Patella.
R	O	T	U	N	D	Chubby, Plump, Podgy, Round, Tubby, Resounding, Resonant, Ringing.

1	2	3	4	5	6	
R	O	U	B	L	E	Basic monetary unit of USSR.
R	O	U	G	E	D	Skin or lips touched by red coloured cosmetic.
R	O	U	N	C	E	Machine used in printing.
R	O	U	N	C	Y	Riding horse.
R	O	U	S	E	D	Stirred, Agitated, Excited, Provoked, Galvanised, Challenged, Stimulated, Rallied.
R	O	U	S	E	R	Inciter, Corker, Dandy, Ripper.
R	O	U	T	E	D	Defeated, Vanquished, Overthrown, Beaten, Cleaned up, Whipped.
R	O	V	I	N	G	Itinerant, Nomadic, Perambulant, Vagabond, Wandering, Wayfaring, Rambling, Ranging.
R	O	W	I	N	G	Sculling, Propelling a boat with oars.
R	O	Y	E	N	A	Genus of Southern African shrub.
R	U	B	B	E	D	Chafed, Eroded, Grazed, Worn, Polished, Furbished, Ruffled, Aggravated.
R	U	B	B	E	R	Substance obtained from latex, Busybody, Snoop.
R	U	B	B	L	E	Broken bricks or masonry from destruction of buildings.
R	U	B	B	L	Y	Resembling rubble.
R	U	B	I	E	D	Made like a ruby in colour.
R	U	B	I	F	Y	To redden.
R	U	B	I	N	E	Reddish.
R	U	B	O	F	F	Incidental effect.
R	U	B	O	U	T	Extinguish, Obliterate.
R	U	B	R	I	C	Titling of book in red.
R	U	C	K	E	R	Crumple, Crimp, Crinkle, Ruck(up), Rumple, Screw, Scrunch, Wrinkle.
R	U	D	D	E	R	Guiding device for a ship or plane.
R	U	D	D	L	E	To mark with red chalk or ochre.
R	U	D	E	L	Y	Insolently, Coarsely, Roughly, Ignorantly, Uncouthly, Discourteously, Inexpertly, Nearly.
R	U	D	E	S	T	Crudest, Roughest, Wildest, Rawest.
R	U	E	F	U	L	Pitiful, Woeful, Doleful, Piteous, Miserable, Mournful, Wretched.
R	U	E	L	L	E	Narrow street or alley.
R	U	F	F	E	D	Trumped (card game).
R	U	F	F	L	E	Pleat, Gather, Blow, Abrade, Annoy, Intimidate, Bother, Provoke.
R	U	F	O	U	S	Ruddy.
R	U	G	A	T	E	Wrinkle, Fold.
R	U	G	G	E	D	Rough, Severe, Harsh, Boorish, Tough, Hard, Scraggy, Formidable.
R	U	G	G	E	R	Rugby football.
R	U	G	O	S	E	Corals.
R	U	G	O	U	S	Wrinkle, Rugous.
R	U	I	N	E	D	Deteriorated, Degenerated, Wrecked, Destroyed, Demolished, Bankrupted, Injured, Damaged.
R	U	I	N	E	R	Vandal, Defacer, Despoiler, Destroyer, Wrecker.
R	U	L	I	N	G	Governing, Edict, Decree, Directive, Central, Overriding, Prevailing, Current.
R	U	M	B	L	E	Growl, Grumble, Roll, Report, Gossip, Hearsay, Reverberate, Rumour.
R	U	M	M	E	R	Large tall drinking glass.
R	U	M	O	U	R	Gossip, Hearsay, Report, Tattle, Grapevine, Talk, Mutter, Undertone.
R	U	M	P	U	S	Commotion, Argument, Contention, Controversy, Dispute, Uproar, Shindig, Furore.
R	U	N	D	L	E	Circle, Sphere, Rung, Drum of windlass.
R	U	N	N	E	L	Creek, Branch, Brook, Rivulet, Stream.
R	U	N	N	E	R	Messenger, Distributor of illegal drugs, Racer (human or horse) Support of drawer or sliding door.
R	U	N	O	F	F	Dash off, Produce by printing press, Decide, Drive off, Portion of land where rain or river runs to the sea.
R	U	N	O	U	T	Expire, Finish, Force to leave, Complete, Exhaust.
R	U	N	W	A	Y	Track, Landing field, Coin.
R	U	S	H	E	D	Hastened, Bolted, Charged, Flew, Dashed, Plunged, Stampeded, Hurried.
R	U	S	S	E	T	Coarse homespun material, Winter apple.
R	U	S	T	E	D	Corroded, Oxidized, Tarnished.
R	U	S	T	I	C	Rural, Pastoral, Farmer, Husbandman, Bumpkin, Bucolic, Hick, Countryman.
R	U	S	T	L	E	Whisper, Haste, Quiver, Dispatch, Hurry, Hustle, Speed, Steal(cattle).
R	U	S	T	R	E	Metal oval or lozenge shape in medieval armour.
R	U	T	I	L	E	Oxide of titanium.
R	U	T	T	E	D	Grooved, Furrowed.
R	U	T	T	L	E	Rattle, Bicker, Clack, Clatter, Shatter.

S

S	A	B	L	E	D	Darkened, Blackened, Furred.
S	A	C	C	O	S	Resembling clerical vestments.
S	A	C	C	U	S	Sack-like pouch.
S	A	C	H	E	T	Small bag containing herbs or perfumed powder.
S	A	C	K	E	D	Dismissed, Pillaged, Plundered, Desecrated, Desolated, Fired, Booted(out), Spoiled.
S	A	C	K	E	R	Marauder, Looter, Plunderer, Freebooter, Raider, Ravisher, Forager, Despoiler.

1	2	3	4	5	6	
S	A	C	R	A	L	Relating to pelvic bone.
S	A	C	R	E	D	Holy, Revered, Venerated, Blessed, Consecrated, Hallowed, Sanctified.
S	A	C	R	U	M	A pelvis bone.
S	A	D	D	E	N	Depress, Oppress, Press, Weigh down, To grieve.
S	A	D	D	L	E	Seat for a horse's back, Burden, Charge, Encumber, Load, Task, Tax, Hamper.
S	A	D	I	S	M	Excessive cruelty, Lustful cruelty.
S	A	D	I	S	T	One who practises sadism, Torturer, Tormenter.
S	A	E	T	E	R	Hut or Pasture in Norwegian mountains.
S	A	F	A	R	I	Caravan, journey or expedition mostly for hunting especially in Africa.
S	A	F	E	L	Y	Surely, Securely, Reliably, Carefully.
S	A	F	E	S	T	Surest.
S	A	F	E	T	Y	Protection, Assurance, Security, Safeguard.
S	A	G	E	L	Y	Knowingly, Wisely, Prudently, Sanely, Sensibly.
S	A	G	E	N	E	Russian unit of length equal to seven feet (2.1 metres).
S	A	G	G	A	R	Pot of fire-clay.
S	A	G	G	E	D	Drooped, Bent, Sunk, Dipped, Declined, Wilted, Dropped, Slumped.
S	A	G	G	E	R	Box for holding fine ceramic pieces to be fired or glazed.
S	A	G	I	N	A	Genus of small herbs.
S	A	G	O	I	N	Marmoset.
S	A	I	L	E	D	Cruised, Swept, Winged, Flown, Darted.
S	A	I	L	O	R	Seaman, Mariner, Salt, Tar, Jack-tar.
S	A	L	A	A	M	Salutation in the East.
S	A	L	A	M	I	Highly seasoned sausage.
S	A	L	A	R	Y	Wage, Emolument, Fee, Hire, Pay, Stipened.
S	A	L	I	F	Y	Impregnate with salt, Salinize.
S	A	L	I	N	E	Salty, Briny, Natural deposit of common salt.
S	A	L	I	T	E	Mineral.
S	A	L	I	V	A	Slaver, Spit, Spittle, Water.
S	A	L	L	E	T	Salad, Light helmet.
S	A	L	L	O	W	Greyish, greenish yellow esp. relating to complexion.
S	A	L	O	O	N	Drawing room, Salon, Bar, Tavern, Taproom.
S	A	L	T	E	D	Preserved, Immune against contagious disease because of prior infection and recovery.
S	A	L	U	K	I	Hunting dog of Southern Arabia.
S	A	L	U	T	E	Address, Accost, Greet, Hail, Greeting, Salutation.
S	A	L	V	E	D	Soothed, Lubricated, Remedied, Rescued.
S	A	L	V	E	R	Tray esp. for use by a butler.
S	A	L	V	I	A	Genus of herb (sage).
S	A	L	V	O	R	Salvage expert.
S	A	M	B	A	L	Condiment of spices for use with curry dishes.
S	A	M	E	L	Y	Unvaried, Monotonous.
S	A	M	I	E	L	Simoon, Dry hot wind.
S	A	M	I	T	E	Silk interwoven with threads of gold or silver.
S	A	M	P	A	N	Chinese skiff.
S	A	M	P	L	E	Specimen, Instance, Case, History, Example, Illustration, Try, Taste.
S	A	N	D	A	L	Shoe usually of a sole fastened by straps or thongs.
S	A	N	E	L	Y	Rationally, Lucidly, Wisely, Prudently, Sensibly.
S	A	N	E	S	T	Soundest.
S	A	N	G	A	R	Rifle pit. Primitive wooden bridge.
S	A	N	I	F	Y	Provide with sanitary conditions and equipment.
S	A	N	I	T	Y	Wit, Lucidity, Wisdom, Normality, Sound mind, Reason, Soundness.
S	A	P	F	U	L	Succulent, Juicy.
S	A	P	P	E	D	Weakened, Debilitated, Enfeebled, Undermined.
S	A	P	P	E	R	Military engineer.
S	A	R	O	N	G	Loose skirt worn in Far East.
S	A	S	H	E	S	Framework of window, Wide dress belt usually of silk.
S	A	T	E	E	N	Smooth lustrous fabric of cotton weave.
S	A	T	I	N	E	Heavy hard lustrous red wood.
S	A	T	I	N	G	Satisfying, Cloying, Filling, Gorging.
S	A	T	I	N	Y	Having soft texture of the smoothness of satin fabric.
S	A	T	I	R	E	Irony, Lampoonery, Raillery, Sarcasm.
S	A	T	I	V	A	Cultivated, Sown(crops).
S	A	T	R	A	P	Viceroy of a sovereign power.
S	A	T	U	R	N	Planet.
S	A	U	C	E	R	Small shallow dish for a cup.
S	A	U	R	I	A	Lizard.
S	A	V	A	G	E	Vicious, Wild, Ferocious, Brutal, Barbaric, Fierce, Inhuman, Cruel.
S	A	V	A	N	T	Sage, Scholar, Professor, Wise man, Scientist.

1	2	3	4	5	6	
S	A	V	A	T	E	Form of boxing where hands and feet are used for blows.
S	A	V	I	N	E	Creeping juniper, Juniper berries used in folk medicine.
S	A	V	I	N	G	Preservation, Conservation, Safekeeping, Salvation, Except, Sparing, Economical, Thrifty.
S	A	V	O	U	R	Taste, Flavour, Relish, Quality, Characteristic, Feature, Mark, Property.
S	A	V	V		Y	Shrewd, Astute, Cagey, Sagacious.
S	A	W	D	E	R	Flatter.
S	A	W	N	E	Y	Fool, Simpleton, Silly.
S	A	W	Y	E	R	Worker who saws timber.
S	A	Y	I	N	G	Adage, Dictum, Byword, Proverb, Word.
S	C	A	B	B	Y	Scaly, Itchy, Mean, Scurrilous, Contemptible.
S	C	A	L	A	R	Stairs, ladder.
S	C	A	L	E	R	Mountain climber, Something or instrument for measuring.
S	C	A	L	E	S	Balance(for weight), Series of musical tones.
S	C	A	M	P	I	Prawns.
S	C	A	N	T	Y	Meagre, Poor, Scrimp, Scarce, Skimpy, Spare, Short, Inadequate.
S	C	A	P	U	S	Stem, Stalk, Column.
S	C	A	R	A	B	Horned beetle, Gem.
S	C	A	R	C	E	Short, Deficient, Inadequate, Insufficient, Infrequent, Occasional, Rare, Seldom, Sporadic.
S	C	A	R	E	D	Afraid, Aghast, Anxious, Fearful, Frightened, Scary, Terrified.
S	C	A	R	R	Y	Scarred, Disfigured.
S	C	A	T	H	E	Lambaste, Blister, Castigate, Flay, Scarify, Scorch, Scourge, Slash.
S	C	A	T	T	Y	Crazy, Mischievous.
S	C	A	Z	O	N	One who limps, Classical verse with halting movement.
S	C	E	N	I	C	Something stressing beauties of nature.
S	C	H	E	L	M	Rascal.
S	C	H	E	M	A	Abridged presentation.
S	C	H	E	M	E	Plan, Design, Project, Strategy, Plot, Conspire, Devise, Intrigue.
S	C	H	I	S	M	Breach, Break, Rupture, Heresy, Chasm, Cleavage, Cleft, Fracture.
S	C	H	I	S	T	Divisible.
S	C	H	O	O	L	Teach, Discipline, Educate, Instruct, Train, Academy, University, Faculty.
S	C	H	U	S	S	A straight high speed run on skis.
S	C	I	E	N	T	Skilful knowing.
S	C	I	L	L	A	Genus of old world bulbous herbs.
S	C	I	O	N	S	Offspring, Brood, Children, Descendants, Issue, Progeny.
S	C	O	L	E	X	Head of a tapeworm.
S	C	O	N	C	E	Head, Protection, Shelter, Belfry, Flat candlestick, Dome, Noggin, Skull.
S	C	O	P	I	C	Observing, Extensive, Broad, Expansive, Extended, Scopious, Wide.
S	C	O	R	C	H	Burn, Singe, Char, Parch, Lambaste, Blister, Castigate, Swelter.
S	C	O	R	E	D	Recorded, Totalled, Gained, Accomplished, Scratched, Prospered, Thrived, Slashed.
S	C	O	R	E	R	One who makes a score (in game or contest), Logger who marks trees to be felled.
S	C	O	R	S	E	Exchange trade.
S	C	O	T	C	H	Score, Scratch, Sparing, Canny, Hinder, Thwart, Economical.
S	C	R	A	P	E	Grate, Rasp, Scratch, Scrimp, Pinch, Screw, Struggle, Stint.
S	C	R	A	W	L	Scribble. Scratch (with pen or pencil), Scrabble, Squiggle.
S	C	R	E	A	M	Screech, Shriek, Shrill, Squeal, Yell, Howl, Cry, Blare.
S	C	R	E	E	D	Fragment, Shred, Diatribe.
S	C	R	E	E	N	Obstruct, Shroud, Defend, Cover, Guard, Shade, Shadow, Hide.
S	C	R	E	E	S	Heap of stones or rocky debris.
S	C	R	E	W	Y	Underhand, Intoxicated, Canned, Drunk, Inebriated, Muddled, Plastered.
S	C	R	I	B	E	Writer, Notary, Write, Engress, Inscribe.
S	C	R	I	M	P	Pinch, Scrape, Stint, Meagre, Spare, Scant.
S	C	R	I	P	T	Handwriting, Calligraphy, Fist, Hand, Penmanship.
S	C	R	I	V	E	Engrave, Write, Inscribe.
S	C	R	O	L	L	List, Roster of names, Register, Flourish.
S	C	R	O	O	P	Rasping sound, Creak, Scrape, Crisp, Rustle of silk.
S	C	R	U	F	F	Nape of the neck, Treat lightly, Dandruff.
S	C	U	L	P	T	To carve, To sculpture, Engraved, Chisel.
S	C	U	M	M	Y	Covered with scum, Contemptible, Mean, Scurvy.
S	C	U	R	F	Y	Having or producing scurf.
S	C	U	R	R	Y	Move briskly, Circulate, Short run, Jumping, Race, Flurry.
S	C	U	R	V	Y	Shabby, Vile, Disease due to vitamin deficiency.
S	C	Y	T	H	E	Implement to mow grass, To cut down.
S	E	A	L	E	D	Confirmed, Shut, Ratified, Decided, Covered to prevent Penetration.
S	E	A	L	E	R	Hunter of seals.
S	E	A	M	A	N	Mariner, Jack-tar, Sailor, Salt, Tar.
S	E	A	M	E	D	Joined, Connected, United, Wrinkled, Furrowed.
S	E	A	M	E	R	Seamstress.

1	2	3	4	5	6	
S	E	A	N	C	E	Meeting for receiving spirit communication.
S	E	A	R	C	H	Seek, Hunt, Quest, Examine, Pursuit, Scour, Comb, Forage.
S	E	A	R	E	D	Scorched, Burnt, Sizzled, Parched, Dehydrated.
S	E	A	S	O	N	Time, Period, Harden, Toughen, Flavour with condiments or herbs.
S	E	A	T	E	D	Sited, Focused, Based, Established.
S	E	A	W	A	Y	Moderate or rough sea, Inland waterway, Ocean traffic lane.
S	E	C	A	L	E	Genus of cereal grasses.
S	E	C	A	N	T	Straight line cutting a curve at two or more points.
S	E	C	E	D	E	Withdraw, Quit, Segregation, Break away.
S	E	C	E	R	N	Discriminate, Secrete, Distinguish.
S	E	C	I	S	H	Relating to secessionist in USA.
S	E	C	O	N	D	Moment, Trice, Flash, Derivative, Assist, Support, Minor, Insignificant.
S	E	C	R	E	T	Clandestine, Covert, Furtive, Obscure, Remote, Deep, Heavy, Profound.
S	E	C	T	O	R	Quarter, District, Precinct, Section, Area, Zone, Division.
S	E	C	U	N	D	Unilateral.
S	E	C	U	R	E	Confident, Obtain, Safe, Reliable, Dependable, Fast, Stable, Sure.
S	E	D	A	T	E	Serious, Earnest, Grave, Solemn, Serene, Calm, Staid, Placid.
S	E	D	E	N	T	Sitting, Inactive, Quiet.
S	E	D	U	C	E	Lure, Decoy, Entice, Tempt, Inveigle, Entrap, Bait, Debauch.
S	E	E	D	E	D	Arrange order of play of certain contestants, To crystallize or form a precipitate.
S	E	E	D	E	R	One who seeds clouds to produce rain, Implement for planting seeds.
S	E	E	I	N	G	Watching, Viewing, Sight, Vision, Because, Considering, Whereas, Since.
S	E	E	K	E	R	Candidate, Inquirer, Applicant, Searcher, Aspirant.
S	E	E	M	E	D	Appeared, Looked, Sounded, Resembled, Suggested.
S	E	E	M	E	R	Pretender.
S	E	E	M	L	Y	Decorous, Becoming, Befitting, Conforming, Correct, Decent, Nice, Proper.
S	E	E	P	E	D	Exuded, Percolated, Bled, Oozed, Strained, Sweated, Wept, Leaked.
S	E	E	S	A	W	Unbalance, Lurch, Pitch, Sway, Tilt, Yaw, Teeter, List.
S	E	E	T	H	E	Boil, Parboil, Simmer, Stew, Soak, Drench, Impregnate, Saturate. Anger, Bristle, Burn, Fume.
S	E	I	N	E	R	One who fishes with a seine net.
S	E	I	Z	E	D	Grasped, Appropriated, Confiscated, Caught, Grabbed, Taken, Commandeered, Caught.
S	E	I	Z	E	R	Snatcher, Thief.
S	E	I	Z	O	R	Bailiff.
S	E	L	D	O	M	Infrequently, Little, Rarely, Few, Occasional, Rare, Scarce, Uncommon.
S	E	L	E	C	T	Chosen, Elect, Exclusive, Choice, Dainty, Elegant, Rare, Prefer.
S	E	L	L	E	R	Salesman, Retailer, Vendor, Vender, Hawker, Pedlar.
S	E	L	V	E	S	Plural of SELF.
S	E	M	I	T	E	Descendant of Shem, son of Noah.
S	E	N	A	R	Y	Group of six.
S	E	N	A	T	E	Council, Assembly, Governing body.
S	E	N	D	A	L	Thin medieval silk.
S	E	N	D	E	R	Despatcher, Consignor, Consigner, Transmitter.
S	E	N	D	U	P	Ridicule, Sentence to imprisonment.
S	E	N	H	O	R	Portugese or Brazilian man.
S	E	N	I	L	E	Doddering, Doting, Infirm, Aged, Enfeebled, Decrepit.
S	E	N	I	O	R	Elder, Older, Superior, Better, Higher-up.
S	E	N	N	I	T	Plaited rope.
S	E	N	O	R	A	Title for married Spanish speaking women.
S	E	N	S	E	D	Felt, Believed, Deemed, Held, Considered, Perceived.
S	E	N	S	O	R	Device designed to respond to a physical stimulus.
S	E	N	T	R	Y	Guard, Sentinel, Picket, Ward, Watchman.
S	E	P	S	I	S	Septicemia, Blood poisoning, Putrefaction.
S	E	P	T	E	T	Group of seven, especially musicians.
S	E	P	T	U	M	Dividing wall or membrane.
S	E	Q	U	E	L	Succession, Alternation, Order, Progression, Sequence, Effect, Outcome, Result, Upshot.
S	E	Q	U	I	N	Spangle, Small metal disc with hole for sewing it on to material.
S	E	R	A	P	E	Blanket worn as cloak or poncho.
S	E	R	A	P	H	Fiery six-winged angel guarding throne of God.
S	E	R	E	N	E	Calm, Collected, Placid, Poised, Tranquil, Self-composed, Self-possessed, Clear.
S	E	R	I	A	L	Consecutive, Sequent, Subsequent, Succeeding, Successional, Successive.
S	E	R	I	E	S	Succession, Progression, Sequence, Order, String, Train, Row, Sequel.
S	E	R	I	P	H	Printing term for short strokes at ends of letters.
S	E	R	M	O	N	Preach, Discourse, Address, Homily.
S	E	R	V	A	L	Wild cat.
S	E	R	V	E	D	Acted, Functioned, Suited, Officiated, Worked(for), Waited, Ministered, Nursed.
S	E	R	V	E	R	Waiter, Sideboard, Trolley, Tray, Implement for serving food.
S	E	S	A	M	E	East Indian herb.

1	2	3	4	5	6	
S	E	T	O	U	T	Design, Arrange, Plan, Head.
S	E	T	T	E	E	Sofa with arms and back.
S	E	T	T	L	E	Ensconce, Calm, Establish, Decide, Negotiate, Soothe, Colonize, Pay(account).
S	E	V	E	R	E	Austere, Stern, Grim, Bleak, Brutal, Hard, Serious, Inclement.
S	E	V	R	E	S	Fine French porcelain.
S	E	W	A	G	E	Refuse liquids and waste matter carried by sewers.
S	E	W	I	N	G	Operation carried out be needle and thread, manually or by machine.
S	E	X	T	E	T	Group of six persons or objects.
S	E	X	T	O	N	Church custodian.
S	E	X	U	A	L	Relating to sex.
S	H	A	B	B	Y	Bedraggled, Decrepit, Squalid, Dilapidated, Contemptible, Despicable, Disreputable.
S	H	A	D	E	D	Shadowed, Umbrageous, Screened, Sheltered.
S	H	A	D	O	W	Shade, Umbrage, Apparition, Phantasm, Wraith, Vestige, Hint, Suggestion.
S	H	A	G	G	Y	Rugged, Unkempt, Rough, Uneven, Tangled.
S	H	A	K	E	N	Agitated, Trembled, Jarred, Jiggled, Oscillated, Lost(pursuer), Appalled, Daunted.
S	H	A	K	E	R	Container with perforated lid.
S	H	A	M	E	D	Ashamed, Chagrined, Mortified, Disgraced, Crestfallen.
S	H	A	N	T	Y	Hut, Box, Cabin, Cottage, Lodge, Shack, Hove, Sea-chant.
S	H	A	P	E	D	Formed, Made, Assembled, Constructed, Fashioned, Forged, Framed, Built.
S	H	A	R	E	D	Divided, Rationed, Common, Communal, Mutual, Public, Parcelled, Joint (use).
S	H	A	R	E	R	Participator, Shareholder, Partaker, Distributor, Divider.
S	H	A	R	I	F	Descendant of prophet Muhammad through his daughter Fatima.
S	H	A	R	P	Y	Shallow draft boat.
S	H	A	V	E	D	Pared, Pruned, Sheared, Trimmed, Reduced, Brushed, Grazed, Skimmed.
S	H	A	V	E	R	Barber, Boy, Youngster, Swindler, Extortioner.
S	H	E	A	F	Y	Resembling a sheaf.
S	H	E	A	R	S	Large scissors, Cuts, Clips, Crops, Pares, Shaves, Trims.
S	H	E	A	T	H	Skin, Scabbard, Connective tissue, Clad, Husk, Pod.
S	H	E	A	V	E	Grooved wheel or pulley.
S	H	E	E	N	Y	Shining, Radiant.
S	H	E	E	R	S	Alternative of shears.
S	H	E	I	K	H	Head of Arab family, clan or tribe.
S	H	E	K	E	L	Various ancient unit of weight.
S	H	E	L	F	Y	Full of sandbanks or flat projecting layers or rock.
S	H	E	L	L	Y	Consisting of shells.
S	H	E	L	V	E	To incline, Defer, Delay, Hold off, Postpone, Prorogue, Stay, Waive.
S	H	E	L	V	Y	Inclining as geological shelf.
S	H	E	R	I	F	Variation of Sharif.
S	H	E	R	R	Y	Fortified wine of Spanish origin.
S	H	E	W	E	L	Scarecrow.
S	H	I	E	L	D	Defend, Armament, Protection, Security, Harbour, Haven, House, Shelter.
S	H	I	F	T	Y	Evasive, Dishonest, Deceitful, Underhand, Devious, Inconstant, Uncertain, Variable.
S	H	I	M	M	Y	Jazz dance with swing steps.
S	H	I	N	D	Y	Shindig, Bash, Commotion, Furore, Rumpus, Uproar.
S	H	I	N	E	R	Black eye, Bootblack.
S	H	I	N	T	O	Indigenous religion of Japan.
S	H	I	R	E	S	Counties in British Isles, Heavy draught horses.
S	H	I	R	T	Y	Angry, Choleric, Heated, Irate, Mad, Wrathful, Indignant.
S	H	I	V	E	R	Shake, Quake, Quiver, Shudder, Tremble, Shatter, Fragment, Splinter.
S	H	O	A	L	Y	Full of shoals.
S	H	O	D	D	Y	Shabby, Run-down, Cheap, Base, Common, Paltry, Rubbishy, Reputable.
S	H	O	G	U	N	Military governor in pre-revolution Japan.
S	H	O	O	E	D	Scared away, Driven away.
S	H	O	R	E	D	Supported, Bolstered, Braced, Propped, Upheld, Underpinned.
S	H	O	R	E	R	One who fixes support for excavations.
S	H	O	R	T	S	By-product of wheat milling, Knee-length trousers, Something less than full length, i.e. lumber.
S	H	O	U	L	D	Want, Must, Ought, Obliged.
S	H	O	V	E	D	Pushed, Driven, Propelled, Poked, Prodded, Elbowed, Hustled, Jostled.
S	H	O	V	E	L	Dig, Excavate, Spade, Scoop, Delve, Shuffle, Scuffle.
S	H	O	V	E	R	One who pushes.
S	H	O	W	E	R	Rain, Spray, Barrage, Broadside, Bathe, Tub, Wash, Distribute.
S	H	R	A	N	K	Contracted, Compressed, Constricted, Failed, Recoiled, Flinched, Quailed, Winced.
S	H	R	E	W	D	Astute, Cagey, Sagacious, Wise, Cunning, Sharp, Canny, Crafty.
S	H	R	I	E	K	Scream, Screech, Shrill, Squeal, Blare, Shout, Yell, Cry.
S	H	R	I	F	T	Confession to a priest, Disclosure of guilt.
S	H	R	I	K	E	Genus of bird that usually impales its prey on thorns.
S	H	R	I	L	L	Acute, High, Piercing, Piping, Sharp, Thin, Treble.

1	2	3	4	5	6	
S	H	R	I	M	P	Small marine crustacean, Puny person.
S	H	R	I	N	E	Sanctuary, Holy place, Sanctorium, Reliquary, Tomb usually containing holy relics.
S	H	R	I	N	K	Contract, Compress, Restrict, Dwindle, Recoil, Blanch, Flinch, Quail.
S	H	R	O	U	D	Enfold, Enclose, Envelop, Veil, Wrap, Screen, Obstruct, Close.
S	H	R	U	N	K	Compressed, Condensed, Dwindled, Restricted, Contracted, Recoiled, Blanched, Quailed.
S	H	Y	I	N	G	Shrinking, Recoiling, Tossing, Throwing.
S	I	C	K	E	N	Upset, Derange, Disorder, Unsettle, Disgust, Repel, Revolt, Nauseate.
S	I	C	K	L	E	Agriculture implement for reaping.
S	I	C	K	L	Y	Unwell, Ailing, Indisposed, Unwholesome, Unhealthy, Morbid, Morose, Noisome.
S	I	D	I	N	G	Short railroad track connected by points, Partisanship.
S	I	D	L	E	D	Edged, Furtive advance.
S	I	E	N	N	A	Earthy substances used as pigment.
S	I	E	R	R	A	Range of mountains with serrated outline.
S	I	E	S	T	A	Nap, Catnap, Forty winks, Snooze, Doze, Afternoon rest.
S	I	F	T	E	D	Screened, Sieved, Sorted, Separated, Winnowed, Explored, Delved, Investigated.
S	I	F	T	E	R	Shaker, Utensil for sieving powdered substances.
S	I	G	H	E	D	Mourned, Exhaled, Longed, Ached, Hungered, Pined, Thirsted.
S	I	G	H	E	R	One that sighs.
S	I	G	L	U	M	Sign, Abbreviation letter character.
S	I	G	N	A	L	Gesture, Motion, Sign, Flag, Noticeable, Arresting, Remarkable, Striking.
S	I	G	N	E	D	Inscribed, Autographed, Transferred, Conveyed, Assigned, Ceded.
S	I	G	N	O	R	Italian man of rank.
S	I	L	A	G	E	Fodder either green or mature.
S	I	L	I	C	A	Hard stone quartz.
S	I	L	K	E	D	Dressed or covered in silk.
S	I	L	K	E	N	Soft, Satiny, Silky, Velvety, Ingratiating, Disarming, Insinuating, Deferential.
S	I	L	T	E	D	Choked or obstructed with sand or debris.
S	I	L	V	A	N	Rustic, Woody, Forest.
S	I	L	V	E	R	White metallic element, Money, Argent, Bright, Lustre.
S	I	M	I	A	N	Relating to monkeys and apes.
S	I	M	I	L	E	Analogy, Metaphor, Likeness, Affinity, Comparison, Resemblance.
S	I	M	M	E	R	Boil gently, Stew, Seethe, Bubble, Churn, Ferment, Stir.
S	I	M	N	E	L	Rich fruit cake with almond paste usually eaten at Easter.
S	I	M	O	O	N	Hot, dry violent wind.
S	I	M	O	U	S	Concave, Snub (nose or beak).
S	I	M	P	E	R	Smirk, Vacuous grin.
S	I	M	P	L	E	Natural, Artless, Plain, Stupid, Retarded, Pure, Easy, Effortless.
S	I	M	P	L	Y	Barely, Just, Merely, Only, Solely, Literally, Sincerely, Modestly.
S	I	N	D	O	N	Linen covering.
S	I	N	E	W	Y	Muscular, Vigorous, Fibrous, Stringy, Wiry, Athletic, Brawny, Sturdy.
S	I	N	F	U	L	Wrong, Bad, Evil, Immoral, Vicious, Blameworthy, Culpable, Guilty.
S	I	N	G	E	D	Scorched, Slightly burned, Embarrassment, Unexpected trouble.
S	I	N	G	E	R	One who sings (human or bird), Songster, Warbler, Chanter, Police informer, Squealer.
S	I	N	G	L	E	Unmarried, Lone, Only, Unattached, Frank, Candid, Sole, Exclusive.
S	I	N	G	L	Y	Apart, Uniquely, Independently, Individually, Separately, Severally.
S	I	N	K	E	R	One who sinks mine shafts, Weight for fishing line.
S	I	N	N	E	D	Wronged, Trespassed, Offended, Transgressed, Erred.
S	I	N	N	E	R	Evil-doer, Criminal, Transgressor, Trespasser, Offender, Reprobate, Scamp.
S	I	P	H	O	N	Pump, Tap, Drain, Conduct, Carry, Channel, Funnel, Pipe.
S	I	P	P	E	D	Taken by the mouth in small draughts.
S	I	P	P	E	R	One who sips.
S	I	P	P	E	T	Fragment, Small piece of bread or toast soaked in milk or broth.
S	I	R	I	N	G	Procreating, Begetting, Fathering (usually domestic animals).
S	I	R	I	U	S	The Dog star.
S	I	S	T	E	R	Female relative of same parents, Nun, Nurse.
S	I	T	T	E	R	One who sits for painter or sculptor, An easy target.
S	I	Z	I	N	G	Sorting or checking by sizes, Part of wheat after milling.
S	I	Z	Z	L	E	Scorch, Fry, Hiss, Buzz, Sear, Sibilate, Deep agitation, Top performance.
S	K	A	T	E	R	One who skates.
S	K	E	T	C	H	Outline, Draught, Portray, Characterize, Draft, Rough out, Map out, Detail.
S	K	E	W	E	R	Impale, Lance, Spear, Spike, Transfix.
S	K	I	M	P	Y	Meagre, Poor, Scanty, Scrimp, Sparse, Short, Deficient, Wanting.
S	K	I	N	N	Y	Lean, Angular, Bony, Gaunt, Lanky, Scrawny, Spare, Rawboned.
S	K	I	V	E	R	Grain side of split sheepskin.
S	L	A	C	K	S	Long trousers for casual wear (also for women).
S	L	A	K	E	D	Quenched.
S	L	A	N	G	Y	Given to vulgarity, Addicted to slang.

1	2	3	4	5	6	
S	L	A	P	U	P	First rate, Fine, Excellent, Elegant, Fancy.
S	L	A	T	E	D	Lambasted, Blistered, Castigated, Lashed, Chided, Upbraided.
S	L	A	T	E	R	Tool or machine for Fleshing hides.
S	L	A	V	E	D	Drudged, Plodded, Slogged, Toiled.
S	L	A	V	E	R	Drool, Dribble, Salivate, Drivel, Slobber, Cower, Cringe, Grovel.
S	L	A	V	E	Y	Slave, Dray horse, Drudge, Galley slave, Peon, Workhorse, Toiler.
S	L	E	A	V	E	Separate into filaments.
S	L	E	A	Z	Y	Limp, Flabby, Flimsy, Cheap, Base, Shabby, Dilapidated, Tacky.
S	L	E	D	G	E	Sleigh, Sled.
S	L	E	E	K	Y	Sleek, Glassy, Glossy, Polished, Smarmy, Smooth.
S	L	E	E	P	Y	Dozy, Drowsy, Somnolent, Soporific, Inactive, Inert, Passive, Narcotic.
S	L	E	E	T	Y	Nature of sleet.
S	L	E	E	V	E	Part of garment covering arm, Tubular part designed to fit over another part.
S	L	E	I	G	H	Sled, Sledge.
S	L	E	U	T	H	Detective, Private eye, Investigator, Sherlock Holmes, Bloodhound.
S	L	E	W	E	D	Twisted, Tipsy, Intoxicated, Canned, Drunk, Inebriated, Muddled, Plastered
S	L	I	C	E	D	Chopped, Pared, Apportioned, Gashed, Slashed, Slit, Split, Severed.
S	L	I	C	E	R	Implement for cutting, Worker who slits turpentine trees.
S	L	I	D	E	R	Sliding part or device.
S	L	I	E	S	T	Most sly, Most crafty, Most cunning.
S	L	I	G	H	T	Thin, Reedy, Slender, Delicate, Neglect, Ignore, Scoff, Overlook.
S	L	I	N	K	Y	Furtively, Sneaky, Creepy, Snaky, Lean.
S	L	I	P	O	N	Easily slipped on, Pullover.
S	L	I	P	P	Y	Sleek, Greasy, Slippery, Slithery, Nimble, Unstable.
S	L	I	P	U	P	Mistake, Error, Blunder, Lapse, Slip, Fluff, Bungle, Boner.
S	L	I	V	E	R	Shave, Shred, Slice, Chop, Mince, Splinter.
S	L	O	G	A	N	Catchword, Byword, Catchphrase, Watchword, War-cry.
S	L	O	K	E	N	Extinguish, Exhaust.
S	L	O	P	E	D	Inclined, Leaning, Oblique, Pitched, Tilted, Tipped, Decamped.
S	L	O	P	P	Y	Slipshod, Careless, Messy, Slovenly, Effusive, Intoxicated, Maudlin.
S	L	O	S	H	Y	Muddy, Mushy, Soppy, Boggy, Watery.
S	L	O	U	C	H	Oaf, Sluggard, Sloth, Lout, Loafer, Droop, Loll, Slump.
S	L	O	U	G	H	Swamp, Bog, Fen, Marsh, Morass, Quagmire, Inlet, Bayou. Hull, Husk, Pod, Discard, Shed.
S	L	O	V	E	N	Uncultivated, Undeveloped, Slut, Slattern.
S	L	O	W	E	R	Comparative of SLOW, Not so fast, Lack of speed.
S	L	O	W	L	Y	Tardily, Sluggishly, Stupidly, Leisurely.
S	L	U	D	G	E	Mud, Ooze, Mire, Slime.
S	L	U	D	G	Y	Muddy, Slushy.
S	L	U	I	C	E	Floodgate, Pour, Flow, Gush, Stream, Surge, Wash, Drench.
S	L	U	I	C	Y	Streaming or falling copiously.
S	L	U	R	R	Y	Watery mixture, Suspension of insoluble matter.
S	L	U	S	H	Y	Trashy, Sentimental, Maudlin, Mawkish, Romantic, Soppy, Tear-jerking.
S	L	Y	E	S	T	Most sly, Most crafty, Most cunning.
S	M	A	R	M	Y	Sleek, Glassy, Polished, Sleeky, Fulsome, Oily, Slick, Unctuous.
S	M	A	R	T	Y	Know-it-all, Wiseacre, Boaster, Wise guy, Exhibitionist, Show-off.
S	M	E	A	R	Y	Greasy, Adhesive, Viscous, Covered by smears.
S	M	E	L	L	Y	Malodorous, Fetid, Noisome, Putrid, Rancid.
S	M	I	D	G	E	Small amount.
S	M	I	L	E	D	Grinned, Simpered, Beamed.
S	M	I	R	C	H	Soil, Begrime, Dirty, Foul, Smudge, Tarnish, Smear, Stain.
S	M	I	T	E	R	One that strikes a heavy blow.
S	M	I	T	H	Y	Workshop of blacksmith.
S	M	O	K	E	D	Exhaled smoke, Fumigated, Cured (meat or fish), Prevented observation.
S	M	O	K	E	R	One who smokes tobacco, Person who dries or preserves food, Apparatus for making smoke.
S	M	O	O	T	H	Even, Flatten, Level, Polish, Perfect, Refine, Hairless, Bald. Easy, Effortless, Simple, Suave, Soft.
S	M	O	U	C	H	Kiss, Osculate, Peck, Steal, Filch, Hook Left, Pilfer.
S	M	U	D	G	E	Soil, Foul, Grime, Smear, Taint, Defile, Stain, Tarnish.
S	M	U	D	G	Y	Stifling, Smothering, Suffocating, Smeary, Stained, Tarnished, Blurred.
S	M	U	G	L	Y	Complacently, Sleekly, Neatly, Primly.
S	M	U	T	C	H	Soil, Smudge, Tarnish, Dirty, Taint, Discolour, Stain, Sully.
S	M	U	T	T	Y	Sooty, Dusky, Obscene, Indecent, Coarse, Vulgar, Filthy.
S	N	A	K	E	D	Stole, Sneaked, Crept, Slithered, Pinched, Swiped, Pilfered.
S	N	A	A	P	D	Tapered, Bevelled.
S	N	A	P	P	Y	Irritable, Petulant, Fast, Rapid, Pungent, Spicy, Stylish, Trendy.
S	N	A	R	E	D	Captured, Caught, Trapped, Netted.
S	N	A	R	E	R	Hunter, Trapper.
S	N	A	T	C	H	Seize, Catch, Clutch, Grab, Nab, Wrench, Kidnap, Abduct.

1	2	3	4	5	6	
S	N	E	E	Z	E	Audible spasmodic expiration through the nose and mouth.
S	N	I	F	F	Y	Disdainful, Supercilious.
S	N	I	T	T	Y	Petty, Mean.
S	N	I	P	E	R	One that fires at exposed people.
S	N	I	P	P	Y	Bluff, Abrupt, Blunt, Brusque, Curt, Gruff, Short-tempered.
S	N	I	T	C	H	Inform, Pimp, Steal, Filch, Lift, Pick, Pinch, Purloin.
S	N	I	V	E	L	Whine, Snuffle, Blubber.
S	N	O	B	B	Y	Pretentious, Haughty, Patronizing, Uncertain, Snooty, High-hat, Condescending, Pompous.
S	N	O	O	T	Y	Snobbish, Haughty, Condescending, Patronizing, Pompous.
S	N	O	O	Z	E	Doze, Siesta, Nap, Catnap, Forty winks, Drowse.
S	N	O	T	T	Y	Viscous, Slimy, Meanly, Contemptible, Snooty, Supercilious, Midshipman (British navy).
S	N	O	U	T	Y	Snoutlike, Having a prominent snout.
S	N	U	B	B	Y	Snub-nosed, Impudent, Vulgar.
S	N	U	F	F	Y	Peevish, Short-tempered, Supercilious, Disdainful, Horrid, Disagreeable.
S	N	U	G	L	Y	Comfortably, Cosily tucked-up.
S	O	A	K	E	D	Wet, Drenched, Saturated, Soaking, Sodden, Sopping, Soused, Dripping.
S	O	A	K	E	R	Drunkard, Boozer, Guzzler, Inebriate, Sot.
S	O	A	P	E	D	Lathered, Flattered.
S	O	A	R	E	D	Ascended, Aspired, Arose, Lifted, Mounted, Towered, Ranged.
S	O	B	B	E	D	Cried, Blubbered, Wailed, Wept, Blubbed.
S	O	B	E	I	T	If, Provided that, As long as.
S	O	C	A	G	E	Tenure of land by various means.
S	O	C	I	A	L	Companionable, Convivial, Gregarious, Genial, Civil, Festive, Hospitable, Cooperative.
S	O	C	K	E	D	Bashed, Belted, Smacked, Whacked, Cuffed, Chopped, Clouted, Punched.
S	O	C	K	E	T	Hollow that serves as a support.
S	O	D	D	E	N	Wet, Drenched, Saturated, Soaked, Soaking, Soused, Impregnate, Seethe.
S	O	D	I	U	M	Silver white soft waxy ductile metallic element.
S	O	F	T	E	N	Depreciate, Relent, Alleviate, Undervalue, Assuage, Mitigate, Mollify, Enervate.
S	O	F	T	E	R	More soft, More gentle, More comfortable, More simple.
S	O	F	T	L	Y	Quietly, Dulcetly, Gently, Pliably.
S	O	I	G	N	E	Modish, Elegantly maintained, Well-groomed, Sleek.
S	O	I	L	E	D	Contaminated, Defiled, Polluted, Tainted, Fouled, Muddied, Stained, Smeared.
S	O	I	R	E	E	Evening reception.
S	O	L	A	C	E	Consolation, Comfort, Cheer, Relief.
S	O	L	A	N	O	Hot oppressive Mediterranean wind.
S	O	L	D	E	R	Metallic alloy used when melted to join metallic surfaces.
S	O	L	E	I	L	Fabric with fancy warp and high lustre finish.
S	O	L	E	L	Y	Solitary, Only, Alone, But, Entirely, Exlusively.
S	O	L	E	M	N	Serious, Earnest, Grave, Ceemonial, Conventional, Formal, Stately, Sombre.
S	O	L	E	R	A	Sherry vats tiered for blending.
S	O	L	E	U	S	Flat muscle in calf of leg.
S	O	L	I	O	N	Electronic detecting and amplifying device.
S	O	L	V	E	D	Fixed, Resolved, Determined, Deciphered, Unfolded, Interpreted, Decoded.
S	O	M	B	R	E	Dark, Dim, Dismal, Gloomy, Obscure, Murky, Serious, Earnest.
S	O	M	I	T	E	Longitudinal body segment of animal.
S	O	N	A	N	T	Syllabic, Voiced, Sound.
S	O	N	A	T	A	Instrumental musical composition.
S	O	N	N	E	T	Poem of fourteen lines.
S	O	O	N	E	R	Before, Earlier, More readily.
S	O	O	T	H	E	Calm, Allay, Balm, Compose, Quieten, Settle, Tranquilize, Palliate.
S	O	P	H	I	C	Skilled, Clever, Wise.
S	O	P	P	E	D	Soaked, Drenched, Drowned, Saturated, Steeped, Mopped up.
S	O	R	B	E	T	Sherbert, Water ice.
S	O	R	D	I	D	Dirty, Foul, Grubby, Slatternly, Dowdy, Base, Despicable, Vile.
S	O	R	E	L	Y	Deeply, Grievously, Sadly, Bitterly, Hardly, Keenly, Resentfully.
S	O	R	E	S	T	Most sore, Most grievous, Most bitter.
S	O	R	R	E	L	Reddish brown, Chestnut coloured horse.
S	O	R	R	O	W	Grieve, Mourn, Woe, Distress, Affliction.
S	O	R	T	E	D	Classified, Grouped, Classed, Typed, Pigeonholed, Separated, Graded.
S	O	R	T	E	R	One who sorts (usually post office mail).
S	O	R	T	I	E	Sally, Mission, Attack.
S	O	T	T	E	D	Become infatuated, Make a fool of.
S	O	U	G	H	T	Hunted, Tried, Quested, Searched, Attempted, Struggld, Endeavoured.
S	O	U	L	E	D	Full of feeling.
S	O	U	P	L	E	Supple silk.
S	O	U	R	C	E	Derivation, Fountain, Origin, Root, Spring, Well, Whence.
S	O	U	R	E	R	More tart, More acid.

1	2	3	4	5	6	
S	O	U	R	L	Y	In a sour manner.
S	O	U	S	I	NG	Wet, Drenched, Dripping, Saturated, Soaked, Soaking, Sodden, Sopping.
S	O	W	I	N	G	Scattering of seed.
S	O	Z	Z	L	E	Muddle, Booze, Splash.
S	P	A	C	E	D	Stretched, Extended, Spread.
S	P	A	R	E	D	Refrained, Saved, Withheld, Exempted, Preserved.
S	P	A	R	E	R	One that reduces destruction.
S	P	A	R	E	S	Extra part of vehicle or machine kept for replacement.
S	P	A	R	K	S	Luminous electric discharges, Radio operator.
S	P	A	R	S	E	Meagre, Poor, Scanty, Scrimp, Thin, Spare.
S	P	A	V	I	N	Swelling, Swollen joint.
S	P	E	C	I	E	In coin, In like manner, Specifically.
S	P	E	C	K	Y	Marked with specks or spots.
S	P	E	E	C	H	Communication, Discourse, Talk, Utterance, Palaver, Oration, Address, Lecture.
S	P	E	E	D	Y	Fast, Breakneck, Fleet, Prompt, Hasty, Brisk, Nimble, Ready.
S	P	E	T	C	H	Patch, Mend.
S	P	E	W	E	D	Vomited, Extruded, Spat.
S	P	H	E	R	E	Orb, Globe, Ball, Round, Field, Province, Terrain, Domain.
S	P	H	E	R	Y	Suggestive of heavenly spheres, Starlike.
S	P	H	I	N	X	Ancient Egyptian image.
S	P	I	C	E	D	Seasoned, Tinged, Aromatic, Scented, Perfumed.
S	P	I	D	E	R	Animal of the order of Araneida (weaver of webs), Cast iron frying pan, Lightweight cart.
S	P	I	F	F	Y	Dappy, Bandbox, Doggy, Native, Spruce, Well-groomed, Smart.
S	P	I	G	O	T	Faucet, Cock, Gate, Stopcock, Tap, Valve.
S	P	I	K	E	D	Skewered, Speared, Impaled, Nullified one's power of hostile action.
S	P	I	N	A	L	Relating to a spine.
S	P	I	N	E	D	Thorny, Spiney, Furnished with a spine.
S	P	I	N	E	T	Small harpsichord, Small electronic organ, Small piano.
S	P	I	N	N	Y	Thorny, Thicket.
S	P	I	R	A	L	Wind, Coil, Corkscrew, Curl, Entwine, Twist, Wreathe.
S	P	I	R	E	D	Having a spire.
S	P	I	R	I	T	Soul, Psyche, Apparition, Phantom, Wraith, Temper, Vigour, Animation. Courage, Heart, Mettle.
S	P	I	T	E	D	Injured, Thwarted, Vexed.
S	P	L	A	S	H	Douse, Slop, Slosh, Spatter, Splosh, Splurge, Swash.
S	P	L	E	E	N	Malice, Grudge, Ill-will, Malevolence, Spite, Anger.
S	P	L	I	C	E	Marry, Hitch, Mate, Tie, Wed, Join.
S	P	L	I	N	T	Small plate or strip of metal for supporting something damaged.
S	P	O	K	E	N	Oral, Traditional, Verbal, Vocal, Articulate, Sonant, Voiced.
S	P	O	N	G	E	Cake, Internal skeleton of marine creature, Cadge, Looter, Parasite, Hanger-on, Leech.
S	P	O	N	G	Y	Soft, Mushy, Pulpy, Squashy, Yielding, Squelchy.
S	P	O	O	K	Y	Weird, Eerie, Uncanny, Unearthly, Nervous, Fidgety, Jumpy, Twittery.
S	P	O	O	N	Y	Simple, Fatuous, Foolish, Silly, Witless.
S	P	O	T	T	Y	Speckled, Dotted.
S	P	O	T	T	ED	Placed in accurate position.
S	P	O	U	S	E	Husband or wife.
S	P	R	A	I	N	Rick, Turn, Wrench, Twist, Stretch, Tear.
S	P	R	A	N	G	Jumped, Leapt, Bounded, Skipped, Vaulted.
S	P	R	A	W	L	Drape, Lounge, Straggle, Spraddle, Spread-eagle, Loll.
S	P	R	E	A	D	Broadcast, Circulate, Disperse, Distribute, Propagate, Open, Expand, Unfold.
S	P	R	I	N	G	Well, Source, Origin, Begin, Puberty, Motive, Cause. Skip, Hop, Jump, Start, Free, Discharge.
S	P	R	I	T	E	Fairie, Brownie, Elf, Fay, Pixie.
S	P	R	O	U	T	Bud, Shoot, Germinate, Scion.
S	P	R	U	C	E	Fir tree, Dapper, Bandbox, Natty, Well-groomed, Dress up, Slick, Smarten.
S	P	R	U	N	G	Liberated, Released, Jumped, Skipped, Hopped.
S	P	R	Y	L	Y	Active, Brisk.
S	P	R	Y	E	R	More agile, Brisker, More nimble.
S	P	U	N	K	Y	Brave, Bold, Courageous, Spirited, Fiery, Plucky, Fearless, Gutsy.
S	P	U	R	G	E	A plant.
S	P	Y	I	N	G	Discerning, Espionage, Watching, Observing, Detecting.
S	Q	U	A	I	L	Throw a weighted stick, disc or counter.
S	Q	U	A	L	L	Blast, Gust, Squawk, Bellow, Bawl, Howl, Quarrel, Altercation.
S	Q	U	A	R	E	Boxlike, Even, Exact, Fair, Equal, Impartial, Conventional, Orthodox. Adapt, Accommodate, Fix.
S	Q	U	A	S	H	Press, Crush, Extinguish, Suppress, Squeeze, A gourd, A game.
S	Q	U	A	W	K	Squall, Caw, Gripe, Bleat, Crab, Fuss, Complain.
S	Q	U	E	A	K	Squeal, Screech, Creak, Grate, Opportunity, Opening, Charge.
S	Q	U	E	A	L	Scream, Screech, Shriek, Inform, Talk, Sing, Yell, Howl.
S	Q	U	E	A	M	Qualm, Compunction, Conscience.

1	2	3	4	5	6	
S	Q	U	I	L	L	Bulbous herb.
S	Q	U	I	N	T	Look or peer obliquely, Squinch.
S	Q	U	I	R	E	Male attendant, Country gentleman, Gallant lover, Escort.
S	Q	U	I	R	M	Squiggle, Wriggle, Wiggle, Worm, Writhe, Agonize, Toss.
S	Q	U	I	R	T	Jet, Spurt, Spout, Spatter, Spray, Eject.
S	T	A	B	L	E	Sure, Fast, Firm, Secure, Durable, Constant, Fixed, Steady. Equable, Even, Lasting, Enduring.
S	T	A	B	L	Y	Solidly, Firmly, Securely.
S	T	A	G	E	D	Produced, Performed, Mounted, Presented.
S	T	A	G	E	R	One that takes part, Actor.
S	T	A	G	E	Y	Theatrical.
S	T	A	K	E	D	Betted, Wagered, Financed, Backed.
S	T	A	L	E	T	Older, Less fresh, More trite, More commonplace, More fusty.
S	T	A	M	E	N	Organ of a flower.
S	T	A	N	C	E	Posture, Attitude, Carriage, Post, Position, Stand.
S	T	A	N	C	H	Stem, Stop.
S	T	A	N	Z	A	Division of poem.
S	T	A	P	E	S	Step, Foot, Bones of inner ear.
S	T	A	P	L	E	Body, Bulk, Core, Mass, Substance, Loop, Eye, Ring.
S	T	A	R	C	H	Rigid, Vigour, Bang, Drive, Get-up, Punch, Snap, Vitality.
S	T	A	R	E	D	Looked, Gaped, Gazed, Goggled, Glared, Gloated, Peered.
S	T	A	R	E	R	One that stares.
S	T	A	R	R	Y	Stellar, Astral, Stellular.
S	T	A	R	V	E	Hunger, Lack, Deprive, Famish.
S	T	A	T	E	D	Regular, Expressed, Related, Announced, Said, Fixed, Settled, Stipulated.
S	T	A	T	E	R	Ancient Grecian gold or silver coin.
S	T	A	T	I	C	Immobile, Stagnant, Stationary, Unmoving, Steady, Rigid.
S	T	A	T	O	R	Stationary member of an electrical machine.
S	T	A	T	U	E	Image, Figurine, Sculpture.
S	T	A	T	U	S	Capacity, Place, Position, Rank, Dignity, Standing, Condition, Posture.
S	T	A	V	E	D	Rebuffed, Delayed, Prevented, Averted, Precluded, Warded(off), Repulsed, Repelled.
S	T	A	V	E	S	Rods, Sticks, Cudgels, Stanzas, Bars of music.
S	T	E	A	D	Y	Sure, Enduring, Constant, Stable, Faithful, Loyal, Resolute, Wholehearted.
S	T	E	E	L	Y	Hard, Firm, Obdurate, Unyielding.
S	T	E	E	P	Y	Precipitous.
S	T	E	M	M	A	Garland, Wreath, Family tree, Pedigree.
S	T	E	N	C	H	Smell, Reek, Stink, Odour.
S	T	E	P	P	E	Vast forestless tract in South Eastern Europe or Asia.
S	T	E	R	E	O	Stereoscopic.
S	T	E	R	O	L	Solid alcohol.
S	T	E	W	E	D	Boiled, Simmered, Seethed, Worried, Fretted, Intoxicated, Inebriated.
S	T	I	C	K	Y	Adhesive, Gummy, Humid, Muggy, Formidable, Sentimental, Mushy.
S	T	I	F	L	E	Suffocate, Asphyxiate, Choke, Muffle, Dampen, Suppress, Stullify, Stagnate.
S	T	I	G	M	A	Blot, Blur, Brand, Disgrace, Tarnish, Slur, Stain, Spot.
S	T	I	L	L	Y	Hush, Noiseless, Silent, Calm, Soundless, Tranquil.
S	T	I	L	T	Y	Stilted, Formal, Stiff.
S	T	I	N	G	Y	Close, Parsimonious, Pinching, Ungenerous, Niggardly, Mean, Mingy, Narrow.
S	T	I	P	E	L	Stipule of a small leaf.
S	T	I	P	E	S	Eyestalk, Supports, Stalks, Strips.
S	T	I	R	P	S	Branch of a family, Ancestor.
S	T	I	T	C	H	Sew, Pain, Ache, Pang, Twinge.
S	T	O	C	K	Y	Chunky, Dumpy, Heavy-set, Sturdy, Stumpy, Robust, Thick-set, Squat.
S	T	O	D	G	E	Satiate, Clay, Fill, Gorge, Plod, Toil, Trudge, Slog.
S	T	O	D	G	Y	Sticky, Adhesive, Gluey, Dull, Dreary, Humdrum, Dowdy, Frumpish.
S	T	O	K	E	D	Fuelled, Fed abundantly.
S	T	O	K	E	R	Locomotive fireman, One who tends and fuels a furnace.
S	T	O	L	E	N	Filched, Purloined, Taken, Appropriated, Pilfered, Swiped, Poached, Rustled.
S	T	O	L	I	D	Impassive, Apathetic, Dry, Phlegmatic, Stoic, Dense, Dull, Stupid.
S	T	O	N	E	D	Intoxicated, Drunk, Inebriated, Muddled, Plastered, Drugged, Doped, High.
S	T	O	N	E	R	One that makes walls of stones.
S	T	O	O	G	E	Tool, Cats-paw, Pawn, Puppet, Dummy, Yes-man, Subordinate, Foil.
S	T	O	R	E	D	Accumulated, Treasured, Garnered, Stockpiled, Supplied, Stocked, Deposited, Cached.
S	T	O	R	E	R	One who stores, Hoarder.
S	T	O	R	E	Y	A floor (building).
S	T	O	R	M	Y	Wild, Rough, Blustery, Raging, Stormy, Tempestuous, Furious, Turbulent.
S	T	O	V	E	R	Cattle fodder, Hay, Stubble.
S	T	O	W	E	D	Packed, Stored, Placed, Loaded, Arranged.
S	T	R	A	F	E	Attack fiercely.

1	2	3	4	5	6	
S	T	R	A	I	N	Try, Distress, Irk, Pain, Stress, Pull, Labour, Strive. Exude, Ooze, Sieve. Mood, Humour, Mind.
S	T	R	A	I	T	Narrow, Dilemma, Juncture, Contingency, Crisis, Emergency, Pass, Zero.
S	T	R	A	N	D	Shore, Bank, Beach, Coast, Shipwreck, Thread, Fibre, Cast-away.
S	T	R	A	T	A	Layer, Level, Bed.
S	T	R	A	T	H	Wide tract of level land.
S	T	R	E	A	K	Hint, Shade, Suspicion, Stripe, Intimation, Suggestion, Run naked.
S	T	R	E	A	M	Creek, Brook, Rivulet, Flow, Current, Flood, Pour.
S	T	R	E	E	T	Way, Artery, Avenue, Boulevard, Highway, Path, Road, Thoroughfare.
S	T	R	E	S	S	Pressure, Strain, Tension, Try, Tax, Emphasize, Feature, Underline.
S	T	R	E	W	N	Scattered, Disseminated, Sprinkled, Spread, Circulated, Dispersed, Distributed, Radiated.
S	T	R	I	C	T	Accurate, exact, precise, rigid, stringent, draconian, true.
S	T	R	I	D	E	Step, Gait, Stalk, March, Slink, Straddle.
S	T	R	I	F	E	Discord, Conflict, Quarrel, Dissent, Variance, Difference, Contest, Competition.
S	T	R	I	K	E	Catch, Clout, Hit, Give, Administer, Deliver, Afflict, Torment. Seize, Attack, Assault. Assume.
S	T	R	I	N	G	Cord, Twine, Line, File, Queue, Succession, Sequence, Order.
S	T	R	I	P	E	Strip, Band, Ribbon, Type, Breed, Line, Stroke, Streak.
S	T	R	I	P	Y	Streaky.
S	T	R	I	V	E	Labour, Drive, Strain, Toil, Try, Attempt, Seek, Struggle.
S	T	R	O	B	E	Tube producing repeated intense flashes of light.
S	T	R	O	D	E	Stalked, Straddled, Stepped, Marched.
S	T	R	O	K	E	Blow, Knock, Heartbeat, Caress, Apoplexy.
S	T	R	O	L	L	Saunter, Amble, Drift, Linger, Ramble, Rove, Walk, Constitutional.
S	T	R	O	N	G	Bold, Lusty, Might, Powerful, Stalwart, Stout, Sturdy, Tough.
S	T	R	O	V	E	Toiled, Tried, Attempted, Vied, Laboured, Strained, Tugged, Worked.
S	T	R	U	C	K	Hit, Collided, Revolted, Clouted, Walked-out, Attacked, Caught, Administered.
S	T	R	U	N	G	Threaded, Queued, Filed.
S	T	U	B	B	Y	Stocky, Chunky, Dumpy, Squat, Stumpy, Blunt, Truncated, Heavy-set.
S	T	U	C	C	O	Plaster covering for walls usually for decoration.
S	T	U	D	I	O	Atelier, Room for broadcasting programmes.
S	T	U	F	F	Y	Airless, Stifling, Close, Prim, Priggish, Prudish, Pompous, Arrogant.
S	T	U	G	G	Y	Stocky, Chunky, Squat, Thick, Dumpy.
S	T	U	M	E	R	Fraud, Sham, Failure, Dud, Wash-out, Worthless, Cheque.
S	T	U	M	P	S	Stubble, Pointed rods used in cricket.
S	T	U	M	P	Y	Stocky, Chumpy, Squat, Chunky, Thick-set.
S	T	U	P	I	D	Dense, Dull, Retarded, Simple, Witless, Dunce, Moron.
S	T	U	P	O	R	Lethargy, Coma, Lassitude, Slumber, Torpor, Dullness, Langour.
S	T	U	R	D	Y	Strong, Stalwart, Stout, Tenacious, Tough, Robust, Vigorous.
S	T	Y	I	N	G	Pen or lodge in a sty.
S	T	Y	L	A	R	Relating to style in writing, Having pillars.
S	T	Y	L	E	D	Fashioned, Designated, Christened.
S	T	Y	L	E	T	Slender surgical probe, Stiletto.
S	T	Y	L	U	S	Pen, Needle (for record), Indicator, Pointer, Cutting tool.
S	T	Y	M	I	E	Block, Check, Thwart.
S	U	B	D	U	E	Conquer, Crush, Defeat, Overpower, Tame, Subjugate, Quell, Vanquish.
S	U	B	I	T	O	Immediately, Suddenly, At once.
S	U	B	L	E	T	Turn over one's right of occupancy to another.
S	U	B	M	I	T	Yield, Capitulate, Defer, Refer, Suggest, Fall, Succumb, Surrender.
S	U	B	O	R	N	Instigate, Bribe, Induce a person to commit perjury.
S	U	B	S	E	T	A set that is an element of a larger set.
S	U	B	T	L	E	Thin, Tenuous, Fine, Delicate, Refined, Logical, Sly, Artful.
S	U	B	T	L	Y	Artfully, Slyly, Astutely, Delicately, Finely, Nicely.
S	U	B	U	R	B	Environ, Outskirt, Fringe, Neighbourhood.
S	U	B	W	A	Y	Underground gallery.
S	U	C	C	I	N	Amber.
S	U	C	C	U	S	Succulent juice.
S	U	C	K	E	D	Absorbed, Imbibed, Licked, Lapped.
S	U	C	K	E	R	Fish, Parasite, Hanger-on, Leech, Lounge-lizard, Fool, Chump, Suction pad.
S	U	C	K	L	E	Nurse, Breast feed, Nourish.
S	U	D	A	R	Y	Shroud, Winding sheet, Veil.
S	U	D	D	E	N	Precipitate, Abrupt, Hasty, Headlong, Hurried, Impetuous, Rushing.
S	U	E	I	N	G	Entreating, Addressing, Prosecuting, Appealing, Courting, Petitioning.
S	U	F	F	E	R	Bear, Brook, Endure, Stomach, Experience, Allow, Leave, Permit.
S	U	F	F	I	X	Add to the end of a word.
S	U	G	A	R	Y	Honeyed, Cloying, Sweet.
S	U	I	T	E	D	Assorted, Adapted, Conformable, Fitted, Matched, Contented, Dressed.
S	U	I	T	O	R	Suppliant, Swain, Wooer, Asker, Beggar, Petitioner, Admirer, Supplicant.
S	U	L	C	U	S	Groove, Fissure.

1	2	3	4	5	6	Clue
S	U	L	L	E	N	Morose, Mumpish, Saturnine, Sulky, Gloomy, Glum, Crabby, Ugly.
S	U	L	T	A	N	King or ruler especially of a Muhammadan state.
S	U	L	T	R	Y	Stuffy, Suffocating, Humid, Sticky, Hot, Sweltering, Sensational, Lurid.
S	U	M	M	E	D	Added, Totted, Summarized, Epitomized, Accepted, Counted.
S	U	M	M	E	R	Season between spring and autumn.
S	U	M	M	I	T	Top, Apex, Crest, Crown, Peak, Culmination, Zenith.
S	U	M	M	O	N	Assemble, Convoke, Call, Convene, Prosecute, Bid.
S	U	N	B	O	W	Arch resembling a rainbow.
S	U	N	D	A	E	Ice cream served with fruit, nuts and/or syrup.
S	U	N	D	A	Y	Christian sabbath observed as a day of rest.
S	U	N	D	E	R	Separate, Divide, Cleave, Carve, Dissect, Sever, Slice, Split.
S	U	N	D	R	Y	Many, Legion, Numerous, Several, Some, Various, Populous, Manifold.
S	U	N	H	A	T	Broad brimmed hat worn for protection against sun's rays.
S	U	N	K	E	N	Submerged, Depressed, Engulfed, Dejected.
S	U	N	L	I	T	Lighted by the sun.
S	U	N	N	E	D	Exposed to the sun.
S	U	N	S	E	T	Evening, Twilight.
S	U	N	T	A	N	Browning of the skin from exposure to the rays of the sun.
S	U	P	E	R	B	Grand, Exalted, Lofty, Splendid, Glorious, Magnificent, Outstanding, Superlative.
S	U	P	I	N	E	Mental or moral lethargy, Abject, Torpid, Inert.
S	U	P	P	E	R	Evening meal.
S	U	P	P	L	E	Elastic, Flexible, Resilient, Lissom, Stretch, Lithe, Adaptable, Pliable.
S	U	P	P	L	Y	Give, Deliver, Dispense, Provide, Stock, Store, Feed, Find.
S	U	R	E	L	Y	Safely, Securely, Certainly, Infallibly, Steadfastly, Assuredly, Really.
S	U	R	E	S	T	Most sure, Safest, Most certain.
S	U	R	E	T	E	Criminal investigation service (French).
S	U	R	E	T	Y	Security, Guarantee, Hostage, Bond, Pledge.
S	U	R	G	E	D	Billowed, Jerked, Strained.
S	U	R	R	E	Y	Four-wheeled 2 seater carriage.
S	U	R	T	A	X	Additional or extra tax.
S	U	R	V	E	Y	Estimate, Appraise, Supervise, Overlook, Superintend, Scrutinize, Examine, Study.
S	U	T	L	E	R	Caterer to army.
S	U	T	T	E	E	Hindu widow who willingly cremates herself on husband's funeral pyre.
S	U	T	U	R	E	Surgical joining of body tissue.
S	V	E	L	T	E	Smooth, Sleek, Sophisticated, Slender, Trim.
S	W	A	G	E	D	Assuaged, Quenched, Shaped, Abated, Decreased.
S	W	A	Y	E	D	Wavered.
S	W	A	M	P	Y	Water-logged, Marshy, Spongy, Morass.
S	W	A	N	K	Y	Boastful, Showy, Trendy, Peacocky.
S	W	A	N	N	Y	Swanlike.
S	W	A	R	D	Y	Grassy.
S	W	A	R	T	H	Crop of grass for hay.
S	W	A	S	H	Y	Wet, Watery, Weak, Insipid.
S	W	A	T	C	H	Collection of samples of cloth.
S	W	A	T	H	E	Envelop, Enwrap, Roll, Swaddle, Enfold, Bind, Bandage.
S	W	A	Y	E	D	Oscillated, Lurched, Swung, Weaved, Wobbled, Vacillated, Affected, Influenced.
S	W	E	A	T	Y	Perspiring, Sweating, Clammy, Sticky, Wet.
S	W	E	E	N	Y	Muscular atrophy of a horse, Waste away, Vanish.
S	W	E	E	P	Y	Sweeping in motion.
S	W	E	R	V	E	Deflect, Dip, Sheer, Skew, Veer, Depart, Deviate, Diverge.
S	W	I	N	G	E	Impetus, Singe, Scorch, Chastise, Power, Authority.
S	W	I	P	E	D	Slogged, Knocked, Swatted, Rapped, Stolen, Pinched, Nicked, Lifted.
S	W	I	P	E	R	One that hits.
S	W	I	P	E	S	Spoiled beer, Small beer, Wild swings especially with a bat.
S	W	I	R	L	Y	Knotted, Twisted, Full of eddies.
S	W	I	T	C	H	Flexible rod, whip or twig, Exchange, Substitute, Swap, Trade, Shunt, Sidetrack.
S	W	I	V	E	L	Ramble, Drift, Turn, Revolve, Pivot, Swing.
S	Y	L	V	A	N	Rustic, Rural, Woodland, Wooded.
S	Y	M	B	O	L	Attribute, Emblem, Token, Sign, Badge, Device, Mark, Character.
S	Y	N	D	I	C	Court assistant, Advocate, Agent of corporation engaged in business enterprise.
S	Y	N	T	A	X	Connected system, Orderly arrangement.
S	Y	P	H	O	N	Used to transfer liquid between containers.
S	Y	R	I	A	N	Relating to Syria.
S	Y	R	I	N	X	Vocal organ of birds.
S	Y	R	T	I	S	Quicksand, Bog.
S	Y	R	U	P	Y	Sugary, Cloying, Sentimental, Dulcet, Maudlin, Mushy, Sticky, Sappy.
S	Y	S	T	E	M	Complex, Whole, Integral, Sum, Method, Order, Pattern, Fashion.

1	2	3	4	5	6
S	Y	Z	Y	G	Y

Yoked together, Dipody, Straight line configuration of three of the celestial bodies during a solar eclipse.

T

T	A	B	A	R	D	Herald's coat, Tunic.
T	A	B	B	E	D	Tagged.
T	A	B	E	R	D	Herald's coat, Tunic.
T	A	B	L	E	D	Catalogued, Tabulated.
T	A	B	L	E	S	Lists usually mathematical.
T	A	B	L	E	T	Flat slab for various inscriptions, Cake, Bar, Pill.
T	A	B	O	U	R	Small drum.
T	A	B	R	E	T	Small stool.
T	A	B	U	L	A	Transverse septa found in coral.
T	A	C	K	E	D	Attached, Stitched, Turned, Yawed (for yacht).
T	A	C	K	E	R	He who tacks.
T	A	C	K	L	E	Attack, Undertake, Grapply, Gear, Equipment, Apparatus, Outfit, Paraphernalia.
T	A	C	T	I	C	Tactile, Tactual, Arrangement, Pattern.
T	A	G	E	N	D	The last part of something.
T	A	G	G	E	D	Marked with a tag or label.
T	A	G	G	E	R	One that tags.
T	A	G	R	A	G	Shabby, Bedraggled, Dilapidated, Dingy, Seedy, Tacky, Threadbare, Run-down.
T	A	G	U	A	N	East Indian flying squirrel.
T	A	I	G	L	E	Catch, Entrap, Delay, Hinder, Fatigue, Loiter, Delay, Entangle.
T	A	I	L	E	D	Followed, Shadowed, Dogged, Trailed, Tagged.
T	A	I	L	O	R	Maker of men's and women's outwear, Adapt, Accomodate, Adjust, Conform, Fit, Suit.
T	A	K	E	I	N	Admit, Receive, Apprehend, Accept, Deceive, Beguile, Betray, Humbug.
T	A	K	I	N	G	Infectious, Catching, Alluring, Attractive.
T	A	L	B	O	T	Hunting dog.
T	A	L	C	K	Y	Relating to talc.
T	A	L	E	N	T	Gift, Aptitude, Faculty, Flair, Genius, Craft, Skill.
T	A	L	I	O	N	Legal retaliation, Punishment.
T	A	L	K	E	D	Spoke, Chatted, Yarned, Reported, Rumoured, Addressed, Lectured.
T	A	L	K	E	R	Gossip, Chatterbox.
T	A	L	L	E	T	Boarded platform, Flooring, Attic.
T	A	L	L	E	R	Sturdier, Loftier, Higher.
T	A	L	L	O	W	Rendered fat of beef and mutton.
T	A	L	M	U	D	Authoritative body of Jewish law and tradition.
T	A	M	A	L	E	Steamed Mexican corn meat roll.
T	A	M	A	R	A	Condiment of mixed spices.
T	A	M	B	A	C	Alloy of copper and zinc used for cheap jewellery.
T	A	M	B	O	R	Red rock fish.
T	A	M	E	L	Y	Meekly, Submissively.
T	A	M	E	S	T	Dullest, Most subdued.
T	A	M	I	N	G	Housetraining, Domesticating, Subduing.
T	A	M	P	A	N	Chicken tick.
T	A	M	P	E	D	Compacted, Rammed, Packed, Crammed.
T	A	M	P	E	R	Bribe, Buy, Fix, Lubricate, Meddle, Interfere, Fool.
T	A	M	P	O	N	Surgical plug to stem bleeding.
T	A	N	D	E	M	One behind the other.
T	A	N	G	E	D	Banged, Flavoured.
T	A	N	G	L	E	Involve, Implicate, Catch, Trap, Entangle, Snarl, Complicate, Muddle.
T	A	N	G	L	Y	Intricate, Entangled, Snarly.
T	A	N	K	E	D	Drunk, Guzzled, Stored, Fuddled, Swilled, Filled.
T	A	N	K	E	R	Steel cargo ship for carrying liquid products in bulk, Vehicle with tank for conveying liquids.
T	A	N	N	E	D	Treated by tanning, Browned by exposure to the sun's rays.
T	A	N	N	E	R	One that tans, hides, Sixpence.
T	A	N	N	I	N	Soluble astringent.
T	A	N	N	O	Y	Amplified loud speaker system.
T	A	P	I	N	G	Binding, Supporting, Recording, Measuring.
T	A	P	P	E	D	To form an internal screw thread, Obtained a loan, Rapped, A spigot for drawing wine from a cask.
T	A	P	P	E	R	One that taps usually on a railroad.
T	A	P	P	E	T	A cam or a lever.
T	A	P	P	I	T	Crested hen, Drinking vessel with a knob on the lid.
T	A	R	G	E	T	Butt mark, Ambition, Aim, Goal, Duty, Function, Objective.
T	A	R	I	F	F	Tax assessment, Duty, Impost, Levy, Price, Charge, Schedule.
T	A	R	I	N	G	Weight of container deducted to obtain actual weight of item.

1	2	3	4	5	6	
T	A	R	M	A	C	Bituminous binder for surfacing roads.
T	A	R	P	O	N	Marine fish.
T	A	R	R	E	D	Asphalted.
T	A	R	S	A	L	Ankle.
T	A	R	T	A	N	Plaid, Textile design.
T	A	R	T	A	R	Cream of tartar found in juice of grapes.
T	A	R	T	L	Y	Sharply, Asperity, Sourly, Acidly, Pungently.
T	A	S	K	E	D	Burdened, Encumbered, Employed, Loaded, Saddled.
T	A	S	K	E	R	One that performs or imposes a task.
T	A	S	L	E	T	Pouch, Part of armour.
T	A	S	S	E	L	Pendant made of bunch of cords.
T	A	S	S	E	T	Armour to cover lower trunk.
T	A	S	S	I	E	Small cup.
T	A	S	T	E	D	Savoured, Touched, Relished.
T	A	S	T	E	R	One that tastes or samples food and drink.
T	A	T	A	M	I	A woven grass mat used in Japan.
T	A	T	T	E	D	Made lace.
T	A	T	T	E	R	Shred, Rag, Hurry, Hasten, Bullet, Fly.
T	A	T	T	I	E	Potato.
T	A	T	T	L	E	Gossip, Blab, Rumour, Talk, Buzz, Cry.
T	A	T	T	O	O	Outdoor military display, Pricking the skin with pigment, Beat on drum rhythmically.
T	A	U	G	H	T	Instructed, Coached, Tutored, Imparted.
T	A	U	R	U	S	Sign of the Zodiac represented by the Bull.
T	A	U	T	E	N	Draw, Drag, Stretch, Strain.
T	A	V	E	R	N	Bar, Saloon, Taproom, Inn, Hostel, Hotel, Lodge, Roadhouse.
T	A	V	E	R	T	Tired, Fatigued, Confused, Stupid, Fuddled.
T	A	W	D	R	Y	Gaudy, Garish, Blatant, Brazen, Flashy, Loud.
T	A	W	E	R	Y	Place where skins are made into white leather.
T	A	W	P	I	E	Foolish, Senseless.
T	A	X	E	M	E	Grammatical selection.
T	A	X	I	E	D	Movement of aeroplane on the ground.
T	A	X	I	N	E	Bitter poisonous alkaloid.
T	A	X	I	N	G	Onerous, Burdensome, Demanding, Tough, Trying, Oppressive, Weighty.
T	E	A	B	A	G	Sachet of tea.
T	E	A	C	U	P	Drinking vessel.
T	E	A	M	E	D	Yoked, Joined forces, Associated, Allied.
T	E	A	P	O	T	Vessel for making tea.
T	E	A	P	O	Y	Three legged stand.
T	E	A	R	E	R	One that tears or rends, Violent storm.
T	E	A	S	E	D	Combed, Plucked, Carded (wool), Worried, Goaded, Plagued, Tormented, Roused.
T	E	A	S	E	L	Bur or wire for raising nap on cloth.
T	E	A	S	E	R	Puzzle, One that tantalizes.
T	E	A	S	E	T	Cups and plates for serving tea.
T	E	A	Z	L	E	Bur or wire for raising nap on cloth.
T	E	B	E	T	H	Fourth month in the Jewish calendar.
T	E	C	T	U	M	Roof.
T	E	D	D	E	D	Spread on, Distribute hay and manure.
T	E	D	D	E	R	Machine for stirring and spreading hay.
T	E	D	E	U	M	Hymn of praise or thanksgiving.
T	E	D	I	U	M	Boredom, Monotony, Ennui, Dullness, Wearisome.
T	E	E	M	E	D	Abounded, Flowed, Swarmed, Abundant.
T	E	E	M	E	R	Workman who controls rate at which stainless steel is poured into moulds.
T	E	E	P	E	E	American Indian conical shaped tent.
T	E	E	T	E	R	Falter, Lurch, Stagger, Stumble, Seesaw, Totter, Topple, Wobble.
T	E	E	T	H	E	To cut one's teeth.
T	E	G	M	E	N	Covering.
T	E	G	U	L	A	Turban shells used for food.
T	E	L	L	E	R	Informer, Narrator, Describer, Bank cashier.
T	E	L	S	O	N	Segment of a tail.
T	E	M	O	R	A	Marine copecods.
T	E	M	P	E	R	Anger, Fury, Passion, Disposition, Mood, Tantrum, Spirit, Strain. Modulate, Restrain, Modify.
T	E	M	P	L	E	House of worship, Church, Chapel, Tabernacle, Part of Head.
T	E	N	A	C	E	Forceps.
T	E	N	A	N	T	Inhabit, Occupy, People, Populate, Lease-holder.
T	E	N	D	E	D	Cared for, Supervised, Watched, Minded, Nursed.
T	E	N	D	E	R	Compassionate, Responsive, Warm, Sympathetic, Offer, Extend, Present, Proffer.
T	E	N	D	O	N	Ligament.

1	2	3	4	5	6	
T	E	N	N	I	S	Game played with rackets and ball.
T	E	N	P	I	N	Bowling game.
T	E	N	S	E	D	Taut, Stretched, Strained, Edgy, Concerned, Nervy.
T	E	N	S	E	R	More uneasy, More strained.
T	E	N	S	O	N	A lyric poem where two opponents speak alternate lines.
T	E	N	S	O	R	A muscle that stretches a part.
T	E	N	T	E	D	Covered by tents.
T	E	N	T	E	R	One that tends a machine in a factory.
T	E	N	U	R	E	Hold, Clamp, Clasp, Clench, Clinch, Clutch, Grapple, Grasp.
T	E	N	U	T	O	Sustained tone or chord in music.
T	E	P	A	R	Y	Drought resistant bean native to S.W. America and Mexico.
T	E	R	A	P	H	Ancient Hebrew household god.
T	E	R	E	D	O	Woodworm.
T	E	R	E	T	E	Approximately cylindrical.
T	E	R	G	A	L	Back, Dorsal.
T	E	R	G	U	M	Back, Dorsal.
T	E	R	M	E	D	Designated, Limited, Terminated.
T	E	R	M	E	R	Person serving a specified term.
T	E	R	M	E	S	White ants, Termites.
T	E	R	M	L	Y	Periodically.
T	E	R	R	E	L	Ring on top of harness pad through which reins pass.
T	E	R	R	O	R	Fear, Alarm, Consternation, Dismay, Dread, Fright, Horror, Panic.
T	E	S	T	E	D	Tried, Experimented, Checked, Examined, Proved.
T	E	S	T	E	R	Frame for canopy of bed, Assayer.
T	E	T	A	N	Y	Appertaining to muscle spasm, Lockjaw, Tetanus.
T	E	T	C	H	Y	Irascible, Cranky, Cross, Ratty, Quick-tempered, Touchy, Grouchy, Irritable.
T	E	T	H	E	R	Tie, Fasten, Stake, Restrain, Secure, Hobble, Fetter.
T	E	T	R	A	D	Group or arrangement of four.
T	E	T	R	A	O	Genus of grouses.
T	E	T	R	Y	L	Pale yellow crystalline explosive.
T	E	T	T	E	R	Pimple, Pustule, Blister, Herpes, Rash.
T	E	T	T	I	X	Genus of grouse locusts.
T	E	U	T	O	N	Ancient Germanic or Celtic people.
T	E	X	T	U	S	Text of the Bible, Tissue.
T	H	A	L	E	R	German dollar.
T	H	A	L	I	A	Genus of American aquatic herbs.
T	H	A	N	K	S	Grace, Benediction, Blessing, Expression of gratitude.
T	H	A	T	C	H	Thick mat of reeds, Rushes, grasses used as roofing material.
T	H	A	W	E	D	Melted, Dissolved, Liquified.
T	H	E	A	V	E	A young ewe.
T	H	E	I	N	E	Caffeine.
T	H	E	I	R	S	Belonging to them.
T	H	E	I	S	M	Belief in God or gods.
T	H	E	I	S	T	Believer in theism.
T	H	E	N	C	E	Away, Hence, Thereof, Therefrom.
T	H	E	O	D	Y	Hymn praising God.
T	H	E	O	R	Y	Belief, Policy, Conjecture, Speculation, Suppose, Suspicion, Perhaps.
T	H	E	S	I	S	Contention, Assumption, Postulate, Premise, Supposition, Discourse, Treatise, Memoir.
T	H	E	T	I	C	Prescribed, Positive, Arbitary.
T	H	E	W	E	D	Mannered, Behaved.
T	H	I	B	E	T	Fine woollen fabric.
T	H	I	B	L	E	Stick or spatula for stirring.
T	H	I	E	V	E	Steal, Filch, Lift, Pilfer, Pinch, Purloin, Swipe, Nip.
T	H	I	N	L	Y	Insufficiently, Sparsely, Scarcity.
T	H	I	R	S	T	Long, Ache, Crave, Hanker, Itch, Lust, Pine, Yearn.
T	H	I	R	T	Y	Cardinal number.
T	H	O	R	A	X	Chest.
T	H	O	R	N	Y	Nettlesome, Prickly, Spiny, Sharp, Brambly, Perplexing, Controversy.
T	H	O	U	G	H	Albeit, Although, Much as, When, Whereas, While.
T	H	R	A	L	L	Bondage, Enslavement, Helotry, Peonage, Serfdom, Servitude, Slavery, Yoke.
T	H	R	A	S	H	Beat, Batter, Lambaste, Pelt, Whip, Smother, Flog, Scourge.
T	H	R	A	V	E	Measure for unthreshed grain.
T	H	R	E	A	D	Filament, Cord, Yarn, Penetrate, Intersperse, Drift, Gist.
T	H	R	E	A	T	Menace, Intimidation, Coercion, Urge, Exert pressure.
T	H	R	E	S	H	Thrash, Beat, Maul, Trounce.
T	H	R	I	C	E	Three times fully, Repeatedly.
T	H	R	I	F	T	Economy, Frugality, Husbandry, Providence, Prudence, Saving.

1	2	3	4	5	6	Definition
T	H	R	I	P	S	Sucking bugs.
T	H	R	I	V	E	Boom, Flourish, Succeed, Prosper, Score.
T	H	R	O	A	T	Jaws, Mouth, Passage, Constriction, Gullet.
T	H	R	O	N	E	Royal seat, Ceremonial seat, Seat of deity, Toilet seat.
T	H	R	O	N	G	Crowd, Crush, Drove, Horde, Multitude, Press, Push, Squash.
T	H	R	O	V	E	Flourished, Prospered.
T	H	R	O	W	S	Hurled, Flung, Cast, Propelled, Tossed, Launched, Pitched.
T	H	R	U	S	H	Fungus disease of the oral cavities.
T	H	R	U	S	T	Drive, force, impel, press, stress.
T	H	U	S	L	Y	In this manner.
T	H	W	A	C	K	Blow, Whack, Thump, Pound, Smack, Welt.
T	H	W	A	R	T	Frustrate, Baffle, Balk, Beat, Circumvent, Foil, Transverse, Crosswise.
T	H	Y	M	O	L	Oil of thyme used in pharmaceutical preparations.
T	H	Y	M	U	S	A glandular structure.
T	I	B	I	A	L	Located near the leg bone.
T	I	C	K	E	D	Marked with ticks, Speckled.
T	I	C	K	E	N	Bed ticking to cover mattress and pillows.
T	I	C	K	E	R	Something that ticks, Watch, Telegraphic receiving instrument for printing stock exchange prices.
T	I	C	K	E	T	Label, Card, Card of admission, Ballot, Vote, Passport, Key, Password.
T	I	C	K	E	Y	S. African threepenny piece.
T	I	C	K	L	E	Excite, Titillate, Stimulate, Provoke, Annoy.
T	I	C	K	L	Y	Ticklish, Risky, Difficult, Pricking.
T	I	C	T	A	C	Signalling system of bookmakers.
T	I	D	B	I	T	Choice morsel of food, Spicy bit of news or information.
T	I	D	D	L	E	Potter, Fidget.
T	I	D	I	E	D	Cleared up, Made things ship shape.
T	I	D	I	L	Y	Neatly, Methodically.
T	I	E	D	U	P	Hampered, Curbed, Fettered, Hobbled, Busy, Shackled.
T	I	E	I	N	G	Confining.
T	I	E	P	I	N	Ornamental pin used to hold ends of neckpiece.
T	I	E	R	C	E	A cask with capacity of Forty Two wine gallons.
T	I	E	R	O	D	Connecting rod usually in engine.
T	I	F	F	I	N	Luncheon, Midday meal.
T	I	G	H	T	S	Skintight garment from neck down or waist down, Stockings combined with pantie.
T	I	K	K	E	R	Interruption in early days of radio.
T	I	L	E	R	Y	Kiln or field where tiles are burned.
T	I	L	I	N	G	The act of one who tiles.
T	I	L	L	E	D	Cultivated, Dressed, Worked, Tended.
T	I	L	L	E	R	Steering gear for ship.
T	I	L	T	E	D	Inclined, Sloped, Tipped, Pitched, Leaned.
T	I	L	T	E	R	Jouster, Seesaw, Teeter.
T	I	M	B	A	L	Cymbal, Kettle-drum.
T	I	M	B	E	R	Forest, Timberland, Weald, Woods, Woodland, Beam, Board.
T	I	M	B	R	E	Temper, Mood, Spirit, Resonance quality, Tone quality.
T	I	M	E	L	Y	Early, Seasonably, Auspicious, Favourable, Opportune, Prosperous, Punctual, Prompt.
T	I	M	I	N	G	Art or practice of regulating speed, Tempo, Clocking.
T	I	N	C	A	N	Food container.
T	I	N	D	E	R	Inflammable substance for use as kindling, Something used to incite and inflame.
T	I	N	E	I	D	Moths.
T	I	N	G	E	D	Coloured, Hinted, Intimated, Tinted, Touched, Imbued, Flavoured.
T	I	N	G	L	E	Thrill, Small nail.
T	I	N	K	E	R	Itinerant repairman who mends kitchen utensils, Fiddle, Doodle, Mess, Potter, Puddle, Putter.
T	I	N	K	L	E	Plink, Tingle, Jingle, Chinkle, Chat, Babble, Chatter, Prattle.
T	I	N	M	A	N	Tinker.
T	I	N	N	E	D	Preserved.
T	I	N	N	E	R	Tin miner, Tinsmith.
T	I	N	P	O	T	Wretched, Inferior.
T	I	N	S	E	L	Gaudy, Blatant, Brazen, Flashy, Garish, Tawdry, Glittering.
T	I	N	T	E	D	Tinged, Imbued, Coloured, Shaded, Toned.
T	I	N	T	E	R	One that mixes paint.
T	I	P	O	F	F	Secret information, Give-away, Hint, Warning.
T	I	P	P	E	D	Overturned, Inclined, Pitched, Sloped, Tilted.
T	I	P	P	E	T	Shoulder cape of fur.
T	I	P	P	L	E	To drink intoxicating liquor.
T	I	P	T	O	E	Standing, or walking on tips of toes, Silent, Cautious, Stealthy.
T	I	P	T	O	P	Top, Summit, Crown, Pinnacle, Excellent, First rate.
T	I	R	A	D	E	Diatribe, Harangue, Rant, Invective.

1	2	3	4	5	6	
T	I	R	I	N	G	Irksome, Boring, Drudging, Tedious, Tiresome.
T	I	R	L	E	D	Twisted, Vibrated.
T	I	S	A	N	E	Herbal drink, Infusion of herbs.
T	I	S	S	U	E	Fine fabric, Aggregate of cells.
T	I	T	B	I	T	Tidbit, Tasty morsel.
T	I	T	H	E	D	Taxed.
T	I	T	H	E	R	One that pays or collects tithes.
T	I	T	L	E	D	Named, Designated, Inscribed, Dubbed.
T	I	T	L	E	R	Card bearing title of cinema film in the making.
T	I	T	T	E	R	Laugh, Chortle, Chuckle, Giggle, Guffaw, Snicker.
T	I	T	T	L	E	Cedilla, Point or small sign used as a punctuation mark, Small particle.
T	I	V	O	L	I	Game resembling bagatelle.
T	O	C	S	I	N	Alarm, Warning, Alert.
T	O	D	D	L	E	Saunter, Totter.
T	O	E	C	A	P	Separate piece of leather or material covering toe of shoe to reinforce or decorate it.
T	O	F	F	E	E	Confection of boiling sugar and butter.
T	O	G	G	E	D	Dressed up, Decked out, Dolled up, Smartened, Spruced.
T	O	G	G	L	E	Wooden or metal pin used with loop to make a fastening.
T	O	I	L	E	D	Worked, Drudged, Laboured, Plodded, Strove, Slogged.
T	O	I	L	E	R	Slave, Labourer, Drudge, Peon, Slavery, Workhouse.
T	O	I	L	E	T	Dress, Attire, Convenience, Latrine, Lavatory, Privy, Water closet.
T	O	L	E	D	O	Finely tempered sword made in Toledo, Spain.
T	O	L	L	E	D	Rang, Knelled, Pealed, Chimed (bells).
T	O	L	L	E	R	Decoy.
T	O	L	L	O	L	Passable, Tolerable.
T	O	L	S	E	Y	Town hall, Borough, Law court.
T	O	L	T	E	C	Early Mexican.
T	O	L	U	I	C	Carbolic acid.
T	O	L	U	O	L	Liquid resembling benzene.
T	O	M	A	T	O	Red globular vegetable.
T	O	M	B	A	C	Copper and zinc alloy for cheap jewellery.
T	O	M	B	E	D	Buried.
T	O	M	B	O	Y	A sporting girl who competes with boys, Gamine, Hoyden.
T	O	M	C	A	T	Male feline.
T	O	M	T	O	M	Small-headed drum usually long and narrow.
T	O	N	G	U	E	Language, Dialect, Speech, Vernacular, Scold, Baste, Berate, Upbraid.
T	O	N	I	N	G	Tinting, Shading.
T	O	N	I	S	H	Fashionable, Stylish.
T	O	N	S	I	L	Lympoid tissue in the throat.
T	O	O	L	E	D	Ornamental work on leather.
T	O	O	T	E	D	Hooted, Blast on horn.
T	O	O	T	E	R	One that toots.
T	O	O	T	H	Y	Having and showing prominent teeth.
T	O	O	T	L	E	Act of tooting.
T	O	P	D	O	G	Leader, Victor, Person in authority.
T	O	P	F	U	L	Brimful.
T	O	P	H	A	T	Topper.
T	O	P	H	E	T	Shrine in ancient Jerusalem where human sacrifices were performed.
T	O	P	H	U	S	Gout.
T	O	P	P	E	D	Filled up, Dominated, Surpassed, Excelled, Headed.
T	O	P	P	L	E	Fall, Plunge, Teeter, Lurch, Stagger, Overturn, Overthrow, Upset.
T	O	R	E	R	O	Matador, Bull-fighter.
T	O	R	O	I	D	Symmetrical, geometrical figure.
T	O	R	O	S	E	Swelling, Knobbed.
T	O	R	P	I	D	Lethargic, Comatose, Heavy, Sluggish, Dopey, Languor, Lassitude.
T	O	R	P	O	R	Lethargy, Coma, Dullness, Languor, Lassitude, Sleep, Stupor, Torpidity.
T	O	R	Q	U	E	A turning or twisting force, Torture, Ancient metal necklace.
T	O	R	R	I	D	Hot, Burning, Blazing, Passionate, Impassioned, Ardent, Flaming, Scorching.
T	O	R	S	E	L	Stone, iron or wood to support end of beam.
T	O	S	S	E	D	Thrown, Pitched, Flung, Hurled, Launched, Heaved, Rolled.
T	O	S	S	E	R	One that tosses.
T	O	S	S	U	P	Matter of luck, Even bet, Choice.
T	O	T	I	N	G	Practice of taking food home from an employer's kitchen.
T	O	T	T	E	D	Added up, Summarized, Figured, Totalized.
T	O	T	T	E	R	Teeter, Falter, Lurch, Stagger, Stumble, Topple, Wobble.
T	O	U	C	A	N	S. American bird with extra large beak, Hornbill.
T	O	U	C	H	E	Acknowledgement of a hit in fencing.

1	2	3	4	5	6	
T	O	U	C	H	Y	Irascible, Choleric, Cranky, Cross, Testy, Delicate, Precarious, Sensitive.
T	O	U	P	E	E	Small wig or section of false hair.
T	O	U	R	E	D	Circled, Journeyed, Proceeded.
T	O	U	S	E	D	Tussled, Racked, Torn, Worried.
T	O	U	S	L	E	Tussle, Tangle, Dishevel, Disorder.
T	O	U	T	E	D	Publicized, Proclaimed, Promoted, Acclaimed.
T	O	U	T	E	R	One who solicits.
T	O	W	A	G	E	Act or process of towing (tugs).
T	O	W	A	R	D	Good, Advantageous, Beneficial, Brave, Helpful, Apropos, About, Against.
T	O	W	E	R	Y	Lofty.
T	O	W	I	N	G	Pulling, Dragging, Hauling, Tugging.
T	O	W	S	E	R	Large dog, Lionhearted, Large rough person especially full of energy.
T	O	X	O	I	D	Detoxidified toxin.
T	O	Y	D	O	G	Tiny dog kept purely as a pet.
T	O	Y	F	U	L	Sportive.
T	O	Y	I	N	G	Trifling, Dallying, Flirting, Fooling.
T	O	Y	I	S	H	Frivlolous, Trivial.
T	O	Y	M	A	N	Maker or dealer of children's toys.
T	R	A	B	A	L	Relating to a beam.
T	R	A	C	E	D	Tracked, Trailed, Found.
T	R	A	C	E	R	Seeker, Investigator.
T	R	A	D	E	D	Bartered, Bargained, Exchanged, Swapped.
T	R	A	G	I	C	Shocking, Disastrous, Fearful, Deplorable, Lamentable, Calamitous.
T	R	A	G	U	S	The prominence in front of the external opening of the ear.
T	R	A	N	C	E	Reverie, Brown study, Muse, Transport, Enrapture, Enravish, Ravish.
T	R	A	P	H	Y	Tricky, Difficult, Treacherous.
T	R	A	S	H	Y	Cheap, Base, Common, Mean, Paltry, Tatty, Rubbishy, Shoddy.
T	R	A	U	M	A	Shock, Stress, Collapse.
T	R	A	V	E	L	Go, Journey, Pass, Proceed, Cover, Track, Traverse, Wend, Move.
T	R	A	V	I	S	Partition between stable stalls.
T	R	E	A	T	Y	Agreement, Concord, Convention, Pact, Contract, Convenant, Alliance.
T	R	E	B	L	E	Triple, Threefold, Acute high piercing piping, Sharp, Shrill, Thin.
T	R	E	B	L	Y	Triply.
T	R	E	M	E	X	Genus of wood wasp.
T	R	E	M	I	E	Funnel for depositing and consolidating concrete underwater.
T	R	E	M	O	R	Earthquake, Shock, Shake, Quiver, Shiver, Shudder, Vibrate, Tremble.
T	R	E	N	C	H	Cut, Ditch, Furrow, Gully, Border, Approach, Verge.
T	R	E	N	D	Y	Stylish, Fashionable, Modish, Swank, Swish.
T	R	E	P	A	N	Operation on skull.
T	R	E	P	I	D	Timorous, Trembling, Quaking.
T	R	E	S	S	Y	Resembling tresses.
T	R	I	A	C	T	Triactinal sponge spicule.
T	R	I	A	G	E	Sorting and first-aid treatment of battle casaulties.
T	R	I	B	A	L	Relating to tribe and customs.
T	R	I	C	A	R	Three wheeled vehicle.
T	R	I	C	K	Y	Sly, Artful, Astute, Crafty, Cunning, Unstable, Delicate, Sensitive.
T	R	I	C	O	T	Knitted fabric.
T	R	I	F	I	D	Trident divided at the base into three lobes.
T	R	I	F	L	E	A dessert of jelly, sponge and custard, Bauble, Novelty, Hint, Suspicion, Dally, Flirt, Philander.
T	R	I	G	L	Y	Tidily, Dandified.
T	R	I	G	O	N	Triangular.
T	R	I	L	B	Y	Hat, Foot.
T	R	I	M	E	R	Compound formed by union of three molecules.
T	R	I	M	L	Y	Neatly, Compactly, With trimness.
T	R	I	N	A	L	Threefold, Trial.
T	R	I	O	D	E	An electron tube.
T	R	I	O	S	E	Two simple sugars, Sweet crystalline compound.
T	R	I	P	L	E	Triad, Threesome, Trinity, Trio, Triumvirate, Troika.
T	R	I	P	O	D	Three-legged.
T	R	I	P	O	S	Honours course or school.
T	R	I	S	T	E	Sad, Dismal, Dull, Depressing.
T	R	I	T	O	N	Minor sea divinity.
T	R	I	T	O	R	Grinding surface of a tooth.
T	R	I	T	Y	L	Crystalline hydrocarbon.
T	R	I	U	N	E	Trinity.
T	R	I	V	E	T	Three-legged stand to hold a kettle near a fire.
T	R	I	V	I	A	Minute, Small change, Triviality.

1	2	3	4	5	6	
T	R	O	C	A	R	Sharp pointed surgical instrument.
T	R	O	C	H	E	Medicinal tablet or lozenge.
T	R	O	G	U	E	Wooden trough forming a mine drain.
T	R	O	I	K	A	Russian sleigh drawn by three horses, Triad, Trio, Triple, Trinity.
T	R	O	J	A	N	Showing pluck, Endurance, Determined, Energy.
T	R	O	L	L	Y	Small wheeled cart.
T	R	O	P	H	I	Mouth of insect.
T	R	O	P	H	Y	Prize, Memento, Keepsake, Relic, Reminder, Souvenir, Memorial, Token.
T	R	O	P	I	C	Relating to or occuring in the tropics.
T	R	O	T	Y	L	Explosive.
T	R	O	U	G	H	Long shallow vessel, often used for feeding animals, Groove, Trench, Furrow.
T	R	O	U	P	E	Company, Band, Corps, Outfit, Party, Troop.
T	R	O	V	E	R	Coming into possession.
T	R	O	W	E	D	Believed, Trusted.
T	R	O	W	E	L	Tool with flat or scoop blade for use in masonry trade or garden.
T	R	U	A	N	T	Vagabond, One who stays away from business or school without permission.
T	R	U	D	G	E	Plod, Slog, Toil, Stodge, Tramp, March.
T	R	U	E	S	T	Most true.
T	R	U	I	S	M	Veracity, Gospel, Truth, Maxim, Commonplace, Cliche, Platitude, Banality.
T	R	U	S	T	Y	Reliable, Dependable, Secure, True, Authentic, Convincing, Credible, Faithful.
T	R	Y	G	O	N	Stingray.
T	R	Y	I	N	G	Tight, Arduous, Onerous, Burdensome, Exacting, Oppressive, Tough, Weighty.
T	R	Y	O	U	T	Exerimental performance or demonstration.
T	S	E	T	S	E	Fly that transmits sleeping sickness.
T	U	A	R	E	G	Tribe of nomads in Sahara.
T	U	B	A	G	E	Inserting a tube usually in a smoothbore gun.
T	U	B	B	E	D	Bathed.
T	U	B	I	N	G	Piping.
T	U	B	U	L	E	A small tube, A slender elongated channel.
T	U	C	K	E	D	Folded, Pleated.
T	U	C	K	E	R	Bib, One that frills.
T	U	C	K	E	T	Fanfare on a trumpet.
T	U	C	K	I	N	A large meal.
T	U	F	F	E	T	A low seat, Hassock.
T	U	F	T	E	R	A deer hound.
T	U	G	G	E	D	Pulled, Dragged, Hauled, Strained, Toiled, Worked, Lugged, Towed.
T	U	G	G	E	R	Portable hoist used in mine.
T	U	I	L	L	E	Thigh armour.
T	U	M	B	L	E	Fall, Plummet, Slump, Discover, Overthrow, Fell, Confuse.
T	U	M	E	F	Y	To swell, Inflate, Distend, Puff up.
T	U	M	O	U	R	Swelling, Protuberance, Cancer, Sarcoma.
T	U	M	T	U	M	Strum, Dogcart.
T	U	M	U	L	T	Commotion, Clamour, Agitation, Hassle, Turmoil, Upheaval, Din, Uproar.
T	U	N	D	R	A	Arctic swamp with frozen sub-soil.
T	U	N	E	I	N	Establish radio contact.
T	U	N	G	U	S	Mongoloid people.
T	U	N	I	N	G	Act or process of putting in tune.
T	U	N	N	E	D	Placed in a cask.
T	U	N	N	E	L	Tube, Shaft, Undermine, Passage, Burrow.
T	U	P	A	I	A	Tree shrew.
T	U	P	E	L	O	Gum-tree.
T	U	R	B	A	N	Head-dress of long cloth wound around a hat.
T	U	R	B	I	D	Muddy, Cloudy, Confused, Disorder, Dark, Dense, Thick, Polluted.
T	U	R	B	O	T	Flat fish.
T	U	R	E	E	N	Covered vessel from which cooked food is served at table.
T	U	R	F	E	D	Covered with turf.
T	U	R	G	I	D	Inflated, Dropside, Flatulent, Rhetorical, Bombastic, Swollen, Flowery, Grandiloquent.
T	U	R	G	O	R	Swollen, Pressure.
T	U	R	K	E	Y	Poultry, Practical action without delay, Theatrical production that fails, Flop.
T	U	R	N	E	D	Shaped in a lathe, Changed direction.
T	U	R	N	E	R	One that shapes things on a lathe.
T	U	R	N	I	N	Deliver, Hand over, Betray, Acquit oneself.
T	U	R	N	I	P	Root vegetable, Thick pocket watch, Dunce, Blockhead, Idiot, Moron, Dimwit, Chump.
T	U	R	N	U	P	Consult, Find, Catch, Relinquish, Abandon, Show up, Come, Arrive.
T	U	R	R	E	T	Tower, Minaret, Pinnacle, Tool holder.
T	U	R	T	L	E	Aquatic reptile.
T	U	S	C	A	N	Classical architecture of Roman origin.

1	2	3	4	5	6	
T	U	S	K	E	D	Having teeth or tusks.
T	U	S	K	E	R	Male elephant with two normally developed tusks.
T	U	S	S	A	H	Silk fabric from Oriental silkworms.
T	U	S	S	I	S	Cough.
T	U	S	S	L	E	Wrestle, Grapple, Scuffle, Contend.
T	U	T	R	I	X	Female tutor.
T	U	T	S	A	N	Plant in Spain from which a healing salve is made.
T	U	X	E	D	O	Dinner jacket.
T	U	Y	E	R	E	A nozzle through which an air blast is delivered.
T	W	A	I	T	E	European shad.
T	W	E	E	N	Y	Between maid.
T	W	E	L	V	E	A dozen.
T	W	E	N	T	Y	A score.
T	W	I	C	E	R	Printer who works as compositor and pressman, A cheat, A crook.
T	W	I	G	G	Y	Delicate, Slight, Thin.
T	W	I	N	E	D	Wound, Coiled, Twisted, Meandered, Curled, Spiralled, Wreathed.
T	W	I	N	E	R	Climbing plant.
T	W	I	N	G	E	Pain, Ache, Misery, Pang, Stitch, Throe, Spasm, Twitch.
T	W	I	T	C	H	Pluck, Jerk, Lug, Lurch, Snap, Yank, Snatch, Pull.
T	W	O	P	L	Y	Consisting of two strands or two boards.
T	W	O	W	A	Y	Involving movement in two directions.
T	Y	C	O	O	N	Business man of exceptional wealth, power and influence.
T	Y	L	O	T	E	Sponge spicule.
T	Y	M	B	A	L	Kettledrum.
T	Y	M	P	A	N	Frames used in a printing press.
T	Y	P	H	O	N	Monster of Greek mythology.
T	Y	P	H	U	S	Severe febrile disease.
T	Y	P	I	F	Y	Represent, Embody, Symbolize, Illustrate, Mirror, Personify, Exemplify.
T	Y	P	I	S	T	One who uses a typewriter.
T	Y	R	A	N	T	Dictator, Despot, Oppressor, Autocrat, Duce.
T	Y	R	I	A	N	Purple colour.
T	Y	S	T	I	E	Black guillemot.

U

1	2	3	4	5	6	
U	B	I	E	T	Y	Position, Location.
U	D	M	U	R	T	Native of Eastern Soviet Russia.
U	G	L	I	F	Y	To make ugly.
U	G	L	I	L	Y	In an ugly manner.
U	G	S	O	M	E	Frightful, Horrid, Loathsome, Gruesome.
U	L	L	A	G	E	Amount necessary to fill a cask.
U	L	S	T	E	R	Long loose overcoat of Irish origin.
U	L	T	I	M	O	In last month.
U	M	B	L	E	S	Entrails of animals.
U	M	B	R	A	S	Ghosts, Phantoms.
U	M	F	A	A	N	Young boy employed to do general work.
U	M	L	A	U	T	Vowel inflection.
U	M	P	I	R	E	Judge, Arbiter, Arbitrator, Referee, Adjudicate.
U	N	A	B	L	E	Incapable, Incompetent, Inefficient, Impotent, Helpless.
U	N	A	W	E	D	Not awed, Undaunted, Undismayed.
U	N	B	E	N	D	Slacken, Undo, Relax, Unknot.
U	N	B	E	N	T	Unbowed, Unsubdued, Unwrinkled.
U	N	B	I	N	D	Untie, Unfasten, Release, Loose, Untangle, Unfetter.
U	N	B	I	T	T	To remove the turns from a bitt.
U	N	B	O	L	T	Unfasten, Unbar, Loosen.
U	N	B	O	R	N	Not born, Non-existent.
U	N	B	R	E	D	Unborn, Ill bred, Untaught, Untrained.
U	N	B	U	R	Y	Disinter, Exhume.
U	N	C	A	G	E	To release from a cage.
U	N	C	A	R	T	To take or discharge from a cart.
U	N	C	A	S	E	Disclose, Uncover, Strip, Undress.
U	N	C	I	A	L	A special script used in manuscripts of the fourth century.
U	N	C	L	A	D	Naked.
U	N	C	L	O	G	To free from obstruction.
U	N	C	O	C	K	Remove hammer from cocked rifle.
U	N	C	O	I	L	Unwind, Release, Unroll.

1	2	3	4	5	6	
U	N	C	O	L	T	Unhorse.
U	N	C	O	R	D	Release from binding.
U	N	C	O	R	K	Release from sealed or pent-up state.
U	N	C	U	R	L	To straighten out.
U	N	D	E	C	K	Remove ornaments.
U	N	D	E	R	N	Afternoon from noon to sundown.
U	N	D	I	E	S	Underwear.
U	N	D	I	N	E	Water nymph, Sylph, Glass vessel for irrigating eye and nasal passages.
U	N	D	O	C	K	Remove a ship from dock.
U	N	D	O	E	R	Destroyer, Seducer.
U	N	D	O	N	E	Not done, Destroyed, Ruined, Unfastened.
U	N	D	R	A	W	To draw aside, Open.
U	N	D	U	K	E	To deprive of dukedom.
U	N	E	A	S	E	Tension, Care, Anxiety, Disquiet, Worry, Misgiving, Embarrassment, Awkwardness.
U	N	E	A	S	Y	Apprehensively, Disturbedly, Restlessly, Fidgetingly, Awkwardly, Precariously.
U	N	E	A	T	H	Not easy, Difficult.
U	N	E	V	E	N	Rough, Craggy, Harsh, Lopsided, Irregular, Unequal, Off balance, Rough, Odd.
U	N	E	Y	E	D	Unseen, Unobserved, Invisible.
U	N	F	A	I	R	Inequitable, Unjust, Dishonest, Foul, Partial, Disproportionate, Unfavourable, Excessive.
U	N	F	E	E	D	Unrewarded, Unpaid, Untipped.
U	N	F	I	N	E	Rough, Inclement, Stormy.
U	N	F	I	R	M	Unsteady, Insecure, Unstable, Weak.
U	N	F	O	L	D	Open, Expand, Extend, Solve, Decipher, Elaborate, Resolve, Unravel.
U	N	F	O	R	M	Destroy, Make formless.
U	N	F	R	E	E	Lacking freedom, Lack of personal liberty.
U	N	F	U	R	L	Release, Open out, Unfold, Unroll, Spread out for display.
U	N	G	A	I	N	Hard to reach, Inaccessable, Inconvenient, Intractable.
U	N	G	E	A	R	Unhitch, Remove harness.
U	N	G	I	L	D	To remove gilding.
U	N	G	I	R	D	Unrestrain, To loosen clothes particularly belts.
U	N	G	I	R	T	Loose, Slack.
U	N	G	L	U	E	Disjoin, Steaming open an envelope.
U	N	G	U	A	L	Nail, Hoof, Claw.
U	N	G	U	I	S	Nail, Hoof, Claw.
U	N	G	Y	V	E	Unfettered.
U	N	H	A	I	R	Remove hair, Work in furriers.
U	N	H	A	N	D	Let go, Release.
U	N	H	A	N	G	Detach from a hanging support.
U	N	H	A	S	P	Unfasten, Open.
U	N	H	E	A	D	Separate the head from the trunk.
U	N	H	E	L	M	Divest of a helmet.
U	N	H	E	W	N	Rough, Unpolished, Crude, Unfashioned, Unfinished, Unformed, Unworked.
U	N	H	I	V	E	To drive from a hive.
U	N	H	O	L	Y	Inpious, Profane, Ungodly, Blameworthy, Culpable, Guilty, Uncivilized.
U	N	H	O	O	K	Disconnect, Unfasten.
U	N	H	U	N	G	Not executed by hanging.
U	N	H	U	R	T	Whole, Entire, Intact, Perfect, Sound, Unbroken, Undamaged, Uninjured.
U	N	H	U	S	K	Expose, Shell.
U	N	I	A	T	E	Union of Greek and Roman Catholic churches.
U	N	I	O	L	A	Genus of American grasses, Sea oat.
U	N	I	P	O	D	One legged support for camera.
U	N	I	Q	U	E	Only, Alone, Sole, Matchless, Exceptional, Extraordinary, Rare, Singular.
U	N	I	S	E	X	For either or both sexes.
U	N	I	S	O	N	Harmony, Concord, Equivalent, Accord.
U	N	I	T	A	L	Unitary, Unique.
U	N	I	T	E	D	Joined, Associated, Combined, Coupled.
U	N	I	T	E	R	One that unites.
U	N	J	U	S	T	Biased, Inequitable, Unfair, Dishonest, Faithless, Wrongful.
U	N	K	E	P	T	Discarded, Neglected, Rejected, Undefended.
U	N	K	I	N	D	Cruel, Harsh, Ungrateful, Rigorous, Cruel, Unfriendly.
U	N	K	I	N	G	To deprive a monarch.
U	N	K	N	I	T	Disperse, Dissolve, Unravel, Relax.
U	N	K	N	O	T	Undo, Untie, Loose.
U	N	L	A	C	E	Untie, Loosen.
U	N	L	A	D	E	Unload, Discharge, Unship, Unstow.
U	N	L	A	I	D	Unplaced, Not pacified.
U	N	L	A	S	H	Loose, Undo, Detach something.

1	2	3	4	5	6	
U	N	L	E	A	D	To remove lead from between lines of type.
U	N	L	E	A	F	Strip of leaves.
U	N	L	E	S	S	Except, But, Save, Saving, Without.
U	N	L	I	K	E	Different, Disparate, Dissimilar, Diverse, Unequal, Various, Divergent.
U	N	L	I	M	E	Delime.
U	N	L	I	N	K	Unfasten, Separate, Detach.
U	N	L	I	V	E	Annul, Reverse, Kill, Not electrified.
U	N	L	O	A	D	Discharge, Off-load, Unship, Relieve, Lighten, Unburden.
U	N	L	O	C	K	Unfasten, Free from restraint, Decode.
U	N	L	O	R	D	Deprive of the rank of lord.
U	N	L	O	V	E	Hate, Absence of love.
U	N	L	U	C	K	Misfortune, Adversity, Mischance, Mishap, Tragedy.
U	N	M	A	D	E	Not made, Uncompleted.
U	N	M	A	K	E	Destroy, Deprive, Dismantle, Demolish, Raze, Wreck, Decimate.
U	N	M	A	S	K	Expose, Discover, Debunk, Undress, Denounce, Reveal, Uncloak.
U	N	M	E	E	T	Unsuitable, Improper, Unfit, Inappropriate, Inapt.
U	N	M	O	O	R	To cast off a boat.
U	N	N	A	I	L	To remove by extracting nails.
U	N	N	E	S	T	To eject or evict.
U	N	P	A	C	K	Unburden.
U	N	P	A	I	D	Outstanding, Uncompensated, Due, Mature, Overdue, Owing, Unsettled.
U	N	P	I	C	K	Unravel, Take out stitches.
U	N	P	I	L	E	Take or disentangle from pile.
U	N	P	L	U	G	Remove an obstruction.
U	N	P	R	O	P	Deprive of support.
U	N	P	U	R	E	Adulterated, Impure.
U	N	R	E	A	D	Illiterate, Ignorant, Unexamined, Not perused.
U	N	R	E	A	L	Fictitious, Fanciful, Fantastic, Fictional, Illusory, Imaginary, Visionary.
U	N	R	E	I	N	Loosen rein, Remove restrictions.
U	N	R	E	N	T	Not torn.
U	N	R	E	S	T	Disquiet, Unease, Ferment, Restlessness, Storm, Stress, Turmoil, Restiveness.
U	N	R	I	P	E	Immature, Young, Callow, Juvenile, Green, Unfledged, Youthful.
U	N	R	O	B	E	Undress, Disrobe.
U	N	R	O	L	L	Uncoil, Extend, Evolve, Open out, Unwind.
U	N	R	O	O	F	Strip off covering of roof.
U	N	R	O	O	T	Eradicate, Uproot.
U	N	R	O	P	E	Unlash, Untie, Go free.
U	N	R	U	D	E	Polite, Civil.
U	N	R	U	L	Y	Fractious, Riotous, Unmanageable, Turbulent, Boisterous, Disorderly, Raucous, Rowdy.
U	N	S	A	F	E	Insecure, Shaky, Risky, Perilous, Uncertain, Hazardous, Erratic.
U	N	S	A	I	D	Tacit, Implicit, Implied, Inferred, Unspoken, Wordless, Understood, Unuttered.
U	N	S	E	A	M	Rip, Unpick.
U	N	S	E	A	T	Throw, Buck, Pitch, Unhorse.
U	N	S	E	E	N	Invisible, Unfamiliar.
U	N	S	O	W	N	Not planted with seed.
U	N	S	P	A	R	Remove stakes or spars.
U	N	S	P	E	D	Not performed or accomplished.
U	N	S	P	I	N	Untwist.
U	N	S	T	E	P	Remove a mast.
U	N	S	T	O	P	Open, Unclose, Undo, Unshut.
U	N	S	T	O	W	Unload, Disburden, Discharge, Off-load.
U	N	S	U	N	G	Neglected, Not praised, Forgotten.
U	N	S	U	R	E	Uncertain, Weak, Shaky, Unstable, Doubtful, Dubious, Unreliable, Untrustworthy.
U	N	T	E	L	L	Nullify passage of time.
U	N	T	E	N	T	Bring out of tent.
U	N	T	I	D	Y	Slovenly, Unkept, Slipshod, Sloppy, Careless, Messy, Slapdash, Dishevelled.
U	N	T	I	E	D	Undone, Unloosed, Unrestricted, Untethered.
U	N	T	I	L	E	Remove tiles from roof.
U	N	T	O	L	D	Huge, Enormous, Immense, Mighty, Mammoth, Innumerable, Countless, Uncountable.
U	N	T	O	M	B	Disinter, Exhume.
U	N	T	O	R	N	Not rent, Not ripped, Whole.
U	N	T	R	I	M	Put in disorder.
U	N	T	R	O	D	Untraversed, Not frequented, Little used.
U	N	T	R	U	E	False, Inaccurate, Incorrect, Wrong, Erroneous, Faithless, Disloyal, Treacherous.
U	N	T	U	C	K	Release from rucking.
U	N	T	U	N	E	Disarrange, Discompose.
U	N	T	U	R	N	Reverse, turn, untwist, Unscrew.

1	2	3	4	5	6	
U	N	U	S	E	D	Vacant, Idle, New, Unaccustomed, Accumulated, Strange.
U	N	V	E	I	L	Uncover, Reveal, Unmask, Disclose, Display, Expose, Betray, Divulge.
U	N	W	A	R	Y	Incautious, Unguarded, Rash, Indiscreet, Credulous, Reckless, Thoughtless, Hasty.
U	N	W	E	L	L	Ailing, Indisposed, Sick, Poorly, Off-colour.
U	N	W	E	P	T	Unlamented.
U	N	W	I	L	Y	Guileless, Simple.
U	N	W	I	N	D	Uncoil, Disentangle, Unroll, Unreel, Relax, Loosen off, Unbend.
U	N	W	I	S	E	Indiscreet, Imprudent, Ill-advised, Ill-judged, Injudicious, Impolitic.
U	N	W	I	S	H	Cancel, Withdraw.
U	N	W	O	R	N	New, Pristine, Unimpaired.
U	N	W	R	A	P	Disclose, Reveal, Uncloak.
U	N	Y	O	K	E	Outspan, Unhitch, Release, Disjoin, Unlink.
U	P	B	E	A	R	Support, Raise, Sustain, Elevate, Bolster, Brace, Carry, Prop.
U	P	B	E	A	T	Optimistic, Cheerful, Happy, Unaccented beat in music.
U	P	B	E	N	D	Forepart of a ski that curves upward.
U	P	C	A	R	D	Playing card turned up to start the game.
U	P	C	A	S	T	Accident, Chance.
U	P	D	A	T	E	Modernise, Renew, Refresh, Refurbish, Rejuvenate, Renovate, Restore.
U	P	F	E	E	D	Supplied with material that is forced upward.
U	P	F	L	O	W	To flow up.
U	P	G	R	O	W	To grow up, Mature.
U	P	H	I	L	L	Hard, Arduous, Difficult, Support, Advocate, Lift, Elevate, Hoist.
U	P	H	U	N	G	Suspended.
U	P	K	E	E	P	Maintain in good condition.
U	P	L	A	N	D	Plateau, Tableland.
U	P	L	E	A	P	To leap up.
U	P	L	I	F	T	Elevate, Hoist, Raise, Uphold, Illuminate, Edify, Enlighten, Improve.
U	P	L	O	C	K	Lock up.
U	P	L	O	O	K	Upward look.
U	P	M	O	S	T	Topmost, Uppermost.
U	P	P	I	S	H	Elated, Uppity, Presumptuous, Brash, Forward, Pushing, Self-assertive.
U	P	P	I	T	Y	Over-weening, Presumptuous, Brash, Forward.
U	P	R	E	A	R	Elevate, Hoist, Build, Construct, Exalt, Glorify, Rise, Aspire.
U	P	R	I	S	E	Ascend, Revolt, Stand up, Roll out, Rise, Turn out.
U	P	R	O	A	R	Riot, Turmoil, Hubbub, Pandemonium, Commotion, Hussle, Tumult, Rumpus.
U	P	R	O	L	L	Wind up.
U	P	R	O	O	T	Annihilate, Abolish, Eradicate, Exterminate, Extirpate, Root out, Wipe out.
U	P	R	U	S	H	Surging upwards.
U	P	S	E	N	D	Send upwards.
U	P	S	H	O	T	Effect, Consequence, Event, Issue, Outcome, Substance, Burden, Purport.
U	P	S	I	D	E	The upper side.
U	P	S	T	A	Y	Sustain, Support.
U	P	T	A	K	E	Lift, Raise, Understand, Comprehend.
U	P	T	E	A	R	Tear up by the roots.
U	P	T	I	L	T	Incline, Sloped.
U	P	T	O	W	N	Upper part of town usually residential district.
U	P	T	U	R	N	Convulsion, Upheaval, Ferment, Clamour, Outcry, Tumult.
U	P	W	A	R	D	Ascending, Uphill.
U	P	W	A	R	P	Broad Anticline.
U	P	W	A	S	H	Upward flow of air.
U	P	W	E	L	L	To flow upward.
U	P	W	I	N	D	Roll, Coil, Face or course against wind.
U	R	A	C	I	L	Crystalline compound.
U	R	A	E	U	S	Representation of sacred asp on ancient Egyptian headdress.
U	R	A	N	I	A	Genus of brightly coloured moths.
U	R	A	N	I	C	Relating to uranium.
U	R	A	N	Y	L	Chemical radical.
U	R	B	A	N	E	Cosmopolitan, Suave, Bland, Civilized, Genteel, Cultivated, Refined, Polished.
U	R	C	E	U	S	Ancient Roman jug with one handle.
U	R	C	H	I	N	Hedgehog, Gamin, Imp, Monkey, Brat.
U	R	E	A	S	E	Enzyme.
U	R	E	I	D	E	Derivative of urea.
U	R	E	T	E	R	Duct that carries urine.
U	R	E	T	I	C	Relating to urine, Urinary, Diuretic.
U	R	G	E	N	T	Pressing, Burning, Clamorous, Imperative, Insistent, Exigent, Importunate, Instart.
U	R	G	I	N	G	Impelling, Pressing, Goading, Prompting, Spurring, Hustling, Pushing, Shoving.
U	R	N	I	N	G	Homosexuality.

1	2	3	4	5	6	
U	R	O	N	I	C	Relating to urine.
U	R	O	P	O	D	Segment of tail fan of lobster.
U	R	S	I	N	E	Characteristic of bear.
U	R	T	I	C	A	Stinging nettle.
U	S	A	B	L	E	Can be used.
U	S	A	G	E	R	Church member accepting Communion.
U	S	A	N	C	E	Usury, Interest.
U	S	E	F	U	L	Practical, Functional, Handy, Beneficial, Convenient, Suitable, Helpful, Proper.
U	S	T	I	O	N	Burn, Cauterization, Combustion.
U	S	U	R	E	R	Money-lender, Loan shark.
U	S	W	A	R	D	Towards us.
U	T	E	R	U	S	Womb.
U	T	M	O	S	T	Extreme, Farthest, Remotest, Maximum, Extreme, Outside, Top, Topmost.
U	T	O	P	I	A	Arcadia, Fairyland, Heaven, Paradise, Wonderland, Dreamland.
U	V	E	O	U	S	Resembling bunch of grapes.
U	V	U	L	A	R	Trilling with back of tongue against uvula.

V

1	2	3	4	5	6	
V	A	C	A	N	T	Empty, Bare, Vacuous, Expressionless, Blank, Idle, Unused, Void.
V	A	C	A	T	E	Clear, Empty, Void, Quit, Rescind, Revoke, Reverse, Repeal.
V	A	C	U	U	M	Void, Vacuity, Emptiness.
V	A	D	I	U	M	Living pledge.
V	A	G	A	R	Y	Whim, Caprice, Fancy, Conceit, Humour, Crotchet, Megrim.
V	A	G	I	N	A	Female genital passage, Sheath.
V	A	G	O	U	S	Wandering, Unsettled, Erratic.
V	A	G	U	E	R	More obscure, More indefinite, More blurred.
V	A	I	L	E	D	Submitted, Tipped.
V	A	I	N	E	R	More conceited, More futile.
V	A	I	N	L	Y	Ineffectually, Emptily, Pettily, Arrogantly.
V	A	K	A	S	S	Clerical vestment of Armenian churchman.
V	A	K	E	E	L	Person of political importance in India.
V	A	L	G	U	S	Bow-legged.
V	A	L	I	N	E	Crystalline amino acid.
V	A	L	I	S	E	Travelling bag, Portmanteau, Holdall.
V	A	L	K	Y	R	Mythological Norse maiden.
V	A	L	L	E	Y	Dale, Glen, Vale, Dell.
V	A	L	L	U	M	Ancient Roman earthwork.
V	A	L	O	U	R	Heroism, Gallantry, Prowess, Valiant, Courage.
V	A	L	U	E	D	Prized, Treasured, Esteemed, Assessed, Rated, Appreciated, Cherished, Surveyed.
V	A	L	U	E	R	Appraiser.
V	A	L	V	E	D	Having valves.
V	A	M	P	E	D	Repaired, Patched, Improvised, Reconditioned, Renovated, Devised, Formulated, Concocted.
V	A	M	P	E	R	Siren, Coquette, Shoe worker.
V	A	N	D	A	L	Destroyer, Wrecker, Defacer, Despoiler, Ruiner, Ruffian, Spoiler, Plunderer.
V	A	N	I	S	H	Disappear, Fade, Depart, Evaporate, Dissolve.
V	A	N	I	T	Y	Conceit, Narcissism, Self-admiration, Vainness, Egotism, Self-esteem, Vainglory.
V	A	N	M	A	N	Van-driver, Pantechnicon worker.
V	A	N	N	E	R	Horse suitable for hauling vans.
V	A	N	N	U	S	Anal lobe of insect's wings.
V	A	P	O	R	S	Nervous dejection.
V	A	P	O	U	R	Steam, Fume, Reek, Smoke, Fog, Mist.
V	A	R	I	E	D	Miscellaneous, Assorted, Diverse, Motley, Mixed, Indiscriminate, Multifarious.
V	A	R	I	E	R	One that varies, Inconsistent person.
V	A	R	L	E	T	Attendant, Menial, Servant, Scoundrel, Rascal, Knave.
V	A	R	S	H	A	Monsoon.
V	A	S	S	A	L	Dependant, Servant, Slave, Retainer, Bondman.
V	A	S	T	E	R	More huge, More colossal.
V	A	S	T	L	Y	Immensely, Widely.
V	A	T	D	Y	E	Water insoluble dye.
V	A	T	T	E	D	Treated in a vat.
V	A	U	L	T	Y	Arched, Concave.
V	A	W	A	R	D	Forefront.
V	E	A	D	A	R	Jewish intercalary month.
V	E	C	T	O	R	To guide.
V	E	D	D	A	H	Aborigine of Sri Lanka (Ceylon).

1	2	3	4	5	6	
V	E	E	R	E	D	Turned, Diverted, Swerved, Deflected, Dipped, Whirled, Averted, Pivoted.
V	E	I	L	E	D	Concealed, Shrouded, Wrapped, Enveloped, Cloaked, Covered, Screened, Secreted.
V	E	I	N	E	D	Streaked, Variegated.
V	E	L	A	T	E	Having a veil.
V	E	L	E	T	A	Ballroom dance in waltz time.
V	E	L	L	O	N	Debased silver.
V	E	L	L	U	M	Vegetable parchment, Parchment from calfskin.
V	E	L	O	C	E	Velocity.
V	E	L	O	U	R	Fabric resembling velvet.
V	E	L	U	R	E	Fabric resembling velvet.
V	E	L	V	E	T	Very soft silky fabric.
V	E	N	D	E	D	Sold, Hawked, Peddled.
V	E	N	D	E	E	Buyer, Purchaser.
V	E	N	D	E	R	Seller, Peddler, Hawker, Packman.
V	E	N	D	O	R	Seller, Peddler, Hawker, Packman.
V	E	N	D	U	E	Public sale, Auction.
V	E	N	E	E	R	Cover, Disguise, Facade, Coating, Layer, Front, Show, Veil.
V	E	N	E	R	Y	Head-keeper.
V	E	N	E	U	R	Superintendent of the chase.
V	E	N	G	E	R	To avenge.
V	E	N	N	E	L	Gutter, Sewer.
V	E	N	O	S	E	Having conspicuous veins.
V	E	N	T	E	D	Discharged, Exhausted, Expressed, Stated, Ventilated, Aired, Released, Loosed.
V	E	N	T	E	R	Abdomen.
V	E	N	T	I	L	Valve in musical wind instrument.
V	E	N	U	L	E	Small branch of a vein of an insect's wings.
V	E	R	B	A	L	Oral, Spoken, Traditional, Unwritten, Verbatim, Literal.
V	E	R	G	E	D	Bordered, Approached, Skirted, Surrounded, Sloped.
V	E	R	G	E	R	Church official.
V	E	R	I	F	Y	Confirm, Authenticate, Identify, Corroborate, Justify, Substantiate, Validate.
V	E	R	I	L	Y	Even, Indeed, Truly, Really, Certainly.
V	E	R	I	S	M	Realistic style of musical composition.
V	E	R	I	S	T	One who practises verism.
V	E	R	I	T	Y	Actuality, Fact, Reality.
V	E	R	M	E	S	Worms.
V	E	R	M	I	N	Noxious, Mischievous, Disgusting animals of small sizes.
V	E	R	N	A	L	Resembling Spring, Springlike.
V	E	R	S	A	L	Universal, Entire, Elaborate capital letter on a manuscript.
V	E	R	S	E	D	Experienced, Practical, Practised, Seasoned, Skilled, Familiar, Accomplished, Veteran.
V	E	R	S	E	R	Poetaster, Bardling, Rhymer, Versificator.
V	E	R	S	E	T	Short interlude or prelude for the pipe organ.
V	E	R	S	U	S	Against, Opposing, Over, At Variance, Contrast, Alternative.
V	E	R	T	E	X	Top, Apex, Crest, Crown, Peak, Acme, Summit, Zenith.
V	E	R	V	E	T	South African monkey.
V	E	S	I	C	A	Bladder.
V	E	S	P	E	R	Evening star.
V	E	S	S	E	L	Receptacle, Container, Utensil.
V	E	S	T	A	L	Virgin, Pure and chaste woman, Nun.
V	E	S	T	E	D	Established, Legalized.
V	E	S	T	R	Y	Storeroom for storage of church vestments and valuables.
V	E	T	O	E	D	Banned, Killed, Denied, Refused.
V	E	T	T	E	D	Scrutinized, Examined, Inspected, Studied, Surveyed, Viewed.
V	E	X	I	N	G	Trying, Annoying, Bothering, Provoking, Fretting, Chafing, Irking, Galling.
V	I	A	B	L	E	Possible, Feasible, Practicable, Workable, Living.
V	I	A	N	D	S	Food, Comestibles, Edibles, Feed, Nurture, Provender, Provisions, Victuals.
V	I	A	T	O	R	Wayfarer, Traveller.
V	I	B	R	A	T	Shake, Vibrate.
V	I	C	T	I	M	Offering, Sacrifice, Casualty, Prey, Underdog, Fool, Dupe, Sucker.
V	I	C	T	O	R	Conqueror, Master, Vanquisher, Winner, Champion, Subduer.
V	I	C	U	N	A	Wild llama.
V	I	D	A	M	E	French feudal temporal officer.
V	I	D	U	A	L	Relating to widows.
V	I	E	L	L	E	Medieval viol, Hurdy gurdy.
V	I	E	W	E	D	Looked, Examined, Analysed, Eyed, Audited, Inspected.
V	I	E	W	E	R	Spectator, Beholder, Bystander, Eye-witness, Observer, Watcher, Witness.
V	I	G	O	U	R	Power, Energy, Force, Drive, Energy, Enterprise, Spirit, Strength.
V	I	H	A	R	A	Buddist temple or monastery.

1	2	3	4	5	6	
V	I	K	I	N	G	Small creek, Sea rover, Scandinavian.
V	I	L	E	L	Y	Basely, Offensively, Ugly, Disgustingly, Botched, Skimped.
V	I	L	E	S	T	Lowest, Basest.
V	I	L	I	F	Y	Malign, Calumniate, Defame, Libel, Slander, Traduce, Disparage.
V	I	L	L	U	S	Shaggy hair.
V	I	N	A	G	E	Adding alcohol to wine.
V	I	N	O	U	S	Caused by or resulting from wine.
V	I	N	T	E	D	Wine made from fruit.
V	I	O	L	E	T	Violet or blue colour.
V	I	O	L	E	T	A colour, Flower.
V	I	O	L	I	N	Bowed string musical instrument.
V	I	R	A	G	O	Fishwife, Harpy, Ogress, Scold, Shrew, Termagant, Vixen, Amazon.
V	I	R	E	N	T	Fresh, Green Verdant.
V	I	R	G	I	N	Maiden, Damsel, Intact, Unspoilt, Untapped, Untouched, Spinster.
V	I	R	I	A	L	Strength, Power, Violence.
V	I	R	I	L	E	Potent, Male, Manly, Masculine, Robust.
V	I	R	O	S	E	Infection with or disease caused by a virus.
V	I	R	T	U	E	Goodness, Morality, Excellence, Quality, Power, Probity, Character.
V	I	S	A	E	D	Ratified, Endorsed (passport).
V	I	S	A	G	E	Aspect, Appearance, Look, Semblance, Face.
V	I	S	C	I	D	Gluey, Sticky, Viscous, Tenacious.
V	I	S	C	I	N	Substance from sap of mistletoe or holly.
V	I	S	C	U	M	Mistletoe.
V	I	S	C	U	S	Entrail.
V	I	S	H	N	U	Hindu god.
V	I	S	I	O	N	Revelation, Oracle, Prophecy, Fancy, Daydream, Fantasy, Seeing, Sight.
V	I	S	I	V	E	Relating to vision.
V	I	S	U	A	L	Ocular, Optic, Visional, Optical, Visible, Perceptible.
V	I	T	A	L	S	Organs necessary for life.
V	I	T	R	I	C	Resembling glass.
V	I	V	A	C	E	Brisk spirited manner (Music).
V	I	V	A	R	Y	Small zoo, Aquarium, Fish pond.
V	I	V	I	F	Y	Quicker, Animate, Enliven, Vivificate.
V	I	Z	A	R	D	Mask, Visor.
V	I	Z	I	E	R	High executive officer of Muslim countries.
V	O	I	C	E	D	Vocal, Articulate, Oral, Sonant, Spoken, Declared, Uttered, Said.
V	O	I	C	E	R	One that voices.
V	O	I	D	E	D	Vacated, Cleared, Empty, Discharged, Abrogated, Left.
V	O	I	D	E	R	Servant that clears table after meals, Tray, Basket.
V	O	L	A	N	T	Flying, Quick, Nimble, Current.
V	O	L	A	T	A	Rapid series of musical notes.
V	O	L	E	N	T	Exercising power of choice.
V	O	L	E	R	Y	Aviary, Flight of birds.
V	O	L	L	E	Y	Barrage, Bombardment, Broadside, Burst, Fusillade, Hail, Shower, Storm.
V	O	L	U	M	E	Book, Tome, Bulk, Mass, Body, Object.
V	O	L	U	T	E	Spiral or scroll-shaped form.
V	O	L	V	O	X	Freshwater algae.
V	O	O	D	O	O	Sorcerer, Jinx, Charm, Magician, Warlock, Wizard, Conjurer.
V	O	R	A	G	O	Abyss, Vortex, Gulf.
V	O	R	A	N	T	To devour.
V	O	R	T	E	X	Eddy, Maelstrom, Whirl, Whirlpool.
V	O	T	A	R	Y	Addict, Buff, Devotee, Fan, Hound, Admirer, Amateur.
V	O	T	I	N	G	Polling, Electing, Balloting.
V	O	T	I	V	E	Offered or erected in fulfillment of a vow, Prayer, Benediction.
V	O	W	I	N	G	Pledging, Promising, Declaring, Consecrating.
V	O	Y	A	G	E	Cruise, Journey, Tour.
V	U	L	C	A	N	Ancient Roman God of fire.
V	U	L	G	A	R	Coarse, Ordinary, Public, Obscene, Barbaric, Indecent, Wild, Profane.

W

W	A	B	B	L	E	Wobble, Stand unsteadily, Lurch, Stagger, Sway, Swing, Weave, Teeter.
W	A	D	D	E	D	Filled, Stuffed.
W	A	D	D	L	E	Toddle, Swaying gait.
W	A	D	I	N	G	Fording.
W	A	F	F	L	E	A cake, Babble, Blather, Drivel, Drool, Gabble, Prattle, Twaddle.

1	2	3	4	5	6	
W	A	F	T	E	D	Waved, Floated, Beckoned, Fanned.
W	A	F	T	E	R	Fan.
W	A	G	G	E	D	Waggled, Waved, Tottered, Swayed, Switched.
W	A	G	G	E	L	Black backed gull.
W	A	G	G	L	E	Vibrate, Wag, Wobble, Lash, Switch, Woggle.
W	A	G	G	O	N	Cart, Dray, Van, Wain.
W	A	G	I	N	G	Betting, Venturing, Conducting.
W	A	H	A	B	I	Member of puritannical Muslim sect.
W	A	H	I	N	E	Maori woman.
W	A	I	L	E	D	Lamented, Cried, Howled, Bawled, Complained, Fussed, Bemoaned, Whined.
W	A	I	L	E	R	Professional mourner.
W	A	I	T	E	D	Ministered, Cared, Nursed, Served, Attended, Tarried, Lingered, Stayed.
W	A	I	T	E	R	Attendant, Servitor, Garcon.
W	A	I	V	E	D	Relinquished, Abandoned, Ceded, Resigned, Surrendered, Delayed, Postponed, Suspended.
W	A	I	V	E	R	Abandoning a claim.
W	A	K	I	N	G	Arising, Rousing, Stirring, Stimulating, Rallying.
W	A	L	I	N	G	Timber brace for trench.
W	A	L	K	E	D	Perambulated, Strolled, Stepped, Trod, Traipsed.
W	A	L	K	E	R	Pedestrian, Hiker.
W	A	L	L	A	H	One in charge in India.
W	A	L	L	E	D	Enclosed, Caged, Fenced, Hedged.
W	A	L	L	E	R	One that builds or repairs walls.
W	A	L	L	E	T	Pouch, Purse, Billfold, Pocketbook.
W	A	L	L	O	P	Blow, Bash, Belt, Impact, Collision, Shock, Beat, Slam.
W	A	L	L	O	W	Welter, Blunder, Flounder, Lurch, Indulge, Luxuriate, Revel, Stumble.
W	A	L	N	U	T	Edible nut.
W	A	L	R	U	S	Mammal of the Bering Sea.
W	A	M	B	L	E	To be nauseated, Squeamish, Sickly.
W	A	M	P	E	E	Asiatic fruit bearing tree.
W	A	M	P	U	M	Shell beads used as money.
W	A	N	D	E	R	Stroll, Meander, Ramble, Drift, Digress, Diverge, Stray, Deviate.
W	A	N	D	L	E	Supple, Fragile.
W	A	N	D	O	O	Australian eucalyptus tree.
W	A	N	G	L	E	Engineer, Machinate, Manoeuvre, Wiggle, Shake, Manipulate, Fake, Finagle.
W	A	N	I	N	G	Ebbing, Declining, Abating, Falling, Failing, Shrinking, Wasting, Dwindling.
W	A	N	N	E	D	Made pale.
W	A	N	T	E	D	Lacked, Needed, Required, Desired, Craved, Liked.
W	A	N	T	E	R	One that wants or is in need, Bachelor.
W	A	N	T	O	N	Fast, Easy, Loose, Uncalled-for, Hussy, Slut, Flirt, Fool.
W	A	P	I	T	I	American elk.
W	A	R	B	L	E	Melody, Quaver, Lay, Strain, Singer, Tune, Songster, Cattle boil caused by eggs of fly.
W	A	R	C	R	Y	Battle-cry, Motto, Slogan, Catchword, Yell.
W	A	R	D	E	D	Deflected, Fended, Parried, Prevented, Averted, Precluded, Repulsed, Forestalled.
W	A	R	D	E	N	Custodian, Curator, Guardian, Keeper, Turnkey, Watch-dog, Gatekeeper, Porter.
W	A	R	I	L	Y	Cautiously, Watchfully, Carefully, Cannily.
W	A	R	M	A	N	Warrior, Soldier.
W	A	R	M	E	R	Hotter, Keener.
W	A	R	M	L	Y	Ardently, Earnestly, Tenderly, Compassionately, Keenly, Zealously, Responsively.
W	A	R	M	T	H	Enthusiasm, Heat, Fervently, Snug.
W	A	R	N	E	D	Cautioned, Forewarned, Informed, Advised, Apprised, Commanded, Charged, Ordered.
W	A	R	N	E	R	One that warns.
W	A	R	P	E	D	Distorted, Perverted, Biased, Debased, Corrupted, Deformed, Misrepresented, Twisted.
W	A	R	P	E	R	A worker that prepares yarn.
W	A	R	R	E	N	Rabbit burrow, Enclosure for game birds and animals.
W	A	R	T	A	X	Tax to help finance war.
W	A	S	A	B	I	Japanese root grated like horseradish.
W	A	S	H	E	D	Laved, Cleansed, Showered, Bathed, Drenched, Saturated, Laundered.
W	A	S	H	E	R	Flat ring of metal or fibre to tighten joints.
W	A	S	H	I	N	Permanent twist of aeroplane wing.
W	A	S	H	U	P	Clean dishes after meal, Exhaust, Finish.
W	A	S	T	E	D	Emaciated, Desecrated, Frittered, Gaunt, Squandered, Devastated, Devoured, Dissipated.
W	A	S	T	E	L	Bread or cake made of very fine flour.
W	A	S	T	E	R	Spendthrift, Spender, Squanderer, Profligate, Idler, Loafer, Prodigal.
W	A	T	E	R	Y	Diluted, Thin, Weak, Pale, Anaemic, Insipid, Bland, Vapid.
W	A	T	T	L	E	Rods or poles used as roof support, Loose skin hanging from throat of bird or reptile.
W	A	V	E	R	Y	Wavering, Unsteady.
W	A	V	I	N	G	Wagging, Swaying, Undulating, Vacillating, Hesitating, Heaving, Flourishing, Swinging.

1	2	3	4	5	6	
W	A	X	E	N	D	Waxed thread used by shoemaker.
W	A	X	I	N	G	Increasing, Building, Enlarging, Expanding, Rising, Surging, Growing.
W	A	Y	L	A	Y	Surprise, Ambush, Intercept, Obstruct, Block.
W	A	Y	M	A	N	Railway worker repairing the tracks.
W	E	A	K	E	N	Dilute, Fail, Decline, Shrink, Impair, Enervate, Lessen, Reduce.
W	E	A	K	E	R	Frailer, Thinner, More diluted, More feeble.
W	E	A	K	L	Y	Delicately, Feebly, Shakily, Wobbly, Incredibly, Thinly, Inadequately, Ineptly.
W	E	A	L	T	H	Assets, Capital, Resources, Riches, Opulence, Abundance, Fortune, Substance.
W	E	A	N	E	D	Estranged, Alienated, Disunited, Withdrawn.
W	E	A	N	L	Y	Childish, Feeble.
W	E	A	P	O	N	Instrument of offensive or defensive combat.
W	E	A	R	E	R	One that wears or carries something as a covering.
W	E	A	S	E	L	Small slender-bodied carnivorous mammal.
W	E	A	V	E	R	One that weaves textiles on a loom.
W	E	A	Z	E	N	Shrunk, Wizered, Shrivelled.
W	E	B	B	E	D	Having toes or fingers webbed skin, Woven, Cobwebbed, Entangled, Ensnared.
W	E	B	F	E	D	Designed to print a continuous roll of paper.
W	E	D	D	E	D	Married, Espoused, Spliced, Conjugal.
W	E	D	G	E	D	Fastened, Compressed, Tightened, Squeezed.
W	E	E	D	E	D	Eradicated, Hoed, Purged, Removed.
W	E	E	D	E	R	Tool for removing weeds.
W	E	E	K	L	Y	Occurring or appearing once a week, Newspaper or Periodical published once a week.
W	E	E	N	E	D	Imagined, Thought, Believed, Expected.
W	E	E	P	E	R	Professional mourner, Widow's veil, Capuchin monkey.
W	E	E	V	E	R	Sting fish.
W	E	E	V	I	L	Destructive beetle.
W	E	I	G	H	T	Load, Burden, Importance, Import, Influence, Doctor, Adulterate, Encumber.
W	E	L	D	E	D	United, Consolidated, Joined, Adhered.
W	E	L	D	E	R	One that welds.
W	E	L	K	I	N	Firmament, Sky, Celestial regions.
W	E	L	L	E	D	Gushed, Spouted.
W	E	L	T	E	D	Edged, Bordered.
W	E	L	T	E	R	Turmoil, Disorder, Wallow, Writhe, Toss, Tumble, Wither, Shrivel.
W	E	N	D	E	D	Journeyed, Proceeded, Departed, Wandered, Gone, Passed, Repaired.
W	E	S	T	E	R	Turn, Veer or shift to West.
W	E	T	H	E	R	Castrated male goat or ram.
W	E	T	T	E	R	Damper, More showery.
W	H	A	L	E	R	Person or ship employed in whaling industry.
W	H	A	L	L	Y	Having light coloured eyes.
W	H	A	T	S	O	Whatever.
W	H	E	E	L	Y	Relating to a wheel or circular movement.
W	H	E	E	Z	E	Puff, Blow, Hiss, Sibilate, Swish, Whisper, Prank, Antic.
W	H	E	E	Z	Y	Inclined to wheeze.
W	H	E	N	A	S	While, Although, Whereas.
W	H	E	N	C	E	From where, Wherefore.
W	H	E	R	R	Y	Type of light boat.
W	H	E	W	E	R	Widgeon, Freshwater duck.
W	H	E	Y	E	Y	Resembling whey.
W	H	I	L	E	D	Passed time pleasantly.
W	H	I	L	E	S	Until.
W	H	I	L	L	Y	Cajole, Wheedle, Persuade.
W	H	I	L	O	M	Formerly, Once, Bygone, Past, Sometime, Erstwhile.
W	H	I	L	S	T	While, Until.
W	H	I	M	S	Y	Caprice, Conceit, Fancy, Freak, Humour, Vagary, Crochet.
W	H	I	N	E	D	Whimpered, Complained, Kicked, Fussed, Repined, Wailed.
W	H	I	N	E	R	One that whines.
W	H	I	N	G	E	Whine, Whimper, Moan.
W	H	I	N	N	Y	Neigh in low or gentle fashion (horse).
W	H	I	P	P	Y	Elastic, Flexible, Resilient, Springy, Stretchy, Supple.
W	H	I	R	R	Y	Hurry.
W	H	I	S	H	T	Silence, Hush, Whish.
W	H	I	S	K	Y	Distilled alcoholic liquor.
W	H	I	T	E	N	Blanch, Bleach, Blench, Palliate, Extenuate, Varnish, Veneer, Lighten.
W	H	I	T	E	R	Purer, Brighter.
W	H	I	T	E	S	Cricket Trousers.
W	H	O	L	L	Y	Well, Entirely, Fully, Utterly, Completely, Roundly, Throughly, Altogether.
W	H	O	M	S	O	Whoso.

1	2	3	4	5	6	
W	H	Y	D	A	H	Weaver bird.
W	I	C	K	E	D	Evil, Dangerous, Perilous, Sinful, Outrageous, Malignant, Malevolent, Ungodly.
W	I	C	K	E	N	Mountain ash, Rowan tree.
W	I	C	K	E	R	Osier used for plaiting basketwork.
W	I	C	K	E	T	Small gate or door.
W	I	C	O	P	Y	Basswood, Willow herb.
W	I	D	E	L	Y	Extensively, Broadly, Greatly, Far.
W	I	D	E	S	T	Broadest, Remotest, More literal, More extensive.
W	I	E	L	D	Y	Strong, Mighty, Powerful.
W	I	E	N	I	E	Frankfurter, Hot-dog.
W	I	F	E	L	Y	Relating to or befitting a wife.
W	I	G	E	O	N	Freshwater duck.
W	I	G	G	E	D	Scolded, Rebuked, Reprimanded, Reproached, Berated, Reviled, Upbraided, Railed.
W	I	G	G	L	E	Waggle, Wriggle, Squiggle, Squirm, Worm, Writhe.
W	I	G	W	A	G	To signal by waving a flag or portable light.
W	I	G	W	A	M	Hut of the American Indian, Lodge.
W	I	L	D	E	R	Bewilder, Perplex, Stray, Wander.
W	I	L	D	L	Y	Fiercely, Recklessly, Furiously, Frantically, Stormily, Madly, Turbulently, Violently.
W	I	L	F	U	L	Obstinate, Perverse, Imperious, Impatient, Unruly, Self-determined, Headstrong, Deliberate.
W	I	L	I	E	R	Craftier, More sly, Cleverer, More cunning, More artful.
W	I	L	I	L	Y	Slyly, Craftily, Obstinately, Shrewdly.
W	I	L	L	E	D	Disposed, Inclined, Resolved, Bequeathed.
W	I	L	L	E	R	One that wields influence e.g. Hypnotist.
W	I	L	L	E	T	Large shore bird of North America.
W	I	L	L	O	W	Economically important tree for bark for tanning, Osier for basketwork, Wood for cricket bats.
W	I	L	T	E	D	Withered, Dried-up, Shrivelled, Collapsed, Succumbed, Drooped, Flagged, Sagged.
W	I	M	B	L	E	Gimlet, Bore, Penetrate.
W	I	M	P	L	E	Veiled headdress, Ripple, Twist, Curve, Bend.
W	I	N	C	E	D	Recoiled, Blanched, Blenched, Flinched, Quailed, Shrunk, Started.
W	I	N	C	E	R	One that winces.
W	I	N	C	E	Y	Wool and cotton mixtures for warm material, usually for night attire.
W	I	N	D	E	D	Short of breath.
W	I	N	D	E	R	Tendril, Winch, Reel, Spool, Key for winding. A step that is wider at one end than at the other.
W	I	N	D	L	E	Measure for wheat.
W	I	N	D	O	W	Casement, Slot, Lattice, Eye.
W	I	N	D	U	P	Close, Complete, Conclude, Terminate, Settle, Finale, Conclusion, Determine.
W	I	N	G	E	D	Lofty, Elevated, Wounded.
W	I	N	G	E	R	Player in wing position (Soccer, Rugby, Hockey).
W	I	N	K	E	D	Flickered, Twinkled, Flashed, Sparkled.
W	I	N	N	E	R	Victor, Champion, Conqueror, Master.
W	I	N	N	O	W	Blow, Fan, Ruffle, Sort, Comb, Separate, Sift, Examine.
W	I	N	T	E	R	Season between December and March in Northern hemisphere.
W	I	N	T	L	E	Stagger, Reel, Roll, Wiggle.
W	I	N	T	R	Y	Cold, Stormy, Dismal, Chilling, Cheerless, Frosty, Icy.
W	I	P	I	N	G	Rubbing, Erasing, Deleting, Blotting.
W	I	R	I	L	Y	In a wiry manner.
W	I	R	I	N	G	Arranging wires for use in electric distribution.
W	I	S	D	O	M	Knowledge, Lore, Information, Sagacity, Sense, Judgement, Insight.
W	I	S	E	L	Y	Sensibly, Shrewdly, Astutely, Sagely, Prudently, Intelligently, Smartly.
W	I	S	E	S	T	Most learned, Most shrews, Most astute.
W	I	S	H	E	D	Desired, Chosen, Coveted, Craved, Wanted, Willed, Elected.
W	I	S	H	E	R	One that wishes.
W	I	S	K	E	T	Straw basket.
W	I	T	H	A	L	Besides, Therewith, Nevertheless.
W	I	T	H	E	R	Shrivel, Welter, Wilt, Wizen, Mummify, Fade, Pine, Languish.
W	I	T	H	I	N	Indoors, Inside, Enclosed, Included, Not exceeding.
W	I	T	H	I	T	Stylish, Fashionable, Modish, Swank, Trendy.
W	I	T	T	E	D	Having understanding.
W	I	Z	A	R	D	Conjurer, Sorcerer, Necromancer, Sage, Magician, Expert, Authority, Professional.
W	O	B	B	L	E	Lurch, Stagger, Topple, Weave, Teeter, Shake, Dither.
W	O	B	B	L	Y	Rickety, Shaky, Weak, Wavering, Vacillating, Tentative, Uncertain.
W	O	E	F	U	L	Afflicted, Doleful, Melancholy, Mournful, Plaintive, Rueful, Deplorable, Grievous.
W	O	L	F	E	R	One that hunts wolves, One that wolfs food or drink.
W	O	L	V	E	S	Crafty rapacious mammals, Philanderers, Mashers, Lady-killers.
W	O	M	B	A	T	Small Australian marsupial.
W	O	N	D	E	R	Marvel, Miracle, Portent, Sensation, Admiration, Amaze, Uncertainty, Prodigy.
W	O	N	I	N	G	Dwelling.

1	2	3	4	5	6	
W	O	N	T	E	D	Usual, Accepted, Accustomed, Chronic, Customary, Habitual, Routine.
W	O	N	T	O	N	Pockets of filled Chinese dough cooked and eaten with soup.
W	O	O	D	E	D	Timbered, Covered with growing trees.
W	O	O	D	E	N	Stiff, Buckram, Awkward, Bumbling, Impassive, Halting, Inept, Maladroit.
W	O	O	F	E	R	Radio speaker for reproducing low pitched sounds.
W	O	O	I	N	G	Addressing, Courting, Pursuing, Sparking.
W	O	O	L	L	Y	Hairy, Fleecy, Hirsute, Pilose, Whiskered.
W	O	R	D	E	D	Expressed, Phrased, Dictated, Reported.
W	O	R	K	E	D	Operated, Used, Cultivated, Laboured, Toiled, Functioned, Performed, Solved.
W	O	R	K	E	R	Labourer, Operative, Artisan, Craftsman, Mechanic, Employee.
W	O	R	K	U	P	Generate, Breed, Engender, Hatch, Induce, Muster.
W	O	R	M	E	D	Insinuated, Crawled, Infiltrated, Wriggled, Squirmed, Writhed.
W	O	R	R	E	L	African monitor lizard.
W	O	R	R	I	T	Trouble, Annoyance.
W	O	R	S	E	N	Deteriorate, Degenerate, Disintegrate, Retrograde, Rot, Sink, Debase, Lower.
W	O	R	S	E	R	More bad, More ill.
W	O	R	T	H	Y	Admirable, Commendable, Deserving, Estimable, Honourable, Noble, Sterling, Laudable.
W	O	U	N	D	Y	Extreme.
W	O	U	W	O	U	Gibbon monkey.
W	O	W	S	E	R	Puritanical person opposed to Sunday sports.
W	R	A	I	T	H	Apparition, Ghost, Phantom, Shadow, Spectre, Spirit.
W	R	A	S	S	E	Fish related to parrot fish.
W	R	A	T	H	Y	Wrathful.
W	R	E	A	T	H	Festoon, Garland, Chaplet.
W	R	E	N	C	H	Wrest, Wring, Strain, Sprain, Rick, Misrepresent, Distort, Extort.
W	R	E	T	C	H	Villain, Vagabond, Blighter, Cur, Scum, Skunk, Snake, Stinker.
W	R	I	G	H	T	Worker in wood, Carpenter, Mechanic.
W	R	I	T	E	R	Author, Scribe, Penman, Scrivener.
W	R	I	T	H	E	Wriggle, Squirm, Toss, Agonize, Wiggle, Squiggle, Worm.
W	Y	V	E	R	N	Heraldic dragon.

X

X	A	N	A	D	U	Pleasure palace of Kubla Khan.
X	E	N	I	A	L	Relating to hospitality between host and guests.
X	E	N	I	U	M	Gift.
X	O	A	N	O	N	Primitive image of wood.
X	R	A	Y	E	D	Irradiated.
X	Y	L	E	N	E	Derivative of benzine.
X	Y	L	O	I	D	Resembling wood.
X	Y	L	O	S	E	Crystalline aldose sugar.
X	Y	S	T	U	S	Scraped, Polished.

Y

Y	A	B	B	E	R	Talk, Language, Conversation, Jabber.
Y	A	F	F	L	E	Green woodpecker, Armful.
Y	A	H	V	E	H	Used as a scholarly transliteration of the Hebrew tetragrammaton.
Y	A	K	S	H	A	Spirit of earth in India regarded as patron of wealth and fertility.
Y	A	M	M	E	R	Wail, Whimper, Grumble, Scold, Whine.
Y	A	N	K	E	D	Jerked, Heaved, Lugged, Twitched, Clutched, Grabbed, Pulled, Extracted.
Y	A	N	K	E	E	Citizen of the U.S.A.
Y	A	O	U	R	T	Yoghurt.
Y	A	P	O	C	K	Aquatic opossum of S. America.
Y	A	P	P	E	D	Yelped, Yupped, Chattered, Complained.
Y	A	R	D	E	D	Confined.
Y	A	R	D	E	R	Donkey engine used to haul logs.
Y	A	R	N	E	D	Chatted, Related, Narrated, Talked, Gossiped.
Y	A	R	P	H	A	Peat bog.
Y	A	R	R	A	N	Small Australian acacia tree.
Y	A	R	R	O	W	Strong scented Eurasian herb.
Y	A	U	P	O	N	Tree leaves used as substitute for tea.
Y	A	W	I	N	G	Deviate erratically from course.
Y	A	W	L	E	D	Howled.
Y	A	W	N	E	D	Gaped.

1	2	3	4	5	6	Definition
Y	C	L	E	P	T	Called, Named.
Y	E	A	N	E	D	Brought forth, a young lamb or goat.
Y	E	A	R	L	Y	Annual, Once a year.
Y	E	A	S	T	Y	Resembling yeast, Frothy, Foamy, Giddy.
Y	E	L	L	E	D	Shouted, Bawled, Screamed, Howled.
Y	E	L	L	O	W	Cowardly, Craven, Gutless.
Y	E	L	P	E	D	Yapped, Barked, Squealed.
Y	E	L	P	E	R	One whose utterance is a sound without sense.
Y	E	M	E	N	I	Citizen of Yemen.
Y	E	O	M	A	N	Farmer, Beefeater, Guard.
Y	E	R	K	E	D	Goaded, Kicked, Thrashed, Hurled.
Y	E	S	M	A	N	Sycophant, Toady.
Y	E	S	T	E	R	Previous, Yesterday.
Y	O	G	I	S	M	Practice of Yoga.
Y	O	I	C	K	S	Cry of encouragement to hunting hounds.
Y	O	J	A	N	A	Hindu measures of distance.
Y	O	K	I	N	G	Contest, Bout, Coupling, Linking, Mugging.
Y	O	L	K	E	D	Having a yolk.
Y	O	N	D	E	R	Somewhere, Distant.
Y	O	N	K	E	R	Nobleman, Young man of high rank.
Y	O	R	K	E	R	Special bowling action in cricket.
Y	O	R	U	B	A	Negro people of Eastern Guinea.
Y	O	U	T	H	Y	Youthful.
Y	O	W	L	E	D	Howled, Yelled, Yelped.

Z

1	2	3	4	5	6	Definition
Z	A	F	F	E	R	Impure cobalt oxide.
Z	A	F	F	R	E	Impure cobalt oxide.
Z	A	N	D	E	R	Pike.
Z	A	N	I	E	S	Clowns, Buffoons, Idiots.
Z	A	R	E	B	A	Enclosure, Pen, Fortified camp.
Z	E	A	L	O	T	Enthusiast, Bigot, Fanatic, Fiend, Freak, Maniac, Nut.
Z	E	C	H	I	N	Sequin.
Z	E	N	A	N	A	Relating to women of the harem.
Z	E	N	I	T	H	Apex, Acme, Climax, Culmination, Peak, Pinnacle, Summit.
Z	E	P	H	Y	R	West wind, Soft breeze.
Z	E	R	E	B	A	Fortified thornbush stockade.
Z	I	A	M	E	T	Land granted for service in Turkish army.
Z	I	G	Z	A	G	Series of short sharp turns.
Z	I	L	L	A	H	Administrative district of India.
Z	I	N	G	E	L	European freshwater fish.
Z	I	N	N	I	A	Flower.
Z	I	P	P	E	D	Breezed, Hurried, Hustled, Whisked, Whizzed.
Z	I	P	P	E	R	Zip fastener.
Z	I	R	C	O	N	Silicate, Semi-precious stone.
Z	I	T	H	E	R	Musical instrument.
Z	O	D	I	A	C	An imaginary belt in the heavens.
Z	O	E	T	I	C	Living, Alive, Animated, Vital.
Z	O	M	B	I	E	Dunce, Moron, Boob, Chump, Eccentric, Character, Oddity, Oaf.
Z	O	N	A	R	Y	Zonal.
Z	O	N	A	T	E	Ringed, Belted.
Z	O	N	I	N	G	Planning, Allocating, Sectioning.
Z	O	N	K	E	D	Intoxicated, Drunk, Inebriated, Tight, Drugged, Doped, Stoned.
Z	O	N	U	L	E	Zone, Belt, Girdle.
Z	O	N	U	R	E	Girdle-tailed lizard.
Z	O	O	Z	O	O	Wood-pigeon.
Z	O	S	T	E	R	Herpes, Shingles.
Z	O	U	A	V	E	Algerian soldier in French infantry.
Z	O	U	N	D	S	Mild oath.
Z	U	F	O	L	O	Little flute.
Z	U	N	I	A	N	Language of Zuni people of New Mexico.
Z	Y	G	I	T	E	Oarsmen in ancient boat.
Z	Y	G	O	S	E	Relating to zygosis (fertilization).
Z	Y	G	O	T	E	Fertilised egg.
Z	Y	M	A	S	E	Complex of enzyme.
Z	Y	T	H	U	M	Ancient type of bear.

A

1	2	3	4	5	6	7	Clue
A	A	R	O	N	I	C	Jewish patriarch and high priest, brother of Moses.
A	B	A	C	A	X	I	Large sweet pineapple.
A	B	A	C	I	S	T	One that uses calculating frame.
A	B	A	C	T	O	R	Cattle thief.
A	B	A	C	U	L	O	Argument using force instead of reason.
A	B	A	D	D	O	N	Place of destruction, Hell.
A	B	A	I	S	S	E	Thin undercrust of pastry.
A	B	A	L	O	N	E	Mollusc.
A	B	A	N	D	O	N	Desert, Forsake, Relinquish, Cede, Resign, Surrender, Waive, Yield.
A	B	A	S	H	E	D	Embarrassed, Confounded, Shamed, Confused, Disconcerted, Rattled, Discomfited.
A	B	A	S	I	N	G	Humbling, Degrading.
A	B	A	X	I	A	L	Facing away from the axis.
A	B	B	O	Z	Z	O	Rough sketch or draft.
A	B	D	O	M	E	N	Belly, Stomach, Tummy, Paunch, Gut.
A	B	D	U	C	E	D	Abducted, Separated.
A	B	E	T	T	E	D	Incited, Instigated, Provoked, Raised, Helped, Assisted.
A	B	E	T	T	E	R	Confederate, Accessory, Accomplice, Conspirator.
A	B	E	Y	A	N	T	Dormant, Latent, Lurking, Potential, Quiescent.
A	B	I	D	I	N	G	Sure, Enduring, Firm, Steadfast, Wholehearted, Residing, Lasting, Durable.
A	B	I	E	N	C	E	Tendency to withdraw from situation.
A	B	I	G	A	I	L	Serving woman, Lady's waiting maid.
A	B	I	L	I	T	Y	Adequacy, Capability, Competence, Qualification, Command, Expertise, Knack, Mastery.
A	B	I	O	T	I	C	Absence of life.
A	B	J	U	D	G	E	Take away by judicial decision.
A	B	J	U	R	E	D	Rejected, Renounced, Recanted, Retracted, Recalled, Withdrawn.
A	B	J	U	R	E	R	One that forswears.
A	B	O	L	I	S	H	Abate, Annihilate, Destroy, Annul, Invalidate, Eradicate, Exterminate, Extinguish.
A	B	R	A	D	E	D	Chafed, Eroded, Grazed, Annoyed, Bothered, Irked, Provoked, Irritated.
A	B	R	A	X	A	S	Amulet, Charm, Talisman.
A	B	R	E	A	S	T	Up-to-date, Contemporary, Familiar, Acquainted, Conversant, Beside one another, Informed.
A	B	R	I	D	G	E	Curtail, Diminish, Lessen, Shorten, Epitomise, Abbreviate, Slash, Summarize.
A	B	R	O	A	C	H	Tapped, In a state to be diffused.
A	B	S	C	E	S	S	Boil, Ulcer, Carbuncle, Pimple, Pustule.
A	B	S	C	I	N	D	Cut, Tear, Shred.
A	B	S	C	I	S	E	Cut off.
A	B	S	C	O	N	D	Withdraw, Flee, Conceal, Escape, Break, Fly, Decamp, Bolt, Quit.
A	B	S	E	N	C	E	Dearth, Lack, Want, Deficiency, Defect, Miss, Privation.
A	B	S	I	N	T	H	Green bitter liqueur.
A	B	S	O	L	V	E	Exempt, Discharge, Dispense, Excuse, Exculpate, Aquit, Exonerate, Vindicate.
A	B	S	T	A	I	N	Refrain, Desist, Deny, Constrain, Curb, Keep, Withold, Forbear.
A	B	U	S	I	N	G	Perverting, Violating, Belittling, Detracting, Discounting, Exploiting, Mistreating, Misusing.
A	B	U	S	I	O	N	Abuse, Misuse, Deception.
A	B	U	S	I	V	E	Invective, Scurrile, Truculent, Vituperous.
A	B	U	T	T	A	L	Boundary of land.
A	B	U	T	T	E	R	One that abuts.
A	B	Y	S	M	A	L	Bottomless, Fathomless, Plumbless, Soundless, Deep, Profound.
A	B	Y	S	S	A	L	Unfathomable.
A	C	A	D	E	M	Y	Institution of higher learning, business skills, or special arts.
A	C	A	D	I	A	N	Inhabitant of Nova Scotia.
A	C	A	L	E	P	H	Jellyfish.
A	C	A	N	T	H	A	Spine of fish.
A	C	A	P	N	I	A	Carbon dioxide deficiency in the blood.
A	C	A	R	I	N	E	Mites, Ticks, Typhus.
A	C	C	E	D	E	D	Ceded, Assented, Succeeded, Acquiesed, Agreed, Consented, Subscribed, Allowed.
A	C	C	E	D	E	R	One who concurs.
A	C	C	L	A	I	M	Commend, Applaud, Compliment, Proclaim, Plaudits, Honour, Reverence.
A	C	C	O	A	S	T	Accost.
A	C	C	O	L	L	E	Collared, Side by side as on a shield or coin.
A	C	C	O	M	P	T	Account.
A	C	C	O	U	N	T	Consider, Bill, Advantage, Worth, Regard, Explanation, Score, Chronicle.
A	C	C	R	E	T	E	Unite, Combine, Adhere, Attached, Grow together.
A	C	C	R	U	E	D	Resulted, Accumulated, Gathered, Collected, Added.

1	2	3	4	5	6	7	
A	C	C	U	R	S	E	Abide, Curse, Anathematize, Consign to destruction, Misery of evil by a curse.
A	C	C	U	S	A	L	Accusation, Indictment.
A	C	C	U	S	E	D	Defendant, Arraigned, Charged, Impeached, Incriminated, Indicted, Taxed.
A	C	C	U	S	E	R	One that accuses.
A	C	E	R	A	T	E	Needlelike.
A	C	E	R	B	I	C	Acid or sour to the taste, Acid in temper, mood or tone, Sarcastic, Critical.
A	C	E	R	O	L	A	Barbados cherry.
A	C	E	R	O	U	S	Without horns.
A	C	E	T	A	T	E	Plastic used in manufacture of film and phonograph records.
A	C	E	T	I	F	Y	To turn into vinegar.
A	C	E	T	O	N	E	Volatile fragrant flammable liquid ketone.
A	C	E	T	O	U	S	Having characteristics of vinegar.
A	C	H	A	E	A	N	Inhabitant of Achaes, Greek.
A	C	H	A	E	T	A	Genus of worms.
A	C	H	I	E	V	E	Perform, Execute, Gain, Accomplish, Attain, Realize, Score, Win.
A	C	H	I	O	T	E	Tropical American tree.
A	C	H	O	L	I	C	Exhibiting deficiency of bile.
A	C	H	T	U	N	G	Beware, Look out.
A	C	I	C	U	L	A	Needle in shape, A needlelike spine, Bristle, Crystal.
A	C	I	D	I	T	Y	Sourness, Tartness.
A	C	I	D	I	Z	E	Treat with acid, Acidify.
A	C	I	D	O	I	D	Like acid.
A	C	I	F	O	R	M	Needle-shaped.
A	C	I	N	O	U	S	Clustered like grapes.
A	C	L	I	N	I	C	Having no inclination, Horizontal.
A	C	O	L	Y	T	E	An ordained cleric, Altar boy, Server, Assistant, Follower.
A	C	O	N	I	T	E	Dried tuberous root of a monkshood.
A	C	O	U	C	H	I	Resin obtained from S. American trees.
A	C	Q	U	I	R	E	Acquire, Acquisition.
A	C	Q	U	I	S	T	Get, Develop, Earn, Gain, Win, Obtain, Procure, Secure.
A	C	R	A	S	I	A	A genus of fungi.
A	C	R	E	A	G	E	Area in acres.
A	C	R	O	B	A	T	Tumbler, Tightrope walker, Trapeze worker.
A	C	R	O	G	E	N	Ferns, Mosses, Liverworts.
A	C	R	O	N	Y	M	Word formed from initial letters.
A	C	R	O	T	E	R	Pedestal.
A	C	R	Y	L	I	C	Relating to acrylic acid or its derivatives.
A	C	T	A	B	L	E	Capable of being acted, Suitable for performance upon a stage.
A	C	T	A	E	O	N	Hunter in Greco-Roman mythology turned into a stag by Diana.
A	C	T	I	N	A	L	Body of starfish.
A	C	T	R	E	S	S	Participant, Performer, Party, Trouper, Thespian.
A	C	T	U	A	R	Y	One trained in mathematics and statistics whose business it is to calculate insurance.
A	C	T	U	A	T	E	Moving into action, putting into motion.
A	C	U	L	E	U	S	Point, Acute, Sting.
A	C	U	S	H	L	A	Darling (Irish).
A	C	U	T	E	L	Y	Keenly, Sharply, Sensitively, Shrilly, Direly, Desperately, Penetratingly, Poignantly.
A	C	Y	S	T	I	C	Not enclosed in a bladder.
A	D	A	M	A	N	T	Inflexible, Inexorable, Obdurate, Relentless, Rigid, Unbending, Unyielding.
A	D	A	M	I	T	E	Nudist.
A	D	A	P	T	E	D	Conformable, Fitted, Matched, Suited, Adjusted, Attuned, Reconciled, Tailored.
A	D	A	P	T	E	R	Music arranger, Fitting, Device.
A	D	A	X	I	A	L	Upper side of leaf stalk.
A	D	D	E	N	D	A	Appendix, Codicil, Rider, Supplement.
A	D	D	L	I	N	G	Becoming rotten, Confusing, Muddling, Spoiling, Bewildering, Distracting.
A	D	D	R	E	S	S	Direct, Send, Apply, Approach, Talk, Lecture, Accost, Court.
A	D	D	U	C	E	D	Advanced, Alleged, Cited, Offered, Presented.
A	D	D	U	C	E	R	One that adduces.
A	D	D	U	L	C	E	Mollify, To bring to agreement.
A	D	E	N	I	N	E	Extracted from glandular organ.
A	D	E	N	O	I	D	Like or relating to glandular tissue.
A	D	E	N	O	M	A	Benign tumour of a glandlike structure or tissue.
A	D	E	N	O	S	E	Like a gland.
A	D	H	E	R	E	D	Stuck, Clung, Cohered, Bonded, Combined, Held, Cleaved, Glued.
A	D	H	I	B	I	T	Summon, Use, Administer, Affix.
A	D	I	N	O	L	E	Dense rock composed chiefly of quartz.
A	D	I	P	O	S	E	Fatty.
A	D	J	O	U	R	N	Defer, Delay, Postpone, Shelve, Suspend, Dissolve, Prorogue, Terminate.

1	2	3	4	5	6	7	
A	D	J	U	D	G	E	Judge, Adjudicate, Arbitrate, Referee, Umpire, Condemn, Decree, Ordain.
A	D	J	U	N	C	T	Appendage, Accessory, Appendix, Appurtenance.
A	D	J	U	R	E	D	Put on oath, Charged or commanded solemnly, Entreated earnestly.
A	D	J	U	R	E	R	One that adjures.
A	D	M	I	R	A	L	Commander in chief of navy.
A	D	M	I	R	E	D	Appreciated, Cherished, Delighted, Relished, Considered, Esteemed, Regarded, Respected.
A	D	M	I	R	E	R	Lover, Beau, Adorer.
A	D	M	I	X	E	D	Mingled, Mixed, Blended.
A	D	O	N	I	Z	E	Beautify.
A	D	O	P	T	E	D	Fathered, Appropriated, Embraced, Espoused, Taken, Usurped, Domesticated, Naturalized.
A	D	O	P	T	E	E	One that is adopted.
A	D	O	R	I	N	G	Worshipping, Loving, Idolizing, Venerating, Lauding, Admiring.
A	D	O	R	N	E	D	Beautified, Bedecked, Decorated, Embellished, Garnished, Ornamented, Trimmed.
A	D	R	E	N	A	L	Kidney glands.
A	D	U	L	A	T	E	Flatter, Cajole, Belaud, Respect.
A	D	U	S	T	E	D	Burned, Scorched, Parched.
A	D	V	A	N	C	E	Encourage, Forward, Elevate, Promote, Lend, Allege, Progress. Advancement, Headway.
A	D	V	E	N	E	D	To become part of something.
A	D	V	E	R	S	E	Antagonistic, Anti, Opposed, Detrimental, Negative, Favourable, Contrary, Hostile.
A	D	V	I	S	E	D	Recommended, Consulted, Designed, Premeditated, Studied, Notified, Informed, Apprised.
A	D	V	I	S	O	R	One that gives advice, Counsellor.
A	D	V	O	W	E	E	One that holds a summons.
A	E	O	L	I	A	N	A soft tone as if made by wind in the trees.
A	E	O	L	I	N	E	A very soft organ stop of mild string quality.
A	E	O	N	I	A	N	Lasting for an immeasurably long period of time.
A	E	R	A	T	E	D	Aerify, Expose to air, Ventilate, Make effervescent or Sparkling.
A	E	R	A	T	O	R	Machine for aerating liquid, Garden tool to remove cores of soil from turf.
A	E	R	O	B	I	A	Organism that only lives in the presence of oxygen.
A	E	R	O	B	U	S	Passenger plane.
A	E	R	O	G	E	L	Gel with gas to avoid shrinking.
A	E	R	O	S	O	L	Container for liquid particles in propellant gas to spray as mist.
A	F	F	A	B	L	E	Gracious, Congenial, Cordial, Genial, Sociable, Benign, Gentle, Amiable.
A	F	F	A	B	L	Y	Cordially, Courteously, Sociably, Amiably.
A	F	F	I	C	H	E	Poster, Placard, Notice.
A	F	F	I	N	A	L	Related by marriage.
A	F	F	I	N	E	D	Connected, Bound by obligation.
A	F	F	I	X	E	D	Fastened, Attached, Fixed, Rivetted, Appended, Annexed.
A	F	F	L	I	C	T	Agonize, Crucify, Excruciate, Harrow, Martyr, Rack, Torment, Torture.
A	F	F	O	R	C	E	Strengthen, Increase.
A	F	F	R	O	N	T	Contumely, Despite, Indignity, Insult, Slap, Outrage, Abuse.
A	F	F	U	S	E	D	Poured.
A	F	F	Y	I	N	G	Betrothing, Confiding, Trusting.
A	F	G	H	A	N	I	Native of Afghanistan.
A	F	R	I	C	A	N	Relating to Africa.
A	G	A	I	N	S	T	Contra, Facing, Fronting, Opposite, Counter, Despite, Toward, Touching.
A	G	A	M	O	U	S	Relating to agamy.
A	G	A	T	I	Z	E	Change to agate.
A	G	E	L	E	S	S	Eternal, Not showing effects of age, Having no limits in time.
A	G	E	L	O	N	G	Everlasting, Unending.
A	G	E	N	D	U	M	Matters of practical duty.
A	G	E	U	S	I	A	Absence or impairment of the sense of taste.
A	G	G	R	A	T	E	To gratify or express gratitude.
A	G	G	R	E	G	E	To aggravate, Make worse.
A	G	G	R	O	U	P	To arrange in a group.
A	G	I	L	E	L	Y	Actively, Quickly, Briskly, Lively, Sprightly, Nimbly.
A	G	I	S	T	E	R	Keeper of Royal forest that controls grazing.
A	G	I	T	A	T	E	Bother, Disturb, Flurry, Fluster, Perturb, Upset, Shake, Argue.
A	G	I	T	A	T	O	Restless and agitated, used in music.
A	G	N	A	T	I	C	Related through male descent.
A	G	N	O	M	E	N	Additional name or epithet.
A	G	N	O	S	I	A	Partial or complete loss of ability to recognize familiar objects by use of senses due to brain damage.
A	G	O	N	I	S	T	One that is engaged in a struggle.
A	G	O	N	I	Z	E	Afflict, Crucify, Harrow, Martyr, Writhe, Squirm, Toss, Torment.
A	G	R	A	F	F	E	Hook and loop fastening for armour or costume.
A	G	R	O	U	N	D	Stranded, Beached, Grounded.
A	I	B	L	I	N	S	Perhaps.
A	I	D	A	N	C	E	Aid, Help, Succour.

7 LETTERS

1	2	3	4	5	6	7	Definition
A	I	D	L	E	S	S	Devoid of help, Helpless.
A	I	L	E	R	O	N	Movable portion of airplane wing, Wing wall.
A	I	L	E	T	T	E	Armoured epaulet.
A	I	L	M	E	N	T	Disease, Complaint, Disorder, Infirmity, Sickness, Unrest, Disquiet, Ferment.
A	I	M	L	E	S	S	Random, Desultory, Haphazard, Pointless, Indiscriminate, Irregular, Unplanned.
A	I	R	B	A	S	E	Base of operations for aircraft.
A	I	R	B	A	T	H	Hygienic exposure of the body to the open air.
A	I	R	B	O	A	T	Shallow draft boat driven by airplane propeller and steered by airplane rudder.
A	I	R	C	E	L	L	Cavity or receptacle for air.
A	I	R	C	O	O	L	Cool by means of air flow.
A	I	R	C	O	R	E	Having no magnetic material in its magnetic circuit.
A	I	R	C	R	E	W	Crew manning an aircraft.
A	I	R	D	O	C	K	Hangar.
A	I	R	D	R	O	P	Drop supplies or troops by parachute.
A	I	R	D	U	C	T	Duct or pipe for conveying air for ventilation.
A	I	R	F	L	O	W	Motion of air relative to the surface of the body.
A	I	R	F	O	I	L	A body designed to provide a desired reaction.
A	I	R	G	L	O	W	Light from nighttime sky originating in high atmosphere.
A	I	R	H	E	A	D	Advance air base.
A	I	R	H	O	L	E	Hole to admit or discharge air, Blowhole, Air pocket.
A	I	R	H	O	R	N	Pneumatic horn.
A	I	R	I	E	S	T	Most airy.
A	I	R	L	E	S	S	Stuffy.
A	I	R	L	I	F	T	Transport by means of aircraft.
A	I	R	L	I	N	E	Aerial transportation.
A	I	R	L	O	C	K	To stop a flow by airlock.
A	I	R	M	A	I	L	Mail transported by airplane.
A	I	R	M	A	R	K	Mark out ground to assist aerial navigation.
A	I	R	M	A	S	S	Body of air extending high into stratosphere.
A	I	R	M	I	L	E	Basic unit of distance in air navigation.
A	I	R	P	A	R	K	Small airport.
A	I	R	P	O	R	T	Land or water maintained for the landing and takeoff of aircraft.
A	I	R	P	U	M	P	Pump for exhausting air from a closed space.
A	I	R	R	A	I	D	Attack by armed aircraft.
A	I	R	S	A	C	S	Parts of bodies of birds that are air filled.
A	I	R	S	H	I	P	Dirirgible, Lighter than air aircraft.
A	I	R	S	P	O	T	Spotting or reporting fall of missiles from aircraft on to target.
A	I	S	L	I	N	G	Poetical description of a vision.
A	J	A	N	G	L	E	Jangling.
A	J	I	V	I	K	A	Member of nontheistic sect.
A	J	U	T	A	G	E	Agitation.
A	K	I	N	E	T	E	Single cell spore.
A	L	A	M	E	D	A	Tree shaded public walk.
A	L	A	N	I	N	E	White crystalline amino acid.
A	L	A	N	T	I	N	Inulin, Starch.
A	L	A	R	M	E	D	Appalled, Alerted, Shocked, Frightened, Daunted, Awed, Scared, Startled.
A	L	A	S	K	A	N	Native of Alaska.
A	L	A	S	T	O	R	Avenging diety.
A	L	B	E	L	A	D	Resin.
A	L	B	U	M	E	N	White of egg.
A	L	B	U	M	I	N	Simple protein.
A	L	C	A	N	N	A	Henna.
A	L	C	A	Z	A	R	Spanish castle.
A	L	C	H	E	M	Y	Medieval chemical science.
A	L	C	O	H	O	L	Liquor, Booze, Drink, Grog, Hooch, Tipple.
A	L	E	C	O	S	T	Tansy scented herb.
A	L	E	M	B	I	C	Glass retort.
A	L	E	N	C	O	N	Fine handmade needlepoint lace.
A	L	E	R	T	E	R	Brisker, More watchful, Brighter, Sharper, Smarter, Keener.
A	L	E	R	T	L	Y	Briskly, Actively, Warily, Vigilantly, Cleverly, Promptly, Smartly.
A	L	E	T	R	I	S	Female slave who ground meal.
A	L	E	W	I	F	E	Herring.
A	L	F	A	L	F	A	Lucerne grown for fodder.
A	L	F	I	O	N	E	Rubberlip perch.
A	L	G	A	T	E	S	Wholly, Completely, Nevertheless, Notwithstanding.
A	L	G	E	B	R	A	Process of reasoning by the use of symbols.
A	L	G	E	S	I	A	Sensitiveness to pain.

1	2	3	4	5	6	7	Definition
A	L	I	D	A	D	E	Part of astrolabe.
A	L	I	E	N	E	E	One to whom the title of property is transferred.
A	L	I	F	O	R	M	Wing shaped.
A	L	I	G	N	E	D	Lined, Ranged, Adjusted, Regulated.
A	L	I	M	E	N	T	Food, Nourishment, Nutriment.
A	L	I	M	O	N	Y	Maintenance.
A	L	I	Q	U	O	T	Contained an exact number of times.
A	L	K	A	M	E	S	Original Italian liqueur.
A	L	K	A	N	E	T	Red dye prepared from root.
A	L	L	A	Y	E	D	Relieved, Assuaged, Eased, Lightened, Mitigated.
A	L	L	E	G	E	D	Ostensible, Pretended, Professed, Purported, Supposed, So-called.
A	L	L	E	G	R	O	Lively fast tempo (music).
A	L	L	E	R	G	Y	Antipathy, Aversion, Rejection, Repulsion, Revulsion, Repugnance.
A	L	L	E	T	T	E	Wing of building.
A	L	L	O	B	A	R	Barometric pressure change.
A	L	L	O	N	G	E	Slip of paper attached to bill of exchange for extra items.
A	L	L	O	N	Y	M	Work published under the name of a person other than the author.
A	L	L	O	W	E	D	Allocated, Apportioned, Assigned, Admitted, Conceded, Granted, Permitted.
A	L	L	O	X	A	N	Crystalline compound formed by oxidation of uric acid.
A	L	L	O	Y	E	D	Debased, Mixed, Compounded, Adulterated, Blended, Tempered.
A	L	L	S	E	E	D	Many-seeded fruit.
A	L	L	T	I	M	E	Full time, Exceeding all others.
A	L	L	U	D	E	D	Referred, Hinted, Implied, Suggested.
A	L	L	U	R	E	D	Enticed, Decoyed, Attracted, Captivated, Enchanted, Fascinated, Charmed.
A	L	L	U	V	I	A	Deposited by water.
A	L	L	W	A	V	E	Multi-wave.
A	L	L	W	I	S	E	Of infinite wisdom.
A	L	L	Y	I	N	G	Betrothing, Banding, Uniting, Associating.
A	L	M	A	N	A	C	Calendar.
A	L	M	O	I	G	N	Charitable endowment.
A	L	M	O	N	E	R	Social-service worker in hospital, One that distributes alms.
A	L	M	O	N	R	Y	Ecclesiastical building set aside for the distribution of alms.
A	L	M	S	B	O	X	Receptacle for receiving alms.
A	L	M	S	F	E	E	Peter's pence.
A	L	M	S	M	A	N	Receiver of alms.
A	L	N	A	G	E	R	Officer to inspect and attest quality of wool.
A	L	O	D	I	U	M	Real estate held in freehold.
A	L	O	E	T	I	C	Medicine from aloes.
A	L	O	G	I	S	M	Illogical statement.
A	L	O	N	G	S	T	Along.
A	L	P	H	O	R	N	Swiss cow horn.
A	L	R	E	A	D	Y	Previously, Before.
A	L	T	E	R	E	D	Changed, Modified, Refashioned, Fixed, Castrated, Gelded.
A	L	T	E	R	N	E	One of a group of adjoining plant communities.
A	L	T	H	A	E	A	Genus of hollyhock, marshmallow.
A	L	T	H	O	R	N	Alto saxhorn.
A	L	T	R	O	S	E	Sugar obtained synthetically as a syrup with glucose.
A	L	U	M	I	N	A	Oxide of aluminium sometimes used as abrasive or catalyst.
A	L	U	M	I	T	E	Alunite.
A	L	U	M	N	A	L	Relating to alumni.
A	L	U	M	N	U	S	College graduate.
A	L	U	N	I	T	E	Mineral occurring massive or in crystals.
A	L	V	E	L	O	S	Milky sap of a Brazilian plant.
A	L	V	E	O	L	E	Small cavity.
A	L	V	E	O	L	I	Socket for tooth, Air cells of the lung.
A	L	Y	S	S	U	M	Edging plant.
A	M	A	L	G	A	M	Alloy, Blend, Composite, Compound, Fusion.
A	M	A	N	D	I	N	Protein of sweet almonds and peach kernels.
A	M	A	N	I	T	A	Poisonous mushroom.
A	M	A	N	O	U	S	Having no hands.
A	M	A	S	S	E	D	Accumulated, Garnered, Stockpiled, Stored, Heaped, Collected.
A	M	A	T	E	U	R	Dabbler, Non-professional, Beginner, Greenhorn, Admirer, Dilettante, Fan.
A	M	A	T	I	V	E	Erotic, Amatory, Amorous, Aphrodisiac.
A	M	A	T	O	R	Y	Erotic, Amative, Amorous, Aphrodisiac.
A	M	A	Z	I	N	G	Marvellous, Astonishing, Astounding, Miraculous, Prodigious, Strange, Surprising.
A	M	B	A	G	E	S	Winding, Circuitous, Secret, Mysterious.
A	M	B	A	R	E	E	Canopied howdah.

1	2	3	4	5	6	7	
A	M	B	I	E	N	T	Enveloping, Encompassing.
A	M	B	I	T	U	S	Exterior edge, Denotation.
A	M	B	L	I	N	G	Sauntering, Drifting, Lingering, Strolling, Easy gait.
A	M	B	O	Y	N	A	Curly grained wood of an Indian tree.
A	M	B	R	E	I	N	Crystalline alcohol from ambergris.
A	M	B	R	O	I	D	Material containing small pieces of amber.
A	M	B	S	A	C	E	Lowest throw of dice, Something worthless or unlucky.
A	M	B	U	L	I	A	Aquarium plants.
A	M	E	N	D	E	D	Corrected, Mended, Rectified, Righted, Improved, Helped, Ameliorated, Repaired.
A	M	E	N	I	T	Y	Cordiality, Geniality, Sweetness, Comfort, Convenience, Facility, Luxury, Courtesy.
A	M	E	N	T	A	L	Devoid of mind, Hospital patient.
A	M	E	N	T	I	A	Mental deficiency.
A	M	E	N	T	U	M	Thong or cord attached to javelin.
A	M	E	R	C	E	D	Fined, Punished.
A	M	H	A	R	I	C	Official Semitic language of Abyssinia.
A	M	I	A	B	L	E	Complaisant, Easy, Good-humoured, Lenient, Gentle, Affable, Genial, Lovable.
A	M	I	A	B	L	Y	Kindly, Charmingly, Easily, Mildly, Gently, Genially.
A	M	I	D	I	N	E	Any strong monobasic containing a protein and amina.
A	M	I	L	D	A	R	Agent manager in India.
A	M	M	E	T	E	R	Instrument for measuring electrical current.
A	M	M	O	N	A	L	Explosive.
A	M	M	O	N	I	A	Colourless gaseous alkaline compound of nitrogen and hydrogen.
A	M	N	E	S	I	A	Loss of memory, Gap in memory.
A	M	N	E	S	T	Y	Pardon, Absolution, Oblivion.
A	M	N	I	O	T	A	Group of vertebrates that develop an amnion in embryonic life.
A	M	O	E	B	I	C	Resembling or relating to amoeba.
A	M	O	E	B	A	N	Resembling or relating to amoeba.
A	M	O	N	G	S	T	Amid, Between, Mingle, During.
A	M	O	R	I	S	T	Gallant, Casanova, Don Juan, Lothario, Paramour, Romeo.
A	M	O	R	O	S	O	With tenderness - (direction in music).
A	M	O	R	O	U	S	Erotic, Amatory, Aphrodisiac, Lustful, Infatuated, Enamoured, Fond, Loving.
A	M	O	R	P	H	A	Genus of Americasn herbs or shrubs, Falso indigo, Leadplant.
A	M	O	S	I	T	E	Mineral used as type of asbestos.
A	M	O	T	I	O	N	Removal of specified object from place or position, Ousted, Deprivation of possession of property.
A	M	P	H	O	R	A	Ancient jar or vase having 2 handles.
A	M	P	L	E	S	T	Most spacious, Most capacious, Most commodious, Most buxom, Most lavish.
A	M	P	L	I	F	Y	Expand, Develop, Elaborate, Enlarge, Dilate, Distend, Inflate, Augment.
A	M	P	O	U	L	E	Flask of glass or earthenware.
A	M	P	U	L	L	A	Flask of glass or earthenware.
A	M	U	S	I	N	G	Entertaining, Diverting, Droll, Deluding, Bemusing, Ludicrous.
A	M	Y	L	A	S	E	Enzyme.
A	M	Y	L	E	N	E	Low boiling hydrocarbons.
A	M	Y	L	O	I	D	Like or containing amylum, Like starch.
A	M	Y	L	O	S	E	Starch or cellulose.
A	N	A	E	M	I	A	Condition of Blood being deficient in red cells lacking vitality.
A	N	A	E	M	I	C	Affected with anaemia.
A	N	A	G	O	G	E	Seeking spiritual significant reference to future life in Heaven.
A	N	A	G	R	A	M	Rearrange letters to discover hidden meaning.
A	N	A	L	O	G	Y	Likeness, Affinity, Resemblance, Similarity, Comparison, Metaphor, Similitude.
A	N	A	L	Y	S	T	One who specializes in interpreting social and political developments, Statistician.
A	N	A	L	Y	Z	E	Resolve, Break, Dissect, Anatomize.
A	N	A	L	Y	S	E	Resolve, Break, Dissect, Anatomize.
A	N	A	N	I	A	S	Liar, Early Christian struck dead for lying to Apostle Peter.
A	N	A	N	I	S	M	Karaism as taught by Anan ben David.
A	N	A	P	E	S	T	Metrical foot of three syllables.
A	N	A	P	S	I	D	Turtle.
A	N	A	R	C	H	Y	Chaos, Lawlessness, Disorder, Misrule, Riot, Confusion, Violence.
A	N	A	T	A	S	E	White pigment in paint and printing inks.
A	N	A	T	M	A	N	Having no soul according to Buddist doctrine.
A	N	A	T	O	M	Y	Histology, Phytotomy, Dissection, Analysis, Skeleton.
A	N	A	U	D	I	A	Loss of voice, Inability to articulate.
A	N	O	M	A	L	Y	Irregular in form.
A	N	C	H	O	V	Y	Small herringlike fish.
A	N	C	I	E	N	T	Aged, Antique, Old, Venerable, Elderly, Olden, Antediluvian, Timeworn.
A	N	C	I	L	L	A	Helper, Assistant, Accessory, Attendant, Striker.
A	N	C	O	N	E	S	Relating to the elbow.
A	N	C	R	E	S	S	Female hermit, Recluse.

1	2	3	4	5	6	7	
A	N	D	A	N	T	E	Moderately slow - (direction in music).
A	N	D	I	R	O	N	Metal support for firewood in grate.
A	N	D	R	O	I	D	Automaton, Robot.
A	N	D	R	O	U	S	Having many.
A	N	E	M	O	N	E	Genus of herbs.
A	N	E	R	O	I	D	Barometer.
A	N	E	S	O	N	E	White anise liqueur.
A	N	E	T	H	O	L	Oil of anise and fennel.
A	N	G	A	R	I	A	Compulsory service.
A	N	G	E	L	I	C	Saintly, Godly, Holy.
A	N	G	E	L	O	T	Angelic, Rich cheese made in Normandy.
A	N	G	E	L	U	S	Roman Catholics using bell for time for devotion.
A	N	G	E	R	E	D	Enraged, Intense, Infuriate, Umbrage, Madden, Bristle, Fume, Rage.
A	N	G	E	R	L	Y	Wrathfully, Eagerly.
A	N	G	E	V	I	N	Inhabitant of Anjou.
A	N	G	I	O	I	D	Resembling a blood vessel or lymph vessel.
A	N	G	I	O	M	A	Tumour composed chiefly of blood vessels or lymph vessels.
A	N	G	L	I	C	E	In readily understood English.
A	N	G	L	I	F	Y	Relating to English.
A	N	G	L	I	N	G	Art of fishing with hook and line.
A	N	G	L	I	S	T	Specialist in English language or literature.
A	N	G	R	I	L	Y	Indignantly, Irately, Madly, Wrathfully, Acrimoniously.
A	N	G	U	I	N	E	Relating to a snake.
A	N	G	U	I	S	H	Sorrow, Affliction, Care, Grief, Heartache, Regret, Rue, Woe.
A	N	G	U	L	A	R	Rude, Crude, Raw, Hewn, Lean, Bony, Gaunt, Scraggy.
A	N	I	D	I	A	N	Formless, Shapeless.
A	N	I	L	I	N	E	Synthetic organic dye.
A	N	I	L	I	T	Y	Old woman, Objectionable quality.
A	N	I	M	A	T	E	Encourage, Hearten, Embolden, Strengthen, Enliven, Fire, Inform, Inspire.
A	N	I	M	I	S	M	Doctrine, according to which the soul is the vital principle.
A	N	I	S	E	E	D	Seed used as flavouring.
A	N	N	A	T	E	S	First fruits of an ecclesiastical benifice.
A	N	N	A	T	T	O	Red or yellowish red dyestuff.
A	N	N	E	L	I	D	Worm.
A	N	N	E	X	E	D	Acquired, Gained, Obtained, Procured, Appropriated, Commandeered, Confiscated, Seized.
A	N	N	O	Y	E	D	Worried, Gnawed, Harassed, Pestered, Plagued, Teased, Bothered, Provoked.
A	N	N	U	I	T	Y	An amount paid at regular intervals.
A	N	N	U	L	A	R	Relating to a ring, Banded, marked or thickened in circles.
A	N	N	U	L	E	T	A little ring, A small moulding or ridge.
A	N	N	U	L	U	S	A ringlike part of structure.
A	N	O	D	I	Z	E	Coating metal with decorative or protective film.
A	N	O	D	Y	N	E	Pain-killer, Opiate, Sedative, Analgesic, Anaesthetic.
A	N	O	E	S	I	S	Want of understanding.
A	N	O	E	S	I	A	Consciousness that is pure passive receptiveness.
A	N	O	E	T	I	C	Relating to anoesis.
A	N	O	L	Y	T	E	Portion of electrolyte.
A	N	O	M	A	L	Y	Inequality, Unevenness, Irregularity, Out of keeping.
A	N	O	P	S	I	A	Blindness, Squint.
A	N	O	S	M	I	A	Loss or impairment to sense of smell.
A	N	O	T	H	E	R	That, Additional, Added, Else, Farther, Fresh, Further, More.
A	N	S	A	T	E	D	Having a handle.
A	N	T	A	C	I	D	Counteractive of acidity.
A	N	T	A	P	E	X	Point of celestial sphere from which the solar system is moving.
A	N	T	B	E	A	R	American mammal.
A	N	T	E	F	I	X	Ornament on the eaves.
A	N	T	E	G	G	S	Pupae of ants dried and used as pet food.
A	N	T	E	N	N	A	Feeler, Sensory appendage of the head, Device for radiating or receiving radio waves.
A	N	T	H	E	R	A	Plant having an anther.
A	N	T	H	E	R	Y	Possession of anthers.
A	N	T	H	I	L	L	A mound thrown up by termites.
A	N	T	H	R	A	X	Carbuncle or malignant pustule, Infectious disease of warm-blooded animal transmissible to man.
A	N	T	I	C	A	L	Bizarre, Frolicsome, Grotesque, Fantastic, Ludicrous.
A	N	T	I	C	L	Y	Foolishly, Comically, Ludicrously, Sprightly, Playfully.
A	N	T	I	C	O	R	Inflammatory swelling caused by pressure or friction of harness on a horse.
A	N	T	I	C	U	M	Front porch.
A	N	T	I	G	E	N	Stimulator of antibodies.
A	N	T	I	Q	U	E	Ancient, Aged, Old, Timeworn, Venerable, Old-fashioned, Archaic, Dated.

1	2	3	4	5	6	7	
A	N	T	L	I	O	N	Insect that digs a pit to catch its prey.
A	N	T	O	N	Y	M	A word of opposite meaning.
A	N	U	R	O	U	S	Being tailless.
A	N	X	I	E	T	Y	Care, Concern, Disquiet, Solicitude, Unease, Worry, Uncertainty, Dread.
A	N	X	I	O	U	S	Afraid, Fearful, Frightened, Scared, Terrified, Impatient, Troubled, Apprehensive.
A	N	Y	B	O	D	Y	A person from an indeterminate number, Unspecified person.
A	N	Y	M	O	R	E	Nowadays, Currently.
A	N	Y	T	I	M	E	Under any circumstances.
A	N	Y	W	A	Y	S	Anywise, To any degree.
A	N	Y	W	H	E	N	At any time.
A	N	Y	W	I	S	E	In any way or form.
A	P	A	G	O	G	E	Abduction, Argument by absurd reasoning.
A	P	A	N	A	G	E	Grant, Perquisite.
A	P	A	N	D	R	Y	Male impotence.
A	P	A	T	I	T	E	Calcium phosphate minerals.
A	P	A	U	M	E	E	Palm of open hand.
A	P	E	L	I	K	E	Imitative, Simian.
A	P	E	T	A	L	Y	Absence of petals.
A	P	H	A	G	I	A	Inability to swallow.
A	P	H	A	K	I	A	Absence of the crystalline lens of the eye.
A	P	H	A	S	I	A	Loss or impairment of the power to use words as symbols of ideas.
A	P	H	A	S	I	C	Relating to aphasia.
A	P	H	E	M	I	A	Loss of speech.
A	P	H	E	S	I	S	Loss of short unaccented vowel at the beginning of a word.
A	P	H	I	D	E	S	Insects injurious to fruit trees.
A	P	H	O	N	I	A	Loss of voice.
A	P	H	O	N	I	C	Silent, Noiseless.
A	P	H	O	T	I	C	Without light.
A	P	H	R	I	T	E	Chalky variety of calcite.
A	P	H	T	H	A	E	Mouth ulcers.
A	P	H	Y	L	L	Y	Absence of leaves.
A	P	I	C	I	A	N	Epicure.
A	P	I	S	H	L	Y	Silly, Affected, Servile imitation.
A	P	L	A	N	A	T	Lens corrected for spherical aberration.
A	P	L	A	S	I	A	Incomplete or faulty development of organ.
A	P	O	C	O	P	E	Loss of sounds or letters at the end of a word.
A	P	O	C	Y	T	E	Multinucleate cell.
A	P	O	G	A	M	Y	Interbreeding within a segregated group.
A	P	O	G	E	A	N	Connected with apogee.
A	P	O	G	E	N	Y	Loss of reproductive function.
A	P	O	L	O	G	Y	Excuse, Regrets, Defence, Justification, Extenuation, Mitigation.
A	P	O	R	O	S	A	Division of corals.
A	P	O	S	T	I	L	Annotation, Marginal note.
A	P	O	S	T	L	E	Disciple of Christ, Messenger.
A	P	O	T	O	M	E	Mathematical difference in semitone (music).
A	P	P	A	R	E	L	Array, Clothe, Garment, Raiment, Clothing, Dress, Garb, Clad.
A	P	P	E	A	C	H	Impeach, Accuse, Cast aspersions.
A	P	P	E	A	S	E	Pacify, Assuage, Conciliate, Mollify, Placate, Satisfy, Content, Gratify.
A	P	P	L	A	U	D	Commend, Acclaim, Compliment, Praise, Cheer, Root, Recommend, Hail.
A	P	P	L	I	E	D	Addressed, Directed, Resorted, Repaired, Exercised, Used.
A	P	P	O	I	N	T	Designate, Make, Name, Nominate, Furnish, Arm, Equip, Outfit.
A	P	P	O	S	E	D	Place opposite or in proximity.
A	P	P	R	I	S	E	Inform, Acquaint, Advise, Notify, Tell, Warn, Post, Clue.
A	P	P	R	I	Z	E	Appreciate, Cherish, Esteem, Prize, Treasure, Value.
A	P	P	R	O	O	F	Proof, Trial, Test, Approval.
A	P	P	R	O	V	E	Accept, Countenance, Favour, Approbate, Accredit, Certify, Endorse, Sanction.
A	P	P	U	L	S	E	Driving or running toward.
A	P	R	I	C	O	T	Fruit, Colour.
A	P	R	O	N	E	D	Wearing an apron.
A	P	R	O	P	O	S	Seasonably, Fitly, Relevant, Concerning, Regarding.
A	P	R	O	T	I	C	Incapable of acting as a proton acceptor or donor.
A	P	S	I	D	A	L	Relating to the apsides of an orbit, Apse of church.
A	P	S	I	D	E	S	Circumference, Orbit.
A	P	T	E	R	A	L	Wingless.
A	P	T	E	R	Y	X	Kiwi, Flightless bird.
A	P	T	N	E	S	S	Fitness, Aptitude, Order, Gift, Bent, Faculty, Flair, Propriety.
A	P	Y	R	O	U	S	Noncombustible.

1	2	3	4	5	6	7	
A	Q	U	A	T	I	C	Living wholly or chiefly in or on water.
A	Q	U	E	O	U	S	Watery.
A	Q	U	I	F	E	R	Water-bearing bed of rock, gravel or sand.
A	R	A	B	I	A	N	Native or inhabitant of Arabia.
A	R	A	B	I	S	M	Characteristic feature of Arabic.
A	R	A	B	I	S	T	Specialist in Arabic language.
A	R	A	C	H	I	S	Peanut.
A	R	A	M	A	I	C	Semitic language.
A	R	A	M	E	A	N	Member of Semitic people that settled in Syria and Mesopotamia.
A	R	B	I	T	E	R	Judge, Referee, Umpire, Arbitrator.
A	R	B	O	R	E	D	Shaded by bower or trees.
A	R	B	U	T	U	S	Genus of evergreen tree or shrub.
A	R	C	A	D	E	D	Lined with arcades.
A	R	C	A	D	I	A	Rural paradise, Utopia, Fairyland, Promised land, Wonderland, Heaven.
A	R	C	A	N	U	M	Secret or mysterious knowledge.
A	R	C	H	A	I	C	Old-fashioned, Antiquated, Antique, Primitive, Underdeveloped, Unevolved, Bygone, Outdated.
A	R	C	H	E	R	Y	Art, skill or practice of shooting with bow and arrow.
A	R	C	H	E	U	S	Vital principle according to followers of Swiss alchemist.
A	R	C	H	I	N	G	Curving, Arcing, Bending, Bowing, Vaulting.
A	R	C	H	W	A	Y	Passage or gate under an arch.
A	R	C	L	A	M	P	Carbon-pole-bridge lamp.
A	R	C	T	I	U	M	Genus of coarse biennial herbs.
A	R	C	T	O	I	D	Family comprising bears, weasels, raccoons.
A	R	C	U	A	T	E	Bend like a bow.
A	R	D	E	N	C	Y	Warmth, Fiery, Intensely.
A	R	D	U	O	U	S	Hard, Difficult, Strenuous, Toilsome, Steep, Abrupt, Tight, Rough.
A	R	E	O	L	A	R	Filled with small spaces.
A	R	G	H	O	O	L	Egyptian musical reed instrument.
A	R	G	U	I	N	G	Debating, Disputing, Bickering, Quibbling, Claiming, Defending, Contending, Vindicating.
A	R	I	D	I	T	Y	Dryness, Sterility, Thirsty, Dusty, Droughty.
A	R	I	E	T	T	A	Short aria.
A	R	I	L	L	E	D	Exterior covering of seeds.
A	R	I	L	L	U	S	Coating or appendage that envelops the seed after fertilization.
A	R	I	P	P	L	E	Rippling (quiet water).
A	R	I	S	I	N	G	Rising, Mounting, Ascending, Springing, Lifting, Soaring.
A	R	M	H	O	L	E	Opening for the arm in a garment.
A	R	M	I	G	E	R	Squire. One entitled to heraldic arms.
A	R	M	I	L	L	A	Gold coronation bracelet.
A	R	M	L	E	S	S	One without arms.
A	R	M	O	I	R	E	Cupboard, Wardrobe, Clothes press.
A	R	M	O	R	I	C	Dialect of natives of Brittany.
A	R	M	O	U	R	Y	Arsenal, Depot, Dump, Magazine.
A	R	N	A	T	T	O	Red or yellowish red dye.
A	R	O	U	S	A	L	Act of arousing or being aroused.
A	R	O	U	S	E	D	Excited, Stimulated, Provoked, Challenged, Rallied, Kindled.
A	R	R	A	I	G	N	Impeach, Accuse, Charge, Incriminate, Inculpate, Indict, Tax.
A	R	R	A	N	G	E	Order, Array, Organize, Design, Plan, Negotiate, Harmonize, Blend.
A	R	R	A	Y	E	D	Ordered, Arranged, Marshalled, Organised, Clothed, Dressed.
A	R	R	E	A	R	S	Debts, Payments, Overdue, Unpaid, Balance.
A	R	R	I	D	E	D	Pleased, Delighted, Gratified, Gladdened.
A	R	R	I	E	R	O	Muleteer.
A	R	R	I	V	A	L	Advent, Coming, Appearance, Attainment.
A	R	S	E	N	A	L	Armoury, Depot, Dump, Magazine, Storehouse.
A	R	S	E	N	I	C	Metalloid element.
A	R	T	I	C	L	E	Essay, Composition, Paper, Theme, Point, Detail, Element, Object.
A	R	T	I	S	A	N	Workman, Operator, Journeyman.
A	R	T	I	S	T	E	Expert, Artist, Authority, Proficient, Virtuoso, Performer, Wizard.
A	R	T	L	E	S	S	Natural, Naive, Simple, Ingenuous, Unaffected, Unsophisticated, Unschooled.
A	R	T	S	M	A	N	Skilled in an art.
A	R	U	S	P	E	X	Soothsayer, Diviner, Prognosticator.
A	S	A	R	O	N	E	Crystalline phenolic found in oil of camphor.
A	S	B	O	L	I	N	Earthy mineral aggregate found in ash.
A	S	C	A	R	I	D	Roundworm.
A	S	C	E	S	I	S	Asceticism, Self-restraint, Self-discipline.
A	S	C	E	T	I	C	Austere, Self-denying, Practices celibacy and Self-mortification.
A	S	C	I	D	I	A	Molluscs.
A	S	C	I	T	E	S	Peritoneal fluid accumulation.

1	2	3	4	5	6	7	
A	S	C	I	T	I	C	Peritoneal fluid accumulation.
A	S	C	R	I	B	E	Accredit, Assign, Attribute, Credit, Impute, Refer, Charge.
A	S	E	P	S	I	S	Sterile, Free of germs.
A	S	E	P	T	I	C	Antiseptic, Sterile, Undemonstrative, Restrained, Retiring, Shrinking, Withdrawn, Unaffable.
A	S	E	X	U	A	L	Having no sex or functional sexual organs, Not relating to sex.
A	S	H	A	M	E	D	Humiliated, Chagrined, Mortified, Disconcerted, Abashed, Confused, Embarrassed.
A	S	H	C	A	K	E	Cake of corn meal baked in hot ashes.
A	S	H	I	V	E	R	Trembling, Shivering, Tremulous, Quaking, Quivering.
A	S	H	T	R	A	Y	Receptacle for cigarette ashes and butts.
A	S	I	A	R	C	H	Roman official in Asia.
A	S	I	A	T	I	C	One of Indian descent.
A	S	I	N	E	G	O	Fool.
A	S	I	N	I	N	E	Simple, Brainless, Fatuous, Foolish, Mindless, Silly, Witless, Obstinate.
A	S	K	A	N	C	E	Awry, Askew, Cockeyed, Crookedly, Distrustfully, Doubtfully, Mistrustfully, Suspiciously.
A	S	P	E	R	G	E	To sprinkle as with hot water.
A	S	P	E	R	S	E	Malign, Calumniate, Defame, Libel, Scandal, Slander, Baptize, Christen.
A	S	P	H	A	L	T	Bitumen.
A	S	P	H	Y	X	Y	Asphyxia, Suffocation.
A	S	P	I	R	E	D	Aimed, Panted, Ascended, Lifted, Mounted, Soared.
A	S	P	I	R	E	R	One that aspires.
A	S	P	I	R	I	N	Salicylic acid used as analgesic.
A	S	P	R	A	W	L	Sprawling.
A	S	P	R	E	A	D	Spreading, Scattering.
A	S	Q	U	I	N	T	Obliquely, Squinting, Glance furtively.
A	S	S	A	G	A	I	Spear.
A	S	S	E	V	E	R	Solemn declaration, Sever, Swear.
A	S	S	H	E	A	D	Blockhead, Ass.
A	S	S	I	E	G	E	Beseige.
A	S	S	I	Z	E	R	Juryman, Inspector of weights and measures.
A	S	S	I	Z	E	S	Courts of jurisdiction, Travelling country courts.
A	S	S	U	A	G	E	Relieve, Allay, Alleviate, Ease, Lighten, Mitigate, Pacify, Placate.
A	S	S	U	M	E	D	Artificial, Affected, Feigned, Spurious, Implied.
A	S	S	U	M	E	R	One that assumes.
A	S	S	U	R	E	D	Confident, Sanguine, Secure, Self-assured, Self-confident, Decided, Definite, Pronounced.
A	S	S	U	R	E	R	One that underwrites insurance.
A	S	S	U	R	O	R	One that underwrites insurance.
A	S	S	W	A	G	E	Assuage.
A	S	T	A	S	I	A	Muscular in co-ordination in standing.
A	S	T	A	T	I	C	Unstable, Unsteady, Lacking, Polarity.
A	S	T	E	R	I	A	Star sapphire.
A	S	T	H	O	R	E	Treasure - as term endearment.
A	S	T	O	U	N	D	Surprise, Amaze, Astonish, Dumbfound, Flabbergast.
A	S	T	R	A	N	D	Stranded.
A	S	T	R	I	C	T	Confine, Constrict, Restrict, Limit, Bind.
A	S	T	R	I	D	E	Bestriding, Straddling, Spanning, Bridging.
A	S	T	R	O	I	D	Shaped like a star.
A	S	T	Y	L	A	R	Without columns.
A	S	U	D	D	E	N	Suddenly, Short, Abruptly, Forthwith, Sudden.
A	S	U	N	D	E	R	Apart, Sky-high.
A	T	A	C	T	I	C	Lacking regularity or co-ordination.
A	T	A	G	H	A	N	A long knife used by Muslims.
A	T	A	R	A	X	Y	Impassiveness, Coolness, Imperturbability, Intellectual, Detachment.
A	T	A	U	N	T	O	Shipshape, Fully rigged.
A	T	A	V	I	S	M	Throwback, Reversion.
A	T	E	B	R	I	N	Used for quinacrine.
A	T	E	L	I	E	R	Studio, Workshop, Fashion designer's establishment.
A	T	H	A	N	O	R	Self-feeding furnace.
A	T	H	E	I	S	M	Disbelief in the existence of God.
A	T	H	E	I	S	T	One who practices atheism.
A	T	H	I	R	S	T	Thirsty, Dry, Eager, Anxious, Ardent, Avid, Impatient, Keen.
A	T	H	L	E	T	E	Contestant, One who takes part in sports, games or physical exercises.
A	T	H	R	I	L	L	Excited.
A	T	H	W	A	R	T	Across, Crosswise, Over, Beyond, Transversely, Askew, Aslant.
A	T	O	K	O	U	S	Anterior sexless part of certain worms.
A	T	O	M	I	S	E	Sprinkle with small particles.
A	T	O	M	I	S	M	Theory of atom.
A	T	O	M	I	S	T	An adherent of atomism.

1	2	3	4	5	6	7	
A	T	O	M	I	Z	E	Demolish, Destruct, Ruin, Shatter, Smash, Wreck, Convert liquid into light spray.
A	T	O	N	I	N	G	Expiating, Compensating, Balancing, Redeeming, Offsetting.
A	T	R	E	S	I	A	Absence or closure of natural opening of body.
A	T	R	O	P	H	Y	Wasting, Deterioration, Decadence, Decline, Degeneration, Downfall.
A	T	R	O	P	I	A	Bella-donna.
A	T	T	A	B	O	Y	Expression of encouragement, approval or admiration.
A	T	T	A	C	H	E	Case, Person attached to another person or group.
A	T	T	A	C	U	S	Genus of tropical moths.
A	T	T	A	I	N	T	Convicted, Accuse, Sully, Contaminate.
A	T	T	E	M	P	T	Endeavour, Essay, Hassle, Try, Aim, Effort, Trial, Undertaking.
A	T	T	I	C	A	L	Athenian style or language.
A	T	T	I	N	G	E	Touch, Contact.
A	T	T	I	R	E	D	Clothed, Arrayed, Clad, Dressed, Garbed.
A	T	T	R	A	C	T	Allure, Bewitch, Captivate, Charm, Enchant, Fascinate, Interest, Appeal.
A	T	T	R	I	S	T	Sadden.
A	T	T	R	I	T	E	Penitent, Contrite, Remorse, Repent, Rue, Worn by friction.
A	T	T	U	N	E	D	Harmonized, Accommodated, Conformed, Integrated, Reconciled.
A	U	B	E	R	G	E	Hotel, Inn, Hospice, Hostel, Tavern, Lodge.
A	U	C	T	I	O	N	Public sale of property going to highest bidder.
A	U	D	I	B	L	E	Capable of being heard, Aural.
A	U	D	I	B	L	Y	Can be heard.
A	U	D	I	E	N	T	Hearer.
A	U	D	I	T	E	D	Examined, Analyzed, Inspected, Checked, Scrutinised, Reviewed.
A	U	D	I	T	O	R	Accountant, Examiner.
A	U	G	I	T	I	C	Relating to mineral augite.
A	U	G	M	E	N	T	Increase, Boost, Enlarge, Expand, Extend, Heighten, Magnify, Multiply.
A	U	G	U	R	A	L	Ominous, Portentous, Auspicious.
A	U	G	U	R	E	D	Presaged, Predicted, Prognosticated, Prophesied, Forebode.
A	U	R	A	L	L	Y	Relating to ear or hearing.
A	U	R	E	A	T	E	Resplendent, Gilded, Golden, Rhetorical, Flowery, Declamatory.
A	U	R	E	I	T	Y	Distinctive properties of gold.
A	U	R	E	L	I	A	Genus of large jellyfishes.
A	U	R	E	O	L	A	Golden halo, Nimbus, Radiance.
A	U	R	E	O	L	E	Golden halo, Nimbus, Radiance.
A	U	R	I	C	L	E	External ear, Chamber of the heart.
A	U	R	I	F	I	C	Producing gold.
A	U	R	O	C	H	S	Wild ox, European bison.
A	U	R	O	R	A	L	Dawn, Rosy, Radiant.
A	U	S	L	A	U	T	Final sound in word or syllable.
A	U	S	P	I	C	E	Augury, Omen, Portent.
A	U	S	T	E	R	E	Severe, Ascetic, Astringent, Stern, Acrid, Grim, Bleak.
A	U	S	T	R	A	L	Southern.
A	U	T	A	R	C	H	Despot, Autocrat.
A	U	T	A	R	K	Y	Self-sufficiency, Independent.
A	U	T	O	B	U	S	Omnibus.
A	U	T	O	C	A	R	Automobile.
A	U	T	O	M	A	T	Robot, Automatic device.
A	U	T	O	P	S	Y	Post-mortem, Necropsy.
A	U	X	E	S	I	S	Growth, Increase of cell size without cell division.
A	U	X	E	T	I	C	Inducing growth.
A	V	A	I	L	E	D	Benefitted, Served, Worked, Helped.
A	V	A	R	I	C	E	Greed, Cupidity, Rapacity, Avariciousness.
A	V	E	N	G	E	D	Revenged, Retaliated, Redressed, Vindicated, Chastened, Chastised.
A	V	E	N	G	E	R	One that avenges.
A	V	E	R	A	G	E	Medium, Indifferent, Intermediate, Mean, Mediocre, Middling, Moderate, Ordinary.
A	V	E	R	N	A	L	Infernal, Hellish, Pandemoniac, Plutonian, Stygian.
A	V	E	R	R	E	D	Vouched, Verified, Affirmed, Alleged, Claimed, Declare, Asserted.
A	V	E	R	T	E	D	Prevented, Turned, Deflected, Diverted, Veered, Forestalled, Precluded, Warded.
A	V	I	A	T	E	D	Flew or navigated an airplane.
A	V	I	A	T	O	R	Aeroplane pilot.
A	V	I	C	I	D	E	Killing of birds.
A	V	I	D	I	T	Y	Greed, Avirice, Voracity, Eagerness, Affinity.
A	V	O	C	A	D	O	Pear-shaped edible fruit with pulpy flesh.
A	V	O	D	I	R	E	Wood of tropical West African tree.
A	V	O	I	D	E	D	Eluded, Escaped, Ducked, Eschewed, Evaded, Shunned.
A	V	O	W	A	N	T	Defendant who justifies taking of goods.
A	V	O	W	I	N	G	Owning, Admitting, Asserting, Declaiming, Professing, Protesting, Allowing, Conceding.

1	2	3	4	5	6	7	Definition
A	W	A	I	T	E	D	Tarried, Expected eagerly, Hoped for, Looked for.
A	W	A	K	I	N	G	Rousing, Bestirring, Knowing.
A	W	A	R	D	E	D	Bestowed, Honoured, Decorated, Allotted, Assigned, Endowed.
A	W	A	R	D	E	R	One that awards.
A	W	A	V	I	N	G	Fluttering.
A	W	E	L	E	S	S	Brave, Bold, Dauntless, Fearless, Intrepid, Valiant, Courageous, Unafraid.
A	W	E	S	O	M	E	Awe-inspiring, Dreadful, Awful, Fearsome, Deeply reverent.
A	W	F	U	L	L	Y	Very, Extremely, Greatly, Hugely, Much, Dreadfully.
A	W	K	W	A	R	D	Clumsy, Gawky, Ungainly, Inept, Inconvenient, Embarrassing, Graceless, Unfortunate.
A	W	L	W	O	R	T	Aquatic plant.
A	W	N	L	E	S	S	Without bristles.
A	X	I	A	L	L	Y	Relating to an axis.
A	X	I	L	L	A	R	Axillary part as vein, nerve or feather.
A	X	L	E	B	O	X	Automobile part.
A	X	O	L	O	T	L	Larval salamander.
A	Z	E	L	A	I	C	Crystalline acid from castor oil.
A	Z	E	L	A	T	E	Salt of azelaic acid.
A	Z	I	L	I	A	N	Pre-Neolithic.
A	Z	I	M	U	T	H	Arc of horizon.
A	Z	T	E	C	A	N	Relating to Aztec people or language.
A	Z	U	L	E	N	E	Blue or green hydrocarbons.
A	Z	U	R	I	N	E	Mineral of translucent pale blue smithsonite.
A	Z	U	R	E	A	N	Sky-blue.
A	Z	U	R	I	T	E	Mineral of blue basic carbonate of copper.
A	Z	Y	G	O	U	S	One, Single, Not in pairs.

B

1	2	3	4	5	6	7	Definition
B	A	A	L	I	S	M	Idolatry.
B	A	A	L	I	T	E	Adherent of baalism.
B	A	B	B	L	E	D	Chattered, Gabbled, Jabbered, Prattled, Jawed, Yammered, Clacked.
B	A	B	B	L	E	R	Bird having loud chattering notes.
B	A	B	U	I	N	A	Female baboon.
B	A	B	Y	I	S	H	Infantile, Childish, Immature, Puerile, Pre-kindergarten.
B	A	C	C	A	R	A	Baccarat, Card game played in casinos.
B	A	C	C	A	T	E	Bearing berry, Pulpy.
B	A	C	C	H	I	C	Revelry, Carousing, Drunkenness.
B	A	C	C	H	U	S	God of wine.
B	A	C	I	L	L	I	Microbes, Bacteria, Long slender wingless stick insects.
B	A	C	K	I	N	G	Auspices, Patronage, Sponsorship, Aid, Support, Assistance, Abetting, Championship.
B	A	C	K	L	O	G	Stockpile, Store, Reservoir, Reserve, Hoard, Accumulation, Inventory.
B	A	C	K	O	F	F	To reverse direction.
B	A	C	K	O	U	T	Withdraw.
B	A	C	K	S	A	W	Short fine-toothed saw.
B	A	C	K	S	E	T	Setback, Check, Reversal, Reverse.
B	A	C	T	R	I	S	Large genus of tropical American spiny palms.
B	A	D	D	I	S	H	Inferior.
B	A	D	L	A	N	D	Waste, Barren, Desert, Wilderness.
B	A	D	N	E	S	S	Evil, Wickedness, Immoral, Sinful, Viciousness.
B	A	F	F	L	E	D	Frustrated, Balked, Beaten, Circumvented, Foiled, Ruined, Thwarted, Mystified.
B	A	F	F	L	E	R	One that baffles.
B	A	G	A	S	S	E	Crushed juiceless remains of milled sugar cane.
B	A	G	G	A	G	E	Trunks, Luggage, Suitcases, Belongings, Wanton, Hussy, Slut, Strumpet.
B	A	G	G	A	L	A	Two-masted trading vessel used in Indian Ocean.
B	A	G	G	I	N	G	Coarse fabric, Filtration through a bag.
B	A	G	P	I	P	E	Musical instrument with melody and drone pipes kept inflated by wind.
B	A	I	L	I	F	F	Sheriff's deputy, Chief officer, Overseer.
B	A	I	L	I	N	G	Confining, Releasing.
B	A	I	T	I	N	G	Molesting, Heckling, Tormenting, Badgering, Hectoring, Luring, Enticing, Seducing.
B	A	K	E	O	U	T	Protracted heating for removing moisture or gas.
B	A	K	L	A	V	A	Dessert of pastry, nuts and honey.
B	A	L	A	N	C	E	Equilibrium, Pose, Symmetry, Harmony, Proportion, Compensate, Outweigh, Redeem.
B	A	L	A	N	U	S	Barnacles.
B	A	L	C	O	N	Y	Gallery, Loggia, Veranda, Piazza, Porch, Portico, Stoop, Overhang.
B	A	L	D	E	S	T	Barest, Plainest, Nudest.
B	A	L	D	I	S	H	Relating to bald, Loss of hair.

1	2	3	4	5	6	7	
B	A	L	D	R	I	C	Richly ornamented sword belt.
B	A	L	E	F	U	L	Sinister, Malignant, Ominous, Fateful, Ill-boding, Harmful, Evil, Noxious.
B	A	L	I	S	T	A	Ancient military engine in form of crossbow.
B	A	L	K	I	N	G	Swerving, Frustrating, Baffling, Foiling, Thwarting, Declining, Refusing, Recoiling.
B	A	L	L	A	D	E	Elaborate musical setting of ballad.
B	A	L	L	A	S	T	Stability, Poise, Steady, Aggregate, Burden Load, Stabilize.
B	A	L	L	B	O	Y	Tennis court attendant who retrieves balls for players.
B	A	L	L	I	N	G	Calibrated in accordance with Balling scale.
B	A	L	L	I	U	M	Wall surrounding keep of fortification.
B	A	L	L	O	O	N	Aerostat without a propelling system, Sphere of light material filled with air.
B	A	L	M	I	L	Y	In a soothing way.
B	A	L	N	E	A	L	Relating to bathing.
B	A	L	O	N	E	Y	Nonsense, Bunkum, Bosh, Bunk, Hogwash, Rot, Rubbish, Horsefeathers.
B	A	L	S	A	M	Y	Like balsam in fragrance.
B	A	M	B	I	N	O	C..d, Infant.
B	A	N	B	U	R	Y	Cake filled with currants and raisins.
B	A	N	D	A	G	E	Strip of fabric used to cover a wound.
B	A	N	D	A	N	A	Large silk handkerchief.
B	A	N	D	B	O	X	Cylindrical box of pasteboard for holding light articles of attire.
B	A	N	D	E	A	U	Band to restrain hair.
B	A	N	D	I	E	D	Exchanged, Discussed, Tossed, Interchanged, Agitated, Retorted, Pitched.
B	A	N	D	I	N	G	Uniting, Confederating.
B	A	N	D	L	E	T	A little band or flat moulding about a column.
B	A	N	D	O	R	E	Ancient bass stringed instrument resembling guitar.
B	A	N	D	R	O	L	Ribbonlike scroll bearing inscription.
B	A	N	D	S	A	W	Saw in form of endless belt.
B	A	N	E	F	U	L	Pernicious, Deadly, Noxious, Pestilent, Ominous, Dire, Threatening, Apocalyptic.
B	A	N	G	I	N	G	Huge, Whopping, Clattering, Overwhelming, Blasting, Bashing, Crashing, Smashing.
B	A	N	K	I	N	G	Relying, Building, Calculating, Trusting, Depending.
B	A	N	K	S	I	A	Genus of Australian trees or shrubs.
B	A	N	N	I	N	G	Forbidding, Proscribing, Barring, Cursing.
B	A	N	N	O	C	K	Unleavened bread of oat and barley flour.
B	A	N	Q	U	E	T	Dinner, Feast, Regale, Spread, Ceremonious meal.
B	A	N	S	H	E	E	Female spirit warning approaching death by wailing.
B	A	N	T	E	N	G	Malayan wild ox.
B	A	N	T	I	N	G	Slimming diet omitting sweets and carbohydrates. Sailing dug-out of Johore.
B	A	P	T	I	S	M	Christening by immersion or sprinkling.
B	A	P	T	I	S	T	Member of Protestant sect.
B	A	P	T	I	Z	E	Christen, Immerse, Sprinkle, Asperse, Name, Denominate, Designate, Style.
B	A	R	B	A	R	Y	North African.
B	A	R	B	A	T	E	Bearded, Bearing long stiff hairs.
B	A	R	B	E	L	L	Bar with adjustable weighted disks used for exercise.
B	A	R	B	I	N	G	Oblique cutting to form sharp points when forming barbed wire.
B	A	R	B	O	L	A	Decoration made from plastic paste.
B	A	R	B	U	L	E	Minute barb, Small beard.
B	A	R	D	A	S	H	Homosexual male.
B	A	R	G	A	I	N	Steal, Contract, Agreement, Bond, Haggle, Higgle, Trade, Exchange.
B	A	R	I	L	L	A	Seaweed.
B	A	R	I	R	O	N	Wrought iron in the form of bars.
B	A	R	K	H	A	N	Long crescent shaped sandhill.
B	A	R	K	I	N	G	Vocal noise of guard dog, Peeling.
B	A	R	M	A	I	D	Female bartender.
B	A	R	M	K	I	N	Outer ramparts of castle.
B	A	R	N	I	N	G	Storing, Garnering, Hoarding.
B	A	R	N	O	W	L	Common owl important factor in rodent control.
B	A	R	O	N	E	T	Young or lesser baron.
B	A	R	O	Q	U	E	Rococo, Whimsical, Odd, Ornate, Flamboyant, Florid, Rich, Luscious.
B	A	R	R	A	C	K	Lodging for soldiers, Jeer, Shout, Booing.
B	A	R	R	A	G	E	Bombardment, Broadside, FUsillade, Hail, Salvo, Volley, Embankment, Dam.
B	A	R	R	I	C	O	Small keg.
B	A	R	R	I	E	R	Bar, Barricade, Blockade, Fierce, Roadblock, Stop, Wall, Railing.
B	A	R	R	I	N	G	Except, Bar, But, Excluding, Saving, Save, Aside from.
B	A	R	R	U	L	Y	Horizontal bars relating to heraldry.
B	A	R	S	H	O	E	Special horseshoe.
B	A	R	W	O	O	D	Hard red dyewood from tropical African tree.
B	A	R	Y	T	E	S	White, yellow or colourless mineral sometimes resembling marble.
B	A	R	Y	T	I	C	Relating to any of several compounds of barium.

1	2	3	4	5	6	7	
B	A	S	B	L	U	E	Blue stocking.
B	A	S	C	A	R	T	Trolley in supermarket for use of shoppers.
B	A	S	C	U	L	E	Balanced drawbridge.
B	A	S	E	B	O	X	Unit of area for tin plate.
B	A	S	E	N	J	I	African breed of dog that hardly ever barks.
B	A	S	H	F	U	L	Self-conscious, Diffident, Timorous, Shy, Coy, Demure, Timid.
B	A	S	H	I	N	G	Belting, Cracking, Smacking, Whacking, Hitting, Beating, Slugging, Coshing.
B	A	S	H	L	Y	K	Protective hood worn by Russian military.
B	A	S	I	L	A	R	Situated at the base.
B	A	S	I	L	I	C	Of great importance, Kingly, Royal.
B	A	S	I	N	E	D	Enclosed in a basin.
B	A	S	I	N	E	T	Perambulator, Basinet, Helmet, Baby carriage.
B	A	S	K	I	N	G	Sunning, Wallowing, Indulging, Luxuriating, Rolling, Revelling.
B	A	S	S	O	O	N	Tenor or bass double reed woodwind instrument.
B	A	S	T	A	R	D	Chance child, Love child, Baseborn, Natural child, Illegitimate, Fatherless, Spurious.
B	A	S	T	I	L	E	Prison, Jail.
B	A	S	T	I	N	G	Coarse stitching, Covering of cooking food with liquid.
B	A	S	T	I	O	N	Projecting part of fortification.
B	A	T	A	T	A	S	Sweet potatoes.
B	A	T	H	B	U	N	Round bun of sweet yeast dough containing raisins, currants, eggs and butter.
B	A	T	H	I	N	G	Act or sport of one who bathes, Giving/having a bath.
B	A	T	H	M	A	T	Mat of washable material used in bathroom.
B	A	T	H	M	I	C	Relating to Bathmism.
B	A	T	H	Y	A	L	Relating to deeper parts of the ocean.
B	A	T	I	S	T	E	Fine soft sheer fabric.
B	A	T	S	M	A	N	Cricketer, One who guides incoming aircraft.
B	A	T	T	E	R	Y	Assault, Cells to produce electrical current, Artillery, Cages for fattening poultry, Series.
B	A	T	T	I	N	G	Wadding for quilting, Cricket.
B	A	T	T	L	E	D	Embattled.
B	A	T	T	L	E	R	One who is supplied with provisions on account whilst living at Oxford university.
B	A	T	T	U	R	E	-Alluvial, Land between low water stage and a levee.
B	A	U	L	K	E	D	Balked, Jibbed, Shied.
B	A	U	S	O	N	D	Badger.
B	A	U	X	I	T	E	Impure mixture that is principal source of aluminium.
B	A	W	C	O	C	K	A fine fellow.
B	A	W	D	I	L	Y	Lewdly, Obscenely, Indecently, Smuttily.
B	A	W	L	I	N	G	Howling, Wailing, Yowling, Yelling.
B	A	Y	O	N	E	T	Steel blade made to attach to muzzle end of shoulder arm.
B	A	Y	S	A	L	T	Solar salt.
B	A	Y	T	R	E	E	Laurel.
B	A	Y	W	O	O	D	Mahogany.
B	A	Z	I	G	A	R	Gypsylike nomadic Muslim people in India.
B	A	Z	O	O	K	A	Light portable weapon.
B	E	A	D	I	N	G	Material that is beaded, Moulding, Decorative trimming.
B	E	A	M	I	L	Y	In a beamy manner.
B	E	A	M	I	N	G	Radiant, Gleaming, Bright, Unreserved joy.
B	E	A	N	F	L	Y	Small dark fly that is a pest of cultivated crops in Australia.
B	E	A	R	D	E	D	Growth of hair, Barbed.
B	E	A	R	D	I	E	Australian cod-like fish, Shaggy collie-like dog.
B	E	A	R	I	N	G	Carriage, Behaviour, Relation, Connection, Influence, Purport, Significance, Supporting.
B	E	A	R	I	S	H	Uncouth, Cranky, Crotchery, Waspish, Declining, Boorish.
B	E	A	S	T	L	Y	Abominable, Brutish, Animal, Bestial, Brutal, Swinish, Disgusting, Distasteful.
B	E	A	T	I	F	Y	Make supremely happy, Canonize.
B	E	A	T	I	N	G	Defeat, Debacle, Drubbing, Licking, Overthrow, Rout, Thrashing.
B	E	A	T	N	I	K	Person of unconventional behaviour and dress.
B	E	B	E	E	R	U	Tropical S. American evergreen tree.
B	E	C	A	U	S	E	As, Being, Considering, For, Seeing, Since, Now, Whereas.
B	E	C	H	A	R	M	Captive, Fascinate, Under a charm.
B	E	C	L	O	U	D	Obscure, Darken, Dim, Eclipse, Fog, Obfuscate, Befuddle, Confuse.
B	E	C	O	M	E	S	Arrives, Graces, Adorns, Befits, Happens.
B	E	D	D	I	N	G	Storing of ores, Adapted, to produce massed effect.
B	E	D	E	A	U	X	System of working and paying of wages by results.
B	E	D	E	M	A	N	Professional prayer, Licensed beggar.
B	E	D	E	V	I	L	Worry, Annoy, Harass, Harry, Pester, Plague, Tantalize, Tease.
B	E	D	E	W	E	D	Sprinkled with dew.
B	E	D	F	A	S	T	Bedridden.
B	E	D	G	O	W	N	Night gown.

1	2	3	4	5	6	7	Definition
B	E	D	I	G	H	T	Equip, Array, Bedeck.
B	E	D	I	Z	E	N	Vulgarly and gaudily dressed.
B	E	D	M	A	T	E	Wife, Mistress, Concubine.
B	E	D	O	U	I	N	Nomadic Arab.
B	E	D	P	O	S	T	Carved support of bed.
B	E	D	R	E	S	T	Continuous confinement to bed.
B	E	D	R	O	C	K	Nadir, Minimum, Basis, Foundation, Root, Substratum, Footing, Under-pinning.
B	E	D	R	O	O	M	Room primarily intended for sleeping.
B	E	D	R	O	P	S	Sprinkled with drops.
B	E	D	S	I	D	E	Conducted at bedside, Light and entertaining literature.
B	E	D	S	O	R	E	Ulceration of tissue caused by prolonged pressure.
B	E	D	T	I	C	K	Tick.
B	E	D	T	I	M	E	Time to go to bed.
B	E	D	W	A	R	D	Towards bed.
B	E	D	W	E	L	L	To inhabit.
B	E	E	B	I	R	D	Birds reputed to eat bees, Fly catchers.
B	E	E	C	H	E	N	Made of beech.
B	E	E	F	T	E	A	Beverage consisting of hot water and meat extract.
B	E	E	G	L	U	E	Propolis, Resinous waxy substance.
B	E	E	H	I	V	E	Home for bees.
B	E	E	L	I	N	E	Straightest, quickest course.
B	E	E	M	O	T	H	Larva of moth that feeds on beeswax and destroys hive.
B	E	E	R	I	L	Y	Maudlin or muddled as if inebriated.
B	E	E	S	W	A	X	Wax produced by honey bee.
B	E	E	T	L	E	D	Scuttled like a beetle.
B	E	E	V	I	S	H	Resembling or suggesting cattle.
B	E	E	W	E	E	D	Any of several bee plants.
B	E	E	Y	A	R	D	Apiary.
B	E	G	G	A	R	S	Impoverish, Reduces to inadequacy.
B	E	G	G	A	R	Y	Poverty, Destitution, Impoverishment, Indigence, Need, Penury, Want, Cadging.
B	E	G	G	I	N	G	Craving, Entreating, Imploring, Invoking, Pleading, Praying, Supplicating, Beseeching.
B	E	G	H	A	R	D	Member of religious order.
B	E	G	L	O	O	M	To make gloomy.
B	E	G	O	N	I	A	Large genus of succulent herbs.
B	E	G	R	I	M	E	Soil, Dirty, Foul, Grime, Smirch, Smudge, Tarnish, Sully.
B	E	G	U	I	L	E	Manipulate, Finesse, Jockey, Deceive, Betray, Bluff, Mislead. To exploit.
B	E	G	U	I	N	E	Woman member of religious order, Rhumba like dance.
B	E	H	A	V	E	D	Comported, Conducted, Disported, Functioned, Operated, Performed, Worked.
B	E	H	E	N	I	C	Crystalline fatty acid from fat, oil or wax.
B	E	H	O	O	V	E	Require, Fitting and proper, Be obliged.
B	E	J	E	W	E	L	Ornament with jewels, Begem.
B	E	K	N	A	V	E	To call a knave.
B	E	L	A	B	O	R	Beat, Batter, Buffet, Pound, Pummel, Thrash, Wallop, Assail.
B	E	L	A	T	E	D	Tardily, Behindhand, Late, Overdue, Unpunctual, Old-fashioned, Antiquated, Archaic.
B	E	L	A	Y	E	D	Fastened, Held, Waylaid, Disregarded, Stopped, Quitted.
B	E	L	C	H	E	D	Erupted, Gushed, Emitted, Ejaculated, Disgorged, Spewed, Expelled, Ejected.
B	E	L	C	H	E	R	Multicoloured handkerchief worn about the neck.
B	E	L	E	P	E	R	Affect with leprosy.
B	E	L	G	A	R	D	A loving look.
B	E	L	G	I	A	N	Of Belgium.
B	E	L	I	B	E	L	Calumniate, Libel, Slander.
B	E	L	I	E	V	E	Accept, Feel, Consider, Credit, Think, Understand, Reckon, Take.
B	E	L	L	H	O	P	One who does messenger service.
B	E	L	L	I	E	D	Possessing a large pronounced belly, Convex, Rounded or bulging surface.
B	E	L	L	I	N	G	Crying or bellowing of animals.
B	E	L	L	J	A	R	Glass vessel to enclose a vacuum.
B	E	L	L	M	A	N	Town crier or night watchman.
B	E	L	L	O	T	A	Acorn of gambel oak.
B	E	L	L	O	W	S	Instrument or machine that draws in and expels air forcibly.
B	E	L	O	V	E	D	Sweetheart, Honey, Girl friend, Boyfriend, Lover, Steady, Favourite, Dear.
B	E	L	T	A	N	E	May day festival.
B	E	L	T	I	N	G	Beating, Blasting, Clobbering, Smashing, Smacking, Thrashing, Slamming, Socking.
B	E	L	Y	I	N	G	Rejecting, Calumniating, Contradicting, Misrepresenting, Counterfeiting.
B	E	M	A	Z	E	D	Bewildered, Stupified.
B	E	M	I	R	E	D	Muddy, Claggy, Miry, Oozy, Soiled, Besmirched.
B	E	M	O	U	T	H	To talk bombastically.
B	E	M	U	S	E	D	Dazed, Benumbed, Paralyzed, Stunned, Stupefied, Perplexed, Puzzled.

1	2	3	4	5	6	7	
B	E	N	C	H	E	R	One that sits on an official bench (judge).
B	E	N	D	I	N	G	Crooked, Curving, Devious, Twisting, Inclining.
B	E	N	D	L	E	T	A narrow band in heraldry.
B	E	N	E	A	T	H	Below, Under, Underneath, Inferior, Subordinate, Beyond, Concealed.
B	E	N	E	F	I	C	Having or making a favourable or benificent, Influence.
B	E	N	E	L	U	X	Belgium, Netherlands and Luxembourg.
B	E	N	G	A	L	I	Relating to Bengal.
B	E	N	I	G	H	T	Obscure, Deprive of light, Envelop in darkness.
B	E	N	I	S	O	N	Benediction, Blessing.
B	E	N	O	T	E	D	To annotate excessively or absurdly.
B	E	N	T	E	A	K	Wood of an East Indian tree.
B	E	N	T	H	O	N	Plankton.
B	E	N	T	H	O	S	Organisms that live at bottom of bodies of water.
B	E	N	Z	E	N	E	Colourless volatile flammable toxic liquid.
B	E	N	Z	O	I	N	Frankincense of Java, A genus of aromatic shrubs.
B	E	N	Z	O	Y	L	Radical of benzoic acid.
B	E	P	A	I	N	T	Paint, gaudily, Smear with paint.
B	E	P	A	P	E	R	Cover with paper, Encumber with papers.
B	E	Q	U	E	S	T	Legacy, Devise, Inheritance.
B	E	R	A	K	A	H	Benediction, Blessing.
B	E	R	A	T	E	D	Scolded, Reviled, Upbraided, Nagged, Chided, Criticized, Reproached.
B	E	R	E	A	V	E	Deprive, Disinherit, Dispossess, Divest, Lose, Oust, Rob, Despoil.
B	E	R	H	Y	M	E	To lampoon in rhyming verse.
B	E	R	L	I	N	E	Enclosed automobile body with glass partition behind driver.
B	E	R	R	I	E	D	Carrying berries, Baccate, Shellfish bearing eggs.
B	E	R	S	E	R	K	Frenzied, Crazed, Mad, Wild, Violent, Erratic behaviour, Ancient Scandinavian warrior.
B	E	R	T	H	E	D	Moored, Situated, Appointed, Placed, Posted.
B	E	S	E	E	C	H	Beg, Appeal, Crave, Entreat, Implore, Importune, Invoke, Plead.
B	E	S	H	R	E	W	Curse.
B	E	S	I	D	E	S	Also, Additionally, Along, Furthermore, Likewise, More, Moreover, Again.
B	E	S	I	E	G	E	Beleaguer, Beset, Blockade, Invest, Importune, Assail, Encircle, Assault.
B	E	S	L	A	V	E	Enslave.
B	E	S	M	E	A	R	Smear, Bedaub, Plaster, Smudge, Taint, Defile, Sully, Stain.
B	E	S	M	O	K	E	Soil with smoke, Cure by smoking (bacon).
B	E	S	P	A	W	L	To spatter with or as if with saliva.
B	E	S	P	A	K	E	Reserve (book in library) Book (play for benefit perrformance) Address, Accost, Ask, Desire.
B	E	S	P	O	K	E	Custom-made wearing apparel, Engaged to be married.
B	E	S	T	A	I	N	Stain, Blot, Discolour, Smut.
B	E	S	T	E	A	D	Placed, Vested, Avail, Assistance, Help.
B	E	S	T	I	A	L	Brutish, Animal, Beastly, Brutal, Swinish, Brute, Ferine, Barbarous.
B	E	S	T	I	N	G	Conquering, Mastering, Overcoming, Defeating, Winning, Surpassing, Outshining.
B	E	S	T	M	A	N	Principal groomsman.
B	E	S	T	R	E	W	Broadcast, Disject, Disseminate, Scatter, Sow, Strew.
B	E	S	T	R	I	D	Mounted, Straddled, Spanned.
B	E	T	A	I	N	E	Crystalline sweet tasting ammonium salt that occurs in beet juice.
B	E	T	A	K	E	N	Granted, Occupied, Committed, Departed.
B	E	T	H	I	N	K	Remember, Cite, Recall, Recollect, Remind, Reminisce, Retain, Revive.
B	E	T	H	U	M	B	Wear or soil as if with thumbs.
B	E	T	H	U	M	P	To beat or pelt soundly.
B	E	T	I	D	E	D	Befell, Forebode, Presaged, Happened, Chanced, Occurred.
B	E	T	I	M	E	S	Seasonally, Early, Soon, Speedily, Occasionally, Timely, Prematurely, Sometimes.
B	E	T	I	T	L	E	To give or call by a title.
B	E	T	O	K	E	N	Indicate, Foreshow, Presage, Announce, Attest, Witness, Auger, Portend.
B	E	T	R	O	T	H	Affiance, Pledge, Intend, Plight, Contract, Espouse.
B	E	T	T	I	N	G	Wagering, Staking, Calling, Raising, Laying.
B	E	T	T	O	N	G	Leaping rat kangaroo.
B	E	T	U	L	O	L	Crystalline (camphor) acid obtained from birch tree.
B	E	T	W	E	E	N	Among, Betwixt, Time, space or interval that separates.
B	E	T	W	I	X	T	Between, Midway position.
B	E	V	E	L	E	D	Bevelled, Edge replaced by sloping plane.
B	E	V	E	L	E	R	One that smooths edges of glass with abrasive wheel.
B	E	W	I	T	C	H	Charm, Enchant, Spell, Attract, Allure, Captivate, Fascinate, Magnetize.
B	E	Z	I	Q	U	E	Card game.
B	I	A	C	U	R	U	Powerfully astringent root of S. American herb.
B	I	A	L	A	T	E	Having two wings.
B	I	A	N	C	H	I	Political faction in Tuscany, Italy.
B	I	A	S	I	N	G	Influencing, Prejudicing, Prepossessing.

(255)

1	2	3	4	5	6	7	
B	I	A	U	R	A	L	Involving function of both ears, Binaural.
B	I	A	X	I	A	L	Having two axis.
B	I	B	B	E	R	Y	Addiction to drinking.
B	I	B	C	O	C	K	Stopcock, Faucet with bent-down nozzle.
B	I	B	E	L	O	T	Trinket, Small household ornament.
B	I	B	E	R	O	N	Drinking vessel with elongated spout.
B	I	B	L	I	S	M	Adherence to the Bible as sole rule of faith.
B	I	B	L	I	S	T	One who practices biblism, Biblical scholar.
B	I	C	H	O	R	D	Having two strings in unison for one note.
B	I	C	O	L	O	R	Printed in two colours.
B	I	C	O	R	N	E	Animal with 2 Horns.
B	I	C	Y	C	L	E	Two wheeled vehicle propelled by rider's feet on pedals.
B	I	D	D	E	R	Y	Pewter used in India for ware inlaid with gold or silver.
B	I	D	D	I	N	G	Commanding, Charging, Dictating, Ordering, Inviting, Asking, Warning, Instructing.
B	I	F	F	I	N	S	Dried apples.
B	I	F	I	D	L	Y	Divided into two equal parts.
B	I	F	I	L	A	R	Double-threaded.
B	I	F	O	C	A	L	Eyeglass lens that has two parts to correct near vision and distant vision.
B	I	G	E	N	E	R	Hybrid.
B	I	G	G	E	S	T	Largest, Greatest.
B	I	G	G	I	S	H	Comparatively big.
B	I	G	H	O	R	N	Wild sheep.
B	I	G	N	E	S	S	State of being big.
B	I	G	O	T	E	D	Illiberal, Hidebound, Intolerant, Narrow-minded, Brassbound, Dogmatic, Small-minded.
B	I	G	O	T	R	Y	Obstinate intolerant zealotry.
B	I	L	B	O	A	S	Finely tempered swords.
B	I	L	B	O	E	S	Finely tempered sword.
B	I	L	I	A	R	Y	Relating to bile ducts or gall bladder.
B	I	L	I	O	U	S	Affected by nausea.
B	I	L	K	I	N	G	Defrauding, Eluding, Disappointing, Cheating, Thwarting, Circumventing, Baffling, Foiling.
B	I	L	L	I	N	G	Invoicing, Presenting, Promoting.
B	I	L	L	I	O	N	A large number.
B	I	L	L	M	A	N	One that posts advertising bills, Billposter.
B	I	L	L	O	W	Y	Surging, Undulating.
B	I	L	O	B	E	D	Divided into two lobes.
B	I	L	T	O	N	G	Dried meat.
B	I	M	A	N	A	L	Two-handed, Ambidextrous.
B	I	M	E	T	A	L	Composed of two different metals.
B	I	N	D	E	R	Y	Place where books are bound.
B	I	N	D	I	N	G	Obligatory, Duty, Responsibility, Conformity, Fabric, Ingredient, Fastening for books.
B	I	N	N	I	N	G	Stowing and aging of bottled wine in a bin.
B	I	N	O	D	A	L	Having two nodes.
B	I	O	C	I	D	E	Pesticide.
B	I	O	G	E	N	Y	Development of life from preexisting life.
B	I	O	L	I	T	H	Rock of organic origin.
B	I	O	L	O	G	Y	Ecology, Science of life.
B	I	O	M	A	S	S	Amount of living matter in a form.
B	I	O	N	T	I	C	Individual.
B	I	O	T	I	T	E	Generally black or dark green form of mica.
B	I	O	T	O	P	E	Uniform habitat and animal and plant population.
B	I	O	T	Y	P	E	Organisms sharing specified genotype.
B	I	O	Z	O	N	E	Fossilfied organisms.
B	I	P	E	D	A	L	Having two feet, Biped.
B	I	P	L	A	N	E	Two-winged aeroplane.
B	I	P	R	I	S	M	Obtuse-angle prism.
B	I	R	C	H	E	D	Caned, Whipped, Flogged.
B	I	R	C	H	E	N	Relating to birch.
B	I	R	D	E	Y	E	Spot resembling an eye in flower's centre.
B	I	R	D	I	N	G	Snaring.
B	I	R	D	M	A	N	Fowler, Ornithologist, Aviator, Airman.
B	I	R	E	T	T	A	Square clerical cap of colours to indicate rank.
B	I	R	L	I	N	G	Sport of log-rolling.
B	I	R	L	I	N	N	Gaelic barge or galley.
B	I	S	C	U	I	T	Hard or crisp dry baked product, Cookie, Cracker.
B	I	S	M	I	T	E	Bismuth trioxide.
B	I	S	M	U	T	H	Metallic element.
B	I	S	T	O	R	T	Plants with twisted roots used as astringents.
B	I	T	T	E	R	N	Small or medium sized heron. Liquid remaining after salt has crystallized.

1	2	3	4	5	6	7	
B	I	T	T	E	R	S	Spirituous liquor.
B	I	T	T	I	N	G	Part of key that activates the lock.
B	I	T	T	I	U	M	Small marine snails.
B	I	T	T	O	C	K	A small bit.
B	I	T	U	M	E	N	Asphalt, Pitch, Tar.
B	I	T	Y	P	I	C	Consisting of two species.
B	I	V	A	L	V	E	Shell of mollusk having two valves.
B	I	V	O	U	A	C	Encampment under little or no shelter.
B	I	Z	A	R	R	E	Strange, Fantastic, Grotesgue, Curious, Outlandish, Peculiar, Unusual, Weird.
B	L	A	B	B	E	D	Chattered, Babbled, Chatted, Gabbled, Jabbered, Tattled, Revealed, Disclosed.
B	L	A	B	B	E	R	Indiscreet, Excessive, Nonsensical talk, Chatterbox, Prattler, Sneak, Jabberer.
B	L	A	C	K	E	D	Obscured, Inked, Fouled, Soiled, Squalid, Sabled.
B	L	A	C	K	E	N	Malign, Asperse, Calumniate, Defame, Decry, Slander, Smear, Vilify.
B	L	A	C	K	E	R	Darker, More sullen.
B	L	A	C	K	E	Y	Blackie, Blackbird, Black duck, Canadian goose.
B	L	A	C	K	L	Y	In a black manner.
B	L	A	D	D	E	R	Organ for collection of urine, Flexible and elastic container.
B	L	A	D	I	N	G	Set of blades in a turbine.
B	L	A	M	I	N	G	Censuring, Reproaching, Condemning, Accusing, Criticizing, Denouncing.
B	L	A	N	D	L	Y	Mildly, Affably, Smoothly, Balmy, Urbanely.
B	L	A	N	K	E	T	Cover, Crown, Overcast, Insulating, Floral display, Enclose, Suppress, Extinguish.
B	L	A	N	K	L	Y	Vacously, Utterly, Completely, Vacantly.
B	L	A	R	I	N	G	Strident, Loud, Piercing, Roaring, Stentorian.
B	L	A	R	N	E	Y	Coax, Cajole, Wheedle, Flattery, Adulation, Incense, Oil, Banter.
B	L	A	S	T	E	D	Withered, Blighted, Ruined, Confounded, Cursed, Damned, Blamed, Blessed.
B	L	A	S	T	E	R	One whose work is blasting with explosive, Golf club.
B	L	A	T	A	N	T	Vociferous, Boisterous, Gaudy, Brazen, Garish, Tawdry, Shameless, Impudent.
B	L	A	T	H	E	R	Babble, Blabber, Blether, Drivel, Gabble, Prate, Twaddle, Prattle.
B	L	A	T	T	E	R	Babble, Blabber, Blether, Drivel, Gabble, Prate, Twaddle, Prattle.
B	L	A	W	O	R	T	Cornflower, Harebell.
B	L	A	Z	I	N	G	Burning, Alight, Conflagrant, Fiery, Flaming, Impassioned, Ardent, Fervent.
B	L	E	A	K	E	R	More exposed, Barer.
B	L	E	A	K	L	Y	Cheerlessly, Drearily, Gloomily, Grimly, Dreary.
B	L	E	E	D	E	R	Haemophiliac, Bloodletter.
B	L	E	M	I	S	H	Injure, Damage, Harm, Impair, Imperfection, Defect, Flaw, Scar.
B	L	E	N	D	E	D	Mixed, Mingled, Amalgamated, Compounded, Fused, Integrated, Unified, Arranged.
B	L	E	N	D	E	R	Machine or device by which materials are blended.
B	L	E	S	B	O	K	S. African antelope.
B	L	E	S	S	E	D	Holy, Hallowed, Extolled, Sanctified, Glorified, Sacred, Cursed, Perfect.
B	L	E	T	H	E	R	Blather, Voluble, Foolish or nonsensical talk.
B	L	E	T	T	E	D	Ripened fruit.
B	L	E	W	I	T	S	Edible mushroom.
B	L	I	G	H	T	Y	One's native land usually England.
B	L	I	N	D	E	D	Stone-blind, Dulled, Sightless, Intoxicated, Bedazzled, Fooled.
B	L	I	N	D	E	R	Blinker, Obstruction to sight.
B	L	I	N	D	L	Y	Without reason or understanding, Mechanically.
B	L	I	N	K	E	D	Twinkled, Flickered, Glanced, Peeped, Winked, Bewitched, Ignored, Recognized.
B	L	I	S	T	E	R	Elevation of skin containing watery liquid.
B	L	O	A	T	E	D	Swollen, Distended, Pompous, Arrogant, Important, Pontifical, Stuffy, Puffy.
B	L	O	A	T	E	R	Large fat herring lightly smoked for a short time.
B	L	O	B	B	E	R	Blubber.
B	L	O	C	K	E	D	Stopped, Barricaded, Blocked, Obstructed, Hindered, Impeded, Intercepted.
B	L	O	O	D	E	D	Entirely or largely of pure blood.
B	L	O	O	M	E	D	Flowered, Blossomed, Flushed, Throve, Glowed, Blushed.
B	L	O	O	M	E	R	Boner, Gross error.
B	L	O	S	S	O	M	Bloom, Bud, Flower, Blow, Burgeon, Unfold, Open.
B	L	O	T	C	H	Y	Splotchy, Patchy, Smeary.
B	L	O	T	T	E	D	Stained, Sullied, Discoloured.
B	L	O	T	T	E	R	Blotting pad.
B	L	O	W	F	L	Y	Blue-bottle.
B	L	O	W	G	U	N	Blow pipe.
B	L	O	W	I	N	G	Noise caused by forcible ejection of air, steam or gas.
B	L	O	W	O	U	T	Extinguished, Clear of contents by blowing, Dissipate by blowing.
B	L	O	W	Z	E	D	Blowsy, Dishevelled, Frowzy, Slatternly.
B	L	U	B	B	E	R	Fat of whales and large marine mammals.
B	L	U	C	H	E	R	A shoe.
B	L	U	E	C	A	P	Blue tit.

1	2	3	4	5	6	7	
B	L	U	E	C	U	P	Cornflower.
B	L	U	E	E	Y	E	Honey-eater bird, Aquarium fish.
B	L	U	E	G	U	M	Eucalyptus.
B	L	U	E	I	N	G	Giving something a blue tint.
B	L	U	E	J	A	Y	A common jay.
B	L	U	F	F	E	D	Deceived, Beguiled, Deluded, Misled, Faked, Feigned, Pretended, Simulated.
B	L	U	F	F	E	R	Deceiver.
B	L	U	F	F	L	Y	In a bluff manner.
B	L	U	N	D	E	R	Error, Bungle, Lapse, Mistake, Waste, Dissipate, Stumble, Botch.
B	L	U	N	G	E	R	Mechanical mixer.
B	L	U	N	T	E	D	Dulled, Bluffed, Desensitize, Numbed, Deaden, Weakened, Disabled, Undermined.
B	L	U	N	T	E	R	More outspoken.
B	L	U	N	T	L	Y	In a blunt manner.
B	L	U	R	R	E	D	Smeared, Obscured, Blemished, Sullied, Stained, Dimmed, Darkened, Smudged.
B	L	U	R	T	E	D	Exclaimed, Ejaculated, Cried out, Abrupt impulsive utterance.
B	L	U	S	H	E	D	Coloured, Glowed, Flushed, Reddened, Blossomed, Crimsoned.
B	O	A	R	D	E	D	Lodged, Housed, Domiciled, Put up, Entrain.
B	O	A	R	D	E	R	Paying guest, Animal not worth its keep.
B	O	A	R	I	S	H	Swinish, Cruel, Lecherous.
B	O	A	S	T	E	R	Braggert.
B	O	A	T	I	N	G	An aquatic sport or pastime.
B	O	A	T	M	A	N	Deckhand, Oarsman.
B	O	B	A	D	I	L	Cowardly braggart.
B	O	B	B	E	R	Y	Row, Brawl, Affray, Fracas, Fray, Melee, Ruction.
B	O	B	B	I	N	G	Curtseying.
B	O	B	B	I	S	H	Hearty, In good spirits.
B	O	B	S	L	E	D	Short sled.
B	O	B	S	T	A	Y	Rope, chain or bar extending from stern of ship to end of bowsprit.
B	O	B	T	A	I	L	Curtail, Abbreviate, Deficient.
B	O	C	L	A	N	D	Freehold land.
B	O	D	E	F	U	L	Portentous, Ominous.
B	O	G	B	E	A	N	Plant that grows in bogs.
B	O	G	G	A	R	T	Goblin, Spectre, Ghost, Scarecrow.
B	O	G	G	L	E	D	Balked, Strained, Demurred, Shied, Haggled, Bungled, Blundered, Perplexed.
B	O	G	L	A	N	D	Marsh, Swamp, Fen.
B	O	G	M	O	S	S	Moss of genus Spaghum.
B	O	G	R	U	S	H	Rush of genus Juncus growing in bogs.
B	O	G	Y	M	A	N	Menacing monstrous imaginary figure used in threatening children.
B	O	I	L	I	N	G	Seething, Churning, Fermenting, Simmering, Stewing, Bristling, Racing, Botting.
B	O	L	D	E	S	T	Bravest, Most intrepid, Cheekiest, Most audacious, Smartest.
B	O	L	E	T	U	S	Genus of fungoid, some poisonous, some edible.
B	O	L	I	V	A	R	Monetary unit of Venezuela.
B	O	L	L	A	R	D	Mooring post, Short post to exclude motor traffic.
B	O	L	O	G	N	A	Large moist sausage.
B	O	L	O	N	E	Y	Baloney, Bunkum, Nonsense, False and insincere, Bosh, Rubbish.
B	O	L	S	T	E	R	Support, Prop, Cushion, Long pillow, Brace, Buttress, Uphold, Sustain.
B	O	L	T	I	N	G	Starting, Rushing, Running, Fleeing, Exclaiming, Gulping, Wolfing, Charging.
B	O	M	B	A	R	D	Blitz, Bomb, Cannonade, Shell, Assault, Barrage, Strafe, Strike.
B	O	M	B	A	S	T	Pretentious, Inflated speech or writing, Rant, Rhapsody, Rhetoric.
B	O	M	B	I	N	G	Bombard, To attack with bombs.
B	O	N	A	G	H	T	Tax formerly imposed by Irish chieftains.
B	O	N	A	N	Z	A	Bounty, Something excessively rich, rewarding or lush, Treasure house.
B	O	N	A	S	U	S	Bison or wild ox.
B	O	N	D	A	G	E	Enslavement, Peonage, Serfdom, Servitude, Thralldom, Yoke, Subjugation, Slavery.
B	O	N	D	I	N	G	Electrical interconnection.
B	O	N	D	M	A	N	Peon, Bondslave, Slave, Chattel, Mancipium.
B	O	N	E	A	C	E	Card game.
B	O	N	E	A	G	E	Prehistoric period characterized by use of bone implements.
B	O	N	E	A	S	H	Residue from bones calcined in air used in pottery making.
B	O	N	E	B	E	D	Terrestial or marine strata containing bone or bone fragments.
B	O	N	F	I	R	E	Funeral pyre, Beacon, Fire made of rubbish.
B	O	N	N	I	L	Y	In a pleasing charming manner.
B	O	O	K	I	N	G	Reservation, Order, Engagement or reserved performance.
B	O	O	K	I	S	H	Pedantic, Academic, Book-learned, Scholastic, Studious, High-brow.
B	O	O	K	L	E	T	Brochure, Pamphlet, Paper-covered publication.
B	O	O	K	M	A	N	Bookdealer, Bookseller, Scholar, Bibliopole.
B	O	O	M	I	N	G	In demand, Banging, Resounding, Cracking, Smashing, Prospering.

1	2	3	4	5	6	7	
B	O	O	M	K	I	N	Bumpkin, Boor, Unsophisticated rustic.
B	O	O	R	I	S	H	Churlish, Coarse, Clownish, Ill-bred, Loutish, Lowbred, Uncultured, Unpolished.
B	O	O	S	I	N	G	Tippling, Drinking, Carousing.
B	O	O	S	T	E	D	Raised, Hiked, Increased, Augmented, Expanded, Extended, Promoted, Advertised.
B	O	O	T	L	E	G	Smuggle, Contraband, Moonshine, Blockade, Hooch, Prohibited sales.
B	O	O	Z	I	N	G	Drinking, Guzzling, Toping, Swilling, Tippling, Imbibing, Carousing, Sousing.
B	O	R	A	C	I	C	Boric, Relating to or derived from boron.
B	O	R	A	S	C	A	Poverty, Destitution, Indigence, Need, Penury, Want.
B	O	R	A	Z	O	N	Crystalline boron nitride.
B	O	R	D	A	G	E	Tenure of services of feudal tenant.
B	O	R	D	U	R	E	Border used in heraldry.
B	O	R	E	D	O	M	Ennui, Pall, Tire, Weary, Tedium, Dullness, Afflicted.
B	O	R	N	E	O	L	Crystalline cyclic terpenoid alcohol from camphor.
B	O	R	N	I	T	E	Sulphide of copper and iron.
B	O	R	O	U	G	H	An urban area.
B	O	R	S	T	A	L	A reform school.
B	O	S	C	A	G	E	Growth, Thicket, Undergrowth.
B	O	S	O	M	E	D	Hidden, Kept in the bosom.
B	O	S	Q	U	E	T	Thicket.
B	O	S	S	A	G	E	Projecting pieces of architecture.
B	O	S	S	I	N	G	Supervising, Overseeing, Superintending, Surveying, Controlling.
B	O	S	S	I	S	M	System of political bosses.
B	O	S	W	E	L	L	Biographer, Memoirist.
B	O	T	A	N	I	C	Relating to plants and flowers.
B	O	T	C	H	E	R	One that does bungling makeshift work.
B	O	T	T	E	G	A	Studio, Artist's workshop.
B	O	T	T	I	N	E	A woman's light boot.
B	O	T	T	L	E	D	Kept in a bottle, Restrained.
B	O	T	T	L	E	R	Machine or person that makes and bottles beverages.
B	O	T	T	O	N	Y	Heraldic decoration of cross.
B	O	T	U	L	I	N	Toxin formed by a bacterium.
B	O	U	C	H	O	N	Bushing for timepiece, Plug and fuse assembly of grenade.
B	O	U	D	O	I	R	Woman's dressing room or private sitting-room.
B	O	U	I	L	L	I	Boiled meat.
B	O	U	L	D	E	R	Large rock.
B	O	U	L	T	E	R	Fishing line with many hooks for use on bottom of ocean.
B	O	U	N	C	E	D	Rebounded, Jumped, Hopped, Discharged, Terminated, Intimidated, Bullied, Hectored.
B	O	U	N	C	E	R	Chucker-out, Lie, Falsehood, Misrepresentation, Hyperbole, Overstatement, Prevarication.
B	O	U	N	D	E	D	Finite, Bound, Limited, Articled, Indentured, Apprenticed, Borderd, Edged.
B	O	U	N	D	E	N	Bound, Fastened, Obliged, Beholden, Obligatory.
B	O	U	N	D	E	R	Cad, Ass, Cur, Rotter, Outsider, Man of objectionable character.
B	O	U	Q	U	E	T	Nosegay, Posy, Compliment, Fragrance, Aroma, Perfume, Scent, Spice.
B	O	U	R	B	O	N	Reactionary, Conservative, Royalist, Diehard, Kentucky whisky.
B	O	U	R	D	O	N	Pip-organ stop of droning or buzzing quality, Lowest bell in carillon.
B	O	U	R	R	E	E	Lively old French dance tune.
B	O	V	I	D	A	E	Family of ruminants containing oxen, sheep, goats and true antelopes.
B	O	W	B	A	C	K	Crooked, Hoop-back.
B	O	W	H	A	N	D	Left hand (archery).
B	O	W	L	D	E	R	Boulder, Large rock.
B	O	W	L	E	S	S	Without a bow.
B	O	W	L	I	N	E	A rope for a square sail, Non-slip knot.
B	O	W	L	I	N	G	Any of several games in which balls are rolled.
B	O	W	S	H	O	T	Effective range of bow.
B	O	X	C	A	L	F	Chrome tanned calfskin.
B	O	X	C	O	A	T	Heavy overcoat.
B	O	X	F	I	S	H	Brightly coloured tropical fish.
B	O	X	H	A	U	L	To put a sailing ship on other tack.
B	O	X	H	E	A	D	Printed head as at head of column in ledger.
B	O	X	K	I	T	E	Kite without a tail used in meteorology.
B	O	X	L	I	K	E	Resembling a box in shape.
B	O	X	L	O	O	M	A loom with more than one shuttle.
B	O	X	R	O	O	M	Small room in a house for storing trunks.
B	O	X	T	O	O	L	Tool holder.
B	O	X	T	R	A	P	Trap with baited trigger where box falls over animal.
B	O	X	T	R	E	E	Tree.
B	O	X	W	O	O	D	Hard tough close grained wood of Boxtree.
B	O	X	W	O	R	K	Mineral-aggregate structure.

1	2	3	4	5	6	7	
B	O	Y	C	O	T	T	Ostracize, Combine against person, employer, group of persons or nation.
B	O	Y	H	O	O	D	State of being a boy.
B	R	A	B	B	L	E	Quarrel, Row, Scrap, Squabble, Tiff, Wrangle, Altercation, Dispute.
B	R	A	C	C	A	E	Shapeless trousers worn by ancient Gauls.
B	R	A	C	C	I	O	Italian unit of length.
B	R	A	C	I	N	G	Invigorating, Animating, Exhilarating, Stimulating, Tonic, Vitalizing, Fortifying, Supporting.
B	R	A	C	K	E	N	Large coarse fern.
B	R	A	C	K	E	T	Brace, Lever, Console, Join, Combine, Connect, Link, Relate.
B	R	A	C	T	E	A	Thin metal plate of silver or gold.
B	R	A	D	A	W	L	Awl with chisel edge to make holes for brads or screws.
B	R	A	G	G	E	D	Boasted, Prated, Blustered, Vaunted, Mouthed, Crowed, Swaggered, Strutted.
B	R	A	H	M	A	N	Member of highest caste in India, Intellectual.
B	R	A	I	D	E	D	Adorned with braid, Entwined, Embroidered, Plaited.
B	R	A	I	L	L	E	System of writing in raised dots for use by the blind.
B	R	A	I	N	E	D	Having a brain of specified character.
B	R	A	I	S	E	D	Cooked in a tightly closed pot.
B	R	A	K	I	N	G	Retarding, Blocking, Hindering, Obstructing, Impeding, Stopping.
B	R	A	M	B	L	E	Blackberry bush.
B	R	A	M	B	L	Y	Full of brambles.
B	R	A	N	C	H	Y	Covered or overgrown with branches.
B	R	A	N	D	E	D	Marked, Stigmatized, Stained, Spotted, Disgraced.
B	R	A	N	G	L	E	Wrangle, Brawl, Squabble.
B	R	A	N	N	E	R	Machine that brans.
B	R	A	S	E	R	O	Brick store built in Mexican kitchens.
B	R	A	S	I	E	R	Brazier, Charcoal pan.
B	R	A	S	S	E	S	Brass musical instruments, Memorial tablet in a church.
B	R	A	S	S	E	T	Armour to protect arm and shoulder.
B	R	A	S	S	I	E	Golf club.
B	R	A	T	T	L	E	Loud clattering.
B	R	A	V	A	D	O	Swagger, Bluster, Overbearing.
B	R	A	V	E	L	Y	Gallantly, Daringly, Courageously, Valiantly, Showy, Gaily, Thrivingly.
B	R	A	V	E	R	Y	Finery, Frippery, Regalia, Display, Valour, Heroism.
B	R	A	V	E	S	T	Most courageous.
B	R	A	V	I	N	G	Daring, Defying.
B	R	A	V	O	E	S	Villain, Desperado, Cutthroat, Hired assassin.
B	R	A	V	U	R	A	Bravado, Show of daring, Stunts, Aggressively confident.
B	R	A	W	L	E	D	Quarrelled, Wrangled, Hassled, Squabbled, Fought, Bickered, Feuded.
B	R	A	W	L	E	R	One that brawls.
B	R	A	Y	I	N	G	Loud harsh cry of donkey.
B	R	A	Z	I	E	R	Pan holding hot coals.
B	R	A	Z	I	N	G	Soldered with an alloy.
B	R	E	A	C	H	Y	Brackish.
B	R	E	A	D	T	H	Distance, Width, Sweep, Scope, Largeness, Generosity.
B	R	E	A	K	E	R	Small water cask, Wave breaking on the shore, Circuit stop.
B	R	E	A	K	I	N	Interruption, House-break, Start an activity.
B	R	E	A	K	U	P	Disruption, Dissolution, Disintegration.
B	R	E	A	M	E	D	Clean a ship's bottom of barnacles.
B	R	E	A	T	H	E	Exhale, Respire, Inhale, Confide, Express, Utter, Evince, Show.
B	R	E	C	C	I	A	Agglomerate deposit of debris.
B	R	E	E	D	E	R	One that produces offspring.
B	R	E	V	I	E	R	Size of type, Point system.
B	R	E	V	I	T	Y	Terseness, Conciseness, Shortness of duration.
B	R	E	W	A	G	E	Something brewed or concocted.
B	R	E	W	E	R	Y	Building where beer is manufactured.
B	R	E	W	I	N	G	Mixing, Plotting, Hatching, Preparing.
B	R	I	B	I	N	G	Influencing people or events with promise of money or a favour.
B	R	I	B	R	I	S	Native of Panama and Costa Rica.
B	R	I	C	K	E	D	Fill up or close with brickwork.
B	R	I	C	K	L	E	Brittle.
B	R	I	C	O	L	E	Rebound of ball in tennis or billiards.
B	R	I	D	G	E	D	Spanned, Transversed, Supported.
B	R	I	D	L	E	D	Restrained, Arrested, Governed, Curbed, Checked.
B	R	I	D	O	O	N	Bit for horse resembling a snaffle.
B	R	I	E	F	E	D	Instructed, Summarized, Coached, Informed, Composed.
B	R	I	E	F	L	Y	Concisely, Laconically, Curtly, Succintly, Tersely, Shortly, Crisply, Precisely.
B	R	I	G	A	D	E	Large body of troops.
B	R	I	G	A	N	D	Marauder, Bandit, Forager, Looter, Pillager, Plunderer, Depredator, Outlaw.

1	2	3	4	5	6	7	
B	R	I	M	F	U	L	Full, Awash, Chock-full, Crammed. Crowded, Jammed, Packed, Teeming.
B	R	I	M	M	E	D	Increased to point of overflowing.
B	R	I	M	M	E	R	A hat with a brim.
B	R	I	N	D	L	E	Streaked yellow and grey.
B	R	I	N	J	A	L	Eggplant.
B	R	I	O	C	H	E	Fancy roll of light yeast dough.
B	R	I	S	K	E	R	Quicker, More sprightly, More lively, More nimble.
B	R	I	S	K	E	T	Breast, Chest of beef animal.
B	R	I	S	K	L	Y	Quickly, Sprightly, Lively, Smartly, Actively.
B	R	I	S	T	L	E	Stiff hair, Anger, Boil, Flare up, Fume, Rage, Seethe.
B	R	I	S	T	L	Y	Belligerent, Prickly.
B	R	I	S	T	O	L	Pottery resembling Delft.
B	R	I	S	U	R	E	Difference.
B	R	I	T	I	S	H	Relating to Britain.
B	R	I	T	T	L	E	Frail, Difficult, Fragile, Brilliant, Perishable, Friable, Crisp, Tense.
B	R	I	T	T	K	A	Long open horse-drawn carriage.
B	R	O	A	D	E	N	Enlarge, Extend, Amplify, Widen, Expand.
B	R	O	A	D	E	R	Wider, Widen, More liberal.
B	R	O	A	D	L	Y	Widely, Openly, Plainly, Liberally, Inclusively, Mainly, Generally.
B	R	O	C	A	D	E	Rich oriental silk fabric with raised patterns.
B	R	O	C	A	R	D	Short proverbial rule.
B	R	O	C	H	A	N	Porridge or gruel.
B	R	O	C	K	E	D	Striped or spotted with black and white.
B	R	O	C	K	E	T	Young male red deer.
B	R	O	I	D	E	R	Embroider, Braid.
B	R	O	I	L	E	D	Grilled, Burned, Roasted, Agitated, Confused, Brawled, Scorched.
B	R	O	I	L	E	R	Grid-iron, Young chicken, Button mushroom.
B	R	O	K	A	G	E	Brokerage.
B	R	O	K	K	I	N	Brokerage, Tricky or dishonest dealing.
B	R	O	M	A	T	E	Salt of bromic acid.
B	R	O	M	I	D	E	Sedative, Bore, Dullard, Commonplace notion.
B	R	O	M	I	N	E	Deep red corrosive toxic liquid.
B	R	O	M	I	S	M	Abnormal state produced by overdose of bromide.
B	R	O	M	O	I	L	Oil pigment photographic prints.
B	R	O	N	C	H	O	Unbroken horse.
B	R	O	N	Z	E	D	Sun-tanned, Coloured film on surface of metal.
B	R	O	O	D	E	D	Moped, Depressed, Meditated, Gloomily distressed.
B	R	O	O	K	E	D	Endured, Tolerated, Allowed, Enjoyed, Swallowed.
B	R	O	O	M	E	D	Cleaned by sweeping.
B	R	O	T	H	E	L	Bordello, Disorderly house, Joyhouse, Whorehouse, Call house.
B	R	O	T	H	E	R	Kinsman, Comrade, Friar.
B	R	O	U	G	H	T	Led, Fetched, Conducted.
B	R	O	W	N	E	D	Tanned, Scorched, Burned.
B	R	O	W	N	E	R	Darker, More dusky, More gloomy.
B	R	O	W	N	I	E	Goblin, Young girl guide, Young girl scout.
B	R	O	W	S	E	D	Grazed, Skimmed, Glanced, Scanned, Thumbed.
B	R	U	C	H	U	S	Genus of small seed-eating weevils.
B	R	U	C	I	N	E	Bitter poisonous crystalline alkaloid.
B	R	U	C	I	T	E	Magnesium hydroxide.
B	R	U	I	S	E	D	Contused, Indented, Injured, Crushed, Squashed.
B	R	U	I	S	E	R	Pugilist, Boxer, Coarse and beefy man.
B	R	U	I	T	E	D	Reported, Publicized, Touted, Rumoured, Advertised, Announced, Proclaimed, Published.
B	R	U	L	Y	I	E	Disturbance, Row, Scuffle.
B	R	U	M	O	U	S	Foggy, Misty.
B	R	U	S	H	E	D	Swept, Grazed, Skimmed, Shaved, Kissed.
B	R	U	S	Q	U	E	Bluff, Abrupt, Blunt, Brief, Crusty, Curt, Gruff, Short.
B	R	U	S	T	L	E	Bristle, Rage, Fume.
B	R	U	T	I	S	H	Animal, Beatly, Bestial, Brutal, Ferine, Swinish.
B	R	U	X	I	S	M	Gritting or grinding the teeth.
B	R	Y	O	N	I	A	Perennial herbaceous tendril-bearing vines.
B	R	Y	O	Z	O	A	Aquatic animals that reproduce by budding.
B	U	B	A	L	I	S	African antelope.
B	U	B	A	L	U	S	Buffalo.
B	U	B	B	L	E	D	Gurgled, Churned, Stirred, Lapped, Washed, Seethed, Boiled, Fermented.
B	U	B	B	L	E	R	Drinking water fountain.
B	U	B	I	N	G	A	Tropical West African tree.
B	U	B	O	N	I	C	Swelling of lymph glands in groin.

1	2	3	4	5	6	7	
B	U	B	U	K	L	E	Pimple, Pustule, Blemish.
B	U	C	C	U	L	A	Double chin, Jowls.
B	U	C	E	R	O	S	Horn-bill.
B	U	C	H	I	T	E	Vitreous metamorphic rock.
B	U	C	K	A	S	S	Low-down, One who obeys without question.
B	U	C	K	E	E	N	An Indian women.
B	U	C	K	E	Y	E	Horse chestnut tree.
B	U	C	K	I	N	G	Balking, Resisting, Contesting, Disputing, Fighting, Opposing, Withstanding, Conveying.
B	U	C	K	I	S	H	Dandified, Foppish, Impetuous.
B	U	C	K	L	E	D	Fastened, Contended, Grappled, Crumpled, Collapsed, Bent, Yielded, Submitted.
B	U	C	K	L	E	R	Small round shield.
B	U	C	K	R	A	M	Stiffened fabric, Rigidity.
B	U	C	K	S	A	W	Frame-saw.
B	U	C	O	L	I	C	Pastoral, Rustic, Arcadian, Rural, Country, Provincial, Countrified.
B	U	D	D	I	N	G	Reproducing asexually, Germinating, Blossoming.
B	U	D	G	I	N	G	Moving, Shifting, Yielding.
B	U	D	L	E	S	S	Sterile, Barren.
B	U	F	F	A	L	O	Wild oxen, Bison.
B	U	F	F	I	N	G	Polishing, Burnishing, Furbishing, Rubbing, Shining.
B	U	F	F	O	O	N	Jester, Clown, Harlequin.
B	U	G	B	A	N	E	Perennial herb with flowers reputed to be distasteful to insects.
B	U	G	B	E	A	R	Goblin, Abomination, Anathema, Hate, Detestation.
B	U	G	L	O	S	S	European annual herb.
B	U	G	S	E	E	D	Herb with flat oval seeds.
B	U	I	L	D	E	D	Built, Erected, Raised.
B	U	I	L	D	E	R	Mason, Contractor, Carpenter.
B	U	I	L	D	U	P	Erect, Construct, Establish, Publicity, Advertising, Promotion.
B	U	I	L	T	I	N	Inherent, Congenital, Constitutional, Essential, Ingrained, Innate.
B	U	I	L	T	U	P	Enlarged, Thickened, Widened, Urban area.
B	U	I	R	D	L	Y	Stalwart, Husky.
B	U	I	S	S	O	N	Fruit tree with very short stem and closely pruned head.
B	U	L	B	I	N	G	Swelling.
B	U	L	B	L	E	T	Small bulb.
B	U	L	B	O	U	S	Bulb-shaped.
B	U	L	G	I	N	G	Jutting, Protruding, Protuberant, Overhanging.
B	U	L	I	M	I	A	Abnormal and constant craving for food.
B	U	L	K	I	E	R	More massive.
B	U	L	K	I	N	G	Swelling, Expanding, Looming.
B	U	L	L	A	C	E	Wild-plum.
B	U	L	L	A	R	Y	Seals, Papal bulls.
B	U	L	L	A	T	E	Blistered, Puckered.
B	U	L	L	B	A	T	Night hawk.
B	U	L	L	D	O	G	Having abnormally undershot jaw. Vice-jaws. Tenacious person.
B	U	L	L	I	E	D	Blustered, Intimidated, Hazed, Browbeawten, Bulldozed, Hectored.
B	U	L	L	I	E	S	Harassers, Hectorers, Intimidators, Annoyers, Hecklers, Persecutors, Tormentors.
B	U	L	L	I	N	G	Dislodging of rock by explosions.
B	U	L	L	I	O	N	Uncoined gold and silver.
B	U	L	L	I	S	H	Obstinate, Optimistic.
B	U	L	L	O	C	K	Young bull, Castrated bull.
B	U	L	L	P	U	P	A special type of rifle.
B	U	L	W	A	R	K	Rampart, Parapet, Breakwater.
B	U	M	B	A	Z	E	Bamboozle, Bewilder, Perplex.
B	U	M	B	L	E	R	Blunderer, Bungler.
B	U	M	B	O	A	T	Small boat carrying provisions to large ships outside port.
B	U	M	I	C	K	Y	Mixture of cement and powdered stone.
B	U	M	M	A	L	O	Bombay duck.
B	U	M	M	I	N	G	Loafing, Cadging, Mooching.
B	U	M	P	I	N	G	Busting, Smashing, Clashing, Colliding, Conflicting, Thumping, Jarring, Knocking.
B	U	M	P	K	I	N	Unsophisticated rustic, Boor, Clodhopper, Hick.
B	U	N	C	H	E	D	Grouped, Bundled, Clustered, Assembled, Concentrated, Crowded.
B	U	N	D	L	E	D	Wrapped, Parcelled, Rolled, Hurried, Hustled.
B	U	N	G	L	E	D	Botched, Blundered, Fluffed, Slipped, Tripped, Mismanaged, Failed.
B	U	N	G	L	E	R	Incompetent, Botcher, Clumsy.
B	U	N	K	E	R	S	Fill a ship's bunkers with coal or oil.
B	U	N	K	I	N	G	Fooling, Decamping, Bolting, Leaving, Deceiving, Misleading.
B	U	N	T	I	N	G	Flags, Festive decoration, Stout-billed bird, Fabric.
B	U	O	Y	A	G	E	System of buoys.

1	2	3	4	5	6	7	
B	U	O	Y	A	N	T	Floating, Light, Elastic, Airy, Bouncy, Expansive, Resilient, Volatile.
B	U	O	Y	I	N	G	Supporting, Bolstering, Sustaining, Upholding.
B	U	R	B	A	R	K	Bark of certain tropical shrubs.
B	U	R	D	O	C	K	Plant with burrs.
B	U	R	E	T	T	E	Graduated glass tube used in laboratory.
B	U	R	G	A	G	E	Property held by burgage tenure.
B	U	R	G	E	O	N	Sprout, Flourish, Develop, Swell, Blossom, Increase, Build, Enlarge.
B	U	R	G	E	S	S	Citizen of British borough, Magistrate.
B	U	R	G	H	A	L	Relating to municipal corporation.
B	U	R	G	H	E	R	Inhabitant of town or city.
B	U	R	G	L	A	R	House-breaker.
B	U	R	G	L	E	D	Robbed, Burglarized.
B	U	R	K	I	N	G	Murdering by suffocation or strangulation, Bypassing, Avoiding.
B	U	R	L	I	N	G	Removing imperfections or knots from fabric.
B	U	R	M	E	S	E	Inhabitant and language of Burma.
B	U	R	N	I	N	G	Blazing, Flaming, Broiling, Sizzling, Feverish, Heated, Impassioned, Pressing.
B	U	R	N	I	S	H	Polish, Buff, Furbish, Gloss, Glance, Glaze, Rub, Shine.
B	U	R	N	O	U	S	Hooded cloak worn by Arabs and Moors.
B	U	R	N	O	U	T	Breakdown of electrical circuit.
B	U	R	R	E	E	D	Plant with globose fruit resembling burrs.
B	U	R	R	H	E	L	Wild sheep of Himalayas and Tibet.
B	U	R	R	I	N	G	Raising a ridge.
B	U	R	S	A	R	Y	Amount granted to needy student by university.
B	U	R	T	H	E	N	Burden.
B	U	R	W	E	E	D	Plant having fruit enclosed in burr.
B	U	R	Y	I	N	G	Burial, Concealing, Entombing, Interring, Covering, Secreting.
B	U	S	H	C	A	T	Serval, Civet, Any small Asian or African Wild cat.
B	U	S	H	I	D	O	Traditional code of Japanese behaviour.
B	U	S	H	I	N	G	Removable sleeve or lining of metal, Threaded plug.
B	U	S	H	M	A	N	Short statured nomadic hunter of Kalahari with low cranial capacity.
B	U	S	H	T	I	T	Titmouse.
B	U	S	K	I	N	G	Preparing, Adorning.
B	U	S	S	I	N	G	Kissing.
B	U	S	S	T	O	P	Point on bus route for stopping.
B	U	S	T	A	R	D	Large game bird.
B	U	S	T	L	E	D	Hurried, Hustled, Struggled, Contended, Hastened, Rushed, Fussed, Whirled.
B	U	S	T	L	E	R	Hustler.
B	U	S	Y	I	N	G	Engaging, Occupying, Working, Bustling, Intruding, Meddling, Interfering.
B	U	T	A	N	O	L	Butyl alcohol derived from butane.
B	U	T	C	H	E	R	Slaughter, Slay, Massacre, Bloodshed, Carnage.
B	U	T	L	E	R	Y	Wine cellar, Pantry.
B	U	T	T	E	N	D	Unused or remaining portion.
B	U	T	T	E	R	Y	Pantry, Larder, Store-room.
B	U	T	T	I	N	G	Abuttal, Boundary.
B	U	T	T	O	C	K	Seat, Rump.
B	U	T	T	O	N	S	Page, Bellboy.
B	U	T	T	O	N	Y	Ornamented with many buttons.
B	U	T	Y	R	I	C	Rancid, Fermentation.
B	U	V	E	T	T	E	Taproom, Bar, Tavern.
B	U	X	O	M	L	Y	Lively, Gaily.
B	U	Z	Z	A	R	D	Bird of Prey.
B	U	Z	Z	S	A	W	Circular saw.
B	Y	A	N	D	B	Y	Presently.
B	Y	E	R	I	T	E	Bituminous coal.
B	Y	G	O	I	N	G	Incidentally.
B	Y	P	L	A	C	E	Odd corner, Out-of-the-way place.
B	Y	R	O	N	I	C	Relating to the poet Byron.
B	Y	S	S	I	N	E	Made of fine linen.
B	Y	S	S	O	I	D	Cottony.
B	Y	W	O	N	E	R	Squatter, Sharecropper.

C

C	A	B	A	R	E	T	Night club, Café, Discotheque, Supper club, Floor show, Entertainment, Tavern, Inn.
C	A	B	B	A	G	E	Leafy garden plant, Money, Steal, Lift, Pinch, Purloin, Appropriate, Nab.
C	A	B	B	A	L	A	Traditional esoteric, occult or secret matter.

1	2	3	4	5	6	7	Definition
C	A	B	E	I	R	I	Ancient Greek deities of Phrygian origin.
C	A	B	I	N	E	D	Confined, Lived within narrow confines.
C	A	B	I	N	E	T	Body of advisers of a soverign or head of state, Cupboard-like compartment, Show-case.
C	A	B	L	I	N	G	Telegraphing, Communicating by cable.
C	A	B	O	O	S	E	Ship's galley, Car at rear of freight-train.
C	A	B	R	A	N	K	Taxi stand.
C	A	C	A	N	N	Y	Slowdown, Deliberate slackening by workmen.
C	A	C	H	E	X	Y	Chronic debased condition of body, mind or outlook.
C	A	C	I	Q	U	E	Native Indian chief in areas dominated by Spanish culture.
C	A	C	K	L	E	D	Chattered, Cry characteristic of goose or hen after laying.
C	A	C	K	L	E	R	One that cackles, Babbler.
C	A	C	O	D	Y	L	Colourless poisonous liquid compound.
C	A	C	O	E	P	Y	Bad pronunciation.
C	A	C	O	N	Y	M	Taxonimic name that is objectionable for linguistic reasons.
C	A	D	A	V	E	R	Corpse, Dead human or animal body intended for dissection.
C	A	D	D	I	C	E	Floss, Cotton wool, Lint, Worsted yarn.
C	A	D	D	I	S	H	Like a cad.
C	A	D	E	L	L	E	Destructive black beetle.
C	A	D	E	N	C	E	Rhythmic sequence or flow.
C	A	D	E	N	C	Y	Status of younger branch of a family.
C	A	D	E	N	Z	A	Parenthetic flourish in course of solo piece.
C	A	D	G	I	N	G	Begging, Sponging.
C	A	D	M	E	A	N	Relating to Cadmus.
C	A	D	M	I	U	M	Tin-white malleable ductile toxic metallic element.
C	A	E	S	I	U	M	Silver-white soft ductile metallic element.
C	A	E	S	U	R	A	Break in flow of sound in verse.
C	A	F	E	N	E	T	Turkish coffeehouse or inn.
C	A	F	F	E	I	C	Yellow crystalline acid.
C	A	F	F	E	I	N	Basic bitter crystalline compound occurs in coffee, tea and maté and acts as a stimulant.
C	A	H	O	O	T	S	Associated, Alliance, Combinaton, Conjunction, Connection, Partnership.
C	A	I	N	I	T	E	Member of sect that honours Cain.
C	A	I	S	S	O	N	Ammunition chest, Two-wheeled cart, Watertight chamber used in construction under water.
C	A	I	T	I	F	F	Captive, Prisoner, Base, Wicked, Cowardly.
C	A	J	E	P	U	T	East Indian tree that yields pungent oil.
C	A	J	O	L	E	D	Coaxed, Wheedled, Beguiled, Tantalized, Inveigled.
C	A	J	U	P	U	T	Pungent oil.
C	A	L	A	B	E	R	Gray fur of Siberian squirrel.
C	A	L	A	M	U	S	Palm of which stem is used for malacca canes, Quill pen.
C	A	L	A	N	D	O	Diminishing - (direction in music).
C	A	L	C	I	F	Y	Harden, Fix, Make inflexible.
C	A	L	C	I	N	E	Heat by high temperature without fusing.
C	A	L	C	I	T	E	Mineral of calcium carbonate crystallized in hexagonal forms.
C	A	L	C	I	U	M	Silver-white soft bivalent metallic element.
C	A	L	C	U	L	I	Stone in bladder or kidneys.
C	A	L	D	E	R	A	Volcanic crater that has collapsed or subsided.
C	A	L	D	R	O	N	Large kettle or boiler.
C	A	L	E	C	H	E	Two-wheeled horse drawn vehicle.
C	A	L	E	N	D	S	First day of ancient Roman month.
C	A	L	I	B	A	N	Person or thing that is slavish, brutal, monstrous or deformed.
C	A	L	I	B	R	E	Rank, Quality, Size, Capacity, Merit, Value, Worth.
C	A	L	I	C	H	E	Sodium nitrate deposits.
C	A	L	I	C	L	E	Small cup-shaped structure.
C	A	L	I	P	E	E	Turtle fat.
C	A	L	I	P	E	R	Measuring instrument.
C	A	L	I	V	E	R	Early handgun.
C	A	L	K	I	N	G	Furnish with calks to prevent slipping.
C	A	L	L	A	N	T	Boy, Lad, Fellow.
C	A	L	L	B	O	Y	Messenger in hotel.
C	A	L	L	I	N	G	Vocation, Profession, Trade, Mission, Business, Employment, Job, Occupation.
C	A	L	L	O	U	S	Unfeeling, Coldhearted, Heartless, Obdurate, Stony, Unsympathetic, Hard.
C	A	L	L	U	N	A	Heather.
C	A	L	M	A	N	T	Sedative.
C	A	L	M	I	N	G	Placating, Relaxing, Soothing, Composing, Lulling, Quietening, Settling, Tranquilizing.
C	A	L	O	M	E	L	White tasteless salt, Mercuric chloride.
C	A	L	O	R	I	C	Relating to heat or food calories.
C	A	L	O	R	I	E	Any of several thermal units.
C	A	L	O	T	T	E	Skullcap, Snow-capped summit or dome.

1	2	3	4	5	6	7	
C	A	L	O	Y	E	R	Monk of Eastern church.
C	A	L	P	A	C	K	High-crowned felt cap worn in Turkey and Iran.
C	A	L	T	R	A	P	Heraldic representation of military caltrop, Plants having stout spines of fruit or flowers.
C	A	L	T	R	O	P	as CALTRAP.
C	A	L	U	M	B	A	Root of African plant used as tonic.
C	A	L	U	M	N	Y	Detraction, Belittlement, Defamation, Depreciation, Disparagement, Scandal, Slander, Tale.
C	A	L	V	A	R	Y	Experience of intense suffering, Trial, Ordeal.
C	A	L	V	I	N	G	Producing a calf.
C	A	L	Y	C	L	E	Cup-shaped structure, Coral cavity.
C	A	M	A	I	E	U	Cameo, Monochrome.
C	A	M	B	I	A	L	Relating to cambium.
C	A	M	B	I	S	M	Theory and practice of exchange in commerce.
C	A	M	B	I	S	T	One who deals in bills of exchange.
C	A	M	B	I	U	M	Cellular tissue responsible for secondary growth.
C	A	M	B	L	E	T	Camel-hair or angora cloth.
C	A	M	B	O	G	E	Air-bricks used for decoration and ventilation.
C	A	M	B	R	E	L	Meat hook.
C	A	M	B	R	I	C	Fine thin closely woven plain white linen fabric.
C	A	M	E	L	O	T	Court of legendary King Arthur.
C	A	M	E	L	R	Y	Camel corps.
C	A	M	M	O	C	K	Hooked stick, Hockey stick.
C	A	M	O	R	R	A	Secret society for dishonest ends.
C	A	M	P	A	N	A	Bell.
C	A	M	P	H	O	R	Crystalline terpenoid ketone.
C	A	M	P	I	N	G	Living in temporary shelter.
C	A	M	P	I	O	N	Bladder plant.
C	A	M	W	O	O	D	Hard red wood of African tree.
C	A	N	A	K	I	N	A small can or drinking vessel.
C	A	N	A	S	T	A	Game played with two packs of cards.
C	A	N	B	U	O	Y	Truncated buoy having a flat top.
C	A	N	C	E	L	S	Revoked, Annul, Invalidate, Neutralize, Offset, Counterbalance, Erase, Obliterate.
C	A	N	D	E	L	A	Candle.
C	A	N	D	E	N	T	White or glowing.
C	A	N	D	I	E	D	Coated or encrusted with sugar.
C	A	N	D	O	C	K	Water lily.
C	A	N	D	O	U	R	Fairness, Frankness, Openness, Impartiality, Candidness.
C	A	N	E	L	L	A	Cinnamon tree.
C	A	N	H	O	O	K	Device to hoist casks.
C	A	N	I	D	A	E	Family comprising dogs, wolves, jackals and foxes.
C	A	N	I	N	U	S	Muscle that elevates the corner of the mouth.
C	A	N	K	E	R	S	Corrupt with a malignancy of mind or spirit, Infested with a spreading sore.
C	A	N	K	E	R	Y	Rusty, Crabbed, Ill-natured.
C	A	N	N	E	R	Y	Factory for the canning of foods.
C	A	N	N	I	E	R	More cautious, More cunning, More wary.
C	A	N	N	I	N	G	Preserving food by sterilising it in cans or jars.
C	A	N	N	U	L	A	Surgical tube inserted for drainage.
C	A	N	O	N	I	C	Belonging to the canon of Scripture.
C	A	N	O	N	R	Y	Office of a canon or canoness.
C	A	N	O	P	I	C	Relating to Canopus.
C	A	N	T	A	T	A	Sacred or secular choral composition.
C	A	N	T	E	E	N	Shop attached to military post, Place of refreshment for industrial workers.
C	A	N	T	H	A	L	Belonging to a canthus.
C	A	N	T	H	U	S	Corner of the eye.
C	A	N	T	I	N	G	Wheedling, Gossipping, Hypocritical, Sanctimonious, Self-righteous, Pharisaic.
C	A	N	T	I	O	N	Song.
C	A	N	T	L	E	T	Piece, Fragment.
C	A	N	T	R	E	D	County division, Hundred.
C	A	N	T	R	I	P	Spell, Witch's trick, Mischievous act.
C	A	N	V	A	S	S	Solicit, Drum up, Discuss, Agitate, Argue, Dispute, Scrutinize, Examine.
C	A	N	Z	O	N	E	Medieval Italian lyric poem.
C	A	P	A	B	L	E	Efficient, Able, Inclusive, Comprehensive, Competent, Good, Proper, Qualified.
C	A	P	A	B	L	Y	Skilfully, Competently, Properly.
C	A	P	A	P	I	E	From head to foot, At all points.
C	A	P	C	A	S	E	Small travelling case.
C	A	P	E	L	I	N	Small salmonoid marine fish.
C	A	P	E	R	E	D	Frolicked, Bounded, Cavorted, Romped, Frisked.
C	A	P	I	R	O	N	Stiffening plate for cutter of carpenter's plane.

1	2	3	4	5	6	7	
C	A	P	I	T	A	L	Assets, Resources, Wealth, Means, Chief, Dominant, Major, Excellent.
C	A	P	I	T	A	N	Hogfish.
C	A	P	I	T	O	L	Building in which a legislative body meets.
C	A	P	O	R	A	L	Coarse tobacco, Foreman on a stock ranch.
C	A	P	P	I	N	G	Topping, Rock overlying mineral body of a mine.
C	A	P	R	A	T	E	Salt of capric acid.
C	A	P	R	I	C	E	Conceit, Crank, Fancy, Freak, Humour, Notion, Vagary, Whim.
C	A	P	R	I	N	E	Like a goat.
C	A	P	R	O	I	N	Glyceryl caproate.
C	A	P	S	I	Z	E	Overturn, Collapse, Upset.
C	A	P	S	T	A	N	Windlass, Winch.
C	A	P	S	U	L	E	Case, Pod, Closed container, Gelatinous envelope.
C	A	P	T	A	I	N	Chief, Leader, Master, Senior office, Senior pilot.
C	A	P	T	I	O	N	Seizure, Cavil, Quibble, Explanatory comment accompanying pictorial illustration.
C	A	P	T	I	V	E	Prisoner, Confined, Captivated, Charmed, Enchanted.
C	A	P	T	U	R	E	Catch, Take, Collar, Apprehend, Secure, Nail, Nab.
C	A	P	U	C	H	E	Hooded cloak.
C	A	P	U	L	I	N	Mexican black cherry tree.
C	A	R	A	B	A	O	Buffalo.
C	A	R	A	B	I	D	Ground beetle.
C	A	R	A	B	U	S	Large ground beetle.
C	A	R	A	C	A	L	Wild cat of Africa and parts of Asia.
C	A	R	A	C	U	L	Pelt of Karakul lamb.
C	A	R	A	M	E	L	Firm chewy candy, Brownish orange.
C	A	R	A	N	N	A	Dark resinous medicinal gum from S. American tree.
C	A	R	A	V	A	N	Covered wagon or motor truck equipped as living quarters, Company of travellers, pilgrims.
C	A	R	A	V	E	L	Any of several sailing vessels.
C	A	R	A	W	A	Y	Aromatic pungent-tasting fruit used in cooking and confectionery.
C	A	R	B	I	D	E	Compound of carbon.
C	A	R	B	I	N	E	Short-barrelled shoulder firearm.
C	A	R	C	A	S	S	Corpse, Body, Cadaver, Remains, Shell, Husk, Framework.
C	A	R	D	E	C	U	Old French silver coin.
C	A	R	D	I	A	C	Relating to the heart.
C	A	R	D	I	N	G	Combing wool or flax.
C	A	R	D	O	O	N	Plant related to the artichoke.
C	A	R	D	U	U	S	Genus of prickly thistle.
C	A	R	E	F	U	L	Cautious, Considerate, Discreet, Wary, Safe, Conscientious, Exact, Meticulous.
C	A	R	F	A	R	E	Fare for carrying passenger on public transport.
C	A	R	F	O	U	R	Place where four roads meet.
C	A	R	G	O	E	S	Load, Freight, Goods for loading.
C	A	R	I	A	M	A	Genus of long-legged S. American bird.
C	A	R	I	B	O	U	Artic reindeer.
C	A	R	I	O	C	A	Ballroom dance originating in Brazil.
C	A	R	I	O	L	E	Light four-wheel one horse carriage.
C	A	R	I	O	U	S	Rotting, Decaying.
C	A	R	I	T	A	S	Charity.
C	A	R	K	I	N	G	Worrying, Vexing, Anxious.
C	A	R	L	I	N	A	Thistle-like herb.
C	A	R	L	I	N	O	Old Italian coin.
C	A	R	L	I	N	E	Witch, Old woman.
C	A	R	L	I	S	H	Churlish.
C	A	R	L	I	S	M	Support for pretender to Spanish throne.
C	A	R	M	I	N	E	Vivid red colour.
C	A	R	N	A	G	E	Slaughter, Butchery, Massacre, Bloodshed.
C	A	R	N	I	F	Y	To make or turn into flesh.
C	A	R	N	O	S	E	Fleshy.
C	A	R	O	C	H	E	Luxurious or stately carriage.
C	A	R	O	L	U	S	Coins issued under monarchs called Charles.
C	A	R	O	T	I	D	Cerebal.
C	A	R	O	T	I	N	Carrot pigment, Vitamin A.
C	A	R	O	U	S	E	Drinking bout, Drunken revel.
C	A	R	P	A	R	K	Area set aside for parking vehicles.
C	A	R	P	I	N	G	Critical, Captious, Caviling, Censorious, Critic, Hypercritical, Overcritical, Objecting.
C	A	R	P	O	R	T	Open-sided roofed automobile shelter.
C	A	R	R	A	C	K	Galleon, Mediterranean merchant ship sometimes fitted out for fighting.
C	A	R	R	I	E	D	Light hearted, Vain, Conveyed, Ferried, Transported, Borne, Conducted, Transmitted.
C	A	R	R	I	E	R	Bearer, Porter, Messenger, Transporter, Conveyor, Emissary, Envoy, Vector.

1	2	3	4	5	6	7	
C	A	R	R	I	O	N	Carcass, Corpse, Vermin, Putrid meat, Something corrupt, vile or rotten.
C	A	R	R	O	T	Y	Resembing carrots in colour.
C	A	R	S	H	O	P	Workshop for construction, maintenance and repair of railroad equipment.
C	A	R	T	A	G	E	Carrying by truck or cart, Hauling.
C	A	R	T	I	N	G	Drive a cart, Transporting.
C	A	R	T	O	O	N	Drawing intended as humour, caricature or satire.
C	A	R	V	I	N	G	Cutting, Cleaving, Dissecting, Severing, Slicing, Splitting.
C	A	R	V	O	N	E	Oily liquid terpenoid ketone having characteristic odour of caraway.
C	A	R	Y	O	T	A	Fishtail palm.
C	A	S	C	A	D	E	Waterfall, Fall of material.
C	A	S	C	A	R	A	Laxative.
C	A	S	E	A	T	E	Become cheesy, Undergo caseation.
C	A	S	E	L	A	W	Law established by legal precedent.
C	A	S	E	O	U	S	Characterized by caseation.
C	A	S	H	I	E	R	One that handles cash payments, Dismiss, Discharge, Sack, Terminate, Discard, Abdicate.
C	A	S	S	A	V	A	Tapioca.
C	A	S	S	I	N	O	Casino, Card game.
C	A	S	S	O	C	K	Long loose cloak.
C	A	S	S	O	N	E	Large Italian chest often decorated with carving or painting.
C	A	S	T	I	N	G	Making casts, Assignment of parts to actors.
C	A	S	T	L	E	D	Move in chess, Castellated.
C	A	S	T	L	E	T	Small castle.
C	A	S	T	O	F	F	Fasten, Unhitch, Loose, Slip, Discarded.
C	A	S	T	R	U	M	Old Roman encampment.
C	A	S	U	I	S	T	One given to casuistry, Quibbler.
C	A	T	A	L	A	N	Relating to Catalonia.
C	A	T	A	L	O	G	List, Register, Inventory, Itemize, Schedule, Book, Enroll, Inscribe.
C	A	T	A	L	P	A	Genus of small American and Asiatic trees.
C	A	T	A	P	A	N	Byzantine emperor.
C	A	T	A	R	R	H	Inflammation of a mucuous membrane.
C	A	T	A	W	B	A	White wine.
C	A	T	B	I	R	D	American songbird.
C	A	T	B	O	A	T	Sailboat.
C	A	T	C	A	L	L	Noise to express disapproval or contempt.
C	A	T	C	H	E	R	One that catches.
C	A	T	C	H	E	S	Captures, Seizes, Snatches, Dupes, Tricks, Hoodwinks, Encounters, Overtakes.
C	A	T	C	H	U	P	Ketchup sauce.
C	A	T	E	C	H	U	Dry, earthy or resinous astringent substance.
C	A	T	E	N	A	S	Connected series of related things.
C	A	T	E	R	A	N	Marauder, Brigand, Looter, Bandit, Pillager, Raider, Freebooter, Plunderer.
C	A	T	E	R	E	D	Indulged, Supplied, Pampered, Spoiled, Coddled.
C	A	T	E	R	E	R	One who arranges and supervises food and service.
C	A	T	E	Y	E	D	Being able to see in the night.
C	A	T	F	A	L	L	Rope or chain used in hoisting the anchor.
C	A	T	F	I	S	H	Barbel.
C	A	T	H	A	R	I	Member of sect that practiced rigorous ascetism.
C	A	T	H	E	A	D	Projection for securing anchor.
C	A	T	H	E	C	T	Invest with libidinal energy.
C	A	T	H	O	D	E	The electrode at which electrons enter a device.
C	A	T	H	O	L	E	Small opening.
C	A	T	L	I	K	E	Stealthly, Noiselessly.
C	A	T	L	I	N	G	Catgut string for a musical instrument.
C	A	T	M	I	N	T	Catnip, Strong scented herb.
C	A	T	S	E	Y	E	Any of various gems, Child's marble, Small reflector on highway.
C	A	T	S	P	A	W	Tool, Pawn, Puppet, Stooge, Dupe.
C	A	T	T	A	L	O	Hybrid between American buffalo and domestic cattle.
C	A	T	T	I	S	H	Spiteful, Catty.
C	A	T	W	A	L	K	Narrow walkway affording passage over an area otherwise inaccessible.
C	A	U	D	A	T	E	Having a tail.
C	A	U	L	I	N	E	Growing on a stem.
C	A	U	L	K	E	D	Rendered watertight.
C	A	U	L	K	E	R	One who makes seams watertight.
C	A	U	L	O	M	E	Stem structure of plant.
C	A	U	S	I	N	G	Occasioning, Obliging, Generating, Producing, Effecting, Making.
C	A	U	S	T	I	C	Scathing, Sarcastic, Acerbic, Corrosive, Mordant, Salty, Ironic, Acrid.
C	A	U	T	E	R	Y	Burning or searing with hot iron or caustic.
C	A	U	T	I	O	N	Warning, Admonition, Forewarning, Prudence, Discretion, Precaution.

1	2	3	4	5	6	7	
C	A	V	A	L	R	Y	Component of an army that fights on horseback.
C	A	V	E	M	A	N	Cave dweller of Stone age.
C	A	V	E	T	T	O	Concave moulding.
C	A	V	I	A	R	E	Processed salted roe of the sturgeon fish.
C	A	Y	E	N	N	E	Pepper.
C	A	Z	I	Q	U	E	Native Indian chief.
C	E	A	S	I	N	G	Stopping, Halting, Quitting, Concluding, Finishing, Terminating, Ending.
C	E	B	I	D	A	E	Family of New World monkeys.
C	E	D	I	L	L	A	Symbol to indicate pronunciation of letters.
C	E	D	R	A	T	E	Citron.
C	E	D	R	E	L	A	Tropical cedar tree.
C	E	D	R	E	N	E	Substance occurring in cedarwood oils.
C	E	I	L	I	N	G	Overhead lining of room, Height above ground for clear vision.
C	E	L	A	D	O	N	Ceramic glaze that originated in China.
C	E	L	L	I	S	T	One that plays the cello.
C	E	L	L	S	A	P	Fluid part of protoplasm.
C	E	L	L	U	L	E	Minute cavity.
C	E	L	S	I	U	S	Centigrade scale.
C	E	M	B	A	L	O	Dulcimer, Harpsichord.
C	E	N	A	C	L	E	Literary or artistic group.
C	E	N	S	I	N	G	Burning incense.
C	E	N	S	U	A	L	Relating to a census.
C	E	N	S	U	R	E	Criticize, Blame, Condemn, Denounce, Rap, Reprehend, Rebuke, Reproach.
C	E	N	T	A	G	E	Percentage.
C	E	N	T	A	U	R	Ancient mythical Greek race with bodies of horses.
C	E	N	T	A	V	O	Monetary unit of some Spanish-American countries.
C	E	N	T	I	M	E	Coin representing one hundredth part of unit.
C	E	N	T	N	E	R	German and Scandinavian hundredweight.
C	E	N	T	R	A	L	Dominant, Important, Main, Cardinal, Pivotal, Middle, Medial, Median.
C	E	N	T	R	E	D	Having a centre, Equidistant.
C	E	N	T	R	I	C	Central, Cylindrical.
C	E	N	T	U	R	Y	Collection of one hundred.
C	E	R	A	M	I	C	Articles made of clay and fired at high temperature.
C	E	R	A	T	E	S	Wax mixed with oil and medicinal ingredients.
C	E	R	E	A	L	S	Plants yielding farinaceous seeds suitable for food.
C	E	R	E	S	I	N	Petroleum wax.
C	E	R	O	T	I	C	Acid occurring in most waxes and some fats.
C	E	R	T	A	I	N	Firm, Settled, Various, Accurate, Dependable, Infallible, Positive, Inevitable.
C	E	R	T	I	F	Y	Attest, Vouch, Witness, Warrant, Guarantee, Approve, Accredit, Endorse.
C	E	R	U	M	E	N	Wax secreted from glands of external ear.
C	E	R	V	I	N	E	Belonging to or resembling deer.
C	E	S	S	I	N	G	Assessing tax, Imposing levy.
C	E	S	S	I	O	N	Yielding, Concession, Compliance, Cede, Transfer, Relinquish, Surrender.
C	E	S	S	P	I	T	Cesspool, Den, Pandemonium, Sty, Pit for disposal of sewage.
C	E	S	T	O	D	E	Tape worm.
C	E	T	A	C	E	A	Whales, Dolphins, Porpoises and related aquatic mammals.
C	H	A	B	L	I	S	Dry white Burgundy table wine.
C	H	A	C	A	T	E	Small Mexican shrub, the bark of which furnishes a brownish red dye.
C	H	A	C	O	N	E	Old Spanish dance in moderate tempo.
C	H	A	F	F	E	D	Irritated, Vexed, Annoyed, Derided, Fretted, Provoked, Rubbed, Bantered.
C	H	A	F	F	E	R	Haggle, Bargain, Patter, Exchange, Banter, Coax, Plead, Higgle.
C	H	A	F	I	N	G	Rubbing, Bothering, Irking, Ruffling, Eroding, Wearing, Galling, Fuming.
C	H	A	G	R	I	N	Depressing, Worrying, Troubling, Grieving, Disconcerting, Crushing, Mortifying, Vexation.
C	H	A	I	N	E	D	Shackled, Fettered, Restrained, Imprisoned, Repressed, Confined.
C	H	A	I	R	E	D	Carried in triumph, Act as presiding officer.
C	H	A	L	A	C	O	A S. American goby used in mosquito control.
C	H	A	L	A	R	A	Genus of imperfect fungi.
C	H	A	L	A	Z	A	Base of ovule where seed stalk is attached.
C	H	A	L	C	I	D	Metallic colour of insects of this genus.
C	H	A	L	D	E	E	Aramaic vernacular.
C	H	A	L	D	E	R	Unit of capacity for dry measure.
C	H	A	L	I	C	E	Goblet, Drinking cup.
C	H	A	L	L	I	S	Lightweight soft clothing fabric.
C	H	A	L	O	N	E	Internal secretion that depresses activity.
C	H	A	M	A	D	E	Drum or trumpet signal for a parley with the enemy.
C	H	A	M	B	E	R	Room, Apartment, Closet, Hall, Cavity, Harbour, Haven, Shelter.
C	H	A	M	F	E	R	Groove, Channel, Flute, Bevel.

1	2	3	4	5	6	7	Definition
C	H	A	M	L	E	T	Camlet, Fabric of camel's hair or Angora wool, Imitation of this fabric.
C	H	A	M	O	I	S	Small goatlike antelope, Soft pliant leather.
C	H	A	M	P	A	C	East Indian tree with yellow flowers which give oil used as perfume.
C	H	A	M	P	E	D	Chewed, Crunched, Munched, Gnashed, Mashed, Scrunched, Masticated, Trampled.
C	H	A	N	C	E	D	Happened, Risked, Gambled, Ventured, Hazarded, Wagered, Befell, Transpired.
C	H	A	N	C	E	L	Area of church used by the clergy.
C	H	A	N	D	O	O	Prepared opium.
C	H	A	N	G	E	D	Altered, Modified, Refashioned, Turned, Varied, Reversed, Transposed, Substituted.
C	H	A	N	G	E	R	Money changer, Record changer, Inconstant.
C	H	A	N	N	E	L	Canal, Conduit, Aqueduct, Course, Duct, Pipeline, Carry, Convey.
C	H	A	N	S	O	N	Music-hall or cabaret song in French or French manner.
C	H	A	N	T	E	D	Sung, Warbled, Intoned, Recited monotonously.
C	H	A	N	T	E	R	Cantor, Chief singer, Reed pipe of a bagpipe.
C	H	A	N	T	R	Y	Chapel, Altar or part of church endowed.
C	H	A	O	T	I	C	Confused, Cluttered, Disordered, Muddled, Snarled, Anarchy, Lawlessness, Unruliness.
C	H	A	P	A	T	I	Pancake-shaped unleavened bread common in N. India.
C	H	A	P	E	A	U	Hat.
C	H	A	P	L	E	T	Wreath, Coronal, Coronet, Crown, Garland.
C	H	A	P	M	A	N	Pedlar, Hawker, Trader, Merchant, Purchaser, Customer.
C	H	A	P	P	E	D	Cracked, Fissured, Roughened, Chopped, Mashed.
C	H	A	P	P	I	E	Fellow, Chap.
C	H	A	P	T	E	R	Main division of book, Regular meeting or assembly.
C	H	A	R	A	C	T	Character.
C	H	A	R	A	D	E	Pretense, Disguise, Make-believe, Pageant, Symbolic action.
C	H	A	R	G	E	D	Encumbered, Saddled, Loaded, Entrusted, Commanded, Directed, Accused, Assigned.
C	H	A	R	G	E	R	Large platter, Cavalry horse.
C	H	A	R	I	L	Y	Carefully, Discreetly, Gingerly, Sparingly, Cautiously, Frugally, Warily, Reluctantly.
C	H	A	R	I	N	G	Odd job or task of housework.
C	H	A	R	I	O	T	Vehicle for conveying persons usually coach of state.
C	H	A	R	I	S	M	Supernatural power or virtue with capacity of eliciting support.
C	H	A	R	I	T	Y	Aid to the needy, Mercy, Benevolence, Alms, Disposition to goodwill.
C	H	A	R	L	E	Y	Night watchman, Short pointed beard, Clown of lubrious pathos.
C	H	A	R	L	I	E	same as CHARLEY.
C	H	A	R	M	E	D	Enamoured, Bewitched, Captivated, Enchanted, Entranced, Fascinated, Attracted.
C	H	A	R	M	E	R	Magician, Conjurer, Necromancer, Sorcerer, Wizard, Enchanter, Siren, Attractive woman.
C	H	A	R	N	E	L	Cemetery, Mortuary.
C	H	A	R	P	O	Y	Indian bed of frame strung with rope.
C	H	A	R	Q	U	I	Dried meat.
C	H	A	R	R	E	D	Scorched, Seared, Burnt, Grilled.
C	H	A	R	T	E	D	Recorded, Delineated, Planned, Projected, Tabulated.
C	H	A	R	T	E	R	Deed, Conveyance, Hire, Lease, Let, Rent, Franchise.
C	H	A	S	I	N	G	Catching, Persecuting, Harassing, Driving, Grooving, Indenting, Engraving.
C	H	A	S	M	A	L	Cavernous, Gaping, Yawning.
C	H	A	S	S	I	S	Frame and Working parts.
C	H	A	S	T	E	N	Punish, Chastise, Correct, Discipline, Humble, Humiliate, Castigate, Afflict.
C	H	A	T	E	A	U	Mansion, Castle, Large country house, Villa.
C	H	A	T	T	E	D	Chattered, Gossiped, Palaver, Prattled, Conversation, Conversed, Dialogue, Parley.
C	H	A	T	T	E	L	Movable property, Belongings, Effects, Goods, Slave, Bondsman.
C	H	A	T	T	E	R	Talk, Prate, Tattle, Babble, Blabber, Gabble, Palaver, Jabber.
C	H	A	W	I	N	G	Chewing, Pondering, Vexing, Embarrassing.
C	H	A	Y	O	T	E	Rounded or pear-shaped fruit of W. Indian vine.
C	H	E	A	P	E	N	Depreciate, Decry, Devaluate, Downgrade, Undervalue, Lower, Mark down, Belittle.
C	H	E	A	P	E	R	Not so expensive, More shoddy, Reduced in price.
C	H	E	A	P	L	Y	Inexpensively, Vulgarly.
C	H	E	A	T	E	D	Defrauded, Swindled, Tricked, Hoaxed, Deceived, Cozened, Duped. Gulled.
C	H	E	C	H	I	A	Cylindrical brimless cap of Arab origin.
C	H	E	C	K	E	D	Arrested, Halted, Interrupted, Restrained, Curbed, Held, Examined, Tested.
C	H	E	C	K	E	R	Vary with differing or contrasting elements, One that marks, counts or tallies.
C	H	E	D	D	A	R	Hard pressed cheese of smooth texture.
C	H	E	E	K	E	D	Flaunted self-assurance, Boldly impudent, Spoken saucily, Teased.
C	H	E	E	P	E	D	Chirped, Peeped, Squeaked.
C	H	E	E	P	E	R	Young quail, grouse or partridge.
C	H	E	E	R	E	D	Applauded, Enlivened, Encouraged, Heartened, Comforted, Consoled.
C	H	E	E	R	E	R	Cheering drink or cup.
C	H	E	E	R	I	O	Farewell, Greeting, Toast.
C	H	E	E	T	A	H	Long-legged swift moving cat with dog-like characteristics.
C	H	E	L	A	T	E	Relating to a cyclic structure.

1	2	3	4	5	6	7	
C	H	E	L	O	N	E	Small genus of perennial herbs.
C	H	E	L	S	E	A	Soft-paste porcelain made in middle eighteenth century.
C	H	E	L	U	R	A	Marine amphipod Crustacea that bore into and can destroy timber.
C	H	E	M	I	S	E	Shift, Smock, Slip, Loose straight-hanging dress.
C	H	E	M	I	S	M	Chemical activity or affinity.
C	H	E	M	I	S	T	Pharmacist, Druggist, Apothecary.
C	H	E	N	I	E	R	Wooded ridge or sandy hummock in a swampy region.
C	H	E	Q	U	E	R	To variegate, Checker.
C	H	E	R	I	S	H	Nurse, Cultivate, Nourish, Appreciate, Esteem, Prize, Treasure, Admire.
C	H	E	R	M	E	S	Genus of aphids.
C	H	E	R	O	O	T	Cigar cut off square at both ends.
C	H	E	R	V	I	L	An aromatic herb.
C	H	E	S	N	U	T	Chestnut, Sweet edible nut, Stale story or joke.
C	H	E	S	S	E	T	Cheese vat.
C	H	E	S	T	E	D	Placed in a coffin.
C	H	E	T	N	I	K	Pan-Serbian guerrilla.
C	H	E	V	A	G	E	Tax or tribute paid to a lord or superior.
C	H	E	V	I	E	D	Chivied, Chased, Pursued, Harried, Hustled.
C	H	E	V	I	O	T	Breed of hardy hornless medium-wooled meat-type sheep.
C	H	E	V	R	O	N	Two diagonal strips meeting at an angle.
C	H	E	W	I	N	G	Munching, Masticating, Crushing, Grinding, Injuring, Destroying, Upbraiding, Reprimanding.
C	H	I	A	N	T	I	Still dry red wine.
C	H	I	A	S	M	A	Source of genetic crossovers.
C	H	I	B	O	U	K	Turkish pipe.
C	H	I	C	A	N	E	Quibble, Dupe, Bamboozle, Fool, Hoax, Hoodwink, Trick, Victimize.
C	H	I	C	K	E	D	Sprouted, Vegetated.
C	H	I	C	K	E	N	Common domestic fowl, Coward, Sissy.
C	H	I	C	O	R	Y	Endive, Thick rooted plant grown for its young leaves which are used as salad greens.
C	H	I	D	D	E	D	Reproved, Censured, Rebuked, Complained, Admonished, Reproached, Scolded.
C	H	I	D	I	N	G	Reproving, Admonishing, Rebuking, Reprimanding, Reproaching, Berating, Scolding.
C	H	I	E	F	L	Y	Generally, Largely, Principally, Mainly, Mostly, Overall, Predominantly, Primarily.
C	H	I	F	F	O	N	Sheer gauzy fabric, Dessert of light delicate texture.
C	H	I	G	G	E	R	Blood sucking mite that transmits disease.
C	H	I	G	N	O	N	Smooth knot, twist or arrangement of hair at back of head.
C	H	I	K	A	R	A	An Indian antelope.
C	H	I	L	D	E	D	Give birth, Bear young.
C	H	I	L	D	L	Y	Childlike, Childish.
C	H	I	L	E	A	N	Relating to Chile.
C	H	I	L	L	E	D	Discouraged, Cold, Depressed, Dampened, Distant, Formal, Unfriendly, Dispiriting.
C	H	I	L	L	E	R	An eerie story, Refrigerator.
C	H	I	L	L	U	M	Part of hookah pipe containing tobacco.
C	H	I	M	E	R	A	She-monster in Greek mythology.
C	H	I	M	I	N	G	Harmonious ringing of bells.
C	H	I	M	N	E	Y	Vertical structure with flue to expel smoke.
C	H	I	N	C	H	A	Sub-division of the Yunca.
C	H	I	N	E	S	E	Relating to China.
C	H	I	N	G	M	A	Bast fibre of Indian mallow used for cordage.
C	H	I	N	I	N	G	Cutting the backbone.
C	H	I	N	K	E	D	Opened a crack, Jingled, Clinked.
C	H	I	N	O	O	K	Indian tribe, Warm moist south west wind of the Pacific region.
C	H	I	N	S	E	D	Caulked in a temporary fashion.
C	H	I	N	T	Z	Y	Decorated with chintz, Gaudy, Cheap.
C	H	I	P	A	Y	A	People of Bolivia.
C	H	I	P	M	A	N	Worker who cleans up metal and wooden chips from machines.
C	H	I	P	P	E	D	Chopped, Designing on glass.
C	H	I	P	P	E	R	Twitter, Machine for reducing something to chips, Lively, Cheerful, Gay, Sprightly.
C	H	I	R	A	T	A	Dried tissue of green gentian used as a tonic.
C	H	I	R	P	E	D	Short sharp sound made by small birds, Peep, Tweet.
C	H	I	R	R	U	P	Soft buzzing sound of insects.
C	H	I	T	O	S	E	Nonfermentable sugar.
C	H	I	T	T	E	D	Germinated, Sprouted.
C	H	I	T	T	E	R	Shiver or chatter with cold.
C	H	L	O	R	A	L	Narcotic.
C	H	L	O	R	I	N	Chlorine, Derivative of chlorophyll.
C	H	O	B	D	A	R	Usher, Attendant.
C	H	O	C	T	A	W	Jargon, Gibberish, Fancy step in skating.
C	H	O	I	R	E	D	Sang in chorus.

1	2	3	4	5	6	7	
C	H	O	K	I	N	G	Suffocating, Strangling, Constricting, Restricting.
C	H	O	L	E	I	C	Relating to bile.
C	H	O	L	E	R	A	Any of several diseases marked by severe gastro-intestinal symptoms.
C	H	O	L	I	N	E	Syrupy liquid base for vitamin B complex.
C	H	O	N	T	A	L	Indian people of Tabasco, Mexico.
C	H	O	O	S	E	R	One that chooses, Voter, Elector.
C	H	O	O	S	E	S	Selects, Wants, Decides, Inclines.
C	H	O	P	I	N	E	Patten, Ladies shoe having high sole to protect feet from mud.
C	H	O	P	P	E	D	Minced, Snapped, Diced, Swooped, Pounced, Felled, Fragmented.
C	H	O	P	P	E	R	Axe, Knife, Cleaver.
C	H	O	R	A	L	E	Hymn or psalm sung by choir.
C	H	O	R	D	A	L	Relating to chord or music, Relating to a spinal cord.
C	H	O	R	D	E	D	Having or combined in chords.
C	H	O	R	E	A	L	Nervous disorder.
C	H	O	R	E	U	S	Trochee.
C	H	O	R	I	O	N	Membrane.
C	H	O	R	I	S	T	Member of choir or chorus.
C	H	O	R	O	I	D	Eye membrane.
C	H	O	R	T	L	E	Laugh, CHuckle, Giggle, Guffaw, Snicker, Sniggle, Titter.
C	H	O	W	D	E	R	Thick stew or soup of seafood.
C	H	R	I	S	M	A	Relating to baptism.
C	H	R	O	M	Y	L	Chrome radical.
C	H	R	O	N	I	C	Habitual, Accustomed, Confirmed, Usual, Accepted, Accustomed, Customary, Routine.
C	H	U	C	K	E	D	Dismissed, Ejected, Discarded, Ousted, Thrown.
C	H	U	C	K	E	R	Operator of machine that trims staves for barrels.
C	H	U	C	K	I	E	Small pebble.
C	H	U	C	K	L	E	Quiet hardly audible laugh.
C	H	U	D	D	A	H	Chador, Combination head covering, veil and shawl used by women among Muslim/Hindu people.
C	H	U	F	F	E	D	Proceeded or operated with chuffs.
C	H	U	G	G	E	D	Proceeded with intermittent explosive sounds.
C	H	U	K	K	E	R	Playing period of polo.
C	H	U	M	M	E	D	To share quarters, Showing affable friendliness.
C	H	U	P	A	T	I	Unleavened bread, Chapati.
C	H	U	R	C	H	Y	Zealous adherence to beliefs of a church.
C	H	U	R	N	E	D	Stirred, Beaten or agitated.
C	H	U	R	R	E	D	Vibrant or whirring noise.
C	H	U	R	R	U	S	Device for drawing water from deep wells.
C	H	U	T	N	E	Y	Condiment with consistency of jam made of fruits.
C	H	U	V	A	S	H	People of Eastern Russia.
C	H	Y	L	O	U	S	Consisting of chyle.
C	H	Y	M	A	S	E	Rennin.
C	H	Y	M	I	F	Y	Partly digested food.
C	H	Y	M	I	S	T	Chemist, Pharmacist, Apothecary.
C	I	C	O	N	I	A	Storks.
C	I	D	A	R	I	S	Sea urchin.
C	I	D	A	R	I	S	Royal tiara of the ancient Persian kings.
C	I	L	I	A	R	Y	Eyelashes.
C	I	L	I	A	T	E	Fringe of hairs, Barbical of feather.
C	I	M	B	R	I	C	Ancient Celtic people.
C	I	M	E	L	I	A	Treasures, Heirlooms, Church treasures.
C	I	M	E	T	E	R	Scimitar.
C	I	N	D	E	R	Y	Full of cinders, Begrimed with cinders.
C	I	N	E	O	L	E	Syrupy liquid of camphorlike odour used as expectorant.
C	I	N	E	R	E	A	Gray matter of nerve tissue.
C	I	N	Z	A	N	O	Vermouth from Turin, Italy used as aperitif.
C	I	P	O	L	I	N	Green marble.
C	I	R	C	A	E	A	Genus of low perennial herbs.
C	I	R	C	E	A	N	Dangerously misleading, Fatally attractive, Lulling.
C	I	R	C	L	E	D	Haloed, Encompassed, Circumvented, Ringed, Revolved, Circulated, Surrounded, Turned.
C	I	R	C	L	E	T	Ring, Coronet, Orb.
C	I	R	C	U	I	T	Circumference, Compass, Perimeter, Tour, Revolution, Rotation, League, Conference.
C	I	R	R	O	S	E	Churled.
C	I	R	R	O	U	S	White filmy cloud.
C	I	S	S	I	N	G	Gathering of wet streaks of varnish into drops or streaks.
C	I	S	S	O	I	D	Geometric curve.
C	I	S	T	E	R	N	Artificial reservoir, Wine cooler, Fluid-containing sac.
C	I	T	A	D	E	L	Fortress, Stronghold, Fastness, Redoubt, Fort, Mission hall of Salvation Army.

1	2	3	4	5	6	7	Definition
C	I	T	A	T	O	R	A record or indexed list of legal decisions and cases.
C	I	T	H	A	R	A	Ancient Greek musical instrument.
C	I	T	I	Z	E	N	Townsman, Burgher, Subject, National citizen, Civilian.
C	I	T	R	A	T	E	Salt of citric acid.
C	I	T	R	I	N	E	Lemon colour.
C	I	T	T	E	R	N	Early guitar.
C	I	V	E	T	T	E	Civet.
C	I	V	I	L	L	Y	Perfunctory politeness, Civil obligations, Civil law, Courteously.
C	I	V	V	I	E	S	Civilian clothes.
C	L	A	B	B	E	R	Sour milk that has thickened or curdled.
C	L	A	C	H	A	N	Hamlet, Small village.
C	L	A	C	K	E	D	Chattered, Clucked, Clicked, Cackled, Clattered, Babbled, Jabbered, Prattled.
C	L	A	C	K	E	R	Gossiping tongue, Rattle to frighten away birds.
C	L	A	D	O	D	E	Having many sprouts.
C	L	A	I	M	E	D	Demanded, Challenged, Requisitioned, Required, Maintained, Asserted, Defended, Vindicated.
C	L	A	I	M	E	R	Claimant, One that asserts rights.
C	L	A	M	A	N	T	Pressing, Burning, Crying, Dire, Imperative, Importunate, Instant, Urgent.
C	L	A	M	B	E	R	Scramble, Scrabble, Sparkle, Climb, Struggle.
C	L	A	M	M	E	D	Gathered clams, Tight-lipped, Close-mouthed person.
C	L	A	M	O	U	R	Hubbub, Rumpus, Protest, Commotion, Bustle, Tumult, Din, Ferment.
C	L	A	M	P	E	D	Held, Clasped, Clenched, Clutched, Grappled, Gripped, Pressed.
C	L	A	M	P	E	R	Patched clumsily or hastily.
C	L	A	N	G	E	D	Banged, Noise like metal struck.
C	L	A	N	K	E	D	Sharp abrupt ringing sound.
C	L	A	P	P	E	R	Tongue of bell, Rattle.
C	L	A	Q	U	E	R	Person hired to applaud.
C	L	A	R	A	I	N	Lustrous layer in coal.
C	L	A	R	I	F	Y	Purify, Clean, Cleanse, Elucidate, Explain, Illuminate, Illustrate, Define.
C	L	A	R	I	O	N	Fair, Clear, Fine, Pleasant, Medieval trumpet.
C	L	A	R	I	T	Y	Clearness, Lucidity, Plainness, Precision, Accuracy, Propriety, Brilliance, Brightness.
C	L	A	R	K	I	A	Small genus of showy annual herbs.
C	L	A	S	H	E	D	Bumped, Collided, Conflicted, Jangled, Mismatched, Opposed, Brawled.
C	L	A	S	P	E	D	Held, Clenched, Clutched, Grappled, Gripped, Embraced, Pressed, Squeezed.
C	L	A	S	P	E	R	Structure modified to assist in copulation.
C	L	A	S	S	E	D	Assorted, Categorized, Classified, Grouped, Pigeonholed, Sorted, Graded, Ranked.
C	L	A	S	S	I	C	Excellent, Capital, Famous, Prime, Superior, Top, Vintage, Typical.
C	L	A	S	S	I	S	Ecclesiastical governing body.
C	L	A	S	T	I	C	Breaking, Destroying, Disintegrating.
C	L	A	T	T	E	R	Clash, Rattle, Commotion, Clamour, Hassle, Tumult, Uproar, Turmoil.
C	L	A	V	A	T	E	Shaped like a club.
C	L	A	V	I	A	L	Violike instrument.
C	L	A	V	I	E	R	Keyboard of musical instrument.
C	L	A	V	I	O	L	Clavial.
C	L	A	W	I	N	G	Pulling, Tearing, Scratching, Scraping, Seizing, Digging.
C	L	A	Y	I	N	G	Daubing with clay, Filtering through clay.
C	L	A	Y	I	S	H	Like clay, Clay colour.
C	L	E	A	N	E	D	Purified, Clarified, Cleansed, Dressed, Gutted, Washed, Scoured.
C	L	E	A	N	E	R	Remover of dirt, More clean.
C	L	E	A	N	L	Y	Immaculate, Spotless, Unsoiled, Deftly executed, Cleverly devised.
C	L	E	A	N	S	E	Clean, Purify, Clarify, Disinfect, Sterilize, Expurgate, Purge, Absolve.
C	L	E	A	N	U	P	Clear, Gain, Make, Cleanse, Settle, Profit, Eliminate enemy.
C	L	E	A	R	E	D	Absolved, Acquitted, Exonerated, Vindicated, Clarified, Eliminated, Gained, Liquidated.
C	L	E	A	R	E	R	Less opaque, More transparent, To enlighten.
C	L	E	A	R	L	Y	Transparently, Translucently, Brightly, Lucidly, Distinctly.
C	L	E	A	V	E	D	Cut, Carved, Dissected, Severed, Sliced, Split, Torn, Rended.
C	L	E	A	V	E	R	Butcher's chopper, One that splits gems for polishing.
C	L	E	M	E	N	T	Forbearing, Charitable, Easy, Indulgent, Lenient, Merciful, Tolerant, Compassionate.
C	L	E	M	M	E	D	To suffer from hunger, thirst and cold.
C	L	E	P	I	N	G	Naming, Calling.
C	L	E	R	I	S	Y	Intelligentsia, Educated, Learned, Academic.
C	L	E	R	K	L	Y	Learned, Scholarly.
C	L	E	R	U	C	H	Citizen of ancient Greece who migrated to conquered lands.
C	L	E	W	I	N	G	Roll into a ball, Giving information.
C	L	I	C	H	E	D	Abounding in cliches, Trite, Hackneyed, Stale, Time-worn.
C	L	I	C	K	E	D	Succeeded, Fitted exactly, Operated efficiently.
C	L	I	C	K	E	R	One that operates a die cutting machine.
C	L	I	C	K	E	T	Latch, Latch-key.

1	2	3	4	5	6	7	
C	L	I	M	A	T	E	Environment, Atmosphere, Weather, Medium, Surroundings.
C	L	I	M	B	E	D	Ascended, Escalated, Mounted, Scaled, Swarmed.
C	L	I	N	K	E	D	Jingled, Chinked, Tingled, Tinkled, Short metallic sound.
C	L	I	N	K	E	R	Residue left in furnace from impurities, Failure, Poor quality.
C	L	I	P	P	E	D	Cut Cropped, Pruned, Shaved, Mown, Reduced, Slashed, Overcharged.
C	L	I	P	P	E	R	Instrument for clipping hair and nails, An electronic circuit.
C	L	I	T	T	E	R	Rattle, Bicker, Clack, Clatter, Shatter, Frictional sound, Stridulate.
C	L	I	V	E	R	S	Goose-grass which cleaves to fur or clothes by its hooks.
C	L	O	A	C	A	L	Concerned with obscenity or indecency.
C	L	O	A	K	E	D	Disguised, Camouflaged, Masked, Veiled, Concealed, Dissembled, Hidden, Screened.
C	L	O	B	B	E	R	Dress, Togs, Hit, Demolish, Crush, Thrash, Smear, Whip.
C	L	O	C	K	E	D	Timed, Registered, Determine timing, Called, Clucked.
C	L	O	C	K	E	R	One that times a race, or measures flow as of traffic.
C	L	O	D	D	E	D	Drive by pelting with clods of earth, Hurled.
C	L	O	G	G	E	D	Encumbered, Hampered, Coalesced, Saddled, Congested, Plugged, Blocked, Hobbled.
C	L	O	G	G	E	R	Clogmaker, Clog dancer.
C	L	O	I	S	O	N	Metal dividing strips used in cloisonné work.
C	L	O	N	K	E	D	Thudded, Clunked, Thumped.
C	L	O	O	T	I	E	Devil, Satan, Beelzebub, Diablo, Fiend, Lucifer.
C	L	O	S	E	L	Y	Secretly, Covertly, Tightly, Intimately, Accurately, Minutely, Strictly, Carefully.
C	L	O	S	E	S	T	Nearest, Tightest.
C	L	O	S	E	U	P	Close proximity, Detailed view from vantage point.
C	L	O	S	I	N	G	Sealing, Blocking, Closure, Last, Concluding, Final, Latest, Terminal.
C	L	O	S	U	R	E	End, Cessation, Conclusion, Ending, Stop, Termination, Completion, Confining.
C	L	O	T	B	U	R	Burdock.
C	L	O	T	H	E	D	Attired, Dressed, Equipped, Draped, Swathed, Invested, Arrayed.
C	L	O	T	T	E	D	Cluttered, Clogged, Choked with thickened assemblages.
C	L	O	T	T	E	R	Clot, Coagulate.
C	L	O	T	U	R	E	Closing or limitation of debate.
C	L	O	U	D	E	D	Doubtful, Dubious, Shady, Uncertain, Unsettled, Obscured, Shadowed, Dimmed.
C	L	O	U	T	E	D	Patched, Struck, Hit, Slogged, Socked, Whacked, Buffeted, Stole.
C	L	O	W	D	E	R	Group of cats.
C	L	O	W	N	E	D	Jest or ridicule grotesquely.
C	L	U	B	B	E	D	Gathered, Combined, United, Contributed, Coshed, Bludgeoned.
C	L	U	B	B	E	R	Member of a club.
C	L	U	B	M	A	N	Wealthy man belonging to exclusive clubs.
C	L	U	M	P	E	D	Grouped, Clustered, Lumped together, Trod noisily.
C	L	U	N	I	A	C	Benedictine monk.
C	L	U	S	T	E	R	Group, Array, Batch, Body, Bunch, Assembly, Band, Party.
C	L	U	T	T	E	R	Confusion, Chaos, Disorder, Muddle, Jumble, Litter, Mess, Scramble.
C	L	Y	P	E	A	L	Plate or shield on insect's head.
C	L	Y	P	E	U	S	Area on front of spider's head bounded by the the eyes.
C	L	Y	S	T	E	R	Purge, Enema.
C	O	A	C	H	E	D	Train intensively by repeated practice and demonstration, Instructed.
C	O	A	C	T	E	D	Interacted, Interplayed, Interreacted, Controlled force, Compelled, Driven, Controlled action.
C	O	A	G	E	N	T	Person, cause, force or other agency working together.
C	O	A	K	I	N	G	Uniting by dowelling.
C	O	A	L	G	A	S	Gas made from coal.
C	O	A	L	I	N	G	Taking on coal for fuel.
C	O	A	L	I	T	E	To unite or associate.
C	O	A	L	O	I	L	Kerosine.
C	O	A	L	P	I	T	Coal mine.
C	O	A	L	T	A	R	Tar extracted by distillation of bituminous coal.
C	O	A	L	T	I	T	Small European tit.
C	O	A	M	I	N	G	Raised frame around floor or roof opening.
C	O	A	P	T	E	D	Closed together, Fastened, Adhered.
C	O	A	R	S	E	N	Roughen.
C	O	A	R	S	E	R	Cruder, Rougher, Ruder, Harsher, Grosser.
C	O	A	S	T	A	L	Relating to a coast.
C	O	A	S	T	E	D	Moved, Traversed, Slid, Glided, Drifted.
C	O	A	S	T	E	R	Vessel engaged in taking cargo from one port to another in the same country.
C	O	A	T	I	N	G	Layer of substance used as cover, protection, decoration or finish.
C	O	A	X	I	A	L	Having common axis.
C	O	A	X	I	N	G	Cajoling, Wheedling, Pestering, Urging, Enticing, Coercing, Luring, Tempting.
C	O	B	B	I	N	G	Striking, Thumping, Surpassing, Excelling, Beating.
C	O	B	B	L	E	D	Mended, patched and repaired in coarse, rough fashion.
C	O	B	B	L	E	R	Maker and repairer of shoes.

1	2	3	4	5	6	7	Clue
C	O	B	I	R	O	N	Iron for supporting a spit.
C	O	B	W	O	R	K	Construction of log cabin.
C	O	C	A	I	N	E	Bitter crystalline alkaloid that acts as local anaesthetic.
C	O	C	H	I	S	E	Belonging to prehistoric culture of South-Eastern Arizona.
C	O	C	H	L	E	A	Conch, Spiral canal in the ear.
C	O	C	K	A	D	E	Rosette or knot of ribbons, Profile like a cock's comb.
C	O	C	K	E	Y	E	Squinting eye, Askew, Confused, Wrong, Incomprehensible, Topsy-turvy, Drunk.
C	O	C	K	I	N	G	Cockfighting.
C	O	C	K	L	E	D	Wrinkled, Puckered, Curled.
C	O	C	K	L	E	R	One that gathers and sells cockles.
C	O	C	K	N	E	Y	A native of London, Effeminate man, Milksop.
C	O	C	K	P	I	T	Place noted for bloody violent or long continued conflict, Compartment for crew of aircraft.
C	O	C	K	S	H	Y	Target, object or person taken as butt of constant or persistent criticism or rididucle.
C	O	C	O	N	U	T	Fruit of coconut palm.
C	O	C	O	T	T	E	Prostitute, Shallow individual baking dish.
C	O	C	O	Y	A	M	Being planted in cocoa groves.
C	O	C	T	I	L	E	Made by baking or exposing to heat.
C	O	C	T	I	O	N	Digestion, Attaining a more mature, perfect and desirable condition.
C	O	D	D	I	N	G	Teasing, Hoaxing, Bantering, Kidding.
C	O	D	D	L	E	D	Catered, Cossetted, Humoured, Indulged, Pampered, Spoiled.
C	O	D	E	I	N	E	Crystalline alkaloid associated in opium with morphine.
C	O	D	F	I	S	H	Flesh of cod often cured and salted.
C	O	D	I	C	E	S	Ancient book, Unbound manuscripts of Scripture, Greek and Latin classics.
C	O	D	I	C	I	L	Appendix to will, Supplement.
C	O	D	I	L	L	A	Mixture of hydrocarbons.
C	O	D	L	I	N	G	Small immature or inferior apple.
C	O	E	L	I	A	C	Abdominal cavity.
C	O	E	L	O	M	E	Concave.
C	O	E	N	U	R	E	Complex tapeworm larva.
C	O	E	Q	U	A	L	Equal with one another.
C	O	E	R	C	E	D	Forced, Compelled, Concussed, Constrained, Made, Obliged, Urged, Intimidated.
C	O	E	X	I	S	T	To live in peace with each other.
C	O	G	E	N	C	E	Compelling power, Convincing, Valid force.
C	O	G	E	N	C	Y	Point, Effectiveness, Force, Punch, Validity, Relevance, Bearing, Concern.
C	O	G	G	I	N	G	A cogged joint.
C	O	G	N	A	T	E	Person related to another on the mother's side.
C	O	G	N	I	S	E	Know, Perceive.
C	O	G	W	O	O	D	Hard tough wood of West Indian tree.
C	O	H	A	B	I	T	To live together as man and wife.
C	O	H	E	R	E	D	Stuck, Adhered, Suited, Blended, Fused, Merged, Combined, United.
C	O	H	E	R	E	R	A radio detector.
C	O	H	I	B	I	T	Restrain, Restrict.
C	O	I	F	F	E	D	To arrange hair by combing, brushing or curling.
C	O	I	L	I	N	G	Winding, Curling, Twining, Twisting, Revolving, Rotating, Rolling.
C	O	I	N	A	G	E	Manufacture of coins, Series of coins.
C	O	I	N	I	N	G	Minting, Striking, Coins, Creating, Inventing.
C	O	J	U	R	O	R	One that vouches for blameless character of another.
C	O	L	A	N	U	T	Kola-nut.
C	O	L	A	T	E	D	Manufactured by dissolving one ingredient in another without the application of heat.
C	O	L	D	E	S	T	Iciest, Frostiest.
C	O	L	D	I	S	H	Somewhat cold.
C	O	L	I	C	K	Y	Resembling colic.
C	O	L	I	T	I	S	Inflammation of the colon.
C	O	L	L	A	G	E	Artistic composition of fragments of material pasted on picture surface.
C	O	L	L	A	T	E	Compare critically, Arrange, Assemble, Bracket, Contrast, Examine.
C	O	L	L	E	C	T	Gather, Assemble, Congregate, Confress, Infer, Conduct, Compose, Amass.
C	O	L	L	E	G	E	Company, Assembly, Buildings used in connection with some specific purpose, Academy.
C	O	L	L	I	D	E	Bump, Clash, Atomize, Crash, Fragment, Pulverize, Shatter.
C	O	L	L	I	E	D	Blackened, Soot.
C	O	L	L	I	E	R	Charcoal maker, Ship transporting coal.
C	O	L	L	I	N	G	Embracing, Petting.
C	O	L	L	O	I	D	Crystalloid emulsion soil.
C	O	L	L	U	D	E	Conspire, Plot, Connive.
C	O	L	O	B	U	S	African monkey.
C	O	L	O	G	N	E	Perfumed toilet water.
C	O	L	O	N	E	L	Highest regimental rank.
C	O	L	O	S	S	I	Colossus, One marked by great scope, size, strength and power.

1	2	3	4	5	6	7	
C	O	L	O	U	R	S	Stand, Point of view, Vitally, Vividness, Interest, Timbre, Distinguishing pennants, Pigments.
C	O	L	T	I	S	H	Undisciplined, Wanton, Frisky, Playful, Sportive.
C	O	L	U	B	E	R	Snake.
C	O	L	U	L	U	S	Vestigial organ of spiders.
C	O	L	U	M	B	A	Genus of pigeon.
C	O	M	B	I	N	E	Join, Bracket, Connect, Embody, Unite, Coalition, Trust, Syndicate.
C	O	M	B	I	N	G	Dressing, Arranging, Scraping, Raking, Sorting, Scouring, Probing, Sifting.
C	O	M	B	U	S	T	Burn, Consume, Obscure, Overpower.
C	O	M	E	T	I	C	Erratic course as a comet.
C	O	M	F	O	R	T	Help, Aid, Assist, Support, Cheer, Console, Upraise, Convenience.
C	O	M	F	R	E	Y	Daisy plant.
C	O	M	I	C	A	L	Laughable, Droll, Farcical, Funny, Ludicrous, Foolish, Ridiculous, Waggish.
C	O	M	I	T	I	A	Ancient Roman assembly.
C	O	M	M	A	N	D	Dictate, Order, Power, Authority, Control, Domination, Ability, Mastery.
C	O	M	M	A	T	A	Plural of comma.
C	O	M	M	E	N	D	Commit, Confide, Consign, Entrust, Acclaim, Applaud, Praise, Recommend.
C	O	M	M	E	N	T	Remark, Note, Dictum, Observation, Cricitism, Notice, Review, Approve.
C	O	M	M	O	D	E	Movable sink or washstand, Chair holding toilet utensil under open seat.
C	O	M	M	O	N	S	Commoners, People, Plebeians, Populace, Rank and file, Plaza, Square, Garden.
C	O	M	M	O	V	E	Agitate, Excite, Impassion, Elate, Inspire, Stimulate, Exhilarate.
C	O	M	M	U	N	E	Commonalty, Commons, Various bodies treated as a unit at law, Group practicing communal living.
C	O	M	M	U	T	E	Exchange, Substitute, Interchange, Change, Alter, Transfer, Translate, Transpose.
C	O	M	P	A	C	T	Pithy, Close, Crowded, Dense, Unify, Concentrate, Contract, Agreement.
C	O	M	P	A	N	Y	Fellowship, Society, Visitors, Gathering, Congregation, Group, Band, Troop.
C	O	M	P	A	R	E	Equate, Match, Contrast, Bracket, Collate, Liken, Parallel, Assimilate.
C	O	M	P	A	R	T	Lay out in parts, Subdivision.
C	O	M	P	A	S	S	Surround, Encircle, Ring, Environ, Secure, Acquire, Apprehend, Understand.
C	O	M	P	E	A	R	Appear, Be visible.
C	O	M	P	E	E	R	Equal with, Match, Colleague, Associate, Compatriot, Confrere.
C	O	M	P	E	N	D	Compendium, Epitome.
C	O	M	P	E	R	E	Master of ceremonies of an entertainment, revue or radio programme.
C	O	M	P	E	T	E	Contend, Contest, Rival, Vie, Emulate, Dispute, Battle, Attempt.
C	O	M	P	I	L	E	List, Enumerate, Collect and assemble, Combine, Arrange, Amass.
C	O	M	P	L	E	X	Composite, Compound, Complicated, Elaborate, Intricate, Involved, Sophisticated, Disturbing.
C	O	M	P	L	I	N	Evening service.
C	O	M	P	L	O	T	Conspiracy, Plot.
C	O	M	P	O	R	T	Behave, Acquit, Act, Conduct, Agree, Accord, Check, Tally.
C	O	M	P	O	S	E	Constitute, Comprise, Make, Create, Calm, Allay, Collect, Restrain.
C	O	M	P	O	S	T	Mixture, Composition, Compound, Potting soil.
C	O	M	P	O	T	E	Fruit cooked in syrup, Small dish.
C	O	M	P	T	E	R	Count.
C	O	M	P	U	T	E	Calculate, Cipher, Estimate, Figure, Reckon.
C	O	M	R	A	D	E	Associate, Companion, Crony, Pal, Mate, Communist, Bolshevik.
C	O	M	T	I	S	M	Positivism.
C	O	M	T	I	S	T	Positivist.
C	O	N	A	C	R	E	Subletting a farm in portions for a single season.
C	O	N	A	T	U	S	Natural tendency, impulse or striving.
C	O	N	C	A	V	E	Hollow, Curved recess, Depression, Scooped, Arched in.
C	O	N	C	E	A	L	Hide, Bury, Cover, Screen, Secrete, Stash, Camouflage, Disguise.
C	O	N	C	E	D	E	Acknowledge, Admit, Allow, Confess, Grant, Accord, Award, Vouchsafe.
C	O	N	C	E	N	T	Consistency, Harmony.
C	O	N	C	E	P	T	Idea, Apprehension, Conceit, Image, Notion, Thought, Perception, Impression.
C	O	N	C	E	R	N	Interest, Affair, Care, Consideration, Uncertainty, Anxiety, Enterprise, Establishment.
C	O	N	C	E	R	T	Negotiate, Arrange, Settle, Agree, Coincide, Concord, Harmony, Chorus.
C	O	N	C	I	S	E	Brief, Curt, Laconic, Succinct, Pithy, Terse, Summary, Short.
C	O	N	C	O	C	T	Contrive, Devise, Formulate, Frame, Invent, Conceive, Envision, Create.
C	O	N	C	O	R	D	Harmony, Accord, Agreement, Rapport, Unity, Treaty, Agree, Convention.
C	O	N	C	U	S	S	Shake, Agitate, Jar, Coerce, Force, Convulse, Compel, Constrain.
C	O	N	D	E	M	N	Criticize, Blame, Condemn, Censure, Reprehend, Sentence, Proscribe, Denunciate.
C	O	N	D	I	G	N	Worthy, Deserved, Merited.
C	O	N	D	I	T	E	Pickle, Preserve.
C	O	N	D	O	L	E	Grieve, Sympathize, Console.
C	O	N	D	O	N	E	Excuse, Forgive, Pardon, Disregard, Forget, Ignore, Overlook.
C	O	N	D	U	C	E	Conduct, Guide, Effect, Tow, Contribute.
C	O	N	D	U	C	T	Guide, Escort, Accompany, Direct, Manage, Channel, Behave, Comport.
C	O	N	D	U	I	T	Channel, Aqueduct, Canal, Course, Pipeline, Passage.
C	O	N	D	Y	L	E	Knuckle, Joint, Fist.

1	2	3	4	5	6	7	Definition
C	O	N	E	L	E	T	A little cone.
C	O	N	F	E	C	T	Comfit, Confection.
C	O	N	F	E	S	S	Acknowledge, Admit, Allow, Avow, Concede, Grant, Own up, Disclose.
C	O	N	F	I	D	E	Commit, Commend, Entrust, Impart, Relegate, Consign, Breathe, Intimate.
C	O	N	F	I	N	E	Limit, Bound, Extent, Scope, Imprison, Intern, Constrain, Restrict.
C	O	N	F	I	R	M	Accede, Assent, Consent, Validate, Authenticate, Verify, Corroborate, Justify.
C	O	N	F	L	U	X	Confluence, Crowd, Assembly, Meeting, Concourse, Combining, Junction.
C	O	N	F	O	R	M	Agree, Correspond, Harmonize, Adapt, Adjust, Reconcile, Integrate, Obey.
C	O	N	F	U	S	E	Embarrass, Bewilder, Puzzle, Confound, Muddle, Misrepresent, Perplex, Fluster.
C	O	N	F	U	T	E	Disprove, Break, Confound, Rebut, Refute, Overcome, Silence, Controvert.
C	O	N	G	E	A	L	Coagulate, Clot, Jellify, Harden, Cake, Dry, Set, Solidify.
C	O	N	G	E	E	D	Dismissed, Ceremoniously bowed.
C	O	N	G	E	S	T	Clog, Choke, Overburden, Collect, Amass, Block, Fill, Obstruct.
C	O	N	G	R	E	E	Agree, In harmony.
C	O	N	G	R	U	E	Same as CONGREE.
C	O	N	I	C	A	L	Having shape of cone.
C	O	N	I	F	E	R	Evergreen pine, Fir tree.
C	O	N	I	I	N	E	Poisonous liquid alkaloid found in hemlock.
C	O	N	J	E	C	T	Speculate, Guess.
C	O	N	J	O	I	N	Join, Associate, Combine, Connect, Couple, Link, Relate, Unite.
C	O	N	J	U	R	E	Invoke, Beg, Appeal, Beseech, Crave, Entreat, Invent, Contrive.
C	O	N	J	U	R	Y	Practice of magic, Conjuring.
C	O	N	N	A	T	E	Congenital, Innate, Indigenous, Natural, Inherent, Constitutional, Related, Allied.
C	O	N	N	E	C	T	Join, Associate, Combine, Couple, Link, Unite, Wed, Yoke.
C	O	N	N	I	N	G	Deceiving, Cheating, Tricking, Fooling, Persuading, Luring, Steering.
C	O	N	N	I	V	E	Plot, Cogitate, Collude, Conspire, Contrive, Devise, Intrigue, Machinate.
C	O	N	N	O	T	E	Suggest, Hint, Imply, Insinuate, Intimate, Mean, Denote, Express.
C	O	N	Q	U	E	R	Crush, Defeat, Overpower, Overthrow, Whip, Win, Subjugate, Vanquish.
C	O	N	S	E	N	T	Assent, Accede, Acquiese, Agree, Subscribe, Approve, Concur, Sanction.
C	O	N	S	I	G	N	Send, Dispatch, Forward, Remit, Route, Transmit, Commit, Confide.
C	O	N	S	I	S	T	Exist, Reside, Agree, Accord, Comport, Conform, Correspond, Subsist.
C	O	N	S	O	L	E	Comfort, Cheer, Solace, Upraise, Soothe, Architectural bracket.
C	O	N	S	O	L	S	Perpetual interest bearing obligations.
C	O	N	S	O	R	T	Accompaniment, Associate, Companion, Fellow, Mate, Spouse, Agree, Accord.
C	O	N	S	T	A	T	Certificate of a record.
C	O	N	S	U	L	T	Confer, Advise, Confabulate, Huddle, Parley, Treat, Deliberate, Examine.
C	O	N	S	U	M	E	Devour, Exhaust, Waste, Expend, Eat, Punish, Monopolize, Dissipate.
C	O	N	T	A	C	T	Closeness, Proximity, Touching, Associating, Union, Reach, Intercourse, Communication.
C	O	N	T	A	I	N	Accommodate, Hold, Include, Comprehend, Encompass, Involve, Compose, Collect.
C	O	N	T	E	M	N	Despise, Disregard, Scorn, Treat with contempt.
C	O	N	T	E	N	D	Strive, Compete, Contest, Rival, Maintain, Argue, Battle, Fight.
C	O	N	T	E	N	T	Satisfy, Appease, Grafity, Delight, Thrill, Tickle, Bewitch, Captivate.
C	O	N	T	E	S	T	Competition, Conflict, Rivalry, Strife, Warfare, Skirmish, Battle, Engagement.
C	O	N	T	E	X	T	Environment, Coherence, Surrounding, Extract.
C	O	N	T	O	R	T	Deform, Distort, Misshape, Torture, Warp, Wind, Writhe, Bend.
C	O	N	T	O	U	R	Outline, Delineation, Figuration, Profile, Silhouette, Graph, Shape, Form.
C	O	N	T	R	O	L	Govern, Direct, Dominate, Manage, Compose, Collect, Power, Authority.
C	O	N	T	U	N	D	Pound, Bruise, Contuse.
C	O	N	T	U	S	E	Bruise, Black, Crush, Injure.
C	O	N	V	E	N	E	Summon, Call, Meet, Open, Assemble, Muster, Convoke.
C	O	N	V	E	N	T	Community of nuns.
C	O	N	V	E	R	T	Transform, Change, Commute, Translate, Transpose, Move, Persuade, Sway.
C	O	N	V	I	C	T	Jailbird, Felon, Sentence, Prove, Repute, Declare guilty.
C	O	N	V	I	V	E	Guest at table, Boon companion.
C	O	N	V	O	K	E	Assemble, Convene, Summon, Call, Collect, Congregate, Gather, Invite.
C	O	O	K	E	R	Y	Art, science, process or practice of cooking.
C	O	O	K	I	N	G	Make fit for eating by use of heat, Broiling, Roasting, Contriving, Devising, Inventing.
C	O	O	L	E	S	T	Calmest, Most cool, Dispassionate.
C	O	O	L	I	N	G	Losing heat, Moderating, Reducing temperature.
C	O	O	L	I	S	H	Somewhat cool.
C	O	O	N	C	A	N	Game of rummy.
C	O	O	N	T	I	E	Tough woody plants whose roots yield arrowroot.
C	O	O	P	E	R	Y	Place where cooper makes casks and tubs.
C	O	O	P	I	N	G	Confining, Restricting, Penning, Obstructing, Inhibiting, ENclosing, Secluding.
C	O	O	P	T	E	D	Preempted, Commandeered, Elected, Chosen.
C	O	P	A	I	B	A	Balsam obtained from S. American tree.
C	O	P	E	P	O	D	Minute aquatic parasitic organism.

1	2	3	4	5	6	7	Definition
C	O	P	I	L	O	T	Assistant to chief pilot.
C	O	P	I	O	U	S	Plentiful, Abundant, Ample, Bounteous, Generous, Liberal, Plenty, Luxuriant.
C	O	P	P	E	R	Y	Like colour in copper.
C	O	P	P	I	C	E	Underwood, Brushwood, Forest originating from shoots.
C	O	P	P	I	N	G	Capturing, Catching, Arresting, Stealing.
C	O	P	U	L	A	R	Relating to a link.
C	O	P	Y	C	A	T	One who slavishly imitates another.
C	O	P	Y	I	N	G	Imitating, Aping, Miming, Mocking.
C	O	P	Y	I	S	M	Act or practice of copying.
C	O	P	Y	I	S	T	Imitator, Plagiarist, Copycat.
C	O	Q	U	I	N	A	Small marine clam used for chowder.
C	O	Q	U	I	T	A	Cordage fibre of palm.
C	O	Q	U	I	T	O	Pinnate-leaved palm.
C	O	R	A	C	L	E	Small boat of wicker covered with hide.
C	O	R	A	N	T	O	Dance, Carouse, Romp.
C	O	R	B	E	A	U	Greenish black.
C	O	R	B	E	I	L	Sculptured basket of flowers or fruit.
C	O	R	C	A	S	S	Marsh or mud flat.
C	O	R	D	A	G	E	Ropes or cords, Number of cords in a given area.
C	O	R	D	A	T	E	Heart-shaped.
C	O	R	D	I	A	L	Gracious, Affable, Congenial, Sociable, Genial, Responsive, Tender, Sincere.
C	O	R	D	I	N	G	Binding, Fastening or connecting with cords, Cord covered with fabric.
C	O	R	D	I	T	E	Smokeless powder composed of nitroglycerin, guncotton and mineral jelly.
C	O	R	D	O	B	A	Monetary unit of Nicaragua.
C	O	R	E	B	O	X	Open box in which a foundry core is formed.
C	O	R	I	N	N	E	Common gazelle.
C	O	R	I	N	T	H	Any of certain red dyes.
C	O	R	I	V	A	L	Competitor.
C	O	R	K	A	G	E	Charge made by hotel or restaurant.
C	O	R	K	I	N	G	Extremely fine, Extraordinary good, Impairment of quality of wine.
C	O	R	K	L	E	G	Artificial leg.
C	O	R	N	C	O	B	Ear of Indian corn.
C	O	R	N	E	A	L	Relating to the eye membrane.
C	O	R	N	I	C	E	Crown, Valance, Ledge, Top moulding.
C	O	R	N	I	F	Y	Convert or change into horny tissue.
C	O	R	N	I	N	G	Granulating, Preserving, Salting, Pickling.
C	O	R	N	I	S	H	Relating to Cornwall, Domestic fowl.
C	O	R	N	L	A	W	Law regulating trade in grain.
C	O	R	N	O	I	L	Yellow oil obtained from corn kernels.
C	O	R	N	U	A	L	Something shaped or resembling a horn.
C	O	R	N	U	T	E	Cuckold, Having horns.
C	O	R	O	L	L	A	Inner set of floral leaves.
C	O	R	O	N	A	L	Circlet, Wreath, Crown, Garland of flowers.
C	O	R	O	N	E	R	Public officer presiding over an inquest.
C	O	R	O	N	E	T	Crown, Sequence of cards.
C	O	R	O	N	I	S	Mark used in Greek over a vowel to indicate contraction.
C	O	R	R	E	C	T	Amend, Mend, Rectify, Right, Punish, Castigate, Chasten, Indulge.
C	O	R	R	O	D	E	Eat, Bite, Erode, Gnaw, Scour, Rust, Canker.
C	O	R	R	O	D	Y	Right of free food, Allowance for charity.
C	O	R	R	U	P	T	Debase, Deprave, Pervert, Crumble, Decompose, Vicious, Infamous, Crooked.
C	O	R	S	A	G	E	Waist or bodice of dress, Arrangement of flowers to be worn as costume accessory.
C	O	R	S	A	I	R	Pirate, Buccaneer, Picaroon, ROver, Sea Robber, Sea dog, Freebooter, Sea rover.
C	O	R	S	L	E	T	Tight-fitting garment covering trunk, Piece of armour for trunk.
C	O	R	T	E	G	E	Train of attendants, Procession of mourners.
C	O	R	T	I	L	E	Open courtyard enclosed by walls of building, Cloister.
C	O	R	V	I	N	E	Resembling a crow.
C	O	R	V	O	I	D	Same as CORVINE.
C	O	R	Y	L	U	S	Genus of shrubs or small trees, Hazel nuts.
C	O	R	Y	P	H	A	Small genus of fan palms.
C	O	S	A	Q	U	E	Cracker.
C	O	S	H	E	R	Y	Entertainment at lodgings.
C	O	S	H	I	N	G	Striking, Assaulting, Bashing, Slugging.
C	O	S	I	E	S	T	Snuggest, Most cosy.
C	O	S	M	I	S	M	Philosophy of cosmic evolution.
C	O	S	S	A	C	K	Russian cavalryman.
C	O	S	T	A	R	D	English cooking apple.
C	O	S	T	A	T	E	Having ribs, Ridged surface.

1	2	3	4	5	6	7	Definition
C	O	S	T	E	A	N	Digging for mineral deposits.
C	O	S	T	I	N	G	Calculating, Recording and allocating of costs.
C	O	S	T	I	V	E	Constipated, Sluggish, Niggardly, Obstructive, Stingy, Parsimonious, Miserly, Mean.
C	O	S	T	R	E	L	Leather, wooden or earthwnare container for liquids.
C	O	S	T	U	M	E	Dress, Uniform, Guise, Outfit, Rig, Livery, Fashion, Mode, Style.
C	O	T	E	R	I	E	Clique, Camp, Circle, Clan, Mob, Ring.
C	O	T	H	U	R	N	Thick-soled laced boot, Stilted spirit of ancient tragedy.
C	O	T	I	D	A	L	Marking or equality in tides.
C	O	T	I	N	G	A	Genus of American bird.
C	O	T	I	S	E	D	Between stripes in heraldry.
C	O	T	L	A	N	D	Land belonging to a peasant above rank of slave.
C	O	T	T	A	G	E	Hut, Shack, Guesthouse, Lodge, Cabin, Shanty, Cot, Caboose.
C	O	T	T	I	C	E	Narrow stripes in heraldry.
C	O	T	T	I	E	R	Peasant farmer.
C	O	T	T	O	N	Y	Downy, Nappy, Woolly, Soft.
C	O	T	Y	L	A	R	Relating to a cotyla, Small kettle, Cup.
C	O	U	C	H	E	D	Overlaid, Inlaid, Located, Bedded.
C	O	U	C	H	E	E	Late evening reception.
C	O	U	C	H	E	R	Coward.
C	O	U	L	D	N	T	Could not.
C	O	U	L	E	U	R	Colour, Colour of first card dealt in card game.
C	O	U	L	O	I	R	Deep gully, Passage, Gangway, Corridor, Hall.
C	O	U	L	O	M	B	Measurement of electric charge.
C	O	U	L	T	E	R	Cutting attachment for plough.
C	O	U	N	C	I	L	Assembly, Club, Society, Association, Ministry, Senate, Organization, Administration.
C	O	U	N	S	E	L	Advice, Advise, Recommend, Barrister, Opinion, Direction, Deliberation, Consultation.
C	O	U	N	T	E	D	Enumerated, Tallied, Numbered, Estimated, Added, Weighed, Signified, Calculated.
C	O	U	N	T	E	R	Contrary, Adverse, Pit, Vie, Match, Opposite, Converse, Opposed.
C	O	U	N	T	R	Y	Region, State, Nation, Fatherland, Homeland, Soil, Motherland, Home.
C	O	U	P	L	E	D	Joined, Bracketed, United, Combined, Hitched, Harnesses, Yoked, Linked.
C	O	U	P	L	E	R	Coupling, Connector, Junction, Union.
C	O	U	P	L	E	T	Two successive lines of verse, Pair, Twins.
C	O	U	R	A	G	E	Fortitude, Resolution, Spirit, Pluck, Heart, Mettle, Valour, Bravery.
C	O	U	R	A	N	T	Newspaper, Running in heraldry, Romp, Caper, Gossipining.
C	O	U	R	I	E	R	Messenger, Bearer, Carrier, Emissary, Envoy, Tourist guide, Espionage agent.
C	O	U	R	L	A	N	Long-billed bird of S. and Central America.
C	O	U	R	S	E	D	Careered, Chased, Raced, Rushed, Sped, Hastened, Hurried, Scampered.
C	O	U	R	S	E	R	War-horse, Charger.
C	O	U	R	S	E	S	Runs, Traverses, Chases, Pulsates, Surges, Races, Sprints.
C	O	U	R	T	E	D	Addressed, Pursued, Wooed, Sued, Charmed, Captivated, Invited, Solicited.
C	O	U	R	T	L	Y	Politely, Civil, Respectful, Urbane, Gallant, Gracious, Stately, Elegant.
C	O	U	T	H	I	E	Pleasant, Kindly, Friendly, Comfortable, Snug.
C	O	U	V	A	D	E	Custom of a primitive male to take his new born child to bed as if he suffered pains of childbirth.
C	O	V	E	R	E	D	Guarded, Protected, Safeguarded, Screened, Shielded, Concealed, Secreted, Buried.
C	O	V	E	R	U	P	Device of strategem of masking, concealing or preventing investigation or discovery.
C	O	V	E	T	E	D	Desired, Craved, Wanted, Wished, Envied.
C	O	W	B	A	N	E	Water hemlock.
C	O	W	B	E	A	N	Cow pea.
C	O	W	B	E	E	T	Mangel-wurzel.
C	O	W	B	E	L	L	Bell to aid location of cow, Percussion instrument.
C	O	W	B	I	N	D	White bryony.
C	O	W	B	I	R	D	Small N. American blackbird.
C	O	W	C	A	L	F	Heifer.
C	O	W	E	R	E	D	Cringed, Shrank, Crouched, Fawned, Toadied, Flinched, Recoiled, Winced.
C	O	W	F	I	S	H	Dolphins and porpoises.
C	O	W	G	A	T	E	Right to pasture one cow on common ground.
C	O	W	G	I	R	L	Girl performing work of cowboy.
C	O	W	G	R	A	M	Chick pea.
C	O	W	H	A	G	E	Tropical woody vine.
C	O	W	H	A	N	D	Man to assist with care of range cattle, Cowboy.
C	O	W	H	E	E	L	Cow or ox foot stewed to jelly.
C	O	W	H	E	R	B	European soapwort.
C	O	W	H	E	R	D	One who tends cows.
C	O	W	H	I	D	E	Leather made of hide of adult bovine animal.
C	O	W	I	T	C	H	Cowhage.
C	O	W	L	I	C	K	Lock or tuft of hair growing in a different direction from the rest of the hair.
C	O	W	L	I	K	E	Having characteristics of a cow.

1	2	3	4	5	6	7	
C	O	W	L	I	N	G	Removable metal covering of an engine.
C	O	W	S	L	I	P	Primrose, Marsh marigold.
C	O	W	T	R	E	E	S. American tree yielding rich milky juice used as food.
C	O	X	C	O	M	B	Fop, Buck, Dandy, Dude, Lounge lizard, Conceited fool.
C	O	Y	N	E	S	S	Shyness, Bashfulness, Timidness.
C	O	Z	E	N	E	D	Cheated, Bilked, Defrauded, Diddled, Swindled, Deluded, Deceived, Wheedled.
C	R	A	B	B	E	D	Morose, Surly, Disparaged, Sullen, Dour, Gloomy, Saturnine, Sulky.
C	R	A	B	I	E	R	Crab eating birds of the Caribbean area.
C	R	A	C	K	E	D	Broken, Snapped, Decoded, Damaged, Flawed, Insane, Lunatic, Crazy.
C	R	A	C	K	E	R	Biscuit, Boaster, Firecracker, Snapper.
C	R	A	C	K	L	E	Sparkle, Effervescence, Small sharp sudden noise, Craze on china.
C	R	A	C	K	U	P	Nervous breakdown, Collapse, Nervous prostration, Crash, Wreck, Debacle, Smash, Decline.
C	R	A	C	O	W	E	Style prevalent in Crakow.
C	R	A	D	L	E	D	Sheltered, Reared, Nurtured, Support protectively.
C	R	A	G	G	E	D	Rough, Craggy, Harsh, Jagged, Rugged, Uneven, Scabrous, Asperous.
C	R	A	K	I	N	G	Harsh cry, Complaining, Fretting.
C	R	A	M	B	U	S	Genus of small moth.
C	R	A	M	M	E	D	Jammed, Stuffed, Studied under pressure, Packed, Brimful, Crowded, Loaded.
C	R	A	M	M	E	R	Instructor or teacher that gives intensive coaching.
C	R	A	M	P	E	D	Confined, Incommodious, Narrow, Tight, Tiny.
C	R	A	M	P	O	N	Spike for climbing ice covered mountain, Grappling iron.
C	R	A	N	A	G	E	Use of crane and price for such where used for loading and unloading ships.
C	R	A	N	I	A	L	Belonging to the skull.
C	R	A	N	I	N	G	Stretching one's neck, Hesitating.
C	R	A	N	I	U	M	Skull, Braincase.
C	R	A	N	K	E	D	Bent, Turned, Wound, Steady, Stiff.
C	R	A	N	K	L	E	Bend, Turn, Twist, Twine, Zigzag.
C	R	A	N	N	O	G	Artificial fortified island constructed in a lake.
C	R	A	P	I	N	G	Draping, Covering, Shrouding, Curling.
C	R	A	P	P	I	E	N. American sunfish.
C	R	A	S	H	E	D	Smashed, Shattered, Failed, Folded.
C	R	A	T	I	N	G	Boxing from a crate.
C	R	A	U	N	C	H	Crunch.
C	R	A	V	I	N	G	Entreating, Longing, Yearning, Desiring.
C	R	A	W	L	E	D	Crept, Trailed, Moved slowly.
C	R	A	W	L	E	R	One that crawls, Child's overall.
C	R	A	Z	I	L	Y	In a crazy manner.
C	R	A	Z	I	N	G	Crushing, Cracking, Smashing, Breaking, Shattering.
C	R	E	A	K	E	D	Grated, Squeaked.
C	R	E	A	M	E	D	Foamed, Frothed, Skimmed cream off milk, Beaten, Lambasted, Removed.
C	R	E	A	N	C	E	Leash for hawk during training.
C	R	E	A	S	E	D	Wrinkled, Corrugated, Crinkled, Folded, Furrowed, Ridge, Rucked.
C	R	E	A	T	E	D	Composed, Constituted, Established, Organized, Procreated, Produced, Spawned, Originated.
C	R	E	A	T	I	C	Relating to or caused by flesh or animal food.
C	R	E	A	T	O	R	Maker, Author, Inventor, Originator, Producer, Father.
C	R	E	D	E	N	T	Confiding, Credible.
C	R	E	E	I	N	G	To soften into a pulpy mass by boiling.
C	R	E	E	P	E	R	One that creeps, Freelance reporter, Climber, Grapnel, A plant that creeps.
C	R	E	E	P	I	E	Low three-legged stool.
C	R	E	M	A	T	E	To reduce to ashes by action of fire, Incinerate.
C	R	E	M	O	N	A	Reed stop on the organ.
C	R	E	N	A	T	E	Having the margin cut in rounded scallops.
C	R	E	O	S	O	L	Colourless aromatic phenol obtained from beechwood tar.
C	R	E	S	S	E	T	Fire basket, Beacon, Torch.
C	R	E	S	T	E	D	Surmounted, Capped, Crowned, Topped, Heraldic device.
C	R	E	T	I	F	Y	Calcify, Convert into chalk, Infiltrate with calcium salts.
C	R	E	T	I	O	N	Act before magistrate by which an outside heir declares his acceptance of succession.
C	R	E	V	I	C	E	Narrow opening, Narrow recess, Crack, Fissure.
C	R	E	W	M	A	N	Member of a crew.
C	R	I	B	B	E	D	Caged, Cramped, Restrained, Pilfered, Purloined, Plagiarized, Copied.
C	R	I	B	B	L	E	Sieve, Strainer, Cover surface with small round holes or dots.
C	R	I	C	K	E	D	Wrenched, Strained.
C	R	I	C	K	E	T	Insect, Metal toy, Small false roof. A game played with bat and ball, Fair and honourable behaviour.
C	R	I	C	O	I	D	Cartilage of the larynx.
C	R	I	M	I	N	E	Used to express surprise.
C	R	I	M	I	N	G	Indict and punish a soldier for a minor infraction of military rules.
C	R	I	M	P	E	D	Crumpled, Crinkled, Rucked, Scrunched, Wrinkled, Restrained, Checked, Constrained.

1	2	3	4	5	6	7	
C	R	I	M	P	L	E	Crimp, Curl, Wave, Crinkle, Ruckle, Screw, Ripple, Rumple.
C	R	I	M	S	O	N	Bloody, Flushed, Violent, Lurid, Blush, Rippen.
C	R	I	N	G	E	D	Fawned, Cowered, Grovelled, Toadied, Blenched, Flinched, Quailed, Winced.
C	R	I	N	G	E	R	One that cringes.
C	R	I	N	G	L	E	Ring or loop for fastening something.
C	R	I	N	I	T	E	Covered or provided with hairy growths.
C	R	I	N	K	L	E	Crumple, Wrinkle, Scrunch, Corrugation, Crease, Fold, Furrow, Ridge.
C	R	I	N	O	I	D	Sea-lily.
C	R	I	O	L	L	A	Relating to Latin America.
C	R	I	O	L	L	O	Same as CRIOLLA.
C	R	I	P	P	L	E	Maim, Dismember, Mutilate, Paralyze, Disable, Weaken, Debilitate, Enfeeble.
C	R	I	S	P	E	D	Curled, Crimped, Rippled, Burned.
C	R	I	S	P	E	R	One that crisps, Closed container in refrigerator.
C	R	I	S	P	I	N	Shoemaker, Cobbler.
C	R	I	S	P	L	Y	Inciseively, Penetratingly, Briskly.
C	R	I	T	T	E	R	Creature, Beast, Animal, Brute.
C	R	I	Z	Z	L	E	Roughened surface.
C	R	O	A	K	E	D	Grumbled, Groused, Muttered, Scolded, Died, Expired, Passed away.
C	R	O	A	K	E	R	Physician, Medicine, Fish, One that grumbles.
C	R	O	C	H	E	T	Interlocking of looped stitch formed with single thread and hooked needle.
C	R	O	C	K	E	D	Intoxicated, Boozed, Broken down, Drunk, Inebriated, Muddled.
C	R	O	C	K	E	T	Ornament used on gable or spire.
C	R	O	E	S	U	S	A very wealthy man.
C	R	O	F	T	E	R	One that rents and works a croft.
C	R	O	O	D	L	E	Low murmuring sound, Cuddle, Snuggle, Cower, Crouch, Burrow.
C	R	O	O	K	E	D	Curved, Winding, Bending, Circuitous, Corrupted, Dishonest, Cheat, Devious.
C	R	O	O	N	E	D	Wailed, Moaned, Lamented, Lulled, Sing in gentl murmuring manner.
C	R	O	O	N	E	R	Singer using soft-voiced technique.
C	R	O	P	P	E	D	Plucked, Trimmed, Cut, Cultivated, Gathered, Harvested.
C	R	O	P	P	E	R	One that raises produce, Severe fall, Worker that cuts hides.
C	R	O	Q	U	E	T	Game played with hoops, ball and sticks.
C	R	O	S	I	E	R	Pastoral staff, Crook, Cross.
C	R	O	S	N	E	S	Chinese artichoke.
C	R	O	S	S	E	D	Denied, Contradicted, Thwarted, Betrayed, Hybridized, Interbred, Intersected, Traversed.
C	R	O	S	S	L	Y	Peevishly, Petulantly.
C	R	O	T	A	L	S	Small spherical metal rattle.
C	R	O	T	T	L	E	Lichen dye.
C	R	O	U	P	O	N	Untanned cattlehide.
C	R	O	U	T	O	N	Bread cube fried crisp.
C	R	O	W	B	A	R	Lever, Jemmy.
C	R	O	W	D	E	D	Pressed, Huddled, Crushed, Thronged, Compressed, Squashed, Crammed, Clustered.
C	R	O	W	D	E	R	Fiddler.
C	R	O	W	D	I	E	Porridge, Gruel of oatmeal and milk.
C	R	O	W	H	O	P	Short quick jump.
C	R	O	W	I	N	G	Exulting, Rejoicing, Boasting, Bragging.
C	R	O	W	N	E	D	Surmounted, Capped, Honoured, Completed, Climaxed, Culminated, Covered, Topped.
C	R	O	W	N	E	R	Coroner, Fall on head, Inspector of shoes.
C	R	O	W	N	E	T	Coronet.
C	R	O	W	T	O	E	Buttercup, Wood hyacinth.
C	R	O	Z	I	E	R	Crosier.
C	R	U	C	I	A	L	Critical, Acute, Decisive, Dire, Desperate, Important, Vital, Pressing.
C	R	U	C	I	F	Y	Martyr, Torment, Torture, Agonize, Afflict, Excruciate, Harrow, Smite.
C	R	U	D	D	L	E	Curdle.
C	R	U	D	E	L	Y	Roughly, Simply, Approximately, Bluntly.
C	R	U	D	E	S	T	Coarsest, Rawest, Roughest.
C	R	U	D	I	T	Y	Rawness, Roughness, Harshness, Impoliteness, Imperfection.
C	R	U	E	L	L	Y	Mercilessly, Extremely, Severely, Inhumanely, Savagely, Harshly.
C	R	U	E	L	T	Y	Inhumanity, Savagery, Barbarity, Inflict pain and suffering, Harshness of discipline.
C	R	U	I	S	E	D	Sailed, Travelled, Explored, Journeyed.
C	R	U	I	S	E	R	Warship, Powerboat, Traveller, Boxer.
C	R	U	I	S	I	E	Iron lamp.
C	R	U	L	L	E	R	Small sweet cake.
C	R	U	M	B	E	D	Broken into crumbs, Shredded, Covered with crumbs.
C	R	U	M	B	L	E	Disintegrate, Collapse, Decay, Fire debris.
C	R	U	M	B	L	Y	Easily crumbled, Friable.
C	R	U	M	P	E	D	Shelled, Bombed, Blasted.
C	R	U	M	P	E	T	Small round cake usually split and toasted.

1	2	3	4	5	6	7	Definition
C	R	U	M	P	L	E	Wrinkle, Crinkle, Ruffle, Crunkle, Scrunch, Ruckle, Give, Bend, Collapse.
C	R	U	N	K	L	E	Crumple, Crimp, Crinkle.
C	R	U	P	P	E	R	Saddle-strap.
C	R	U	S	A	D	E	Expedition for religious purpose, Remedial activity.
C	R	U	S	A	D	O	Old Portugese gold coin.
C	R	U	S	H	E	D	Pressed, Mashed, Squashed, Pulverized, Crowded, Conquered, Subjugated, Crammed.
C	R	U	S	H	E	R	Machine for crushing rocks, oilseeds, grapes and other materials.
C	R	U	S	I	L	Y	Sprinkled with cross-crosslet in heraldry.
C	R	U	S	T	A	E	Something prepared for inlaying or applying.
C	R	U	S	T	E	D	Covered with incrustation, Formed a crust, Having adhering layer or deposit.
C	R	Y	B	A	B	Y	One who cries or complains easily or often.
C	R	Y	O	G	E	N	Substance for obtaining low temperatures.
C	R	Y	P	T	I	C	Dark, Enigmatic, Mystifying, Obscure, Murky, Opaque, Vague, Incomprehensible.
C	R	Y	S	T	A	L	Transparent quartz, Clear, Lucent, Lucid, Luminous, Pellucid, Translucent, Unblurred.
C	T	E	N	O	I	D	Having the margin toothed like a comb, Scales with ctenoid margins.
C	U	B	B	I	N	G	Confine, Shut up, Hunting of young foxes.
C	U	B	B	I	S	H	Awkward, Uncouth.
C	U	B	I	C	A	L	Cubic, Relating to volume.
C	U	B	I	C	L	E	Small room, Compartment.
C	U	B	I	T	U	S	Forearm, Ulna.
C	U	B	I	T	A	L	Cubital, Primary vein of insect's wing.
C	U	C	K	O	L	D	Husband of adulteress.
C	U	C	K	O	O	S	Cuckoo.
C	U	D	B	E	A	R	Colouring matter prepared from lichens.
C	U	D	D	L	E	D	Caressed, Fondled, Petted, Snuggled, Burrowed, Nestled, Nuzzled, Embraced.
C	U	D	W	E	E	D	Any of plants with silky or woolly foliage.
C	U	E	B	A	L	L	Ball struck with billiard cue.
C	U	F	F	I	N	G	Fighting, Striking, Scuffling, Slapping, Smacking, Spanking, Punching, Socking.
C	U	I	R	A	S	S	Armour covering body from neck to girdle.
C	U	I	S	I	N	E	Manner of preparing food, Style of cooking.
C	U	I	T	T	L	E	Coax, Wheedle, Cajole.
C	U	L	I	C	I	D	Relating to mosquito.
C	U	L	L	I	N	G	Garnering, Extracting, Choosing, Gathering, Selecting, Gleaning, Discriminating, Amassing.
C	U	L	L	I	O	N	Orchid.
C	U	L	P	R	I	T	Accused person, Guilty one, Criminal, Delinquent, Offender.
C	U	L	T	I	S	T	Devotee or practitioner of a cult.
C	U	L	T	U	R	E	Breeding, Cultivation, Polish, Refinement, Education, Gentility, Class, Elegance.
C	U	L	V	E	R	T	Transverse drain or waterway, Small bridge.
C	U	M	B	E	N	T	Recumbent, Lying down.
C	U	M	F	R	E	Y	Comfrey.
C	U	M	Q	U	A	T	Kumquat, Small orange citrus fruits with acid pulp used in preserves.
C	U	M	S	H	A	W	Gratuity, Largess, Perquisite, Tip, Gift, Present.
C	U	M	U	L	U	S	Heap, Accumulation, Massy cloud form.
C	U	N	E	A	T	E	Wedge-shaped.
C	U	N	N	I	N	G	Artfulness, Craft, Slyness, Deceit, Duplicity, Guile, Adroitness, Dexterity.
C	U	P	F	U	L	L	As much as a cup wil hold.
C	U	P	M	A	T	E	Drinking companion.
C	U	P	P	I	N	G	Curving into a hollow, Place as if in a cup.
C	U	P	R	A	T	E	Insoluble solid obtained by heating copper oxide.
C	U	P	R	I	T	E	Copper ore.
C	U	P	R	O	U	S	Relating to copper.
C	U	R	A	B	L	E	Capable of being cured.
C	U	R	A	C	A	O	Orange-flavoured liqueur.
C	U	R	A	T	O	R	Overseer, Guardian, Manager, Steward, Custodian, Keeper, Warden.
C	U	R	B	I	N	G	Hampering, Restraining, Shackling, Denying, Checking, Holding, Withholding, Repressing.
C	U	R	C	U	M	A	Arrowroot, Turmeric.
C	U	R	D	I	N	G	Coagulating, Thickening, Congealing.
C	U	R	D	L	E	D	Spoiled, Addled, Soured, Embittered, Congealed, Frozen, Coagulated.
C	U	R	E	A	L	L	Panacea, Remedy for all diseases.
C	U	R	E	T	T	E	Scoop, ring or loop used as a scraper of a bodily cavity.
C	U	R	I	O	S	A	Curiosities, Rareties, Pornography, Erotica, Strange or unusual books or objects.
C	U	R	I	O	S	O	Collection of curios or objects d'arts.
C	U	R	I	O	U	S	Elaborate, Inquisitive, Chary, Cautious, Prying, Snoopy, Strange, Bizarre.
C	U	R	L	I	N	G	Winding, Coiling, Rolling, Twining, Twisting, Spiralling, Spinning stones on ice.
C	U	R	R	A	C	K	Wicker pannier.
C	U	R	R	A	G	H	Coracle, Wicker boat covered with hide.
C	U	R	R	A	N	T	Dried seedless raisin used in cooking. Plant with fruit with acid edible juice used in jam making.

1	2	3	4	5	6	7	
C	U	R	R	E	N	T	Running, Flowing, Moving, Fluent, Present, Existent, Prevailing, Widespread.
C	U	R	R	I	E	D	Groomed(horse), Thrashed, Dressed, Arranged, Gained favour.
C	U	R	R	I	E	R	One that grooms horses, One that dresses hides.
C	U	R	R	I	N	G	Cooing(doves), Purring(cats).
C	U	R	R	I	S	H	Mongrel, Base, Meanspirited.
C	U	R	S	I	N	G	Blaspheming, Swearing, Cussing, Imprecating, Objurgating, Execrating.
C	U	R	S	I	V	E	Running, Coursing, Flowing, Easy, Effortless, Smooth.
C	U	R	S	O	R	Y	Superficial, Shallow, Sketchy, Uncritical, Hasty, Haphazard, Random, Hurried.
C	U	R	T	A	I	L	Shorten, Abbreviate, Abridge, Cut, Retrench, Diminish, Lessen, Minify.
C	U	R	T	A	I	N	Window drape, Screen, Conceal, Barrier, Protect, Restrict.
C	U	R	T	A	T	E	Shortened, Reduced, Abbreviated.
C	U	R	T	E	S	T	Briefest, Shortest, Bluntest.
C	U	R	T	S	E	Y	Act of respect or reverence made by women dropping the body by bending the knees.
C	U	R	V	I	N	G	Bending, Twisting, Bowing, Diverting, Deviating, Swerving, Coiling, Winding.
C	U	R	V	I	T	Y	Curvature, Curve.
C	U	S	H	I	O	N	Pillow, Pad, Hassock, Palliate, Absorb, Protect, Check.
C	U	S	P	U	L	E	Small tubercle on surface of tooth.
C	U	S	S	I	N	G	Swearing, Damning, Cursing, Execrating, Imprecating.
C	U	S	T	A	R	D	Sweetened mixture of milk and eggs that is baked, boiled or frozen.
C	U	S	T	O	D	E	Custodian, Watchman, Guardian, Warden, Keeper, Steward, Overseer, Supervisor.
C	U	S	T	O	D	Y	Care, Guardianship, Safekeeping, Trust, Imprisonment, Duress.
C	U	S	T	O	M	S	Duties imposed on merchandise, Habits, Manners, Practices, Uses.
C	U	S	T	R	E	L	Squire of a knight.
C	U	T	A	W	A	Y	Having parts cut away, Pictorial prsentation in which inner details are made apparent.
C	U	T	B	A	C	K	Reduce, Retrench, Prune, Eliminate, Decrease, Abolish, Lessen, Diminish.
C	U	T	I	C	L	E	Skin, Pellicle, Membrane, Integument.
C	U	T	L	A	S	S	Short heavy curving sword, Machete.
C	U	T	L	E	R	Y	Cutting tools as shears, knives, surgical implements, Implements for use in cutting.
C	U	T	T	I	N	G	Sectioning, Incisive, Biting, Crisp, Penetrating, Trenchant, Piercing, Probing.
C	U	T	W	E	E	D	Marine algae.
C	U	T	W	O	R	K	Embroidery, Lace-making.
C	U	T	W	O	R	M	Caterpillar pest.
C	U	V	E	T	T	E	Small tube or basin used in scientific research, Cameo.
C	Y	A	N	A	T	E	A salt or ester of cyanic acid.
C	Y	A	N	I	D	E	Compound of cyanogen.
C	Y	A	N	I	N	E	Unstable dyes important in photography.
C	Y	A	N	I	T	E	Mineral of aluminium silicate.
C	Y	C	L	I	N	G	Riding a bicycle, Passing through a cycle of changes.
C	Y	C	L	I	S	T	One that rides a bicycle.
C	Y	C	L	O	I	D	Circular, Arranged or progressing in circles.
C	Y	C	L	O	N	E	Tornado, Hurricane, Typhoon, Twister.
C	Y	C	L	O	P	S	Race of giants in Greek mythology with a single eye in middle of the forehead.
C	Y	M	R	A	E	G	The Welsh language.
C	Y	N	I	C	A	L	Disparaging, Ironical, Sardonic, Wry, Pessimistic, Misogynic, Faultfinding, Sneering.
C	Y	P	E	R	U	S	Papyrus, Umbrella plant.
C	Y	P	R	E	S	S	Coniferous tree, Branches of tree used as symbol of mourning.
C	Y	P	R	I	A	N	Lewd person, Prostitute, Licentious.
C	Y	P	R	I	N	E	Variety of idocrase that is coloured blue by copper.
C	Y	P	R	I	O	T	Relating to Cyprus.
C	Y	S	T	I	N	E	Colourless crystalline amino acid.
C	Y	S	T	O	I	D	Like a bladder, Mass resembling a cyst but lacking a membrane.
C	Y	S	T	O	M	A	Tumour containing cysts.
C	Y	T	I	D	I	N	Crystalline nucleoside.
C	Y	T	I	S	U	S	Genus of broom plant.
C	Z	A	R	D	A	S	Hungarian dance.
C	Z	A	R	D	O	M	Territory ruled by a czar.
C	Z	A	R	I	N	A	Wife of Russian czar.
C	Z	A	R	I	S	M	Autocratic rule, Despotism.

D

1	2	3	4	5	6	7	
D	A	B	B	I	N	G	Stabbing, Pecking Piercing, Patting, Daubing, Tapping.
D	A	B	B	L	E	D	Spattered, Splashed, Sprinkled, Tampered, Meddled, Trifled.
D	A	B	B	L	E	R	Amateur, Dilettante, Non-professional, Tyro, Uninitiate.
D	A	B	S	T	E	R	Expert, Adept, Authority, Master, Professional, Proficient.
D	A	C	O	I	T	Y	Robbery by gang of brigands (dacoits).

1	2	3	4	5	6	7	
D	A	D	A	I	S	M	Practice in art of following negation of laws of beauty and social organization.
D	A	D	D	L	E	D	Loitered, Delayed.
D	A	F	T	E	S	T	Silliest, Craziest, Foolishest, Maddest.
D	A	G	G	I	N	G	Removing matted wool, Cutting into jagged strips.
D	A	G	G	L	E	D	Clothing soiled, wet and muddied.
D	A	G	L	O	C	K	Dirty or matted lock of fur, hair or wool.
D	A	G	O	M	B	A	Negroid people of Ghana.
D	A	L	L	I	E	D	Played, Sported, Trifled, Dawdled, Lingered, Tarried, Delayed, Loitered.
D	A	M	A	G	E	D	Flawed, Impaired, Injured, Marred, Spoiled, Broken, Unsound, Blemished.
D	A	M	B	R	O	D	Checkerboard.
D	A	M	M	I	N	G	Blocking, Barring, Impeding, Obstructing, Suppressing, Partitioning, Hindering, Banking.
D	A	M	N	I	F	Y	Damage, Injure, Wrong.
D	A	M	N	I	N	G	Condemning, Cursing, Swearing, Execrating, Conclusive.
D	A	M	O	S	E	L	Damsel, Damozel, Girl, Maiden, Lass.
D	A	M	P	I	N	G	Choking, Stifling, Extinguishing, Checking, Restraining, Retarding, Depressing, Moistening.
D	A	M	P	I	S	H	Moist, Damp, Dank, Wettish, Humid.
D	A	N	A	K	I	L	Afar, Hamitic people of N.E. Ethiopia.
D	A	N	C	E	R	Y	Place of entertainment providing facilities for dancing.
D	A	N	C	I	N	G	Prancing, Pirouetting, Capering, Tripping, Flitting, Fluttering, Hovering, Flickering.
D	A	N	D	I	F	Y	Fastidious, Smarten, Beautify, Attention to dress.
D	A	N	D	L	E	D	Caress, Cosset, Cuddle, Fondle, Love, Pet.
D	A	N	E	L	A	W	Part of England under control of Danes.
D	A	N	G	L	E	D	Hung, Depended, Slung, Suspended, Swung.
D	A	N	K	I	S	H	Damp, Dark, Moist.
D	A	N	S	K	E	R	Dane.
D	A	N	T	E	A	N	Relating to Dante.
D	A	N	T	I	S	T	Dante scholar.
D	A	P	H	N	I	A	Genus of minute freshwater crustaceans.
D	A	P	H	N	I	D	Water fleas.
D	A	P	H	N	I	N	Bitter crystalline glucoside occurring in laurel plants.
D	A	P	P	I	N	G	Fishing with bait, Rebounding, Skipping, Bouncing.
D	A	P	P	L	E	D	Variegated, Motley, Multicoloured, Multihued, Varicoloured, Parti-coloured, Versicolour.
D	A	R	B	I	E	S	Handcuffs.
D	A	R	I	O	L	E	Rich pastry filled with cream and jam.
D	A	R	K	E	S	T	Most secret, Blackest.
D	A	R	K	I	S	H	Somewhat dark, Dusky, Gloomy, Murky.
D	A	R	L	I	N	G	Beloved, Dear, Sweetheart, Honey, Delightful, Adorable, Luscious, Heavenly.
D	A	R	N	I	N	G	Mending with interlacing stitches.
D	A	R	R	E	I	N	Last, Final.
D	A	R	T	I	N	G	Throwing, Casting, Quick, Volatile.
D	A	S	H	I	N	G	Lively, Alert, Bright, Keen, Stylish, Exclusive, Fashionable, Splashing.
D	A	S	H	P	O	T	Device for cushioning a shock.
D	A	S	T	A	R	D	Coward, Craven, Funk, Poltroon, Quitter, Dullard.
D	A	S	Y	P	U	S	Genus of armadillos.
D	A	S	Y	U	R	E	Carnivorous marsupial.
D	A	T	A	B	L	E	Containing a date.
D	A	T	I	S	C	A	Genus of hemp herbs.
D	A	T	I	V	A	L	Relating to the dative case.
D	A	U	B	E	R	Y	Crude work, Mystifying action.
D	A	U	B	I	N	G	Smearing, Dabbling, Smudging, Speckled, Spotted, Dappled, Flecked.
D	A	U	N	T	E	D	Dismayed, Appalled, Horrified, Shaken, Intimated, Baffled, Foiled, Thwarted.
D	A	U	P	H	I	N	Eldest son of the King of France.
D	A	W	D	L	E	D	Idled, Lazed, Loafed, Loitered, Delayed, Dallied, Tarried, Ambled.
D	A	W	D	L	E	R	Laggard, Lingerer, Loiterer, Slow coach, Straggler.
D	A	W	N	I	N	G	Dawn, Daybreak, Daylight, Sunrise, Beginning, Commencement, Opening, Outset.
D	A	Y	B	O	O	K	Diary, Journal, Ledger recording daily transactions.
D	A	Y	G	A	T	E	Inner grating used while a safety vault is open.
D	A	Y	G	I	R	L	Day student at girl's boarding school.
D	A	Y	L	E	S	S	Lacking daylight.
D	A	Y	L	I	L	Y	Plantain.
D	A	Y	L	O	N	G	Lasting all day.
D	A	Y	M	A	R	K	Marker visible to pilots as a navigation guide in daylight.
D	A	Y	R	O	O	M	Room fitted up for reading, writing and recreation.
D	A	Y	S	I	D	E	Staff working on afternoon shift of newspaper.
D	A	Y	S	T	A	R	Morning star.
D	A	Y	T	I	M	E	Time during daylight.
D	A	Y	W	O	R	K	Work paid for at a unit of time.

1	2	3	4	5	6	7	Definition
D	A	Z	Z	L	E	D	Dazed, Blinded, Bewildered, Reflected, Confused, Mystified.
D	E	A	D	E	N	D	Blind alley, Cul-de-sac, Impasse, Pocket, Deadlock, Halt, Standstill, Bottleneck.
D	E	A	D	E	Y	E	Wooden block with holes to receive a lanyard, Dead shot.
D	E	A	D	I	S	H	Dull, Somewhat dead.
D	E	A	D	M	E	N	Buried logs serving as anchors, Empty bottles.
D	E	A	D	P	A	N	Expressionless, Blank, Empty, Inexpressive, Vacant.
D	E	A	D	S	E	T	Determined effort, Attitutde of fixed hostility.
D	E	A	F	A	I	D	Hearing aid.
D	E	A	F	I	S	H	Hard of hearing.
D	E	A	F	N	U	T	Nut with no kernel, A thing without profit.
D	E	A	L	A	T	E	Insect divested of wings usually after nuptial flight.
D	E	A	L	I	N	G	Handling, Paying, Negotiating, Playing, Serving, Directing, Controlling, Administering.
D	E	A	N	E	R	Y	Office or position of dean, Residence of a dean.
D	E	A	R	E	S	T	Most costly, Most expensive, Most loved.
D	E	A	T	H	L	Y	Corpselike, Dead, Deadly, Fatal, Lethal, Mortal, Pestilent, Ghastly.
D	E	B	A	C	L	E	Defeat, Beating, Drubbing, Overthrow, Rout, Collapse, Crash, Wreck.
D	E	B	A	S	E	D	Corrupted, Debauched, Depraved, Perverted, Vitiate, Decadent, Degenerate, Dissolute.
D	E	B	A	S	E	R	One that debases.
D	E	B	A	T	E	D	Argued, Disputed, Controverted, Rebutted, Refuted, Heeded, Applied, Considered, Studied.
D	E	B	A	T	E	R	One that debates.
D	E	B	A	U	C	H	Debase, Bastardfize, Brutalize, Corrupt, Demoralize, Seduce, Deprave, Pervert.
D	E	B	I	T	E	D	Entered on left hand of an account consisting of a debt.
D	E	B	I	T	O	R	Debtor, One that owes.
D	E	B	O	U	C	H	March out into open ground, Emerge, Discharge.
D	E	C	A	D	A	L	Of or belonging to a group of ten.
D	E	C	A	D	I	C	Relating to the decimal system.
D	E	C	A	G	O	N	Polygon of ten angles and ten sides.
D	E	C	A	L	I	N	Used for decahydronapthalene.
D	E	C	A	N	A	L	High boiling liquid aldehyde.
D	E	C	A	P	O	D	Crustacea such as shrimps, lobsters and crabs having five pairs of thoracic appendages.
D	E	C	A	Y	E	D	Corrupted, Decomposed, Tainted, Spoiled, Bad, rotten, Putrid, Overripe.
D	E	C	E	A	S	E	Expire, Die, Depart, Pass away, Demise, Succumb, Drop, Go.
D	E	C	E	I	V	E	Beguile, Betray, Delude, Mislead, Mock, Cheat, Defraud, Dupe.
D	E	C	E	N	C	Y	Decorum, Dignity, Etiquette, Propriety, Seemliness, Fitness, Formality.
D	E	C	I	A	R	E	Metric unit equal to ten square metres.
D	E	C	I	B	E	L	Unit expressing electric or acoustic power.
D	E	C	I	D	E	D	Assured, Definite, Pronounced, Resolved, Certain, Positive, Explicit, Obvious.
D	E	C	I	D	E	R	One that decides.
D	E	C	I	M	A	L	Numbered or proceeding by tens.
D	E	C	K	I	N	G	Adorning, Beautifying, Decorating, Embellishing, Trimming, Garnishing, Ornamenting.
D	E	C	K	L	E	D	Limit width of paper by using a wooden frame.
D	E	C	L	A	I	M	Orate, Harangue, Perorate, Rant, Rave, Assert, Inveigh, Rhetorical, Display.
D	E	C	L	A	R	E	Announce, Advertise, Broadcast, Proclaim, Profess, Protest, Affirm, Deliver.
D	E	C	L	A	S	S	Degrade, Break, Bust, Demerit, Demote, Disgrade, Downgrade, Reduce.
D	E	C	L	I	N	E	Dip, Sink, Fail, Languish, Deteriorate, Descend, Refuse, Reject.
D	E	C	O	D	E	D	Deciphered, Broken, Cracked, Translated, Resolved, Solved, Elucidated, Worked out.
D	E	C	O	D	E	R	Cryptographer.
D	E	C	O	R	U	M	Decency, Dignity, Etiquette, Propriety, Convention, Order, Correctness, Orderliness.
D	E	C	O	Y	E	D	Lured, Snared, Enticed, Inveigled, Seduced, Snared, Tempted, Trapped.
D	E	C	R	E	E	D	Dictated, Imposed, Ordained, Prescribed, Set, Compelled, Forced, Demanded.
D	E	C	R	E	E	T	Court judgment.
D	E	C	R	I	A	L	Depreciation.
D	E	C	R	I	E	R	One that decries.
D	E	C	R	O	W	N	Discrown, Dethrone.
D	E	C	U	M	A	N	Huge wave, Tenth cohort (chief gate of a Roman camp).
D	E	C	U	P	L	E	Tenfold, Taken by tens or groups of ten.
D	E	D	I	M	U	S	Judicial commission.
D	E	D	U	C	E	D	Concluded, Reasoned, Inferred, Collected, Derived, Gathered, Judged, Deemed.
D	E	E	D	F	U	L	Active, Stirring.
D	E	E	D	I	L	Y	Actively, Industriously, Earnestly.
D	E	E	D	I	N	G	Convey or transfer by deed.
D	E	E	M	I	N	G	Considering, Accounting, Feeling, Believing, Knowing, Thinking, Holding, Expecting.
D	E	E	P	E	S	T	Bottomless, Profoundest, Heaviest, Craftiest, Trickiest, Lowest.
D	E	E	P	F	R	Y	To cook by immersing in hot fat.
D	E	E	P	S	E	A	In parts of ocean far from land.
D	E	F	A	C	E	D	Disfigured, Destroyed, Effaced, Erased, Defamed, Outshone, Discredited, Imapired.
D	E	F	A	C	E	R	One that spoils and mutilates.

1	2	3	4	5	6	7	
D	E	F	A	M	E	D	Maligned, Dishonoured, Caluminated, Denigrated, Slandered, Vilified, Misrepresented.
D	E	F	A	M	E	R	One that defames.
D	E	F	A	U	L	T	Omit, Failure, Deliquency, Dereliction, Neglect, Oversight, Deficiency, Fault, Imperfection.
D	E	F	E	N	C	E	Armour, Guard, Protection, Safeguard, Security, Apology, Justification, Excuse.
D	E	F	I	A	N	T	Challenge, Dared, Defied, Stubborn, Provocative.
D	E	F	I	C	I	T	Failure, Defalcation, Deficiency, Inadequacy, Insufficiency, Lack, Scantiness, Shortage.
D	E	F	I	L	E	D	Impure, Common, Desecrated, Polluted, Unclean, Contaminated.
D	E	F	I	L	E	R	One that defiles.
D	E	F	I	N	E	D	Prescribed, Assigned, Circumscribed, Limited, Designated, Described, Bordered, Etched.
D	E	F	I	N	E	R	One that defines.
D	E	F	L	A	T	E	Puncture, Collapse, Sag, Contract.
D	E	F	L	E	C	T	Turn, Avert, Divert, Pivot, Veer, Ward, Fend, Parry.
D	E	F	O	R	C	E	Withhold wrongfully, Deprive wrongfully, Oppose or resist forcibly to prevent execution of the law.
D	E	F	R	A	U	D	Cheat, Beat, Bilk, Cozen, Swindle, Hoax, Trick, Circumvent.
D	E	F	U	N	C	T	Dead, Deceased, Departed, Extinct, Inanimate, Lifeless, Bygone, Vanished.
D	E	F	Y	I	N	G	Challenging, Flouting, Daring, Venturing, Facing, Bearding, Braving, Mocking.
D	E	G	A	U	S	S	To make a ship nonmagnetic.
D	E	G	L	A	Z	E	Remove glaze from pottery or porcelain to make a dull finish.
D	E	G	R	A	D	E	Break, Demerit, Demote, Downgrade, Reduce, Debase, Humble, Humiliate.
D	E	H	I	S	C	E	Gape, Yawn.
D	E	I	C	I	D	E	Act of killing a divine being.
D	E	I	C	I	N	G	Removing ice.
D	E	I	C	T	I	C	Showing or proving directly.
D	E	I	F	I	E	D	Made a god, Idolized, Exalted.
D	E	I	F	O	R	M	Godlike.
D	E	I	G	N	E	D	Condescended, Stooped, Vouchsafed.
D	E	I	S	T	I	C	Professing deism.
D	E	J	E	C	T	A	Excrements.
D	E	L	A	I	N	E	Lightweight dress fabric.
D	E	L	A	T	E	D	Deferred, Accused, Denounced, Reported, Related.
D	E	L	A	T	O	R	Accuser, Professional informer.
D	E	L	A	Y	E	D	Detained, Retarded, Slackened, Procrastinated, Loitered, Dawdled, Dallied, Lagged.
D	E	L	A	Y	E	R	One that delays, Procrastinator.
D	E	L	E	T	E	D	Erased, Destroyed, Annihilated, Expunged, Eliminated, Cancelled, Obliterated, Excluded.
D	E	L	I	G	H	T	Exult, Glory, Jubilate, Triumph, Please, Gladden, Pleasure, Enjoyment.
D	E	L	I	M	I	T	Demarcate, Bound, Delimitate, Determine, Limit, Measure, Confine, Restrict.
D	E	L	I	V	E	R	Rescue, Save, Disperse, Bear, Birth, Declare, Give, Administer.
D	E	L	O	U	S	E	Remove lice, To free from something unpleasant or harmful.
D	E	L	P	H	I	C	Prophetic, Oracular, Relating to Delphi-characterised by obscurity and ambiguity.
D	E	L	P	H	I	N	Relating to the Delphin classics.
D	E	L	T	A	I	C	Typical of a delta, Arising or originating in the Nile delta.
D	E	L	T	O	I	D	Triangular, Shoulder muscle.
D	E	L	U	D	E	D	Deceived, Beguiled, Betrayed, Bluffed, Misled, Humbug, Juggled, Gulled.
D	E	L	U	D	E	R	One that deludes.
D	E	L	U	G	E	D	Engulfed, Flooded, Drowned, Inundated, Swamped.
D	E	L	V	I	N	G	Inquest, Inquisition, Investigating, Probing, Questing, Researching, Digging, Exploring.
D	E	M	E	N	T	I	Official or formal denial of the truth of a report.
D	E	M	E	R	I	T	Imperfection, Deficiency, Fault, Short-coming, Sin.
D	E	M	E	S	N	E	Estate, Territory, Land attached to a country mansion, Realm, Province.
D	E	M	I	G	O	D	Mythological divine person.
D	E	M	I	R	E	P	Demimondaine, Courtesan.
D	E	M	I	S	E	C	Drier that doux, sweeter than sec.
D	E	M	I	S	E	D	Bequeathed, Willed, Cessation, Death, Transference of sovereignty.
D	E	M	O	D	E	D	Out-of-date, Old fashioned.
D	E	M	O	N	I	C	Fiendish, Devilish, Diabolic, Satanic, Serpentine, Unhallowed, Insane, Maniac.
D	E	M	O	T	I	C	Popular, Common, Relating to the people, Enchorial, Belonging to written forms.
D	E	N	D	R	O	N	Dendrite of nerve cell, Branching figure resembling a tree produced in a mineral or stone.
D	E	N	I	Z	E	N	Inhabitant, Dweller, Occupier, Resident, Citizen, National subject, Habitué.
D	E	N	O	T	E	D	Expressed, Intended, Indicated, Signified, Spelled, Announced, Proved.
D	E	N	S	E	L	Y	Closely, Thickly, Solidly.
D	E	N	S	E	S	T	Thickest, Closest.
D	E	N	S	I	T	Y	Distribution of quantity, Compactness, Closeness of texture.
D	E	N	T	A	R	Y	Either of a pair of membrane bones of the lower jaw.
D	E	N	T	A	T	E	Having toothlike projections.
D	E	N	T	I	N	E	Calcerous material similar to bone but harder and denser.
D	E	N	T	I	N	G	Breaking, Indenting, Weakening, Notching.
D	E	N	T	I	S	T	One whose profession is to treat diseases of teeth and oral tissues.

1	2	3	4	5	6	7	Definition
D	E	N	T	O	I	D	Resembling a tooth.
D	E	N	T	U	R	E	Artificial replacement of teeth.
D	E	N	U	D	E	D	Stripped, Bared, Divested, Disrobed, Exposed, Naked, Peeled, Deprived.
D	E	N	Y	I	N	G	Disclaiming, Disowning, Repudiating, Refusing, Withholding, Curbing, Refraining, Contradicting.
D	E	O	D	A	N	D	A forfeit to the English crown prior to 1846.
D	E	P	E	T	E	R	Finish for plastered wall by pressing small stones in the soft plaster.
D	E	P	L	A	N	E	Descend from a plane after a flight.
D	E	P	L	E	T	E	Drain, Draw, Exhaust, Impoverish, Debilitate, Sap, Decrease, Diminish.
D	E	P	L	O	R	E	Bemoan, Bewail, Grieve, Lament, Moan, Weep, Mourn, Sorrow.
D	E	P	L	U	M	E	To pluck off feathers, To strip of possessions or honours.
D	E	P	O	S	E	D	Testified, Deposed, Mounted, Sworn.
D	E	P	O	S	A	L	Act of deposing, especially from a throne.
D	E	P	O	S	E	D	Overthrew, Subverted, Dismissed, Ejected, Ousted, Affirmed, Asserted, Testified.
D	E	P	O	S	I	T	Bank, Store, Slow, Sediment, Grounds, Precipitate, Settle, Security.
D	E	P	R	A	V	E	Debase, Bestialize, Corrupt, Debauch, Demoralize, Pervert, Warp, Vitiate.
D	E	P	R	E	S	S	Lower, Droop, Sink, Sadden, Trouble, Torment, Discourage, Disturb.
D	E	P	R	I	V	E	Strip, Bare, Denudate, Bereave, Disinherit, Dispossess, Divest, Rob.
D	E	P	U	T	E	D	Appointed, Devoted, Delegated, Authorized, Deputized, Commissioned.
D	E	R	A	I	G	N	Discharge from a religious order.
D	E	R	A	N	G	E	Disorder, Disarray, Distract, Disturb, Unsettle, Upset, Unhinge, Madden.
D	E	R	A	T	E	D	Reduced or eliminated rated capability.
D	E	R	I	D	E	D	Ridiculed, Mocked, Taunted, Chaffed, Ribbed, Jeered, Scorned, Lampooned.
D	E	R	I	V	E	D	Traced, Originated, Evolved, Concluded, Stemmed, Secondary, Developed, Inferred.
D	E	R	M	O	I	D	Resembling skin.
D	E	R	N	I	E	R	Last, Final, A column on a roulette layout.
D	E	R	N	I	N	G	Hiding, Concealing, Secreting.
D	E	R	R	I	C	K	Rig, Hoisting apparatus, Tower over an oil well, Support for a crane.
D	E	R	V	I	S	H	Muslim monk, Fakir, Something that whirls or dances with abandon.
D	E	S	C	A	N	T	Discourse, Discuss, Dissert, Sermonize, Melody, Strain, Tune, Warble.
D	E	S	C	E	N	D	Fall, Drop, Lower, Stoop, Sink, Deteriorate, Decline, Degenerate.
D	E	S	C	E	N	T	Drop, Fall, Discomfiture, Ancestry, Lineage, Origin, Decline, Declivity.
D	E	S	E	R	V	E	Earn, Merit, Justify, Win, Rate, Gain, Demand, Get.
D	E	S	I	R	E	D	Appropriate, Fitting, Proper, True, Craved, Wished, Hankered, Asked.
D	E	S	I	R	E	R	One that desires.
D	E	S	K	I	L	L	To mechanize or break down so that little or no skill is necessary to perform the operation.
D	E	S	M	I	N	E	Stilbite zeolitic mineral.
D	E	S	P	A	I	R	Defeat, Abandon, Relinquish, Resign, Surrender, Yield, Hopelessness, Futility.
D	E	S	P	I	S	E	Abhor, Disdain, Scorn, Detest, Loathe, Reject, Spurn, Shun.
D	E	S	P	I	T	E	Against, Notwithstanding, Regardless of, Malice, Grudge, Defiance, Contempt, Affront.
D	E	S	P	O	I	L	Ravage, Depredate, Desecrate, Desolate, Devastate, Devour, Pillage, Sack.
D	E	S	P	O	N	D	Despair, Give up, Droop, Sag, Languish, Mope, Brood, Dejectedness.
D	E	S	S	E	R	T	Course of fruit, pastry, pudding, ice cream or cheese served at end of meal.
D	E	S	T	I	N	E	Preordain, Predetermine, Designate, Dedicate, Foreordain, Appoint, Intend.
D	E	S	T	I	N	Y	Fate, Doom, Fortune, Circumstance, Kismet, Lot, Portion, Objective.
D	E	S	T	R	O	Y	Kill, Finish, Slay, Annihilate, Decimate, Destruct, Dissolve, Pulverize.
D	E	T	E	N	T	E	Release, Easing of strained relations.
D	E	T	E	R	G	E	Cleanse.
D	E	T	E	R	M	A	Central American tree with valuable light strong wood.
D	E	T	I	N	U	E	Detention of something, Writ for common-law action for recovery of personal chattel.
D	E	T	R	A	C	T	Decry, Belittle, Disparage, Defame, Discount, Depreciate, Minimize, Derogate.
D	E	T	R	A	I	N	To remove from a railroad train.
D	E	T	R	U	D	E	To thrust or force down, out or away.
D	E	U	T	Z	I	A	Genus of ornamental shrubs.
D	E	V	A	L	U	E	Depreciate, Devalorize, Devaluate, Lower, Mark down, Under-rate, Undervalue, Write down.
D	E	V	E	L	O	P	Unfold, Expand, Mature, Ripen, Acquire, Happen, Transpire, Enlarge.
D	E	V	I	A	T	E	Swerve, Depart, Digress, Diverge, Err, Stray, Wander.
D	E	V	I	L	E	D	Highly seasoned dish of fried chops or meaty bones, Grill with cayenne pepper.
D	E	V	I	L	R	Y	Witchcraft, Extreme wickedness, Act of studied malignancy, Cruelty, Vicious conduct.
D	E	V	I	O	U	S	Obscure, Remote, Crooked, Twisting, Erratic, Wandering, Underhand, Indirect.
D	E	V	I	S	E	D	Planned, Arranged, Designed, Contrived, Plotted, Concocted, Willed, Bequeathed.
D	E	V	O	L	V	E	Voluble, Transfer, Pass by succession, Impose.
D	E	V	O	T	E	D	Loving, Affectionate, Dear, Doting, Fond, Constant, Faithful, Loyal.
D	E	V	O	T	E	E	Zealous follower, Votary, Ardent supporter.
D	E	W	A	N	N	Y	Right to collect revenues in certain districts of India.
D	E	W	C	L	A	W	Vestigial digit not reaching to the ground.
D	E	W	D	R	O	P	Drop of dew, Glass or crystal bead.
D	E	W	F	A	L	L	Time when dew begins to deposit.

1	2	3	4	5	6	7	Definition
D	E	W	P	O	N	D	Shallow artificial pond kept filled by condensation of dew and mist.
D	E	W	W	O	R	M	Earthworm suitable for use as bait.
D	E	X	T	R	A	D	Toward the right.
D	E	X	T	R	A	L	Right-handed.
D	E	X	T	R	A	N	Plasma substitute.
D	E	X	T	R	I	N	Starch gum.
D	H	O	O	T	I	E	Loincloth worn by Hindu men.
D	H	U	R	R	I	E	Thick cotton cloth or carpet made in India.
D	I	A	B	A	S	E	Variously defined rock types.
D	I	A	B	O	L	O	Game.
D	I	A	G	R	A	M	Sketch, Drawing, Graph, Chart.
D	I	A	L	E	C	T	Language, Idiom, Speech, Tongue, Vernacular, Terminology, Patois, Jargon.
D	I	A	L	L	E	D	Manipulated a dial.
D	I	A	M	I	D	E	Any compound containing two amido groups.
D	I	A	M	O	N	D	Bright, Sparkling, Crystallized carbon.
D	I	A	P	A	S	M	Perfume of powdered aromatic herbs.
D	I	A	P	S	I	D	Subclass of reptile as crocodiles, lizards and snakes.
D	I	A	R	C	H	Y	Government in which power is vested in two rulers.
D	I	A	R	I	E	S	Daily records of personal activities.
D	I	A	R	I	S	T	One who keeps a diary.
D	I	A	R	I	Z	E	To record in a diary.
D	I	A	S	T	E	R	Stage in division of a cell.
D	I	A	T	O	M	S	Seaweed.
D	I	A	X	O	N	E	Nerve cell with two axons.
D	I	B	A	S	I	C	Having two atoms.
D	I	B	A	T	A	G	Small gazelle.
D	I	B	B	I	N	G	To fish by letting the bait bob and dip lightly.
D	I	B	B	L	E	D	Planting in holes made in the ground.
D	I	C	E	B	O	X	Box from which dice are thrown.
D	I	C	E	I	N	G	Playing dice games.
D	I	C	E	R	A	T	Clams.
D	I	C	K	I	T	E	Mineral consisting of a basic silicate of aluminium.
D	I	C	L	I	N	Y	Having the stamens and pistils in separate flowers.
D	I	C	T	A	T	E	Decree, Impose, Ordain, Prescribe, Command, Behest, Mandate, Order.
D	I	C	T	I	O	N	Wording, Parlance, Phrase, Enunciation, Pronunciation, Phrasing, Verbalism, Wordage.
D	I	D	D	L	E	D	Jiggled, Dawdled, Loafed, Swindled, Cheated, Hoaxed, Deluded, Idled.
D	I	D	D	L	E	R	Cheat, Swindler, Defrauder, Trickster, Confidence man.
D	I	D	I	N	A	E	Family of extinct flightless birds, Dodo.
D	I	E	A	W	A	Y	Languishing, Gradual fading out.
D	I	E	C	A	S	E	Matrix case.
D	I	E	C	A	S	T	To make by forcing molten metal into a die.
D	I	E	H	A	R	D	Irreconcilable opponent of change, Extreme conservative.
D	I	E	T	A	R	Y	Rules of diet. Allowance of food.
D	I	E	T	I	N	G	Regulating amount of food eaten, Eating sparingly.
D	I	E	W	I	S	E	In the shape of a die, Cubically.
D	I	F	F	O	R	M	Unlike, Dissimilar, Anomalous, Lopsided, Uneven, Asymmetric, Disproportional, Unequal.
D	I	F	F	U	S	E	Wordy, Confused, Difficult, Widestread, Verbose, Scatter, Extend, Copious.
D	I	G	A	M	M	A	A letter of the original Greek alphabet which fell into disuse.
D	I	G	G	I	N	G	Delving, Excavating, Scooping, Thrusting, Plunging, Poking, Prodding, Probing.
D	I	G	I	T	A	L	Relating to fingers, Relating to calculating by numerical methods, Key to be played by a finger.
D	I	G	L	Y	P	H	Projecting ornamental face having two grooves.
D	I	G	N	I	F	Y	Enoble, Exalt, Erect, Honour, Magnify, Distinguish, Aggrandize.
D	I	G	N	I	T	Y	Status, Consequence, Position, Prestige, Rank, Standing, Decorum, Decency.
D	I	G	R	A	P	H	A group of two successive letters whose phonetic value is a single sound.
D	I	G	R	E	S	S	Swerve, Depart, Deviate, Diverge, Ramble, Stray, Wander, Drift.
D	I	G	Y	N	I	A	Plants with two pistils.
D	I	K	E	R	I	A	Two-branched candlestick used in Eastern Orthodox Church.
D	I	L	A	T	E	D	Expanded, Distended, Inflated, Swollen, Amplified, Discoursed, Discussed, Flattened.
D	I	L	A	T	O	R	Instrument for expanding a tube, duct or cavity.
D	I	L	A	T	E	R	Same as DILATER.
D	I	L	E	M	M	A	Predicament, Quandary, Plight, Fix, Hole, Scrape, Pickle, Spot.
D	I	L	L	I	N	G	Youngest child of the family, Weakest pig of the litter.
D	I	L	L	I	S	K	Coarse red seaweed.
D	I	L	L	O	I	L	Essential oil derived from the common dill and used as flavouring agent.
D	I	L	U	E	N	T	Thinners, Inert substance added to reduce concentration.
D	I	L	U	T	E	D	Cut, Thinned, Weakened, Watered-down, Reduced, Adulterated, Impaired, Altered.
D	I	L	U	T	E	E	Unskilled worker.

1	2	3	4	5	6	7	
D	I	L	U	T	E	R	One that dilutes.
D	I	M	E	D	O	N	Crystalline diketone.
D	I	M	E	T	E	R	A line consisting of two metrical feet.
D	I	M	M	E	S	T	Least bright, Dullest, Most boring.
D	I	M	M	I	N	G	Boring, Dulling, Obscuring, Eclipsing, Fogging, Clouding, Darkening, Blurring.
D	I	M	M	I	S	H	Somewhat dim.
D	I	M	N	E	S	S	Quality of being dim.
D	I	M	P	L	E	D	Having conical depressions, Having natural indentation on some part of body or face.
D	I	N	E	T	T	E	Small space for informal dining.
D	I	N	G	I	N	G	Thrashing, Dashing, Flinging, Driving, Bouncing, Beating, Damning, Surpassing.
D	I	N	G	O	E	S	Australian wild dogs.
D	I	N	G	I	L	Y	In a dingy manner.
D	I	N	M	O	N	T	Whether between one and two years old or between first and second shearing.
D	I	N	N	I	N	G	Assailing, Clamouring, Impressing by insistent repetition, Resounding.
D	I	N	T	I	N	G	Striking, Beating, Imprinting.
D	I	O	C	E	S	E	Extent of a bishop's jurisdiction, Sphere of authority.
D	I	O	C	O	E	L	Cavity of the developing diencephalon that later gives rise to the third ventricle of the brain.
D	I	O	D	I	N	E	Iodine x-ray preparation.
D	I	O	E	C	I	A	Class of plants having staminate and pistillate flowers on different individuals.
D	I	O	P	S	I	S	Genus of two-winged flies.
D	I	O	P	T	E	R	Unit of measurement of the refractive power of a lens.
D	I	O	P	T	R	E	Same as DIOPTER.
D	I	O	R	A	M	A	Scenic representation, Panorama.
D	I	O	X	A	N	E	Flammable irritating water-soluble liquid.
D	I	O	X	I	D	E	An oxide containing two atoms of oxygen in the molecule.
D	I	P	L	O	I	D	Isometric crystalline form having twice the number of chromosones.
D	I	P	L	O	M	A	Letter or writing conferring honour or privilege, Record of graduation.
D	I	P	L	O	N	T	On organism with somatic cells having diploid chromosones.
D	I	P	O	L	A	R	Having two poles.
D	I	P	P	I	N	G	Plunging, Immersing, Ducking, Implicating, Saluting, Dunking, Sousing, Ladling.
D	I	P	T	E	R	A	A large order of winged insects.
D	I	P	T	O	T	E	Noun with only two cases.
D	I	P	T	Y	C	H	Two-leaved hinged tablet folding to protect writing.
D	I	R	E	F	U	L	Fearful, Appalling, Awful, Dreadful, Ominous, Baleful, Ill-boding, Inauspicious.
D	I	R	K	I	N	G	Stabbing with a dirk.
D	I	R	T	B	E	D	Buried soil containing leaves and stems in state of partial decay.
D	I	R	T	I	E	D	Soiled, Sullied, Begrimed, Contaminated, Defiled, Polluted, Tainted, Fouled.
D	I	R	T	I	E	R	Grubbier, More Soiled, More polluted.
D	I	R	T	I	L	Y	In a foul or filthy manner, Sordidly, Despicably.
D	I	S	A	B	L	E	Disqualify, Incapacitate, Disparage, Weaken, Paralyze, Cripple, Immobilize, Undermine.
D	I	S	A	G	I	O	Charge for exchanging foreign money.
D	I	S	A	L	L	Y	Sever, Free from an alliance.
D	I	S	A	V	O	W	Disclaim, Deny, Disallow, Disown, Repudiate, Negate, Refuse, Decline.
D	I	S	B	A	N	D	Dissolve, Discharge, Disperse, Scatter, Dissect, Divide, Divorce, Separate.
D	I	S	C	A	N	T	Descant, Discourse, Dilate, Dissert, Expatiate.
D	I	S	C	A	R	D	Ditch, Dump, Cast, Chuck, Reject, Scrap, Abdicate, Jettison.
D	I	S	C	A	S	E	Undress, Strip.
D	I	S	C	E	P	T	Debate, Discuss, Disagree, Agitate, Canvass, Argue, Moot, Thrash out.
D	I	S	C	E	R	N	See, Behold, Distinguish, Observe, Know, Extricate, Separate, Discriminate, Dismember.
D	I	S	C	O	I	D	Shaped like a disc.
D	I	S	C	O	R	D	Conflict, Difference. Disunity, Division, Strife, Mischief, Variance.
D	I	S	C	O	U	S	Flat like a disc.
D	I	S	C	U	S	S	Discourse, Expatiate, Dilate, Dissert, Elucidate, Debate, Argue, Dispute.
D	I	S	D	A	I	N	Despise, Abhor, Scorn, Contemn, Spurn, Ignore.
D	I	S	E	A	S	E	Malady, Complaint, Ailment, Disorder, Infirmity, Sickness, Syndrome, Debility.
D	I	S	E	D	G	E	Blunt, Dull.
D	I	S	E	U	S	E	Professional and skilled woman reciter.
D	I	S	F	O	R	M	Deform, To change or lose form or order.
D	I	S	G	U	S	T	Nauseate, Repel, Repulse, Revolt, Sicken, Offend, Outrage, Vexation.
D	I	S	H	E	L	M	Deprive a person of a helmet.
D	I	S	H	F	U	L	The content of a dish usually of ice cream.
D	I	S	H	I	N	G	Serving, Hollowing, Frustrating, Cheating, Chatting, Chattering, Dithering, Babbling.
D	I	S	H	O	M	E	Deprive of a home.
D	I	S	H	O	R	N	Remove horns.
D	I	S	J	O	I	N	Separate, Break up, Disjoint, Disunite, Divide, Divorce, Part, Sunder.
D	I	S	J	U	N	E	Breakfast.
D	I	S	L	E	A	F	Strip of leaves.

1	2	3	4	5	6	7	
D	I	S	L	E	A	L	Disloyal, Perfidious.
D	I	S	L	I	K	E	Aversion, Disfavour, Discord, Disapprobation, Disapproval, Distaste, Indisposition.
D	I	S	L	I	M	B	Dismember.
D	I	S	L	I	M	N	Vanished.
D	I	S	L	I	N	K	Disunite, Uncouple, Separate, Unlink.
D	I	S	L	O	A	D	Unload, Disburden.
D	I	S	M	A	L	S	Low spirits, Depression, Swamp.
D	I	S	M	A	S	K	Unmask.
D	I	S	M	A	S	T	Carry away or break off mast of ship.
D	I	S	M	I	S	S	Decline, Refuse, Reject, Cashier, Discharge, Chase, Evict, Sack.
D	I	S	O	B	E	Y	Transgress, Refuse, Disregard, Infringe, Rebel, Neglect.
D	I	S	O	M	I	C	Having one or more chromosones duplicated.
D	I	S	O	M	U	S	Two-bodied monster.
D	I	S	P	A	R	K	To throw open a private park.
D	I	S	P	A	R	T	Separate, Divide.
D	I	S	P	E	N	D	Dispense, Distribute, Spend, Expend.
D	I	S	P	L	A	Y	Show, Brandish, Exhibit, Expose, Flaunt, Parade, Exhibition, Demonstration.
D	I	S	P	O	N	E	Dispose, Grant, Transfer.
D	I	S	P	O	R	T	Play, Diversion, Fun, Recreation, Sport, Merriment, Amuse, Entertain.
D	I	S	P	O	S	E	Incline, Bend, Bias, Discard, Complete, Dispatch, Destroy, Demeanour.
D	I	S	P	U	T	E	Debate, Wrangle, Fight, Contest, Quarrel, Struggle, Bicker, Resist.
D	I	S	R	A	N	K	To throw into disorder.
D	I	S	R	A	T	E	Demote, Reduce to lower rank, class or rating.
D	I	S	R	O	B	E	Undress, Strip, Deprive, Dismantle, Divest, Denude, Unclothe.
D	I	S	R	O	O	T	Uproot, Dislodge from a fixed position.
D	I	S	R	U	P	T	Rupture, Break up, Disintegrate, Breach, Open disorder, Disorganize.
D	I	S	S	E	A	T	Unseat.
D	I	S	S	E	C	T	Separate, Disjoint, Divide, Part, Sever, Cut, Carve, Analyse, Resolve.
D	I	S	S	E	N	T	Nonagreement, Disagreement, Nonconcurrence, Differ, Discord, Divide, Heresy, Misbelief.
D	I	S	S	E	R	T	Discourse, Descant, Dilate, Discuss, Expatiate, Sermonize.
D	I	S	T	A	F	F	Staff for holding unspun flax, Female side of family.
D	I	S	T	A	I	N	Stain, Discolour, Defile, Dishonour, Sully.
D	I	S	T	A	N	T	Far-away, Remote, Far, Different, Unequal, Unsociable, Reserved, Withdrawn.
D	I	S	T	E	N	D	Dilate, Swell, Expand, Amplify, Enlarge, Increase, Extend, Lengthen.
D	I	S	T	E	N	T	Spread out, Breadth, Distention.
D	I	S	T	I	C	H	Strophic unit or unit of verse consisting of two lines.
D	I	S	T	O	M	A	Small bandage, Genus of worms.
D	I	S	T	O	R	T	Misrepresent, Garble, Pervert, Twist, Deform, Contort, Torture, Warp.
D	I	S	T	U	N	E	Put out of tune.
D	I	S	T	U	R	B	Agitate, Trouble, Alarm, Discompose, Disorder, Interruption, Alteration, Commotion.
D	I	S	T	Y	L	E	Marked by columniation with two columns across the front.
D	I	S	U	S	E	D	Obsolete, Neglected, Dead, Extinct, Outmoded, Outworn, Passé, Superseded.
D	I	T	C	H	E	D	Crash-landed, Discarded, Failed examination, Dismissed.
D	I	T	C	H	E	R	Workman who repairs and digs ditches.
D	I	T	H	E	R	Y	Nervous, Agitated, Tremulous.
D	I	T	T	A	N	Y	Small aromatic herb, Bastard.
D	I	T	T	I	E	D	Set to music.
D	I	T	T	I	E	S	Sonnets, Shanties.
D	I	U	R	N	A	L	Daybook, Diary, Journal.
D	I	V	E	R	G	E	Swerve, Depart, Deviate, Digress, Excurse, Ramble, Stray, Wander.
D	I	V	E	R	S	E	Different, Dissimilar, Distant, Divergent, Unalike, Various, Distinct, Separate.
D	I	V	I	D	E	D	Apportioned, Separated, Divorced, Disjoined, Severed, Dissected, Distributed, Disagreed.
D	I	V	I	D	E	R	Compass, Nipper, Something serving as a partition, Device that splits dough into equal portions.
D	I	V	I	N	E	R	Predictor, Magician, Seer.
D	I	V	I	S	O	R	Number by which the dividend is divided.
D	I	V	O	R	C	E	Separation, Dissolution, Partition, Rupture, Disjoint, Divide, Dismiss, Sever.
D	I	V	U	L	G	E	Reveal, Betray, Disclose, Discover, Give away, Spill, Tell, Gossip.
D	I	V	U	L	S	E	To rend, To tear apart (usually in surgery).
D	I	V	I	N	A	L	Examination in biblical literature.
D	I	Z	E	N	E	D	Dress gaudily and with finery.
D	I	Z	Z	A	R	D	Blockhead, Nitwit.
D	I	Z	Z	I	E	D	Confused, Stupified, Bewildered, Dazed.
D	I	Z	Z	I	E	R	Giddier, More dazed, More confused.
D	I	Z	Z	I	L	Y	Confusedly, Giddily.
D	J	I	B	B	A	H	Eastern garment.
D	O	C	E	T	A	E	Early Christian sect that practised docetism.
D	O	C	E	T	I	C	Relating to the Docetist.

1	2	3	4	5	6	7	Definition
D	O	C	I	B	L	E	Docile, Easily taught, Tractable, Amenable.
D	O	C	I	O	U	S	Docile, Placid, Pliant.
D	O	C	K	A	G	E	Charge for the use of a dock, A deduction taken or withheld as compensation for some defect.
D	O	C	K	I	N	G	Removing part of an animal's tail, Abridging, Lessening, Reducing.
D	O	C	K	I	Z	E	Equip with docks.
D	O	C	Q	U	E	T	Docket.
D	O	D	D	I	N	G	Lopping or clipping wool.
D	O	D	G	E	R	Y	Tricky, Artifice, Expedient.
D	O	D	G	I	N	G	Avoiding, Evading, Parrying, Shirking, Sidestepping, Ducking, Hedging, Eluding.
D	O	E	S	K	I	N	Soft glove leather, Tanned skin from sheep and lambs.
D	O	F	F	I	N	G	Removing, Dousing, Putting off, Taking off, Undressing.
D	O	G	B	A	N	E	Tropical herbs and shrubs having a milky juice.
D	O	G	B	O	D	Y	Square-sterned boat.
D	O	G	B	O	L	T	Long slim bolt for uniting two parts at right angles.
D	O	G	C	A	R	T	Two-wheeled cart drawn by dogs.
D	O	G	D	A	Y	S	Period between July and early September when weather is hot and sultry.
D	O	G	F	A	C	E	Infantryman.
D	O	G	F	A	L	L	Draw, Tie, Inconclusive fall in wrestling.
D	O	G	F	I	S	H	Small shark.
D	O	G	G	I	N	G	Hunting, Tracking, Hounding.
D	O	G	G	I	S	H	Currish, Snappish, Sulky, Dashing.
D	O	G	G	O	N	E	Damned.
D	O	G	G	R	E	L	Burlesque or comic verse, Trivial or bad poetry.
D	O	G	H	E	A	D	Hammer of a gunlock.
D	O	G	H	O	L	E	A mean, miserable abode.
D	O	G	L	I	K	E	Characteristic of a dog, especially in dumb devotion.
D	O	G	M	A	T	A	Something held as an established opinion.
D	O	G	N	A	I	L	Nail with a head that fits flush in a countersink.
D	O	G	R	O	S	E	Common European wild rose.
D	O	G	S	E	A	R	Corner of page of book turned down.
D	O	G	S	K	I	N	Glove leather.
D	O	G	S	T	A	R	Sirius.
D	O	G	T	I	C	K	Any of several ticks infesting dogs and other animals.
D	O	G	T	R	O	T	Quick easy gait.
D	O	G	V	A	N	E	Small vane carried on weather rail of a ship.
D	O	G	W	O	O	D	Flowering shrub of genus of boxwood.
D	O	L	E	F	U	L	Downcast, Creastfallen, Dejected, Depressed, Dispirited, Downhearted, Woeful, Sorrowful.
D	O	L	L	I	E	D	Laundered, Crushed, Convey on a dolly (camera).
D	O	L	L	I	E	R	Worker who scours or polishes with a dolly.
D	O	L	P	H	I	N	Porpoise, Small toothed whale.
D	O	L	T	I	S	H	Stupid, Blockhead, Dense, Dull, Dumb, Thick, Stolid, Witless.
D	O	M	A	T	I	C	Belonging to a crystallographic class of symmetry characterised by a dome.
D	O	M	I	C	A	L	Shaped like a dome.
D	O	M	I	N	A	L	Principal as distinguished from an agent.
D	O	N	A	T	O	R	Donor.
D	O	N	N	I	N	G	Putting on, Dressing, Assuming, Clothing oneself.
D	O	N	N	I	S	H	Academic, Pedantic.
D	O	N	N	I	S	M	Donnish attitude.
D	O	N	S	H	I	P	Possession of the title or rank of don.
D	O	O	M	I	N	G	Condemning, Pssing judgment, Inflicting disaster.
D	O	O	R	M	A	T	Mat just inside door, One that submits supinely to abuse.
D	O	O	R	W	A	Y	Portal, Entrance, Gaining access to enjoyable condition.
D	O	R	H	A	W	K	Common European nightjar.
D	O	R	K	I	N	G	English breed of large domestic fowl.
D	O	R	L	A	C	H	Bundle, Package, Suitcase.
D	O	R	M	A	N	T	Latent, Abeyant, Lurking, Potential, Prepatent, Quiescent.
D	O	R	M	I	C	E	Mice that become torpid in cold weather.
D	O	R	N	I	C	K	Coarse damask of wool and silk.
D	O	R	T	O	U	R	Dormitory.
D	O	S	S	I	E	R	Accumulation of records, reports or documents.
D	O	T	T	I	E	R	More foolish, More absurd.
D	O	T	T	I	N	G	Spotting, Stipling, Speckling.
D	O	U	B	L	E	D	Duplicated, Folded, Escaped, Avoided, Eluded, Turned, Repeated, Agumented.
D	O	U	B	L	E	T	Man's close fitting garment for the upper body consisting of two idential parts.
D	O	U	B	T	E	D	Mistrusted, Concerned, Questioned, Disputed, Suspected, Challenged.
D	O	U	B	T	E	R	Skeptic, Doubting Thomas, Unbeliever.
D	O	U	C	E	L	Y	Modestly, Neatly, Tidily, Sedately, Cheerfully.

1	2	3	4	5	6	7	
D	O	U	C	E	T	S	Sweet dishes.
D	O	U	C	E	U	R	Amiability, Compliment, Gratuity, Present, Tip.
D	O	U	C	I	N	E	Ornamental curved moulding.
D	O	U	G	H	T	Y	Brave, Bold, Fearless, Dauntless, Able, Unafraid, Valiant, Strong.
D	O	U	P	I	O	N	Large uneven silk thread reeled from double cocoon for shantung and pongee fabrics.
D	O	U	R	E	S	T	Harshest, Grimmest, Hardest, Surliest, Ugliest.
D	O	U	R	I	N	E	Contagious horse disease transmitted during breeding.
D	O	U	S	I	N	G	Immersing, Throwing, Extinguishing, Ducking, Splashing, Quenching, Spattering, Submerging.
D	O	U	T	I	N	G	Extinguishing, Dousing, Putting out, Quenching.
D	O	V	E	C	O	T	Raised house or box for domestic pigeons, Settled or harmonious group.
D	O	V	E	K	I	E	Small short-billed auk.
D	O	V	E	L	E	T	Small or immature dove.
D	O	V	E	R	E	D	Dozed off, Lost consciousness momentarily, Cat-napped, Snoozed.
D	O	W	A	B	L	E	Legally entitled to dower.
D	O	W	A	G	E	R	Matriarch, Matron, Widow in enjoyment of inheritance from late husband.
D	O	W	D	I	L	Y	Slatternly, Drably, Sordidly.
D	O	W	E	R	E	D	Endowed, Appointed, Gifted, Furnished, Outfitted.
D	O	W	N	I	N	G	Swallowing, Defeating, Taking, Felling, Dropping.
D	O	W	S	I	N	G	Flattening, Killing, Destroying.
D	O	Y	E	N	N	E	Senior lady in position of importance.
D	O	Z	E	N	T	H	Twelfth.
D	R	A	B	B	E	R	Duller, Colourless, Bleaker, More dingy.
D	R	A	B	B	L	E	Draggle, Befoul, Wet and muddy.
D	R	A	B	L	E	R	Additional sail.
D	R	A	C	H	M	A	Ancient Greek unit of weight, Basic monetary unit of modern Greece.
D	R	A	C	U	L	A	Vampire depicted in novel by Bram Stoker, One that saps physical and emotional strengh of another.
D	R	A	F	T	E	D	Sketched, Blocked, Conscripted, Outlined, Characterized, Formulated, Framed, Prepared.
D	R	A	G	B	A	R	Hinged yoke on mine car to prevent accident if cable breaks.
D	R	A	G	G	E	D	Hauled, Pulled, Lugged, Towed, Tugged, Delayed, Dawdled, Loitered.
D	R	A	G	G	L	E	Drag, Trail, Traipse, Besmirch, Drabble, Shuffle, Soak.
D	R	A	G	M	A	N	A man who drags something, Fisherman, Hunter, Conveyor-operator.
D	R	A	G	N	E	T	Trawling net, Measures taken by police to apprehend a suspect.
D	R	A	G	O	O	N	Mounted infantryman, Cavalryman, Dragon, Persecute by the harsh use of troops.
D	R	A	I	N	E	D	Effete, Depleted, Exhausted, Spent, Worn-out, Washed-up, Siphoned, Impoverished.
D	R	A	I	N	E	R	Colander, Draining vat.
D	R	A	P	E	R	Y	Store dealing in cloth, clothing, haberdashery and dry goods, Hangings, Curtains.
D	R	A	P	I	N	G	Enveloping, Swathing, Wrapping, Swaddling, Enwrapping, Rolling, Enfolding.
D	R	A	P	P	I	E	A small amount of liquid usually whisky.
D	R	A	S	T	I	C	Rigorous, Severe, Vigorous, Forcible, Acting with harshness.
D	R	A	T	T	E	D	Damned, Blasted, Blessed, Confounded, Dang, Darn, Doggone, Infernal.
D	R	A	U	G	H	T	Draft, Conscript, Pull Traction, Draw, Breeze, Dose, Outline.
D	R	A	W	B	A	R	Removable bar in a fence.
D	R	A	W	B	O	Y	Boy who operated the harness cords of a hand loom.
D	R	A	W	I	N	G	Sketching, Pulling, Siphoning, Attracting, Taking, Collecting, Extending, Inhaling.
D	R	A	W	L	E	D	Spoke slowly, Loitered, Drawn-out.
D	R	A	W	N	E	T	Net once used for catching large wild birds.
D	R	A	W	O	F	F	Tap or spigot by which liquid is drawn off.
D	R	A	Y	A	G	E	Charge for draying of goods.
D	R	A	Y	M	A	N	Man who drives a dray.
D	R	E	A	D	E	D	Frightened, Alarmed, Horrified, Terrified, Dismayed, In fearful apprehension.
D	R	E	A	M	E	D	Longed, Craved, Hankered, Hungered, Lusted, Thirsted, Dreamt, Imagined.
D	R	E	A	M	E	R	Visionary, Castle-builder, Idealist, Utopian, Wishful-thinker.
D	R	E	D	G	E	D	Scooped, Removed, Deepened, Searched, Sprinkled.
D	R	E	D	G	E	R	Machine or boat for dredging, Table-shaker.
D	R	E	E	I	N	G	Enduring, Suffering, Dreading, Fearing.
D	R	E	S	D	E	N	Meissen porcelain.
D	R	E	S	S	E	D	Clothed, Bandaged, Bound, Cleaned, Altered, Clad, Tilled, Cultivated.
D	R	E	S	S	E	R	Table, Sideboard, Cupboard, Wardrobe mistress.
D	R	I	B	B	E	D	Dribble.
D	R	I	B	L	E	T	Trifling sum, Pittance, Insignificant quantity, Globule, Falling drop.
D	R	I	F	T	E	D	Floated, Sauntered, Ambled, Lingered, Strolled, Wandered, Rambled, Ranged.
D	R	I	F	T	E	R	Rover, Wanderer, Rambler, Roamer, Vagabond, Hobo, Vagrant, Tramp.
D	R	I	L	L	E	D	Perforated, Bored, Punctured, Exercised, Rehearsed, Accustomed, Penetrated, Disciplined.
D	R	I	N	K	E	R	Reveller, Toper, Carouser, Vessel to provide water for domestic animals or poultry.
D	R	I	P	D	R	Y	To dry with few or no wrinkles when hung dripping wet.
D	R	I	P	P	E	D	Dribble emitted in steady drops, Leaked, Trickled, Dropped, Wept, Oozed.
D	R	I	V	E	I	N	Business where patrons are served while remaining in their automobiles.

1	2	3	4	5	6	7	
D	R	I	V	I	N	G	Energetic, Active, Enterprising, Lively, Forcing, Urging, Navigating, Launching.
D	R	I	Z	Z	L	E	Sprinkle, Fine rain, Slow trickle, Dribble.
D	R	O	G	H	E	R	Sailing barge, Carrier, Porter.
D	R	O	I	L	E	D	Drudge.
D	R	O	L	L	E	D	Jested, Sported, Clowned, Made fun, Influenced by raillery.
D	R	O	L	L	E	R	More laughable, Funnier, Odder.
D	R	O	M	O	N	D	Large medieval fast-sailing galley.
D	R	O	N	I	N	G	Humming, Buzzing, Spending in idleness.
D	R	O	N	I	S	H	Indolent, Slow.
D	R	O	O	L	E	D	Slavered, Drivel, Twaddled, Dribbled.
D	R	O	O	P	E	D	Slouched, Slumped, Lowered, Depressed, Sunk, Flagged, Wilted, Languished.
D	R	O	P	L	E	T	A drip, Bead of moisture.
D	R	O	P	O	U	T	One who ceases activities before achieving the goal.
D	R	O	P	P	E	D	Fallen, Plunged, Slumped, Toppled, Tumbled, Floored, Withdraw, Crouched.
D	R	O	P	P	E	R	Glass tube with rubber bulb to measure liquids by drops.
D	R	O	S	E	R	A	Sundew.
D	R	O	S	H	K	Y	Russian four-wheeled open carriage.
D	R	O	U	G	H	T	Aridity, Dryness, Lack of moisture, Chronic shortage of something.
D	R	O	U	T	H	Y	Thirsty, Dry, Drought.
D	R	O	W	N	E	D	Suffocated in water, Sunk in water, Extinguished, Overwhelmed, Soaked, Drenched.
D	R	O	W	S	E	D	Inactive, Half asleep, Light slumber, Dozed.
D	R	U	B	B	E	D	Basted, Battered, Belabored, Pounded, Thrashed, Lambasted, Lashed, Whipped.
D	R	U	C	K	E	N	Drunken.
D	R	U	D	G	E	D	Performed hard menial rasks, Plodded, Toiled, Slaved.
D	R	U	G	G	E	D	Administered a drug, Stupefied.
D	R	U	G	G	E	R	Druggist.
D	R	U	G	G	E	T	Fabric of wool or wool mixed with linen or silk, Rug.
D	R	U	I	D	I	C	Relating to the druids.
D	R	U	M	L	I	N	Oval hill of glacial drift.
D	R	U	M	M	E	D	Vibrated, Solicited, Canvassed, Expelled.
D	R	U	M	M	E	R	One who plays a drum, Large cockroach, Travelling salesman.
D	R	U	N	K	E	N	Drunk, Drenched, Intoxicated, Wobbly, Inebriated, Tipsy.
D	R	Y	B	O	N	E	Smithsonite.
D	R	Y	C	E	L	L	Type of battery.
D	R	Y	D	O	C	K	Dock that can be dry during repair work.
D	R	Y	N	E	S	S	Lack of emotional warmth, Monotony, Sardonic humour, Aridity, Thirst, Lacking moisutre.
D	R	Y	R	E	N	T	Rent, Seck.
D	R	Y	S	A	L	T	To treat skins and hides with salt.
D	R	Y	S	H	O	D	Having dry shoes on, Not wetting shoes or feet.
D	U	A	L	I	S	M	Doctrine that the universe is under dominion of two opposing principles one is good one evil.
D	U	A	L	I	S	T	Adherent of dualism.
D	U	A	L	I	T	Y	Being made up of two elements, Doubleness, Dichotomy.
D	U	A	L	I	Z	E	Make dual.
D	U	A	R	C	H	Y	Government of two rulers having equal power.
D	U	B	B	I	N	G	Substituting dialogue in a film, Conferring knighthood, Giving a nickname, Rerecording.
D	U	B	I	E	T	Y	Dubiousness, Uncertainty, Doubtful, Skeptical, Mistrust, Suspicion, Wonder, Hesitancy.
D	U	B	I	O	U	S	Debatable, Doubtful, Questionable, Uncertain, Suspect, Undecided, improbable, Unlikely.
D	U	C	A	L	L	Y	In the style of a duke.
D	U	C	H	E	S	S	Wife of a duke.
D	U	C	K	I	N	G	Dousing, Immersing, Submerging, Dipping, Stooping, Dodging, Fencing, Escaping.
D	U	C	T	I	L	E	Plastic, Adaptable, Malleable, Pliable, Pliant, Supple, Tractable.
D	U	C	T	U	L	E	A small duct.
D	U	D	G	E	O	N	Offense, Huff, Resentment, Umbrage, Ill humour.
D	U	E	B	I	L	L	Written acknowledgment of debt due.
D	U	E	L	I	S	T	One who engages in duels.
D	U	E	L	L	E	D	Fought in a duel.
D	U	E	N	E	S	S	Quality or state of being due.
D	U	F	F	I	N	G	Faking, Cheating, Furbishing.
D	U	K	E	D	O	M	Duchy, Territory ruled by a duke or duchess.
D	U	L	C	I	F	Y	Make sweet, Mollify, Appease.
D	U	L	L	A	R	D	Stupid person, Dunce, Dumbbell, Idiot, Dummy, Moron, Simpleton, Blockhead.
D	U	L	L	E	S	T	Bluntest, Most obtuse, Most cloudy, Dimmest.
D	U	L	L	I	N	G	Making indistinct, Blunting, Numbing, Stupefying.
D	U	L	L	I	S	H	Somewhat dull.
D	U	L	N	E	S	S	Stupidity, Apathy, Drowsiness, Bluntness, Monotony, Lacklustre.
D	U	L	O	S	I	S	Enslavement by an insect.
D	U	M	B	E	S	T	Most silent, Most taciturn.

DUMPING **7 LETTERS** **EARRING**

1	2	3	4	5	6	7	
D	U	M	P	I	N	G	Plunging, Dropping, Tipping, Discarding, Scrapping, Riddance, Junking.
D	U	M	P	I	S	H	Dull, Stupid, Sad, Melancholy, Dejected.
D	U	N	B	I	R	D	Pochard duck.
D	U	N	C	E	R	Y	Stupidity.
D	U	N	C	I	F	Y	To cause to appear stupid.
D	U	N	C	I	S	H	Like a dunce.
D	U	N	E	D	I	N	City in New Zealand.
D	U	N	F	I	S	H	Fish cured by dunning.
D	U	N	G	E	O	N	Close dark prison or vault.
D	U	N	N	A	G	E	Packing timber, Padding in container.
D	U	N	N	I	N	G	Persistence in making demands for money owing, Curing codfish by salting.
D	U	N	N	I	S	H	Dark brown grayish colour.
D	U	N	N	O	C	K	Hedge sparrow.
D	U	O	T	O	N	E	Process for making prints typically in two shades of same colour.
D	U	O	T	Y	P	E	Process for making prints in two colours.
D	U	P	A	B	L	E	Can be duped, Credulous, Gullible.
D	U	R	A	B	L	E	Lasting, Enduring, Permanent, Stable, Stout, Strong, Tenacious, Diuturnal.
D	U	R	A	B	L	Y	Lastingly, Strongly.
D	U	R	A	M	E	N	Heartwood.
D	U	R	A	N	C	E	Continuance, Endurance, Restraint, Confinement, Durability.
D	U	R	A	N	T	E	Everlasting, During.
D	U	R	M	A	S	T	European oak valued for its dark heavy tough elastic wood.
D	U	S	K	I	E	R	More swarthy, Blackish, More gloomy, More obscure.
D	U	S	K	I	L	Y	Obscurely.
D	U	S	K	I	S	H	Rather dark, Partially obscured.
D	U	S	T	B	I	N	Trashcan, Receptacle for rubbish.
D	U	S	T	I	L	Y	In a dusty condition.
D	U	S	T	I	N	G	Sprinkling, Beating, Buffeting, Powdering.
D	U	S	T	M	A	N	Garbage collector.
D	U	S	T	P	A	N	Pan for receiving and conveying dirt from floor.
D	U	T	E	O	U	S	Respectful, Deferential, Dutiful, Regardful.
D	U	T	I	F	U	L	Respectful, Deferential, Duteous, Sense of duty, Obedient.
D	U	U	N	V	I	R	One of two Roman magistrates.
D	V	A	N	D	V	A	Compound words.
D	W	A	R	F	E	D	Eclipsed, Stunted, Suppressed.
D	W	E	L	L	E	D	Sojourned, Resided, Lived, Consisted, Existed.
D	W	E	L	L	E	R	Inhabitant, Denizen, Liver, Occupyer, Occupant, Resident, Inmate, Indigene.
D	W	I	N	D	L	E	Decrease, Abate, Diminish, Lessen, Reduce, Taper, Fail, Shrink.
D	Y	A	R	C	H	Y	Government where power is vested in two rulers.
D	Y	E	W	E	E	D	Woodwaxer.
D	Y	E	W	O	O	D	Wood from which colouring matter is extracted.
D	Y	N	A	M	I	C	Active, Operative, Vigorous, Energetic, Lusty, Vital, Intense, Vehement.
D	Y	N	A	S	T	Y	A succession of rulers of the same line of descent.
D	Y	P	N	O	N	E	Liquid ketone.

E

1	2	3	4	5	6	7	
E	A	G	E	R	L	Y	Avidly, Ardently, Fervently, Impatiently, Keenly, Thirstily, Intently, Enthusiastically.
E	A	R	A	C	H	E	Pain in the ear, Otalgia.
E	A	R	B	A	S	H	Harangue, Lecture.
E	A	R	C	L	I	P	Earring with a clip fastener.
E	A	R	D	R	O	P	Fuchsia plant, Buckwheat vine.
E	A	R	D	R	U	M	Tympanum.
E	A	R	H	E	A	D	Ear of grain.
E	A	R	L	D	O	M	Territory of earl or countess.
E	A	R	L	E	S	S	Lacking ears, Tone-deaf as regards music.
E	A	R	L	I	E	R	Previously, Before, Sooner, Already, Formerly, Beforehand.
E	A	R	L	I	K	E	Projecting like an ear.
E	A	R	L	O	B	E	Pendant part of the pinna of the ear.
E	A	R	L	O	C	K	Lock or curl of hair hanging in front of the ear.
E	A	R	M	A	R	K	Mark of identification on the ear of a domestic animal, Designate, Allocate.
E	A	R	N	E	S	T	Pledge, Intentness, Serious, Grave, Sedate, Sober, Solemn, Steady.
E	A	R	N	I	N	G	Profit, Gain, Lucre, Proceeds, Return, Wage, Dividend, Compensation.
E	A	R	P	I	C	K	Device for removing wax or foreign bodies from the ear.
E	A	R	P	L	U	G	Ornament for lobe of the ear, Device as protection against water or to deaden sound.
E	A	R	R	I	N	G	Ear ornament.

1	2	3	4	5	6	7	
E	A	R	S	H	O	T	The range within which something may be heard without mechanical aid.
E	A	R	T	H	E	D	Hidden, Banked, Ridged, Gone to ground.
E	A	R	T	H	E	N	Made of fired clay.
E	A	R	T	H	L	Y	Realistic, Factual, Terrestrial, Mundane, Worldly, Likely, Probably, Conceivable.
E	A	S	E	F	U	L	Restful, Comfortable, Cozy, Cushy, Easy, Snug, Soft, Comfy.
E	A	S	I	E	S	T	Lightest, Smoothest, Plainest, Kindest, Softest, Mildest, Politest, Simplest.
E	A	S	T	E	R	N	Inhabitant of the East, Oriental.
E	A	T	A	B	L	E	Fit to be eaten, Pleasant to eat, Edible, Comestible, Esculent.
E	B	B	T	I	D	E	Tide at ebb, Period or state of decline.
E	B	O	N	I	T	E	Hard rubber.
E	B	O	N	I	Z	E	To make or stain black.
E	C	B	O	L	I	C	Drug to increase uterine contraction and facilitate delivery.
E	C	C	R	I	N	E	Produced by an eccrine gland.
E	C	D	Y	S	I	S	Act of moulting or shedding outer skin or shell.
E	C	H	A	P	P	E	One of the positions of the feet in ballet.
E	C	H	E	L	L	E	Lacing of ribbons on a 17th century costume, Diffraction, Grating.
E	C	H	E	L	O	N	Staggered formation of troops or planes, File, Queue, Rank, Row.
E	C	H	I	D	N	A	Australian ant-eater.
E	C	H	I	M	Y	S	Rodents of South and Central America.
E	C	H	I	N	A	L	Relating to a sea urchin.
E	C	H	I	N	U	S	Sea urchin, Decoration of Greek Doric and Ionic Columns.
E	C	H	O	I	N	G	Repeating, Reflecting, Repeating, Imitating.
E	C	H	O	I	S	M	Onomatopoeia.
E	C	L	I	P	S	E	Obscure, Bedim, Dark, Dim, Surpass, Shroud, Overshadow, Murk.
E	C	L	O	G	U	E	Bucolic, Idyll, Pastoral poem featuring shepherds in conversation.
E	C	O	C	I	D	E	Polluting the environment whether by accident or design.
E	C	O	L	O	G	Y	Branch of science concerned with interrelationship of organisms and their environments.
E	C	O	N	O	M	Y	Thrifty, Frugality, Saving, Providence, Discretion, Husbandry, Organization, Prudence.
E	C	O	T	O	N	E	Transition area between plant communities.
E	C	S	T	A	S	Y	Rapture, Transport, Rhapsody, Exhilaration, Pleasure, Blissfulness, Exaltation, Inspiration.
E	C	T	A	S	I	A	Expansion of tubular or hollow organ.
E	C	T	A	S	I	S	Lengthening of a short syllable.
E	C	T	A	T	I	C	Relating to ectasia.
E	C	T	H	Y	M	A	Skin rash, Sore mouth of sheep.
E	C	T	O	P	I	A	Abnormal or cogenital or acquired position of an organ.
E	C	T	O	P	I	C	Occurring in an abnormal position.
E	C	T	O	Z	O	A	External animal parasites.
E	C	T	Y	P	A	L	Having the characteristics of a copy of an original.
E	D	A	C	I	T	Y	Voracity, Rapacity, Appetite, Greed, Devour.
E	D	A	P	H	O	N	Animal and plant life present in soils.
E	D	D	Y	I	N	G	Swirling, Vortical, Whirling, Circular, Turning.
E	D	E	N	I	T	E	Light-coloured variety of a luminous amphibole.
E	D	E	N	T	A	L	Lacking teeth as sloths, armadillos, anteaters and pangolins.
E	D	I	C	T	A	L	Relating to a decree.
E	D	I	F	I	C	E	Magnificent or massive building, Erection, Structure.
E	D	I	F	I	E	D	Improved spiritually.
E	D	I	T	I	O	N	Impression, Origin, Printing, Issue, Creation, Reissue, Reproduction.
E	D	U	C	A	T	E	Teach, School, Train, Discipline, Instruct, Cultivate, Nurture, Inform.
E	D	U	C	I	N	G	Eliciting, Extracting, Evolving, Evincing, Extorting, Wresting, Wringing, Deriving.
E	D	U	C	T	O	R	Ejector, Device for mixing two fluids.
E	E	L	B	O	A	T	Dutch canal boat.
E	E	L	F	A	R	E	Migration of young eels up a stream.
E	E	L	P	O	U	T	Various marine fishes resembling blennies.
E	E	L	W	O	R	M	Plant-parasitic earthworm.
E	F	F	A	B	L	E	Capable of being uttered or expressed.
E	F	F	A	C	E	D	Eliminated, Erased, Annulled, Cancelled, Eradicated, Expunged, Obliterated, Excluded.
E	F	F	E	C	T	S	Personal belongings, Results, Causes, Produces, Induces, Performs, Fulfils.
E	F	F	E	N	D	I	Title of respect for a Turkish official.
E	F	F	O	R	C	E	Force.
E	F	F	U	L	G	E	Radiate, Gleam, Glisten, Shine, Glorious.
E	F	F	U	S	E	D	Diffused, Emanated, Gushed, Expanded, Unrestrained, Slobbered.
E	G	A	L	I	T	Y	Social or political equality.
E	G	E	S	T	E	D	Ejected, Cast out.
E	G	G	B	I	R	D	Sooty tern.
E	G	G	C	E	L	L	Female germ cell.
E	G	G	H	E	A	D	Intellectual, Highbrow, Theorist.
E	G	O	T	I	S	M	Vanity, Selfishness, Conceit, Self-centredness, Boasting, Bragging, Megalomania, Arrogance.

1	2	3	4	5	6	7	Definition
E	G	O	T	I	S	T	One marked by boastfulness.
E	G	O	T	I	Z	E	Refer unduly to oneself.
E	I	D	E	T	I	C	One having vivid mental images.
E	I	D	O	L	O	N	Apparition, Ghost, Phantasm, Phantom, Shadow, Spectre, Spirit, Spook.
E	I	R	E	N	I	C	Irenic, Harmony, Peace, Moderation, Nonviolent, Pacifist.
E	J	E	C	T	E	D	Banished, Dispossessed, Expelled, Ousted, Evicted, Dismissed, Chased, Excluded.
E	J	E	C	T	O	R	Mechanism of firearm that ejects the empty cartridge, A device to eject finished work from a mould.
E	L	A	I	D	I	N	Glycerol ester of elaidic acid.
E	L	A	N	C	E	D	Threw, Launched.
E	L	A	P	S	E	D	Passed, Outstayed, Outlasted, Expired, Ran out, Glided, Slid away, Overstay.
E	L	A	S	T	I	C	Flexible, Expansive, Resilient, Buoyant, Volatile, Effervescent, Stretchy, Supple.
E	L	A	S	T	I	N	Protein similar to collagen.
E	L	A	T	I	N	E	Genus of aquatic or amphibious creeping herbs.
E	L	A	T	I	N	G	Exalting, Intoxicating, Stimulating, Exciting, Inspiring, Elevating.
E	L	A	T	I	O	N	Self-exaltation, Buoyancy, Joy, Exhilaration, Euphoria, Happiness, Rapture, Gratification.
E	L	B	O	W	E	D	Pushed, Jostled, Nudged, Forced, Hustled, Pressed, Shoved, Shouldered.
E	L	D	E	R	L	Y	Aged, Ancient, Old, Aging, Declining, Out-moded, Old-fashioned, Advanced in years.
E	L	E	A	T	I	C	Relating to school of Greek philosophers.
E	L	E	C	T	E	D	Chosen, Designated, Marked, Picked, Selected, Decided, Balloted, Voted.
E	L	E	C	T	O	R	One that chooses, German prince.
E	L	E	G	A	N	T	Excellent, Fine Splendid, Polished, Select, Superior, Tasteful, Cultured.
E	L	E	G	I	A	C	Poem expressing sorrow, Plaintive, Nostalgic, Melancholy.
E	L	E	G	I	S	T	Composer of an elegy.
E	L	E	G	I	Z	E	Lament or celebrate in elegy.
E	L	E	M	E	N	T	Substance, Component, Ingredient, Integrant, Factor, Particle, Constituent, Segment.
E	L	E	V	A	T	E	Raise, Erect, Ennoble, Exhalt, Refine, Exhilarate, Elate, Excite.
E	L	F	B	O	L	T	Flint arrowhead.
E	L	F	L	A	N	D	Fairyland.
E	L	F	L	O	C	K	Tangled hair.
E	L	F	W	O	R	T	Coarse large herbs.
E	L	I	D	I	N	G	Annulling, Ignoring, Omitting, Suppressing, Curtailing, Shortening, Reducing, Diminishing.
E	L	I	S	I	O	N	Omission, Cut.
E	L	K	W	O	O	D	Soft wood of the umbrella tree.
E	L	L	I	P	S	E	A regular oval.
E	L	L	W	A	N	D	Measuring rod.
E	L	O	G	I	U	M	Inscriptions on tombstones.
E	L	O	G	I	E	S	Same as ELOGIUM.
E	L	O	H	I	S	M	Worshipping of minor divinities of ancient Canaanites.
E	L	O	H	I	S	T	Priestly writer.
E	L	O	P	I	N	G	Escaping, Fleeing, Running away, Bolting, Decamping.
E	L	U	D	I	N	G	Baffling, Frustrating, Evading, Escaping, Avoiding, Shunning, Foiling, Thwarting.
E	L	U	S	I	O	N	Illusion, Evasion, Avoidance, Escaping, Eschewing, Shunning,
E	L	U	S	I	V	E	Evasive, Baffling, Deceptive, Illusory, Intangible, Fugitive, Mysterious, Incomprehensible.
E	L	U	S	O	R	Y	Evasive, Elusive, Intangible, Nebulous, Vague, Unsolved.
E	L	U	T	I	N	G	Extract, Remove, Wash out.
E	L	Y	S	I	A	N	Sweetly blissful, Beatific, Heavenly, Delightful.
E	L	Y	S	I	U	M	Paradise, Zion, Heaven, Nirvana, Bliss.
E	L	Y	T	R	A	L	Relating to wings or scales giving protection.
E	L	Y	T	R	O	N	Wing sheath of beetles, Shielding dorsal scales of a certain worm.
E	L	Y	T	R	U	M	Same as ELYTRON.
E	L	Z	E	V	I	R	Publication from 16th and 17th century Dutch family printers and publishers.
E	M	A	N	A	N	T	Emerging from.
E	M	A	N	A	T	E	Come out, Emit, Spring, Arise, Birth, Derive, Originate, Issue.
E	M	B	A	L	E	D	Baled, Wrapped.
E	M	B	A	R	G	O	Retain, Seize, Requisition, Prohibition, Veto.
E	M	B	A	S	S	Y	Official residence and office of an ambassador.
E	M	B	A	T	H	E	Bathe, Immerse, Drench.
E	M	B	A	Y	E	D	Encircled, Surrounded.
E	M	B	L	A	Z	E	Embellish, Emblazon, Ignite, Illuminate, Kindle.
E	M	B	L	E	M	A	Featured picture is mosaic, Separate ornament done in relief.
E	M	B	O	I	T	E	Ballet step with feet interlocked.
E	M	B	O	L	I	C	Relating to an embolus.
E	M	B	O	L	U	S	Wedge, Bubble of air in bloodstream.
E	M	B	O	S	O	M	Shelter, Enclose, Cherish, Foster, Surround, Embrace, Enfold, Hug.
E	M	B	O	W	E	R	Enclose or shelter in a bower.
E	M	B	O	X	E	D	Enclose in a box.
E	M	B	R	A	C	E	Hug, Encircle, Enclose, Enfold, Welcome, Encompass, Include, Cover.

1	2	3	4	5	6	7	
E	M	B	R	A	V	E	Brighten, Inspire with courage.
E	M	B	R	O	I	L	Confuse, Disorder, Distract.
E	M	B	R	O	W	N	Darken, Cause leaves to turn brown.
E	M	B	R	U	E	D	In heraldry.
E	M	B	R	Y	O	N	An embryo.
E	M	E	N	D	E	D	Amended, Corrected, Bettered, Improved, Altered, Changed.
E	M	E	R	A	L	D	Variety of rich green coloured beryl.
E	M	E	R	G	E	D	Revealed, Manifested, Appeared, Derived, Originated, Materialized, Emanated, Proceeded.
E	M	E	R	I	T	A	Bait bug, Female variation of emeritus.
E	M	E	R	I	Z	E	Nap a fabric surface to resemble suede.
E	M	E	T	I	N	E	Alkaloid extracted from ipecac root.
E	M	G	A	L	L	A	African warthog.
E	M	I	N	E	N	T	Conspicuous, Evident, Noteworthy, Protruding, Lofty, Towering, Important, Valuable.
E	M	I	R	A	T	E	State of an emir.
E	M	I	T	T	E	D	Exuded, Oozed, Vented, Exhaled, Ejected, Transmitted, Discharged, Released.
E	M	I	T	T	E	R	Electrode or substance that emits particles.
E	M	O	T	I	O	N	Turmoil, Agitation, Feeling, Passion, Affection, Sentiment, Sensation, Responsiveness.
E	M	O	T	I	V	E	Emotional, Affective, Moving.
E	M	P	A	L	E	D	Impaled, Transfixed.
E	M	P	A	T	H	Y	Sympathy, Compassion, Accord, Affinity, Compatibility, Concord, Rapport, Understanding.
E	M	P	E	R	O	R	Sovereign, Supreme monarch, Commander.
E	M	P	I	R	I	C	Quack, Charlatan.
E	M	P	L	A	C	E	To place in position, To put.
E	M	P	L	A	N	E	Board a plane for purpose of travel.
E	M	P	L	U	M	E	To feather.
E	M	P	O	W	E	R	Commission, Authorize, Enable.
E	M	P	R	E	S	S	Wife or widow of an emperor.
E	M	P	R	I	S	E	Undertaking, Enterprise.
E	M	P	T	I	E	D	Uninhabited, Vacated, Deprived, Divested, Evacuated, Drained, Depleted.
E	M	P	T	I	E	R	More vacuous, Blanker, More inane.
E	M	P	T	I	O	N	Purchase.
E	M	U	L	A	T	E	Imitate, Envy, Strive, Endeavour, Rival, Envy.
E	M	U	L	O	U	S	Compete, Challenge, Vie, Striving to equal or be superior.
E	M	U	W	R	E	N	Australian warbler.
E	N	A	B	L	E	D	Endowed, Allowed, Authorized, Commissioned, Empowered, Licensed, Permitted, Qualified.
E	N	A	C	T	E	D	Chronicled, Represented, Played, Constituted, Established, Impersonated, Proclaimed, Made.
E	N	A	C	T	O	R	One that enacts (new laws).
E	N	A	M	O	U	R	Charm, Captivate, Infatuate, Bewitch, Enchant, Fascinate, Entrance.
E	N	A	R	M	E	D	Equipped with arms or armour.
E	N	A	T	I	O	N	Outgrowth from the surface of an organ, Kinship on the maternal side.
E	N	C	A	G	E	D	Caged, Cooped.
E	N	C	A	S	E	D	Enclosed, Put in, Mounted.
E	N	C	A	V	E	D	Hidden in a cave.
E	N	C	H	A	F	E	Chafe, Heat, Excite.
E	N	C	H	A	I	N	Fetter, Bind, Shackle, Restrain, Attract and hold, Link.
E	N	C	H	A	N	T	Bewitch, Delight, Attract, Captivate, Charm, Fascinate, Enthrall, Thrill.
E	N	C	H	A	S	E	Encase, Enclose, Ornament, Decorate, Inlay, Enshrine, Set (jewel), Engrave.
E	N	C	H	E	E	R	Cheer.
E	N	C	H	Y	M	A	Cellular, Tissue.
E	N	C	L	A	S	P	Clasp, Seize and hold.
E	N	C	L	A	V	E	Enclose within, Surrounded by alien or foreign territory.
E	N	C	L	O	S	E	Surround, Envelop, Enfold, Confine, Fence, Pen, Corral, Cage.
E	N	C	O	I	L	S	Kinky or crinkled hair.
E	N	C	O	R	E	D	Repeated by request.
E	N	C	R	U	S	T	Form a crust on surface, Overlay, Inlay, Coat.
E	N	D	A	R	C	H	Used of a primary xylem of its development.
E	N	D	E	M	I	C	Indigenous, Native, Exotic, Aboriginal, Local.
E	N	D	G	A	M	E	Last stage in playing bridge, Final phase of board game.
E	N	D	G	A	T	E	Tailboard.
E	N	D	L	E	S	S	Boundless, Infinite, Limitless, Eternal, Immeasurable, Everlasting, Continual, Perpetual.
E	N	D	L	O	N	G	Lengthwise.
E	N	D	M	O	S	T	Farthest.
E	N	D	N	O	T	E	Footnote, Note placed at end of text.
E	N	D	O	G	E	N	Plant that develops by growing from inside.
E	N	D	O	R	S	E	Underwrite, Favour, Inscribe, Acknowledge, Certify, Sanction, Authenticate, Uphold.
E	N	D	O	W	E	D	Enriched, Heightened, Enhance, Credit, Bequeathed, Bestowed, Granted, Furnished.
E	N	D	S	E	A	L	Gummed label placed over ends of wrapper.

1	2	3	4	5	6	7	
E	N	D	U	I	N	G	Investing, Transfusing.
E	N	D	U	R	E	D	Allowed, Permitted, Countenanced, Tolerated, Borne, Continued, Brooked, Accepted.
E	N	D	U	R	E	R	One that patiently endures.
E	N	D	W	A	Y	S	Lengthwise, Ahead.
E	N	D	Y	S	I	S	Developing a new coat of hair or new set of feathers.
E	N	E	R	G	I	C	Energetic, Active.
E	N	F	A	C	E	D	Written or printed on the face of a draft.
E	N	F	E	O	F	F	Invest with a fee.
E	N	F	I	L	E	D	Passed through in heraldry.
E	N	F	L	E	S	H	To clothe with flesh.
E	N	F	O	R	C	E	Encourage, Inspire, Assail, Assault, Constrain, Compel, Implement, Oblige.
E	N	G	A	G	E	D	Occupied, Employed, Pledged, Betrothed, Earnest, Fitted, Framed, Meshed.
E	N	G	A	G	E	R	Guarantor, Surety, Employer.
E	N	G	I	N	E	D	Equipped with an engine.
E	N	G	L	I	S	H	Of England.
E	N	G	L	O	B	E	To enclose in a globe, Ingest.
E	N	G	O	R	G	E	Devour, Engulf, Swallow with greediness.
E	N	G	R	A	C	E	To endure with grace.
E	N	G	R	A	F	T	Graft.
E	N	G	R	A	I	L	To indent in heraldry, Roughen, Ornament.
E	N	G	R	A	I	N	Ingrain, Dye Permeat.
E	N	G	R	A	V	E	Chisel, Cut, Represent, Carve, Etch, Chase, Impress, Inscribe, Instil.
E	N	G	R	O	S	S	Amass, Collect, Monopolize, Absorb, Consume, Inscribe, Engage, Immerse.
E	N	H	A	N	C	E	Raise, Lift, Extol, Advance, Augment, Elevate, Heighten, Increase.
E	N	I	S	L	E	D	Placed apart as on an island.
E	N	J	O	Y	E	D	Liked, Amused, Entertained, Rejoiced, Relished, Fancied, Possessed, Retained.
E	N	L	A	C	E	D	Encircled, Enfolded, Entangled, Entwined, Interlaced.
E	N	L	A	R	G	E	Magnify, Expand, Increase, Dilate, Expatiate, Extend, Amplify, Augment.
E	N	L	I	V	E	N	Animate, Quicken, Arouse, Refresh, Renew, Restore, Galvanize, Invigorate.
E	N	N	O	B	L	E	Elevate, Exalt, Raise, Aggrandize, Dignify, Erect, Glorify, Honour.
E	N	N	U	I	E	D	Bored, Palled, Wearied.
E	N	O	L	O	G	Y	Science that treats of winemaking.
E	N	O	U	N	C	E	Enunciate, Set forth.
E	N	P	L	A	N	E	To board an aeroplane for purpose of travel.
E	N	Q	U	I	R	E	Inquire, Investigate, Ask, Examine, Interrogate, Query, Question, Scrutinize.
E	N	Q	U	I	R	Y	Inquiry, Question, Search, Inquest, Investigation, Probe, Research, Examination.
E	N	R	A	G	E	D	Infuriated, Exasperated, Incensed, Maddened, Angered, Steamed up, Exacerbated.
E	N	R	O	B	E	D	Attired, Coated, Invested, Clothed, Arrayed.
E	N	R	O	U	G	H	Roughen.
E	N	S	I	L	E	D	Prepared fodder by silage.
E	N	S	K	I	E	D	Elevated as if to Heaven, Raised to the skies.
E	N	S	L	A	V	E	Subjugate, Capture, Enthral, Oppress, Shackle, Yoke.
E	N	S	N	A	R	E	Catch, Entangle, Entrap, Snare, Tangle, Trap, Decoy, Entice.
E	N	S	N	A	R	L	Entangle, Perplex, Snarl, Tangle, Enmesh, Trammel.
E	N	S	T	A	M	P	Impress, Imprint.
E	N	S	T	E	E	L	Make hard and strong.
E	N	S	T	Y	L	E	To call, To name.
E	N	S	U	I	N	G	Imitating, Succeeding, Resulting, Accruing.
E	N	S	U	R	E	D	Assured, Affianced, Guaranteed, Insured, Secured, Certified, Established, Provided.
E	N	S	W	E	E	P	Sweep over, Sweep across.
E	N	T	A	S	I	S	Slight convexity in the shaft of a column.
E	N	T	E	N	T	E	Written international understanding. Coalition of parties.
E	N	T	E	R	E	D	Engaged, Penetrated, Joined, Started, Pierced, Begun, Trained, Initiated.
E	N	T	E	R	E	R	One that enters or makes entries.
E	N	T	E	R	I	C	Intestinal, Related to medicinal preparation for treating Disease, in the intestines.
E	N	T	E	R	O	N	Alimentary system.
E	N	T	H	R	A	L	Enslave, Charm, Captivate, Fascinate, Engage, Mesmerize, Spellbound, Absorb.
E	N	T	H	U	S	E	Enthusiastic, Thrill, Electrify, Send, Rhapsodize, Rave.
E	N	T	I	C	E	D	Incited, Instigated, Allured, Attracted, Lured, Tempted, Decoyed, Seduced.
E	N	T	I	T	L	E	Assign, Impute, Ascribe, Qualify, Allow, Designate, Style, Authorize.
E	N	T	O	M	I	C	Relating to insects.
E	N	T	O	P	I	C	Occurring in the usual place.
E	N	T	O	T	I	C	Relating to the interior of the ear.
E	N	T	O	Z	O	A	Internal animal parasites.
E	N	T	R	A	I	N	To board a train for the purpose of travel.
E	N	T	R	A	N	T	One that enters, Competitor.
E	N	T	R	E	A	T	Persuade, Treat, Discourse, Plead, Beg, Appeal, Implore, Supplicate.

1	2	3	4	5	6	7	
E	N	T	R	O	P	Y	A measure of the efficiency of a system.
E	N	T	R	U	S	T	Commit, Charge, Trust, Commend, Confide, Consign, Relegate, Allocate.
E	N	T	W	I	N	E	Encircle, Wreathe, Interweave, Attach, Involve, Twist, Around, Coil, Spiral.
E	N	T	W	I	S	T	Corkscrew, Twist, Wreathe, Plait.
E	N	T	U	I	N	G	Inuring, Using familiarizing disciplining, Training.
E	N	V	E	L	O	P	Enclose, Enwrap, Shroud, Veil, Swathe, Drape, Roll, Hedge.
E	N	V	E	N	O	M	Taint, Impregnate with substance harmful to life, Make poisonous, Embitter, Infuse malice.
E	N	V	I	O	U	S	Jealous, Emulous, Covetous, Grasping, Greedy, Resentful, Longing, Begrudging.
E	N	V	I	R	O	N	Encircle, Envelop, Vibrate, Gyrate, Surround, Encompass, Gird, Enclose.
E	N	V	Y	I	N	G	Begrudging, Resenting, Coveting, Craving, Hankering, Longing, Wanting, Yearning.
E	N	W	O	U	N	D	To wind about, Encircle, Enfold.
E	N	W	O	V	E	N	Interwoven.
E	P	A	C	R	I	D	Plant of the family of Australian heathlike shrubs, small shrubs and woody vines.
E	P	A	G	O	G	E	Induction by simple enumeration.
E	P	A	R	C	H	Y	Diocese in the Eastern Orthodox church.
E	P	A	U	L	E	T	Ornamental gold-fringed shoulder pad on a uniform.
E	P	A	X	I	A	L	Located above or on the dorsal side of the axis.
E	P	H	E	B	I	C	Adult.
E	P	H	E	L	I	S	Freckle.
E	P	I	B	O	L	Y	Growing of one part about another during embryogenesis.
E	P	I	C	A	R	P	Rind of fruit.
E	P	I	C	E	D	E	Funeral song or ode, Dirge, Elegy.
E	P	I	C	E	N	E	Effeminate, Sexless, Delicate, Intersexual.
E	P	I	C	H	I	L	Terminal lobe of the labellum in some orchids.
E	P	I	C	I	S	T	An epic poet.
E	P	I	C	U	R	E	Sybarite, Gourmet, Glutton, Gastronome, Connoisseur, Bon vivant.
E	P	I	C	Y	T	E	The investing membrane of a cell.
E	P	I	D	O	T	E	Yellowish green mineral.
E	P	I	G	E	A	L	Growing above the surface of the ground.
E	P	I	G	E	N	E	Not natural to the substance in which it is found.
E	P	I	G	O	N	E	An imitative follower.
E	P	I	G	R	A	M	Short poem involving witticism.
E	P	I	H	Y	A	L	An element of the hyoid arch.
E	P	I	M	E	R	E	Mesothelial-wall zone.
E	P	I	O	T	I	C	Part of the temporal bone.
E	P	I	S	O	D	E	Incident, Scene, Occurrence, Circumstance, Event, Happening, Occasion, Thing.
E	P	I	S	T	L	E	Letter, Missive, Note, Communication, Part of New Testament.
E	P	I	T	A	P	H	Funeral oration, Inscription on a tombstone.
E	P	I	T	A	X	Y	Growth of crystalline substance.
E	P	I	T	H	E	M	Lotion, Poultice.
E	P	I	T	H	E	T	Descriptive term or expression.
E	P	I	T	O	M	E	Abridgment, Abstract, Embodiment, Synopsis, Summary, Résumé, Breviary, Ultimate.
E	P	I	Z	O	I	C	Parasite carried by an animal.
E	P	I	Z	O	O	N	Animal parasite.
E	P	O	C	H	A	L	Momentous, Unparalleled, Outstanding, Remarkable, Important, Unmatched, Unique.
E	P	O	N	Y	M	Y	The derivation of a name for something from that of a person.
E	P	O	X	I	D	E	Plastic resin.
E	Q	U	A	B	L	E	Steady, Serene, Calm, Uniform, Constant, Stable, Orderly, Invariable.
E	Q	U	A	B	L	Y	Uniformly, Justly, Calmly.
E	Q	U	A	L	L	Y	Justly, Impartially, Uniformly, Evenly, Likewise, Alike, Similarly, Squarely.
E	Q	U	A	T	E	D	Equalised, Evened, Compared, Assimilated, Likened, Matched, Paralleled, Balanced.
E	Q	U	A	T	O	R	Great circle midway between the poles of rotation of a planet star or other celestial body.
E	Q	U	E	R	R	Y	Regular attendant of a member of royalty.
E	Q	U	I	N	A	L	Relating to a horse.
E	Q	U	I	N	I	A	Fatal disease of cattle.
E	Q	U	I	N	O	X	When sun crosses the equator and day and night are equal length.
E	Q	U	I	T	E	S	Eques, Ancient Romans below rank of senator.
E	R	A	S	I	N	G	Obliterating, Annulling, Neutralizing, Eliminating, Expunging, Effacing, Deleting, Cancelling.
E	R	A	S	I	O	N	Erasure, Surgical removal of diseased tissue by scraping, Obliteration, Deletion.
E	R	E	C	T	E	D	Built, Raised, Exalted, Magnified, Established, Created, Constructed, Uplifted.
E	R	E	C	T	L	Y	Uprightly, Nobly, Rigidly.
E	R	E	C	T	O	R	One that erects or supervises, Derrick, Shipfitter.
E	R	E	L	O	N	G	Soon.
E	R	E	M	I	T	E	Hermit, Recluse.
E	R	E	P	S	I	N	Enzme obtained from intestinal juice.
E	R	G	O	T	I	C	Of, Relating to, or produced by ergot.
E	R	I	C	O	I	D	Resembling heath.

1	2	3	4	5	6	7	Definition
E	R	I	N	E	U	M	Abnormal felty growth of hairs from leaf epidermis of plant caused by mites.
E	R	I	N	I	T	E	Mineral consisting of emeral-green basic copper arsenate.
E	R	I	S	T	I	C	Controversialist dialectical apodictic.
E	R	M	E	L	I	N	Ermine.
E	R	M	I	N	E	D	Trimmed or lined with ermine.
E	R	M	I	N	E	S	Heraldic fur consisting of white ermine spots on a black field.
E	R	O	D	I	N	G	Corroding, Destroying, Deteriorating, Wearing, Disappearing, Decaying, Scouring, Undermining.
E	R	O	S	I	O	N	Corrosion, Depletion, Deterioration, Denudation, Surface destruction, Disintegration.
E	R	O	S	I	V	E	Erodible, Soil-exposing, Gnawing, VIrulent, Acid.
E	R	O	T	I	C	A	Ponographic literature.
E	R	O	T	I	Z	E	Invest with erotic significance.
E	R	R	A	B	L	E	Liable to error, Fallible, Errant.
E	R	R	A	T	I	C	Wandering, Nomadic, Unpredictable, Capricious, FLuctuating, Uneven, Eccentric, Strange.
E	R	R	A	T	U	M	Error in something published.
E	R	R	H	I	N	E	Medical snuff.
E	R	U	D	I	T	E	Learned, Pedantic, Bookish, Scholarly, Studious, Lettered.
E	R	U	P	T	E	D	Exploded, Burst, Expelled, Ejected, Pustule on skin or mucous membrane.
E	S	C	A	P	E	D	Avoided, Eluded, Evaded, Absconded, Decamped, Shunned, Disappeared, Leaked.
E	S	C	A	P	E	R	One that escapes from enemy custody.
E	S	C	H	A	R	A	Coral.
E	S	C	H	E	A	T	Confiscation, Forfeiture, Plundering.
E	S	C	R	I	B	E	To draw a circle touching one side of a triangle externally and other two sides internally.
E	S	C	R	I	P	T	A written document.
E	S	C	R	O	L	L	A heraldic scroll.
E	S	C	U	A	G	E	The military service required of a knight.
E	S	C	U	L	I	N	Crystalline glucoside from the inner bark of the horse chestnut.
E	S	E	R	I	N	E	Physostigmine used in biology.
E	S	K	I	M	O	S	Group of people of Northern Canada, Greenland, Alaska and Eastern Siberia.
E	S	O	T	E	R	Y	Esotericism (secret knowledge).
E	S	P	A	D	O	N	Swordfish.
E	S	P	A	R	T	O	Spanish and Algerian grass of which shoes and baskets are made.
E	S	P	L	E	E	S	Profits or products that land yields.
E	S	P	O	U	S	E	Wed, Betroth, Marry, Adopt, Embrace, Champion, Advocate, Uphold.
E	S	P	Y	I	N	G	Seeing, Perceiving, Discovering, Watching, Finding, Discerning, Noticing, Distinguishing.
E	S	Q	U	I	R	E	Accompany or escort in public.
E	S	S	A	Y	E	D	Assayed, Tested, Tried, Attempted, Endeavoured, Strived, Struggled, Ventured.
E	S	S	E	N	C	E	Element, Entity, Perfume, Odour, Scent, Elixir, Essential, Indispensable.
E	S	S	O	I	G	N	Excuse for not appearing in court at appointed time.
E	S	T	I	V	A	L	Belonging to summer.
E	S	T	O	I	L	E	Heraldic star.
E	S	T	R	A	D	E	Platform, Dias.
E	S	T	R	E	A	T	True copy, Duplicate or extract.
E	S	T	U	A	R	Y	Water passage where the tide meets the current of a stream.
E	S	U	R	I	N	E	Voracious.
E	T	A	G	E	R	E	Cabinet consisting of a tier of open shelves.
E	T	A	T	I	S	M	State socialism.
E	T	C	H	A	N	T	Solution of acid used in etching.
E	T	C	H	I	N	G	Producing pictures by printing from a metal plate.
E	T	E	R	N	A	L	Ceaseless, Unchanging, Interminable, Unchangeable, Infinite, Forever, Immortal, Continual.
E	T	H	I	C	A	L	Moral, Noble, Principled, Righteous, Virtuous, Upright, Moralistic, Upstanding.
E	T	H	I	O	P	E	Black in complexion.
E	T	H	M	O	I	D	Relating to the nasal cavity.
E	T	O	N	I	A	N	Relating to Eton college.
E	U	C	A	I	N	E	Local anaesthetic.
E	U	C	H	L	R	E	Made slightly tart by an acid or spice.
E	U	C	L	A	S	E	Rare brittle silicate.
E	U	C	R	I	T	E	A meteorite composed essentially of anorthite and augite.
E	U	G	E	N	I	A	Large genus of tropical trees and shrubs.
E	U	G	E	N	I	C	Relating to or fitted for the production of good offspring.
E	U	G	E	N	O	L	Clove oil.
E	U	L	A	L	I	A	Ornamental grasses.
E	U	L	O	G	I	A	Praise, Blessing, Gift, Applaud.
E	U	L	O	G	I	C	Eulogistic.
E	U	P	E	P	S	Y	Good digestion.
E	U	P	H	O	N	Y	Pleasing or sweet sounds, Melody, Tuneful.
E	U	P	H	R	O	E	Tent-slide.
E	U	R	I	P	U	S	Strait, Channel having violent tides or currents, Condition of rapid or dangerous fluctuation.

1	2	3	4	5	6	7	
E	U	R	Y	A	L	E	Genus of basket stars.
E	U	S	T	Y	L	E	Having columns.
E	U	T	A	X	I	C	Relating to stratified ore deposits.
E	U	T	E	R	P	E	Tropical American palm with pea-sized fruit.
E	U	T	O	C	I	A	Normal parturition.
E	V	A	C	U	E	E	Person displaced by war measures.
E	V	A	D	I	N	G	Eluding, Escaping, Avoiding, Parrying, Baffling, Dodging, Circumventing, Foiling.
E	V	A	N	G	E	L	The Gospel, Announcement, Good news.
E	V	A	N	I	S	H	Vanish, Disappear, To cease to be.
E	V	A	S	I	O	N	Avoidance, Elusion, Eschewal, Shunning, Evading, Excuse, Subterfuge, Escape.
E	V	A	S	I	V	E	Equivocal, Shifty, Elusive, Vague, Nebulous, Prevaricative, Shuffling, Sly.
E	V	E	N	I	N	G	Afternoon, Dusk, Soiree, Gloaming, Nightfall, Twilight, Sundown, Sunset.
E	V	E	R	T	E	D	Overthrown, Disproved, Broke, Upset, Confounded, Confuted, Refuted, Rebutted.
E	V	I	C	T	E	D	Ejected, Ousted, Expelled, Proved, Chucked, Chased, Dismissed, Dispossessed.
E	V	I	C	T	O	R	One that evicts.
E	V	I	D	E	N	T	Discernible, Obvious, Manifest, Apparent, Conclusive, Patent, Clear, Distinct, Palpable.
E	V	I	L	E	Y	E	Glance believed to be capable of inflicting injury.
E	V	I	N	C	E	D	Convinced, Confuted, Proved, Confirmed, Exhibited, Revealed, Expressed, Provoked.
E	V	I	R	A	T	E	Castrate, Emasculate.
E	V	O	C	A	T	E	Invocate, Summoning, Spell.
E	V	O	K	I	N	G	Invoking, Educing, Evincing, Extorting, Extracting, Arousing, Exciting, Stimulating.
E	V	O	L	U	T	E	Evolve, Develop, Grow.
E	V	O	L	V	E	D	Unfolded, Emitted, Derived, Educed, Developed, Elaborated, Matured, Grew.
E	X	A	C	T	E	D	Extorted, Pinched, Wrested, Demanded, Wrenched, Levied, Challenged, Imposed.
E	X	A	C	T	L	Y	Accurately, Entirely, Precisely, All, Altogether, Expressly, Even, Squarely.
E	X	A	L	T	E	D	Elevated, Extolled, Magnified, Glorified, Heightened, Intensified, Concentrated.
E	X	A	M	I	N	E	Investigate, Scrutinize, Inquire, Inspect, Study, Survey, Check, Query.
E	X	A	M	P	L	E	Instance, Model, Pattern, Sample, Illustration, Representative, Problem, Specimen.
E	X	A	R	A	T	E	Grooved, Furrowed.
E	X	C	E	R	P	T	Extract, Glean, Pick, Cull, Select, Single, Cite, Quote.
E	X	C	I	P	L	E	Saucer shaped rim around hymenium of various lichens.
E	X	C	I	S	E	D	Overcharged, Amputated, Resected, Entirpated, Removed, Eradicated, Slashed, Cut out.
E	X	C	I	T	E	D	Stimulated, Provoked, Elated, Exhilarated, Animated, Delighted, Enthusiastic.
E	X	C	I	T	E	R	Dynamo, Battery, Electric oscillator.
E	X	C	I	T	O	N	Concentration of energy.
E	X	C	I	T	O	R	An afferent nerve arousing increased action of the part that it supplies.
E	X	C	L	A	I	M	Cry, Ejaculate, Blurt, Vociferate, Burst, Roar, Snort.
E	X	C	L	A	V	E	Portion of country surrounded by politically alien territory.
E	X	C	L	U	D	E	Debar, Eliminate, Suspend, Prohibit, Preclude, Ban, Prevent, Ostracize, banish.
E	X	C	R	E	T	A	Waste matter eliminated or separated from an organism.
E	X	C	R	E	T	E	To eliminate from blood, tissues or organs.
E	X	C	U	R	S	E	Digress, Ramble, Wander, Depart, Diverge, Stray.
E	X	C	U	S	E	D	Overlooked, Exculpated, Justified, Condoned, Pardoned, Forgiven, Released, Exonerated.
E	X	E	C	U	T	E	Perform, Effect, Conduct, Play, Kill, Administer, Fulfil, Transact.
E	X	E	D	E	N	T	Wasting, Ulcerating.
E	X	E	D	R	A	E	A room for conversation furnished with seats.
E	X	E	G	E	T	E	One who studies critical interpretation of the gospel.
E	X	E	R	G	U	E	Space for date on coin or medal.
E	X	E	R	T	E	D	Emitted, Showed, Revealed, Exercised, Wielded, Applied, used.
E	X	H	A	L	E	D	Emitted, Evaporated, Emanated, Breathed, Expired.
E	X	H	A	U	S	T	Evacuate, Drain, Deplete, Discharge, Empty, Expend, Impoverish, Consume.
E	X	H	I	B	I	T	Show, Display, Picture, Bring, Administer, Explain, Manifest, Expose.
E	X	H	U	M	E	D	Disinterred, Dug up, Unearthed.
E	X	H	U	M	E	R	One that exhumes.
E	X	I	G	E	N	T	Pressing, Critical, Demanding, Exacting, Urgent, Importunate, Imperative, Insistent.
E	X	I	L	I	A	N	Relating or belonging to exile.
E	X	I	L	I	N	G	Banishing, Displacing, Deporting, Expelling, Relegating, Evacuating, Dispossessing.
E	X	I	L	I	T	Y	Smallness, Meagreness, Slenderness, Fineness, Thinness.
E	X	I	S	T	E	D	Lived, Lasted, Subsisted, Consisted, Dwelled, Resided, Breathed.
E	X	I	T	I	A	L	Destructive, Fatal.
E	X	O	C	O	N	E	Relating to compound of insect's eyes.
E	X	O	D	E	R	M	Outer cell layer.
E	X	O	D	I	S	T	Emigrant.
E	X	O	G	A	M	Y	Mixed marriage, Sexual reproduction between organisms not closely related.
E	X	P	A	N	S	E	Firmament, Space, Breadth, Distance, Spread, Stretch, Range, Scope.
E	X	P	A	R	T	E	One one side only, Biased, Prejudiced.
E	X	P	E	N	S	E	Spending, Extravagance, Consumption, Cost, Sacrifice, Charge, Outlay, Toll.

1	2	3	4	5	6	7	
E	X	P	I	A	T	E	Cleanse, Avert, Atone, Compensate, Correct, Rectify, Redress, Remedy.
E	X	P	I	R	E	D	Ceased, Terminated, Ended, Stopped, Concluded, Exhaled, Emitted, Passed.
E	X	P	L	A	I	N	Expound, Disclose, Interpret, Clarify, Unfold, Expand, Rationalize, Elucidate.
E	X	P	L	O	D	E	Detonate, Burst, Discharge, Erupt, Discredit, Shoot, Disprove, Puncture.
E	X	P	L	O	I	T	Work, Cultivate, Utilise, Feat, Deed, Act, Employ, Exercise.
E	X	P	L	O	R	E	Investigate, Examine, Search, Prospect, Delve, Enquire, Burrow, Probe.
E	X	P	O	S	E	D	Displayed, Exhibited, Ridiculed, Satirized, Shown, Revealed, Stripped, Uncovered.
E	X	P	O	S	E	R	One that exposes.
E	X	P	O	U	N	D	Interpret, State, Present, Teach, Construe, Gloss, Unfold, Explicate.
E	X	P	R	E	S	S	Delineate, Depict, State, Utter, Vent, Broach, Recount, Describe.
E	X	P	U	N	G	E	Exclude, Discard, Erase, Omit, Annihilate, Eradicate, Annul, Obliterate.
E	X	S	C	I	N	D	Excise, Cut out, Remove.
E	X	T	I	N	C	T	Extinguished, Dead, Deceased, Superseded, Obsolete, Defunct, Departed, Bygone.
E	X	T	R	A	C	T	Summary, Outline, Excerpt, Quotation, Essence, Concentrate, Extort, Juice.
E	X	T	R	E	M	E	Uncompromising, Radical, Fanatical, Last, Final, Farthest, Excessive, Maximum.
E	X	T	R	U	D	E	Eject, Expel, Protrude, Project, Emerge, Evict, Dismiss, Chase.
E	X	U	L	T	E	D	Gladdened, Delighted, Gloried, Triumphed, Boasted, Rejoiced, Celebrated, Crowded.
E	X	U	R	B	I	A	Generalised region of exurbs.
E	X	U	V	I	A	E	Put on, Natural covering of an animal after sloughing.
E	X	U	V	I	A	L	Relating to cast off skins.
E	Y	E	B	A	L	L	Globular capsule of the eye.
E	Y	E	B	A	L	M	Goldseal, Perennial American herb.
E	Y	E	B	A	T	H	Eyecup shaped for fitting snugly into the orbit of the eye for bathing it.
E	Y	E	B	E	A	M	Beam as folk etymology.
E	Y	E	B	O	L	T	Bolt with a looped head.
E	Y	E	B	R	O	W	Arc or ridge over the eye, Hair growing on this ridge.
E	Y	E	H	O	L	E	One of the orbits of the skull, Peephole.
E	Y	E	L	A	S	H	Fringe of hair that edges the eyelid.
E	Y	E	L	E	S	S	Blinded, Lacking sight, Moving or acting blindly.
E	Y	E	S	H	O	T	Markings on a butterfly's wings resembling an eye.
E	Y	E	S	H	O	T	Range of the eye.
E	Y	E	S	O	R	E	Something offensive to the eye.
E	Y	E	S	P	O	T	Ocellus, Small visual organ in many invertebrates consisting of pigmented cells.
E	Y	E	W	A	S	H	Giving a misleading appearance, Prettify.
E	Y	E	W	I	N	K	Wink of the eye, Look, Glance.
E	Y	E	W	O	R	T	Any of herbs once regarded as remedies for eye ailments.

F

F	A	B	E	L	L	A	Small fibrocartilage ossified in many animals.
F	A	B	L	I	A	U	Metrical tales usually coarse and cynical in their treatment of women.
F	A	B	L	I	N	G	Romancing, Prevarication.
F	A	C	E	T	E	D	Cut facets upon, usually relating to a diamond.
F	A	C	O	N	N	E	Pattern or a figure on a fabric.
F	A	C	T	I	C	E	Used for a vulcanized oil.
F	A	C	T	I	O	N	Combination, Party, Clique, Action, Deed, Behaviour, Dispute, Quarrel.
F	A	C	T	O	R	Y	Workshop, Mill, Works, Building for manufacture of goods.
F	A	C	T	U	A	L	Actual, Absolute, Genuine, Positive, Authentic, Legitimate, Valid, Unquestionable.
F	A	C	T	U	R	E	Execution, Invoice.
F	A	C	U	L	A	E	Bright regions of the sun's photosphere.
F	A	C	U	L	T	Y	Means, Property, Resources, Competence, Gift, Position, Disposition, Talent.
F	A	D	D	I	N	G	Fading.
F	A	D	D	I	S	H	Inclined to take up fads, Collecting of stamps, antiques.
F	A	D	D	I	S	T	One inclined to take up fads.
F	A	D	E	D	L	Y	In the manner of one that has faded.
F	A	D	E	O	U	T	Vanishing, Disappearing, Closing scene of film.
F	A	D	G	I	N	G	Suiting, Agreeing, Succeeding, Thriving.
F	A	G	G	I	N	G	Tiring, Flagging, Drudgery, Toiling, Forcing to be a servant, usually in a public school.
F	A	H	L	E	R	Z	Copper crystal ore.
F	A	I	E	N	C	E	Earthenware decorated with opaque coloured glazes.
F	A	I	L	I	N	G	Lacking, Dwindling, Fault, Feeble, Shortcoming, Short, Inadequate, Unsuccessful.
F	A	I	L	U	R	E	Deficiency, Lack, Absence, Neglect, Miscarriage, Dereliction, Nonexistence, Bankruptcy.
F	A	I	N	I	N	G	Willing, Disposing, Inclining, Predisposing.
F	A	I	N	T	E	D	Discouraged, Swooned, Declined, Depressed, Enfeebled, Weaken, Languished.
F	A	I	N	T	E	R	More cowardly, More indistinct, Dimmer, More obscure.
F	A	I	N	T	L	Y	Slightly, Indistinctly, Weakly, Mutedly, Sotto voce, Dimly.

1	2	3	4	5	6	7	
F	A	I	R	E	S	T	Quietest, Clearest, Purest, Finest, Mildest, Lightest, More just.
F	A	I	R	I	E	S	Brownies, Elves, Pixies, Sprites, Gnomes, Goblins.
F	A	I	R	I	L	Y	Lightly, Delicately.
F	A	I	R	I	N	G	Souvenir, Present or cake bought at a fair.
F	A	I	R	I	S	H	Tolerably good.
F	A	I	R	W	A	Y	Navigable part of river, Clear or open space, Unobstructed channel.
F	A	I	T	O	U	R	Cheat, Impostor.
F	A	L	B	A	L	A	Flounce or trimming for a woman's garment.
F	A	L	C	A	T	A	Genus of North American and Asian vines.
F	A	L	C	A	T	E	Hooked, Curved.
F	A	L	C	U	L	A	Curved and sharp-pointed claw.
F	A	L	D	A	G	E	Foldage, Right of the lord of the manor to have his tenant's sheep graze on his land to manure it.
F	A	L	L	A	C	Y	Guile, Trickery, Deception, Erroneousness, Falsehood, Untruth, Delusion, Sophism.
F	A	L	L	A	L	S	Ornaments or trimmings especially in dress.
F	A	L	L	I	N	G	Dropping, Sinking, Slumping, Subsiding, Descending, Lowering, Plunging, Plummeting.
F	A	L	L	O	U	T	Descent of radioactive particles resulting from a nuclear explosion.
F	A	L	S	E	L	Y	Wrongly, Incorrectly, Dishonestly, Deceitly, Insincerely, Fallaciously.
F	A	L	S	E	S	T	Most disloyal, Most dishonest.
F	A	L	S	I	E	S	Breast-shaped fabric or rubber cup used to pad a brassiere.
F	A	L	S	I	F	Y	Confute, Counterfeit, Forge, Adulterate, Disappoint, Frustrate, Misrepresent, Distort.
F	A	L	S	I	T	Y	Untruth, Deceitfulness, Untrustworthiness, Faithlessness, Falsehood, Lie, Sham, Fabrication.
F	A	M	U	L	U	S	Private secretary or attendant especially to a scholar or magician.
F	A	N	A	T	I	C	Crazed, Extravagant, Unreasonable, Lunatic, Religious maniac, Enthusiast, Zealot, Bigot.
F	A	N	C	I	E	D	Imagined, Unreal, Favourite, Chosen, Fanciful, Bizarre, Shadowy, Grotesque.
F	A	N	C	I	E	R	Enthusiast, Expert, Breeder, Artistic designer, Devotee, Fan.
F	A	N	C	I	F	Y	To make something ornate, elaborate or fancy, To indulge in fancies.
F	A	N	C	I	L	Y	Elaborately, Ornately.
F	A	N	F	A	R	E	Flourish, Sounding of trumpets, Showy outward display, Panoply, Parade, Pomp.
F	A	N	G	L	E	D	Fashioned, Dressed up-to-date, Latest mode.
F	A	N	M	A	I	L	Letter sent to a public figure by an admirer.
F	A	N	N	I	N	G	Winnowing of grain, Coarse tea siftings, Beating, Whipping, Stimulating, Directing a current of air.
F	A	N	P	A	L	M	Palm having simple fan-shaped leaves.
F	A	N	T	A	I	L	Tail with the shape of a fan, Pigeon, Flycatcher, Goldfish, Wild horse.
F	A	N	T	A	S	M	Phantasm, Spook, Ghost, Apparition.
F	A	N	T	A	S	T	Visionary, Dreamer, Eccentric person.
F	A	N	T	A	S	Y	Fancy, Imagine, Daydream, Nightmare, Vision, Imagination, Illusion, Imaginativeness.
F	A	R	A	D	A	Y	Unit of electrolysis.
F	A	R	A	D	I	C	Relating to an asymmetric alternating current of electricity.
F	A	R	A	W	A	Y	Dreamy, Abstract, Remote in time, Something remote from vision, Unknown.
F	A	R	C	E	U	R	Joker, Wag, Person skilled in farce.
F	A	R	C	E	R	T	Maker of farces.
F	A	R	M	E	R	Y	Building and yards of a farm, Farmstead.
F	A	R	M	E	R	G	Renting, Cultivating, Collect and take fees due.
F	A	R	M	O	S	T	Farthest.
F	A	R	N	E	S	S	State of being far off, Remote state or situation.
F	A	R	R	A	G	O	Mixed fodder, Mixture, Medley, Confused, Disordered and irrational.
F	A	R	R	I	E	R	Blacksmith who shoes horses.
F	A	R	R	U	C	A	Spanish gypsy dance, Having sudden changes of mood and temper.
F	A	R	T	H	E	R	Further.
F	A	S	C	E	T	S	Tools used in glass making.
F	A	S	C	I	A	E	Name boards over the fronts of shops.
F	A	S	C	I	A	L	Relating to a fascia.
F	A	S	C	I	N	E	Bundle of wooden sticks bound together and used for filling ditches, Cover, Protect and strengthen.
F	A	S	C	I	S	M	Setting up a dictatorial regime.
F	A	S	C	I	S	T	One who advocates, practices or adheres to fascism.
F	A	S	H	E	R	Y	Annoyance, Bother, Unnecessary ornament or ceremony.
F	A	S	H	I	O	N	Style, Shape, Manner, Bearing, Behaviour, Fad, Vogue, Mode.
F	A	S	T	D	A	Y	Day set aside for fasting and praying.
F	A	S	T	E	S	T	Swiftest, Fleetest, Closest.
F	A	S	T	I	N	G	Act of abstaining from food.
F	A	S	T	I	S	H	Rather fast.
F	A	T	A	L	L	Y	Mortally, Irrevocably, Disastrously, Irresistibly, Deathly, Calamitously.
F	A	T	B	A	C	K	Type of hog, Strip of fat from back of hog carcass.
F	A	T	B	O	D	Y	Mass of fatty tissue in amphibians and insects.
F	A	T	E	F	U	L	Ominous, Prophetic, Deadly, Catastrophic, Baleful, Direful, Ill-boding, Threatening.
F	A	T	H	E	A	D	Slow-witted or stupid person, Fool, Idiot, Chump, Dolt, Dunce, Booby.
F	A	T	I	D	I	C	Fate, Prophetic.

1	2	3	4	5	6	7	Definition
F	A	T	I	G	U	E	Tire, Daze, Weary, Exhaustion, Enervation, Lassitude, Langour, Feebleness.
F	A	T	L	I	N	G	Young animal such as calf, lamb or kid fattened for slaughter.
F	A	T	N	E	S	S	Corpulence, Obesity, Fertility, Fruitfulness, Adiposity, Fleshiness.
F	A	T	T	E	S	T	Most obese, Most corpulent, Fleshiest.
F	A	T	T	I	N	G	Fattening.
F	A	T	T	I	S	H	Rather plump, Adipose.
F	A	T	U	I	T	Y	Foolishness, Inanity, Absurdity, Stupidity, Imbecility, Idiocy, Silly, Dementia.
F	A	T	U	O	U	S	Imbecile, Demented, Illusory, Asinine, Foolish, Witless, Idiotic, Moronic.
F	A	U	C	I	A	L	Relating to narrow passage from the mouth to the pharynx.
F	A	U	L	T	E	D	Marked by faults, Faulty.
F	A	U	L	T	E	R	Wrongdoer especially against the church.
F	A	U	N	I	S	T	Naturalist.
F	A	V	O	U	R	S	Emblems, Badges, Small gifts given out at a celebration, Acts of kindness or helpfulness.
F	A	W	N	I	N	G	Servilely, Abject, Sycophantic, Cringing, Grovelling.
F	A	Y	E	N	C	E	Faience, Earthenware decorated with opaque coloured glaze.
F	E	A	R	F	U	L	Awful, Dreadful, Frightful, Terrible, Horrible, Dire, Formidable.
F	E	A	R	I	N	G	Shocking, Appalling, Dreading, Alarming, Frightening, Terrifying, Foreboding.
F	E	A	S	T	E	D	Dined richly, Enjoyed an unusual pleasure, Delighted, Gratified.
F	E	A	T	H	E	R	Quill, Plumage, Attire, Dress, Clothes, Something extremely light, Mood, Condition, Spirit.
F	E	A	T	U	R	E	Element, Part, Constituent, Face, Countenance, Peculiarity, Characteristic, Lineament.
F	E	A	Z	I	N	G	Becoming frayed, Becoming rough or jagged at edges.
F	E	B	R	I	L	E	Feverish.
F	E	D	A	Y	E	E	Member of Arab commando group operating against Israel.
F	E	D	E	R	A	L	Relating to treaty or league, Compact between states, Association.
F	E	E	D	I	N	G	Suckling, Eating, Subsisting, Supplying emotional, intellectual or spiritual sustenance.
F	E	E	F	A	R	M	Land held in perpetual fixed rent.
F	E	E	L	I	N	G	Affection, Emotion, Sentiment, Passion, Affect, Sensation, Awareness, Opinion.
F	E	E	R	I	N	S	Furrowed land.
F	E	E	T	A	I	L	Estate with restrictions.
F	E	E	Z	I	N	G	Driving away, Twisting, Tightening by twisting.
F	E	I	G	N	E	D	Fictitious, Imaginary, Insincere, False, Pretended, Counterfeit, Disguised, Simulated.
F	E	I	N	T	E	D	Lured, Deceived, Tricked, Hoaxed, Cheated, Faked, Resorted, Manoeuvred.
F	E	L	I	D	A	E	Cat genus.
F	E	L	I	N	A	E	Same as FELIDAE.
F	E	L	L	I	N	G	Knocking down, Cutting down, Killing, Slaughtering, Bringing to state of exhaustion.
F	E	L	O	N	R	Y	Felons, Convict population of a penal colony.
F	E	L	S	I	T	E	Dense macrocrystalline igneous rock.
F	E	L	S	P	A	R	Feldspar, Minerals closely related in crystalline form.
F	E	L	T	I	N	G	When fibres of fabric mat together.
F	E	L	U	C	C	A	Narrow sailing ship peculiar to Mediterranean area.
F	E	L	W	O	R	T	Herb with thick woolly leaves.
F	E	M	I	N	A	L	Feminine.
F	E	M	O	R	A	L	Relating to the thigh.
F	E	N	C	I	N	G	Repelling, Excluding, Protecting, Evading, Parrying, Shielding, Dodging, Enclosing.
F	E	N	D	I	N	G	Defending, Protecting, Shoving, Supporting, Struggling, Managing, Providing, Repelling.
F	E	N	F	I	R	E	Will o' the wisp.
F	E	N	L	A	N	D	Area of low marshy ground.
F	E	N	S	T	E	R	Erosional opening through rock exposing underlying rock.
F	E	N	T	I	N	G	Chinese porcelain.
F	E	O	D	A	R	Y	Confederate, Accomplice, Vassal, Subject, Dependent, Servant.
F	E	O	F	F	E	E	Trustee invested with a freehold estate.
F	E	O	F	F	O	R	One who grants fief.
F	E	R	I	N	G	I	European, Eurasian of Porguese-Indian blood.
F	E	R	M	A	T	A	A prolongation at the discretion of the performer of a musical note or chord beyond its time.
F	E	R	M	E	N	T	Agitation, Inflame, Excitement, Tumult, Enzyme, Unrest, Disquiet, Commotion.
F	E	R	M	I	O	N	A particle (electron, proton or neutron).
F	E	R	M	I	U	M	A radioactive metallic element artificially produced.
F	E	R	N	E	R	Y	A place where ferns are growing.
F	E	R	N	O	W	L	Nightjar.
F	E	R	R	A	R	A	Style prevalent in Ferrara, Italy.
F	E	R	R	A	T	E	Class of compound containing iron and oxygen.
F	E	R	R	I	E	D	Transported, Conveyed, Crossed, Carried, Toted, Borne.
F	E	R	R	I	E	S	Ferry-boats, Service for carrying people or goods, Air transportation.
F	E	R	R	I	T	E	Compound formed by treating hydrated ferric oxide with metallic oxide.
F	E	R	R	O	U	S	Relating to or containing iron.
F	E	R	R	U	L	E	Protective knob or cap, Edge or corner covering of a book.
F	E	R	T	I	L	E	Productive, Creative, Inventive, Numerous, Teeming, Fruitful, Prolific, Fecund.

1	2	3	4	5	6	7	
F	E	R	U	L	E	D	Punished with cane or switch.
F	E	R	V	E	N	T	Enthusiastic, Zealous, Impassioned, Ardent, Fiery, Blazing, Devout, Earnest.
F	E	R	V	O	U	R	Passion, Earnestness, Passion, Ardour, Enthusiasm, Devoutness, Piety, Sincerity.
F	E	S	T	I	V	E	Joyous, Merry, Sportive, Convivial, Gay, Jocund, Jovial, Blithe.
F	E	S	T	O	O	N	Garland, Decorative chain, Swag, Adorn, Swathe, Drape.
F	E	S	T	U	C	A	Genus of mostly tufted perennial grasses.
F	E	T	C	H	E	D	Derived, Deduced, Elicted, Convinced, Attracted, Reached, Brought, Filched.
F	E	T	L	O	C	K	Tuft of long hair on the back side of the leg above the hoof of the horse and similar animals.
F	E	U	D	I	N	G	Quarelling, Battling, Bickering, Disputing, Squabbling, Arguing, Combating, Contesting.
F	E	U	D	I	S	T	One who is party to a hostile feud, Specialist in feudal law.
F	E	U	D	U	T	Y	The annual rent paid by tenant.
F	E	V	E	R	E	D	Heated, Agitated, Febrile, Fiery, Burning, Hectic, Fervid.
F	E	W	N	E	S	S	Paucity, Smallness in amount or quantity.
F	I	A	N	C	E	E	Woman engaged to be married.
F	I	B	B	E	R	Y	Falsehood, Practice of fibbing.
F	I	B	B	I	N	G	Beating, Pummelling, Telling lies.
F	I	B	R	O	I	D	Benign tumour of the uterine wall.
F	I	B	R	O	I	N	Insoluble protein of silk comprising the filaments of the raw fibre held together by sericin.
F	I	B	R	O	M	A	Benign tumour consisting mainly of fibrous tissue.
F	I	B	R	O	S	E	Fibrous.
F	I	B	R	O	U	S	Consisting of fibres.
F	I	B	S	T	E	R	One who tells fibs.
F	I	B	U	L	A	R	Smaller of two bones below the knee.
F	I	C	A	R	I	A	Small genus of European herbs closely related to buttercups.
F	I	C	T	I	L	E	Pliable, Moulded of earth, clay or other soft material, Capable of being led or directed.
F	I	C	T	I	O	N	Figment, Fabrication, Fable, Assumption, Novel, Fantasy, Narrative, Concotion.
F	I	C	T	I	V	E	Imaginary, Feigned.
F	I	D	D	L	E	D	Meddled, Tampered, Tinkered, Trifled, Played on a fiddle.
F	I	D	D	L	E	R	Violinist.
F	I	D	D	L	E	Y	Uppermost part of the stokehole of a steamship.
F	I	D	G	E	T	Y	Restless, Uneasy, Fussy, Jittery, Jumpy, Nervy, Twittery, Nervous.
F	I	E	L	D	E	D	Handled the ball in cricket or baseball.
F	I	E	L	D	E	R	Opposition to the batting side.
F	I	E	R	C	E	R	Merciless, More cruel, More ferocious, More savage.
F	I	E	R	I	L	Y	In a fiery manner, Ardently, Torridly, Spiritedly.
F	I	G	B	I	R	D	Australian orioles that feed chiefly on figs and other fruits.
F	I	G	G	I	N	G	Dressing, Adorning richly.
F	I	G	H	T	E	R	Warrior, Soldier, Boxer, Prizefighter, Serviceman, Pugnacious individual.
F	I	G	L	E	A	F	Leaf of fig tree, Something that conceals, masks or camouflages.
F	I	G	M	E	N	T	Fiction, Fabrication, Fable, Something contrived, Creation, Daydream.
F	I	G	T	R	E	E	Tree of the warmer regions of Old and New Worlds with edible fruit.
F	I	G	U	R	A	L	Figurate, Consisting wholly of human or animal figures.
F	I	G	U	R	E	D	Portrayed, Symbolized, Calculated, Estimated, Solved, Decided, Concluded, Considered.
F	I	L	A	R	I	A	Parasitic worms.
F	I	L	B	E	R	T	Thick-shelled, sweet-flavoured nut, Hazelnut.
F	I	L	C	H	E	D	Stolen, Pilfered, Swiped, Pinched, Purloined, Lifted.
F	I	L	C	H	E	R	Thief, Larcenist, Pilferer, Prig, Purloiner, Stealer.
F	I	L	I	A	T	E	Affiliate.
F	I	L	I	C	A	L	Order of climbing plants, True ferns.
F	I	L	I	C	E	S	True ferns.
F	I	L	I	N	G	S	Fragments or particles rubbed off in filing.
F	I	L	L	I	N	G	Providing, Loading, Putting, Satisfying, Distending, Surfeiting, Stocking, Replenishing.
F	I	L	M	F	A	N	Devotee of the cinema, Ardent admirer of film stars.
F	I	L	M	I	N	G	Making of a motion picture from a scenario, Photographing.
F	I	M	B	R	I	A	Bordering fringe.
F	I	N	A	B	L	E	Subject to the payment of a fine.
F	I	N	A	L	L	Y	Eventuality, Ultimately, Conclusively, Decisively, Irrevocably, Lastly.
F	I	N	A	N	C	E	Management of funds, Settlement, Resources, Provide funds.
F	I	N	B	A	C	K	Whalebone whale.
F	I	N	D	I	N	G	Devising, Inventing, Detecting, Regarding, Contriving, Discovering, Perceiving, Encountering.
F	I	N	E	C	U	T	Tobacco cut into small shreds for chewing or smoking.
F	I	N	E	S	S	E	Subtlety, Refinement, Cunning, Strategy, Trick, Manoeuvre.
F	I	N	F	I	S	H	True fish.
F	I	N	F	O	O	T	Grebe, Bird that is an expert diver and able to swim long distances under water.
F	I	N	G	E	N	T	Pliable, Flexible, Yielding.
F	I	N	I	C	A	L	Finiky, Nice.

1	2	3	4	5	6	7	Definition
F	I	N	L	E	S	S	Devoid of fins.
F	I	N	N	A	G	E	Whole set of fins of a fish.
F	I	N	N	I	S	H	Relating to Finland.
F	I	N	N	O	C	K	European sea trout.
F	I	O	R	I	T	E	Opal occurring near hot springs.
F	I	R	E	A	R	M	Weapon from which a shot is discharged by gunpowder.
F	I	R	E	B	A	R	Bar of a grate or boiler furnace.
F	I	R	E	B	O	X	Chamber that contains a fire.
F	I	R	E	B	U	G	Incendiary, Pyromaniac, Fire patrol in a mine. Firefly.
F	I	R	E	D	O	G	Andiron, Metal support for firewood in a grate.
F	I	R	E	F	L	Y	Winged nocturnal light-producing insect.
F	I	R	E	M	A	N	One who fights fires, Stoker, One who tends or feeds fires.
F	I	R	E	N	E	W	Brand new.
F	I	R	E	P	O	T	Pot that holds a fire.
F	I	R	M	I	N	G	Compacting, Establishing, Settling, Tightening, Hardening, Confirming, Establishing.
F	I	R	R	I	N	G	Furring, Application of thin wood, metal or brick to form a flat surface.
F	I	S	H	D	A	Y	Fast day when fish is eaten instead of flesh.
F	I	S	H	E	R	Y	Place for catching fish, Place for breeding and studying fish.
F	I	S	H	F	L	Y	Small insect.
F	I	S	H	G	I	G	Fish spear having two or more barbed prongs.
F	I	S	H	I	F	Y	To change into a fish.
F	I	S	H	I	L	Y	In a fishy manner.
F	I	S	H	I	N	G	Occupation or pastime of catching fish.
F	I	S	H	M	A	W	Air-bladder of a fish.
F	I	S	H	O	I	L	Fatty oil from body of fishes used as drying oil in paint and varnish.
F	I	S	H	W	A	Y	Fish ladder to enable fish to pass a dam.
F	I	S	S	I	L	E	Capable of being split, cleft or divided in the direction of the grain.
F	I	S	S	I	O	N	Process of cleaving, splitting or breaking into parts, Reproduction by spontaneous division.
F	I	S	S	I	V	E	Relating or tending to fission.
F	I	S	S	U	R	E	Narrow opening, chasm or crack, Cleavage, Division.
F	I	S	T	F	U	L	Handful, Collection.
F	I	S	T	I	N	G	Clenching hands into a fist, Handling.
F	I	S	T	U	L	A	Reed instrument or pipe, Abnormal congenital or acquired passage from one organ to another.
F	I	T	C	H	E	D	Fidgeted.
F	I	T	C	H	E	E	Pointed lower extremity of a cross.
F	I	T	C	H	E	T	Pole-cat.
F	I	T	M	E	N	T	Equipment, Furnishing, Built-in furniture, Shop furniture.
F	I	T	N	E	S	S	Quality or state of being fit, Eligibility, Soundness, Capacity, Appropriateness, Propriety.
F	I	T	T	I	N	G	Appropriate, Suitable, Proper, Accessory, Adjunct, Attachment, Coupling, Valve.
F	I	T	W	E	E	D	Tropical American herbaceous feverweed.
F	I	X	A	B	L	E	Capable of being fixed.
F	I	X	E	D	L	Y	In a fixed manner.
F	I	X	T	U	R	E	Institution, Appointment, Engagement, Shelving, Machinery, Chattel.
F	I	Z	Z	I	N	G	Effervescing, Exciting, Hissing.
F	I	Z	Z	L	E	D	Failed, Petered, Ended, Feebly, Sputtered, Hissed.
F	L	A	C	C	I	D	Flabby, Limp, Flimsy, Floppy, Sleazy, Enfeebled, Sapped, Enervated.
F	L	A	C	K	E	R	Flutter, Palpitate, Flap, Flick.
F	L	A	F	F	E	R	Flap, Flutter.
F	L	A	G	D	A	Y	Day when contributions for a charity are solicited and small flags are given in return.
F	L	A	G	G	E	D	Signalled, Drooped, Weakened, Enervated, Waved, Failed, Faded, Declined.
F	L	A	G	M	A	N	A person who signals with a flag.
F	L	A	K	I	N	G	Separating into flakes, Peeling, Scaling.
F	L	A	M	I	N	G	Blazing, Burning, Kindling, Exciting, Glowing, Ardent, Fervent, Impassioned.
F	L	A	M	M	E	D	Deceived, Tricked, Cheated.
F	L	A	N	E	U	R	Aimless, Self centred and superficial person, Intellectual trifler, Man-about-town.
F	L	A	N	G	E	D	Widened, Spread.
F	L	A	N	K	E	D	Sheltered, Protected, Situated at the side, Bordered.
F	L	A	N	K	E	R	Something that adjoins on the side, Protector of the flank.
F	L	A	N	N	E	L	Soft twilled fabric.
F	L	A	P	P	E	R	Young woman who aggressively manifests freedom from constraint and conventions.
F	L	A	R	I	N	G	Streaming, Fluttering, Flaming, Funnel-shaped, Glaring, Glowing, Fiery.
F	L	A	S	H	E	D	Glanced, Gleamed, Glimmed, Glinted, Flickered, Twinkled, Displayed, Flaunted.
F	L	A	S	H	E	R	Flashy or showy person, Signal by flashing, Blinker.
F	L	A	S	K	E	T	Small flask.
F	L	A	T	L	E	T	Small compact flat.
F	L	A	T	T	E	D	Levelled, Razed, Flattened, Divided into flats.
F	L	A	T	T	E	N	Prostrate, Depress, Deject, Level, Smooth, Dispirit, Even, Knock down.

1	2	3	4	5	6	7	
F	L	A	T	T	E	R	Become, Enhance, Suit, Adorn, Beautify, Embellish, Beguile, Smooth.
F	L	A	U	N	T	Y	Ostentatious, Given to flaunting.
F	L	A	V	E	D	O	Outer coloured layer of citrus fruit.
F	L	A	V	I	A	N	Relating to ancient Roman generals.
F	L	A	V	I	N	E	Yellow acridine dye used in medicine.
F	L	A	V	O	N	E	Colourless crystalline ketone found as dust on yellow primroses.
F	L	A	V	O	U	R	Odour, Fragrance, Aroma, Taste, Relish, Savour.
F	L	A	W	I	N	G	Violating, Nullifying, Cracking, Breaking.
F	L	A	Y	I	N	G	Stripping of skin, Censuring, Castigating, Lashing, Scourging, Lambasting, Scorching.
F	L	E	A	B	A	G	Inferior hotel room, Flea-ridden animal, Slatternly old woman.
F	L	E	C	K	E	D	Streaked, Striped, Variegated, Spotted.
F	L	E	C	K	E	R	To spot, To dapple.
F	L	E	D	G	E	D	Attained majority, Ready for flight, Covered with feathers.
F	L	E	E	C	E	D	Sheared, Stripped, Plundered, Despoiled, Cheated, Clipped, Shorn, Overcharged.
F	L	E	E	C	E	R	One who fleeces, Cheat, Rogue.
F	L	E	E	I	N	G	Abandoning, Forsaking, Vanishing, Escaping, Flying, Running, Bolting, Absconding.
F	L	E	E	R	E	D	Sneered, Mocked, Scoffed, Gibed, Leered, Derided.
F	L	E	E	R	E	R	Derider, Scoffer.
F	L	E	E	T	E	D	Floated, Drifted, Vanished, Fluctuated, Solved, Hastened, Flitted, Flew.
F	L	E	E	T	L	Y	Nimbly, Rapidly, Swiftly, Speedily.
F	L	E	M	I	N	G	Native of Flanders.
F	L	E	M	I	S	H	Relating to Flanders.
F	L	E	N	S	E	D	Stripped of blubber or skin.
F	L	E	S	H	E	D	Gratified, Satiated, Glutted, Fattened.
F	L	E	S	H	E	R	Butcher.
F	L	E	S	H	L	Y	Bodily, Carnal, Sensual, Lascivious, Wordly.
F	L	E	T	T	O	N	Yellowish red brick made in Huntingdonshire.
F	L	E	U	R	E	T	Fencing foil, Small sword.
F	L	E	U	R	O	N	Flower-shaped ornament, Printer's type floral ornament.
F	L	E	X	I	L	E	Tractable, Manageable, Pliable, Elastic, Resilient, Flexible, Supple.
F	L	E	X	I	N	G	Bending, Stretching, Extending, Turning.
F	L	E	X	I	O	N	Bend, Fold, Inflexion, Turning.
F	L	E	X	U	R	E	Turning, Flection, Turn, Bend, Fold, Pliancy.
F	L	I	C	K	E	D	Flipped, Fluttered, Struck, Lightly, Jerked.
F	L	I	C	K	E	R	Flutter, Waver unsteadily, Twinkle, Scintillate, Brief movement.
F	L	I	G	H	T	Y	Fleeting, Swift, Transient, Volatile, Skittish.
F	L	I	N	G	E	R	Baseball pitcher.
F	L	I	P	P	E	D	Flicked, Filliped, Propelled, Twitched, Turned over.
F	L	I	P	P	E	R	Broad flat fore-limb adapted for swimming, Flat rubber shoe for skin-diving.
F	L	I	R	T	E	D	Coquetted, Flicked, Mocked, Flipped, Darted, Trifled.
F	L	I	T	T	E	R	Flutter, Tatter, Flake.
F	L	O	A	T	E	D	Drifted, Wafted, Suspended, Buoyed up by liquid, Spread on surface.
F	L	O	A	T	E	R	Something that drifts on fluid, Illegal voter, Vagrant, Tramp.
F	L	O	C	C	U	S	Tuft of woolly hairs on a plant, Small mass making a certain cloud formation.
F	L	O	C	K	E	D	Crowded, Thronged, Coated with flock, Swarmed.
F	L	O	G	G	E	D	Lashed, Punished, Driven, Exhausted, Scourged, Thrashed, Whipped.
F	L	O	G	G	E	R	One that flogs, Foundry worker.
F	L	O	O	D	E	D	Inundated, Deluged, Overflowed, Splashed, Swamped, Drowned, Streamed, Poured.
F	L	O	O	R	E	D	Silenced, Defeated, Flattened, Knocked down.
F	L	O	O	R	E	R	Workman who lays floors, Something that discomfits or confuses one.
F	L	O	P	P	E	D	Flapped, Failed, Dropped with heavy clumsiness, Struck heavily, Plumped, Retired.
F	L	O	R	I	S	T	One who raises flowers and plants for financial gain.
F	L	O	R	U	I	T	Period during which something flourished most.
F	L	O	T	A	G	E	Act or state of floating, Flotsam.
F	L	O	T	S	A	M	Wreckage of a ship or its cargo found floating on the sea, Floating population, Vagrants.
F	L	O	U	N	C	E	State of emotional turmoil, Turned, Twisted, Flounder, Struggle, Gathered strip of fabric.
F	L	O	U	R	E	D	Milled, Pulverized, Coated with flour, Powdered.
F	L	O	U	T	E	D	Mocked, Insulted, Sneered, Scoffed, Disregarded, Repudiated, Spurned, Defied.
F	L	O	U	T	E	R	Scoffer, Mocker.
F	L	O	W	A	G	E	Flooding, Overflowing, Current, Discharge.
F	L	O	W	E	R	Y	Relating to a flower, Ornate and florid.
F	L	O	W	I	N	G	Streaming, Fluent, Copious, Proceeding, Flooding, Inundating, Springing.
F	L	U	E	N	C	Y	Smoothness, Ease, Volubility.
F	L	U	F	F	E	D	Blundered, Bungled, Slipped, Tripped, Botched, Muffed, Misplayed, Failed.
F	L	U	I	D	I	C	Having characteristics of fluid.
F	L	U	I	D	L	Y	With fluidity.
F	L	U	M	M	O	X	Confound, Disconcert, Collapse, Embarrass, Fail.

1	2	3	4	5	6	7	Definition
F	L	U	M	P	E	D	Plumped, Flopped, Dropped, Plopped.
F	L	U	N	K	E	Y	Footman, Liveried servant, Ship's steward, General labourer, Cringing person.
F	L	U	S	H	E	D	Blushed, Coloured, Glowed, Reddened, Evened, Executed, Animated, Smoothed.
F	L	U	S	H	E	R	Tanker for flushing dirt from roadways.
F	L	U	S	T	E	R	Befuddle, Confuse, Muddle, Bewilder, Discompose, Bother, Perturb, Upset.
F	L	U	S	T	R	A	Sea-mat, Genus of marine bryozoans.
F	L	U	T	I	N	G	Playing on a flute, Forming flutes.
F	L	U	T	I	S	T	Flute player.
F	L	U	T	T	E	R	Flit, Quake, Quiver, Flicker, Vibrate, Confusion, Disorder, Flurry.
F	L	U	V	I	A	L	Relating to rivers.
F	L	U	X	I	L	E	Inconstant, Variable.
F	L	U	X	I	O	N	Something that flows, Continuing motion or change, Fusion, Variation.
F	L	Y	A	W	A	Y	Volatile, Flighty, Loose and floating, Ready to fly.
F	L	Y	B	A	C	K	Term used in electronics, Return of second hand on a stop-watch.
F	L	Y	B	L	O	W	Taint, Contaminate.
F	L	Y	B	O	A	T	Fast boat, Flat-bottomed coasting boat.
F	L	Y	B	O	M	B	Flying bomb, Robot bomb.
F	L	Y	B	O	O	K	Case in form of book for storing anglers' flies.
F	L	Y	F	L	A	P	Device such as fan for driving away or killing flies.
F	L	Y	H	A	L	F	Football player.
F	L	Y	L	E	A	F	Blank leaf at beginning or end of book.
F	L	Y	L	I	N	E	Habitual line of flight of a bird group in its migrations.
F	L	Y	O	V	E	R	Overpass, Prearranged low-altitude flight over a public gathering.
F	L	Y	P	A	S	T	Flight by aircraft usually on special occasions.
F	L	Y	R	A	I	L	Bracket to support hinged leaf of table, Support railing on theatre stage.
F	L	Y	T	I	M	E	Season of the year when flies are troublesome.
F	L	Y	T	R	A	P	Device for catching flies, Pitcher plant, Venus's fly-trap.
F	O	A	L	I	N	G	Mare giving birth.
F	O	A	M	I	N	G	Frothing, Raging, Expanding, Whipping, Lathering, Bubbling, Gushing.
F	O	B	B	I	N	G	Deceiving, Cheating, Imposing.
F	O	C	U	S	E	D	Concentrated, Converged, Fastened, Met, Fixed, Put, Riveted.
F	O	D	I	E	N	T	Fitted for digging or burrowing.
F	O	E	L	E	S	S	Having no enemy.
F	O	G	B	A	N	K	Mass of fog resting on the sea.
F	O	G	B	E	L	T	Area where fog is encountered.
F	O	G	G	A	G	E	Winter grazing.
F	O	G	G	I	E	R	More obscured, More confused, More muddled, More vague, More blurred.
F	O	G	G	I	L	Y	Mistily, Vaguely.
F	O	G	G	I	N	G	Obscuring, Confusing, Blurring, Muddling.
F	O	G	H	O	R	N	Horn used as warning of fog, Hoarse voice.
F	O	G	L	A	M	P	Yellow headlight designed to penetrate fog.
F	O	G	L	E	S	S	Absence of fog.
F	O	G	Y	I	S	H	Antiquated, Out-of-date, Orthodox, Traditionalistic.
F	O	G	Y	I	S	M	Old fashioned ideas, Conservative behaviour.
F	O	I	L	I	N	G	Defeating, Repulsing, Baffling, Frustrating, Beating, Thwarting, Curbing, Restraining.
F	O	I	N	I	N	G	Thrusting, Lunging.
F	O	I	S	T	E	D	Insinuated, Infiltrated, Imposed, Palmed off, Deceived, Misled, Duped, Inflicted.
F	O	I	S	T	E	R	Cheat, Rogue.
F	O	L	D	A	G	E	Right of the lord of the manor to the sheep of his tenants for manuring his meadows.
F	O	L	D	I	N	G	Pleating, Bending, Creasing, Furrowing, Ridging, Corrugating.
F	O	L	I	A	G	E	Mass of leaves, Verdure, Herbage, Vegetation.
F	O	L	I	A	T	E	Beat into thin leaf, Laminated.
F	O	L	I	O	E	D	Having each page numbered.
F	O	L	I	O	L	E	Leaflet, Small leaf-shaped organ.
F	O	L	I	O	S	E	Leafy, Resembling a leaf.
F	O	L	I	O	U	S	Having leaves.
F	O	L	L	I	E	S	Indulgences, Inanities, Thoughtless acts, Whims.
F	O	M	I	T	E	S	Inanimate objects such as towels that may transmit infection.
F	O	N	D	A	N	T	Cooked or uncooked sugar paste.
F	O	N	D	E	S	T	Most loving, Most affectionate, Most infatuated, Most doting.
F	O	N	D	I	N	G	Beguiling, Fondling, Caressing.
F	O	N	D	L	E	D	Caressed, Cuddled, Embraced, Petted, Hugged, Nestled, Clasped, Snuggled.
F	O	N	D	L	E	R	One that fondles.
F	O	N	T	I	N	A	Soft cooked ripened cheese.
F	O	O	L	E	R	Y	Absurdity, Clowning, Buffoonery, Act of foolishness.
F	O	O	L	I	N	G	Philandering, Joking, Trifling, Flittering, Hoodwinking, Beguiling, Skylarking, Rowdiness.
F	O	O	L	I	S	H	Idiotic, Simple, Feebleminded, Absurd, Ridiculous, Preposterous, Abashed, Nonplussed.

1	2	3	4	5	6	7	Definition
F	O	O	T	A	G	E	Length expressed in feet.
F	O	O	T	B	O	Y	Serving boy, Page, Attendant.
F	O	O	T	H	O	T	Hastily, Speedily.
F	O	O	T	I	N	G	Foothold, Status, Stable position of feet, Basis, Social relationship, Position, Substructure.
F	O	O	T	L	E	D	Talked or acted foolishly.
F	O	O	T	M	A	N	Liveried male servant, Doorman, Assistant to butler.
F	O	O	T	P	A	D	Hold-up man who robs pedestrians.
F	O	O	T	R	O	T	Disease affecting stem of plants.
F	O	O	T	T	O	N	Measure of energy used in various jobs.
F	O	O	T	W	A	Y	Footpath, Sidewalk.
F	O	O	Z	L	E	D	Bungled, Worked hurriedly, Played unskillfully.
F	O	P	L	I	N	G	Absurd man of fashion, Ladies' man.
F	O	P	P	E	R	Y	Folly, Absurdity, Vanity, Coxcombry, Affectation.
F	O	P	P	I	S	H	Finical, Absurd in style of dress, Overdressed.
F	O	R	A	G	E	D	Plundered, Ravaged, Raided, Rummaged, Pillaged, Searched, Ransacked, Searched.
F	O	R	A	G	E	R	Pillager, Looter, Plunderer, Raider, Spoiler, Ravisher, Sacker.
F	O	R	A	M	E	N	Small opening, perforation or orifice.
F	O	R	A	Y	E	D	Ravaged, Pillaged, Invaded, Raided, Overran, Harried, Harassed, Marauded.
F	O	R	A	Y	E	R	One in vanguard, Harbinger.
F	O	R	B	A	D	E	Prohibited, Interdicted, Excluded, Hindered, Banned, Enjoined, Inhibited, Proscribed.
F	O	R	B	E	A	R	Endure, Shun, Abstain, Decline, Forgo, Restrain, Abstain, Cease.
F	O	R	B	O	R	E	Sacrificed, Eschewed, Bridled, Curbed, Avoided, Evaded, Refrained, Withheld.
F	O	R	C	E	P	S	Pincers, Tongs, Pliers, Instruments for delicate operations.
F	O	R	C	I	N	G	Compelling, Coercing, Constraining, Obliging, Spoiling, Violating, Making.
F	O	R	D	I	N	G	Crossing at lowest level of water.
F	O	R	D	I	Z	E	Standardize operations to improve efficiency and institute mass production.
F	O	R	D	O	N	E	Killed, Abolished, Destroyed, Undone, Ruined, Terminated, Exhausted.
F	O	R	E	A	R	M	Arm of fore-limb between elbow and wrist.
F	O	R	E	B	A	Y	Discharging end of pond or millrace.
F	O	R	E	D	I	D	Terminated, Exhausted.
F	O	R	E	E	N	D	Front end, Stock of firearm under the barrel.
F	O	R	E	G	U	T	Front portion of the alimentary canal of animal.
F	O	R	E	I	G	N	Inappropriate, Extrinsic, Alien, Exotic, Strange, Incompatible, Extraneous, Inconsistent.
F	O	R	E	L	A	Y	Ambush, Hinder, Obstruct, Intend.
F	O	R	E	L	E	G	Front pair of legs of a quadruped, Front leg of chair or cabinet.
F	O	R	E	M	A	N	Leader, Overseer, Supervisor, Ganger boss.
F	O	R	E	R	U	N	Precede, Forestall, Announce, Anticipate, Herald, Presage, Antecede, Predate.
F	O	R	E	S	A	W	Anticipated, Foreknew, Apprehended, Prophesied, Perceived, Visualized, Predicted.
F	O	R	E	S	A	Y	Predict, Foretell.
F	O	R	E	S	E	E	Anticipate, Apprehend, Divine, Forefeel, Foreknow, Previse, See, Visualize.
F	O	R	E	T	O	P	Crown of the head, Forelock of horse, Platform at top of foremast.
F	O	R	E	V	E	R	Eternity, Always, Eternally, Evermore.
F	O	R	F	E	I	T	Misdeed, Crime, Penalty, Fine, Lose, Drop, Sacrifice, Foreclose.
F	O	R	F	E	N	D	Forbid, Prohibit, Avert, Prevent, Protect, Preserve, Secure.
F	O	R	G	A	V	E	Excused, Pardoned, Absolved, Condoned, Granted relief.
F	O	R	G	E	R	Y	Invention, Feigning, Fiction, Counterfeiting.
F	O	R	G	I	N	G	Fashioning, Making, Producing, Progressing, Advancing, Shaping, Building, Constructing.
F	O	R	G	I	V	E	Excuse, Remit, Condone, Absolve, Pardon.
F	O	R	G	O	N	E	Quitted, Left, Resigned, Sacrificed, Foreborne, Renounced, Abdicated, Abandoned.
F	O	R	K	F	U	L	As much as a fork will hold.
F	O	R	K	I	N	G	Dividing into two, Contributing, Turning, Pitching, Disbursing.
F	O	R	L	O	R	N	Ruined, Doomed, Forsaken, Destitute, Bereft, Miserable, Wretched, Despondent.
F	O	R	M	A	N	T	Pitch of pronunciation of a vowel.
F	O	R	M	A	T	E	Salt of formic acid, To join or fly in formation.
F	O	R	M	F	U	L	Exhibiting, Special form as in a sport.
F	O	R	M	I	N	G	Framing, Constructing, Making, Fashioning, Developing, Acquiring, Forging, Contracting.
F	O	R	M	U	L	A	Recipe, Prescription, Milk mixture for babies, Rule, Principle.
F	O	R	N	E	N	T	Opposite, Beside, Against.
F	O	R	P	I	N	E	Waste or pine away as from suffering.
F	O	R	S	A	K	E	Leave, Desert, Abandon.
F	O	R	S	O	O	K	Left, Abandoned, Deserted, Quitted, Renounced, Abdicated, Spurned, Resigned.
F	O	R	T	I	F	Y	Strengthen, Invigorate, Refresh, Confirm, Encourage, Brace, Reinforce, Restore.
F	O	R	T	L	E	T	Small fort.
F	O	R	T	U	N	E	Success, Mishap, Chance, Riches, Wealth, Happen, Destiny, Fate.
F	O	R	W	A	R	N	Forbid, Prohibit.
F	O	R	W	A	R	D	Eager, Ready, Brash, Bold, Indecorous, Early, Extreme, Radical.
F	O	R	W	E	N	T	Quitted, Left, Sacrificed, Abandoned, Abdicated.

1	2	3	4	5	6	7	
F	O	R	W	O	R	N	Tattered, Exhausted by effort, Greatly tired.
F	O	S	S	I	C	K	Rummage, Prospect, Search, Ferret out.
F	O	U	G	A	D	E	Land mine, Fougasse.
F	O	U	L	A	R	D	Silk fabric printed with a small pattern.
F	O	U	L	D	E	R	Flash.
F	O	U	L	I	N	G	Incrustation, Soiling, Polluting, Dishonouring, Obstructing, Blocking, Decomposing, Rotting.
F	O	U	N	D	E	D	Originated, Initiated, Established, Instituted, Organized, Based.
F	O	U	N	D	E	R	Collapsed, Fail, Wreck, Damage, Sink, Submerge, Architect, Creator.
F	O	U	N	D	R	Y	Building where metal or glass founding is carried on.
F	O	U	R	G	O	N	Wagon for carrying baggage.
F	O	V	E	A	T	E	Pitted, Pocked.
F	O	V	E	O	L	A	Pit in embryonic gastric mucosa from which the gastric glands develop.
F	O	W	L	I	N	G	Seeking, killing, catching or netting wild fowl for sport or food.
F	O	X	H	O	L	E	Defensive depression in the ground for use during combat as protection against enemy fire.
F	O	X	I	E	S	T	Slyest, Most cunning, Craftiest.
F	O	X	T	A	I	L	Tail of the fox.
F	O	X	T	R	O	T	Ballroom dance.
F	O	Y	A	I	T	E	Nephelite-syenite rock.
F	R	A	C	T	E	D	Broken, In heraldry having a part displaced.
F	R	A	G	I	L	E	Weak, Tenuous, Unsubstantial, Diaphanous, Shortlived, Evanescent, Brittle, Infirm.
F	R	A	I	L	L	Y	In a frail manner.
F	R	A	I	L	T	Y	Insubstantiality, Tenuousness, Infirmity, Susceptibility, Fault.
F	R	A	I	S	E	D	Enlarged.
F	R	A	K	T	U	R	Illuminated writing on scrolls.
F	R	A	M	E	U	P	A plot to involve innocent people, Make-up, Fabricate evidence, Invent.
F	R	A	M	I	N	G	Devising, Contriving, Planning, Formulating, Constructing, Regulating, Arranging, Shaping.
F	R	A	N	C	I	C	Frankish, Relating to the Franks.
F	R	A	N	I	O	N	Idler, Reveller.
F	R	A	N	K	E	D	Marked with an official signature or stamp, To make immune.
F	R	A	N	K	L	Y	Generously, Unreservedly, Openly, Plainly, Clearly, Bluntly, Forthrightly, Indeed, Undoubtedly.
F	R	A	N	T	I	C	Furious, Delirious, Insane, Frenzied, Extreme, Raving, Rabid, Wild.
F	R	A	P	P	E	D	Struck, Beaten, Tightened.
F	R	A	T	C	H	Y	Peevish.
F	R	A	U	G	H	T	Laden, Freighted, Burdened, Menaced, Endangered, Threatened, Accompanied, Attended.
F	R	A	Y	I	N	G	Fretted, Worn, Peeling, Shredding.
F	R	A	Z	Z	L	E	Fray, Wear, Fatigued, Exhausted, Tattered.
F	R	E	A	K	E	D	Streaked, Variegated.
F	R	E	C	K	L	E	Sprinkle with small spots, Spot, Discolouration.
F	R	E	C	K	L	Y	Marked with freckles.
F	R	E	E	D	O	M	Independence, Generosity, Magnanimity, Ease, Facility, Right, Privilege, Franchise.
F	R	E	E	I	N	G	Releasing, Liberating, Emancipating, Delivering, Discharging, Removing, Disentangling.
F	R	E	E	M	A	N	One enjoying civil and political liberty, Citizen with full Rights.
F	R	E	E	S	I	A	Genus of sweet scented African herbs.
F	R	E	E	W	A	Y	Expressway with controlled access.
F	R	E	E	Z	E	R	Insulated cabinet equipped to freeze perishable foods.
F	R	E	I	G	H	T	Cargo, Load, Burden.
F	R	E	N	A	T	E	Butterfly or moth.
F	R	E	S	H	E	N	Refresh, Desalinate, Revive, Improve, Restore, Invigorate.
F	R	E	S	H	E	R	More pure, More active, More sober, More invigorating.
F	R	E	S	H	E	S	Flush, Spring, Stream of pool of fresh water.
F	R	E	S	H	E	T	Overflowing of stream, Sudden inundation.
F	R	E	S	H	L	Y	Newly, Recently, Strongly, Vigorously, Brightly, Vividly, Strikingly, Impudently.
F	R	E	T	F	U	L	Gnawing, Corrosive, Irritating, Peevish, Impatient, Restless, Angry, Troubled.
F	R	E	T	S	A	W	Narrow-bladed fine-toothed saw held under tension in a frame.
F	R	E	T	T	E	D	Interlaced with one another.
F	R	E	T	T	E	R	One that frets.
F	R	I	A	B	L	E	Easily crumbled, pulverized or reduced to powder.
F	R	I	A	R	L	Y	Relating to friars.
F	R	I	B	B	L	E	Act frivolously, Totter, Stammer, Falter, Trifling, Captious.
F	R	I	E	Z	E	D	Make a nap on a cloth.
F	R	I	G	A	T	E	Warship smaller than a cruiser larger than a destroyer.
F	R	I	J	O	L	E	Kidney bean.
F	R	I	L	L	E	D	Decorated with a frill, Pleated edge.
F	R	I	N	G	E	D	Adorned with a fringe.
F	R	I	P	P	E	R	One who deals in old clothes or finery.
F	R	I	S	E	U	R	Hairdresser.
F	R	I	S	I	A	N	Relating to Friesland.

1	2	3	4	5	6	7	
F	R	I	S	K	E	D	Leapt, Skipped, Danced, Searched a person, Romped, Gambolled.
F	R	I	S	K	E	R	One that frolics, Police officer that searches people.
F	R	I	S	K	E	T	Light frame used in printing to hold a sheet of paper.
F	R	I	S	U	R	E	Style of curling or dressing the hair.
F	R	I	T	T	E	D	Fused by heat.
F	R	I	T	T	E	R	Diminish, Consume, Dissipate, Waste, Squander, Dwindle, Fragment.
F	R	I	Z	I	N	G	Forming hair into tight curls.
F	R	I	Z	Z	E	D	Curled, Crisped.
F	R	I	Z	Z	L	E	Curl or crisp hair with heat.
F	R	I	Z	Z	L	Y	Frizzy.
F	R	O	C	K	E	D	Clothed in a frock, Made a cleric.
F	R	O	G	B	I	T	European aquatic floating herb.
F	R	O	G	E	Y	E	Leaf disease.
F	R	O	G	G	E	D	Caught frogs.
F	R	O	G	M	A	N	Special type of underwater swimmer.
F	R	O	N	D	E	D	Furnished with fronds.
F	R	O	N	T	A	L	Belonging to the front, Direct, Attack on main point.
F	R	O	N	T	E	D	Furnished with a special front.
F	R	O	N	T	O	N	Pediment over door or window, Court for playing jai alai.
F	R	O	S	T	E	D	Ornamented with frosting, Etched with sand, Arrogant, Stuck-up, Dim with age.
F	R	O	T	H	E	D	Foamed, Vented, Voiced.
F	R	O	U	N	C	E	Curl, Frizzle.
F	R	O	W	A	R	D	Perverse, Adverse, Unfavourable, Contrary, Beyond control.
F	R	O	W	N	E	D	Scowled, Wrinkled the brow in displeasure, Facial expression expressing strong feelings.
F	R	O	W	S	T	Y	Musty and stuffy.
F	R	U	C	T	E	D	Use of heraldic tree or plant.
F	R	U	I	T	E	D	Borne fruit, Developed fruit.
F	R	U	I	T	E	R	Ship for carrying fruit, Tree or plant that bears fruit.
F	R	U	M	P	E	D	Insulted, Flouted, Mocked, Snubbed, Provoked, Irritated, Vexed, Sulked.
F	R	U	S	T	U	M	Part of a cone-shaped solid next to the base.
F	U	C	A	L	E	S	Order of brown algae.
F	U	C	H	S	I	A	Genus of decorative shrubs.
F	U	C	H	S	I	N	Brilliant bluish red dye.
F	U	D	D	L	E	D	Tippled, Intoxicated, Muddled, Stupefied.
F	U	D	D	L	E	R	Drunkard.
F	U	D	G	I	N	G	Resulting, Cheating, Hedging, Distorting, Welshing, Embellishing, Dodging.
F	U	E	H	R	E	R	Leader, Tyrant.
F	U	E	L	L	E	R	One that supplies fuel or feeds fires.
F	U	F	F	I	N	G	Panting, Raging, Smoking.
F	U	G	U	I	S	T	One who composes or performs fugues.
F	U	L	C	R	U	M	Prop, Support.
F	U	L	G	E	N	T	Radiant, Dazzlingly bright, Shine, Flash, Luminous, Beaming, Incandescent.
F	U	L	G	O	R	A	Genus of family of plant-feeding insects.
F	U	L	L	E	S	T	More swollen, More replete, More occupied, more distended.
F	U	L	L	I	N	G	Process of shrinking and thickening woollen fabric.
F	U	L	N	E	S	S	Quality of being full.
F	U	L	S	O	M	E	Plump, Fat, Nauseating, Sickening, Repulsive, Disgusting.
F	U	L	V	O	U	S	Tawny, Dull brownish yellow.
F	U	M	A	R	I	A	Genus of annual herbs.
F	U	M	B	L	E	D	Blundered, Misplayed, Mumbled, Groped, Muttered, Messed, Muffed.
F	U	M	B	L	E	R	One that fumbles.
F	U	M	E	T	T	E	Concentrated essence of game or fish, herbs and spices to flavour a sauce.
F	U	N	A	R	I	A	Genus of mosses.
F	U	N	D	I	N	G	Accumulating, Providing a fund, Financing, Endowing, Subsidizing.
F	U	N	E	R	A	L	Memorial service, Requiem, Service for the dead.
F	U	N	F	A	I	R	Amusement park.
F	U	N	G	A	T	E	Assume a fungous form, Grow rapidly like a fungus.
F	U	N	G	O	I	D	Mushroom growths.
F	U	N	I	C	L	E	Umbilical cord, Column, Fibre, Ligament.
F	U	N	K	I	N	G	Emitting an offensive smell or smoke.
F	U	N	N	I	L	Y	Oddly, Laughably, In a funny manner.
F	U	N	N	I	N	G	Hoaxing, Teasing, Tricking, Joking, Fooling.
F	U	R	B	I	S	H	Burnish, Polish, Renovate, Revive, Buff, Gloss, Shine, Glaze.
F	U	R	C	A	T	E	Branch like a fork.
F	U	R	C	U	L	A	Wishbone, Forked Structure.
F	U	R	I	O	S	O	Fanatic, Furious or insane man.
F	U	R	I	O	U	S	Fierce, Violent, Stormy, Turbulent, Energetic, Vigorous, Extravagant, Fanatical.

1	2	3	4	5	6	7	
F	U	R	L	A	N	A	Forlana, Old Italian dance.
F	U	R	L	I	N	G	Curling, Wrinkling, Covering, Wrapping, Enfolding, Rolling.
F	U	R	L	O	N	G	Unit of distance, one eighth of a statute mile.
F	U	R	M	E	T	Y	Cereal dessert made in a mould.
F	U	R	N	I	S	H	Ornament, Decorate, Contribute, Yield, Equip, Outfit, Appoint, Provide.
F	U	R	R	I	N	G	Incrustation of fur, Deposit from water on a boiler, Coating.
F	U	R	R	O	W	Y	Furrowed.
F	U	R	T	H	E	R	Farther, Additional, Moreover, Promote, Advance.
F	U	R	T	I	V	E	Secret, Surreptitious, Stolen, Thievish, Clandestine, Sneaky, Sly, Stealthy.
F	U	S	C	O	U	S	Lighter colour than chocolate brown, slightly redder than mouse gray.
F	U	S	I	B	L	E	Capable of being fused, Capable of being liquefied by heat.
F	U	S	S	I	E	R	More meticulous, More ornate, More irritable.
F	U	S	S	I	L	Y	In a fussy manner.
F	U	S	S	I	N	G	Bustling, Puttering, Fretting, Worrying, Nagging, Scolding, Chiding, Protesting.
F	U	S	S	P	O	T	One who frets over trifles.
F	U	S	T	I	A	N	Cotton fabric, Exaggerated, Bombast, Good-for-nothing, Worthless.
F	U	S	T	I	E	R	Mustier, Mouldier.
F	U	T	C	H	E	L	Wood or metal socket for pole of carriage.
F	U	T	T	O	C	K	Curved timber that is part of the rib of a ship.
F	U	T	U	N	A	N	Polynesian people.
F	U	Z	Z	I	E	R	Vaguer, More confused, More muddled, More blurred.
F	U	Z	Z	I	L	Y	In a fuzzy manner.

G

1	2	3	4	5	6	7	
G	A	B	B	A	R	D	Small ship such as lighter or barge.
G	A	B	B	I	N	G	Rapid chatter, Thoughtless talk.
G	A	B	B	L	E	D	Jabbered, Chattered, Babbled.
G	A	B	B	L	E	R	Chatterer, Babbler.
G	A	B	E	L	L	E	Impost of salt prior to 1790.
G	A	D	D	I	N	G	Running wild, Roving, Wandering, Gallivanting, Dashing about.
G	A	D	G	E	T	Y	Fond of gadgets.
G	A	D	R	O	O	N	Ornament produced by notching or carving a rounded moulding.
G	A	D	W	A	L	L	Grayish brown duck.
G	A	F	F	I	N	G	Hooking a heavy fish, Deceiving, Tricking, Fleecing, Fixing.
G	A	G	G	I	N	G	Preventing speaking, Obstructing, Choking Heaving, Retching, Balking, Making witty remarks.
G	A	G	G	L	E	D	Bunch, Gang, Cackled, Gabbled.
G	A	H	N	I	T	E	Dark green mineral consisting of oxide of zinc and aluminium.
G	A	I	N	F	U	L	Profitable, Remunerative, Advantageous, Lucrative, Worthwhile, Lush, Rich, Satisfying.
G	A	I	N	I	N	G	Reaching, Attaining, Increasing, Accomplishing, Achieving, Realizing, Scoring, Winning.
G	A	I	N	S	A	Y	Contradict, Controvert, Oppose, Resist, Deny, Traverse, Combat, Withstand.
G	A	I	T	E	R	S	Overshoe reaching to the ankle, Cloth or leather leg covering.
G	A	L	A	H	A	D	Gallant.
G	A	L	A	T	E	A	British man-of-war, Striped cotton cloth.
G	A	L	E	A	T	E	Hooded.
G	A	L	E	E	N	Y	Guinea fowl.
G	A	L	E	N	I	C	Relating to Galen, a Greek physician and medical writer.
G	A	L	E	T	T	E	Flat round cake of pastry sprinkled with sugar.
G	A	L	I	L	E	E	Chapel or porch at the entrance of an English church.
G	A	L	I	L	E	O	Eminent astronomer.
G	A	L	L	A	N	T	Fine, Wonderful, Excellent, Stately, Splendid, Civil, Gentleman, Escort.
G	A	L	L	A	T	E	Salt of gallic acid.
G	A	L	L	E	O	N	Heavily built fortified ship.
G	A	L	L	E	R	Y	Ambulatory portico, Colonnade, Balcony, Verandah, Porch.
G	A	L	L	F	L	Y	Insect that deposits its eggs in plants.
G	A	L	L	I	N	G	Chafing, Irritating, Eroding, Grazing, Rubbing, Annoying, Ruffling, Wearing.
G	A	L	L	I	O	T	Swift galley used in Mediterranean and moved by sails and motor.
G	A	L	L	I	U	M	Rare bluish white metallic element.
G	A	L	L	N	U	T	Swelling on plant resembling a nut.
G	A	L	L	O	W	S	Structure used for hanging condemned persons.
G	A	L	O	P	I	N	Kitchen helper.
G	A	L	U	M	P	H	Move with clumsy bumbling, Progress clumsily.
G	A	M	B	A	D	O	A long boot, Long gaiter, Caper, Gambol.
G	A	M	B	I	A	N	Native of Gambia.
G	A	M	B	I	E	R	Yellowish catecho obtained from a Malayan woody vine.
G	A	M	B	I	S	T	Performer on a viola de gamba.

1	2	3	4	5	6	7	
G	A	M	B	L	E	D	Played game of chance, Staked something of value on an uncertain event.
G	A	M	B	L	E	R	Gamester, Speculator, Punter.
G	A	M	B	O	G	E	Orange to brown gum resin that becomes bright yellow when powdered.
G	A	M	B	R	E	L	Crooked stick used by butchers in suspending slaughtered animals.
G	A	M	E	B	A	G	Pouch used by bird hunters for carrying their take.
G	A	M	E	L	A	N	South East Asian orchestra.
G	A	M	E	T	A	L	Derived from a mature germ cell.
G	A	M	E	T	I	C	Relating to a gamete.
G	A	N	C	H	E	D	Executed or killed by impaling or hanging on hooks.
G	A	N	G	I	N	G	Assembling in groups, Going travelling.
G	A	N	G	S	A	W	Thin-toothed saw blades in gang mill.
G	A	N	G	W	A	Y	Aisle, Passage in or out, Opening in ship for passengers.
G	A	N	O	I	D	S	Primitive looking fishes.
G	A	N	O	S	I	S	Process of toning down the glare of marble.
G	A	N	T	L	E	T	Stretch of railroad where two lines overlap.
G	A	N	T	R	E	E	Bridge carrying a travelling crane, A frame used for supporting barrels.
G	A	P	P	I	N	G	Breaching, Notching, Separating, Fracturing, Cleaving, Dividing.
G	A	R	B	A	G	E	Offal, Refuse, Rubbish, Waste, Debris, Junk, Trash, Litter.
G	A	R	B	L	E	D	Distorted, Mutilated, Disarranged, Jumbled, Obscured, Beclouded, Misrepresented, Twisted.
G	A	R	B	L	E	R	One that misstates, Spice sifter.
G	A	R	B	O	I	L	Turmoil, Disturbance, Uproar.
G	A	R	B	U	R	E	Thick soup of bacon and cabbage with cheese and stale bread.
G	A	R	D	A	N	T	Guardant, Guardian, Keeper, Heraldic beast full face.
G	A	R	F	I	S	H	Fish resembling a pike.
G	A	R	G	L	E	D	Cleansed or disinfected mouth and throat with liquid.
G	A	R	L	A	N	D	Wreath, Chaplet, Coronet, Festoon, Anthology, Album, Omnibus.
G	A	R	L	I	O	N	Hybrid vegetable a cross between onion and garlic.
G	A	R	M	E	N	T	Clothing, Apparel, Array, Attire, Clad, Dress, Garb, Raiment.
G	A	R	N	I	S	H	Embellish, Adorn, Decorate, Furnish, Deck, Trim, Beautify.
G	A	R	O	T	T	E	Throttle, Strangle, Choke, Garrote.
G	A	R	P	I	K	E	Fish of the pike family.
G	A	S	B	U	O	Y	Metal buoy with light fed by compressed gas.
G	A	S	C	O	A	L	Coal used for making gas by distillation.
G	A	S	C	O	K	E	Coke made in a gas retort.
G	A	S	E	I	T	Y	Effervescence.
G	A	S	E	O	U	S	Having the form of gas, Superheated, Tenuous, Lacking substance or solidity.
G	A	S	F	I	R	E	Heating appliance using gas.
G	A	S	H	F	U	L	Ghastly, Frightful.
G	A	S	H	I	N	G	Cutting, Slashing.
G	A	S	L	A	M	P	Lamp burning illuminating gas.
G	A	S	L	I	M	E	After being used to purify gas, hydrated lime used as dressing for soil.
G	A	S	M	A	S	K	Respirator, Protection against poisonous gases.
G	A	S	P	I	N	G	Laborious breathing, Catching the breath convulsively, Panting, Puffing, Huffing.
G	A	S	P	I	P	E	Pipe for conveying gas.
G	A	S	R	I	N	G	Portable gas burner with a stand.
G	A	S	S	I	N	G	Fumigating, Poisoning of persons by gas.
G	A	S	T	A	N	K	Fuel tank for storage of gas.
G	A	S	T	R	I	C	Relating to the stomach.
G	A	T	E	A	G	E	Use of gates for control as water in sluice.
G	A	T	E	M	A	N	Attendant at a gate such as toll or railway.
G	A	T	E	W	A	Y	Limited area for entering or leaving.
G	A	U	D	E	R	Y	Fripperies, Finery, Ostentatious display.
G	A	U	D	I	E	R	More tawdry, More garish, Flashier.
G	A	U	D	I	L	Y	Showily, Garishly, Brazenly.
G	A	U	F	F	E	R	Crimp, Plait, Flute, Curl, Crimp.
G	A	U	F	R	E	D	Embossed.
G	A	U	G	I	N	G	Appraising, Judging, Measuring, Checking.
G	A	U	L	I	S	H	Relating to the Gauls.
G	A	U	M	I	N	G	Behaving in a stupid or awkward manner.
G	A	U	N	T	L	Y	Bonily, Lankly, Haggardly, Desolately, Leanly.
G	A	V	O	T	T	E	French dance in quick time.
G	A	Y	N	E	S	S	Gaiety, Hilarity.
G	A	Y	S	O	M	E	Blithe, Cheery, Jolly, Vivacious.
G	A	Z	E	L	L	E	Variety of African and Asian antelopes.
G	A	Z	E	T	T	E	Newspaper, Journal, Record.
G	E	A	R	B	O	X	Transmission.
G	E	A	R	I	N	G	Providing or fitting with gears, Harnessing, Meshing.

1	2	3	4	5	6	7	
G	E	D	R	I	T	E	Mineral of aluminous variety of anthophyllite.
G	E	H	E	N	N	A	Hell, Place or state of misery.
G	E	L	A	T	I	N	Animal jelly, Isinglass, Edible jelly.
G	E	L	D	I	N	G	Castrated male horse.
G	E	L	I	D	L	Y	Icy, Extremely cold, Frigid.
G	E	M	M	A	T	E	Reproducing by a bud.
G	E	M	M	E	R	Y	Science of gems.
G	E	M	M	I	N	G	Budding.
G	E	M	M	U	L	E	Bud produced by asexual reproduction, Small bud, Minute self-multiplying particles.
G	E	M	S	B	O	K	Male antelope.
G	E	N	A	P	P	E	To subject worsted yarns to singeing.
G	E	N	E	R	A	L	Prevalent, Usual, Widespread, Broad, Catholic, Comprehensive, Universal, Generic.
G	E	N	E	R	I	C	Universal, Characteristic, Collective, General.
G	E	N	E	S	I	S	Origin, Development into being by growth or evolution, Dawning, Opening.
G	E	N	E	T	I	C	Casual, Historical, Evolutionary.
G	E	N	E	T	T	E	Civet, Wild cat.
G	E	N	E	V	A	N	Native or resident of Geneva, Calvinist.
G	E	N	I	P	A	P	Tree of West Indies and South America with edible orange-sized fruit.
G	E	N	I	S	T	A	Large genus of broom.
G	E	N	I	T	A	L	Generative, Relating to a sexual organ.
G	E	N	I	T	O	R	Father, Parent.
G	E	N	O	E	S	E	Native or resident of Genoa, Italy.
G	E	N	T	E	E	L	Stylish, Fashionable, Cultivated, Cultured, Civil, Courteous, Polite, Prim.
G	E	N	T	I	A	N	Plant genus.
G	E	N	T	I	L	E	Not a Jew, Christian, Pagan, Heathen.
G	E	N	T	L	E	R	Kinder, More amiable, More courteous, More distinguished.
G	E	N	U	I	N	E	Native, Natural, Pure, Authentic, True, Sincere, Frank, Veritable.
G	E	O	D	E	S	Y	Branch of applied mathematics that surveys and measures the earth.
G	E	O	G	O	N	Y	Science or theory of the formation of the earth.
G	E	O	I	D	A	L	Surface within and around the earth that is everywhere normal to the direction of gravity.
G	E	O	L	O	G	Y	Science that deals with history of the earth usually through study of rocks.
G	E	O	N	O	M	A	Genus of tropical American palms with berry fruit.
G	E	O	R	A	M	A	Hollow globe containing map of world inside to be examined by a person in the interior.
G	E	O	R	D	I	E	Native of Scotland or Northern England.
G	E	O	R	G	I	C	Rustic, Relating to agriculture.
G	E	R	M	A	N	E	Compound of germanium and hydrogen.
G	E	R	M	U	L	E	A small germ.
G	E	R	U	S	I	A	The Spartan senate of ancient Greece.
G	E	R	V	A	I	S	Trademark of cheese and milk products.
G	E	S	T	A	L	T	Complete and total structure.
G	E	S	T	A	P	O	Secret police of the Nazi regime.
G	E	S	T	A	T	E	Carry in the uterus during pregnancy, Conceive and develop in the mind.
G	E	S	T	U	R	E	Notable or expressive action, Something done as a symbol or token.
G	E	T	A	B	L	E	Attainable, Obtainable.
G	E	T	A	W	A	Y	Escape, Flight, Break-out, Depart, Exit, Leave, Slip, Go.
G	E	T	T	I	N	G	Acquiring, Gaining, Obtaining, Securing, Earning, Reaching, Catching, Moving.
G	H	A	S	T	L	Y	Frightening, Terrifying, Deathlike, Pale, Wan, Terrible, Grisly, Hideous.
G	H	E	R	K	I	N	Small cucumber of a trailing vine usually pickled.
G	H	I	L	L	I	E	Fishing and hunting guide, Shoe with special lacing.
G	H	O	S	T	L	Y	Spiritual, Spectral, Shadowy, Ghastly, Cadaverous, Copselike, Deathlike, Ghostlike.
G	I	A	N	T	L	Y	Like a giant.
G	I	B	B	O	S	E	Gibbous.
G	I	B	B	O	U	S	Rounded, Protruberant, Humpbacked.
G	I	B	L	E	T	S	Edible viscera of a domestic bird, such as gizzard, liver and heart.
G	I	D	D	I	L	Y	In a giddy manner.
G	I	F	T	I	N	G	Investing, Endowing with power, Presenting with a gift.
G	I	G	M	I	L	L	Textile mill using gigs.
G	I	L	B	E	R	T	Unit of magnetomotive force.
G	I	L	D	I	N	G	Adorning, Brightening, Overlaying with thin covering of gold, Embellishing.
G	I	M	M	I	C	K	Gadget, Catch, Joker, Ingenious device.
G	I	N	G	E	R	Y	Sharp, Spicy, High-spirited, Peppy, Mettlesome, Flavoured with ginger.
G	I	N	M	I	L	L	Bar, Saloon.
G	I	N	N	I	N	G	Separating cotton fibres from seeds and waste plant material.
G	I	N	S	E	N	G	Aromatic root valued as a medicine in China.
G	I	N	T	R	A	P	Trap used for catching rabbits.
G	I	P	P	I	N	G	Gaping, Yawning, Gutting fish.
G	I	P	S	I	E	S	Gypsies, Itinerant nomands, Fortune-tellers, Romanies.

1	2	3	4	5	6	7	Definition
G	I	R	A	F	F	E	African ruminant mammal that is the tallest quadruped, with exceptionally long neck.
G	I	R	A	S	O	L	Jerusalem artichoke, Fire opal.
G	I	R	D	I	N	G	Encircling, Binding, Surrounding, Mocking, Jesting, Rushing, Flouting, Bracing.
G	I	R	D	L	E	D	Confined, Restrained, Encircled, Ringed, Hemmed, Surrounded, Encompassed, Banded.
G	I	R	D	L	E	R	Maker of girdles, Insect that feeds on bark and gnaws grooves about stems.
G	I	R	L	I	S	H	Having characteristics of a girl, Maidenly.
G	I	R	N	I	N	G	Snaring, Trapping, Grimacing, Snarling, Sneering, Whimpering, Whining, Complaining.
G	I	R	T	H	E	D	Encircled, Bound with a girth.
G	I	T	T	E	R	N	Medieval stringed instrument of the guitar family.
G	I	Z	Z	A	R	D	Muscular enlargement of the alimentary canal of birds that follows the crop.
G	L	A	C	I	A	L	Icy, Frigid, Freezing, Chilling, Arctic, Frosty, Aloof, Emotionless.
G	L	A	C	I	E	R	Moving ice field.
G	L	A	D	D	E	N	Please, Delight, Gratify, Comfort, Console, Solace, Invigorate, Enliven.
G	L	A	D	D	E	R	More satisfied, More pleased, Happier, More cheerful, More joyful.
G	L	A	D	E	Y	E	Welcoming glance, Pleasant friendly glance sometimes with sexual overtones.
G	L	A	D	I	U	S	Pen.
G	L	A	I	K	I	T	Foolish, Silly, Giddy.
G	L	A	I	R	E	D	Sizing liquid of egg white and vinegar applied to book covers or edges before gilding.
G	L	A	M	O	U	R	Bewitchment, Allure, Charm, Appeal, Charisma, Magnetism, Fascination.
G	L	A	N	C	E	D	Grazed, Skimmed, Brushed, Scraped, Shaved, Gleamed, Sparkled, Flashed.
G	L	A	R	I	N	G	Glowering, Scowling, Garish, Gaudy, Flagrant, Conspicuous, Noticeable, Blatant.
G	L	A	S	S	E	S	Spectacles, Goggles, Binoculars.
G	L	A	U	C	U	S	Sea-lizard.
G	L	A	Z	I	E	R	Worker who cuts and sets window glass, Worker who seals ends of glass tubes.
G	L	A	Z	I	N	G	Act or process of providing with glass.
G	L	E	A	M	E	D	Shone, Beamed, Radiated, Flashed, Glanced, Glimmered, Glistened, Sparkled.
G	L	E	A	N	E	D	Gathered, Acquired, Learned, Ascertained, Culled, Extracted, Concluded, Sifted.
G	L	E	A	N	E	R	One that follows the reaper.
G	L	E	E	F	U	L	Glad, Mirthful, Merry, Jocund, Jovial, Lighthearted, Delight, Merriment.
G	L	E	E	M	A	N	Professional entertainer, Singer, Reciter.
G	L	E	N	O	I	D	Having form of smooth shallow depression.
G	L	I	A	D	I	N	Prolamin found in wheat and rye.
G	L	I	D	I	N	G	Stealing, Creeping, Slipping, Glancing, Flying, Sailing, Slinking.
G	L	I	M	M	E	R	Gleam, Shimmer, Flicker, Intimation, Inkling, Vague manifestation, Glint, Flash.
G	L	I	M	P	S	E	Peep, Glance, Peek.
G	L	I	N	T	E	D	Glittered, Sparkled, Gleamed, Peeped, Glimpsed, Shimmered, Twinkled, Glazed.
G	L	I	R	I	N	E	Genus of rodents, Dormouse.
G	L	I	S	T	E	N	Flash, Glance, Gleam, Glimmer, Glitter, Shimmer, Sparkle, Twinkle.
G	L	I	S	T	E	R	Glisten.
G	L	O	A	M	E	D	Darken, Dusk, Became twilight.
G	L	O	A	T	E	D	Revelled, Gazed with self-satisfaction, Looked with passionate gratification.
G	L	O	B	A	T	E	Globular.
G	L	O	B	I	N	G	Forming into a globe.
G	L	O	B	O	I	D	Spheroid.
G	L	O	B	O	S	E	Globular.
G	L	O	B	O	U	S	Globuse.
G	L	O	B	U	L	E	Minute spherical mass, Tiny globe or ball.
G	L	O	O	M	E	D	Frowned, Lowered, Brooded, Moped, Obscured, Scowled, Glowered, Saddened.
G	L	O	R	I	E	D	Exulted, Boasted, Delighted, Jubilated, Triumphed.
G	L	O	R	I	F	Y	Extol, Praised, Celebrate, Laud, Magnify, Dignify, Ennoble, Honour.
G	L	O	S	S	E	D	Whitewashed, Palliated, Polished, Buffed, Burnished, Furbished, Glazed, Shone.
G	L	O	T	T	I	C	Glottal, Relating to the throat.
G	L	O	T	T	I	S	The space between the vocal fold and aryteroid, Larynx.
G	L	O	W	I	N	G	Blazing, Impassioned, Passionate, Fervent, Passionate, Blushing, Flushing, Ruddy, Florid.
G	L	O	Z	I	N	G	Glossing, Palliating, Brightening, Fawning, Flattering.
G	L	U	C	I	D	E	Any of the classes of carbohydrates comprising both the glycoses and the glycosides.
G	L	U	C	O	S	E	An aldose sugar.
G	L	U	E	P	O	T	Double boiler designed to melt glue.
G	L	U	M	M	E	R	More dismal, More dreary, More gloomy, More overcast, More dejected.
G	L	U	T	A	E	I	Muscles of the buttocks.
G	L	U	T	T	E	D	Swallowed greedily, Gulped down, Wolfed.
G	L	U	T	T	O	N	Epicure, One given to excessive eating and drinking.
G	L	Y	C	I	N	E	Sweet crystalline amino acid.
G	L	Y	O	X	A	L	A reactive yellow low-melting aldehyde.
G	L	Y	P	H	I	C	Resembling a symbolic figure or character.
G	L	Y	P	T	I	C	Carving or engraving especially on gems.
G	M	E	L	I	N	A	Small genus of Australasian trees and shrubs.

1	2	3	4	5	6	7	
G	N	A	R	I	N	G	Snarling, Growling.
G	N	A	R	L	E	D	Cross-grained, Knotty, Warped, Twisted, Hard-bitten, Crabbed disposition.
G	N	A	R	R	E	D	Snarled, Growled.
G	N	A	S	H	E	D	Ground teeth together.
G	N	A	T	H	I	C	Relating to the jaw.
G	N	A	T	T	E	R	Talk rapidly or idly, Nibble, Peevish, Grumble.
G	N	A	W	I	N	G	Chewing, Biting, Harassing, Plaguing, Worrying, Pestering, Annoying, Corroding.
G	N	O	C	C	H	I	Dumpling of a pasta often made with cheese.
G	N	O	S	T	I	C	Intellectual, Knowing, Shrewd, Clever.
G	O	A	D	I	N	G	Stinging, Driving, Inciting, Spurring, Urging, Stimulating.
G	O	A	H	E	A	D	Enterprising, Energy, Spirit, Green-light, Up-and-coming.
G	O	A	T	I	S	H	Having characteristics of a goat, Lascivious, Lecherous, Libidinous, Passionate, Satyric.
G	O	B	B	L	E	R	One that eats greedily, Reads rapidly, Turkey-cock.
G	O	B	E	L	I	N	French tapestry noted for its pictorial designs.
G	O	D	D	E	S	S	Divinity of the female sex, Woman of extraordinary physical beauty.
G	O	D	E	T	I	A	Small genus of Western plants.
G	O	D	H	E	A	D	State of being divine deity.
G	O	D	H	O	O	D	Godhead, Position of being a god.
G	O	D	L	E	S	S	Ungodly, Impious, Wicked, Infidel, Atheistic, Agnostic.
G	O	D	L	I	E	R	More pious, More righteous, More devout.
G	O	D	L	I	K	E	Divine, Having qualities of a god.
G	O	D	L	I	L	Y	In a godly fashion.
G	O	D	L	I	N	G	Inferior or local deity, Supernatural being midway between a god and a fetish.
G	O	D	S	E	N	D	Something needed that comes unexpectedly, Welcome event.
G	O	D	W	A	R	D	With reference to God, Directed toward God.
G	O	G	G	L	E	D	Stare with wide or protruberant eyes.
G	O	G	G	L	E	S	Eye covering like spectacles but with side shields.
G	O	I	T	R	E	D	Affected with a goitre.
G	O	L	D	C	U	P	Buttercup, Marsh marigold.
G	O	L	D	I	S	H	Having a tinge of gold.
G	O	L	F	I	N	G	Playing the game with clubs and a tough-covered ball.
G	O	L	I	A	R	D	Wandering student acting as a minstrel.
G	O	L	I	A	T	H	Giant.
G	O	M	B	E	E	N	Usury.
G	O	M	E	R	I	L	Simpleton, Fool.
G	O	N	D	O	L	A	Venetian flat-bottomed boat used on the canals, Elongated car underneath an airship.
G	O	N	G	I	N	G	Sounding a gong.
G	O	N	I	T	I	S	Inflammation of the knee.
G	O	N	O	P	O	D	The appendage of an insect to serve as an organ for copulation.
G	O	O	D	B	Y	E	Contraction of "God be with you" as a farewell expression.
G	O	O	D	D	A	Y	Convential greeting on meeting or parting.
G	O	O	D	I	N	G	Asking for alms and wishing good to the donors.
G	O	O	D	I	S	H	Moderately good, Rather good.
G	O	O	D	M	A	N	Head of family or household, Husband, Landlord.
G	O	O	D	N	O	W	Expression of surprise.
G	O	O	N	D	I	E	Hut of Australian aborigine.
G	O	P	U	R	A	M	Gateway of an Indian temple.
G	O	R	C	O	C	K	Male red grouse.
G	O	R	C	R	O	W	Carrion crow.
G	O	R	D	I	A	N	Genus of roundworms.
G	O	R	G	I	N	G	Satiating, Cramming, Devouring, Filling, Guzzling, Stuffing, Gobbling, Bolting.
G	O	R	I	L	L	A	Large anthrapoid ape. Ugly brutish man.
G	O	R	M	A	N	D	Gourmand, Glutton.
G	O	R	S	E	D	D	Mock druidical institution.
G	O	S	H	A	W	K	Long-tailed short-winged hawk.
G	O	S	L	I	N	G	Young goose, Foolish or callow person, Catkin.
G	O	S	S	I	P	Y	Full of gossip, Spread rumours.
G	O	S	S	O	O	N	Boy, Youth, Serving boy.
G	O	U	A	C	H	E	Water-colour painting.
G	O	U	G	I	N	G	Cutting Holes, Forcing out, Overcharging, Exploiting, Swindling.
G	O	U	L	A	S	H	Stew of mixed ingredients, Highly seasoned stew, Method of dealing cards, Mish-mash.
G	O	U	R	A	M	I	Brightly coloured tropical fish.
G	O	U	R	M	E	T	Connoisseur in eating and drinking, Epicure.
G	R	A	B	B	A	G	Bag of small articles or special collection.
G	R	A	B	B	E	D	Seized, Clutched, Captured, Restrained, Nabbed, Grappled, Snatched, Taken.
G	R	A	B	B	E	R	One that snatches unscrupulously.
G	R	A	B	B	L	E	Grope, Sprawl, Grovel, Feel, Fumble.

1	2	3	4	5	6	7	Definition
G	R	A	B	M	A	N	Clipper in a coal mine.
G	R	A	C	I	L	E	Thin, Slight, Slender, Graceful.
G	R	A	C	I	N	G	Gratifying, Delighting, Adorning, Embellishing, Ornamenting.
G	R	A	C	K	L	E	Blackbirds, Hill mynahs.
G	R	A	D	A	T	E	Serial arrangement having equal variation between adjacent members.
G	R	A	D	E	L	Y	God, Desirable, Upstanding, Worthy, Good-looking, Promising, Healthy, Approporiate.
G	R	A	D	I	N	E	Low steps or seats raised one above the other, Altar shelf for flowers and candlesticks.
G	R	A	D	I	N	G	Classing, Sorting, Graduating, Grouping, Ranking, Notching, Categorizing, Classifying.
G	R	A	D	U	A	L	Step-by-step, Deliberate, Piecemeal, Imperceptible, Change proceeding slowly.
G	R	A	F	T	E	D	Implanted, United, Joined, Fastened, Woven together.
G	R	A	F	T	E	R	Hardworking person.
G	R	A	I	N	E	D	Linear arrangement, Roughness or ridges on surface, Granulated, Strangled, Choked.
G	R	A	I	N	E	R	Printing worker, Worker who grains metal or wood.
G	R	A	L	L	A	E	Wading birds.
G	R	A	M	A	R	Y	Necromancy, Magic, Enchantment.
G	R	A	M	M	A	R	Study of classes of words, their inflections and functions.
G	R	A	M	P	U	S	Killer whale.
G	R	A	N	A	R	Y	Storehouse for grain.
G	R	A	N	D	A	M	Grandmother.
G	R	A	N	D	E	E	Spanish or Portugese nobleman.
G	R	A	N	D	E	R	Greater, More imposing, More impressive, More lavish.
G	R	A	N	D	L	Y	In a majestic manner.
G	R	A	N	D	M	A	Grandmother.
G	R	A	N	G	E	R	Farmer, Grain-carrying railroad.
G	R	A	N	I	T	E	Rock of crystalline texture, Unyielding.
G	R	A	N	T	E	D	Allowed, Accorded, Agreed, Given, Bestowed, Acknowledged, Conceded, Awarded.
G	R	A	N	T	E	E	One to whom a grant is made.
G	R	A	N	T	E	R	One that grants.
G	R	A	N	T	O	R	One that extends credit, Guarantor.
G	R	A	N	U	L	E	Little grain, Particle, Sugar-coated pill.
G	R	A	P	E	R	Y	Area or building where grape vines are cultivated.
G	R	A	P	H	I	C	Written, Pictorial, Vivid, Engraved, Clear, Lucid, Photographic, Cogent.
G	R	A	P	N	E	L	Grappel, Small anchor with four of five hooks.
G	R	A	P	P	L	E	Wrestle, Clamp, Clasp, Clutch, Grasp, Hold, Scuffle, Tussle.
G	R	A	S	P	E	D	Grabbed, Clutched, Embraced, Grappled, Seized, Held, Understood, Comprehended.
G	R	A	S	P	E	R	One that clutches.
G	R	A	S	S	E	D	Turfed, Furnished with pasture, Felled.
G	R	A	S	S	E	R	Beef animal fed solely on pasture, Calfskin taken from an underfed animal.
G	R	A	T	I	F	Y	Requite, Remunerate, Satisfy, Appease, Indulge, Please, Adorn, Welcome.
G	R	A	T	I	N	G	Covering or frame of latticed bars, Harsh, Hoarse, Jarring, Rasping, Raucous, Rough, Strident.
G	R	A	V	E	D	O	Cold in the head.
G	R	A	V	E	L	Y	Containing gravel, Harsh, Irritating, Unpleasant.
G	R	A	V	E	S	T	Most serious, Most sombre, Most severe, Grimmest, Saddest, Most dangerous.
G	R	A	V	I	E	D	Covered or dressed with gravy.
G	R	A	V	I	N	G	Engraving.
G	R	A	V	I	T	Y	Attraction of the earth's mass, Importance, Significance, Weight, Seriousness, Influence.
G	R	A	V	U	R	E	Photogravure, Producing by grooving or etching.
G	R	A	Z	I	E	R	Owner or rancher of cattle.
G	R	A	Z	I	N	G	Feeding on growing grass, Brushing, Rubbing, Chafing, Skimming, Glancing, Shaving.
G	R	E	A	S	E	D	Lubricated, Bribed, Facilitated, Expedited.
G	R	E	A	T	E	N	Enlarge, Magnify, Increase, Exalt, Ennoble.
G	R	E	A	T	E	R	Ampler, Larger, Fatter, Bigger, More famous, Heavier, Weightier, Grander.
G	R	E	A	T	L	Y	Very, Nobly, Magnamiously, Highly.
G	R	E	A	V	E	S	Groves, Hickets, Leg armour.
G	R	E	C	I	A	N	Characteristic of the Greeks.
G	R	E	C	I	S	M	Mode of thought or action of ancient Greece.
G	R	E	C	I	Z	E	To mould in the way of Greece.
G	R	E	E	N	E	D	Grown green, Hoaxer, Acquired green colour.
G	R	E	E	N	E	R	Younger, Fresher, Tender, More inexperienced, More gullible.
G	R	E	E	N	T	H	Verdure, Green growth.
G	R	E	E	T	E	D	Hailed, Welcomed, Met, Encountered, Accosted, Saluted, Addressed.
G	R	E	M	I	A	L	Relating to lap or bosom.
G	R	E	M	L	I	N	Unaccountable disruptive influence.
G	R	E	N	A	D	E	High explosive missile, Glass bottle containing volatile chemicals for throwing to extinguish fires.
G	R	E	Y	L	A	G	Common gray wild goose.
G	R	I	D	D	E	D	Covered with a grid, Distribute by means of a grid.
G	R	I	D	D	L	E	Flat surface on which food is placed to cook over dry heat.

1	2	3	4	5	6	7	
G	R	I	E	V	E	D	Distressed, Sorrowed, Mourned, Constrained, Hurt, Injured, Endured, Pained.
G	R	I	F	F	I	N	Heraldic animal, White person new to East.
G	R	I	F	F	O	N	Breed of small dogs of Belgian origin.
G	R	I	L	L	E	D	Broiled, Afflicted, Cross-examined.
G	R	I	M	A	C	E	Distortion of face, Contort face, Wry face, Affectation, Sham, Pretense.
G	R	I	M	M	E	R	More uncompromising, Fiercer, Crueler, More savage, More gruesome, Bleaker, Harsher.
G	R	I	N	D	E	R	Molar tooth, Worker who pulverizes material.
G	R	I	N	N	E	D	Laughed broadly, Gaped open.
G	R	I	P	I	N	G	Painful, Distressing, Clutching, Grasping, Avaricious.
G	R	I	P	P	E	D	Seized, Held, Enthralled, Fascinated, Mesmerized, Clamped, Clasped, Clutched.
G	R	I	P	P	E	R	Device that holds something.
G	R	I	P	P	L	E	Greedy and Grasping, Avaricious, Grapple, Grasp.
G	R	I	Q	U	A	S	Mixed race people of Griqualand.
G	R	I	S	K	I	N	Steak, Pork chop.
G	R	I	S	L	E	D	Streaked with gray.
G	R	I	S	T	L	E	Cartilage, Strength of character.
G	R	I	S	T	L	Y	Containing gristle.
G	R	I	T	T	E	D	Grated, Ground, Spread with grit.
G	R	I	Z	Z	L	E	Gripe, Grumble, Whimper, Complain, Mourn, Grieve, Lament.
G	R	I	Z	Z	L	Y	Streaked with gray.
G	R	O	A	N	E	D	Moaned, Bewailed, Annoyed, Creaked, Voiced, Disapproved, Rasped.
G	R	O	B	I	A	N	Boor, Lout.
G	R	O	C	E	R	Y	Articles of food and produce sold by a grocer.
G	R	O	G	R	A	M	Coarse loosely woven fabric of silk or silk and mohair.
G	R	O	I	N	E	D	Built with high vaulted roof.
G	R	O	M	M	E	T	Eyelet, Gasket, Washer, Grummet.
G	R	O	O	M	E	D	Maintained health and condition, Readied, Prepared.
G	R	O	O	V	E	D	Furrowed, Wrinkled, Scooped, Ingrained.
G	R	O	P	I	N	G	Handling, Fumbling, Feeling, Touching, Searching, Exploring.
G	R	O	S	S	E	R	Coarser, Rougher, Plainer, Bigger, Denser, Thicker, Cheaper, Cruder.
G	R	O	S	S	L	Y	Flagrantly, Vulgarly.
G	R	O	T	I	A	N	Relating to theories of Grotius a Dutch salesman.
G	R	O	U	N	D	S	Foundations, Reasons, Dregs, Backgrounds, Fields, Proof, Subjects, Bases.
G	R	O	U	P	E	D	Clustered, Classified, Collected, Assembled, Gathered, Compared, Graded.
G	R	O	U	P	E	R	Solitary bottom fish that usually attains great size.
G	R	O	U	S	E	D	Complained, Grumbled, Grunted, Muttered, Scolded, Growled.
G	R	O	U	S	E	R	Habitual grumbler or complainer, Crank, Grouch.
G	R	O	U	T	E	D	Spaces between tiles, bricks or masonry filled with thin mortar fluid.
G	R	O	W	I	N	G	Thriving, Springing up, Producing, Raising, Maturing, Developing, Escalating, Expanding.
G	R	O	W	L	E	D	Rumbled, Grumbled, Rolled.
G	R	O	W	L	E	R	Four-wheeled carriage, Container for beer. Small iceberg.
G	R	O	W	N	U	P	Adult, Matured, Mellowed.
G	R	U	B	B	E	D	Toiled, Drudged, Scraped, Burrowed, Dug, Poked, Rooted, Foraged.
G	R	U	B	B	E	R	Digger, Drudge, Cultivator, Chisel.
G	R	U	B	B	L	E	Grope.
G	R	U	D	G	E	D	Complained, Grumbled, Begrudged, Envied, Denied, Refused.
G	R	U	F	F	E	R	Harsher, Surlier, Hoarser, Rougher, More severe.
G	R	U	F	F	L	Y	In an ungracious manner.
G	R	U	M	B	L	E	Complain, Growl, Rumble, Complaint, Grouse, Squawk, Grouch, Scold.
G	R	U	M	M	E	T	Eyelet, Grommet, Gasket, Washer, Cabin boy, Awkward lad.
G	R	U	M	O	S	E	Formed of clustered grains.
G	R	U	M	O	U	S	Thick, Clotted.
G	R	U	N	T	E	R	Sea bream of S. Africa, One that grunts.
G	R	U	Y	E	R	E	Pressed whole-milk cheese with small holes.
G	R	Y	L	L	I	D	Cricket.
G	R	Y	P	H	O	N	Griffin, Heraldic animal.
G	R	Y	S	B	O	K	Small reddish antelope.
G	U	A	J	I	R	A	Cuban peasant dance.
G	U	A	N	A	C	O	S. American animal related to the camel but without a hump.
G	U	A	N	A	S	E	Enzyme present in most animal tissues.
G	U	A	R	A	N	A	Dried paste from Brazilian climbing shrub and made into a drink.
G	U	A	R	D	E	D	Defended, Shielded, Escorted, Restrained, Warned, Safeguarded, Protected, Screened.
G	U	D	G	E	O	N	Pivot, Journal, Iron pin, Cheat, Dupe, Bait, Allure, Fool.
G	U	E	N	O	N	S	African monkeys.
G	U	E	R	D	O	N	Reward, Recompense.
G	U	E	R	E	Z	A	Colobus monkey.
G	U	E	R	I	T	E	Turret or shelter on a watch tower.

1	2	3	4	5	6	7	Definition
G	U	E	S	S	E	D	Conjectured, Estimated, Surmised, Assumed, Deduced, Inferred, Gathered, Conceived.
G	U	E	S	S	E	R	One that guesses.
G	U	E	S	T	E	N	For guests.
G	U	E	S	T	E	R	To be a guest.
G	U	I	C	H	E	T	Grilled opening, Ticket office.
G	U	I	D	I	N	G	Conducting, Piloting, Instructing, Advising, Leading, Directing, Escorting, Steering.
G	U	I	L	D	E	R	Dutch gold coin, Member of a guild.
G	U	I	L	D	R	Y	Municipal corporation of a royal Scottish burgh.
G	U	I	N	E	A	N	Inhabitant of Guinea.
G	U	I	P	U	R	E	Thick heavy lace.
G	U	I	S	A	R	D	Mummer.
G	U	L	L	E	R	Y	Trickery, Deception, Breeding place of gulls.
G	U	L	L	I	E	D	Eroded.
G	U	L	L	I	E	S	Miniature gorges, Ravines, Gutters, Drains, Swords, Large knives.
G	U	L	L	I	N	G	Deceiving, Cheating, Duping, Bamboozling, Hoaxing, Fooling.
G	U	M	B	O	I	L	Abscess in the gum.
G	U	M	B	O	O	T	Rubber boot.
G	U	M	D	R	O	P	Candy made from corn syrup and coated with sugar crystals.
G	U	M	M	I	N	G	Chewing without teeth, Using adhesive, Cementing.
G	U	M	M	O	U	S	Composed of gum.
G	U	M	S	H	O	E	Rubber overshoe, Detective, Policeman, Investigator, Snoop, Pry, Lurk, Slink.
G	U	M	T	R	E	E	Tree that yields gum.
G	U	M	W	O	O	D	Shrub.
G	U	N	B	O	A	T	Armed ship of shallow draught, Catamaran.
G	U	N	D	E	C	K	Deck carrying ship's guns.
G	U	N	F	I	R	E	Firing of guns.
G	U	N	L	I	N	E	Line or cable one end of which can be shot by a gun device.
G	U	N	L	O	C	K	Mechanism of a firearm.
G	U	N	N	E	R	Y	Instruction in the use of guns.
G	U	N	N	I	N	G	Shooting of game.
G	U	N	P	O	R	T	Opening through which a gun can be fired.
G	U	N	R	O	O	M	Apartment on a warship used by junior officers.
G	U	N	S	H	O	T	Range of a gun, Shot fired from a gun.
G	U	N	W	A	L	E	Part of a vessel where topsides and deck meet.
G	U	R	G	L	E	D	Rippled, Burbled, Bubbled, Chuckled with a throaty sound.
G	U	R	N	A	R	D	Marine scorpaenid fishes with shells and are considered edible.
G	U	S	H	I	N	G	Pouring, Flowing, Effusive, Slobbering, Flushing, Surging.
G	U	S	T	I	L	Y	With great relish, In a manner suggesting a gust of wind.
G	U	T	T	A	T	E	Having spots, Lose moisture by exudation.
G	U	T	T	I	N	G	Eviscerating, Removing entrails, Extracting.
G	U	T	T	L	E	D	Eaten and drank noisily and greedily, Guzzled.
G	U	T	T	U	L	E	Small spot shaped like a drop.
G	U	T	W	E	E	D	Perennial sow thistle.
G	U	Z	Z	L	E	D	Gulped, Swigged, Swilled, Bolted, Crammed, Gobbled, Sloshed, Wolfed.
G	U	Z	Z	L	E	R	One that eats and drinks greedily, Device for preserving water for game birds in an arid region.
G	W	I	N	I	A	D	Welsh fish related to lake whitefish.
G	Y	M	N	A	S	T	Expert in gymnastics.
G	Y	R	A	T	E	D	Revolved, Spiralled, Twisted, Turned, Swung back and forth.
G	Y	R	O	N	N	Y	Heraldic coat of arms divided into triangular forms.
G	Y	T	R	A	S	H	Spectre or ghost in the form of an animal.

H

1	2	3	4	5	6	7	Definition
H	A	B	I	T	A	T	Haunt, Home, Locality, Range, Environment, Locale, Territory, Surroundings.
H	A	B	I	T	E	D	Inhabited, Accustomed.
H	A	B	I	T	U	E	One who frquents a place, Customer, Patron, Addict, Fan, Devotée.
H	A	C	H	U	R	E	Contour line on a relief map.
H	A	C	K	E	R	Y	Bullock cart.
H	A	C	K	I	N	G	Heckling, Kicking, Mangling, Slashing, Chipping, Mutilating, Trimming.
H	A	C	K	L	E	D	Covered with natural animal coat, Combed flax, jute or hemp, Chopped roughly.
H	A	C	K	L	E	R	Worker who separates fibres of flax, jute or hemp.
H	A	C	K	L	O	G	Chopping block.
H	A	C	K	N	E	Y	Nag, Horse suitable for driving or riding, Trite, Vulgar, Commonplace, Make sophisticated.
H	A	C	K	S	A	W	Fine-toothed saw with blade under tension in a frame.
H	A	D	D	O	C	K	Important food fish that appears on both sides of the Atlantic.
H	A	D	R	O	M	E	The part of the mestome that conducts water.

1	2	3	4	5	6	7	
H	A	F	F	E	T	S	Cheeks, Temples, Hair growing at the temples.
H	A	F	F	L	I	N	Immature.
H	A	F	N	I	U	M	Metallic element used for filaments for incandescent lamps.
H	A	F	T	I	N	G	Established pasture, Furnishing a knife or dagger with a handle.
H	A	G	F	I	S	H	Related to the lamprey, Parasitic fish.
H	A	G	G	A	D	A	Explanatory matter in Jewish literature.
H	A	G	G	A	R	D	Careworn, Drawn, Pinched, Gaunt, Lank, Scraggy, Faded, Fatigued.
H	A	G	G	I	N	G	Goading, Harassing, Harrying, Nagging, Tiring, Fatiguing.
H	A	G	G	I	S	H	Resembling a witch.
H	A	G	G	L	E	D	Wrangled, Bargained, Hacked, Bartered, Traded, Argued, Higgled, Quibbled.
H	A	G	G	L	E	R	Huckster.
H	A	G	S	E	E	D	Offspring of a witch.
H	A	G	W	O	R	M	Adder, Viper, Blindworm.
H	A	I	L	I	N	G	Pouring hail, Saluting, Greeting, Accosting, Acclaiming, Praising, Summoning, Complimenting.
H	A	I	R	C	U	T	Hairstyle achieved by cutting and shaping the hair.
H	A	I	R	N	E	T	Open net worn to keep hair in place.
H	A	I	R	P	I	N	Pin to hold the hair in place.
H	A	I	T	I	A	N	Relating to the island of Haiti.
H	A	L	A	K	A	H	Particular Jewish law or custom prescribed by the legal codices.
H	A	L	A	V	A	H	Jewish sweetmeat of crushed sesame seeds in a base of honey.
H	A	L	B	E	R	D	Old-time weapon of a battle-axe and pike mounted on a six feet handle.
H	A	L	C	Y	O	N	Serene, Happy, Prosperous, Golden, Affluent, Calm, Placid, Untroubled.
H	A	L	F	O	N	E	Golf handicap.
H	A	L	F	W	A	Y	Midway, Amenably, Partially, Almost, More or less.
H	A	L	F	W	I	T	Foolish person, Dolt, Blockhead.
H	A	L	I	B	U	T	One of the largest flatfish.
H	A	L	L	I	O	N	Scamp, Scoundrel.
H	A	L	O	G	E	N	One of the five elements forming part of group VIIA.
H	A	L	T	E	R	E	One of modified second pair of wings in Diptera that function as flight instruments.
H	A	L	T	I	N	G	Lame, Limping, Dragging, Uncertain, Faltering, Awkward, Fumbling.
H	A	L	V	I	N	G	Dividing into two equal parts, Reducing to one half.
H	A	L	Y	A	R	D	Rope or tackle for hoisting or lowering sail, flags or spars.
H	A	M	B	L	E	D	Limped, Stumbled.
H	A	M	B	U	R	G	From city of Hamburg, Embroidered edging for women's clothes, Domestic fowl.
H	A	M	I	T	I	C	Language of descendants of Ham, one of the sons of Noah.
H	A	M	M	O	C	K	Bed of netting or canvas slung between supports.
H	A	M	S	T	E	R	Rodent of burrowing habits.
H	A	M	U	L	A	R	Hooked, Bent.
H	A	M	U	L	U	S	Little hook terminating the barbicel of a feather.
H	A	N	A	P	E	R	Small wicker case used as a repository for legal documents.
H	A	N	D	B	A	G	Woman's bag used for personal articles.
H	A	N	D	F	U	L	As much as a hand will contain, Small quantity, As much as one can control.
H	A	N	D	I	E	R	More convenient, Cleverer, More adroit, More dexterous.
H	A	N	D	I	L	Y	Dexterously, Easily, Conveniently.
H	A	N	D	I	N	G	Manipulating, Conducting, Leading, Transmitting, Giving, Compelling, Conceding, Passing.
H	A	N	D	J	A	R	Short curved dagger of Muslim countries.
H	A	N	D	L	E	D	Seized, Manipulated, Wielded, Managed, Controlled, Held, Touched, Directed.
H	A	N	D	L	E	R	One in immediate physical charge of an animal, Publicity agent.
H	A	N	D	O	U	T	Food, clothing or money given to a beggar.
H	A	N	D	S	A	W	Saw able to be used with one hand.
H	A	N	D	S	E	L	Luck, Augury, Earnest, Foretaste, First experience.
H	A	N	D	S	E	T	Telephone mouthpiece, earpiece, Microphone and speaker mounted on a single handle.
H	A	N	G	D	O	G	Despicable or miserable fellow.
H	A	N	G	I	N	G	Executing, Holding, Suspending, Dangling, Floating, Hovering, Clinging, Leaning.
H	A	N	G	M	A	N	Public executioner.
H	A	N	K	I	E	S	Handkerchiefs.
H	A	N	K	I	N	G	Folding, Coiling, Making into a hank or skein.
H	A	N	K	L	E	D	Twisted, Entangled, Lured, Enticed.
H	A	N	S	A	R	D	Official published report of proceedings in the British parliament.
H	A	N	U	K	A	H	Jewish festival.
H	A	N	U	M	A	N	Indian monkey protected as a protegé of a monkey god.
H	A	P	L	E	S	S	Unfortunate, Unlucky, Misfortuned, Unhappy, Ill-fated, Woeful, Wretched.
H	A	P	L	O	I	D	Having half the number of chromosones characteristic of somatic cells.
H	A	P	L	O	N	T	Organism having somatic cells with the haploid chromosone number.
H	A	P	O	R	T	H	Halfpennyworth.
H	A	P	P	I	E	R	More fortunate, More prosperous, More favourable, More congenial.
H	A	P	P	I	L	Y	Fortunately, Luckily, Haply, Successfully, Appropriately, Felicitously.

1	2	3	4	5	6	7	
H	A	P	P	I	N	G	Clothing, Covering, Wrapping.
H	A	R	B	O	U	R	Haven, Refuge, Asylum, Shelter, Contain, Cherish, Entertain, Live.
H	A	R	D	E	S	T	Firmest, Most compact, Tightest, Strongest, Roughest, Coarsest, Harshest, Strictest.
H	A	R	D	I	E	R	Bolder, Braver, Stronger, More audacious, More brazen, More resolute.
H	A	R	D	I	L	Y	Boldly, Stoutly.
H	A	R	D	I	S	H	Rather hard.
H	A	R	D	O	C	K	Burdock.
H	A	R	D	P	A	N	Compacted soil.
H	A	R	D	S	E	T	Hard pressed, Firm, Fixed in rigidity.
H	A	R	D	T	O	P	Automobile with a metal top.
H	A	R	E	I	N	G	Running, Fleeting.
H	A	R	E	L	I	P	Cleft tip.
H	A	R	I	C	O	T	Ripe seed of a bean.
H	A	R	K	I	N	G	Listening, Attending, Marking, Minding, Noting.
H	A	R	L	I	N	G	Special way of angling for salmon.
H	A	R	M	A	L	A	Herb of India and the Levant that yields alkaloids used as a vermifuge and stimulant.
H	A	R	M	F	U	L	Damaging, Troublesome, Injurious.
H	A	R	M	I	N	G	Hurting, Damaging, Injuring, Impairing, Spoiling, Ruining.
H	A	R	M	O	N	Y	Melody, Integration, Rhythm, Agreement, Accord, Tranquillity.
H	A	R	N	E	S	S	Tackle, Gear, Equipment, Arm, Utilize.
H	A	R	P	I	N	G	Dwelling on a subject, Repeating a theme with tiresome frequency.
H	A	R	P	I	S	T	Harp player.
H	A	R	P	O	O	N	Barbed whaling gun.
H	A	R	R	I	E	D	Assaulted, Devastated, Ravaged, Tormented, Desecrated, Pillaged, Worried, Annoyed.
H	A	R	R	I	E	R	Hunting dog, Hawk.
H	A	R	S	H	E	N	To make harsh.
H	A	R	S	H	E	R	Rougher, Coarser, Sharper, Hoarser, Bleaker, Grimmer.
H	A	R	V	E	S	T	Season for gathering agriculture crop.
H	A	S	B	E	E	N	Obsolete, Passed peak of effectiveness.
H	A	S	H	I	N	G	Chopping, Jumbling, Slashing, Reviewing, Considering.
H	A	S	H	I	S	H	Narcotic drug derived from hemp, Cannabis.
H	A	S	S	O	C	K	Small kneeling cushion, Footstool, Tussock.
H	A	S	T	A	T	E	Shaped like an arrow with flaring barbs.
H	A	S	T	I	E	R	Quicker, More eager, More rash, Faster.
H	A	S	T	I	L	Y	Hurriedly, Rashly.
H	A	S	T	I	N	G	Hasten, Hurry.
H	A	T	A	B	L	E	Detestable, Being hated.
H	A	T	B	A	N	D	Band of fabric, leather or cord around the crown of a hat above the brim.
H	A	T	C	H	E	D	Produced young from the egg, Brooded, Originated, Produced.
H	A	T	C	H	E	L	Hackle.
H	A	T	C	H	E	R	One that hatches, One that produces or originates.
H	A	T	C	H	E	S	Produces young from eggs.
H	A	T	C	H	E	T	Short-handled axe.
H	A	T	E	F	U	L	Malicious, Repulsive, Uncongenial, Annoying, Distasteful, Abhorrent, Obnoxious.
H	A	T	L	E	S	S	Being without a hat.
H	A	T	R	A	C	K	Wooden framework with pegs to hold outer clothing.
H	A	U	B	E	R	K	Long tunic of chain mail.
H	A	U	G	H	T	Y	Arrogant, Proud, Noble, Lofty.
H	A	U	L	A	G	E	Process of transporting goods by road.
H	A	U	L	I	E	R	One who carries on business of hauling.
H	A	U	L	I	N	G	Transporting goods in a truck.
H	A	U	N	C	H	Y	Having large haunches.
H	A	U	N	T	E	D	Frequented, Troubled, Molested, Lingered.
H	A	U	N	T	E	R	Frequent visitor.
H	A	U	S	T	U	S	Right to draw water from a well or spring on another's land.
H	A	U	T	B	O	Y	Oboe, Pipe-organ stop similar to oboe, Strawberry.
H	A	U	T	E	U	R	Haughtiness, Assumption of superiority, Arrogant, Condescending manner.
H	A	U	T	P	A	S	Dais, Raised part of floor.
H	A	V	E	N	O	T	One that is poor in material wealth, Under-privileged.
H	A	W	K	B	I	T	Dandelion.
H	A	W	K	I	N	G	Falconry.
H	A	W	K	O	W	L	Large diurnal owl.
H	A	Y	C	O	C	K	Conical pile of hay.
H	A	Y	F	O	R	K	Fork for pitching hay.
H	A	Y	L	O	F	T	Loft or scaffold for hay.
H	A	Y	R	I	C	K	Haystack.
H	A	Y	S	E	E	D	Seed shattered from hay, Yokel, Bumpkin, Hick, Rustic.

1	2	3	4	5	6	7	
H	A	Y	W	A	R	D	Keeper of a town's common herd of cattle.
H	A	Y	W	I	R	E	Flimsy, Broken-down, Inadequate, Tangled, Mixed-up, Upset, Emotionally excited.
H	A	Z	E	L	L	Y	Covered with hazels, Light yellowish-brown colour.
H	A	Z	I	E	S	T	Vaguest, Cloudiest, Foggiest, Dreamiest, Muzziest.
H	E	A	D	I	L	Y	Rashly, Headlong, Dizzily.
H	E	A	D	I	N	G	Lopping, Leading, Surpassing, Setting a course, Rising, Intercepting, Originating.
H	E	A	D	M	A	N	Chief, Overseer, Foreman.
H	E	A	D	W	A	Y	Advance, Progress, March, Proficiency.
H	E	A	L	A	L	L	Self-heal, Panacea, Green orchis.
H	E	A	L	I	N	G	Curing, Remedial, Remedying, Restoring, Curative, Eliminating, Mending.
H	E	A	L	T	H	Y	Viable, Prosperous, Flourishing, Desirable, Positive, Beneficial, Robust, Wholesome.
H	E	A	P	I	N	G	Amassing, Piling, Accumulating, Stacking, Mounding, Collecting, Packing, Loading.
H	E	A	R	I	N	G	Apprehending sound, Audition, Audience, Preaching, Granting, Consenting, Yielding.
H	E	A	R	K	E	N	Listen, Hear.
H	E	A	R	S	A	Y	Report, Rumour.
H	E	A	R	S	E	D	Buried, Entombed, Shrouded.
H	E	A	R	T	E	D	Hearten, Encouraged, Inspired, Seated in the heart.
H	E	A	R	T	E	N	Inspire, Rouse, Strengthen, Encourage, Energize.
H	E	A	T	H	E	N	Pagan, Idolator, Gentile, Irreligious person.
H	E	A	T	H	E	R	Member of heath family.
H	E	A	T	I	N	G	Raising temperature, Exciting, Inflaming, Becoming hot.
H	E	A	V	E	R	S	Labourers handling freight.
H	E	A	V	E	T	O	Bring ship to standstill.
H	E	A	V	I	E	R	Deeper, Graver, Weightier, Steeper, More oppressive, More acute.
H	E	A	V	I	L	Y	Dully, Severely, Dejectedly, Injuriously.
H	E	A	V	I	N	G	Lifting, Raising, Tossing, Hurling, Casting, Throwing.
H	E	B	R	A	I	C	Relating to Hebrew.
H	E	C	K	L	E	D	Hackled, Badgered, Molested, Interfered, Meddled, Disturbed, Challenged.
H	E	C	K	L	E	R	One that badgers a public speaker.
H	E	C	T	A	R	E	Metric unit of 10,000 square metres.
H	E	D	E	O	M	A	Small genus of American herbs.
H	E	D	E	R	I	N	Crystalline antibiotic glycoside found in ivy which is active against fungi and bacteria.
H	E	D	G	I	N	G	Enclosing, Encircling, Protecting, Guarding, Hindering, Evading, Trimming, Modifying.
H	E	D	O	N	I	C	Relating to pleasure.
H	E	E	D	F	U	L	Attentive, Mindful, Careful, Observant.
H	E	E	D	I	N	G	Concerning, Paying attention, Minding, Noticing, Regarding.
H	E	E	L	I	N	G	Tipping, Leaning, Canting, Listing, Tilting, Providing.
H	E	F	T	I	E	R	Mightier, Heavier, Larger, Bigger, More powerful.
H	E	F	T	I	L	Y	Strongly, Mightily.
H	E	G	U	M	E	N	Head of a religious community in the Eastern church.
H	E	I	G	H	H	O	Expression of encouragement or boredom, weariness or sadness.
H	E	I	N	O	U	S	Abominable, Execrable, Outrageous, SHockingly evil.
H	E	I	R	D	O	M	Heritage.
H	E	I	R	E	S	S	Female heir to great wealth.
H	E	L	I	C	A	L	Cylindrically spiral.
H	E	L	I	C	E	S	Plural of helix- land snails.
H	E	L	I	C	O	N	Large brass tuba.
H	E	L	I	X	E	S	Something spiral in form.
H	E	L	I	X	I	N	Family of land snails.
H	E	L	L	B	O	X	Receptacle for damaged or discarded printer's type material.
H	E	L	L	C	A	T	Witch, Shrew, Tormentor.
H	E	L	L	E	N	E	Greek.
H	E	L	L	I	E	R	Tiler or slater of roof.
H	E	L	L	I	S	H	In an execrable manner.
H	E	L	P	F	U	L	Useful, Salutary, Constructive, Encouraging.
H	E	L	P	I	N	G	Serving (of food), Relieving, Curing, Mending, Aiding, Assisting, Supporting, Befriending.
H	E	L	V	I	N	G	Fitting with a handle.
H	E	L	V	I	T	E	Silicate mineral.
H	E	M	I	O	L	A	Rhythmic alteration in musical notes.
H	E	M	L	O	C	K	Poisonous herb with small white flowers.
H	E	M	M	I	N	G	Finishing edge of article with stitching.
H	E	N	B	A	N	E	Poisonous herb similar to belladona.
H	E	N	N	A	E	D	Dyed with henna.
H	E	N	N	E	R	Y	Poultry farm.
H	E	N	P	E	C	K	Persistent nagging and domination of husband.
H	E	N	T	I	N	G	Seizing, Catching, Reaching.
H	E	N	W	I	F	E	Woman who raised poultry.

1	2	3	4	5	6	7	Definition
H	E	P	A	R	I	N	Polysaccharide sulfuric acid ester found in liver, lung and other tissues.
H	E	P	A	T	I	C	Relating to the liver.
H	E	P	T	A	N	E	Liquid normal hydrocarbon found in petroleum.
H	E	P	T	O	D	E	Vacuum tube.
H	E	P	T	O	S	E	Class of monosaccharides.
H	E	R	B	A	G	E	Pasture grass, Succulent parts of herbaceous plants.
H	E	R	B	I	S	H	Resembling herbs.
H	E	R	B	L	E	T	Small herb.
H	E	R	B	O	U	S	Herby.
H	E	R	D	I	N	G	Associating, Feeding and running together, Taking care of livestock.
H	E	R	E	O	U	T	Hence.
H	E	R	E	T	I	C	Dissenter from established church dogma, Unorthodox.
H	E	R	I	T	O	R	Inheritor.
H	E	R	L	I	N	G	Sea trout.
H	E	R	O	I	N	E	Woman admired for her achievements.
H	E	R	O	I	S	M	Qualities of courage, bravery, self-sacrifice and unselfishness.
H	E	R	O	I	Z	E	Treat as a hero.
H	E	R	O	N	R	Y	Community of herons.
H	E	R	R	I	N	G	Valuable food fish.
H	E	R	S	E	L	F	Female reflexive pronoun.
H	E	R	S	H	I	P	Warlike raid to steal cattle.
H	E	S	S	I	A	N	German mercenary, Burlap.
H	E	S	S	I	T	E	Mineral.
H	E	T	A	I	R	A	Mistress, Courtesan, Ancient Greek prostitute.
H	E	X	A	G	O	N	Plane polygon of six sides.
H	E	X	A	P	L	A	Edition or work in six texts.
H	E	X	A	P	O	D	Six-footed relating to insects.
H	E	X	A	R	C	H	Having six radiating vascular strands.
H	E	X	E	R	E	I	Witchcraft.
H	I	B	A	C	H	I	Charcoal brazier.
H	I	C	A	T	E	E	West Indian freshwater tortoise.
H	I	C	K	O	R	Y	American nut tree, Switch or cane for punishing children.
H	I	D	A	L	G	O	Member of the lower nobility of Spain.
H	I	D	E	O	U	S	Frightful, Terrible, Monstrous, Embarrassing, Ludicrous, Dismaying, Grisly.
H	I	D	E	O	U	T	Place of refuge, Retreat, Concealment.
H	I	G	G	L	E	D	Haggled, Argued.
H	I	G	G	L	E	R	Itinerant pedlar, Hawker.
H	I	G	H	D	A	Y	Holy day, Feast day.
H	I	G	H	E	S	T	Loftiest, Tallest, Richest, Shrillest, Gayest, Keenest, Smelliest.
H	I	G	H	H	A	T	Beaver, Snob, Swell, Supercilious, Snobbish, Arrogant, Aristocratic, Snub.
H	I	G	H	L	O	W	Ankle-high laced boot, Poker game.
H	I	G	H	U	P	S	Persons of high rank or status.
H	I	G	H	W	A	Y	Public road, Main direct road, Primary aspect.
H	I	L	A	R	I	A	Genus of Mexican grasses, Mesquite.
H	I	L	D	I	N	G	Immoral person.
H	I	L	L	I	E	R	Steeper.
H	I	L	L	I	N	G	Heaping earth.
H	I	L	L	M	A	N	Person living in mountainous area.
H	I	L	L	O	C	K	Small hill, Mound.
H	I	L	L	T	O	P	Summit of a hill.
H	I	M	S	E	L	F	Male reflective pronoun.
H	I	N	D	G	U	T	Posterior part of alimentary canal of a vertebrate embryo.
H	I	N	T	I	N	G	Suggesting, Presaging, Foreshadowing, Implying, Insinuating, Indicating, Soliciting, Seeking.
H	I	P	B	A	T	H	Sitting bath.
H	I	P	L	O	C	K	Wrestling manoeuvre.
H	I	P	P	I	N	G	Throwing in wrestling, Carrying on the hips.
H	I	P	P	O	I	D	Like a horse.
H	I	P	R	O	O	F	Roof having sloping ends and sloping sides.
H	I	P	S	H	O	T	Dislocation of hip, Having one hip lower than the other.
H	I	P	S	T	E	R	Devotee of jazz.
H	I	R	A	B	L	E	Available for hire.
H	I	R	C	I	N	E	Relating to a goat.
H	I	R	S	U	T	E	Hairy, Shaggy.
H	I	R	U	D	I	N	Anticoagulant preparation prepared from buccal glands of the leech.
H	I	S	S	I	N	G	Making sibilant noise, Audible disapproval in the theatre, Buzzing.
H	I	S	T	O	N	E	Water soluble proteins.
H	I	S	T	O	R	Y	Chronological record of events.

1	2	3	4	5	6	7	
H	I	S	T	R	I	O	Actor.
H	I	T	C	H	E	D	Jerked, Twitched, Hooked, Connected, Hobbled, Caught, Attached.
H	I	T	T	I	N	G	Striking, Censuring, Discovering, Stressing, Emphasizing, Attacking.
H	I	T	T	I	T	E	Ancient people of Eastern Asia Minor.
H	I	V	E	B	E	E	Domestic honeybee.
H	O	A	R	D	E	D	Collected, Accumulated, Kept, Secreted, Preserved, Garnered, Stored.
H	O	A	T	Z	I	N	Crested bird of tropical S. American.
H	O	A	X	I	N	G	Deluding, Duping, Misleading, Victimizing, Fooling, Hoodwinking, Gulling, Tricking.
H	O	B	B	I	S	M	Philosophical system of Hobbes.
H	O	B	B	I	S	T	Advocate of Hobbism.
H	O	B	B	L	E	D	Restricted movement of the legs, Moved unsteadily, Hampered, Obstructed, Impeded.
H	O	B	B	L	E	R	Unlicensed boat pilot.
H	O	B	N	A	I	L	Short nail with large head to stud soles of heavy shoes, Clodhopper.
H	O	B	O	I	S	M	Condition of being a hobo.
H	O	C	K	D	A	Y	Old English festival on second Tuesday after Easter.
H	O	C	K	I	N	G	Hamstringing.
H	O	E	C	A	K	E	Small cornmeal cake cooked before an open fire.
H	O	G	B	A	C	K	Arched back, Ridge, Crest.
H	O	G	G	E	R	S	Stockings without a foot used as a gaiter.
H	O	G	G	I	N	G	Consuming voraciously.
H	O	G	G	I	S	H	Piggish, Swinish.
H	O	G	H	E	R	D	Herd of pigs.
H	O	G	P	L	U	M	Tropical American tree with yellow fruit which resembles plums.
H	O	G	S	K	I	N	Pigskin.
H	O	G	W	A	S	H	Swill, Flavourless, Insipid, Worthless.
H	O	G	W	E	E	D	Various weeds and coarse plants.
H	O	I	S	T	E	D	Raised, Lifted, Elevated, Uplifted.
H	O	I	S	T	E	R	Mechanical apparatus for lifting.
H	O	L	D	A	L	L	Travelling case.
H	O	L	D	I	N	G	Gripping, Clasping, Detaining, Enthralling, Accommodating, Reserving, Retaining.
H	O	L	I	D	A	Y	Holy day, Festivity, Celebration, Vacation.
H	O	L	I	E	S	T	Most hallowed, Most sacred, Most godly, Most pious.
H	O	L	L	A	N	D	Netherlands.
H	O	L	M	I	U	M	Trivalent metallic element.
H	O	L	M	O	A	K	Evergreen oak.
H	O	L	S	T	E	R	Leather case for a pistol.
H	O	L	Y	D	A	Y	Day of special religious significance.
H	O	M	A	G	E	R	One that pays homage.
H	O	M	B	U	R	G	Man's hat.
H	O	M	E	R	A	Y	European ray.
H	O	M	E	R	I	C	Relating to the Greek poet Homer.
H	O	M	I	N	I	D	Manlike creature.
H	O	M	O	N	Y	M	Two or more words spelled the same but different in meaning.
H	O	N	E	S	T	Y	Integrity, Truthfulness, Sincerity, Chastity, Virtue, Reliability, Dependability, Morality.
H	O	N	E	Y	E	D	Flattered, Fawned, Liquid, Mellifluent, Mellow, Golden.
H	O	N	I	T	O	N	Bobbin lace.
H	O	N	K	I	N	G	Cry of a goose.
H	O	O	D	I	N	G	Covering, Obscuring, Hiding.
H	O	O	D	L	U	M	Thug, Ruffian, Mobster, Ruffian.
H	O	O	F	I	N	G	Walking, Kicking, Trampling, Ejecting, Booting, Dancing.
H	O	O	K	I	N	G	Crooking, Stealing, Pilfering, Slicing, Goring, Leaving, Pinching, Departing.
H	O	O	P	A	S	H	Black ash.
H	O	O	P	I	N	G	Clasping, Enclosing, Surrounding.
H	O	O	T	I	N	G	Shouting loudly, Making the sound of an owl, Expressing disapproval or contempt.
H	O	P	B	A	C	K	Brewing vat.
H	O	P	B	I	N	E	Hop vine.
H	O	P	E	F	U	L	Confident, Expectant, Optimistic, Cheerful, Promising, Eager.
H	O	P	E	I	T	E	Mineral.
H	O	P	K	I	L	N	Kiln for drying hops.
H	O	P	L	I	T	E	Ancient Greek soldier in heavy armour.
H	O	P	P	I	N	G	Flitting about, Intensely active, Extremely violent, Bustling, Fussy, Lively, Popping.
H	O	P	P	L	E	D	Hobbled, Fettered.
H	O	P	P	L	E	S	Fetters.
H	O	P	T	R	E	E	Small American tree.
H	O	P	V	I	N	E	Hop plant, Twining hop plant.
H	O	P	Y	A	R	D	Hop field.
H	O	R	D	E	I	N	Prolamin found in the seeds of barley.

1	2	3	4	5	6	7	
H	O	R	D	E	U	M	Widely distributed genus of grasses, Barley.
H	O	R	I	Z	O	N	Apparent visible junction of the earth and the sky, Goal, Prospect.
H	O	R	M	O	N	E	Organic product of living cells.
H	O	R	N	E	R	O	Baker bird.
H	O	R	N	I	N	G	Cuckolding, Butting and goring with horns.
H	O	R	N	I	S	T	Performer on the French horn.
H	O	R	N	I	T	O	Mound in volcanic regions that emits smoke and vapours.
H	O	R	N	O	W	L	Horned owl.
H	O	R	R	E	N	T	Bristled, Bristling.
H	O	R	R	I	F	Y	Strike with horror, Dismay, Appal, Daunt, Shake.
H	O	S	A	N	N	A	Acclamation, Adoration, Applaud.
H	O	S	E	M	A	N	One who uses, tends or repairs hoses.
H	O	S	I	E	R	Y	Hose, Knitwear.
H	O	S	P	I	C	E	Establishment providing rest and entertainment for travellers.
H	O	S	T	A	G	E	Pledge, Security, Guarantee.
H	O	S	T	E	S	S	Woman who receives and entertains guests socially.
H	O	S	T	I	L	E	Inimicable, Unfriendly, Argumentative, Contrary, Disapproving, Unfavourable, Belligerent.
H	O	S	T	L	E	R	Groom, Stableman, One who services locomotives.
H	O	T	F	O	O	T	Hasten, Hurry, Insult, Taunt, Annoy, Goad.
H	O	T	H	E	A	D	Fiery, Impetuous or hasty person.
H	O	T	N	E	S	S	State of being hot, High temperature, Sensation of heat.
H	O	T	S	P	O	T	Spot hotter than surrounding area, Centre of night-life.
H	O	T	S	P	U	R	A rash, hotheaded impetuous man.
H	O	T	T	E	S	T	Most fiery, Most urgent, Most feverish, Most peppery, Most ardent.
H	O	T	T	R	O	D	Scottish hunt with hounds across the border.
H	O	T	W	A	L	L	Wall equipped with heating for ripening fruit.
H	O	U	B	A	R	A	Ruffled bustard.
H	O	U	G	H	E	D	Hamstrung.
H	O	U	N	D	E	D	Baited, Chased, Hunted, Badgered, Heckled, Dogged, Hectored.
H	O	U	S	I	N	G	Sheltering, Lodging, Dwelling, Enclosing, Encasing, Protecting.
H	O	V	E	R	E	D	Waited, Lingered, Suspended, Fluttered, Flickered, Floated, Cowered, State of uncertainty.
H	O	V	E	R	E	R	One that hovers.
H	O	W	B	E	I	T	Although.
H	O	W	E	V	E	R	Nevertheless, Notwithstanding, Yet, Still, How.
H	O	W	L	I	N	G	Shrieking, Wailing, Doleful sound, Rampaging, Yelping, Squealing, Bawling.
H	U	D	D	L	E	D	Crowded, Crouched, Assembled, Bunched, Consulted, Parleyed, Gathered, Advised.
H	U	D	D	L	E	R	One that huddles.
H	U	E	L	E	S	S	Colourless.
H	U	F	F	I	L	Y	In a huffy manner.
H	U	F	F	I	N	G	Blowing, Panting, Snapping, Storming, Blustering, Ranting, Flouncing, Puffing.
H	U	F	F	I	S	H	Arrogant, Sulky, Irritable.
H	U	G	G	I	N	G	Clutching, Congratulating, Cherishing, Keeping, Crushing, Crowding, Embracing, Staying close.
H	U	L	K	I	N	G	Moving ponderously, Looming, Bulky, Husky, Massive.
H	U	L	L	I	N	G	Shucking, Removing shells.
H	U	M	A	N	L	Y	Viewpoint of man, Within the range of human capacity, In a human manner.
H	U	M	B	L	E	D	Degraded, Abased, Debased, Humiliated, Lowered, Mortified, Embarrassed.
H	U	M	B	L	E	R	More humble, Meeker, Simpler, Quieter, Baser, Meaner, Lower.
H	U	M	D	R	U	M	Monotonous, Workaday, Prosaic.
H	U	M	E	R	A	L	Relating to the shoulder.
H	U	M	E	R	U	S	Long bone of the upper arm.
H	U	M	E	T	T	Y	Coupled at the extremities.
H	U	M	I	D	L	Y	Wetly.
H	U	M	M	I	N	G	Droning, Buzzing, Booming, Brisk.
H	U	M	M	O	C	K	Conical, Hillock, Slight knoll, Ridge of ice.
H	U	M	O	R	A	L	Involving a bodily humour.
H	U	M	U	L	U	S	Genus of herbaceous vines.
H	U	N	C	H	E	D	Huddled, Squatted, Pushed, Jostled, Crooked, Arched, Shoved.
H	U	N	D	R	E	D	The square of ten.
H	U	N	G	E	R	S	Longs, Desires, Hankers, Craves, Lusts, Pines.
H	U	N	K	E	R	S	Crouches, Squats.
H	U	N	T	I	N	G	Chasing, Shooting, Following, Tracking, Driving, Pursuing, Searching, Trailing.
H	U	R	D	L	E	D	Overcame, Surmounted.
H	U	R	D	L	E	R	One that runs in a hurdle race.
H	U	R	L	I	N	G	Pitching, Throwing, Flinging, Rushing, Hurtling, Impelling, Thrusting, Driving.
H	U	R	R	I	E	D	Fast, Tumultuous, Hasty, Harassed, Expedited, Rushed, Accelerated, Scurried.
H	U	R	R	I	E	R	One that hurries or causes to hurry.
H	U	R	T	F	U	L	Damaging, Painful, Harmful, Detrimental, Injurious, Aching, Afflictive, Deleterious.

7 LETTERS

1	2	3	4	5	6	7	
H	U	R	T	L	E	D	Collided, Clattered, Crashed, Rushed, Shot, Catapulted, Flung.
H	U	S	B	A	N	D	Married man, Hoarder, Save, Cultivate, Manage, Conserve.
H	U	S	H	A	B	Y	To soothe a child to sleep.
H	U	S	H	I	N	G	Lulling, Silencing, Calming, Quieting, Stilling.
H	U	S	K	I	E	S	Heavy coated Eskimo working dogs.
H	U	S	K	I	N	G	Peeling, Stripping.
H	U	S	S	I	E	S	Lewd women, Saucy girls, Minxes.
H	U	S	S	I	T	E	Member of Bohemian religious movement started by John Huss.
H	U	S	T	I	N	G	Court held before Lord Mayor of London.
H	U	S	T	L	E	D	Jostled, Shoved, Gathered, Earned, Cheated, Swindled.
H	U	S	T	L	E	R	Go-getter, Live wire, Prostitute, Pickpocket's accomplice, Swindler, Professional gambler.
H	U	T	C	H	E	D	Stored in a hutch.
H	U	T	M	E	N	T	Encampment, Hut, Prefabricated army housing unit.
H	U	T	T	I	N	G	Housing, Billetting, Sheltering.
H	Y	A	L	I	N	E	Resembling glass, Transparent, Glassy.
H	Y	A	L	I	T	E	Colourless opal, Translucent.
H	Y	A	L	O	I	D	Glassy, Transparent.
H	Y	D	N	O	I	D	Genus of fungi.
H	Y	D	R	A	N	T	Discharge pipe and valve for water usually for fire-fighting.
H	Y	D	R	A	T	E	Compound formed by union with water.
H	Y	D	R	I	A	E	Greek or Roman water jugs.
H	Y	D	R	O	I	D	Genus of polyps or jellyfishes.
H	Y	D	R	O	U	S	Watery.
H	Y	G	E	I	A	N	Relating to health or medical practice.
H	Y	G	I	E	N	E	Science of maintaining health.
H	Y	G	R	O	M	A	Cystic tumour.
H	Y	M	N	A	R	Y	Relating to a hymn.
H	Y	M	N	I	N	G	Extolling, Singing praises.
H	Y	M	N	I	S	T	Writer of hymns.
H	Y	M	N	O	D	Y	Singing, writing and stydying of hymns.
H	Y	P	E	R	O	N	Elementary particle that is greater in mass than the proton or neutron.
H	Y	P	N	O	I	D	Relating to sleep or hypnosis, Resembling moss.
H	Y	P	O	G	E	A	Underground cellar, Catacomb.
H	Y	P	O	P	U	S	Nonfeeding migratory larva of mites.
H	Y	P	O	X	I	A	A deficiency of oxygen reaching tissues of the body.
H	Y	P	P	I	S	H	Hypochondriac, Depressed, Melancholic.
H	Y	P	U	R	A	L	Lower backbone of certain fishes.
H	Y	S	T	R	I	X	Genus of perennial grasses, Bottle brush grass.

I

1	2	3	4	5	6	7	
I	A	M	B	I	C	S	Satiric verses in ancient Ionian Greek style.
I	A	M	B	I	S	T	One who writes iambic verse.
I	B	E	R	I	A	N	Relating to Spain and Portugal.
I	C	A	R	I	A	N	Rashly headlong, Incapable of fulfilling ambition.
I	C	E	B	E	L	T	Ice foot.
I	C	E	B	E	R	G	Mass of land ice broken from glacier, Emotionally cold person.
I	C	E	B	I	R	D	Sea birds that frequent ice floes.
I	C	E	B	O	A	T	Sailboat with runners to travel on ice.
I	C	E	F	A	L	L	Frozen waterfall.
I	C	E	F	L	O	E	Flat free mass of floating sea ice in Arctic regions.
I	C	E	F	O	O	T	Ice frozen on shore at or below low-water mark.
I	C	E	F	R	E	E	Port navigable all the year round, Not frozen in winter.
I	C	E	L	A	I	D	Deposited by ice.
I	C	E	P	A	C	K	Crushed ice packed in container and applied to body.
I	C	E	P	I	C	K	Hand tool with spike for chipping ice.
I	C	E	S	H	E	D	Glacial divide from which ice moves in opposite directions.
I	C	H	A	B	O	D	Used to express regret for departed glory.
I	C	H	N	I	T	E	Fossil footprint.
I	C	H	T	H	Y	S	Pagan fertility talisman resembling a fish, Christian Greek symbol for Jesus Christ.
I	C	I	N	E	S	S	A frigid quality.
I	C	T	E	R	I	C	Relating to jaundice.
I	C	T	E	R	U	S	Jaundice.
I	C	T	O	N	Y	X	Family of weasels.
I	D	A	L	I	A	N	Ancient Cyprian town that was centre of worship of Aphrodite.
I	D	E	A	L	L	Y	Perfectly, Classically, Mentally, Intellectually.

1	2	3	4	5	6	7	
I	D	E	N	T	I	C	Identical form, Duplicate, Equal, Tantamount.
I	D	I	O	T	C	Y	Utter folly.
I	D	I	O	T	I	C	Foolish, Senseless, Ridiculous, Absurd, Fatuous, Inane, Witless.
I	D	L	E	S	S	E	Idleness.
I	D	O	L	I	S	M	Worship of idols.
I	D	O	L	I	S	T	Idolater, One who worhips idols.
I	D	O	L	I	Z	E	Love to excess, Adoration, Worship, Dote.
I	D	Y	L	L	I	C	Naturally picturesque, Pleasing in simplicity, Pastoral, Poetic.
I	G	N	E	O	U	S	Relating to fire, Fiery, Suggestive of volcanoes.
I	G	N	I	T	E	D	Kindled, Excited, Inflamed, Fired, Inspired, Agitated.
I	G	N	I	T	E	R	Device for igniting fuel mixture.
I	G	N	O	B	L	E	Plebeian, Common, Lowly, Despicable, Abject, Humble, Base, Mean.
I	G	N	O	B	L	Y	In a despicable manner.
I	G	N	O	R	E	D	Neglected, Disregarded, Overlooked, Evaded, Slighted, Avoided, Forgotten, Omitted.
I	J	O	L	I	T	E	Granular igneous rock.
I	L	E	I	T	I	S	Inflammation of the ileum.
I	L	L	A	P	S	E	Influx, Accession, Flow, Glide, Slip.
I	L	L	B	R	E	D	Impolite, Impertinent, Uncivil, Rude, Loutish, Boorish, Churlish, Discourteous.
I	L	L	E	G	A	L	Unlawful, Illicit, Criminal, Wrongful, Forbidden, Outlawed, Felonious, Proscribed.
I	L	L	E	I	S	M	Excessive use of pronoun "he".
I	L	L	E	I	S	T	One who makes excessive use of pronoun "he" in reference to himself.
I	L	L	F	A	M	E	Bad repute, Notoriety, Reputation for immorality.
I	L	L	I	C	I	T	Unlawful, Criminal, Illegitimate, Illegal, Lawless, Wrongful.
I	L	L	N	E	S	S	Malady, Sickness, Infirmity, Infection, Indisposition, Disorder, Affliction, Disease.
I	L	L	O	C	A	L	Not confined to a particular locality.
I	L	L	U	D	E	D	Deceived, Deluded, Betrayed, Double-crossed, Eluded, Humbugged, Beguilded.
I	L	L	U	M	E	D	Enlightened, Illuminated, Edified, Improved, Irradiated, Uplifted.
I	L	L	U	S	E	D	Maltreated, Abused, Ill-treated, Mistreated, Misused, Outraged.
I	L	L	W	I	L	L	Malice, Hostility, Animosity, Grudge, Spite, Rancour, Venom, Malevolence.
I	L	V	A	I	T	E	Silicate of iron and calcium.
I	M	A	G	E	R	Y	Images, Statues, Ornate and florid written description.
I	M	A	G	I	N	E	Mental image, Fabricate, Suppose, Think, Guess, Fancy, Conceive, Vision.
I	M	A	G	I	N	G	Imagining.
I	M	A	M	A	T	E	Region ruled by an imam.
I	M	B	I	B	E	D	Soaked, Assimilated, Absorbed, Drunk, Swallowed, Tippled, Quaffed, Guzzled.
I	M	B	I	B	E	R	One that drinks usually to excess.
I	M	B	O	S	O	M	Embosom, Caress.
I	M	B	O	U	N	D	Embound, Impound.
I	M	B	R	U	E	D	Drenched.
I	M	B	R	U	T	E	Brutalize, Sink to the level of a brute, Become bestial.
I	M	B	U	I	N	G	Permeating, Impregnating, Infusing, Penetrating deeply.
I	M	I	T	A	N	T	Counterfeit, Substitute.
I	M	I	T	A	T	E	Copy, Reproduce, Mimic, Mock, Attempt, Parody, Endeavour, Duplicate.
I	M	M	E	N	S	E	Huge, Colossal, Enormous, Gigantic, Mighty, Monstrous, Tremendous, Vast.
I	M	M	E	R	G	E	Immerse, Plunge into.
I	M	M	E	R	S	E	Plunge, Dip, Include, Sink, Bury, Absorb, Saturate, Soak.
I	M	M	I	X	E	D	Mixed, Intimately, Commingled.
I	M	M	O	R	A	L	Wicked, Licentious, Impure, Unchaste, Wrong, Evil, Sinful, Vicious.
I	M	M	U	R	E	D	Enclosed, Imprisoned, Incarcerated, Entombed, Cooped, Fenced, Penned, Walled.
I	M	P	A	I	N	T	Paint, Depict.
I	M	P	A	L	E	D	Pierced, Deflated by biting wit, Skewered, Lanced, Transfixed, Perforated, Stabbed.
I	M	P	A	N	E	L	Enroll, Join on a panel.
I	M	P	A	S	S	E	Blind alley, Deadlock, Predicament, Boxed in, Plight.
I	M	P	A	S	T	E	Make into a paste, Decorate with paste.
I	M	P	A	S	T	O	Thick application of paint to raise surface for decoration.
I	M	P	A	V	I	D	Fearless, Undaunted.
I	M	P	E	A	C	H	Accuse, Charge, Arraign, Criminate, Inculpate, Tax, Indict.
I	M	P	E	A	R	L	Adorn with pearls.
I	M	P	E	D	E	D	Interfered, Blocked, Obstructed, Hindered, Detracted, Embarrassed, Disconcerted, Rattled.
I	M	P	E	R	I	L	Endanger, Jeopardize, Compromise, Hazard, Menace, Risk, Peril.
I	M	P	E	T	U	S	Impulse, Incentive, Stimulus, Encouragement, Goad, Incitement, Motivation, Spur.
I	M	P	I	E	T	Y	Irreverence, Ungodliness, Profanity, Undutiful.
I	M	P	I	N	G	E	Strike, Dash, Contact, Encroach, Infringe, Impress Collide, Touch upon.
I	M	P	I	O	U	S	Irreverent, Profane, Irreligious, Blasphemous, Contempt, Sacrilegious, Depredation.
I	M	P	L	A	N	T	Insert, Inculcate, Instill, Infuse, Ingrain, Impregnate, Pervade, Inspire.
I	M	P	L	E	A	D	Accuse, Impeach, Sue, Prosecute, Incorporate, Institute a law suit.
I	M	P	L	I	E	D	Included, Suggested, Hinted, Inferred, Insinuated, Indicated, Called, Pointed.

1	2	3	4	5	6	7	
I	M	P	L	O	R	E	Beseech, Entreat, Pray, Beg, Crave, Importune, Plead, Appeal.
I	M	P	O	N	E	D	Staked, Wagered.
I	M	P	O	S	E	D	Charged, Imputed, Subjected, Inflicted, Prescribed, Dictated, Deposited, Placed.
I	M	P	O	S	E	R	Stoneman.
I	M	P	O	U	N	D	Confine, Enclose, Appropriate, Seize and hold, Confiscate.
I	M	P	R	E	G	N	Impregnate.
I	M	P	R	E	S	S	Engrave, Inscribe, Affect, Influence, Inspire, Pound, Stamp, Fix.
I	M	P	R	E	S	T	Loan or advance of money.
I	M	P	R	I	N	T	Impress, Stamp, Inscribe, Indent, Print, Influence.
I	M	P	R	O	V	E	Increase, Augment, Enlarge, Intensify, Employ, Use, Occupy, Help.
I	M	P	U	L	S	E	Thrust, Impetus, Drive, Push, Incentive, Motive, Goad, Motivation.
I	M	P	U	T	E	D	Accused, Credited, Ascribed, Imparted, Gave, Reckoned, Considered, Regarded.
I	N	A	N	D	I	N	Inbreeding.
I	N	A	N	E	L	Y	Insubstantially, Vacantly, Silly, Fatuously, Insipidly.
I	N	A	N	I	T	Y	Emptiness, Hollowness, Shallowness, Vapid, Pointless, Foolish, Stupidity, Trivial.
I	N	A	P	T	L	Y	Ineptly, Inadequately, Unskilfully, Awkwardly, Insipidly, Inexpertly, Untimely, Improperly.
I	N	B	O	A	R	D	Toward centre line of ship or aircraft.
I	N	B	O	U	N	D	Inward bound.
I	N	B	R	E	A	K	Inroad, Invasion, Incursion.
I	N	B	R	E	E	D	Produce, Generate, Crossbreed, Breed together.
I	N	B	R	I	N	G	To bring into court.
I	N	B	U	I	L	T	Built in, Fixture.
I	N	C	E	N	S	E	Perfumed smoke, Fragrance, Homage, Flattery, Burn, Inflame, Arouse, Excite.
I	N	C	H	A	S	E	Enchase, Engrave.
I	N	C	H	I	N	G	Moving by small degrees, Sparingly, Dealing out small amounts.
I	N	C	I	P	I	T	Beginning, Explicit, Introduction.
I	N	C	I	S	E	D	Cut-in, Carved, Engrave, Margined.
I	N	C	I	S	O	R	Cutting tooth.
I	N	C	I	T	E	D	Instigated, Fomented, Abetted, Provoked, Inflamed, Roused, Agitated, Encouraged.
I	N	C	I	T	E	R	Instigator, Agitator.
I	N	C	I	V	I	L	Rude, Barbarous.
I	N	C	L	A	S	P	Enclasp, Embrace.
I	N	C	L	I	N	E	Bow, Lean, Interest, Influence, Tend, Slant, Bias, Dispose.
I	N	C	L	O	S	E	Enclose, Envelop, Wrap.
I	N	C	L	U	D	E	Comprehend, Contain, Embrace, Encompass, Involve, Embody, Admit, Cover.
I	N	C	O	M	E	R	Immigrant, Stranger.
I	N	C	R	U	S	T	Encrust, Coat.
I	N	C	U	B	U	S	Nightmare, Oppress, Burden.
I	N	C	U	R	V	E	Curve, Crook.
I	N	C	U	S	E	D	Punched, Stamped, Impressed.
I	N	D	I	C	A	N	Colourless crystalline glucoside, Indigo.
I	N	D	I	C	E	S	Plural of index.
I	N	D	I	C	I	A	Indications, Signs, Tokens, Criterions, Identifications.
I	N	D	I	T	E	D	Composed, Wrote, Dictated.
I	N	D	I	T	E	R	Author, Writer, Composer.
I	N	D	O	O	R	S	Inside a building.
I	N	D	O	R	S	E	Endorse, Countersign, Ratify.
I	N	D	O	X	Y	L	Yellow crystalline phenolic compound.
I	N	D	R	A	F	T	Inland, Inward flow of current of air or water.
I	N	D	R	A	W	N	Drawn in, Reserved, Taciturn, Egocentric.
I	N	D	U	C	E	D	Influenced, Persuaded, Introduced, Caused, Aroused, Prevailed, Incited, Motivated.
I	N	D	U	C	E	R	Part that feeds air into impeller of fan.
I	N	D	U	I	N	G	Enduing, Endowing, Investing.
I	N	D	U	L	G	E	Gratify, Undertake, Pamper, Humour, Spoil, Mollycoddle, Satisfy, Regale.
I	N	D	W	E	L	L	Inner activating power.
I	N	E	A	R	T	H	Bury, Inter.
I	N	E	P	T	L	Y	Inappropriately, Inadequately, Awkwardly, Clumsily, Inexpertly, Unseemly.
I	N	E	R	T	I	A	Inertness, Inactivity, Sleepy, Idleness, passiveness, Quietly, Impotence, Stolidness.
I	N	E	R	T	L	Y	Passively, Lifelessly, Stolidly, Idly, Sleepily.
I	N	E	X	A	C	T	Indefinite, Indeterminate, Indistinct, Inaccurate, Untrue.
I	N	F	A	M	E	D	Defamed, Libelled, Slandered.
I	N	F	A	N	C	Y	Minority, Early childhood, Immaturity, Early period of existence.
I	N	F	A	N	T	A	Daughter of king and queen of Spain and Portugal.
I	N	F	A	N	T	E	Any son other than the eldest of the king and queen of Spain and Portugal.
I	N	F	A	R	C	T	Coagulation necrosis of tissue resulting from thrombus or embolus.
I	N	F	A	U	S	T	Unlucky, Unpropitious.
I	N	F	E	R	N	O	Fire, Conflagration, Holocaust, Hell, Abyss, Hades, Perdition, Blazes.

1	2	3	4	5	6	7	Definition
I	N	F	I	D	E	L	Non-Christian, Unbeliever, Heathen, Pagan, Profane.
I	N	F	I	E	L	D	Cultivated field.
I	N	F	I	X	E	D	Instilled, Fastened, Inculcated, Impressed, Pierced.
I	N	F	L	A	M	E	Intensify, Rouse, Kindle, Irritate, Exasperate, Incense, Provoke, Enrage.
I	N	F	L	A	T	E	Swell, Distend, Elate, Expand, Extend, Amplify.
I	N	F	L	E	C	T	Bend, Curve, Conjugate, Decline, Modulate.
I	N	F	L	I	C	T	Impose, Afflict, Give, Administer, Deal, Deliver, Strike, Punish.
I	N	F	U	L	A	E	Tokens, Badges, Fillets.
I	N	F	U	S	E	D	Introduced, Insinuated, Suggested, Inspired, Imbued, Animated, Ingrained, Filled.
I	N	F	U	S	E	R	Device for infusing tea leaves.
I	N	G	E	N	U	E	Debutante, Soubrette, Youthful character, Sweet.
I	N	G	E	S	T	A	Food and other materials taken into the body by way of the digestive tract.
I	N	G	O	I	N	G	Entering, Penetrating, Thorough.
I	N	G	R	A	F	T	Engraft, Instil, Introduce.
I	N	G	R	A	I	N	Saturate, Imbue, Infuse.
I	N	G	R	A	T	E	An ungrateful person.
I	N	G	R	E	S	S	Entrance, Ingredient, Access, Door, Admission, Entry, Way, Admittance.
I	N	G	R	O	S	S	Engross, Monopolize, Absorb, Copy.
I	N	H	A	B	I	T	Occupy, Dwell, Live, Populate, Tenant, Settle, Abide.
I	N	H	A	L	E	D	Breathed in, Drawn in, Swallowed, Inspired, Consumed.
I	N	H	A	L	E	R	Device by means of which various materials can be inhaled.
I	N	H	A	U	S	T	Inhale, Imbibe.
I	N	H	E	R	E	D	Belonged, Inherent, Fixed, Element, Consisted, Resided, Dwelled, Existed.
I	N	H	E	R	I	T	Possess, Receive, Succeed.
I	N	H	I	B	I	T	Forbid, Interdict, Repress, Restrain, Retard, Prevent, Reduce, Prohibit.
I	N	H	U	M	A	N	Cruel, Barbarous, Savage, Cold, Impersonal, Mechanical, Superhuman, Fierce.
I	N	I	T	I	A	L	Incipient, First, Beginning, Introductory, Elementary, Early, Basic, Primary.
I	N	J	O	I	N	T	Join.
I	N	J	U	R	E	D	Harmed, Hurt, Damaged, Impaired, Marred, Offended, Spoiled, Wronged.
I	N	J	U	R	E	R	One that injures.
I	N	K	H	O	R	N	Small portable container for ink.
I	N	K	L	I	N	G	Undertone, Rumour, Hint, Intimation, Notion, Suggestion, Clue, Hint.
I	N	K	W	E	L	L	Container for writing ink.
I	N	L	A	W	E	D	Placed under protection of the law.
I	N	L	A	Y	E	R	Inner layer or sheathing.
I	N	M	E	A	T	S	Inner parts of an animal used for human consumption.
I	N	N	E	R	V	E	Invigorate, Stimulate.
I	N	N	I	N	G	S	Division of a cricket match.
I	N	Q	U	E	S	T	Inquiry, Investigation, Judicial examination.
I	N	Q	U	I	R	E	Investigate, Examine, Interrogate, Question, Ask, Query, Probe, Search.
I	N	Q	U	I	R	Y	Research, Investigation, Inquisition, Inquest, Probe, Search, Delving, Scrutiny.
I	N	S	C	U	L	P	Engrave, Sculpture.
I	N	S	H	O	R	E	Situated or carried toward shore.
I	N	S	I	D	E	R	Recognized member of an organization.
I	N	S	I	G	H	T	Discernment, Penetration, Understanding, Inspection, Look, Wisdom, Sagacity, Intuition.
I	N	S	I	P	I	D	Tasteless, Flavourless, Vapid, Flat, Inane, Banal, Uninteresting, Commonplace.
I	N	S	N	A	R	E	Ensnare.
I	N	S	O	O	T	H	Truly, Actually, Factually.
I	N	S	P	E	C	T	Scrutinize, Examine, Check, Study, Survey, Review, Inquire, Question.
I	N	S	P	I	R	E	Encourage, Impel, Motivate, Inhale, Arouse, Provoke, Produce, Incite.
I	N	S	T	A	L	L	Induct, Initiate, Inaugurate, Invest, Ensconce, Settle.
I	N	S	T	A	N	T	Moment, Pressing, Urgent, Insistent, Current, Immediate, Direct, Occasion.
I	N	S	T	A	T	E	Install, Invest, Endow, Bestow, Confer.
I	N	S	T	E	A	D	Substitute, In lieu, Alternative, Rather.
I	N	S	T	E	E	P	Steep, Soak, Imbue, Impregnate.
I	N	S	T	I	L	L	Implant, Introduce, Drop by drop, Inseminate.
I	N	S	T	Y	L	E	Call, Denominate.
I	N	S	U	L	A	R	Insulated, Isolated, Detached, Prejudice, Illiberal, Limited, Narrow, Circumscribed.
I	N	S	U	L	I	N	Protein, Pancreatic, Hormone used to control diabetes.
I	N	S	U	R	E	D	Assured, Underwritten, Ensured, Secured, Guarded, Protected.
I	N	S	U	R	E	R	One that guarantees, One that contracts to indemnify.
I	N	T	E	G	E	R	Any of the natural numbers, Complete entity.
I	N	T	E	N	S	E	Considerable, Concentrated, Desperate, Fierce, Furious, Vehement, Vicious.
I	N	T	E	R	I	M	Meantime, Interval, Break, Compromise, Temporary supply.
I	N	T	E	R	N	E	Intern, Detain, Restrain, Confine.
I	N	T	H	R	A	L	Enthrall, Fascinate, Enslave, Subjugate.
I	N	T	I	T	L	E	Entitle, Name, Designate, Allow, Enable.

1	2	3	4	5	6	7	
I	N	T	O	N	E	D	Recited in sing-song tones, Chanted.
I	N	T	R	A	N	T	Entrant, Student, Lay preacher.
I	N	T	R	E	A	T	Entreat, Beg, Appeal, Beseech.
I	N	T	R	O	I	T	Psalm, Anthem or hymn at the beginning of Communion.
I	N	T	R	U	D	E	Encroach, Trespass, Infringe, Invade, Insinuate, Impose, Presume, Interject.
I	N	T	R	U	S	T	Entrust, Commit, Commend, Relegate.
I	N	T	W	I	N	E	Entwine, Coil, Wreathe.
I	N	T	W	I	S	T	Entwist, Spiral, Curl.
I	N	U	L	A	S	E	An enzyme.
I	N	U	R	I	N	G	Accustoming, Accruing, Hardening, Training, Using, Disciplining, Familiarizing.
I	N	U	T	I	L	E	Useless, Unusable.
I	N	V	A	D	E	D	Overran, Assaulted, Infringed, Entrenched, Trespassed, Permeated, Penetrated, Engulfed.
I	N	V	A	D	E	R	Plunderer, Trespasser.
I	N	V	A	L	I	D	Indefensible, Unjustified, Irrational, Illogical, Void, Inadequate, Weak, Unreasonable.
I	N	V	E	I	G	H	Rail, Object, Expostulate, Protest, Remonstrate, Except.
I	N	V	E	R	S	E	Opposite, Reverse, Transpose, Turn, Revert, Change.
I	N	V	I	O	U	S	Lacking roads, Trackless.
I	N	V	I	T	E	D	Enticed, Tempted, Encouraged, Welcomed, Courted, Called, Solicited, Lured.
I	N	V	I	T	E	R	One that invites.
I	N	V	O	I	C	E	Inventory, Bill, Account, Reckoning, Score, Statement.
I	N	V	O	K	E	D	Entreated, Implored, Conjured, Petitioned, Enforced, Implemented, Caused, Excited.
I	N	V	O	K	E	R	Petitioner, One that invokes.
I	N	V	O	L	V	E	Engage, Employ, Envelop, Shroud, Entangle, Implicate, Entwine, Connect.
I	N	W	A	R	D	S	Towards centre or inside, Homeward, Internally, Toward inner being.
I	N	W	E	A	V	E	Insert, Interlace.
I	N	W	O	V	E	N	Interwoven, Entwined.
I	O	D	I	Z	E	D	Treated with iodine.
I	O	N	I	Z	E	D	Converted into ions.
I	P	O	M	A	E	A	Herbaceous vine, Morning glory, Sweet potato, Convolvulus.
I	P	S	E	I	T	Y	Individual identity.
I	R	A	C	U	N	D	Irascible, Easily provoked to anger.
I	R	A	N	I	A	N	Relating to Iran.
I	R	E	N	I	C	S	Theology concerned with securing Christian unity.
I	R	I	C	I	S	M	Irishism.
I	R	I	D	I	Z	E	Make irridescent.
I	R	I	S	H	R	Y	Irish character or trait.
I	R	K	S	O	M	E	Fatiguing, Wearisome, Stupid, Drudging, Exhausting, Irritating, Tedious, Boring.
I	R	O	N	I	E	S	Sarcasms, Mockery, Ridicule.
I	R	O	N	I	N	G	Smoothing or pressing with an iron.
I	R	O	N	I	S	T	One given to irony.
I	S	A	G	O	G	E	Scholarly introduction to a branch of study or research.
I	S	C	H	I	U	M	Group of bones of the pelvic area.
I	S	H	M	A	E	L	Son of Abraham.
I	S	I	D	I	U	M	Lichens.
I	S	L	A	M	I	C	Relating to Islam.
I	S	L	E	M	A	N	Islander.
I	S	O	B	A	S	E	Imaginary line on a map for land measurements.
I	S	O	B	A	T	H	Imaginary line on a chart for sea measurements.
I	S	O	C	Y	A	N	Containing the univalent group.
I	S	O	D	O	N	T	Having very even teeth.
I	S	O	D	R	I	N	Insecticide.
I	S	O	E	T	E	S	Marsh ferns.
I	S	O	G	A	M	Y	Gamete reproduction.
I	S	O	G	R	A	M	Line on map linking areas with similar temperature, pressure or rainfall.
I	S	O	H	Y	E	T	Line on map linking similar rainfall figures.
I	S	O	L	A	T	E	Insulate, Segregate, Separate, Sequester, Abstract, Detach, Divide, Remove.
I	S	O	N	E	P	H	Line on map connecting points with similar percentage of cloudiness.
I	S	O	N	O	M	Y	Equal in the eyes of the law.
I	S	O	P	A	C	H	Line connecting points of equal thickness of geological strata.
I	S	O	P	O	D	A	Parasitical crustaceans.
I	S	O	T	A	C	H	Line on map connecting points of equal wind speed.
I	S	O	T	O	N	E	Nuclides having same number of neutrons.
I	S	O	T	O	P	E	Species of atom of the same chemical element.
I	S	O	T	R	O	N	Electromagnetic apparatus.
I	S	O	Z	O	N	E	Animals, plant or group common to two or more life regions.
I	S	R	A	E	L	I	Native of Israel.
I	S	S	U	A	N	T	Rising upward.

1	2	3	4	5	6	7	Definition
I	S	S	U	I	N	G	Emerging, Accuring, Resulting, Emitting, Discharging, Emanating, Publishing.
I	S	T	H	M	U	S	Strip of land surrounded on three sides by water.
I	T	A	C	I	S	M	Particular Greek pronunciation.
I	T	A	L	I	A	N	Relating to Italy.
I	T	A	L	I	C	S	Written characters in a particular way to give emphasis.
I	T	C	H	I	N	G	Irritating, Vexing, Craving, Urging, Longing, Seething, Lusting.
I	T	E	M	I	Z	E	Analyse, Specify, Inventory, Specialize, List, Document, Count, Cite.
I	T	E	R	A	N	T	Repetitive, Reiterate.
I	T	E	R	A	T	E	Repeat, Recapitulate.
I	V	O	R	O	I	D	Resembling ivory.
I	X	O	D	O	I	D	Relating to ticks.

J

1	2	3	4	5	6	7	Definition
J	A	B	B	I	N	G	Stabbing, Thrusting, Poking, Punching, Prodding.
J	A	C	A	M	A	R	Tropical insect-catching bird.
J	A	C	I	N	T	H	Tawny colour.
J	A	C	K	A	S	S	Donkey, Fool, Dolt.
J	A	C	K	D	A	W	Bird related to a crow and is a clever mimic.
J	A	C	K	I	N	G	Raising, Increasing, Bolstering, Reprimanding, Lifting, Tilting.
J	A	C	K	P	O	T	Winning combination at cards or on a slot machine.
J	A	C	K	T	A	R	Sailor.
J	A	C	O	B	I	N	Dominican, Political extremist or radical.
J	A	C	O	B	U	S	Unite.
J	A	C	O	N	E	T	Lightweight cotton cloth.
J	A	D	E	D	L	Y	Worn out, Exhausted, Satiated.
J	A	D	E	I	T	E	Monoclinic mineral.
J	A	G	G	I	N	G	Stabbing, Jabbing, Pricking, Thrusting, Slashing.
J	A	G	H	I	R	E	Grant of public revenues to a person with the power to collect same.
J	A	H	V	I	S	T	Jahwist, Relating to the Old Testament.
J	A	I	L	I	N	G	Imprisoning, Gaoling.
J	A	I	N	I	S	M	Religion of India.
J	A	L	A	P	I	N	Cathartic glucosidic constituent of true jalap resin and scammony resin.
J	A	L	O	U	S	E	Suspect, Surmise, Jealous.
J	A	M	A	D	A	R	Officer in the Indian army.
J	A	M	B	O	N	E	Hand of cards in euchre.
J	A	M	M	I	N	G	Squeezing, Obstructing, Packing, Crushing, Pushing, Ramming, Pressing, Squashing.
J	A	N	E	I	T	E	A fan of Jan Austen.
J	A	N	G	A	D	A	Brazilian raft of balsa wood, Catamaran.
J	A	N	G	L	E	D	Babbled, Chattered, Wrangled, Altercated, Clashed, Conflicted.
J	A	N	G	L	E	R	One that jangles.
J	A	N	I	T	O	R	Doorkeeper, Cleaner of offices or flats.
J	A	N	N	O	C	K	Upright, Decent.
J	A	N	U	A	R	Y	First month of ancient Roman year.
J	A	R	G	O	O	N	Colourless or pale yellow or smoky zircon.
J	A	R	H	E	A	D	Army mule.
J	A	R	K	M	A	N	Counterfeiter of licences, passes and documents.
J	A	R	R	I	N	G	Grating, Rattling, Clashing, Bickering, Unsettling, Colliding, Jangling, Shaking.
J	A	S	M	I	N	E	Plant with sweet scented flowers.
J	A	S	P	E	R	Y	Resembling or containing jasper.
J	A	U	N	D	E	R	Prattle, Gabble.
J	A	U	N	T	E	D	Trudged, Tripped, Journeyed, Strolled, Ambled.
J	A	U	P	I	N	G	Splashing, Spattering.
J	A	V	E	L	I	N	Light spear cast by hand.
J	A	W	B	O	N	E	Mandible.
J	A	W	F	O	O	T	Maxilliped, One of three pairs of appendages of a crustacean.
J	A	W	R	O	P	E	Rope holding the jaws of the gaff to the mast.
J	A	Y	W	A	L	K	Crossing the street without due care, Wandering on the street in an irresponsible manner.
J	A	Z	Z	I	N	G	Enlivening, Popularizing, Accelerating, Gadding.
J	E	A	L	O	U	S	Vigilant, Envious, Resentful, Suspicious, Possesive, Covetous, Grudging, Mistrustful.
J	E	C	O	R	I	N	Complex lipoidal substance isolated from liver tissue.
J	E	E	R	I	N	G	Deriding, Mocking, Scoffing, Ridiculing, Flouting, Jesting, Quipping, Sneering.
J	E	J	U	N	U	M	First two fifths of the small intestine.
J	E	L	L	I	E	D	Gelatinized, Set.
J	E	L	L	I	F	Y	Coagulate, Clot, Congeal, Gell, Gelatinize, Reduce to slackness.
J	E	M	A	D	A	R	Officer in the Indian army.

1	2	3	4	5	6	7	
J	E	O	F	A	I	L	Mistake or oversight in legal pleading.
J	E	O	P	A	R	D	Jeopardize, Endanger, Hazard.
J	E	R	K	I	N	G	Snapping, Twitching, Yanking, Lurching, Dragging, Wrenching.
J	E	R	V	I	N	E	Crystalline alkaloid.
J	E	S	S	A	M	Y	Jasmine, Dandy, Fop.
J	E	S	T	I	N	G	Taunting, Mocking, Quipping, Ridiculing, Bantering, Wisecracking, Joking.
J	E	T	T	I	E	D	Projected, Jutted.
J	E	T	T	I	N	G	Intruding, Encroaching, Gushing, Spurting, Spouting.
J	E	W	E	L	R	Y	Ornamental pieces such as rings, brooches and necklaces.
J	E	W	S	E	A	R	Widely distributed edible fungus.
J	E	Z	E	B	E	L	Impudent, Shameless, Wanton woman.
J	I	B	B	I	N	G	Balking, Demurring, Gagging, Straining, Stumbling.
J	I	B	B	O	O	M	A spar which serves as an extension of the bowsprit.
J	I	B	D	O	O	R	A door made flush with the wall.
J	I	G	A	J	O	G	Jig-jog, Bounce jerkily.
J	I	G	G	E	R	S	Repeated tugs.
J	I	G	G	I	N	G	Jerking up and down.
J	I	G	G	I	S	H	Suitable for a jig.
J	I	G	G	L	E	D	Moved with quick little jerks.
J	I	L	T	I	N	G	Cast off, Rejecting.
J	I	M	C	R	O	W	Offensive description of a negro.
J	I	M	J	A	M	S	Delirium tremens, Depressed condition, Apprehension, Jitters.
J	I	N	G	L	E	D	Tingled, Tinkled, Clinked, Chinked, Clattered.
J	I	N	G	L	E	T	Ball clapper of a sleigh bell.
J	I	N	K	I	N	G	Dodging, Twisting, Weaving, Cheating, Tricking.
J	I	T	T	E	R	S	Extreme nervousness, Sense of panic.
J	I	T	T	E	R	Y	Suffering from the jitters.
J	O	B	B	E	R	Y	Official corruption, Political intrigue or graft.
J	O	B	B	I	N	G	Doing odd jobs or casual work, Speculating.
J	O	B	L	E	S	S	Unemployed.
J	O	C	U	L	A	R	Jesting, Witty, Playful, Merry, Humorous, Jovial, Comic, Laughable.
J	O	G	G	I	N	G	Jostling, Nudging, Reminding, Trudging, Agitating, Shaking, Plodding, Journeying.
J	O	G	G	L	E	D	Jostled, Jiggled.
J	O	G	G	L	E	S	Masonry joints.
J	O	G	T	R	O	T	Slow regular gait, Easygoing action.
J	O	I	N	D	E	R	Conjunction, Joining, Putting together.
J	O	I	N	E	R	Y	Carpentry.
J	O	I	N	I	N	G	Associating, Fastening, Uniting, Coupling, Binding, Bracketing, Combining, Linking.
J	O	I	N	T	E	D	United, Combined, Articulated, Coalesced.
J	O	I	N	T	E	R	Tool for smoothing joints or filing points.
J	O	I	N	T	L	Y	Together, Unitedly, Mutually.
J	O	I	S	T	E	D	To supply with supporting material.
J	O	L	L	I	E	R	Person who flatters or banters, Worker on a shoe machine.
J	O	L	L	I	F	Y	Carouse, Merrymaker.
J	O	L	L	I	L	Y	Cheerfully.
J	O	L	L	I	T	Y	Gaiety, Merriment, Jocularity, Cheer, Joviality, Frolic, Hilarity.
J	O	L	T	I	N	G	Jerking, Bouncing, Colliding, Crashing, Bumping.
J	O	N	Q	U	I	L	Perennial bulbous herb with sweet scented flowers.
J	O	O	K	E	R	Y	Trickery, Swindling, Cheating, Deceiving.
J	O	T	T	I	N	G	Writing down, Brief notes.
J	O	U	N	C	E	D	Fell, Bounced, Collided, Jarred, Bumped.
J	O	U	R	N	A	L	Logbook, Ledger, Magazine, Newspaper, Periodical, Diary, Shaft that turns on a bearing.
J	O	U	R	N	E	Y	Trip, Travel, Expedition, Excursion, Tour, Cruise, Voyage, Pilgrimage, Safari.
J	O	U	S	T	E	D	Tilted, Competed, Contest between lance-carrying knights on horseback.
J	O	Y	A	N	C	E	Pleasure, Delight, Jubilation, Gaiety, Fruition, Festivity.
J	O	Y	R	I	D	E	Action taken with no heed of consequences or danger.
J	U	B	I	L	E	E	Completion of significant specified number of years.
J	U	D	A	I	C	A	Written material devoted to Judaism.
J	U	D	A	I	S	M	Religion of the Jewish people.
J	U	D	A	I	S	T	Believer in Judaism.
J	U	D	A	I	Z	E	Become Jewish.
J	U	D	C	O	C	K	Jacksnipe, Sandpiper.
J	U	D	G	I	N	G	Trying, Condemning, Governing, Deciding, Determining, Inferring, Ruling, Umpiring.
J	U	G	A	T	E	D	Conjoined, Overlapping, Paired.
J	U	G	G	I	N	G	Stewing game meat, Confining.
J	U	G	G	I	N	S	Simpleton, Dolt, Fool.
J	U	G	G	L	E	D	Cheated, Tricked, Jiggled, Beguiled, Betrayed, Deluded, Misled.

1	2	3	4	5	6	7	
J	U	G	G	L	E	R	One practiced in manual dexterity.
J	U	G	G	L	E	S	Blocks of timber of specified size.
J	U	G	L	A	N	S	Walnut trees.
J	U	G	U	L	A	R	Relating to throat and neck.
J	U	G	U	L	U	M	Breast and neck region of birds.
J	U	J	I	T	S	U	Method of self-defence without use of weapons.
J	U	J	U	T	S	U	same as JUJITSU.
J	U	K	E	B	O	X	Mechanical record player that operates by placing a coin in a slot.
J	U	M	B	L	E	D	Disordered, Muddled, Confused, Disorganized, Disturbed, Tangled.
J	U	M	E	L	L	E	Objects made in pairs.
J	U	M	P	I	N	G	Springing, Leaping, Hopping, Skipping, Risking, Anticipating, Clearing, Rising.
J	U	N	I	P	E	R	Coniferous tree.
J	U	N	K	I	N	G	Abandoning, Scrapping, Jettisoning, Rejecting.
J	U	N	K	M	A	N	A person who deals in discarded and second-hand articles.
J	U	P	I	T	E	R	A planet.
J	U	R	A	L	L	Y	Legally, Rightly, Lawfully.
J	U	R	Y	M	A	N	Person summoned to serve on a jury.
J	U	S	S	I	V	E	Command.
J	U	S	T	I	C	E	Fairness, Integrity, Honesty, Equity, Impartiality.
J	U	S	T	I	F	Y	Vindicate, Confirm, Support, Verify, Explain, Maintain, Claim, Defend.
J	U	T	T	I	N	G	Bulging, Pouching, Projecting, Protruding, Overhanging.
J	U	V	E	N	A	L	Youth.
J	Y	N	G	I	N	E	Genus of woodpeckers.

K

K	A	B	B	A	L	A	Occult or secret matter, Group of persons plotting intrigue.
K	A	C	H	I	N	A	Rain-making spirit of the Hopi Indians.
K	A	D	D	I	S	H	Ancient Jewish prayer.
K	A	I	N	I	T	E	A natural salt.
K	A	K	A	T	O	E	Cockatoo.
K	A	L	E	N	D	S	Calends, First day of the ancient Roman month.
K	A	L	M	U	C	K	Member of a Buddhist Mongol people.
K	A	M	E	R	A	D	Companion, Comrade.
K	A	M	P	O	N	G	Malay village.
K	A	N	D	Y	A	N	Relating to Kandy, Sri Lanka.
K	A	N	T	I	S	T	Follower of Kant.
K	A	N	T	I	S	M	Kantionism, A philosophy.
K	A	R	A	I	T	E	An adherent of Karaism.
K	A	R	A	K	U	L	Astrakhan, Persian lamb, Broadtail.
K	A	R	A	T	A	S	Genus of tropical American plants.
K	A	T	Y	D	I	D	Grasshopper.
K	E	B	B	O	C	K	A whole cheese.
K	E	C	K	L	E	D	Prevented chafing by wrapping around with rope.
K	E	D	G	I	N	G	Moving a ship to another position.
K	E	D	L	O	C	K	White mustard.
K	E	E	K	I	N	G	Peeping.
K	E	E	L	A	G	E	Port toll.
K	E	E	L	I	N	G	Large codfish.
K	E	E	L	M	A	N	Crew member of a keel-boat.
K	E	E	L	S	O	N	Strengthening plates of a ship.
K	E	E	N	I	N	G	Mourning, Wailing.
K	E	E	P	I	N	G	Preserving, Maintaining, Tending, Holding, Detaining, Storing, Saving, Reserving.
K	E	I	T	L	O	A	Black rhinocerous.
K	E	N	N	I	N	G	Knowing, Recognising, Little.
K	E	N	O	S	I	S	Renouncing wordly things to follow teachings of Christ.
K	E	N	O	T	I	C	same as KENOSIS.
K	E	N	T	I	S	H	Relating to the county of Kent, England.
K	E	R	A	S	I	N	Cerebroside occurring in Gaucher's disease.
K	E	R	A	T	I	N	Fibrous proteins forming hair and horn.
K	E	R	M	E	S	S	Dutch fair.
K	E	R	N	I	N	G	Forming kernels.
K	E	R	N	I	T	E	Mineral that is an important source of borax.
K	E	S	T	R	E	L	Small falcon.
K	E	T	C	H	U	P	Catsup, Tomato sauce.
K	E	T	O	S	I	S	Abnormal increase of ketone bodies in the body.

1	2	3	4	5	6	7	
K	E	T	O	T	I	C	Relating to Ketosis.
K	E	V	A	L	I	N	Someone liberated from mundane things.
K	E	Y	B	O	L	T	Bolt secured at one end by a key.
K	E	Y	C	O	L	D	Lacking warmth.
K	E	Y	H	O	L	E	Hole in lock for inserting a key, Intimate details revealed in a scandal magazine.
K	E	Y	N	O	T	E	Fundamental tone of a scale.
K	E	Y	S	E	A	T	A groove in machine to receive a key.
K	E	Y	W	O	R	D	Word that is important for understanding, especially in a discussion.
K	H	A	L	I	F	A	Caliph.
K	H	A	M	S	I	N	Hot wind blowing from Sahara desert.
K	H	A	N	A	T	E	Under the rule of a khan.
K	H	E	D	I	V	E	Viceroy of Sultan of Turkey who ruled Egypt in late nineteent century.
K	I	B	B	L	E	D	Ground coarsely.
K	I	B	B	U	T	Z	Collective farm in Israel.
K	I	B	I	T	K	A	Russian covered vehicle on wheels or runners.
K	I	C	K	I	N	G	Striking with foot, Thrusting, Driving, Rebelling, Raising objections, Protesting, Opposing.
K	I	C	K	O	F	F	Begin the proceedings or game.
K	I	D	D	I	E	S	Small children.
K	I	D	D	I	N	G	Deceiving, Fooling, Joking, Hoaxing, Tricking, Duping, Fooling, Gulling.
K	I	D	S	K	I	N	Leather from skin of young goat.
K	I	K	U	M	O	N	Chrysanthemum.
K	I	L	L	D	E	E	Plover.
K	I	L	L	I	C	K	Anchor.
K	I	L	L	I	N	G	Murder, Homicide, Manslaughter, Foul play, Slaughtering, Butchering, Slaying, Tiring.
K	I	L	L	J	O	Y	One that spoils fun, Pessimist.
K	I	L	L	O	C	K	Small anchor.
K	I	L	N	D	R	Y	To season timber in a kiln.
K	I	L	O	V	A	R	Volt-amperes unit.
K	I	L	T	I	N	G	Gathering up the skirts.
K	I	N	D	E	S	T	Fondest, Friendliest, Most gentle, Most lenient, Most charitable.
K	I	N	D	L	E	D	Ignited, Aroused, Inspired, Instituted, Illuminated, Inflamed, Provoked, Instigated.
K	I	N	D	L	E	R	Kindling.
K	I	N	D	R	E	D	People, Population, Congenial, Related, Affinity.
K	I	N	E	T	I	C	Active, Lively, Energizing, Dynamic.
K	I	N	G	C	U	P	Buttercup, Marsh marigold.
K	I	N	G	D	O	M	Realm, Empire, Principality, Monarchy, Dominion.
K	I	N	G	L	E	T	Weak or petty king, Ruler of a small territory, Small birds.
K	I	N	G	P	I	N	Chief executive in a company, Decision-taking official.
K	I	N	K	I	N	G	Winding, Twisting, Looping.
K	I	N	L	E	S	S	Having no relatives.
K	I	N	S	H	I	P	Close relationship.
K	I	N	S	M	A	N	Someone related by blood or marriage.
K	I	P	S	K	I	N	Skin of a young calf.
K	I	R	G	H	I	Z	Mongolian race.
K	I	R	I	M	O	N	An imperial badge of Japan.
K	I	R	T	L	E	D	Wrapped in a skirt.
K	I	S	S	I	N	G	Pressing with the lips, Caressing with the lips, Gently touching.
K	L	I	P	D	A	S	Hyrax of Southern Africa.
K	L	I	P	P	E	N	Isolated outcrop of rock.
K	N	A	C	K	E	R	One that buys years old domestic animals usually horses for use as fertiliser and cat's meat.
K	N	A	P	P	E	D	Rapped, Snapped, Cropped.
K	N	A	P	P	E	R	One that dresses flints.
K	N	A	R	R	E	D	Gnarled, Knotty.
K	N	A	V	E	R	Y	Fraud, Trickery, Roguery.
K	N	A	V	I	S	H	Dishonest, Fraudulent, Rascally.
K	N	E	A	D	E	D	Manipulated, Mixed, Massaged.
K	N	E	A	D	E	R	One that mixes dough.
K	N	E	E	C	A	P	Patella.
K	N	E	L	L	E	D	Tolled, Warned.
K	N	E	S	S	E	T	Israeli Parliament.
K	N	I	F	I	N	G	Stabbing, Slashing, Wounding, Trimming, Cutting, Undermining.
K	N	I	T	T	E	D	United, Joined, Consolidated, Interlocked, Knotted, Interlaced, Contracted, Linked.
K	N	I	T	T	L	E	Provoke, Sting, Nettle, Incite, Irritate.
K	N	O	B	B	E	D	Ending in a knob, Provided with knobs.
K	N	O	B	B	L	E	A small lump.
K	N	O	B	B	L	Y	Covered with small knobs.
K	N	O	C	K	E	D	Rapped, Collided, Bumped, Bustled, Struck, Tapped, Criticized, Blamed.

1	2	3	4	5	6	7	Definition
K	N	O	C	K	E	R	Critic, Faultfinder, Ornamental fixture on a door, Troublemaker.
K	N	O	C	K	O	N	Line of play in rugby, Result of collision of a neutron.
K	N	O	C	K	U	P	Improvised, Rouse, Summon, Destroy, Make, Achieve, Disturb, Bother.
K	N	O	L	L	E	D	Mound, Hillock.
K	N	O	P	P	E	R	An oak gall used in tanning and dyeing.
K	N	O	T	T	E	D	Tied, Fastened, Connected, Entangled, Netted, Laced, Meshed, Tangled.
K	N	O	W	A	L	L	One who thinks he knows everything, Wiseacre.
K	N	O	W	H	O	W	Expertise to complete the work, Ability, Expertness, Adroitness, Dexterity, Skill.
K	N	O	W	I	N	G	Shrewd, Astute, Appreciating, Apprehending, Grasping, Understanding, Discerning.
K	N	U	C	K	L	E	Yield, Capitulate, Joint where ends of two bones meet, Defer, Submit.
K	O	L	A	N	U	T	Seed of kola nut that is chewed as a condiment and stimulant.
K	O	L	K	H	O	Z	Collective farm of U.S.S.R.
K	O	M	A	T	I	K	Eskimo sledge.
K	O	R	A	N	I	C	Relating to the Koran.
K	O	T	O	W	E	D	Cowered, Cringed, Grovelled, Toadied, Fawned.
K	O	U	M	I	S	S	Fermented beverage made from milk.
K	R	E	M	L	I	N	Central government of U.S.S.R.
K	R	I	M	M	E	R	Gray fur resembling astrakhan.
K	R	I	S	H	N	A	Hindu god.
K	R	Y	P	T	O	N	Colourless inert gaseous element.
K	U	M	Q	U	A	T	Small yellow-orange citrus fruit.
K	U	R	B	A	S	H	Hide whip used for punishment.
K	U	R	D	I	S	H	Relating to the Kurds.
K	U	W	A	I	T	I	Native of Kuwait.
K	Y	A	N	I	T	E	Cyanite.
K	Y	A	N	I	Z	E	Preserving wood.

L

1	2	3	4	5	6	7	Definition
L	A	B	A	R	U	M	Imperial standard of Roman Emperors.
L	A	B	I	A	T	E	Having lips.
L	A	B	R	O	I	D	Fish resembling wrasse.
L	A	C	C	A	S	E	Blue copper-containing oxidase.
L	A	C	C	A	T	E	Having a lacquered or varnished finish.
L	A	C	E	R	T	A	Genus of lizards.
L	A	C	I	N	I	A	Segment of a leaf.
L	A	C	K	I	N	G	Wanting, Failing, Needing, Requiring, Missing.
L	A	C	L	A	K	E	Indian lake.
L	A	C	O	N	I	C	Spartan, Curt, Terse, Undemonstrative, Pithy, Brief, Concise, Brusque.
L	A	C	Q	U	E	R	Spirit varnish, Shellac, Synthetic coating.
L	A	C	Q	U	E	Y	Lackey, Flunky, Footman, Servant, Toady.
L	A	C	T	A	S	E	Enzyme found in yeasts and intestines of young mammals.
L	A	C	T	A	T	E	Salt of lactic acid, To secrete milk.
L	A	C	T	E	A	L	Lymphatic vessels.
L	A	C	T	I	F	Y	Transform by lactic fermentation.
L	A	C	T	O	N	E	Ester of hydroxy carboxylic acids.
L	A	C	T	O	S	E	Sugar present in milk.
L	A	C	T	U	C	A	Genus of milky-juiced herbs.
L	A	C	U	N	A	E	Gap, Hole, Defect, Flaw, Break.
L	A	C	U	N	A	L	Lacunary.
L	A	C	U	N	A	R	Recessed panel forming part of a vault or ceiling.
L	A	D	A	N	U	M	Oleoresin obtained from rock roses.
L	A	D	L	I	N	G	Dipping with a ladle.
L	A	D	Y	B	U	G	Small hemispherical beetle.
L	A	D	Y	D	A	Y	Annunciation day.
L	A	D	Y	I	S	H	Somewhat like a lady.
L	A	G	G	A	R	D	Loiterer, Lingerer, Backward, Behindhand, Dilatory, Sluggish, Slow.
L	A	G	G	I	N	G	Covering, Insulating.
L	A	G	O	P	U	S	Genus of game birds comprising ptarmigans and red grouse.
L	A	I	C	I	S	M	Nonclerical administration.
L	A	I	C	I	T	Y	Control by the laity.
L	A	K	E	L	E	T	A little lake.
L	A	L	I	Q	U	E	Decorated glassware with specialised ornamentation.
L	A	L	L	A	N	D	Lowland.
L	A	M	A	I	S	M	Form of Buddhism.
L	A	M	A	I	S	T	An adherent of Lamaism.

1	2	3	4	5	6	7	
L	A	M	B	A	L	E	English feast held about Whitsuntide.
L	A	M	B	E	N	T	Wavering, Flickering, Bright, Brilliant, Luminous, Lustrous, Beaming, Radiant.
L	A	M	B	E	R	T	Measurement of unit of brightness.
L	A	M	B	I	N	G	Giving birth to a lamb.
L	A	M	B	K	I	N	Little lamb, Innocent child.
L	A	M	E	L	L	A	Thin plate or scale.
L	A	M	E	T	E	R	Cripple.
L	A	M	I	N	A	R	Flake, Layer.
L	A	M	M	I	N	G	Thrashing, Striking, Whacking, Scramming, Fleeing.
L	A	M	P	A	R	A	Fishing net resembling a purse.
L	A	M	P	I	N	G	Shining, Flashing.
L	A	M	P	I	O	N	Small lamp.
L	A	M	P	L	I	T	Lighted by a lamp.
L	A	M	P	O	O	N	Ridicule, Satirize.
L	A	M	P	R	E	Y	Eel-like fish.
L	A	N	A	T	E	D	Woolly.
L	A	N	C	E	R	S	Old fashioned dance.
L	A	N	C	I	N	G	Piercing, Opening, Launching, Hurling, Flinging, Transfixing, Spearing, Impaling.
L	A	N	D	I	N	G	Disembarking, Setting down, Winning, Gaining, Capturing, Arriving, Settling, Acquiring.
L	A	N	D	L	E	R	Austrian dance.
L	A	N	D	M	A	N	Countryman.
L	A	N	D	T	A	X	Assessment for tax.
L	A	N	G	A	H	A	Snake.
L	A	N	G	I	T	E	Copper based mineral.
L	A	N	G	L	E	Y	Measurement of a unit of solar radiation.
L	A	N	G	U	E	D	Heraldic animal with a visible tongue.
L	A	N	G	U	E	T	Latchet, Something resembling a tongue.
L	A	N	G	U	I	D	Slack, Weak, Listless, Slow, Lackadaisical, Spiritless, Enervated, Limp.
L	A	N	G	U	O	R	Lassitude, Dreaminess, Sluggishness, Dullness, Stagnation, Letharge, Torpor, Slumber.
L	A	N	I	A	R	Y	Canine.
L	A	N	I	A	T	E	To tear in pieces.
L	A	N	K	I	E	R	Scantier, Droopier, Thinner, Leaner, Bonier, Skinnier, More gangling.
L	A	N	O	L	I	N	Cream refined from wool grease.
L	A	N	T	A	N	A	Genus of verbena shrubs.
L	A	N	T	E	R	N	Portable lamp.
L	A	N	Y	A	R	D	Rope for fastening something in a ship.
L	A	O	C	O	O	N	Someone who struggles valiantly against great difficulties.
L	A	O	T	I	A	N	Inhabitant of Laos.
L	A	P	I	L	L	I	Volcanic cinder.
L	A	P	I	L	L	O	Small fragment of lava.
L	A	P	P	I	N	G	Surrounding, Swathing, Winding, Nestling, Folding.
L	A	P	P	I	S	H	Relating to Lapland.
L	A	P	S	I	N	G	Backsliding, Subsiding, Relapsing, Terminating, Forfeiting, Slipping, Disappearing, Passing.
L	A	P	U	T	A	N	Absurd, Visionary.
L	A	P	W	I	N	G	Crested plover.
L	A	R	C	E	N	Y	Embezzlement, Theft, Pinch, Purloining, Stealing, Thieving.
L	A	R	D	I	N	G	Dressing meat before cooking with fat.
L	A	R	D	O	I	L	Olein expressed from lard and used for lubrication.
L	A	R	D	O	O	N	Strip of fat pork for larding.
L	A	R	G	E	L	Y	Extensively, Abundantly, Generally, Comprehensively, Chiefly, Pompously, Mainly, Mostly.
L	A	R	G	E	S	S	Liberal, Giving assistance, Gratuities, Tipping, Free gift, Support, Benevolence.
L	A	R	G	I	S	H	Rather large.
L	A	R	I	G	O	T	Flageolet.
L	A	R	K	I	N	G	Frolicsome, Giddy, Teasing, Sporting.
L	A	R	M	I	E	R	Drip.
L	A	R	N	I	T	E	Mineral calcium silicate.
L	A	R	V	A	T	E	Covered, Concealed, Masked.
L	A	S	A	G	N	A	Broad flat noodles baked and served with a savoury sauce.
L	A	S	H	I	N	G	Whipping, Binding with rope, cord or chain.
L	A	S	H	K	O	?	Relating to city of Lashkar, India.
L	A	S	S	O	E	D	Caught with a running noose.
L	A	S	S	O	E	S	Rope or thong of leather with a running noose.
L	A	S	T	A	G	E	Duty paid at port for loading a ship.
L	A	S	T	I	N	G	Enduring, Durable, Abiding, Continuance, Duration, Permanent, Stable, Eternal.
L	A	T	A	K	I	A	Turkish smoking tobacco.
L	A	T	C	H	E	D	Fastened with a latch.
L	A	T	C	H	E	S	Devices for fastening doors.

1	2	3	4	5	6	7	
L	A	T	C	H	E	T	Thong, Loop, Gurnard fish.
L	A	T	E	B	R	A	White yolk in a bird's egg.
L	A	T	E	N	C	Y	Lying dormant.
L	A	T	E	R	A	L	Relating to the side, Horizontal.
L	E	T	T	E	R	N	Lectern.
L	A	T	H	I	N	G	Lining with laths.
L	A	T	R	A	N	T	Barking, Snarling, Complaining.
L	A	T	R	I	N	E	Pit closet.
L	A	T	T	I	C	E	Framework made by criss-crossing strips of wood or metal.
L	A	T	V	I	A	N	Relating to Latvia.
L	A	U	D	I	N	G	Acclaiming, Extolling, Praising, Glorifying, Blessing, Adoring, Admiring, Venerating.
L	A	U	G	H	E	D	Expressed mirth, Chortled, Chuckled, Giggled, Tittered, Whooped.
L	A	U	N	D	E	R	Wash clothes, Purify, Cleanse, Remove dirt, Sluice.
L	A	U	N	D	R	Y	Room or building set aside for washing clothes.
L	A	U	R	E	L	S	Crown of laurel leaves for victor or conqueror.
L	A	U	R	I	T	E	Mineral of iron-black ruthenium sulfide.
L	A	V	O	L	T	A	Early French dance.
L	A	W	B	O	O	K	Book dealing with laws.
L	A	W	C	A	L	F	Calfskin used for binding lawbooks.
L	A	W	L	E	S	S	Without laws, Unruly, Disorderly.
L	A	W	L	O	R	D	Member of House of Lords acting as appeal judge.
L	A	W	S	U	I	T	Case before a court.
L	A	X	N	E	S	S	Looseness, Carelessness, Slackness.
L	A	Y	B	A	C	K	Receding nose and undershot jaw, as in a bulldog.
L	A	Y	D	A	Y	S	Delay day in port.
L	A	Y	E	R	E	D	Arranged in layers.
L	A	Y	E	T	T	E	Complete outfit of clothing awaiting birth of baby.
L	A	Y	L	O	C	K	Lilac.
L	A	Y	L	O	R	D	A lord who is not a law-lord.
L	A	Z	A	R	E	T	Hospital for contagious diseases, Quarantine ship.
L	A	Z	A	R	U	S	Leprous beggar.
L	A	Z	I	E	S	T	Idlest, Most sluggish, Most indolent, Most slothful.
L	A	Z	Y	B	E	D	Small plot on rocky ground tilled by hand.
L	E	A	C	H	E	D	Extracted, Removed, Drawn out, Separated.
L	E	A	D	I	N	G	Taking, Conveying, Guiding, Directing, Shepherding, Escorting, Foremost, Principal.
L	E	A	D	O	F	F	Starting, Opening, Commence, Embark, Inter, Inaugurate, Launch, Start.
L	E	A	F	A	G	E	Foliage, Umbrage, Verdure.
L	E	A	F	F	A	T	Abdominal and kidney fat of a hog.
L	E	A	F	I	N	G	Producing leaves, Covering with leaves, Overlapping.
L	E	A	F	L	E	T	Folded sheet containing printed or written advertisement or instructions.
L	E	A	G	U	E	D	United in a league, Combined.
L	E	A	G	U	E	R	Old Dutch unit of liquid capacity, Member of a league.
L	E	A	K	A	G	E	Process of leaking.
L	E	A	K	I	N	G	Escaping through a hole, Urinating, Becoming public information.
L	E	A	N	E	S	T	Poorest, Scantiest, Most gaunt, Most scrawny, Skinniest.
L	E	A	N	I	N	G	Sloping, Inclination, Penchant, Flair, Propensity, Proclivity.
L	E	A	P	I	N	G	Hopping, Vaulting, Rushing, Bounding, Springing, Jumping, Throbbing, Bouncing.
L	E	A	R	N	E	D	Pedantic, Bookish, Scholastic, Erudite, Cultivated, Scholarly, Cultured.
L	E	A	R	N	E	R	Student, Apprentice, Trainee.
L	E	A	S	H	E	D	Controlled, Restrained, Hampered, Curbed, Shackled, Fettered.
L	E	A	S	I	N	G	Letting, Holding, Renting.
L	E	A	T	H	E	R	Skin, Hide, Thrash.
L	E	A	V	I	N	G	Bequeathing, Devising, Deserting, Desisting, Abandoning, Forsaking, Ceasing.
L	E	C	T	E	R	N	Reading desk in church or lecture hall.
L	E	C	T	U	R	E	Rebuke, Reprimand, Talk, Address, Speak.
L	E	E	C	H	E	D	Cured, Healed, Drained, Exhausted.
L	E	E	C	H	E	E	Litchi, Fruit of a Chinese tree.
L	E	E	F	A	N	G	Traveller.
L	E	E	R	I	L	Y	In a distrustful way, Warily.
L	E	E	R	I	N	G	Slinking, Sneaking, Giving a lascivious look, Sneering, Ogling.
L	E	E	W	A	R	D	Downwind.
L	E	G	A	L	L	Y	Lawfully, Legitimately.
L	E	G	A	T	E	E	One to whom a legacy is bequeathed.
L	E	G	B	A	I	L	Flight, Escape by flight.
L	E	G	G	I	N	G	One that pushes a barge through a tunnel.
L	E	G	G	I	N	S	Covering made for the legs.
L	E	G	H	O	R	N	From the city of Leghorn, Italy, Straw hat, Domestic fowl.

1	2	3	4	5	6	7	Definition
L	E	G	I	B	L	E	Capable of being read, Decipherable.
L	E	G	I	B	L	Y	Clearly written, Easily understood.
L	E	G	I	R	O	N	Shackles, Fetters.
L	E	G	I	T	I	M	Portion of estate reserved for the children upon the death of the Father.
L	E	G	L	E	S	S	Having no legs.
L	E	G	P	U	L	L	Deception, Hoax.
L	E	G	U	M	E	S	Vegetables such as beans and peas.
L	E	I	S	T	E	R	Fish spear with barbed prongs.
L	E	I	S	U	R	E	Spare time, Rest, Ease, Relaxation, Repose.
L	E	M	M	A	T	A	Word or phrase explained in a glossary.
L	E	M	M	I	N	G	Small rodent.
L	E	M	N	I	A	N	Relating to the island of Lemnos.
L	E	M	P	I	R	A	Basic monetary unit of Honduras.
L	E	M	U	R	E	S	Hostile spirits of the unburied dead exorcised in ancient Roman times.
L	E	N	D	I	N	G	Furnishing, Affording, Providing, Supplying, Accommodating, Offering, Money given.
L	E	N	G	T	H	Y	Overlong, Extended, Drawn-out, Prolonged, Protracted, Dragging.
L	E	N	I	E	N	T	Assuasive, Emollient, Indulgent, Merciful, Forbearing, Soft, Tolerant, Charitable.
L	E	N	T	I	G	O	Freckle.
L	E	N	T	I	S	K	Mastic tree.
L	E	N	T	O	I	D	Lens-shaped structure.
L	E	O	N	E	S	E	Native of León.
L	E	O	N	I	N	E	Relating to a lion.
L	E	O	P	A	R	D	Strong feline with a tawny hide speckled with black rosettes.
L	E	P	R	O	M	A	Nodular lesion of leprosy.
L	E	P	R	O	S	E	Scurfy, Scaly.
L	E	P	R	O	S	Y	Chronic disease resulting in deformities and mutilations.
L	E	P	R	O	U	S	Infected with leprosy.
L	E	P	T	O	M	E	Part of the mestome that conducts food materials.
L	E	S	B	I	A	N	Erotic, Homosexual relations between women.
L	E	S	O	T	H	O	Formerly Basuto (Southern Africa).
L	E	T	C	H	E	S	Bogs, Swamps, Cravings, Sexual desires.
L	E	T	D	O	W	N	Lower, Forsake, Betray, Disappoint, Fail, Dilute, Relax, Discouragement.
L	E	T	H	E	A	N	Relating to forgetfulness.
L	E	T	T	I	N	G	Making, Causing, Renting, Leasing, Releasing, Spilling, Allowing, Permitting.
L	E	T	T	I	S	H	Latvian.
L	E	T	T	U	C	E	Common garden vegetable used in salads.
L	E	U	C	I	N	E	White crystalline amino acid.
L	E	U	C	I	T	E	White or gray mineral of potassium aluminium silicate.
L	E	U	C	O	M	A	Dense white opacity in the cornea of the eye.
L	E	V	A	T	O	R	Muscle that raises a body part.
L	E	V	E	L	E	R	Scraper to level the ground.
L	E	V	E	L	L	Y	In a level manner.
L	E	V	E	R	E	D	Worked with a lever, Operated as a lever.
L	E	V	E	R	E	T	Young hare.
L	E	V	I	T	I	C	Relating to the Levites.
L	E	V	Y	I	N	G	Imposing, Collecting, Exacting, Making, Enlisting, Waging, Enforcing, Taxing.
L	E	X	I	C	A	L	Vocabulary as opposed to grammar.
L	E	X	I	C	O	N	Dictionary, Words in alphabetical order.
L	I	A	I	S	O	N	Relationship, Intercommunication, Intrigue, Illicit sexual affair.
L	I	A	S	S	I	C	Geological timetable.
L	I	B	B	I	N	G	Castrating.
L	I	B	E	R	A	L	Abundant, Bountiful, Ample, Large, Full, Conservative, Radical, Licentious.
L	I	B	E	R	T	Y	Freedom, Unrestrained privilege, Exemption, Franchise, Leave, Independence, Permission.
L	I	B	R	A	R	Y	Building or room given over to books, Collection of reference material.
L	I	B	R	A	T	E	Value of a pound a year, Vibrate, Balance, Weigh.
L	I	C	E	N	S	E	Permission, Responsibility, Grant, Permit, Allow, Let, Accredit, Enable.
L	I	C	E	N	C	E	Freedom, Liberty, Laxity, Slackness, Relaxation.
L	I	C	H	O	W	L	Barn owl.
L	I	C	I	T	L	Y	Legally.
L	I	C	K	I	N	G	Passing the tongue over, Beating, Thrashing, Defeating, Overcoming, Whipping, Overwhelming.
L	I	E	A	B	E	D	Someone who stays in bed later than is normal practice.
L	I	F	T	M	A	N	One who operates a lift/elevator.
L	I	F	T	I	N	G	Elevating, Rescinding, Plagiarizing, Transporting, Stealing, Rising, Hoisting, Warping.
L	I	G	A	T	E	D	Tied with rope, bandage or strap.
L	I	G	H	T	E	D	Brightened, Ignited, Kindled, Illuminated, Animated, Burning, Flaring, Blazing.
L	I	G	H	T	E	N	Illuminate, Enlighten, Brighten, Lessen, Gladden, Cheer, Alleviate, Relieve.
L	I	G	H	T	E	R	Trivial, Inconsiderable, Faint, Indistinct, Frivolous, Giddy, Buoyant, Fluffy.

1	2	3	4	5	6	7	
L	I	G	H	T	L	Y	Buoyantly, Gently, Easily, Readily, Nimbly, Swiftly, Smoothly, Faintly.
L	I	G	N	I	F	Y	Convert into wood.
L	I	G	N	I	T	E	Variety of coal.
L	I	G	R	O	I	N	Petroleum naptha product.
L	I	G	U	L	A	R	Shaped like a strap.
L	I	K	A	B	L	E	Amiable, Attractive disposition, Lovable.
L	I	K	E	N	E	D	Represented, Compared, Equated, Matched, Parallel.
L	I	L	Y	P	A	D	Water lily leaf.
L	I	M	A	C	E	L	Small internal shell of slugs.
L	I	M	A	C	O	N	Plane curve drawn inside a circle.
L	I	M	B	A	T	E	Having a different coloured border or edging.
L	I	M	B	I	N	G	Dismember, To strip felled tree of its branches.
L	I	M	E	P	I	T	Limestone quarry.
L	I	M	I	N	A	L	Relating to the threshold of the subconscious, Minimal quantity.
L	I	M	I	T	E	D	Prescribed, Confined, Restricted, Definite, Ineffectual, Qualified, Fixed, Precise.
L	I	M	I	T	E	R	Electronic device for limiting electrical oscillation.
L	I	M	N	I	N	G	Drawing or painting on a canvas or flat surface, Delineate.
L	I	M	N	I	T	E	Bog iron ore.
L	I	M	P	I	N	G	Hobbling, Faltering, Stumbling, Proceeding with difficulty, Shuffling, Staggering.
L	I	M	P	K	I	N	Wading bird.
L	I	N	C	T	U	S	Syrupy expectorant.
L	I	N	E	A	G	E	Origin, Ancestry, Background, Descent, Pedigree, Family, Clan, Race.
L	I	N	E	A	T	E	Marked with lines or stripes.
L	I	N	E	M	A	N	Electrician, Post office employee working with communication links.
L	I	N	E	O	U	T	A certain movement in the game of rugby.
L	I	N	G	U	A	L	Relating to the tongue.
L	I	N	K	A	G	E	United, Fitted together, Bond, Relationship, Coupled, Connected, Linked, Joined.
L	I	N	K	B	O	Y	Torch bearing attendant for night travellers.
L	I	N	K	I	N	G	Coupling, Connecting, Looping, Associating, Combining, Uniting, Joining, Relating.
L	I	N	K	M	A	N	Doorman or porter who attends to vehicles of patrons or guests.
L	I	N	N	A	E	A	Genus of creeping evergreen shrubs.
L	I	N	O	X	Y	N	Elastic solid from linseed oil that is used in adhesives.
L	I	N	S	A	N	G	Genus of Asian mammals resembling long-tailed cats.
L	I	N	S	E	E	D	Seed of the flax plant.
L	I	O	N	C	E	L	Heraldic representation of a small lion.
L	I	O	N	C	U	B	Very young lion.
L	I	O	N	E	S	S	Female lion.
L	I	O	N	I	S	E	To lionize.
L	I	O	N	I	Z	E	Extoll, Laud, Praise, Eulogize, Glorify, Magnify.
L	I	P	E	M	I	A	Excess fat or cholestrol in the blood.
L	I	P	P	I	N	G	Deformed bone at joint as in arthritis.
L	I	Q	U	A	T	E	Liquefy, Dissolve, Separate.
L	I	Q	U	E	F	Y	Reduce to a liquid state, Dissolve, Flux, Fuse, Melt, Run, Thaw.
L	I	Q	U	E	U	R	Alcoholic drink made by distilling flavouring in spirit.
L	I	R	E	L	L	A	Spore-bearing depression of a lichen with a furrow along the middle.
L	I	S	P	I	N	G	Stammering, Stuttering, Pronouncing sibilants imperfectly.
L	I	S	S	O	M	E	Slender, Lithe, Nimble, Supple.
L	I	S	T	F	U	L	Attentive.
L	I	S	T	I	N	G	Tilting, Slanting, Inclining, Sloping, Itemizing, Enumerating, Specifying, Recording.
L	I	T	E	R	A	L	Actual, Obvious, Verbatim, Plain, Unadorned, Prosaic, Exact, Unimaginative.
L	I	T	H	E	L	Y	Flexibly, Resiliently, Leanly, Serenely, Gently.
L	I	T	H	I	U	M	Soft silver-white univalent element that is the lightest metal known.
L	I	T	H	O	I	D	Resembling a stone.
L	I	T	H	O	P	S	Genus of Southern African succulent with a stonelike body.
L	I	T	O	T	E	S	Figure of speech, Understatement, Inverted compliment.
L	I	T	T	E	R	Y	Untidy, Covered with litter.
L	I	T	U	A	T	E	Forked.
L	I	T	U	I	T	E	Fossil of mollusk.
L	I	T	U	R	G	Y	Ritual, Rite, Service or ceremonial worship.
L	I	V	A	B	L	E	Bearable, Endurable, Viable, Habitable, Tenantable, Snug, Acceptable, Tolerable.
L	I	V	E	N	E	D	Enlivened, Animated, Inspired, Encouraged, Quickened.
L	I	V	E	O	A	K	American evergreen oak.
L	I	V	E	R	E	D	Thickened, Rubberized, Gellitinized.
L	L	A	N	E	R	O	South American herdsman.
L	O	A	D	I	N	G	Burdening, Packing, Stowing, Encumbering, Oppressing, Taxing, Conveying, Adulterating.
L	O	A	F	I	N	G	Idling, Dawdling, Lazing, Loitering, Lolling.
L	O	A	M	I	N	G	Filling in with soil.

1	2	3	4	5	6	7	
L	O	A	N	I	N	G	Lending, Advancing, Borrowing.
L	O	A	T	H	E	D	Detested, Abhorred, Hated, Rejected, Repudiated, Spurned.
L	O	A	T	H	E	R	One that hates or loathes something.
L	O	A	T	H	L	Y	Loathsome, Repulsive, Detestable.
L	O	B	B	I	E	D	Tried to obtain favours or attempted to influence policy decision.
L	O	B	B	I	E	S	Corridors, Halls, Vestibules, Passageways, Foyers.
L	O	B	B	I	N	G	Throwing, Hitting, Moving slowly.
L	O	B	C	O	C	K	Lout, Stupid person, Uncouth person.
L	O	B	E	L	E	T	Small lobe.
L	O	B	E	L	I	A	Genus of herbaceous plant.
L	O	B	I	P	E	D	Having lobate toes.
L	O	B	S	T	E	R	Large marine decapod crustaen used for food.
L	O	B	U	L	A	R	Resembling a lobule.
L	O	B	U	L	E	S	Lobe, Lobule.
L	O	B	W	O	R	M	Lugworm.
L	O	C	A	L	L	Y	Nearby, In area of origin, In the vicinity of a particular place.
L	O	C	A	T	E	D	Settled, Situated, Positioned, Sited, Set, Stationed, Determined position.
L	O	C	A	T	E	R	One that discovers or decides position.
L	O	C	K	A	G	E	Toll paid when passing along locks of a canal.
L	O	C	K	I	A	N	Theories and philosophy of John Locke.
L	O	C	K	I	N	G	Fastening, Securing, Overcoming, Fixing, Holding fast.
L	O	C	K	J	A	W	Early symptom of tetanus.
L	O	C	K	M	A	N	Lock keeper on a canal.
L	O	C	K	O	U	T	To prevent striking employees from entering place of employment.
L	O	C	K	R	A	M	Coarse French linen fabric.
L	O	C	O	I	S	M	Disease of horses, cows and sheep caused by poisoning with locoweeds.
L	O	C	U	L	A	R	Composed of loculi.
L	O	C	U	L	U	S	Small cavity, Cell, Egg sac, Small sinus in a bone.
L	O	C	U	S	T	S	Grasshoppers.
L	O	D	G	I	N	G	Dwelling, Habitation, Camp, Accommodation, Apartment, Flat, Room, Suite.
L	O	F	T	I	E	R	Nobler, Prouder, Higher, More grandiose, More pretentious.
L	O	F	T	I	L	Y	In a supercilious or proud manner, Scornfully, Stately.
L	O	F	T	I	N	G	Promoting, Lifting, Raising, Hitting, Throwing.
L	O	G	B	O	O	K	Official record of speed, performance or ownership.
L	O	G	C	H	I	P	Ship's instrument to gauge velocity of a current.
L	O	G	G	A	T	S	Loggets, English game where pieces of wood are thrown at a stake in the ground.
L	O	G	G	I	N	G	Sawing into logs, Recording speed, progress or performance, Arriving at a pre-destined place.
L	O	G	I	C	A	L	Rational, Intelligent, Sensible, Sound, Analytical, Clear, Cogent, Valid.
L	O	G	L	I	N	E	Line with a log-chip attached for measuring speed of ship.
L	O	G	R	E	E	L	Small wooden reel for holding logline.
L	O	G	R	O	L	L	Influencing passage of legislation.
L	O	G	S	H	I	P	Log-chip.
L	O	G	W	O	O	D	Hard wood from Central America and West Indies from which a dye is prepared.
L	O	K	S	H	E	N	Noodles.
L	O	L	L	A	R	D	Religious sect in Netherlands in the fourteenth century.
L	O	L	L	I	N	G	Drooping, Dangling, Slouching, Slumping, Idling, Lazing, Loafing, Lounging.
L	O	M	A	T	I	A	Chilean and Australian trees from which furniture dyes are extracted.
L	O	M	B	A	R	D	Banker, Moneylender, Pawnbroker.
L	O	N	G	A	G	O	In the past.
L	O	N	G	B	O	W	Extra long bow drawn by hand.
L	O	N	G	E	S	T	Lengthiest, Tallest, Largest, Farthest.
L	O	N	G	H	O	P	Special flight of a cricket ball.
L	O	N	G	I	N	G	Craving, Desiring, Lusting, Pining, Yearning, Aching, Dreaming, Hankering.
L	O	N	G	I	S	H	Not excessively long.
L	O	N	G	L	E	G	Position of a fielder in cricket.
L	O	N	G	O	I	L	Varnish with high content of drying oil.
L	O	N	G	R	U	N	Time for results to be evaluated.
L	O	O	K	I	N	G	Examining, Seeking, Expecting, Observing, Watching, Noticing, Perceiving, Staring.
L	O	O	K	O	U	T	Sentry, Sentinel, Guard, Scout, Watchman, Crow's nest, Watchtower, Observer.
L	O	O	K	S	E	E	Investigation, Inspection.
L	O	O	M	I	N	G	Appearing, Emerging, Showing, Gathering, Lowering, Towering, Impending, Threatening.
L	O	O	P	E	R	S	Hairless caterpillars.
L	O	O	P	I	N	G	Curving, Connecting, Ringing, Coiling, Circling, Hooking, Girdling, Surrounding.
L	O	O	S	E	L	Y	Slackly, Vaguely.
L	O	O	S	I	N	G	Releasing, Undoing, Unbinding, Dissolving, Relaxing, Detaching, Freeing, Discharging.
L	O	O	T	I	N	G	Plundering, Sacking, Robbing, Ransacking, Relieving, Rifling.
L	O	P	P	I	N	G	Trimming, Curtailing, Cutting, Drooping, Flopping, Bounding.

1	2	3	4	5	6	7	
L	O	R	D	I	N	G	Putting on airs, Knighting, Ennobling, Swaggering, Pretending.
L	O	R	E	L	E	I	Siren, Seductress, Temptress.
L	O	R	E	T	T	E	Courtesan.
L	O	R	G	N	O	N	Lorgnette, Eyeglasses with a handle.
L	O	R	I	M	E	R	Loriner, Saddler and harness-maker.
L	O	S	A	B	L	E	Easily mislaid, Capable of being lost.
L	O	T	T	E	R	Y	Game of chance.
L	O	T	T	I	N	G	Allotting, Apportioning, Casting lots, Drawing lots.
L	O	U	D	E	S	T	Noisiest, Hoarsest, Coarsest, Most offensive.
L	O	U	N	D	E	R	Severe blow.
L	O	U	N	G	E	D	Loafed, Lolled, Sauntered, Dawdled, Lazed, Idled, Loitered, Reclined.
L	O	U	N	G	E	R	Idler, Loafer.
L	O	U	S	I	L	Y	Contemptibly, Meanly, Vilely, Abominably, Repulsively.
L	O	U	T	I	S	H	Coarse, Boorish.
L	O	V	A	B	L	E	Attracting love.
L	O	V	E	M	A	N	Cleavers.
L	O	V	E	R	L	Y	In the manner of a lover.
L	O	W	B	E	L	L	Small bell around the neck of a sheep or cow.
L	O	W	B	O	R	N	Of humble birth.
L	O	W	B	R	E	D	Boorish, Churlish, Cloddish, Vulgar, Loutish, Uncivilised, Uncultured.
L	O	W	B	R	O	W	Lacking strong intellectual interests.
L	O	W	C	O	S	T	Cheap, Inexpensive, Popular, Reasonable.
L	O	W	D	O	W	N	Inside information, Actual facts, Base, Despicable, Mean, Scurvy, Servile, Wretched.
L	O	W	E	R	E	D	Degraded, Diminished, Decreased, Depreciated, Devaluated, Depressed, Submerged.
L	O	W	L	A	N	D	Level country.
L	O	W	L	I	F	E	Wretch, Villian, Rascal, Rogue, Scoundrel, Knave.
L	O	W	L	I	L	Y	Humbly, Meekly, Humility.
L	O	W	N	E	S	S	Dejection, Depression.
L	O	W	T	I	D	E	Tide at its lowest ebb.
L	O	Y	A	L	L	Y	Faithfully, Devotedly.
L	O	Y	A	L	T	Y	Fidelity, Fealty, Allegiance, Devotion, Faithfulness.
L	O	Z	E	N	G	E	Pastille, Heraldic diamond-shaped figure.
L	O	Z	E	N	G	Y	Heraldic figure divided into diamond shapes.
L	U	C	A	N	U	S	Genus of beetles.
L	U	C	A	R	N	E	Dormer window.
L	U	C	E	N	C	Y	Luminosity, Radiancy.
L	U	C	E	R	N	E	Important plant for fodder.
L	U	C	I	D	L	Y	Clearly, Transparently, Understandably.
L	U	C	I	F	E	R	Satan, A match.
L	U	C	I	G	E	N	Oil lamp giving a bright light.
L	U	C	K	I	E	R	More fortunate, Happier.
L	U	C	K	I	L	Y	Fortunately.
L	U	F	F	I	N	G	Sailing on the windward side.
L	U	G	G	A	G	E	Baggage, Personal belongings packed in a suitcase or trunk.
L	U	G	G	I	N	G	Dragging, Pulling, Conveying, Packing, Toting, Transporting.
L	U	G	S	A	I	L	Four-sided sail.
L	U	G	W	O	R	M	Sand-burrowing worm used as bait.
L	U	L	L	A	B	Y	A song to soothe children and help them to go to sleep.
L	U	L	L	I	N	G	Soothing, Calming, Composing, Quieting, Settling.
L	U	M	B	A	G	O	Rheumatism affecting the lumbar region.
L	U	M	I	N	A	L	Narcotic, Sleeping tablet.
L	U	M	P	I	E	R	Bumpier, More awkward.
L	U	M	P	I	N	G	Putting up with something, Gathering together as a whole.
L	U	M	P	I	S	H	Clumsy, Awkward, Lumbering, Boorish, Clownish, Loutish.
L	U	M	P	S	U	M	Single payment of cash.
L	U	N	A	T	I	C	Mad, Giddy, Maniac, Madman, Paranoid, Screwball, Psychopath, Nut.
L	U	N	E	T	T	E	Crescent shape, Window opening, Specially shaped spectacle lens.
L	U	N	U	L	A	R	Having crescent shaped markings.
L	U	N	U	L	E	T	Crescent shaped ornament.
L	U	P	U	L	I	N	Yellow powder on pistils of flower of hop plant.
L	U	R	C	H	E	D	Rolled Tipped, Canted, Pitched, Jerked, Lunged, Blundered, Stumbled.
L	U	R	C	H	E	R	Loiterer, Hoodlum, Crossbred dog often used by poachers.
L	U	R	K	I	N	G	Prowling, Skulking, Sneaking, Stealing, Slinking, Creeping, Awaiting.
L	U	S	H	I	N	G	Drinking excessively, Swilling, Toping.
L	U	S	T	F	U	L	Lecherous, Libidinous, Lusty, Licentious, Lewd, Libertine, Passionate, Satyric.
L	U	S	T	I	E	R	Merrier, Sturdier, More joyous, More robust, Stronger.
L	U	S	T	I	L	Y	Vigorously, Enthusiastically.

1	2	3	4	5	6	7	
L	U	S	T	I	N	G	Desiring, Craving, Yearning, Aching, Hungering.
L	U	S	T	R	A	L	Used for purification.
L	U	S	T	R	U	M	Period of five years.
L	U	T	E	O	U	S	Spectrum of colours from light to moderate greenish yellow.
L	U	T	H	E	R	N	Dormer window.
L	U	T	R	I	N	E	Relating to otters.
L	U	X	A	T	E	D	Displaced, Dislocated.
L	Y	C	H	N	I	S	Large genus of herbs.
L	Y	C	O	P	O	D	Genus of moss.
L	Y	C	O	S	I	D	Spider.
L	Y	D	D	I	T	E	High explosive composed chiefly of picric acid.
L	Y	I	N	G	I	N	Awaiting birth, Imminent confinement.
L	Y	I	N	G	L	Y	Falsely, Fabricating.
L	Y	M	N	A	E	A	Genus of snails.
L	Y	N	C	E	A	N	Relating to a lynx, Sharp-sighted.
L	Y	N	C	H	E	D	Hanged or killed by a mob, Scorned, Defamed, Ridiculed.
L	Y	N	C	H	E	T	Strip of uncultivated land marking a boundary.
L	Y	R	A	T	E	D	Shaped like a lyre.
L	Y	R	I	C	A	L	Musically poetic expression of emotions and thoughts.

M

M	A	C	A	B	R	E	Horrible, Distressing, Unpleasant, Hideous, Terrible, Gruesome, Ghastly, Grim.
M	A	C	A	C	U	S	Monkey.
M	A	C	A	D	A	M	Broken stones used in making a roadway.
M	A	C	A	Q	U	E	Genus of monkeys.
M	A	C	C	H	I	A	Maquis.
M	A	C	E	R	A	L	Fragment of plant debris found in coal.
M	A	C	H	A	I	R	Low-lying field.
M	A	C	H	E	T	E	Heavy knife with a broad blade.
M	A	C	H	I	N	E	Erection, Appliance, Device, Engine Apparatus.
M	A	C	R	A	M	E	Decorative work made by knotting cords.
M	A	C	U	L	A	E	Blotches, Spots, Stains, Anatomical spot differing from the surrounding tissue.
M	A	C	U	L	E	D	Marked with spots.
M	A	D	D	E	S	T	Craziest, Most insane, Angriest, Giddiest.
M	A	D	D	I	N	G	Frenzied, Raving.
M	A	D	E	I	R	A	Dessert wine, Mahogany wood.
M	A	D	L	I	N	G	Fool, Simpleton, Dolt, Lunatic, Madman, Maniac.
M	A	D	N	E	S	S	Insanity, Rashness, Enthusiasm, Ecstacy, Inaneness, Distraction, Lunacy.
M	A	D	O	N	N	A	Representation of the Virgin Mary.
M	A	D	O	Q	U	A	Small African antelopes.
M	A	D	R	O	N	E	Madrono, Evergreen shrub or tree of the Pacific coast of N. America having edible red berries.
M	A	D	W	E	E	D	Mad-dog, Skullcap, Genus of herbs.
M	A	D	W	O	R	T	Alyssum plant.
M	A	E	S	T	R	O	Master or teacher of an art, Expert in one of the arts.
M	A	F	F	I	C	K	Noisy celebrations.
M	A	F	F	L	E	D	Confused, Bewildered, Muddled.
M	A	G	E	N	T	A	Deep purplish red colour.
M	A	G	G	O	T	Y	Something infested with maggots, Freakish, Crochety, Fanciful.
M	A	G	I	C	A	L	Mystic, Supernatural, Phenomenal, Bewitching, Enchanting, Extraordinary.
M	A	G	I	N	O	T	Line of defence giving false sense of security.
M	A	G	N	A	T	E	Industrial executive with great influence, Person of exceptional wealth and power in the business.
M	A	G	N	E	T	O	Alternator used to generate current.
M	A	G	N	I	F	Y	Intensify, Heighten, Exaggerate, Extol, Laud, Increase, Augment, Enlarge.
M	A	H	A	L	E	B	Wild cherry sometimes used for making a dye or a cordial.
M	A	H	A	T	M	A	Very wise Indian or Tibetan usually very self-disciplined.
M	A	H	D	I	S	M	Belief in the Muslim tradition of the coming of a messiah.
M	A	H	D	I	S	T	Adherent of Mahdist.
M	A	H	J	O	N	G	Game of Chinese origin.
M	A	H	S	E	E	R	Large Indian freshwater fish.
M	A	I	L	B	A	G	Sack or pouch for carrying mail.
M	A	I	L	B	O	X	Receptacle for receiving either incoming or outgoing mail.
M	A	I	L	I	N	G	Posting.
M	A	I	M	I	N	G	Mutilating, Disabling, Disfiguring, Breaking, Crippling, Battering, Mauling, Mangling.
M	A	I	N	O	U	R	A thief caught red-handed with his booty.
M	A	I	N	T	O	P	Platform at top of mainmast.

1	2	3	4	5	6	7	Definition
M	A	I	S	T	E	R	Master.
M	A	J	E	S	T	Y	Kingly, Regally, Princely, Grandeur, Authority, Stateliness.
M	A	K	A	I	R	A	Genus of large fishes, Marlin.
M	A	K	A	T	E	A	Coral reef in South Pacific.
M	A	L	A	B	A	R	Relating to Malabar, India.
M	A	L	A	C	C	A	Cane made from the rattan palm found in Asia.
M	A	L	A	C	I	A	Tissue becoming abnormally soft.
M	A	L	A	C	O	N	A form of zircon.
M	A	L	A	I	S	E	Disease, Unhealthiness, Infirmity, Sickness, Decrepitude, Debility, Ill-health.
M	A	L	A	R	I	A	Disease transmitted by mosquitoes.
M	A	L	A	Y	A	N	Relating to Malaya.
M	A	L	E	F	I	C	Malicious, Noxious, Sinister, Criminal, Baleful, Malign.
M	A	L	I	S	O	N	Curse, Malediction, Injury, Hostility.
M	A	L	L	A	R	D	Common duck.
M	A	L	L	E	A	L	Relating to malleus.
M	A	L	L	E	I	N	Test for disease of glanders.
M	A	L	L	E	U	S	Mammalian ear.
M	A	L	M	S	E	Y	Sweet Madeira wine.
M	A	L	T	A	S	E	An enzyme.
M	A	L	T	E	S	E	Relating to Malta.
M	A	L	T	I	N	G	Adding malt or malt extract.
M	A	L	T	M	A	N	Maltster, Brewer.
M	A	L	T	O	S	E	Sugar formed by chemical action from malt.
M	A	M	E	L	O	N	Dome-shaped, Rounded hill, Fortified mound.
M	A	M	M	A	R	Y	Relating to the glands secreting milk.
M	A	M	M	A	T	E	Having breasts.
M	A	M	M	O	C	K	Litter, Mess, Shred, Fragment, Scrap, Disarrange, Mangle.
M	A	M	M	O	S	E	Young sturgeon.
M	A	M	M	O	T	H	Extinct elephant, Giant, Enormous, Immense, Gargantuan, Monstrous, Colossal, Leviathan.
M	A	M	M	U	L	A	Consisting of nipples.
M	A	N	A	C	L	E	Fetter, Handcuff, Bind, Shackle, Hamper, Restrain, Tether, Confine.
M	A	N	A	G	E	D	Conducted, Administered, Cultivated, Trained, Controlled, Manipulated, Supervised.
M	A	N	A	G	E	R	Executive, Administrator, Official.
M	A	N	A	K	I	N	Dwarf, Pygmy, Diminutive, Puny, Manikin, Small birds.
M	A	N	A	T	E	E	Tropical aquatic mammal.
M	A	N	C	H	E	T	Bread roll, Piece of white bread.
M	A	N	D	A	T	E	Decree, Injunction, Order, Dictate, Command, Authorization, Behest, Bidding.
M	A	N	D	I	O	C	Manioc, Cassava.
M	A	N	D	O	L	A	Lute, Forerunner of the mandolin.
M	A	N	D	R	E	L	Axle or spindle, Part of a lathe.
M	A	N	D	R	I	L	Large baboon.
M	A	N	E	T	T	I	China rose.
M	A	N	G	A	B	Y	African monkey.
M	A	N	G	L	E	D	Maimed, Hacked, Lacerated, Rent, Torn, Injured, Butchered, Defaced.
M	A	N	G	L	E	R	One that operates a mangle for laundry.
M	A	N	G	O	L	D	Mangel-wurzel.
M	A	N	H	O	L	E	Entrance and exit for underground workers.
M	A	N	H	O	O	D	Maturity, Virility, Courage, Bravery, Resolution, Ideal.
M	A	N	H	O	U	R	Amount of pay due for each unit of work.
M	A	N	H	U	N	T	Intensive search for criminal or lost persons.
M	A	N	I	H	O	T	Cassava.
M	A	N	I	K	I	N	Manakin, Dwarf, Pigmy, Puny, Diminutive.
M	A	N	I	L	L	A	Ornaments and coins of copper alloy or iron.
M	A	N	I	L	L	E	Second highest trump card in various card games.
M	A	N	I	P	L	E	Ecclesiastical scarf.
M	A	N	I	T	O	U	Red Indian spirit.
M	A	N	K	I	N	D	The human race.
M	A	N	L	E	S	S	Without a man, Unaccompanied woman.
M	A	N	L	I	K	E	Resembling man, Masculine, Vigorous.
M	A	N	M	A	D	E	Manufactured, Constructed, Synthetic.
M	A	N	N	I	N	G	Managing, Escorting, Crewing, Fortifying, Bracing.
M	A	N	N	I	S	H	Masculine, Unwomanly, Male.
M	A	N	N	I	T	E	Mannitol.
M	A	N	N	O	S	E	An aldose sugar.
M	A	N	R	O	P	E	Side rope used as an handrail.
M	A	N	S	I	O	N	Large house, Opulent residence, Villa, Chateau, Hall, Castle.
M	A	N	T	L	E	D	Covered with a mantle, Enfolded, Enveloped.

1	2	3	4	5	6	7	
M	A	N	T	L	E	T	Short cape or cloak, Movable shelter.
M	A	N	T	R	A	P	Something likely to cause injury or difficulty.
M	A	N	U	M	I	T	Liberate, Set free, Freedom from slavery.
M	A	N	U	R	E	D	Applied manure or fertilizer.
M	A	N	U	R	E	R	One who distributes manure.
M	A	N	X	C	A	T	A tail-less cat.
M	A	N	Z	A	N	A	Measurement of area of land.
M	A	P	P	I	N	G	Charting features of territory.
M	A	R	A	B	O	U	African stork.
M	A	R	A	C	A	N	A Brazilian macaw.
M	A	R	A	T	H	I	An Indian language.
M	A	R	B	L	E	D	Mottled, Streaked, Blotched, Veined, Covered with marble.
M	A	R	B	L	E	R	One that marbles edges of books.
M	A	R	C	A	T	O	Direction in music - strong accent.
M	A	R	C	H	E	D	Advanced, Moved with steady stride, Tramped in accord.
M	A	R	C	H	E	N	Folk tale.
M	A	R	C	H	E	R	A lord having certain rights.
M	A	R	C	H	E	S	Rhythmic strides, Advances, Traverses.
M	A	R	E	M	M	A	Coastland swamp.
M	A	R	G	O	S	A	East Indian tree, the bark used for a tonic and oil extracted from fruit and seed.
M	A	R	I	M	B	A	Primitive xylophone.
M	A	R	I	N	E	R	Sailor, Seaman, Seafarer.
M	A	R	I	T	A	L	Relating to marriage, Conjugal.
M	A	R	K	H	O	R	Wild goat.
M	A	R	K	I	N	G	Labelling, Picking, Choosing, Branding, Electing, Indicating, Selecting, Distinguishing.
M	A	R	L	I	N	E	Tarred rope.
M	A	R	L	I	T	E	Marl resistant to the action of air.
M	A	R	L	P	I	T	Claypit.
M	A	R	M	I	T	E	Vegetable and yeast extract used for flavouring.
M	A	R	M	O	S	E	Genus of opossums.
M	A	R	P	L	O	T	One who prevents culmination of plans through ineptness.
M	A	R	Q	U	E	E	Large tent erected for outdoor celebrations.
M	A	R	Q	U	I	S	Nobleman of inherited rank.
M	A	R	R	A	N	O	One who converts to another religions under persecution.
M	A	R	R	I	E	D	Espoused, Wed, Spliced.
M	A	R	R	I	N	G	Spoiling, Impairing, Injuring, Damaging, Harming, Hurting, Tarnishing, Bruising.
M	A	R	R	O	W	Y	Full of marrow, Pithy.
M	A	R	S	A	L	A	Sweet wine.
M	A	R	S	H	A	L	Order, Arrange, Array, Dispose, Organize, Guide, Shepherd, Usher.
M	A	R	T	E	X	T	Blundering and careless preacher.
M	A	R	T	I	A	L	Relating to army, Warlike, Military, Aggressive, Belligerent.
M	A	R	T	I	N	I	Cocktail of gin and vermouth.
M	A	R	T	I	T	E	Hematite.
M	A	R	T	L	E	T	Heraldic device representing a fourth son.
M	A	R	X	I	A	N	Influence of the doctrines of Karl Marx.
M	A	R	X	I	S	M	Theory and practice of socialism.
M	A	R	X	I	S	T	Adherent of Marxism.
M	A	R	Y	B	U	D	Marsh marigold.
M	A	S	C	A	R	A	Cosmetic preparation for use on eyelashes and eyebrows.
M	A	S	C	L	E	D	Covered with lozenge-shaped discs.
M	A	S	C	U	L	Y	Lozenge-shaped division in heraldry.
M	A	S	H	I	N	G	Crushing, Smashing, Crowding, Pulping, Squashing, Squeezing, Pushing.
M	A	S	H	L	U	M	Mixed agriculture crop of cereal and a legume.
M	A	S	H	T	U	B	Large container for processing malt or other grains.
M	A	S	K	I	N	G	Disguising, Concealing, Camouflaging, Screening, Veiling, Shielding, Cloaking, Guarding.
M	A	S	O	N	I	C	Connected to Freemasonry.
M	A	S	O	N	R	Y	Something constructed of brick, stone, concrete or tiles.
M	A	S	S	A	G	E	Rub, Knead, Manipulate, Stroke, Tapping.
M	A	S	S	I	N	G	Assembling, Collecting, Concentrating, Gathering, Accumulating, Heaping.
M	A	S	S	I	V	E	Heavy, Ponderous, Weighty, Gigantic, Grand, Immense, Mighty, Monstrous.
M	A	S	T	A	B	A	Egyptian tomb.
M	A	S	T	E	R	Y	Control, Dominion, Sway, Superiority, Command, Power, Ability, Expertise.
M	A	S	T	I	C	H	Mastic, Resin exuded from mastic tree and used in varnish.
M	A	S	T	I	F	F	Large powerful dog favoured as a watchdog.
M	A	S	T	I	N	G	Masts of the ship.
M	A	S	T	O	I	D	Ear bone.
M	A	T	A	D	O	R	Bullfighter, Game of dominoes.

1	2	3	4	5	6	7	
M	A	T	C	H	E	D	Arrayed, Pitted, Opposed, Compared, Likened, Rivalled, Equalled, Equated.
M	A	T	C	H	E	S	Contests, Competitions.
M	A	T	C	H	E	T	Machete, Chopping knife with a broad blade.
M	A	T	E	L	O	T	Sailor.
M	A	T	E	R	I	A	Study of drugs used in medicine.
M	A	T	I	N	A	L	Relating to early morning.
M	A	T	I	N	E	E	Afternoon performance of a show or concert.
M	A	T	R	A	S	S	Distilling flask.
M	A	T	R	I	C	E	Matrix tissue.
M	A	T	R	O	S	S	Gunner's mate.
M	A	T	T	E	R	Y	Infection causing pus.
M	A	T	T	I	N	G	Interweaving, Surface without a shine.
M	A	T	T	I	N	S	Matins, Early morning prayers.
M	A	T	T	O	C	K	Type of axe used for digging and chopping.
M	A	T	T	O	I	D	Dangerous mentally unstable person.
M	A	T	U	R	E	D	Ripened, Full-grown, Adult, Developed, Due Payable, Ready, Outstanding.
M	A	U	D	L	I	N	Tearful, Weeping, Fuddled, Sentimental, Mushy, Romantic, Slushy, Confused.
M	A	U	L	I	N	G	Mangling, Beating, Bruising, Battering, Lashing, Whipping, Abusing, Molesting.
M	A	U	N	D	E	R	Grumble, Progress slowly, Ramble, Speak indistinctly.
M	A	U	R	I	S	T	Benedictine monk.
M	A	U	T	H	E	R	Awkward clumsy young girl.
M	A	W	K	I	S	H	Squeamish, Cloying, Sentimental, Maudlin, Mushy, Romantic, Slushy.
M	A	W	W	O	R	M	Parisitic worm of the stomach and intestine, Sanctimonious hypocrite.
M	A	X	I	L	L	A	Upper jaw-bone.
M	A	X	I	M	A	L	Highest, Greatest, Most effective.
M	A	X	I	M	E	D	Expressed as a proverb.
M	A	X	I	M	U	M	Highest value, Greatest quantity.
M	A	X	W	E	L	L	Measurement of unit of magnetic flux.
M	A	Y	B	I	R	D	Birds that appear in Spring such as thrushes.
M	A	Y	D	U	K	E	Cherry.
M	A	Y	F	I	S	H	Oviparous fish.
M	A	Y	L	A	D	Y	Queen for the festivities of First day of May.
M	A	Y	L	I	L	Y	Lily of the Valley.
M	A	Y	L	O	R	D	May King for May day festival.
M	A	Y	O	R	A	L	Relating to a mayor.
M	A	Y	P	O	L	E	Pole with streamers for Mayday dancing.
M	A	Y	T	I	M	E	Month of May.
M	A	Y	W	E	E	D	Highly scented wild camomile.
M	A	Z	A	H	U	A	Member of Mexican Indian people.
M	A	Z	A	R	I	N	Deep fish, Blue colour.
M	A	Z	D	E	A	N	Persian religion renouncing evil of all kinds.
M	A	Z	E	D	L	Y	Utterly confused, Bewildered.
M	A	Z	E	F	U	L	Confusing.
M	A	Z	U	R	K	A	Polish dance.
M	A	Z	Z	A	R	D	Mazard, Head, Face.
M	E	A	D	O	W	Y	Grassland.
M	E	A	L	M	A	N	One dealing in meal.
M	E	A	N	D	E	R	Ramble, Drift, Wander, Gallivant, Roam, Range, Rove, Traipse.
M	E	A	N	I	N	G	Purport, Intent, Purpose, Aim, Object, Significance, Point, Essence.
M	E	A	S	L	E	D	Infected with measles.
M	E	A	S	L	E	S	Contagious virul disease manifesting red spots.
M	E	A	S	U	R	E	Regulate, Weigh, Apportion, Determine, Limit, Gauge, Calculate, Scale.
M	E	A	T	F	L	Y	Blow-fly.
M	E	A	T	T	E	A	English high tea.
M	E	C	C	A	N	O	Metal constructional toy for children.
M	E	C	H	L	I	N	Bobbin lace.
M	E	D	A	L	E	T	Small medal.
M	E	D	D	L	E	D	Disturbed, Interfered, Tampered, Mingled, Intruded, Pried, Snooped, Trespassed.
M	E	D	D	L	E	R	Busybody, Snooper.
M	E	D	I	A	C	Y	Being in the middle.
M	E	D	I	A	N	T	A special note in the musical scale.
M	E	D	I	A	T	E	Instrumental, Acting through a third person.
M	E	D	I	C	A	L	Relating to medicine and physicians.
M	E	D	I	N	A	N	Relating to N. American geological timetable.
M	E	D	U	L	L	A	Bone marrow, Compendium, Summary, Central core.
M	E	D	U	S	A	E	Jellyfish.
M	E	D	U	S	A	N	Relating, to Medusa.

1	2	3	4	5	6	7	Definition
M	E	E	R	K	A	T	Mongoose.
M	E	E	T	I	N	G	Coming together, Confluence, Congress, Competition, Conference, Intersection, Junction.
M	E	G	A	P	O	D	Australian brush turkey.
M	E	G	A	R	O	N	Central hall of an ancient Greek house.
M	E	G	A	T	O	N	Explosive force equal to a million tons of TNT.
M	E	G	R	I	M	S	Vertigo, Dizziness, Migraine, Fancy, Whim, Humour, Conceit, Caprice.
M	E	I	O	S	I	S	Litotes, Understatement, Complex nuclear changes.
M	E	I	S	S	E	N	European porcelain.
M	E	L	A	N	G	E	Mixture, Silken pillow lace, Patchwork, Sale lots of diamonds, Assortment, Jumble, Medley.
M	E	L	A	N	I	C	Black and brown-skinned people.
M	E	L	A	N	I	N	Brown or black pigments.
M	E	L	A	S	M	A	Pigmentation of the skin caused by a disease.
M	E	L	I	L	O	T	Genus of clover.
M	E	L	I	S	M	A	Song, Tune, Cadenza.
M	E	L	I	S	S	A	Genus of herbs, Balm.
M	E	L	L	I	T	E	Honey-coloured mineral, Medicine containing honey.
M	E	L	L	O	W	Y	Mellow, Softly.
M	E	L	O	D	I	A	Song, Melody, Organ stop for wood pipes and flutes.
M	E	L	O	D	I	C	Melodious, Musical, Tuneful, Sweet, Euphonic.
M	E	L	T	I	N	G	Dissolving, Disintegrating, Liquefying, Softening, Weakening, Enervating, Blending, Fusing.
M	E	M	E	N	T	O	Relic, Trace, Memorial, Keepsake, Reminder, Souvenir, Memory, Remembrance.
M	E	N	A	C	E	D	Threatened, Alarmed, Scared, Tormented, Imperilled.
M	E	N	A	C	M	E	Period of woman's life when menstruation is occurring.
M	E	N	D	I	N	G	Rectifying, Repairing, Patching, Rebuilding, Remodelling, Curing, Ameliorating, Correcting.
M	E	N	F	O	L	K	Male sex, Men of a family or community.
M	E	N	O	P	O	N	Bird lice.
M	E	N	O	R	A	H	Candelabrum used in Jewish religious services.
M	E	N	T	H	O	L	Crystalline racemic sometimes made synthetically and used in medicine.
M	E	N	T	I	O	N	Speak, Name, Instance, Specify, Cite, Allude, Remark, State.
M	E	R	A	N	T	I	Wood from a Malayasian tree.
M	E	R	C	E	R	Y	Shop dealing in textile fabrics.
M	E	R	C	I	E	S	Acts of leniency and clemency, Showing charitable intents.
M	E	R	C	U	R	Y	Heavy silver-white metallic element, Planet, Messenger of the Gods.
M	E	R	G	I	N	G	Immersing, Amalgamating, Mixing, Consolidating, Blending, Fusing, Compounding, Mingling.
M	E	R	I	S	I	S	Growth by increase in cells.
M	E	R	I	T	E	D	Rewarded, Deserved, Earned, Rated, Awarded, Justified, Warranted, Repaid.
M	E	R	M	A	I	D	Ficticious marine creature having trunk of a woman with the tail of a fish.
M	E	R	R	I	E	R	Happier, Gayer, More vivacious, Jollier.
M	E	R	R	I	L	Y	Gaily, Jolly, Happily, Joyously.
M	E	S	A	R	C	H	Internal and external mataxylem developed to the protoxylem.
M	E	S	E	E	M	S	Seems to me.
M	E	S	H	I	N	G	Entangling, Engaging, Interlocking, Co-ordinating, Harmonizing.
M	E	S	S	A	G	E	Missive, Errand, Communication, Directive, Memo, Note, Dispatch, Report.
M	E	S	S	I	A	H	Expected deliverer, Promised king.
M	E	S	S	I	N	G	Disarranging, Muddling, Bungling, Damaging, Spoiling, Jumbling, Dabbling, Trifling.
M	E	S	S	T	I	N	Tin for holding servings of food and forming part of a soldier's kit.
M	E	S	T	E	N	O	Wild horse.
M	E	S	T	I	Z	O	Person of mixed ancestry.
M	E	T	A	Y	E	R	One that cultivates the land for a share in the profit.
M	E	T	A	Z	O	A	Higher multicelled animals.
M	E	T	H	A	N	E	Colourless odourless flammable gas produced by decomposition of organic matter and from coal.
M	E	T	H	O	N	E	Crystalline diketone.
M	E	T	O	N	Y	M	An associated word that is substituted for the correct one.
M	E	T	O	P	I	C	Frontal, Relating to the forehead.
M	E	T	O	P	O	N	Narcotic drug derived from morphine.
M	E	T	R	I	C	S	Standards of measurement according to the metric system.
M	E	T	R	I	F	Y	Change into metre.
M	E	T	R	I	S	T	Student of metrics.
M	E	T	T	L	E	D	Of the character or spirit.
M	E	W	L	I	N	G	Whimpering, Whining.
M	E	X	I	C	A	N	Relating to Mexico.
M	E	Z	Q	U	I	T	Mesquite.
M	I	A	S	M	A	L	Fog, Mist, Fuggy, Vapourish.
M	I	A	O	W	E	D	Mewed, Meowed, Caterwauled.
M	I	C	E	L	L	E	Structural chemical particles.
M	I	C	H	I	N	G	Meeching, Skulking, Sneaking, Loitering.
M	I	C	R	O	B	E	Minute organism, Bacillus.

1	2	3	4	5	6	7	Definition
M	I	C	R	O	H	M	One millionth of an ohm (electrical).
M	I	D	D	E	S	T	In the exact middle.
M	I	D	I	D	A	E	Family of S. American monkeys, Marmosets.
M	I	D	I	R	O	N	Iron golf club.
M	I	D	L	A	N	D	Inland, Interior.
M	I	D	L	I	F	E	Middle age.
M	I	D	M	O	S	T	In the exact middle.
M	I	D	N	O	O	N	Midday.
M	I	D	R	A	S	H	Ancient Jewish narrative.
M	I	D	R	I	F	F	Diaphragm, Middle of the trunk, Waistline.
M	I	D	S	H	I	P	Middle of the ship exactly between bow and stern.
M	I	D	T	E	R	M	Half way in the scholastic term.
M	I	D	W	I	F	E	Woman who assists at childbirth.
M	I	G	R	A	N	T	One who transfers to another area or country.
M	I	G	R	A	T	E	To leave one region or country to work or settle in another.
M	I	L	D	E	S	T	Kindest, Softest, Smoothest, Blandest, Most lenient.
M	I	L	D	E	W	Y	Affected with mildew.
M	I	L	E	A	G	E	Distance travelled, Travelling allowance.
M	I	L	F	O	I	L	Genus of herbs, Yarrow.
M	I	L	I	A	R	Y	Small eruptions that accompany a sickness.
M	I	L	I	O	L	A	Small shellfish resembling seeds.
M	I	L	I	T	I	A	Military service, All males of a certain age liable for conscription.
M	I	L	K	B	A	R	Shop with bar-like counter serving dairy products such as milk and ice cream.
M	I	L	K	I	L	Y	In a milky fashion, Opaque liquid.
M	I	L	K	M	A	N	One who delivers milk to customers.
M	I	L	K	R	U	N	Something done with monotonous and boring regularity.
M	I	L	K	S	O	P	Effeminate youth, Weak or vapid individual.
M	I	L	L	A	G	E	A certain rate of tax.
M	I	L	L	D	A	M	Millpond.
M	I	L	L	I	A	D	A thousand million.
M	I	L	L	I	N	G	Grinding, Stamping, Crushing, Grooving, Thrashing, Rolling.
M	I	L	L	I	O	N	One thousand thousand, A great number.
M	I	L	T	I	N	G	Impregnating fish eggs with male reproductive secretion.
M	I	L	V	A	G	O	Genus of brown and white S. American caracaras.
M	I	M	E	S	I	S	Imitation, Mimicry, Impersonation.
M	I	M	E	T	I	C	Imitative, Mimic, Onomatopoeic, Stimulating, Impersonating, Resembling.
M	I	M	I	C	A	L	Mimic.
M	I	M	I	C	R	Y	Imitation, Superficial, Resemblance, Apery, Mockery, Parody.
M	I	M	U	L	U	S	Genus of American herbs.
M	I	N	A	R	E	T	Slender tower usually attached to a mosque.
M	I	N	C	I	N	G	Chopping, Cutting, Minimizing, Genteel, Affected way of talking or walking, Pretentious.
M	I	N	D	F	U	L	Aware, Apprehensive, Awake, Conscious, Conversant, Heedful, Observant, Attentive.
M	I	N	D	I	N	G	Remembering, Noticing, Tending, Looking after, Protecting, Worrying, Obeying, Attending.
M	I	N	E	R	A	L	Solid Crystalline element.
M	I	N	E	T	T	E	Dark igneous rock composed chiefly of biolite and orthoclase.
M	I	N	E	V	E	R	White fur previously ermine used on ceremonial robes.
M	I	N	G	L	E	D	Mixed, Melded, Merged, Socialized, Combined, Concocted.
M	I	N	I	A	T	E	To paint with red, Illuminate a manuscript.
M	I	N	I	B	U	S	Vehicle accommodating small number of passengers.
M	I	N	I	K	I	N	Affected, Diminutive, Miniature, Tiny.
M	I	N	I	M	A	L	Least possible quantity, Insignificant.
M	I	N	I	M	U	M	Smallest allowable amount, Lowest degree.
M	I	N	I	M	U	S	The smallest size, Little finger or toe.
M	I	N	I	V	E	R	Minever.
M	I	N	O	R	C	A	Island in the Mediterranean off the coast of Spain.
M	I	N	S	T	E	R	Church or monastery, Large cathedral.
M	I	N	T	A	G	E	Minting of coins, Fabrication of something, Impressing.
M	I	N	T	I	N	G	Attempting, Venturing, Daring, Insinuating, Suggesting.
M	I	N	U	E	N	D	Subtraction.
M	I	N	U	T	E	D	Timed, Noted, Recorded.
M	I	O	C	E	N	E	Geological period.
M	I	R	A	C	L	E	Extraordinary event, Supernatural wonder.
M	I	R	A	D	O	R	Watchtower, Turret, Bay window, Enclosed balcony.
M	I	R	A	T	E	D	Expressed surprise or admiration.
M	I	R	I	F	I	C	Marvellous, Outstanding, Wondrous.
M	I	S	C	A	L	L	Misname, Abuse, Revile.
M	I	S	C	A	S	T	In the wrong occupation or role (theatre).

1	2	3	4	5	6	7	
M	I	S	C	I	T	E	Misquote.
M	I	S	C	O	P	Y	To copy inaccurately.
M	I	S	C	U	E	D	Actor mistaking his cue.
M	I	S	D	A	T	E	Dating documents incorrectly.
M	I	S	D	E	A	L	Mistake when dealing cards.
M	I	S	D	E	E	D	Criminal action, Immoral, Offense.
M	I	S	D	E	E	M	Misjudge, Mistaken opinion, Make a mistake.
M	I	S	D	O	E	R	Petty criminal, Delinquent.
M	I	S	D	O	N	E	Something done ineptly or inexpertly.
M	I	S	E	R	L	Y	Grasping, Mean, Stingy, Niggardly, Parsimoniously, Tightfisted, Close, Penurious.
M	I	S	F	I	R	E	Failure of the gun to fire, Failure of a plan or scheme.
M	I	S	G	I	V	E	Suspicious, Fearful, Apprehensive.
M	I	S	H	N	A	H	Traditional doctrine of the Jews.
M	I	S	K	N	O	W	Misunderstand, Fail to recognize.
M	I	S	L	A	I	D	Misplaced, Temporarily lost.
M	I	S	L	E	A	D	Deceive, Betray, Beguile, Delude, Misguide, Entice, Inveigle, Lure.
M	I	S	L	I	K	E	Dislike, Aversion.
M	I	S	L	I	N	E	Printing or copying error.
M	I	S	L	U	C	K	Misfortune.
M	I	S	M	A	D	E	Faulty manufacture.
M	I	S	N	A	M	E	Abuse, Miscall.
M	I	S	P	L	A	Y	Playing error.
M	I	S	R	E	A	D	Misinterpret, Misunderstand, Misconstrue, Misconceive.
M	I	S	R	U	L	E	Anarchy, Disorder, Riot, Disquiet.
M	I	S	S	E	E	M	False appearance.
M	I	S	S	E	N	T	Wrongly addressed.
M	I	S	S	E	N	D	Same as MISSEND.
M	I	S	S	I	L	E	Weapon projected from its station, Self-propelling weapon.
M	I	S	S	I	N	G	Absent, Lacking, Lost, Omitting, Failing, Overlooking, Escaping, Avoiding.
M	I	S	S	I	S	H	Prim, Affected, Maudlin.
M	I	S	S	I	V	E	Letter, Note, Brief, Epistle.
M	I	S	S	T	E	P	False step, Lapse, Blunder, Error, Slip.
M	I	S	T	A	K	E	Mix, Blunder, Misconstrue, Misunderstood, Misinterpret, Misjudge, Underestimate.
M	I	S	T	E	R	M	Designate incorrectly, Mislead.
M	I	S	T	E	R	Y	Mystery.
M	I	S	T	F	U	L	Misty.
M	I	S	T	I	C	O	Small sailing ship.
M	I	S	T	I	L	Y	Vaguely, Obscurely, Hazily.
M	I	S	T	I	M	E	Inopportune, Untimely, Inaccurately timed.
M	I	S	T	R	A	L	Violent cold seasonal wind of France.
M	I	S	U	S	E	D	Misapplied, Misemployed, Outraged, Abused, Mistreated, Mishandled, Perverted, Maltreated.
M	I	S	W	O	R	D	Wrong use of a word.
M	I	T	O	S	I	S	Complex nuclear division of a cell.
M	I	T	R	A	T	E	Resembling a mitre or headdress.
M	I	T	R	I	N	G	Making an angled join.
M	I	X	A	B	L	E	Possible to combine.
M	I	X	E	D	L	Y	Variety of types together.
M	I	X	T	U	R	E	Mixing.
M	I	X	T	U	R	E	Proportion, Alloy, Blend, Mélange, Combination, Brew, Composite, Confection.
M	I	Z	M	A	Z	E	Confusion, Maze, Tangle, Whirl, Labyrinth, Jungle, Snarl, Web.
M	I	Z	Z	L	E	D	Confused, Muddled, Misinformed, Decamped, Speckled, Spotted.
M	O	A	B	I	T	E	Tribe living in the time of the Old Testament.
M	O	A	N	F	U	L	Plaintive, Sad.
M	O	A	N	I	N	G	Lamenting, Complaining, Groaning, Deploring, Grieving, Weeping.
M	O	B	B	I	N	G	Abusing, Scolding, Crowding, Rioting.
M	O	B	B	I	S	H	Lawless, Terrorizing.
M	O	B	I	L	E	S	Free-moving ornaments, Delicately balanced sculptures.
M	O	B	S	M	A	N	Pickpocket, Swindler, Rogue.
M	O	B	S	T	E	R	Criminal, Gangster, Ruffian, Hoodlum.
M	O	C	K	A	D	O	Woollen fabric, Imitation velvet.
M	O	C	K	E	R	Y	Derision, Counterfeit, Scorn, Ridicule, Jest, Burlesque, Sham, Caricature.
M	O	C	K	I	N	G	Deriding, Deceiving, Deluding, Imitating, Scorning, Ridiculing, Copying, Defying.
M	O	C	K	O	R	E	Zinc ore.
M	O	C	K	S	U	N	Sun spots, Haloes around the sun.
M	O	D	A	L	L	Y	Typically, Provisionally, Conditionally.
M	O	D	E	S	T	Y	Moderation, Chastity, Propriety.
M	O	D	I	C	U	M	Small portion, Limited quantity, Particle, Grain, Jot, Scrap.

1	2	3	4	5	6	7	
M	O	D	I	S	T	E	Dressmaker and milliner.
M	O	D	U	L	A	R	In standard unit form.
M	O	D	U	L	U	S	Value of a complex number, Factor.
M	O	E	L	L	O	N	Wool grease.
M	O	F	E	T	T	E	Fissures in volcanic ground.
M	O	H	I	C	A	N	American Indian tribe.
M	O	I	D	O	R	E	Seventeenth century gold coin of Portugal and Brazil.
M	O	I	L	I	N	G	Toiling, Hardworking, Industrious, Noisy, Turbulent.
M	O	I	S	T	E	N	Dampen, Saturate, Sprinkle.
M	O	L	A	S	S	E	Swiss fossil deposits.
M	O	L	E	R	A	T	Rodent resembling a mole.
M	O	L	I	M	E	N	Pre-menstrual tension.
M	O	L	L	I	F	Y	Conciliate, Pacify, Assuage, Appease, Ameliorate, Soften, Relent, Pacify.
M	O	L	L	U	S	K	Shellfish.
M	O	M	E	N	T	A	Masses having velocity of continued motion.
M	O	N	A	C	I	D	One hydroxyl group.
M	O	N	A	D	I	C	Individual atomistic unitary.
M	O	N	A	R	C	H	Emperor, Czar, King, Queen, Kaiser, Sovereign.
M	O	N	A	X	O	N	With a single axis.
M	O	N	E	P	I	C	Consisting of one word.
M	O	N	E	R	A	L	Bacteria, Algae, Living organisms lacking nuclei.
M	O	N	E	R	A	N	Same as MONERAL.
M	O	N	E	R	O	N	Same as MONERAL.
M	O	N	E	Y	E	D	Affluent, Wealthy, Rich, Opulent.
M	O	N	E	Y	E	R	Worker in the mint making coins.
M	O	N	G	R	E	L	Mixed breed of people or animals.
M	O	N	I	K	E	R	Name, Nickname, Byname, Byword, Appellation, Denomination, Designation, Title.
M	O	N	I	T	O	R	Mentor, Advisor, Lizard, Checker, Regulator, Tester.
M	O	N	K	E	R	Y	Monastery, Tramps.
M	O	N	K	E	Y	S	Members of order of primates.
M	O	N	K	I	S	H	Monastic, Resembling monks, Ascetic.
M	O	N	O	C	L	E	Eye-glass for one eye.
M	O	N	O	D	I	C	Relating to a dirge or funeral song, Solo.
M	O	N	O	D	O	N	Genus of arctic cetaceans, Narwhal.
M	O	N	O	M	E	R	Chemical compound of low molecular weight.
M	O	N	S	O	N	I	Tribe of Canadian Indians.
M	O	N	S	O	O	N	Season of heavy rainfall in India.
M	O	N	S	T	E	R	Prodigy, Enormous, Freak, Giant, Mammoth, Huge, Gargantuan, Titanic.
M	O	N	T	A	G	E	Composition of several photographs, sound effects or voices.
M	O	N	T	A	N	E	Area just below the timber-line.
M	O	N	T	E	R	O	Huntsman, Forester, Ranger, Hunting cap.
M	O	N	T	H	L	Y	Relating to the period of one month.
M	O	N	T	U	R	E	Setting, Mounting, Frame.
M	O	O	C	H	E	D	Ambled, Sauntered, Slunk, Sponged, Cadged, Prowled, Slouched, Begged.
M	O	O	D	I	L	Y	Gloomily, Dismally.
M	O	O	L	V	I	E	Learned Muslim.
M	O	O	N	E	Y	E	Moon blindness.
M	O	O	N	I	N	G	Day-dreaming.
M	O	O	N	I	S	H	Variable, Fickle, Capricious, Doltish.
M	O	O	N	L	I	T	Illuminated by moonlight.
M	O	O	N	S	E	T	The time when the moon sets.
M	O	O	R	H	E	N	Female grouse.
M	O	O	R	I	L	L	Cattle dysentery.
M	O	O	R	I	N	G	Anchorage, Making fast a ship.
M	O	O	R	I	S	H	Relating to the Moors.
M	O	O	T	I	N	G	Discussing, Debating, Suggesting, Broaching, Ventilating, Introducing, Arguing, Disputing.
M	O	O	T	M	A	N	A law student debating.
M	O	P	P	I	N	G	Wiping, Dabbing, Whipping, Beating, Licking, Overwhelming, Clobbering, Lombasting.
M	O	R	A	I	N	E	Debris left behind by movement of a glacier.
M	O	R	A	L	E	R	One who moralizes.
M	O	R	A	L	L	Y	Virtually, Ethically, Practically.
M	O	R	A	S	S	Y	Marshy, Swampy, Boggy, Maze, Labyrinth, Confusion, Something that impedes progress.
M	O	R	C	E	A	U	Morsel, Musical piece, Short literary piece.
M	O	R	D	A	N	T	Burning, Pungent, Incisive, Keen, Caustic, Scathing, Salty, Trenchant.
M	O	R	D	E	N	T	A musical trill.
M	O	R	E	L	L	O	Cherry.
M	O	R	E	S	C	O	Morisco, Moor residing in Spain in the time of the occupation.

1	2	3	4	5	6	7	Definition
M	O	R	I	C	H	E	Miriti palm having edible fruits and giving wine from the sap.
M	O	R	I	N	G	A	Genus of East Indian and African trees.
M	O	R	N	I	N	G	Break of day, Dawn, Beginning, Daybreak, Daylight, Sunrise, Forenoon.
M	O	R	O	C	C	O	Country in North West Africa.
M	O	R	P	H	E	W	Genus or fungi, Skin condition.
M	O	R	P	H	I	A	Morphine.
M	O	R	P	H	I	C	Having a form.
M	O	R	R	H	U	A	Codfish.
M	O	R	R	I	C	E	Morris dance.
M	O	R	S	U	R	E	Take a bite.
M	O	R	T	I	C	E	Mortise, Hole, Groove, Slot, Joined or fastened by a tenon.
M	O	R	T	I	E	R	Ceremonial hat worn in France.
M	O	R	T	I	F	Y	Decay, Destroy, Putrify, Humiliate, Embarrass, Vex.
M	O	S	A	I	C	S	Ancient Hebrew laws reputed to have been handed down by Moses.
M	O	S	C	H	U	S	Genus of Asiatic musk deer.
M	O	S	E	L	L	E	German white wine.
M	O	S	S	H	A	G	Marsh where peat has been removed.
M	O	T	A	C	I	L	Genus of birds, Wagtail.
M	O	T	H	E	R	Y	Resembling mother, Maternal.
M	O	T	T	L	E	D	Blotched, Dappled, Spotted.
M	O	T	T	O	E	S	Favours, Appropriate captions.
M	O	U	F	L	O	N	Wild sheep.
M	O	U	I	L	L	E	Sound in Old French.
M	O	U	L	A	G	E	Impression, Mould, Taking a cast for comparison.
M	O	U	L	D	E	D	Fenced, Manipulated, Designed, Cast, Shaped, Persuaded.
M	O	U	L	D	E	R	Molder, Disintegrate, Decay, Waste, Brickmaker.
M	O	U	L	T	E	D	Shed hair, feathers, shell, horns or skin.
M	O	U	L	V	I	E	Maulvi, Learned Muslim.
M	O	U	N	D	E	D	Heaped, Banked, Piled, Fortified, Stacked, Barricaded, Fenced, Enclosed.
M	O	U	N	T	E	D	Increased, Climbed, Rose, Grew, Intensified, Advanced, Ascended, Enhanced.
M	O	U	N	T	E	R	One who sets jewels, Optical worker.
M	O	U	R	N	E	D	Grieved, Wailed, Drooped, Sorrowed, Pined, Protested.
M	O	U	R	N	E	R	One who attends a funeral.
M	O	U	S	I	N	G	Hunting mice, Snooping, Prying, Poking, Stealing, Gliding, Sliding, Creeping.
M	O	U	T	H	E	D	Declaimed, Ranted, Orated, Raved, Boasted, Bragged, Betrayed, Revealed.
M	O	U	T	H	E	R	One who declaims or raves.
M	O	V	A	B	L	E	Mobile, Unstable, Unsteady, Changeable, Unrestricted.
M	O	Z	A	R	A	B	Christian Spaniard under Muslim rule in Spain.
M	O	Z	E	T	T	A	Ecclesiastical cape.
M	U	C	I	G	E	N	Substance easily converted into mucins.
M	U	C	K	I	N	G	Stable cleaning, Botching, Bungling, Complicating, Tangling, Snarling.
M	U	D	B	A	T	H	Mineral bath for relief of rheumatism or beauty treatment.
M	U	D	B	O	A	T	Dredger.
M	U	D	D	I	E	D	Soiled, Stained, Fouled, Dirtied, Confused, Clouded.
M	U	D	D	I	N	G	Plastering with mud.
M	U	D	D	L	E	D	Confused, Intoxicated, Cloudy, Vague, Jumbled, Incoherent, Disjointed, Cluttered.
M	U	D	D	L	E	R	Utensil for crushing or mixing.
M	U	D	F	I	S	H	Fish that burrows in the mud.
M	U	D	F	L	A	T	Bank of land exposed at low-tide.
M	U	D	H	O	L	E	Depression containing more mud than water.
M	U	D	L	A	R	K	To romp in the mud.
M	U	D	S	I	L	L	Lowest point of a structure, Low-born person.
M	U	D	W	O	R	T	Genus of herb.
M	U	E	Z	Z	I	N	Muslim priest who calls from the mosque for holy prayers.
M	U	F	F	I	N	G	Bungling, Fluffing, Fumbling, Botching.
M	U	F	F	L	E	D	Covered, Enveloped, Shrouded, Stifled, Subdued, Silenced, Suppressed, Repressed.
M	U	F	F	L	E	R	Cloak, Scarf, Mask, Facade, Veil, Veneer, Baffler, Disguise.
M	U	F	F	L	O	N	Mouflon, Wild sheep.
M	U	G	G	I	E	R	Damper, More humid, Moister.
M	U	G	G	I	N	G	Cramming, Swotting, Assaulting with intent to rob.
M	U	G	G	I	N	S	Claiming a score, Dolt, Dope, Simpleton, Idiot, Blockhead, Dunce.
M	U	G	I	E	N	T	Bellowing as cattle.
M	U	G	W	O	R	T	Plant of the wormwood.
M	U	G	W	U	M	P	Notable, Big chief, Heavyweight, Leader, Politician with no obvious leaning.
M	U	L	A	T	T	O	Child of a Negro and White person.
M	U	L	C	H	E	D	Applied top dressing to soil, Protective cover for plants.
M	U	L	C	T	E	D	Fined, Penalised, Forfeited, Punished, Swindled.

1	2	3	4	5	6	7	Clue
M	U	L	E	T	T	A	Portugese sailing ship with an eye painted on its bow.
M	U	L	L	I	N	G	Pondering, Deliberating, Musing, Blunting, Dulling, Confusing, Lingering, Delaying.
M	U	L	L	I	O	N	Thin division between panes of glass in doors and windows.
M	U	L	L	I	T	E	Mineral silicate of aluminium.
M	U	L	L	O	C	K	Mess, Rubbish, Litter, Refuse, Dirt, Waste, Spoil.
M	U	L	S	H	E	D	Same as MULCHED.
M	U	L	T	U	R	E	Payment for grinding grain.
M	U	M	B	L	E	D	Muttered, Whispered.
M	U	M	B	L	E	R	One who talks in an inarticulate fashion.
M	U	M	E	S	O	N	A meson with a mass two hundred times of an electron.
M	U	M	M	E	R	Y	Ridiculous actions, Hypercritical performance, Hocus-pocus, Mumbo-jumbo.
M	U	M	M	I	E	D	Mummified, Withered, Shrivelled.
M	U	M	M	I	F	Y	Embalm, Preserve, Envelop in bandages.
M	U	M	M	I	N	G	Masking, Impersonating, Mimicry.
M	U	M	M	O	C	K	Mammock, Shred, Scrap, Fragment.
M	U	M	P	I	N	G	Mumbling, Grimacing, Murmuring, Muttering, Cheating, Begging, Sponging, Cadging.
M	U	M	P	I	S	H	Sullen, Sulky.
M	U	N	C	H	E	D	Chewed noisily, Champed, Chomped, Crunched, Scrunched.
M	U	N	C	H	E	R	One that masticates audibly.
M	U	N	D	A	N	E	Earthy, Worldly, Secular, Materialistic, Sensual, Temporal, Prosaic, Commonplace.
M	U	N	D	I	F	Y	Cleanse, Purify.
M	U	N	J	E	E	T	Indian madder, East Indian plant used in the Orient for dye.
M	U	N	N	I	O	N	Mullion, Division between window or door panes.
M	U	N	T	I	N	G	Strip separating panes of glass.
M	U	N	T	J	A	K	Small Asian deer, Barking deer.
M	U	R	A	E	N	A	Moray eel.
M	U	R	E	X	A	N	Nitrogenous cyclic compound.
M	U	R	E	X	E	S	Shellfish valued in ancient Tyre for the purple dye it yielded.
M	U	R	G	E	O	N	Grimace.
M	U	R	I	A	T	E	Chloride.
M	U	R	I	C	E	S	Same as MUREXES.
M	U	R	K	I	E	R	Cloudier, Vaguer, Duller, Muddier, Dimmer, Foggier, Mistier, Darker.
M	U	R	K	I	L	Y	Darkly, Vaguely, Luridly, Duskily.
M	U	R	R	A	I	N	Plague, Anthrax.
M	U	R	R	I	N	A	Horse disease prevalent in Central America.
M	U	R	T	H	E	R	Murder.
M	U	S	C	A	R	I	Grape hyacinth.
M	U	S	C	I	T	E	Genus of fossil plant that resembles tree moss.
M	U	S	C	L	E	D	Intruded, Pushed, Forced, Shoved, Reinforced, Trespassed.
M	U	S	C	O	I	D	House-fly.
M	U	S	E	F	U	L	Pensive, Meditative, Bemused, Day-dreaming.
M	U	S	E	T	T	E	Oboe, Small bagpipe, Reed organ stop, Gavotte.
M	U	S	H	I	N	G	Sleighing with a dog team.
M	U	S	I	C	A	L	Harmonious, Symphonic, Melodious, Songful, Tuneful, Blending.
M	U	S	I	M	O	N	Mouflon, Wild sheep.
M	U	S	K	B	A	G	Gland of male musk deer producing an odour to attract the female.
M	U	S	K	C	A	T	Animal with a musk-gland, Civet, Genet.
M	U	S	K	I	E	R	Stronger odour of musk.
M	U	S	K	R	A	T	Musquash, Aquatic rodent.
M	U	S	T	A	N	G	Wild horse.
M	U	S	T	A	R	D	Pungent condiment, Stimulant.
M	U	S	T	E	L	A	Weasel, Otter, Mink, Polecat, Wolverine.
M	U	S	T	I	L	Y	Sourly, Mouldily, Fustily.
M	U	T	A	B	L	E	Changeable, Fickle, Inconstant, Unstable, Wavering, Capricious, Uncertain, Volatile.
M	U	T	A	B	L	Y	Variably, Uncertainly, Inconstantly, Unsteadily, Slippery.
M	U	T	A	G	E	N	Something that may produce an alteration.
M	U	T	T	O	N	Y	Resembling mutton.
M	U	Z	Z	I	L	Y	Dizzily, Confusedly.
M	U	Z	Z	L	E	D	Restrained from talking, Prevented from biting, Gagged.
M	Y	A	L	G	I	A	Muscle pain.
M	Y	A	L	G	I	C	Affected with pains in the muscles.
M	Y	A	L	I	S	M	West Indian cult of sorcery and magic rituals.
M	Y	C	E	L	I	A	Filaments of a mushroom.
M	Y	C	E	T	E	S	Genus of monkeys, Howler monkeys.
M	Y	C	O	S	I	S	Disease caused by fungus.
M	Y	C	O	T	I	C	Relating to mycosis.
M	Y	E	L	O	I	D	Bone marrow.

1	2	3	4	5	6	7	Clue
M	Y	E	L	O	M	A	Malignant tumour of the bone marrow.
M	Y	I	A	S	I	S	Infested by fly maggots.
M	Y	L	O	D	O	N	Prehistoric sloth.
M	Y	N	H	E	E	R	Dutch gentleman, Polite title.
M	Y	O	C	O	E	L	Myotome cavity.
M	Y	O	C	Y	T	E	Muscle cell.
M	Y	O	G	R	A	M	Measurement of muscle contractions.
M	Y	O	L	O	G	Y	Scientific study of muscles.
M	Y	O	M	E	R	E	Segment of a muscle.
M	Y	O	N	E	M	E	Protozoan fibril.
M	Y	O	T	O	M	Y	Muscle separation.
M	Y	O	T	O	M	Y	Muscle division.
M	Y	O	X	I	N	E	Relating to dormice.
M	Y	R	I	N	G	A	Membrane of the ear-drum.
M	Y	R	R	H	I	C	Relating to myrrh.
M	Y	R	R	H	I	S	Genus of perennial herbs.
M	Y	S	T	E	R	Y	Conundrum, Enigma, Puzzle, Riddle, Poser, Problem, Perplexity.
M	Y	S	T	I	C	S	Advocates of the theory of mysticism, Initiates of a mystery, Visionaries.
M	Y	S	T	I	F	Y	Bewilder, Puzzle, Perplex.
M	Y	T	I	L	U	S	Genus of mussels.

N

1	2	3	4	5	6	7	Clue
N	A	B	B	I	N	G	Grabbing, Seizing, Catching, Apprehending, Stealing.
N	A	C	A	R	A	T	Geranium lake, Brilliant red.
N	A	C	E	L	L	E	Enclosed shelter on an aircraft.
N	A	C	R	I	T	E	Clay mineral.
N	A	C	R	O	U	S	Pearly.
N	A	G	G	I	N	G	Scolding, Faultfinding, Carping, Harassing, Badgering, Vexing, Goading, Hectoring.
N	A	I	A	D	E	S	Water nymphs of Greek and Roman mythology, Young of dragonflies.
N	A	I	L	I	N	G	Spiking, Fastening, Capturing, Securing, Seizing, Clutching, Striking, Nabbing.
N	A	I	L	R	O	D	Iron strip for making nails.
N	A	I	V	E	L	Y	Innocently, Simply, Artlessly, Naturally.
N	A	I	V	E	T	E	Ingenuousness, Artlessness.
N	A	I	V	E	T	Y	Simplicity, Innocence, Freshness.
N	A	K	E	D	L	Y	Baldly, Openly, Simply, Barely, Manifestly, Poorly, Inadequately.
N	A	M	A	B	L	E	Nameable, Memorable, Noteworthy, Identifiable.
N	A	M	A	Q	U	A	Coastal region in Southwest Africa/Namibia.
N	A	N	D	I	N	E	Civet cat.
N	A	N	D	U	T	I	Patterned lace made in Paraguay.
N	A	N	K	E	E	N	Cotton fabric of a yellowish colour made in China.
N	A	O	L	O	G	Y	Study of sacred and religious structures and shrines.
N	A	P	H	T	H	A	Voatile flammable liquids.
N	A	P	L	E	S	S	Threadbare.
N	A	P	P	I	N	G	Dozing, Snoozing, Catnapping, Drowsing, Grabbing, Nabbing.
N	A	R	C	O	M	A	Coma induced by narcotics.
N	A	R	C	O	S	E	Narcous, In a stupor.
N	A	R	D	I	N	E	Genus of plants often used in pharmacy.
N	A	R	R	A	T	E	Relate, Describe, Recount, Recite, Discourse.
N	A	R	T	H	E	X	Vestibule of a church.
N	A	R	W	H	A	L	An arctic cetacean.
N	A	S	A	L	I	S	Small nasal muscle.
N	A	S	A	L	L	Y	In a nasal manner.
N	A	S	C	E	N	T	Originating, Incipient, Birth.
N	A	S	T	I	E	R	Cheaper, Viler, Dirtier, Meaner.
N	A	S	T	I	L	Y	Offensively.
N	A	T	T	I	L	Y	Smartly, Neatly, Sprucely.
N	A	T	U	R	A	L	Innate, Congenital, Indigenous, Native, Regular, General, Common, Normal.
N	A	T	U	R	E	D	Having a specified nature, temper or disposition.
N	A	U	G	H	T	Y	Wicked, Ill-behaved, Disobedient, Perverse, Wayward, Disorderly, Contrary, Relcalcitrant.
N	A	V	A	R	C	H	Ancient Grecian fleet commander.
N	A	V	A	R	H	O	Aircraft navigation system.
N	A	V	A	R	I	N	Mutton stew with vegetables.
N	A	V	E	T	T	E	Marquise.
N	A	V	V	I	E	S	Unskilled labourers, Roadworkers.
N	A	Y	W	O	R	D	By-word, Watch-word.

1	2	3	4	5	6	7	
N	A	Z	I	I	S	M	German socialism.
N	E	A	R	E	S	T	Closest, Most direct, Narrowest, Shortest, Stingiest.
N	E	A	R	I	N	G	Approaching, Approximaing, Equalling, Matching, Rivalling, Touching, Forthcoming.
N	E	A	T	E	S	T	Brightest, Deftest, Tidiest, Trimmest, Snuggest, Cleanest, Plainest.
N	E	B	U	L	A	E	Galaxies, Interstellar, Gaseous matter.
N	E	B	U	L	A	R	Cloudy, Vague, Hazy.
N	E	C	K	I	N	G	Kissing, Fondling, Petting.
N	E	C	K	L	E	T	Choker, Ornamental neck jewellery.
N	E	C	K	T	I	E	Cravat, Hangman's noose.
N	E	C	T	A	R	Y	Nectar-secreting gland.
N	E	E	D	F	U	L	Essential, Requisite, Money, Indispensable, Necessary, Imperative, Vital, Lacked.
N	E	E	D	I	E	R	In dire straits.
N	E	E	D	I	N	G	Requiring, Lacking, Hankering, Hungering, Desiring, Wanting, Demanding, Exacting.
N	E	I	T	H	E	R	Not either, Not the one, Nor.
N	E	L	U	M	B	O	Lotus, Water lily.
N	E	M	A	T	I	C	First cooling of substance when molecules are in parallel lines.
N	E	M	E	S	I	S	Avenger, Destroyer, Fearful retribution, Justice, Inevitable result.
N	E	M	O	R	A	L	Relating to a grove of trees.
N	E	O	C	E	N	E	Prehistoric period.
N	E	O	L	I	T	H	Neolithic stone implement, Flint.
N	E	O	L	O	G	Y	Use of a new word or expression.
N	E	O	T	E	N	Y	Retention of immature character into adulthood.
N	E	O	Z	O	I	C	Geological system.
N	E	P	H	R	I	C	Relating to the kidneys, Renal.
N	E	P	H	R	O	N	Single excretory tube.
N	E	P	O	T	I	C	Relating to family favouritsism.
N	E	P	T	U	N	E	God of the sea, Planet.
N	E	R	I	T	I	C	Shallow coastal undersea shelf.
N	E	R	V	A	T	E	Support, Inspire, Encourage.
N	E	R	V	I	N	E	Tranquilizing, Quietening, Nerve tonic, Soothing, Lulling. Removal of inflamed nerve.
N	E	R	V	O	U	S	Timid, Fearful, Jittery, Jumpy, Agitated, Excitable, Irritable.
N	E	R	V	U	L	E	Small nerve.
N	E	R	V	U	R	E	Vein.
N	E	S	T	E	G	G	Savings or fund put away for emergency or use in the future.
N	E	S	T	I	N	G	Building a nest, Settling, Stacking.
N	E	S	T	L	E	D	Cuddled, Snuggled, Burrowed, Buzzled.
N	E	S	T	L	E	R	One that nestles, Young bird.
N	E	T	B	A	L	L	Game similar to basketball.
N	E	T	S	U	K	E	Small Japanese figurine carved in ivory or wood.
N	E	T	T	I	N	G	Snaring, Material of crossed, twisted or knotted threads.
N	E	T	T	L	E	D	Incited, Irritated, Exasperated, Provoked, Agitated, Disturbed, Upset, Riled.
N	E	T	T	L	E	R	One that provokes or agitates.
N	E	T	W	O	R	K	Any system interconnected like a mesh or grid.
N	E	U	R	I	N	E	Poisonous ammonium hydroxide.
N	E	U	R	I	T	E	Nerve cell process, Axon.
N	E	U	R	O	I	D	Resembling a nerve or nerve tissue.
N	E	U	R	O	M	A	Nerve tumour.
N	E	U	R	U	L	A	One stage of embryo development.
N	E	U	S	T	I	C	Relating to neuston.
N	E	U	S	T	O	N	Minute aquatic organisms.
N	E	U	T	R	A	L	Indifferent, Neuter, Unbiased, Normal, Not involved in hostilities, Unstressed.
N	E	U	T	R	O	N	Uncharged elementary particle.
N	E	V	A	D	A	N	Characteristic of Nevada.
N	E	W	B	O	R	N	Recently born, Born anew (religion).
N	E	W	C	O	M	E	Just arrived, Recently come.
N	E	W	F	I	S	H	Australian salmon.
N	E	W	M	A	D	E	Recently introduced, Recently fabricated, Neoteric, Novel, Fresh.
N	E	W	S	B	O	Y	Youth who delivers or sells newspapers.
N	E	W	S	M	A	N	Journalist, Reporter.
N	I	A	G	A	R	A	Waterfall between Canada and U.S.A., Torrent, Cataract, Deluge.
N	I	B	B	L	E	D	Gently bit, Take in morsels, Trimmed cautiously with small cuts, Carped, Niggled.
N	I	B	B	L	E	R	Paper cutting machine.
N	I	B	L	I	C	K	Iron golf club.
N	I	C	K	I	N	G	Notching, Chipping, Recording, Scoring, Defrauding, Indenting, Pilfering, Stealing.
N	I	C	O	T	I	N	Tobacco.
N	I	C	T	A	T	E	Wink.
N	I	D	G	I	N	G	Shaking, Quivering, Dressing stone.

1	2	3	4	5	6	7	
N	I	D	U	L	U	S	Centre.
N	I	F	T	I	E	R	Smarter, Cleverer, Handier, More stylish.
N	I	G	E	L	L	A	Genus of European herbs, Love-in-a-mist.
N	I	G	G	A	R	D	Stingy, Mean, Miserly, Scanty, Covetous, Penurious, Tight.
N	I	G	G	L	E	D	Trifled, Carped, Gnawed, Irritated, Vexed, Provoked.
N	I	G	G	L	E	R	Petty faultfinder.
N	I	G	H	T	E	D	Remained through the night.
N	I	G	H	T	I	E	Nightgown.
N	I	G	H	T	L	Y	Every night.
N	I	G	R	I	N	E	Black mineral.
N	I	L	L	I	N	G	Rejecting, Refusing, Unwilling, Preventing.
N	I	L	O	T	I	C	Relating to people and language in the Nile area.
N	I	M	B	L	E	R	More agile, Livelier, Brisker, Lighter, Handier, Slicker.
N	I	M	I	E	T	Y	Excess, Redundancy, Over-abundance.
N	I	N	E	P	I	N	Wooden pin in a game resembling skittles.
N	I	O	B	A	T	E	Salt of noibic acid.
N	I	O	B	I	U	M	Metallic element used in alloys.
N	I	O	B	O	U	S	Containing niobium.
N	I	P	P	E	R	S	Pincers, Pliers, Crab-claw, Young children.
N	I	P	P	I	E	R	Frostier, Quicker, Snappier, Sharper, Chillier, Colder.
N	I	P	P	I	N	G	Squeezing, Clamping, Securing, Pinching, Snatching, Sipping, Hurrying, Biting.
N	I	R	V	A	N	A	Paradise, Oblivion, Salvation, Dream, Harmony.
N	I	T	H	I	N	G	Coward, Miser.
N	I	T	R	A	T	E	Salt of nitric acid.
N	I	T	R	I	D	E	Compound of nitrogen.
N	I	T	R	I	F	Y	Combine with nitrogen.
N	I	T	R	I	L	E	Organic cyanide.
N	I	T	R	O	U	S	Containing nitrogen.
N	I	V	E	O	U	S	Snowy.
N	J	O	R	O	A	N	Prehistoric implements found in Kenya.
N	O	B	B	L	E	D	Swindled, Cheated, Tampered with a racehorse.
N	O	B	B	L	E	R	One that interferes with the performance of a racehorse, Swindler.
N	O	B	L	E	S	T	Grander, Most famous, Most aristocratic, Impressive.
N	O	C	T	U	I	D	Moth.
N	O	C	T	U	L	E	Bat.
N	O	C	T	U	R	N	Relating to night.
N	O	C	U	O	U	S	Harmful, Damaging.
N	O	D	A	T	E	D	Knotted.
N	O	D	D	I	N	G	Drooping, Pendulous, Drowsy.
N	O	D	I	C	A	L	Relating to astronomical nodes.
N	O	D	U	L	A	R	Having nodules.
N	O	D	U	L	E	D	Occurring in the form of nodules.
N	O	D	U	L	U	S	Nodule.
N	O	G	G	I	N	G	Brickwork.
N	O	I	S	I	L	Y	Loudly, Rowdily, Uproariously.
N	O	I	S	O	M	E	Noxious, Harmful, Disgusting, Distasteful, Offensive, Foul, Repulsive, Horrid.
N	O	M	A	D	I	C	Wandering, Rover, Vagrant, Roaming.
N	O	M	A	N	C	Y	Divination by words.
N	O	M	A	R	C	H	Magistrate in ancient Egypt.
N	O	M	B	L	E	S	Numbles, Offal.
N	O	M	B	R	I	L	Centre point in heraldic escutcheon.
N	O	M	I	N	A	L	Formal, Apparent, Ostensible, Alleged, Pretended, Professed.
N	O	M	I	N	E	E	Candidate, Person named as a recipient.
N	O	N	A	C	I	D	Alkali, Non-caustic.
N	O	N	A	G	E	D	Minor, Under legal age.
N	O	N	A	G	O	N	Nine-sided figure.
N	O	N	P	L	U	S	Astound, Bewilder, Perplex, Baffle, Stump, Frustrate, Thwart, Confound.
N	O	N	S	K	I	D	Tread of tyres to prevent skidding, Corrugated surface.
N	O	N	S	T	O	P	Without stopping, Perpetual motion.
N	O	N	S	U	C	H	Superb, Matchless, Unequalled, Unrivalled, Peerless, Unique, Alone.
N	O	N	S	U	I	T	Law suit lost due to lack of evidence.
N	O	N	T	E	R	M	Law court vacation.
N	O	N	U	P	L	E	Relating to nine, Ninefold.
N	O	O	L	O	G	Y	Study of the mind, Psychology, Knowledge of mental processes.
N	O	O	N	D	A	Y	Midday.
N	O	O	N	I	N	G	Lunchtime meal or siesta.
N	O	O	S	I	N	G	Entrapping, Hanging, Lassoing, Tying, Snaring.

1	2	3	4	5	6	7	Definition
N	O	R	F	O	L	K	Pertaining to Norfolk, England.
N	O	R	I	M	O	N	Palanquin carried by Japanese men.
N	O	R	L	A	N	D	North country.
N	O	R	T	H	E	R	North wind suddenly gusting.
N	O	R	W	I	C	H	Relating to Norwich, England.
N	O	S	E	B	A	G	Pouch containing feed hung over a horse's muzzle.
N	O	S	E	G	A	Y	Posy, Small bouquet, Dainty collection.
N	O	S	T	R	I	L	External nasal passage.
N	O	S	T	R	U	M	Panacea, Quack medicine, Old wives' remedy.
N	O	T	A	B	L	E	Striking, Conspicuous, Memorable, Important, Distinguished, Prominent, Notorious.
N	O	T	A	B	L	Y	Eminently, Exceptionally, Extremely, Remarkably, Strikingly, Exceedingly, Greatly, Highly.
N	O	T	A	E	U	M	Upper back portion of a bird's body.
N	O	T	A	N	D	A	Notes, Reminders, Memoranda, Chits, Memos.
N	O	T	C	H	E	D	Nicked, Slit, Defiled, Indented, Scored, Gashed, Graded, Staged.
N	O	T	E	D	L	Y	Markedly, Eminently, Particularly.
N	O	T	E	L	E	T	Little note, Brief epistle.
N	O	T	H	I	N	G	Zero, Nought, Nil, Nonentity, Worthless, Valueless.
N	O	T	I	C	E	D	Seen, Discerned, Distinguished, Marked, Recognized, Observed, Perceived, Acknowledged.
N	O	T	I	T	I	A	Ecclesiastical register.
N	O	U	M	E	N	A	Object that cannot be connected with any of the physical senses, Soul.
N	O	U	R	I	S	H	Nurture, Nurse, Cherish, Foster, Rear, Strengthen, Feed, Fertilize.
N	O	V	A	L	I	A	Reclaimed land.
N	O	V	E	L	L	A	Story with a complex plot.
N	O	V	E	L	T	Y	New, Unusual, Gimmick, Innovation, Fashion, Trinket, Bauble, Sport.
N	O	W	H	E	R	E	Nonexistent, Obscurity, Wilderness, Unknown place.
N	O	X	I	O	U	S	Unwholesome, Distasteful, Injurious, Pernicious, Sickly, Deadly, Pestilent, Putrid.
N	O	Y	A	D	E	S	Mass drownings.
N	O	Z	Z	L	E	D	Using a nozzle to eject something.
N	U	C	L	E	A	L	Relating to nuclear.
N	U	C	L	E	A	R	Central atom, Relating to atomic energy in weaponry.
N	U	C	L	E	I	N	Substance obtained from cell nuclei.
N	U	C	L	E	O	N	Proton or neutron.
N	U	C	L	E	U	S	Kernel, Centre, Core, Focus, Embryo, Seen, Ring, Central star.
N	U	C	L	I	D	E	Special type of atom, Isotope.
N	U	D	G	I	N	G	Prodding, Jostling, Elbowing, Poking, Jabbing, Punching, Digging.
N	U	L	L	I	F	Y	Annul, Negate, Abolish, Abrogate, Neutralize, Limit, Invalidate, Annihilate.
N	U	L	L	I	T	Y	Annulment, Invalidity, Voided, Nonentity, Nonexistence, Nothing, Zero, Vacuity.
N	U	M	B	E	R	S	Complement, Several, Multitude, Period, Quantity, Ciphers, Digits.
N	U	M	B	I	N	G	Stupefying, Deadening, Blunting, Desensitizing, Dulling, Chilling, Freezing.
N	U	M	B	L	E	S	Offal, Edible internal organs of an animal.
N	U	M	E	R	A	L	Designate by number.
N	U	M	E	R	I	C	Numerical.
N	U	M	M	A	R	Y	Relating to coins, Monetary, Numismatic.
N	U	N	A	T	A	K	Arctic glacial mound.
N	U	N	B	U	O	Y	Conical buoy indicating starboard channel.
N	U	N	D	I	N	E	Ancient Roman custom of holding a market at nine day intervals.
N	U	N	H	O	O	D	Entering a convent.
N	U	N	N	E	R	Y	Convent.
N	U	N	N	I	S	H	Characteristic of a nun.
N	U	P	T	I	A	L	Relating to marriage, Conjugal, Connubial, Marital, Wedding, Bridal.
N	U	R	A	G	H	E	Sardinian structure dating from the bronze age.
N	U	R	S	E	R	Y	Room or building set aside for babies and children, A place for growing and selling plants.
N	U	R	S	I	N	G	Suckling, Nourishing, Rearing, Attending.
N	U	R	T	U	R	E	Feed, Cherish, Foster, Cultivate, Educate, Train, Support, Sustain.
N	U	T	C	A	K	E	Cake containing nuts.
N	U	T	G	A	L	L	Nutlike gall produced on an oaktree.
N	U	T	H	O	O	K	Old fashioned crook for gathering nuts.
N	U	T	M	E	A	T	Kernel of a nut.
N	U	T	P	I	N	E	Swiss pine.
N	U	T	T	I	N	G	Gathering nuts.
N	U	T	T	E	R	Y	Orchard of nut trees.
N	U	Z	Z	L	E	D	Rooted, Rubbed, Snuggled, Nestled, Nudged, Pushed, Cuddled.
N	Y	L	O	N	E	D	Wearing nylon stockings.
N	Y	M	P	H	A	E	Thick muscle of shellfish.
N	Y	M	P	H	A	L	Relating to larva of dragon-flies.

O

1	2	3	4	5	6	7	Definition
O	A	F	L	I	K	E	Stupid, Clownish, Loutish, Idiotic.
O	A	K	F	E	R	N	Common fern.
O	A	K	G	A	L	L	Nodule caused by larvae of parasitic insect.
O	A	K	L	I	N	G	Oak sapling.
O	A	R	F	I	S	H	Ribbon fish.
O	A	R	L	O	C	K	Rowlock, Support for oar.
O	A	R	S	M	A	N	Rower.
O	A	T	C	A	K	E	Flat cake made of oatmeal.
O	A	T	M	E	A	L	Ground oats, Rolled oats, Porridge.
O	B	C	O	N	I	C	Inverted cone shape.
O	B	D	U	C	E	D	Covered, Enveloped.
O	B	D	U	R	E	D	Hardhearted, Inflexible, Relentless.
O	B	E	L	I	O	N	Back portion of the head.
O	B	E	L	I	S	K	Sharp-pointed monolithic pillar, Needle-like.
O	B	E	L	I	Z	E	Indicate something as false or misleading.
O	B	E	S	I	T	Y	Corpulence, Fat, Overweight.
O	B	E	Y	I	N	G	Complying, Conforming, Keeping, Following, Agreeing, Observing, Acquiesing, Acceding.
O	B	I	T	U	A	L	Obituary.
O	B	L	I	G	E	D	Pleased, Gratified, Accommodated.
O	B	L	I	G	E	E	One under an obligation to another.
O	B	L	I	G	E	R	One who accommodates another.
O	B	L	I	G	O	R	One who bonds himself to another.
O	B	L	I	Q	U	E	Slantwise, Leaning, Pitched, Sloped, Tilted, Tipped, Indirect, Underhand.
O	B	L	O	Q	U	Y	Censure, Abuse, Invective, Vituperation, Calumny, Slander, Disgrace.
O	B	O	V	A	T	E	Egg shaped.
O	B	O	V	O	I	D	Same as OBOVATE.
O	B	S	C	E	N	E	Coarse, Repulsive, Vile, Offensive, Disgusting, Hideous, Horrible, Repugnant.
O	B	S	C	U	R	E	Indistinct, Dark, Dim, Dusky, Murky, Shadowy, Clouded.
O	B	S	E	Q	U	Y	Funeral rite, Burial ceremony.
O	B	S	E	R	V	E	Heed, See, Notice, Remark, Mark, Espy, Obey, Regard.
O	B	T	R	U	D	E	Push, Extrude, Instruct, Interfere, Infringe, Impose.
O	B	V	E	R	S	E	Front of medal or token, Head of a coin, Converse.
O	B	V	I	A	T	E	Prevent, Avert, Preclude, Ward, Interfere, Intervene, Forestall.
O	B	V	I	O	U	S	Open, Subject, Evident, Patent, Distinct, Manifest, Palpable, Clear.
O	C	A	R	I	N	A	Wind instrument.
O	C	C	I	P	U	T	Back portion of the skull.
O	C	C	L	U	D	E	Obstruct, Close, Block, Choke, Clog, Congest, Plug, Stopper.
O	C	E	A	N	I	C	Relating to the ocean.
O	C	E	L	L	A	R	Rock structure with eye-like strata.
O	C	E	L	L	U	S	Eye-like spot, Resembling an eye.
O	C	H	R	O	I	D	An ochre-like colour.
O	C	R	E	A	T	E	Wearing leggings.
O	C	T	A	G	O	N	Eight-sided figure.
O	C	T	A	M	E	R	Chemical compound formed from eight molecules.
O	C	T	A	P	L	A	Text in eight columns.
O	C	T	E	T	T	E	Group of eight musicians.
O	C	T	O	B	E	R	Tenth month.
O	C	T	O	P	O	D	Octopus, Having eight limbs.
O	C	T	O	P	U	S	Eight-limbed marine creature, Multi-branch concern.
O	C	T	U	P	L	E	Eightfold.
O	C	U	L	A	T	E	Having spots or holes resembling eyes.
O	C	U	L	I	S	T	Specialist dealing with diseases of the eye.
O	C	Y	P	O	D	E	Crab resembling fiddler crabs.
O	D	A	L	I	S	K	Female slave or concubine in a harem.
O	D	D	B	A	L	L	Eccentric person, Peculiar, Odd, Original.
O	D	D	M	E	N	T	Remnant, Sundries, Etceteras, Odds and ends, Motley, Miscellany, Medley, Assortment.
O	D	D	N	E	S	S	Eccentric, Peculiar, Bizarre.
O	D	O	N	T	I	A	Condition of the teeth, Genus of fungi.
O	D	O	R	A	N	T	Substance with an odour.
O	D	O	R	A	T	E	Scented.
O	D	O	R	O	U	S	Malodorous, Emitting an odour, Scented, Fragrant, Pungent, Smelling, Redolent, Reeking.
O	D	Y	S	S	E	Y	Long adventure-filled journey.
O	E	D	I	P	U	S	Sexual love for a parent by a child.

1	2	3	4	5	6	7	Definition
O	E	N	O	M	E	L	Ancient Greek beverage of milk and honey.
O	E	R	S	T	E	D	Unit of magnetic field.
O	E	S	T	R	U	M	Pertaining to a bitch in heat.
O	E	S	T	R	U	S	Biting or tormenting fly.
O	F	F	B	E	A	T	Unconventional, Unorthodox, Unusual, Advanced, Downbeat.
O	F	F	C	O	M	E	Outcome, Excuse.
O	F	F	E	N	S	E	Resentment, Misdeed, Crime, Trangression, Misdemeanor, Infringement, Attack, Assault.
O	F	F	E	R	E	D	Proposed, Suggested, Extended, Tendered, Displayed, Attempted, Exhibited, Advanced.
O	F	F	E	R	E	R	One that communicates terms of a contract or lease.
O	F	F	H	A	N	D	Casual, Informal, Impromptu, Unrehearsed, Extemporaneous.
O	F	F	I	C	E	R	Constable, Bailiff, SHeriff, One in position of authority.
O	F	F	L	I	N	E	Located away from public transport.
O	F	F	S	A	L	E	Selling alcoholic beverages for consumption off the premises.
O	F	F	S	I	D	E	A certain rule in football.
O	F	F	W	A	R	D	Leaning away from something.
O	G	H	A	M	I	C	Constituting ogham- old Irish alphabetic writing.
O	G	R	E	I	S	H	Like an ogre, Frightening.
O	G	Y	G	I	A	N	Primeval, Ancient, Prehistoric, Legendary.
O	I	L	B	A	T	H	Bath of oil for lubrication or preservation.
O	I	L	B	I	R	D	Bird of S. America akin to the owl that has very fatty young.
O	I	L	C	A	K	E	Residue after expressing oil and used as cattle feed.
O	I	L	G	O	L	D	Gilding a surface coated with oil.
O	I	L	M	E	A	L	Oil cake ground for cattle feed or fertilizer.
O	I	L	M	I	L	L	Machine to crush oil seed.
O	I	L	P	A	L	M	African oil palm.
O	I	L	S	E	E	D	Seeds grown for oil.
O	I	L	S	K	I	N	Waterproofed material.
O	I	L	W	E	L	L	Well from which petroleum is extracted.
O	J	I	B	W	A	Y	Various tribes of American Indians.
O	L	D	N	E	S	S	Age, Antiquity, Senility.
O	L	D	S	T	E	R	Oldtimer, Experienced person.
O	L	D	T	I	M	E	In times past.
O	L	E	F	I	N	E	Alkene, Hydrocarbon.
O	L	I	F	A	N	T	Made from elephant ivory.
O	L	I	G	I	S	T	Hematite.
O	L	I	T	O	R	Y	Home grown herbs and vegetables.
O	L	I	V	A	R	Y	Shaped like an olive.
O	L	I	V	I	N	E	Mineral, Peridot, Demantoid.
O	L	Y	M	P	I	C	Characteristic of Olympic games.
O	M	E	N	I	N	G	Auguring, Presaging, Divining, Foretelling, Prophesying.
O	M	E	N	T	A	L	Formed from abdominal structure.
O	M	E	N	T	U	M	Same as OMENTAL.
O	M	I	C	R	O	N	Letter of the Greek alphabet.
O	M	I	N	O	U	S	Fateful, Unpropitious, Portentous, Inauspicious, Dire, Doomful, Unlucky, Evil.
O	M	I	T	T	E	D	Left out, Neglected, Absent, Gone, Lacked, Missed, Wanted, Ignored.
O	M	N	E	I	T	Y	Encompassing all things.
O	M	N	I	B	U	S	Public vehicle, Compendium, Including many items.
O	M	N	I	F	I	C	All-creating.
O	N	A	N	I	S	M	Self-satisfaction, Masturbation, Coitus interruptus.
O	N	C	O	S	T	S	Overheads, Indirect expenses.
O	N	D	A	T	R	A	Genus of rodents, Muskrats.
O	N	E	E	Y	E	D	Vision limited to one eye, Narrow-minded, Bigoted.
O	N	E	F	O	L	D	Complete in its entirety.
O	N	E	I	R	I	C	Pertaining to dreams and their interpretation.
O	N	E	N	E	S	S	Integrity, Uniqueness, Identity, Harmony, Concord, Wholeness, Entirety, Sameness.
O	N	E	R	O	U	S	Troublesome, Oppressive, Exacting, Burdensome, Weighty, Trying, Demanding.
O	N	E	S	E	L	F	Me, You, Himself, Herself.
O	N	E	S	H	O	T	Successful first time, Single performance, Only one attempt.
O	N	E	S	T	E	P	Ballroom dance.
O	N	E	T	I	M	E	Former, Sometime, Previous, Bygone, Past, Old, Late.
O	N	G	O	I	N	G	Progress, Development, Growing, Advancing, Headway, Proficiency.
O	N	M	A	R	C	H	To advance forward.
O	N	O	C	L	E	A	Genus of ferns.
O	N	S	H	O	R	E	Near or on the shore.
O	N	S	T	A	G	E	In the centre of the stage, Call for performers.
O	N	S	T	E	A	D	Farmstead.
O	N	W	A	R	D	S	Forward, Ahead, Along, Forth.

1	2	3	4	5	6	7	
O	N	Y	C	H	I	A	Inflammation of the cuticle of finger or toe nail, Whitlow.
O	N	Y	G	E	N	A	Genus of fungi.
O	N	Y	M	O	U	S	Something bearing name of author or creator.
O	O	E	C	I	U	M	Brood pouch of aquatic moss.
O	O	M	A	N	C	Y	Making prophecies by using eggs.
O	O	M	E	T	E	R	Instrument for measuring eggs.
O	O	P	H	Y	T	E	Sexual reproduction of mosses and ferns, Development of sexual organs.
O	O	P	L	A	S	M	Cytoplasm of an egg, Surrounding the nucleus.
O	O	S	P	E	R	M	Fertilised egg.
O	O	S	P	O	R	E	Fertilised spore.
O	O	T	H	E	C	A	Hard egg case as of a cockroach.
O	O	Z	O	O	I	D	Fertile segmented larva that reproduces by budding.
O	P	A	C	I	T	Y	Obscurity, Darkness, Vague, Unintelligible, Ambiguity.
O	P	A	C	O	U	S	Opaque, Obscure, Uncertain, Unclear, Vague.
O	P	A	L	I	N	E	Opalescent, Milky iridescence.
O	P	A	L	I	Z	E	Become irridescent.
O	P	E	N	A	I	R	Outdoors, Not in a building, Alfresco, Outside.
O	P	E	N	E	N	D	Allowing for increase in measurement.
O	P	E	N	I	N	G	Aperture, Breach, Door, Orifice, Outlet, Gap, Break, Opportunity.
O	P	E	N	J	A	W	Round trip ticket finishing at a different place from the commencement.
O	P	E	R	A	N	T	Effective.
O	P	E	R	A	T	E	Perform, Work, Function, Act, Handle, Manage, Drive, Pilot.
O	P	E	R	O	S	E	Industrious, Busy, Diligent, Arduous, Formidable, Severe, Strenuous, Difficult.
O	P	E	R	O	U	S	Operose.
O	P	H	I	D	I	A	Snakes.
O	P	H	I	U	R	A	Genus of starfish.
O	P	I	A	T	E	D	Drugged, Doped, Deadened.
O	P	I	N	A	N	T	One who forms or expresses an opinion.
O	P	I	N	I	N	G	Stating, Expressing, Judging.
O	P	I	N	I	O	N	Approval, Esteem, View, Belief, Conviction, Sentiment, Notion, Conjecture.
O	P	O	S	S	U	M	American marsupial.
O	P	P	I	D	A	N	Townsman, University student not living in residence.
O	P	P	O	S	E	D	Confronted, Pitted, Matched, Resisted, Antagonistic, Arrayed, Combated, Disputed.
O	P	P	O	S	E	R	One that opposes a registration of a trademark.
O	P	P	R	E	S	S	Suppress, Quell, Harass, Distress, Crush, Trample, Overcome, Ravish.
O	P	S	O	N	I	C	Relating to anti-bodies, Corpuscles attacking foreign bodies in the blood.
O	P	S	O	N	A	L	Same as OPSONIC.
O	P	T	I	C	A	L	Pertaining to vision. Aids to correct defects of vision.
O	P	T	I	C	O	N	Brain zone of insect connected to compound eye.
O	P	T	I	M	U	M	Most favourable, Best value, Greatest degree.
O	P	U	L	E	N	T	Rich, Affluent, Wealthy, Lavish, Extravagant, Ostentatious, Showy, Plush.
O	P	U	N	T	I	A	Prickly pear.
O	R	A	N	I	A	N	Prehistoric blades found in Morocco.
O	R	A	R	I	O	N	Ecclesiastical stole worn in the Eastern church.
O	R	A	R	I	U	M	Same as ORARION.
O	R	A	T	I	N	G	Haranguing, Spouting, Declaiming, Ranting, Raving, Sermonizing.
O	R	A	T	I	O	N	Petition, Prayer, Clamour, Uproar, Speech, Address, Harangue.
O	R	A	T	O	R	Y	Chapel, Elocution, Rhetoric.
O	R	A	T	R	I	X	Lady speaker.
O	R	B	I	T	A	L	Circling, Revolve in orbit.
O	R	B	L	E	S	S	Without an orb.
O	R	C	H	A	R	D	Area of fruit or nut-bearing trees planted to design.
O	R	C	I	N	O	L	Crystalline extract from lichens.
O	R	D	E	R	E	D	Arranged, Disposed, Marshalled, Organized, Adjusted, Regulated, Commanded, Arrayed.
O	R	D	E	R	E	R	Controller, Manager.
O	R	D	E	R	L	Y	Methodical, Regular, Systematic, Accurate, Precise, Neat, Tidy, Trim.
O	R	D	I	N	A	L	Of a specified order, Order of succession.
O	R	D	I	N	E	E	Young inexperienced clergyman.
O	R	E	C	T	I	C	Pertaining to desires, Gratification.
O	R	G	A	N	I	C	Instrumental, Fundamental, Inherent, Vital, Radical, Functional, Constitutional.
O	R	G	A	N	U	M	Association or group formed to acquire knowledge.
O	R	G	A	N	O	N	Same as ORGANON.
O	R	G	I	A	S	T	One who takes an active part in orgies.
O	R	I	E	N	C	Y	Brilliancy.
O	R	I	F	I	C	E	Aperture, Hole, Vent, Opening, Outlet.
O	R	I	G	A	M	I	Japanese paper sculpture.
O	R	O	G	E	N	Y	Geological movement creating mountains.

1	2	3	4	5	6	7	Definition
O	R	O	L	O	G	Y	Science of mountains.
O	R	O	T	U	N	D	Resonant, Resounding, Ringing, Rotund, Loud, Stentorian, Rhetorical, Bombastic.
O	R	P	H	E	A	N	Orphic, Relating to Orpheus and music.
O	R	P	H	E	U	S	God of music.
O	R	P	H	I	S	M	Belief in the purification of the soul through a cycle of reincarnation.
O	R	P	H	R	E	Y	Embroidered border.
O	R	T	H	I	T	E	Allanite occurring in slender prismatic crystals.
O	R	T	H	R	O	S	Morning service in the Eastern church.
O	R	T	O	L	A	N	European bird.
O	S	A	Z	O	N	E	Basic compound containing two adjacent hydrazone groupings.
O	S	C	I	N	E	S	Suborder of singing birds.
O	S	C	U	L	A	R	Concerned with kissing.
O	S	C	U	L	U	M	Small mouth, Orifice of a sponge.
O	S	I	E	R	E	D	A grove of osiers.
O	S	M	A	N	L	I	Turkish.
O	S	M	A	T	I	C	Sense of smell used for orientation.
O	S	M	I	U	M	S	High melting metallic element.
O	S	M	O	S	I	S	Process of absorption of diffusion.
O	S	M	O	T	I	C	Having the property of osmosis.
O	S	M	U	N	D	A	Genus of large ferns.
O	S	S	E	L	E	T	Bony growth on a horse's leg.
O	S	S	E	O	U	S	Composed of bone.
O	S	S	I	C	L	E	Any of the small bones in the skeleton.
O	S	S	I	F	I	C	Pertaining to bone.
O	S	S	U	A	R	Y	Vault for interment of bones.
O	S	T	E	O	I	D	Having a skeleton of bone.
O	S	T	E	R	I	A	Snack bar, Restaurant, Hostelry, Coffee shop, Cafe.
O	S	T	I	A	R	Y	Doorkeeper.
O	S	T	I	O	L	E	Orifice, Vent, Opening, Outlet, Pore.
O	S	T	R	I	C	H	Largest flightless bird.
O	T	A	L	G	I	A	Earache.
O	T	A	L	G	I	C	Remedy for earache.
O	T	A	R	I	N	E	Relating to seals.
O	T	I	D	I	N	E	Referring to bustards.
O	T	O	C	Y	S	T	Earlike organ of a fish containing fluid and stones.
O	T	O	L	I	T	H	Calcified secretion in the ear.
O	T	O	L	O	G	Y	Science of the ear and related diseases.
O	T	T	O	M	A	N	Divan, Ribbed fabric of silk and wool mixture.
O	U	A	B	A	I	N	Southern African tree from which poison is obtained.
O	U	R	S	E	L	F	Referring to the individual.
O	U	T	B	A	C	K	Australian wilderness, Far from Civilisation.
O	U	T	B	U	L	K	Larger mass.
O	U	T	B	U	R	N	To destroy by burning.
O	U	T	C	A	M	P	Not the main base camp.
O	U	T	C	A	S	T	Friendless, Despised, Exile, Derelict, Leper, Vagabond, Castaway, Untouchable.
O	U	T	C	O	M	E	Effect, Result, Sequel, Consequence, Aftermath, Event, Issue, Conclusion.
O	U	T	C	R	O	P	Coming into the open, Rock above surrounding ground.
O	U	T	D	A	R	E	Challenge, Defy, Venture, Outdo.
O	U	T	D	A	T	E	Outmode, Superannuate, Obsolesce, Replace, Supersede, Age.
O	U	T	D	O	N	E	Surpassed, Eclipsed, Defeated, Exceeded, Provoked, Vexed.
O	U	T	D	O	O	R	Open-air, Outside, Alfresco, Roofless.
O	U	T	D	R	A	W	Attracting a larger audience, Aim gun faster than opponent.
O	U	T	F	A	C	E	Confront, Challenge, Defy, Stare down, Dare, Beard.
O	U	T	F	A	L	L	Outlet, Vent, Discharge of sewer, Raid, Sortie.
O	U	T	F	L	O	W	Flowing out, Outlet, Disseminate.
O	U	T	F	O	O	T	Outstrip, Speedier, Outpace, Superior.
O	U	T	G	A	M	E	More courageous, Braver.
O	U	T	G	A	T	E	Exit, Way out.
O	U	T	G	O	E	R	One making an exit, Outgoing tenant.
O	U	T	G	R	O	W	Grow faster, Grow too large, Exceed limitations or expectations.
O	U	T	G	U	S	H	Spurting out, Deluge.
O	U	T	H	A	U	L	Rope used in sailing.
O	U	T	J	E	S	T	To laugh at misfortune.
O	U	T	K	I	C	K	To outshine opponent in football.
O	U	T	L	A	N	D	Foreign country, Provinces, Outlying districts.
O	U	T	L	A	S	T	Survive, Outlive.

1	2	3	4	5	6	7	
O	U	T	L	E	A	P	Angry retort.
O	U	T	L	I	E	R	Someone or something away from main centre of activities or location.
O	U	T	L	I	N	E	Contour, Delineation, Profile, Sketch, Draft, Shape, Open, Silhouette.
O	U	T	L	I	V	E	Outlast, Overcome, Survive, Outstay.
O	U	T	L	O	O	K	Lookout, Perspective, Prospect, Scene, View, Angle, Future, Direction.
O	U	T	M	O	D	E	Outdate, Antiquate, Unfashionable, Obsolete, Unstylish, Supersede.
O	U	T	M	O	S	T	Furthest out, Extreme, Remotest, Utmost, Farther, Furthermost.
O	U	T	N	E	S	S	Objectiveness.
O	U	T	P	A	C	E	Outdo, Outdistance, Outstrip, Outrun.
O	U	T	P	A	S	S	Exceed, Excel in a movement in rugby and football.
O	U	T	P	L	A	Y	Outshine, Outstrip the opponent, More skilful.
O	U	T	P	O	L	L	Obtain more votes in an election.
O	U	T	P	O	R	T	Small harbour.
O	U	T	P	O	S	T	Frontier fort or camp as vanguard of army, Distant branch of a company.
O	U	T	P	O	U	R	Spout, Gush, Flow, Spurt.
O	U	T	P	R	A	Y	To surpass in prayer.
O	U	T	R	A	G	E	Rape, Maltreat, Injury, Damage, Harm, Ravish, Insult, Persecute.
O	U	T	R	A	N	K	Precede, To be of a higher office.
O	U	T	R	I	D	E	Outstrip, Outdistance, Outpace, Ride as escort.
O	U	T	R	I	N	G	To sound louder in comparison.
O	U	T	R	O	A	D	A border raid.
O	U	T	R	O	A	R	Roar louder, Uproar.
O	U	T	R	O	O	T	Uproot, Extract, Eradicate.
O	U	T	R	U	S	H	Outflow, Gushing, Pouring.
O	U	T	S	A	I	L	Outstrip in sailing.
O	U	T	S	E	L	L	To be top salesman, Exceed record sales.
O	U	T	S	E	R	T	Extra leaflet or pages.
O	U	T	S	H	O	T	Lean-to, Small building addition.
O	U	T	S	I	D	E	Maximum, Extraneous, Outer, Remote, Open-air, Exterior, External, Utmost.
O	U	T	S	I	Z	E	Larger than average.
O	U	T	S	O	A	R	To fly out of range.
O	U	T	S	P	A	N	Unharness, Unyoke, Unhitch.
O	U	T	S	T	A	Y	Remain longer than expected, Surpass in staying power.
O	U	T	S	T	E	P	Overstep, Exceed, Overrun.
O	U	T	T	A	L	K	To talk until the opposition is silenced.
O	U	T	T	U	R	N	Output, Yield, Production, Turnout.
O	U	T	V	I	E	D	Surpassed, Overwhelmed.
O	U	T	V	O	T	E	To defeat a candidate by polling more votes.
O	U	T	W	A	L	K	Outpace, Outstride.
O	U	T	W	A	L	L	Outer wall, Clothing on the body.
O	U	T	W	A	R	D	Exterior, External, Outer, Outside, Ostensible, Apparent.
O	U	T	W	A	S	H	Silt washed down by rainwater or glacial stream.
O	U	T	W	E	A	R	Exhaust, Outgrow, Outlive, Outlast, Prostrate, Endure.
O	U	T	W	E	L	L	Well out, Pour, Gush, Spurt, Flow.
O	U	T	W	E	N	T	Outstripped, Departed.
O	U	T	W	I	N	D	To be out of breath.
O	U	T	W	I	N	G	Outstrip in flying, Outflank.
O	U	T	W	I	T	H	Except, Beyond scope.
O	U	T	W	O	R	E	Exhausted, Outlasted, Endured, Held up.
O	U	T	W	O	R	K	High productivity.
O	U	T	W	O	R	N	Outmoded, Obsolete.
O	U	T	Y	E	L	L	Ranting and raving more than the opposition.
O	V	A	R	I	A	L	Pertaining to an ovary.
O	V	A	R	I	A	N	Relating to an ovary.
O	V	A	T	I	O	N	Fiery exultation, Enthusiastic reception, Enthralled applause.
O	V	E	R	A	C	T	Exaggerated actions, Overplay, Rant, Spout, Declaim, Over-theatrical.
O	V	E	R	A	G	E	To old to be serviceable, Older than normal.
O	V	E	R	A	L	L	Everywhere, Generally, Comprehensive, Global, Sweeping, Total, Mainly, Chiefly.
O	V	E	R	A	R	M	Activity with arm above the shoulder.
O	V	E	R	A	W	E	Intimidate, Daunt, Cow, Terrorize, Startle.
O	V	E	R	B	I	D	Successful bid at auction, Bid in bridge.
O	V	E	R	B	U	Y	To buy in excess of necessity.
O	V	E	R	D	U	E	Tardy, Outstanding debt in excess of time allotted.
O	V	E	R	D	Y	E	Excess of colour in dyeing.
O	V	E	R	E	A	T	Gorge, Guzzle, Gourmandize, Stuff.
O	V	E	R	F	L	Y	Overshoot, To pass intended landing point.
O	V	E	R	L	A	P	Lap over, Extend and partly cover, Adjoining portion, Overhang.

1	2	3	4	5	6	7	Definition
O	V	E	R	L	A	Y	Superimpose, Cover, Overburden, Encumber, Overcast, Overspread, Blanket.
O	V	E	R	L	I	E	Rest upon, Smother.
O	V	E	R	M	A	N	Too many crew, Too many workers, Foreman, Chief.
O	V	E	R	P	A	Y	Pay too much, Excessive compensation.
O	V	E	R	P	L	Y	Overwork, Overexert.
O	V	E	R	R	U	N	Overwhelm, Overpower, Crush, Infest, Invade, Overflow, Foray, Thrash.
O	V	E	R	S	E	A	Across the sea.
O	V	E	R	S	E	E	Survey, Overlook, Superintend, Supervise, Examine, Disregard, Neglect, Chaperon.
O	V	E	R	S	E	T	Upset, Overturn, Subvert, Topple, Overthrow, Tumble, Unhorse.
O	V	E	R	S	E	W	Overcast, Overhand, Joining pages of a book.
O	V	E	R	T	A	X	Overload, Overburden, Overcharge, Overweight.
O	V	E	R	T	L	Y	Manifestly, Publicly, Openly.
O	V	E	R	T	O	P	Override, Obscure, Superior, Taller, Higher in rank.
O	V	I	C	E	L	L	Brood pouch of aquatic moss-like organisms.
O	V	I	C	I	D	E	Insecticide that is capable of killing eggs.
O	V	I	D	I	A	N	Pertaining to the Roman poet Ovid.
O	V	I	D	U	C	T	Uterus, Internal tube for the passage of eggs.
O	V	I	F	O	R	M	Egg-shaped, Resembling a sheep.
O	V	O	I	D	A	L	Egg-shaped.
O	V	U	L	A	R	Y	Lower part of flower where fertilisation is effected.
O	V	U	L	I	S	T	One holding the theory of ovism.
O	W	E	N	I	T	E	Follower of Robert Owen.
O	W	L	L	I	K	E	Resembling an owl.
O	W	N	N	E	S	S	Belonging to oneself.
O	X	A	L	A	T	E	Salt of oxalic acid.
O	X	B	L	O	O	D	Reddish brown colour.
O	X	B	R	A	K	E	Frame to hold oxen when being shod.
O	X	H	E	A	R	T	Variety of large cherries, Cabbages with conical heads.
O	X	I	D	A	N	T	Oxidising agent.
O	X	I	D	A	S	E	Enzyme.
O	X	I	D	I	S	E	Combine with oxygen, Oxygenate, Remove electrons, Rust.
O	X	I	M	A	T	E	Convert into an oxime.
O	X	O	N	I	A	N	Native or resident of Oxford, England.
O	X	Y	A	E	N	A	Genus of extinct primitive mammals.
O	X	Y	N	T	I	C	Acid-secreting glands.
O	X	Y	O	P	I	A	Having unusually high quality of vision.
O	X	Y	T	O	N	E	Placing stress on pronunciation of the last syllable of a word.
O	Z	O	N	I	D	E	Chemical compound.
O	Z	O	N	I	F	Y	Ozonise.
O	Z	O	N	I	Z	E	Combine with ozone.
O	Z	O	N	O	U	S	Ozonic.

P

1	2	3	4	5	6	7	Definition
P	A	B	U	L	U	M	Food, Nutrient, Nourishment, Grist, Thought-provoking material.
P	A	C	H	I	S	I	Ancient game resembling backgammon.
P	A	C	H	Y	M	A	Genus of fungi.
P	A	C	I	F	I	C	Peaceful, Calm, Tranquil, Conciliatory, Peaceable, Irenic, Appeasing, Gentle.
P	A	C	K	A	G	E	Bundle, Parcel, Bale, Container, Composite, Combination.
P	A	C	K	I	C	E	Sea ice crushed by movement.
P	A	C	K	I	N	G	Stowing, Parcelling, Baling, Jamming, Stuffing, Compressing, Finishing, Congregating.
P	A	C	K	M	A	N	Pedlar, Travelling hawker.
P	A	C	K	W	A	X	Tendon in an animal's neck.
P	A	C	K	W	A	Y	Path used by mules or packhorses.
P	A	C	T	I	O	N	Bargain, Compact, Agreement, Convenant, Bond.
P	A	D	D	I	N	G	Stuffing, Muffling, Exaggerating, Overstating, Magnifying, Trudging, Overcharging, Stretching.
P	A	D	D	L	E	D	Rowed, Propelled, Thrashed, Thwacked, Spanked, Toddled, Dabbled.
P	A	D	D	L	E	R	Paddle-steamer, One who paddles a canoe or raft.
P	A	D	D	O	C	K	Enclosed field, Pasture, Grassland, Turfed enclosure, Frog, Toad.
P	A	D	L	O	C	K	Heavy portable lock.
P	A	D	R	O	N	E	Innkeeper, Landlord, Patron, Master, Gangland boss, Racketeer.
P	A	E	N	U	L	A	Ancient Roman cloak.
P	A	E	O	N	I	A	Genus of perennial herbs, Peony.
P	A	E	O	N	I	C	Verse in metre of three to two.
P	A	G	E	A	N	T	Show, Spectacle, Exhibition, Stage, Platform, Part, Role, Ceremonial.
P	A	G	I	N	A	L	Consisting of pages.

1	2	3	4	5	6	7	
P	A	H	L	E	V	I	Iranian gold coin.
P	A	I	L	F	U	L	As much as a bucket can hold.
P	A	I	L	L	O	N	Thin sheet of metal foil for decoration.
P	A	I	N	F	U	L	Sore, Grievous, Hurtful, Vexatious, Annoying, Irksome, Upsetting, Troublesome.
P	A	I	N	I	N	G	Hurting, Suffering, Provoking, Aching, Distressing, Crucifying, Tormenting, Afflicting.
P	A	I	N	T	E	D	Daubed, Coloured, Portrayed, Produced by pigment, Adorned.
P	A	I	N	T	E	R	Artist, One who applies paint, Rope, Line for a ship.
P	A	I	R	I	N	G	Mating, Coupling, Uniting, Arranging in pairs.
P	A	J	A	M	A	S	Pyjamas, Loose fitting trouser suit, Nightwear.
P	A	K	T	O	N	G	Alloy of nickel, zinc and copper.
P	A	L	A	D	I	N	Protagonist, Legendary hero.
P	A	L	A	M	A	E	Webbings on the feet of aquatic birds.
P	A	L	A	T	A	L	Pertaining to the soft palate.
P	A	L	A	V	E	R	Conference, Discussion, Conversation, Chatter, Affair, Jargon, Parley, Cajole.
P	A	L	E	A	T	E	Covered with chaffy scales.
P	A	L	E	R	M	O	Style prevalent in Palermo, Sicily.
P	A	L	E	T	O	T	Overcoat, Woman's jacket worn with a crinoline.
P	A	L	E	T	T	E	Artist's board to hold tools and paint.
P	A	L	F	R	E	Y	Light horse suitable for a lady rider.
P	A	L	I	N	A	L	Retrogressive, Backward movement.
P	A	L	L	I	A	L	Relating to the cerebral cortex.
P	A	L	L	I	N	G	Failing, Daunting, Appalling, Satiating, Cloying, Gorging, Disgusting, Wearying.
P	A	L	L	I	U	M	Cloak, Altar cloth, Cerebral cortex, Sheet of clouds.
P	A	L	L	O	N	E	Italian ball-game similar to tennis.
P	A	L	M	A	R	Y	Outstanding, Superior, Worthy, Rewarding.
P	A	L	M	A	T	E	Resembling outspread hand, Webbed.
P	A	L	M	E	R	Y	Place for growing palms.
P	A	L	M	I	N	G	Concealing in the hand, Bribing, Tipping, Pilfering.
P	A	L	M	I	S	T	Fortune-teller who examines the palms of the client's hands.
P	A	L	M	O	F	F	Foist, Deceive by trickery, Dispose of by trickery, Substituted by guile.
P	A	L	M	O	I	L	Edible fat extracted from the fruit of the African oil palm.
P	A	L	M	Y	R	A	Fan palm that yields hard wood and sap rich in sugar.
P	A	L	O	O	K	A	Oaf, Clumsy, inept person, Incompetent boxer.
P	A	L	P	A	T	E	Medically examine by touch.
P	A	L	S	H	I	P	Comradeship, Esprit between bosom pals.
P	A	L	S	I	E	D	Paralyzed.
P	A	L	U	D	A	L	Marshy.
P	A	M	P	E	R	O	Cold wind that blows over the S. American grasslands.
P	A	N	A	C	E	A	Universal remedy, Cure-all, Elixir, Relief.
P	A	N	A	C	H	E	Verve, Swagger, Self-esteem, Flamboyance, Self-confidence.
P	A	N	A	G	I	A	Morning service to honour the Virgin Mary.
P	A	N	C	A	K	E	Very thin fried batter cake, Flatten, Forced landing.
P	A	N	D	E	A	N	Pertaining to Pan, god of music.
P	A	N	D	E	C	T	Complete code of Roman civil laws.
P	A	N	D	I	O	N	Genus of fish-eating hawks, Osprey.
P	A	N	D	O	R	A	Woman in Greek mythology who let loose misfortunes on mankind, Shellfish.
P	A	N	D	O	U	R	Austrian mercenary.
P	A	N	D	U	R	A	Ancient stringed instrument like a lute.
P	A	N	E	I	T	Y	State of being bread.
P	A	N	F	I	S	H	Edible fish caught with hook and line, Gamefish.
P	A	N	G	A	N	E	Leaf fibre used for ropes.
P	A	N	G	I	N	G	Cramming, Stuffing, Tamping, Ramming.
P	A	N	I	C	K	Y	Jumpy, Nervous, Fearful, Alarmed.
P	A	N	I	C	L	E	Flower cluster.
P	A	N	I	C	U	M	Genus of grasses.
P	A	N	N	A	G	E	Legal right for pigs to feed in a forest, Food for swine.
P	A	N	N	I	E	R	Pair of baskets carried by a beast or on a yoke.
P	A	N	N	I	N	G	Scouring for gold, Washing, Criticizing severely.
P	A	N	N	O	S	E	Texture of woollen cloth or felt.
P	A	N	O	C	H	A	Mexican raw sugar, Fudge made with brown sugar.
P	A	N	O	P	L	Y	Ceremonial attire, Complete set of armour, Pomp, Dress uniform.
P	A	N	P	I	P	E	Primitive wind instrument.
P	A	N	S	I	E	D	Covered with pansies.
P	A	N	T	H	E	R	Leopard of a black colour, Cougar, Jaguar.
P	A	N	T	I	E	S	Undergarments.
P	A	N	T	I	L	E	Roof tile, Sea biscuit, Dutch paving stone.
P	A	N	T	I	N	G	Breathing spasmodically, Throbbing, Pulsating.

1	2	3	4	5	6	7	
P	A	N	T	L	E	R	Butler.
P	A	P	E	R	E	D	Sand-papered, Covered with wallpaper, Written down on paper.
P	A	P	E	R	E	R	Paper-hanger.
P	A	P	H	I	A	N	Wanton, Harlot, Courtesan, Whore, Prostitute, Illicit love.
P	A	P	I	L	I	O	Swallow-tailed butterflies.
P	A	P	I	L	L	A	Nipple-like protuberances on the tongue.
P	A	P	O	O	S	E	Young child of N. American Indians.
P	A	P	P	I	N	G	Feeding with pap.
P	A	P	P	O	S	E	Furnished with a pappus, Downy, Early growth of a beard.
P	A	P	R	I	K	A	Dried ground pimento, Reddish orange colour.
P	A	P	U	L	A	E	Papule, Pimple.
P	A	P	U	L	A	R	Characterized by pimples.
P	A	P	Y	R	U	S	Pith of water reed to make parchment for writing.
P	A	R	A	B	L	E	Comparison, Similitude, Allegory.
P	A	R	A	D	E	D	Exhibited, Marshalled, Shown off, Masqueraded.
P	A	R	A	D	O	S	Parapet, Bank of earth.
P	A	R	A	D	O	X	Contrary proposition, Contradictory statement which contains a true fact.
P	A	R	A	G	O	N	Ideal, Model, Epitome, Quintessence, Ultimate, Exemplar, Lovely, Champion.
P	A	R	A	P	E	T	Rampart, Low wall, Bulwark, Bastion.
P	A	R	A	S	O	L	Light-weight umbrella used as a sunshade.
P	A	R	B	O	I	L	Partially cooked, Blanched, Scalded, Simmer.
P	A	R	C	H	E	D	Scorched, Dehydrated, Dried, Dessicated.
P	A	R	C	I	T	Y	Frugality, Scantiness, Paucity, Lack.
P	A	R	D	I	E	U	In truth - used as a mild oath.
P	A	R	D	I	N	E	Spotted like a leopard.
P	A	R	E	I	R	A	Brazilian plant used medicinally.
P	A	R	E	R	G	A	Taking on extra jobs, Moonlighting.
P	A	R	E	S	I	S	Slight or partial paralysis.
P	A	R	E	T	I	C	Individual afflicted with Paresis.
P	A	R	F	A	I	T	Layered dessert of ice cream, fruit and whipped cream.
P	A	R	G	I	N	G	Gilding, Ornamenting, Plastering.
P	A	R	I	S	O	N	Evenly balanced sentence, Incomplete glass object.
P	A	R	I	T	O	R	Apparitor, Bailiff, Herald.
P	A	R	K	I	N	G	To keep a vehicle standing in a designated place.
P	A	R	L	O	U	R	Reception room, Living room, Sitting room.
P	A	R	L	O	U	S	Difficult, Perilous, Dangerous, Critical, Precarious, Hazardous.
P	A	R	O	D	I	C	Imitating in a satirical manner.
P	A	R	O	L	E	D	Freed on probation, Released under certain conditions.
P	A	R	O	L	E	E	One released on parole.
P	A	R	O	T	I	A	Birds of paradise.
P	A	R	O	T	I	C	Adjacent to the ear, Auricular.
P	A	R	O	T	I	D	Salivary gland.
P	A	R	Q	U	E	T	Laying wood blocks in a set pattern, Inlaid with wood, Decorative veneers.
P	A	R	R	I	E	D	Evaded, Warded, Fended, Dodged, Shirked, Deflected, Prevented, Forestalled.
P	A	R	S	I	N	G	Grammatical dissecting of parts of speech.
P	A	R	S	L	E	Y	Culinary herb.
P	A	R	S	N	I	P	Cultivated root vegetable.
P	A	R	T	A	K	E	Share, Participate, Consume, Receive, Accept, Devour, Eat, Ingest.
P	A	R	T	I	A	L	Biased, Partisan, Incomplete, Fractional, Fragmentary, Warped, Part, Prejudiced.
P	A	R	T	I	E	S	Sides, Combinations, Litigants, Participants, Factions, Groups, Outfits, Individuals.
P	A	R	T	I	N	G	Departure, Leave-taking, Farewell, Separating, Final, Cracking, Diverging, Breaking.
P	A	R	T	I	T	E	Partially divided into sections.
P	A	R	T	L	E	T	Hen, Modesty vest for low neckline dresses.
P	A	R	T	N	E	R	Colleague, Associate, Assistant, Helper, Comrade, Companion, Husband, Wife.
P	A	R	U	L	I	S	Gumboil, Abscess.
P	A	R	V	E	N	U	Nouveau rich, Upstart, Social climber.
P	A	R	V	I	S	E	Court, Enclosed garden, Colonnade, Portico, Church porch.
P	A	R	V	U	L	E	Tiny pill.
P	A	S	C	H	A	L	Passover, Easter.
P	A	S	C	U	A	L	Grazing land, Pasture.
P	A	S	Q	U	I	L	Political satire, Lampoon, Criticism, Burlesque.
P	A	S	Q	U	I	N	Same as PASQUIL.
P	A	S	S	A	D	E	Flirtation.
P	A	S	S	A	D	O	Fencing manoeuvre.
P	A	S	S	A	G	E	Transit, Migration, Pass, Route, Way, Enactment, Course, Corridor.
P	A	S	S	A	N	T	Heraldic lion with upraised paw.
P	A	S	S	I	N	G	Transient, Fleeting, Superficial, Death, Exceeding, Decease, Overtaking, Proceeding.

1	2	3	4	5	6	7	Definition
P	A	S	S	I	O	N	Suffering, Ardour, Fervour, Enthusiasm, Zeal, Desire, Craving, Emotion.
P	A	S	S	I	V	E	Inactive, Lethargic, Inert, Apathetic, Impassive, Acquiescent, Resigned, Submissive.
P	A	S	S	K	E	Y	Skeleton key, Master key.
P	A	S	S	M	A	N	Student enrolled at a British university.
P	A	S	T	E	R	N	Ankle joint below fetlock of a horse or cow.
P	A	S	T	E	U	P	Combining several literary articles for production as a whole.
P	A	S	T	I	E	S	Meat, vegetables or fish enclosed in half-moon shaped cases of pastry.
P	A	S	T	I	M	E	Recreation, Diversion, Sport, Hobby.
P	A	S	T	I	N	G	Sticking, Spreading, Striking, Beating, Pounding, Thrashing, Gumming.
P	A	S	T	O	S	E	Thick layer of paint.
P	A	S	T	U	R	E	Herbage, Grazing, Meadow, Nourish, Feed.
P	A	T	A	M	A	R	Indian coasting vessel.
P	A	T	B	A	L	L	Gentle game with a bat and ball.
P	A	T	C	H	E	D	Mended, Repaired, Fixed, Reconditioned, Overhauled, Reconstructed, Rebuilt, Doctored.
P	A	T	C	H	E	R	One that repairs by patching.
P	A	T	E	L	L	A	Knee-cap, Limp, Disk-like fungus.
P	A	T	E	R	A	E	Ancient Roman sacrificial saucer, Decorative disc.
P	A	T	H	W	A	Y	Footpath, Way, Track, Trail.
P	A	T	I	E	N	T	Forbearance, Resignation, Long-sufferance, Self-control, Enduring, Passive, Composed.
P	A	T	N	E	S	S	Suitability, Aptness, Opportuneness.
P	A	T	O	N	C	E	Heraldic curved cross.
P	A	T	R	I	A	L	National identity.
P	A	T	R	I	C	O	Patercove, Evangelist.
P	A	T	R	I	O	T	Compatriot, Loyalist, Nationalist.
P	A	T	R	O	O	N	Landlord of grant of land under old Dutch American rule.
P	A	T	T	E	R	N	Model, Example, Ideal, Figure, Design, Device, Outline, Plan.
P	A	T	T	I	E	S	Pasties, Small pies, Flat filled chocolates.
P	A	T	T	I	N	G	Tapping, Smoothing, Flattening, Stroking, Applauding, Approving, Encouraging.
P	A	T	U	L	I	N	Antibiotic.
P	A	T	U	R	O	N	End section of a spider's front leg.
P	A	U	C	I	T	Y	Scarcity, Exiguity, Dearth, Insufficiency, Poverty, Scant, Lack.
P	A	U	L	I	N	E	St Paul the apostle.
P	A	U	N	C	H	Y	Potbellied, Stout, Overweight, Obese.
P	A	U	S	I	N	G	Lingering, Hesitating, Tarrying, Remaining, Lulling, Waiting, Lapsing, Suspending.
P	A	V	I	O	U	R	Paving slab.
P	A	W	N	I	N	G	Pledging, Staking, Wagering, Mortgaging, Bonding.
P	A	X	I	L	L	A	Spine in types of starfishes.
P	A	X	I	U	B	A	Brazilian palm.
P	A	Y	A	B	L	E	Due, Profitable, Mature, Unpaid, Outstanding, Unsettled, Owing, Overdue.
P	A	Y	B	A	C	K	Profit-taking.
P	A	Y	B	O	O	K	Identity book of a member of the armed services.
P	A	Y	D	I	R	T	Soil containing profitable mineral deposits, Profitable idea.
P	A	Y	L	O	A	D	reight, Portion of a plane's cargo that brings in income, Instruments and explosive in Rocket head.
P	A	Y	M	E	N	T	Return, Requital, Recompense, Reward, Discharge of a debt, Punishment, Chastisement.
P	A	Y	R	O	L	L	List of wages and salaries to be paid, Total wages payable.
P	A	Y	S	A	G	E	Landscape.
P	E	A	C	H	E	D	Betrayed, Informed, Squealed, Ratted, Divulged.
P	E	A	C	O	A	T	Pea jacket, Short overcoat worn by seamen.
P	E	A	C	O	C	K	Male bird known by fan-like tail, Swagger, Vain person, Swank.
P	E	A	C	R	A	B	Minute crab found in mussels and cockles.
P	E	A	F	O	W	L	Ornamental fowl.
P	E	A	K	I	N	G	Sickly, Fading, Petering, Mean, Sneaking, Rising to a point, Reaching maximum.
P	E	A	L	I	N	G	Resounding, Chiming, Tolling, Ringing.
P	E	A	R	L	E	D	Decorated with pearls, Beaded, Ground to small round grains.
P	E	A	R	L	I	N	Trimming of lace and pearls.
P	E	A	S	A	N	T	Rustic, Yokel, Hillbilly, Farm labourer, Bumpkin, Countryperson, Ethnic.
P	E	A	S	C	O	D	Pea pod.
P	E	A	S	O	U	P	Soup made of dried peas.
P	E	A	T	B	O	G	Area where peat is found.
P	E	A	T	E	R	Y	Area from which peat has been cut.
P	E	A	V	I	E	S	Tool used by workers handling cut logs.
P	E	B	B	L	E	D	Covered with small round stones.
P	E	B	R	I	N	E	Silk-worm and caterpillar disease.
P	E	C	C	A	N	T	Corrupt, Diseased, Unwholesome, Criminal, Sinning.
P	E	C	C	A	R	Y	Wild pig-like animal of the New World.
P	E	C	C	A	V	I	Confession, Statement of sins or errors.
P	E	C	K	I	N	G	Piercing, Picking up, Kissing, Smoochin, Carping, Scolding, Nagging.

1	2	3	4	5	6	7	Definition
P	E	C	K	I	S	H	Hungry, Famished, Ravenous, Starved, Irritable.
P	E	C	T	A	S	E	Plant enzme that forms gel.
P	E	C	T	A	T	E	Salt of pectic acid.
P	E	C	T	I	Z	E	Change to a gel.
P	E	C	T	O	S	E	Pectic substance of plants that is not soluble in water.
P	E	D	D	L	E	D	Hawked, Circulated, Retailed.
P	E	D	D	L	E	R	Pedlar, Hawker, Itinerant vendor.
P	E	D	E	S	I	S	Movement of particles caused by molecular impact.
P	E	D	I	C	E	L	Small stalk, Narrow joining section of an organ or appendage.
P	E	D	I	C	L	E	Same as PEDICEL.
P	E	D	I	W	A	K	Malayan sailing boat.
P	E	D	O	C	A	L	Soil that has layer of carbonates.
P	E	D	R	A	I	L	Tractor wheel with circular feet fastened on the rim.
P	E	E	K	I	N	G	Glimpsing, Glancing, Peeping.
P	E	E	L	I	N	G	Paring, Skinning, Exposing, Opening, Baring, Stripping.
P	E	E	L	I	T	E	Follower of Sir Robert Peel in the 19th century.
P	E	E	N	I	N	G	Hammering metal or leather.
P	E	E	P	I	N	G	Cheeping, Chirping, Squeaking, Peering, Peeking, Spying, Glancing, Snooping.
P	E	E	R	A	G	E	Book containing pertinent information of aristocrats.
P	E	E	R	E	S	S	Lady peer, Wife or widow of a peer.
P	E	E	R	I	N	G	Staring, Gazing, Gaping, Glaring, Gloating, Goggling, Prying, Snooping.
P	E	E	V	E	R	S	Hopscotch.
P	E	E	V	I	S	H	Querulous, Irritable, Fretful, Contrary, Fractious, Huffy, Critical, Petulant.
P	E	G	A	S	U	S	Winged horse of Greek mythology, Fish, Constellation.
P	E	G	G	I	N	G	Fastening with pegs, Restricting, Nailing down, Hammering, Striking, Plugging, Plodding.
P	E	G	W	O	O	D	Sticks for cleaning works of a watch.
P	E	H	L	E	V	I	Pahlavi, Iranian gold coin.
P	E	I	S	H	W	A	Chief minister of an Indian prince.
P	E	L	A	G	I	C	Living in the deep sea.
P	E	L	A	M	Y	D	Young tuna.
P	E	L	A	S	G	I	Early inhabitants of Greece.
P	E	L	I	C	A	N	Large bird with a very large pouch under its bill.
P	E	L	I	S	S	E	Fur cloak or coat, Coat or cloak trimmed or lined with fur.
P	E	L	L	A	E	A	Small ferns growing amongst rocks.
P	E	L	O	R	I	A	Abnormality in flower structure.
P	E	L	O	R	I	C	Having peloria.
P	E	L	O	R	U	S	Navigational dial.
P	E	L	O	T	O	N	Platoon, Coiled filaments in fungi.
P	E	L	T	A	S	T	Ancient Greek soldier with a light shield.
P	E	L	T	A	T	E	Leaf stem.
P	E	L	T	I	N	G	Beating, Hurrying, Battering, Thrashing, Flying, Hastening, Hammering, Pounding.
P	E	N	A	E	I	D	Prawn.
P	E	N	A	L	L	Y	Acting in a legal fashion.
P	E	N	A	L	T	Y	Fine, Punishment, Forfeit, Handicap, Retribution, Costs.
P	E	N	A	N	C	E	Humiliation, Attrition, Contrition, Remorse, Repentance, Sorrow, Distress, Mortification.
P	E	N	D	A	N	T	Neck ornament hanging on a chain, Pennant.
P	E	N	D	E	N	T	Floating, Suspended, Overhanging, Pending, Dangling.
P	E	N	D	I	N	G	Impending, Imminent, During, Undecided, Unsettled.
P	E	N	F	O	L	D	Pinfold, Pound for animals.
P	E	N	G	U	I	N	Flightless aquatic birds of the Antarctic.
P	E	N	N	A	G	E	Breeding flock of poultry with only one male.
P	E	N	N	A	M	E	Author's pseudonym, Nom de plume.
P	E	N	N	A	N	T	Nautical flag.
P	E	N	N	A	T	E	Pinnate, Winged.
P	E	N	N	I	E	D	Having pennies.
P	E	N	N	I	E	S	More than one penny.
P	E	N	N	I	N	E	Mineral of chlorite group.
P	E	N	N	I	N	G	Enclosing, Restraining, Confining, Restricting.
P	E	N	S	I	L	E	Overhanging, Hanging, Pendant, Pendent.
P	E	N	S	I	O	N	Annuity, Regular payment for services rendered, Retirement pay, accommodation establishment.
P	E	N	S	I	V	E	Thoughtful, Meditative, Musing, Wistful, Preoccupied, Withdrawn.
P	E	N	T	A	C	T	Five-rayed.
P	E	N	T	A	I	L	Tree shrew.
P	E	N	T	A	N	E	Paraffin hydrocarbons found in petroleum and natural gas.
P	E	N	T	I	C	E	Penthouse.
P	E	N	T	O	D	E	Vacuum tube with five electrodes.
P	E	N	T	O	S	E	Monosacharides.

1	2	3	4	5	6	7	
P	E	N	T	Z	I	A	Southern African shrubs.
P	E	N	U	C	H	E	Fudge containing brown sugar and nuts.
P	E	O	N	A	G	E	Bonded labour in agriculture.
P	E	O	N	I	S	M	Same as PEONAGE.
P	E	O	N	I	E	S	Herbaceous or shrubby plants cultivated for their showy blooms.
P	E	O	P	L	E	D	Populated, Inhabited, Occupied.
P	E	P	P	E	R	Y	Pungent, Spicy, Irascible, Choleric, Cranky, Hot-tempered, Passionate, Fiery.
P	E	P	P	I	L	L	Stimulant in a pill form.
P	E	P	S	I	N	E	Pepsin, Gastric juice.
P	E	P	T	A	L	K	Encouraging or inspiring talk or advice.
P	E	P	T	I	C	S	Digestive organs.
P	E	P	T	I	D	E	Class of amides.
P	E	P	T	O	N	E	Protein derivatives.
P	E	R	A	C	I	D	An acid.
P	E	R	B	E	N	D	Large stone or brick acting as a bonding stone.
P	E	R	C	A	L	E	Fine smooth cotton fabric.
P	E	R	C	E	N	T	Whole divided into one hundred parts.
P	E	R	C	E	P	T	Something that is perceived.
P	E	R	C	H	E	D	Stationed, Alighted, Landed, Roosted, Sat.
P	E	R	C	H	E	R	Bird that roosts.
P	E	R	C	O	I	D	Fish of perch-type.
P	E	R	C	U	S	S	Striking or tapping the body to aid diagnosis.
P	E	R	D	U	R	E	Endure, Persist, Continue, Last.
P	E	R	E	I	O	N	Thorax of a crustacea.
P	E	R	F	E	C	T	Flawless, Intact, Unblemished, Absolute, Expert, Proficient, Pure, Total.
P	E	R	F	I	D	Y	Treachery, Betrayal, Deception, Disloyalty, Faithlessness, Infidelity, Treason.
P	E	R	F	O	R	M	Fulfill, Implement, Enact, Present, Function, Execute, Accomplish, Achieve.
P	E	R	F	U	M	E	Fragrance, Scent, Pleasant odour, Liquid essence of flowers.
P	E	R	F	U	S	E	Suffuse, Diffuse, Permeate.
P	E	R	G	O	L	A	Trellis, Bower, Arbour, Colonnade for supporting climbing plants.
P	E	R	H	A	P	S	Maybe, Perchance, Possibly, Conceivably, Feasibly.
P	E	R	I	A	P	T	Charm, Talisman, Amulet.
P	E	R	I	D	O	T	Mineral consisting of a silicate of magnesium and iron used as a gem.
P	E	R	I	G	E	E	Lowest point of an earth orbit.
P	E	R	I	Q	U	E	Strong-flavoured tobacco.
P	E	R	I	W	I	G	Wig, Peruke.
P	E	R	J	U	R	E	Violate an oath, Deceive, Delude, Mislead, Trick, Lie, Prevaricate.
P	E	R	J	U	R	Y	False testimony, False swearing, False statement, Breach of an oath.
P	E	R	K	I	E	R	Brisker, Jauntier, Cockier, Sprightlier.
P	E	R	K	I	L	Y	Saucily, Impudently, Airily, Jauntily, Briskly, Sprightly.
P	E	R	K	I	N	G	Asserting, Sticking up, Freshening, Animating, Improving, Gaining, Mending.
P	E	R	L	I	T	E	Vitreous rock used for insulating material when expanded.
P	E	R	M	I	A	N	Geological period.
P	E	R	M	U	T	E	Re-arrange, Transform, Change.
P	E	R	O	R	A	L	Using the mouth.
P	E	R	O	S	I	S	Dietary disorder of poultry.
P	E	R	P	E	N	D	Reflect, Consider, Cogitate, Ponder, Contemplate, Study, Weigh, Think about.
P	E	R	P	L	E	X	Complicate, Puzzle, Bewilder, Confuse, Entangle, Perturb, Thwart, Surprise.
P	E	R	R	I	E	R	Mechanical catapult.
P	E	R	S	A	L	T	Acidic salt.
P	E	R	S	E	I	D	Group of meteors.
P	E	R	S	E	U	S	Warrior of ancient Greek mythology.
P	E	R	S	I	A	N	Relating to Persia, now Iran.
P	E	R	S	I	S	T	Continue, Persevere, Press, Endure, Abide, Prevail, Last.
P	E	R	S	O	N	A	Person.
P	E	R	S	P	E	X	Acrylic plastic.
P	E	R	T	A	I	N	Concern, Belong, Apply, Relate, Associate, Combine, Connect, Join.
P	E	R	T	U	R	B	Derange, Unsettle, Disquiet, Discompose, Agitate, Bother, Dismay, Trouble.
P	E	R	U	S	A	L	Study carefully.
P	E	R	U	S	E	D	Read intently.
P	E	R	V	A	D	E	Permeate, Traverse, Impregnate, Penetrate, Saturate, Percolate, Imbue, Transfuse.
P	E	R	V	E	R	T	Corrupt, Misuse, Debase, Brutalize, Abuse, Outrage, Debauch, Demoralize.
P	E	S	K	I	L	Y	In a troublesome way.
P	E	S	T	L	E	D	Beaten, Pounded, Pulverized, Crushed.
P	E	S	T	L	E	S	Thin pliable internal portion of the leg of a lobster or prawn.
P	E	T	A	S	U	S	Hat worn by ancient Greeks and Romans, Winged hat as in pictures of Mercury.
P	E	T	E	R	E	D	Diminished, Disappeared, Exhausted, Decreased, Dwindled, Receded, Lessened.

1	2	3	4	5	6	7	Definition
P	E	T	I	O	L	E	Leafstalk, Waistlike section of an insect.
P	E	T	R	A	R	Y	Military catapult.
P	E	T	R	I	F	Y	Calcify, Deaden, Paralyze, Stupefy, Daze, Dumbfound, Stun, Benumb.
P	E	T	R	I	N	E	Relating to St. Peter the apostle.
P	E	T	R	O	U	S	Rocky, Hard front portion of the skull.
P	E	T	T	I	L	Y	Futily, Paltry, Measly, Irritably, Peevishly.
P	E	T	T	I	N	G	Caressing, Pampering, Indulging, Cuddling, Fondling, Embracing.
P	E	T	T	I	S	H	Fretful, Peevish, Irritable, Fractious, Querulous, Petulant, Snappish, Huffy.
P	E	T	U	N	I	A	Genus of American herbs cultivated for the colourful flowers.
P	E	T	Z	I	T	E	Mineral of silver gold, Telluride.
P	E	W	R	E	N	T	Payment for use of a church pew.
P	F	E	N	N	I	G	German low value coin.
P	H	A	E	T	O	N	Four-wheeled carriage, Dangerous driver.
P	H	A	L	A	N	X	Closed formation of warriors, Massed arrangement.
P	H	A	L	L	I	C	Symbol of male sexual organ.
P	H	A	L	L	U	S	Representation of male sex organ, Penis.
P	H	A	N	T	O	M	Apparition, Spirit, Ghost, Illusory, Elusive, Spectre, Spirit, Shadow.
P	H	A	R	A	O	H	Ruler of ancient Egypt.
P	H	A	R	Y	N	X	Gullet, Upper respiratory organs.
P	H	A	S	I	N	G	Adjusting, Performing, Guiding.
P	H	E	L	L	E	M	Cell-layer built up by plant tissue.
P	H	E	N	A	T	E	Salt of phenol.
P	H	I	D	I	A	N	Characteristic of work of Greek sculptor Phidias.
P	H	I	L	T	R	E	Magic portion, Love drug or charm.
P	H	O	C	I	A	N	Relating to the ancient Greek state of Phocis.
P	H	O	C	I	N	E	Resembling seals.
P	H	O	E	N	I	X	Legendary bird represented as symbol of immortality, Paragon.
P	H	O	N	A	T	E	Enunciate, Articulate, Pronounce, Speak.
P	H	O	N	E	M	E	Distinguishing sound.
P	H	O	N	I	C	S	Acoustics, Science of sound, Learning to read by sounds.
P	H	O	N	I	N	G	Telephoning, Contact by telephone.
P	H	O	R	O	N	T	Animals or insects that are transported by another kind of animal.
P	H	O	R	O	N	E	Solvent condensed for acetone.
P	H	O	T	I	A	N	Relating to belief that split the Eastern and Western churches.
P	H	O	T	I	C	S	Science of light.
P	H	O	T	I	S	M	Ability to see by using other senses.
P	H	R	A	G	M	A	Dividing membrane.
P	H	R	A	S	E	D	Worded, Termed, Styled, Expressed.
P	H	R	A	S	E	R	Humorist, Wit, One given to flowery but meaningless talk.
P	H	R	A	T	R	Y	Kinship, Tribal affinity, Clannish.
P	H	R	E	N	I	C	Relating to the mind or diaphragm.
P	H	R	E	N	S	Y	Frenzy, Delirium, Madness.
P	H	Y	S	I	C	K	Science of medicine, Cures, Medicines.
P	H	Y	T	O	I	D	Plant-like.
P	I	A	F	F	E	R	Particular movement of a horse in dressage.
P	I	A	N	I	N	O	Small piano.
P	I	A	N	I	S	M	Piano playing, Composing or arranging music for the piano.
P	I	A	N	I	S	T	One skilled in the art of piano playing.
P	I	A	N	O	L	A	Automatic piano that uses music rolls.
P	I	A	R	I	S	T	Member of 17th century religious school.
P	I	A	S	T	R	E	Monetary unit of many countries.
P	I	B	R	O	C	H	Bagpipe music based on a folk song.
P	I	C	A	D	O	R	Horseman in a bullfight who plants banderillas in the bull.
P	I	C	C	O	L	O	Small flute pitched higher than an ordinary one.
P	I	C	I	D	A	E	Family of birds, Woodpeckers.
P	I	C	C	A	G	E	Rent paid by fairs to erect booths.
P	I	C	K	I	N	G	Plucking, Penetrating, Choosing, Electing, Marking, Preferring, Pecking, Taking.
P	I	C	K	L	E	D	Preserved, Steeped in a vinegar solution, Intoxicated.
P	I	C	O	L	E	T	Automatic correction of flight stability.
P	I	C	O	T	E	E	Flowers speckled or edged with another colour.
P	I	C	Q	U	E	T	Picket, Stake, post or peg with sharpened point used for fencing or edging.
P	I	C	R	A	T	E	Salt of picric acid.
P	I	C	R	I	T	E	Peridot without feldspar.
P	I	C	T	I	S	H	Pertaining to the Picts.
P	I	C	T	U	R	E	Portrait, Pictorial representation, Illustration, Symbol, Copy, Pattern, Show, Movie.
P	I	D	D	L	E	D	Trifled, Dawdled, Urinated.
P	I	D	D	O	C	K	Mollusc.

1	2	3	4	5	6	7	Clue
P	I	E	B	A	L	D	Marked in two different colours.
P	I	E	C	I	N	G	Patching, Joining, Uniting, Agreeing, Assembling.
P	I	E	R	A	G	E	Wharfage, Harbour charges.
P	I	E	R	C	E	D	Penetrated, Incised, Impaled, Transfixed, Stabbed, Bored, Perforated, Entered.
P	I	E	R	C	E	R	Instrument for making holes.
P	I	E	R	I	A	N	Relating to learing or poetry, Of the region of Pieria in ancient Macedonia.
P	I	E	R	I	N	E	Genus of evergreen shrubs.
P	I	E	R	R	O	T	Buffoon, Clown, Minstrel, Traditional pantomime character.
P	I	E	T	I	S	M	Religious movement that advocated simpler devotions.
P	I	E	T	I	S	T	Adherent of pietism.
P	I	E	W	O	O	L	Inferior wool.
P	I	F	F	E	R	O	Old Italian wind instrument.
P	I	F	F	L	E	D	Trifled, Twaddled, Acted in an inept manner.
P	I	G	D	E	E	R	Babirusa, East Indian hog-like mammal.
P	I	G	E	Y	E	D	Having small deep-set eyes.
P	I	G	F	I	S	H	Salt-water grunts, Fish.
P	I	G	G	E	R	Y	Pigsty.
P	I	G	G	I	N	G	Living in Squalor.
P	I	G	G	I	S	H	Messy, Dirty, Greedy, Mean, Stubborn.
P	I	G	H	T	L	E	Barnyard.
P	I	G	I	R	O	N	Crude iron, Cast iron.
P	I	G	L	E	A	D	Lead ingots.
P	I	G	M	E	N	T	Colouring substance to mix with liquid for paint, enamel, inks and plastics.
P	I	G	M	I	E	S	Pygmies, Dwarfs, People of small stature.
P	I	G	N	O	N	S	Fir-cones.
P	I	G	S	K	I	N	Leather from skin of pigs used for shoes, wallets, saddles and bookbinding.
P	I	G	T	A	I	L	Hair in a plait.
P	I	G	W	A	S	H	Swill.
P	I	K	E	L	E	T	Crumpet, Small round thick pancake.
P	I	K	E	M	A	N	Soldier armed with a pike.
P	I	L	C	H	E	R	A scabbard.
P	I	L	E	A	T	E	Crested bird.
P	I	L	F	E	R	Y	Petty theft.
P	I	L	G	R	I	M	Traveller, Wayfarer, One who visits shrines or holy places.
P	I	L	I	O	U	S	Hairy.
P	I	L	L	A	G	E	Sack, Robbery, Ravage, Depredate, Desecrate, Devour, Usurp, Confiscate.
P	I	L	L	B	O	X	Small round box for pills, Woman's small hat resembling a pillbox.
P	I	L	L	I	N	G	Making into pills.
P	I	L	L	I	O	N	Passenger seat or cushion behind the driver on a motor cycle or a horse.
P	I	L	L	O	R	Y	Frame for public punishment, Expose to ridicule or scorn.
P	I	L	L	O	W	Y	Soft, Yielding.
P	I	L	O	T	E	D	Conducted, Escorted, Coached, Managed, Steered, Directed, Led, Guided.
P	I	L	U	L	A	R	Characteristic of a pill.
P	I	L	U	L	E	S	Little pill.
P	I	M	B	I	N	A	Cranberry.
P	I	M	E	L	E	A	Genus of Australian and New Zealand shrubs.
P	I	M	E	N	T	A	Tropical American aromatic tree.
P	I	M	E	N	T	O	Allspice, Thick-fleshed pepper.
P	I	M	P	L	E	D	Spotted or covered with pimples.
P	I	N	A	C	O	L	Liquid glycol.
P	I	N	B	A	L	L	Game of bagatelle played on an electrical machine.
P	I	N	B	O	N	E	Hipbone of a quadruped.
P	I	N	B	U	S	H	Australian needlebush.
P	I	N	C	E	R	S	Pliers, large grasping claws of a crab or lobster.
P	I	N	C	H	E	D	Squeezed, Nipped, Compressed, Constricted, Extorted, Wasted, Stolen, Arrested.
P	I	N	C	H	E	R	One that steals or nips.
P	I	N	C	H	E	S	Squeezes, Nips, Compresses, Arrests, Steals, Constricts.
P	I	N	D	A	R	I	Indian bandit.
P	I	N	E	O	I	L	Oil from pine tree or conifer.
P	I	N	E	T	U	M	Plantation of pine trees.
P	I	N	F	I	R	E	Explosive mechanism of a firearm.
P	I	N	F	I	S	H	Grunt fish with sharp dorsal spines.
P	I	N	F	O	L	D	Confine, Pound for animals.
P	I	N	G	I	N	G	Sharp metallic sound.
P	I	N	G	U	I	D	Fat, Fatty.
P	I	N	H	E	A	D	Small, Insignificant, Dull, Stupid, Fool.
P	I	N	H	O	L	E	Tiny aperture, Defect in a glaze, Beetle-hole in timber.

1	2	3	4	5	6	7	Definition
P	I	N	K	E	Y	E	Conjunctivitis.
P	I	N	K	I	N	G	Serrating edge of fabric or paper with special shears, Knocking sound in a car engine.
P	I	N	K	I	S	H	Tending toward the left in politics.
P	I	N	N	A	C	E	Ship's boat.
P	I	N	N	A	T	E	Resembling a feather.
P	I	N	N	I	N	G	Foundation, Propping, Supporting, Fastening with a pin.
P	I	N	N	O	C	K	A small bridge.
P	I	N	N	U	L	A	Barb of a feather.
P	I	N	N	U	L	E	Same as PINNULA.
P	I	N	T	A	D	O	Painted or printed chintz made in India.
P	I	N	T	A	I	L	River duck.
P	I	N	T	P	O	T	Pint measure for ale or beer.
P	I	N	W	O	R	M	Parasitic worm, Plant burrowing insect.
P	I	O	N	E	E	R	Explore, Settle, Forerunner, Earliest, Initial, Original, Pilot, Primary.
P	I	O	N	I	N	G	Digging, Excavating.
P	I	O	U	S	L	Y	Devoutly, Religiously, Priestly.
P	I	P	E	M	M	A	Signal code meaning afternoon.
P	I	P	E	T	T	E	Glass tubes used in a laboratory for operations with liquids.
P	I	P	P	I	N	G	Defeating, Killing, Winning by a small margin, Breaking shell of egg when hatching.
P	I	Q	U	A	N	T	Stinging, Provocative, Cutting, Pungent, Stimulating, Poignant, Spicy, Peppery.
P	I	Q	U	I	N	G	Nettling, Irritating, Provoking, Aggravating, Exasperating, Peeving, Riling, Rousing.
P	I	R	A	G	U	A	Canoe made of a hollowed tree trunk Dug-out.
P	I	R	A	T	E	D	Infringement of a copywright, Lured workers, To use in violation of exclusive assignment.
P	I	R	A	T	I	C	Being a pirate, Resembling a pirate.
P	I	R	O	G	U	E	Dug-out canoe.
P	I	S	C	A	R	Y	Fishery, Fishing place.
P	I	S	C	I	N	A	Ancient Roman tank used as pool or fish pond.
P	I	S	M	I	R	E	Ant, Insignificant or contemptible person.
P	I	S	O	N	E	S	Indian people of Northeastern Mexico.
P	I	S	T	O	L	E	Old European gold coin.
P	I	T	A	P	A	T	Pitter-patter, Pattering sound, Palpitation.
P	I	T	C	H	E	D	Thrown, Flung, Directed, Narrated, Encamped, Plunged, Sloped, Dipped.
P	I	T	C	H	E	R	Jug.
P	I	T	C	O	A	L	Coal mined from the earth.
P	I	T	E	O	U	S	Pitiful, Pathetic, Poor, Rueful, Beseeching, Entreating, Imploring, Plaintive.
P	I	T	F	A	L	L	Trap, Snare, Hidden danger, Booby trap, Hazard, Peril, Bait, Lure.
P	I	T	H	E	A	D	Top of a mine-shaft.
P	I	T	H	I	L	Y	Concisely, Briefly, Tersely.
P	I	T	H	I	N	G	Extracting sap or marrow, Severing the spinal cord.
P	I	T	H	R	A	Y	Root or stem cell.
P	I	T	I	F	U	L	Contemptible, Wretched, Pathetic, Piteous, Rueful, Miserable, Woeful.
P	I	T	M	I	R	K	Intense darkness.
P	I	T	T	I	N	G	Making indentations, Opposing, Striving.
P	I	T	T	I	T	E	Theatregoer who sits in the pit.
P	I	T	U	I	T	A	Pituitary body.
P	I	T	U	I	T	E	Same as PITUITA.
P	I	T	Y	I	N	G	Feeling pity, Commiserating, Soothing, Sympathizing.
P	I	V	O	T	A	L	Functioning as a pivot, Vital, Cardinal, Overruling, Essential.
P	I	V	O	T	E	D	Oscillated, Turned, Hinged, Diverted, Wheeled, Wound.
P	L	A	C	A	R	D	Poster, Sign, Advertise.
P	L	A	C	A	T	E	Appease, Pacify, Conciliate, Assuage, Mollify, Comfort, Tranquilise, Propitiate.
P	L	A	C	E	B	O	Harmles medicent given for psychological reasons, Something to soothe.
P	L	A	C	I	N	G	Arranging, Disposing, Setting, Fixing, Investing, Estimating, Ranking, Assigning.
P	L	A	C	K	E	T	Slit, Opening into a pocket.
P	L	A	C	O	D	E	Plate-like thickening of embryonic ectoderm.
P	L	A	C	O	I	D	Fish.
P	L	A	C	U	L	A	Flattened blastula.
P	L	A	C	U	N	A	Windowpane oyster.
P	L	A	F	O	N	D	Elaborately decorated ceiling, Bridge game.
P	L	A	G	I	U	M	Kidnapping, Abducting.
P	L	A	G	U	E	D	Tormented, Scourged, Worried, Annoyed, Harassed, Badgered, Afflicted, Hectored.
P	L	A	G	U	E	Y	Troublesome.
P	L	A	G	U	L	A	Hard plate on the underside of a spider.
P	L	A	I	D	E	D	Wearing a tartan.
P	L	A	I	N	E	R	Smoother, Clearer, Balder, More obvious, Franker, Blunter, Coarser, More simple.
P	L	A	I	N	L	Y	Distinctly, Clearly, Obviously, Frankly, Simply, Unpretentiosly, Candidly, Baldly.
P	L	A	I	T	E	D	Braided, Interwoven, Involved, Devious.

1	2	3	4	5	6	7	
P	L	A	N	I	N	G	Gliding, Smoothing, Evening, Levelling, Laying.
P	L	A	N	I	S	H	Polish, Hammer smooth.
P	L	A	N	K	E	D	Laid down, Floored, Deposited, Covered with boards.
P	L	A	N	N	E	D	Designed, Intended, Sketched, Schemed, Arranged, Outlined, Formulated, Proposed.
P	L	A	N	N	E	R	Designer, Projector.
P	L	A	N	T	A	D	Toward the sole of the foot.
P	L	A	N	T	A	E	The whole of the plant kingdom.
P	L	A	N	T	A	R	Of the sole of the foot.
P	L	A	N	T	E	D	Cultivated, Populated, Grew, Established, Sown, Hidden, Buried, Secreted.
P	L	A	N	T	E	R	Farmer, Plantation owner, Grower, Settler, Container for decorative plants.
P	L	A	N	U	L	A	Young free-swimming larva.
P	L	A	N	X	T	Y	Irish melody written for a harp.
P	L	A	S	H	E	D	Dashed, Spattered, Speckled, Dabbled.
P	L	A	S	M	I	C	Plasmatic.
P	L	A	S	M	I	N	Enzyme that dissolves the fibrin of blood clots.
P	L	A	S	M	O	N	Cytoplasm.
P	L	A	S	T	E	R	Coat, Soothe, Alleviate, Remedy, Smear, Bedaub, Smudge, Saturate.
P	L	A	S	T	I	C	Creative, Formative, Elastic, Pliable, Yielding, Flexible, Adaptable, Supple.
P	L	A	S	T	I	D	Cell constituent.
P	L	A	T	A	N	E	Plane-tree.
P	L	A	T	E	A	U	Tableland, Highland, Stable period or condition, Level off.
P	L	A	T	I	N	A	Crude platinum, Pale bluish grey colour.
P	L	A	T	I	N	G	Thin coating usually of metal.
P	L	A	T	O	O	N	Group, Battery, Lot, Cluster, Array, Bunch, Set, Batch.
P	L	A	T	T	E	D	Planned, Arranged as of town planning.
P	L	A	T	T	E	R	Large shallow plate, Broad flat object.
P	L	A	U	D	I	T	Applause, Approbation, Praise, Acclaim.
P	L	A	Y	A	C	T	Professional actor, Make-believe, Impersonate, Insincere behaviour.
P	L	A	Y	B	O	X	Box for storage of childrens' toys.
P	L	A	Y	B	O	Y	Wealthy young man leading a life of indolence.
P	L	A	Y	D	A	Y	Holiday from work, Informal school athletic meeting.
P	L	A	Y	F	U	L	Sportive, Humorous, Jocular, Frisky, Prankish, Roguish, Frolicsome, Mischievous.
P	L	A	Y	I	N	G	Sporting, Running, Disporting, Romping, Entertaining, Using, Manipulating, Gambling.
P	L	E	A	D	E	D	Appealed, Litigated, Begged, Implored, Defended, Beseeched, Craved, Entreated.
P	L	E	A	D	E	R	Advocate, Intercessor.
P	L	E	A	S	E	D	Placated, Satisfied, Gratified, Delighted, Regaled, Rejoiced, Contented, Suited.
P	L	E	A	S	E	R	One that pleases.
P	L	E	A	T	E	D	Folded over, Furrowed, Wrinkled, Creased.
P	L	E	B	I	A	N	Plebeian, Ignoble, Common, Humble, Lowly, Base, Homely.
P	L	E	C	T	R	E	Plectrum.
P	L	E	D	G	E	D	Pawned, Secured, Guaranteed, Promised, Assured, Warranted, Bonded, Toasted.
P	L	E	D	G	E	E	One who holds bond.
P	L	E	D	G	E	T	Compress of gauze for a wound.
P	L	E	I	A	D	S	Seven stars in the constellation Taurus.
P	L	E	N	A	R	Y	Absolute, Perfect, Unqualified, Complete, Entire.
P	L	E	N	I	S	H	Replenish, Provide, Equip, Furnish.
P	L	E	O	P	O	D	Abdominal limb of a crustacean.
P	L	E	R	O	M	A	Plenitude, Abundance, Fullness.
P	L	E	R	O	M	E	The stelar region in a root tip.
P	L	E	U	R	A	L	Relating to the lungs.
P	L	E	U	R	O	N	Lateral part of a thoracic segment of an insect.
P	L	E	X	U	R	E	Weaving together.
P	L	I	A	B	L	E	Flexible, Supple, Complaisant, Adaptable, Compliant, Ductile, Manipulable, Plastic.
P	L	I	A	B	L	Y	Docily, Flexibly, Lithely.
P	L	I	A	N	C	Y	Flexibility, Complaisance.
P	L	I	C	A	T	E	Plaited, Folded, Ridged, Wrinkled, Furrowed, Corrugated.
P	L	I	M	M	E	D	Swelled, Inflated, Distended.
P	L	I	S	K	I	E	Practical joke, Trick.
P	L	O	D	D	E	D	Trudged, Drudged, Tramped, Slogged, Toiled, Stamped, Wallowed, Floundered.
P	L	O	D	D	E	R	Person who walks slowly, One who works at a steady pace.
P	L	O	P	P	E	D	Dropped heavily, Splashed, Plumped.
P	L	O	S	I	V	E	Explosive.
P	L	O	T	T	E	D	Conspired, Planned, Schemed, Intrigued, Measured, Devised, Concocted, Contrived.
P	L	U	M	B	I	C	Containing lead.
P	L	U	M	B	U	M	Lead.
P	L	U	M	C	O	T	Hybrid fruit between the plum and apricot.
P	L	U	M	E	R	Y	Plumes, Plumage.

1	2	3	4	5	6	7	Definition
P	L	U	M	I	N	G	Showing self-satisfaction, Depriving, Despoiling, Taking credit.
P	L	U	M	M	E	T	Plumb bob, Drop sharply, Fall abruptly.
P	L	U	M	O	S	E	Having feathers or plumes, Feathery.
P	L	U	M	P	E	D	Fattened, Distended, Swelled.
P	L	U	M	P	E	R	Rounder, Chubbier, Fatter, Stouter.
P	L	U	M	P	L	Y	Firmly, Directly, In a plumb manner.
P	L	U	M	U	L	E	Primary plant bud, A down feather.
P	L	U	N	D	E	R	Pillaging, Spoil, Booty, Loot, Baggage, Freight, Ransack, Rob.
P	L	U	N	G	E	D	Submerged, Immersed, Sunk, Thrust, Pitched, Rammed, Shoved, Lunged.
P	L	U	N	G	E	R	Diver, Reckless, Speculator, Rod carrying valves, Pump part.
P	L	U	V	I	A	L	Relating to rain, Ceremonial robe.
P	L	Y	W	O	O	D	Layers of thin veneer woods glued together.
P	O	A	C	E	A	E	Granimeae, Grasses, Bamboo, Cereals.
P	O	A	C	H	E	D	Cooked in a liquid.
P	O	A	C	H	E	R	One that trespasses and steals, One who kills game or fish illegally.
P	O	C	H	A	R	D	Heavy bodied diving duck.
P	O	C	H	O	I	R	Stencil colour process.
P	O	D	A	G	R	A	Gout.
P	O	D	A	L	I	C	By means of the feet.
P	O	D	D	I	N	G	To produce pods.
P	O	D	E	S	T	A	Chief magistrate.
P	O	D	O	M	E	R	Part of a limb of an arthropod, such as crustacean or spider.
P	O	E	T	E	S	S	Female poet.
P	O	E	T	I	C	S	Treatise on poetry, Poetic theory, Poetic feelings.
P	O	E	T	I	S	E	To write poetry, Speak poetically.
P	O	I	N	D	E	D	Taken forceful possession. Impounded.
P	O	I	N	T	E	D	Sharpened, Punctuated, Indicated, Exact, Precise, Aimed, Suggested, Turned.
P	O	I	N	T	E	R	Tip, Point, Steer, Tip-off, Indicator.
P	O	I	S	I	N	G	Counterbalancing, Bracing, Balancing, Hanging.
P	O	I	T	R	E	L	Decorated horse armour.
P	O	L	A	C	C	A	Polonaise.
P	O	L	A	R	O	N	Conducting electron.
P	O	L	D	E	R	S	Reclaimed land.
P	O	L	E	C	A	T	European carnivorous mammal.
P	O	L	E	M	I	C	Controversial discussion, Disputant, Contentious.
P	O	L	E	N	T	A	Mush made of cornmeal or semolina.
P	O	L	I	C	E	D	Governed, Kept order, Supervised.
P	O	L	I	G	A	R	Indian village chief.
P	O	L	I	T	E	S	Skipper butterflies.
P	O	L	I	T	I	C	Expedient, Advisable, Prudent, Tactical, Wise, Astute, Shrewd, Diplomatic.
P	O	L	L	A	C	K	Atlantic food fish.
P	O	L	L	A	R	D	Foreign coin of little value, Cow or sheep, Pruned tree, Bran.
P	O	L	L	A	X	E	Pole-axe, Axe with hammer opposite cutting edge.
P	O	L	L	I	N	G	Clipping, Cropping, Fleecing, Robbing, Enumerating, Canvassing, Casting vote.
P	O	L	L	T	A	X	Tax levied on adults, Head tax.
P	O	L	L	U	T	E	Corrupt, Defile, Desecrate, Profane, Dirty, Taint, Befoul, Contaminate.
P	O	L	O	I	S	T	Polo player.
P	O	L	Y	A	C	T	Having many rays.
P	O	L	Y	G	O	N	Closed figure of straight lines joined by angles.
P	O	L	Y	M	E	R	Natural or synthetic chemical compound.
P	O	L	Y	P	E	D	Animal having many feet.
P	O	L	Y	P	O	D	Having many feet or abdominal limbs, Insect larva.
P	O	L	Y	P	U	S	Genus of octopuses.
P	O	L	Y	Z	O	A	Bryozoa, Cestode.
P	O	M	A	T	U	M	Ointment, Perfumed unguent for the hair and scalp.
P	O	M	F	R	E	T	Black flat licorice confection.
P	O	M	P	A	N	O	American food fish.
P	O	M	P	I	O	N	Pumpkin.
P	O	M	P	O	S	O	Pompously, Imposingly.
P	O	M	P	O	U	S	Self-important, Grandiose, Arrogant, Bloated, Important, Proud, Egocentric.
P	O	N	C	E	A	U	Rec colour, Small bridge or culvert.
P	O	N	D	A	G	E	Storage capacity of a pond.
P	O	N	D	I	N	G	Creating a dam to form a pond.
P	O	N	I	A	R	D	Dagger with slender triangular blade.
P	O	N	T	A	G	E	Payment in lieu of personal service.
P	O	N	T	I	F	F	High priest or chief religious figure.
P	O	N	T	I	N	E	Relating to a bridge, Pontile, Area between Rome and Naples.

1	2	3	4	5	6	7	Clue
P	O	N	T	O	O	N	Portable float for constructing a temporary bridge.
P	O	O	H	B	A	H	Character in a Gilbert and Sullivan opera, One holding many public offices.
P	O	O	L	I	N	G	Put together to share, Reserve of material.
P	O	O	P	I	N	G	Tooting, Gulping, Shipping water, Exhausting, Ceasing.
P	O	O	R	B	O	X	Box for alms for the poor.
P	O	O	R	E	S	T	Scantiest, Leanest, Thinnest, Most needy, Sparsest, Most pathetic, Meanest, Cheapest.
P	O	O	R	I	S	H	Rather poor in comparison.
P	O	O	R	L	A	W	Law regulating public relief for the needy.
P	O	P	C	O	R	N	Corn popped by heat.
P	O	P	E	D	O	M	Office or tenure of the Pope.
P	O	P	E	Y	E	D	Having eyes that bulge.
P	O	P	O	V	E	R	Quick bread cooked in high heat.
P	O	P	P	I	E	D	Drowsy, Indolent, Narcotic.
P	O	P	P	I	N	G	Protruding, Bulging, Intermittent, Occasional, Sporadic, Bustling, Lively, Busy.
P	O	P	P	L	E	D	Tossed about, Agitated, Bubbled.
P	O	P	S	H	O	P	Pawnshop.
P	O	P	U	L	A	R	Plebeian, Inexpensive, Crowded, Approved, Prevalent, Widespread, Familiar, Current.
P	O	P	U	L	U	S	Poplar tree.
P	O	P	W	E	E	D	Bladderwort, Bladder wrack.
P	O	R	C	A	T	E	Furrowed for draining.
P	O	R	C	I	N	E	Piggy, Swinish.
P	O	R	I	T	E	S	Coral.
P	O	R	K	P	I	E	Pie of raised pastry containing port pieces, Hat of pie shape.
P	O	R	O	S	I	S	Bone condition.
P	O	R	O	T	I	C	Medicine favouring the formation of callus, Marked by porous structure.
P	O	R	P	H	I	N	Deep purple crystalline compound.
P	O	R	R	E	C	T	Extend, Present, Tender.
P	O	R	T	A	G	E	Carry, Pack, Haul canoes or rafts over land between non-navigable portions of a river.
P	O	R	T	E	N	D	Bode, Presage, Forecast, Predict, Indicate, Signify, Extend, Foretell.
P	O	R	T	E	N	T	Omen, Sign, Marvel, Prodigy, Wonder, Augury, Miracle, Phenomenon.
P	O	R	T	I	C	O	Covered entrance, Balcony, Porch.
P	O	R	T	I	N	G	Intake or exhaust opening of an engine.
P	O	R	T	I	O	N	Part, Share, Division, Allotment, Quota, Slice, Parcel, Segment.
P	O	R	T	R	A	Y	Delineate, Depict, Enact, Represent, Describe, Picture, Copy, Reproduce.
P	O	R	Z	A	N	A	Genus of short-billed rails.
P	O	S	A	U	N	E	Trombone, Reed stop in an organ for trombone sound.
P	O	S	I	T	E	D	Disposed, Set, Fixed, Presupposed.
P	O	S	S	E	S	S	Occupy, Inhabit, Have, Control, Dominate, Retain, Enjoy, Hold.
P	O	S	T	A	G	E	Postal fees for carrying mail.
P	O	S	T	B	A	G	Mailbag for the carrying of letters and parcels.
P	O	S	T	B	O	X	Box for incoming or outgoing mail.
P	O	S	T	B	O	Y	Postilion, Postrider.
P	O	S	T	D	A	M	Extension of a denture to make a full set.
P	O	S	T	E	E	N	Sheepskin jacket from Afghanistan.
P	O	S	T	E	R	N	Private gate, Obscure entrance or exit, Subterranean passage.
P	O	S	T	F	I	X	Suffix, To add a letter or syllable at the end of a word.
P	O	S	T	I	N	G	Stationing, Assigning, Placing, Setting, Recording, Mailing, Depositing, Furnishing.
P	O	S	T	M	A	N	Carrier of mail for delivery.
P	O	S	T	U	R	E	Pose, Attitude, Position.
P	O	S	T	W	A	R	Period after the war.
P	O	T	A	B	L	E	Beverage, Drinkable.
P	O	T	A	G	E	R	Cook whose speciality is making soups and broths.
P	O	T	A	M	I	C	Relating to rivers and navigation of rivers.
P	O	T	A	R	C	H	Kiln for preheating clay pots.
P	O	T	A	S	S	A	Potash.
P	O	T	B	A	N	K	Place where pottery is made.
P	O	T	C	H	E	R	Paper-pulp machine.
P	O	T	E	N	C	E	Potent.
P	O	T	E	N	C	Y	Force, Power, Authority, Ability, Influence, Energy, Strength, Virtue.
P	O	T	H	E	A	D	Hermetically sealed terminal.
P	O	T	H	E	E	N	Illicitly distilled Irish whiskey.
P	O	T	H	E	R	B	Herb used as a vegetable.
P	O	T	H	O	L	E	Deep cave, Circular hole in river bed made by the current.
P	O	T	H	O	O	K	Hook for hanging kettle or pot over an open fire.
P	O	T	I	C	H	E	Vase with separate cover.
P	O	T	L	E	A	D	Graphite.
P	O	T	L	I	N	E	Electrolytic cells used in production of aluminium.

1	2	3	4	5	6	7	
P	O	T	L	U	C	K	Have no choice but to accept what is available.
P	O	T	O	R	O	O	Rat kangaroo.
P	O	T	S	H	O	T	Shot taken at random, Remark made on chance.
P	O	T	T	A	G	E	Vegetables and meat cooked to a mush.
P	O	T	T	E	R	Y	Shop or factory where earthen, china, glaze or ceramic vessels are made.
P	O	T	T	I	N	G	Making of pottery, Canning, Preserving.
P	O	U	C	H	E	D	Protruded, Pocketed, Bagged, Marsupial, Swallowed.
P	O	U	L	A	R	D	Sterilized pullet.
P	O	U	L	T	E	R	Poulterer, One that deals in poultry.
P	O	U	L	T	R	Y	Domesticated birds.
P	O	U	N	C	E	D	Pricked, Pierced, Seized, Assaulted, Sprang, Swooped, Grabbed.
P	O	U	N	D	A	L	Unit of force.
P	O	U	N	D	E	D	Impounded, Pulverized, Crushed, Thumped, Lumbered, Tramped, Thundered, Pelted.
P	O	U	R	I	N	G	Diffusing, Discharging, Streaming, Gushing, Sluicing, Flooding, Cascading, Inundating.
P	O	U	S	S	I	N	Young chicken.
P	O	U	T	I	N	G	Sulking, Protruding, Grumping, Mumping, Jutting, Overhanging, Projecting, Poking.
P	O	V	E	R	T	Y	Privation, Want, Scarcity, Dearth, Inferiority, Feebleness, Emaciation.
P	O	W	D	E	R	Y	Crumbling, Friable, Dusty, Chalky, Fine, Pulverized, Impalpable, Floury.
P	O	W	E	R	E	D	Engined, Energized, Strengthened, Armed, Supplied, Impelled, Functioned.
P	R	A	C	T	I	C	Practical, Cunning, Deceitful, Realistic, Hard, Pragmatic, Utilitarian.
P	R	A	E	S	E	S	Chairman.
P	R	A	E	T	O	R	Ancient Roman magistrate.
P	R	A	I	R	I	E	Plain, Pampa, Savanna, Steppe, Treeless grassy expanse.
P	R	A	I	S	E	D	Applauded, Extolled, Commended, Lauded, Magnified, Appraised, Acclaimed, Hailed.
P	R	A	K	R	I	T	Modern Indic languages.
P	R	A	L	I	N	E	Almonds roasted in sugar, Fudge with nuts.
P	R	A	N	C	E	D	Capered, Bounded, Ostentatious walk, Swaggered, Danced, Flounced, Prinked, Minced.
P	R	A	N	G	E	D	Hit, Struck, Collided, Clashed, Bumped, Crashed, Wrecked, Smashed.
P	R	A	N	K	E	D	Pranced, Played a malicious trick, Performed magic.
P	R	A	N	K	E	R	Prankster, One who plays practical jokes.
P	R	A	T	I	E	S	Potatoes.
P	R	A	T	T	L	E	Chattering foolishly, Babbling, Boasting, Gossiping maliciously.
P	R	A	T	T	L	E	Idle chatter, Babble, Drivel, Blabber, Palaver.
P	R	A	Y	I	N	G	Entreating, Imploring, Craving, Begging, Inviting, Appealing, Beseeching, Bracing.
P	R	E	A	C	H	Y	Didactic, Tedious moralizing.
P	R	E	B	E	N	D	Stipend paid to member of officiating clergy from estate of the church.
P	R	E	C	E	D	E	Exceed, Surpass, Introduce, Preface, Usher, Herald, Antecede, Lead.
P	R	E	C	E	P	T	Law, Decree, Edict, Maxim, Behest, Regulation, Rule, Statute.
P	R	E	C	I	S	E	Legal writ.
P	R	E	C	I	S	E	Absolute, Exact, Accurate, Scrupulous, Restricted, Definite, Fixed, Correct.
P	R	E	D	A	T	E	Ante-date, Earlier in time, Precede.
P	R	E	D	I	A	L	Pertaining to land.
P	R	E	D	I	C	T	Prophesy, Foretell, Portend, Presage, Augur, Forecast, Surmise, Conjecture.
P	R	E	D	O	O	M	Condemn, Prejudge.
P	R	E	E	C	H	O	Sound fault on a defective record.
P	R	E	E	M	P	T	Appropriate, Annex, Commandeer, Confiscate, Expropriate, Seize, Assume, Usurp.
P	R	E	E	N	E	D	Tidied up, Dressed, Arranged clothing and hair, Groomed, Gloated, Sleeked.
P	R	E	F	A	C	E	Foreword, Prologue, Preliminary, Precede, Herald, Overture, Preamble, Prelude.
P	R	E	F	E	C	T	Chief officer, Chief magistrate, Student monitor.
P	R	E	F	I	N	E	Limit, Determine.
P	R	E	F	O	R	M	Predetermine, State of manufacture between primary and finished.
P	R	E	H	E	A	T	Heat beforehand, Raise to required temperature.
P	R	E	L	A	C	Y	Church government, Office of a prelate.
P	R	E	L	A	T	E	Church dignitary, Superior, Chief leader, Chaplain.
P	R	E	L	E	C	T	Lecture, Discourse publicly.
P	R	E	L	U	D	E	Introduction, Preface.
P	R	E	M	I	E	R	Chief, Principal, Leading, Earliest, First night of play, Foremost, Head.
P	R	E	M	I	S	E	Presupposition, Assumption, Postulation, Presumption, Thesis, Assume, Presume, Stipulate.
P	R	E	M	I	S	S	Stipulation, Logical premise, Taken for granted.
P	R	E	M	I	U	M	Award, Bonus, Fee, Reward, Bounty, Dividend, Prize, Superior.
P	R	E	N	D	R	E	Right of seizure.
P	R	E	O	R	A	L	In front of the mouth.
P	R	E	P	A	C	K	Transparent package of food prepared in advance.
P	R	E	P	A	I	D	Deferred charge, Paid in advance.
P	R	E	P	A	R	E	Make ready, Provide, Make, Educate, Train, Compose, Fit, Qualify.
P	R	E	P	U	C	E	Foreskin.
P	R	E	P	U	P	A	Stage of insect before changing to pupa.

(372)

1	2	3	4	5	6	7	
P	R	E	R	U	P	T	Break up, Precipitous, Steep, Abrupt.
P	R	E	S	A	G	E	Omen, Prognostic, Foreboding, Presentiment, Prediction, Foretell, Augury, Forecast.
P	R	E	S	E	L	L	Promote sales by an advertising campaign.
P	R	E	S	E	N	T	Donation, Gift, Introduce, Accuse, Perform, Offer, Contemporary, Attentive.
P	R	E	S	I	D	E	Direct, Rule, Conduct, Control, Manage, Operate, Administer, Supervise.
P	R	E	S	S	E	D	Assailed, Harassed, Expressed, Constrained, Urged, Emphasized, Stressed, Squeezed.
P	R	E	S	S	E	R	Apparatus that presses clothing, food or article.
P	R	E	S	S	O	R	Raising blood pressure.
P	R	E	S	T	E	R	Neck vein swollen with anger.
P	R	E	S	U	M	E	Anticipate, Expect, Assume, Infer, Suppose, Guess, Conjecture, Impose.
P	R	E	T	E	N	D	Fake, Feign, Sham, Simulate, Deceive, Delude, Suppose, Surmise.
P	R	E	T	E	X	T	Excuse, Alibi, Plea, Mask, Masquerade, Guise, Cloak, Cover.
P	R	E	T	O	N	E	Sound or syllable before accented one.
P	R	E	T	Z	E	L	Thin brittle twisted cracker.
P	R	E	V	A	I	L	Triumph, Predominate, Obtain, Persist, Induce, Convince, Persuade, Prompt.
P	R	E	V	E	N	E	Precede.
P	R	E	V	E	N	T	Frustrate, Circumvent, Forestall, Preclude, Obviate, Avert, Ward, Hinder.
P	R	E	V	I	E	W	Foretaste, Glimpse, Presentation in advance of public showing.
P	R	E	V	I	S	E	Foresee, Warn.
P	R	E	W	A	R	N	Forewarn, Give notice of.
P	R	E	Y	I	N	G	Plundering, Ravaging, Robbing, Wasting.
P	R	I	A	P	U	S	Phallus, God of fertility.
P	R	I	C	I	N	G	Costing, Valuing, Rating, Charging.
P	R	I	C	K	E	D	Pierced, Perforated, Urged, Punctured, Drilled, Exhorted, Goaded, Prodded.
P	R	I	C	K	E	R	Awl, Briar, Thorn.
P	R	I	C	K	E	T	Spike on candlestick to anchor the candle, Young buck or deer.
P	R	I	C	K	L	E	A little prick, Pierce, Prod, Cause tingling, Thorn.
P	R	I	C	K	L	Y	Stinging, Vexations, Easily irritated.
P	R	I	D	I	A	N	Former.
P	R	I	D	I	N	G	Glorifying, Adorning, Esteeming, Preening, Boasting, Crowing, Vaunting, Valuing.
P	R	I	G	G	E	D	Stolen, Clouted, Filched, Pilfered.
P	R	I	G	G	E	R	Thief.
P	R	I	M	A	C	Y	First, Precedence, Preeminence, Superiority, Ecclesiastical primate.
P	R	I	M	A	G	E	Extra payment to captain for extra special care of goods.
P	R	I	M	A	R	Y	Initial, Chief, Principal, Basic, Fundamental, Independent, Original, Primitive.
P	R	I	M	A	T	E	Leader, Bishop, Member of monkey family, Principal.
P	R	I	M	E	L	Y	Excellently, Originally.
P	R	I	M	E	R	O	Old fashioned card game.
P	R	I	M	E	U	R	Early crop of fruit or vegetables.
P	R	I	M	I	N	G	Positioning explosive, Applying first coat of paint, Stimulating, Moving.
P	R	I	M	M	E	D	Adopted prim expression to express disapproval.
P	R	I	M	S	I	E	Prim, Demure.
P	R	I	M	U	L	A	Genus of herb with showy flowers, Primrose.
P	R	I	N	K	E	D	Dressed up, Dolled up, Smartened, Primped.
P	R	I	N	K	E	R	One dressed in an eye-catching outfit.
P	R	I	N	T	E	D	Published, Issued, Stamped, Impressed, Produced from a negative.
P	R	I	N	T	E	R	Compositor or pressman, Typographer.
P	R	I	S	A	G	E	English crown levy on imported wine.
P	R	I	S	E	R	E	Primary succession of vegetational stages.
P	R	I	S	I	N	G	Pressing, Forcing with a lever, Forcing, Packing.
P	R	I	S	T	I	S	Genus of fish, Swordfish.
P	R	I	T	H	E	E	Polite request.
P	R	I	V	A	C	Y	Seclusion, Isolation, Secrecy, Solitude, Retreat.
P	R	I	V	A	T	E	Restricted, Personal, Civilian, Alone, Secret, Confidential, Discreet, Concealed.
P	R	I	V	I	L	Y	Privately, Secretly.
P	R	I	V	I	T	Y	Secrecy, Seclusion, Privacy, Cognizance.
P	R	I	Z	I	N	G	Appraising, Pricing, Rating, Esteeming highly, Appreciating, Cherishing, Treasuring.
P	R	O	B	A	N	G	Whalebone and sponge medical swab.
P	R	O	B	A	T	E	Testimony, Proving a will.
P	R	O	B	I	N	G	Searching, Exploring, Penetrating, Prodding, Thrusting, Entering, Delving, Questing.
P	R	O	B	I	T	Y	Integrity, Uprightness, Rectitude, Honesty, Sincerity, Virtue, Goodness, Morality.
P	R	O	B	L	E	M	Mystery, Query, Enigma, Question, Puzzle, Conundrum, Bugbear.
P	R	O	C	A	R	P	Female reproductive branch of red algae.
P	R	O	C	E	E	D	Issue, Continue, Happen, Occur, Advance, Spring, Process, Journey.
P	R	O	C	E	S	S	Operation, Course, Procedure, Fashion, Method, System, Technique, Routine.
P	R	O	C	T	O	R	Attorney acting on behalf of client, Supervisor, Monitor, Adviser.
P	R	O	C	U	R	E	Obtain, Acquire, Gain, Win, Effect, Contrive, Induce, Get.

1	2	3	4	5	6	7	
P	R	O	C	Y	O	N	Genus of raccoon family.
P	R	O	D	D	E	D	Jostled, Nudged, Pricked, Urged, Goaded, Shoved, Propelled, Prompted.
P	R	O	D	D	E	R	Stimulator, Goader.
P	R	O	D	I	G	Y	Marvel, Wonder, Miracle, Phenomenon, Portent, Stunner, Sensation.
P	R	O	D	U	C	E	Procreate, Stage, Effect, Fabricate, Generate, Construct, Yield, Breed.
P	R	O	D	U	C	T	Handiwork, Consequence, Outcome, Result, Fruit, Harvest, Proceeds, Manifestation.
P	R	O	F	A	C	E	Salutation, Drinking a toast.
P	R	O	F	A	N	E	Desecrate, Pollute, Abuse, Defile, Violate, Impious, Secular, Infidel.
P	R	O	F	E	S	S	Proclaim, Aver, Assert, Affirm, Protest, Declare, Avouch, Depose.
P	R	O	F	F	E	R	Tender, Volunteer, Offer, Extend, Present, Propose, Invite, Suggest.
P	R	O	F	I	L	E	Outline, Contour, Silhouette, Lineament, Figuration, Sketch, Drawing, Graph.
P	R	O	F	U	S	E	Copious, Lavish, Exuberant, Lush, Luxuriant, Opulent, Riotous, Generous.
P	R	O	G	E	N	Y	Offspring, Children, Kin, Outcome, Product, Issue, Seed, Scions.
P	R	O	G	G	E	D	Goaded, Prodded, Poked, Prowled, Foraged, Filched.
P	R	O	G	R	A	M	Programme, Syllabus, Curriculum, Schedule, Prospectus, Agenda, Timetable, Policy.
P	R	O	J	E	C	T	Draft, Pattern, Proposal, Idea, Plan, Design, Enterprise, Undertaking.
P	R	O	L	A	T	E	Extended.
P	R	O	L	E	G	S	Fleshy leg found on abdominal segments of larva of some butterflies and insects.
P	R	O	L	I	N	E	Heterocyclic amino acid.
P	R	O	L	O	N	G	Continue, Protract, Lengthen, Elongate, Delay, Postpone, Endure, Persist.
P	R	O	M	I	S	E	Pledge, Agreement, Consideration, Contract, Pact, Guarantee, Token, Vow.
P	R	O	M	O	T	E	Further, Raise, Encourage, Launch, Advance, Foster, Upgrade, Elevate.
P	R	O	N	A	O	S	Portico of ancient Greek temple.
P	R	O	N	A	T	E	Rotate hand or forearm.
P	R	O	N	E	L	Y	Aptly, Likely, Willingly, Readily, Recumbently, Lying down.
P	R	O	N	G	E	D	Stabbed, Pierced, Forked.
P	R	O	N	O	U	N	Word replacing a noun.
P	R	O	O	F	E	D	Tested, Examined, Made a proof.
P	R	O	O	T	I	C	Bone in relation to the ear section.
P	R	O	P	A	L	E	Divulge.
P	R	O	P	A	N	E	Flammable gaseous paraffin hydrocarbon that is heavier than air.
P	R	O	P	E	N	D	Incline, Tend, Hand downward, Lean forward.
P	R	O	P	E	N	E	Propylene, Flammable gaseous olefin hydrocarbon.
P	R	O	P	H	E	T	Seer, Predictor, Preacher, Foreteller, Soothsayer, Divinely inspired spokesman.
P	R	O	P	I	N	E	Tip, Gratuity, Reward, Disbursement, Pledge.
P	R	O	P	O	S	E	Intend, Suggest, Propound, Confront, Image, Offer, Present, Submit.
P	R	O	P	P	E	D	Supported, Shored, Sustained, Strengthened, Braced, Upheld, Bolstered, Buttressed.
P	R	O	R	A	T	A	Share in proportion.
P	R	O	R	A	T	E	Divide or distribute proportionately.
P	R	O	R	U	P	T	Protuberant.
P	R	O	S	A	I	C	Factual, Literal, Commonplace, Dull, Colourless, Humdrum, Ordinary, Mundane.
P	R	O	S	I	F	Y	Turn into prose.
P	R	O	S	I	L	Y	Tediously.
P	R	O	S	I	N	G	Lifeless or mundane conversation.
P	R	O	S	O	D	Y	Rhythmic aspect of language, Theory of writing poetry.
P	R	O	S	P	E	R	Flourish, Succeed, Score, Thrive, Multiply, Produce, Yield, Augment.
P	R	O	T	E	A	N	Exceedingly variable, Versatile, Acting many parts.
P	R	O	T	E	C	T	Defend, Shield, Guard, Cover, Secure, Safeguard, Preserve, Shelter.
P	R	O	T	E	G	E	Someone under the protection of a sponsor, Pupil.
P	R	O	T	E	I	D	Protein, Important constituent in nourishment.
P	R	O	T	E	I	N	Same as PROTEID.
P	R	O	T	E	N	D	Extend, Protrude.
P	R	O	T	E	S	T	Object, Exclaim, Aver, Publish, Remonstrate, Assert, Declare, Combat.
P	R	O	T	E	U	S	God of the sea, Amoeba, Changeable, Having diverse interests or abilities.
P	R	O	T	I	D	E	Compounds comprising amino acids and proteides.
P	R	O	T	I	U	M	Hydrogen isotope.
P	R	O	U	D	E	R	Haughtier, More arrogant, Loftier, Vainer, More elated, More gratified.
P	R	O	U	D	L	Y	Imperiously, Pompously, Loftily, Arrogantly.
P	R	O	V	A	N	D	Provisions.
P	R	O	V	E	R	B	Adage, Parable, Maxim, Epigrammatic, Saying, Byword.
P	R	O	V	I	D	E	Give, Deliver, Dispense, Prepare, Afford, Yield, Equip, Supply.
P	R	O	V	I	N	E	Layer.
P	R	O	V	I	N	G	Testing, Establishing, Demonstrating, Trying, Showing, Checking, Examining, Determining.
P	R	O	V	I	S	O	Condition, Provision, Reservation, Stipulation, Terms.
P	R	O	V	O	K	E	Enrage, Rouse, Infuriate, Arouse, Evoke, Excite, Quicken, Stimulate.
P	R	O	V	O	S	T	Person of authority, Magistrate.
P	R	O	W	E	S	S	Gallantry, Valour, Skill, Dexterity, Excellence, Heroism, Adroitness, Deftness.

1	2	3	4	5	6	7	Definition
P	R	O	W	L	E	D	Roamed, Roved, Slunk, Paced stealthily.
P	R	O	W	L	E	R	Sneak thief, Stalker.
P	R	O	X	I	M	E	Proximate, Close, Next, Imminent.
P	R	O	X	I	M	O	In the next month.
P	R	U	D	E	N	T	Frugal, Provident, Discreet, Cautious, Wise, Sage, Expedient, Politic.
P	R	U	D	E	R	Y	State of being prudish, Primness, Excessive modesty.
P	R	U	D	I	S	H	Prim, Priggish.
P	R	U	N	I	N	G	Reducing, Clipping, Trimming, Lopping, Retrenching, Paring, Shaving, Eliminating.
P	R	U	R	I	G	O	Chronic inflammatory skin disease marked by pimples.
P	R	Y	T	A	N	Y	Athenian council division.
P	S	A	L	T	E	R	Translation of the Psalms.
P	S	C	H	E	N	T	Royal crown of Upper and Lower Egypt.
P	S	O	A	T	I	C	Relating to the muscle of the loin.
P	S	Y	C	H	A	L	Relating to the mind.
P	S	Y	C	H	I	C	Not physical or organic, Marked by sensitivity.
P	T	A	R	M	I	C	Substance that causes sneezing.
P	T	E	R	I	O	N	Craniology.
P	T	E	R	O	M	A	Front portion of Greek temple.
P	T	Y	A	L	I	N	Salivary enzyme.
P	U	B	E	R	A	L	Pertaining to puberty.
P	U	B	E	R	T	Y	Reaching sexual maturity.
P	U	B	L	I	S	H	Disclose, Circulate, Censure, Advertise, Declare, Disseminate, Utter, Print.
P	U	C	H	E	R	O	Latin American stew of meat and vegetables.
P	U	C	K	E	R	Y	Causing a wrinkle, Like a furrow.
P	U	C	K	I	S	H	Impish, Whimsical, Mischievous.
P	U	D	D	I	N	G	Baked or boiled sweetened dessert.
P	U	D	D	L	E	D	Puttered, Urinated, Befuddled, Confused, Saturated the soil when hosing.
P	U	D	D	L	E	R	One who converts pig iron into wrought iron.
P	U	D	E	N	C	Y	Modesty, Prudishness, Bashfulness.
P	U	E	R	I	L	E	Boyish, Childish, Immature, Youthful, Immature, Infantile, Babyish.
P	U	F	F	E	R	Y	Advertising extravagant claims.
P	U	F	F	I	N	G	Panting, Blustering, Erupting, Exploding, Expanding, Popping, Inflating, Overrating.
P	U	F	F	I	L	Y	Gustily, Pompously, Showily.
P	U	G	A	R	E	E	Turban worn in India.
P	U	G	G	I	N	G	Making clay workable, Deafening.
P	U	G	G	R	E	E	Scarf worn around a sun helmet.
P	U	G	M	I	L	L	Cement mixer.
P	U	G	N	O	S	E	Snub nose.
P	U	L	L	I	N	G	Dragging, Hauling, Tugging, Towing, Gathering, Plucking, Impelling, Extracting.
P	U	L	L	M	A	N	Comfortably furnished passenger coach.
P	U	L	L	O	U	T	Printed matter easily removed from magazine or book.
P	U	L	P	I	F	Y	To make pulp of something.
P	U	L	P	I	N	G	Forming into pulp, Pulverizing.
P	U	L	P	O	U	S	Pulpy, Mashy, Mushy.
P	U	L	S	A	T	E	Beat, Throb, Palpitate, Quiver, Oscillate, Vibrate, Pump, Pound.
P	U	L	S	I	N	G	Throbbing, Oscillating, Vibrating, Pumping, Beating, Pounding.
P	U	L	S	I	O	N	Propulsion, Pushing, Driving.
P	U	M	P	A	G	E	Amount raised by pumping.
P	U	M	P	I	N	G	Ejecting, Forcing, Pulsating, Draining, Siphoning, Drawing, Tapping, Driving.
P	U	M	P	K	I	N	Firm-rinded vine squash used as vegetable and cattle feed.
P	U	M	P	R	O	D	Piston rod.
P	U	N	C	H	E	D	Pushed, Struck, Jabbed, Nudged, Hit, Slapped, Prodded, Punctured.
P	U	N	C	H	E	R	Operator of a press, Cowboy.
P	U	N	C	T	U	M	Dot, Punctuate.
P	U	N	G	E	N	T	Caustic, Stinging, Biting, Poignant, Spicy, Snappy, Piquant, Acrid.
P	U	N	J	A	B	I	Native of Punjab region of N. Western India.
P	U	N	N	I	N	G	Quipping, Pounding, Making play with words.
P	U	N	S	T	E	R	One skilled in making puns.
P	U	N	T	G	U	N	Gun firing shot used for hunting waterfowl.
P	U	N	T	I	N	G	Propelling a punt, Gambling, Betting, Kicking a ball in soccer.
P	U	P	A	T	E	D	Formed a chrysalis.
P	U	R	A	N	I	C	Pertaining to Indian legends.
P	U	R	F	L	E	D	Trimmed, Bordered, Decorated.
P	U	R	G	I	N	G	Cleaning, Pruning, Elinating, Ridding, Purifying, Removing, Expelling, Dismissing.
P	U	R	I	T	A	N	Adherent to rigorous and severe religious movement.
P	U	R	L	I	E	U	Haunt, Environ, Neighbourhood.
P	U	R	L	I	N	E	Timber supports in a roof.

1	2	3	4	5	6	7	Clue
P	U	R	L	O	I	N	Filch, Steal, Render ineffectual.
P	U	R	P	L	E	D	Dyed purple, Exalted station, Great wealth.
P	U	R	P	L	E	S	Fabrics dyed purple, Ceremonial robes.
P	U	R	P	O	R	T	Intenton, Substance, Meaning, Import, Message, Sense, Drift, Gist.
P	U	R	P	O	S	E	Intent, Aim, Resolution, Determination, Talk, Plan, Propose, Resolve.
P	U	R	P	U	R	A	Skin haemorrhage, Genus of marine snails that yield purple dye.
P	U	R	P	U	R	E	Heraldic purple.
P	U	R	R	I	N	G	Low vibrating murmur of a cat.
P	U	R	S	I	N	G	Enclosing, Puckering, Knitting, Confining.
P	U	R	S	U	E	D	Persecuted, Bedevilled, Continued, Prosecuted, Followed, Accomplished, Hunted, Practised.
P	U	R	S	U	E	R	Plaintiff, One that chases.
P	U	R	S	U	I	T	Chase, Search, Calling, Business, Work, Employment, Occupation, Job.
P	U	R	V	I	E	W	Extent, Scope, Preamble, Proviso, Saving, Clause, Range, Orbit.
P	U	S	H	F	U	L	Zealous, Energetic, Enterprising, Aggressive, Assertive, Militant, Brash, Imposing.
P	U	S	H	I	N	G	Vigorous, Jostling, Thrusting, Crowding, Crushing, Bunching, Crowding, Operating.
P	U	S	H	P	I	N	Children's game.
P	U	S	H	R	O	D	Rod that activates valves of an engine.
P	U	S	T	U	L	E	Pimple, Abscess, Boil, Blister, Wart, Swelling, Skin erruption.
P	U	T	A	M	E	N	Tough membrane lining of an egg, Layer of grey matter in lentil nucleus.
P	U	T	R	E	F	Y	Putrify, Decay, Decompose, Disintegrate, Moulder, Rot, Taint, Turn rotten.
P	U	T	T	E	E	S	Bandage covering or leather legging for protection of lower leg.
P	U	T	T	I	E	D	Applied putty.
P	U	T	T	I	E	R	Glazier.
P	U	T	T	I	N	G	Striking the golf ball on the green toward the hole.
P	U	T	T	O	C	K	Buzzard.
P	U	Z	Z	L	E	D	Confounded, Bewildered, Confused, Perplexed, Complicated, Entangled, Mystified.
P	U	Z	Z	L	E	R	Person that spends time to solve puzzles.
P	Y	A	E	M	I	A	Septic blood-poisoning with multiple abscesses.
P	Y	C	N	I	T	E	Pillar-shaped topaz.
P	Y	C	N	I	U	M	Rust, Fungi infection.
P	Y	G	M	E	A	N	Pygmy, Small statured person.
P	Y	G	O	P	O	D	Relating to diving birds.
P	Y	J	A	M	A	S	Pajamas, Night wear, Loose trouser suit.
P	Y	L	O	R	I	C	Relating to lower section of the stomach.
P	Y	L	O	R	U	S	Opening from stomach into the intestine.
P	Y	R	A	M	I	D	Figure of four triangles meeting in a peak at the apex, Series of business operations.
P	Y	R	E	N	I	N	Substance of the true nucleolus.
P	Y	R	E	T	I	C	Febrile, Pertaining to fever.
P	Y	R	E	X	I	A	Abnormally high blood temperature.
P	Y	R	E	X	I	N	Nitrogenous factor which may cause fever when allied with inflammation.
P	Y	R	I	T	E	S	Common mineral of iron disulfide.
P	Y	R	I	T	I	C	Resembling pyrites.
P	Y	R	O	G	E	N	Fever-producing substance.
P	Y	R	O	S	I	S	Heartburn.
P	Y	R	R	H	I	C	Suffering heavy losses in order to win.
P	Y	R	R	O	L	E	Colourless toxic liquid heterocyclic compound.
P	Y	T	H	I	A	D	Games held every four years in Pytho- now Delphi- in ancient times.
P	Y	T	H	I	A	N	Relating to Apollo as patron god of Delphi, Ecstatic, Phrenetic.
P	Y	X	I	D	E	S	Decorated toilet box used in ancient Rome and Greece.

Q

1	2	3	4	5	6	7	Clue
Q	U	A	B	I	R	D	Night heron.
Q	U	A	C	K	E	D	Made the noise of a duck, Posed as medical practitioner, Boasted.
Q	U	A	C	K	L	E	Suffocate, Choke.
Q	U	A	D	R	A	T	Game played by printers, Small plot of land for scientific studies.
Q	U	A	D	R	E	L	Square block of brick, tile or plastic.
Q	U	A	D	R	I	C	Relating to the second degree (geometry).
Q	U	A	F	F	E	D	Drank copiously, Swilled, Guzzled.
Q	U	A	F	F	E	R	One who drinks freely.
Q	U	A	H	A	U	G	American clam.
Q	U	A	I	L	E	D	Cowered, Flinched, Blenched, Recoiled, Winced, Cringed, Wasted, Declined.
Q	U	A	K	E	R	S	Members of an austere religious sect.
Q	U	A	K	I	N	G	Shaking, Vibrating, Trembling, Shuddering, Wavering, Fluctuating, Dithering, Quivering.
Q	U	A	L	I	F	Y	Entitle, Regulate, Authorize, Signalize, Characterize, Distinguish, Mark, License.
Q	U	A	L	I	T	Y	Trait, Attribute, Feature, Merit, Stature, Value, Worth, Status.

1	2	3	4	5	6	7	Definition
Q	U	A	M	A	S	H	Genus of Camas plant having edible bulbs.
Q	U	A	N	T	U	M	Quantity, Amount, Portion, Aggregate, Bulk, Allowance, Ration, Allotment.
Q	U	A	R	R	E	L	Dispute, Strife, Aversion, Dislike, Wrangle, Altercation, Squabble, Bickering.
Q	U	A	R	T	A	N	Occurring every fourth day, Malaria recurring at seventy two hour intervals.
Q	U	A	R	T	E	R	Fourth part, District, Region, Residence, Forbearance, Mercy, Dismember, Section in heraldry.
Q	U	A	R	T	E	T	Musical composition for four players, Group of four performers, Foursome.
Q	U	A	R	T	I	C	Of the fourth degree.
Q	U	A	R	T	Z	Y	Quartzose, Resembling quartz.
Q	U	A	S	A	R	S	Quasi-stellar radio sources.
Q	U	A	S	H	E	D	Voided, Abated, Annulled, Overthrew, Dissolved, Discharged, Vacated, Crushed.
Q	U	A	S	S	I	A	Genus of trees and shrubs yielding a bitter tonic, remedy for parasitic worms.
Q	U	A	S	S	I	N	Bitter crystalline extract of quassia.
Q	U	A	T	U	O	R	Quartet.
Q	U	A	V	E	R	Y	Trembling, Vibrating, Shaking, Wavering, Dithering, Vacillating, Hesitating, Faltering.
Q	U	A	Y	A	G	E	Wharfage, Charge for use of quays at the harbour.
Q	U	E	A	C	H	Y	Boggy, Marshy, Swampy.
Q	U	E	E	N	E	D	Played the queen, Lorded it over people, False sense of superiority.
Q	U	E	E	N	L	Y	Majestic, Regal, Haughty, Dignified.
Q	U	E	E	R	E	D	Jeopardized, Harmed, Disrupted, Spoiled.
Q	U	E	E	R	E	R	Stranger, More bizarre, Odder, More peculiar.
Q	U	E	E	R	L	Y	Dubiously, Strangely, Oddly.
Q	U	E	L	L	E	D	Quenched, Crushed, Killed, Slaughtered, Pacified, Extinguished, Suppressed, Conquered.
Q	U	E	L	L	E	R	Victor, Conqueror, Peace-maker.
Q	U	E	R	C	U	S	Oak tree.
Q	U	E	R	E	L	A	Court action, Complaint.
Q	U	E	R	E	N	T	One who consults an astrologer, Complainant, Plaintiff.
Q	U	E	R	I	E	D	Asked, Challenged, Inquired, Interrogated, Examined, Questioned.
Q	U	E	R	I	S	T	Questioner, Interrogator.
Q	U	E	S	T	E	D	Asked, Howled, Wailed, Demanded, Hunted, Searched, Probed, Pursued.
Q	U	E	S	T	E	R	Searcher, Hunter.
Q	U	E	S	T	O	R	A Roman official in ancient times in charge of monies.
Q	U	E	T	Z	A	L	Mexican bird with brilliant plumage.
Q	U	I	B	B	L	E	Cavil, Carp, Bicker, Prevaricate, Criticize, Dispute, Hassle, Wrangle.
Q	U	I	C	K	E	N	Rouse, Expedite, Animate, Enliven, Energize, Provoke, Galvanize, Motivate.
Q	U	I	C	K	E	R	Faster, Swifter, Fleeter, Brisker, Prompter, Smarter, Wiser, Slicker.
Q	U	I	C	K	I	E	Something done or made in a hurry sometimes of inferior quality.
Q	U	I	C	K	L	Y	Rapidly, Speedily, Hastily, Swiftly, Promptly, Keenly, Smartly.
Q	U	I	D	D	I	T	Quibbling, Subtley.
Q	U	I	D	D	L	E	Dawdle, Fussy.
Q	U	I	E	S	C	E	Be still, Calm, Silent.
Q	U	I	E	T	E	D	Pacified, Calmed, Lulled, Soothed, Silenced, Hushed, Composed, Settled.
Q	U	I	E	T	E	N	Silence, Shush, Still, Allay, Compose, Pacify, Settle, Soothe.
Q	U	I	E	T	E	R	More secluded, More hushed, More silent, More placid.
Q	U	I	E	T	L	Y	Calmly, Silently, Peacefully, Serenely.
Q	U	I	E	T	U	S	Final, Discharge, Extinction, Release, Death, Silence, Dissolution, Passing.
Q	U	I	L	L	E	D	Removed quills, Pierced with quills, Frilled, Crimped, Fluted.
Q	U	I	L	L	E	T	Small paper tube.
Q	U	I	L	L	O	N	Arm of cross guard of a sword.
Q	U	I	L	T	E	D	Padded and stitched.
Q	U	I	L	T	E	R	Sewing machine attachment for quilting.
Q	U	I	N	A	R	Y	Arranged or grouped in fives, Based on counting by fingers.
Q	U	I	N	A	T	E	Composed of sets of five.
Q	U	I	N	I	N	A	Extract from cinchona bark used medicinally.
Q	U	I	N	N	A	T	King salmon.
Q	U	I	N	O	N	E	Isomeric cyclic compounds from dihydro-benzene.
Q	U	I	N	T	A	L	Metric unit of one hundred kilogrammes.
Q	U	I	N	T	A	N	Occurring every fifth day or after four similar units.
Q	U	I	N	T	E	T	Musical composition for five performers, Group of five musicians or singers.
Q	U	I	N	T	I	C	Of the fifth degree, Having five links.
Q	U	I	N	T	U	S	Fifth voice in medieval music.
Q	U	I	P	P	E	D	Scoffed, Gibed, Joked, Jested, Flouted, Jeered, Sneered, Taunted.
Q	U	I	R	I	N	G	Folding or making paper to a special size.
Q	U	I	T	T	A	L	Acquittal.
Q	U	I	T	T	E	D	Released, Relieved, Discharged, Acquitted, Relinquished, Abandoned, Deported, Left.
Q	U	I	T	T	E	R	Coward, Shirker, Deserter.
Q	U	I	T	T	O	R	Chronic inflammation of horses' feet.
Q	U	I	V	I	V	E	Challenge, Alert, Look-out.

1	2	3	4	5	6	7	
Q	U	I	X	O	T	E	Chivalrous person, Idealist, Romantic.
Q	U	I	Z	Z	E	D	Ridiculed, Derided, Mocked, Taunted, Asked, Examined, Inquired, Queried.
Q	U	I	Z	Z	E	R	Questioner usually on a radio or television programme.
Q	U	O	N	D	A	M	Former, Onetime, Bygone, Late, Past, Sometime.
Q	U	O	T	I	N	G	Noticing, Marking, Citing, Repeating, Pricing.

R

R	A	B	B	I	T	Y	Resembling a rabbit, Timid, Shy.
R	A	B	B	L	E	R	Iron-worker.
R	A	B	B	O	N	I	Jewish title for a master or teacher.
R	A	B	I	D	L	Y	Furiously, Virulently, Frantically, Maniacally, Madly, Crazily, Insanely.
R	A	B	I	N	E	T	Ancient gun.
R	A	B	I	O	U	S	Fierce, Rabid.
R	A	C	C	O	O	N	Carnivorous nocturnal mammal.
R	A	C	E	M	E	D	Bearing a flower spray like the lily-of-the-valley.
R	A	C	E	M	I	C	Derived from recemic acid, Grape acid.
R	A	C	E	W	A	Y	Canal for current of water, Channel designed for electric wires or cables.
R	A	C	K	E	T	Y	Noisy, Exciting, Gay, Dissipated, Rowdy, Raffish, Rickety.
R	A	C	K	I	N	G	Stepping end bricks to join at a corner, Motion on a knitting machine.
R	A	C	Q	U	E	T	Racket, Bat strung with gut for tennis or squash or badminton, Paddle-like bat for table tennis.
R	A	D	D	L	E	D	Scarred, Interweave, Beaten, Thrashed, Confused, Worn, Befuddled, Broken-down.
R	A	D	I	A	L	E	Bone or cartilage in the wrist that pivots on the arm-bone.
R	A	D	I	A	N	T	Glowing, Brilliant, Bright, Beaming, Incandescent, Luminous, Glad, Cheerful.
R	A	D	I	A	T	E	Irradiate, Disseminate, Diffuse, Spread, Circulate, Disperse, Distribute, Propagate.
R	A	D	I	C	A	L	Original, Fundamental, Inherent, Extreme, Drastic, Liberal, Basis, Foundation.
R	A	D	I	C	L	E	Extremity or root portion, Rootlike beginning of a body, vessel or part.
R	A	D	I	O	E	D	Transmitted or communicated by radio.
R	A	D	U	L	A	R	Band of minute teeth in mollusks.
R	A	F	F	I	N	G	Rip-roaring.
R	A	F	F	I	S	H	Tawdry, Unkempt, Rakish.
R	A	F	F	L	E	D	Awarded, Prize won by drawing tickets or lots.
R	A	F	F	L	E	R	Organiser of a lottery.
R	A	F	T	D	O	G	Iron bar to fasten floating logs into a raft.
R	A	F	T	I	N	G	Making into a raft, Floating on a raft.
R	A	G	B	O	L	T	Barbed shank holding fast.
R	A	G	E	F	U	L	Furious, Angered.
R	A	G	F	A	I	R	Second-hand clothing market.
R	A	G	G	E	T	Y	Ragged, Tattered.
R	A	G	G	I	N	G	Scolding, Tormenting, Annoying, Teasing, Chaffing, Ranting, Joking, Ribbing.
R	A	G	T	I	M	E	Syncopation.
R	A	G	W	E	E	D	Tansy ragwort, American weedy herbaceous plant causing hay fever and asthma.
R	A	G	W	O	R	T	Tansy ragwort.
R	A	I	D	I	N	G	Marauding, Pillaging, Foraying, Invading, Assaulting, Attacking.
R	A	I	L	B	U	S	Passenger car that can operate on rails.
R	A	I	L	C	A	R	Self-propelled railroad car carrying combination of passenger and freight.
R	A	I	L	I	N	G	Reviling, Ranting, Upbraiding, Berating, Fencing, Scolding, Nagging.
R	A	I	L	W	A	Y	Railroad, Tracks permanently laid for transporting freight and passengers.
R	A	I	M	E	N	T	Clothing, Garments, Vesture.
R	A	I	N	B	O	W	Refraction and reflection of sun's rays in drops of rain that give an arc of primary colours.
R	A	I	N	I	N	G	Pouring, Showering, Water descending in drops.
R	A	I	S	I	N	G	Lifting, Elevating, Hoisting, Inciting, Erecting, Building, Growing, Constructing.
R	A	K	E	O	F	F	Percentage of winnings retained by agent, operator or gang boss.
R	A	L	L	I	E	D	Reunited, Collected, Assembled, Mobilized, Mustered, Kindled, Marshalled, Recovered.
R	A	L	L	I	E	S	Reuniting of forces, Recovery of prices, Mass meeting, Long distance fun for automobiles.
R	A	L	L	I	N	E	Resembling rails.
R	A	M	A	D	A	N	Sacred month of Muhammadan year.
R	A	M	A	Z	A	N	Same as RAMADAN.
R	A	M	B	L	E	D	Wandered, Meandered, Roved, Strayed, Ranged, Digressed, Sauntered, Strolled.
R	A	M	B	L	E	R	One that rambles or wanders.
R	A	M	E	K	I	N	Individual baking dish for cheese or egg dishes.
R	A	M	E	N	T	A	Thin brownish scales on young shoots of ferns, Shaving, Scraping.
R	A	M	E	O	U	S	Branch, Right or left side.
R	A	M	H	E	A	D	Blockhead, Stupid or dullwitted person, Crane hook.
R	A	M	L	I	N	E	Line to mark a straight middle line.
R	A	M	M	I	N	G	Pounding, Crashing, Cramming, Butting, Packing, Forcing, Plunging, Stabbing.

1	2	3	4	5	6	7	
R	A	M	M	I	S	H	Resembling a ram.
R	A	M	P	A	G	E	Violent, Riotous, Unruly, Destructive, Turmoil, Uproar, Orgy, Splurge.
R	A	M	P	A	N	T	Unbridled, Rank, Excessive, Prevailing, Current, Popular, Ruling, Widespread.
R	A	M	P	A	R	T	Bulwark, Bastion, Parapet, Fortification, Defence, Protection.
R	A	M	P	I	C	K	Dead tree, Splintered stump.
R	A	M	P	I	K	E	Same as RAMPICK.
R	A	M	P	I	N	G	Raging, Storming, Climbing, Creeping, Bounding.
R	A	M	P	I	O	N	European bellflower with edible tuberous root and leaves used in salads.
R	A	M	S	O	N	S	Garlics.
R	A	M	S	O	T	A	M	Headstrong, Reckless.
R	A	M	U	L	U	S	Small branch, Branchlet.
R	A	N	C	H	E	D	Worked on a ranch.
R	A	N	C	H	E	R	One who owns or operates a ranch.
R	A	N	C	O	U	R	Deep-seated enmity, Inveterate malevolence, Animosity, Hostility, Antipathy, Virulence.
R	A	N	G	E	R	S	Royal parkkeepers, Forest rangers, Those who look after straying animals.
R	A	N	G	I	E	R	More open, More spacious, More mountainous, More slender.
R	A	N	G	I	N	G	Placing, Ranking, Aligning, Positioning, Extending, Wandering, Inclining, Classifying.
R	A	N	K	E	S	T	Most rancid, Most foul, Coarsest, Most indecent, Most Gross.
R	A	N	K	I	N	G	Arranging, Identifying, Classifying, Rating, Grading, Preceding, Sorting.
R	A	N	K	L	E	D	Festered, Inflamed, Irritated, Aggravated, Plagued, Tormented, Harassed, Vexed.
R	A	N	S	A	C	K	Rummage, Search, Seek, Plunder, Pillage, Rifle, Comb, Forage.
R	A	N	T	I	N	G	Carousing, Railing, Revelling, Bombasting, Declaiming, Blistering, Raging, Scolding.
R	A	P	E	O	I	L	Cole-seed oil used as lubricant, illuminant and food.
R	A	P	F	U	L	L	Sailing under a full sail.
R	A	P	H	I	D	E	Needle-shaped crystal irritating to mucous membrane.
R	A	P	I	D	L	Y	Speedily, Swiftly, Hastily, Quickly, Briskly, Nimbly, Hurriedly, Expediously.
R	A	P	L	O	C	H	Coarse, Rough.
R	A	P	P	I	N	G	Knocking, Hitting, Beating, Tapping, Criticizing, Censuring, Denouncing, Condemning.
R	A	P	P	O	R	T	Relation, Harmony, Concord, Unity.
R	A	P	T	U	R	E	Paroxysm, Ecstasy, Bliss, Rhapsody, Transport.
R	A	R	E	B	I	T	Welsh rabbit, Cheese sauce on toast.
R	A	S	O	R	E	S	Order of birds, Pigeons, Grouse.
R	A	S	P	I	N	G	Grating, Rubbing, Coarse voice, Scratching.
R	A	T	A	B	L	E	Taxable value. Rated or estimated.
R	A	T	A	B	L	Y	Distribute proportionally.
R	A	T	A	F	I	A	Liqueur flavoured with plum, peach or apricot kernels, Almond paste biscuit.
R	A	T	A	T	A	T	Sharp repeated knocking.
R	A	T	C	H	E	D	Stretched, Rent.
R	A	T	C	H	E	T	Toothed blade to turn toothed wheels to prevent reverse motion.
R	A	T	H	O	L	E	Narrow opening or passageway, Hole that seems bottomless.
R	A	T	I	T	A	E	Genus of flightless bird, Ostrich, Emu.
R	A	T	L	I	N	E	Ship's rope.
R	A	T	L	I	N	G	Same as RATLINE.
R	A	T	R	A	C	E	Vicious circle, Confusing activities.
R	A	T	T	A	I	L	Slender and tapering, Resembling a rat's tail.
R	A	T	T	I	N	G	Informing, Deserting for personal gain.
R	A	T	T	L	E	D	Clattered, Scolded, Agitated, Disconcerted, Embarrassed, Roused, Irritated, Chattered.
R	A	T	T	L	E	R	Rattlesnake.
R	A	T	T	O	O	N	Sugarcane sucker.
R	A	T	T	R	A	P	Trap for rats, Dirty ramshackle structure.
R	A	U	C	I	T	Y	Being strident, Noisy, Hoarse.
R	A	U	C	O	U	S	Hoarse, Strident, Disorderly, Boisterous, Turbulent, Grating, Rowdy, Rough.
R	A	V	A	G	E	D	Devastated, Wasted, Sacked, Pillaged, Despoiled, Desperate, Desecrate, Devour.
R	A	V	A	G	E	R	Bandit, Brigand, Plunderer.
R	A	V	E	L	I	N	Part of a fort consisting of detached embankments.
R	A	V	E	N	E	D	Devoured eagerly, Consumed eagerly, Wolfed, Plundered, Ravished.
R	A	V	E	N	E	R	Robber, Glutton, Ravisher.
R	A	V	I	N	E	D	Gullied, Crossed with ravines or gorges.
R	A	V	I	O	L	I	Pasta shells containing savoury fillings.
R	A	W	B	O	N	E	Lean, Gaunt, Angular, Scrawy, Skinny, Spare.
R	A	W	H	E	A	D	Spectre, Mischievous spirit.
R	A	W	H	I	D	E	Leather made from untanned cattle hide.
R	A	W	N	E	S	S	Uncooked, Immature, Unprocessed.
R	A	Y	L	E	S	S	Having no rays, Dark, Blind.
R	E	A	C	H	E	D	Extended, Snatched, Arrived, Gained, Accomplished, Approached, Contacted, Attained.
R	E	A	C	H	E	R	One who hands in.
R	E	A	C	T	E	D	Responded, Acted, Behaved, Functioned, Operated, Performed, Returned, Reverted.

1	2	3	4	5	6	7	Definition
R	E	A	C	T	O	R	Apparatus for chain reaction of fissionable material.
R	E	A	D	I	E	D	Prepared, Primed, Qualified, Adjusted, Fortified, Strengthened, Fixed.
R	E	A	D	I	E	R	More inclined, More disposed, Prompter, Quicker.
R	E	A	D	I	L	Y	Willingly, Easily, Cheerfully, Effortlessly, Freely, Smoothly, Lightly.
R	E	A	D	I	N	G	Studying, Interpretation, Rendering, Version, Observing.
R	E	A	D	M	I	T	Admit again, Receive again, Recognize again.
R	E	A	G	E	N	T	Substance that reacts to stimulus.
R	E	A	L	G	A	R	Orange-red Mineral that consists of arsenic sulfide.
R	E	A	L	I	S	M	Naturalism, Preoccupied with fact, Idealism, Preoccupation with trivia.
R	E	A	L	I	S	T	Advocate of realism.
R	E	A	L	I	T	Y	Fact, Actuality, Materiality, Actual, Nature.
R	E	A	L	I	Z	E	Accomplish, Gain, Achieve, Attain, Think, Reach, Score, Win.
R	E	A	L	L	O	T	Re-assign, Allocate again.
R	E	A	L	T	O	R	Real estate agent.
R	E	A	M	I	N	G	Countersink, Cheating, Victimizing, Diddling, Enlarging.
R	E	A	N	N	E	X	To annex again, Re-unite.
R	E	A	P	I	N	G	Gleaning, Gathering, Garnering, Harvesting, Cropping.
R	E	A	P	P	L	Y	To apply again, Try again.
R	E	A	R	G	U	E	Argue again, Dispute again.
R	E	A	R	I	N	G	Constructing, Producing, Originating, Elevating, Raising, Towering, Lifting, Nursing.
R	E	A	R	I	S	E	Arise again, Ascend again.
R	E	A	R	M	E	D	Equipped again with military material, Armed again.
R	E	A	V	I	N	G	Plundering, Pillaging, Robbing, Despoiling, Seizing, Removing.
R	E	A	W	A	K	E	To awake again, Rouse again.
R	E	B	A	T	E	D	Diminished, Lessened, Blunted, Decreased, Dwindled, Reduced, Discounted.
R	E	B	I	R	T	H	Renaissance, Revival, Spiritual regeneration.
R	E	B	O	U	N	D	Reverberating, Resounding.
R	E	B	O	U	N	D	Leap, Spring, Return, Recoil, Recovery, Resilience, Echo.
R	E	B	U	I	L	D	Reconstruct, Re-create, Remodel, Mend, Overhaul, Repair, Recondition, Revamp.
R	E	B	U	I	L	T	Reconstructed, Remodelled, Re-erected, Reconditioned, Revamped.
R	E	B	U	K	E	D	Reproved, Admonished, Chided, Reprimanded, Reproached, Lectured, Scolded, Checked.
R	E	B	U	K	E	R	One that reprimands.
R	E	C	E	D	E	D	Departed, Withdrew, Contracted, Diminished, Retreated, Retracted, Retired, Ebbed.
R	E	C	E	I	P	T	Recipe, To acknowledge payment or delivery, Receptacle.
R	E	C	E	I	V	E	Contain, Hold, Greet, Harbour, Catch, Intercept, Accept, Admit.
R	E	C	E	N	C	Y	State of being recent, Up-to-date.
R	E	C	H	E	A	T	Sound of horn to recall hounds of the hunt.
R	E	C	I	T	A	L	Enumeration, Discourse, Story, Public performance of entertainment.
R	E	C	I	T	E	D	Enumerated, Related, Described, Narrated, Recounted, Reported, Stated, Told.
R	E	C	I	T	E	R	One that recites.
R	E	C	K	I	N	G	Considering, Deeming, Caring, Regarding, Concerning, Taking heed.
R	E	C	L	A	I	M	Recall, Subdue, Tame, Object, Protest, Rescue, Regain, Rehabilitate.
R	E	C	L	A	M	E	Publicity, Vogue, Showmanship, Notoriety.
R	E	C	L	I	N	E	Lean, Rest, Lie, Repose, Incline, Slope, Tilt, Tip.
R	E	C	L	U	S	E	Cloistered, Solitary, Remote, Secluded, Hermit, Anchorite.
R	E	C	O	U	N	T	Narrate, Relate, Tell, Report, State, Rehearse.
R	E	C	O	V	E	R	Rescue, Deliver, Cure, Heal, Reclaim, Retrieve, Recoup, Recruit.
R	E	C	R	O	S	S	Traverse again, Cross again.
R	E	C	R	U	I	T	Muster, Raise, Repair, Replenish, Recuperate, Recover, Enlist, Regain.
R	E	C	T	I	F	Y	Remedy, Amend, Straighten, Correct, Redress, Rebuild, Repair, Right.
R	E	C	T	I	O	N	Government.
R	E	C	T	O	R	Y	Parsonage, Rectorship.
R	E	C	T	R	I	X	Quill feather of the tail for controlling flight.
R	E	D	B	O	O	K	19th century court guide.
R	E	D	B	U	C	K	Impala.
R	E	D	C	E	N	T	Trivial amount, Penny.
R	E	D	C	L	A	Y	Soil containing oxide of iron.
R	E	D	C	O	A	T	British soldier who fought in American War of Independence.
R	E	D	C	O	C	K	Male of the red grouse.
R	E	D	D	E	E	R	Common stag.
R	E	D	D	E	S	T	Most red, Most revolutionary, Most ruddy.
R	E	D	D	I	N	G	Redden.
R	E	D	D	I	S	H	Tinged with red.
R	E	D	D	R	U	M	Fish, Channel bass.
R	E	D	E	Y	E	S	Fish with red eyes, Rock bass, Copperhead.
R	E	D	F	I	S	H	Salmon, Channel bass.
R	E	D	H	A	N	D	Heraldic hand that is erect, open and couped at the wrist.

1	2	3	4	5	6	7	
R	E	D	H	E	A	D	Person having red hair, American duck.
R	E	D	L	E	A	D	Orange red to brick lead oxide.
R	E	D	L	E	G	S	Purple sandpiper, Bacterial disease of frogs.
R	E	D	N	E	S	S	Quality of being red.
R	E	D	O	U	B	T	Temporary fortification, Stronghold.
R	E	D	O	U	N	D	Contribute, Conduce, Tend, Accrue, Rebound, Reflect, Predominate, Overflow.
R	E	D	P	O	L	L	Finch, Warbler.
R	E	D	R	A	F	T	Revision, Revised copy, Bill of exchange dishonoured by the drawer.
R	E	D	R	A	W	N	Drawn again, Revised, Redrafted, Revamped, Rewritten.
R	E	D	R	E	S	S	Repair, Remedy, Compensate, Heal, Rectify, Avenge, Counteract, Correct.
R	E	D	R	O	O	T	Perennial herb used as a source of a dye, Buckthorn.
R	E	D	R	U	S	T	Fungi disease, Red spider infestation.
R	E	D	S	E	E	D	Red feed.
R	E	D	S	K	I	N	North American Indian.
R	E	D	T	A	I	L	Brazilian shrimp, Common rodent-eating hawk.
R	E	D	T	A	P	E	Government procedure that seems to hamper and hinder the common people.
R	E	D	U	C	E	D	Condensed, Lessened, Curtailed, Abridged, Lowered, Slashed, Depreciated, Degraded.
R	E	D	U	C	E	R	Valve that reduces pressure.
R	E	D	W	E	E	D	Corn poppy.
R	E	D	W	I	N	G	Southern African francolin, Redwing blackbird.
R	E	D	W	O	O	D	Any of various timbers of a reddish brown colour.
R	E	E	D	I	F	Y	Rebuild.
R	E	E	D	I	N	G	Thatching, Decorating with reeds.
R	E	E	F	I	N	G	Reducing area of sail.
R	E	E	K	I	N	G	Smoking, Emanating, Issuing, Rising, Exhaling, Emitting, Venting, Exuding.
R	E	E	L	I	N	G	Winding, Rolling up, Whirling, Wavering, Recoiling, Staggering, Vacillating, Careening.
R	E	E	N	T	R	Y	Retaking possession, Return to earth's atmosphere after space flight.
R	E	E	Q	U	I	P	Supply with arms again, Outfit again.
R	E	E	V	I	N	G	Passing a rope through a hole or opening, Threading.
R	E	F	E	R	E	E	Judge, Arbiter, Umpire, Adjudge, Adjudicate, Arbitrate, Umpire.
R	E	F	I	N	E	D	Purified, Polished, Smoothed, Cultivated, Fastidious, Precise, Exact, Genteel.
R	E	F	I	N	E	R	Machine that gives final finish to paper.
R	E	F	L	A	S	H	Rekindling and bursting into flame.
R	E	F	L	E	C	T	Deflect, Divert, Reconsider, Reproduce, Rebound, Recoil, Think, Deliberate.
R	E	F	O	R	G	E	Fashion or fabricate anew.
R	E	F	R	A	C	T	Divide, Bend at an angle.
R	E	F	R	A	I	N	Curb, Govern, Avoid, Shun, Keep, Deny, Check, Interrupt.
R	E	F	R	A	M	E	Provide with a new frame, Change the order.
R	E	F	R	E	S	H	Revive, Cheer, Replenish, Renovate, Renew, Refurbish, Restore, Regenerate.
R	E	F	U	G	E	D	Took sanctuary.
R	E	F	U	G	E	E	Displaced person, Evacuee, Fugitive, Exile, Expatriate.
R	E	F	U	S	A	L	Denial, Declination, Rejection.
R	E	F	U	S	E	D	Declined, Disapproved, Dismissed, Rejected, Repudiated, Spurned, Shunned, Avoided.
R	E	F	U	S	E	R	One that refuses.
R	E	F	U	T	E	D	Confuted, Disproved, Confounded, Controverted, Rebuffed.
R	E	F	U	T	E	R	One that refutes.
R	E	G	A	L	E	D	Refreshed, Entertained sumptiously, Pleased, Feasted, Dined lavishly.
R	E	G	A	L	I	A	Ceremonial robes, jewels and insignia.
R	E	G	A	L	L	Y	In a regal manner, Royally, Stately, Kingly.
R	E	G	A	T	T	A	Organized series of races for small boats.
R	E	G	E	N	C	Y	Period of rule by a regent.
R	E	G	I	M	E	N	Governing, Rule, Administration, Management, Guidance, Natural process, Systematic, Diet.
R	E	G	L	A	Z	E	Replace damaged windows.
R	E	G	N	A	N	T	Reigning, Dominant, Prevalent, Paramount, Current, Prevailing, Popular, Rife.
R	E	G	O	R	G	E	Disgorge, Vomit, Throw back, Swallow again, Suck back.
R	E	G	R	A	D	E	Assign a new category, Regroup.
R	E	G	R	A	N	T	Renew a licence.
R	E	G	R	A	S	P	Seize. Hold again.
R	E	G	R	A	S	S	Relaid turf.
R	E	G	R	A	T	E	Remove outer surface to improve appearance.
R	E	G	R	E	D	E	Retrograde.
R	E	G	R	E	E	T	Return a salutation.
R	E	G	R	E	S	S	Withdrawal, Revert, Cease operating or functioning.
R	E	G	U	L	A	R	Symmetrical, Orderly, Methodical, Normal, Standard, Correct, Complete, Typical.
R	E	G	U	L	U	S	Metallic substance beneath slag remaining after melting, Coarse metal.
R	E	I	G	N	E	D	Governed, Ruled, Predominated, Prevailed, Administered, Dominated.
R	E	I	N	I	N	G	Restraining, Curbing, Controlling, Repressing, Subduing, Smothering.

1	2	3	4	5	6	7	
R	E	I	T	B	O	K	Reedbuck.
R	E	J	O	I	C	E	Gladden, Please, Exult, Have, Own, Possess, Feel delight, Experience gladness.
R	E	J	O	I	N	T	Fill up open joints, Reunite.
R	E	J	U	D	G	E	Review, Re-examine.
R	E	L	A	P	S	E	Sink, Subside, Lapse, Revert, Backslide, Withdraw, Recurrence.
R	E	L	A	T	E	D	Told, Asserted, Reputed, Recited, Recounted, Narrated, Described, Stated.
R	E	L	A	T	O	R	Narrator.
R	E	L	A	T	E	R	Same as RELATER.
R	E	L	A	X	E	D	Slackened, Relieved, Rested, Abated, Eased, Unbend.
R	E	L	A	Y	E	D	Transmitted, Divided, Pumped, Passed along.
R	E	L	E	A	S	E	Alleviate, Relinquish, Surrender, Resign, Quit, Free, Mitigate, Liberate, Unshackle. To renew a lease.
R	E	L	I	A	N	T	Dependent, Trusting, Confident, Contingent, Relative, Conditional, Self-assured.
R	E	L	I	E	V	E	Rescue, Deliver, Mitigate, Lessen, Alleviate, Rob, Deprive, Succeed.
R	E	L	I	E	V	O	In relief.
R	E	L	I	G	H	T	To illuminate again, To re-kindle.
R	E	L	I	V	E	D	Recalled to life, Revived, Remember past experiences.
R	E	L	U	M	E	D	Rekindled, Illuminated again.
R	E	L	Y	I	N	G	Trusting, Depending, Calculating, Reckoning, Trusting, Entrusting, Banking, Belonging.
R	E	M	A	I	N	S	Remainder, Balance, Leavings, Remnants, Residue, Corpse, Carcass.
R	E	M	A	N	E	T	Postponed court hearing.
R	E	M	E	R	C	Y	Thank.
R	E	M	I	C	L	E	Small quill feather of a bird's wing.
R	E	M	I	P	E	D	Having feet or legs used as oars.
R	E	M	I	S	E	D	Replaced, Returned, Granted, Surrendered, Deeded, Conveyed, Ceded, Alienated.
R	E	M	N	A	N	T	Remainder, Rest, Unsold portion, Survivor, Residue, Fragment, Balance.
R	E	M	O	D	E	L	Reconstruct, Refashion, Remake, Redesign.
R	E	M	O	R	S	E	Self-reproach, Compassion, Penitence, Anguish, Contrition, Compunction, Penance.
R	E	M	O	U	N	T	Mount again, Furnish a fresh horse.
R	E	M	O	V	A	L	Being removed, Displaced, Dismissal, Shift of location.
R	E	M	O	V	E	D	Shifted, Transferred, Assassinated, Eradicated, Eliminated, Disappeared, Dislodged.
R	E	M	O	V	E	R	Transfer of proceeding.
R	E	N	A	M	E	D	Name again, Rechristened, Retitled.
R	E	N	D	I	N	G	Wrenching, Wresting, Cleaning, Disintegrating, Tearing, Ripping, Splitting, Severing.
R	E	N	E	G	E	D	Denied, Renounced, Deserted, Retracted, Refused, Declined, Revoked, Welshed.
R	E	N	E	W	A	L	Repetition, Replacement, Re-establish, Revival.
R	E	N	E	W	E	D	Refreshed, Regenerated, Re-invigorated, Revived, Recalled, Renovated, Reinstated.
R	E	N	E	W	E	R	Renovator.
R	E	N	T	I	E	R	One who lives on a fixed income from investments.
R	E	N	T	I	N	G	Endowing, Letting, Leasing, Possession for paying rent.
R	E	O	R	D	E	R	Repeat an order of goods already supplied, Re-organize, Re-arrange, Reconstruct.
R	E	P	A	I	N	T	Paint over, Another coat of paint.
R	E	P	A	P	E	R	A palindrome.
R	E	P	I	N	E	D	Complained, Whined, Wailed, Fretted, Fussed, Envied.
R	E	P	I	N	E	R	One that complains.
R	E	P	I	Q	U	E	Score in game of piquet.
R	E	P	L	A	C	E	Succeed, Supplant, Displace, Supersede, Reinstate, Restitute, Substitute, Change.
R	E	P	L	E	A	D	File a new legal plea.
R	E	P	L	E	T	E	Surfeited, Gorged, Complete, Crammed, Overflowing, Teeming, Loaded.
R	E	P	L	E	V	Y	Recover goods by court order.
R	E	P	L	I	C	A	Reproduction, Facsimile, Copy, Duplicate, Imitation.
R	E	P	L	I	E	D	Answered, Rejoined, Responded, Retorted, Returned, Echoed.
R	E	P	L	I	E	R	One who answers or returns fire.
R	E	P	L	U	M	E	To preen.
R	E	P	O	N	E	D	Rehabilitated.
R	E	P	O	S	A	L	Reposing of trust.
R	E	P	O	S	E	D	Laid at rest, Composed, Relied, Relaxed, Reclined, Settled.
R	E	P	O	S	I	T	Deposit, Store, Replace.
R	E	P	R	E	S	S	Control, Curb, Subdue, Quell, Crush, Check, Restrain, Compose.
R	E	P	R	I	N	T	Subsequent identical printing of a book already published.
R	E	P	R	I	S	E	Deduction made yearly, Repeat, Reiterate, Renew, Recapitulation, Repetition.
R	E	P	R	O	O	F	Censure, Rebuke, Reprimand, Refutation, Admonition, Chiding, Reproach.
R	E	P	R	O	V	E	Condemn, Disprove, Refute, Chide, Admonish, Lambaste, Scold.
R	E	P	T	A	N	T	Repent.
R	E	P	T	I	L	E	Animal that moves or crawls on its belly, Amphibian, Creeping, Reptant, Low, Malignant.
R	E	P	U	L	S	E	Rebuff, Refuse, Reject, Disgust, Denial, Deter, Revolt, Fend.
R	E	P	U	T	E	D	Reputable, Alleged, Putative, Deemed, Reckoned, Respectable, Supposed, Creditable.
R	E	Q	U	E	S	T	Entreaty, Petition, Demand, Ask, Solicit, Appeal, Pray, Sue.

1	2	3	4	5	6	7	Definition
R	E	Q	U	I	E	M	Dirge or Service for the dead.
R	E	S	C	A	L	E	Formulate on a smaller scale.
R	E	S	C	I	N	D	Annul, Cancel, Remove, Revoke, Repeal, Squash, Dismantle, Reverse.
R	E	S	C	O	R	E	Arrange a musical composition.
R	E	S	C	U	E	D	Saved, Delivered, Redeemed, Ransomed, Reclaimed, Freed, Liberated, Released.
R	E	S	C	U	E	R	Liberator, One who rescues.
R	E	S	E	I	Z	E	Confiscate again by legal right.
R	E	S	E	R	V	E	Spare, Save, Remain, Store, Stock, Secret, Hoard, Reserve.
R	E	S	H	A	P	E	Take on a new form, Remould.
R	E	S	I	A	N	T	Resident.
R	E	S	I	D	E	D	Remained, Stayed, Lived, Sojourned, Lodged, Tenanted, Occupied, Inhabited.
R	E	S	I	D	E	R	Resident, Tenant.
R	E	S	I	D	U	E	Remnant, Remainder, Rest, Unit, Balance, Leavings, Surplus.
R	E	S	I	L	E	D	Recoiled, Retracted, Retreated, Receded, Rebounded, Reneged, Welshed.
R	E	S	O	L	V	E	Analyze, Decide, Solve, Settle, Determine, Resolution, Decipher, Dispel.
R	E	S	O	U	N	D	Ring, Echo, Reverberate, Extol, Praise, Celebrate, Glorify, Laud. Echo.
R	E	S	P	E	A	K	Echo, Resound, Repeat, Reply.
R	E	S	P	E	C	T	Relevance, Honour, Consideration, Reputation, Motive, Interest, Regard, Anticipate.
R	E	S	P	I	R	E	Revive, Breathe, Inhale, Exhale.
R	E	S	P	I	T	E	Delay, Reprieve, Leisure, Postponement, Opportunity, Rest, Suspend, Recess.
R	E	S	P	O	N	D	Answer, Reply, Accord, Rejoinder, Retort, Return.
R	E	S	T	A	F	F	Provide with new workers.
R	E	S	T	A	R	T	Resume operation.
R	E	S	T	A	T	E	To declaim again.
R	E	S	T	A	U	R	Legal recourse of insurers.
R	E	S	T	D	A	Y	Sabbath, Day of rest in many religions.
R	E	S	T	F	U	L	Placid, Tranquil, Relaxed, Comfortable, Quiescent.
R	E	S	T	I	F	F	Restive.
R	E	S	T	I	N	G	Dormant, Quiescent, Reposing, Relaxing, Leaning, Reclining, Lounging, Loafing.
R	E	S	T	I	V	E	Inactive, Sluggish, Persistent, Stubborn, Inflexible, Fractious, Tense, Uneasy.
R	E	S	T	O	C	K	Provide new stock of plants, animals or articles.
R	E	S	T	O	R	E	Return, Renew, Rebuild, Reconstruct, Renovate, Reinstate, Repair, Heal.
R	E	S	T	Y	L	E	Refashion.
R	E	S	U	I	N	G	Preparation for mining a narrow vein.
R	E	S	U	M	E	D	Reoccupied, Reiterated, Summarized, Epitomized, Renewed, Continued, Recommenced.
R	E	S	U	R	G	E	Become resurrected, Surge back and forth.
R	E	T	A	B	L	E	Raised shelf behind the altar.
R	E	T	A	K	E	N	Recaptured, Re-photographed.
R	E	T	A	K	E	R	One that retakes.
R	E	T	I	A	R	Y	Armed with a net, Skilled in using a net.
R	E	T	I	C	L	E	Grid system to aid focussing of gunsight, telescope or microscope.
R	E	T	I	N	A	L	Pertaining to the retina.
R	E	T	I	N	U	E	Entourage, Escort, Bodyguard, Suite, Train of attendants.
R	E	T	I	R	A	L	Retreat, Withdrawal, Retirement.
R	E	T	I	R	E	D	Recalled, Withdrawn, Gone, Retreated, Receded, Resigned, Removed, Terminated.
R	E	T	O	U	C	H	Revise, Colour up to improve appearance.
R	E	T	R	A	C	E	Recall, Reinspect, Trace ancestors, Reverse direction.
R	E	T	R	A	C	T	Prevent, Restrain, Recant, Disavow, Recall, Recede, Abjure, Revoke.
R	E	T	R	E	A	D	Replace worn tread of a tyre by vulcanizing.
R	E	T	R	E	A	T	Refuge, Asylum, Evacuate, Recess, Withdraw, Remove, Recoil, Vacate.
R	E	T	R	I	A	L	Second trial.
R	E	T	R	U	D	E	Thrust back.
R	E	T	T	E	R	Y	Place where flax is soaked to loosen fibre.
R	E	T	T	I	N	G	Soaking of flax to release fibre.
R	E	U	N	I	F	Y	Restoring unity.
R	E	U	N	I	O	N	Social gathering, Meeting of persons, Peace-making.
R	E	U	N	I	T	E	Rejoin, Reconcile, Bring together.
R	E	V	A	L	U	E	Reappraise, Re-assess.
R	E	V	E	L	R	Y	Noisy party, Carousal, Roistering, Boisterous festivity, Gaiety.
R	E	V	E	N	G	E	Punish, Retaliate, Vindicate, Redress, Inflict injury in return.
R	E	V	E	N	U	E	Income from investment, Taxes, Earning, Wages, Proceeds, Profit, Returns, Yield.
R	E	V	E	R	E	D	Venerated, Worshipped, Adored, Respected, Admired, Esteemed, Cherished, Appreciated.
R	E	V	E	R	E	E	Miniature pink.
R	E	V	E	R	I	E	Daydream, Trance, Vision, Absorption, Muse, Meditation, Abstraction.
R	E	V	E	R	S	E	Contrary, Opposite, Misfortune, Check, Defeat, Return, Recoil, Revoke.
R	E	V	E	R	S	I	Card game.
R	E	V	E	R	S	O	To go back, Revert, Revoke, Restore, Annul, Invert, Reverse.

1	2	3	4	5	6	7	Definition
R	E	V	I	L	E	D	Abused, Scolded, Villified, Railed, Calumniated, Defamed, Maligned, Slandered.
R	E	V	I	L	E	R	One that reviles.
R	E	V	I	S	A	L	Revision.
R	E	V	I	S	E	D	Examined, Improved, Amended, Altered, Redrawn, Revamped, Rewritten, Restyled.
R	E	V	I	S	E	R	Proof-reader.
R	E	V	I	S	I	T	Visit again, Check again.
R	E	V	I	V	A	L	Restoration, Recall, Reanimation, Renaissance, Resurrection, Reactivated, Renewal.
R	E	V	I	V	E	D	Restored, Resuscitated, Gained, Improved, Recuperated, Reinstated, Renewed, Renovated.
R	E	V	I	V	E	R	Stimulant, Renovator.
R	E	V	I	V	O	R	Revival in English law of a law suit that is invalid.
R	E	V	O	K	E	D	Restrained, Reverted, Rescinded, Cancelled, Repealed, Retracted, Recovered, Annulled.
R	E	V	O	L	V	E	Rotate, Turn, Gyrate, Ponder, Study, Spin, Whirl, Circle.
R	E	V	O	M	I	T	To vomit again.
R	E	V	V	I	N	G	Incrasing speed of revolutions.
R	E	W	A	K	E	N	To waken again.
R	E	W	R	I	T	E	Revise, Revamp, Rework, Alter, Restyle.
R	E	Y	N	A	R	D	Fox.
R	H	A	B	D	O	M	Rodlike structure in compound eye of insects or spiders.
R	H	A	E	T	I	C	Ancient language of Roman province south of Danube area.
R	H	A	G	A	D	E	Crack or fissure of the skin.
R	H	A	M	N	U	S	Genus of trees or shrubs with a stone fruit, Buckthorn.
R	H	A	T	A	N	Y	Dried root of Peruvian shrub that yields an astringent.
R	H	E	M	I	S	H	Pertaining to Reims, France.
R	H	E	N	I	S	H	Pertaining to area of Germany along the Rhine river.
R	H	E	N	I	U	M	Heavy metallic element that resembles manganese.
R	H	E	T	I	A	N	Rhaetian.
R	H	E	U	M	E	D	Rheumy, Affected with catarrh or rheumatism.
R	H	I	N	I	O	N	Relating to the nasal bones.
R	H	I	Z	I	N	A	Rhizoid, Root-like structure, Fungi.
R	H	I	Z	O	M	E	Tuber-shaped or elongated root-structure.
R	H	I	Z	O	M	A	Same as RHIZOME.
R	H	I	Z	O	T	A	Order of Rotifers, Minute aquatic animals.
R	H	I	Z	O	T	E	Same as RHIZOTA.
R	H	O	D	I	A	N	Relating to island of Rhodes.
R	H	O	D	I	U	M	Bright white metallic element of the platinum metals.
R	H	O	D	O	R	A	Shrub related to the Rhododendron.
R	H	O	M	B	I	C	Equilateral parallelogram, Aerial antenna.
R	H	O	N	C	U	S	Wheezing from obstructed bronchial tubes.
R	H	U	B	A	R	B	Plant with edible stalks used as a dessert, Dried root used in the East as a purgative.
R	H	Y	M	I	N	G	Forming rhymes, Making verse, Harmonize.
R	H	Y	M	I	S	T	Poet.
R	H	Y	N	C	H	O	Snout as used in zoology.
R	H	Y	T	I	N	A	Family of aquatic mammals. Dugong, Manatee, Sea-cow.
R	I	B	B	A	N	D	Timber used in ship-building.
R	I	B	B	I	N	G	Strengthening, Enclosing with ribs, Knitting stitch forming ridges, Poking fun, Ridiculing.
R	I	B	B	O	N	S	Flat or tubular lengths of fabric used for trimming or decorating, Reins, Pieces, Fragments.
R	I	B	L	I	K	E	Resembling a rib.
R	I	B	W	O	R	T	Ribgrass.
R	I	C	E	H	E	N	Aquatic birds from Florida.
R	I	C	I	N	U	S	Castor-oil plant.
R	I	C	K	E	R	S	Poles, Spars.
R	I	C	K	E	T	S	Bone complaint due to diet deficiency.
R	I	C	K	E	T	Y	Tottering, Feeble joints, Shaky, Unsound, Wobbly, Unstable, Weak.
R	I	C	K	I	N	G	Wrenching, Spraining, Turning, Twisting.
R	I	C	K	S	H	A	Rickshaw, Light two-wheeled vehicle drawn by a man.
R	I	C	O	T	T	A	Cottage cheese made of skim milk.
R	I	D	A	B	L	E	Fit for riding, Road or ford suitable for travelling over.
R	I	D	D	I	N	G	Dispatching, Clearing, Purging, Removing, Cleansing, Eliminating, Losing, Liberating.
R	I	D	D	L	E	D	Screened, Sifted, Seized, Permeated, Corrupted, Penetrated, Pierced.
R	I	D	D	L	E	R	One who sifts with a riddle.
R	I	D	E	R	E	D	Used to describe a fence in relation to horse riding.
R	I	D	O	T	T	O	Public entertainment, Abridgment of a musical score.
R	I	E	T	B	O	K	Reedbuck.
R	I	F	F	L	E	R	Small file with curved ends.
R	I	F	L	I	N	G	Ransacking, Plundering, Robbing, Pillaging, Despoiling, Stealing, Searching, Boring.
R	I	F	T	I	N	G	Cleaving, Splitting, Dividing, Fracturing, Renting, Breaching.
R	I	G	A	R	E	E	Ornamentation in glass forming lines.

7 LETTERS

1	2	3	4	5	6	7	
R	I	G	G	I	N	G	Network of ropes or wires.
R	I	G	G	I	S	H	Wanton.
R	I	G	H	T	E	D	Justified, Redressed, Rectified, Adjusted, Recovered, Fixed, Overhauled, Reconditioned.
R	I	G	H	T	E	N	Straighten.
R	I	G	H	T	E	R	One that sees justice done.
R	I	G	H	T	L	Y	Fairly, Appropriately, Fitly, Properly, Correctly, Accurately, Exactly, Justly.
R	I	G	I	D	L	Y	Stiffly, Severely, Strictly, Staunchly, Inflexibly.
R	I	L	I	E	V	O	Relievo, In relief.
R	I	L	L	I	N	G	Flowing, Rippling.
R	I	M	F	I	R	E	Percussion compound, Leaf disease caused by lack of potash.
R	I	M	L	E	S	S	Having no frame.
R	I	M	M	I	N	G	Enclosing, Bordering, Edging, Hemming, Outlining, Surrounding.
R	I	N	D	I	N	G	Removing the rind.
R	I	N	G	E	N	T	Gaping, Opening wide.
R	I	N	G	H	A	L	Spitting cobra.
R	I	N	G	I	N	G	Encircling, Surrounding, Pealing, Tolling, Banding, Shackling, Resounding, Chiming.
R	I	N	G	L	E	T	Long curl of hair, Small circle.
R	I	N	G	M	A	N	Boxer.
R	I	N	G	N	E	T	Fishing net.
R	I	N	G	P	I	N	Pin with a ring for a head to attach a label.
R	I	N	K	I	N	G	Skating at a rink.
R	I	N	S	I	N	G	Cleansing, Sluicing.
R	I	O	T	I	N	G	Disorder, Roustering, Despoiling, Attacking.
R	I	O	T	I	S	E	Excess revelry, Licentiousness.
R	I	O	T	O	U	S	Profligate, Wanton, Turbulent, Exuberant, Abundant, Profuse, Lavish, Luxuriant.
R	I	P	C	O	R	D	Cord to release a parachute.
R	I	P	E	N	E	D	Matured, Ready, Developed.
R	I	P	I	E	N	O	Supplementary musical instrument.
R	I	P	O	S	T	E	Retort, Repartee, Deliver a counterblow.
R	I	P	P	I	N	G	Grand, Swell, Tearing, Splitting, Slashing, Rending, Attacking.
R	I	P	P	L	E	D	Rilled, Lightly ruffled, Dimpled, Fretted, Waved.
R	I	P	P	L	E	R	One that ripples.
R	I	P	S	A	C	K	Gray whale.
R	I	P	T	I	D	E	Destructive vortex.
R	I	S	I	B	L	E	Disposed to laugh, Funny, Ridiculous, Laughable.
R	I	S	K	I	E	R	More hazardous, More daring, Bolder, More dangerous.
R	I	S	K	I	N	G	Venturing, Endangering, Jeopardizing, Menacing, Daring, Confronting, Gambling, Chancing.
R	I	S	O	T	T	O	Seasoned rice cooked in meat stock.
R	I	S	S	O	L	E	Minced meat patty fried in deep fat.
R	I	V	A	L	R	Y	Competition, Antagonism, Contest, Conflict, Strife. Warfare emulation.
R	I	V	E	R	E	T	Rivulet.
R	I	V	E	T	E	D	Fastened, Affixed, Attached, Concentrated, Focused.
R	I	V	E	T	E	R	Worker inserting rivets.
R	I	V	I	E	R	A	Mediterranean resort area.
R	I	V	I	E	R	E	Diamond necklace.
R	I	V	U	L	E	T	Brook, Runnel, Streamlet, Creek, Burn.
R	O	A	D	B	E	D	Ballast on a railroad.
R	O	A	D	H	O	G	Selfish and inconsiderate driver.
R	O	A	D	I	N	G	Highway construction and maintenance.
R	O	A	D	M	A	N	Builder and maintainer of public roads, Peddler, Canvasser, Travelling salesman.
R	O	A	D	M	A	P	Plan of road network.
R	O	A	D	W	A	Y	Road for vehicular traffic.
R	O	A	M	I	N	G	Roving, Wandering, Rambling, Going, Proceeding, Meandering, Ranging, Gallivanting.
R	O	A	S	T	E	D	Cooked, Parched, Ridiculed, Criticized, Burned, Baked, Broiled, Scorched.
R	O	A	S	T	E	R	Device for roasting.
R	O	B	B	E	R	Y	Larceny, Theft, Piracy, Pillage, Burglary.
R	O	B	B	I	N	G	Stealing, Plundering, Looting, Thieving, Ransacking, Filching, Pilfering, Cheating.
R	O	C	K	E	E	L	Gunnel.
R	O	C	K	E	R	Y	Rock garden.
R	O	C	K	I	E	R	More rocky, Harder, More steadfast.
R	O	C	K	I	N	G	Swaying, Rolling, Back and forth movement.
R	O	C	K	O	I	L	Petroleum.
R	O	C	K	O	O	N	Small rocket carried to high altitude by a balloon and then fired.
R	O	C	K	O	I	L	Petroleum.
R	O	D	L	I	K	E	Resembling a rod.
R	O	E	B	U	C	K	Male Roe deer.
R	O	E	D	E	E	R	Small European and Asiatic deer.

7 LETTERS

1	2	3	4	5	6	7	Definition
R	O	G	U	E	R	Y	Knavery, Conduct of a rogue.
R	O	G	U	I	S	H	Dishonest, Unprincipled, Impish, Mischievous, Coy, Shifty, Playful.
R	O	I	L	I	N	G	Romping or playing in a rough manner.
R	O	I	S	T	E	R	Revel, Carouse, Frolic, Riot, Noisy festivities, Drunken romp, Disorder.
R	O	K	E	L	A	Y	Long cloak.
R	O	L	L	I	C	K	Frolic, Romp, Play, Escapade, Lark, Caper, Cavort, Gambol.
R	O	L	L	I	N	G	Lurching, Swaying, Wallowing, Resounding, Reverberating, Staggering, Recurring, Coiling.
R	O	L	L	M	O	P	Pickled herring.
R	O	L	L	O	C	K	Rowlock, Support for oars.
R	O	L	L	W	A	Y	Landing, Incline, Slope for rolling logs into a river.
R	O	M	A	I	K	A	Modern Greek folk dance.
R	O	M	A	I	N	E	Cos lettuce.
R	O	M	A	N	C	E	Fictional love stories, Love affair, Sentimental, Mushy.
R	O	M	A	N	I	C	Romance, Descended from the Roman people.
R	O	M	A	U	N	T	Romance, Exaggeration.
R	O	M	E	I	T	E	Mineral consisting of yellow oxide of calcium, iron, manganese sodium and antimony.
R	O	M	M	A	N	Y	Romany, Gipsy.
R	O	M	P	E	R	S	Child's one piece garment.
R	O	M	P	I	N	G	Gambolling, Playing, Capering, Cavorting.
R	O	M	P	I	S	H	Romping, Frolicsome, Frisky.
R	O	N	D	E	A	U	Fixed form of verse, Medieval French song.
R	O	N	D	I	N	O	Short Rondo.
R	O	N	G	E	U	R	Surgical forceps for removing small pieces of bone.
R	O	N	Q	U	I	L	Marine fish.
R	O	N	T	G	E	N	Roentgen, International unit of X radiation and Gamma radiation.
R	O	O	F	I	N	G	Material suitable for the construction of a roof.
R	O	O	F	L	E	T	Small roof.
R	O	O	I	B	O	K	Impala.
R	O	O	I	N	E	K	Description of a British soldier from time of the Boer War.
R	O	O	K	E	R	Y	Breeding place of rooks, penguins and seals.
R	O	O	K	I	N	G	Defrauding, Cheating, Swindling, Fleecing.
R	O	O	M	A	G	E	Space, Accommodation.
R	O	O	M	F	U	L	As many as a room will hold.
R	O	O	M	I	E	R	More spacious, More elbowroom, More leeway.
R	O	O	M	I	L	Y	Spaciously, Capaciously.
R	O	O	S	T	E	D	Perched, Lodged, Settled, Alighted, Seated.
R	O	O	S	T	E	R	Male domestic fowl, Male person displaying cocky tendencies.
R	O	O	T	C	A	P	Protective cap at terminal of root.
R	O	O	T	E	R	Y	Plants set on a pile of roots and soil.
R	O	O	T	I	N	G	Planting, Lodging, Searching, Settling, Cheering, Lauding, Encouraging.
R	O	O	T	L	E	D	Rummaged, Grubbed, Dug, Scrabbled.
R	O	O	T	L	E	T	Small root.
R	O	P	A	L	I	C	Rhopalic, Each successive word is longer by one syllable than its predecessor.
R	O	P	E	W	A	Y	Aerial cable, Cableway.
R	O	R	Q	U	A	L	A whale.
R	O	S	A	L	E	S	Genus of cacti.
R	O	S	A	L	I	A	Melody which rises by half tone as it is repeated.
R	O	S	E	A	T	E	Resembling a rose, Optimistic, Looking through rose-tinted spectacles.
R	O	S	E	B	A	Y	Oleander.
R	O	S	E	B	I	T	Rose countersink or reamer.
R	O	S	E	B	O	X	Strainer for the end of the suction pipe of a pump.
R	O	S	E	B	U	D	Partly-opened flower of a rosebush.
R	O	S	E	C	U	T	Special cut for a diamond.
R	O	S	E	E	A	R	A dog's ear that folds backward.
R	O	S	E	H	A	W	Ripe fruit of a wild rose.
R	O	S	E	H	I	P	Same as ROSE-HAW.
R	O	S	E	L	L	A	Australian parrakeet.
R	O	S	E	L	L	E	East Indian herb cultivated for use in tarts and jellies and the fibre being substituted for hemp.
R	O	S	E	O	L	A	Rubella, German measles.
R	O	S	E	R	E	D	Colour of clear red.
R	O	S	E	T	T	E	Ribbon gathered into a circle and worn to denote a prize or membership of a particular group.
R	O	S	I	E	S	T	Most blushing, Healthier, Most optimistic, Most promising, Ruddier.
R	O	S	I	N	E	D	Rubbed with rosin.
R	O	S	K	O	P	F	Special type of watch.
R	O	S	O	L	I	O	Cordial made from spirits and sugar and flavoured with rose petals or orange blossom.
R	O	S	S	I	N	G	Removing scaly outside of bark.
R	O	S	T	R	A	L	Pertaining to a platform at the front of an ancient ship.

1	2	3	4	5	6	7	
R	O	S	T	R	U	M	Platform of ancient Roman orators, Ship's prow, Relating to bill, beak or snout.
R	O	T	A	L	I	A	Genus of minute aquatic organisms.
R	O	T	A	T	E	D	Revolved, Spun, Twirled, Gyrated, Rolled, Alternated, Exchanged, Relieved.
R	O	T	A	T	O	R	Machine or mechanical part that causes rotation.
R	O	T	I	F	E	R	Microscopic many-celled aquatic animals.
R	O	T	O	N	D	A	Rotunda, Round bulding covered with a domed ceiling and a domed roof.
R	O	T	T	I	N	G	Decomposing, Decaying, Deteriorating, Degenerating, Joking, Corrupting, Teasing, Debasing.
R	O	T	U	L	A	R	Patella, Kneecap.
R	O	T	U	N	D	A	Round building with a domed ceiling and covered by a dome.
R	O	U	G	H	E	D	Manhandled, Beaten, Pushed, Acted violently, Outlined, Sketched, Unpolished.
R	O	U	G	H	E	N	Made rough, Made coarse, Made hoarse.
R	O	U	G	H	E	R	Harsher, Coarser, Ruder, Tougher, Cruder, Blunter, Gruffer.
R	O	U	G	H	L	Y	Harshly, Violently, Severely, Coarsely, Approximately, Grossly, Rudely, Improperly.
R	O	U	G	I	N	G	Blushing, Painting the cheeks with rouge.
R	O	U	L	A	D	E	Musical trill, Rolled slice of meat braised.
R	O	U	L	E	A	U	Decorative piping for clothing, Roll of coins.
R	O	U	N	D	E	D	Curved, Trimmed, Encircled, Mellow, Shapely, Polished, Finished, Complete.
R	O	U	N	D	E	L	Circular group, Ring of things or persons, Glass disc.
R	O	U	N	D	E	R	Wastrel, Travelling Methodist preacher.
R	O	U	N	D	L	Y	Completely, Fully, Wholly, Boldly, Openly, Plainly, Promptly, Smartly.
R	O	U	N	D	U	P	Collect cattle for branding, Camber, Gathering of persons, Brief resumé of news.
R	O	U	P	I	N	G	Croaking, Calling, Shouting, Selling at an auction.
R	O	U	S	A	N	T	Rising as the heraldic swan.
R	O	U	S	I	N	G	Awakening, Stirring, Intensifying, Stimulating, Ranting, Exciting, Inflaming, Mounting.
R	O	U	S	T	E	R	Roustabout, Dock worker, Unskilled labourer, Circus worker, Vagabound.
R	O	U	T	I	N	E	Act, Ordinary, Usual, System, Groove, Customary, Habitual, Wonted.
R	O	U	T	I	N	G	Bawling, Bellowing, Rooting, Rummaging, Rousting, Stampeding, Conquering, Overwhelming.
R	O	W	A	B	L	E	Capable of being rowed.
R	O	W	B	O	A	T	Small boat propelled by oars.
R	O	W	D	I	E	R	Noisier, Rougher, More vulgar, More unruly.
R	O	W	D	I	L	Y	Boisterously, Vulgarly, Noisily, Turbulently, Stubbornly.
R	O	W	L	O	C	K	Support for oars, Course of bricks with ends exposed.
R	O	W	P	O	R	T	Opening in the side of a small sailing ship.
R	O	Y	A	L	L	Y	With pomp and ceremony, Grandly, Gloriously, Indulgently, Regally, Imperially, Magnificently.
R	O	Y	A	L	T	Y	Sovereignity, Realm, Glory, Magnificence, Majesty, Nobility, Bonus, Payment for copyright.
R	O	Y	N	I	S	H	Mangy, Scabby, Base, Coarse.
R	O	Z	E	L	L	E	Roselle.
R	U	B	A	D	U	B	Sound of drumbeats.
R	U	B	A	S	S	E	Red quartz.
R	U	B	B	I	N	G	Grating, Chafing, Scouring, Tracing, Grazing, Provoking, Polishing, Buffing.
R	U	B	B	I	S	H	Rubble, Trash, Debris, Litter, Garbage, Nonsense, Bosh, Rot.
R	U	B	D	O	W	N	To massage well, To dry all over with a towel.
R	U	B	E	L	L	A	Contagious disease with red skin eruptions, German measles.
R	U	B	E	O	L	A	Measles.
R	U	B	I	C	O	N	Boundary, Limit, The time or place of no return.
R	U	B	I	D	I	C	Relating to Rubidium.
R	U	B	I	O	U	S	Ruby red.
R	U	B	R	E	N	E	Orange-red crystalline hydrocarbon.
R	U	B	Y	I	N	G	Making red.
R	U	C	H	I	N	G	Strip of material gathered into a frill, Fluted trimming.
R	U	C	K	I	N	G	Puckering, Wrinkling, Creasing, Making furrows.
R	U	C	K	L	E	D	Made a hoarse rattling sound.
R	U	C	T	I	O	N	Contention, Dissension, Friction, Uproar, Turmoil, Disturbance, Brawl, Commotion.
R	U	D	D	I	E	D	Reddened.
R	U	D	D	I	E	R	Redder, Rosier.
R	U	D	D	I	L	Y	Glowingly, Rosily.
R	U	D	D	L	E	D	Reddened, Flushed, Blushed, Rouged, Coloured with red ochre.
R	U	D	D	O	C	K	Robin.
R	U	D	E	R	A	L	Plant growing in waste ground, Weed introduced into a disturbed area.
R	U	D	E	S	B	Y	Boisterous uncouth person.
R	U	E	L	L	I	A	Genus of tropical American trees or shrubs.
R	U	F	F	I	A	N	Bully, Rowdy, Brutal, Tough, Hoodlum, Hooligan, Thug, Desperado.
R	U	F	F	I	N	G	To make into a ruff, Ruffling, Teasing the hair.
R	U	F	F	L	E	D	Grazed, Distracted, Troubled, Attacked, Bullied, Swaggered, Gathered, Pleated.
R	U	F	F	L	E	R	Sewing machine attachment for making ruffles.
R	U	G	G	I	N	G	Covering with a blanket.
R	U	I	N	A	T	E	Destroy, Annihilate, Demolish, Raze, Smash, Wreck.

1	2	3	4	5	6	7	
R	U	I	N	I	N	G	Devasting, Overthrowing, Bankrupting, Improverishing, Destroying, Demolishing, Mutilating.
R	U	I	N	O	U	S	Ruined, Destructive, Disastrous, Pernicious, Calamitous, Fatal, Catastrophic, Shattering.
R	U	L	A	B	L	E	Permissable according to the rules.
R	U	L	L	I	O	N	Large rough-looking person or creature.
R	U	M	B	L	E	D	Reverberated, Growled, Grumbled, Boomed, Blasted, Crashed, See through a trick.
R	U	M	B	L	E	R	Operator of a tumbling machine.
R	U	M	I	N	A	L	Relating to the rumen, First stomach of a ruminant.
R	U	M	M	A	G	E	Uproar, Ransack, Disorder, Stir, Seek, Discover, Disarrange, Disorganize.
R	U	M	M	I	E	R	Queer, Peculiar, Eccentric.
R	U	M	N	E	S	S	Oddness, Idiosyncrasy, Eccentricity.
R	U	M	P	L	E	D	Wrinkled, Creased, Crumpled, Tousled, Mussed, Scrunched.
R	U	M	S	H	O	P	Saloon bar, Commercial establishment where alcoholic beverages are sold.
R	U	N	A	W	A	Y	Fugitive, Deserter, Renegade, Out of control, Cinch, Setup, Conquest.
R	U	N	D	A	L	E	Strip of land between small farms as a boundary.
R	U	N	D	L	E	T	Small barrel or keg.
R	U	N	D	O	W	N	Dilapidated, Exhausted, Weak, Shabby, Dingy, Derogate, Detract, Decry.
R	U	N	N	I	N	G	Fleeing, Retreating, Escaping, Functioning, Working, Hastening, Managing.
R	U	N	O	V	E	R	Overflow, Exceed a limit, Examine, Continue.
R	U	P	T	U	R	E	Breach, Break, Fracture, Separate, Broken, Disrupt, Divide, Rift.
R	U	R	A	L	L	Y	In a rural manner, Rustically.
R	U	S	H	I	N	G	Dashing, Tearing, Shooting, Overpowering, Careering, Hurrying, Stampeding, Streaming.
R	U	S	H	N	U	T	Edible nut-like tuber.
R	U	S	S	E	T	Y	Reddish brown colour.
R	U	S	S	I	A	N	Member of Slavic Great Russian ethnic group.
R	U	S	S	I	F	Y	To conform to characteristics of Russian mode.
R	U	S	S	U	L	A	Genus of fungi.
R	U	S	T	I	E	R	More rusty, Disused, Out of practice, More surly.
R	U	S	T	I	L	Y	In a rusty manner, Fustily.
R	U	S	T	I	N	G	Tarnishing, Corroding, Impairing by disuse, Withering, Oxidizing.
R	U	S	T	L	E	D	Crackled, Stirred, Foraged, Stole, Hustled.
R	U	S	T	L	E	R	Cattle thief.
R	U	S	T	R	E	D	Lozenge-shaped pertaining to medieval armour.
R	U	T	H	F	U	L	Pitiful, Tender, Woeful, Rueful.
R	U	T	T	I	N	G	Period when animals are sexually active, Furrowing.
R	U	T	T	I	S	H	Lustful, Salacious.

S

1	2	3	4	5	6	7	
S	A	B	B	A	T	H	Observed as a day of rest in many religions.
S	A	B	E	L	L	A	Tube-dwelling marine worm.
S	A	B	R	I	N	G	Killing with a sabre or sword.
S	A	B	R	E	U	R	Cavalryman.
S	A	B	U	R	R	A	Sand colic, Disease of stomach and intestines of horses and cows.
S	A	C	A	T	O	N	Coarse grass for hay-making. Early culture in Arizona.
S	A	C	C	A	D	E	To check a horse with the reins.
S	A	C	C	A	T	E	Being enclosed in a pouch, Cyst.
S	A	C	C	U	L	E	Small bag, Inner part of the ear.
S	A	C	E	L	L	A	Small chapels.
S	A	C	K	A	G	E	Pillage, Looting, Plundering.
S	A	C	K	B	U	T	Medieval trombone.
S	A	C	K	F	U	L	As much as would fill a sack.
S	A	C	K	I	N	G	Plundering, Looting, Desecrating, Devastating, Foraging, Dismissing, Terminating, Expelling.
S	A	C	R	A	R	Y	Holy place or temple.
S	A	C	R	I	N	G	Consecrating.
S	A	C	R	I	S	T	Sexton, Officer of the church in charge of the treasures.
S	A	D	D	E	S	T	Gravest, Gloomiest, Most downcast, Sorriest, Most depressing.
S	A	D	D	L	E	D	Burdened, Encumbered, Loaded, Taxed, Hampered, Impeded, Restricted, Weighed.
S	A	D	D	L	E	R	One that makes, repairs or sells saddles.
S	A	D	I	R	O	N	Flat iron pointed at each end.
S	A	D	N	E	S	S	Sorrowfulness, Unhappiness, Gloominess, Depression, Melancholy, Dejection, Blues.
S	A	D	W	A	R	E	Flatware of pewter of a poor quality.
S	A	F	F	I	A	N	Brightly coloured goatskin or sheepskin leather.
S	A	F	F	R	O	N	Dried stigmas of flowers used to colour and flavour food and medicine.
S	A	G	A	M	A	N	Bard, One who relates long historical stories and legends.
S	A	G	A	T	H	Y	Fine twilled worsted fabric.
S	A	G	G	I	N	G	Downward drooping, Declining, Sinking, Dipping downward, Flagging.

1	2	3	4	5	6	7	Definition
S	A	G	I	T	T	A	Measurement of an arc, Part of the ear of a fish, Arrowworm.
S	A	G	U	A	R	O	New World giant cactus bearing edible fruit.
S	A	I	L	I	N	G	Travelling on a ship, Cruising, Yachting, Achieving without apparent effort, Gliding.
S	A	I	M	I	R	I	Squirrel monkey.
S	A	I	N	T	E	D	Beatified, Canonized, Enshrined.
S	A	I	N	T	L	Y	Holy, Pious.
S	A	I	V	I	S	M	The worship of one of the Indian deities, Siva.
S	A	L	A	B	L	E	Marketable, Vendible, Venal.
S	A	L	C	H	O	W	Special jump in figure skating.
S	A	L	I	A	N	T	Salient, Noticeable, Arresting, Important, Pertinent, Heraldic leaping beast.
S	A	L	I	C	I	N	Bitter white crystalline betaglucoside from willow and poplar trees used in medicine.
S	A	L	I	E	N	T	Protruberant, Prominent, Striking, Noticeable, Outstanding, Conspicuous, Significant.
S	A	L	I	V	A	L	Salivary.
S	A	L	L	I	E	D	Issued, Spurted, Sprung, Gushed, Erupted.
S	A	L	L	O	W	Y	Being a greenish yellow colour.
S	A	L	M	I	A	C	Sal Ammoniac.
S	A	L	M	I	N	E	Protamine from fish sperm used to reverse anti-coagulant effect of heparin.
S	A	L	P	I	N	X	Pertaining to tube, Eustachian tune, Fallopian tube.
S	A	L	S	I	F	Y	European biennial herb with an edible root.
S	A	L	S	O	L	A	Genus of Old World herbs and shrubs, Thistle.
S	A	L	T	A	N	T	Dancing, Leaping, Mutant strain produced in a fungal or bacterial culture.
S	A	L	T	A	T	E	Move by leaps and jumps.
S	A	L	T	B	O	X	Type of New England house.
S	A	L	T	C	A	T	Salt, meal and lime mixture attractive to pigeons.
S	A	L	T	E	R	N	Saltworks.
S	A	L	T	I	E	R	More salty, Wittier.
S	A	L	T	I	N	E	Cracker biscuit sprinkled with salt.
S	A	L	T	I	N	G	Land flooded regularly by tides, Curing, Preserving, Planting material or ore with intent to fraud.
S	A	L	T	I	R	E	Saint Andrew's cross.
S	A	L	T	I	S	H	Impregnated with salt.
S	A	L	T	P	A	N	Pan for making salt by evaporation.
S	A	L	T	P	I	T	Pit for evaporating sea water.
S	A	L	U	T	E	D	Greeted, Recognized, Honoured, Addressed, Accosted, Hailed.
S	A	L	V	A	G	E	Save, Compensation, Deliver, Rescue, Reclaim, Recover, Retrieve, Regain.
S	A	L	V	I	N	G	Anointing, Healing, Curing, Soothing, Allaying, SOlving, Assuaging, Resolving.
S	A	M	B	H	U	R	Large Asiatic Deer.
S	A	M	B	U	C	A	Triangle, Ancient harp.
S	A	M	I	S	E	N	Japanese stringed musical instrument.
S	A	M	N	I	T	E	People of central Italy in ancient times.
S	A	M	O	G	O	N	Illicitly distilled Russian vodka.
S	A	M	O	L	U	S	Genus of tropical herbs, Primula, Primrose.
S	A	M	O	V	A	R	Russian tea-urn.
S	A	M	O	Y	E	D	Siberian thick-coated working dog.
S	A	M	P	L	E	D	Symbolized, Copied, Tested, Experienced, Skimmed, Represented, Tasted.
S	A	M	P	L	E	R	Example of different embroidery stitches, One that prepares samples.
S	A	M	U	R	A	I	Professional Japanese soldier, Aristocratic warrior.
S	A	N	C	T	U	M	Sacred place, Place of retreat, Study, Office.
S	A	N	C	T	U	S	Opening of a hymn.
S	A	N	D	B	A	G	Bag filled with sand used as fortication or as a weapon.
S	A	N	D	B	A	R	Bar of sand caused by tide or current.
S	A	N	D	B	O	X	Box containing sand for children to play in.
S	A	N	D	B	O	Y	Peddler of sand, Proverbially a person who is very light-hearted.
S	A	N	D	B	U	G	Common bait bug.
S	A	N	D	B	U	R	Weeds growing in waste ground.
S	A	N	D	D	A	B	Flatfish.
S	A	N	D	E	E	L	Slender soft-finned fish.
S	A	N	D	E	R	S	Red sandalwood.
S	A	N	D	F	L	Y	Small biting fly.
S	A	N	D	I	N	G	Smoothing by grinding or rubbing with sandpaper, Covering with sand.
S	A	N	D	J	E	T	Sandblast.
S	A	N	D	L	O	B	Lugworm.
S	A	N	D	M	A	N	Gentle fairy-story man who sprinkles sleep over the eyes of children.
S	A	N	D	P	I	T	Pit for procuring sand.
S	A	N	D	R	A	T	Rodent native to a desert. Gopher, Mole-rat.
S	A	N	G	S	U	E	Leech.
S	A	N	I	C	L	E	Plant reputed to possess healing powers, Root used in folk medicine.
S	A	N	K	H	Y	A	System of Hindu philosophy.

1	2	3	4	5	6	7	
S	A	P	A	J	O	U	Spider monkey.
S	A	P	E	R	D	A	Genus of long-horned beetles.
S	A	P	H	E	A	D	Weak-minded, Stupid person.
S	A	P	H	E	N	A	Chief vein.
S	A	P	I	E	N	T	Wise, Judicious, Prudent, Sage, Sane, Sensible, Learned, Scholarly.
S	A	P	L	E	S	S	Dry, Lifeless, Feeble, Insipid, Bland, Inane, Innocuous, Vapid.
S	A	P	L	I	N	G	Young forest tree, Youth.
S	A	P	O	N	I	N	Glycoside that occurs in plants.
S	A	P	P	H	I	C	Erotic, Relating to special type of poetry.
S	A	P	P	I	N	G	Undermining, Diminishing, Exhausting, Weakening, Crippling, Disabling, Depleting, Draining.
S	A	P	P	L	E	S	Soapsuds.
S	A	P	R	O	B	E	Living in organic matter without oxygen.
S	A	P	S	A	G	O	Hard green cheese made from skim milk.
S	A	P	W	O	O	D	Inner layer of wood next to nucleus.
S	A	R	A	C	E	N	Arabian people.
S	A	R	C	A	S	M	Taunt, Caustic wit, Bitter humour, Satire, Mockery, Ridicule, Scorn, Acrimony.
S	A	R	C	I	N	A	Genus of bacteria.
S	A	R	C	O	D	E	Protoplasm.
S	A	R	C	O	I	D	Nodule disease of horses and mules, Flesh-like.
S	A	R	C	O	M	A	Malignant tumour of bone joint.
S	A	R	C	O	U	S	Muscle tissue, Fleshy.
S	A	R	D	A	N	A	Catalan dance.
S	A	R	D	I	N	E	Young pilchard.
S	A	R	D	I	U	S	Relating to ancient city of Sardis in Asia Minor.
S	A	R	I	N	D	A	Indian bowed stringed musical instrument.
S	A	R	K	I	N	G	Roof boarding under the slates or shingles.
S	A	R	M	E	N	T	Cutting, Runner.
S	A	R	P	L	E	R	Measurement of weight of a bale of wool, Wrapper of cloth, Sackcloth.
S	A	R	S	N	E	T	Sarsenet, Soft fine silk.
S	A	S	H	I	N	G	Providing a door or window frame, Fastening with a sash.
S	A	S	S	A	B	Y	Large South African antelope.
S	A	S	S	I	N	G	Cheeking, Talking Disrespectfully, Answering impudently.
S	A	T	A	N	I	C	Diabolical, Fiendish, Ghoulish, Infernal, Awful, Demoniac, Hideous, Derisive.
S	A	T	C	H	E	L	Leather or canvas bag with a shoulder strap.
S	A	T	I	A	T	E	Surfeit, Cloy, Pall, Saturate, Glut, Gorge, Stuffed, Replete.
S	A	T	I	E	T	Y	Fullness, Surfeit, Overindulged, Excessively, Gratified.
S	A	T	I	N	E	T	Imitation silk, Satinette.
S	A	T	I	R	I	C	Ridiculing, Lampooning, Bantering, Caustic, Ironic, Mocking, Parodying, Farcical.
S	A	T	I	S	F	Y	Discharge, Settle, Suit, Gratify, Please, Convince, Persuade, Fulfill.
S	A	T	R	A	P	Y	Sphere of influence of a powerful individual.
S	A	T	S	U	M	A	Japanese province, Cultivated mandarin tree.
S	A	T	Y	R	I	C	Having the characteristics of a satyr.
S	A	U	C	I	E	R	More impudent, Bolder, Smarter, Brasher, More brazen.
S	A	U	C	I	L	Y	Impudently, Archly, Pertly, Frivolously, Insolently, Smartly, Boldly, Brazenly.
S	A	U	C	I	N	G	Fluid combination of ingredients to give relish to a dish.
S	A	U	N	T	E	R	Dawdle, Idle, Stroll, Meander, Ramble, Roam, Loiter, Tarry.
S	A	U	R	I	A	N	Lizard-like.
S	A	U	R	O	I	D	Relating to ganoid fishes.
S	A	U	S	A	G	E	Minced meat packed in a skin covering.
S	A	U	T	O	I	R	Long gold chain with a pendant.
S	A	V	A	B	L	E	Capable of being saved.
S	A	V	A	G	E	D	Treated brutally, Attacked violently, Trampled furiously.
S	A	V	A	N	N	A	Treeless grassland.
S	A	V	A	R	I	N	Brioche baked in a ring mould covered with nuts and fruits.
S	A	V	E	A	L	L	Miserly, Stingy, Mean, Niggardly, Parsimonious, Something to prevent waste.
S	A	V	E	L	O	Y	Cooked dry sausage.
S	A	V	I	N	G	S	Nest-egg, Sparing, Canny, Chary, Economical, Provident, Thrifty, Wary.
S	A	V	I	O	U	R	Messiah, One that preserves from danger or destruction, One that brings salvation.
S	A	W	B	A	C	K	Mountain range with sharp peaks.
S	A	W	B	I	L	L	Bird with a serrated beak.
S	A	W	B	U	C	K	Sawhorse.
S	A	W	D	U	S	T	Dust from cutting timber with a saw.
S	A	W	F	I	S	H	Several large elongated fishes.
S	A	W	M	I	L	L	Plant for sawing logs.
S	A	W	W	H	E	T	Small North American owl.
S	A	W	W	O	R	T	Plant with leaves that yield a yellow dye.
S	A	X	H	O	R	N	Brass wind musical instrument.

1	2	3	4	5	6	7	
S	A	X	O	N	I	C	Relating to the Anglo-Saxons.
S	A	Y	A	B	L	E	Capable of being said.
S	C	A	B	B	E	D	Covered with a scab, Acted as a scab, Mean, Contemptible, Sheathed.
S	C	A	B	B	L	E	Dressing stone, Working stone in the quarry.
S	C	A	B	I	E	S	Itch or mange caused by mites.
S	C	A	B	R	I	D	Rough texture.
S	C	A	D	D	L	E	Fierce, Wild, Skittish.
S	C	A	L	A	D	E	Escalade, Scaling a mountain or wall.
S	C	A	L	A	D	O	Same as SCALADE.
S	C	A	L	D	E	D	Burnt with hot liquid or steam, Blanched, Parboiled, Scorched, Tormented.
S	C	A	L	D	E	R	Cannery worker who sterilises fruit or other produce.
S	C	A	L	D	I	C	Relating to Norse legends and poetry.
S	C	A	L	E	N	E	Triangle with unequal sides.
S	C	A	L	I	N	G	Peeling, Husking, Skimming, Sailing, Flaking, Graduating, Measuring, Ascending.
S	C	A	L	L	E	D	Scalded.
S	C	A	L	L	O	P	Half circle edged trimming, Marine bivalve mollusk, Type of baking on shells.
S	C	A	L	O	P	S	Scalopus, Mole, Insectivore.
S	C	A	L	P	E	D	Cut scalp from the head, Remove top layer, Humiliated.
S	C	A	L	P	E	L	Sharp straight surgical knife.
S	C	A	L	P	E	R	Flat tool used in wood engraving.
S	C	A	M	B	L	E	Sprawl, Shamble, Collect, Botch, Mess up.
S	C	A	M	P	E	D	Skimped, Scanty.
S	C	A	M	P	E	R	Scoot, Skip, Run, Bolt, Flee, Scuddle, Hasten.
S	C	A	N	D	A	L	Disgrace, Infamy, Discredit, Detraction, Defamation, Slander, Disrepute, Malign.
S	C	A	N	D	I	X	Small genus of Eurasian herbs.
S	C	A	N	N	E	D	Scrutinized, Perused, Examined, Inspected, Surveyed, Observed, Reviewed, Audited.
S	C	A	N	N	E	R	Device that automatically checks a process.
S	C	A	N	T	E	D	Limited, Narrowed, Reduced, Stinted, Skimped.
S	C	A	N	T	L	E	Adjust.
S	C	A	N	T	L	Y	Barely, Scarcely.
S	C	A	P	N	E	T	Scoop net for catching bait.
S	C	A	P	P	L	E	Scabble, Dressing stone.
S	C	A	P	U	L	A	Shoulder blade.
S	C	A	R	C	E	R	Rarer, Scantier, Less plentiful, Shorter, Sparser.
S	C	A	R	F	E	D	Removed defects from unfinished steel, Timber united by a special joint.
S	C	A	R	I	F	Y	Scratch, Cut, Scar, Frighten, Disfigure, Criticize, Lambast, Castigate.
S	C	A	R	I	N	G	Frightening, Alarming, Daunting, Terrifying, Startling, Petrifying, Terrorizing.
S	C	A	R	L	E	T	Red.
S	C	A	R	O	I	D	Parrot fish.
S	C	A	R	P	E	D	Cut into a precipice, Steep sided ditch.
S	C	A	R	R	E	D	Marred, Disfigured, Blemished, Flawed.
S	C	A	R	V	E	S	Cravats, Kerchiefs, Military sashes.
S	C	A	T	H	E	D	Harmed, Injured, Damaged, Scorched, Scourged, Lambasted, Blistered.
S	C	A	T	T	E	R	Squander, Broadcast, Disseminate, Diffuse, Sprinkle, Strew, Disperse, Dispel.
S	C	A	U	P	E	R	Scorper, Flat tool for wood engraving.
S	C	E	N	E	R	Y	View, Landscape, Setting, Decor, Furnishings, Picturesque spot.
S	C	E	N	T	E	D	Smelt, Perfumed, Suspected.
S	C	E	P	S	I	S	Sceptical outlook.
S	C	E	P	T	I	C	One inclined to disbelieve, Doubting, Questioning.
S	C	E	P	T	R	E	Sovereignty, Baton or mace carried by Sovereign as symbol of authority.
S	C	H	A	P	P	E	Fabric of spun silk.
S	C	H	E	L	L	Y	Gwyniad, Welsh whitefish.
S	C	H	E	M	E	D	Devised, Contrived, Designed, Plotted, Planned, Employed, Projected, Proposed.
S	C	H	E	M	E	R	Plotter, Intriguer, Projector.
S	C	H	E	P	E	L	Dutch unit of capacity.
S	C	H	E	P	E	N	Dutch municipal officer.
S	C	H	E	R	Z	O	Lively instrumental musical composition.
S	C	H	E	S	I	S	Habitude, Relation.
S	C	H	I	N	U	S	Genus of tropical American Tree, Pepper tree.
S	C	H	I	S	M	A	Interval between acoustical pure and tempered fifth.
S	C	H	L	I	C	H	Slime.
S	C	H	L	O	S	S	German manor house, German beer house.
S	C	H	N	A	P	S	Distilled liqueur, Hollands gin.
S	C	H	O	L	A	R	Pupil, Student, Scholarship holder.
S	C	H	O	R	L	Y	Mingled with tourmaline.
S	C	I	A	T	I	C	Sciatic part as a nerve or artery in lower back area.
S	C	I	E	N	C	E	Possessing knowledge, Information, Lore, Wisdom, Education, Erudition, Learning, Study.

1	2	3	4	5	6	7	Clue
S	C	I	O	L	T	O	Music instruction to play with abandon.
S	C	I	R	P	U	S	Large genus of sedges, Bulrush.
S	C	I	S	S	E	L	Metal scrap clippings.
S	C	I	S	S	O	R	Hold in a crossed position, Minimize, Reduce, Cut, Snip.
S	C	I	U	R	I	D	Rodents, Squirrels, Marmots.
S	C	L	E	R	A	L	Relating to sclerosis, Hardening of tissue.
S	C	L	E	R	I	A	Genus of sedges, Razor grass, Nut grass.
S	C	O	F	F	E	D	Jeered, Sneered, Flouted, Mocked, Ridiculed, Quipped, Derided, Guzzled.
S	C	O	F	F	E	R	One that jeers, One that eats greedily.
S	C	O	L	D	E	D	Upbraided, Reviled, Rated, Berated, Vituperated, Reproved, Abused, Lambasted.
S	C	O	L	D	E	R	One that reproves.
S	C	O	L	I	T	E	Tubular structures found in rocks.
S	C	O	L	L	O	P	Scallop.
S	C	O	M	B	E	R	Atlantic mackerel.
S	C	O	O	P	E	D	Dipped, Gathered, Excavated, Beat, Glided, Ladled, Shovelled, Gouged.
S	C	O	O	P	E	R	Grain unloader.
S	C	O	O	T	E	D	Darted, Scudded, Decamped, Hurried, Rushed, Scampered, Scurried, Spurted.
S	C	O	O	T	E	R	Child's toy, Light motorcycle, Ice sled.
S	C	O	P	A	T	E	Resembling a brush.
S	C	O	P	I	N	E	Crystalline heterocyclic amino alcohol.
S	C	O	P	O	L	A	Dried rhizome of herb yielding atropine and hyoscyamine drugs.
S	C	O	P	O	N	E	Card game.
S	C	O	P	U	L	A	Web-making hair on feet of spiders.
S	C	O	R	I	A	C	Volcanic ashes, Slag, Dross.
S	C	O	R	I	F	Y	Reduce to ashes or dross.
S	C	O	R	I	N	G	Recording, Charging, Counting, Listing, Reckoning, Scratching, Grooving.
S	C	O	R	N	E	D	Mocked, Derided, Disdained, Scoffed, Despised, Jeered, Ridiculed, Taunted.
S	C	O	R	N	E	R	Mocker.
S	C	O	R	P	E	R	Flat tool used for wood engraving, Jeweller's chisel for engraving.
S	C	O	R	P	I	O	Sign of the Zodiac, Scorpion.
S	C	O	T	I	S	M	Doctrine of Duns Scotus, Separation of philosophy and theology.
S	C	O	T	I	S	T	Adherent of Scotism.
S	C	O	T	O	M	A	Blind or dark spot.
S	C	O	T	O	M	Y	Dizziness with dimness of sight.
S	C	O	U	R	E	D	Rubbed hard, Purged, Combed, Ransacked, Corroded, Gnawed, Rummaged, Searched.
S	C	O	U	R	E	R	One who polishes and cleans.
S	C	O	U	R	G	E	Whip, Punish, Plague, Curse, Pestilence, Flog, Lash, Ravage.
S	C	O	U	T	E	D	Observed, Reconnoitred, Explored, Probed, Surveyed, Examined, Inspected, Derided.
S	C	O	U	T	E	R	Member of Boy Scouts.
S	C	O	W	L	E	D	Frowned, Glowered, Pulled a face to express annoyance or displeasure.
S	C	R	A	G	G	Y	Rugged, Jagged, Knotted, Bony, Meagre, Scrawny, Lean, Gaunt.
S	C	R	A	N	C	H	Crunch.
S	C	R	A	P	E	D	Erased, Expunged, Scratched, Rasped, Chafed, Abraded, Scrimped, Pinched.
S	C	R	A	P	E	R	Edged blade on a tool for removing a layer, Miser, Skinflint, Fiddler, Barber.
S	C	R	A	P	I	E	Virus sheep disease.
S	C	R	A	P	P	Y	Fragmentary, Quarrelsome, Brawling, Belligerent, Pugnacious, Truculent.
S	C	R	A	T	C	H	Scrape, Scribble, Lacerate, Grate, Rasp, Scrabble, Scrawl, Score.
S	C	R	A	W	L	Y	Sprawling, Scribbled, Awkwardly irregular.
S	C	R	A	W	N	Y	Lean, Thin, Rawboned, Angular, Gaunt, Lank, Skinny, Spare.
S	C	R	E	A	M	Y	Given to screaming.
S	C	R	E	E	C	H	Shrill piercing cry.
S	C	R	E	E	V	E	Write begging letters, Ooze, Leak.
S	C	R	E	W	E	D	Twisted, Squinted, Crumpled, Fastened with a screw, Extorted, Exacted, Squeezed.
S	C	R	E	W	E	R	Extortioner.
S	C	R	I	B	A	L	Relating to a writer.
S	C	R	I	B	E	D	Written, Inscribed.
S	C	R	I	B	E	R	Sharp pointed tool for marking off material.
S	C	R	I	E	V	E	Move quickly and smoothly, Write, Inscribe.
S	C	R	I	N	G	E	Cringe, Flinch, Beat the water when fishing.
S	C	R	I	T	C	H	Screech.
S	C	R	O	L	L	Y	Ornately decorated.
S	C	R	O	O	C	H	Crouch, Huddle.
S	C	R	O	O	G	E	Miser.
S	C	R	O	T	A	L	Relating to the scrotum.
S	C	R	O	T	U	M	External pouch containing male testicles.
S	C	R	O	U	G	E	Crowd, Crush, Press.
S	C	R	U	B	B	Y	Stunted, Runty, Poor, Inferior, Shabby, Bedraggled, Dingy, Seedy.

1	2	3	4	5	6	7	
S	C	R	U	F	F	Y	Shabby, Miserable, Seedy, Tattered, Threadbare, Tacky, Moth-eaten, Run-down
S	C	R	U	N	C	H	Crunch, Crush, Contract, Hunch, Crouch, Squeeze, Champ, Chomp.
S	C	R	U	P	L	E	Compunction, Qualm, Demur, Apology, Particle, Fragment, Conscience, Balk.
S	C	R	Y	I	N	G	Crystal gazing, Divination.
S	C	U	D	D	E	D	Moved swiftly, Darted, Skimmed, Sailed, Glided.
S	C	U	D	D	L	E	Hurry, Scuttle, Scurry, Dart, Skim, Hasten.
S	C	U	F	F	L	E	Scurry, Scuff, Shuffle, Shamble, Wrestle, Grapple, Tussle, Brawl.
S	C	U	L	L	E	D	Propelled a boat.
S	C	U	L	L	E	R	Metallurgical worker who removes slag.
S	C	U	L	P	I	N	Scorpion fish, Worthless creature.
S	C	U	M	B	L	E	Overlay painting to diminish brilliance, Soften outline.
S	C	U	M	M	E	R	Utensil for removing scum.
S	C	U	N	N	E	R	State or irritation.
S	C	U	P	P	E	R	Ambush, Defeat, Destroy, Spoil.
S	C	U	P	P	I	T	Small shovel.
S	C	U	T	A	G	E	Tax on a tenant in feudal times.
S	C	U	T	A	T	E	Covered by bony or horny plates or scales, Peltate.
S	C	U	T	T	E	R	Scurry, Scramble.
S	C	U	T	T	L	E	Shallow open receptacle, Opening with a lid, Damage, Destroy, Abandon.
S	C	Y	P	H	U	S	Ancient Grecian drinking vessel. Cup-shaped centre of lichens.
S	C	Y	T	A	L	E	Ancient Spartan code for sending messages.
S	C	Y	T	H	E	D	Mown, Cut with a scythe.
S	C	Y	T	H	I	C	Relating to ancient Scythia.
S	E	A	B	A	N	K	Seashore, Seawall.
S	E	A	B	A	S	S	Marine fish.
S	E	A	B	E	A	N	Large tropical beans carried by ocean currents.
S	E	A	B	E	A	R	Polar bear.
S	E	A	B	E	E	T	Forerunner of garden beet but without a bulbous root, Sea Lavender.
S	E	A	B	E	L	T	Kelp.
S	E	A	B	I	R	D	Any marine bird, Albatrosses, Peguins, Gulls, Petrels.
S	E	A	B	O	A	T	A ship fit to sail on the open sea.
S	E	A	B	O	R	N	Originating or born from the sea.
S	E	A	C	A	L	F	Harbour seal.
S	E	A	C	A	R	D	The card of a mariner's compass.
S	E	A	C	L	A	M	Surf clam.
S	E	A	C	O	A	L	Pulverized bituminous coal.
S	E	A	C	O	O	T	Guillemot.
S	E	A	C	O	R	N	Eggs of the Whelks (marine snails).
S	E	A	C	R	O	W	Cormorant, Coot, Oyster catcher.
S	E	A	D	A	T	E	Mussel.
S	E	A	D	O	V	E	Black guillemot.
S	E	A	D	U	C	K	Eider duck.
S	E	A	F	I	R	E	Marine phosphorescence.
S	E	A	F	O	A	M	Froth on the sea.
S	E	A	F	O	L	K	Mariners.
S	E	A	F	O	O	D	Edible fish and shellfish.
S	E	A	G	A	T	E	Rolling swell of the sea.
S	E	A	G	I	R	T	Surrounded by the sea.
S	E	A	H	A	R	E	Squid-like creature.
S	E	A	H	A	W	K	Skua.
S	E	A	K	A	L	E	European perennial herb.
S	E	A	K	I	N	G	Viking, Prehistoric king of Crete.
S	E	A	L	A	C	E	Seaweed.
S	E	A	L	A	R	K	Sandpiper, Plover.
S	E	A	L	E	G	S	To become used to the movement of a ship.
S	E	A	L	E	R	Y	Seal fishery.
S	E	A	L	I	K	E	Resembling the sea.
S	E	A	L	I	L	Y	Crinoid.
S	E	A	L	I	N	E	Line for measuring the depth of the sea.
S	E	A	L	I	N	G	Impression made on wax to prevent intrusion of privacy, Hunting of seals.
S	E	A	L	I	O	N	Large-eared seal.
S	E	A	L	O	F	F	Close tightly to prevent entry or exit.
S	E	A	M	A	I	D	Mermaid, Sea nymph.
S	E	A	M	A	R	K	Mark of tide limit on a beach, Beacon, Landmark.
S	E	A	M	I	L	E	Nautical mile, 6080 feet, 1853 metres.
S	E	A	M	I	N	G	Stitching or welding a seam.
S	E	A	M	I	N	K	King whiting.

1	2	3	4	5	6	7	Definition
S	E	A	M	O	N	K	Monk seal.
S	E	A	M	O	S	S	Seaweed.
S	E	A	M	S	E	T	Tool for flattening seams in leather or metalwork.
S	E	A	P	A	S	S	Sea letter.
S	E	A	P	E	A	R	Stalked ascidian.
S	E	A	P	I	K	E	Barracuda.
S	E	A	P	I	N	K	Marsh pink.
S	E	A	P	O	R	K	Ascidian.
S	E	A	P	O	R	T	Harbour, port or town on the seacoast.
S	E	A	R	I	N	G	Parching, Shrivelling, Dessicating, Burning, Cauterizing, Scorching, Browning, Grilling.
S	E	A	R	O	O	M	Space to manoeuvre without danger.
S	E	A	S	I	C	K	Sickness or nausea caused by the movement of a ship.
S	E	A	S	I	D	E	Country adjoining the sea.
S	E	A	S	L	U	G	Naked marine gastropod.
S	E	A	T	A	N	G	Tang, Seaweed.
S	E	A	T	I	N	G	Act of providing seats.
S	E	A	T	O	A	D	Fishes of grotesgue or heavy body.
S	E	A	T	U	R	N	Wind that brings mist.
S	E	A	W	A	L	L	Wall or embankment to hold back the sea.
S	E	A	W	A	R	D	Toward the sea, Facing the beach.
S	E	A	W	A	R	E	Sea-wrack used as manure.
S	E	A	W	E	E	D	Growth of marine plants, Algae, Kelp, Sea lettuce.
S	E	A	W	H	I	P	Sea-fan, Gorgonian.
S	E	A	W	I	F	E	Wrasses, Marine fishes.
S	E	A	W	O	L	F	Elephant seal, Pirate, Corsair, Submarine.
S	E	B	I	L	L	A	Wooden receptacle used by stonecutters and ore assayers.
S	E	B	U	N	D	Y	Sepoy, Indian infantryman in British army.
S	E	C	E	D	E	D	Withdrew, Quit, Separated, Divided.
S	E	C	E	D	E	R	Member of the Secession Church of Scotland.
S	E	C	H	I	U	M	Genus of herbaceous vines, Cucumber, Squash.
S	E	C	L	U	D	E	Confine, Isolate, Hide, Secrete, Protect, Screen, Retire, Cloister.
S	E	C	O	N	A	L	A proprietary name of a hypnotic and sporific barbiturate.
S	E	C	O	N	D	O	Second voice, Lower part in a piano duet.
S	E	C	R	E	C	Y	Privacy, Seclusion, Trust, Silence, Covertness, Concealment, Stealth, Subterfuge.
S	E	C	T	A	R	Y	Dissenter from the Church of England, Zealous follower of a particular cult.
S	E	C	T	I	L	E	Cut into small divisions, Mosaic of large pieces of marble.
S	E	C	T	I	O	N	Profile, Part, Division, Member, Portion, District, Sector, Segment.
S	E	C	T	I	S	T	Sectarian, Dissenter.
S	E	C	U	L	A	R	Mundane, Civil, Nonclerical, Lay, Profane, Cyclical, Temporal.
S	E	C	U	R	E	D	Guarded, Assured, Guaranteed, Pinioned, Prevented, Defended, Ensured, Fastened.
S	E	D	I	L	I	A	Seats in chancel of a church for officiating clergy.
S	E	D	U	C	E	D	Coaxed, Lured, Decoyed, Misled, Enslaved, Overwhelmed, Debauched, Ravished.
S	E	D	U	C	E	R	One that induces a female to surrender her chastity.
S	E	E	A	B	L	E	Visible.
S	E	E	D	A	G	E	Method of propagating plants by means of seeds or spores.
S	E	E	D	B	E	D	Soil prepared for planting of seeds.
S	E	E	D	B	O	X	North American Swamp herb.
S	E	E	D	F	U	L	Generative, Capable of reproducing, Fertile.
S	E	E	D	I	L	Y	In a shabby or furtive way.
S	E	E	D	I	N	G	Spawning, Sowing seed, Treating clouds to produce rain.
S	E	E	D	L	A	C	Granular resinous material obtained from stick lac.
S	E	E	D	L	I	P	Basket or container in which seed is carried before being broadcast.
S	E	E	K	I	N	G	Pursuing, Entreating, Requesting, Searching, Hunting, Rummaging, Ransacking, Scouring.
S	E	E	L	I	N	G	Depriving of sight.
S	E	E	M	I	N	G	Apparent, Ostensible, Appearing, Feigning, Semblance, Looking, Illusive, Illusory.
S	E	E	P	A	G	E	Oozing, Leakage, Drainage, Weepage.
S	E	E	T	H	E	D	Boiled, Stewed, Soaked, Churned, Fermented, Agitated, Bristled, Churned.
S	E	G	M	E	N	T	Portion, Section, Division, Parcel, Piece, Separate, Slice, Part.
S	E	I	N	I	N	G	Catching fish with a seine net.
S	E	I	S	I	N	G	Taking possession, Grasping, Seizing.
S	E	I	S	M	A	L	Seismic, Vibration of an earthquake.
S	E	I	Z	I	N	G	Clutching, Afflicting, Taking, Arresting, Capturing, Apprehending, Abducting.
S	E	I	Z	U	R	E	Seizing, Possession, Ownership, Hold, Grip, Sudden attack of disease or sickness.
S	E	L	E	N	I	C	Relating to the moon, Containing selenium.
S	E	L	F	I	S	H	Egocentric, Self centred, Self-seeking, Mean, Ungenerous, Concentration on self-interest.
S	E	L	F	I	S	T	Selfish person.
S	E	L	L	I	N	G	Marketing, Vending, Bartering, Trading, Hawking, Betraying, Crossing, Splitting.

1	2	3	4	5	6	7	
S	E	L	T	Z	E	R	Mineral water from Selters, Germany.
S	E	L	V	A	G	E	Firm edge of fabric to prevent fraying.
S	E	M	A	T	I	C	A warning of danger.
S	E	M	E	I	O	N	Either of two divisions of the foot.
S	E	M	I	A	P	E	Lemur.
S	E	M	I	N	A	L	Original, Germinative, Seeds of later development.
S	E	M	I	N	A	R	Group of advanced students, Conference, Briefing session, Scheduled meeting.
S	E	M	I	P	E	D	Metrical half-foot.
S	E	M	I	T	I	C	Jewish.
S	E	N	A	T	O	R	Member of a legislative body.
S	E	N	D	I	N	G	Thrusting, Despatching, Emitting, Driving, Impelling, Transmitting, Remitting, Shipping.
S	E	N	D	O	F	F	Farewell party, Organised demonstration of goodwill for the beginning of a new venture.
S	E	N	D	O	U	T	Amount distributed.
S	E	N	E	G	A	L	State in West Africa.
S	E	N	S	A	T	E	Sensation, Feel or apprehend through the senses.
S	E	N	S	I	L	E	Sentient, Capable of sensation, Felt or sensed.
S	E	N	S	I	N	G	Anticipating, Expounding, Testing, Grasping, Realizing, Examining, Analyzing, Comprehending
S	E	N	S	I	S	M	Sensationalism, Hedonistic resort to the sensuous.
S	E	N	S	O	R	Y	Relating to senation or to the senses, Conveying nerve impulses.
S	E	N	S	U	A	L	Sensory, Carnal, Fleshly, Wordly, Irreligious, Materialistic, Sensuous, Hedonistic.
S	E	P	I	O	L	A	Small squid, Cuttlefish.
S	E	P	P	U	K	U	Hara-kiri, Suicide by disembowelling.
S	E	P	T	A	T	E	Divided by a septum, wall or membrane.
S	E	P	T	I	E	R	Setier, Old French measurement.
S	E	P	T	I	L	E	Relating to Sepla.
S	E	P	T	I	M	E	Guard position in fencing.
S	E	P	T	U	L	A	Small perforation in a cell wall.
S	E	Q	U	E	L	A	Consequence, Secondary result.
S	E	Q	U	E	N	T	Consequent, Sequel.
S	E	Q	U	O	I	A	Coniferous tree, Redwood.
S	E	R	B	I	A	N	Member of former Balkan country, now Yugoslavia.
S	E	R	E	N	E	D	Tranquilized, Soothed, Lulled, Calmed.
S	E	R	E	N	O	A	Small genus of fan palm of Florida.
S	E	R	F	A	G	E	Serfdom.
S	E	R	F	D	O	M	Slavery, Peonage, Agriculture bondage.
S	E	R	F	I	S	M	Social strata where bondage is allowed.
S	E	R	I	A	T	E	Arranged in series, Crystals that vary gradually in shape.
S	E	R	I	C	I	N	Gelatinous protein that joins filaments in silk.
S	E	R	I	E	M	A	Cariama, Bird related to cranes, bustards or herons.
S	E	R	I	N	G	A	Mock orange, Brazilian rubber tree.
S	E	R	I	N	U	S	Finch, Canary.
S	E	R	I	O	L	A	Genus of fishes, Amberfish.
S	E	R	I	O	U	S	Devoted, Important, Significant, Emphatic, Grave, Solemn, Sedate, Sober.
S	E	R	P	E	N	T	Snake, Crocodile, Devil, Bass wind instrument, Satan, Lucifer.
S	E	R	P	H	I	D	Wasp.
S	E	R	P	I	G	O	Spreading skin disease, Ringworm.
S	E	R	P	U	L	A	Genus of small marine worms.
S	E	R	R	A	T	E	Notched, Tooth-edged, Saw-edged, Jagged peaks.
S	E	R	R	I	E	D	Crowded, Pressed, Dense, Concise, Serrated.
S	E	R	R	U	L	A	Toothed keel, Serrated edge of a spider's leg.
S	E	R	T	U	L	E	Sertulum, Collection of scientifically studied plants.
S	E	R	V	A	N	T	Retainer, Menial, Maid, Butler, One that performs household duties.
S	E	R	V	I	A	N	Serbian.
S	E	R	V	I	C	E	Action, Combat, Favour, Courtesy, Dispensation, Avail, Fitness, Relevance.
S	E	R	V	I	L	E	Subservient, Menial, Obeisant, Slavish, Obsequious, Submissive, Abject, Ignoble.
S	E	R	V	I	N	G	Satisfying, Sufficing, Attending, Feeding, Availing, Suiting, Covering, Firing.
S	E	R	V	I	T	E	Order of Florentine friars.
S	E	S	A	M	U	M	Genus of tropical African and Indian herbs, Sesame.
S	E	S	O	T	H	O	Language of Southern African country, Basutoland.
S	E	S	S	I	L	E	Attached to base, Sedentary, Permanently attached.
S	E	S	S	I	O	N	Constructive assembly, Term, Court, Group of people for particular type of entertainment.
S	E	S	T	I	N	A	Special lyrical form developed by 12th century Provencal troubadours.
S	E	S	T	O	L	E	Sextuplet, One of a group of six.
S	E	T	A	R	I	A	Genus of grasses, Millet, Parasitic worms.
S	E	T	B	A	C	K	Checking of progress, Defeat, Reverse, Withdrawal, Hinder.
S	E	T	D	O	W	N	Reproof, Snub.
S	E	T	L	I	N	E	Long fishing line for bottom fishing.

1	2	3	4	5	6	7	
S	E	T	T	I	N	G	Fixing, Placing, Directing, Spreading, Provoking, Hardening, Coagulating, Sinking.
S	E	T	T	L	E	D	Colonized, Planted, Consolidated, Resolved, Compounded, Calmed, Decided, Subdued.
S	E	T	T	L	E	R	Colonist, Separator.
S	E	T	W	A	L	L	Garden heliotrope.
S	E	T	W	O	R	K	Tapestry embroidery, Boatbuilding, Plastering.
S	E	V	E	N	T	H	Number seven, Seventh part.
S	E	V	E	N	T	Y	Ten times seven.
S	E	V	E	R	A	L	Diverse, Various, Respective, Distinct, Many, Sundry, Considerable, Different.
S	E	V	E	R	E	D	Parted, Distinguished, Cleaved, Separated, Dissected, Jointed, Carved, Divided.
S	E	V	E	R	E	R	Stricter, Simpler, More stringent, More difficult.
S	E	X	F	O	I	L	Flower with six petals, Group of six.
S	E	X	L	E	S	S	Lacking sex, Neuter.
S	E	X	T	A	I	N	Sestina, Stanza of six lines.
S	E	X	T	A	N	S	Ancient Roman bronze coin.
S	E	X	T	A	N	T	Instrument for determining position of ship or plane by comparing position of celestial bodies.
S	E	X	T	I	L	E	Measured by 60 degrees.
S	E	X	U	A	L	E	Bisexual aphids.
S	H	A	C	K	E	D	Shambled, Went sluggishly.
S	H	A	C	K	L	E	Fetter, Chain, Couple, Join, Hamper, Curb, Hobble, Leash.
S	H	A	D	F	L	Y	Insects that appear when shad enter the rivers.
S	H	A	D	I	E	R	Darker, More suspect, More doubtful, More disreputable, Quieter, Shadowier.
S	H	A	D	I	L	Y	In a dishonourable manner, Shabbily, Shoddily.
S	H	A	D	I	N	G	Sheltering, Screening, Eclipsing, Protecting, Veiling, Obscuring, Tinting, Covering.
S	H	A	D	O	O	F	Egyptian device to raise water for irrigation.
S	H	A	D	O	W	Y	Fleeting, Imaginary, Ghostly, Spectral, Faint, Dim, Fuzzy, Indistinct.
S	H	A	F	T	E	D	Fitted with a shaft, Beamed.
S	H	A	G	G	E	D	Chased, Fetched, Followed, Loped, Jagged.
S	H	A	H	E	E	N	Indian falcon.
S	H	A	I	T	A	N	Evil spirit.
S	H	A	K	E	U	P	Makeshift, Arouse with a shake, Hurry, Re-organize, Re-arrange.
S	H	A	K	I	L	Y	Precarioiusly, Untrustworthy, Rickety, Insecure, Dubiously, Unsteadily.
S	H	A	K	I	N	G	Trembling, Quivering, Fluttering, Agitating, Rocking, Convulsing, Weakening, Scattering.
S	H	A	L	L	O	N	Lightweight twilled fabric.
S	H	A	L	L	O	P	Small open boat.
S	H	A	L	L	O	T	Bulbous perennial herb with small bulbs used for salads and seasoning, Green onion.
S	H	A	L	L	O	W	Superficial, Weak, Cursory, Sketchy, Paltry, Trivial, Hollow, Vain.
S	H	A	M	B	L	E	Shuffle, Walk awkwardly, Scuffle.
S	H	A	M	I	N	G	Dishonouring, Disgracing, Embarrassing, Mortifying.
S	H	A	M	M	E	D	Faked, Assumed, Deceived, Cheated, Tricked, Malingered, Counterfeited, Feigned.
S	H	A	M	M	E	R	Imposter, Malingerer, Cheat.
S	H	A	M	P	O	O	Wash or clean hair, animals or articles with a wet or dry shampoo.
S	H	A	N	D	R	Y	Light carriage.
S	H	A	N	K	E	D	Walked, Decayed at footstalk, Hit a golf ball, Cut a person deeply with a knife.
S	H	A	P	E	L	Y	Symmetrical, Curvaceous, Statuesque, Trim, Well-proportioned, Comely, Pleasing, Rounded.
S	H	A	P	I	N	G	Forming, Creating, Moulding, Appointing, Adapting, Regulating, Adjusting, Making.
S	H	A	R	D	E	D	Having scales or hard wing cover as beetles.
S	H	A	R	I	N	G	Dividing, Apportioning, Participating, Partaking, Allowing, Rationing, Parting, Assigning.
S	H	A	R	K	E	D	Fished for sharks, Preyed on others.
S	H	A	R	K	E	R	Cheat, Fraud.
S	H	A	R	P	E	D	Sharpened, Tricked, Swindled, Pilfered, Sung or played above true pitch.
S	H	A	R	P	E	N	Make sharper, Hone, Whet.
S	H	A	R	P	E	R	Swindler, Cardsharper, Cheat, Trickster, Diddler.
S	H	A	R	P	I	E	Long narrow shallow-draft boat.
S	H	A	R	P	L	Y	Acutely, Keenly, Prickly, Fiery, Furiously, Severely, Harshly, Distinctly.
S	H	A	S	T	R	A	Sacred scriptures of Hinduism.
S	H	A	T	T	E	R	Fracture, Smash, Scatter, Ruin, Wreck, Disintegrate, Break, Demolish.
S	H	A	V	I	N	G	Removing hair with a blade, Flaking, Chipping, Scraping, Reducing.
S	H	E	A	R	E	D	Cut, Clipped, Severed, Pruned, Cleaved, Manicured, Pared, Trimmed.
S	H	E	A	R	E	R	One that uses shears.
S	H	E	A	T	H	E	Scabbard, Connective tissue, Narrow straight unbelted dress, Encase, Cover, Envelop, Wrap.
S	H	E	A	T	H	Y	Resembling a sheath.
S	H	E	A	V	E	D	Gathered and bound into a sheaf.
S	H	E	B	A	N	G	Hut, Establishment, Contrivance, Affair, Concern, Thing.
S	H	E	B	E	E	N	Unlicensed drinking establishment.
S	H	E	D	D	E	R	One that sheds something, Carrier crab that has just lost its shell.
S	H	E	E	R	E	D	Deviated, Swerved, Turned, Averted, Deflected, Pivoted, Deverted, Wheeled.
S	H	E	E	T	E	D	Extended a sail.

1	2	3	4	5	6	7	
S	H	E	L	L	A	C	Purified lac resin, Lacquer, Varnish, Polishing wax.
S	H	E	L	L	E	D	Shucked, Stripped, Removed, Bombarded.
S	H	E	L	L	E	R	Operator of a shelling device.
S	H	E	L	T	E	R	Refuge, Screen, Housing, Structure, Protection, Harbour, Asylum, Haven.
S	H	E	L	T	I	E	Shetland pony or sheepdog.
S	H	E	L	V	E	D	Inclined, Delayed, Postponed, Dismissed, Stayed, Prorogued, Waived.
S	H	E	L	V	E	S	Ledges, Thin timber fixed to walls to hold books or objects
S	H	E	M	I	T	E	Semite, Shem son of Noah.
S	H	E	R	B	E	T	Cooling drink made of diluted fruit juice, Water ice.
S	H	E	R	E	E	F	Sharif, Islamic aristocrat.
S	H	E	R	I	A	T	Islamic law.
S	H	E	R	I	F	F	County officer in Britain and U.S. representing law and order.
S	H	E	W	I	N	G	Showing, Demonstrating, Displaying.
S	H	I	F	T	E	D	Moved, Transferred, Changed, Distributed, Escaped, Dislodged, Consumed, Disturbed.
S	H	I	F	T	E	R	One that resorts to evasion in reasoning.
S	H	I	I	T	E	S	Muslim of the Shi'a branch of Islam.
S	H	I	K	A	R	I	Professional hunter or guide.
S	H	I	L	P	I	T	Puny, Weak, Insipid, Feeble.
S	H	I	M	M	E	D	Hoed or weeded with a shim, Filled up with putty.
S	H	I	M	M	E	R	Glimmer, Scintillate, Flicker, Wavering, Subdued, Sparkle, Sheen, Glisten.
S	H	I	N	D	I	G	Social gathering, Festive occasion, Elaborate celebration.
S	H	I	N	G	L	E	Coarse gravel. Beach stones, Small thin piece of building material, Small signboard.
S	H	I	N	G	L	Y	Beach with gravelly sand and pebbles.
S	H	I	N	I	N	G	Gleaming, Lustrous, Glowing, Resplendent, Burnished, Glossy, Glistening, Polished.
S	H	I	N	N	E	D	Climbed, Moved rapidly.
S	H	I	P	B	O	Y	Cabin attendant.
S	H	I	P	L	A	P	Steel plating or planks on the sides and deck of a ship.
S	H	I	P	M	A	N	Seaman. Sailor.
S	H	I	P	P	E	D	Transported by ship, Took into a ship, Sent, Embarked.
S	H	I	P	P	E	N	Shed for livestock.
S	H	I	P	P	E	R	Consignor of goods by ship, Shipping clerk.
S	H	I	P	W	A	Y	Slipway where ship is built, Supports for a ship in a dry dock.
S	H	I	R	K	E	D	Sponged, Scamped, Shifted, Sneaked, Dodged, Evaded, Avoided, Skulked.
S	H	I	R	K	E	R	Slacker, Malingerer, Dodger.
S	H	I	R	R	E	D	Material gathered with fine elastic for decoration.
S	H	I	R	T	E	D	Clothed with a shirt.
S	H	I	T	T	A	H	Hard yellowish brown wood from which the Ark is believed to have been constructed.
S	H	I	T	T	I	M	Cascara tree, Buckthorn.
S	H	I	V	E	R	Y	Brittle, Flaky, Tremulous, Chilling, Cold, Frosty, Shaky, Nippy.
S	H	I	Z	O	K	U	Japanese Samurai social class.
S	H	O	A	L	E	D	Became shallow, Driven to shallow water.
S	H	O	C	K	E	D	Offended, Astonished, Scandalized, Assailed, Collided, Astounded, Startled, Outraged.
S	H	O	C	K	E	R	Dreadful, Horrifying.
S	H	O	E	I	N	G	Supplying with shoes, Cover for protection.
S	H	O	E	P	A	C	Moccasin, Waterproof high boot.
S	H	O	G	G	E	D	Jolted, Shaken, Jostled, Shoved.
S	H	O	O	I	N	G	Driving away, Chasing, Dispelling, Scaring away.
S	H	O	O	K	E	D	Packed in a barrel.
S	H	O	O	T	E	R	One that shoots a missile-discharging device, Plant that grows rapidly, Fire-arm.
S	H	O	P	M	A	N	Any worker in a retail shop.
S	H	O	P	P	E	D	Betrayed, Arrested, Imprisoned, Searched, Hunted, Examined.
S	H	O	P	P	E	R	Customer, Consumer, Purchaser.
S	H	O	R	I	N	G	Supporting, Strengthening.
S	H	O	R	T	E	D	Cheated, Shortchanged, Short circuited.
S	H	O	R	T	E	N	Abbreviate, Abridge, Curtail, Retrench, Decrease, Diminish, Lessen, Reduce.
S	H	O	R	T	E	R	Lower, Curter, Crisper, Conciser, Briefer, Scantier, Scarcer, Blunter.
S	H	O	T	G	U	N	Double-barrelled smoothbore shoulder weapon.
S	H	O	T	P	U	T	Putting the shot, a field event in athletics.
S	H	O	T	T	E	D	Loaded with shot, Weighted with shot as skirts or curtains.
S	H	O	T	T	E	N	Weakened, Dispirited, Good-for-nothing.
S	H	O	U	T	E	D	Cried out, Whooped, Yelled, Exclaimed, Howled, Bawled, Bellowed, Blared.
S	H	O	U	T	E	R	Member of North American Negro religious sect.
S	H	O	V	I	N	G	Driving, Thrusting, Compelling, Peddling, Leaving, Pushing, Poking, Prodding.
S	H	O	W	B	O	X	Box for peep show.
S	H	O	W	E	R	Y	Raining in showers, Producing showers.
S	H	O	W	I	L	Y	In a striking manner, Flashily, Gaudily, Dramatically.
S	H	O	W	I	N	G	Offering, Appearing, Manifesting, Demonstrating, Displaying, Performing, Exhibiting.

1	2	3	4	5	6	7	
S	H	O	W	M	A	N	Person able to dramatize events, Producer of an entertainment.
S	H	O	W	O	F	F	Exhibitionist.
S	H	R	E	D	D	Y	Ragged.
S	H	R	I	L	L	Y	High pitched tone, High strung, Sharply insistent manner.
S	H	R	I	N	E	D	Enshrined, Placed in a shrine.
S	H	R	I	V	E	L	Wrinkle, Shrink, Corrugate, Wither, Mummify, Parch, Fossilize, Wizen.
S	H	R	I	V	E	N	Given absolution, Pardoned, Purged, Imposed penance, Confessed.
S	H	R	O	U	D	S	Winding-sheets, Protects, Enfolds, Envelops, Screens, Obstructs, Veils, Encloses.
S	H	R	U	B	B	Y	Covered with shrubs, Scrubby.
S	H	U	C	K	E	R	Worker who shells or shucks produce.
S	H	U	D	D	E	R	Shiver, Tremble, Quaver, Quiver, Shake, Tremor, Twitter, Grate.
S	H	U	F	F	L	E	Dodge, Evade, Scuffle, Shamble, Drag, Stumble, Limp, Muddle.
S	H	U	N	N	E	D	Eschewed, Escaped, Shied away, Avoided deliberately, Evaded, Eluded, Refused, Snubbed.
S	H	U	N	T	E	D	Sidetracked, Switched, Shifted, Shuttled, Switched, Diverted, Turned, Averted.
S	H	U	N	T	E	R	Switchman.
S	H	U	T	E	Y	E	Sleep, Slumber.
S	H	U	T	T	E	R	Movable cover, Louvre, Rotating element.
S	H	U	T	T	L	E	Shunt, Travel back and forth, Transport.
S	H	Y	L	O	C	K	Rapacious moneylender.
S	H	Y	N	E	S	S	Timidity, Diffidence, Bashfulness, Coyness.
S	H	Y	S	T	E	R	Professionally unscrupulous lawyer or politician.
S	I	A	M	A	N	G	Black gibbon of Sumatra.
S	I	A	M	E	S	E	Pertaining to Thailand.
S	I	B	L	I	N	G	Children of the same parent, Brothers and sisters.
S	I	C	K	B	A	Y	Compartment in ship used as a hospital or dispensary.
S	I	C	K	B	E	D	Bed in which a sick person is confined.
S	I	C	K	E	S	T	Most queasy, Most sick.
S	I	C	K	L	E	D	Reaped with a sickle.
S	I	C	K	P	A	Y	Salary or wages paid to an employee who is sick.
S	I	C	L	I	K	E	Suchlike.
S	I	D	E	A	R	M	Weapon worn at the side or in the belt.
S	I	D	E	B	O	X	Box or enclosed seat on the side of a theatre.
S	I	D	E	C	A	R	Passenger accommodation on the side of a motor cycle, A cocktail.
S	I	D	E	C	U	T	Intersecting way, Breakdown.
S	I	D	E	R	O	D	Coupling rod.
S	I	D	L	I	N	G	Sideling, Oblique, Sloping, Steep.
S	I	E	N	E	S	E	Characteristics of Sienna, Italy.
S	I	F	F	L	E	D	Whistled, Hissed.
S	I	F	T	I	N	G	Screening, Winnowing, Probing, Sieving, Filtering.
S	I	G	H	F	U	L	Mournful.
S	I	G	H	I	N	G	Lamenting, Grieving, Yearning, Mourning, Exhaling, Groaning, Sobbing, Pining.
S	I	G	H	T	E	D	Aimed, Looked carefully, Presented, Viewed, Seen, Glimpsed.
S	I	G	H	T	E	R	Sighting shot, One who tests accuracy of small arms sights.
S	I	G	H	T	L	Y	Pleasing, Handsome.
S	I	G	M	A	T	E	Forming, a tense or plural by adding a suffix.
S	I	G	M	O	I	D	Curved.
S	I	G	N	A	T	E	Designated, Identified.
S	I	G	N	I	F	Y	Denote, Indicate, Portend, Imply, Announce, Intimate, Express, Intend.
S	I	G	N	I	N	G	Marking, Consecrating, Affixing a signature, Subscribing, Motioning, Gesturing.
S	I	G	N	O	R	A	Title of married Italian lady.
S	I	G	N	O	R	Y	Lordship.
S	I	K	H	I	S	M	Indian religion.
S	I	L	E	N	C	E	Quietness, Noiselessness, Soundlessness, Stillness, Calm, Hush, Secrecy, Dissolution.
S	I	L	E	N	U	S	Minor woodland god of Greek mythology.
S	I	L	E	S	I	A	Former Prussian province, Lightweight cotton fabric.
S	I	L	I	C	I	C	Derived from silica or silicon.
S	I	L	I	C	L	E	Narrow many-seeded capsule of nearly equal length and width.
S	I	L	I	C	O	N	Tetravalent nonmetallic element.
S	I	L	I	Q	U	A	Roman silver coin.
S	I	L	I	Q	U	E	Silicle.
S	I	L	K	I	E	R	Softer, Smoother, Glossier, Sleeker, More lustrous.
S	I	L	K	I	N	G	Covering with silk.
S	I	L	K	M	A	N	One who sells or makes silk.
S	I	L	L	A	G	O	Percoid fishes, Whiting.
S	I	L	L	I	E	R	Weaker, Simpler, More foolish, More inane, More absurd.
S	I	L	L	I	L	Y	Ridiculously, Foolishly, Absurdly, Giddily, Dizzily, Crazily.
S	I	L	L	O	C	K	Young pollack, Fish resembling a cod.

1	2	3	4	5	6	7	
S	I	L	T	I	N	G	Choking, Obstructing, Filling, Covering.
S	I	L	U	R	E	S	People occupying ancient Wales.
S	I	L	U	R	U	S	Catfish.
S	I	L	V	E	R	N	Silvery.
S	I	L	V	E	R	Y	Lustrous, Made of silver, Resonant tone.
S	I	M	A	R	R	E	Renaissance dress style, Shift.
S	I	M	I	L	A	R	Comparable, Corresponding, Like, Counterpart, Parallel, Uniform.
S	I	M	I	O	U	S	Simian, Monkey, Ape.
S	I	M	P	L	E	R	Plainer, More naive, Easier, Sillier, More primitive, More stupid.
S	I	M	U	L	A	R	Counterfeit, Imitative, One concealing the truth.
S	I	M	U	R	G	H	Legendary Persian bird.
S	I	N	A	P	I	S	Genus comprising cruciferous herbs, Mustard.
S	I	N	C	E	R	E	Real, True, Honest, Pure, Genuine, Hearty, Candid, Faithful.
S	I	N	E	W	E	D	Sinewy, Tough.
S	I	N	G	I	N	G	Vocal art, Chanting, Serenading, Crooning, Intoning, Vocalizing.
S	I	N	G	L	E	D	Parted, Separated, Withdrew, Concentrated, Chosen, Culled, Selected, Picked.
S	I	N	G	L	E	S	Tennis court play for two players.
S	I	N	G	L	E	T	Undershirt or athletic vest.
S	I	N	G	U	L	T	Sob, Sigh.
S	I	N	K	A	G	E	Sinking, Depression, Concavity, Deep, Sag, Hollow.
S	I	N	K	I	N	G	Submerging, Settling, Subsiding, Descending, Falling, Degenerating, Collapsing, Immersing.
S	I	N	L	E	S	S	Free from sin, Holy, Impeccable.
S	I	N	N	I	N	G	Violating religious or social law. Evildoing, Wrongdoing, Trespassing, Offending, Trangressing.
S	I	N	O	P	I	A	Red pigment made from clay.
S	I	N	S	Y	N	E	Ago.
S	I	N	U	A	T	E	Sinuous, Wavy, Tortuous, Undulate, Wind, Bend, Curve.
S	I	N	U	O	U	S	Bending, Serpentine, Winding, Intricate, Complex, Wriggling, Undulating.
S	I	N	W	A	R	D	Toward sin.
S	I	P	P	I	N	G	Drinking a small quantity, Tasting.
S	I	R	E	N	I	A	Large aquatic herbivorous mammals, Manatee, Dugong, Sea cow.
S	I	R	E	N	I	C	Melodious, Alluring, Deceptive.
S	I	R	G	A	N	G	Cissa, Green or blue magpies of Southeast Asia.
S	I	R	L	O	I	N	Cut of beef from the hindquarters.
S	I	R	O	C	C	O	Hot desert wind in the Mediteranean area.
S	I	S	T	I	N	E	Colours of the painted ceiling in the Sistine chapel.
S	I	S	T	R	U	M	Musical instrument played like a rattle, Ancient Egyptian percussion instrument.
S	I	T	F	A	S	T	Sore on a horse's back caused by chafing of the saddle.
S	I	T	T	I	N	E	Genus of small birds, Nuthatch.
S	I	T	T	I	N	G	Resting on the buttocks, Brooding, Perching, Squatting, Meeting, Setting, Ensconcing.
S	I	T	U	A	T	E	Locate, Place, Position, Site, Localize, Assign.
S	I	V	A	I	T	E	Supreme Hindu god.
S	I	X	F	O	L	D	Having six parts, Being six times as great.
S	I	X	T	E	E	N	Square of four.
S	I	Z	A	B	L	E	Reasonable bulk, Considerable, Large, Bulky, Respectable, Sensible.
S	I	Z	Z	L	E	D	Burned, Seared, Strong language, In a state of deep anger, In top form, Swished, Hissed.
S	J	A	M	B	O	K	Heavy leather whip often of animal hide.
S	K	E	E	T	E	R	Trapshooter.
S	K	E	L	D	E	R	Dishonesty, Begging, Fraud, Cheating, Swindling.
S	K	E	L	L	U	M	Scoundrel, Scamp, Rascal.
S	K	E	L	T	E	R	Bustling rush, Scurry.
S	K	E	P	F	U	L	Unit of capacity based on a bushel-sized basket, Beehive.
S	K	E	P	T	I	C	Doubting and incredulous person.
S	K	E	T	C	H	Y	Vaguely outlined, Roughly drafted, Slight, Superficial, Cursory, Shallow.
S	K	E	W	G	E	E	Askew, Aslant, Crooked.
S	K	I	D	D	E	D	Slid, Skewed, Veered, Sheered.
S	K	I	D	P	A	N	Place where motorists learn advanced driving.
S	K	I	J	U	M	P	Steep slope for ski-ing.
S	K	I	L	F	U	L	Displaying skill, Ability, Well versed, Proficiency, Accomplished.
S	K	I	L	I	F	T	Mechanical seats or device to cary skiers to top of the slope.
S	K	I	L	L	E	D	Understood, Comprehended, Expert, Proficient, Adroit.
S	K	I	L	L	E	T	Frying pan, Small kettle on feet.
S	K	I	M	M	E	D	Removed something from the surface, Glided, Grazed, Brushed, Shaved, Browsed, Scanned.
S	K	I	M	M	E	R	Perforated scoop.
S	K	I	M	P	E	D	Stinted, Scrimped, Pinched, Scraped, Screwed.
S	K	I	N	F	U	L	Intoxicating amount of alcohol, Satisfying quantity.
S	K	I	N	K	E	R	Tapster, Barman.
S	K	I	N	N	E	D	Peeled, Stripped, Fleeced, Criticized, Pared, Flayed.

1	2	3	4	5	6	7	Definition
S	K	I	N	N	E	R	One that deals in hides.
S	K	I	P	P	E	D	Capered, Gambolled, Hopped, Frisked, Loped, Tripped, Skimmed, Bolted.
S	K	I	P	P	E	R	Master of a ship, Captain of an aircraft.
S	K	I	P	P	E	T	Small box for covering and protecting a seal.
S	K	I	R	L	E	D	Uttered a shrill note as a bagpipe, Screamed, Twisting, Curving.
S	K	I	R	R	E	T	Asiatic herb cultivated for its sweet edible tuberous roots.
S	K	I	R	T	E	D	Bordered, Defined, Edged, Fringed, Bypassed, Circumvented, Sidestepped, Detoured.
S	K	I	R	T	E	R	Hunter or hound that goes around obstacles instead of over them.
S	K	I	S	U	I	T	Warm outfit designed for winter sports.
S	K	I	T	T	E	R	Scurry, Skip, Scamper, Rustle, Lope, Spring, Trip, Hop.
S	K	I	T	T	L	E	One of the wooden pins in a game.
S	K	I	V	I	N	G	Splitting leather, Shaving, Paring, Decamping.
S	K	O	P	T	S	Y	Dissenter from Russian Orthodox Church who practises strict celibacy.
S	K	U	L	K	E	D	Sneaked, Hid, Lurked, Shirked, Stole, Slipped, Malingered, Concealed.
S	K	U	L	K	E	R	Shirker, Malingerer.
S	K	U	L	P	A	N	Skullcap.
S	K	Y	B	L	U	E	Azure, Cerulean.
S	K	Y	H	I	G	H	Unusually high level, Enthusiastic manner, Apart.
S	K	Y	L	A	R	K	Frolic, High jinks, Fool around.
S	K	Y	L	I	N	E	Horizon, Outline of mountains or buildings.
S	K	Y	P	O	R	T	Landing pad for a helicopter.
S	K	Y	S	A	I	L	A sail in a special position.
S	K	Y	W	A	R	D	Upward, Toward the sky.
S	L	A	B	B	E	D	Covered with slabs, Cut in thick slices, Specially cut railroad tie.
S	L	A	B	B	E	R	Drool, Dribble, Salivate, Slobber, Gorge, Bolt.
S	L	A	C	K	E	D	Loosened, Eased, Relaxed, Abated.
S	L	A	C	K	E	N	Abate, Moderate, Retard, Loosen, Delay, Detain, Wane, Mitigate.
S	L	A	C	K	E	R	Shirker, Slinker, Idler, Loafer, Malingerer.
S	L	A	C	K	L	Y	Loosely, Carelessly, Inadequately.
S	L	A	I	N	T	E	Salutation, Toast.
S	L	A	K	I	N	G	Abating, Moderating, Crumbling, Disintegrating, Diminishing, Easing, Mitigating, Satisfying.
S	L	A	M	M	E	D	Knocked, Banged, Criticized, Bashed, Crashed, Pounded, Smacked, Struck.
S	L	A	N	D	E	R	Detraction, Defame, Malign, Charge, Blame, Calumny, Depreciation, Scandal.
S	L	A	N	G	E	D	Cheated, Swindled, Duped, Abused, Censured in coarse language.
S	L	A	N	T	E	D	Sloped, Angled, Biased, Inclined, Tilted, Leaned, Bevelled, Diagonal.
S	L	A	N	T	L	Y	Slantingly, Slopingly, Aslope, Aside, Sideways, Obliquely, Aslant.
S	L	A	P	P	E	D	Struck, Smacked, Spanked, Cuffed, Clouted, Clipped, Rebuffed, Insulted.
S	L	A	P	P	E	R	Canvas device for driving cattle.
S	L	A	S	H	E	D	Lashed, Whipped, Gashed, Slit, Hacked, Lambasted, Scourged, Reduced.
S	L	A	S	H	E	R	Weapon, Cutting tool.
S	L	A	T	H	E	R	Spread thickly, Waste, Squander.
S	L	A	T	I	N	G	Roofing with slates, Berating, Recording, Scheduling, Appointing, Hounding, Censuring.
S	L	A	T	T	E	R	Worker in a soap factory.
S	L	A	V	D	O	M	Area under the influence of Slavs.
S	L	A	V	E	R	Y	Drudgery, Subservience, Bondage, Servitude, Serfdom, Enslavement, Thralldom, Grind.
S	L	A	V	I	N	G	Toiling, Drudging, Plodding, Slogging.
S	L	A	V	I	S	H	Spineless, Menial, Obeisant, Emulative, Imitative, Subservient, Wretched, Servile.
S	L	A	Y	I	N	G	Murdering, Stabbing, Throttling, Slaughtering, Eradicating, Suppressing, Overwhelming.
S	L	E	A	V	E	D	Separated into filaments.
S	L	E	D	D	E	D	Transported with a sled.
S	L	E	D	G	E	D	Travelled on a sleigh.
S	L	E	E	K	E	D	Slicked, Glossed.
S	L	E	E	K	E	N	To smooth, To polish.
S	L	E	E	K	E	R	Flashier, Slicker, Glossier, Smoother, Silkier, More lustrous.
S	L	E	E	K	I	T	Crafty, Deceitful.
S	L	E	E	K	L	Y	Silky, Glossy, Slickly, Flashy, Smoothly.
S	L	E	E	P	E	R	One that sleeps, Timber support, Beam, Ships timber, Railway tie, Dormouse.
S	L	E	E	T	E	D	Showered sleet.
S	L	E	I	D	E	D	Untwisted silk.
S	L	E	I	G	H	T	Cunning, Trickery, Dexterity, Knack, Deftness, Skill, Adroitness, Artifice.
S	L	E	N	D	E	R	Thin, Slim, Slight, Reedy, Lithe, Svelte, Scanty, Meagre.
S	L	E	W	I	N	G	Twisting, Basketwork.
S	L	E	Y	I	N	G	Operations in weaving.
S	L	I	C	I	N	G	Cutting, Slitting, Dividing, Hitting a ball, Slashing, Carving, Severing, Cleaving.
S	L	I	C	K	E	R	Swindler, Cheat, Trickster, Diddler, Smarter, More deft, Rogue.
S	L	I	D	D	E	R	Slither, Slide, Slip.
S	L	I	D	I	N	G	Varying, Gliding, Slipping, Slithering, Flowing, Slumping, Skidding, Shifting.

1	2	3	4	5	6	7	
S	L	I	M	I	L	Y	Vilely, Vulgarly, Viscously, Scummy.
S	L	I	M	M	E	R	Thinner, Meaner, Craftier, Cleverer, More adroit, Sharper, Smaller, Scarcer.
S	L	I	N	G	E	R	Rigger.
S	L	I	P	P	E	D	Glided, Escaped, Disengaged, Lapsed, Deteriorated, Declined, Eluded, Released.
S	L	I	P	P	E	R	Soft shoe for indoor wear.
S	L	I	P	W	A	Y	Inclined way for shipbuilding.
S	L	I	T	H	E	R	Slide, Glide, Undulate, Creep, Sidle, Lurk, Prowl, Sneak.
S	L	I	T	T	E	D	Slashed, Cut, Split, Severed, Gashed, Incised.
S	L	I	T	T	E	R	Wheel for slitting or sawing precious stones.
S	L	O	B	B	E	R	Drool, Slaver, Dribble, Salivate.
S	L	O	C	K	E	N	Quench, Extinguish.
S	L	O	E	G	I	N	Reddish liqueur of grain spirits flavoured with sloeberries.
S	L	O	G	G	E	D	Toiled, Socked, Scored, Plodded, Tramped, Plugged, Struck, Clouted.
S	L	O	G	G	E	R	Plodder, Slugger.
S	L	O	P	I	N	G	Travelling, Walking, Leaning, Bending, Curving, Slanting, Tilting, Inclining.
S	L	O	P	P	E	D	Splashed, Spilt, Dished clumsily, Gobbled, Gushed, Doused, Guzzled, Trudged.
S	L	O	S	H	E	D	Floundered, Gurgled, Splashed, Struck, Guzzled, Swilled, Bashed, Punched.
S	L	O	T	T	E	D	Cut a slit, Made slots, Pass through a slot, Grooved.
S	L	O	T	T	E	R	Slotting machine.
S	L	O	U	C	H	Y	Slovenly, Slackly, Ungainly.
S	L	O	U	G	H	Y	Marshy, Muddy, Swampy, Presence of dead tissue.
S	L	O	V	E	N	E	Characteristic of the Slovenes.
S	L	O	W	E	S	T	Most stupid, Dullest, Steadiest, Slackest, Lowest, Most gentle, Most deliberate.
S	L	O	W	I	N	G	Retarding, Plodding, Dragging, Braking, Halting, Delaying, Dawdling, Flagging.
S	L	U	B	B	E	R	Become muddied, Stain, Sully, Worker on woollen thread.
S	L	U	D	G	E	R	Sand pump, Shovel for clearing drains.
S	L	U	G	G	E	D	Loitered, Delayed, Hindered, Struck, Smashed, Clobbered, Coshed.
S	L	U	I	C	E	D	Drenched, Washed, Scoured, Flushed, Doused, Poured, Surged, Soaked.
S	L	U	M	B	E	R	Sleep, Hibernate, Doze, Drowse, Lethargy, Coma, Stupor.
S	L	U	M	P	E	D	Collapsed, Declined, Sagged, Fell, Slipped, Settled, Pitched, Plunged.
S	L	U	R	R	E	D	Slurped, Slid, Slipped, Dragged, Shuffled, Maligned, Defamed, Neglected.
S	L	U	S	H	E	D	Sluiced, Lubricated, Grouted, Sloshed, Waded.
S	L	Y	N	E	S	S	Shrewdness, Craftiness, Furtiveness, Artfulness, Foxiness, Wiliness, Cunning.
S	M	A	C	K	E	D	Tasted, Struck, Slapped, Spanked, Threw, Kissed, Resembled, Suggested.
S	M	A	C	K	E	R	One that smacks, Dollar (slang).
S	M	A	R	T	E	D	Pained, Suffered, Ached, Burned, Tingled, Pricked.
S	M	A	R	T	E	N	Brighten, Primp, Enliven, Invigorate, Spruce, Prink, Deck out.
S	M	A	R	T	E	R	Brighten, Brisker, Brainier, Sharper, Wiser, Quicker, Bolder, Saucier.
S	M	A	R	T	L	Y	Vigorously, Smartly, Curtly, Severely, Considerably, Neatly, Trimly, Precisely.
S	M	A	S	H	E	D	Shattered, Battered, Destroyed, Pressed, Crushed, Wrecked, Demolished, Ruined.
S	M	A	S	H	E	R	Something large or fine, Smashing machine, Skilled tennis player.
S	M	A	S	H	U	P	Complete collapse, Motor vehicle collision.
S	M	A	T	T	E	R	Slight superficial knowledge, Shatter, Babble, Chatter, Spatter, Sprinkle, Fragment, Few.
S	M	E	A	R	E	D	Besmirched, Sullied, Daubed, Smudged, Stained, Repulsed, Slandered, Frustrated.
S	M	E	A	R	E	R	One that blackens a reputation.
S	M	E	C	T	I	C	Purifying, Detergent.
S	M	E	D	D	U	M	Powder, Dust of ground malt, Spunk, Spirit, Vigour.
S	M	E	L	L	E	D	Smelt, Inhaled, Sniffed, Savoured, Scented, Snuffed, Reeked, Stunk.
S	M	E	L	L	E	R	Expert in a perfume factory, Spirit blender.
S	M	E	L	T	E	R	Foundry, Ore-worker.
S	M	I	C	K	E	R	To ogle, Leer, Smirk, Simper.
S	M	I	C	K	E	T	A woman's smock.
S	M	I	D	G	E	N	Small amount, Trifle, Mite, Particle, Atom, Iota, Jot, Speck.
S	M	I	L	I	N	G	Smirking, Looking with favour, Bestowing approval, Beaming, Grinning, Simpering
S	M	I	R	K	E	D	Simpered, Affected smile, Sneered.
S	M	I	T	I	N	G	Striking, Killing, Injuring, Clouting, Slogging, Afflicting, Tormenting, Torturing.
S	M	I	T	H	A	M	Fine particles of ore obtained by sifting.
S	M	I	T	T	E	N	Afflicted, Tormented, Agonized, Struck, Injured, Crucified.
S	M	I	T	T	L	E	Infect with a contagious disease, Grasp, Seize.
S	M	O	K	I	E	R	Emitting more smoke, Obscuring, Smelling of smoke.
S	M	O	K	I	L	Y	Hazily, Foggily, Unstable.
S	M	O	K	I	N	G	Steaming, Inhaling cigarette smoke, Comprehending, Absconding, Fumigating, Ridiculing.
S	M	O	L	D	E	R	Smoulder, Burn or smoke without flames, State of agitation.
S	M	O	T	H	E	R	Suffocate, Stifle, Suppress, Quench, Overwhelm, Choke, Restrain, Compose.
S	M	U	D	G	E	D	Begrimed, Soiled, Smeared, Daubed, Wiped, Blurred, Splotched, Smothered.
S	M	U	D	G	E	R	Worker who tends frost-dispelling equipment in an orchard.
S	M	U	G	G	E	R	Better groomed, More complacent, Neater, Smarter.

1	2	3	4	5	6	7	
S	M	U	G	G	L	E	Import articles in violation of the customs laws, Bootleg, Contraband.
S	M	Y	T	R	I	E	Miscellaneous collection of small creatures or things, Bunch.
S	N	A	F	F	L	E	Part of a horse's bridle, Steal, Rob, Restrain, Pinch, Purloin.
S	N	A	G	G	E	D	Caught on a projection, Progress interrupted by unexpected hitch.
S	N	A	G	G	E	R	Foundry worker.
S	N	A	I	L	E	R	Operator of a polishing machine for watch wheels.
S	N	A	K	I	N	G	Coiling, Winding, Wriggling, Slithering, Crawling, Gliding.
S	N	A	K	I	S	H	Reptilian, Sinuous, Wriggly, Wavy.
S	N	A	P	P	E	D	Jerked, Yanked, Pounced, Snatched, Broken, Scintillated, Sparkled, Snarled.
S	N	A	P	P	E	R	Castanets, Cracker, Double-sided fastener, Clipper, Young fish.
S	N	A	R	I	N	G	Capturing, Catching, Entrapping, Trapping, Tangling, Seducing, Tempting, Involving.
S	N	A	R	L	E	D	Ensnared, Entangled, Complicated, Muddled, Perplexed, Tangled, Expressed disgust.
S	N	A	R	L	E	R	One that snarls.
S	N	A	T	C	H	Y	Interrupted, Spasmodic, Irregular.
S	N	E	A	K	E	R	Canvas shoe with a runner sole, Peson acting in a furtive manner.
S	N	E	C	K	E	D	Latched, Fastened.
S	N	E	C	K	U	P	To absent oneself.
S	N	E	E	R	E	D	Derided, Declaimed, Leered, Smirked, Scoffed, Jeered, Belittled, Disparaged.
S	N	E	E	R	E	R	Taunter.
S	N	E	E	Z	E	D	Violent spasmodic audible expiration of breath through nose and mouth.
S	N	I	C	K	E	R	Laugh in derision, Snigger, Giggle, Chuckle, Chortle, Guffaw, Titter.
S	N	I	D	E	S	T	Meanest, Basest, Lowest, Cheapest, Most spurious, Most dishonest.
S	N	I	F	F	E	D	Inhaled, Smelled.
S	N	I	F	F	L	E	Snivel, Sniff repeatedly, Nasal congestion.
S	N	I	F	T	E	R	Small drink of liquor, Small dose of narcotic, Specially shaped brandy goblet.
S	N	I	G	G	E	R	Snicker, Chuckle, Titter, Guffaw, Chortle.
S	N	I	G	G	L	E	Creep, Crawl, Snare.
S	N	I	P	I	N	G	Shooting from a concealed position.
S	N	I	P	P	E	R	Worker who trims edges of hides or metal.
S	N	I	P	P	E	T	Small part, Brief quotation, Cutting, Fragment.
S	N	I	R	T	L	E	Laugh with a snort.
S	N	O	O	D	E	D	Having hair confined in a net bag.
S	N	O	O	K	E	R	Game similar to billiards, Thwart, Defeat, Hinder.
S	N	O	O	P	E	R	A prying meddler, Nosy parker.
S	N	O	O	T	E	D	Treated with disdain.
S	N	O	O	Z	E	R	One that dozes, Fellow, Scamp.
S	N	O	R	K	E	L	Tube for air intake on a submarine, Plastic breathing tube for underwater swimmer.
S	N	O	R	T	E	R	Something remarkable, Humdinger.
S	N	O	T	T	E	R	Part of rigging.
S	N	O	U	T	E	D	Dug with a snout, Grubbed.
S	N	O	W	F	L	Y	Minute insect that appears on the snow in large numbers.
S	N	O	W	I	C	E	Glacial ice, Porous ice formed by the freezing of half melted snow.
S	N	O	W	M	A	N	Figure moulded from snow.
S	N	O	W	O	W	L	Snowy owl, Large diurnal arctic owl.
S	N	U	B	B	E	D	Rebuked, Upbraided, Scolded, Slighted, Ostracized, Overlooked, Restrained, Humiliated.
S	N	U	B	B	E	R	Miner.
S	N	U	D	G	E	D	Snugged, Nestled.
S	N	U	F	F	E	D	Extinguished, Killed, Died, Croaked, Sniffed, Scented, Smelled.
S	N	U	F	F	E	R	Device for extinguishing candles.
S	N	U	F	F	L	E	Snivel, Whimper, Nasal catarrh, Sniffle.
S	N	U	G	G	L	E	Cuddle, Nestle, Lie in a comfortable position.
S	N	U	G	Z	L	E	Cuddle, Nestle.
S	O	A	K	A	G	E	Absorbtion, Seepage, Being soaked.
S	O	A	K	I	N	G	Steeping, Immersing, Percolating, Permeating, Penetrating, Saturating, Submerging.
S	O	A	N	D	S	O	Cover up for a profanity, Vague definition.
S	O	A	P	B	O	X	Stand for amateur orators in public places.
S	O	A	P	I	N	G	Rubbing soap, Scouring, Flattering, Complimenting for an ulterior motive.
S	O	A	R	I	N	G	Flying upward, Operating a glider.
S	O	B	B	I	N	G	Crying noisily, Weeping with convulsive catching of the breath, Lamentation, Blubbering.
S	O	B	E	R	E	D	Became serious, Became neutral in colour, Subdued, Composed, Disciplined.
S	O	B	E	R	L	Y	Seriously, Earnestly, Gravely, Sedately, Earnestly, Moderately, Staidly.
S	O	C	A	G	E	R	Tenant of a farm paying rent in cash and kind.
S	O	C	C	A	G	E	Tenure of land with rent in cash or kind but not military service.
S	O	C	I	E	T	Y	Company, Guild, Relationship, Community, Association, Fraternity, Union, Elite.
S	O	C	K	E	Y	E	Small Pacific salmon.
S	O	C	K	I	N	G	Hitting, Striking, Punching, Clouting, Belting, Whacking, Smashing, Bashing.
S	O	D	A	A	S	H	Commercial sodium carbonate.

1	2	3	4	5	6	7	
S	O	D	D	I	N	G	Covering with pieces of turf.
S	O	F	A	B	E	D	Studio couch, Couch able to be converted into a bed.
S	O	F	T	E	S	T	Calmest, Kindest, Mildest, Most gentle, Silkiest, Smoothest, Cushiest, Silliest.
S	O	F	T	I	S	H	Squashy, Balmy, Flabby, Slushy, Cushy.
S	O	G	G	I	N	G	Soaking.
S	O	I	G	N	E	E	Modish, Stylish, Fashionable.
S	O	I	L	A	G	E	Green crops cut for animal fodder.
S	O	I	L	I	N	G	Polluting, Corrupting, Dirtying, Smudging, Disgracing, Sullying, Contaminating, Tainting.
S	O	I	L	U	R	E	Stain, Smidge.
S	O	J	O	U	R	N	Reside, Stay as resident, Visit, Stay, Tarry, Linger, Abide.
S	O	K	E	M	A	N	Socager.
S	O	L	A	C	E	D	Comforted, Consoled, Allayed, Assuaged, Amused, Entertained, Diverted.
S	O	L	A	N	U	M	Genus of plants cultivated for food and decoration, Potato, Jerusalem cherry, Egg plant.
S	O	L	D	I	E	R	Serviceman, Private, Warrior, Fighter, Trooper.
S	O	L	I	C	I	T	Manage, Forward, Require, Incite, Entreat, Importune, Request, Accost.
S	O	L	I	D	L	Y	Strongly, Firmly, Securely, Seriously, Intensively, Wholly, Unanimously.
S	O	L	I	D	U	M	Whole.
S	O	L	I	D	U	S	Ancient Roman gold coin.
S	O	L	I	P	E	D	Animal with a single hoof, Horse, Mule, Ass.
S	O	L	O	I	S	T	Lone performer.
S	O	L	O	M	O	N	Personification of wisdom.
S	O	L	O	N	I	C	Relating to Solon, an ancient Athenian law giver.
S	O	L	P	U	G	A	Hairy spider of Madagascar and Australia.
S	O	L	U	B	L	E	Emulsifiable, Dispersible, Solvable, Capable of being dissolved.
S	O	L	V	E	N	D	Solute, Dissolved substance.
S	O	L	V	E	N	T	Substance used in dissolving or dispersing, Thinner, Something that dissipates.
S	O	L	V	I	N	G	Dissolving, Elucidating, Resolving, Unfolding, Unravelling, Deciphering, Deciding, Settling.
S	O	M	A	T	I	C	Physical, Corporal, Bodily.
S	O	M	E	D	A	Y	Some time in the future.
S	O	M	E	H	O	W	One way or another, Someway.
S	O	M	E	O	N	E	Somebody, Some person unspecified.
S	O	M	E	W	A	Y	Somehow.
S	O	M	N	I	A	L	Pertaining to sleep or dreams.
S	O	N	A	N	C	E	Sound, Noise.
S	O	N	C	H	U	S	Genus of Old World herbs, Sow thistle.
S	O	N	D	A	G	E	Trial excavation.
S	O	N	D	E	L	I	Muskshrew.
S	O	N	G	F	U	L	Melodious, Joyful.
S	O	N	G	M	A	N	Male chorister.
S	O	N	L	E	S	S	Having no son.
S	O	N	S	H	I	P	Relationship of son to father.
S	O	O	R	K	E	E	Brickdust mixed with lime to form a mortar.
S	O	O	T	H	E	D	Calmed, Composed, Quietened, Placated, Mollified, Alleviated, Consoled, Tranquilized.
S	O	O	T	H	E	R	One that calms or comforts.
S	O	O	T	H	L	Y	Truly.
S	O	O	T	I	N	G	Smudging, Soiling with soot.
S	O	P	H	I	S	M	Specious reasoning, Fallacy, Deception, Delusion, Equivocation, Illogicality, Invalidity.
S	O	P	H	I	S	T	One who submits illogical reasoning.
S	O	P	H	O	R	A	Japanese pagoda tree.
S	O	P	P	I	N	G	Soaking, Steeping, Mopping.
S	O	P	R	A	N	O	High treble voice.
S	O	R	B	E	N	T	A substance that absorbs.
S	O	R	B	I	A	N	Wendis, Germanic Slavs.
S	O	R	B	I	T	E	A constituent of steel.
S	O	R	B	O	S	E	Sweet crystalline unfermentable sugar.
S	O	R	C	E	R	Y	Witchcraft, Necromancy, Magic, Bewitching, Conjuring, Enchantment, Incantation.
S	O	R	D	I	N	E	A mute for a trumpet.
S	O	R	D	I	N	O	Sourdine, Obsolete musical instruments of a low tone.
S	O	R	G	H	U	M	Grain used for fodder and also a drink.
S	O	R	I	T	E	S	Collection of related things, items or facts, Deductive logical analysis.
S	O	R	N	I	N	G	Imposing, Cadging, Sponging.
S	O	R	O	R	A	L	Sisterly.
S	O	R	O	S	I	S	A club for women.
S	O	R	R	I	L	Y	Unhappily, Doefully, Mournfully.
S	O	R	T	I	N	G	Classifying, Analyzing, Separating, Sifting, Screening, Choosing, Selecting, Picking.
S	O	T	H	I	A	C	Relating to the ancient Egyptian calendar.
S	O	T	T	I	N	G	Tippling, Guzzling, Bemusing, Boozing, Stultifying.

1	2	3	4	5	6	7	
S	O	T	T	I	S	H	Doltish, Stupid, Drunken.
S	O	U	B	I	S	E	White or brown onion sauce.
S	O	U	F	F	L	E	Light puffy dessert mainly of eggs, Something light and happy, Fluffy.
S	O	U	G	H	E	D	Made a moaning sound, Died, Sighed deeply.
S	O	U	L	F	U	L	Sentimental, Emotional.
S	O	U	N	D	E	D	Summoned, Appeared, Seemed, Declared, Advertised, Announced, Published, Proclaimed.
S	O	U	N	D	E	R	Healthier, Fitter, Saner, Better, Firmer, More rational, More stable, More secure.
S	O	U	N	D	L	Y	Thoroughly, Securely, Deeply, Profoundly, Correctly, Violently, Severely.
S	O	U	P	C	O	N	Trace, Touch, Taste, Whiff, Hint, Suggestion, Sprinkling, Streak.
S	O	U	R	E	S	T	Rankest, Most bitter, Most rotten, Most unpleasant, Harshest, Most disagreeable.
S	O	U	R	I	N	G	Fermenting, Rotting, Disappointing, Disillusioning, Exacerbating, Irritating, Deteriorating.
S	O	U	R	I	S	H	Acidulous, Vinagery, Acrid, Bitter.
S	O	U	R	S	O	P	Small tropical American tree with slightly acid fleshy fruit.
S	O	U	S	I	N	G	Pickling, Plunging, Drenching, Saturating, Soaking, Submerging, Sloshing, Pouring.
S	O	U	T	A	N	E	Cassock worn by Roman Catholic clergy.
S	O	U	T	H	E	R	Wind shifting to the south, Southerly wind.
S	O	V	K	H	O	Z	Russian state-owned farm.
S	O	W	B	A	C	K	Mountain ridge.
S	O	W	B	A	N	E	Herb considered poisonous to pigs.
S	O	Y	B	E	A	N	Annual legume, the seeds of which yield valuable products.
S	O	Z	Z	L	E	D	Drunk, Splashed, Soused, Lounged, Lolled, Tipsy.
S	P	A	C	I	A	L	Spatial, Relating to space.
S	P	A	C	I	N	G	Placing at intervals, Separating.
S	P	A	D	G	E	R	House sparrow.
S	P	A	D	I	N	G	Digging with a spade, Any operation using a spade.
S	P	A	D	I	S	H	With a direct or blunt attitude.
S	P	A	E	M	A	N	Wizard, Prophet, Fortune-teller.
S	P	A	I	R	G	E	Sparge, Sprinkle, Bespatter.
S	P	A	L	L	E	D	Chipped, Splintered, Reduced, Flaked.
S	P	A	N	C	E	L	Fetter, Shackle, Restrain, Hobble.
S	P	A	N	D	E	X	Synthetic textile elastic fibres.
S	P	A	N	G	L	E	Glistening shape of metal used as decoration, Small shining object.
S	P	A	N	G	L	Y	Glistening, Flashy, Glittery, Sparkling, Twinkling.
S	P	A	N	I	E	L	Special breed of dog, Frolic, Sport, Follow with devotion.
S	P	A	N	I	S	H	Characteristic of Spain.
S	P	A	N	K	E	D	Struck, Smacked, Clouted, Cuffed, Slapped, Socked, Punched, Belted.
S	P	A	N	K	E	R	Sail, Mast, Horse capable of a good speed.
S	P	A	N	N	E	D	Stretched, Traversed, Seized, Spread, Bridged.
S	P	A	N	N	E	R	Wrench.
S	P	A	N	N	E	W	Brand-new.
S	P	A	R	E	L	Y	Sparingly, Sparsely, Meagerly, Leanly.
S	P	A	R	G	E	D	Sprinkled, Bespattered, Plastered, Sprayed.
S	P	A	R	G	E	R	Sprinkler for irrigation.
S	P	A	R	I	N	G	Saving, Frugal, Reticent, Meagre, Scanty, Thrifty, Economical, Scrimping.
S	P	A	R	K	E	D	Activated, Incited, Stimulated.
S	P	A	R	K	L	E	Scintillate, Flash, Glisten, Gleam, Glimmer, Glint, Shimmer, Twinkle.
S	P	A	R	O	I	D	Sea bream.
S	P	A	R	R	E	D	Fought, Wrangled, Boxed, Disputed, Contested.
S	P	A	R	R	O	W	Genus of bird distributed throughout the world, Person of small stature, Active person.
S	P	A	R	T	A	N	Austere, Self-disciplined, Leading a life of simplicity with no luxury.
S	P	A	S	T	I	C	Characterised by spasmodic movement and activity.
S	P	A	T	H	E	D	Having a floral bract.
S	P	A	T	H	I	C	Having foliage, shells or large showy blooms.
S	P	A	T	I	A	L	Relating to space.
S	P	A	T	T	E	R	Splash, Sprinkle, Spot, Defame, Splutter, Spurt, Drop.
S	P	A	T	T	L	E	Spatula.
S	P	A	T	U	L	A	Thin flexible dull-edged implement for spreading or mixing a soft substance.
S	P	A	T	U	L	E	Spatula.
S	P	A	W	L	E	D	Spat, Chipped, Flaked.
S	P	A	W	N	E	D	Produced eggs, Planted mushroom spores, Generated, Reproduced.
S	P	A	W	N	E	R	Mature female fish.
S	P	A	Y	I	N	G	Removing ovaries from a female animal, Sterilising.
S	P	E	A	K	E	R	One that speaks, A man that addresses an audience, Presiding officer.
S	P	E	A	R	E	D	Pierced, Struck, Impaled, Thrust.
S	P	E	A	R	E	R	One that pierces.
S	P	E	C	I	A	L	Uncommon, Noteworthy, Extraordinary, Peculiar, Unique, Individual, Specific, Distinctive.
S	P	E	C	I	E	S	Group, Genus, Class, Kind, Humanity, Coin, Breed, Order.

1	2	3	4	5	6	7	
S	P	E	C	I	F	Y	Mention, Indicate, Detail, Cite, Name, Enumerate, Specialize, Itemize.
S	P	E	C	K	E	D	Spotted, Speckled.
S	P	E	C	K	L	E	Spotted, Marked with dots, Small splotch.
S	P	E	C	T	R	A	Spectrum, Apparition, Refracted through a prism.
S	P	E	C	T	R	E	Ghost, Phantom, Spirit, Phantasm.
S	P	E	C	U	L	A	Speculum, Ancient mirror, Tubular instrument for visual inspection of passages of the body.
S	P	E	E	D	E	D	Prospered, Succeeded, Executed, Advanced, Furthered, Satisfied, Accelerated, Hurried.
S	P	E	E	D	E	R	Device for regulating speed of a machine or part.
S	P	E	L	L	E	R	Stretch, Sprawl.
S	P	E	L	L	E	D	Discovered, Comprehended, Understood, Formed, Composed, Asked, Hinted, Signified.
S	P	E	L	L	E	R	Book for teaching spelling.
S	P	E	L	T	E	R	Zinc slabs for commercial use.
S	P	E	N	C	E	R	Fitted jacket of waist length, Sails.
S	P	E	N	D	E	R	Spendthrift, One that wastes natural resources.
S	P	E	R	R	A	E	Hoped for, Hoping to be paid.
S	P	E	R	M	A	L	Having seeds.
S	P	E	W	E	N	G	Vomiting, Exuding, Gushing, Flooding, Spurting, Ejecting, Cascading, Belching.
S	P	H	E	R	A	L	Resembling a sphere, Harmonious.
S	P	H	E	R	E	D	Placed in a sphere, Completed, Perfected, Rounded, Surrounded, Circulated.
S	P	H	E	R	I	C	Resembling a sphere, Orbital.
S	P	H	Y	R	N	A	Genus of large sharks.
S	P	I	C	A	T	E	Pointed, Spiky.
S	P	I	C	E	R	Y	Storage space for spices.
S	P	I	C	I	L	Y	Pungently.
S	P	I	C	I	N	G	Seasoning.
S	P	I	C	U	L	E	Prickle.
S	P	I	C	U	L	E	Spikelet, Fleshy point or appendage, Spikelike organ.
S	P	I	D	E	R	Y	Resembling a spider, Infested with spiders, Composed of weblike threads.
S	P	I	G	N	E	L	Spicknel, European perennial herb.
S	P	I	K	I	N	G	Suppressing, Quashing, Piercing, Impaling, Adding liquor to a non-alcohol drink.
S	P	I	L	I	N	G	Plugging a hole with a bung, Drawing liquor from a cask, Piling, Underpinning.
S	P	I	L	I	T	E	Fine-grained extrusive rock.
S	P	I	L	L	E	D	Wasted, Squandered, Ruined, Spoiled, Divulged, Perished, Deteriorated, Tumbled.
S	P	I	L	L	E	R	Fishing line with many hooks.
S	P	I	N	A	C	H	Annual potherb cultivated for its edible leaves, Repellent, Obnoxious, Spurious, Unwanted.
S	P	I	N	A	T	E	Spiniform, Having a spine.
S	P	I	N	D	L	E	Axis, Tapered stick to twist yarn in spinning, Bobbin pin or rod, Shaft, Axle.
S	P	I	N	D	L	Y	Long and thin, Weakling, Undernourished.
S	P	I	N	N	E	R	Mayfly, Spinning machine, Candymaker, Fishing lure.
S	P	I	N	N	E	Y	Small wood with undergrowth.
S	P	I	N	O	F	F	Business transfer, By-product, Off-shoot, Derivative.
S	P	I	N	O	I	D	Spinelike.
S	P	I	N	O	S	E	Full of spines.
S	P	I	N	O	U	S	Bristling, Sharp, Thorny.
S	P	I	N	U	L	E	Small spine.
S	P	I	O	N	I	D	Marine worm.
S	P	I	R	A	E	A	Genus of shrubs with pink or white flowers.
S	P	I	R	A	N	T	Sibilant, Fricative consonant.
S	P	I	R	I	N	G	Germinating, Sprouting, Tapering, Mounting, Soaring.
S	P	I	R	I	T	Y	Lively, Spirited, Alert, Animate, Rousing, Sprightly, Vivacious.
S	P	I	R	T	E	D	Spurted, Gushed, Surged, Spouted.
S	P	I	R	T	L	E	Splatter, Splash.
S	P	I	R	U	L	A	Cuttlefish.
S	P	I	T	B	O	X	Spittoon.
S	P	I	T	T	N	G	Disliking, Hating, Treating maliciously.
S	P	I	T	T	E	D	Impaled, Cooked on a spit.
S	P	I	T	T	E	R	One that ejects saliva, Short fuse, Spitting snake.
S	P	I	T	T	L	E	Saliva.
S	P	L	A	S	H	Y	Mussy, Showy, Sensational, Ostentatious display.
S	P	L	A	Y	E	D	Expanded, Spread outward, Sloped, Slanted, Extended apart.
S	P	L	E	E	N	Y	Peevish, Irritable, Complaining.
S	P	L	E	N	I	C	Located in a spleen.
S	P	L	I	C	E	D	Fastened together, United, Attached, Fixed, Joined in, Married, Interwoven.
S	P	L	I	N	T	S	Thin strips of wood or plastic to immobilise and protect damaged parts, Supports, Braces.
S	P	L	O	D	G	E	Splash, Splosh.
S	P	L	O	D	G	Y	Splotchy.
S	P	L	O	T	C	H	Blot, Blotch, Daub, Smear, Spot, Stain.

1	2	3	4	5	6	7	Definition
S	P	L	U	R	G	E	Burst of activity, Showy display, Self-indulgence, Extravagance, Binge, Orgy, Rampage.
S	P	L	U	R	G	Y	Orgy of spending, Extravagent squandering.
S	P	O	D	I	U	M	Bone or animal charcoal.
S	P	O	I	L	E	D	Stripped, Tainted, Damaged, Flawed, Impaired, Marred, Decayed, Putrid.
S	P	O	I	L	E	R	Plunderer, Robber, Corrupter.
S	P	O	N	D	E	E	Poetic foot as used with solemn music.
S	P	O	N	G	E	D	Erased, Obliterated, Effaced, Drained, Soaked, Cadged, Imposed, Depended.
S	P	O	N	G	E	R	Parasite, Cadger, Leech, Free-loader, Barnacle, Bloodsucker, Hanger-on, Sucker.
S	P	O	N	G	I	N	Skeletal fibres of sponges.
S	P	O	N	S	A	L	Spousal, Matrimonial, Nuptial.
S	P	O	N	S	O	N	Projection from side of a ship.
S	P	O	N	S	O	R	Surety, Patron, Champion, Backer, Supporter, Champion, Promoter, Benefactor.
S	P	O	O	F	E	D	Deluded, Hoaxed, Hoodwinked, Tricked, Bamboozled, Duped, Cheated, Fooled.
S	P	O	O	L	E	D	Wound on a spool or drum.
S	P	O	O	N	E	D	Transferred something in a spoon, Petted, Courted, Necked, Boat driven before the wind.
S	P	O	O	N	E	Y	Spoony, Silly, Foolish, Emotional, Sentimental, Indulgent, Amorous.
S	P	O	O	R	E	R	Animal tracker.
S	P	O	R	O	I	D	Resembling a spore.
S	P	O	R	O	N	T	Sporozoan, Intracellular parasite that reproduces by spores.
S	P	O	R	R	A	N	Large skin pouch used as a purse and worn with a kilt.
S	P	O	R	T	E	D	Diverted, Amused, Cheered, Wagered, Mocked, Played, Disported, Wore.
S	P	O	R	T	E	R	Sportsman, Spendthrift.
S	P	O	R	U	L	E	A small spore.
S	P	O	T	T	E	D	Identified, Sullied, Tarnished, Detected, Noticed, Recognized, Dotted, Located.
S	P	O	T	T	E	R	Watcher, Look-out, Investigator.
S	P	O	U	S	A	L	Conjugal, Matrimonial, Nuptial, Wedlock.
S	P	O	U	T	E	D	Declaimed, Spurted, Pawned, Orated, Ejected, Gushed, Harangued.
S	P	O	U	T	E	R	Voluble speaker, Whale that spouts.
S	P	R	A	I	N	G	Decorate with bright stripes.
S	P	R	A	Y	E	D	Scattered, Sprinkled, Spumed, Spread about.
S	P	R	A	Y	E	Y	Branching out like sprays, Twiggy.
S	P	R	E	A	G	H	Foray, Raid, Plunder, Pillage.
S	P	R	I	G	G	Y	Having sprigs or small branches.
S	P	R	I	G	H	T	Sprite, Ghost, Fairy, Elf, Phantom, Goblin, Pixie.
S	P	R	I	N	G	E	Snare, Trap, Supple, Agile.
S	P	R	I	N	G	Y	Spongy, Lively, Resilient, Elastic, Flexible.
S	P	R	I	N	T	S	Dashes, Runs, Races, Scampers, Scoots, Scurries.
S	P	R	U	C	E	D	Smartened, Trimmed, Groomed, Prinked, Slicked, Dressed up.
S	P	R	Y	E	S	T	Liveliest, Most agile, Most active, Most nimble, Most sprightly.
S	P	U	L	Z	I	E	Plunder, Loot, Booty.
S	P	U	M	I	N	G	Frothing, Foaming, Lathering.
S	P	U	M	O	I	D	Relating to the upper jaw where teeth are positioned.
S	P	U	N	H	A	Y	Twisted hay.
S	P	U	R	D	O	G	Dogfish.
S	P	U	R	I	A	E	Feathers of the bastard wing of a bird.
S	P	U	R	N	E	D	Depised, Scorned, Declined, Rejected, Repudiated, Dismissed, Refused, Disdained.
S	P	U	R	N	E	R	One that spurns.
S	P	U	R	R	E	D	Urged, Stimulated, Incited, Urged, Goaded, Prodded, Prompted, Propelled.
S	P	U	R	T	E	D	Spouted, Gushed, Sprouted, Squirted, Ejected, Hastened, Rushed.
S	P	U	R	T	L	E	Implement similar to a spatula for stirring food.
S	P	U	T	T	E	R	Splutter, Spit, Ejaculate, Eject, Bluster, Heckle, Hector, Rant.
S	Q	U	A	B	B	Y	Squab, Dumpy, Plump, Broad, Thick, Tubby.
S	Q	U	A	C	C	O	Small crested heron.
S	Q	U	A	L	I	D	Filthy, Neglected, Dirty, Contemptible, Sordid, Crude, Slovenly, Unkempt.
S	Q	U	A	L	L	Y	Gusty, Stormy.
S	Q	U	A	L	O	R	Corruption, Foul, Crassness, Degradation, Filth, Dirt.
S	Q	U	A	L	U	S	Genus of sharks.
S	Q	U	A	R	E	D	Multiplied by itself, Adjusted, Regulated, Shaped, Formed exact right angle.
S	Q	U	A	S	H	Y	Boggy, Very soft, Pulpy, Mushy, Spongy, Squelchy, Yielding, Pappy.
S	Q	U	A	T	T	Y	Dumpy, Thickset.
S	Q	U	A	W	K	Y	Harsh, Discordant, Raucous.
S	Q	U	E	A	K	Y	Emitting squeaks.
S	Q	U	E	A	M	Y	Squeamish, Queasy, Nauseated, Distant, Cold, Prudish, Shocked, Fastidious.
S	Q	U	E	E	Z	E	Compress, Press, Crush, Pinch, Nip, Embrace, Clasp, Extort.
S	Q	U	E	E	Z	Y	Cramped, Confined, Incommodious.
S	Q	U	E	L	C	H	Blow, Buffet, Thud, Suppress, Muffle, Repress, Shush, Strangle.
S	Q	U	I	D	G	Y	Clammy, Damp.

1	2	3	4	5	6	7	Definition
S	Q	U	I	F	F	Y	Intoxicated, Drunk, Tipsy, Boozed.
S	Q	U	I	N	C	H	Support in masonry, Contort the face, Flinch, Squint, Squeeze.
S	Q	U	I	N	N	Y	Squinty.
S	Q	U	I	R	E	D	Accompanied, Escorted, Attended, Acted as a squire.
S	Q	U	I	R	M	Y	Wriggly, Fidgety.
S	Q	U	I	S	H	Y	Soft, Yielding, Damp, Clammily viscous.
S	Q	U	I	T	C	H	Couch grass.
S	R	A	D	D	H	A	Hindu ceremony performed for departed ancestors.
S	T	A	B	B	E	D	Wounded with a dagger, Pierced, Punctured, Driven, Pricked, Jabbed, Stuck, Plunged.
S	T	A	B	B	E	R	Awl, Marlinspike.
S	T	A	B	I	L	E	Stationary, Steady, Abstract sculpture.
S	T	A	B	L	E	D	Housed horses.
S	T	A	B	L	E	R	One that keeps a stable.
S	T	A	B	L	E	S	Buildings where domestic animals are housed.
S	T	A	C	H	Y	S	Genus of herbs, Hedge nettle.
S	T	A	C	K	E	D	Heaped, Loaded, Piled, Assigned planes waiting to land, Curvaceous, Rounded, Well-developed.
S	T	A	C	K	E	R	One who stacks goods for transportation.
S	T	A	D	D	L	E	Lower part of a stack, Supporting frame.
S	T	A	D	I	U	M	An arena, Running track, Gymnasium, Coliseum.
S	T	A	F	F	E	D	Provided necessary workers.
S	T	A	G	E	R	Y	Stagecraft.
S	T	A	G	G	E	R	Sway, Tremble, Vibrate, Totter, Perplex, Reel, Lurch, Wobble, Teeter.
S	T	A	G	I	N	G	Scaffolding, Producing, Structure, Mounting, Assembling of troops.
S	T	A	I	D	L	Y	Soberly, Gravely, Sedately, Seriously, Solemnly, Weighty, Coolly.
S	T	A	I	N	E	D	Discoloured, Soiled, Sullied, Tainted, Spotted, Dyed, Defiled, Corrupted.
S	T	A	I	N	E	R	Worker who applies furniture stain or processes dyes.
S	T	A	I	T	H	E	Coal wharf.
S	T	A	K	I	N	G	Impaling, Transfixing, Wagering, Venturing, Supporting, Stretching, Claiming.
S	T	A	L	E	L	Y	Mustily, Uninterestingly, Fustily, Smelly, Rankly, Stenchy, Tritely.
S	T	A	L	E	S	T	Most stuffy, Most fusty, Most smelly, Most rank, Most trite, Most tired.
S	T	A	L	K	E	D	Stole, Slipped, Pursued, Tracked, Followed, Ambushed, Marched, Investigated.
S	T	A	L	K	E	R	Tracker, Hunter, Investigator.
S	T	A	L	L	E	D	Satiated, Arranged, Assigned, Checked, Stopped, Interrupted, Halted, Arrested.
S	T	A	M	I	N	A	Fundamental parts, Elements, Vigour, Strength, Courage, Perserverance, Tolerance, Durability.
S	T	A	M	M	E	L	Bright red cloth.
S	T	A	M	M	E	R	Stutter, Hammer, Falter, Hesitate, Stumble, Splutter, Jabber, Falter.
S	T	A	M	N	O	S	Ancient Greek wine jar.
S	T	A	M	P	E	D	Pounded, Crushed, Struck, Beat, Extinguished, Eradicated, Impressed, Trampled.
S	T	A	M	P	E	R	Worker who stamps identifying information.
S	T	A	N	D	B	Y	Substitute, Emergency equipment, One to be relied upon.
S	T	A	N	D	E	R	Base, Support.
S	T	A	N	D	I	N	Alternate, Replacement, Surrogate, Assistant, Second.
S	T	A	N	D	U	P	Erect, Upright, Exchanging blows, Enduring stress or strain, Fail to keep an appointment.
S	T	A	N	I	N	E	Aptitude score for aviation students.
S	T	A	N	K	I	E	Gallinule, Marsh hen.
S	T	A	N	N	I	C	Containing tin.
S	T	A	N	N	U	M	Alloy of silver and lead.
S	T	A	P	L	E	D	Sorted, Graded, Connected together.
S	T	A	P	L	E	R	Machine that inserts stapled.
S	T	A	R	C	H	Y	Containing starch, Prudish, Aloof, Crusty, Crotchety.
S	T	A	R	D	O	M	Being a top performer, Body of stars.
S	T	A	R	I	N	G	Looking, Glaring, Gazing, Gaping, Goggling, Gloating, Peering.
S	T	A	R	K	E	N	Stiffen.
S	T	A	R	K	E	R	Nuder, Bleaker, Emptier, Firmer, Stiffer, More vacant.
S	T	A	R	K	L	Y	Completely, Absolutely, Sturdily, Stoutly.
S	T	A	R	L	E	T	Junior actress intended for stardom.
S	T	A	R	L	I	T	By the light of the stars.
S	T	A	R	R	E	D	Adorned with stars, Featured, Performed outstandingly.
S	T	A	R	T	E	D	Darted, Jumped, Recoiled, Began, Commenced, Originated, Flinched, Winced.
S	T	A	R	T	E	R	One that starts a race, Controller, One that starts an operation.
S	T	A	R	T	L	E	Frighten, Alarm, Surprise, Bolt, Jump, Spring, Scare, Terrify.
S	T	A	R	V	E	D	Hungry, Famished, Ravenous, Underfed, Weakened, Emaciated.
S	T	A	S	I	M	A	Choral odes in a Greek tragedy.
S	T	A	T	A	N	T	Heraldic beast seen in profile with all feet on the ground.
S	T	A	T	E	L	Y	Haughty, Courtly, Ceremonious, Unapproachable, Majestic, Grand, Convential, Formal.
S	T	A	T	I	C	E	Genus of coastal herbs, Sea lavender.
S	T	A	T	I	C	S	Dynamics, Study of equilibrium.

1	2	3	4	5	6	7	
S	T	A	T	I	N	G	Settling, Fixing, Reciting, Reporting, Framing, Phrasing, Asserting, Declaring.
S	T	A	T	I	O	N	Place, Location, Point, Position, Situation, Site, Depot, Rank.
S	T	A	T	I	S	M	Concentration of all economic controls in hands of government.
S	T	A	T	I	S	T	Advocating statism.
S	T	A	T	I	V	E	Expressing a bodily or mentality state.
S	T	A	T	O	H	M	Unit of resistance.
S	T	A	T	U	E	D	Adorned with statues.
S	T	A	T	U	R	E	Standing posture, Natural height, Prestige, Quality, Merit, Value, Calibre, Virtue.
S	T	A	T	U	T	E	Constitution, Decree, Edict, Ordinance.
S	T	A	U	N	C	H	Substantial, Watertight, Sound, Steady, True, Faithful.
S	T	A	V	I	N	G	Powerful, Excellent, Extremely, Hurrying, Rushing, Casing of staves.
S	T	A	Y	I	N	G	Pausing, Ceasing, Living, Lodging, Visiting, Delaying, Abstaining, Abiding.
S	T	A	Y	P	U	T	Remain permanently, Firmly fixed or attached.
S	T	E	A	L	E	R	Robber.
S	T	E	A	L	T	H	Furtiveness, Secret, Slyness, Surreptitious, Crafty, Cunning, Wily, Skulk, Slink.
S	T	E	A	M	E	D	Travelled by steam, Vaporized, Condensed, Reeked, Boiled.
S	T	E	A	M	E	R	Double cooking vessel, Steamship.
S	T	E	A	R	I	C	Resembling stearin or tallow.
S	T	E	A	R	I	N	Ester of glycerol and stearic acid, Solid portion of any fat.
S	T	E	E	L	E	D	Made of steel, Edged, tipped or armoured with steel.
S	T	E	E	P	E	D	Soaked, Infused, Macerated, Bathed, Immersed, Moistened, Saturated, Drenched.
S	T	E	E	P	E	N	To make steeper, To increase in incline or height.
S	T	E	E	P	E	R	Loftier, Taller, Higher, More precipitous, More sheer, More abrupt, More arduous.
S	T	E	E	P	L	E	Tall structure rising to a point.
S	T	E	E	P	L	Y	Abruptly, Precipitously, Sharply, Swiftly.
S	T	E	E	R	E	D	Guided, Managed, Controlled, Wended, Directed, Escorted, Piloted, Conducted.
S	T	E	E	R	E	R	Tout, A person who guides gullible persons to a swindler.
S	T	E	E	V	E	D	Pressed together, Stowed, Stuffed, Packed, Stored, Inclined upward.
S	T	E	L	L	A	R	Astral, Derived from the stars, Characteristics of stars, Outstanding, First-rate.
S	T	E	M	L	E	T	Slender young stem.
S	T	E	M	M	E	D	Furnished with a stem.
S	T	E	M	P	L	E	Stempel, Crossbar of wood in a mine shaft.
S	T	E	M	S	O	N	Piece of curved ship's timber.
S	T	E	N	C	H	Y	Stinking, Malodorous, Fetid, Noisome, Putrid, Rancid, Reeking, Smelly.
S	T	E	N	C	I	L	Perforated pattern plate, Printing process.
S	T	E	N	T	E	R	Tenter, Frame for stretching and drying cloth.
S	T	E	N	T	O	N	A mining operation.
S	T	E	N	T	O	R	Protozoan with a trumpet-shaped body, Howler monkey.
S	T	E	P	I	N	S	Women's elastic panties.
S	T	E	P	N	E	Y	Spare-wheel with inflated tyre.
S	T	E	P	P	E	D	Arranged or constructed in steps, Walked, Departed, Performed, Placed, Trod.
S	T	E	P	P	E	R	Horse with high stepping gait.
S	T	E	P	S	O	N	Son of one's husband or wife by a previous marriage.
S	T	E	R	E	I	D	Plant cell.
S	T	E	R	I	L	E	Barren, Impotent, Unfruitful, Infertile, Unproductive, Desolate, Uninspired, Dry.
S	T	E	R	L	E	T	Small sturgeon.
S	T	E	R	N	A	D	Toward the sternum, Breastbone.
S	T	E	R	N	A	L	Involving the sternum.
S	T	E	R	N	E	R	More exacting, More inflexible, More austere, Stouter.
S	T	E	R	N	L	Y	Cruelly, Harshly, Severely, Stoutly.
S	T	E	R	N	U	M	Breastbone.
S	T	E	R	O	I	D	Any of a class of compounds of polycyclic structure.
S	T	E	R	T	O	R	Producing a snoring sound.
S	T	E	T	S	O	N	Broad-brimmed hat, Cowboy hat.
S	T	E	W	A	R	D	Bailiff, Head manager, Waiter on a passenger liner, One who directs catering operations.
S	T	E	W	I	N	G	Boiling, Simmering, In a state of agitation, Sweating.
S	T	E	W	P	A	N	Saucepan with a long handle.
S	T	E	W	P	O	T	Saucepan with two hand grips.
S	T	H	E	N	I	C	Active, Strong, Nervous energy, Excessive vitality.
S	T	I	B	I	A	L	Antimonial, Containing antimony.
S	T	I	B	I	N	E	Colourless poisonous gaseous compound of antimony and hydrogen.
S	T	I	B	I	U	M	Antimony, Used in ancient Egypt as eye-colouring.
S	T	I	C	H	I	C	Arranged or divided by lines, Succession.
S	T	I	C	H	I	D	Red algae.
S	T	I	C	H	O	S	Line, Verse, Stich, Measured part of something written.
S	T	I	C	K	E	R	Slaughterhouse worker, Poultry killer, One that persists or endures, Adhesive label.
S	T	I	C	K	L	E	Hesitate, To feel scruples, Demur, Contend, Agitation, Perplexity.

1	2	3	4	5	6	7	Definition
S	T	I	F	F	E	N	Tauten, Immobilize, Benumb, Restrict, Harden, Formalize, Thicken, Solidify.
S	T	I	F	F	E	R	More rigid, Harder, Tauter, More stark, More tense, More severe.
S	T	I	F	F	L	Y	Rigidly, Firmly, Starkly, Obstinately, Subbornly, Woodenly, Steeply, Extremely.
S	T	I	F	L	E	D	Suffocated, Asphyxiated, Smothered, Muffled, Silenced, Concealed, Suppressed.
S	T	I	L	L	E	D	Allayed, Pacified, Settled, Overcome, Lulled, Soothed, Hushed, Comforted.
S	T	I	L	L	E	R	One that comforts or soothes.
S	T	I	L	T	E	D	Raised on stilts, Limped, Pompous, Lofty, Formal, Stiff, Rhetorical.
S	T	I	L	T	O	N	Two year old blue-veined cheese.
S	T	I	M	U	L	I	Incentives, Goads, Impulses, Motivations, Spurs, Stimulants.
S	T	I	N	G	E	R	Sharp blow or remark, Sharp organ for offence or defense used by insects and animals.
S	T	I	N	K	E	R	An offensive person, Petrel that feeds on carrion, Disgustingly low quality.
S	T	I	N	T	E	D	Stopped, Stunted, Confined, Restricted, Bound, Divided, Limited, Restrained.
S	T	I	N	T	E	R	One that shares frugally.
S	T	I	P	E	N	D	Salary, Living allowance, Scholarship, Wage, Emolument, Fee, Hire, Payment.
S	T	I	P	P	L	E	Design engraved by dots and licks, Speckle, Fleck, Streak.
S	T	I	P	U	L	A	Leaflike or membranous appendages at the base of a leaf.
S	T	I	P	U	L	E	Same as STIPULA.
S	T	I	R	P	E	S	Persons from whom the family is descended, Group of animals, Variety of plants.
S	T	I	R	R	E	D	Agitated, Roused, Incited, Rallied, Exerted, Disturbed, Mixed, Provoked.
S	T	I	R	R	E	R	Workman who stirs substances, Long spoon.
S	T	I	R	R	U	P	Mounting support attached to a saddle, Something that goes under the instep.
S	T	I	V	I	N	G	Crowding, Stifling, Suffocating.
S	T	O	C	K	E	D	Invested, Equipped, Furnished, Supplied, Hoarded, Carried, Stockpiled, Reserved.
S	T	O	I	C	A	L	Impassive, Apathetic, Phlegmatic, Stolid, Aloof, Indifferent, Unconcerned, Spartan.
S	T	O	K	I	N	G	Feeding the fire, Poking the fire, Supplying the fuel, Eating a hearty meal.
S	T	O	L	L	E	N	Sweet yeast bread.
S	T	O	M	A	C	H	Organ linked between gullet and intestine, Nauseate, Disgust, Enrage, Resent.
S	T	O	M	A	T	A	Stoma, Minute openings in cells and spores, Surgical permanent opening in abdominal wall.
S	T	O	M	I	O	N	Midpoint of lips when closed.
S	T	O	M	I	U	M	Thin-walled cells of fern spores.
S	T	O	N	I	E	D	Stupefied, Stunned.
S	T	O	N	I	F	Y	Petrify.
S	T	O	N	I	L	Y	Dumbly, Callously, Heartlessly.
S	T	O	N	I	N	G	Pelting, Hurling stones, Removing fruit stones.
S	T	O	O	G	E	D	Acted as a dupe for a comedian, Patrolled slowly in flight.
S	T	O	O	K	E	D	To arrange in sheaves.
S	T	O	O	K	I	E	Fool.
S	T	O	O	L	I	E	Informer, Betrayer, Stool pigeon, Squealer, Tipster.
S	T	O	O	P	E	D	Leaned, Bent, Bowed, Submitted, Ducked, Dipped, Descended, Deigned.
S	T	O	O	T	E	R	Old Dutch silver coin.
S	T	O	P	G	A	P	Makeshift, Temporary, Filling a gap, Substitute, Resource, Expedient, Refuge, Provisional.
S	T	O	P	I	N	G	Process in mining.
S	T	O	P	P	E	D	Hindered, Obstructed, Choked, Intercepted, Pushed, Restrained, Baffled, Ceased.
S	T	O	P	P	E	R	Check, Baseball pitcher, Plug.
S	T	O	P	P	L	E	Same as STOPPER.
S	T	O	R	A	G	E	Space for storing, Amount stored, Fee for caretaking furniture, Reversal of chemical reactions.
S	T	O	R	I	E	D	Illustrations of a story, Structure above ground floor.
S	T	O	R	I	E	S	Narratives of important events, Anecdotes, Traditions, Legends, Romances, Lies.
S	T	O	R	I	N	G	Providing, Supplying, Filling, Stowing, Hoarding, Stocking, Reserving, Accumulating.
S	T	O	R	M	E	D	Raged, Raved, Assaulted, Assailed, Attacked violently.
S	T	O	R	M	E	R	Blusterer.
S	T	O	T	T	E	D	Bounced, Jumped, Rebounded.
S	T	O	T	T	E	R	Stumble, Stagger.
S	T	O	U	T	E	R	Braver, Fiercer, Heavier, Fatter, Weightier, Bolder, More portly, Stronger.
S	T	O	U	T	L	Y	Resolutely, Stubbornly, Solidly, Strongly, Vigorously, Sturdily, Stalwartly.
S	T	O	V	I	N	G	Drying in an oven, Treating with heat, Smashing, Destroying, Hurrying, Rushing.
S	T	O	W	A	G	E	Stowing, Storage, Packing, Loading.
S	T	O	W	I	N	G	Placing, Lodging, Housing, Confining, Arranging, Packing, Loading, Crowding.
S	T	R	A	I	K	S	Soothing, Caressing, Stroking, Smoothing, Whetting.
S	T	R	A	N	G	E	Foreign, Alien, New, Unfamiliar, Unusual, Extraordinary, Exceptional, Unaccountable.
S	T	R	A	T	A	L	Relating to layers.
S	T	R	A	T	U	M	Layers of rack, Thin sheet of sedimentary rock, Vertical layer of vegetation.
S	T	R	A	T	U	S	Cloud formation.
S	T	R	A	W	E	D	Covered with straw, Provided with straw.
S	T	R	A	Y	E	D	Wandered, Roved, Deviated, Meandered, Erred, Rambled, Roamed, Digressed.
S	T	R	A	Y	E	R	Roamer, Wanderer, Rover.
S	T	R	E	A	K	Y	Variegate, Stripy, Mixed quality, Apprehensive, Variable, Unreliant.

1	2	3	4	5	6	7	
S	T	R	E	A	M	Y	Resembling a stream.
S	T	R	E	T	C	H	Extend, Expand, Pull, Strain, Hang, Reach, Exaggerate, Prolong.
S	T	R	E	T	T	O	Musical direction to play more quickly, Quick and sharp.
S	T	R	E	W	E	D	Scattered, Sow, Broadcast, Dispersed, Circulated, Diffused, Distributed, Sprinkled.
S	T	R	I	A	T	E	Striped, Band, Line.
S	T	R	I	D	O	R	Harsh noise, Creaking, Harsh vibrating sound in the throat.
S	T	R	I	G	E	S	Genus of owls.
S	T	R	I	G	I	L	Ancient Grecian or Roman skin scraper, Comb-like structure on insect's front leg.
S	T	R	I	K	E	R	Batsman, Player in a variety of games, Striking clock, Worker on hides, Blacksmith.
S	T	R	I	N	G	Y	Consisting of strings, Fibrous, Filaments, Sinewy, Wiry, Gluey, Ropy, Viscid.
S	T	R	I	O	L	A	Minute streak, Scratch.
S	T	R	I	P	E	D	Streaked, Striated.
S	T	R	I	P	E	S	Long narrow bands, Braiding.
S	T	R	I	P	I	N	Stripped photographic material.
S	T	R	I	V	E	D	Striven, Contested, Contended, Struggled, Competed, Attempted, Endeavoured, Tried.
S	T	R	I	V	E	R	One that struggles.
S	T	R	O	B	I	C	Having a spinning motion.
S	T	R	O	K	E	D	Caressed, Soothed, Ruffled, Rubbed gently, Smoothed, Whetted, Honed.
S	T	R	O	K	E	R	Soother.
S	T	R	O	P	H	E	Rhythmic turning or system, Stanza, Part of a Greek choral ode.
S	T	R	U	D	E	L	Paper-thin dough rolled up with various fillings.
S	T	U	B	B	E	D	Struck a toe, Lamed a horse, Cut down, Blunted knife, Extinguished.
S	T	U	B	B	L	E	Stalks of cultivated plants left after harvesting, Short beard growth.
S	T	U	C	K	U	P	Conceited, Vainglorious, Arrogant, Pompous, Vain.
S	T	U	D	D	E	D	Adorned with studs, Mark or set with various objects.
S	T	U	D	D	L	E	Prop or stud used in timbering, Muddy water by stirring it.
S	T	U	D	E	N	T	Pupil, Person engaged in study.
S	T	U	D	I	E	D	Knowledgeable, Learned, Thoughtful, Deliberated, Perused, Examined.
S	T	U	F	F	E	D	Stocked, Crammed, Plugged, Crowded, Furnished, Padded, Thrust, Tucked.
S	T	U	F	F	E	R	Worker in skins and hides, Worker who puts articles in envelopes or containers.
S	T	U	M	B	L	E	Err, Trip, Slip, Blunder, Lurch, Stagger, Scruple, Stammer.
S	T	U	M	B	L	Y	Given to stumbling.
S	T	U	M	M	E	L	Bowl and shank of a tobacco pipe.
S	T	U	M	P	E	D	Trimmed, Reduced, Perplexed, Confounded, Stubbed, Nonplussed, Lumped, Stumbled.
S	T	U	M	P	E	R	Wicketkeeper, Poser, Operator of a felting machine.
S	T	U	N	N	E	D	Lost consciousness, Benumbed, Bewildered, Dazed, Perplexed, Confounded, Stupefied.
S	T	U	N	T	E	D	Checked progress, Hindered growth, Arrested development, Performed stunts.
S	T	U	P	E	F	Y	Benumb, Blunt, Dull, Petrify, Rattle, Stun, Astound, Daze.
S	T	U	P	E	N	T	Confused, Bewildered, Dumbfounded.
S	T	U	P	O	S	E	Having tufted or matted fibres.
S	T	U	R	N	U	S	Genus of birds, Starlings.
S	T	U	T	T	E	R	Stammer, Speech with spasmodic repetition, Hesitate.
S	T	Y	G	I	A	N	Hellish, Infernal, Gloomy, Deathly, Inviolable.
S	T	Y	L	A	T	E	Having the form of an insect, Bearing a style or stylet.
S	T	Y	L	I	N	G	Naming, Designating, Calling, Christening, Titling, Improving.
S	T	Y	L	I	S	H	Fashionable, Elegant, Chic, Exclusive, Modish, Dapper, Smart, Dashing.
S	T	Y	L	I	S	T	Eminent writer, Literary critic, Designer, Star sportsman.
S	T	Y	L	I	T	E	Hermit of ancient Syria living on top of a pillar.
S	T	Y	L	I	Z	E	Conform to a style, Convential, Design according to tradition.
S	T	Y	L	O	I	D	Styliform, Something very thin and slender.
S	T	Y	L	O	P	S	Genus of parasitic insects with protuberant eyes, Bees.
S	T	Y	M	I	E	D	Stopped, Blocked, Checked, Thwarted, Hindered, Obstructed, Puzzled.
S	T	Y	P	S	I	S	Application of styptic.
S	T	Y	P	T	I	C	Astringent to check bleeding, Harsh, Acrid, Acid.
S	U	A	S	I	V	E	Persuasive.
S	U	A	V	E	L	Y	Smoothly, Pleasantly, Blandly, Urbane, Worldly, Courtly, Tactfully, Cordially.
S	U	A	V	I	T	Y	Mildness, Pleasantness, Fragrance, Amenity, Affability.
S	U	B	A	C	I	D	Moderately sour, Somewhat biting, Containing less than normal amount of acid.
S	U	B	A	R	I	D	Moderately or slightly arid.
S	U	B	B	A	S	S	16 foot or 32 foot stop used in a pedal organ.
S	U	B	B	I	N	G	Serving as a substitute.
S	U	B	C	O	X	A	Segment of a primitive leg of an insect.
S	U	B	D	E	A	N	Deputy or substitute of dean.
S	U	B	D	U	A	L	Act of subduing.
S	U	B	D	U	C	T	Withdraw, Subtract, Deduct, Remove.
S	U	B	D	U	E	D	Routed, Overwhelmed, Vanquished, Crushed, Curbed, Conquered, Tamed, Controlled.
S	U	B	D	U	E	R	Conqueror.

7 LETTERS

1	2	3	4	5	6	7	Clue
S	U	B	E	D	I	T	Copyread.
S	U	B	E	R	I	N	Complex fatty substance in cork cell walls.
S	U	B	F	U	S	C	Drab, Dingy, Murky, Muddy.
S	U	B	H	E	A	D	Heading or title in a newspaper or magazine.
S	U	B	J	E	C	T	Dependent, Citizen, Thesis, Topic, Subservient, Problem, Reason, Motive.
S	U	B	J	O	I	N	To annex, Appendix, Add something, Combine, Unite.
S	U	B	L	A	T	E	Negate, Deny, Cancel, Eliminate.
S	U	B	L	I	M	E	Elevate, Grand, Lofty, Notable, Haughty, Splendid, Proud, Supreme.
S	U	B	R	E	N	T	To rent or lease from a tenant.
S	U	B	R	O	S	A	Covertly, Privately, Confidentially, Secret, Clandestine, Stealthy, Undercover.
S	U	B	S	I	D	E	Settle, Precipitate, Descend, Ease, Sink, Abate, Slacken, Wane.
S	U	B	S	I	D	Y	Appropriation, Grant, Tax, Gift, Reward, Dole, Monetary aid, Compensation.
S	U	B	S	I	S	T	Exist, Breathe, Live, Persist, Continue, Feed, Maintain, Obtain.
S	U	B	S	I	Z	E	Less than average size.
S	U	B	S	O	I	L	Level of soil under top soil.
S	U	B	S	U	M	E	Include, Comprehend, Contain, Embrace, Encompass, Involve, Classify, Summarize.
S	U	B	T	A	C	K	Sublease under Scottish law.
S	U	B	T	E	E	N	Range of cloting designed for young people up to fourteen years of age.
S	U	B	T	E	N	D	Delimit, Lie opposite, Mark off, Embrace, Enfold.
S	U	B	T	I	L	E	Cunning, Subtle, Elusive, Artful, Wily, Crafty, Perceptive.
S	U	B	T	I	L	L	To experiment on sub-soil.
S	U	B	T	L	E	R	More delicate, More elusive, More intangible, More skilful, More ingenious, Wilier.
S	U	B	T	Y	P	E	Subordinate type.
S	U	B	U	R	B	S	Outlying areas of a town, Periphery, Environs, Residential area within commuting distance.
S	U	B	V	E	R	T	Overthrow, Undermine, Demolish, Alienate, Pervert, Corrupt, Destroy, Sabotage.
S	U	B	V	O	L	A	Interval between the second and fifth fingers.
S	U	C	C	A	D	E	Fruit preserve, Crystallised or candied fruit.
S	U	C	C	E	E	D	Follow, Prevail, Flourish, Achieve, Prosper, Thrive, Inherit, Result.
S	U	C	C	E	S	S	Consequence, Issue, Lineage, Arrival, Accomplishment, Triumph, Victory, Attainment.
S	U	C	C	I	S	A	Genus of European herbs, Blue Scabious.
S	U	C	C	O	R	Y	Chicory.
S	U	C	C	U	B	I	Fiends, Demons, Strumpets, Whores.
S	U	C	C	U	M	B	Yield, Die, Capitulate, Submit, Abandon, Resign, Relinquish, Collapse.
S	U	C	K	I	N	G	Before weaning, Very young, Lapping, Licking, Nursing, Exhausting, Drawing by suction.
S	U	C	K	L	E	D	Nursed, Reared, Fostered, Nourished, Breast-fed, Sucked.
S	U	C	K	L	E	R	Mammal, Animal that suckles its young.
S	U	C	R	O	S	E	Water-soluble crystalline sugar obtained from vegetables, fruits or plants.
S	U	C	T	I	O	N	Sucking, Exerting force by reason of reduced air pressure, Drawing in.
S	U	D	A	N	I	C	Inhabitant or native of Sudan.
S	U	D	E	T	E	N	Borders of Czechoslovakia.
S	U	F	F	E	C	T	Substitute consul in ancient Rome.
S	U	F	F	E	T	E	Chief magistrate of ancient Carthage.
S	U	F	F	I	C	E	Satisfy, Replenish, Furnish, Serve, Suit, Competent, Capable, Satiate.
S	U	F	F	U	S	E	Flush, Fill, Infuse, Permeate, Impregnate, Innoculate, Invest, Imbue.
S	U	G	A	R	E	D	Sweetened, Sugarcoated, Palliated, Extenuated, Whitened.
S	U	G	G	E	S	T	Urge, Tempt, Seduce, Arouse, Evoke, Hint, Intimate, Imply.
S	U	I	C	I	D	E	Self-destruction, Hara-kiri, Self-violence, Self-slaughter.
S	U	I	F	O	R	M	Relating to pigs, peccaries, Hippopotamuses.
S	U	I	M	A	T	E	Chess problem.
S	U	I	T	I	N	G	Agreeing, Pleasing, Adjusting, Accommodating, Fitting, Adapting, Serving, Conforming.
S	U	K	K	O	T	H	Succoth, Jewish religious festival of thanksgiving.
S	U	L	C	A	T	E	Furrowed, Grooved.
S	U	L	F	A	T	E	Combine with sulfuric acid, Sulphate.
S	U	L	F	I	D	E	Salt of hydrogen sulfide.
S	U	L	F	O	N	E	Produce by oxidation.
S	U	L	K	I	E	R	Moodier, Duller, Gloomier.
S	U	L	K	I	L	Y	Moodily, Dully, Sullenly, Gloomily.
S	U	L	K	I	N	G	Sluggish, Inactive, Sullen, Glum, Morose, Surly, Sour, Crabbed.
S	U	L	L	A	G	E	Sewage, Silt, Scum on molten metal.
S	U	L	L	E	N	S	Sulks, Morose, Glum.
S	U	L	L	I	E	D	Stained, Soiled, Tarnished, Besmirched, Shamed, Defiled, Defamed, Tainted.
S	U	L	P	H	U	R	Non-metallic element occurring free, in crystals or with other minerals.
S	U	L	T	A	N	A	Sultan's wife, Pale yellow seedless grape used for wine and dried fruit, Marsh bird.
S	U	M	A	T	R	A	Island in Indonesia.
S	U	M	L	E	S	S	Uncountable, Incalculable, Inestimable.
S	U	M	M	A	R	Y	Recapitulation, Brief, Terse, Compacted, Concise, Immediate, Curt, Laconic.
S	U	M	M	E	R	Y	Relating to summer.

1	2	3	4	5	6	7	
S	U	M	M	I	N	G	Summary, Counting, Calculating, Reaching the expected goal, Attaining, Revising.
S	U	M	M	I	S	T	One who writes a thesis or treatise.
S	U	M	M	O	N	S	Legal writ, Command, Subpoena, Order to appear in court.
S	U	M	P	T	E	R	Pack, Saddlebag, Beast of burden, Mule, Horse, Oxen, Ass.
S	U	N	B	A	C	K	Clothes having a low back for summer wear.
S	U	N	B	A	T	H	Exposure to sunlight or sun lamp.
S	U	N	B	E	A	M	Beam or ray of light of the sun, Bright and merry personality.
S	U	N	B	I	R	D	Genus of birds resembling humming-birds.
S	U	N	B	U	R	N	Burn or discolour by the sun.
S	U	N	D	A	R	I	Sundri, East Indian tree with a bark rich in tannin and used in boat-building.
S	U	N	D	I	A	L	Instrument to show the time of the day by throwing a shadow on the dial.
S	U	N	D	O	W	N	Setting of the sun.
S	U	N	F	I	S	H	Very large genus of American fish, To buck as a horse.
S	U	N	G	L	O	W	Flush in the sky seen before sunrise or after sunset due to solar rays scattered by particles.
S	U	N	L	A	M	P	Electric lamp ultra-violet to ultra-red used for therapy or tanning.
S	U	N	L	E	S	S	Cheerless, Dank.
S	U	N	L	I	K	E	Resembling the sun.
S	U	N	N	I	N	G	Exposing to the rays of the sun, Irradiating, Illuming, Basking in the sun.
S	U	N	N	I	S	M	Religious system of Sunni.
S	U	N	N	I	T	E	Muslim belonging to Sunni branch of Islam.
S	U	N	P	A	I	N	Intermittent neuralgic headache.
S	U	N	R	I	S	E	When the sun is visible on the horizon.
S	U	N	R	O	S	E	Heliathemum, Sunflower.
S	U	N	S	P	O	T	Freckle, Dark spot on the surface of the sun.
S	U	N	W	A	R	D	Toward the sun.
S	U	N	W	I	S	E	Clockwise.
S	U	N	Y	A	T	A	Buddism, Transcendental void.
S	U	P	E	R	E	D	Reinforced.
S	U	P	P	I	N	G	Evening meal, Providing supper.
S	U	P	P	L	E	D	Reduced violence, Made complaisant, Made flexible.
S	U	P	P	O	R	T	Maintain, Sustain, Bolster, Prop, Brace, Advocate, Tolerate, Accompany.
S	U	P	P	O	S	E	Anticipate, Assume, Believe, Think, Presume, Conceive, Imagine, Suspect.
S	U	P	R	E	M	E	Loftiest, Diminant, Outstanding, Vital, Final, Crucial, Incomparable, Maximum.
S	U	R	A	M	I	N	Drug administered in early stage of sleeping sickness.
S	U	R	A	N	A	L	Above the anus.
S	U	R	B	A	S	E	Moulding above base of a wall, Cornice on top of base of podium.
S	U	R	C	O	A	T	Medieval coat or robe often with a fur lining, Sleeveless tunic worn over chain mail.
S	U	R	F	A	C	E	Exterior, Outside, Top, Superficial, Rise, Come-up, Cover-up.
S	U	R	F	E	I	T	Excess, Superfluity, Cloy, Satiate, Gorge, Pall, Surplus, Overabundance.
S	U	R	F	M	A	N	Lifesaver with U.S. Coast Guard.
S	U	R	G	E	N	T	Surging, Swelling in waves.
S	U	R	G	E	O	N	Medical specialist qualified to perform surgical operations.
S	U	R	G	E	R	Y	Office for medical consultations, Operation.
S	U	R	G	I	N	G	Rising and falling in waves, Swelling, Heaving, Electric current flowing in an abnormal fashion.
S	U	R	L	I	E	R	Haughtier, More gloomy, More menacing, More sullen, More threatening, More arrogant.
S	U	R	L	I	L	Y	Rudely, Morosely, Glumly, Dourly, Irritably.
S	U	R	M	I	S	E	Guess, Suppose, Conjecture, Suspicion, Conclusion, Think, Theorize, Consider.
S	U	R	N	A	M	E	Family name, Designate.
S	U	R	P	A	S	S	Exceed, Overstep, Transcent, Outdo, Eclipse, Outstrip, Overshadow, Pass.
S	U	R	P	L	U	S	Excess, Overflow, Plethora, Oversupply, Extra, Spare, Superfluous, Surfeit.
S	U	R	T	O	U	T	Man's fitted coat, Woman's mantle with a hood.
S	U	R	V	I	V	E	Outlive, Outlast, Continue, Endure, Recover, Revive, Persist.
S	U	S	C	E	P	T	Host for a parasitic organism.
S	U	S	P	E	C	T	Distrust, Doubtful, Dubious, Uncertain, Doubt, Assume, Conceive, Problematic.
S	U	S	P	E	N	D	Debar, Withdraw, Discontinue, Exclude, Defer, Interrupt, Shelve, Postpone.
S	U	S	P	I	R	E	Sigh, Breathe, Yearn, Crave, Hanker, Lust, Pine, Thirst.
S	U	S	T	A	I	N	Maintain, Preserve, Support, Brace, Prop, Bear, Suffer, Prolong.
S	U	T	L	E	R	Y	Relating to a shopkeeper attached to an army post.
S	U	T	U	R	A	L	Connective, Relating to a suture or seam.
S	U	T	U	R	E	D	United, Secured or fastened by means of sutures.
S	W	A	B	B	E	D	Cleaned with a mop, Mopped, Applied with a swab, Drew out with a swab.
S	W	A	B	B	E	R	Sailor, Worker on hides, One that cleans screens of an oil well.
S	W	A	B	I	A	N	Native of former German duchy of Swabia.
S	W	A	D	D	L	E	Wrap in bandages, Swathe, Envelop.
S	W	A	G	G	E	D	Swayed, Lurched, Tilted, Drooped, Sagged, Vacillated, Festooned, Adorned.
S	W	A	G	G	E	R	Arrogant, Swank, Strut, Bluster, Brandish, Flourish, Brag, Bully.
S	W	A	G	M	A	N	Vagrant, Vagabond, Tramp, Roadster, Drifter, Hobo.

1	2	3	4	5	6	7	Definition
S	W	A	H	I	L	I	Bantu language of East Africa.
S	W	A	L	I	N	G	Wavering, Swaying.
S	W	A	L	L	E	T	Underground stream.
S	W	A	L	L	O	W	Envelop, Engulf, Devour, Displace, Comprehend, Appropriate, Endure, Eat.
S	W	A	M	P	E	D	Inundated, Submerged, Engulfed, Flooded, Defeated, Ruined, Overwhelmed, Overpowered.
S	W	A	N	K	E	D	Swaggered, Snubbed, Lorded.
S	W	A	N	K	I	E	Active strapping fellow, Inferior beer or cider.
S	W	A	N	P	A	N	Chinese abacus, Suan pan.
S	W	A	P	P	E	D	Exchanged, Bartered, Swooped, Pounced, Substituted, Switched, Traded, Bargained.
S	W	A	R	D	E	D	Turfed.
S	W	A	R	F	E	D	Swooned.
S	W	A	R	M	E	D	Teemed, Abounded, Gathered, Migrated, Assembled, Covered.
S	W	A	R	T	H	Y	Dusky, Dark complexioned.
S	W	A	S	H	E	D	Blustered, Swaggered, Splashed, Sploshed, Bullied.
S	W	A	S	H	E	R	Swashbuckler, Adventurer.
S	W	A	T	H	E	D	Wrapped, Enveloped, Covered, Swaddled, Surrounded.
S	W	A	T	H	E	R	Implement for harvesting crops.
S	W	A	T	T	E	R	Device for killing insects.
S	W	A	Y	I	N	G	Bending, Swinging, Lurching, Wobbling, Weaving, Ruling, Affecting, Influencing.
S	W	E	A	L	E	D	Burned, Guttered, Singed, Scorched.
S	W	E	A	R	E	R	One that takes an oath.
S	W	E	A	T	E	D	Perspired, Drudged, Fermented, Strained, Laboured, Steamed, Exuded, Fleeced.
S	W	E	A	T	E	R	Woollen jacket or jumper, Knitted pullover.
S	W	E	D	I	S	H	Characteristic of Sweden.
S	W	E	E	P	E	R	Device that cleans by sweeping, Minesweeper.
S	W	E	E	T	E	N	Refine, Appease, Mollify, Cleanse, Purify, Relieve, Solace, Lighten.
S	W	E	E	T	E	R	More fragrant, More pleasant, More fair, More delectable, More luscious, More balmy.
S	W	E	E	T	I	E	Candy, Sweet, Sweetheart.
S	W	E	E	T	L	Y	Agreeably, Comfortably, Pleasantly, Graciously, Charmingly, Finely, Greatly, Smoothly.
S	W	E	L	L	E	D	Dilated, Distended, Bulged, Protruded, Expanded, Augmented, Inflated, Bloated.
S	W	E	L	T	E	R	Sweat, Perspire, Burn, Bake, Melt, Roast, Scorch.
S	W	E	L	T	R	Y	Sweltering, Sultry, Humid, Oppressive.
S	W	E	R	V	E	D	Veered, Deviated, Departed, Digressed, Wavered, Strayed, Skewed.
S	W	E	R	V	E	R	One that digresses.
S	W	I	F	T	E	R	More alert, Faster, Readier, More sudden, Speedier, Nimbler, Quicker.
S	W	I	F	T	L	Y	Rapidly, Promptly, Suddenly, Hastily, Speedily, Fleetly, Expeditiously.
S	W	I	G	G	E	D	Guzzled, Imbibed, Soaked, Swilled, Tippled, Gulped, Swayed, Rocked.
S	W	I	G	G	E	R	Guzzler, Toper, Drunkard, Inebriate, Tippler, Sot, Boozer.
S	W	I	M	M	E	R	One that swims.
S	W	I	N	D	L	E	Fraud, Cheat, Deceive, Bilk, Fake, Hoax, Imposture.
S	W	I	N	E	R	Y	Place where swine are kept, Pigsty.
S	W	I	N	G	E	D	Beaten, Scourged, Lashed, Thrashed.
S	W	I	N	G	E	R	One that swings, Whopper.
S	W	I	N	G	L	E	Loose end of a flail.
S	W	I	N	I	S	H	Beastly, Sensual, Glutton, Brutish, Brutal, Bestial, Hoggish.
S	W	I	N	K	E	D	Drudged, Toiled, Slaved, Laboured.
S	W	I	P	I	N	G	Striking, Hitting, Cutting, Snatching, Filching, Stealing.
S	W	I	R	L	E	D	Twisted, Eddied, Convoluted, Turned, Gurgled, Whorled.
S	W	I	S	H	E	D	Agitated, Hissed, Sizzled, Wheezed, Whooshed, Lashed, Flogged.
S	W	I	S	H	E	R	Flogger.
S	W	I	T	H	E	R	Doubt, Waver, Hesitate.
S	W	I	T	Z	E	R	Swiss.
S	W	I	Z	Z	L	E	Cocktail stirrer.
S	W	O	L	L	E	N	Bulging, Puffy, Protuberant, Distended, Rhetorical, Expanded, Bombastic, Pompous.
S	W	O	O	N	E	D	Fainted, Floated, Faded.
S	W	O	O	P	E	D	Brushed, Swept, Descended, Pounced, Alighted, Dropped, Caught, Snatched.
S	W	O	T	T	E	D	Studied constantly.
S	Y	C	O	N	E	S	Genus of primitive sponges.
S	Y	C	O	S	I	S	Inflammatory disease of a bearded face involving pustules, Barber's itch.
S	Y	E	N	I	T	E	Ancient Egyptian granite, Rock of feldspar.
S	Y	L	L	A	B	I	Plural of syllabus.
S	Y	L	P	H	I	D	Young girl of light and graceful carriage.
S	Y	L	V	I	I	D	Genus of birds, Thrushes.
S	Y	L	V	I	T	E	Mineral of potassium chloride.
S	Y	M	B	I	O	N	Organisms living together as host and parasite.
S	Y	M	P	T	O	M	Sign, Trace, Indication, Evidence, Mark, Token.
S	Y	N	A	P	S	E	Nerve junction, Function of communication between neutrons.

1	2	3	4	5	6	7	
S	Y	N	A	P	T	E	Litany of Eastern Orthodox Church.
S	Y	N	A	X	I	S	Congregation in the early Church.
S	Y	N	C	H	R	O	Adapted at synchronization, System of motor, generator and multiple wiring.
S	Y	N	E	R	G	Y	Combined actions or operations.
S	Y	N	E	S	I	S	Grammatical construction according to usage.
S	Y	N	N	E	M	A	Erect bunch of hyphae.
S	Y	N	O	D	A	L	Constitution made in a synod.
S	Y	N	O	N	Y	M	Word having same meaning as another.
S	Y	N	O	V	I	A	Lubricating fluid in a joint.
S	Y	N	T	A	G	M	Systematic collection of writings.
S	Y	N	T	H	O	L	Synthetic motor fuel made by heating water gas under pressure.
S	Y	N	T	O	N	Y	Being in harmony with the surroundings.
S	Y	R	I	N	G	A	Genus of Old World shrubs, Mock orange blossom.
S	Y	R	I	N	G	E	Device to inject into or draw from fluids of the body.
S	Y	S	T	O	L	E	Shortened syllable, Contracted heart.
S	Y	S	T	Y	L	E	Intercolumniation of two diameters.

T

1	2	3	4	5	6	7	
T	A	B	A	N	I	D	Genus of Fly.
T	A	B	A	N	U	S	Genus of horseflies and green-bottle flies.
T	A	B	E	L	L	A	Medicated lozenge or tablet.
T	A	B	E	T	I	C	One affected by syphylis involving bottom of the spinal cord.
T	A	B	I	N	E	T	Silk and worsted fabric with a moiré lustre.
T	A	B	L	E	A	U	Image, Picture, Arrangement, Scene.
T	A	B	L	I	N	G	Providing, Feeding, Placing on agenda.
T	A	B	L	O	I	D	Brief, Synopsis, Small newspaper.
T	A	B	O	O	E	D	Put apart as sancrosant, Prescribed, Shunned, Forbidden, Interdicted, Prohibited.
T	A	B	O	R	E	R	One that plays on a tabor.
T	A	B	O	R	E	T	Small portable stand, Small cabinet.
T	A	B	U	L	A	R	Flat, Laminar, Plateau, Arranged in a table.
T	A	C	I	T	L	Y	Silently, Implicitly, Acquiescently, Wordlessly.
T	A	C	K	I	E	R	More sticky, More adhesive, More clinging, More binding, More tenacious.
T	A	C	K	I	F	Y	Improve the adhesive properties.
T	A	C	K	I	N	G	Attaching, Fastening, Stitching, Connecting, Basting, Hitching, Linking, Changing direction.
T	A	C	K	L	E	D	Seized, Held, Grappled, Obstructed, Undertaken, Dealt with, Approached.
T	A	C	K	R	A	G	Cloth for removing dirt prior to painting.
T	A	C	T	F	U	L	Diplomatic, Sensitive, Fitting, Suave, Adroit, Perceptive, Deft, Considerate.
T	A	C	T	I	C	S	Science of warfare, Method, Study of grammar, Decision-making, Planning with forethought.
T	A	C	T	I	L	E	Tangible, Palpable, Touchable, Tactual, Sense of touch.
T	A	C	T	O	I	D	Virus that appears as spindle-shaped when magnified.
T	A	C	T	U	A	L	Relating to sense or organs of touch, Tactile.
T	A	D	P	O	L	E	Frog or toad embryo.
T	A	D	Z	H	I	K	Tajic, Ancient Iranian people of Caucasian appearance.
T	A	E	N	I	T	E	Mineral of nickel-iron alloy found in meteoric iron.
T	A	F	F	E	T	A	Fine crisp lustrous fabric, Taffety.
T	A	G	A	L	O	G	Language of Philippines.
T	A	G	E	T	E	S	Genus of tropical American herbs, Marigold.
T	A	G	G	I	N	G	Labelling, Identifying, Branding, Appending, Trailing, Saddling, Following, Ticketing.
T	A	G	M	E	M	E	Grammatical forms that function in isolation and cannot be analyzed.
T	A	I	L	E	N	D	Behind, Buttocks, Rump, Hindmost, Conclusion, Rear, End.
T	A	I	L	I	N	G	Following, Shadowing, Watching, Driving.
T	A	I	L	P	I	N	Pin to lift a large stringed instrument off the floor when being played.
T	A	I	L	Z	I	E	Entail.
T	A	I	N	T	E	D	Rotted, Putrified, Corrupted, Defiled, Depraved, Stained, Contaminated, Discredited.
T	A	I	P	I	N	G	Chinese rebel against Manchu dynasty.
T	A	K	E	A	L	L	Destructive fungus disease of cereal grasses.
T	A	K	E	O	F	F	Remove, Release, Discontinue, Reproduce, Portray, Detract, Decrease, Depart.
T	A	K	H	A	A	R	Backveld Boer.
T	A	K	I	N	G	S	Cash payments, Booking office receipts.
T	A	L	A	R	I	A	Mythological winged shoes as Mercury is wearing in pictures.
T	A	L	A	Y	O	T	Prehistoric stone tower of the Balearic islands.
T	A	L	C	O	S	E	Containing talc.
T	A	L	I	P	E	S	Clubfoot.
T	A	L	I	P	O	T	Showy fan palm.
T	A	L	I	S	A	Y	Java almond.

1	2	3	4	5	6	7	
T	A	L	I	T	O	L	Crystalline polyhydroxy alcohol.
T	A	L	K	I	E	S	Motion sound films.
T	A	L	K	I	N	G	Prating, Discoursing, Saying, Uttering, Discussing, Speaking, Conversing, Chattering.
T	A	L	L	A	G	E	Feudal tax or fee.
T	A	L	L	B	O	Y	High chest of drawers, Clothes press.
T	A	L	L	E	S	T	Loftiest, Highest, Longest, Most improbable.
T	A	L	L	I	E	D	Tabulated, Recorded, Totalled, Reckoned, Matched, Agreed, Balanced, Enumerated.
T	A	L	L	I	S	H	Taller than average, Above normal height.
T	A	L	L	I	T	H	Hebrew praying shawl.
T	A	L	L	O	W	Y	Sebaceous, Resembling tallow or its colour.
T	A	L	L	Y	H	O	Hunting cry.
T	A	L	O	N	E	D	Possessing talons or claws.
T	A	L	P	O	I	D	Related to moles.
T	A	L	Q	U	A	L	Just as they come.
T	A	M	A	B	L	E	Capable of being tamed.
T	A	M	A	R	I	N	South American marmoset.
T	A	M	B	O	U	R	Drum, Drum shaped, Embroidery hoops.
T	A	M	M	A	N	Y	Political organisation of New York city.
T	A	M	P	I	N	G	Plugging, Compacting, Packing, Cramming, Stuffing, Concentrating.
T	A	M	P	I	O	N	Plug, Stopper, Cover for muzzle of a gun.
T	A	N	A	G	E	R	Genus of American birds.
T	A	N	A	G	R	A	Genus of small fruit-eating tropical tangers, Small terracotta statuette.
T	A	N	D	A	V	A	Energetic dance of India.
T	A	N	G	E	N	T	Touching at a single point, Erratic, Contiguous, Digression, Irrelevancy.
T	A	N	G	H	I	N	Virulent poison from kernels of the fruit from the ordeal tree of Madagascar.
T	A	N	G	I	N	G	Stinging, Affecting the taste. Having a sharp flavour.
T	A	N	G	L	E	D	Involved, Entrapped, Interwoven, Jumbled, Implicated, Snarled, Complicated, Trapped.
T	A	N	G	R	A	M	Chinese puzzle.
T	A	N	J	O	N	G	Cape, Point, Headland, Promontory.
T	A	N	K	A	G	E	Contents of a tank. Fee for storage in tanks.
T	A	N	K	A	R	D	Beer mug of silver or pewter often with a lid.
T	A	N	K	C	A	R	Railroad car for bulk liquid or gas transport.
T	A	N	K	I	N	G	Flowing into a tank, Treating in a tank.
T	A	N	L	I	N	G	One tanned by the sun.
T	A	N	N	A	G	E	Result of tanning.
T	A	N	N	A	S	E	Enzyme that accelerates the hydrolysis of tannin.
T	A	N	N	A	T	E	Compound of a tannin.
T	A	N	N	E	R	Y	Place where tanning of hides is carried out.
T	A	N	N	I	N	G	Sunbathing, Browning, Severe whipping.
T	A	N	R	I	D	E	Riding track.
T	A	N	S	P	U	D	Tool used for stripping bark from trees.
T	A	N	T	A	R	A	Fanfare, Blare of trumpet or horn.
T	A	N	T	I	V	Y	Headlong dash, Gallop, Impetuous rush.
T	A	N	T	R	U	M	Burst of bad temper, Petulance, Ill humour, Sulks.
T	A	N	Y	A	R	D	Place where tanning vats are housed.
T	A	O	T	I	E	H	Mythical animal's face that appears on ancient Chinese objects of art.
T	A	P	B	O	L	T	Screw bolt.
T	A	P	E	R	E	D	Diminished, Became smaller towards the pinnacle, Dwindled, Reduced, Decreased.
T	A	P	E	R	E	R	One that carries a candle in a religious procession.
T	A	P	E	T	U	M	Layer of membrane of the retina of the eye, Layer of nerve fibres of the brain.
T	A	P	I	O	C	A	Processed Cassava for use as food or in industry.
T	A	P	I	R	U	S	Genus of ungulates, Tapirs.
T	A	P	L	A	S	H	Dregs of a cask, Weak or stale beer.
T	A	P	P	I	N	G	Rapping, Beating, Hitting, Hammering, Striking, Thudding, Thumping, Selecting.
T	A	P	R	O	O	M	Room where alcohol liquors are kept on tap.
T	A	P	R	O	O	T	Prominent central root.
T	A	P	S	T	E	R	Tapsman, Barman.
T	A	R	B	U	S	H	Tarboosh, Red hat resembling a fez.
T	A	R	D	I	E	R	Slower, Later, More sluggish, More dilatory.
T	A	R	D	I	L	Y	Slowly, Late, Slackly, Dilatory, Sluggishly, Reluctantly.
T	A	R	N	I	S	H	Soil, Stain, Taint, Sully, Dissipate, Deteriorate, Diminish, Blemish.
T	A	R	R	I	E	D	Delayed, Hindered, Procrastinated, Dawdled, Stayed, Lingered, Waited, Sojourned.
T	A	R	R	I	N	G	Smearing with tar, Defiling, Staining, Defaming.
T	A	R	S	I	E	R	Nocturnal mammals relating to lemurs.
T	A	R	T	I	N	E	Slice of bread, butter and jam.
T	A	R	T	I	S	H	Somewhat caustic, Sourish.
T	A	R	T	L	E	T	Small tart.

1	2	3	4	5	6	7	
T	A	S	H	L	I	K	Orthodox Jewish rite.
T	A	S	K	I	N	G	Burdening, Charging, Encumbering, Loading, Saddling, Weighing.
T	A	S	T	I	E	R	More palatable, More savoury, More tasteful.
T	A	S	T	I	L	Y	In a tasteful manner.
T	A	S	T	I	N	G	Liking, Appreciating, Enjoying, Relishing, Experiencing, Savouring, Knowing.
T	A	T	A	R	I	C	Manchurian or Mongolian inhabitant of part of U.S.S.R.
T	A	T	O	U	A	Y	A large armadillo.
T	A	T	T	E	R	Y	Ragged, Tattered.
T	A	T	T	I	N	G	Handmade lace, Patting.
T	A	T	T	L	E	D	Chattered, Prated, Gossiped, Rumoured, Reported, Talked.
T	A	T	T	L	E	R	Squealer, Informer, Rumour-monger.
T	A	U	N	T	E	D	Jeered, Mocked, Ridiculed, Upbraided, Provoked, Insulted, Censured, Derided.
T	A	U	N	T	E	R	Reviler, Mocker.
T	A	U	R	I	N	E	Relating to a bull, Bovine, Crystalline compound found in bile of cattle. Taurine.
T	A	U	T	E	S	T	Tightest, Tensest, Most high-strung, Firmest, Trimmest, Most severe, Strictest, Closest.
T	A	X	A	B	L	E	Liable for tax, Capable of being taxed, Subject to taxation.
T	A	X	C	A	R	T	Spring cart that was liable to a small tax in England.
T	A	X	F	R	E	E	Exempt from tax.
T	A	X	I	C	A	B	Commercial passenger-carrying vehicle for which payment is determined by a meter.
T	A	X	I	I	N	G	A plane manoeuvring into position for either take-off or landing.
T	A	X	I	M	A	N	Driver of a taxicab.
T	A	X	L	E	S	S	Untaxed.
T	E	A	C	A	K	E	Cookie.
T	E	A	C	H	E	R	Instructor, Religious instructor, Tutor.
T	E	A	C	O	S	Y	Padded cover to keep a pot of tea hot.
T	E	A	G	O	W	N	Semi-formal gown for afternoon entertaining.
T	E	A	L	E	A	D	Metal alloy used to line tea chests.
T	E	A	M	I	N	G	Yoking, Joining, Conveying, Hauling, Allying.
T	E	A	M	M	A	N	Teamster, Professional truck driver.
T	E	A	R	A	G	E	Allowance for removal of short-fibre in shorn wool.
T	E	A	R	F	U	L	Weeping, Causing tears.
T	E	A	R	G	A	S	Substance that disperses in the atmosphere and irritates the eyes without damaging them.
T	E	A	R	I	N	G	Lacerating, Rending, Dividing, Ripping, Cleaving, Splitting, Destroying, Hurrying.
T	E	A	R	O	S	E	Hybrid rose of range yellowish to pinkish.
T	E	A	R	P	I	T	Sebaceous gland beneath lower eyelid of deer and antelope.
T	E	A	S	H	O	P	Tearoom, Cafe.
T	E	A	S	I	N	G	Ruffling, Goading, Tormenting, Worrying, Pestering, Importuning, Coaxing, Provoking.
T	E	A	T	I	M	E	Usually around four to five o' clock in the afternoon.
T	E	A	T	R	A	Y	Tray used for serving tea.
T	E	A	T	R	E	E	A shrub, the leaves of which act as a substitute for tea.
T	E	C	H	N	I	C	Technical, Technique.
T	E	C	T	R	I	X	Covert, Underhand.
T	E	D	D	I	N	G	Scatter, Spread out to dry.
T	E	D	I	O	U	S	Tiresome, Slow, Dilatory, Dull, Boring.
T	E	E	M	F	U	L	Productive, Fruitful.
T	E	E	M	I	N	G	Conceiving, Abounding, Swarming, Pouring.
T	E	E	N	A	G	E	Relating to young people in the teens.
T	E	G	U	L	A	R	Relating to a tile.
T	E	I	N	I	T	E	Mineral consisting of hydrous sulfate and tellurate of copper.
T	E	K	T	I	T	E	Glassy rounded body of probable meteoritic origin.
T	E	L	A	M	O	N	Masculine figure as a supporting column.
T	E	L	E	O	S	T	Genus of jawed fishes.
T	E	L	E	R	G	Y	Telepathy, Transmission of thought.
T	E	L	E	S	M	E	Talisman.
T	E	L	L	I	N	G	Narrating, Recounting, Informing, Reporting, Saying, Uttering, Impressive, Revealing.
T	E	L	O	M	E	R	Product of a chemical reaction.
T	E	L	P	H	E	R	Aerial cable car.
T	E	L	S	T	A	R	Television satellite.
T	E	M	A	C	H	A	Persian comic.
T	E	M	E	N	O	S	Temple enclosure in ancient Greece.
T	E	M	P	E	A	N	Pertaining to a place of natural beauty.
T	E	M	P	E	R	A	Painting where water-based paint is used.
T	E	M	P	E	S	T	Storm, Agitate, Thunderstorm, Tumult, Uproar, Rout, Rage, Commotion.
T	E	M	P	L	A	R	Barrister or student of law having chambers in Temple, London.
T	E	M	P	L	E	D	Provided with a temple.
T	E	M	P	L	E	T	To mark or lay off a pattern or template.
T	E	M	P	T	E	D	Seduced, Provoked, Incited, Persuaded, Lured, Enticed, Induced, Attracted.

1	2	3	4	5	6	7	
T	E	M	P	T	E	R	Devil.
T	E	N	A	B	L	E	Defensible, Reasonable, Secure, Justifiable, Excusable, Credible, Plausible.
T	E	N	A	N	C	Y	Tenure, Holding of an estate, Temporary possession of property belonging to another.
T	E	N	D	I	N	G	Listening, Awaiting, Cultivating, Fostering, Serving, Minding, Offering, Extending, Inclining.
T	E	N	D	R	I	L	Spirally coiling stem, Twining shoot, Something clinging.
T	E	N	E	R	A	L	Moulting stage of insect when it is soft and immature.
T	E	N	F	O	L	D	Ten times as much.
T	E	N	O	N	E	D	United or held in place by tenon, Cut for insertion in a mortise.
T	E	N	O	N	E	R	One that makes tenon joints.
T	E	N	P	I	N	S	Bowling game.
T	E	N	S	E	L	Y	Tightly, Tautly, Nervy, Edgy, Jittery, Anxiously, Uneasily.
T	E	N	S	E	S	T	Stiffest, Closest, Tautest, Most anxious, Most rigid.
T	E	N	S	I	L	E	Ductile, Pliant, Flexible, Malleable, Tractable, Compliant, Plastic, Adaptable.
T	E	N	S	I	O	N	Stress, Tautness, Pressure, Strain, Unease, Anxiety, Nervousness, Agitation.
T	E	N	S	I	T	Y	Tenseness.
T	E	N	S	I	V	E	Causing tension.
T	E	N	T	B	E	D	Field bed, Camp bed.
T	E	N	T	F	U	L	Tent fully occupied.
T	E	N	T	I	N	G	Living in a tent, Sheltering in a tent.
T	E	N	T	U	R	E	Grasp, Hold.
T	E	N	U	I	T	Y	Meagreness, Poverty, Slenderness, Thinness, Faintness, Feebleness.
T	E	N	U	O	U	S	Flimsy, Insignificant, Rare, Slender, Slim, Weak, Hazy, Vague.
T	E	Q	U	I	L	A	Mexican liquor.
T	E	R	B	I	U	M	Metallic element.
T	E	R	E	B	R	A	Battering ram used by the ancient Romans.
T	E	R	E	F	A	H	Food unfit for Jewish consumption.
T	E	R	G	A	N	T	Heraldic position showing the back.
T	E	R	G	I	T	E	Dorsal plate of an articulate animal.
T	E	R	M	F	E	E	Periodic payment stipulated by law.
T	E	R	M	I	N	G	Expressing, Stating, Phrasing, Calling, Naming, Designating.
T	E	R	M	I	N	E	Determine, Limit.
T	E	R	M	I	N	I	That may come or be brought to an end.
T	E	R	M	I	T	E	Destructive wood-eating insect.
T	E	R	N	A	R	Y	Threefold, Triple, Relating to three.
T	E	R	N	A	T	E	Arranged in threes.
T	E	R	N	E	R	Y	Breeding place of terns.
T	E	R	N	I	O	N	Triad, Trio.
T	E	R	P	E	N	E	Isomeric hydrocarbons found in pine oils, Camphor.
T	E	R	R	A	C	E	Promenade, Gallery, Porch, Balcony, Deck, Portico, Open paved area.
T	E	R	R	A	I	N	Region, Territory, Ground, Contour, Topography, Area.
T	E	R	R	A	N	E	Rock formation.
T	E	R	R	A	Z	O	Mosaic flooring of marble or granite chips set in concrete.
T	E	R	R	E	N	E	Mundane, Earthy, Terrestrial, Earth, Terrain.
T	E	R	R	I	E	R	Small type of dogs often bred for hunting.
T	E	R	R	I	F	Y	Deter, Intimidate, Harrass, Torment, Frighten, Startle, Petrify, Stupefy.
T	E	R	R	I	N	E	Tureen, Casserole in which foods are cooked and served, Vegetable dish for table use.
T	E	R	S	E	L	Y	Briefly, Curtly, Concisely, Laconically, Shortly, Succintly, Precisely, Abruptly.
T	E	R	T	I	A	L	Relating to flight feathers.
T	E	R	T	I	A	N	Occurring every second day.
T	E	S	S	E	R	A	Small tablet used by ancient Romans for identification.
T	E	S	T	A	C	Y	State of being testate.
T	E	S	T	A	T	E	Having made a will, Covered with shell or hard husk.
T	E	S	T	B	A	N	Agreement to restrict nuclear weapons.
T	E	S	T	I	E	R	More irritable, More crotchety, More irascible, More peevish.
T	E	S	T	I	F	Y	Affirm, Prove, Avow, Depose, Swear, Indicate, Attest, Witness.
T	E	S	T	I	L	Y	Peevishly, Petulantly.
T	E	S	T	I	N	G	Examining, Trial, Trying, Validating, Proving, Analyzing, Exploring, Determining.
T	E	S	T	O	O	N	Old Italian silver coin.
T	E	S	T	U	D	O	Genus of the giant tortoises, Arched ceiling, Protective screen of shields.
T	E	T	A	N	A	L	Relating to tetanus.
T	E	T	A	N	I	C	Same as TETANAL.
T	E	T	A	N	U	S	Acute infectious disease introduced through a wound, Lockjaw.
T	E	T	R	A	C	T	Having four rays.
T	E	T	R	O	D	E	Vacuum tube with four electrodes.
T	E	T	R	O	S	E	Class of monosaccharides containing four carbon atoms.
T	E	X	T	I	L	E	Cloth, Fabric, Woven material, Household furnishings.
T	E	X	T	U	A	L	Based on the text of something.

1	2	3	4	5	6	7	Definition
T	E	X	T	U	R	E	Substance, Nature, Character, Essence, Structure, Composition, Fibre, Fabric.
T	H	A	L	I	A	N	Comic, Relating to comedy.
T	H	A	L	L	U	S	Plant bodies of the Thallophytes, Large marine algae and fungi.
T	H	A	L	W	E	G	Contour line following lowest part of valley even under a river, Middle of navigable waterway.
T	H	A	M	E	N	G	Thamin, Deer of the Malay peninsula.
T	H	A	N	A	G	E	Pertaining to a thane, Retainer of a lord in Anglo-Saxon times.
T	H	A	N	K	E	D	Expressed gratitude, Acknowledged courtesy.
T	H	A	P	S	I	A	Small genus of herbs of the Mediterranean, Deadly carrot.
T	H	A	S	I	A	N	Inhabitant of the island of Thasos in the Aegean Sea.
T	H	A	W	I	N	G	Melting, Nullifying, Unbending, Changing, Dissolving, Reversing hostility.
T	H	E	A	T	R	E	Structure for the performing arts, Playhouse, Building for showing motion pictures, Exhibition.
T	H	E	B	A	I	C	Relating to ancient Egyptian city of Thebes.
T	H	E	C	A	T	A	Leptomedusae, Jellyfish.
T	H	E	C	A	T	E	Having a sac, capsule, spore case or sheath, Testate.
T	H	E	C	I	U	M	Hymenium, Spore-bearing layer in fungi.
T	H	E	E	L	I	N	Estrone.
T	H	E	E	L	O	L	Estriol.
T	H	E	L	I	O	N	Central point of the nipple.
T	H	E	O	R	B	O	Obsolete stringed musical instrument.
T	H	E	O	R	E	M	Statement in mathematics that has been proved.
T	H	E	O	R	I	C	Theory, Speculation.
T	H	E	R	A	P	Y	Treatment for the handicapped or maladjusted.
T	H	E	R	E	A	T	At that place or point, On that account.
T	H	E	R	E	B	Y	By that, Beside, Therabouts, Connected with, In consequence.
T	H	E	R	E	I	N	Into that place, In that respect.
T	H	E	R	E	O	F	Thence, Of that, From that cause.
T	H	E	R	E	O	N	On that, On it.
T	H	E	R	E	T	O	To that.
T	H	E	R	I	A	C	Medicinal, Cure-all, Panacea.
T	H	E	R	M	A	E	Public baths in ancient Greece or Rome.
T	H	E	R	M	A	L	Relating to heat, Warm, Hot, Pertaining to hot springs or geysers.
T	H	E	R	M	I	T	Mixture of aluminium powder and powdered iron oxide.
T	H	E	R	M	O	S	Trade name of vacuum flask.
T	H	E	U	R	G	Y	Appeal to a divine being, Miracle.
T	H	I	A	M	I	N	Antineuritic member of the Vitamin B complex.
T	H	I	C	K	E	N	Make stronger, Confirm, Intensify, Broaden, Blur, Obscure, Curdle, Coagulate.
T	H	I	C	K	E	R	More stocky, Broader, Wider, Compacter, Denser, Tighter, More concentrated.
T	H	I	C	K	E	T	Dense growth of shrubbery, Coppice, Tangle.
T	H	I	C	K	L	Y	Broadly, Widely, Densely, Tightly, Massively, Closely, Dully, Dumbly.
T	H	I	E	V	E	D	Stolen, Robbed, Purloined.
T	H	I	G	G	E	D	Begged.
T	H	I	G	G	E	R	Beggar.
T	H	I	L	L	E	R	Horse used to pull a vehicle.
T	H	I	M	B	L	E	Finger protector when sewing, Thimble-shaped cup.
T	H	I	N	K	E	R	One that thinks in a specified way.
T	H	I	N	N	E	D	Diluted, Pruned, Attenuated, Reduced, Diffused, Refined, Edited, Abridged.
T	H	I	N	N	E	R	Volatile liquid to thin paint or lacquer. More thin.
T	H	I	R	S	T	Y	Dry, Parched, Arid, Longing, Very absorbent.
T	H	I	S	T	L	E	Prickly plant.
T	H	I	S	T	L	Y	Prickly, Thorny.
T	H	I	T	H	E	R	There, Yon, Hither, There.
T	H	O	L	I	N	G	Enduring, Bearing.
T	H	O	M	I	S	M	System of Thomas Aquimis' teaching that philosophy and theology have separate spheres.
T	H	O	M	I	S	T	Adherent of Thomism.
T	H	O	R	I	T	E	Rare mineral resembling zircon.
T	H	O	R	I	U	M	Radioactive tetravalent metallic element.
T	H	O	U	G	H	T	Meditated, Reflected, Attended, Regarded, Imagined, Concern, Care, Deliberated.
T	H	O	U	I	N	G	Addressing in second person singular in poetic language.
T	H	R	E	A	D	Y	Consisting of fibres or filaments, Thin, Slight.
T	H	R	E	T	T	Y	A dial, Form of thirty.
T	H	R	I	F	T	Y	Thriving, Provident, Saving, Sparse, Sparing, Frugal, Economical, Prosperous.
T	H	R	I	V	E	D	Succeeded, Waxed, Flourished, Boomed, Developed, Grew, Increased, Prospered.
T	H	R	O	A	T	Y	Guttural, Thick deep sound in the throat.
T	H	R	O	N	E	D	Enthroned, Crowned, Exalted, In power.
T	H	R	O	U	G	H	Clear, Unobstructed, Direct, Straight, Completed, Concluded, Via, Round.
T	H	R	O	W	E	R	One that pitches, Worker who throws clay on a potter's wheel.
T	H	R	U	M	M	Y	Having a shaggy or downy surface.

1	2	3	4	5	6	7	Clue
T	H	U	L	I	T	E	Norwegian mineral of rose-red zoisit used for jewellery.
T	H	U	L	I	U	M	Trivalent metallic element.
T	H	U	L	U	T	H	Arabic and Persian script.
T	H	U	M	B	E	D	Examined, Sorted, Browsed, Glanced, Skimmed, Scanned, Riffled.
T	H	U	M	P	E	D	Pounded, Knocked, Hammered, Thrased, Whipped, Beat heavily, Clonked.
T	H	U	M	P	E	R	Something large or heavy.
T	H	U	N	D	E	R	Storm, Bombastic shouting, Bang, Rumble, Violent, Loud reverberation.
T	H	U	R	I	F	Y	Cense, To perfume by burning incense.
T	H	W	A	I	T	E	Forest land cleared for use as a pasture.
T	H	Y	M	I	N	E	Crystalline pyrimidine base obtained from fish sperm.
T	H	Y	M	O	M	A	Tumour of the thymus.
T	H	Y	R	I	T	E	Electrical resistance material.
T	H	Y	R	O	I	D	Cartilage of the larynx.
T	H	Y	R	S	U	S	Staff decorated with vine or ivy leaves and berries carried at Bacchalanian revels.
T	H	Y	S	E	L	F	Respectively of yourself and used in poetic language.
T	I	B	E	T	A	N	Native of Tibet.
T	I	C	K	I	N	G	Making a regular muted noise, Operating or functioning, Marking with a tick, Checking.
T	I	C	K	L	E	D	Had a tingling sensation, Excited surface nerves, Stimulated, Annoyed, Provoked, Amused.
T	I	C	K	L	E	R	Record book kept to refresh the memory.
T	I	D	D	L	E	R	Small fish, Stickleback, Small child.
T	I	D	E	R	I	P	Swift tidal current.
T	I	D	E	W	A	Y	Rush of tidal water through a channel. Onrush.
T	I	D	I	E	S	T	Neatest, Fairest, Sprucest, Trimmest, Sleekest, Most Orderly.
T	I	D	I	N	G	S	Messages, News, Advice, Information, Intelligence.
T	I	E	B	A	C	K	Decorative strap to hold back curtains.
T	I	E	B	E	A	M	Beam used as rafter support.
T	I	E	R	C	E	L	Male of hawk and falcon family.
T	I	E	R	C	E	T	Tercet, Three-line stanza, Measure in an Italian sonnet.
T	I	F	F	A	N	Y	Thin transparent fabric, Delicate, Filmy, Fragile, Gossamer, Sheer, Gauzy.
T	I	G	E	L	L	A	Short stem.
T	I	G	H	T	E	N	Make tighter, Become tense, Improve, Become complete, Become more adequate.
T	I	G	H	T	E	R	Firmer, Tauter, Closer, Rougher, Stingier, Drunker, More dense, More trying.
T	I	G	H	T	L	Y	Hard, Fast, Firmly, Fixedly, Solidly, Steadfastly, Stingily, Securely.
T	I	G	R	E	S	S	Female tiger.
T	I	G	R	I	N	E	Resembling a tiger.
T	I	G	R	O	I	D	Resembling the markings of a tiger.
T	I	L	B	U	R	Y	Light two-wheeled carriage.
T	I	L	E	O	R	E	Earthy cuprite sometimes mixed with iron oxide.
T	I	L	E	R	E	D	Reddish brown.
T	I	L	L	A	G	E	Cultivated area.
T	I	L	L	I	N	G	Cultivating, Ploughing, Harrowing, Preparing, Researching, Improving by study.
T	I	L	L	I	T	E	Rock of clay subsoil.
T	I	L	S	E	E	D	Sesame seed.
T	I	L	T	I	N	G	Inclining, Slanting, Tipping, Leaning, Listing, Pitching, Rushing, Bursting.
T	I	M	A	L	I	A	Genus of birds.
T	I	M	B	A	L	E	Pastry shell fried with a timbale iron and filled with sweet or savoury mixture.
T	I	M	B	R	E	L	Small hand drum or tambourine.
T	I	M	E	F	U	L	Seasonable, Timely.
T	I	M	E	L	A	G	Interval of time between two related items, as cause and effect.
T	I	M	I	D	L	Y	Shyly, Coyly, Modestly, Gently, Mildly, Nervously, Cowardly, Uncertainly.
T	I	M	O	T	H	Y	European grass grown in U.S.A. and Europe for hay.
T	I	M	P	A	N	I	Set of two or three kettle drums played by one performer.
T	I	N	A	M	O	U	Genus of game birds, Pheasant, Quail, Grouse, Turkey.
T	I	N	C	H	E	L	Ring of hunters driving deer.
T	I	N	D	A	L	O	Timber tree of the Phillipines.
T	I	N	D	E	R	Y	Highly inflammable, Inflammatory writings.
T	I	N	E	I	N	A	Group of small moths.
T	I	N	E	O	I	D	Group of clothes moths, carpet moths.
T	I	N	E	O	L	A	Same as TINEOID.
T	I	N	F	I	S	H	Torpedo.
T	I	N	F	O	I	L	Thin aluminium sheeting, Silver paper.
T	I	N	G	I	N	G	Chinking, Tinkling, Jingling.
T	I	N	G	L	E	D	Prickled, Tickled, Stimulated, Stirred.
T	I	N	I	E	S	T	Smallest, Most tiny, Most minute.
T	I	N	K	L	E	D	Jingled, Chattered, Tingled, Jangled, Clinked, Chattered, Rattled.
T	I	N	K	L	E	R	Tinker, Roving man who repairs kitchen utensils, Gypsy, Bungler.
T	I	N	N	I	N	G	Plating with tin, Preserving in tin cans, Lining of tin.

1	2	3	4	5	6	7	
T	I	N	T	A	C	K	Small tack coated with tin.
T	I	N	T	I	N	G	Colouring of photo prints, To add a slight tinge of colour.
T	I	N	T	Y	P	E	Ferro-type, Positive photograph, Making a glossy surface.
T	I	N	W	A	R	E	Utensils made of tinplate.
T	I	P	C	A	R	T	Cart that can be tipped to empty the contents.
T	I	P	H	I	I	D	Wasp.
T	I	P	P	I	N	G	Attaching a point, Removing the points, Leaning, Slanting, Toppling, Topping.
T	I	P	P	L	E	D	Drunk, Squandered, Guzzled, Imbibed, Swilled, Soaked.
T	I	P	P	L	E	R	Boozer, Pigeon, Tumbler.
T	I	P	S	I	F	Y	Intoxicate.
T	I	P	S	I	L	Y	Unsteadily, Drunkenly.
T	I	P	S	T	E	R	Informer, Racing tout, Betrayer.
T	I	P	T	O	E	D	Crept, Sneaked, Stole, Silent, Stealthy.
T	I	Q	U	E	U	R	One subject to a tic, Twitching of muscles.
T	I	R	A	S	S	E	Pedal coupler in an organ.
T	I	R	E	D	L	Y	Wearily.
T	I	R	L	I	N	G	Rattling, Twirling.
T	I	R	R	I	N	G	Undressing, Stripping.
T	I	S	S	U	E	D	Woven into tissue, Embroidered by weaving.
T	I	T	A	N	I	A	Titanium dioxide used as a pigment.
T	I	T	A	N	I	C	Colossal, Gigantic, Huge, Enormous, Gargantuan, Mighty, Monstrous, Tremendous.
T	I	T	H	I	N	G	Giving tenth part of income to the church, Paying taxes, Decimating.
T	I	T	I	L	L	A	Stimulating love play on male genitilia.
T	I	T	L	A	R	K	Pipit.
T	I	T	L	I	N	G	Terming, Styling, Endowing with a title, Providing a title for a book.
T	I	T	M	I	C	E	Small insect-eating birds, Blue tits.
T	I	T	O	I	S	M	Policies of Tito, one time Premier of Yugoslavia.
T	I	T	R	A	T	E	Standardize, Analyze.
T	I	T	T	I	N	G	Jerking, Tugging, Switching.
T	I	T	T	U	P	Y	Rickety, Shaky, Unsteady.
T	I	T	U	L	A	R	Nominal, Existing in name only, Formed, Having limited powers.
T	I	Z	Z	I	C	K	Phthisic, Suffering from tuberculosis.
T	O	A	D	I	E	D	Fawned, Ingratiating deference, Unctuously cringed for favours.
T	O	A	D	I	E	S	Sycophants, Footlickers, Yes-men.
T	O	A	D	I	S	H	Suggestive of toads.
T	O	A	S	T	E	D	Crisped, Browned, Heated, Warmed.
T	O	A	S	T	E	R	Device for toasting bread.
T	O	B	A	C	C	O	Genus of plant Nicotiana cultivated for its leaves that are processed for smoking or chewing.
T	O	B	Y	M	A	N	Highwayman.
T	O	C	C	A	T	A	Musical composition for pipe organ to be played in rapid trills.
T	O	D	D	L	E	D	Tottered, Sauntered, Progressed slowly.
T	O	D	D	L	E	R	Young child learning to walk.
T	O	E	H	O	L	D	Support for feet when climbing, Progress by influence.
T	O	E	N	A	I	L	Nail on toe of foot.
T	O	F	T	M	A	N	Owner of a small holding.
T	O	G	A	T	E	D	Wearing a toga, Dignified, Stately.
T	O	G	G	E	R	Y	Ceremonial uniform, Official clothing.
T	O	G	G	L	E	D	Fastened with a toggle, a wooden peg.
T	O	I	L	F	U	L	Laborious, Arduous, Tedious, Toilsome, Difficult, Strenuous, Uphill, Hard.
T	O	I	L	I	N	G	Labouring, Driving, Straining, Striving, Drudging, Plodding, Slogging, Working.
T	O	K	E	N	E	D	Signified, Symbolized, Indicated, Pledged, Secured.
T	O	L	L	A	G	E	Payment of toll.
T	O	L	L	B	A	R	Gate used to control traffic at a tollhouse.
T	O	L	L	I	N	G	Sounding, Pealing, Chiming.
T	O	L	L	M	A	N	Collector of tolls at gate.
T	O	L	U	E	N	E	Liquid aromatic hydrocarbon used in aviation fuel.
T	O	M	B	O	L	A	Game of chance, Bingo.
T	O	M	F	O	O	L	Buffoon, Blockhead, Dolt, Fool.
T	O	M	O	S	I	S	Disease of cotton plant.
T	O	M	P	I	O	N	Tampion, Plug, Stopper.
T	O	M	T	A	T	E	Genus of grunt fishes.
T	O	N	E	M	I	C	Dealing with intonations, Tone languages.
T	O	N	E	T	T	E	Simple end-blown flute.
T	O	N	G	U	E	D	Scolded, Abused, Talked, Chattered, Joined by tongue and groove.
T	O	N	I	C	A	L	Relating to a tonic.
T	O	N	I	G	H	T	On this present night.
T	O	N	N	A	G	E	Duty or levy based on cargo capacity of a ship.

1	2	3	4	5	6	7	
T	O	N	N	E	A	U	Carriage, Rear seating of a limousine.
T	O	N	S	I	L	E	Pertaining to clipping of hair.
T	O	N	S	U	R	E	Shaving of head according to religious rites.
T	O	N	T	I	N	E	Financial arrangement for a select group.
T	O	O	L	B	A	R	Frame at rear of tractor for attaching various implements.
T	O	O	L	B	O	X	Box or chest to hold tools.
T	O	O	L	I	N	G	Driving, Conveying, Lettering or ornamenting a book, Proceeding Equipping a factory.
T	O	O	T	H	E	D	Indented, Jagged, Bit, Roughened, Geared, Meshed.
T	O	O	T	I	N	G	Peeping, Gazing, Spying, Hooting, Advertising, Broadcasting.
T	O	O	T	L	E	D	Tooted, Continuously, Wrote nonsense, Twaddled, Dawdled, Meandered.
T	O	P	A	R	C	H	Minor ruler or prince.
T	O	P	B	O	O	T	High boot worn by riders and liveried footmen.
T	O	P	C	O	A	T	Overcoat.
T	O	P	D	O	W	N	Closely organized controlled and directed planned society.
T	O	P	F	U	L	L	Brimful.
T	O	P	H	O	L	E	Excellent, First-class, Capital, Prime, Superior.
T	O	P	I	A	R	Y	Art of training, cutting and shaping shrubs into ornamental shapes.
T	O	P	I	C	A	L	Of local or temporary interest, Particular. Presently in the news.
T	O	P	K	N	O	T	Ornament forming a head-dress, Tuft of hair, Small European flounder fish.
T	O	P	L	E	S	S	Without a top, Supreme, Exposing top of body.
T	O	P	M	A	S	T	Special mast.
T	O	P	M	O	S	T	Uppermost, Highest of all.
T	O	P	O	N	Y	M	Place name.
T	O	P	P	I	N	G	Pruning the top, Stripping, Skimming, Tipping, Excelling, Surpassing, Dominating.
T	O	P	P	L	E	D	Tumbled, Tottered, Overturned, Upset, Overthrew, Plunged, Slumped.
T	O	P	S	A	I	L	Special sail.
T	O	P	S	I	D	E	Top of ship, Highest level of authority.
T	O	P	S	M	A	N	Hangman.
T	O	P	S	O	I	L	Surface soil, The most fertile.
T	O	R	C	H	E	D	Set fire to, Burned, Seared, Wiped, Plastered.
T	O	R	C	H	E	R	One that points slate roofs.
T	O	R	C	H	O	N	Coarse lace used for edgings and trimmings.
T	O	R	E	N	I	A	Genus of tropical Asian and African herbs.
T	O	R	G	O	C	H	Saibling, Trout.
T	O	R	M	E	N	T	Torture, Agony, Plague, Afflict, Distress, Disturb, Harass, Trouble.
T	O	R	N	A	D	E	Envoy of an Italian canzone.
T	O	R	N	A	D	O	Whirlwind, Squall, Cyclone, Hurricane, Tempest, Dynamo, Spate, Rush.
T	O	R	N	O	T	E	Sponge spicule having both ends pointed.
T	O	R	P	E	D	O	Weapon to destroy ships, Explosive enclosed in a container, Railway detonating cartridge.
T	O	R	P	I	F	Y	Daze, Benumb, Stupefy.
T	O	R	R	E	F	Y	Parch, Scorch, Roast, Dehydrate.
T	O	R	R	E	N	T	Violent stream, Rush, Outpouring, Flood, Deluge, Overflow, Spate, Inundation.
T	O	R	R	E	Y	A	Genus of Asiatic and N. American tree, California nutmeg.
T	O	R	S	A	D	E	Wreath of twisted ribbon as a hat ornament.
T	O	R	S	A	L	O	Botfly that attacks mammals including man.
T	O	R	S	I	O	N	Turning, Twisting, Stress.
T	O	R	T	E	A	U	A roundel depicted in heraldry.
T	O	R	T	I	L	E	Coiled, Twisted, Sinuous.
T	O	R	T	O	N	I	Ice cream with almonds and cherries.
T	O	R	T	R	I	X	Genus of moths.
T	O	R	T	U	R	E	Afflict, Torment, Agonize, Crucify, Excruciate, Rack, Persecute, Mutilate.
T	O	R	U	L	U	S	Antenna socket of an insect.
T	O	R	Y	I	S	M	Conservatism.
T	O	S	S	I	N	G	Heaving, Jettisoning, Agitating, Vibrating, Shunting, Restless, Flinging, Hurling.
T	O	S	S	P	O	T	Drunkard, Toper, Sot.
T	O	S	T	A	D	A	Tortilla deep fried in fat.
T	O	T	A	L	L	Y	Completely, Wholly, Entirely, Altogether, Exactly, Utterly.
T	O	T	E	M	R	Y	Humanising animals as emblems of the family.
T	O	T	T	E	R	Y	Shaky, Unsteady.
T	O	T	T	I	N	G	Summarizing, Totalling, Adding, Costing.
T	O	U	C	H	E	D	Palpated, Contacted, Tactile experience, Aroused, Pushed, Adjoined, Handled, Eccentric.
T	O	U	C	H	E	R	Bowl which touches the jack.
T	O	U	G	H	E	N	Become tough, Harden, Acclimatize, Season, Develop, Strengthen.
T	O	U	G	H	L	Y	Stubbornly, Tenaciously, Stiffly, Militantly, Aggressively, Ruffianly, Strongly, Robustly.
T	O	U	R	A	C	O	Various African birds with a coloured bill.
T	O	U	R	I	N	G	Going, Proceeding, Turning, Journeying, Travelling, Visiting.
T	O	U	R	I	S	M	Business of catering for tourists.

1	2	3	4	5	6	7	
T	O	U	R	I	S	T	One that travels from place to place on vacation and for pleasure.
T	O	U	R	N	E	Y	Croupier in charge of the roulette wheel in a casino.
T	O	U	S	I	N	G	Tussling, Dishevelling, Teasing, Pulling, Tangling.
T	O	U	S	L	E	D	Tumbled, Disordered, Dishevelled.
T	O	U	T	I	N	G	Canvassing, Soliciting, Spying, Tipping, Pestering.
T	O	W	A	R	D	S	Coming soon, Facing, In the direction, About, Approximately, Near.
T	O	W	B	O	A	T	Tugboat, Pushboat.
T	O	W	E	R	E	D	Rose, Overshadowed, Soared, Elevated, Dominated, Overlooked.
T	O	W	I	R	O	N	Harpoon with a line attached.
T	O	W	L	I	N	E	Hawser used in whale-hunting.
T	O	W	N	I	S	H	Characteristic of life and style of town living, Appropriate for town.
T	O	W	P	A	T	H	Path alongside a canal for men and animals involved with towing of barges.
T	O	W	R	O	P	E	Rope or cable used for towing.
T	O	X	E	M	I	A	Blood poisoning.
T	O	X	E	M	I	C	Same as TOXEMIA.
T	O	X	I	C	A	L	Toxic, Poisonous.
T	O	X	O	T	A	E	Public slaves in ancient Athens.
T	O	X	O	T	E	S	Family of percoid fishes.
T	O	Y	W	O	R	T	Shepherd's purse.
T	R	A	B	A	N	T	Armed attendant.
T	R	A	B	U	C	O	Blunderbuss, Spanish cigar.
T	R	A	C	E	R	Y	Decorative openwork.
T	R	A	C	H	E	A	Main tube for air passing to and from the lungs.
T	R	A	C	H	L	E	Dishevel, Bedraggle, Drudge, Bother, Overexert, Overwork.
T	R	A	C	I	N	G	Sketching, Outlining, Delineating, Traversing, Trudging, Investigating, Rambling, Copying.
T	R	A	C	K	E	D	Trailed, Traced, Travelled, Traversed, Walked.
T	R	A	C	K	E	R	One that has the ability to read and follow tracks.
T	R	A	C	T	O	R	Vehicle with caterpillar treads for towing agriculture implements.
T	R	A	D	E	I	N	To receive credit for a used article when purchasing a new one.
T	R	A	D	I	N	G	Engaged in commercial business, Buying and selling.
T	R	A	D	U	C	E	Violate, Misrepresent, Libel, Slander, Malign, Defame, Denigrate, Vilify.
T	R	A	F	F	I	C	Business, Exchange, Cargo, Commerce, Dealings, Patronage, Custom, Trade.
T	R	A	G	E	D	Y	Calamity, Disaster, Misfortune, Catastrophe, Misadventure, Shock, Curse, Woe.
T	R	A	I	L	E	D	Dragged, Plodded, Trudged, Drifted, Hauled, Pulled, Pursued, Followed.
T	R	A	I	L	E	R	Hunter, Creeper, Caravan.
T	R	A	I	N	E	D	Trailed, Dragged, Protracted, Instructed, Drilled, Taught, Associated, Travelled.
T	R	A	I	N	E	E	Apprentice, Learner.
T	R	A	I	N	E	R	One that educates or drills, Tutor.
T	R	A	I	P	S	E	Wander, Walk, Tramp, Drift, Ramble, Rove, Meander, Drag.
T	R	A	I	T	O	R	One that betrays trust, One that commits treason.
T	R	A	J	E	C	T	Act or place of crossing.
T	R	A	M	C	A	R	Passenger vehicle that travels on rails in the roadway.
T	R	A	M	M	E	L	Net for catching birds or fish.
T	R	A	M	P	E	D	Walked with a heavy tread, Trudged, Marched, Footslogged, Plodded, Stamped.
T	R	A	M	P	E	R	Vagrant, Hiker.
T	R	A	M	P	L	E	Tread heavily, Tyranize, Oppress, Crush, Spurn, Squelch, Pound, Override.
T	R	A	M	W	A	Y	Line of rails for a tramcar, and the vehicles.
T	R	A	N	C	E	D	Benumbed, Petrified, Entranced, Dreamlike, Transported.
T	R	A	N	C	H	E	Slice, Section, Portion.
T	R	A	N	E	E	N	Trifle, Something of little or no value.
T	R	A	N	G	A	M	Trinket, Gimcrack.
T	R	A	N	S	I	T	Journey, Passage, Change, Transition, Conveyance, Carrying, Transport, Travel.
T	R	A	N	S	O	M	Crosspiece, Lintel, Fanlight.
T	R	A	N	T	E	R	Pedlar with a horse and cart.
T	R	A	P	E	Z	E	Acrobatic apparatus similar to a swing.
T	R	A	P	P	E	D	Ensnared, Caught, Confined, Engangled, Held, Stopped, Lured, Enticed.
T	R	A	P	P	E	R	One whose business is trapping animals.
T	R	A	S	H	E	D	Restrained, Hindered, Stripped, Trudged, Tramped, Fatigued.
T	R	A	V	A	I	L	Labour, Toil, Drudgery, Lash, Effort, Agony, Torment, Work.
T	R	A	V	E	L	S	Journeys, Tours, Trips, Traffic, Narration of a trip.
T	R	A	V	O	I	S	Primitive sled used by American Indians.
T	R	A	W	L	E	D	Trolled, Caught fish with a dragnet.
T	R	A	W	L	E	R	Craft for trawl fishing.
T	R	E	A	C	L	E	Molasses, Dark syrup, Sentimental trash.
T	R	E	A	C	L	Y	Cloying, Sticky.
T	R	E	A	D	E	R	One that treads automobile tyres, Grape presser.
T	R	E	A	D	L	E	Treddle, Device for working with the foot to operate a machine.

1	2	3	4	5	6	7	
T	R	E	A	S	O	N	Perfidy, Treachery, Disloyalty, Deceit, Duplicity, Faithlessness.
T	R	E	A	T	E	D	Negotiated, Discoursed, Argued, Arranged, Entertained, Bribed, Handled, Dealt, given.
T	R	E	A	T	E	R	Negotiator.
T	R	E	B	L	E	D	Three times as much.
T	R	E	E	I	N	G	Taking refuge in a tree, Cornering, Putting at a disadvantage.
T	R	E	F	O	I	L	Represented by cluster of three.
T	R	E	G	E	R	G	One trillion ergs.
T	R	E	H	A	L	A	Sweet edible substance from the pupal covering of an Asiatic beetle.
T	R	E	K	K	E	D	Migrated by ox-wagon, Plodded, Pulled.
T	R	E	K	K	E	R	One that travels by ox-wagon.
T	R	E	L	L	I	S	Structure of lattice-work.
T	R	E	M	B	L	E	Shiver, Shudder, Quiver, Quake, Shake, Tremor, Vibrate, Oscillate.
T	R	E	M	B	L	Y	Unsteady, Shaky, Tottery, Shivery, Tremulous, Shy, Timid.
T	R	E	M	O	L	O	Tremulous effect in music.
T	R	E	N	A	I	L	Treenail, Wooden peg or pin.
T	R	E	N	D	E	D	Bent, Curved, Shifted, Moved, Inclined, Gravitated.
T	R	E	N	D	L	E	Wooden tub or trough.
T	R	E	N	T	A	L	Thirty Roman Catholic masses for the dead.
T	R	E	P	A	N	G	Wormlike aquatic creatures that are dried and considered a delicacy in China.
T	R	E	S	S	E	D	Braided, Plaited.
T	R	E	S	S	E	L	Trestle, Support, Braced frame.
T	R	E	V	I	S	S	Traverse, Penetrate, Lying across something else.
T	R	I	A	B	L	E	Provable.
T	R	I	A	C	I	D	Able to react with three molecules, Containing three hydrogen atoms.
T	R	I	A	D	I	C	Constituting a triad.
T	R	I	A	E	N	E	Sponge spicule with three divergent rays.
T	R	I	A	R	C	H	Having three xylem strands or groups.
T	R	I	B	U	N	E	Roman official, Military commander.
T	R	I	B	U	T	E	Payment, Tax, Rental, Duty, Tariff, Offering, Gift, Recognition.
T	R	I	C	E	P	S	Great extensor muscle along back of upper arm arising from three heads.
T	R	I	C	I	N	G	Hauling, Lashing, Securing, Raising with a line.
T	R	I	C	K	E	D	Decorated, Deceived, Defrauded, Cheated, Duped, Hoaxed, Hoodwinked, Fooled.
T	R	I	C	K	E	R	Trickster.
T	R	I	C	K	L	E	Flow gently, Drops, Diminish slowly, Ooze, Dribble, Weep, Trill.
T	R	I	C	K	L	Y	Marked by trickling.
T	R	I	C	K	S	Y	Prankish, Uncertain, Evasive, Deceiving, Deceptive, Trying.
T	R	I	C	O	R	N	Cocked hat.
T	R	I	D	E	N	T	Three-pronged spear, Symbol of naval power.
T	R	I	D	I	U	M	Term of three days.
T	R	I	F	L	E	D	Flirted, Played, Loitered, Dallied, Twiddled, Toyed, Fooled, Fiddled.
T	R	I	F	L	E	R	Idler, Shallow frivolous person.
T	R	I	F	O	R	M	Having a triple form.
T	R	I	G	A	M	Y	Having three spouses at the same time.
T	R	I	G	G	E	D	Stuffed, Crammed, Trotted, Run, Wedged, Restrained.
T	R	I	G	G	E	R	Piece connected with a catch, Part of the action of a firearm.
T	R	I	G	L	O	T	Book or edition in three languages.
T	R	I	G	O	N	A	Genus of stingless honeybees.
T	R	I	G	O	N	E	Triangular body part.
T	R	I	G	R	A	M	Figure made by three lines or elements.
T	R	I	L	E	T	E	Trigonous, Genus of spores with triangular apertures.
T	R	I	L	I	T	H	A form of megalithic monument consisting of two upright stones supporting another crosswise.
T	R	I	L	L	E	D	Vibrated, Shaken, Quavered, Warbled.
T	R	I	L	O	B	E	Having three lobes.
T	R	I	L	O	G	Y	Three dramas or musical compositions.
T	R	I	M	E	R	A	Pseudotrimera, Genus of beetles.
T	R	I	M	M	E	D	Decorated, Adorned, Chastised, Thrashed, Defrauded, Cheated, Swindled, Stabilized.
T	R	I	M	M	E	R	Neater, More gay, One that puts the finishing touches to articles in production.
T	R	I	N	A	R	Y	Threefold, Triad.
T	R	I	N	A	T	E	Celebrate three masses in one day.
T	R	I	N	D	L	E	Metal plate for shaping a book for trimming.
T	R	I	N	G	L	E	Narrow straight moulding, Fillet.
T	R	I	N	I	T	Y	Union of three persons or hypostases.
T	R	I	N	K	E	T	Trifle, Ornament, Cheap jewellery.
T	R	I	N	K	L	E	Trickle, Flow by drops.
T	R	I	O	B	O	L	Ancient Greek coin.
T	R	I	O	D	D	A	Genus of grasses.
T	R	I	O	D	O	N	Genus of puffer fish having fused teeth in the lower jaw.

1	2	3	4	5	6	7	Definition
T	R	I	O	L	E	T	Poem or stanza of eight lines.
T	R	I	O	N	A	L	Hypnotic sulfone.
T	R	I	O	N	E	S	Chemical compounds.
T	R	I	P	A	C	K	Combination of three superposed but separable films.
T	R	I	P	A	R	A	Woman who has borne three children.
T	R	I	P	E	R	Y	Place where tripe is prepared and sold.
T	R	I	P	L	E	D	Trebled, Three times as great.
T	R	I	P	L	E	R	Circuit associated with a vacuum tube.
T	R	I	P	L	E	T	Collection of three of a kind.
T	R	I	P	L	E	X	Having three parts, Building containing three apartments.
T	R	I	P	L	U	M	Musical composition for three voices.
T	R	I	P	O	D	Y	Group of three feet.
T	R	I	P	O	L	I	Earth containing deposits of silica.
T	R	I	P	P	E	D	Slipped, Stumbled, Capered, Erred, Skipped, Hopped, Halted, Obstructed.
T	R	I	P	P	E	R	Tourist, One on an excursion.
T	R	I	P	T	O	N	Suspended non-living debris.
T	R	I	R	E	M	E	Ancient galley having three banks of oars.
T	R	I	S	E	C	T	Divide into three equal parts.
T	R	I	S	E	M	E	Syllable of three morae.
T	R	I	S	M	U	S	Lockjaw, Spasm of jaw muscles.
T	R	I	S	U	L	A	Three pointed emblem associated with the god Siva.
T	R	I	T	E	L	Y	Corny, Musty, Ordinarily, Dully, Vapidly, Hackneyed.
T	R	I	T	I	U	M	Radioactive isotope.
T	R	I	T	O	M	A	Genus of showy African herbs, Kniphofia.
T	R	I	T	O	N	E	Musical interval of three whole steps.
T	R	I	U	M	P	H	Exultation, Victory, Success, Prevail, Flourish, Conquer, Gain, Jubilation.
T	R	I	V	I	A	L	Commonplace, Ordinary, Flimsy, Minor, Slight, Petty, Insignificant, Negligible.
T	R	I	V	I	U	M	Three liberal arts of grammar, rhetoric and logic.
T	R	O	C	H	A	L	Resembling a wheel.
T	R	O	C	H	E	E	Long and short or stressed and unstressed syllables.
T	R	O	C	H	U	S	Genus of marine gastropod with beautiful shells.
T	R	O	D	D	E	N	Strolled, Trampled, Trailed, Tracked.
T	R	O	G	G	I	N	Pedlar's wares.
T	R	O	L	A	N	D	Photon unit of light.
T	R	O	L	L	E	D	Bowled, Rocked, Fished, Circuited, Rolled, Spoken rapidly, Trolley, Round.
T	R	O	L	L	E	R	Singer in a roundelay.
T	R	O	L	L	E	Y	Small wheeled cart, Small mine truck, Pushcart.
T	R	O	L	L	O	P	Slattern, Wanton, Slump, Bedraggle, Slouch, Droop, Tramp, Hussy, Prostitute.
T	R	O	M	M	E	L	Mining sieve.
T	R	O	M	P	I	L	Aperture in forge bellows.
T	R	O	N	A	G	E	Medieval duty for compulsory weighing of coarse goods.
T	R	O	O	P	E	D	Assembled, Walked, Associated, Thronged, Stepped, Traipsed.
T	R	O	O	P	E	R	Mounted man, Cavalryman, Paratrooper, Mounted policeman.
T	R	O	P	H	I	C	Nutritional, Tropically.
T	R	O	P	I	C	S	Areas of latitude between Tropic of Capricorn and Tropic of Cancer.
T	R	O	P	I	N	E	Poisonous crystalline heterocyclic amino alcohol.
T	R	O	P	I	S	M	Tendency to turn toward, Innate tendence to react to stimuli.
T	R	O	T	T	E	R	Horse trained for harness racing, Errand boy, Hoof of a pig used as food.
T	R	O	T	T	I	E	Small child, Toddler.
T	R	O	U	B	L	E	Worry, Bother, Mistreat, Check, Disarrange, Uneasiness, Annoyance, Exertion.
T	R	O	U	N	C	E	Thrash, Punish, Flog, Cudgel, Defeat, Indict, Sue, Tramp.
T	R	O	U	P	E	R	Member of a troupe, Actor.
T	R	O	W	I	N	G	Hoping, Expecting, Thinking, Supposing, Belief, Creed, Opinion.
T	R	U	A	N	C	Y	Playing truant.
T	R	U	C	I	A	L	19th Century maritime truce between Britain and some Arab states.
T	R	U	C	K	E	D	Swapped, Bartered, Exchanged, Trafficked.
T	R	U	C	K	E	R	One that barters, Pedlar, Transport driver.
T	R	U	C	K	L	E	Small wheel, Pulley, Roll-a-way bed, Yield, Submit.
T	R	U	D	G	E	D	Walked wearily, Plodded, Tramped.
T	R	U	D	G	E	N	Swimming stroke.
T	R	U	F	F	L	E	Edible European fungi.
T	R	U	M	E	A	U	Central pillar supporting portico of medieval building, Large mirrored overmantel.
T	R	U	M	P	E	D	Outdone, Topped, Defeated.
T	R	U	M	P	E	T	Wind instrument.
T	R	U	N	C	A	L	Relating to the trunk of the body.
T	R	U	N	C	U	S	Trunk.
T	R	U	N	D	L	E	Spin, Convey, Push, Haul, Wheel, Roll, Travel, Lumber.

1	2	3	4	5	6	7	
T	R	U	S	S	E	D	Bundled, Packed, Bound, Tied, Dressed, Supported by a truss, Poultry dressed ready for cooking.
T	R	U	S	T	E	D	Entrusted, Depended, Believed, Credited, Relied, Hoped.
T	R	U	S	T	E	E	Guardian, Custodian, Supervisor, Country supervising trust territory.
T	R	U	S	T	E	R	One that believes, One that creates a trust.
T	R	Y	P	S	I	N	Preparation from the pancreatic juice.
T	R	Y	P	T	I	C	Produced by trypsin.
T	R	Y	S	A	I	L	Fore-and-aft sail.
T	R	Y	S	T	E	D	Met, Negotiated, Visited, Agreed to assignation.
T	R	Y	S	T	E	R	One that is a party to an assignation.
T	S	A	D	D	I	K	Zaddick, A righteous and saintly person.
T	S	A	N	T	S	A	Shrunken head prepared by a Jivaro Indian.
T	S	A	R	I	N	A	Wife of a czar.
T	S	A	T	L	E	E	Raw silk from China.
T	S	Q	U	A	R	E	Ruler with a crosspiece for drawing straight parallel lines and accurate angles.
T	S	U	N	A	M	I	Tidal wave, Great sea wave produced by submarine earth movement.
T	U	A	T	A	R	A	Large reptile of New Zealand.
T	U	B	B	I	N	G	Washing or bathing in a tub, Storing in a tub.
T	U	B	B	I	S	H	Rather tubby or plump, Fleshy.
T	U	B	F	I	S	H	Gurnard.
T	U	B	I	F	E	X	Genus of worms.
T	U	B	S	I	Z	E	Use a tub for sizing articles.
T	U	B	U	L	A	R	Made up of tubes, Fistulous, Tube-shaped.
T	U	C	K	B	O	X	Box of extra treats for boarding school pupils from their homes.
T	U	C	K	I	N	G	Gathering into a fold, Eating, Making snug.
T	U	C	K	O	U	T	Large meal, Spread.
T	U	E	S	D	A	Y	Day of Ares, God of war, Day after Monday.
T	U	F	T	I	N	G	Weaving with tufts.
T	U	G	B	O	A	T	Powerful boat used for towing and pushing.
T	U	G	G	I	N	G	Struggling, Labouring, Contending, Dragging, Hauling, Lugging, Pulling, Towing.
T	U	G	H	R	I	K	Tugrik, Monetary unit of Mongolia.
T	U	I	T	I	O	N	Tutoring, Teaching, Training, Advising, Education, Instruction, Schooling, Tutelage.
T	U	L	A	P	A	I	Fermented corn beverage of the Apache Indians.
T	U	L	C	H	A	N	Stuffed calfskin to induce a cow to give milk.
T	U	M	B	A	K	I	Coarse Middle East tobacco.
T	U	M	B	L	E	D	Fallen, Rolled, Dropped, Keeled, Slumped, Discovered, Learned, Overthrew.
T	U	M	B	L	E	R	Acrobat, Roly-poly, Device for drying washing, Drum for cleaning stones, Pigeon.
T	U	M	B	R	E	L	Farmer's wagon, Vehicle that conveyed French aristocrats to the guillotine during the Revolution.
T	U	M	I	D	L	Y	Bombastically, Pompously, In a swollen manner.
T	U	M	U	L	A	R	Relating to an artificial hillock.
T	U	M	U	L	U	S	Artificial mound.
T	U	N	A	B	L	E	Tuneful, Attuned, Concordant.
T	U	N	A	B	L	Y	Tunefully, Concordantly, Harmoniously.
T	U	N	D	I	S	H	Funnel, Pouring basin.
T	U	N	E	F	U	L	Melodious.
T	U	N	G	O	I	L	Pale yellow pungent drying oil.
T	U	N	I	C	I	N	Substance in marine animals that resembles plant cellulose.
T	U	N	I	C	L	E	Ecclesiastical vestment, Covering membrane, Mantle.
T	U	N	N	A	G	E	Tonnage, Cargo duty imposed on vessels.
T	U	P	P	I	N	G	Breeding appertaining to sheep.
T	U	R	A	C	I	N	Red pigment obtained from the feathers of the touraco.
T	U	R	A	C	O	U	Genus of birds, Touracas.
T	U	R	B	A	R	Y	Peat bog, Relating to domestic hogs and sheep of prehistoric times.
T	U	R	B	I	N	E	Rotary engine.
T	U	R	D	O	I	D	Thrushlike.
T	U	R	F	I	N	G	Covering with turf, Burying, Ejecting, Kicking, Throwing.
T	U	R	F	I	T	E	Turfman, Devotee of horse racing, One who owns and races horses.
T	U	R	G	E	N	T	Swollen.
T	U	R	K	I	S	H	Relating to Turkey.
T	U	R	M	O	I	L	Tumult, Agitation, Commotion, Confusion, Unease, Discord, Unrest, Distress.
T	U	R	N	C	A	P	Chimney cap that turns with the wind.
T	U	R	N	E	R	Y	Fashioning articles on a lathe.
T	U	R	N	I	N	G	Wrenching, Inverting, Unsettling, Ploughing, Curdling, Revolving, Spinning, Twirling.
T	U	R	N	K	E	Y	Jailer, Warden.
T	U	R	N	O	U	T	Strike, Gathering of people, Equipage, Get out, Equipment, Rig, Output, Product.
T	U	R	N	U	P	S	Disturbances, Rows, Disorders. Trouser hem pleats.
T	U	R	P	E	T	H	Root of tropical Asiatic and Australian vine formerly used as a purgative.
T	U	R	T	L	E	R	One that hunts turtles, Turtle dealer.

1	2	3	4	5	6	7	
T	U	S	S	I	V	E	Caused by a cough.
T	U	S	S	L	E	D	Scuffled, Struggled, Wrestled, Grappled, Sparred, Hassled.
T	U	S	S	O	C	K	Small hummock of solid ground in a marsh.
T	U	S	S	O	R	E	Natural silk fabric.
T	U	T	A	N	I	A	Silver-white alloy of tin with other metals used for tableware.
T	U	T	E	L	A	R	Tutelary, Guardian, Protector.
T	U	T	O	R	E	D	Taught, Trained, Instructed, Educated, Coached, Informed, Guided.
T	U	T	W	O	R	K	Piecework, Payment by unit.
T	W	A	D	D	L	E	Gabble, Empty silly talk, Prate, Babble.
T	W	A	I	N	E	D	Divided, Parted.
T	W	A	N	G	E	D	Plucked a stringed instrument, Vibrated, Throbbed, Twitched.
T	W	A	N	G	L	E	Twanging sound.
T	W	A	T	T	L	E	Twaddle, Babble, Prate.
T	W	E	A	K	E	D	Pinched, Jerked, Jogged, Snatched, Twitched.
T	W	E	E	D	L	E	Pipe, Chirp, Entice by music.
T	W	E	E	N	I	E	Betweenmaid.
T	W	E	E	T	E	R	Small loudspeaker reproducing high pitched sounds only.
T	W	E	L	F	T	H	Number twelve in a countable series, Musical interval of an octave and a fifth.
T	W	I	B	I	L	L	Double-headed battle-axe, Reaping hook.
T	W	I	D	D	L	E	Fiddle, Jiggle, Quiver, Twirl, Turn.
T	W	I	G	G	E	D	Switched, Pulled, Twitched, Noticed, Observed, Perceived, Watched, Understood.
T	W	I	G	G	E	N	Covered with wickerwork.
T	W	I	N	G	E	D	Plucked, Twitched, Pricked.
T	W	I	N	I	N	G	Braiding, Weaving, Interlacing, Wrapping, Twisting, Wrenching, Coiling, Squirming.
T	W	I	N	K	L	E	Scintillate, Flash, Glitter, Sparkle, Shine, Flicker, Gleam, Wink.
T	W	I	N	N	E	D	Parted, Divided, Linked, Coupled, Joined, Duplicated, Matched, Paralleled.
T	W	I	N	T	E	R	Sheep and cattle of two years of age.
T	W	I	R	L	E	D	Revolved, Spun, Undulated, Rotated, Twisted, Flourished, Coiled, Pitched.
T	W	I	R	L	E	R	One that flourishes a baton, Whirling toys.
T	W	I	S	T	E	D	Plaited, Wreathed, Entwined, Coiled, Sprained, Perverted, Tortured, Warped.
T	W	I	S	T	E	R	Tornado, Textile machine, Torture machine, Shifty person, Rogue.
T	W	I	S	T	L	E	Wrench, Twist.
T	W	I	T	T	E	D	Ridiculed, Reproached, Taunted, Jeered, Scoffed.
T	W	I	T	T	E	N	A narrow lane.
T	W	I	Z	Z	L	E	Spin, Twirl.
T	W	O	F	O	L	D	Twice as much, Doubled, Dual, Binary, Twice as large.
T	W	O	L	I	N	E	Twice the depth or point size of the type named.
T	W	O	N	E	S	S	Duality.
T	W	O	S	O	M	E	Couple, Duo, Group of two persons or things.
T	W	O	S	T	E	P	Ballroom dance.
T	W	O	T	I	M	E	Betray by having an affair. Double-cross.
T	Y	C	H	I	S	M	Theory based on chance.
T	Y	C	H	I	U	S	Genus of weevils.
T	Y	I	N	G	I	N	Attaching a new yarn.
T	Y	L	A	R	U	S	Pad on the undersurface of a bird's toe.
T	Y	L	O	P	O	D	Mammal, Camel.
T	Y	L	O	S	I	S	Forming a callus.
T	Y	L	O	T	I	C	Relating to tylosis.
T	Y	M	P	A	N	O	Drum, Membrane.
T	Y	M	P	A	N	Y	Resonance on percussion, Bombastic.
T	Y	P	E	B	A	R	Bar on a typewriter that carries printing type.
T	Y	P	H	O	I	D	Communicable disease.
T	Y	P	H	O	O	N	Tropical cyclone.
T	Y	P	H	O	U	S	Resembling typhus.
T	Y	P	I	C	A	L	Emblematic, Prefigurative, Regular, Classic, Exemplary, Ideal, Model, Representative.
T	Y	P	O	N	Y	M	Name based on type.
T	Y	R	A	N	N	Y	Autocracy, Despotism, Dictatorship, Totalitarianism, Fascism, Terrorism, Oppression.
T	Z	A	D	D	I	K	Zaddik.
T	Z	I	G	A	N	E	Gipsy.
T	Z	O	L	K	I	N	Maya sacred year.

U

U	I	N	T	J	I	E	Edible corn that when boiled tastes like chestnut.
U	I	T	S	P	A	N	Outspan, Unhitch.
U	K	U	L	E	L	E	Small Hawaiian guitar.

1	2	3	4	5	6	7	
U	L	E	X	I	N	E	Cytisine from furze seeds.
U	L	E	X	I	T	E	Mineral of hydrous sodium calcium borate.
U	L	N	A	R	I	A	Bones of the forearm.
U	L	T	I	M	U	S	Pertaining to feudal law when property reverted to the sovereign in absence of heirs.
U	L	U	L	A	N	T	Howling, Wailing.
U	L	U	L	A	T	E	Howl, Wail, Cry.
U	M	B	E	L	L	E	Flower cluster.
U	M	B	E	R	E	D	Stained brown, Darkened.
U	M	B	I	L	I	C	Centre point.
U	M	B	O	N	A	L	Having a projection or rounded elevation.
U	M	B	O	N	E	D	Umbonal.
U	M	B	R	A	G	E	Shadow, Shelter, Suspicion, Hint, Displeasure, Offense, Resentment, Annoyance.
U	M	B	R	I	A	N	People of Umbria in ancient Italy.
U	M	B	R	I	N	E	Umbra, Darkness, Shadow, Mediterrean food fish.
U	M	B	R	O	U	S	Shady, Shadowed.
U	M	P	I	R	E	D	Supervised, Arbitrated, Judged, Refered.
U	M	P	T	E	E	N	Indefinitely numerous, Unable to be counted.
U	N	A	C	T	E	D	Not performed.
U	N	A	I	D	E	D	Accomplished without assistance, Single-handed.
U	N	A	I	R	E	D	Not exposed to fresh air, Not expressed.
U	N	A	L	I	S	T	Holder of one benefice.
U	N	A	P	T	L	Y	Unsuitably, Inappropriately, Slowly, Dully. Inaptly.
U	N	A	R	M	E	D	Having no weapon, Lacking a natural means of defence or attack.
U	N	A	S	K	E	D	Uninvited, Not requested. Unbidden.
U	N	A	W	A	R	E	Unconscious, Ignorant, Oblivious, Unfamiliar, Unacquainted, Uninformed, Unwitting.
U	N	B	A	T	E	D	Unabated, Incessantly.
U	N	B	E	G	U	N	Not yet begun.
U	N	B	L	I	N	D	Free from blindness or illusion.
U	N	B	L	O	C	K	To release, Special play of a card game.
U	N	B	L	O	W	N	Sheltered from the wind. Not fly-blown.
U	N	B	O	S	O	M	Disclose, Reveal, Display, Betray, Divulge, Tell, Uncover.
U	N	B	O	U	N	D	Not confined, Loose pages of a book to be bound.
U	N	B	O	W	E	D	Not subdued, Defiant, Not conquered.
U	N	B	R	A	C	E	Weaken, Remove support.
U	N	B	R	A	I	D	Separate the strands, Unravel.
U	N	B	U	I	L	D	Demolish, Raze.
U	N	B	U	I	L	T	Not yet constructed, Area without buildings.
U	N	B	U	R	N	T	In a natural state, Not burned.
U	N	C	A	G	E	D	Released from confinement.
U	N	C	A	N	N	Y	Eerie, Mysterious, Weird, Spooky, Supernatural, Unnatural, Unearthy.
U	N	C	A	S	E	D	Disclosed, Uncovered, Displayed.
U	N	C	H	A	I	N	Release, Set loose.
U	N	C	H	A	R	M	To free from infatuation or attraction.
U	N	C	H	A	R	Y	Not cautious or reserved, Heedless.
U	N	C	H	E	C	K	Not supervised. Undiscipline.
U	N	C	H	O	K	E	To clear of obstruction.
U	N	C	I	N	A	L	Hooklike.
U	N	C	I	N	U	S	Hooked.
U	N	C	I	V	I	L	Barbarous, Savage, Ill-mannered, Impolite, Rude, Disrespectful, Coarse, Impertinent.
U	N	C	L	A	S	P	Open a clasp or lock, Reveal.
U	N	C	L	E	A	N	Wicked, Dirty, Filthy, Impure, Muddled, Immoral, Squalid, Defiled.
U	N	C	L	E	A	R	Indistinct, Obscure, Confuse, Vague, Ambiguous, Unexplicit, Problematic, Unsure.
U	N	C	L	O	A	K	Remove the cover, Reveal, Unmask.
U	N	C	L	O	S	E	Open, Disclose, Reveal.
U	N	C	L	O	U	D	Free from clouds, Clear, Cloudless, Pleasant, Sunny.
U	N	C	O	U	T	H	Outlandish, Rugged, Strange, Bizarre, Curious, Eccentric, Quaint, Erratic.
U	N	C	O	V	E	R	Disclose, Reveal, Expose, Remove, Betray, Divulge, Open, Tell.
U	N	C	R	O	S	S	Change position.
U	N	C	R	O	W	N	Depose, Dethrone.
U	N	C	T	I	O	N	Consecrating, Religious rite, Soothing balm, Ointment, Salve, Unguent.
U	N	D	A	T	E	D	Having no limit, Having no specified time or date.
U	N	D	E	I	F	Y	To degrade from exalted position.
U	N	D	E	R	D	O	Underact, Insufficient cooking, Work below capacity.
U	N	D	E	R	G	O	Endure, Suffer, Sustain, Experience, Tolerate, Yield, Submit, Abide.
U	N	D	O	I	N	G	Destruction, Ruin, Cancellation, Loosing, Unfastening, Downfall, Bane, Unravelling.
U	N	D	R	A	P	E	Uncover, Unveil.
U	N	D	R	A	W	N	Not extended, Not pulled, Not in a drawing, Not tapped.

1	2	3	4	5	6	7	
U	N	D	R	E	S	S	Divest, Strip, Expose, Unmask.
U	N	D	R	I	E	D	Not dried.
U	N	E	A	R	T	H	Exhume, Disinter, Uncover, Discover, Determine, Learn, Exhibit, Expose.
U	N	E	A	T	E	N	Not consumed.
U	N	E	Q	U	A	L	Irregular, Unlike, Variable, Uneven, Partial, Different, Dissimilar, Diverse.
U	N	E	X	A	C	T	Inexact, Indefinite, Indistinct, Indeterminate.
U	N	F	A	D	E	D	Fresh, Clear, Distinct.
U	N	F	A	I	T	H	Disbelief, Opposed to religious faith.
U	N	F	I	L	E	D	Unpolished, Not placed on a file.
U	N	F	I	R	E	D	Not baked, Not exploded, Undischarged, Lacking stimulus, Not aroused, Uninspired.
U	N	F	I	T	L	Y	Unsuitably, Inappropriately.
U	N	F	I	X	E	D	Detached, Free, Undetermined, Unstable, Vague.
U	N	F	L	E	S	H	To deprive of flesh.
U	N	F	O	U	N	D	Remaining unknown, Undiscovered.
U	N	F	R	O	C	K	To divest clergy of ecclesiastical office, Degrade, Depose, Discharge.
U	N	F	U	M	E	D	Not fumigated.
U	N	F	U	S	E	D	Not joined, Not blended by melting.
U	N	G	I	V	E	N	Not given.
U	N	G	L	O	V	E	Removing a glove.
U	N	G	L	U	E	D	Disjoined, Prised apart, Moved by force.
U	N	G	O	D	L	Y	Impious, Irreligious, Sinful, Wicked, Indecent, Outrageous, Profane.
U	N	G	R	A	C	E	Lacking in grace.
U	N	G	U	A	R	D	Leave unprotected.
U	N	G	U	E	N	T	Ointment, Salve, Cerate, Balm, Cream, Unction, Chrism.
U	N	G	U	L	A	R	Nail, Hoof, Claw.
U	N	G	Y	V	E	D	Unfettered, Unshackled.
U	N	H	A	N	D	Y	Incovenient, Unwieldy, Awkward, Incompetent, Inapt, Cumbersome, Inept, Clumsy.
U	N	H	A	P	P	Y	Miserable, Unfortunate, Melancholy, Wretched, Cheerless, Dreary, Misfortune, Hapless.
U	N	H	A	R	D	Y	Delicate, Not robust.
U	N	H	A	S	T	Y	Leisurely, Slow.
U	N	H	E	A	R	D	Not able to be heard.
U	N	H	E	E	D	Y	Heedless, Careless, Rash, Feckless, Uncaring.
U	N	H	I	N	G	E	Disrupt, Disorder, Derange, Sway, Unsettle, Crack, Dismember, Agitate.
U	N	H	I	R	E	D	Not hired.
U	N	H	I	T	C	H	Unfasten.
U	N	H	I	V	E	D	Driven from the hive.
U	N	H	O	P	E	D	Unexpected.
U	N	H	O	R	S	E	Dislodge, Overthrow, Unseat, Pitch, Tumble, Topple, Overturn.
U	N	H	O	U	S	E	Eject from shelter, Deprived of protection.
U	N	H	U	M	A	N	Inhuman.
U	N	I	A	X	A	L	Having one axis, Affecting one axis.
U	N	I	C	I	T	Y	Unique, Oneness, Singleness, Uniquity.
U	N	I	C	O	R	N	Animal depicted with single horn in centre of forehead.
U	N	I	D	E	A	L	Lacking ideals or ideal qualities.
U	N	I	F	I	E	D	Integrated, Consolidated, Concentrated, Compacted, United, Organized, Harmonized
U	N	I	F	I	E	R	One that unites.
U	N	I	F	O	R	M	Steady, Consonant, Alike, Comparable, Corresponding, Parallel, Equable.
U	N	I	O	N	I	D	Freshwater mussel.
U	N	I	O	V	A	L	Monovular.
U	N	I	T	A	G	E	Specification of the amount of a unit, Amount in units.
U	N	I	T	A	R	Y	Monistic, Characterized by unity, System of government as opposed to federal.
U	N	I	T	I	N	G	Connecting, Combining, Conjoining, Co-operating, Joining, Coupling, Marrying, Linking.
U	N	I	T	I	O	N	Junction.
U	N	I	T	I	V	E	Tending to produce union.
U	N	I	T	I	Z	E	To aggregate elements into a whole, Divide and package into units for easier handling.
U	N	J	O	I	N	T	Disjoint, Severed at a joint, Dislocated.
U	N	K	E	M	P	T	Dishevelled, Rough, Slipshod, Slovenly, Messy, Sloppy, Untidy, Uncombed.
U	N	K	N	O	W	N	Strange, Unfamiliar, Incalculable, Inexpressible, Ignorant, Nameless, Uncelebrated.
U	N	L	A	C	E	D	Unrestrained.
U	N	L	A	D	E	D	Unloaded.
U	N	L	A	T	C	H	To open or loose by lifting a latch.
U	N	L	E	A	R	N	Unteach, Forget, Discard acquired knowledge.
U	N	L	E	A	S	H	Free from a leash, Let loose from control.
U	N	L	E	V	E	L	Uneven.
U	N	L	I	M	E	D	Delime.
U	N	L	I	N	E	D	Constructed without a lining, Not traced with lines.
U	N	L	O	O	S	E	Relax a grip, Release, Disengage, Unbind, Undo, Unfasten, Unfix, Unloosen.

1	2	3	4	5	6	7	
U	N	L	O	V	E	D	Not loved.
U	N	L	U	C	K	Y	Ill-omened, Regrettable, Disastrous, Unfortunate, Hapless, Luckless, Dire, Ominous.
U	N	M	A	N	L	Y	Cowardly, Effeminate, Craven, Gutless, Poltroon, Sissy.
U	N	M	A	R	R	Y	Divorce, Annulled.
U	N	M	E	A	N	T	Unintentional.
U	N	M	E	R	G	E	Dissolve a merger.
U	N	M	I	X	E	D	Unadulterated, Pure, Plain, Neat, Absolute, Sheer, Simple, Unalloyed.
U	N	M	O	I	S	T	Not moist.
U	N	M	O	R	A	L	Immoral, Licentious.
U	N	M	O	U	L	D	Remove gelatined food from a mould, Remove sculpture at casting.
U	N	M	O	V	E	D	Calm, Indifferent, Undisturbed, Impassive, Serene, Quiet.
U	N	N	A	M	E	D	Unidentified, Unspecified.
U	N	N	E	R	V	E	Denervate, Unman, Emasculate, Frighten, Intimidate, Undermine, Weaken.
U	N	N	O	B	L	E	Common, Plebian, Ordinary, Not high-born.
U	N	N	O	T	E	D	Unobserved, Disregarded.
U	N	O	F	T	E	N	Seldom.
U	N	O	I	L	E	D	Not lubricated.
U	N	O	W	N	E	D	Unacknowledged, Not owned.
U	N	P	A	G	E	D	Pages being without numbers.
U	N	P	A	V	E	D	Without paving stones, No pavement.
U	N	P	E	R	C	H	Remove from a perch.
U	N	P	L	A	I	T	Undo the plaits.
U	N	P	L	U	M	E	Strip of feathers, Pluck.
U	N	P	R	I	M	E	Not first class.
U	N	Q	U	E	E	N	Divest of the rank of queen.
U	N	Q	U	I	E	T	Agitated, Disturbed, Turbulent, Uneasy.
U	N	Q	U	O	T	E	End a quotation by the insertion of closing quotes.
U	N	R	A	K	E	D	Not tilled.
U	N	R	A	V	E	L	Disentangle, Reverse, Undo, Solve, Resolve, Extricate, Decipher, Untangle.
U	N	R	E	A	D	Y	Unprepared, Unwilling, Slow-witted.
U	N	R	E	E	V	E	Withdraw a ship's rope.
U	N	R	I	V	E	N	Untorn, Unbroken.
U	N	R	I	V	E	T	Detach, Undo, Unloose.
U	N	R	O	B	E	D	Disrobed, Undressed, Stripped.
U	N	R	O	U	G	H	Beardless.
U	N	R	O	Y	A	L	Not royal.
U	N	R	U	L	E	D	Unlined writing paper, Ungoverned.
U	N	S	A	T	E	D	Not satisfied, Insatiable.
U	N	S	C	R	E	W	Draw the screws out, Remove lid by turning.
U	N	S	E	N	S	E	Make insensible.
U	N	S	E	X	E	D	Deprived of sexual power, Impotent. Not branded male or female.
U	N	S	H	E	L	L	Remove the husk.
U	N	S	H	O	R	N	Not clipped, Not reaped.
U	N	S	H	O	W	N	Not on display.
U	N	S	I	G	H	T	Prevent from seeing.
U	N	S	I	Z	E	D	Not fashioned to a set size, Not treated with size.
U	N	S	L	A	T	E	Remove slates from a roof.
U	N	S	L	E	P	T	Not used for sleeping.
U	N	S	L	I	N	G	Detach, Unhitch.
U	N	S	N	A	R	L	Undo, Release, Untangle.
U	N	S	O	B	E	R	Intoxicated, Immoderate, Excessive.
U	N	S	O	L	I	D	Lacking substance.
U	N	S	O	U	N	D	Unhealthy, Diseased, Stale, Rotten, False, Inaccurate, Dangerous, Insane.
U	N	S	P	E	L	L	Release from a spell, Exorcise.
U	N	S	P	E	N	T	Unexpended, Not consumed.
U	N	S	P	I	K	E	Remove a spike.
U	N	S	P	L	I	T	Not split, Not divided.
U	N	S	T	A	C	K	Removed from a pile.
U	N	S	T	A	I	D	Uncontrolled, Unrestrained.
U	N	S	T	A	T	E	Deprive of state dignity or rank.
U	N	S	T	E	E	L	Disarm by gentleness, Make soft or penetrable.
U	N	S	T	I	C	K	Release, Unfasten, Cause to draw apart.
U	N	S	T	U	C	K	Prised apart, State of disorder, Disorganization, Unseated.
U	N	S	T	U	F	F	Remove the stuffing.
U	N	S	W	E	A	R	Retract an oath, Recant sworn statement.
U	N	S	W	E	E	T	Distasteful, Foul, Dry, Unplesant, Disagreeable.
U	N	S	W	E	P	T	Not swept, Unbrushed.

1	2	3	4	5	6	7	
U	N	S	W	O	R	N	Not verified on oath, Not bound by an oath.
U	N	T	A	K	E	N	Not taken.
U	N	T	A	M	E	D	Wild, Savage, Unsubdued, Not humbled, Not submissive.
U	N	T	A	X	E	D	Not subject to taxation. Not weakened.
U	N	T	H	I	N	K	To dismiss a thought, Reverse a thought process.
U	N	T	I	L	E	D	Not supplied with tiles.
U	N	T	I	R	E	D	Not worn out, Capable of action.
U	N	T	O	O	T	H	To remove the teeth.
U	N	T	R	A	C	K	Cause to get going.
U	N	T	R	A	I	N	To undo the training, Reverse the instruction.
U	N	T	R	E	A	D	.Retrace.
U	N	T	R	I	E	D	Not proved by experience.
U	N	T	R	I	P	E	Disembowel.
U	N	T	R	U	L	Y	In an untrue manner.
U	N	T	R	U	S	S	Untie, Unfasten, Undress.
U	N	T	R	U	T	H	Disloyalty, Unfaithfulness, Falsity, Falsehood, Lie, Prevarication.
U	N	T	U	N	E	D	Made discordant.
U	N	T	W	I	N	E	Dissolve, Disentangle, Unclasp, Unwound.
U	N	T	W	I	S	T	Untwine, Frustrate, Free.
U	N	U	R	G	E	D	Voluntarily.
U	N	U	S	U	A	L	Exceptional, Remarkable, Peculiar, Strange, Extraordinary, Rare, Singular, Unique.
U	N	V	A	L	U	E	Negative value.
U	N	V	E	X	E	D	Calm, Serene, Free from disturbance.
U	N	V	I	T	A	L	Inconsequently, Inanimate.
U	N	V	O	C	A	L	Inarticulate, Unmusical.
U	N	V	O	I	C	E	Devoice.
U	N	V	O	W	E	D	Not bound by an oath.
U	N	W	A	T	E	R	Drain.
U	N	W	E	A	R	Y	Unflagging, Unspent.
U	N	W	E	A	V	E	Disentangle, Ravel, Dismantle.
U	N	W	I	P	E	D	Smeary.
U	N	W	I	R	E	D	Not equipped with electrical circuits.
U	N	W	I	T	C	H	Free from a spell, Unbewitch.
U	N	W	I	T	T	Y	Senseless, Silly, Not wise or clever.
U	N	W	I	V	E	D	Wifeless, Being without a wife.
U	N	W	O	O	E	D	Not wooed.
U	N	W	O	R	T	H	Poverty, Lack of merit or value, Unworthiness.
U	N	W	O	U	N	D	Not wound, Released from a coiled state.
U	N	W	O	V	E	N	Not woven.
U	N	W	R	I	T	E	Expunge, Rescind, Obliterate from writing.
U	N	W	R	U	N	G	Unmoved, Not painfully affected.
U	N	Y	O	K	E	D	Unhitched, Unrestrained, Released, Unlinked, Disjoined.
U	N	Z	O	N	E	D	Unrestricted.
U	P	B	L	A	S	T	Force of blast exerting upward.
U	P	B	L	O	W	N	Inflated.
U	P	B	O	U	N	D	Travelling in an up direction.
U	P	B	R	A	I	D	Criticize, Scold, Berate, Lash, Revile, Vituperate.
U	P	B	R	E	A	K	Eruption, Outburst.
U	P	B	U	I	L	D	To build up.
U	P	C	H	E	C	K	Satisfactory result in a test.
U	P	C	L	I	M	B	Ascend.
U	P	C	U	R	V	E	An upward curve.
U	P	E	N	D	E	D	Turned upside down, Beaten, Overwhelmed, Trounced.
U	P	G	L	I	D	E	Upward glide.
U	P	G	R	A	D	E	Increase, Rise, Advance, Elevate, Promote, Hike, Boost, Wax.
U	P	H	E	A	V	E	Lift, Raise, Force upward.
U	P	H	O	A	R	D	To hoard up.
U	P	L	Y	I	N	G	Situated on high land.
U	P	R	A	I	S	E	Lift, Elevate, Cheer, Hoist, Uphold, Uplift, Comfort, Console.
U	P	R	I	G	H	T	Erect, Raised, Honest, Just, Sc rupulous, Right, Ethical, Perpendicular.
U	P	R	I	V	E	R	Nearer the source of the river.
U	P	R	O	U	S	E	To rouse up.
U	P	S	H	I	F	T	Shift into a higher gear.
U	P	S	H	O	O	T	Raise.
U	P	S	T	A	G	E	To steal the show, Superiority of manner, Haughty, Snobbish, High-class.
U	P	S	T	A	N	D	Rise to a standing position.
U	P	S	T	A	R	T	One risen from a low position to wealth or power, Presumptuous, Social climber.

1	2	3	4	5	6	7	Definition
U	P	S	U	R	G	E	Augment, Increase, Enlarge, Expand, Rise, Multiply, Wax, Heighten.
U	P	S	W	E	E	P	Upward curving, Increase in elevation, Marked increase in activity.
U	P	S	W	E	L	L	To swell up.
U	P	T	H	R	O	W	Upward displacement, Upheaval of the earth's crust.
U	P	T	I	G	H	T	Tense, Edgy, Nervy, Restive, Uneasy.
U	P	T	R	A	I	N	Rear, Bring up.
U	P	T	R	E	N	D	Upward tendency in economic factors.
U	P	W	A	R	D	S	Above, Increasing, Ascending, Upstream, Rising.
U	P	W	H	I	R	L	To whirl upward.
U	R	A	C	H	A	L	Relating to a urachus.
U	R	A	C	H	U	S	Functionless remnant of embryo duct.
U	R	A	E	M	I	A	Uremia. Toxic condition of the blood.
U	R	A	L	I	T	E	Fibrous and dark-green amphibole.
U	R	A	N	A	T	E	Compound formed by reaction of a uranyl salt.
U	R	A	N	I	A	N	Heavenly, Celestial, Astronomical, Relaiting to planet Uranus.
U	R	A	N	I	D	E	Uranian.
U	R	A	N	I	S	M	Homosexual condition.
U	R	A	N	I	S	T	Homosexual.
U	R	A	N	I	U	M	Radioactive metallic element.
U	R	A	N	O	U	S	Relating to uranium.
U	R	C	E	O	L	E	Vessel used in religious rites.
U	R	E	D	I	U	M	Spore bearing rust fungi.
U	R	G	E	N	C	Y	Insistence, Pressure, Urge, Importunity, Entreaty, Goading, Impelling.
U	R	G	R	U	N	D	Ultimate cosmic principle.
U	R	H	E	E	N	S	Chinese fiddle.
U	R	I	C	A	S	E	Enzyme that promotes oxidation of uric acid.
U	R	I	D	I	N	E	Crystalline nucleoside.
U	R	I	N	A	N	T	In heraldy to be head down.
U	R	I	N	A	R	Y	Relating to urine.
U	R	I	N	A	T	E	To discharge urine.
U	R	O	C	Y	O	N	Genus of mammals, American gray foxes.
U	R	O	C	Y	S	T	The urinary bladder.
U	R	O	G	R	A	M	X-ray for urinary tract.
U	R	O	H	Y	A	L	Bony element of hyoid arch of a fish.
U	R	O	L	I	T	H	Stone in urinary tract.
U	R	O	L	O	G	Y	Branch of medicine concerned with urinary tract.
U	R	O	N	I	D	E	A glycosidic compound.
U	R	O	P	Y	G	I	Genus of scorpions.
U	R	S	I	D	A	E	Family of carnivores including bears.
U	R	U	N	D	A	Y	S. American timber trees.
U	S	E	L	E	S	S	Ineffectual, Inefficient, Unserviceable, Futile, Impracticable, Worthless, Unproductive.
U	S	H	E	R	E	D	Introduced, Preceded, Prefaced, Led, Entered, Conducted.
U	S	U	A	L	L	Y	Habitually, Customarily, Ordinarily, Consistently, Commonly, Frequently, Normally.
U	S	U	R	P	E	D	Appropriated, Supplanted, Seized, Occupied, Arrogated, Assumed, Commandeered, Displaced.
U	S	U	R	P	E	R	One that encroaches upon the rights of others.
U	T	E	N	S	I	L	Article used in a household, Implement, Instrument, Tool.
U	T	E	R	I	N	E	Related by blood through the mother, Situated in the uterus.
U	T	I	L	I	T	Y	Appropriateness, Serviceableness, Usefulness, Applicability, Fitness, Relevance, Service.
U	T	I	L	I	Z	E	Apply, Bestow, Employ, Exercise, Exploit, Handle, Use, Promote.
U	T	O	P	I	A	N	Visionary, Impossible, Impracticable, Idealistic, Abstract, Grandiose, Lofty, Pretentious.
U	T	O	P	I	S	M	Unrealistic.
U	T	O	P	I	S	T	One advocating impractically ideal schemes.
U	T	R	I	C	L	E	Air cell of seaweed, Small sacs of an animal or plant body.
U	T	T	E	R	E	D	Pronounced, Spoke, Disclosed, Revealed, Divulged, Discharged, Ejected, Emitted.
U	T	T	E	R	L	Y	Absolutely, Altogether, Entirely, Fully, Thoroughly, Totally, Completely, Wholly.
U	V	E	I	T	I	S	Inflammation of the iris of the eye.
U	X	O	R	I	A	L	Having the characteristics of a wife.

V

1	2	3	4	5	6	7	Definition
V	A	C	A	N	C	Y	Void, Blank, Loneliness, Vacuity, Emptiness.
V	A	C	A	T	E	D	Left, Annulled, Abrogated, Discharged, Voided, Repealed, Rescinded, Revoked.
V	A	C	A	T	U	R	Order of court vacating a legal proceeding.
V	A	C	C	I	N	E	Preparation of organisms to produce immunity to a particular disease.
V	A	C	U	A	T	E	Evacuate.
V	A	C	U	I	S	T	One who maintains there are vacuums in nature.

1	2	3	4	5	6	7	Definition
V	A	C	U	I	T	Y	Void, Gap, Vacuum, Inanity, Blankness, Hollowness, Cavity, Hollow.
V	A	C	U	O	L	E	Small space in tissue containing air or fluid.
V	A	C	U	O	M	E	Vacuolar system.
V	A	C	U	O	U	S	Empty, Dull, Stupid, Idle, Null, Void, Superficial, Inane.
V	A	E	S	I	T	E	Mineral of sulfide of nickel.
V	A	G	I	N	A	L	Resembling a vagina, Thecal.
V	A	G	N	E	R	A	Smilacina, Genus of American and Asian plants.
V	A	G	R	A	N	T	Wanderer, Vagabond, Derelict, Tramp, Itinerant, Nomadic, Hobo.
V	A	G	U	E	L	Y	Indistinctly, Vacantly, Shadowly, Obscurely, Uncertainly, Cloudily, Dimly, Hazily.
V	A	G	U	E	S	T	Most obscure, Most uncertain, Dimmest, Haziest, Most nebulous.
V	A	I	L	I	N	G	Falling, Descending, Sinking, Yielding, Submitting, Humbling, Abasing.
V	A	I	N	E	S	T	Emptiest, Most idle, Most unsuccessful, Most fooled, Silliest.
V	A	L	A	N	C	E	Gathered or pleated drapery as decoration or trimming.
V	A	L	E	N	C	E	Degree of combining power of an element.
V	A	L	E	N	C	Y	Same as VALENCE.
V	A	L	E	R	Y	L	Univalent radical of a valeric acid.
V	A	L	E	T	R	Y	Occupation or service of a valet.
V	A	L	I	A	N	T	Courageous, Intrepid, Fearless, Heroic, Excellent, Noteworthy, Brave, Bold.
V	A	L	I	D	L	Y	With legal force, Justifiably, Pertinently, Effectively, Strongly, Soundly.
V	A	L	L	A	R	Y	Gold circlet surmounted by flat pointed strips.
V	A	L	L	A	T	E	Having a raised edge surrounding a depression.
V	A	L	O	N	I	A	Dried acorn cups used in tanning industry, Genus of marine green algae.
V	A	L	S	O	I	D	Resembling perithecia, Like fungi.
V	A	L	U	I	N	G	Appraising, Evaluating, Prizing, Esteeming, Appreciating, Estimating.
V	A	L	V	A	T	E	Meeting at the edges.
V	A	L	V	I	N	G	Arrangement of valves.
V	A	L	V	U	L	E	Structure resembling a fold.
V	A	M	O	O	S	E	Depart quickly, Decamp.
V	A	M	P	I	N	G	Patching, Inventing, Fabricating, Concocting, Tramping, Plodding, Flirting.
V	A	M	P	I	R	E	Bloodsucker, Extortioner, One who preys mercilessly on others.
V	A	M	P	I	S	H	Having the characteristics of a vamp.
V	A	N	A	D	I	C	Containing vanadium.
V	A	N	A	D	Y	L	Either of two radicals composed of vanadium and oxygen.
V	A	N	D	Y	K	E	Wide lace collar, Scalloped edge, Stagger, Weave, Wander, Zigzag.
V	A	N	E	S	S	A	Genus of brightly coloured butterflies.
V	A	N	I	L	L	A	Genus of tropical Americal climging orchids, Pod of plant used as flavouring.
V	A	N	N	I	N	G	Carrying in a van.
V	A	N	T	A	G	E	Superiority, Advantage, Profit, Allowance, Draw, Handicap.
V	A	N	W	A	R	D	Advanced, Forward.
V	A	P	I	D	L	Y	Insipidly, Inertly, Languidly, Inanely, Weakly.
V	A	P	O	U	R	S	Depressed or hysterical nervous condition.
V	A	P	O	U	R	Y	Misty, Vague.
V	A	Q	U	E	R	O	Herdsman, Cowboy, Apache.
V	A	R	A	N	I	D	Relating to varanus.
V	A	R	A	N	U	S	Genus of Old World lizards.
V	A	R	I	A	N	T	Variable, Fickle, Variegated, Mutation, Different, Diverse.
V	A	R	I	A	T	E	Break, Irregular.
V	A	R	I	C	E	S	Abnormally dilated vein or artery, Abnormal swelling.
V	A	R	I	E	T	Y	Species, Assortment, Race, Breed, Strain, Stock, Diversity, Medley.
V	A	R	I	O	L	A	Disease marked by a pustular eruption, Smallpox.
V	A	R	I	O	L	E	Whitish spherules embedded in rock.
V	A	R	I	O	U	S	Variable, Changeable, Inconstant, Multifarious, Unlike, Several, Numerous, Many.
V	A	R	M	I	N	T	Vermin, Rascal, Rogue.
V	A	R	N	I	S	H	Coating, Glaze, Gloss, Palliate, Extenuate, Veneer, Whiten, Whitewash.
V	A	R	S	I	T	Y	University, First team of players.
V	A	R	V	E	L	S	Vervels, Ring attached to a bird's leg to secure it to a perch.
V	A	R	Y	I	N	G	Diversifying, Differing, Deviating, Departing, Swerving, Changing, Altering, Modifying.
V	A	S	T	E	S	T	Most huge, Most enormous, Most gigantic, Biggest, Largest, Broadest, Widest, Most ample.
V	A	T	I	C	A	N	Pertaining to Papal power.
V	A	T	T	I	N	G	Treating in a vat.
V	A	U	D	O	I	S	Inhabitant of the Swiss canton of Vaud.
V	A	U	L	T	E	D	Arched, Covered with a vault, Jumped, Hurdled, Surmounted, Cleaned, Negotiated.
V	A	U	L	T	E	R	Pole-vaulter.
V	A	U	N	T	E	D	Bragged, Boasted, Crowed, Mouthed, Displayed, Exhibited, Flaunted, Paraded.
V	A	U	N	T	E	R	Braggart, Boaster.
V	A	V	A	S	O	R	Feudal tenant with a rank below a baron.
V	E	D	A	N	G	A	One of Sanskrit works.

1	2	3	4	5	6	7	Definition
V	E	D	A	N	T	A	An orthodox Hindu philosophy.
V	E	D	D	O	I	D	Relating to the aboriginal people of Sri Lanka.
V	E	D	E	T	T	E	Mounted sentinel.
V	E	E	R	I	N	G	Paying out a rope, Swerving, Turning, Shifting, Variable, Altering course.
V	E	G	E	T	A	L	Relating to vegetables or vegetation.
V	E	H	I	C	L	E	Conveyance, Transport, Agency, Channel, Instrument, Medium, inert substance.
V	E	I	L	I	N	G	Covering with a veil, Enshrouding, Enwrapping, Cloaking, Screening, Concealing, Secreting.
V	E	I	N	I	N	G	Patterning with veins, Striating, Spreading.
V	E	I	N	L	E	T	Small vein.
V	E	I	N	O	U	S	Veined.
V	E	I	N	U	L	E	Veinlet.
V	E	L	A	M	E	N	Thick membrane covering aerial roots of an orchid.
V	E	L	A	R	I	C	Having a vela, Inner closure.
V	E	L	A	T	E	D	Veiled.
V	E	L	O	U	R	S	Fabrics with a pile or napped surface.
V	E	L	O	U	T	E	White sauce made of chicken or veal stock.
V	E	L	V	E	T	Y	Soft and smooth to taste or touch.
V	E	N	A	L	L	Y	In a saleable manner, Open to bribery.
V	E	N	A	T	I	C	Used in hunting.
V	E	N	D	A	C	E	Whitefish found in lakes of the United Kingdom.
V	E	N	D	A	G	E	Harvest time of grapes.
V	E	N	D	I	N	G	Selling, Hawking, Peddling, Publishing abroad.
V	E	N	E	R	E	R	Hunter.
V	E	N	I	S	O	N	Edible flesh of a game animal taken in hunting.
V	E	N	T	A	G	E	Vent, Small hole, Arrangement for venting.
V	E	N	T	A	I	L	Lower movable front of a medieval helmet.
V	E	N	T	I	L	E	Waterproof fabric designed to allow free circulation of air.
V	E	N	T	I	N	G	Ventilating, Expelling, Evacuating, Loosing, Emitting, Expressing, Uttering, Drawing.
V	E	N	T	O	S	E	Flatulent, Windy.
V	E	N	T	R	A	D	Toward the ventral side.
V	E	N	T	R	A	L	Relating to the belly, Abdominal, Located on the lower surface.
V	E	N	T	U	R	E	Hazard, Risk, Chance, Endanger, Imperil, Jeopardize, Brave, Trust.
V	E	N	T	U	R	I	Short tube designed for use in taking various measurements.
V	E	N	U	L	A	R	Involving small veins.
V	E	R	A	N	D	A	Balcony, Porch, Piazza, Outside gallery.
V	E	R	B	E	N	A	Genus of sweet-scented American herbs.
V	E	R	B	I	F	Y	To make into a verb.
V	E	R	B	I	L	E	One whose mental imagery consists of words.
V	E	R	B	O	S	E	Loquacious, Prolix, Wordiness, Pedantic, Long-winded, Flowery, wordy.
V	E	R	D	A	N	T	Coloured green, Covered with vegetation, Unsophisticated, Raw.
V	E	R	D	I	C	T	Decision, Judgment, Finding.
V	E	R	D	U	R	E	Vigorous growth, Good health, Freshness, Strength, Tapestry with garden design.
V	E	R	G	I	N	G	Bordering, Edging, Trimming, Sinking, Moving, Extending, Inclining.
V	E	R	G	L	A	S	Thin film of ice on rock.
V	E	R	I	E	S	T	Truest, Mere, Bare, Most sheer, Absolute, Utter, Special, Particular.
V	E	R	M	E	I	L	Bright red.
V	E	R	M	I	A	N	Resembling the worms.
V	E	R	M	U	T	H	White wine flavoured with herbs.
V	E	R	N	A	N	T	Vernal, Springlike.
V	E	R	N	I	E	R	Slide rule for measuring graduated scale divisions.
V	E	R	O	N	A	L	Barbital.
V	E	R	R	U	C	A	Wart.
V	E	R	S	A	N	T	Concerned, Interested, Occupied, Experienced, Practiced, Conversant, Familiar, Inclination.
V	E	R	S	I	F	Y	To write poetry.
V	E	R	S	I	N	E	Relating to an angle.
V	E	R	S	I	N	G	Turning into verse.
V	E	R	S	I	O	N	Translation, Rendering, Clarification, Interpretation, Account, Chronicle, History, Narrative.
V	E	R	T	I	G	O	Dizziness, Confusion, Giddiness, Disturbed Equilibrium.
V	E	R	V	A	I	N	Verbena.
V	E	R	V	E	L	S	Ring around a bird's leg to secure it to a perch.
V	E	S	I	C	A	L	Relating to the urinary bladder.
V	E	S	I	C	I	C	Same as VESICAL.
V	E	S	P	I	N	E	Resembling a wasp.
V	E	S	P	O	I	D	Related to the wasps.
V	E	S	T	I	G	E	Footstep, Track, Mark, Memento, Relic, Shadow, Trace, Spoor.
V	E	S	T	I	N	G	Giving, Granting, Endowing, Investing, Authorizing, Empowering, Belonging, Pertaining.
V	E	S	T	I	N	I	Ancient Sabine people of central Italy.

1	2	3	4	5	6	7	Definition
V	E	S	T	L	E	T	Organism that has a tough tube about the body, Sea-anemone.
V	E	S	T	R	A	L	Relating to a vestry.
V	E	S	T	U	R	E	Clothing, Apparel, Costume, Vestment, Covering, Garment, Dress.
V	E	T	E	R	A	N	Old-timer, Expert, Master, Experienced, Practiced, Seasoned, Skilled, Worldly.
V	E	T	I	V	E	R	Khuskhus, Aromatic grass that yields a perfumery oil from the fragrant roots.
V	E	T	O	I	N	G	Negating, Prohibiting, Denying, Disallowing, Defeating, Refusing, Rejecting.
V	E	T	T	I	N	G	Scrutinizing, Checking, Examining, Inspecting, Surveying, Viewing.
V	E	T	T	U	R	A	Italian four-wheeled carriage.
V	I	A	D	U	C	T	Bridge having high supportive arches.
V	I	A	J	A	C	A	Small Cuban freshwater food fish.
V	I	B	R	A	N	T	Pulsing, Alive, Vital, Sensitive, Sonorous, Resonant, Resounding, Ringing.
V	I	B	R	A	T	E	Shake, Quake, Tremble, Tremor, Oscillate, Alternate, Quiver, Swing.
V	I	B	R	A	T	O	Tremulous effect given to vocal or instrumental rendering of music.
V	I	B	R	I	O	N	Curved rod-shaped bacterium.
V	I	C	E	R	O	Y	Governor who rules as representative of the monarch.
V	I	C	I	L	I	N	Globulin associated with legumes as peas, beans or lentils.
V	I	C	I	N	A	L	Local, Neighbouring, Confined to a limited district.
V	I	C	I	O	U	S	Debased, Depraved, Malicious, Spiteful.
V	I	C	T	O	R	Y	Conquest, Triumph, Control, Dominion, Mastery, Supremacy, Superiority, Overwhelm.
V	I	C	T	R	I	X	Victress, Female victor.
V	I	C	T	U	A	L	Edible food, Provisions, Supplies of food.
V	I	D	E	T	T	E	Vedette, Mounted sentinel.
V	I	D	I	C	O	N	Small camera tube for transmitting television picture signals.
V	I	D	I	M	U	S	Official or legal inspection of a document.
V	I	D	U	A	G	E	Widowhood.
V	I	E	W	I	N	G	Inspecting, Scrutinizing, Observing, Seeing, Checking, Examining, Surveying, Scanning.
V	I	L	A	Y	E	T	Province of Turkey.
V	I	L	L	A	G	E	Settlement, Municipal unit. Larger than Hamlet, Smaller than town.
V	I	L	L	A	I	N	Scoundrel, Knave, Rascal, Rogue, Scamp, Miscreant, Rapscallion, Reprobate.
V	I	L	L	E	I	N	Freeman of a village, Serf.
V	I	L	L	O	T	E	Detached dwelling unit.
V	I	L	L	O	U	S	Villous, Shaggy, Resembling pile of velvet or bristles of a brush.
V	I	L	L	O	S	E	Covered with long soft hair.
V	I	N	A	S	S	E	Dregs remaining after distillation of liquors.
V	I	N	E	G	A	R	Sour liquid used as condiment or preservative obtained by acetic fermentatio.
V	I	N	G	T	U	N	Vingt-et-un, A card game twenty one.
V	I	N	T	A	G	E	Wine or grape crop of a certain year, Maturity, Age, Old-fashioned, Dated, Classic, Venerable.
V	I	N	T	N	E	R	Wine merchant, Person who specialises in making wines.
V	I	O	L	A	T	E	Transgress, Disregard, Profane, Desecrate, Contravene, Infringe, Offend, Rape.
V	I	O	L	E	N	T	Intense, Concentrated, Desperate, Fierce, Furious, Terrible, Forceful, Vicious.
V	I	O	L	I	N	E	Violet colour.
V	I	O	L	I	S	T	One who plays the viola.
V	I	O	L	O	N	E	A viol of contrabass size and range.
V	I	P	E	R	I	N	Resembling a viper, Venomous.
V	I	R	E	L	A	Y	Old French verse form.
V	I	R	E	M	I	A	Presence of virus in the blood.
V	I	R	G	A	T	E	A quarter of an acre, Slender rod, To branch in diverging lines.
V	I	R	G	U	L	A	Axial support of carbonized fossils.
V	I	R	G	U	L	E	Earliest form of a comma, Diagonal, Indication of division of a word at the end of a line.
V	I	R	I	D	I	N	Crystalline fungistatic antibiotic.
V	I	R	I	L	I	A	The male genitals.
V	I	R	O	S	I	S	Infection caused by a virus.
V	I	R	T	U	A	L	Implicit, Constructive, Practical, Basic, Essential, Fundamental.
V	I	S	A	G	E	D	Having a special appearance or facial expression.
V	I	S	A	V	I	S	Face-to-face, Escort, Date, Counterpart, Opposite number, Tete-a-tete.
V	I	S	C	E	R	A	Internal organs of the body.
V	I	S	C	O	U	S	Gelatinous, Gluey, Sticky, Glutinous, Slimy, Semi-fluid, Tenacious.
V	I	S	E	I	T	E	Mineral of phosphate and silicate of aluminium and calcium.
V	I	S	I	B	L	E	Available, Conspicuous, Discoverable, Recognizable, Visual, Ocular.
V	I	S	I	B	L	Y	Obviously, Noticeably.
V	I	S	I	T	E	D	Comforted, Afflicted, Inflicted, Imposed, Stayed, Sojourned, Searched, Called.
V	I	S	I	T	O	R	Caller, Guest, Tourist, Traveller, Trustee, Visitant.
V	I	S	N	O	M	Y	Physiognomy.
V	I	S	O	R	E	D	Masked, Disguised.
V	I	S	T	A	E	D	Made to form a vista.
V	I	S	V	I	V	A	Calculation of the force of a moving body.

1	2	3	4	5	6	7	
V	I	T	A	L	L	Y	Notably, Extremely, Very, Exceedingly, Hugely, Remarkably, Strikingly, Surpassingly.
V	I	T	A	M	I	N	Various organic substances believed to be essential to growth and nourishment.
V	I	T	I	A	T	E	Impair, Contaminate, Spoil, Corrupt, Deprave, Pervert, Debase, Invalidate.
V	I	T	R	A	I	L	Stained glass.
V	I	T	R	A	I	N	Constituent of bituminous coal.
V	I	T	R	I	F	Y	Change into glass.
V	I	T	R	I	N	A	Genus of land snails.
V	I	T	R	I	O	L	Sulfate of a metal, Caustic quality, Virulence of speech or feeling.
V	I	T	T	A	T	E	Striped lengthwise.
V	I	V	E	R	R	A	Genus of civets.
V	I	V	I	D	L	Y	Animatedly, Brilliantly, Freshly, Lively, Actively, clearly.
V	I	V	I	F	I	C	Reviving, Enlivening, Animating.
V	O	C	A	B	L	E	Term, Name, Word, Individual sound.
V	O	C	A	L	I	C	Consisting of vowels, Characterized by a vowel change.
V	O	C	A	L	L	Y	In a vocal manner, By voice.
V	O	C	O	D	E	R	Electronic mechanism that scrambles and unscrambles speech signals.
V	O	G	L	I	T	E	Mineral of hydrous carbonate of uranium, calcium, and copper.
V	O	I	C	I	N	G	Uttering, Electing, Expressing.
V	O	I	D	I	N	G	Something that is voided, Dung, Excrement.
V	O	I	T	U	R	E	Light carriage, Light open automobile.
V	O	I	V	O	D	E	Vaivode, Military commander of a province in Slavic countries.
V	O	L	A	D	O	R	Flying gurnard, Various sailfishes.
V	O	L	A	N	T	E	Direction in music, Moving with light rapidity, Two-wheeled carriage.
V	O	L	A	P	U	K	Artificial international language.
V	O	L	C	A	N	O	Vent in the earth's crust from which molten rock and steam issue, Suppressed force.
V	O	L	T	A	G	E	Electric potential, Effectiveness, Power.
V	O	L	T	A	I	C	Producing direct electric current by chemical action, Galvanic.
V	O	L	U	B	L	E	Talkative, Vocal, Glib, Fluent, Rotating, Revolving, Changeable, Unstable.
V	O	L	U	B	L	Y	Glibly.
V	O	L	U	M	E	D	Rolled in volume, Collected, Rounded mass, Massive, Great.
V	O	L	U	T	E	D	Having a spiral or scroll, Scroll-shaped.
V	O	L	V	E	L	L	Old contrivance for astronomical measurements.
V	O	M	I	T	U	S	Vomit.
V	O	T	A	B	L	E	Capable of being decided by vote.
V	O	U	C	H	E	D	Proved, Substantiated, Vouchsafed, Certified, Attested, Witnessed, Verified, Assured.
V	O	U	C	H	E	E	One called into court to warrant.
V	O	U	C	H	E	R	Proof, Certificate, Credential, Authority, Evidence, Witness.
V	O	Y	A	G	E	D	Travelled, Sailed, Traversed, Cruised, Toured, Journeyed.
V	O	Y	A	G	E	R	Traveller.
V	R	I	E	S	E	A	Genus of herbs.
V	U	L	G	A	T	E	An edition or copy of the Latin bible, Common speech.
V	U	L	P	I	N	E	Resembling a fox, Crafty, Marked by slyness or predatoriness.
V	U	L	T	U	R	E	Family of large birds that subsist mainly on carrion.
V	U	L	V	A	T	E	Vulvar, Relating to the external genital parts of a female.

W

W	A	B	B	L	E	R	Wobbler, One that wobbles.
W	A	B	S	T	E	R	Webster, Weaver.
W	A	D	A	B	L	E	Capable of being waded, Fordable.
W	A	D	D	I	N	G	Wads of material used for padding.
W	A	D	D	L	E	D	Walked with short steps swinging from side to side, Moved clumsily.
W	A	D	H	O	O	K	Wormer, Extractor.
W	A	E	S	U	C	K	Used to express grief or pity.
W	A	F	E	R	E	D	Sealed, closed or fastened with a wafer.
W	A	F	T	A	G	E	Act of wafting, Conveyance, Carriage.
W	A	F	T	I	N	G	Beckoning, Moving lightly.
W	A	F	T	U	R	E	Beckoning.
W	A	G	E	R	E	D	Risked, Ventured, Gambled, Staked, Competed.
W	A	G	G	E	R	Y	Pleasantry, Jocularity, Impishness, Jest, Roguery, Devilment, Mischief, Witticism.
W	A	G	G	I	N	G	Moving, Stirring, Waggling, Oscillating, Switching, Waving.
W	A	G	G	I	S	H	Frolicsome, Sportive, Humorous.
W	A	G	G	L	E	D	Jerked back and forth or up and down, Wobbled.
W	A	G	O	N	E	D	Transported by wagon.
W	A	G	O	N	E	R	Driver of a wagon. Wagoneer.
W	A	G	T	A	I	L	Genus of long tailed birds.

1	2	3	4	5	6	7	
W	A	H	H	A	B	I	Puritanical Muslim sect.
W	A	I	L	F	U	L	Sorrowful, Mournful.
W	A	I	L	I	N	G	Lamenting, Weeping, Complaining, Bewailing, Crying, Howling, Bawling, Whining.
W	A	I	N	A	G	E	Implements of feudal husbandry.
W	A	I	S	T	E	D	Having a definite waist, Shaped like a waist.
W	A	I	S	T	E	R	Inefficient seaman stationed in the waist of a ship.
W	A	I	T	I	N	G	Staying, Lingering, Abiding, Remaining, Tarrying, Anticipaing, Expecting, Serving.
W	A	I	V	I	N	G	Relinquishing, Abandoning, Ceding, Resigning, Surrendering, Delaying, Granting, Allowing.
W	A	K	E	F	U	L	Watchful, Vigilant, Sleepless, Restless.
W	A	K	E	N	E	D	Became Active, Animated, Stirred, Excited, Stimulated.
W	A	K	E	N	E	R	One that causes to waken.
W	A	L	K	I	N	G	Perambulating, Promenading, Strolling, Hiking, Tramping, Stepping, Traipsing, Pacing.
W	A	L	K	O	U	T	Strike, Leave as an expression of disapproval.
W	A	L	L	A	B	A	Valuable timber tree of Northern Brazil.
W	A	L	L	A	B	Y	Small kangaroo.
W	A	L	L	A	C	H	Vlach, Chiefly herdsman speaking Romanian dialect.
W	A	L	L	E	Y	E	Eye having an opaque white cornea, Cross-eyed, Leucoma.
W	A	L	L	I	N	G	Material for a wall, Wall.
W	A	L	L	O	O	N	Belgian Flemish, French dialect of Walloon.
W	A	L	L	R	U	E	Small delicate spleen-wort found on a cliff.
W	A	L	T	Z	E	D	Danced a waltz, Flounced, Breezed, Marched, Carried, Lugged.
W	A	L	T	Z	E	R	One that dances a waltz.
W	A	M	B	L	E	D	Felt nauseau, Rolled, Spun, Revolved, Moved unsteadily.
W	A	M	P	I	S	H	Fluctuate, Swing.
W	A	N	G	L	E	D	Wiggled, Faked, Engineered, Manoeuvred, Machinated.
W	A	N	I	G	A	N	Chest for supplies, Mobile shelter.
W	A	N	N	E	S	S	Being pale.
W	A	N	N	I	N	G	Becoming sickly or pallid.
W	A	N	T	A	G	E	Amount wanting, Shortage.
W	A	N	T	I	N	G	Craving, Liking, Desiring, Wishing, Choosing, Short, Deficient, Absent.
W	A	N	T	W	I	T	Fool.
W	A	R	A	T	A	H	Australian plant.
W	A	R	B	L	E	D	Sang in a trilling manner, Babbled, Trilled.
W	A	R	B	L	E	R	Singer, Songster, Old World singing birds.
W	A	R	B	L	E	S	Sings, Trills.
W	A	R	D	I	N	G	Confinement in a prison, Fending.
W	A	R	F	A	R	E	Hostilities, War, Contest, Competition, Conflict, Rivalry, Strife.
W	A	R	H	E	A	D	Section of a missile containing the explosive.
W	A	R	I	E	S	T	Most cautious, Most economical, Most provident.
W	A	R	I	S	O	N	A bugle call to attack.
W	A	R	L	I	K	E	Bellicose, Military, Martial.
W	A	R	L	O	C	K	Sorcerer, Wizard, Conjurer, Wizard.
W	A	R	L	O	R	D	Military governer excising civil power.
W	A	R	M	E	S	T	Most ardent, Most fervent, Most affable, Most cordial, Most sincere.
W	A	R	M	I	N	G	Thrashing, Trouncing, Heating.
W	A	R	N	I	N	G	Cautioning, Informing, Admonition, Calling, Summons.
W	A	R	P	A	T	H	Warlike expedition of Red Indians.
W	A	R	P	I	N	G	Twisting, Bending, Curving, Perverting, Contorting, Deforming, Corrupting, Debauching.
W	A	R	R	A	N	T	Assure, Authorize, Secure, Attest, Guarantee, Justify, Defend, Vindicate.
W	A	R	R	I	N	G	Contending, Battling, Rioting, Fighting, Attempting, Striving, Struggling, Challenging.
W	A	R	R	I	O	R	Soldier, Fighter, Serviceman.
W	A	R	S	H	I	P	Battleship, Cruiser, Ship armed for combat.
W	A	R	T	H	O	G	African wild hog.
W	A	R	W	O	L	F	Werewolf.
W	A	R	W	O	R	N	Ruined, Ravaged, Wasted by war.
W	A	S	H	D	A	Y	A day set aside with regularity for washing household linen and clothes.
W	A	S	H	I	N	G	Cleansing, Rubbing, Obliterating, Saturating, Drenching, Suffusing.
W	A	S	H	O	U	T	Washing away of earth, Failure, Flop.
W	A	S	H	P	O	T	Pot for boiling the washing.
W	A	S	H	T	U	B	Tub in which clothes and linen are washed.
W	A	S	P	F	L	Y	Various syrphus flies that resemble wasps.
W	A	S	P	I	S	H	Snappish, Testy, Irritable, Fractious, Peevish, Petulant, Querulous, Impatient.
W	A	S	S	A	I	L	Revelry, A toast, Carouse.
W	A	S	T	A	G	E	Losses, Decrease, Destruction, Decayed, Erosion, Leakage.
W	A	S	T	I	N	G	Devastating, Desolation, Atrophy, Losing, Squandering.
W	A	S	T	R	E	L	Profligate, Vagabond, Waif, Spendthrift, Waster, Worthless, Knave, Rascal.
W	A	T	C	H	E	D	Observed, Guarded, Tended, Examined, Inspected, Scrutinized, Attended.

1	2	3	4	5	6	7	
W	A	T	C	H	E	R	Watchman, Guard, Observer, Viewer.
W	A	T	C	H	E	T	Light blue.
W	A	T	E	R	E	D	Irrigated, Soaked, Diluted, Drenched, Saturated.
W	A	T	E	R	E	R	One that irrigates, Device supplying water to stock or poultry.
W	A	T	T	L	E	D	Enfolded, Built of wattle, Interlaced.
W	A	U	L	I	N	G	Howling, Bawling, Squalling.
W	A	V	E	L	E	T	A little wave, Ripple.
W	A	V	E	R	E	D	Vacillated, Varied, Hesitated, Dithered, Staggered.
W	A	V	E	R	E	R	Vacillating or indecisive person.
W	A	V	E	S	O	N	Flotsam, Goods that float on the sea after a shipwreck.
W	A	X	B	E	A	N	Various kidney beans.
W	A	X	B	I	L	L	Old World birds with bills of a waxy appearance.
W	A	X	D	O	L	L	French doll.
W	A	X	M	O	T	H	Bee moth.
W	A	X	P	A	L	M	A palm that yields wax.
W	A	X	T	R	E	E	A tree yielding wax.
W	A	X	W	I	N	G	American and Eurasian passerine birds.
W	A	X	W	O	R	K	Effigy in wax for exhibition.
W	A	Y	B	I	L	L	Traveller's itinerary, Document prepared by the carrier.
W	A	Y	F	A	R	E	Journey, Travel.
W	A	Y	L	E	S	S	Without a road or path.
W	A	Y	M	A	R	K	Sign-post for travellers.
W	A	Y	P	O	S	T	Guidepost.
W	A	Y	S	I	D	E	The side of a road or path, Adjacent to the highway.
W	A	Y	W	A	R	D	Wilful, Capricious, Contrary, Fickle, Unstable, Inconstant, Restive, Erratic.
W	A	Y	W	I	S	E	Experienced, Well-trained horse.
W	A	Y	W	O	D	E	Military governer, Vaivode.
W	A	Y	W	O	R	N	Travel-weary.
W	E	A	K	E	S	T	Frailest, Most fragile, Most infirm, Most decrepit, Puniest, Thinnest.
W	E	A	L	T	H	Y	Opulent, Affluent, Ample, Full, Abundant, Rich, Moneyed.
W	E	A	N	I	N	G	Ceasing to depend on mother's milk, Reconciling to a loss.
W	E	A	R	I	E	D	Tired, Fatigued, Jaded, Weary, Worn.
W	E	A	R	I	E	R	More tired, More jaded, More fatigued.
W	E	A	R	I	L	Y	Tediously, Tiredly.
W	E	A	R	I	N	G	Exhausting, Deteriorating, Using, Diminishing.
W	E	A	R	I	S	H	Tasteless, Insipid, Sickly, Withered, Squeamish.
W	E	A	S	A	N	D	Windpipe, Throat, Gullet, Trachea, Esophagus.
W	E	A	Z	A	N	D	Same as WEASAND.
W	E	A	T	H	E	R	Climate, State of atmosphere, Rain, Storm, Disintegrate, Discolour, Deteriorate.
W	E	A	V	I	N	G	Interlacing, Swaying, Lurching, Staggering, Wobbling, Reeling, Rocking, Oscillating.
W	E	B	B	I	N	G	Narrow woven or braided fabric.
W	E	B	F	O	O	T	Having webbed toes.
W	E	B	S	T	E	R	Weaver.
W	E	B	W	O	R	M	Caterpillar that spins a large web.
W	E	D	D	I	N	G	Marrying, Pledging, Wagering, Espousal, Nuptial, Existing in close association.
W	E	D	G	I	N	G	Forcing a wedge, Squeezing, Crowding, Cramming, Packing.
W	E	D	L	O	C	K	Marriage, Matrimony.
W	E	E	D	A	G	E	Weeds.
W	E	E	D	E	R	Y	Place full of weeds.
W	E	E	D	I	N	G	Clearing weeds, Culling, Removing something considered harmful.
W	E	E	K	D	A	Y	Workday, Any day except the Sabbath.
W	E	E	K	E	N	D	Period between close of one week and beginning of the next.
W	E	E	N	I	N	G	Believing, Conceiving, Imagining, Supposing, Expecting.
W	E	E	P	I	N	G	Bewailing, Lamenting, Crying, Exuding, Dripping, Leaking, Discharging, Drooping.
W	E	E	V	I	L	Y	Infested with weevils.
W	E	F	T	I	N	G	Weaving a weft.
W	E	I	G	H	E	D	Esteemed, Regarded, Counter-balanced, Evaluated, Pondered, Measured, Courted, Raised.
W	E	I	G	H	E	R	Worker who weighs out ingredients, Customs inspector.
W	E	I	G	H	I	N	Weighing a contestant.
W	E	I	G	H	T	Y	Earnest, Solemn, Corpulent, Burdensome, Grievous, Onerous, Powerful, Telling.
W	E	I	R	D	E	R	More mysterious, Odder, More unusual, More fantastic, More eerie, More uncanny.
W	E	I	R	D	L	Y	Ghostly, Eerily, Unusually, Mysteriously, Spookily, Strangely.
W	E	L	C	H	E	R	Welsher, One that cheats by non payment.
W	E	L	C	O	M	E	Greeting of pleasure, Salutation, Agreeable, Congenial, Good, Cordially invited, Plesant.
W	E	L	D	I	N	G	Junction made by welding, United metals, Form into a single unit, Adhesion of tissues.
W	E	L	F	A	R	E	Advantage, Benefit, Good, Interest, Prosperity, Well-being, Fortune.
W	E	L	L	I	N	G	Rising, Flowing, Springing, Pouring.

1	2	3	4	5	6	7	
W	E	L	L	O	F	F	In favourable circumstances, Prosperous, Well-to-do.
W	E	L	L	S	E	T	Firmly established, Strongly built.
W	E	L	S	H	E	D	Cheated by avoiding payment of debts, Decamped, Absconded.
W	E	L	S	H	E	R	Dishonest bookie, One who cheats on obligations.
W	E	L	T	I	N	G	Having welts, Trimming along edges, Beating.
W	E	N	C	H	E	D	Consorted with lewd women.
W	E	N	D	I	N	G	Departing, Proceeding, Travelling, Directing, Passing, Journeying.
W	E	N	D	I	S	H	Medieval Slavic people of eastern Germany.
W	E	N	L	O	C	K	Prehistoric division of Europe.
W	E	R	G	I	L	D	Value of life of a murdered man according to Anglo-Saxon law.
W	E	R	G	E	L	D	Same as WERGILD.
W	E	S	T	E	R	N	Occidental, Relating to cowboy lore of U.S.A.
W	E	S	T	I	N	G	Difference in longitude to the west from last point of reckoning.
W	E	T	D	O	C	K	A dock filled with water in order that a ship can float.
W	E	T	L	A	N	D	Swamp or bog.
W	E	T	N	E	S	S	Dampness, Something wet.
W	E	T	S	A	L	T	To treat hides with wet salt.
W	E	T	S	H	O	D	Having feet or shoes wet.
W	E	T	T	I	N	G	Moistening, Dampening, Soaking, Drenching, Saturating, Urinating.
W	E	T	T	I	S	H	Moist, Rather wet.
W	E	T	T	E	S	T	Dampest, Most moist, Most soaked, Most saturated, Most drenched.
W	E	T	W	O	O	D	Wood with high-water content.
W	H	A	C	K	E	D	Struck, Defeated, Hit, Slogged, Socked, Exhausted, Fatigued, Wearied.
W	H	A	C	K	E	R	Drover.
W	H	A	I	S	L	E	Wheeze.
W	H	A	L	E	R	Y	Processing factory for whale carcasses.
W	H	A	L	I	N	G	Catching whales, Thrashing, Beating, Whacking, Very, Extremely.
W	H	A	N	G	E	E	Chinese bamboo, Cane made of Chinese bamboo.
W	H	A	P	P	E	D	Whopped, Struck, Thrashed, Vanquished.
W	H	A	R	F	E	D	Docked, Berthed.
W	H	A	R	V	E	S	Docks, Piers, Quays, Berths, Jetties, Levees.
W	H	A	T	N	O	T	Set of shelves for displaying small ornaments or personal treasures.
W	H	A	T	T	E	N	What kind of.
W	H	E	A	T	E	N	Relating to wheat.
W	H	E	E	D	L	E	Coax, Cajole, Influence, Inveigle, Con, Blandish.
W	H	E	E	L	E	D	Revolved, Swayed, Reeled, Rotated, Circled, Reversed, Averted, Pivoted.
W	H	E	E	L	E	R	Worker who trucks loads, Maker of wheels, Wheelwright.
W	H	E	E	P	L	E	Whistle.
W	H	E	E	Z	E	D	Breathed with difficult, Difficult respiration.
W	H	E	E	Z	L	E	Wheeze.
W	H	E	L	K	E	D	Twisted, Convoluted.
W	H	E	L	P	E	D	Gave birth to pups.
W	H	E	M	M	L	E	Stumble, Overturn.
W	H	E	R	E	A	S	Since, Although, While.
W	H	E	R	E	A	T	Whereupon.
W	H	E	R	E	B	Y	Through which, whereupon, In consequence of which.
W	H	E	R	E	I	N	Where, In what particular or regard.
W	H	E	R	E	O	F	Of what, Of whom.
W	H	E	R	E	O	N	Whereupon, Following which.
W	H	E	R	E	S	O	Wheresoever.
W	H	E	R	E	T	O	To what place or purpose.
W	H	E	R	R	E	T	Tease, Worry.
W	H	E	T	H	E	R	Whichever, Either.
W	H	E	T	T	E	D	Sharpened, Rubbed, Incited, Aroused, Stimulated, Excited.
W	H	E	T	T	E	R	One that sharpens or stimulates.
W	H	E	W	I	N	G	Whistling.
W	H	E	Y	I	S	H	Resembling whey.
W	H	I	F	F	E	D	Puffed, Fanned, Blew, Intimated, Hinted.
W	H	I	F	F	E	T	Very small dog, Unimportant person, Whippersnapper.
W	H	I	F	F	L	E	Flicker, Flutter, Vacillate, Flourish, Emit a whistling sound.
W	H	I	L	E	R	E	Some time before.
W	H	I	L	I	N	G	Passing the time pleasantly.
W	H	I	M	P	E	R	Whining sound, Plaintive cry, Wail, Petulant complaining.
W	H	I	M	S	E	Y	Whimsy, Whim, Caprice, Vagary, Fanciful device.
W	H	I	N	D	L	E	Whimper or whine.
W	H	I	N	G	E	R	Whinyard, Short sword.
W	H	I	N	I	N	G	Uttering a high pitched cry, Complaining, Snivelling, Lamenting, Moaning.

1	2	3	4	5	6	7	
W	H	I	P	P	E	D	Flogged, Lashed, Spanked, Aroused, Incited, Abused, Confounded, Beaten.
W	H	I	P	P	E	R	One that uses a whip.
W	H	I	P	P	E	T	Small dog of greyhound type.
W	H	I	P	R	A	Y	Sting-ray.
W	H	I	P	S	A	W	Cut with a whipsaw, Two-man crosscut saw.
W	H	I	P	T	O	P	Whipping top, Top spun by whipping.
W	H	I	R	L	E	D	Circled, Revolved, Rotated, Sped, Rushed, Reeled, Twisted, Turned.
W	H	I	R	R	E	D	Flew or revolved with a monotonous drone.
W	H	I	R	R	E	R	Dervish, Whirling table for coating photographic plates.
W	H	I	R	T	L	E	Perforated steel die through which wires or tubes are drawn.
W	H	I	S	H	E	D	Sibilant sound, Moved fast, Whizzed.
W	H	I	S	K	E	D	Frisked, Zipped, Moved nimbly, Flicked, Whipped, Hurried, Brushed.
W	H	I	S	K	E	R	Hair growing on the face.
W	H	I	S	K	E	Y	Distilled alcoholic liquor made from fermented grain or potatoes.
W	H	I	S	P	E	R	Speak softly, Hiss, Sibilate, Confide, Murmur, Mutter, Rumour, Suspicion.
W	H	I	S	T	L	E	Shrill sound made by blowing air out through pursed lips.
W	H	I	S	T	L	Y	Resembling a whistle.
W	H	I	T	E	L	Y	Whitish, Pale.
W	H	I	T	E	S	T	Purest, Lightest, Most decent, Most innocent.
W	H	I	T	H	E	R	To what place, Whereunto, Whereto.
W	H	I	T	I	N	G	Various marine food fishes.
W	H	I	T	I	S	H	Pale, Dilute, Somewhat white.
W	H	I	T	L	O	W	Severe infection of the finger around the nail.
W	H	I	T	S	U	N	Pentecost.
W	H	I	T	T	L	E	Shave. Erode. Fashion, form by knife-work.
W	H	I	Z	Z	E	D	Moved swiftly with a hissing or buzzing sound, Rotated rapidly.
W	H	I	Z	Z	E	R	One what whizzes, Something notable.
W	H	O	E	V	E	R	Whatever person.
W	H	O	L	I	S	M	Holism.
W	H	O	O	P	E	D	Shouted, Hallooed, Boomed, Cheered, Expressed.
W	H	O	O	P	E	E	Boisterous convivial fun.
W	H	O	O	P	E	R	Whooping crane.
W	H	O	P	P	E	D	Beaten, Struck, Thrashed, Overcome, Vanquished.
W	H	O	P	P	E	R	Something unusually large.
W	H	O	R	I	S	H	Lewd, Resembling a whore.
W	H	O	R	L	E	D	Coiled, Spiralled, Swirled, Whirled.
W	I	C	K	I	N	G	Twisting, Braiding, Material used for wicks.
W	I	C	K	I	U	P	Hut used by nomadic American Indians.
W	I	D	E	N	E	D	Broadened, Expanded, Enlarged.
W	I	D	E	N	E	R	Reamer.
W	I	D	G	E	O	N	Freshwater duck.
W	I	D	O	W	E	D	Bereft of spouse, Survived as a widow.
W	I	D	O	W	E	R	Man who has survived his wife.
W	I	E	L	D	E	D	Managed, Handled, Manipulated, Controlled, Governed, Expressed.
W	I	E	L	D	E	R	One that handles a weapon or implement.
W	I	G	G	E	R	Y	Dealing in wigs.
W	I	G	G	I	N	G	Scolding, Reprimand, Upbraiding, Ranting, Berating, Reviling, Bawling.
W	I	G	G	L	E	D	Jiggled, Oscillated, Wriggled, Wormed, Squiggled, Writhed.
W	I	G	G	L	E	R	Larva or pupa of the mosquito.
W	I	G	H	T	L	Y	Strongly, Swiftly.
W	I	G	L	E	S	S	Wearing no wig.
W	I	L	D	A	S	S	Equine mammals that resemble the domestic donkey.
W	I	L	D	C	A	T	Various small or medium wild feline, Lynx, Ocelot, An illegal strike.
W	I	L	D	E	S	T	Shyest, Roughest, Most desolate, Most unruly, Most reckless, Most barbaric.
W	I	L	D	I	N	G	Uncultivated plant, Wild, Escape.
W	I	L	D	I	S	H	Somewhat wild.
W	I	L	D	O	A	T	Wild grass, Youthful indiscretions, Male promiscuity.
W	I	L	I	E	S	T	Craftiest, Cleverest, Most astute, Most artful, Trickiest, Most foxy.
W	I	L	L	I	N	G	Ready, Voluntary, Disposed, Inclined, Predisposed, Prone, Compliant, Agreeable.
W	I	L	L	O	C	K	Genus of birds, Guillemot, Puffin, Razorbill.
W	I	L	L	O	W	Y	Gracefully tall and slender, Delicate, Supple.
W	I	L	T	I	N	G	Sagging, Collapsing, Flagging, Succumbing, Ebbing, Fading, Drooping.
W	I	M	B	L	E	D	Bored, Twisted, Penetrated.
W	I	M	B	R	E	L	Whimbrel, European curlew.
W	I	M	P	L	E	D	Wearing a medieval head-covering, Covered, Veiled, Wrapped, Meandered, Twisted.
W	I	N	C	H	E	D	Reeled, Hoisted, Hauled.
W	I	N	D	A	G	E	Space between the bore and the bullet, Air friction.

1	2	3	4	5	6	7	Definition
W	I	N	D	B	A	G	Pompous person who talks too much and knows little.
W	I	N	D	E	G	G	Imperfect egg.
W	I	N	D	G	U	N	Air rifle.
W	I	N	D	I	E	R	More gusty, More stormy, Violent, More verbose.
W	I	N	D	I	L	Y	Stormily, Breezily, Briskly.
W	I	N	D	I	N	G	Rambling, Staggering, Reeling, Coiling, Twisting, Curving, Tortuous.
W	I	N	D	R	O	W	Something placed in rows.
W	I	N	D	S	O	R	Principal residence of the British monarch.
W	I	N	E	C	U	P	Fringed poppy mallow.
W	I	N	G	I	N	G	Flying, Dispatching, Sailing, Wounding, Fleeting, Sweeping.
W	I	N	G	L	E	T	Very small wing.
W	I	N	K	E	R	S	Blinkers, Eyes, Flashing lights.
W	I	N	K	I	N	G	Shutting one eye, briefly, Glancing, Blinking, Twinkling, Squinting, Conniving.
W	I	N	N	I	N	G	Prevailing, Succeeding, Acquiring, Beating, Overcoming, Triumphing, Gaining, Accomplishing.
W	I	N	N	O	C	K	Whimper.
W	I	N	S	O	M	E	Agreeable, Pleasant, Cheerful, Sweet, Engaging, Adorable, Lovable.
W	I	N	T	E	R	Y	Wintry, Cold, Stormy, White, Chilling, Aged, Cheerless.
W	I	P	E	O	F	F	Special effect during projecting a film.
W	I	R	E	B	A	R	Ingot for making wire.
W	I	R	E	C	U	T	Shaped as if cut by a taut wire.
W	I	R	E	M	A	N	Lineman, Artisan who installs, maintains and repairs electrical wiring and equipment.
W	I	R	E	T	A	P	To tap a telephone or telegraph wire.
W	I	R	E	W	A	Y	Channel for the installation of wires.
W	I	R	I	E	S	T	Sinewy, Flexible, Tense, Leanest, Supple, Highest pitch of tones.
W	I	R	L	I	N	G	Stunted or puny creature.
W	I	S	E	G	U	Y	Conceited know-all, Cocky person, Smart Aleck.
W	I	S	H	F	U	L	Hopeful, Longing, Eager, Desirous, Fanciful, Craving.
W	I	S	P	I	L	Y	Insubstantial, Wispy, Tenuous, Fleetingly.
W	I	S	T	F	U	L	Melancholy, Yearning, Pensive, Mournful, Musing, Meditative.
W	I	S	T	I	T	I	Marmoset.
W	I	T	C	H	E	D	Bewitched.
W	I	T	C	H	E	N	Rowan tree.
W	I	T	H	E	R	S	Between base of the neck and shoulder bones in various animals.
W	I	T	H	O	U	T	Outside, Beyond, Past, Lacking, Minus, Wanting, Except, Unless.
W	I	T	L	E	S	S	Foolish, Heedless, Insane, Stupid, Simple, Brainless, Silly, Daft.
W	I	T	L	O	O	F	Chicory, Endive.
W	I	T	N	E	S	S	Testimony, Evidence, Attest, Testify, Proof, Spectator, Observer, Bystander.
W	I	T	T	I	E	R	Cleverer, More jocular, More humourous, Droller.
W	I	T	T	I	L	Y	Humourously, Jocularly, Entertainingly, Facetiously, Scintillating.
W	I	T	T	I	N	G	Cognizant, Conscious, Intentional, Aware, Knowing, Sensible, Deliberate, Willing.
W	I	T	W	A	L	L	Woodpecker.
W	I	Z	E	N	E	D	Withered, Shrivelled, Mummified, Dwindled.
W	O	B	B	L	E	D	Rocked, Staggered, Lurched, Swayed, Teetered, Faltered, Tottered, Quivered.
W	O	B	B	L	E	R	One that staggers or dithers.
W	O	L	F	D	O	G	Large dog for hunting wolves, A dog resembling a wolf.
W	O	L	F	I	S	H	Ravenous, Ferocious, Barberous, Cruel, Grim, Inhuman, Savage.
W	O	L	F	R	A	M	Tungsten.
W	O	M	A	N	E	D	Made into a woman, Staffed with women.
W	O	M	A	N	L	Y	Gently, Feminine, Graceful, Mature.
W	O	M	M	E	R	A	Throwing stick used by Australian aborigines.
W	O	N	G	H	A	I	Asiatic tree.
W	O	O	D	A	N	T	Termite.
W	O	O	D	C	U	T	Engraving on wood, Letterpress printing surface.
W	O	O	D	I	E	R	More overgrown with forest.
W	O	O	D	M	A	N	Tree feller, Woodcutter.
W	O	O	D	O	I	L	An oil yielded by wood, Balsam, Pine oil, Tung oil.
W	O	O	D	O	W	L	An owl living in trees.
W	O	O	D	S	I	A	Genus of small or medium-sized rock inhabiting ferns.
W	O	O	D	T	A	R	Pine tar, Creosote.
W	O	O	D	T	I	N	Cassiterite occurring in fibrous form.
W	O	O	L	D	E	D	Wound a chain, Wrapped a rope.
W	O	O	L	D	E	R	A stick to tighten a rope at the knot.
W	O	O	L	L	E	N	Fabric woven from wool, Yarn spun from wool.
W	O	O	L	M	A	N	Dealer in wool.
W	O	O	L	S	E	Y	Lindsey - Woolsey, Fabric of mixture of wool and linen.
W	O	O	M	E	R	A	Same as WOMMERA.
W	O	O	Z	I	L	Y	In a befuddled manner, Dizzily, Vaguely, Blurry.

1	2	3	4	5	6	7	
W	O	R	D	A	G	E	Diction, Parlance, Phrase, Verbalism, Verbage.
W	O	R	D	I	L	Y	In a talkative manner, Repetitious, Garrulity, Rhetoric.
W	O	R	D	I	N	G	Phrasing, Phraseology, Diction, Parlance, Phrasing, Verbalism, Language, Mode, Style.
W	O	R	D	I	S	H	Verbal, Verbose, Wordy, Having to do with words.
W	O	R	K	B	A	G	Bag holding implements and materials.
W	O	R	K	B	O	X	A box holding necessities for needlework.
W	O	R	K	D	A	Y	A day for performing work.
W	O	R	K	I	N	G	Operating, Functioning, Forging, Shaping, Solving, Contriving, Arranging, Acting.
W	O	R	K	M	A	N	Artisan, Craftsman, Labourer, Operator, Mechanic, Employee.
W	O	R	K	O	U	T	Practice game, Test for determining ability.
W	O	R	K	S	H	Y	Lazy, Unwilling to work.
W	O	R	L	D	L	Y	Earthly, Mundane, Terrestrial, Materialistic, Sensual, Sophisticated, Disillusioned.
W	O	R	M	I	N	G	Digging for worms, Wriggling, Insinuating, Foisting, Infiltrating, Squiggling, Squirming.
W	O	R	N	O	U	T	Dilapidated, Dissipated, Depleted, Stale, Trite, Hackneyed, Exhausted.
W	O	R	R	I	E	D	Harassed, Distraught, Distracted, Distressed, Tormented, Troubled, Annoyed, Pestered.
W	O	R	R	I	E	R	One that worries.
W	O	R	S	H	I	P	Honour, Venerate, Adore, Idolize, Love.
W	O	R	S	T	E	D	Overthrew, Defeated, Bested, Outdone. Closely woven fabric.
W	O	U	L	D	B	E	Desiring to be, Aspiring to self improvement, Unsuccessful.
W	O	U	L	D	S	T	Will.
W	O	U	N	D	E	D	Cut, Stabbed, Pierced, Lacerated, Injured.
W	R	A	P	P	E	D	Covered, Enveloped, Encompassed, Swathed, Draped, Intent, Absorbed, Preoccupied.
W	R	A	P	P	E	R	Paper cover, Cover for something, Sheet of paper for wrapping newspapers or magazines.
W	R	A	W	L	E	D	Cried, Howled, Bawled.
W	R	E	A	K	E	D	Avenged, Indulged, Gratified, Expended, Caused, Inflicted.
W	R	E	A	T	H	E	Twist, Contort, Interweave, Encircle, Adorn, Crown, Writhe, Wind.
W	R	E	A	T	H	Y	Wreathed, Twisted, Curled, Spiral.
W	R	E	C	K	E	D	Shipwrecked, Shattered, Destroyed, Damaged, Disabled, Crashed.
W	R	E	C	K	E	R	One that wrecks ships by enticing them to rocks with false signals.
W	R	E	N	B	O	Y	Costumed male singer of a group that visits houses the day after Xmas.
W	R	E	N	T	I	T	Small brown Californian bird resembling a wren.
W	R	E	S	T	E	D	Pull, Moved, Forced, Wrenched, Confiscated, Extorted, Squeezed, Gouged.
W	R	E	S	T	E	R	Perverter.
W	R	E	S	T	L	E	Grapple, Tussle, Scuffle, Fight, Contend, Struggle, Exert.
W	R	I	G	G	L	E	Squirm, Writhe, Worm, Flow, Meander, Twist, Ooze, Slide.
W	R	I	N	G	E	R	Device for wringing moisture from linen or clothes.
W	R	I	N	K	L	E	Corrugation, Crease, Ridge, Technique, Suggestion, Hint, Fault, Pucker.
W	R	I	N	K	L	Y	Corrugated, Puckered, Furrowed.
W	R	I	T	E	I	N	Insert in a document, Cast a vote, Write to a source of supply.
W	R	I	T	E	U	P	Write an account, Increase book value of assets.
W	R	I	T	H	E	D	Wrenched, Intertwined, Contorted, Wrested, Agonized, Squirmed, Recoiled, Twisted.
W	R	I	T	H	E	N	Intertwined, Writhed, Twisted, Contorted, Coiled, Looped.
W	R	I	T	I	N	G	Art of forming letters, Use of characters to record ideas, Style of composition.
W	R	I	T	T	E	N	Inscribed, Recorded, Dictated, Drafted, Formed characters, Scrawled, Scribbled.
W	R	I	Z	L	E	D	Wrinkled.
W	R	O	N	G	E	D	Deprived, Violated, Defrauded, Dispossessed, Impaired, Spoiled, Maligned, Injured.
W	R	O	N	G	E	R	One that abuses or violates.
W	R	O	N	G	L	Y	Improperly, Inappropriately, Inaccurately, Incorrectly, Mistakenly.
W	R	O	S	T	L	E	Wrestle.
W	R	O	U	G	H	T	Created, Fashioned, Shaped, Formed, Embellished, Manufactured, Finished, Hammered.
W	R	Y	B	I	L	L	New Zealand plover with a deflected bill.
W	R	Y	N	E	C	K	Woodpecker that controls its neck.
W	R	Y	T	H	E	N	Treat in a perverse or distorted fashion.
W	U	R	R	U	N	G	A special type of Australian wallaby.
W	U	S	T	I	T	E	Artificial mineral consisting of ferrous oxide.
W	Y	A	N	D	O	T	Member of a tribe of American Indians.
W	Y	C	H	E	L	M	Witch elm tree.
W	Y	E	T	H	I	A	Genus of plants that resemble sunflowers.

X

X	A	N	T	H	I	C	Something of a yellow colour.
X	A	N	T	H	I	N	Carotenoid pigment.
X	A	N	T	H	Y	L	Univalent radical.
X	E	N	O	P	U	S	Genus of African aquatic frogs.
X	E	N	U	R	U	S	Genus of armadillos.

1	2	3	4	5	6	7	Definition
X	E	R	A	F	I	N	Portugese silver coin.
X	E	R	A	R	C	H	Ecologically developing in a dry place.
X	E	R	O	S	I	S	Abnormal dryness of a part of the body or tissue.
X	I	M	E	N	I	A	Small genus of tropical shrubs or trees, Sour plum.
X	I	P	H	I	A	S	Swordfish.
X	I	P	H	O	I	D	Related to the swordfish.
X	Y	L	E	N	O	L	Crystalline isomeric phenols.
X	Y	L	I	T	O	L	Sweet crystalline pentahydroxy alcohol.
X	Y	L	O	P	I	A	Genus of tropical American trees or shrubs, Guinea pepper.
X	Y	L	O	S	M	A	Genus of American and Asiatic evergreen trees and shrubs.

Y

1	2	3	4	5	6	7	Definition
Y	A	C	H	T	E	D	Raced or cruised in a yacht.
Y	A	H	W	I	S	M	Religion of the Israelites.
Y	A	H	W	I	S	T	Adherent of the old religion of Judah.
Y	A	M	A	M	A	I	Large Japanese silkworm.
Y	A	N	K	I	N	G	Jerking, Pulling, Lurching, Twitching, CLutching, Grabbing, Snatching.
Y	A	P	P	I	N	G	Yelping, Snapping, Barking, Chattering, Scolding.
Y	A	R	D	A	G	E	Livestock enclosure supplied by the railroad.
Y	A	R	D	A	N	G	Ridge eroded by wind.
Y	A	R	D	A	R	M	End of spar on a square-rigged sailing ship.
Y	A	R	D	I	N	G	Herding, Penning, Congregating, Collecting.
Y	A	R	D	M	A	N	Sailor, Worker in a railroad yard with livestock.
Y	A	R	N	I	N	G	Telling a long story, Chatting, Gossip.
Y	A	S	H	M	A	K	Veil worn by Muslim women to cover the face except for the eyes.
Y	A	U	P	I	N	G	Yawping, Yelling.
Y	A	W	L	I	N	G	Howling, Screaming.
Y	A	W	N	I	N	G	Gaping, Opening the jaws wide.
Y	A	W	P	I	N	G	Squawking, Yelling, Complaining, Yammering, Gaping, Staring.
Y	E	A	N	I	N	G	Lambing, Giving birth to young sheep or goat.
Y	E	A	R	N	E	D	Craved, Longed, Ached, Hankered, Hungered, Lusted, Pined, Desired.
Y	E	G	G	M	A	N	Robber, Safecracker.
Y	E	L	L	I	N	G	Shouting, Crying, Whooping, Howling, Screaming, Squealing, Lamenting, Wailing.
Y	E	L	L	O	W	Y	Yellowish, Sallowy.
Y	E	L	P	I	N	G	Squealing, Calling, Yapping.
Y	E	R	K	I	N	G	Thrashing, Goading, Jerking, Hurting, Kicking.
Y	E	S	T	E	R	N	Relating to yesterday.
Y	E	W	T	R	E	E	Evergreen tree.
Y	I	D	D	I	S	H	Relating to east European language of the Jews.
Y	I	E	L	D	E	D	Rewarded, Delivered, Relinquished, Abandoned, Surrendered, Succumbed, Resigned.
Y	I	E	L	D	E	R	One that surrenders.
Y	O	D	E	L	E	R	One that yodels.
Y	O	G	H	U	R	T	Fermented slightly acid milk food.
Y	O	K	E	L	R	Y	Gullible countryfolk, Yokels.
Y	O	R	K	I	S	T	Supporter of the English royal house of York.
Y	O	U	N	G	E	R	Junior, Offspring, Young person, Inferior in age.
Y	O	U	N	G	L	Y	In an immature manner.
Y	O	U	N	K	E	R	Youngster, Child, Junior seaman.
Y	O	U	T	H	L	Y	Youthful, Fresh, Vigorous, Juvenile, Puerile, Boyish, Virginal, Maidenly.
Y	O	W	L	I	N	G	Wailing, Howling, Screaming, Squealing, Bawling, Squalling.
Y	P	E	R	I	T	E	Mustard gas.
Y	U	C	A	T	E	L	French yellow.
Y	U	L	E	L	O	G	Large log brought in as a tradition on Christmas Eve.

Z

1	2	3	4	5	6	7	Definition
Z	A	C	A	T	O	N	Several grasses of the dry regions of the U.S.A. and Mexico.
Z	A	K	U	S	K	A	Hors d'oeuvre, Tasty little snacks served with drinks before a meal.
Z	A	M	A	R	R	A	Sheepskin coat worn by Spanish shepherds.
Z	A	M	O	U	S	E	Bush cow.
Z	A	N	C	L	U	S	Genus of marine fishes.
Z	A	N	J	E	R	O	Officer in charge of irrigation ditches.
Z	A	N	O	N	I	A	Genus of Indo-Malayan herbaceous vines with three-valved fruits, Bandoleer fruit.
Z	A	N	Y	I	N	G	Clowning, Fooling, Behaving in a crazy fashion.

1	2	3	4	5	6	7	
Z	A	N	Y	I	S	M	Buffoonery.
Z	A	P	A	T	E	O	Spanish or Latin-American dance.
Z	E	A	L	O	U	S	Enthusiastic, Keen, Warm, Ardent, Fervent, Avid, Eager, Obsessed.
Z	E	B	R	A	S	S	Hybrid bred from a zebra and an ass.
Z	E	B	R	I	N	E	Resembling markings of a zebra.
Z	E	B	R	U	L	A	Zebroid.
Z	E	D	O	A	R	Y	Fragrant drug derived from a rhizome.
Z	E	L	K	O	V	A	A small genus of shrubs and trees.
Z	E	M	I	R	O	T	Religious Hebrew songs.
Z	E	O	L	I	T	E	Hydrous silicates.
Z	E	R	O	I	N	G	Concentrating, Training, Adjusting, Closing, Directing, Aiming, Casting, Pointing.
Z	E	S	T	F	U	L	Showing keen enjoyment.
Z	E	S	T	I	N	G	Relishing, Enjoying.
Z	E	T	E	T	I	C	Skeptic, Seeker, Inquiry.
Z	E	U	G	I	T	E	A structure in which nuclear fusion occurs.
Z	E	U	Z	E	R	A	Genus of moths.
Z	I	M	A	R	R	A	Black cassock and trimmings worn by Roman Catholic prelates.
Z	I	M	O	C	C	A	Harsh commercial sponge found in the Mediterranean Sea.
Z	I	N	C	I	F	Y	Coat with zinc, Galvanize.
Z	I	N	C	I	T	E	Brittle hexagonal mineral of zinc oxide.
Z	I	N	C	O	I	D	Resembling zinc.
Z	I	N	C	O	U	S	Zincic, Relating to zinc.
Z	I	O	N	I	S	M	Plan for setting up a Jewish community in Palestine.
Z	I	O	N	I	S	T	Advocating Zionism.
Z	I	O	N	I	T	E	Citizen of Zion.
Z	I	P	H	I	I	D	Ziphioid, Genus of toothed whales.
Z	I	P	H	I	U	S	Genus of beaked whales.
Z	I	P	P	I	N	G	Closing or opening a zip fastener, Hurrying, Bustling.
Z	I	Z	A	N	I	A	Genus of tall grasses, Wild rice.
Z	O	A	R	I	T	Y	Member of 19th century communal sect of German Protestant separatists.
Z	O	A	R	I	U	M	Colony of colonial bryozoans.
Z	O	C	C	O	L	O	Socle, Plinth.
Z	O	I	S	I	T	E	Orthorhombic mineral related to epidote.
Z	O	N	A	L	L	Y	Girdled, Belted, Banded.
Z	O	N	U	L	A	R	Relating to a little zone, girdle or belt.
Z	O	O	I	D	A	L	Single entity that does not reproduce by sexual methods, Coral.
Z	O	O	L	O	G	Y	Science that deals with animals.
Z	O	O	M	I	N	G	Moving with a low hum, Movement with a camera lense keeping the subject in focus.
Z	O	O	N	O	M	Y	Physiology, Natural science.
Z	O	O	T	O	M	Y	Dissection of animals.
Z	O	O	T	Y	P	Y	Zoological classification.
Z	O	R	I	L	L	A	Itonyx, Skunk.
Z	O	R	I	L	L	O	Tropical American shrub that has an offensive skunklike odour.
Z	O	S	T	E	R	A	Small genus of marine plants.
Z	U	F	F	O	L	O	Litte flute.
Z	Y	G	O	S	I	S	Union of gametes.
Z	Y	G	O	T	I	C	Existing as a zygote.
Z	Y	M	O	G	E	N	An inactive protein precursor.
Z	Y	M	O	S	I	S	Fermentation.
Z	Y	M	O	T	I	C	Relating to fermentation, Causing an infectious or contagious disease.
Z	Y	M	U	R	G	Y	Chemistry that deals with brewing or wine making.

A

Word	Definition
A A R D V A R K	Ant-eater.
A A R D W O L F	Hyenalike mammal.
A A R O N I T E	Priestly descendant of Aaron.
A A S V O G E L	Vulture.
A B A C U L U S	Tile used in mosaic.
A B A M P E R E	Electromagnetic unit of electric current.
A B A S H I N G	Disconcerting, Discomfiting, Embarrassing, Confusing, Abasing, Demeaning, Rattling.
A B A T A B L E	Capable of being abolished.
A B A T J O U R	Skylight.
A B A T T O I R	Slaughter-house.
A B A T V O I X	Device for reflecting sound.
A B B A T I A L	Belonging to an abbey, abbot or abbess.
A B B E T D I N	Vice-president of the supreme council of ancient Jewish nation.
A B D E R I A N	Foolish, Belonging to ancient city of Abdera.
A B D E R I T E	Simpleton, Scoffer.
A B D I C A T E	Disown, Disinherit, Surrender, Discard, Renounce.
A B D U C E N T	Abducting.
A B D U C I N G	Abducting.
A B D U C T E D	Kidnapped, Separated.
A B D U C T O R	One that carries off a person by force.
A B E L M O S K	Bushy herb of tropical Asia and East Indies whose seeds are used in perfumery and coffee.
A B E R D E E N	From the city of Aberdeen, Scotland.
A B E R R A N T	Deviant, Deviate, Abnormal, Unrepresentative, Eccentric, Odd, Strange, Unusual.
A B E T M E N T	Act of abetting a crime.
A B E T T I N G	Inciting, Encouraging, Instigating, Assisting in a purpose.
A B E Y A N C E	Dormancy, Interruption, Intermission, Suspension, Break, Interval, Pause.
A B H I N A Y A	Expressive use of face and hands in Indian dance.
A B H O R R E D	Detested, Loathed, Avoided, Scorned, Rejected, Hated, Disdained.
A B H O R R E R	One who signed an address to Charles the Second of England.
A B I D A N C E	Continuance, Compliance, Staying.
A B I E T E N E	Hydrocarbon mixture.
A B I N I T I O	From the beginning.
A B J E C T L Y	In a degraded manner, Servilely, Despicably.
A B J U R I N G	Rejecting, Renouncing, Recanting, Retracting, Forswearing, Avoiding, Renouncing.
A B L A T I O N	Removal of an organ by surgery.
A B L A T I V E	Grammatical case.
A B L E G A T E	Envoy on a papal mission.
A B L E N E S S	Capable, Worthy, Tending, Favouring, Liable, Ability, Skill.
A B L U T I O N	Washing, Cleansing, Purification, Baptism.
A B N E G A T E	Surrender, Relinquish, Deny, Renounce, Forgo, Adjure.
A B N O R M A L	Irregular, Unusual, Excessive, Exceptional, Subnormal, Odd, Unnatural, Monstrous.
A B O M A S U M	The fourth or true digestive stomach of a ruminant.
A B O R D A G E	Boarding a ship in an attack.
A B O R N I N G	Being born or produced.
A B O R T I N G	Premature birth, Stopping before fruition, Terminate prematurely, Checked development.
A B O R T I O N	Miscarriage, Monstrosity, Arrest of development.
A B O R T I V E	Miscarrying, Fruitless, Unsuccessful, Rudimentary.
A B R A D A N T	Abrasive.
A B R A D I N G	Eroding, Chafing, Irritating, Grazing, Rubbing, Galling, Annoying, Irking.
A B R A S I O N	Wearing away by friction, Scraping.
A B R A S I V E	Substances used to grind, scour, clean or rub.
A B R I D G E D	Curtailed, Diminished, Lessened, Limited, Narrowed, Reduced, Restricted, Minimized.
A B R O G A T E	Abolish, Annul, Repeal, Nullify, Void, Discharge, Dissolve, Vacate.
A B R U P T E D	Separated.
A B S C I S S A	Geometrical theory.
A B S E N T E D	Kept away, Omitted, Lost.
A B S E N T E E	One that absents himself.
A B S E N T L Y	Preoccupied, Lacking, Inattentive, Dreamily, Vaguely.
A B S I N T H E	Green bitter liqueur once flavoured with wormwood.
A B S O L U T E	Absolved, Free, Perfect, Pure, Outright, Positive, Peremptory, Unquestionable.
A B S O L V E D	Resolved, Acquitted, Pardoned, Exculpated, Exempted, Exonerated, Vindicated, Released.
A B S O L V E R	One that pardons.
A B S O N A N T	Discordant, Contrary, Unreasonable.

1	2	3	4	5	6	7	8	
A	B	S	O	R	B	E	D	Engulfed, Assimilated, Incorporated, Monopolized, Intent, Imbibed, Engaged, Preoccupied.
A	B	S	T	E	R	G	E	Cleanse, Purge.
A	B	S	T	R	A	C	T	Abstruse, Ideal, Formal, Removed, Separate, Hypothetical, Theoretical, Detach.
A	B	S	T	R	U	S	E	Reconcile, Deep, Esoteric, Occult, Profound, Secret, Complex, Intricate.
A	B	S	U	R	D	L	Y	Irrationally, Foolishly, Ridiculously.
A	B	U	N	D	A	N	T	Rich, Ample, Plentiful, Copious, Generous, Liberal, Lavish, Profuse.
A	B	U	S	A	B	L	E	Violable, Capable of being abused.
A	B	U	T	I	L	O	N	Genus of mostly tropical plants, Indian mallow.
A	B	U	T	M	E	N	T	Support structure, Anchorage for cables of a suspension bridge.
A	B	U	T	T	A	L	S	Boundaries of lands in relation to adjoining properties.
A	B	U	T	T	I	N	G	Adjacent.
A	C	A	D	E	M	I	A	Academic environment.
A	C	A	D	E	M	I	C	Scholarly, Visionary, Conventional, Pedantic, Bookish, Impractical, Utopian, Speculative.
A	C	A	L	E	P	H	S	Class of jellyfishes.
A	C	A	N	T	H	U	S	Genus of prickly herbs, Corinthian decoration.
A	C	A	R	I	D	E	A	Genus of parasitic mites.
A	C	A	R	I	D	A	E	Large and widely distributed family of mites.
A	C	A	R	P	O	U	S	Sterile, Not producing fruit.
A	C	A	U	D	A	T	E	Without a tail.
A	C	A	U	L	I	N	E	Stemless.
A	C	C	E	D	I	N	G	Approaching, Associating, Assenting, Acquiescing, Agreeing, Consenting, Subscribing.
A	C	C	E	N	T	E	D	Inflected, Intoned, Emphasised, Stressed, Throbbed.
A	C	C	E	N	T	O	R	Genus of bird, European hedge sparrow.
A	C	C	E	P	T	E	D	Received, Acknowledged, Recognized, Understood, Approved, Endured, Believed.
A	C	C	E	P	T	E	R	One that accepts an order or bill of exchange.
A	C	C	E	P	T	O	R	Substance capable of being combined with another.
A	C	C	I	D	E	N	T	Fortune, Hazard, Casualty, Mischance, Disaster, Mishap, Misadventure, Calamity.
A	C	C	O	L	A	D	E	Award, Embrace, Knighthood, Honour, Decoration, Distinction, Laurels.
A	C	C	O	R	D	E	D	Reconciled, Harmonized, Allowed, Conceded, Awarded, Allotted, Agreed, Granted.
A	C	C	O	S	T	E	D	Addressed, Called, Hailed, Saluted, Confronted, Approached, Pestered, Worried.
A	C	C	O	U	N	T	S	Bills, Invoices, Scores, Statements, Values, Regards, Explanations, Chronicles.
A	C	C	O	U	P	L	E	Join, Couple, Link.
A	C	C	O	U	T	R	E	Dress, Furnish, Equip, Military dress.
A	C	C	R	E	D	I	T	Credit, Approve, Ascribe, Authorize, Certify, Endorse, Sanction, Attest.
A	C	C	R	E	T	E	D	United, Combined, Adhered.
A	C	C	R	O	A	C	H	Assume, Appropriate, Usurp, Commandeer, Preempt, Arrogate, Annex, Confiscate.
A	C	C	R	U	I	N	G	Gathering, Accumulating, Adding, Compounding, Resulting, Collecting.
A	C	C	U	R	A	C	Y	Correctness, Exactness, Precise, Definitiveness.
A	C	C	U	R	A	T	E	Correct, Exact, Nice, Precise, Proper, Right, Rigorous, Careful.
A	C	C	U	R	S	E	D	Doomed, Execrable, Cursed, Damnable, Abhorrent, Detestable, Offensive, Repugnant.
A	C	C	U	S	A	N	T	One that accuses.
A	C	C	U	S	I	N	G	Betraying, Charging, Indicting, Impeaching, Arraigning. Accusing, Incriminating.
A	C	C	U	S	T	O	M	Habituate, Familiarize, Inure, Use, Wont, Accommodate, Adapt, Adjust.
A	C	E	L	D	A	M	A	Field of bloodshed, Place of highly disagreeable association.
A	C	E	N	T	R	I	C	Lacking a centromere.
A	C	E	P	H	A	L	A	Clams, Oysters, Mussels.
A	C	E	R	B	A	T	E	Irritated, Exasperated, Harsh, Embitter.
A	C	E	R	B	I	T	Y	Acidity, Astringency of manner.
A	C	E	R	V	A	T	E	Growing in heaps or closely compacted clusters.
A	C	E	S	C	E	N	T	Turning sour.
A	C	H	A	T	I	N	A	Genus of very large African land snails.
A	C	H	E	N	I	U	M	Single-seeded fruit.
A	C	H	E	T	O	U	S	Having no bristles.
A	C	H	I	E	V	E	D	Accomplished, Reached, Attained, Performed, Executed, Gained, Concluded, Perfected.
A	C	H	O	R	I	O	N	Genus of imperfect fungi.
A	C	H	R	O	M	I	A	Absence of normal pigmentation.
A	C	I	C	U	L	A	E	Needlelike spine, crystal or bristle.
A	C	I	C	U	L	A	R	Slender and pointed like a needle.
A	C	I	D	N	E	S	S	State of being acid.
A	C	I	D	O	S	I	S	Decreased alkalinity of the blood and tissues.
A	C	I	D	O	T	I	C	Characterised by acidosis.
A	C	I	E	R	A	G	E	Process of coating the surface of a metal plate.
A	C	I	L	I	A	T	E	Without cilia.
A	C	I	N	O	N	Y	X	Cheetahs.
A	C	O	E	M	E	T	I	Monks of the 5th and 6th century Eastern monastries.
A	C	O	N	I	T	I	C	Characteristics of aconite.
A	C	O	N	I	T	U	M	Genus of poisonous herbs.

1	2	3	4	5	6	7	8	Clue
A	C	O	R	N	C	U	P	Cupule of an acorn.
A	C	O	U	S	T	I	C	Relating to hearing or sound, Auditory, Aural, Audible, Sonic measuring.
A	C	Q	U	A	I	N	T	Introduce, Inform, Present, Advise, Apprise, Notify, Disclose, Divulge.
A	C	Q	U	I	R	E	D	Gained, Possessed, Controlled, Attained, Obtained, Procured, Achieved, Accumulated.
A	C	R	I	D	I	N	E	Colourless compound used in dyes and synthetics.
A	C	R	I	D	I	A	N	Locust, Grasshopper.
A	C	R	I	D	I	T	Y	Irritating, Extreme bitterness, Sharpness.
A	C	R	I	M	O	N	Y	Sharpness, Rancour, Causticity, Asperity, Bitterness, Malice, Malevolence, Spite.
A	C	R	O	L	E	I	N	Toxic colourless mobile liquid aldehyde.
A	C	R	O	L	I	T	H	Statue with metal drapery.
A	C	R	O	M	I	O	N	The scapula and clavicle.
A	C	R	O	S	T	I	C	Composition of verse, Acronym, Play on words.
A	C	T	I	F	I	E	R	Part of the equipment for liquid purification of gases.
A	C	T	I	N	I	D	E	Chemical element.
A	C	T	I	N	I	S	M	Property of radiant energy.
A	C	T	I	N	I	U	M	Darkening effect of light on some zinc sulfide.
A	C	T	I	N	O	I	D	Radial symmetry.
A	C	T	I	N	O	S	T	Small bones supporting rays of some fishes.
A	C	T	I	V	A	T	E	Vitalize, Energize, Arouse, Awaken, Rally, Rouse, Wake.
A	C	T	I	V	E	L	Y	Effectively, Lively, Nimbly, Energetically, Seriously, Earnestly.
A	C	T	I	V	I	S	M	Philosophical doctrines, Actualism.
A	C	T	I	V	I	S	T	Advocating activism.
A	C	T	I	V	I	T	Y	Liveliness, Agility, Exercise, Exertion.
A	C	T	U	A	L	L	Y	Really, Very, Genuinely, Truly, Veritably.
A	C	T	U	A	T	E	D	Moved, Impelled, Mobilized, Propelled, Circulated, Galvanized, Aroused, Vitalized.
A	C	U	L	E	A	T	E	One of the bees, wasps or ants.
A	D	A	P	T	I	N	G	Acclimatizing, Suiting, Adjusting, Accommodating, Conforming, Reconciling, Adapting.
A	D	A	P	T	I	V	E	Adjustable, Conformable.
A	D	D	E	N	D	U	M	Addition, Supplement, Accessory, Appurtenance, Appendix, Codicil, Rider, Supplement.
A	D	D	I	C	T	E	D	Surrendered, Devoted, Prone, Inclined, Disposed, Habituated, Attached, Craved.
A	D	D	I	T	I	O	N	Increase, Augmentation, Alternation, Increment, Raise, Accessory, Adjunct, Supplement.
A	D	D	I	T	I	V	E	Added, Involving, Cumulative, Accumulative, Component, Constituent, Chain, Summative.
A	D	D	O	R	S	E	D	In heraldry back to back.
A	D	D	U	C	E	N	T	Adducting, Bringing together.
A	D	D	U	C	I	N	G	Bringing forward, Offering, Presenting, Citing.
A	D	D	U	C	T	O	R	A powerful muscle with drawing powers, Muscle of an oyster.
A	D	E	N	O	I	D	S	Abnormally enlarged mass of lymphatic tissue at the back of the throat.
A	D	E	Q	U	A	C	Y	Ability, Capability, Capacity, Competence, Qualified, Sufficiency.
A	D	E	Q	U	A	T	E	Sufficient, Comfortable, Competent, Decent, Enough, Satisfactory, Sufficiency, Suitable.
A	D	H	E	R	E	N	T	Follower, Cohort, Disciple, Partisan, Supporter, Satellite, Champion, Upholder, Backer.
A	D	H	E	R	I	N	G	Sticking, Cleaning, Clinging, Combining, Joining, Linking, Uniting.
A	D	H	E	S	I	O	N	Adherence, Bond, Cling, Cohesion, Sticking, Attachment, Constancy, Loyalty.
A	D	H	E	S	I	V	E	Sticky, Gluey, Gummy, Stodgy.
A	D	I	A	N	T	U	M	Genus of plants, Maidenhair fern.
A	D	I	P	O	S	I	S	Obesity, Degeneration of a heart or liver.
A	D	J	A	C	E	N	T	Abutting, Touching, Adjoining, Contiguous, Juxtaposed, Bordering.
A	D	J	O	I	N	E	D	Jointed, Added, United, Linked.
A	D	J	O	I	N	E	D	Joined, Attached, Touched, Abutted, Bordered, Communicated, Marched, Verged.
A	D	J	U	R	I	N	G	Swearing an oath, Commanding, Entreating, Begging.
A	D	J	U	S	T	E	R	One that investigates complaints.
A	D	J	U	T	A	G	E	Tube or nozzle to regulate discharge of water.
A	D	J	U	T	A	N	T	General assistant to commandant in the armed services.
A	D	J	U	V	A	N	T	Serving to aid, An ingredient that modifies the action of a principal ingredient.
A	D	M	E	D	I	A	L	Near the median plane.
A	D	M	I	R	I	N	G	Wondering, Enjoying, Marvelling Appreciating, Cherishing, Delighting, Adoring.
A	D	M	I	T	T	E	D	Conceded, Acknowledged, Permitted, Allowed, Received, Entered, Installed, Introduced.
A	D	M	I	X	I	N	G	Mingling, Mixing, Blending.
A	D	M	O	N	I	S	H	Reprove, Chide, Rebuke, Reprimand, Reproach, Caution, Warn.
A	D	N	A	T	I	O	N	Grown together.
A	D	O	N	I	D	I	N	Mixture of glucosides once used as a cardiac stimulant.
A	D	O	N	I	T	O	L	A crystalline pentahydroxy alcohol.
A	D	O	P	T	I	N	G	Maintaining, Supporting, Embracing, Espousing, Assuming, Arrogating, Usurping.
A	D	O	P	T	I	O	N	Espousal, Embracing.
A	D	O	P	T	I	V	E	Acquired by adoption.
A	D	O	R	A	B	L	E	Delightful, Lovable, Charming, Delectable, Heavenly, Luscious, Delicious.
A	D	O	R	A	B	L	Y	Delightfully, Heavenly, Deliciously, Charmingly.
A	D	O	R	N	I	N	G	Decorating, Embellishing, Beautifying, Decking, Garnishing.

1	2	3	4	5	6	7	8	Definition
A	D	R	E	C	T	A	L	A gland adjacent to the rectum of certain mollusks.
A	D	R	O	I	T	L	Y	Cleverly, Dexterously, Deftly, Nimbly, Skillfully, Shrewdly.
A	D	S	C	R	I	P	T	Irremovably attached, Written immediately after another character.
A	D	S	O	R	B	E	D	Taken up by physical and chemical forces of gases or substances.
A	D	U	L	A	R	I	A	Moonstone.
A	D	U	L	A	T	E	D	Flattered excessively, Fawned, Acclaimed.
A	D	U	L	A	T	O	R	One that flatters or acclaims.
A	D	U	L	T	E	R	Y	Fornication, Extra-marital cohabitation, Unchastity, Idolatry.
A	D	V	A	N	C	E	D	Furthered, Marched, Increased, Promoted, Progressed, Approached.
A	D	V	A	N	C	E	R	Promoter.
A	D	V	E	N	I	N	G	Adding to something, Becoming part of something.
A	D	V	E	R	T	E	D	Paid heed, Directed attention, Alluded, Referred.
A	D	V	I	S	I	N	G	Cautioning, Warning, Informing, Counselling, Notifying, Inducing, Coaxing, Persuading.
A	D	V	I	S	O	R	Y	Exercising power to advise, Giving advice, Giving counsel.
A	D	V	O	C	A	A	T	Eggnog made from brandy, sugar, eggs and flavouring.
A	D	V	O	C	A	C	Y	Profession of an advocate, Supporting, Defending.
A	D	V	O	C	A	T	E	Barrister, Defender, Counsellor, Attorney, Support, Recommend.
A	D	V	O	W	S	O	N	Proposing an applicant for an ecclesiastical vacancy.
A	D	Y	N	A	M	I	A	Debility caused by disease.
A	D	Y	N	A	M	I	C	Relating to weakness.
A	E	C	I	D	I	U	M	Cup-shaped fungi.
A	E	D	E	A	G	U	S	Phallus, Organ of a male insect.
A	E	D	I	L	I	T	Y	Superintendence of public buildings and works.
A	E	G	E	R	I	I	D	Clearwing moth.
A	E	G	O	L	I	U	S	Genus of small northern owls.
A	E	G	R	O	T	A	T	Certificate for degree given to a student unable to sit examinations due to ill-health.
A	E	O	L	I	G	H	T	Gas-discharge glow lamp used in optical sound recording.
A	E	Q	U	O	R	E	A	Genus of jellyfish.
A	E	R	A	T	I	N	G	Supplying with oxygen, Ventilating, Making effervescent.
A	E	R	A	T	I	O	N	Exposing to air.
A	E	R	I	A	L	L	Y	Atmospherically, Lofty, Ethereal, Imaginary, By means of aircraft.
A	E	R	I	F	I	E	D	Aerated, Vaporized.
A	E	R	I	F	O	R	M	Gaseous, Intangible, Lacking substance.
A	E	R	O	B	I	C	S	Exercises designed to stimulate circulation and breathing.
A	E	R	O	B	I	U	M	Aerobe, Organism that only lives in oxygen, Bacterium.
A	E	R	O	D	Y	N	E	Heavy-than-air aircraft.
A	E	R	O	F	O	I	L	Airfoil.
A	E	R	O	G	R	A	M	Air-letter, Message sent by wireless telegraph, aircraft or radio.
A	E	R	O	L	I	T	E	Stony meteorite.
A	E	R	O	L	O	G	Y	Meteorology dealing with effects of wind on kites, airplanes, balloons and clouds.
A	E	R	O	N	A	U	T	One that travels in an airship or balloon.
A	E	R	O	S	T	A	T	Balloon or airship.
A	E	S	C	U	L	I	N	Esculin, Crystalline glucoside from the inner bark of the horse chestnut.
A	E	S	T	H	E	T	E	Professed beauty lover.
A	E	S	T	I	V	A	L	Belonging to summer.
A	F	E	B	R	I	L	E	Free from fever, Not marked by fever.
A	F	F	E	C	T	E	D	Fancied, Pretended, Assumed, Frequented, Influenced, Impressed, Swayed, Allotted.
A	F	F	E	E	R	E	D	Assessed.
A	F	F	E	R	E	N	T	Conveying nervous impulses toward a nerve centre.
A	F	F	I	A	N	C	E	Betroth, Engage.
A	F	F	I	N	A	G	E	Refining metal.
A	F	F	I	N	I	N	G	Refining as raw sugar.
A	F	F	I	N	I	T	Y	Relationship, Kinship, Alliance, Attraction, Sympathy, Likeness, Resemblance, Accord.
A	F	F	I	R	M	E	D	Validated, Confirmed, Asserted, Declared, Deposed, Certified, Guaranteed, Witnessed.
A	F	F	I	X	I	N	G	Fastening, Attaching, Adding, Subjoining, Impressing, Appending.
A	F	F	L	A	T	U	S	Inspiration, Supernatural, Impulse, Ecstacy.
A	F	F	L	U	E	N	T	Abundant, Copious, Wealthy, Rich, Opulent, Acquisitive, Grasping.
A	F	F	O	R	C	E	D	Strengthened.
A	F	F	O	R	D	E	D	Managed to pay, Gave, Furnished, Incurred the cost.
A	F	F	O	R	E	S	T	To plant a forest.
A	F	F	R	I	G	H	T	Frighten, Alarm, Sudden terror.
A	F	F	R	O	N	T	É	Heraldic figures face to face or full face, Gardant.
A	F	F	U	S	I	N	G	Pouring.
A	F	F	U	S	I	O	N	Pouring a liquid, (Baptism).
A	F	T	E	R	N	W	A	A desert shrub.
A	F	T	E	R	W	I	T	Perception that comes too late to be useful.
A	G	A	L	A	X	I	A	The failure of milk secreting glands in mammals.

1	2	3	4	5	6	7	8	Definition
A	G	A	L	I	N	I	S	Genus of flaxlike American herbs.
A	G	A	L	W	O	O	D	Aggalloch, Soft resinous wood of an East Indian tree burnt as a perfume by Orientals.
A	G	A	M	I	D	A	E	Family of Old World lizards.
A	G	A	P	E	T	A	E	Nuns who lived in the same house as monks under vows of celibacy.
A	G	A	R	A	G	A	R	Extract of red algae.
A	G	A	S	T	R	I	C	Having no stomach or digestive canal.
A	G	A	T	I	Z	E	D	Changed into agate.
A	G	E	N	E	S	I	S	Complete absence of an organ or part due to embryonic cell disorder.
A	G	E	N	T	I	A	L	Expressive of an agency.
A	G	G	R	I	E	V	E	Grieve, Distress, Oppress, Wrong.
A	G	I	O	T	A	G	E	Exchange business, Speculative buying or selling of stocks.
A	G	I	S	T	A	G	E	Grazing for a specified time at a fixed rate.
A	G	I	T	A	B	L	E	Excitable, Capable of being agitated.
A	G	I	T	A	T	E	D	Quivering, Shaking, Disturbed, Excited, Bothered, Flustered, Irritated, Provoked.
A	G	I	T	A	T	O	R	One who stirs up political, religious, economic or other social agitation.
A	G	L	I	M	M	E	R	Glimmering.
A	G	L	O	S	S	A	L	Minus a tongue.
A	G	M	A	T	I	N	E	Base formed from arginine in putrefaction.
A	G	N	A	T	H	I	A	Congenital complete or partial absence of one or both jaws.
A	G	N	A	T	I	O	N	Relationship of male descendants.
A	G	N	O	S	T	I	C	Freethinker, One who doubts the existence of a supreme being.
A	G	O	N	I	A	D	A	Bark of a S. American shrub yielding a bitter crystalline glucoside.
A	G	O	N	I	Z	E	D	Tortured, Struggled, Writhed, Afflicted, Harrowed, Tormented, Distressed, Squirmed.
A	G	R	A	P	H	I	A	Pathologic loss of the ability to write.
A	G	R	A	R	I	A	N	Relating to the land.
A	G	R	E	E	I	N	G	Consenting, Admitting, Arranging, Harmonizing, Suiting, Concurring, Granting, Assenting.
A	G	R	E	S	T	A	L	Wild, Uncultivated.
A	G	R	E	S	T	I	C	Rustic.
A	G	R	I	M	O	N	Y	Various plants, Hemp.
A	G	R	O	C	I	T	Y	Group of collective farms in the U.S.S.R.
A	G	R	O	L	O	G	Y	Branch of agriculture dealing with analysis of soils and crop production.
A	G	R	O	M	Y	Z	A	Genus of flies.
A	G	R	O	N	O	M	Y	Soil management and crop production.
A	G	R	O	S	T	I	S	Genus of grasses including pasture, hay and lawn.
A	G	R	Y	P	N	I	A	Vigil in the Eastern Church.
A	G	U	E	C	A	K	E	Enlarged hard spleen of chronic malaria.
A	G	U	E	T	R	E	E	Sassafras, Small genus of N. American and Asiatic aromatic trees.
A	H	A	N	K	A	R	A	A principle of Hinduism and Jainism.
A	I	G	R	E	T	T	E	Spray of feathers, Hair ornament.
A	I	L	E	T	T	E	S	Shoulder protection for a coat of mail.
A	I	R	B	O	R	N	E	Supported by aerodynamic and aerostatic forces.
A	I	R	B	R	A	K	E	A brake operated by compressed air.
A	I	R	B	R	I	C	K	Perforated brick used for ventilation.
A	I	R	B	R	U	S	H	Device for spraying paint by compressed air.
A	I	R	C	R	A	F	T	Weight carrying flying machines.
A	I	R	E	D	A	L	E	A large terrier dog.
A	I	R	F	I	E	L	D	Landing field of an airport.
A	I	R	F	L	E	E	T	Group of military aircraft.
A	I	R	F	L	O	A	T	Air sac.
A	I	R	F	R	A	M	E	Structure of an aircraft.
A	I	R	G	R	A	P	H	Air mail letter.
A	I	R	I	N	E	S	S	Sprightliness, Delicacy, Gaiety.
A	I	R	L	I	N	E	R	Commercial aircraft carrying passengers and freight.
A	I	R	P	I	L	O	T	A flyer.
A	I	R	P	L	A	N	E	Fixed wing aircraft.
A	I	R	P	O	W	E	R	Potential craft for attack or defence.
A	I	R	S	C	R	E	W	Airplane propeller.
A	I	R	S	H	A	F	T	Air well.
A	I	R	S	P	A	C	E	Area of space above a country considered under its jurisdiction.
A	I	R	S	T	R	I	P	Runway without usual commercial facilities.
A	I	R	T	I	G	H	T	Impenetrable, Impermeable.
A	K	E	L	D	A	M	A	Alceldama.
A	K	I	N	E	S	I	A	Loss or impairment of voluntary ability.
A	K	I	N	E	T	I	C	Relating to akinesia.
A	L	A	B	A	R	C	H	Chief magistrate of the Jews in ancient Egypt.
A	L	A	C	R	I	T	Y	Briskness, Eagerness, Promptness, Expedition, Quickness, Readiness, Enthusiasm.
A	L	A	R	M	I	N	G	Disturbing, Frightening, Scaring, Startling, Terrifying, Amazing, Surprising.

1	2	3	4	5	6	7	8	Definition
A	L	A	R	M	I	S	T	One that spreads panic.
A	L	B	A	C	O	R	E	Large pelagic fish, Tuna.
A	L	B	A	N	I	A	N	Relating to a country in the Balkan peninsula.
A	L	B	I	C	O	R	E	Same as ALBACORE.
A	L	B	I	N	I	S	M	Lacking pigment.
A	L	B	O	R	A	D	A	Instrumental serenade played on a bagpipe or oboe.
A	L	B	U	R	N	U	M	Sapwood.
A	L	C	A	H	E	S	T	Belief of alchemists that a universal solvent is possible.
A	L	C	A	T	R	A	S	Large water bird, Pelican, Frigate.
A	L	C	H	E	M	I	C	Concerned with alchemy.
A	L	D	E	H	Y	D	E	Organic compound.
A	L	D	E	R	M	A	N	Magistrate, Chief officer of the City of London.
A	L	D	I	M	I	N	E	Chemical compound.
A	L	D	O	L	A	S	E	A crystalline enzyme.
A	L	D	O	L	I	Z	E	Convert into an aldol.
A	L	E	A	T	O	R	Y	Relating to good and bad luck, Depending on an uncertain event.
A	L	E	B	E	N	C	H	Bench in an alehouse.
A	L	E	G	R	I	A	S	Solo flamenco dance performed by a woman.
A	L	E	H	O	U	S	E	Premises for consumption of ale.
A	L	E	M	B	E	R	T	System of betting in gambling games.
A	L	E	R	T	I	N	G	Alarming, Awakening, Arousing, Warning, Cautioning.
A	L	E	U	R	O	N	E	Ergastic protein matter.
A	L	F	R	E	S	C	O	In the open air.
A	L	G	E	R	I	N	E	Pirate, Algerian.
A	L	G	I	D	I	T	Y	Chilly, Coldness, Clammy.
A	L	G	O	L	O	G	Y	Study or science of algae.
A	L	G	O	N	K	I	N	Canadian Indian.
A	L	G	O	R	I	S	M	System of Arabic numerals, Arithmetic.
A	L	G	R	A	P	H	Y	Lithographic process using an aluminium plate.
A	L	I	C	A	N	T	E	From the city of Alicante, Spain.
A	L	I	E	N	A	G	E	Status of an alien.
A	L	I	E	N	A	T	E	Estrange, Cede, Convey, Disunite, Transfer, Assign, Relinquish, Hostile.
A	L	I	E	N	I	S	M	Status of an alien.
A	L	I	E	N	I	S	T	One that treats diseases of the mind, Psychiatrist.
A	L	I	G	H	T	E	D	Dismounted, Lodged, Landed, Settled, Dropped, Tumbled, Rested.
A	L	I	G	N	I	N	G	Adjusting, Arraying, Ranging, Regulating.
A	L	I	N	A	S	A	L	Relating, to the lateral portions of the nose.
A	L	I	Q	U	A	N	T	Being a part of a number but not dividing it.
A	L	I	T	R	U	N	K	Portion of the thorax of an insect that bears its wings.
A	L	I	Z	A	R	I	N	Orange or red crystalline compound.
A	L	J	A	M	A	D	O	Inhabitant of a Jewish community in medieval Spain.
A	L	K	A	H	E	S	T	Same as ALCAHEST.
A	L	K	A	L	I	E	S	Make alkaline.
A	L	K	A	L	I	F	Y	Same as ALKALIES.
A	L	K	A	L	I	N	E	Having the properties of an alkali.
A	L	K	A	L	O	I	D	Group of organic bases containing nitrogen.
A	L	K	E	R	M	E	S	Italian brandy liqueur flavoured with many herbs and spices.
A	L	K	O	X	I	D	E	Base formed from an alcohol.
A	L	K	Y	L	A	T	E	To introduce one or more alkyl groups into a compound.
A	L	L	A	N	I	T	E	Silicate mineral.
A	L	L	A	Y	I	N	G	Alleviating, Abating, Relieving, Pacifying, Appeasing, Quelling, Calming, Mitigating.
A	L	L	C	L	E	A	R	Indication to the populace that raiding aircraft have left the area.
A	L	L	E	G	I	N	G	Citing, Presenting, Advancing, Affirming, Asserting, Avowing, Stating, Declaring.
A	L	L	E	G	O	R	Y	Emblem, Figuration, Symbolism, Typification, Fable, Parable, Myth.
A	L	L	E	L	U	I	A	Hallelujah, Hymn of praise.
A	L	L	E	R	G	E	N	A substance that induces allergy.
A	L	L	E	R	G	I	C	Disagreeably sensitive, Antipathy, Aversion, Repugnance.
A	L	L	E	Y	W	A	Y	Narrow passageway between houses or cabins on a ship.
A	L	L	F	I	R	E	D	Extremely, Excessively, Infernal, Blasted, Blessed, Dashed, Deuced.
A	L	L	F	O	U	R	S	Using two arms and two legs for progress, Various card games.
A	L	L	I	A	N	C	E	Union, Affinity, Connection, Association, Affiliation, Combination, Partnership, Coalition.
A	L	L	I	O	N	I	A	Genus of chiefly American herbs.
A	L	L	I	S	I	O	N	Running of a ship into another ship that is stationary.
A	L	L	O	C	A	T	E	Ration, Share, Allot, Apportion, Assign, Give, Designate, Earmark.
A	L	L	O	D	I	A	L	Freehold land held without restriction.
A	L	L	O	D	I	U	M	Allodial.
A	L	L	O	G	A	M	Y	Cross fertilization.

1	2	3	4	5	6	7	8	Definition
A	L	L	O	P	A	T	H	Relating to allopathy, To combat disease by producing effects different from disease produced.
A	L	L	O	S	O	M	E	An atypical chromosone.
A	L	L	O	T	T	E	D	Assigned, Apportioned, Ordained, Appointed, Allocated, Gave, Dispensed, Accorded.
A	L	L	O	T	T	E	E	One that receives an allotment.
A	L	L	O	T	Y	P	E	A type specimen of the opposite sex to the holotype.
A	L	L	O	W	I	N	G	Approving, Sanctioning, Accepting, Acknowledging, Admitting, Conceding, Supposing.
A	L	L	O	Y	A	G	E	Act of alloying.
A	L	L	O	Y	I	N	G	Moderating, Mixing, Tempering, Allaying, Adulterating, Blending, Compounding, Fusing.
A	L	L	S	P	I	C	E	The berry of a tree yielding a pungent and aromatic spice.
A	L	L	U	D	I	N	G	Referring, Implying, Intimating, Suggesting, Pointing.
A	L	L	U	R	I	N	G	Luring, Attracting, Captivating, Charming, Drawing, Fascinating, Deluding, Magnetizing.
A	L	L	U	S	I	O	N	Reference, Indication.
A	L	L	U	S	I	V	E	Figurative, Symbolical, Making puns.
A	L	L	U	V	I	A	L	Deposits of various soils made by running water or floods.
A	L	L	U	V	I	O	N	Wash of water, Overflowing, Inundation, Flood, Alluvium.
A	L	L	U	V	I	U	M	Geological deposits of various kinds made by streams or floods.
A	L	L	Y	L	A	T	E	To introduce allyl into a substance.
A	L	M	A	C	I	G	A	Philippine timber tree yielding a resin.
A	L	M	A	G	E	S	T	Medieval treatise on a branch of knowledge.
A	L	M	E	N	D	R	O	Malabar almond.
A	L	M	E	R	I	A	N	Pertaining to prehistoric Spanish cultures.
A	L	M	I	G	H	T	Y	Absolute power, God, Unlimited power, Extreme.
A	L	M	S	D	E	E	D	Act of giving alms.
A	L	M	U	E	R	Z	O	Substantial lunch-time meal eaten in Spain around noon-time.
A	L	N	E	B	D	R	O	Almond tree.
A	L	O	C	A	S	I	A	Genus of tropical Asiatic herbs.
A	L	O	C	I	N	M	A	Genus of Asiatic snails that serve as hosts of the Chinese liver fluke.
A	L	O	P	E	C	I	A	Baldness, Loss of hair, wool or feathers.
A	L	O	U	A	T	T	A	Genus of monkeys, Howler monkeys.
A	L	P	H	A	B	E	T	Set of letters arranged in a set order.
A	L	P	I	N	I	S	T	A mountain climber specialising in difficult and very high terrain.
A	L	S	A	T	I	A	N	German shepherd dog.
A	L	S	A	T	I	A	S	Regions without law, Asylums or refuges for criminals.
A	L	S	T	O	N	I	A	Genus of trees or shrubs found in tropical Asia, Australia and Polynesia.
A	L	T	A	R	A	G	E	Payment to priests for altar services and for a mass for the dead.
A	L	T	E	R	A	N	T	Something that alters.
A	L	T	E	R	E	G	O	Trusted friend, Confidential representative, Guardian spirit.
A	L	T	E	R	I	N	G	Becoming different, Varying, Changing.
A	L	T	E	R	I	T	Y	Quality of being other.
A	L	T	E	R	N	A	T	Allocating of diplomatic precedence, Special distribution of signed treaties.
A	L	T	H	A	E	I	N	Crystalline pigment obtained from the hollyhock.
A	L	T	H	O	U	G	H	Though, Notwithstanding, In spite of the fact, Supposing that.
A	L	T	I	T	U	D	E	Height, Eminence, Elevation, Apex, Peak, Summit, Pomposity, Exalted position.
A	L	T	O	C	L	E	F	Position of middle C in music notation.
A	L	T	R	I	C	E	S	Young being hatched in an immature and helpless condition.
A	L	T	R	U	I	S	M	Devotion to the interest of others.
A	L	T	R	U	I	S	T	One that practices altruism.
A	L	U	M	I	N	I	C	Relating to aluminium.
A	L	U	M	I	N	U	M	Aluminium, Bluish silver-white trivalent metallic element.
A	L	U	N	O	G	E	N	Mineral consisting of a white fibrous aluminium sulfate.
A	L	U	R	G	I	T	E	Manganese mica.
A	L	V	E	O	L	A	E	Small depression or pits, Pores of fungi.
A	L	V	E	O	L	A	R	Relating to that part of the jaw where the teeth are situated, Air cells, Sacs.
A	L	V	E	O	L	U	S	Small cavity, Air cell, Tooth socket.
A	M	A	C	R	I	N	E	Unipolar nerve cell found in the retina.
A	M	A	D	A	V	A	T	Avadavat, Small weaverbird.
A	M	A	N	D	I	N	E	Prepared or served with almonds.
A	M	A	R	A	N	T	H	Red acid azo dye used for food colouring and pharmaceutical preparations.
A	M	A	R	E	L	L	E	Cultivated cherries.
A	M	A	R	E	T	T	O	Italian liqueur flavoured with almonds.
A	M	A	R	I	L	L	O	Tropical American timber trees.
A	M	A	S	S	I	N	G	Accumulating, Collecting, Gathering, Assembling, Stockpiling, Garnering.
A	M	A	Z	E	D	L	Y	Confusedly, Astonishment, Bewildered.
A	M	B	E	R	I	N	A	19th Century American glassware of red and amber shades.
A	M	B	I	E	N	C	E	Atmosphere, Environment, Climate, Surroundings, Medium.
A	M	B	I	T	I	O	N	Aspiration, Initiative, Energy, Drive, Pretension, Keenness, Enterprise, Motive.
A	M	B	I	V	E	R	T	Type of person balanced between extrovert and introvert.

1	2	3	4	5	6	7	8	
A	M	B	L	Y	P	O	D	Extinct hoofed mammals resembling elephants.
A	M	B	R	E	T	T	E	French dessert pear.
A	M	B	R	O	S	I	A	Mythical food of the Greek and Roman gods, Something pleasing to the taste.
A	M	B	R	O	S	I	N	13th or 14th Century Milanese gold or silver coin.
A	M	B	U	L	A	N	T	Walking, Itinerant, Moving from place to place.
A	M	B	U	L	A	T	E	Move from place to place, Walk.
A	M	B	U	S	H	E	D	Surprised, Waylaid, Assailed, Assaulted, Attacked, Ensnared, Entrapped. Lurked.
A	M	E	I	O	T	I	C	Abnormal cell and chromosome activity, Without meiosis.
A	M	E	N	A	B	L	E	Answerable, Accountable, Responsive, Tractable, Obedient, Responsible, Liable, Docile.
A	M	E	N	A	B	L	Y	Obediently, Responsively.
A	M	E	N	A	N	C	E	Behaviour, Bearing.
A	M	E	N	D	I	N	G	Correcting, Rectifying, Restoring, Mending, Improving, Repairing, Helping, Promoting.
A	M	E	R	C	I	N	G	Punishing by inflicting a fine at the discretion of the court.
A	M	E	R	I	C	A	N	Inhabitant of America.
A	M	E	T	H	Y	S	T	Clear purple crystallized quartz.
A	M	E	T	R	O	P	E	A person with an abnormal condition of the retina.
A	M	I	A	N	T	U	S	Fine silky asbestos.
A	M	I	C	A	B	L	E	Peaceable, Neighbourly, Friendly, Understanding, Sympathetic, Agreeing, Harmonious.
A	M	I	C	A	B	L	Y	In a friendly manner.
A	M	I	S	S	I	O	N	Lost.
A	M	I	T	O	S	I	S	Cell division.
A	M	I	T	O	T	I	C	Involving amitosis.
A	M	M	O	B	I	U	M	Small genus of Australian herbs.
A	M	M	O	D	Y	T	E	Sand lance.
A	M	M	O	N	I	A	C	Aromatic gum resin.
A	M	M	O	N	I	T	E	Fossil shells.
A	M	M	O	N	I	U	M	Ion or radical derived from ammonia.
A	M	N	I	O	T	I	C	Pertaining to the fluid-filled membranous sac surrounding an embryo.
A	M	O	E	B	A	E	A	Subclass of protozoans.
A	M	O	E	B	I	A	N	Common amoebas of soil and water.
A	M	O	E	B	O	I	D	Relating to amoebas.
A	M	O	R	E	T	T	O	Cupid, Cherub.
A	M	O	R	T	I	Z	E	Gradual reduction of a mortgage or bond, Lower value of assets gradually in profit/loss account.
A	M	O	U	N	T	E	D	Attained in significance, Numbered, Included, Rated, Comprised.
A	M	P	E	L	I	T	E	Black earth rich in pyrites.
A	M	P	H	I	B	I	A	Amphibians, Able to live on the land and in the water.
A	M	P	H	O	R	A	E	Ancient Greek jars.
A	M	P	H	O	R	I	C	Resembling the sound made by blowing across the mouth of an empty bottle.
A	M	P	L	E	X	U	S	Mating of frog or toad when eggs are shed and fertilized.
A	M	P	L	I	A	T	E	Widened, Enlarged.
A	M	P	O	N	G	U	E	Woolly lemur.
A	M	P	U	L	L	A	R	Relating to an ampulla.
A	M	P	U	T	A	T	E	Cut off, Lop off, Prune.
A	M	U	L	E	T	I	C	Functioning as an amulet.
A	M	U	S	E	T	T	E	Light rifled fieldpiece.
A	M	Y	G	D	A	L	A	One of the tonsils of the pharanx.
A	M	Y	G	D	U	L	E	One of the rounded nodules in volcanic rock.
A	M	Y	N	O	D	O	N	Genus of prehistoric animal related to the rhinoceros.
A	N	A	B	A	E	N	A	Genus of freshwater algae.
A	N	A	B	A	S	I	S	Advance, Marching up.
A	N	A	B	A	T	I	C	Ascending, Upward moving.
A	N	A	B	L	E	P	S	Genus of tropical American saltwater and freshwater fishes.
A	N	A	B	O	L	I	C	Characterised by anabolism.
A	N	A	C	O	N	D	A	Large snake of the boa family.
A	N	A	E	R	O	B	E	An organism that does not require air to maintain life.
A	N	A	G	L	Y	P	H	Sculpture chased or embossed as a cameo.
A	N	A	G	O	G	I	C	Having a spiritual meaning.
A	N	A	L	E	C	T	S	Leftovers from a feast, Collection of literary excerpts or passages.
A	N	A	L	E	M	M	A	Astronomical instrument.
A	N	A	L	O	G	O	N	Analogue, Something similar, Parallel, Weather chart.
A	N	A	L	Y	S	E	D	Resolved, Dissected, Anatomized, Divided, Parted, Separated, Classified, Inspected.
A	N	A	L	Y	S	E	R	Tester for electronic equipment.
A	N	A	L	Y	S	I	S	Separation, Examination, Audit, Inspection, Scrutiny, Survey, Breakdown, Dissection.
A	N	A	L	Y	T	I	C	Relating to analysis.
A	N	A	P	A	E	S	T	Special measure in verse.
A	N	A	P	H	A	S	E	Mitosis in chromosomes.
A	N	A	P	H	O	R	A	Repetition for rhetorical or poetic effect.

1	2	3	4	5	6	7	8	Definition
A	N	A	P	L	A	S	M	Anaplasma, Genus of micro-organisms found in red blood cells.
A	N	A	R	C	H	I	C	Tending towards anarchy.
A	N	A	S	A	R	C	A	Oedema, Edema, Swelling of tissue by increase of fluid content, Dropsy.
A	N	A	S	T	A	T	E	Anabolite.
A	N	A	S	T	R	A	L	Used of achromatic figures.
A	N	A	T	E	X	I	S	Dissolving of plutonic rocks.
A	N	A	T	H	E	M	A	Imprecation, Curse, Malediction, Censure, Condemnation, Denunciation, Abomination.
A	N	A	U	X	I	T	E	Mineral of hydrous aluminium silicate.
A	N	A	X	O	N	I	A	Organism that has no distinct axis.
A	N	C	H	E	N	I	A	Genus of ruminants, Camels.
A	N	C	E	S	T	O	R	Forerunner, Prototype, Progenitor, Forefather, Antecedent, Precursor, Predecessor.
A	N	C	E	S	T	R	Y	Descent, Lineage, Origin, Pedigree, Kindred, Line, Race.
A	N	C	H	O	R	E	D	Fastened, Caught, Moored, Secured, Fixed, Rested, Stopped.
A	N	C	O	N	E	A	L	Relating to the elbow.
A	N	C	O	N	O	I	D	Resembling an elbow.
A	N	C	Y	L	I	T	E	Mineral of hydrous basic carbonate of strontium and cerum.
A	N	D	E	S	I	N	E	Feldspar.
A	N	D	E	S	I	T	E	Dark grayish rock.
A	N	D	I	R	O	N	S	Metal supports for firewood on a hearth.
A	N	D	O	R	R	A	N	Inhabitant of Andorra.
A	N	D	R	O	G	E	N	Male sex hormone.
A	N	E	C	D	O	T	E	Short narrative.
A	N	E	C	H	O	I	C	Rooms with sound absorbent walls.
A	N	E	M	O	S	I	S	Wind shake.
A	N	E	R	O	B	I	C	Living in the absence of free oxygen.
A	N	E	S	T	H	Y	L	Mixture of ethyl and methal chloride for production of local anesthesia.
A	N	E	S	T	R	U	S	Period of sexual inactivity.
A	N	E	U	R	I	S	M	Localized abnormal dilatiation of a blood vessel forming a pulsating tumour.
A	N	E	U	R	Y	S	M	Same as ANEURISM.
A	N	G	A	R	E	E	B	Canopied bed without posts.
A	N	G	E	L	I	C	A	Cultivated herbs having stalks that are candied for decoration in confectionery.
A	N	G	E	R	I	N	G	Inflaming, Infuriating, Flaming, Ranting, Incensing, Enraging.
A	N	G	L	I	C	A	N	Connected with the Church of England.
A	N	G	R	I	E	S	T	More irate, Most indignant.
A	N	G	S	T	R	O	M	Unit of wavelength.
A	N	G	U	L	A	T	E	Formed with corners, Angled.
A	N	H	E	D	R	A	L	Allotriomorphic.
A	N	I	C	O	N	I	C	Symbolic or suggestive, Opposed to the use of idols and images.
A	N	I	M	A	L	L	Y	In a beastly manner, Behaving in an inhuman way.
A	N	I	M	A	T	E	D	Encouraged, Brought to life, Stimulated, Enlivened, Motivated, Incited, Prompted.
A	N	I	M	A	T	O	R	One that produces animated cartoons.
A	N	I	R	I	D	I	A	Cogenital absence or defect of the iris.
A	N	I	S	E	T	T	E	Sweet liqueur derived from aniseed.
A	N	K	Y	L	O	S	E	Unite to a rigid joint, Fused into one.
A	N	K	Y	R	O	I	D	Shaped like a hook.
A	N	N	A	L	I	S	T	Historian.
A	N	N	A	M	E	S	E	Vietnamese, Mongolian people.
A	N	N	E	A	L	E	D	Strengthened, Toughened, Heated, Tempered.
A	N	N	E	L	I	D	A	Worms.
A	N	N	E	X	I	N	G	Attaching, Expropriating, Seizing, Joining, Linking, Uniting, Acquiring, Confiscating.
A	N	N	O	T	A	T	E	Add comment, Elucidate, Explain, Commentate, Remark, Expound.
A	N	N	O	U	N	C	E	Proclaim, Foretell, Declare, Advertise, Blazon, Broadcast, Promulgate, Publish.
A	N	N	O	Y	I	N	G	Provoking, Vexing, Irking, Worrying, Bothering, Chafing, Disturbing, Perturbing.
A	N	N	U	A	L	L	Y	Occurring, appearing or acted upon once a year.
A	N	N	U	L	A	R	Y	Ring finger.
A	N	N	U	L	A	T	E	Ringlike characteristics.
A	N	N	U	L	L	E	D	Neutralized, Obliterated, Abolished, Nullified, Voided, Cancelled, Invalidated, Dissolved.
A	N	N	U	L	L	E	R	One that annuls.
A	N	N	U	L	O	S	A	Worms.
A	N	O	D	I	S	E	D	Subjected to electrolytic action.
A	N	O	I	N	T	E	D	Rubbed over with oil, Applied oil, Consecrated.
A	N	O	P	L	U	R	A	An order or suborder of insects, the bugs, unarmed.
A	N	O	R	E	T	I	C	Causing loss of appetite.
A	N	O	R	E	X	I	A	Pathological loss of appetite.
A	N	O	R	T	H	I	C	Having unequal oblique axes.
A	N	O	X	E	M	I	A	Condition of subnormal oxygenation of the arterial blood.
A	N	S	E	R	I	N	E	Pertaining to a goose, Silly, Stupid.

1	2	3	4	5	6	7	8	
A	N	S	E	R	O	U	S	Same as ANSERINE.
A	N	S	I	F	O	R	M	Shaped like a hoop.
A	N	S	W	E	R	E	D	Replied, Responded, Rejoined, Retorted, Observed, Rebutted, Solved, Disproved.
A	N	T	E	A	T	E	R	A snouted mammal that feeds on ants, Ant-bear, Aardvark.
A	N	T	E	C	E	D	E	Precede, Antedate, Forerun, Predate, Pace.
A	N	T	E	D	A	T	E	Predate, Anticipate, Accelerate, Precede in time.
A	N	T	E	F	I	X	A	Ornament to either conceal joints or act as water gutters at roof level.
A	N	T	E	L	O	P	E	Old World ruminant mammal, Buck, Gazelle.
A	N	T	E	M	A	S	K	Antimasque, Small masquerade as introduction or contrast for the main performance.
A	N	T	E	N	A	T	I	Person born before a date applicable to eligibility of certain rights.
A	N	T	E	N	N	A	S	Feelers of insects, Rod or wire for radiating or receiving radio waves.
A	N	T	E	P	A	S	T	Foretaste, Appetizer.
A	N	T	E	P	O	R	T	An outer gate or door.
A	N	T	E	R	I	O	R	Situated toward the front, Antecedent, Prior.
A	N	T	E	R	O	O	M	Foyer to a waiting room or sitting room.
A	N	T	E	V	E	R	T	Displace so that centre is farther forward than normal.
A	N	T	H	E	L	I	A	Luminous rings appearing opposite the sun.
A	N	T	H	E	L	I	X	Curved cartilage at edge of ear, Antihelix.
A	N	T	H	E	M	I	S	Genus of Old World herbs, Camomile.
A	N	T	H	E	R	A	L	Part of the stamen that produces pollen.
A	N	T	H	E	S	I	S	Blooming of a flower.
A	N	T	H	O	Z	O	A	Corals, Sea anemones.
A	N	T	H	R	O	N	E	Substance related to anthracene, a fluorescent hydrocarbon.
A	N	T	I	A	C	I	D	An alkali or absorbent to neutralize or counteract acidity.
A	N	T	I	A	R	I	N	Crystalline glycoside that is a powerful cardiac poison.
A	N	T	I	B	O	D	Y	Body globulins produced in response to infection or toxic substances.
A	N	T	I	D	O	T	E	Remedy, Corrective, Counteractive, Cure, Countermeasure, Neutralizer, Nullifier.
A	N	T	I	H	A	L	O	Preventing halation.
A	N	T	I	I	C	E	R	Device to prevent the formation of ice.
A	N	T	I	L	O	G	Y	Contradiction in terms or ideas.
A	N	T	I	L	O	P	E	Beast represented in heraldry.
A	N	T	I	M	A	S	K	Additional masque introduced as contrast.
A	N	T	I	M	O	N	Y	Metallic silvery white crystalline element used in alloys and for smelting.
A	N	T	I	N	O	D	E	Region of maximum aplitude relating to radio wave interference.
A	N	T	I	N	O	M	Y	Contradiction within a law, Paradox, Conflict, Contrast.
A	N	T	I	P	H	O	N	Response, Answer, Liturgy.
A	N	T	I	P	O	D	E	Persons dwelling at a directly opposite position of the world, Exactly opposite.
A	N	T	I	P	O	L	E	Same as ANTIPODE.
A	N	T	I	P	O	P	E	One claiming to be pope in opposition to the chosen pope.
A	N	T	I	S	T	E	S	Prelate in the church.
A	N	T	I	T	A	N	K	Device or obstacle to destroy or check and attack by tanks.
A	N	T	I	T	Y	P	E	Opposite type.
A	N	T	I	T	Y	P	Y	Resistance offered to alteration or change.
A	N	T	I	Z	O	E	A	Larva of a crab.
A	N	T	L	E	R	E	D	Having antlers.
A	N	T	R	O	R	S	E	Directed forward or upward.
A	N	U	R	E	S	I	S	Unable to excrete urine.
A	N	U	S	V	A	R	A	Sign used in writng Sanskrit.
A	N	Y	T	H	I	N	G	Something or other, Aught.
A	N	Y	W	H	E	R	E	At, it or to any position, Anyplace.
A	N	Z	A	N	I	T	E	Elamite, Ancient people of an area of Babylon.
A	O	R	I	S	T	I	C	Indefinite, Indeterminate.
A	O	R	T	I	T	I	S	Inflammation of the aorta.
A	P	A	G	O	G	I	C	Involving a apogoge, reducing an argument to an absurdity.
A	P	A	T	E	T	I	C	Imitative in colour or form.
A	P	E	R	I	E	N	T	Laxative.
A	P	E	R	I	T	I	F	Appetizer, Wine or snack taken to stimulate the appetite.
A	P	E	R	T	U	R	E	Hole, Gap, Cleft, Chasm, Slit, Orifice, Breach.
A	P	E	X	B	E	A	T	Position of heart-beat easily felt or heard.
A	P	H	A	N	I	T	E	Close textured dark rock.
A	P	H	E	L	I	O	N	Point or orbit of planet or comet furthest from the sun.
A	P	H	L	E	B	I	A	Abnormality found in fossil ferns.
A	P	H	O	D	I	U	S	Genus of dung beetles.
A	P	H	O	R	I	S	M	Concise statement, Adage, Maxim.
A	P	H	O	R	I	S	T	One who repeats aphorisms.
A	P	H	O	R	I	Z	E	Express terse general opinions.
A	P	H	R	A	S	I	A	Inability to articulate words in intelligible order.

1	2	3	4	5	6	7	8	Definition
A	P	H	T	H	O	I	D	Disease resembling the thrush.
A	P	H	T	H	O	U	S	Relating to a disease of the mucous membranes, Thrush.
A	P	I	A	R	I	A	N	Relating to beekeeping.
A	P	I	A	R	I	S	T	Beekeeper.
A	P	I	C	A	L	L	Y	At the apex, tip or summit, Phonetics using the tip of the tongue.
A	P	I	C	U	L	U	S	Small point or tip.
A	P	I	G	E	N	I	N	Yellowish crystalline compound occurring in various plants.
A	P	I	K	O	R	O	S	A Jew who does not believe in Judaism, Skeptic, Atheist.
A	P	I	O	L	O	G	Y	Study of honeybees.
A	P	I	O	S	O	M	A	Babesia, Tick fever.
A	P	L	A	S	T	I	C	No change in structure.
A	P	L	U	S	T	R	E	Curved ornamented stern of an ancient Greek or Roman ship.
A	P	N	E	U	S	I	S	Ability to prolong inhalation of air.
A	P	O	C	R	I	N	E	Produced by an apocrine gland.
A	P	O	D	I	D	A	E	Family of birds, Swifts.
A	P	O	D	O	S	I	S	Conclusion.
A	P	O	G	A	E	I	C	Apogean, Measurement of point of astronomical orbit.
A	P	O	G	O	N	I	D	Genus of marine percoid fishes.
A	P	O	G	R	A	P	H	Copy, Transcript.
A	P	O	L	I	S	T	A	People of S. American Indians of Bolivia.
A	P	O	L	L	Y	O	N	Devil.
A	P	O	L	O	G	I	A	An apology.
A	P	O	L	O	G	U	E	Allegory, Legend, Narrative with a moral.
A	P	O	L	Y	S	I	S	Shedding of reproductive segments by a tapeworm.
A	P	O	M	I	X	I	S	Reproduction not dependent on fertilization.
A	P	O	P	H	Y	G	E	Curve at top and bottom of classical column.
A	P	O	P	L	E	X	Y	Stroke, Cerebral Hemorrhage, Cerebral thrombosis.
A	P	O	R	E	T	I	C	Skeptical.
A	P	O	R	I	D	E	A	Parasitic tapeworms in swans.
A	P	O	S	T	A	S	Y	Renunciation of religious faith.
A	P	O	S	T	A	C	Y	Same as APOSTASY.
A	P	O	S	T	A	T	E	Renegade, Abandonment of allegiance.
A	P	O	S	T	E	M	E	Abscess, Pus-filled swelling.
A	P	O	T	H	E	G	M	Pithy saying, Terse precept.
A	P	O	T	Y	P	I	C	Varying from type.
A	P	P	A	L	L	E	D	Dismayed, Shocked, Horrified, Astonished, Daunted, Awed.
A	P	P	A	N	A	G	E	Provide an endowment.
A	P	P	A	R	E	N	T	Seeming, Ostensible, Illusory, Clear, Distinct, Evident, Obvious, Perceivable.
A	P	P	E	A	L	E	D	Invoked, Prayed, Entreated, Implored, Petitioned, Asked, Requested, Charmed.
A	P	P	E	A	L	E	R	Appellant.
A	P	P	E	A	R	E	D	Emerged, Loomed, Arrived, Emanated, Issued, Materialized, Seemed, Looked.
A	P	P	E	A	S	E	D	Calmed, Settled, Assuaged, Allayed, Conciliated, Satisfied, Pacified, Placated.
A	P	P	E	A	S	E	R	One that mollifies.
A	P	P	E	L	L	E	E	Respondent to an appeal.
A	P	P	E	L	L	O	R	Appellant.
A	P	P	E	N	D	E	D	Added, Attached, Annexed, Subjoined.
A	P	P	E	N	D	I	X	Appendage, Codicil, Addendum, Rider, Supplement, Accessory, Adjunct.
A	P	P	E	S	T	A	T	Neural centre believed to regulate the appetite.
A	P	P	E	T	E	N	T	Longing, Eager, Anxious, Ardent, Impatient, Keen, Thirsty, Craving.
A	P	P	E	T	I	T	E	Desire to eat, Taste, Liking, Preference, Hunger, Voracity, Urge, Fondness.
A	P	P	I	N	I	T	E	Group of various rocks.
A	P	P	L	A	U	S	E	Approval expressed by clapping hands, Commendation.
A	P	P	L	E	P	I	E	Perfect, Excellent, First-rate.
A	P	P	L	I	Q	U	E	Cut-out design of material stitched on base material.
A	P	P	L	Y	I	N	G	Imposing, Adhering, Handling, Devoting, Undertaking, Employing, Using, Exploiting.
A	P	P	O	S	I	T	E	Relevant, Apt, Applicable, Apropos, Pertinent, Opportune, Timely, Suitable.
A	P	P	R	A	I	S	E	Estimate, Assess, Evaluate, Rate, Survey, Value, Esteem, Judge.
A	P	P	R	I	S	E	D	Informed, Advised, Notified, Told, Warned, Announced, Communicated, Declared.
A	P	P	R	I	Z	E	D	Appreciated, Cherished, Esteemed, Treasured, Valued, Adjudged.
A	P	P	R	O	A	C	H	Approximate, Near, Achieve, Reach, Accost, Consult, Advance, Border.
A	P	P	R	O	V	A	L	Approbation, Sanction, Applause, Commendation, Acceptance, Endorsement.
A	P	P	R	O	V	E	D	Accepted, Sanctioned, Endorsed, Accredited, Certified, Upheld, Sustained, Commended.
A	P	P	R	O	V	E	R	One that approves.
A	P	P	U	L	S	E	S	Driving toward, Running toward, Striking against, Close encounter.
A	P	R	E	S	S	K	I	Relaxation after snow sports.
A	P	R	O	N	M	A	N	Workman, Tradesman.
A	P	T	E	R	I	A	L	Relating to a bare space between feathered areas on the body of a bird.

1	2	3	4	5	6	7	8	
A	P	T	E	R	O	U	S	Lacking wings.
A	P	T	I	T	U	D	E	Aptness, Fitness, Quick-wittedness, Capacity, Inclination, Disposition, Readiness.
A	P	Y	R	E	X	I	A	Without fever, Febrile.
A	P	Y	R	E	X	I	A	Absence or intermission of fever.
A	Q	U	A	C	A	D	E	Programme of water entertainments.
A	Q	U	A	L	U	N	G	Cylinder of compressed air for breathing underwater.
A	Q	U	A	R	I	U	M	Tank for housing an aquatic collection.
A	Q	U	A	R	I	U	S	11th Sign of the Zodiac, Water-carrier.
A	Q	U	A	S	T	A	T	Thermostat for regulating temperature of water heated by a furnace or boiler.
A	Q	U	A	T	I	N	T	Process of etching where the finished result resembles a water colour.
A	Q	U	A	T	I	O	N	Replacement by water molecules in a co-ordination complex.
A	Q	U	A	T	O	N	E	Offset printing method.
A	Q	U	E	D	U	C	T	Artificial channel for conveying water.
A	Q	U	I	L	I	N	E	Prominent, Curving or hooked like an eagle's beak.
A	Q	U	I	N	I	S	T	Specialist in the study of St Thomas Aquinas.
A	Q	U	O	S	I	T	Y	Moistness, Wetness, Wateriness.
A	R	A	B	I	T	O	L	Sweet crystalline pentahydroxy alcohol.
A	R	A	C	A	N	G	A	Scarlet macaw.
A	R	A	C	H	I	D	E	Peanut.
A	R	A	C	H	N	I	D	Class of arthropods including scorpions, spiders, mites and related forms.
A	R	A	M	A	I	S	M	Characteristic feature of Aramaic occurring in another language.
A	R	A	N	E	I	D	A	Spiders.
A	R	A	N	E	O	U	S	Arachnoid, Thin membrane of the brain and spinal cord, Resembling a spider's web.
A	R	A	P	A	N	G	A	Bellbird.
A	R	B	A	L	E	S	T	Crossbow.
A	R	B	I	T	R	A	L	Concerning arbitration.
A	R	B	O	R	E	A	L	Resembling a tree.
A	R	B	O	R	E	T	A	Botanic gardens for the scientific study of trees and shrubs.
A	R	B	O	R	I	S	T	Specialist in all aspects of planting and maintenance of trees.
A	R	B	O	R	O	U	S	Relating to trees.
A	R	B	U	S	C	L	E	A dwarf tree or treelike shrub.
A	R	B	U	S	T	U	M	Copse, Orchard.
A	R	B	U	T	E	A	N	Genus of evergreen trees.
A	R	C	A	D	I	A	N	Idealized representation of pastoral life.
A	R	C	A	D	I	N	G	Series of arches or arcades used in the construction of buildings.
A	R	C	A	N	I	T	E	Potassium sulfate.
A	R	C	A	T	U	R	E	Imitation arcade for decoration.
A	R	C	H	A	E	A	N	Archean, Prehistoric rocks.
A	R	C	H	A	E	U	S	Paracelsian principle of good health.
A	R	C	H	A	I	S	M	Use of absolute or old-fashioned diction, idiom or style in writing, speaking or the arts.
A	R	C	H	A	I	Z	E	To appear archaic or antique.
A	R	C	H	D	U	K	E	A prince usually of royal lineage.
A	R	C	H	E	L	O	N	Family of large extinct marine turtles.
A	R	C	H	I	V	A	L	Constituting archives or records.
A	R	C	H	I	V	E	S	Repositories for historical documents and artifacts, Public records.
A	R	C	H	L	U	T	E	A large lute.
A	R	C	H	N	E	S	S	Playful slyness, Roguishness, Coyness.
A	R	C	H	P	O	E	T	Chief poet.
A	R	C	T	O	M	Y	S	Marmota, Genus of large rodents that resemble badgers.
A	R	C	T	O	N	Y	X	Genus that consists of the hognosed badger.
A	R	C	T	O	T	I	S	African daisy.
A	R	D	E	N	T	L	Y	Eagerly, Zealously, Devotedly, Extremely, Faithfully, Warmly, Passionately.
A	R	E	N	A	R	I	A	Genus of low-tufted herbs, Thyme-leaved Sandwort.
A	R	E	O	L	A	T	E	Divided by small spaces or cracks.
A	R	E	T	H	U	S	A	Genus of bog orchids.
A	R	G	E	M	O	N	E	Genus of American herbs, Prickly poppy.
A	R	G	E	N	T	A	N	Needlepoint lace with bold designs.
A	R	G	E	N	T	I	C	Relating to silver.
A	R	G	E	N	T	U	M	Silver.
A	R	G	I	L	L	I	C	Relating to clay and clay minerals.
A	R	G	I	N	A	S	E	Crystalline enzyme obtained from the liver.
A	R	G	I	N	I	N	E	A crystalline basic amino acid.
A	R	G	O	N	A	U	T	Member of the crew of the legendary Jason, Adventurer following a set idea.
A	R	G	O	S	I	E	S	Richly laden merchant ships, Storehouses.
A	R	G	U	A	B	L	E	Open to question, Debatable, In dispute.
A	R	G	U	F	I	E	D	Disputed, Debated, Wrangled, Bickered, Hassled, Quibbled.
A	R	G	U	M	E	N	T	Dispute, Discussion, Proof, Contention, Controversy, Debate, Dissension, Topic.

1	2	3	4	5	6	7	8	Definition
A	R	G	U	T	E	L	Y	Shrewdly, Shrilly, Piercing, Acutely.
A	R	I	A	N	I	S	M	A theological movement in the 4th century Eastern church.
A	R	I	D	N	E	S	S	Dryness, Aridity.
A	R	I	S	T	A	T	E	Having a slender tip.
A	R	I	S	T	I	D	A	Genus of grasses.
A	R	M	A	G	N	A	C	Dry brown brandy from Southern France.
A	R	M	A	M	E	N	T	War equipment, Munitions, Arms, Guns.
A	R	M	A	R	I	U	M	Pantry, Church, Sacristy, Store cupboard.
A	R	M	A	T	U	R	E	Armor, Supporting bars, Dynamo part.
A	R	M	C	H	A	I	R	Chair with arm rests.
A	R	M	E	N	I	A	N	Native of Armenia, Indo-European language.
A	R	M	E	N	O	I	D	Member of the Eastern branch of the Alpine subrace.
A	R	M	I	G	E	R	O	One entitled to armorial bearings, Squire of a knight.
A	R	M	I	N	I	A	N	Doctrine of theologian Arminius.
A	R	M	O	R	I	A	L	Bearing heraldic arms.
A	R	M	O	R	I	S	T	Specialist in the study of heraldry.
A	R	M	O	U	R	E	D	Equipped or protected with armour or armour-plate.
A	R	M	O	U	R	E	R	Specialist in firearms, One responsible for weapons on an aricraft.
A	R	M	O	Z	E	E	N	Heavy black silk taffeta fabric used for clerical robes.
A	R	M	O	Z	I	N	E	Same as ARMOZEEN.
A	R	M	Y	W	O	R	M	Crop-destroying larval moth.
A	R	N	I	M	I	T	E	A mineral basic copper carbonate.
A	R	O	M	A	T	I	C	Fragrant, Sweet-scented, Spicy smell, Pungent taste.
A	R	O	U	S	I	N	G	Exciting, Stimulating, Stirring, Kindling, Rallying, Inflaming, Challenging, Awakening.
A	R	P	E	G	G	I	O	Musical direction to play a chord in succession.
A	R	Q	U	E	B	U	S	15th Century heavy matchlock gun.
A	R	R	A	N	G	E	D	Disposed, Settled, Placed, Planned, Orchestrated, Marshalled, Organized.
A	R	R	A	N	G	E	R	One that adapts music for a particular performer or performance.
A	R	R	A	N	T	L	Y	Shamelessly, Extremely, Utterly, Absolutely, Completely, Impudently, Totally, Blatantly.
A	R	R	A	S	E	N	E	Embroidery cord resembling chenille.
A	R	R	A	S	T	R	E	Process of dragging a dead bull away after the bullfight.
A	R	R	A	Y	I	N	G	Marshalling, Adorning, Attiring, Dressing, Organizing.
A	R	R	E	S	T	E	D	Stopped, Halted, Checked, Hindered, Interrupted, Seized, Captured, Frustrated.
A	R	R	E	S	T	E	R	One empowered to make a legal arrest.
A	R	R	I	C	C	I	O	First coat of plaster in fresco painting.
A	R	R	I	D	I	N	G	Pleasing, Gratifying, Delighting, Entertaining, Diverting.
A	R	R	I	V	I	N	G	Attaining, Coming, Reaching, Showing, Succeeding, Prospering Thriving, Scoring.
A	R	R	O	G	A	N	T	Proud, Disdainful, Haughty, Insolent, Supercilious, Superior, Affected, Showy.
A	R	R	O	G	A	T	E	Claim, Seize, Appropriate, Ascribe, Attribute, Assume, Commandeer, Annex.
A	R	S	E	N	A	T	E	Salt or ester of an arsenic acid.
A	R	S	E	N	I	D	E	Binary compound of arsenic with a more positive element.
A	R	S	E	N	I	T	E	Salt or ester of an arsenious acid.
A	R	S	O	N	A	T	E	Salt or ester of arsonic acid.
A	R	S	O	N	I	S	T	One that wilfully or maliciously burns building or property, Firebug.
A	R	S	O	N	I	U	M	A univalent radical containing arsenic.
A	R	T	E	R	I	A	L	Relating to an artery, Freeway for through traffic.
A	R	T	E	S	I	A	N	Upward movement of water under pressure from the rocks.
A	R	T	F	U	L	L	Y	Craftily, Skilfully, Dexterously, Slyly, Cunningly, Wily, Tricky.
A	R	T	I	C	L	E	D	Bound by articles as an apprenticeship, Stipulated.
A	R	T	I	F	A	C	T	Simple tool or ornament.
A	R	T	I	F	I	C	E	Cunning, Trickery, Guile, Insincerely, Ingenuity, Inventiveness, Art, Stratagem.
A	R	T	I	S	T	I	C	Aesthetic, Tasteful, Good taste, Skilful discrimination, Expert judgment of the arts.
A	R	T	I	S	T	R	Y	Artistic ability.
A	R	V	I	C	O	L	A	Genus of rodent, Water voles.
A	R	V	I	C	O	L	E	Same as ARVICOLA.
A	R	Y	A	N	I	S	M	Doctrine of the Nazis of the superiority of the Aryan peoples.
A	R	Y	A	N	I	S	T	Adherent of Aryanism.
A	R	Y	A	N	I	Z	E	To clear of non-Aryan influence.
A	S	A	R	O	T	U	M	Ancient Roman painted pavement.
A	S	B	E	S	T	I	C	Fibrous sand mixed with asbestos and used with lime to form Fireproof wall plaster.
A	S	B	E	S	T	O	S	Mineral of flexible fibres used where uncombustible, non-conducting material is required.
A	S	C	A	P	H	U	S	Genus of N. American toads.
A	S	C	A	R	I	D	S	Parasitical worms.
A	S	C	A	R	O	P	S	Stomach worm that infests swine.
A	S	C	E	N	D	E	D	Mounted, Climbed, Scaled, Escalated, Clambered, Lifted, Soared, Surmounted.
A	S	C	E	N	D	E	R	Ascending letter or character.
A	S	C	E	N	S	O	R	Funicular railway used on steep ascents.

1	2	3	4	5	6	7	8	Definition
A	S	C	I	D	I	A	N	Tunicate with minute active tadpole as a larva.
A	S	C	I	D	I	U	M	Pitcher shaped appendage of a plant.
A	S	C	O	N	O	I	D	Sponges.
A	S	C	R	I	B	E	D	Attributed, Assigned, Referred, Charged, Imputed, Connected, Guessed, Alleged.
A	S	H	P	L	A	N	T	Ash sapling.
A	S	H	S	T	O	N	E	Rock composed of tiny particles of volcanic ash.
A	S	I	L	I	D	A	E	Genus of large two-winged fly, Robber fly.
A	S	P	E	R	A	T	E	Rough or harsh to the touch.
A	S	P	E	R	G	E	S	Ceremony of sprinkling holy water.
A	S	P	E	R	I	T	Y	Acrimony, Severity, Hardship, Difficulty, Vicissitude, Austerity, Grimness, Inequality.
A	S	P	E	R	S	E	D	Sprinkled, Maligned, Defamed, Denigrated, Libelled, Derided, Mocked, Taunted.
A	S	P	H	O	D	E	L	Old world perennial herbs, Daffodil, Lily.
A	S	P	H	Y	X	I	A	Suffocation, Smothered, Stifled, Choked.
A	S	P	I	D	I	U	M	Genus of ferns.
A	S	P	I	R	A	N	T	One who is ambitious for success in endeavour, Candidate.
A	S	P	I	R	A	T	E	Emphasize the sound of the "H", To remove noxious substances from the body by suction.
A	S	P	I	R	I	N	G	Yearning, Longing, Rising, Ascending, Soaring, Aiming, Pining, Straining.
A	S	P	O	R	O	U	S	Without true spores.
A	S	S	A	I	L	E	D	Assaulted, Attacked, Struck, Buffeted, Pounded.
A	S	S	A	M	E	S	E	Native of Assam, India.
A	S	S	A	R	T	E	D	Removed trees and shrubs for cultivating the land.
A	S	S	A	S	S	I	N	Hire killer, Fanatic who commits murder.
A	S	S	A	Y	I	N	G	Trying, Attempting, Essaying, Estimating, Endeavouring, Seeking, Appraising, Striving.
A	S	S	E	M	B	L	E	Gather, Convene, Convoke, Summon, Congregate, Congress, Muster, Cluster.
A	S	S	E	M	B	L	Y	Collection, Gathering, Crowd, Group, Association, Faction, Sect, Fraternity.
A	S	S	E	N	T	E	D	Consented, Sanctioned, Agreed, Acquiesced, Adopted, Tolerated, Yielded, Embraced.
A	S	S	E	R	T	E	D	Declared, Professed, Affirmed, Protested, Avowed, Avouched, Warranted, Defended.
A	S	S	E	S	S	E	D	Estimated, Determined, Valued, Imposed, Calculated, Computed, Weighed, Rated.
A	S	S	E	S	S	O	R	One authorized to assess property for taxation.
A	S	S	I	E	T	T	E	Hors d'oeuvres or cold cuts of meat served on one plate, Mixture used for gilding books.
A	S	S	I	G	N	A	T	Currency issued during the French Revolution.
A	S	S	I	G	N	E	D	Allotted, Ascribed, Specified, Designated, Endowed, Prescribed, Transferred, Deeded.
A	S	S	I	G	N	E	E	Agent, Representative.
A	S	S	I	G	N	E	R	One that transfers a legal interest or right.
A	S	S	I	S	T	E	D	Helped, Supported, Joined, Attended, Raised, Aided, Escorted, Accompanied.
A	S	S	I	Z	I	N	G	Regulating or fixing a price.
A	S	S	O	N	A	N	T	Relating to the resemblance of sound in words or syllables.
A	S	S	O	N	A	T	E	To correspond in sound.
A	S	S	O	R	T	E	D	Miscellaneous, Heterogeneous, Matched, Suited, Fitted, Varied, Selected, Coupled.
A	S	S	U	A	G	E	D	Allayed, Mitigated, Eased, Mollified, Pacified, Abated, Subsided.
A	S	S	U	M	I	N	G	Pretentious, Presumptuous, Postulating, Surmising.
A	S	S	U	R	I	N	G	Securing, Ensuring, Reassuring, Encouraging, Promising, Convincing, Persuading.
A	S	S	Y	R	I	A	N	Pertaining to Assyria, an ancient empire of western Asia.
A	S	T	A	C	E	I	N	Red pigment found in boiled lobster shell.
A	S	T	A	C	O	I	D	Family of freshwater crayfish and true lobsters.
A	S	T	A	T	I	N	E	Radioactive element.
A	S	T	A	T	I	Z	E	To render unstable, Not static.
A	S	T	E	R	I	A	S	Genus of starfishes.
A	S	T	E	R	I	O	N	Point behind the ear where the various bones meet.
A	S	T	E	R	I	S	K	Star-shaped character used in printing for various reasons.
A	S	T	E	R	I	S	M	Constellation, Small group of stars.
A	S	T	E	R	N	A	L	Having no sternum, Not sternal.
A	S	T	E	R	O	I	D	Celestial body resembling a star, Small planet.
A	S	T	H	E	N	I	A	Debility, Deficient in vitality.
A	S	T	H	E	N	I	C	Weak, Debilitated, Slender, Lacking in muscle.
A	S	T	I	G	M	A	T	An astigmatic person, Having prejudices.
A	S	T	O	G	E	N	Y	Marked change as colony of zooids age.
A	S	T	O	N	I	E	D	Astonished, Dazed, Stunned, Paralyzed.
A	S	T	O	N	I	S	H	Stun, Daze, Bewilder, Confuse, Surprise, Alarm, Dumbfound, Astound.
A	S	T	R	A	G	A	L	Convex or rounded moulding.
A	S	T	R	I	N	G	E	Constrict, Compress, Bind together, Draw together.
A	S	T	R	O	I	T	E	Star-shaped mineral or fossil.
A	S	T	U	C	I	T	Y	Astuteness.
A	S	T	U	T	E	L	Y	Shrewdly, Cleverly, Craftily, Cunningly, Wily.
A	S	T	Y	A	N	A	X	Genus of brightly coloured tropical fishes.
A	S	Y	S	T	O	L	E	Failure or weakening of the systole, Contraction of the heart.
A	T	A	B	R	I	N	E	Quinacrine.

1	2	3	4	5	6	7	8	
A	T	A	R	A	X	I	A	Imperturbability, Stoic attitude, Calmness, Intellectual detachment.
A	T	H	E	I	Z	E	D	Became an atheist, Non-believer, Skeptic.
A	T	H	E	L	I	N	G	Prince of a royal family, Crown prince, Heir-apparent.
A	T	H	E	N	I	A	N	Inhabitant of Athens, Greece.
A	T	H	E	R	I	N	E	European food fish.
A	T	H	E	R	O	M	A	Disease of the inner lining of the arteries.
A	T	H	L	E	T	I	C	Strong, Muscular, Robust, Vigorous, Agile, Active, Energetic, Brawny.
A	T	L	A	N	T	E	S	Male figures used as supporting columns.
A	T	L	A	N	T	I	C	One of the more important oceans.
A	T	M	O	P	H	I	L	Having a tendency to occur in the atmosphere.
A	T	O	M	I	C	A	L	Concerned with atoms, Resulting from an atom bomb.
A	T	O	M	I	Z	E	D	Reduced to minute particles, Vaporized.
A	T	O	M	I	Z	E	R	An instrument that atomizes perfume or disinfectant.
A	T	O	N	A	B	L	E	Amendable, Able to be atoned for.
A	T	R	E	M	A	T	A	Shellfish.
A	T	R	E	M	B	L	E	Trembling, Quivering.
A	T	R	I	P	L	E	X	Genus of herbs.
A	T	R	O	C	I	T	Y	Enormity, Heinousness, Brutal or cruel deed.
A	T	R	O	P	H	I	C	Characterised by wasting away.
A	T	R	O	P	I	N	E	Poisonous white crystalline alkaloid.
A	T	R	O	P	O	U	S	Not inverted.
A	T	T	A	C	H	E	D	Seized, Connected, Bound, Fastened, Tied, Ascribed, Adhered, Associated.
A	T	T	A	C	K	E	D	Assaulted, Raped, Ravished, Tackled, Assailed, Stormed, Bombarded, Raided.
A	T	T	A	I	N	E	D	Reached, Gained, Achieved, Accomplished, Obtained, Caught, Realized, Scored.
A	T	T	E	N	D	E	D	Escorted, Conjoined, Associated, Heeded, Listened, Watched, Supervised, Directed.
A	T	T	E	N	T	A	T	Unsuccessful attempt at a political crime.
A	T	T	E	S	T	E	D	Certified, Manifested, Testified, Indicated, Invoked, Witnessed, Confirmed, Verified.
A	T	T	I	C	I	S	M	Witty remark, Attachment to style of ancient Athens.
A	T	T	I	C	I	Z	E	To favour the Athenians.
A	T	T	I	N	G	E	D	Touched, Influenced, Affected.
A	T	T	I	R	I	N	G	Dressing, Arraying, Adorning, Clothing, Garbing, Outfitting, Equipping.
A	T	T	I	T	U	D	E	Posture, Carriage, Air, Demeanour, Position, Stance, Stand, Bias.
A	T	T	O	R	N	E	D	Tenancy transferred.
A	T	T	O	R	N	E	Y	Agent, Deputy, Proxy, Lawyer.
A	T	T	R	I	T	E	D	Worn by penitence, Abraded, Erased.
A	T	T	R	I	T	U	S	Pulverized matter.
A	T	T	U	N	I	N	G	Harmonizing, Accommodating, Conforming, Integrating, Regulating, Balancing, Agreeing.
A	U	B	U	S	S	O	N	16th Century Tapestry, Carpet or rug with design resembling the tapestry.
A	U	D	A	C	I	T	Y	Temerity, Assurance, Hardiness, Effrontery, Impudence, Resolution, Spirit.
A	U	D	I	E	N	C	E	Hearing, Following, Interview, Admirers, Fans, Clientele, Listeners.
A	U	D	I	T	I	N	G	Examining and verifying books of account, Scrutinizing.
A	U	D	I	T	I	O	N	Power of hearing, Critical hearing, Trial performance.
A	U	D	I	T	I	V	E	Auditory, Relating to hearing.
A	U	D	I	T	O	R	Y	Relating to hearing.
A	U	D	I	V	I	S	E	Transmit or receive by audivision.
A	U	G	I	T	I	T	E	An olivine-free basaltic rock.
A	U	G	I	T	I	T	E	Extrusive porphyritic rock.
A	U	G	U	R	A	T	E	To divine from signs and omens.
A	U	G	U	R	I	E	S	Signs and omens believed to foretell the future, Portents, Premonitions.
A	U	G	U	R	I	N	G	Predicting the future by portents and signs.
A	U	G	U	S	T	A	N	Roman colony in Germany.
A	U	G	U	S	T	L	Y	In a dignified manner.
A	U	L	A	R	I	A	N	Belonging to an English university hall.
A	U	R	A	M	I	N	E	Bright yellow kentonimine dye.
A	U	R	A	N	T	I	A	Poisonous red-brown crystalline alcohol-soluble dye.
A	U	R	E	L	I	A	N	Golden in colour, Collection and breeding of moths and butterflies.
A	U	R	E	O	L	E	D	Haloed, Surrounded by radiance, Glorified.
A	U	R	I	C	U	L	A	Ellobium, Type genus of snails, Auricular, Appendix of the heart.
A	U	R	I	F	O	R	M	Shaped like the human ear.
A	U	R	O	R	E	A	N	Auroral, Rosy, Radiant.
A	U	R	U	L	E	N	T	Golden in colour.
A	U	S	O	N	I	A	N	Italian, Poetic.
A	U	S	T	R	I	A	N	Characteristic of Austria.
A	U	T	A	C	O	I	D	Hormone, Organic substance.
A	U	T	A	R	C	H	Y	Absolute sovereignty, Autocratic rule.
A	U	T	A	R	K	I	C	Free, Self-sufficient, Independent.
A	U	T	I	S	T	I	C	Withdrawn to escape from reality.

1	2	3	4	5	6	7	8	
A	U	T	O	B	A	H	N	Double carriageway in Germany.
A	U	T	O	C	A	D	E	Cavalcade of automobiles.
A	U	T	O	C	A	R	P	Self-fertilized fruit.
A	U	T	O	C	R	A	T	One that rules with absolute power.
A	U	T	O	D	A	F	E	Burning of a pronounced heretic by the Inquisition.
A	U	T	O	D	Y	N	E	Special heterodyne generating auxiliary current.
A	U	T	O	E	T	T	E	Motor cycle with three wheels and box used for making deliveries.
A	U	T	O	G	A	M	Y	Self-fertilization.
A	U	T	O	G	E	N	Y	Self-generation.
A	U	T	O	G	Y	R	O	Type of helicopter.
A	U	T	O	L	I	T	H	Crystallised portion of rock encased in similar rock that solidified later.
A	U	T	O	L	Y	Z	E	Self-digestion occurring in plant and animal tissue.
A	U	T	O	M	A	T	A	Robots, Automatic devices performing routine tasks.
A	U	T	O	M	A	T	E	Replacing human operators with machines.
A	U	T	O	N	O	M	Y	Independent, Free, Self-government.
A	U	T	O	P	T	I	C	Seen with one's own eyes.
A	U	T	O	S	L	E	D	Convertible sled that can operate on snow and ice or a road.
A	U	T	O	S	O	M	E	Chromosome other than a sex chromosome.
A	U	T	O	T	O	M	Y	Separation, Amputation.
A	U	T	O	T	Y	P	E	Making carbon copies.
A	U	T	O	T	Y	P	Y	Same as AUTOTYPE.
A	U	T	U	M	N	A	L	Autumn harvesting, Serene, Calm, Mature.
A	U	T	U	N	I	T	E	Radio-active lemon-yellow mineral.
A	U	X	I	L	I	A	R	Auxiliary.
A	U	X	I	M	O	N	E	Certain substances considered essential for growth.
A	U	X	O	C	Y	T	E	Gamete-forming cell.
A	V	A	I	L	I	N	G	Profiting, Using, Serving, Working, Satisfying, Answering.
A	V	E	L	L	A	N	E	Relating to the hazel nut.
A	V	E	N	G	I	N	G	Revenging, Retaliation, Counterblow, Reprisal, Vengeance, Retribution.
A	V	E	N	T	A	I	L	Ventail, Lower opening in a medieval helmet.
A	V	E	N	T	U	R	E	Adventure.
A	V	E	R	A	G	E	D	Proportional, Equated, Divided according to a given number.
A	V	E	R	M	E	N	T	Verification, Affirmation, Justification.
A	V	E	R	N	I	A	N	Infernal, Demoniac, Plutonic, Stygian, Hellish.
A	V	E	R	R	I	N	G	Avouching, Verifying, Asserting, Claiming, Declaring, Professing, Protesting, Justifying.
A	V	E	R	S	E	L	Y	Reluctantly, Unwillingly.
A	V	E	R	S	I	O	N	Repugnance, Revulsion, Dislike, Antagonism, Displeasure, Distaste, Hostility, Fear.
A	V	I	A	R	I	S	T	One who keeps caged birds.
A	V	I	A	T	I	N	G	Piloting an aircraft.
A	V	I	A	T	I	O	N	Manufacture and operation of aircraft.
A	V	I	F	A	U	N	A	Classification of regional birds.
A	V	I	O	N	I	C	S	Pertaining to electrical and electronic devices in aviation.
A	V	O	I	D	I	N	G	Escaping, Eluding, Evading, Shunning, Diverting, Preventing, Defeating, Vacating.
A	V	O	U	C	H	E	D	Affirmed, Guaranteed, Accepted, Confessed, Asserted, Declared, Deposed, Confirmed.
A	V	O	W	E	D	L	Y	Openly, Frankly, Admittedly.
A	V	U	L	S	I	O	N	Forcible separation, Isolating, Surgically tearing apart.
A	W	A	I	T	I	N	G	Attending, Expecting, Staying.
A	W	A	K	E	N	E	D	Stirred, Roused, Challenged, Inflamed, Rallied.
A	W	A	K	E	N	E	R	One that awakens.
A	W	A	N	T	I	N	G	Wanting.
A	W	A	R	D	I	N	G	Judging, Deciding, Granting, Adjudging, Bestowing, Allocating, Assigning, Conferring.
A	W	E	A	R	I	E	D	Wearied, Tired, Jaded.
A	W	E	A	T	H	E	R	Toward the weather or windward side.
A	X	H	A	M	M	E	R	Axhammer, Tool for dressing rough stone.
A	X	I	L	L	A	R	Y	Relating to an angle in the branch, Armpit, Special group of feathers.
A	X	I	O	L	I	T	E	A spherulitic aggregate rock.
A	X	I	O	L	O	G	Y	Theory of values.
A	X	L	E	T	R	E	E	Fixed beam for wheels of carriage or cart.
A	X	O	I	D	E	A	N	Relating to the axis, Vertebra.
A	X	O	P	L	A	S	M	Protoplasm of an axon.
A	Z	O	T	E	M	I	A	Kidney disease.
A	Z	O	T	U	R	I	A	Excess of urea in the urine.
A	Z	Z	A	T	A	M	E	Arab people.

B

B	A	B	A	K	O	T	O	Large short-tailed lemur of Madagascar.

1	2	3	4	5	6	7	8	
B	A	B	B	L	I	N	G	Prattling, Chattering, Jabbering, Gabbling, Blabbering, Prating, Waffling, Clacking.
B	A	B	E	L	I	S	M	Confusion of sense, Medley of sounds.
B	A	B	E	L	I	Z	E	Confound.
B	A	B	I	R	U	S	A	Piglike deer with tusks native to the East Indies.
B	A	B	I	S	H	L	Y	Acting in a childish fashion, Babyisly, Infantile.
B	A	B	O	U	C	H	E	Oriental slipper-like mule.
B	A	B	U	S	H	K	A	Grandmother, Head-kerchief worn tied under the chin.
B	A	B	Y	F	A	C	E	A face that conveys youth and innocence.
B	A	B	Y	F	A	R	M	A creche of a low standard of child-care.
B	A	B	Y	H	O	O	D	Infancy.
B	A	C	C	A	R	A	T	Card game played in casinos.
B	A	C	C	H	A	N	T	Pertaining to revelry and drunkenness as orgies held in honour of Bacchus.
B	A	C	H	E	L	O	R	Unmarried male of marriageable age, Holder of the lowest degree conferred by a college.
B	A	C	I	L	L	U	S	Rod-shaped bacteria, many important for natural decay and others that transmit disease.
B	A	C	K	B	A	N	D	A band that a horse wears to support vehicle shafts, Outside moulding of door or window.
B	A	C	K	B	E	N	D	Gymnastic or acrobatic position where the body is arched backwards.
B	A	C	K	B	O	N	D	Method of acknowledging sole trusteeship.
B	A	C	K	B	O	N	E	Spine, Spinal column, Principal support, Fortitude, Nerve, Spunk, Resolution, Mainstay.
B	A	C	K	C	H	A	T	Impudence, Repartee, Banter, Badinage.
B	A	C	K	D	O	O	R	Kitchen entrance, Surreptitious, Underhand or illegal means.
B	A	C	K	D	R	O	P	Scenic curtain at the back of a stage, Background.
B	A	C	K	F	A	L	L	Musical direction, Paper pulp machine.
B	A	C	K	F	I	L	L	To refill an excavation or trench.
B	A	C	K	F	I	R	E	A fire used to try and check the spread of a runaway fire, Explosion of fuel mixture in a car.
B	A	C	K	F	L	A	P	Flap of back cover of a book that folds inside.
B	A	C	K	F	L	O	W	Returning to the source.
B	A	C	K	G	E	A	R	Part of a lathe to reduce the speed of the spindle.
B	A	C	K	H	A	N	D	To hit with the back of the hand, Handwriting sloping backwards.
B	A	C	K	H	A	U	L	Return trip of a transport vehicle.
B	A	C	K	H	E	E	L	A movement in wrestling.
B	A	C	K	K	I	C	K	Kickback, Rebate, Underhand commission.
B	A	C	K	L	A	S	H	Recoil, Jar, Reaction.
B	A	C	K	M	O	S	T	Farthest back.
B	A	C	K	P	A	C	K	Knapsack carried by campers or hikers.
B	A	C	K	P	A	L	M	Conjuror or card - sharper concealing cards or coins in the hand.
B	A	C	K	R	A	K	E	Rake.
B	A	C	K	R	E	S	T	Support for a person confined to bed.
B	A	C	K	R	O	O	M	Room situated at the rear, Place where important activities or decisions take place.
B	A	C	K	R	O	P	E	Rope or chain on each side of a sailing ship.
B	A	C	K	S	E	A	T	Inferior position.
B	A	C	K	S	I	D	E	Buttocks, Behind, Bottom, Posterior, Rear, Rump, Seat.
B	A	C	K	S	P	I	N	Backward rotary movement given to a ball that causes it to recoil.
B	A	C	K	S	T	O	P	Support, Bolster, A stop that prevents a backward movement.
B	A	C	K	V	E	L	D	Backcountry.
B	A	C	K	W	A	R	D	Toward the back, Reverse, Reminiscing, Mentally retarded, Reactionary, Unprogressive.
B	A	C	K	W	A	S	H	Backward flow, Sequel, Aftermath, Repercussion.
B	A	C	O	N	I	A	N	Relating to Frances Bacon or his doctrines.
B	A	C	T	E	R	I	A	Bacterium, Microorganism.
B	A	C	T	R	I	A	N	Two-humped camel, One of the ancient Iranian people.
B	A	C	U	L	I	T	E	Extinct ammonoids having a shell straight like a tapering rod.
B	A	D	E	N	I	T	E	Metal consisting of cobalt, nickel and iron bismuth-arsenide.
B	A	D	G	E	R	E	D	Harassed, Pestered, Baited, Heckled, Hectored, Hounded, Plagued, Teased.
B	A	D	I	N	A	G	E	Banter, Backchat, Repartee, Chaffing, Kidding.
B	A	E	D	E	K	E	R	Guidebook devoted to Europe, Handbook.
B	A	E	T	U	L	U	S	Roughly shaped stone held sacred or worshipped.
B	A	F	F	L	I	N	G	Disconcerting, Perplexing, Frustrating, Cheating, Tricking, Disappointing, Foiling.
B	A	G	P	I	P	E	R	Player of bagpipes.
B	A	G	U	E	T	T	E	Long-shaped gem, Small moulding, Beading, Narrow watch movement.
B	A	I	L	A	B	L	E	Entitled to bail.
B	A	I	L	B	O	N	D	Bond posted to cover the bail.
B	A	I	L	I	E	R	Y	Jurisdiction of a bailie.
B	A	I	L	M	E	N	T	Act of bailing a prisoner or person accused.
B	A	I	L	S	M	A	N	One who gives bail, Surety.
B	A	K	E	L	I	T	E	Synthetic resins and plastics.
B	A	K	E	M	E	A	T	A meat pie.
B	A	K	S	H	I	S	H	Baksheesh, Tip, Alms, Commission.
B	A	K	U	P	A	R	I	Brazilian tree with an edible fruit.

1	2	3	4	5	6	7	8	
B	A	L	A	G	H	A	T	Tableland above mountain passes.
B	A	L	A	N	C	E	D	Compensated, Counterpoised, Redeemed, Settled, Adjusted, Harmonized, Stabilized.
B	A	L	A	N	C	E	R	Electronic appliance used with a direction finder.
B	A	L	A	N	I	T	E	Fossil balanoid shell.
B	A	L	C	O	N	E	T	Railing or balcony on the outside of a window.
B	A	L	D	C	O	O	T	Old world coot resembling a duck.
B	A	L	D	H	E	A	D	Head lacking hair, Pigeon, Abnormality of seedlings.
B	A	L	D	N	E	S	S	State of being bald.
B	A	L	D	P	A	T	E	Baldhead, White-crowned widgeon.
B	A	L	D	R	I	C	K	Richly ornamented belt worn over one shoulder and supporting a sword.
B	A	L	E	A	R	I	C	Group of islands in the Mediterranean Sea off the coast of Spain.
B	A	L	E	F	I	R	E	Beacon, Bonfire, Signal fire.
B	A	L	E	S	T	R	A	A move in fencing.
B	A	L	I	N	G	E	R	Small British seagoing ship of the 15th to 17th centuries.
B	A	L	I	S	T	E	S	Marine fishes.
B	A	L	I	S	T	I	D	Relating to long-snouted marine fishes.
B	A	L	K	L	I	N	E	Relating to the game of billiards.
B	A	L	L	A	D	I	C	Pertaining to a ballad.
B	A	L	L	C	L	A	Y	Pipe clay.
B	A	L	L	C	O	C	K	Float valve with a spherical float.
B	A	L	L	E	T	I	C	Suitable for ballet.
B	A	L	L	I	S	T	A	Ancient military weapon in the form of a crossbow for hurling missiles.
B	A	L	L	O	N	E	T	Gas tight compartment for controlling ascent and descent of a balloon or airship.
B	A	L	L	O	T	E	D	Voted by ballot, Decided by ballot, Selected by ballot.
B	A	L	L	R	O	O	M	A large room or hall set aside for dancing.
B	A	L	L	Y	H	O	O	Publicity, Bunkum, Trumpet, Flamboyant display, Nonsense, False talk.
B	A	L	L	Y	R	A	G	Bulldoze, Badger, Bait, Torment, Abuse, Scold, Harass.
B	A	L	M	O	R	A	L	Special type of shoe, Round flat cap.
B	A	L	N	E	A	R	Y	Relating to a bath or bathroom.
B	A	L	S	A	M	I	C	Soothing, Healing, Restorative, Balmy.
B	A	L	U	S	T	E	R	Balustrade of stair rail.
B	A	N	A	L	I	T	Y	Commonplace, Cliche, Platitude, Truism.
B	A	N	D	A	G	E	D	Covered with a bandage, Bound, Dressed.
B	A	N	D	A	N	N	A	Large cotton or silk kerchief.
B	A	N	D	E	A	U	X	Wide bands to control the hair, Fillets, Ribbons, Stripes.
B	A	N	D	E	L	E	T	Flat moulding around a column.
B	A	N	D	E	R	O	L	Flag, Banner, Ensign Pennant, Streamer.
B	A	N	D	F	I	S	H	Ribbonfish.
B	A	N	D	I	T	T	I	Brigands, Gangsters, Outlaws, Robbers, Assassins, Thugs, Marauders, Villains.
B	A	N	D	S	M	A	N	Musician, Member of a band.
B	A	N	D	Y	I	N	G	Exchanging, Striving, Pitching, Tossing, Answering, Retorting, Repaying.
B	A	N	D	Y	M	A	N	Driver of a bullock cart.
B	A	N	E	W	O	R	T	Belladonna.
B	A	N	G	A	L	A	Y	Bastard Mahogany (Australia).
B	A	N	G	A	L	O	W	Australian palm.
B	A	N	G	S	T	E	R	Shooting, Violent action.
B	A	N	G	S	T	R	Y	Bully, Roughneck.
B	A	N	G	T	A	I	L	Racehorse, Wild horse, Short stubby tail used for identifying cattle.
B	A	N	I	S	H	E	D	Exiled, Ostracized, Deported, Displaced, Ejected, Expelled, Ousted, Discharged.
B	A	N	I	S	T	E	R	Support of a staircase handrail.
B	A	N	J	O	I	S	T	One that plays a banjo.
B	A	N	K	A	B	L	E	Acceptable to a bank.
B	A	N	K	B	I	L	L	Bank note, Obsolete Bank of England note.
B	A	N	K	B	O	O	K	Book in which the bank records transactions of the depositor.
B	A	N	K	N	O	T	E	Promissory note issued by the bank.
B	A	N	K	R	A	T	E	Discount rate fixed by a central bank.
B	A	N	K	R	U	P	T	Impoverished, Broken, Ruined, Finished, Depleted, Sterile, Deprived.
B	A	N	K	S	M	A	N	Overseer at a section of a mine.
B	A	N	L	I	E	U	E	Environs, Suburbs.
B	A	N	N	E	R	E	D	Furnished with a banner, Given extreme prominence.
B	A	N	N	E	R	E	T	Civil officer in a Swiss canton or Italian republic.
B	A	N	N	E	R	O	L	Banner displayed at a funeral and draped over the tomb.
B	A	N	T	A	Y	A	N	Look out, Signal tower.
B	A	N	T	E	R	E	D	Jested, Dared, Challenged, Wheedled, Teased, Exchanged.
B	A	N	T	L	I	N	G	Infant.
B	A	N	X	R	I	N	G	Tree shrew.
B	A	P	H	O	M	E	T	Idol.

1	2	3	4	5	6	7	8	
B	A	P	T	I	Z	E	D	Christened, Purified, Cleansed, Immersed, Sprinkled, Named, Designated Styled.
B	A	R	A	B	A	R	A	Turf hut in the Arctic region.
B	A	R	A	R	I	T	E	Mineral consisting of ammonium flurosilicate.
B	A	R	A	T	H	E	A	Broken twill weave fabric with a pebbly surface.
B	A	R	B	A	R	E	A	Small genus of yellow-flowered herbs, Winter Cress.
B	A	R	B	A	R	I	C	Barbarous, Graceless, Vulgar, Wild, Tasteless, Coarse, Crude, Tawdry.
B	A	R	B	A	S	C	O	Wild cinnamon, Plant used by S. American Indians to make fish poison.
B	A	R	B	A	T	E	D	Bearded, Bristled.
B	A	R	B	E	C	U	E	Food cooked over an open fire in the out-doors.
B	A	R	B	E	I	R	O	Red-spotted bug of the American tropics that transmits Chagas' disease.
B	A	R	B	E	R	R	Y	Shrub, Dried rhizome and roots used as a tonic.
B	A	R	B	E	T	T	E	Nun's face band, Protecting armour of a gun-turret.
B	A	R	B	I	C	A	N	Defensive tower at a gate or bridge.
B	A	R	B	I	T	O	N	Ancient Greek lyre.
B	A	R	B	I	Z	O	N	Natural style of French painting.
B	A	R	C	L	A	M	P	Clamps on a bar used in cabinet-making.
B	A	R	D	L	I	N	G	Poetaster, Versifier, Writer of inferior verse.
B	A	R	D	I	E	S	T	Most insolent, Most forward, Boldest.
B	A	R	E	B	A	C	K	To ride a horse without using a saddle.
B	A	R	E	B	O	A	T	Finalisation of a charter contract for a ship.
B	A	R	E	F	O	O	T	Not wearing shoes or stockings.
B	A	R	E	S	A	R	K	Berserker, Frenzied, Crazed, Mad, Wild.
B	A	R	G	E	M	A	N	Crew member on a barge.
B	A	R	G	H	E	S	T	Ghost or goblin sometimes in the form of a large dog said to foretell disaster.
B	A	R	I	T	O	N	E	Male singing voice of a range between bass and tenor, Viola Bastarda, Saxhorn.
B	A	R	K	P	E	E	L	To peel the bark from a tree.
B	A	R	N	A	C	L	E	Small shellfish that cements itself to rocks or ships. Unprogressive.
B	A	R	N	D	O	O	R	Special light panel used for TV work.
B	A	R	N	Y	A	R	D	Fenced area adjoining a barn.
B	A	R	O	N	A	G	E	Nobility, Collection of barons or peers.
B	A	R	O	N	E	S	S	Wife or widow of a baron, Woman who holds a baronial title in her own right.
B	A	R	O	N	I	A	L	Splendid, Stately, Spacious, Sumptuous, Ample.
B	A	R	O	U	C	H	E	Four-wheeled carriage.
B	A	R	R	A	B	L	E	Capable of being barred.
B	A	R	R	A	C	K	S	Permanent buildings for housing soldiers or workers.
B	A	R	R	A	N	C	A	Barranco, Steep bank.
B	A	R	R	A	T	O	R	One who engages in barratry.
B	A	R	R	A	T	R	Y	Fraudulent breach of duty by the master of a ship, Encouraging litigation, Prolongong quarrels.
B	A	R	R	E	N	L	Y	Fruitlessly, Sterilely, Desolately, Unprofitability, Dully.
B	A	R	R	I	C	O	E	Small cask, Keg.
B	A	R	R	U	L	E	T	Small bar in heraldry.
B	A	R	T	E	R	E	D	Exchanged, Traded, Bargained, Swapped, Trafficked, Trucked.
B	A	R	T	H	I	A	N	Adherent of the theology of Karl Barth.
B	A	R	T	I	Z	A	N	Defense lookout, Turret, Tower.
B	A	R	T	O	N	I	A	Genus of small herbs with yellow flowers, Mentzelia.
B	A	S	A	L	T	I	C	Formed of basalt.
B	A	S	A	N	I	T	E	Touchstone, An extrusive-igneous rock.
B	A	S	C	I	N	E	T	Basinet, A light helmet worn under a battle helmet.
B	A	S	E	B	A	L	L	Outdoor ball game played in a square.
B	A	S	E	B	O	R	N	Lowly, Plebeian, Spurious, Ignoble, Illegitimate, Meanspirited, Bastard.
B	A	S	E	L	E	S	S	Groundless, Without foundation, Unfounded, Unwarranted, False, Unjustifiable, Idle, Vain.
B	A	S	E	L	I	N	E	A base from which to take measurements, Quantity for use as a control.
B	A	S	E	M	E	N	T	Part of a building wholly or partly underground.
B	A	S	E	N	E	S	S	Meanness, Wickedness of character.
B	A	S	E	P	L	U	G	Electric plug socket near the floor.
B	A	S	I	C	I	T	Y	Degree of being a base, Reaction of an acid in an experiment.
B	A	S	I	D	I	A	L	Consisting of a basidium.
B	A	S	I	D	I	U	M	Structure on a fungus in which nuclear fusion occurs.
B	A	S	I	F	I	E	R	Alkaline base.
B	A	S	I	L	E	U	S	Ruler of the Eastern Roman empire.
B	A	S	I	L	I	A	N	Relating to the monastic rule of St Basil.
B	A	S	I	L	I	C	A	Roman Catholic cathedral, Ancient Roman place of assembly, Early Christian church.
B	A	S	I	L	I	S	K	Legendary reptile, American lizard, Large cannon.
B	A	S	K	E	T	E	D	Thrown into a basket.
B	A	S	K	E	T	R	Y	Art of weaving wickerwork.
B	A	S	O	P	H	I	L	Substance easily stained, White blood cell.
B	A	S	Q	U	I	N	E	Rich outer petticoat worn by Basque or Spanish women.

1	2	3	4	5	6	7	8	
B	A	S	S	D	R	U	M	Large two-headed drum that gives a deep booming note.
B	A	S	S	H	O	R	N	Tuba.
B	A	S	S	I	N	E	T	Perambulator for an infant, Crib.
B	A	S	S	O	R	I	N	Substnce from gum that is insoluble in water but swells to form a gel.
B	A	S	S	V	I	O	L	Contrabass.
B	A	S	S	W	O	O	D	Linden, Tulip tree.
B	A	S	T	A	A	R	D	Person of mixed blood, Griqua.
B	A	S	T	A	R	D	Y	Illegitimacy.
B	A	S	T	I	L	L	E	Place of detention, Prison, Jail.
B	A	T	A	V	I	A	N	Inhabitant of ancient Low Countries.
B	A	T	E	L	E	S	S	That cannot be blunted.
B	A	T	H	E	T	I	C	Characterised by an anticlimax.
B	A	T	H	M	I	S	M	A hypothetical growth force.
B	A	T	H	O	R	S	E	Packhorse in a military campaign.
B	A	T	H	R	O	B	E	Dressing gown.
B	A	T	H	R	O	O	M	Room containing bath, basin and toilet.
B	A	T	O	I	D	E	I	Order of flatfishes, Skates, Rays.
B	A	T	O	N	I	S	T	Conductor.
B	A	T	T	A	L	I	A	Battle array.
B	A	T	T	E	L	E	D	Account for provisions supplied at Oxford University.
B	A	T	T	E	N	E	D	Fastened, Secured.
B	A	T	T	E	R	E	D	Beat, Pounded, Mangled, Disabled, Mutilated, Shattered, Thrashed, Wrecked.
B	A	T	T	E	R	I	E	A leg movement in ballet.
B	A	T	T	L	I	N	G	Fighting, Struggling, Forcing, Contending, Thrusting, Driving, Assaulting, Contesting.
B	A	U	D	E	K	I	N	Baldachin, Rich fabric for church vestments, Ornate canopy over an altar.
B	A	U	D	R	O	N	S	Cat.
B	A	U	L	K	I	N	G	Balking, Recoiling, Frustrating, Quibbling, Halting, Avoiding.
B	A	V	A	R	I	A	N	Characeristic of Bavaria.
B	A	Y	A	D	E	R	E	A fabric with horizontal stripes.
B	A	Y	B	E	R	R	Y	Bay rum, Wax myrtle.
B	D	E	L	L	I	U	M	Gum resin similar to myrrh.
B	E	A	C	H	I	N	G	Running a ship ashore, Mooring, Anchoring, Stranding.
B	E	A	C	O	N	E	D	Lit as a beacon, Inspired, Guided.
B	E	A	D	R	O	L	L	Rosary, Long list.
B	E	A	D	S	M	A	N	Inmate of an almshouse that prays for the souls of the benefactors.
B	E	A	D	T	R	E	E	Tree that has scarlet seeds used for necklaces, Red sandalwood.
B	E	A	D	W	O	R	K	Ornamental work made with beads.
B	E	A	K	H	E	A	D	Forward space of a ship where the latrines of the crew are situated.
B	E	A	K	I	R	O	N	Bickiron, The taper end of an anvil.
B	E	A	L	L	A	C	H	Mountain pass.
B	E	A	M	B	I	R	D	Spotted flycatcher.
B	E	A	M	T	R	E	E	Whitebeam.
B	E	A	N	B	A	L	L	Baseball deliberately pitched at a batter's head.
B	E	A	N	K	I	N	G	Bean.
B	E	A	R	A	B	L	E	Tolerable, Sufferable, Supportable, Acceptable, Admissible, Allowable, Livable, Satisfactory.
B	E	A	R	A	B	L	Y	Endurably.
B	E	A	R	B	I	N	D	Bearbine, Convolvulus.
B	E	A	R	D	I	N	G	Beardlike growth, Forward edge of a rudder.
B	E	A	R	I	N	G	S	Relative situation or position.
B	E	A	R	S	E	A	R	Auricular.
B	E	A	R	S	K	I	N	Article made of the skin of the bear, Head-dress of a guardsman.
B	E	A	R	W	A	R	D	Bear keeper.
B	E	A	S	T	I	E	S	Animals, Small creatures.
B	E	A	S	T	I	L	Y	Bestially.
B	E	A	T	I	F	I	C	Saintly, Angelic, Seraphic.
B	E	A	U	T	I	E	S	Lovelies, Ideals, Perfect attributes.
B	E	A	U	T	I	F	Y	Embellish, Adorn, Decorate, Garnish, Ornament, Bedeck, Trim.
B	E	A	U	X	I	T	E	Bauxite.
B	E	C	A	L	M	E	D	Motionless, Soothed, Tranquilized, Cessation of activity.
B	E	C	H	A	M	E	L	White sauce.
B	E	C	H	A	N	C	E	Happen, Befall.
B	E	C	K	I	R	O	N	Horned anvil.
B	E	C	K	O	N	E	D	Gestured, Signalled, Invited, Waved, Welcomed.
B	E	C	O	M	I	N	G	Emerging, Happening, Adorning, Befitting, Graceful, Suitable, Seemly.
B	E	D	A	B	B	L	E	Soil by dabbling, Sprinkling with wet.
B	E	D	A	U	B	E	D	Soiled with someting thick or sticky, Bedizened, Decorated gaudily.
B	E	D	E	C	K	E	D	Adorned richly, Decorated in an opulent fashion.

1	2	3	4	5	6	7	8	
B	E	D	E	G	U	A	R	Gall-like moss produced on rosebushes.
B	E	D	E	S	M	A	N	Beadsman.
B	E	D	E	W	I	N	G	Moistening with dew, Crying tears.
B	E	D	I	M	M	E	D	Obscured, Reduced available light, Made dim.
B	E	D	L	I	N	E	N	Sheets and pillowcases and related articles.
B	E	D	P	L	A	T	E	Supporting plate or frame, Part of a papermaking beater.
B	E	D	S	T	A	F	F	Bed slat.
B	E	D	S	T	E	A	D	Framework of a bed.
B	E	D	S	T	O	C	K	Structure supporting bed slats.
B	E	D	S	T	R	A	W	Straw used as a substitute for a mattress or to stuff a mattress.
B	E	D	W	A	R	D	S	Toward bed.
B	E	E	B	R	E	A	D	Bitter yellowish brown pollen, used mixed with honey as food by the bees.
B	E	E	E	A	T	E	R	Brightly coloured tropical Old World birds.
B	E	E	F	I	E	S	T	Heaviest, Thickset, Heftiest.
B	E	E	F	W	O	O	D	Heavy reddish tropical woods.
B	E	E	R	P	U	M	P	Pump for drawing up beer from casks, Beerpull.
B	E	E	S	W	I	N	G	Film of shiny scales of tartar formed in port and wines.
B	E	E	T	L	I	N	G	Scuttling like a beetle.
B	E	E	T	R	O	O	T	Pigweed, Red root used as salad vegetable.
B	E	F	I	T	T	E	D	In harmony, Suited, Agreed, Suitable.
B	E	F	O	G	G	E	D	Obscured, Made indistinct, Confused, Puzzled.
B	E	F	O	O	L	E	D	Duped. Deceived, Fooled, Hoaxed, Tricked, Victimized.
B	E	F	O	U	L	E	D	Slandered, Calumniated, Disgraced, Blackened, Denigrated, Defamed, Maligned, Smeared.
B	E	F	R	I	E	N	D	Show kindness, sympathy and understanding, To act friendly, Patronized, Aided.
B	E	F	R	I	N	G	E	Border with a fringe.
B	E	F	U	R	R	E	D	Adorned with fur.
B	E	G	E	T	T	E	R	One that procreates or produces.
B	E	G	G	A	R	E	D	Impoverished, Rendered penniless.
B	E	G	G	A	R	L	Y	Contemptible, Cheap, Despicable, Mean, Pitiable, Paltry, Shabby, Wretched.
B	E	G	I	N	N	E	R	Young or inexperienced person, Tyro.
B	E	G	I	R	D	E	D	Surrounded, Encompassed, Enveloped.
B	E	G	I	R	D	L	E	Encircle as with a girdle.
B	E	G	O	T	T	E	N	Procreated.
B	E	G	R	I	M	E	D	Sullied, Tarnished, Corrupted, Soiled, Fouled, Dirtied.
B	E	G	R	U	D	G	E	Envy, Give reluctantly, Concede with displeasure.
B	E	G	U	I	L	E	D	Diverted, Disappointed, Deceived, Hoodwinked, Cheated, Charmed, Manipulated.
B	E	G	U	I	L	E	R	Deceiver.
B	E	H	A	T	T	E	D	Wearing a hat.
B	E	H	A	V	I	N	G	Conducting, Comporting, Acquitting, Demeaning, Acting, Directing, Managing, Operating.
B	E	H	E	A	D	A	L	Beheading.
B	E	H	E	A	D	E	D	Decapitated, Severed the head.
B	E	H	E	M	O	T	H	Something of a monstrous size, Oppressive.
B	E	H	O	L	D	E	N	Obligated to return a favour, Indebted, Dependent.
B	E	H	O	L	D	E	R	Spectator, Bystander, Eyewitness, Observer, Onlooker, Viewer, Watcher, Witness.
B	E	H	O	V	I	N	G	Fitting, Proper, Requiring, Necessary.
B	E	J	E	S	U	I	T	To make Jesuitic.
B	E	K	I	S	S	E	D	Kissed intensely or excessively.
B	E	L	A	B	O	U	R	Assail, Attack, Beat, Work diligently, Work to absurd lengths.
B	E	L	A	M	O	U	R	One who is loved.
B	E	L	A	T	I	N	G	Delaying, Retarding.
B	E	L	A	U	D	E	D	Praised excessively or unduly.
B	E	L	A	Y	I	N	G	Cancelling, Disregarding, Stopping, Securing a rope in mountain climbing.
B	E	L	C	H	I	N	G	Expelling gas from the stomach through the mouth, Erupting. Ejaculating, Exploding.
B	E	L	F	R	I	E	S	Towers in which bells are hung.
B	E	L	I	E	V	E	D	Credited, Convinced, Accepted, Trusted, Admitted, Supposed.
B	E	L	I	E	V	E	R	Devotee, Christian, Adherent to a religious faith.
B	E	L	I	T	T	L	E	Disparage, Depreciate, Decry, Derogate, Detract, Diminish, Discount, Discredit.
B	E	L	L	B	I	N	E	Bell-bine, Bindweed.
B	E	L	L	B	I	R	D	A bird whose notes are bell-like, Honey eater, Wood thrush.
B	E	L	L	B	U	O	Y	Buoy marking a shoal or rocks with the ringing of a bell.
B	E	L	L	C	O	T	E	Small jutting belfry.
B	E	L	L	E	R	I	C	The fruit of the bathera.
B	E	L	L	L	Y	R	A	A glockenspiel mounted in a portable frame.
B	E	L	L	O	W	E	D	Bawled, Roared, Blustered, Routed, Clamoured, Wailed.
B	E	L	L	P	U	L	L	Cord or wire hanging for operating a bell.
B	E	L	L	P	U	S	H	A button to push for ringing a bell.
B	E	L	L	R	O	P	E	Rope attached to bell of tongue of bell.

1	2	3	4	5	6	7	8	
B	E	L	L	W	O	O	D	Silver Bell.
B	E	L	L	W	O	R	T	Plant of family Campanulaceae, Having flowers shaped like bells.
B	E	L	L	Y	F	U	L	More than be comfortably tolerated.
B	E	L	L	Y	G	O	D	Glutton.
B	E	L	L	Y	I	N	G	Swelling, Filling, Bulging, Moving on the belly.
B	E	L	O	N	G	E	D	Became, Suited, Agreed, Matched, Corresponded, Pertained, Attributed.
B	E	L	T	L	I	N	E	Production line, Waistline.
B	E	L	T	W	I	S	E	Resembling a belt.
B	E	M	A	S	T	E	R	Bring under control.
B	E	M	I	R	I	N	G	Covering or soiling with mud.
B	E	M	I	S	T	E	D	Involved, Confused, Obscured, Muddled.
B	E	M	O	A	N	E	D	Lamented, Deplored, Bewailed, Grieved, Wept, Complained, Regretted.
B	E	M	U	F	F	L	E	Muffle up.
B	E	M	U	S	I	N	G	Bewildering, Paralyzing, Petrifying, Stupefying, Perplexing, Dazing, Puzzling, Stunning.
B	E	N	C	H	I	N	G	Seating on a bench, Removing a player from the field.
B	E	N	D	A	B	L	E	Capable of being bent, Pliable, Not rigid.
B	E	N	D	W	I	S	E	Diagonally in heraldry.
B	E	N	E	A	P	E	D	Neaped.
B	E	N	E	D	I	C	K	Married man who has been a bachelor many years.
B	E	N	E	D	I	C	T	Blessed, Benign, Mild.
B	E	N	E	F	I	C	E	Rectory, Vicarage, Tenancy for life, Gift, Ecclesiastical post.
B	E	N	G	A	L	E	E	Small tropical songbird often kept in a cage.
B	E	N	I	G	N	L	Y	Graciously, Kindly, Salutary, Favourably.
B	E	N	I	T	I	E	R	Holy water stoup.
B	E	N	J	A	M	I	N	Balsam, Man's overcoat.
B	E	N	O	T	I	N	G	Annotating absurdly.
B	E	N	T	W	O	O	D	Furniture made of wood that is shaped into curves.
B	E	N	U	M	B	E	D	Deadened, Stupefied, Dazed, Blunted, Dulled, Petrified.
B	E	N	Z	O	A	T	E	Salt or ester of benzoic acid.
B	E	P	O	W	D	E	R	Cover with powder.
B	E	P	R	A	I	S	E	To praise excessively.
B	E	P	U	F	F	E	D	Very puffy or swollen.
B	E	Q	U	E	A	T	H	Will, Entrust, Commend, Transmit, Devise, Legate, Leave.
B	E	R	A	T	I	N	G	Criticizing, Scolding, Reviling, Upbraiding, Rating, Vituperating.
B	E	R	B	E	R	I	S	Barberry.
B	E	R	B	E	R	R	Y	Same as BARBERRY.
B	E	R	E	A	V	E	D	Deprived, Stripped, Dispossessed, Lost, Ousted, Robbed, Divested, Bereft.
B	E	R	G	A	M	O	T	Orange that yields oil necessary for perfumery.
B	E	R	G	D	A	M	A	Branch of the Damara.
B	E	R	G	E	N	I	A	Genus of perennial spring-blooming herbs.
B	E	R	G	H	A	A	N	Eagle of Southern Africa.
B	E	R	H	Y	M	E	D	Lampooned in rhyming verse.
B	E	R	I	B	E	R	I	Deficiency disease caused by lack of Vitamin B.
B	E	R	L	O	Q	U	E	Drumbeat, Trumpet call.
B	E	R	N	I	C	L	E	Barnacle goose.
B	E	R	R	E	T	T	A	Biretta, Ecclesiastic square head covering coloured according to rank.
B	E	R	R	Y	I	N	G	Producing, Gathering or picking berries.
B	E	R	T	H	A	G	E	Reserved space at a wharf for mooring, Dock fees.
B	E	R	T	H	I	N	G	Wooden planking of a ship, Mooring, Anchoring.
B	E	R	Y	L	L	I	A	Beryllium oxide.
B	E	S	C	R	E	E	N	Screen, Shelter, Seclude.
B	E	S	E	E	M	E	D	Befitted, Became.
B	E	S	I	E	G	E	D	Beleaguered, Blockaded, Invested, Assaulted, Attacked, Surrounded, Trapped, Encircled.
B	E	S	I	E	G	E	R	One who assails.
B	E	S	I	L	V	E	R	Cover with silver.
B	E	S	L	A	V	E	D	Enslaved.
B	E	S	M	I	R	C	H	Sully, Soil, Tarnish, Stain, Defile, Discolour, Taint, Smear.
B	E	S	O	R	T	E	D	Suited, Fitted.
B	E	S	O	T	T	E	D	Infatuated, Obsessed, Stupid, Dull-witted, Doltish, Dazed, Enamoured, Muddled.
B	E	S	O	U	G	H	T	Beseeched.
B	E	S	P	O	K	E	N	Custom-made, Made to order, Engaged to be married.
B	E	S	P	R	E	A	D	Overspread, Broadcast, Disseminate.
B	E	S	S	E	M	E	R	Special furnace used in a steel process.
B	E	S	T	I	A	R	Y	Medieval book describing real and legendary beasts.
B	E	S	T	O	W	A	L	Presentation, Storage.
B	E	S	T	O	W	E	D	Applied, Put, Placed, Located, Stowed, Gave, Granted, Conferred.
B	E	S	T	O	W	E	R	One that makes a presentation.

1	2	3	4	5	6	7	8	
B	E	S	T	R	E	A	K	Cover with streaks.
B	E	S	T	R	E	W	N	Objects scattered about.
B	E	S	T	R	I	D	E	Mount, Straddle, Dominate, Tower over.
B	E	S	T	R	O	D	E	Mounted, Dominated.
B	E	T	A	C	I	S	M	Inability to pronounce "b" and "v" distinctly.
B	E	T	A	F	I	T	E	Mineral of Madagascar consisting of an oxide of niobium, titanium and uranium.
B	E	T	A	K	I	N	G	Granting, Taking oneself.
B	E	T	A	R	A	Y	S	Stream of beta particles.
B	E	T	A	T	R	O	N	Accelerator in which electrons are propelled.
B	E	T	E	L	N	U	T	Astringent seed of the betal palm used as a vermifuge and myotic, also for chewing.
B	E	T	I	D	I	N	G	Befalling, Foreboding, Presaging, Happening.
B	E	T	O	S	S	E	D	Agitated.
B	E	T	R	A	Y	A	L	Being betrayed, Treachery.
B	E	T	R	A	Y	E	D	Misled, Deceived, Beguiled, Deluded, Ensnared, Informed, Revealed, Divulged.
B	E	T	R	A	Y	E	R	Informer, Telltale, Squealer, Seducer.
B	E	T	T	E	R	E	D	Improved, Exelled, Exceeded.
B	E	V	E	L	I	N	G	Sloping the edge, Cutting across, Slanting, Inclining, Deviating.
B	E	V	E	L	L	E	D	Having a slanted edge, Inclined, Diagonal, Biased.
B	E	V	E	R	A	G	E	Liquid other than water for drinking purposes.
B	E	W	A	I	L	E	D	Deplored, Lamented, Bemoaned, Grieved, Wept.
B	E	W	A	R	I	N	G	Avoiding, Being wary, Taking care, Watching, Noticing, Heeding.
B	E	W	I	G	G	E	D	Wearing a wig.
B	E	W	I	L	D	E	R	Perplex, Confuse, Puzzle, Confound, Baffle, Muddle, Fluster, Distract.
B	E	W	R	A	Y	E	D	Divulged, Disclosed, Revealed.
B	E	Y	E	R	I	T	E	Mineral of rare calcium bismuth oxide and carbonate.
B	E	Z	E	L	L	E	D	Bevelled.
B	H	A	G	A	W	A	T	Lord, used as an epithet.
B	H	E	A	S	T	I	E	Water carrier of a household or regiment.
B	I	B	A	C	I	T	Y	Addiction to drink, Tippling.
B	I	B	A	T	I	O	N	Tippling, Imbibing.
B	I	B	I	O	N	I	D	Family of two-winged flies.
B	I	B	L	I	C	A	L	Relating to the Bible.
B	I	B	U	L	O	U	S	Inclined to drink, Addicted to tippling.
B	I	C	A	U	D	A	L	Having two tails.
B	I	C	K	E	R	E	D	Fought, Wrangled, Flickered, Argued, Disputed, Hassled, Battled, Squabbled.
B	I	C	O	L	O	U	R	Having two colours, Two-tone.
B	I	C	O	N	V	E	X	Lens being convex on both sides.
B	I	C	R	U	R	A	L	Having two legs.
B	I	C	U	S	P	I	D	Ending in two points or teeth.
B	I	C	Y	C	L	E	D	Rode a bicycle, Direct transmission of a television programme.
B	I	D	D	A	B	L	E	Obedient.
B	I	E	N	N	I	A	L	Occurring every two years.
B	I	F	A	C	I	A	L	Hand axe of flint.
B	I	F	O	R	A	T	E	Having two perforations.
B	I	G	A	M	I	S	T	One taking part in another marriage while still legally married to the first spouse.
B	I	G	A	M	O	U	S	Involving bigamy.
B	I	G	A	R	A	D	E	Sour orange.
B	I	G	B	O	N	E	D	Having a large skeletal structure.
B	I	G	G	O	N	E	T	Woman's cap or coif of linen.
B	I	G	M	O	U	T	H	Variety of fishes having large mouths, Gossipy person.
B	I	G	N	O	N	I	A	Small genus of American and Japanese woody vines.
B	I	J	U	G	A	T	E	Having two pairs of leaves.
B	I	K	A	N	E	R	I	Indian breed of sheep.
B	I	L	A	B	I	A	L	Between the lips.
B	I	L	A	N	D	E	R	Small two-masted merchant ship.
B	I	L	B	E	R	R	Y	Whortleberry, Sweet edible bluish-black fruit.
B	I	L	I	N	E	A	R	Relating to two lines, Algebraic form.
B	I	L	L	E	T	E	D	Lodged, Located, Boarded, Quartered, Bedded.
B	I	L	L	F	I	S	H	Fishes having long slender jaws, Sailfish.
B	I	L	L	F	O	L	D	Wallet.
B	I	L	L	H	E	A	D	Invoice with sellers name printed on the top.
B	I	L	L	H	O	O	K	Large bladed tool with a hook used for pruning.
B	I	L	L	I	A	R	D	A shot in the game of billiards.
B	I	L	L	O	W	E	D	Surged, Undulated, Swelled.
B	I	L	L	Y	B	O	Y	Flat-bottomed river or coasting boat.
B	I	L	L	Y	C	A	N	Can for carrying liquid.
B	I	L	O	B	A	T	E	Divided into two lobes.

1	2	3	4	5	6	7	8	Definition
B	I	M	A	N	O	U	S	Two-handed.
B	I	M	A	N	U	A	L	Requiring the use of two hands.
B	I	M	A	S	T	I	C	Having two breasts.
B	I	M	E	S	T	E	R	Period of two months.
B	I	N	A	U	R	A	L	Pertaining to the function of two ears.
B	I	N	D	W	E	E	D	Genus of plants that mat together.
B	I	N	N	A	C	L	E	Box or stand containing a ship's compass and a lamp.
B	I	N	O	M	I	A	L	Mathematical expression, Having two names.
B	I	N	O	X	I	D	E	Dioxide.
B	I	O	A	S	S	A	Y	Determination of the relative effective strength of a substance.
B	I	O	B	L	A	S	T	Altmann's Granule.
B	I	O	C	H	O	R	E	Group of similar biotopes.
B	I	O	C	Y	C	L	E	Group of related biochores.
B	I	O	C	Y	T	I	N	Colourless crystalline peptide.
B	I	O	G	E	N	I	C	Produced by the action of living organisms, Essential to life and its maintenance.
B	I	O	G	R	A	P	H	To write a biographical sketch.
B	I	O	L	O	G	I	C	Relating to life and living things.
B	I	O	L	Y	S	I	S	Death and bodily disintegration.
B	I	O	L	Y	T	I	C	Decomposition by living organisms of sewage.
B	I	O	M	E	T	E	R	Device for measuring carbon dioxide given off by living matter.
B	I	O	M	E	T	R	Y	Biometrics.
B	I	O	N	O	M	I	C	Relating to ecology.
B	I	O	P	H	O	R	E	Ultimate supramolecular vital unit in Weismann' theory of life processes.
B	I	O	P	L	A	S	M	Living protoplasm.
B	I	O	S	C	O	P	E	Motion-picture projector.
B	I	O	V	U	L	A	R	Derived from two ova, used of fraternal twins.
B	I	P	A	L	I	U	M	Genus of flatworms.
B	I	P	A	R	O	U	S	Bringing forth two young at birth.
B	I	P	H	A	S	I	C	Having two phases.
B	I	P	L	A	N	A	R	Lying in two planes.
B	I	Q	U	A	R	T	Z	A quartz plate used in detecting polarization.
B	I	R	A	C	I	A	L	Involving members of two races.
B	I	R	A	D	I	A	L	Having both bilateral and radia symmetry.
B	I	R	A	M	O	U	S	Consisting of two branches.
B	I	R	C	H	I	N	G	Caning, Beating, Whipping.
B	I	R	D	B	A	T	H	Garden ornament providing a place for birds to bathe.
B	I	R	D	B	O	L	T	Short blunt missile.
B	I	R	D	C	A	G	E	A cage for confining birds.
B	I	R	D	C	A	L	L	A sound made imitating the cry of a bird.
B	I	R	D	E	Y	E	D	Having eyes like a bird, Skittish, Easily frightened.
B	I	R	D	L	I	F	E	Avifauna, Activities and habits of birds.
B	I	R	D	L	I	K	E	Resembling a bird.
B	I	R	D	L	I	M	E	Adhesive used on tree branches to trap birds.
B	I	R	D	S	E	E	D	Mixture of small seed used chiefly for feeding cage birds.
B	I	R	D	S	E	Y	E	Aerial view, Panoramic, General, Cursory, Superficial.
B	I	R	D	S	O	N	G	Song of a bird.
B	I	R	T	H	D	A	Y	Anniversary of one's birth, The day on which a person is born.
B	I	R	T	H	D	O	M	Domain by birthright, Native land.
B	I	S	C	A	Y	A	N	Basque.
B	I	S	E	C	T	E	D	Divided into two equal parts, Separated.
B	I	S	E	C	T	O	R	A straight line that bisects an angle or a line segment.
B	I	S	E	R	I	A	L	Characterized by an arrangement in two rows or series.
B	I	S	E	T	O	S	E	Having two bristles.
B	I	S	E	X	U	A	L	Hermaphroditic, Possessing characters typical of both sexes.
B	I	S	H	O	P	E	D	Confirmed, Sanctioned, Approved formally.
B	I	S	T	E	R	E	D	Swarthy of complexion.
B	I	S	T	O	U	R	Y	Small slender straight or curved surgical knife.
B	I	T	A	N	H	O	L	Tropical tree of Philippines with bark and seeds that yield an aromatic resin and bitter oil.
B	I	T	E	G	M	I	C	Having two integuments, Having two covers.
B	I	T	E	W	I	N	G	Special dental X-ray film.
B	I	T	I	N	G	L	Y	In a cutting, caustic manner.
B	I	T	T	A	C	L	E	Binnacle.
B	I	T	T	E	R	E	D	Embittered.
B	I	T	T	E	R	L	Y	Sourly, Acridly.
B	I	V	A	L	E	N	T	Having a valence of two, Pair of synaptic chromosomes.
B	I	W	E	E	K	L	Y	Occurring every two weeks, Fortnightly.
B	I	X	A	C	E	A	E	Family of tropical shrubs or trees.

1	2	3	4	5	6	7	8	Clue
B	I	X	B	Y	I	T	E	Mineral consisting of an iron maganese oxide.
B	L	A	B	B	I	N	G	Chattering, Gabbling, Jabbering, Prattling.
B	L	A	C	K	A	R	M	Leaf spot disease of cotton.
B	L	A	C	K	B	O	X	Flight recorder on an aircraft.
B	L	A	C	K	C	A	P	Head cloth worn by a British judge when passing the death sentence.
B	L	A	C	K	F	L	Y	Small two-winged biting fly, Greenhouse thrips.
B	L	A	C	K	G	U	M	A tree of the genus Nyssa of the U.S. having close-grained wood.
B	L	A	C	K	I	N	G	Paste or liquid for shining black shoes.
B	L	A	C	K	I	S	H	Somewhat black.
B	L	A	C	K	L	E	G	Strikebreaker, Worker hostile to a trade union, Professional gambler.
B	L	A	C	K	N	E	B	Carrion crow, Sympathizer with the French Revolution, Blackleg.
B	L	A	C	K	O	U	T	Envelop in darkness, Loss of consciousness, Cease to operate.
B	L	A	C	K	R	O	D	Usher to the House of Lords.
B	L	A	D	D	E	R	Y	Puffy, Inflated.
B	L	A	M	A	B	L	E	Reprehensible, Blameworthy.
B	L	A	M	A	B	L	Y	In a censurable way.
B	L	A	M	E	F	U	L	Disapproval, Blame, Punishment.
B	L	A	N	C	H	E	D	Bleached, Whitened, Decolourized, Blenched, Whitewashed.
B	L	A	N	C	H	E	R	To cause to turn aside.
B	L	A	N	D	E	S	T	Gentlest, Dullest, Softest, Most suave, Smoothest, Creamiest.
B	L	A	N	D	I	S	H	Coax, Cajole, Wheedle, Banter, Flatter, Beguile, Charm.
B	L	A	N	K	E	S	T	Blindest, Most disconcerted, Most intense, Most vacant.
B	L	A	N	K	I	N	G	Obstructing, Obscuring, Blotting, Fading.
B	L	A	S	T	E	M	A	Mass of living substance capable of growth.
B	L	A	S	T	I	N	G	Withering, Blighting, Shrivelling, Wrecking, Ruining.
B	L	A	S	T	O	F	F	Act of beginning to travel used for rockets and missiles.
B	L	A	T	A	N	C	Y	In a conspicuous manner, Brazen, Vulgary.
B	L	A	U	W	B	O	K	An extinct antelope.
B	L	A	Z	O	N	E	D	Displayed, Decked, Embellished, Advertised, Announced, Broadcast, Proclaimed, Published.
B	L	A	Z	O	N	E	R	One that displays.
B	L	A	Z	O	N	R	Y	Artistic display, Ornamental covering.
B	L	E	A	C	H	E	D	Decolourized, Blanched, Lightened, Whitened.
B	L	E	A	C	H	E	R	A worker who bleaches materials.
B	L	E	A	K	E	S	T	Palest, Coldest, Rawest, Grimmest, Most austere, Most dismal.
B	L	E	A	T	I	N	G	Whimpering, Whining, Blathering, Griping, Fussing, Squawking.
B	L	E	E	D	I	N	G	Haemorrhaging, Oozing, Flowing, Drawing off, Extracting.
B	L	E	N	C	H	E	D	Paled, Flinched, Quailed, Shrunk, Recoiled, Winced, Started.
B	L	E	N	D	I	N	G	Mixing, Mingling, Uniting, Harmonizing, Compounding, Fusing, Melding, Resolving.
B	L	E	N	N	I	I	D	Large family of small carnivorous fishes, Blennies.
B	L	E	P	H	A	R	A	One of the peristome teeth of a moss.
B	L	E	S	S	I	N	G	Praising, Glorifying, Guarding, Thanks, Grace, Approbation, Approval, Benediction.
B	L	E	T	T	I	N	G	Ripening and softening of certain fruits in storage.
B	L	I	G	H	T	E	D	Deteriorated, Blasted, Ruined, Frustrated.
B	L	I	G	H	T	E	R	Worthless or contemptible person, Fellow, Guy.
B	L	I	M	B	I	N	G	Carambola, Acid fruit used in Chinese cookery.
B	L	I	N	D	A	G	E	Large deep dugout.
B	L	I	N	D	E	S	T	Most blind, Blankest, Dullest, Dimmest.
B	L	I	N	D	I	N	G	Confusing, Dazzling, Obscuring, Dazzling, Depriving of sight.
B	L	I	N	K	A	R	D	Stupid, Slow witted person.
B	L	I	N	K	E	R	S	Eye shades for horses, Hoodwinks.
B	L	I	N	K	I	N	G	Winking, Peeping, Glancing, Flickering, Ignoring, Twinkling.
B	L	I	S	S	F	U	L	Very happy, Ecstasy, Rapturous.
B	L	I	S	T	E	R	Y	Marred by blisters.
B	L	I	T	H	E	L	Y	Joyfully, Cheerfully, Gaily, Merrily, Joyously.
B	L	I	T	H	E	S	T	Merriest, Most joyful, Most vivacious.
B	L	I	T	Z	I	N	G	Making a vigorous attack, Hustling, Moving, Stampeding.
B	L	I	Z	Z	A	R	D	Intensely strong cold wind filled with snow, Severe snowstorm, Unexpected occurrence.
B	L	O	A	T	I	N	G	Swelling, Inflating, Stuffing.
B	L	O	C	K	A	D	E	Block, Obstruct, Isolation, Besiege, Beleaguer.
B	L	O	C	K	I	N	G	Hindering, Braking, Impeding, Obstructing, Intercepting, Plugging, Clogging, Closing.
B	L	O	C	K	I	S	H	Stupid, Doltish.
B	L	O	C	K	O	U	T	Reproduction of a photographic of which a part has been blocked out.
B	L	O	C	K	T	I	N	Solid tin not tinplate.
B	L	O	E	D	I	T	E	Mineral consisting of a hydrous sodium magnesium sulfate.
B	L	O	N	D	I	N	E	To bleach hair to a blond colour.
B	L	O	N	D	I	S	H	Rather light in colour.
B	L	O	O	D	I	E	D	Made bloody, Stained with blood.

1	2	3	4	5	6	7	8	Definition
B	L	O	O	D	I	L	Y	In a bloody manner.
B	L	O	O	D	I	N	G	Staining with blood, Bloody, Giving new soldiers first experience in battle, Exasperate.
B	L	O	O	D	R	E	D	Having the colour of blood.
B	L	O	O	M	E	R	S	Loose trousers gathered at the knee, Underpants worn by school girls.
B	L	O	O	M	E	R	Y	Furnace and forge in which wrought iron blooms were made.
B	L	O	O	M	I	N	G	Flowering, Thriving in health, beauty and vigour, Freshness of youth.
B	L	O	S	S	O	M	Y	Flowery, Full of blossoms.
B	L	O	T	C	H	E	D	Marred with blotches.
B	L	O	T	L	E	S	S	Immaculate.
B	L	O	T	T	I	N	G	Obliterating, Mopping, Disgracing, Staining, Spoiling, Discolouring, Caluminating.
B	L	O	W	B	A	L	L	Fluffy seed ball, Dandelion.
B	L	O	W	D	O	W	N	Severe wind storm that blows down structures and trees.
B	L	O	W	F	I	S	H	Walleyed pike.
B	L	O	W	H	O	L	E	Breathing hold in the ice for whales and seals.
B	L	O	W	L	A	M	P	Blowtorch.
B	L	O	W	L	I	N	E	A light fishing line for being blown by the wind out over the stream.
B	L	O	W	P	I	P	E	Small tubular instrument for directing a jet of air, Blowgun.
B	L	U	D	G	E	O	N	Beat, Overbear, Bully, Cudgel, Baton, Intimidate, Bluster, Hector.
B	L	U	E	B	A	C	K	Fishes of a bluish colour, Herring, Young hooded seal.
B	L	U	E	B	I	R	D	N. American songbird related to the robin.
B	L	U	E	B	O	O	K	Government publication, Register of persons of social prominence.
B	L	U	E	C	O	A	T	One that is a student of an English charity school.
B	L	U	E	E	Y	E	D	Having blue eyes, Favoured, Preferred, Favourite, Pet, Beloved, Precious.
B	L	U	E	F	I	S	H	Active and voracious food fish, Black sea bass.
B	L	U	E	G	I	L	L	Common sunfish.
B	L	U	E	G	O	W	N	Beadsman.
B	L	U	E	N	E	S	S	State of being blue.
B	L	U	E	N	O	S	E	Puritan, One who advocates a rigorous moral code.
B	L	U	E	P	I	L	L	Pill of prepared mercury used as an aperient.
B	L	U	E	W	E	E	D	Coarse prickly weed, Chicory.
B	L	U	E	W	I	N	G	Blue-winged teal.
B	L	U	F	F	E	S	T	Most gruff, Most brusque, Most curt, Surliest, Roughest.
B	L	U	F	F	I	N	G	Misleading, Deceiving, Dissuading, Frightening, Feigning, Shamming.
B	L	U	N	G	I	N	G	Amalgamating, Blending, Mixing in water, Beating.
B	L	U	N	T	E	S	T	Roughest, Dullest, Plainest, Most abrupt.
B	L	U	N	T	I	N	G	Dulling, Deadening, Weakening, Diluting, Numbing, Undermining.
B	L	U	R	R	I	N	G	Sullying, Smearing, Blotting, Staining, Dimming, Darkening.
B	L	U	R	T	I	N	G	Exclaiming, Ejaculating, Uttering impulsively.
B	L	U	S	H	F	U	L	Ruddy, Rose.
B	L	U	S	H	I	N	G	Flushing, Colouring, Blooming, Reddening.
B	L	U	S	T	E	R	Y	Stormy, Wild, Coarse, Furious, Raging, Rough, Tempestuous.
B	O	A	R	D	I	N	G	Entering, Mounting, Embarking, Entraining, Billeting, Entertaining, Lodging, Harbouring.
B	O	A	R	F	I	S	H	Tropical percoid fishes.
B	O	A	S	T	F	U	L	Vaunting, Braggart, Self-glorifying.
B	O	A	S	T	I	N	G	Exulting, Bragging, Vaunting, Crowing, Preening, Aggrandizing, Swaggering, Flaunting.
B	O	A	T	A	B	L	E	A waterway navigable for small craft.
B	O	A	T	B	I	L	L	Broadbill related to Night herons.
B	O	A	T	H	O	O	K	Hook fixed on a long pole to manoeuvre boats.
B	O	A	T	L	O	A	D	Indefinitely large number, As much or many as a boat can hold.
B	O	A	T	R	O	P	E	A support rope used by the crew when leaving or getting aboard, Painter.
B	O	B	B	I	N	E	T	Machine made net.
B	O	B	H	O	U	S	E	Small shack on runners used for fishing through the ice.
B	O	B	O	L	I	N	K	Common American songbird, Ricebird, Deer.
B	O	B	W	H	I	T	E	Quail.
B	O	C	A	C	C	I	O	Rockfish of the Pacific coast.
B	O	C	C	O	N	I	A	Plume poppy.
B	O	C	K	B	E	E	R	Heavy dark rich beer.
B	O	C	K	L	A	N	D	Bookland, Land granted by charter in Anglo-Saxon England.
B	O	D	E	M	E	N	T	Omen, Foreboding, Presentiment, Prediction, Prophecy.
B	O	D	I	A	N	U	S	Genus of stout-bodied percoid fishes.
B	O	D	I	E	R	O	N	Californian sea trout.
B	O	D	I	L	E	S	S	Lacking substance, Incorporeal, Having no body.
B	O	D	L	E	I	A	N	Belonging to the Bodleian Library of Oxford University.
B	O	D	Y	L	I	N	E	A special type of bowling in cricket.
B	O	D	Y	W	A	L	L	External surface of the body enclosing the body cavity.
B	O	D	Y	W	O	R	K	Vehicle body.
B	O	E	H	M	I	A	N	Relating to mystical teaching of Böhme which influenced Quakerism.

1	2	3	4	5	6	7	8	
B	O	E	O	L	I	A	N	Dull, Loutish.
B	O	G	E	A	R	T	H	Compost of partly decomposed vegetable fibre.
B	O	G	E	Y	M	A	N	Menace, Imaginary figure used to frighten naughty children.
B	O	G	G	L	I	N	G	Dumbfounding, Haggling, Bungling, Blundering, Startling, Perplexing, Demurring, Harassing.
B	O	H	E	M	I	A	N	Unconventional, Nonconformist, Eccentric, Original, Dropout.
B	O	I	G	I	D	A	E	Family of venomous snakes, African boomslang.
B	O	I	L	D	O	W	N	Condensation, Abridgment.
B	O	I	L	O	V	E	R	Overflow of boiling liquid.
B	O	I	S	E	R	I	E	Carved wood panelling.
B	O	L	D	F	A	C	E	Forward and impudent person, Typeface with heavy downstrokes.
B	O	L	D	N	E	S	S	Insolence, Disrespect, Hardihood, Impertinence, Impudence.
B	O	L	I	V	I	A	N	Native of Bolivia.
B	O	L	L	W	O	R	M	Moth larvae feeding on cotton boils.
B	O	L	O	B	O	L	O	West African tree fibre resembling jute.
B	O	L	T	H	E	A	D	The head of a bolt, End of a rifle bolt.
B	O	L	T	H	O	L	E	Way of escape.
B	O	L	T	R	O	P	E	Strong hemp rope stitched to the edges of a sail to strengthen it.
B	O	M	B	A	R	D	E	Powerful reed stop in a pipe organ.
B	O	M	B	A	Z	E	T	Thin worsted cloth with a smooth finish.
B	O	M	B	I	D	A	E	Family of black and yellow hairy bees, Bumblebees, Honeybees.
B	O	M	B	I	L	L	A	Small tube with a strainer at one end used in drinking maté.
B	O	M	B	Y	C	I	D	Silkworm or silkworm moth.
B	O	N	A	F	I	D	E	Sincere, Genuine, Authentic, Indubitable, Real, True, Veritable.
B	O	N	A	I	L	I	E	Stirrup cup.
B	O	N	A	R	O	B	A	Courtesan, Prostitute.
B	O	N	D	A	G	E	R	One bound to a tenant farmer to do farm labour.
B	O	N	D	S	M	A	N	One who guarantees a bond, Surety.
B	O	N	E	D	U	S	T	Bone meal.
B	O	N	E	F	I	S	H	Slender silvery small-scaled fishes, outstanding as game and food fishes.
B	O	N	E	H	E	A	D	Blockhead, Numbskull.
B	O	N	E	L	L	I	A	Genus of marine worms.
B	O	N	E	L	A	C	E	Bobbin lace.
B	O	N	E	L	E	S	S	Being without bones, Weak, Impotent, Inadequate.
B	O	N	H	O	M	I	E	Warm geniality, Good cheer, Friendliness.
B	O	N	I	F	A	C	E	Saloonkeeper, Hotelier, Innkeeper, Publican, Taverner.
B	O	N	I	F	O	R	M	Promoting, Perceiving.
B	O	N	N	E	T	E	D	Wearing a hat or hood, Crushed a person's headgear around the head.
B	O	N	S	P	I	E	L	A match between curling clubs.
B	O	N	T	E	B	O	K	Southern African antelope.
B	O	N	Y	T	A	I	L	A minnow of the Colorado river system.
B	O	O	G	E	R	E	D	A frightened or startled animal that shied.
B	O	O	H	O	O	E	D	Wept loudly, Wailed, Cried, Blubbered, Sobbed.
B	O	O	K	C	A	S	E	Cabinet with shelves and doors in which to store books.
B	O	O	K	C	L	U	B	An association to promote literary intersts.
B	O	O	K	D	E	B	T	Amount owed on a current account.
B	O	O	K	L	E	S	S	Unlearned, Illiterate.
B	O	O	K	L	O	R	E	Book learning.
B	O	O	K	M	A	R	K	Narrow strip of material to mark a place in a book.
B	O	O	K	P	O	S	T	Special postal rates for sending books through the mail.
B	O	O	K	S	H	O	P	Bookstore, Place of business where books are the main items for sale.
B	O	O	K	W	O	R	M	Larvae of various moths that damage books, Someone who is an avid reader.
B	O	O	S	T	I	N	G	Raising, Plugging, Lifting, Increasing, Augmenting, Enlarging, Expanding, Promoting.
B	O	O	T	H	I	T	E	Mineral consisting of hydrous copper sulfate.
B	O	O	T	H	O	O	K	Long hook used to pull on riding boots by the straps.
B	O	O	T	H	O	S	E	Stockings worn with or in place of boots.
B	O	O	T	J	A	C	K	Device for removing boots.
B	O	O	T	L	A	C	E	Lace for a boot, Shoelace.
B	O	O	T	L	E	S	S	Incurable, Fruitless, Frustrating, No advantage.
B	O	O	T	L	I	C	K	Fawning, Toadying, Sycophant, Parasite, Cultivating favour.
B	O	O	T	T	R	E	E	Shoe tree, Bootjack.
B	O	R	A	C	H	I	O	Drunkard.
B	O	R	A	C	I	T	E	Mineral consisting of borate and chloride of magnesium.
B	O	R	A	Z	O	L	E	A colourless volatile liquid.
B	O	R	D	E	A	U	X	Table wine from the Gironde area of France.
B	O	R	D	E	R	E	D	Bound, Adjoined, Limited, Verged, Defined, Hemmed, Enclosed, Framed.
B	O	R	D	R	O	O	M	A space off a bord from which the coal is being mined.
B	O	R	E	C	O	L	E	Kale.

1	2	3	4	5	6	7	8	
B	O	R	R	A	C	H	A	Grades of crude Para rubber.
B	O	R	R	E	L	I	A	Genus of small flexible spirochets parasitic to man and warm-blooded animals.
B	O	R	R	O	W	E	D	Received temporary, Appropriate, Lent, Derive by way of a loan.
B	O	R	R	O	W	E	R	One that borrows.
B	O	R	S	T	A	L	L	Pathway up a steep hill.
B	O	R	U	N	D	U	K	Barunduki, Russian ground squirrel.
B	O	S	T	A	N	J	I	Turkish imperial guard.
B	O	T	A	N	I	S	T	Specialist in botany, Professional student of plants.
B	O	T	A	N	I	Z	E	To collect plants for botanical investigation.
B	O	T	C	H	E	R	Y	To repair or mend in a clumsy or inept fashion.
B	O	T	C	H	I	N	G	Bungling, Spoiling, Ruining, Messing.
B	O	T	H	E	R	E	D	Flustered, Puzzled, Mystified, Vexed, Irritated, Irked, Annoyed, Worried.
B	O	T	H	I	D	A	E	Family of flatfishes.
B	O	T	H	R	O	P	S	Genus of venomous pit vipers.
B	O	T	R	Y	O	S	E	A formation resembling a bunch of grapes.
B	O	T	R	Y	O	I	D	Botryoidal, Resembling a bunch of grapes.
B	O	T	R	Y	T	I	S	A form genus of imperfect fungi.
B	O	T	S	W	A	N	A	Was Bechuanaland, Southern Africa.
B	O	T	T	L	I	N	G	Putting in a bottle, Preserving, Pickling, Checking, Restraining, Cornering.
B	O	T	T	O	M	E	D	Provided a foundation, Based, Established, Plumbed, Fathomed, Finished, Exhausted.
B	O	T	T	O	M	R	Y	Special mortgage with the ship as surety.
B	O	T	U	L	I	S	M	Acute food poisoning.
B	O	U	F	F	A	N	T	Voluminous, Flaring, Puffed out.
B	O	U	G	H	T	E	N	Bought.
B	O	U	I	L	L	O	N	Meat broth, Stock made from lean meat.
B	O	U	N	C	I	N	G	Scolding, Bullying, Blustering, Swaggering, Boasting, Dismissing, Healthy, Vigorously.
B	O	U	N	D	A	R	Y	Something that fixes a limit, A bounding or separating line.
B	O	U	N	D	I	N	G	Enclosing, Circumscribing, Limiting, Determining.
B	O	U	R	E	T	T	E	Irregular slubbed yarn made of silk waste.
B	O	U	R	G	E	O	N	Burgeon, Sprout, Blossom, Flourish.
B	O	V	A	R	I	S	M	Split personality.
B	O	W	D	R	I	L	L	Drill worked by bow and string to make a fire or bore holes.
B	O	W	G	R	A	C	E	Fender of rope to protect a ship from damage by floating ice.
B	O	W	I	N	G	L	Y	In a courteous fashion, Subserviently.
B	O	W	S	P	R	I	T	A large spar.
B	O	X	D	R	A	I	N	A drain that is square and has a lid.
B	O	X	F	R	A	M	E	Window frame having hollow spaces for sash weights.
B	O	X	P	L	E	A	T	Pleat formed with two folded edges facing opposite sides and making an inverted pleat.
B	O	X	T	H	O	R	N	Matrimony vine.
B	O	Y	I	S	H	L	Y	Acting in an immature fashion, Youthfully.
B	O	Y	S	L	E	T	T	Wormwood.
B	O	Z	Z	E	T	T	O	A small clay model of a large sculpture.
B	R	A	B	B	L	E	D	Squabbled.
B	R	A	C	E	L	E	T	Ornament worn around the wrist.
B	R	A	C	H	I	A	L	Relating to the arm.
B	R	A	C	K	I	S	H	Undrinkable water, Unpalatable, Distasteful.
B	R	A	C	O	N	I	D	Family of parasitic flies.
B	R	A	C	T	E	A	L	Leaf formation pertaining to the reproductive structures.
B	R	A	D	B	U	R	Y	British pound note.
B	R	A	D	S	H	A	W	Timetable of the British railroad system.
B	R	A	D	Y	P	U	S	Family of true sloths.
B	R	A	G	G	A	R	T	Bragger, Boaster, Vaunter, Blusterer, Loudmouth, Raver, Windbag.
B	R	A	G	G	I	N	G	Boasting, Defying, Challenging, Vaunting, Crowing.
B	R	A	I	D	I	N	G	Plaiting, Intermingling, Mixing, Trimming.
B	R	A	I	L	I	N	G	Taking in a sail, Restraining, Hoisting.
B	R	A	I	N	F	A	G	Mental fatigue.
B	R	A	I	N	I	N	G	Banging on the head, Smashing the skull.
B	R	A	I	N	I	S	H	Impetuous, Mentally unstable, Delirious, Hot-headed, Demented, Deranged.
B	R	A	I	S	I	N	G	Slow cooking in a covered pot.
B	R	A	K	E	M	A	N	Railway worker assisting train crew.
B	R	A	K	E	V	A	N	Railway compartment where braking equipment is available.
B	R	A	M	I	D	A	E	Family of deep-bodied percoid fishes.
B	R	A	N	C	H	E	D	Diverged, Adding, Enlarging, Sprung out, Extending, Arranging, Forking, Sectioning.
B	R	A	N	C	H	E	R	Young bird old enough to leave the nest, One that makes artificial flower arrangements.
B	R	A	N	D	I	E	D	Preserved in brandy.
B	R	A	N	D	I	N	G	Placing a brand, Stigmatize, Impressing indelibly, Exposing dishonesty.
B	R	A	N	D	I	S	E	Trivet.

1	2	3	4	5	6	7	8	
B	R	A	N	D	I	S	H	Flourish, Wave, Swing, Display, Exhibit, Expose, Flaunt, Parade.
B	R	A	N	D	N	E	W	Conspicuously new and unused, Fresh from the manufacturer.
B	R	A	N	G	L	E	D	Squabbled, Wrangled.
B	R	A	S	H	I	N	G	Removing the lower branches.
B	R	A	S	S	A	G	E	Cost to individual for minting gold or silver.
B	R	A	S	S	A	R	D	Protective armour for the arm, Armband for identification purposes.
B	R	A	S	S	A	R	T	Same as BRASSARD.
B	R	A	S	S	H	A	T	Person holding a high position in the armed services or civil life.
B	R	A	S	S	I	C	A	Genus of herbs, Cabbages, Cauliflowers, Turnips, Mustard.
B	R	A	T	L	I	N	G	A little brat.
B	R	A	T	T	I	C	E	Temporary partition of cloth or planks.
B	R	A	T	T	I	S	H	Spoiled, Pettish.
B	R	A	T	T	L	E	D	Clattered, Rushed, Rattled.
B	R	A	U	N	I	T	E	Mineral consisting of manganese silicate.
B	R	A	V	O	I	T	E	Mineral consisting of a nickel sulfide.
B	R	A	W	L	I	N	G	Quarrelsome, Wrangling, Rioting, Rowing, Reviling.
B	R	A	Y	E	R	I	N	Kosin.
B	R	A	Z	E	N	E	D	Faced with resolution, Defiant, Impudent.
B	R	A	Z	E	N	L	Y	Insolently, Boldly, Intensely, Extremely.
B	R	A	Z	I	L	I	N	White or pale yellow phenolic compund once used in dyeing.
B	R	E	A	C	H	E	D	Smashed a gap, Effected an opening, Broke, Violated.
B	R	E	A	D	N	U	T	Nut of a Jamaican or Mexican tree that is roasted and ground into a bread flour.
B	R	E	A	K	A	G	E	Loss caused by breaking, Compensation for breaking.
B	R	E	A	K	I	N	G	Smashing, Infringing, Ploughing virgin land, Shattering.
B	R	E	A	K	O	U	T	Escape, Flight, Releasing from restraint.
B	R	E	A	M	I	N	G	Cleaning the bottom of a ship.
B	R	E	A	S	T	E	D	Faced, Confronted, Ascended, Pressed forward.
B	R	E	A	T	H	E	D	Respired, Inhaled and exhaled, Lived, Uttered, Expressed, Evinced, Exhausted.
B	R	E	A	T	H	E	R	A rest period.
B	R	E	E	C	H	E	D	Put into breeches.
B	R	E	E	C	H	E	S	Pants, Trousers.
B	R	E	E	D	I	N	G	Producing, Engendering, Nurturing, Training, Impregnating, Procreating, Generating.
B	R	E	E	Z	I	N	G	Freshening, Hurrying, Hastening, Waltzing, Skimming, Slipping.
B	R	E	L	O	Q	U	E	Seal or charm for a watch chain.
B	R	E	M	S	U	N	G	Sudden slowing down of a moving charged particle.
B	R	E	S	C	I	A	N	16th Century school of Italian painting.
B	R	E	T	H	R	E	N	Used in a formal form in an association or society.
B	R	E	V	I	A	R	Y	Abridgment, daily canonical prayers, Brief, Condensation, Prayer book.
B	R	E	V	I	A	T	E	Compendium, Summary, Abstract, Synopsis.
B	R	E	V	I	G	E	R	A friar carrying a licence for begging.
B	R	E	V	I	P	E	S	Having short legs.
B	R	E	W	S	T	E	R	Brewer.
B	R	I	B	A	B	L	E	Capable of being bribed, Open to corruption.
B	R	I	C	K	B	A	T	Fragment of brick, Insult, Uncomplimentary remark.
B	R	I	C	K	I	N	G	Building with bricks.
B	R	I	C	K	R	E	D	Dark red.
B	R	I	C	K	T	E	A	Small brick of tea leaves.
B	R	I	D	E	B	E	D	Bed in which a couple spend their wedding night.
B	R	I	D	G	I	N	G	Providing a bridge, Shunting, Making an electrical connection.
B	R	I	E	F	I	N	G	Composing a brief, Giving final instructions, Coaching thoroughly.
B	R	I	G	A	D	E	D	Formed into a brigade.
B	R	I	G	H	T	E	N	Enliven, Shining, More cheerful, More lively.
B	R	I	G	H	T	L	Y	Brilliantly, Sharply, Clearly.
B	R	I	G	U	I	N	G	Plotting, Scheming, Intriguing.
B	R	I	M	L	E	S	S	Being without a brim.
B	R	I	M	M	I	N	G	Becoming full to overflowing.
B	R	I	N	D	I	S	I	A drinking or toasting song.
B	R	I	N	D	L	E	D	Streaked or blotched, Blurred.
B	R	I	N	E	P	A	N	Pan in which brine is evaporated to form salt.
B	R	I	N	G	I	N	G	Leading, Moving, Attending, Carrying, Conducting, Selling, Attracting, Escorting.
B	R	I	S	A	N	C	E	Measuring of the crushing effect of an explosive.
B	R	I	S	C	O	L	A	Italian card game.
B	R	I	S	K	I	N	G	Enlivening, Animating, Sharpening, Quickening.
B	R	I	S	L	I	N	G	Small herring resembling a sardine.
B	R	I	S	T	L	E	D	Assumed an aggressive stance, Angered, Boiled, Burned, Fumed, Raged, Ruffled, Seethed.
B	R	I	T	C	H	E	L	Brittle.
B	R	I	T	C	H	E	S	Breeches, Pants, Trousers.

1	2	3	4	5	6	7	8	Definition
B	R	I	T	Z	S	K	A	Britska, Open horse-drawn carriage.
B	R	O	A	C	H	E	D	Pierced, Tapped, Introduced, Presented, Announced, Suggested, Ventilated.
B	R	O	A	C	H	E	R	One that works with a broach.
B	R	O	A	D	A	X	E	Large axe with a broad blade, Battle-axe.
B	R	O	A	D	E	S	T	Most spacious, Most liberal, Plainest, Most open, Deepest, Widest.
B	R	O	A	D	I	S	H	Tending towards broadness.
B	R	O	C	A	D	E	D	Patterns woven into fabric with gold or silver thread.
B	R	O	C	A	T	E	L	Stiff decorating brocade fabric.
B	R	O	C	C	O	L	I	Branching type of cauliflower.
B	R	O	C	H	U	R	E	Pamphlet, Booklet.
B	R	O	D	E	R	I	E	Pottery decoration originating in Rouen, France.
B	R	O	I	D	E	R	Y	Embroidery.
B	R	O	I	L	I	N	G	Grilling, Agitating, Embroiling, Brawling, Quarrelling.
B	R	O	K	E	N	L	Y	In a subdued fashion, Unsteady from shock or emotion.
B	R	O	K	E	R	L	Y	To act as a broker.
B	R	O	M	E	L	I	A	Genus of plant, Bromeliad.
B	R	O	M	E	L	I	N	Proteinase obtained from the juice of the pineapple.
B	R	O	M	I	D	I	C	Pertaining to sedatives, Dull, Tiresome, Uninteresting.
B	R	O	M	L	I	T	E	Alstonite.
B	R	O	M	V	O	E	L	Large Southern African hornbill, Turkey buzzard.
B	R	O	N	C	H	I	A	Two main divisions of the trachae leading to the lungs.
B	R	O	N	T	E	U	M	Device used in ancient Greek and Roman theatre for simulating the noise of thunder.
B	R	O	N	T	I	D	E	Low muffled sound heard at sea level believed to be light earth tremors.
B	R	O	N	T	O	P	S	Extinct mammals.
B	R	O	N	Z	I	N	G	Coating with bronze, Suntanning.
B	R	O	N	Z	I	T	E	Mineral with a bronze-like lustre.
B	R	O	O	D	I	N	G	Hatching, Hovering, Thinking, Pondering, Meditating.
B	R	O	O	D	S	A	C	Brood pouch.
B	R	O	O	K	I	N	G	Enduring, Bearing, Tolerating, Stomaching, Suffering, Taking, Swallowing.
B	R	O	O	K	I	T	E	Mineral consisting of titanium dioxide.
B	R	O	O	K	L	E	T	Rivulet, Rill, Little stream.
B	R	O	O	M	I	N	G	Sweeping, Cleansing, Applying with a broom.
B	R	O	U	G	H	A	M	Light closed carriage, Electrically driven two-door sedan.
B	R	O	U	H	A	H	A	Uproar, Furore, Commotion, Hubbub, Din, Babel, Tumult, Clamour.
B	R	O	W	B	A	N	D	Band to cross the forehead, Part of a bridle.
B	R	O	W	B	E	A	T	Bully, Intimidate, Bludgeon, Bluster, Bulldoze, Hector.
B	R	O	W	L	E	S	S	Unabashed, Lacking eyebrows.
B	R	O	W	N	I	N	G	Becoming brown, Scorching, Discolouration of cut tissue in fruit and vegetables.
B	R	O	W	N	I	S	H	Somewhat brown.
B	R	O	W	N	I	S	T	Adherent of Brownism, the teachings of congregationalist Robert Browne.
B	R	O	W	S	I	N	G	Grazing, Skimming through a book, Scanning, Glancing, Perusing, Studying, Examining.
B	R	U	I	S	I	N	G	Disabling, Contusing, Battering, Indenting, Wounding, Injuring, Crushing.
B	R	U	N	E	T	T	E	Brown or black-haired, Brown or olive-skinned.
B	R	U	S	H	B	O	X	Australian shade-tree.
B	R	U	S	H	I	N	G	Applying or removing with a brush, Dismiss summarily, Gently touching.
B	R	U	S	H	I	T	E	Mineral of calcium hydrogen phosphate.
B	R	U	S	H	O	U	T	Sample application of paint for testing.
B	R	U	S	S	E	L	S	Carpets, Sprouts, miniatue cabbages.
B	R	U	T	A	L	L	Y	Brutishly, Beastly, Harshly.
B	R	Y	A	C	E	A	E	Family of mosses.
B	R	Y	A	N	I	T	E	Member of a Methodist order.
B	R	Y	O	L	O	G	Y	Science of mosses.
B	U	B	B	L	I	N	G	Gurgling, Effervescent, Churning, Boiling, Seething, Fermenting, Simmering.
B	U	C	C	A	L	L	Y	Toward the cheek.
B	U	C	C	A	N	E	D	Cooked over an open fire.
B	U	C	C	H	E	R	O	Ancient undecorated pottery found in Italy.
B	U	C	C	I	N	U	M	Genus of shellfish, Whelks.
B	U	C	E	L	L	A	S	Portugese white wine.
B	U	C	H	N	E	R	A	Genus of herbs, Bluehearts.
B	U	C	K	A	R	O	O	Cowboy.
B	U	C	K	B	E	A	N	A plant that grows in bogs.
B	U	C	K	E	T	E	D	Lifted in a bucket, Drove hurriedly, Hustled, Hurried.
B	U	C	K	E	Y	E	D	Poisoned by buckeye or one of its products.
B	U	C	K	H	O	R	N	Horn of a buck, Deerhorn.
B	U	C	K	J	U	M	P	To jump like a bucking horse.
B	U	C	K	L	I	N	G	Grappling, Contending, Yielding, Cringing, Applying, Devoting, Capitulating, Directing.
B	U	C	K	R	A	K	E	Horse-drawn rake for hay-making.

1	2	3	4	5	6	7	8	
B	U	C	K	S	H	E	E	Gratuity, Windfall.
B	U	C	K	S	H	O	T	Coarse lead shot.
B	U	C	K	S	K	I	N	Soft pliable suede-finished deerskins.
B	U	C	R	A	N	I	A	Classical ornamental frieze composed of ox-skulls and garlands or ribbons in sculpture.
B	U	D	D	H	I	S	M	Religion of the East from the teachings of Buddha.
B	U	D	D	H	I	S	T	An adherent of Buddhism.
B	U	D	D	L	I	N	G	Washing ore on a buddle.
B	U	D	G	E	R	E	E	Good, Fine, Pretty.
B	U	D	G	E	T	E	D	Planned expenditure, Formulate provision for spending.
B	U	F	F	C	O	A	T	17th Century military coat.
B	U	F	F	E	T	E	D	Battered, Cuffed, Slapped, Contended, Struggled, Clouted, Thrashed, Slapped.
B	U	F	O	N	I	T	E	Fossilized teeth or bones of prehistoric fish.
B	U	H	L	W	O	R	K	Inlay work.
B	U	I	L	D	I	N	G	Constructing, Fashioning, Developing, Creating, Making, Forming, Tailoring.
B	U	L	G	A	R	I	C	Bulgarian.
B	U	L	I	M	O	I	D	Resembling land snails.
B	U	L	K	H	E	A	D	Upright partition separating compartments.
B	U	L	L	D	O	Z	E	Bully, Intimidate, Bluster, Browbeat, Hector, Menace, Threaten, Harass.
B	U	L	L	D	U	S	T	Coarse dust or silt.
B	U	L	L	E	T	I	N	Public notice, Brief statement, Announcement, Progress report.
B	U	L	L	F	R	O	G	Deep-voiced frog.
B	U	L	L	H	E	A	D	Family of large-headed fishes, Headstrong or stubborn person.
B	U	L	L	N	O	S	E	Conditions arising from facial wounds of swine.
B	U	L	L	O	C	K	Y	Management of cattle.
B	U	L	L	R	I	N	G	Arena for a bullfight, Ring through the nose of a bull.
B	U	L	L	S	E	Y	E	A round opening, Small porthole, Deadlight, Centre of a target, Lantern, Daisy.
B	U	L	L	W	E	E	D	Knapweed.
B	U	L	L	W	H	I	P	Extra long rawhide plaited whip.
B	U	L	L	W	O	R	K	Hard manual work.
B	U	L	L	Y	I	N	G	Intimidating, Blustering, Domineering, Browbeating, Hectoring, Threatening, Tormenting.
B	U	L	L	Y	I	S	M	Bullying behaviour.
B	U	L	L	Y	R	A	G	Bulldoze, Bludgeon, Bait, Badger, Chivy, Heckle, Hound, Ride.
B	U	L	R	U	S	H	Y	Having bullrushes.
B	U	M	B	L	I	N	G	Stupid, Awkward, Blundering, Gauche, Inept, Wooden, Heavy-handed.
B	U	M	M	A	L	O	W	Bombay duck.
B	U	M	P	B	A	L	L	A special type of ball play in cricket.
B	U	N	C	H	I	N	G	Protruding, Gathering, Assembling, Clustering, Banding, Crowding, Clumping.
B	U	N	D	L	I	N	G	Compressing, Hurrying, Hustling, Grouping.
B	U	N	F	I	G	H	T	Tea party.
B	U	N	G	A	L	O	W	Single-storey house.
B	U	N	G	A	R	U	M	Genus of exceedingly venomous snakes related to the cobra.
B	U	N	G	A	R	U	S	Same as BUNGARUM.
B	U	N	G	H	O	L	E	Opening in a cask for filling or emptying.
B	U	N	G	L	I	N	G	Mishandling, Botching, Goofing, Muffing.
B	U	N	K	E	R	E	D	A ship's bunkers filled with fuel, Entangled in difficulties. Unable to progress.
B	U	N	O	D	O	N	T	Family of mammals including hogs and hippopotami.
B	U	N	T	L	I	N	E	Rope attached to a square sail.
B	U	O	Y	A	N	C	Y	Ability to float, Lightheartedness, Sprightliness, Springiness, Ebullience.
B	U	R	B	E	R	R	Y	Weatherproof coat.
B	U	R	D	E	N	E	D	Encumbered, Overloaded, Saddled, Charged, Taxed, Lumbered, Afflicted, Oppressed.
B	U	R	G	A	M	O	T	Bergamot, Citron oil used in perfumery.
B	U	R	G	L	A	R	Y	Housebreaking, Felony, Robbery, Stealing.
B	U	R	G	L	I	N	G	Burglarizing, Forcing entrance to rob.
B	U	R	G	R	A	V	E	Hereditary ruler of a German castle and estates.
B	U	R	G	U	N	D	Y	Red or white French wines stronger flavoured than Bordeaux.
B	U	R	H	I	N	U	S	Long-legged wading birds.
B	U	R	I	N	I	S	T	Engraver.
B	U	R	K	E	I	T	E	Mineral consisting of a carbonate-sulfate of sodium.
B	U	R	L	E	T	T	A	18th Century musical comic opera.
B	U	R	N	A	B	L	E	Combustible.
B	U	R	N	O	O	S	E	Burnous, Loose flowing hooded cloak worn by the Arabs.
B	U	R	R	K	N	O	T	Abnormal growth on trunk and roots of some trees.
B	U	R	R	O	W	E	D	Tunnelled, Excavated, Snuggled, Nestled, Progressed through the earth.
B	U	R	R	O	W	E	R	Animal that makes a hole underground to live in.
B	U	R	S	I	C	L	E	Pouched receptacle.
B	U	R	S	I	T	I	S	Painful inflammation of shoulder or elbow joints.
B	U	R	S	T	I	N	G	Exploding, Opening, Unfolding, Launching, Plunging, Erupting, Blasting, Gusting.

1	2	3	4	5	6	7	8	
B	U	S	H	B	A	B	Y	Small African lemurs.
B	U	S	H	B	U	C	K	Southern African antelope.
B	U	S	H	E	L	E	R	Worker in a furnace.
B	U	S	H	R	O	P	E	Liana.
B	U	S	H	V	E	L	D	Southern African veld of shrub and thorny vegetation.
B	U	S	I	N	E	S	S	Occupation, Position, Trade, Patronage, Task, Chore, Mission, Assignment.
B	U	S	K	I	N	E	D	Relating to tragedy.
B	U	S	T	L	I	N	G	Busy, Fussy, Hopping, Struggling, Hustling, Lively, Teeming, Hurrying.
B	U	S	Y	B	O	D	Y	Snooper, Meddler, Interfering person, Officious person.
B	U	S	Y	N	E	S	S	State of being busy.
B	U	T	A	C	E	A	E	Family of herbs resembling cacti with a poisonous milky juice.
B	U	T	A	N	O	N	E	Methyl ethyl ketone.
B	U	T	C	H	E	R	Y	Slaughterhouse, Place where meat is processed and sold, Botch, Bungle, Massacre.
B	U	T	C	H	I	N	G	Slaughtering, Butchering, Botching.
B	U	T	H	I	D	A	E	Family of scorpions.
B	U	T	O	X	I	D	E	A binary compound of butoxyl.
B	U	T	T	E	R	E	D	Spread with butter, Flattered, Praised.
B	U	T	T	E	R	I	S	Steel instrument for paring the hoofs of horses.
B	U	T	T	O	N	E	D	Fastened with buttons, Kept the lips closed, Secretive.
B	U	T	T	R	E	S	S	Support, Prop, Brace, Column, Shore, Stay, Underpinning.
B	U	T	Y	L	A	T	E	Butoxide.
B	U	T	Y	L	E	N	E	Isomeric flammable liquefiable gaseous hydron carbons.
B	U	T	Y	R	A	T	E	Salt or ester of butyric acid.
B	U	T	Y	R	O	U	S	Butyraceous, Resembling butter.
B	U	X	A	C	E	A	E	Small family of widely distributed shrubs, trees and herbs.
B	Y	B	I	D	D	E	R	One who bids at an auction on behalf of the owner to run up the prices.
B	Y	M	O	T	I	V	E	A hidden motive.
B	Y	P	A	S	S	E	D	Detoured, Deviated, Digressed, Avoided, Evaded, Skirted, Circumnavigated.
B	Y	R	O	N	I	S	M	The characteristics of the poet Byron.
B	Y	S	T	R	E	E	T	Side street, Street off main thoroughfare.
B	Y	S	T	R	O	K	E	Using devious methods to achieve results.
B	Y	T	H	E	W	A	Y	Incidentally, Casual, Offhand.

C

1	2	3	4	5	6	7	8	
C	A	A	T	I	N	G	A	Sparse forest area in Brazil.
C	A	B	A	L	I	S	M	Esoteric doctrine.
C	A	B	A	L	I	S	T	One skilled in esoteric doctrine.
C	A	B	A	L	L	E	D	United in a secret society or plot.
C	A	B	A	L	L	E	R	One involved in an intrigue.
C	A	B	A	Z	O	N	E	Genus of scorpion fish.
C	A	B	B	A	G	E	D	Compressed metal.
C	A	B	E	C	E	R	A	Chief city of a Spanish speaking province.
C	A	B	I	N	B	O	Y	Young male servant of ship's officers and passenger.
C	A	B	I	N	I	N	G	Living in a cabin, Confining within a narrow space.
C	A	B	L	E	W	A	Y	Cables supported on towers for conveying passenger-carrying cabins or goods.
C	A	B	O	C	E	E	R	West African native chief.
C	A	B	O	C	H	O	N	Convex gem, polished but not faceted.
C	A	B	O	O	D	L	E	Collection, Lot.
C	A	B	O	S	H	E	D	Caboched, Use of an animal's head without a neck in heraldry.
C	A	B	O	T	A	G	E	Coasting trade.
C	A	B	R	I	O	L	E	Curved leg used in furniture, A ballet leap.
C	A	B	S	T	A	N	D	Place where taxi-cabs wait for hire.
C	A	C	H	A	L	O	T	Sperm whale.
C	A	C	H	E	P	O	T	Ornamental cover for a flower-pot.
C	A	C	H	E	X	I	A	General physical wasting caused by a chronic disease.
C	A	C	H	U	C	H	A	Andalusian solo dance.
C	A	C	K	L	I	N	G	Chattering, Laughing with a harsh noise, Noise made by a hen after laying an egg.
C	A	C	O	D	O	X	Y	Heterodoxy, Heresy, Unorthodox.
C	A	C	O	L	O	G	Y	Bad diction or pronunciation.
C	A	D	A	L	E	N	E	A colourless liquid hydrocarbon.
C	A	D	A	S	T	R	E	Official register of value of an estate for tax purposes.
C	A	D	E	N	C	E	D	Put into rhythm.
C	A	D	I	N	E	N	E	An oily hydrocarbon.
C	A	D	R	E	M	A	N	Member of a military cadre.
C	A	D	U	C	E	U	S	Symbolic staff, Symbol of physician or medical corps.

1	2	3	4	5	6	7	8	Definition
C	A	D	U	C	I	T	Y	Senility, Old age, Lapse, Transitoriness, Feebleness.
C	A	D	U	C	O	U	S	Deciduous, Lapsed, Early falling of petals or leaves.
C	A	E	C	I	D	A	E	Family of minute marine mollusks.
C	A	E	S	I	O	U	S	Having a blue colour.
C	A	E	S	U	R	A	L	Relating to a caesura, a break in the flow of sound in verse.
C	A	F	F	E	A	T	E	Salt or ester of caffeic acid.
C	A	F	F	E	I	N	E	Basic bitter crystalline compound.
C	A	G	E	L	I	N	G	A caged bird.
C	A	G	E	W	O	R	K	Openwork.
C	A	I	A	R	A	R	A	Amazonian arboreal monkey.
C	A	I	S	S	O	N	S	Two-wheeled vehicle for artillery ammunition, Watertight chamber for construction work.
C	A	J	O	L	E	R	Y	Flattery, Deluding, Enticing, Deceiving with false promises.
C	A	J	O	L	I	N	G	Coaxing, Deceiving, Wheedling.
C	A	K	E	W	A	L	K	High stepping dance step derived from a Negro competition that had a cake as a prize.
C	A	L	A	B	A	S	H	Gourd, Tropical American tree.
C	A	L	A	B	A	Z	A	Same as CALABASH.
C	A	L	A	D	I	U	M	Small genus of tropical American plants.
C	A	L	A	M	A	R	Y	Giant squid.
C	A	L	A	M	B	A	C	Agallach, Soft resinous wood.
C	A	L	A	M	I	N	E	Pink powder mixture of zinc oxide with ferric oxide used in medication for skin treatment.
C	A	L	A	M	I	N	T	Genus of mint, Aromatic plant, Basil thyme.
C	A	L	A	M	I	T	E	Genus of fossil plants.
C	A	L	A	M	I	T	Y	Disaster, Cataclysm, Catastrophe, Tragedy, Ruin, Wreck, Affliction, Tribulation.
C	A	L	A	N	D	R	A	Genus of weevils.
C	A	L	A	N	T	A	S	Kalantas, Philippine cedar.
C	A	L	A	N	T	H	E	Genus of terrestrial showy orchids.
C	A	L	A	T	H	E	A	Genus of tropical American herbs.
C	A	L	A	T	H	U	S	A flared fruit basket, carried on the head as a symbol, in art of fruitfulness.
C	A	L	C	I	N	E	D	Converted to a powder by heating.
C	A	L	C	I	N	E	R	Burner, Kiln that calcines.
C	A	L	C	S	P	A	R	Calcite.
C	A	L	C	T	U	F	F	Calcareous tufa.
C	A	L	C	U	L	U	S	Solid concretion composed of mineral salts found in passages and ducts, Gall stones.
C	A	L	E	N	D	A	R	Almanac, Register of day, weeks and months and official holidays, List of events & activities.
C	A	L	E	N	D	E	R	To press between rollers.
C	A	L	F	L	E	S	S	Being without a calf.
C	A	L	F	L	O	V	E	Puppy love, Adolescent love.
C	A	L	F	S	K	I	N	Leather made of the skin of a calf.
C	A	L	I	D	U	C	T	Duct to convey hot air, hot water or steam for heating.
C	A	L	I	F	A	T	E	Dominion of a caliph.
C	A	L	I	N	A	G	O	Carib of the Lesser Antilles.
C	A	L	I	P	A	S	H	The fatty substance under the upper shell of the turtle.
C	A	L	I	P	E	R	S	Measuring instrument having two legs for adjustment.
C	A	L	I	P	P	U	S	Genus of dwarf horse of prehistoric America.
C	A	L	I	X	T	I	N	A member of a Hussite body.
C	A	L	L	A	B	L	E	Subject to a demand for payment of a debt before due date.
C	A	L	L	B	I	R	D	Decoy bird.
C	A	L	L	G	I	R	L	A prostitute called by telephone to visit customers.
C	A	L	L	L	O	A	N	A loan payable on demand.
C	A	L	L	N	O	T	E	A note used by a bird to call another.
C	A	L	L	O	S	A	L	Relating to brain fibres.
C	A	L	L	O	S	U	M	Same as CALLOSAL.
C	A	L	L	O	V	E	R	Meeting of bookmakers relating to details of races.
C	A	L	L	U	S	E	D	Having calluses.
C	A	L	M	E	C	A	C	Aztec school for sons of nobles.
C	A	L	M	N	E	S	S	Tranquillity, Serenity, Placidness.
C	A	L	O	R	I	S	T	One that holds to the caloric theory of heat.
C	A	L	O	R	I	Z	E	Special process of coating metal with aluminium.
C	A	L	O	T	Y	P	E	Early photographic-negative process.
C	A	L	T	H	R	O	P	Sponge spicule with rays of equal length.
C	A	L	V	A	R	I	A	Incomplete skull.
C	A	L	V	A	T	I	A	Genus of fungi.
C	A	L	Y	C	I	N	E	Resembling a cup.
C	A	L	Y	C	L	E	D	Calyx-like.
C	A	L	Y	M	E	N	E	Genus of extinct marine arthropods.
C	A	L	Y	P	T	R	A	Thin membrane, Caplike covering.
C	A	M	A	L	O	T	E	Water lily.

1	2	3	4	5	6	7	8	
C	A	M	A	S	S	I	A	A genus of scapose herbs having edible bulbs.
C	A	M	A	T	I	N	A	Unripe acorns and cups used for tanning when dried.
C	A	M	B	E	R	E	D	Curved, Bent, Arched.
C	A	M	B	I	A	T	A	Nonharmonic note of a melody.
C	A	M	B	O	G	I	A	Gum resin obtained from various Asian trees.
C	A	M	B	R	I	A	N	Welsh.
C	A	M	E	L	E	E	R	Driver and tender of a camel.
C	A	M	E	L	E	O	N	Chameleon.
C	A	M	E	L	I	N	E	Twilled camel's hair fabric.
C	A	M	E	L	L	I	A	Genus of tropical Asiatic evergreen shrub, Thea.
C	A	M	E	R	A	T	E	Divided into chambers.
C	A	M	I	S	A	D	O	An attack by night.
C	A	M	I	S	A	D	E	Same as CAMISADE.
C	A	M	I	S	A	R	D	French Protestant rebel of the 18th century.
C	A	M	I	S	O	L	E	Short vest-like garment worn under thin clothing.
C	A	M	O	M	I	L	E	Genus of plant having strong-scented foliage & flower heads that contain a medicinal principle.
C	A	M	P	A	I	G	N	Military operation, Period of activity leading to a desired result.
C	A	M	P	F	I	R	E	Fire built outside, Social gathering of members of a society or league.
C	A	M	P	H	A	N	E	Bornane.
C	A	M	P	H	E	N	E	Terpene related to camphor.
C	A	M	P	H	I	N	E	Oil of turpentine.
C	A	M	P	H	I	R	E	Camphor.
C	A	M	P	H	O	I	D	Solution of pyroxylin in a alcoholic solution.
C	A	M	P	I	L	A	N	Kampilan, Long straight-edged sheathed cutlass.
C	A	M	P	O	D	E	A	Genus of wingless elongated insects.
C	A	M	P	O	O	D	Y	An Indian village.
C	A	M	P	O	R	E	E	Gathering of boy scouts.
C	A	M	P	S	H	E	D	Facing of piles to protect a river bank.
C	A	M	P	S	I	T	E	Place used for a camp.
C	A	M	S	H	A	F	T	Shaft to which a cam is fastened.
C	A	M	S	T	O	N	E	Limestone containing much clay.
C	A	M	W	H	E	E	L	Wheel shaped to act as a cam.
C	A	N	A	D	I	A	N	Inhabitant of Canada.
C	A	N	A	I	G	R	E	A large dock of the southwestern U.S. having a root rich in tannin.
C	A	N	A	L	I	N	E	Crystalline amino acid.
C	A	N	A	L	I	Z	E	Build a canal, Provide with an outlet, To drain.
C	A	N	A	P	I	N	A	Fine silky strong fibre of the Indian mallow.
C	A	N	A	R	E	S	E	Kanarese, Kanada-speaking people of Mysore, S. India.
C	A	N	A	R	I	U	M	Java almond.
C	A	N	A	S	T	E	R	Smoking tobacco.
C	A	N	C	E	L	L	I	Screens used in a church.
C	A	N	C	R	O	I	D	Resembling a crab, Skin cancer.
C	A	N	D	I	D	L	Y	Frankly, Bluntly, Openly, Honestly.
C	A	N	D	Y	I	N	G	Coating with sugar, Sweetening, Crystallizing.
C	A	N	E	P	H	O	R	Maiden carrying a basket on her head in an early Greek festival.
C	A	N	E	W	A	R	E	Yellowish Wedgewood stoneware.
C	A	N	I	C	U	L	E	Dog days, Relating to rising of Sirius, Dog star.
C	A	N	I	S	T	E	L	Orange-yellow sweet fruit of a tropical tree, Egg-fruit.
C	A	N	I	S	T	E	R	Container for storage of dry goods in a kitchen, Metal drum.
C	A	N	I	T	I	E	S	Gray or white hair.
C	A	N	K	E	R	E	D	Corrupted, Infested with canker, Debased, Demoralized, Debauched.
C	A	N	N	A	B	I	N	Greenish black resin extracted from dried leaves of hemp plant, Cannabis.
C	A	N	N	A	B	I	S	Genus of hemp plant, Hashish, Marihuana.
C	A	N	N	E	L	O	N	Baked puff paste with savoury or cream filling, Baked or fried roll of highly seasoned meat.
C	A	N	N	I	B	A	L	Human being that eats human flesh, Animal that devours its own kind.
C	A	N	N	I	K	I	N	Small can.
C	A	N	N	O	N	E	D	Rebounded after colliding, A shot in billiards.
C	A	N	N	U	L	A	R	Tubular.
C	A	N	O	E	I	S	T	One that paddles a canoe.
C	A	N	O	I	D	E	A	Arctoidea, Family comprising Bears, Weasels and Raccoons.
C	A	N	O	N	I	S	T	One skilled in canon law.
C	A	N	O	N	I	Z	E	To put in the catalogue of saints.
C	A	N	O	N	L	A	W	Body of religuous law governing conduct of members of a religious faith.
C	A	N	O	O	D	L	E	Pet, Caress, Fondle.
C	A	N	O	P	I	E	D	Covered with a canopy.
C	A	N	O	R	O	U	S	Suggestive of melody or song.
C	A	N	S	T	I	C	K	Candlestick.

1	2	3	4	5	6	7	8	Definition
C	A	N	T	A	N	D	O	Cantabile, direction in music.
C	A	N	T	E	R	E	D	Rode at a canter.
C	A	N	T	H	O	O	K	Wooden lever with a blunt end instead of a hook.
C	A	N	T	I	C	L	E	Song, Poem, Hymn.
C	A	N	T	L	I	N	E	Contline, space between the strands on the outside of a rope.
C	A	N	T	L	I	N	G	Portioning, Dividing, Fragmenting, Sectioning.
C	A	N	T	O	N	A	L	Relating to a canton.
C	A	N	T	O	N	E	D	Divided, Quartered.
C	A	N	T	O	R	I	A	Choir gallery in an Italian church.
C	A	N	T	O	R	I	S	Cantorial.
C	A	N	Z	O	N	E	T	Light and graceful song.
C	A	P	A	C	I	T	Y	Ability, Capability, Competence, Cavity, Volume, Stature, Qualification.
C	A	P	E	C	A	R	T	Two-wheeled vehicle drawn by two horses.
C	A	P	E	L	I	N	E	Small skull cap of metal worn by medieval soldiers, Shaped bandage, Woman's hat.
C	A	P	E	R	I	N	G	Prancing, Cavorting, Frisking, Gambolling, Romping, Dancing.
C	A	P	E	R	O	S	E	Common cultivated caper.
C	A	P	E	T	I	A	N	French dynasty.
C	A	P	I	B	A	R	A	S. American rodent related to the guinea pig.
C	A	P	Y	B	A	R	A	Same as CAPIBARA.
C	A	P	I	L	L	U	S	A hair of the head, The bore of a capillary tube.
C	A	P	I	T	A	N	O	Swaggering, cowardly character in an Italian comedy.
C	A	P	I	T	A	T	E	Forming a head, Abruptly enlarged and globose.
C	A	P	I	V	A	R	A	Capybara.
C	A	P	O	N	I	Z	E	Castrate.
C	A	P	P	A	R	I	S	Genus of shrubs and small trees, Caper.
C	A	P	R	E	L	L	A	Genus of small shellfish resembling a praying mantis and found in seaweed.
C	A	P	R	E	T	T	O	Meat of a kid.
C	A	P	R	I	D	A	E	Family consisting of sheep and goats.
C	A	P	R	I	F	I	G	Wild fig used for pollination of the edible fig.
C	A	P	R	I	O	L	E	Caper, A special jump of a trained horse.
C	A	P	R	O	A	T	E	Salt or ester of caproic acid, found in butter.
C	A	P	R	Y	L	I	C	Pungent body odour.
C	A	P	R	Y	L	I	N	Glycerol caproate.
C	A	P	R	Y	L	Y	L	Radical of caprylic acid, Octanoyl.
C	A	P	S	C	R	E	W	Tap bolt.
C	A	P	S	E	L	L	A	Genus of weeds, Shepherd's purse.
C	A	P	S	I	C	U	M	Genus of perennial shrubby plants, Cayenne pepper, Hot pepper used as intestinal stimulant.
C	A	P	S	T	O	N	E	Coping, Climax, Acme, Crowning point. Important element.
C	A	P	S	U	L	A	R	Relating to a capsule, Capsulate.
C	A	P	S	I	C	I	N	Red crystalline carotenoid pigment in a Guinea pepper.
C	A	P	T	I	O	U	S	Entangle, Perplex, Discomfit, Critical, Demanding, Exacting, Contrary, Perverse.
C	A	P	T	R	E	S	S	Female captor.
C	A	P	T	U	R	E	D	Caught, Gained, Secured, Taken, Apprehended, Seized, Controlled, Dominated.
C	A	P	U	C	H	I	N	Franciscan friar, Woman's hooded cloak, S. American monkey.
C	A	R	A	M	I	N	E	Quince yellow.
C	A	R	A	B	E	E	N	Australian shade tree.
C	A	R	A	B	O	I	D	Genus of beetle.
C	A	R	A	C	A	R	A	Large S. American hawk.
C	A	R	A	C	O	L	E	Spiral staircase, Prancing, Capering.
C	A	R	A	N	D	A	Y	Espavé, S. American timber tree with reddish soft wood.
C	A	R	A	P	A	C	E	Shell of shield covering, Hard protective outer covering.
C	A	R	A	P	A	T	O	Carrapato, S. American ticks, parasitic to man and animals.
C	A	R	B	A	N	I	L	Phenyl isoyanate.
C	A	R	B	A	S	U	S	Surgical gauze, Lint.
C	A	R	B	I	N	O	L	Methanol.
C	A	R	B	I	N	Y	L	Methyl.
C	A	R	B	I	T	O	L	Used for a high-boiling ether-alcohol.
C	A	R	B	O	N	I	T	Mineral consisting of a carbonaceous, ocherous or pitchy substances.
C	A	R	B	O	L	I	C	Phenyl.
C	A	R	B	O	L	O	Y	Hard metallic substance.
C	A	R	B	O	N	I	C	Relating to carbon dioxide.
C	A	R	B	O	N	Y	L	Compound of the carbonyl radical with a metal.
C	A	R	B	U	R	A	N	A pitchlike hydrocarbon containing uranium.
C	A	R	B	U	R	E	T	Carbide.
C	A	R	C	A	N	E	T	Ornamental jewelled collar or necklace.
C	A	R	D	A	M	O	M	The aromatic capsular of an East Indian herb.
C	A	R	D	A	N	O	L	Nonvesicant oily liquid obtained from the shells of cashew nuts.

1	2	3	4	5	6	7	8	Definition
C	A	R	D	I	G	A	N	Sweater or jacket that opens the full length of the centre front, Welsh corgi dog.
C	A	R	D	I	N	A	L	Chief, Primary, Essential, Fundamental, Vital, Central, Pivotal, Ruling.
C	A	R	D	I	O	I	D	Heart-shaped closed curve on a geometrical figure.
C	A	R	D	I	T	I	S	Inflammation of the heart muscle, Myocarditis.
C	A	R	E	E	N	E	D	Lurched, Swayed, Staggered, Wobbled, Wove, Swung.
C	A	R	E	E	R	E	D	Charged, Pranced, Caracoled, Run recklessly, Drove headlong, Raced, Dashed.
C	A	R	E	F	R	E	E	Happy, Light-hearted, Irresponsible, Incautious, Feckless, Reckless.
C	A	R	E	L	E	S	S	Feckless, Heedless, Irresponsible, Negligent, Incautious, Remiss, Slipshod, Unkempt.
C	A	R	E	S	S	E	D	Loved, Cuddled, Dandled, Fondled, Embraced, Cherished, Pampered.
C	A	R	E	W	O	R	N	Distressed, Haggard, Drawn, Troubled, Exhausted, Jaded, Pinched.
C	A	R	G	A	D	O	R	Porter, Stevedore.
C	A	R	I	B	E	E	R	Hybrid between the caribou and the reindeer.
C	A	R	I	L	L	O	N	Set of fixed bells pitched in chromatic series.
C	A	R	I	N	A	T	E	Keeled, Ridged.
C	A	R	I	N	U	L	E	Small carina.
C	A	R	I	T	I	V	E	Abessive, Lack, Absence.
C	A	R	L	I	C	U	E	Curlicue, Fancifully curved or spiral.
C	A	R	N	A	L	L	Y	In a carnal fashion.
C	A	R	N	A	U	B	A	A fan palm with an edible root.
C	A	R	N	E	O	L	E	Carnelian, Chalcedony of deep-red or reddish-white that polishes well and is used for seals.
C	A	R	N	I	F	E	X	Public execution in ancient Rome.
C	A	R	N	I	V	A	L	Merrymaking, Travelling amusement park, Festival, Programme of entertainment.
C	A	R	O	L	I	N	E	Swedish coin, Bavarian gold coin, Germanic coins.
C	A	R	O	L	L	E	D	Sang carols, Sang cheerfully, Warbled.
C	A	R	O	T	E	N	E	Orange or red crystalline pigments occurring in plants. Vitamin 'A'.
C	A	R	O	U	S	A	L	Carrousel, Merry-go-round.
C	A	R	O	U	S	E	D	Went on a drinking spree.
C	A	R	O	U	S	E	L	Carrousel.
C	A	R	O	U	S	E	R	Reveller.
C	A	R	P	E	T	E	D	Furnished with carpets, Spread with carpet, Reprimanded.
C	A	R	P	I	N	U	S	Genus of small trees, Beech nut.
C	A	R	R	A	W	A	Y	White flowered herb, Aromatic pungent-tasting fruit used in cooking and confectionery.
C	A	R	R	I	A	G	E	Transport, Conveyance, Deportment, Management, Execution, Administration, Vehicle.
C	A	R	R	I	O	L	E	Light four-wheeled carriage.
C	A	R	R	I	T	C	H	Catechism.
C	A	R	R	Y	I	N	G	Conveying, Conducting, Escorting, Leading, Guiding, Moving, Swaying, Bearing.
C	A	R	T	L	O	A	D	As much as will fill a cart.
C	A	R	T	O	U	C	H	Ornamental frame in baroque style, Oval shield.
C	A	R	U	C	A	G	E	Old English tax on every plough or ploughland.
C	A	R	U	C	A	T	E	Old English unit of land.
C	A	R	U	N	C	L	E	Fleshy outgrowth on a bird or insect, Colyledon.
C	A	R	Y	A	T	I	C	Relating to a caryatid.
C	A	R	Y	A	T	I	D	Statue of a draped female figure used as a support instead of a column.
C	A	R	Y	O	C	A	R	Genus of S. American tree having strong wood for furniture or ship-building.
C	A	S	A	N	O	V	A	Lover, A promiscuous man.
C	A	S	C	A	B	E	L	Part of a cannon, Vicious rattlesnake, Jingle bell.
C	A	S	C	A	D	E	D	Fell, Poured, Spilled, Disgorged, Spouted.
C	A	S	C	A	V	E	L	Cascabel.
C	A	S	E	A	R	I	A	Tropical trees with bark and leaves used for medicine and fruit yielding fish poison.
C	A	S	E	M	A	T	E	Fortified position for cannons to be placed for firing.
C	A	S	E	M	E	N	T	A window sash that opens on hinges.
C	A	S	E	S	H	O	T	Balls or metal fragments enclosed in a case and fired by artillery.
C	A	S	E	W	O	R	M	An insect-larva that makes a case for its body.
C	A	S	H	M	E	R	E	Fine yarn made of the wool of the Kashmir goat, Soft lightweight wool fabric.
C	A	S	I	M	E	R	E	Cassimere, Fancy weave fabric of fine wool.
C	A	S	K	E	T	E	D	Enclosed in a casket.
C	A	S	S	E	T	T	E	Casket, Magazine for film or tape.
C	A	S	S	I	O	P	E	Genus of low tufted shrubs, Erica.
C	A	S	T	A	B	L	E	Material with bonding agent that can be mixed with water and set in a mould.
C	A	S	T	A	N	E	A	Genus of rough-barked trees, Chestnut.
C	A	S	T	A	N	E	T	Shell-shaped instrument held in the hand by dancers and clicked to emphasize the rhythm.
C	A	S	T	A	W	A	Y	Rejected, Outcast, Thrown away, Left without friends or resources, Shipwrecked person.
C	A	S	T	E	L	E	T	A small castle.
C	A	S	T	I	L	L	A	Castilloa, Genus of tropical American trees.
C	A	S	T	I	R	O	N	Commercial alloy of iron, carbon and silicon, Rigid, Strict, Inflexible.
C	A	S	T	L	I	N	G	A move with the king in chess.
C	A	S	T	R	A	T	E	Emasculate, Geld, Deprive of the testes or ovaries, Spay, Expurgate, Mutilate, Sterilize.

1	2	3	4	5	6	7	8	Definition
C	A	S	T	R	A	T	O	A male singer castrated in youth to preserve the range of his voice.
C	A	S	U	A	L	L	Y	Accidentally, Haphazardly, Informally, Easily, Incidentally, Indifferently.
C	A	S	U	A	L	T	Y	Injury from an accident, Victim, Mischance, Disaster, Misadventure, Mishap, Fatality.
C	A	T	A	C	O	M	B	Crypt, Vault, Subterranean cemetery.
C	A	T	A	L	A	S	E	Red crystalline enzyme consisting of a protein complex.
C	A	T	A	L	I	N	A	A movement in synchronized swimming.
C	A	T	A	L	U	F	A	Brightly coloured marine fishes.
C	A	T	A	L	Y	S	T	Any substance that initiates a reaction, Stimulus, Goad, Incentive, Motivation, Impulse.
C	A	T	A	L	Y	Z	E	Same as CATALYST.
C	A	T	A	P	U	L	T	Slingshot, Any mechanical device for hurling or launching objects.
C	A	T	A	R	A	C	T	Waterfall, Cascade, Chute, Deluge Spate, Torrent, Inundation, Flood.
C	A	T	B	L	O	C	K	Heavy block to use bringing up the anchor.
C	A	T	C	H	A	L	L	Collection of miscellaneous articles.
C	A	T	C	H	C	R	Y	Distinctive word or slogan to attract attention or rally support.
C	A	T	C	H	F	L	Y	Plants which have sticky stems to trap insects.
C	A	T	C	H	I	N	G	Trapping, Finding, Detecting, Seizing, Snatching, Taking, Arresting, Capturing.
C	A	T	E	C	H	I	N	White crystalline pheno-alcohol.
C	A	T	E	C	H	O	L	Same as CATECHIN.
C	A	T	E	G	O	R	Y	Group, Class, Classification, Grade, League.
C	A	T	E	N	A	R	Y	Cable suspended between two points, Decoration of a chain or chord hanging in a curve.
C	A	T	E	N	A	T	E	Link, Connect by links or ties.
C	A	T	E	N	O	I	D	Rotation of a catenary about its axis, Filliform.
C	A	T	E	R	E	S	S	A female experienced in catering.
C	A	T	E	R	I	N	G	To organize and provide food, service and entertainment for parties, wedding and socials.
C	A	T	H	E	D	R	A	Official chair or throne of a bishop.
C	A	T	H	E	T	E	R	Medical tube for insertion into the body.
C	A	T	H	E	X	I	S	Using emotional or psychic energy.
C	A	T	H	I	S	M	A	Kathisma, Use of psalter in the Eastern Orthodox Church.
C	A	T	H	O	D	I	C	Relating to a cathode.
C	A	T	H	O	L	I	C	General, Universal, Global, Planetary, Ecumenical, Cosmopolitan, Inclusive, Comprehensive.
C	A	T	I	O	N	I	C	Relating to cations, positively charged ions.
C	A	T	O	C	T	I	N	Residual hill or ridge rising above a pereplain.
C	A	T	O	N	I	A	N	Austere, Harsh.
C	A	T	S	F	O	O	T	Ground ivy.
C	A	T	S	L	I	D	E	Side of a roof that slopes very low.
C	A	T	S	T	A	I	L	Grasses, Timothy.
C	A	T	S	T	I	C	K	A stick or club used as a bat.
C	A	T	T	L	E	Y	A	Genus of tropical orchids.
C	A	U	D	A	T	E	D	Having a tail.
C	A	U	D	I	C	E	S	Stems of palms or tree ferns covered with persistent leaf bases.
C	A	U	D	I	C	L	E	Slender stalklike appendage of the pollen masses in orchids.
C	A	U	L	D	R	O	N	Caldron, Large kettle or boiler, Being in a state of ferment.
C	A	U	L	I	C	L	E	Stem of a young seedling.
C	A	U	L	K	I	N	G	Making seams watertight, Tightening a joint.
C	A	U	L	O	M	I	C	Stem structure.
C	A	U	S	A	B	L	E	Capable of being caused.
C	A	U	S	A	L	L	Y	Marked by cause and effect.
C	A	U	S	E	R	I	E	Chat, Small talk, Light conversation.
C	A	U	S	E	U	S	E	Tête-a-tête, A small sofa for two persons.
C	A	U	S	E	W	A	Y	Raised road across a swamp, Paved highway.
C	A	U	T	I	O	U	S	Wary, Calculating, Chary, Circumspect, Careful, Discreet, Guarded, Safe.
C	A	V	A	L	I	E	R	Debonair, Arrogant, Supercilious, Aristocrat, Proud, Disdainful, Insolent, Haughty.
C	A	V	A	T	I	N	A	Operatic solo briefer than an aria.
C	A	V	A	Y	A	R	D	Remuda, Herd of chosen saddle horses.
C	A	V	E	A	T	E	D	Warned, Cautioned.
C	A	V	E	A	T	O	R	One that files a legal notice.
C	A	V	E	B	E	A	R	Large extinct bear.
C	A	V	E	R	N	E	D	Formed a cavern, Large underground chamber.
C	A	V	E	S	S	O	N	Noseband made of metal for a horse.
C	A	V	I	C	O	R	N	Having hollow horns.
C	A	V	I	L	L	E	D	Raised frivolous objections, Hypercriticized, Quibbled.
C	A	V	I	T	A	R	Y	Characterized by cavitation.
C	A	V	I	T	A	T	E	To form a cavity.
C	A	V	I	T	O	M	A	Weakening of cotton fibre due to micro-organisms.
C	A	V	O	R	T	E	D	Pranced, Frisked, Bounded, Gambolled, Capered, Romped.
C	A	Y	U	M	I	T	O	Star apple.
C	A	Y	T	O	N	I	A	Genus of fossil plants.

1	2	3	4	5	6	7	8	Definition
C	E	L	A	T	I	O	N	Concealment of pregnancy or childbirth.
C	E	L	E	R	I	A	C	Variety of celery.
C	E	L	E	R	I	T	Y	Promptness, Alacrity, Swiftness, Speed, Haste, Hurry, Hustle, Rapidity.
C	E	L	I	B	A	C	Y	Chastity, Abstention from sexual intercourse.
C	E	L	I	B	A	T	E	Relating to celibacy.
C	E	L	L	A	R	E	R	Official in charge of buying, storing and distributing provisions.
C	E	L	L	A	R	E	T	Sideboard with a small wine storage area.
C	E	L	L	O	C	U	T	Artist's print made from a plastic plate.
C	E	L	L	U	L	A	R	Dealing with cells, Porous, In related sections or units.
C	E	L	L	U	L	I	N	Celluloselike carbohydrate of animal origin but also found in fungi.
C	E	M	B	A	L	O	S	Harpsichord, Dulcimer.
C	E	M	E	N	T	E	D	Adhered, Joined, Bound together, Stuck, Cohered, Glued, United.
C	E	M	E	N	T	I	N	Intercellular material uniting the borders of certain cells.
C	E	M	E	N	T	U	M	Bony layer enclosing the dentine of the part of the tooth normally in the gum.
C	E	M	E	T	E	R	Y	Graveyard, Area for burial.
C	E	N	O	B	I	T	E	Member of religious order living in common.
C	E	N	O	T	A	P	H	Monument erected in honour of persons usually buried elsewhere.
C	E	N	O	Z	O	I	C	Relating to a grand division of geological history.
C	E	N	S	O	R	E	D	Altered, Banned, Deleted, Excised, Purged, Restricted, Forbidden.
C	E	N	S	U	R	E	D	Judged, Criticized, Disapproved, Condemned, Denounced, Rebuked, Blamed.
C	E	N	T	A	U	R	Y	Old world herb used as a tonic, Knapweed.
C	E	N	T	E	R	E	D	Focused, Clustered at a focal point, Collected, Concentrated.
C	E	N	T	E	T	E	S	Spines on the back, Tenrec, Spiny insect-eating mammals.
C	E	N	T	I	A	R	E	Centare, Square metre.
C	E	N	T	I	B	A	R	Unit of atmospheric pressure.
C	E	N	T	I	D	A	Y	Period of 14 mins, 24 secs used in the study of plant growth.
C	E	N	T	R	I	N	G	Gathering around a focal point.
C	E	N	T	R	I	S	T	Moderate.
C	E	N	T	R	O	I	D	Centre of mass, Centre of gravity.
C	E	N	T	U	P	L	E	Hundred-fold.
C	E	P	H	A	L	I	C	Relating to the head.
C	E	P	H	A	L	I	N	Various acidic phosphotides that are similar to lecithins.
C	E	P	H	A	L	O	B	Member of a family of nematode worms.
C	E	R	A	M	I	C	S	Articles made from clay and then fired at high temperatures.
C	E	R	A	M	I	S	T	One engaged in the manufacture of ceramics.
C	E	R	A	S	T	E	S	Horned viper.
C	E	R	A	T	I	T	E	Fossil of a shellfish.
C	E	R	A	T	I	U	M	Species of plankton.
C	E	R	A	T	O	I	D	Hornlike.
C	E	R	A	T	O	P	S	Type genus of American dinosaurs.
C	E	R	A	T	O	S	A	Keratosa, Horny sponges.
C	E	R	B	E	R	U	S	Watchdog, Gatekeeper, Genus of East Indian water snakes.
C	E	R	C	O	P	I	D	Froghopper.
C	E	R	C	O	P	O	D	Cercus, Appendages at posterior end of some insects.
C	E	R	E	A	L	I	N	Relating to cereals.
C	E	R	E	B	R	A	L	Pertaining to the brain, Mental.
C	E	R	E	B	R	U	M	Brain.
C	E	R	E	M	E	N	T	A waxed shroud.
C	E	R	E	M	O	N	Y	Form, Formality, Liturgy, Ritual, Observance, Service, Rite, Solemn act.
C	E	R	E	S	I	N	E	Hard brittle wax, Petroleum wax.
C	E	R	I	N	T	H	E	Genus of Eurasian herbs, Honeywort.
C	E	R	N	U	O	U	S	Pendulous, Drooping, Inclining, Nodding.
C	E	R	U	L	E	A	N	Resembling the blue colour of the sky, Azure.
C	E	R	U	L	E	I	N	Coerulein, A xanthene dye.
C	E	R	U	S	I	T	E	Native lead carbonate.
C	E	R	V	E	L	A	T	Spiced smoked sausages.
C	E	R	V	I	C	A	L	Relating to a neck.
C	E	R	V	I	C	U	M	Joint between head and thorax of an insect.
C	E	R	V	I	N	E	S	Antlered mammals, Deer, Elk, Moose.
C	E	R	V	U	L	U	S	Muntiacus, Asian deer.
C	E	S	A	R	E	A	N	Birth of young through an incision of the abdomen.
C	E	S	S	P	O	O	L	Underground drain allowing waste liquid to seep into the soil, where there is no sewer pipes.
C	E	S	T	O	D	E	S	Cestoda, Tapeworms.
C	E	T	A	C	E	A	N	Relating to marine mammals, Whales, Dolphins, Porpoises.
C	E	T	O	L	O	G	Y	Branch of zoology pertaining to whales.
C	E	T	O	N	I	I	D	Family of scarab beetles.
C	E	T	R	A	R	I	A	Iceland moss.

1	2	3	4	5	6	7	8	Definition
C	H	A	C	O	N	N	E	Old Spanish dance, Musical composition with a special rhythm.
C	H	A	D	L	O	C	K	Charlock, Wild mustard.
C	H	A	E	T	U	R	A	Genus of swifts.
C	H	A	F	E	W	A	X	A Chancery officer that prepares wax for sealing documents, a position now abolished.
C	H	A	F	F	E	R	S	Exchange, Barter, Haggle, Beg, Coax, Plead, Bargain.
C	H	A	F	F	I	N	G	Bantering, Jesting, Kidding, Razzing.
C	H	A	F	F	R	O	N	Chamron, Headpiece of a horse's armour.
C	H	A	F	F	W	A	X	Chafewax.
C	H	A	I	N	I	N	G	Fastening with a chain, Shackling, Fettering, Repressing, Confining.
C	H	A	I	N	L	E	T	A small chain.
C	H	A	I	R	B	E	D	Chair with a retractable seat able to be converted into a bed.
C	H	A	I	R	I	N	G	Carrying on the shoulders, Installing as a presiding officer.
C	H	A	I	R	M	A	N	Presiding officer, Supervisor, Director, Chief officer.
C	H	A	L	A	Z	A	L	Facing towards the base of an ovule.
C	H	A	L	D	A	I	C	Chaldean, Ancient Semitic people.
C	H	A	L	D	R	O	N	Old units of measure.
C	H	A	L	I	C	E	D	Having a cup-shaped blossom.
C	H	A	L	K	I	N	G	Preparing with chalk, Marking with chalk, Applying chalk to a billiard cue.
C	H	A	L	K	O	N	E	Chalcone, Yellow crystalline ketone.
C	H	A	M	F	R	O	N	Band of armour for a horse's head.
C	H	A	M	I	S	A	L	Shrubby vegetation.
C	H	A	M	O	R	R	O	People of the Mariana islands.
C	H	A	M	P	I	N	G	Gnashing, Mashing, Trampling, Biting, Chomping.
C	H	A	M	P	I	O	N	Warrior, Fighter, Combatant, Supporter, Advocate, Uphold, Battle, Contend.
C	H	A	N	C	E	R	Y	Judicial administration, Record office, Court of equity.
C	H	A	N	C	I	N	G	Happening, Venturing, Risking, Occurring, Gambling, Hazarding, Wagering, Transpiring.
C	H	A	N	D	L	E	R	Dealer that supplies provisions.
C	H	A	N	G	I	N	G	Transforming, Converting, Reversing, Altering, Turning, Modifying, Refashioning, Varying.
C	H	A	N	T	E	U	R	Singer of ballads.
C	H	A	N	T	I	N	G	Singing, Vocalizing, Warbling, Intoning, Reciting monotonously.
C	H	A	P	A	T	T	I	Flat unleavened bread made in India.
C	H	A	P	B	O	O	K	Small books that were sold by old-time pedlars.
C	H	A	P	E	L	R	Y	District with its own chapel.
C	H	A	P	E	R	O	N	15th Century head-dress, Older person accompanying young people to ensure proper behaviour.
C	H	A	P	I	T	E	R	The capital of a column.
C	H	A	P	L	A	I	N	A percon chosen to conduct religious services.
C	H	A	P	L	E	S	S	Having no lower jaw.
C	H	A	P	P	I	N	G	Chopping, Pounding, Splitting, Cracking, Striking, Beating, Knocking, Rapping.
C	H	A	P	T	R	E	L	Impost, Tax, Tribute, Duty, Support for an arch.
C	H	A	R	A	C	I	N	White substance found in fatty algae.
C	H	A	R	A	L	E	S	Algae.
C	H	A	R	A	N	G	O	Small guitar with body made of an animal shell.
C	H	A	R	B	R	A	Y	American cross-bred cattle.
C	H	A	R	C	O	A	L	Dark porous form of carbon made from animal or vegetable matter.
C	H	A	R	G	I	N	G	Burdening, Encumbering, Loading, Taxing, Weighing, Choking, Commanding, Accusing.
C	H	A	R	I	S	M	A	Charm, Allure, Appeal, Fascination, Glamour, Magnetism, Witchery.
C	H	A	R	L	A	D	Y	A cleaning woman.
C	H	A	R	L	O	C	K	Wild mustard that infests grainfields.
C	H	A	R	M	I	N	G	Pleasing, Delighting, Fascinating, Attracting, Captivating, Bewitching, Enchanting.
C	H	A	R	R	I	N	G	House or office cleaning.
C	H	A	R	T	I	N	G	Planning, Projecting, Delineating, Arranging, Designing, Devising, Mapping, Recording.
C	H	A	R	T	I	S	M	19th Century reformers advocating improved conditions for workers.
C	H	A	R	T	I	S	T	One that makes studies and predictions from charts and graphs.
C	H	A	S	A	B	L	E	Fit for hunting.
C	H	A	S	S	E	U	R	Hunter, Huntsman, Hotel employee.
C	H	A	S	T	E	L	Y	In a modest manner, Decently.
C	H	A	S	T	I	S	E	Reprove, Rebuke, Scold, Castigate, Chasten, Punish, Discipline, Thrash.
C	H	A	S	T	I	T	Y	Decency, Modesty, Celibate, Purity.
C	H	A	S	U	B	L	E	Outer ecclesiastical vestment.
C	H	A	T	E	L	E	T	Small castle.
C	H	A	T	T	E	L	S	Tangible items of property.
C	H	A	T	T	I	N	G	Prattling, Approaching, Chattering.
C	H	A	T	T	I	L	Y	In a chatty manner.
C	H	A	U	D	R	O	N	Antique red.
C	H	A	U	F	F	E	R	Portable stove.
C	H	A	U	N	T	E	R	Chanter.
C	H	A	U	S	S	E	S	Hose for lower trunk and legs, Armour fitting like chausses.

1	2	3	4	5	6	7	8	
C	H	A	V	I	C	O	L	Colourless oily phenol.
C	H	A	Y	R	O	O	T	Root of an East Indian herb.
C	H	E	A	T	E	R	Y	Cheating swindling.
C	H	E	A	T	I	N	G	Defrauding, Swindling, Deceiving, Hoaxing, Tricking, Bilking, Fleecing, Extorting.
C	H	E	C	H	A	K	O	A tenderfoot in Alaska.
C	H	E	C	K	E	R	S	Discs used in the game of checkers.
C	H	E	C	K	I	N	G	Rebuking, Reprimanding, Blocking, Arresting, Restraining, Tallying, Verifying, Agreeing.
C	H	E	E	K	I	N	G	Teasing, Speaking impudently, Being saucy.
C	H	E	E	P	I	N	G	Chirping, Peeping, Squeaking.
C	H	E	E	R	F	U	L	Glad, Merry, Blithe, Lively, Carefree, Jaunty, Vivacious, Animated.
C	H	E	E	R	I	L	Y	Cheerfully.
C	H	E	E	R	I	N	G	Comforting, Inspiring, Invigorating, Rejoicing, Encouraging, Consoling, Strengthening.
C	H	E	L	A	T	E	D	Combined with metal to form a chelate ring.
C	H	E	L	I	F	E	R	Genus of scorpion.
C	H	E	L	L	E	A	N	Relating to Chelles, France.
C	H	E	L	O	N	I	A	Genus of green turtles.
C	H	E	L	O	N	U	S	Genus of small flies parasitic on lepidopterous larvae.
C	H	E	L	Y	D	R	A	Genus of snapping turtles.
C	H	E	M	I	C	A	L	Operated by chemical means, Related to science of chemistry.
C	H	E	M	O	S	I	S	Swelling of tissue around the cornea.
C	H	E	M	O	T	I	C	Relating to chemosis.
C	H	E	M	U	R	G	Y	Branch of chemistry dealing with organic materials.
C	H	E	N	I	L	L	E	Tufted yarn used for soft furnishings.
C	H	E	R	U	B	I	C	Resembling a cherub.
C	H	E	R	U	B	I	M	Cupid, Beautiful young angel.
C	H	E	S	H	I	R	E	American breed of white swine.
C	H	E	S	H	V	A	N	Heshvan, Date in ecclesiastical year of Jewish calendar.
C	H	E	S	S	M	A	N	Pieces used in the game of chess.
C	H	E	S	T	I	N	G	Placing in a coffin.
C	H	E	S	T	N	U	T	Sweet edible nut produced by tree of the genus Castanea, Stale joke, story.
C	H	E	T	O	P	O	D	Large marine worm.
C	H	E	V	A	I	N	E	European freshwater bass.
C	H	E	V	E	R	E	L	Kid leather, Soft leather.
C	H	E	V	E	R	I	L	Same as CHEVEREL.
C	H	E	V	I	L	L	E	Padding for a sentence or verse, Peg of a stringed instrument.
C	H	E	V	R	O	N	Y	In heraldry to be divided into chevrons.
C	H	E	V	Y	I	N	G	Chasing, Pursuing, Harassing, Baiting.
C	H	I	A	S	M	U	S	Inversion of the order of syntactical elements.
C	H	I	C	A	N	E	D	Tricked by legalistic subterfuge, Cheated, Duped, Cavilled, Quibbled.
C	H	I	C	A	N	E	R	One that deceives or defrauds.
C	H	I	C	C	O	R	Y	Chicory, Endive, Salad vegetable, Dried, roasted and then ground to mix with coffee.
C	H	I	C	H	I	P	E	Mexican cactus with edible red fruits.
C	H	I	C	K	I	N	G	Sprouting.
C	H	I	C	K	E	R	Y	Poultry hatchery.
C	H	I	C	K	P	E	A	Asiatic herb with pods containing seeds that are important to diet.
C	H	I	E	F	E	R	Y	Chieftaincy, Tributes due to the chief.
C	H	I	E	F	D	O	M	Leadership.
C	H	I	G	E	T	A	I	Mongolian wild ass.
C	H	I	L	D	B	E	D	Woman in child-birth, Parturition, Lying-in.
C	H	I	L	D	I	N	G	Productive, Fruitful, Pregnant, Fecund, Fertile, Prolific, Spawning.
C	H	I	L	D	I	S	H	Immature, Puerile, Petty.
C	H	I	L	D	R	E	N	Young persons.
C	H	I	L	I	A	S	M	Doctrine that Christ will return in a visible form and usher in the millennium.
C	H	I	L	I	A	S	T	Millenarian, One that believes in Chiliasm.
C	H	I	L	L	I	E	R	Colder, More unfriendly, Cooler.
C	H	I	L	L	I	N	G	Making cold, Discouraging, Depressing, Dampening, Checking.
C	H	I	L	O	D	O	N	Genus of freshwater ciliates, that destroy the skin and gills of certain fishes.
C	H	I	L	T	E	R	N	Special type of English loamy soils in dry areas.
C	H	I	M	A	E	R	A	Mythical she-monster, Illusion.
C	H	I	M	E	R	I	C	Unrealistic, Illusory, Absurd, Fanciful, Imaginary, Delusive, Preposterous, Fictional.
C	H	I	N	A	M	A	N	Native of China, Manufacturer of porcelain.
C	H	I	N	A	M	P	A	Mexican artificially made floating garden.
C	H	I	N	B	O	N	E	Mandible, Lower jaw.
C	H	I	N	C	H	I	N	Expression of greeting or farewell, Drinking toast, Salutation, Chatter.
C	H	I	N	K	I	N	G	Filling in chinks, Striking together with a metallic sound, Gasping.
C	H	I	N	O	T	T	O	Sour orange.
C	H	I	O	L	I	T	E	A mineral resembling cryolite in colour and composition.

1	2	3	4	5	6	7	8	
C	H	I	P	M	U	N	K	Small striped American squirrels.
C	H	I	P	P	I	N	G	Chopping, Hacking, Cracking, Germinating, Checking.
C	H	I	P	S	H	O	T	Special approach shot in golf.
C	H	I	R	A	G	R	A	Pain in the hand.
C	H	I	R	I	M	I	A	High-pitched oboe of Spanish and Spanish America.
C	H	I	R	I	Q	U	I	Prehistoric culture of Panama.
C	H	I	R	P	I	N	G	Chirruping, Cheering, Enlivening.
C	H	I	R	R	I	N	G	Purring, Trilling repetitively.
C	H	I	R	R	U	P	Y	Chatty, Cheerful, Lively, Chirpy.
C	H	I	S	E	L	E	D	Clean-cut, Carved, Cheated, Intruded.
C	H	I	S	E	L	E	R	Petty crook, Cheat, Gouger.
C	H	I	T	C	H	A	T	Gossip, Small talk.
C	H	I	T	O	S	A	N	A substance formed from chitin.
C	H	I	V	A	L	R	Y	Gallantry, Generosity, Protectiveness.
C	H	L	O	A	S	M	A	Discolouration of the skin.
C	H	L	O	R	A	T	E	A salt of chloric acid.
C	H	L	O	R	I	D	E	Ester of hydrochloric acid.
C	H	L	O	R	I	N	E	Common nonmetallic univalent and polyvalent element used extensively for water purification.
C	H	L	O	R	I	T	E	Monoclinic mineral that is Hydrous silicate and resembles mica.
C	H	L	O	R	O	M	A	Leukemia originating in the bone marrow.
C	H	O	A	N	A	T	E	Sponge having internal nares.
C	H	O	C	A	L	H	O	A Brazilian rattle.
C	H	O	I	C	E	L	Y	Carefully, Discriminatingly, Daintily, Exquisitely.
C	H	O	I	R	B	O	Y	Boy member of a church choir.
C	H	O	I	R	I	N	G	Singing in concert.
C	H	O	L	E	A	T	E	Ester of choleic acid.
C	H	O	L	E	R	I	C	Hot-tempered, Irascible, Angry, Irate, Wrathful, Touchy, Angry, Indignant.
C	H	O	L	I	A	M	B	Special iambic metre of verse.
C	H	O	L	U	R	I	A	Presence of bile in urine.
C	H	O	N	D	R	A	L	Relating to cartilage.
C	H	O	N	D	R	I	N	Horny substance obtainable from cartilage similar to gelatin.
C	H	O	N	D	R	U	S	Genus of red algae, Irish moss.
C	H	O	O	S	I	N	G	Selecting, Electing, Wanting, Picking, Deciding, Preferring, Considering.
C	H	O	P	C	H	O	P	Quickly, Promptly.
C	H	O	P	P	I	N	G	Cutting, Felling, Mincing, Dicing, Hitting, Striking, Reducing, Retarding.
C	H	O	P	S	U	E	Y	Form of Chinese cooking of bean sprouts, bamboo shoots, meat or fish, soy sauce.
C	H	O	R	A	G	I	C	Honouring a successful choragus.
C	H	O	R	A	G	U	S	Leader of a chorus, choir, group or movement.
C	H	O	R	A	G	O	S	Same as CHORAGUS.
C	H	O	R	D	A	T	A	Animals having dorsally situated nervous system.
C	H	O	R	D	I	N	G	Harmonizing together, Playing an accompaniment, Making chords.
C	H	O	R	D	O	I	D	Like a chorda, Genus of brown algae.
C	H	O	R	E	G	U	S	Choragus.
C	H	O	R	I	A	M	B	Special metre in classical prosody.
C	H	O	R	I	S	I	S	Separation of a leaf or floral organ during development.
C	H	O	R	T	L	E	D	Chuckled, Giggled, Laughed, Guffawed, Snickered, Tittered.
C	H	O	R	U	S	E	D	Sang in chorus, Uttered together, Echoed, Spoke simultaneously.
C	H	O	U	L	T	R	Y	Inn, Hostelry, Pillared hall of a temple.
C	H	O	U	S	I	N	G	Cheating, Tricking, Defrauding, Chasing, Harassing.
C	H	O	W	C	H	O	W	Assorted, Mixed, Miscellaneous, Hodgepodge, Confection of preserved fruit, Mixed pickles.
C	H	O	W	M	E	I	N	Thick stew of diced meat, mushrooms and vegetables served with fried noodles.
C	H	R	E	S	A	R	D	Soil water available for plant growth.
C	H	R	I	S	M	A	L	Relating to chrism, consecrated oil, Vessel to hold the chrism.
C	H	R	I	S	M	O	N	Christian monogram.
C	H	R	I	S	T	E	N	Baptize, Name, Denominate, Designate, Style, Term, Title, Immerse.
C	H	R	I	S	T	L	Y	Like Christ, Generalized term of disparagement.
C	H	R	O	M	A	T	E	Ester of chromic acid.
C	H	R	O	M	I	D	E	Small brightly coloured African fishes.
C	H	R	O	M	I	T	E	Mineral consisting of oxide of iron and chromium.
C	H	R	O	M	I	U	M	Blue-white multivalent metallic element hard and brittle.
C	H	R	O	M	O	U	S	Derived from chromium.
C	H	R	O	N	I	S	T	Chronicler.
C	H	R	Y	S	E	N	E	White chrystalline hydrocarbon obtained from coal-tar.
C	H	T	H	O	N	I	C	Living in the Underworld, Infernal, Ghostly.
C	H	U	C	K	I	E	S	Small pebble used in the game of checkstones.
C	H	U	C	K	I	N	G	Patting under the chin, Tossing, Dismissing, Ejecting, Quitting, Yielding, Ditching.
C	H	U	C	K	L	E	D	Laughed, Chortled, Giggled, Guffawed, Sniggled, Snickered, Tittered.

1	2	3	4	5	6	7	8	Definition
C	H	U	M	M	A	G	E	Lodging people in the same room together.
C	H	U	M	M	E	R	Y	Living quarters of friends sharing.
C	H	U	M	M	I	N	G	Attracting fish with chopped bait.
C	H	U	N	K	I	L	Y	In a chunky fashion.
C	H	U	P	A	T	T	I	Chapati.
C	H	U	R	I	N	G	A	Object of wood or stone considered sacred by Australian aborigines.
C	H	U	R	L	I	S	H	Rustic, Vulgar, Mean, Base, Rude, Ill-bred, Intractable, Boorish.
C	H	U	R	N	I	N	G	Agitating, Stirring, Rotating, Seething, Boiling, Fermenting, Simmering.
C	H	Y	L	O	S	I	S	Converting in chyle, milky looking lympth.
C	H	Y	M	O	S	I	S	Chylification.
C	H	Y	M	O	S	I	N	Rennin.
C	I	B	A	C	R	O	N	Fibre-reactive dyes.
C	I	B	A	R	I	A	L	Relating to the mouthparts of an insect.
C	I	B	A	R	I	A	N	Same as CIBARIAN.
C	I	B	A	T	I	O	N	Feeding alchemical crucible with fresh material during course of operation.
C	I	B	O	R	I	U	M	Goblet-shaped ecclesiastical vessel, Canopy over the high altar.
C	I	C	A	T	R	I	X	Scar.
C	I	C	E	R	O	N	E	Guide, Mentor, Showing the sights, Museum guide.
C	I	C	I	S	B	E	O	Recognised lover of a married woman in the 18th century.
C	I	C	U	R	A	T	E	To tame.
C	I	D	E	R	K	I	N	Weak cider made by using residue of apples after cider making.
C	I	L	I	A	T	E	D	Having eyelashes.
C	I	M	B	O	R	I	O	Lantern built over the crossing of a Gothic cathedral.
C	I	M	B	R	I	A	N	Ancient Celtic or Teutonic invaders defeated by the Romans.
C	I	M	I	C	O	I	D	Resembling the family of bloodsucking bugs, Bedbugs.
C	I	M	I	N	I	T	E	An extrusive rock marked by presence of olivine.
C	I	M	O	L	I	T	E	A mineral consisting of a hydrous aluminium silicate.
C	I	N	C	H	I	N	G	Binding closely, Fastening tightly, Tightening, Guaranteeing, Ensuring, Assuring, Securing.
C	I	N	C	H	O	N	A	Dried bark of trees containing alkaloids, quinine and used as antipyretic and tonic.
C	I	N	C	T	U	R	E	Girding, Encompassing, Enclosure, Belt, Encircle.
C	I	N	E	R	A	R	Y	Receptacle for the ashes of the cremated dead.
C	I	N	E	R	E	A	L	Like ashes, Consisting of ashes.
C	I	N	E	R	O	U	S	Light bluish grey.
C	I	N	G	U	L	A	R	Annular.
C	I	N	G	U	L	U	M	Band, Zone, Ridge, Fibres, Raised spiral.
C	I	N	N	A	B	A	R	Mineral consisting of mercuric sulfide, Vermilion pigment.
C	I	N	N	A	M	O	N	Highly aromatic oil from bark of a tree.
C	I	N	Q	U	A	I	N	Five line verse form.
C	I	O	P	P	I	N	O	Dish of fish and shellfish seasoned with spices, wine and cooked in tomato sauce.
C	I	P	H	E	R	E	D	Calculated, Computed, Reckoned, Resolved, Estimated, Figured, Solved, Coded.
C	I	R	C	L	I	N	G	Enclosing, Forming a circle, Revolving, Moving in a circle, Meandering, Surrounding.
C	I	R	C	U	I	T	Y	Detailed plan of an electric circuit.
C	I	R	C	U	L	A	R	Indirect, Round, Oblique, Roundabout.
C	I	R	R	A	T	E	D	Leaf with a curled tendril at the tip.
C	I	R	R	H	O	U	S	Same as CIRRHOSE.
C	I	R	R	I	P	E	D	Parasitic barnacles.
C	I	T	A	T	I	O	N	Summon, Mention, Enumeration, Award, Eulogy, Salutation, Tribute.
C	I	T	A	T	O	R	Y	Relating to citing, Summoning.
C	I	T	R	E	O	U	S	Citron, Yellow in colour.
C	I	T	R	I	N	I	N	A Toxic antibiotic.
C	I	T	Y	H	O	O	D	State of being citified.
C	I	V	E	T	C	A	T	Small carnivorous mammal.
C	I	V	E	T	O	N	E	A crystalline ketone.
C	I	V	I	L	I	A	N	Non-military, Not an active list.
C	I	V	I	L	I	S	T	Civilian.
C	I	V	I	L	I	T	Y	Propriety, Convential behaviour, Social behaviour, Politeness, Courtesy.
C	I	V	I	L	I	Z	E	Socialize, Educate, Uplift from savagery, Cultural development.
C	L	A	C	K	I	N	G	Clicking, Chattering, Clattering, Cackling, Babbling, Blabbing.
C	L	A	D	D	I	N	G	Clothing, Sheathing, Facing, Covering, Overlaying, Coating.
C	L	A	D	O	N	I	A	Genus of lichens, Reindeer moss.
C	L	A	G	G	I	N	G	Clogging, Clotting, Adhering, Bedaubing, Sticking.
C	L	A	I	M	A	N	T	One that asserts a claim.
C	L	A	I	M	I	N	G	Proclaiming, Naming, Annoucing, Maintaining, Demanding, Requiring, Challenging.
C	L	A	M	B	A	K	E	Clambake.
C	L	A	M	B	A	K	E	Seashore picnic where clams and fish are baked over the fire, Political rally.
C	L	A	M	M	I	S	H	Coldly dampish.
C	L	A	M	M	I	N	G	Groping, Clutching, Sticking, Harvesting clams.

1	2	3	4	5	6	7	8	
C	L	A	M	P	I	N	G	Fastening, Holding, Grasping, Clenching, Clutching, Grappling, Clasping.
C	L	A	N	G	I	N	G	Resounding loudly, Ringing.
C	L	A	N	G	O	U	R	Noisy and resounding, Din, Clamour.
C	L	A	N	K	I	N	G	Clanging, Clashing.
C	L	A	N	N	I	S	H	Associating with members of the same ideas or way of life.
C	L	A	N	S	H	I	P	Belonging to a clan, Sticking together.
C	L	A	N	S	M	A	N	One belonging to a clanlike group.
C	L	A	P	D	I	S	H	Begging bowl with a lid to clap to attract attention.
C	L	A	P	N	E	T	T	Net dropped over a pool to trap water birds.
C	L	A	P	P	I	N	G	Beating one's hands together, Applauding, Banging, Smashing, Booming, Cracking.
C	L	A	P	T	R	A	P	Nonsense, Baloney, Bunkum, Drivel, Humbug, Twaddle, Trash.
C	L	A	Q	U	E	U	R	Member of a group of demonstraters or professional applauders.
C	L	A	R	E	N	C	E	Closed four-wheeled carriage, Growler.
C	L	A	R	I	N	E	T	Single-reed wood wind instrument, 8ft reed organ stop.
C	L	A	S	H	I	N	G	Bumping, Colliding, Conflicting, Jangling, Jarring, Grating, Dashing, Slamming.
C	L	A	S	P	I	N	G	Embracing, Clinching, Enfolding, Hugging, Pressing, Squeezing, Taking, Grasping.
C	L	A	S	P	N	U	T	Split nut that grips its mating screw when closed.
C	L	A	S	S	I	E	R	Superior, Finer, More stylish, More high-class.
C	L	A	S	S	I	F	Y	To group into categories, Sort, Assort, Pigeonhole, Evaluate, Grade, Rank, Rate.
C	L	A	S	S	I	N	G	Dividing, Distributing, Grading, Sorting, Grouping.
C	L	A	U	D	I	A	N	Characteristic of Roman emperors.
C	L	A	U	S	U	L	A	Cadence in ancient Latin prose rhythm.
C	L	A	U	S	U	R	E	Closure.
C	L	A	V	A	R	I	A	Genus of fungi.
C	L	A	V	A	T	E	D	Shaped like a club.
C	L	A	V	E	C	I	N	Harpsichord.
C	L	A	V	I	C	L	E	Collarbone, One of the two bones fused into the wishbone of a bird.
C	L	A	V	I	G	E	R	Custodian, Warden.
C	L	A	V	I	L	U	X	Instrument for throwing varying patterns of light on to a screen.
C	L	A	W	B	A	C	K	Flatterer, Sycophant, Toady.
C	L	A	W	F	O	O	T	Foot on furniture representing a claw, Deformity of the foot.
C	L	A	W	H	A	N	D	Deformity of the hand.
C	L	A	W	L	E	S	S	Having no claws.
C	L	A	Y	M	A	R	L	Whitish smooth chalky clay.
C	L	A	Y	M	I	L	L	Pug mill.
C	L	A	Y	M	O	R	E	Two-handed sword used by Scottish highlanders.
C	L	A	Y	W	A	R	E	Articles made of fired clay, Crockery, Bricks.
C	L	A	Y	W	E	E	D	Coltsfoot.
C	L	E	A	D	I	N	G	Lining or covering of non-conducting material, Insulating, Lagging.
C	L	E	A	M	I	N	G	Smearing, Daubing, Spreading, Adhering, Sticking.
C	L	E	A	N	I	N	G	Washing, Scraping, Purifying, Cleansing, Wiping, Gutting, Dressing, Pruning.
C	L	E	A	N	S	E	D	Freed, Purified, Absolved, Healed, Purged, Scrubbed, Eradicated, Scavenged.
C	L	E	A	N	S	E	R	Preparation for cleaning, Scouring or eradicating.
C	L	E	A	R	A	G	E	Clearance.
C	L	E	A	R	C	U	T	To remove all timber from an area.
C	L	E	A	R	E	S	T	Most lucid, Most distinct, Most transparent, Purest.
C	L	E	A	R	I	N	G	Absolving, Justifying, Vindicating, Settling, Paying, Discharging, Disappearing, Vanishing.
C	L	E	A	V	A	G	E	Parting, Division.
C	L	E	A	V	E	R	S	Goose grass, Catchweed.
C	L	E	A	V	I	N	G	Adhering, Tearing, Splitting, Dividing, Penetrating, Piercing, Forcing, Severing.
C	L	E	C	K	I	N	G	Hatching.
C	L	E	M	A	T	I	S	Genus of woody vines.
C	L	E	M	E	N	C	Y	Merciful, Compassionate, Mildness, Moderateness, Leniency.
C	L	E	N	C	H	E	D	Clutched, Clinched, Clamped, Clasped, Grappled, Gripped.
C	L	E	R	I	C	A	L	Characteristic of the clergy, Pertaining to office work.
C	L	E	R	K	E	S	S	A female clerk.
C	L	E	R	K	I	N	G	Working as a clerk.
C	L	E	R	K	I	S	H	Suggesting the work of a clerk, Overprecise of detail.
C	L	E	R	U	C	H	Y	Settlement of ancient Greeks in conquered territory.
C	L	E	V	E	I	T	E	Uraninite.
C	L	E	V	E	R	E	R	More adroit, More deft, More astute, More cunning, More intelligent.
C	L	E	V	E	R	L	Y	Fully, Completely, Entirely, Quite, Satisfactorily, Conveniently.
C	L	I	C	K	I	N	G	A sharp noise, Agreeing exactly, Operating efficiently, Succeeding, Forging.
C	L	I	E	N	T	A	L	Relating to a client.
C	L	I	M	A	T	I	C	Relating to a climate.
C	L	I	M	A	X	E	D	Came to a climax, Culminated, Crowned, Satisfied, Terminated.
C	L	I	M	B	I	N	G	Ascending, Mounting, Scaling, Escalating, Rising.

1	2	3	4	5	6	7	8	
C	L	I	N	C	H	E	D	Embraced, Clasped, Enfolded, Hugged, Pressed, Clenched, Gripped, Squeezed.
C	L	I	N	C	H	E	R	Trump card, Trump, Decisive fact, Powerful argument.
C	L	I	N	G	I	N	G	Adherence, Holding tenaciously, Bonding, Cohesion, Sticking, Attaching, Resisting pressure.
C	L	I	N	I	C	A	L	Direct observance of the living patient, Applying objective views.
C	L	I	N	N	I	D	E	Family of fishes, Blennies.
C	L	I	N	K	I	N	G	Making a sharp metallic sound, Jingling, Slapping, Striking.
C	L	I	P	P	E	R	S	Instrument for clipping hair, nails or wool of sheep.
C	L	I	P	P	I	N	G	Severing, Removing, Excising, Curtailing, Restraining, Diminishing, Cropping, Shaving.
C	L	I	Q	U	I	S	H	Forming a clique, Divide into cliques.
C	L	I	Q	U	I	S	M	Tendency to form a clique.
C	L	I	T	C	H	E	D	Clutched, Adhered.
C	L	I	T	O	R	A	L	Relating to the clitoris.
C	L	I	T	O	R	I	A	Genus of woody vines, Butterfly pea.
C	L	I	T	O	R	I	S	Small female organ homologous to the male penis.
C	L	O	A	K	I	N	G	Hiding, Disguising, Screening, Veiling, Covering, Clothing, Secreting.
C	L	O	C	H	A	R	D	Tramp, Bum, Hobo.
C	L	O	C	K	I	N	G	Timing, Registering time, Punching, Ornamenting with figured work.
C	L	O	D	D	I	N	G	Pelting with clods of earth, Hurling.
C	L	O	D	D	I	S	H	Heavy, Spiritless, Stolid, Boorish, Churlish, Loutish, Ill-bred, Unpolished.
C	L	O	D	P	A	T	E	Dunce, Blockhead, Numskull, Muttonhead, Thickskull, Bonehead.
C	L	O	D	P	O	L	L	Dimwit, Dolt, Clodpate, Dumbbell.
C	L	O	G	G	A	G	E	Condition of being clogged.
C	L	O	G	G	I	N	G	Halting, Retarding, Hampering, Curbing, Choking, Congesting, Obstructing, Plugging.
C	L	O	G	W	O	O	D	Wood used for making clogs.
C	L	O	I	S	T	E	R	A covered passage having a wall on one side and an open arcade on the other.
C	L	O	S	E	T	E	D	Secluded, Shut up, In secret consultation.
C	L	O	T	H	I	E	R	Tailor, Retailer of men's clothes.
C	L	O	T	H	I	N	G	Wearing apparel, Covering, Fitting out, Couching, Presenting, Portraying.
C	L	O	T	P	O	L	L	Clodpoll.
C	L	O	T	T	I	N	G	Coagulating, Congealing, Jellifying, Gelatinizing.
C	L	O	U	D	A	G	E	Mass of clouds.
C	L	O	U	D	I	L	Y	Indistinctly, Obscurely, Mistily, Blurred, Befogged.
C	L	O	U	D	I	N	G	Blurring, Obscuring, Misting, Billowing, Confusing, Dulling, Impairing, Distorting.
C	L	O	U	D	L	E	T	A small cloud.
C	L	O	U	R	I	N	G	Battering, Thumping.
C	L	O	U	T	I	N	G	Mending, Patching, Striking, Hitting, Cuffing, Punching, Pulling.
C	L	O	W	N	A	G	E	The function of a clown.
C	L	O	W	N	E	R	Y	Buffoonery, Behaviour of a clown.
C	L	O	W	N	I	N	G	Jesting, Ridiculing, Performing in burlesque.
C	L	O	W	N	I	S	H	Boorish, Resembling a clown.
C	L	O	Y	L	E	S	S	That does not cloy.
C	L	O	Y	S	O	M	E	Tending to cloy, excess of sweetness or sentimentality.
C	L	U	B	B	I	N	G	Striking with a club, Associating, Uniting, Combining, Fraternising, Contributing.
C	L	U	B	B	I	S	H	Tending to frequent clubs.
C	L	U	B	B	I	S	T	Member of a revolutionary club.
C	L	U	B	F	O	O	T	Congenital deformity of the foot.
C	L	U	B	H	A	N	D	Deformity of the hand.
C	L	U	B	H	A	U	L	Steering manoeuvre of a ship.
C	L	U	B	L	A	N	D	Area where many social clubs are situated.
C	L	U	B	M	O	S	S	Genus of moss with club-shaped strobiles.
C	L	U	B	R	O	O	M	Room set aside for exclusive use of club members.
C	L	U	B	R	O	O	T	Plant disease.
C	L	U	B	R	U	S	H	Bulrush.
C	L	U	B	S	T	E	R	Stoat.
C	L	U	B	W	E	E	D	Knapweed.
C	L	U	C	K	I	N	G	Clicking sound to express alarm, distress or concern, Urging.
C	L	U	M	P	I	N	G	Treading noisily, Clustering, Grouping, Striking heavily.
C	L	U	M	S	I	E	R	More awkward, More tactless.
C	L	U	M	S	I	L	Y	Awkwardly, Tactlessly, Heavily, Inefficiently.
C	L	U	P	E	O	I	D	Family of fishes, Herrings.
C	L	U	S	T	E	R	S	Bunches, Groups, Batches, Clumps, Gathers, Assembles, Bands, Collects.
C	L	U	T	C	H	E	D	Clenched, Grasped, Held, Taken.
C	L	Y	P	E	A	T	E	Having a protective shell or shield
C	N	I	D	A	R	I	A	Jellyfishes, Corals, Sea anemones.
C	O	A	C	H	B	O	X	Driver's seat on a couch.
C	O	A	C	H	D	O	G	Dalmation, A dog that used to run alongside a coach.
C	O	A	C	H	I	N	G	Touring in a coach, Receiving instruction from a coach.

1	2	3	4	5	6	7	8	Definition
C	O	A	C	H	M	A	N	Driver of a coach.
C	O	A	C	T	I	N	G	Forcing, Compelling, Driving, Controlling, Co-operative, Co-efficient.
C	O	A	C	T	I	O	N	Joint action.
C	O	A	C	T	I	V	E	Restrictive.
C	O	A	D	J	U	S	T	Adjust by mutual adaptation.
C	O	A	G	E	N	C	Y	Combined agency.
C	O	A	G	U	L	I	N	Tissue constituent that assists clotting.
C	O	A	G	U	L	U	M	Coagulated substance, Clot, Curd.
C	O	A	L	F	I	S	H	Genus of blackish fish, Pollack, Cobia.
C	O	A	L	H	O	L	E	Outside opening to allow coal to be delivered into a cellar.
C	O	A	L	E	S	C	E	Unite, Join, Mix, Connect, Link, Relate, Blend, Fuse.
C	O	A	L	P	O	R	T	Porcelain produced at Coalport in the 19th century.
C	O	A	M	I	N	G	S	Raised frames around hatchways or skylights.
C	O	A	P	P	E	A	R	Appear simultaneously.
C	O	A	R	S	E	L	Y	Vulgarly, Roughly, Stormily, Harshly, Brutally.
C	O	A	R	S	E	S	T	Most granular, Lumpiest, Crudest, Rudest, Dirtiest, Roughest, Wildest.
C	O	A	S	T	I	N	G	Skirting, Approaching, Drifting, Sliding, Freewheeling, Gliding.
C	O	A	T	C	A	R	D	Face card.
C	O	A	T	R	O	O	M	Cloakroom.
C	O	A	T	T	A	I	L	Rear flap of a man's coat.
C	O	A	U	T	H	O	R	A writer who collaborates with another in the production of a literary work.
C	O	B	A	L	T	I	C	Containing cobalt.
C	O	B	B	L	I	N	G	Mending, Patching, Repairing.
C	O	B	N	O	S	E	D	Having a large bulbous nose.
C	O	B	W	E	B	B	Y	Suggesting cobwebs, Musty, Stagnant, Cobwebbed, Festooned.
C	O	C	C	A	G	E	E	Cider apple.
C	O	C	C	I	D	A	E	Genus of insects, Mealybugs.
C	O	C	C	I	D	I	A	Parasites of the intestinal wall.
C	O	C	C	U	L	I	N	Picrotoxin, poison of the vine berry.
C	O	C	C	U	L	U	S	Small genus of slender woody vine, Very poisonous bean-shaped berry of the vine.
C	O	C	H	L	E	A	R	Pertaining to the labyrinth of the ear. Spoon used in the Eastern Church for serving wine.
C	O	C	I	N	E	R	A	Cook.
C	O	C	K	A	D	E	D	Wearing a rosette of ribbons on the hat.
C	O	C	K	A	N	D	Y	Puffin.
C	O	C	K	A	T	O	O	Large Australasian parrot with a colourful crest.
C	O	C	K	A	Y	N	E	Cockaigne, Imaginary land of luxury and ease.
C	O	C	K	B	E	L	L	Icicle.
C	O	C	K	B	I	L	L	Suspend an anchor.
C	O	C	K	B	I	R	D	Male bird.
C	O	C	K	B	O	A	T	A small boat.
C	O	C	K	C	R	O	W	Dawn, Sound suggesting crowing of a cock.
C	O	C	K	E	R	E	D	Indulged, Pampered.
C	O	C	K	E	R	E	L	Young male domestic fowl.
C	O	C	K	E	Y	E	D	Askew, Wrong, Awry, Confused, Incomprehensible, Drunk, Topsy-turvy.
C	O	C	K	H	E	A	D	Top of grinding spindle supporting the stone.
C	O	C	K	L	I	N	G	Producing cockles in fabric or paper, Rippling, Wobbling.
C	O	C	K	L	O	F	T	Small attic under the roof used for storage.
C	O	C	K	S	H	U	T	Twilight when fowls are confined to their roosts.
C	O	C	K	S	P	U	R	Spiny tree.
C	O	C	K	S	U	R	E	Sure, Certain, Positive, Confident, Convinced.
C	O	C	K	T	A	I	L	Short iced drink of spirits mixed with flavouring and liquor and served cold with a garnish.
C	O	C	O	A	N	U	T	Fruit of the coconut palm.
C	O	C	O	B	O	L	O	Genus of valuable American timber trees.
C	O	D	D	L	I	N	G	Pampering, Cooking gently, Treating with extreme care.
C	O	D	I	A	L	E	S	Siphonales, Marine and freshwater algae.
C	O	D	I	F	I	E	D	Reduced to a code, Systematized, Classified.
C	O	E	D	I	T	O	R	Part of a team concerned with editing a publication.
C	O	E	M	P	T	I	O	Ceremony symbolizing the sale of a woman to a man.
C	O	E	N	Z	Y	M	E	Nonprotein compound.
C	O	E	R	C	I	O	N	Force, Sanctions, Compulsion, Constraint, Duress, Violence, Menacing, Threat.
C	O	E	R	C	I	V	E	Compelling.
C	O	F	A	C	T	O	R	Factor occurring in multiplication, Substance acting with another substance.
C	O	F	F	E	R	E	D	Hoarded, Stored, Treasured, Secured.
C	O	F	F	E	R	E	R	Treasurer.
C	O	F	F	I	N	E	D	Enclosed in a coffin.
C	O	G	E	N	T	L	Y	Convincingly, Potently.
C	O	G	I	T	A	T	E	Think, Deliberate, Reason, Reflect, Speculate, Plan, Plot, Ponder.

1	2	3	4	5	6	7	8	Clue
C	O	G	N	A	T	U	S	Related by blood on the mother's side.
C	O	G	N	O	M	E	N	Surname.
C	O	G	N	O	S	C	E	Determine judicially with respect to sanity.
C	O	G	W	H	E	E	L	Wheel with cogs.
C	O	H	E	N	I	T	E	A tin-white crystalline mineral.
C	O	H	E	R	E	N	T	Adhered, Consistent, Connected, United.
C	O	H	E	R	I	N	G	Sticking, Adhering, Fitting together, Bonding, Clinging, Uniting, Connecting, Suiting.
C	O	H	E	S	I	O	N	Solidarity, Togetherness, Adherence, Bond, Cling.
C	O	H	E	S	I	V	E	Causing to cohere, Producing cohesion.
C	O	H	O	B	A	T	E	Redistillation.
C	O	I	F	F	E	U	R	A male hairdresser.
C	O	I	F	F	U	R	E	Hair styling, Arranging the hair, Headdress.
C	O	I	N	C	I	D	E	Concord, Agree, Concur, Identical, Correspond, Harmonize, Equal, Match.
C	O	I	N	S	U	R	E	To insure a property jointly with others.
C	O	I	N	T	I	S	E	Lady's scarf worn as a favour on a knight's helmet.
C	O	I	S	T	R	E	L	Groom for the horses of a knight, A mean creature, Varlet.
C	O	K	E	R	N	U	T	Edible seed similar to a small coconut in the fruit of the coquito palm.
C	O	L	A	M	I	N	E	Ethanolamine.
C	O	L	A	N	D	E	R	Bowl with perforations used as a strainer.
C	O	L	A	T	U	R	E	Removing solids from liquids by straining through a filter paper.
C	O	L	A	T	I	O	N	Straining.
C	O	L	D	C	O	C	K	To knock unconscious.
C	O	L	D	D	E	C	K	Cheat, Defraud, Swindle.
C	O	L	D	N	E	S	S	Chilly, Frigidness, Bleakness, Frosty, Emotionless, Indifference.
C	O	L	D	S	H	U	T	Freezing the surface of liquid metal during pouring or casting, Imperfect weld.
C	O	L	D	T	Y	P	E	A printing method.
C	O	L	E	O	N	Y	X	Genus of lizards, Ground geckos.
C	O	L	E	S	E	E	D	Seed of the rape.
C	O	L	E	S	L	A	W	Salad of raw chopped cabbage.
C	O	L	E	W	O	R	T	A young cabbage.
C	O	L	I	C	I	N	S	Antibacterial substances produced by intestinal bacteria.
C	O	L	I	F	O	R	M	Colon bacillus.
C	O	L	I	I	D	A	E	Family of birds, Colies.
C	O	L	I	N	E	A	R	Lying in the same straight line.
C	O	L	I	S	E	U	M	Stadium, Large building for sports or games with provision for many spectators.
C	O	L	L	A	G	E	N	Insoluble fibrous protein found in skin and tendons.
C	O	L	L	A	P	S	E	Crumble, Disintegrate, Yield, Shatter, Succumb, Wilt, Droop, Fail.
C	O	L	L	A	R	E	D	Stolen, Captured, Tackled, Banned, Grasped, Grabbed, Cornered, Clouted.
C	O	L	L	A	R	E	T	Necklace, Jewelled collar.
C	O	L	L	A	T	E	D	Compared, Contrasted, Bracketed, Gathered, Verified, Assembled, Arranged, Examined.
C	O	L	L	A	T	O	R	One that gathers or assembles data.
C	O	L	L	E	T	E	R	Sticky hairs on buds as horse chestnut.
C	O	L	L	E	T	I	A	Genus of spiny S. American shrubs, Anchor plant.
C	O	L	L	E	T	I	N	Plate armour for neck and shoulders.
C	O	L	L	I	C	L	E	Prominence.
C	O	L	L	I	D	E	D	Bumped, Banged, Smashed, Crashed, Jolted, Fragmented, Disagreed, Pulverized.
C	O	L	L	I	E	R	Y	Coal mine.
C	O	L	L	O	G	U	E	Intrigue, Conspire, Confer, Cogitate, Connive, Devise, Consult, Parley.
C	O	L	L	O	Q	U	Y	Conversation, Dialogue, Conference, Seminar.
C	O	L	L	U	D	E	D	Conspired, Plotted, Connived, Contrived, Devised, Schemed.
C	O	L	L	Y	I	N	G	Blackening with soot.
C	O	L	O	B	I	U	M	Short-sleeved tunic worn as an ecclesiastical vestment, Coronation robe.
C	O	L	O	B	O	M	A	Fissure of the eye.
C	O	L	O	N	A	T	E	Status of being a colony.
C	O	L	O	N	I	S	T	One that colonizes or settles in a new country.
C	O	L	O	N	I	Z	E	To establish a colony with migrants, Settle.
C	O	L	O	P	E	X	Y	Suturing operation in the abdomen.
C	O	L	O	P	H	O	N	Identifying symbol of publisher or printer in a book.
C	O	L	O	R	A	N	T	Dye, Pigment.
C	O	L	O	R	F	U	L	Striking, Exaggerated, Attractive, Bright, Vivid, Gaudy, Showy, Florid.
C	O	L	O	S	S	A	L	Huge, Elephantine, Gargantuan, Gigantic, Mammoth, Monstrous, Vast.
C	O	L	O	S	S	U	S	Larger than life size statue.
C	O	L	O	T	O	M	Y	Surgical incision of the colon.
C	O	L	O	U	R	E	D	Painted, Dyed, Shaded, Stained, Distorted, Shaped, Excused, Palliated.
C	O	L	P	I	T	I	S	Inflammation of a sheath, tendon or vagina.
C	O	L	U	M	B	I	C	Derived from the calumba root.
C	O	L	U	M	N	E	D	Having columns.

1	2	3	4	5	6	7	8	
C	O	L	U	S	I	T	E	Mineral consisting of a sulfide of copper and arsenic.
C	O	L	Y	M	B	U	S	Family of aquatic birds, Grebes.
C	O	M	A	C	I	N	E	Member of a medieval Italian guild of masons.
C	O	M	A	T	O	S	E	In a coma, Lethargic, Torpid, Drowsy, Dull, Inactive.
C	O	M	B	I	N	E	D	Joined, Associated, Coalesced, Connected, Linked, Related, United, Blended.
C	O	M	B	I	N	E	R	Machine that produces laminated board.
C	O	M	E	B	A	C	K	Repartee, Answer, Retort, Return of unsatisfactory merchandise.
C	O	M	E	D	I	A	N	Actor who plays comedy or farce, Amusing individual.
C	O	M	E	D	I	S	T	One who writes comedies.
C	O	M	E	D	O	W	N	Setback, Humiliation, Disappointment, Demotion.
C	O	M	E	L	I	L	Y	In a pleasing fashion, Behaving with propriety, Dignified.
C	O	M	E	T	A	R	Y	Relating to a comet.
C	O	M	I	N	G	I	N	Entrance, Beginning, Income, Revenue.
C	O	M	I	T	I	A	L	Assembly in ancient Rome.
C	O	M	M	A	N	D	O	Military unit trained for hit and run tactics.
C	O	M	M	A	T	I	C	Relating to a musical comma.
C	O	M	M	E	N	C	E	Begin, Start, Originate, Embark, Inaugurate, Launch, Initiate.
C	O	M	M	E	R	C	E	Trade, Traffic, Communion, Contact, Intercourse, Business, Industry, Interchange.
C	O	M	M	I	X	E	D	Mix, Comingle, Compound, Intermingle, Meld, Merge, Blend, Mingle.
C	O	M	M	O	N	E	D	Participated, Shared.
C	O	M	M	O	N	E	R	Member of the House of Commons, Not of the nobility.
C	O	M	M	O	N	L	Y	Usually, Ordinarily, Frequently, Generally.
C	O	M	M	O	N	T	Y	Right of ownership held by more than two persons with servitudes.
C	O	M	M	O	V	E	D	Agitated, Excited, Impassioned.
C	O	M	M	U	N	A	L	Shared, Owned or used by the whole community.
C	O	M	M	U	N	E	D	Associated together, Communicated earnestly.
C	O	M	M	U	T	E	D	Exchanged, Substituted, Interchanged, Altered, Compensated, Travelled regularly.
C	O	M	M	U	T	E	R	One who commutes between suburban residence and place of work in the city.
C	O	M	P	A	D	R	E	A close friend, Buddy.
C	O	M	P	A	G	E	S	Complex structure, Large geographic region.
C	O	M	P	A	R	E	D	Equated, Likened, Matched, Collaged, Bracketed, Contrasted, Rivalled, Scrutinized.
C	O	M	P	A	T	H	Y	Shared feeling, whether good or bad.
C	O	M	P	E	R	E	D	Acted as Master of Ceremonies of an entertainment, revue radio or television programmes.
C	O	M	P	E	S	C	E	Restrain.
C	O	M	P	E	T	E	D	Contended, Contested, Disputed, Battled, Rivalled, Emulated, Struggled, Vied.
C	O	M	P	I	L	E	D	Collected, Assembled, Listed, Enumerated, Piled up, Put together.
C	O	M	P	I	L	E	R	Person who assembles items of information for publication.
C	O	M	P	L	A	I	N	Lament, Bewail, Repine, Grumble, Grouse, Gripe, Croak, Squawk.
C	O	M	P	L	E	C	T	Intertwine, Embrace, Interweave, Plait together.
C	O	M	P	L	E	T	E	Balanced, Concluded, Thorough, Accomplish, Execute, Fulfill, Consummate, Close.
C	O	M	P	L	I	C	E	A partner in crime.
C	O	M	P	L	I	E	D	Obeyed, Conformed, Followed, Observed, Adapted.
C	O	M	P	L	I	E	R	One that conforms or adapts.
C	O	M	P	L	I	N	E	Last prayer of the day before retiring.
C	O	M	P	O	N	E	D	Divided into segments in heraldry.
C	O	M	P	O	S	E	D	Fashioned, Constituted, Created, Produced, Written, Calmed, Settled, Adjusted.
C	O	M	P	O	S	E	R	One that writes music, Author, Writer.
C	O	M	P	O	T	U	S	Medieval calculating tables.
C	O	M	P	O	U	N	D	Combine, Unite, Augment, Agree, Compromise, Join, Connect, Couple.
C	O	M	P	R	E	S	S	Constrict, Close, Squeeze, Embrace, Repress, Restrain, Condense, Contract.
C	O	M	P	R	I	S	E	Cover, Contain, Seize, Enclose, Fold, Constitute, Consist, Make.
C	O	M	P	U	T	E	D	Calculated, Reckoned, Estimated, Figured.
C	O	M	P	U	T	E	R	Calculator designed for solving complex mathematical problems.
C	O	N	A	C	R	E	D	To sub-let land.
C	O	N	A	R	I	A	L	Relating to the pineal gland.
C	O	N	A	R	I	T	E	Mineral consisting of hydrous nickel silicate.
C	O	N	A	R	I	U	M	Same as CONARIAL.
C	O	N	A	T	I	O	N	Conscious drive to perform volitional acts.
C	O	N	A	T	I	V	E	Denoting an attempt to perform an action.
C	O	N	C	A	U	S	E	One of several causes acting together.
C	O	N	C	A	V	E	D	Curved in, Arched in, Bowl-like depression.
C	O	N	C	E	D	E	D	Allowed, Permitted, Surrendered, Admitted, Acknowledged, Confessed, Yielded, Granted.
C	O	N	C	E	I	V	E	Impregnate, Originate, Envisage, Feature, Imagine, Visualize, Cogitate, Speculate.
C	O	N	C	E	R	T	O	Composition for one or more voices with organ or orchestral accompaniment.
C	O	N	C	E	T	T	O	Conceit, Pomposity.
C	O	N	C	H	O	I	D	Geometric figure.
C	O	N	C	L	A	V	E	Secret meeting, Conference, Convention, Gathering.

1	2	3	4	5	6	7	8	Definition
C	O	N	C	L	U	D	E	Terminate, End, Close, Infer, Complete, Determine, Resolve, Settle.
C	O	N	C	O	U	R	S	Contest, Public competition, Conflict, Meeting.
C	O	N	C	R	E	T	E	Solidify, Congeal, Combine, Blend, Fuse, Unite, Harden, Set.
C	O	N	D	E	N	S	E	Abridge, Compress, Contract, Concentrate, Constrict, Shrink, Compact, Consolidate.
C	O	N	D	I	T	E	D	Pickled, Preserved, Embalmed.
C	O	N	D	O	L	E	D	Grieved, Sympathized, Commiserated, Expressed formal regrets.
C	O	N	D	O	N	E	D	Overlooked, Pardoned, Forgiven, Excused, Permitted, Ignored, Forgotten, Disregarded.
C	O	N	D	U	C	E	D	Effected, Contributed, Tended.
C	O	N	E	L	R	A	D	System for preventing an enemy from using radio signals to guide aircraft or missiles.
C	O	N	F	E	R	V	A	Genus of green algae that forms scum in sluggish freshwater.
C	O	N	F	E	T	T	I	Tiny coloured paper discs used at carnivals, parties or weddings.
C	O	N	F	I	D	E	D	Trusted, Entrusted, Committed, Intimated, Consigned, Relegated, Whispered.
C	O	N	F	I	N	E	D	Imprisoned, Secured, Enclosed, Fastened, Limited, Restricted, Circumscribed, Constrained.
C	O	N	F	I	N	E	R	Neighbour, Inhabitant.
C	O	N	F	L	A	T	E	Assembled, Blended, Consolidated, Fuse, Collect, Merge, Confuse.
C	O	N	F	L	I	C	T	Clash, Competition, Antagonism, Struggle, Contest, Discord, Warfare, Strife.
C	O	N	F	O	C	A	L	Use of conic sections.
C	O	N	F	O	U	N	D	Baffle, Spoil, Corrupt, Discomfit, Abash, Stupefy, Perplex, Confuse.
C	O	N	F	R	E	R	E	Colleague, Fellow, Comrade.
C	O	N	F	R	O	N	T	Face, Affront, Oppress, Meet, Encounter, Challenge, Defy, Flout.
C	O	N	F	U	S	E	D	Disconcerted, Flustered, Misled, Bewildered, Perplexed, Blurred, Confounded, Embarrassed.
C	O	N	F	U	T	E	D	Overcome, Silenced, Disproved, Confounded, Rebutted, Controverted.
C	O	N	G	E	N	E	R	Member of the same genus, Person or thing resembling another.
C	O	N	G	I	A	R	Y	Present made to soldiers or people in ancient Rome.
C	O	N	G	L	O	B	E	To form into a ball.
C	O	N	G	R	E	E	T	Mutual greeting.
C	O	N	G	R	E	S	S	Association, Club, Fellowship, Fraternity, Guild, League, Society, Union.
C	O	N	I	C	I	T	Y	State of being conical.
C	O	N	I	C	O	I	D	Quadric, A surface of second degree.
C	O	N	I	F	O	R	M	Shaped like a form.
C	O	N	J	O	I	N	T	United, Conjoined, Combined, Simultaneous.
C	O	N	J	U	G	A	L	Matrimonial, Connubial, Nuptial, Married, Spousal, Wedded.
C	O	N	J	U	N	C	T	Joined, United, Communal, Mutual, Public, Shared.
C	O	N	J	U	R	E	D	Implored, Beseeched, Invented, Contrived, Conspired, Juggled, Charmed, Supplicated.
C	O	N	J	U	R	E	R	Magician, Juggler, Wizard.
C	O	N	J	U	R	O	R	Same as CONJURER.
C	O	N	N	A	R	U	S	Genus of tropical shrubs bearing one-seeded pods, Zebrawood.
C	O	N	N	I	V	E	D	Conspired, Intrigued, Condoned, Ignored, Overlooked, Tolerated, Machinated, Devised.
C	O	N	N	I	V	E	R	Conspirator.
C	O	N	N	O	T	E	D	Meant, Signified, Implied, Suggested, Denoted, Expressed, Hinted, Insinuated.
C	O	N	O	I	D	A	L	Resembling the shape of a cone.
C	O	N	Q	U	E	S	T	Conquer, Vanquish, Victory, Triumph, Win, Defeating, Overthrow, Rout.
C	O	N	S	E	R	V	E	Save, Preserve, Maintain, Support, Sustain, Jam, Confiture, Hoard.
C	O	N	S	I	D	E	R	Respect, Esteem, Regard, Account, Reckon, Deem, Contemplate, Study.
C	O	N	S	O	L	E	D	Comforted, Soothed, Cheered, Relieved, Tranquilized, Heartened.
C	O	N	S	O	M	M	E	Meat broth cleared and strained.
C	O	N	S	P	I	R	E	Plot, Plan, Contrive, Collogue, Collude, Connive, Devise, Intrigue.
C	O	N	S	P	U	E	D	Spurned with contempt.
C	O	N	S	T	A	N	T	Steady, Uniform, Immovable, Solid, Positive, Certain, Faithful, Fixed.
C	O	N	S	T	R	U	E	Explain, Explicate, Expound, Interpret, Construct, Understand.
C	O	N	S	U	L	A	R	Duties or powers of a consul.
C	O	N	S	U	M	E	D	Destroyed, Squandered, Expended, Engrossed, Perished, Monopolized, Dissipated.
C	O	N	S	U	M	E	R	Customer, One that utilizes economic goods.
C	O	N	S	U	M	P	T	Consumption.
C	O	N	T	A	N	G	O	Premium or interest paid on a fixed day for a certain consideration.
C	O	N	T	E	M	P	T	Disdain, Scorn, Disgrace, Shame, Disparagement, Aversion, Distate, Repugnance.
C	O	N	T	E	N	T	S	Topics, Ideas, Facts, Statements, Things contained, Capacity.
C	O	N	T	I	N	U	E	Persevere, Endure, Persist, Last, Abide, Outlast, Survive, Remain.
C	O	N	T	R	A	C	T	Agreement, Bargain, Compact, Covenant, Constrict, Concentrate, Compress, Shrink.
C	O	N	T	R	A	I	L	Streaks of condensed water vapour created in the air by an airplane or rocket.
C	O	N	T	R	A	R	Y	Perverse, Restive, Wayward, Cantankerous, Unfavourable, Antagonistic, Discordant.
C	O	N	T	R	A	S	T	Divergence, Comparison, Collate.
C	O	N	T	R	A	T	E	Having gear teeth set on face of wheel and perpendicular to its plane.
C	O	N	T	R	I	T	E	Remorseful, Apologetic, Attritional, Penitent, Regretful, Repentant, Sorry.
C	O	N	T	R	I	V	E	Devise, Invent, Frame, Concoct, Consume, Pass, Manipulate, Formulate.
C	O	N	T	U	S	E	D	Bruised, Injured, Disorganized, Pounded, Beaten.
C	O	N	V	E	N	E	D	Met, Assembled, Mustered, Summoned, Convoked.

1	2	3	4	5	6	7	8	
C	O	N	V	E	N	E	R	The chairman of an organized body of persons.
C	O	N	V	E	R	G	E	Meet, Join, Concentrate focus.
C	O	N	V	E	R	S	E	Speak, Associate, Obverse, Reverse, Talk, Contrary, Dialogue, Opposite.
C	O	N	V	E	X	E	D	Bowed outward in a curve, Curved exterior, Arched up, Bulging out.
C	O	N	V	E	Y	E	D	Carried, Transmitted, Stolen, Conducted, Transported, Ferried, Transferred, Assigned.
C	O	N	V	E	Y	E	R	One that carries, transmits or transfers.
C	O	N	V	E	Y	O	R	Same as CONVEYER.
C	O	N	V	I	N	C	E	Confute, Demonstrate, Prove, Assure, Persuade, Satisfy, Induce, Prevail.
C	O	N	V	O	K	E	D	Summoned, Assembled, Convened, Congregated, Gathered, Collected, Invited, Requested.
C	O	N	V	O	L	V	E	Roll together, Twist, Writhe, Circulate.
C	O	N	V	O	Y	E	D	Accompanied, Conducted, Attended, Escorted, Defended, Guarded, Protected, Shielded.
C	O	N	V	U	L	S	E	Shake, Agitate, Rock, Concuss, Laugh violently.
C	O	N	Y	R	I	N	E	An oily base obtained as a decomposition produce of conine.
C	O	O	K	A	B	L	E	Foodstuff to be cooked.
C	O	O	K	R	O	O	M	Kitchen, Galley.
C	O	O	K	S	H	O	P	Eating house, Shop supplying or serving cooked food.
C	O	O	L	A	M	O	N	Australian wooden bowl for carrying water.
C	O	O	L	N	E	S	S	Chilliness, Calmness, Self-possession, Self-assurance, Equanimity, Imperturbability.
C	O	O	N	R	O	O	T	Bloodroot.
C	O	O	N	S	K	I	N	Article made of the pelt of a racoon.
C	O	O	N	T	A	I	L	Hornwort.
C	O	O	P	E	R	E	D	Secured with hoops, Packed in barrels, Spoiled, Ruined.
C	O	O	P	E	R	I	A	Genus of Amaryllis, Genus of nematode worms.
C	O	O	P	T	I	N	G	Choosing, Electing, Appointing, Preempting, Commandeering.
C	O	O	S	S	I	F	Y	Growing together of bones.
C	O	P	A	L	C	H	I	Shrub or tree having medicinal bark.
C	O	P	A	T	A	I	N	A sugarloaf hat.
C	O	P	E	P	O	D	A	Minute aquatic organisms.
C	O	P	H	A	S	A	L	Having the same phase.
C	O	P	L	A	N	A	R	Lying in the same plane.
C	O	P	P	E	R	A	S	Green ferrous sulfate heptahydrate.
C	O	P	P	E	R	E	D	Coated or treated with copper.
C	O	P	R	I	N	U	S	Genus of black-spored mushrooms.
C	O	P	R	O	S	M	A	Genus of shrubs found in New Zealand, Australia and Hawaii.
C	O	P	U	L	A	T	E	Join, Unite, Sexual intercourse, Engage in coitus, Fuse permanently.
C	O	P	Y	B	O	O	K	Book used for practising penmanship, Conventional.
C	O	P	Y	H	O	L	D	Out-of-date condition of land tenure.
C	O	Q	U	E	T	R	Y	Flirting, Philandering, Trifling, Dallying.
C	O	Q	U	E	T	T	E	A flirt, Vamp.
C	O	R	A	C	I	A	S	Genus of birds resembling the kingfishers.
C	O	R	A	C	I	T	E	Uraninite.
C	O	R	A	C	O	I	D	Cartilage bone of the shoulder girdle.
C	O	R	A	L	L	I	C	Like coral.
C	O	R	A	L	L	U	M	Entire skeleton of a compound coral.
C	O	R	A	M	I	N	E	Used for nikethamide.
C	O	R	D	A	T	E	D	Shaped like a heart.
C	O	R	D	E	L	L	E	Towline for a boat.
C	O	R	D	O	V	A	N	Soft fine-grained coloured leather.
C	O	R	D	U	R	O	Y	Cotton, ribbed, cut-pile fabric, Road of logs across a swamp.
C	O	R	D	W	A	I	N	Cordovan leather.
C	O	R	D	W	O	O	D	Wood sold for firewood.
C	O	R	E	M	I	U	M	Imperfect fungi.
C	O	R	I	A	R	I	A	Genus of shrubs with a purplish fruit.
C	O	R	I	N	D	O	N	Aluminium oxide.
C	O	R	K	L	I	N	E	Upper edge of a net with corks to give it buoyancy.
C	O	R	K	T	R	E	E	Cork oak, Prickly Australian coral tree.
C	O	R	K	W	I	N	G	European wrasse.
C	O	R	K	W	O	O	D	Tropical American or Australian trees and shrubs having lightweight or corky wood.
C	O	R	N	B	A	L	L	Ball of popped corn and molasses.
C	O	R	N	B	E	E	F	Corned beef.
C	O	R	N	B	I	N	D	Corn bindweed.
C	O	R	N	C	A	K	E	Corn bread baked in a pan in the oven.
C	O	R	N	E	O	U	S	Horny.
C	O	R	N	E	R	E	D	Driven into a corner, Commanded the market, Captured, Caught, At bay, Controlled.
C	O	R	N	E	T	C	Y	Commission of a cornet, lowest rank of officer.
C	O	R	N	F	L	A	G	Genus of gladiolus, Yellow iris.
C	O	R	N	I	C	H	E	Road built along the face of the cliff.

8 LETTERS

1	2	3	4	5	6	7	8	Definition
C	O	R	N	I	C	L	E	A little horn.
C	O	R	N	I	F	I	C	Forming horn.
C	O	R	N	L	A	N	D	Land suitable for growing corn.
C	O	R	N	L	O	F	T	Granary.
C	O	R	N	M	E	A	L	Meal made from white or yellow corn.
C	O	R	N	M	I	L	L	Flour mill.
C	O	R	N	M	I	N	T	An European mint.
C	O	R	N	P	O	N	E	Corn bread often made without milk or eggs and fried on a griddle.
C	O	R	N	U	T	E	D	Cuckolded, Husband deceived by an adulterous wife.
C	O	R	O	N	A	C	H	Dirge, Lamentation for the dead played on the bagpipes.
C	O	R	O	N	A	D	O	Amberjack, Large sport fish.
C	O	R	O	N	A	R	Y	Forming a crown, Involving the heart.
C	O	R	O	N	A	T	E	Crown.
C	O	R	O	N	I	O	N	Tip of the coronoid process of the jaw.
C	O	R	O	N	I	U	M	A hypothetical chemical element.
C	O	R	O	N	O	I	D	Indicating the coronoid process.
C	O	R	O	N	U	L	E	Ring of spines on the shells of some diatoms.
C	O	R	P	O	R	A	L	Belonging to the body, Material, Physical, Bodily, Non-commissioned officer.
C	O	R	R	A	N	T	O	Romp, Carouse.
C	O	R	R	I	D	O	R	Passageway, Gallery, Narrow strip of land, Open strip.
C	O	R	R	I	V	A	L	Rival, Competitor.
C	O	R	R	O	D	E	D	Eaten, Gnawed, Worn, Eroded, Scoured, Weakened, Diminished.
C	O	R	S	E	L	E	T	Tight-fitting garment covering the trunk, Armour for the upper trunk.
C	O	R	S	I	C	A	N	Relating to the island of Corsica.
C	O	R	T	I	C	A	L	The outer cover of something, Mental as opposed to sensory.
C	O	R	U	N	D	U	M	Aluminium oxide as coloured gems.
C	O	R	V	E	T	T	E	Escort ship smaller than a warship.
C	O	R	V	I	D	A	E	Family of birds including ravens, crows, magpies and jays.
C	O	R	Y	B	A	N	T	Relating to the goddess Cybele, Priests of Cybele.
C	O	R	Y	D	I	N	E	A crystalline alkaloid.
C	O	R	Y	D	O	R	A	Small catfishes.
C	O	R	Y	P	H	E	E	Chorus girl, Ballerina, Danseuse, Dancing girl.
C	O	S	E	C	A	N	T	Geometrical diagram for describing angles.
C	O	S	H	E	R	E	D	Lived at the expense of another, Sponged, Pampered.
C	O	S	H	E	R	E	R	One that cadges or sponges.
C	O	S	I	N	E	S	S	Coziness, Snugness, Warmness.
C	O	S	M	E	T	I	C	Beautifying, Correcting defects, Preparation for beautifying the human body.
C	O	S	M	I	C	A	L	Relating to the terrestrial world, Cosmic.
C	O	S	S	E	T	E	D	Petted, Fondled, Pampered.
C	O	S	T	A	R	D	S	Strip or slice, Chip.
C	O	S	T	A	T	E	D	Ridged.
C	O	S	T	B	O	O	K	Shareholders book pertaining to a mine.
C	O	S	T	L	E	S	S	Costing nothing.
C	O	S	T	L	I	E	R	More costly, More expensive, More extravagant, Dearer.
C	O	S	T	M	A	R	Y	A tansy-scented herb.
C	O	S	T	P	L	U	S	Addition of percentage or fixed free to a contract price as profit.
C	O	S	T	U	M	E	D	Provided with a costume, Designing costumes for a specific use.
C	O	S	T	U	M	E	R	One that specialises in costumes for stage or fancy-dress.
C	O	S	U	R	E	T	Y	To act as surety with another person or company.
C	O	T	C	H	I	N	G	Catching.
C	O	T	E	N	A	N	T	Being a tenant jointly with another.
C	O	T	E	R	E	L	L	Cotter.
C	O	T	H	O	U	S	E	Cottage.
C	O	T	I	L	L	O	N	Ballroom dance that resembles the quadrille.
C	O	T	O	N	I	E	R	Sycamore.
C	O	T	Q	U	E	A	N	Wife of a cotter.
C	O	T	S	W	O	L	D	English breed of a long-wooled sheep.
C	O	T	T	A	G	E	R	Cotter, Rural labourer, Peasant, Resident of a cottage.
C	O	T	T	O	N	E	D	Coddled, Succeeded, Agreed, Fraternized, Taken, Understood, Toadied, Perceived.
C	O	T	Y	L	O	I	D	Relating to cup-shaped socket of the hip joint, Acetabular.
C	O	U	C	H	A	N	T	Prone, Lying down with the head up in heraldry.
C	O	U	C	H	I	N	G	Reclining, Phrasing, Composing, Kneeling, Lurking.
C	O	U	D	I	E	R	E	Elbow guard in armour.
C	O	U	G	H	I	N	G	An explosive noise. Expelling air from the lungs, Single shot.
C	O	U	L	I	S	S	E	Side scene of a stage, Lobby or corridor.
C	O	U	M	A	L	I	N	Pyrone or any of the derivatives.
C	O	U	M	A	R	A	N	A colourless oil.

1	2	3	4	5	6	7	8	Clue
C	O	U	M	A	R	I	N	Toxic white crystalline lactone with an odour of new mown hay found in tonka-beans.
C	O	U	M	A	R	O	U	The tonka-bean tree.
C	O	U	N	T	E	S	S	Wife or widow of an earl or count.
C	O	U	N	T	I	N	G	Tallying, Reckoning, Numbering, Accounting, Enumerating, Relying.
C	O	U	N	T	O	U	T	Exclude, Boxing knock-out, False return of votes.
C	O	U	P	L	I	N	G	Joining, Linking, Connecting, Recording, Uniting, Combining, Harnessing, Yoking.
C	O	U	R	A	N	T	E	A dance of Italian origin, Romp, Carouse.
C	O	U	R	S	I	N	G	Pursuing, Chasing, Running, Trouncing, Racing, Pulsating, Surging, Hunting.
C	O	U	R	T	D	A	Y	A day when the court is in session.
C	O	U	R	T	E	S	Y	Well-mannered behaviour, Gallantry, Attention, Chivalry, Civility, Dispensation.
C	O	U	R	T	I	E	R	Attendant at the royal court.
C	O	U	R	T	I	N	G	Paying homage, Paying attention with a view to marriage, Wooing.
C	O	U	S	C	O	U	S	A N. African dish of steamed cracked wheat with meat and vegetables or fruits and nuts.
C	O	U	S	I	N	L	Y	Becoming a cousin.
C	O	U	S	I	N	R	Y	Body of cousins.
C	O	U	V	E	R	T	E	Hard procelain glaze.
C	O	V	A	L	E	N	T	Characterized by covalence.
C	O	V	E	N	A	N	T	Contract, Promise, Bond, Pact, Vow, Pledge, Plight, Swear.
C	O	V	E	N	T	R	Y	Being ostracized or excluded by society for objectionable behaviour.
C	O	V	E	R	A	G	E	Insurance, Ground cover, Circulation of a publication.
C	O	V	E	R	A	L	L	An outer garment worn to protect other clothing, Comprehensive.
C	O	V	E	R	I	N	G	Guarding, Protecting, Commanding, Concealing, Blanketing, Enveloping, Filming.
C	O	V	E	R	L	E	T	Bedspread.
C	O	V	E	R	L	I	D	Same as COVERLET.
C	O	V	E	R	T	L	Y	Secretly, Clandestinely, Furtively, Privately, Stealthily, Surreptitiously.
C	O	V	E	T	I	N	G	Wishing, Craving, Desiring, Choosing, Wanting, Envying.
C	O	V	E	T	O	U	S	Greedy, Grasping, Acquisitive, Avaricious, Envious, Desirous, Rapacious, Ravenous.
C	O	V	I	N	O	U	S	Collusive, Fraudulent, Tricking, Deceiving, Conspiring, Scheming, Plotting.
C	O	W	A	R	D	L	Y	Cravenly, Dastardly, Gutless, Unmanly, Afraid, Panicky.
C	O	W	B	E	R	R	Y	Mountain cranberry.
C	O	W	E	R	I	N	G	Shrinking, Cringing, Squatting, Bending down, Flinching, Wincing, Quailing, Recoiling.
C	O	W	G	R	A	S	S	Red clover.
C	O	W	H	I	D	E	D	Flogged with a cowhide whip.
C	O	W	H	O	U	S	E	A barn for cows.
C	O	W	O	R	K	E	R	A Fellow worker.
C	O	W	P	I	L	O	T	Sergeant major.
C	O	W	W	H	E	A	T	A herb considered a weed in European wheat fields.
C	O	X	A	L	G	I	A	Hip-joint disease, Pain in the hip.
C	O	X	I	E	L	L	A	Genus of small micro-organism occurring in biting ticks and causing transmission of disease.
C	O	X	S	W	A	I	N	A sailor who steers a small power or rowing boat.
C	O	Z	E	N	A	G	E	Fraud, Practising deception, Artifice.
C	O	Z	E	N	I	N	G	Cheating, Defrauding, Deluding, Deceiving, Tricking.
C	R	A	B	B	I	N	G	Angering, Irritating, Spoiling, Ruining, Grousing, Complaining, Criticizing, Scratching.
C	R	A	B	T	R	E	E	Crab-apple tree.
C	R	A	B	W	O	O	D	A tree of West Indies and Florida that contains a poisonous juice.
C	R	A	B	Y	A	W	S	Thickening of the skin on the soles of the feet with fissures and ulcers as result of lesion.
C	R	A	C	K	I	N	G	Breaking, Wrecking, Ruining, Slapping, Bursting, Bragging, Extolling, Failing.
C	R	A	C	K	J	A	W	Hard to pronounce, Jawbreaking.
C	R	A	C	K	L	E	D	Sparkled, Crushed, Crazed, Covered with minute cracks.
C	R	A	C	K	L	O	O	A gambling game.
C	R	A	C	K	N	E	L	A hard brittle biscuit.
C	R	A	C	K	P	O	T	Someone given to lunatic ideas or eccentric notions, Impractical person.
C	R	A	D	L	I	N	G	Sheltering, Rearing, Holding closely, Cuddling.
C	R	A	F	T	I	E	R	Slyer, More cunning, Wilier, More ingenious.
C	R	A	F	T	I	L	Y	Skilfully, Artfully, Slyly.
C	R	A	G	S	M	A	N	Expert cliff climber.
C	R	A	M	F	U	L	L	Overflowing, As full as can be.
C	R	A	M	M	I	N	G	Jamming, Stuffing, Bolting, Packing, Brimming, Thrusting, Driving, Tutoring.
C	R	A	M	O	I	S	Y	Crimson cloth.
C	R	A	M	P	I	N	G	Compressing, Restraining, Confining, Shackling.
C	R	A	M	P	O	N	S	Grappling irons, Climing iron for use on boots on ice.
C	R	A	N	E	F	L	Y	Resembling mosquitoes that do not not bite but produce larvae destructive to grassroots.
C	R	A	N	K	I	N	G	Winding, Turning, Zigzagging, Operating by a crank.
C	R	A	N	K	I	S	H	Freakish, Crackpot, Perverse.
C	R	A	N	K	P	I	N	Bearing support on a crank shaft.
C	R	A	N	N	I	E	D	Full of crannies, Penetrated through crevices.
C	R	A	N	N	I	E	S	Niches, Crevices, Clefts, Fissures, Corners, Nooks, Cracks.

1	2	3	4	5	6	7	8	
C	R	A	S	H	I	N	G	Smashing, Shattering, Gnashing, Failing, Breaking, Banging, Clapping, Blasting.
C	R	A	S	S	U	L	A	Genus of S. African succulent herb.
C	R	A	T	A	E	V	A	Small genus of tropical shrubs, Garlic pear.
C	R	A	T	C	H	E	S	Gratings, Mangers, Frames, Racks for fodder.
C	R	A	T	E	R	A	L	Belonging to a crater.
C	R	A	T	E	R	E	D	Full of craters.
C	R	A	V	E	N	L	Y	Cowardly, Abjectly.
C	R	A	W	C	R	A	W	Skin disease caused by infiltration of skin by minute worms that cause intense irritation.
C	R	A	W	F	I	S	H	Crayfish, Spiny lobster.
C	R	A	W	L	I	N	G	Creeping, Trailing, Sliding, Grovelling, Worming, Teeming, Flowing, Swarming.
C	R	A	Y	F	I	S	H	Crustacean resembling a small lobster.
C	R	A	Y	O	N	E	D	Drawing coloured or decorated with a crayon.
C	R	A	Z	I	E	S	T	Frailest, Wildest, Oddest, Most unusual, Most eccentric, Weirdest.
C	R	E	A	K	I	N	G	Croaking, Grating, Squeaking.
C	R	E	A	M	E	R	Y	Dairy, Place where butter and cheese are processed and sold.
C	R	E	A	M	I	N	G	Blending, Foaming, Frothing, Whipping, Removing the best part, Beating, Blasting.
C	R	E	A	M	N	U	T	Brazil nut.
C	R	E	A	S	I	N	G	Grooving, Ridging, Folding, Furrowing, Crinkling, Ruckling, Corrugating, Wrinkling.
C	R	E	A	S	O	T	E	Creosote.
C	R	E	A	T	I	N	E	White crystalline compound found in muscles, blood and meat extracts.
C	R	E	A	T	I	N	G	Producing, Appointing, Inventing, Griping, Generating, Making, Establishing, Originating.
C	R	E	A	T	I	O	N	Universe, Cosmos, Nature, World, Act of devising, Original work of art.
C	R	E	A	T	I	V	E	Productive, Imaginative, Ingenious, Innovative, Original.
C	R	E	A	T	R	I	X	Female author, inventor or founder.
C	R	E	A	T	U	R	E	Person, Beast, Animal, Brute, Toady, Individual, Mortal Sycophant.
C	R	E	B	R	I	T	Y	Frequency.
C	R	E	D	E	N	C	E	Belief, Credit, Faith, Trustworthiness, Reliability, Acceptance, Reliance, Admitting.
C	R	E	D	E	N	D	A	Articles of faith.
C	R	E	D	E	N	Z	A	Server, sideboard, buffet or bookcase without legs.
C	R	E	D	I	B	L	E	Trustworthy, Believable, Plausible, Satisfying, Solid, Convincing, Authentic, Valid.
C	R	E	D	I	B	L	Y	Validly, Believably, Authentically, Genuinely.
C	R	E	D	I	T	E	D	Accepted, Honoured, Acknowledged, Recognized, Entrusted, Ascribed, Assigned.
C	R	E	D	I	T	O	R	One to whom money or an obligation is owed, Mortgagee, Lender.
C	R	E	E	D	I	T	E	A mineral consisting of hydrous calcium aluminium flouride with calcium sulfate.
C	R	E	E	P	A	G	E	Leakage of electricity, Slow spreading of rust.
C	R	E	E	P	I	L	Y	Eerily, Uncannily.
C	R	E	E	P	I	N	G	Crawling, Stealing, Cringing, Sliding, Snaking, Wriggling, Slithering, Sneaking.
C	R	E	M	A	T	O	R	Attendant in a crematorium.
C	R	E	N	A	T	E	D	Having the margin cut into rounded scallops.
C	R	E	N	E	L	L	E	An opening in the parapet of a fortified building used for defence.
C	R	E	O	D	O	N	T	Extinct primitive mammals.
C	R	E	O	L	I	T	E	Californian jasper.
C	R	E	O	L	I	Z	E	Adopt Creole customs.
C	R	E	O	S	O	T	E	Oily liquid obtained by the distillation of wood tar and used as an expectorant.
C	R	E	P	A	N	C	E	Injury to a horse's leg caused by interference.
C	R	E	P	I	T	U	S	Crepitation, Grating or crackling sound or sensation.
C	R	E	S	C	E	N	T	Shape of the new moon, Figure defined by a convex and concave edge.
C	R	E	S	C	I	V	E	Increasing, Growing.
C	R	E	S	T	I	N	G	Topping, Crowning, Surmounting, Ornamental crest.
C	R	E	S	Y	L	I	C	Derived from creosote.
C	R	E	T	A	C	I	C	Chalky.
C	R	E	T	O	N	N	E	Strong unglazed cotton or linen fabric.
C	R	E	U	T	Z	E	R	Kretzer, Small silver or copper coin of Austria, Germany or Hungary.
C	R	E	V	A	L	L	E	Cavalla, Food fish.
C	R	E	V	A	S	S	E	Opening, Chasm, Split in the earth.
C	R	E	V	I	C	E	D	Having a crevice.
C	R	I	B	B	A	G	E	A card game.
C	R	I	B	B	I	N	G	Pilfering, Purloining, Stealing, Plagiarizing, Cheating.
C	R	I	B	B	L	E	D	Made a pattern of small round holes or dots.
C	R	I	B	R	O	S	E	Like a sieve.
C	R	I	B	R	O	U	S	Perforated.
C	R	I	B	W	O	R	K	Framework made with logs.
C	R	I	C	E	T	I	D	Family of rodents, Lemmings, Voles, Rats, Mice.
C	R	I	C	E	T	U	S	Genus of mammals, Hamsters.
C	R	I	M	E	F	U	L	Marked by crime, Criminal.
C	R	I	M	I	N	A	L	Reprehensible, Blameworthy, Disgraceful, Excessive, Extortionate, Felon, Convict.
C	R	I	M	P	A	G	E	Money paid to a crimp for his services.

1	2	3	4	5	6	7	8	
C	R	I	M	P	I	N	G	Wrinkling, Creasing, Waving, Curling, Gashing, Corrugating, Inhibiting, Cramping.
C	R	I	M	S	O	N	Y	Tinged with crimson.
C	R	I	N	G	I	N	G	Shrinking, Huddling, Crouching, Fawning, Contracting, Contorting, Abject, Servile.
C	R	I	N	K	L	E	D	Turned, Rippled, Rustled, Curled, Winding, Folded.
C	R	I	P	P	L	E	D	Hobbled, Halted, Maimed, Weakened, Disabled, Incapacitated.
C	R	I	S	P	A	T	E	Crisped, Irregularly curled.
C	R	I	S	P	I	N	G	Curling, Crimping, Wrinkling, Crackling, Folding.
C	R	I	S	T	A	T	E	Crested.
C	R	I	T	E	R	I	A	Standards of judgment.
C	R	I	T	I	C	A	L	Crucial, dangerous, censorious, desperate, dire, disparaging.
C	R	I	T	I	Q	U	E	Criticize, Review.
C	R	O	A	K	I	N	G	Hoarse, Raucous voice, Complaining, Protesting.
C	R	O	C	E	O	U	S	Saffron.
C	R	O	C	K	A	R	D	13th Century English base metal coin worth a half-penny.
C	R	O	C	K	E	R	Y	Earthenware, China articles for domestic use.
C	R	O	C	K	I	N	G	Disabling, Breaking down, Becoming impaired.
C	R	O	C	O	I	T	E	Mineral of native lead, chromate in monoclinic crystals.
C	R	O	F	T	I	N	G	Exposing on a grass for bleaching, Living in a croft.
C	R	O	M	L	E	C	H	Circle of monoliths.
C	R	O	M	O	R	N	A	8 foot pitch reed organ stop.
C	R	O	N	Y	I	S	M	Appointing hangers-on without qualifications to political offices.
C	R	O	O	D	L	E	D	Made a low murmuring sound, Snuggled, Cuddled, Nested, Nestled.
C	R	O	O	K	E	R	Y	Crooked dealings or practices.
C	R	O	O	K	I	N	G	Bending, Misapplying, Cheating, Manipulating, Curving, Bowing, Bilking, Swindling.
C	R	O	O	N	I	N	G	Lamenting, Wailing, Moaning, Lowing, Lulling, Special type of singing.
C	R	O	P	P	I	N	G	Cutting, Lopping, Pruning, Trimming, Shearing, Plucking, Reaping, Harvesting.
C	R	O	P	S	I	C	K	Sick from overeating or drinking to excess.
C	R	O	S	S	A	R	M	A member fastened at right angles to the upright.
C	R	O	S	S	B	A	R	Horizontal brace of a cross, Rung, Top bar of a cycle frame.
C	R	O	S	S	B	I	T	Rock drill for mining.
C	R	O	S	S	B	O	W	A bow with a mechanical device to draw back the string.
C	R	O	S	S	C	U	T	To cut transversely, Intersect, Divide, Cross section.
C	R	O	S	S	I	N	G	Intersecting, Blessing, Eradicating, Thwarting, Contradicting, Traversing, Obstructing.
C	R	O	S	S	L	E	T	Crucible, Small Greek cross, A cross in heraldry.
C	R	O	S	S	R	I	B	An arch supporting and strengthening a vault.
C	R	O	S	S	R	O	W	The alphabet.
C	R	O	S	S	S	E	A	A choppy sea in which the waves run in different directions.
C	R	O	S	S	T	I	E	A railway sleeper.
C	R	O	S	S	W	A	Y	Crossroad.
C	R	O	T	A	L	I	C	Relating to rattlesnakes.
C	R	O	T	A	L	I	D	Pit viper.
C	R	O	T	A	L	I	N	Venom of a rattlesnake.
C	R	O	T	A	L	U	M	One of a pair of small cymbals used by dancers in ancient times.
C	R	O	T	C	H	E	D	Notched, Married, Spliced, A certain play in billiards.
C	R	O	T	C	H	E	T	Small hooked instrument, Whim, Peculiarity, Trick, Dodge, Device.
C	R	O	T	E	S	C	O	Grotesque.
C	R	O	T	O	N	Y	L	The univalent radical of crotonic acid.
C	R	O	T	O	X	I	N	A crystalline neurotoxin obtained from the venom of a rattlesnake.
C	R	O	T	T	L	E	S	Hare droppings, Lichens used in dyeing.
C	R	O	U	C	H	E	D	Stooped with limbs close to the body, Bent, Cringed, Fawned, Bowed.
C	R	O	U	P	A	D	E	A leap of a horse with the hind legs well under its belly.
C	R	O	U	P	I	E	R	Employee of a casino officiating at a gaming table.
C	R	O	U	P	O	U	S	Resembling croup.
C	R	O	W	B	A	I	T	A worn-out emaciated horse.
C	R	O	W	B	I	L	L	Conical arrowhead made of horn.
C	R	O	W	D	I	N	G	Hurrying, Forcing, Thronging, Compressing, Cramming, Pushing, Jostling, Packing.
C	R	O	W	F	O	O	T	Genus of flowers resembling a bird's foot.
C	R	O	W	L	I	N	G	Stunting, Dwarfing.
C	R	O	W	N	I	N	G	Enriching, Adorning, Climaxing, Culminating, Cresting, Surmounting, Capping, Topping.
C	R	O	W	N	S	A	W	A saw for cutting round holes.
C	R	O	W	S	O	A	P	Soapwort.
C	R	U	C	I	A	T	E	Cross-shaped, Cruciform, Crossing.
C	R	U	C	I	B	L	E	A vessel used in a laboratory for melting a substance.
C	R	U	C	I	F	E	R	One that crucifies.
C	R	U	C	I	F	I	X	A representation of Christ on the cross, A gymnastic stunt.
C	R	U	D	I	T	E	S	A selection of raw vegetable snacks.
C	R	U	E	L	E	S	T	Most sadistic, Fiercest, Most severe, Sternest, Grimmest.

8 LETTERS

1	2	3	4	5	6	7	8	
C	R	U	I	S	I	N	G	Sailing from port to port, Voyaging at random, Travelling at a speed for maximum operation.
C	R	U	M	B	I	N	G	Covering food with crumbs before cooking.
C	R	U	M	B	L	E	D	Disintegrated, Collapsed, Decayed, Ruined, Broken into small pieces.
C	R	U	M	E	N	A	S	A pouch or purse.
C	R	U	M	M	O	C	K	A staff with a crooked head.
C	R	U	M	P	L	E	D	Rumpled, Creased, Collapsed, Wrinkled.
C	R	U	N	C	H	E	D	Ground, Pressed, Crushed, Bitten with a crushing noise.
C	R	U	S	A	D	E	D	Attacked with zest, Worked hard to support a cause.
C	R	U	S	A	D	E	R	Ardent campaigner.
C	R	U	S	H	I	N	G	Pressing, Squeezing, Forcing, Hugging, Suppressing, Quenching, Squashing.
C	R	U	S	T	I	L	Y	In a surly fashion.
C	R	U	S	T	O	S	E	Forming a thin brittle crust.
C	R	U	T	C	H	E	D	Supported, Propped, Mixed, Caught.
C	R	U	Z	E	I	R	O	Basic monetary unit of Portugal.
C	R	Y	O	L	I	T	E	A mineral consisting of sodium-aluminium fluoride found in Greenland.
C	R	Y	O	L	O	G	Y	Study of snow and ice, The science of refrigeration.
C	R	Y	O	S	T	A	T	An apparatus for maintaining a constant low temperature.
C	R	Y	O	T	R	O	N	A device performing some of the functions of an electron tube.
C	T	E	N	I	Z	I	D	A family of large burrowing spiders.
C	T	E	N	O	D	U	S	Genus of dipnoan fishes.
C	U	B	A	L	A	Y	A	A fowl of Cuban breed.
C	U	B	A	N	I	T	E	A bronze-yellow copper-iron sulfide.
C	U	B	A	T	U	R	E	Determination of cubic contents, Volume.
C	U	B	I	F	O	R	M	Shape of a cube.
C	U	B	O	I	D	A	L	Relating to a cubical structure.
C	U	C	U	B	A	N	O	A large luminous click beetle of the West Indies.
C	U	C	U	L	I	N	E	Relating to the cuckoos.
C	U	C	U	L	L	U	S	Anterior dorsal shield of pseudoscorpions.
C	U	C	U	M	B	E	R	A succulent fruit of a vine.
C	U	C	U	R	B	I	T	A vessel used in distillation.
C	U	D	D	L	I	N	G	Fondling, Hugging, Nestling, Snuggling.
C	U	F	F	L	I	N	K	Jewellery fastening for cuffs of a shirt.
C	U	L	D	E	S	A	C	Blind alley, Dead end, Point where further progress is impossible.
C	U	L	I	N	A	R	Y	Relating to cooking or kitchen.
C	U	L	L	Y	I	N	G	Tricking, Cheating, Deceiving.
C	U	L	P	A	B	L	E	Blameworthy, Censurable, Guilty, Reprehensible, Criminal.
C	U	L	P	A	B	L	Y	Reprehensibly, Deserving of blame or censure.
C	U	L	T	I	G	E	N	An organism of a kind that has originated and persisted under cultivation.
C	U	L	T	R	A	T	E	Sharp-edged and pointed, Pruning knife.
C	U	L	T	U	R	A	L	Relating to artistic and intellectual aspects of human activity.
C	U	L	T	U	R	E	D	Cultivated, Grown, Well-educated, Polished, Urbane, Refined, Man-made, Artificially produced.
C	U	L	V	E	R	I	N	15th Century long cannon.
C	U	M	A	R	O	N	E	Heavy oily compound present in solvent naptha.
C	U	M	B	E	R	E	D	Defeated, Harassed, Troubled, Hindered, Bothered, Burdened, Saddled, Taxed.
C	U	M	B	R	I	A	N	Cumberland, Ancient Celtic.
C	U	M	B	R	O	U	S	Vexatious, Unwieldy, Clogging, Cumbersome, Heavy, Ponderous, Hampering, Hindering.
C	U	M	U	L	A	T	E	Accumulate, Gather, Collect, Amass, Garner, Stockpile, Store, Secure.
C	U	M	U	L	O	S	E	Heap of accumulated organic matter.
C	U	N	A	B	U	L	A	Beginnings, Infancy, Record or example of early human endeavour.
C	U	N	E	A	T	E	D	Shaped like a wedge, Narrowed triangular.
C	U	N	I	F	O	R	M	Cuneiform, Wedge-shaped, Wrist bone.
C	U	N	J	E	V	O	I	Family of mollusks used as bait.
C	U	N	J	E	V	O	I	Large Australian plant with poisonous juice.
C	U	P	B	O	A	R	D	Small closet, Buffet, Shelf for cups and dishes.
C	U	P	I	D	I	T	Y	Greed, Rapacity, Avarice, Voracity, Craving, Desire, Infatuation, Lust.
C	U	P	J	O	I	N	T	Ball and spigot joint.
C	U	P	R	E	I	N	E	A crystalline alkaloid closely related to quinine.
C	U	P	R	E	O	U	S	Resembling copper.
C	U	P	U	L	A	T	E	Shaped like a cupule.
C	U	R	A	R	I	N	E	Alkaloid obtained from curare.
C	U	R	A	R	I	S	E	Bring under the influence of curare.
C	U	R	A	S	S	O	W	Large game and food birds of South and Central America distantly related to the domestic fowl.
C	U	R	A	T	I	V	E	Relating to the cure of diseases.
C	U	R	A	T	O	R	Y	Body of curators.
C	U	R	B	L	I	N	E	Boundary between the pavement and the roadway.
C	U	R	B	R	O	O	F	Roof with a ridge at the centre and a double slope at each side.
C	U	R	C	U	L	I	O	Genus of destructive weevils.

1	2	3	4	5	6	7	8	
C	U	R	D	L	I	N	G	Congealing, Freezing, Spoiling, Addling, Coagulating, Souring, Embittering, Fermenting.
C	U	R	L	I	C	U	E	Fancy curved figure or letter.
C	U	R	R	E	N	C	Y	Circulation, Prevalence, Money, Cash, Coin.
C	U	R	R	I	C	L	E	Two-wheeled chaise drawn by two horses.
C	U	R	R	Y	I	N	G	Grooming a horse, Treating leather, Beating, Thrashing, Cooking with curry powder.
C	U	R	S	E	D	L	Y	Intensely, Damnably, Bitterly.
C	U	R	S	I	T	O	R	Courier.
C	U	R	S	O	R	E	S	Certain groups of long-legged birds, Wolf spiders.
C	U	R	T	N	E	S	S	Shortness of speech, Terseness, Abruptness.
C	U	R	T	S	I	E	D	Dropped the body and bent the knees in a gesture of respect.
C	U	S	H	C	U	S	H	American tropical yam with edible tubers.
C	U	S	P	I	D	A	L	Relating to a cusp, point or apex.
C	U	S	P	I	D	O	R	Spittoon.
C	U	S	T	O	M	A	L	Written collection of local customs.
C	U	S	T	O	M	E	D	Accustomed.
C	U	S	T	O	M	E	R	Client, Buyer of goods or services.
C	U	T	A	N	E	A	L	Relating to the skin.
C	U	T	G	L	A	S	S	Ornamented glass with the design cut into the surface.
C	U	T	P	U	R	S	E	Thief who cut purses from girdles, Pickpocket.
C	U	T	W	A	T	E	R	Front of a ship's stern, Sharpened edge of the building.
C	Y	A	N	O	G	E	N	Univalent radical, A flammable colourless poisonous gas.
C	Y	A	N	O	S	I	S	Bluish or purplish discolouration of the skin due to lack of oxygen.
C	Y	A	N	O	T	I	C	Related to cyanosis.
C	Y	C	L	A	D	I	C	Relating to Minoan culture of ancient times.
C	Y	C	L	A	M	E	N	Small genus of widely cultivated Eurasian plants.
C	Y	C	L	A	M	I	N	White amorphous saponin of the root of the cyclamen.
C	Y	C	L	E	C	A	R	Small three-wheeled motor driven vehicle.
C	Y	C	L	I	C	A	L	Caused by a business cycle, Influence of recurring economic fluctuation.
C	Y	C	L	I	T	I	S	Inflammation of the ciliary body.
C	Y	C	L	I	T	O	L	An alicyclic polyhydroxy.
C	Y	C	L	O	N	I	C	Resembling the violence of a cyclone.
C	Y	C	L	O	P	I	C	Massive, Huge, Stone construction without using mortar.
C	Y	C	L	O	S	I	S	Circulatory movement.
C	Y	C	L	O	T	I	C	Exhibiting cyclosis.
C	Y	L	I	N	D	E	R	Drum shaped object, Solid or hollow roller.
C	Y	M	A	T	I	U	M	A crowning moulding in classic architecture.
C	Y	M	O	G	E	N	E	A flammable easily condensable gaseous petroleum product.
C	Y	N	I	C	I	S	M	Faultfinding, Sneering, Distrustfulness, Disbelief.
C	Y	N	O	D	O	N	T	Having small pulp cavities.
C	Y	N	O	S	U	R	E	Centre of attraction, Something that commands attention.
C	Y	P	R	I	N	I	D	Family of freshwater fishes, Barbels, Breams, Carps.
C	Y	R	E	N	A	I	C	Follower of the school of philosophers believing pleasure is the chief aim of life.
C	Y	R	I	L	L	I	C	Invention of the alphabet being the foundation of the Slavic languages.
C	Y	R	T	O	P	I	A	Larvae of crustaceans.
C	Y	S	T	I	T	I	C	Afflicted with cystitis.
C	Y	S	T	I	T	I	S	Inflammation of the urinary bladder.
C	Y	T	A	S	T	E	R	An accessory aster not associated with the chromosomes.
C	Y	T	I	D	I	N	E	A crystalline nucleoside.
C	Y	T	I	S	I	N	E	A bitter crystalline very poisonous alkaline found in plants of the pea family.
C	Y	T	O	G	E	N	E	A self-duplicating cytoplasmic gene.
C	Y	T	O	L	Y	S	E	Pathological disintegration of cells.
C	Y	T	O	L	O	G	Y	Study of the cells.
C	Y	T	O	P	H	I	L	Having affinity for cells.
C	Y	T	O	P	Y	G	E	Point of waste discharge from the protozoan body.
C	Y	T	O	S	I	N	E	A crystalline primidine base.
C	Y	T	O	S	O	M	E	The cytoplasmic portion of a cell.
C	Y	T	O	Z	O	I	C	Parasitic within a cell.
C	Y	T	T	A	R	I	A	Genus of fungi.
C	Z	E	C	H	I	S	H	Relating to Czechoslovakia.

D

1	2	3	4	5	6	7	8	
D	A	B	B	L	I	N	G	Spattering, Splashing, Sprinkling, Tampering, Meddling, Ungifted, Amateurish, Unskilled.
D	A	B	C	H	I	C	K	A small grebe.
D	A	C	T	Y	L	A	R	Relating to a dactylus.
D	A	C	T	Y	L	I	A	Condition of having digits.

1	2	3	4	5	6	7	8	Definition
D	A	C	T	Y	L	I	C	Consisting of dactyls.
D	A	C	T	Y	L	I	S	Genus of spiky grasses.
D	A	C	T	Y	L	U	S	Joints of the leg of an insect.
D	A	E	D	A	L	E	A	Genus of tough spore fungi.
D	A	E	D	A	L	I	C	Suggesting escape by flying.
D	A	E	M	O	N	I	C	Demonic, Fiendish, Devilish, Diabolical, Satanic.
D	A	F	F	O	D	I	L	Genus of flower growing from a bulb with a trumpet-like flower.
D	A	F	T	N	E	S	S	Foolishness, Silliness, Madness, Craziness, Stupidity.
D	A	G	G	E	R	E	D	Stabbed with a dagger, Marked with a printing dagger.
D	A	G	G	L	I	N	G	Dragging, Soiling, Muddying, Sprinkling, Splashing with mud.
D	A	H	A	B	E	A	H	A Nile houseboat.
D	A	H	L	L	I	T	E	Carbonate-apatite.
D	A	I	M	I	A	T	E	Territory of a Japanese feudal baron.
D	A	I	N	T	I	L	Y	Delicately, Elegantly, Exquisitely, Lovely, Deliciously.
D	A	I	Q	U	I	R	I	Cocktail of rum and lime with lemon juice and sugar.
D	A	I	R	Y	I	N	G	Conducting a dairy business.
D	A	I	R	Y	M	A	N	One who works in a dairy or is connected with dairy farming.
D	A	L	E	S	M	A	N	Inhabitant of the river valleys of Northern England.
D	A	L	L	Y	I	N	G	Playing, Lingering, Delaying, Tarrying, Toying, Wasting, Trifling, Petting.
D	A	L	M	A	T	I	C	Relating to Dalmatia now included in Yugoslavia.
D	A	M	A	G	I	N	G	Hurting, Injuring, Impairing, Harming, Spoiling, Tarnishing, Destroying, Demolishing.
D	A	M	A	S	K	E	D	Decorated in a way characteristic of Damask, Defaced a seal with a hammer.
D	A	M	E	W	O	R	T	Dame's violet.
D	A	M	N	A	B	L	E	Detestable, Execrable, Cursed, Abhorred, Abominable, Blamed, Hateful, Odious.
D	A	M	P	E	N	E	D	Depressed, Deadened, Dulled, Moistened, Muffled, Stifled, Muted.
D	A	M	P	E	N	E	R	Device for dampening cloth in a laundry.
D	A	M	P	N	E	S	S	Moistness, Wetness.
D	A	N	A	I	D	A	E	Family of tropical butterflies.
D	A	N	A	L	I	T	E	Mineral consisting of silicate with sulfide of iron and beryllium.
D	A	N	C	E	T	T	E	Having indentations in heraldry.
D	A	N	D	E	R	E	D	Sauntered, Idled.
D	A	N	D	I	E	S	T	Finest, Niftiest, Grandest, Keenest, Most glorious, Gaudiest.
D	A	N	D	L	I	N	G	Tossing up and down gently, Pampering, Petting, Trifling, Playing.
D	A	N	D	R	U	F	F	White scales forming on the scalp and being shed.
D	A	N	D	Y	I	S	H	Foppish, Dressing in an ostentatious fashion.
D	A	N	D	Y	I	Z	E	Dandify, Acting in a foppish manner.
D	A	N	D	Y	I	S	M	Extravagant fashion in speech, attire and manner of living.
D	A	N	E	G	E	L	D	Annual tax in ancient England at the time of the Danish invasion.
D	A	N	E	L	A	G	H	Law of the part of England held by the Danes.
D	A	N	E	W	E	E	D	Dwarf herbaceous elder having an unpleasant odour.
D	A	N	E	W	O	R	T	Same as DANEWEED.
D	A	N	G	L	I	N	G	Hanging, Depending, Slinging, Suspending, Swinging.
D	A	N	K	N	E	S	S	Wetness, Moistness, Rankness, Humidity.
D	A	N	S	E	U	S	E	Female ballet dancer.
D	A	N	U	B	I	A	N	Pertaining to prehistoric Neolithic culture of the Danube basin.
D	A	P	E	D	I	U	S	Genus of prehistoric ganoid fishes.
D	A	P	H	N	E	A	N	Shy, Bashful.
D	A	P	H	N	I	T	E	Mineral of a basic aluminosilicate of magnesium iron.
D	A	P	P	E	R	L	Y	Sprucely, Smartly, Lively, Briskly, Jauntily.
D	A	P	P	L	I	N	G	Variegating with spots, Streaks or patches, Mottling.
D	A	R	B	Y	I	S	M	Doctrine of the Plymouth Brethren.
D	A	R	I	N	G	L	Y	Adventurously, Risking, Boldly, Strikingly.
D	A	R	K	E	N	E	D	Obscured, Tainted, Tarnished, Dimmed, Eclipsed, Overshadowed, Fogged.
D	A	R	K	L	I	N	G	In the dark, Dusky, Deeply shadowed.
D	A	R	K	N	E	S	S	Blackness, Gloom, Ignorance, Wickedness, Iniquity, Blindness, Privacy, Secrecy.
D	A	R	K	R	O	O	M	Room with a safelight for processing film.
D	A	R	K	S	O	M	E	Obscure, Sombre, Mysterious.
D	A	R	T	R	O	S	E	Fungus disease of potato and tomato plants.
D	A	S	T	A	R	D	Y	Dastardliness, Cowardly, Cravenly.
D	A	S	Y	U	R	I	D	Family of polyprotodont marsupials.
D	A	S	Y	U	R	U	S	Genus of carnivorous marsupials of Australia and Tasmania.
D	A	T	E	B	O	O	K	Diary of news events kept by a newspaper editor.
D	A	T	E	L	E	S	S	Endless, Immemorial, Timeless, Foolish.
D	A	T	E	L	I	N	E	Hypothetical line on the earth's surface where each calendar day commences.
D	A	T	E	P	A	L	M	Tall tree with pinnate leaves bearing a fruit that is a staple food for people of N. Africa.
D	A	T	E	P	L	U	M	Persimmon.
D	A	T	O	L	I	T	E	Mineral consisting of a basic calcium borosilicate.

1	2	3	4	5	6	7	8	Clue
D	A	U	B	S	T	E	R	An unskilled painter of poor quality work.
D	A	U	G	H	T	E	R	Female child, Maiden, Female descendant.
D	A	U	N	T	I	N	G	Conquering, Subduing, Discouraging, Intimidating, Appalling, Bullying, Horrifying.
D	A	U	P	H	I	N	E	Balls of mashed potatoes fried in deep fat.
D	A	V	A	I	N	E	A	Family of tapeworms.
D	A	V	A	L	L	I	A	Genus of tropical ferns.
D	A	V	I	E	S	I	A	Genus of Australasian Shrubs.
D	A	V	Y	L	A	M	P	Early safety lamp for the mines.
D	A	W	D	L	I	N	G	Loitering, Delaying, Wasting, Idling, Lazing, Loafing, Tarrying, Dallying.
D	A	W	S	O	N	I	A	Large tufted erect mosses.
D	A	Y	B	R	E	A	K	Dawn.
D	A	Y	D	R	E	A	M	Fantasy, Vision, Imagining.
D	A	Y	L	I	G	H	T	Light as opposed to dark, Understanding, Openness, Publicity.
D	A	Y	S	H	I	F	T	Work crew that does the daytime term.
D	A	Y	T	O	D	A	Y	Daily, One day at a time.
D	A	Y	W	O	M	A	N	Deywoman, Dairymaid.
D	A	Z	Z	L	I	N	G	Shining, Reflecting, Eclipsing, Impressing deeply, Confounding, Blinding.
D	E	A	D	B	E	A	T	Man without financial resources, Sponger, Cadger, Exhausted.
D	E	A	D	B	O	R	N	Stillborn.
D	E	A	D	E	N	E	D	Blunted, Retarded, Obscured, Deafened, Killed, Numbed, Dulled, Stunned.
D	E	A	D	F	A	L	L	Trap, Pit, Crooked gambling den, Windfall, Pitfall, Booby trap.
D	E	A	D	F	I	R	E	Saint Elmo's fire.
D	E	A	D	H	E	A	D	Gatecrasher, One unsuitable or unwilling for promotion, Bollard.
D	E	A	D	H	E	A	T	A result where there is no single winner.
D	E	A	D	L	I	E	R	More lethal, More fatal.
D	E	A	D	L	I	F	T	A direct lift without mechanical assistance.
D	E	A	D	L	I	N	E	A fixed limit, Boundary.
D	E	A	D	L	O	C	K	Standstill, Stalemate, Dilemma, Predicament, Quandary, Inaction.
D	E	A	D	M	E	L	T	Keeping metal molten until bubbling ceases.
D	E	A	D	N	E	S	S	State of being dead, Dullness, Inactivity.
D	E	A	D	R	I	S	E	Measurement of the rise of the bottom of a ship.
D	E	A	D	R	O	P	E	A rope that is not controlled by a ring or block.
D	E	A	D	W	A	L	L	A wall without openings.
D	E	A	D	W	O	O	D	Dead branches, Inefficient personnel.
D	E	A	D	W	O	R	K	Work which must be done for future operations.
D	E	A	F	E	N	E	D	Deprived of hearing, Soundproofing, Stunned with noise.
D	E	A	F	M	U	T	E	Unable to hear or speak.
D	E	A	F	N	E	S	S	Lack of ability to hear.
D	E	A	L	A	T	E	D	Divested of the wings.
D	E	A	L	B	A	T	E	Covered with opaque white powder.
D	E	A	L	F	I	S	H	Ribbon-like fish of deep sea areas.
D	E	A	R	N	E	S	S	Being beloved, Lovableness, Fondness, Endearing quality, Costliness.
D	E	A	T	H	B	E	D	Last hours of a person's life. The bed in which they die.
D	E	A	T	H	D	A	Y	The day or anniversary of a person's death.
D	E	A	T	H	F	U	L	Deadly, Murderous, Mortal, Destructive, Bloody.
D	E	A	U	R	A	T	E	Gild.
D	E	B	A	R	K	E	D	Disembarked, Removed bark from a tree, Removed vocal chords from a dog.
D	E	B	A	R	R	E	D	Excluded, Deprived, Eliminated, Suspended, Hindered, Impeded, Obstructed.
D	E	B	A	S	I	N	G	Depraving, Corrupting, Debauching, Perverting, Depreciating, Brutalizing, Degrading.
D	E	B	A	T	I	N	G	Fighting, Contending, Quarreling, Discussing, Arguing, Disputing.
D	E	B	I	L	I	T	Y	Infirmity, Disease, Malaise, Weakness, Feebleness.
D	E	B	I	T	I	N	G	Charging the debtor, Entering on the debit side of account.
D	E	B	I	T	T	E	R	To remove bitterness from an edible substance.
D	E	B	O	N	A	I	R	Courteous, Gracious, Light-hearted, Carefree.
D	E	B	O	U	C	H	E	Opening or passage to serve as an outlet.
D	E	B	T	L	E	S	S	Free from debt, Not owing any money.
D	E	B	U	N	K	E	D	Exposed an exaggerated claim, Discovered, Uncloaked, Unmasked.
D	E	B	U	T	A	N	T	One making first public appearance, Beginning a professional career.
D	E	C	A	D	E	N	T	Marked by decay or decline, Becoming less prominent, Degenerate.
D	E	C	A	G	R	A	M	Metric unit of mass and weight equal to 10 grams.
D	E	C	A	L	A	G	E	Difference between wing angles of a biplane.
D	E	C	A	M	P	E	D	Departed, Ran away, Escaped, Absconded, Quit, Evaded, Cleared out, Shunned.
D	E	C	A	N	N	Y	L	Capryl, The univalent radical derived from 2-octanol and 1-methyl-heptyl.
D	E	C	A	N	T	E	D	Poured, Transferred, Unloaded.
D	E	C	A	N	T	E	R	Ornamental glass bottle for serving wine.
D	E	C	A	P	O	D	A	Order of crustaceans, Prawns, Shrimps, Lobsters, Crabs.
D	E	C	A	P	P	E	R	Instrument for removing a cap from a cartridge case.

1	2	3	4	5	6	7	8	Definition
D	E	C	A	R	C	H	Y	A governing body of ten members.
D	E	C	A	T	I	N	G	A textile process for adding lustre to cloth.
D	E	C	A	Y	I	N	G	Decomposing, Rotting, Putrefying, Spoiling, Disintegrating, Perishing, Crumbling.
D	E	C	E	A	S	E	D	Departed from life, Dead.
D	E	C	E	D	E	N	T	A deceased person.
D	E	C	E	I	V	E	D	Misled, Deluded, Beguiled, Betrayed, Cheated, Duped, Defrauded, Ensnared, Duped.
D	E	C	E	I	V	E	R	Cheat, Trickster.
D	E	C	E	M	B	E	R	Twelfth month of the Gregorian calendar.
D	E	C	E	M	V	I	R	Member of an ancient Roman council of ten than framed the laws.
D	E	C	E	N	T	L	Y	Correctly, Properly, Rightly, Chastely, Modestly, Purely, Nobly, Respectably.
D	E	C	E	R	N	E	D	Decreed by judicial sentence.
D	E	C	I	D	I	N	G	Resolving, Ruling, Determining, Settling, Concluding, Gathering, Judging, Surmising.
D	E	C	I	D	U	A	L	Having a mucous membrane of the uterus.
D	E	C	I	G	R	A	M	Metric unit of mass and weight equal to one tenth of a gram.
D	E	C	I	M	A	T	E	To kill every tenth hostage, One tenth for tax, Take one tenth of the whole, Destroy.
D	E	C	I	M	O	L	E	Decuplet, Group of ten notes in music.
D	E	C	I	P	H	E	R	Detect, Discover, Unravel, Reveal, Solve, Delineate, Portray, Decide.
D	E	C	I	S	I	O	N	Settlement, Conclusion, Resolution, Agreement, Understanding, Compromise.
D	E	C	I	S	I	V	E	Determined, Resolute, Unmistakeable, Conclusive, Unquestionable, Assured, Steadfast.
D	E	C	K	H	A	N	D	A sailor working on the deck.
D	E	C	K	H	E	A	D	The ceiling of a compartment of a ship.
D	E	C	K	L	I	N	G	Limiting the size of paper by use of a wooden frame.
D	E	C	L	A	R	E	D	Explained, Broadcast, Proclaimed, Published, Asserted, Affirmed, Announced.
D	E	C	L	A	S	S	E	Of inferior status, Fallen in circumstances, Low-grade, Mean, Poor, Second-class.
D	E	C	L	I	N	E	D	Rejected, Refused, Repudiated, Spurned, Failed, Faded, Languished, Weakened.
D	E	C	L	I	N	E	R	One that refuses.
D	E	C	L	U	T	C	H	To disengage a clutch.
D	E	C	O	C	T	E	D	Extracted flavour by boiling, Concentrated by boiling away.
D	E	C	O	C	T	U	M	Decoction.
D	E	C	O	D	I	N	G	Deciphering, Translating, Solving, Interpreting, Explaining, Rendering, Elucidating.
D	E	C	O	L	O	U	R	Bleach, Remove colour.
D	E	C	O	R	A	T	E	Adorn, Beautify, Bedeck, Embellish, Garnish, Ornament, Trim.
D	E	C	O	R	I	S	T	One noted for artistic restraint.
D	E	C	O	R	O	U	S	Decent, Seemly, Proper, Demure, Civilized, Correct, Respectable, Convential.
D	E	C	O	Y	I	N	G	Enticing, Alluring, Entrapping, Baiting, Tempting, Deceiving, Seducing.
D	E	C	R	E	A	S	E	Lessen, Dwindle, Reduce, Abate, Decline, Recede, Curtail, Minimize.
D	E	C	R	E	P	I	T	Wasted, Weak, Shabby, Threadbare, Feeble, Fragile, Ancient, Unsound.
D	E	C	R	E	T	A	L	Decree, Decisive, Final.
D	E	C	R	Y	I	N	G	Depreciating, Lowering, Undervaluing, Disparaging, Derogating, Minimizing, Detracting.
D	E	C	U	M	A	R	Y	A woody vine of South East U.S.A.
D	E	C	U	P	L	E	D	Became ten times as much or as many.
D	E	C	U	P	L	E	T	Combination of ten of a kind.
D	E	C	U	R	I	O	N	Member of the great council in an Italian city or town.
D	E	C	U	R	T	E	D	Curtailed.
D	E	C	U	R	V	E	D	Curved downward, Bent down.
D	E	D	E	N	D	U	M	Root of a gear tooth.
D	E	D	I	C	A	N	T	One that dedicates.
D	E	D	I	C	A	T	E	Devote, Consecrate, Hallow, Direct, Surrender, Commit, Entrust, Assign.
D	E	D	I	T	I	O	N	Surrender, Yield.
D	E	D	O	L	E	N	T	Callous, Bereft of feeling, Unemotional.
D	E	D	U	C	I	N	G	Inferring, Conducting, Concluding, Deriving, Gathering, Judging, Presuming, Conceiving.
D	E	D	U	C	T	E	D	Subtracted, Discounted, Decreased, Diminished, Lessened, Reduced, Abated, Retracted.
D	E	E	D	L	E	S	S	Inactive.
D	E	E	D	P	O	L	L	Deed made and executed by only one party.
D	E	E	M	S	T	E	R	Justice of common-law court in the Isle of Man.
D	E	E	P	D	Y	E	D	Thorough, Unrelieved, Ingrained.
D	E	E	P	E	N	E	D	Intensified, Aggravated, Enhanced, Heightened, Magnified, Mounted, Redoubled.
D	E	E	P	M	O	S	T	Deepest.
D	E	E	P	N	E	S	S	State of being deep, Profoundness.
D	E	E	R	F	O	O	D	Water shield.
D	E	E	R	F	O	O	T	Wild vanilla.
D	E	E	R	H	A	I	R	Small club rush with filiform stems.
D	E	E	R	H	E	R	D	A keeper of deer.
D	E	E	R	H	O	R	N	Horny material of the antlers of a deer, A large freshwater mussel.
D	E	E	R	S	K	I	N	Leather of the skin of a deer.
D	E	F	A	C	I	N	G	Disfiguring, Destroying, Demolishing, Mutilating, Defaming, Discrediting, Impairing.
D	E	F	A	M	I	N	G	Maligning, Libelling, Slandering, Disgracing, Discrediting, Denigrating, Misrepresenting.

1	2	3	4	5	6	7	8	Definition
D	E	F	E	A	T	E	D	Conquered, Crushed, Overpowered, Subdued, Subjugated, Vanquished, Repulsed.
D	E	F	E	C	A	T	E	Clarify, Purify, Cleanse, Refine, Purge, Empty the bowels.
D	E	F	E	C	T	E	D	Failed, Deserted, Repudiated, Forsaken, Rejected, Spurned.
D	E	F	E	N	C	E	D	Fortified, Impeded.
D	E	F	E	N	D	E	D	Protected, Shielded, Guarded, Upheld, Prevented, Justified, Opposed, Resisted.
D	E	F	E	N	D	E	R	Protector, Advocate, Champion, Vindication, Upholder.
D	E	F	E	N	S	E	D	Fortified.
D	E	F	E	R	E	N	T	Honouring, Respectful.
D	E	F	E	R	R	E	D	Postponed, Suspended, Waited, Procrastinated, Prolonged, Delayed, Adjourned, Waived.
D	E	F	E	R	R	E	R	One that procrastinates.
D	E	F	I	A	N	C	E	Challenge, Dare, Command, Contempt, Stubbornness, Rebelliousness, Bravado.
D	E	F	I	L	A	D	E	Utilising natural cover as protection against fire or observation.
D	E	F	I	L	I	N	G	Befouling, Ravishing, Violating, Polluting, Contaminating, Tarnishing, Desecrating.
D	E	F	I	N	I	N	G	Concluding, Settling, Deciding, Determining, Describing, Expounding, Explaining.
D	E	F	I	N	I	T	E	Limited, Fixed, Real, Actual, Explicit, Cogent, Precise, Restricted.
D	E	F	L	A	T	E	D	Contracted, Punctured, Collapsed, Sagged, Reduced.
D	E	F	L	A	T	O	R	Percentage by which monetary quantities are reduced to eliminate effect of higher prices.
D	E	F	L	E	X	E	D	Deflected, Turned downward.
D	E	F	L	O	W	E	R	Ravage, Despoil, Rape, Violate, Defile, Outrage, Desecrate, Ravish.
D	E	F	L	U	E	N	T	Flowing down.
D	E	F	O	R	C	E	D	Withheld forcefully, Ejected, Opposed, Resisted.
D	E	F	O	R	E	S	T	To clear of forests.
D	E	F	O	R	M	E	D	Disfigured, Defaced, Distorted, Monstrous, Warped, Gnarled, Tortured, Crippled.
D	E	F	R	A	Y	A	L	Act of defraying, Payment.
D	E	F	R	A	Y	E	D	Disbursed, Requited, Satisfied, Reimbursed, Averted, Appeased.
D	E	F	T	N	E	S	S	Dexterity, Neatness, Quickness, Adroitness, Prowess, Skill, Agility, Nimbleness.
D	E	G	A	U	S	S	E	Neutralize the magnetism of a ship to afford protection from magnetic mines.
D	E	G	R	A	D	E	D	Demoted, Deposed, Debased, Distorted, Contaminated, Vulgarized, Downgraded, Reduced.
D	E	G	R	E	A	S	E	To remove dirt and grease.
D	E	G	U	E	L	I	N	Derris, Woody vines and shrubs yielding poison and insecticide.
D	E	H	O	R	N	E	D	Removed horns, Prevented growth of horns.
D	E	I	F	Y	I	N	G	Making a god, Transfiguring, Glorifying, Exalting, Becoming divine.
D	E	I	G	N	I	N	G	Condescending, Stooping, Allowing.
D	E	I	N	O	D	O	N	Variety of extinct American dinosaurs.
D	E	J	E	C	T	E	D	Downcast, Crestfallen, Depressed, Disconsolate, Dispirited, Mournful, Downhearted.
D	E	J	E	C	T	L	Y	Sadly, Dispiritedly, Disconsolately.
D	E	J	E	U	N	E	R	Breakfast or a light lunch.
D	E	L	A	T	I	N	G	Accusing, Denouncing, Reporting, Relating, Delegating, Referring, Transferring.
D	E	L	A	T	I	O	N	Accusation, Denouncement.
D	E	L	A	T	I	V	E	Moving down as used in a grammatical case.
D	E	L	A	Y	I	N	G	Postponing, Retarding, Slowing, Slackening, Detaining, Impeding, Obstructing.
D	E	L	E	C	T	U	S	Book for persons learning Latin or Greek.
D	E	L	E	G	A	C	Y	Delegation, Appointed as delegate.
D	E	L	E	G	A	T	E	Deputy, Representative, Commissioner, Deputize, Appoint, Designate, Choose, Select.
D	E	L	E	T	E	R	Y	Poisonous, Antidote.
D	E	L	E	T	I	N	G	Erasing, Expunging, Annulling, Effacing, Obliterating, Eliminating, Excluding.
D	E	L	E	T	I	O	N	Erasure, Deficiency, Destruction, Extinction.
D	E	L	I	B	A	T	E	Dabble, Sip, Take a little.
D	E	L	I	C	A	C	Y	Dainty, Morsel, Pleasure, Banquet, Feast, Indulgence, Luxury, Frailty.
D	E	L	I	C	A	T	E	Delightful, Dainty, Exquisite, Airy, Fragile, Frail, Flimsy, Tactful.
D	E	L	I	M	I	N	G	Removing lime in hide processing.
D	E	L	I	R	I	U	M	Mania, Frenzy, Enthusiasm, Fervour, Passion, Zeal, Ecstasy, Rapture.
D	E	L	I	V	E	R	Y	Birth, Bearing, Supply, Dispatch, Transfer of goods.
D	E	L	O	U	S	E	D	Removed lice, Freed from something unpleasant.
D	E	L	P	H	I	A	N	Relating to Delphi, Prophetic, Oracular, Ambiguous.
D	E	L	P	H	I	N	E	Pertaining to dolphins.
D	E	L	T	A	I	T	E	A mineral consisting of a basic hydrous phosphate of calcium and aluminium.
D	E	L	U	D	I	N	G	Deceiving, Mocking, Evading, Eluding, Frustrating, Disappointing, Duping, Misleading.
D	E	L	U	G	I	N	G	Inundating, Flooding, Drenching, Swamping, Overpowering, Submerging, Drowning.
D	E	L	U	S	I	O	N	Halluciation, Illusion, Mirage, Phantasm, Deception, Trickery, Fake, Fantasy.
D	E	L	U	S	I	V	E	Deceptive, Beguiling, Misleading, False, Fantastic, Imagery, Ostensible, Illusionary.
D	E	L	U	S	O	R	Y	Deceptive.
D	E	L	U	V	I	U	M	Flooding.
D	E	M	A	G	O	G	Y	Rabble-rousing, Inciting, Agitating, Making extravagant promises.
D	E	M	A	N	D	E	D	Exacted, Claimed, Required, Requisitioned, Solicited, Requested, Commanded.
D	E	M	A	N	S	I	A	Genus of snakes comprising the venomous Australian brown snake and related forms.
D	E	M	A	R	C	H	E	Proceeding, Move, Countermove, Manoeuvre, Formal statement by a public officer.

1	2	3	4	5	6	7	8	Clue
D	E	M	E	A	N	E	D	Humbled, Abased, Debased, Degraded, Humiliated, Belittled, Derogated, Detracted.
D	E	M	E	N	T	E	D	Deranged, Insane, Crazed, Lunatic, Maniac, Unbalanced, Unsound, Delirious.
D	E	M	E	N	T	I	A	Madness, Insanity, Deteriorated mentality.
D	E	M	E	R	S	A	L	Organisms living on the bottom of the sea.
D	E	M	I	J	O	H	N	Narrow-necked bottle enclosed in wickerwork, Carboy.
D	E	M	I	L	U	N	E	Distinctive group of cells in the salivary glands.
D	E	M	I	S	I	N	G	Deceasing, Passing by descent or bequest.
D	E	M	I	S	T	E	R	Device for removing condensation from a windscreen.
D	E	M	I	T	I	N	T	Medium tone, Half-tint.
D	E	M	I	T	O	N	E	Semitone.
D	E	M	I	T	T	E	D	Dismissed, Resigned, Withdrew, Relinquished.
D	E	M	I	U	R	G	E	Lesser god, Something conceived as a decisive power.
D	E	M	I	W	O	L	F	Offspring of a dog and a wolf.
D	E	M	O	B	B	E	D	Demobilized, Discharged from the armed services.
D	E	M	O	C	R	A	T	Advocate of democracy, Member of a democratic political party.
D	E	M	O	L	I	S	H	Shatter, Smash, Raze, Destroy, Decimate, Ruin, Wreck, Crush.
D	E	M	O	N	I	A	C	Produced by a demon, Fiendish, Devilish, Possessed by an evil spirit.
D	E	M	O	N	I	Z	E	Convert into a demon, Instill the power of a demon.
D	E	M	O	T	I	S	T	Student of demotic writings.
D	E	M	P	S	T	E	R	An officer who pronounces the doom of the court.
D	E	M	U	R	E	L	Y	Modestly, Primly, Sedately, Shyly, Daintily.
D	E	M	U	R	R	E	D	Balked, Boggled, Remonstrated, Delayed, Hesitated, Objected, Stumbled, Faltered.
D	E	M	U	R	R	E	R	Objection, Exception.
D	E	M	Y	S	H	I	P	Scholarship at Magdalen College, Oxford.
D	E	N	A	R	I	U	S	Silver or gold coin of ancient Rome.
D	E	N	A	T	U	R	E	Change the nature of something, Adulterate.
D	E	N	A	Z	I	F	Y	To be cleared of the charge of advocating Nazism.
D	E	N	D	R	I	T	E	Branching figure produced in a mineral, A crystallized arborescent form.
D	E	N	D	R	O	I	D	Resembling a tree in form.
D	E	N	E	H	O	L	E	Ancient excavation found in chalk cliffs in South England and France.
D	E	N	I	A	B	L	E	Refutable, Open to denial.
D	E	N	O	T	A	T	E	Denote, Signify, Imply.
D	E	N	O	T	I	N	G	Indicating, Designating.
D	E	N	O	U	N	C	E	Criticize, Blame, Censure, Condemn, Accuse, Charge, Incriminate, Impeach.
D	E	N	T	A	T	E	D	Had teeth or pointed conical projections.
D	E	N	T	E	L	L	E	Lace, Lacework, Decoration of pointed outlines.
D	E	N	T	I	C	L	E	Small tooth, Conical pointed projection.
D	E	N	T	I	N	A	L	Relating to the enamel of a tooth.
D	E	N	U	D	A	N	T	An agent that denudes.
D	E	N	U	D	A	T	E	Lay bare, Strip, Divest, Deprive.
D	E	N	U	D	I	N	G	Stripping, Depriving, Divesting, Weakening, Disrobing, Undressing, Dismantling.
D	E	P	A	R	T	E	D	Gone, Swerved, Deviated, Left, Perished, Divided, Retired, Withdrew.
D	E	P	E	N	D	E	D	Hinged, Turned, Hung, Based, Inclined, Leaned, Relied, Banked.
D	E	P	I	L	A	T	E	To remove hair.
D	E	P	I	L	O	U	S	Devoid of hair.
D	E	P	L	E	T	E	D	Exhausted, Emptied, Lessened, Impoverished, Drained, Spent, Enfeebled.
D	E	P	L	O	R	E	D	Lamented, Grieved, Wept, Mourned, Sorrowed, Regretted, Repented, Bewailed.
D	E	P	L	O	Y	E	D	Extended, Placed, Arranged.
D	E	P	L	U	M	E	D	Plucked, Deprived of plumage, Stripped of possessions or honours.
D	E	P	O	L	I	S	H	To roughen, To destroy smoothness.
D	E	P	O	N	E	N	T	One who gives evidence in writing.
D	E	P	O	N	I	N	G	Testifying, Swearing, Asserting under oath.
D	E	P	O	R	T	E	D	Carried, Demeaned, Conducted, Transported, Banished, Behaved, Displaced, Acquitted.
D	E	P	O	R	T	E	E	One who has been deported.
D	E	P	O	S	I	N	G	Dethroning, Divesting of authority, Dispossessing, Swearing, Affirming, Testifying.
D	E	P	R	A	V	E	D	Depreciated, Maligned, Perverted, Debased, Deprived, Corrupted, Debauched, Warped.
D	E	P	R	A	V	E	R	Reprobate, Debaucher.
D	E	P	R	A	V	E	D	Finish for a plastered wall made by pressing pebbles in the soft plaster.
D	E	P	R	I	V	E	D	Removed, Destroyed, Divested, Bereaved, Depressed, Disadvantaged, Ousted, Underprivileged.
D	E	P	R	I	V	E	R	One that deprives.
D	E	P	U	R	A	T	E	Purify, Cleanse, Clarify.
D	E	P	U	T	I	N	G	Delegating, Commissioning, Deputizing, Authorizing, Charging.
D	E	P	U	T	I	Z	E	Entrust, Appoint, Substitute, Act for another.
D	E	R	A	I	L	E	D	Interrupted, Off the lines, Thrown off course, Diverted.
D	E	R	A	I	L	E	R	A device for preventing accidents on the railway.
D	E	R	A	N	G	E	D	Disordered, Disarranged, Unbalanced, Crazy, Insane, Mad, Unsound, Disturbed.
D	E	R	A	T	I	N	G	Reducing the amount of liability for rates.

1	2	3	4	5	6	7	8	Definition
D	E	R	A	T	I	O	N	Eliminating the necessity to ration or restrict supply of a commodity.
D	E	R	E	L	I	C	T	Run-down, Unused, Drifter, Outcast, Abandoned, Forgotten, Desolate, Dilapidated.
D	E	R	I	D	I	N	G	Ridiculing, Mocking, Taunting, Chaffing, Kidding, Razzing, Jeering.
D	E	R	I	S	I	O	N	Ridicule, Mockery, Scorn, Laughingstock, Jest, Butt, Joke, Sport.
D	E	R	I	S	I	V	E	Causing derision, Jeering.
D	E	R	I	S	O	R	Y	Derisive, Ridiculing.
D	E	R	I	V	A	T	E	Derived, Obtained, Received.
D	E	R	I	V	I	N	G	Taking, Receiving, Deducing, Transmitting, Originating, Stemming, Evolving, Emanating.
D	E	R	O	G	A	T	E	Disparage, Decry, Belittle, Detract, Minimize, Diminish, Depreciate, Decrease.
D	E	R	R	I	E	R	E	Buttocks, Rump, Behind, Back, Direction in ballet.
D	E	S	C	R	I	A	L	Discovery, Disclosure of a secret.
D	E	S	C	R	I	B	E	Express, Signify, Denote, Relate, Narrate, Recount, Report, State.
D	E	S	E	R	T	E	D	Abandoned, Left, Forsaken, Withdrawn, Inhospitable, Rejected, Renounced, Quit.
D	E	S	E	R	T	E	R	One who forsakes a duty or cause.
D	E	S	E	R	V	E	D	Earned, Merited, Rated, Gained, Won, Demanded, Just, Appropriate.
D	E	S	E	R	V	E	R	One who merits.
D	E	S	I	G	N	E	D	Conceived, Planned, Devoted, Consigned, Destined, Intended, Contemplated, Proposed.
D	E	S	I	G	N	E	R	Planner, Creater, Producer.
D	E	S	I	L	V	E	R	Remove silver, Extract silver.
D	E	S	I	R	I	N	G	Longing, Requesting, Craving, Wanting, Wishing, Entreating, Asking, Hankering.
D	E	S	I	R	O	U	S	Solicitous, Covetous, Desirable, Delectable, Acquisitive, Grasping, Greedy, Eager.
D	E	S	I	S	T	E	D	Refrained, Ceased, Discontinued, Stopped, Halted, Yielded, Abstained, Relinquished.
D	E	S	K	W	O	R	K	Work performed at a desk.
D	E	S	M	O	D	U	S	Genus of bloodsucking bats, Vampires.
D	E	S	M	O	G	E	N	Vascular cell tissue.
D	E	S	O	L	A	T	E	Deserted, Abandoned, Dissolute, Bereaved Forsaken, Derelict, Solitary, Inconsolable.
D	E	S	P	A	T	C	H	Dispatch, Dismiss, Discharge, Hasten, Kill, End.
D	E	S	P	I	S	A	L	Intense dislike, Contempt.
D	E	S	P	I	S	E	D	Disdained, Detested, Scorned, Loathed, Spurned, Disliked, Ignored, Rejected.
D	E	S	P	I	S	E	R	One that regards another as inferior.
D	E	S	P	I	T	E	D	Showed contempt.
D	E	S	P	O	T	A	T	State ruled by a despot.
D	E	S	P	O	T	I	C	Belonging to absolute ruler, Domineering, Arbitrary.
D	E	S	T	I	N	E	D	Preordained, Predetermined, Designated, Assigned, Dedicated, Fated, Intended, Directed.
D	E	S	T	O	N	E	R	Worker operating a machine that removes hard particles from vegetables to be frozen.
D	E	S	T	R	I	E	R	War-horse.
D	E	S	T	R	U	C	T	Destroy.
D	E	S	T	R	U	D	O	Death wish.
D	E	S	Y	A	T	I	N	Russian unit of land area.
D	E	T	A	C	H	E	D	Disengaged, Alone, Parted, Severed, Removed, Uncoupled, Disconnected.
D	E	T	A	I	L	E	D	Relayed, Reported, Specified, Enumerated, Furnished, Circumstantial, Itemized.
D	E	T	A	I	L	E	R	One that makes detail drawings.
D	E	T	A	I	N	E	D	Apprehended, Withheld, Delayed, Stopped, Kept, Retained, Retarded, Reserved.
D	E	T	A	I	N	E	R	Detention in custody.
D	E	T	E	C	T	E	D	Demodulated, Rectified, Encountered, Met, Discovered, Found out, Unmasked, Uncovered.
D	E	T	E	C	T	O	R	Device to prevent tampering with a lock, Device for indicating malfunction of an operation.
D	E	T	E	R	G	E	D	Cleansed, Washed away.
D	E	T	E	R	R	E	D	Dissuaded, Prevented, Inhibited, Discouraged, Diverted, Hindered, Impeded, Averted.
D	E	T	E	S	T	E	D	Abhorred, Loathed, Hated, Disliked, Abominated, Rejected, Repudiated, Spurned.
D	E	T	H	R	O	N	E	Depose, Displace, Uncrown, Disthrone.
D	E	T	O	N	A	T	E	Explode, Burst.
D	E	T	O	R	T	E	D	Twisted, Distorted, Perverted.
D	E	T	O	X	I	F	Y	Destroying poison or removing the effects.
D	E	T	R	A	Q	U	E	Deranged, Psychopathic.
D	E	T	R	I	T	A	L	Resulting from disintegration of rock.
D	E	T	R	I	T	E	D	Worn down, Resulting from disintegration.
D	E	T	R	I	T	U	S	Product of disintegration.
D	E	T	R	U	D	E	D	Forced down, Thrust away.
D	E	T	R	U	S	O	R	Muscles of the bladder-wall.
D	E	U	C	E	A	C	E	A throw of the dice.
D	E	U	C	E	D	L	Y	Very, Remarkably, Extremely, Damnably, Devilishly.
D	E	U	T	E	R	O	N	The nucleus of the deuterium atom that consists of one proton and one nucleus.
D	E	U	T	O	V	U	M	Inactive incompletely developed larva of a mite.
D	E	V	A	C	H	A	N	State intermediate between two earth lives.
D	E	V	A	L	O	K	A	Heaven in Buddism and Hinduism.
D	E	V	A	L	U	E	D	Reduction in the exchange value of a currency, Declined.
D	E	V	E	L	O	P	E	Expound, Explain, Disclose, Reveal, Detect, Discover, Evolve, Mature.

1	2	3	4	5	6	7	8	Definition
D	E	V	E	S	T	E	D	Alienated, Divested, Discarded, Abandoned.
D	E	V	I	A	B	L	E	Capable of being defected.
D	E	V	I	A	N	C	E	Deviation.
D	E	V	I	A	T	E	D	Diverged, Turned aside, Strayed, Swerved, Departed, Erred, Wandered.
D	E	V	I	A	T	O	R	Someone or something that causes deviation.
D	E	V	I	L	D	O	M	Realm of the devil.
D	E	V	I	L	I	N	G	Teasing, Pesky, Importunate.
D	E	V	I	L	I	S	H	Diabolical, Evil, Vicious, Extreme, Excessive, Fiendish, Satanic, Nefarious.
D	E	V	I	L	I	S	M	Devilish practice.
D	E	V	I	L	I	Z	E	Cause to become devilish.
D	E	V	I	L	K	I	N	Little devil, Imp.
D	E	V	I	L	L	E	D	Teased, Tormented, Annoyed, Hazed, Food chopped and mixed with a hot seasoning.
D	E	V	I	L	T	R	Y	Devilry, Witchcraft, Works of the devil.
D	E	V	I	S	I	N	G	Contriving, Inventing, Planning, Scheming, Supposing, Imagining, Guessing, Plotting.
D	E	V	O	L	U	T	E	Devolve, Deteriorate, Decline, Degenerate.
D	E	V	O	L	V	E	D	Transferred, Rolled, Flowed, Succeeded.
D	E	V	O	N	I	A	N	Period of prehistoric plant growth and preservation of fossils.
D	E	V	O	T	I	N	G	Consecrating, Dedicating, Hallowing, Sanctifying, Vowing, Giving, Donating, Bestowing.
D	E	V	O	T	I	O	N	Reverence, Piety, Oblation, Zeal, Ardour, Fidelity, Purpose, Mission.
D	E	V	O	U	R	E	D	Consumed, Engulfed, Wasted, Annihilated, Absorbed, Eaten, Exhausted, Ravaged.
D	E	V	O	U	R	E	R	Destroyer, An avid reader, A glutton.
D	E	V	O	U	T	L	Y	Reverently, Sincerely, Earnestly, Deeply.
D	E	W	B	E	R	R	Y	Several sweet edible berries resembling blackberries.
D	E	W	I	N	E	S	S	Suggesting freshness or purity.
D	E	W	P	O	I	N	T	Temperature at which a vapour begins to condense.
D	E	X	T	R	I	N	S	Water soluble gummy polysaccharides obtained from starch, used as adhesives, sizes.
D	E	X	T	R	O	S	E	Glucose from starch and used in foods and beverages, Corn sugar, Grape sugar.
D	E	X	T	R	O	U	S	Dexterous, Skilful, Crafty, Expert, Clever, Adroit, Deft, Handy.
D	I	A	B	A	S	I	C	Resembling diabase, Ophitic.
D	I	A	B	A	T	I	C	Involving the transfer of heat.
D	I	A	B	E	T	E	S	Disease characterized by excessive production of sugar and abnormal discharge of urine.
D	I	A	B	E	T	I	C	Resulting from diabetes.
D	I	A	B	O	L	I	C	Relating to the devil, Derived from the devil, Devilish, Fiendish.
D	I	A	C	E	T	Y	L	Containing two acetyl groups.
D	I	A	C	O	E	L	E	The third ventricle of the brain.
D	I	A	C	O	N	A	L	Relating to a deacon.
D	I	A	C	T	I	N	E	A sponge spicule having two pointed arms.
D	I	A	D	E	M	E	D	Adorned with a diadem, ornamental or jewelled headband.
D	I	A	G	L	Y	P	H	Intaglio, Sunk relief.
D	I	A	G	N	O	S	E	Identify, Determine the cause.
D	I	A	G	O	N	A	L	From corner to corner, Biased, Slanted, Inclined, Slantwise.
D	I	A	G	R	A	P	H	A drawing instrument combining a protractor and scale.
D	I	A	L	A	B	L	E	Capable of being dialed.
D	I	A	L	L	I	N	G	Measuring with a dial, Operating a dial.
D	I	A	L	O	G	I	C	Characterized by dialogue.
D	I	A	L	O	G	U	E	Conversation, Exchange of ideas, Chat, Colloquy, Converse, Parley.
D	I	A	L	Y	S	I	S	Separation of substances in solution.
D	I	A	L	Y	T	I	C	Capable of dissolution.
D	I	A	L	Y	Z	E	D	Diffused through a suitable membrane.
D	I	A	M	E	T	E	R	Thickness of a circular object, Length of a line passing through centre of a circle.
D	I	A	N	T	H	U	S	Genus of herbs including carnations and pinks.
D	I	A	P	A	S	O	N	Melody, Strain, A principal foundation organ stop, Tuning fork, Full deep outburst of sound.
D	I	A	P	A	U	S	E	Period of dormancy.
D	I	A	P	E	N	T	E	The interval of the fifth in ancient music.
D	I	A	P	E	R	E	D	Ornamented with a specialised design.
D	I	A	P	H	A	N	E	Diaphanous, Fine textured fabric, Chiffon, Georgette, Ethereal, Insubstantial, Vague.
D	I	A	P	H	O	N	E	Special trill peculiar to some languages, Fog signal resembling a siren, Powerful pipe-organ.
D	I	A	P	S	I	D	A	Subclass of reptiles including extinct dinosaurs, crocodiles, lizards and snakes.
D	I	A	R	I	S	E	D	Recorded in a diary.
D	I	A	S	P	O	R	A	Exile, Scattering, Migration.
D	I	A	S	P	O	R	E	Mineral consisting of aluminium hydrogen.
D	I	A	S	T	A	S	E	A mixture of amylases obtained from malt.
D	I	A	S	T	E	M	A	A space between teeth in a jaw.
D	I	A	S	T	O	L	E	Expansion, Passive rhythmical dilatation of heart cavities while filling with blood.
D	I	A	S	T	Y	L	E	Intercolumniation of three diameters.
D	I	A	T	O	M	I	C	Consisting of two atoms, Having two replaceable radicals.
D	I	A	T	O	N	I	C	Relating to a standard major or minor scale of eight tones.

1	2	3	4	5	6	7	8	Definition
D	I	A	T	R	I	B	E	Bitter, abusive lengthy speech or piece of writing, Ironical criticism.
D	I	A	T	R	Y	M	A	Extinct flightless birds of Mexico related to bustards.
D	I	B	B	L	I	N	G	Working with a small implement for making planting holes.
D	I	B	O	R	A	N	E	A gaseous compound of boron and hydrogen.
D	I	B	S	T	O	N	E	The game of jacks.
D	I	C	A	C	I	T	Y	Raillery, Biting wit.
D	I	C	A	R	Y	O	N	Dikaryon, A pair of associated but unfused haploid nuclei.
D	I	C	E	N	T	R	A	Genus of herbs, Bleeding heart, Dutchman's breeches.
D	I	C	E	R	I	O	N	Dikerion, Two-branched candlebra used by Eastern Orthodox Church.
D	I	C	H	L	O	N	E	A yellow crystalline compound used as a fungicide.
D	I	C	H	R	O	I	C	Having two colours.
D	I	C	K	E	R	E	D	Haggled, Bargained.
D	I	C	R	A	N	U	M	A large genus of mosses.
D	I	C	R	O	T	I	C	Having a double beat, Relating to the second expansion of the artery during diastole of heart.
D	I	C	T	A	T	E	D	Spoken, Recited, Transcribed, Prescribed, Commanded, Enjoined, Imposed, Decreed.
D	I	C	T	A	T	O	R	One ruling absolutely with brutality and ruthless oppression.
D	I	C	T	Y	O	T	A	Brown algae.
D	I	C	Y	C	L	I	C	Biennial, Having two maxima of population each year as plankton.
D	I	D	A	C	T	I	C	Teaching, Conveying information, Dry, Erudite, Pompously dull, Moralistic, Instructive.
D	I	D	A	C	T	Y	L	Having only two digits at each extremity.
D	I	D	A	P	P	E	R	Small grebe.
D	I	D	D	E	R	E	D	Quivered, Shook, Trembling.
D	I	D	D	L	I	N	G	Loafing, Dawdling, Swindling, Cheating, Hoaxing, Deluding, Idling, Bilking.
D	I	D	I	N	I	U	M	Genus of carnivorous protozoans.
D	I	D	R	A	C	H	M	Ancient Greek silver coin.
D	I	D	U	C	T	O	R	Muscle that opens a shell.
D	I	D	Y	M	I	U	M	Mixture of rare-earth elements used in colouring glass for optical filters.
D	I	D	Y	M	O	U	S	Grouping in pairs, Twin, Twofold.
D	I	E	L	D	R	I	N	A white crystalline insecticide.
D	I	E	M	E	N	I	A	Demansia, Genus of Australian brown snakes.
D	I	E	S	T	A	M	P	Form for sheet stock or emboss by means of a die.
D	I	E	S	T	O	C	K	A stock for holding dies used for cutting threads.
D	I	E	T	E	T	I	C	Composing special diets.
D	I	F	F	E	R	E	D	Varied, Disagreed, Dissented, Disputed, Quarrelled, Divided, Differentiated, Clashed.
D	I	F	F	R	A	C	T	To break, Separate into two parts.
D	I	F	F	U	S	E	D	Poured, Extended, Scattered, Broadcast, Distributed, Spread, Circulated, Dispersed.
D	I	F	F	U	S	E	R	A device for deflecting a substance, light or gas.
D	I	F	F	U	S	O	R	Same as DIFFUSER.
D	I	G	E	N	I	T	E	A mineral consisting of isometric copper sulfide.
D	I	G	E	S	T	E	D	Classified, Distributed, Assimilated, Brooked, Comprehended, Decomposed, Compressed.
D	I	G	E	S	T	E	R	A medicine or food that aids digestion.
D	I	G	G	I	N	G	S	Place of excavating, Place, Premises, Lodgings.
D	I	G	I	T	A	T	E	Having fingers, Resembling fingers.
D	I	G	I	T	I	Z	E	To put data into digital notation.
D	I	G	O	N	I	U	M	Primitive germ cell.
D	I	G	Y	N	I	A	N	Order of plants having flowers with two pistils.
D	I	G	Y	N	O	U	S	Same as DIGYNIAN.
D	I	H	E	D	R	A	L	Mathematical figure formed by two intersecting planes.
D	I	H	Y	B	R	I	D	Individual or strain that has genes of two members.
D	I	I	O	D	I	D	E	Compound containing two atoms of iodine combined with a radical.
D	I	K	E	T	E	N	E	An unsaturated pungent liquid lactone.
D	I	K	E	T	O	N	E	A chemical compound containing two ketonic carbonyl groups.
D	I	L	A	T	A	N	T	Swelling, Increasing in viscosity.
D	I	L	A	T	I	N	G	Widening, Extending, Swelling, Expanding, Discoursing, Stretching, Distending, Inflating.
D	I	L	A	T	I	O	N	Expansion, Stretching, Distension, Amplification, Narration, Recitation.
D	I	L	A	T	I	V	E	Causing dilation.
D	I	L	A	T	O	R	Y	Delay, Slow, Tardy, Laggard, Leisured, Neglectful, Remiss, Slack.
D	I	L	I	G	E	N	T	Busy, Careful, Observant, Heedful, Assiduous, Industrious, Persevering Persistent.
D	I	L	L	E	N	I	A	Genus of East Indian trees and shrubs.
D	I	L	L	S	E	E	D	Seed of the dill plant used for flavouring pickles.
D	I	L	L	W	E	E	D	Mayweed, Dill.
D	I	L	L	Y	B	A	G	Mesh bag kept closed with a drawstring.
D	I	L	L	U	I	N	G	Mine worker.
D	I	L	U	E	N	D	O	Dying away, direction in music.
D	I	L	U	T	A	N	T	Diluting.
D	I	L	U	T	I	N	G	Reducing, Debasing, Thinning, Weakening, Liquefying, Adulterating, Impairing.
D	I	L	U	T	I	O	N	Act of reducing the strength or value.

1	2	3	4	5	6	7	8	Definition
D	I	L	U	V	I	A	H	Flooding, Deluging.
D	I	L	U	V	I	U	M	Geological deposit produced by a massive flooding.
D	I	M	E	D	O	N	E	A crystalline diketone.
D	I	M	E	R	O	U	S	Quality of having two parts.
D	I	M	E	R	O	U	S	Consisting of two parts, joints or members.
D	I	M	E	T	R	I	C	Hexagonal or tetragonal.
D	I	M	I	N	I	S	H	Decrease, Taper, Disparage, Dwindle, Belittle, Curtail, Lessen, Wane.
D	I	M	P	L	I	N	G	Producing conical depressions, Rippling.
D	I	M	Y	A	R	I	A	Bivalve mollusks.
D	I	N	G	D	O	N	G	Ringing sound on a bell or any metallic object, Working hard, Scolding insistently.
D	I	N	G	H	I	E	S	Small rowboats, yachts or rubber rafts.
D	I	N	G	I	E	S	T	Dirtiest, Shabbiest, Most squalid, Dullest.
D	I	N	O	H	Y	U	S	Genus of extinct giant pigs.
D	I	N	O	R	N	I	S	Genus of extinct giant birds related to the emu.
D	I	N	O	S	A	U	R	A large extinct reptile.
D	I	O	C	E	S	A	N	Being the seat of a bishop.
D	I	O	I	C	O	U	S	Having staminate and pistillate flowers on separate plants.
D	I	O	M	E	D	E	A	Genus of albatrosses.
D	I	O	N	Y	S	I	A	An ancient Greek festival.
D	I	O	P	S	I	D	E	A pyroxene that contains calcium and magnesium sometimes used in jewellery.
D	I	O	P	T	R	A	L	Relating to focal power in diopters.
D	I	O	P	T	R	I	C	Refractive.
D	I	O	R	A	M	I	C	Peculiar to a diaroma.
D	I	O	S	C	U	R	I	Twin gods.
D	I	P	H	A	S	I	C	Having two phases.
D	I	P	H	E	N	A	N	A crystalline ester used in the treatment of pin worms.
D	I	P	H	E	N	Y	L	Diphenol, A chemical compound containing two phenyl groups.
D	I	P	H	Y	L	L	A	Genus of bloodsucking bats.
D	I	P	L	A	S	I	C	Two to one in proportion.
D	I	P	L	E	G	I	A	Paralysis on both sides of the body.
D	I	P	L	E	X	E	R	A combining network allowing operation of two functions.
D	I	P	L	O	D	I	A	A large form genus of imperfect fungi.
D	I	P	L	O	M	A	T	Ambassador, Envoy, Negotiator.
D	I	P	L	O	P	I	A	Disorder of the eye resulting in double vision.
D	I	P	L	O	P	O	D	Millipede.
D	I	P	L	O	S	I	S	Increasing amount of precious metal by transmutation.
D	I	P	M	E	T	E	R	Geological measuring instrument.
D	I	P	N	O	O	U	S	Having lungs and gills.
D	I	P	S	A	C	U	S	Genus of prickly herbs, Teasels.
D	I	P	S	T	I	C	K	Rod for measuring level of liquid in a tank or container.
D	I	P	T	E	R	A	L	Comprising a double row of identical columns.
D	I	P	T	E	R	A	N	Genus of winged insects, Flies, Mosquitoes, Gnats, Midges.
D	I	P	T	E	R	O	N	Same as DIPTERAN.
D	I	P	T	E	R	O	S	A building having two wings at each end of main structure.
D	I	P	T	E	R	Y	X	Genus of tropical American trees, Tonka bean.
D	I	R	E	C	T	E	D	Assigned, Allotted, Addressed, Aimed, Pointed, Applied, Turned, Trained.
D	I	R	E	C	T	L	Y	Exactly, Shortly, Straight, Verbatim, Literally, Immediately, Instantly, Presently.
D	I	R	E	C	T	O	R	Head, Chief, Supervisor, Producer, Conductor, Manager, Controller.
D	I	R	E	N	E	S	S	Calamity, Horror, Frightfulness, Dismalness, Gloominess.
D	I	R	G	E	F	U	L	Mournful, Lamentful, Funereal.
D	I	R	H	I	N	I	C	Affecting both nostrils together.
D	I	R	T	I	E	S	T	Filthiest, Foulest, Nastiest, Dingiest.
D	I	R	T	Y	I	N	G	Sullying, Tarnishing, Fouling, Smudging, Tainting, Staining, Besmirching.
D	I	S	A	B	L	E	D	Incapacitated, Disqualified, Weakened, Disparaged, Paralyzed, Debilitated, Crippled.
D	I	S	A	B	U	S	E	Undeceive, Rid, Purge, Amend, Correct, Rectify, Enlighten, Liberate.
D	I	S	A	G	R	E	E	Dissent, Differ, Unsuitable, Vary, Discord, Divide.
D	I	S	A	L	L	O	W	Refuse, Reject, Disclaim, Veto, Deny, Withhold, Disavow, Repudiate.
D	I	S	A	N	N	E	X	Disunite, Release from annexation.
D	I	S	A	R	M	E	D	Deprived of arms, Made harmless, Charmed, Captivated, Immobilized, Won over.
D	I	S	A	R	R	A	Y	Confusion, Clutter, Disorder, Muddle, Disarrange, Disorganize, Disturb, Jumble.
D	I	S	A	S	T	E	R	Calamity, Catastrophe, Portent, Fiasco, Cataclysm, Misadventure, Tragedy, Fatality.
D	I	S	B	O	W	E	L	Disembowel, Eviscerate, Remove the substance.
D	I	S	B	U	R	S	E	Pay out, Defray, Spend, Distribute, Dispense, Partition, Outlay, Disperse.
D	I	S	C	A	N	D	Y	Melt, Dissolve.
D	I	S	C	A	S	E	D	Undressed.
D	I	S	C	I	N	C	T	Loose, Negligent.
D	I	S	C	I	P	L	E	Follower, Convinced adherent, Partisan, Zealot, Enthusiast.

1	2	3	4	5	6	7	8	
D	I	S	C	L	A	I	M	Disavow, Renounce, Deny, Repudiate, Dispute, Disallow, Contradict, Disacknowledge.
D	I	S	C	L	O	S	E	Reveal, Display, Expose, Reveal, Betray, Discover, Divulge, Confess.
D	I	S	C	O	U	N	T	Allowance, Reduction, Deduction, Drawback, Hindrance, Minimize, Depreciate.
D	I	S	C	O	V	E	R	Exhibit, Display, Manifest, Find, Discern, Reveal, Detect, Determine.
D	I	S	C	R	E	E	T	Prudent, Circumspect, Tactful, Unpretentious, Modest, Restrained, Polite, Civil.
D	I	S	C	R	E	T	E	Detached, Separate, Distinct, Diverse, Different, Several, Various, Merged.
D	I	S	C	R	O	W	N	Deprive of a crown, Depose.
D	I	S	E	A	S	E	D	Sickly, Fevered, Disordered, Unwholesome, Decrepitude, Afflicted.
D	I	S	E	D	G	E	D	Deprived of an edge, Blunted, Dulled.
D	I	S	E	D	I	F	Y	To injure the piety or morals, Shock the religious feelings.
D	I	S	E	N	D	O	W	To strip of an endowment.
D	I	S	E	N	J	O	Y	To take no pleasure, Bored with.
D	I	S	F	A	I	T	H	Distrust, Lack of faith.
D	I	S	F	R	O	C	K	Unfrock.
D	I	S	G	A	V	E	L	To deprive of common-law tenure of land.
D	I	S	G	O	R	G	E	Vomit, Discharge violently, Empty, Discharge contents, Relinquish ill-gotten gains.
D	I	S	G	R	A	C	E	Discredit, Upbraid, Revile, Loss of honour, Misfortune, Dishonesty, Infamy, Shame.
D	I	S	G	R	A	D	E	Degrade, Lower in quality or position.
D	I	S	G	U	I	S	E	Disfigure, Cloak, Mask, Dissemble, Deform, Conceal, Camouflage, Falsify.
D	I	S	H	A	U	N	T	Absent oneself.
D	I	S	H	E	R	I	T	Disinherit.
D	I	S	H	E	V	E	L	Fall in disorder, Cause disarray.
D	I	S	H	F	A	C	E	An animal with a concave face.
D	I	S	H	O	A	R	D	To put money or goods back into circulation.
D	I	S	H	O	R	S	E	Dismount.
D	I	S	H	O	U	S	E	To clear an area of houses.
D	I	S	I	N	T	E	R	Exhume, Unearth, Dig, Remove from concealment.
D	I	S	J	O	I	N	T	Separate, Break, Divide, Dislocate, Disunite, Sever, Sunder, Upset.
D	I	S	J	U	N	C	T	Discontinuous, Separation, Melodic progression interval larger than a major second.
D	I	S	L	E	A	V	E	Strip of leaves.
D	I	S	L	I	K	E	D	Hated, Disapproved, Displeased, Detested, Loathed.
D	I	S	L	I	K	E	N	Disguise.
D	I	S	L	O	D	G	E	To drive out, Force to leave, Shift, Move.
D	I	S	L	O	Y	A	L	Faithless, Lacking adherence, False, Treacherous, Perfidious, Traitorous, Unloyal.
D	I	S	M	A	L	L	Y	Drearily, Desolately, Gloomily.
D	I	S	M	A	Y	E	D	Daunted, Disenchanted, Disillusioned, Upset, Perturbed, Alarmed, Appalled, Horrified.
D	I	S	M	O	U	N	T	Descend, Alight, Degrade, Disassemble.
D	I	S	O	R	B	E	D	Thrown out of its orbit.
D	I	S	O	R	D	E	R	Disarrange, Disorganize, Unsettle, Disturb, Derange, Jumble, Confuse, Upset.
D	I	S	O	W	N	E	D	Repudiated, Denied, Disclaimed, Disavowed.
D	I	S	P	A	T	C	H	Hasten, Kill, End, Dismiss, Discharge, Consign, Post, Transmit.
D	I	S	P	E	A	C	E	Dissension, Strife, Turmoil, Discord, Conflict.
D	I	S	P	E	N	S	E	Disharmony, Difference, Distribute, Provide, Give, Administer, Handle, Release, Exempt.
D	I	S	P	E	R	S	E	Scatter, Dispel, Disseminate, Dissipate, Radiate, Spread, Diffuse, Strew.
D	I	S	P	E	T	A	L	Remove petals.
D	I	S	P	I	R	I	T	Discourage, Demoralize, Dishearten, Deject, Disparage, Depress, Chill.
D	I	S	P	L	A	C	E	Banish, Discharge, Depose, Supplant, Replace, Deport, Exile, Remove.
D	I	S	P	L	A	N	T	Uproot, Displace, Supplant.
D	I	S	P	L	U	M	E	Deplume, Strip of plumage, Pluck feathers.
D	I	S	P	O	N	E	D	Dispose, Grant, Transfer.
D	I	S	P	O	N	E	E	One to whom property is disponed.
D	I	S	P	O	P	E	D	To remove from the office of Pope.
D	I	S	P	O	R	U	M	Genus of herbs with leafy branching stems.
D	I	S	P	O	S	A	L	Administration, Dispensation, Bestowal, Destruction, Discarding, Relegation, Scrapping.
D	I	S	P	O	S	E	D	Willing, Inclined, Predisposed, Prone, Ready.
D	I	S	P	O	S	E	R	Manager, Director, Electrical device in a sink to dispose of garbage.
D	I	S	P	R	E	A	D	To spread out, Open out, Expand.
D	I	S	P	R	I	Z	E	Despise, Underestimate.
D	I	S	P	R	O	O	F	Confutation, Rebuttal, Evidence that disproves.
D	I	S	P	R	O	V	E	Refute, Disallow, Confute, Rebut, Controvert, Confound, Contravene, Overturn.
D	I	S	P	U	N	G	E	To pour down upon, Expunge.
D	I	S	P	U	T	E	D	Debated, Wrangled, Discussed, Maintained, Contested, Controverted, Opposed, Argued.
D	I	S	P	U	T	E	R	Quarrelsome person, Debater.
D	I	S	Q	U	I	E	T	Discompose, Anxiety, Uneasiness, Restlessness, Agitate, Bother, Perturb, Fluster.
D	I	S	R	A	T	E	D	Demoted, Downgraded.
D	I	S	R	O	B	E	D	Undressed, Divested, Stripped, Denuded, Bankrupted, Dismantled.
D	I	S	R	O	B	E	R	One that assists with ceremonial robing.

1	2	3	4	5	6	7	8	Definition
D	I	S	S	E	I	Z	E	To deprive of, To oust without legality.
D	I	S	S	E	R	V	E	Injure, Damage, Harm.
D	I	S	S	E	V	E	R	Sever, Separate, Part, Disunite.
D	I	S	S	O	L	V	E	Decompose, Destroy, Kill, Undo, Melt, Liquefy, Vanish, Disappear.
D	I	S	S	U	A	D	E	Peter, Discourage, Divert, Advise, Counsel, Exhort, Prevail, Disincline.
D	I	S	T	A	L	I	A	Any of the remote row of carpal or tarsal bones.
D	I	S	T	A	L	L	Y	Toward the end.
D	I	S	T	A	N	C	E	Difference, Disparity, Interval, Coldness, Reserve, Space, Length, Area.
D	I	S	T	A	S	T	E	Disgust, Nauseate, Offend, Displace, Alienation, Aversion, Abhorrence, Repulsion.
D	I	S	T	I	N	C	T	Notable, Unusual, Clear, Individual, Particular, Obvious, Specific, Manifest.
D	I	S	T	O	M	U	M	Liver flukes.
D	I	S	T	R	A	C	T	Divide, Separate, Disperse, Puzzle, Harass, Confound, Bewilder, Derange.
D	I	S	T	R	A	I	N	Confiscate, Seize for a debt.
D	I	S	T	R	A	I	T	Inattentive, Distraught, Distracted, Frantic, Crazed, Worried, Absentminded, Tormented.
D	I	S	T	R	E	S	S	Pain, Suffering, Constraint, Compulsion, Misfortune, Misery, Agony, Affliction.
D	I	S	T	R	I	C	T	Territorial division, Precinct, Section, Sector, Locality, Vicinity, Neighbourhood.
D	I	S	T	R	U	S	T	Suspicion, Wariness, Doubt, Suspect, Disbelieve, Discredit.
D	I	S	T	U	N	E	D	Put out of tune.
D	I	S	U	N	I	F	Y	Estrange, Alienate, Disunite, Wean, Separate.
D	I	S	U	N	I	O	N	Detachment, Dissolution, Division, Partition, Rupture, Dissent, Discord, Conflict.
D	I	S	U	N	I	T	E	Separate, Disjoin, Divide, Sunder, Part, Estrange.
D	I	S	U	N	I	T	Y	Discord, Conflict, Contention, Dissension, Strife, Variance.
D	I	S	U	S	A	G	E	Disuse, Discard, Abandon, Cessation of use.
D	I	S	U	S	I	N	G	Abandoning, Discarding, Ceasing to use.
D	I	S	V	A	L	U	E	Depreciate, Disesteem, Undervalue.
D	I	T	C	H	B	U	R	Cocklebur.
D	I	T	C	H	I	N	G	Discarding, Crash-landing, Chucking, Rejecting, Jettisoning, Hiding, Concealing.
D	I	T	H	E	I	S	M	Theory of the existence of two gods, one good and one evil.
D	I	T	H	E	I	S	T	Adherent of Ditheism.
D	I	T	H	E	R	E	D	Shivered, Trembled, Wavered, Vacillated, Babbled, Dazed, Faltered, Hesitated.
D	I	T	H	I	O	I	C	Containing two atoms of sulfur replacing two oxygen atoms in the molecule of acid.
D	I	T	O	K	O	U	S	Producing two young or two eggs at a time.
D	I	T	T	Y	B	A	G	Small bag used by sailors to hold needles, thread, tape, etc.
D	I	T	T	Y	B	O	X	Box used for the same purpose as a ditty-bag.
D	I	U	R	E	T	I	C	An agent to increase the flow of urine.
D	I	V	A	G	A	T	E	Ramble, wander, digress.
D	I	V	A	L	E	N	T	Bivalent, Double.
D	I	V	E	B	O	M	B	To bomb by making a steep dive.
D	I	V	E	R	G	E	D	Deflected, Swerved, Deviated, Digressed, Divided, Disagreed, Rambled, Wandered.
D	I	V	E	R	S	E	D	Deviated, Digressed, Deflected, Distracted, Entertained, Amused, Dissuaded, Turned.
D	I	V	E	S	T	E	D	Undressed, Stripped, Abandoned, Deprived, Dismantled, Bared, Plundered, Spoiled.
D	I	V	I	D	E	N	D	Bonus, Reward, Prize, Share of profit.
D	I	V	I	D	I	N	G	Separating, Classifying, Distinguishing, Distributing, Grading, Sharing, Partaking.
D	I	V	I	D	I	V	I	Small tree of tropical America.
D	I	V	I	D	U	A	L	Separate, Distinct, Divisible, Dividend.
D	I	V	I	N	E	L	Y	Excellently, Supremely well, Godly, Marvellous.
D	I	V	I	N	I	F	Y	To make divine, Deify.
D	I	V	I	N	I	T	Y	Deity, God, Celestial being, Theology, Science of divine things.
D	I	V	I	N	I	Z	E	Exalt, Glorify, Deify.
D	I	V	I	S	I	O	N	Partition, Apportionment, Separation, Disunity, Disaggreement, Variance, Dissolution.
D	I	V	I	S	I	V	E	Distributive, Analytical, Creating disunity.
D	I	V	O	R	C	E	D	Separated legally, Removed, Banished, Divided, Severed, Dissolution, Annulled, Dismissed.
D	I	V	O	R	C	E	E	A divorced person.
D	I	V	O	R	C	E	R	One that divorces.
D	I	V	U	L	G	E	D	Revealed, Betrayed, Disclosed, Discovered, Spilled, Proclaimed, Made public.
D	I	V	U	L	S	E	D	Pulled apart, Torn apart, Rent.
D	I	X	E	N	I	T	E	A maganese arsenate and silicate.
D	I	Z	Z	Y	I	N	G	Confusing, Bewildering, Dazzling, Brilliant.
D	O	C	E	T	I	S	M	An early Christian doctrine that Christ only appeared in a spiritual body.
D	O	C	E	T	I	S	T	Adherent of Docetism.
D	O	C	H	M	I	A	C	Dochmius, A foot of five syllables having two short and three long.
D	O	C	I	L	E	L	Y	Obediently, Submissively, Pliantly.
D	O	C	I	M	A	S	Y	Practice of assaying ores, To determine whether a dead baby was stillborn.
D	O	C	K	I	Z	E	D	Equipped with a harbour.
D	O	C	K	Y	A	R	D	Naval shipyard, Area for shipbuilding and repairs.
D	O	C	O	S	A	N	E	A paraffin hydrocarbon.
D	O	C	T	O	R	A	L	Characteristic of a doctor or doctorate.

1	2	3	4	5	6	7	8	
D	O	C	T	O	R	E	D	Mended, Repaired, Adapted, Modified, Adulterated, Overhauled, Reconstructed, Debased.
D	O	C	T	O	R	L	Y	Like a doctor.
D	O	C	T	R	I	N	E	Tenet, Dogma, Learning, Knowledge.
D	O	C	U	M	E	N	T	Proof, Evidence, Record, Testimony.
D	O	D	D	E	R	E	D	Trembled, Shook, Tottered, Quaked, Unsteadily, Shattered.
D	O	D	D	E	R	E	R	A person enfeebled from age or weakness.
D	O	D	E	C	A	N	E	Any of the oily paraffin hydrocarbons.
D	O	D	O	N	E	A	N	Relating to the ancient oracle of Zeus at Dodona.
D	O	G	B	E	R	R	Y	Blundering official, Policeman, Constable, Small fruits unfit for human consumption.
D	O	G	B	R	I	A	R	Same as DOG-BRIER.
D	O	G	B	R	I	E	R	Dog rose.
D	O	G	C	H	E	A	P	Cheaply, A low price.
D	O	G	E	A	R	E	D	When a corner of a book's page is turned over.
D	O	G	G	E	D	L	Y	Belligerently, Determinedly, Obstinately.
D	O	G	G	E	R	E	L	Trivial, comic poetry.
D	O	G	G	O	N	E	D	Damned, Confounded.
D	O	G	G	R	A	S	S	Couch grass.
D	O	G	H	O	U	S	E	Kennel, Caboose, Imaginary place to go when one is out of favour.
D	O	G	L	E	E	C	H	Quack, One that treats diseases of dogs.
D	O	G	M	A	T	I	C	Dictatorial, Arbitrary, Authoritarian, Dictative, Deductive, Derivable, Reasoned.
D	O	G	S	B	A	N	E	Wolfsbane.
D	O	G	S	H	O	R	E	Short timber to support a ship before launching.
D	O	G	S	L	E	E	P	Dozing, Fitful sleep.
D	O	G	S	M	E	A	T	Meat fit only for a dog, Carrion, Offal.
D	O	G	S	N	O	S	E	A mixed drink of malt liquor and spirits, Hot spiced porter.
D	O	G	T	O	O	T	H	Canine tooth, Architectural ornament in early English Gothic.
D	O	G	T	R	I	C	K	A dishonest trick.
D	O	G	W	A	T	C	H	Short watch on a ship on a rotating basis.
D	O	G	W	H	E	L	K	Thick-shelled marine snails.
D	O	L	D	R	U	M	S	Blues, Quandary, Tedium, Boredom, Dejection, Depression, Gloom, Apathy.
D	O	L	E	F	U	L	S	Blues.
D	O	L	E	R	I	T	E	A coarse basalt, Diabase.
D	O	L	E	S	O	M	E	Doleful, Dismal. Rueful.
D	O	L	I	C	H	O	S	Genus of tropical vines.
D	O	L	I	T	T	L	E	Idler, Loafer.
D	O	L	L	E	D	U	P	Made more attractive, Dressed elegantly.
D	O	L	L	F	A	C	E	Person having a smooth pretty face resembling a doll.
D	O	L	L	Y	M	O	P	Strumpet, Drab.
D	O	L	L	Y	T	U	B	A washtub for washing with a dolly.
D	O	L	O	M	I	T	E	A mineral consisting of a calcium magnesium carbonate.
D	O	L	O	R	O	S	O	Sorrowful, Plaintive, Used as a direction in music.
D	O	L	O	R	O	U	S	Deplorable, Lamentable, Woeful, Lugubrious, Distressing, Wretched, Grievous, Miserable.
D	O	M	A	N	I	A	L	Belonging to a particular domain.
D	O	M	A	I	N	A	L	Same as DOMAINAL.
D	O	M	E	S	T	I	C	Internal, Tame, Household, Family, Civic, Personal, Municipal, Submissive.
D	O	M	I	C	I	L	E	Abode, Residence, Habitation, Dwelling, Lodge, House, Home, Harbour.
D	O	M	I	F	I	E	D	Divided the Zodiac into twelve positions, Specified the Zodiac planets.
D	O	M	I	N	A	N	T	Predominant, Paramount, Preponderant, Sovereign, Superior, Prevalent, Supreme.
D	O	M	I	N	A	T	E	Govern, Control, Direct, Handle, Manage, Rule, Overlook, Domineer.
D	O	M	I	N	E	E	R	Rule, Prevail, Reign, Dominate, Swagger.
D	O	M	I	N	I	C	K	Dominique, American breed of domestic fowl.
D	O	M	I	N	I	O	N	Dominance, Rule, Power, Supremacy, Sovereignty, Ascendancy, Ownership, Possession.
D	O	M	I	N	I	U	M	Ownership, Property rights.
D	O	M	I	N	O	E	S	A game played with blocks, Masquerade costume.
D	O	N	A	T	A	R	Y	Receiver of a donation.
D	O	N	A	T	I	N	G	Giving, Bestowing, Devoting, Presenting, Supplying, Emitting, Loaning, Transferring.
D	O	N	A	T	I	O	N	Alms, Charity, Allowance, Contribution, Offering, Bequest, Grant, Subsidy.
D	O	N	A	T	I	S	M	Early Christian doctrine that believed in rebaptism before acceptance into their church.
D	O	N	C	E	L	L	A	Brightly coloured wrasses, Ladyfish, West Indian timber tree.
D	O	N	D	E	R	E	D	Dazed, Stupefied.
D	O	O	D	L	I	N	G	Cheating, Dawdling, Toying, Scribbling.
D	O	O	M	B	O	O	K	Ancient code of laws.
D	O	O	M	P	A	L	M	Large African fan palm that yields material for rope and has useful edible fruit.
D	O	O	M	S	D	A	Y	Day of final judgment, Day of death.
D	O	O	M	S	M	A	N	One invested with authority as a judge.
D	O	O	R	B	E	L	L	Bell, gong or chimes to be rung by a push button on a door.
D	O	O	R	C	A	S	E	Doorframe.

1	2	3	4	5	6	7	8	Definition
D	O	O	R	H	E	A	D	Upper horizontal timber of a doorframe.
D	O	O	R	K	N	O	B	A knob to be turned to release a latch on a door.
D	O	O	R	L	E	S	S	Having no door.
D	O	O	R	N	A	I	L	Large-headed nail for using on door battens.
D	O	O	R	P	O	S	T	Upright piece of a doorframe.
D	O	O	R	S	I	L	L	Lower horizontal member of a doorframe.
D	O	O	R	S	T	E	P	A step on the outside of a door.
D	O	O	R	S	T	O	P	A device to prevent a door banging against a wall or a piece of furniture.
D	O	O	R	Y	A	R	D	An area of yard outside a door.
D	O	P	E	S	T	E	R	One who publishes forecasts of sporting or political events.
D	O	R	I	C	I	S	M	A phrase or idiom in ancient Greek.
D	O	R	M	A	N	C	Y	Suspension, Doldrums, Quiescence, Latency, Abeyance, Inactivity.
D	O	R	M	O	U	S	E	Small rodent that feeds on nuts and hibernates during the winter.
D	O	R	O	S	O	M	A	Genus of fishes.
D	O	R	S	A	L	I	S	Arteries in the back.
D	O	R	S	A	L	L	Y	Toward the back.
D	O	R	Y	L	I	N	E	Relating to army ants.
D	O	S	S	E	R	E	T	Obvious block resting on the top of a column.
D	O	T	T	E	R	E	L	A plover, Congener, Stupid foolish person.
D	O	U	A	N	I	E	R	A customs officer.
D	O	U	B	L	E	T	S	16th Century upper torso garments for men usually embroidered and jewelled, Pairs.
D	O	U	B	L	I	N	G	Increasing by an equal quantity, Twice as great, Reinforcing, Folding, Bending.
D	O	U	B	L	O	O	N	Old gold Spanish coin.
D	O	U	B	L	U	R	E	Ornamental lining of a book cover.
D	O	U	B	T	F	U	L	Perilous, Fearful, Wavering, Hesitating, Undecided, Dubious, Questionable, Problematic.
D	O	U	B	T	I	N	G	Distrusting, Suspecting, Questioning, Challenging, Disputing, Querying.
D	O	U	C	H	I	N	G	Spraying a body cavity, Drenching.
D	O	U	G	H	B	O	Y	Flour dumpling, Bread dough fried in deep fat, Infantryman.
D	O	U	G	H	N	U	T	Yeast cake fried in deep fat.
D	O	U	M	P	A	L	M	Doom-palm.
D	O	U	N	D	A	K	E	The back of a country fig once used as an astringent and febrifuge.
D	O	U	R	N	E	S	S	Sullenness, Grimness, Bleakness, Harshness, Gloominess, Surliness, Sulkiness.
D	O	V	E	C	O	T	E	Small raised house for tame birds, Harmonious group.
D	O	V	E	E	Y	E	D	Having soft gentle eyes.
D	O	V	E	L	I	K	E	Mild, Gentle, Pure, Lovable.
D	O	V	E	R	I	N	G	Dozing.
D	O	V	E	T	A	I	L	A woodwork joint resembling a dove's tail.
D	O	W	D	Y	I	S	H	Slatternly, Slovenly, Frumpish, Unstylish.
D	O	W	E	L	L	E	D	Fastened with a round rod.
D	O	W	E	R	I	N	G	Endowing, Supplying with a dowry.
D	O	W	F	N	E	S	S	Listless, Apathetic, Dullness.
D	O	W	N	B	E	A	R	Depress, Press upon.
D	O	W	N	B	E	A	T	Stress, Depressed condition, Pessimistic, Gloomy, Unhappy.
D	O	W	N	B	E	N	D	Depression in the earth's crust.
D	O	W	N	C	A	S	T	Crestfallen, Dejected, Doleful, Dull, Sad, Oppressed, Morose, Troubled.
D	O	W	N	C	O	M	E	Downfall, Overthrow.
D	O	W	N	F	A	L	L	Ruin, Destruction, Descent, Abyss, Debacle, Decadence, Decline, Discomfiture.
D	O	W	N	H	A	U	L	Rope or line for hauling down a sail.
D	O	W	N	H	I	L	L	Descent, Declivity, Descending gradient.
D	O	W	N	I	E	S	T	Softest, Fluffiest.
D	O	W	N	L	A	N	D	Gentle rolling hills.
D	O	W	N	L	I	N	E	The railway line running south.
D	O	W	N	P	I	P	E	Outside pipe to channel rainwater from the roof.
D	O	W	N	P	O	U	R	Heavy drenching rain.
D	O	W	N	S	I	D	E	Under or lower side, Downward trend in prices.
D	O	W	N	S	M	A	N	A person that lives on the downs.
D	O	W	N	T	I	M	E	Period when a factory is not producing during working hours.
D	O	W	N	T	O	W	N	Lower or business area of a town.
D	O	W	N	T	R	O	D	Oppressed by a tyrant.
D	O	W	N	T	U	R	N	Decline, Decrease.
D	O	W	N	W	A	R	D	Descending from an ancestor, Dejected, Toward a lower standard.
D	O	W	N	W	I	N	D	Leeward, The direction in which the wind is blowing.
D	O	Z	I	N	E	S	S	Drowsiness, Sluggishness, Sleepiness.
D	R	A	B	B	L	E	D	Draggled, Muddied, Sullied, Soiled by mud.
D	R	A	B	B	L	E	R	Piece of canvas laced to a sail.
D	R	A	C	A	E	N	A	Genus of Old World tropical shrubs and trees, Dragon's blood.
D	R	A	C	H	M	A	L	Relating to a drachma, an ancient Greek unit of weight.

1	2	3	4	5	6	7	8	Clue
D	R	A	C	O	N	I	C	Relating to a dragon.
D	R	A	F	T	I	N	G	Outlining, Sketching, Drawing, Composing, Preparing, Framing, Devising, Formulating.
D	R	A	G	B	O	L	T	Coupler.
D	R	A	G	G	I	N	G	Searching, Pulling, Hauling, Drawing, Lugging, Dredging, Lingering, Tedious.
D	R	A	G	G	L	E	D	Traipsed, Trailed, Besmirched, Shuffled, Dirty, Unkempt, Untidy, Soaked.
D	R	A	G	H	U	N	T	A hunt where a live animal is not chased.
D	R	A	G	O	M	A	N	An interpreter, A tourist guide in the Middle East.
D	R	A	G	O	N	E	T	Genus of small brightly coloured scaleless food fish.
D	R	A	G	R	O	P	E	Mooring line.
D	R	A	G	S	H	O	E	A brake.
D	R	A	G	S	M	A	N	Driver of a drag.
D	R	A	I	L	I	N	G	Fishing with special hooks.
D	R	A	I	N	A	G	E	Draining, Sewage, Removal of excess water from the land.
D	R	A	I	N	I	N	G	Filtering, Exhausting, Venting, Emptying, Dwindling, Discharging, Firing, Depleting.
D	R	A	M	A	T	I	C	Theatrical, Thespian, Histrionic, Pertaining to drama.
D	R	A	M	B	U	I	E	Liqueur from whisky.
D	R	A	M	M	O	C	K	Distasteful gruel porridge.
D	R	A	M	S	H	O	P	Room where intoxicating drinks were sold.
D	R	A	U	G	H	T	S	Board-game, Checkers.
D	R	A	U	G	H	T	Y	Currents of air causing discomfort.
D	R	A	W	B	A	C	K	Refund, Kickback, Defect, Hindrance, Disadvantage, Handicap, Detriment.
D	R	A	W	B	O	L	T	Bolt with a washer and nut.
D	R	A	W	B	O	R	E	Enlarge the bore with a tool.
D	R	A	W	G	E	A	R	Device to couple up railway trucks or carriages.
D	R	A	W	L	I	N	G	Lagging, Slow-moving, Droning.
D	R	A	W	L	I	N	K	Drawbar on a railroad coach.
D	R	A	W	T	U	B	E	Telescoping tube as contained in the eyepiece of optical instruments.
D	R	E	A	D	F	U	L	Frightening, Revolting, Horrible, Tragic, Extreme, Fearful, Appalling, Shocking.
D	R	E	A	D	I	N	G	Fearing, Trepidation, Frightening, Apprehensive.
D	R	E	A	M	E	R	Y	Impractical fantasies.
D	R	E	A	M	F	U	L	Dreamy.
D	R	E	A	M	I	L	Y	Vaguely, Unworldly.
D	R	E	A	M	I	N	G	Having a dream, The mind running in an idle reverie, Imagining.
D	R	E	A	R	I	L	Y	Depressingly, Dismally, Discouragingly.
D	R	E	D	G	I	N	G	Gathering up in a dredger, Searching.
D	R	E	N	C	H	E	D	Drowned, Submerged, Steeped, Saturated, Pervaded, Soaked, Impregnated.
D	R	E	N	C	H	E	R	A delimer who uses bran drench.
D	R	E	S	S	I	N	G	Erecting, Clothing, Cultivating, Tending, Aligning, Packing, Wearing.
D	R	I	B	B	L	E	D	Trickled, Drooled, Frittered, Wasted, Blundered, Consumed, Squandered, Spent.
D	R	I	B	B	L	E	R	Worker in a glassworks.
D	R	I	B	B	L	E	T	A trifling sum of money, A falling drop of water.
D	R	I	F	T	A	G	E	Drifting caused by the action of wind and water, Deviation from course.
D	R	I	F	T	I	C	E	Fragments of an ice floe blown by wind currents.
D	R	I	F	T	I	N	G	Floating, Sauntering, Ambling, Lingering, Wandering, Rambling.
D	R	I	F	T	N	E	T	A large fishing net that drifts with the tide and is buoyed up by floats.
D	R	I	F	T	W	A	Y	Driveway, Private lane or country road.
D	R	I	L	L	B	O	W	Small bow used for turning a bow drill.
D	R	I	L	L	I	N	G	Boring, Disciplining, Exercising, Practicing, Perforating, Piercing, Rehearsing, Puncturing.
D	R	I	N	K	I	N	G	Absorbing, Imbibing, Quaffing, Sipping, Swallowing, Toasting, Pledging.
D	R	I	P	P	I	N	G	Fats and juices from meat during the cooking, Wet, Drenched, Saturated, Soaking, Sopping.
D	R	I	Z	Z	L	E	D	Rained lightly, Showered, Sprinkled, Dribbled slowly, Slow steady issue of ideas.
D	R	O	I	L	I	N	G	Drudge.
D	R	O	L	L	I	N	G	Drollery.
D	R	O	L	L	E	R	Y	Jest, Humour, Joke, Comedy, Wisecrack, Quip, Witticism.
D	R	O	L	L	I	S	H	Jesting, Sporting, Laughable, Whimsical.
D	R	O	M	I	C	A	L	In the form of a racehorse.
D	R	O	M	I	C	I	A	Genus of marsupials.
D	R	O	N	E	F	L	Y	Two-winged fly resembling the drone-bee.
D	R	O	O	L	I	N	G	Slavering, Drivelling, Talking nonsense, Slobbering, Dribbling, Raving, Enthusing.
D	R	O	O	P	I	N	G	Languishing, Flagging, Wilting, Sagging, Lolling, Depressing, Falling, Sinking.
D	R	O	P	G	O	A	L	Goal scored in rugby by a dropkick.
D	R	O	P	H	E	A	D	Newspaper headline, Convertible automobile.
D	R	O	P	K	I	C	K	A special kick in football and rugby.
D	R	O	P	P	I	N	G	Falling, Sinking, Retreating, Unloading, Depositing, Leaving, Dismissing, Curtsying.
D	R	O	P	S	H	O	T	A ball or shuttlecock that is struck in a way that return is impossible.
D	R	O	P	W	I	S	E	Adding a solution drop by drop.
D	R	O	P	W	O	R	T	Genus of Eurasean herbs.

1	2	3	4	5	6	7	8	Definition
D	R	O	U	G	H	T	Y	Dry, Arid, Lacking moisture, Thirsty.
D	R	O	W	N	I	N	G	Suffocating in water, Soaking, Drenching, Extinguishing, Stunning, Deluging, Overcoming.
D	R	O	W	S	I	L	Y	Indolently, Sleepily, Dozily.
D	R	O	W	S	I	N	G	Sleeping, Dozing, Slumbering.
D	R	U	B	B	I	N	G	Pummeling, Thrashing Berating, Censuring, Stamping, Tapping, Drumming, Pounding.
D	R	U	D	G	E	R	Y	Slavery, Labour, Work, Toil, Travail, Tedium.
D	R	U	D	G	I	N	G	Grinding, Slaving, Plodding, Slogging, Toiling, Plugging, Performing, Pegging away.
D	R	U	G	G	I	N	G	Poisoning with a drug, Doping, Using a narcotic, Administering medicinal drugs, Sedating.
D	R	U	G	G	I	S	T	Chemist, Pharmacist, Apothecary.
D	R	U	I	D	E	S	S	A female druid.
D	R	U	I	D	I	S	M	Early Celtic religion with belief in the immortality of the soul.
D	R	U	M	F	I	R	E	Continuous artillery barrage.
D	R	U	M	F	I	S	H	Genus of American fish making a drumming noise.
D	R	U	M	H	E	A	D	Tympanic membrane, Drumskin, A skin stretched over each end of a drum.
D	R	U	M	M	I	N	G	Stirring interest, Soliciting, Canvassing, Vibrating, Beating, Throbbing, Tapping, Driving.
D	R	U	M	S	K	I	N	Various plant and animal membranes.
D	R	U	N	K	A	R	D	One suffering from chronic alcoholism, Boozer, Inebriate, Tippler, Toper.
D	R	U	P	E	L	E	T	Individual part of an aggregate fruit such as rasberry and like fruits.
D	R	U	T	H	E	R	S	Preference.
D	R	Y	B	E	L	L	Y	Botulism of cattle.
D	R	Y	C	L	E	A	N	To clean with solvents as opposed to water.
D	R	Y	G	O	O	D	S	Textiles, Drapery, Goods other than food.
D	R	Y	P	L	A	T	E	Photographic plate.
D	R	Y	P	O	I	N	T	Engraving made with a needle.
D	R	Y	S	T	E	A	M	Steam without free water particles.
D	R	Y	S	T	O	V	E	Hothouse with low relative humidity.
D	R	Y	W	A	X	E	D	Made in such a way that the wax is almost all driven into the paper.
D	U	A	L	I	Z	E	D	Made dual.
D	U	B	I	T	A	T	E	Doubt.
D	U	C	A	T	O	O	N	16th Century silver coin.
D	U	C	H	E	S	S	E	18th Century chaise longue, Fine satin or rayon fabric, Small cream puff.
D	U	C	K	B	I	L	L	Platypus, Having a bill shaped like a duck.
D	U	C	K	F	O	O	T	Mollusk, Shovel attached to a cultivator.
D	U	C	K	H	A	W	K	American falcon.
D	U	C	K	L	I	N	G	A young duck.
D	U	C	K	M	O	L	E	Platypus.
D	U	C	K	S	E	G	G	The egg of a duck.
D	U	C	K	S	H	O	T	Lead shot used in duck hunting.
D	U	C	K	W	E	E	D	Small floating aquatic plant.
D	U	C	T	I	B	L	E	Ductile, Pliant, Flexible, Malleable, Amenable.
D	U	C	T	L	E	S	S	Without a duct.
D	U	C	T	W	O	R	K	A system of ducts.
D	U	E	L	L	I	N	G	Fighting in a duel.
D	U	E	L	L	I	S	T	One who fights in a duel.
D	U	E	T	T	I	S	T	A participant in a duet.
D	U	K	E	L	I	N	G	An insignificant duke.
D	U	L	C	I	M	E	R	Wire stringed instrument played with hammers.
D	U	L	L	H	E	A	D	Blockhead, Dullard.
D	U	L	L	N	E	S	S	Stupidity, Apathy, Drowsiness, Bluntness, Monotony, Lethargy, Slumber, Languor.
D	U	M	B	B	E	L	L	Exercise appliance, One that is dull and stupid.
D	U	M	B	C	A	N	E	Tropical American herb that if it is chewed causes the tongue to swell.
D	U	M	B	N	E	S	S	Muteness, Silence, Inability to speak, Stupidity, Dullness.
D	U	M	B	S	H	O	W	Pantomime, Dramatic performance with only signs and gestures.
D	U	M	P	L	I	N	G	Small amount of unleavened dough boiled or steamed.
D	U	N	D	I	V	E	R	Female or immature diving duck.
D	U	N	G	A	R	E	E	Work overall made from heavy coarse cotton twill.
D	U	N	G	H	I	L	L	Heap of dung, Degraded or vile situation.
D	U	O	D	E	N	A	L	Relating to the duodenum.
D	U	O	D	E	N	U	M	Beginning of the small intestine.
D	U	O	L	O	G	U	E	Dialogue reserved for two people.
D	U	O	P	S	O	N	Y	Market manipulation of supply and demand by two rival buyers.
D	U	R	A	B	L	E	S	Household appliances expected to be in use for a number of years.
D	U	R	A	T	I	O	N	Term, Span, Time, Run, Continuation, Endurance, Persistence.
D	U	R	A	T	I	V	E	Continuing, Imperfect.
D	U	S	K	E	N	E	D	Becoming dusk.
D	U	S	T	B	A	L	L	Concretion of matter found in the intestine.
D	U	S	T	B	A	N	D	Plate in a watch to exclude dust.

8 LETTERS

1	2	3	4	5	6	7	8	Definition
D	U	S	T	C	A	R	T	Vehicle for collection of household refuse.
D	U	S	T	C	O	A	T	Coat of lightweight cotton worn to protect clothing.
D	U	S	T	H	E	A	P	Pile of refuse.
D	U	T	C	H	M	A	N	Hollander, Native of the Netherlands.
D	U	T	I	A	B	L	E	Subject to duty.
D	U	T	Y	F	R	E	E	Not liable for duty.
D	W	A	R	F	I	N	G	Stunting in growth, Hindering development.
D	W	A	R	F	I	S	H	Resembling a dwarf.
D	W	A	R	F	I	S	M	Condition of stunted growth.
D	W	E	L	L	I	N	G	Living, Residing, Abode, Habitation, Consisting, Existing, Domicile, House, Residence.
D	W	I	N	D	L	E	D	Decreased, Diminished, Declined, Abated, Lessened, Reduced, Subsided, Disappeared.
D	Y	A	R	C	H	I	C	Pertaining to government by two rulers.
D	Y	E	H	O	U	S	E	Building where dyeing operations are carried out.
D	Y	E	S	T	U	F	F	Dye.
D	Y	N	A	M	I	C	S	Driving physical, moral or intellectual forces, Pattern of change.
D	Y	N	A	M	I	S	M	Theory that explains the universe in terms of forces.
D	Y	N	A	M	I	S	T	An adherent of dynamism.
D	Y	N	A	M	I	T	E	Solid blasting explosive, Something that has great potential.
D	Y	N	A	M	O	U	S	Having developing power.
D	Y	N	A	S	T	E	S	Genus of beetle, Rhinocerus beetle.
D	Y	N	A	S	T	I	C	Belonging to a dynasty.
D	Y	N	A	T	R	O	N	A four-electrode vacuum tube.
D	Y	S	E	R	G	I	A	Inability to exert oneself, Difficulty in working.
D	Y	S	G	E	N	I	C	Biologically defective.
D	Y	S	G	O	N	I	C	Growing with difficulty on an artificial media.
D	Y	S	L	A	L	I	A	Unable to articulate due to malformation of organs.
D	Y	S	L	E	X	I	A	Difficulty in reading.
D	Y	S	L	O	G	I	A	Difficulty in expressing ideas through speech caused by impairment in power of reasoning.
D	Y	S	L	U	I	T	E	A brown variety of gahnite.
D	Y	S	O	D	I	L	E	A hydrocarbon mineral.
D	Y	S	P	A	T	H	Y	Lack of sympathy.
D	Y	S	P	E	P	S	Y	Dyspepsia, Disturbed digestion, Heartburn.
D	Y	S	P	N	O	E	A	Difficulty in breathing.
D	Y	S	S	O	D	I	A	Small genus of prairie herbs.
D	Y	S	T	O	C	I	A	Difficult childbirth.
D	Y	S	T	O	N	I	A	A state of disordered tonicity of tissues.

E

1	2	3	4	5	6	7	8	Definition
E	A	G	L	E	O	W	L	Genus of large horned owls.
E	A	G	L	E	R	A	Y	Large stingray.
E	A	R	D	R	O	P	S	Ear medication to be inserted by means of a dropper.
E	A	R	J	E	W	E	L	Jewelweed.
E	A	R	L	S	H	I	P	The rank of earl.
E	A	R	L	Y	I	S	H	Somewhat early.
E	A	R	P	H	O	N	E	Device that transmits sound waves and is worn over or in the ear.
E	A	R	P	I	E	C	E	Sidepiece of spectacles, Anything to protect the ear.
E	A	R	R	E	A	C	H	Range within which an unaided voice may be heard.
E	A	R	S	H	E	L	L	Abalone.
E	A	R	S	P	O	O	L	Earplug worn in the lobe of the ear by primitive people.
E	A	R	T	H	H	O	G	Aardvaark.
E	A	R	T	H	I	N	G	Hiding in the earth, Burrowing, Burying, Guiding electrical current to earth.
E	A	R	T	H	M	A	N	Human resident of the planet Earth.
E	A	R	T	H	N	U	T	Truffle, Edible root or tuber, Peanut.
E	A	R	W	I	G	G	Y	Full of earwigs.
E	A	S	E	L	E	S	S	Unceasing, Subject to no relief or rest.
E	A	S	E	M	E	N	T	Alleviation, Mitigation, Relief, Entertainment, Servitude, Privilege.
E	A	S	I	N	E	S	S	Kindness, Relaxed easy poise, Credulity, Freedom from harshness.
E	A	S	T	E	R	L	Y	Toward the east, Wind blowing from the east.
E	A	S	T	L	A	K	E	Machine-made furniture of a sturdy character.
E	A	S	T	M	O	S	T	The farthest point in the East.
E	A	S	T	S	I	D	E	The eastern side of Manhatten.
E	A	S	T	W	A	R	D	Toward the east.
E	A	S	T	W	E	S	T	Along a line of geographic latitude.
E	A	S	Y	L	I	K	E	Gently, Cautiously.
E	A	U	D	E	V	I	E	Spirit distilled from fruit or fruit juice, Brandy.

1	2	3	4	5	6	7	8	Meaning
E	B	E	N	A	L	E	S	An order of shrubs and trees.
E	B	E	N	E	Z	E	R	A memorial, Anger, Temper.
E	B	I	O	N	I	S	M	Principles and practices of the Ebionites.
E	B	I	O	N	I	T	E	One of a Judaistic Christian Gnostic sect of the 2nd century.
E	B	O	N	I	Z	E	D	Stained black to imitate ebony.
E	B	U	R	N	E	A	N	Resembling ivory in colour.
E	C	A	U	D	A	T	E	Minus a tail.
E	C	C	L	E	S	I	A	An assembly of ancient Athenian citizens, A local organization of the Christadelphians.
E	C	D	E	M	I	T	E	A yellow or green lead arsenate and chloride.
E	C	D	Y	S	I	A	L	Relating to moulting or shedding outer covering.
E	C	G	O	N	I	N	E	A crystalline alkaloid.
E	C	H	A	P	P	E	E	An escape note.
E	C	H	E	N	E	I	D	Genus of fish, Remora.
E	C	H	E	N	E	I	S	Same as ECHENEID.
E	C	H	I	N	A	T	E	Covered with spines, Prickly like a hedgehog.
E	C	H	I	N	I	T	E	A fossil sea urchin.
E	C	H	I	N	O	I	D	A sea urchin.
E	C	H	I	N	O	P	S	A large genus of Mediterranean herbs, Thistles.
E	C	H	I	U	R	U	S	Common genus of marine worms.
E	C	H	O	G	R	A	M	Record made by a sonic depth finder.
E	C	H	O	L	E	S	S	Producing no echo.
E	C	L	E	C	T	I	C	A free choice of the best on offer.
E	C	L	I	P	S	E	D	Obscured, Extinguished, Darkened, Dimmed, Overshadowed, Reduced in rank.
E	C	L	I	P	S	E	R	Occulting screen for a light in a lighthouse.
E	C	L	I	P	S	I	S	Suppression of words or sound.
E	C	L	I	P	T	I	C	Relating to an eclipse.
E	C	L	O	G	I	T	E	Metamorphic rock.
E	C	L	O	S	I	O	N	Hatching from an egg or emerging from pupa.
E	C	O	N	O	M	I	C	Household management, Having practical use, Sparing, Profitable.
E	C	O	P	H	E	N	E	Ecad, An acquired character organism modified by environment.
E	C	O	S	T	A	T	E	A leaf having no midvein or midrib.
E	C	P	H	O	R	I	A	The rousing of an engram from a latent to an active state.
E	C	S	T	A	T	I	C	Rapturous, Exhilarated, Blissful, Joyful, Intoxicated, Euphoric.
E	C	T	O	C	Y	S	T	The external walls of a cyst, cell or coral.
E	C	T	O	D	E	R	M	Outer cellular membrane of a jellyfish.
E	C	T	O	L	O	P	H	Top of molar teeth.
E	C	T	O	S	A	R	C	A grass cell before change.
E	C	T	O	Z	O	I	C	Relating to external animal parasites.
E	C	U	M	E	N	I	C	Worldwide, Universal, General, Tending toward worldwide Christian unity.
E	D	A	C	I	O	U	S	Voracious, Devouring, Gluttonous, Rapacious, Ravenous.
E	D	D	I	S	H	E	S	Taro.
E	D	E	N	T	A	T	A	Mammals with a few teeth, Sloths, Armadillos, Anteaters, Pangolins, Aardvaaks.
E	D	E	N	T	A	T	E	Lacking teeth.
E	D	G	E	L	E	S	S	Lacking an edge, Dull, Blunted, Blurred.
E	D	G	E	R	A	I	L	Guardrail laid alongside the main rail at a switch.
E	D	G	E	S	H	O	T	Having a planed edge.
E	D	G	E	T	O	O	L	A tool with a cutting edge.
E	D	G	E	W	A	Y	S	With the edge toward, By an edge, Barely.
E	D	G	E	W	I	S	E	Same as EDGEWAYS.
E	D	G	I	N	E	S	S	A sharply defined outline, Nervousness.
E	D	I	F	Y	I	N	G	Organizing, Uplifting, Elevating, Establishing, Improving, Enlightening, Instructing.
E	D	I	T	R	E	S	S	A female editor.
E	D	U	C	A	B	L	E	Capable of being educated.
E	D	U	C	A	T	E	D	Reared, Informed, Accustomed, Skilled, Taught, Instructed, Trained, Literate.
E	D	U	C	A	T	O	R	Teacher, Educationist, Education administrator.
E	D	U	C	I	B	L	E	Capable of being evoked.
E	D	U	C	T	I	O	N	Inference, Action of eliciting.
E	E	L	G	R	A	S	S	Submerged marine plant.
E	E	L	S	P	E	A	R	A barbed spear for catching eels.
E	E	R	I	N	E	S	S	Weirdness, Creepiness, Strangeness.
E	F	F	A	C	I	N	G	Eradicating, Destroying, Overshadowing, Annulling, Deleting, Obliterating, Expunging.
E	F	F	E	C	T	E	D	Produced, Accomplished, Executed, Performed, Created, Generated, Achieved, Realized.
E	F	F	E	C	T	O	R	One that creates.
E	F	F	E	R	E	N	T	Conducting outward from a part or organ, Centrifugal, Motor, Blood vessel, Nerve centre.
E	F	F	I	C	A	C	Y	Effectiveness, Power to produce an effect.
E	F	F	I	G	I	A	L	Resembling an effigy.
E	F	F	I	G	I	E	S	Full or partial representations of persons, Portraits on coins.

1	2	3	4	5	6	7	8	Definition
E	F	F	L	U	E	N	T	Something that flows out, Emanating, Outgoing.
E	F	F	L	U	V	I	A	Emanation, Exhaust, Unpleasant smell, Waste product, Noxious gases.
E	F	F	O	R	C	E	D	Forced.
E	F	F	U	L	G	E	D	Radiated.
E	F	F	U	S	I	N	G	Radiating, Shedding, Emanating, Pouring out.
E	F	F	U	S	I	O	N	Poured out, Extravasation, Flow of gas, Unrestrained delight.
E	F	F	U	S	I	V	E	Pouring freely, Gushing, Demonstrative, Expansive, Profuse, Unrestrained, Unreserved.
E	F	T	S	O	O	N	S	Quickly, Often.
E	G	E	S	T	I	N	G	Ridding the body of waste matter by any normal route.
E	G	E	S	T	I	O	N	Excretion of waste substances.
E	G	G	A	P	P	L	E	Eggplant.
E	G	G	D	A	N	C	E	An old English dance among eggs performed by dancer with a blindfold on.
E	G	G	F	R	U	I	T	Edible fruit of certain plants.
E	G	G	P	L	A	N	T	Hairy woody perennial herb, Brinjal, Aubergine.
E	G	G	S	H	E	L	L	Hard exterior covering of an egg, Special finish to paper.
E	G	G	T	O	O	T	H	Sharp prominence on beak or nose of baby birds and reptiles with which they break their shells.
E	G	L	A	T	E	R	E	Eglantine, Dog rose.
E	G	L	O	M	I	S	E	Painted glass with a gilded picture showing through from the back.
E	G	O	I	S	T	I	C	Egocentric, Self-centred, Selfish, Self-satisfied, Individualistic, Self-absorbed.
E	G	O	P	H	O	N	Y	Change in voice caused by certain chest diseases.
E	G	O	T	I	S	T	S	Someone who suffered self-conceit.
E	G	R	E	S	S	E	D	Went out, Issued, Exodus, Emerged, Exited, Departed, Escaped.
E	G	Y	P	T	I	A	N	Relating to ancient Egypt.
E	G	Y	P	T	I	A	N	Inhabitant of Egypt.
E	I	C	O	S	A	N	E	Any of the isomeric hydrocarbons.
E	I	G	H	T	E	E	N	One more than seventeen, One and a half dozen.
E	I	G	H	T	H	L	Y	In the eighth place.
E	J	E	C	T	I	N	G	Expelling, Ousting, Dispossessing, Emitting, Evicting, Displacing, Eliminating, Discharging.
E	J	E	C	T	I	O	N	Expulsion, Discharge, Dismissal.
E	J	E	C	T	I	V	E	Causing ejection.
E	L	A	N	C	I	N	G	Launching, Throwing, Hurling.
E	L	A	P	H	I	N	E	Resembling the red deer.
E	L	A	P	S	I	N	G	Passing, Expiring, Going, Gliding, Emanating, Finishing.
E	L	A	S	T	A	S	E	An enzyme obtained from the pancreas that decomposes elastin and collagen.
E	L	A	T	E	D	L	Y	Exultant, Excitedly, Enrapturous, Ecstatic.
E	L	A	T	E	R	I	D	A genus of beetles Click beetle.
E	L	A	T	E	R	I	N	A bitter white crystalline poisonous cathartic substance.
E	L	B	O	W	I	N	G	Pushing, Jostling, Nudging, Forcing, Turning, Hustling, Pressing, Shoving.
E	L	D	O	R	A	D	O	A place of fabulous wealth, abundance or opportunity, End of the rainbow.
E	L	D	R	I	T	C	H	Weird, Eerie, Uncanny.
E	L	E	C	T	I	N	G	Choosing, Designating, Picking, Deciding, Determining, Judging, Balloting, Nominating.
E	L	E	C	T	I	O	N	Choice, Freewill, Acceptance, Alternative, Preference.
E	L	E	C	T	I	V	E	Optional, Discretionary, Facultative, Assigned by popular selection.
E	L	E	C	T	R	E	T	A dielectric body in which a permanent state of electric polarization has been set up.
E	L	E	C	T	R	I	C	Charged by an electric potential, Stimulated.
E	L	E	C	T	R	O	N	One of the constituent elementary particles of an atom.
E	L	E	C	T	R	U	M	Natural pale yellow alloy of gold and silver.
E	L	E	G	A	N	C	E	Dignity, Grace, Culture, Polish, Sophistication, Taste, Richness, Refinement.
E	L	E	G	A	N	C	Y	Elegance, Dignity, Propriety.
E	L	E	G	A	N	T	E	A fashionable woman.
E	L	E	G	I	A	S	T	Elegist, Composer of an elegy.
E	L	E	G	I	S	E	D	Lamented, Celebrated in elegy.
E	L	E	M	E	N	E	S	A liquid ether.
E	L	E	N	C	H	U	S	Refutation.
E	L	E	N	C	T	I	C	Serving to refute.
E	L	E	O	T	R	I	D	Large family of widely distributed small fishes.
E	L	E	P	H	A	N	T	Giant mammal, Mammoth.
E	L	E	U	S	I	N	E	Genus of grasses.
E	L	E	V	A	T	E	D	Excited, Noble, Refined, Exhilarated, Formal, Dignified, Tipsy, Intoxicated.
E	L	E	V	A	T	O	R	Something that raises or lifts anything.
E	L	E	V	E	N	T	H	One of an eleventh equal part.
E	L	F	A	R	R	O	W	Flint arrowhead.
E	L	F	C	H	I	L	D	Changeling.
E	L	I	C	I	T	E	D	Drawn out, Evinced, Evoked, Extorted, Extracted, Fetched.
E	L	I	G	I	B	L	E	Advantageous, Preferable, Desirable, Possible, Acceptable, Capable, Qualified, Marriageable.
E	L	I	G	I	B	L	Y	In an eligible manner.
E	L	L	I	P	S	I	S	Omission of one or more words necessary for grammatical accuracy, Suspension.

1	2	3	4	5	6	7	8	
E	L	L	I	P	T	I	C	Summary, Brief, Concise, Condensed, Enigmatic, Cryptic, Oblique, Obscure.
E	L	L	O	B	I	U	M	Genus of snails.
E	L	O	C	U	L	A	R	Having only one cavity.
E	L	O	N	G	A	T	E	Depart, Recede, Extend, Lengthen, Prolong, Protract, Stretch.
E	L	O	Q	U	E	N	T	Expressive, Vocal, Articulate, Fluent, Forceful, Potent, Voluble, Meaningful.
E	L	S	E	W	I	S	E	Otherwise.
E	L	U	V	I	A	T	E	The downward soil movement during heavy rainfall.
E	L	V	I	S	H	L	Y	Mischievously, Spitefully, Impishly, Irritatingly.
E	L	Y	T	R	O	I	D	Resembling the protective wing cover of beetles.
E	M	A	C	I	A	T	E	Waste away, Decline, Weaken, Enfeeble, Attenuate.
E	M	A	N	A	T	E	D	Emitted, Arisen, Born, Derived, Issued, Originated, Proceeded, Stemmed.
E	M	A	N	A	T	O	R	One that emanates.
E	M	B	A	L	I	N	G	Wrapping, Baling.
E	M	B	A	L	M	E	D	Preserved, Treated, Perfumed, Protected from decay.
E	M	B	A	L	M	E	R	A person who prepared the dead for burial.
E	M	B	A	N	K	E	D	Build up a mound usually at the side of a river or canal.
E	M	B	A	R	K	E	D	Boarded a boat or plane, Invested, Commenced.
E	M	B	A	R	R	E	D	Enclosed, Imprisoned, Barred, Impeded.
E	M	B	A	T	T	L	E	Fortify with battlements, Castellate.
E	M	B	A	Y	I	N	G	Sheltering, Encircling, Surrounding.
E	M	B	E	D	D	E	D	Enclosed, Surrounded tightly, Entrenched, Ingrained, Rooted, Lodged.
E	M	B	E	R	I	Z	A	Genus of passerine birds, Finched.
E	M	B	E	Z	Z	L	E	Lessen, Weaken, Squander, Dissipate, Appropriate, Fraudently.
E	M	B	I	O	D	E	A	Embiodea, Small order of tropical insects.
E	M	B	I	T	T	E	R	Exacerbate, Acerbate, Make bitter or sour.
E	M	B	L	A	Z	E	D	Illuminated, Kindled.
E	M	B	L	A	Z	O	N	To adorn with heraldic designs, Celebrate, Extol.
E	M	B	O	D	I	E	D	Organized, Personified, Coalesced.
E	M	B	O	D	I	E	R	One that embodies.
E	M	B	O	G	G	E	D	Sink down, Mire, Bog down.
E	M	B	O	L	D	E	N	Encourage, Animate, Cheer, Hearten, Strengthen, Inspire, Venture, Hazard.
E	M	B	O	L	I	S	M	Obstruction in a blood vessel usually a blood clot, Intercalation.
E	M	B	O	L	I	T	E	A mineral consisting of native silver chloride and bromite.
E	M	B	O	L	I	U	M	Narrow edge on wings of bugs.
E	M	B	O	L	I	Z	E	To lodge in and obstruct.
E	M	B	O	R	D	E	R	To edge with a border.
E	M	B	O	S	S	E	D	Inflated, Raised device or decoration in relief.
E	M	B	O	S	S	E	R	Operator of a machine for forming raised designs.
E	M	B	O	W	I	N	G	Arching, Vaulting.
E	M	B	R	A	C	E	D	Hugged, Encircled, Enclosed, Encompassed, Enfolded, Included, Covered, Adopted.
E	M	B	R	A	C	E	R	One that embraces.
E	M	B	R	A	V	E	D	Brightened, Inspired.
E	M	B	R	U	T	E	D	Degraded to the level of a brute, Brutalized.
E	M	B	R	Y	O	I	D	Resembling an embryo.
E	M	B	R	Y	O	U	S	Embryonic.
E	M	B	U	S	Q	U	E	Shirker, Slacker, A person seeking to avoid military service.
E	M	B	U	S	S	E	D	Boarded a bus.
E	M	E	N	D	A	T	E	Emend, Correct, Improve, Rectify, Right.
E	M	E	N	D	I	N	G	Correcting, Improving, Editing, Altering, Retouching.
E	M	E	R	G	E	N	T	Emerging, Issuing, Suddenly appearing, Urgent.
E	M	E	R	G	I	N	G	Appearing, Looming, Showing, Deriving, Originating, Issuing, Stemming, Materializing.
E	M	E	R	I	T	E	D	Retired from occupation or service.
E	M	E	R	I	T	U	S	One retired from professional life but permitted an honorary title of his last rank.
E	M	E	R	S	I	O	N	Reappearance of a planet after an eclipse.
E	M	E	T	I	C	A	L	A substance that will cause vomiting.
E	M	I	G	R	A	N	T	A person who leaves a country to establish a new life somewhere else.
E	M	I	G	R	A	T	E	Leave a country for residence elsewhere.
E	M	I	N	E	N	C	E	Superior rank, Position of distinction, Prestige, Prominence, Renown, Dignity, Dignitary.
E	M	I	N	E	N	C	Y	Outstanding quality, Prominence.
E	M	I	S	S	A	R	Y	Agent, Representative, Spy, Undercover agent, Messenger, Courier, Carrier.
E	M	I	S	S	I	L	E	Capable of being protruded used for certain worms.
E	M	I	S	S	I	O	N	Emanation, Ejaculate, Effluvium, Circulatize.
E	M	I	S	S	I	V	E	Emitted.
E	M	I	T	T	I	N	G	Discharging, Releasing, Transmitting, Expressing, Delivering, Oozing, Exhaling, Venting.
E	M	M	A	R	B	L	E	To make like marble.
E	M	P	A	L	I	N	G	Impaling, Tranfixing.
E	M	P	A	N	A	D	A	A turnover filled with meat.

1	2	3	4	5	6	7	8	
E	M	P	E	O	P	L	E	Populate.
E	M	P	E	T	R	U	M	Genus of low shrubs having flowers scattered, Crowberry.
E	M	P	H	A	S	I	S	Forcefulness, Prominence, Stress, Importance, Distinct, Vividness, Insistence, Accent.
E	M	P	H	A	T	I	C	Prominent, Insistent, Striking, Conspicuous, Assertive, Aggressive, Vigorous, Accented.
E	M	P	I	E	R	C	E	Penetrate.
E	M	P	I	R	I	S	M	Quackery, Charlatanry, Pragmatism.
E	M	P	L	A	C	E	D	Placed in position.
E	M	P	L	A	N	E	D	Boarded a plane.
E	M	P	L	O	Y	E	D	Used, Occupied, Implied, Busied, Enclosed, Engaged, Utilized, Working.
E	M	P	L	O	Y	E	E	Worker engaged for a salary or wage.
E	M	P	L	O	Y	E	R	One that employs something or somebody.
E	M	P	L	U	M	E	D	Furnished with plumes.
E	M	P	O	I	S	O	N	Embitter.
E	M	P	O	R	I	U	M	Market-place, Mart, Commercial centre, Departmental store.
E	M	P	T	Y	I	N	G	Removing, Depriving, Evacuating, Divesting, Depriving, Clearing, Depleting, Vacating.
E	M	P	U	R	P	L	E	Redden, Flushed.
E	M	P	Y	R	E	A	L	Celestial, Sublime.
E	M	P	Y	R	E	A	N	Heavens, Firmament, Divine, Spiritual.
E	M	U	L	A	T	E	D	Imitated, Rivalled, Endeavoured, Competed, Challenged, Contested.
E	M	U	L	A	T	O	R	Imitator, Rival.
E	M	U	L	G	E	N	T	Something that drains, An organ or part that strains substances, such as kidneys.
E	M	U	L	S	I	O	N	Milky fluid, Mixture of two miscible liquids.
E	M	U	L	S	I	V	E	Yielding an emulsion.
E	M	U	L	S	O	I	D	A colloidal system consisting of a liquid dispersed in a liquid.
E	M	Y	D	I	D	A	E	Family of chelonians, Freshwater aquatic tortoises, Terrapins.
E	N	A	B	L	I	N	G	Allowing, Endowing, Authorizing, Licensing, Permitting, Sanctioning, Qualifying, Letting.
E	N	A	C	T	I	N	G	Chronicling, Representing, Performing, Executing, Establishing, Making, Proclaiming.
E	N	A	C	T	U	R	E	Resolution, Enactment.
E	N	A	N	T	H	E	M	An eruption upon a mucous surface.
E	N	A	R	C	H	E	D	In heraldry bent into an arch or curve.
E	N	A	S	C	E	N	T	Nascent, Origin.
E	N	C	A	E	N	I	A	Annual university ceremony.
E	N	C	A	G	I	N	G	Confining in a cage.
E	N	C	A	M	P	E	D	Formed into a camp.
E	N	C	A	R	P	U	S	Decoration on frieze of festoons of fruit or flowers.
E	N	C	A	S	H	E	D	Cashed, Converted into cash.
E	N	C	A	S	I	N	G	Enclosing, Providing with a case.
E	N	C	A	S	T	R	E	To castrate.
E	N	C	A	V	I	N	G	Hiding in a cave.
E	N	C	E	I	N	T	E	Pregnant, Fortification surrounding a castle.
E	N	C	H	A	R	G	E	Entrust.
E	N	C	H	A	S	E	D	Ornamented, Decorated, Engraved, Inlaid, Enshrined, Enclosed.
E	N	C	I	P	H	E	R	To convert into a cipher.
E	N	C	I	R	C	L	E	Surround, Encompass, Girdle, Ring, Hem, Gird, Environ.
E	N	C	L	I	S	I	S	Inclined, Accentuated in grammar.
E	N	C	L	I	T	I	C	Same as ENCLISIS.
E	N	C	L	O	S	E	D	Surround, Envelop, Enfold, Confine, Hold, Fence, Pen, Coop.
E	N	C	L	O	S	E	R	One that holds.
E	N	C	L	O	T	H	E	To cover with clothing.
E	N	C	O	F	F	I	N	To shut up as if in a coffin.
E	N	C	O	L	U	R	E	The mane of a horse.
E	N	C	O	M	I	U	M	Eulogy, Citation, Panegyric, Salutation, Tribute, Praise, Accaim, Accolade.
E	N	C	O	R	I	N	G	Request for a repeat performance by audience acclaimation.
E	N	C	R	I	N	A	L	Relating to fossil crinoids.
E	N	C	R	I	N	I	C	Same as ENCRINAL.
E	N	C	R	O	A	C	H	Trespass, Intrude, Entrench, Infringe, Invade, Interpose, Intervene, Meddle.
E	N	C	U	M	B	E	R	Burden, Hinder, Impede, Hamper, Load, Saddle, Inconvenience, Obstruct.
E	N	C	Y	C	L	I	C	Important missive of grave importance and intended for intensive publication.
E	N	C	Y	S	T	E	D	Enclosed as in a cyst or capsule.
E	N	D	A	M	A	G	E	Harm, Injure.
E	N	D	A	N	G	E	R	Compromise, Hazard, Imperil, Jeopardize, Menace, Risk, Expose, Venture.
E	N	D	B	R	A	I	N	Anterior subdivision of the forebrain.
E	N	D	E	A	R	E	D	Beloved, Made fond of, Esteemed.
E	N	D	E	M	I	A	L	Endemic, Indigenous, Native.
E	N	D	E	N	I	Z	E	Naturalize.
E	N	D	E	R	M	I	C	Acting through the skin, Direct application to the skin.
E	N	D	O	C	A	R	P	Inner skin of a fruit.

1	2	3	4	5	6	7	8	Definition
E	N	D	O	C	Y	S	T	Inner membrane.
E	N	D	O	D	E	R	M	Innermost of three primary germ layers of an embryo.
E	N	D	O	F	O	R	M	A rust producing spores in the aecia.
E	N	D	O	G	A	M	Y	Marriage within a specific group as required by custom or law.
E	N	D	O	G	E	N	Y	Growth from a deep-seated layer.
E	N	D	O	M	E	R	E	A blastomere forming endoderm.
E	N	D	O	R	S	E	D	Approved, Underwritten, Accredited, Certified, Sanctioned, Authenticated, Vouched.
E	N	D	O	R	S	E	E	One to whom a bill is endorsed.
E	N	D	O	S	A	R	C	Endoplasm, The semifluid part of the protoplasm of amoebas.
E	N	D	O	S	O	M	E	The inner part of the body of a sponge, Central body of a vesicular nucleus.
E	N	D	O	W	I	N	G	Enriching, Heightening, Enhancing, Crediting, Bestowing, Awarding, Financing, Subsidizing.
E	N	D	O	Z	O	I	C	Involving passing through an animal.
E	N	D	P	A	P	E	R	A folded sheet of paper being pasted down on one side and forming a flyleaf on the other side.
E	N	D	P	L	A	T	E	A flat terminal plate, Complex treelike bunching of motor nerve fibre.
E	N	D	U	R	I	N	G	Lasting, Strengthening, Suffering, Allowing, Permitting, Bearing, Continuing, Tolerating.
E	N	E	R	G	E	I	A	Energy.
E	N	E	R	G	I	S	M	Self-realizationism.
E	N	E	R	G	I	S	T	Adherent of energism.
E	N	E	R	G	I	Z	E	Strengthen, Vitalize.
E	N	E	R	V	A	T	E	Enfeeble, Weaken, Unnerve, Unstring, Debilitate, Disable, Exhaust, Fatigue.
E	N	F	A	C	I	N	G	Facing forward, Opposite, Write or print on a draft.
E	N	F	E	E	B	L	E	Weaken, Attenuate, Blunt, Cripple, Disable, Sap, Undermine, Exhaust.
E	N	F	E	T	T	E	R	To shackle in fetters.
E	N	F	I	L	A	D	E	Arrangement in opposite and parallel rows.
E	N	F	O	L	D	E	D	Contained, Enveloped, Embraced, Enclosed, Enwrapped, Clasped, Shrouded, Veiled.
E	N	F	O	R	C	E	D	Reinforced, Implemented, Assaulted, Compelled, Constrained, Effected, Obliged.
E	N	F	O	R	C	E	R	One that uses force.
E	N	F	O	R	E	S	T	To convert into a forest.
E	N	F	R	A	M	E	D	Placed in a frame.
E	N	G	A	G	I	N	G	Attractive, Sweet, Exhorting, Persuading, Occupying, Participating, Attracting, Promising.
E	N	G	E	N	D	E	R	Procreate, Propagate, Produce, Originate, Stem, Breed, Multiply, Develop.
E	N	G	I	L	D	E	D	Gilded, Brightened.
E	N	G	I	N	E	E	R	Arrange, Contrive, Devise, Plot, Intrigue, Manage, Manipulate, Negotiate.
E	N	G	I	N	E	R	Y	Machinery, Plant, Tools, Mechanical devices.
E	N	G	I	N	I	N	G	Equipping with an engine.
E	N	G	I	R	D	E	D	Encompassed, Enveloped.
E	N	G	I	R	D	L	E	Girdle, Circle, Surround.
E	N	G	L	O	B	E	D	Enclosed as if in a globe.
E	N	G	O	R	G	E	D	Devoured, Engulfed, Crammed, Satiated, Filled.
E	N	G	O	U	L	E	D	Congestion, Hyperemia.
E	N	G	R	A	M	M	E	Protoplasmic change in relation to persistence of memory.
E	N	G	R	A	V	E	D	Etched, Incised, Carved, Inscribed, Impressed, Instilled, Entrenched, Imprinted.
E	N	G	R	A	V	E	R	Producer of engraving.
E	N	G	R	O	O	V	E	Fit into a groove.
E	N	G	U	L	F	E	D	Overwhelmed, Overpowered, Drowned, Inundated, Overflowed, Flooded, Submerged.
E	N	H	A	N	C	E	D	Intensified, Aggravated, Extolled, Advanced, Augmented, Elevated, Ornamented.
E	N	H	A	N	C	E	R	One that embellishes.
E	N	H	A	R	D	E	N	Harden.
E	N	H	O	R	R	O	R	Horrify.
E	N	H	U	N	G	E	R	To make hungry.
E	N	H	Y	D	R	O	S	A hollow nodule of chalcedony containing water.
E	N	J	A	I	L	E	D	Confined as if in jail.
E	N	J	A	M	B	E	D	Running over of a sentence from one line into another.
E	N	J	O	I	N	E	D	Forbade, Prohibited, Commanded, Directed, Instructed, Ordered, Told, Warned.
E	N	J	O	Y	I	N	G	Rejoicing, Having, Liking, Amusing, Entertaining, Contemplating, Appreciating, Possessing.
E	N	K	I	N	D	L	E	Cause to ignite, Flame, To make bright and glowing.
E	N	L	A	C	I	N	G	Encircling, Enfolding, Entangling, Entwining, Interlacing.
E	N	L	A	R	D	E	D	Larded.
E	N	L	A	R	G	E	D	Magnified, Expanded, Dilated, Expatiated, Increased, Augmented, Heightened, Multiplied.
E	N	L	A	R	G	E	R	Optical projecter used to produce a photographic enlargement.
E	N	L	I	N	K	E	D	Connected by links.
E	N	L	I	S	T	E	D	Engaged in military service for a set period, Attracted, Participated.
E	N	L	O	C	K	E	D	Locked up.
E	N	M	A	R	B	L	E	Emmarble.
E	N	M	E	S	H	E	D	Caught, Entangled.
E	N	N	E	A	D	I	C	Relating to an ennead, a group of nine.
E	N	N	O	B	L	E	D	Exalted, Aggrandized, Dignified, Erected, Glorified, Honoured, Magnified.

1	2	3	4	5	6	7	8	
E	N	O	R	M	I	T	Y	Abnormality, Hugeness, Immensity, Monstrous, Outrageous.
E	N	O	R	M	O	U	S	Extremely, Very, Inordinate, Huge, Colossal, Gigantic, Immense, Titanic.
E	N	O	U	N	C	E	D	Enunciated, Stated.
E	N	P	L	A	N	E	D	Boarded a plane.
E	N	Q	U	I	R	E	D	Inquired.
E	N	R	A	G	I	N	G	Exacerbating, Maddening, Raging, Exasperating, Infuriating, Angering, Incensing.
E	N	R	A	V	I	S	H	Enrapture.
E	N	R	I	C	H	E	D	Adorned, Decked, Fertilized, Complemented, Added value, Improved, Increased, Expanded.
E	N	R	I	C	H	E	R	One that increases value or quality.
E	N	R	I	D	G	E	D	Wavy, Furrowed, Corrugated.
E	N	R	I	N	G	E	D	Encircled, Surrounded.
E	N	R	O	B	I	N	G	Attiring, Coating, Adorning.
E	N	R	O	L	L	E	D	Registered, Inserted, Recorded, Enlisted, Enfolded, Coiled, Listed, Entered.
E	N	R	O	L	L	E	E	A person who is registered or enlisted.
E	N	R	O	O	T	E	D	Established, Implanted.
E	N	S	A	L	A	D	A	Spanish burlesque madrigal.
E	N	S	A	M	P	L	E	Example, Pattern, Model, Instance.
E	N	S	C	O	N	C	E	Conceal, Place, Hide, Establish, Settle, Plant, Install, Locate.
E	N	S	C	R	O	L	L	Inscribe, Record.
E	N	S	E	A	L	E	D	Ratified.
E	N	S	E	A	M	E	D	Marked as if with seams.
E	N	S	E	M	B	L	E	Aggregate, Complete costume, Group of persons or things producing an effect.
E	N	S	H	I	E	L	D	To shield.
E	N	S	H	R	I	N	E	Preserve, Cherish, Care for.
E	N	S	H	R	O	U	D	Cover, Enfold, Enwrap, Veil, Envelop, Invest, Wrap, Conceal.
E	N	S	I	F	O	R	M	Sword-shaped, Tapering to a point.
E	N	S	I	G	N	C	Y	Rank or office of an ensign.
E	N	S	I	G	N	E	D	Distinguished by a mark, Surmounted with a mark.
E	N	S	I	L	A	N	G	Preparing fodder by chopping and excluding air by compression.
E	N	S	L	A	V	E	D	Subjugated, Enthralled, Oppressed, Disfranchised, Shackled, Yoked, Captive.
E	N	S	L	A	V	E	R	Captor, One who deals in slaves.
E	N	S	N	A	R	E	D	Caught, Captured, Netted, Entangled, Trapped, Bagged, Enticed, Inveigled.
E	N	S	O	U	L	E	D	Cherished in the soul, Imbued with a soul.
E	N	S	P	H	E	R	E	Envelop, Encircle, Sphere, Ball, Conglobe, Encompass, Surround.
E	N	S	T	Y	L	E	D	Named, Designated, Styled.
E	N	S	U	R	I	N	G	Assuring, Betrothing, Guranteeing, Insuring, Marrying, Securing, Certifying, Warranting.
E	N	S	W	A	T	H	E	Swathe, Envelop, Drape, Roll, Swaddle, Wrap, Cloak.
E	N	T	A	I	L	E	D	A restricted or limited inheritance, Burdened, Fastened, Imposed, Attached, Settled.
E	N	T	A	I	L	E	R	One that burdens an inheritance.
E	N	T	A	N	G	L	E	Snarl, Confuse, Entrap, Twist, Perplex, Bewilder, Complicate, Enmesh.
E	N	T	E	L	L	U	S	Hanuman, A sacred Indian monkey.
E	N	T	E	M	P	L	E	Enshrine.
E	N	T	E	N	D	E	R	To inspire tenderness.
E	N	T	E	R	I	N	G	Coming, Joining, Engaging, Starting, Registering, Inserting, Penetrating, Probing.
E	N	T	H	R	A	L	L	Charm, Captivate, Master, Subdue, Fascinate, Mesmerize, Spellbind, Absorb.
E	N	T	H	R	O	N	E	Exalt, Elevate, Install, Worship, Respect.
E	N	T	H	U	S	E	D	Thrilled, Electrified, Rhapsodized.
E	N	T	I	C	I	N	G	Alluring, Attracting, Tempting, Luring, Fetching, Beguiling, Enchanting, Bewitching.
E	N	T	I	R	E	L	Y	Altogether, Completely, Fully, Perfectly, Thoroughly, Utterly, Solely, Earnestly.
E	N	T	I	R	E	T	Y	Total, Sum, Whole, Completeness, Unity, Integrity, Universality, Aggregate.
E	N	T	I	T	L	E	D	Assigned, Imputed, Ascribed, Designated, Authorized, Qualified, Empowered, Allowed.
E	N	T	O	C	O	N	E	Part of an upper molar tooth.
E	N	T	O	D	E	R	M	Endoderm.
E	N	T	O	H	Y	A	L	Basibranchial, relating to the gill area of fishes.
E	N	T	O	I	L	E	D	Ensnared, Entrapped.
E	N	T	O	L	O	M	A	Pink-spored poisonous fungus.
E	N	T	O	M	B	E	D	Buried, Planted, Enshrined, Interred, Inhumed.
E	N	T	O	M	E	R	E	Endomere.
E	N	T	O	M	I	O	N	Part of the parietal bone of the skull.
E	N	T	O	P	S	I	C	Lying within the eyeball.
E	N	T	O	S	A	R	C	Endosarc.
E	N	T	O	Z	O	I	C	Living within an animal.
E	N	T	O	Z	O	O	N	Internal animal parasite.
E	N	T	R	A	C	T	E	Interval or piece of music between two acts of a play.
E	N	T	R	A	I	L	S	Internal parts of something, Viscera, Bowels, Guts.
E	N	T	R	A	N	C	E	Ingress, Admission, Enrapture, Transport, Please, Attract, Bewitch, Captivate.
E	N	T	R	E	A	T	Y	Plea, Prayer, Appeal, Imploration, Petition, Imprecation, Application, Supplication.

1	2	3	4	5	6	7	8	Definition
E	N	T	R	E	M	E	S	Short comic piece in Spanish theatre.
E	N	T	R	E	N	C	H	Strengthen, Trespass, Embed, Lodge, Establish, Invade, Encroach, Infringe.
E	N	T	R	E	P	O	T	A transhipment place for the collection and distribution of goods.
E	N	T	R	E	S	O	L	Mezzanine, Balcony or intermediate floor between ground and first floors.
E	N	T	W	I	N	E	D	Twisted, Encircled, Wreathed, Involved, Entangled, Coiled, Spiralled, Interlaced.
E	N	T	Y	L	O	M	A	Genus of parasitic fungi.
E	N	U	R	E	S	I	S	Incontinence, Involuntary discharge of urine.
E	N	V	A	S	S	A	L	To reduce to serfdom, Bondage, Enslave.
E	N	V	E	I	G	L	E	Inveigle, Lure, Seduce.
E	N	V	E	L	O	P	E	A cover, Wrapper, Container, Receptacle, Jacket.
E	N	V	I	A	B	L	E	Attracting envy, Highly desirable.
E	N	V	I	A	B	L	Y	Covetously, Grudgingly.
E	N	V	I	R	O	N	S	Boundaries, Limits, Vicinity, Neighbourhood, Surroundings, Outskirts, Suburbs, Districts.
E	N	V	I	S	A	G	E	Conceive, Contemplate, Foresee, Think, Regard, Envision, Feature, Imagine.
E	N	V	I	S	I	O	N	Envisage, Foresee, Think.
E	N	Z	O	O	T	I	C	Endemic, Disease peculiar to a certain locality.
E	O	D	I	S	C	I	D	Prehistoric minute organisms.
E	O	L	I	E	N	N	E	A lustrous lightweight dress fabric.
E	O	L	I	P	I	L	E	Aeolipe, An apparatus invented in the second century, believed to be the first steam engine.
E	O	L	I	T	H	I	C	Relating to the earliest period of the Stone age.
E	P	A	L	P	A	T	E	Lacking feelers.
E	P	A	P	P	O	S	E	Beardless or lacking bristles.
E	P	E	N	D	Y	M	A	A tumour in the brain membrane or canal of the spinal cord.
E	P	H	E	B	E	U	M	A place for gymnastics in ancient Greece or Rome.
E	P	H	E	M	E	R	A	A genus of mayflies with transparent wings.
E	P	H	E	S	I	A	N	A boon companion.
E	P	H	E	S	T	I	A	Genus of small moths that feed on stored food products.
E	P	H	O	R	A	T	E	A body of magistrates in ancient Sparta.
E	P	H	Y	R	U	L	A	Free-swimming larva of a jellyfish.
E	P	I	B	I	O	N	T	An organism that lives on the body surface of another.
E	P	I	B	L	A	S	T	The outer layer of the blastoderm.
E	P	I	B	L	E	M	A	Superficial layer of tissue in roots and stems of submerged aquatic plants.
E	P	I	B	O	L	I	C	Relating to the growth of one part about another in the embryo stage.
E	P	I	C	A	L	Y	X	A substitute calyx.
E	P	I	C	A	R	I	D	Minute parasitic crustaceans.
E	P	I	C	A	U	T	A	Genus of blister beetles.
E	P	I	C	O	E	L	E	Anterior part of the fourth ventricle of the brain.
E	P	I	C	O	L	I	C	Situated over the colon.
E	P	I	C	O	T	Y	L	Portion of the axis of a plant embryo.
E	P	I	C	Y	C	L	E	Circulating cycle.
E	P	I	D	E	M	I	C	Common, Pandemic, Contagious, Outbreak, Plague.
E	P	I	F	A	G	U	S	Genus of leafless herbs, Beechdrops.
E	P	I	G	A	M	I	C	Tending to attract the opposite sex during the breeding season.
E	P	I	G	R	A	P	H	Inscription, Quotation, Motto.
E	P	I	G	Y	N	U	M	Genital opening of a female spider.
E	P	I	L	E	P	S	Y	Chronic nervous disorder producing convulsions.
E	P	I	L	O	G	U	E	Conclusion, Ending, Sequel, Postscript.
E	P	I	M	E	R	A	L	Relating to an epimeron.
E	P	I	M	E	R	O	N	Leg-joint segment of an insect.
E	P	I	N	A	S	T	Y	The movement by which a plant is bent by the opening of a bud.
E	P	I	P	H	A	N	Y	A Christian feast celebrated on January 6th, Twelfth night.
E	P	I	P	H	O	R	A	Watering of the eye.
E	P	I	P	H	Y	L	L	A parasitic plant growing on a leaf.
E	P	I	P	H	Y	T	E	A plant that grows on a building or another plant, Air plant.
E	P	I	P	L	A	S	M	Residual cytoplasm left after spore formation.
E	P	I	P	L	O	I	C	Relating to the peritoneum.
E	P	I	P	R	O	C	T	A plate above the anus of certain insects.
E	P	I	P	U	B	I	S	Pair of bones attached in front of the pubis.
E	P	I	S	C	O	P	E	A projector for images of opaque objects.
E	P	I	S	O	D	I	C	Incidental, Temporary, Ephemeral, Occasional, Capricious.
E	P	I	S	P	O	R	E	Outer membrane of a spore.
E	P	I	S	P	E	R	M	Testa, Hard external coating of a seed.
E	P	I	S	T	L	E	R	A writer of epistles.
E	P	I	S	T	O	M	E	Region between the antennae and the mouth of a crustacean.
E	P	I	S	T	Y	L	E	Architrave.
E	P	I	T	A	S	I	S	The part of a Greek tragedy leading to the catastrophe.
E	P	I	T	H	E	C	A	An external clacareous layer on corals.

1	2	3	4	5	6	7	8	Definition
E	P	I	T	H	E	M	A	A horny protuberance on the bill of some birds.
E	P	I	T	R	I	T	E	A foot in Greek and Latin prosody.
E	P	I	V	A	L	V	E	The calcareous part of a coral.
E	P	I	Z	O	O	T	Y	Epidemic of an animal disease.
E	P	S	O	M	I	T	E	Epsom salts.
E	Q	U	A	L	I	T	Y	The state of being equal, Uniformity, Sameness.
E	Q	U	A	L	I	Z	E	Make equal, Reach a score equal to one's opponent.
E	Q	U	A	L	L	E	D	Levelled, Matched, Rivalled, Measured, Met, Corresponded, Evened.
E	Q	U	A	T	I	N	G	Equalising, Comparing, Balancing, Matching, Relating, Representing, Treating.
E	Q	U	A	T	I	O	N	Identification, Adjusting, Factor, Balance, Allowance.
E	Q	U	I	F	O	R	M	Uniform, Similar.
E	Q	U	I	N	I	T	Y	Equine nature or character.
E	Q	U	I	P	A	G	E	Equipment, Outfit, Uniform, Trappings, Retinue, Style, Pomp, Service.
E	Q	U	I	P	P	E	D	Provided, Supplied, Prepared, Fitted, Qualified, Furnished, Appointed, Armed.
E	Q	U	I	T	A	N	T	Overlapping at the base as of a flower, Iris.
E	Q	U	I	V	O	K	E	Pun, Double meaning, Wordplay.
E	Q	U	O	I	D	A	E	Hippoedea, Related to horses, Zebras, Asses.
E	R	A	D	I	A	T	E	Radiate.
E	R	A	S	A	B	L	E	Capable of being erased without damage.
E	R	A	S	T	I	A	N	Doctrine that the state is supreme over the church.
E	R	E	C	T	I	L	E	Capable of being raised to an erect position, Cavernous.
E	R	E	C	T	I	N	G	Building, Raising, Creating, Constituting, Constructing, Fabricating, Fashioning, Framing.
E	R	E	C	T	I	O	N	Construction, Establishment, Edifice.
E	R	E	M	I	T	I	C	Solitary, Relating to a hermit, A life of ascetic solitude.
E	R	E	M	U	R	U	S	A small genus of Asiatic herbs.
E	R	E	T	H	I	S	M	Abnormal irritability or responsiveness to stimulation.
E	R	E	W	H	I	L	E	Some time ago, A little while before.
E	R	G	A	S	T	I	C	Constituting the nonliving by-products of protoplasm activity.
E	R	G	A	T	I	V	E	Denoting agency in a grammatical case.
E	R	G	A	T	O	I	D	Having wingless fertile sexual individuals of either sex.
E	R	G	O	T	I	N	E	A crystalline tripeptical alkaloid from ergot.
E	R	G	O	T	I	S	M	A toxic condition produced by eating grain products infected with ergot fungus.
E	R	G	O	T	I	Z	E	To argue logically or sophistically.
E	R	I	C	E	T	A	L	Containing heaths.
E	R	I	G	E	R	O	N	A widely distributed genus of herbs resembling asters.
E	R	I	O	N	I	T	E	A mineral consisting of zeolitic aluminosilicates of sodium potassium and calcium.
E	R	M	I	N	O	I	S	Heraldic fur consisting of black ermine spots on a golden field.
E	R	O	D	I	B	L	E	Capable of being eroded.
E	R	O	T	Y	L	I	D	A family of oval hairy beetles having larvae that live in fungi.
E	R	R	A	N	T	L	Y	Deviously, Straying, Roving, Naughty, Arbitrary, Whimsically.
E	R	R	A	N	T	R	Y	Wandering, Roving.
E	R	R	O	R	I	S	T	One who holds to and propagates error.
E	R	U	C	T	A	T	E	To belch, Erupt violently.
E	R	U	M	P	E	N	T	Breaking out, Bursting forth.
E	R	U	P	T	I	N	G	Releasing suddenly, Bursting, Exploding, Expelling, Ejecting, Burgeoning.
E	R	U	P	T	I	O	N	Outburst, Outbreak, Rash, Irruption, Explosion, Flare-up.
E	R	U	P	T	I	V	E	Tending to erupt, Produced by eruption, Explosive.
E	R	Y	N	G	I	U	M	A genus of coarse bristly herbs.
E	R	Y	S	I	M	U	M	Small genus of Old World herbs, Wallflower.
E	R	Y	T	H	E	M	A	Abnormal redness of the skin due to capillary congestion.
E	R	Y	T	H	R	O	L	A liquid unsaturated dihydroxy alcohol.
E	R	Y	T	H	R	O	N	A body organ consisting of red blood cells.
E	S	C	A	L	A	D	E	Scaling, Climb up and over.
E	S	C	A	L	A	D	O	Escalade.
E	S	C	A	L	A	T	E	Ascend or carry up on a moving staircase or conveyor belt, Increase in activity or effect.
E	S	C	A	L	L	O	P	Scallop, Decoration in the form of a scallop shell.
E	S	C	A	M	B	I	O	An out-of-date requirement for transferring money overseas.
E	S	C	A	P	A	D	E	Escape, Evasion, An adventure, Mischief, Experience, Caper, Lark, Prank.
E	S	C	A	P	I	N	G	Avoiding, Eluding, Evading, Shunning, Absconding, Decamping, Fleeing, Dodging.
E	S	C	A	P	I	S	M	Diversion, Entertainment, Evasion of unpleasant facts.
E	S	C	A	P	I	S	T	A man who writes about life without participating in it.
E	S	C	A	R	G	O	T	Edible snail.
E	S	C	A	R	O	L	E	Endive, a salad plant.
E	S	C	A	R	P	E	D	A steeply sloped hill.
E	S	C	H	A	L	O	T	Shallot.
E	S	C	H	E	W	A	L	Shunning, Avoidance.
E	S	C	H	E	W	E	D	Shunned, Escaped, Eluded, Evaded, Sacrificed, Abstained, Refrained, Avoided.

1	2	3	4	5	6	7	8	Definition
E	S	C	O	B	I	T	A	Californian plant.
E	S	C	O	P	E	T	A	A short musket.
E	S	C	O	R	T	E	D	Accompanied, Conducted, Guided, Taken, Chaperoned, Steered, Convoyed, Shepherded.
E	S	C	R	O	W	E	D	Gave a certificate confirming receipt of trust money.
E	S	C	U	L	E	N	T	Edible.
E	S	D	R	A	G	O	L	Estragole, Liqiuid ether with an odour like aniseed.
E	S	E	P	T	A	T	E	Having no septum.
E	S	O	C	I	D	A	E	Family of voracious fishes, Pikes.
E	S	O	T	E	R	I	C	Abstruse, Private, Confidential, Recondite, Hermetic, Occult, Profound, Secret.
E	S	P	A	L	I	E	R	A plant trained to grow flat against a wall, Railing or trellis for training plants to grow flat.
E	S	P	A	R	C	E	T	Sainfoin, A perennial herb.
E	S	P	E	C	I	A	L	Special, Unusual, Notable, Exceptional, Particular, Peculiar, Intimate, Specific.
E	S	P	I	E	G	L	E	Roguish, Frolicsome.
E	S	P	O	U	S	A	L	Betrothal, Nuptials, Marriage, Adopting a cause.
E	S	P	O	U	S	E	D	Wed, Adopted, Embraced, Accepted, Backed, Championed, Supported, Upheld.
E	S	P	O	U	S	E	R	Supporter, Partisan.
E	S	P	U	N	D	I	A	Infection of upper respiratory tissues prevalent in Central and South America.
E	S	Q	U	I	M	A	U	Eskimo.
E	S	Q	U	I	R	E	D	Accompanied or escorted in public.
E	S	S	A	Y	I	N	G	Trying, Attempting, Striving, Struggling, Toiling, Venturing, Labouring, Seeking.
E	S	S	A	Y	I	S	T	A writer of essays.
E	S	S	E	N	C	E	D	Scented, Perfumed.
E	S	S	E	N	I	S	M	Brotherhood of Jews in Palestine in second century B.C. that advocated community living.
E	S	S	E	X	I	T	E	Granular intrusive igneous rocks.
E	S	S	O	I	N	E	D	Made an excuse for non-appearance in court.
E	S	S	O	I	N	E	E	One whose excuse is accepted.
E	S	S	O	I	N	E	R	One that makes an excuse for another.
E	S	S	O	N	I	T	E	A variety of garnet.
E	S	T	A	M	P	I	E	12th Century slow stamping dance.
E	S	T	A	N	C	I	A	S. American cattle ranch.
E	S	T	E	E	M	E	D	Appraised, Respected, Prized, Believed, Regarded, Admired, Revered, Venerated.
E	S	T	E	R	A	S	E	A class of enzymes that accelerates the hydrolysis of esters of low fatty acids.
E	S	T	E	R	I	F	Y	To convert into an ester.
E	S	T	H	E	R	I	A	A genus of small crustaceans.
E	S	T	H	E	S	I	A	Capacity for sensation, Sensibility.
E	S	T	H	E	S	I	S	Sensation.
E	S	T	H	E	T	I	C	Aesthetic, Artistic, Beautiful.
E	S	T	I	M	A	T	E	Value, Evaluate, Rate, Assay, Appraise, Calculate, Measure, Reckoning.
E	S	T	I	V	A	T	E	Aestivate, Summer vacation, Pass the summer in a state of inactivity.
E	S	T	O	C	A	D	A	Final kill at a bullfight.
E	S	T	O	F	A	D	O	Gilded finish of wood sculpture.
E	S	T	O	L	I	D	E	Class of long-chain esters.
E	S	T	O	N	I	A	N	Relating to Estonia.
E	S	T	O	P	P	E	D	Precluded, Barred, Prohibited, Forbidden.
E	S	T	O	P	P	E	L	A legal preclusion.
E	S	T	O	V	E	R	S	Wood belonging to a landlord that a tenant is allowed to use for specific reasons.
E	S	T	R	A	N	G	E	Alienate, Wean, Disunite, Divide, Divorce, Part, Separate, Split.
E	S	T	R	A	Y	E	D	Something that has wandered away.
E	S	T	R	I	A	T	E	Not striated.
E	S	T	R	O	G	E	N	A sex hormone produced in the ovaries.
E	S	U	R	I	E	N	T	Voracious, Greedy, Predatory.
E	T	C	E	T	E	R	A	Additional items, Odds and ends.
E	T	E	R	N	I	T	Y	Immortality, Ages, Endlessness, Perpetuity, Timelessness.
E	T	E	R	N	I	Z	E	Perpetuate, Immortalize, Eternalize.
E	T	H	E	R	A	T	E	A compound with an ether.
E	T	H	E	R	E	A	L	Celestial, Heavenly, Dainty, Exquisite, Airy, Immaterial.
E	T	H	E	R	I	F	Y	To convert into an ether.
E	T	H	E	R	I	Z	E	Anaesthetize.
E	T	H	I	C	I	S	T	A specialist in ethics.
E	T	H	I	C	I	Z	E	To make ethical.
E	T	H	I	O	P	I	C	A Semitic language formerly spoken in Ethiopia.
E	T	H	N	A	R	C	H	A provincial governor.
E	T	H	N	I	C	A	L	Relating to ethnic division of people according to race or religion.
E	T	H	O	L	O	G	Y	Study of the formation of human character and of animal behaviour.
E	T	H	Y	L	A	T	E	To introduce one ethyl group into a compound.
E	T	H	Y	L	E	N	E	A colourless flammable gaseous olefin hydrocarbon found in coal gas.
E	T	I	O	L	A	T	E	To weaken by depriving a plant of sunlight, To make pale and sickly.

1	2	3	4	5	6	7	8	Definition
E	T	I	O	L	O	G	Y	Dealing with causes.
E	T	R	U	M	E	U	S	Genus of small fishes, Japanese herring.
E	T	R	U	R	I	A	N	Relating to ancient Etruria.
E	T	R	U	S	C	A	N	Same as ETRURIAN.
E	T	T	E	R	C	A	P	Spider, Ill-tempered or spiteful person.
E	U	A	R	C	T	O	S	Genus of bears.
E	U	C	A	L	Y	P	T	Eucalyptus tree.
E	U	C	A	R	I	D	A	Group of crustaceans.
E	U	C	A	R	P	I	C	Reproducing as a fungi or algae.
E	U	C	H	A	R	I	S	Genus of S. American herbs, Amazon lily.
E	U	C	H	O	R	D	A	Division of Chordate, animals with a nervous system.
E	U	C	O	L	I	T	E	A mineral similar to eudialyte but optically negative.
E	U	C	R	A	S	I	A	A normal state of health.
E	U	C	T	I	C	A	L	Supplicatory.
E	U	C	Y	C	L	I	C	Comprised of alternate whorls.
E	U	D	E	S	M	O	L	Crystalline sequiterpenoid alcohol found in eucalyptus and used in perfumery.
E	U	D	O	R	I	N	A	Genus of green algae.
E	U	G	E	N	I	C	S	Science for the improvement of race.
E	U	G	E	N	I	S	T	One that believes in eugenics.
E	U	H	E	D	R	A	L	Idiomorphic, Having normal shape.
E	U	L	A	C	H	A	N	Candlefish, An oily food fish that can be dried and used as a candle.
E	U	L	O	G	I	S	T	One that extols in writing or speech.
E	U	L	O	G	I	U	M	Eulogy.
E	U	L	O	G	I	Z	E	To praise excessively.
E	U	L	Y	T	I	T	E	A mineral consisting of a bismuth silicate.
E	U	M	Y	C	E	T	E	A fungus.
E	U	N	E	C	T	E	S	Genus of snakes comprising the anaconda.
E	U	N	I	C	E	A	N	Genus of marine worms.
E	U	O	N	Y	M	I	N	Dry powdered extract of the wahoo plant.
E	U	O	N	Y	M	U	S	Genus of evergreen shrubs, Dried bark used as a cathartic.
E	U	P	A	T	O	R	Y	Hemp agrimony.
E	U	P	A	T	R	I	D	Hereditary aristocrat of ancient Athens who made the laws.
E	U	P	E	P	S	I	A	A good digestion.
E	U	P	E	P	T	I	C	Cheerful, Optimistic, Pleasant disposition relating to good health.
E	U	P	H	O	N	I	A	Smooth and pleasant pronunciation.
E	U	P	H	O	N	I	C	Relating to euphony, Harmonious.
E	U	P	H	O	R	I	A	Feeling of well-being or elation.
E	U	P	H	R	A	S	Y	An eye-bright plant formerly thought to cure eye ailments.
E	U	P	H	U	I	S	M	Affected and artificial style of language.
E	U	P	H	U	I	S	T	A person using an affected style of conversation.
E	U	P	H	U	I	Z	E	To use high-flown diction.
E	U	P	L	O	I	D	Y	A state of having three or more identical genomes.
E	U	P	R	A	X	I	A	Normally co-ordinated muscular performance.
E	U	P	T	E	L	E	A	Genus of Asiatic shrubs.
E	U	P	Y	R	E	N	E	Having a normal nucleus.
E	U	P	Y	R	I	O	N	An early 19th century match.
E	U	R	A	S	I	A	N	Of mixed European and Asiatic origin.
E	U	R	H	O	D	O	L	A class of dyes.
E	U	R	O	P	E	A	N	Belonging to Europe.
E	U	R	O	P	I	U	M	A bivalent and trivalent metallic element of the rare-earth group.
E	U	R	O	P	O	I	D	Caucasoid.
E	U	R	O	P	O	U	S	Relating to compounds of europium.
E	U	R	Y	A	L	A	E	Basket stars, Starfish.
E	U	R	Y	P	Y	G	A	Genus of tropical birds, Sun-grebes.
E	U	R	Y	S	O	M	A	Having a thickset build of body.
E	U	R	Y	T	H	M	Y	Harmonious body movement.
E	U	S	E	B	I	A	N	A follower of Eusebuis, Bishop of Nicomedia.
E	U	S	T	A	T	I	C	Relating to a world-side change of sea-level.
E	U	S	U	C	H	I	A	Members of the family of crocodiles and alligators.
E	U	T	A	M	I	A	S	Genus of rodents comprising the chipmunks.
E	U	T	E	C	T	I	C	Alloy or solution having its melting point the lowest possible.
E	U	T	H	A	M	I	A	Genus of composite herbs with flat-topped flowers.
E	U	T	H	E	R	I	A	Genus of placental mammals.
E	U	T	R	O	P	H	Y	Healthy nutrition.
E	U	X	E	N	I	T	E	A brownish black mineral.
E	V	A	C	U	A	N	T	Emptying, Emetic, Diuretic, Purgative, Cathartic.
E	V	A	C	U	A	T	E	Nullify, Vacate, Void, Exhaust, Remove, Abandon, Forsake, Withdrawn, Deprive.

1	2	3	4	5	6	7	8	Definition
E	V	A	L	U	A	T	E	Value, Appraise, Rate, Estimate, Interpretation,Assess, Class, Criticize.
E	V	A	N	E	S	C	E	Vanish, Disappear, Evaporate, Fade, Disintegrate, Scatter, Dissipate, Dissolve.
E	V	E	C	T	I	O	N	The movement of the moon due to the attraction of the sun.
E	V	E	N	F	A	L	L	Beginning of the evening.
E	V	E	N	N	E	S	S	Fairness, Impartiality, Fairly, Justly, Quietly, Unemotionally, Smoothly, Uniformly.
E	V	E	N	S	O	N	G	Evening worship service.
E	V	E	N	T	F	U	L	Momentous, Deeply important, Stirring.
E	V	E	N	T	I	D	E	Evening, Dusk, Gloaming, Twilight, Owl-light.
E	V	E	N	T	U	A	L	Change, Conditional, Ultimate, Final, Concluding, Terminal, Latest, Inevitable.
E	V	E	R	M	O	R	E	Always, Forever, Certainly, Definitely.
E	V	E	R	S	I	O	N	Destriction.
E	V	E	R	T	I	N	G	Overthrowing, Upsetting, Disproving, Confounding, Confuting, Refuting.
E	V	E	R	Y	D	A	Y	Ordinary day, Usual routine.
E	V	E	R	Y	M	A	N	A typical man.
E	V	E	R	Y	O	N	E	Everybody.
E	V	E	R	Y	W	A	Y	In every respect.
E	V	I	C	T	I	N	G	Ejecting, Dismissing, Extruding, Dislodging, Proving.
E	V	I	C	T	I	O	N	Ejectment, Ouster, Proof, Dispossession.
E	V	I	D	E	N	C	E	Indication, Proof, Testimony, Prominent, Conspicuous, Display, Evince, Illustrate.
E	V	I	L	D	O	E	R	Criminal, Malefactor, Felon.
E	V	I	L	N	E	S	S	Badness, Wickedness, Foulness.
E	V	I	N	C	I	N	G	Proving, Confirming, Showing, Provoking, Demonstrating, Signifying, Exhibiting, Illustrating.
E	V	I	N	C	I	V	E	Demonstrative.
E	V	I	T	A	B	L	E	Avoidable.
E	V	O	C	A	T	O	R	One that evokes.
E	V	O	L	V	I	N	G	Deriving, Obtaining, Advancing, Unfolding, Developing, Elaborating, Progressing, Maturing.
E	V	U	L	G	A	T	E	Publish, Divulge.
E	V	U	L	S	I	O	N	Plucking out, Casting or rooting out.
E	X	A	C	T	I	N	G	Wresting, Extorting, Wringing, Correcting, Demanding, Onerous, Taxing, Trying.
E	X	A	C	T	I	O	N	Extortion, Contribution, Demand.
E	X	A	L	T	I	N	G	Magnifying, Concentrating, Extolling, Glorifying, Elevating, Aggrandizing, Boosting.
E	X	A	M	I	N	E	D	Investigated, Inspected, Searched, Scrutinized, Studied, Surveyed, Viewed, Tested.
E	X	A	M	I	N	E	E	A person who is examined.
E	X	A	M	I	N	E	R	A person conducting examinations.
E	X	A	M	P	L	A	R	Exemplar, One that serves as a model.
E	X	A	N	T	H	E	M	Eruptive disease, Smallpox, Measles.
E	X	C	A	V	A	T	E	Dig, Delve, Shovel, Gouge, Scoop, Scrape, Expose to view.
E	X	C	E	E	D	E	D	Surpassed, Predominated, Excelled, Outdone, Outstripped, Presumed, Transcended.
E	X	C	E	E	D	E	R	One that surpasses.
E	X	C	E	P	T	E	D	Objected, Excluded, Debarred, Eliminated, Suspended, Rejected, Omitted, Exempted.
E	X	C	E	R	N	E	D	Discharged, Excreted.
E	X	C	E	S	S	E	S	State of exceeding the limits.
E	X	C	H	A	N	G	E	Trade, Barter, Substitute, Alter, Bargain, Change, Replace, Switch.
E	X	C	I	S	I	N	G	Resecting, Extirpating, Erasing, Amputating, Removing, Slashing, Eradicating, Deleting.
E	X	C	I	S	I	O	N	Destruction, Erasure, Resection.
E	X	C	I	T	A	N	T	Something that excites, A stimulant.
E	X	C	I	T	I	N	G	Provoking, Stimulating, Activating, Arousing, Exhilarating, Inspiring, Interesting, Intriguing.
E	X	C	I	T	R	O	N	A single-anode mercury-arc rectifier.
E	X	C	L	U	D	E	D	Eliminated, Disbarred, Suspended, Banned, Prevented, Obviated, Prohibited, Ostracized.
E	X	C	U	R	S	E	D	Digressed, Rambled, Made an excursion.
E	X	C	U	R	S	U	S	Digression, Supplementary exposition of a topic in a certain work.
E	X	C	U	S	I	N	G	Condoning, Pardoning, Forgiving, Overlooking, Exempting, Exculpating, Justifying.
E	X	C	U	S	S	E	D	Discarded, Discussed, Preceded, Repossession.
E	X	E	C	R	A	T	E	Denounce, Revile!, Abhor, Damn, Curse, Swear, Objurgate.
E	X	E	C	U	T	E	D	Performed, Carried out, Effected, Conducted, Completed, Killed, Played, Administered.
E	X	E	G	E	S	I	S	Exposition, Explanation, Critical interpretation of a portion of Scripture.
E	X	E	G	E	T	I	C	Explanatory, Expository.
E	X	E	M	P	L	A	R	Model, Example, Typical specimen, Manuscript, Universal.
E	X	E	M	P	T	E	D	Removed, Excluded, Released, Delivered, Excused, Absolved, Dispersed, Relieved.
E	X	E	Q	U	I	A	L	Relating to funerals.
E	X	E	Q	U	I	E	S	Funeral procession.
E	X	E	R	C	I	S	E	Exercising, Practicing.
E	X	E	R	C	I	S	E	Study, Practice, Vex, Harass, Drill, Train, Condition, Exhibition.
E	X	E	R	E	S	I	S	Surgical removal of a part or organ.
E	X	E	R	G	U	A	L	Relating to the space for the date on a coin or medal.
E	X	E	R	T	I	N	G	Exercising, Wielding, Applying, Employing, Using, Throwing, Striving, Plying.
E	X	E	R	T	I	O	N	Effort, Exercise, Application, Employment, Operation, Use, Strain.

1	2	3	4	5	6	7	8	
E	X	H	A	L	A	N	T	Emissive, An exhaling duct.
E	X	H	A	L	I	N	G	Breathing out, Evaporating, Emanating, Oozing, Percolating through a membrane.
E	X	H	O	R	T	E	D	Incited, Advised, Warned, Preached, Urged, Goaded, Stimulated, Prodded.
E	X	H	O	R	T	E	R	Preacher.
E	X	H	U	M	A	T	E	Exhume, Disinter, Dig, Uncover, Remove.
E	X	H	U	M	I	N	G	Digging, Uncovering, Reviving, Disinterring.
E	X	I	G	E	A	N	T	Pressing, Critical, Demanding, Exacting, Imperative, Importunate, Insistent, Urgent.
E	X	I	G	E	N	C	Y	Pressure, Urgency, Demands, Requirement, Juncture, Contingency, Crisis, Emergency.
E	X	I	G	I	B	L	E	Requirable, Demandable.
E	X	I	G	U	I	T	Y	Scantiness, Smallness, Sparseness, Inadequateness.
E	X	I	G	U	O	U	S	Meagre, Narrow, Scanty, Spare, Skimpy, Limited, Little, Restricted.
E	X	I	L	A	R	C	H	Third century Jewish ruler of Babylonian exiles.
E	X	I	M	I	O	U	S	Select, Choice, Excellent.
E	X	I	S	T	E	N	T	Existing, Present, Contemporary, Current, Extant, Entity, Actual, Living.
E	X	I	S	T	I	N	G	Alive, Around, Existent, Living.
E	X	I	T	I	O	U	S	Destructive, Fatal.
E	X	L	I	B	R	I	S	Bookplate.
E	X	O	C	O	E	L	E	Space between thread-like organs of a genus of coral.
E	X	O	C	R	I	N	E	Glands that discharge their secretion through a duct.
E	X	O	N	U	M	I	A	Collection of trivia, such as labels, bus tickets, etc.
E	X	O	P	L	A	S	M	Ectoplasm, Emanation from a spiritual medium.
E	X	O	R	A	B	L	E	Lenient, Capable of applying mercy.
E	X	O	R	C	I	S	M	The act of driving away evil spirits, Purifying.
E	X	O	R	C	I	S	T	One who drives away evil spirits by use of holy rites.
E	X	O	R	C	I	Z	E	To get rid of something troublesome.
E	X	O	R	D	I	A	L	Introductory.
E	X	O	R	D	I	U	M	Beginning, Introduction, Overture, Preamble, Preface, Prelude, Preliminary, Prologue.
E	X	O	S	P	O	R	E	An asexual spore as from a fungi.
E	X	O	S	T	O	M	E	Outer part of the peristome of a moss.
E	X	O	T	E	R	I	C	Popular, External, Exterior, Publicly known.
E	X	O	T	O	X	I	N	Soluble poisonous substance transmitted by bacilli.
E	X	P	A	N	D	E	D	Outstretched, Unfolded, Open, Displayed, Enlarged, Amplified, Inflated, Distended.
E	X	P	E	C	T	E	D	Awaited, Supposed, Believed, Hoped, Anticipated, Thought, Understood, Assured.
E	X	P	E	D	I	T	E	Hasten, Facilitate, Quick, Speedy, Prompt, Issue, Dispatch, Accelerate.
E	X	P	E	L	L	E	E	Emigree, Exile, Expatriate.
E	X	P	E	L	L	E	R	A screw press.
E	X	P	E	N	D	E	D	Spent, Distributed, Consumed, Used up, Exhausted, Finished.
E	X	P	E	R	T	L	Y	Adroitly, Adeptly, Skilfully.
E	X	P	I	A	B	L	E	Atonable.
E	X	P	I	A	T	E	D	Cleansed, Averted, Amended, Compensated, Corrected, Rectified, Remedied, Redressed.
E	X	P	I	A	T	O	R	One that remedies.
E	X	P	I	R	I	N	G	Terminating, Dying, Exhaling, Emitting, Concluding, Departing, Passing, Elapsing.
E	X	P	L	I	C	I	T	Definite, Specific, Express, Categorical, Unequivocal, Outspoken, Certain, Distinct.
E	X	P	L	O	D	E	D	Detonated, Blasted, Discharged, Erupted, Flared, Burst, Discredited, Punctured.
E	X	P	L	O	D	E	R	A blasting machine.
E	X	P	L	O	R	E	D	Investigated, Examined, Searched, Penetrated, Delved, Inquired, Probed, Tested.
E	X	P	L	O	R	E	R	One that travels and investigates.
E	X	P	O	N	E	N	T	Explaining, Advocate, Supporter, Champion, Promoter, Defender, Upholder.
E	X	P	O	R	T	E	D	Removed, Carried, Transmitted, Conveyed, Sent abroad.
E	X	P	O	R	T	E	R	A wholesaler who sells to consumers in foreign countries.
E	X	P	O	S	I	N	G	Exhibiting, Displaying, Showing, Uncovering, Subjecting, Endangering, Jeopardizing.
E	X	P	O	S	U	R	E	Liability, Vulnerability, Helplessness, Danger, Jeopardy, Peril, Presentation, Risk.
E	X	P	U	N	G	E	D	Vanquished, Erased, Annulled, Annihilated, Eradicated, Deleted, Obliterated, Excluded.
E	X	S	E	C	T	E	D	Cut out, Excised, Extirpated.
E	X	S	E	R	T	E	D	Protruded, Projected.
E	X	S	H	E	A	T	H	Used when certain larval escape from residual membrane.
E	X	T	E	N	D	E	D	Expanded, Strained, Distended, Adulterated, Granted, Lengthened, Prolonged, Advanced.
E	X	T	E	N	D	E	R	Substance added as a diluent, adulterant or modifier.
E	X	T	E	N	S	O	R	A muscle that serves to extend a body part.
E	X	T	E	R	I	O	R	External, Outer, Outside.
E	X	T	E	R	N	A	L	Bodily, Physical, Visible, Superficial, Accidental, Peripheral, Outward, Outer.
E	X	T	O	L	L	E	R	One that lauds or glorifies.
E	X	T	O	R	T	E	D	Forced, Exacted, Educed, Wrenched, Wrested, Secured, Fleeced, Evoked.
E	X	T	R	A	D	O	S	Exterior curve of an arch.
E	X	T	R	E	M	U	M	Stationary value of a mathematical function that is either a maximum or a minimum.
E	X	T	R	O	R	S	E	Turned away from the axis of growth.
E	X	T	R	U	D	E	D	Protruded, Projected, Emerged, Ejected, Expelled, Evicted, Dismissed, Thrown out.

1	2	3	4	5	6	7	8	
E	X	T	U	B	A	T	E	To surgically remove a tube.
E	X	U	L	T	A	N	T	Jubilant, Triumphant, Overjoyed, Elated, Flushed with victory.
E	X	U	L	T	I	N	G	Gladdening, Delighting, Rejoicing, Celebrating, Boasting, Bragging, Glorying.
E	X	U	V	I	A	T	E	Moulting or shedding of natural covering of an animal.
E	Y	E	G	L	A	S	S	Eyepiece of an optical instrument, Monocle, Lens for spectacles.
E	Y	E	P	I	E	C	E	The lens at the end of an optical instrument, Transparent shield for the eyes fitted in a helmet.
E	Y	E	S	H	I	N	E	Reflection of light from the inner surface of an eye.
E	Y	E	S	I	G	H	T	Ability to see, Sight, Vision, Observation.
E	Y	E	S	T	A	L	K	The peduncle bearing the eye of a decapod crustacean, such as crab or lobster.
E	Y	E	T	O	O	T	H	Canine tooth of the upper jaw, Something of value.
E	Y	E	W	A	T	E	R	Tears, An eyewash.

F

F	A	B	A	C	E	A	E	Legumes, Peas, Beans.
F	A	B	I	F	O	R	M	Shaped like a bean.
F	A	B	L	I	A	U	X	Short metrical tale often coarse and cynical about women.
F	A	B	U	L	I	S	T	Liar, Prevaricator.
F	A	B	U	L	I	Z	E	Fable, To give a false account of.
F	A	B	U	L	O	U	S	Fictitious, Belonging to fables, Outstanding.
F	A	B	U	R	D	E	N	Fauxbourdon, A sacred homophonic choral composition.
F	A	C	E	C	A	R	D	Playing card bearing a picture, Court card.
F	A	C	E	L	E	S	S	Unidentifiable, Member of a category lacking individuality.
F	A	C	E	L	I	F	T	Operation to remove facial wrinkles, Restyling, Alteration.
F	A	C	E	P	A	C	K	Cosmetic paste applied to the face.
F	A	C	E	T	I	A	E	Witty or humorous writings or saying, Erotica.
F	A	C	E	T	I	N	G	Cutting facets on a diamond.
F	A	C	I	A	L	L	Y	Superficially.
F	A	C	I	L	I	T	Y	Ease, Dexterity, Readiness, Skill, Wit, Aptitude, Amenity.
F	A	C	T	I	O	U	S	Seditious, Insubordinate, Mutinous, Rebellious, Estranged, Belligerent, Quarrelsome.
F	A	C	T	O	T	U	M	General servant, A Person having many duties.
F	A	C	U	L	O	U	S	Bright regions seen near the edge of the sun.
F	A	D	E	L	E	S	S	Not susceptible to fading.
F	A	D	I	N	G	L	Y	Resembling one that is fading.
F	A	G	A	C	E	A	E	Family of shrubs and trees.
F	A	G	G	O	T	E	D	Twigs bound together, Drawn thread work in embroidery.
F	A	G	O	T	I	N	G	Drawn thread embroidery.
F	A	I	N	E	A	N	T	Irresponsible person, Sluggard, Loafer, Slouch, Lazy, Indolent, Apathetic, Impassive.
F	A	I	N	T	E	S	T	Dimmest, Spiritless, Weakest.
F	A	I	N	T	I	N	G	Depressed, Swooning, Declining, Loss of consciousness.
F	A	I	R	C	O	P	Y	A neat and exact copy.
F	A	I	R	L	E	A	D	Guide for a ship's rope.
F	A	I	R	N	E	S	S	Impartiality, Reasonableness.
F	A	I	R	P	L	A	Y	Justice, Equitable treatment, Impartial judgment.
F	A	I	R	Y	I	S	M	Resembling a fairy.
F	A	I	T	H	F	U	L	Loyal, Conscientious, Accurate, Reliable, Exact, Credible, Constant, Staunch.
F	A	K	E	M	E	N	T	Something faked, A device used to deceive.
F	A	L	A	N	A	K	A	A viverrine mammal closely related to the Asiatic palm civet.
F	A	L	C	A	T	E	D	The moon or a planet when less than half is illuminated.
F	A	L	C	H	I	O	N	Broad-bladed slightly curved sword.
F	A	L	C	O	N	E	R	A person who breeds or trains hawks for taking birds or game.
F	A	L	C	O	N	E	T	A smaller type of falcon.
F	A	L	C	O	N	R	Y	The art of training falcons.
F	A	L	C	U	L	A	R	Indicating a sharp-pointed claw.
F	A	L	D	E	R	O	L	Folderol, Trifle, Gegaw, Useless ornament.
F	A	L	I	S	C	A	N	Relating to the ancient city of Falerii in Etruria.
F	A	L	L	I	B	L	E	Liable to err, Careless, Liable to be inaccurate, Errant, Faulty.
F	A	L	L	I	B	L	Y	Heedlessly, Erroneously, Inaccurately, Carelessly.
F	A	L	L	O	W	E	D	Ploughed but not sown, to rest the soil or destroy the weeds.
F	A	L	L	T	R	A	P	A trap with a door or weight that falls on the victim.
F	A	L	S	E	T	T	O	An artificially produced singing voice that extends above the range of a tenor.
F	A	L	T	B	O	A	T	A small collapsible boat.
F	A	L	T	E	R	E	D	Stumbled, Staggered, Loitered, Hesitated, Stammered, Wavered, Flinched, Declined.
F	A	M	E	L	E	S	S	Obscure, Undistinguished.
F	A	M	I	L	I	A	L	Congential, Hereditary.
F	A	M	I	L	I	A	R	Intimate, Social, Common, Ordinary, Close, Thick, Presumptuous, Confidential.

1	2	3	4	5	6	7	8	Clue
F	A	M	I	L	I	S	T	Member of a mystical set of 16th and 17th century Europe.
F	A	M	I	S	H	E	D	Starved, Hungry, Peckish, Ravenous.
F	A	M	O	U	S	L	Y	Notably, Excellently, Very, Eminently, Prominently, Honourably.
F	A	N	A	G	A	L	O	A pidgin language used in South African mines for communication among various tribes.
F	A	N	C	I	F	U	L	Imaginary, Shadowy, Fictitious, Legendary, Mythical, Bizarre, Fantastic, Grotesgue.
F	A	N	C	Y	I	N	G	Liking, Enjoying, Devising, Imagining, Thinking, Endorsing, Approving.
F	A	N	D	A	N	G	O	A lively Spanish dance performed with castanets, Improper behaviour.
F	A	N	F	A	R	O	N	Braggart, Swaggerer, Fanfare.
F	A	N	G	L	E	S	S	Having no fangs, Having lost the power to harm.
F	A	N	L	I	G	H	T	A semicircular window with radiating ribs placed over a door or window.
F	A	N	T	A	S	I	A	Medley of operatic or folk airs, Something strange or foreign, Unreal qualities.
F	A	N	W	H	E	E	L	The wheel of a fan blower.
F	A	R	A	D	A	I	C	Relating to the alternating current of electricity produced by an induction coil.
F	A	R	A	D	I	S	M	Application of a current of electricity for therapeutic purposes.
F	A	R	C	E	U	S	E	An actress skilled in playing farce.
F	A	R	C	I	C	A	L	Laughable, Resembling farce, Receiving laughter.
F	A	R	C	Y	B	U	D	A swollen subcutaneous lymph gland characteristic of cutaneous glanders.
F	A	R	D	E	L	E	D	Bundled.
F	A	R	E	W	E	L	L	Goodbye, Adieu, Leave-taking, Parting, Departing, Valedictory.
F	A	R	F	L	U	N	G	Widely spread or distributed, Remote, Distant.
F	A	R	I	N	O	S	E	Yielding farina, Mealy.
F	A	R	M	Y	A	R	D	Barnyard, Area adjoining a homestead and enclosed by fencing.
F	A	R	O	U	C	H	E	Lacking social graces, Shy, Uncultured, Wild, Disorderly.
F	A	R	R	I	E	R	Y	The art of being a blacksmith.
F	A	R	R	O	W	E	D	When a sow has given birth.
F	A	R	T	H	E	S	T	Remotest, Latest, Most distant, Ultimate, Most remote in time.
F	A	R	T	H	I	N	G	A quarter of a penny, Mite.
F	A	S	C	I	A	T	E	Broadly banded in colour.
F	A	S	C	I	C	L	E	A small collection, A division of a book published in parts.
F	A	S	C	I	O	L	A	A narrow band of colour, Genus of parasitic worms including common liver flukes.
F	A	S	C	I	O	L	E	A band of spines on sea urchins.
F	A	S	C	I	S	T	A	Member of an organization similar to the Italian Fasciti.
F	A	S	C	I	S	T	I	Members of an Italian organisation dedicated to nationalism.
F	A	S	H	I	O	U	S	Troublesome, Annoying, Vexatious, Provocative.
F	A	S	S	A	I	T	E	A mineral consisting of a pale to dark green variety of augite.
F	A	S	T	E	N	E	D	Confirmed, Established, Ratified, Affixed, Attached, Connected, Adhered, Joined.
F	A	S	T	N	E	S	S	Stronghold, Fort, Fortress, Castle, Retreat, Shelter, Protection, Sanctum.
F	A	T	A	L	I	S	M	A belief in the inevitable.
F	A	T	A	L	I	S	T	One whose conduct is regulated by the belief that everything is ordained by fate.
F	A	T	A	L	I	T	Y	Condition of causing death, Mortality, Lethality, Deadliness, Malignancy, Casualty.
F	A	T	H	E	R	L	Y	Paternally kind, Benignly.
F	A	T	H	O	M	E	D	Measured, Understood, Probed, Investigated, Comprehended.
F	A	T	I	G	U	E	D	Tired, Depleted, Exhausted, Weakened, Debilitated, Wearied, Weary, Disabled.
F	A	T	T	E	N	E	D	Made bigger, Made fleshy or plump, Stuffed.
F	A	T	T	E	N	E	R	Stock to be fattened for slaughter.
F	A	T	T	R	E	L	S	Ends of ribbons.
F	A	U	B	O	U	R	G	Suburb of a French city, A city quarter.
F	A	U	C	H	A	R	D	A long-handled medieval weapon with a long convex edge.
F	A	U	L	T	F	U	L	Full of faults.
F	A	U	L	T	I	L	Y	In an imperfect manner.
F	A	U	L	T	I	N	G	Blundering, Failing, Blaming, Scolding, Censuring, Bungling, Liability, Sinning.
F	A	U	N	A	T	E	D	Possessing intestinal micro-organisms.
F	A	U	T	E	U	I	L	Upholstered chair with open arms, A stall in the theatre.
F	A	U	V	E	T	T	E	Any of several small singing birds.
F	A	V	E	O	L	A	E	Resembling a honeycomb in structure.
F	A	V	O	N	I	A	N	Mild, Bland.
F	A	V	O	U	R	E	D	Spared, Encouraged, Countenanced, Approved, Accepted, Endorsed, Sanctioned, Valued.
F	A	V	O	U	R	E	R	One that promotes.
F	A	Y	A	L	I	T	E	A mineral consisting of an iron silicate isomeric with olivine.
F	E	A	B	E	R	R	Y	Gooseberry.
F	E	A	R	L	E	S	S	Bold, Courageous, Dauntless, Unafraid, Assured, Sure, Confident, Sanguine.
F	E	A	R	S	O	M	E	Awe-inspiring, Timid, Timorous Arousing terror.
F	E	A	S	I	B	L	E	Suitable, Reasonable, Likely, Possible, Practicable, Viable, Workable, Profitable.
F	E	A	S	I	B	L	Y	Suitably, Likely, Possibly, Viably.
F	E	A	S	T	D	A	Y	A periodic religious festival.
F	E	A	S	T	F	U	L	Festive, Devoted to feasting.
F	E	A	S	T	I	N	G	Enjoying an unusual pleasure, Delighting, Gratifying, Entertaining lavishly.

1	2	3	4	5	6	7	8	Definition
F	E	A	T	H	E	R	Y	Light and delicate, Fluffy, Marked by delicate tracery, Almost weightless.
F	E	A	T	N	E	S	S	The quality of being dexterous.
F	E	A	T	U	R	E	D	Displayed, Advertised, Well-shaped, Favoured, Conceived, Envisaged, Emphasized.
F	E	B	R	I	F	I	C	Producing fever.
F	E	B	R	U	A	R	Y	The second month of the Gregorian calendar.
F	E	C	K	L	E	S	S	Helpless, Incompetent, Inefficient, Meaningless, Purposeless, Unreliable, Irresponsible.
F	E	C	U	L	E	N	T	Foul, Covered with filth, Fetid, Turbid, Coated with noxious matter.
F	E	D	E	L	I	N	I	Small type of vermicelli.
F	E	D	E	R	A	C	Y	Alliance, Confederacy, Federation.
F	E	D	E	R	A	T	E	Forming an alliance.
F	E	E	B	L	I	S	H	Somewhat weak, Rather fragile.
F	E	E	D	B	A	C	K	Return to the input of a part of the output, Partial reversion of the effects of a given process.
F	E	E	D	H	E	A	D	Excess of metal left above a mould during casting to compensate for shrinkage.
F	E	E	D	P	I	P	E	Pipe supplying material to machines.
F	E	E	D	P	U	M	P	A force pump for supplying water to a steam boiler.
F	E	I	G	N	I	N	G	Pretending, Alleging, Dissembling, Counterfeiting, Assuming, Imaging, Shamming, Faking.
F	E	I	N	T	I	N	G	Pretending, Tricking, Playing, Hoodwinking, Cheating, Hoaxing, Shifting.
F	E	L	D	S	P	A	R	Mineral that is aluminium silicates with potassium sodium calcium or barium.
F	E	L	I	C	I	D	E	Killing of a cat.
F	E	L	I	C	I	T	Y	Success, Grace, Aptness, Happiness, Good fortune, Bliss, Fortunate, Achievement.
F	E	L	I	N	I	T	Y	Characteristics of a feline.
F	E	L	L	A	H	I	N	A peasant in Arabic-speaking countries.
F	E	L	L	N	E	S	S	Extreme cruelty, Harshness, Destruction.
F	E	L	L	O	W	E	D	Matched, Equalled.
F	E	L	L	O	W	L	Y	Sociable, Companionable.
F	E	L	L	S	I	D	E	Hillside, Mountainside.
F	E	L	O	D	S	E	E	Self-destruction, Suicide.
F	E	L	O	I	D	E	A	Family of cats, civets, hyenas.
F	E	L	S	T	O	N	E	Dense macrocrystalline igneous rock.
F	E	L	S	I	T	I	C	Felsite.
F	E	L	T	E	R	E	D	Intertwined, Matted together.
F	E	L	T	L	I	K	E	Soft and matted, Having a fuzzy appearance.
F	E	L	T	S	I	D	E	The side of the paper not in contact with the machine, Top side.
F	E	L	T	W	O	R	K	A fibrous network.
F	E	L	T	W	O	R	T	A mullein with thick woolly leaves.
F	E	M	E	R	E	L	L	Louvre, Open structure on the roof for ventilation.
F	E	M	I	N	I	N	E	Female, Woman, Passive, Gentle.
F	E	M	I	N	I	S	M	Theory of the political, economic and social equality of the sexes, Removing discrimination.
F	E	M	I	N	I	S	T	Adherent of feminism.
F	E	M	I	N	I	Z	E	To give a feminine quality, Composed mostly of females.
F	E	N	C	H	E	N	E	Isomeric liquid terpene.
F	E	N	C	H	O	N	E	An oily terpenoid ketone.
F	E	N	C	I	B	L	E	A late 18th century, early 19th century soldier enlisted for home defence during war.
F	E	N	E	S	T	R	A	A small opening, An opening like a window cut in bone such as an operation on the ear.
F	E	N	N	O	M	A	N	Finnish partisan of the 19th century.
F	E	O	F	F	I	N	G	Possessing a freehold.
F	E	R	E	T	O	R	Y	Ornate receptacle for relics of a saint.
F	E	R	N	B	U	S	H	A low densely branched very leafy white-flowered shrub.
F	E	R	N	G	A	L	E	Sweetfern.
F	E	R	N	L	I	K	E	Resembling a fern.
F	E	R	N	S	E	E	D	Dustlike asexual spores of ferns.
F	E	R	O	C	I	T	Y	Fury, Ardour, Savage, Wildness, Cruelty, Savagery, Rapacity.
F	E	R	R	E	O	U	S	Containing iron.
F	E	R	R	E	T	E	D	Hunted, Extracted, Worried, Harried, Searched carefully, Pursued, Quested.
F	E	R	R	E	T	E	R	One that ferrets or seeks.
F	E	R	R	I	A	G	E	Transporting by ferry and fee due for the journey.
F	E	R	R	I	T	E	S	Compounds formed by heating ferric oxide with a metallic oxide.
F	E	R	R	I	T	I	N	Amber-coloured crystalline protein found in the liver and spleen where iron is stored.
F	E	R	R	U	L	E	D	Ringed or capped to prevent splitting and to strengthen a join.
F	E	R	R	Y	I	N	G	Conveying over a body of water, Transporting, Shipping, Flying from point to point.
F	E	R	R	Y	M	A	N	A person operating a ferry.
F	E	R	U	L	I	N	G	Punishing with a cane, rod, switch or ruler.
F	E	R	V	E	N	C	Y	Fervour, Zeal, Passion, Ardour, Sincerity, Warmth.
F	E	R	V	I	D	L	Y	Passionately, Intensely, Zealously, Warmly.
F	E	S	T	A	L	L	Y	Festivity for a religious feast day, Joyously, Merrily.
F	E	S	T	E	R	E	D	Inflamed, Putrified, Rankled, Corrupted, Generated ill-feeling, Irritated.
F	E	S	T	I	V	A	L	Feast, Merrymaking, Cultural events, Fair, Gaiety, Conviviality, Celebration.

1	2	3	4	5	6	7	8	
F	E	T	C	H	I	N	G	Attractive, Alluring, Enticing, Tempting, Bringing.
F	E	T	E	R	I	T	A	Grain sorghum.
F	E	T	I	S	H	E	S	Natural or artificial objects believed to protect the owner from evil, Fixations.
F	E	T	T	E	R	E	D	Shackled, Tethered, Hampered, Hindered, Restrained, Deprived of freedom, Bound, Hobbled.
F	E	T	T	L	I	N	G	Mending, Repairing, Arraying, Arranging, Dressing, Cleaning.
F	E	V	E	R	F	E	W	Perennial European herb, Chrysanthemum.
F	E	V	E	R	I	N	G	Heating, Agitating.
F	E	V	E	R	I	S	H	Agitated, Ardent, Abnormally hot, Hectic, Unstable, Fiery, Devoutness.
F	E	V	E	R	O	U	S	Feverish.
F	E	W	T	R	I	L	S	Odds and ends, Trifles.
F	I	B	E	R	I	S	E	To reduce to fibres by crushing or beating.
F	I	B	R	I	L	L	A	Small thread or fibre.
F	I	B	R	O	S	I	S	Fibrous degeneration.
F	I	B	R	O	S	E	S	Same as FIBROSIS.
F	I	B	U	L	A	R	E	Bones of the heel and ankle.
F	I	D	D	L	I	N	G	Meddling, Tampering, Tinkering, Cheating, Swindling, Tampering, Petty, Trifling.
F	I	D	E	L	I	T	Y	Loyalty, Exactness, Allegiance, Fealty, Devotion, Piety, Constancy, Reliability.
F	I	D	G	E	T	E	D	Worried, Fiddled, Tinkered nervously, Moved uneasily, Fretted, Chafed.
F	I	D	U	C	I	A	L	Founded on faith or trust, Confidence, Honesty.
F	I	E	L	D	B	E	D	Four-poster bed with an arched canopy, A bed used in the field.
F	I	E	L	D	D	A	Y	A day when troop manoeuvres are held, An occasion marked by fun, An outdoor sports day.
F	I	E	L	D	I	N	G	Putting into action either in war or in sport.
F	I	E	N	D	I	S	H	Cruel, Wicked, Diabolical, Devilish, Satanic, Infernal, Malignant.
F	I	E	R	C	E	L	Y	Terribly, Awfully, Frantically, Furiously, Hardly, Madly, Tumultously, Violently.
F	I	E	R	C	E	S	T	Most violent, Most savage, Cruellest, Most barbarous.
F	I	F	E	R	A	I	L	Railing around the bulwarks of a quarterdeck.
F	I	F	T	I	E	T	H	One of fifty equal parts, Number fifty in a countable series.
F	I	G	H	T	I	N	G	Contending, Waging, Contesting, Battling, Striving, Struggling, Disputing, Squabbling.
F	I	G	S	H	E	L	L	Shell of a mollusk.
F	I	G	U	R	A	N	T	Member of a dancing troupe that only performs in group dancing.
F	I	G	U	R	A	T	E	Relating to a figure, Florid.
F	I	G	U	R	I	N	E	Small statuette.
F	I	G	U	R	I	N	G	Portraying, Symbolizing, Computing, Reckoning, Understanding, Calculating, Thinking.
F	I	G	U	R	I	S	T	One that believes in the figurative presence of Christ in the Eucharist.
F	I	L	A	G	R	E	E	Filigree, Ornamental openwork of a delicate design.
F	I	L	A	M	E	N	T	Fibre, Thread of a spider's web, Slender wire.
F	I	L	A	R	I	A	L	Infested with parasitic worms.
F	I	L	A	R	I	I	D	Slender nematode worms.
F	I	L	A	T	U	R	E	The reeling of silk from the cocoons.
F	I	L	C	H	I	N	G	Pilfering, Stealing, Pinching, Swiping, Purloining, Snitching.
F	I	L	E	F	I	S	H	Fishes with rough granulated leathery skins, Triggerfish.
F	I	L	I	A	L	L	Y	Relating to a son or daughter.
F	I	L	I	A	T	E	D	Declared the offspring of a particular parent.
F	I	L	I	C	I	D	E	Murdering of a son or daughter, Parent who murders their child.
F	I	L	I	C	I	T	E	Fossil fern.
F	I	L	I	F	O	R	M	An extremely slender medical instrument for introduction into tubular passages of the body.
F	I	L	I	G	R	E	E	Ornamental openwork of an intricate design.
F	I	L	I	P	I	N	O	Native of the Philippine islands.
F	I	L	L	E	T	E	D	Bound with a fillet, Rounded off a corner, Cut into fillets.
F	I	L	L	I	P	E	D	Flipped a nail against the hand, Urged, Stimulated, Snapped.
F	I	L	M	G	O	E	R	A regular patron of the movie theatre.
F	I	L	T	E	R	E	D	Strained, Percolated, Infiltrated, Purified.
F	I	L	T	H	I	E	R	Dirtier, More obscene, More vile.
F	I	L	T	H	I	L	Y	Nastily, Sloppily, Repulsively, Offensively, Obscenely.
F	I	L	T	R	A	T	E	Something that has been filtered or diffused.
F	I	M	B	R	I	A	L	Marked by a bordering fringe.
F	I	N	A	G	L	E	R	Cheat, Swindler.
F	I	N	A	L	I	S	M	A belief in final causes.
F	I	N	A	L	I	S	T	A contestant in the final round of a competition.
F	I	N	A	L	I	T	Y	Conclusion, Inevitability, Ultimate, Closure, Eventuality.
F	I	N	A	N	C	E	D	Provided funds, Sold on credit, Endowed, Subsidized, Sponsored, Supported.
F	I	N	E	C	O	M	B	Search thoroughly.
F	I	N	E	L	E	S	S	Endless.
F	I	N	E	N	E	S	S	Clearness, Purity, Elegance, Delicacy, Acuity, Subtlety, Sensitivity.
F	I	N	E	S	P	U	N	Performed or produced with extreme skill, care, delicacy or ingenuity.
F	I	N	E	S	S	E	D	Manoeuvred, Played a card, Evaded, Tricked.
F	I	N	G	E	R	E	D	Handled, Purloined, Identified, Indicated, Designated, Shadowed, Extended.

1	2	3	4	5	6	7	8	
F	I	N	I	S	H	E	D	Terminated, Completed, Closed, Concluded, Halted, Accomplished, Consumed, Destroyed.
F	I	N	I	S	H	E	R	A worker who performs the finishing steps in manufacture.
F	I	N	I	T	E	L	Y	Limited.
F	I	N	I	T	U	D	E	Quality or state of being finite.
F	I	N	W	H	A	L	E	Finback.
F	I	R	E	A	R	M	S	Weapons from which a shot is discharged.
F	I	R	E	B	A	C	K	Asiatic pheasant, Back lining of a fireplace.
F	I	R	E	B	A	L	L	A ball of fire, Ball filled with powder, Cloud resulting from a nuclear explosion.
F	I	R	E	B	A	R	S	Bars of a grate or boiler furnace.
F	I	R	E	B	O	A	T	Boat equipped with apparatus for fighting fires.
F	I	R	E	B	O	T	E	Right of a tenant to take a reasonable amount of wood for domestic use.
F	I	R	E	C	L	A	Y	Clay that will withstand high temperatures.
F	I	R	E	C	O	C	K	A cock to supply water for extinguishing fires.
F	I	R	E	D	A	M	P	A combustible gas that is formed in mines by decomposition of coal that consists of methane.
F	I	R	E	E	Y	E	D	Having glowing eyes.
F	I	R	E	F	I	S	H	Small scarlet and orange banded coral fish with venomous spines.
F	I	R	E	H	O	O	K	A pole with a hook for ripping away material as an aid for fighting fires.
F	I	R	E	L	E	S	S	Having no fire.
F	I	R	E	L	O	C	K	Flintflock, Wheel lock.
F	I	R	E	P	L	U	G	A hydrant for drawing water from the mains for extinguishing fires.
F	I	R	E	S	A	F	E	Protected from fire.
F	I	R	E	S	H	I	P	A ship carrying explosives sent among enemy's ships to set them alight.
F	I	R	E	S	I	D	E	A place near the hearth, Household, Informal, Intimate.
F	I	R	E	S	T	E	P	Firing step.
F	I	R	E	T	A	I	L	Birds with reddish tails.
F	I	R	E	T	R	A	P	A building that would be dangerous for the inhabitants in the case of a fire.
F	I	R	E	W	A	R	D	Fire warden, An officer responsible for fire control.
F	I	R	E	W	E	E	D	Troublesome weeds in clearings and burnt areas.
F	I	R	E	W	O	O	D	Wood for fuel.
F	I	R	E	W	O	R	K	Pyrotechnic, Device for making a striking display with explosive or flammable substances.
F	I	R	E	W	O	R	M	Larva of moths that eat leaves of the cranberry vine, Glowworm.
F	I	R	M	L	A	N	D	Terra firma.
F	I	R	M	N	E	S	S	Steadiness, Strength, Steadfastness, Solidity, Resolution, Stability.
F	I	R	S	T	A	I	D	Emergency medical treatment.
F	I	R	S	T	D	A	Y	A day when new postage stamps are issued.
F	I	S	H	A	B	L	E	Legally open for fishing.
F	I	S	H	B	A	L	L	Ball of cooked fish and mashed potatoes fried in oil.
F	I	S	H	B	E	A	M	A beam with one side bulging and resembling the belly of a fish.
F	I	S	H	B	O	W	L	A bowl for keeping live fish, Something open to inspection from every angle.
F	I	S	H	C	A	K	E	A fish-ball flattened into a patty.
F	I	S	H	G	L	U	E	Gelatinous substance obtained from fish waste products, Isinglass.
F	I	S	H	H	A	W	K	Osprey.
F	I	S	H	H	O	O	K	A hook for catching fish.
F	I	S	H	M	E	A	L	Ground dried fish used as fertilizer and animal feeds.
F	I	S	H	P	O	N	D	A pond stocked with edible or ornamental fish.
F	I	S	H	T	A	I	L	A shape that resembles the tail of a fish, To swing the tail of a plane to reduce speed.
F	I	S	H	W	E	I	R	A dam or weir to control the movements of fish.
F	I	S	H	W	I	F	E	An abusive woman or trampish woman.
F	I	S	S	I	P	E	D	Having a cloven hoof.
F	I	S	S	U	R	E	D	Cracked, Fractured, Divided, Breached, Rent, Ruptured, Gashed, Split.
F	I	S	T	I	A	N	A	The world of boxing.
F	I	S	T	M	E	L	E	A measurement of the hand used in archery to determine the correct height of a bow string.
F	I	S	T	U	L	A	R	Fistulous, Having a fistula.
F	I	T	F	U	L	L	Y	Variably, Impulsively, Spasmodically, Desultory, Intermittently, Inconstantly.
F	I	V	E	F	O	L	D	Five times as large, Increased by five times.
F	I	V	E	L	E	A	F	Cinquefoil.
F	I	V	E	S	O	M	E	A group of five persons.
F	I	X	A	T	I	O	N	Focussing, Obsession, Concentration, Craze, Fascination, Infatuation.
F	I	X	A	T	I	V	E	Stabilizer, Varnish for protection, Substance to fix living tissue.
F	I	Z	Z	L	I	N	G	Hissing, Sputtering, Failing, Petering out.
F	L	A	B	B	I	L	Y	Feebly, Limply, Slackly, Weakly.
F	L	A	G	G	I	N	G	Signalling, Decorating, Identifying, Drooping, Declining, Fading, Weakening, Wilting.
F	L	A	G	P	O	L	E	A pole used for raising a flag.
F	L	A	G	R	A	N	T	Bold, Conspicuous, Shocking, Shameful.
F	L	A	G	S	H	I	P	The finest ship of the line, The ship that carries the commander of the fleet.
F	L	A	K	E	L	E	T	A small snowflake.
F	L	A	M	B	E	A	U	Flaming torch, Ornamental candlestick, Kettle used for boiling sugar.

1	2	3	4	5	6	7	8	
F	L	A	M	E	C	U	T	To cut metal with a gas flame.
F	L	A	M	E	L	E	T	A small flame.
F	L	A	M	E	N	C	O	A dance of the Andalusian gypsies.
F	L	A	M	I	N	G	O	Long-legged aquatic bird.
F	L	A	M	M	I	N	G	Deceiving, Tricking, Cheating.
F	L	A	M	M	U	L	E	A small flame depicted in a Chinese or Japanese picture.
F	L	A	N	C	H	E	D	Flared, Slanted outwards.
F	L	A	N	E	U	S	E	A self-centred woman behaving in the fashion of a playboy.
F	L	A	N	E	R	I	E	Aimless, Idle, Lounging.
F	L	A	N	K	I	N	G	Sheltering, Protecting, Escaping, Evading, Bordering, Situating at the side.
F	L	A	P	J	A	C	K	Griddle cake, Fruit turnover.
F	L	A	P	P	I	N	G	Flinging, Beating, Striking, Clapping, Agitating, Dithering, Fluttering, Waving.
F	L	A	S	H	I	L	Y	Gaudily, Brightly, Garishly, Loudly, Ornately, Floridly.
F	L	A	S	H	I	N	G	Rushing, Glittering, Scintillating, Blinking, Dazzling, Sparkling, Twinkling, Displaying.
F	L	A	T	B	O	A	T	Boat with a flat bottom for negotiating shallow water.
F	L	A	T	F	I	S	H	A fish with a compressed body and having both eyes on the upper side.
F	L	A	T	F	O	O	T	A foot condition where the arch of the instep has dropped, Policeman.
F	L	A	T	H	E	A	D	N. American Indians that practiced head-flattening.
F	L	A	T	I	R	O	N	Sadiron, An iron with a smooth surface heated on a fire or stove used for smoothing clothes.
F	L	A	T	L	A	N	D	Region where the land is flat, A city area with many hi-rise apartments.
F	L	A	T	N	E	S	S	State or quality of being flat.
F	L	A	T	R	A	C	E	A race without hurdles or obstacles.
F	L	A	T	T	E	R	Y	Adulation, Insincere praise, Blandishment, Cajolery, Fawning, Ingratiation, Toadying.
F	L	A	T	T	E	S	T	Smoothest, Lowest, Dullest, Most insipid.
F	L	A	T	T	I	N	G	Flattening, Razing.
F	L	A	T	T	I	S	H	Comparatively flat.
F	L	A	T	U	O	U	S	Flatulent.
F	L	A	T	W	A	R	E	Platters, Shallow dishes, Serving utensils, Cutlery.
F	L	A	T	W	I	S	E	With the flat side downward.
F	L	A	T	W	O	R	M	Tapeworm.
F	L	A	U	N	T	E	D	Displayed, Flouted, Paraded, Exposed, Boasted, Revealed, Flourished, Advertised.
F	L	A	U	N	T	E	R	One that desires to be the centre of attraction.
F	L	A	U	T	I	N	O	Piccolo, Small accordion, Small flute.
F	L	A	U	T	I	S	T	One that plays a flute.
F	L	A	V	E	R	I	A	Genus of tropical American herbs.
F	L	A	V	O	N	O	L	Hydroxy derivative of flavone.
F	L	A	W	L	E	S	S	Perfect, Intact, Unblemished, Undamaged, Unimpaired, Inpeccable, Faultless, Ideal.
F	L	A	X	B	I	R	D	Goldfinch.
F	L	A	X	C	O	M	B	Hackle, Comb with long teeth for dressing the fibres of flax.
F	L	A	X	L	I	L	Y	New Zealand flax.
F	L	A	X	S	E	E	D	The seed that yields linseed oil.
F	L	A	X	S	I	C	K	Soil infested with fungi.
F	L	A	X	W	E	E	D	Toadflax.
F	L	E	A	B	A	N	E	A plant that is supposed to drive away fleas.
F	L	E	A	B	I	T	E	Bite of a flea, Small irritation, Trifling annoyance, Minute amount.
F	L	E	A	S	E	E	D	Oak-leaf gall that moves about due to activity of insect larva enclosed within.
F	L	E	A	W	O	R	T	A plant with a smell that is supposed to be repugnant to fleas.
F	L	E	A	W	O	R	T	A plantain the seeds of which are used as a mild laxative.
F	L	E	C	K	I	N	G	Streaking, Stippling, Variegating, Dappling, Spotting.
F	L	E	C	T	I	O	N	Turning, Bend, Fold, Turn, Inflection, Angle, Bow.
F	L	E	E	C	I	N	G	Extorting, Despoiling, Plundering, Cheating, Defrauding, Swindling.
F	L	E	E	R	I	N	G	Sneering, Mocking, Gibing, Scoffing, Grimacing, Smirking, Leering.
F	L	E	E	T	E	S	T	Fastest, Most nimble, Most agile, Quickest, Swiftest.
F	L	E	E	T	I	N	G	Fluctuating, Dissolving, Vanishing, Skimming, Hastening, Momentary, Transient, Volatile.
F	L	E	N	C	H	E	D	Skinned, Stripped blubber from a whale.
F	L	E	N	S	I	N	G	Skinning.
F	L	E	S	H	F	L	Y	Bluebottle or blowfly whose maggots feed on flesh.
F	L	E	S	H	I	N	G	Thrusting into flesh, Covering as if with flesh, Fattening, Tights.
F	L	E	S	H	O	U	T	Shoe leather used with the grain side against the foot.
F	L	E	S	H	P	O	T	Life of luxury, High-living.
F	L	E	T	C	H	E	D	Feathered arrows.
F	L	E	T	C	H	E	R	A maker of arrows.
F	L	E	X	I	B	L	E	Pliable, Mangeable, Tractable, Resilient, Springy, Supple, Docile, Amenable.
F	L	E	X	I	B	L	Y	Stretchily, Springily.
F	L	E	X	U	O	U	S	Zigzag, Wavy, Flexible, Adaptable, Flickering, Undulating.
F	L	I	C	H	T	E	R	Flutter, Flicker, Quiver, Throb, Palpitate.
F	L	I	C	K	I	N	G	Striking lightly, Fluttering, Waving.

1	2	3	4	5	6	7	8	
F	L	I	G	H	T	E	D	Birds risen from feeding grounds, Fletched.
F	L	I	M	F	L	A	M	Freak, Trifle, Conceit, Deception, Trick, Trifling, Nonsense, Deception.
F	L	I	M	S	I	E	S	Something transparent, Thin paper, Women's lightweight clothing.
F	L	I	M	S	I	L	Y	Weakly, Unsubstantially, Trifling, Slightly, Fraility.
F	L	I	N	C	H	E	D	Winced, Started, Recoiled, Withdrew, Blanched, Quailed, Evaded, Retreated.
F	L	I	N	C	H	E	R	One that flinches.
F	L	I	N	D	E	R	S	Splinters, Fragments, Pieces.
F	L	I	N	G	I	N	G	Hurling, Throwing, Discarding, Casting, Heaving, Launching, Tossing, Rushing.
F	L	I	N	K	I	T	E	Mineral consisting of a greenish brown basic manganese arsenate.
F	L	I	N	T	I	F	Y	To convert into flint.
F	L	I	N	T	I	L	Y	Harshly, Sternly.
F	L	I	P	F	L	A	P	Repeated sound and motion of something loose being moved in a regular fashion.
F	L	I	P	F	L	O	P	Same as FLIPFLAP.
F	L	I	P	P	A	N	T	Talkative, Voluble, Frivolous, Flighty, Volatile, Saucy, Mischievous, Playful.
F	L	I	P	P	I	N	G	Flicking over, Flapping, Moving jerkily, Skimming.
F	L	I	R	T	I	N	G	Flipping, Flicking, Tossing, Teasing amorously, Mocking.
F	L	I	R	T	I	S	H	Flirtatious.
F	L	I	T	T	E	N	S	Rags, Tatters, Fragments.
F	L	I	T	T	I	N	G	Fluttering, Hovering, Teetering, Quivering, Transitory, Brief, Evanescent.
F	L	I	X	W	E	E	D	A branching annual tansy mustard.
F	L	O	A	T	A	G	E	Something or wreckage floating on a body of water.
F	L	O	A	T	A	N	T	Same as FLOATAGE.
F	L	O	A	T	I	N	G	Lacking the usual attachment, Operating smoothly, Wavering, Negotiating, Resting on fluid.
F	L	O	C	C	O	S	E	Covered with tufts of soft woolly hairs.
F	L	O	C	C	U	L	E	Small mass of material floating in a liquid.
F	L	O	C	K	B	E	D	Mattress stuffed with flock.
F	L	O	C	K	I	N	G	Design or decorative work in flock.
F	L	O	G	G	I	N	G	Whipping, Lashing, Punishing, Driving, Chastising, Exhausting, Scourging, Thrashing.
F	L	O	O	D	I	N	G	Inundating, Deluging, Covering, Overwhelming, Splashing, Overflowing, Swamping.
F	L	O	O	D	L	I	T	Illuminated with artificial lights.
F	L	O	O	R	A	G	E	Floor space.
F	L	O	O	R	I	N	G	Material for laying floors.
F	L	O	P	P	I	L	Y	Limply, Flabbily, Flaccidly.
F	L	O	P	P	I	N	G	Flapping, Throwing oneself down heavily, Failing.
F	L	O	R	A	L	L	Y	Associated with flowers, Concerned with flora.
F	L	O	R	E	N	C	E	From the city of Florence, Florentine.
F	L	O	R	I	A	T	E	Being decorated with flowers.
F	L	O	R	I	C	A	N	Indian bustard.
F	L	O	R	I	D	L	Y	Flowery, Ruddily, Ornately.
F	L	O	T	I	L	L	A	Small fleet of boats, Group of ships.
F	L	O	U	N	C	E	D	Floundered, Struggled, Twisted, Minced, Pranced, Prinked, Strutted.
F	L	O	U	N	D	E	R	Stumble, Muddle, Wallow, Lurch, Strive, Struggle, Toil.
F	L	O	U	R	I	N	G	Grinding, Pulverizing, Sprinkling or coating with flour, Chalking.
F	L	O	U	R	I	S	H	Prosper, Blossom, Thrive, Boast, Brag, Ornament, Succeed, Fanfare.
F	L	O	U	T	I	N	G	Mocking, Insulting, Sneering, Scoffing, Jeering, Jesting, Quipping, Spurning.
F	L	O	W	E	R	E	D	Bloomed, Blossomed, Burgeoned, Adorned with flowers.
F	L	O	W	E	R	E	R	A person who makes representations of flowers in pottery or embroidery.
F	L	O	W	L	I	N	E	Differences in arrangements through a flow occurring in liquid rock or metal.
F	L	U	E	N	T	L	Y	Freely, Easily, Smoothly, Vocally.
F	L	U	F	F	I	N	G	Bungling, Failing, Erring, Blundering, Lapsing, Tripping.
F	L	U	I	D	I	F	Y	To make fluid, Accumulate liquid.
F	L	U	I	D	I	T	Y	A liquid or gaseous state, Flexibility, Unstable quality, Adaptability.
F	L	U	I	D	R	A	M	Unit of liquid capacity.
F	L	U	M	E	R	I	N	A dark red powder with a greenish fluorescence.
F	L	U	M	M	E	R	Y	A soft porridge, Cold dessert with fruit and nuts, Humbug, Foolish deceptive language.
F	L	U	O	R	E	N	E	A colourless crystalline cyclic hydrocarbon.
F	L	U	O	R	I	D	E	A binary compound of fluorine.
F	L	U	O	R	I	N	E	A non-metallic univalent element belonging to the halogens.
F	L	U	O	R	I	T	E	A transparent or translucent mineral consisting of calcium fluoride.
F	L	U	O	R	O	I	D	Tetrahexahedron.
F	L	U	R	R	I	E	D	Agitated, Disconcerted, Excited, Stirred, Confused, Discomposed, Disturbed, Embarrassed.
F	L	U	S	H	I	N	G	Blushing, Exciting, Glowing, Animating.
F	L	U	X	I	B	L	E	Inconstant, Variable.
F	L	U	X	W	E	E	D	Tansy mustard.
F	L	Y	B	L	O	W	N	Tainted, Infested with flyblows.
F	L	Y	P	A	P	E	R	Paper coated with a poisonous sticky substance for killing flies.
F	L	Y	S	H	E	E	T	Handbill, Canvas or nylon tent cover, Two or four page tract.

1	2	3	4	5	6	7	8	Definition
F	L	Y	W	H	E	E	L	A heavy metal wheel for governing the speed of an engine.
F	O	A	L	F	O	O	T	A plant with large rounded leaves once used as a flavouring agent, Coltsfoot.
F	O	C	A	L	I	Z	E	Bring into focus, Converge, Concentrate, Confine to a limited area.
F	O	C	U	S	I	N	G	Concentrating, Converging, Adjusting one's eye or camera to a certain range.
F	O	G	B	O	U	N	D	Unable to move because of fog, Surrounded by fog.
F	O	G	G	I	E	S	T	Vaguest, Murkiest, Dimmest.
F	O	I	L	S	M	A	N	Fencer.
F	O	I	S	T	I	N	G	Palming, Tricking, Infiltrating, Imposing, Insinuating, Deluding, Misleading, Hoaxing.
F	O	L	D	A	B	L	E	Able to be folded.
F	O	L	D	E	R	O	L	Trifle, Gegaw, Piffle, Nonsense, Impractical frippery.
F	O	L	D	L	E	S	S	Without a crease or fold.
F	O	L	D	Y	A	R	D	Enclosure for sheep and cattle.
F	O	L	I	A	G	E	D	Decorated with leaves.
F	O	L	I	A	T	E	D	Ornamented with foils, Having numbered leaves.
F	O	L	K	L	A	N	D	Land held in early England by customary law.
F	O	L	K	L	O	R	E	Traditional customs, beliefs, dances, songs or tales.
F	O	L	K	M	O	T	E	A general assembly, court or council.
F	O	L	K	S	I	L	Y	In a sociable and friendly manner.
F	O	L	K	S	O	N	G	A traditional song.
F	O	L	K	T	A	L	E	A traditional tale.
F	O	L	L	E	T	T	O	Imp, Goblin, Fairy.
F	O	L	L	I	C	L	E	A small cavity, A small lymph node, An air sac.
F	O	L	L	O	W	E	D	Pursued, Chased, Trailed, Ensued, Succeeded, Conformed, Obeyed.
F	O	L	L	O	W	E	R	Adherent, Disciple, Partisan, Supporter, Devotee, Admirer, Advocate.
F	O	L	L	O	W	O	N	To go in for a second innings in cricket.
F	O	L	L	O	W	U	P	Pursue closely, Exploit, Relating to a repeated act, Seeking further details.
F	O	M	E	N	T	E	D	Roused, Incited, Encouraged, Instigated, Provoked, Goaded, Spurred, Cultivated.
F	O	M	E	N	T	E	R	One that provokes trouble.
F	O	N	D	L	I	N	G	Pampering, Coddling, Caressing.
F	O	N	D	N	E	S	S	Prosperity, Relish, Affection, Attachment, Devotion, Inclination, Taste.
F	O	N	T	A	N	E	L	An ulcer, Gap in the brain covering at birth.
F	O	N	T	A	N	G	E	Commode.
F	O	O	D	L	E	S	S	Lacking food or nutrition.
F	O	O	L	S	C	A	P	Dunce cap, Large size writing paper.
F	O	O	T	B	A	L	L	Soccer.
F	O	O	T	B	A	T	H	A small tub for cleansing, warming or disinfecting feet.
F	O	O	T	F	A	L	L	The sound of a footstep.
F	O	O	T	G	E	A	R	Covering for the feet.
F	O	O	T	H	I	L	L	A hilly region at the base of a mountain.
F	O	O	T	H	O	L	D	A hold for feet, A safe footing.
F	O	O	T	I	R	O	N	Step of a carriage, Bracket for securing scenery to the stage floor.
F	O	O	T	L	E	S	S	Lacking foundation, Unsubstantial, Clumsy, Stupid, Inept, Useless, Futile.
F	O	O	T	L	I	N	G	Floorboard of a boat, Foolish, Silly, Trivial, Insignificant.
F	O	O	T	L	O	C	K	A grip secured by the feet in climbing a rope.
F	O	O	T	M	A	R	K	A footprint.
F	O	O	T	M	U	F	F	A lined bag for keeping the feet warm.
F	O	O	T	N	O	T	E	A note of reference, explanation or comment at the bottom of a text.
F	O	O	T	P	A	C	E	Walking pace, Raised floor on which an altar stands.
F	O	O	T	P	A	T	H	Footway, Sidewalk, Pavement, Pedestrian path.
F	O	O	T	P	I	C	K	A pointed pole with headgrips and footpiece for digging in hard or stony ground.
F	O	O	T	P	O	S	T	A bottom bed post.
F	O	O	T	R	A	C	E	A walking or running race.
F	O	O	T	R	O	P	E	A rope as a foothold on a sailing ship.
F	O	O	T	R	U	L	E	A stick twelve inches long.
F	O	O	T	S	O	R	E	Having sore or tender feet from excessive walking or standing.
F	O	O	T	S	T	E	P	Footfall, Tread, Pace, Track.
F	O	O	T	W	E	A	R	Wearing apparel for feet excluding hosiery.
F	O	O	T	W	O	R	K	The management and work of the feet in boxing, football, tennis and dancing.
F	O	O	Z	L	I	N	G	Bungling, Playing unskilfully.
F	O	R	A	G	I	N	G	Supplying animals with fodder, Ravaging, Raiding, Rummaging, Searching.
F	O	R	A	M	I	N	A	Small openings, Orifices.
F	O	R	A	Y	I	N	G	Ravaging, Pillaging, Raiding, Invading, Harassing, Harrying, Overrunning, Marauding.
F	O	R	B	O	R	N	E	Endured, Forgone, Abstained, Declined, Refrained, Restrained, Avoided, Withheld.
F	O	R	C	E	D	L	Y	Compulsorily, Unnaturally, Involuntarily.
F	O	R	C	E	F	U	L	Forcible, Mighty, Effective, Powerful, Potent, Intense, Violent, Militant.
F	O	R	C	I	B	L	E	Powerful, Impressive, Convincing, Efficacious, Aggressive, Self-assertive, Coercive.
F	O	R	D	O	I	N	G	Killing, Abolishing, Destroying, Undoing, Ruining, Terminating, Exhausting, Concluding.

1	2	3	4	5	6	7	8	
F	O	R	E	B	E	A	R	Ancestor, Forefather.
F	O	R	E	B	O	D	E	Foretell, Portend, Presage, Predict, Augur, Prognosticate.
F	O	R	E	B	O	D	Y	Forward part of a ship, Thorax.
F	O	R	E	C	A	S	T	Foretell, Guess, Calculate, Predict, Anticipate, Prophesy, Conjecture.
F	O	R	E	D	A	T	E	Antedate.
F	O	R	E	D	E	C	K	Forepart of the main deck of a ship.
F	O	R	E	D	O	N	E	Previously done.
F	O	R	E	D	O	O	M	To consign to a particular fate.
F	O	R	E	D	O	O	R	Front door of a house.
F	O	R	E	D	U	N	E	A sand dune stablized by vegetation.
F	O	R	E	E	D	G	E	The edge of a book.
F	O	R	E	F	E	E	L	Anticipate, Have a presentiment.
F	O	R	E	F	E	L	T	Anticipated.
F	O	R	E	F	O	O	T	Front foot of a quadruped, Forward part of a ship where stern and keel meet.
F	O	R	E	G	I	F	T	Lease premium, Payment in advance.
F	O	R	E	G	O	E	R	Example, Predecessor, Ancestor.
F	O	R	E	G	O	N	E	Previous.
F	O	R	E	H	A	N	D	A working foreman, Advantage, Prior, Anticipative, A stroke in tennis.
F	O	R	E	H	E	A	D	Brow, Part of the face between the brow and scalp, Front of something.
F	O	R	E	H	O	O	K	Timber to strengthen a ship.
F	O	R	E	K	N	O	W	To have previous knowledge.
F	O	R	E	L	A	D	Y	A woman supervisor in a factory.
F	O	R	E	L	A	I	D	Ambushed, Waylaid, Hindered, Obstructed, Planned.
F	O	R	E	L	A	N	D	Headland, Cape, Promontory, Point.
F	O	R	E	L	O	C	K	Lock of hair that grows in the middle of the forehead, Centre of a horse's mane between ears.
F	O	R	E	M	A	S	T	Mast nearest the bow of a sailing ship.
F	O	R	E	M	I	L	K	First drawn milk usually contaminated.
F	O	R	E	M	O	S	T	First, Chief, Pre-eminent, Inaugural, Initial, Leading, Principal, Premier.
F	O	R	E	N	A	M	E	Baptismal name, Christian name.
F	O	R	E	N	O	O	N	Morning between breakfast and noon.
F	O	R	E	N	S	I	C	Used in legal proceedings, Argumentative, Rhetorical.
F	O	R	E	P	A	R	T	Front of something, Earlier part of a period of time.
F	O	R	E	P	E	A	K	Extreme forward lower compartment of a ship.
F	O	R	E	P	L	A	Y	Sexual stimulation that often leads to sexual intercourse.
F	O	R	E	P	L	O	T	To plan in advance.
F	O	R	E	P	O	L	E	System devised to cross quicksand or unstable ground.
F	O	R	E	P	O	S	T	Outpost.
F	O	R	E	R	I	B	S	Best cut of beef for roasting, Prime ribs.
F	O	R	E	S	A	I	D	Spoken previously.
F	O	R	E	S	A	I	L	A sail on a square-rigged ship.
F	O	R	E	S	E	E	N	Anticipated, Divined, Looked forward.
F	O	R	E	S	E	E	R	Soothsayer, Prophet.
F	O	R	E	S	H	I	P	Forward part of a ship.
F	O	R	E	S	H	O	T	The forerun in the distillation of whiskey.
F	O	R	E	S	H	O	W	Foretell.
F	O	R	E	S	I	D	E	Front.
F	O	R	E	S	T	A	L	Fronstall, An old English law against highwaymen.
F	O	R	E	S	T	A	Y	Support in front.
F	O	R	E	S	T	E	R	A person in charge of a timber growing area.
F	O	R	E	S	T	R	Y	Management of growing timber.
F	O	R	E	T	A	L	K	Preface.
F	O	R	E	T	E	L	L	Predict, Forecast, Prophesy, Augur, Presage, Forebode, Prognosticate, Portend.
F	O	R	E	T	I	M	E	Time before the present.
F	O	R	E	T	O	L	D	Prophesied.
F	O	R	E	T	U	R	N	Twist of yarn or wire forming a rope.
F	O	R	E	W	A	R	N	To give previous information, Advance warning.
F	O	R	E	W	E	N	T	Preceded.
F	O	R	E	W	O	R	D	Preface.
F	O	R	E	Y	A	R	D	A yard in front of a building.
F	O	R	F	A	I	R	N	Forlorn, Bereft, Exhausted, Worn out, Wilted.
F	O	R	G	E	M	A	N	A smith.
F	O	R	G	I	V	E	N	Absolved, Pardoned, Excused, Condoned, Overlooked, Remitted.
F	O	R	G	I	V	E	R	One that forgives.
F	O	R	G	O	I	N	G	Eschewing, Sacrificing, Abstaining, Renouncing, Resigning, Relinquishing, Forsaking.
F	O	R	K	E	D	L	Y	Ambiguously, Equivocally, Horned, Cuckolded, Having a double meaning.
F	O	R	K	H	E	A	D	An arrowhead with prongs facing outward, Forked end of a rod.
F	O	R	K	L	E	S	S	Having no fork.

1	2	3	4	5	6	7	8	
F	O	R	K	T	A	I	L	Any of various fork-tailed animals, birds or fishes, Swordfish, Kites.
F	O	R	M	A	B	L	E	Capable of being formed.
F	O	R	M	A	L	I	N	Solution of formaldehyde used for disinfecting and preserving.
F	O	R	M	A	L	L	Y	Expressly, Explicitly, Ceremoniously, Conventially, Solemnly, Methodically, Decorously.
F	O	R	M	A	Z	A	N	A hypothetical hydrazone related to formic acid.
F	O	R	M	E	R	L	Y	Beforehand, First, Once, Previously, Earlier, Erstwhile, Already.
F	O	R	M	I	C	A	L	Relating to ants.
F	O	R	M	L	E	S	S	Shapeless, Immaterial, Lacking a regular shape, Chaotic, Obscure.
F	O	R	M	U	L	A	E	Set words in ceremonies or rituals, Recipes, Prescriptions, Principles.
F	O	R	N	E	N	S	T	Opposite, Alongside, Beside, Against, Near to.
F	O	R	R	A	D	E	R	Forward.
F	O	R	S	A	K	E	N	Renounced, Left, Deserted, Abandoned, Spurned, Abdicated, Desolate, Solitary.
F	O	R	S	L	A	C	K	Neglect.
F	O	R	S	O	O	T	H	Certainly, Indeed.
F	O	R	S	P	E	A	K	Asperse, Bewitch, To cast a spell.
F	O	R	S	P	E	N	T	Exhausted, Worn out.
F	O	R	S	W	E	A	R	Reject, Renounce, Abjure, Deny upon oath.
F	O	R	S	W	O	R	N	Perjured.
F	O	R	T	H	I	N	K	Regret, Have a change of mind.
F	O	R	T	I	S	A	N	Lightweight fabric used for parachutes, clothing, curtains and bandages.
F	O	R	T	R	E	S	S	Stronghold, Permanent fortification, Refuge, Protected place.
F	O	R	T	U	I	T	Y	A chance event or occurrence.
F	O	R	T	U	N	E	D	Provided with a fortune, Happened, Chanced.
F	O	R	W	A	R	D	S	Forward, Onward.
F	O	R	Z	A	N	D	O	Sforzando, Direction in music for an accented sound.
F	O	S	S	A	R	I	A	Genus of small freshwater snails.
F	O	S	S	E	T	T	E	A little hollow.
F	O	S	T	E	R	E	D	Nursed, Nourished, Cared for, Encouraged, Cultivated.
F	O	S	T	E	R	E	R	One that fosters.
F	O	T	H	E	R	E	D	Covered a leak in the hull of a ship.
F	O	U	G	A	S	S	E	A land mine covered with stones and loose missiles.
F	O	U	L	H	O	O	K	To hook a fish anywhere but in the mouth.
F	O	U	L	M	A	R	T	A contemptible person.
F	O	U	L	N	E	S	S	Filth, Unclean, Pollution, Obscenity, Repulsiveness, Vulgarity, Squalidness, Nastiness.
F	O	U	L	P	L	A	Y	Violence, Unfair, Dishonest or treacherous conduct.
F	O	U	N	D	I	N	G	Building, Originating, Initiate, Establishing, Instituting, Creating, Organizing, Basing.
F	O	U	N	T	A	I	N	Spring of water, Source, Reservoir, Origin, Root, Inception, Wellhead.
F	O	U	N	T	F	U	L	Full of springs.
F	O	U	R	C	H	E	E	In heraldry having the end of each arm divided.
F	O	U	R	F	O	L	D	Quadruple, Being four times as large.
F	O	U	R	L	I	N	G	A twin crystal consisting of four individuals.
F	O	U	R	S	O	M	E	A group of four, Quartet, Two couples.
F	O	U	R	T	E	E	N	Seven times two, One more than thirteen.
F	O	X	B	E	R	R	Y	Mountain cranberry.
F	O	X	G	L	O	V	E	Plant of the genus Digitalis.
F	O	X	G	R	A	P	E	Native grape of N. America that is the ancestor of most of the American cultivated grapes.
F	O	X	H	O	U	N	D	Large, swift powerful hound used in foxhunting.
F	O	X	I	N	E	S	S	Slyness, Cleverness, Alertness, Smartness.
F	O	Z	I	N	E	S	S	Sponginess, Obesity, Fatheadedness.
F	R	A	C	T	I	O	N	Part of a whole, Scrap, Portion, Section, Fragment, Discord, Disharmony, Rupture.
F	R	A	C	T	U	R	E	Break, Violate, Rift, Breach, Rent, Fissure, Split, Schism.
F	R	A	G	A	R	I	A	Genus of strawberries.
F	R	A	G	M	E	N	T	A part broken off, Detached portion, Part, Small, Insignificant.
F	R	A	G	R	A	N	T	Having a fragrance, Marked by a fragrance.
F	R	A	M	A	B	L	E	Capable of being framed.
F	R	A	M	E	M	A	N	A telephone worker who connects terminals on a wire-distributing frame.
F	R	A	N	C	I	E	N	Middle-age French that was basis of present day French language.
F	R	A	N	C	I	U	M	A radioactive element of the alkali metal group.
F	R	A	N	G	U	L	A	Bark of frangula used as a laxative, Alder, Buckthorn.
F	R	A	N	K	I	N	G	To mark indicating payment of postage, Exempting, Freeing.
F	R	A	N	K	I	S	H	Relating to the Franks.
F	R	A	N	K	L	I	N	An old English landowner who was not an aristocrat.
F	R	A	P	P	I	N	G	Securing with ropes, Binding.
F	R	A	S	N	I	A	N	Relating to prehistoric fossil period.
F	R	A	U	D	F	U	L	Fraudulent.
F	R	A	U	L	E	I	N	Unmarried German girl, German governess.
F	R	A	V	A	S	H	I	Immortal spirit guardian of each individual.

8 LETTERS

1	2	3	4	5	6	7	8	Definition
F	R	A	X	E	T	I	N	A yellow crystalline compound derived from coumarin.
F	R	A	X	I	N	U	S	Genus of trees, Ash.
F	R	A	Z	Z	L	E	D	Frayed, Worn, Exhausted, Prostrated, Ragged, Tattered, Fatigued.
F	R	E	A	K	I	S	H	Whimsical, Capricious, Abnormal, Erratic, Wayward, Vagarious.
F	R	E	C	K	L	E	D	Marked with freckles, Spotted, Speckled.
F	R	E	E	B	O	R	N	Not born into slavery.
F	R	E	E	C	I	T	Y	Self-governing city, Semi-autonomous city and adjacent area.
F	R	E	E	D	M	A	N	Former slave, A negro slave freed as a result of the Civil War.
F	R	E	E	H	A	N	D	A drawing made without any mechanical aid, Unrestrained.
F	R	E	E	H	O	L	D	Property or estate held in fee simple.
F	R	E	E	L	O	A	D	To impose upon the generosity or hospitality of another.
F	R	E	E	L	O	V	E	Sexual intercourse or cohabitation without a legal wedding.
F	R	E	E	N	E	S	S	Freedom.
F	R	E	E	P	O	R	T	Foreign trade zone where duties are not levied, Free trade area.
F	R	E	E	R	E	E	D	A reed in a musical wind instrument often used in a concertina.
F	R	E	E	S	O	I	L	Anti-slavery movement.
F	R	E	E	W	I	L	L	Voluntary, Spontaneous, Ability and opportunity to choose.
F	R	E	E	Z	E	U	P	The period of the year when lakes and dams freeze over.
F	R	E	E	Z	I	N	G	Being at or below freezing point.
F	R	E	G	A	T	A	E	Family of web-footed sea birds.
F	R	E	M	I	T	U	S	Vibration felt in parts of the body during speech.
F	R	E	N	E	T	I	C	Frenzied, Frantic, Hectic, Furious, Delirious, Mad, Rabid, Wild.
F	R	E	N	U	L	U	M	A connecting fold of membrane, Bristles of the wings of butterflies.
F	R	E	N	Z	I	E	D	Driven to madness, Furious, Rabid, Wild, Frantic, Maddened.
F	R	E	Q	U	E	N	T	Full, Common, Familiar, Current, Usual, Habitual, Persistent, Intimate.
F	R	E	S	C	A	D	E	A cool walk, Shady place.
F	R	E	S	C	O	E	D	Painted in frescoe, Decorated heavily.
F	R	E	S	H	M	A	N	First year student of a college or university.
F	R	E	T	S	O	M	E	Annoying, Irritating, Bothersome.
F	R	E	T	T	I	N	G	Decorating with interlacing designs, Enriching, Rubbing, Chafing, Disturbing, Agitating.
F	R	E	T	W	O	R	K	Ornamental openwork.
F	R	E	U	D	I	A	N	Relating to the theories of Sigmund Freud and his system of psychoanalysis.
F	R	I	B	B	L	E	D	Acted frivolously, Trifled, Giddily, Dizzily.
F	R	I	C	A	N	D	O	Specially cooked veal.
F	R	I	C	T	I	O	N	Attrition, Stimulation, Sliding, Rubbing, Rolling, Disagreement, Abrasion, Clashing of views.
F	R	I	E	N	D	E	D	Befriended, Aided, Served.
F	R	I	E	N	D	L	Y	Favourable, Amicable, Neighbourly, Intimately, Affectionately, Lovingly, Devotedly.
F	R	I	E	S	I	A	N	Relating to Friesland.
F	R	I	G	H	T	E	D	Scared, Alarmed.
F	R	I	G	H	T	E	N	Terrify, Amaze, Appall, Terrorize, Alarm, Shock, Horrify.
F	R	I	G	I	D	L	Y	Coldly, Chilly, Frosty, Icy, Indifferently, Unresponsively, Glacially.
F	R	I	L	L	I	N	G	Decorating with a frill, Crimping, Pleating.
F	R	I	N	G	I	N	G	Forming a fringe.
F	R	I	P	P	E	R	Y	Trifling, Contemptible, Finery, Ostentation.
F	R	I	S	E	T	T	E	Fringe of curls worn on the forehead by women.
F	R	I	S	K	I	L	Y	Gaily, Playfully.
F	R	I	S	K	I	N	G	Leaping, Skipping, Dancing, Searching, Capering, Gambolling, Romping.
F	R	I	T	T	A	G	E	Mosaic.
F	R	I	T	T	I	N	G	Fusing (by heat).
F	R	I	Z	Z	L	E	D	Curled, Crisped, Fried, Burned, Scorched, Seared.
F	R	O	C	K	I	N	G	Clothing, Creating a cleric.
F	R	O	G	F	I	S	H	Toadfish.
F	R	O	G	G	E	R	Y	A gathering of frogs.
F	R	O	G	G	I	N	G	Ornamented with braid loops for fastening.
F	R	O	G	L	I	N	G	Small or young frog.
F	R	O	G	S	K	I	N	A dollar bill.
F	R	O	G	S	P	I	T	An algae that forms slimy masses on ponds.
F	R	Ö	H	L	I	C	H	A direction in music, joyous, happy.
F	R	O	M	W	A	R	D	From.
F	R	O	N	D	A	G	E	Leafy foliage.
F	R	O	N	D	E	N	T	Having fronds.
F	R	O	N	D	E	U	R	Rebel, Malcontent, Dissident.
F	R	O	N	D	O	S	E	Resembling fronds, Thalloid.
F	R	O	N	T	A	G	E	A portion of land that fronts a road, stream, river or the sea.
F	R	O	N	T	I	E	R	Border, Boundary, Zone, Region, Barrier.
F	R	O	N	T	I	N	G	Facing in a specified direction, Confronting, Acting as an advocate, Introductory, Prefacing.
F	R	O	N	T	L	E	T	Frontal, Browband, A short valance over an altar frontal.

1	2	3	4	5	6	7	8	
F	R	O	P	P	I	S	H	Peevish, Fretful.
F	R	O	S	T	I	L	Y	Chilly, reserved or distant manner.
F	R	O	S	T	I	N	G	Icing, Trimming on a garment, Matt finish of glass or metal.
F	R	O	T	H	I	L	Y	Foaming, Bubbly.
F	R	O	T	H	I	N	G	Foaming, Venting, Lathering.
F	R	O	T	T	A	G	E	Rubbing, Polishing.
F	R	O	T	T	O	L	A	Homophonic song of 15th and 16th century Italy.
F	R	O	U	F	R	O	U	Rustling, Frilly trimming, Fussy details, Excessive ornamentation.
F	R	O	U	N	C	E	D	Curled, Frizzled.
F	R	O	W	Z	L	E	D	Dishevelled, Unkempt.
F	R	U	C	T	I	F	Y	Make productive, Bear fruit, To make fruitful.
F	R	U	C	T	O	S	E	A ketose sugar.
F	R	U	G	A	L	L	Y	Meanly, Thriftily, Economically, Sparingly.
F	R	U	I	T	A	G	E	Process of bearing fruit, Offspring, Progeny.
F	R	U	I	T	B	U	D	A bud that produces flowers and if fertilized, fruit.
F	R	U	I	T	E	R	Y	Fruit.
F	R	U	I	T	F	L	Y	Genus of small fly whose larvae feed on fruit and decaying vegetable matter.
F	R	U	I	T	F	U	L	Productive, Abundant, Fertile, Fecund, Prolific, Breeding Reproducing, Propagating.
F	R	U	I	T	I	N	G	Producing fruit.
F	R	U	I	T	I	O	N	Enjoyment Realization, Accomplishment, Conclusion, Pleasure.
F	R	U	I	T	I	V	E	Enjoying, Possessing, Fruitful.
F	R	U	I	T	L	E	T	Small fruit, Unit of collective fruit.
F	R	U	M	E	N	T	Y	A dessert of wheat boiled in milk, flavoured with sugar spice and raisins.
F	R	U	M	P	I	N	G	Insulting, Flouting, Mocking, Provoking, Irritating, Sulking, Vexing.
F	R	U	M	P	I	S	H	Dowdy, Dull, Old-fashioned.
F	R	U	S	T	U	L	E	Shell of a diatom composed of two valves that overlap.
F	R	U	T	I	L	L	A	Chilean strawberry.
F	U	C	H	S	I	N	E	Brilliant bluish red dye for wool or silk.
F	U	C	H	S	I	T	E	A mineral consisting of a common mica.
F	U	C	O	I	D	I	N	A sulfuric ester of fucosan obtained from brown algae.
F	U	D	D	L	I	N	G	Tippling, Drinking, Intoxicating, Muddling.
F	U	E	L	L	I	N	G	To fill with fuel, Supporting, Stimulating.
F	U	G	A	C	I	T	Y	Transience, Instability, Uncertainty.
F	U	G	I	T	I	V	E	Fleeing, Perishable, Refugee, Exile, Runaway.
F	U	G	L	E	M	A	N	Leader, Drill leader.
F	U	L	C	R	A	T	E	Having a fulcrum, a part that serves as hinge support or axis.
F	U	L	G	E	N	C	Y	Resplendence, Brilliant lustre.
F	U	L	G	U	R	A	L	Relating to lightning.
F	U	L	L	A	G	E	D	Reached mature age or legal majority.
F	U	L	L	B	A	C	K	Defense player in soccer, rugby or hockey.
F	U	L	L	F	A	C	E	Front face.
F	U	L	L	N	E	S	S	Being full, Repletion, Profusion.
F	U	L	L	S	T	O	P	Punctuation point.
F	U	L	L	T	I	M	E	Employed for normal working hours.
F	U	L	M	I	N	E	D	Fulminated, Detonated, Exploded, Censured, Denounced.
F	U	M	A	G	I	N	E	Fungi that causes a sooty mould on greenhouse plants.
F	U	M	A	R	A	S	E	A crystalline enzyme that occurs in animal and plant tissues.
F	U	M	A	R	A	T	E	An ester of fumaric acid.
F	U	M	A	R	I	N	E	Protopine, a crystalline alkaline found in opium and plants.
F	U	M	A	R	O	L	E	A hole in volcanic regions from which gases and vapours are emitted.
F	U	M	A	R	O	Y	L	The radical of fumaric acid.
F	U	M	B	L	I	N	G	Groping, Blundering, Floundering, Mumbling, Bungling, Muffing, Misplaying, Muttering.
F	U	M	E	L	E	S	S	Free from fumes.
F	U	M	E	W	O	R	T	Plant related to the fumitories.
F	U	M	I	G	A	N	T	A gaseous chemical used as a disinfectant or pesticide.
F	U	M	I	G	A	T	E	To apply smoke to preserve, to treat for disease or pests, To remove something offensive.
F	U	M	I	T	O	R	Y	A common European herb.
F	U	M	O	S	I	T	Y	Something emitting fumes.
F	U	N	C	T	I	O	N	Occupation, Role, Duty, Purpose, Behaviour, Performance, Operation, Office.
F	U	N	D	L	E	S	S	Being without funds or finance.
F	U	N	D	U	L	U	S	Genus of carnivorous fishes.
F	U	N	E	R	A	L	S	Mortuary, Funeral, Burial.
F	U	N	E	R	E	A	L	Belonging to a funeral, Gloomy, Dismal.
F	U	N	G	A	L	E	S	Fungi.
F	U	N	G	I	B	L	E	Commodities that can be weighed, measured, counted, consumed, used or enjoyed.
F	U	N	G	U	S	E	D	Infected with fungus.
F	U	N	K	H	O	L	E	Dugout, Place of retreat especially for cowards.

1	2	3	4	5	6	7	8	
F	U	N	M	A	K	E	R	Humorist, Comedian.
F	U	N	T	U	M	I	A	Genus of tropical African trees.
F	U	R	A	N	O	I	D	Resembling furan in chemical structure.
F	U	R	A	N	O	S	E	A glucose sugar.
F	U	R	B	E	L	O	W	Ruffle, Flounce, A showy trimming.
F	U	R	C	A	T	E	D	Branched like a fork.
F	U	R	C	I	L	I	A	Intermediate larva of a shrimp.
F	U	R	C	U	L	A	R	Wishbone, Forked appendages of insects.
F	U	R	F	U	R	A	L	Liquid aldehyde.
F	U	R	F	U	R	A	N	Furan.
F	U	R	F	U	R	Y	L	The univalent radical derived from furfuryl alcohol.
F	U	R	I	B	U	N	D	Frenzied, Raging, Furious, Mad.
F	U	R	L	O	U	G	H	Leave of absence usually for state-employed personnel including the armed services.
F	U	R	M	E	N	T	Y	Frumenty.
F	U	R	R	I	E	R	Y	Art of the furrier, Trade in furs.
F	U	R	R	O	W	E	D	Cultivated, Cleaved, Ploughed, Wrinkled, Grooved, Ridged, Corrugated.
F	U	R	T	H	E	S	T	Farthest, Most distant, Remotest.
F	U	R	U	N	C	L	E	Bacterial infection of the skin causing a boil. Carbuncle.
F	U	S	A	R	O	L	E	A moulding at the top of classical pillars.
F	U	S	E	L	A	G	E	The central body portion of an aeroplane.
F	U	S	E	L	O	I	L	An acrid oily liquid that is a by-product of alcohol fermentation.
F	U	S	I	F	O	R	M	Shaped like a spindle, Tapering at each end.
F	U	S	I	L	E	E	R	A member of a British regiment that was once armed with a fusil, a light flintlock musket.
F	U	S	I	L	I	E	R	Same as FUSILEER.
F	U	S	I	N	I	T	E	Opaque carbonised cell structure found in fusain.
F	U	S	I	O	N	A	L	Characterized by fusion.
F	U	T	I	L	E	L	Y	Ineffectively, Frivolously, Ineffectually, Uselessly, Vainly, Unsatisfactorily, Inefficiently.
F	U	T	I	L	I	T	Y	Uselessness, Frivolity, Abortive attempt, Useless gesture.
F	U	T	U	R	A	M	A	A preview of a future project or a model.
F	U	T	U	R	E	L	Y	In future.
F	U	T	U	R	I	S	M	Wishful thinking, Utopianism, Rejection of traditional forms of culture.
F	U	T	U	R	I	S	T	One who believes that biblical prophecies are still to be fulfilled.
F	U	T	U	R	I	T	Y	Future, Posterity.
F	U	Z	Z	B	A	L	L	Puffball.
F	U	Z	Z	T	A	I	L	A wild horse.

G

1	2	3	4	5	6	7	8	
G	A	B	B	L	I	N	G	Chattering, Jabbering, Blabbing, Prattling, Gibbering.
G	A	B	B	R	O	I	D	Resembing granular igneous rock.
G	A	B	I	O	N	E	D	Built up with gabions.
G	A	B	L	E	E	N	D	The end wall of a building furnished with a gable.
G	A	D	A	B	O	U	T	One who never settles, Wanderer, Playboy.
G	A	D	G	E	T	R	Y	Small devices to assist in a particular type of work.
G	A	D	H	E	L	I	C	Division of the Celtic languages.
G	A	D	Z	O	O	K	S	A mild oath.
G	A	G	G	L	I	N	G	Cackling, Gabbling.
G	A	G	T	O	O	T	H	A projecting tooth.
G	A	I	E	T	I	E	S	Entertainments, Festivities, Liveliness.
G	A	I	L	L	A	R	D	Galliard, A 16th century dance in quick time.
G	A	I	N	C	O	P	E	To intercept by a short cut.
G	A	I	N	L	E	S	S	Unprofitable, Unavailing, Unsuccessful, Unproductive.
G	A	I	N	S	A	I	D	Denied, Contradicted, Opposed, Resisted, Subverted, Contravened, Crossed, Withstood.
G	A	L	A	B	I	E	H	Loose cloak worn by Arabic speaking people.
G	A	L	A	C	T	A	N	Polysaccharides that yield galactose on hydrolysis.
G	A	L	A	C	T	I	A	Genus of twining herbs.
G	A	L	A	C	T	I	C	Relating to a galaxy, Huge.
G	A	L	A	C	T	I	N	Lactogenic hormone.
G	A	L	A	F	A	T	E	Black sea bream.
G	A	L	A	L	I	T	H	Hornlike plastic made from casein and formaldehyde.
G	A	L	A	N	G	A	L	Pungent aromatic rhizome produced in eastern Asia by a ginger-related plant.
G	A	L	A	T	I	A	N	Inhabitant of Galatia in Asia Minor.
G	A	L	A	X	I	T	E	A black mineral consisting of an oxide of manganese and aluminium.
G	A	L	B	A	N	U	M	Aromatic bitter gum resin that contains oil and is used in medicine and incense.
G	A	L	B	U	L	U	S	Spherical closed fleshy cone of the cypress.

1	2	3	4	5	6	7	8	
G	A	L	E	A	T	E	D	Helmet-shaped, Hooded.
G	A	L	E	G	I	N	E	Bitter crystalline base derived from guanidine.
G	A	L	E	I	D	A	E	Genus of sharks.
G	A	L	E	N	I	S	M	Galenic system of medical practice.
G	A	L	E	N	I	S	T	Follower of the ancient physician, Galen.
G	A	L	E	N	I	T	E	Galena.
G	A	L	E	N	O	I	D	Resembling galena.
G	A	L	E	S	A	U	R	Reptile fossil.
G	A	L	I	L	E	A	N	Relating to Galileo, founder of experimental physics and astronomy.
G	A	L	I	P	I	N	E	A crystalline alkaloid derived from quinoline and found in angostura bark.
G	A	L	L	E	A	S	S	A 17th century armed galley.
G	A	L	L	I	A	R	D	Lively, Hardy, Valiant.
G	A	L	L	I	A	S	S	Same as GALLEASS.
G	A	L	L	I	C	A	N	Gallic, Relating to Gaul.
G	A	L	L	I	P	O	T	Small earthenware pot, Druggist, Apothecary.
G	A	L	L	I	V	A	T	An East Indian ship propelled by sails and oars often used by pirates.
G	A	L	L	O	M	A	N	Bibliomania, Francophile.
G	A	L	L	O	P	E	D	Rode at full speed, Rode at a gallop.
G	A	L	L	O	P	E	R	A horse or rider that travels at full speed, A light field gun.
G	A	L	L	O	W	A	Y	A large pony, A breed of hornless beef cattle native to Scotland.
G	A	L	L	S	I	C	K	An animal sickness transmitted by ticks.
G	A	L	T	O	N	I	A	Small genus of Southern African bulbous plants, Summer hyacinth.
G	A	L	V	A	N	I	C	Producing a direct current of electricity, Arousing interest, Stimulating activity.
G	A	M	A	S	H	E	S	Coloured or embossed leather.
G	A	M	B	A	D	O	S	Long leggings.
G	A	M	B	E	S	O	N	Protective medieval tunic of quilted leather.
G	A	M	B	L	I	N	G	Wagering, Chancing, Betting Staking, Risking, Venturing, Jeopardizing.
G	A	M	B	U	S	I	A	A genus of topminnows that are valuable exterminators of the larvae of mosquitoes.
G	A	M	E	B	I	R	D	A bird that can be legally hunted.
G	A	M	E	C	O	C	K	A male game fowl, A plucky indomitable person.
G	A	M	E	L	O	T	E	A genus of grass.
G	A	M	E	N	E	S	S	Endurance, Pluck.
G	A	M	E	S	O	M	E	Gay, Sportive, Playful, Frolicsome, Merry.
G	A	M	E	S	T	E	R	Athlete, One who plays games of chance.
G	A	M	M	A	R	I	D	A genus of swimming amphipod crustaceas, Beach fleas.
G	A	M	M	A	R	U	S	Same as GAMMARID.
G	A	M	M	O	N	E	D	Pretended, Feigned, Deceived, Fooled.
G	A	M	O	B	I	U	M	Sexual reproducing generation in metagenesis.
G	A	M	O	D	E	M	E	Isolated breeding community of organisms.
G	A	M	O	G	E	N	Y	Gamogenesis.
G	A	M	O	G	O	N	Y	Multiple fission producing sporozoan gametes.
G	A	N	D	O	U	R	A	A long loose gown worn in Northern Africa.
G	A	N	G	D	A	Y	S	Rogation days, The three days before Ascension day for supplication.
G	A	N	G	E	T	I	C	Relating to the Ganges.
G	A	N	G	L	A	N	D	Relating to organized crime, Underworld.
G	A	N	G	L	I	A	L	Relating to a ganglion.
G	A	N	G	L	I	N	G	Spindly, Having an awkwardly long growth.
G	A	N	G	L	I	O	N	Enlargement or knot on nerve.
G	A	N	G	P	L	O	W	A twin plough for parallel furrows.
G	A	N	G	R	E	N	E	Death of local tissue due to loss of blood supply, Pervasive deeply rooted moral or social evil.
G	A	N	G	S	T	E	R	Gunman, Thug, Racketeer, One of a gang of criminals.
G	A	N	I	S	T	E	R	Fine-grained quartzite used in the manufacture of silica brick.
G	A	N	N	E	T	R	Y	A breeding colony for gannets.
G	A	N	O	D	O	N	T	Fossil mammals.
G	A	N	O	I	D	E	I	Variety of extinct and living fishes, Sturgeon, Paddlefishes.
G	A	N	T	L	I	N	E	A running line for a sail or clothes line.
G	A	N	Y	M	E	D	E	Cupbearer in Roman mythology.
G	A	P	I	N	G	L	Y	Widely open. Importantly.
G	A	R	A	G	I	N	G	Keeping cars enclosed in garages.
G	A	R	B	A	G	E	D	Eviscerated, Scavenged.
G	A	R	B	A	N	Z	O	Chick-pea.
G	A	R	B	L	I	N	G	Refining, Culling, Distorting, Mutilating, Jumbling, Disarranging.
G	A	R	B	O	A	R	D	Plank or steel plate lying next to the keel of a ship.
G	A	R	C	I	N	I	A	A large genus of tropical Asiatic trees.
G	A	R	D	E	N	E	R	One employed to care for gardens.
G	A	R	D	E	N	I	A	Genus of tropical trees and shrubs having fragrant blooms, Cape jasmine.
G	A	R	E	F	O	W	L	Great Auk.

1	2	3	4	5	6	7	8	Definition
G	A	R	G	A	N	E	Y	A European teal.
G	A	R	G	L	I	N	G	Cleansing or disinfecting of mouth or throat by moving liquid about in them.
G	A	R	G	O	Y	L	E	A water-spout having the form of a grotesque figure.
G	A	R	I	S	H	L	Y	Flashily, Glaringly, Gaudily, Blatantly, Tawdrily.
G	A	R	L	I	C	K	Y	Smelling or tasting of garlic.
G	A	R	N	E	R	E	D	Stored, Earned, Reaped, Accumulated, Collected, Harvested.
G	A	R	R	E	T	E	D	Galleted, Fill in mortar with chips of stones.
G	A	R	R	I	S	O	N	Stronghold, Military post, Station, Occupy, Accommodate.
G	A	R	R	O	T	T	E	Instrument of strangulation.
G	A	R	R	U	L	U	S	A large genus of Old World Jays.
G	A	R	T	E	R	E	D	Fastened with a garter.
G	A	S	B	L	A	C	K	Channel black.
G	A	S	E	L	I	E	R	Gasolier, A chandelier with gaslights.
G	A	S	I	F	I	E	D	Converted into gas.
G	A	S	I	F	O	R	M	In the form of gas, Gaseous.
G	A	S	L	I	G	H	T	Light yielded by combustion of illuminating gas.
G	A	S	M	E	T	E	R	An instrument for recording the quantity of gas passing through a particular outlet.
G	A	S	O	G	E	N	E	A portable apparatus for carbonating liquids.
G	A	S	O	L	I	E	R	A chandelier equipped with gaslights.
G	A	S	O	L	I	N	E	A volatile flammable liquid hydrocarbon mixture used as fuel. Petrol.
G	A	S	T	A	L	D	O	A steward in a nobleman's household.
G	A	S	T	H	A	U	S	A German inn or tavern.
G	A	S	T	I	G	H	T	Impervious to gas.
G	A	S	T	R	A	E	A	Primordial organism.
G	A	S	T	R	U	L	A	An early metazoan embryo.
G	A	S	W	O	R	K	S	A plant for manufacturing gas.
G	A	T	E	F	O	L	D	Folded insert in a book that is larger than the page.
G	A	T	E	L	E	S	S	Without a gate.
G	A	T	E	P	O	S	T	A post that supports a gate.
G	A	T	H	E	R	E	D	Collected, Concentrated, Accumulated, Assembled, Plucked, Harvested, Picked, Deduced.
G	A	U	L	D	I	N	G	Heron.
G	A	U	M	L	E	S	S	Dull and stupid, Lacking comprehension.
G	A	U	N	T	L	E	T	A large cuffed glove to protect the hand.
G	A	V	E	L	M	A	N	A person paying gavel.
G	A	V	E	L	O	C	K	Javelin, Iron crowbar, Lever.
G	A	Z	E	T	T	A	L	An act of gazetting.
G	A	Z	E	T	T	E	D	Published in gazette, Announced publicly.
G	A	Z	O	G	E	N	E	Gasogene.
G	A	Z	P	A	C	H	O	A cold soup made of vegetables with garlic and vinegar.
G	E	A	S	T	R	U	M	Genus of fungi.
G	E	D	A	N	I	T	E	A fossil resin similar to amber.
G	E	G	E	N	I	O	N	Counterion, An ion having a charge opposite to the substance with which it is associated.
G	E	L	A	S	I	A	N	Relating to Pope Gelasius.
G	E	L	A	S	T	I	C	Risible, Laughable, Funny, Ridiculous.
G	E	L	A	T	I	N	E	Glutinous material obtained from animal tissue by prolonged boiling.
G	E	L	A	T	I	O	N	Process of freezing.
G	E	L	I	D	I	T	Y	Icy, Extremely cold.
G	E	L	I	D	I	U	M	Genus of red algae.
G	E	M	A	R	I	S	T	Specialist in the study of Gemara, Talmud.
G	E	M	A	T	R	I	A	Explanation of Hebrew scriptures by means of the cryptographic significance of the words.
G	E	M	E	I	N	D	E	A German municipality.
G	E	M	E	L	L	U	S	Hip muscle.
G	E	M	I	N	A	T	E	Binate, Growing in pairs.
G	E	M	I	N	O	U	S	Doubled, Paired.
G	E	M	S	H	O	R	N	Pipeorgan stop between a string tone and a reed tone.
G	E	N	D	A	R	M	E	Policeman in France, Pinnacle of rock, A flaw in a precious stone.
G	E	N	D	E	R	E	D	Bred, Copulated.
G	E	N	E	R	A	T	E	Procreate, Beget, Originate, Produce, Create, Multiply, Induce, Provoke.
G	E	N	E	R	O	U	S	Magnanimous, Benevolent, Kindly, Liberal, Considerate, Charitable, Unselfish, Munificent.
G	E	N	E	T	I	C	S	Study of heredity, evolution and organisms, Evolutionary, Historical.
G	E	N	E	T	R	I	X	Mother.
G	E	N	E	V	E	S	E	Belonging to Geneva.
G	E	N	I	A	L	L	Y	Cheerfully, Pleasantly, Naturally, Affably, Graciously, Cordially, Friendly, Jolly.
G	E	N	I	S	A	R	O	Rain tree.
G	E	N	I	S	T	I	N	Pale yellow glucoside from soybean.
G	E	N	I	T	A	L	S	Sexual organs.
G	E	N	I	T	I	V	E	Possessive case, A word expressing a relationship.

1	2	3	4	5	6	7	8	
G	E	N	I	T	U	R	E	Nativity, Birth.
G	E	N	I	Z	E	R	O	Genisaro, Genizaro.
G	E	N	O	C	I	D	E	Intention to exterminate a racial, political cultural group of people or their language or religion.
G	E	N	O	M	E	R	E	Hypothetical subsection of a gene.
G	E	N	O	S	O	M	E	A portion of a chromosome that is coextensive with a given gene.
G	E	N	O	T	Y	P	E	Genetic constitution of an individual or group.
G	E	N	T	H	I	T	E	A mineral consisting of a soft amorphous nickel magnesium silicate.
G	E	N	T	I	A	N	A	Genus of herbs, Gentian.
G	E	N	T	I	L	I	C	Tribal, Racial, National, With ethnic connotation.
G	E	N	T	I	S	I	N	Yellow pigment obtained from the root of the gentian.
G	E	N	T	R	I	C	E	Rank.
G	E	O	B	I	O	N	T	Soil organism.
G	E	O	C	A	R	P	Y	Producing fruit beneath the surface, Peanut.
G	E	O	C	L	I	N	E	The gradation in variation of organisms along geographical lines.
G	E	O	D	E	S	I	C	Shortest line between two points on a mathematically derived surface.
G	E	O	D	E	T	I	C	Relating to geometry of geodetic lines.
G	E	O	G	N	O	S	T	Specialist in geognosy.
G	E	O	G	N	O	S	Y	Branch of geology that deals with materials, general exterior and interior constitution of earth.
G	E	O	G	O	N	I	C	Relating to theory of the formation of the earth.
G	E	O	M	A	N	C	Y	Fortune-telling by connecting dots on paper.
G	E	O	M	A	T	I	C	Mathematics of the earth.
G	E	O	M	E	T	E	R	Specialist in geometry, Moth.
G	E	O	M	E	T	R	Y	Mathematics that deal with measurements, relationships of points, lines, angles and surfaces.
G	E	O	P	H	A	G	Y	Practice of primitive people by eating soil, believed to alleviate lack of essential elements in diet.
G	E	O	P	H	I	L	A	Group of gastropods, Land snails, Slugs.
G	E	O	P	H	O	N	E	Instrument for detecting vibrations passing through rocks, soil or ice.
G	E	O	P	H	O	T	O	Aerial photograph used in geologic investigations.
G	E	O	P	H	Y	T	E	Perennial bulb that has buds beneath the surface.
G	E	O	P	O	N	I	C	Agriculture, Relating to tillage.
G	E	O	R	D	I	E	S	Natives of Scotland or Northern England.
G	E	O	R	G	I	A	N	Relating to state of Georgia, Characteristic of the reigns of kings of England known as George.
G	E	O	S	C	O	P	Y	Knowledge gained from inspection of soil.
G	E	O	T	A	X	I	S	A taxis in which the force of gravity is the directive factor.
G	E	P	H	Y	R	E	A	Marine worms.
G	E	R	A	N	I	A	L	Genus of plants, Geraniums, Cranesbills, Flaxes.
G	E	R	A	N	I	O	L	Fragrant liquid unsaturated alcohol used in perfumery and soap manufacture.
G	E	R	A	N	I	U	M	Widely distributed genus of plants.
G	E	R	A	R	D	I	A	Genus of herbs, False foxglove.
G	E	R	A	T	I	N	G	In heraldry, spotting a shield with roundels.
G	E	R	M	A	N	I	C	Teutonic, Pertaining to Germany.
G	E	R	M	I	N	A	L	Incipient, Embryonic.
G	E	R	O	N	T	A	L	Relating to old age or decadence.
G	E	R	O	N	T	I	C	Same as GERONTAL.
G	E	R	O	U	S	I	A	Gerusia, Council of elders in ancient Sparta.
G	E	R	R	I	D	A	E	Family of true bugs, Family of tropical marine food fishes.
G	E	R	T	R	U	D	E	Infant's cotton slip buttoned on each shoulder.
G	E	S	T	U	R	A	L	Consisting of gestures.
G	E	S	T	U	R	E	D	Expressed intentions by actions, Used motions, Indicated, Signalled.
G	H	A	N	A	I	A	N	Inhabitant of Ghana.
G	H	A	W	A	Z	E	E	Egyptian dancing girls.
G	H	E	T	T	O	E	S	Part of a city where minority racial or cultural groups live.
G	H	O	R	K	H	A	R	Indian wild ass.
G	H	O	S	T	I	N	G	Haunting, Sailing quietly, Moving silently, Writing for and in the name of another person.
G	H	O	U	L	I	S	H	Gruesome, Evil, Fiendish, Act of preying on the misfortune of others.
G	I	A	N	T	E	S	S	Unusually large woman.
G	I	A	N	T	I	S	M	State of being very large, Concentration of economic power.
G	I	B	B	S	I	T	E	Mineral consisting of translucent aluminum hydroxide.
G	I	B	I	N	G	L	Y	Scoffingly, Scornfully, Mockingly, Reproachfully, Jeeringly.
G	I	D	D	I	E	S	T	Dizziest, Most thoughtless, Most hare-brained, Wildest.
G	I	D	D	Y	I	N	G	Making giddy.
G	I	F	F	G	A	F	F	Banter, Repartee.
G	I	F	T	B	O	O	K	Illustrated book published in the 19th century U.S. intended as a gift.
G	I	G	A	N	T	I	C	Giantism, Huge, Colossal, Enormous, Gargantuan, Immense, Mammoth, Stupendous.
G	I	G	E	L	I	R	A	Xylophone.
G	I	G	E	R	I	U	M	Gizzard.
G	I	G	G	L	I	N	G	Sniggering, Laughing in an affected or silly fashion, Tittering.
G	I	L	L	A	R	O	O	Irish trout.

1	2	3	4	5	6	7	8	Definition
G	I	L	L	E	N	I	A	Genus of American herbs, Indian physic.
G	I	L	L	I	V	E	R	Gillyflower, Clove, Pink, Wallflower.
G	I	L	T	E	D	G	E	Of the best quality, Safe investment.
G	I	L	T	H	E	A	D	Marine food fish.
G	I	M	C	R	A	C	K	Gadget, Trifle, Frivolous, Flimsy, Unsubstantial, Gewgaw, Shoddy, Fop.
G	I	M	L	E	T	E	D	Pierced, Penetrated.
G	I	M	M	A	L	E	D	Made of interlocked rings or links.
G	I	N	G	E	L	L	Y	Sesame seed.
G	I	N	G	E	R	L	Y	Cautiously, Carefully, Warily, Chary, Calculating, Discreetly, Circumspectly, Guardedly.
G	I	N	G	I	V	A	L	Relating to the gums.
G	I	N	H	O	U	S	E	A building where cotton is ginned.
G	I	N	O	R	I	T	E	A mineral consisting of hydrous borate of calcium.
G	I	R	A	S	O	L	E	Jerusalem artichoke, Fire opal.
G	I	R	D	L	I	N	G	Encircling, Surrounding, Belting, Banding, Circling, Ringing, Encompassing.
G	I	R	L	H	O	O	D	Condition of being a girl.
G	I	R	T	H	I	N	G	Encircling, Extending around, Measuring the girth, Determining the weight of an animal.
G	I	R	T	L	I	N	E	Gantline.
G	I	V	E	A	W	A	Y	A game where the object is to lose, A betrayal, A radio or TV programme where prizes are given.
G	I	V	E	T	I	A	N	Prehistoric period.
G	I	Z	Z	E	N	E	D	Dried out, Wizened, Shrivelled.
G	L	A	B	E	L	L	A	Smooth prominence of the forehead.
G	L	A	B	R	A	T	E	Smooth even surface, Hairless, Bald, Free of roughness.
G	L	A	B	R	O	U	S	Same as GLABRATE.
G	L	A	C	I	A	T	E	Cover with glaciers, Cover with ice and snow, Freeze.
G	L	A	D	D	E	S	T	Merriest, Happiest, Jolliest, Brightest, Cheeriest.
G	L	A	D	D	I	N	G	Pleasing.
G	L	A	D	I	A	T	E	Shaped like a sword, Ensiform.
G	L	A	D	I	O	L	E	Gladiolus.
G	L	A	D	I	O	L	I	Plant of the genus, Gladiolus.
G	L	A	D	L	E	S	S	Devoid of happiness and joy.
G	L	A	D	N	E	S	S	Happiness, Joyfulness, Jolliness.
G	L	A	D	R	A	G	S	Formal dress, Finery, Frippery, Regalia, Sunday best.
G	L	A	D	S	O	M	E	Glad.
G	L	A	I	R	I	N	G	Applying glair, sizing liquid made from egg white and vinegar.
G	L	A	N	C	I	N	G	Hitting, Striking, Glossing, Peeping, Browsing, Grazing, Rebounding.
G	L	A	N	D	E	R	S	Highly contagious animal disease.
G	L	A	N	D	U	L	E	A small gland, Swelling of the neck glands.
G	L	A	R	E	O	L	A	Genus of Old World shorebirds.
G	L	A	R	E	O	U	S	Viscid, Slimy, Sticky.
G	L	A	S	S	E	Y	E	Walleyed pike.
G	L	A	S	S	F	U	L	Quantity of liquid held by a drinking glass.
G	L	A	S	S	I	L	Y	In an apathetic fashion.
G	L	A	S	S	I	N	G	Glazing, Enclosing with glass, Reflecting.
G	L	A	S	S	I	T	E	An 18th century Christian sect denying the authority of a civil magistrate in a church.
G	L	A	S	S	P	O	T	A small crucible used in small glass-making operations.
G	L	A	U	C	I	U	M	A small genus of Eurasian herbs.
G	L	A	U	C	O	M	A	An eye disease.
G	L	A	U	C	O	P	E	A person with fair hair and blue eyes.
G	L	A	U	C	O	U	S	Having a powdery or waxy covering.
G	L	E	A	M	I	N	G	Reflecting, Glistening, Shining, Glossy, Burnished, Lustrous, Polished.
G	L	E	A	N	I	N	G	Gathering, Garnering, Reaping, Learning, Ascertaining, Extracting, Concluding, Deducing.
G	L	E	E	S	O	M	E	Gleeful, Lively.
G	L	I	B	N	E	S	S	Offhandness, Casualness, Shallowness, Volubleness, Slickness.
G	L	I	D	D	E	R	Y	Slippery.
G	L	I	M	P	S	E	D	Glanced, Peeped, Peeked, Took a brief look.
G	L	I	N	T	I	N	G	Sparkling, Flashing, Gleaming, Twinkling, Glistening, Glancing, Shimmering, Glimmering.
G	L	I	O	C	Y	T	E	Neurogial cell.
G	L	I	R	I	D	A	E	Genus of rodents, Dormice.
G	L	I	S	S	A	D	E	Controlled slide, A gliding step in ballet.
G	L	I	T	T	E	R	Y	Glittering, Having much glitter.
G	L	O	A	M	I	N	G	Twilight, Dusk.
G	L	O	A	T	I	N	G	Goggling, Peering, Staring, Revelling, Envying, Grudging.
G	L	O	B	A	T	E	D	Formed into a globe.
G	L	O	B	U	L	A	R	Having the shape of a globe, Globose, Whole, Entire, Global.
G	L	O	B	U	L	E	T	A minute globule.
G	L	O	B	U	L	I	N	Simple protein almost completely insoluble in pure water that occurs in plant and animal tissue.
G	L	O	O	M	I	L	Y	Despondently, Drearily, Bleakly, Sullenly, Dourly, Sulky.

1	2	3	4	5	6	7	8	
G	L	O	O	M	I	N	G	Dark, Gloomy.
G	L	O	R	I	O	L	E	Aureole. A genus of bird.
G	L	O	R	I	O	S	A	Genus of tropical African and Asiatic tuberous herbs resembling lilies.
G	L	O	R	I	O	U	S	Illustrious, Praiseworthy, Resplendent, Magnificent, Splendid, Wonderful, Sublime.
G	L	O	R	Y	I	N	G	Exulting, Revelling, Boasting, Delighting, Jubilating, Triumphing.
G	L	O	R	Y	P	E	A	A vine cultivated for its bright red blooms.
G	L	O	S	S	A	R	Y	An explanatory list of words or terms.
G	L	O	S	S	E	M	E	The smallest unit.
G	L	O	S	S	I	L	Y	Smoothly, Sleekly, Glibly.
G	L	O	S	S	I	N	A	An African genus of flies, Tsetse flies.
G	L	O	S	S	I	N	G	Hiding, Extenuating, Varnishing, Veneering, Whitewashing, Justifying, Falsifying, Extenuating.
G	L	O	S	S	I	S	T	Glossarist, One that compiles a glossary.
G	L	O	W	E	R	E	D	Scowled, Brooded, Frowned, Stared, Lowered.
G	L	O	W	L	A	M	P	A gas discharge tube used in stroboscopes and sound-film recording.
G	L	O	W	W	O	R	M	Luminous insects, Firefly.
G	L	O	X	I	N	I	A	Small genus of American herbs.
G	L	U	C	A	G	O	N	A crystalline protein obtained from the pancreas.
G	L	U	C	I	N	U	M	Beryllium.
G	L	U	C	I	T	O	L	A hexahydric alcohol formed by a reduction of glucose.
G	L	U	C	I	T	Y	L	A univalent radical derived from glucitol.
G	L	U	C	O	S	A	N	Intramolecular anhydrides of glucose.
G	L	U	C	O	S	Y	L	A glycosyl radical derived from glucose.
G	L	U	M	M	E	S	T	Most dismal, Most dreary, Most sullen.
G	L	U	M	N	E	S	S	State of being sullen, ill-humoured or displeased.
G	L	U	M	P	I	S	H	Somewhat grumpy.
G	L	U	T	A	R	Y	L	The bivalent radical of glutaric acid.
G	L	U	T	E	L	I	N	Simple protein that occurs in the seeds of cereal.
G	L	U	T	E	N	I	N	Glutelin found in wheat.
G	L	U	T	T	I	N	G	Gorging, Surfeiting, Satiating, Saturating.
G	L	U	T	T	O	N	Y	Excess in eating and drinking, Greedy.
G	L	Y	C	E	R	I	A	Genus of perennial grasses.
G	L	Y	C	E	R	I	N	Glycerol.
G	L	Y	C	E	R	O	L	Sweet syrupy hygroscopic trihydroxy alcohol.
G	L	Y	C	E	R	Y	L	A trivalent radical derived from glycerol.
G	L	Y	C	I	D	O	L	A liquid alcohol obtained from glycerol.
G	L	Y	C	I	N	I	N	A globulin found in the seeds of the soybean.
G	L	Y	C	O	G	E	N	A white tasteless polysaccharide by which carbohydrate is stored in animal tissues.
G	L	Y	C	O	N	I	C	A variable verse or rhythmic system.
G	L	Y	C	O	S	Y	L	A univalent radical derived from a cyclic form of glucose.
G	L	Y	O	X	I	M	E	Oxime of glyoxal.
G	N	A	R	L	I	N	G	Twisting, Contorting, Deforming.
G	N	A	R	R	I	N	G	Snarling, Growling.
G	N	A	S	H	I	N	G	Grinding the teeth together, Biting.
G	N	A	T	H	I	O	N	Midpoint of the lower jaw, Chin.
G	N	A	T	H	I	S	M	Projection of the upper jaw.
G	N	A	T	H	I	T	E	A mouth appendage of an arthropod.
G	N	A	T	H	O	U	S	Having a jaw.
G	N	A	T	L	I	N	G	Small or insignificant person.
G	N	A	T	S	N	A	P	A small bird that feeds on insects.
G	N	O	M	O	N	I	C	Relating to gnomon of the sundial.
G	O	A	L	L	E	S	S	Having no goal scored by either team.
G	O	A	L	L	I	N	E	A line marking each end of field of play.
G	O	A	L	P	O	S	T	One of two vertical posts that with a crossbar forms the goal.
G	O	A	T	H	E	R	D	One who tends the goats.
G	O	A	T	L	I	N	G	A young goat.
G	O	A	T	M	O	T	H	Wood-boring larva of a moth.
G	O	A	T	S	K	I	N	Leather made from the skin of a goat.
G	O	A	T	S	R	U	E	Tall blue-flowered European perennial plant.
G	O	B	B	L	I	N	G	Guttural noise made by a male turkey, Gulping, Bolting, Guzzling, Wolfing.
G	O	B	I	I	D	A	E	A family of bony fishes.
G	O	B	L	I	N	R	Y	Acts of goblins.
G	O	B	S	T	I	C	K	A stick for removing the hook from the gullet of a fish.
G	O	D	C	H	I	L	D	One for whom a godparent stands sponsor at baptism.
G	O	D	S	A	C	R	E	Churchyard, Cemetery, Burial ground.
G	O	D	S	M	I	T	H	Maker of idols.
G	O	D	S	P	E	E	D	A parting wish for success and a prosperous journey.
G	O	E	T	H	E	A	N	Pertaining to the works of the poet Goethe.

1	2	3	4	5	6	7	8	
G	O	E	T	H	I	T	E	A mineral consisting of an iron hydrogen oxide.
G	O	F	F	E	R	E	D	Crimped, Plaited, Fluted, Curled, Crimped.
G	O	G	E	T	T	E	R	Enterprising, pushing aggressive person, Hustler.
G	O	G	G	L	I	N	G	Looking, Gaping, Ogling, Gazing, Glaring, Gloating, Peering, Squinting.
G	O	I	N	G	S	O	N	Actions, Events, Happenings.
G	O	I	T	E	R	E	D	Enlargement of the thyroid gland.
G	O	I	T	R	O	U	S	Affected with a goitre.
G	O	L	C	O	N	D	A	A source of great wealth.
G	O	L	D	D	U	S	T	Particles of gold.
G	O	L	D	F	I	S	H	Yellow or orange carp used as an aquarium or pond fish.
G	O	L	D	F	O	I	L	Gold beaten or rolled very thin.
G	O	L	D	L	A	C	E	Lace or braid of gold silk used on uniforms to denote rank.
G	O	L	D	L	E	A	F	Sheet gold used for gilding and lettering on glass.
G	O	L	D	L	E	S	S	Lacking gold.
G	O	L	D	M	I	N	E	Location where gold is mined, A source of something rich.
G	O	L	D	R	U	S	H	A rush to newly discovered gold deposits.
G	O	L	D	S	I	Z	E	Adhesive for gold leaf.
G	O	L	D	T	A	I	L	White moths with yellow abdominal tufts.
G	O	L	D	W	O	R	K	Work done in gold.
G	O	L	F	C	L	U	B	Long shafted club with a head in wood or iron to hit the ball.
G	O	L	L	I	W	O	G	Gollywog, A black doll dressed as a male.
G	O	L	O	S	H	E	S	Galoshes, Rubber overshoes.
G	O	M	A	R	I	S	T	Gomarian, Follower of Dutch Calvinistic theologian, Gomarus.
G	O	M	A	R	I	T	E	Same as GOMARIST.
G	O	M	B	R	O	O	N	A white semi-porcelain.
G	O	M	O	N	T	I	A	Genus of branching algae.
G	O	N	D	O	L	E	T	A small gondola.
G	O	N	E	N	E	S	S	Faintness, State of exhaustion.
G	O	N	F	A	L	O	N	A flag that hangs from a crosspiece.
G	O	N	I	D	I	A	L	Containing a gonidium.
G	O	N	I	D	I	U	M	Reproductive granules of bacteria, Green chlorophyll-bearing cells of lichen.
G	O	N	I	O	D	E	S	Genus of biting lice that attacks various wild and domestic animals.
G	O	N	O	C	O	E	L	The body cavity that contains the gonads.
G	O	N	O	C	Y	T	E	A cell that produces gametes.
G	O	N	O	D	U	C	T	The duct of a gonad.
G	O	N	O	M	E	R	E	A pronucleus retaining its identity for a time during cleavage.
G	O	N	O	P	O	R	E	A genital pore.
G	O	N	O	S	O	M	E	The totality of reproductive zooids of a hydroid.
G	O	N	O	T	O	M	E	The portion of a somite that participates in gonad formation.
G	O	O	D	F	O	L	K	Fairies.
G	O	O	D	L	A	C	K	Expression of surprise or objection.
G	O	O	D	N	E	S	S	Virtue, Benevolence, Generosity, Morality, Probity, Rectitude, Honesty, Integrity.
G	O	O	D	W	I	F	E	Mistress of an inn, Landlady.
G	O	O	D	W	I	L	L	Friendliness, Amity, Kindliness, Charity, Helpfulness, Sympathy, Alacrity, Readiness.
G	O	O	D	Y	E	R	A	Genus of small orchids.
G	O	O	G	L	I	E	S	Offbreaks in cricket with a leg-break action.
G	O	O	R	A	N	U	T	Kola-nut.
G	O	O	S	E	C	A	P	A silly person, A flighty young girl.
G	O	O	S	E	E	G	G	Zero, Nothing, Failure.
G	O	R	D	I	O	I	D	Freshwater forms parasitic as larvae.
G	O	R	G	O	N	I	A	Genus of evergreen shrubs, Genus of extinct reptiles.
G	O	R	G	E	O	U	S	Magnificent, Showy, Dazzling, Flamboyant, Resplendent, Terrific, Superb, Colourful.
G	O	R	G	O	N	I	N	Family of common sea fans.
G	O	R	G	O	N	I	N	A complex protein containing iodine.
G	O	S	P	E	L	E	R	An evangelist.
G	O	S	S	A	M	E	R	Fine, filmy substance, Gauzy veiling, Light, Delicate, Tenuous, Cobwebby.
G	O	S	S	I	P	E	D	Retailed rumours, Repeated spicy tales.
G	O	S	S	I	P	R	Y	Chitchat, Gossip.
G	O	S	S	Y	P	I	N	A glucoside occurring in cotton flowers and hibiscus flowers.
G	O	U	R	M	A	N	D	Epicure, Gourmet, Glutton, Greedy or ravenous eater.
G	O	U	T	W	E	E	D	A coarse European plant.
G	O	V	E	R	N	E	D	Administered, Manipulated, Determined, Guided, Regulated, Restrained, Controlled.
G	O	V	E	R	N	O	R	Commandant, Director, Guardian, Controller, God, Deity, One that exercises authority.
G	O	W	N	S	M	A	N	Civilian, One that wears a special habit relating to his profession.
G	R	A	B	B	I	N	G	Seizing, Clutching, Restraining, Capturing, Snatching, Taking, Catching.
G	R	A	A	C	U	P	L	A cup used in drinking a final health after the grace at the end of a meal.
G	R	A	C	E	F	U	L	Pleasing, Attractive, Elegant, Dignified, Affable, Polite, Benign.

1	2	3	4	5	6	7	8	Definition
G	R	A	C	I	L	I	S	Muscle of the inner thigh.
G	R	A	C	I	O	S	O	A buffoon or comic character in Spanish comedy.
G	R	A	C	I	O	U	S	Pious, Godly, Lucky, Fortunate, Happy, Cordial, Affable, Genial.
G	R	A	D	A	T	E	D	Blended, Arranged in steps, grades or ranks.
G	R	A	D	I	E	N	T	Inclination, Slope, Grade, Ramp, Slant, Leaning, Tilt.
G	R	A	D	U	A	N	D	Candidate for a degree.
G	R	A	D	U	A	T	E	One that has received a degree, Arranged by degrees, To qualify as proficient.
G	R	A	F	F	I	T	I	Scribblings on walls.
G	R	A	F	F	I	T	O	Design scratched on rocks or walls.
G	R	A	F	T	I	N	G	Uniting, Forming a graft, Implanting.
G	R	A	I	N	I	N	G	Ingraining, Granulating, Forming into grains.
G	R	A	L	L	I	N	A	Genus of birds, Magpie, Lark.
G	R	A	L	L	O	C	H	Entrails of a deer.
G	R	A	M	A	R	Y	E	Necromancy, Magic, Enchantment.
G	R	A	N	D	D	A	D	Grandfather.
G	R	A	N	D	E	S	T	Most majestic, Most stately, Most magnificent.
G	R	A	N	D	E	U	R	Dignity, Personal greatness, Stately.
G	R	A	N	D	I	S	H	Grandness.
G	R	A	N	D	S	O	N	The son of a daughter or son.
G	R	A	N	I	T	I	C	Resembling granite in hardness.
G	R	A	N	T	I	N	G	Allowing, According, Conceding, Vouchsafing, Awarding, Giving, Bestowing.
G	R	A	N	U	L	A	R	Consisting of granules, Grainy.
G	R	A	P	H	I	C	S	Pictures, maps or graphs used for illustration or demonstration.
G	R	A	P	H	I	T	E	A mineral consisting of soft black lustrous carbon.
G	R	A	P	H	I	U	M	Form genus of imperfect fungi.
G	R	A	P	P	L	E	D	Seized, Held, Dragged, Fastened, Clamped, Clasped, Grasped, Snatched.
G	R	A	P	S	O	I	D	Relating to a family of crabs.
G	R	A	S	P	I	N	G	Clutching, Grappling, Embracing, Taking, Comprehending, Understanding, Apprehending.
G	R	A	S	S	I	N	G	Providing cattle with grazing, Covering with grass, Felling, Turfing.
G	R	A	S	S	N	U	T	Peanut.
G	R	A	T	E	F	U	L	Appreciative, Pleasant, Thankful, Obliged, Gratified, Agreeable, Pleasureable, Welcome.
G	R	A	T	I	O	L	A	Genus of small herbs.
G	R	A	T	U	I	T	Y	Alms, Benefaction, Contribution, Donation, Offering, Reward, Largesse, Wages.
G	R	A	V	A	M	E	N	Grievance.
G	R	A	V	E	L	L	Y	Containing gravel, Caused by gravel, Harsh, Irritating, Unpleasant.
G	R	A	V	I	F	I	C	Tending to produce weight.
G	R	A	Y	L	I	N	G	Salmonoid fishes related to the trouts, Grayish or brownish butterflies.
G	R	A	Z	I	O	S	O	Direction in music, graceful and smooth.
G	R	E	A	S	I	L	Y	Shiftily, Slippery, Unreliably, Unctuously.
G	R	E	A	S	I	N	G	Lubricating, Persuading, Smoothing, Facilitating, Expediting, Bribing, Tipping.
G	R	E	A	T	E	S	T	Largest, Biggest, Fattest, Heaviest, Weightiest, Most eminent.
G	R	E	C	I	Z	E	D	To make Grecian in quality.
G	R	E	E	D	I	L	Y	In a voracious manner.
G	R	E	E	N	E	R	Y	Verdure, Green foliage or plants.
G	R	E	E	N	I	N	G	Growing green, Making fun of, Hoaxing, Green appearance of oysters.
G	R	E	E	N	I	S	H	Having a tinge of green.
G	R	E	E	N	T	E	A	Tea that is light in colour from incomplete fermentation.
G	R	E	E	T	I	N	G	Salutation, Salute, Address, Hail, Hello, Welcome, Paying respects.
G	R	E	F	F	I	E	R	Registrar, Recorder.
G	R	E	G	A	R	I	A	A phase in the life cycle of migratory or plague grasshoppers.
G	R	E	M	L	I	N	S	Unaccountable disruptive influences.
G	R	E	Y	F	I	S	H	A small percoid food fish.
G	R	I	D	B	I	A	S	A small constant compound of the grid potential negative for control.
G	R	I	D	E	L	I	N	Dark purplish red.
G	R	I	D	I	R	O	N	Iron grating for cooking food over coals, A network of pipes, roads, etc.
G	R	I	E	V	O	U	S	Oppressive, Hurtful, Distressing, Injurious, Severe, Serious, Deplorable, Bitter.
G	R	I	G	G	L	E	S	Inferior apples left on the trees after harvesting.
G	R	I	L	L	A	D	E	Something that is grilled, usually to a special order.
G	R	I	L	L	A	G	E	Framework of beams for crossing marshy ground and resembling a grill.
G	R	I	L	L	I	N	G	Broiling on an open grill, Pressing with questions.
G	R	I	M	A	C	E	D	Distortion of expression, Affected, Sham, Pretended.
G	R	I	M	A	L	D	I	Prehistorical remains found in Liguria, Italy.
G	R	I	M	M	E	S	T	Fiercest, Sternest, Cruelest, Harshest, Bleakest.
G	R	I	M	N	E	S	S	Bleakness, Savageness, Hardness, Coldness, Rigidness, Firmness, Hideousness.
G	R	I	M	O	I	R	E	A magician's manual.
G	R	I	N	D	I	N	G	Crushing, Polishing, Sharpening, Harassing, Grating.
G	R	I	N	N	I	N	G	Drawing the lips back from the teeth.

1	2	3	4	5	6	7	8	
G	R	I	P	P	I	N	G	Seizing, Fastening, Grasping, Enthralling, Fascinating, Holding, Taking.
G	R	I	S	E	O	U	S	Grizzled, White mottled with brown or gray.
G	R	I	S	S	I	N	O	A long slender crusty breadstick.
G	R	I	T	T	I	N	G	Spreading with grit, Grinding.
G	R	I	Z	Z	L	E	D	Fretted, Complained, Whimpered, Mourned, Lamented, Grieved, Streaked with gray.
G	R	O	A	N	F	U	L	Dismal and sad.
G	R	O	A	N	I	N	G	Making a deep strangled sound expressing unpleasantness, Complaining.
G	R	O	G	G	E	R	Y	A liquor store.
G	R	O	G	G	I	N	G	Soaking a liquor cask with hot water to draw out the spirits in the wood.
G	R	O	G	S	H	O	P	Low-class barroom.
G	R	O	I	N	I	N	G	Building with ribs at the edge of a vaulted ceiling.
G	R	O	M	W	E	L	L	Genus of herbs, Millet.
G	R	O	O	M	I	N	G	Conditioning, Making a clean and neat appearance, Polishing, Preparing, Refining, Readying.
G	R	O	O	V	I	N	G	Providing with a groove, Furrowing, Settling in a groove.
G	R	O	S	B	E	A	K	Finches with large conical bills.
G	R	O	S	C	H	E	N	A German or Austrian coin.
G	R	O	T	H	I	T	E	Mineral, Sphene.
G	R	O	T	T	O	E	S	Picturesque caves.
G	R	O	U	N	D	E	D	Forced to the ground, Supplying a foundation of knowledge, Falling to the ground.
G	R	O	U	N	D	E	R	A ball that rolls along the ground.
G	R	O	U	P	I	N	G	Clustering, Classifying, Arranging, Belonging, Harmonizing, Gathering, Mustering, Collecting.
G	R	O	U	T	I	N	G	Placing thin mortar in joints.
G	R	O	U	T	I	T	E	Mineral consisting of manganese, hydrogen and oxygen.
G	R	O	W	A	B	L	E	Capable of being grown.
G	R	O	W	L	I	N	G	Making a deep throaty guttural sound. Grumbling.
G	R	U	B	B	I	L	Y	Slovenly, Dirtily, Grimy, Squalid.
G	R	U	B	B	I	N	G	Digging up, Rooting up, Extricating with difficulty, Delving.
G	R	U	B	B	L	E	D	Groped.
G	R	U	D	G	I	N	G	Unwilling, Reluctant, Illiberal, Ungenerous, Parsimonious.
G	R	U	E	S	O	M	E	Fearful, Grisly, Hideous, Ghastly, Horrible, Lurid, Macabre, Terrible.
G	R	U	M	B	L	E	D	Groused, Grunted, Muttered, Scolded, Complained, Growled, Whined, Moaned.
G	R	U	M	B	L	E	R	Grouch, Complainer, Faultfinder, Grouser, Malcontent, Sorehead.
G	R	U	M	P	H	I	E	Sow.
G	R	Y	S	B	O	C	K	Small reddish antelope.
G	U	A	C	H	A	R	O	Oilbird.
G	U	A	I	A	C	O	L	Liquid or crystalline solid with an aromatic odour.
G	U	A	I	A	C	U	M	Genus of tropical American trees and shrubs.
G	U	A	R	A	C	H	A	Lively Spanish or Cuban dance.
G	U	A	R	A	N	T	Y	Guarantee, Surety.
G	U	A	R	D	A	N	T	In heraldry the head turned forward, Guardian, Keeper.
G	U	A	R	D	I	A	N	Adviser, Leader, Custodian, Keeper, Warden, Watchdog, Curator.
G	U	A	R	D	I	N	G	Protecting, Defending, Shielding, Escorting, Safeguarding.
G	U	A	T	A	M	B	U	Brazilian timber tree.
G	U	A	Y	A	C	A	N	South and Central American timber trees.
G	U	B	B	I	N	G	S	Gadgets, Bits and pieces, Simpleton.
G	U	E	R	I	D	O	N	Small ornately carved table.
G	U	E	R	I	L	L	A	One who carries on an irregular war.
G	U	E	R	N	S	E	Y	One of the Channel islands.
G	U	E	S	S	I	N	G	Estimating, Surmising, Assuming, Deducing, Imagining, Supposing, Believing, Presuming.
G	U	E	S	T	I	N	G	Appearing as a guest artist on an entertainment programme.
G	U	G	G	L	I	N	G	Gurgling.
G	U	I	D	A	B	L	E	Tractable.
G	U	I	D	A	N	C	E	Direction, Leading, Steering, Shepherding, Showing, Escorting.
G	U	I	L	D	I	T	E	A mineral that is a basic hydrated sulfate of copper and iron.
G	U	I	L	E	F	U	L	Sly, Treacherous, Deceitful, Cunning.
G	U	I	L	T	I	L	Y	Liability for penalty.
G	U	I	M	B	A	R	D	Jew's harp.
G	U	J	A	R	A	T	I	Language of north western region of India.
G	U	L	C	H	I	N	G	Falling heavily.
G	U	L	F	W	E	E	D	Seaweed with berrylike air vesicles.
G	U	L	L	I	B	L	E	Easily deceived, Naive, Susceptible, Easy, Can be duped.
G	U	L	L	Y	I	N	G	Eroding, Making gullies.
G	U	L	O	S	I	T	Y	Excessive appetite, Greediness.
G	U	M	P	H	I	O	N	A funeral banner.
G	U	M	P	T	I	O	N	Common sense, Initiative, Resolution, Astuteness, Wisdom, Judgment, Shrewdness.
G	U	M	R	E	S	I	N	Mixture of gum and resin obtained from the juice of a plant.
G	U	N	F	L	I	N	T	A flint for the spark to ignite priming of a flintlock.

1	2	3	4	5	6	7	8	Definition
G	U	N	H	O	U	S	E	Enclosure of light armour to protect guns of a ship.
G	U	N	K	H	O	L	E	A cove or channel blocked by mud or vegetation.
G	U	N	L	A	Y	E	R	A sailor who aims the guns of a ship.
G	U	N	M	A	K	E	R	A manufacturer of guns.
G	U	N	M	E	T	A	L	Metal or alloy used for cannon.
G	U	N	S	M	I	T	H	The occupation of desiging, making and repairing small arms.
G	U	N	S	T	I	C	K	Device used to determine the fall of a tree before felling.
G	U	N	S	T	O	C	K	The stock to which the barrel and mechanism of a firearm are secured.
G	U	N	S	T	O	N	E	Canonball, In heraldry a roundel sable.
G	U	R	G	E	O	N	S	Coarse meal.
G	U	R	G	L	I	N	G	Chuckling sound, Bubbling, Burbling, Sloshing.
G	U	R	M	U	K	H	I	Alphabet of the sacred texts of the Sikhs.
G	U	S	T	A	B	L	E	Appetizing, Savoury, Tasty.
G	U	T	T	A	T	E	D	Lost moisture by exuding drop by drop.
G	U	T	T	E	R	E	D	Made channels, Furrowed, Provided with gutters.
G	U	T	T	L	I	N	G	Eating or drinking merrily.
G	U	T	T	U	R	A	L	Relating to a throaty sound.
G	U	Z	M	A	N	I	A	Large genus of tropical American herbs.
G	U	Z	Z	L	I	N	G	Drinking or eating greedily, Using greedily.
G	Y	M	K	H	A	N	A	A sports meeting especially for horses and riders.
G	Y	M	N	A	S	I	A	Buildings equipped for sports activities.
G	Y	M	N	O	T	I	D	Cyprinoid fishes, Eels.
G	Y	M	N	O	T	U	S	Same as GYMNOTID.
G	Y	N	A	N	D	E	R	Mosaic individual made up of female and male portions from an extra egg or sperm nucleus.
G	Y	N	A	N	D	R	Y	Hermaproditism, Intersexuality.
G	Y	N	A	R	C	H	Y	Government by women.
G	Y	N	E	C	O	I	D	Typical of a woman, Having characteristics of a woman.
G	Y	N	E	C	I	U	M	Pistils of a flower.
G	Y	N	O	P	A	R	A	Aphid that produces the sexual generation of various aphids.
G	Y	P	A	E	T	U	S	Genus of vultures.
G	Y	P	S	E	O	U	S	Consisting of gypsum.
G	Y	P	S	Y	I	S	M	Life and ways of gypsies.
G	Y	R	A	T	I	N	G	Revolving, Moving spirally about an axis.
G	Y	R	A	T	I	O	N	Whirling, Revolution, Whorl of a spiral shell.
G	Y	R	A	T	O	R	Y	Rotary, Revolving, Moving in a circle or spiral.
G	Y	R	O	D	Y	N	E	Intermediate aircraft between a helicopter and an autogyro.
G	Y	R	O	I	D	A	L	Arranged in spirals or whorls.
G	Y	R	O	L	I	T	E	Mineral consisting of hydrous calcium silicate.
G	Y	R	O	S	T	A	T	A stabilizing device for a ship or aircraft.

H

1	2	3	4	5	6	7	8	Definition
H	A	B	A	N	E	R	A	Slow Cuban dance.
H	A	B	D	A	L	A	H	A Jewish religious ceremony marking close of Sabbath or holidays.
H	A	B	E	N	D	U	M	A limiting part of a deed of an estate.
H	A	B	I	L	I	T	Y	Expertness.
H	A	B	I	T	A	N	T	Inhabitant, Resident.
H	A	B	I	T	I	N	G	Clothing, Dressing, Accustoming, Living, Abiding.
H	A	B	I	T	U	A	L	Customary, Usual, Inborn, Accepted, Routine, Confirmed.
H	A	B	I	T	U	D	E	Relation, Respect, Familiarity, Habit, Custom, Manner, Practice, Usage.
H	A	C	I	E	N	D	A	Large estate in a Spanish-speaking country, Plantation.
H	A	C	K	L	I	N	G	Combing flax, hemp or jute fibres with a hackle.
H	A	E	M	O	P	I	S	Genus of large aquatic leeches.
H	A	F	T	A	R	A	H	A biblical selection read in the Jewish synagogue service.
H	A	G	B	E	R	R	Y	European bird cherry.
H	A	G	G	A	D	A	H	Explanatory matter in rabbinical literature.
H	A	G	G	A	D	I	C	Same as HAGGADAH.
H	A	G	G	L	I	N	G	Wrangling, Bargaining, Nagging, Cutting clumsily, Bartering, Bickering, Quibbling.
H	A	G	T	A	P	E	R	Muellein, A plant that is a weed.
H	A	I	L	S	H	O	T	Small shot that scatters like hail.
H	A	I	R	L	A	C	E	A fillet of netting for the hair.
H	A	I	R	L	E	S	S	Bald.
H	A	I	R	L	I	K	E	Resembling a hair, An elongated slender filament.
H	A	I	R	L	I	N	E	A very thin line, Thin, Close, Precise.
H	A	I	R	S	A	L	T	Epsomite when in silky fibres.
H	A	I	R	S	L	I	P	Loosening of hair from an improperly cured hide.

1	2	3	4	5	6	7	8	Definition
H	A	I	R	T	A	I	L	Cutlass fish.
H	A	I	R	W	E	E	D	A filamentous green algae.
H	A	I	R	W	O	R	K	Making wigs and switches.
H	A	I	R	W	O	R	M	Nematode worm.
H	A	K	A	F	O	T	H	A ceremony in a Jewish synagogue.
H	A	L	A	P	E	P	E	A tree of the Pacific islands having lily-like blooms and wood used for carving.
H	A	L	A	T	I	O	N	A bright ring of light in a photograph or on a television screen.
H	A	L	E	N	E	S	S	State of being robust and healthy.
H	A	L	F	B	A	C	K	Position of a player in soccer, rugby or hockey.
H	A	L	F	B	O	O	T	Ankle-high boot.
H	A	L	F	B	R	E	D	Offspring of two different races, Hybrid.
H	A	L	F	C	O	C	K	Inadequately prepared, Confused.
H	A	L	F	D	E	C	K	A deck extending half the length of a ship.
H	A	L	F	L	I	F	E	Time required for radioactivity of a substance to decrease by half.
H	A	L	F	L	I	N	E	A straight line in mathematics extending indefinitely in one direction only.
H	A	L	F	L	I	N	G	Immature.
H	A	L	F	L	O	O	P	An aerial acrobatic manoeuvre.
H	A	L	F	M	A	S	T	Flag lowered halfway down as a sign of mourning.
H	A	L	F	M	O	O	N	The moon when half the disc is illuminated, Lunule of a finger-nail.
H	A	L	F	N	O	T	E	Musical note of half value.
H	A	L	F	P	A	C	E	The landing of a staircase.
H	A	L	F	P	I	K	E	A pike with a short shaft.
H	A	L	F	R	I	P	E	A half-grown tree or shrub.
H	A	L	F	T	I	D	E	Time betwen flood or ebb.
H	A	L	F	T	I	M	E	Intermission in a game, Work and pay for half-day only.
H	A	L	F	T	I	N	T	A tint between high light and deep shade.
H	A	L	F	T	O	N	E	Shade between darkest and the lightest parts of a photographic image.
H	A	L	I	C	O	R	E	Dugong.
H	A	L	I	O	T	I	S	Genus of mollusks, Abalone.
H	A	L	L	C	I	S	T	Large earth-covered corridors used in ancient tombs.
H	A	L	L	I	A	R	D	Halyard, A rope or tackle for hoisting and lowering.
H	A	L	L	M	A	R	K	An official stamp marked on gold and silver articles to attest their purity.
H	A	L	L	M	O	O	T	Private court of the lord of the manor.
H	A	L	L	O	O	E	D	Uttered loudly.
H	A	L	L	O	W	E	D	Consecrated, Venerated, Revered, Sacred, Blessed.
H	A	L	O	F	O	R	M	A compound derived from methane.
H	A	L	O	S	A	U	R	Member of the family of extinct sea fishes.
H	A	L	O	S	E	R	E	An ecological sere originating in a saline habitat.
H	A	L	O	X	E	N	E	An organism tolerating a saline habitat.
H	A	L	T	E	R	E	D	Bridled, Fettered, Hampered, Restrained, Tethered.
H	A	L	T	E	R	E	S	Flight wings of insects.
H	A	L	U	C	K	E	T	Half-witted, Wild, Giddy.
H	A	M	B	L	I	N	G	Limping, Stumbling.
H	A	M	I	F	O	R	M	Hooked.
H	A	M	I	N	O	E	A	Common genus of bubble shells.
H	A	M	M	E	R	E	D	Pounded, Fashioned, Formed, Shaped, Battered.
H	A	M	M	E	R	E	R	One that hammers.
H	A	M	P	E	R	E	D	Impeded, Curbed, Restrained, Shackled, Clogged, Manacled, Encumbered, Disrupted.
H	A	N	A	H	I	L	L	A sea bass.
H	A	N	D	B	A	L	L	A game similar to squash but without using a raquet.
H	A	N	D	B	E	L	L	Small bell with a handle.
H	A	N	D	B	I	L	L	An advertising sheet distributed by hand.
H	A	N	D	B	O	O	K	Concise reference book, Manual.
H	A	N	D	C	A	R	T	A cart pushed by hand.
H	A	N	D	C	U	F	F	Manacle, A metal circlet fastening around a wrist.
H	A	N	D	F	A	S	T	Betroth, Closefisted.
H	A	N	D	F	I	S	H	A fish with pectoral fins that resemble hands.
H	A	N	D	F	L	A	G	A signalling flag used in semaphore.
H	A	N	D	G	R	I	P	Handle, Something for the hand to grasp as a support, Hilt.
H	A	N	D	H	O	L	D	Hold, Grip, Something to hold for safety.
H	A	N	D	H	O	L	E	A shallow manhole.
H	A	N	D	I	C	A	P	Disadvantage imposed on a stronger contestant, Something that limits capacity to work.
H	A	N	D	L	A	I	D	Made by hand.
H	A	N	D	L	E	S	S	Having no hands, Inefficient, Clumsy, Incompetent.
H	A	N	D	L	I	N	E	Fishing line.
H	A	N	D	L	I	N	G	Touching, Fingering, Pawing, Manipulating, Operating, Testing, Trying, Feeling.
H	A	N	D	L	I	S	T	Brief reference list.

1	2	3	4	5	6	7	8	
H	A	N	D	L	O	C	K	Manacle, Handcuff.
H	A	N	D	L	O	O	M	Weaving loom operated by hand or foot not machinery.
H	A	N	D	M	A	D	E	Made by hand.
H	A	N	D	M	A	I	D	Personal maid, Female attendant.
H	A	N	D	P	I	C	K	To select personally, Select very carefully.
H	A	N	D	R	A	I	L	A supporting rail.
H	A	N	D	S	A	L	E	A sale made binding by a handshake.
H	A	N	D	S	O	M	E	Suitable, Beautiful, Liberal, Adroit, Accomplished, Ample, Apt, Good-looking.
H	A	N	D	W	O	R	K	Work done with the hands.
H	A	N	D	Y	M	A	N	One with a variety of skills used in the repair and maintenance of buildings.
H	A	N	G	A	B	L	E	Capable of being hanged, Punishable by hanging.
H	A	N	G	B	I	R	D	Oriole that suspends its nest from a branch.
H	A	N	G	E	R	O	N	Parasite, A person that hangs around in anticipation of personal gain.
H	A	N	G	F	I	R	E	To delay a plan, To have second thoughts.
H	A	N	G	N	A	I	L	A piece of skin hanging loose at the side of the nail.
H	A	N	G	N	E	S	T	A bird's nest suspended from the branches of a tree.
H	A	N	G	O	V	E	R	Something that remains from what is passed, Disagreeable after-effects.
H	A	N	K	E	R	E	D	Yearned, Desired, Longed, Ached, Craved, Hungered, Thirsted, Coveted.
H	A	P	L	O	M	I	D	Relating to an order of teleost fishes.
H	A	P	L	O	S	I	S	Halving of the somatic chromosome number by meiosis.
H	A	P	P	E	N	E	D	Occurred, Chanced, Transpired, Befell, Developed, Passed, Met, Tumbled.
H	A	P	T	E	R	O	N	A discoid outgrowth or swelling of the stem by which a plant attaches itself to a rock.
H	A	Q	U	E	T	O	N	A padded jacket worn under armour.
H	A	R	A	K	I	R	I	A traditional Japanese method of suicide by disembowelment.
H	A	R	A	N	G	U	E	Oration, Declamation, Lecture, Scolding, Rant, Rave.
H	A	R	A	S	S	E	D	Raided, Harried, Exhausted, Fatigued, Plagued, Bedevilled, Badgered, Worn-out.
H	A	R	D	B	A	C	K	A book bound in hard covers.
H	A	R	D	B	A	K	E	Sweetmeat of sugar and almonds.
H	A	R	D	B	O	O	T	A person devoted to horse racing.
H	A	R	D	C	A	S	E	An intractable person, A tough customer.
H	A	R	D	C	O	R	E	Stubbornly resisting change or reform, Unrepentant, Unwavering.
H	A	R	D	E	N	E	D	Unfeeling, Callous, Confirmed, Inveterate, Veteran.
H	A	R	D	E	N	E	R	A worker who hardens steel objects, Substance added to impart hardness.
H	A	R	D	F	E	R	N	Deer fern.
H	A	R	D	H	A	C	K	An American shrub.
H	A	R	D	I	E	S	T	Bravest, Strongest, Boldest, Most robust, Most resolute.
H	A	R	D	N	E	S	S	Property of solids, Hardship, Difficulty, Asperity, Rigour, Vicissitude.
H	A	R	D	S	H	I	P	Suffering, Privation, Difficulty, Adversity, Misfortune, Danger, Hazard, Affliction.
H	A	R	D	T	A	C	K	A hard biscuit in the rations of a serviceman.
H	A	R	D	W	A	R	E	Fittings, trimmings, cutlery, machine parts made of metal.
H	A	R	D	W	O	O	D	The wood of an angiospermous tree.
H	A	R	E	B	E	L	L	A slender herb, Bluebell, Wood hyacinth.
H	A	R	E	F	O	O	T	A long narrow close-toed foot of some dogs.
H	A	R	E	S	E	A	R	European annual herb.
H	A	R	E	W	O	O	D	Greenish gray figured cabinet wood resulting from the dyeing of sycamore maple.
H	A	R	I	K	A	R	I	Hara-kiri.
H	A	R	L	O	T	R	Y	Prostitution, Obscenity, Vulgarity.
H	A	R	M	A	L	O	L	A brown crystalline phenolic alkaloid.
H	A	R	M	L	E	S	S	Innocent, Innocuous, Inoffensive, Safe, Non-toxic, Guiltless.
H	A	R	M	O	N	I	A	Harmonic suture.
H	A	R	M	O	N	I	C	Musical, Congruous, Progression, Integration.
H	A	R	R	I	D	A	N	Worn-out horse, Tall lean ugly woman, Hag.
H	A	R	R	I	S	I	A	Genus of slender spiny tropical American cacti.
H	A	R	R	O	W	E	D	Ploughed, Cultivated, Lacerated, Agonized, Excruciated, Tormented, Tortured, Pestered.
H	A	R	R	O	W	E	R	One that harrows.
H	A	R	R	U	M	P	H	Protest.
H	A	R	R	Y	I	N	G	Assaulting, Devastating, Ravaging, Raiding, Looting, Attacking, Tormenting, Annoying.
H	A	R	T	O	G	I	A	Agathosma, Genus of southern African shrub that yields a sulphur-containing oil for medicine.
H	A	R	U	S	P	E	X	Soothsayer.
H	A	S	K	A	L	A	H	An intellectual enlightenment movement among 18th and 19th century Eastern European Jews.
H	A	S	S	L	I	N	G	Arguing, Fighting, Disputing.
H	A	S	T	E	N	E	D	Hurried, Accelerated, Shaken, Hustled, Flew, Rushed, Ran.
H	A	S	T	E	N	E	R	One that hurries.
H	A	S	T	I	N	G	S	Early ripening of fruit and vegetables.
H	A	T	C	H	E	R	Y	A place for hatching eggs of fowls or fish.
H	A	T	C	H	I	N	G	Breeding, Incubating, Originating, Producing, Propagating.
H	A	T	C	H	W	A	Y	An opening equipped with a hatch and giving access to a room or cellar, A passageway.

1	2	3	4	5	6	7	8	
H	A	T	E	A	B	L	E	Detestable.
H	A	T	H	O	R	I	C	Relating to the Egyptian goddess of love.
H	A	T	S	T	A	N	D	A stand with hooks for holding hats and coats.
H	A	T	T	E	R	I	A	Genus of reptiles.
H	A	T	T	R	I	C	K	A skilful manoeuvre.
H	A	U	L	O	V	E	R	Portage.
H	A	U	N	C	H	E	D	Having haunches.
H	A	U	N	T	I	N	G	Frequenting, Troubling, Molesting, Lingering, Affecting, Resorting.
H	A	U	R	I	A	N	T	Drain, Devour, Exhaust, In heraldry with the head up.
H	A	U	S	F	R	A	U	Housewife.
H	A	U	S	T	R	U	M	A recess in the colon.
H	A	V	E	R	I	N	G	Devious.
H	A	V	I	L	A	N	D	Porcelain tableware made at Limoges, France.
H	A	V	I	L	D	A	R	Non-commissioned officer, sergeant, in the Indian army.
H	A	V	O	C	K	E	D	Devastated, Destroyed.
H	A	W	A	I	I	A	N	Relating to the Hawaii islands.
H	A	W	F	I	N	C	H	A common finch.
H	A	W	K	B	E	L	L	Small bell attached to leg of a hawk.
H	A	W	K	E	Y	E	D	Sharp-sighted, Scrutinized.
H	A	W	K	M	O	T	H	Genus of large moths.
H	A	W	K	W	E	E	D	Of a composite plant.
H	A	W	T	H	O	R	N	Spring-flowering shrub or tree with small red fruits.
H	A	Y	F	E	V	E	R	An allergy associated with pollen.
H	A	Y	F	I	E	L	D	A field of grass or legumes grown for hay.
H	A	Y	K	N	I	F	E	Long-bladed knife for trimming a haystack.
H	A	Y	M	A	K	E	R	Machine for curing hay, A powerful knockout blow.
H	A	Y	S	T	A	C	K	Hay rick, Stack of hay.
H	A	Z	A	R	D	E	D	Gambled, Bet, Ventured, Risked, Chanced, Wagered, Endangered, Compromised.
H	A	Z	A	R	D	E	R	Gamester.
H	A	Z	E	L	H	E	N	European woodland grouse.
H	A	Z	E	L	N	U	T	Nuts from the hazel tree.
H	A	Z	I	N	E	S	S	State of being hazy, Vagueness, Uncertainty.
H	E	A	D	A	C	H	E	Pain inside the head, Vexatious situation, Baffling problem, Sourse of worry.
H	E	A	D	A	C	H	Y	Causing a headache.
H	E	A	D	B	A	N	D	Ornamental band.
H	E	A	D	F	A	S	T	Mooring hawser at the head of a ship.
H	E	A	D	G	E	A	R	Covering for the head, Head harness, Drilling gear at the top of a mine or oilwell.
H	E	A	D	H	U	N	T	To kill and decapitate enemies. To seek to deprive political enemies of their positions.
H	E	A	D	I	E	S	T	Most rash, Giddiest, Most violent, Smartest.
H	E	A	D	L	A	M	P	Headlight.
H	E	A	D	L	A	N	D	Portion of high land jutting out to the sea or lake.
H	E	A	D	L	E	S	S	Beheaded, Leaderless, Lacking good sense or prudence, Foolish, Stupid.
H	E	A	D	L	I	N	E	Head of a newspaper story usually printed in large type, Banner.
H	E	A	D	L	O	C	K	A wrestling hold.
H	E	A	D	L	O	N	G	Headfirst, Rashly, Recklessly, Heedlessly, Unswervingly.
H	E	A	D	M	A	R	K	Distinguishing mark, Credit given to a pupil.
H	E	A	D	M	O	S	T	Leading, Most advanced.
H	E	A	D	N	O	T	E	Explanation at the head of a page, Explanatory notes on the ruling of a decided legal case.
H	E	A	D	P	O	S	T	A top bedpost.
H	E	A	D	R	A	C	E	Turbine or waterwheel for conveying water for power.
H	E	A	D	R	E	S	T	Attachment for supporting the head.
H	E	A	D	R	I	N	G	Decorated ring worn by married warriors of some black African tribes.
H	E	A	D	S	I	L	L	Top member of door or window frame.
H	E	A	D	S	K	I	N	Tough elastic fat covering the head of a sperm whale beneath the skin.
H	E	A	D	T	I	R	E	Headdress.
H	E	A	D	W	A	L	L	A steep slope forming the head of a valley.
H	E	A	D	W	I	N	D	Wind blowing against the course of a ship or plane.
H	E	A	D	W	O	R	D	Word or term at the beginning of a chapter.
H	E	A	D	W	O	R	K	Mental work, Ornmentation of an arch.
H	E	A	L	A	B	L	E	Capable of being healed.
H	E	A	R	A	B	L	E	Capable of being heard.
H	E	A	R	T	I	L	Y	Vigorously, Wholeheartedly, Completely, Thoroughly, Exceedingly, Sincerely.
H	E	A	R	T	R	O	T	Disintegration of the central part of a plant or plant organ.
H	E	A	T	H	E	R	Y	Covered with heather, Resembling heather.
H	E	A	T	H	H	E	N	Female black grouse.
H	E	A	T	H	P	E	A	European leguminous herb bearing small edible tubers used in Scotland to flavour whisky.
H	E	A	T	L	E	S	S	Lacking heat or a heating appliance.

1	2	3	4	5	6	7	8	
H	E	A	T	U	N	I	T	British thermal unit, Calorie.
H	E	A	T	W	A	V	E	Wave of thermal radiation.
H	E	A	V	E	N	L	Y	Celestial, Sacred, Blessed, Divine, Delightful, Enchanting, Exceedingly, Ambrosial.
H	E	A	V	I	E	S	T	Weightiest, Harshnest, Most serious, Deepest, Most intense, Most clumsy, Fattest.
H	E	B	D	O	M	A	D	A group of seven.
H	E	B	E	T	A	T	E	Make dull, Blunting, Become obtuse, Stupefy.
H	E	B	E	T	U	D	E	Dullness, Lethargy, Coma, Languour, Lassitude, Slumber, Stupor, Torpor.
H	E	B	R	A	I	C	A	Collection of early Hebrew historical material.
H	E	B	R	A	I	S	M	Characteristic of the early Hebrews.
H	E	B	R	A	I	S	T	Specialist in Hebrew studies.
H	E	B	R	A	I	Z	E	To follow Hebraism.
H	E	C	A	T	O	M	B	Sacrifice or slaughter of many victims, Ancient Greek or Roman sacrifice of 100 beasts.
H	E	C	K	L	I	N	G	Challenging, Gibing, Harassing with questions, Badgering, Molesting, Annoying, Interfering.
H	E	C	T	O	R	E	D	Blustered, Bullied, Hounded, Intimidated, Browbeaten, Terrorized, Baited, Badgered.
H	E	D	G	E	H	O	G	Nocturnal insectivorous mammal covered with prickles.
H	E	D	G	E	H	O	P	To fly an aeroplane at a very low altitude.
H	E	D	G	E	P	I	G	Hedgehog.
H	E	D	G	E	R	O	W	Row of shrubs and trees acting as a boundary.
H	E	D	O	N	I	C	S	A theory of ethics based on the relation of duty to pleasure.
H	E	D	O	N	I	S	M	An ethical doctrine that asserts that pleasure and happiness is the sole purpose of life.
H	E	D	O	N	I	S	T	One who practices hedonism.
H	E	E	D	L	E	S	S	Inattentive, Unmindful, Careless, Unobservant, Feckless, Oblivious, Thoughtless.
H	E	E	L	A	M	A	N	Hieleman, wooden shield used by Australian aborigines.
H	E	E	L	B	A	L	L	Composition of wax and lampblack used by shoe-makers and also to take brass rubbings.
H	E	E	L	P	O	S	T	The post to which a door or gate is hinged.
H	E	E	L	W	O	R	K	Dance technique emphasising accents with the heels.
H	E	F	T	I	E	S	T	Mightiest, Heaviest, Weightiest, Most powerful, Most massive, Biggest.
H	E	G	E	L	I	A	N	Relating to Hegel and objective idealism.
H	E	G	E	M	O	N	Y	Leadership, Dominance.
H	E	I	G	H	T	E	N	Augment, Amplify, Deepen, Intensify, Highlight, Strengthen, Elevate, Increase.
H	E	I	R	L	E	S	S	Having no heir.
H	E	I	R	L	O	O	M	Something having special intrinsic or financial value to a family.
H	E	I	R	S	H	I	P	Right of inheritance, Heritage.
H	E	L	E	I	D	A	E	Family of biting midges.
H	E	L	E	P	O	L	E	Ancient siege engine consisting of a tower covering a battering ram.
H	E	L	I	A	C	A	L	Relating to the sun.
H	E	L	I	C	I	N	A	Genus of land snails.
H	E	L	I	C	O	I	D	Arranged in a spiral.
H	E	L	I	C	T	I	S	Genus of mammals, Ferret-badgers.
H	E	L	I	O	D	O	N	Device for simulating sun and shadow orientation for a planned building.
H	E	L	I	O	D	O	R	Southern African golden-yellow beryl.
H	E	L	I	O	S	I	S	Sunstroke, Exposure to the sun.
H	E	L	I	O	Z	O	A	Freshwater protozoans.
H	E	L	I	P	O	R	T	Place for landing and take-off for a helicopter.
H	E	L	I	S	O	M	A	Genus of freshwater snails.
H	E	L	L	A	D	I	C	Relating to Bronze Age culture of Greece.
H	E	L	L	B	E	N	T	Reckless, Stubborn, Wilful.
H	E	L	L	E	N	I	C	Classical Greek culture.
H	E	L	L	F	I	R	E	Fire and brimstone, Torment.
H	E	L	L	H	O	L	E	Place of extreme discomfort, Notorious place of immoral activities.
H	E	L	L	I	C	A	T	A giddy girl, An irresponsible and wild person.
H	E	L	L	K	I	T	E	One that shows abominable cruelty.
H	E	L	L	R	O	O	T	Small Broomrape.
H	E	L	L	W	A	R	D	Progress to damnation.
H	E	L	L	W	E	E	D	Hedge bindweed.
H	E	L	M	E	T	E	D	Wearing a helmet.
H	E	L	M	I	N	T	H	Parasitic worm.
H	E	L	M	L	E	S	S	Lacking a helm.
H	E	L	M	S	M	A	N	One who steers a ship.
H	E	L	O	N	I	A	S	Genus of bog herbs.
H	E	L	O	T	I	S	M	Serfdom.
H	E	L	O	T	I	U	M	Fungi.
H	E	L	P	L	E	S	S	Defenseless, Futile, Powerless, Involuntary, Bewildered, Desolate, Impotent, Feeble.
H	E	L	P	M	A	T	E	Wife, One serving as companion, partner or assistant.
H	E	L	P	M	E	E	T	Helpmate.
H	E	L	V	E	L	L	A	Genus of fungi.
H	E	L	V	E	T	I	A	Switzerland.

1	2	3	4	5	6	7	8	
H	E	L	V	E	T	I	C	A Swiss Protestant.
H	E	L	V	E	T	I	I	Early Celtic inhabitants of Switzerland in the time of the ancient Romans.
H	E	M	A	T	E	I	N	Crystalline phenolic quinonoid.
H	E	M	A	T	I	T	E	Mineral consisting of ferric oxide.
H	E	M	I	D	O	M	E	A dome that has only two like faces.
H	E	M	I	F	O	R	M	A rust in which only the uredinial and telial stages are known.
H	E	M	I	O	L	I	C	Relating to a proportion of three to two.
H	E	M	I	O	P	I	A	Blindness in one half of the visual field of one or both eyes.
H	E	M	I	P	O	D	E	Button quail.
H	E	M	I	T	Y	P	E	Imperfectly typical.
H	E	M	I	Z	O	I	C	Having chlorophyll-bearing chromatophores.
H	E	M	O	L	I	Z	E	To cause red blood cells to dissolve.
H	E	M	O	P	T	O	E	Haemorrhage from the lungs.
H	E	M	O	S	T	A	T	An instrument for compressing a bleeding vessel.
H	E	M	O	Z	O	O	N	An animal parasite that lives in the blood.
H	E	M	P	P	A	L	M	Dwarf fan palms.
H	E	M	P	S	E	E	D	The seed of the hemp that yields oil used in soft soap, paint and varnishes.
H	E	N	C	H	M	A	N	Retainer, Adherent, Right-hand man, Violent member of a gang.
H	E	N	D	E	C	Y	L	An alkyl radical derived from liquid paraffin hydrocarbons.
H	E	N	E	Q	U	E	N	Henequin, strong hard fibre derived from leaves of a tropical plant.
H	E	N	P	A	R	T	Y	Party for women only.
H	E	N	R	O	O	S	T	A place for fowls to roost.
H	E	P	A	T	I	C	A	Small genus of perennial herbs, Ranunculus.
H	E	P	A	T	I	T	E	A barite that becomes fetid when rubbed or heated.
H	E	P	A	T	I	Z	E	To become solidified tissue.
H	E	P	A	T	O	M	A	A maglignant tumour of the liver.
H	E	P	T	A	G	O	N	A plane polygon having seven sides and seven angles.
H	E	P	T	A	N	A	L	Pungent oily compound obtained from castor-oil and used in making artificial cognac.
H	E	P	T	A	R	C	H	One ruler of a heptarchy, a government of seven.
H	E	P	T	I	T	O	L	A hepta-hydroxy alcohol.
H	E	R	A	L	D	E	D	Announced, Signalled, Publicized, Preceded, Foreshadowed, Trumpeted, Hailed, Touted.
H	E	R	A	L	D	I	C	Relating to heraldry.
H	E	R	A	L	D	R	Y	Devising and granting of armorial insignia, Pageantry.
H	E	R	B	A	L	E	S	Broomrape.
H	E	R	B	L	E	S	S	Lacking herbage.
H	E	R	C	U	L	E	S	Man of great physical strength.
H	E	R	D	B	O	O	K	Official record of pedigrees of livestock.
H	E	R	D	S	M	A	N	Manager, tender or breeder of livestock.
H	E	R	E	A	W	A	Y	Hereabout.
H	E	R	E	D	I	T	Y	Inheritance, Tradition, Transmission of qualities from generation to generation.
H	E	R	E	G	E	L	D	A feudal tribute.
H	E	R	E	S	I	E	S	Noncomformities, Schisms, Infidelities, Defections from dominant beliefs.
H	E	R	E	U	N	T	O	To this writing or document.
H	E	R	E	U	P	O	N	As a sequel to this.
H	E	R	E	W	I	T	H	With this, By this.
H	E	R	I	T	A	G	E	Property that descend to an heir, Legacy, Tradition, Birthright, Inheritance.
H	E	R	M	A	E	A	N	Relating to Hermes.
H	E	R	M	E	T	I	C	Relating to something obscure and mysterious, Recondite, Alchemist.
H	E	R	M	I	T	R	Y	Isolation.
H	E	R	N	I	A	R	Y	Relating to hernia or its treatment.
H	E	R	N	I	A	T	E	Rupture, Protrude through an abnormal body opening.
H	E	R	O	I	C	A	L	Noble, Dauntless, Courageous, Fearless, Extreme, Intrepid, Unafraid, Radical.
H	E	R	O	I	C	L	Y	Boldly, Bravely, Valiantly, Enormously, Mightily.
H	E	R	O	I	Z	E	D	Represented as a hero.
H	E	R	P	E	T	I	C	Relating to herpes, blisters arising from a virus.
H	E	R	T	Z	I	A	N	Developed by the physicist Hertz.
H	E	S	I	O	D	I	C	Relating to the poet Hesiod and his theology.
H	E	S	I	T	A	N	T	Disinclined, Afraid, Averse, Indisposed, Loath, Reluctant, Unwilling, Vacillating.
H	E	S	I	T	A	T	E	Waver, Vacillate, Falter, Halt, Stagger, Boggle, Balk, Dawdle.
H	E	S	P	E	R	I	A	Genus of skipper butterfly.
H	E	S	P	E	R	I	D	Same as HESPERIA.
H	E	S	P	E	R	I	S	Genus of Eurasian herb, Dame's violet.
H	E	T	E	R	I	S	M	Variability of animals and plants.
H	E	T	E	R	O	M	I	A small order of eellike deep-sea teleost fishes.
H	E	X	A	F	O	I	L	A triangular sign put on a barn to ward off evil spirits.
H	E	X	A	G	R	A	M	Figure formed by completing externally an equilateral triangle on each side of a hexagon.
H	E	X	A	N	O	Y	L	Caproyl.

1	2	3	4	5	6	7	8	Clue
H	E	X	A	P	L	A	R	A work in six texts.
H	E	X	A	P	O	D	S	Typical insects.
H	E	X	O	X	I	D	E	An oxide containing six atoms of oxygen in the molecule.
H	E	X	U	L	O	S	E	A ketose containing six carbon atoms in the molecule.
H	E	X	Y	L	E	N	E	Liquid isomeric hydrocarbon.
H	I	B	E	R	N	A	L	Relating to winter, Wintry.
H	I	B	I	S	C	U	S	Large genus of herbs, shrubs or trees, China rose.
H	I	C	C	O	U	G	H	Spasmodic movement of the diaphragm.
H	I	C	C	U	P	E	D	Suffered from hiccoughs.
H	I	C	K	S	I	T	E	Member of Quakers.
H	I	C	K	W	A	L	L	Green woodpecker.
H	I	D	A	T	I	O	N	Assessing by hides.
H	I	D	D	E	N	L	Y	Furtively, Covertly, Obscurely.
H	I	D	E	A	W	A	Y	Refuge, Secluded place of entertainment, Concealed.
H	I	D	E	R	O	P	E	Rope plaited from strips of green hide.
H	I	D	R	O	S	I	S	Perspiration.
H	I	D	R	O	T	I	C	Causing perspiration.
H	I	E	L	A	M	A	N	An elongated wooden shield used by Australian aborigines.
H	I	E	R	A	R	C	H	High priest.
H	I	E	R	A	T	I	C	Associating with priestly functions.
H	I	G	G	L	I	N	G	Bargaining, Haggling, Chaffing.
H	I	G	H	B	A	L	L	Railroad signal, To drive at full speed.
H	I	G	H	B	O	R	N	An aristocrat, Of noble birth.
H	I	G	H	B	R	O	W	Person with pretensions to superiority, Strong intellectual interests.
H	I	G	H	J	U	M	P	A jump for height in a track or field contest.
H	I	G	H	L	A	N	D	Elevated or mountainous land.
H	I	G	H	L	I	N	E	High-voltage electric transmission line, Line or cable strung between ships to move cargo.
H	I	G	H	M	A	S	S	A mass with more ceremony than a low mass.
H	I	G	H	N	E	S	S	Elevation, Loftiness, Person of honour.
H	I	G	H	R	O	A	D	Highway, An easy way.
H	I	G	H	S	T	E	P	To move with a high step.
H	I	G	H	T	A	I	L	To move at full speed, Making a getaway.
H	I	G	H	T	I	D	E	Culminating point, Climax.
H	I	G	H	T	O	N	E	Dignified, Aristocratic, Pretentious, High-flown.
H	I	G	H	V	E	L	D	High plateau.
H	I	J	A	C	K	E	D	Stopped in transit and forced to change course, Kidnapped, Coerced, Forced.
H	I	J	A	C	K	E	R	One that hi-jacks.
H	I	L	A	R	I	T	Y	Cheer, Cheerfulness, Gaiety, Merriment, Mirth, Jocularity, Joviality.
H	I	L	L	S	M	A	N	A man inhabiting an isolated hilly region.
H	I	L	L	O	C	K	Y	Having small mounds.
H	I	L	L	S	I	D	E	A portion of a hill between summit and base.
H	I	N	D	E	R	E	D	Impaired, Retarded, Hampered, Prevented, Checked, Blocked, Obstructed, Arrested.
H	I	N	D	M	O	S	T	Towards the rear, Most remote, Last.
H	I	N	D	N	E	C	K	Nape-used chiefly of birds.
H	I	N	D	U	I	S	M	Religious beliefs of India, marked by social and cultural practices and noted for caste system.
H	I	N	G	E	I	N	G	Attaching by hinges, Using a jointed device to attach a swinging part.
H	I	N	N	I	T	E	S	Genus of scallops.
H	I	P	J	O	I	N	T	Articulation between the femur and the innominate bone.
H	I	P	P	O	D	E	S	A mythical animal with the body of a man and legs of a horse.
H	I	P	P	U	R	I	S	Genus of aquatic herbs.
H	I	R	A	G	A	N	A	Japanese symbols.
H	I	R	E	L	E	S	S	Receiving no wages or remuneration, Voluntary.
H	I	R	E	L	I	N	G	One who is hired, Mercenary.
H	I	R	E	N	O	L	A	Auricularia, free swimming larva of the sea cucumber.
H	I	R	P	L	I	N	G	Limping, Hobbling.
H	I	R	S	E	L	E	D	Slithered, Scrambled.
H	I	R	S	U	T	A	L	Relating to the hair.
H	I	R	T	E	L	L	A	Genus of tropical American trees and shrubs.
H	I	S	P	A	N	I	C	Relating to Spain, Portugal and Latin-America.
H	I	S	T	E	R	I	D	Relating to a family of shining beetles.
H	I	S	T	I	O	I	D	Histoid, resembling normal tissue.
H	I	S	T	O	G	E	N	Zone of primary tissue from which parts of a plant organ are produced.
H	I	S	T	O	R	I	C	True to history, Having considerable significance.
H	I	S	T	R	I	O	N	Theatrical, Stage, Deliberately affected.
H	I	T	C	H	I	N	G	Hobbling, Fastening, Moving jerkily, Attaching, Harnessing, Coupling, Yoking.
H	I	T	H	E	R	T	O	Up to this time, As yet, Until now, Previous.
H	I	V	E	L	E	S	S	Having no hives.

1	2	3	4	5	6	7	8	
H	O	A	C	T	Z	I	N	Hoatzin, Crested bird of South America.
H	O	A	R	D	I	N	G	Collecting, Accumulating, Amassing, Saving, Stashing, Garnering, Stockpiling, Reserving.
H	O	A	R	S	E	L	Y	Raucously, Harshly, With a raucous tone.
H	O	B	B	L	I	N	G	Hampering, Limping, Fettering, Moving laboriously, Obstructing, Curbing, Impeding.
H	O	B	B	Y	I	S	T	One that cultivates hobbies.
H	O	C	H	M	O	O	R	Growing on acid peats or peaty soils.
H	O	C	K	S	H	O	P	Pawnshop.
H	O	C	K	T	I	D	E	Hockday, Second Tuesday after Easter.
H	O	C	U	S	S	E	D	Deceived, Drugged, Cheated, Adulterated.
H	O	D	M	A	D	O	D	Scarecrow.
H	O	G	F	R	A	M	E	A trussed frame used to strengthen American river and lake steamers.
H	O	G	G	E	R	E	L	A young sheep.
H	O	G	M	A	N	A	Y	Traditional Scottish celebration for New Year.
H	O	G	S	H	E	A	D	A large cask or barrel.
H	O	G	S	T	E	E	R	A three year old wild boar.
H	O	I	S	T	I	N	G	Raising, Lifting, Elevating, Uplifting, Upholding, Rearing.
H	O	I	S	T	M	A	N	Engine-man.
H	O	I	S	T	W	A	Y	A passage through which something is hoisted.
H	O	L	D	B	A	C	K	A device for holding something back, Tieback, Withholding part payment.
H	O	L	D	F	A	S	T	Something that secures, supports or holds in place.
H	O	L	I	N	E	S	S	Sanctity, Saintliness, Title for a high religious dignitary.
H	O	L	L	A	N	D	S	Gin made in the Netherlands.
H	O	L	L	E	R	E	D	Shouted, Griped, Complained, Grumbled, Cried out, Summoned.
H	O	L	L	O	W	E	D	Excavated, Formed a concave, Channelled, Curved, Gouged, Scooped.
H	O	L	L	O	W	L	Y	Reverberantly, Gloomily, Vainly, Emptily, Cavernously.
H	O	L	M	G	A	N	G	A duel on an island.
H	O	L	O	G	A	M	Y	Fusion of mature cells in fungi.
H	O	L	O	P	T	I	C	Having compound eyes as in a fly.
H	O	L	O	S	I	D	E	A glycoside that yields only glycoses on hydrolysis.
H	O	L	O	S	T	E	I	An order of ganoid fishes.
H	O	L	O	T	Y	P	E	Single specimen designated by an author as the type of a species.
H	O	L	O	Z	O	I	C	Obtaining food by ingesting complex organic matter.
H	O	L	Y	W	E	E	K	The week before Easter.
H	O	L	Y	W	R	I	T	A writing that is taken to be as sacred as the Bible.
H	O	M	A	G	I	N	G	Paying homage, Deferring, Honouring.
H	O	M	A	X	I	A	L	Having all axes equal.
H	O	M	E	B	O	D	Y	Stay-at-home, One whose life centres around activities in the home.
H	O	M	E	B	O	R	N	Indigenous.
H	O	M	E	B	R	E	D	Unsophisticated, Homeborn.
H	O	M	E	F	E	L	T	Inward, Private.
H	O	M	E	L	A	N	D	Country of origin, Native land, Mother country.
H	O	M	E	L	E	S	S	Having no permanent place of residence.
H	O	M	E	L	I	K	E	Simple, comfortable and wholesome accommodation.
H	O	M	E	M	A	D	E	Prepared on the premises, Native, Domestic origin or manufacture.
H	O	M	E	R	I	A	N	Relating to the poet Homer.
H	O	M	E	R	U	L	E	Self government.
H	O	M	E	S	I	C	K	Longing for home and family.
H	O	M	E	S	P	U	N	Spun or made at home, Folksy, Plebeian, Unsophisticated, Unpretentious, Straightforward.
H	O	M	E	W	A	R	D	In the direction of one's home.
H	O	M	E	W	O	R	K	Work done at home either for financial reward or on an assignment given to a student.
H	O	M	I	C	I	D	E	Murderer, Killer, Slayer, Murder, Manslaughter, Killing, Foul play.
H	O	M	I	L	I	S	T	One who delivers a homily, discourse on a religious theme.
H	O	M	I	L	I	T	E	Same as HOMILETE.
H	O	M	I	N	O	I	D	An animal resembling man.
H	O	M	O	D	O	N	T	Having all the teeth similar in form.
H	O	M	O	D	Y	N	E	Detecting a radio wave with a locally generated current of exactly the same frequency.
H	O	M	O	G	A	M	Y	Having flowers alike, Maturing of stamens and pistils simultaneously.
H	O	M	O	G	E	N	Y	Similarity often attributable to common origin.
H	O	M	O	L	O	G	Y	Same as HOMOGENY.
H	O	M	O	N	Y	M	Y	Same word used to denote different things.
H	O	M	O	O	S	I	S	Development of a structure in a different part of the organ than is usual.
H	O	M	O	T	Y	P	Y	The relation existing between homotypes.
H	O	N	D	U	R	A	N	A native of Honduras.
H	O	N	E	S	T	L	Y	Genuinely, Sincerely, Truly, Justly, Openly, Truthfully, Candidly, Uprightly.
H	O	N	E	W	O	R	T	Perennial herb, Stone parsley.
H	O	N	E	Y	B	A	G	Honey sac.
H	O	N	E	Y	B	E	E	Social honey-producing bee.

1	2	3	4	5	6	7	8	Clue
H	O	N	E	Y	D	E	W	Sweet secretion from aphids, scales or fungi found on plants.
H	O	N	E	Y	P	O	D	Pod of a mesquite.
H	O	N	E	Y	P	O	T	A waxen vessel constructed by wild bees, A glass or crockery container for honey.
H	O	N	O	R	A	R	Y	Conferring distinction, Commemorative, Titular, Voluntary.
H	O	N	O	U	R	E	D	Praised, Exalted, Recognised, Respected, Saluted, Unremunerative, Distinguished.
H	O	N	O	U	R	E	R	One that honours.
H	O	O	D	W	I	N	K	Blindfold, Fool, Gull, Deceive, Impose, Dupe, Hoax, Trick.
H	O	O	F	B	E	A	T	Sound of a hoof striking the ground.
H	O	O	F	P	I	C	K	A hooked implement used to remove foreign objects from a hoof.
H	O	O	K	N	O	S	E	An aquiline nose.
H	O	O	K	W	O	R	M	Parasitic worms that attach themselves by means of buccal Hooks.
H	O	O	L	I	G	A	N	Hoodlum, Vandal, Thug, Ruffian.
H	O	O	P	I	R	O	N	Thin iron for barrel hoops.
H	O	O	P	W	O	O	D	Black ash.
H	O	P	E	L	E	S	S	Despairing, Incurable, Desperate, Despondent, Forlorn, Gloomy, Glum, Morose.
H	O	P	I	N	G	L	Y	Trustingly.
H	O	P	P	L	I	N	G	Fettering the feet.
H	O	R	A	T	I	A	N	Resembling the poetic style of Horace.
H	O	R	M	O	G	O	N	Filaments of blue-green algae that became detached as reproductive bodies.
H	O	R	M	O	N	A	L	Relating to hormones.
H	O	R	N	B	E	A	M	A tree with smooth gray bark resembling the beech.
H	O	R	N	B	I	L	L	Arboreal bird with an enormous bill surmounted by a horny casque.
H	O	R	N	B	O	O	K	Child's primer, Rudimentary treatise.
H	O	R	N	F	I	S	H	Family of marine fishes that frequent the sandy bottom and feed on mollucks.
H	O	R	N	L	E	S	S	Having no horn.
H	O	R	N	P	I	P	E	Single reed instrument, A lively folk dance.
H	O	R	N	T	A	I	L	Sawflies.
H	O	R	N	W	O	R	T	A perennial herb.
H	O	R	O	L	O	G	Y	Science of measuring time, the art of clock-making.
H	O	R	R	I	B	L	E	Fearful, Disagreeable, Unpleasant, Ghastly, Grim, Gruesome, Hideous, Terrible.
H	O	R	R	I	B	L	Y	Unpleasantly, Dreadfully, Terribly, Nastily, Offensively.
H	O	R	R	I	D	L	Y	Nastily, Alarmingly.
H	O	R	R	I	F	I	C	Horrible, Fearful, Horrifying, Awful, Frightful.
H	O	R	S	E	B	O	X	A trailer or car for transporting horses.
H	O	R	S	E	B	O	Y	Hostler.
H	O	R	S	E	C	A	R	Car drawn by horses or fitted for transporting horses.
H	O	R	S	E	F	L	Y	Family of flies, the female of which sucks the blood of animals inflicting a painful wound.
H	O	R	S	E	H	O	E	Horse drawn cultivator.
H	O	R	S	E	M	A	N	One skilled in the management of horses.
H	O	R	S	E	P	O	X	Virus disease of horses related to cowpox.
H	O	R	T	U	L	A	N	Pertaining to a garden.
H	O	S	E	B	I	R	D	Rascal, Rapscallion.
H	O	S	A	N	N	A	H	Cry of entreaty chanted in the synagogue.
H	O	S	P	I	T	A	L	Place for sick and injured people, Clinic, Sanatorium.
H	O	S	P	O	D	A	R	A governor of Walachia under Turkish rule.
H	O	S	T	E	L	R	Y	Inn, Hotel, A place where accommodation and meals are available.
H	O	T	C	H	P	O	T	Mixing of property for equal division of property to heirs.
H	O	T	E	L	D	O	M	Hotel and hotel workers.
H	O	T	E	L	I	E	R	Hotelkeeper.
H	O	T	H	O	U	S	E	A building where the temperature is maintained at a certain figure for a specific reason.
H	O	T	P	L	A	T	E	Heated iron plate on a stove or a plate heated by electricity.
H	O	T	P	R	E	S	S	A machine where paper or cloth is glossed between hot metal plates and glazed boards.
H	O	T	S	H	O	R	T	Used to describe metal when heated beyond red heat.
H	O	T	T	O	N	I	A	Genus of aquatic herbs.
H	O	T	W	A	T	E	R	Trouble, Difficulty, Predicament, Dilemma, Fix, Hole, Jam, Pickle.
H	O	U	G	H	I	N	G	Hamstringing.
H	O	U	N	D	I	N	G	Hunting, Chasing, Tracking, Pursuing, Baiting, Harassing, Heckling, Hectoring.
H	O	U	R	H	A	N	D	The index showing the hour on a timepiece.
H	O	U	S	E	B	O	Y	Houseman.
H	O	U	S	E	D	O	G	Dog trained to guard a house.
H	O	U	S	E	F	L	Y	A two-winged fly found in most parts of the world and that transmits diseases.
H	O	U	S	E	M	A	N	One hired to perform general duties about a house, An attendant in a gambling house.
H	O	V	E	L	L	E	R	Aided a ship to unload.
H	O	V	E	L	L	E	R	An unlicensed boatman who helps out with salvage.
H	O	V	E	R	I	N	G	Suspended, Fluttering, Uncertain, Poised, Floating, Cowering, Lingering.
H	O	W	I	T	Z	E	R	A short cannon.

1	2	3	4	5	6	7	8	
H	U	C	K	S	T	E	R	Hawker, Pedlar, Middleman, Showman.
H	U	D	D	L	I	N	G	Crowding, Bunching, Assembling, Massing, Ganging, Conferring, Crouching, Consulting.
H	U	G	E	N	E	S	S	Vastness, Enormity, Immensity, Magnitude.
H	U	G	U	E	N	O	T	A French Protestant in the 16th and 17th centuries.
H	U	I	A	B	I	R	D	A bird of New Zealand related to the starling.
H	U	M	A	N	E	L	Y	Charitably, Kindly, Gently, Benevolently.
H	U	M	A	N	I	S	M	Devotion to human welfare.
H	U	M	A	N	I	S	T	One who has concern for his fellow man.
H	U	M	A	N	I	T	Y	Compassion, Benevolence, Generous disposition, Mankind.
H	U	M	A	N	I	Z	E	To represent as human, Soften, Refine, Civilize.
H	U	M	B	L	I	N	G	Deflating, Abasing, Degrading, Humiliating, Lowering, Demeaning, Mortifying
H	U	M	I	D	I	F	Y	Moisten.
H	U	M	I	D	I	T	Y	Moisture, Dampness, Moderate degree of wetness.
H	U	M	I	F	I	E	D	Converted into humus.
H	U	M	I	L	I	T	Y	Freedom from pride or arrogance, Meekness.
H	U	M	M	O	C	K	Y	Uneven, Abounding in hummocks.
H	U	M	O	R	I	S	T	Eccentric person, Joker, Wag, Jester, Comedian, Comic, Quipster.
H	U	M	O	R	O	U	S	Capricious, Whimsical, Jocular, Funny, Sense of humour, Witty.
H	U	M	O	U	R	E	D	Indulged, Pampered, Gratified, Coddled, Spoiled.
H	U	M	P	B	A	C	K	Hunchback, A crooked back.
H	U	M	P	L	E	S	S	Having no hump.
H	U	M	S	T	R	U	M	A crude fiddle, An out-of-tune instrument, Hurdy-gurdy.
H	U	N	G	E	R	E	D	Longed, Forced by hunger, Hankered, Craved, Lusted, Pined, Sighed, Yearned.
H	U	N	G	R	I	L	Y	Longingly, Eagerly.
H	U	N	K	E	R	E	D	Crouched, Squatted.
H	U	N	T	R	E	S	S	A female hunter, One who follows the chase.
H	U	N	T	S	M	A	N	A manager of the hunt.
H	U	R	D	L	I	N	G	Overcoming, Surmounting, Negotiating, Vaulting, Springing, Throwing.
H	U	R	O	N	I	O	N	Relating to an early prehistoric period.
H	U	R	R	Y	I	N	G	Speeding, Harassing, Rushing, Hastening, Quickening, Whirling.
H	U	R	T	L	E	S	S	Harmless, Unhurt, Incapable of inflicting injury.
H	U	R	T	L	I	N	G	Colliding, Clattering, Crashing, Rushing, Shooting, Flinging, Catapulting, Propelling.
H	U	S	H	H	U	S	H	Secret, Confidential, Secrecy, Suppression, Censorship.
H	U	S	T	I	N	G	S	A court held in London before the Lord Mayor and his retinue.
H	U	S	T	L	I	N	G	Jostling, Shoving, Working, Robbing, Cheating, Pushing, Pressing, Swindling.
H	U	T	C	H	I	N	G	Hoarding, Storing.
H	U	T	U	K	H	T	U	A Lamaist dignitary.
H	U	Z	Z	A	I	N	G	Applauding, Cheering.
H	Y	A	C	I	N	T	H	A bulbous plant with blossoms that yield an outstanding fragrance, A red zircon.
H	Y	A	L	I	T	H	E	An opaque glass that resembles porcelain and is sometimes used as a gem stone.
H	Y	A	L	O	G	E	N	Insoluble substances found in cysts and sponges.
H	Y	B	L	A	E	A	N	Mellifluous, Honeyed.
H	Y	B	O	D	O	N	T	A shark.
H	Y	D	A	T	I	N	A	Genus of stout-bodied naked rotifers.
H	Y	D	R	A	N	T	H	A nutritive zooid of a hydroid colony.
H	Y	D	R	A	T	E	D	Combined with water, Proportion of fluid in the body.
H	Y	D	R	I	D	A	E	Family of aquatic snakes.
H	Y	D	R	O	G	E	L	A gel in which the liquid is water.
H	Y	D	R	O	G	E	N	A nonmetallic univalent element that is the simplest and lightest of the elements.
H	Y	D	R	O	I	D	A	Asexual polyp.
H	Y	D	R	O	M	E	L	A liquor consisting of fermented honey, Mead.
H	Y	D	R	O	M	Y	S	Genus of rodents, Australian beaver rats.
H	Y	D	R	O	P	I	C	Exhibiting hydrops, Cellular degeneration.
H	Y	D	R	O	P	S	Y	Edema, Distention with fluid.
H	Y	D	R	O	S	O	L	A sol in which the liquid is water.
H	Y	D	R	O	X	Y	L	The univalent group of radicals consisting of one atom of hydrogen and one of oxygen.
H	Y	D	R	O	Z	O	A	Family of polyps and jellyfishes.
H	Y	D	R	U	R	G	A	Genus of mammals, Leopard seal.
H	Y	D	R	U	R	U	S	Sticky foul-smelling feathery greenish brown plantlike tufts that thrive in cold flowing water.
H	Y	G	I	E	N	I	C	Healthful, Good, Salubrious, Wholesome, Sanitary, Healthy.
H	Y	L	O	Z	O	I	C	Relating to the doctrine that all matter is animated.
H	Y	M	E	N	E	A	L	Relating to marriage, Nuptial.
H	Y	M	E	N	E	A	N	Hymen.
H	Y	M	E	N	I	U	M	Spore-bearing layer in fungi.
H	Y	M	N	B	O	O	K	Hymnal, Book containing hymns.
H	Y	O	I	D	E	A	N	Relating to the hyoid bone.
H	Y	O	S	C	I	N	E	Scopolamine, poisonous alkyloid used as a sedative and to prevent motion sickness.

1	2	3	4	5	6	7	8	Definition
H	Y	P	A	X	I	A	L	Beneath the axis of the vertebral column.
H	Y	P	E	R	G	O	L	Hypergolic fluid propellant.
H	Y	P	H	A	E	N	E	Genus of tropical African fan palms.
H	Y	P	H	E	N	E	D	Connected with a hyphen.
H	Y	P	H	E	N	I	C	Relating to hyphens.
H	Y	P	N	O	S	I	S	A state resembling sleep that is induced by suggestion.
H	Y	P	N	O	T	I	C	Soporific, Narcotic, Opiate, Sleepy, Somnolent.
H	Y	P	O	C	H	I	L	The lower part of the labellum in orchids.
H	Y	P	O	C	O	N	E	Principal rear inner cusp of a mammalian upper molar.
H	Y	P	O	D	E	R	M	Tissue underlying epidermis of a plant.
H	Y	P	O	G	A	M	Y	Marriage into a lower caste, class or social group.
H	Y	P	O	G	E	A	L	Occurring beneath the surface of the soil.
H	Y	P	O	G	E	A	N	Same as HYPOGEAL.
H	Y	P	O	G	E	N	E	Plutonic, Formed, crystallized or lying beneath the earth's surface.
H	Y	P	O	G	E	U	M	Cellar, Underground portion of a building, Catacomb.
H	Y	P	O	H	Y	A	L	Relating to the area of the hyoid arch of most fishes.
H	Y	P	O	N	O	M	E	Swimming funnel as a water siphon of the octopus and squid.
H	Y	P	O	P	Y	O	N	A collection of pus in the anterior chamber of the eye.
H	Y	P	O	T	H	E	C	Pledge by the debtor without transference of title to the creditor.
H	Y	P	O	Z	O	I	C	Lying under the fossiliferous systems.
H	Y	R	A	C	E	U	M	A substance secreted by the hydrax formerly used for folk medicine.
H	Y	S	S	O	P	U	S	Genus of perennial herbs.
H	Y	S	T	E	R	I	A	Nervous disorder producing violent outbursts of emotion.
H	Y	S	T	E	R	I	C	An overemotional or unstable person.

I

1	2	3	4	5	6	7	8	Definition
I	A	N	T	H	I	N	A	Genus of pelagic snails having a thin spiral purple shell.
I	A	T	R	I	C	A	L	Relating to healing and medical treatment.
I	B	I	S	B	I	L	L	A bluish gray bird of central Asia resembling a lapwing.
I	B	O	G	A	I	N	E	A crystalline alkaloid obtained from root, bark and leaves of a plant.
I	B	S	E	N	I	S	M	Dramatic invention characteristic of Ibsen.
I	C	E	B	L	I	N	K	A yellowish or whitish glare in the sky over an ice field.
I	C	E	B	O	U	N	D	Immobilized by ice, Constricted by inhibitions or taboos.
I	C	E	C	R	A	F	T	Skill in travelling on an ice surface.
I	C	E	C	R	E	A	M	Frozen dessert containing cream, butter, eggs and flavouring.
I	C	E	F	I	E	L	D	Large body of glacial ice.
I	C	E	H	O	U	S	E	A building for storing ice.
I	C	E	P	L	A	N	T	An Old World annual herb.
I	C	E	Q	U	A	K	E	The concussion of the breaking of an ice mass.
I	C	E	S	H	E	E	T	Glacial ice cover.
I	C	E	W	A	T	E	R	Chilled or iced drinking water.
I	C	E	Y	A	C	H	T	Iceboat.
I	C	H	O	R	O	U	S	Thin, Watery, Serous, Sanious.
I	C	H	T	H	Y	I	C	Relating to fishes or having the form of fishes.
I	C	O	S	T	E	U	S	Genus of typical ragfishes.
I	C	T	E	R	I	D	S	Family of American birds, Orioles, Blackbirds, Meadowlarks.
I	C	T	E	R	O	I	D	Resembling jaundice.
I	D	E	A	L	I	S	M	Theory that affirms that mind or the spiritual and ideal of central importance in reality.
I	D	E	A	L	I	S	T	One that places ideals before practical considerations, Visionary, Dreamer.
I	D	E	A	L	I	T	Y	Something imagined or ideal, Unrealistic.
I	D	E	A	L	I	Z	E	Attribute ideal characteristics.
I	D	E	A	T	I	N	G	Conceiving, Preconceiving, Prefiguring.
I	D	E	A	T	I	O	N	Process of entertaining and relating ideas.
I	D	E	A	T	I	V	E	Ideational, Conceptual, Notional.
I	D	E	N	T	I	F	Y	Determine, Diagnose, Distinguish, Finger, Place, Recognize, Establish.
I	D	E	N	T	I	T	Y	Oneness, Sameness, Agreement, Likeness, Resemblance, Similarity, Correspondence.
I	D	E	O	G	R	A	M	A picture or a symbol that represents a thing not a word, Logogram.
I	D	E	O	L	O	G	Y	Branch of knowledge concerned with the origin and nature of ideas.
I	D	I	O	S	O	M	E	Sex chromosome.
I	D	I	O	T	I	S	M	Idiom, Imbecility, Inanity.
I	D	I	O	T	I	Z	E	To make a fool of, Cause to behave like an idiot.
I	D	L	E	H	O	O	D	Idleness.
I	D	L	E	N	E	S	S	Indolence, Laziness, Slothfulness, Sluggishness.
I	D	O	C	R	A	S	E	A mineral that is a silicate of calcium, magnesium, iron and aluminium.
I	D	O	L	A	T	O	R	One that worships idols or something not usually considered a subject of worship.

8 LETTERS

1	2	3	4	5	6	7	8	Definition
I	D	O	L	A	T	R	Y	Adoration, Worship, Immoderate attachment, Excessive devotion.
I	D	O	L	I	Z	E	D	Adored, Worshipped, Doted, Revered, Loved to excess.
I	D	O	L	I	Z	E	R	One that dotes upon something or someone.
I	D	O	N	E	I	T	Y	Suitability, Fitness.
I	G	N	A	T	I	A	N	Relating to St Ignatius, Bishop of Antioch.
I	G	N	I	T	I	N	G	Kindling, Burning, Setting aflame, Heating, Exciting, Flaming, Blazing, Flaring.
I	G	N	I	T	I	O	N	Method of igniting a fuel mixture.
I	G	N	I	T	R	O	N	Half-way rectifier tube containing mercury.
I	G	N	O	M	I	N	Y	Dishonour, Disgrace, Discredit, Disrepute, Mortification, Infamy, Contempt, Scorn.
I	G	N	O	R	A	N	T	Uninformed, Incivilized, Illiterate, Uneducated, Untutored, Unlearned, Uncultured, Crude.
I	G	N	O	R	I	N	G	Neglecting, Disregarding, Failing, Forgetting, Overlooking, Omitting, Avoiding, Evading.
I	G	U	A	N	I	A	N	A lizard like an iguana.
I	L	L	A	E	N	U	S	Genus of extinct marine arthropods.
I	L	L	A	P	S	E	D	Glided, Slipped.
I	L	L	A	T	I	O	N	Inference, Deduction, Judgment, Conclusion.
I	L	L	A	T	I	V	E	Introducing an inference.
I	L	L	B	L	O	O	D	Bad-blood, Enmity, Discord.
I	L	L	F	A	T	E	D	Unsuccessful, Inauspicious.
I	L	L	F	A	T	E	D	Unlucky, Hapless, Luckless, Misfortunate, Unhappy.
I	L	L	G	U	I	D	E	Mismanage.
I	L	L	I	C	I	U	M	Small genus of evergreen trees, Chinese anise.
I	L	L	I	N	I	U	M	Chemical element.
I	L	L	I	Q	U	I	D	Having no liquid assets, Lacking capital.
I	L	L	K	E	M	P	T	Slovenly, Careless, Dishevelled, Messy, Sloppy, Slipshod, Uncombed, Untidy.
I	L	L	T	I	M	E	D	Unseasonable, Inopportune, Mistimed, Improper, Inappropriate, Inept, Unbecoming.
I	L	L	T	R	E	A	T	Abuse, Maltreat, Mistreat, Outrage, Harass, Molest, Aggrieve, Pervert.
I	L	L	U	D	I	N	G	Deluding, Deceiving, Eluding, Mocking, Deriding, Betraying, Misleading, Bluffing.
I	L	L	U	M	I	N	E	Illuminate, Irradiate, Enlighten.
I	L	L	U	M	I	N	G	Illuminating.
I	L	L	U	S	A	G	E	Maltreatment, Abusive treatment.
I	L	L	U	S	I	O	N	Apparition, Hallucination, Delusion, Misconception, Fancy, Mirage, Phantasm.
I	L	L	U	S	O	R	Y	Apparent, Illusory, Ostensible, Semblant.
I	L	L	U	S	I	V	E	Fictitious, Fanciful, Fictional, Imaginary, Unreal, Deceptive, Apparent.
I	L	L	U	V	I	A	L	Marked by accumulation of dissolved or suspended soil.
I	L	L	Y	R	I	A	N	Characteristic of ancient Illyria.
I	L	M	E	N	I	T	E	Iron-black mineral of sub-metallic luster.
I	M	A	G	I	N	A	L	Relating to an image.
I	M	A	G	I	N	E	D	Fabricated, Supposed, Guessed, Thought, Conceived, Envisioned, Understood, Assumed.
I	M	A	G	I	N	E	R	One that imagines or has flights of fancy.
I	M	B	A	U	B	A		Trumpetwood.
I	M	B	E	C	I	L	E	Feeble-minded, Retarded, Backward, Dull, Half-witted, Moronic, Fool, Simpleton.
I	M	B	E	D	D	E	D	Fixed firmly.
I	M	B	E	L	L	I	C	Not warlike.
I	M	B	I	B	I	N	G	Soaking, Assimilating, Absorbing, Drinking, Quaffing, Incorporating, Guzzlingly, Tippling.
I	M	B	R	U	I	N	G	Drenching, Saturating.
I	M	B	R	U	T	E	D	Brutalized, Degenerated.
I	M	B	U	R	S	E	D	Supplied with money.
I	M	I	T	A	B	L	E	Capable of being imitated or copied.
I	M	I	T	A	N	C	Y	Imitativeness.
I	M	I	T	A	T	E	D	Copied, Reproduced, Mocked, Mimed, Duplicated, Invested, Aped, Parodied.
I	M	I	T	A	T	O	R	One that impersonates.
I	M	M	A	N	E	N	T	Inherent, Intrinsic, Subjective, Imminent.
I	M	M	A	N	I	T	Y	Monstrosity.
I	M	M	A	N	T	L	E	To cover with a cloak.
I	M	M	A	S	K	E	D	Disguised.
I	M	M	A	T	U	R	E	Young, Juvenile, Unfledged, Premature, Unripe, Infantile, Crude, Unfinished.
I	M	M	E	R	G	E	D	Plunged, Obscured.
I	M	M	E	R	S	E	D	Plunged, Dipped, Embedded, Included, Sunk, Buried, Absorbed, Inundated.
I	M	M	E	S	H	E	D	Enmeshed, Entangled, Implicated.
I	M	M	I	N	E	N	T	Impending, Proximate, Approaching, Pending, Probable, Menacing, Ominous, Sinister.
I	M	M	I	N	G	L	E	Blend, Mix, Intermingle, Meld.
I	M	M	I	T	T	E	D	Injected, Admitted, Introduced.
I	M	M	I	X	I	N	G	Commingling, Compounding, Interfusing, Intermingling, Mingling, Mixing.
I	M	M	O	B	I	L	E	Immovable, Fixed, Stable, Unmoving, Motionless, Static, Stationary, Stagnant.
I	M	M	O	D	E	S	T	Brazen, Indecent, Indelicate, Coarse, Bold, Improper, Presumptuous, Pert.
I	M	M	O	L	A	T	E	Kill, Destroy, Sacrifice, Victimize, Surrender.
I	M	M	O	R	T	A	L	Imperishable, Abiding, Deathless, Enduring, Eternal, Indestructible, Perpetual, Everlasting.

1	2	3	4	5	6	7	8	
I	M	M	U	N	I	T	Y	Exemption, Freedom, Impunity, Lack of susceptibility.
I	M	M	U	N	I	Z	E	To cause to produce antibodies, To make immune.
I	M	M	U	R	I	N	G	Enclosing, Incarcerating, Punish by entombing.
I	M	P	A	C	T	E	D	Clashed, Impinged, Collided, Jolted, Shocked, Bumped, Crashed.
I	M	P	A	I	R	E	D	Damaged, Lessened, Deteriorated, Injured, Marred, Tarnished, Blemished, Spoiled.
I	M	P	A	I	R	E	R	One or something that impairs.
I	M	P	A	L	I	N	G	Staking, Piercing, Transfixing, Perforating, Confining, Encircling.
I	M	P	A	N	A	T	E	Pertaining to the body of Christ in the Eucharistic bread.
I	M	P	A	R	I	T	Y	Inequality, Disparity.
I	M	P	A	R	K	E	D	Enclosed.
I	M	P	A	R	L	E	D	Conferred in a dispute.
I	M	P	A	R	T	E	D	Communicated, Transmitted, Disclosed, Given, Bestowed, Conveyed, Divulged.
I	M	P	A	S	T	E	D	Made into dough.
I	M	P	A	W	N	E	D	Put into pawn.
I	M	P	E	D	I	N	G	Blocking, Hindering, Blocking, Braking, Obstructing, Disconcerting, Embarrassing, Rattling.
I	M	P	E	L	L	E	D	Propelled, Moved, Mobilized, Activated, Compelled, Constrained, Forced, Goaded.
I	M	P	E	L	L	E	R	Rotor.
I	M	P	E	L	L	O	R	Same as IMPELLER.
I	M	P	E	N	D	E	D	Menaced, Loomed, Gathered.
I	M	P	E	R	A	T	A	Genus of tropical grasses.
I	M	P	E	R	A	T	E	Command, Govern.
I	M	P	E	R	I	A	L	Royal, Sovereign, Imperious, Haughty, Regal, Grandiose, Commanding.
I	M	P	E	R	I	U	M	Supreme power, Territory, Empire, Jurisdiction, Sovereignty.
I	M	P	E	S	T	E	R	Entangle, Embarrass.
I	M	P	E	T	I	G	O	Acute contagious skin disease transmitted by contact.
I	M	P	I	N	G	E	D	Encroached, Infringed, Impacted, Collided, Jolted, Shocked, Smashed, Jarred.
I	M	P	I	N	G	E	R	Instrument for collecting samples of dust.
I	M	P	I	S	H	L	Y	Mischievously, Playfully, Archly, Saucily, Giddily, Casually.
I	M	P	L	E	A	C	H	Interweave.
I	M	P	L	E	D	G	E	Pledge.
I	M	P	L	I	C	I	T	Interwoven, Implied, Potential, Unquestioning, Whole-hearted, Tacit, Inferred, Understood.
I	M	P	L	O	R	E	D	Beseeched, Entreated, Prayed, Begged, Appealed, Conjured, Craved, Importuned.
I	M	P	L	U	M	E	D	Furnished with plumes.
I	M	P	L	U	N	G	E	Plunge.
I	M	P	L	Y	I	N	G	Including, Suggesting, Hinting, Indicating, Pointing, Insinuating, Asserting, Intimating.
I	M	P	O	C	K	E	T	Keep in the pocket.
I	M	P	O	L	I	C	Y	State of impolitic, Inexpediency.
I	M	P	O	L	I	T	E	Not polite, Rude, Discourteous, Disrespectful, Ill-bred, Ungracious, Ill-mannered, Incivil.
I	M	P	O	N	E	N	T	One that imposes.
I	M	P	O	N	I	N	G	Staking, Wagering.
I	M	P	O	R	O	U	S	Not porous.
I	M	P	O	R	T	E	D	Denoted, Purported, Signified, Expressed, Intended, Counted, Meant, Weighed.
I	M	P	O	R	T	E	R	One whose business is the importation and sale of goods from a foreign country.
I	M	P	O	S	I	N	G	Inflicting, Creating, Dictating, Levying, Depositing, Commanding, Deceptive, Treacherous.
I	M	P	O	S	T	O	R	Pretender, Fraud, Humbug, Phoney, Deceiver, Cheat, Trickster, Hypocrite.
I	M	P	O	T	E	N	T	Sterile, Weak, Powerless, Crippled, Disabled, Inadequate, Spineless, Ineffectual.
I	M	P	R	I	M	I	S	In the first place.
I	M	P	R	I	S	O	N	Confine, Limit, Restrain, Confine, Incarcerate, Restrict, Check, Curb.
I	M	P	R	O	P	E	R	Incorrect, Inaccurate, Indecent, Indecorous, Ill-timed, Inapt, Unbecoming, Infitting.
I	M	P	R	O	V	E	D	Increased, Augmented, Enlarged, Intensified, Employed, Corrected, Rectified, Remedied.
I	M	P	R	O	V	E	R	A final-year apprentice not yet accepted into a union.
I	M	P	U	D	E	N	T	Insolent, Shameless, Disrespectful, Forward, Audacious, Saucy, Blatant, Brazen.
I	M	P	U	G	N	E	D	Opposed, Resisted, Denied, Gainsaid, Contradicted, Contravened, Assailed, Attacked.
I	M	P	U	N	I	T	Y	Freedom from punishment, Exemption, Immunity.
I	M	P	U	R	E	L	Y	Unchastely, Lewdly, Obscenely, Filthy, Uncleanly, Vilely, Dirtily, Unholy.
I	M	P	U	R	I	T	Y	Something impure.
I	M	P	U	R	P	L	E	Empurple.
I	M	P	U	T	I	N	G	Considering, Regarding, Reckoning, Ascribing, Imparting, Giving, Assigning, Accusing.
I	N	A	C	T	I	O	N	Idleness, Lethargy.
I	N	A	C	T	I	V	E	Sedentary, Indolent, Sluggish, Idle, Passive, Supine, Quiescent, Dormant.
I	N	A	S	M	U	C	H	In view of the fact, Since, Because, For the reason that.
I	N	B	O	R	N			Inherited, Hereditary, Innate.
I	N	C	A	R	N	E	D	Become healed, Covered with flesh.
I	N	C	A	S	I	N	G	Encasing.
I	N	C	E	N	S	E	D	Angered, Enraged, Infuriated, Inflamed, Maddened, Scented, Perfumed, Flattered.
I	N	C	E	P	T	O	R	One that begins or introduces.
I	N	C	H	M	E	A	L	Gradually, Little by little.

1	2	3	4	5	6	7	8	
I	N	C	H	O	A	T	E	Start, Formless, Shapeless.
I	N	C	I	D	E	N	T	Happening, Occurrence, Factor, Liable, Circumstance, Episode, Event, Occasion.
I	N	C	I	S	I	N	G	Engraving, Carving, Gashing, Piercing, Slashing, Etching, Slicing, Slitting.
I	N	C	I	S	I	O	N	Resembling a typical incisor tooth, Shaped for cutting.
I	N	C	I	S	I	V	E	Clear-cut, Crisp, Trenchant, Cutting, Biting, Penetrating, Acute, Sharp.
I	N	C	I	S	O	R	Y	Sharp.
I	N	C	I	S	U	R	E	Notch, Cleft, Fissure of an organ.
I	N	C	I	T	A	N	T	Inciting, Causative, Stimulating.
I	N	C	I	T	I	N	G	Stirring, Spurring, Instigating, Fomenting, Abetting, Provoking, Agitating, Exciting.
I	N	C	I	V	I	S	M	Lack of patriotism.
I	N	C	L	I	N	E	D	Leaned, Sloped, Willing, Disposed, Prone, Apt, Given, Liable.
I	N	C	L	I	N	E	R	One that inclines.
I	N	C	L	O	S	E	D	Enclosed.
I	N	C	L	U	D	E	D	Enclosed, Confined, Embraced, Encompassed, Involved, Numbered, Embodied, Subsumed.
I	N	C	O	M	I	N	G	Arriving, Revenue, Accruing, Starting, Beginning, Entering.
I	N	C	R	E	A	S	E	Grow, Advance, Wax, Enlarge, Augment, Multiply, Compound, Boost.
I	N	C	R	E	A	T	E	Uncreated, Self-existent.
I	N	C	R	O	A	C	H	Encroach.
I	N	C	R	U	E	N	T	Unbloody.
I	N	C	U	B	A	T	E	Brood, Develop, Give form and substance.
I	N	C	U	B	O	U	S	Overlapping like shingles.
I	N	C	U	D	A	T	E	Having an incus, small ear-bone.
I	N	C	U	M	B	E	R	Encumber.
I	N	C	U	R	R	E	D	Contracted, Acquired, Induced, Entailed, Brought.
I	N	C	U	R	V	E	D	Curved, Crooked, Bent.
I	N	C	U	S	I	N	G	Stamping, Punching-as in old coins.
I	N	D	A	G	A	T	E	Investigate.
I	N	D	A	M	I	N	E	Class of organic base that is amino-phenyl derivative.
I	N	D	A	N	G	E	R	Endanger.
I	N	D	A	Z	O	L	E	A feebly basic crystalline bicyclic compound.
I	N	D	E	B	T	E	D	Beholden, Obliged, Obligated, Duty-bound, Honour-bound.
I	N	D	E	C	E	N	T	Unseemly, Unsightly, Uncomely, Indecorous, Improper.
I	N	D	E	N	T	E	D	Notched, Duplicated, Marginal cut.
I	N	D	E	V	O	U	T	Not devout.
I	N	D	E	X	I	N	G	Listing, Indicating.
I	N	D	I	A	M	A	N	A large sailing ship used in trade with India.
I	N	D	I	C	A	N	T	Something that serves to indicate.
I	N	D	I	C	A	T	E	Betoken, Attest, Argue, Prove, Point, Hint, Imply, Suggest.
I	N	D	I	C	T	E	D	Accused, Charged, Arraigned, Incriminated, Inculpated, Taxed, Impeached.
I	N	D	I	C	T	E	E	One that is indicted.
I	N	D	I	G	E	N	E	Deficiency, Native, Neediness.
I	N	D	I	G	E	N	T	Impoverished, Poor, Needy, Deficient, Impecunious, Penniless, Penurious.
I	N	D	I	G	O	I	D	Resembling indigo.
I	N	D	I	R	E	C	T	Roundabout, Deceitful, Dishonest, Oblique, Circular, Crooked, Devious, Twisting.
I	N	D	I	T	I	N	G	Composing, Writing, Inscribing.
I	N	D	O	C	I	L	E	Unruly, Fractious, Intractable, Recalcitrant, Wild, Undisciplined, Unmangeable.
I	N	D	O	L	E	N	T	Lazy, Easygoing, Slothful, Slowgoing, Work-shy, Apathetic.
I	N	D	O	R	S	E	D	Endorsed.
I	N	D	R	E	N	C	H	Drench, Drown, Saturate.
I	N	D	U	C	I	N	G	Influencing, Persuading, Effecting, Causing, Prevailing, Convincing, Procuring, Motivating.
I	N	D	U	C	T	E	D	Installed, Conducted, Initiated, Inaugurated, Invested.
I	N	D	U	C	T	O	R	One who installs another.
I	N	D	U	L	G	E	D	Pampered, Humoured, Spoiled, Mollycoddled, Bestowed, Gratified, Obliged, Delighted.
I	N	D	U	L	G	E	R	One that indulges.
I	N	D	U	L	I	N	E	Class of blue or violet dyes related to the safranines.
I	N	D	U	R	A	T	E	Make hardy, Confirm, Harden, Callousness, Obstinacy, Obdurateness, Sclerosis.
I	N	D	U	S	I	A	L	Relating to a membranic covering.
I	N	D	U	S	I	U	M	Cuplike fringe, Fleshy ring of a fungi.
I	N	D	U	S	T	R	Y	Skill, Cleverness, Business, Commerce, Trade, Traffic.
I	N	E	D	I	B	L	E	Not edible, Unfit for food.
I	N	E	D	I	T	E	D	Unpublished.
I	N	E	Q	U	I	T	Y	Injustice, Unfairness, Unjustness, Wrong.
I	N	E	R	R	A	N	T	Unerring, Infallible, Sure, Accurate, Correct, Precise, Reliable, Trustworthy.
I	N	E	R	T	I	O	N	Inertness, Quietude.
I	N	E	X	P	E	R	T	Inskilled, Unpracticed, Unseasoned, Incompetent, Inefficient, Untried, Unversed, Inapt.
I	N	F	A	M	I	N	G	Defaming.
I	N	F	A	M	I	Z	E	To make infamous.

1	2	3	4	5	6	7	8	
I	N	F	A	M	O	U	S	Detestable, Abhorrent, Vicious, Contemptible, Villainous, Notorious, Atrocious, Scandalous.
I	N	F	A	N	T	R	Y	Foot-soldiers.
I	N	F	E	C	T	E	D	Contaminated, Tainted, Affected, Induced to support.
I	N	F	E	C	T	U	M	Category of tenses in Latin.
I	N	F	E	C	U	N	D	Unfruitful, Infertile, Unproductive, Sterile, Barren, Impotent.
I	N	F	E	R	I	O	R	Lower, Nether, Mediocre, Second-rate, Lesser, Minor, Subordinate, Indifferent.
I	N	F	E	R	N	A	L	Hellish, Diabolical, Fiendish, Damnable, Damned, Plutonic, Devilish, Cursed.
I	N	F	E	R	R	E	D	Deduced, Concluded, Judged, Gathered, Hinted, Indicated, Surmised, Derived.
I	N	F	E	S	T	E	D	Overrun, Haunted, Worried, Annoyed, Swarmed, Crawled, Beset, Plagued.
I	N	F	E	S	T	E	R	To cause to fester.
I	N	F	A	C	E	T	E	Heavy-footed, Not witty.
I	N	F	I	L	T	E	R	Filter, Sift.
I	N	F	I	N	I	T	E	Boundless, Immeasurable, Vast, Immense, Endless, Inexhaustible, Eternal, Perpetual.
I	N	F	I	N	I	T	Y	Boundless, Unlimited capacity, Nonexistent limit, Eternity, Endless, Indefinite.
I	N	F	I	R	M	E	D	Deprived of strength, Invalidated.
I	N	F	I	R	M	L	Y	Feebly, Insecurely.
I	N	F	L	A	M	E	D	Kindled, Excited, Exasperated, Irritated, Incensed, Enraged, Provoked, Aggravated.
I	N	F	L	A	M	E	R	One that inflames.
I	N	F	L	A	T	E	D	Expanded, Dilated, Elated, Increased, Bombastic, Pompous, Exaggerated, Turgid.
I	N	F	L	A	T	O	R	Hand air pump.
I	N	F	L	A	T	U	S	Afflatus, Inspiration.
I	N	F	L	E	X	E	D	Turned or bent inward or downward.
I	N	F	L	U	E	N	T	Affluent, Flowing water contributing to stability of water table, Determining factor in ecology.
I	N	F	O	L	D	E	D	Enfolded, Folded inward.
I	N	F	O	R	M	A	L	Unofficial, Casual, Unceremonious, Spontaneous, Simple, Easy-going, Relaxed, Natural.
I	N	F	O	R	M	E	D	Acquainted, Apprised, Advised, Notified, Advertised, Told, Warned, Betrayed.
I	N	F	O	R	M	E	R	Busybody, Gossip, Betrayer, Squealer, Tattler, Tipster, Stool pigeon.
I	N	F	R	A	D	I	G	Undignified.
I	N	F	R	A	R	E	D	Thermal radiation of wavlengths longer than those of visible light.
I	N	F	R	I	N	G	E	Destroy, Defeat, Frustrate, Confute, Impair, Weaken, Violate, Transgress.
I	N	F	U	M	A	T	E	Clouded with blackish colour.
I	N	F	U	S	I	N	G	Introducing, Insinuating, Suggesting, Inspiring, Imbuing, Animating, Instilling, Suffusing.
I	N	F	U	S	I	O	N	Act of introducing, Steeping or soaking in a liquid.
I	N	F	U	S	I	V	E	Inspiring, Influencing.
I	N	F	U	S	O	R	Y	Relating to minute organisms found in infusions of decaying organic matter.
I	N	G	A	T	H	E	R	Assemble.
I	N	G	E	S	T	E	D	Swallowed, Absorbed, Eaten.
I	N	G	I	V	I	N	G	Handing in thread to a loom.
I	N	G	R	O	W	T	H	Something that grows inward.
I	N	G	U	I	N	A	L	Abdominal region, Relating to area of the groin.
I	N	H	A	L	A	N	T	A medicinal substance that is inhaled.
I	N	H	A	L	I	N	G	Breathing in, Consuming greedily.
I	N	H	E	R	E	N	T	Intrinsic, Essential, Congenital, Constitutional, Ingrained, Inborn, Inbred.
I	N	H	E	R	I	N	G	Belonging, Consisting, Existing, Residing, Dwelling.
I	N	H	E	S	I	O	N	Inherence.
I	N	H	O	O	P	E	D	Enclosed in a hoop.
I	N	H	U	M	I	N	G	Burying, Interring.
I	N	I	M	I	C	A	L	Hostile, Unfriendly, Adverse, Prejudicial.
I	N	I	Q	U	I	T	Y	Wickedness, Gross injustice, Sin, Evil, Crime, Wrongdoing.
I	N	I	T	I	A	T	E	Begin, Commence, Enter, Inaugurate, Launch, Introduce, Institute, Originate.
I	N	J	E	C	T	E	D	Forced, Introduced, Driven, Thrown, Congested.
I	N	J	E	C	T	O	R	Jet pump.
I	N	J	U	R	A	N	T	An injurious substance.
I	N	J	U	R	I	N	G	Harming, Hurting, Damaging, Impairing, Spoiling, Marring, Offending, Prejudicing.
I	N	K	I	N	E	S	S	State of being inky or murky.
I	N	K	S	T	A	N	D	A stand with a container for holding ink for pens.
I	N	L	A	N	D	E	R	One that lives inland.
I	N	L	A	W	I	N	G	Placing under the protection of the law.
I	N	L	A	Y	I	N	G	Fusing of material into an incised cavity of another material.
I	N	N	A	T	E	L	Y	Naturally, Constitutionally, Elementally, Normally, Regularly.
I	N	N	E	R	V	E	D	Invigorated, Stimulated.
I	N	N	O	C	E	N	T	Blameless, Pure, Candid, Artless, Unsuspecting, Innocuous, Harmless, Guiltless.
I	N	N	O	V	A	T	E	Change, Invent, Originate, Create, Introduce.
I	N	N	U	E	N	D	O	Hint, Insinuation, Allusion.
I	N	O	C	U	L	A	R	Inserted in a notch in the corner of the eye.
I	N	O	C	U	L	U	M	Laboratory material for use in innoculation.
I	N	O	R	N	A	T	E	Unadorned.

1	2	3	4	5	6	7	8	
I	N	O	S	I	T	O	L	Crystalline stereoisomeric cyclic hexahydroxy alcohol.
I	N	Q	U	I	R	E	D	Asked, Investigated, Probed, Researched, Examined, Interrogated, Questioned, Scrutinized.
I	N	Q	U	I	R	E	R	Questioner.
I	N	S	A	N	E	L	Y	Absurdly, Ridiculously, Foolishly, Crazily, Silly.
I	N	S	A	N	I	T	Y	Lunacy, Psychosis, Mania, Dementia, Delirium, Hysteria, Craziness, Inanity.
I	N	S	C	I	E	N	T	Based on ignorance.
I	N	S	C	R	I	B	E	Write, Engrave, Print, Enrol, List, Catalogue, Etch, Impress.
I	N	S	C	R	O	L	L	Enscroll.
I	N	S	E	A	M	E	D	An inner seam, A hidden seam.
I	N	S	E	C	T	E	D	Segmented.
I	N	S	E	C	U	R	E	Uncertain, Unstable, Unsure, Unassured, Unconfident, Hesitant, Questioning.
I	N	S	E	R	T	E	D	Introduced, Interpolated, Insinuated, Interposed, Interjected.
I	N	S	E	T	T	E	D	Set in, Placed in an insert.
I	N	S	H	R	I	N	E	Enshrine.
I	N	S	I	G	N	I	A	Distinctive marks, badges or signs, Badge, Emblem.
I	N	S	I	S	T	E	D	Persevered, Persisted, Asserted, Forced, Pressed, Maintained, Urged.
I	N	S	I	T	I	O	N	Adding by means of a graft.
I	N	S	N	A	R	E	D	Ensnared.
I	N	S	O	L	A	T	E	Exposed to the sun's rays.
I	N	S	O	L	E	N	T	Overbearing, Extravagant, Excessive, Proud, Impertinent, Supercilious, Disdainful, Uncivil.
I	N	S	O	M	N	I	A	Prolonged inability to sleep.
I	N	S	O	M	U	C	H	In as much.
I	N	S	P	H	E	R	E	Ensphere.
I	N	S	P	I	R	E	D	Encouraged, Inhaled, Aroused, Provoked, Motivated, Impelled, Affected, Incited.
I	N	S	P	I	R	E	R	One that inspires.
I	N	S	P	I	R	I	T	Animate, Hearten, Encourage, Cheer, Embolden, Nerve, Inform, Strengthen.
I	N	S	T	A	B	L	E	Unstable.
I	N	S	T	A	N	C	E	Instigation, Suggestion, Case, Illustration, Example, Sample, Specimen, Item.
I	N	S	T	A	N	C	Y	Urgency, Insistence, Imminence.
I	N	S	T	A	T	E	D	Installed, Bestowed, Conferred.
I	N	S	T	I	N	C	T	Filled, Charged, Impulse, Natural or inherent attitude or capacity.
I	N	S	T	R	U	C	T	Teach, Command, Educate, Apprise, Prepare, Train, Discipline, Direct.
I	N	S	T	Y	L	E	D	Called, Denominated.
I	N	S	U	C	K	E	N	Being bound by a milling rule.
I	N	S	U	L	A	T	E	Separate, Shield, Segregate, Isolate, Sterilize.
I	N	S	U	L	T	E	D	Affronted, Attached, Assaulted, Assailed, Abused, Offended, Annoyed, Vaunted.
I	N	S	U	L	T	E	R	One that insults.
I	N	S	U	R	A	N	T	Holder of life insurance policy.
I	N	S	U	R	I	N	G	Assuring against a loss. Ensuring, Underwriting, Guarding, Protecting, Shielding.
I	N	T	A	G	L	I	O	Design in sunk relief.
I	N	T	A	R	S	I	A	Wood mosaic, Marquetry.
I	N	T	E	G	R	A	L	Constitutent, Inherent, Complete, Composite, Entire, Perfect, Totality.
I	N	T	E	N	D	E	D	Apphrehended, Signified, Meant, Designed, Proposed, Maintained, Asserted, Extended.
I	N	T	E	N	D	E	R	A person who intends.
I	N	T	E	N	T	L	Y	Closely, Searchingly, Sharply, Hard, Earnestly, Seriously.
I	N	T	E	R	A	C	T	Have reciprocal effect, Collaborate, Co-operate, Combine, Join, Merge, Unite.
I	N	T	E	R	C	O	M	Intercommunication system.
I	N	T	E	R	E	S	T	Affect, Concern, Stake, Claim, Business, Benefit, Profit, Curiosity.
I	N	T	E	R	I	O	R	Inside, Inner, Inland, Internal, Inward, Intimate, Heart.
I	N	T	E	R	L	A	P	Overlap.
I	N	T	E	R	L	A	Y	Placed between two outer agents.
I	N	T	E	R	M	I	T	Discontinue, Interrupt, Suspend, Defer, Delay, Postpone, Check, Arrest.
I	N	T	E	R	M	I	X	Mix, Blend, Commingle, Mingle, Admix, Interfuse, Intermingle.
I	N	T	E	R	N	A	L	Inward, Interior, Inner, Private, Subjective, Domestic, Home, Municipal.
I	N	T	E	R	N	E	D	Confined, Imprisoned, Constrained, Incarcerated, Jailed.
I	N	T	E	R	N	E	E	A person interned.
I	N	T	E	R	R	E	D	Buried, Inhumed, Deposited in the earth.
I	N	T	E	R	R	E	X	One who exercises power during a break in monarchy or government.
I	N	T	E	R	S	E	T	Set between other things.
I	N	T	E	R	S	E	X	An intergrade between the sexes.
I	N	T	E	R	T	I	E	Connect or fasten mutually.
I	N	T	E	R	V	A	L	Intermission, Pause, Break, Lull, Interlude, Gap, Breach, Interim.
I	N	T	E	R	W	A	R	Lying between wars.
I	N	T	E	R	W	E	D	Intermarry.
I	N	T	E	X	I	N	E	The inner membrane of a pollen grain.
I	N	T	I	M	A	C	Y	Acquaintance, Experience, Familiarity, Inwardness.
I	N	T	I	M	A	T	E	Inherent, Essential, Ingrained, Familiar, Confidential, Affectionate, Devoted, Secret.

1	2	3	4	5	6	7	8	
I	N	T	I	M	I	T	Y	Intimate, Privacy.
I	N	T	O	N	A	T	E	Intone, Utter.
I	N	T	O	N	I	N	G	Reciting in singing tones, Chanting.
I	N	T	R	A	D	O	S	Inner surface of a vault, Interior curve of an arch.
I	N	T	R	E	N	C	H	Entrench.
I	N	T	R	E	P	I	D	Brave, Bold, Courageous, Audacious, Dauntless, Fearless, Valiant, Unafraid.
I	N	T	R	I	G	U	E	Beguile, Plot, Scheme, Appeal, Attract, Excite, Connive, Conspire.
I	N	T	R	O	M	I	T	Admit, Introduce, Insert, Meddle, Interfere.
I	N	T	R	O	R	S	E	Facing inward.
I	N	T	R	U	D	E	D	Encroached, Trespassed, Infringed, Invaded, Insinuated, Intervened, Interjected, Disturbed.
I	N	T	R	U	D	E	R	Trespasser, Interloper.
I	N	T	U	B	A	T	E	To introduce a tube into a hollow organ.
I	N	U	N	D	A	N	T	Flooding, Inundating.
I	N	U	N	D	A	T	E	Flood, Submerge, Overwhelm, Swamp, Engulf, Overflow, Deluge.
I	N	U	R	B	A	N	E	Rude, Discourteous, Disrespectful, Ill-bred, Ill-mannered, Impolite, Incivil, Ungracious.
I	N	U	R	N	I	N	G	Entombing.
I	N	U	S	T	I	O	N	Cauterization.
I	N	V	A	D	I	N	G	Encroaching, Infringing, Permeating, Penetrating, Engulfing, Trespassing, Assailing.
I	N	V	A	S	I	O	N	Assault, Intrusion, Foray, Incursion, Raid, Aggression, Offensive, Transgression.
I	N	V	A	S	I	V	E	Tending to invade healthy tissue, Tending to spread.
I	N	V	E	C	K	E	D	Scalloped, Edged by convex semicircles.
I	N	V	E	C	T	E	D	Same as INVECKED.
I	N	V	E	I	G	L	E	Entice, Cajole, Lure, Decoy, Entice, Seduce, Tempt, Bait.
I	N	V	E	I	L	E	D	Enveiled.
I	N	V	E	N	T	E	D	Devised, Originated, Found, Discovered, Initiated, Instituted, Formulated, Contrived.
I	N	V	E	N	T	O	R	Originator.
I	N	V	E	R	S	E	D	Reversed, Inverted.
I	N	V	E	R	T	E	D	Reversed, Transposed, Changed, Reverted, Transplaced, Topsy-turvy, Homosexual.
I	N	V	E	R	T	E	R	Device for converting direct current to alternating current.
I	N	V	E	R	T	O	R	A muscle that turns a part inward.
I	N	V	E	S	T	E	D	Initiated, Inaugurated, Installed, Endowed, Authorized, Enclosed, Infused, Blockaded.
I	N	V	E	S	T	O	R	One that seeks to invest funds for a profit with a minimum of risk.
I	N	V	I	A	B	L	E	Incapable of surviving.
I	N	V	I	N	A	T	E	To make present as in the eucharistic wine.
I	N	V	I	T	I	N	G	Offering, Enticing, Tempting, Encouraging, Welcoming, Asking, Summoning, Soliciting.
I	N	V	O	C	A	T	E	Pray, To make a supplication.
I	N	V	O	I	C	E	D	Billed, Submitted a statement of monies owed for goods or services.
I	N	V	O	K	I	N	G	Enforcing, Implementing, Instigating, Employing, Begging.
I	N	V	O	L	U	T	E	Curled spirally, Disappear, Appealing, Pleading, Imploring.
I	N	V	O	L	V	E	D	Engaged, Entangled, Implicated, Included, Absorbed, Embroiled, Contained, Embraced.
I	N	W	A	L	L	E	D	Enclosed with a wall.
I	N	W	A	R	D	L	Y	Mentally, Spiritually, Fully, Intimately, Inaudibly, Secretly, Internally.
I	O	D	A	T	I	N	G	Treating with iodine or an iodide.
I	O	D	O	F	O	R	M	Yellow crystalline volatile compound with a penetrating persistent odour.
I	O	D	O	N	I	U	M	Univalent cation derived from hydrogen iodine.
I	O	D	Y	R	I	T	E	Yellowish or greenish hexagonal mineral.
I	O	N	I	C	I	T	Y	An Ionic feature.
I	O	N	I	C	I	S	E	To make Ionic.
I	O	N	I	S	I	N	G	Converting into ions.
I	O	T	A	C	I	S	M	Excessive use of "I".
I	R	E	F	U	L	L	Y	Angrily, Furiously, Wrathfully.
I	R	E	N	I	C	A	L	Tranquil, Peaceful, Harmonious, Conciliatory.
I	R	E	N	I	C	O	N	Eirenicon.
I	R	I	S	A	T	E	D	Iridescent.
I	R	I	S	H	I	S	M	Characteristic of the Irish.
I	R	I	S	H	M	A	N	Inhabitant of Ireland.
I	R	O	N	B	A	C	K	Plate of iron for the back of a fireplace.
I	R	O	N	B	A	R	K	Australian eucalyptus tree having hard grey bark and useful timber.
I	R	O	N	C	L	A	D	An armoured naval vessel.
I	R	O	N	G	R	A	Y	Dark grayish colour.
I	R	O	N	I	C	A	L	Sarcastic, Satirical, Cynical, Caustic, Scathing.
I	R	O	N	S	A	N	D	Sand rich in iron ore.
I	R	O	N	S	I	D	E	Man of great strength and bravery.
I	R	O	N	W	A	R	E	Household articles such as cooking vessels made of iron.
I	R	O	N	W	O	O	D	Trees with exceptionally hard or tough wood.
I	R	O	N	W	O	R	K	Decorative work in iron.
I	R	R	I	G	A	T	E	Wet, Moisten, Imbibe, Supplying water for cultivation.

1	2	3	4	5	6	7	8	Definition
I	R	R	I	S	I	O	N	Derision.
I	R	R	I	T	A	N	T	Making null and void, Provoking, Something that irritates or excites.
I	R	R	I	T	A	T	E	Aggravate, Provoke, Exasperate, Annoy, Stimulate, Rile, Nettle, Peeve.
I	R	R	O	R	A	T	E	Moisten, Sprinkled with dew, Speckled.
I	R	R	U	P	T	E	D	Intruded, Erupted.
I	S	A	B	E	L	L	A	Moderate yellowish brown colour.
I	S	A	G	O	G	I	C	Introductory studies.
I	S	A	R	I	T	H	M	A line drawn on a map or chart to connect points having equal numerical values.
I	S	A	T	O	G	E	N	A parent compound isomeric with isatin.
I	S	C	H	E	M	I	A	Localized tissue anemia due to obstruction of the inflow of arterial blood.
I	S	I	D	I	O	I	D	Resembling an outgrowth of lichens.
I	S	L	A	M	I	S	M	The faith, doctrine and cause of Islam.
I	S	L	A	M	I	S	T	Scholar of Islamics.
I	S	L	A	M	I	T	E	Muslim.
I	S	L	A	M	I	Z	E	To bring under the control of Islam.
I	S	L	A	N	D	E	D	Made into a island, Isolated.
I	S	L	A	N	D	E	R	Inhabitant of an island.
I	S	L	E	S	M	A	N	Same as ISLANDER.
I	S	O	B	A	R	I	C	Showing equal barometric pressure.
I	S	O	B	R	O	N	T	A line on a chart marking simultaneous development of a thunderstorm.
I	S	O	B	U	T	Y	L	The primary alkyl radical.
I	S	O	C	H	E	I	M	A line joining points on the earth's surface having the same mean winter temperature.
I	S	O	C	H	E	L	A	A chelate spicule having both ends alike.
I	S	O	C	H	O	R	E	A line representing the variation of pressure with temperature when the volume is constant.
I	S	O	C	O	L	O	N	The use of equal cola in immediate succession.
I	S	O	C	R	A	C	Y	Equality of power or rule.
I	S	O	C	R	Y	M	E	A line on a map connecting points having the same temperature for the coldest time of the year.
I	S	O	D	O	M	O	N	Masonry having blocks of equal length and thickness.
I	S	O	D	O	M	U	M	Same as ISODOMON.
I	S	O	G	O	N	A	L	Having equal angles.
I	S	O	G	O	N	I	C	Same as ISOGONAL.
I	S	O	G	R	A	P	H	Electronic calculator for finding roots of algebraic equations.
I	S	O	L	A	T	E	D	Detached, Separated, Alone, Apart, Removed, Secluded, Unaccompanied, Withdrawn.
I	S	O	L	A	T	O	R	Device that absorbs or prevents transmission of noise or vibration.
I	S	O	L	O	G	U	E	A compound isologous with one or more other compounds.
I	S	O	M	E	R	I	C	Relating to the phenomenon exhibited by two or more chemical compounds, radicals or ions.
I	S	O	M	O	R	P	H	Something identical with or similar to something else in form or shape.
I	S	O	N	I	T	R	O	Acid bivalent group.
I	S	O	P	H	E	N	E	A line on a map connecting places where a particular biological phenomenon occurs.
I	S	O	P	L	E	T	H	A line on a map connecting points where a given variable has a specified constant value.
I	S	O	P	L	O	I	D	Having an even number of genomes in somatic cells.
I	S	O	P	R	E	N	E	A flammable liquid diolefin hydrocarbon.
I	S	O	P	T	E	R	A	Order of termites.
I	S	O	S	P	O	R	A	Parasitic organisms.
I	S	O	S	T	A	S	Y	State of being subjected to equal pressure on all sides.
I	S	O	S	T	E	R	E	A line on a chart connecting points of equal atmospheric pressure.
I	S	O	T	H	E	R	E	A line on a map connecting points having the same summer temperature.
I	S	O	T	H	E	R	M	A line on a chart connecting points having the same temperature at the same time.
I	S	O	T	O	N	I	C	Having the same or equal osmotic pressure.
I	S	O	T	O	P	I	C	Having the relationship of an isotope.
I	S	S	U	A	B	L	E	Authorized for issue.
I	S	S	U	A	N	C	E	Issue.
I	S	T	H	M	I	A	N	Relating to the Isthmus of Corinth in ancient Greece.
I	T	A	L	I	O	T	E	A Greek inhabitant of ancient Italy.
I	T	C	H	M	I	T	E	Minute parasitic mite that burrows into the skin of man and animal and causes an itch.
I	T	E	R	A	N	C	E	Repetition, Reiteration, Recurrence.
I	T	E	R	A	T	E	D	Reoeated.
I	V	O	R	Y	N	U	T	Applenut.

J

1	2	3	4	5	6	7	8	Definition
J	A	B	A	L	I	N	A	Peccary, New World wild swine.
J	A	B	B	E	R	E	D	Chattered, Babbled, Gibbered, Gabbled.
J	A	B	B	E	R	E	R	Chatterbox, Blabbermouth, Prattler, Gossiper.
J	A	C	I	N	T	H	E	Hyacinth, An orange coloured gem.
J	A	C	K	E	R	O	O	Unskilled worker on an Australian sheep ranch.

1	2	3	4	5	6	7	8	Clue
J	A	C	K	B	I	R	D	Bird of New Zealand resembling the starling.
J	A	C	K	B	O	O	T	Heavy black leather military boot with a flaring top.
J	A	C	K	E	T	E	D	Dressed in a jacket, Having an outside covering.
J	A	C	K	F	I	S	H	Pike.
J	A	C	K	F	L	A	G	Small flag of nationality flown by a ship.
J	A	C	K	F	O	O	L	Tomfool.
J	A	C	K	S	T	A	Y	Support for sails, Rigging.
J	A	C	K	W	O	O	D	Wood of the jackfruit tree.
J	A	C	K	Y	A	R	D	A spar to extend a for-and-aft topsail.
J	A	C	O	B	E	A	N	Relating to the time of James and First of England.
J	A	C	O	B	I	T	E	A Stuart supporter after the revolution.
J	A	C	Q	U	A	R	D	Special loom to weave a raised design.
J	A	G	G	E	D	L	Y	Roughly, Harshly, Ragged, Unevenly.
J	A	I	L	B	A	I	T	A temptation to commit an offence punishable by a jail sentence.
J	A	I	L	B	I	R	D	One confined in jail.
J	A	L	O	U	S	I	E	Louvred window, Venitian blind, Slatted shutter.
J	A	L	P	A	I	T	E	A mineral consisting of cupriferous argentite.
J	A	M	A	I	C	A	N	Characteristic of the island of Jamaica.
J	A	M	B	E	A	U	X	Medieval armour for the lower legs.
J	A	M	B	O	R	E	E	Mixed programme of entertainment, Spree, Rally, International assembly of boy scouts.
J	A	N	G	L	I	N	G	Arguing, Wrangling, Altercating, Babbling, Chattering, Jarring, Conflicting, Clashing.
J	A	N	I	C	E	P	S	A mythical monster with two faces.
J	A	N	I	F	O	R	M	Having a face on each of its two sides.
J	A	P	A	N	E	S	E	Relating to Japan.
J	A	P	A	N	I	S	M	Japanese nationalism.
J	A	P	A	N	N	E	D	Having a smooth glossy black enamelled surface.
J	A	P	A	N	N	E	R	A worker who enamels or varnishes to achieve a japanned finish.
J	A	P	A	N	W	A	X	A yellowish fat obtained from sumac berries and used in polishes and textile finishes.
J	A	P	H	E	T	I	C	Derived from Japheth, a son of Noah.
J	A	P	O	N	I	C	A	Camellia.
J	A	R	A	R	A	C	A	S. American pit viper.
J	A	R	O	S	I	T	E	A mineral consisting of basic sulfate of potassium and iron.
J	A	R	O	V	I	Z	E	Vernalize, Hastening the blossoming of flowers and the ripening of fruit and vegetables.
J	A	S	P	A	T	E	D	Speckled.
J	A	S	P	O	N	Y	X	An onyx part whose layers consist of jasper.
J	A	S	S	I	D	A	E	Family of leafhoppers, Pests of cultivated plants which transmit plant diseases.
J	A	T	R	O	P	H	A	Genus of herbs, Physic nut.
J	A	U	N	D	I	C	E	Disease of the liver that produces excessive bile in the blood.
J	A	U	N	T	I	E	R	More stylish, More sprightly, More carefree.
J	A	U	N	T	I	L	Y	Airily, In a light and carefree fashion.
J	A	U	N	T	I	N	G	Making a journey for pleasure or sightseeing.
J	A	V	A	N	E	S	E	Inhabitant of the island of Java.
J	A	V	E	L	I	N	A	Jabalina.
J	A	W	S	M	I	T	H	A professional talker.
J	A	Z	E	R	A	N	T	Armour made of small overlapping plates mounted on a lining.
J	E	B	U	S	I	T	E	Member of Canaanite people living around ancient city of Jebus on the site of Jerusalem.
J	E	C	O	R	I	Z	E	To impart some of the properties of cod liver-oil.
J	E	H	O	V	I	S	T	Jahwist.
J	E	L	L	Y	B	A	G	A bag of cheese cloth used as a strainer for jelly.
J	E	L	U	T	O	N	G	Malayan tree yielding a milky juice used in rubber compound and chewing gum.
J	E	O	P	A	R	D	Y	Trick, Danger, Hazard, Peril, Risk, Accident, Compromise, Exposure.
J	E	R	E	M	I	A	D	A doleful story, Lament, Tirade, Complaint.
J	E	R	O	B	O	A	M	Oversize wine bottle.
J	E	R	O	M	I	A	N	Relating to St Jerome or his works.
J	E	R	R	Y	C	A	N	Five gallon fluid container.
J	E	S	T	B	O	O	K	Book containing jests and jokes, Jokebook.
J	E	S	U	I	T	I	C	Relating to the Jesuits.
J	E	S	U	I	T	R	Y	Principles ascribed to the Jesuits.
J	E	T	B	L	A	C	K	A very intense black.
J	E	T	C	R	A	F	T	An aircraft with jet propulsion.
J	E	T	P	L	A	N	E	Same as JET-CRAFT.
J	E	T	T	I	S	O	N	Casting overboard, abandon, Discard, Abdicate, Cast, Reject, Scrap, Shed.
J	E	T	T	Y	I	N	G	Projecting, Jutting, Extending.
J	E	W	E	L	L	E	D	Adorned or trimmed with jewels, Beautified in a natural fashion.
J	E	W	E	L	L	E	R	One who designs, manufactures, repairs and sells jewellery.
J	E	W	I	S	H	L	Y	Characteristic of the Jewish way of life.
J	E	W	S	H	A	R	P	A small lyre shaped instrument played by holding it in the teeth and plucking the strings.

1	2	3	4	5	6	7	8	
J	E	Z	E	K	I	T	E	Mineral consisting of a basic aluminium calcium sodium fluophosphate.
J	I	G	G	E	R	E	D	Jerked up and down, Rearranged, Altered.
J	I	G	G	L	I	N	G	Moving in a jerky fashion.
J	I	N	G	L	I	N	G	Clinking, Tinkling, Chinkling.
J	I	N	G	O	I	S	H	Tending to arrogant nationalism.
J	I	N	G	O	I	S	M	Belligerent foreign policy.
J	O	A	C	H	I	S	M	Adherence to the doctrines of the Joachimites.
J	O	B	A	T	I	O	N	Scolding, Lecture.
J	O	C	K	E	Y	E	D	Outwitted, Tricked, Gulled, Manipulated, Manoeuvred, Exploited, Beguiled.
J	O	C	O	S	E	L	Y	Jokingly, Wittily, Funnily, Amusingly.
J	O	C	O	S	I	T	Y	Sportive, Whimsical, Joviality.
J	O	C	U	N	D	L	Y	Merrily, Lively, Cheerfully, Gaily.
J	O	D	H	P	U	R	S	Breeches cut full on the hips and close-fitting at the ankles for horse-riding.
J	O	G	G	L	I	N	G	Shaking, Jostling, Tottering, Jiggling.
J	O	I	N	T	I	N	G	Making a joint, Uniting, Caulking joints.
J	O	I	N	T	O	I	L	Synovia, Viscid lubricating fluid of the articulated body parts.
J	O	I	N	T	U	R	E	Union, Juncture, Joint tenancy of an estate.
J	O	I	S	T	I	N	G	Supporting with joists.
J	O	K	I	N	G	L	Y	Jestingly, Banteringly, Joviality.
J	O	L	L	I	E	S	T	Merriest, Blithest, Happiest.
J	O	L	T	H	E	A	D	Dunce, Booby, Blockhead.
J	O	N	G	L	E	U	R	Accompanist for a medieval troubadour, Itinerant medieval minstrel.
J	O	R	D	A	N	O	N	Microspecies.
J	O	R	O	B	A	D	O	Moorfish.
J	O	S	T	L	I	N	G	Pushing, Shoving, Agitating, Disturbing, Hustling, Pressing, Elbowing, Crowding.
J	O	U	N	C	I	N	G	Jolting, Impacting, Bumping, Jarring, Shocking.
J	O	U	S	T	I	N	G	Tilting, Competing in a tournament, Jockeying for an answer to a problem.
J	O	V	I	A	L	L	Y	Merrily, Jolly, Lightheartedly, Humorously.
J	O	Y	F	U	L	L	Y	Gladly, Happily, Joyously.
J	O	Y	O	U	S	L	Y	Rapturously, Ecstatically.
J	O	Y	S	T	I	C	K	Control stick.
J	U	B	I	L	A	N	T	Exultant, Triumphant.
J	U	B	I	L	A	T	E	Exult, Delight, Glory, Triumph.
J	U	B	I	L	E	A	N	Relating to a jubilee.
J	U	D	A	H	I	T	E	Member of the kingdom of Judah.
J	U	D	A	I	Z	E	D	Converted to Judaism.
J	U	D	A	I	Z	E	R	Early Jewish Christian efforts to enforce conformity by all Christians.
J	U	D	G	M	E	N	T	Sentence, Censure, Criticism, Decree, Inference, Deduction, Conclusion, Appraisal.
J	U	D	I	C	I	A	L	Critical, Conventional, Legitimate, Legislative.
J	U	D	I	C	I	U	M	Judgment.
J	U	G	G	L	E	R	Y	Art of a juggler.
J	U	G	G	L	I	N	G	Manual dexterity, Cheating, Trickery, Beguiling, Twisting and turning.
J	U	L	I	E	N	N	E	A clear soup containing vegetables cut into thin strips.
J	U	M	B	L	I	N	G	Mixing, Confusing, Disarranging, Disorganizing, Mussing, Disturbing, Messing.
J	U	M	P	S	E	A	T	Folding or collapsible seat, usually in a plane or car.
J	U	N	K	E	T	E	D	Feasted, Banqueted, Toured, Celebrated.
J	U	N	K	R	I	N	G	A ring forming a base for a piston.
J	U	N	O	N	I	A	S	A rare volute mollusk sought by collectors for the beautiful shell.
J	U	R	A	S	S	I	C	Relating to a prehistoric era.
J	U	R	A	T	O	R	Y	Expressed in an oath.
J	U	R	I	S	T	I	C	Recognized in law.
J	U	R	Y	M	A	S	T	Temporary replacement for a broken mast.
J	U	S	T	L	I	N	G	Jostling.
J	U	S	T	N	E	S	S	Fairness, Rightness, Soundness, Validity, Accuracy, Precision, Righteousness, Nicety.
J	U	V	E	N	I	L	E	Young, Immature, Childish, Unfledged, Youthful, Youngster, Infant, Child.

K

K	A	B	B	A	L	A	H	Written certificate issued by a rabbi.
K	A	F	F	I	Y	A	H	Arab headdress.
K	A	I	L	Y	A	R	D	Sentimental description of the way of life of the Scottish peasant.
K	A	K	A	R	I	K	I	Green parakeet, Green lizard of New Zealand.
K	A	K	E	M	O	N	O	Japanese painting on a hanging scroll of silk.
K	A	L	A	A	Z	A	R	Severe infectious Asian disease, Black fever.
K	A	L	E	N	D	A	R	Ecclesiastical calendar.
K	A	L	E	R	U	N	T	The stem of kale.

1	2	3	4	5	6	7	8	Definition
K	A	L	E	Y	A	R	D	Kallyard.
K	A	L	I	N	I	T	E	A mineral consisting of a fibrous and birefringent hydrous sulfate of potassium and aluminium.
K	A	L	U	M	P	I	T	Philippine tree that yields soft wood and fleshy fruit used for preserves.
K	A	M	A	C	I	T	E	A mineral consisting of a nickel-iron alloy.
K	A	M	A	R	U	P	A	Form assumed by the kama after a person's death.
K	A	M	I	K	A	Z	E	Pilot flying on a suicidal mission.
K	A	M	P	I	L	A	N	Long straight-edged sheathed cutlass.
K	A	N	A	R	E	S	E	Script used in writing Kannada.
K	A	N	D	E	L	I	A	Genus of East Indian tree related to the common mangrove.
K	A	N	G	A	R	O	O	Herbivorous leaping marsupial mammal.
K	A	N	T	I	K	O	Y	Cantico.
K	A	O	L	I	N	I	C	Resembling kaolin.
K	A	P	P	A	R	A	H	A symbolic ceremony performed by Orthodox Jews on the eve of Yom Kippur.
K	A	R	A	B	A	G	H	Small Caucasian rug.
K	A	R	A	K	U	R	T	A venomous spider.
K	A	R	E	L	I	A	N	A region of north western U.S.S.R. and Finnish borders.
K	A	R	Y	O	T	I	N	Stainable material of the cell nucleus.
K	A	S	H	M	I	R	I	Inhabitant of Kashmir.
K	A	S	O	L	I	T	E	A mineral consisting of a hydrous uranium lead silicate.
K	A	T	A	K	A	N	A	A set of Japanese writing symbols.
K	A	U	R	I	G	U	M	A secretion from the kauri tree used in making varnishes and linoleum.
K	E	C	K	L	I	N	G	Winding with rope to prevent chafing.
K	E	D	G	E	R	E	E	Cooked flaked fish, rice, eggs and seasoning.
K	E	E	L	B	O	A	T	Shallow covered river boat.
K	E	E	L	H	A	U	L	To severly rebuke a person.
K	E	E	N	N	E	S	S	Eagerness, Astuteness, Sharpness, Shrewdness, Discrimination, Incisiveness.
K	E	E	P	S	A	K	E	Something given as a memento, Giftbook.
K	E	E	S	H	O	N	D	Breed of small heavy-coated dogs used on barges in Holland as watch-dogs.
K	E	M	A	L	I	S	T	A follower of Ataturk.
K	E	M	A	N	C	H	A	Arabian violin.
K	E	N	O	T	R	O	N	A high vacuum diode used as a rectifer in appliances.
K	E	R	A	T	O	S	A	Horny.
K	E	R	A	T	O	S	E	Horny sponges including commercial sponges.
K	E	R	C	H	I	E	F	A folded square of cloth worn as a head covering.
K	E	R	M	E	S	S	E	A local outdoor festival of the Low Countries for the purpose of raising money for charity.
K	E	R	N	E	L	L	Y	Resembling kernels.
K	E	R	O	S	E	N	E	A flammable hydrocarbon oil that is less volatile than gasoline.
K	E	T	O	X	I	M	E	An oxime of a ketone.
K	E	Y	B	L	O	C	K	Key plate.
K	E	Y	B	O	A	R	D	A bank of keys to operate a musical instrument, a typewriter or a typesetting machine.
K	E	Y	B	U	G	L	E	A bugle having six keys and a chromatic range of about two octaves.
K	E	Y	F	R	U	I	T	Samara.
K	E	Y	M	O	N	E	Y	A bribe paid by a prospective tenant to obtain possession of housing.
K	E	Y	P	L	A	T	E	Part of a stove top in which the lids are placed. Protective plate surrounding a keyhole.
K	E	Y	P	U	N	C	H	A machine actuated by a keyboard and used to cut notches or holes in punched cards.
K	E	Y	S	T	O	N	E	The stone at the crown of an arch, Bondstone in masonry.
K	I	B	I	T	Z	E	R	An onlooker who offers unwanted advice at a card game.
K	I	C	K	A	B	L	E	Deserving to be kicked.
K	I	C	K	D	O	W	N	A change to lower gear.
K	I	C	K	P	I	P	E	A short length of pipe to protect a cable where it emerges from the floor.
K	I	D	G	L	O	V	E	Marked by courtesy and delicate handling.
K	I	E	L	B	A	S	A	Uncooked smoked sausage.
K	I	L	L	C	R	O	P	A greedy baby.
K	I	L	L	D	E	E	R	A plover.
K	I	L	L	O	G	I	E	Sheltered space before a kiln fire.
K	I	L	L	T	I	M	E	An occupation that fills in an idle period.
K	I	L	O	G	R	A	M	Basic metric unit of mass and weight.
K	I	L	O	V	O	L	T	A unit of electric motive force equal to one thousand volts.
K	I	L	O	W	A	T	T	A unit of power equal to one thousand watts.
K	I	N	D	L	E	S	S	Disagreeable, Unsympathetic, Uncongenial, Repellant, Ungenial, Aversive.
K	I	N	D	L	I	E	R	More charitable, More compassionate.
K	I	N	D	L	I	N	G	Igniting, Lighting, Flaring, Provoking, Stimulating, Inciting.
K	I	N	D	N	E	S	S	Courtesy, Indulgence, Service, Favour, Sympathy, Clemency, Affection, Love.
K	I	N	E	S	I	C	S	Systematic study of body language and gestures.
K	I	N	E	T	I	C	S	Branch of dynamics that deals with the effects of forces upon the motions of material bodies.
K	I	N	G	B	I	R	D	Genus of birds, Flycatchers.
K	I	N	G	C	R	A	B	The largest of the edible crabs.

1	2	3	4	5	6	7	8	Clue
K	I	N	G	F	I	S	H	A marine percoid fish.
K	I	N	G	H	O	O	D	Kingship, Majesty.
K	I	N	G	L	E	S	S	Lacking a king.
K	I	N	G	S	H	I	P	Majesty, Monarchy, State of being a king.
K	I	N	G	W	A	N	A	Dialect of Swahili.
K	I	N	G	W	O	O	D	Brazilian wood.
K	I	N	K	A	J	O	U	Nocturnal animal of the raccoon family.
K	I	N	S	F	O	L	K	Kinfolk, Relatives.
K	I	P	P	E	R	E	D	Cured by smoking.
K	I	R	K	Y	A	R	D	Churchyard.
K	I	R	O	U	M	B	O	A coloured bird of Madagascar related to the rollers.
K	I	S	S	A	B	L	E	Attractive enough to be kissed.
K	I	S	S	C	U	R	L	A loose curl on the forehead.
K	I	S	T	V	A	E	N	Prehistorical burial chamber.
K	I	T	T	E	N	E	D	Had a litter of kittens.
K	I	T	T	L	I	S	H	Ticklish.
K	L	Y	S	T	R	O	N	An electron tube converting stream of electrons to high-frequency waves.
K	N	A	P	P	I	N	G	Snapping, Cropping, Rapping, Chattering.
K	N	A	P	S	A	C	K	Bag or case of canvas carried on the back supported by straps over the shoulders.
K	N	A	P	W	E	E	D	A weedy perennial plant.
K	N	E	A	D	I	N	G	Working and pressing with the hands, Manipulating, Massaging.
K	N	E	E	D	E	E	P	Sunk to the knees, Overwhelmed.
K	N	E	E	H	I	G	H	Reaching to the knees.
K	N	E	E	L	I	N	G	Genuflection, Bending at the knees.
K	N	E	I	F	F	I	A	Genus of North American day-blooming herbs, Sundrops.
K	N	E	L	L	I	N	G	Ringing, Tolling, Sounding a warning.
K	N	I	C	K	E	R	S	Bloomers, Underpants.
K	N	I	F	E	B	O	Y	A scullery boy caring for the cutlery.
K	N	I	G	H	T	E	D	To dub a knight, To induct into the order of knighthood.
K	N	I	G	H	T	L	Y	Chivalrous, Relating to a knight.
K	N	I	T	B	A	C	K	A coarse branching hairy comfrey.
K	N	I	T	T	I	N	G	Cementing, Consolidating, Interlacing of yarn by needles to form a fabric.
K	N	I	T	W	E	A	R	Knitted clothing.
K	N	O	C	K	I	N	G	Rapping, Cricitizing, Censuring, Denouncing, Hitting, Swiping, Blaming, Condemning.
K	N	O	C	K	O	U	T	Exhaust, Prostrate, Dispatch, Eliminate, Crush, Squash, Demolish, Destroy.
K	N	O	T	H	E	A	D	Fool, dullard, stupid.
K	N	O	T	H	O	L	E	A hole in a board where a knot has come out.
K	N	O	T	L	E	S	S	Devoid of knots.
K	N	O	T	T	I	E	R	More complex, More intricate, More difficult, Tougher.
K	N	O	T	T	I	N	G	Tieing, Fastening, Connecting, Entangling, Equalizing, Binding, Uniting.
K	N	O	U	T	I	N	G	Flogging with a knout, a lash of leather thongs twisted with wire.
K	N	O	W	A	B	L	E	Capable of being known.
K	N	O	W	A	L	L	S	Wiseacres, Busybodies.
K	N	U	C	K	L	E	D	Yielded, Capitulated, Deferred, Submitted, Projected, Protruded, Struck.
K	O	F	T	G	A	R	I	Indian damascene work in which steel is inlaid with gold.
K	O	H	E	K	O	H	E	A New Zealand tree whose wood is used for furniture.
K	O	H	I	N	O	O	R	A famous diamond that is part of the British crown jewels.
K	O	H	L	E	R	I	A	A genus of rhizomatous tropical American herbs.
K	O	H	L	R	A	B	I	Cabbage with a turnip-shaped stem.
K	O	K	T	A	I	T	E	A mineral consisting of a hydrous sulfate of calcium and ammonium.
K	O	L	I	N	S	K	Y	Pelt of an Asiatic mink.
K	O	T	O	W	I	N	G	Fawning, Cowering, Cringing, Grovelling, Toadying, Kneeling in homage.
K	O	U	R	B	A	S	H	Turkish or Egyptian leather thonged whip.
K	O	Y	E	M	S	H	I	Indian clowns that are credited with being healers.
K	R	A	U	S	I	T	E	A mineral consisting of a hydrous sulfate of potassium and iron.
K	R	E	U	T	Z	E	R	A small Germanic silver coin.
K	R	O	M	E	S	K	Y	A croquette wrapped in bacon, dipped in batter and fried.
K	U	K	U	K	U	K	U	People of Papua, New Guinea.
K	U	R	V	E	Y	O	R	Travelling trader in Southern Africa using an ox-wagon.
K	Y	A	N	I	Z	E	D	Preserving wood by steeping in a solution of corrosive sublimate.
K	Y	P	H	O	S	I	S	Abnormal backward curvature of the spine.

L

1	2	3	4	5	6	7	8	Clue
L	A	B	D	A	N	U	M	Oleoresin obtained from rockroses and used as a fixative in perfumery.
L	A	B	E	L	L	E	D	Ticketed, Tagged, Marked, Designated, Distinguished, Classified.

1	2	3	4	5	6	7	8	Definition
L	A	B	E	L	L	U	M	The lower petal of an orchid.
L	A	B	I	A	L	L	Y	By means of the lips.
L	A	B	I	A	T	E	D	Having lips, having fleshy margins.
L	A	B	I	L	I	T	Y	Unstability, Being changeable, Adaptability.
L	A	B	O	U	R	E	D	Worked, Tired, Distressed, Burdened, Suffered, Cultivated, Arduous, Difficult.
L	A	B	O	U	R	E	R	Worker, Hand, Operative, Workman.
L	A	B	R	I	D	A	E	Family of percoid fishes, Wrasse.
L	A	B	R	U	S	C	A	Forerunner of American cultivated grapes.
L	A	B	U	R	N	U	M	Small genus of Eurasian poisonous shrubs and trees.
L	A	C	C	I	F	E	R	Insects that secrete a resinous substance that is used in the form of shellac.
L	A	C	E	B	A	R	K	An Australian Kurrajong with interlaced baste fibres.
L	A	C	E	L	E	A	F	Lattice plant.
L	A	C	E	R	A	T	E	Tear, Rend, Jagged, Wound, Pierce, Harrow, Torment.
L	A	C	E	R	T	I	D	Genus of lizards.
L	A	C	E	W	I	N	G	Insects having delicate lacy wing venation.
L	A	C	E	W	O	R	K	Something resembling lace.
L	A	C	H	E	S	I	S	American pit viper.
L	A	C	I	N	U	L	A	A narrow flap.
L	A	C	K	A	D	A	Y	Used to express sorrow or regret.
L	A	C	K	E	Y	E	D	Attending, Toadied, Fawned.
L	A	C	O	N	I	A	N	Relating to Laconia, a region of ancient Greece.
L	A	C	O	N	I	S	M	Concise, Brief, Compendiary, Curt, Short, Terse, Succint, Brusque.
L	A	C	R	I	M	A	L	Lachrymal, Marked by tears.
L	A	C	R	O	S	S	E	A game played with long-handled racquets.
L	A	C	T	E	N	I	N	A nitrogenous substance present in milk that inhibits bacterial growth.
L	A	C	T	E	O	U	S	Milky, White.
L	A	C	T	I	F	I	C	Producing milk.
L	A	C	U	N	A	R	Y	Relating to lacunae, Pits.
L	A	C	U	N	O	M	E	Spaces in a typical plant cell.
L	A	D	D	E	R	E	D	Harrowed, Runged, Run in knitted fabric.
L	A	D	L	E	F	U	L	The quantity held by a ladle.
L	A	D	Y	B	I	R	D	Small hemispherical brightly coloured beetle.
L	A	D	Y	F	E	R	N	Widely distributed ferns.
L	A	D	Y	F	I	S	H	Crimson and gold wrasse.
L	A	D	Y	H	E	L	P	Female domestic help accepting low wages in return for acceptance as a social equal.
L	A	D	Y	H	O	O	D	State of being a lady.
L	A	D	Y	L	I	K	E	Well-bred female, Weak, Soft, Yielding.
L	A	D	Y	L	O	V	E	Sweetheart, Mistress.
L	A	D	Y	S	H	I	P	Having the rank of a lady.
L	A	G	T	H	I	N	G	Upper section of the Norwegian parliament.
L	A	I	C	I	Z	E	D	Put under the direction of laymen.
L	A	I	T	A	N	C	E	Scum forming on surface of improperly mixed concrete.
L	A	K	E	L	A	N	D	A region with many lakes.
L	A	K	E	S	I	D	E	On the shore of a lake.
L	A	M	A	N	I	T	E	Descendant of Laman, son of Jewish prophet Lehi.
L	A	M	A	N	T	I	N	Manatee.
L	A	M	A	S	E	R	Y	A monastery of lamas.
L	A	M	B	D	O	I	D	Relating to a suture connecting the occipital and parietal bones.
L	A	M	B	E	N	C	Y	State of wavering or flickering, Brightness.
L	A	M	B	K	I	L	L	A plant that can be poisonous to grazing sheep.
L	A	M	B	L	I	K	E	Gently, Meekly.
L	A	M	B	L	I	N	G	A little young lamb, An innocent child.
L	A	M	B	S	K	I	N	Fine soft leather made from lab or sheepskin.
L	A	M	E	D	U	C	K	Victim, Ne'er-do-well, A person who never achieves great heights, in business of life.
L	A	M	E	L	L	A	S	Resembling plates.
L	A	M	E	N	E	S	S	Weakness, State of being lame.
L	A	M	E	N	T	E	D	Deplored, Sorrowed, Wailed, Wept, Mourned.
L	A	M	E	N	T	E	R	One that laments.
L	A	M	I	N	A	R	Y	In thin layers.
L	A	M	I	N	A	T	E	Unite in layers.
L	A	M	P	H	O	L	E	Inspection shaft between manholes of sewers.
L	A	M	P	P	O	S	T	Post supporting an outdoor lamp.
L	A	M	P	Y	R	I	D	Family of beetles, Glowworms.
L	A	N	A	R	K	I	A	Genus of Silurian fossils.
L	A	N	C	E	G	A	Y	A medieval lance.
L	A	N	C	E	L	E	T	Small marine animals that burrow into sand.
L	A	N	D	C	R	A	B	An edible crab that breeds in the sea and lives on land.

1	2	3	4	5	6	7	8	Definition
L	A	N	D	F	A	L	L	First sight of land after a long voyage.
L	A	N	D	G	I	R	L	A woman farm-hand releasing a male for active service during the war.
L	A	N	D	L	A	D	Y	A woman who rents or leases accommodation to others.
L	A	N	D	L	E	S	S	Having no property.
L	A	N	D	L	I	N	E	A line of transportation or communication.
L	A	N	D	L	O	C	K	Enclosed by land.
L	A	N	D	L	O	R	D	A man who rents or leases property to others, The owner of an inn.
L	A	N	D	M	A	R	K	A conspicuous object serving as a guide.
L	A	N	D	M	I	N	E	A mine placed just below the surface to be detonated by vehicles or troops.
L	A	N	D	S	H	I	P	Covered wagon.
L	A	N	D	S	L	I	P	Landslide.
L	A	N	D	S	M	A	N	One who lives on the land, A newly emigrated Eastern European Jew.
L	A	N	D	W	A	R	D	Rural, Being toward the land.
L	A	N	D	W	E	H	R	Experienced continental soldiers forming second line of defence.
L	A	N	D	W	I	N	D	Land breeze.
L	A	N	G	L	A	U	F	Cross-country running, Racing on skis.
L	A	N	G	O	O	T	Y	Piece of cloth hanging from a waistband worn by lower class people in India.
L	A	N	G	O	S	T	A	Spiny lobster.
L	A	N	G	R	A	G	E	Shot once used in naval warfare.
L	A	N	G	S	H	A	N	Asiatic breed of black or white fowls.
L	A	N	G	S	Y	N	E	A distant time in the past.
L	A	N	G	U	A	G	E	Audible, Articulate, Meaningful sound produced by action of the vocal organ, Tongue.
L	A	N	G	U	I	S	H	Fade, Spiritless, Decline, Deteriorate, Flag, Weaken.
L	A	N	I	A	T	E	D	Torn in pieces.
L	A	N	K	I	E	S	T	Most bony, Most lanky, Leanest.
L	A	N	K	N	E	S	S	Leanness, Scragginess, Gauntness.
L	A	N	N	E	R	E	T	Male falcon.
L	A	N	O	L	I	N	E	Refined wool grease.
L	A	N	T	H	A	N	A	Lanthanum oxide obtained as a white powder.
L	A	N	T	H	O	R	N	Lantern.
L	A	P	A	C	H	O	L	Yellow crystalline colouring matter.
L	A	P	A	C	T	I	C	Cathartic, Laxative.
L	A	P	B	O	A	R	D	A firm board used where a table or desk is not available.
L	A	P	E	L	L	E	D	Clothing made with lapel fronts.
L	A	P	I	D	A	R	Y	A cutter, polisher or engraver of precious stones other than diamonds.
L	A	P	I	D	A	T	E	To pelt or kill with stones.
L	A	P	I	D	I	F	Y	Petrify, Turn into stone.
L	A	P	I	D	I	S	T	Lapidary.
L	A	P	I	L	L	U	S	Small stone or glass fragment of lava, Otolith.
L	A	P	J	O	I	N	T	Joint made by overlapping the edges and securing.
L	A	P	O	L	A	P	U	Philippine grouper.
L	A	P	O	R	T	E	A	Genus of perennial stinging herbs or trees.
L	A	P	P	E	T	E	D	With flaps.
L	A	P	S	A	B	L	E	Liable to slip or to make an error.
L	A	P	S	T	O	N	E	A stone or plate used by a shoemaker for hammering leather soft or pliable.
L	A	R	B	O	A	R	D	Left hand side of a ship.
L	A	R	C	E	N	E	R	Larcenist.
L	A	R	D	E	R	E	R	One in charge of a larder.
L	A	R	G	E	S	S	E	Generosity, Liberality, Gift, Benevolence, Compliment, Favour, Present, Gratuity.
L	A	R	I	I	D	A	E	Bruchidae. Family of small beetles whose larvae infests legumes.
L	A	R	K	S	P	U	R	A cultivated annual plant.
L	A	R	R	I	D	A	E	A family of digger wasps that nest in sandy soil.
L	A	R	R	I	G	A	N	A moccasin favoured by trappers.
L	A	R	R	I	K	I	N	Hoodlum, Rowdy, Boisterous.
L	A	R	V	A	T	E	D	Concealed by a mask.
L	A	R	Y	N	G	A	L	Relating to the larynx.
L	A	S	E	R	I	N	G	A device that utilises the natural oscillation of atoms.
L	A	S	H	I	N	G	S	Much, Lot, Mass, Mountain, Power, Barrel.
L	A	S	I	U	R	U	S	A genus of bats.
L	A	S	S	L	O	R	N	Being rejected by a sweetheart.
L	A	T	A	N	I	A	S	Small genus of fan palms.
L	A	T	C	H	K	E	Y	A front door key.
L	A	T	E	N	E	S	S	Tardiness, Slowness.
L	A	T	E	N	T	L	Y	Secretly, Dormantly.
L	A	T	E	R	I	T	E	A residual product of rock decay.
L	A	T	H	E	R	E	D	Frothed, Foamed, Flogged, Excited, Agitated.
L	A	T	H	R	A	E	A	Genus of parasitic plants.

1	2	3	4	5	6	7	8	
L	A	T	I	N	I	S	M	Characteristic of Latin.
L	A	T	I	N	I	S	T	A person skilled in Latin.
L	A	T	I	N	I	T	Y	Manner of speaking or writing Latin.
L	A	T	I	N	I	Z	E	To give a Latin form.
L	A	T	I	N	X	U	A	A system for romanization of the Chinese language.
L	A	T	I	T	U	D	E	Breadth, Width, Angular distance north or south from the equator.
L	A	T	R	I	D	A	E	Small family of marine percoid fishes, Trumpeters.
L	A	T	T	E	R	L	Y	At a subsequent time.
L	A	T	T	I	C	E	D	Arranged in strips resembling lattice work.
L	A	U	D	A	B	L	E	Commendable, Healthy, Worthy, Admirable, Estimable, Deserving, Praiseworthy.
L	A	U	D	A	B	L	Y	Healthily, Admirably.
L	A	U	D	A	N	U	M	Opium preparation.
L	A	U	G	H	I	N	G	Laughable, Merry, Jocular.
L	A	U	G	H	T	E	R	Amusement, Exuberance.
L	A	U	N	C	H	E	D	Shot, Flung, Commenced, Initiated, Introduced, Plunged, Pitched, Tossed.
L	A	U	R	E	A	T	E	Relating to a prizewinner, Crowned with laurel.
L	A	V	A	L	A	V	A	Rectangular cloth worn like a kilt by the Polynesian people.
L	A	V	A	T	I	O	N	Washing, Cleansing.
L	A	V	A	T	O	R	Y	Water closet, A room with conveniences for washing and a toilet.
L	A	V	E	N	D	E	R	Mediterranean mint cultivated for its aromatic leaves and blooms.
L	A	V	E	R	O	C	K	Lark.
L	A	V	I	S	H	E	D	Squandered, Wasted, Overdoing.
L	A	V	I	S	H	L	Y	Wastefully, Profusely, Grandly, Sumptuously.
L	A	W	F	U	L	L	Y	Legally, Legitimately, Rightfully.
L	A	W	G	I	V	E	R	Legislator.
L	A	W	M	A	K	E	R	One that makes laws.
L	A	W	Y	E	R	L	Y	Lawyerlike.
L	A	X	A	T	I	O	N	Relaxing.
L	A	X	A	T	I	V	E	A medication to relieve constipation, Loose, Unrestrained.
L	A	Y	A	B	O	U	T	Lazy, Good-for-nothing, Tramp, Loafer.
L	A	Y	C	L	E	R	K	Member of a choir in an Anglican cathedral.
L	A	Y	E	L	D	E	R	Presbyterian elder.
L	A	Y	E	R	I	N	G	Shading of the areas between contour lines on a map.
L	A	Y	S	T	A	L	L	A rubbish tip.
L	A	Z	A	R	I	S	T	Roman Catholic missionary.
L	A	Z	I	N	E	S	S	Slackness, Idleness, Indolence, Sluggishness.
L	A	Z	U	L	I	N	E	Colour of lapis lazuli.
L	A	Z	U	L	I	T	E	An azure-blue mineral.
L	A	Z	U	R	I	T	E	A mineral occurring as the chief constituent of lapis lazuli.
L	E	A	C	H	I	N	G	Process of separating the soluble components from a mixture by percolation, Dissolving.
L	E	A	D	S	M	A	N	A man using a sounding lead to determine the depth of water.
L	E	A	F	L	A	R	D	Lard made from leaf fat.
L	E	A	F	L	E	S	S	Lacking leaves.
L	E	A	G	U	I	N	G	Besieging, Encamping.
L	E	A	N	N	E	S	S	Slenderness, Gauntness, Thinness, Lacking fat.
L	E	A	P	F	R	O	G	Pass or go ahead in turn one after another, To evade by a bypass.
L	E	A	P	Y	E	A	R	The year when an extra day is inserted at the end of February.
L	E	A	R	N	I	N	G	Gaining knowledge, Receiving instruction, Education, Erudition.
L	E	A	S	A	B	L	E	Capable of being leased.
L	E	A	S	H	I	N	G	Controlling, Restraining, Tying together.
L	E	A	T	H	E	R	N	Suggestive of leather, Consisting of leather.
L	E	A	T	H	E	R	Y	Tough, Resembling leather.
L	E	A	V	E	N	E	D	Aerated, Infused.
L	E	A	V	I	N	G	S	Remnants, Relics, Remainder, Balance.
L	E	B	A	C	H	I	A	Genus of fossil conifers.
L	E	B	A	N	E	S	E	Style prevalent in Lebanon.
L	E	C	A	N	O	R	A	Genus of lichens.
L	E	C	I	T	H	A	L	Having a yolk.
L	E	C	I	T	H	I	N	Commercially produced mixture of phosphatides.
L	E	C	T	U	R	E	D	Talked, Addressed, Spoken, Rebuked, Reprimanded.
L	E	C	T	U	R	E	R	One giving a lecture course at a college or university.
L	E	C	Y	T	H	U	S	A shaped vase used in ancient Greece for oils and ointments.
L	E	E	B	O	A	R	D	Wood or metal planes attached outside a ship's hull as stabilisers.
L	E	E	C	H	I	N	G	Curing, Healing, Draining, Exhausting, Hanging-on, Sponging.
L	E	E	F	A	N	G	E	Traveller.
L	E	E	S	H	O	R	E	Source of peril, Cause of ruin.
L	E	F	T	W	A	R	D	Toward the left.

8 LETTERS

1	2	3	4	5	6	7	8	Definition
L	E	F	T	W	I	N	G	Political division favouring leftist principles and practices.
L	E	G	A	C	I	E	S	Bequests, Inheritances, Birthrights.
L	E	G	A	L	I	S	M	Adherence to the letter of the law as distinguished from the spirit.
L	E	G	A	L	I	S	T	One that advocates theological legalism.
L	E	G	A	L	I	T	Y	Lawfulness, Being legal.
L	E	G	A	L	I	Z	E	Sanction, To give legal validity, Authenticate a document.
L	E	G	A	T	A	R	Y	Legatee, Relating to a legacy.
L	E	G	A	T	I	N	E	Enacted under the authority of a legate.
L	E	G	A	T	I	O	N	Embassy, Diplomatic mission.
L	E	G	B	R	E	A	K	Special type of bowled ball in cricket.
L	E	G	E	R	I	T	Y	Nimbleness, Mental or physical agility.
L	E	G	G	I	E	R	O	Direction in music, lightly, gracefully.
L	E	G	I	O	N	E	D	Formed into a large military force.
L	E	G	U	A	N	I	D	Genus of fossil birds.
L	E	I	S	U	R	E	D	Having leisure.
L	E	M	O	N	A	D	E	Beverage of diluted sweetened lemon juice.
L	E	M	U	R	I	N	E	Genus of arboreal nocturnal mammals, Lemurs.
L	E	M	U	R	O	I	D	Lemurine.
L	E	N	D	A	B	L	E	Available for lending.
L	E	N	G	T	H	E	N	Prolong, Protract, Elongate, Extend, Stretch.
L	E	N	I	E	N	C	E	Indulgent, Merciful.
L	E	N	I	E	N	C	Y	Same as LENIENCE.
L	E	N	I	N	I	S	M	Social principles advocated by Lenin.
L	E	N	I	N	I	S	T	Adherent of Leninism.
L	E	N	I	N	I	T	E	Same as LENINIST.
L	E	N	I	T	I	V	E	Alleviating pain or acrimony, Palliative, Assuasive, Mitigating, Soothing, Gentle.
L	E	N	S	H	O	O	D	Shade for a camera lens.
L	E	N	T	A	N	D	O	Used as a direction in music, in a retarding manner.
L	E	N	T	I	C	E	L	A pore that is common in the stems of woody plants.
L	E	N	T	I	C	L	E	Lentil, A geological lens of moderate length.
L	E	N	T	L	I	L	Y	Daffodil, Madonna lily.
L	E	N	Z	I	T	E	S	Genus of bracket fungi.
L	E	P	I	D	O	T	E	Covered with scurf or scurfy scales.
L	E	P	O	R	I	N	E	Resembling a hare.
L	E	P	R	O	M	I	N	Human leprous tissue used in a skin test for leprosy infection.
L	E	P	R	O	S	I	S	Disease of the sweet orange.
L	E	S	S	E	N	E	D	Decreased, Curtailed, Diminished, Clipped, Abated, Dwindled, Reduced, Truncated.
L	E	T	H	A	R	G	Y	Lassitude, Apathy, Langour, Stupor, Laziness, Torpidity, Torpor, Dullness.
L	E	T	T	E	R	E	D	Printed, Inscribed, Set down in letters, Learned.
L	E	U	C	E	T	T	A	Genus of sponges.
L	E	U	C	I	T	I	C	Resembling leucite.
L	E	U	C	O	R	Y	X	Large pale brownish antelope of north Africa.
L	E	U	C	O	S	I	N	Whitish lumps of carbohydrate in yellowish-green algae.
L	E	U	C	O	S	I	S	Leukosis, Leukemia, Disturbed blood formation.
L	E	V	A	N	T	E	D	Leather with the look of Morocco leather.
L	E	V	A	N	T	E	R	Strong easterly Mediterranean wind, Leather dresser.
L	E	V	E	L	L	E	D	Flattened, Smoothed, Directed, Aimed, Inclined, Pointed, Turned, Grounded.
L	E	V	E	L	L	E	R	Something to reduce or eliminate differences among men.
L	E	V	E	R	A	G	E	Effectiveness, Power, Influence.
L	E	V	E	R	I	N	G	Prying with a lever, Exerting pressure, Raised with a lever.
L	E	V	I	A	B	L	E	Taxable, Can be levied upon.
L	E	V	I	G	A	T	E	To grind to a smooth powder.
L	E	V	I	R	A	T	E	Ancient custom of the marriage of a widow to a brother or heir of her deceased husband.
L	E	V	I	T	A	T	E	Suspend or cause to move in the air, Rise.
L	E	V	I	T	I	E	S	Follies, Frivolities.
L	E	V	U	L	O	S	E	Fructose derived from insulin from dahlia tubers or Jerusalem artichokes.
L	E	W	D	N	E	S	S	Baseness, Evilness, Wickedness.
L	E	W	D	S	T	E	R	A lewd person.
L	E	W	I	S	I	T	E	A mineral consisting of a titain romeite.
L	I	B	A	T	I	O	N	An offering of wine, A ceremonious drink.
L	I	B	E	L	L	E	D	Spread defamation, Maligned.
L	I	B	E	L	L	E	R	One that libels.
L	I	B	E	R	A	T	E	Release, Free, Separate, Disengage, Steal, Emancipate, Detach, Untangle.
L	I	B	E	R	I	A	N	Inhabitant of Liberia.
L	I	B	R	A	T	E	D	Vibrated, Balanced, Weighed.
L	I	B	R	E	T	T	O	Text of an opera or an extended choral composition.
L	I	C	E	N	S	E	D	Authorized, Commissioned, Enabled, Allowed, Permitted, Empowered, Certified, Sanctioned.

1	2	3	4	5	6	7	8	Definition
L	I	C	E	N	S	E	E	One holding a license.
L	I	C	E	N	S	E	R	One that grants licenses.
L	I	C	E	N	S	O	R	Same as LICENSER.
L	I	C	H	E	N	E	S	Major category of lichens.
L	I	C	H	E	N	I	N	Gelatinous polysaccharide composed of glucose units.
L	I	C	H	G	A	T	E	Lych-gate.
L	I	C	K	E	R	I	N	Drum of cylinder in a carding machine.
L	I	C	K	S	P	I	T	Parasite, Hanger-on, Toady.
L	I	C	O	R	I	C	E	Dried root of gummy texture used in confectionery and pharmaceutical products.
L	I	E	G	E	M	A	N	Devoted follower.
L	I	E	N	A	B	L	E	Capable of being the subject of a lien.
L	I	F	E	B	E	L	T	A buoyant belt used as an aid to someone in distress in water.
L	I	F	E	B	O	A	T	Buoyant boat used for rescue work.
L	I	F	E	B	U	O	Y	A buoyant float used to support persons in water.
L	I	F	E	F	O	R	M	Body from characterizing a species at maturity.
L	I	F	E	H	O	L	D	Held for life.
L	I	F	E	L	E	S	S	Dead, Inanimate, Colourless, Dull, Extinct, Defunct, Departed, Drab.
L	I	F	E	L	I	K	E	Representing real life.
L	I	F	E	L	I	N	E	A line to which people cling to try to save their lives, Something for distressed people to use.
L	I	F	E	L	O	N	G	Enduring, Long-lived, Until death, Perennial.
L	I	F	E	P	E	E	R	A British peer with a conferred title for only his or hers lifetime.
L	I	F	E	R	A	F	T	Buoyant raft usually used in case of a shipwreck.
L	I	F	E	R	E	N	T	Personal servitude.
L	I	F	E	S	I	Z	E	A representation equal in size to the original.
L	I	F	E	S	P	A	N	The length of an individual's existence under certain conditions.
L	I	F	E	T	I	M	E	Duration of existence of a living being.
L	I	F	E	W	O	R	K	Work extending over a lifetime.
L	I	F	T	A	B	L	E	Capable of being lifted.
L	I	G	A	M	E	N	T	Tough band of tissue to connect or support parts and organs of the body, Bond, Knot.
L	I	G	A	T	I	N	G	Tying with a ligature.
L	I	G	A	T	I	O	N	Connection, Tying up a blood vessel.
L	I	G	A	T	U	R	E	Surgical material used for binding or tying, Something to unite or connect.
L	I	G	H	T	F	U	L	Bright.
L	I	G	H	T	I	N	G	Brightening, Ignition, Kindling, Illuminating, Animating, Perching, Roosting, Settling.
L	I	G	H	T	I	S	H	Rather light in colour or complexion.
L	I	G	N	E	O	U	S	Made of wood, Woody.
L	I	G	N	I	T	I	C	Variety of coal in which original wood is still visible.
L	I	G	N	O	S	A	E	All plants classified as woody.
L	I	G	R	O	I	N	E	Petroleum naphtha fractions with a wide boiling range.
L	I	G	U	L	A	T	E	Shaped like a strap.
L	I	G	U	L	O	I	D	Genus of tapeworms.
L	I	G	U	R	I	T	E	Apple-green variety of sphene.
L	I	K	E	A	B	L	E	Likable, Attracts regard.
L	I	K	E	N	E	S	S	Resemblance, Similarity, Appearance, Form, Guise, Shape, Effigy, Copy.
L	I	K	E	N	I	N	G	Comparing.
L	I	K	E	W	I	S	E	Similarly, Moreover, Besides, In like manner.
L	I	L	I	A	L	E	S	An order of plants with complete trimerous flowers.
L	I	L	L	I	P	U	T	Extremely small, Miniature.
L	I	L	Y	I	R	O	N	Harpoon used for hunting swordfish.
L	I	L	Y	L	I	K	E	Resembling a lily, Pure, Fragile, Fair, Virginal.
L	I	M	A	C	I	N	E	Sluglike.
L	I	M	A	C	O	I	D	Same as LIMACINE.
L	I	M	A	T	I	O	N	Filing, Polishing.
L	I	M	A	W	O	O	D	Soluble red wood from a Peruvian tree and used in dyeing.
L	I	M	B	E	R	L	Y	Nimbly, Lithely, Pliably, Springy, Agilely.
L	I	M	E	K	I	L	N	A furnace for reducing limestone and shells to lime.
L	I	M	E	R	I	C	K	A humorous poem of five lines.
L	I	M	E	T	T	I	N	A colourless crystalline compound from oil of lemons and limes.
L	I	M	E	T	W	I	G	Trap, Snare, A branch covered with bird lime.
L	I	M	E	W	A	S	H	Solution of lime and water as a cheap substitute for paint on walls.
L	I	M	E	W	O	O	D	Wood of the linden tree.
L	I	M	I	N	A	R	Y	Introductory, Preliminary.
L	I	M	I	T	A	R	Y	Enclosing, Limiting, Demarcating.
L	I	M	I	T	I	N	G	Bounding, Restrictive, Determining, Allotting, Prescribing, Circumscribing, Confining.
L	I	M	N	A	E	I	D	Genus of freshwater snails.
L	I	M	N	E	T	I	C	Inhabiting deep area of fresh water.
L	I	M	N	E	T	I	S	Genus of crustaceans.

1	2	3	4	5	6	7	8	Clue
L	I	M	O	N	E	N	E	Liquid terpene hydrocarbon that has a lemon-like odour.
L	I	M	O	N	I	T	E	Hydrous ferric oxide.
L	I	M	O	N	I	U	M	Genus of shrubby herbs, Sea lavender.
L	I	M	O	N	I	U	S	Genus of click beetles.
L	I	N	A	C	E	A	E	Genus of herbs, Flax.
L	I	N	A	R	I	T	E	Basic lead copper sulfate.
L	I	N	C	H	P	I	N	Locking device, Something that serves to hold together.
L	I	N	E	A	L	L	Y	Hereditary, Directly, In a direct line.
L	I	N	E	A	R	L	Y	Same as LINEALLY.
L	I	N	E	S	M	A	N	An official assisting a referee, A soldier of the line.
L	I	N	G	B	I	R	D	Meadow pipit.
L	I	N	G	E	R	E	D	Delayed, Loitered, Tarried, Dawdled, Hesitated, Postponed, Protracted, Prolonged.
L	I	N	G	E	R	E	R	Loiterer.
L	I	N	G	E	R	I	E	Women's underwear of fine sheer fabrics.
L	I	N	G	U	A	L	E	Midpoint of the lower jaw.
L	I	N	G	U	I	S	T	An expert in languages.
L	I	N	I	M	E	N	T	Embrocation.
L	I	N	O	L	E	I	N	A glycerol ester of linoleic acid.
L	I	N	O	L	E	U	M	Floor covering made by laying solidified linseed oils with additives on a backing of canvas.
L	I	N	O	T	Y	P	E	Typesetting machine operated by a keyboard.
L	I	N	S	T	O	C	K	Pointed stick for holding lighted match to ignite a cannon.
L	I	O	N	I	Z	E	D	Treated as a celebrity.
L	I	P	A	R	I	T	E	Acid volcanic rock.
L	I	P	E	U	R	U	S	Genus of parasitic bird lice.
L	I	P	O	G	R	A	M	A writing composed of words where a certain letter is omitted.
L	I	P	O	I	D	A	L	Fatlike substance.
L	I	P	O	S	O	M	E	A fatty droplet in the cytoplasm.
L	I	P	I	Z	Z	A	N	Lippizaner.
L	I	P	S	T	I	C	K	Waxy solid cosmetic for colouring the lips.
L	I	Q	U	A	T	E	D	Separated by application of heat.
L	I	Q	U	I	D	L	Y	Fluidly, Watery, Smoothly.
L	I	Q	U	I	D	U	S	Curve on a diagram indicating temperatures where only a liquid phase exists.
L	I	Q	U	O	R	E	D	Treated with a liquid substance.
L	I	R	I	P	O	O	P	Part of a medieval headdress.
L	I	S	T	A	B	L	E	Taxable.
L	I	S	T	E	N	E	D	Heard, Heeded, Sounded, Attended, Hearkened.
L	I	S	T	E	N	E	R	One that sets themselves to hear.
L	I	S	T	L	E	S	S	Languid, Spiritless, Enervated, Limp, Lackadaisical, Apathetic, Heedless, Thoughtless.
L	I	T	E	R	A	C	Y	Ability to read and write.
L	I	T	E	R	A	R	Y	Well-read, Expert in literature, Formal.
L	I	T	E	R	A	T	E	Able to read and write, Educated, Cultured, Polished, Lucid.
L	I	T	E	R	A	T	I	Educated class, Intelligentsia, Intellectuals, Men of letters, Avant garde.
L	I	T	H	A	R	G	E	Lead monoxide.
L	I	T	H	E	M	I	A	A condition in which the blood contains excess uric acid.
L	I	T	H	O	D	E	S	Deep sea crab.
L	I	T	H	U	R	I	A	Excess of uric acid in the urine.
L	I	T	I	G	A	N	T	One engaged in a lawsuit.
L	I	T	I	G	A	T	E	Contest in law, Prosecute or defend in court.
L	I	T	O	R	I	N	A	Genus of marine periwinkles.
L	I	T	T	E	R	E	D	Cluttered, Jumbled, Spread rubbish, Produced a litter of young.
L	I	T	T	O	R	A	L	Growing near a seashore, Composed of material deposited on or near a shore.
L	I	T	U	R	A	T	E	Spotted.
L	I	V	E	A	B	L	E	Endurable, Bearable, Suitable for living in.
L	I	V	E	A	X	L	E	Driving axle of a self-propelled vehicle.
L	I	V	E	L	I	L	Y	Freshly, Gaily, Springtly.
L	I	V	E	L	O	N	G	Whole, Entire, Complete.
L	I	V	E	N	I	N	G	Becoming more lively.
L	I	V	E	R	I	E	D	Wearing distinctive clothing.
L	I	V	E	R	I	E	S	Uniforms, Garments of a special work.
L	I	V	E	R	I	S	H	Bilious, Crabbed, Melancholy, Suffering from a liver disorder, Jaundiced, Irritable.
L	I	V	E	W	E	L	L	A well in a boat for keeping fish alive.
L	I	V	E	W	I	R	E	An energised electrical conductor, Hustler, An alert active aggressive person.
L	I	V	I	D	I	T	Y	Discolouration, Resembling bruising, Luridly.
L	I	V	I	N	G	L	Y	Vitally, Realistically.
L	I	X	I	V	I	A	L	Alkaline, Extracting by washing or percolation.
L	I	X	I	V	I	U	M	Solution obtained by leaching.
L	O	A	D	L	I	N	E	Line on a ship's hull to show safety limit for loading.

1	2	3	4	5	6	7	8	
L	O	A	I	A	S	I	S	Eye disease caused by a minute worm.
L	O	A	N	A	B	L	E	Available for loan.
L	O	A	N	W	O	R	D	A word borrowed or adopted from another language.
L	O	A	T	H	F	U	L	Shrinking, Reluctant, Bashful.
L	O	A	T	H	I	N	G	Antipathy, Abhorrence, Repulsion, Detestation, Hatred, Revulsion, Repugnance, Aversion.
L	O	B	B	Y	I	N	G	Attempting to secure a desired objective by personal contact.
L	O	B	B	Y	I	S	T	One who lobbies.
L	O	B	E	L	I	N	E	A poisonous crystalline alkaloid obtained from lobelia.
L	O	B	L	O	L	L	Y	Mudhole, An unsightly mess, Thick gruel.
L	O	B	O	T	O	M	Y	A brain operation.
L	O	C	A	L	I	S	M	Placing local interests above national needs.
L	O	C	A	L	I	S	T	One concerned with local matters.
L	O	C	A	L	I	T	Y	Situation, Particular place, Position, District.
L	O	C	A	L	I	Z	E	To assign to a particular place.
L	O	C	A	T	I	N	G	Positioning, Situating, Placing, Siting.
L	O	C	A	T	I	O	N	Place, Point, Position, Site, Spot, Station, Tract.
L	O	C	A	T	I	V	E	A grammatical case that denotes place.
L	O	C	H	E	T	I	C	Lying in wait for prey.
L	O	C	K	F	A	S	T	Made fast by a lock.
L	O	C	K	L	E	S	S	Having no lock.
L	O	C	K	S	M	A	N	Turnkey, Lockkeeper.
L	O	C	K	S	P	I	T	Demarcation by a small trench for future digging.
L	O	C	O	F	O	C	O	Nineteenth century match or cigar ignited by friction, Democrat.
L	O	C	U	L	A	T	E	Divided into cells.
L	O	C	U	S	T	A	L	Relating to locusts.
L	O	C	U	T	I	O	N	Speech, Form of expression, Phraseology, Discourse.
L	O	D	E	S	T	A	R	A star that leads or guides.
L	O	D	G	I	N	G	S	Dwellings, Habitations, Sleeping accommodations, Temporary places to stay in.
L	O	D	G	M	E	N	T	Occupation and holding of a position in enemy territory.
L	O	D	I	C	U	L	E	A delicate membranous stamen scale of a grass.
L	O	G	G	L	A	S	S	Small hourglass used to time the running out of a log-line.
L	O	G	I	C	I	A	N	One skilled in logic.
L	O	G	I	C	I	S	M	Philosophical system with special emphasis on logic.
L	O	G	I	C	I	Z	E	Reason, Convert to a logical form.
L	O	G	I	S	T	I	C	Relating to logic.
L	O	G	O	G	R	A	M	Letter, character or graphic sign to represent an entire word.
L	O	G	O	T	Y	P	E	Single print plate faced with a trademark.
L	O	G	S	L	A	T	E	Folding slate for preliminary notes.
L	O	I	T	E	R	E	D	Dawdled, Lingered, Delayed, Lagged, Procrastinated, Tarried, Idled, Lolled.
L	O	I	T	E	R	E	R	Laggard, Straggler.
L	O	K	E	L	A	N	I	Small fragrant pink or red rose of Hawaii.
L	O	L	L	A	R	D	Y	Principles of the Lollards.
L	O	L	L	I	P	O	P	A disc of candy on a stick.
L	O	L	L	O	P	E	D	Slouched, Lurched, Drooped, Slumped.
L	O	M	A	T	I	N	E	Lobed.
L	O	M	E	N	T	U	M	Dry one-celled fruit.
L	O	M	O	N	I	T	E	White monoclinic mineral consisting of a hydrous calcium and aluminium silicate.
L	O	N	D	O	N	E	R	Native of London.
L	O	N	E	N	E	S	S	Isolation.
L	O	N	E	S	O	M	E	Alone, Unfrequented, Remote, Solitary, Forlorn, Obscure, Removed, Secret.
L	O	N	G	B	O	A	T	Largest boat carried by a merchant sailing ship.
L	O	N	G	E	R	O	N	Supporting parts of an aeroplane fuselage.
L	O	N	G	E	V	A	L	Long lasting.
L	O	N	G	H	A	N	D	Handwriting in the usual fashion.
L	O	N	G	L	E	G	S	Stilt, Daddy longlegs.
L	O	N	G	M	O	S	S	Spanish moss.
L	O	N	G	S	H	I	P	Ship similar to an ancient Norse galley.
L	O	N	G	S	O	M	E	Tediously long.
L	O	N	G	S	P	U	R	Long-clawed birds of the Arctic regions.
L	O	N	G	S	T	O	P	Fielding position in cricket.
L	O	N	G	T	A	I	L	An animal that has an uncut tail.
L	O	N	G	T	I	M	E	Involving a relatively long period of time.
L	O	N	G	W	A	Y	S	A folk dance with the couples facing each other.
L	O	N	G	W	I	S	E	Lengthwise.
L	O	N	I	C	E	R	A	Genus of climbing shrubs, Honeysuckle.
L	O	O	K	E	R	O	N	Onlooker, Spectator, Observer.
L	O	O	P	H	O	L	E	Small opening, A means to escape, An omission by which a debt can be prescribed.

1	2	3	4	5	6	7	8	
L	O	O	S	E	B	O	X	Box-stall.
L	O	O	S	E	N	E	D	Released, Relaxed, Slackened, Undone, Liberated, Freed, Discharged, Emancipated.
L	O	O	S	E	N	E	R	One that loosens.
L	O	P	A	R	I	T	E	A perovskite containing alkalies and cerium.
L	O	P	E	A	R	E	D	Having drooping ears.
L	O	P	E	Z	I	T	E	A mineral consisting of a dichromate of potassium.
L	O	P	O	L	I	T	H	Mass of igneous rock with a basin-shaped base.
L	O	P	S	I	D	E	D	Leaning to one side, Lacking a balance.
L	O	P	S	T	I	C	K	A tree specially trimmed to act as a landmark.
L	O	R	D	L	I	K	E	Lordly.
L	O	R	D	L	I	N	G	A petty lord.
L	O	R	D	O	S	I	S	Abnormal forward curving of the spine.
L	O	R	D	S	D	A	Y	Sunday, According to Christian belief Christ arose from the dead on Sunday.
L	O	R	D	S	H	I	P	Dominion, Sovereignty, Control over a domain.
L	O	R	I	C	A	T	E	Cover with a protective substance.
L	O	R	I	K	E	E	T	Small Australian parrot.
L	O	S	E	Y	I	T	E	Mineral composed of a basic carbonate of manganese and zinc.
L	O	T	H	A	R	I	O	Libertine, Rake, Seducer, Casanova, Gallant, Don Juan, Romeo.
L	O	U	D	N	E	S	S	Resonance, Resounding, Strident.
L	O	U	N	G	I	N	G	Loafing, Lolling, Sauntering, Dawdling, Lazing, Indolent, Slack, Reclining.
L	O	V	E	B	I	R	D	Small parrot, Budgerigar.
L	O	V	E	K	N	O	T	Decorative knot used as an emblem of love.
L	O	V	E	L	E	S	S	Unloving, Unloved.
L	O	V	E	L	I	E	S	Professional beauties, Objects of beauty.
L	O	V	E	L	I	F	E	Romantic side of existence.
L	O	V	E	L	I	L	Y	In a lovely manner.
L	O	V	E	L	O	C	K	A long curl of hair hanging over one shoulder.
L	O	V	E	L	O	R	N	Without a lover.
L	O	V	E	N	E	S	T	A place where illicit lovers meet.
L	O	V	E	S	I	C	K	Yearning for love, Pining away for love.
L	O	V	E	S	O	M	E	Charming, Winsome, Beautiful, Friendly, Affectionate, Amorous, Adorable, Devoted.
L	O	V	I	N	G	L	Y	Fondly, Affectionately, Painstakingly, Attentively, Tenderly, Fervently.
L	O	W	E	R	I	N	G	Frowning, Gloomily, Threateningly, Decreasing, Diminishing, Reducing, Degrading.
L	O	W	K	E	Y	E	D	Subdued, Restrained.
L	O	W	W	A	T	E	R	Low state of water, Depressed, Degraded, Embarassed.
L	O	X	O	C	O	S	M	Device for demonstrating inclination of the earth's axis.
L	O	X	O	D	O	N	T	Having shallow hollows between the ridges of the molar teeth.
L	O	Y	A	L	I	S	T	A person who remains loyal, Patriot.
L	U	B	B	E	R	L	Y	Clumsy, Lazy, Loutish, Stupid, Oaf.
L	U	C	E	R	N	A	L	Relating to a lamp.
L	U	C	I	D	I	T	Y	Clarity, Clearness, Limpidity, Reason, Saneness, Sanity, Soundness, Perspicuity.
L	U	C	K	I	E	S	T	Happiest, Most fortunate, Most profitable.
L	U	C	K	L	E	S	S	Unfortunate, Unlucky.
L	U	C	K	Y	B	A	G	Locker on a warship where lost articles wait to be claimed.
L	U	C	K	Y	D	I	P	A container with wrapped mystery parcels.
L	U	C	U	L	E	N	T	Brilliant, Shining, Convincing, Evident, Illustrious, Resplendent, Luminous, Translucent.
L	U	K	E	W	A	R	M	Tepid, Halfhearted, Indifferent, Unenthusiastic, Unresolved, Uncertain, Hesitant, Undecided.
L	U	M	B	E	R	E	D	Encumbered, Burdened, Charged, Loaded, Saddled, Clumped, Stumped, Trudged.
L	U	M	B	E	R	E	R	One employed in the lumber business.
L	U	M	I	N	A	R	Y	Illumination, Celebrity, Notability, Leader, Eminence, Successful person, Leading light.
L	U	M	I	N	A	T	E	Illuminate.
L	U	M	I	N	O	U	S	Clear, Translucent, Enlightened, Incandescent, Radiant, Understandable, Beaming, Lucid.
L	U	M	P	F	I	S	H	Soft clumsy marine fish.
L	U	N	A	R	I	A	N	An authority on lunar astronomy.
L	U	N	A	T	I	O	N	Period between two new moons.
L	U	N	C	H	E	O	N	A light midday meal.
L	U	N	C	H	I	N	G	Eating lunch.
L	U	N	G	E	I	N	G	Plunging, Surging, Bursting, Driving, Pitching.
L	U	N	G	E	O	U	S	Ill-tempered.
L	U	N	G	F	I	S	H	A fish that breathes by a modified lunglike air bladder.
L	U	N	G	L	E	S	S	Having no lungs.
L	U	N	G	W	O	R	M	Parasitic worms that infest lungs of mammals.
L	U	N	G	W	O	R	T	A lichen once used to treat bronchitis but now useful in perfumes.
L	U	N	U	L	A	T	E	Resembling a small crescent.
L	U	P	I	F	O	R	M	Resembling a skin disease.
L	U	P	I	N	I	N	E	A crystalline poisonous alkaloid.

1	2	3	4	5	6	7	8	
L	U	P	U	L	I	N	E	Resembling a cluster of hops.
L	U	P	U	L	O	N	E	A bitter crystalline antibiotic effective against fungi and various bacteria.
L	U	R	C	H	I	N	G	Prowling, Sneaking, Pitching, Careening, Staggering, Teetering, Reeling, Tottering.
L	U	S	C	I	O	U	S	Toothsome, Aromatic, Cloying, Voluptuous, Seductive, Florid, Delightful, Scrumptious.
L	U	S	T	I	E	S	T	Strongest, Most virile, Most robust, Most vigorous, Most dynamic.
L	U	S	T	R	A	T	E	Purify, Cleanse, Expurgate, Purge.
L	U	S	T	R	I	N	G	Finishing process for surface of material.
L	U	S	T	R	O	U	S	Gleaming, Luminous, Brilliant, Glamorous, Illustrous, Bright, Glossy, Splendid.
L	U	T	A	N	I	S	T	One who plays a lute.
L	U	T	E	C	I	U	M	Lutetium.
L	U	T	E	O	L	I	N	Yellow crystalline pigment.
L	U	T	E	T	I	U	M	A trivalent metallic element of the rare-earth group.
L	U	T	H	E	R	A	N	Adherent of the doctrines of Luther.
L	U	T	I	D	I	N	E	Dimethyl derivative associated with bases of coal tar.
L	U	T	R	A	R	I	A	Genus of edible clams.
L	U	T	R	E	O	L	A	Genus of mammals, Minks.
L	U	X	A	T	I	N	G	Displacing, Dislocating.
L	U	X	A	T	I	O	N	Displacement, Dislocation.
L	U	X	M	E	T	E	R	Device to measure illuminance.
L	U	X	U	R	I	E	S	Extravagances, Expensive trifles, Non-essential pleasures. Comforts, Delicacies.
L	Y	C	H	G	A	T	E	A roofed gate of a churchyard.
L	Y	C	O	P	E	N	E	A red crystalline open chain unsaturated hydrocarbon that is colouring matter of tomatoes.
L	Y	C	O	R	I	N	E	Poisonous crystalline alkaloid found in daffodil and amaryllis bulbs.
L	Y	C	T	I	D	A	E	Family of wood-boring beetles.
L	Y	G	O	D	I	U	M	Genus of tropical ferns.
L	Y	G	O	S	O	M	A	Genus of lizards lacking limbs.
L	Y	M	P	H	O	I	D	Pertaining to tissue of the lymph glands.
L	Y	N	C	H	I	N	G	Hanging without a trial by a mob.
L	Y	N	C	H	L	A	W	Court of the mob inflicting punishment without recourse to law.
L	Y	N	X	E	Y	E	D	Sharp-sighted, Eagle-eyed, Hawk-eyed.
L	Y	O	N	E	T	I	A	Family of moths.
L	Y	R	E	B	I	R	D	Australian bird distinguished by the long tail feathers of the male bird.
L	Y	R	I	C	I	S	M	Lyric composition, Songfulness, Unrestrained enthusiasm.
L	Y	S	I	L	O	M	A	Genus of tropical American trees.
L	Y	S	O	Z	Y	M	E	An enzyme found in tears, being slightly antiseptic.

M

1	2	3	4	5	6	7	8	
M	A	C	A	R	O	N	I	Pasta in the form of slender tubes, Fop, Dandy, Exquisite.
M	A	C	A	R	O	O	N	Small almond biscuit.
M	A	C	E	R	A	T	E	Waste away, Steep, Rot away, Soften.
M	A	C	H	I	L	I	S	Genus of very primitive insects.
M	A	C	H	I	N	A	L	Mechanical, Relating to machines.
M	A	C	H	I	N	E	D	Produced by machine, Conformed to a certain pattern.
M	A	C	K	E	R	E	L	Small herring-like fish.
M	A	C	L	E	A	Y	A	Genus of Asiatic herbs.
M	A	C	O	N	I	T	E	Vemiculite.
M	A	C	R	O	P	U	S	Type genus of kangaroos and wallabies.
M	A	C	U	L	A	T	E	Blotched, Besmirched, Defiled.
M	A	D	D	E	N	E	D	Driven mad, Crazed, Enraged, Deranged, Distracted, Unbalanced, Frenzied, Unhinged.
M	A	D	H	O	U	S	E	An insane asylum, Scene of utter confusion, Bedlam.
M	A	D	R	I	G	A	L	Medieval short lyrical poem.
M	A	D	S	T	O	N	E	A stony concretion supposed to counteract effects of the bite of animals.
M	A	E	C	E	N	A	S	A generous benefactor, A patron of the arts.
M	A	E	N	A	D	I	C	Unnaturally distraught or excited woman.
M	A	E	S	T	O	S	O	Majestic, Stately, Direction in music, moderate in tempo.
M	A	F	F	L	I	N	G	Mumbling, Stammering.
M	A	G	A	D	I	S	E	To sing or play in octaves.
M	A	G	A	Z	I	N	E	Warehouse, Depository, Arsenal, Review, Periodical, Journal, Newspaper, Dump.
M	A	G	D	A	L	E	N	A reformed prostitute, A refuge for prostitutes.
M	A	G	I	C	I	A	N	Conjurer, Sorcerer, Enchanter, Wizard, Soothsayer, Prophet, Medium.
M	A	G	I	S	T	E	R	A teacher in ancient Rome or a medieval university.
M	A	G	M	A	T	I	C	Derived from magma, molten matter under the earth's crust.
M	A	G	N	E	T	I	C	Power to attract, Arresting, Captivating, Attractive, Bewitching, Fascinating, Irrestible.
M	A	G	N	I	F	I	C	Illustrious, High-sounding, Munificent, Exalted, Pompous, Majestic, Grandiose, Imposing.
M	A	H	A	R	A	J	A	A Hindu prince.

1	2	3	4	5	6	7	8	
M	A	H	A	R	A	N	I	The wife of an Indian rajah.
M	A	H	O	G	A	N	Y	Hard and heavy wood of a tropical tree.
M	A	I	D	E	N	L	Y	Gentle, Modest, Timid, Virginal.
M	A	I	D	H	O	O	D	Occupation of a maidservant.
M	A	I	E	U	T	I	C	Method used by Socrates to clarify ideas of others.
M	A	I	L	A	B	L	E	Legally admissible as mail.
M	A	I	L	B	O	A	T	A ship under contract to convey mail.
M	A	I	L	C	A	R	T	Cart for carrying mail, Children's push cart.
M	A	I	L	C	L	A	D	Protected by a coat of mail.
M	A	I	N	D	E	C	K	Principal deck of a ship.
M	A	I	N	L	A	N	D	Chief part of a continent.
M	A	I	N	M	A	S	T	Principal mast of a sailing ship.
M	A	I	N	S	A	I	L	Principal sail.
M	A	I	N	S	T	A	Y	Chief support.
M	A	I	N	Y	A	R	D	The yard of a mainsail.
M	A	J	E	S	T	I	C	Imperial, Regal, Grand, August, Grandioso, Lordly, Noble, Royal.
M	A	J	O	L	I	C	A	Earthenware covered with an opaque tin glaze.
M	A	J	O	R	A	N	A	Genus of herbs.
M	A	J	O	R	I	T	Y	Superiority, Full legal age, Edge, Margin, Deciding vote.
M	A	K	E	B	A	T	E	One that provokes quarrels and causes discord.
M	A	K	E	L	E	S	S	Having no match.
M	A	K	E	W	O	R	K	Work devised to provide employment for people that would otherwise be out-of-work.
M	A	K	H	O	R	K	A	Coarse tobacco grown in the Ukraine.
M	A	K	I	M	O	N	O	Japanese wall scroll with a pictured story painted on it.
M	A	K	O	M	A	K	O	A New Zealand tree with a berry used for making wine.
M	A	L	A	C	E	A	E	Family of trees, Apples, Pears, Quince.
M	A	L	A	C	O	I	D	Abnormally soft tissue.
M	A	L	A	D	I	E	S	Diseases, Disorders, Ailments, Complaints, Infirmities, Syndromes, Afflictions, Illnesses.
M	A	L	A	G	A	S	Y	Region of Madagascar.
M	A	L	A	P	E	R	T	Saucy, Impudent, Minx, Hussy, Jade, Slut, Insolent, Bold.
M	A	L	A	P	R	O	P	Misapplication of a word, Ludicrous use of a similar sounding word.
M	A	L	A	R	I	A	L	Infected with malaria.
M	A	L	D	E	M	E	R	Seasickness.
M	A	L	E	F	E	R	N	A fern producing an oleoresin used for expelling tapeworms.
M	A	L	E	F	I	C	E	Evil spell, Enchantment, Mischief, Evil deed.
M	A	L	E	T	O	L	T	Medieval customs duty.
M	A	L	E	T	O	T	E	Same as MALETOLT.
M	A	L	I	G	N	E	D	Resented, Begrudged, Calumniated, Aspersed, Vilified, Defamed, Slandered, Libelled.
M	A	L	I	N	G	E	R	Dodge, Pretend illness or exaggerate incapacity to avoid duty or work.
M	A	L	L	E	A	T	E	Beat, Mark, Dent, Hammer, Pound.
M	A	L	L	O	M	Y	S	Genus of New Guinea giant rats.
M	A	L	O	D	O	U	R	An offensive smell, Stench, Stink, Putrid, Fetid, Foul, Noxious.
M	A	L	T	H	I	T	E	Black viscid substance between pertroleum and asphalt.
M	A	L	T	R	E	A	T	Abuse, Misuse, Mistreat, Outrage, Ill-treat, Harm, Injure.
M	A	L	T	W	O	R	M	Tippler, Toper, Drunkard, Alcoholic.
M	A	L	U	N	I	O	N	Incomplete or faulty union.
M	A	L	V	A	S	I	A	A grape that yields malmsey wine.
M	A	L	V	I	D	I	N	Violet brown crystalline chloride from plants and grapes.
M	A	M	M	A	L	I	A	Highest class of mammals that nourish their young at the breast.
M	A	M	M	I	F	E	R	Mammal.
M	A	M	M	I	L	L	A	Nipple.
M	A	M	P	A	L	O	N	Mammal of Malaysia resembling an otter.
M	A	N	A	C	L	E	D	Shackled, Fettered, Restrained, Hampered, Handcuffed, Tethered, Shackled, Leashed.
M	A	N	A	G	I	N	G	Training, Handling, Conducting, Manipulating, Directing, Operating, Controlling, Governing.
M	A	N	C	H	I	L	D	A son, Male child.
M	A	N	C	I	P	L	E	Steward or purveyor in a college or monastery.
M	A	N	D	A	E	A	N	Member of a sect that regards John the Baptist as the Messiah.
M	A	N	D	A	M	U	S	Mandate of the sovereign under early English law.
M	A	N	D	A	R	I	N	Public officer of the Chinese empire, Chief dialect of China, Tangerine.
M	A	N	D	A	T	O	R	One that gives a mandate.
M	A	N	D	A	T	U	M	Mandate.
M	A	N	D	I	B	L	E	Lower jaw.
M	A	N	D	I	N	G	O	People of West Africa centering in the Upper Niger Valley.
M	A	N	D	I	O	C	A	Manioc.
M	A	N	D	O	L	I	N	Pear-shaped stringed instrument.
M	A	N	D	O	R	L	A	A panel in the shape of an almond, Almond-shaped auriole.
M	A	N	D	R	A	K	E	A herb with a large forked root which is the subject of many superstitions.

1	2	3	4	5	6	7	8	
M	A	N	D	R	I	L	L	Large fierce baboon.
M	A	N	E	A	T	E	R	Animal, fish or reptile that kills human beings.
M	A	N	E	L	E	S	S	Having no mane.
M	A	N	F	U	L	L	Y	Resolutely, Bravely, Boldly, Valiantly.
M	A	N	G	A	B	E	Y	Long-tailed African monkey.
M	A	N	G	L	I	N	G	Whittling, Chewing, Hacking, Mutilating, Maiming, Battering, Disfiguring, Lacerating.
M	A	N	G	O	N	E	L	Military engine for throwing missiles.
M	A	N	G	R	O	V	E	Maritime tree bearing fruit that germinates on the tree.
M	A	N	H	A	T	E	R	A person who hates mankind, One that avoids the society of men.
M	A	N	H	O	U	R	S	Units of work per person per hour.
M	A	N	I	A	C	A	L	Mad, Insane, Frantic, Violent, Demented, Lunatic, Delirious, Frenzied.
M	A	N	I	C	U	R	E	To groom the fingernails.
M	A	N	I	F	E	S	T	Apparent, Distinct, Evident, Patent, Disclosed, Show, Demonstrate.
M	A	N	I	F	O	L	D	Diverse, Increase, Aggrandize, Augment, Compound, Enlarge, Expand, Magnify.
M	A	N	N	E	R	L	Y	Civil, Respectable, Polite, Courteous, Genteel, Well-mannered.
M	A	N	N	I	K	I	N	Dwarf, Pygmy.
M	A	N	N	I	T	O	L	Slightly sweet crystalline hexahydroxy alcohol.
M	A	N	O	F	W	A	R	A warship.
M	A	N	O	R	I	A	L	Relating to a manor.
M	A	N	O	S	T	A	T	A device for automatically maintaining constant pressure within an enclosure.
M	A	N	P	O	W	E	R	Unit of power which is the rate at which a man can perform mechanical work.
M	A	N	S	I	Z	E	D	Large scale.
M	A	N	S	O	N	I	A	Genus of mosquitoes.
M	A	N	S	U	E	T	E	Gentle, Tame, Mild.
M	A	N	T	E	L	E	T	Short cape or cloak.
M	A	N	T	I	D	A	E	Family of carnivorous insects.
M	A	N	T	I	L	L	A	Headdress of lace worn over a high comb by Spanish women.
M	A	N	T	I	S	S	A	Decimal part of a common logarithm.
M	A	N	T	L	I	N	G	Covering, Coating, Blushing, Colouring, Spreading.
M	A	N	T	O	M	A	N	Frank, Candid, Straightforward, Unreserved.
M	A	N	U	A	L	L	Y	With the hands.
M	A	N	U	C	O	D	E	Bird of paradise.
M	A	N	U	R	I	N	G	Training, Enriching, Fertilizing, Developing.
M	A	O	R	I	H	E	N	Weka, Flightless bird of New Zealand.
M	A	Q	U	E	T	T	E	Small preliminary model of an intended sculpture.
M	A	R	A	B	O	U	T	Muslim holy man or hermit.
M	A	R	A	S	M	U	S	Progressive wasting due to malnutrition.
M	A	R	A	T	H	O	N	A race of great length.
M	A	R	A	U	D	E	D	Raided, Pillaged, Harassed, Invaded, Looted, Plundered, Ravaged, Sacked.
M	A	R	A	U	D	E	R	Bandit, Brigand, Pirate, Wrecker, Looter, Raider, Depredator, Forager.
M	A	R	A	V	E	D	I	An old Moorish gold coin.
M	A	R	B	L	I	N	G	Streaking, Blotching, Mottling, Veining.
M	A	R	C	A	N	D	O	Direction in music, strongly accented.
M	A	R	C	H	E	S	A	Marchioness.
M	A	R	C	H	I	N	G	Travelling, Tramping, Striding, Stalking, Advancing, Proceeding, Traversing.
M	A	R	C	O	T	T	E	Layering by binding rooting medium to the plant.
M	A	R	G	A	R	I	N	A glycerol ester of margaric acid, Substitute butter.
M	A	R	G	I	N	A	L	A note printed in the margin, Situated in a border, Minimum, Lower limit.
M	A	R	G	I	N	E	D	Provided with a border, Formed a border, Edged.
M	A	R	G	R	A	V	E	Military governor of a German border province.
M	A	R	I	A	C	H	I	Itinerant Mexican folk singers.
M	A	R	I	G	O	L	D	Widely distributed plant having orange flowers.
M	A	R	I	G	R	A	M	Record from a tide-gauge.
M	A	R	I	N	A	D	E	Mixture of wine or vinegar with herbs for steeping food to enhance the flavour.
M	A	R	I	N	A	T	E	To soak in a marinade.
M	A	R	I	T	I	M	E	Relating to commerce of the sea, Bordering on the sea.
M	A	R	J	O	R	A	M	Fragrant herb used in cooking.
M	A	R	K	E	D	L	Y	Noticeably, Plainly.
M	A	R	K	E	T	E	D	Sold, Exposed for sale in a market.
M	A	R	K	S	M	A	N	Expert in target shooting.
M	A	R	K	W	E	E	D	Poison Ivy.
M	A	R	M	O	S	E	T	Soft-furred monkey with claws instead of nails.
M	A	R	O	C	A	I	N	A crepe dress fabric made of a rayon mixture.
M	A	R	O	N	I	T	E	Arabic-speaking member of the Uniate church.
M	A	R	O	O	N	E	D	Having been put ashore on a desolate part, Left in isolation.
M	A	R	O	O	N	E	R	Buccaneer, Pirate.

1	2	3	4	5	6	7	8	
M	A	R	O	Q	U	I	N	Morocco.
M	A	R	Q	U	E	S	S	Aristocrat with an hereditary title.
M	A	R	Q	U	I	S	E	A special cut of a gem stone.
M	A	R	R	I	A	G	E	Wedlock, Espousal, Wedding.
M	A	R	R	Y	I	N	G	Uniting in wedlock, Uniting two wines.
M	A	R	S	H	G	A	S	Methane gas from decaying vegetable matter in marshy ground.
M	A	R	S	H	H	E	N	Moorhen, Bittern.
M	A	R	S	H	T	I	T	A grayish Old World titmouse.
M	A	R	T	A	B	A	N	A large green glazed pottery jar made in Burma and used for domestic storage.
M	A	R	T	I	N	E	T	A strict discliplinarian.
M	A	R	T	Y	N	I	A	Genus of herbs with perennial downy heads.
M	A	R	T	Y	R	E	D	Put to death for adhering to a belief, Tortured to death.
M	A	R	Z	I	P	A	N	Confection of crushed almonds with sugar and whites of eggs.
M	A	S	C	A	R	O	N	Mask.
M	A	S	H	G	I	A	H	An inspector who checks on adherence to Kosher principles in shops and eating houses.
M	A	S	O	R	I	T	E	One of the scribes who wrote down the Masorah.
M	A	S	S	A	C	R	E	Slaughter, Mangle, Mutilate, Bloodshed, Butchery, Carnage, Decimation, Genocide.
M	A	S	S	A	G	E	D	Rubbed, Kneaded, Stroked, Manipulated, Tapped.
M	A	S	S	B	O	O	K	Missal, Book of devotions.
M	A	S	S	E	T	E	R	Large muscle that raises the lower jaw for mastication.
M	A	S	S	E	U	S	E	A female masseur.
M	A	S	S	I	C	O	T	Lead monoxide.
M	A	S	T	E	R	E	D	Conquered, Overcame, Subdued, Tamed, Surmounted, Dominated, Governed, Ruled.
M	A	S	T	E	R	L	Y	Proficient, Domineering, Adept, Expert, Skilled, Supreme, Superlative, Dexterously.
M	A	S	T	H	E	A	D	The top of a mast.
M	A	S	T	I	T	I	S	Inflammation of the breast or udder caused by infection.
M	A	S	T	L	E	S	S	Having no mast.
M	A	S	T	O	D	O	N	Huge extinct mammals resembling elephants, Giant.
M	A	S	T	O	M	Y	S	Genus of rodents, Multimammate mice.
M	A	S	U	R	I	U	M	Chemical element.
M	A	T	A	C	H	I	N	Member of a group of Mexican Indian dancers who perform ritual dances.
M	A	T	A	D	O	R	E	Bullfighter who has the principal role of killing the bull.
M	A	T	A	M	A	T	A	Brazilian turtle whose eggs yield an edible oil.
M	A	T	A	S	A	N	O	White sapota.
M	A	T	C	H	B	O	X	A box holding matches.
M	A	T	C	H	I	N	G	Equalling, Competing, Pitting, Arraying, Adapting, Suiting, Rivalling.
M	A	T	E	L	O	T	E	Sauce made of wine, onions, seasoning and fish stock.
M	A	T	E	R	I	A	L	Physical, Substantial, Essential, Relevant, Pertinent, Solid, Sensible, Objective.
M	A	T	E	R	I	E	L	Equipment, Military apparatus and supplies, Outfit.
M	A	T	E	R	N	A	L	Motherly, Motherhood, On the mother's side.
M	A	T	E	S	H	I	P	Fellowship.
M	A	T	G	R	A	S	S	Matweed, Spiny rolling grass, Knotgrass.
M	A	T	H	E	S	I	S	Science, Learning, Mathematics.
M	A	T	H	E	T	I	C	Relating to science and learning.
M	A	T	H	U	R	I	N	Trinitarian.
M	A	T	R	O	N	A	L	Matronly.
M	A	T	R	O	N	L	Y	Having the characteristics of a matron, Mature female.
M	A	T	T	E	R	E	D	Imported, Signified, Valued, Counted, Meant, Weighed.
M	A	T	T	R	E	S	S	Resilient pad for resting or sleeping.
M	A	T	U	R	A	T	E	Ripen, Maturate, Age, Develop, Grow, Mellow.
M	A	T	U	R	E	L	Y	Mellowly, Progressively, Wisely.
M	A	T	U	R	I	N	G	Ripening, Aging, Developing, Growing, Mellowing.
M	A	T	U	R	I	T	Y	Fullness, Readiness, Deliberateness, Ripeness, Becoming due for payment.
M	A	T	U	T	I	N	E	Rising just before the dawn.
M	A	U	R	I	T	I	A	Large Peuto Rican magnolia that yields high-grade lumber and an essential oil.
M	A	V	E	R	I	C	K	Relcalcitrant member of a political group, Unmarked stray animal, Unorthodox.
M	A	X	I	M	I	S	T	An enthusiast over maxims.
M	A	X	I	M	I	Z	E	Increase to a maximum.
M	A	Y	A	P	P	L	E	N. American herb that has a poisonous rootstock but the fruit is edible.
M	A	Y	B	L	O	B	S	Marsh marigolds.
M	A	Y	B	L	O	O	M	Hawthorn.
M	A	Y	Q	U	E	E	N	A young girl chosen as queen for the May Day festivities.
M	A	Y	O	R	E	S	S	Wife or hostess of a mayor.
M	A	Z	A	G	R	A	N	Cold diluted sweetened coffee served in a glass.
M	A	Z	A	R	I	N	E	Deep dish often used as a liner in a serving dish.
M	A	Z	D	A	I	S	M	Religion founded in Persia, Zoroastrianisy.
M	E	A	G	R	E	L	Y	Poorly, Inadequately, Sparsely, Scantily.

1	2	3	4	5	6	7	8	
M	E	A	L	T	I	M	E	The usual time of taking a meal.
M	E	A	L	W	O	R	M	Various beetles whose larvae pollute grain products.
M	E	A	L	Y	B	U	G	Plant pests.
M	E	A	N	N	E	S	S	Baseness, Stinginess.
M	E	A	N	T	I	M	E	Meanwhile.
M	E	A	S	U	R	E	D	Regulated, Weighed, Contended, Contested, Rhythmical, Limited, Calculated, Determined.
M	E	A	S	U	R	E	R	A worker that measures material before processing.
M	E	A	T	B	A	L	L	Small fried ball of ground meat, Clumsy or dull person.
M	E	A	T	L	E	S	S	Lacking meat, Vegetarian.
M	E	A	T	S	A	F	E	Small cupboard for storing meat.
M	E	C	H	A	N	I	C	Artisan, Machinist, Base, Vulgar, Automatic, Uninspired, Agile, Inventive.
M	E	C	O	N	I	U	M	Foetal excrement.
M	E	D	A	L	L	I	C	Tablet or window bearing a portrait, Decoration on a carpet or lace.
M	E	D	D	L	I	N	G	Interfering, Tampering, Disturbing, Combining, Mingling, Dealing, Obtruding, Prying.
M	E	D	I	A	T	E	D	Conveyed, Interposed, Interceded, Interfered, Intervened, Reconciled.
M	E	D	I	A	T	O	R	Intercessor, Peacemaker.
M	E	D	I	C	A	T	E	To treat with medicine, To impregnate with a medicinal substance.
M	E	D	I	C	E	A	N	Relating to the Medici family.
M	E	D	I	C	I	N	E	Remedy, Cure, Medicant, Physic, Medication, Pharmacon.
M	E	D	I	E	V	A	L	Relating to the middle ages, Antiquated, Outmoded.
M	E	D	I	O	C	R	E	Indifferent, Ordinary, Middle quality, Medium, Average, Commonplace, Intermediate.
M	E	D	I	T	A	T	E	Ponder, Reflect, Consider, Contemplate, Intend, Purpose, Ruminate.
M	E	D	U	L	L	A	E	Inner parts of organs and structures, Bone marrows.
M	E	D	U	S	O	I	D	Like a jellyfish.
M	E	E	K	E	N	E	D	Became meek.
M	E	E	K	N	E	S	S	Humility, Submissiveness, Mildness, Weakness.
M	E	E	T	N	E	S	S	Fitness, Order, Appropriateness, Aptness, Propriety, Suitability.
M	E	G	A	L	I	T	H	Prehistoric monument constructed of huge stones, Monolith.
M	E	G	A	L	O	P	S	Final larval stage of crabs.
M	E	G	A	P	O	D	E	Australasian bird that makes a nest by heaping debris.
M	E	G	A	T	R	O	N	Lighthouse tube.
M	E	G	A	V	O	L	T	One million volts.
M	E	G	A	W	A	T	T	One million watts, One thousand kilowatts.
M	E	H	A	R	I	S	T	One riding a swift dromedary.
M	E	I	O	N	I	T	E	A mineral consisting of aluminosilicate of calcium.
M	E	I	O	T	A	X	Y	Suppression of a complete whorl of leaves.
M	E	L	A	M	I	N	E	A white crystalline high-melting organic base, Plastic made from melamine resin.
M	E	L	A	N	I	S	M	Dark or black pigmentation.
M	E	L	A	N	I	T	E	A black garnet of the variety andradite.
M	E	L	A	N	O	I	D	Darkened by melanins.
M	E	L	A	N	O	M	A	Malignant tumour that starts in a black mole.
M	E	L	A	N	O	S	E	A disease of the grapevine caused by a fungus.
M	E	L	A	N	O	U	S	Having black hair and a dark complexion.
M	E	L	A	T	O	P	E	The point in an interference figure.
M	E	L	A	X	U	M	A	Plant disease causing black bark cankers.
M	E	L	I	L	I	T	E	A mineral occurring in small tetragonal crystals that is a silicate of sodium, calcium and iron.
M	E	L	I	N	I	T	E	A high explosive similar to lyddite.
M	E	L	L	E	O	U	S	Resembling or containing honey.
M	E	L	L	O	W	E	D	Matured, Aged, Ripened, Honeyed, Liquid, Enriched.
M	E	L	L	O	W	L	Y	Softly, Sweetly, Gently.
M	E	L	O	D	E	O	N	American organ.
M	E	L	O	D	I	S	T	Singer, Composer of melodies.
M	E	L	O	D	I	Z	E	Compose a melody, Set to melody.
M	E	L	O	I	D	A	E	Family of cylindrical beetles, Blister beetle.
M	E	M	B	E	R	E	D	Divided into members, In heraldry, having legs different from the body.
M	E	M	B	R	A	N	E	Thin soft pliable sheet of animal or vegetable origin.
M	E	M	O	R	I	A	L	Relic, Trace, Commemoration, Memorandium, Note, Keepsake, Memento, Souvenir.
M	E	M	O	R	I	Z	E	Record, Mention, Remember, Commemorate, Learn, Study.
M	E	M	P	H	I	A	N	Egyptian, Resident of Memphis.
M	E	M	P	H	I	T	E	Relating to Memphite in ancient Egypt.
M	E	M	S	A	H	I	B	The wife of an official or a white man in India.
M	E	N	A	C	I	N	G	Threatening, Endangering, Imminent, Lowering, Overhanging, Tormenting, Frightening.
M	E	N	H	A	D	E	N	A marine fish.
M	E	N	I	L	I	T	E	An impure opal in brown or dull grayish concretions.
M	E	N	I	N	G	E	S	Meninx, Membranes that enclose the brain and spinal cord.
M	E	N	I	S	C	U	S	Crescent-shaped.

1	2	3	4	5	6	7	8	Definition
M	E	N	O	L	O	G	Y	An ecclesiastical calendar of festivals related to saints.
M	E	N	S	U	R	A	L	Capable of being measured.
M	E	N	T	A	L	I	S	A muscle that raises the chin and pushes up the lower lip.
M	E	N	T	A	L	L	Y	Inwardly, Intellectually, Ideologically, Pertaining to the mind.
M	E	N	T	H	A	N	E	Isomeric liquid saturated cyclic hydrocarbons.
M	E	N	T	H	E	N	E	Oily unsaturated hydrocarbon.
M	E	N	T	H	O	N	E	Liquid ketone.
M	E	N	Z	E	L	I	A	Genus of scabrous and bristly western American herbs.
M	E	P	H	I	T	I	C	Noxious, Pestilential, Offensive smell.
M	E	P	H	I	T	I	S	Stench, Poisonous smell, Malodorous, Fetid, Musty, Noisome, Toxic, Stinking.
M	E	R	A	S	P	I	S	A late larva of a trilobite.
M	E	R	C	H	A	N	T	Storekeeper, Customer, Purveyor, Specialist, Trader, Buyer, Seller, Dealer.
M	E	R	C	I	F	U	L	Clement, Compassionate, Lenient, Forbearing, Charitable, Indulgent, Kind, Tolerant.
M	E	R	C	U	R	I	C	Containing mercury.
M	E	R	E	N	G	U	E	Dominican and Haitian ballroom dance with a limping step.
M	E	R	G	E	N	C	E	Condition of being merged.
M	E	R	I	C	A	R	P	One of the two carpels that resemble achenes.
M	E	R	I	D	I	A	N	Relating to midday, A great circlel, Consummate, Extreme.
M	E	R	I	N	G	U	E	Mixture of beaten egg whites and sugar used in confectionery.
M	E	R	I	O	N	E	S	A genus of gerbils.
M	E	R	I	S	T	E	M	A formative plant tissue.
M	E	R	I	S	T	I	C	Divided into segments.
M	E	R	I	T	I	N	G	Earning, Deserving, Rewarding, Recompensing, Repaying, Entitling, Justifying, Warranting.
M	E	R	O	G	A	M	Y	Microgamy.
M	E	R	O	T	O	M	Y	Division into parts.
M	E	R	O	X	E	N	E	A mineral consisting of a biotite.
M	E	R	R	Y	M	A	N	Buffoon, Jester.
M	E	R	S	A	L	Y	L	An organic mercurial.
M	E	S	D	A	M	E	S	Plural of Madam or Madame.
M	E	S	H	W	O	R	K	Meshes, Network.
M	E	S	M	E	R	I	C	Fascinating, Irresistible, Attractive, Alluring, Magnetic, Bewitching, Captivating, Enchanting.
M	E	S	N	A	L	T	Y	The estate of a mesne lord.
M	E	S	O	C	A	R	P	Middle layer of a pericarp.
M	E	S	O	D	E	R	M	The middle of the three primary germ layers of an embryo.
M	E	S	O	E	N	A	S	Genus of birds of Madagascar.
M	E	S	O	L	I	T	E	A zeolitic mineral.
M	E	S	O	M	E	R	E	A primitive segment.
M	E	S	O	S	A	U	R	An extinct aquatic reptile.
M	E	S	O	S	O	M	A	Middle region of the body of various invertebrates.
M	E	S	O	T	R	O	N	An unstable nuclear particle.
M	E	S	O	Z	O	I	C	Divisions of prehistoric time and ecological zones.
M	E	S	Q	U	I	T	E	A spiny deep-rooted tree of America and Mexico.
M	E	S	S	M	A	T	E	An associate in a messroom.
M	E	S	S	R	O	O	M	Dining-room on a naval vessel.
M	E	S	S	U	A	G	E	A dwelling house with outbuildings and adjoining land.
M	E	T	A	B	O	L	A	Insects that undergo a transformation.
M	E	T	A	B	O	L	E	A physical change.
M	E	T	A	C	O	N	E	Cusps of upper molars.
M	E	T	A	L	L	E	D	Covered with metal, Having a hard surface, Macadamized.
M	E	T	A	L	L	I	C	Being a metal or alloy, Reflective, Sharp, Harsh, Grating, Stark, Mechanical.
M	E	T	A	L	M	A	N	Worker in a metal recycling plant.
M	E	T	A	L	O	P	H	Crest on a molar.
M	E	T	A	M	I	C	T	Uncrystallized because of the disruption by radiation.
M	E	T	A	N	O	I	A	Spiritual conversion.
M	E	T	A	P	H	O	R	A compressed simile, An implied comparison.
M	E	T	A	S	O	M	A	Hind regions of mollusks and arachnids.
M	E	T	A	S	O	M	E	The replacing mineral where one mineral grows at the expense of another.
M	E	T	A	T	Y	P	E	Homeotype determined by the original author of its species.
M	E	T	A	Y	A	G	E	The metayer system of farming land.
M	E	T	A	Z	O	A	N	Animal bodies of numerous cells differentiated into tissues and organs.
M	E	T	A	Z	O	O	N	One of the Metazoa.
M	E	T	E	O	R	I	C	Derived from the earth's atmosphere, Resembling a meteor, An amazing rise to success.
M	E	T	E	W	A	N	D	Measuring rod.
M	E	T	E	Y	A	R	D	Same as METEWAND.
M	E	T	H	A	N	O	L	A light volatile pungent flammable poisonous liquid alcohol.
M	E	T	H	I	N	K	S	It seems to me.
M	E	T	H	O	D	I	C	Methodical, Systematic.

1	2	3	4	5	6	7	8	Definition
M	E	T	H	Y	L	A	L	A volatile flammable liquid acetal.
M	E	T	H	Y	L	I	C	Containing methyl.
M	E	T	O	N	Y	M	Y	Using the name of one thing for that of something which is associated with it.
M	E	T	O	O	I	S	M	Policies of a me-tooer.
M	E	T	O	P	I	O	N	Point situated between frontal eminences of the skull.
M	E	T	O	P	I	S	M	Having a persistent union line on the forehead.
M	E	T	R	I	C	A	L	Capable of being defined by a metric.
M	E	T	R	I	T	I	S	Inflammation of the uterus.
M	E	U	N	I	E	R	E	Served with browned butter.
M	E	Z	E	R	E	O	N	A small European shrub with fragrant lilac purple flowers.
M	I	A	S	M	A	T	A	Heavy vaporous atmosphere, Pervasive corrupting influence.
M	I	C	R	A	N	E	R	A very small male ant.
M	I	C	R	O	B	A	R	Unit of pressure.
M	I	C	R	O	B	I	C	Developed from microbes.
M	I	C	R	O	P	U	S	Genus of birds, Swifts.
M	I	C	R	O	D	O	T	A photographic copy, greatly reduced in size.
M	I	C	R	O	T	U	S	Genus of rodents, Voles.
M	I	C	R	O	X	E	A	A microsclere having the form of an oxea.
M	I	C	R	U	R	G	Y	Using miniature tools in a magnified area.
M	I	D	D	L	I	N	G	Intermediate, Mediocre, Second-rate, Moderately, Rather, Fairly, Average, Indifferent.
M	I	D	N	I	G	H	T	Twelve o'clock at night, Deep darkness, Gloom.
M	I	D	P	L	A	N	E	A plane dividing something into symmetrical halves.
M	I	D	P	O	I	N	T	A point at centre of an area or period of time.
M	I	D	S	H	I	P	S	Middle part of a ship.
M	I	E	R	S	I	T	E	A mineral consisting of silver copper iodide.
M	I	G	H	T	I	L	Y	Earnestly, Powerfully, Vigorously, Energetically, Forcefully, Laboriously, Hardly, Strongly.
M	I	G	R	A	I	N	E	Severe recurrent headaches accompanied by nausea.
M	I	G	R	A	T	E	D	Left, Transferred, Ranged, Roamed, Wandered.
M	I	G	R	A	T	O	R	A migratory bird.
M	I	L	A	N	E	S	E	Fine warp-knitted fabric, Native to Milan.
M	I	L	D	E	W	E	D	Affected with mildew.
M	I	L	D	N	E	S	S	Kindness, Graciousness, Blandness, Tameness.
M	I	L	E	P	O	S	T	A roadside stone showing distance to or from an important town.
M	I	L	E	S	I	A	N	Irishman.
M	I	L	I	T	A	N	T	Aggressive, Combative, Fighting, Belligerent, Contentious, Assertive, Truculent.
M	I	L	I	T	A	R	Y	Martial, Warlike, Soldierly, Troop, Armed forces, Servicemen.
M	I	L	I	T	A	T	E	Engage in warfare, To fight, Oppose, Contend, Combat.
M	I	L	K	F	I	S	H	A large active silvery herbivorous food fish.
M	I	L	K	M	A	I	D	Dairymaid.
M	I	L	K	T	R	E	E	A tree having abundant latex, Cow tree.
M	I	L	K	W	A	R	M	Lukewarm.
M	I	L	K	W	E	E	D	A plant that secretes latex.
M	I	L	K	W	O	R	T	An European plant, Milk parsley.
M	I	L	K	Y	W	A	Y	A galaxy of faint stars.
M	I	L	L	E	P	E	D	Millipede.
M	I	L	L	I	A	R	D	A thousand millions.
M	I	L	L	I	B	A	R	Unit of atmospheric pressure.
M	I	L	L	I	G	A	L	Unit of acceleration.
M	I	L	L	I	L	U	X	One thousandth of a lux.
M	I	L	L	I	N	E	R	One who designs, makes and sells women's hats.
M	I	L	L	I	P	E	D	An insect with a cylindrical many-segmented body having legs on each segment.
M	I	L	L	P	O	N	D	A stream dammed to produce a volume of water to operate a mill.
M	I	L	L	P	O	S	T	A large post supporting a windmill.
M	I	L	L	R	A	C	E	A canal where water flows to drive a mill.
M	I	L	L	T	A	I	L	Flow of water after turning the wheel of the mill.
M	I	L	L	W	O	R	K	Operating mill machinery.
M	I	L	T	O	N	I	C	Characteristic of John Milton.
M	I	M	E	T	I	T	E	A lead arsenate and chloride.
M	I	M	I	C	K	E	D	Ridiculed, Simulated, Copied, Aped, Burlesqued, Mocked. Parodied, Impersonated.
M	I	M	O	S	I	N	E	A crystalline amino acid.
M	I	N	A	T	O	R	Y	Threatening, Menacing.
M	I	N	C	E	P	I	E	A pie filled with mincemeat.
M	I	N	D	L	E	S	S	Stupid, Unintelligent, Unthinking, Uninterested, Unattentive, Asinine, Foolish, Witless.
M	I	N	G	L	I	N	G	Combining, Mixing, Concocting, Melding, Merging, Socializing.
M	I	N	I	A	T	E	D	Painted with red lead, Rubicated, Illuminated.
M	I	N	I	F	I	E	D	Lessened, Reduced, Decreased, Diminished.
M	I	N	I	M	I	Z	E	Decry, Depreciate, Reduce, Belittle, Derogate, Discount, Disparage, Dwarf.

1	2	3	4	5	6	7	8	
M	I	N	I	S	T	E	R	Serve, Administer, Care, Nurse, Treat, Pander, Parson, Preacher.
M	I	N	I	S	T	R	Y	Agency, Channel, Instrument, Medium, Organ, Vehicle, Function, Office.
M	I	N	O	R	I	T	Y	Lesser, Smaller in number.
M	I	N	S	T	R	E	L	Itinerant entertainer, Bard, Troubadour, Singer.
M	I	N	T	M	A	R	K	Identification mark on a coin.
M	I	N	U	T	E	L	Y	Exactly, Precisely, Continual, Unceasing, Constant, Particularly, Continuous, Incessant.
M	I	N	U	T	E	S	T	Tiniest, Smallest, Most trifling, Most petty.
M	I	N	U	T	I	A	E	Small things, Precise details.
M	I	N	U	T	I	A	L	Being of a minor detail.
M	I	N	U	T	I	N	G	Timing, Recording, Noting.
M	I	R	E	C	R	O	W	Black-headed gull.
M	I	R	E	P	O	I	X	Seasoned vegetables placed under meat while it is braising.
M	I	R	I	N	E	S	S	State of being muddy or soiled.
M	I	R	R	O	R	E	D	Reflected, Represented, Epitomized, Illustrated, Embodied, Typified, Symbolized.
M	I	R	T	H	F	U	L	Full of merriment.
M	I	S	A	I	M	E	D	Aimed incorrectly, Misdirected.
M	I	S	A	P	P	L	Y	Misuse, Misspend, Squander, Misemploy, Mishandle, Pervert, Misappropriate, Mismanage.
M	I	S	A	R	R	A	Y	Disarray.
M	I	S	B	R	A	N	D	To brand in a misleading way.
M	I	S	C	A	R	R	Y	Die, Perish, Fail, Go wrong, Misfire, Abort, Be unsuccessful.
M	I	S	C	E	L	L	A	A solution or mixture containing an extracted oil or grease.
M	I	S	C	H	I	E	F	Discord, Dissension, Injury, Damage, Harm, Hurt, Outrage, Roguery.
M	I	S	C	I	B	L	E	Mixable, Compatible.
M	I	S	C	O	U	N	T	Miscalculate.
M	I	S	C	R	E	E	D	A false creed.
M	I	S	C	U	I	N	G	Making an error or mistake, Making a slip.
M	I	S	D	A	T	E	D	Used the wrong date.
M	I	S	D	E	A	L	T	Playing cards dealt incorrectly.
M	I	S	D	O	I	N	G	Wrongdoing, Misbehaviour, Misconduct, Misdemeanour, Misdeed.
M	I	S	D	O	U	B	T	Distrust, Mistrust, Suspect, Suspicion, Apprehensive, Fear, Dread.
M	I	S	E	N	I	T	E	A mineral consisting of a native acid potassium sulfate.
M	I	S	E	R	E	R	E	A prayer, exclamation or speech appealing for mercy.
M	I	S	F	I	E	L	D	Make an error in the field when playing rugby or cricket.
M	I	S	F	I	R	E	D	Failed to fire, Miscarried, Missed.
M	I	S	G	U	I	D	E	Spoil, Injure, Abuse, Misdirect, Mislead, Lead astray.
M	I	S	H	E	A	R	D	Heard wrongly, Misunderstood what was said.
M	I	S	H	M	A	S	H	Hodgepodge, Miscellany, Medley, Mélange, Potpourri, Clutter, Jumble, Muddle.
M	I	S	H	N	A	I	C	Rabbinical tenets of the early days of Christianity.
M	I	S	J	U	D	G	E	A mistaken estimation, Unjust opinion, Miscalculate, Misreckon, Misconstrue, Misinterpret.
M	I	S	L	A	B	E	L	Falsely charged.
M	I	S	L	A	Y	E	R	An untidy person.
M	I	S	L	I	K	E	D	Displeased, Disliked, Disapproved.
M	I	S	M	A	T	C	H	Incompatible, Wrongly paired, Unsuitably matched, Conflict, Discord, Jangle.
M	I	S	N	A	M	E	D	Abused, Miscalled.
M	I	S	N	O	M	E	R	Use of a wrong name, Incorrect designation.
M	I	S	O	G	A	M	Y	Hatred of marriage.
M	I	S	O	G	Y	N	Y	Hatred of women.
M	I	S	O	R	D	E	R	Confusion, Clutter, Disarray, Disorder, Muddle, Untidy.
M	I	S	P	L	A	C	E	Mislay, Lose, Displace.
M	I	S	P	L	E	A	D	An omission in a plea.
M	I	S	P	O	I	N	T	To punctuate wrongly.
M	I	S	P	R	I	N	T	A mistake in printed matter, To leave uneven footprints.
M	I	S	P	R	I	S	E	Misdemeanour, To conceal a felon, Clerical error in a court proceeding.
M	I	S	P	R	I	Z	E	Neglect, Undervalue, Neglect of official duty, Belittle.
M	I	S	Q	U	O	T	E	To quote incorrectly.
M	I	S	R	U	L	E	D	A state of anarchy and rebellion developed.
M	I	S	S	H	A	P	E	Deform, Give an unnatural form.
M	I	S	S	P	E	A	K	Express oneself imperfectly, Speak incorrectly.
M	I	S	S	P	E	L	L	Spell incorrectly.
M	I	S	S	P	E	L	T	Used incorrect spelling.
M	I	S	S	P	E	N	D	Squander, Waste.
M	I	S	S	T	A	T	E	Give a false or exaggerated account.
M	I	S	T	A	K	E	N	Misunderstood, Misconceived, Erroneous, Misguided, Misinformed, Confused, Deceived.
M	I	S	T	E	A	C	H	To teach badly.
M	I	S	T	H	I	N	K	To think unfavourably.
M	I	S	T	I	B	L	U	A grayish blue colour.
M	I	S	T	I	M	E	D	Unseasonable, Inopportune, Untimely.

1	2	3	4	5	6	7	8	
M	I	S	T	R	A	I	N	To train incorrectly.
M	I	S	T	R	E	A	T	Abuse, Ill-treat, Outrage, Misuse, Ill-use.
M	I	S	T	R	E	S	S	Girlfriend, Lover, Paramour, Concubine, Bedmate, Sweetheart, A woman wielding power.
M	I	S	T	R	I	A	L	Legal effect cancelled through error or misconduct.
M	I	S	T	R	U	S	T	Distrust, Suspicion, Uncertainty, Doubt, Suspect, Alarm, Dismay, Challenge.
M	I	S	T	R	Y	S	T	To fail to keep an engagement.
M	I	S	T	U	N	E	D	Made discordant.
M	I	S	U	S	A	G	E	Abuse, Wrong use, Disemploy, Mishandle, Pervert.
M	I	S	U	S	I	N	G	Misapplying, Using a grant of authority unlawfully, Profaning.
M	I	S	V	A	L	U	E	Undervalue.
M	I	S	W	R	I	T	E	Make a mistake in writing.
M	I	T	H	R	A	I	C	Relating to Mithras, Persian god of light.
M	I	T	I	C	I	D	E	Acaricide, a substance that kills mites.
M	I	T	I	G	A	N	T	Alleviating, Relieving, Easing.
M	I	T	I	G	A	T	E	Mollify, Soften, Lessen Relieve, Lighten, Allay, Extenuate, Palliate.
M	I	T	O	S	O	M	E	One assumed to be derived from middle of sperm cell.
M	I	T	T	I	M	U	S	Warrant, Writ for deployment of records, Discharge, Dismissal.
M	I	X	O	L	O	G	Y	Skill of preparing mixed drinks in a bar.
M	I	Z	Z	L	I	N	G	Confused, Muddled, Decamped, Speckled, Spotted, Sprinkled, Drizzled, Distracted.
M	N	E	M	O	N	I	C	An assistance to memory i.e. rhyme or formula.
M	O	B	I	L	I	T	Y	Movability, Versatility, Capacity of movement, Fickleness, Unsteady.
M	O	B	I	L	I	Z	E	Circulate, Organize, Marshal, Rally, Assemble, Activate, Propel.
M	O	B	O	C	R	A	T	One who favours rule by mobs or gangs, Anarchist.
M	O	C	A	S	S	I	N	Heelless shoe of soft leather that was favoured by the American Indians.
M	O	D	A	L	I	S	M	A theological doctrine relating to the Holy Trinity.
M	O	D	A	L	I	S	T	An adherent of modalism.
M	O	D	A	L	I	T	Y	Form, Pattern, Being typical.
M	O	D	E	L	L	E	D	Shaped, Fashioned, Constructed, Designed.
M	O	D	E	L	L	E	R	One that models, Carver of leather for parts of shoes.
M	O	D	E	R	A	T	E	Calm, Reasonable, Mediocre, Temperate, Sober, Modest, Gentle, Average.
M	O	D	E	R	A	T	O	Direction in music to indicate a moderate tempo.
M	O	D	E	S	T	L	Y	Humbly, Shyly, Meekly, Demurely, Timidly, Primly, Decently, Cleanly.
M	O	D	I	F	I	E	D	Qualified, Changed, Altered, Refashioned, Turned, Limited, Reserved, Varied.
M	O	D	I	F	I	E	R	One that moderates or tempers.
M	O	D	I	O	L	A	R	Relating to the modiolus of the ear.
M	O	D	I	O	L	U	S	A central bony column on the cochlea of the ear.
M	O	D	I	S	H	L	Y	Fashionably, Stylishly, Exclusively, Smartly.
M	O	D	U	L	A	T	E	Intone, Sing, Adjust, Temper, Soften, Vary, Restrain.
M	O	F	U	S	S	I	L	Rural districts of India.
M	O	H	A	R	R	A	M	A muslim festival.
M	O	H	N	S	E	E	D	Poppy seed.
M	O	I	S	T	F	U	L	Moist, Damp, Wet, Humid, Clammy.
M	O	I	S	T	U	R	E	A condensed liquid, Precipitation, Damp, Wettish.
M	O	K	I	H	A	N	A	A Hawaiian tree with fragrant fruits.
M	O	L	A	L	I	T	Y	Relating to the ratio of solute to solvent.
M	O	L	A	R	I	T	Y	Molar concentration.
M	O	L	A	S	S	E	S	Thick syrup left during processing of raw sugar.
M	O	L	E	C	A	S	T	Molehill.
M	O	L	E	C	U	L	E	A unit of matter that is the smallest particle of an element, Fraction, Fragment.
M	O	L	E	H	I	L	L	Earth thrown up by a mole tunnelling beneath the surface.
M	O	L	E	S	K	I	N	Garment made of moleskin, Heavy durable cotton fabric.
M	O	L	E	S	T	E	D	Inconvenienced, Harassed, Plagued, Afflicted, Annoyed, Persecuted, Disturbed, Raided.
M	O	L	E	S	T	E	R	A sexual pervert or bully.
M	O	L	I	N	I	S	T	Advocate of molinism.
M	O	L	L	U	S	C	A	Family of invertebrate animals, Snails, Mussels, Oysters, Gastropods, Octopuses.
M	O	L	O	S	S	I	C	Relating to a measure, Foot of three long syllables.
M	O	L	Y	B	D	I	C	Containing molybdenum a metallic element resembling chromium.
M	O	M	E	N	T	L	Y	From moment to moment, At any moment.
M	O	M	E	N	T	U	M	Force of motion acquired by a moving body, Impetus.
M	O	N	A	C	H	A	L	Monastic.
M	O	N	A	N	D	R	Y	A marriage custom in which a woman has only one husband at a time.
M	O	N	A	R	C	H	Y	Absolute sovereignty, Undivided rule, Absolute, Constitutional, Hereditary rule.
M	O	N	A	S	T	I	C	Pertaining to a monastery.
M	O	N	A	U	R	A	L	Designed for use with one ear.
M	O	N	A	X	I	A	L	Based on a single axis.
M	O	N	A	Z	I	T	E	A mineral consisting of phosphate of the cerium metals and thorium.
M	O	N	D	A	I	N	E	Worldy, Sophisticated, Fashionable, Knowing, Blasé, Disentranced.

1	2	3	4	5	6	7	8	
M	O	N	E	T	A	R	Y	Pertaining to money, Pecuniary, Financial, Fiscal, Numismatic.
M	O	N	E	T	I	Z	E	Establish as legal tender, To coin into money.
M	O	N	E	Y	B	O	X	A box for saving coins at home.
M	O	N	G	E	R	E	D	Peddled, Purveyed, Dealt, Spread, Hawked, Vended.
M	O	N	G	O	L	I	C	Mongoloid.
M	O	N	G	O	O	S	E	Viverrine mammal that feeds on snakes and rodents.
M	O	N	I	L	I	A	L	Infected by a fungus of the genus, Candida.
M	O	N	I	L	I	I	D	Secondary dermatitis caused by an infection, Thrush.
M	O	N	I	M	E	N	T	A person acting in a ridiculous fashion.
M	O	N	I	S	T	I	C	Of one type or character.
M	O	N	I	T	I	O	N	Admonition, Warning, Caution, Summons, Citation, Ecclesiastical Order, Forewarning.
M	O	N	I	T	O	R	Y	Warning, Admonishing, Cautioning, Advisory, Remonstratory, Counselling, Moralizing
M	O	N	K	E	Y	E	D	Fooled, Trifled, Tampered, Meddled, Interfered.
M	O	N	K	F	I	S	H	Bottom-dwelling sharks that resemble skates or rays.
M	O	N	K	H	O	O	D	Profession of a monk.
M	O	N	K	S	E	A	L	Endangered species of hair seal.
M	O	N	O	B	A	T	H	Single solution with ingredients for multi-processing of film.
M	O	N	O	B	L	O	C	Made in one casting.
M	O	N	O	C	A	R	P	Annual fruiting and then dying.
M	O	N	O	C	L	E	D	Wearing a monocle.
M	O	N	O	C	R	A	T	Autocrat, One who governs alone.
M	O	N	O	C	Y	T	E	A leukocyte with an oval or horseshoe-shaped nucleus.
M	O	N	O	D	I	S	T	Writer, singer or composer of monody.
M	O	N	O	D	O	N	T	Having one tooth.
M	O	N	O	G	A	M	Y	Marriage with one person at any set time.
M	O	N	O	G	E	N	Y	The descent of man from a single created pair.
M	O	N	O	G	O	N	Y	Asexual reproduction.
M	O	N	O	G	R	A	M	Cipher composed of interwoven letters representing an initial used on clothing.
M	O	N	O	G	Y	N	Y	Having one wife at a time, Having one chief or leader.
M	O	N	O	L	I	T	H	A single great stone, Colossus.
M	O	N	O	L	O	G	Y	Monologue, Habit of soliloquizing.
M	O	N	O	M	A	R	K	A system for a firm or person registering a combination of letters as an identifying mark.
M	O	N	O	M	I	A	L	A single word or term.
M	O	N	O	M	I	C	T	Rock of a single mineral species.
M	O	N	O	P	O	D	E	Having only one foot.
M	O	N	O	P	O	L	Y	Domination of all aspects of the market, Exclusive possession, Cartel, Syndicate.
M	O	N	O	R	A	I	L	Single rail for railway cars.
M	O	N	O	T	I	N	T	A single colur, Monochrome.
M	O	N	O	T	O	N	E	Speaking or chanting in an unvaried tone, Humdrum, Intone.
M	O	N	O	T	O	N	Y	Lack of variety, Sameness, Depressing uniformity.
M	O	N	O	T	Y	P	E	Single species, Used for a typesetting apparatus.
M	O	N	O	X	I	D	E	An oxide containing one atom of oxygen in the molecule.
M	O	N	O	X	I	M	E	A compound containing one oxime grouping.
M	O	N	S	I	E	U	R	Mister, A courtesy title used for a Frenchman.
M	O	N	S	T	E	R	A	A genus of tropical American climbing plants.
M	O	N	T	E	I	T	H	A large silver punch bowl with a scalloped rim.
M	O	N	T	I	C	L	E	A little hill.
M	O	N	U	M	E	N	T	Commemorate, Document, Record, Memorial, Testimonial, Memento, Tribute, Headstone.
M	O	O	C	H	I	N	G	Ambling, Sauntering, Slinking, Sponging, Cadging, Sneaking, Stealing.
M	O	O	N	B	E	A	M	Ray of light from the moon.
M	O	O	N	C	A	L	F	Monster, Dolt, Simpleton.
M	O	O	N	E	Y	E	D	An eye affected with moon blindness, American freshwater fish, Bloater.
M	O	O	N	F	A	C	E	A face as round as a full moon.
M	O	O	N	G	L	O	W	Moonlight.
M	O	O	N	L	E	S	S	Having no moonlight.
M	O	O	N	S	A	I	L	A light sail of a clipper ship.
M	O	O	N	S	E	E	D	A plant having crescent-shaped seeds and bluish black fruits.
M	O	O	N	T	Y	P	E	A system of large embossed letters to assist the blind but differing from braille.
M	O	O	N	W	O	R	T	A fern, Honesty.
M	O	O	R	B	A	L	L	A globular mass of filaments of a green algae.
M	O	O	R	C	O	C	K	A male red grouse.
M	O	O	R	E	I	T	E	A mineral consisting of a hydrous basic sulfate of magnesium, zinc and manganese.
M	O	O	R	F	O	W	L	Red grouse.
M	O	O	R	G	A	M	E	Same as MOORFOWL.
M	O	O	R	H	A	W	K	Marsh harrier.
M	O	O	R	L	A	N	D	An infertile area of land usually covered with heather and bracken.
M	O	O	R	W	O	R	T	Bog rosemary.

1	2	3	4	5	6	7	8	Definition
M	O	O	T	A	B	L	E	Debatable.
M	O	O	T	H	A	L	L	Town hail.
M	O	O	T	H	I	L	L	A hill used as a meeting place.
M	O	O	T	N	E	S	S	Used of a case before a court.
M	O	P	E	Y	E	D		Nearsighted.
M	O	Q	U	E	T	T	E	Upholstery fabric with a pile.
M	O	R	A	L	I	S	T	One who leads a moral life, One concerned with moral principles.
M	O	R	A	L	I	T	Y	Goodness, Probity, Rectitude, Righteousness, Rightness, Virtue, Ethics.
M	O	R	A	L	I	Z	E	Preach, Sermonize, Lecture, Pontificate.
M	O	R	A	T	O	R	Y	Authorizing delay in payment of an obligation.
M	O	R	A	V	I	A	N	Descendant of medieval Slavic people.
M	O	R	B	I	D	L	Y	Gloomily, Sickly, Morosely, Moodily, Sullenly.
M	O	R	B	I	F	I	C	Diseased.
M	O	R	D	A	N	C	Y	Incisiveness, Harshness, Sharply, Critical feeling.
M	O	R	E	O	V	E	R	Besides, Further.
M	O	R	E	S	Q	U	E	Characteristic of Moorish art.
M	O	R	I	B	U	N	D	Dormant, Approaching death, Expiring, Decadent, Deteriorating, Regressing.
M	O	R	I	L	L	O	N	European duck.
M	O	R	M	Y	R	U	S	Genus of fishes comprising oily fleshed edible fishes and including the sacred fishes.
M	O	R	O	C	C	O		Morocco red.
M	O	R	O	C	C	A	N	Inhabitant of Morocco.
M	O	R	O	N	I	T	Y	Stupidity.
M	O	R	O	S	E	L	Y	Sullenly.
M	O	R	O	X	I	T	E	Bluish variety of apatite.
M	O	R	P	H	E	A	N	Producing sleep.
M	O	R	P	H	E	U	S	Something that prolongs sleep.
M	O	R	P	H	I	N	E	A bitter crystalline narcotic habit-forming base.
M	O	R	T	A	L	L	Y	Grievously, Awfully, Extremely, Intensely, Dreadfully, Fatally, Vitally, Terribly.
M	O	R	T	A	R	E	D	Plastered.
M	O	R	T	G	A	G	E	Pledge, Security, Binding obligation.
M	O	R	T	I	S	E	D	Fastened securely.
M	O	R	T	L	I	N	G	Wool taken from a dead sheep.
M	O	R	T	M	A	I	N	An inalienable possession of lands by an ecclesiastical or other corporation.
M	O	R	T	U	A	R	Y	A place where dead bodies are kept. Funeral home, Characteristic of death.
M	O	S	Q	U	I	T	O	A two-winged insect, the female of which transmits diseases.
M	O	S	S	B	A	C	K	An old turtle with a mosslike growth on its back.
M	O	S	S	L	I	K	E	Resembling moss.
M	O	S	S	P	I	N	K	A low-tufted perennial phlox.
M	O	S	S	R	O	S	E	A variety of cabbage rose.
M	O	T	H	B	A	L	L	A ball of naphthalene to prevent moths, Preserve, Inactivate.
M	O	T	H	E	R	E	D	Produced, Escorted, Ministered.
M	O	T	I	L	I	T	Y	Contractility.
M	O	T	I	O	N	A	L	Kinetic, Characterized by motion.
M	O	T	I	O	N	E	D	Proposed, Recommended, Signalled, Gestured, Signalled.
M	O	T	I	O	N	E	R	One that proposes or instigates.
M	O	T	I	V	A	T	E	Impel, Incite, Provoke, Excite, Galvanize, Rouse, Stimulate.
M	O	T	I	V	I	T	Y	Producing motion, Available energy.
M	O	T	O	R	B	U	S	Automotive omnibus, Motorcoach.
M	O	T	O	R	C	A	R	Automobile.
M	O	T	O	R	I	A	L	Motor.
M	O	T	O	R	I	N	G	Driving of automobiles.
M	O	T	O	R	I	S	T	One who drives a car.
M	O	T	O	R	I	Z	E	Equip with a motor.
M	O	T	O	R	M	A	N	An operator of a motor-driven vehicle.
M	O	T	O	R	W	A	Y	Superhighway.
M	O	T	T	L	I	N	G	Mingling of other colours, Spotting, Dappling, Speckling.
M	O	U	C	H	I	N	G	Mooching.
M	O	U	F	F	L	O	N	A wild mountain sheep.
M	O	U	L	D	I	N	G	Shaping, Forming, Making, Fashioning, Fancy trimming for walls and doors.
M	O	U	L	T	I	N	G	Losing plumage, Shedding skin or shell.
M	O	U	N	D	I	N	G	Banking, Heaping, Fortifying, Piling, Fencing, Gathering, Bounding.
M	O	U	N	T	A	I	N	Steep elevation, High land mass, Heap, Hunk, Crisis, Pile, Quantity.
M	O	U	N	T	A	N	T	An adhesive used for fastening a print or drawing to a mount, Specimen between glass sides
M	O	U	N	T	I	E	S	Members of the Royal Canadian Mounted Police.
M	O	U	N	T	I	N	G	Frame, Support, Embellishment, Astounding, Climbing, Escalating, Scaling, Rising.
M	O	U	R	N	F	U	L	Sad, Doleful, Dispirited, Dismal, Regrettable, Melancholy, Depressing, Lamentable.
M	O	U	R	N	I	N	G	Grieving, Sorrowing, Pining, Drooping, Bewailing, Protesting.

1	2	3	4	5	6	7	8	Definition
M	O	U	S	E	E	A	R	European hawkweed.
M	O	U	T	H	F	U	L	A quantity that fills the mouth.
M	O	U	T	H	I	N	G	Grimace, Oration, Accustoming a horse to the bridle.
M	O	V	A	B	L	E	S	Pieces of property that are not fixed.
M	O	V	E	L	E	S	S	Motionless, Fixed, Immobile.
M	O	V	E	M	E	N	T	Manoeuvre, Action, Activity, Tendency, Trend, Motion, Time, Tempo. Affiliation.
M	O	V	I	N	G	L	Y	Touchingly, Affectingly, Emotionally, Poignantly, Eloquently.
M	O	V	I	N	G	U	I	West-African leguminous tree having straw-coloured wood.
M	O	W	B	U	R	N	T	Hay or straw damaged through being stored while still damp.
M	O	Z	Z	E	T	T	A	Short ecclesiastical cape.
M	U	C	E	D	I	N	E	Mould, Fungus.
M	U	C	H	A	C	H	A	A young girl, A female servant.
M	U	C	H	N	E	S	S	Very extensive, Huge quantity.
M	U	C	I	L	A	G	E	A gelatine obtained from seaweeds, Viscid solution of gum.
M	U	C	I	N	O	I	D	Resembling mucin.
M	U	C	I	N	O	U	S	Mucoid.
M	U	C	K	H	E	A	P	A pile of manure.
M	U	C	K	H	I	L	L	Same as MUCK-HEAP.
M	U	C	K	R	A	K	E	To ferret out scandal. To publicly expose corruption and misconduct.
M	U	C	K	W	O	R	M	A worm found in manure. Guttersnipe.
M	U	C	O	C	E	L	E	A sac or hollow organ distended with mucus.
M	U	C	O	S	I	T	Y	Being mucous.
M	U	C	U	L	E	N	T	Mucoid.
M	U	D	D	L	I	N	G	Bungling, Jumbling, Confusing, Befuddling, Bewildering, Disarranging.
M	U	D	D	Y	I	N	G	Soiling, Begriming, Dirtying, Smudging, Tarnishing, Clouding, Dulling, Confusing.
M	U	D	G	U	A	R	D	A protective shield against flying stones on the fenders of cars.
M	U	D	S	T	O	N	E	Shale produced by the consolidation of mud.
M	U	F	F	L	I	N	G	Enveloping, Blindfolding, Suppressing, Silencing, Dulling, Stifling, Deadening, Wrapping.
M	U	G	H	O	U	S	E	Alehouse.
M	U	H	A	R	R	A	M	A Muslim festival.
M	U	I	S	H	O	N	D	Weasels of Southern Africa that emit a fetid odour when disturbed.
M	U	L	B	E	R	R	Y	A tree with edible acid berrylike dark purple fruit.
M	U	L	C	H	I	N	G	Layering mulch on the soil.
M	U	L	C	T	I	N	G	Punishing, Penalizing, Fining, Milking, Swindling, Bleeding, Extorting, Defrauding.
M	U	L	E	D	E	E	R	A long-eared deer.
M	U	L	E	T	E	E	R	A driver in charge of a team of mules.
M	U	L	I	S	H	L	Y	Stubbornly, Obstinately.
M	U	L	L	I	G	A	N	A stew of meat, fish, vegetables or any available foodstuffs.
M	U	L	T	E	I	T	Y	Multiplicity, Variety, Diversity, Multifariousness.
M	U	L	T	I	F	I	D	Cleft into many parts.
M	U	L	T	I	P	E	D	Any animal with more than one foot.
M	U	L	T	I	P	L	E	Many, Manifold, Several, Repeated, Various, Complex, Collective, Numerous.
M	U	L	T	I	P	L	Y	Increase, Augment, Amplify, Spread, Boost, Enlarge, Expand, Magnify.
M	U	M	B	L	I	N	G	Muttering, Fumbling, Murmuring, Stuttering, Stumbling.
M	U	M	M	Y	I	N	G	Mummifying, Embalming.
M	U	N	C	H	I	N	G	Crunching, Noisy chewing, Eating with relish, Masticating, Chomping, Scrunching.
M	U	N	G	O	O	S	E	Mongoose.
M	U	N	I	M	E	N	T	Title deeds, Charters, Judgments.
M	U	N	I	T	I	O	N	War material, Armament.
M	U	R	D	E	R	E	D	Slaughtered, Killed, Destroyed, Mutilated, Teased, Tormented, Mangled, Assassinated.
M	U	R	D	E	R	E	R	Assassin, Manslayer, Homicide, Killer.
M	U	R	E	N	G	E	R	One in charge of a wall of a town and responsible for its maintenance.
M	U	R	E	X	I	D	E	A red crystalline compound having a green lustre and once used as a dye.
M	U	R	I	A	T	E	D	Pickled in brine.
M	U	R	I	C	A	T	E	Roughened with sharp hard points.
M	U	R	I	F	O	R	M	Resembling a mouse or a rat.
M	U	R	K	S	O	M	E	Quite murky.
M	U	R	M	U	R	E	D	Grumbled, Muttered, Rumoured, Whispered, Complained, Accused, Reported, Repined.
M	U	R	M	U	R	E	R	One that murmurs.
M	U	R	R	H	I	N	E	Made of murra.
M	U	S	C	A	D	I	N	A young French fop. A royalist sympathiser during the French Revolution.
M	U	S	C	A	T	E	L	A sweet dessert wine.
M	U	S	C	I	D	A	E	A family of two-winged flies including the house-fly.
M	U	S	C	U	L	A	R	Sinewy, Brawny, Mighty, Vigorous, Forceful, Sturdy, Strong, Fibrous.
M	U	S	H	R	O	O	M	Illiterate, Uncultured.
M	U	S	H	R	O	O	M	Fungi, Expand, Grow, Burst, Detonate.
M	U	S	I	C	A	L	E	Social entertainment with musical performances.

1	2	3	4	5	6	7	8	
M	U	S	I	C	I	A	N	One who is a skilled performer in one of the arts of music.
M	U	S	I	N	G	L	Y	Contemplatively.
M	U	S	K	C	A	V	Y	Hutia, A rodent almost extinct.
M	U	S	K	D	E	E	R	A small deer.
M	U	S	K	D	U	C	K	A duck that exudes a musky odour during breeding season.
M	U	S	K	E	T	R	Y	Technique of using small-arms and automatic rifles.
M	U	S	K	R	O	O	T	A plant with an aromatic root.
M	U	S	K	W	O	O	D	The timber of this tree is used as a substitute for mahogany.
M	U	S	L	I	N	E	T	A heavy muslin fabric.
M	U	S	Q	U	A	S	H	The fur of the musk-rat.
M	U	S	T	A	C	H	E	Moustache.
M	U	S	T	E	R	E	D	Enlisted, Enrolled, Convened, Assembled, Collected, Accumulated, Congregated.
M	U	S	T	E	R	E	R	A ranch hand who rounds up livestock.
M	U	T	A	T	I	O	N	Significant alteration, Change, Modification, Turn, Variation, Permutation, Innovation.
M	U	T	A	T	I	V	E	Factive.
M	U	T	C	H	K	I	N	Scotch unit of liquid capacity.
M	U	T	E	N	E	S	S	Dumbness, Speechless, Voiceless.
M	U	T	I	C	A	T	E	Growing without a point.
M	U	T	I	L	A	T	E	Cripple, Dismember, Injure, Spoil, Sterilize, Deface, Damage, Maim.
M	U	T	I	L	L	I	D	A wasp, Velvet ant.
M	U	T	I	N	E	E	R	Rebel, Anarchist, Insurgent, Malcontent, Revolter.
M	U	T	I	N	I	E	D	Revolted, Insurrected, Rebelled.
M	U	T	I	N	O	U	S	Rebellious, Turbulent, Unruly, Insubordinate, Seditious, Factious.
M	U	T	T	E	R	E	D	Grumbled, Growled, Murmured, Mumbled, Rumoured, Whispered.
M	U	T	T	E	R	E	R	One that mutters.
M	U	T	U	A	L	L	Y	Together, Conjointly, Jointly, Reciprocally.
M	U	Z	Z	L	I	N	G	Gagging, Nuzzling, Restraining, Silencing, Muffling.
M	Y	A	T	O	N	I	A	Muscular flabbiness, Lack of muscle tone.
M	Y	C	E	L	I	U	M	Spore filaments of fungi.
M	Y	C	E	T	O	I	D	Fungoid.
M	Y	C	E	T	O	M	A	Invasion of deep tissue with fungi.
M	Y	C	E	T	O	M	E	One of a pair of insect organs.
M	Y	C	O	C	I	D	E	A fungicide that destroys mould.
M	Y	C	O	L	O	G	Y	A branch of botany dealing with fungi.
M	Y	E	L	I	T	I	S	Inflammation of the spinal cord or the bone marrow.
M	Y	E	L	O	N	I	C	Relating to the spinal cord.
M	Y	E	L	O	S	I	S	Leukemia.
M	Y	O	B	L	A	S	T	Undifferentiated cell capable of giving rise to muscle cells.
M	Y	O	G	E	N	I	C	Cardiac muscular contraction.
M	Y	O	G	R	A	P	H	Recording device.
M	Y	O	P	A	T	H	Y	Disorder of muscle tissue or muscles.
M	Y	O	P	H	O	R	E	Part of a shell adapted for the attachment of a muscle.
M	Y	O	S	I	T	I	S	Excessive discomfort, Muscular pain from an infection or an unknown cause.
M	Y	O	S	M	I	N	E	A heterocyclis liquid base formed during smoking.
M	Y	O	S	O	T	I	S	A large genus of herbs, Forget-me-not.
M	Y	O	T	A	T	I	C	Stretching of a tendon followed by a reflex contraction of a muscle.
M	Y	R	I	A	P	O	D	Centipede.
M	Y	R	I	A	R	C	H	An ancient Grecian commander of ten thousand men.
M	Y	R	M	I	D	O	N	Hireling, Loyal retainer, Attendant.
M	Y	R	R	H	I	N	E	Murrhine.
M	Y	R	T	A	L	E	S	Order of shrubs, herbs or trees.
M	Y	S	T	I	C	A	L	Cryptic, Enigmatic, Obscure, Furtive, Secret, Unintelligible, Clandestine, Covert.
M	Y	S	T	I	Q	U	E	Complex of transcendental beliefs developing around an object.
M	Y	T	A	C	I	S	M	Excessive or wrong use of the letter "m" or of the sound it represents.
M	Y	T	H	I	C	A	L	Imaginary, Fancied, Fictitious, Fabulous, Legendary, Visionary, Fanciful, Created.
M	Y	X	E	D	E	M	A	Severe hypothyroidism.
M	Y	X	O	C	O	E	L	A body cavity that is only partly of coelomic origin.
M	Y	X	O	C	Y	T	E	A stellate cell that is characteristic of mucous tissue.
M	Y	X	O	P	O	D	A	Protozoa.

N

1	2	3	4	5	6	7	8	
N	A	C	R	E	O	U	S	Pearly.
N	A	D	O	R	I	T	E	A mineral consisting of lead chloride and stibnite.
N	A	I	L	F	I	L	E	A manicure implement for keeping nail growth controlled.
N	A	I	L	H	E	A	D	A flat head of a nail used for decoration.

1	2	3	4	5	6	7	8	
N	A	I	L	W	O	R	T	Whitlow grasses.
N	A	I	N	S	O	O	K	A soft lightweight cotton fabric.
N	A	I	S	S	A	N	T	Issuant, In heraldry-rising from the middle.
N	A	M	E	A	B	L	E	Identifiable, Memorable, Noteworthy.
N	A	M	E	L	E	S	S	Obscure, Bastard, Unidentifiable.
N	A	M	E	S	A	K	E	One named after another person.
N	A	P	H	T	H	O	L	Compounds derived from betanapthol.
N	A	P	I	F	O	R	M	Turnip-shaped.
N	A	P	O	L	E	O	N	French gold coin, Rich pastry, Card game.
N	A	R	C	E	I	N	E	Bitter crystalline narcotic alkaloid found in opium.
N	A	R	C	I	S	S	I	Genus of bulbous herbs.
N	A	R	C	O	S	I	S	Stupor, Insensibility, Unconsciousness.
N	A	R	C	O	T	I	C	Drug, Dope, Opiate, Anodyne, Soporific, Hypnotic, Somnific, Somnolent.
N	A	R	G	H	I	L	E	A pipe resembling a hookah.
N	A	R	I	C	O	R	N	Horny segment covering nostrils of some birds.
N	A	R	I	N	G	I	N	A bitter crystalline glucoside found in the blossoms or fruit of the grapefruit.
N	A	R	R	A	T	E	D	Told, Related, Recited, Recounted.
N	A	R	R	A	T	E	R	One that narrates.
N	A	R	R	O	W	E	D	Contracted, Decreased, Restricted, Limited, Constricted, Cramped, Fixed, Limited.
N	A	R	R	O	W	E	R	Closer, Nearer.
N	A	R	R	O	W	L	Y	Barely, Carefully, Intensely, Closely, Tightly, Nearly, Scarcely.
N	A	S	A	L	I	T	Y	Being nasal in utterance.
N	A	S	A	L	I	Z	E	To speak in a nasal manner.
N	A	S	C	E	N	C	Y	Birth, Origin.
N	A	S	I	C	O	R	N	Having a horn on the nose, Rhinoceros.
N	A	T	A	L	I	T	Y	Birthrate.
N	A	T	A	N	T	I	A	Suborder of Decapoda, SHrimps, Prawns.
N	A	T	A	T	I	O	N	Art of swimming.
N	A	T	A	T	O	R	Y	Used for swimming.
N	A	T	H	L	E	S	S	Nevertheless, Notwithstanding.
N	A	T	I	C	O	I	D	Snail.
N	A	T	I	O	N	A	L	Public, Civic, Civil, Domestic, Internal, Municipal, Native.
N	A	T	I	V	E	L	Y	Innately, Naturally.
N	A	T	I	V	I	S	M	Policy of favouring the indigenous people.
N	A	T	I	V	I	T	Y	Christmas, Festival to commemorate the birth of Christ.
N	A	T	T	E	R	E	D	Chattered, Babbled, Clacked, Jawed, Prattled.
N	A	T	T	I	E	S	T	Smartest, Sprucest.
N	A	T	U	R	I	S	M	Nudism.
N	A	T	U	R	I	S	T	Adherent of Naturism.
N	A	U	P	L	I	U	S	Curstacean larva in first stage after leaving the egg.
N	A	U	S	E	A	N	T	Expectorant.
N	A	U	S	E	A	T	E	Abhor, Loathe, Disgust, Reluct, Repel, Repulse, Revolt, Sicken.
N	A	U	S	E	O	U	S	Nauseated, Sickening, Loathsome, Disgusting.
N	A	U	T	I	C	A	L	Associated with the sea and navigation.
N	A	U	T	I	L	U	S	Shellfish.
N	A	V	A	L	I	S	M	Dominance of naval policies.
N	A	V	I	C	E	R	T	Official permit to prevent seizure of goods during a naval blockade.
N	A	V	I	C	U	L	A	Boat-shaped diatoms.
N	A	V	I	G	A	T	E	Move, Walk, Negotiate, Travel, Steer, Pass, Direct, Voyage.
N	A	V	Y	B	L	U	E	Dark dull blue favoured for naval uniforms.
N	A	Z	A	R	E	N	E	Christian.
N	A	Z	A	R	I	T	E	Man of ancient Israel or Judal consecrated to God for a set time.
N	A	Z	I	F	I	E	D	Subject to Nazi control.
N	E	A	R	C	T	I	C	Greenland and adjacent regions.
N	E	A	R	H	A	N	D	Adjacent, Nearby.
N	E	A	R	M	I	S	S	Just failed, Just short of success.
N	E	A	R	N	E	S	S	Close relationship, Intimacy, Frugality, Stinginess.
N	E	A	T	H	E	R	D	Cowherd, Herdsman.
N	E	A	T	N	E	S	S	Orderliness, Shipshape, Tidiness, Trimness, Spotless, Correctness, Systematic.
N	E	B	U	L	I	Z	E	Reduce to a fine spray.
N	E	B	U	L	O	U	S	Hazy, Indistinct, Turbid, Clouded, Nobular, Misty.
N	E	B	U	L	O	S	E	Same as NEBULOSE.
N	E	C	K	B	A	N	D	Part of a shirt to which the collar is sewn, Ornamental band worn about the neck.
N	E	C	K	L	A	C	E	String of beads, Chain or band, Trimming or decoration that belongs around the neck.
N	E	C	K	W	E	A	R	Article of clothing work around the neck, collars, ties, scarves.
N	E	C	R	O	P	S	Y	Postmortem examination.

1	2	3	4	5	6	7	8	Definition
N	E	C	R	O	S	I	N	A toxic substance that hastens blood coagulation.
N	E	C	R	O	T	I	C	Characterized by producing necrosis, Death of tissue.
N	E	C	T	A	R	E	D	Mingled with nectar, Deliciously sweet.
N	E	C	T	O	P	O	D	A limb adapted for swimming.
N	E	E	D	F	I	R	E	Purificatory fire traditionally kindled to ward off evil spirits.
N	E	E	D	L	E	S	S	Unnecessary, Gratuitious, Superfluous.
N	E	E	D	L	I	N	G	Irritating, Goading, Prodding, Worrying, Harassing, Pestering, Plaguing, Teasing.
N	E	G	A	T	I	N	G	Denying, Contravening, Nullifying, Abolishing, Invalidating, Frustrating, Neutralizing.
N	E	G	A	T	I	O	N	Denial, Contradiction, Gainsaying.
N	E	G	A	T	I	V	E	Adverse, Detrimental, Unfavourable.
N	E	G	A	T	R	O	N	Electron.
N	E	G	L	I	G	E	E	A woman's long flowing dressing gown, Informal attire.
N	E	G	R	I	T	I	C	Resembling negroes.
N	E	G	R	I	T	O	S	Negro people of small stature found in south eastern part of Asia.
N	E	G	R	O	I	S	M	To advocate equal rights for negroes, Distinctive of negroes.
N	E	I	G	H	I	N	G	Loud prolonged calling typical of a horse whinnying.
N	E	M	A	L	I	N	E	Fibrous.
N	E	M	A	L	I	O	N	Genus of wormlike branching algae.
N	E	M	A	L	I	T	E	A fibrous brucite.
N	E	M	A	T	O	D	A	Parasitic roundworms.
N	E	M	A	T	O	I	D	Relating to the Nematoda.
N	E	M	E	R	T	E	A	Soft-bodied worms that burrow in sand or mud.
N	E	M	O	B	I	U	S	Genus of crickets which inhabit open fields.
N	E	N	U	P	H	A	R	Water lily, Egyptian lotus.
N	E	O	B	L	A	S	T	Various cells of worms that regenerate lost parts.
N	E	O	L	A	T	I	N	New Latin, Romance.
N	E	O	L	O	G	I	C	Relating to neology.
N	E	O	M	Y	C	I	N	An antibiotic active against a wide variety of bacteria.
N	E	O	N	A	T	A	L	Affecting the newborn and the first month of life.
N	E	O	P	H	R	O	N	Genus of Old World vultures.
N	E	O	P	H	Y	T	E	A new convert to the church.
N	E	O	P	L	A	S	M	Malignant tumour.
N	E	O	T	E	N	I	C	A termite colony having a new king or queen.
N	E	P	A	L	E	S	E	Relating to Nepal.
N	E	P	E	N	T	H	E	Narcotic, Opiate, Drug causing oblivion.
N	E	P	H	R	I	T	E	A form of jade once thought to be remedy for kidney disease.
N	E	P	H	R	O	I	D	Reniform, Bean-shaped.
N	E	P	H	R	O	M	A	Malignant tumour of the renal cortex.
N	E	P	H	R	O	P	S	Genus of lobsters.
N	E	P	I	O	N	I	C	Immature larval.
N	E	P	O	T	I	S	M	Showing favouritism to relatives especially in the field of employment.
N	E	P	O	T	I	S	T	One who practices nepotism.
N	E	R	O	N	I	A	N	Resembling Nero.
N	E	R	O	N	I	Z	E	Tyrannize in the manner of Nero.
N	E	R	V	A	T	E	D	Supported.
N	E	S	C	I	E	N	T	Ignorant, Agnostic.
N	E	S	T	L	I	N	G	Settling, Sheltering, Snuggling, Cuddling, Embedding, Occupying a nest.
N	E	T	H	I	N	I	M	Servants performing low menial services in an ancient Jewish tabernacle.
N	E	T	T	A	P	U	S	Genus of geese with legs so short as to be almost useless on land.
N	E	T	T	L	I	N	G	Provoking, Inciting, Irritating, Angering, Displeasing, Exasperating, Peeving, Riling.
N	E	U	R	A	L	G	Y	Neuralgia.
N	E	U	R	I	T	I	S	Inflammation of a nerve.
N	E	U	R	O	P	I	L	Delicate terminal branch of a nerve fibre.
N	E	U	R	O	S	I	S	Functional disorder of the central nervous system manifested by anxiety.
N	E	U	R	O	T	I	C	Nervous, Relating to neurosis.
N	E	U	T	R	I	N	O	An uncharged elementary particle with a zero rest mass.
N	E	W	C	O	M	E	R	Novice, Immigrant, Apprentice, Beginner, Freshman, Novitiate, Tenderfoot, Neophyte.
N	E	W	M	O	D	E	L	Reorganize, Remodel.
N	E	W	S	H	A	W	K	Reporter for a news agency, newspaper or periodical.
N	E	W	S	R	O	O	M	Office where news is processed for publication or presentation.
N	I	B	B	L	I	N	G	Biting piece by piece, Trimming, Shaping, Carping, Trifling.
N	I	C	E	L	I	N	G	An overfastidious person.
N	I	C	E	N	E	S	S	State of being nice.
N	I	C	K	E	L	I	C	Containing nickel.
N	I	C	K	N	A	C	K	Knicknack, Small or trivial article, Trifle, Petty trick.
N	I	C	K	N	A	M	E	Misapply the name of someone, A familiar form of a proper name.
N	I	C	O	T	I	N	E	A very poisonous volatile weakly basic liquid alkaloid.

1	2	3	4	5	6	7	8	Definition
N	I	D	U	L	A	N	T	Embedded, Nestling.
N	I	D	U	L	A	T	E	Same as NIDULANT.
N	I	F	F	N	A	F	F	Trifle.
N	I	G	E	R	I	A	N	Relating to Nigeria.
N	I	G	G	L	I	N	G	Carping, Gnawing, Petty, Measly, Paltry, Trifling, Pettifogging.
N	I	G	H	N	E	S	S	Closeness, Nearness.
N	I	G	H	T	C	A	P	A head covering to wear in bed, The last drink, The final race.
N	I	G	H	T	J	A	R	Nocturnal bird.
N	I	G	H	T	M	A	N	A night worker, Watchman.
N	I	G	H	T	O	W	L	A person who keeps late hours.
N	I	H	I	L	I	S	M	Extreme doctrine that no reality exists, Terrorism.
N	I	H	I	L	I	S	T	Terrorist.
N	I	H	I	L	I	T	Y	Nullity, Trifle, Amounting to nothing.
N	I	M	B	A	T	E	D	Haloed, Having a nimbus.
N	I	M	B	L	E	S	T	Liveliest, Most agile.
N	I	N	E	E	Y	E	S	Lamprey.
N	I	N	E	F	O	L	D	Being nine times as large, Having nine parts.
N	I	N	E	P	I	N	S	A bowling game played without the headpin.
N	I	N	E	T	E	E	N	Being one more than eighteen, Used to designate the years of the twentieth century.
N	I	N	E	V	I	T	E	Inhabitant of the ancient city of Nineveh.
N	I	T	I	D	I	T	Y	Brilliance, Sheen.
N	I	T	R	A	T	E	D	Converted into a nitro compound.
N	I	T	R	O	G	E	N	A common nonmetallic element colourless odourless tasteless insoluble inert diatomic gas.
N	I	T	R	O	L	I	M	Calcium cyanamide.
N	I	T	R	O	X	Y	L	Nitryl.
N	I	Z	A	M	A	T	E	Territory of a soverign of Hyderabad, India.
N	O	A	C	H	I	A	N	Ancient, Aged, Antiquated, Related to the time of Noah, Antediluvian.
N	O	B	B	L	I	N	G	Stealing, Taking, Swindling, Cheating, Drugging a racehorse, Bribing.
N	O	B	E	L	I	U	M	Artificially produced radioactive element.
N	O	B	I	L	I	T	Y	Superiority, Aristocracey, Eminence, High-born.
N	O	B	L	E	M	A	N	Peer, Belonging to the nobility, Aristocrat.
N	O	B	L	E	S	S	E	Noble birth.
N	O	C	T	I	L	I	O	Genus of American fish-eating mastiff bats.
N	O	C	T	U	A	R	Y	Journal of nocturnal incidents.
N	O	C	T	U	R	N	E	Dreamy, pensive composition for the piano, Painting of a night scene.
N	O	D	I	C	O	R	N	Having a nodose antennae.
N	O	D	I	F	O	R	M	Resembling a node.
N	O	D	O	S	I	T	Y	Protuberance, Swelling, Node.
N	O	D	U	L	I	Z	E	Convert into nodules.
N	O	D	U	L	O	S	E	Having minute nodules.
N	O	E	M	A	T	I	C	Involved in intellectual or abstract reasoning.
N	O	I	S	E	T	T	E	Meat cooked and served in small rounds.
N	O	M	A	D	I	S	M	Roving, Wandering, Wayfaring, Vagrancy.
N	O	M	A	D	I	Z	E	To live like a vagabond.
N	O	M	A	R	C	H	Y	Department of modern Greece.
N	O	M	I	N	A	T	E	Designate, Name, Specify, Propose, Appoint, Present, Proffer, Tender.
N	O	M	I	S	T	I	C	Conforming to moral law.
N	O	M	O	L	O	G	Y	The science of the laws of the mind.
N	O	N	B	E	I	N	G	Void, Nonexistence.
N	O	N	C	L	A	I	M	Failure to claim within the time-limit designated.
N	O	N	E	N	T	R	Y	Failure to enter.
N	O	N	E	S	U	C	H	Paragon, Matchless, Unequalled, Unrivalled.
N	O	N	G	R	A	T	A	Unwelcome.
N	O	N	H	U	M	A	N	Other than a human being.
N	O	N	I	O	N	I	C	Detergent.
N	O	N	J	U	R	O	R	A person refusing to take an oath of allegiance.
N	O	N	M	E	T	A	L	A chemical element not exhibiting typical metallic properties.
N	O	N	M	O	R	A	L	Amoral, Not in the sphere of morals or ethics.
N	O	N	P	A	R	T	Y	Nonpartisan, Not affliated with any political party.
N	O	N	P	O	L	A	R	Lacking a dipole, Having a low dielectric.
N	O	N	R	I	G	I	D	Maintaining form by pressure of contained gas.
N	O	N	S	E	N	S	E	Babble, Drivel, Jabber, Rubbish, Trash, Tomfoolery, Twaddle, Humbug.
N	O	N	T	O	X	I	C	Not poisonous for indicated agents.
N	O	N	U	N	I	O	N	Failure to unite.
N	O	N	V	O	C	A	L	Silent, No voice.
N	O	N	Y	L	E	N	E	Liquid isomeric hydrocarbon of ethylene series.
N	O	O	N	T	I	D	E	Midday, Apex, Acme, Climax, Culmination, Peak, Pinnacle, Summit.

1	2	3	4	5	6	7	8	
N	O	P	I	N	E	N	E	A terpene associated with alph-pinene in turpentine oils.
N	O	R	M	A	L	C	Y	Normality, Being normal.
N	O	R	M	A	L	L	Y	Commonly, Usually, Customary, Naturally, Typically, Regularly.
N	O	R	S	E	M	A	N	Ancient Scandinavian.
N	O	R	T	H	E	R	N	Lying north.
N	O	R	T	H	I	N	G	Going north.
N	O	R	T	H	M	A	N	Inhabitant of a northern region.
N	O	S	E	B	A	N	D	Part of the bridle of a horse.
N	O	S	E	C	L	I	P	A small clamp to prevent water entering the nose of a swimmer.
N	O	S	E	D	I	V	E	To plunge headlong, Sudden drop.
N	O	S	E	L	E	A	F	Skin on the nose of certain bats.
N	O	S	E	L	E	S	S	Lacking a nose.
N	O	S	E	L	I	T	E	Mineral that is a sodium aluminosilicate and sulfa.
N	O	S	E	R	I	N	G	A ring in the nose of an animal for control.
N	O	S	O	L	O	G	Y	A classification of diseases.
N	O	T	A	L	I	A	N	Relating to south temperate marine realm.
N	O	T	A	N	D	U	M	Note, Memorandum.
N	O	T	A	R	I	A	L	Executed by a notary.
N	O	T	A	T	I	O	N	Note, Observation, Memo, Notandum.
N	O	T	A	T	I	V	E	Suggesting things denoted.
N	O	T	C	H	I	N	G	Indenting, Nicking, Incising, Cutting, Gashing.
N	O	T	E	B	O	O	K	A book with blank pages for entering notes.
N	O	T	E	L	E	S	S	Undistinguished, Not noticed, Unmusical.
N	O	T	I	C	I	N	G	Recognizing, Greeting, Marking, Alluding, Notifying, Discerning, Observing, Perceiving.
N	O	T	I	F	I	E	D	Observed, Informed, Advised, Apprised, Posted, Told, Warned, Published.
N	O	T	I	O	N	A	L	Theoretical, Visionary, Imaginary, Unreal, Whimsical, Fanciful, Shadowy, Ideal.
N	O	T	O	G	E	A	N	Area of Australasia and adjacent islands.
N	O	T	O	R	N	I	S	Genus of flightless birds of New Zealand.
N	O	T	R	O	P	I	S	Genus of N. American fishes.
N	O	T	T	U	R	N	O	Serenade, Nocturne.
N	O	U	M	E	I	T	E	Variety of silicate mineral.
N	O	U	M	E	N	A	L	An unknowable object such as a soul.
N	O	U	M	E	N	O	N	An object conceived in the mind.
N	O	V	A	T	I	A	N	A member of a puritannical Early Christian sect.
N	O	V	A	T	I	O	N	Innovation, Substitution of a new legal obligation for an old one.
N	O	V	E	L	E	S	E	The use of trite expressions and poor quality language in a certain type of novel.
N	O	V	E	L	I	S	H	Novelistic, Typical style of a novel.
N	O	V	E	L	I	S	T	Writer of novels.
N	O	V	E	L	I	Z	E	To convert into a novel, Fictionalize.
N	O	V	E	M	B	E	R	The eleventh month of the Gregorian calendar.
N	O	V	E	N	A	R	Y	Novena, a devotion of Catholicism.
N	O	V	E	R	C	A	L	Characteristic of a stepmother.
N	O	W	A	D	A	Y	S	At the present time.
N	U	B	E	C	U	L	A	A cloudy condition of the urine, A speck in the eye.
N	U	B	I	L	I	T	Y	Physically attractive in a sexual way.
N	U	B	I	L	O	U	S	Cloudy, Foggy, Misty, Obscure, Vague, Unclear, Uncertain, Ambiguous.
N	U	C	A	M	E	N	T	Ament, Catkin.
N	U	C	E	L	L	A	R	Relating to a nucellus.
N	U	C	E	L	L	U	S	Cell mass of the centre of an ovule.
N	U	C	I	F	O	R	M	Shaped like a nut.
N	U	C	L	E	A	S	E	Enzymes found in plants and animals.
N	U	C	L	E	A	T	E	Cluster, form into a nucleus.
N	U	C	L	E	O	L	E	Nucleolus, Any undifferentiated nuclear body other than a chromosone.
N	U	C	L	E	O	M	E	The entire nuclear content of a protoplast.
N	U	C	U	L	A	N	A	Type genus of beaked cockles.
N	U	C	U	L	O	I	D	Family of marine bivalve mollusks.
N	U	D	I	C	A	U	L	Having leafless stems.
N	U	G	A	T	O	R	Y	Worthless, Invalid, Vain.
N	U	I	S	A	N	C	E	Harm, Injury, Pest, Annoyance, Bother, Exasperation, Irritant, Plague.
N	U	M	B	E	R	E	D	Computed, Estimated, Included, Tallied, Counted, Apportioned, Divided, Enumerated.
N	U	M	B	E	R	E	R	Enumerator.
N	U	M	B	N	E	S	S	Stupefaction, Lacking feeling, Reduced sensitivity.
N	U	M	E	R	A	T	E	Enumerate, List, Count, Number, Tally, Tell, Classify, Index.
N	U	M	E	R	O	U	S	Many, Multifarious, Populous, Several, Sundry, Various, Plentiful, Large.
N	U	M	I	N	O	U	S	Magical, Supernatural, Sacred, Holy, Spiritual, Mysterious, Incomprehensible.
N	U	M	M	U	L	A	R	Marked by circular or oval lesions.
N	U	M	S	K	U	L	L	Bonehead, Dunce, Blockhead, Woodenhead, Stupid, Dense, Thick.

1	2	3	4	5	6	7	8	Definition
N	U	N	C	H	E	O	N	Mid-morning or mid-afternoon snack of bread, cheese and beer.
N	U	N	D	I	N	A	L	Relating to a special market-day in ancient Rome.
N	U	P	T	I	A	L	S	Weddings, Marriages, Ceremonies relating to marriage.
N	U	R	S	L	I	N	G	One that is cared for, A nursing mammal.
N	U	R	T	U	R	E	D	Fostered, Nursed, Nourished, Educated, Civilized.
N	U	T	A	T	I	O	N	Spiral course of apex of growing plant, Involuntary nodding of the head.
N	U	T	B	R	O	W	N	Brown as a nut.
N	U	T	H	A	T	C	H	Family of small birds with long wings and short tails that creep over branches of trees.
N	U	T	H	O	U	S	E	Lunatic asylum.
N	U	T	R	I	E	N	T	Nutritious, Nourishing, Nutritive, Promoting growth.
N	U	T	S	H	E	L	L	Shell of a kernel, Something small.
N	U	Z	Z	L	I	N	G	Snuggling, Burrowing, Cuddling, Nestling.
N	Y	C	T	E	R	I	S	Genus of bats.
N	Y	M	P	H	A	E	A	Water lilies.
N	Y	M	P	H	I	S	H	Resembling a nymph.
N	Y	S	T	A	T	I	N	Yellow crystalline antibiotic active against fungi.

O

1	2	3	4	5	6	7	8	Definition
O	A	K	A	P	P	L	E	An oak gall caused by the larva of a wasp.
O	A	T	G	R	A	S	S	Wild oat.
O	B	D	U	C	I	N	G	Enveloping, Covering.
O	B	D	U	R	A	C	Y	Callousness, Heartless, Inflexibility, Relentlessly, Rigidly.
O	B	D	U	R	A	T	E	Inflexible, Unyielding, Harsh, Rugged, Rough, Unfeeling, Coldhearted, Adamant.
O	B	E	D	I	E	N	T	Subservient, Docile, Tractable, Biddable, Compliant, Submissive, Dutiful, Loyal.
O	B	E	I	S	A	N	T	Menial, Obsequious, Servile, Slavish, Deferential, Bowing in homage.
O	B	E	L	I	Z	E	D	Marked as doubtful or spurious.
O	B	I	T	U	A	R	Y	Notice of a person's death combined with a short biographical account.
O	B	J	E	C	T	E	D	Protested, Remonstrated, Expostulated, Dissented, Challenged, Kicked, Balked, Complained.
O	B	J	E	C	T	O	R	One that objects.
O	B	L	A	T	I	O	N	Offering or sacrifice of something without life.
O	B	L	A	T	O	R	Y	Relating to oblation.
O	B	L	I	G	A	N	T	Surety for a bond, Person bonded under a surety bond.
O	B	L	I	G	A	T	E	Bound, Restricted, Bind, Fasten, Pledge, Essential, Necessary, Initiate.
O	B	L	I	G	A	T	O	A noisy accompaniment.
O	B	L	I	G	I	N	G	Amiable, Good-tempered, Pleasing, Accommodating, Favouring, Gratifying, Forcing.
O	B	L	I	Q	U	E	D	Advanced at an angle.
O	B	L	I	V	I	O	N	Oblivious.
O	B	L	I	V	I	T	Y	Forgetfulness, Insensibleness.
O	B	N	O	U	N	C	E	Portend, To tell of an ill omen, Forewarn.
O	B	R	O	G	A	T	E	To modify or repeal a law.
O	B	R	O	T	U	N	D	Having the form of a flattened cylinder.
O	B	S	C	U	R	E	D	Concealed, Hidden, Darkened, Eclipsed, Clouded, Overshadowed, Disguised, Screened.
O	B	S	C	U	R	E	R	One that obscures.
O	B	S	E	R	V	E	D	Heeded, Obeyed, Remarked, Watched, Conformed, Celebrated, Commemorated.
O	B	S	E	R	V	E	R	Representative sent to observe and listen.
O	B	S	E	S	S	E	D	Bewitched, Dominated, Gripped, Possessed, Dogged, Harassed, Haunted, Plagued.
O	B	S	I	D	I	A	N	Volcanic glass.
O	B	S	O	L	E	T	E	Disused, Neglected, Outmoded, Reduced, Effaced, Extinct, Outworn, Superseded.
O	B	S	T	A	C	L	E	Obstruction, Impediment, Snag, Hindrance, Hurdle, Handicap, Encumbrance.
O	B	S	T	R	U	C	T	Retard, Impede, Hinder, Block, Brake, Screen, Close, Plug.
O	B	T	A	I	N	E	D	Held, Kept, Possessed, Attained, Reached, Succeeded, Acquired, Secured.
O	B	T	A	I	N	E	R	One that obtains.
O	B	T	E	C	T	E	D	Enclosed, Covered, Hidden.
O	B	T	E	M	P	E	R	Submit, Comply, Obey.
O	B	T	E	S	T	E	D	Beseeched, Supplicated, Protested, Invoked as a witness.
O	B	T	R	U	D	E	D	Extruded, Intruded, Imposed, Infringed, Presumed.
O	B	T	R	U	D	E	R	One that obtrudes.
O	B	T	U	N	D	E	D	Dulled, Blunted, Turned, Lacked an edge.
O	B	T	U	R	A	T	E	Obstruct, Close.
O	B	T	U	S	E	L	Y	Dully, Stupidly, Stolidly.
O	B	T	U	S	I	T	Y	Condition of being blunted.
O	B	V	E	R	T	E	D	Turned, Confronted.
O	B	V	I	A	T	E	D	Prevented, Avoided, Averted, Deterred, Forestalled, Anticipated, Precluded, Warded.
O	B	V	O	L	U	T	E	Overlapping, Contorted, Convolute.
O	C	C	A	M	I	S	M	Doctrine of Occam.

1	2	3	4	5	6	7	8	
O	C	C	A	M	I	S	T	Doctrine of Occam.
O	C	C	A	S	I	O	N	Opportunity, Happening, Requirement, Opening, Cause, Obligation, Occurrence, Episode.
O	C	C	I	D	E	N	T	West, Opposite to Orient.
O	C	C	I	S	I	O	N	Slaughter.
O	C	C	L	U	D	E	D	Closed, Obstructed, Blocked, Choked, Clogged, Congested, Obstructed, Plugged.
O	C	C	L	U	D	E	R	A body part that closes or blocks another.
O	C	C	U	L	T	E	D	Concealed, Undisclosed, Eclipsed, Buried, Ensconced, Secreted, Stashed, Hidden.
O	C	C	U	L	T	L	Y	Secretly.
O	C	C	U	P	A	N	T	Tenant, Resident, Inhabitant, Dweller, Habitant.
O	C	C	U	P	I	E	D	Seized, Engrossed, Engaged Immersed, Populated, Inhabited, Employed, Working.
O	C	C	U	P	I	E	R	One holding possession of property.
O	C	C	U	R	R	E	D	Appeared, Happened, Chanced, Developed, Transpired, Struck.
O	C	E	A	N	I	A	N	Inhabitant of Oceania.
O	C	E	A	N	I	T	Y	Degree to which the ocean affects the climate of adjacent land.
O	C	E	L	L	A	T	E	Eyelike.
O	C	H	E	R	O	U	S	Resembling the yellow of ochre.
O	C	H	I	D	O	R	E	Shore crab.
O	C	O	T	I	L	L	O	A desert shrub.
O	C	T	A	P	O	D	Y	Octameter, Having eight metrical feet.
O	C	T	O	B	A	S	S	A huge contrabass with three strings.
O	C	T	O	D	O	N	T	Having eight teeth.
O	C	T	O	N	A	R	Y	A group of eight verses.
O	C	T	O	P	O	D	A	Mollusks with eight arms, Octopuses.
O	C	T	O	P	O	L	E	A system of eight electric charges arranged in two quadrupoles.
O	C	T	O	R	O	O	N	A person with one-eighth Negro ancestry.
O	C	T	U	P	L	E	T	A combination of eight of a kind.
O	C	U	L	A	R	L	Y	Visually, Visibly.
O	D	I	O	U	S	L	Y	Hatefully, Offensively.
O	D	O	G	R	A	P	H	Instrument for plotting course and distance travelled by a vehicle.
O	D	O	M	E	T	E	R	Instrument for measuring distance traversed by a vehicle.
O	D	O	N	T	O	I	D	Toothlike.
O	D	O	N	T	O	M	A	Tumour originating from a tooth and containing dental tissue.
O	E	D	I	P	E	A	N	Relating to the Oedipus complex.
O	E	N	A	N	T	H	E	Small genus of Old World passerine birds.
O	E	N	O	L	O	G	Y	Enology, Science of wine making.
O	E	R	L	I	K	O	N	Automatic aircraft or antiaircraft cannon.
O	E	S	T	R	O	U	S	Estrous, Being on heat, Ready for mating.
O	F	F	B	R	E	A	K	Bowled ball in cricket.
O	F	F	E	N	D	E	D	Trespassed, Transgressed, Violated, Breached, Contravened, Infringed, Affronted.
O	F	F	E	N	D	E	R	Transgressor.
O	F	F	E	R	I	N	G	Tendering, Proposing, Extending, Presenting, Alleging, Trying, Attempting, Showing.
O	F	F	G	O	I	N	G	Departure, Exit, Egress, Exodus, Withdrawal.
O	F	F	I	C	I	A	L	Authorized, Certified, Cleared, Endorsed, Approved, Sanctioned.
O	F	F	L	Y	I	N	G	Outlying, Remote.
O	F	F	P	R	I	N	T	An excerpt separately printed.
O	F	F	S	H	O	O	T	Outgrowth, Derived branch, descendant or member.
O	F	F	S	H	O	R	E	Situated off the shore.
O	F	F	S	T	A	G	E	Away from the stage, Unofficially.
O	F	F	W	H	I	T	E	A colour resembling white but having a tinge of gray or cream.
O	F	T	T	I	M	E	S	Often.
O	H	M	M	E	T	E	R	An instrument for indicating directly resistance in ohms.
O	I	L	C	L	O	T	H	Linoleum, Fabric made waterproof by coating with oily preparations.
O	I	L	F	I	E	L	D	A region of petroleum deposits.
O	I	L	F	I	R	E	D	Using oil as a fuel.
O	I	L	G	L	A	N	D	A gland that secretes oil.
O	I	L	I	N	E	S	S	State of being oily.
O	I	L	P	A	P	E	R	Paper soaked in oil to render it waterproof.
O	I	L	P	R	O	O	F	Impervious to oil.
O	I	L	S	K	I	N	S	Suit made of oilskins usually for marine use.
O	I	L	S	T	O	N	E	Whetstone used with oil for sharpening metal.
O	I	N	T	M	E	N	T	A medicinal or antiseptic salve with a greasy base for application to the skin.
O	I	T	I	C	I	C	A	S. American tree with a pecan-like nut that yields oil.
O	K	O	L	E	H	A	O	A pot-still used in Hawaii.
O	L	D	T	I	M	E	R	Veteran, Old-hand, Antique, Oldster, Elder, Senior citizen.
O	L	D	W	E	N	C	H	Queen triggerfish.
O	L	D	W	O	R	L	D	Old-fashioned, Picturesque.
O	L	E	A	C	E	A	E	Family of shrubs.

OLEACINA   8 LETTERS   OPIFICER

1	2	3	4	5	6	7	8	Clue
O	L	E	A	C	I	N	A	Genus of West Indian carnivorous land snails.
O	L	E	A	N	D	E	R	Ornamental evergreen shrub with fragrant flowers.
O	L	E	A	S	T	E	R	Wild tree of the cultivated olive.
O	L	E	O	C	Y	S	T	Oil-containing organ of a portugese man-of-war.
O	L	E	O	S	O	M	E	Fatty inclusion in cytoplasm.
O	L	I	B	A	N	U	M	Frankincense.
O	L	I	P	H	A	N	T	A hunter's horn made from an elephant tusk.
O	L	I	V	E	O	I	L	Non-drying oil obtained from the pulp of the olives.
O	L	Y	M	P	I	A	D	Four year period between Olympic games.
O	L	Y	M	P	I	A	N	Lofty, Superlative, Olympic.
O	L	Y	M	P	I	C	S	Olympic games.
O	M	A	D	H	A	U	N	Fool, Idiot, Simpleton.
O	M	E	L	E	T	T	E	Dish made of beaten eggs cooked in butter.
O	M	I	S	S	I	O	N	Oversight, Lapse, Slip, Failure, Disregard, Break, Gap, Overlook.
O	M	I	T	T	I	N	G	Failing to include, Leaving undone, Neglecting, Forbearing.
O	M	M	A	T	E	U	M	Compound eye.
O	M	N	I	T	U	D	E	Totality, Universality.
O	M	N	I	V	O	R	A	A group comprising the pigs and hippopotamuses.
O	M	O	D	Y	N	I	A	Pain in the shoulder.
O	M	O	H	Y	O	I	D	Muscle in the shoulder.
O	M	O	I	D	E	U	M	Upper jaw bones of birds.
O	M	O	P	L	A	T	E	Scapula, Shoulder blade.
O	M	P	H	A	L	I	C	Relating to the navel.
O	M	P	H	A	L	O	S	Focal point, Umbilicus, Navel.
O	N	C	E	O	V	E	R	Single swift examination, Rapid survey.
O	N	C	I	C	O	L	A	Genus of parasitic worms.
O	N	C	I	D	I	U	M	Genus of American orchid.
O	N	C	O	G	E	N	Y	The process of tumour formation.
O	N	C	O	L	O	G	Y	The study of tumours.
O	N	C	O	M	I	N	G	Approaching, Moving forward, Rising, Emergent, Approach.
O	N	C	O	T	O	M	Y	Surgical incision of a swelling.
O	N	E	H	O	R	S	E	Inferior, Inadequate, Second-rate, Trivial, Insular.
O	N	E	S	I	D	E	D	Partial, Unjust, Unfair, Unilateral.
O	N	E	T	R	A	C	K	Unimaginitive mind, Single interest, Limited in scope, Lacking initiative, Undiversified.
O	N	L	I	N	E	S	S	The only one of its kind.
O	N	L	O	O	K	E	R	A passive spectator, Observer.
O	N	O	M	A	N	C	Y	Divination from the letters of a name.
O	N	R	U	S	H	E	D	Rushing forward rapidly.
O	N	S	T	R	E	A	M	Going into operation.
O	N	T	O	G	E	N	Y	The biological development of an individual organism.
O	N	T	O	L	O	G	Y	Science of being.
O	N	Y	C	H	I	U	M	Fingernail, Toenail.
O	N	Y	C	H	O	I	D	Resembling a fingernail in shape or texture.
O	O	G	A	M	E	T	E	A female gamete.
O	O	G	A	M	O	U	S	Fusion of small mobile male gamete and large immobile female gamete.
O	O	G	O	N	I	U	M	Descendant of a primordial germ cell.
O	O	K	I	N	E	T	E	A motile zygote, as a malaria parasite.
O	O	L	O	G	I	S	T	Collector of bird's eggs.
O	O	P	H	O	R	O	N	Ovary.
O	O	S	P	H	E	R	E	Ovum.
O	P	A	L	E	S	C	E	Iridescence.
O	P	A	L	I	S	E	D	Convert into opal.
O	P	E	N	C	A	S	T	Mine with surface excavation.
O	P	E	N	D	O	O	R	Accessible, Public, Unrestricted.
O	P	E	N	E	Y	E	D	Watchful.
O	P	E	N	N	E	S	S	Exposure, Liability, Vulnerability.
O	P	E	N	W	O	R	K	Work that is perforated or pierced, Lacy.
O	P	E	R	A	H	A	T	A top hat with a crown that can be collapsed.
O	P	E	R	A	T	E	D	Performed, Worked, Initiated, Acted, Traded, Managed, Functioned, Steered.
O	P	E	R	A	T	I	C	Performance of an opera, Exaggerated display of emotional temperament.
O	P	E	R	A	T	O	R	Driver, Fraud, Cheat.
O	P	E	R	C	L	E	D	Having a gill cover.
O	P	E	R	E	T	T	A	A light musical production with spoken drama and dancing and singing.
O	P	H	I	D	I	A	N	Snakelike.
O	P	H	I	D	I	I	D	Eels.
O	P	H	I	U	R	A	N	Starfish.
O	P	I	F	I	C	E	R	Workman, Maker.

1	2	3	4	5	6	7	8	
O	P	I	N	A	B	L	E	Constituting an object of opinion.
O	P	I	U	M	D	E	N	A place where opium is bought and smoked.
O	P	O	P	O	N	A	X	Odorous gum resin used in medicine.
O	P	P	I	L	A	T	E	Obstruct, Block up.
O	P	P	O	N	E	N	S	Digit muscles of the hand and foot.
O	P	P	O	N	E	N	T	Antagonist, Adversary, Opposer, Enemy, Foe, Competitor, Rival, Combatant.
O	P	P	O	S	I	N	G	Contesting, Matching, Pitting, Confronting, Resisting, Disputing, Fighting, Combating.
O	P	P	O	S	I	T	E	Facing, Contrary, Contrast, Contradictory, Antagonistic, Polar, Reverse, Different.
O	P	P	U	G	N	E	D	Withstood, Contended, Controverted, Battled, Tugged.
O	P	P	U	G	N	E	R	Challenger.
O	P	S	O	N	I	Z	E	To modify by the action of opsonin.
O	P	T	A	T	I	V	E	Expressing desire or wish.
O	P	T	I	C	I	A	N	Maker or dealer in optical instruments and items.
O	P	T	I	C	O	E	L	The cavity of the optic vesicle.
O	P	T	I	M	A	C	Y	Aristocracy.
O	P	T	I	M	I	S	M	Doctrine that reality is essentially good, Sanguinity, Buoyancy, Positivism, Happiness.
O	P	T	I	M	I	S	T	Idealist, Positivist.
O	P	T	I	M	I	Z	E	To make the best of.
O	P	T	I	O	N	A	L	Not compulsory, Discretionary, Voluntary, Alternative, Free.
O	P	U	L	E	N	C	E	Wealth, Riches, Affluence, Plenty, Profusion, Amplitude, Lavishness, Extravagance.
O	P	U	L	E	N	C	Y	Same as OPULENCE.
O	P	U	S	C	U	L	E	A small or petty work, Minor work.
O	R	A	B	A	S	S	U	S. American monkeys.
O	R	A	C	U	L	A	R	Forecasting, Divining.
O	R	A	N	G	E	L	O	Hybrid citrus fruit produced by crossing an orange and a pomelo.
O	R	A	N	G	E	R	Y	Greenhouse for growing oranges.
O	R	A	T	O	R	I	O	Musical composition based on a scriptual or religious subject.
O	R	B	I	C	U	L	E	Spherical body or pellets found in granites or rocks.
O	R	C	A	D	I	A	N	Relating to the Orkney islands.
O	R	C	H	E	S	I	S	Dancing in the Greek chorus.
O	R	D	A	I	N	E	D	Arranged, Ordered, Regulated, Managed, Conducted, Instituted, Enacted, Dictated.
O	R	D	A	I	N	E	R	One that ordains.
O	R	D	E	R	I	N	G	Arranging, Directing, Marshalling, Commanding, Organizing, Disposition, Distribution.
O	R	D	I	N	A	N	D	A person about to be ordained.
O	R	D	I	N	A	N	T	A person who ordains.
O	R	D	I	N	A	R	Y	Routine, Normal, Common, Abundant, Plain, Usual, Natural, Casual.
O	R	D	I	N	A	T	E	Arranged in rows.
O	R	D	N	A	N	C	E	Military supplies.
O	R	E	A	M	N	O	S	Mountain goat.
O	R	G	A	N	D	I	E	Fine transparent plain-woven muslin with a crisp finish.
O	R	G	A	N	I	S	M	Something felt to resemble a living plant or animal, System.
O	R	G	A	N	I	S	T	An organ player.
O	R	G	A	N	I	Z	E	Found, Integrate, Unionize, Create, Establish, Institute, Arrange, Dispose.
O	R	I	C	H	A	L	C	A yellow metallic substance considered precious by the ancient Greeks.
O	R	I	E	N	T	A	L	Belonging to the East, Asiatic.
O	R	I	E	N	T	E	D	Faced to the East, Position defined in relation to the East, Directed to a given position.
O	R	I	G	I	N	A	L	Initial, Primary, Pristine, Fresh, New, Creative, Fertile, Novel.
O	R	I	L	L	I	O	N	A projection built out at the corner of a bastion.
O	R	I	N	A	S	A	L	Pronounced through mouth and nose.
O	R	N	A	M	E	N	T	Adjunct, Decoration, Embellish, Beautify, Bedeck, Trim, Garnish, Enrich.
O	R	N	A	T	E	L	Y	Flamboyantly, Floridly.
O	R	N	I	T	H	I	C	Relating to birds.
O	R	O	G	R	A	P	H	A machine that makes topographical maps.
O	R	O	M	E	T	E	R	An aneroid barometer that also gives elevation above sea-level.
O	R	P	H	A	N	C	Y	Orphanhood.
O	R	P	H	A	N	E	D	Deprived of parents.
O	R	P	I	M	E	N	T	Mineral consisting of arsenic trisulfide.
O	R	T	H	I	C	O	N	Type of camera tube.
O	R	T	H	O	D	O	X	Conservative, Conventional, Accepted, Traditionalistic, Sanctioned, Customary, Approved.
O	R	T	H	O	E	P	Y	Study of pronunciation.
O	R	Y	Z	E	N	I	N	A glutelin found in the seeds of rice.
O	R	Y	Z	O	M	Y	S	Genus of rodents, Rice rats.
O	S	C	I	N	I	N	E	Relating to singing birds.
O	S	C	I	T	A	N	T	Yawning with drowsiness, Lazy, Stupid.
O	S	C	U	L	A	N	T	Embracing, Connecting link between two groups.
O	S	C	U	L	A	T	E	Kiss, Have characters in common with two groups.
O	S	N	A	B	U	R	G	Rough coarse durable cotton fabric.

1	2	3	4	5	6	7	8	
O	S	S	I	A	N	I	C	Resembling the legendary Irish bard Ossian.
O	S	S	I	F	I	E	D	Fixed, Hardened, Ultraconservative, Changed to bone.
O	S	T	E	I	T	I	S	Inflammation of bone.
O	S	T	I	N	A	T	O	Recurrent musical figure in a composition.
O	S	T	I	O	L	A	R	Orifice in seaweed, sponges, fungus or lichens.
O	S	T	R	A	C	E	A	Oysters.
O	S	T	R	A	C	O	D	Crustacea enclosed in a bivalve shell.
O	S	T	R	A	K	O	N	Fragment of pottery containing a written inscription.
O	S	T	R	E	G	E	R	Falconer who keeps goshawks.
O	S	T	R	E	O	I	D	Resembling an oyster.
O	T	I	D	I	D	A	E	Family of Old World birds.
O	T	I	O	S	I	T	Y	Functionless, Profitless.
O	T	O	L	O	G	I	C	Relating to otology, science that deals with the ear and its diseases.
O	T	O	R	R	H	E	A	Discharge from the outer ear.
O	T	O	S	C	O	P	E	Magnifying instrument with a light to examine internal ears.
O	T	O	S	C	O	P	Y	Examination of the ear.
O	U	I	S	T	I	T	I	Marmoset.
O	U	R	I	C	U	R	I	An important Brazilian feather palm.
O	U	T	B	L	O	O	M	Blossom, Burgeon, Flower.
O	U	T	B	L	U	F	F	To oudo in bluffing.
O	U	T	B	O	A	R	D	Outside the line of a ship's hull.
O	U	T	B	O	U	N	D	Outward bound traffic.
O	U	T	B	R	A	V	E	To resist defiantly, Exceed in courage.
O	U	T	B	R	E	A	K	Sudden increase, Insurrection, Revolt.
O	U	T	B	R	E	E	D	Eliminate characteristics by breeding.
O	U	T	B	U	R	S	T	Intense surge of activity, Eruption, Explosion.
O	U	T	C	A	S	T	E	One considered outside society.
O	U	T	C	L	A	S	S	To excel or surpass.
O	U	T	C	R	O	S	S	Hybrid.
O	U	T	D	A	R	E	D	Defied.
O	U	T	D	A	T	E	D	Antiquated, Outmoded, Ancient, Old-fashioned, Obsolete, Archaic, Old-time, Superseded.
O	U	T	D	O	I	N	G	Defeating, Exceeding, Excelling, Surpassing, Overcoming.
O	U	T	D	O	O	R	S	Out of a building, In the open air.
O	U	T	D	W	E	L	L	To live in a remote area.
O	U	T	F	A	C	E	D	Stared down, Challenged, Bearded, Braved, Dared, Defied, Ventured.
O	U	T	F	I	E	L	D	A field far away from the farmhouse.
O	U	T	F	L	A	N	K	Bypass.
O	U	T	F	L	A	S	H	Outshine.
O	U	T	F	L	U	N	G	Thrown wide.
O	U	T	G	A	R	T	H	Outer yard.
O	U	T	G	O	I	N	G	Issue, Demonstrative, Expansive, Unreserved, Outlay, Expenditure.
O	U	T	G	R	O	W	N	Grown too large, Exceeded rate of growth.
O	U	T	G	U	A	R	D	Guard at an outpost.
O	U	T	G	U	E	S	S	To anticipate future events correctly.
O	U	T	G	U	I	D	E	A card placed in a file where material has been temporarily removed.
O	U	T	H	E	R	O	D	Exceedingly violent or extravagant.
O	U	T	H	O	U	S	E	Outbuilding, Outside toilet.
O	U	T	L	A	W	E	D	Forbidden, Banned, Enjoined, Prohibited, Inhibited, Interdicted, Banished.
O	U	T	L	A	W	R	Y	Making something illegal, Freedom from legal or conventional restraint.
O	U	T	L	E	A	P	T	Jumped over.
O	U	T	L	E	A	R	N	Surpass in learning.
O	U	T	L	I	N	E	D	Defined, Bound, Bordered, Edged, Surrounded, Sketched, Drafted, Skeletonized.
O	U	T	L	I	V	E	D	Outlasted, Survived, Outworn, Outstayed.
O	U	T	L	Y	I	N	G	Extraneous, Extrinsic, Remote, Distant, Removed, Far-off, Far-away.
O	U	T	M	A	R	C	H	Surpass in marching.
O	U	T	M	A	R	R	Y	To marry a person in a superior class.
O	U	T	M	A	T	C	H	Outdo, Surpass.
O	U	T	M	O	D	E	D	Obsolete, Old-fashioned, Archaic, Old-time, Veteran, Vintage.
O	U	T	P	A	C	E	D	Surpassed in speed, Outdone.
O	U	T	P	O	I	N	T	Obtain more points in a contest.
O	U	T	R	A	G	E	D	Raped, Defiled, Ravished, Violated, Abused, Maltreated, Persecuted, Oppressed.
O	U	T	R	A	N	G	E	Surpass in range, Excel.
O	U	T	R	E	A	C	H	Exceed, Overreach, Outwit, Outmanoeuvre, Outsmart, Outjockey, Outfox.
O	U	T	R	I	D	E	R	Attendant, Motor-cyclist, Scout, Harbinger, Portent, Forerunner, Herald, Precursor.
O	U	T	R	I	G	H	T	Completely, Utter, Absolute, Downright, Perfect, Positive, Whole, Total.
O	U	T	R	I	V	A	L	To outdo in competition.
O	U	T	S	C	O	R	E	To score more points.

1	2	3	4	5	6	7	8	
O	U	T	S	H	I	N	E	Excel, Surpass, Beat, Better, Exceed, Outstrip, Top, Transcend.
O	U	T	S	H	O	N	E	Surpassed, Excelled in splendour.
O	U	T	S	I	D	E	R	Stranger, Alien, Foreigner, One who is isolated, A competitor with little chance of winning.
O	U	T	S	I	G	H	T	Perception, Capacity to observe.
O	U	T	S	K	I	R	T	Border, Fringe, Environ, Suburb, Somewhere remote.
O	U	T	S	L	E	E	P	To sleep later.
O	U	T	S	L	E	P	T	Slept later.
O	U	T	S	M	A	R	T	Outwit, Outjockey, Outmanoeuvre, Outthink, Undo.
O	U	T	S	P	E	A	K	To speak out forcefully.
O	U	T	S	P	E	N	T	Exhausted.
O	U	T	S	P	O	R	T	To go beyond the limits in sport.
O	U	T	S	T	A	N	D	Contradict, Resist stubbornly, To stand out clearly.
O	U	T	S	T	A	R	E	Outface, Stare down.
O	U	T	S	T	A	R	T	Beginning, Dawning, Onset, Opening, Outset.
O	U	T	S	T	R	I	P	Exceed, Excel, Surpass, Outpace, Outrun, Outdistance, Outshine, Beat.
O	U	T	S	W	E	A	R	To surpass in swearing.
O	U	T	S	W	E	L	L	To exceed in swelling.
O	U	T	T	O	O	U	T	Measured from outer edge to outer edge.
O	U	T	V	A	L	U	E	To be worth more.
O	U	T	V	O	T	E	D	Defeated in a contest which depended on casting votes.
O	U	T	W	A	R	D	S	Towards the outside, Externally.
O	U	T	W	A	T	C	H	To maintain a longer vigil.
O	U	T	W	E	I	G	H	Exceed in weight, value or importance, Overbalance, Compensate, Redeem.
O	V	A	R	I	O	L	E	Ovararian tube of an insect.
O	V	A	R	I	T	I	S	Inflammation of an ovary, Oophoritis.
O	V	E	R	A	G	E	D	Regarded as too old, Overstocked, Oversupplied.
O	V	E	R	A	L	L	S	Protective clothing.
O	V	E	R	A	R	C	H	Dominate.
O	V	E	R	A	W	E	D	Inspired awe, Restrained by fear.
O	V	E	R	B	E	A	R	Overwhelm, Overcome by force, To bear to excess.
O	V	E	R	B	L	O	W	Blow away, Distend, Swell.
O	V	E	R	B	O	I	L	Boil over.
O	V	E	R	B	O	L	D	Presumptuous, Impudent.
O	V	E	R	B	O	W	L	A long throw in bowls.
O	V	E	R	B	R	I	M	Overflow.
O	V	E	R	B	U	R	N	To burn too much.
O	V	E	R	C	A	L	L	To overbid in bridge.
O	V	E	R	C	A	S	T	Overthrow, Cloud, Overspread, Darken, Overshadow, Obscure, Cover, Blanket, Whipstitch.
O	V	E	R	C	O	A	T	Topcoat for winter wear, Protective coat of paint or varnish.
O	V	E	R	C	O	M	E	Subdue, Conquer, Overwhelm, Overpower, Defeat, Master, Prevail, Triumph.
O	V	E	R	C	R	O	W	Overbear, Triumph, Boast, Overpower.
O	V	E	R	D	A	T	E	To overstamp with a new date.
O	V	E	R	D	E	A	R	Too costly.
O	V	E	R	D	E	C	K	To adorn extravagantly.
O	V	E	R	D	O	N	E	Exaggerated, Exhausted, Fatigued, Overcooked.
O	V	E	R	D	O	S	E	An excessive or toxic dose.
O	V	E	R	D	R	A	W	To draw cheques in excess of amount available in account, Overstatement.
O	V	E	R	F	A	L	L	Waterfall, Water turbulence caused by winds and opposing currents.
O	V	E	R	F	E	E	D	To eat too much.
O	V	E	R	F	I	L	L	Become full to overflowing.
O	V	E	R	F	I	S	H	To fish to the depletion of the shoals.
O	V	E	R	F	L	O	W	Inundate, Surplus, Excess, Deluge, Overwhelm, Submerge, Swamp, Cascade.
O	V	E	R	F	O	L	D	To fold over.
O	V	E	R	F	U	L	L	Excessively, Extremely, Inordinately, Overmuch, Unduly.
O	V	E	R	G	R	O	W	Outgrow, Overburden, Overcome.
O	V	E	R	H	A	N	D	The upper hand, Advantage, Overarm, Handicap, Allowance.
O	V	E	R	H	A	N	G	Project, Suspend, Bulge, Jetty, Beetle, Pouch, Protrude, Jut.
O	V	E	R	H	A	U	L	Clean, Disentangle, Mend, Doctor, Patch, Rebuild, Recondition, Repair.
O	V	E	R	H	E	A	D	Over, Above, Aloft, On the floor above.
O	V	E	R	H	E	A	R	To hear something without the speaker's intention.
O	V	E	R	H	E	A	T	Excessive heat, Raise the temperature beyond the limit.
O	V	E	R	J	U	M	P	To jump too far.
O	V	E	R	K	I	L	L	Excess, Overabundance, Overflow, Overmuch, Superfluity, Surplus, Surfeit.
O	V	E	R	K	I	N	D	Excessively kind.
O	V	E	R	K	I	N	G	King who has supreme sovereignty.
O	V	E	R	K	N	E	E	Extending above the knee.
O	V	E	R	L	A	D	E	Overload.

1	2	3	4	5	6	7	8	
O	V	E	R	L	A	I	D	Superimposed, Covered, Encumbered, Overpowered, Obscured, Smothered.
O	V	E	R	L	A	I	N	Rested upon.
O	V	E	R	L	A	N	D	Upon or across land.
O	V	E	R	L	E	A	F	Other side of the page.
O	V	E	R	L	E	A	P	Omit, Ignore.
O	V	E	R	L	I	N	E	Identifying line of type. Title above a picture or cartoon.
O	V	E	R	L	I	V	E	Outlive, Live too long.
O	V	E	R	L	O	A	D	An excessive load.
O	V	E	R	L	O	C	K	Interlock, Overcast by machine.
O	V	E	R	L	O	N	G	Extremely long, Too long a time.
O	V	E	R	L	O	O	K	Inspect, Survey, Oversee, Supervise, Neglect, Ignore, Dominate, Disregard.
O	V	E	R	L	O	R	D	Tyrannize, Supreme rule.
O	V	E	R	M	O	S	T	Uppermost, Highest.
O	V	E	R	M	U	C	H	Excessive, Very, Great, Extremely, Immensely, Overfill, Ever, Inordinately, Unduly.
O	V	E	R	N	A	M	E	Name in a series.
O	V	E	R	N	I	C	E	Too fastidious, Too scrupulous.
O	V	E	R	P	A	I	D	Paid in excess of required amount.
O	V	E	R	P	A	S	S	Surmount, Discount, Surpass, Transgress, Disregard, Neglect, Cross, Forget.
O	V	E	R	P	A	S	T	Ended, Past, Over.
O	V	E	R	P	E	E	R	Overlook, Look down on.
O	V	E	R	P	L	A	Y	Overact, Magnify, Overemphasize, Accentuate, Dramatize, Overwork, Exaggerate.
O	V	E	R	P	L	U	S	Excess, Surplus, Overmuch, Plethora, Surfeit, Overskill, Superfluity, Overflow.
O	V	E	R	R	A	N	K	Too luxuriant growth.
O	V	E	R	R	A	T	E	Estimate too highly, Overvalue, Overprize, Overestimate.
O	V	E	R	R	I	D	E	Pass, Vanquish, Conquer, Annul, Supersede, Overlap, Trample, Dominate.
O	V	E	R	R	I	P	E	Decadent, Decayed, Degenerate, Flamboyant, Ornate, Sugary.
O	V	E	R	R	U	L	E	Govern, Prevail, Overcome, Supremacy, Reign, Sway, Set aside.
O	V	E	R	S	A	I	L	Project beyond the base.
O	V	E	R	S	E	A	M	Overcast seam.
O	V	E	R	S	E	A	S	Abroad, Colonial.
O	V	E	R	S	E	E	N	Mistaken, Rash.
O	V	E	R	S	E	E	R	Supervisor, Superintendent, Foreman, Boss.
O	V	E	R	S	E	L	L	To sell more than can be delivered, To make excessive claims.
O	V	E	R	S	E	W	N	Overcast sewing by machine.
O	V	E	R	S	H	O	E	Protective shoe worn over ordinary shoes in wet weather, Galosh.
O	V	E	R	S	H	O	T	Mistaken, Deceived, The upper jaw extending beyond the lower.
O	V	E	R	S	I	D	E	Over the side of a ship, Other side of a record.
O	V	E	R	S	I	Z	E	Larger than normal, Big, Fat, Great, Husky, Obese.
O	V	E	R	S	K	I	P	Omit, Pass over lightly.
O	V	E	R	S	L	I	P	Omit, Neglect, Escape.
O	V	E	R	S	M	A	N	Foreman, Chief, Umpire, Arbiter.
O	V	E	R	S	O	L	D	Share prices unrealistically low due to heavy selling.
O	V	E	R	S	O	U	L	Spiritual being having an ideal nature.
O	V	E	R	S	P	I	N	Special spin given to a cricket ball.
O	V	E	R	S	T	A	Y	To stay beyond the time limit.
O	V	E	R	S	T	E	P	Transgress, Infringe, Trespass.
O	V	E	R	S	W	A	Y	Dominate, Govern, Induce, Argue, Convince, Persuade, Prevail, Prompt.
O	V	E	R	T	A	K	E	Catch, Overhaul, Take, Seize, Involve, Captivate, Ensnare, Intoxicate.
O	V	E	R	T	I	L	T	Upset.
O	V	E	R	T	I	M	E	In excess of the set time, Additional payment for extra work performed after normal hours.
O	V	E	R	T	O	I	L	Overwork.
O	V	E	R	T	O	N	E	Harmonic, Implication, Suggestion, Connotation, Hint, Dominate, Drown.
O	V	E	R	T	R	I	P	Trip over nimbly.
O	V	E	R	T	U	R	E	Disclosure, Discovery, Revelation, Prelude, Commencement, Introduction, Foreword.
O	V	E	R	T	U	R	N	Upset, Capsize, Upturn, Prostrate, Overthrow, Topple, Subvert, Tumble.
O	V	E	R	V	E	I	L	To veil over, Shroud.
O	V	E	R	V	I	E	W	Survey, Inspect.
O	V	E	R	W	E	A	R	Exhaust by wearing too much, Wear out.
O	V	E	R	W	E	E	N	Egotistic, Arrogant, Rash, Conceited.
O	V	E	R	W	I	N	D	To wind too tightly.
O	V	E	R	W	I	S	E	Too wise.
O	V	E	R	W	O	R	K	Overdo, Overelaborate, Overplay, Overuse.
O	V	E	R	W	O	R	N	Spent, Exhausted, Stale, Obsolete, Overworked.
O	V	E	R	Y	E	A	R	Superannuate.
O	V	I	C	I	D	A	L	Relating to an ovicide.
O	V	I	D	U	C	A	L	Relating to an oviduct.
O	V	I	P	O	S	I	T	To lay eggs.

1	2	3	4	5	6	7	8	Clue
O	V	O	P	L	A	S	M	Ooplasm.
O	W	L	I	G	H	T		Dusk.
O	X	I	D	A	B	L	E	Capable of being oxidized.
O	X	I	D	I	Z	E	D	Combined with oxygen.
O	X	I	D	I	Z	E	R	The oxidizing agent.
O	X	I	M	E	T	E	R	A measuring instrument for oxygen saturation of circulating blood.
O	X	P	E	C	K	E	R	Small African bird that feeds on ticks removed from backs of cattle or wild mammals.
O	X	Y	C	A	N	U	S	Genus of moths.
O	X	Y	A	S	T	E	R	Sponge spicule.
O	X	Y	M	O	R	O	N	Combination of contradictory words.
O	X	Y	T	O	C	I	C	Hastening childbirth.
O	X	Y	T	O	C	I	N	A synthetic hormone to stimulate labour contractions.
O	Z	O	K	E	R	I	T	A waxlike mineral used in making candles.
O	Z	O	N	I	Z	E	D	Converted into ozone.
O	Z	O	N	I	Z	E	R	An apparatus for converting oxygen into ozone.

P

1	2	3	4	5	6	7	8	Clue
P	A	C	I	F	I	E	D	Appeased, Propitiated, Placated, Soothed, Mollified, Conciliated, Settled, Alleviated.
P	A	C	I	F	I	E	R	Nipple-shaped device for babies to suck or bite upon, Dummy.
P	A	C	I	F	I	S	M	Opposition to war or violence.
P	A	C	I	F	I	S	T	Adherent of pacifism, Pacific.
P	A	C	K	E	T	E	D	Made up into a parcel.
P	A	C	K	F	O	N	G	Paktong, Alloy of nickel, zinc and copper.
P	A	D	C	L	O	T	H	Saddlecloth, A cloth placed under a saddle.
P	A	C	K	S	A	C	K	Knapsack.
P	A	D	D	L	I	N	G	Rowing gently, Swimming gently, Travelling by paddlesteamer, Thrashing, Spanking.
P	A	D	I	S	H	A	H	Sovereign, Mogul, Powerful important personage.
P	A	D	S	T	O	N	E	Stone template to support the end of girder in a wall.
P	A	D	U	A	S	O	Y	A rich heavy corded silk fabric.
P	A	G	A	N	I	S	H	Heathenish.
P	A	G	A	N	I	S	M	Pagan beliefs or practices.
P	A	G	A	N	I	Z	E	To act in a pagan way.
P	A	G	A	T	P	A	T	A tree growing in mangrove swamps.
P	A	G	I	N	A	T	E	To mark with consecutive numbers.
P	A	G	O	D	I	T	E	Agalmatolite, Stone used for carving miniature pagodas.
P	A	G	U	R	I	A	N	A hermit crab.
P	A	I	N	L	E	S	S	Not experiencing pain.
P	A	I	N	T	B	O	X	A box for artists that holds tubes or cakes of paints.
P	A	I	N	T	I	N	G	Applying paint, Paintwork, Picture or design.
P	A	I	N	T	O	U	T	Obliterate by covering with paint.
P	A	I	N	T	P	O	T	Receptacle for holding paint.
P	A	I	T	R	I	C	K	Partridge.
P	A	K	I	S	T	A	N	A republic in the Indian sub-continent.
P	A	L	A	E	M	O	N	Genus of prawns.
P	A	L	M	A	T	E	D	Web-footed.
P	A	L	O	M	I	N	O	Palomino.
P	A	L	A	P	E	R	S	Documents.
P	A	L	A	T	I	A	L	Magnificent, Luxurious, Deluxe, Opulent, Plush, Luscious, Rich, Sumptuous.
P	A	L	A	T	I	N	E	Relating to a Germanic ruler, Possessing royal privileges.
P	A	L	A	T	I	O	N	Pertaining to the hard palate.
P	A	L	E	B	U	C	K	Oribi.
P	A	L	E	F	A	C	E	Caucasian, White person.
P	A	L	E	N	E	S	S	Pallor.
P	A	L	E	S	T	R	A	Gymnasium, Stadium.
P	A	L	I	F	O	R	M	Resembling a palus.
P	A	L	I	L	O	G	Y	Repetition of a word for emphasis.
P	A	L	I	N	O	D	E	Retraction.
P	A	L	I	N	O	D	Y	Same as PALINODE.
P	A	L	I	S	A	D	E	Strong defensive fence of stakes.
P	A	L	L	I	A	T	E	Cloak, Shelter, Hide, Extenuate, Excuse, Lessen, Mitigated, Alleviated.
P	A	L	L	I	D	L	Y	Wanly, Palely, Dully.
P	A	L	L	M	A	L	L	A seventeenth century game played with a wooden ball and mallet.
P	A	L	M	A	R	I	S	Muscles of the palm of the hand.
P	A	L	M	A	T	E	A	A group consisting of the web-footed birds.
P	A	L	M	E	L	L	A	Terrestrial and freshwater green algae.

1	2	3	4	5	6	7	8	
P	A	L	M	E	T	T	E	Ancient ornament resembling an Egyptian lotus.
P	A	L	M	E	T	T	O	Low-growing fan palms.
P	A	L	M	I	L	L	A	A soap plant.
P	A	L	M	I	P	E	D	Web-footed.
P	A	L	M	I	S	T	E	Cabbage palm.
P	A	L	M	I	T	I	N	An ester of glycerol and palmitic acid.
P	A	L	M	L	I	K	E	Like a palm.
P	A	L	M	O	D	I	C	Twitching, Jerkiness, Palpitation.
P	A	L	O	M	E	T	A	Californian pompano fishes.
P	A	L	O	M	I	N	O	Light tan or cream horse.
P	A	L	P	A	B	L	E	Tangible, Noticeable, Patent, Plain, Distinct, Obvious, Evident, Manifest.
P	A	L	P	A	B	L	Y	Perceptible by one of the senses.
P	A	L	P	A	T	E	D	Examined by touch.
P	A	L	P	E	B	R	A	Eyelid.
P	A	L	P	I	F	E	R	The lobe of the upper jaw of an insect.
P	A	L	P	L	E	S	S	Lacking palps.
P	A	L	P	O	C	I	L	Tactile hair.
P	A	L	S	T	A	F	F	Bronze Celtic axe designed for a split handle.
P	A	L	S	Y	I	N	G	Paralyzing.
P	A	L	T	E	R	E	D	Equivocated, Acted deceitfully, Lied, Played fast and loose.
P	A	L	T	E	R	E	R	One who acts insincerely.
P	A	L	T	R	I	L	Y	In a despicable fashion.
P	A	L	U	D	I	N	A	Viviparis, Freshwater snails.
P	A	L	U	D	I	S	M	Malaria.
P	A	L	U	D	O	U	S	Marshy.
P	A	M	A	Q	U	I	N	A toxic antimalarial drug.
P	A	M	P	E	R	E	D	Treated with extreme care, Coddled, Cossetted, Indulged, Regaled, Spoiled, Mollycoddled.
P	A	M	P	E	R	E	R	One that pampers.
P	A	M	P	H	L	E	T	Brochure, Printed unbound publication, Religious or political tract.
P	A	N	A	C	H	E	D	Variegated with stripes of colour.
P	A	N	A	T	E	L	A	A long slender cigar.
P	A	N	C	A	K	E	D	Flattened, A forced landing.
P	A	N	C	H	A	M	A	Member of the lowest caste group in India, Untouchable.
P	A	N	C	H	E	O	N	A large earthenware vessel.
P	A	N	C	R	E	A	S	A gland secreting digestive ferments.
P	A	N	D	A	L	U	S	Genus of deepwater prawns.
P	A	N	D	A	N	U	S	Tropical trees, Screw pines of Malaysia.
P	A	N	D	A	R	U	S	Genus of fish lice that attacks marine fish.
P	A	N	D	E	M	I	C	An epidemic of unusual extent and severity.
P	A	N	D	E	N	U	A	Same as PANDENUA.
P	A	N	D	E	R	E	D	Procured, Ministered, Gratified, Encouraged.
P	A	N	D	O	R	E	A	Genus of tropical Old World woody vines.
P	A	N	D	O	W	D	Y	Deep dish apple dessert.
P	A	N	E	G	Y	R	Y	A festival in honour of a god.
P	A	N	E	L	E	S	S	Lacking window panes.
P	A	N	E	L	I	S	T	Member of a discussion or advisory panel.
P	A	N	E	L	L	E	D	Decorated with panels.
P	A	N	E	L	S	A	W	A handsaw for cutting thin wood.
P	A	N	F	O	R	T	E	A holiday bread made with honey and nuts.
P	A	N	G	O	L	I	N	An ant-eater covered with scales that rolls itself into a ball when disturbed.
P	A	N	H	U	M	A	N	Relating to all humanity.
P	A	N	I	C	K	E	D	Alarmed, Terrorized, Frightened, Horrified, Fearful.
P	A	N	I	C	L	E	D	Flowers clustered in pyramid formation.
P	A	N	I	O	N	I	C	Gathering of ancient Greeks to worship Poseidon.
P	A	N	M	I	X	I	A	Nonselective mating within a closed society.
P	A	N	N	I	K	I	N	Small pan or cup made of tin.
P	A	N	O	P	T	I	C	Permitting everything to be seen.
P	A	N	O	R	A	M	A	Range, A picture that unrolls before the viewer.
P	A	N	S	O	P	H	Y	System of universal knowledge.
P	A	N	T	H	E	O	N	A temple dedicated to the gods.
P	A	N	T	O	N	A	L	Giving equal importance to each of the twelve semitones of the octave.
P	A	P	A	B	I	L	E	Qualified to become a pope.
P	A	P	A	L	I	S	M	The papal system.
P	A	P	A	L	I	S	T	Adherent of papalism.
P	A	P	A	L	I	Z	E	To make papal.
P	A	P	A	R	C	H	Y	Government by a pope.
P	A	P	E	R	B	O	Y	A young boy employed to sell and deliver newspapers.

1	2	3	4	5	6	7	8	
P	A	P	E	R	I	N	G	Lining with paper, Covering with wallpaper.
P	A	P	I	L	L	A	E	Nipples, Taste buds on the tongue.
P	A	P	I	L	L	A	R	Same as PAPILLAE.
P	A	P	I	S	T	I	C	Relating to Roman Catholicism.
P	A	P	I	S	T	R	Y	Same as PAPISTIC.
P	A	P	U	L	O	S	E	Covered with papulae.
P	A	P	Y	R	I	N	E	Vegetable parchment.
P	A	R	A	B	E	M	A	Prothesis, Preparation of the bread and wine in the Eastern Church.
P	A	R	A	B	L	E	D	Used as a parable.
P	A	R	A	B	O	L	A	Bowl-shaped antenna to receive and transmit radio waves.
P	A	R	A	C	H	O	R	Measurement of surface volume and determination of partial structure.
P	A	R	A	C	O	N	E	Cusps of a primitive upper molar.
P	A	R	A	D	I	G	M	Example, Pattern, Model, Ideal, Mirror, Standard.
P	A	R	A	D	I	N	G	Assembling, Marshalling, Advertising, Exhibiting, Flaunting, Revealing, Displaying.
P	A	R	A	D	I	S	X	Heaven, Zion, A state where souls live in eternal bliss, State of happiness.
P	A	R	A	D	O	X	Y	State of being parodoxical.
P	A	R	A	F	F	I	N	Mixture of hydrocarbons of the methane series.
P	A	R	A	F	O	R	M	Formaldehyde.
P	A	R	A	G	O	G	E	Addition of sound or syllable to the end of a word for emphasis.
P	A	R	A	G	R	A	M	A pun made by changing the letters of a word.
P	A	R	A	K	E	E	T	Parrakeet, Small parrot.
P	A	R	A	L	L	A	X	Distortion of an image caused by an apparent displacement.
P	A	R	A	L	L	E	L	Extending in the same direction but not meeting, Equate, Alike, Comparable, Similar.
P	A	R	A	L	Y	Z	E	Cripple, Disable, Disarm, Immobilize, Incapacitate, Enfeeble, Weaken, Daze.
P	A	R	A	M	E	R	E	A paired structure of an insect.
P	A	R	A	M	I	T	A	One of the perfect virtues that must be practiced before entering in Buddahood.
P	A	R	A	N	O	I	A	Delusions of persecution, Suspiciousness, Distrustful, Hallucinations.
P	A	R	A	N	O	I	D	Characterized by suspiciousness, megalomania. Afflicted with schizophrenia.
P	A	R	A	P	S	I	S	Lateral piece of thorax shield of an insect.
P	A	R	A	S	A	N	G	Ancient unit of distance.
P	A	R	A	S	H	O	T	One trained in para-shooting.
P	A	R	A	S	I	T	E	Barnacle, Bloodsucker, Leech, Hanger-on, Sponger, Sycophant, Idler.
P	A	R	A	S	T	A	S	Enclosing portico of an ancient Greek building.
P	A	R	A	T	O	M	Y	Reproduction by fission.
P	A	R	A	V	A	I	L	The lowest tenant in the feudal system.
P	A	R	A	V	A	N	E	Underwater protective device for cutting mines loose.
P	A	R	A	V	E	N	T	A screen to protect from the wind.
P	A	R	A	X	I	A	L	Located on each side of the axis.
P	A	R	C	E	N	E	R	A joint heir.
P	A	R	C	H	I	N	G	Toasting, Scorching, Drying, Shrivelling, Dehydrating, Dessicating, Burning, Searing.
P	A	R	C	L	O	S	E	Screen used to separate the chapel from main body of the church.
P	A	R	D	O	N	E	D	Excused, Tolerated, Condoned, Forgiven, Remitted, Freed, Liberated, Released.
P	A	R	D	O	N	E	R	A medieval preacher raising money by selling indulgences.
P	A	R	E	N	T	A	L	Paternal, Maternal, Originator, Source.
P	A	R	E	R	G	O	N	Ornamental accessory, Embellishment, An extra job done in addition to normal employment.
P	A	R	F	O	C	A	L	Having corresponding focal points in the same plane.
P	A	R	G	E	T	E	D	Coated with plaster, Gilded, Whitewashed.
P	A	R	G	E	T	E	R	Plasterer.
P	A	R	H	E	L	I	C	Mock sun.
P	A	R	I	E	T	A	L	Relating to special bones of the skull, Appearing on a wall.
P	A	R	I	E	T	E	S	Walls of cavities or hollows, Middle part of a barnacle shell.
P	A	R	I	S	I	A	N	Native of Paris.
P	A	R	I	S	I	T	E	A mineral consisting of a carbonate and fluorides.
P	A	R	L	A	N	C	E	Speech, Wording, Diction, Phrase, Phraseology, Phrasing, Verbalism, Wordage.
P	A	R	L	A	N	D	O	Singing in an unmusical fashion.
P	A	R	L	E	Y	E	D	Uttered, Spoke, Addressed, Conferred, Consulted, Conversed, Discussed, Discoursed.
P	A	R	M	E	L	I	A	Genus of alpine lichens.
P	A	R	M	E	S	A	N	Very hard cheese grated to flavour other foods.
P	A	R	O	D	I	E	D	Burlesqued, Composed a parody.
P	A	R	O	D	I	S	T	A writer of literary parodies.
P	A	R	O	Q	U	E	T	Parrakeet.
P	A	R	O	S	E	L	A	Dalea, Genus of herbs.
P	A	R	O	U	S	I	A	Second Advent, The presence of a Platonic idea in something.
P	A	R	O	X	Y	S	M	Spasm, Convulsion, Fit, Violent action, Eruption, Earthquake.
P	A	R	R	Y	I	N	G	Warding, Evading, Dodging, Avoiding, Shirking, Preventing, Sidestepping, Forestalling.
P	A	R	S	O	N	I	C	Clerical.
P	A	R	T	A	K	E	R	Participant, Partner, Supporter.

1	2	3	4	5	6	7	8	Clue
P	A	R	T	E	R	R	E	A formal garden, Theatre floor behind the orchestra.
P	A	R	T	H	I	A	N	Fighting on horseback with a bow and arrow.
P	A	R	T	I	B	L	E	Divisible, Separable.
P	A	R	T	I	C	L	E	Molecule, Atom, Electron, Small portion, Minute quantity, Tiny fragment, Crumb.
P	A	R	T	I	S	A	N	Adherent, Zealous advocate, Guerrilla, Patriot, Follower, Champion, Devoted, Fanatic.
P	A	R	T	N	E	R	S	Partakers, Associates, Colleagues, Assistants, Comrades, Companions, Helpers, Cohorts.
P	A	R	T	S	O	N	G	A fifteenth century German song for several voice parts.
P	A	R	T	T	I	M	E	Employed for less time than a normal working day.
P	A	R	T	Y	I	S	M	Devoted to a political party.
P	A	S	C	O	I	T	E	A mineral consisting of a hydrous calcium vanadate.
P	A	S	H	A	L	I	K	Territory governed by a pasha.
P	A	S	P	A	L	U	M	Genus of perennial grasses.
P	A	S	S	A	B	L	E	To pass inspection, Tolerable, Able to qualify.
P	A	S	S	A	B	L	Y	Moderately, Tolerably.
P	A	S	S	B	O	O	K	Bankbook.
P	A	S	S	E	D	I	X	A game played with three dice.
P	A	S	S	E	R	B	Y	One who passes by an event by chance.
P	A	S	S	E	R	E	S	Family of singing birds.
P	A	S	S	I	B	L	E	Impressionable.
P	A	S	S	L	E	S	S	Impassable.
P	A	S	S	O	V	E	R	Agricultural festival that commemorates the liberation of the Hebrews from slavery in Egypt.
P	A	S	S	P	O	R	T	Document of identification necessary for international travel.
P	A	S	S	W	O	R	D	Watchword, Identifying word to be used to a security official for egress and exit to areas.
P	A	S	T	I	C	H	E	Musical selection, Potpourri, Hodgepodge, Medley, Miscellany, Mélange, Assortment.
P	A	S	T	I	L	L	E	An aromatic sweet of gum, A medicated lozenge.
P	A	S	T	O	R	A	L	Rural, Innocent, Idyllic, Bucolic, Countrified, Rustic, Agrarian, Provincial.
P	A	S	T	O	R	L	Y	Appropriate to a pastor.
P	A	S	T	R	A	M	I	Highly seasoned smoked beef.
P	A	S	T	R	I	E	S	Confectionery, Small fancy sweet cakes usually decorated with cream or icing.
P	A	S	T	U	R	E	D	Grazed, Fed, Nourished.
P	A	T	A	G	I	U	M	Wing membrane, Fold of skin on flying squirrels and lizards.
P	A	T	A	G	I	A	L	Same as PATAGIAL.
P	A	T	A	S	H	T	E	Tropical American tree resembling cacao and yielding a chocolate substitute.
P	A	T	C	H	B	O	X	Small fancy box for holding face patches fashionable in seventeenth and eighteenth centuries.
P	A	T	C	H	E	R	Y	Patchwork, Untidy or inept repair job.
P	A	T	C	H	I	N	G	Mending, Covering, Repairing, Fixing, Overhauling, Reconditioning, Reconstructing.
P	A	T	E	L	L	A	R	Involving the knee cap, Genus of European limpet.
P	A	T	E	L	L	I	D	Family of mollusks, Limpets.
P	A	T	E	N	T	E	D	Licenced, Secured by patient, Exclusive right to make, vend or use.
P	A	T	E	N	T	E	E	One receiving a patent.
P	A	T	E	N	T	O	R	One that grants a patent.
P	A	T	E	R	E	R	O	Pedrero, Medieval catapult.
P	A	T	E	R	N	A	L	Relating to a father, Fatherly, Inherited from a father.
P	A	T	H	E	T	I	C	Passionate, Affecting, Pitiable, Moving, Pitiful, Poor, Rueful, Commiserable.
P	A	T	H	L	E	S	S	Untrod, Trackless.
P	A	T	H	O	S	I	S	A diseased state, An abnormal condition.
P	A	T	I	E	N	C	E	Steadfastness, Forbearance, Resignation, Composure, Equanimity, Endurance, Sufferance.
P	A	T	I	N	A	E	D	Having a patina, Coated with patina.
P	A	T	I	N	A	T	E	Same as PATINAED.
P	A	T	R	I	K	I	N	Paternal relatives.
P	A	T	R	O	N	A	L	Relating to a patron or patron saint.
P	A	T	T	A	M	A	R	A coasting ship used for trade on the Indian coast.
P	A	T	T	E	R	E	D	Tapped, Struck, Patted, Chatted, Babbled.
P	A	T	T	E	R	E	R	One that talks patter.
P	A	T	T	Y	P	A	N	Muffinpan, A pan for baking small cakes.
P	A	T	U	L	O	U	S	Distended, Spread widely apart, Expanded, Spread out.
P	A	T	U	P	O	R	U	A short Maori club.
P	A	U	L	D	R	O	N	Shoulder armour.
P	A	U	N	C	H	E	D	Wounded in the stomach, Eviscerated.
P	A	U	R	O	P	O	D	Minute arthropods.
P	A	V	E	M	E	N	T	Covered surface of a pedestrian walkway, Sidewalk, Tiled interior floor.
P	A	V	I	L	I	O	N	Ornamental structure for entertainment in a park or garden. Structure for an exhibition.
P	A	V	I	S	A	D	E	A continuous defensive screen.
P	A	V	O	N	I	N	E	Resembling the peacock, Iridescent.
P	A	W	N	S	H	O	P	The shop of a pawnbroker.
P	A	X	I	L	L	U	S	Genus of rusty-spored mushrooms.
P	A	Y	C	H	E	C	K	Wages or salary paid by cheque.

8 LETTERS

1	2	3	4	5	6	7	8	Clue
P	A	Y	S	A	N	N	E	Food prepared in a simple style.
P	A	Y	S	H	E	E	T	Payroll.
P	E	A	B	E	R	R	Y	A coffeeberry with a seed resembling a pea.
P	E	A	C	E	F	U	L	Quiet, Calm, Composed, Cool, Unruffled, Equable, Steady, Nonviolent.
P	E	A	C	H	I	C	K	The chick of the peafowl.
P	E	A	C	H	I	N	G	Betraying, Blabbing, Tattling, Informing.
P	E	A	G	R	E	E	N	A variable green colour.
P	E	A	K	L	O	A	D	Maximum load carried at a given time.
P	E	A	R	L	A	S	H	Potassium carbonate.
P	E	A	R	L	E	Y	E	A bird's eye suggestive of a pearl.
P	E	A	R	L	I	E	S	Costumes covered with pearl buttons worn by London costermongers.
P	E	A	R	L	I	N	G	Trimming of silk lace.
P	E	A	R	L	I	T	E	Lamellar mixture of ferrite and cementite.
P	E	A	S	E	C	O	D	A pea pod.
P	E	A	S	H	O	O	T	To shoot with a peashooter.
P	E	A	S	T	O	N	E	Pisolite.
P	E	A	T	M	O	S	S	Sphagmum, Any moss from which peat has been formed.
P	E	A	T	R	E	E	K	The smoke of burning peat.
P	E	C	C	A	B	L	E	Susceptible to temptation, Prone to sin.
P	E	C	C	A	N	C	Y	Offense, Fault.
P	E	C	O	R	I	N	O	Romano cheese made of ewe's milk.
P	E	C	T	I	N	A	L	Located near the pubic bone.
P	E	C	T	O	R	A	L	Situated on the chest, Breastplate on an ecclesiastical vestment.
P	E	C	U	L	A	T	E	Steal, Embezzle, Defraud, Misappropriate.
P	E	C	U	L	I	A	R	Separate, Independent, Special, Singular, Strange, Curious, Distinctive, Characteristic.
P	E	C	U	L	I	U	M	Exclusive right to a fund or property.
P	E	D	A	G	O	G	Y	Instruction, Education, Science of teaching.
P	E	D	A	L	F	E	R	A soil that lacks a hardened layer of accumulated carbonates.
P	E	D	A	L	I	E	R	Pedal keyboard of an organ.
P	E	D	A	L	I	N	E	Strawy material with a hemp or cotton core made into braid.
P	E	D	A	L	L	E	D	Rode a cycle, Worked a pedal of a musical instrument.
P	E	D	A	L	I	U	M	A genus of smooth annual musky herbs.
P	E	D	A	N	T	I	C	Unimaginitive, Pedestrian, Formalistic, Academic, Bookish, Scholastic, Erudite, Learned.
P	E	D	A	N	T	R	Y	Priggishness, Dull presentation of material by a teacher.
P	E	D	D	L	E	R	Y	The trade of a peddler.
P	E	D	D	L	I	N	G	Travelling about with wares for sale, Hawking, Retailing.
P	E	D	E	R	E	R	O	Medieval catapult.
P	E	D	E	S	T	A	L	Support of a column, Separate bearing, Supporting part.
P	E	D	I	C	U	L	E	Pedicel, A slender-plant stalk.
P	E	D	I	C	U	R	E	Grooming of the feet, toes and nails.
P	E	D	I	G	R	E	E	Lineage, Descent, Register of ancestors, Recorded purity of breed.
P	E	D	I	M	E	N	T	Triangular space forming a gable.
P	E	D	I	P	A	L	P	Whip scorpions.
P	E	D	O	L	O	G	Y	Scientific study of soils.
P	E	D	U	N	C	L	E	A stalk that bears a flower-cluster.
P	E	E	K	A	B	O	O	A game to amuse a baby.
P	E	E	P	H	O	L	E	A hole in a door through which one can peer.
P	E	E	P	S	H	O	W	A small show viewed through a magnifying glass.
P	E	E	R	L	E	S	S	Matchless, Incomparable, Unequalled, Unique, Unmatched, Sovereign, Paramount.
P	E	E	S	W	E	E	P	Lapwing.
P	E	E	T	W	E	E	T	Spotted sandpiper.
P	E	G	A	S	E	A	N	Related to a mythical winged horse, Pegasus, Swift, Highly imaginative, Poetic.
P	E	I	G	N	O	I	R	Loose dressing gown or wrapper.
P	E	J	O	R	A	T	E	Depreciate, Worsen, Derogate, Disparage, Detract, Slight.
P	E	K	I	N	E	S	E	Breed of very small dog originating in China two thousand years ago and having a flat face.
P	E	L	A	G	I	A	N	Living in the open sea.
P	E	L	A	R	G	I	C	Relating to the stork.
P	E	L	A	S	G	I	C	Relating to very early inhabitants of ancient Greece.
P	E	L	E	L	I	T	E	Pumiceous lava from the throat of a volcano.
P	E	L	E	M	E	L	E	Pell-mell, Disorder.
P	E	L	E	R	I	N	E	Woman's narrow cape with long ends hanging in front.
P	E	L	L	A	G	R	A	Kwashiokor, Disease associated with lack of nutrition.
P	E	L	L	I	C	L	E	Thin membrane, Pellicule.
P	E	L	L	M	E	L	L	Disorder, Confusion, Helter-skelter, Indiscriminately, Haste, Medley.
P	E	L	L	U	C	I	D	Translucent, Transparent, Clear, Shining, Iridescent, Limpid, Crystal, Unblurred.
P	E	L	O	R	I	Z	E	To affect with an abnormal regularity of structure.
P	E	L	T	A	T	E	D	Having the stem attached to the lower surface instead of a base.

1	2	3	4	5	6	7	8	
P	E	L	T	W	O	O	L	Wool removed from a dead sheep.
P	E	L	U	S	I	T	S	Genus of freshwater turtles.
P	E	L	V	E	T	I	A	Genus of rockweeds.
P	E	M	B	R	O	K	E	Small four-legged table having drop-leaf sides.
P	E	M	M	I	C	A	N	Dried food used as emergency rations.
P	E	N	A	L	I	Z	E	Inflict a penalty on.
P	E	N	C	H	A	N	T	Leaning, Liking, Disposition, Predilection, Tendency, Inclining, Bent, Propensity.
P	E	N	C	R	A	F	T	Penmanship, Authorship, SKill in writing.
P	E	N	D	E	N	C	Y	The state of pending, undecided or unsettled.
P	E	N	D	U	L	A	R	Resembling movement of a pendulum by swinging back and forth.
P	E	N	D	U	L	U	M	Suspended body that swings or rotates freely.
P	E	N	E	I	D	A	E	Family of prawns and shrimps.
P	E	N	E	I	D	E	S	Same as PENEIDAE.
P	E	N	E	L	O	P	E	Genus of guans, game birds resembling turkeys.
P	E	N	I	F	O	R	M	Resembling a penis.
P	E	N	I	T	E	N	T	Remorseful, Apologetic, Contrite, Regretful, Sorry, Attritional, Repentant.
P	E	N	K	N	I	F	E	Small pocketknife with folding blades.
P	E	N	N	A	R	I	A	Genus of hydroids.
P	E	N	N	O	R	T	H	Pennyworth.
P	E	N	O	L	O	G	Y	Study of punishment for crime.
P	E	N	S	T	O	C	K	Sluice gate or valve regulating flow of liquid.
P	E	N	T	A	C	I	D	Containing five hydrogen atoms.
P	E	N	T	A	C	L	E	Five-pointed star used as a symbol of the occult.
P	E	N	T	A	G	O	N	Polygon having five sides.
P	E	N	T	A	R	C	H	Having five protoxylem groups.
P	E	N	T	E	L	I	C	Pertaining to Mount Pentelicus, Greece.
P	E	N	T	E	N	Y	L	Radicals derived from pentenes by the removal of one hydrogen atom.
P	E	N	T	O	S	A	N	Any of a class of polysaccharides.
P	E	N	T	R	O	O	F	A roof sloping one way only.
P	E	N	U	M	B	R	A	Fringe, Aura, Nimbus, Borderland, Shade, Shadow.
P	E	N	W	O	M	A	N	Authoress.
P	E	O	P	L	I	N	G	Filling with people, Inhabitating, Settling with immigrants, Populating.
P	E	P	E	R	O	N	I	Highly seasoned sausage.
P	E	P	P	E	R	E	D	Sprinkled with pepper, Thrashed, Showered with particles or shot, To make provocative.
P	E	P	Y	S	I	A	N	Relating to Samuel Pepys or his diary.
P	E	R	A	C	U	T	E	Very acute and violent disease.
P	E	R	A	M	I	U	M	Genus of N. American orchids.
P	E	R	C	E	I	V	E	Discern, Realize, Note, Observe, See, Behold, Distinguish, Espy.
P	E	R	C	H	I	N	G	Alighting, Sitting, Settling, Stationery, Landing, Roosting.
P	E	R	C	L	O	S	E	Parclose, Screen used to separate a chapel from the main body of the church.
P	E	R	D	E	N	D	O	Direction in music, dying away.
P	E	R	D	U	R	E	D	Continued to exist, Lasted.
P	E	R	E	Z	O	N	E	Low lying land undergoing erosion beyond the low tide mark.
P	E	R	F	O	R	C	E	Forcibly, Willy-nilly, Helplessly, Inescapably, Inevitably, Unavoidably.
P	E	R	F	U	M	E	D	Sweet, Ambrosial, Aromatic, Balmy, Fragrant, Scented.
P	E	R	F	U	M	E	R	An expert in blending perfumes.
P	E	R	F	U	S	E	D	Suffused, Diffused.
P	E	R	I	A	G	U	A	A canoe made from a hollowed out tree trunk.
P	E	R	I	A	N	A	L	Located in the region of the anus.
P	E	R	I	A	N	T	H	External envelope of a flower.
P	E	R	I	B	L	E	M	Cell tissue of the root tip.
P	E	R	I	C	A	R	P	Ripened wall of a plant ovary.
P	E	R	I	C	O	P	E	Selection from the Bible to be read in church.
P	E	R	I	C	Y	S	T	Fibrous tissue of the host enclosing various parasites.
P	E	R	I	C	Y	T	E	cell of connective tissue about small blood vessels.
P	E	R	I	D	E	R	M	Protective layer of tissue in stems and roots.
P	E	R	I	D	E	S	M	Conjunctive tissue about a vascular bundle in astelic stems.
P	E	R	I	D	I	U	M	Outer envelope of the sporophore of many fungi.
P	E	R	I	G	E	A	L	Relating to perigee.
P	E	R	I	G	E	A	N	Same as PERIGEAL.
P	E	R	I	G	O	N	E	The external cover of the flower of a liverwort.
P	E	R	I	G	Y	N	Y	Having stamens and petals borne on a ring.
P	E	R	I	L	L	E	D	Exposed to danger, Risked, Hazarded, Compromised, Jeopardized, Menaced.
P	E	R	I	L	O	U	S	Hazardous, Dreadful, Dangerous, Risky, Treacherous, Unhealthy, Wicked, Unstable.
P	E	R	I	O	T	I	C	Situated around the ear.
P	E	R	I	P	E	T	Y	Sudden or unexpected reversal of the situation.
P	E	R	I	P	L	U	S	Circuit, Circumnavigation.

8 LETTERS

1	2	3	4	5	6	7	8	
P	E	R	I	S	A	R	C	Outer covering of a hydroid.
P	E	R	I	S	C	I	I	Polar people whose shadows move entirely round during summer.
P	E	R	I	S	H	E	D	Destroyed, Ruined, Spoiled, Squandered, Wasted, Deceased, Expired.
P	E	R	I	S	O	M	E	Body wall of an invertebrate.
P	E	R	I	S	S	A	D	An element of odd atomic number.
P	E	R	J	U	R	E	D	Violated an oath, Deceived, Forsworn, Equivocated, Deluded, Prevaricated, Misled, Lied.
P	E	R	L	E	C	H	E	Inflammatory condition of the corners of the mouth.
P	E	R	L	I	T	I	C	Having a texture like perlite.
P	E	R	M	E	A	N	T	Permeating.
P	E	R	M	E	A	T	E	Penetrate, Diffuse, Pervade, Impregnate, Saturate, Invade, Infuse, Infiltrate.
P	E	R	M	U	T	E	D	Transformed, Changed the order, Innovate, Altered.
P	E	R	N	A	N	C	Y	Receiving something such as rents or profits.
P	E	R	O	N	A	T	E	Having a woolly covering resembling a boot or stocking.
P	E	R	O	N	E	A	L	Relating to the fibula.
P	E	R	O	N	E	U	S	Muscles of the lower leg.
P	E	R	O	R	A	T	E	Deliver an oration, Declaim.
P	E	R	O	X	I	D	E	An oxide containing a relatively high proportion of oxygen.
P	E	R	R	U	Q	U	E	Peruke, Wig.
P	E	R	S	I	C	O	T	A liqueur made from brandy flavoured with peach or apricot kernels.
P	E	R	S	O	N	A	L	Affecting one individual, Bodily, Present in person. Distinctive.
P	E	R	S	P	I	R	E	Pass off by evaporation or exhalation, Secrete through the skin, Emit, exhale through pores.
P	E	R	S	U	A	D	E	Induce, Coax, Convince, Prevail, Prompt, Impress, Reason, Assure.
P	E	R	T	H	I	T	E	A feldspar rock.
P	E	R	T	N	E	S	S	Sauciness, Boldness, Audaciously, Brazenly, Vivaciously, Sprightlyness.
P	E	R	U	S	I	N	G	Examining, Considering, Surveying, Reading, Scrutinising.
P	E	R	U	V	I	A	N	Inhabitant of Peru.
P	E	R	V	A	D	E	D	Traversed, Permeated, Impenetrated, Impregnated, Penetrated, Transfused, Percolated.
P	E	R	V	E	R	S	E	Corrupt, Wicked, Improper, Vicious, Depraved, Putrid, Unhealthy, Obstinate.
P	E	R	V	I	O	U	S	Intelligible, Perforate, Penetrable, Porous, To permit access.
P	E	S	S	I	M	A	L	Worst.
P	E	S	S	U	L	U	S	A bony bar at the end of the windpipe of a bird.
P	E	S	T	E	R	E	D	Obstructed, Impeded, Annoyed, Bothered, Vexed, Worried, Plagued, Harassed.
P	E	S	T	E	R	E	R	One that annoys or obstructs.
P	E	S	T	L	I	N	G	Beating, Pounding, Pulverizing.
P	E	T	A	L	I	N	E	Resembling a petal.
P	E	T	A	L	I	S	M	Ostracism, Ancient Syracusan method of banishing a dissident for five years.
P	E	T	A	L	I	T	E	A white mineral consisting of a lithium aluminium silicate.
P	E	T	A	L	O	D	Y	Metamorphosis of various floral organs into petals.
P	E	T	A	L	O	I	D	Resembling a flower petal.
P	E	T	A	L	O	U	S	Having petals.
P	E	T	E	C	H	I	A	Spots that appear with some infectious diseases.
P	E	T	E	R	I	N	G	Diminishing, Ceasing, Tapering, Lessening, Decreasing, Abating, Dwindling, Receding.
P	E	T	E	R	M	A	N	Fisherman, Safecracker.
P	E	T	I	O	L	A	R	Supported upon a slender stem.
P	E	T	I	T	I	O	N	Entreaty, Supplication, Complaint, Prayer, Appeal, Application, Beseech, Plead.
P	E	T	I	T	O	R	Y	Relating to a civil suit arising from ownership of property or damages.
P	E	T	R	I	F	I	C	Petrifying.
P	E	T	R	O	B	I	A	Genus of mites.
P	E	T	R	O	N	E	L	A portable firearm resembling a large calibre carbine.
P	E	T	R	O	S	A	L	Petrous, Hard, Stony.
P	E	T	T	I	F	O	G	Cavil, Bicker, Niggle, Peddle, Trifle.
P	E	T	U	L	A	N	T	Peevish, Irritable, Fractious, Fretful, Huffy, Snappish, Grouchy, Sulky.
P	E	T	U	N	T	S	E	China stone.
P	E	W	T	E	R	E	R	One that makes pewter utensils or vessels.
P	E	Z	I	Z	O	I	D	Resembling a fungus.
P	H	A	C	E	L	I	A	Genus of American herbs, California bluebell.
P	H	A	C	E	L	L	A	Filaments of the gastric cavity of some jellyfishes.
P	H	A	L	A	N	G	E	A segment of an insect's tarsus.
P	H	A	N	T	A	S	M	Illusion, Deception, Spectre, Spirit, Fantasy, Dream, Delusion, Fancy.
P	H	A	N	T	A	S	Y	Fantasy, Fancy.
P	H	A	R	I	S	E	E	Member of a strict and formal party of ancient Jews.
P	H	A	R	M	A	C	Y	Administering of drugs, Dispensing drugs and medicines.
P	H	E	A	S	A	N	T	Long-tailed brightly coloured birds reared in semidomestication.
P	H	E	N	G	I	T	E	A translucent or transparent stone, Variety of muscovite.
P	H	E	N	O	L	I	C	Containing phenolic resin, Plastic.
P	H	I	A	L	I	N	E	Flask-shaped.
P	H	I	L	A	B	E	G	Kilt.

1	2	3	4	5	6	7	8	
P	H	I	L	I	B	E	G	Same as PHILABEG.
P	H	I	L	O	M	E	L	Nightingale.
P	H	L	E	G	M	O	N	Abscess.
P	H	O	C	A	E	N	A	Genus of porpoises.
P	H	O	L	A	D	I	D	Genus of bivalve mollusks, Piddocks.
P	H	O	L	I	O	T	A	Genus of brown-spored agarics growing on decaying wood.
P	H	O	N	A	T	E	D	Produced speech sounds, Used the voice, Articulated, Enunciated, Pronounced.
P	H	O	N	E	M	I	C	Phonemic, Distinctive.
P	H	O	N	E	T	I	C	Relating to speech sounds, Employing for sound.
P	H	O	R	E	S	I	S	Transmission.
P	H	O	R	I	D	A	E	Family of small two-winged flies.
P	H	O	R	M	I	U	M	Genus of herbs, New Zealand flax.
P	H	O	R	O	N	I	S	Genus of small wormlike marine animals.
P	H	O	S	G	E	N	E	Colourless gaseous compound used as a poison gas in World War One.
P	H	O	S	P	H	O	R	Anything that exhibits phosporescence or flourescent materials.
P	H	O	T	I	N	I	A	Genus of small shrubs cultivated as ornamentals.
P	H	R	A	S	I	N	G	Expressing in words, Terming, Styling, Wording.
P	H	R	O	N	I	M	A	Type of hermit crab.
P	H	R	Y	G	I	A	N	Relating to the ancient country of Phrygia.
P	H	T	H	A	L	I	N	Group of colourless compounds.
P	H	T	H	I	S	I	C	Consumption, Pulmonary tuberculosis.
P	H	Y	L	A	R	C	H	Magistrate in the Asiatic provinces of the Roman Empire.
P	H	Y	L	E	T	I	C	Racial.
P	H	Y	L	L	I	T	E	A foliated rock.
P	H	Y	L	L	A	R	Y	Bract subtending the flower head of a plant.
P	H	Y	L	L	I	U	M	Genus of Asiatic leaf insects.
P	H	Y	L	L	O	D	E	A form of leaf.
P	H	Y	L	L	O	D	Y	The changing of a plant organ into a foliage leaf.
P	H	Y	L	L	O	I	D	Resembling a leaf.
P	H	Y	L	L	O	M	E	Plant part that is a leaf.
P	H	Y	M	A	T	I	D	Family of carnivorous bugs.
P	H	Y	S	A	L	I	A	Genus of siphonophones, Portugese man-of-war.
P	H	Y	S	A	L	I	S	Genus of low-growing American herbs, Cape gooseberry, Chinese lantern.
P	H	Y	S	A	R	I	A	Genus of herbs.
P	H	Y	S	A	R	U	M	Genus of slime moulds.
P	H	Y	S	E	T	E	R	Genus of sperm whales.
P	H	Y	S	I	C	A	L	Ill, Material, Natural, Carnal, Lusty, Bodily, Sensible, Substantial.
P	H	Y	S	I	Q	U	E	Build, Constitution, Habit, Anatomy, Structure, Configuration, Shape, Body.
P	H	Y	T	E	R	A	L	Recognizable plant forms and fossils in coal.
P	H	Y	T	O	M	E	R	A structural unit that makes up the body of a plant.
P	H	Y	T	O	S	I	S	An infection with a disease caused by a parasitic plant.
P	H	Y	T	O	Z	O	A	Zoophyte.
P	I	A	C	U	L	A	R	Sacrificial, Expiatory, Sinful, Heinous.
P	I	A	C	U	L	U	M	Expiatory offering.
P	I	A	N	E	T	T	E	Pianino.
P	I	A	S	S	A	B	A	Fibre from a Brazilian palm.
P	I	A	S	S	A	V	A	Same as PIASSABA.
P	I	A	Z	Z	A	E	D	Furnished with a piazza.
P	I	C	A	D	U	R	A	Cut tobacco for cigarettes.
P	I	C	A	R	I	A	E	Order of birds, Woodpeckers, Parrots, Cuckoos.
P	I	C	A	R	O	O	N	Pirate, Corsair, Brigand.
P	I	C	A	Y	U	N	E	A coin of little value, Petty, Trifling, Narrow, Small-minded, Paltry, Measly.
P	I	C	I	F	O	R	M	Woodpecker.
P	I	C	K	A	D	I	L	Old-fashioned high winged collar.
P	I	C	K	E	R	E	L	Genus of fishes, Pike.
P	I	C	K	E	T	E	D	Enclosed, Fastened, Fenced, Tethered, Acted as pickets in a strife.
P	I	C	K	L	I	N	G	Preserving in a vinegar solution.
P	I	C	K	L	O	C	K	One that picks a lock, Burglar, Thief.
P	I	C	K	M	E	U	P	Tonic, Bracer, Stimulant, Something that restores.
P	I	C	O	L	I	N	E	Liquid pyridine bases found in coaltar, ammonia liquor and bone oil.
P	I	C	O	T	I	T	E	Variety of spinel containing chromium and iron.
P	I	C	R	O	T	I	N	A non-poisonous bitter crystalline compound.
P	I	C	T	U	R	E	D	Depicted, Illustrated, Portrayed, Represented, Described, Interpreted, Rendered, Shown.
P	I	E	C	R	U	S	T	Pastry shell of a pie.
P	I	E	D	N	E	S	S	Variegation.
P	I	E	R	C	I	N	G	Boring, Perforating, Penetrating, Sharp, Acute, Stabbing, Loud, Blaring.
P	I	E	R	H	E	A	D	Outer end of a wharf.

1	2	3	4	5	6	7	8	Definition
P	I	F	F	L	I	N	G	Trifling, Twaddling, Petty, Trivial, Measly, Niggling, Peddling, Gabbling.
P	I	G	E	O	N	E	D	Gulled, Duped, Bamboozled, Fooled, Hoaxed, Hoodwinked, Victimized.
P	I	G	E	O	N	R	Y	Dovecote, Roost for pigeons.
P	I	G	S	T	I	E	S	Enclosures for pigs, Dirty dwellings.
P	I	G	S	W	A	S	H	Pig-swill.
P	I	L	A	S	T	E	R	Square architectural column.
P	I	L	C	H	A	R	D	A food fish that resembles a herring, Sardine.
P	I	L	E	A	T	E	D	Capped.
P	I	L	E	W	O	R	K	Work consisting of piles.
P	I	L	E	W	O	R	M	Shipworm.
P	I	L	E	W	O	R	T	Variable fireweed.
P	I	L	F	E	R	E	D	Plundered, Robbed, Filched, Stolen, Cribbed, Pinched, Purloined, Appropriated.
P	I	L	F	E	R	E	R	Thief, Filcher, Larcener, Purloiner, Stealer.
P	I	L	I	D	I	U	M	Free-swimming hat-shaped larva of various worms.
P	I	L	L	A	G	E	D	Looted, Sacked, Plundered, Ravaged, Desecrated, Devoured, Despoiled, Depredated.
P	I	L	L	A	G	E	R	Robber, Bandit, Marauder, Looter, Plunderer, Raider, Ravisher, Sacker.
P	I	L	L	A	R	E	D	Supported by pillars, Strenghtened with pillars, Represented by a pillar.
P	I	L	L	O	W	E	D	Cushioned, Served as a pillow.
P	I	L	L	W	O	R	T	Genus of water fern.
P	I	L	O	S	E	L	Y	Hairily.
P	I	L	O	S	I	T	Y	Hairiness.
P	I	L	O	T	A	G	E	Guidance by a pilot, Navigation of a ship or plane.
P	I	L	O	T	I	N	G	Guiding, Conducting, Escorting, Steering, Coaching, Managing, Directing, Shepherding.
P	I	M	I	E	N	T	O	Pimento, Conical thick-fleshed sweet peppers.
P	I	M	P	L	I	N	G	Covering with pimples.
P	I	N	A	B	E	T	E	Central American fir trees.
P	I	N	A	C	E	A	E	Family of coniferous trees and shrubs.
P	I	N	A	C	O	I	D	Crystal form consisting of two parallel and opposite faces.
P	I	N	A	F	O	R	E	A protective apron.
P	I	N	A	S	T	E	R	Cluster pine.
P	I	N	C	E	N	E	Z	Eyeglasses clipped to the nose by a spring.
P	I	N	C	E	T	T	E	Small pair of forceps used in surgery.
P	I	N	C	H	E	R	S	Pincers.
P	I	N	C	H	I	N	G	Act of stealing, Squeezin, Nipping.
P	I	N	D	A	R	I	C	Loose irregular verses.
P	I	N	E	C	O	N	E	Cone seed of the pine tree.
P	I	N	E	W	E	E	D	Orange grass.
P	I	N	E	W	O	O	D	Wood of pines.
P	I	N	G	P	O	N	G	Table tennis.
P	I	N	I	N	G	L	Y	Longingly.
P	I	N	I	O	N	E	D	Having wings or pinions, Bound, Fettered.
P	I	N	K	E	Y	E	D	Conjunctivitis, Acute highly contagious eye inflammation.
P	I	N	K	R	O	O	T	A perennial woodland herb.
P	I	N	K	S	T	E	R	Whitsuntide.
P	I	N	M	A	K	E	R	One who makes pins.
P	I	N	M	O	N	E	Y	Pocket money.
P	I	N	N	A	C	L	E	Apex, Climax, Culmination, Summit, Acme, Raise or rear, Zenith, Meridian, Peak.
P	I	N	N	A	T	E	D	Feathered, Plumed, Having parts arranged on opposite sides to resemble feathers.
P	I	N	N	I	P	E	D	Seal, Walrus.
P	I	N	N	O	I	T	E	A hydrous magnesium borate.
P	I	N	O	C	H	L	E	A card game played with forty eight cards.
P	I	N	O	L	I	N	E	Rosin spirit.
P	I	N	P	A	T	C	H	Periwinkle.
P	I	N	P	O	I	N	T	Something small, Identify, Diagnose, Distinguish, Recognize, Spot, Precise, Emphasize.
P	I	N	P	R	I	C	K	Small puncture, petty irritation, Antagonistic action.
P	I	N	T	A	B	L	E	A pinball machine.
P	I	N	U	L	A	T	E	Having one projecting ray.
P	I	N	W	H	E	E	L	Revolving toy resembling a windmill, A firework that revolves when the fuse is lit.
P	I	P	E	C	L	A	Y	White clay used for making pipes and for whitening military equipment.
P	I	P	E	F	I	S	H	A long slender fish.
P	I	P	E	L	I	N	E	Line of pipe for conveying liquids, gases or finely divided solids, Direct channel for information.
P	I	P	E	R	A	C	K	A rack for holding pipes.
P	I	P	E	R	I	N	E	A crystalline alkaloid that is an active constituent of pepper.
P	I	P	E	R	O	L	L	Statement of treasury expenses as written up to the nineteenth century in Britain.
P	I	P	E	S	T	E	M	A very thin arm or leg.
P	I	P	E	T	R	E	E	Shrub having wood once used for pipe stems.
P	I	P	E	V	I	N	E	A genus of climbing plant, Dutchman's pipe.

1	2	3	4	5	6	7	8	Clue
P	I	P	E	W	O	O	D	Shrub from the wood of which pipe bowls are made.
P	I	P	E	W	O	R	T	Genus of herbs.
P	I	P	R	I	D	A	E	Family of birds.
P	I	P	T	U	R	U	S	Genus of Australian woody plants.
P	I	Q	U	A	N	C	Y	Pungency, Raciness, Spicily, Flavoursome.
P	I	R	A	T	I	N	G	Robbing, Poaching staff, Infringing of copyright.
P	I	R	I	F	O	R	M	Pear-shaped.
P	I	S	A	N	I	T	E	Mineral consisting of a hydrous iron copper sulfate.
P	I	S	C	A	T	O	R	Fisherman, Angler.
P	I	S	C	I	D	I	A	Genus of shrubs the leaves and bark of which are poisonous to fish.
P	I	S	C	I	N	A	L	Reservoir, fishpond or swimming pool in ancient Rome.
P	I	S	I	F	O	R	M	Resembling a pea in size and shape.
P	I	S	O	L	I	T	E	A limestone composed of globular concretions the size of a pea.
P	I	S	S	O	D	E	S	Genus of small weevils that feed on coniferous trees.
P	I	S	T	A	C	I	A	Small genus of trees.
P	I	S	T	O	L	E	T	A gold coin from one of the European countries.
P	I	T	C	H	I	N	G	Throwing, Casting, Flinging, Heaving, Hurling, Launching, Tossing, Slinging.
P	I	T	H	E	C	U	S	Genus of Old World monkeys.
P	I	T	H	L	E	S	S	Devoid of pith.
P	I	T	I	A	B	L	E	Pitiful, Contemptible, Pathetic, Poor, Rueful, Despicable, Miserable, Wretched.
P	I	T	I	A	B	L	Y	In a deplorable manner.
P	I	T	I	L	E	S	S	Merciless, Unfeeling, Unpitying, Heartless, Stony, Barbarous, Brutal, Inhumane.
P	I	T	T	A	N	C	E	Alms, Mite, Scrap, Trace, Inadequacy, Insuffiency, Smidgen.
P	I	T	U	I	T	R	Y	Pituitary body.
P	I	V	O	T	I	N	G	Turning, Oscillating, Wheeling, Whirling, Diverting, Veering.
P	I	Z	Z	E	R	I	A	An establishment where pizzas are sold.
P	L	A	C	A	B	L	E	Tractable, Peaceable, Quiet, Placid.
P	L	A	C	A	T	E	D	Appeased, Soothed, Mollified, Pacified, Assuaged, Conciliated, Tranquillized, Comforted.
P	L	A	C	A	T	E	R	Mediator.
P	L	A	C	E	M	A	N	Political appointee.
P	L	A	C	E	N	T	A	The lining of the uterus during gestation, Afterbirth.
P	L	A	C	I	D	L	Y	Calmly, Phlegmatically, Complacently, Quietly, Peacefully, Serenely, Tranquilly.
P	L	A	G	I	A	R	Y	Using the ideas or words of another without acknowledgment.
P	L	A	G	U	I	N	G	Tormenting, Troubling, Harassing, Hampering, Burdening, Bothering, Nagging, Worrying.
P	L	A	I	T	I	N	G	Intertwining, Braiding, Interlacing.
P	L	A	N	C	H	E	T	Small metal disc to be stamped as a coin.
P	L	A	N	G	E	N	T	Resonant, Expressive, Consonant, Resounding, Ringing, Rotund, Round, Vibrant.
P	L	A	N	K	I	N	G	Laying a floor of planks.
P	L	A	N	K	T	O	N	Minute swimming animals that are an important link in the marine food chain.
P	L	A	N	L	E	S	S	Taking place without a plan.
P	L	A	N	N	I	N	G	Designing, Arranging, Charting, Devising, Intending, Scheming, Contemplating, Proposing.
P	L	A	N	T	A	I	N	A genus of plants, Roadside weeds, Starchy fruit similar in appearance to the banana.
P	L	A	N	T	I	N	G	Cultivating, Introducing, Sowing, Scattering, Broadcasting, Concealing, Entombing.
P	L	A	N	T	L	E	T	A little plant.
P	L	A	N	T	U	L	E	An embryo plant.
P	L	A	N	U	L	A	E	Free-swimming larva of a jellyfish, coral or sponge.
P	L	A	S	H	I	N	G	Splashing, Spattering, Speckling.
P	L	A	S	M	O	D	E	Type genus of malarial parasite.
P	L	A	S	T	E	R	Y	Resembling plaster.
P	L	A	S	T	I	D	S	Small bodies of specialized protoplasm.
P	L	A	S	T	I	F	Y	To make plastic.
P	L	A	S	T	R	O	N	Metal breastplate, Ventral part of the shell of a tortoise or turtle.
P	L	A	T	A	E	A	N	Relating to Plataea, a city in ancient Greece.
P	L	A	T	A	N	N	A	A Southern African frog that has strongly clawed feet.
P	L	A	T	B	A	N	D	Architrave, A flat arch, Lintel.
P	L	A	T	E	F	U	L	Generous serving of food.
P	L	A	T	E	L	E	T	Minute flattened body.
P	L	A	T	F	O	R	M	Horizontal flat surface higher than adjoining area, Base for a gun, Design, Pattern, Scheme.
P	L	A	T	I	N	I	C	Containing platinum.
P	L	A	T	I	N	U	M	Heavy precious metallic element that is typically grayish white.
P	L	A	T	O	N	I	C	Relating to the Greek philosopher, Plato.
P	L	A	T	T	I	N	G	Plaiting, Material that is plaited.
P	L	A	T	Y	O	P	E	An individual with a broad face.
P	L	A	T	Y	P	U	S	A small aquatic mammal of Australasia.
P	L	A	T	Y	S	M	A	A broad thin layer of muscle on each side of the neck.
P	L	A	U	S	I	V	E	Applauding, Pleasing, Agreeable.
P	L	A	Y	A	B	L	E	Suitable for being played.

1	2	3	4	5	6	7	8	Definition
P	L	A	Y	B	I	L	L	Theatre programme, Poster advertising a theatrical performance.
P	L	A	Y	B	O	O	K	A play in book form.
P	L	A	Y	D	E	B	T	A gambling debt.
P	L	A	Y	G	O	E	R	An inveterate theatre-goer.
P	L	A	Y	M	A	T	E	A companion in play.
P	L	A	Y	R	O	O	M	Nursery, Rumpus room.
P	L	A	Y	S	O	M	E	Playful, Sportive, Wanton.
P	L	A	Y	T	I	M	E	A time for recreation.
P	L	E	A	C	H	E	D	Interlaced, Interwoven, Plaited.
P	L	E	A	D	I	N	G	Wrangling, Begging, Appealing, Beseeching, Craving, Entreating, Imploring, Praying.
P	L	E	A	S	A	N	T	Agreeable, Merry, Well-mannered, Grateful, Welcome, Congenial, Joyful, Cherry.
P	L	E	A	S	I	N	G	Charming, Palatable, Favourable, Congenial, Gratifying, Enchanting, Winning, Delightful.
P	L	E	A	S	U	R	E	Fancy, Inclination, Liking, Delight, Enjoyment, Felicity, Happiness, Joy.
P	L	E	A	T	I	N	G	Folding, Creasing on a fold.
P	L	E	B	E	I	A	N	Commonplace, Everyday, Homely, Undistinguished, Ignoble, Base, Humble, Lowly.
P	L	E	C	T	R	U	M	Small thin shape of material like ivory, metal plastic used to pluck the strings of an instrument.
P	L	E	D	G	I	N	G	Depositing, Toasting, Promising, Plighting, Undertaking, Mortgaging, Binding, Vowing.
P	L	E	N	A	R	T	Y	State of a benefice when occupied.
P	L	E	O	N	A	S	M	Tautology, Repetition, Superfluity.
P	L	E	S	S	I	T	E	A mineral consisting of an intimate intergrowth of kamacite and taenite in meteorites.
P	L	E	T	H	O	R	A	Profusion, Excess, Overflow, Overabundance, Overkill, Surfeit, Surplus, Deluge.
P	L	E	U	R	I	S	Y	Inflammation of the pleura.
P	L	E	U	S	T	O	N	Floating algae.
P	L	I	A	N	T	L	Y	Flexibility, Lithely, Aptly, Suitability, Adaptability.
P	L	I	C	A	T	E	D	Folded, Pleated.
P	L	I	G	H	T	E	D	Engaged, Promised.
P	L	I	M	M	I	N	G	Increasing, Swelling, Distending.
P	L	I	M	S	O	L	L	Light shoe of canvas with a rubber sole.
P	L	I	O	C	E	N	E	Pre-historic era.
P	L	I	O	S	A	U	R	Pre-historic reptile.
P	L	I	O	T	R	O	N	High vacuum tube containing cathode anode and control grid.
P	L	O	D	D	I	N	G	Trudging, Dull, Pedestrian, Drudging, Travelling slowly, Walking heavily, Monotonously.
P	L	O	P	P	I	N	G	Falling with the sound of droping in water, Dropping heavily.
P	L	O	T	T	I	N	G	Planning, Dileanating, Conspiring, Contriving, Devising, Intriguing, Manoeuvering.
P	L	O	U	G	H	E	D	Cultivated, Break, Furrowed, Ridged, Trenched, Harrowed, Raked, Plodded.
P	L	O	U	G	H	E	R	Plowman.
P	L	U	C	K	I	L	Y	Courageously, Bravely, Resolutely, Distinctly, Sharply.
P	L	U	C	K	I	N	G	Twitching, Pulling.
P	L	U	G	G	I	N	G	Stopping, Advertising, Filling, Closing, Choking, Clogging, Congesting, Promoting.
P	L	U	G	U	G	L	Y	Tough, Roughneck, Political intimidator, Ruffian, Bullyboy, Rowdy, Thug.
P	L	U	M	B	A	G	O	Genus of herbs and woody climbing plants.
P	L	U	M	B	A	N	E	Compound of lead and hydrogen.
P	L	U	M	B	A	T	E	A salt formed by reaction of lead oxide with basic oxides.
P	L	U	M	B	B	O	B	Metal bob of a plumbline.
P	L	U	M	B	E	R	Y	Work of a plumber, Leadworker.
P	L	U	M	B	I	N	G	Sealing with lead, Working upon a plumbing system, Testing with a plumbline.
P	L	U	M	B	I	S	M	Lead poisoning.
P	L	U	M	C	A	K	E	Rich cake with raisins and currants.
P	L	U	M	D	U	F	F	Steamed or boiled pudding with raisins.
P	L	U	M	E	L	E	T	A small plume.
P	L	U	M	E	T	I	S	Lighweight dress fabric woven with an embroidered effect.
P	L	U	M	I	P	E	D	Having feet covered with feathers.
P	L	U	M	M	I	N	G	Rising, Swellin, Spoiling of a photograph.
P	L	U	M	P	E	S	T	Roundest, Most buxom, Fattest, Most chubby.
P	L	U	M	P	I	N	G	Very large, Of exceptional size.
P	L	U	N	G	I	N	G	Immersing, Submerging, Diving, Thrusting, Lunging, Pitching, Rushing, Flinging.
P	L	U	R	A	L	L	Y	More than once.
P	L	U	S	S	A	G	E	Increasing.
P	L	U	T	A	R	C	H	Biographer.
P	L	U	T	O	N	I	C	Originating from deep in the earth.
P	L	U	V	I	O	S	E	In an area receiving regular rainfall.
P	L	Y	M	E	T	A	L	Plywood sheathed in aluminium used in construction of airplanes.
P	O	A	C	H	I	N	G	Poking, Stealing, Hunting illegally, Trampling, Trespassing.
P	O	C	H	E	T	T	E	Small handbag, Small envelope for holding one stamp of a collection.
P	O	C	K	E	T	E	D	Put away, Stole, Accepted, Suppressed, Collected in a pocket.
P	O	D	A	G	R	A	L	Condition of gout in the big toe.
P	O	D	A	G	R	I	C	Condition of gout in the big toe.

1	2	3	4	5	6	7	8	Definition
P	O	D	A	R	G	U	S	Family of Oriental and Australian birds, Frogmouths.
P	O	D	A	U	G	E	R	An auger having a pod.
P	O	D	E	T	I	A	L	Resembling a stalk.
P	O	D	E	T	I	U	M	Lichen stalk.
P	O	D	I	C	E	P	S	Genus of aquatic birds, Grebes, Loons.
P	O	D	O	C	A	R	P	Genus of evergreen trees.
P	O	D	O	D	E	R	M	Covering of a foot of a hoofed animal.
P	O	D	O	G	O	N	A	Recinulei, Genus of ticks living and fossil.
P	O	D	O	L	I	T	E	Carbonate-Apatite.
P	O	D	O	L	O	G	Y	Scientific study of physiology of the feet.
P	O	D	O	M	E	R	E	Leg segment of an arthropod, Spiders, Millipedes.
P	O	E	M	A	T	I	C	Poetic.
P	O	E	T	I	C	A	L	Poetic, Idealized, Rhyming, Imaginative, Flowery rhetoric.
P	O	E	T	I	Z	E	D	Wrote poetry, Spoke poetically.
P	O	I	G	N	A	N	T	Pungent, Piercing, Keen, Stinging, Cutting, Incisive, Penetrating, Pressing.
P	O	I	G	N	A	R	D	Poniard, Dagger with a slender blade.
P	O	I	N	D	I	N	G	A creditor seizing property of a debtor.
P	O	I	N	T	I	N	G	Sharpening, Punctuating, Directing, Aiming, Addressing, Indicating, Turning, Training.
P	O	I	S	O	N	E	D	Killed by poison, Tainted, Infected, Corrupted, Vitiated, Perverted, Debased, Debauched.
P	O	I	S	O	N	E	R	One that poisons.
P	O	L	A	R	I	T	Y	United opposites, Attraction toward a particular object.
P	O	L	E	J	U	M	P	Vaulting using a pole.
P	O	L	E	M	A	S	T	Mast formed from one spar.
P	O	L	E	M	I	C	S	Aggressive attacks, Controversial discussions.
P	O	L	E	S	T	A	R	The conspicuous star nearest the celestial north pole, Directing principle.
P	O	L	I	C	I	E	S	Courses, Procedures, Programmes, Methods of action, Certificates of insurance.
P	O	L	I	C	I	N	G	Governing, Controlling by police, Supervising.
P	O	L	I	S	H	E	D	Burnished, Perfected, Matured, Glazed, Buffed, Smoothed, Refined, Improved.
P	O	L	I	S	H	E	R	One that polishes.
P	O	L	I	T	E	L	Y	Tactfully, Courteously, Mannerly, Considerately, Civilly, Urbanely.
P	O	L	I	T	I	C	O	Politician.
P	O	L	I	T	I	C	S	Art or science of government.
P	O	L	L	B	O	O	K	Official register of electors entitled to vote.
P	O	L	L	E	V	I	L	Inflammation located on the poll of a horse.
P	O	L	L	I	W	O	G	Tadpole, One who crosses the equator for the first time and undergoes an initiation.
P	O	L	L	S	T	E	R	One that conducts a public poll.
P	O	L	L	U	T	E	D	Unclean, Impure, Defiled, Corrupted, Tainted, Profaned, Intoxicated, Inebriated.
P	O	L	L	U	T	E	R	One that pollutes.
P	O	L	L	Y	W	O	G	Same as POLLIWOG.
P	O	L	O	C	Y	T	E	Polar body.
P	O	L	O	N	I	U	M	A radioactive metallic element that occurs in pitchblende.
P	O	L	T	R	O	O	N	Craven, Dastard, Cowardly, Quitter, Chicken, Gutless, Unmanly, Spunkless.
P	O	L	Y	A	R	C	H	Having many tissues.
P	O	L	Y	A	X	O	N	Having many axes.
P	O	L	Y	B	R	I	D	Heterogen.
P	O	L	Y	C	L	A	D	Flatworm.
P	O	L	Y	C	Y	T	E	A blood granulocyte with a segmented nucleus found in various infections.
P	O	L	Y	F	O	I	L	Multifoil.
P	O	L	Y	G	A	M	Y	A form of marriage in which more than one wife or husband is allowed at the same time.
P	O	L	Y	G	L	O	T	One who speaks or writes many languages, Confusion of languages.
P	O	L	Y	G	R	A	M	A figure determined by many lines.
P	O	L	Y	M	A	T	H	Learned in many fields.
P	O	L	Y	M	E	R	Y	Having many similar parts.
P	O	L	Y	O	D	O	N	Genus of fishes, Paddlefishes.
P	O	L	Y	O	P	I	A	Multiple vision.
P	O	L	Y	P	A	R	Y	A structure in which polyps of coral are embedded.
P	O	L	Y	P	I	D	E	Polyp, An individual zooid.
P	O	L	Y	P	O	D	E	Insect larva having abdominal legs.
P	O	L	Y	P	O	D	Y	Genus of ferns.
P	O	L	Y	P	O	I	D	Resembling a polyp.
P	O	L	Y	P	O	R	E	Pore fungus.
P	O	L	Y	P	O	S	E	Like a polyp.
P	O	L	Y	P	O	U	S	Same as POLYPOSE.
P	O	L	Y	S	E	M	Y	Multiplicity of meaning.
P	O	L	Y	S	O	M	Y	Condition of being polysomic, Having deviation in number of chromosomes.
P	O	L	Y	T	E	N	E	Multiple in relation to chromosomes.
P	O	L	Y	T	O	M	A	Genus of flagellates distributed in stagnant freshwater.

1	2	3	4	5	6	7	8	Definition
P	O	L	Y	T	O	N	E	Spoken in a varied tone or pitch.
P	O	L	Y	T	Y	P	E	One of several polymophic crystal structures.
P	O	L	Y	U	R	I	A	Excessive secretion of urine in pathologic conditions.
P	O	L	Y	Z	O	A	N	Bryozoan.
P	O	L	Y	Z	O	I	C	Containing many kinds of animals.
P	O	L	Y	Z	O	O	N	Polypide.
P	O	M	A	N	D	E	R	A clove-studded orange perfumed with aromatic substances used to perfume a clothes closet.
P	O	M	I	F	O	R	M	Shaped like an apple.
P	O	M	O	L	O	G	Y	Science of the cultivation of fruits.
P	O	M	P	E	I	A	N	Characteristic of the ancient city of Pompeii.
P	O	M	P	I	L	U	S	Genus of fishes.
P	O	N	C	I	R	U	S	Genus of low thorny Chinese citrus tree.
P	O	N	D	E	R	A	L	Relating to weight.
P	O	N	D	E	R	E	D	Meditated, Considered, Studied, Weighed, Appraised, Deliberated, Evaluated, Ruminated.
P	O	N	D	E	R	E	R	One that ponders.
P	O	N	D	F	I	S	H	Small America freshwater sunfish.
P	O	N	D	L	I	L	Y	Water lily.
P	O	N	D	W	E	E	D	Aquatic plant.
P	O	N	G	I	D	A	E	Family of primates, Gorillas, Chimpanzees, Gibbons.
P	O	N	T	A	N	I	A	Genus of sawflies.
P	O	N	T	I	F	E	X	High priest, Pontiff, Pope.
P	O	N	T	I	F	I	C	Episcopal, Pompous, Dogmatic.
P	O	N	T	I	N	A	L	Relating to a bridge.
P	O	N	Y	T	A	I	L	A style where long hair is drawn back and tied to resemble the tail of a pony.
P	O	O	H	P	O	O	H	An expression of disbelief, contempt or impatience.
P	O	O	L	R	O	O	M	A public room where pool is played and bookmaking activities flourish.
P	O	O	R	J	O	H	N	Small dried and salted cod or haddock, Plain food.
P	O	O	R	L	A	W	S	Old-fashioned rigorous laws that controlled aid to the poor.
P	O	O	R	N	E	S	S	State of poverty.
P	O	O	R	R	A	T	E	A tax for the relief of the poor.
P	O	P	E	J	O	A	N	A card game resembling fan-tan.
P	O	P	E	L	I	N	E	A silk/wool mixture fabric resembling poplin.
P	O	P	E	L	I	N	G	A petty or deputy pope.
P	O	P	E	S	E	Y	E	The lymphatic gland in the thigh of an ox or sheep.
P	O	P	E	S	H	I	P	Popedom.
P	O	P	I	N	J	A	Y	Green woodpecker, Fop, Dandy, Dude, Coxcomb, Beau Brummel.
P	O	P	I	S	H	L	Y	In the manner of a pope.
P	O	P	P	L	I	N	G	Heaving, Tossing, Bobbing about.
P	O	P	U	L	A	C	E	Common people, Rand and file, Plebeians.
P	O	P	U	L	A	T	E	Inhabit, Occupy, People, Tenant, Propagate.
P	O	P	U	L	I	S	T	Member of a political party that represents the working class.
P	O	P	U	L	O	U	S	Numerous, Crowded, Many, Legion, Several, Sundry, Various.
P	O	R	I	F	E	R	A	Family of sponges.
P	O	R	I	F	O	R	M	Resembling a pore.
P	O	R	K	L	I	N	G	Piglet.
P	O	R	O	C	Y	T	E	A large tubular cell that is a constituent of a sponge.
P	O	R	O	G	A	M	Y	Entrance of the pollen tube of a seed.
P	O	R	O	P	O	R	O	Kangaroo apple.
P	O	R	O	R	O	C	A	A tidal bore at the mouth of the Amazon river.
P	O	R	O	S	I	T	Y	Something that is porous.
P	O	R	P	H	Y	R	A	Genus of red algae.
P	O	R	P	H	Y	R	Y	Egyptian rock consisting of feldspar crystals embedded in a groundmass and much prized.
P	O	R	P	O	I	S	E	Small gregarious toothed whale having a blunt rounded snout.
P	O	R	R	I	D	G	E	Soft food made by boiling oats in milk or water.
P	O	R	T	A	B	L	E	Easily transported, Light enough to be moved.
P	O	R	T	A	G	U	E	A sixteenth century Portugese gold coin.
P	O	R	T	F	I	R	E	A slow-burning fuse, Incendiary cord.
P	O	R	T	H	O	L	E	A window in the side of a ship or aeroplane, A loophole in a wall for shooting at aggressors.
P	O	R	T	I	E	R	E	A curtain hanging across a doorway.
P	O	R	T	L	A	N	D	Yellowish limestone.
P	O	R	T	L	A	S	T	Upper edge of the gunwale of a ship.
P	O	R	T	M	O	T	E	Local government of a seaport.
P	O	R	T	O	I	S	E	Portlast.
P	O	R	T	O	L	A	N	Medieval navigational manual with charts.
P	O	R	T	R	A	I	T	Picture, Image, Painting, Bust, Statue, Sculpture, Similitude, Description.
P	O	R	T	R	E	S	S	Female doorkeeper in a convent or apartment house, Charwoman.
P	O	S	H	T	E	E	N	Afghan pelisse made of leather with the fleece on.

1	2	3	4	5	6	7	8	
P	O	S	I	N	G	L	Y	Puzzlingly.
P	O	S	I	T	I	N	G	Disposing, Presupposing, Fixing, Affirming, Assuming, Presuming.
P	O	S	I	T	I	O	N	Assertion, Statement, Stand, Employment, Vocation, Attitude, Location, Capacity.
P	O	S	I	T	I	V	E	Self-assured, Dogmatic, Sheer, Absolute, Downright, Concrete, Genuine, Sure.
P	O	S	I	T	R	O	N	Positive electron.
P	O	S	O	L	O	G	Y	A branch of medical science concerned with dosage.
P	O	S	S	I	B	L	E	Feasible, Viable, Workable, Expedient, Attainable, Available, Likely, Potential.
P	O	S	S	I	B	L	Y	Perhaps, Maybe, Perchance.
P	O	S	T	A	L	L	Y	On postage stamps.
P	O	S	T	C	A	R	D	A card for sending a message through the mail without an envelope.
P	O	S	T	D	A	T	E	Subsequent date, A date on a document later than the actual date.
P	O	S	T	F	A	C	E	A brief explanation at the end of a publication.
P	O	S	T	F	A	C	T	Subsequent deed or occurrence.
P	O	S	T	F	I	N	E	Early English licence paid to levy a fine.
P	O	S	T	F	R	E	E	Postpaid.
P	O	S	T	G	E	N	A	Part of the skull of an insect.
P	O	S	T	H	O	L	E	A shallow oil well.
P	O	S	T	H	O	R	N	A horn used by postillions of horse-coaches.
P	O	S	T	I	C	H	E	False hair, Switch, Toupee.
P	O	S	T	I	C	U	M	Portico behind an ancient Greek or Roman temple.
P	O	S	T	L	U	D	E	A concluding piece of music.
P	O	S	T	M	A	R	K	Mark of postal service showing place, date and time of posting.
P	O	S	T	N	A	T	I	Used of persons born after a designated event.
P	O	S	T	N	O	T	E	Bank note payable on a specified date in the future.
P	O	S	T	O	B	I	T	Taking effect after death.
P	O	S	T	O	R	A	L	Situated behind the mouth.
P	O	S	T	O	T	I	C	Behind the ear vesicle.
P	O	S	T	P	A	I	D	Postage prepaid for a reply, Postage paid by the seller.
P	O	S	T	P	O	N	E	Defer, Delay, Subordinate, Prorogue, Shelve, Suspend, Hold up, Adjourn.
P	O	S	T	T	O	W	N	A town having the main post office of the area.
P	O	S	T	U	R	A	L	Involving posture.
P	O	S	T	U	R	E	D	Posed, Sat, Attitudinized, Masqueraded, Passed off.
P	O	S	T	U	R	E	R	Poseur, Contortionist.
P	O	T	A	R	I	T	E	Mineral consisting of a natural alloy compound of palladium and mercury.
P	O	T	A	T	I	O	N	An alcoholic brew, Draft.
P	O	T	A	T	O	E	S	Edible starchy tubers used as a vegetable.
P	O	T	A	T	O	R	Y	Given to drinking.
P	O	T	A	U	F	E	U	French thick soup of meat and vegetables.
P	O	T	B	E	L	L	Y	Enlarged, swollen or protruding belly.
P	O	T	E	N	T	L	Y	Powerfully, Forcibly, Strongly, Lustily, Robustly.
P	O	T	E	S	T	A	S	Legal authority of a Roman citizen over his family and household.
P	O	T	E	S	T	A	T	Same as POTESTAS.
P	O	T	H	E	R	E	D	Troubled, Disturbed, Perplexed, Fussed, Worried, Concerned, Puzzled, Fretted.
P	O	T	H	O	U	S	E	Alehouse, Tavern.
P	O	T	L	A	T	C	H	To give a present in anticipation of a favour in return.
P	O	T	M	E	T	A	L	Cast iron or an alloy of lead and copper for making pots.
P	O	T	O	M	A	T	O	A plant obtained by grafting a tomato slip on to a potato plant.
P	O	T	O	R	O	U	S	Genus of marsupial mammal, Rat kangaroo.
P	O	T	P	L	A	N	T	An ornamental plant grown in a pot.
P	O	T	R	O	A	S	T	Meat roasted in a pot on top of the stove.
P	O	T	S	H	E	R	D	Fragment of pottery usually from an earlier civilization.
P	O	T	S	T	I	C	K	A stick for stirring a pot.
P	O	T	S	T	I	L	L	A still used for the distillation of Scotch and Irish whiskey.
P	O	T	S	T	O	N	E	A mineral used in prehistoric times for making cooking vessels.
P	O	T	T	E	R	E	D	Puttered, Idled, Fiddled, Doodled, Messed around, Tinkered, Frittered, Muddled.
P	O	T	T	E	R	E	R	One that acts in an ineffective manner.
P	O	U	C	H	I	N	G	Protruding, Puffing out, Pocketing, Swallowing.
P	O	U	L	A	I	N	E	A shoe with a long pointed toe.
P	O	U	L	A	R	D	E	A pullet that has been sterilized.
P	O	U	L	T	I	C	E	A hot mass laid on lint and used to allay inflammation.
P	O	U	N	C	I	N	G	Seizing, Springing, Swooping, Plunging, Leaping, Attacking.
P	O	U	N	D	A	G	E	Commission, A charge made by weight.
P	O	U	N	D	I	N	G	Pulverizing, Crushing, Beating, Hammering, Lumbering, Tramping, Thumping, Pelting.
P	O	U	R	A	B	L	E	Capable of being poured.
P	O	U	T	E	R	I	A	Genus of tropical American timber trees with edible fruit.
P	O	W	D	E	R	E	D	Scattered, Bestrewn, Pulverized, Spiced, Ground, Chalked, Seasoned, Dusty.
P	O	W	E	R	F	U	L	Strong, Compelling, Capable, Influential, Stimulating, Considerable, Mighty, Dynamic.

1	2	3	4	5	6	7	8	
P	O	W	E	R	G	A	S	A commercial gas for providing power.
P	R	A	C	T	I	C	E	Use, Employ, Train, Drill, Operate, Proceed, Drill, Exercise.
P	R	A	C	T	I	C	K	Practical, Cunning.
P	R	A	C	T	I	S	E	Execute, Negotiation, Intrigue, Plot, Habit, Usage, Pursue, Scheme.
P	R	A	E	C	I	P	E	A legal writ commanding a person to do something.
P	R	A	E	D	I	U	M	A tenement of land.
P	R	A	E	F	E	C	T	Prefect, Magistrate.
P	R	A	I	S	I	N	G	Extolling, Commending, Applauding, Honouring, Eulogizing, Acclaiming, Complimenting.
P	R	A	M	N	I	A	N	Strong ancient Greek wine.
P	R	A	N	C	I	N	G	Springing, Bounding, Dancing, Capering, Swaggering, Flouncing, Strutting, Mincing.
P	R	A	N	D	I	A	L	Relating to a meal.
P	R	A	N	G	I	N	G	Damaging or destroying by bombing, Crashing an aeroplane, Striking, Hitting.
P	R	A	N	K	I	N	G	Playing tricks, Gambolling, Adorning, Decking, Spangling.
P	R	A	N	K	I	S	H	Frolicsome.
P	R	A	T	I	Q	U	E	Permission for a ship to resume normal activities after health clearance.
P	R	A	T	T	L	E	D	Babbled, Chattered, Clacked, Jawed, Waffled, Drooled, Twaddled.
P	R	A	T	T	L	E	R	Chatterbox.
P	R	E	A	C	H	E	D	Proclaimed, Discoursed, Inculcated, Delivered, Sermonized, Addressed, Moralized.
P	R	E	A	C	H	E	R	Clergyman, Cleric, Ecclesiastic, Minister, Parson, Reverend.
P	R	E	A	M	B	L	E	Introduction, Preface, Preliminary, Foreword, Overture, Prelude, Prologue, Prelusion.
P	R	E	A	X	I	A	L	Situated in front of the axis of the body.
P	R	E	B	O	U	N	D	A book given a durable binding.
P	R	E	C	E	D	E	D	Prefaced, Introduced, Outranked, Heralded, Foreshadowed, Announced, Presaged, Led.
P	R	E	C	I	N	C	T	District, Domain, Enclosure, Section, Sector, Sphere, Region, Territory.
P	R	E	C	I	O	U	S	Costly, Invaluable, Priceless, Choice, Exquisite, Rare, Fine, Great.
P	R	E	C	L	U	D	E	Hinder, Stop, Impede, Prevent, Avert, Forestall, Obviate, Discontinue.
P	R	E	C	U	R	S	E	Something that predicts a future event.
P	R	E	D	A	T	E	D	To be earlier in time than the actual date.
P	R	E	D	A	T	O	R	Carnivore, One that preys, devours or destroys.
P	R	E	D	E	L	L	A	The step or platform of an altar.
P	R	E	E	N	I	N	G	Dressing, Grooming, Tidying, Gloating, Self-congratulatory.
P	R	E	E	X	I	S	T	To exist earlier than a designated time.
P	R	E	F	A	C	E	D	Introduced, Preceded, Heralded, Led, Ushered, Announced, Presaged.
P	R	E	F	A	C	E	R	Writer of a preface.
P	R	E	F	I	N	E	D	Limited, Determined or defined beforehand.
P	R	E	F	I	X	E	D	Predetermined.
P	R	E	G	N	A	N	T	Carrying unborn young, Fertile, Significant, Inventive, Expressive, Meaningful, Weighty.
P	R	E	H	N	I	T	E	A pale green mineral that occurs in crystalline aggregates.
P	R	E	H	U	M	A	N	A primate regarded as an ancestor of man.
P	R	E	J	U	D	G	E	To anticipate the judgment.
P	R	E	L	A	R	V	A	A newly hatched larva.
P	R	E	L	A	T	I	C	Episcopal, Relating to a prelacy.
P	R	E	L	U	D	E	D	Preformed a prelude, Introduced, Foreshadowed.
P	R	E	L	U	D	E	R	One that introduces.
P	R	E	M	I	A	T	E	To give a prize or premium.
P	R	E	M	I	E	R	E	First night of a theatrical performance, The chief actress or dancer.
P	R	E	M	I	S	E	D	Presupposed, Assumed, Presumed.
P	R	E	M	I	S	E	S	Property, Buildings, Institutions, Places of employment.
P	R	E	M	O	L	A	R	Milk teeth.
P	R	E	M	O	R	A	L	Before the existence of a moral code in society.
P	R	E	M	O	R	S	E	Bitten off, Terminated abruptly.
P	R	E	N	A	S	A	L	Situated in front of the nasal bones.
P	R	E	N	A	T	A	L	Taking place before birth.
P	R	E	N	O	D	A	L	At the base of the wings of an insect.
P	R	E	N	O	M	E	N	The first name of a person.
P	R	E	N	T	I	C	E	Apprentice, Learner.
P	R	E	O	P	T	I	C	Situated in part of the optic region.
P	R	E	O	R	D	E	R	To arrange beforehand.
P	R	E	P	A	R	E	D	Educated, Trained, Produced, Made, Qualified, Drafted, Equipped, Readied.
P	R	E	P	A	R	E	R	One who performs initial step in manufacturing process.
P	R	E	P	E	N	S	E	Deliberate, Premeditated, Considered, Designed, Studied.
P	R	E	P	U	B	I	C	In front of the pubis.
P	R	E	S	A	G	E	D	Foreshadowed, Portended, Preindicated, Foretold, Predicted, Announced, Heralded.
P	R	E	S	A	G	E	R	One that presages.
P	R	E	S	C	I	N	D	Sever, Cut short, Detach, Cut off, Abstract, Separate.
P	R	E	S	C	O	R	E	To record sound effects or dialogue before filming the action.
P	R	E	S	E	N	C	E	Bearing, Address, Air, Demeanour, Deportment, Mien, Appearance, Aspect.

1	2	3	4	5	6	7	8	
P	R	E	S	E	R	V	E	Protect, Save, Guard, Defend, Maintain, Keep, Pickle, Sustain.
P	R	E	S	I	D	E	D	Controlled, Directed, Regulated, Ruled, Conducted, Managed, Supervised, Administered.
P	R	E	S	S	B	E	D	A bed that folds into a cupboard.
P	R	E	S	S	B	O	X	Seating reserved for news presenters at special events.
P	R	E	S	S	I	N	G	Ironing, Compressing, Forcing, Thrusting, Urging, Harassing, Expressing, Depressing.
P	R	E	S	S	I	O	N	Pressing, Pressure.
P	R	E	S	S	M	A	N	Newspaperman.
P	R	E	S	S	U	R	E	Pushing, Squeezing, Compression, Image, Stamp, Stress, Strain, Tension.
P	R	E	S	T	I	G	E	Influence, Reputation, Honour, Status, Dignity, Postition, Eminence, Authority.
P	R	E	S	U	M	E	D	Expected, Anticipated, Assumed, Inferred, Supposed, Implied, Conjectured, Presupposed.
P	R	E	S	U	M	E	R	One that presumes.
P	R	E	T	A	S	T	E	Foretaste.
P	R	E	T	E	N	S	E	Cover, Pretext, Excuse, Claim, Disguise, Charade, Deceit, Deception.
P	R	E	T	E	R	I	T	Bygone, Former, Relating to an action in the past.
P	R	E	T	E	X	T	A	A white robe with a purple border worn by an ancient Roman magistrate.
P	R	E	T	R	I	A	L	A conference of legal representatives before a trial to save time and expense.
P	R	E	T	T	I	F	Y	Adorn, Soften, Beautify, Palliate.
P	R	E	T	T	I	L	Y	Charmingly, Pointedly, Aptly.
P	R	E	V	I	O	U	S	Earlier, Preceding, Prior, Hasty, Premature, Before, Ahead, Formerly.
P	R	I	C	K	I	N	G	Piercing, Inciting, Puncturing, Goading, Urging, Impelling, Boring, Perforating.
P	R	I	C	K	L	E	D	Tingled, Stung.
P	R	I	D	E	F	U	L	Haughty, Elated.
P	R	I	E	D	I	E	U	Small kneeling bench in a church for use when praying.
P	R	I	E	S	T	L	Y	Becoming to a priest.
P	R	I	G	G	E	R	Y	Priggishness.
P	R	I	G	G	I	S	H	Complacent. Conceited, Affected, Rigidness.
P	R	I	G	G	I	S	M	Puritanism, Obnoxious conceit.
P	R	I	M	A	T	E	S	Bishops, Prelates, Large apes.
P	R	I	M	E	V	A	L	Primitive, Aboriginal, Primary, Early age of the world.
P	R	I	M	M	I	N	G	Decking, Prinking, Dressing demurely, Affecting a demure demeanour.
P	R	I	M	N	E	S	S	State of being prim.
P	R	I	M	P	I	N	G	Smartening, Sprucing, Dressing up.
P	R	I	M	R	O	S	E	Genus of a hybrid plant, Flowery, Gay, Choice, Prime, Elite.
P	R	I	N	C	E	L	Y	Kingly, Noble, Stately, Magnificent, Grand, August, Imposing, Grandiose.
P	R	I	N	C	E	P	S	First edition, One that is first, Chief official.
P	R	I	N	C	E	S	S	Female member of a royal family, Daughter of a reigning monarch.
P	R	I	N	C	O	C	K	Coxcomb.
P	R	I	N	K	I	N	G	Mincing, Walking in an affected manner, Strutting, Primping.
P	R	I	N	T	I	N	G	Publishing, Impressing, Imprinting, Stamping.
P	R	I	O	N	A	C	E	Genus of sharks.
P	R	I	O	R	A	T	E	Office of a prior, Religious community under a prior.
P	R	I	O	R	E	S	S	Head of a convent.
P	R	I	O	R	I	T	Y	Precedence, Arrangement, Order, Ascendancy, Supremacy, Superiority.
P	R	I	S	M	O	I	D	A prismatoid whose bases have the same number of sides.
P	R	I	S	O	N	E	D	Imprisoned, Confined, Constrained, Incarcerated, Interned, Jailed.
P	R	I	S	O	N	E	R	Convict, Lag, A person arrested and confined.
P	R	I	S	T	A	N	E	A saturated liquid hydrocarbon obtained from the liver oils of sharks.
P	R	I	S	T	I	N	E	Original, Primitive, Uncorrupted, Innocence, Fresh and clean.
P	R	I	Z	E	M	A	N	Winner of an academic prize.
P	R	O	A	T	L	A	S	Bone between skull and vertebra.
P	R	O	B	A	B	L	E	Possible, Likely, Conceivable, Earthly, Credible, Mortal, Plausible, Reasonable.
P	R	O	B	A	B	L	Y	Preumably, Likely, Doubtless.
P	R	O	B	A	T	O	R	Approver.
P	R	O	C	A	I	N	E	A local anesthetic less toxic than cocaine.
P	R	O	C	E	E	D	S	Yield, Return, Results, Produce, Profit, Earnings, Gain, Revenue.
P	R	O	C	H	E	I	N	Next.
P	R	O	C	I	N	C	T	Readiness.
P	R	O	C	L	A	I	M	Announce, Denounce, Publish, Extol, Declare, Advertise, Broadcast, Disseminate.
P	R	O	C	L	I	V	E	Prone, Inclined.
P	R	O	C	U	R	A	L	Action of acquiring something.
P	R	O	C	U	R	E	D	Obtained, Acquired, Gained, Won, Possessed, Induced, Secured, Convinced.
P	R	O	C	U	R	E	R	Pimp, One that exploits women for prostitution.
P	R	O	D	D	I	N	G	Poking, Digging, Jabbing, Jogging, Nudging, Urging, Goading, Spurring.
P	R	O	D	I	G	A	L	Spendthrift, Squanderer, Repentant wastrel, Profligate.
P	R	O	D	I	T	O	R	Traitor.
P	R	O	D	R	O	M	E	A symptom giving warning of a disease.
P	R	O	D	U	C	E	D	Exhibited, Generated, Yielded, Prolonged, Procreated, Constructed, Mounted, Originated.

1	2	3	4	5	6	7	8	Definition
P	R	O	D	U	C	E	R	One that produces, usually theatrical or movie productions.
P	R	O	E	M	I	A	L	Introductory, Prefatory, Preliminary, Inductive, Preludial, Preparatory, Prelusive.
P	R	O	F	A	N	E	D	Violated, Desecrated, Polluted, Abused, Defiled, Vulgarized, Debased, Impure.
P	R	O	F	A	N	E	R	One that profanes.
P	R	O	F	I	L	E	D	Outlined, Silhouetted.
P	R	O	F	I	T	E	D	Advanced, Improved, Gained, Benefitted, Aided, Furthered, Served, Availed.
P	R	O	F	I	T	E	R	One that profits.
P	R	O	F	O	R	M	A	Memorandum invoice sent prior to the shipment of goods.
P	R	O	F	O	U	N	D	Complete, Deep, Abstruse, Esoteric, Abysmal, Occult, Intense, Intensive.
P	R	O	F	U	N	D	A	Deep-seated arteries or veins.
P	R	O	G	G	I	N	G	Poking, Searching, Foraging, Prowling, Wandering, Begging.
P	R	O	G	R	E	S	S	Journey, Advance, Tour, Headway, Proficiency, Development, Evolution, Growth.
P	R	O	H	I	B	I	T	Forbid, Debar, Preclude, Prevent, Ban, Enjoin, Interdict, Outlaw.
P	R	O	L	A	M	I	N	A class of simple proteins found in seeds.
P	R	O	L	A	P	S	E	The slipping of a body part from its usual position.
P	R	O	L	I	F	I	C	Fruitful, Fecund, Fertile, Abundant, Profuse, Productive, Spawning, Proliferant.
P	R	O	L	I	X	L	Y	Wordily, Verbosity.
P	R	O	L	O	G	O	S	The very first part of an ancient Greek play.
P	R	O	L	O	G	U	E	Introduction, Preface, Foreword, Overture, Preamble, Prelude, Exordium.
P	R	O	L	O	N	G	E	A rope with a hook and toggle for dragging a gun carriage.
P	R	O	M	E	R	I	T	To win or deserve the favour.
P	R	O	M	I	S	E	D	Assured, Warranted, Pledged, Plighted, Contracted, Betrothed, Undertaken, Bargained.
P	R	O	M	I	S	E	E	A person to whom a promise is made.
P	R	O	M	I	S	E	R	One that makes a promise.
P	R	O	M	I	S	O	R	Promittor.
P	R	O	M	O	T	E	D	Raised, Encouraged, Launched, Advanced, Elevated, Upgraded, Advertised, Fostered.
P	R	O	M	O	T	E	E	One that is upgraded.
P	R	O	M	O	T	E	R	One that promotes.
P	R	O	M	P	T	E	D	Incited, Provoked, Urged, Suggested, Induced, Convinced, Exhorted, Prevailed.
P	R	O	M	P	T	E	R	One responsible for prompting actors during performances.
P	R	O	M	P	T	L	Y	Immediately, Quickly, Expeditiously, Fleetly, Hastily, Posthaste, Swiftly, Rapidly.
P	R	O	M	U	L	G	E	Promulgate, Proclaim.
P	R	O	N	A	T	E	D	Rotated the arm and having the palm facing downward or upward.
P	R	O	N	A	T	O	R	A muscle that rotates a limb.
P	R	O	N	G	H	O	E	A hoe with curved prongs.
P	R	O	N	O	T	U	M	Dorsal plate of the first segment of an insect's body.
P	R	O	N	Y	M	P	H	The state of a larva being cocooned in a thin membrane.
P	R	O	O	F	I	N	G	Proofreading, Making impervious to moisture or chemical action.
P	R	O	P	A	N	O	L	Propyl alcohol.
P	R	O	P	E	N	S	E	Inclined, Prone, Disposed, Penchant, Tending.
P	R	O	P	E	N	Y	L	A univalent unsaturated radical.
P	R	O	P	E	R	L	Y	Suitably, Fitly, Correctly, Strictly, Individually, Intrinsically, Inherently, Extremely.
P	R	O	P	E	R	T	Y	Quality, Affection, Attribute, Wealth, Fortune, Resources, Possession, Dominion.
P	R	O	P	H	A	G	E	Various bacterial viruses which are harmless to the host and act as a protection.
P	R	O	P	H	A	S	E	Cell division in which chromosomes are condensed and split.
P	R	O	P	H	E	C	Y	Foretelling, Prediction, Revelation, Oracle, Vision, Prognosis.
P	R	O	P	H	E	S	Y	Foretell, Augur, Forecast, Portend, Predict, Presage, Prognosticate, Soothsay.
P	R	O	P	H	Y	L	L	A plant structure resembling a leaf.
P	R	O	P	L	A	S	M	A preliminary model, Matrix.
P	R	O	P	O	L	I	S	Waxy resin collected by bees and used by them as cement.
P	R	O	P	O	S	A	L	Suggestion, Motion, Invitation, Recommendation, Idea, Plan, Project, Outline.
P	R	O	P	O	S	E	D	Intended, Suggested, Propounded, Exhibited, Contemplated, Presented, Tendered.
P	R	O	P	O	S	E	R	One who proposes.
P	R	O	P	O	U	N	D	Propose, Pose, Prefer, Proposition, Put, Suggest, Proffer.
P	R	O	P	P	I	N	G	Shoring, Supporting, Sustaining, Strengthening, Bolstering, Bracing, Upholding, Carrying.
P	R	O	P	R	I	U	M	Property, Attribute.
P	R	O	P	Y	L	O	N	Outer monumental gateway before a main gateway.
P	R	O	R	A	T	E	D	Divided, Distributed, Apportioned, Parcelled, Shared.
P	R	O	R	O	G	U	E	Prolong, Protract, Defer, Postpone, Adjourn, Suspend, Delay, Recess.
P	R	O	S	A	I	S	M	Commonplace, Banality, Bromide, Platitude.
P	R	O	S	A	I	S	T	A writer of prose.
P	R	O	S	E	M	A	N	Same as PROSAIST.
P	R	O	S	I	M	I	I	Sub-order of primates, Lemurs.
P	R	O	S	O	D	U	S	A small canal in a sponge.
P	R	O	S	O	P	I	S	Genus of shrubs, Mesquite, Family of small black hairy bees.
P	R	O	S	P	O	R	E	A cell in which spores are formed.
P	R	O	S	P	E	C	T	Anticipation, Vision, Foresight, Explore, Vista, Outlook, Perspective, Investigate.

1	2	3	4	5	6	7	8	Definition
P	R	O	S	T	A	T	E	Relating to the prostate gland.
P	R	O	T	A	G	O	N	A white crystalline powder consisting of a mixture of lipides obtained from the brain.
P	R	O	T	A	S	I	S	The first part of an ancient drama introducing the characters.
P	R	O	T	A	T	I	C	Introductory.
P	R	O	T	A	X	I	S	Initial uplift of a mountain range.
P	R	O	T	E	A	S	E	A digestive enzyme.
P	R	O	T	E	G	E	E	One under the protection of a patron or country.
P	R	O	T	E	I	D	A	Aquatic salamanders.
P	R	O	T	E	I	D	E	Large class of extremely complex combinations of amino acids.
P	R	O	T	E	I	D	S	Same as PROTEIDE.
P	R	O	T	E	L	E	S	Genus of mammals, Aardwolf.
P	R	O	T	E	O	S	E	Derivatives of proteins.
P	R	O	T	H	E	C	A	First-formed part of calyculus of coral.
P	R	O	T	I	S	T	A	Unicellular and acellular organisms, Bacteria, Viruses, Algae, Fungi.
P	R	O	T	O	C	O	L	Original record, Treaty, Correct procedure.
P	R	O	T	O	P	O	D	Part of a limb of a crustacean, Early stage of an insect embryo.
P	R	O	T	O	Z	O	A	Sub-kingdom of animals that are found in almost every habitat, Amoebas, Parasites.
P	R	O	T	R	A	C	T	Continue, Prolong, Extend, Elongate, Lengthen, Stretch.
P	R	O	T	R	U	D	E	Bulge, Project, Thrust, Stick out, Pouch, Pout, Beetle, Overhang.
P	R	O	U	D	I	S	H	Somewhat proud.
P	R	O	V	A	B	L	E	Capable of being proved.
P	R	O	V	A	B	L	Y	Verifiably.
P	R	O	V	I	A	N	T	Provender.
P	R	O	V	I	D	E	D	Equipped, Furnished, Prepared, Yielded, Afforded, Stipulated, Dispensed, Supplied.
P	R	O	V	I	D	E	R	Purveyor, Supplier.
P	R	O	V	I	N	C	E	Administrative region, District, Sphere, Territory, Function, Business, Duty, Role.
P	R	O	V	I	N	E	S	Layering plants.
P	R	O	V	I	S	O	R	Purveyor, Steward, Guardian.
P	R	O	V	O	K	E	D	Aroused, Stimulated, Excited, Irritated, Aggravated, Inflamed, Riled, Fomented.
P	R	O	W	L	I	N	G	Roving, Slinking, Wandering stealthily, Roaming, Searching, Pacing restlessly.
P	R	O	X	I	M	A	L	Situated close, Immediate, Near, Imminent, Impending, Approximate, Nearby, Nigh.
P	R	U	D	E	N	C	E	Foresight, Caution, Discretion, Precaution, Acumen, Astuteness, Wisdom, Insight.
P	R	U	I	N	O	S	E	Covered with whitish dust.
P	R	U	I	N	O	U	S	Frosty, Covered with frost.
P	R	U	N	E	L	L	A	A genus of passerine birds that resemble thrushes.
P	R	U	N	E	L	L	E	Sweet brown French liqueur with a grape brandy base and flavoured with the sloe.
P	R	U	N	E	L	L	O	Small yellow dried plum packed without the skin.
P	R	U	R	I	E	N	T	Restless craving, Intense curiosity, Lusty, Sensual, Passionate, Lascivious, Erotic, Lewd.
P	R	U	R	I	T	I	C	Irritation at point of sensory nerve endings.
P	R	U	R	I	T	U	S	Same as PRURITIC.
P	R	Y	I	N	G	L	Y	Inquisitively.
P	S	A	L	M	I	S	T	Composer of sacred songs.
P	S	A	L	M	O	D	Y	Collection of psalms.
P	S	A	L	T	E	R	Y	An ancient and medieval stringed instrument.
P	S	A	M	M	I	T	E	Sandstone.
P	S	E	P	H	I	S	M	Decree of an ancient popular assembly.
P	S	I	L	O	S	I	S	Loss of hair, Depilation.
P	S	I	L	O	T	U	M	Genus of tropical ferns.
P	S	I	T	T	A	C	I	Relating to zgodactyl birds, Parrots, Macaws, Cockatoos.
P	S	O	C	I	D	A	E	Family of winged insects related to book lice.
P	S	O	R	O	S	I	S	Virus disease of citrus trees.
P	S	Y	C	H	I	C	S	Study of psychic, mental or spiritual phenomena and laws.
P	S	Y	C	H	I	S	M	Psychical research.
P	S	Y	L	L	I	U	M	Fleawort.
P	T	A	R	M	I	C	A	Sneezewort.
P	T	E	R	E	T	I	S	Genus of ferns, Ostrich fern.
P	T	E	R	O	M	Y	S	Family of rodents, Flying squirrels.
P	T	E	R	O	P	O	D	Class of mollusks.
P	T	E	R	O	T	I	C	Skull bone of a fish.
P	T	I	L	I	N	U	M	A head organ of flies that pierces the pupa case.
P	T	I	L	O	P	O	D	Having the feet feathered.
P	T	I	L	O	S	I	S	Having plumage.
P	T	I	N	I	N	A	E	Family of small beetles that live on dead animals.
P	T	O	M	A	I	N	E	Putrefaction, Decay caused by bacterial action, Disintegration.
P	T	Y	A	L	I	S	M	Excessive flow of saliva.
P	U	B	C	R	A	W	L	Making the rounds of a series of bars.
P	U	B	L	I	C	A	N	Innkeeper, One estranged from the church.

1	2	3	4	5	6	7	8	Definition
P	U	B	L	I	C	L	Y	Openly, Obviously, Communally.
P	U	C	K	E	R	E	D	Furrowed, Wrinkled, Contracted, Constricted, Pleated, Screwed up.
P	U	D	D	L	I	N	G	Mixing of wet earth or concrete, Planting in thin mud.
P	U	D	I	C	I	T	Y	Modesty, Chastity.
P	U	E	R	A	R	I	A	Genus of woody vines.
P	U	E	R	P	E	R	A	A woman in childbirth.
P	U	F	F	B	A	L	L	Genus of fungi.
P	U	F	F	B	I	R	D	A bird related to the parrot.
P	U	F	F	I	N	U	S	Genus of oceanic birds.
P	U	G	E	T	T	I	A	Genus of spider crabs.
P	U	G	G	A	R	E	E	A light scarf wrapped around a sun helmet.
P	U	G	I	L	I	S	M	Boxing.
P	U	G	I	L	I	S	T	A professional boxer, Fighter.
P	U	I	S	S	A	N	T	Strong, Powerful, Forceful, Mighty, Potent, Influential, Commanding, Ruling.
P	U	L	E	G	O	N	E	Fragrant liquid ketone that yields menthol.
P	U	L	I	C	I	D	E	An agent used for destroying fleas.
P	U	L	I	N	G	L	Y	Fretfully, Whiningly, Feebly.
P	U	L	L	B	A	C	K	Check, Drawback, Restraining force, Reactionary, Withdrawal, Closing hook for a window.
P	U	L	L	B	O	A	T	Flatboat used to pull logs to the bank of a river.
P	U	L	L	O	V	E	R	A sweater without a fastening and is put on by being pulled over the head.
P	U	L	M	O	N	I	A	Genus of European herbs.
P	U	L	M	O	N	I	C	Pertaining to the lungs.
P	U	L	P	I	T	E	R	Preacher.
P	U	L	P	W	O	O	D	Timber used for making pulp for the manufacturing of paper.
P	U	L	S	A	T	O	R	Beater, Striker, Something that throbs or beats.
P	U	L	S	I	F	I	C	Exciting the pulse.
P	U	L	V	I	N	A	R	Cushion.
P	U	L	V	I	N	U	S	Cushion-like arrangement at the base of a stalk.
P	U	M	P	D	A	L	E	Discharge spout of a bilge pump.
P	U	M	P	R	O	O	M	A hall or casino at a spa for the social activities of the patrons.
P	U	M	P	W	E	L	L	Well.
P	U	N	C	H	E	O	N	A pointed tool for working on stone, Figured stamp, die or punch used for engraving, Large cask.
P	U	N	C	H	I	N	G	Striking, Cuffing, Buffeting, Clouting, Poking, Jabbing, Prodding, Slapping.
P	U	N	C	T	A	T	E	Ending in a point, Small like a dot, Depression of a skin.
P	U	N	C	T	U	A	L	Careful, Conscientious, Exact, Fussy, Prompt, Timely, Accentuate, Emphasize.
P	U	N	C	T	U	R	E	Perforate, Pierce, Bore, Drill, Prick, Discredit, Destroy, Shoot.
P	U	N	G	E	N	C	E	Pungency.
P	U	N	G	E	N	C	Y	Keennees, Sharpness, Poignancy.
P	U	N	I	N	E	S	S	Feebleness, Frailty.
P	U	N	I	S	H	E	D	Chastised, Corrected, Penalized, Castigated, Disciplined, Avenged, Lambasted.
P	U	N	I	S	H	E	R	One that inflicts punishment.
P	U	N	I	T	I	V	E	Disciplinary, Punishing, Correctional, Penal, Punitory.
P	U	N	I	T	O	R	Y	Having the nature of a punishment.
P	U	N	T	I	L	L	A	A dagger used in bullfighting.
P	U	N	T	S	M	A	N	Punter, One who manages a punt.
P	U	P	A	R	I	A	L	Relating to the pupal covering when an insect turns into a chrysalis.
P	U	P	A	R	I	U	M	Same as PUPARIAL.
P	U	P	A	T	I	O	N	Process of pupation.
P	U	P	I	F	O	R	M	Shaped like a pupa.
P	U	P	I	L	A	R	Y	Being like a pupil.
P	U	P	I	L	L	A	R	Relating to a pupil or ward.
P	U	P	I	L	A	T	E	Ocelated, Colour spot resembling an eye.
P	U	P	I	P	A	R	A	Genus of ticks the young of which are born as mature maggots.
P	U	P	P	E	T	R	Y	Creation of puppets or a puppet theatre.
P	U	P	P	Y	I	S	H	Characteristic of the behaviour of a puppy.
P	U	P	P	Y	I	S	M	State of being a puppy.
P	U	R	B	L	I	N	D	Partly blind, Dim-sighted, Short-sighted, Myopic, Obtuse.
P	U	R	C	H	A	S	E	Win, Earn, Buy, Procure, Effect, Gain, Acquire, Leverage.
P	U	R	E	N	E	S	S	Purity.
P	U	R	F	L	I	N	G	Inlaid border of a musical instrument.
P	U	R	I	F	I	E	D	Clarified, Cleansed, Filtered, Refined, Expurgated, Purged, Atoned, Expiated.
P	U	R	I	F	O	R	M	Purulent, Resembling pus.
P	U	R	I	S	T	I	C	Marked by being oversolicitous about nicety.
P	U	R	I	T	A	N	O	A medium-sized cigar that is pointed at both ends.
P	U	R	L	I	C	U	E	Concluding a discourse or service.
P	U	R	P	A	R	T	Y	Share of an estate.
P	U	R	P	L	I	N	G	To become purple.

1	2	3	4	5	6	7	8	Clue
P	U	R	P	L	I	S	H	Having a tinge of purple.
P	U	R	P	O	S	E	D	Proposed, Determined, Intended, Proceeded, Aimed, Considered, Contemplated, Designed.
P	U	R	P	U	R	I	C	Affected with purpura.
P	U	R	S	E	F	U	L	All that can be carried in a purse.
P	U	R	S	E	I	N	E	A special large fishing net set by two boats.
P	U	R	S	L	A	N	E	Genus of fleshy herb cultivated as a salad plant.
P	U	R	S	U	A	N	T	Conformance to an agreement.
P	U	R	S	U	I	N	G	Chasing, Following, Persecuting, Harassing, Persisting, Baiting, Badgering, Hounding.
P	U	R	U	L	E	N	T	Formation of pus.
P	U	R	V	E	Y	E	D	Supplied provisions, Conveyed something, Procured, Retailed.
P	U	R	V	E	Y	O	R	Caterer, Victualer, One supplying provisions.
P	U	S	E	Y	I	S	M	Tractarianism.
P	U	S	E	Y	I	T	E	High churchman.
P	U	S	H	B	A	L	L	A game involving an inflated leather-covered ball.
P	U	S	H	B	I	K	E	Pedal cycle.
P	U	S	H	C	A	R	T	Barrow or cart pushed by hand.
P	U	S	H	O	V	E	R	An opponent easy to defeat, An effortless victory.
P	U	S	H	P	U	L	L	An arrangement of two electron tubes.
P	U	S	S	M	O	T	H	Light-coloured European moth.
P	U	S	S	Y	T	O	E	Cat, Pussy willow, Rabbit foot clover.
P	U	S	T	U	L	A	R	Covered with pustules, Eruptions.
P	U	T	A	T	I	V	E	Reputed, Supposed, Inferred, Conjectural, Hypothetical, Reputed, Alleged.
P	U	T	T	Y	I	N	G	Applying putty.
P	U	Z	Z	L	I	N	G	Mystifying, Perplexing, Bewildering, Distracting, Baffling, Befuddling, Confounding, Confusing.
P	Y	C	N	O	S	I	S	Degenerative condition of a cell nucleus.
P	Y	E	L	I	T	I	S	Inflammation of the pelvis or a kidney.
P	Y	G	I	D	I	U	M	Terminal tergite of the abdomen of an insect.
P	Y	O	D	E	R	M	A	Inflammatory skin disease marked by pustules.
P	Y	O	G	E	N	I	C	Producing pus.
P	Y	O	M	E	T	R	A	Accumulation of pus in the uterine cavity.
P	Y	O	R	R	H	E	A	Discharge of pus.
P	Y	R	A	M	E	I	S	Family of brightly coloured butterflies.
P	Y	R	A	N	O	N	E	Characterised by the presence of the furan ring.
P	Y	R	A	N	O	S	E	A glycose sugar.
P	Y	R	A	U	S	T	A	Genus of coloured moths with larvae that bore into plant stems.
P	Y	R	A	Z	O	L	E	A crystalline feeble heterocyclic base.
P	Y	R	E	N	O	I	D	Genus of algae.
P	Y	R	E	X	I	A	L	Abnormally high body temperature.
P	Y	R	I	D	I	N	E	A toxic water-soluble flammable liquid heterocyclic base derived from coal tar.
P	Y	R	I	F	O	R	M	Pear-shaped.
P	Y	R	I	T	I	S	E	To convert into pyrite.
P	Y	R	I	T	O	U	S	Pyritic.
P	Y	R	O	N	E	M	A	Genus of soil fungi.
P	Y	R	O	S	O	M	A	Genus of tropical free-swimming marine animals whose colony forms a hollow cylinder.
P	Y	R	O	S	T	A	T	A device for warning of fire or smoke.
P	Y	R	O	X	E	N	E	A mineral constituting a common constituent of igneous rock.
P	Y	R	R	O	L	Y	L	Any of three univalent radicals.
P	Y	R	U	V	A	T	E	An ester of pyruvic acid.
P	Y	T	H	O	N	I	C	Oracular, Pretending to foretell events, Huge, Monstrous.
P	Y	X	I	D	A	T	E	Resembling a pyxidium.
P	Y	X	I	D	I	U	M	A capsular fruit with an upper portion that falls off like a cap.

Q

1	2	3	4	5	6	7	8	Clue
Q	U	A	C	K	E	R	Y	Charlatanry.
Q	U	A	C	K	I	N	G	The cry of a duck, Making loud pretensions, Pretending to be able to cure ailments.
Q	U	A	C	K	I	S	H	Boasting and fraudulent.
Q	U	A	C	K	I	S	M	Quackery.
Q	U	A	C	K	L	E	D	Suffocated, Choked.
Q	U	A	D	R	A	N	S	Ancient Roman bronze coin.
Q	U	A	D	R	A	N	T	The shape of a quarter-circle.
Q	U	A	D	R	A	T	E	Perfect, Ideal, An arrangement of a cross in heraldry.
Q	U	A	D	R	I	G	A	An ancient Roman chariot drawn by four horses abreast.
Q	U	A	D	R	O	O	N	One with one quarter aboriginal or negro blood.
Q	U	A	D	R	U	A	L	Relating to nouns or pronouns denoting four.
Q	U	A	D	R	U	L	A	Genus of freshwater mussels.

1	2	3	4	5	6	7	8	Definition
Q	U	A	E	S	T	O	R	Agent of the pope.
Q	U	A	F	F	I	N	G	Drinking deeply or freely.
Q	U	A	G	M	I	R	E	Soft wet miry land.
Q	U	A	G	M	I	R	Y	Quaggy, Swamp-like, Treacherous.
Q	U	A	I	L	I	N	G	Withering, Declining, Wincing, Flinching, Weakening, Recoiling, Cowing, Daunting.
Q	U	A	I	N	T	E	R	More picturesque, Odder, Stranger.
Q	U	A	I	N	T	L	Y	In a fastidious fashion, Strangely, Oddly.
Q	U	A	K	E	R	L	Y	Characteristic of a member of the sect of the Friends.
Q	U	A	L	M	I	S	H	Nauseated, Squeamish.
Q	U	A	N	D	A	N	G	A small Australian tree with edible nuts.
Q	U	A	N	D	A	R	Y	Dilemma, Predicament, Difficulty, Troubled.
Q	U	A	N	T	I	F	Y	Qualify, Making explicit.
Q	U	A	N	T	I	T	Y	Aggregate, Amount, Budget, Bulk, Total, Lot, Measure.
Q	U	A	R	R	I	E	D	Excavated, Plucked, Dug, Mined, Delved.
Q	U	A	R	R	I	E	R	Quarrieman, A worker in a quarry.
Q	U	A	R	R	I	E	S	Excavations, Open mines.
Q	U	A	R	T	E	R	N	Quarter, Fourth part.
Q	U	A	R	T	E	R	S	One of four equal parts, Living accommodation, Lodgings.
Q	U	A	S	H	I	N	G	Voiding, Abating, Annulling, Overthrowing, Subduing, Quelling, Crushing, Squashing.
Q	U	A	T	E	N	U	S	As, In the capacity of.
Q	U	A	T	O	R	Z	E	A special hand held in a card game of piquet.
Q	U	A	T	R	A	I	N	A verse unit of four lines.
Q	U	A	V	E	R	E	D	Trembled, Vibrated, Shook, Vacillated, Dithered, Shuddered, Hesitated, Twittered.
Q	U	A	Y	S	I	D	E	Land adjacent to a quay.
Q	U	E	A	S	I	L	Y	Squeamishly.
Q	U	E	B	R	A	D	A	Ravine.
Q	U	E	E	N	B	E	E	Fully developed fertile female bee. A woman who dominates a social group.
Q	U	E	E	N	D	O	M	Territory ruled by a queen.
Q	U	E	E	N	I	N	G	Winter apple, Acting like a queen.
Q	U	E	E	R	I	L	Y	Queerly.
Q	U	E	E	R	I	N	G	Jeopardizing, Harming, Disrupting, Spoiling, Disarranging, Embarrassing, Putting in a bad light.
Q	U	E	E	R	I	S	H	Rather queer or eccentric.
Q	U	E	L	L	I	N	G	Overpowering, Suppressing, Extinguishing, Quieting, Allaying, Pacifying, Crushing, Killing.
Q	U	E	N	C	H	E	D	Extinguished, Cooled, Slaked, Inhibited, Subdued, Overcame, Killed, Crushed.
Q	U	E	N	C	H	E	R	A satisfying drink.
Q	U	E	N	E	L	L	E	A portion of forcemeat boiled and served as a garnish.
Q	U	E	R	Y	I	N	G	Asking, Examining, Inquiring, Questioning, Challenging, Objecting.
Q	U	E	S	T	E	U	R	French financial officer in charge of senate payments.
Q	U	E	S	T	I	N	G	Seeking, Asking, Examining, Pursuing, Demanding, Searching, Hunting.
Q	U	E	S	T	I	O	N	Inquiry, Interrogation, Query, Problem, Issue, Demur, Challenge, Objection.
Q	U	E	S	T	M	A	N	One legally entitled to solicit alms, Sidesman.
Q	U	I	A	Q	U	I	A	A small fish of the mackerel family.
Q	U	I	B	B	L	E	D	Cavilled, Carped, Bickered, Criticized in a peevish manner.
Q	U	I	B	B	L	E	R	One that quibbles.
Q	U	I	C	K	E	S	T	Fastest, Speediest.
Q	U	I	C	K	I	E	S	Something done in a hurry, Cheaply produced film or book, Hurried trip.
Q	U	I	C	K	S	E	T	Living slip or cutting of a plant, Unauthorized brief strike, Something that sets quickly.
Q	U	I	D	D	A	N	Y	Jelly or syrup made from fruit.
Q	U	I	D	D	I	N	G	Dropping chewed food from the mouth.
Q	U	I	D	D	I	T	Y	Eccentricity, Quibbling.
Q	U	I	D	D	L	E	D	Dawdled, Trifled.
Q	U	I	D	N	U	N	C	Busybody, Gossip.
Q	U	I	E	S	C	E	D	Became quiet, Calm or silent.
Q	U	I	E	T	E	S	T	Calmest, Most silent, Most still.
Q	U	I	E	T	I	S	M	State of calmness and passivity.
Q	U	I	E	T	I	S	T	Advocate of quietism.
Q	U	I	E	T	I	V	E	Sedative, Tranquillizer.
Q	U	I	E	T	U	D	E	Quietness.
Q	U	I	L	L	A	J	A	Genus of S. American trees, Soapbark.
Q	U	I	L	L	I	N	G	Piercing with quills, Winding on a quill.
Q	U	I	L	T	I	N	G	Stitched padding, Sewing between two pieces of material.
Q	U	I	N	C	U	N	X	A special arrangement of five things.
Q	U	I	N	D	E	N	E	The fourteenth day after a church festival.
Q	U	I	N	E	L	L	A	A betting pool.
Q	U	I	N	I	T	O	L	A crystalline cyclic glycol.
Q	U	I	N	O	L	Y	L	A univalent radical.
Q	U	I	N	O	V	I	N	Bitter crystalline glycoside found in barks.

1	2	3	4	5	6	7	8	
Q	U	I	N	T	A	I	N	An object used in a tilting contest.
Q	U	I	N	T	I	L	E	Division into five classes.
Q	U	I	N	T	O	L	E	Quintuplet.
Q	U	I	P	P	I	N	G	Scoffing, Gibing, Jeering, Jesting, Sneering, Flouting.
Q	U	I	P	P	I	S	H	A witty or taunting response.
Q	U	I	R	K	I	L	Y	Whimsically.
Q	U	I	R	K	I	N	G	Flourishing, Jerking, Flicking, Crooking, Twisting.
Q	U	I	S	L	I	N	G	A traitor who works with invaders of his country.
Q	U	I	T	R	E	N	T	A small sum paid as rent in lieu of services due.
Q	U	I	T	T	I	N	G	Releasing, Leaving, Stopping, Discharging, Resigning, Abandoning, Deserting.
Q	U	I	V	E	R	E	D	Trembled, Shook.
Q	U	I	X	O	T	I	C	Idealistic, Impractical, Imaginary, Rash, Romantic.
Q	U	I	X	O	T	R	Y	Same as QUIXOTIC.
Q	U	I	Z	Z	I	N	G	Mocking, Peering, Ridiculing, Taunting, Questioning, Deriding, Testing, Chaffing.
Q	U	O	T	A	B	L	E	Suitable for a quotation.
Q	U	O	T	I	E	N	T	Answer to a division sum.

R

1	2	3	4	5	6	7	8	
R	A	B	B	E	T	E	D	Joined by a recessed joint, Grooved.
R	A	B	B	I	N	I	C	Relating to rabbis.
R	A	B	B	I	T	E	R	One whose business is trapping and destroying rabbits.
R	A	B	I	D	I	T	Y	Furiously, Raving, Frenzy, Virulently.
R	A	B	I	F	O	R	M	Resembling rabies.
R	A	C	E	G	O	E	R	One who attends racecourses regularly.
R	A	C	E	L	I	N	E	Artificial channel for conveying water.
R	A	C	E	M	A	S	E	Enzymes that catalyze racemizations and occur in bacteria.
R	A	C	E	M	A	T	E	Salt or ester of racemic acid.
R	A	C	E	M	O	S	E	Compound with freely branching ducts resembling a bunch of grapes.
R	A	C	H	I	D	I	A	Condition of the spine.
R	A	C	H	I	L	L	A	The axis of a spikelet of a grass.
R	A	C	H	I	T	I	C	Affected by rickets, Rickety.
R	A	C	H	I	T	I	S	Rickets.
R	A	C	I	N	E	S	S	Vigorous, Liveliness, Freshness, Naturalness.
R	A	C	K	E	T	E	R	One who plays a sport using a racket.
R	A	C	K	E	T	R	Y	Uproar, Excitement.
R	A	C	K	R	E	N	T	Excessively high rent.
R	A	C	K	W	O	R	K	A mechanism having a rack.
R	A	C	O	V	I	A	N	Relating to seventeenth centre of the intellectuals in Rakow, Poland.
R	A	D	A	R	M	A	N	Operator of a radar device.
R	A	D	I	A	L	L	Y	Resembling the spokes of a wheel.
R	A	D	I	A	N	C	E	Brightness, Splendour, Glory, Glitter, Sheen, Brilliance, Luminosity, Incandescence.
R	A	D	I	A	N	C	Y	Same as RADIANCE.
R	A	D	I	A	T	E	D	Shone, Burned, Gleamed, Spread, Circulated, Diffused, Dispersed, Distributed.
R	A	D	I	A	T	O	R	Various devices for heating rooms.
R	A	D	I	C	A	N	D	The quantity under a radical sign.
R	A	D	I	C	A	T	E	To take root, Plant firmly, Establish firmly.
R	A	D	I	C	O	L	A	Plant lice that attacks roots.
R	A	D	I	C	U	L	A	Nasturtium.
R	A	D	I	O	I	N	G	Communicating by radio.
R	A	D	I	O	N	I	C	Electronic.
R	A	D	U	L	A	T	E	Rasping tongue of a mollusk.
R	A	F	F	L	I	N	G	A lottery usually decided by means of drawing tickets.
R	A	F	T	D	U	C	K	Scaup duck.
R	A	F	T	E	R	E	D	Supported by timber logs.
R	A	F	T	P	O	R	T	A large square port in a ship for unloading or loading bulky goods.
R	A	F	T	S	M	A	N	One who travels on a raft.
R	A	G	A	B	A	S	H	Riffraff.
R	A	G	G	E	D	L	Y	Roughly, Shaggily, Irregularly, Stragglingly, Unevenly, Unco-ordinated.
R	A	G	I	N	G	L	Y	Violently, Wildly, Extraordinarily, Tremendously.
R	A	G	P	A	P	E	R	Paper made from rags.
R	A	G	S	T	O	N	E	A hard rock.
R	A	I	L	B	I	R	D	A racing enthusiast who sits on the rail watching the workouts.
R	A	I	L	H	E	A	D	The end of a railway track.
R	A	I	L	L	E	R	Y	Banter, Chaffing, Mocking, Jest, Satire, Lampoonery, Ridicule, Pleasantry.
R	A	I	L	R	O	A	D	Railway, A railed track for freight and passenger trucks.

1	2	3	4	5	6	7	8	
R	A	I	N	B	A	N	D	A dark band in the solar spectrum caused by watery vapour and used in weather predictions.
R	A	I	N	B	I	R	D	Genus of bird believed to cry when rain is expected.
R	A	I	N	C	O	A	T	Waterproofed coat to wear in inclement weather.
R	A	I	N	D	R	O	P	A drop of rain.
R	A	I	N	F	A	L	L	Amount of rain that has fallen in a certain area at a certain time according to the recording.
R	A	I	N	L	E	S	S	Lacking precipitation.
R	A	I	N	W	A	S	H	The washing away of material by rain.
R	A	I	N	W	E	A	R	Waterproofed clothing.
R	A	I	N	W	O	R	M	An earthworm that appears above ground after heavy rain.
R	A	K	E	H	E	L	L	Dissolute, Licentious, Rascally, Wild, Gay, Rakish, Sporty, Fast.
R	A	K	I	S	H	L	Y	Smartly, Sportily, Raffishly.
R	A	K	S	H	A	S	A	A demon in Hindu mythology.
R	A	L	L	Y	I	N	G	Reuniting, Reassembling, Stirring, Reviving, Mobilizing, Mustering, Organizing, Bracing.
R	A	M	A	L	I	N	A	Genus of lichens used for dyes and perfumes.
R	A	M	A	S	S	E	D	Gathered.
R	A	M	B	L	I	N	G	Roving, Wandering, Roaming, Strolling, Exploring, Sauntering, Meandering, Diverging.
R	A	M	B	U	T	A	N	Bright red Malayan fruit that has a pleasant acid pulp and covered with long soft spines.
R	A	M	E	N	T	U	M	Scraping, Shaving, Scales.
R	A	M	I	C	O	R	N	Having branched antennae.
R	A	M	I	F	I	E	D	Separated into divisions, Split up into branches, Branched out.
R	A	M	O	N	E	U	R	Chimney sweep.
R	A	M	P	A	G	E	D	Rushed, Stormed, Splurged, Raged, Created havoc, Romped, Gambolled, Rioted.
R	A	M	P	A	N	C	Y	Extravagance.
R	A	M	R	O	D	D	Y	Inflexibly, Stiffly.
R	A	M	S	H	O	R	N	Genus of aquatic ofted used as a scavenger in an aquarium.
R	A	M	U	L	O	S	E	Having many small branches.
R	A	M	U	L	O	U	S	Same as RAMULOSE.
R	A	N	A	L	I	A	N	Relating to Ranunculas.
R	A	N	C	H	E	R	O	Rancher.
R	A	N	C	H	I	N	G	Breeding and tending animals on a ranch.
R	A	N	C	H	M	A	N	Rancher.
R	A	N	C	I	D	L	Y	Sourly, Odiously, Obnoxiously.
R	A	N	D	O	M	L	Y	Haphazardly, Casually, Anyhow, Helter-skelter, Aimlessly, Indiscriminately.
R	A	N	G	I	F	E	R	Genus consisting of domestic and wild reindeer and caribous.
R	A	N	K	L	I	N	G	Festering, Insiduously irritating, Inflaming, Smouldering.
R	A	N	K	N	E	S	S	Overgrown, Foulness, Grossness.
R	A	N	S	O	M	E	D	Expiated, Rescued, Bought, Recovered, Retrieved, Released, Liberated, Extracted.
R	A	N	S	O	M	E	R	One that pays for the release of a hostage.
R	A	P	A	C	I	T	Y	Cupidity, Avarice, Greed, Voracity.
R	A	P	E	C	A	K	E	Cattle feed made from residue left after expressing oil.
R	A	P	E	S	E	E	D	Seed of rape, genus of herbs.
R	A	P	H	A	N	U	S	Genus of herbs. Radish.
R	A	P	H	I	D	A	E	Genus of extinct flightless birds, Dodos.
R	A	P	H	I	D	E	S	Crystals found in plants.
R	A	P	I	D	I	T	Y	Swiftness, Celerity, Velocity, Speed, Pace, Quickness, Rapidness.
R	A	P	P	A	R	E	E	Plunderer, Vagabond.
R	A	P	T	O	R	E	S	Genus of flesh-eating birds, Falcons.
R	A	P	T	U	R	E	D	Enraptured, Transported, Ecstatic.
R	A	R	E	F	I	E	D	Esoteric, Abstuse, Made thin.
R	A	R	E	N	E	S	S	Rarity.
R	A	R	E	R	I	P	E	Ripening early, Ripe before others of the same type.
R	A	S	C	A	L	L	Y	Meanly, Mischievously, Roguishly, Knavish, Dishonestly.
R	A	S	H	N	E	S	S	Carelessness, Foolishnss, Impulsiveness, Unwariness, Foolhardiness, Brashness.
R	A	S	O	R	I	A	L	Birds that scratch the ground for food.
R	A	T	A	P	L	A	N	Beat of a drum, Hoofbeats of a horse.
R	A	T	C	H	E	T	Y	Jerky, Irregular, Creaky.
R	A	T	C	H	I	N	G	Operating with a ratchet.
R	A	T	E	A	B	L	E	Taxable, Proportionable rate, Assessable.
R	A	T	G	O	O	S	E	Brant goose.
R	A	T	H	R	I	P	E	Precocious.
R	A	T	I	F	I	E	D	Confirmed, Verified, Authorized, Approved, Endorsed, Licensed, Sanctioned, Validated.
R	A	T	I	F	I	E	R	One that ratifies.
R	A	T	I	O	N	A	L	Reasoning, Intelligent, Sensible, Reasonable, Logical, Sound, Sober, Prudent.
R	A	T	I	O	N	E	D	Distributed, Divided, Apportion, Use sparingly.
R	A	T	S	B	A	N	E	Genus of plants that are supposed to be poisonous to rats.
R	A	T	S	N	A	K	E	Family of rat-eating snakes.
R	A	T	T	L	I	N	G	Clattering, Short sharp noises, Clacking, Agitating, Disconcerting, Embarrassing, Rousing.

1	2	3	4	5	6	7	8	
R	A	V	A	G	I	N	G	Devastating, Pillaging, Raiding, Despoiling, Sacking, Desecrating, Looting, Plundering.
R	A	V	E	H	O	O	K	A hooked tool.
R	A	V	E	L	L	E	D	Twisted, Entangled, Tangled, Complicated, Muddled, Snarled, Perplexed.
R	A	V	E	N	I	N	G	Devouring, Seizing by violence, Consuming greedily.
R	A	V	E	N	O	U	S	Rapacious, Voracious, Craving, Gluttonous, Hungry, Starving, Famished.
R	A	V	I	G	O	T	E	Vinegar herbed dressing coloured with spinach puree.
R	A	V	I	N	G	L	Y	Wildly, Incoherently, Irrationally.
R	A	V	I	S	H	E	D	Raped, Abducted, Violated, Plundered, Robbed, Despoiled, Corrupted, Outraged.
R	A	V	I	S	H	E	R	Rapist.
R	A	W	B	O	N	E	D	Gaunt, Lean, Angular, Bony, Scrawny, Skinny, Scraggy, Lank.
R	A	W	H	I	D	E	S	Prospector, Small-scale miner, Harsh taskmaster.
R	A	Y	O	N	I	S	M	A Russian style of painting.
R	A	Z	Z	M	A	T	A	Z	Z	Razzle-dazzle.
R	E	A	B	S	O	R	B	To absorb again, Soak up again.
R	E	A	C	C	E	D	E	Return.
R	E	A	C	H	I	N	G	Extending, Thrusting, Stretching, Snatching, Grasping, Attaining, Acquiring, Gaining.
R	E	A	C	T	A	N	T	Initial factor in a chemical reaction.
R	E	A	C	T	I	O	N	Recoil, Catalysis, Chemcial transformation, Counteracting force.
R	E	A	C	T	I	V	E	Response to stimulus.
R	E	A	D	A	B	L	E	Pleasant or easy to read, Legible.
R	E	A	D	A	B	L	Y	In a legible condition.
R	E	A	D	J	U	S	T	Reorganize, Rearrange, Reconstitute, Reorient, Reshuffle, Modify, To accept changes.
R	E	A	F	F	I	R	M	Affirm again in order to confirm or strengthen.
R	E	A	G	E	N	C	Y	Stimulus for an experiment.
R	E	A	L	I	Z	E	D	Thought, Accomplished, Gained, Achieved, Attained, Conceived, Envisaged, Visualized.
R	E	A	L	L	E	G	E	To allege again.
R	E	A	L	N	E	S	S	Reality.
R	E	A	P	P	E	A	R	To make a return appearance, Recurr, Reoccur.
R	E	A	R	M	I	N	G	Equipping with improved weaponry.
R	E	A	R	M	O	S	T	Last, Farthest in the rear.
R	E	A	R	R	E	S	T	To arrest again.
R	E	A	R	W	A	R	D	Backward, Located at the end.
R	E	A	S	C	E	N	D	To go up again.
R	E	A	S	C	E	N	T	A fresh climb.
R	E	A	S	O	N	E	D	Thought, Cogitated, Deliberated, Reflected, Speculated.
R	E	A	S	O	N	E	R	One that debates or discourses.
R	E	A	S	S	E	R	T	To assert again.
R	E	A	S	S	E	S	S	Revalue.
R	E	A	S	S	I	G	N	To designate different tasks.
R	E	A	S	S	U	R	E	To free from fear, Comfort, Console, Pacify, Cheer.
R	E	A	T	T	A	C	H	To join again.
R	E	A	T	T	A	I	N	To acquire again.
R	E	B	A	T	I	N	G	Diminishing, Lessening, Blunting, Dulling, Dwindling, Removing, Reducing, Tapering.
R	E	B	E	L	L	E	D	Opposed, Disobeyed, Resisted, Renounced, Revolted, Mutinied, Feel revulsion.
R	E	B	E	L	L	E	R	Mutineer, Insurgent.
R	E	B	O	I	L	E	D	Boiled again.
R	E	B	O	I	L	E	R	Piece of equipment for supplying additional heat.
R	E	B	U	F	F	E	D	Snubbed, Repulsed, Rejected, Repelled, Fended, Staved off.
R	E	B	U	K	I	N	G	Reprimanding, Checking, Repulsing, Reproving, Admonishing, Scolding, Chiding.
R	E	B	U	R	I	E	D	Re-interred.
R	E	B	U	T	T	A	L	Refutation, Retort.
R	E	B	U	T	T	E	D	Contradicted, Disproved, Confounded, Confuted, Refuted, Repelled.
R	E	B	U	T	T	E	R	One that answers evidence given by the plaintiff.
R	E	C	A	L	L	E	D	Remembered, Reminded, Retained, Extracted, Recollected, Recanted, Withdrew, Revoked.
R	E	C	A	N	T	E	D	Withdrew, Repudiated, Revoked, Abjured, Renunciated, Foreswore, Retracted.
R	E	C	A	P	T	O	R	One that recovers something.
R	E	C	A	S	I	N	G	Re-binding a book without disturbing the pages.
R	E	C	E	D	I	N	G	Departing, Withdrawing, Retiring, Retreating, Regressing, Diminishing, Shrinking.
R	E	C	E	I	V	E	D	Possessed, Accepted, Caught, Intercepted, Held, Admitted, Taken, Sanctioned.
R	E	C	E	I	V	E	R	One who knowingly accepts and sells stolen property.
R	E	C	E	N	T	L	Y	Lately, Newly, Afresh, Of late.
R	E	C	E	S	S	E	D	Concealed in a recess, Terminated, Adjourned, Dissolved.
R	E	C	E	S	S	E	S	Vacations, Recessions, Alcoves, Clefts.
R	E	C	E	S	S	U	S	Recess.
R	E	C	H	A	R	G	E	Make a new attack, Reload, To give a boost.
R	E	C	I	S	I	O	N	Cancellation, Rescinding.
R	E	C	I	T	I	N	G	Relating, Describing, Narrating, Recounting, Reporting, Stating, Rehearsing, Enumerating.

1	2	3	4	5	6	7	8	
R	E	C	K	L	E	S	S	Foolhardy, Rash, Careless, Neglectful, Thoughtless, Heedless, Daring, Headstrong.
R	E	C	K	L	I	N	G	Weakling.
R	E	C	K	O	N	E	D	Enumerated, Computed, Calculated, Estimated, Figured, Numbered, Considered, Judged.
R	E	C	K	O	N	E	R	Aid to calculating.
R	E	C	L	I	N	E	D	Rested, Recumbent, Slanted, Inclined, Reposed, Stored, Canted, Tilted.
R	E	C	L	I	N	E	R	A reclining dial.
R	E	C	L	O	S	E	R	A switch or circuit breaker to reactivate power after an interruption.
R	E	C	O	A	L	E	D	Supplied with a fresh supply of coal.
R	E	C	O	I	L	E	D	Retreated, Balked, Flinched, Winced, Blenched, Quailed, Faltered, Wavered.
R	E	C	O	I	N	E	D	Melted down obsolete coinage to mint new ones.
R	E	C	O	L	O	U	R	To repaint or retint.
R	E	C	O	M	M	I	T	To entrust again, To consign again.
R	E	C	O	N	V	E	Y	To restore property to its owner, To return back to its original position.
R	E	C	O	R	D	E	D	Indicated, Marked, Read, Registered, Copied, Noted, Entered, Folioed.
R	E	C	O	R	D	E	R	One that records progress of work, A device that records.
R	E	C	O	U	P	E	D	Deducted, Reimbursed, Indemnified, Recovered, Regained, Recruited, Repossessed.
R	E	C	O	U	R	S	E	Resort, Access, Expedient, Makeshift, Refuge, Shift, Substitute, Stopgap.
R	E	C	O	V	E	R	Y	Cure, Remedy, Convalesce, Improve, Recuperate, Heal, Resume, Restore.
R	E	C	R	E	A	N	T	Craven, False, Cowardly, Unfaithful, Faithless, Disloyal, Perfidious, Treacherous.
R	E	C	R	E	A	T	E	Amuse, Divert, Entertain, Restore, Refresh, Cheer, Revive, Rejuvenate.
R	E	C	T	O	R	A	L	Referring to God as a ruler of men.
R	E	C	U	M	B	E	D	Reclined, Reposed.
R	E	C	U	R	R	E	D	Returned, Resorted, Reacted, Reverted, Applied, Repaired, Reiterated, Repeated.
R	E	C	U	R	V	E	D	Curved backward or inward.
R	E	C	U	S	A	N	T	Non-conformist, Refusal to conform to authority.
R	E	D	A	C	T	O	R	Editor.
R	E	D	A	R	G	U	E	Disprove.
R	E	D	B	E	L	L	Y	Red grouper, Red-bellied terrapin.
R	E	D	C	E	D	A	R	An American juniper.
R	E	D	C	H	A	L	K	Red ochre.
R	E	D	C	O	R	A	L	Coral of a delicate shade of pink used for jewellery.
R	E	D	C	R	O	S	S	International humanitarian organization.
R	E	D	D	E	N	D	O	Specifying duty owed to a superior.
R	E	D	D	E	N	E	D	Blushed, Made red.
R	E	D	E	A	R	T	H	Hard red deep clays of a tropical climate.
R	E	D	E	E	M	E	D	Repurchased, Liberated, Cleared, Justified, Purified, Reformed, Compensated, Reclaimed.
R	E	D	E	E	M	E	R	One that redeems.
R	E	D	E	M	A	N	D	To demand again.
R	E	D	E	P	L	O	Y	To transfer troops and arms from one area to another.
R	E	D	F	A	C	E	D	Flushed with anger or embarrassment.
R	E	D	I	G	E	S	T	To digest again.
R	E	D	O	L	E	N	T	Aromatic, Rich, Distinctive, Scented, Smelling, Evocative, Reminiscent, Perfumed.
R	E	D	O	U	B	L	E	Double, Intensify, Duplicate, Resound, Aggravate, Deepen, Enhance, Magnify.
R	E	D	S	H	A	N	K	Common bird with pale red legs, Highlander.
R	E	D	S	H	I	R	T	Member of the Garibaldi organization that wears a red shirt as part of a uniform.
R	E	D	S	H	O	R	T	Metal that is brittle when red-hot.
R	E	D	S	T	A	R	T	A small European singing bird related to the redbreast.
R	E	D	U	C	I	N	G	Restricting, Demolishing, Overcoming, Demoting, Condensing, Consolidating.
R	E	D	U	V	I	I	D	Type genus of blood-sucking insects.
R	E	E	C	H	O	E	D	Reverberated, Resounded.
R	E	E	D	B	I	R	D	Sedge warbler.
R	E	E	D	F	I	S	H	Slender West African freshwater fish that resembles an eel.
R	E	E	D	L	E	S	S	A pipe organ lacking a reed but producing a reedlike tone.
R	E	E	D	L	I	N	G	Bearded tit.
R	E	E	D	M	A	C	E	Cat's tail.
R	E	E	D	P	I	P	E	Musical instrument made of a reed.
R	E	E	D	S	T	O	P	Set of reed pipes in a pipe organ that imitates orchestral instruments.
R	E	E	D	W	R	E	N	Reed warbler.
R	E	E	F	B	A	N	D	A piece of canvas to strengthen a sail.
R	E	E	F	K	N	O	T	A square knot used in tying reef points.
R	E	E	F	L	I	N	E	Reef point.
R	E	E	L	A	B	L	E	Able to be wound on a reel.
R	E	E	L	R	A	L	L	Disturbance, Fuss.
R	E	E	L	S	E	A	T	The part of a fishing rod where the reel is mounted.
R	E	E	M	B	O	D	Y	Reshape, Reorganize, Reincorporate.
R	E	E	M	E	R	G	E	To emerge after concealment or suppression.
R	E	E	N	L	I	S	T	To sign up again in the armed forces after a tour of duty has ended.

1	2	3	4	5	6	7	8	
R	E	E	X	P	O	R	T	A re-exported commodity.
R	E	F	A	S	T	E	N	To fasten again.
R	E	F	E	R	E	N	T	Someone that is consulted.
R	E	F	E	R	R	E	D	Related, Recurred, Ascribed, Assigned, Imputed, Submitted, Alluded, Quoted.
R	E	F	E	R	R	E	R	One that refers.
R	E	F	I	G	U	R	E	To figure again.
R	E	F	I	L	L	E	D	Replenished.
R	E	F	I	N	E	R	Y	A building with equipment for refining or purifying metals or oils.
R	E	F	I	N	I	N	G	The process of removing impurities.
R	E	F	I	T	T	E	D	Fitted out. Replenished, Renovated.
R	E	F	L	E	X	E	D	Thrown back, Produced by reflection, Bent or curved backward or downward.
R	E	F	L	E	X	L	Y	By means of reflexes.
R	E	F	L	O	W	E	D	Flowed back, Ebbed.
R	E	F	L	O	W	E	R	To flourish again, Blossom again.
R	E	F	L	U	E	N	T	Ebbing, Subsiding.
R	E	F	O	R	E	S	T	Replanting forest cover.
R	E	F	O	R	G	E	D	Making over into a new form.
R	E	F	O	R	M	E	D	Emended, Improved, Corrected, Pruned, Rectified, Remodelled, Restored.
R	E	F	O	R	M	E	R	An advocate of political reform.
R	E	F	R	A	M	E	D	Put into a few frame.
R	E	F	R	E	E	Z	E	To freeze again after thawing.
R	E	F	U	N	D	E	D	Given back, Repaid, Reimbursed, Put back, Returned a payment.
R	E	F	U	S	I	N	G	Declining, Rejecting, Denying, Renouncing, Disapproving, Dismissing, Repudiating.
R	E	F	U	T	I	N	G	Disproving, Confuting, Breaking, Confounding, Controverting, Rebutting.
R	E	G	A	I	N	E	D	Recovered, Recouped, Recruited, Repossessed, Retrieved.
R	E	G	A	L	I	N	G	Entertaining sumptuously, Feeding, Pleasing, Banqueting, Refreshing, Indulging.
R	E	G	A	L	I	S	M	Doctrine of royal supremacy in church affairs.
R	E	G	A	L	I	T	Y	A royal grant, Sovereignty over a territory.
R	E	G	A	R	D	E	D	Considered, Evaluated, Judged, Respected, Gazed, Admired, Esteemed.
R	E	G	A	R	D	E	R	A forester in medieval England who checked on violations of the law.
R	E	G	A	T	H	E	R	Reunite, Regroup, Recollect.
R	E	G	I	C	I	D	E	The killing or murder of a king.
R	E	G	I	L	D	E	D	Brightened, Freshened.
R	E	G	I	M	E	N	T	A military unit, To organize into groups, Subject to strict discipline.
R	E	G	I	O	N	A	L	Relating to a geographical region, Sectional, Local, Provincial.
R	E	G	I	O	N	E	D	Divided into regions.
R	E	G	I	S	T	E	R	A written record, List, Catalogue, Schedule, Roster, Enroll, Indicate, Read.
R	E	G	I	S	T	R	Y	Registration, Enrollment, Agency.
R	E	G	N	A	N	C	Y	Sovereignty, Rule.
R	E	G	O	R	G	E	D	Vomited, Disgorged, Swallowed again, Thrown back.
R	E	G	R	A	D	E	D	Assigned to a new category, Regrouped.
R	E	G	R	A	T	E	D	Sold at retail for a profit, Removed outer surface to freshen the appearance.
R	E	G	R	O	W	T	H	A product of regrowing, Vegetation that appears after clearing the land.
R	E	G	U	L	A	T	E	Adjust, Discipline, Rectifying, Direct, Govern, Organize, Moderate, Temper.
R	E	H	A	N	D	L	E	Give a new treatment.
R	E	H	A	S	H	E	D	Presented or used again, Restated without any new ideas.
R	E	H	E	A	R	S	E	Narrate, Recount, Relate, Tell, Practice, Recite, Train.
R	E	H	E	A	T	E	D	Heated again.
R	E	H	O	B	O	A	M	Very large wine bottle.
R	E	H	O	U	S	E	D	To be moved into better type of housing.
R	E	I	G	N	I	N	G	Governing, Ruling, Prevailing, Predominating, Dominating, Preponderating, Swaying.
R	E	I	M	P	O	S	E	To impose again, Retax.
R	E	I	N	D	E	E	R	A deer of Northern areas, often domesticated, Caribou, Elk, Moose.
R	E	I	N	F	O	R	M	To notify again.
R	E	I	N	L	E	S	S	Unchecked, Unrestrained, Uncontrolled, Lacking guidance.
R	E	I	N	S	E	R	T	To insert again.
R	E	I	N	S	M	A	N	A skilful jockey or harness driver.
R	E	I	N	S	U	R	E	To transfer business to another insurance compay. To provide increased insurance cover.
R	E	I	N	V	E	S	T	To invest again usually when investment reaches maturity.
R	E	I	S	S	U	E	D	Published again, Reprinted, A repeated issue.
R	E	J	E	C	T	E	D	Refused, Discarded, Ejected, Declined, Dismissed, Repudiated, Spurned, Disapproved.
R	E	J	O	I	C	E	D	Gladdened, Pleased, Feel great joy, Exulted, Gloried, Delighted.
R	E	J	O	I	C	E	S	One that rejoices.
R	E	J	O	I	N	E	D	Made a reply, Reunited, Answered.
R	E	J	U	D	G	E	D	Reviewed, Re-examined.
R	E	K	I	N	D	L	E	Revitalize, Retrieve, Revive, Renew, Renovate, Resurrect, Reactivate.
R	E	L	A	P	S	E	D	Backslid, Slipped back, Sunk, Subsided, Lapsed, Withdrew.

1	2	3	4	5	6	7	8	Definition
R	E	L	A	P	S	E	R	One that relapses.
R	E	L	A	S	T	E	R	A worker who puts shoes on a finishing last.
R	E	L	A	T	I	N	G	Telling, Saying, Asserting, Reputing, Rehearsing, Recounting, Describing, Reporting.
R	E	L	A	T	I	O	N	Narration, Recitation, Kinsman, Kinswoman, Relative, Connection, Reference, Respect.
R	E	L	A	T	I	V	E	Relative, Relation, Kinswoman, Relevant, Pertitent, Pertaining, Comparative, Corresponding.
R	E	L	A	X	A	N	T	Something that relieves tension, Laxative.
R	E	L	A	X	I	N	G	Slackening, Resting, Easing, Loosening, Unbending, Unwinding, Loosing.
R	E	L	A	Y	I	N	G	Transmitting, Relieving.
R	E	L	E	A	S	E	D	Alleviated, Surrendered, Relinquished, Quitted, Freed, Mitigated, Discharged, Liberated.
R	E	L	E	A	S	E	E	One who is released.
R	E	L	E	A	S	E	R	A stimulus that initiates a change of behaviour.
R	E	L	E	G	A	T	E	Banish, Degrade, Demote, Commit, Deport, Displace, Exile, Expel.
R	E	L	E	A	S	E	E	One who is given a release.
R	E	L	E	A	S	O	R	One giving a release.
R	E	L	E	V	A	N	T	Material, Pertinent, Applicable, Proportional, Commensurate, Valid, Sufficient, Apropos.
R	E	L	I	A	B	L	E	Dependable, Trustworthy, Trusty, Tried, Secure, Safe, Proven, Validated.
R	E	L	I	A	B	L	Y	Dependably, Trustily, Safely, Unerringly, Convincingly, Accurately.
R	E	L	I	A	N	C	E	Dependence, Confidence, Mainstay, Trust, Faith, Hope.
R	E	L	I	C	T	E	D	Widowed, Survived, Remained behind.
R	E	L	I	E	V	E	D	Rescued, Delivered, Mitigated, Lessened, Alleviated, Robbed, Deprived, Allayed.
R	E	L	I	E	V	E	R	Something that relieves pain or distress.
R	E	L	I	G	I	O	N	Faith, Creed, Communion, Denomination, Sect, Cult, Persuasion, Doctrine.
R	E	L	I	N	I	N	G	Fitting a new lining.
R	E	L	I	S	H	E	D	Liked, Savoured, Enjoyed, Delighted, Appreciated, Cherished.
R	E	L	I	V	I	N	G	Living over again, Reviving, Recollecting.
R	E	L	O	A	D	E	D	Act of loading, Worthless securities sold to someone who has already bought.
R	E	L	U	C	E	N	T	Radiant, Shining, Refulgent.
R	E	L	U	M	I	N	E	Rekindle.
R	E	M	A	I	N	E	D	Stayed, Lingered, Tarried, Waited, Left over, Stopped.
R	E	M	A	K	I	N	G	Transforming, Rebuilding, Giving a different image.
R	E	M	A	N	E	N	T	Supplementary, Further, Residue.
R	E	M	A	N	N	E	D	Manned again, Renewed the staff.
R	E	M	A	R	K	E	D	Observed, Perceived, Noted, Stated, Said, Discerned, Noticed, Mentioned.
R	E	M	A	R	K	E	R	One that remarks.
R	E	M	A	R	Q	U	E	Drawn, Etched, Sketch, Proof.
R	E	M	E	D	I	A	L	Intended as a remedy, A correction for a fault, Healing, Curative.
R	E	M	E	D	I	E	D	Cured, Relieved, Repaired, Corrected, Healed, Restored, Adjusted, Rectified.
R	E	M	E	M	B	E	R	Recollect, Recall, Remind, Reminisce, Retain, Revive, Revoke, Cite.
R	E	M	I	N	D	E	D	Remembered, Cited, Recalled, Recollected, Retained, Revived, Hinted, Intimated.
R	E	M	I	N	D	E	R	Expression, Gesture, Indication, Sign, Souvenir, Token, Keepsake, Memento.
R	E	M	I	S	I	N	G	Replacing, Returning, Releasing a claim, Surrender by deed.
R	E	M	I	S	S	L	Y	Carelessly, Negligently, Lazily, Heedlessly, Slovenly.
R	E	M	I	T	T	A	L	Remission.
R	E	M	I	T	T	E	D	Pardoned, Forgiven, Surrendered, Released, Remanded, Postponed, Mitigated, Resigned.
R	E	M	I	T	T	E	E	One to whom a remittance is sent.
R	E	M	O	L	A	D	E	A mayonnaise-type dressing with savoury herbs.
R	E	M	O	T	E	L	Y	Distantly, Obscurely, Deviously.
R	E	M	O	T	I	O	N	Remoteness, Removal.
R	E	M	O	V	I	N	G	Dislodging, Shifting, Transferring, Assassinating, Eradicating, Eliminating, Disappearing.
R	E	M	U	R	M	U	R	Repeat, Echo, Murmur repeatedly.
R	E	N	A	M	I	N	G	To give another name.
R	E	N	D	E	R	E	D	Delivered, Transmitted, Yielded, Emitted, Repaid, Imparted, Administered, Translated.
R	E	N	D	E	R	E	R	One that operates a rendering plant.
R	E	N	D	I	B	L	E	Capable of being torn.
R	E	N	E	G	A	D	E	Turncoat, Traitor, One who changes their religious faith, Deserter.
R	E	N	E	G	A	D	O	Renegade.
R	E	N	E	G	A	T	E	Renegade.
R	E	N	E	G	I	N	G	Refusing, Declining, Revoking, Reversing, Backing out, Crying off, Breaking a promise.
R	E	N	E	W	I	N	G	Re-establishing, Reviving, Resuming, Resuscitating, Rebuilding, Repeating, Replacing.
R	E	N	I	F	O	R	M	Bean-shaped, Resembling a kidney
R	E	N	I	T	E	N	T	Recalcitrant, Resisting constraint, Persistently opposed.
R	E	N	O	U	N	C	E	Abandon, Disclaim, Repudiate, Adjure, Revoke, Refuse, Decline.
R	E	N	O	V	A	T	E	Revive, Regenerate, Renew, Restore, Rekindle, Refurnish, Modernize, Update.
R	E	N	O	W	N	E	D	Celebrated, Famous, Distinguished, Eminent, Famed, Great, Illustrious, Notable.
R	E	N	O	W	N	E	R	One that gives renown.
R	E	N	T	A	B	L	E	Available for rent.
R	E	N	T	F	R	E	E	Can be occupied without paying rent.

1	2	3	4	5	6	7	8	
R	E	N	T	L	E	S	S	Not torn.
R	E	N	T	R	O	L	L	A detailed register of tenants and rents due and paid.
R	E	N	U	M	B	E	R	To number again with different numbers.
R	E	N	V	E	R	S	E	Reverse, Overturn, Overthrow, A movement in ballet.
R	E	O	C	C	U	P	Y	Occupy again, Repossess, Retake, Reassume, Resume.
R	E	O	P	E	N	E	D	Continued, Resumed, Begun again, Recommenced, Renewed, Restarted.
R	E	O	R	I	E	N	T	To get one's bearings again, Finding the right direction again.
R	E	P	A	I	R	E	D	Fixed, Mended, Renewed, Revived, Remedied, Overhauled, Patched, Reconditioned.
R	E	P	A	I	R	E	R	One who specialises in making repairs.
R	E	P	A	R	T	E	E	Wit, Adroitness, Clever retorts, Comeback, Riposte, Banter, Backchat, Badinage.
R	E	P	A	S	S	E	D	Returned, Passed again in the opposite direction, Passed through.
R	E	P	A	S	T	E	D	Fed, Feasted.
R	E	P	A	Y	I	N	G	Profitable, Rewarding.
R	E	P	E	A	L	E	D	Revoked, Abrogated, Annulled, Abandoned, Renounced, Dismantled, Rescinded, Reversed.
R	E	P	E	A	L	E	R	One that repeals.
R	E	P	E	A	T	E	D	Recited, Reiterated, Presented, Reproduced, Renewed, Retold, Duplicated, Imitated.
R	E	P	E	A	T	E	R	A watch or clock that chimes the hours or minutes when a spring is pressed.
R	E	P	E	L	L	E	D	Repulsed, Repressed, Discouraged, Disgusted, Resisted, Combated, Contested, Disputed.
R	E	P	E	L	L	E	R	One that repels.
R	E	P	E	N	T	E	D	Regretted, Deplored, Rued.
R	E	P	E	O	P	L	E	Repopulate, Restock.
R	E	P	E	T	E	N	D	Repeated or recurrent sound, Refrain.
R	E	P	I	N	I	N	G	Complaining, Fretting, Fussing, Murmuring, Wailing, Whining.
R	E	P	L	A	C	E	D	Displaced, Supplanted, Superseded, Restitute, Restored, Reinstated, Changed, Shifted.
R	E	P	L	A	C	E	R	One that replaces.
R	E	P	L	E	D	G	E	To remove from the jurisdiction of another court to one's own.
R	E	P	L	E	V	I	N	Returning property wrongfully seized, Putting up bail.
R	E	P	L	Y	I	N	G	Answering, Resounding, Responding, Rejoining, Retorting, Returning, Saluting, Addressing.
R	E	P	O	N	I	N	G	Rehabilitating.
R	E	P	O	R	T	E	D	Narrated, Related, Told, Chronicled, Declared, Stated, Commented, Reviewed.
R	E	P	O	R	T	E	R	Commentator, One who makes a shorthand record.
R	E	P	O	S	I	N	G	Resting, Relaxing, Reclining, Stretching.
R	E	P	O	T	T	E	D	Transferring a plant to a new pot.
R	E	P	O	U	S	S	E	Ornamented with a pattern in relief made by pressing on the wrong side.
R	E	P	R	I	E	V	E	Suspension of sentence, Delay, Postpone, Temporary relief, Respite.
R	E	P	R	I	S	A	L	Resorting to force, Compensation, Retaliation, Reparation, Redress, Indemnity.
R	E	P	R	O	A	C	H	Upbraid, Censure, Scold, Reprove, Disapprove, Rebuke, Admonition, Discredit.
R	E	P	R	O	V	E	D	Censured, Condemned, Disproved, Refuted, Reprimanded, Reproached, Chided.
R	E	P	R	O	V	E	R	One that reproves.
R	E	P	T	I	L	I	A	Family of snakes, lizards and turtles.
R	E	P	U	B	L	I	C	Democratic state, Government by citizens entitled to vote.
R	E	P	U	G	N	E	D	Objected, Opposed, Resisted, Refuted, Rejected, Repelled, Contended, Disputed.
R	E	P	U	L	S	E	D	Rebuffed, Refused, Rejected, Disgusted, Nauseated, Revolted, Rebutted, Sickened.
R	E	P	U	T	I	N	G	Accounting, Esteeming, Thinking.
R	E	Q	U	I	R	E	D	Demanded, Exacted, Requested, Lacked, Needed, Wanted, Challenged, Claimed.
R	E	Q	U	I	R	E	R	One that requires.
R	E	Q	U	I	T	A	L	Repayment for something, Compensation, Retaliation.
R	E	Q	U	I	T	E	D	Repaid, Rewarded, Avenged, Reciprocated, Compensated, Recompensed, Retaliated.
R	E	Q	U	I	T	E	R	One that requites something.
R	E	R	A	I	L	E	D	Replaced on the rails.
R	E	R	E	F	I	E	F	A fee due under medieval tenure.
R	E	R	E	W	A	R	D	Rear-guard.
R	E	R	O	L	L	E	R	A textile worker who winds cloth.
R	E	S	A	I	L	E	D	Sailed back or again.
R	E	S	A	L	U	T	E	To salute in return.
R	E	S	C	O	R	E	D	Re-arrange a musical score.
R	E	S	C	R	I	B	E	Rewrite.
R	E	S	C	R	I	P	T	A written answer from a Roman emperor to a pope.
R	E	S	C	U	I	N	G	Saving, Delivering, Redeeming, Ransoming, Reclaiming, Liberating, Extricating.
R	E	S	E	A	R	C	H	Inquiry, Inquest, Inquisition, Investigation, Probing, Quest.
R	E	S	E	A	T	E	D	Equipped with new seats, Sat down again after rising.
R	E	S	E	I	Z	E	D	Seized again.
R	E	S	E	I	Z	I	N	Possession by a feudal lord after a tenant's death.
R	E	S	E	M	B	L	E	Liken, Compare, Represent, Portray, Depict, Symbolize, Appear, Simulate.
R	E	S	E	N	T	E	D	Resisted, Objected strongly, Displeased.
R	E	S	E	R	V	E	D	Kept, Remained, Excepted, Saved, Retained, Held, Preserved, Reticent.
R	E	S	E	R	V	E	R	One that reserves.

1	2	3	4	5	6	7	8	Definition
R	E	S	E	T	T	E	R	One that assists criminals, A receiver of stolen goods.
R	E	S	E	T	T	L	E	To settle in a new place, To repopulate an area.
R	E	S	H	A	P	E	D	Given a new form.
R	E	S	I	A	N	C	E	Residence, Abode, Dwelling place.
R	E	S	I	D	E	N	T	Occupier, Inhabitant, Dweller, Resider, Denizen.
R	E	S	I	D	U	A	L	Remainder, Residue, Balance, Leavings, Remains, Rest.
R	E	S	I	D	U	U	M	Residue, Deposit, Sediment.
R	E	S	I	G	N	E	D	Relinquished, Renounced, Quitted, Surrendered, Ceded, Committed, Abdicated, Abandoned.
R	E	S	I	G	N	E	E	A person who resigns from something.
R	E	S	I	G	N	E	R	One that resigns.
R	E	S	I	L	I	U	M	Part of the ligament hinge of a bivalve, Shell fish.
R	E	S	I	L	I	N	G	Recoiling, Retracting, Retreating, Rebounding, Returning to the original position.
R	E	S	I	N	A	T	E	Ester of a resin acid.
R	E	S	I	N	I	F	Y	To form a gummy material, Evaporation of oil to resin.
R	E	S	I	N	O	I	D	Gum resin, Flower essences used in perfumery industry.
R	E	S	I	S	T	E	D	Opposed, Contested, Disputed, Fought, Balked, Frustrated, Thwarted, Repelled.
R	E	S	I	S	T	E	R	One that resists.
R	E	S	I	S	T	O	R	Device used in an electric circuit for protection.
R	E	S	M	O	O	T	H	To give a smoothness to the surface again.
R	E	S	O	L	U	T	E	Determined, Resolved, Bold, Firm, Steady, Ardent, Faithful, Constant.
R	E	S	O	L	V	E	D	Analyzed, Decided, Solved, Fixed, Deciphered, Dissolved, Unfolded, Determined.
R	E	S	O	L	V	E	R	One that resolves.
R	E	S	O	N	A	N	T	Resounding, Ringing, Vibrant, Sonorous, Mellow, Profound, Reverberant, Strident.
R	E	S	O	N	A	T	E	Vibrate, Oscillate, Ring, Resound, Pulsate, Throb, Boom.
R	E	S	O	R	B	E	D	Swallowed again, reassimilated a substance, Reabsorbed.
R	E	S	O	R	C	I	N	Crystalline phenol obtained from various resins.
R	E	S	O	R	T	E	D	Repaired, Reverted, Returned, Referred, Used, Employed, Devoted, Utilized.
R	E	S	O	R	T	E	R	One that frequently visits resorts.
R	E	S	O	U	R	C	E	Expedient, Shift, Substitute, Surrogate, Refuge, Manner, Method, System.
R	E	S	O	W	I	N	G	To plant seed again in the same area.
R	E	S	P	E	C	T	S	Admires, Esteems, Considers, Venerates, Honours, Compliments, Regards, Heeds.
R	E	S	P	I	R	E	D	Revived, Breathed, Exhaled, Inhaled.
R	E	S	P	I	R	I	T	Renew courage.
R	E	S	P	I	T	E	D	Delayed, Postponed, Reprieved, Suspended, Rested, Desisted.
R	E	S	P	L	E	N	D	To be outstanding.
R	E	S	P	O	N	S	E	Answer, Reply, Reaction, Rejoinder, Retort, Return.
R	E	S	P	R	I	N	G	To replace worn out springs.
R	E	S	T	A	T	E	D	Stated again.
R	E	S	T	B	A	L	K	A ridge of land between furrows.
R	E	S	T	C	U	R	E	Enforced rest necessary in the cure of some diseases.
R	E	S	T	L	E	S	S	Uneasy, Unceasing, Unsettled, Changeful, Disturbed, Fidgety, Discontented, Jumpy.
R	E	S	T	O	R	E	D	Rebuilt, Reconstructed, Reinstated, Renewed, Revived, Refreshed, Renovated, Reclaimed.
R	E	S	T	O	R	E	R	One that restores something to its original condition.
R	E	S	T	R	A	I	N	Check, Curb, Bridle, Inhibit, Arrest, Prevent, Hinder, Impede.
R	E	S	T	R	I	C	T	Hamper, Diminish, Limit, Restrain, Circumscribe, Bind, Delimit, Tie.
R	E	S	T	R	I	K	E	To strike again.
R	E	S	T	R	I	N	G	To fit with new strings.
R	E	S	U	B	M	I	T	To offer again.
R	E	S	U	L	T	E	D	Terminated, Ended, Rebounded, Recoiled, Reverted, Issued.
R	E	S	U	M	I	N	G	Reoccupying, Reiterating, Summarizing, Epitomizing, Recouping, Repossessing, Retaking.
R	E	S	U	M	M	O	N	To summon again.
R	E	S	U	P	I	N	E	Lying on the back again.
R	E	T	A	I	L	E	D	Sold direct to the consumer, Related.
R	E	T	A	I	L	E	R	One who sells direct to the consumer.
R	E	T	A	I	N	E	D	Kept, Held, Owned, Possessed, Detained, Reserved, Withheld, Remembered.
R	E	T	A	I	N	E	R	Fee paid to a professional person for services to be rendered, Dependant, Servant.
R	E	T	A	K	I	N	G	Recapturing, Re-photographing.
R	E	T	A	R	D	E	D	Delayed, Slackened, Slowed, Hampered, Backward, Imbecile, Slow-witted, Simple.
R	E	T	A	R	D	E	R	Restrainer, Braking device.
R	E	T	E	M	P	E	R	To mix concrete or mortar again after initial set has taken place.
R	E	T	E	N	T	O	R	A retaining muscle.
R	E	T	I	C	E	N	T	Silent, Reserved, Taciturn, Uncommunicative, Close-mouthed, Restrained, Quiet.
R	E	T	I	C	U	L	E	A small drawstring bag used by a woman as a carryall.
R	E	T	I	C	U	L	A	Netlike, Connective tissue cells of the framework of the lymphatic cells.
R	E	T	I	N	E	N	E	A light-yellow crystalline compound related to Vitamin A and formed from rhodopsin.
R	E	T	I	N	I	T	E	A fossil resin.
R	E	T	I	N	O	I	D	Resembling a resin.

1	2	3	4	5	6	7	8	
R	E	T	I	N	U	L	A	Part of a single facet of the compound eye of an arthropod.
R	E	T	I	R	A	C	Y	Retirement, Seclusion.
R	E	T	I	R	A	D	E	Fortification of two faces making an angle.
R	E	T	I	R	I	N	G	Withdrawing, Shy, Bashful, Unassertive, Departing, Resigning, Receding, Discharging.
R	E	T	O	R	T	E	D	Returned, Repaid, Reverberated, Reflected, Retaliated, Answered, Replied, Responded.
R	E	T	O	R	T	E	R	One that replies.
R	E	T	O	S	S	E	D	Tossed again.
R	E	T	R	A	C	E	D	Recalled, Going back over a previous route, Reinspect.
R	E	T	R	A	X	I	T	Withdrawal by a plaintiff of his suit in court.
R	E	T	R	E	N	C	H	Lessen, Reduce, Curtail, Intercept, Excise, Omit, Economize, Shorten.
R	E	T	R	I	E	V	E	Rescue, Salvage, Regain, Repossess, Recuperate, Recover, Repair, Correct.
R	E	T	R	O	A	C	T	React.
R	E	T	R	O	F	I	T	Modification to include more modern changes of the model.
R	E	T	R	O	R	S	E	Bent backward or downward.
R	E	T	R	U	D	E	D	Thrust backward out of natural position.
R	E	T	R	Y	I	N	G	Placing people on trial again for the same reason as previously.
R	E	T	U	N	D	E	D	Blunted, Made impotent or ineffective, Refuted.
R	E	T	U	R	N	E	D	Gone back, Come back, Reverted, Reacted, Answered, Replied, Restored, Replaced.
R	E	T	U	R	N	E	E	One returned to native land from abroad.
R	E	T	U	R	N	E	R	One that fastens metal bands around bales of cotton.
R	E	U	N	I	T	E	D	Rejoined, Brought together.
R	E	U	S	A	B	L	E	In a fit condition to be used again.
R	E	V	A	L	U	E	D	Reappraised, Made a new value.
R	E	V	A	M	P	E	D	Renovated, Reconstructed, Revised, Mended, Overhauled, Reconditioned, Restyled.
R	E	V	A	N	C	H	E	Revenge, Retaliation, Reprisal, Requital, Retribution, Vengeance.
R	E	V	E	A	L	E	D	Disclosed, Divulged, Told, Betrayed, Unveiled, Uncovered, Displayed, Exposed.
R	E	V	E	A	L	E	R	One that betrays.
R	E	V	E	H	E	N	T	Carrying back.
R	E	V	E	I	L	L	E	Signal for beginning the duties of the day, Signal to arise.
R	E	V	E	L	L	E	D	Indulged, Delighted, Feasted, Frolicked, Roistered, Caroused, Luxuriated, Wallowed.
R	E	V	E	L	L	E	R	Roisterer.
R	E	V	E	N	A	N	T	Recurring, Coming back, Returning, Ghost, Spectre, Wraith.
R	E	V	E	N	G	E	D	Avenged, Redressed, Vindicated, Defended, Justified, Retaliated, Repaid, Requited.
R	E	V	E	N	G	E	R	Avenger, Vindicator.
R	E	V	E	R	E	N	D	Characteristic of the clergy, Clergyman, Minister, Parson, Preacher, Venerable.
R	E	V	E	R	E	N	T	Profoundly respectful, Expressing veneration.
R	E	V	E	R	I	N	G	Venerating, Worshipping, Adoring, Honouring, Admiring, Respecting, Esteeming, Exalting.
R	E	V	E	R	I	S	T	One who indulges in reveries, A dreamer.
R	E	V	E	R	S	A	L	Change, Inversion, Changeabout, Reverse, Setback, Check, Turning, Volte-face.
R	E	V	E	R	S	E	D	Subverted, Annulled, Voided, Recoiled, Returned, Revoked, Transposed, Transferred.
R	E	V	E	R	S	E	R	A device for reversing an electric current.
R	E	V	E	R	T	E	D	Revoked, Annulled, Restored, Returned, Regressed, Degenerated, Relapsed, Declined.
R	E	V	E	S	T	E	D	Resumed, Reinstate, Reverted to a former owner.
R	E	V	E	T	T	E	D	Built up an embankment.
R	E	V	I	E	W	A	L	Revision, Criticism, Literary review, Comment, Notice, Critique.
R	E	V	I	E	W	E	D	Reconsidered, Re-examined, Reweighed, Revised, Surveyed, Re-evaluated, Criticized.
R	E	V	I	E	W	E	R	One that examines publication critically.
R	E	V	I	L	I	N	G	Abusing, Scolding, Railing, Swearing, Upbraiding, Defaming, Maligning, Vilifying.
R	E	V	I	S	I	N	G	Reflecting, Correcting, Redrafting, Restyling, Rewriting, Re-organizing, Polishing, Perfecting.
R	E	V	I	S	I	O	N	Review, Redraft, Amendment, Correction, Rectification, Re-examination, Studying past notes.
R	E	V	I	S	O	R	Y	Making a revision.
R	E	V	I	V	I	F	Y	Resuscitate, Reactivate, Reinvigorate, Reanimate, Restore, Rekindle, Renew, Retrieve.
R	E	V	O	K	I	N	G	Repeating, Rescinding, Recalling, Reneging, Cancelling, Retracting, Abrogating, Erasing.
R	E	V	O	L	T	E	D	Deserted, Mutinied, Disgusted, Shocked, Repelled, Nauseated, Sickened.
R	E	V	O	L	T	E	R	Rebel, Anarchist, Insurgent, Mutineer.
R	E	V	O	L	U	T	E	Rolled backward or downward, Revolutionize.
R	E	V	O	L	V	E	D	Rotated, Turned, Pondered, Considered, Deliberated, Meditated, Ruminated, Gyrated.
R	E	V	O	L	V	E	R	A handgun having a cylinder of several chambers.
R	E	V	U	L	S	E	D	Affected with revulsion.
R	E	W	A	R	D	E	D	Recompensed, Compensated, Paid, Remunerated, Requited, Repaid.
R	E	W	A	R	D	E	R	One that gives a reward.
R	E	W	A	R	P	E	R	A textile worker who rewinds yarn from the warp beam.
R	E	W	O	R	D	E	D	Rephrased, Translated, Altered the wording.
R	H	A	B	D	I	T	E	Minute rod-like structure produced in certain cells.
R	H	A	B	D	O	I	D	Resembling a minute parasitic worm.
R	H	A	B	D	O	M	E	Minute rod-like structure in compound-eyes.

8 LETTERS

1	2	3	4	5	6	7	8	Definition
R	H	A	E	T	I	A	N	Relating to an ancient Roman province.
R	H	A	G	A	D	E	S	Fissures of the skin.
R	H	A	G	O	D	I	A	Genus of Australian herbs.
R	H	A	M	N	O	S	E	A crystalline aldose sugar.
R	H	A	P	S	O	D	E	Rhapsodist.
R	H	A	P	S	O	D	Y	Medley, Jumble, Highly emotional delivery of a literary work.
R	H	E	A	D	I	N	E	A nonpoisonous crystalline alkaloid found in poppies.
R	H	E	O	B	A	S	E	The minimal electrical current required to excite a tissue.
R	H	E	O	L	O	G	Y	A science dealing with the deformation and flow of matter.
R	H	E	O	S	T	A	T	A resistor for regulating a current.
R	H	E	T	O	R	I	C	Eloquence, Verbosity, Bombast, Discourse, Speech, Elocution, Oratory, Rhapsody.
R	H	I	N	I	T	I	S	Inflammation of the mucous membrane of the nose.
R	H	I	Z	O	G	E	N	Producing roots.
R	H	I	Z	O	M	Y	S	Genus of rodents, Oriental bamboo rats.
R	H	I	Z	O	P	O	D	Creeping protozoans, Amoebina.
R	H	O	D	E	O	S	E	Fucose, An aldose sugar.
R	H	O	D	I	T	E	S	Minerals consisting of native alloys of rhodium and gold.
R	H	O	D	N	I	U	S	Genus of bugs that are hosts to parasites causing Chaga's disease.
R	H	O	M	B	O	I	D	A parallelogram with oblique angles and adjacent sides unequal.
R	H	O	N	C	H	U	S	Sound heard in the chest when air channels are partly obstructed.
R	H	O	P	A	L	I	C	A metre in verse having each successive word longer than its predecessor.
R	H	Y	O	L	I	T	E	Acid volcanic rock.
R	H	Y	T	H	M	I	C	Regularly recurrent, Cadenced, Harmonious, Lilting.
R	H	Y	T	H	M	U	S	Rhythm, Beat, Measure, Metre, Rhyme, Swing.
R	I	B	A	L	D	R	Y	Offensively, Coarsely, Vulgarly, Debauchery, Lewdly.
R	I	B	B	O	N	E	D	Decorated or adorned with ribbon, Ripped to shreds.
R	I	B	G	R	A	S	S	Plantain with long narrow ribbed leaves.
R	I	B	O	S	I	D	E	A glycoside that yields ribose.
R	I	B	R	O	A	S	T	Cut of meat containing the rib eye and with or without the rib bone.
R	I	B	U	L	O	S	E	A ketose that is formed from ribose.
R	I	C	I	N	I	N	E	A crystalline compound obtained from castor beans.
R	I	C	E	B	I	R	D	Java sparrow.
R	I	C	E	G	L	U	E	Cement made by boiling ground rice and used like papier-maché.
R	I	C	E	M	E	A	L	By-product of rice milling and used as stock-feed.
R	I	C	H	L	I	N	G	A rich youth.
R	I	C	H	N	E	S	S	The state of being rich, Opulence.
R	I	C	K	R	A	C	K	Zig-zag braid used for decoration on clothing and linen.
R	I	C	K	S	H	A	W	Two-wheeled passenger vehicle powered by a man or by a man using a bicycle.
R	I	C	O	C	H	E	T	Rebound, Glance, Graze, Skim, Skip, Recoil.
R	I	D	D	A	N	C	E	Clearance, Deliverance, Relief, Disposal, Discarding. Dumping, Jettison, Scrapping.
R	I	D	D	L	I	N	G	Sifting, Screening, Puncturing full of holes, Corrupting, Permeating, Debasing.
R	I	D	E	A	B	L	E	Capable of being ridden.
R	I	D	G	E	C	A	P	Cover for the ridge of a roof.
R	I	D	I	C	U	L	E	Deride, Mock, Taunt, Rally, Jeer, Scoff, Sneer, Mimic.
R	I	E	S	L	I	N	G	Dry white wine resembling Rhine wine.
R	I	F	E	N	E	S	S	State of being prevalent, common or abundant.
R	I	F	F	R	A	F	F	Disreputable, Refuse, Rubbish, Trash, Rabble, Common, Unconvential.
R	I	F	L	E	M	A	N	Soldier armed with a rifle.
R	I	G	A	D	O	O	N	A lively dance popular in the 17th and 18th centuries.
R	I	G	A	T	I	O	N	Irrigation.
R	I	G	H	T	F	U	L	Righteous, Upright, Legitimate, Equitable, Fitting, Proper, Legal, Due.
R	I	G	H	T	I	N	G	Justifying, Vindicating, Adjusting, Repairing, Correcting, Amending, Rectifying.
R	I	G	I	D	I	T	Y	Harshness, Inflexibility, Firmness, Hardness, Severity, Sternly.
R	I	G	O	R	I	S	M	Austerity of life, Rigid principles.
R	I	G	O	R	O	U	S	Strict, Rigid, Draconian, Stringent, Unpermissive.
R	I	G	O	R	O	U	S	Inexorable, Exact, Precise, Rigid, Ascetic, Oppressive, Brutal, Inclement.
R	I	L	L	E	T	T	E	Highly seasoned potted pork.
R	I	M	A	T	I	O	N	Having a fissure, cleft or crack.
R	I	M	O	S	I	T	Y	Having numerous clefts, cracks or fissures.
R	I	M	U	L	O	S	E	Having small chinks or fissures.
R	I	N	G	B	A	R	K	Girdle with a cut.
R	I	N	G	B	I	L	L	Ring-necked duck.
R	I	N	G	B	O	L	T	An eyebolt with a ring through its eye.
R	I	N	G	B	O	N	E	A disease of a foot bone of a horse.
R	I	N	G	D	I	A	L	A portable dial for telling the time.
R	I	N	G	D	O	V	E	Common European pigeon.
R	I	N	G	L	O	C	K	Combination lock where grooved rings must be arranged in a set order to operate the lock.

1	2	3	4	5	6	7	8	Definition
R	I	N	G	N	E	C	K	A ringed-neck bird or animal.
R	I	N	G	R	O	A	D	A highway built to avoid crossing suburban housing estates.
R	I	N	G	R	O	P	E	An anchor rope.
R	I	N	G	S	I	D	E	Closest to the area where the action is taking place.
R	I	N	G	T	A	I	L	Immature Golden eagle.
R	I	N	G	W	A	L	L	A fence that completely encircles the area.
R	I	N	G	W	O	R	M	Contagious fungi disease that manifests itself by round scaly patches.
R	I	P	A	R	I	A	N	Living on the bank of a body of water.
R	I	P	E	N	E	S	S	Quality of being ripe, Maturity, Perfection, Completeness, Mellowness.
R	I	P	E	N	I	N	G	Maturing, Developing, Becoming fit for use, Maturating, Improving, Enhancing.
R	I	P	P	L	I	N	G	Ruffling, Flowing in small waves, Undulating.
R	I	S	K	I	E	S	T	Most reckless, Most chancy, Most dangerous.
R	I	T	E	L	E	S	S	Devoid of ceremony.
R	I	T	E	N	U	T	O	Direction in music to indicate an abrupt slowing down.
R	I	T	U	A	L	L	Y	As a ritual, According to formality, Ceremoniously.
R	I	V	A	L	I	T	Y	Rivalry.
R	I	V	A	L	I	Z	E	To act as a rival.
R	I	V	A	L	L	E	D	Competed, Emulated, Matched, Surpassed, Equalled, Contested, Corresponded, Struggled.
R	I	V	E	R	B	E	D	Channel occupied by a river.
R	I	V	E	R	G	O	D	A deity supposed to preside over a river.
R	I	V	E	R	H	O	G	African wild hog that lives by streams.
R	I	V	E	R	A	I	N	Relating to the bank of a river.
R	I	V	E	R	I	N	E	Situated on the banks of a river.
R	I	V	E	R	M	A	N	One who lives and works along a river.
R	I	V	E	T	I	N	G	Fastening with rivets, Concentrating, Focusing, Fixing, Attracting.
R	I	V	U	L	O	S	E	Marked with irregular, narrow, sinuous or crooked lines.
R	I	Z	Z	A	R	E	D	Process of drying or curing in the sun.
R	O	A	D	B	O	O	K	Guidebook devoted to routes and distances.
R	O	A	D	H	E	A	D	End of a road.
R	O	A	D	L	E	S	S	Having no roads.
R	O	A	D	S	I	D	E	The side of a road.
R	O	A	D	S	M	A	N	Roadman, One who works on roads, Peddler, Travelling salesman.
R	O	A	D	S	T	E	R	Road horse, Highwayman, Tramp, Automobile with an open body.
R	O	A	D	W	O	R	K	Work done on a road.
R	O	A	S	T	I	N	G	Cooking in an oven, Lambasting, Blistering, Castigating, Scathing, Slashing.
R	O	B	O	T	I	Z	E	Make automatic, Turn into a robot.
R	O	B	U	S	T	L	Y	Sturdily, Stoutly, Lustily, Powerfully, Roughly, Rudely, Healthily.
R	O	C	A	I	L	L	E	Rococo, 18th century ornamentation based on shellwork.
R	O	C	C	E	L	L	A	A genus of maritime rock-inhabiting lichens.
R	O	C	K	A	W	A	Y	A carriage.
R	O	C	K	B	I	R	D	A sea-bird that breeds in rocky cliffs.
R	O	C	K	C	A	K	E	A small fruit bun.
R	O	C	K	C	O	R	K	Mountain cork.
R	O	C	K	C	R	A	B	A crab inhabiting rocky beaches or sea bottoms.
R	O	C	K	D	O	V	E	Rock pigeon.
R	O	C	K	E	T	E	D	Attacked with rockets, Soared, Surged, Mounted, Ascended, Hurried, Whizzed.
R	O	C	K	E	T	E	R	A game bird that rockets.
R	O	C	K	E	T	R	Y	The study of rockets.
R	O	C	K	F	I	S	H	Fish that live among rocks, Groupers, Bass.
R	O	C	K	G	O	A	T	Ibex.
R	O	C	K	H	A	I	R	Tufted lichen that lives on rocks and is used in dyeing.
R	O	C	K	L	A	R	K	Rock pipit.
R	O	C	K	L	E	S	S	Land without rocks.
R	O	C	K	L	I	L	Y	Tropical American club moss, Australian orchid, Rock-loving herbs, Columbine.
R	O	C	K	L	I	N	G	Small marine cod-fish.
R	O	C	K	M	O	S	S	Rock-loving lichen.
R	O	C	K	R	O	S	E	Succulent plant used in rockeries.
R	O	C	K	S	A	L	T	Common salt occurring in solid form as a mineral.
R	O	C	K	S	E	A	L	Harbour seal.
R	O	C	K	S	O	A	P	Mountain soap.
R	O	C	K	W	E	E	D	A coarse seaweed.
R	O	C	K	W	O	R	K	Rockery garden, Artificial rock ledges and waterfalls.
R	O	C	K	W	R	E	N	An American or Mexican wren.
R	O	D	E	N	T	I	A	An order of gnawing rodents, Rats, squirrels, Mice.
R	O	D	O	M	O	N	T	Braggart, Boaster, Vaunter.
R	O	E	N	T	G	E	N	The international unit of X radiation or gamma radiation.
R	O	E	S	T	O	N	E	Oolite.

1	2	3	4	5	6	7	8	Definition
R	O	G	A	T	I	O	N	Litany, Supplication, Three days before Ascension.
R	O	G	A	T	O	R	Y	Seeking information, Authorized to examine witnesses.
R	O	I	S	T	I	N	G	Roistering, Carousing, Revelling.
R	O	I	T	E	L	E	T	A petty king.
R	O	L	L	B	A	C	K	Push back, Reduce in price because of government legislation.
R	O	L	L	C	A	L	L	Calling a list of names for checking attendance.
R	O	L	Y	P	O	L	Y	A game played by rolling a ball, A pudding of dough rolled with a filling and baked.
R	O	M	A	N	C	E	D	Exaggerated, Invented.
R	O	M	A	N	C	E	R	Writer of romantic novels.
R	O	M	A	N	I	A	N	Characteristic of Romania.
R	O	M	A	N	I	S	H	Relating to the Roman Catholic church.
R	O	M	A	N	I	S	T	Adhering to Roman Catholicism.
R	O	M	A	N	I	Z	E	Become adapted to customs of Rome.
R	O	M	A	N	S	C	H	Dialect of a province of Switzerland.
R	O	M	A	N	T	I	C	Fanciful, Exotic, Strange, Sentimental, Maudlin, Mawkish, Mushy, Imaginary.
R	O	M	E	S	C	O	T	Peter's pence.
R	O	M	E	W	A	R	D	Toward Roman Catholicism.
R	O	N	C	A	D	O	R	Family of croaker, Yellowfin.
R	O	N	D	A	V	E	L	A round hut of Southern Africa made of mud with a thatched roof.
R	O	N	D	E	L	E	T	A modified rondeau running on two rhymes.
R	O	N	D	E	L	L	E	The crust on molten metal in the crucible.
R	O	O	D	A	R	C	H	The arch between the nave and the chancel immediately above the rood.
R	O	O	D	B	E	A	M	The entrance beam of the chancel that supports a crucifix.
R	O	O	D	E	B	O	K	Impala.
R	O	O	D	L	O	F	T	The loft above the rood-screen in a medieval church.
R	O	O	F	L	E	S	S	Having no roof, Homeless.
R	O	O	F	T	R	E	E	Ridge-pole of a roof.
R	O	O	M	S	O	M	E	Roomy, Spacious.
R	O	O	S	T	I	N	G	Perching, Lodging, Landing, Alighting, Boarding, Rooming.
R	O	O	T	B	E	E	R	A sweetened effervescent beverage of extractions of herbs, roots and aromatic oils.
R	O	O	T	C	R	O	P	A crop of enlarged roots used as vegetables, Carrots, Turnips, Sweet potatoes.
R	O	O	T	H	A	I	R	Hairlike outcrops found on roots.
R	O	O	T	H	O	L	D	When a plant anchors itself to the ground by spreading roots.
R	O	O	T	K	N	O	T	Plant disease caused by eelworms.
R	O	O	T	L	E	S	S	Unstable, Lacking firmness, Vacillating, Wavering, Shaky, Fluctuant, Insecure.
R	O	P	E	R	I	P	E	Punishable by hanging, Villian, Knave, Rogue, Miscreant.
R	O	P	E	W	A	L	K	A long space for rope to be laid out during manufacture.
R	O	P	E	Y	A	R	N	Yarn or thread for the manufacture of rope.
R	O	P	I	N	E	S	S	A stringy condition, Stringiness, Slimy condition due to bacterial contamination.
R	O	Q	U	E	T	E	D	A hit as described in croquet.
R	O	R	I	D	U	L	A	An insect-eating shrub of Southern Africa.
R	O	R	T	I	E	S	T	Dashing, Flamboyant, Gay.
R	O	S	A	C	E	A	N	Made of roses.
R	O	S	A	L	I	N	E	A lace with rose designs.
R	O	S	A	R	I	A	N	A cultivator of roses.
R	O	S	A	R	I	U	M	A rose garden.
R	O	S	A	S	I	T	E	A mineral consisting of a basic carbonate of copper and zinc.
R	O	S	E	B	U	S	H	A shrubby rose.
R	O	S	E	D	U	S	T	A grayish red to reddish brown.
R	O	S	E	F	I	S	H	A large marine food fish.
R	O	S	E	L	I	T	E	A mineral consisting of a rose-red arsenate of calcium, cobalt and manganese.
R	O	S	E	M	A	R	Y	A fragrant shrubby mint used as a culinary herb.
R	O	S	E	P	I	N	K	A variable pink colour.
R	O	S	E	R	O	O	T	A perennial fleshy herb with rose-scented roots.
R	O	S	E	T	R	E	E	A tree rose.
R	O	S	E	T	T	E	D	To form in dense clusters.
R	O	S	E	W	O	O	D	Tropical trees that yield valuable dark red cabinet woods.
R	O	S	E	W	O	R	M	Larva of a small brown moth that nests in rose bushes and devours leaves and buds.
R	O	S	E	W	O	R	T	Roseroot.
R	O	S	I	N	A	T	E	Mixture of salts and ester prepared from rosin.
R	O	S	I	N	E	S	S	A rosy colour or complexion, Cheerful outlook.
R	O	S	I	N	O	I	L	Liquid oil distilled from rosin.
R	O	S	I	N	O	U	S	Resembling rosin.
R	O	S	O	G	L	I	O	A cordial made from spirits and flavoured sugar.
R	O	S	O	L	I	T	E	Pink variety of garnet.
R	O	S	O	R	I	A	L	Gnawing.
R	O	S	T	R	A	T	E	Having a rostrum, Raised platform.

1	2	3	4	5	6	7	8	Definition
R	O	T	A	L	I	A	N	Protozoan.
R	O	T	A	R	I	A	N	Member of a service club (Rotary).
R	O	T	A	T	I	N	G	Circling, Circumducting, Gyrating, Revolving, Rolling, Exchanging, Following, Alternating.
R	O	T	A	T	I	O	N	Revolution, Circuit, circulation, Gyration, Turn, Wheel, Whirl.
R	O	T	A	T	I	V	E	Turning like a wheel, Occuring in a regular series.
R	O	T	G	R	A	S	S	Marsh plants believed to be harmful to sheep.
R	O	T	I	F	E	R	A	Microscopic aquatic animals having the appearance of wheels.
R	O	T	I	F	O	R	M	Rotate.
R	O	T	T	E	N	L	Y	Abominably, Putridly, Disagreeably, Foully, Sourly, Viciously, Unhappily, Corruptly.
R	O	T	T	L	E	R	A	Kamala tree that yields substances for dyeing and a veterinary vermifuge.
R	O	T	U	R	I	E	R	A rich person of plebian origin, Nouveau riche.
R	O	U	G	H	A	G	E	Coarse bulky food high in fibre to stimulate the intestines.
R	O	U	G	H	D	R	Y	To dry the laundry without smoothing or ironing.
R	O	U	G	H	H	E	W	Roughcast, To hew or form crudely and roughly.
R	O	U	G	H	I	N	G	Ruffling, Manhandling, Beating, Sketching, Drafting, Outlining, Blocking.
R	O	U	G	H	I	S	H	Somewhat rough.
R	O	U	L	E	A	U	X	A decorative piping or rolled trimming for women's clothing, A roll of coins in paper.
R	O	U	L	E	T	T	E	A gambling game using a wheel that spins.
R	O	U	N	D	A	R	M	An outward swing of the arm, especially in ball games.
R	O	U	N	D	E	R	S	An English game that resembles baseball.
R	O	U	N	D	I	N	G	Encircling, Encompassing.
R	O	U	N	D	I	S	H	Somewhat round.
R	O	U	N	D	L	E	T	Disk, A little circlet or round object.
R	O	U	N	D	M	A	N	A worker in a slaughterhouse.
R	O	U	N	D	T	O	P	A round platform at the masthead.
R	O	U	T	E	I	N	G	Planning an itinerary, Directing, Diverting, Sending.
R	O	W	D	Y	D	O	W	Hubbub, Noisy excitement, Boisterous party, Spree.
R	O	W	D	Y	I	S	H	Tending to be crude or noisy.
R	O	W	D	Y	I	S	M	Rowdy, Riotous, Noisy.
R	O	W	E	L	L	E	D	Spurred, Dug into, Troubled, Pricked, Rended.
R	O	X	B	U	R	G	H	County in Scotland.
R	O	Y	A	L	I	S	M	Monarchism.
R	O	Y	A	L	I	S	T	Adherent of a king, Cavalier.
R	O	Y	A	L	I	Z	E	To make royal.
R	U	B	B	I	S	H	Y	Trashy, Worthless.
R	U	B	I	A	L	E	S	Order of plants having opposite leaves.
R	U	B	I	C	U	N	D	Ruddy, Red.
R	U	B	I	D	I	U	M	A soft silvery metallic element of the alkali metal group.
R	U	B	R	I	C	A	L	Coloured, written, printed or marked with red, Red-letter.
R	U	B	S	T	O	N	E	Whetstone, Grit for scouring, polishing or sharpening.
R	U	B	Y	T	A	I	L	Common European insect with a red abdomen.
R	U	B	Y	W	O	O	D	Red sandal-wood.
R	U	C	E	R	V	U	S	A type of deer.
R	U	C	K	L	I	N	G	Raking into a heap, Wrinkling.
R	U	C	K	S	A	C	K	Knapsack.
R	U	C	T	I	O	U	S	Quarrelsome, Contentious, Unruly, Vexed, Belligerent, Militant, Pugnacious, Bellicose.
R	U	D	D	L	I	N	G	Flushing, Reddening, Rougeing, Rubifying.
R	U	D	E	N	E	S	S	Crudeness, Roughness, Coarseness, Harshness, Surliness, Savageness.
R	U	D	I	M	E	N	T	Basic element, Vestige, Essential, Fundimental, Part and parcel, Grammar.
R	U	E	F	U	L	L	Y	Woefully, Pitiably, Sorrowfully, Regretfully, Sadly, Mournfully.
R	U	F	F	L	I	N	G	Distracting, Troubling, Vexing, Attacking, Blustering, Swaggering, Gathering, Pleating.
R	U	F	O	S	I	T	Y	Being reddish.
R	U	G	B	E	I	A	N	A pupil of Rugby school.
R	U	G	G	E	D	L	Y	Shaggily, Jaggedly, Unevenly, Severely, Bitterly, Harshly, Hardily, Inclemently, Huskily.
R	U	G	O	S	E	L	Y	Wrinkled.
R	U	G	U	L	O	S	E	Finely wrinkled.
R	U	I	N	A	T	E	D	Demolished, Destroyed, Overthrown, Degraded, Dishonoured, Subverted, Crashed.
R	U	L	E	L	E	S	S	Lawless.
R	U	M	A	N	I	A	N	Romanian.
R	U	M	B	L	I	N	G	A low heavy rolling sound, Grumbling, Growling, Roaring, Thundering, Resounding.
R	U	M	I	N	A	N	T	A mammal that chews the cud.
R	U	M	I	N	A	T	E	Reflect, Consider, Ponder, Deliberate, Cogitate, Meditate, Masticate, Chew.
R	U	M	M	A	G	E	D	Stirred, Ransacked, Disarranged, Disorganized, Disrupting, Disturbing, Jumbling, Foraged.
R	U	M	M	A	G	E	R	One that searches for contraband.
R	U	M	O	R	O	U	S	Murmuring.
R	U	M	O	U	R	E	D	Reported, Gossiped, Mumbled, Muttered.
R	U	M	O	U	R	E	R	One that spreads rumours.

1	2	3	4	5	6	7	8	Definition
R	U	M	P	L	E	S	S	Tailless.
R	U	M	P	L	I	N	G	Folding, Wrinkling.
R	U	N	A	B	O	U	T	Vagabond, Stray, Straggler, Speedboat.
R	U	N	A	G	A	T	E	Renegade, Fugitive, Runaway, Vagabond, Wanderer.
R	U	N	N	E	R	U	P	A competitor that does not win first prize but is awarded a credit or prize.
R	U	N	O	L	O	G	Y	The study of runes and runic writings.
R	U	P	I	C	O	L	A	Genus of birds.
R	U	R	A	L	I	S	M	State of being rural.
R	U	R	A	L	I	S	T	Farmer, One supporting the advantages of life in the country, Country bumpkin.
R	U	R	A	L	I	T	Y	A rural place.
R	U	R	A	L	I	Z	E	Rusticate, Give a rural appearance.
R	U	S	H	H	O	U	R	The time of the day when traffic and travelling commuters reach their maximum numbers.
R	U	S	H	L	I	K	E	Resembling a rush.
R	U	S	H	T	O	A	D	Natterjack.
R	U	S	S	E	L	I	A	Genus of nearly leafless Mexican shrubs, Coral plant.
R	U	S	T	I	C	A	L	Rustic, Sylvan.
R	U	S	T	L	I	N	G	Sound of movement, Stealing of cattle.
R	U	S	T	M	I	T	E	Small mites that attack citrus trees.
R	U	T	A	B	A	G	A	A turnip.
R	U	T	H	E	N	I	C	Compounds of the metallic element, ruthenium.
R	U	T	H	L	E	S	S	Merciless, Pitiless, Relentless, Unsparing, Implacable, Unyielding, Unflinching, Savage.
R	U	T	I	L	A	N	T	Shining, Having a reddish glow.
R	U	T	I	L	A	T	E	Shine.
R	U	T	I	O	D	O	N	A genus of subaquatic reptiles.
R	Y	E	G	R	A	S	S	Genus of grass with many-flowered spikelets.
R	Y	O	T	W	A	R	I	System of collecting rents from tenant farmers in India.
R	Y	O	T	W	A	R	Y	Same as RYOT-WARI.

S

1	2	3	4	5	6	7	8	Definition
S	A	B	B	A	T	I	A	Genus of North American herb, Marsh pink.
S	A	B	B	A	T	I	C	Period of rest or renewal.
S	A	B	B	A	T	O	N	A piece of armour for the foot.
S	A	B	I	N	A	N	E	Thujane, evergreen shrub.
S	A	B	I	N	E	N	E	Liquid bicyclic unsaturated terpene hydrocarbon found in savin oil.
S	A	B	O	T	A	G	E	Wreck, Destroy, Damage, Subvert, Undermine, Frustrate, Hamper, Obstruct.
S	A	B	O	T	E	U	R	One that engages in sabotage.
S	A	B	O	T	I	E	R	One that makes sabots.
S	A	B	U	L	O	S	E	Sandy, Gritty.
S	A	B	U	L	O	U	S	Same as SABULOSE.
S	A	C	A	L	A	I	T	Killifish.
S	A	C	B	R	O	O	D	Virus disease of the honeybee.
S	A	C	C	A	D	I	C	Jerky.
S	A	C	C	A	T	E	D	Encysted.
S	A	C	C	U	L	A	R	Being like a sac.
S	A	C	C	U	L	U	S	Saccule, Small chamber of the ear.
S	A	C	E	L	L	U	M	A small monumental chapel in a church.
S	A	C	K	L	E	S	S	Unmolested, Weak, Dispirited, Harmless.
S	A	C	K	R	A	C	E	A race where competitors have their legs in sacks.
S	A	C	R	E	D	L	Y	In a sacred manner.
S	A	C	R	I	S	T	Y	Vestry, A room attached to a church where the vestments and sacred utensils are stored.
S	A	D	D	E	N	E	D	Depressed, Oppressed, Weighed down, Melancholy, Mournful, Sorry, Dispirited, Unhappy.
S	A	D	D	L	E	R	Y	Saddles and other equipment for riding horses.
S	A	D	D	L	I	N	G	Placing a saddle on, Burdening, Encumbering, Loading, Taxing, Inflicting, Weighing.
S	A	D	D	U	C	E	E	A member of a sect of the Jews of the second century.
S	A	D	I	S	T	I	C	Delight in inflicting pain and cruelty.
S	A	F	E	H	O	L	D	A refuge from attack.
S	A	F	F	R	O	N	Y	Yellowish.
S	A	F	R	A	N	I	N	Red or blue azine dyes.
S	A	G	A	C	I	T	Y	Insight, Wisdom, Perception, Sensitivity, Grasp, Understanding, Prudence, Comprehension.
S	A	G	A	M	I	T	E	Hulled Indian corn.
S	A	G	A	M	O	R	E	American Indian chief.
S	A	G	E	C	O	C	K	Male sage grouse.
S	A	G	E	K	I	N	G	Mythological ruler of pre-historic China.
S	A	G	E	N	E	S	S	Insight, Wisdom.
S	A	G	E	N	I	T	E	A mineral consisting of an acicular rutile found embedded in quartz.

1	2	3	4	5	6	7	8	Definition
S	A	G	I	N	A	T	E	Fatten.
S	A	G	I	T	T	A	L	Shaped like an arrow or arrowhead.
S	A	G	O	P	A	L	M	A palm tree that yields sago.
S	A	I	B	L	I	N	G	Sunapee trout.
S	A	I	L	B	O	A	T	A boat propelled by sail.
S	A	I	L	F	I	S	H	A large pelagic fish having a very large dorsal fin.
S	A	I	L	L	E	S	S	Having no sails.
S	A	I	L	L	O	F	T	A room where sails are cut and made.
S	A	I	L	Y	A	R	D	A spar on which a sail is spread.
S	A	I	N	F	O	I	N	A Eurasian perennial herb.
S	A	I	N	T	I	S	H	Somewhat saintly.
S	A	L	A	C	I	T	Y	Obscenity, Lewdly, Lecherously.
S	A	L	A	D	O	I	L	Edible vegetable oil used in a salad dressing.
S	A	L	A	D	I	N	G	Vegetables or herbs for a salad.
S	A	L	A	M	B	A	T	A large Phillipine fishing net.
S	A	L	A	R	I	A	T	Persons earning salaries as opposed to wage-earners.
S	A	L	A	R	I	E	D	Receiving a salary.
S	A	L	D	I	D	A	E	Family of aquatic bugs.
S	A	L	E	A	B	L	E	Marketable, Vendible.
S	A	L	E	R	O	O	M	A place where auction sales are held.
S	A	L	E	S	I	T	E	A mineral consisting of a basic copper iodate.
S	A	L	E	S	M	A	N	A male employed to sell goods or services.
S	A	L	I	E	N	C	E	Protrusion, Projection, Emphasis, Highlight.
S	A	L	I	F	I	E	D	Salinized, Impregnated with salt, Converted into a salt.
S	A	L	I	N	I	T	Y	Saltiness, A concentration of salt.
S	A	L	I	V	A	N	T	Causing saliva to flow, Mouth-watering.
S	A	L	I	V	A	R	Y	Relating to saliva or the glands producing saliva.
S	A	L	I	V	A	T	E	Drivel, Drool, Slaver, To produce an abnormal flow of saliva.
S	A	L	I	V	O	U	S	Made up of saliva.
S	A	L	L	Y	I	N	G	Leaping, Rushing, Bounding, Springing, Spurting, Issuing, Bursting forth, Dashing.
S	A	L	M	O	N	I	D	Genus of fishes, Salmon, Trout, Whitefish.
S	A	L	O	P	I	A	N	Inhabitant of Shropshire, England.
S	A	L	P	I	D	A	E	Small family of tunicates.
S	A	L	S	I	L	L	A	A tropical American plant with edible tubers.
S	A	L	T	B	U	S	H	Genus of shrubby plants used for forage.
S	A	L	T	C	A	K	E	An hydrous sodium sulfate.
S	A	L	T	I	C	I	D	A jumping spider.
S	A	L	T	J	U	N	K	Dried salt beef.
S	A	L	T	L	E	S	S	Insipid, Lacking flavour.
S	A	L	T	L	I	C	K	Rock or soil impregnated with salt where animals come to lick.
S	A	L	T	M	I	N	E	Mine for rock-salt.
S	A	L	T	N	E	S	S	Salinity, Pungency.
S	A	L	T	S	I	C	K	Cattle suffering from a cobalt deficiency.
S	A	L	T	W	E	L	L	A well bored to obtain brine.
S	A	L	T	W	O	R	K	A plant for producing salt on a commercial scale.
S	A	L	T	W	O	R	T	Genus of plant used in the manufacture of soda ash.
S	A	L	U	T	A	R	Y	Curative, Restorative, Healthful, Remedial, Hygienic, Salubrious, Wholesome, Tonic.
S	A	L	U	T	I	N	G	Addressing, Signalling respect, A military token, Greeting, Salutation.
S	A	L	V	A	B	L	E	Salvageable, Capable of being saved.
S	A	L	V	A	G	E	D	Rescued, Saved, Delivered, Reclaimed, Recovered, Retrieved, Salved, Ransomed.
S	A	L	V	I	F	I	C	Having the intent to admit to salvation.
S	A	L	V	I	N	I	A	A small genus of water ferns. Floating moss.
S	A	M	A	D	E	R	A	Genus of East African and Indian trees.
S	A	M	A	R	I	U	M	A pale gray lustrous metallic element of the rare-earth group.
S	A	M	B	U	C	U	S	Genus of shrubs or trees with red or black berrylike fruit.
S	A	M	E	N	E	S	S	Identity, Similarity, Monotony, Uniformity, Unity, Parity, Resemblance.
S	A	M	P	H	I	R	E	A fleshy European sea-coast plant.
S	A	M	P	L	I	N	G	Testing, Trial, Survey, Investigating, Example, Specimen, Illustration, Representative.
S	A	N	A	T	I	O	N	Process of healing.
S	A	N	A	T	I	V	E	Beneficial, Restorative, Curing, Healing.
S	A	N	A	T	O	R	Y	Curative, Curing, Remedial, Healing, Vulnerary, Wholesome.
S	A	N	C	T	I	F	Y	Consecrate, Hallow, Purify, Bless, Unprofane, To make sacred.
S	A	N	C	T	I	O	N	Approve, Accredit, Certify, Endorse, Authorize, Commission, License, Permit.
S	A	N	C	T	I	T	Y	Saintliness, Godliness, Sacredness, Inviolability, Uprightness, Holiness.
S	A	N	D	A	R	A	C	A tree yielding aromatic resin used in making varnish and incense.
S	A	N	D	B	A	N	K	Deposit of sand in a shoal.
S	A	N	D	B	A	T	H	A pan of sand used in a laboratory for heating vessels.

1	2	3	4	5	6	7	8	
S	A	N	D	C	A	S	T	Cast in a mould of sand.
S	A	N	D	C	O	C	K	Redshank.
S	A	N	D	C	R	A	B	Australian swimming crab.
S	A	N	D	D	U	N	E	A ridge of sand.
S	A	N	D	E	V	E	R	Glass gall.
S	A	N	D	F	I	S	H	Fish of the north Pacific that burrow in the sand.
S	A	N	D	F	L	A	G	Sandstone split to make flag stones.
S	A	N	D	F	L	E	A	A flea found in sandy places, Chigoe.
S	A	N	D	H	I	L	L	Ridge of sand, Dune.
S	A	N	D	I	V	E	R	Glass gall.
S	A	N	D	L	A	R	K	Sandpiper or plover.
S	A	N	D	M	I	T	E	A mite that is a serious pest of vegetable crops.
S	A	N	D	M	O	L	E	Mole rat.
S	A	N	D	P	E	E	P	A very small sandpiper.
S	A	N	D	P	U	M	P	A pump for removing wet sand, mud or silt.
S	A	N	D	R	E	E	D	Beach grass, Sand sedge.
S	A	N	D	R	E	E	L	Windlass to raise and lower the bailer in well-boring rig.
S	A	N	D	R	O	L	L	A roll to guide newly-woven cloth.
S	A	N	D	S	H	O	E	Canvas shoe.
S	A	N	D	S	O	A	P	Gritty soap for cleansing.
S	A	N	D	S	T	A	R	Starfish.
S	A	N	D	T	R	A	P	An artificial hazard on a golf course, Bunker.
S	A	N	D	W	A	S	P	A wasp that burrows in the sand.
S	A	N	D	W	E	L	D	To weld with a flux of fused sand which is hammered.
S	A	N	D	W	I	C	H	Two slices of bread with a filling.
S	A	N	D	W	O	R	M	A worm that builds a tube of sand, Lugworm.
S	A	N	D	W	O	R	T	A plant that grows in sandy soil.
S	A	N	E	N	E	S	S	Wit, Lucidity, Mind, Reason, Perception, Comprehension, Understanding.
S	A	N	G	A	R	E	E	A long cool drink of wine served with crushed ice and flavoured with nutmeg.
S	A	N	G	L	I	E	R	A wild boar.
S	A	N	G	R	A	D	O	Quack, One who pretends to be a doctor.
S	A	N	G	U	I	F	Y	To change into blood.
S	A	N	G	U	I	N	E	Bloody, Gory, Ruddy, Florid, Confident, Assured, Secure, Hopeful.
S	A	N	I	C	U	L	A	Genus of American herbs having fruit covered with hooked bristles.
S	A	N	I	D	I	N	E	Glassy fedspar.
S	A	N	I	T	A	R	Y	Healthful, Hygienic, Disinfected, Sterilized.
S	A	N	I	T	A	T	E	To provide with sanitary appliances.
S	A	N	I	T	I	Z	E	Sterilize.
S	A	N	S	K	R	I	T	Classical language of India.
S	A	N	T	A	L	I	N	Red crystalline compound constituting the chief colouring matter in red sandalwood.
S	A	N	T	A	L	O	L	A mixture of two liquid isomeric sesquiterpene alcohols.
S	A	N	T	A	L	U	M	A small genus of Indo-malayan parasitic trees.
S	A	N	T	O	N	I	N	A poisonous slightly bitter crystalline compound.
S	A	P	G	R	E	E	N	Dull green lake prepared from buckthorn berries.
S	A	P	I	D	I	T	Y	Taste, Savour, Savouriness.
S	A	P	I	E	N	C	E	Wisdom, Sageness, Sagacity, Insight, Perception.
S	A	P	I	N	D	U	S	A genus of tropical and sub-tropical trees.
S	A	P	I	U	T	A	N	Anoa, Small wild ox.
S	A	P	O	N	A	R	Y	Soapwort.
S	A	P	O	N	I	F	Y	To convert into soap.
S	A	P	O	N	I	T	E	A mineral consisting of a hydrous magnesium aluminosilicate.
S	A	P	O	R	O	U	S	Palatable, Appetizing, Mouth-watering, Relishing, Sapid, Savoury, Tasty, Toothsome.
S	A	P	P	H	I	R	E	Precious stone of blue conundrum.
S	A	P	R	E	M	I	A	Blood poisoning often accompanying gangrene.
S	A	P	R	O	B	I	C	An environment rich in organic matter and relatively free from oxygen.
S	A	P	R	O	G	E	N	An organism living upon nonorganic matter.
S	A	P	R	O	P	E	L	A slimy sediment of decaying organic matter.
S	A	P	S	T	A	I	N	A discolouration in sapwood caused by a fungus.
S	A	P	U	C	A	I	A	Hard, heavy durable timber.
S	A	R	A	B	A	N	D	A stately court dance resembling the minuet.
S	A	R	A	T	O	G	A	A card game.
S	A	R	C	E	L	L	E	Teal.
S	A	R	C	E	N	E	T	Soft thin silk.
S	A	R	C	O	C	O	L	A small genus of shrubs.
S	A	R	C	O	D	I	C	Resembling protoplasm.
S	A	R	D	E	L	L	E	Sardine.
S	A	R	D	O	N	I	C	Sarcastic, Cynical, Ironic, Wry, Scornful, Derisive, Saturnine, Sneering.

1	2	3	4	5	6	7	8	
S	A	R	D	O	N	Y	X	An onyx marked by parallel layers of sard.
S	A	R	G	A	S	S	O	Mass of floating vegetation and seaweed.
S	A	R	P	L	I	E	R	Wrapper or covering of coarse cloth.
S	A	R	R	A	Z	I	N	Buckwheat.
S	A	R	S	E	N	E	T	Sarcenet, Fine thin silk.
S	A	S	S	A	N	I	D	Architecture of an ancient Persian dynasty.
S	A	S	S	O	L	I	N	A mineral consisting of native boric acid.
S	A	T	A	N	I	S	M	Affinity for evil, Worship of Satan.
S	A	T	A	N	I	S	T	One inherently evil, An adherent of Satan, Anti-Christ.
S	A	T	A	N	I	T	Y	Satanism.
S	A	T	E	L	E	S	S	Insatiate.
S	A	T	I	A	T	E	D	Glutted, Gorged, Bored.
S	A	T	I	R	I	S	T	A satirical writer.
S	A	T	I	R	I	Z	E	To write satires, Censure, Ridicule.
S	A	T	U	R	A	N	T	Impregnating, Saturating, Permeating.
S	A	T	U	R	A	T	E	Surfeit, Sate, Soak, Steep, Permeate, Neutralize, Drenched, Sodden.
S	A	T	U	R	D	A	Y	The seventh day of the week, following Friday.
S	A	T	U	R	N	I	A	Genus of wild silk moths.
S	A	T	Y	R	I	N	E	Relating to a genus of butterfly.
S	A	U	C	E	B	O	X	A saucy impudent person.
S	A	U	C	E	P	A	N	A deep cooking utensil with a long handle and used for stewing or boiling.
S	A	U	C	I	S	S	E	A tube of paper or canvas filled with powder and used as a fuse.
S	A	U	R	U	R	U	S	Genus of herbs.
S	A	U	T	E	R	N	E	Semisweet golden-coloured table wine produced from overripe grapes.
S	A	V	A	G	E	L	Y	In a savage manner.
S	A	V	A	G	E	R	Y	Wildness, Viciousness, Uncivilized, Ferocity, Rapacity.
S	A	V	A	G	I	N	G	Attacking, Maltreating, Destroying.
S	A	V	A	G	I	S	M	Savagery.
S	A	V	A	N	N	A	H	Treeless plain, A grassland.
S	A	V	E	A	B	L	E	Savable, Able to be saved.
S	A	V	I	N	G	L	Y	In a saving manner, Frugally, Redeeming.
S	A	V	O	U	R	E	D	Tasted, Relished, Felt.
S	A	V	O	U	R	L	Y	With keen understanding.
S	A	V	O	Y	A	R	D	Characteristic of Savoy, France.
S	A	W	B	O	N	E	S	A physician or surgeon, usually attached to the navy.
S	A	W	F	L	I	E	S	Family of insects having females that lay their eggs in leaves and stems.
S	A	W	F	R	A	M	E	Stretching frame for saws.
S	A	W	G	R	A	S	S	Sedge grass with serrated leaves.
S	A	W	H	O	R	S	E	A rack supporting wood while it is being sawn.
S	A	W	T	A	B	L	E	A saw-bench.
S	A	X	I	C	O	L	A	Growing among rocks.
S	A	X	I	C	O	L	E	Same as SAXITILE.
S	A	X	O	N	I	A	N	Saxon.
S	A	X	O	N	I	S	M	Anglo-saxonism.
S	A	X	O	N	I	S	T	A specialist in Old English or in Saxon history.
S	A	X	O	N	I	Z	E	Anglo-saxonize.
S	A	Y	O	N	A	R	A	Goodbye in Japanese.
S	C	A	B	B	A	R	D	A leather or metal sheath to protect a blade.
S	C	A	B	B	L	E	D	Shaped stone in the quarry.
S	C	A	B	I	O	S	A	A large genus of Old World herbs.
S	C	A	B	I	O	U	S	A plant, Fleabane, Horseweed, Blue scabious, Scabby.
S	C	A	B	L	A	N	D	Shallow-soiled rocky land.
S	C	A	B	M	I	T	E	A mite that causes scab.
S	C	A	B	R	O	U	S	Difficult, Knotty, Scaly, Prickly, Scurfy, Scabby, Rough, Grimy.
S	C	A	F	F	O	L	D	Temporary or movable platform.
S	C	A	L	A	B	L	E	Capable of being scaled.
S	C	A	L	A	R	I	A	Marine mollusks with a spiral shell.
S	C	A	L	A	W	A	G	Rascal, Scamp, Reprobate, Rogue, Villain, Devil, Miscreant, Knave.
S	C	A	L	D	I	N	G	Blanching, Boiling, Scorching, Worrying, Broiling, Scathing, Sizzling, Hot.
S	C	A	L	E	N	U	S	Neck muscles.
S	C	A	L	L	I	O	N	Shallot, Leek.
S	C	A	L	P	I	N	G	Depriving of a scalp, Removing a top layer, Humiliating.
S	C	A	M	B	L	E	D	Sprawled, Shambled, Collected, Scraped together.
S	C	A	M	B	L	E	R	Sponger.
S	C	A	M	M	O	N	Y	A twining plant native to Asia Minor.
S	C	A	M	O	Z	Z	I	Variation of Ionic style column.

1	2	3	4	5	6	7	8	Definition
S	C	A	M	P	I	N	G	Skimping, Shirking, Stinting, Scrimping.
S	C	A	M	P	I	S	H	Roguish.
S	C	A	N	D	I	U	M	A white trivalent metallic element.
S	C	A	N	N	I	N	G	Checking, Scrutinizing, Browsing, Skimming, Perishing, Examining, Observing.
S	C	A	N	S	I	O	N	An analysis of a rhythmic structure.
S	C	A	N	T	I	E	S	Abbreviated panties for women.
S	C	A	N	T	I	L	Y	In a scanty manner.
S	C	A	N	T	I	N	G	Providing with an inadequate allowance, Slighting.
S	C	A	N	T	L	E	D	Having a supply cut down.
S	C	A	P	A	N	U	S	Mole.
S	C	A	P	H	I	T	E	A fossil cephalopod.
S	C	A	P	H	O	I	D	Boat-shaped.
S	C	A	P	P	L	E	D	Rough-hewn.
S	C	A	P	U	L	A	R	Shoulder-blade.
S	C	A	R	A	B	E	E	Scarab.
S	C	A	R	C	E	L	Y	Barely, Just, Hardly.
S	C	A	R	C	I	T	Y	Parsimony, Penury, Poverty, Inadequacy, Rareness, Shortage, Dearth, Absence.
S	C	A	R	E	B	U	G	Bugbear.
S	C	A	R	F	I	N	G	Uniting, Removing defects.
S	C	A	R	F	P	I	N	Tiepin.
S	C	A	R	I	D	A	E	Family of marine percoid fishes, Parrot-fish.
S	C	A	R	I	O	U	S	Thin and membranous in texture.
S	C	A	R	L	E	S	S	Leaving no scar.
S	C	A	R	P	H	E	D	Scarfed.
S	C	A	R	R	I	N	G	Marring, Disfiguring, Blemishing, Flawing, Defacing, Damaging, Wounding, Injuring.
S	C	A	T	H	I	N	G	Harming, Injuring, Damaging, Assailing, Lambasting, Scourging, Blistering, Castigating.
S	C	A	T	T	E	R	Y	Scattered.
S	C	A	V	E	N	G	E	Hunt, Collect, Search.
S	C	A	W	T	I	T	E	A mineral consisting of a silicate and carbonate of calcium.
S	C	E	L	E	R	A	T	Villain, Rogue, Criminal, Miscreant.
S	C	E	N	A	R	I	O	Screenplay, Synopsis of a play.
S	C	E	N	E	M	A	N	Scene shifter.
S	C	E	N	I	C	A	L	Imaginary, Unreal, Resembling a stage performance.
S	C	E	N	T	B	A	G	Sachet, A small scented bag.
S	C	E	P	T	R	A	L	Relating to a sceptre or royal authority.
S	C	E	P	T	R	E	D	Royal, Regal, Invested with sovereign authority.
S	C	H	E	D	U	L	E	Catalogue, Inventory, List, Register, Roll-call, Roster, Agenda, Calendar.
S	C	H	E	M	I	N	G	Planning, Devising, Contriving, Plotting, Planning, Conniving, Conspiring, Intriguing.
S	C	H	E	M	I	S	T	An advocate of a particular scheme.
S	C	H	I	E	D	A	M	A strongly flavoured gin.
S	C	H	I	L	L	E	R	Iridescent colouration.
S	C	H	I	S	T	I	C	Having the structure of a metamorphic crystalline rock.
S	C	H	I	Z	A	E	A	Genus of small ferns.
S	C	H	I	Z	O	I	D	Split personality.
S	C	H	I	Z	O	N	T	Multi-nucleate cell in some sporozoans.
S	C	H	L	A	G	E	R	A long duelling sword used by German students.
S	C	H	M	A	L	T	Z	Sentimentalism in artistic expression, Florid or showy.
S	C	H	M	E	L	Z	E	Decorative glasses.
S	C	H	N	A	P	P	S	Various distilled liquors, Strong Holland gin.
S	C	H	O	E	N	U	S	Genus of stout sedges.
S	C	H	O	L	I	A	N	A pedantic or academic expression.
S	C	H	O	L	I	O	N	Explanatory remark or comment, A marginal annotation.
S	C	H	O	L	I	U	M	Same as SCHOLION.
S	C	H	O	O	L	E	D	Educated, Trained, Instructed, Informed, Guided, Shown, Cultivated, Disciplined.
S	C	H	O	O	N	E	R	A sailing boat.
S	C	H	R	A	D	A	N	An almost odourless viscous liquid used in insecticide.
S	C	I	A	T	I	C	A	Pain in the area of the sciatic nerve usually caused by pressure or inflammation.
S	C	I	E	N	T	E	R	Knowingly, Wilfully, Deliberately.
S	C	I	E	N	T	I	A	Philosophy.
S	C	I	L	I	C	E	T	Namely, To wit.
S	C	I	M	I	T	A	R	A curved sword favoured by Arabs and Turks.
S	C	I	N	C	O	I	D	Resembling skink.
S	C	I	O	L	I	S	M	A show of learning without substantial foundation.
S	C	I	O	L	I	S	T	One with a superficial education.
S	C	I	O	L	O	U	S	Lacking knowledge.
S	C	I	O	P	T	I	C	Relating to the formation of images in a darkened room.
S	C	I	R	R	H	U	S	A hard cancerous tumour.

1	2	3	4	5	6	7	8	
S	C	I	S	S	I	L	E	Capable of being easily split.
S	C	I	S	S	I	O	N	Division, Cleavage, Cutting, Dividing, Splitting, Dissension.
S	C	I	S	S	O	R	S	Cutting instruments of two blades on a movable pivot.
S	C	I	S	S	U	R	E	Cleft, Elongated opening.
S	C	I	U	R	O	I	D	Resembling the tail of a squirrel.
S	C	L	A	R	E	O	L	A liquid bicyclic diterpenoid alcohol.
S	C	L	E	R	E	I	D	A cell of a higher plant having diameters essentially alike.
S	C	L	E	R	I	T	E	A hard calcareous plate, piece or spicule.
S	C	L	E	R	O	I	D	Hard tissue.
S	C	L	E	R	O	M	A	Rinoscleroma, Chronic inflammatory disease of the nasal tissues.
S	C	L	E	R	O	U	S	Hard, Indurated.
S	C	O	F	F	I	N	G	Jeering, Gibing, Girding, Sneering, Flouting, Quipping, Deriding, Mocking.
S	C	O	F	F	L	A	W	One who violates a law.
S	C	O	L	D	I	N	G	Berating, Jawing, Bawling, Railing, Reviling, Reproving, Criticizing, Ranting.
S	C	O	L	O	P	A	X	Genus of birds, Woodcock.
S	C	O	L	Y	T	U	S	Type genus of bark beetles.
S	C	O	O	P	N	E	T	A net for sweeping the bottom of a river.
S	C	O	O	P	I	N	G	Dipping, Ladling, Gathering, Lifting, Bailing, Gouging, Excavating, Digging.
S	C	O	O	T	I	N	G	Darting, Scudding, Squirting, Hurrying, Bustling, Rushing, Dashing, Scampering.
S	C	O	P	A	R	I	N	The yellow crystalline colouring matter of the flowers of the broom.
S	C	O	P	H	O	N	Y	A television system using mechanical and optical devices.
S	C	O	P	I	D	A	E	Family of African wading birds.
S	C	O	P	I	O	U	S	Spacious, Extensive, Broad, Expansive, Extended, Wide.
S	C	O	R	C	H	E	D	Burnt, Parched, Charred, Devastated, Seethed, Stewed, Scourged, Blistered.
S	C	O	R	C	H	E	R	One that drives at an excessive speed, One that creates a sensation.
S	C	O	R	D	I	U	M	Water germander.
S	C	O	R	I	O	U	S	Containing dross, slag, ash or larva.
S	C	O	R	N	F	U	L	Contemptuous, Disdainful, Despising.
S	C	O	R	N	I	N	G	Disdaining, Despising, Ignoring, Scoffing, Ridiculing, Taunting, Mocking.
S	C	O	R	P	I	O	N	Arachnid carrying a venomous sting in its tail.
S	C	O	T	C	H	E	D	Hindered, Thwarted, Impeded, Blocked, Wedged, Hampered.
S	C	O	T	F	R	E	E	Unharmed, Nothing to pay.
S	C	O	T	O	P	I	A	Vision in dim light when the eyes are adjusted to the lack of light.
S	C	O	T	O	P	S	Y	Same as SCOTOPIA.
S	C	O	T	S	M	A	N	Native of Scotland.
S	C	O	T	T	I	F	Y	In a Scotch manner.
S	C	O	T	T	I	S	H	Scotch.
S	C	O	U	R	G	E	D	Lashed, Flogged, Devastated, Ravaged, Desecrated, Despoiled, Wasted, Pillaged.
S	C	O	U	R	I	N	G	Scrubbing, Corroding, Gnawing, Removing, Punishing, Purging, Rushing, Seeking.
S	C	O	U	R	W	A	Y	Area gouged by strong flow of water.
S	C	O	U	T	H	E	R	A light shower, A light fall of snow.
S	C	O	U	T	I	N	G	Reconnoitering, Searching, Exploring, Observing, Spying, Mocking, Scoffing, Rejecting.
S	C	O	W	L	I	N	G	Frowning, Glowering.
S	C	R	A	B	B	L	E	Scrawl, Scribble, Scratch, Claw, Scramble. A board game using letter tiles to construct words.
S	C	R	A	G	G	E	D	Choked, Manhandled, Killed, Murdered, Strangled, Throttled.
S	C	R	A	G	G	L	Y	Ragged, Unkempt, Straggly, Scrawny.
S	C	R	A	M	B	L	E	Clamber, Scrabble, Sprawl, Ramble, Jumble, Struggle, Scurry, Scuttle.
S	C	R	A	N	B	A	G	A bag for left-over food, Receptacle for articles found lying about on a ship.
S	C	R	A	N	N	E	L	Unmelodious, Thin and grating noise.
S	C	R	A	P	I	N	G	Erasing, Expunging, Scratching, Grating, Rasping, Abrading, Scuffing, Chafing.
S	C	R	A	P	P	E	D	Disposed, Abandoned, Jettisoned, Rejected, Scuttled, Fought, Quarrelled, Brawled.
S	C	R	A	P	P	L	E	A stewed meat mush, moulded and fried when sliced.
S	C	R	A	T	C	H	Y	Tingling, Itching, Irritating, Prickly, Scant, Meagre, Ragged.
S	C	R	A	T	T	L	E	Scratch, Scramble.
S	C	R	A	W	L	E	D	Scribbled, Scrabbled, Scratched, Squibbled, Doodled.
S	C	R	A	W	L	E	R	A device for marking fields for planting.
S	C	R	E	A	M	E	D	Screeched, Shrieked, Squealed, Yelled, Caterwauled, Howled, Wailed, Howled.
S	C	R	E	A	M	E	R	One that screams.
S	C	R	E	E	C	H	Y	Shrilly.
S	C	R	E	E	N	E	D	Concealed, Secluded, Defended, Covered, Protected, Secured, Shielded, Shaded.
S	C	R	E	E	V	E	R	Writer of begging letters. A beggar who collects money by chalking pictures on the pavement.
S	C	R	E	W	I	N	G	Twisting, Tightening, Adjusting, Squinting, Crumpling, Extorting, Wresting, Wringing.
S	C	R	E	W	K	E	Y	A wrench or spanner for turning a screw or nut.
S	C	R	E	W	P	O	D	Screw bean, sweet pod used for fodder.
S	C	R	I	B	B	L	E	Illegible writing, Scrawl, Scrabble, Squiggle, Writing carelessly.
S	C	R	I	B	I	S	M	Activities of the Jewish scribes in the time of Christ.
S	C	R	I	G	G	L	E	Wriggle, Twist, Squirm.

1	2	3	4	5	6	7	8	Definition
S	C	R	I	M	P	E	D	Pinched, Scraped, Skimped, Stinted, Saved, Economized.
S	C	R	I	P	T	E	R	Scriptwriter.
S	C	R	I	V	A	N	O	Scribe.
S	C	R	O	F	U	L	A	Tuberculosis of the lymph glands.
S	C	R	O	L	L	E	D	Formed into scrolls, Curved.
S	C	R	O	U	G	E	D	Crowded, Pressed.
S	C	R	O	U	N	G	E	Find, Salvage, Forage, Hunt, Cadge, Wheedle, Sponge.
S	C	R	U	B	B	E	D	Rubbed, Scratched, Cancelled, Eliminated, Cleansed, Polished, Scoured, Buffed.
S	C	R	U	B	B	E	R	An apparatus for removing impurities.
S	C	R	U	B	O	A	K	Small size trees growing in inferior soil.
S	C	R	U	P	L	E	D	Demurred, Hesitated, Troubled, Fretted, Questioned, Balked, Strained, Stumbled.
S	C	R	U	P	L	E	R	One that scruples.
S	C	R	U	T	I	N	Y	Examination, Investigation, Surveillance, Analysis, Audit, Inspection, Review, Scan.
S	C	U	D	D	I	N	G	Scraping.
S	C	U	F	F	L	E	D	Scurried, Wrestled, Grappled, Tussled, Cuffed, Shuffled, Shambled, Scuffed.
S	C	U	F	F	L	E	R	Cultivator.
S	C	U	L	L	E	R	Y	Room adjacent to kitchen for preparation and cleaning.
S	C	U	L	L	I	N	G	Propelling a boat by using the scull in a special way.
S	C	U	L	L	I	O	N	Kitchen helper for washing up and preparing vegetables.
S	C	U	L	P	T	O	R	One that produces sculptures.
S	C	U	M	B	L	E	D	Reducing the brilliance of colour, Softening the lines or colour of a drawing.
S	C	U	R	R	I	E	D	Scuttled, Ran, Dashed, Scampered, Scooted, Sprinted, Skeltered, Scuttered.
S	C	U	R	R	I	E	S	Flurries.
S	C	U	R	R	I	L	E	Abusive, Truculent, Vituperative, Coarse, Vulgar, Obscene, Foul, Insulting.
S	C	U	R	V	I	L	Y	Contemptibly, Shabbily, Meanly, Despicably, Beggarly.
S	C	U	T	C	H	E	D	Whipped, Beaten.
S	C	U	T	C	H	E	R	A worker who tends a machine doing scutching.
S	C	U	T	E	L	L	A	Sea urchin.
S	C	U	T	I	P	E	D	Have a scaly foot.
S	C	U	T	T	L	E	D	Sank, Abandoned, Scurried, Damaged, Destroyed, Ran, Bolted, Scooted.
S	C	U	T	T	L	E	R	One that destroys, A runner in a race.
S	C	Y	P	H	U	L	A	Hypothetical ancestral jellyfishes.
S	C	Y	T	H	I	A	N	Ancient country by the Black Sea.
S	C	Y	T	H	I	S	M	The paganism developed by the Scythians.
S	E	A	A	C	O	R	N	Acorn barnacle.
S	E	A	A	D	D	E	R	Genus of pipefishes.
S	E	A	A	R	R	O	W	Flying squid.
S	E	A	B	E	A	C	H	Beach lying adjacent to the sea.
S	E	A	B	E	A	R	D	A green marine alga that grows in thick tufts.
S	E	A	B	E	L	L	S	A bindweed with pink bell flowers that grows on the coast.
S	E	A	B	O	A	R	D	Seacoast.
S	E	A	B	O	R	N	E	Carried over or on the sea.
S	E	A	B	O	U	N	D	Going to sea.
S	E	A	B	R	A	N	T	A wild goose.
S	E	A	B	R	E	A	M	Genus of fishes.
S	E	A	C	O	A	S	T	The shore adjacent to the sea.
S	E	A	C	R	A	F	T	Being skilled in navigation at sea, A sea-worthy ship.
S	E	A	D	A	I	S	Y	A thrift, A tufted scapose herb growing at the coast.
S	E	A	D	E	V	I	L	Monkfish, Ray, Stonefish.
S	E	A	D	R	A	K	E	Cormorant, Male eider.
S	E	A	E	A	G	L	E	Eagles that feed on fish.
S	E	A	F	A	R	E	R	A mariner, Sailor, Seaman.
S	E	A	F	I	G	H	T	A naval engagement, A battle between ships.
S	E	A	F	R	O	N	T	A promenade or built-up area alongside the beach.
S	E	A	F	R	O	T	H	The foam of the sea.
S	E	A	G	A	T	E	S	Long rolling swells, Gates to protect from the sea.
S	E	A	G	O	I	N	G	Making voyages out to sea, Designed for sailing on the sea.
S	E	A	G	O	O	S	E	Dolphin.
S	E	A	G	R	A	P	E	Gulfweed.
S	E	A	G	R	A	S	S	Eelgrass, Seaweed, Green alga.
S	E	A	G	R	E	E	N	A moderate green colour.
S	E	A	H	E	A	T	H	Genus of perennial herb growing in seasand.
S	E	A	H	O	L	L	Y	An evergreen herb.
S	E	A	H	O	R	S	E	A small pipe fish with a head resembling a horse and that swims in an upright position.
S	E	A	H	O	U	N	D	Dog-fish.
S	E	A	J	E	L	L	Y	Jellyfish.
S	E	A	L	E	M	O	N	Family of mollusks having a smooth convex yellow body.

1	2	3	4	5	6	7	8	
S	E	A	L	E	V	E	L	Level midway between average high and low tides.
S	E	A	L	O	U	S	E	Fish louse.
S	E	A	L	R	I	N	G	A ring set with an engraved stone, Signet ring.
S	E	A	L	S	K	I	N	The skin of a fur seal.
S	E	A	L	U	N	G	S	Jellyfish.
S	E	A	L	W	O	R	T	A pearlwort.
S	E	A	M	A	N	L	Y	Seamanlike.
S	E	A	M	I	E	S	T	Most unpleasant, Most disreputable.
S	E	A	M	L	E	S	S	Circular knit, Woven without seams.
S	E	A	M	L	I	K	E	Forming a linear joint.
S	E	A	M	O	U	N	T	A submarine mountain in the deep depths of the ocean.
S	E	A	M	O	U	S	E	Marine worm, Sea-urchin, Sandpiper.
S	E	A	M	R	E	N	T	Wearing ragged garments.
S	E	A	M	S	T	E	R	Tailor.
S	E	A	O	N	I	O	N	Small delicate herb with fragrant blue flowers.
S	E	A	O	T	T	E	R	A large marine otter.
S	E	A	O	X	E	Y	E	Scrubby coastal plants, Sea marigold.
S	E	A	P	E	A	C	H	A tunicate having a velvety surface and the colour of a ripe peach.
S	E	A	P	E	R	C	H	Sea bass.
S	E	A	P	I	E	C	E	A painting of a scene at sea, Seascape.
S	E	A	P	L	A	N	E	Flying boat.
S	E	A	P	O	W	E	R	Pertaining to the strength of a country's naval power.
S	E	A	P	U	R	S	E	Egg-case of a skate or shark.
S	E	A	Q	U	A	I	L	Turnstone, Family of migratory birds related to the sandpipers.
S	E	A	Q	U	A	K	E	Seismic disturbance under the sea.
S	E	A	R	A	V	E	N	Scorpion fish.
S	E	A	R	C	H	E	D	Looked, Scrutinized, Investigated, Foraged, Hunted, Inspected, Ransacked, Rummaged.
S	E	A	R	C	H	E	R	Seeker, Inspector.
S	E	A	R	O	B	I	N	Gurnard, Fish with a pectoral fin used for walking on the sea bottom.
S	E	A	R	O	V	E	R	Pirate, Buccaneer.
S	E	A	S	C	A	P	E	A picture of a scene at sea.
S	E	A	S	H	E	L	L	The hard covering of a marine animal.
S	E	A	S	H	O	R	E	Foreshore, Land adjacent to the sea.
S	E	A	S	H	R	U	B	Sea-fan.
S	E	A	S	N	A	I	L	Creeping marine gastropod, Whelk.
S	E	A	S	N	A	K	E	Venomous aquatic sea serpent.
S	E	A	S	N	I	P	E	Shore bird.
S	E	A	S	O	N	A	L	Relating to a particular season.
S	E	A	S	O	N	E	D	Experienced, Skilled, Versed, Practiced, Acclimatized, Practical, Hardened, Flavoured.
S	E	A	S	O	N	E	R	A worker that seasons hides or leather.
S	E	A	S	W	I	N	E	Porpoise.
S	E	A	T	H	O	N	G	Brown seaweed.
S	E	A	T	L	E	S	S	Having or requiring no seat.
S	E	A	T	M	I	L	E	Measurement for passenger transport.
S	E	A	T	R	O	U	T	A trout that lives in the sea but moves to a river to spawn.
S	E	A	T	W	O	R	M	Parasitic worm that infests human intestines.
S	E	A	W	A	T	E	R	Salt water, Water of the sea.
S	E	A	W	R	A	C	K	Seaweed.
S	E	B	A	C	A	T	E	Ester of sebacic acid.
S	E	B	E	S	T	E	N	East Indian tree with an edible fruit.
S	E	B	U	N	D	E	E	Native soldiers in the time when India was under British rule.
S	E	C	A	L	O	S	E	A polysaccharide of frutose units from green rye and oats.
S	E	C	A	M	O	N	E	Genus of Old World tropical woody vines.
S	E	C	A	T	E	U	R	Scissors, Shears usually pertaining to gardening tools.
S	E	C	E	D	I	N	G	Withdrawing, Quitting, Retiring.
S	E	C	E	R	N	E	D	Separating, Distinguishing, Discriminating.
S	E	C	L	U	D	E	D	Secreted, Hidden, Isolated, Protected, Screened, Sequestered, Solitary, Cloistered.
S	E	C	O	D	O	N	T	Having teeth adapted for cutting.
S	E	C	O	N	D	E	D	Attended, Assisted, Accompanied, Confirmed, Followed, Supported, Repeated, Aided.
S	E	C	O	N	D	E	R	Supporter.
S	E	C	R	E	T	E	D	Concealed, Cloaked, Hidden, Buried, Ensconsed, Screened, Stashed, Produced.
S	E	C	R	E	T	I	N	Hormone found in the upper intestine that stimulates the action of the pancreas and liver.
S	E	C	R	E	T	L	Y	Inaudibly, Covertly, Furtively, Privately, Stealthily, Surreptitiously, Clandestinely.
S	E	C	T	A	T	O	R	Disciple, Follower, Adherent, Cohort, Partisan, Supporter.
S	E	C	U	N	D	L	Y	Unilaterally.
S	E	C	U	N	D	U	M	According to law.
S	E	C	U	R	E	L	Y	Trustingly, Firmly, Certainly, Safely, Tightly, Reliably, Staunchly, Confidently.

1	2	3	4	5	6	7	8	
S	E	C	U	R	I	N	G	Ensuring, Assuring, Catching, Fastening, Anchoring, Capturing, Acquiring, Gaining.
S	E	C	U	R	I	T	Y	Safety, Confidence, Assurance, Firmness, Stability, Guarantee, Dependability, Pledge.
S	E	D	A	T	E	L	Y	Quietly, Calmly, Seriously, Soberly, Placidly, Serenely, Seemly, Solemnly.
S	E	D	A	T	I	V	E	Calmative, Tranquilizer, Sleeping pill, Pacifier.
S	E	D	A	R	U	N	T	Session of an ecclesiastical assembly.
S	E	D	G	E	H	E	N	Family of wading birds.
S	E	D	I	M	E	N	T	Material settled at the bottom of liquid, Dregs, Grounds.
S	E	D	I	T	I	O	N	Insurrection, Treason, Mutiny, Rebellion, Alienation, Strike, Revolt, Uprising.
S	E	D	U	C	I	N	G	Luring, Enticing, Inveigling, Decoying, Tempting, Trapping, Deceiving, Raping.
S	E	D	U	L	I	T	Y	Diligence, Industry.
S	E	D	U	L	O	U	S	Busy, Assiduous, Diligent, Industrious, Active, Hustling, Persevering, Persistent.
S	E	E	D	B	I	R	D	Pied wagtail.
S	E	E	D	C	A	K	E	A cake containing aromatic seeds such as caraway or sesame.
S	E	E	D	C	A	S	E	Pod.
S	E	E	D	C	O	A	T	Outer protective cover of a seed.
S	E	E	D	D	O	W	N	To sow with grass or legume seed.
S	E	E	D	F	I	S	H	A fish full of ripe spawn.
S	E	E	D	G	A	L	L	A gall that resembles a seed.
S	E	E	D	L	E	A	F	A broadleaf tobacco used in cigars.
S	E	E	D	L	E	S	S	Without seeds or pips.
S	E	E	D	L	I	N	G	A tree grown from a seed.
S	E	E	D	N	E	S	S	The action of sowing.
S	E	E	D	P	L	O	T	Seedbed.
S	E	E	D	T	I	C	K	The larva of a tick.
S	E	E	D	T	I	M	E	The season for sowing seeds.
S	E	E	D	Y	T	O	E	An abnormality of a horse's foot.
S	E	E	P	W	E	E	D	A glabrous undershrub that is believed to indicate groundwater.
S	E	E	R	F	I	S	H	Genus of large fishes related to the mackerel.
S	E	E	R	S	H	I	P	The functions of a seer.
S	E	E	S	A	W	E	D	Moved back and forth, Lurched, Pitched, Teetered, Rocked, Swayed, Tilted.
S	E	E	T	H	I	N	G	Boiling, Stewing, Fermenting, Agitated, Intense, Violent, Churning, Simmering.
S	E	G	R	E	A	N	T	In heraldry, to have the wings expanded.
S	E	I	G	N	E	U	R	Feudal lord, Lord, Gentleman.
S	E	I	G	N	I	O	R	Feudal lord of the manor.
S	E	I	N	E	N	E	T	A type of fishing net.
S	E	I	R	F	I	S	H	Seerfish.
S	E	L	A	D	A	N	G	A wild ox.
S	E	L	E	C	T	E	D	Chosen, Culled, Elected, Marked, Picked, Preferred, Exclusive, Singled.
S	E	L	E	C	T	O	R	A mechanical or electrical device for sorting or choosing.
S	E	L	E	N	A	T	E	Ester of selenic acid.
S	E	L	E	N	I	D	E	A binary compound of selenium.
S	E	L	E	N	I	T	E	Variety of gypsum.
S	E	L	E	N	I	U	M	A nonmetallic element resembling sulphur.
S	E	L	F	B	O	R	N	Arising within the self.
S	E	L	F	E	A	S	E	Bodily comfort.
S	E	L	F	H	E	A	L	Plants thought to have healing properties.
S	E	L	F	H	E	L	P	Providing facilities for people to help themselves.
S	E	L	F	H	O	O	D	Possessing an individual identity, Selfishness.
S	E	L	F	L	E	S	S	Unselfish.
S	E	L	F	L	I	F	E	Selfish living.
S	E	L	F	L	O	V	E	Conceit, Love of oneself.
S	E	L	F	M	A	D	E	To improve oneself by one's own efforts.
S	E	L	F	N	E	S	S	Personality, Selfishness, Egoism.
S	E	L	F	P	I	T	Y	To feel sorry for oneself.
S	E	L	F	S	A	M	E	Identical, Same, Exact, Alike.
S	E	L	F	W	I	L	L	Obstinacy, Pig-headedness.
S	E	L	F	W	I	S	E	Having a high opinion of one's intelligence.
S	E	L	L	A	B	L	E	Able to be sold.
S	E	L	V	A	G	E	E	A skein of rope yarns wound round with marline.
S	E	L	V	E	D	G	E	Border, Edge, Margin, Specially woven edge on fabric to prevent fraying.
S	E	M	A	N	T	I	C	Relating to meaning in language.
S	E	M	B	L	A	N	T	Countenance, Face, Aspect, Apparition, Image, Likeness, Similarity, Appearance.
S	E	M	E	S	T	E	R	A half year, Six months session, Term of instruction.
S	E	M	I	D	O	M	E	A roof covering a semi-circular room or recess.
S	E	M	I	F	O	R	M	An imperfect form.
S	E	M	I	H	A	R	D	Not very hard.
S	E	M	I	N	A	R	Y	Professional school giving training in religion.

1	2	3	4	5	6	7	8	
S	E	M	I	N	A	T	E	Inseminate.
S	E	M	I	N	O	L	E	American Indian tribe.
S	E	M	I	O	P	A	L	An impure opal.
S	E	M	I	O	S	I	S	The process in which something functions as a sign for an organism.
S	E	M	I	O	T	I	C	Theory of signs and symbols.
S	E	M	I	O	V	A	L	The shape of a half oval.
S	E	M	I	P	U	P	A	Insect at a stage between the larva and the pupa.
S	E	M	I	T	I	S	M	Semitic character.
S	E	M	I	T	I	S	T	A scholar of Semitic languages.
S	E	M	I	T	O	N	E	Half-tone, Half-step.
S	E	M	O	L	I	N	A	Coarse middlings used for porridge or puddings.
S	E	M	P	L	I	C	E	Direction in music, simple, unaffected.
S	E	M	P	S	T	E	R	Seamster.
S	E	N	A	R	I	U	S	A verse in Latin prosody.
S	E	N	D	D	O	W	N	Suspend, Expel, Down-grade.
S	E	N	G	R	E	E	N	Houseleek.
S	E	N	I	L	I	T	Y	Old age, Dotage, Decline.
S	E	N	N	I	G	H	T	Week, Seven days and nights.
S	E	N	O	N	I	A	N	Relating to inhabitants of prehistoric Gaul.
S	E	N	O	R	I	T	A	Respectful title of an unmarried Spanish woman.
S	E	N	S	E	F	U	L	Significant, Judicious.
S	E	N	S	I	B	L	E	Aware, Material, Perceptible, Wise, Persuaded, Tangible, Physical, Intelligent.
S	E	N	S	I	B	L	Y	Significantly, Intelligently, Discreetly, Judiciously, Appreciably, Sanely, Wisely, Logically.
S	E	N	S	I	B	L	E	Something which is perceptible.
S	E	N	S	U	O	U	S	Sensual, Luxurious, Voluptuous, Sybaritic.
S	E	N	T	E	N	C	E	Period, Proposition, Clause, Doom, Maxim, Punishment.
S	E	N	T	I	E	N	T	Aware, Alive, Awake, Conscious, Knowing, Sensible, Emotional, Feeling.
S	E	N	T	I	N	E	L	Sentry, Soldier, Watchguard, Warden, Picket, Ward, Look-out.
S	E	N	T	R	Y	G	O	Changing of the guard.
S	E	P	A	L	I	N	E	Resembling a petal.
S	E	P	A	L	O	D	Y	The changing of floral parts into petals.
S	E	P	A	L	O	I	D	Resembling a sepal.
S	E	P	A	L	O	U	S	Having sepals.
S	E	P	A	R	A	T	E	Discriminate, Detach, Distinguish, Segregate, Scatter, Extract, Withdraw, Sunder.
S	E	P	I	I	D	A	E	Cuttlefishes.
S	E	P	I	M	E	N	T	A hedge or fence that encloses an area.
S	E	P	S	I	D	A	E	Family of shiny black flies that develop in decaying matter.
S	E	P	T	A	R	C	H	A plant stem having seven tissue groups.
S	E	P	T	A	R	I	A	Nodules of limestone or ironstone.
S	E	P	T	A	T	E	D	Divided by a septum.
S	E	P	T	E	T	T	E	Group or set of seven.
S	E	P	T	E	N	E	R	Same as SEPTENAR.
S	E	P	T	F	O	I	L	Ornamental leaf having seven lobes.
S	E	P	T	I	E	M	E	Mutation stop of an organ.
S	E	P	T	O	R	I	A	Genus of imperfect fungi.
S	E	P	T	U	L	U	M	A small septum.
S	E	Q	U	E	N	C	E	Series, Succession, Order, Progression, Sequel, Order.
S	E	Q	U	I	T	U	R	An inference that follows from a premises.
S	E	R	A	B	E	N	D	A Persian rug.
S	E	R	A	G	L	I	O	Harem, Brothel, Bordello, A residence of a sultan.
S	E	R	A	P	H	I	C	Angelic, Sublime, Pure, Resembling a seraph.
S	E	R	A	P	H	I	N	Fossil giant crab.
S	E	R	A	P	I	A	S	Genus of orchids.
S	E	R	E	N	A	D	E	A love song performed at night under the lady's window.
S	E	R	E	N	A	T	A	Serenade, Cantata.
S	E	R	E	N	E	L	Y	Calmly, Placidly, Tranquilly, Restfully.
S	E	R	E	N	E	S	T	Calmest, Most tranquil, Most peaceful.
S	E	R	E	N	I	T	Y	Calm, Peacefulness, Repose.
S	E	R	G	E	A	N	T	Non-commissioned officer.
S	E	R	I	A	L	L	Y	In serial form, In sequence.
S	E	R	I	A	T	I	M	Serially.
S	E	R	I	C	I	T	E	A scaly variety of muscovite.
S	E	R	I	N	G	A	L	A collection of trees yielding rubber.
S	E	R	J	A	N	I	A	A genus of tropical American woody tendril-bearing vines.
S	E	R	J	E	A	N	T	Sergeant.
S	E	R	M	O	N	I	C	Given to sermonizing, Didactic.
S	E	R	O	L	O	G	Y	A science of serums and their reactions.

1	2	3	4	5	6	7	8	Definition
S	E	R	O	S	I	T	Y	Resembling serum.
S	E	R	O	T	I	N	E	Late developing or flowering, Common European brown bat.
S	E	R	P	H	O	I	D	Minute wasp.
S	E	R	P	O	L	E	T	Wild thyme.
S	E	R	R	A	N	I	D	Genus of carnivorous marine percoid fishes, Sea bass.
S	E	R	R	A	N	U	S	Genus of highly toxic small sea basses.
S	E	R	R	A	T	E	D	Notched, Saw-edged, Saw-toothed, Jagged.
S	E	R	R	A	T	U	S	Muscles of the trunk.
S	E	R	T	U	L	U	M	A collection of scientifically studied plants.
S	E	R	V	I	E	N	T	Servile, Serving, Instrumental, Subordinate, Subject.
S	E	R	V	I	T	O	R	Menial, Male servant.
S	E	S	A	M	O	I	D	Nodular mass of bone or cartilage in a tendon where it passes over a joint.
S	E	S	B	A	N	I	A	A small genus of pinnate-leaved shrubs, herbs or trees.
S	E	S	T	E	R	C	E	An ancient Roman coin.
S	E	S	T	O	L	E	T	Sextuplet.
S	E	T	A	S	I	D	E	Reserved, Earmarked for a special purpose.
S	E	T	I	F	O	R	M	Like a bristle.
S	E	T	P	I	E	C	E	A precisely planned operation, A composition of formal pattern of the arts.
S	E	T	S	C	R	E	W	A machine screw designed to prevent movement.
S	E	T	T	L	I	N	G	Planting, Colonizing, Installing, Ensconcing, Establishing, Resolving, Placing, Concluding.
S	E	T	U	L	O	S	E	Covered with small hairs or bristles.
S	E	V	E	R	E	L	Y	With severity, Badly, Harshly, Painfully, Rigorously, Roughly, Seriously, Gravely.
S	E	V	E	R	I	N	G	Separating, Dissecting, Dividing, Parting, Cutting, Carving, Cleaving, Slicing.
S	E	V	E	R	I	T	Y	Austerity, Harshness.
S	E	W	E	L	L	E	L	Mountain beaver.
S	E	W	E	R	A	G	E	Drainage of domestic wastes.
S	E	X	O	L	O	G	Y	Study of the interaction of the sexes.
S	E	X	T	E	T	T	E	Group of six.
S	E	X	T	U	P	L	E	Sixfold, Being in six parts, Group of six.
S	E	X	U	A	L	L	Y	In a sexual manner.
S	E	Y	M	E	R	I	A	Genus of widely distributed herbs, Mullein foxglove.
S	F	O	R	Z	A	T	O	Direction in music, an accented chord.
S	H	A	B	B	I	E	R	Poorer, More ragged, More dilapidated, More neglected.
S	H	A	B	B	I	L	Y	Meanly, Unfairly, Dishonourably, Despicably, Slovenly.
S	H	A	B	R	A	C	K	A saddlecloth that was used by the European light cavalry.
S	H	A	C	K	I	N	G	Tramping slowly, Plodding.
S	H	A	C	K	L	E	D	Fettered, Chained, Joined, Coupled, Hampered, Curbed, Strapped, Manacled.
S	H	A	D	B	I	R	D	A common sandpiper.
S	H	A	D	B	U	S	H	Juneberry.
S	H	A	D	D	O	C	K	Citrus fruit related to the grapefruit.
S	H	A	D	F	R	O	G	Leopard frog.
S	H	A	D	O	W	E	D	Darkened, Clouded, Obscured, Concealed, Symbolized, Screened, Overcast, Hazed.
S	H	A	F	T	I	N	G	Fitting with a shaft.
S	H	A	G	G	I	N	G	Shredding, Roughing, Making shaggy.
S	H	A	G	R	E	E	N	Untanned leather with a special decoration.
S	H	A	K	E	O	U	T	Downturn in share prices, A slowing down of commercial activity.
S	H	A	L	L	O	O	N	Lightweight fabric used for lining uniforms and coats.
S	H	A	M	A	N	I	C	A belief in trances and ancestral spirits.
S	H	A	M	B	L	E	S	Wreckage, Mess, Hash, Muddle, Botch, Ruin, Slaughter-house, Disorder.
S	H	A	M	E	F	U	L	Disgraceful, Indecent, Ashamed, Disreputable, Dishonourable, Shoddy, Ignominious.
S	H	A	M	M	I	N	G	Cheating, Faking, Assuming, Bluffing, Counterfeiting, Simulating, Feigning, Pretending.
S	H	A	M	R	O	C	K	Trifoliolate plant used as a floral emblem of Ireland.
S	H	A	N	G	H	A	I	Forcing men to serve on ships, Kidnapping, Tricking into a dangerous position.
S	H	A	N	T	I	E	S	Rough crude dwelling places, Seasongs.
S	H	A	N	T	U	N	G	A plain weave fabric with an irregular surface due to wild silk fibres.
S	H	A	P	A	B	L	E	Shapely, Able to be shaped.
S	H	A	R	E	M	A	N	A farmer who shares expenses and produce.
S	H	A	R	K	L	E	T	A small or young shark.
S	H	A	R	P	C	U	T	Cut or engraved with a well-defined impression.
S	H	A	R	P	I	N	G	Pilfering, Raising the pitch in music by a half-step.
S	H	A	R	P	S	E	T	Set at a sharp angle, Ravenous.
S	H	A	S	H	L	I	K	Kabob, Kebab, Cubed meat and vegetables cooked on skewers.
S	H	A	T	T	E	R	Y	Easily shattered.
S	H	A	W	F	O	W	L	Scarecrow.
S	H	E	A	D	I	N	G	One of the divisions of the Isle of Man under the jurisdiction of a chief constable.
S	H	E	A	L	I	N	G	Husked grain.
S	H	E	A	R	H	O	G	A sheep after the first shearing.

1	2	3	4	5	6	7	8	Definition
S	H	E	A	R	I	N	G	Clipping, Severing, Separating, Divesting, Paring, Trimming, Stripping, Shaving.
S	H	E	A	R	M	A	N	One who earns his living by shearing.
S	H	E	A	T	H	E	D	Enclosed, Covered, Plunged, Buried, Blunted, Dulled, Surrounded, Wrapped.
S	H	E	A	T	R	E	E	A rough-barked tropical African tree of hard heavy dark red wood and yielding one fatty nut.
S	H	E	A	V	I	N	G	Gathering and binding into sheaves.
S	H	E	B	E	E	C	H	An Australian timber tree with aromatic wood.
S	H	E	D	D	I	N	G	Dividing, Segregating, Imparting, Releasing, Diffusing, Departing, Scattering, Falling.
S	H	E	E	L	I	N	G	Shielding, A shelter for shepherds, Summer pasture.
S	H	E	E	P	D	I	P	A disinfecting solution for destroying parasites on sheep.
S	H	E	E	P	D	O	G	A dog trained to guide, drive and guard sheep.
S	H	E	E	P	F	L	Y	A fly having destructive larvae that feed on the flesh of live sheep.
S	H	E	E	P	I	S	H	Bashful, Meek, Simple, Timid, Stupid, Embarrassed, Self-conscious.
S	H	E	E	P	N	U	T	Jojoba, A small tree with seeds that yield a valuable oil.
S	H	E	E	P	P	O	D	Locoweed.
S	H	E	E	R	I	N	G	Turning, Deviating, Swerving, Diverting, Deflecting, Pivotting, Whirling, Wheeling.
S	H	E	E	R	L	E	G	One of two spars secured together.
S	H	E	E	T	F	E	D	Description of a printing press.
S	H	E	E	T	I	N	G	Material woven very wide to be used for making sheets.
S	H	E	I	L	I	N	G	Sheeling.
S	H	E	K	I	N	A	H	A belief by Jews and Christians of phenomena manifesting the presence of God.
S	H	E	L	D	U	C	K	Sheldrake, European duck slightly larger than a mallard.
S	H	E	L	L	I	C	E	Ice formed on a sheet of water and remaining when the water is withdrawn.
S	H	E	L	L	I	N	G	Stripping, Hulling, Shucking, Separating, Scaling, Husking, Bombarding.
S	H	E	L	T	E	R	Y	A structure that affords shelter.
S	H	E	L	V	I	N	G	A collection of shelves, Placing on a shelf, Inclining, Dismissing, Sloping.
S	H	E	M	I	T	I	C	Semitic.
S	H	E	P	H	E	R	D	One that tends a flock of sheep, Pastor.
S	H	E	R	A	T	O	N	Style of graceful and elegant inlaid furniture with little or no carving.
S	H	I	E	L	D	E	D	Harboured, Defended, Covered, Fended, Guarded, Protected, Screened, Secured.
S	H	I	E	L	D	E	R	One that shields.
S	H	I	E	L	I	N	G	Sheeling.
S	H	I	F	T	I	L	Y	Elusively, Trickily, Furtively Evasively, Deceitfully, Shadily, Dishonestly, Deviously.
S	H	I	F	T	I	N	G	Moving, Transferring, Distributing, Changing, Altering, Disturbing, Removing, Shuffling.
S	H	I	L	L	I	N	G	A monetary unit.
S	H	I	M	M	I	N	G	Levelling, Filling out, Filling up with putty.
S	H	I	N	B	O	N	E	Bone of the lower leg.
S	H	I	N	G	L	E	D	Covered with shingles, Hair cut and shaped to the nape of the neck, Overlapped.
S	H	I	N	G	L	E	S	Herpes Zoster, Acute inflammation of nerves caused by a virus infection.
S	H	I	N	N	I	N	G	Climbing by using arms and legs without help of a ladder or rope.
S	H	I	P	L	E	S	S	Lacking a ship.
S	H	I	P	L	O	A	D	A Load or cargo of a ship, An indefinitely large amount.
S	H	I	P	M	A	T	E	A fellow sailor.
S	H	I	P	M	E	N	T	Commodity, Consignment, Cargo.
S	H	I	P	P	I	N	G	Passage on a ship, A fleet of ships.
S	H	I	P	W	O	R	M	A marine clam that resembles a worm and is very destructive to wooden wharves or ships.
S	H	I	P	Y	A	R	D	A place where ships are built or repaired.
S	H	I	R	K	I	N	G	Sneaking, Dodging, Frauding, Parrying, Sidestepping, Bilking, Skulking, Cadging.
S	H	I	R	T	I	N	G	A fabric suitable for making men's shirts.
S	H	I	V	E	R	E	D	Shook, Quivered, Trembled, Shattered, Broken, Vibrated, Fragmented, Smashed.
S	H	O	A	L	I	N	G	Becoming shallow.
S	H	O	C	K	I	N	G	Stunning, Fearful, Outraging, Astonishing, Startling, Surprising, Jolting, Insulting.
S	H	O	E	B	I	L	L	A large wading bird related to the storks and herons.
S	H	O	E	H	O	R	N	A curved instrument to aid in putting on a shoe, Foist, Squeeze.
S	H	O	E	L	A	C	E	A thin cord or thong for securing shoes.
S	H	O	E	L	E	S	S	Having no shoe.
S	H	O	G	G	I	N	G	Jolting, Shaking, Jostling, Shoving.
S	H	O	O	T	I	N	G	Discharging, Darting, Wrecking, Firing, Launching, Triggering, Blasting, Destroying.
S	H	O	O	T	O	U	T	A fight to the death.
S	H	O	P	G	I	R	L	Saleswoman.
S	H	O	P	L	I	F	T	To steal goods from a shop.
S	H	O	P	P	I	N	G	Buying produce, Betraying, Arresting, Imprisoning, Hunting.
S	H	O	P	W	O	R	N	Faded, soiled or impaired goods in a store, Bedraggled, Jaded, Trite.
S	H	O	R	T	A	G	E	Deficiency, Failure, Inadequacy, Lack, Curtailment, Pinch, Shortfall.
S	H	O	R	T	A	N	D	Ampersand.
S	H	O	R	T	C	U	T	Bypass, Detour, Shorter route, Quick way to complete a task.
S	H	O	R	T	I	T	E	A mineral consisting of a carbonate of sodium and calcium.
S	H	O	R	T	L	E	G	A fielding position in cricket.

1	2	3	4	5	6	7	8	Definition
S	H	O	R	T	R	U	N	Relatively short period of time, Manufacture of a small quantity.
S	H	O	R	T	S	E	A	Coastwise shipping between ports.
S	H	O	T	F	R	E	E	Scot-free.
S	H	O	T	H	O	L	E	A hole drilled for an explosive charge.
S	H	O	T	T	I	N	G	Making metal shot, Producing wrought iron.
S	H	O	U	L	D	E	R	Part of the body on each side of the neck, Jostle, Hustle, Press, Shove, Push, Bulldoze.
S	H	O	U	T	I	N	G	Yelling, Screaming, Roaring, Bellowing, Hollering, Vociferating, Bawling, Exclaiming loudly.
S	H	O	W	B	I	L	L	Advertising poster.
S	H	O	W	C	A	R	D	Display card.
S	H	O	W	C	A	S	E	Exhibit, Cabinet for displaying wares.
S	H	O	W	D	O	W	N	Final settlement of a dispute.
S	H	O	W	E	R	E	D	Rained, Sprayed, Bathed in a shower, Spattered.
S	H	O	W	R	O	O	M	A place where merchandise is displayed either for sale or on exhibition.
S	H	O	W	Y	A	R	D	A yard for exhibiting livestock.
S	H	R	A	P	N	E	L	Fragments of a shell that has been fired.
S	H	R	E	D	D	E	D	Cut into fine strips, Slivered, Ripped, Lopped.
S	H	R	E	D	D	E	R	A utensil used for cutting, tearing or scraping.
S	H	R	E	W	D	L	Y	Severely, Hutfully, Intensely, Astutely, Knowingly, Wisely, Cannily, Cleverly.
S	H	R	E	W	I	S	H	Ill-tempered, Intractable.
S	H	R	I	E	K	E	D	Screamed, Screeched, Shrilled, Squealed, Squawked, Cried.
S	H	R	I	E	V	A	L	Relating to a sheriff.
S	H	R	I	L	L	E	D	Screeched, Squealed, Screamed, Shrieked.
S	H	R	I	M	P	E	D	Caught shrimps.
S	H	R	I	M	P	E	R	A shrimp fisherman.
S	H	R	I	N	I	N	G	Enshrining.
S	H	R	I	N	K	E	R	One that puts things through a shrinking process.
S	H	R	I	V	I	N	G	Giving absolution, Hearing confession, Pardoning, Purging, Imposing a penance.
S	H	R	O	U	D	E	D	Veiled, Covered, Obscured, Enclosed, Enveloped, Wrapped, Buried, Hidden.
S	H	R	O	V	I	N	G	Merrymaking.
S	H	R	U	G	G	E	D	Gesture of indifference, Raised the shoulders, Fidget, Cowered, Bunched up.
S	H	U	C	K	I	N	G	Peeling, Removing, Stripping, Discarding, Ditching, Rejecting, Shedding, Sloughing.
S	H	U	F	F	L	E	D	Jumbled, Scuffled, Shambled, Dodged, Evaded, Disarranged, Disrupted, Stumbled.
S	H	U	F	F	L	E	R	One that shuffles a pack of playing cards.
S	H	U	N	N	I	N	G	Escaping, Evading, Avoidance, Ducking, Eluding, Rejecting, Despising, Eschewal.
S	H	U	N	P	I	K	E	A side road used to avoid paying toll on a turnpike.
S	H	U	N	T	I	N	G	Sidetracking, Shuttling, Shifting, Switching, Shoving, Turning, Averting, Deflecting.
S	H	U	S	H	I	N	G	Quietening, Silencing, Hushing, Suppressing, Muffling, Repressing, Stilling.
S	H	U	T	D	O	W	N	Suspension, Cessation, Temporary stoppage, Discontinuance.
S	H	U	T	T	I	N	G	Closing, Locking, Sealing, Battening, Bolting, Fastening.
S	I	A	L	I	D	A	E	Family of large insects.
S	I	B	E	R	I	A	N	Characteristic of Siberia.
S	I	B	E	R	I	T	E	Rubellite from Siberia.
S	I	B	E	R	S	K	I	A settler in Siberia.
S	I	B	I	L	A	N	T	Hiss, Whistle, Buzz.
S	I	B	I	L	A	T	E	Same as SIBILANT.
S	I	B	I	L	O	U	S	Sibilant.
S	I	B	Y	L	L	I	C	Sibylline, Prophetic, Mysterious.
S	I	C	E	L	I	O	T	An ancient Greek colony in Italy.
S	I	C	I	L	I	A	N	Characteristic of Sicily.
S	I	C	K	C	A	L	L	Daily roll-call which enables people to report sickness or injury.
S	I	C	K	E	N	E	D	Diseased, Nauseated, Weakened, Impoverished, Impaired, Revolted, Disgusted, Unsettled.
S	I	C	K	E	N	E	R	Overdose, A sickening blow.
S	I	C	K	F	L	A	G	A flag flown to denote quarantine.
S	I	C	K	L	I	E	D	Made sickly.
S	I	C	K	L	I	L	Y	In a sickly fashion.
S	I	C	K	L	I	S	T	A list of people who are sick or indisposed.
S	I	C	K	N	E	S	S	Illness, Malady, Nausea, Queasiness, Vomit, Affliction, Disorder, Infirmity, Disability.
S	I	C	U	L	I	A	N	Relating to an ancient people who inhabited Sicily.
S	I	D	A	L	C	E	A	Genus of mallows.
S	I	D	E	B	E	A	M	Walking beam of a side-lever engine.
S	I	D	E	C	O	M	B	An ornamental comb for a woman's hair.
S	I	D	E	D	I	S	H	A food served as a relish or extra adjunct to main course.
S	I	D	E	D	R	U	M	Snare drum.
S	I	D	E	H	O	L	D	A hold in mountain climbing, A special hold in wrestling.
S	I	D	E	L	I	N	E	An extra money-making occupation in addition to the main position.
S	I	D	E	L	I	N	G	Sideways, Sidelong, Steep, Abrupt, Arduous, Precipitate, Obliquely.
S	I	D	E	L	O	C	K	Lock of hair falling at the side of the face.

8 LETTERS

1	2	3	4	5	6	7	8	
S	I	D	E	L	O	N	G	Laterally, Obliquely, Sideways, Sloping, Sidewise.
S	I	D	E	N	O	T	E	Note of reference put in the margin as an explanation.
S	I	D	E	R	E	A	L	Relating to stars or constellation.
S	I	D	E	R	I	S	M	Phenomenon similar to animal magnetism.
S	I	D	E	R	I	T	E	A native ferrous carbonate.
S	I	D	E	S	H	O	W	Small shows subordinate to the main attraction at fairs and shows.
S	I	D	E	S	L	I	P	To skid sideways.
S	I	D	E	S	M	A	N	Assistant to the churchwarden.
S	I	D	E	S	P	I	N	A special throw of a ball.
S	I	D	E	S	T	E	P	Avoid, Evade, Dodge, Equivocate, Hedge, Skirt, Duck, Parry.
S	I	D	E	T	O	N	E	The sound of a speaker's voice in his own ears.
S	I	D	E	V	I	E	W	A view in profile, A view from the side.
S	I	D	E	W	A	L	K	A pavement for pedestrians.
S	I	D	E	W	A	Y	S	Obliquely, Laterally, Sidelong, Indirectly, Aside, Aslant, Aslope, Slantwise.
S	I	D	E	W	I	N	D	Indirect attack, Illegitimate.
S	I	D	E	W	I	R	E	To fasten with a side stitch.
S	I	D	E	W	I	S	E	Sideways.
S	I	F	F	L	E	U	R	A whistler, An animal that makes a whistling noise.
S	I	F	F	L	I	N	G	Whistling, Hissing.
S	I	G	A	T	O	K	A	A serious leaf spot disease of bananas.
S	I	G	H	T	I	N	G	Aiming, Viewing, Seeing, Presenting, Looking through.
S	I	G	M	A	T	I	C	Forming a tense.
S	I	G	M	O	D	O	N	Genus of rodents, American cotton rats.
S	I	G	N	A	B	L	E	Suitable to be signed.
S	I	G	N	A	L	L	Y	Notably, Unmistakably, Remarkably.
S	I	G	N	I	F	E	R	Standard-bearer.
S	I	G	N	I	F	I	C	Acting as a sign or signal.
S	I	G	N	L	E	S	S	Having no algebraic sign.
S	I	G	N	P	O	S	T	A guidepose on a road, Guide, Beacon.
S	I	K	I	N	N	I	S	A grotesque dance of ancient Greece.
S	I	L	E	N	C	E	D	Stilled, Repressed, Suppressed, Hushed, Quietened, Muffled, Muted, Quelled.
S	I	L	E	N	C	E	R	A device to muffle noise.
S	I	L	E	N	T	L	Y	Noiselessly.
S	I	L	I	C	A	T	E	Insoluble complex metal salts that contain silicon and oxygen.
S	I	L	I	C	I	D	E	A binary compound of silicon.
S	I	L	I	C	I	F	Y	To impregnate with silicate.
S	I	L	I	C	I	U	M	Silicon.
S	I	L	I	C	O	N	E	An organic compound analogous to a ketone.
S	I	L	I	C	U	L	A	Silicle, A pod.
S	I	L	I	C	U	L	E	Same as SILICULA.
S	I	L	K	E	N	E	D	Made silklike, Covered with silk.
S	I	L	K	W	O	R	M	A moth larva that spins a large amount of silk in constructing its cocoon.
S	I	L	L	A	B	U	B	Syllabub.
S	I	L	L	Y	H	O	W	A caul on a newborn infant.
S	I	L	P	H	I	U	M	An extinct plant that was used medicinally by the ancient Greeks.
S	I	L	U	R	I	A	N	Pre-historic era.
S	I	L	U	R	I	S	T	A native of Breckonshire, Wales.
S	I	L	V	E	R	L	Y	An appearance of silver or a silvery sound.
S	I	L	V	I	C	A	L	Relating to the study of forest trees.
S	I	M	A	R	U	B	A	Simarouba, A genus of tropical American shrubs, Marupa.
S	I	M	I	I	D	A	E	Family of primates, Gorillas, Chimpanzees.
S	I	M	I	L	I	Z	E	Liken, Compare.
S	I	M	M	E	R	E	D	Stewed, Boiled, Fermented, Seethed, Bubbled, Churned, Agitated.
S	I	M	O	N	I	A	C	The buying and selling of church office.
S	I	M	P	E	R	E	D	Smirked, Whimpered.
S	I	M	P	E	R	E	R	One that simpers.
S	I	M	P	L	I	F	Y	Abridge, Streamline, Clarify, Explain, Simple, Reduce, Shorten, Disentangle.
S	I	M	P	L	I	S	H	Simple.
S	I	M	P	L	I	S	M	Oversimplification.
S	I	M	U	L	A	T	E	Feign, Imitate, Resemble, Pretend, Assume, Affect, Bluff, Sham.
S	I	N	A	I	T	I	C	Relating to Mount Sinai.
S	I	N	A	P	I	S	M	Mustard plaster.
S	I	N	C	I	P	U	T	Forehead.
S	I	N	E	A	T	E	R	A person hired to eat food placed near a corpse in order to assume the sins of the dead person.
S	I	N	E	C	U	R	E	A remunerative position that requires little work.
S	I	N	E	W	I	N	G	Strengthening.
S	I	N	E	W	O	U	S	Sinewy, Tendinous, Tough, Strong and firm.

1	2	3	4	5	6	7	8	
S	I	N	F	O	N	I	A	Symphony.
S	Y	N	F	U	L	L	Y	Wickedly, Culpably, Unreasonably.
S	I	N	G	A	B	L	E	Suitable for singing.
S	I	N	G	E	I	N	G	Scorching, Burning, Searing.
S	I	N	G	E	R	I	E	Design, decoration or picture in which monkeys are included.
S	I	N	G	L	I	N	G	Parting, Separating, Withdrawing, Concentrating, Selecting, Distinguishing, Picking.
S	I	N	G	S	I	N	G	A West African waterbuck.
S	I	N	G	S	O	N	G	Community singing, Something delivered in a monotonous chant. In a droning fashion.
S	I	N	G	U	L	A	R	Rare, Valuable, Peculiar, Eccentric, Strange, Uncommon, Eminent, Extraordinary.
S	I	N	I	C	I	S	M	Something peculiar to the Chinese.
S	I	N	I	C	I	Z	E	To modify by Chinese influence.
S	I	N	I	G	R	I	N	A crystalline glucoside found in the seeds of black mustard.
S	I	N	I	S	T	E	R	Prejudicial, Evil, Bad, Corruptive, Fraudulent, Portentous, Ominous, Dangerous.
S	I	N	K	H	O	L	E	A hollow place, Depression, Cesspool, Unprofitable venture.
S	I	N	N	F	E	I	N	A militant Irish home-rule society.
S	I	N	O	G	R	A	M	A Chinese written character.
S	I	N	O	L	O	G	Y	The study of Chinese culture and language.
S	I	N	O	P	H	I	L	A fondness for all things Chinese.
S	I	N	U	A	T	E	D	Wound, Bent, Curved, Intricate.
S	I	P	H	O	N	A	L	Resembling a siphon.
S	I	P	H	O	N	E	D	Drained, Sucked, Drawn off, Withdrew, Pumped, Conveyed, Conducted, Carried.
S	I	P	H	O	N	E	T	Honey tube of a aphid.
S	I	P	H	O	N	I	C	Relating to a siphon.
S	I	R	E	L	E	S	S	Fatherless.
S	I	R	E	N	I	A	N	Family of large aquatic mammals, Dugong, Manatee.
S	I	R	E	N	O	I	D	Relating to the order of Sirenian.
S	I	R	I	A	S	I	S	Sunstroke.
S	I	R	V	E	N	T	E	Moral or religious song of Provencal troubadours.
S	I	S	C	O	W	E	T	Large lake trout found in the Greak Lakes.
S	I	S	T	E	R	L	Y	In the manner of a sister, Affectionate, Platonic.
S	I	T	O	L	O	G	Y	Science of nutrition and dietetics.
S	I	T	U	A	T	E	D	Located, Circumstanced, Positioned, Set, Sited.
S	I	T	Z	B	A	T	H	A hip bath, A bath used for therapeutic effect.
S	I	X	P	E	N	C	E	A coin representing half a shilling.
S	I	X	P	E	N	N	Y	Something cheap and trashy.
S	I	X	T	I	E	T	H	Number of sixty, One of sixty equal parts.
S	I	Z	E	A	B	L	E	Considerable, Large.
S	I	Z	I	N	E	S	S	Viscousness.
S	I	Z	I	N	G	U	P	Evaluating something, Estimating.
S	I	Z	Z	L	I	N	G	Very hot, Burning, Searing, Hissing, Scorcher, Agitating.
S	K	A	N	D	H	A	S	The five transitory personal elements of body perception.
S	K	E	A	N	D	H	U	A dagger formerly worn by Scottish Highlanders.
S	K	E	L	E	T	A	L	Skeleton, Emaciated.
S	K	E	L	E	T	O	N	Bony framework, Protective structure, Outline, A shameful secret.
S	K	E	L	L	O	C	H	Scream.
S	K	E	T	C	H	E	D	Drew, Described, Outlined, Roughed, Simulated, Characterized, Depicted, Designed.
S	K	E	T	C	H	E	R	One that sketches.
S	K	E	W	B	A	C	K	A course of masonry involving a segmental arch.
S	K	E	W	B	A	L	D	Variegated.
S	K	E	W	E	R	E	D	Transfixed, Pierced, Impaled, Lanced, Speared, Spiked.
S	K	I	A	G	R	A	M	Radiograph.
S	K	I	D	D	I	N	G	Sliding, Slueing, Skewing, Plummeting, Dipping, Dropping, Plunging, Tumbling.
S	K	I	L	L	E	S	S	Lacking knowledge or skill.
S	K	I	L	L	I	N	G	Old fashioned Scandanavian monetary unit.
S	K	I	M	M	I	L	K	Milk from which the cream has been removed.
S	K	I	M	M	I	N	G	Scanning, Grazing, Glancing, Kissing, Skipping, Removing from the top.
S	K	I	M	M	I	T	Y	A public ridiculing of a henpecked, deceived or unfaithful husband or a shrewish wife.
S	K	I	M	P	I	N	G	Scrimping, Scamping, Stinting, Scraping, Sparing, Pinching.
S	K	I	N	D	E	E	P	Superficial, Not thorough or lasting.
S	K	I	N	L	E	S	S	Having no skin or casing, Sensitive, Easily moved.
S	K	I	N	N	I	N	G	Peeling, Scraping, Rubbing, Paring, Flaying, Fleecing, Stripping, Criticizing.
S	K	I	N	T	L	E	D	Bricks stacked for drying.
S	K	I	N	W	O	O	L	Inferior wool taken from a dead sheep.
S	K	I	P	D	E	N	T	An openwork fabric woven by a special process.
S	K	I	P	E	T	A	R	An Albanian.
S	K	I	P	J	A	C	K	A young conceited fop, Family of fishes that play on the surface.
S	K	I	P	P	I	N	G	Capering, Scooting, Cavorting, Hopping, Skimming, Jumping, Misfiring, Scampering.

1	2	3	4	5	6	7	8	
S	K	I	R	L	I	N	G	Shrieking, Shrill tone, Screaming, Playing the bagpipes.
S	K	I	R	M	I	S	H	Clash, Affray, Brush, Fray, Melee, Assault, Ambush, Encounter.
S	K	I	R	T	I	N	G	Bordering, Defining, Edging, Fringing, Surrounding, Bypassing, Circumventing, Sidestepping.
S	K	I	T	T	I	S	H	Capricious, Irresponsible, Variable, Unstable, Restive, Coy, Bashful, Shy.
S	K	I	T	T	L	E	S	A game played by rolling a ball to knock down pins.
S	K	U	A	G	U	L	L	A large and aggressive gull.
S	K	U	L	K	I	N	G	Sneaking, Lurking, Malingering, Slinking, Shirking, Slipping, Creeping, Stealing.
S	K	U	L	L	C	A	P	A close-fitting brimless cap.
S	K	Y	L	I	G	H	T	An opening in a roof or deck with a translucent cover to improve the quality of light.
S	K	Y	P	I	L	O	T	Chaplain, Clergyman.
S	K	Y	S	C	A	P	E	A picture of mostly sky.
S	K	Y	S	H	A	D	E	A screen on a camera to reduce the light from the sky.
S	L	A	B	B	I	N	G	A process in coal-mining.
S	L	A	B	L	I	N	E	A line on a ship to haul a sail.
S	L	A	C	K	I	N	G	Loosening, Relaxing, Easing, Untightening, Slowing down.
S	L	A	I	S	T	E	R	Slop around, Messing around.
S	L	A	M	M	I	N	G	Banging, Knocking, Beating, Striking, Slapping, Bashing, Pounding, Whacking.
S	L	A	N	G	I	L	Y	In a slangy manner.
S	L	A	N	G	I	N	G	Cheating, Swindling, Abusing, Censuring, coarsely, Duping.
S	L	A	N	T	I	N	G	Glancing, Sloping, Trending, Angling, Cutting, Striking, Diagonal, Biased.
S	L	A	P	B	A	N	G	Precipitately, Rough manner, Excessive force.
S	L	A	P	D	A	S	H	Haphazard, Slipshod, Sloppy, Directly, Right, Smack.
S	L	A	P	J	A	C	K	Pancake, Flapjack, A card game.
S	L	A	P	P	I	N	G	Censuring, Striking, Cuffing, Smacking, Spanking, Swatting, Boxing, Socking.
S	L	A	S	H	I	N	G	Lashing, Whipping, Cracking, Shortening, Cutting, Exercising, Pelting, Dashing.
S	L	A	T	T	E	R	N	An untidy slovenly person, Slut, Prostitute.
S	L	A	V	E	R	E	D	Drooled, Slobbered, Salivated, Fawned, Flattered, Dribbled, Cringed, Cowered.
S	L	A	V	O	N	I	C	Slavic.
S	L	E	A	V	I	N	G	Separating into filaments.
S	L	E	D	D	I	N	G	Sledging, Using a sledge.
S	L	E	D	G	I	N	G	Transporting on a sledge.
S	L	E	E	K	I	N	G	Covering up, Glossing over, Slicking.
S	L	E	E	P	F	U	L	Marked by sleep.
S	L	E	E	P	I	L	Y	In a sleepy fashion.
S	L	E	E	P	I	N	G	In a state of torpor, Slumbering, Dozing, Napping, Reposing, Comatose.
S	L	E	E	T	I	N	G	Showering with sleet.
S	L	I	C	K	I	N	G	Polishing, Levelling, Plastering, Sprucing, Grooming, Slipping, Refining, Smartening.
S	L	I	C	K	E	N	S	Thin layer of fine silt deposited by flood waters.
S	L	I	D	A	B	L	E	Capable of being slid.
S	L	I	G	H	T	E	D	Neglected, Disregarded, Discounted, Failed, Forgotten, Ignored, Despised, Overlooked.
S	L	I	M	E	P	I	T	A pit in which ore slimes are deposited.
S	L	I	M	M	I	N	G	Giving an impression of slenderness, Loafing, Loosing weight, Slenderizing.
S	L	I	M	N	E	S	S	State of being slim.
S	L	I	N	G	I	N	G	Suspending, Cutting, Throwing, Casting, Heaving, Launching, Pitching, Tossing.
S	L	I	N	K	I	N	G	Creeping, Stealing, Lurking, Moving furtively, Stealing, Skulking, Sneaking.
S	L	I	P	K	N	O	T	A knot that slips along the rope.
S	L	I	P	O	V	E	R	Sweater, A pullover that slips over the head.
S	L	I	P	P	E	R	Y	Greasy, Slick, Slithery, Changeable, Shifty, Uncertain, Unstable, Unsteady.
S	L	I	P	P	I	N	G	Sliding, Slinking, Creeping, Skidding, Declining, Plummetting, Crashing, Eluding.
S	L	I	P	R	A	I	L	Set of movable rails that can be used as a gateway.
S	L	I	P	S	H	O	D	Shabby, Slovenly, Slovenly, Unkempt, Dishevelled, Sloppy, Bedraggled, Careless.
S	L	I	P	S	L	O	P	Twaddle, Inane, Wishy-washy, Nonsense, Claptrap, Bunk, Poppy-cock, Drivel.
S	L	I	T	H	E	R	Y	Having a slippery surface, Slick, Greasy, Slippery, Slippy.
S	L	I	T	T	I	N	G	Slashing, Severing, Shredding, Cutting, Gashing, Piercing, Slicing, Splitting.
S	L	I	V	E	R	E	D	Sliced, Splintered, Fragmented, Shaved, Minced, Pulverized, Crushed, Mashed.
S	L	O	B	B	E	R	Y	Muddy, Slushy, Dirty, Slack, Slovenly, Effusive, Gushing, Sloppy.
S	L	O	G	G	I	N	G	Striking, Beating, Scoring, Driving, Clouting, Plodding, Toiling, Trudging.
S	L	O	M	M	A	C	K	Messy, Untidy, Awkward, Uncouth.
S	L	O	P	B	O	W	L	A small basin on the table to hold the dregs of tea or coffee from the cups.
S	L	O	P	P	A	I	L	A pail for household slops.
S	L	O	P	P	I	N	G	Spilling, Splashing, Gushing, Gobbling, Sloshing, Spattering, Guzzling, Wolfing.
S	L	O	P	S	H	O	P	A shop that sells cheap ready-made clothes.
S	L	O	P	W	O	R	K	Manufacture of cheap ready-made clothes.
S	L	O	S	H	I	N	G	Floundering, Guzzling, Swilling, Bashing, Striking, Slamming.
S	L	O	T	H	F	U	L	Inactive, Indolent, Laziness, Idling, Languor, Lethargy, Torpidity.
S	L	O	T	T	I	N	G	Cutting into slices, Slitting, Grooving, Putting into a slot.
S	L	O	U	C	H	E	D	Slumped, Drooped, Bent, Depressed, Lolled, Loafed, Lounged, Stooped.

1	2	3	4	5	6	7	8	
S	L	O	U	G	H	E	D	Shed, Shelled, Husked, Abandoned, Discarded, Skinned, Moulted, Rejected.
S	L	O	V	E	N	L	Y	Negligently, Unkempt, Carelessly, Messily, Sloppily, Untidy.
S	L	O	V	E	N	R	Y	Slovenliness.
S	L	O	W	D	O	W	N	To reduce capacity or productivity, Slackening, Downtrend, Inactivity, Strike, Walkout.
S	L	O	W	N	E	S	S	Tardiness, Inactivity, Sluggishness, Slackness.
S	L	O	W	W	O	R	M	Blindworm.
S	L	U	B	B	I	N	G	Drawing out and twisting yarns to weave an uneven surface.
S	L	U	G	G	A	R	D	Lazy, Idler, Inactive, Loafer, Laggard, Dawdler, Lazybones, Slow-coach.
S	L	U	G	G	I	N	G	Loitering, Delaying, Striking, Fighting, Slamming, Smashing, Walloping, Clobbering.
S	L	U	G	G	I	S	H	Torpid, Indolent, Lethargic, Dull, Stagnant, Comatose, Stupid, Slow.
S	L	U	G	H	O	R	N	Horn, Trumpet.
S	L	U	I	C	I	N	G	Flushing, Dousing, Pouring, Flowing, Gushing, Streaming, Surging, Drenching.
S	L	U	M	B	E	R	Y	Slumberous.
S	L	U	M	M	I	N	G	To visit the slums in vulgar curiosity.
S	L	U	M	P	I	N	G	Falling, Sinking, Collapsing, Declining, Sagging, Slipping, Settling, Toppling.
S	L	U	R	R	I	E	D	Smeared, Smirched.
S	L	U	R	R	I	N	G	Slipping, Sliding, Skidding, Neglecting, Discounting, Slighting, Maligning, Defaming.
S	L	U	S	H	I	N	G	Sluicing, Giving a protective coating, Sloshing.
S	L	U	T	T	E	R	Y	Sluttishness.
S	L	U	T	T	I	S	H	Slovenly, Disorderly, Drab, Bedraggled, Slatternly.
S	L	Y	B	O	O	T	S	A tricky person, Scamp, Cunning, Mischievous.
S	L	Y	G	O	O	S	E	Sheldrake.
S	M	A	C	K	I	N	G	Smelling, Suggesting, Stinking, Kissing, Slapping, Cuffing, Clouting, Spanking.
S	M	A	L	L	A	L	E	A weak ale with little malt and no hops.
S	M	A	L	L	E	S	T	Youngest, Slightest, Least, Narrowest, Most limited, Meanest, Remotest.
S	M	A	L	L	E	R	S	Minor, Lesser, Unimportant.
S	M	A	L	L	I	S	H	Small, Little, Petite, Trivial, Minor, Secondary, Paltry.
S	M	A	L	L	P	O	X	An acute contagious virus disease.
S	M	A	L	T	I	N	E	A tin-white or gray isometric mineral of metallic lustre.
S	M	A	L	T	I	T	E	Same as SMALTINE.
S	M	A	R	T	I	N	G	Stinging, Pricking, Tingling, Hurting.
S	M	A	S	H	H	I	T	A highly popular book, film, actor, song or any form of art, fashion or entertainment.
S	M	A	S	H	I	N	G	Shattering, Splitting, Battering, Mashing, Pressing, Executing, Destroying, Demolishing.
S	M	E	A	R	I	N	G	Daubing, Besmirching, Dullying, Smothering, Plastering, Coating, Tainting, Defaming.
S	M	E	L	L	I	N	G	Inhaling, Scenting, Sniffing, Stinking, Detecting, Perceiving, Savouring, Reeking.
S	M	E	L	L	O	U	T	To ferret out.
S	M	E	L	T	E	R	Y	Foundry.
S	M	E	L	T	I	N	G	Melting, Fusing, Refining, Reducing.
S	M	I	R	C	H	E	D	Sullied, Soiled, Tarnished, Smeared, Stained, Discredited, Begrimed, Into disrepute.
S	M	I	R	K	I	N	G	Simpering, Smiling in an affected way, Grinning, Leering, Sneering.
S	M	I	T	H	E	R	Y	A smithy where a blacksmith follows his trade.
S	M	I	T	H	I	N	G	Working with metal, Forging metal on an anvil.
S	M	I	T	H	I	T	E	A mineral consisting of a silver arsenic sulfide.
S	M	O	C	K	I	N	G	Embroidering with a special type of gathering stitch.
S	M	O	K	A	B	L	E	Fit for smoking.
S	M	O	K	E	B	O	X	Part of a steam boiler between flue and chimney.
S	M	O	K	E	D	R	Y	To cure or dry by smoking.
S	M	O	O	T	H	E	D	Levelled, Evened, Refined, Polished, Soothed, Palliated, Flattened, Sleeked.
S	M	O	O	T	H	E	N	Even, Flatten, Flush, Level, Plane.
S	M	O	O	T	H	E	R	Milder, Blander, More suave.
S	M	O	O	T	H	L	Y	Evenly, Flatly, Uniformly, Easily, Effortlessly, Freely, Lightly, Readily.
S	M	O	R	Z	A	T	O	Direction in music, dying away, softer and softer.
S	M	O	T	H	E	R	Y	Stifling, Smothering.
S	M	O	U	L	D	E	R	To burn and smoke without a flame, Try to suppress anger.
S	M	U	D	G	I	N	G	Soiling, Begriming, Daubing, Dirtying, Fouling, Tarnishing, Smearing, Tainting.
S	M	U	G	G	I	N	G	Smartening, Sprucing.
S	M	U	G	G	L	E	D	Imported or exported secretly and in violation of the law.
S	M	U	G	G	L	E	R	One that smuggles.
S	M	U	G	N	E	S	S	State of being smug, Self-satisfied.
S	M	U	T	B	A	L	L	The spore mass where the host's ovary is converted.
S	M	U	T	C	H	E	D	Soiled, Blotted, Smutted, Sooted, Grimed, Defiled, Sullied, Tainted.
S	N	A	C	K	B	A	R	A public eating bar where food and drink is consumed standing at a counter.
S	N	A	F	F	L	E	D	Equipped with a snaffle bridle, Restrained, Checked, Purloined, Stolen, Robbed, Filched.
S	N	A	G	B	O	A	T	Inland steamboat equipped to clear debris from its path.
S	N	A	G	G	I	N	G	Trimming roughly, Catching, Hooking, Interfering, Interrupting.
S	N	A	I	L	E	R	Y	A place where edible snails are bred and fattened for market.
S	N	A	K	E	E	E	L	Family of scaleless eels often resembling venomous sea snakes.

1	2	3	4	5	6	7	8	Definition
S	N	A	P	P	I	N	G	Barking, Snarling, Growling, Grumbling, Snorting, Yanking, Jerking, Lurching.
S	N	A	P	P	I	S	H	Irritable, Fractious, Querulous, Waspish, Testy, Irascible, Cutting, Morose.
S	N	A	P	S	H	O	T	A casual photograph.
S	N	A	P	W	E	E	D	Jewelweed.
S	N	A	R	L	I	N	G	Growling, Scolding, Complaining, Snapping, Barking, Complicating, Entangling, Muddling.
S	N	A	T	C	H	E	D	Grasped, Seized, Clutched, Grabbed, Wrenched, Yanked, Kidnapped, Abducted.
S	N	A	T	C	H	E	R	Kidnapper, Thief.
S	N	A	Z	Z	I	E	R	More flashy, More outstanding in style.
S	N	E	A	K	C	U	P	One who fails to drink his share.
S	N	E	A	K	I	N	G	Furtive, Underhand, Mean, Niggardly, Paltry, Lurking, Slinking.
S	N	E	E	R	I	N	G	Leering, Smirking, Scoffing, Mocking, Jeering, Taunting, Belittling, Facial contortion.
S	N	E	E	Z	I	N	G	Spasmodic nasal expiration of breath, Despising.
S	N	I	C	K	I	N	G	To make a clicking sound, Snippy.
S	N	I	F	F	I	N	G	Smelling with audible inhalation, Expressing disdain, Be contemptuous, Inhaling.
S	N	I	G	G	L	E	D	Crept, Crawled, Sneaked.
S	N	I	P	P	I	N	G	Clipping, Snatching, Filching, Chipping, Curbing, Checking.
S	N	I	P	S	N	A	P	Clever quick repartee.
S	N	I	T	C	H	E	R	Informer, Stool-pigeon.
S	N	I	V	E	L	L	Y	Tearful, Whiny, Whimpery.
S	N	O	B	B	E	R	Y	Snobbishness.
S	N	O	B	B	I	S	H	Characteristic of a snob. Feeling of superiority.
S	N	O	B	B	I	S	M	Snobbery.
S	N	O	B	L	I	N	G	Young or petty snob.
S	N	O	O	P	I	N	G	Prying, Looking, Searching, Poking, Peeking, Peeping, Peering, Interfering.
S	N	O	O	Z	I	N	G	Dozing, Drowsing, Sleeping, Napping, Catnapping.
S	N	O	R	T	I	N	G	Forcing air through the nose. Exclaiming, Expressing strong feelings by puffing.
S	N	O	W	B	A	L	L	Small round mass of snow pressed hard together by hands.
S	N	O	W	B	A	N	K	Slope of snow.
S	N	O	W	B	I	R	D	Ivory gull, A finch, Cocaine addict, Skier.
S	N	O	W	B	O	O	T	A boot designed for wear in the snow.
S	N	O	W	D	R	O	P	A bulbous European herb bearing white flowers that appears in the very early spring.
S	N	O	W	F	A	L	L	A fall of snow measured in a specific time period.
S	N	O	W	L	I	N	E	The area above which snow remains throughout the year.
S	N	O	W	S	H	E	D	A shelter to protect against snowslides.
S	N	O	W	S	H	O	E	A device worn to prevent sinking into the snow when walking.
S	N	O	W	S	L	I	P	An avalanche of snow.
S	N	O	W	S	U	I	T	A one-piece winter suit similar to ski-clothing.
S	N	O	W	W	O	R	M	A genus of worm that lives in or on snow.
S	N	U	B	B	I	N	G	Rebuking, Scolding, Upbraiding, Ostracizing, Ignoring, Checking, Suppressing, Sneering.
S	N	U	B	B	I	S	H	Somewhat snub.
S	N	U	B	N	O	S	E	A short blunt nose that is slightly turned up at the tip.
S	N	U	F	F	B	O	X	A small box used for holding snuff.
S	N	U	F	F	L	E	D	Sniffed, Snivelled, Whimpered, Spoke in a nasal manner.
S	N	U	F	F	L	E	R	One that snuffles.
S	N	U	F	F	L	E	S	Respiratory disorder in animals characterized by sniffling.
S	N	U	G	G	E	R	Y	A snug cosy place.
S	N	U	G	G	I	N	G	Nestling, Snuggling, Hiding.
S	N	U	G	G	L	E	D	Cuddled, Nestled, Burrowed, Croodled, Nuzzled.
S	N	U	G	N	E	S	S	State of being snug, Warm and comfortable.
S	O	A	P	B	A	R	K	The bark of a tree that yields a soapy lather.
S	O	A	P	F	I	S	H	A family of fishes with scales that are soapy to the touch.
S	O	A	P	R	O	C	K	Steatite.
S	O	A	P	S	U	D	S	Froth on soapy water.
S	O	A	P	T	E	S	T	Testing the hardness of water with a soap solution.
S	O	A	P	T	R	E	E	A tree that yields saponin.
S	O	A	P	W	E	E	D	Soap plant.
S	O	A	P	W	O	O	D	Wild pear.
S	O	A	P	W	O	R	T	European perennial herb, Cowherb.
S	O	B	E	R	I	Z	E	To become sober.
S	O	B	R	A	L	I	A	Genus of tropical American terrestial orchids.
S	O	B	R	I	E	T	Y	State of being sober.
S	O	B	S	T	O	R	Y	Sentimental story to evoke sympathy.
S	O	B	S	T	U	F	F	Sob story designed to make a strong emotional appeal.
S	O	C	A	L	L	E	D	Commonly named, Named to deceive.
S	O	C	I	A	B	L	E	Affable, Companionable, Friendly, Congenial, Cordial, Genial, Convivial, Gregarious.
S	O	C	I	A	B	L	Y	In a sociable manner.
S	O	C	I	A	L	L	Y	In a social manner.

1	2	3	4	5	6	7	8	Definition
S	O	C	I	A	T	R	Y	Group psychotherapy of a special type.
S	O	C	I	E	T	A	L	Social.
S	O	C	I	N	I	A	N	Relating to Socinus.
S	O	C	K	E	T	E	D	Secured in a socket.
S	O	C	M	A	N	R	Y	Sokemanry, A medieval tenure of land.
S	O	C	R	A	T	I	C	A follower of Socrates.
S	O	D	A	L	I	M	E	Granular mixture of calcium hydroxide with sodium hydroxide.
S	O	D	A	L	I	T	E	A mineral consisting of a sodium aluminium silicate with some chlorine.
S	O	D	A	L	I	T	Y	Brotherhood, Community, Fraternity, Club.
S	O	D	A	M	I	D	E	Sodium amide.
S	O	D	A	S	O	A	P	Hard soap made with sodium hydroxide.
S	O	D	D	E	N	E	D	Soaked, Saturated, Caused hardship, Drenched, Seethed, Impregnated, Soused, Steeped.
S	O	F	T	E	N	E	D	Assuaged, Mitigated, Mollified, Enervated, Lowered, Devaluated, Depreciated, Underrated.
S	O	F	T	E	N	E	R	A worker who softens hides or skins.
S	O	F	T	L	I	N	G	Weakling, Soft and delicate.
S	O	F	T	N	E	S	S	Gentleness, Smoothness, Mildness, Sleekness.
S	O	F	T	S	H	O	E	Tap dancing in soft shoes without metal taps.
S	O	F	T	S	O	A	P	Semi-liquid soap.
S	O	F	T	W	A	R	E	Data necessary for the operation of computers.
S	O	F	T	W	O	O	D	Wood of a coniferous tree.
S	O	I	L	L	E	S	S	Carried on without soil.
S	O	I	L	P	I	P	E	Sewage pipe.
S	O	L	A	C	I	N	G	Consoling, Comforting, Entertaining, Amusing, Allaying, Assuaging, Soothing, Cheering.
S	O	L	A	N	D	E	R	A protective case for books and documents.
S	O	L	A	N	I	N	E	A bitter crystalline glycosidal alkaloid.
S	O	L	A	R	I	S	M	Interpretation of legends in connection with the sun.
S	O	L	A	R	I	U	M	A room where sunlight penetrates and is used for health, cosmetic and medical reasons.
S	O	L	A	R	I	Z	E	Expose to sunlight.
S	O	L	A	S	T	E	R	A type genus of starfishes.
S	O	L	A	T	I	U	M	Compensation.
S	O	L	D	E	R	E	D	United, Adhered, Closed, Repaired.
S	O	L	D	E	R	E	R	A worker who repairs with solder.
S	O	L	D	I	E	R	Y	Military, A body of soldiers.
S	O	L	E	C	I	S	M	An ungrammatical combination of words in a sentence, Deviation from the normal.
S	O	L	E	C	I	Z	E	Speaking incorrectly.
S	O	L	E	M	N	L	Y	Formally, Grandly, Seriously, Earnestly, Gravely, Sedately, Soberly.
S	O	L	E	N	E	S	S	State of being sole, Singleness.
S	O	L	E	N	I	A	L	Involving a runner of a plant.
S	O	L	F	A	I	S	T	User of the tonic sol-fa system in music.
S	O	L	I	D	A	R	Y	Characterized by community of interests.
S	O	L	I	D	I	F	Y	Harden, Congeal, Indurate, Set, Compress, Contract.
S	O	L	I	D	I	S	H	Comparatively solid.
S	O	L	I	D	I	T	Y	Density, Compactness, Volume, Being solid.
S	O	L	I	T	A	R	Y	Single, Individual, Sole, Alone, Reserved, Distant.
S	O	L	I	T	U	D	E	Isolation, Seclusion, Uniqueness, Remote, Dearth, Withdrawal, Detachment, Quarantine.
S	O	L	L	E	R	E	T	Flexible steel shoe that was part of a medieval armour.
S	O	L	O	D	I	Z	E	To develop through dealkalized processes.
S	O	L	O	D	I	A	N	Constituting solod.
S	O	L	O	N	I	A	N	Relating to Solon, the Athenian law-giver.
S	O	L	S	T	I	C	E	Furthest or highest point, Limit, Ecliptic point.
S	O	L	U	T	I	O	N	Explanation, Answer, Result, Deliverance, Disruption, Discharge, Break, Dispersion.
S	O	L	U	T	I	V	E	Laxative.
S	O	L	V	A	B	L	E	Soluble.
S	O	L	V	E	N	C	Y	State of being solvent, Able to meet all financial commitments.
S	O	M	A	T	I	S	T	One who treats mental disorders by investigating brain lesions and physical conditions.
S	O	M	A	T	O	M	E	Somite, The body segment of an animal.
S	O	M	B	R	E	R	O	A felt or straw hat with a wide rolled brim.
S	O	M	B	R	O	U	S	Sombre, Gloomy, Doleful.
S	O	M	E	B	O	D	Y	Indeterminate person, Person of some importance.
S	O	M	E	G	A	T	E	Somehow, Somewhere.
S	O	M	E	R	S	E	T	Somersault.
S	O	M	E	T	I	M	E	Once, Occasionally, Formerly, Bygone, Erstwhile, Late, Onetime, Past.
S	O	M	E	W	H	A	T	Something unspecified, Slightly.
S	O	M	E	W	H	E	N	Sometime.
S	O	M	N	I	F	I	C	Somniferous, Soporific, Sleep-inducing.
S	O	N	A	N	T	A	L	Syllabic.
S	O	N	A	T	I	N	A	A short sonata.

1	2	3	4	5	6	7	8	
S	O	N	A	T	I	O	N	Sounding, Making noise.
S	O	N	G	B	I	R	D	A bird that utters musical notes, A female singer.
S	O	N	G	B	O	O	K	A collection of songs or hymns.
S	O	N	G	L	E	S	S	Not given to song.
S	O	N	G	S	T	E	R	A skilled singer, Poet.
S	O	N	I	N	L	A	W	The husband of one's daughter.
S	O	N	O	B	U	O	Y	A buoy equipped with instruments to detect unusual noise and to transmit information.
S	O	N	O	R	I	T	Y	Resonance.
S	O	N	O	R	O	U	S	Resonant, Consonant, Resounding, Ringing, Vibrant, Rhetorical, Bombastic, Flowery.
S	O	O	T	H	I	N	G	Placating, Mollifying, Alleviating, Palliating, Calming, Composing, Consoling, Tranquilizing.
S	O	O	T	H	S	A	Y	Predict, Foretell, Prophesy, Omen, Portent.
S	O	P	H	E	R	I	C	Relating to literature of scribes.
S	O	P	H	E	R	I	M	Scribe.
S	O	P	O	R	O	S	E	Sleepiness.
S	O	R	B	A	R	I	A	Small genus of Asiatic shrubs.
S	O	R	B	I	T	A	N	An inner anhydride of sorbitol.
S	O	R	B	I	T	O	L	A crystalline faintly sweet hexahydroxy alcohol.
S	O	R	B	O	N	N	E	University of Paris.
S	O	R	C	E	R	E	R	Magician, Wizard, Conjurer, Enchanter, Warlock, Necromancer.
S	O	R	D	I	D	L	Y	Ignobly, Basely, Slatternly, Grubbily, Meanly, Scurvily, Foully.
S	O	R	E	D	I	U	M	Vegetative buds on lichens.
S	O	R	E	H	E	A	D	A person easily angered, Grouch, Complainer, Grouser, Grumbler, Malcontent.
S	O	R	E	N	E	S	S	Painfulness, Distress, Violence, Severity.
S	O	R	I	C	I	N	E	Relating to a shrew.
S	O	R	O	R	A	T	E	The marriage of a man with a sister or sisters of his first wife.
S	O	R	O	R	I	T	Y	Sisterhood, Club of girls.
S	O	R	O	R	I	Z	E	Fellowship of girls.
S	O	R	P	T	I	O	N	Absorption.
S	O	R	R	O	W	E	D	Grieved, Lamented, Mourned, Groaned, Moaned, Sobbed.
S	O	R	R	O	W	E	R	Mourner.
S	O	R	T	A	B	L	E	Suitable, Befitting, Proper.
S	O	R	T	M	E	N	T	Assortment.
S	O	T	A	D	E	A	N	Characteristic of ancient Green satirical and licentious poet.
S	O	T	E	R	I	A	L	Relating to salvation.
S	O	U	C	H	O	N	G	Chinese black tea leaves.
S	O	U	G	H	I	N	G	Moaning, Sighing, Humming, Whistling, Chanting.
S	O	U	L	B	E	L	L	Passing bell.
S	O	U	L	L	E	S	S	Spiritless, Having no soul.
S	O	U	L	S	C	O	T	Mortuary fee, Present to clergy from a deceased estate.
S	O	U	L	S	H	O	T	Same as SOUL-SCOT.
S	O	U	L	S	I	C	K	Spiritually ill, Dejected, Depressed.
S	O	U	N	D	B	O	W	The part of the bell struck by the clapper.
S	O	U	N	D	I	N	G	Resounding, Summoning, Playing, Striking, Inclining, Emitting, Reverberating, Proclaiming.
S	O	U	R	B	A	L	L	A peevish person, Grouch. A sweet with a tart flavour.
S	O	U	R	B	U	S	H	French Mulberry.
S	O	U	R	C	A	K	E	A sour leavened cake of oatmeal or rye.
S	O	U	R	D	O	C	K	Dock with sour juice, Sheep sorrel.
S	O	U	R	J	A	C	K	Jackfruit.
S	O	U	R	N	E	S	S	Acidity, Discontent, Peevishness, Asperity, Tartness, Unhappiness, Sharpness, Bitterness.
S	O	U	T	H	E	R	N	Coming from the South.
S	O	U	T	H	I	N	G	Difference in latitude to the south from the last point of reckoning.
S	O	U	V	E	N	I	R	Keepsake, Memory, Recollection, Memento, Relic, Token, Trophy, Memorial.
S	O	W	B	E	L	L	Y	Fat salt pork.
S	O	W	B	R	E	A	D	A common wild cyclamen.
S	O	Y	B	E	A	N	S	Annual legume whose seeds yield valuable products.
S	O	Z	Z	L	I	N	G	Intoxicating, Splashing, Sousing, Lolling, Lounging.
S	P	A	C	E	B	A	R	A bar on a typewriter which moves the carriage one space for each depression.
S	P	A	C	E	M	A	N	Visitor to earth from outer space, Astronaut.
S	P	A	C	I	O	U	S	Vast, Roomy, Wide, Expansive, Comprehensive, Ample, Commodious, Extensive.
S	P	A	D	I	L	L	E	The highest trump in the card game of solo.
S	P	A	D	R	O	O	N	A light sword suitable for cutting and thrusting.
S	P	A	G	Y	R	I	C	Alchemic, Chemical.
S	P	A	L	L	I	N	G	Breaking with a hammer, Exfoliating.
S	P	A	L	P	E	E	N	Common labourer, Migratory worker, Rascal.
S	P	A	N	D	R	E	L	Ornamented space between arches or on walls.
S	P	A	N	D	R	I	L	Same as SPANDREL.
S	P	A	N	G	L	E	D	Sparkled, Glistened, Glimmered, Twinkled, Shimmered, Glittered, Scintillated, Gleamed.

1	2	3	4	5	6	7	8	
S	P	A	N	G	L	E	R	One that spangles.
S	P	A	N	I	A	R	D	Inhabitant of Spain, A spear grass of New Zealand.
S	P	A	N	K	I	N	G	Slapping, Smacking, Clouting, Awfully, Extremely, Whacking, Whopping, Dashing.
S	P	A	N	L	O	N	G	The length of a span.
S	P	A	N	N	I	N	G	Traversing, Encompassing, Bridging, Seizing, Grasping, Extending, Measuring, Arching.
S	P	A	N	R	O	O	F	A common roof having two slopes with one ridge.
S	P	A	R	A	B	L	E	A small headless nail used to repair soles of shoes.
S	P	A	R	D	E	C	K	Upper deck above the main deck.
S	P	A	R	E	R	I	B	A cut of pork.
S	P	A	R	G	I	N	G	Sprinkling, Bespattering, Spraying, Agitating, Stirring.
S	P	A	R	H	A	W	K	Sparrow hawk.
S	P	A	R	K	I	N	G	Sparkling, Activating, Inciting, Stimulating, Pursuing, Wooing.
S	P	A	R	K	I	S	H	Gay, Showy, Dapper.
S	P	A	R	K	L	E	R	Diamond, Brilliant performer, A witty vivacious person, A hand-held firework.
S	P	A	R	K	L	E	T	Tiny point of light, A small glittery ornament.
S	P	A	R	L	I	N	G	European smelt.
S	P	A	R	R	I	N	G	Argument, Dispute, Wrangling, Fighting, Boxing.
S	P	A	R	S	E	L	Y	Scantily, Thinly, Skimpy, Meagrely.
S	P	A	R	T	I	N	A	Genus of salt marsh grass.
S	P	A	T	H	O	S	E	Spathic, Foliated.
S	P	A	V	I	N	E	D	Lame, Maimed.
S	P	A	W	L	I	N	G	Spitting.
S	P	A	W	N	I	N	G	Generating, Producing eggs, Depositing eggs, Reproducing.
S	P	E	A	K	I	N	G	Talking, Statement, Revealing, Saying, Speech, Discourse, Conversing, Hailing.
S	P	E	A	R	I	N	G	Piercing, Striking, Impaling, Thrusting, A small lizard fish.
S	P	E	A	R	M	A	N	A soldier having a spear as a weapon.
S	P	E	C	I	F	I	C	Explicit, Special, Individual, Particular, Categorical, Definitive, Express, Set.
S	P	E	C	I	M	E	N	Instance, Sample, Individual, Case, Example, Illustration, Representative type.
S	P	E	C	I	O	U	S	Showy, Plausible, False, Erroneous, Inaccurate, Unsound, Untrue, Apparent.
S	P	E	C	K	I	N	G	Spotting, Dotting.
S	P	E	C	K	L	E	D	Marked with spots, Dotted.
S	P	E	C	T	R	A	L	False, Illusory, Ghostly, Spooky, Shadowy, Phantom, Unearthly, Ghastly.
S	P	E	C	T	R	U	M	Apparition, Spectre, Haunt, Phantasm, Spirit.
S	P	E	C	U	L	A	R	Reflected, Mirrorlike, Providing a good view.
S	P	E	C	U	L	U	M	A tubular instrument for medical examination or medication.
S	P	E	E	D	F	U	L	Rapid, Speedy.
S	P	E	E	D	I	E	R	Quicker, Faster, Swifter.
S	P	E	E	D	I	L	Y	Quickly, Rapidly, Promptly, Soon, Swiftly, Hastily, Posthaste, Fast.
S	P	E	E	D	W	A	Y	Expressway, A racecourse for automobiles or motorcycles.
S	P	E	L	D	R	I	N	Stockfish.
S	P	E	L	D	R	O	N	Same as SPELDRIN.
S	P	E	L	L	I	N	G	Formation of words, Orthography, Sequence of letters forming a word, Composing.
S	P	E	N	D	A	L	L	Spendthrift.
S	P	E	N	D	I	N	G	Distributing, Consuming, Disbursing, Expending, Paying, Contributing, Exhausting
S	P	E	O	T	Y	T	O	Genus of owls.
S	P	E	R	G	U	L	A	Small genus of annual herbs, Corn spurry.
S	P	E	R	M	A	R	Y	An organ in which sperm are developed.
S	P	E	R	M	O	I	L	Yellow oil found in the head cavities of the sperm whale.
S	P	H	A	G	N	U	M	A large genus of mosses which contribute to forming peat.
S	P	H	E	C	I	U	S	Genus of large solitary wasps.
S	P	H	E	C	O	I	D	Relating to the order of bees.
S	P	H	E	N	O	I	D	Wedge-shaped.
S	P	H	E	R	I	C	S	Sperical geometry and trigonometry.
S	P	H	E	R	O	I	D	A figure resembling a sphere but not identical to one.
S	P	H	E	R	O	M	E	Cytonie, Functional unit of a sperm cell.
S	P	H	E	R	U	L	E	A little sphere.
S	P	H	I	N	D	I	D	Family of beetles living in dry fungi.
S	P	H	I	N	G	I	D	Hawk-moth.
S	P	H	Y	G	M	I	C	Relating to the circulatory pulse.
S	P	H	Y	R	I	O	N	Malleolar point, Rounded ankle bone.
S	P	I	C	A	T	E	D	Pointed, Spiked.
S	P	I	C	C	A	T	O	Direction in music for stringed instruments.
S	P	I	C	E	B	O	X	A box fitted with small boxes for storing spices.
S	P	I	C	I	E	S	T	Most spicy, Most exciting in an indecent fashion.
S	P	I	C	K	N	E	L	A European perennial herb with aromatic leaves.
S	P	I	C	U	L	A	R	Prickly, Divided into small spikes.
S	P	I	C	U	L	U	M	Small spiky organs of animals.

1	2	3	4	5	6	7	8	Definition
S	P	I	F	F	I	N	G	Grooming, Smartening, Sprucing.
S	P	I	G	E	L	I	A	A large genus of American herbs.
S	P	I	K	E	L	E	T	Flowering spike head of grass.
S	P	I	L	I	K	I	N	Jackstraw, A game played with straws, Genus of birds.
S	P	I	L	L	I	N	G	Wasting, Slopping, Spoiling, Upsetting, Dribbling, Overflowing, Revealing, Betraying.
S	P	I	L	L	W	A	Y	A channel for overflow, Passage for surplus water.
S	P	I	N	A	C	E	A	Spinach.
S	P	I	N	A	C	I	A	Same as SPINACEA.
S	P	I	N	D	L	E	D	Tapered, Thin and useless.
S	P	I	N	I	F	E	X	Genus of Australian grasses.
S	P	I	N	N	E	R	Y	A spinning mill.
S	P	I	N	N	I	N	G	Making fibres into yarn or thread, Rapid rotation.
S	P	I	N	S	T	E	R	An unmarried woman.
S	P	I	N	S	T	R	Y	The occupation of spinning.
S	P	I	R	A	C	L	E	Vent, Air-hole, Breathing orifice, Blowhole of a whale.
S	P	I	R	A	L	L	Y	Coiled, Twisted, Whorled.
S	P	I	R	E	L	E	T	Coiled thread in the coating of a seed.
S	P	I	R	I	F	E	R	Fossil shellfish.
S	P	I	R	I	T	E	D	Lively, Animated, Sprightly, Vivacious, Fiery, Intrepid, Resolute, Valiant.
S	P	I	R	I	T	U	S	Breathing.
S	P	I	R	T	I	N	G	Spouting, Spurting, Squirting, Jetting, Surging, Gushing, Shooting.
S	P	I	T	C	U	R	L	A curl of hair plastered down with saliva.
S	P	I	T	E	F	U	L	Malicious, Malignant, Hateful, Malevolent, Hostile, Revengeful, Vindictive, Vicious.
S	P	I	T	F	I	R	E	Quick-tempered, Fiery, Violent, Emotional, Quarrelsome.
S	P	I	T	T	I	N	G	Expectorating, Sputtering, Salivating, Splattering, Throwing, Spattering.
S	P	I	T	T	O	O	N	A receptacle for spit from chewers of tobacco.
S	P	I	Z	E	L	L	A	Genus of small American finches.
S	P	L	A	S	H	E	D	Doused, Spattered, Slopped, Spurtled, Sprayed, Sprinkled, Soaked, Drenched.
S	P	L	A	S	H	E	R	A guard to prevent splashes.
S	P	L	A	S	H	E	S	Splash, Slop, Slosh, Spatter, Splosh, Sprinkle.
S	P	L	A	Y	I	N	G	Spreading, Expanding, Sloping, Slanting, Clumsy, Ungainly, Lumbering, Awkwardly.
S	P	L	E	E	N	E	D	Angered.
S	P	L	E	N	D	I	D	Sumptuous, Radiant, Illustrious, Distinguished, Excellent, Praiseworthy, Glorious.
S	P	L	E	N	I	A	L	Thin membrane splint-like bone in the jaw of some animals.
S	P	L	E	N	I	U	M	Thick rounded fold in the brain area.
S	P	L	E	N	I	U	S	Muscle in the back neck and thoracic area in humans.
S	P	L	I	C	I	N	G	Fastening, Uniting, Hitching, Joining, Twisting, Tying, Connecting, Marrying.
S	P	L	I	N	T	E	R	Sliver, Chip, Fragment, Splint, Shiver, Shatter, Split, Secede.
S	P	L	I	T	S	A	W	Ripsaw.
S	P	L	I	T	T	E	R	Operator of a hide-splitting machine.
S	P	L	O	T	C	H	Y	Covered with spots or stains, Smeared, Daubed.
S	P	L	U	R	G	E	D	Splashed, Squandered, Sploshed, Sloshed, Splattered, Indulged in extravagance.
S	P	L	U	T	T	E	R	Sputter, Spatter, Spit, Bustle, Stammer, Speak hastily.
S	P	O	F	F	I	S	H	Fussy, Officious.
S	P	O	I	L	A	G	E	Something wasted, Food decay caused by bacterial or fungal infection.
S	P	O	I	L	I	N	G	Decaying, Injuring, Indulging, Plundering, Damaging, Desecrating, Marring, Impairing.
S	P	O	L	I	A	T	E	Ravage, Depredate, Desecrate, Desolate, Plunder, Pillage, Devour, Destroy.
S	P	O	N	D	A	I	C	Spondee.
S	P	O	N	D	E	A	N	Direction in music.
S	P	O	N	D	E	E	S	Same as SPONDEAN.
S	P	O	N	D	I	A	S	Small genus of tropical trees.
S	P	O	N	D	Y	L	E	Spiny oyster.
S	P	O	N	G	I	A	E	Sponges.
S	P	O	N	G	I	L	Y	Springily, Porously.
S	P	O	N	G	I	N	G	Draining, Cadging, Soaking, Swabbing, Sopping, Erasing, Sprucing, Obliterating.
S	P	O	N	G	I	U	M	Network of cells.
S	P	O	N	G	O	I	D	Sponge-like animal or fossil.
S	P	O	N	S	I	O	N	Act of becoming surety.
S	P	O	N	T	O	O	N	Truncheon.
S	P	O	O	F	E	R	Y	Kidding, Ribbing, Ridiculing.
S	P	O	O	F	I	N	G	Deluding, Hoaxing, Kidding, Duping, Bamboozling, Fooling, Hoodwinking, Tricking.
S	P	O	O	K	I	S	H	Ghostly, Frightening, Terrifying.
S	P	O	O	L	I	N	G	Winding on to a spool or reel.
S	P	O	O	N	F	U	L	The amount a spoon can hold.
S	P	O	O	N	I	L	Y	Foolishly, Amorously, Soppily.
S	P	O	O	N	I	N	G	Courting, Necking, Wooing, Petting, Nestling, Cuddling.
S	P	O	R	A	D	I	C	Separate, Single, Isolated, Desultory, Infrequent, Occasional, Scarce, Uncommon.

1	2	3	4	5	6	7	8	Definition
S	P	O	R	O	S	A	C	Simple degenerate gonophore.
S	P	O	R	O	Z	O	A	Intracellular parasites.
S	P	O	R	T	F	U	L	Entertaining, Diverting, Playful, Frolicsome, Sportive, Jesting, Teasing, Jocose.
S	P	O	R	T	I	N	G	Diverting, Amusing, Cheering, Wagering, Betting, Mocking, Generous.
S	P	O	R	T	I	V	E	Gay, Playful, Merry, Lusty, Wanton, Frisky, Impish, Mischievous.
S	P	O	R	U	L	A	R	Relating to a small spore.
S	P	O	T	B	A	L	L	Cue ball in the game of billiards.
S	P	O	T	L	E	S	S	Immaculate, Pure, Unblemished, Blameless, Irreproachable, Clear, Unsullied, Hygienic.
S	P	O	T	T	I	L	Y	In an irregular fashion.
S	P	O	T	T	I	N	G	Dotting, Identifying, Speckling, Sprinkling, Staining, Mottling, Finding, Detecting.
S	P	O	U	T	I	N	G	Spewing, Spurting, Gushing, Blowing, Declaiming, Cascading, Orating, Ejecting.
S	P	R	A	D	D	L	E	Straddle, Sprawl, Spread-eagle.
S	P	R	A	G	G	E	D	Propped with timber, Restrained with a sprag.
S	P	R	A	I	N	E	D	Wrenched, Twisted, Ricked, Turned, Strained, Stretched, Ruptured, Dislocated.
S	P	R	A	I	N	T	S	The dung of an otter.
S	P	R	A	N	G	L	E	Straggle, Diffuse, Ramify, Spread out, Rough up.
S	P	R	A	W	L	E	D	Spraddled, Spread-eagled, Lolled, Lounged, Slouched, Ungainly, Slumped, Draped.
S	P	R	A	W	L	E	R	Genus of moths.
S	P	R	A	Y	I	N	G	Sprinkling, Jetting, Atomizing, Vaporizing, Scattering, Discharging.
S	P	R	E	A	D	E	R	Implement for spreading, diffusing or scattering.
S	P	R	I	G	G	E	D	Secured with sprigs, Stripped of sprigs, Something decorated with sprigs of flowers.
S	P	R	I	N	G	A	L	A young man, Stripling.
S	P	R	I	N	G	E	R	A supporting stone of an arch, Springbok.
S	P	R	I	N	K	L	E	Scatter in drops, Dust, Powder, Speckle, Dot, Freckle, Stipple, Bedew.
S	P	R	I	N	T	E	D	Dashed, Ran, Speeded, Scampered, Scooted, Shinned.
S	P	R	I	N	T	E	R	One that sprints, Racer.
S	P	R	I	T	T	E	D	Sprouted, Germinated, Budded.
S	P	R	I	T	Z	E	R	A drink of white wine and soda water.
S	P	R	O	C	K	E	T	A cog.
S	P	R	U	C	E	L	Y	Neatly, Tidily, Smartly, Nattily.
S	P	R	U	C	I	N	G	Grooming, Cleaning, Tidying, Refurbishing, Dressing, Decking out, Smartening up.
S	P	R	U	N	T	E	D	Sprinted, Jumped, Ran.
S	P	U	I	L	Z	I	E	Plundered, Looted, Pillaged, Ravaged, Devastated.
S	P	U	N	K	I	N	G	Leaking out information, Mustering, Inciting.
S	P	U	N	Y	A	R	N	Textile yarn, Loosely-twisted rope.
S	P	U	R	G	A	L	L	Injure, Harass.
S	P	U	R	G	E	A	R	Toothed gear wheel.
S	P	U	R	I	O	U	S	False, Counterfeit, Forged, Illogical, Fraudulent, Illegitimate, Artificial, Substitute.
S	P	U	R	L	E	S	S	Without a spur.
S	P	U	R	N	I	N	G	Declining, Rejecting, Disapproving, Dismissing, Refusing, Despising, Repudiating.
S	P	U	R	R	I	E	R	One that makes spurs.
S	P	U	R	R	I	N	G	Inciting, Goading, Urging, Stimulating, Exhorting, Prodding, Prompting, Rallying.
S	P	U	R	R	I	T	E	A mineral consisting of a calcium silicate and carbonate.
S	P	U	R	T	I	N	G	Forcing, Expelling, Jetting, Spouting, Squirting, Gushing.
S	P	U	R	T	L	E	D	Sprinkled, Spattered, Streamed.
S	P	Y	G	L	A	S	S	A telescope.
S	Q	U	A	B	A	S	H	Lambaste, To crush with criticism.
S	Q	U	A	B	B	E	D	Crushed, Squashed, Stuffed.
S	Q	U	A	B	B	L	E	Wrangle, Bicker, Dispute, Quarrel.
S	Q	U	A	B	P	I	E	Pigeon pie.
S	Q	U	A	D	D	E	D	Arranged in squads.
S	Q	U	A	D	R	O	N	A unit of military personnel Group of military vehicles, ships or aircraft.
S	Q	U	A	L	E	N	E	A liquid acrylic triterpene hydrocarbon found in shark liver oil.
S	Q	U	A	L	I	D	S	Family of sharks.
S	Q	U	A	L	L	E	D	Screamed, Squawked, Yelled.
S	Q	U	A	L	L	E	R	A child that cries excessively.
S	Q	U	A	L	O	I	D	Resembling a shark.
S	Q	U	A	M	A	T	A	Order of reptiles including snakes and lizards.
S	Q	U	A	M	A	T	E	Scaly.
S	Q	U	A	M	O	S	E	Same as SQUAMATE.
S	Q	U	A	M	O	U	S	Covered with scales.
S	Q	U	A	M	U	L	A	A scalelike lobe of the thallus of a lichen.
S	Q	U	A	M	U	L	E	Same as SQUAMULA.
S	Q	U	A	N	D	E	R	Scatter, Dissipate, Roam, Wander, Waste, Lavish, Fritter, Consume.
S	Q	U	A	R	E	L	Y	Justly, Honestly, Evenly, Accurately, Exactly, Precisely, Right, Sharp.
S	Q	U	A	R	I	N	G	Agreeing, Adjusting, Regulating, Shaping, Fixing, Conforming, Balancing, Angling.
S	Q	U	A	R	I	S	H	Somewhat square in form.

1	2	3	4	5	6	7	8	Definition
S	Q	U	A	R	S	O	N	A landowner who is also a clergyman.
S	Q	U	A	S	H	E	D	Crushed, Suppressed, Disconcerted, Squelched, Squeezed, Pressed, Crowded, Quelled.
S	Q	U	A	T	T	E	D	Crouched, Hunched, Stooped, Sat cross-legged.
S	Q	U	A	T	T	E	R	A person who settles on land illegally and without permission.
S	Q	U	A	T	T	L	E	Settle.
S	Q	U	A	W	K	E	D	Complained, Squalled, Griped, Bleated, Fussed, Yammered.
S	Q	U	A	W	K	E	R	Informer, Betrayer, Squealer, Stool-pigeon.
S	Q	U	A	W	M	A	N	A white man married to an Indian woman and living within her tribe.
S	Q	U	E	A	K	E	D	Squealed, Grated, Screeched, Screamed, Squeaked, Talked, Informed.
S	Q	U	E	A	K	E	R	Informer, Betrayer, Tipster, Stool-pigeon.
S	Q	U	E	A	L	E	D	Screamed, Screeched, Shrieked, Creaked, Grated, Informed, Snitched.
S	Q	U	E	E	G	E	E	A kitchen device consisting of a sponge on a handle that is used to wipe a surface.
S	Q	U	E	E	Z	E	D	Compressed, Hugged, Forced, Thrust, Crowded, Extorted, Pressed, Crushed.
S	Q	U	E	E	Z	E	R	A device for expressing fruit or vegetable juice.
S	Q	U	E	G	G	E	D	Irregular oscillating.
S	Q	U	I	B	B	E	D	Disputed in a petty fashion, Lampooned, Fired.
S	Q	U	I	G	G	L	E	Squirm, Wiggle, Scribble.
S	Q	U	I	N	T	E	D	Deviated from a straight line, Looked obliquely, Cross-eyed, Peered.
S	Q	U	I	R	E	E	N	A gentleman in a low position.
S	Q	U	I	R	E	L	Y	Resembling a squire.
S	Q	U	I	R	I	N	G	Escorting, Accompanying.
S	Q	U	I	R	M	E	D	Twisted, Wormed, Wriggled, Writhed, Extricated, Tossed.
S	Q	U	I	R	R	E	L	A rodent with a bushy tail that feeds on nuts.
S	Q	U	I	R	T	E	D	Ejected, Spurted, Forced, Gushed, Streamed, Darted, Poured, Surged.
S	Q	U	I	R	T	E	R	One that squirts.
S	T	A	B	B	I	N	G	Piercing, Thrusting, Puncturing, Driving, Plunging, Ramming, Sinking, Sharp.
S	T	A	B	L	I	N	G	Accommodation for domestic animals.
S	T	A	B	L	I	S	H	Establish.
S	T	A	C	C	A	T	O	Disjointed, Cut short, Abrupt.
S	T	A	C	K	I	N	G	Loading, Heaping, Piling, Banking.
S	T	A	F	F	I	N	G	Supplying with staff, Manning, Providing personnel.
S	T	A	G	G	A	R	D	Male red deer.
S	T	A	G	G	E	R	Y	Unsteady, Reeling walk.
S	T	A	G	H	O	R	N	The horn of a stag used for ornamental purposes.
S	T	A	G	N	A	N	T	Motionless, Stale, Static, Immobile, Stationary, Unmoving.
S	T	A	G	N	A	T	E	Motionless, Stale, Dull, Vegetate, Stultify, Constipate, Stifle, Trammel.
S	T	A	G	W	O	R	M	Larva of a botfly that infests the stag.
S	T	A	H	L	I	A	N	Relating to a doctrine of animism.
S	T	A	I	N	I	N	G	Discolouring, Spotting, Corrupting, Defiling, Tainting, Soiling, Smearing, Tingeing.
S	T	A	I	R	R	O	D	A rod for holding stair carpet in place on the treads.
S	T	A	I	R	W	A	Y	Flights of stairs connecting levels.
S	T	A	K	E	N	E	T	A net held in position by stakes.
S	T	A	L	K	I	N	G	Stealing, Slipping, Haunting, Dogging, Pursuing, Tracking, Ambushing, Striding.
S	T	A	L	L	A	G	E	Rent paid to enable one to erect a stall at a fair.
S	T	A	L	L	F	E	D	Keeping an animal in a stall and fattening it.
S	T	A	L	L	I	N	G	Arresting, Halting, Interrupting, Braking, Satiating, Filling, Gorging, Palling.
S	T	A	L	L	I	O	N	A male horse used for breeding, A male noted for his virility.
S	T	A	L	L	M	A	N	One who sells goods from a stall.
S	T	A	L	W	A	R	T	Stout, Sturdy, Brave, Resolute, Valiant, Strong, Tenacious, Muscular.
S	T	A	M	E	N	E	D	Having stamens.
S	T	A	M	I	N	A	L	Consisting of a stamen.
S	T	A	M	P	E	D	E	Headlong rush, Rout, Pell-mell, Bolt, Charge, Hurry, Shoot, Tear.
S	T	A	M	P	I	N	G	Pounding, Crushing, Striking, Beating, Clomping, Impressing, Hammering, Imprinting.
S	T	A	N	C	H	E	D	Staunched, Checked, Stopped, Quenched, Extinguished.
S	T	A	N	C	H	E	L	Stanchion.
S	T	A	N	C	H	E	R	Styptic.
S	T	A	N	D	A	R	D	Criterion, Gauge, Banner, Flag, Model, Example, Ideal, Pattern.
S	T	A	N	D	I	N	G	Rising to an erect position, Resisting, State, Status, Position, Rank, Term, Footing.
S	T	A	N	D	O	F	F	Draw, Deadlock, Dogfall, Stalemate, Neutralization.
S	T	A	N	D	O	U	T	Something outstanding, Superb, Magnificent, Superlative.
S	T	A	N	D	P	A	T	Stubbornly conservative, Die-hard, Fundamentalist, Tory.
S	T	A	N	H	O	P	E	A light carriage.
S	T	A	N	K	H	E	N	Gallinule, Aquatic bird.
S	T	A	N	N	A	N	E	A compound of tin and hydrogen.
S	T	A	N	N	A	R	Y	A region of England containing a tinwork.
S	T	A	N	N	A	T	E	A salt of stannic acid.
S	T	A	N	N	I	D	E	Compound of tin.

1	2	3	4	5	6	7	8	Definition
S	T	A	N	N	I	T	E	A mineral consisting of a sulfide of copper, iron and tin.
S	T	A	N	N	O	U	S	Containing tin.
S	T	A	N	Z	A	I	C	Relating to stanzas.
S	T	A	N	Z	A	E	D	Same as STANZAED.
S	T	A	P	E	L	I	A	A large genus of evil-smelling plants, Carrion-flower.
S	T	A	P	L	I	N	G	Securing, Sorting, Grading, Converting.
S	T	A	R	C	H	E	D	Stiffened, Formal, Precise.
S	T	A	R	C	H	E	R	A laundry worker who does the starching.
S	T	A	R	C	H	L	Y	Formally, Precisely, Rigidly, Punctiliously.
S	T	A	R	D	U	S	T	A vast number of small stars resembling dust particles, Cosmic dust, Gossamer, Twinkling.
S	T	A	R	F	I	S	H	An aquatic animal shaped like a star with five arms that feeds largely on mollusks.
S	T	A	R	G	A	Z	E	To day-dream, Absentmindedness, Indulging in impractical ideas.
S	T	A	R	L	E	S	S	Without stars.
S	T	A	R	L	I	K	E	Resembling a star, Shining like a star, Radiated like a star.
S	T	A	R	L	I	N	G	Genus of birds, A structure to protect a pier.
S	T	A	R	N	O	S	E	A semiaquatic mole.
S	T	A	R	R	I	L	Y	In a starlike fashion.
S	T	A	R	R	I	N	G	Bespangling, Featuring, Sprinkling with stars, Playing a lead part.
S	T	A	R	T	E	R	S	A dish for the beginning of a meal.
S	T	A	R	T	I	N	G	Darting, Jumping, Flinching, Recoiling, Beginning, Commencing, Originating, Opening.
S	T	A	R	T	L	E	D	Frightened, Bolted, Jumped, Shocked, Jolted, Alarmed, Scared, Astonished.
S	T	A	R	T	L	E	R	One that startles.
S	T	A	R	T	U	R	N	The most important performer or act in a show.
S	T	A	R	V	I	N	G	Dying, Perishing, Hungry, Famished, Depriving, Ravenous, Craving.
S	T	A	R	W	O	R	M	Genus of marine worms.
S	T	A	R	W	O	R	T	Chickweed.
S	T	A	S	I	M	O	N	Ode sung by the choir in a Greek tragedy.
S	T	A	T	A	B	L	E	Capable of being stated.
S	T	A	T	E	D	L	Y	Regularly, As an established practice.
S	T	A	T	I	C	A	L	Stable, Stagnant, Unchanging, Stationary, Immobile, Constant.
S	T	A	T	U	A	R	Y	A collection of statues.
S	T	A	T	U	R	E	D	Pertaining to physical posture or height.
S	T	A	Y	B	O	L	T	A bolt used to protect against pressure.
S	T	A	Y	L	A	C	E	A lace for securing a corset to allow for adjustment.
S	T	A	Y	S	A	I	L	A fore-and-aft sail.
S	T	E	A	D	I	E	D	Calmed, Composed, Stabilized, Firmed, Poised.
S	T	E	A	D	I	L	Y	Evenly, Constantly, Uniformly, Reliably, Calmly, Soberly.
S	T	E	A	D	I	N	G	A small farm or homestead.
S	T	E	A	L	I	N	G	Pilfering, Filching, Purloining, Sneaking, Smuggling, Enticing, Pinching, Swiping.
S	T	E	A	L	T	H	Y	Furtive, Secret, Clandestine, Covert, Crafty, Cunning, Wily, Skulking.
S	T	E	A	M	I	N	G	Giving off vapour, Exhaling, Reeking, Boiling.
S	T	E	A	M	T	U	G	A small vessel used for towing or guiding ships.
S	T	E	A	P	S	I	N	Enzyme of the pancreas that breaks down fat.
S	T	E	A	R	A	T	E	Ester of stearic acid.
S	T	E	A	R	I	N	E	Ester of glycerol and stearic acid.
S	T	E	A	R	O	Y	L	The radical of stearic acid.
S	T	E	A	T	I	T	E	A grayish green or brown talc, Soapstone.
S	T	E	A	T	O	M	A	A sebaceous cyst, Lipoma.
S	T	E	E	L	I	F	Y	Convert into steel.
S	T	E	E	L	I	N	G	Bracing, Preparing, Fortifying, Strengthening, Hardening, Rallying, Encouraging, Heartening.
S	T	E	E	N	I	N	G	Lining an excavation to prevent caving in.
S	T	E	E	P	I	N	G	Soaking, Infusing, Immersing, Saturating, Moistening, Bathing, Sousing, Suffusing.
S	T	E	E	P	L	E	D	Risen high into the air, Arranged in the form of a steeple.
S	T	E	E	R	A	G	E	Cheapest and inferior accommodation on a passenger ship, Direction, Management.
S	T	E	E	R	I	N	G	Controlling, Guiding, Wending, Hinting, Conducting, Escorting, Piloting, Shepherding.
S	T	E	E	V	I	N	G	Stowing, Stuffing, Storing, Packing.
S	T	E	G	O	D	O	N	A prehistoric mammal related to the elephant.
S	T	E	G	O	M	U	S	A prehistoric five-toed reptile.
S	T	E	I	N	B	O	K	Steenbok.
S	T	E	I	N	I	N	G	Steening.
S	T	E	L	L	A	R	Y	Stellar, Relating to stars.
S	T	E	L	L	A	T	E	Shaped like a star.
S	T	E	L	L	I	T	E	Alloy composed of cobalt and chromium.
S	T	E	M	F	L	O	W	Rainfall reaching the ground by draining down the trunks of trees.
S	T	E	M	H	E	A	D	Top of a ship's stem.
S	T	E	M	L	E	A	F	A leaf growing on the upper part of a stem.
S	T	E	M	L	E	S	S	Having no stem.

1	2	3	4	5	6	7	8	
S	T	E	M	M	I	N	G	Springing, Tracing the origin or development.
S	T	E	N	O	S	E	D	Affected with stenosis.
S	T	E	N	O	S	I	S	Constriction of a tube, passage or orifice.
S	T	E	N	O	T	I	C	Relating to stenosis.
S	T	E	P	D	A	M	E	Stepmother.
S	T	E	P	P	I	N	G	Treading, Walking, Advancing, Dancing, Traversing, Performing, Pacing, Prancing.
S	T	E	P	W	I	S	E	Gradual.
S	T	E	R	E	O	M	E	Rigid cellular tissue of a plant.
S	T	E	R	I	G	M	A	Spore-bearing stalks of fungi.
S	T	E	R	L	I	N	G	Genuine, Honourable, Estimable, Noble, Worthy, Pure, True.
S	T	E	R	N	I	T	E	Thoracic segment of an insect.
S	T	E	R	N	W	A	Y	A ship moving stern first or backwards.
S	T	I	B	B	L	E	R	A student of divinity.
S	T	I	B	I	O	U	S	Compound containing antimony.
S	T	I	B	N	I	T	E	A mineral consisting of native antimony trisulfide.
S	T	I	C	H	O	U	S	Having rows or sides.
S	T	I	C	K	I	N	G	Stabbing, Puncturing, Piercing, Adhering, Impaling, Hesitating, Remaining, Baffling.
S	T	I	C	K	J	A	W	A candy that is difficult to chew.
S	T	I	C	K	L	E	D	Contended, Held out, Scrupled, Demurred.
S	T	I	C	K	L	E	R	Poser, Meddler, One that refuses to compromise.
S	T	I	F	F	I	S	H	Rigid, Inflexible, Steep, Inclined to be formal.
S	T	I	F	L	I	N	G	Oppressive, Suffocating, Muffling, Silencing, Restraining, Discouraging, Inhibiting.
S	T	I	G	M	A	T	A	Marks appearing on one's body without physical cause that correspond to Christ's wounds.
S	T	I	L	B	E	N	E	An aromatic hydrocarbon.
S	T	I	L	B	I	T	E	A mineral of the zeolite family.
S	T	I	L	E	T	T	O	A slender pointed dagger.
S	T	I	L	L	A	G	E	A small table sometimes with wheels.
S	T	I	L	L	I	N	G	A rack for storing casks in a brewery.
S	T	I	L	L	I	O	N	Same as STILLING.
S	T	I	M	U	L	U	S	Incentive, Catalyst, Goad, Impetus, Boost, Spur, Encouragement, Instigation.
S	T	I	N	G	I	L	Y	Miserly, Parsimoniously, Tightly, Meanly, Sparingly.
S	T	I	N	G	I	N	G	Pricking, Piercing, Wounding with a poisonous process, Goading, Cheating, Overcharging.
S	T	I	N	G	R	A	Y	Family of fishes with dangerous whiplike tails.
S	T	I	N	K	A	R	D	Mean or contemptible person.
S	T	I	N	K	P	O	T	A pot with offensive smelling substances in it.
S	T	I	N	T	I	N	G	Stopping, Stunting, Confining, Restraining, Restricting, Desisting, Sparing.
S	T	I	P	P	L	E	D	Engraved with dots or small strokes, Speckled, Streaked, Flecked.
S	T	I	P	P	L	E	R	A painter who stipples a surface.
S	T	I	P	U	L	E	D	Growing like stipules.
S	T	I	P	U	L	E	S	Stipulate.
S	T	I	R	L	E	S	S	Motionless.
S	T	I	R	R	I	N	G	Agitating, Exerting, Disturbing, Inciting, Arousing, Evoking, Movement, Quickening.
S	T	I	T	C	H	E	D	Sewn, Embroidered, Fastened, United, Mended.
S	T	I	T	C	H	E	R	One that stitches.
S	T	I	Z	I	D	A	E	Family of sphecoid wasps.
S	T	O	C	C	A	D	O	Stab, Thrust with a rapier.
S	T	O	C	K	A	D	E	An enclosure made with stakes.
S	T	O	C	K	I	E	R	Thicker, Stouter build.
S	T	O	C	K	I	L	Y	In a stocky manner, Thickset.
S	T	O	C	K	I	N	G	A close-fitting covering for leg and foot.
S	T	O	C	K	I	S	H	Stupid, Blockish.
S	T	O	C	K	I	S	T	One that stocks goods.
S	T	O	C	K	M	A	N	Cowherd, Shepherd, A ranch owner, One who keeps records.
S	T	O	C	K	P	O	T	A pot in which stock is prepared.
S	T	O	I	C	I	S	M	Impassiveness, Insensibility, Fortitude, Pluck, Stolidity, Resignation, Phlegm, Apathy.
S	T	O	K	E	S	I	A	Genus of erect perennial herbs.
S	T	O	L	I	D	L	Y	Impassively, Obtusely, Passivity.
S	T	O	L	Z	I	T	E	A mineral consisting of a native lead tungstate isomorphous.
S	T	O	M	A	T	I	C	Constituting a stoma, minute openings.
S	T	O	M	O	X	Y	S	Genus of blood-sucking flies.
S	T	O	N	E	B	O	W	Crossbow or catapault for shooting stones.
S	T	O	N	E	F	L	Y	Winged insects with nymphs that are aquatic.
S	T	O	N	E	O	I	L	Petroleum.
S	T	O	O	K	I	N	G	Stacking sheaves of corn.
S	T	O	O	L	I	N	G	Informing, Squealing, Defecating, Luring.
S	T	O	O	P	I	N	G	Bending, Leaning, Bowing, Submitting, Lowering, Prostrating, Debasing, Degrading.
S	T	O	P	B	A	C	K	Disease of peach and pear nursery stock.

1	2	3	4	5	6	7	8	
S	T	O	P	B	A	T	H	An acid rinse bath used in photography.
S	T	O	P	C	O	C	K	A tap for controlling the flow of liquid through a pipe.
S	T	O	P	O	V	E	R	An interruption in a journey, Stopping place on a trip.
S	T	O	P	P	A	G	E	Strike, Deduction from pay, Obstruction of a body function.
S	T	O	P	P	I	N	G	Halting, Plugging, Intercepting, Restraining, interrupting, Arresting, Parrying, Baffling.
S	T	O	P	P	L	E	D	Stoppered, Closed with a stopper.
S	T	O	P	W	O	R	K	A device to prevent overwinding a watch or clock.
S	T	O	R	A	B	L	E	That may be stored.
S	T	O	R	E	R	I	A	A common harmless American snake.
S	T	O	R	M	I	L	Y	Angrily, Tempestuously, Passionately.
S	T	O	R	M	I	N	G	Attacking, Assaulting, Ranting, Rushing, Assailing.
S	T	O	R	Y	I	N	G	Telling a story, Telling a lie.
S	T	O	T	I	N	K	A	Monetary unit of Bulgaria.
S	T	O	U	T	I	S	H	Inclined to be corpulent.
S	T	O	W	A	W	A	Y	A person who hides on a ship to take an illegal journey, Hiding place.
S	T	R	A	D	D	L	E	Sprawl, Bestride, Spread-eagle, Scramble.
S	T	R	A	G	G	L	E	Rove, Stray, Wander, Drift, Meander, Ramble, Roam, Range.
S	T	R	A	I	G	H	T	Upright, Immediately, Direct, Uninterrupted, Steep, Correct, Undiluted, Severe.
S	T	R	A	I	N	E	D	Sprained, Constricted, Wrenched, Oozed, Exuded, Forced, Tense, Tight.
S	T	R	A	I	N	E	R	A sieve, Filter.
S	T	R	A	I	T	E	N	Confine, Constrict, Make narrow, Tighten.
S	T	R	A	I	T	L	Y	Strictly, Narrowly.
S	T	R	A	M	A	S	H	Disturbance, Commotion, Racket, Broil, Brawl, Crash, Smashup.
S	T	R	A	M	M	E	L	Straw.
S	T	R	A	N	D	E	D	Beached, Shipwrecked, Wrecked, Aground, Piled up, Left behind.
S	T	R	A	N	G	E	R	Foreigner, Alien, Unfamiliar, Outsider, Transient, Abnormal, Crazier.
S	T	R	A	N	G	L	E	Throttle, Choke to death, Suppress, Muffle, Quelch, Reppress, Shush.
S	T	R	A	P	P	E	D	Bound, Stropped, Constricted, Groomed, Busied, Beggared, Poor, Destitute.
S	T	R	A	P	P	E	R	One that takes care of stables and horses.
S	T	R	A	T	E	G	Y	Tactics, Plan, Blueprint, Design, Game, Project, Scheme.
S	T	R	A	T	I	F	Y	Arrange in strata, Divide into classes, Segregate, Grade.
S	T	R	A	T	O	S	E	Arranged in strata.
S	T	R	A	T	O	U	S	Resembling stratus clouds.
S	T	R	A	V	A	I	G	Saunter, Stroll, Wander.
S	T	R	A	W	H	A	T	A hat of plaited or woven straw.
S	T	R	A	Y	I	N	G	Wandering, Roving, Straying, Meandering, Deviating, Roaming, Straggling, Digressing.
S	T	R	E	A	K	E	D	Rubbed, Smeared, Grizzled, Striated, Sick, Upset.
S	T	R	E	A	K	E	R	Yellow bass.
S	T	R	E	A	M	E	D	Flowed, Exuded, Poured, Washed, Gushed, Surged, Sluiced, Rolled.
S	T	R	E	A	M	E	R	Festoon, Banner, Pennant.
S	T	R	E	N	G	T	H	Fortitude, Integrity, Vitality, Influence, Power, Energy, Force, Muscle.
S	T	R	E	P	E	R	A	Genus of Australian birds.
S	T	R	E	P	Y	A	N	Relating to an early culture using primitive type of flints.
S	T	R	E	S	S	E	D	Distressed, Emphasized, Accented.
S	T	R	E	T	C	H	Y	Being able to be stretched.
S	T	R	E	W	I	N	G	Scattering, Disseminating, Sowing, Broadcasting, Spreading, Circulating, Propagating.
S	T	R	I	A	T	E	D	Streaked, Striped, Straked.
S	T	R	I	A	T	U	M	Brain matter.
S	T	R	I	C	K	E	N	Incapacitated, Afflicted, Wounded, Hit, Overwhelmed by misfortune.
S	T	R	I	C	K	L	E	Template, A straight edge fed with an abrasive and used as a knife sharpener.
S	T	R	I	C	T	L	Y	Closely, Precisely, Rigorously, Stringently, Positively.
S	T	R	I	D	D	L	E	Straddle, Standing astride, Stride.
S	T	R	I	D	E	N	T	Discordant, Harsh, Shrill, Blatant, Grating, Creaking.
S	T	R	I	D	I	N	G	Straddling, Stalking, Marching, Clumping, Stomping, Tramping.
S	T	R	I	G	A	T	E	Parasitic worms.
S	T	R	I	G	I	N	E	Owllike.
S	T	R	I	G	O	S	E	Striated, Marked with grooves.
S	T	R	I	G	O	U	S	Same as STRIGOSE.
S	T	R	I	K	I	N	G	Clouting, Whacking, Noticeable, Arresting, Conspicuous, Outstanding, Prominent.
S	T	R	I	N	G	E	D	Equipped with strings, Tensed.
S	T	R	I	N	G	E	R	A line of specified objects.
S	T	R	I	N	K	L	E	Sprinkle.
S	T	R	I	P	I	N	G	Making or affixing stripes, Lashing with a rod.
S	T	R	I	P	P	E	D	Bared, Removed, Plucked, Dismantled, Plundered, Disassembled, Denuded, Divested.
S	T	R	I	P	P	E	R	One who strips tobacco leaves, Stripteaser.
S	T	R	I	V	I	N	G	Conflicting, Contesting, Rivalry, Fighting, Attempting, Trying, Endeavouring, Competing.
S	T	R	O	B	I	L	E	The segments forming the body of a tapeworm.

1	2	3	4	5	6	7	8	Definition
S	T	R	O	C	K	L	E	A shovel used by glassworkers.
S	T	R	O	K	I	N	G	Marking with a line, Caressing, Hitting, Propelling.
S	T	R	O	L	L	E	D	Sauntered, Rambled, Wandered, Drifted, Lingered, Moped, Walked.
S	T	R	O	L	L	E	R	Vagrant, Tramp, A folding baby carriage.
S	T	R	O	M	B	U	S	A genus of marine mollusks, Conch.
S	T	R	O	N	G	L	Y	Powerfully, Forcibly, Firmly, Boldly, Emphatically, Mightily.
S	T	R	O	N	T	I	A	Strontium oxide.
S	T	R	O	P	H	I	C	Relating to strophes.
S	T	R	O	P	P	E	D	Sharpened on a strop.
S	T	R	U	G	G	L	E	Strive, Contend, Try, Contest, Compete, Attempt, Endeavour, Undertake.
S	T	R	U	M	M	E	D	Thrummed, Played in a careless fashion.
S	T	R	U	M	O	S	E	Having a glandular swelling.
S	T	R	U	M	O	U	S	Goitrous.
S	T	R	U	M	P	E	T	Prostitute, Harlot, Wanton woman, Slattern, Slut.
S	T	R	U	T	H	I	O	A genus of African ostriches.
S	T	R	U	T	T	E	D	Swaggered, Strode, Paraded, Flaunted, Supported.
S	T	R	U	T	T	E	R	One that struts.
S	T	U	B	B	I	N	G	Cutting down, Crushing, Guarding, Pulverizing, Uprooting.
S	T	U	B	B	L	E	D	Covered with stubble, Bristled.
S	T	U	B	B	O	R	N	Determined, Dogged, Resistant, Obstinate, Headstrong, Unyielding, Inflexible, Adamant.
S	T	U	C	C	O	E	D	Decorated with plaster work.
S	T	U	D	B	O	L	T	A bolt with threads on both ends.
S	T	U	D	B	O	O	K	Official record of a pedigree of an animal.
S	T	U	D	D	I	N	G	Covering or protecting with stud, Uprights of wall framing of a building.
S	T	U	D	F	A	R	M	A farm where horses are bred.
S	T	U	D	I	O	U	S	Learning, Deliberate, Diligent, Advised, Considered, Designed, Premeditated, Planned.
S	T	U	D	M	A	R	E	A mare kept for breeding purposes.
S	T	U	D	W	O	R	K	Ornamented with studs.
S	T	U	D	Y	I	N	G	Learning, Considering, Contemplating, Pondering, Scrutinizing, Surveying, Examining.
S	T	U	F	F	I	N	G	Padding, Cramming, Stocking, Filling, Plugging, Crowding, Gorging.
S	T	U	L	T	I	F	Y	Frustrate, Nullify, Stagnate, Style, Trammel, Inhibit, Stunt, Dull.
S	T	U	M	B	L	E	D	Fell, Blundered, Tottered, Stammered, Staggered, Tripped, Balked, Lurched.
S	T	U	M	B	L	E	R	One who blunders or totters.
S	T	U	M	M	I	N	G	Reviving wine by mixing with must.
S	T	U	M	P	I	N	G	Trimming, Perplexing, Confounding, Digging out, Lumbering, Barging, Beating.
S	T	U	N	D	I	S	M	A religious movement.
S	T	U	N	D	I	S	T	Member of a Russian denomination of Protestants.
S	T	U	N	N	I	N	G	Surprising, Astonishing, Astounding, Sensational, Splendid, Handsome, First rate.
S	T	U	N	S	A	I	L	Studding sail.
S	T	U	N	T	I	N	G	Performing stunts, Dwarfing, Checking, Hindering growth, Suppressing, Curbing.
S	T	U	P	E	O	U	S	Having long loose scales or matted filaments.
S	T	U	P	I	D	L	Y	Dumbly, Crassly, Foolishly, Slowly, Sluggishly, Senselessly.
S	T	U	P	R	A	T	E	Rape.
S	T	U	R	D	I	L	Y	Strongly, Stoutly, Solidly, Robustly.
S	T	U	R	G	E	O	N	Genus of large fish valued for its roe which is made into caviar.
S	T	U	R	N	I	N	E	Relating to a starling.
S	T	U	R	N	O	I	D	Same as STURNINE.
S	U	A	S	I	B	L	E	Easily persuaded.
S	U	A	S	O	R	I	A	Ancient Roman oration dealing with the problem of conscience.
S	U	B	A	C	U	T	E	Moderately acute, Having a tapering form.
S	U	B	A	G	E	N	T	A person delegated by an agent.
S	U	B	A	H	D	A	R	A native military officer in the former British Indian Army.
S	U	B	B	I	F	I	D	Somewhat forked.
S	U	B	C	L	A	S	S	A sub-division of a class, Less than first class.
S	U	B	C	O	S	T	A	Subcostal vein of an insect's wing.
S	U	B	C	R	U	S	T	A layer underneath the top one.
S	U	B	D	U	I	N	G	Conquering, Vanquishing, Crushing, Defeating, Overpowering, Suppressing, Reducing.
S	U	B	D	U	R	A	L	Occurring under the membrane enveloping the brain.
S	U	B	E	N	T	R	Y	An entry in a ledger made under a general entry.
S	U	B	E	Q	U	A	L	Not exactly equal.
S	U	B	E	R	A	T	E	Ester of suberic acid.
S	U	B	E	R	E	C	T	Ascending, Standing or growing in an erect position.
S	U	B	E	R	I	T	E	Genus of sponges.
S	U	B	E	R	I	Z	E	The conversion of plant-cell walls into corky tissue.
S	U	B	E	R	O	N	E	Oily saturated cyclic hydrocarbon.
S	U	B	E	R	O	S	E	Having a corky texture.
S	U	B	E	R	O	U	S	Same as SUBEROSE.

1	2	3	4	5	6	7	8	Clue
S	U	B	F	A	U	N	A	A localized fauna.
S	U	B	F	L	O	O	R	Rough floor as a base for finished floor.
S	U	B	F	L	O	R	A	A localized flora.
S	U	B	F	O	C	A	L	Not clearly conscious.
S	U	B	G	A	L	E	A	A segment of the maxilla of an insect.
S	U	B	G	E	N	U	S	A category below a genus but above a species.
S	U	B	G	I	A	N	T	A bright star that does not qualify as a giant star.
S	U	B	G	R	A	D	E	A layer beneath the principal layer, Not first grade.
S	U	B	G	R	O	U	P	A group division.
S	U	B	H	U	M	A	N	Failing to attain the level of a human.
S	U	B	I	M	A	G	O	An intermediate stage in the development of an insect.
S	U	B	I	N	D	E	X	Index to a division of a main classification.
S	U	B	L	A	T	E	D	Removed, Eliminated, Cancelled, Negated, Denied.
S	U	B	L	E	A	S	E	A lease given by a tenant.
S	U	B	L	I	M	E	D	Exalted, Ennobled, Aggrandized, Glorified, Honoured, Magnified.
S	U	B	L	U	N	A	R	Situated beneath the moon. Within the orbit of the moon.
S	U	B	M	E	R	G	E	Inundate, Dip, Plunge, Impregnate, Saturate, Soak, Deluge, Drown.
S	U	B	M	E	R	S	E	Dip, Douse, Souse, Sink, Founder, Submerge, Duck, Dunk.
S	U	B	O	R	D	E	R	Subdivision of an order.
S	U	B	O	R	N	E	D	Incited, Instigated, Equipped, Adorned.
S	U	B	O	R	N	E	R	One that persuades a person to break the law.
S	U	B	O	V	A	T	E	Not quite oval in shape.
S	U	B	P	L	A	T	E	A plate placed for protection or support.
S	U	B	P	O	E	N	A	A court order commanding attendance or evidence.
S	U	B	P	O	L	A	R	Subartic, Subantartic, The fringe of the polar regions.
S	U	B	P	R	E	S	S	A small press for delicate work.
S	U	B	P	R	I	O	R	An assistant to a prior.
S	U	B	R	I	G	I	D	Having flexibility to resist shock.
S	U	B	S	E	N	S	E	A subordinate division of a sense.
S	U	B	S	E	R	V	E	To function in a lesser position.
S	U	B	S	I	D	E	D	Settled, Precipitated, Descended, Sunk, Eased, Fell, Abated, Slackened.
S	U	B	S	O	L	A	R	Situated at the equator between the tropics.
S	U	B	S	O	N	I	C	A speed less than the sound of air.
S	U	B	S	T	A	G	E	Subdivision of a geological stage.
S	U	B	S	T	Y	L	E	A line of a sundial.
S	U	B	S	U	M	E	D	Included, Comprehended, Contained, Embodied, Embraced, Encompassed, Summarized.
S	U	B	T	E	N	S	E	To measure by observation of the angle.
S	U	B	T	I	T	L	E	Showing a translation of a foreign dialogue beneath a motion picture.
S	U	B	T	L	E	T	Y	Skilfully, Ingeniously, Deviously, Wiliness, Artfulness, Cunningly.
S	U	B	T	O	N	I	C	Seventh degree of the musical scale.
S	U	B	T	O	T	A	L	The sum of part of a series of figures.
S	U	B	T	R	A	C	T	Take away, Withhold, Remove, Deduct, Discount, Withdraw.
S	U	B	T	R	I	B	E	Subdivision of a tribe.
S	U	B	U	L	A	T	E	Tapering to a fine point.
S	U	B	U	R	B	A	N	On the outskirts, Relating to the environs, Provincial.
S	U	B	U	R	B	I	A	The suburbs of a city.
S	U	B	V	O	C	A	L	Thinking of the words without uttering or uttering in an inaudible fashion.
S	U	C	C	I	N	C	T	Brief, Concise, Curt, Laconic, Short, Summary, Blunt, Brusque.
S	U	C	C	O	R	E	D	Aided, Helped, Relieved, Alleviated, Cured, Mitigated, Sheltered, Assisted.
S	U	C	C	U	B	U	S	Demon, Fiend, Strumpet, Whore.
S	U	C	H	L	I	K	E	Similar.
S	U	C	H	N	E	S	S	Essential quality.
S	U	C	H	W	I	S	E	In such a manner.
S	U	C	K	E	N	E	R	A tenant bound to grind his corn at a mill he is tenured to.
S	U	C	K	E	R	E	D	Provided with suckers.
S	U	C	K	L	I	N	G	A child or young animal still fed on the milk of its mother.
S	U	D	A	M	I	N	A	A temporary eruption caused by excessive sweating.
S	U	D	A	N	E	S	E	Inhabitant of the Sudan.
S	U	D	A	R	I	U	M	Handkerchief, A linen square carried by ancient Romans to wipe away perspiration.
S	U	D	A	T	I	O	N	Sweating.
S	U	D	A	T	O	R	Y	Producing sweating.
S	U	D	D	E	N	L	Y	Hastily, Abruptly, Quickly, Forthwith, Short, Unawares.
S	U	F	F	E	R	E	D	Allowed, Permitted, Tolerated, Submitted, Sustained, Experienced, Subjected.
S	U	F	F	E	R	E	R	One that endures.
S	U	F	F	I	C	E	D	Replenished, Furnished, Appeased, Served, Suited.
S	U	F	F	I	X	A	L	Being a suffix.
S	U	F	F	I	X	E	D	Added to the end of a word.

1	2	3	4	5	6	7	8	
S	U	F	F	L	A	T	E	Inflated, Inspired.
S	U	F	F	R	A	G	E	Approval, Sanction, Vote, Consensus, Ballot, Franchise.
S	U	F	F	R	A	G	O	Knee, The hock of a horse.
S	U	F	F	U	S	E	D	Flushed, Filled, Poured, Infused, Imbued, Steeped, Innoculated, Introduced.
S	U	F	I	S	T	I	C	Relating to an ascetic Islamic mysticism.
S	U	G	A	R	I	N	G	Sweetening, Granulating, Coating with sugar, Palliating, Extenuating, Whitewashing.
S	U	I	C	I	D	A	L	Self-destructive.
S	U	I	T	A	B	L	E	Appropriate, Proper, Right, Apt, Qualified, Fit, Deserved Merited.
S	U	I	T	A	B	L	Y	Well, Acceptably, Adequately, Simply, Appropriately, Becomingly, Fittingly, Properly.
S	U	I	T	C	A	S	E	Travelling bag that is rigid, flat and rectangular.
S	U	K	I	Y	A	K	I	Meat, soybean curd and vegetables cooked in the pan at the table.
S	U	L	C	A	T	E	D	Scored with furrows lengthwise.
S	U	L	C	U	L	U	S	A small furrow.
S	U	L	F	A	T	I	C	Containing a sulfate.
S	U	L	F	O	N	Y	L	The bivalent group of radical occurring in sulfones.
S	U	L	L	E	N	L	Y	Gloomily, Morosely, Sulkily, Dourly.
S	U	L	L	Y	I	N	G	Besmirching, Staining, Defiling, Soiling.
S	U	L	P	H	A	T	E	Sulfate.
S	U	L	P	H	I	D	E	Sulfide.
S	U	L	P	H	I	T	E	Sulfite.
S	U	L	T	A	N	I	C	Characteristic of a sultan.
S	U	M	E	R	I	A	N	An inhabitant of the ancient region of lower Babylonia.
S	U	M	M	E	R	E	D	Carried through the summer, Protected, Cherished.
S	U	M	M	O	N	E	D	Convoked, Cited, Conjured, Aroused, Called, Assembled, Commanded, Enjoined.
S	U	M	M	O	N	E	R	One that summons.
S	U	M	P	I	T	A	N	A Malaysian blowpipe.
S	U	N	B	A	T	H	E	To bare the body in the sunlight.
S	U	N	B	L	I	N	D	Awning to provide shade from the sun.
S	U	N	B	U	R	N	T	Affected by sunburn.
S	U	N	B	U	R	S	T	A sudden flash of sunlight, A decoration resembling the rays of sun.
S	U	N	C	R	A	C	K	A crack in sun-dried mud.
S	U	N	D	E	R	E	D	Separated, Severed, Disjointed, Disunited, Divided, Divorced, Parted, Cleaved.
S	U	N	D	R	I	E	S	Items, Miscellany, Oddments, Notions, Details.
S	U	N	G	L	A	D	E	The bright reflection of the sun on a large area of water.
S	U	N	L	I	G	H	T	Light of the sun.
S	U	N	N	I	T	E	S	Moslems that are adherents of the Sunni branch of Islam.
S	U	N	P	R	O	O	F	Resistant to damage caused by the light or heat of the sun.
S	U	N	S	C	A	L	D	An injury to woody plants caused by heat and light of sun.
S	U	N	S	H	A	D	E	Parasol, Awning.
S	U	N	S	H	I	N	E	The direct rays of the sun.
S	U	N	S	H	I	N	Y	Joyous, Resplendent, Happily, Brightly.
S	U	N	S	T	O	N	E	Feldspar.
S	U	P	E	R	A	D	D	To add over and above, Something out of the ordinary, Extra.
S	U	P	E	R	B	L	Y	Richly, Elegantly, Magnificently, Gorgeously, Grandly, Opulently, Splendidly, Proudly.
S	U	P	E	R	H	E	T	Inaudible oscillation for the reproduction of sound in a telephone receiver.
S	U	P	E	R	I	O	R	Higher, Choice, Haughty, Primary, Miraculous, Proud, Exceptional, Excellent.
S	U	P	E	R	M	A	N	Superhuman, Demigod, A person of extraordinary powers or achievements.
S	U	P	E	R	N	A	L	Heavenly, Ethereal, Spiritual, Celestial, Situated at the top.
S	U	P	E	R	T	A	X	Surtax, A tax in addition to normal tax levied on extra large incomes.
S	U	P	I	N	E	L	Y	Abjectly, Lethargy, Languidly, Inactively, Inertly, Sluggishly.
S	U	P	P	L	A	N	T	Replace, Supersede, Substitute, Usurp, Uproot, Oust, Displace, Expel.
S	U	P	P	L	I	E	D	Gave, Delivered, Dispensed, Fed, Found, Provided, Transferred, Fulfilled.
S	U	P	P	L	I	E	R	A country, area or person that supplies a substance or produce in demand.
S	U	P	P	O	S	A	L	Hypothesis, Something supposed, Conjecture, Supposition, Theory.
S	U	P	P	O	S	E	D	Imagined, Accepted, Believed, Understood, Pretended, Alleged, Intended, Permitted.
S	U	P	P	O	S	E	R	One that surmises.
S	U	P	P	R	E	S	S	Subdue, Crush, Compress, Annihilate, Extinguish, Squash, Quell, Squench.
S	U	R	B	A	S	E	D	The position of the curve centre in arches and vaults.
S	U	R	C	E	A	S	E	Abandon, Discontinue, Cessation, Desist, Stop, Refrain, Halt, Quit.
S	U	R	C	U	L	U	S	Sucker.
S	U	R	E	F	I	R	E	Dependable, Reliable, Infallible, Certain, Sure, Unfailing.
S	U	R	E	N	E	S	S	Certainty, Assurance, Certitude, Confidence, Surety, Reliability.
S	U	R	E	T	I	E	S	Guarantees, Sponsors, Warranties, Backers.
S	U	R	F	A	C	E	D	Brought to the surface, Applied a surface.
S	U	R	F	B	I	R	D	A shorebird resembling the golden plover.
S	U	R	F	B	O	A	T	A boat built to operate safely in heavy surf.
S	U	R	F	D	U	C	K	Scoter.

1	2	3	4	5	6	7	8	Definition
S	U	R	G	E	N	C	Y	Noted for quickness and cleverness.
S	U	R	G	I	C	A	L	Concerned with surgery.
S	U	R	I	C	A	T	A	A Southern African mammal that burrows and is related to the mongoose.
S	U	R	I	C	A	T	E	Same as SURICATA.
S	U	R	M	I	S	E	D	Guess, Supposed, Conjectured, Presumed, Pretended, Thought, Considered, Theorized.
S	U	R	M	I	S	E	R	One that presumes.
S	U	R	M	O	U	N	T	Excel, Overcome, Conquer, Crown, Top, Outstrip, Master, Hurdle.
S	U	R	N	A	M	E	D	Given a family name, Designated.
S	U	R	P	L	I	C	E	Loose white ecclesiastical vestment worn as an overtunic.
S	U	R	P	R	I	N	T	Overprint, Superimpose on a film.
S	U	R	P	R	I	S	E	Astonishment, Wonder, Captivate, Overcome, Amaze, Astound, Capture, Seize.
S	U	R	R	E	B	U	T	A reply in common law pleading of a plaintiff.
S	U	R	R	O	U	N	D	Overflow, Inundate, Encircle, Encompass, Envelop, Girdle, Enclose, Throng.
S	U	R	R	O	Y	A	L	Part of the antler of a four-year old stag.
S	U	R	V	E	Y	A	L	Survey.
S	U	R	V	E	Y	E	D	Appraised, Estimated, Evaluated, Supervised, Investigated, Considered, Viewed, Observed.
S	U	R	V	E	Y	O	R	A government official having the responsibility of inspection.
S	U	R	V	I	V	A	L	Outliving others, Continuance, Escaping extinction.
S	U	R	V	I	V	E	D	Outlived, Outlasted, Continued, Endured, Lasted, Persisted, Recovered, Revived.
S	U	R	V	I	V	O	R	One continuing to exist.
S	U	S	P	E	N	S	E	Anxiety, Apprehension, Indecisiveness, Doubtful, Hesitant, Uncertainty, Cautious.
S	U	S	P	I	R	E	D	Sighed, Respired, Longed for something.
S	U	S	U	R	R	U	S	Whispering, rustling or murmuring sound.
S	U	T	U	R	I	N	G	Uniting or fastening with sutures.
S	U	Z	E	R	A	I	N	Overlord, Dominant state.
S	W	A	B	B	I	N	G	Mopping, Wiping up, Sopping.
S	W	A	D	D	L	E	D	Wrapped, Enveloped, Swathed, Restrained, Confined, Restricted.
S	W	A	D	D	L	E	R	Protestant, Methodist preacher.
S	W	A	D	E	S	H	I	An Indian movement to boycott foreign goods.
S	W	A	G	G	I	N	G	Swaying, Vacillating, Drooping, Sagging, Lurching, Tilting, Seesawing, Pitching.
S	W	A	I	N	I	S	H	Boorish, Unrefined, Lacking culture, Ill-bred, Loutish, Lumpish, Churlish, Clownish.
S	W	A	M	P	I	N	G	Inundating, Submerging, Engulfing, Flooding, Ruining, Overpowering, Overwhelming.
S	W	A	M	P	O	A	K	An Australian shrub resembling broom.
S	W	A	M	P	O	R	E	Bog iron ore.
S	W	A	N	H	E	R	D	One who counts and supervises the swans.
S	W	A	N	K	I	N	G	Swaggering, Strutting, Behaving ostentatiously, Pontificating, Showing off.
S	W	A	N	L	I	K	E	Graceful, Sinuous.
S	W	A	N	M	A	R	K	Identification mark cut on the beak of a swan.
S	W	A	N	N	E	C	K	Having a curve resembling the neck of a swan.
S	W	A	N	N	E	R	Y	A place where swans are kept.
S	W	A	N	N	I	N	G	Dallying, Sweeping majestically, Putting on airs and graces.
S	W	A	N	S	H	O	T	Shot used in hunting small game and wildfowl.
S	W	A	N	S	K	I	N	Skin of the swan with the feathers attached, Soft flannel fabric.
S	W	A	N	S	O	N	G	Farewell appearance, Final act, The last word.
S	W	A	P	P	I	N	G	Exchanging, Bartering, Swopping, Pouncing, Substituting, Switching, Trading, Bargaining.
S	W	A	R	D	I	N	G	Covering with turf.
S	W	A	R	M	I	N	G	Migrating, Teeming, Assembling, Abounding, Gathering, Crawling, Flowing, Thronged.
S	W	A	S	H	I	N	G	Swaggering, Sloshing, Burbling, Splashing, Splurging, Shopping, Spattering, Gurgling.
S	W	A	S	H	W	A	Y	A channel between sandbanks.
S	W	A	S	T	I	K	A	A symbol, decoration or ornament in the form of a Greek cross with arms extended.
S	W	A	T	H	I	N	G	Swaddling, Wrapping, Bandaging, Draping, Enveloping, Rolling, Enfolding, Covering.
S	W	A	T	T	I	N	G	Hitting, Striking, Biffing, Clouting, Whacking, Slapping, Slogging.
S	W	E	A	L	I	N	G	Burning, Melting, Scorching, Singeing, Guttering.
S	W	E	A	R	I	N	G	Taking an oath, Making a solemn promise, Testifying, Affirming, Deponing, Cursing.
S	W	E	A	T	I	L	Y	Perspiringly, Laboriously.
S	W	E	A	T	I	N	G	Perspiring, Oozing, Exuding, Fleecing, Fermenting, Putrefying, Steaming, Seeping.
S	W	E	A	T	O	U	T	Endure, Wait, Work painfully or tediously to a solution.
S	W	E	E	P	I	N	G	Brushing, Removing, Collecting, Extensive, Indiscriminate, Dragging, Passing, Cleaning.
S	W	E	E	P	N	E	T	A large fishing net.
S	W	E	E	T	B	A	Y	Laurel, American magnolia.
S	W	E	E	T	G	U	M	A North American tree yielding reddish brown lumber used as imitation mahogany.
S	W	E	E	T	I	N	G	A sweet apple.
S	W	E	E	T	I	S	H	Somewhat sweet, Sickeningly sweet.
S	W	E	E	T	O	I	L	Mild edible oil, Olive oil.
S	W	E	E	T	P	E	A	A climbing garden plant with fragile scented blooms.
S	W	E	E	T	S	O	P	Tropical American tree, Custard apple.
S	W	E	L	L	D	O	M	High society, The world of fashion.

1	2	3	4	5	6	7	8	SYNOPSIS
S	W	E	L	L	I	N	G	Enlarging, Rising, Expansive, Bombastic, Pompous, Rhetorical, Dilating, Flowery.
S	W	E	L	L	I	S	H	Stylish.
S	W	E	L	L	M	O	B	Gangsters who dress well and promote an image of respectability.
S	W	E	R	V	I	N	G	Deviating, Wavering, Veering, Digressing, Diverging, Shifting, Sheering, Deflecting.
S	W	I	F	T	E	S	T	Fastest, Fleetest, Quickest, Most nimble, Most ready, Most hasty.
S	W	I	F	T	L	E	T	The swift that produces the edible bird's nest.
S	W	I	G	G	I	N	G	Swilling, Drinking, Swaying, Rocking, Quaffing, Draining, Hauling.
S	W	I	L	L	I	N	G	Washing, Drenching, Rinsing, Flushing, Guzzling, Pouring, Feeding greedily, Flowing.
S	W	I	M	M	I	N	G	Propelling oneself in water, Floating, Surmounting difficulties, Swaying, Wavering.
S	W	I	M	S	U	I	T	Bathing suit.
S	W	I	N	D	L	E	D	Cheated, Defrauded, Tricked, Bilked, Diddled, Victimized, Gyped.
S	W	I	N	D	L	E	R	Cheat, Swindler.
S	W	I	N	E	P	O	X	Mild virus disease of young pigs.
S	W	I	N	E	S	T	Y	Pigsty.
S	W	I	N	G	I	N	G	Moving through an arc, Rotating, Turning, Oscillating, Waving, Revolving, Rocking.
S	W	I	N	G	L	E	D	Separated by beating.
S	W	I	N	K	I	N	G	Labouring, Toiling, Slaving.
S	W	I	R	L	I	N	G	Whirling, Eddying, Turning, Whorling, Gushing, Swooshing, Surging, Boiling.
S	W	I	S	H	I	N	G	Hissing, Fizzing, Sizzling, Buzzing, Sibilating, Wheezing, Whishing, Flogging.
S	W	I	T	C	H	E	D	Diverted, Shifted, Changed, Shunted, Moved, Lashed, Swung, Struck.
S	W	I	T	C	H	E	L	A drink of molasses or syrup with rum and water and flavoured with ginger and vinegar.
S	W	I	Z	Z	L	E	D	Guzzled, Mixed with a swizzle stick.
S	W	O	O	N	I	N	G	Fainting, Losing consciousness.
S	W	O	O	P	I	N	G	Moving haughtily, Descending, Dislodging, Catching, Swapping, Swallowing, Pouncing.
S	W	O	R	D	A	R	M	The right arm.
S	W	O	T	T	I	N	G	Studying hard and constantly.
S	Y	B	A	R	I	T	E	A person devoted to luxury and pleasure, Voluptuary.
S	Y	C	A	M	I	N	E	Mulberry.
S	Y	C	A	M	O	R	E	A large spreading tree.
S	Y	C	O	N	I	U	M	A fleshy fruit with hollow receptacle for the ovaries.
S	Y	E	N	I	T	I	C	Containing a type of feldspar.
S	Y	L	L	A	B	I	C	Denoting syllables.
S	Y	L	L	A	B	L	E	Unit of spoken language.
S	Y	L	L	A	B	U	B	A milk and cream dessert flavoured with wine.
S	Y	L	L	A	B	U	S	Summary, Treatise, Course of study.
S	Y	L	V	A	T	I	C	Occurring in wild animals.
S	Y	M	B	A	T	I	C	Increasing or decreasing together though not in the same proportions.
S	Y	M	B	O	L	I	C	Expressed in symbols, Representative.
S	Y	M	M	E	T	R	Y	Balance, Harmony, Proportion, Order, Agreement, Conformity, Evenness, Regularity.
S	Y	M	M	I	X	I	S	Material with coarse and fine particles before segregation.
S	Y	M	P	A	T	H	Y	Pity, Compassion, Commiseration, Condolence, Empathy, Kindness, Sensitivity.
S	Y	M	P	H	I	L	E	An insect living in the nest of another type, and giving secretions as food in return for food.
S	Y	M	P	H	O	N	Y	Harmony of sounds, Orchestra, Sinfonia.
S	Y	M	P	H	Y	L	A	A small class of minute arthropods that are rarely seen.
S	Y	M	P	L	A	S	M	A mass of fused bacteria.
S	Y	M	P	L	A	S	T	A multi-nucleate mass of protoplasm.
S	Y	N	A	N	T	H	Y	Coalescence of normally separate flowers.
S	Y	N	A	P	S	I	D	Fossil reptile.
S	Y	N	A	P	S	I	S	Contact of the nerve cell.
S	Y	N	A	P	T	I	C	Same as SYNAPSIS.
S	Y	N	A	R	C	H	Y	Joint rule, Joint sovereignty.
S	Y	N	A	S	T	R	Y	Co-incidence of birth signs in astrology.
S	Y	N	C	L	I	N	E	A trough of stratified rock.
S	Y	N	C	O	P	A	L	Characterized by syncope, fainting.
S	Y	N	D	E	S	I	S	Pertaining to synapsis.
S	Y	N	D	E	T	I	C	Connecting, Connective.
S	Y	N	D	R	O	M	E	Group of symptoms typical of a disease, disturbance or condition in animals or plants.
S	Y	N	E	C	H	I	A	Disease of the eye.
S	Y	N	E	R	G	I	C	Co-operating, Co-operative.
S	Y	N	E	R	E	S	E	Become dense with the loss of fluid.
S	Y	N	G	A	M	I	C	Involving sexual reproduction.
S	Y	N	G	A	M	I	D	Family of parasitic nematode worms.
S	Y	N	G	A	M	U	S	Same as SYNGAMID.
S	Y	N	G	R	A	P	H	A written contract signed and sealed.
S	Y	N	O	D	I	S	T	One who supports a synod.
S	Y	N	O	N	Y	M	E	Synonym, Words having the same meaning.
S	Y	N	O	P	S	I	S	Condensed statement, Brief outline, Summary, Abridgment, Epitome, Breviary.

1	2	3	4	5	6	7	8	
S	Y	N	O	P	T	I	C	Comprehensive, Presentation of a physical theory.
S	Y	N	O	V	I	A	L	Relating to the lubricating fluid of joints and tendons.
S	Y	N	T	A	X	I	C	Relating to a mode of experience.
S	Y	N	T	A	X	I	S	Syntax, Relating to grammar.
S	Y	N	T	E	X	I	C	Originating of magma by melting of rocks.
S	Y	N	T	O	N	I	C	Being in harmony with one's environment.
S	Y	P	H	A	C	I	A	Genus of parasitic nematode worms.
S	Y	S	T	E	M	I	C	Common to a system, Affecting the whole body.
S	Y	S	T	O	L	I	C	Contraction of the heart keeping up the circulation.
S	Y	Z	Y	G	I	A	L	Relating to a syzygy.

T

T	A	B	A	N	U	C	O	Candlewood.
T	A	B	A	R	D	E	D	Wearing a tabard.
T	A	B	A	S	H	I	R	Siliceous growth in the joints of bamboo valued as a medicine.
T	A	B	B	I	N	E	T	Tabinet, Silk and worsted fabric similar to poplin.
T	A	B	B	Y	C	A	T	A cat with a striped or streaked coat.
T	A	B	L	E	A	U	X	Images, Pictures, Arrangements, Scenes, Artistic grouping.
T	A	B	L	E	C	U	T	Custom made, Individually made.
T	A	B	L	E	F	U	L	As much as a table can hold or as many as a table will accommodate.
T	A	B	L	I	N	U	M	A room in a Roman house for storing family records.
T	A	B	O	O	I	N	G	Prohibiting, Banning, Shunning, Avoiding, Interdicting, Outlawing, Inhibiting.
T	A	B	O	R	I	N	E	Tabret, Tambourine.
T	A	B	O	R	I	N	G	Striking or tapping repetitively.
T	A	B	O	R	I	T	E	Member of radical wing of the Hussites.
T	A	B	U	L	A	T	A	An artificial group of stony corals.
T	A	B	U	L	A	T	E	Enumerate, Catalogue, Summarize, Condense.
T	A	C	H	I	N	I	D	Family of specialized two-winged flies.
T	A	C	I	T	U	R	N	Laconic, Reticent, Dour, Silent, Reserved, Wordless, Uncommunicative, Brooding.
T	A	C	K	L	I	N	G	Seizing, Holding, Attacking, Undertaking, Grasping, Solving, Confronting, Challenging.
T	A	C	K	S	M	A	N	Lessee.
T	A	C	T	I	C	A	L	Short range planning, Expedient, Tactful, Diplomatic, Prudent, Advisable, Politic, Strategic.
T	A	C	T	L	E	S	S	Inconsiderate, Undiplomatic, Blunt, Inept, Brash, Rude, Impolite, Bungling.
T	A	E	N	I	A	D	A	Parasitic flatworm.
T	A	E	N	I	A	T	E	With longitude stripes.
T	A	F	F	R	A	I	L	The upper flat part of the stern of a wooden ship.
T	A	G	I	L	I	T	E	A mineral consisting of a hydrous basic copper phosphate.
T	A	G	M	O	S	I	S	Division of the arthropod body.
T	A	I	L	B	A	N	D	Footband.
T	A	I	L	B	O	O	M	Boom.
T	A	I	L	C	O	A	T	A man's full dress coat with tails.
T	A	I	L	G	A	T	E	A rear gate, Back door of rear loading vehicle.
T	A	I	L	I	N	G	S	Gruffs.
T	A	I	L	L	E	S	S	Having no tail.
T	A	I	L	O	R	E	D	Fashioned, Made by a tailor, Adapted for a special purpose, Fitted, Styled.
T	A	I	L	R	A	C	E	A channel for conveying industrial water from point of use.
T	A	I	L	R	O	P	E	A rope attached to the rear end.
T	A	I	L	S	P	I	N	Chaos, Demoralization, Depression, Disorder.
T	A	I	N	T	I	N	G	Tinting, Anointing, Corrupting, Defiling, Depraving, Staining, Rotting, Contaminating.
T	A	I	N	T	U	R	E	Defilement, Stain.
T	A	K	E	O	V	E	R	To acquire control, Taking possession, Displacing someone.
T	A	K	E	R	O	F	F	Mimic, One that takes something off.
T	A	K	I	N	G	L	Y	Attractively, Engagingly, Captivatingly, Winningly.
T	A	L	A	P	O	I	N	A Western African monkey.
T	A	L	A	V	E	R	A	Spanish glazed and decorated earthenware.
T	A	L	E	N	T	E	D	Accomplished, Gifted, Skilled, Genius, Expert.
T	A	L	E	S	M	A	N	Person summoned for jury duty.
T	A	L	I	S	M	A	N	A charm against evil, Amulet, Fetish, Mascot.
T	A	L	K	A	B	L	E	Disposed to friendly conversation.
T	A	L	K	D	O	W	N	Disparage, Belittle, To bring an aeroplane to a safe landing by radioed instructions.
T	A	L	L	N	E	S	S	The state of being tall.
T	A	L	L	O	W	E	D	Greased with tallow.
T	A	L	L	Y	I	N	G	Tabulating, Recording, Matching, Agreeing, Reckoning, Totalling, Listing, Checking.
T	A	L	L	Y	M	A	N	One who sells goods on instalments.
T	A	L	M	U	D	I	C	Characteristic of the Talmud.

1	2	3	4	5	6	7	8	Definition
T	A	M	A	N	D	U	A	A South American ant-eater.
T	A	M	A	N	O	I	R	Ant-bear.
T	A	M	A	R	A	C	K	A tree of the American larch family.
T	A	M	A	R	I	N	D	Tropical tree with flowers that are eaten in India and that yields a very useful fruit.
T	A	M	A	R	I	S	K	A flowering shrub.
T	A	M	B	O	U	R	A	Four-stringed instrument from India, resembling a lute.
T	A	M	B	O	U	T	I	An African tree with hard slightly fragrant wood.
T	A	M	E	A	B	L	E	Capable of being tamed.
T	A	M	E	L	E	S	S	Not capable of being tamed.
T	A	M	E	N	E	S	S	Being tame.
T	A	M	P	E	R	E	D	Meddled, Interfered, Intervened, Doctored, Manipulated, Bribed, Squared, Lubricated.
T	A	M	P	E	R	E	R	Busybody, Meddling person.
T	A	N	G	E	L	O	S	Hybrid fruit of a tangerine and lemon.
T	A	N	G	E	N	C	Y	Touching, Being in contact.
T	A	N	G	I	B	L	E	Palpable, Tactile, Touchable, Physical, Material, Real, Perceptible, Substantial.
T	A	N	G	I	B	L	Y	Obviously, Perceptibly, Materially.
T	A	N	G	L	I	N	G	Entrapping, Complicating, Uniting, Hampering, Obstructing, Interweaving, Involving.
T	A	N	H	O	U	S	E	A building where tanning is carried out.
T	A	N	I	S	T	R	Y	Early Irish law of succession.
T	A	N	T	A	L	U	M	A hard ductile metallic element that has a very high melting point.
T	A	N	T	A	L	U	S	Genus of storks, Ibis.
T	A	N	T	I	E	M	E	Share of the profits, Bonus.
T	A	N	T	R	I	S	M	School of Buddhism.
T	A	P	A	C	O	L	O	Small terrestrial bird of Chile and Argentina.
T	A	P	A	D	E	R	A	A leather cover attached to a stirrup to protect boots.
T	A	P	D	A	N	C	E	A rhythm dance that is tapped out with shoes fitted with metal tips.
T	A	P	E	L	I	N	E	Tape measure.
T	A	P	E	R	I	N	G	Diminishing, Decreasing, Abating, Closing, Dwindling, Lessening, Reducing, Draining.
T	A	P	E	S	T	R	Y	Hand woven fabric made on a loom.
T	A	P	E	W	O	R	M	A parasitic worm.
T	A	P	H	R	I	N	A	Genus of parasitic fungi.
T	A	P	I	N	O	M	A	Genus of small ants with a pungent odour.
T	A	P	I	R	O	I	D	Relating to a tapir.
T	A	R	A	K	I	H	I	Pacific food fish, Sea carp.
T	A	R	A	X	E	I	N	A substance found in the blood of schizophrenic persons.
T	A	R	B	A	G	A	N	A marmot of central Asia.
T	A	R	B	O	O	S	H	A red hat similar to a fez.
T	A	R	G	E	T	E	D	Made a target of. Determined a set course.
T	A	R	G	U	M	I	C	Relating to Aramaic translations of parts of the Old Testament.
T	A	R	I	F	F	E	D	Levied a tariff, Set a fixed price.
T	A	R	L	A	T	A	N	Stiff cotton fabric used mostly in theatrical costumes.
T	A	R	O	G	A	T	O	Hungarian musical instrument.
T	A	R	P	E	I	A	N	A cliff used by the ancient Romans for execution of criminals.
T	A	R	R	A	G	O	N	The foliage of a perennial wormwood used for the manufacture of vinegar and pickles.
T	A	R	R	Y	I	N	G	Delaying, Hindering, Wasting, Procrastinating, Staying, Dawdling, Idling, Loitering.
T	A	R	S	I	O	I	D	Related to the lemur.
T	A	R	S	I	P	E	S	Genus of marsupial mammals, Honey possum.
T	A	R	T	A	R	I	C	Derived from tartaric acid.
T	A	R	T	A	R	I	N	Sacred baboon.
T	A	R	T	A	R	U	S	Nether regions, Hell, Hades.
T	A	R	T	N	E	S	S	Sharpness, With asperity.
T	A	R	T	R	A	T	E	An ester of tartaric acid.
T	A	R	W	A	T	E	R	Tar soaked in cold water and once regarded as a medicine to cure all afflictions.
T	A	S	K	W	O	R	K	Piece work, Hard work, Drudgery.
T	A	S	T	A	B	L	E	Capable of being tasted.
T	A	S	T	E	B	U	D	Tiny organs of taste on the tongue.
T	A	S	T	E	F	U	L	Showing good taste, Elegant, Stylish, Appetizing, Savoury, Restrained, Subdued.
T	A	T	T	E	R	E	D	Torn in shreds.
T	A	T	T	L	I	N	G	Chattering, Telling tales, Gossiping.
T	A	T	T	O	O	E	D	Having a design pricked on the skin with coloured ink.
T	A	T	T	O	O	E	R	One earning a living by forming or removing tattoos.
T	A	T	U	K	I	R	A	A small S. American biting fly believed to carry disease.
T	A	U	N	T	I	N	G	Insulting, Upbraiding, Ridiculing, Deriding, Mocking, Provoking, Scorning, Offending.
T	A	U	R	A	N	G	A	New Zealand bush sickness.
T	A	U	T	E	N	E	D	Tightened, Stretched, Tensed, Closed, Firmed, Strained.
T	A	U	T	N	E	S	S	Tightness, Tenseness, Firmness.
T	A	V	E	R	N	E	R	An innkeeper.

1	2	3	4	5	6	7	8	Definition
T	A	W	D	R	I	L	Y	Gaudily, Flashily, Garishly.
T	A	X	A	C	E	A	E	Evergreen shrubs and trees.
T	A	X	A	T	I	O	N	Raising revenue by imposing tax.
T	A	X	I	A	R	C	H	A commander of a unit of the ancient Greek army.
T	A	X	O	D	I	U	M	Tall deciduous trees with drooping branches, Bald Cypress.
T	A	X	O	L	O	G	Y	Classification of animals and plants.
T	A	X	O	N	O	M	Y	Same as TAXOLOGY.
T	A	X	P	A	Y	E	R	One liable for the payment of tax.
T	E	A	B	O	A	R	D	A tray for serving tea.
T	E	A	C	A	D	D	Y	A canister for storing tea.
T	E	A	C	H	E	S	T	A square wooden case used for the transporting of tea.
T	E	A	C	H	I	N	G	Instructing, Doctrine, Guiding, Directing, Educating, Training, Coaching, Tuition.
T	E	A	L	L	I	T	E	A mineral consisting of a sulfide of tin and lead.
T	E	A	M	S	T	E	R	One whose occupation is driving a team of horses or a motortruck.
T	E	A	M	W	O	R	K	Co-operation of a group to bring a project to efficient fruition.
T	E	A	R	D	R	O	P	A tear, Something resembling the shape of a dropping tear.
T	E	A	R	D	U	C	T	A duct in the corner of the eye.
T	E	A	R	L	E	S	S	Free from tears.
T	E	C	H	N	I	C	S	Technology, Technical terms or details.
T	E	C	T	O	N	I	C	Relating to building or constructing, Study of the deformation of the earth's crust.
T	E	E	N	A	G	E	R	A young person in their teens.
T	E	E	T	E	R	E	D	Faltered, Lurched, Staggered, Stammered, Stumbled, Toppled, Tottered, Wobbled.
T	E	E	T	H	I	N	G	The breaking through of the first set of teeth through the gums.
T	E	E	T	O	T	A	L	Total abstinence from alcoholic drinks.
T	E	E	T	O	T	U	M	A small spinning top.
T	E	G	U	E	X	I	N	Genus of lizards.
T	E	G	U	M	E	N	T	A covering membrane.
T	E	L	A	B	L	E	M	Membrane covering young spore of mushrooms.
T	E	L	E	C	A	S	T	Broadcast by television.
T	E	L	E	C	I	N	E	Televised motion picture.
T	E	L	E	F	I	L	M	Motion picture produced for televising.
T	E	L	E	G	O	N	Y	Influence believed to be exerted by the first mate of a dam on the offspring by later sires.
T	E	L	E	G	R	A	M	A message by telegraph.
T	E	L	E	S	T	I	C	Mystical.
T	E	L	E	T	A	P	E	A special fast transmission of telegraph tape.
T	E	L	E	T	H	O	N	A television programme lasting longer than usual.
T	E	L	E	T	Y	P	E	A message sent on a Teletype machine.
T	E	L	E	V	I	E	W	To watch a television show on a receiver.
T	E	L	E	V	I	S	E	Broadcast by television.
T	E	L	L	T	A	L	E	Informer, Gossip, Sandalmonger, Hint, Clue, Indication, Inkling, Suggestion.
T	E	L	L	U	R	I	C	Terrestrial.
T	E	L	O	O	G	O	O	Dravidian language of the Telegu people.
T	E	L	O	T	Y	P	E	Automatically printed telegram.
T	E	M	E	R	I	T	Y	Audacity, Nerve, Effrontery, Cheek, Gall, Brashness, Reckless, Hardihood.
T	E	M	P	E	R	E	D	Moderated, Temperate, Restrained, Modulated, Softened, Pacified, Adjusted, Diluted.
T	E	M	P	L	A	T	E	Pattern, Guide, Guage.
T	E	M	P	O	R	A	L	Temporary, Transitory, Terrestrial, Civil, Political, Mundane, Worldly, Secular.
T	E	M	P	T	I	N	G	Seducing, Provoking, Inciting, Persuading, Testing, Prompting, Alluring, Rousing.
T	E	N	A	C	I	T	Y	Determination, Firmness, Persistence, Adhesiveness, Resistance, Retentiveness.
T	E	N	A	I	L	L	E	A rampart between bastions of a fortification.
T	E	N	A	N	T	E	D	Inhabited, Held, Occupied, Possessed, Dwelt, Populated.
T	E	N	A	N	T	R	Y	Tenancy, Occupying as a tenant.
T	E	N	D	A	N	C	E	Ministration, Giving attention, Service, Homage.
T	E	N	D	E	N	C	Y	Bias, Inclination, Trend, Drift, Current, Habit, Usage, Propensity.
T	E	N	D	E	R	E	D	Offered, Proffered, Extended, Gave, Proposed, Purposed, Submitted, Suggested.
T	E	N	D	E	R	L	Y	Gently, Softly, Leniently, Cautiously, Warmly.
T	E	N	E	B	R	A	E	A church service during the final part of Holy Week.
T	E	N	E	M	E	N	T	Residence, Dwelling, Habitation, Apartment, Flat.
T	E	N	E	S	M	U	S	Painful and ineffectual urge to perform natural evacuation functions.
T	E	N	O	N	I	N	G	Uniting by a tenon, fixing with a tenon joint.
T	E	N	O	R	I	S	T	One who sings tenor or plays a tenor instrument.
T	E	N	O	R	I	T	E	A mineral that is native cupric oxide.
T	E	N	O	T	O	M	E	A delicate surgical instrument.
T	E	N	S	I	B	L	E	Capable of being extended.
T	E	N	T	A	C	L	E	Feeler, Stalks, Tendril, Long flexible slender organ of feeling, Sensitive hairs.
T	E	N	T	E	R	E	D	Fabric hung or stretched on a rack to dry.
T	E	N	U	R	I	A	L	Relating to tenure of land.

1	2	3	4	5	6	7	8	Definition
T	E	O	C	A	L	L	I	An ancient temple of Mexico built upon a mound.
T	E	O	S	I	N	T	E	A large annual grass of Central American from which it is believed Indian corn was developed.
T	E	P	E	T	A	T	E	Caliche, Nitrate-bearing gravel or rock.
T	E	P	I	D	I	T	Y	Lukewarmness, Lifeless, Spiritless, Dullness.
T	E	R	A	P	H	I	M	Images representing primitive household gods of ancient Jews.
T	E	R	A	T	I	S	M	Monstrosity, Worship of monsters.
T	E	R	A	T	O	M	A	A tumour composed of various tissues.
T	E	R	A	T	O	D	E	Same as TERATOID.
T	E	R	C	E	R	O	N	Quadroon.
T	E	R	E	B	E	N	E	A liquid mixture of tepenes.
T	E	R	F	E	Z	I	A	Genus of fungi resembling truffles.
T	E	R	M	I	N	A	L	Lateral, Concluding, Final, Ultimate, Last, Latter, Hindmost, Eventual.
T	E	R	M	I	N	U	S	End, Starting point, Term, Extremity, Tip, Period, Termination, Cessation.
T	E	R	M	L	E	S	S	Unconditioned, Boundless, Unending, Unconditional.
T	E	R	P	E	N	I	C	Derived from a terpene.
T	E	R	R	A	C	E	D	Being in terraces.
T	E	R	R	A	P	I	N	Family of turtles.
T	E	R	R	A	Z	Z	O	Surface or floor of a type of mosaic.
T	E	R	R	I	B	L	E	Frightening, Terrifying, Bad, Destructive, Awful, Disreputable, Obnoxious, Fearful.
T	E	R	R	I	B	L	Y	Awesomely, Extremely, Tensely, Appallingly, Dreadfully, Exceedingly, Highly, Remarkably.
T	E	R	R	I	F	I	C	Powerful, Severe, Magnificent, Marvellous, Fearful, Astounding, Tremendous, Awful.
T	E	R	T	I	A	R	Y	Of the third rank or order.
T	E	R	U	T	E	R	O	South American lapwing.
T	E	R	Y	L	E	N	E	Fabric of synthetic fibres.
T	E	R	Z	E	T	T	O	Musical composition for three voices.
T	E	S	S	E	L	L	A	Piece of mosaic or small tile, Identifying token.
T	E	S	S	E	R	A	E	Same as TESSELLA.
T	E	S	S	E	R	A	L	Same as TESSELLA.
T	E	S	T	A	B	L	E	Qualified to bear witness or make a will.
T	E	S	T	A	C	E	A	Lower form of aquatic animal with a shell.
T	E	S	T	A	M	U	R	A certificate for a pass in a University examination.
T	E	S	T	A	T	O	R	A person leaving a valid will.
T	E	S	T	C	A	S	E	A case that will test judgment and serve as a precedent.
T	E	S	T	I	C	L	E	Male genital gland.
T	E	S	T	T	U	B	E	A tube of glass used for simple tests in science.
T	E	T	A	N	I	Z	E	To induce tetanus.
T	E	T	A	N	O	I	D	Resembling tetanus.
T	E	T	C	H	I	L	Y	Touchily, Irritability, Crossly.
T	E	T	H	E	R	E	D	Bound, Restrained by a rope or thong, Restricted, Tied, Fastened.
T	E	T	R	A	D	I	C	Relating to a group of four.
T	E	T	R	A	L	I	N	Tetrahydronapthalene.
T	E	T	R	A	P	L	A	A polygot book with four texts in parallel columns.
T	E	T	R	A	P	O	D	A four-footed animal, Quadruped, Something with four arms or projections.
T	E	T	R	A	R	C	H	Groups of four in ruling or management.
T	E	T	R	A	X	O	N	A sponge spicule.
T	E	T	R	I	G	I	D	Family of leaping insects, Grouse locust.
T	E	T	R	I	T	O	L	Tetrahydroxy alcohol.
T	E	T	R	O	B	O	L	Ancient Grecian silver coin.
T	E	T	R	O	D	O	N	Tropical marine fishes.
T	E	U	T	O	N	I	C	Germanic.
T	E	X	T	B	O	O	K	A book published for the study of a specific subject.
T	E	X	T	H	A	N	D	Style of handwriting using large letters.
T	E	X	T	U	R	A	L	Marked by texture.
T	E	X	T	U	A	R	Y	A biblical scholar.
T	H	A	L	A	M	I	C	Involving the thalamus.
T	H	A	L	A	M	U	S	Part of the brain.
T	H	A	L	L	I	U	M	Metallic element.
T	H	A	N	E	D	O	M	Land held by a thane.
T	H	A	N	K	F	U	L	Grateful, Glad, Well pleased, Obliged.
T	H	A	N	K	I	N	G	Expressing gratitude, Acknowledging gratefully.
T	H	A	T	C	H	E	D	Covered or roofed with thatch.
T	H	A	T	C	H	E	R	One that thatches.
T	H	E	A	R	C	H	Y	Divine sovereignty, System of ruling by gods.
T	H	E	B	A	I	N	E	A poisonous crystalline alkaloid found in opium.
T	H	E	I	T	S	E	E	Black varnish tree.
T	H	E	I	S	T	I	C	Relating to the belief in one God.
T	H	E	M	A	T	I	C	Relating to the stem of a word, Subject of artistic or cultural expression.

1	2	3	4	5	6	7	8	Clue
T	H	E	O	C	R	A	T	One who lives under a government of rule by priests or clergy.
T	H	E	O	D	I	C	Y	Philosophy.
T	H	E	O	G	O	N	Y	Mythology dealing with the origin and descent of gods.
T	H	E	O	L	O	G	Y	Study of a doctrine or religious practices.
T	H	E	O	R	I	E	S	Beliefs, Policies, Procedures, Conjectures, Speculations, Assumptions, Hunches.
T	H	E	O	R	I	S	T	One who formulates theories.
T	H	E	O	R	I	Z	E	To form opinions solely by theories.
T	H	E	O	S	O	P	H	Theosophist, A person inspired by mysticism.
T	H	E	R	B	L	I	G	Analyzing of manual operations in industry.
T	H	E	R	E	F	O	R	Therefore, Then, Accordingly, Hence, Consequently.
T	H	E	R	E	O	U	T	Therefrom, From that, From it.
T	H	E	R	I	A	C	A	An antidote for poison consisting of certain drugs mixed with honey.
T	H	E	R	M	I	O	N	An electrically charged particle.
T	H	E	S	P	I	A	N	Dramatic, Relating to acting, Theatrical.
T	H	E	U	R	G	I	C	Magical.
T	H	E	V	E	T	I	A	Genus of tropical American shrubs and trees, Oleander.
T	H	E	V	E	T	I	N	A poisonous crystalline cardiac glucoside from oleander seeds.
T	H	E	W	L	E	S	S	Thowless, Feeble, Lazy, Spiritless, Weak, Inanimate, Languid, Listless.
T	H	I	A	M	I	N	E	Belonging to vitamin B complex.
T	H	I	A	Z	I	N	E	Compound of four carbon atoms, one sulfur atom and one nitrogen atom.
T	H	I	A	Z	O	L	E	Compound that has an odour resembling pyridine.
T	H	I	C	K	E	S	T	Broadest, Widest, Most stocky, Most massive, Most stupid.
T	H	I	C	K	I	S	H	Rather thickset.
T	H	I	C	K	S	E	T	Burly, Stocky, Planted closely.
T	H	I	E	V	E	R	Y	Theft.
T	H	I	E	V	I	N	G	Stealing, Robbing, Filching, Purloining, Pilfering, Larceny, Pinching, Lifting.
T	H	I	E	V	I	S	H	Larcenous, Stealthy, Sly.
T	H	I	G	G	I	N	G	Begging.
T	H	I	N	K	I	N	G	Conceiving, Imagining, Assuming, Envisaging, Featuring, Realizing, Understanding.
T	H	I	N	N	E	S	S	Slimness, Leanness, Lankness, Gauntness, Smallness, Slenderness.
T	H	I	N	N	E	S	T	Lankest, Leanest, Slimmest.
T	H	I	N	N	I	N	G	Attenuating, Extenuating, Diminishing, Reducing, Diluting, Weakening, Cutting, Pruning.
T	H	I	N	N	I	S	H	Meagre, Spare, Rather slender.
T	H	I	O	A	C	I	D	An acid in which sulfur replaces oxygen.
T	H	I	O	N	A	T	E	Ester of a thionic acid.
T	H	I	O	N	I	N	E	A dye used as a biological stain.
T	H	I	O	P	H	E	N	Heterocyclic compound.
T	H	I	O	U	R	E	A	A bitter crystalline compound that resembles urea.
T	H	I	R	L	A	G	E	A feudal servitude.
T	H	I	R	S	T	E	D	Craved, Longed, Ached, Hankered, Hungered, Lusted, Pined, Yearned.
T	H	I	R	T	E	E	N	One more than twelve.
T	H	I	S	N	E	S	S	Reality.
T	H	O	L	E	P	I	N	A pair of pins in place of an oarlock.
T	H	O	M	I	S	I	D	A crab spider.
T	H	O	R	A	C	I	C	Pertaining to the chest and related organs.
T	H	O	R	I	A	T	E	To impregnate an electron-tube cathode with thoria.
T	H	O	R	O	U	G	H	Complete, Exhaustive, Absolute, Circumstantial, Detailed, Minute, Particular, Full.
T	H	O	U	S	A	N	D	A hundred multiplied by a hundred, A large number.
T	H	R	A	L	D	O	M	Slavery, Bondage, Serfdom, Yoke, Peonage, Servitude, Enslavement.
T	H	R	A	N	I	T	E	The highest position in a group of three rowers.
T	H	R	A	P	P	L	E	Throat or windpipe of a horse.
T	H	R	A	S	H	E	D	Threshing, Pounding, Flogging, Drubbing, Beating, Flailing, Overthrowing, Trouncing.
T	H	R	A	S	H	E	R	Thresher, Family of birds.
T	H	R	A	W	A	R	D	Stubborn, Perverse, Crooked, Twisted.
T	H	R	E	A	D	E	D	Penetrated, Passed, Through, Pierced, Strung.
T	H	R	E	A	D	E	N	Made of thread.
T	H	R	E	A	D	E	R	A device for threading a needle.
T	H	R	E	A	P	E	D	Pressed, Disputed, Wrangled.
T	H	R	E	A	T	E	N	Warn, Menace, Browbeat, Intimidate, Cow, Forebode, Caution, Forewarn.
T	H	R	E	E	P	L	Y	Having three strands or layers.
T	H	R	E	N	O	D	Y	A song of lamentation for a dead person.
T	H	R	E	N	O	D	E	Same as THRENODE.
T	H	R	E	P	T	I	C	Relating to the rearing of young by ants and other social insects.
T	H	R	E	S	H	E	D	Beat grain, Thrashed, Struck, Flailed, Rubbed, Discussed.
T	H	R	E	S	H	E	R	A threshing machine.
T	H	R	I	L	L	E	D	Enthused, Electrified, Animated, Excited, Stimulated, Inspired, Aroused, Galvanized.
T	H	R	I	L	L	E	R	A book, film or play that is full of suspense.

1	2	3	4	5	6	7	8	
T	H	R	I	P	P	L	E	An extension rail used on a hay wagon.
T	H	R	I	V	I	N	G	Succeeding, Prospering, Advancing, Flourishing, Developing, Growing, Increasing.
T	H	R	O	B	B	E	D	Pulsated, Palpitated, Vibrated, Beat, Thumped, Resonated.
T	H	R	O	M	B	I	N	An enzyme that assists the blood to clot.
T	H	R	O	M	B	U	S	A blood clot within a blood vessel.
T	H	R	O	N	G	E	D	Crowded, Compressed, Squeezed, Packed, Jammed, Abounding, Overflowing, Swarming.
T	H	R	O	N	I	N	G	Enthroning, Raising to power.
T	H	R	O	P	P	L	E	Throttle.
T	H	R	O	S	T	L	E	Thrush, Old-fashioned cotton spinning device.
T	H	R	O	T	T	L	E	Choke, Strangle, Garrote, Repress, Smother, Extinguish, Squash, Silence.
T	H	R	O	W	I	N	G	Casting, Flinging, Heaving, Hurling, Launching, Pitching, Slinging, Tossing.
T	H	R	O	W	O	U	T	Eject, Discard, Jettison, Scrap, Dismiss, Evict, Extrude, Shed.
T	H	R	U	M	M	E	D	Strummed.
T	H	R	U	M	M	E	R	A strolling player.
T	H	R	U	S	T	E	R	Pusher, One that intrudes himself.
T	H	U	D	D	I	N	G	Striking, Thumping, Clunking, Pounding.
T	H	U	G	G	E	R	Y	The actions of professional gangsters.
T	H	U	M	B	I	N	G	Leafing or paging through a book, Browsing, Hitching a lift.
T	H	U	M	B	N	U	T	A nut designed to be turned by hand, Wing-nut.
T	H	U	M	B	P	O	T	Tiny flower pot used for seedlings.
T	H	U	M	P	I	N	G	Pounding, Knocking, Hammering, Thrashing, Whipping, Thudding.
T	H	U	N	D	E	R	Y	Likely to produce thunder, Ominous, Threatening.
T	H	U	R	I	B	L	E	A censer used in religious services.
T	H	U	R	I	F	E	R	One who carries a censer.
T	H	U	R	S	D	A	Y	The fifth day of the week.
T	H	U	S	W	I	S	E	Thus, So.
T	H	W	A	C	K	E	D	Thruck, Whacked, Beaten, Packed, Punished, Defeated, Rebuked, Satirized.
T	H	W	A	R	T	E	D	Opposed, Baffled, Contravened, Frustrated, Quarrelled, Clashed, Obstructed, Hampered.
T	H	W	A	R	T	E	R	One who obstructs or hinders.
T	H	Y	R	S	O	I	D	In the form of a thyrse.
T	I	A	R	E	L	L	A	Small genus of N. American herbs.
T	I	B	I	A	L	I	S	Muscle of the calf of the leg.
T	I	C	K	B	E	A	N	Horsebean having small seeds shaped like a tick.
T	I	C	K	E	T	E	D	Labelled, Classified, Booked, Designated, Described.
T	I	C	K	L	I	N	G	Exciting the surface nerves, Titillation, Stimulating, Annoying, Tormenting, Provoking.
T	I	C	K	L	I	S	H	Touchy, Unsteady, Unstable, Over-sensitive, Unreliable, Delicate, Critical, Inconstant.
T	I	C	K	T	A	C	K	Secret signalling of bookmakers on the racecourse.
T	I	C	K	T	I	C	K	The repeated ticking of a clock or watch.
T	I	C	K	T	O	C	K	Same as TICK-TICK.
T	I	D	E	G	A	T	E	A gate to control flow of tidal water.
T	I	D	E	L	E	S	S	Having no tides.
T	I	D	E	L	O	C	K	A lock to enable ships to pass through canals and harbours regardless of the level of tides.
T	I	D	E	M	A	R	K	Mark left by either high or low tide.
T	I	D	E	M	I	L	L	A mill operated by tidal currents.
T	I	D	E	S	M	A	N	Customs officer working at dockside or aboard ships.
T	I	D	E	W	A	V	E	Rise and fall of water within the earth's movement.
T	I	D	I	N	E	S	S	Neatness, Trimness, Sleekness, Spruceness.
T	I	G	E	R	C	A	T	A moderately sized wild cat, Serval, Ocelot.
T	I	G	E	R	E	Y	E	Yellow-brown chatoyant stone used in jewellery.
T	I	G	E	R	I	S	H	Resembling a tiger in grace, voracity or ferocity.
T	I	G	E	R	I	S	M	Showy ostentation.
T	I	G	H	T	I	S	H	Close-fitting.
T	I	G	H	T	W	A	D	A miserly person, Parsimonious.
T	I	L	L	A	B	L	E	Arable land, Able to be tilled.
T	I	L	L	E	R	E	D	Shaped to correct a curvature.
T	I	L	T	Y	A	R	D	A place for tilting.
T	I	M	B	E	R	E	D	Constructed of timber.
T	I	M	E	B	A	L	L	A large ball on a mast.
T	I	M	E	B	I	L	L	A bill of exchange payable on a designated future date.
T	I	M	E	B	O	M	B	A bomb that explodes at a fixed time, An explosive situation.
T	I	M	E	B	O	O	K	A time record of hours taken for a job.
T	I	M	E	C	A	R	D	A card for an employee to record time of arrival and departure.
T	I	M	E	F	U	S	E	A detonating fuse that operates after a certain time has elapsed.
T	I	M	E	L	E	S	S	Eternal, Interminable, Unending, Dateless, Ageless, Changeless, Continual, Ceaseless.
T	I	M	E	W	O	R	K	Work paid for by the piece or the time spent.
T	I	M	E	W	O	R	N	Ancient, Aged, Hackneyed, Decayed, Weatherbeaten.
T	I	M	I	D	I	T	Y	Shyness, Gentleness, Mildness, Cautiously, Nervousness, Uncertainty.

1	2	3	4	5	6	7	8	
T	I	M	O	N	E	E	R	Helmsman.
T	I	M	O	N	I	S	M	Misanthropy.
T	I	M	O	R	O	S	O	Direction in music, hesitating, Timid.
T	I	M	O	R	O	U	S	Afraid, Apprehensive, Timid, Fearful.
T	I	N	C	T	U	R	E	Pigment, Stain, Tint, Extract, Cast, Touch, Hint, Trace.
T	I	N	E	I	D	A	E	A family of small coloured moths.
T	I	N	G	E	I	N	G	Tinting, Casting, Touching, Colouring, Shading, Toning, Sprinkling, Suggestion.
T	I	N	G	L	I	N	G	Stinging, Pricking, Tinkling, Stirring, Stimulating, Chiming, Jingling, Thrilling.
T	I	N	G	T	A	N	G	A special chime in a clock.
T	I	N	K	E	R	E	D	Repaired or adjusted in an inefficient manner, Fiddled, Doodled, Pottered, Puttered.
T	I	N	K	L	I	N	G	Clinking, Chinking, Rhyming, Chatting, Babbling, Clacking, Prattling, Gabbing.
T	I	N	N	I	T	U	S	Ringing, roaring or hissing noise in the ears.
T	I	N	P	L	A	T	E	Thin sheet metal coated with tin.
T	I	N	S	E	L	L	Y	Tinseled, Tawdry.
T	I	N	S	M	I	T	H	One who makes or repairs metal objects.
T	I	N	S	T	O	N	E	Cassiterite, Brown or black mineral that consists of tin dioxide.
T	I	N	T	A	M	A	R	Uproar, Din, Babel, Clamour, Hubbub, Pandemonium, Racket, Tumult.
T	I	N	T	L	E	S	S	Lacking colour.
T	I	P	P	L	I	N	G	Squandering, Drinking, Boozing, Guzzling, Imbibing, Swilling, Swigging, Soaking.
T	I	P	S	T	A	F	F	A metal-tipped staff carried as a badge of offce, Constable, Bailiff.
T	I	R	E	L	E	S	S	Indefatigable, Inexhaustible, Untiring, Active, Enthusiastic.
T	I	R	E	S	O	M	E	Tedious, Wearisome, Boring, Drudging, Tiring, Onerous, Oppressive, Difficult.
T	I	R	O	D	I	T	E	A mineral consisting of a basic silicate of magnesium.
T	I	R	O	N	I	A	N	Relating to Tiro.
T	I	R	R	I	V	I	E	Commotion, Outburst.
T	I	S	S	U	I	N	G	Weaving into tissue, Embroidering or interweaving.
T	I	T	A	N	A	T	E	Various compounds that are multiple oxides.
T	I	T	A	N	E	S	S	A female giant.
T	I	T	A	N	I	A	N	Containing titanium.
T	I	T	A	N	I	S	M	Headlong revolt against limits, Freedom from all restraints.
T	I	T	A	N	I	T	E	Sphene, A mineral that is a silicate of calcium and titanium.
T	I	T	H	A	B	L	E	Liable to payment of tithes.
T	I	T	H	O	N	I	A	A genus of tall herbs, Mexican sunflower.
T	I	T	I	V	A	T	E	Dressing up, Sprucing, Smartening, Adorning.
T	I	T	M	O	U	S	E	Small passerine birds, Blue tit, Marsh tit.
T	I	T	R	A	T	E	D	Standardized, Analyzed.
T	I	T	T	A	T	T	O	The game of noughts and crosses.
T	I	T	T	E	R	E	D	Laughed lightly or in a nervous manner, Chortled, Chuckled, Snickered, Giggled.
T	I	T	T	E	R	E	L	Whimbrel, European curlew.
T	I	T	T	U	P	P	Y	Rickety, Shaky, Unsteady.
T	I	T	U	B	A	N	T	Wavering, Vacillating, Unsteady.
T	I	T	U	B	A	T	E	Stagger, Totter, Reel, Lurch, Wobble.
T	I	T	U	L	A	R	Y	Holding a title.
T	L	A	C	H	T	L	I	An ancient Aztec game still played today with a solid rubber ball.
T	O	A	D	F	I	S	H	Various marine fishes, some of which have venomous spines.
T	O	A	D	F	L	A	X	Common European herb.
T	O	A	D	P	I	P	E	Horsetail.
T	O	A	D	S	P	I	T	Cuckoo spit.
T	O	A	D	Y	I	N	G	Fawning, Bootlicking, Cringing, Cowering, Groveling, Kowtowing, Parasitic.
T	O	A	D	Y	I	S	H	Sycophantic.
T	O	A	D	Y	I	S	M	Behaviour of a toady.
T	O	A	S	T	I	N	G	Heating, Browning, Drinking to health or good luck.
T	O	B	O	G	G	A	N	A light sled for travelling over snow.
T	O	C	O	L	O	G	Y	The sicence of obstretrics.
T	O	D	D	L	I	N	G	Walking with short tottery steps.
T	O	E	B	O	A	R	D	Support or protection for toes at the base of something.
T	O	E	P	L	A	T	E	A metal tab on the toe of a shoe for protection against extra heavy wear.
T	O	G	E	T	H	E	R	Collected, Grouped, Gathered, Mutually, Reciprocally, Simultaneously, Consecutively.
T	O	H	U	B	O	H	U	Chaos, Confusion.
T	O	I	L	E	T	T	E	Formal or fashionable style of dressing.
T	O	I	L	S	O	M	E	Arduous, Laborious, Wearisome, Difficult, Strenuous, Uphill.
T	O	I	L	W	O	R	N	Showing the effects of drudgery.
T	O	K	O	N	O	M	A	A niche or recess in a Japanese house where a silk painted wall hanging is on show.
T	O	L	B	O	O	T	H	Tollbooth, Customhouse, An office where tolls are paid.
T	O	L	E	R	A	N	T	Enduring, Forbearing, Indulgent, Liberal, Advanced, Progressive, Radical, Lenient.
T	O	L	E	R	A	T	E	Endure, Bear, Accept, Condone, Countenance, Allow, Suffer, Swallow.
T	O	L	L	D	I	S	H	A measure for the miller's share of the grain ground for a customer.

1	2	3	4	5	6	7	8	
T	O	L	L	G	A	T	E	A point where the toll is paid.
T	O	L	T	E	C	A	N	Early inhabitants of Mexico.
T	O	M	A	H	A	W	K	A light axe used by the American Indians.
T	O	M	A	L	L	E	Y	Lobster liver.
T	O	M	A	T	I	N	E	A crystalline antibiotic glycoside alkaloid that is active against fungi.
T	O	M	A	T	O	E	S	Round globular fruits of a S. American herb widely grown for cooking and for use in salads.
T	O	M	B	L	E	S	S	Having no tomb.
T	O	M	E	N	T	U	M	Stuffing for a cushion.
T	O	M	M	Y	B	A	R	A small lever for turning bolts and screws.
T	O	M	M	Y	G	U	N	Submachine gun.
T	O	M	M	Y	R	O	T	Foolishness, Nonsense, Balderdash, Bilge, Bosh, Rot, Rubbish, Trash.
T	O	M	N	O	D	D	Y	Fool, Dunce, Atlantic puffin.
T	O	M	O	G	R	A	M	X-ray photograph.
T	O	M	O	R	R	O	W	The day after today.
T	O	N	A	L	I	T	E	A granular igneous rock.
T	O	N	A	L	I	T	Y	The quality of having a keynote or tonic.
T	O	N	E	D	E	A	F	Inability to distinguish musical pitch.
T	O	N	E	L	E	S	S	Lacking in tone, modulation or expression.
T	O	N	G	U	I	N	G	Scolding, Abusing, Talking, Chattering, Articulating, Voiced.
T	O	N	I	C	I	T	Y	Vigour, Healthy, Healthiness.
T	O	N	S	U	R	E	D	Having the head shaved.
T	O	O	T	H	F	U	L	A small drink of liquor, A small bite or mouthful.
T	O	O	T	L	I	N	G	Tooting gently on a wind instrument.
T	O	P	A	R	C	H	Y	A district consisting of a few cities.
T	O	P	A	Z	I	N	E	Resembling a topaz in colour.
T	O	P	B	O	O	T	S	High boots usually worn by riders.
T	O	P	D	R	E	S	S	Scatter fertilizer or manure.
T	O	P	H	E	A	V	Y	Top part too heavy, Unstable, Overcapitalized, Having too many officers or bosses.
T	O	P	L	O	F	T	Y	Disdainful, Supercilious, Proud, Arrogant, Haughty, Insolent, Superior, Egotistic.
T	O	P	N	O	T	C	H	Excellent, Capital, Fine, First-rate, Prime, Superior, First-class.
T	O	P	O	L	O	G	Y	The study of a region by the charting of natural and man-made features.
T	O	P	O	N	Y	M	Y	The study of the place-naming of a region.
T	O	P	O	T	Y	P	E	Specimen from the area where an original was found.
T	O	P	P	L	I	N	G	Tumbling, Tottering, Pitching, Slumping, Teetering, Faltering, Overturning.
T	O	P	S	H	E	L	F	Of the highest social level, Top-drawer.
T	O	P	S	H	E	L	L	A marine snail with a spiral conical shell.
T	O	P	S	T	O	N	E	Capstone.
T	O	Q	U	I	L	L	A	Flexible fibre used to make panama hats.
T	O	R	C	H	E	R	E	Ornamental stand for a candlestick. Standard lamp.
T	O	R	C	H	I	N	G	Illuminating with a torch.
T	O	R	C	U	L	A	R	The point where the brain sinuses meet.
T	O	R	E	A	D	O	R	Bullfighter.
T	O	R	E	U	T	I	C	Relating to metalwork embossed or chased.
T	O	R	N	A	D	I	C	Relating to a tornado.
T	O	R	N	A	R	I	A	Free-swimming larva.
T	O	R	O	I	D	A	L	Dough-nut shaped.
T	O	R	O	T	O	R	O	Kingfisher of New Guinea.
T	O	R	P	I	D	L	Y	Numbly, Dully, Dormantly.
T	O	R	Q	U	A	T	E	Collared.
T	O	R	T	I	L	L	A	A round thin cake of cornmeal bread eaten with a savoury filling.
T	O	R	T	I	O	U	S	Improper, Mistaken.
T	O	R	T	O	I	S	E	Reptile with a shell, Turtle, Laggard, Slow moving, Tardy.
T	O	R	T	U	O	U	S	Winding, Twisting, Devious, Circuitous, Involved, Tricky, Meandering, Sinuous.
T	O	R	T	U	R	E	D	Punished, Coerced, Plagued, Afflicted, Crucified, Tormented, Persecuted, Mutilated.
T	O	R	T	U	R	E	R	One that tortures.
T	O	R	U	L	O	S	E	Having knobs.
T	O	R	U	L	O	U	S	Same as TORULOSE.
T	O	T	A	L	I	T	Y	Entirety, Unity, Whole, Completeness, Integral, Sum, Total, Gross.
T	O	T	A	L	I	Z	E	Add, Cast, Figure, Foot, Sum, Summate, Tot, Total.
T	O	T	E	M	I	S	M	Belief in kinship with a totem.
T	O	T	T	E	R	E	D	Wavered, Swayed, Staggered, Wobbled, Teetered, Faltered, Lurched, Staggered.
T	O	U	C	H	I	L	Y	Peevishly, Petulantly.
T	O	U	C	H	I	N	G	Concerning, Perceiving, Pushing, Contacting, Brushing, Patting, Stroking, Feeling.
T	O	U	C	H	P	A	N	The pan of a flintlock.
T	O	U	G	H	E	S	T	Strongest, Stoutest, Hardest, Stiffest, Harshest, Strictest, Hardiest, Fittest.
T	O	U	G	H	I	S	H	Rather tough.
T	O	U	R	E	L	L	E	Turret, Small tower.

8 LETTERS

1	2	3	4	5	6	7	8	Clue
T	O	U	R	I	S	T	Y	Pertaining to the tourist trade.
T	O	U	R	N	U	R	E	Pad worn under the rear of a dress, Bustle.
T	O	U	S	L	I	N	G	Tangling, Dishevel, Pulling, Dragging, Ruffling, Rumpling, Making untidy.
T	O	W	A	R	D	L	Y	Advantageous, Propitious, Docilely, Promisingly, Obligingly, Beneficial, Pleasant, Affable.
T	O	W	E	R	I	N	G	Imposing, Surpassing, Overwhelming, Soaring, Excessive, Overweening, Elevating, Rising.
T	O	W	N	H	A	L	L	The chief public building of a town or city.
T	O	W	N	L	A	N	D	A township.
T	O	W	N	S	H	I	P	A district or residential area designated as a municipality.
T	O	W	N	S	M	A	N	A person born and bred in a city.
T	O	W	N	T	A	L	K	Public gossip, Subject of rumour.
T	O	X	A	E	M	I	A	Blood-poisoning.
T	O	X	I	C	A	N	T	Poisonous, Toxic, Venomous, Virulent.
T	O	X	I	C	I	T	Y	The state of being poisonous.
T	O	X	I	F	E	R	A	A group of venomous marine snails.
T	O	X	O	D	O	N	T	Large mammal or fossil with distinctive teeth.
T	O	Y	I	S	H	L	Y	Frivolously, Triviality, Playfully.
T	R	A	C	H	E	A	L	Relating to the windpipe from the larynx.
T	R	A	C	H	O	M	A	Chronic contagious conjunctivitis.
T	R	A	C	H	Y	T	E	Light coloured volcanic rock.
T	R	A	C	K	A	G	E	Towage.
T	R	A	C	K	I	N	G	Trailing, Following, Tracing, Travelling, Walking, Going, Drawing, Towage.
T	R	A	C	K	W	A	Y	Roadway, Layer of material for easy passage of vehicles.
T	R	A	C	T	A	T	E	Treatise, Dissertation, Essay, Discourse.
T	R	A	C	T	I	L	E	Ductile, Can be stretched.
T	R	A	C	T	I	O	N	Drawing, Pulling, Attraction, Towing, Tension.
T	R	A	C	T	I	T	E	Tractarian.
T	R	A	C	T	I	V	E	Exerted in drawing or pulling.
T	R	A	C	T	R	I	X	A curve.
T	R	A	D	E	F	U	L	Commercial.
T	R	A	D	I	T	O	R	Traitor, Early Christian informer.
T	R	A	D	U	C	E	D	Debased, Perverted, Violated, Betrayed, Maligned, Disgraced, Exposed to shame.
T	R	A	D	U	C	E	R	Calumniator.
T	R	A	G	I	C	A	L	Disastrous, Shocking, Grievous, Deplorable.
T	R	A	G	O	P	A	N	Genus of brilliantly coloured Asiatic pheasants.
T	R	A	G	U	L	I	D	Family of ruminant mammals, Mouse deer.
T	R	A	I	L	I	N	G	Trudging, Plodding, Losing, Straggling, Pursuing, Shadowing, Following, Hauling.
T	R	A	I	L	N	E	T	A net trailed between two boats, Trawl.
T	R	A	I	N	I	N	G	Teaching, Associating, Instructing, Coaching, Drilling, Protracting, Exercising, Directing.
T	R	A	I	N	O	I	L	Whale oil, Oil from marine animals.
T	R	A	I	P	S	E	D	Walked, Tramped, Wandered, Meandered, Rambled, Ranged, Roamed, Trooped.
T	R	A	M	P	I	N	G	Treading, Hiking, Plodding, Marching, Thudding, Trudging, Stamping, Stomping.
T	R	A	M	P	L	E	D	Tramped, Pounded, Tread, Stamped, Override, Crushed, Tyrannized, Extinguished.
T	R	A	M	R	O	A	D	Roadway with rails for trams to travel on.
T	R	A	N	C	I	N	G	Prancing, Moving briskly.
T	R	A	N	Q	U	I	L	Quiet, Peaceful, Steady, Stable, Serene, Calm, Composed, Poised.
T	R	A	N	S	A	C	T	Negotiate, Transmit, Transfer, Effect, Perform, Handle, Exchange, Conduct.
T	R	A	N	S	E	C	T	Cut transversely, Sample area of vegetation for study.
T	R	A	N	S	E	P	T	The aisle of a church that crosses the main nave.
T	R	A	N	S	F	E	R	Transport, Remove, Transmit, Change, Shift, Deliver, Cede, Assign.
T	R	A	N	S	F	I	X	Impale, Skewer, Spear, Spike, Transpierce.
T	R	A	N	S	H	I	P	Transfer from one ship to another.
T	R	A	N	S	I	R	E	A customs document for clearing of coasting vessels.
T	R	A	N	S	M	I	T	Send, Convey, Disseminate, Communicate, Carry, Consign, Dispatch, Remit.
T	R	A	N	S	U	D	E	Exude, Bleed, Ooze, Seep, Strain, Sweat, Weep.
T	R	A	N	T	L	U	M	Trifle, Trinket.
T	R	A	P	B	A	L	L	An old ball game.
T	R	A	P	D	O	O	R	A door for an opening in a ceiling or floor.
T	R	A	P	E	S	E	D	Traipsed.
T	R	A	P	E	Z	I	A	A quadrilateral having no two sides parallel.
T	R	A	P	F	A	L	L	Pitfall.
T	R	A	P	I	C	H	E	Wine press, Sugar mill.
T	R	A	P	P	I	N	G	Ensnaring, Entrapping, Entangling, Confining, Catching, Stopping, Holding, Snagging.
T	R	A	P	P	I	S	T	Member of a Roman Catholic order.
T	R	A	P	P	O	I	D	Resembling traprock.
T	R	A	P	U	N	T	O	Embroidered quilting.
T	R	A	S	H	E	R	Y	Trash, Rubbish.
T	R	A	S	H	I	L	Y	Worthless.

1	2	3	4	5	6	7	8	Definition
T	R	A	U	L	I	S	M	Stammering, Stuttering.
T	R	A	V	A	T	E	D	Divided into traves.
T	R	A	V	E	R	S	E	Crosspiece, Transom, Bar, Barrier, Obstacle, Adversity, Passage, Crossing.
T	R	A	V	E	S	T	Y	Parody, Sham, Make-up, Disguise, Mockery, Caricature.
T	R	A	W	L	I	N	G	Trolling, Fishing with a trawl net.
T	R	E	A	C	L	E	D	Sweetened or spread with treacle.
T	R	E	A	D	I	N	G	Stepping, Walking, Following, Pursuing, Beating, Pacing, Trampling, Stamping.
T	R	E	A	D	L	E	D	Operated a machine by using the foot control.
T	R	E	A	S	U	R	E	Hoard, Appreciate, Wealth, Prize, Catch, Cherish, Esteem, Value.
T	R	E	A	S	U	R	Y	Gallery, Museum, Repository, Depository, Chest, Coffer, Exchequer, Eldorado.
T	R	E	A	T	I	N	G	Negotiating, Arranging, Expounding, Discussing, Using, Entertaining, Feasting, Handling.
T	R	E	A	T	I	S	E	A thesis dealing with a specific subject, Dissertation, Memoir, Argument.
T	R	E	B	L	I	N	G	Multiply by three, Increase threefold.
T	R	E	C	E	N	T	O	The fourteenth century period in Italian literature and art.
T	R	E	C	U	L	I	A	Genus of African trees, Breadfruit.
T	R	E	E	B	I	N	E	Cultivated woody vines, Marine ivy.
T	R	E	E	C	A	L	F	Calfskin dyed and with a tree design on it.
T	R	E	E	C	R	A	B	Mangrove crab.
T	R	E	E	F	E	R	N	Ferns that grow in or about trees.
T	R	E	E	F	I	S	H	A Californian rockfish.
T	R	E	E	F	R	O	G	A tailless amphibian.
T	R	E	E	L	E	S	S	Lacking trees, Usually grassy plains.
T	R	E	E	N	A	I	L	Wooden peg used for fastening planking.
T	R	E	K	K	I	N	G	Travelling by ox-wagon, Making one's way slowly, Migrating.
T	R	E	M	A	N	D	O	Direction in music, trembling.
T	R	E	M	B	L	E	D	Quivered, Shook, Shivered, Shuddered, Quaked, Dithered, Vibrated.
T	R	E	M	B	L	E	R	Family of West Indian birds, Vibrating hammer.
T	R	E	M	E	T	O	L	Unsaturated alcohol.
T	R	E	N	C	H	E	D	Carved, Incised, Entrenched, Verged, Bordered.
T	R	E	N	C	H	E	R	A wooden plate or dish.
T	R	E	N	D	I	N	G	Truncating, Bordering, Bending.
T	R	E	P	H	I	N	E	Surgical instrument for cutting out circles of bone.
T	R	E	P	H	O	N	E	Various substances that promote the growth of cells.
T	R	E	S	P	A	S	S	Encroach, Entrench, Infringe, Invade, Err, Sin, Offend, Lapse.
T	R	E	S	S	U	R	E	An inner ornamented circle surrounding a device on a coin or medal.
T	R	E	V	A	L	L	Y	A food fish of tropical seas.
T	R	I	A	D	I	S	M	Threefold division or constitution.
T	R	I	A	L	A	T	E	Having three wings.
T	R	I	A	L	I	S	M	Federation or union of three states.
T	R	I	A	L	I	S	T	One that competes in a trial contest.
T	R	I	A	N	G	L	E	Polygon having three sides, Situation involving three persons.
T	R	I	A	P	S	A	L	A building having three apses.
T	R	I	A	R	C	H	Y	Triumvirate, A country with three rulers.
T	R	I	A	S	S	I	C	Prehistoric geological period.
T	R	I	A	S	T	E	R	Abnormal three part cell-division.
T	R	I	A	X	I	A	L	Having three components.
T	R	I	A	Z	A	N	E	Compound containing a ring of three carbon and three nitrogen atoms.
T	R	I	A	Z	O	L	E	Compound containing a ring of two carbon and three nitrogen atoms.
T	R	I	B	A	L	L	Y	Being a tribe.
T	R	I	B	A	S	I	C	Having three hydrogen atoms.
T	R	I	B	E	L	E	T	A small tribe.
T	R	I	B	R	A	C	H	Three-branched ornament.
T	R	I	B	U	L	U	S	Genus of tropical herbs.
T	R	I	B	U	N	A	L	Court, Lawcourt, Forum of justice.
T	R	I	B	U	T	E	D	Paid as a tribute.
T	R	I	B	U	T	E	R	A miner that receives payment for his labour in ore.
T	R	I	C	H	I	N	A	A parasitic worm.
T	R	I	C	H	I	T	E	A hairlike crystallite.
T	R	I	C	H	O	D	E	A chain of cells.
T	R	I	C	H	O	I	D	Hairlike, Capillary.
T	R	I	C	H	O	M	A	Chain of cells as in bacteria or algae.
T	R	I	C	H	O	M	E	Same as TRICHOMA.
T	R	I	C	H	O	R	D	A specially tuned piano.
T	R	I	C	K	E	R	Y	Deception, Cheat, Fraud, Sharp practice, Craftiness.
T	R	I	C	K	I	L	Y	Artfully, Cunningly, Craftily, With difficulty.
T	R	I	C	K	I	N	G	Deceiving, Imposing, Cheating, Arranging, Hoaxing, Ornamenting, Decorating, Duping.
T	R	I	C	K	L	E	D	Oozed, Dripped, Moved slowly, Dissipated slowly, Flowed in drops.

1	2	3	4	5	6	7	8	
T	R	I	C	K	L	E	T	A thin stream, Rill.
T	R	I	C	O	L	O	N	Period in classical prosody.
T	R	I	C	O	L	O	R	Having three colours, The flag of France.
T	R	I	C	O	R	N	E	Having three corners.
T	R	I	C	T	R	A	C	A game resembling backgammon.
T	R	I	C	Y	C	L	E	A three-wheeled cycle.
T	R	I	D	A	C	N	A	Genus of marine bivalves, Giant clam.
T	R	I	D	A	I	L	Y	Three times a day or every three days.
T	R	I	F	L	I	N	G	Dallying, Loitering, Toying, Chit-chat, Fooling, Petty, Badinage, Flirting.
T	R	I	F	O	C	A	L	Having three focal lengths.
T	R	I	G	G	I	N	G	Trotting, Running.
T	R	I	G	L	Y	P	H	An architectural ornament.
T	R	I	G	N	E	S	S	Trimness, Spruceness, Smartness, Stylishness.
T	R	I	G	O	N	A	L	Triangular.
T	R	I	G	O	N	I	A	Genus of Australian mollusk with a pearly shell.
T	R	I	G	O	N	I	D	Part of a lower molar.
T	R	I	G	O	N	O	N	A triangle.
T	R	I	G	R	A	P	H	Cluster of three successive letters.
T	R	I	L	E	M	M	A	Argument having three alternatives.
T	R	I	L	L	I	N	G	Turning, Twirling, Rolling, Revolving, Trickling, Quavering, Vibrating, Shaking.
T	R	I	L	L	I	O	N	A very large number.
T	R	I	L	L	I	U	M	Genus of N. American herbs.
T	R	I	L	O	B	E	D	Divided into three lobes.
T	R	I	M	A	R	A	N	A sailing vessel with three hulls.
T	R	I	M	E	T	E	R	A line of three measures in verse.
T	R	I	M	M	I	N	G	Decorating, Adorning, Chastising, Thrashing, Defrauding, Cheating, Clipping, Cutting.
T	R	I	M	N	E	S	S	Neatness, Tidiness, Orderliness, Cleanliness.
T	R	I	M	O	R	P	H	Crystalline form of a trimorphos substance.
T	R	I	N	G	I	N	E	Relating to sandpipers.
T	R	I	N	G	O	I	D	Same as TRINGINE.
T	R	I	N	I	T	R	O	Containing three nitro groups in the molecule.
T	R	I	N	K	U	M	S	Trinkets, Frippery.
T	R	I	N	O	D	A	L	Having three nodes.
T	R	I	O	D	I	O	N	Prayer book used prior to Easter having three odes.
T	R	I	O	L	E	I	N	Oily liquid triglyceride of oleic acid found in olive oil.
T	R	I	O	X	A	N	E	A crystalline combustible heterocyclic trimer of formaldehyde.
T	R	I	O	X	I	D	E	An oxide containing three atoms of oxygen.
T	R	I	P	H	A	N	E	Monoclinic mineral.
T	R	I	P	H	O	R	A	Genus of American terrestrial orchids.
T	R	I	P	L	A	N	E	An aeroplane with three wings.
T	R	I	P	L	I	N	G	Multiplying by three, Three times as much.
T	R	I	P	L	I	T	E	Monoclinic basic phosphate of manganese, iron, magnesium and calcium.
T	R	I	P	L	O	I	D	Threefold in arrangement.
T	R	I	P	O	D	A	L	Having three legs or feet, Forming a tripod.
T	R	I	P	O	L	A	R	Having three poles.
T	R	I	P	P	A	N	T	In heraldry, passant, walking with front paw raised.
T	R	I	P	P	E	R	Y	Touristy.
T	R	I	P	P	I	N	G	Light-footed, Nimble, Quick, Skipping, Hopping, Springing, Stumbling, Hopping.
T	R	I	P	S	I	L	L	A timber to assist closing a dam.
T	R	I	P	T	A	N	E	Liquid hydrocarbon used as a blender for aviation fuel.
T	R	I	P	T	O	T	E	A noun having three cases.
T	R	I	P	T	Y	C	H	A decorated three-part altar screen.
T	R	I	P	W	I	R	E	A concealed wire used to trigger explosives or used as a warning to trespassers.
T	R	I	S	E	M	I	C	Equal to three short syllables.
T	R	I	S	K	E	L	E	Figure of three curved or bent branches radiating from centre.
T	R	I	S	O	M	I	C	Relating to triploid chromosomes.
T	R	I	S	T	E	Z	A	Infectious disease of grafted citrus trees.
T	R	I	S	T	F	U	L	Sad, Melancholy.
T	R	I	S	T	I	C	H	Stanza of three lines.
T	R	I	T	I	C	A	L	Trite.
T	R	I	T	I	C	U	M	Genus of cereal grasses.
T	R	I	T	O	L	Y	L	Containing three tolyl radicals in the molecule.
T	R	I	T	O	N	I	A	Genus of S. African bulbous plants, Montbretia.
T	R	I	T	U	R	U	S	Genus of aquatic salamanders.
T	R	I	U	M	V	I	R	One of a body of three members.
T	R	I	U	N	I	T	Y	Trinity.
T	R	I	V	A	L	V	E	Having three valves.

1	2	3	4	5	6	7	8	Clue
T	R	I	Z	O	N	A	L	Concerned with three administrative areas.
T	R	O	C	H	A	I	C	A foot in classical prosody containing two short syllables.
T	R	O	C	H	I	L	I	Family of hummingbirds.
T	R	O	C	H	I	T	E	Wheel-like joint of a fossil stem.
T	R	O	C	H	L	E	A	Part of anatomy that works like a pulley.
T	R	O	C	H	O	I	D	Pivot, Cycloid, Rotation on an axis.
T	R	O	I	L	I	T	E	A mineral that is a native ferrous sulfide.
T	R	O	L	L	I	N	G	Bowling, Rolling, Singing loudly, Circulating, Wagging, Fishing with a dragging line.
T	R	O	L	L	I	U	S	Genus of herbs, Ranunculus.
T	R	O	L	L	O	P	Y	Behaving like a trollop.
T	R	O	M	B	O	N	E	Brass wind instrument with a movable slide.
T	R	O	N	A	D	O	R	Woody herb yielding fibre for nets and ropes.
T	R	O	O	P	I	A	L	Genus of brightly coloured orioles.
T	R	O	O	P	I	N	G	Assembling, Gathering, Collecting, Marching, Thronging, Swarming, Walking, Pacing.
T	R	O	P	A	I	O	N	Ancient Greek or Roman monument commemorating a military victory.
T	R	O	P	H	E	M	A	The uterine blood that nourishes the embryo.
T	R	O	P	H	I	E	S	Memorials, Relics, Reminders, Souvenirs, Tokens, Ornaments, Medals, Keepsakes.
T	R	O	P	I	C	A	L	Region between Tropics of Capricorn and Cancer.
T	R	O	T	C	O	Z	Y	Covering for head and shoulders worn by riders.
T	R	O	T	T	E	U	R	Woman's tailored garment to be worn outdoors.
T	R	O	T	T	I	N	G	A pace between a walk and a run.
T	R	O	T	T	O	I	R	Footpath, Sidewalk, Pavement.
T	R	O	U	B	L	E	D	Worried, Bothered, Agitated, Disarranged, Distraught, Distrait, Harassed, Tormented.
T	R	O	U	B	L	E	R	One that agitates or torments.
T	R	O	U	N	C	E	D	Thrashed, Punished, Whipped, Defeated, Overthrew, Routed, Flogged, Censured.
T	R	O	U	P	I	A	L	Troopial, Brilliantly coloured oriole bird.
T	R	O	U	S	E	R	S	Garment from waist to ankle covering each leg separately, Trews, Breeches.
T	R	O	U	T	I	N	G	Fishing for trout.
T	R	O	U	V	E	R	E	Troubadour, French school of poets.
T	R	O	W	S	E	R	S	Trousers.
T	R	U	A	N	T	L	Y	Shirking, Lazily, Evasively, Neglectful.
T	R	U	A	N	T	R	Y	Truancy.
T	R	U	C	K	A	G	E	Conveyance of freight by trucks.
T	R	U	C	K	I	N	G	Transporting by truck, Shuffling dance step.
T	R	U	C	K	L	E	D	Submitted, Yielded, Acted in a subservient manner.
T	R	U	C	K	L	E	R	One that acts in a servile manner.
T	R	U	D	G	I	N	G	Walking wearily, Marching steadily, Plodding, Tramping.
T	R	U	E	B	L	U	E	Loyal faithful person.
T	R	U	E	B	O	R	N	Of legitimate birth.
T	R	U	E	B	R	E	D	Purebred.
T	R	U	E	L	O	V	E	Sweetheart, Steady, Beloved, Inamorata, Boyfriend, Girlfriend.
T	R	U	E	N	E	S	S	Honesty, Truthfulness, Scrupulous, Voracity, Authenticity.
T	R	U	I	S	T	I	C	Relating to a self-evident truth.
T	R	U	M	P	E	R	Y	Bric-a-brac, Paraphernalia, Twaddle, Cheap, Common, Rubbishy, Claptrap, Nonsense.
T	R	U	M	P	I	N	G	Outdoing, Topping, Surpassing, Excelling, Capping, Outstripping, Passing, Besting.
T	R	U	N	C	A	T	E	Crop, Abridge, Lop, Abbreviate, Cut off.
T	R	U	N	D	L	E	D	Spun, Bowled, Rolled, Hauled, Revolved, Transported, Travelled, Churned, Lumbered.
T	R	U	N	K	F	U	L	As much as a trunk will hold.
T	R	U	N	N	I	O	N	Pin or pivot for rotating or tilting something.
T	R	U	S	S	I	N	G	Binding, Tying, Securing, Strengthening, Fastening, Supporting, Bundling, Packing.
T	R	U	S	T	F	U	L	Confiding.
T	R	U	S	T	I	F	Y	To form a trust.
T	R	U	S	T	I	L	Y	Reliably, Staunchly, Dependably.
T	R	U	S	T	I	N	G	Depending, Hoping, Entrusting, Crediting, Relying, Committing, Consigning, Charging.
T	R	Y	P	E	T	I	D	Relating to the Mediterranean fruit fly and other fruit pests.
T	R	Y	P	T	O	N	E	A peptone produced by the action of trypsin.
T	R	Y	S	T	I	N	G	Meeting in secret, Negotiating, Visiting, Making an assignation.
T	U	B	E	R	C	L	E	A small rough prominence, a small knob, Nodule, A small lump, Tissue reaction.
T	U	B	E	R	O	S	E	A Mexican bulbous herb that has flowers resembling small lilies.
T	U	B	E	R	O	U	S	Knobbed, Resembling a tuber.
T	U	B	E	W	E	L	L	A well driven by machinery.
T	U	B	I	C	O	L	A	Tube worms.
T	U	B	I	F	O	R	M	A tubular shape.
T	U	B	I	P	O	R	A	Organ-pipe corals.
T	U	B	S	I	Z	E	D	Paper passed through a size solution in a vat.
T	U	B	U	L	A	T	E	Having the form of a tube.
T	U	B	U	L	U	R	E	Short tubular opening.

1	2	3	4	5	6	7	8	Clue
T	U	B	W	H	E	E	L	A drum for tumbling hides and skins.
T	U	C	K	A	H	O	E	A plant with edible roots used by American Indians.
T	U	C	K	S	H	O	P	A small shop with a wide choice of goods usually attached to a school or hospital.
T	U	C	O	T	U	C	O	American burrowing rodents resembling gophers.
T	U	C	U	N	A	R	E	S. American river fishes resembling bass and providing sport and food.
T	U	G	O	F	W	A	R	Struggle for supremacy, Contest, Competition, Rivalling, Strife.
T	U	K	U	T	U	K	U	Decorative latticework made by the Maori people.
T	U	M	B	L	I	N	G	Rolling, Turning, Rumpling, Dishevelling, Jumbling, Muddling, Falling, Scrambling.
T	U	M	E	F	I	E	D	Swollen, Produced a tumour.
T	U	M	I	D	I	T	Y	Inflation, Pomposity.
T	U	M	P	L	I	N	E	A strap around the head or over the chest for carrying bundles.
T	U	M	U	L	A	R	Y	Placed over a tomb.
T	U	M	U	L	O	S	E	Full of small hills or mounds.
T	U	N	B	E	L	L	Y	Potbellied.
T	U	N	E	A	B	L	E	Tuneful, Harmonious.
T	U	N	E	L	E	S	S	Lacking musical quality.
T	U	N	G	S	T	E	N	High-melting ductile hard polybalent metallic element.
T	U	N	G	S	T	I	C	Wolframic, Containing tungsten.
T	U	N	I	C	A	R	Y	Covered with a tunic or mantle, Coated with layers.
T	U	N	I	C	A	T	E	Same as TUNICARY.
T	U	N	I	S	I	A	N	Native of Tunis or Tunisia.
T	U	R	A	N	I	A	N	Constituting various Asian languages.
T	U	R	A	N	O	S	E	Crystalline reducing disaccharide sugar.
T	U	R	B	A	N	E	D	Having the appearance of wearing a turban.
T	U	R	B	I	D	L	Y	Muddiness, Confusion, Obscurity.
T	U	R	B	I	N	A	L	Bony plates of the nasal chambers.
T	U	R	B	O	J	E	T	Using exhaust gases to turn a turbine as a method of propulsion.
T	U	R	C	O	M	A	N	People of Turkic stock living in Republics of the U.S.S.R.
T	U	R	K	O	M	A	N	Same as TURCOMAN.
T	U	R	D	I	D	A	E	Widely distributed family of singing birds.
T	U	R	G	I	D	L	Y	Pompously, Ostentatiously.
T	U	R	L	O	U	G	H	A winter lake that is marshy in summer.
T	U	R	M	E	R	I	C	Dried and powdered rhizome of an East Indian herb used as a condiment in pickles and curries.
T	U	R	N	C	O	A	T	Renegade, Defector, Deserter, Betrayer, Quisling, Traitor.
T	U	R	N	C	O	C	K	A plug for opening and closing the supply of water to any pre-determined point.
T	U	R	N	D	O	W	N	Rejection, Declined, Fold down.
T	U	R	N	O	V	E	R	Upset, Shift, Reversal, Re-organization, Shake-up, A pastry with a savoury or sweet filling.
T	U	R	N	P	I	K	E	Tollgate, A main highway.
T	U	R	N	S	I	C	K	Giddy.
T	U	R	N	S	O	L	E	Plants with flowers that are believed to face the sun, Sunflowers.
T	U	R	N	S	P	I	T	A rotating spit.
T	U	R	R	E	T	E	D	Having turrets.
T	U	R	R	I	D	A	E	Family of marine snails.
T	U	S	S	O	C	K	Y	Covered with tussocks or tufts.
T	U	T	E	L	A	G	E	Guardianship, Protection, Dependence, Teaching, Training, Instruction, Education.
T	U	T	E	L	A	R	Y	Guarding, Protective.
T	U	T	O	R	A	G	E	Tutorship, Tuition.
T	U	T	O	R	E	S	S	A female tutor.
T	U	T	O	R	I	A	L	A small class enabling a tutor to give individual tuition.
T	U	T	O	R	I	N	G	Teaching, Guiding, Instructing, Educating, Training, Coaching, Informing, Directing.
T	W	A	D	D	L	E	D	Prated, Babbled, Gabbled, Chattered.
T	W	A	D	D	L	E	R	One that talks nonsense.
T	W	A	N	G	I	N	G	Quick harsh ringing sound, Plucking a stringed instrument, Vibrating, Throbbing, Twitching.
T	W	A	N	G	L	E	D	Twanged.
T	W	A	T	T	L	E	D	Chattered, Babbled, Prated.
T	W	E	A	K	I	N	G	Jerking, Pinching, Pulling, Snatching, Twitching, Snapping, Yanking, Nipping.
T	W	E	E	D	L	E	D	Piped, Chirped.
T	W	E	E	Z	E	R	S	Small pincers-type instruments for plucking or manipulating.
T	W	E	L	V	E	M	O	The size of a sheet of paper cut twelve from a sheet.
T	W	I	D	D	L	E	D	Fiddled, Jiggled, Quivered, Twirled, Turned, Twisted.
T	W	I	G	G	I	N	G	Noticing, Observing, Perceiving, Watching, Comprehending, Understanding.
T	W	I	L	I	G	H	T	The half-light before darkness.
T	W	I	L	L	I	N	G	Making fabric with a twilled weave.
T	W	I	N	B	O	R	N	Born at the same time.
T	W	I	N	K	I	N	G	Twitching, Plucking, Tweaking.
T	W	I	N	K	L	E	D	Scintillated, Flashed, Glittered, Sparkled, Flickered, Gave off radiance.
T	W	I	N	K	L	E	R	A person who becomes a star.

1	2	3	4	5	6	7	8	Definition
T	W	I	R	L	I	N	G	Revolving, Spinning, Turning, Undulating, Twisting.
T	W	I	S	T	I	N	G	Entwining, Plaiting, Wreathing, Coiling, Warping, Distorting, Diverting, Deflecting.
T	W	I	T	C	H	E	D	Plucked, Jerked, Snatched, Yanked, Clutched, Grasped, Piched, Nipped.
T	W	I	T	C	H	E	R	One that twitches.
T	W	I	T	T	I	N	G	Ridiculing, Taunting, Reproaching, Deriding, Mocking, Chiding, Blaming, Censuring.
T	W	O	E	D	G	E	D	Double-edged.
T	W	O	F	A	C	E	D	False, Double-dealing, Ambiguous.
T	W	O	P	E	N	N	Y	Twopence, Cheap, Mean, Worthless.
T	W	O	P	I	E	C	E	Two separate pieces of clothing that match and are intended to be worn together.
T	Y	C	H	O	N	I	C	Relating to a system of astronomy.
T	Y	L	O	S	O	I	D	A callus formed in a resin canal of a conifer.
T	Y	L	O	T	A	T	E	Knobbed at both ends.
T	Y	M	P	A	N	I	C	Relating to the eardrum.
T	Y	M	P	A	N	U	M	The membrane separating the outer and middle ear.
T	Y	P	E	C	A	S	T	To cast an actor in the same type of role many times.
T	Y	P	E	F	A	C	E	Printed impression of type.
T	Y	P	E	H	I	G	H	Having a regular size of type.
T	Y	P	H	O	E	A	N	Resembing a mythical giant.
T	Y	P	H	O	N	I	C	Resembling a typhoon.
T	Y	P	I	F	I	E	D	Represented by an image, form, model or resemblance.
T	Y	P	O	L	O	G	Y	A doctrine or theory of types.
T	Y	R	A	M	I	N	E	A crystalline phenolic amine.
T	Y	R	O	L	E	A	N	Characteristic of the Tyrol.
T	Y	R	O	L	E	S	E	Tyrolean.
T	Y	R	O	L	I	T	E	A mineral that is a hydrous hydroxide arsenate and carbonate of copper and calcium.
T	Y	R	T	A	E	A	N	Styled in the manner of a seventh century Spartan poet.
T	Z	E	D	A	K	A	H	Charity.

U

1	2	3	4	5	6	7	8	Definition
U	B	I	Q	U	I	T	Y	Presence everywhere.
U	D	O	M	E	T	E	R	A rain guage.
U	G	L	I	F	I	E	D	Made ugly.
U	G	L	I	N	E	S	S	Unsightliness, Sordidness, Gloominess, Vileness.
U	I	N	T	A	I	T	E	Black lustrous asphalt occurring in Utah and useful in the arts.
U	L	C	E	R	O	U	S	Affected with ulcers, Ulcerated.
U	L	O	T	H	R	I	X	Genus of green algae.
U	L	T	E	R	I	O	R	Further, Remote, Hidden, Indirect, Buried, Concealed, Obscured, Ambiguous.
U	L	T	I	M	A	T	A	Plural of ultimatum.
U	L	T	I	M	A	T	E	Farthest, Earliest, Final, Eventual, Extreme, Utmost, Complete, Conclude.
U	L	T	I	M	A	C	Y	Ultimate, Fundimental.
U	L	T	R	A	I	S	M	The principle of those who advocate extreme measures.
U	L	T	R	A	I	S	T	Characteristic of ultraism.
U	L	U	L	A	T	E	D	Howled, Wailed, Mournful lamentation, Roared.
U	M	B	E	L	L	E	T	Flower cluster resembling an umbrella.
U	M	B	O	N	A	T	E	Forming an umbo, Rounded elevation with a corresponding depression on the other side.
U	M	B	R	A	T	E	D	Drawn indistinctly.
U	M	B	R	A	T	I	C	Secluded, Retiring, Shadowy, Indistinct.
U	M	B	R	E	L	L	A	A small cloth canopy on a ribbed frame for protection against inclement weather.
U	M	B	R	E	T	T	E	Hammerkop, African wading bird.
U	M	B	R	I	D	A	E	A family of small bottom-dwelling freshwater fishes.
U	M	B	U	R	A	N	A	S. American timber tree.
U	M	P	I	R	A	G	E	An act of umpiring.
U	N	A	B	A	T	E	D	At full strength or full force.
U	N	A	C	H	I	N	G	Not aching.
U	N	A	C	T	I	V	E	Inactive.
U	N	A	D	O	R	E	D	Not adored, Unloved.
U	N	A	F	R	A	I	D	Confident, Brave, Fearless, Bold, Audacious, Dauntless, Intrepid, Valiant.
U	N	A	I	M	I	N	G	Indiscriminating, Without a fixed target, Not aiming.
U	N	A	L	L	I	E	D	Not allied, Having no connection.
U	N	A	M	A	Z	E	D	Not surprised.
U	N	A	M	U	S	E	D	Not amused.
U	N	A	N	C	H	O	R	Loosen from an anchor.
U	N	A	N	E	L	E	D	Not having received extreme unction.
U	N	A	R	G	U	E	D	Undisputed, Being without debate.
U	N	A	R	T	F	U	L	Artless, Natural, Ingenuous, Naive, Simple, Unsophisticated.

1	2	3	4	5	6	7	8	Definition
U	N	A	T	O	N	E	D	Unexpiated.
U	N	A	V	O	W	E	D	Not affirmed or declared.
U	N	A	W	A	R	E	S	Suddenly, Unexpectedly, Without warning, Short, Unprepared, Unready.
U	N	B	A	C	K	E	D	Unbroken, Unaided, Not supported.
U	N	B	A	G	G	E	D	Removed from a bag.
U	N	B	A	N	N	E	D	Unrestricted, Permitted.
U	N	B	A	R	B	E	D	Without barbs.
U	N	B	A	R	R	E	D	Unlocked, Unbolted, Open.
U	N	B	A	T	H	E	D	Not bathed, Unwashed.
U	N	B	E	A	T	E	N	Undefeated.
U	N	B	E	D	D	E	D	Removed from a bed, Uprooted.
U	N	B	E	H	E	L	D	Unseen.
U	N	B	E	L	I	E	F	Incredulity, Skepticism, Witholding of belief.
U	N	B	E	N	I	G	N	Malignant, Malevolent.
U	N	B	E	R	E	F	T	Not bereaved.
U	N	B	E	S	E	E	M	To be unbecoming, Unbefitting.
U	N	B	I	A	S	E	D	Fair, Dispassionate, Equal, Unprejudiced, Just, Objective, Aloof, Nondiscriminatory.
U	N	B	I	D	D	E	N	Uninvited, Unasked, Unrequested, Unsought.
U	N	B	I	T	T	E	D	Uncontrolled, Unbridled.
U	N	B	I	T	T	E	R	Not bitter, Having no feelings of malice, resentment or revenge.
U	N	B	L	A	M	E	D	Not blamed.
U	N	B	L	O	O	D	Y	Bloodless.
U	N	B	O	D	I	E	D	Formless, Disembodied, Metaphysical, Immaterial, Discarnate.
U	N	B	O	I	L	E	D	Not boiled.
U	N	B	O	L	T	E	D	Unfastened, Unlocked, Open.
U	N	B	O	N	N	E	T	Remove one's hat or cap.
U	N	B	O	U	G	H	T	Not bought.
U	N	B	O	Y	I	S	H	Uncharacteristic of a boy.
U	N	B	R	A	C	E	D	Relaxed, Tension-free, Weakened, Disabled, Undermined, Blunted, Crippled.
U	N	B	R	E	E	C	H	Removing breeches.
U	N	B	R	I	B	E	D	Uncorrupted by bribery.
U	N	B	R	I	D	L	E	Free, Set loose.
U	N	B	R	O	K	E	N	Whole, Intact, Complete, Untamed, Unsubdued, Entire, Perfect, Undamaged.
U	N	B	U	C	K	L	E	Unfasten, Loosen a buckle.
U	N	B	U	R	D	E	N	Rid, Clear, Discharge, Unload, Relieve from a burden.
U	N	B	U	R	I	E	D	Uninterred.
U	N	B	U	R	N	E	D	Not burned.
U	N	B	U	T	T	O	N	Unfasten by loosing buttons.
U	N	C	A	G	I	N	G	Releasing from a cage.
U	N	C	A	L	L	E	D	Not invited.
U	N	C	A	N	D	I	D	Cautious, Reserved, Secretive.
U	N	C	A	R	T	E	D	Discharged from a cart.
U	N	C	A	S	I	N	G	Displaying, Uncovering, Unpacking.
U	N	C	A	U	G	H	T	Free, Being at large.
U	N	C	A	U	S	E	D	Self-existent.
U	N	C	H	A	N	C	Y	Unsafe, Unlucky, Illfated, Dangerous, Ill-omened.
U	N	C	H	A	R	G	E	Acquit.
U	N	C	H	A	S	T	E	Lacking in chastity, Impure, Lewd, Dirty, Immoral, Unclean, Wanton, Loose.
U	N	C	H	U	R	C	H	Excommunicate.
U	N	C	I	F	O	R	M	Hooklike, Uncinate.
U	N	C	I	N	A	T	E	Hooked.
U	N	C	L	E	N	C	H	Relax, Release from a grip, Open a fist.
U	N	C	L	I	N	C	H	Unclench.
U	N	C	L	O	S	E	D	Not closed or settled, Not concluded, Unblocked, Opened.
U	N	C	L	O	T	H	E	Undress, Uncover, Strip, Disrobe, Disclose, Display, Expose, Reveal.
U	N	C	L	O	U	D	Y	Sunny, Sunshiny, Fine, Not obscured, Clear.
U	N	C	L	U	T	C	H	Unclench, Release a grip.
U	N	C	O	A	T	E	D	Not having a coating.
U	N	C	O	I	L	E	D	Unwound, Become straight, Unrolled.
U	N	C	O	I	N	E	D	Not minted, Natural, Not fabricated, Not artificial.
U	N	C	O	M	B	E	D	Unkempt, Slovenly, Slipshod, Sloppy, Untidy, Dishevelled.
U	N	C	O	M	E	L	Y	Plain, Homely, Unattractive, Improper, Inappropriate, Unsuitable, Ugly, Unsightly.
U	N	C	O	M	M	O	N	Infrequent, Rare, Outstanding, Exceptional, Scarce, Seldom, Sporadic, Singular.
U	N	C	O	O	K	E	D	Raw, Not processed.
U	N	C	O	O	L	E	D	Still heated, Warm.
U	N	C	O	R	D	E	D	Released from cords, Unbound.
U	N	C	O	R	K	E	D	Have the cork drawn, Released from tension.

1	2	3	4	5	6	7	8	Definition
U	N	C	O	S	T	L	Y	Inexpensive, Cheap, Low-priced, Popular, Reasonable, Low-cost.
U	N	C	O	U	P	L	E	Release, Detach, Disconnect, Disassociate, Unfix, Disengage.
U	N	C	O	W	L	E	D	Removed a cowl or covering.
U	N	C	R	E	A	T	E	Deprive of existence, Annihilate.
U	N	C	T	U	O	U	S	Fatty, Greasy, Oily, Smooth, Plastic, Slick, Soapy, Ingratiating.
U	N	C	U	L	L	E	D	Not culled, Not reduced in numbers.
U	N	C	U	R	B	E	D	Not retrained, Not confined, Loosed.
U	N	C	U	R	L	E	D	Unrolled, Straightened.
U	N	C	U	R	S	E	D	Not cursed.
U	N	D	A	M	P	E	D	Not depressed, Not stifled, Not checked, Dry.
U	N	D	A	S	H	E	D	Undaunted, Undiluted, Undismayed, Brave, Valiant, Intrepid, Courageous, Bold.
U	N	D	E	C	E	N	T	Indecent, Offensive.
U	N	D	E	C	K	E	D	Unadorned, Without a deck, Not decorated.
U	N	D	E	E	D	E	D	Not exploited in deeds.
U	N	D	E	F	I	N	E	Vague, Primitive, Ambiguous, Obscure, Unclear, Dim, Indistinct, Faint.
U	N	D	E	N	I	E	D	Not contested, Undisputed.
U	N	D	E	R	A	C	T	Perform with restraint, Unskilled performance.
U	N	D	E	R	A	G	E	Immature, Under legal age, Shortage, Deficit, Failure, Inadequacy, Lack.
U	N	D	E	R	A	R	M	Placed between arm and body, Style of bowling a ball.
U	N	D	E	R	B	I	D	Undervalue, Offer too little.
U	N	D	E	R	B	U	Y	To buy too little, To obtain at a bargain price.
U	N	D	E	R	C	U	T	Cut beneath, Accept a lower price, Carving in relief.
U	N	D	E	R	D	I	D	Underacted, Did less than expected.
U	N	D	E	R	D	O	G	The victim in a power struggle, Weaker contestant, Casualty, Prey.
U	N	D	E	R	F	E	D	Not fed enough, Short rations.
U	N	D	E	R	L	A	P	Something laid under the edge of a top layer.
U	N	D	E	R	L	A	Y	Complete layer for protection under top and final layer.
U	N	D	E	R	L	E	T	Let at an uneconomic rent, To sub-let.
U	N	D	E	R	L	I	E	Support, Concealed, Submit, Foundation, Slope.
U	N	D	E	R	L	I	P	The lower lip.
U	N	D	E	R	M	A	N	A person in an inferior position, Support man for an acrobatic group.
U	N	D	E	R	P	A	Y	Insufficient wages, Incomplete payment.
U	N	D	E	R	P	I	N	Strengthen foundations, Support, Substantiate.
U	N	D	E	R	R	U	N	Pass under, Undercurrent, A run of goods less than quantity ordered.
U	N	D	E	R	S	E	T	Underpin, Place underneath.
U	N	D	E	R	T	O	W	Tidal current just beneath the surface.
U	N	E	A	R	N	E	D	Unmerited, Received in advance of service rendered.
U	N	E	A	S	I	L	Y	Apprehensively, Disturbedly, Awkwardly, Restlessly, Precariously, Uncomfortably.
U	N	E	N	D	I	N	G	Endless, Continuous, Everlasting, Timeless, Undying, Interminable, Eternal, Extravagant.
U	N	E	N	V	I	E	D	Not envied, Inspiring no envious feelings, Not coveted.
U	N	E	R	R	I	N	G	Infallible, Inerrant, Sure.
U	N	E	S	P	I	E	D	Passing unseen.
U	N	E	V	E	N	L	Y	Irregularly, Unfairly, Oddly, Unequally, Unjustly, Not uniformly.
U	N	E	V	O	K	E	D	Not enforced, Dormant.
U	N	E	X	P	E	R	T	Unexperienced, Inefficient, Incapable, Incompetent, Inept, Unskilled, Unworkmanlike.
U	N	F	A	B	L	E	D	Real, Actual.
U	N	F	A	D	I	N	G	Not loosing colour or freshness, Not losing value, importance, effectiveness or appeal.
U	N	F	A	I	R	L	Y	Inequitably, Unjustly, Unreasonably.
U	N	F	A	L	L	E	N	Not morally fallen, Virtuous.
U	N	F	A	S	T	E	N	Unpin, Unbuckle, Undo, Detach, Untie, Weaken, Unbind, Disengage.
U	N	F	A	U	L	T	Y	Blameless, Innocent.
U	N	F	E	A	R	E	D	Unafraid, Bold, Courageous, Fearless.
U	N	F	E	N	C	E	D	Unguarded, Not enclosed.
U	N	F	E	T	T	E	R	Unshackle, Liberate, Emancipate.
U	N	F	I	L	I	A	L	Undutiful, Rebellious.
U	N	F	I	L	L	E	D	Empty, Blank.
U	N	F	I	L	M	E	D	Not yet made into a motion picture.
U	N	F	I	R	M	L	Y	Unsteadily, Insecurely.
U	N	F	I	X	I	N	G	Disengaging, Unsettling, Dissolving, Loosening.
U	N	F	L	A	W	E	D	Perfect, Flawless.
U	N	F	L	O	W	E	R	To strip, To empty.
U	N	F	O	L	D	E	D	Expanded, Opened out, Unwrapped, Revealed, Blossomed, Spread, Developed, Perfected.
U	N	F	O	O	T	E	D	Untrod, Not walked on.
U	N	F	O	R	C	E	D	Voluntary, Willing, Deliberate, Intentional, Easy, Natural, Spontaneous.
U	N	F	O	R	K	E	D	Not forked.
U	N	F	O	R	M	A	L	Informal, Casual, Unconventional.
U	N	F	O	R	M	E	D	Undeveloped, Immature, Unpolished, Shapeless, Crude, Rough, Unfashioned, Unworked.

1	2	3	4	5	6	7	8	
U	N	F	O	U	G	H	T	Uncontested.
U	N	F	O	U	L	E	D	Disentangled.
U	N	F	R	A	M	E	D	Not provided with a frame.
U	N	F	R	E	E	Z	E	To thaw, To free from strict control, To release funds.
U	N	F	R	I	E	N	D	Enemy.
U	N	F	R	O	Z	E	N	Not frozen, Thawed.
U	N	F	R	U	G	A	L	Extravagant, Lavish.
U	N	F	U	E	L	E	D	Unfed, Self-sustained.
U	N	F	U	N	D	E	D	Not funded, Floating.
U	N	F	U	R	L	E	D	Cast loose, Unfolded, Unrolled, Spread out, Released.
U	N	G	A	I	N	L	Y	Coarse, Ugly, Unwieldy, Clumsy, Gawky, Lumbering, Blundering, Maladroit.
U	N	G	E	A	R	E	D	Unhitched, Disconnected, Disrupted.
U	N	G	E	N	I	A	L	Disagreeable, Aversive, Repugnant, Repellent, Unsympathetic, Uncongenial.
U	N	G	E	N	T	L	E	Harsh, Rough.
U	N	G	E	N	T	L	Y	Harshly, Roughly, Unkindly.
U	N	G	I	F	T	E	D	Lacking talent.
U	N	G	I	L	D	E	D	Not ornamented with gilt.
U	N	G	I	R	D	E	D	Loosened, Unrestrained, Released, Untethered.
U	N	G	I	V	I	N	G	Frugal, Stingy, Adamant, Inflexible, Rigid, Parsimonious.
U	N	G	L	A	Z	E	D	Not glazed, Without glass panes fitted.
U	N	G	L	O	V	E	D	Removed gloves.
U	N	G	L	U	I	N	G	Disjoining, Detaching, Separating.
U	N	G	O	T	T	E	N	Not obtained.
U	N	G	O	W	N	E	D	Not gowned, Not wearing a ceremonial robe.
U	N	G	R	A	C	E	D	Graceless, Awkward.
U	N	G	R	O	U	N	D	Not ground, Not milled.
U	N	G	U	I	D	E	D	Not being led or directed, Uncontrolled.
U	N	G	U	I	L	T	Y	Innocent.
U	N	G	U	L	A	T	A	Hoofed mammals.
U	N	G	U	L	A	T	E	Having hoofs.
U	N	G	U	M	M	E	D	Not having adhesive.
U	N	H	A	I	L	E	D	Not hailed, Not called.
U	N	H	A	I	R	E	D	Deprived of hairs.
U	N	H	A	L	L	O	W	To make profane.
U	N	H	A	N	D	E	D	Removed the hand, Let go, Released from a grip.
U	N	H	A	N	G	E	D	Not executed by hanging.
U	N	H	A	R	M	E	D	Safe, Unscathed, Not injured, Immune, Undamaged.
U	N	H	A	S	P	E	D	Opened, Unfastened a hasp.
U	N	H	E	A	D	E	D	Removed the top.
U	N	H	E	A	T	E	D	Not heated.
U	N	H	E	D	G	E	D	Unprotected, Unqualified.
U	N	H	E	E	D	E	D	Disregarded, Ignored, Neglected, Overlooked.
U	N	H	E	L	M	E	D	Removed a helmet.
U	N	H	E	L	P	E	D	Unaided, Not assisted.
U	N	H	E	M	M	E	D	Not hemmed, Having a raw edge.
U	N	H	E	R	O	I	C	Timid, Unimpressive.
U	N	H	I	N	G	E	D	Disrupted, Disordered, Deranged, Unsettled, Swayed, Cracked, Discomposed, Upset.
U	N	H	I	V	I	N	G	Driving from a hive.
U	N	H	O	N	E	S	T	Dishonest.
U	N	H	O	O	D	E	D	Removed a hood, Exposed.
U	N	H	O	O	K	E	D	Removed from a hook, Unfastened by undoing hooks.
U	N	H	O	R	N	E	D	Not having a horn.
U	N	H	O	R	S	E	D	Dislodged, Unseated, Put out of action.
U	N	H	O	U	S	E	D	Ejected from a house.
U	N	H	U	M	B	L	E	Not humble.
U	N	H	U	N	T	E	D	Not hunted, Protected.
U	N	H	U	S	K	E	D	Stripped of husks.
U	N	I	A	X	I	A	L	Having one axis, Monaxial.
U	N	I	C	Y	C	L	E	Vehicle with one wheel.
U	N	I	D	E	A	E	D	Deficient in ideas, Lacking in originality of thought.
U	N	I	F	Y	I	N	G	Integrating, Consolidating, Compacting, Concentrating, Articulating, Organizing, Binding.
U	N	I	O	N	I	S	M	Policy of forming a union, Workers combining in industry.
U	N	I	O	N	I	S	T	Advocate of religious union.
U	N	I	O	N	I	Z	E	Form into a labour union.
U	N	I	P	H	A	S	E	Single phase.
U	N	I	P	O	L	A	R	Produced by a single magnetic or electrical pole.
U	N	I	Q	U	E	L	Y	Exceptionally, Peculiarly, Solitary, Extraordinary.

1	2	3	4	5	6	7	8	
U	N	I	Q	U	I	T	Y	Uniqueness, Singularity, Singleness, Unicity.
U	N	I	S	O	N	A	L	Harmonious, Alike in nature, Concordant.
U	N	I	T	E	D	L	Y	Jointly, Concertedly, Cojointly.
U	N	I	T	I	Z	E	D	Converted into a unit, Divided and packaged into smaller units.
U	N	I	V	A	L	V	E	Having one valve.
U	N	I	V	E	R	S	E	Cosmos, The whole body, The world, The earth.
U	N	I	V	O	C	A	L	Having only one meaning, Uniform, Clear, Distinct, Evident, Obvious, Plain.
U	N	J	O	I	N	E	D	Separated, Not joined, Uncoupled, Detached.
U	N	J	O	Y	O	U	S	Gloomy, Glum, Melancholy, Miserable.
U	N	J	U	S	T	L	Y	Wrongfully, Unfairly.
U	N	K	E	N	N	E	D	Unknown, Strange.
U	N	K	E	N	N	E	L	Bring into the open, Discover, Disclose.
U	N	K	I	N	D	L	Y	Harshly, Unfriendly, Cruelly, Rigorously, Inconsiderately.
U	N	K	I	N	G	E	D	Removed a king, Deprived of a monarch.
U	N	L	A	C	I	N	G	Untying laces, Loosening, Freeing from restraint.
U	N	L	A	P	P	E	D	Uncovered.
U	N	L	A	S	H	E	D	Untied the restraining ropes, Loosed binding.
U	N	L	A	W	F	U	L	Irregular, Illegal, Illicit, Criminal, Wrongful, Nefarious, Improper, Objectionable.
U	N	L	A	X	I	N	G	Relaxing, Releasing tension.
U	N	L	A	Y	I	N	G	Untwisting.
U	N	L	E	A	R	N	T	Not learned.
U	N	L	I	C	K	E	D	Immature, Ungainly, Naive, Unpolished.
U	N	L	I	K	E	L	Y	Improbable, Disagreeable, Doubtful, Questionable, Dubious, Unpromising, Unbelievable.
U	N	L	I	M	B	E	R	To prepare for action.
U	N	L	I	N	K	E	D	Disconnected, Separated, Uncoupled, Detached.
U	N	L	I	V	E	L	Y	Dull, Cheerless, Lacking animation.
U	N	L	O	A	D	E	D	Delivered, Discharged, Removed, Relieved from pressure, Dumped, Discarded.
U	N	L	O	C	K	E	D	Unbolted, Unfastened, Opened, Furnished a key to solve something.
U	N	L	O	O	K	E	D	Unheeded, Lacking attention.
U	N	L	O	O	S	E	D	Released from restraints, Relaxed from strain.
U	N	L	O	O	S	E	N	Unloose.
U	N	L	O	R	D	E	D	Deprived of the rank of a lord.
U	N	L	O	R	D	L	Y	Not lordly, Not arbitrary.
U	N	L	O	V	E	L	Y	Unpleasant, Disagreeable, Unattractive, Unsightly, Hideous.
U	N	L	O	V	I	N	G	Not loving, Cold, Not affectionate.
U	N	M	A	I	M	E	D	Not maimed.
U	N	M	A	K	I	N	G	Destroying, Deposing.
U	N	M	A	N	N	E	D	Not guided by men.
U	N	M	A	N	T	L	E	Uncover.
U	N	M	A	P	P	E	D	Uncharted.
U	N	M	A	R	K	E	D	Not having a marker, Unobserved.
U	N	M	A	R	R	E	D	Not marred, Not sullied.
U	N	M	A	R	T	Y	R	To deprive of martyrdom.
U	N	M	A	S	K	E	D	Exposed, Revealed, Discovered, Debunked, Undressed, Uncloaked.
U	N	M	E	E	T	L	Y	Improperly, Unsuitably.
U	N	M	E	L	T	E	D	Not melted.
U	N	M	E	S	H	E	D	Disentangled, Release a gear from a mesh.
U	N	M	I	L	K	E	D	Not milked.
U	N	M	I	L	L	E	D	Not milled.
U	N	M	I	N	D	E	D	Ignored, Unheeded.
U	N	M	I	S	S	E	D	Not missed.
U	N	M	O	D	E	S	T	Immodest.
U	N	M	O	D	I	S	H	Unfashionable.
U	N	M	O	O	R	E	D	Raised the anchor to loose from moorings.
U	N	M	O	V	I	N	G	Impassive, Motionless, Unemotional.
U	N	M	U	F	F	L	E	To free from something that muffles.
U	N	M	U	Z	Z	L	E	To remove a muzzle, To allow free speech.
U	N	N	E	E	D	E	D	Unnecessary.
U	N	N	E	R	V	E	D	Castrated, Enfeebled, Undermined, Weakened, Bewildered, Distracted, Agitated, Upset.
U	N	O	P	E	N	E	D	Closed.
U	N	P	A	C	K	E	D	Unwrapped, Removed, Emptied.
U	N	P	A	C	K	E	R	One that empties cartons.
U	N	P	A	I	N	E	D	Feeling no pain.
U	N	P	A	I	R	E	D	Not matched or mated.
U	N	P	A	R	T	E	D	Unseparated, Not parted.
U	N	P	A	W	N	E	D	Not pawned.
U	N	P	E	E	L	E	D	With outer skin intact.

1	2	3	4	5	6	7	8	
U	N	P	E	G	G	E	D	Removed a peg.
U	N	P	E	N	N	E	D	Released from a pen.
U	N	P	E	O	P	L	E	Depopulate.
U	N	P	I	C	K	E	D	Unsorted, Not picked, Not chosen.
U	N	P	I	N	I	O	N	Free from restraint.
U	N	P	I	N	N	E	D	Removed pins.
U	N	P	I	T	I	E	D	Pitiless, Merciless.
U	N	P	L	A	C	E	D	Not in the first three or four.
U	N	P	L	I	A	N	T	Obstinate, Unpliable, Not easily managed.
U	N	P	L	U	M	E	D	Stripped of plumes.
U	N	P	O	E	T	I	C	Not poetic, Prosaic.
U	N	P	O	I	S	E	D	Unbalanced, Not poised.
U	N	P	O	L	I	S	H	Deprive of polish.
U	N	P	O	L	I	T	E	Impolite.
U	N	P	O	L	L	E	D	Not included in a poll.
U	N	P	R	A	Y	E	D	Unsolicited, Uninvited.
U	N	P	R	E	A	C	H	Retract by preaching.
U	N	P	R	E	T	T	Y	Ugly, Not pretty, Reprehensible.
U	N	P	R	I	E	S	T	Unfrock.
U	N	P	R	I	S	O	N	To free from prison.
U	N	P	R	I	Z	E	D	Not properly valued.
U	N	P	R	O	P	E	R	Improper.
U	N	P	R	O	V	E	D	Not proved.
U	N	P	U	R	G	E	D	Not purged.
U	N	R	A	I	L	E	D	Not enclosed with railings.
U	N	R	A	I	S	E	D	Not raised.
U	N	R	E	A	S	O	N	Madness, Irrationality, Chaos, Confusion.
U	N	R	E	E	L	E	D	Unwound, Unrolled.
U	N	R	E	I	N	E	D	Loosened the reins, Removed restraint.
U	N	R	E	P	A	I	D	Not repaid.
U	N	R	E	P	A	I	R	Disrepair.
U	N	R	I	D	D	L	E	Solve.
U	N	R	I	F	L	E	D	Undespoiled, Unrobbed.
U	N	R	I	G	G	E	D	Unclothed, Undressed, Dismantled.
U	N	R	I	P	P	E	D	Disclosed, Revealed.
U	N	R	O	B	I	N	G	Disrobing, Undressing.
U	N	R	O	L	L	E	D	Uncoiled, Spread out, Extended, Unwound.
U	N	R	O	O	F	E	D	Stripped off the roof.
U	N	R	O	O	T	E	D	Eradicated, Uprooted, Rootless.
U	N	R	O	U	T	E	D	Not routed, Orderly.
U	N	R	U	F	F	L	E	Calm, Quiet.
U	N	R	U	I	N	E	D	Not ruined.
U	N	S	A	D	D	L	E	Unhorse, Remove the saddle.
U	N	S	A	F	E	T	Y	Insecurity.
U	N	S	A	L	T	E	D	Not salted.
U	N	S	A	Y	I	N	G	Recalling, Recanting, Retracting.
U	N	S	C	A	R	E	D	Not scared.
U	N	S	E	A	L	E	D	Not sealed, Not confirmed.
U	N	S	E	A	M	E	D	Opened the seam.
U	N	S	E	A	T	E	D	Deposed, Not seated, Dislodged from a position.
U	N	S	E	C	R	E	T	Disclose, Reveal.
U	N	S	E	E	D	E	D	Not selectively placed in a draw for a tournament.
U	N	S	E	E	I	N	G	Blind, Unobservant, Unsuspecting.
U	N	S	E	E	M	L	Y	Indecent, Inappropriate, Unseasonable, Unbecoming, Indecorous, Coarse, Crude.
U	N	S	E	I	Z	E	D	Not grasped.
U	N	S	E	R	V	E	D	Given no attention.
U	N	S	E	T	T	L	E	Disturb, Discompose, Disorder, Disarrange, Disorganize, Jumble, Upset.
U	N	S	H	A	D	E	D	Exposed, Not darkened.
U	N	S	H	A	D	O	W	Expose, Reveal.
U	N	S	H	A	K	E	N	Firm, Steady, Sure, Fixed, Steadfast, Unfaltering, Unwavering, Abiding.
U	N	S	H	A	M	E	D	Unashamed.
U	N	S	H	A	P	E	N	Unshaped.
U	N	S	H	A	R	E	D	Not shared.
U	N	S	H	A	V	E	D	Not shaved.
U	N	S	H	A	V	E	N	Having the stubble of a beard, Not shaved.
U	N	S	H	R	O	U	D	Expose, Uncover.
U	N	S	I	F	T	E	D	Not inspected or scrutinized.

1	2	3	4	5	6	7	8	
U	N	S	L	A	K	E	D	Not lessened.
U	N	S	L	U	I	C	E	Open to sluice.
U	N	S	M	O	K	E	D	Not exposed to smoke, Uncured.
U	N	S	M	O	O	T	H	Rough, Harsh.
U	N	S	O	C	I	A	L	Not social, Antisocial.
U	N	S	O	C	K	E	T	Take from a socket.
U	N	S	O	I	L	E	D	Not dirtied, Not sullied.
U	N	S	O	L	D	E	R	Divide, Separate.
U	N	S	O	L	E	M	N	Not solemn.
U	N	S	O	L	V	E	D	Not solved.
U	N	S	O	R	T	E	D	Not classified.
U	N	S	O	U	G	H	T	Not sought, Unsolicited.
U	N	S	O	U	R	E	D	Not soured.
U	N	S	P	H	E	R	E	Displace.
U	N	S	P	I	K	E	D	Removed a spike.
U	N	S	P	O	I	L	T	Not spoilt, Undamaged.
U	N	S	P	O	K	E	N	Tacit, Unexpressed, Silent.
U	N	S	P	R	U	N	G	Not equipped with springs.
U	N	S	T	A	B	L	E	Movable, Irregular, Vacillating, Unconstant, Mobile, Rocky, Insecure, Weak.
U	N	S	T	A	T	E	D	Not stated or set forth.
U	N	S	T	A	Y	E	D	Not firmly supported, Not steadfast, Not hindered, Not fastened.
U	N	S	T	E	A	D	Y	Unstable, Vacillating, Mobile, Moving, Changeable, Fluid, Unsettled, Variable.
U	N	S	T	R	A	I	N	To relieve from strain.
U	N	S	T	R	E	S	S	A syllable having a relatively weak stress.
U	N	S	T	R	I	N	G	To remove a string, Enervate, Emasculate, Unnerve.
U	N	S	T	R	U	N	G	Unnerved, Discomposed.
U	N	S	U	I	T	E	D	Unfit, Ill-adapted, Inappropriate, Inapt, Inadmissable, Disappointing, Objectionable.
U	N	S	U	N	N	E	D	Not exposed to sunlight, Not sun-burned, Not open to the public.
U	N	S	U	R	E	T	Y	Uncertainty, Insecurity.
U	N	S	W	A	T	H	E	To unbandage, Unwrap.
U	N	S	W	A	Y	E	D	Not influenced, Unbiased, Unprejudiced.
U	N	T	A	C	K	L	E	Remove tackle or harness.
U	N	T	A	N	G	L	E	Disentangle, Extricate, Straighten out, Disencumber, Unscramble, Disembarrass, Untwine.
U	N	T	A	N	N	E	D	Not put through a tanning process.
U	N	T	A	P	P	E	D	Not utilized, Unspoiled, Untouched, Virginal.
U	N	T	A	S	T	E	D	Not tried, Not eaten, Not sampled.
U	N	T	A	U	G	H	T	Ignorant, Untutored, Naive, Natural, Spontaneous.
U	N	T	E	N	A	N	T	Leave, Quit, Remove a tenant.
U	N	T	E	N	D	E	D	Neglected, Uncared-for.
U	N	T	E	N	D	E	R	Tough, Not gentle, Unsympathetic, Not easily hurt.
U	N	T	E	N	T	E	D	Not attended to, Unheeded.
U	N	T	E	S	T	E	D	Not tested, Untried, Unpracticed, Unproved, Undemonstrated.
U	N	T	H	A	W	E	D	Not thawed, Frozen.
U	N	T	H	R	E	A	D	Take out a thread, Loosen threads.
U	N	T	H	R	I	F	T	Extravagance, Wastefulness, Spendthrift, Wastrel.
U	N	T	H	R	O	N	E	Dethrone, Remove from a throne.
U	N	T	I	D	I	L	Y	Carelessly, Sloppily, Messily.
U	N	T	I	L	L	E	D	Not cultivated.
U	N	T	I	M	E	L	Y	Inopportune, Early, Premature, Previous, Unseasonable, Ill-timed, Improper, Inopportune.
U	N	T	I	N	G	E	D	Not coloured.
U	N	T	I	R	I	N	G	Unwearying, Indefatigable, Tireless, Unflagging, Inexhaustible.
U	N	T	I	T	L	E	D	Having no title.
U	N	T	O	G	G	L	E	Unfasten by removing a toggle from its loop.
U	N	T	O	M	B	E	D	Unburied, Not supplied with a tomb.
U	N	T	O	W	A	R	D	Unruly, Unfortunate, Unlucky, Adverse, Improper, Indelicate, Indecorous, Fractious.
U	N	T	R	A	C	E	D	Loosed from a trace, Not found.
U	N	T	R	A	D	E	D	Uncommon, Unusual.
U	N	T	R	U	I	S	M	Falsehood, Lie, Misrepresentation, Fib, Prevarication, Untruth.
U	N	T	R	U	S	T	Y	Untrustworthy, Dubious, Undependable, Questionable, Unsure.
U	N	T	U	C	K	E	D	Released from a tuck.
U	N	T	U	F	T	E	D	Not having tufts.
U	N	T	U	N	I	N	G	Disarranging, Discomposing, Bothering, Agitating, Unhinging, Disturbing, Flustering.
U	N	T	U	R	N	E	D	Not turned.
U	N	T	W	I	N	E	D	Disentangled, Unclasped, Dissolved, Extricated, Disembroiled, Untied, Unscrambled.
U	N	U	N	I	T	E	D	Disunited.
U	N	U	R	B	A	N	E	Churlish, Vulgar.
U	N	U	S	A	B	L	E	Impractical, Non-functional, Unserviceable, Useless, Unworkable.

1	2	3	4	5	6	7	8	
U	N	V	A	L	U	E	D	Disregarded, Insignificant, Not important.
U	N	V	E	I	L	E	D	Open, Revealed, Disclosed, Displayed, Exposed, Uncovered, Unclothed.
U	N	V	E	N	T	E	D	Not vented.
U	N	V	E	R	S	E	D	Ignorant, Inexperienced, Callow, Fresh, Raw, Unpractical, Unseasoned, Untried.
U	N	V	O	I	C	E	D	Silent, Stifled, Voiceless, Tacit, Unexpressed, Unuttered, Wordless.
U	N	V	U	L	G	A	R	Refined.
U	N	W	A	L	K	E	D	Not walked.
U	N	W	A	L	L	E	D	Not enclosed, Open, Exposed.
U	N	W	A	N	I	N	G	Constant, Perpetual.
U	N	W	A	N	T	E	D	Superfluous, Unnecessary, Faulty, Undesirable, Ill-favoured, Unwelcome, Unsought.
U	N	W	A	R	I	L	Y	Carelessly, Incautiously.
U	N	W	A	R	M	E	D	Not subjected to heat or stimulation.
U	N	W	A	R	N	E	D	Receiving no warning, Not rebuked.
U	N	W	A	R	P	E	D	Undistorted.
U	N	W	A	S	H	E	D	Not washed, Ignoble, Baseborn, Humble, Lowborn, Lowly, Mean, Plebeian.
U	N	W	A	S	T	E	D	Undiminished, Unravaged.
U	N	W	E	A	N	E	D	Not weaned.
U	N	W	E	D	D	E	D	Not married, Single.
U	N	W	E	E	D	E	D	Not weeded.
U	N	W	I	E	L	D	Y	Awkward, Cumbersome, Ungainly, Ponderous, Inconvenient, Uncontrollable, Massive.
U	N	W	I	L	L	E	D	Involuntary, Unintentional.
U	N	W	I	N	G	E	D	Wingless.
U	N	W	I	S	D	O	M	Recklessness, Foolishness, Lack of wisdom.
U	N	W	I	S	E	L	Y	Senselessly, Foolishly, Ill-advisedly.
U	N	W	O	N	T	E	D	Rare, Unusual, Unused, Exceptional, Extraordinary, Singular, Uncommon.
U	N	W	O	O	D	E	D	Treeless.
U	N	W	O	R	K	E	D	Crude, Raw, Unexplored, Untapped, Rough, Unfashioned, Unfinished, Unpolished.
U	N	W	O	R	T	H	Y	Poor, Worthless, Base, Dishonourable, Undeserving, Unjustified, Unmerited, Valueless.
U	N	Y	O	K	I	N	G	Outspanning, Unhitching, Releasing, Disjoining, Unlinking.
U	P	C	O	M	I	N	G	Forthcoming, Approaching.
U	P	C	U	R	L	E	D	Curled up.
U	P	F	U	R	L	E	D	Furled upward, Rolled upward.
U	P	G	R	O	W	T	H	Development, Process.
U	P	H	E	A	P	E	D	Accumulated.
U	P	H	E	A	V	A	L	Agitation, Disorder, Convulsion, Commotion, Ferment, Clamour, Outcry, Tumult.
U	P	H	E	A	V	E	D	Lifted, Raised.
U	P	H	O	L	D	E	R	Upholsterer, Undertaker, Supporter, Defender.
U	P	L	I	F	T	E	D	Elevated, Hoisted, Upheld, Upraised, Illuminated, Enlightened, Improved, Irradiated.
U	P	M	A	K	I	N	G	Action of making up.
U	P	P	E	R	C	U	T	Powerful upward blow.
U	P	P	E	R	T	E	N	Upper class, Members of the highest social class.
U	P	R	A	I	S	E	D	Lifted, Elevated, Uplifted, Comforted, Consoled, Cheered, Solaced.
U	P	R	I	S	I	N	G	Rebellion, Insurrection, Revolt.
U	P	R	O	O	T	E	D	Eradicated, Displaced, Destroyed, Exterminated, Annihilated, Abolished, Demolished.
U	P	S	T	A	I	R	S	Up the stairway, Go to a higher floor.
U	P	S	T	A	Y	E	D	Sustained, Supported.
U	P	S	T	R	E	A	M	Toward the source of a stream.
U	P	S	T	R	O	K	E	An upward stroke of a pen.
U	P	T	H	R	O	W	N	Displaced upward in a geologic fault.
U	P	T	H	R	U	S	T	Uplift of the earth's crust in a fault.
U	P	T	U	R	N	E	D	Overturned, Upheaved, Face upward.
U	P	W	A	R	D	L	Y	Rising, Ascending, Increasingly.
U	R	B	A	N	I	S	M	Characteristic way of life of those who live in an urban area, City planning.
U	R	B	A	N	I	T	E	One who lives in a city.
U	R	B	A	N	E	L	Y	Suavely, Smoothly, Blandly, Civilly, Graciously.
U	R	B	A	N	I	Z	E	To incorporate into an urban area.
U	R	C	E	O	L	U	S	Part of a plant shaped like an urn.
U	R	E	T	H	A	N	E	A crystalline ester-amide used as an anaesthetic for animals.
U	R	G	E	N	T	L	Y	Pressingly, Insistently, Demandingly, Impellingly.
U	R	O	B	I	L	I	N	Brown pile pigments found in human waste.
U	R	O	C	H	O	R	D	Minute marine animal.
U	R	O	D	A	E	U	M	Part of a bird's anatomy where ureters empty.
U	R	O	G	L	E	N	A	Genus of colonial plantlike flagellates united in a spherical colony.
U	R	O	L	O	G	I	C	Relating to the urinary tract.
U	R	O	M	E	R	E	S	An abdominal segment of an arthropod.
U	R	O	S	C	O	P	Y	Diagnostic examination of urine.
U	R	O	S	T	E	G	E	A scale on the underside of the tail of a snake.

1	2	3	4	5	6	7	8	
U	R	O	S	T	Y	L	E	Tip of the vertebral column of frogs and toads.
U	R	S	I	F	O	R	M	In the shape of a bear.
U	R	S	U	L	I	N	E	Member of a teaching order of nuns.
U	R	T	I	C	A	N	T	Stinging, Itching.
U	R	T	I	C	A	T	E	Same as URTICANT.
U	R	T	I	C	O	S	E	Abounding with nettles.
U	R	U	S	H	I	Y	E	Japanese colour print.
U	S	E	F	U	L	L	Y	Functionally, Handily, Conveniently, Suitably, Beneficially, Utility.
U	S	H	E	R	I	N	G	Introducing, Preceding, Conducting, Guiding.
U	S	T	I	L	A	G	O	A genus of smut fungi.
U	S	U	F	R	U	C	T	The right to use or enjoy something.
U	S	U	R	I	O	U	S	Charging illegal and exorbitant rates of interest on loans.
U	S	U	R	P	I	N	G	Seizing, Occupying, Supplanting, Appropriating, Assuming, Displacing, Commandeering.
U	T	I	L	I	Z	E	D	Used, Promoted, Employed, Exploited, Handled, Exercised, Applied, Bestowed.
U	T	T	E	R	I	N	G	Selling, Vending, Pronouncing, Say, Speaking, Disclosing, Divulging, Revealing.
U	V	U	L	A	R	I	A	Genus of N. American herbs.
U	X	O	R	I	O	U	S	Characterised by doting and submission to a wife.

V

1	2	3	4	5	6	7	8	
V	A	C	A	N	T	I	A	Goods without an owner.
V	A	C	A	T	I	N	G	Voiding, Annulling, Leaving, Discharging, Dissolving, Clearing, Repealing, Emptying.
V	A	C	A	T	I	O	N	Intermission, Rest, Holiday, Annulment, Recess, Respite, Furlough.
V	A	C	C	A	R	I	A	A small genus of Eurasian herbs.
V	A	C	C	I	N	A	L	Relating to vaccination.
V	A	C	C	I	N	I	A	Cowpox.
V	A	G	A	B	O	N	D	Wandering, Nomadic, Worthless, Vagrant, Truant, Tramp, Hobo, Derelict.
V	A	G	A	R	I	E	S	Capers, Frolics, Fancies, Humours, Whims, Fantasies, Daydreams, Quirks.
V	A	G	I	L	I	T	Y	Power of movement, Competing successfully in the struggle for existence.
V	A	G	I	N	A	N	T	Sheathing.
V	A	G	I	N	A	T	E	Invested with a sheath.
V	A	G	I	N	U	L	A	Part of a moss sheath.
V	A	G	O	T	O	M	Y	Surgical cutting of the vagus nerve.
V	A	G	R	A	N	C	Y	Vagary, Wandering, Rambling, Roving, Roaming.
V	A	I	N	N	E	S	S	Vanity, Conceit, Inanity, Futility, Idleness.
V	A	L	A	N	C	E	D	Decorated with pleated drapery.
V	A	L	E	R	I	A	N	A drug consisting of the dried rhizome and roots of the garden heliotrope.
V	A	L	E	T	I	N	G	Working as a valet.
V	A	L	H	A	L	L	A	A place of honour, Shrine, Resting place of heroes.
V	A	L	I	A	N	C	E	Valiancy, Heroism, Prowess.
V	A	L	I	A	N	C	Y	Bravery, Valour, Gallantry, Valorousness.
V	A	L	I	D	A	T	E	Verify, Substantiate, Ratify, Confirm, Corroborate, Support, Authenticate, Justify.
V	A	L	I	D	I	T	Y	Point, Cogency, Effectiveness, Force, Punch, Validness, Fallacy, Falsity.
V	A	L	K	Y	R	I	E	A maiden in Norse mythology.
V	A	L	L	A	T	E	D	Having a raised edge surrounding a depression.
V	A	L	O	R	I	Z	E	To set a price by governmental intervention.
V	A	L	O	R	O	U	S	Brave, Courageous, Audacious, Bold, Dauntless, Fearless, Intrepid, Valiant.
V	A	L	U	A	B	L	E	Costly, Worthy, Estimable, Precious, Priceless, Appreciated, Prized, Esteemed.
V	A	L	U	A	T	O	R	Appraiser, Assessor.
V	A	L	V	U	L	A	R	Having the function of a valve.
V	A	M	B	R	A	C	E	Medieval armour to protect the forearm.
V	A	M	O	O	S	E	D	Decamped, Ran out, Departed quickly.
V	A	M	P	H	O	R	N	Megaphone used in churches during the 18th and 19th centuries.
V	A	M	P	I	R	I	C	Bloodsucking, Parasitic.
V	A	M	P	L	A	T	E	A round iron plate on a spear to protect the hand.
V	A	N	A	D	A	T	E	An ester derived from vanadium pentoxide.
V	A	N	A	D	I	U	M	A malleable ductile polyvalent metallic element.
V	A	N	A	D	O	U	S	Containing vanadium.
V	A	N	D	A	L	I	C	Barbarous, Savage.
V	A	N	D	Y	K	E	D	Sharply pointed.
V	A	N	G	U	A	R	D	Forefront, Advance, Leader.
V	A	N	I	L	L	I	N	A crystalline phenolic aldehyde.
V	A	N	I	S	H	E	D	Evaporated, Disappeared, Extinct, Bygone, Defunct, Departed, Expired, Perished.
V	A	N	Q	U	I	S	H	Conquer, Overcome, Control, Subdue, Subjugate, Overpower, Crush, Defeat.
V	A	P	I	D	I	T	Y	Dullness, Insipidy, Inanity.
V	A	P	O	R	I	Z	E	Convert into vapour, Dissipate.

1	2	3	4	5	6	7	8	Definition
V	A	P	O	R	O	U	S	Ethereal, Unsubstantial, Vague, Filmy, Hazy, Cloudy, Misty, Airy.
V	A	P	O	U	R	E	D	Evaporated, Bullied, Depressed, Bored, Fumed, Steamed, Bragged, Boasted.
V	A	P	O	U	R	E	R	Braggart.
V	A	R	G	U	E	R	O	Decorative writing desk of Spanish origin.
V	A	R	I	A	B	L	E	Changeable, Shifting, Fickle, Unsteady, Inconstant, Mobile, Unstable, Capricious.
V	A	R	I	A	B	L	Y	Changeably, Fitfully, Unsteadily, Uncertainly.
V	A	R	I	A	N	C	E	Difference, Deviation, Discrepancy, Discord, Fluctuation, Contention, Disunity, Strife.
V	A	R	I	A	T	E	D	Variegated, Altered, Changed.
V	A	R	I	C	O	I	D	Resembling an abnormal swelling in a vein or artery.
V	A	R	I	C	O	S	E	Abnormally dilated or swollen.
V	A	R	I	E	T	A	L	Relating to a variety.
V	A	R	I	F	O	R	M	Having various forms.
V	A	R	I	O	L	A	R	Relating to smallpox.
V	A	R	I	O	R	U	M	A classical work with notes by various persons.
V	A	R	I	S	T	O	R	An electrical resistor.
V	A	R	L	E	T	R	Y	Rabble, Crowd, Mob.
V	A	R	T	A	B	E	D	A celibate preacher in the Armenian clergy.
V	A	S	C	U	L	A	R	Relating to a tube carrying body fluid.
V	A	S	C	U	L	U	M	A special box for collecting plant specimens.
V	A	S	E	L	I	N	E	Petroleum jelly.
V	A	S	I	C	I	N	E	A crystalline alkaloid found in the leaves of the Malabar nut.
V	A	S	I	F	O	R	M	Having the form of a vase.
V	A	S	S	A	L	E	D	Bonded to an employer or landlord, Slavery, Servitude.
V	A	S	S	A	L	R	Y	Feudal system, Bondage.
V	A	S	T	N	E	S	S	Enormity, Hugeness, Immensity, Magnitude.
V	A	T	E	R	I	T	E	A mineral that consists of a relatively unstable form of calcium carbonate.
V	A	T	I	C	I	D	E	The murderer of a prophet.
V	A	U	L	T	A	G	E	A vaulted place, An arched cellar.
V	A	U	L	T	I	N	G	Leaping upwards, Stretching, Construction of vaults.
V	A	U	N	T	E	R	Y	Bravado, Boasting, Bragging.
V	A	U	N	T	F	U	L	Boastful, Vainglorious, Swaggering, Ostentatious.
V	A	U	N	T	I	N	G	Bragging, Boasting, Self-glorifying, Brandishing, Flaunting, Parading, Exhibiting.
V	A	U	N	T	L	A	Y	Relating to the releasing of dogs on a hunt.
V	A	V	A	S	O	R	Y	The fee paid under the feudal system.
V	A	V	A	S	O	U	R	A feudal tenant in rank directly below a peer or baron.
V	E	A	L	S	K	I	N	A large calfskin.
V	E	D	A	N	T	I	C	Relating to a Hindu philosophy.
V	E	G	E	T	A	T	E	Stagnate, Hibernate, Idle, Languish.
V	E	G	E	T	I	V	E	Vegetable.
V	E	H	E	M	E	N	T	Emphatic, Pronounced, Lively, Strenuous, Truculent, Fervent, Zealous, Heated.
V	E	I	L	L	E	S	S	Unscreened, Exposed.
V	E	I	N	L	E	S	S	Having no veins.
V	E	L	A	R	I	U	M	An awning over an ancient Roman theatre.
V	E	L	A	T	I	O	N	Act of veiling or screening.
V	E	L	L	E	I	T	Y	Desire, Inclination, Will, Fancy, Liking, Volition, Pleasure, Wish.
V	E	L	L	I	N	C	H	An instrument for taking a sample from a cask.
V	E	L	L	O	Z	I	A	A genus of Brazilian plants.
V	E	L	O	C	I	T	Y	Swiftness, Speed, Celerity, Rapidity, Impetus, Haste, Gait, Momentum.
V	E	L	U	T	I	N	A	Genus of marine gastropods.
V	E	L	V	E	R	E	T	A velveteen fabric having printed designs.
V	E	L	V	E	T	E	D	Covered with velvet or something resembling velvet.
V	E	N	A	L	I	T	Y	Willing to be bribed or corrupted.
V	E	N	A	T	I	O	N	Arrangement of veins.
V	E	N	D	A	V	A	L	A gusty southwest winter wind in the Straits of Gibraltar.
V	E	N	D	E	T	T	A	Prolonged fued, Dispute, Quarrel, Conflict, Vengeance.
V	E	N	D	E	U	S	E	Saleswoman.
V	E	N	D	I	B	L	E	Available or suitable for sale.
V	E	N	E	E	R	E	D	Overlaid, Glued together, Given an attractive surface.
V	E	N	E	N	A	T	E	Poisoned, Poisonous.
V	E	N	E	R	A	T	E	Revere, Adore, Reverence, Worship, Honour, Idolize.
V	E	N	E	R	E	A	N	Relating to Venus.
V	E	N	E	R	E	A	L	Same as VENEREAN.
V	E	N	E	S	E	C	T	To open a vein for letting blood.
V	E	N	E	T	I	A	N	Characteristic of Venice.
V	E	N	G	E	F	U	L	Revengeful, Vindictive, Antagonistic, Hostile, Inimical.
V	E	N	I	A	L	L	Y	Trivially, Insignificantly, Harmlessly.
V	E	N	O	G	R	A	M	An X-ray to follow the progress of an opaque substance injected into a vein.

1	2	3	4	5	6	7	8	Definition
V	E	N	O	M	I	N	G	Corrupting, Poisoning.
V	E	N	O	M	O	U	S	Poisonous, Virulent, Baneful, Malignant, Spiteful, Toxic, Malevolent, Evil.
V	E	N	O	S	I	T	Y	State of being venous.
V	E	N	O	U	S	L	Y	Veined.
V	E	N	T	H	O	L	E	An opening that is used or made for a outlet.
V	E	N	T	U	R	E	D	Risked, Chanced, Jeopardized, Hazarded, Gambled, Wagered, Endangered, Challenged.
V	E	N	T	U	R	E	R	Adventurer.
V	E	N	U	S	I	A	N	Relating to the planet Venus.
V	E	R	A	C	I	T	Y	Truthfulness, Correctness, Truth, Accuracy, Honesty, Sincerity, Frankness, Verity.
V	E	R	A	N	D	A	H	Balcony, Piazza, Porch.
V	E	R	A	T	R	U	M	A genus of coarse herbs.
V	E	R	A	T	R	Y	L	The univalent radical of the alcohol corresponding to veratraldehyde.
V	E	R	B	A	L	L	Y	Orally, By word of mouth, Wordily, Literally.
V	E	R	B	A	T	I	M	Direct, Directly, Literally, Accurately, Exactly, Precisely, Literal, Faithful.
V	E	R	B	I	A	G	E	Verbosity, Wordiness, Tautology, Repetition, Floridity, Wording, Phrase, Diction.
V	E	R	B	O	T	E	N	Forbidden, Banned, Prohibited, Outlawed, Taboo, Disapproved, Unauthorized, Unlicensed.
V	E	R	D	A	N	C	Y	Greenness.
V	E	R	D	E	R	E	R	An English officer having control of the forest of the king.
V	E	R	D	I	T	E	R	Green pigment.
V	E	R	G	E	N	C	Y	Tendency, Inclination.
V	E	R	I	F	I	E	D	Confirmed, Substantiated, Corroborated, Validated.
V	E	R	I	F	I	E	R	One that confirms or substantiates.
V	E	R	J	U	I	C	E	Sour juice of crab apples or other unripe fruit, Having an acid dispostion.
V	E	R	M	O	U	T	H	A white wine flavoured with herbs.
V	E	R	N	I	C	L	E	A handkerchief belonging to St. Veronica.
V	E	R	O	N	E	S	E	A resident of Verona.
V	E	R	O	N	I	C	A	A genus of herbs, Speedwell.
V	E	R	S	E	L	E	T	A little verse.
V	E	R	S	I	C	L	E	A short verse said or sung in public worship by a priest.
V	E	R	T	E	B	R	A	A bone in the spinal column.
V	E	R	T	I	C	A	L	Perpendicular, Plumb, Upright, Erect, Steep.
V	E	R	T	I	C	E	S	Plural of vertex, Zeniths, Summits.
V	E	R	T	I	C	I	L	A circle or whorl of similar body parts.
V	E	S	I	C	A	N	T	A drug or substance that produces blisters.
V	E	S	I	C	A	T	E	Blister.
V	E	S	I	C	U	L	A	A small blister, A fluid-filled sac.
V	E	S	P	E	R	A	L	An insect active in the evening, Glow-worm.
V	E	S	P	I	A	R	Y	A nest of social wasps.
V	E	S	T	I	A	R	Y	Vestry, Cloakroom, Robing room.
V	E	S	T	M	E	N	T	Ecclesiastical robes, Ceremonial garb.
V	E	S	T	U	R	A	L	Relating to clothing.
V	E	S	T	U	R	E	R	Sexton, One in charge of religious vestments.
V	E	S	U	V	I	A	N	Resembling the volcano Vesuvius, Furious, A match to light a cigar.
V	E	T	I	V	O	N	E	A bicyclic sesquiterpenoid ketone.
V	E	X	A	T	I	O	N	Irritation, Troubling, Annoyance, Harassment, Provokation, Irking, Tormenting.
V	E	X	I	L	L	U	M	A square flag used by the ancient Roman cavalry, Standard.
V	E	X	I	N	G	L	Y	Annoyingly, Provokiningly.
V	I	A	T	I	C	U	M	A travelling allowance.
V	I	B	R	A	T	E	D	Quivered, Swung, Oscillated, Alternated, Shook, Trembled, Quaked, Shivered.
V	I	B	R	A	T	O	R	A device that causes vibration, often used for massage.
V	I	B	R	I	S	S	A	Whisker, Bristle.
V	I	B	U	R	N	U	M	Large genus of widely distributed shrubs and trees.
V	I	C	A	R	A	G	E	The house supplied for the use of a vicar.
V	I	C	A	R	E	S	S	The nun in rank immediately below the Mother superior.
V	I	C	A	R	I	A	L	Delegated, Deputed.
V	I	C	E	K	I	N	G	Regent, Viceroy.
V	I	C	E	N	A	R	Y	Containing twenty.
V	I	C	H	Y	I	T	E	A French collaborator in World War Two.
V	I	C	I	A	N	I	N	A crystalline glycoside found in the seeds of a vetch.
V	I	C	I	N	A	G	E	Neighbourhood, Vicinity.
V	I	C	I	N	I	S	M	Natural cross-pollination between two species of two varieties of plants.
V	I	C	I	N	I	T	Y	Proximity, Locality, Area, District, Neighbourhood, Order, Extent, Matter.
V	I	C	T	O	R	I	A	A four-wheel carriage.
V	I	C	T	R	E	S	S	A female victor.
V	I	C	T	U	A	L	S	Provisions, Supplies of food.
V	I	E	T	M	I	N	H	Adherent of the Vietnamese communist movement.
V	I	E	W	A	B	L	E	Capable of being seen or inspected.

1	2	3	4	5	6	7	8	
V	I	E	W	L	E	S	S	Invisible, Expressing no views or opinions.
V	I	G	I	L	A	N	T	Watchful, Awake, Alert, Unsleeping, Anxious, Acute, Attentive, Keen.
V	I	G	N	E	R	O	N	Winegrower.
V	I	G	N	E	T	T	E	A running decoration in a book, A picture on a postage stamp, A brief word-sketch.
V	I	G	O	R	O	S	O	Direction in music, energetic in style.
V	I	G	O	R	O	U	S	Energetic, Strenuous, Lusty, Virile, Dynamic, Vital, Zealous, Robust.
V	I	L	E	N	E	S	S	Meanness, Baseness, Sordidness, Squalidness, Ugliness, Coarseness, Foulness.
V	I	L	I	F	I	E	D	Degraded, Maligned, Defamed, Slandered, Abused, Mistreated, Outraged, Dishonoured.
V	I	L	I	F	I	E	R	One that maligns.
V	I	L	I	P	E	N	D	Depreciate, Condemn, Hold as of small importance.
V	I	L	L	A	G	E	R	Inhabitant of a village.
V	I	L	L	A	I	N	Y	Fraud, Depravity, Rascality, Wrongdoing, Wickedness, Viciousness, Atrocity, Evilness.
V	I	L	L	A	T	I	C	Rural, Relating to a village.
V	I	L	L	I	C	U	S	Steward of a farm in medieval times.
V	I	N	A	G	R	O	N	A whip scorpion.
V	I	N	C	H	U	C	A	Genus of blood-sucking bugs.
V	I	N	C	I	B	L	E	Surmountable, Capable of being subdued, Within control.
V	I	N	C	U	L	U	M	Fibres uniting tendons of a bird's foot.
V	I	N	E	G	A	R	Y	Tart, Sour, Crabbed, Astringent, Peppery, Choleric, Cantankerous, Crotchery.
V	I	N	E	L	A	N	D	Land especially good for the cultivation of vines.
V	I	N	E	Y	A	R	D	An area planted with grape vines, An area of physical or mental occupation.
V	I	N	I	F	E	R	A	Relating to a common European grape.
V	I	N	O	S	I	T	Y	Distinctive qualities of a wine.
V	I	N	T	A	G	E	R	One that takes part in a vintage.
V	I	N	Y	L	A	T	E	To introduce a vinyl radical into a compound.
V	I	N	Y	L	E	N	E	A bivalent radical derived from ethylene.
V	I	N	Y	L	I	T	E	Vinyl resin.
V	I	O	L	A	B	L	E	Liable to be violated.
V	I	O	L	A	N	I	N	An anthocyanin that is obtained from the pansy.
V	I	O	L	A	T	E	D	Desecrated, Contravened, Infringed, Trangressed, Offended, Raped, Defiled, Outraged.
V	I	O	L	A	T	O	R	Rapist, Transgressor.
V	I	O	L	E	N	C	E	Passion, Fury, Force, Compulsion, Constraint, Frenzy, Savagery, Onslaught.
V	I	O	L	E	T	T	A	A small viol, An ornament resembling a violet.
V	I	O	L	O	T	T	A	A special viol extending the range.
V	I	P	E	R	I	N	E	Relating to a viper, Venomous.
V	I	P	E	R	I	S	H	Spitefully, Abusive.
V	I	P	E	R	O	U	S	Treacherous, Malignant, Venomous.
V	I	R	E	M	E	N	T	Administrative transfer of budgetary funds.
V	I	R	G	I	L	I	A	Genus of Southern African trees, Yellowwood.
V	I	R	G	I	N	A	L	Pristine, Unsullied, Youthful, Intact, Unspoiled, Untouched, Chaste, Pure.
V	I	R	G	I	N	I	A	Tobacco, Genus of climbing plant.
V	I	R	I	C	I	D	E	An agent that destroys viruses.
V	I	R	I	D	I	A	N	Blue-green colour.
V	I	R	I	D	I	T	Y	Colour of grass, Appearing to be young, fresh and innocent.
V	I	R	I	L	I	S	M	Appearance of secondary masculine characteristics in a male or female.
V	I	R	I	L	I	T	Y	Manhood, Energy, Decisiveness, Forcefulness, Potency, Masculinity, Manly vigour.
V	I	R	O	L	O	G	Y	Branch of science dealing with viruses.
V	I	R	T	U	O	S	E	Relating to an expert in an artistic field.
V	I	R	T	U	O	S	O	One skilled in the fine arts.
V	I	R	T	U	O	U	S	Chaste, Pure, Moral, Effective, Ethical, Noble, Principled, Righteous.
V	I	R	U	C	I	D	E	An agent that kills viruses.
V	I	R	U	L	E	N	T	Deadly, Noxious, Malignant, Toxic, Venomous, Bitter, Antagonistic, Hostile.
V	I	S	C	A	C	H	A	S. American burrowing rodent related to the chinchilla.
V	I	S	C	E	R	A	L	Physical, Bodily, Inner, Internal, Instinctive, Intuitive, Intimate, Raw.
V	I	S	C	O	U	N	T	A peer of Great Britain ranking below an earl but above a baron.
V	I	S	I	G	O	T	H	Fourth century barbarians.
V	I	S	I	O	N	A	L	Unreal, Imaginary, Visual, Ocular, Optic, Optical, Visionary.
V	I	S	I	T	A	N	T	Pilgrim, Tourist, Visitor, Guest, Migrant, Caller.
V	I	S	I	T	I	N	G	Inspecting, Searching, Calling, Haunting, Afflicting, Punishing, Chatting, Frequenting.
V	I	T	A	L	I	S	M	A doctrine that maintains that functions of a living organism are due to a vital principle.
V	I	T	A	L	I	S	T	A believer in vitalism.
V	I	T	A	L	I	T	Y	Vigour, Animation, Liveliness, Pulse, Endurance, Energy, Spirit, Drive.
V	I	T	A	L	I	S	E	Energize, Activate, Provoke, Animate, Actify, Enliven, Invigorate, Stimulate.
V	I	T	E	L	L	I	N	Phosphoprotein constituting the principal protein in egg yolk.
V	I	T	E	L	L	U	S	Egg yolk.
V	I	T	I	A	T	E	D	Impaired, Contaminated, Depraved, Perverted, Debauched, Debased, Injured, Spoilt.
V	I	T	I	A	T	O	R	One that perverts.

1	2	3	4	5	6	7	8	
V	I	T	I	L	I	G	O	A skin complaint with loss of pigment in patches.
V	I	T	R	E	L	L	A	A cell of the eye of an insect.
V	I	T	R	E	O	U	S	Resembling glass.
V	I	T	T	A	R	I	A	Genus of tropical ferns.
V	I	T	U	L	I	N	E	Like a calf or veal.
V	I	V	A	C	I	T	Y	Animation, Liveliness, Sprightliness, Brilliance, Keenly, Gaily, Sprightly, Vibrantly.
V	I	V	A	R	I	U	M	A glassed-in enclosure for animals.
V	I	V	A	V	O	C	E	Vocal, Articulate, Oral, Spoken, Voiced, Orally.
V	I	V	E	R	R	I	D	Family of catlike carnivores, Civets, Genets, Mongooses.
V	I	V	I	D	I	T	Y	Vividness.
V	I	V	I	F	I	E	D	Quickened, Animated, Enlivened, Refreshed, Renewed, Restored, Excited, Galvanized.
V	I	V	I	P	A	R	A	Genus of freshwater snails.
V	I	V	I	P	A	R	Y	Development of vegetative shoots among the reproductive organs of a flower.
V	I	V	I	S	E	C	T	To practice vivisection.
V	I	X	E	N	I	S	H	Ill-tempered, Shrewish, Snappish, Quarrelsome.
V	O	C	A	L	I	S	E	An exercise for singers.
V	O	C	A	L	I	S	M	Singing, Vocal technique, Exercise of vocal organs.
V	O	C	A	L	I	S	T	Singer.
V	O	C	A	L	I	T	Y	Exercise of vocal powers.
V	O	C	A	L	I	Z	E	Utter, Sing, To change a consonant to a vowel.
V	O	C	A	T	I	O	N	Calling, Task, Trade, Craft, Profession, Mission, Lifework, Occupation.
V	O	C	A	T	I	V	E	Voluble, Garrulous, Loquacious, Glib, Talkative, Slick, Chatty, Smooth-talking.
V	O	G	U	E	I	S	H	Fashionable, Smart.
V	O	I	D	A	B	L	E	Capable of being invalidated, Can be annulled.
V	O	I	D	A	N	C	E	Voiding, Emptying, Ejecting, Evacuating, Annulling.
V	O	I	D	N	E	S	S	Nullity, Vacuity, Vacancy, Blankness, Emptiness.
V	O	L	A	D	O	R	A	Small S. American characin fishes.
V	O	L	A	T	I	L	E	Lively, Airy, Elastic, Fickle, Changeable, Transitory, Explosive, Evanescent.
V	O	L	C	A	N	I	C	Relating to a volcano, Eruptive, Violent, Volatile, Emotional.
V	O	L	I	T	A	N	T	Able to fly, Flying, Moving about.
V	O	L	I	T	I	O	N	Choosing, Deciding, Will, Choice, Option, Selection, Desire, Preference.
V	O	L	I	T	I	V	E	Expressing a wish.
V	O	L	L	E	Y	E	D	Discharged, Kicked, Uttered rapidly, Stormed.
V	O	L	P	L	A	N	E	Glide, Sail or coast through the air.
V	O	L	T	A	I	S	M	Galvanism, Direct electrical current.
V	O	L	T	Z	I	T	E	A mineral consisting of a zinc oxysulfide.
V	O	L	U	T	I	O	N	Twist, Convolution, Rolling, Revolving.
V	O	L	V	A	R	I	A	Genus of agarics.
V	O	L	V	U	L	U	S	Twisting of the intestine which causes an obstruction.
V	O	M	B	A	T	I	D	Australian marsupial resembling a small bear.
V	O	M	B	A	T	U	S	Same as VOMBATID.
V	O	M	E	R	I	N	E	Pertaining to a bone in the skull.
V	O	M	I	C	I	N	E	A crystalline alkaloid occurring with brucine and strychnine.
V	O	M	I	T	I	N	G	Retching, Gushing, Ejecting, Spewing, Heaving, Disgorging, Expelling, Cascading.
V	O	M	I	T	I	O	N	Vomiting.
V	O	M	I	T	I	V	E	Causing vomiting, Emetic.
V	O	M	I	T	O	R	Y	Entrance through seats in a theatre, Portal.
V	O	R	A	C	I	T	Y	Rapacity, Greed, Avidness, Gluttony.
V	O	R	T	E	X	E	S	Whirlpools, Whirlwinds, Maelstroms, Tornadoes, Eddies, Spirals.
V	O	R	T	I	C	A	L	Resembling a whirlpool.
V	O	R	T	I	C	E	S	Vortexes.
V	O	T	A	R	E	S	S	A female pledged by solemn vows to a religious life.
V	O	T	A	R	I	S	T	Votary.
V	O	U	C	H	I	N	G	Proving, Substantiating, Warranting, Attesting, Declaring, Certifing, Upholding, Confirming.
V	O	U	S	S	O	I	R	Wedges forming an arch.
V	O	W	E	L	I	S	E	To cause by means of vowels, Make vocalic.
V	O	W	E	L	L	E	D	Furnished with vowels.
V	O	Y	A	G	E	U	R	A man employed by a fur company in Northwest territories.
V	U	L	C	A	N	I	C	Relating to working with iron. Volcanic.
V	U	L	G	A	R	L	Y	Coarsely, Crudely, Boorishly, Roughly, Obscenely, Smuttily, Basely, Rudely.
V	U	L	S	E	L	L	A	Tweezers, Surgical forceps.

1	2	3	4	5	6	7	8	
W	A	B	B	L	I	N	G	Wobbling.
W	A	D	D	L	I	N	G	Moving clumsily, Awkward walking, Swaying gait.

1	2	3	4	5	6	7	8	
W	A	E	S	U	C	K	S	Used to express grief or pity.
W	A	F	E	R	I	N	G	Sealing with a wafer.
W	A	F	F	L	I	N	G	Blathing, Babbling, Gabbling, Prattling, Twaddling, Prating.
W	A	G	E	L	E	S	S	Unpaid.
W	A	G	E	R	I	N	G	Betting, Staking, Chancing, Venturing, Gambling.
W	A	G	G	L	I	N	G	Switching, Waving, Moving, Beating, Lashing, Swaying, Waddling, Wobbling.
W	A	G	G	O	N	E	R	Driver of a wagon.
W	A	G	O	N	A	G	E	Payment for conveyance by wagon.
W	A	G	O	N	F	U	L	Wagonload.
W	A	G	O	N	I	N	G	Transporting by wagon.
W	A	G	O	N	L	I	T	Railroad sleeping car.
W	A	I	N	S	C	O	T	Timber panelling of lower portion of wall.
W	A	I	T	A	B	I	T	Bramble plant with hooked thorns.
W	A	I	T	R	E	S	S	A girl or woman who waits at table.
W	A	K	E	N	I	N	G	Awakening, Rousing, Stimulating.
W	A	K	E	R	I	F	E	Watchful, Alert.
W	A	L	D	H	O	R	N	Natural horn.
W	A	L	H	A	L	L	A	Valhalla.
W	A	L	K	A	B	L	E	Capable of being traversed on foot.
W	A	L	K	M	I	L	L	Fulling mill.
W	A	L	K	O	V	E	R	Something easily accomplished.
W	A	L	L	A	R	O	O	Large kangaroo.
W	A	L	L	E	Y	E	D	Having an eye showing an abnormal amount of white, Cross-eyed.
W	A	L	L	K	N	O	T	Interweaving rope for a double knot.
W	A	L	L	O	P	E	D	Beat, Lambasted, Pounded, Slugged, Socked, Trounced, Belaboured, Belted.
W	A	L	L	O	W	E	D	Floundered, Grovelled, Sprawled, Rolled, Tumbled, Cuddled, Lurched, Stumbled.
W	A	L	L	O	W	E	R	One that flounders.
W	A	L	L	T	R	E	E	A tree trained to grow against a wall.
W	A	L	L	W	O	R	T	A plant that grows on a wall.
W	A	L	T	Z	I	N	G	Dancing, Meandering, Flouncing, Breezing, Advancing easily, Marching, Carrying.
W	A	M	B	L	I	N	G	Feeling nausea, Spinning, Revolving, Weaving, Tottering, Reeling, Weak, Ineffective.
W	A	N	D	E	R	E	D	Strayed, Circulated, Erred, Roamed, Straggled, Rambled, Ranged, Strolled.
W	A	N	D	E	R	E	R	Rover, Drifter, Rambler, Roamer.
W	A	N	D	E	R	O	O	Langur monkey.
W	A	N	G	L	I	N	G	Shaking, Wiggling, Faking, Engineering, Manoeuvring, Outflanking, Finagling.
W	A	N	T	L	E	S	S	Without desire.
W	A	N	T	O	N	E	D	Dallied, Luxuriated, Trifled, Flirted, Fooled.
W	A	N	T	O	N	L	Y	Inhumanely, Extravagantly, Capriciously.
W	A	R	B	L	I	N	G	Trilling, Babbling, Quavering.
W	A	R	D	A	N	C	E	A vigorous tribal dance in preparation for an attack.
W	A	R	D	E	N	C	Y	The powers of a warden.
W	A	R	D	M	O	T	E	Assembly of the citizens of a ward.
W	A	R	D	R	O	B	E	A cupboard for storing clothes.
W	A	R	D	R	O	O	M	Living quarters for commissioned officers aboard a warship.
W	A	R	D	S	H	I	P	Guardianship.
W	A	R	D	W	I	T	E	A feudal fine.
W	A	R	E	R	O	O	M	Store, Shop.
W	A	R	F	A	R	I	N	A crystalline compound used in medicine as an anticoagulant.
W	A	R	H	O	R	S	E	Charger, A powerful horse used in military service, A retired military officer of high rank.
W	A	R	I	N	E	S	S	Watchfulness, Caution.
W	A	R	M	N	E	S	S	Warmth, Cosiness.
W	A	R	P	A	I	N	T	Pigment put on before going to war, Regalia, Finery, Make-up.
W	A	R	P	L	A	N	E	A military aeroplane.
W	A	R	R	A	G	A	L	A wild horse, Dingo.
W	A	R	R	A	N	T	Y	Guarantee, Bail, Bond, Security, Surety.
W	A	R	R	E	N	E	R	Gamekeeper, Australian shells.
W	A	R	T	L	E	S	S	Free from warts.
W	A	R	T	W	E	E	D	A plant believed to cure warts.
W	A	R	T	W	O	R	T	Lichen.
W	A	R	W	E	A	R	Y	Tired or depressed by war.
W	A	R	W	H	O	O	P	A war cry of the American Indians.
W	A	S	H	A	B	L	E	Fabric that can be washed without damage.
W	A	S	H	A	W	A	Y	Washout.
W	A	S	H	B	A	L	L	A ball of toilet soap.
W	A	S	H	B	O	W	L	Washbasin, A large bowl used for washing hands and face.
W	A	S	H	D	I	R	T	Earth washed in panning gold.
W	A	S	H	R	O	O	M	Lavatory, A room for washing hands and face.

1	2	3	4	5	6	7	8	
W	A	S	T	E	F	U	L	Destructive, Lavish, Prodigal, Squandered.
W	A	T	C	H	B	O	X	Sentry box.
W	A	T	C	H	D	O	G	Custodian, Guardian, Keeper, Warden.
W	A	T	C	H	F	U	L	Vigilant, Wide-awake, Alert, Cautious, Wary, Prompt. Ready.
W	A	T	C	H	I	N	G	Guarding, Vigil, Observing, Waiting, Overseeing, Seeing, Policing, Tending.
W	A	T	C	H	K	E	Y	A special key that was used to wind watches.
W	A	T	C	H	M	A	N	Guard, Sentinel, Lookout, Sentry, Picket, Ward, Watch, Custodian.
W	A	T	E	R	A	G	E	Fee paid for transporting goods by water.
W	A	T	E	R	B	E	D	A bed filled with water.
W	A	T	E	R	B	U	G	Aquatic insects or bugs.
W	A	T	E	R	D	O	G	A hunting dog used for retrieving waterfowl.
W	A	T	E	R	F	L	Y	A fly that is found over water, Dragonfly.
W	A	T	E	R	G	A	S	A poisonous flammable gaseous mixture of carbon monoxide and hydrogen.
W	A	T	E	R	H	E	N	Aquatic birds, Coot, Gallinule.
W	A	T	E	R	I	C	E	A frozen dessert of water, sugar and flavouring, Sherbet, Sorbet.
W	A	T	E	R	I	N	G	Irrigating, Supplying water for cultivation, Soaking, Drenching.
W	A	T	E	R	I	S	H	Resembling water, Pale, Dilute, Thin, Sloppy, Flat, Flavourless, Insipid.
W	A	T	E	R	L	O	G	Saturate, Soak, Drench, Impregnate, Sodden, Souse, Steep.
W	A	T	E	R	M	A	N	Boatman, Oarsman.
W	A	T	E	R	P	O	T	A vessel for holding or conveying water.
W	A	T	E	R	R	A	T	An amphibious rodent, Muskrat, Beaver rat. Waterfront loafer.
W	A	T	E	R	R	U	G	A shaggy or rough-coated water dog.
W	A	T	E	R	T	A	P	A spigot for controlling the flow of water.
W	A	T	E	R	W	A	Y	A navigable passage or area of water.
W	A	T	T	H	O	U	R	Unit of work and energy.
W	A	T	T	L	I	N	G	Plaiting, Hurdling, Uniting, Interweaving.
W	A	V	E	B	A	N	D	Range of radio-wave frequencies, Channel.
W	A	V	E	F	O	R	M	A graph of a wave producing medium.
W	A	V	E	L	E	S	S	Calm, Smooth, Unruffled.
W	A	V	E	L	I	K	E	Resembling a wave.
W	A	V	E	M	A	R	K	Wavemark, Small ridge of sand left by receding wave.
W	A	V	E	R	I	N	G	Vacillating, Varying, Reeling, Tottering, Fluttering, Quivering, Shaking, Hesitating.
W	A	V	E	T	R	A	P	A device to eliminate interference in a radio-receiver.
W	A	V	E	W	O	R	N	Attrition due to wave movement.
W	A	V	I	N	E	S	S	State of being wavy.
W	A	X	C	L	O	T	H	A fabric waterproofed with wax or paraffin.
W	A	X	L	I	G	H	T	Wax candle, Taper.
W	A	X	P	A	P	E	R	Waxed paper.
W	A	X	P	L	A	N	T	A cultivated twining plant, Begonia with shiny leaves.
W	A	X	W	O	R	K	S	A display of wax effigies of well-known people.
W	A	Y	B	R	E	A	D	Genus of plants that grow by the roadside.
W	A	Y	F	A	R	E	R	Traveller, Tourist, Tripper, Pilgrim.
W	A	Y	G	O	I	N	G	Departure.
W	A	Y	G	O	O	S	E	An annual outing for printers.
W	A	Y	L	E	A	V	E	Servitude, Right-of-way.
W	A	Y	M	A	K	E	R	One that makes a road.
W	A	Y	S	H	A	F	T	Rockshaft.
W	A	Y	T	H	O	R	N	A common buckthorn.
W	A	Y	T	R	A	I	N	A train that stops at all wayside stations.
W	A	Y	W	I	S	E	R	A device to measure distance travelled.
W	E	A	K	E	N	E	D	Enfeebled, Debilitated, Undermined, Sapped, Crippled, Disabled, Minimized, Reduced.
W	E	A	K	E	N	E	R	One that weakens.
W	E	A	K	L	I	N	G	Doormat, Baby, Milksop, Namby-pamby, Sop, Pushover, Sucker, Misfit.
W	E	A	K	N	E	S	S	Lacking vigour, Fault, Defect, Feebleness, Fragility, Puniness, Unstability.
W	E	A	N	L	I	N	G	A child or animal that is recently weaned.
W	E	A	P	O	N	E	D	Armed, Equipped with weapons.
W	E	A	R	A	B	L	E	Suitable to be worn.
W	E	A	R	I	F	U	L	Tedious, Vexatious, Wearied, Arid, Dusty, Insipid.
W	E	A	R	Y	I	N	G	Something that wearies.
W	E	D	G	W	O	O	D	A fine hardware like procelain.
W	E	E	D	H	O	O	K	A curved hook to clear weeds.
W	E	E	D	L	E	S	S	Free from weeds.
W	E	E	T	W	E	E	T	European sandpiper.
W	E	E	V	I	L	E	D	Infested with weevils.
W	E	F	T	W	I	S	E	Crosswise, Running across the warp.
W	E	H	R	L	I	T	E	A bismuth and tellurium alloy mineral.
W	E	I	G	H	A	G	E	A fee for weighing merchandise.

1	2	3	4	5	6	7	8	
W	E	I	G	H	I	N	G	Balancing, Esteeming, Regarding, Considering, Studying, Encumbering, Contemplating.
W	E	I	G	H	O	U	T	Weighing jockeys and equipment before a horse race.
W	E	I	G	H	T	E	D	Loaded, Given due weight.
W	E	I	S	S	I	T	E	A mineral consisting of a massive bluish black copper telluride.
W	E	L	C	O	M	E	D	Greeted, Hailed, Saluted.
W	E	L	C	O	M	E	R	One that welcomes.
W	E	L	D	A	B	L	E	Capable of being welded.
W	E	L	D	M	E	N	T	A unit formed by welding together an assortment of pieces.
W	E	L	L	A	D	A	Y	An expression of lament.
W	E	L	L	A	W	A	Y	Same as WELLADAY.
W	E	L	L	B	O	A	T	A boat with a well in which fish are stored.
W	E	L	L	B	O	R	N	Born into a family of high social standing.
W	E	L	L	B	R	E	D	Cultivated, Refined, Cultured, Well-behaved, Having a good pedigree, Genteel.
W	E	L	L	D	E	C	K	A space on the weather deck of a ship.
W	E	L	L	H	E	A	D	The plant of the source of a spring, Fountainhead, Principal source.
W	E	L	L	H	O	L	E	The shaft of a lift, The centre of a stairway.
W	E	L	L	K	N	I	T	Firmly and strongly constructed, Compacted.
W	E	L	L	N	I	G	H	Almost.
W	E	L	L	R	E	A	D	Characterized by extensive reading, Well-informed.
W	E	L	L	T	O	D	O	Prosperous, Comfortable, Substantial, Financially stable, Affluent.
W	E	L	L	W	O	R	N	Trite, Commonplace, Stale, Threadbare, Stereotyped, Tired, Worn-out.
W	E	L	S	H	I	N	G	To cheat by avoiding payment or obligation.
W	E	L	S	H	M	A	N	Inhabitant of Wales.
W	E	L	T	E	R	E	D	Writhed, Tossed, Tumbled, Reeled, Staggered, Wallowed, Tossed, Involved.
W	E	R	E	G	I	L	D	Ancient law of compensation paid for a life.
W	E	R	E	W	O	L	F	A person transformed temporarily into a wolf and then acts in a savage fashion.
W	E	S	L	E	Y	A	N	Relating to the Methodist Wesley Brothers.
W	E	S	T	E	R	L	Y	Toward the west.
W	E	S	T	W	A	R	D	In a westward direction.
W	E	T	N	U	R	S	E	A woman who suckles an infant not born to her, Excessive care, To coddle.
W	H	A	C	K	I	N	G	Striking, Catching, Slogging, Socking, Beating, Smacking, Hitting, Defeating.
W	H	A	L	E	M	A	N	A man employed on a whaling ship.
W	H	A	L	E	O	I	L	A versatile oil obtained from the blubber of a whale.
W	H	A	N	G	H	E	E	Chinese bamboo.
W	H	A	N	G	I	N	G	Flogging, Beating, Thrashing, Striking, Propelling, Attacking.
W	H	A	R	F	A	G	E	Charge for the use of a wharf.
W	H	A	R	F	I	N	G	Docking.
W	H	A	T	E	V	E	R	Anything, Everything, No matter what, Anything at all.
W	H	E	A	T	E	A	R	A small bird related to the stonechat.
W	H	E	A	T	E	E	L	Wheatworm.
W	H	E	A	T	F	L	Y	A fly whose larvae lives in wheat stems.
W	H	E	E	D	L	E	D	Coaxed, Cajoled, Persuaded, Conned, Allured, Deluded, Inveigled, Influenced.
W	H	E	E	L	A	G	E	A toll on wheeled vehicles.
W	H	E	E	L	I	N	G	Revolving, Swaying, Reeling, Circling, Rotating, Pivoting, Turning, Curving.
W	H	E	E	L	M	A	N	Helmsman, Vehicle driver.
W	H	E	E	L	O	R	E	The mineral bournonite.
W	H	E	E	Z	I	L	Y	Asthmatically, Gaspingly.
W	H	E	E	Z	I	N	G	Tattling, Whistling, Sibilant breathing.
W	H	E	L	M	I	N	G	Burying, Submerging, Covering, Overpowering, Overwhelming, Engulfing, Flooding.
W	H	E	L	P	I	N	G	Giving birth to young.
W	H	E	N	E	V	E	R	In every instance, At any time, No matter when.
W	H	E	R	E	O	U	T	Whence.
W	H	E	R	E	V	E	R	In any circumstances.
W	H	E	T	T	I	N	G	Sharpening, Honing, Goading, Inciting, Arousing, Exciting, Stimulating, Kindling.
W	H	E	Y	F	A	C	E	Weakling, Sickly-looking, Pale.
W	H	I	F	F	I	N	G	Puffing, Fanning, Blowing, Exhaling, Expelling, Whistling, Sniffing, Gusting.
W	H	I	F	F	L	E	R	One that changes his opinion often.
W	H	I	G	G	E	R	Y	Policies associated with the eighteenth century political party, Whigs.
W	H	I	G	G	I	S	H	Inclined toward whiggery.
W	H	I	G	G	I	S	M	Whiggery.
W	H	I	M	B	R	E	L	European curlew.
W	H	I	M	S	I	E	D	Whimsical, Arbitary, Capricious, Erratic, Freakish, Wayward.
W	H	I	M	W	H	A	M	Trifle, Trinket, Notion, Fancy, Whimsical object.
W	H	I	N	C	H	A	T	A small European saxicoline bird.
W	H	I	N	N	I	E	D	Neighed, Whickered, Nickered.
W	H	I	N	N	O	C	K	Whimper.
W	H	I	N	Y	A	R	D	A short sword.

1	2	3	4	5	6	7	8	
W	H	I	P	C	O	R	D	A twilled fabric with a diagonal rib, Marine brown algae, Seaweed.
W	H	I	P	H	A	N	D	Advantage, Superiority, Upper hand, Control, Mastery.
W	H	I	P	L	A	S	H	Neck injury due to violent oscillation of the head, Lash of a whip.
W	H	I	P	P	I	N	G	Snatching, Jerking, Flogging, Sparking, Driving, Forcing, Urging, Abusing.
W	H	I	P	T	A	I	L	Whip scorpion, A lizard.
W	H	I	R	L	B	A	T	A woman's belt, A leather band worn on the hand by boxers in ancient Rome.
W	H	I	R	L	I	N	G	Circling, Spinning, Revolving, Rotating, Speeding, Rushing, Reeling, Impelling.
W	H	I	R	R	I	N	G	Flying, Revolving, Moving rapidly.
W	H	I	S	K	E	R	S	Hair growth on the face, Moustache, Bristles on an animal's face.
W	H	I	S	K	I	N	G	Zipping, Flicking, Whipping, Frisking, Speeding, Brushing, Swishing, Hurrying.
W	H	I	S	T	L	E	D	Uttered a shrill note through puckered lips, Piped.
W	H	I	S	T	L	E	R	One that whistles, A player of a pipe or flute, Australian bird related to the shrike.
W	H	I	T	E	A	N	T	Wood-boring termite.
W	H	I	T	E	B	O	Y	A favoured person, Pet, Member of an eighteenth century militant Irish group.
W	H	I	T	E	H	O	T	Being extremely hot, Ardently fervid.
W	H	I	T	E	N	E	D	Made white, Bleached, To give an innocent appearance, Palliated, Blanched.
W	H	I	T	E	N	E	R	A bleach.
W	H	I	T	E	O	U	T	A surface weather condition in the polar regions where there is no variation of light and shade.
W	H	I	T	L	I	N	G	A large sea trout.
W	H	I	T	S	T	E	R	A bleacher of linen.
W	H	I	T	T	L	E	D	Pare, Shaped, Cut, Shaved, Chipped.
W	H	I	T	T	R	E	T	Weasel.
W	H	I	Z	Z	I	N	G	Moving swiftly with a hissing sound, Projecting.
W	H	O	D	U	N	I	T	A mystery thriller as a book, play or film.
W	H	O	M	E	V	E	R	Whoever.
W	H	O	O	P	I	N	G	Shouting, Hallooing, Hooting, Roaring, Booming, Exciting, Boosting, Carousing.
W	H	O	P	P	I	N	G	Extraordinary, Extravagant, Outrageous, Beating, Striking, Extremely, Immensely.
W	H	U	R	R	I	N	G	Making a throaty sound, Purring, Snarling, Roaring.
W	I	C	K	E	D	L	Y	Viciously, Maliciously, Poisonously, Dangerously, Terribly, Outrageously, Atrociously.
W	I	C	K	E	R	E	D	Covered with wickerwork.
W	I	D	E	E	Y	E	D	Amazed, Naive, Staring, Struck with wonder, Gullible, Astonished.
W	I	D	E	N	E	S	S	Breadth, Width.
W	I	D	E	N	I	N	G	Expanding, Increasing in width, Broadening.
W	I	D	O	W	I	N	G	Causing to become a widow, Bereaving a spouse, Depriving.
W	I	E	L	D	I	N	G	Managing, Handling, Manupulating, Controlling, Governing, Running, Dispensing.
W	I	F	E	H	O	O	D	The state of being a wife.
W	I	F	E	L	E	S	S	Having no wife.
W	I	F	E	L	I	K	E	Wifely.
W	I	G	B	L	O	C	K	A round block for storing and dressing wigs.
W	I	G	G	L	I	N	G	Jiggling, Oscillating, Jerking, Wriggling, Worming, Twisting, Turning, Writhing.
W	I	G	M	A	K	E	R	One that makes and dresses wigs.
W	I	L	D	B	O	A	R	A wild hog.
W	I	L	D	B	O	R	E	A woollen dress fabric.
W	I	L	D	D	U	C	K	An undomesticated duck, Mallard.
W	I	L	D	E	R	E	D	Bewildered, Perplexed, Wandered, Strayed.
W	I	L	D	F	I	R	E	A destructive fire, Something that spreads quickly through a crowd of people as rumour.
W	I	L	D	F	O	W	L	Gamebird.
W	I	L	D	L	A	N	D	Uncultivated land, Wasteland, Desert.
W	I	L	D	N	E	S	S	Wilderness, Not being tame.
W	I	L	D	W	O	O	D	A wood unfrequented by man.
W	I	L	F	U	L	L	Y	Obstinately, Perversely, Stubbornly, Unruly, Deliberately.
W	I	L	I	N	E	S	S	Craftiness, Artfulness, Subtlely.
W	I	L	L	O	W	E	D	Opened and cleaned.
W	I	M	B	L	I	N	G	Twisting, Boring, Penetrating, Piercing.
W	I	M	P	L	I	N	G	Veiling, Wrapping, Meandering, Twisting, Winding, Rippling.
W	I	N	C	H	M	A	N	A worker who operates a winch.
W	I	N	D	B	A	N	D	A band composed of wind instruments, A military band.
W	I	N	D	B	E	L	L	A cluster of small pieces of glass or metal that tinkle as they blow in the wind.
W	I	N	D	B	I	L	L	Bill for accommodation.
W	I	N	D	F	A	L	L	Something blown down by the wind. An unexpected gain.
W	I	N	D	G	A	L	L	A soft tumour on a horse's leg.
W	I	N	D	L	A	S	S	A turning device for hauling and hoisting.
W	I	N	D	L	E	S	S	Absence of wind.
W	I	N	D	M	I	L	L	A mill operated by vanes turned by the action of the wind.
W	I	N	D	O	W	E	D	Provided with windows.
W	I	N	D	P	I	P	E	The air passage from the larynx to the lungs, Tracheas.
W	I	N	D	P	U	M	P	A pump operated by a windmill.

1	2	3	4	5	6	7	8	
W	I	N	D	R	O	O	T	Butterfly weed.
W	I	N	D	R	O	S	E	A European poppy, Prickly poppy, Corn poppy.
W	I	N	D	S	A	I	L	Funnel of canvas used to ventilate part of a ship.
W	I	N	D	W	A	R	D	Sailing against the wind, Weatherly, The direction from which the wind is blowing.
W	I	N	E	L	E	E	S	Dregs of wine.
W	I	N	E	S	K	I	N	A bag made from an animal skin to hold wine.
W	I	N	G	C	A	S	E	Elytron, A thick scale to protect the wings of an insect, Marine bivalve.
W	I	N	G	L	E	S	S	Having no wings, Slow moving, Pedestrian.
W	I	N	G	S	H	O	T	A shot at a flying target.
W	I	N	N	O	W	E	D	Separated, Deleted, Selected, Sifted, Fanned, Sorted, Combed, Removed.
W	I	N	N	O	W	E	R	A machine for winnowing grain.
W	I	N	T	E	R	E	D	Fed in the winter, Managed to survive in winter, Changed living quarters in winter.
W	I	N	T	E	R	L	Y	Wintry, Cheerless.
W	I	R	E	D	R	A	W	Elongate, Distort, Wrench, Attenuate, Draw, Stretch.
W	I	R	E	L	E	S	S	Having no wires, Relating to radio.
W	I	R	E	M	A	R	K	Resembling a watermark on paper.
W	I	R	E	R	O	P	E	A rope formed of wires, Cable.
W	I	R	E	S	I	D	E	The side of the paper in contact with the mould during manufacture.
W	I	R	E	W	O	O	L	Pad of fine wool for scouring pots and pans.
W	I	R	E	W	O	R	M	A worm with a hard coat, A garden pest, Millipede.
W	I	R	I	N	E	S	S	Toughness, Fibrous, Sinewy.
W	I	S	E	A	C	R	E	Smart aleck, Know-it-all.
W	I	S	E	L	I	N	G	Wiseacre, Simpleton.
W	I	S	H	B	O	N	E	A forked bone from the breast of a fowl and once believed to be lucky.
W	I	S	H	W	A	S	H	Insipid talk, Weak drink, Claptrap, Twaddle, Nonsense.
W	I	S	T	A	R	I	A	Genus of woody vines grown for showy drooping flowers.
W	I	T	C	H	E	L	M	Wych elm, Witch Hazel, A tree where the bark yields an alcohol solution used cosmetically.
W	I	T	C	H	I	N	G	Bewitching, Fascinating, Magic, Conjuring, Sorcery, Enchantment, Necromancy.
W	I	T	H	D	R	A	W	Remove, Disengage, Abjure, Recant, Retract, Depart, Retire, Quit.
W	I	T	H	D	R	E	W	Retreaded, Departed, Retired, Quailed, Recoiled, Receded, Shrunk, Recalled.
W	I	T	H	E	R	E	D	Decayed, Declined, Faded, Paralyzed, Stunned, Wrinkled, Crumbled, Wasted.
W	I	T	H	E	R	O	D	N. American viburnum resembling osier.
W	I	T	H	H	E	L	D	Held, Reserved, Curbed, Bridled, Denied, Refused, Abstained, Detained.
W	I	T	H	H	O	L	D	Check, Restrain, Keep, Forbear, Detain, Refrain, Inhibit, Constrain.
W	I	T	H	W	I	N	D	Bindweed.
W	I	Z	A	R	D	L	Y	Weird, Relating to a wizard.
W	I	Z	A	R	D	R	Y	Sorcery, Witchcraft, Magic.
W	I	Z	E	N	I	N	G	Withering, Shrivelling, Mummifying, Decreasing, Dwindling, Wrinkling.
W	O	E	F	U	L	L	Y	Mournfully, Deplorabley, Wretchedly.
W	O	L	F	F	I	S	H	Large marine fish noted for its ferocity.
W	O	L	F	L	I	K	E	Having the savage characteristics of the wolf.
W	O	L	F	S	K	I	N	The skin of a wolf.
W	O	M	A	N	I	S	H	Female, Feminine, Resembling a woman.
W	O	M	M	E	R	A	H	An aboriginal throwing stick.
W	O	N	D	E	R	E	D	Marvelled, Speculated, Awed, Surprised, Curious, Pondered, Puzzled, Cogitated.
W	O	N	D	E	R	E	R	One that wonders.
W	O	N	D	R	O	U	S	Wonderful, Astonishing, Marvellous, Amazing, Strange, Miraculous, Spectacular.
W	O	N	T	L	E	S	S	Unaccustomed.
W	O	O	D	B	I	N	D	European twining shrub, Honeysuckle.
W	O	O	D	B	I	N	E	Same as WOODBIND.
W	O	O	D	C	H	A	T	Family of Asiatic birds.
W	O	O	D	C	O	A	L	Charcoal.
W	O	O	D	C	O	C	K	Genus of Old World bird, Woodpecker.
W	O	O	D	D	O	V	E	Wood pigeon.
W	O	O	D	I	B	I	S	A large wading bird.
W	O	O	D	K	E	R	N	An Irish robber or brigand living in a forest.
W	O	O	D	L	A	N	D	Covered with trees, Forest.
W	O	O	D	L	A	R	K	A small European lark.
W	O	O	D	L	E	S	S	Treeless.
W	O	O	D	L	I	C	E	Termite, Garden pest.
W	O	O	D	L	I	L	Y	Lily of the valley.
W	O	O	D	L	O	C	K	A piece of wood fitted to keep a rudder from rising.
W	O	O	D	M	I	T	E	Mites that live under stones or in moss in shady areas.
W	O	O	D	M	O	T	E	A forest court.
W	O	O	D	N	O	T	E	A sound or call natural in a wood.
W	O	O	D	O	P	A	L	Wood petrified with opal.
W	O	O	D	P	U	L	P	Wood that is pulped and manufactured into cellulose.

1	2	3	4	5	6	7	8	
W	O	O	D	R	E	E	D	Genus of tall perennial grasses.
W	O	O	D	R	U	F	F	Genus of Old World herbs.
W	O	O	D	S	E	R	E	Cuckoo spit.
W	O	O	D	S	H	E	D	A shed for storing firewood.
W	O	O	D	S	I	D	E	Country bordering on a wood.
W	O	O	D	S	K	I	N	Bark from which canoes are made.
W	O	O	D	S	M	A	N	One who lives and works in a forest.
W	O	O	D	T	I	C	K	A tick that fastens on an animal and causes troublesome sores.
W	O	O	D	W	A	L	E	Golden oriole, Green woodpecker.
W	O	O	D	W	A	L	L	Same as WOODWALE.
W	O	O	D	W	A	R	D	An English forest officer who guards a forest.
W	O	O	D	W	O	R	K	Work in carpentry or joinery.
W	O	O	D	W	O	R	M	Worm that is the larva of a wood borer.
W	O	O	D	W	R	E	N	Wood warbler.
W	O	O	I	N	G	L	Y	Attractively, Alluringly.
W	O	O	L	B	A	L	L	A hairball of a sheep.
W	O	O	L	D	I	N	G	Twisting a rope or chain to strengthen something.
W	O	O	L	D	Y	E	D	Dyed in the wool.
W	O	O	L	F	E	L	L	Sheepskin from which the wool has not been removed.
W	O	O	L	P	A	C	K	A canvas wrapper used to pack fleeces for shipment.
W	O	O	L	S	A	C	K	A sack for wool, The office of a judge.
W	O	O	L	S	K	I	N	Sheepskin with the wool on it.
W	O	O	L	W	A	R	D	Wearing wool next to the skin.
W	O	O	L	W	O	R	K	Needlework made with wool.
W	O	R	D	B	O	O	K	Vocabulary, Dictionary, Lexicon.
W	O	R	D	L	E	S	S	Silent, Speechless, Tacit, Implied, Undeclared, Mute, Unsaid, Unspoken.
W	O	R	D	L	O	R	E	Study or information about words.
W	O	R	D	P	L	A	Y	Verbal wit based on different meanings expressed by one word.
W	O	R	D	S	I	G	N	Symbol representing a word or words, Logogram.
W	O	R	K	A	B	L	E	Capable of being worked.
W	O	R	K	B	O	O	K	A manual setting out methods of work, A time-record of work performed.
W	O	R	K	F	O	L	K	Farm workers.
W	O	R	K	G	I	R	L	A girl employed in manual labour in industry.
W	O	R	K	H	E	A	D	The head of a lath that holds the work.
W	O	R	K	R	O	O	M	A room used for manual work.
W	O	R	K	S	H	O	P	A small manufacturing industry.
W	O	R	M	C	A	S	T	Minute heap of earth passed through an earthworm.
W	O	R	M	G	E	A	R	Gear wheels working together.
W	O	R	M	H	O	L	E	A minute hole made by a pest.
W	O	R	M	L	I	K	E	Resembling a worm.
W	O	R	M	S	E	E	D	Any plant whose seeds possess anthelmintic properties.
W	O	R	M	W	E	E	D	Pinkroot.
W	O	R	M	W	O	O	D	European woody herb, Something bitter or grievous, Bitterness.
W	O	R	R	I	C	O	W	Devil, Hobgoblin, Bugaboo.
W	O	R	R	Y	I	N	G	Harassing, Tormenting, Annoying, Nagging, Plaguing, Pestering, Bothering, Teasing.
W	O	R	S	E	N	E	D	Deteriorated, Impaired, Declined, Degenerated, Blighted, Degraded, Tainted, Fouled.
W	O	R	S	T	I	N	G	Defeating, Overthrowing, Besting, Outdoing.
W	O	R	T	H	F	U	L	Honourable, Worthy, Esteemed, Valuable.
W	O	R	T	H	I	L	Y	Honourably, Admirably, Commendably, Nobly.
W	O	U	N	D	I	L	Y	Extremely, Excessively.
W	O	U	N	D	I	N	G	Cutting, Stabbing, Piercing, Lacerating, Tearing, Hurting, Maiming, Injuring.
W	R	A	C	K	F	U	L	Destructive, Injurious.
W	R	A	C	K	I	N	G	Destroying, Decimating, Demolishing, Ruining, Razing, Wrecking.
W	R	A	N	G	L	E	D	Disputed, Quarrelled, Brawled, Altercated, Bickered, Scrapped, Squabbled.
W	R	A	N	G	L	E	R	Antagonist, Opponent.
W	R	A	P	P	A	G	E	Wrapping material.
W	R	A	P	P	I	N	G	Covering, Enveloping, Enclosing, Concealing, Enshrouding, Camouflaging, Cloaking.
W	R	A	T	H	F	U	L	Angry, Vindictive, Bitter.
W	R	A	T	H	I	L	Y	Furiously, Indignantly, Irately.
W	R	A	W	L	I	N	G	Crying, Howling, Mewling.
W	R	E	A	K	F	U	L	Revengeful, Vindictive, Vengeful.
W	R	E	A	K	I	N	G	Avenging, Punishing, Indulging, Gratifying, Visiting, Expending, Inflicting, Imposing.
W	R	E	A	T	H	E	D	Writhed, Twisted, Contorted, Interwoven, Encircled, Adorned, Crowned, Wound.
W	R	E	A	T	H	E	N	Interlaced, Intertwined.
W	R	E	C	K	A	G	E	Debris, Driftwood, Flotsam, Jetsam.
W	R	E	C	K	F	U	L	Destructive, Ruinous, Wrackful, Shattering, Annihilative.
W	R	E	C	K	I	N	G	Destroying, Demolishing, Ruining, Despoiling, Plundering, Sabotaging, Undermining.

1	2	3	4	5	6	7	8	
W	R	E	N	C	H	E	D	Wrested, Distorted, Extorted, Bent, Sprained, Ricked, Rent, Torn.
W	R	E	S	T	I	N	G	Exacting, Pinching, Confiscating, Usurping, Arrogating, Distorting, Forcing.
W	R	E	S	T	L	E	D	Grappled, Writhed, Squirmed, Tussled, Scuffled, Contended, Endeavoured, Struggled.
W	R	E	S	T	L	E	R	One that engages in the sport of wrestling.
W	R	E	T	C	H	E	D	Dejected, Distressed, Squalid, Dismal, Foul, Meagre, Paltry, Shabby.
W	R	I	G	G	L	E	D	Squirmed, Writhed, Insinuated, Extricated, Oozed, Slid, Slipped.
W	R	I	G	G	L	E	R	One that wriggles.
W	R	I	N	G	I	N	G	Squeezing, Twisting, Oppressing, Wrenching, Extorting, Contorting, Screwing, Coiling.
W	R	I	N	K	L	E	D	Puckered, Furrowed, Corrugated, Creased, Ridged, Waved.
W	R	I	S	T	L	E	T	Close-fitting knitted band for the wrist.
W	R	I	S	T	P	I	N	A pin for a connecting rod.
W	R	I	T	E	O	F	F	Cancel, Reduce, Derogate, Devaluate, Destroy, Kill, Lower, Depreciate.
W	R	I	T	H	I	N	G	Twisting, Wrenching, Wringing, Intertwining, Squirming, Agonizing, Flinching, Recoiling.
W	R	I	T	H	L	E	D	Wrinkled, Shrivelled.
W	R	O	N	G	F	U	L	Injurious, Unjust, Unfair, Unlawful, Illegitimate, Criminal, Illegal, Illicit.
W	R	O	N	G	I	N	G	Violating, Impairing, Spoiling, Defrauding, Dispossessing, Persecuting, Aggrieving.
W	R	O	N	G	O	U	S	Iniquitous, Wrongful, Illegal, Unlawful, Unfitting.
W	R	Y	M	O	U	T	H	Large eellike fish.
W	U	R	T	Z	I	T	E	Mineral that consists of zinc sulfide.

X

1	2	3	4	5	6	7	8	
X	A	N	C	I	D	A	E	A family of gastropod mollusks.
X	A	N	T	H	A	T	E	A compound that is an ester of a xanthic acid.
X	A	N	T	H	E	N	E	A white crystalline heterocyclic compound obtained by reduction of zanthone.
X	A	N	T	H	I	A	N	Relating to the ancient town of Xanthis of Lycia.
X	A	N	T	H	I	N	E	A feebly based crystalline nitrogenous compound.
X	A	N	T	H	I	S	M	Colouring of the skin by yellow pigment.
X	A	N	T	H	I	U	M	A genus of coarse, rough spiny herbs, Cocklebur.
X	A	N	T	H	O	M	A	A condition where the skin is marked by yellow patches or nodules.
X	A	N	T	H	O	N	E	A crystalline ketone that is a parent of yellow pigments.
X	A	N	T	H	O	U	S	Having reddish, yellowish or auburn hair, Marked by yellow colouration.
X	E	N	A	R	C	H	I	An order of fishes that comprise pirate perches.
X	E	N	O	G	A	M	Y	Fertilization by cross-pollination.
X	E	N	O	L	I	T	H	A fragment of rock embedded in another rock.
X	E	N	O	T	I	M	E	A mineral that is a phosphate of yttrium.
X	E	R	A	P	H	I	N	An old Portugese silver coin.
X	E	R	O	P	H	I	L	Living in a dry environment.
X	E	R	O	S	E	R	E	Dry-land succession.
X	I	P	H	I	O	I	D	Related to the swordfish.
X	I	P	H	O	D	O	N	An extinct two-toed animal.
X	Y	L	E	U	T	E	S	Genus of moths.
X	Y	L	O	C	O	P	A	A genus of carpenter bees.
X	Y	L	O	C	A	R	P	A hard woody fruit.
X	Y	L	O	L	O	G	Y	Dealing with the gross and the minute structure of wood.
X	Y	L	O	N	I	T	E	Trademark used for plastic.
X	Y	L	O	S	I	D	E	A glycoside that yields xylose.
X	Y	L	O	T	I	L	E	A mineral that is a hydrous iron magnesium.
X	Y	L	O	T	O	M	Y	Art of preparing wood for microscopic examination.
X	Y	L	O	T	R	Y	A	A genus of marine bivalves.
X	Y	L	U	L	O	S	E	A ketose sugar.

Y

1	2	3	4	5	6	7	8	
Y	A	C	H	T	I	N	G	Racing or cruising in a yacht.
Y	A	H	O	O	I	S	M	Rowdyism.
Y	A	M	M	E	R	E	D	Wailed, Whimpered, Whined, Grumbled, Scolded, Complained, Griped, Fussed.
Y	A	R	D	B	I	R	D	An untrained enlisted man.
Y	A	R	D	L	A	N	D	Virgate, An old English unit of land measure.
Y	A	R	D	W	A	N	D	Yardstick.
Y	A	T	A	G	H	A	N	A long knife common among Muslim people.
Y	E	A	N	L	I	N	G	A lamb or kid.
Y	E	A	R	B	O	O	K	A book of facts published once a year, Annual.
Y	E	A	R	L	I	N	G	An animal one year old.
Y	E	A	R	L	O	N	G	Lasting through a year.

1	2	3	4	5	6	7	8	Definition
Y	E	A	R	N	F	U	L	Mournful, Distressing.
Y	E	A	R	N	I	N	G	Longing, Craving, Desiring, Grieving, Aching, Pining, Hankering, Coveting.
Y	E	L	L	O	W	E	D	Turned yellow, Tinged with yellow.
Y	E	O	M	A	N	L	Y	Bravely, Sturdily, Staunchly.
Y	E	O	M	A	N	R	Y	An eighteenth century force of voluntary defenders.
Y	E	S	T	R	E	E	N	Last evening, Last night.
Y	I	E	L	D	I	N	G	Relinquishing, Abandoning, Surrendering, Flexible, Soft, Mushy, Spongy, Passive.
Y	O	D	E	L	L	E	D	Vocalized in a manner peculiar to the Swiss.
Y	O	G	A	C	A	R	A	Buddhist philosopy.
Y	O	K	E	L	I	S	H	Rude, Uncouth.
Y	O	K	E	M	A	T	E	Mate, Fellow, Partner.
Y	O	K	E	T	O	E	D	Having two toes in front and two toes behind.
Y	O	K	O	H	A	M	A	Characteristic of the city of Yokohama, Japan.
Y	O	M	A	W	O	O	D	Wood of Asiatic padauk.
Y	O	U	N	G	E	S	T	Most youthful, Last born in a family.
Y	O	U	N	G	I	S	H	Juvenile, Characteristic of a young person.
Y	O	U	R	S	E	L	F	Reflexive pronoun.
Y	O	U	T	H	F	U	L	Appropriate for youth, Callow, Immature, Unfledged.
Y	T	T	E	R	B	I	C	Relating to ytterbium.
Y	U	G	O	S	L	A	V	Inhabitant of Yugoslavia.
Y	U	L	E	T	I	D	E	Christmastime.

Z

1	2	3	4	5	6	7	8	Definition
Z	A	D	O	K	I	T	E	An early Jewish sect that settled in Damascus in the second century.
Z	A	L	O	P	H	U	S	Genus of small-eared seals.
Z	A	M	I	N	D	A	R	An absentee landlord in India after independence.
Z	A	M	P	O	G	N	A	Panpipe, Bagpipe.
Z	A	N	T	I	O	T	E	Resident of Zante.
Z	A	P	A	T	E	R	O	A tropical American timber tree.
Z	A	R	A	T	I	T	E	A hydrous basic nickel carbonate.
Z	A	R	Z	U	E	L	A	A Spanish opera having spoken dialogue.
Z	E	A	L	L	E	S	S	Lifeless, Lacking zeal, Apathetic.
Z	E	A	L	O	T	R	Y	Fanatical devotion.
Z	E	C	C	H	I	N	O	Sequin.
Z	E	M	I	N	D	A	R	Zamindar.
Z	E	M	I	R	O	T	H	Religious Hebrew songs sung at table at the Sabbath meal.
Z	E	N	I	T	H	A	L	Located near the zenith.
Z	E	O	L	I	T	I	C	Relating to silicates.
Z	E	P	P	E	L	I	N	A rigid airship.
Z	E	R	O	I	Z	E	D	Atmospheric conditions reducing ceiling and visibility to zero.
Z	I	B	E	L	I	N	E	A soft lustrous woollen fabric.
Z	I	G	G	U	R	A	T	An ancient Babylonian temple.
Z	I	M	B	A	L	O	N	Cimbalon, Hungarian gipsy dulcimer.
Z	I	N	G	I	B	E	R	Genus of tropical Asiatic and Polynesian plants, Ginger.
Z	I	O	N	W	A	R	D	Heavenward.
Z	I	P	H	I	O	I	D	Whale.
Z	I	R	C	O	N	I	A	Zirconium, Oxide.
Z	I	R	C	O	N	Y	L	The bivalent radical of zirconium and oxygen.
Z	I	R	I	C	O	T	E	A Mexican tree having brown wood streaked with dark lines.
Z	I	Z	I	P	H	U	S	A large genus of spiny shrubs, Christ's thorn.
Z	O	A	N	T	H	U	S	Large genus of marine polyps resembling anemones.
Z	O	D	I	A	C	A	L	Within the zodiac.
Z	O	E	T	R	O	P	E	An optical toy with a revolving cylinder.
Z	O	L	O	T	N	I	K	A Russian unit of weight.
Z	O	N	A	T	I	O	N	Distribution of kinds of organisms.
Z	O	N	E	L	E	S	S	Ungirt, Lacking a girdle.
Z	O	O	C	H	O	R	E	A plant distributed by living animals.
Z	O	O	G	E	N	I	C	Associated with animals or their activities.
Z	O	O	G	L	E	A	L	Growth of bacteria in a fluid media.
Z	O	O	G	R	A	F	T	Animal tissue used in a surgical graft.
Z	O	O	L	A	T	E	R	One that practices zoolatry.
Z	O	O	L	A	T	R	Y	Animal worship.
Z	O	O	M	E	T	E	R	An animal whose activities are used to predict population variations of another animal.
Z	O	O	M	O	R	P	H	Something in the form of an animal.
Z	O	O	N	O	S	I	S	A disease that can be communicated from animals to man.

1	2	3	4	5	6	7	8
Z	O	O	N	O	T	I	C
Z	O	O	P	H	A	G	A
Z	O	O	P	H	I	L	E
Z	O	O	P	H	I	L	Y
Z	O	O	P	H	Y	T	E
Z	O	O	S	P	E	R	M
Z	O	O	S	P	O	R	E
Z	O	O	S	T	U	I	T
Z	O	U	C	H	S	N	I
Z	W	I	E	B	A	C	K
Z	Y	G	A	D	E	N	E
Z	Y	G	O	C	I	T	Y
Z	Y	G	O	D	O	N	T
Z	Y	G	O	T	E	N	E
Z	Y	M	O	L	O	G	Y

Constituting a zoonosis.
Family of flesh-eating mammals.
An individual having a preference for animals.
An erotic fixation on animals.
Marine animals as corals, sea anaemones, sponges.
Zoospore.
Assexual spore of alga or lower fungus.
A flashy suit of extreme cut.
A summer squash.
Sweetened bread enriched with eggs, baked then sliced and toasted.
Genus of herbs.
Twin formation.
Pertaining to molar teeth.
Synaptic stage in meiosis.
Science that deals with fermentation.

A

ABANDONED	Deserted, Renounced, Discarded, Relinquished, Derelict, Forsaken, Dissolute.
ABATEMENT	Deduction, Subraction, Discount, Decrease, Rebate, Reduction.
ABHORRENT	Repellent, disgusting, contrary.
ABOLITION	Annulment, Act of bringing to an end, Voiding.
ABOMINATE	Abhor, Loathe, Hate, Detest, Execrate, Strong dislike.
ABORIGINE	Primitive, Indigenous, Native.
ABSTAINED	Curbed, Refrained, Declined, Rejected, Spurned, Denied, Refused, Constrained.
ABSTAINER	One that practices self-restraint and usually refrains from drinking alcohol.
ABSTINENT	Temperate, Continent, Sober, Abstentious, Self-restraining.
ABUNDANCE	Thriving, Plenty, Lavishness, Profusion, Prosperity, Easy, Affluence, Rich.
ACANTHOID	Spiny, similar to a thorn.
ACAPPELLA	Style of singing without an instrumental accompaniment.
ACARIASIS	Infested with ticks and mites.
ACAROLOGY	The study of ticks and mites.
ACCESSORY	Accompaniment, Accretion, Addition, Adjunct, Appendix, Confederate.
ACCIPITER	Birds of the hawk and falcon family.
ACCLIMATE	Adapt, Harden, Season, Toughen, Acclimatize.
ACCOMPANY	Combine, Join, Safeguard, Link, Chaperon, Escort, Attend, Convoy.
ACCORDING	Harmonious, In mutual agreement, Congruous.
ACCORDION	Small portable keyboard wind instrument operated by bellows.
ACCRETION	Growing together, Increasing by external addition.
ACCRETIVE	Organic growth, Extraneous addition.
ACIDULOUS	Made acid, Sour, Acerbic, Tart, Dry, Piquant, Sharp, Cutting.
ACQUIESCE	Accede, accept, agree, consent.
ACQUITTAL	Discharge, Deliverance from a charge.
ACROBATIC	Gymnastic.
ACROPETAL	From base to apex.
ACROPOLIS	Citadel of ancient Greece.
ACROSPIRE	First showing of a germinating grain seed.
ACTUALITY	Reality, Realism, Existence, Achievement, Attainment.
ACUMINATE	Pointed, Acute, Sharp, Piked, Tapered, Sharpened.
ADDICTIVE	Enthusiastic devotion, Applying habitually, Compulsive uncontrolled use.
ADDICTION	Causing addiction.
ADIABATIC	Occurring with constant temperature.
ADJACENCY	Nearby place, Neighbouring place.
ADJECTIVE	Additional, Dependent, Qualifying.
ADJOINING	Adjacent, Touching, Abutting, Bordering, Juxtaposed, Contiguous.
ADMIRABLE	Excellent, Estimable, Wonderful, Surprising.
ADMIXTURE	Mingled, A compound, An ingredient.
ADORATION	Worship, Idolization, Passion, Infatuation, Devotion.
ADRENALIN	Hormone secreted by adrenal glands.
ADSORBENT	Capacity to adsorb, Substance that holds by adsorption.
ADULATION	Excessive flattery, Blandishment, Acclaim, Praise effusively.
ADUMBRATE	Outline, Overshadow, Typify, Predict, Shade, Darken, Presage.
ADVANCING	Approaching, Going forward, Making progress, Promoting, Assisting, Encouraging.
ADVANTAGE	Superiority, Victory, Allowance, Benefit, Prosperity, Use, Service, Fitness.
ADVENTURE	Enterprise, Exploit, Feat, Hazard, Risk, Wager, Imperil, Daring activity.
ADVERBIAL	Qualifying or modifying part of speech.
ADVERSARY	Opponent, Antagonist, Opposer, Enemy, Foe, Contestant.
ADVERTISE	Notify, Report, Warn, Inform, Proclaim, Announce, Broadcast, Publicize.
ADVISABLE	Expedient, Recommended, Prudent.
AEPYORNIS	Genus of extinct flightless birds.
AERIALIST	Entertainer who performs on a high wire or trapeze.
AERODROME	An open space for movement of aircraft.
AEROMETER	Device to establish weight and density of air or gas.
AEROPAUSE	Atmosphere level where an aircraft is unable to function.
AESTHETIC	Appreciation of culture and beauty.
AETIOLOGY	Study of causes or origins, especially of diseases.
AFFECTING	Touching, Moving, Impressive, Poignant, Disturbing.
AFFECTION	Emotion, Love, Devotion, Concern, Passion, Warmth, Tenderness, Goodwill.
AFFECTIVE	Emotional.
AFFIANCED	Betrothed, Promised in marriage, Plighted, Contracted.
AFFIDAVIT	Statement made under oath.

1	2	3	4	5	6	7	8	9	
A	F	F	I	L	I	A	T	E	Attach, Connect, Adopt, Trace, Ally, Associate, Combine.
A	F	O	R	E	S	A	I	D	Mentioned previously.
A	F	T	E	R	M	A	T	H	Results, Consequences, Outcome.
A	F	T	E	R	N	O	O	N	Part of the day between noon and dusk.
A	G	G	R	A	V	A	T	E	Exasperate, Irritate, Peeve, Provoke, Magnify, Intensify, Deepen, Redouble.
A	G	G	R	E	G	A	T	E	Amount, Accumulation, Bulk, Quantity, Total, Sum.
A	G	G	R	I	E	V	E	D	Distressed, Hurt, Injured, Abused, Outraged, Wronged, Persecuted, Tormented.
A	G	I	S	T	M	E	N	T	Money paid for grazing for cattle.
A	G	I	T	A	T	I	O	N	Commotion, Disturbance, Shaking, Bouncing, Turbulence, Turmoil, Confusion.
A	G	R	E	E	A	B	L	E	Pleasant, Conformable, Congenial, Compatible, Gratifying, Sympathetic.
A	G	R	E	E	M	E	N	T	Harmony, Accord, Understanding, Contract, Bargain, Bond, Compact, Covenant.
A	G	R	O	L	O	G	I	C	Study of illiterate people.
A	G	R	O	N	O	M	I	C	Relating to agriculture.
A	I	L	A	N	T	H	U	S	Small genus of East Indian and Chinese trees.
A	I	M	L	E	S	S	L	Y	Without aim or direction, Randomly, Desultory, Haphazardly.
A	L	A	B	A	S	T	E	R	A pure granular gypsum rock.
A	L	B	A	T	R	O	S	S	Long-winged oceanic bird.
A	L	B	E	S	C	E	N	T	Becoming white, Fading into white.
A	L	C	H	E	M	I	S	T	One that studied chemical sciences in medieval times.
A	L	C	O	H	O	L	I	C	One addicted to the excessive drinking of alcohol.
A	L	D	E	B	A	R	A	N	Bright reddish star in the constellation of Taurus.
A	L	E	R	T	N	E	S	S	State of being vigilant.
A	L	G	A	R	R	O	B	A	Carob.
A	L	I	G	N	M	E	N	T	Act of aligning, Formation on a straight line.
A	L	I	M	E	N	T	A	L	Nourishing, Furnishing sustenance.
A	L	K	A	L	I	S	E	D	Increased alkalinity content.
A	L	L	A	N	T	O	I	D	Sausage-shaped plant.
A	L	L	E	G	O	R	I	C	Relating to a figurative story.
A	L	L	E	M	A	N	D	E	A type of Germanic dance.
A	L	L	E	V	I	A	T	E	Relieve, Moderate, Lighten, Lessen, Extenuate, Assuage, Allay, Mitigate.
A	L	L	O	C	A	T	E	D	Assigned, Allowed, Designated, Reserved, Apportioned.
A	L	L	O	G	R	A	P	H	Written character representing a sound.
A	L	L	O	P	A	T	H	Y	Medical remedies having opposite effects of the disease to be cured.
A	L	L	O	P	H	A	N	E	A formless clay mineral.
A	L	L	O	T	M	E	N	T	Allowance, Cut, Lot, Share, Portion, Quota, Ration.
A	L	L	O	T	R	O	P	E	Crystal form of an element differing from another.
A	L	M	A	N	D	I	N	E	Purple Indian garnet.
A	L	O	P	E	C	O	I	D	Like a fox, Vulpine.
A	L	T	E	R	C	A	T	E	Wrangle, Dispute.
A	L	T	E	R	N	A	T	E	Arrange, Perform, Interchange, Succeed, Periodical, Recurrent, Substitute.
A	L	T	I	M	E	T	E	R	Instrument for measuring height.
A	L	T	I	P	L	A	N	O	High plateau, Plain.
A	L	T	I	S	S	I	M	O	The highest pitch - as in music.
A	M	A	U	R	O	S	I	S	Partial or total loss of sight from disease but without an obvious change in the eye.
A	M	A	Z	E	M	E	N	T	Wonder, Admiration, Surprise, Astonishment, Confoundment.
A	M	A	Z	O	N	I	T	E	A blue-green semi-precious stone.
A	M	B	E	R	G	R	I	S	Wax-like substance found in the sperm whale and used in perfumery.
A	M	B	I	G	U	I	T	Y	Double-meaning, Evasion, Subterfuge, Vagueness, Uncertainty, Cavil.
A	M	B	I	G	U	O	U	S	Obscure, Opaque, Unclear, Unintelligible, Dubious, Doubtful, Suspect, Unsure.
A	M	B	I	T	I	O	U	S	Aspiring, Enterprising, Energetic, Keen, Indefatigable, Audacious, Pretentious.
A	M	B	U	L	A	N	C	E	Vehicle equipped for transporting sick, wounded or injured people or animals.
A	M	B	U	S	C	A	D	E	Ambush.
A	M	E	N	D	M	E	N	T	Correction, Reformation, Improvement, Betterment.
A	M	E	R	I	C	I	U	M	Artificially made metallic radio-active element.
A	M	E	T	R	O	P	I	A	Imperfection of sight.
A	M	I	A	N	T	H	U	S	Asbestos.
A	M	I	D	S	H	I	P	S	Middle of the ship.
A	M	O	R	O	U	S	L	Y	Affectionately, Fondly, Romantically, Lovingly.
A	M	O	R	P	H	O	U	S	Formless, Shapeless, Unclassifiable, Not crystalline.
A	M	P	E	R	S	A	N	D	A sign standing for the word "and".
A	M	P	H	I	B	I	A	N	Animal or plant that can live on land and in water, Operates on land and in water.
A	M	P	L	I	F	I	E	R	Equipment for increasing current or power.
A	M	P	L	I	T	U	D	E	Abundance, Fullness, Breadth, Measurement of distance or displacement.
A	M	U	S	E	M	E	N	T	Entertainment, Distraction, Diversion, Recreation.
A	N	A	B	O	L	I	S	M	Complex molecules formed from simpler living ones.
A	N	A	C	L	I	T	I	C	Characterized by dependence.
A	N	A	C	R	U	S	I	S	Preliminary to poetry, music or dancing.

1	2	3	4	5	6	7	8	9	Definition
A	N	A	E	R	O	B	I	C	Ability to exist without oxygen.
A	N	A	P	L	A	S	T	Y	Plastic surgery.
A	N	A	L	G	E	S	I	C	A pain-killer.
A	N	A	L	O	G	O	U	S	Similar, Parallel.
A	N	A	R	C	H	I	S	T	One who uses violence to overthrow established order.
A	N	A	R	T	H	R	I	A	Inability to speak.
A	N	A	T	O	M	I	S	E	Detailed analysis, dissection.
A	N	A	T	O	M	I	S	T	Expert and/or student of Anatomy.
A	N	C	E	S	T	R	A	L	Relating to ancestors, Forerunner, Prototype.
A	N	C	H	O	R	A	G	E	Lying at anchor.
A	N	C	H	O	R	I	T	E	Hermit, Recluse.
A	N	C	I	L	L	A	R	Y	Subordinate, Auxiliary, Supplementary, Related, Subsidiary, Satellite, Contributory.
A	N	C	I	P	I	T	A	L	Double-edged.
A	N	E	M	O	L	O	G	Y	Study of the winds.
A	N	G	L	E	S	I	T	E	Lead sulfate formed by oxidation of galena.
A	N	G	O	S	T	U	R	A	Aromatic bitter bark used as a tonic.
A	N	H	Y	D	R	I	D	E	A compound derived from another compound by the removal of water.
A	N	H	Y	D	R	O	U	S	Substances having no water.
A	N	I	M	A	L	I	S	M	Doctrine that considers human beings as mere animals.
A	N	I	M	A	T	I	O	N	Spirited, Dash, Esprit, Verve, Enlivening, Lively, Inspiration, Incitement.
A	N	I	M	O	S	I	T	Y	Enmity, Antagonism, Hostility, Rancour, Antipathy, Illwill, Resentment.
A	N	K	Y	L	O	S	I	S	Stiffness of a joint, Fusion, Uniting of bones.
A	N	N	E	A	L	I	N	G	Tempering, Strengthening, Toughening.
A	N	N	O	U	N	C	E	R	Official who introduces programmes usually on television and radio.
A	N	N	O	Y	A	N	C	E	Vexation, Irritation, Nuisance, Provocation, Exasperation, Harassment, Irritant.
A	N	N	U	L	A	T	E	D	Marked with rings.
A	N	N	U	L	M	E	N	T	Nullification, Cancellation.
A	N	O	M	A	L	O	U	S	Abnormal, Irregular, Unnatural, Deviant, Strange, Divergent, Aberrant.
A	N	O	N	Y	M	O	U	S	Nameless, Undesignated, Unknown, Incognito, Unspecified, Unrecognized.
A	N	O	P	H	E	L	E	S	Genus of mosquito that transmits malaria.
A	N	T	E	N	N	U	L	E	Pair of small antennae of crustaceans.
A	N	T	H	E	L	I	O	N	Sun spots.
A	N	T	H	E	M	I	O	N	Honeysuckle ornament in relief sculpture or painting.
A	N	T	H	O	L	O	G	Y	Selected collection of poems, literary passages, paintings or sculpture.
A	N	T	I	C	L	I	N	E	Arch-like fold in levels of rock opposite to the crest.
A	N	T	I	P	A	S	T	O	Hors d'oeuvre, Titbits served as an appetizer.
A	N	T	I	P	A	T	H	Y	Repugnance, Distaste, Enmity, Animosity, Hostility, Eschewal, Allergy, Evasion.
A	N	T	I	P	O	D	A	L	Diametrically opposed, Contradictory, Counter, Reverse.
A	N	T	I	P	O	D	E	S	Exact opposite or contrary, Persons dwelling at a directly opposite point of the earth.
A	N	T	I	Q	U	A	R	Y	One with a great interest in antiques.
A	N	T	I	Q	U	I	T	Y	Ancient times.
A	N	T	I	T	O	X	I	N	A substance that neutralizes a toxin.
A	N	T	I	V	E	N	I	N	Antidote to a venom.
A	N	T	I	V	I	R	A	L	Acting to make a virus ineffective.
A	P	A	R	T	H	E	I	D	Separation of the races.
A	P	A	R	T	M	E	N	T	Single room, Small flat.
A	P	A	T	H	E	T	I	C	Impassive, Phlegmatic, Stoic, Stolid, Sluggish, Torpid, Limp, Spiritless.
A	P	E	T	A	L	O	U	S	Having no petals.
A	P	I	C	U	L	A	T	E	Having a sharp point.
A	P	I	V	O	R	O	U	S	Feeding on bees.
A	P	O	L	O	G	I	Z	E	Offer an excuse, Acknowledge a fault, Expression of regret.
A	P	P	A	L	L	I	N	G	Shocking, Frightful, Fearful, Awful, Dreadful, Formidable, Horrific, Daunting.
A	P	P	A	L	O	O	S	A	American saddle horse of Spanish origin.
A	P	P	A	R	A	T	U	S	Equipment, Gear, Machinery, Outfit, Paraphernalia, Tackle, Utensils, Implements.
A	P	P	A	R	I	T	O	R	Herald, Usher, One who serves an officer or authority.
A	P	P	E	A	L	I	N	G	Attractive, Pleasing, Pleading, Imploring, Alluring, Bewitching, Cativating.
A	P	P	E	A	R	I	N	G	Emerging, Looming, Showing, Arriving, Materializing, Rising, Manifesting.
A	P	P	E	A	S	I	N	G	Pacifying, Soothing, Satisfying, Placating, Propitiating, Assuaging, Gratifying.
A	P	P	E	L	L	A	T	E	Appealing, One who appeals to higher courts.
A	P	P	E	N	D	A	G	E	Adjunct, Appurtenance, Accessory, Supplement, Collateral, Extra.
A	P	P	E	R	T	A	I	N	Belong, Pertain, Bear, Apply, Relate, Relevant.
A	P	P	E	T	I	Z	E	R	Something to stimulate the appetite.
A	P	P	L	A	U	D	E	D	Expressed approval by clapping hands, Praised, Commended.
A	P	P	L	E	J	A	C	K	Apple brandy.
A	P	P	L	I	A	N	C	E	Apparatus, Implement, Machine, Device, Attachment, Utensil, Instrument, Tool.
A	P	P	L	I	C	A	N	T	One who makes a formal request.
A	P	P	O	R	T	I	O	N	Allot, Portion, Ration, Assign, Share, Allocate, Divide, Administer.

1	2	3	4	5	6	7	8	9	
A	P	P	R	A	I	S	A	L	Estimate, Assessment, Estimation, Valuation, Judgment.
A	P	P	R	E	H	E	N	D	Accept, Comprehend, Conceive, Arrest, Detain, Foresee, Anticipate, Fathom.
A	P	P	R	O	B	A	T	E	Approve, Accept, Countenance, Favour, Sanction.
A	P	R	O	S	E	X	I	A	Abnormal inability to sustain attention.
A	Q	U	A	R	E	L	L	A	Watercolour drawing or painting in transparent colours.
A	Q	U	I	L	E	G	I	A	Genus of herbs, Columbine.
A	R	A	B	E	S	Q	U	E	Intricate ornamentation, Musical passage, Position in ballet.
A	R	A	B	I	N	O	S	E	Crystalline aldose sugar.
A	R	A	C	H	N	O	I	D	Thin membrane of the brain and spinal cord.
A	R	A	U	C	A	R	I	A	Small genus of South American and Australian trees.
A	R	B	I	T	R	A	R	Y	Imperious, Despotic, Tyrannical, Absolute, Capricious, Erratic, Whimsical.
A	R	B	I	T	R	A	T	E	Judge, Adjudicate, Referee, Umpire, Intermediate, Intervene, Soothe, Placate.
A	R	B	O	R	E	O	U	S	Having the characteristics of a tree.
A	R	B	O	R	E	T	U	M	Botanic garden for the study of trees and shrubs.
A	R	C	H	A	N	G	E	L	Angel of the highest rank. Plant of the mint family.
A	R	C	H	E	T	Y	P	E	Original, Prototype, Universal symbol, Example, Ideal, Model, Pattern, Standard.
A	R	C	H	F	I	E	N	D	Devil, Demon, Satan.
A	R	C	H	I	T	E	C	T	Generator, Inventor, Author, Creator, Founder, Maker, Originator, Designer.
A	R	C	H	I	V	I	S	T	Keeper of archives.
A	R	C	H	I	V	O	L	T	Inner curve of an arch.
A	R	D	U	O	U	S	L	Y	Laboriously, Difficulty, Strenuously, Toilsomely, Hard, Steeply.
A	R	E	N	I	C	O	L	A	Genus of burrowing worms, Lugworms.
A	R	M	I	L	L	A	R	Y	Pertaining to bracelets.
A	R	M	I	S	T	I	C	E	Agreement to cease hostilities, Truce, Cease-fire.
A	R	R	I	V	I	S	T	E	Upstart, Aggressive, unscrupulous person who uses any means to gain success.
A	R	R	O	G	A	N	C	E	Hauteur, Loftiness, Superciliousness, Disdain.
A	R	R	O	W	R	O	O	T	Nutritive powder used to nourish invalids and children.
A	R	S	E	N	I	O	U	S	Containing arsenic.
A	R	T	H	R	I	T	I	C	Affected with arthritis.
A	R	T	H	R	I	T	I	S	Inflammation of the joints caused by a variety of causes.
A	R	T	I	C	H	O	K	E	An edible thistle-like herb.
A	R	T	I	C	U	L	A	R	Pertaining to the joints.
A	R	T	I	F	I	C	E	R	Skilled or artistic worker, Designer, Inventor, Armourer.
A	R	T	I	L	L	E	R	Y	Guns larger than small arms, Cannons.
A	R	T	L	E	S	S	L	Y	Naturally, Naively, Trustingly, Simply.
A	S	C	E	N	D	A	N	T	Rising, Predominant, Superior, Preeminent, Controlling, Supremacy.
A	S	C	E	N	D	I	N	G	Rising, Escalating, Mounting, Scaling, Surmounting, Scrambling.
A	S	C	E	R	T	A	I	N	Determine, Unearth, Appraise, Discover, Learn, See, Inspect, Study.
A	S	C	O	S	P	O	R	E	Spore developed in a sac-like body.
A	S	P	A	R	A	G	U	S	An edible plant of the lily family.
A	S	P	E	R	S	I	O	N	Slur, Stricture, Abuse, Lampoon, Libel, Defamation, Vituperation, Invective.
A	S	S	A	I	L	A	N	T	Attacker, Aggressor, Assassin.
A	S	S	E	R	T	I	O	N	Affirmation, Positive statement.
A	S	S	E	R	T	I	V	E	Insistent, Aggressive, Emphatic, Forceful, Militant, Pushing, Resounding, Dogmatic.
A	S	S	I	D	U	O	U	S	Industrious, Hardworking, Diligent, Indefatigable, Zealous.
A	S	S	I	S	T	A	N	T	Helper, Aid, Attendant, Aide-de-camp, Agent, Deputy, Proxy, Minion.
A	S	S	I	S	T	I	N	G	Helping, Aiding, Escorting, Accompanying, Co-operating, Relieving, Comforting.
A	S	S	O	C	I	A	T	E	Partner, Confederate, Accomplice, Collaborator, Join, Combine, Connect, Unite.
A	S	S	O	N	A	N	C	E	Resemblance of sound in words or syllables.
A	S	S	U	A	S	I	V	E	Calming, Soothing.
A	S	S	U	R	A	N	C	E	Guarantee, Pledge, Promise, Certainty, Surety, Safety, Confidence, Aplomb.
A	S	S	U	R	E	D	L	Y	Confidently, Surely, Certainly.
A	S	T	H	M	A	T	I	C	Relating to asthma.
A	S	T	O	U	N	D	E	D	Surprised, Astonished, Amazed, Dumbfounded, Flabbergasted, Shocked.
A	S	T	R	O	D	O	M	E	Dome-shaped window in a plane used by the navigator.
A	S	T	R	O	L	A	B	E	Forerunner of the sextant.
A	S	T	R	O	L	O	G	Y	Making prediction on the supposed effect of the stars on human lives.
A	S	T	R	O	N	A	U	T	A traveller in space.
A	S	T	R	O	N	O	M	Y	Study of celestial bodies.
A	S	Y	M	M	E	T	R	Y	Lack of proportion, Lack of co-ordination.
A	T	A	V	I	S	T	I	C	Reversion to characteristics of remote ancestors.
A	T	H	E	I	S	T	I	C	Irreverent, Impious, Godless, Unbelieving.
A	T	M	O	M	E	T	E	R	Device for measuring the rate of water evaporation.
A	T	O	N	E	M	E	N	T	Reconciliation, Satisfaction, Expiation.
A	T	R	O	C	I	O	U	S	Scandalous, Outrageous, Heinous, Iniquitous, Vicious, Abominable, Despicable.
A	T	R	O	P	H	I	E	D	Deteriorated, Declined, Degenerated, Downgraded, Wasted.
A	T	T	E	N	D	A	N	T	Assistant, Helper, Servant.

1	2	3	4	5	6	7	8	9	
A	T	T	E	N	T	I	O	N	Consideration, Notice, Attentiveness.
A	T	T	E	N	T	I	V	E	Observant, Intent, Heedful, Courteous, Polite, Thoughtful, Considerate.
A	T	T	E	N	U	A	T	E	Thin, Lessen, Dissipate, Constrict, Deflate, Weaken, Debilitate, Enfeeble.
A	T	T	R	I	B	U	T	E	Characteristic, Feature, Mark, Trait, Speciality, Ascribe, Credit, Impute.
A	T	T	R	I	T	I	O	N	Penance, Remorse, Repentance, Penitence, Contrition, Friction, Abrasion.
A	U	B	E	R	G	I	N	E	Brinjal, Eggplant.
A	U	B	R	I	E	T	I	A	Genus of Mediterranean herbs having purplish flowers.
A	U	D	A	C	I	O	U	S	Brave, Bold, Courageous, Fearless, Intrepid, Valiant, Daring, Reckless.
A	U	R	I	C	U	L	A	R	Audible, Aural, Pertaining to the ear.
A	U	S	T	E	R	I	T	Y	Severity, Ascetic practice, Harshness, Severely simple.
A	U	T	H	E	N	T	I	C	Genuine, Veritable, Credible, Authoritative, Convincing, Valid, Real, Original.
A	U	T	H	O	R	I	T	Y	Citation, Testimony, Dominion, Jurisdiction, Basis, Government, Warrant.
A	U	T	H	O	R	I	Z	E	Commission, Enable, Empower, Approve, Promote, Entitle, Qualify, Accredit.
A	U	T	O	C	R	A	C	Y	Despotism, Dictatorship, Tyranny, Totalitarionism.
A	U	T	O	G	R	A	P	H	Signature, Subscribe, Sign.
A	U	T	O	L	Y	T	U	S	A genus of marine annelids.
A	U	T	O	M	A	T	I	C	Mechanical, Perfunctory, Spontaneous, Impulsive, Instinctive, Involuntary.
A	U	T	O	M	A	T	O	N	Robot, Machine, Android.
A	U	X	I	L	I	A	R	Y	Aid, Support, Accessory, Ancillary, Subservient, Subsidiary, Collateral, Assisting.
A	V	A	I	L	A	B	L	E	Obtainable, Securable, Attainable, Accessible, Convenient, Purchasable.
A	V	A	L	A	N	C	H	E	A mass of snow moving down a mountain.
A	V	O	C	A	T	I	O	N	Diversion, Distraction, Hobby.
A	V	O	I	D	A	N	C	E	Vacancy, Outlet, Annulment, Evasion.
A	V	U	N	C	U	L	A	R	Relating to an uncle, Benevolent, Condescending.
A	W	A	K	E	N	I	N	G	Stirring, Rousing.
A	W	A	R	E	N	E	S	S	Consciousness, Alertness.
A	W	K	W	A	R	D	L	Y	Clumsily, Embarrassingly, Ineptly.
A	X	I	O	M	A	T	I	C	Self-evident, Aphoristic.

B

1	2	3	4	5	6	7	8	9	
B	A	B	A	C	O	O	T	E	A large Madagascan short-tailed lemur.
B	A	C	C	H	A	N	A	L	Relating to drunken revels.
B	A	C	C	H	A	N	T	E	Priestess of Bacchus.
B	A	C	C	I	F	O	R	M	Berry-shaped.
B	A	C	I	L	L	A	R	Y	Shaped like a rod.
B	A	C	K	B	I	T	E	R	One that defames or slanders.
B	A	C	K	W	A	R	D	S	In the direction of the rear, In reverse.
B	A	C	K	W	O	O	D	S	Wooden area in outlying parts.
B	A	C	T	E	R	I	U	M	Genus of straight rod-shaped bacteria.
B	A	G	A	T	E	L	L	E	Trifle, Mere nothing, Short piece of music.
B	A	I	L	I	W	I	C	K	Under control of bailiff.
B	A	L	A	B	O	S	T	A	Competent Jewish hostess.
B	A	L	A	C	L	A	V	A	Knitted hood covering head, neck and part of the shoulders.
B	A	L	A	E	N	O	I	D	Whalebone whale.
B	A	L	A	L	A	I	K	A	A Russian stringed instrument similar to a guitar.
B	A	L	D	A	C	H	I	N	Ornamental canopy.
B	A	L	L	E	R	I	N	A	Female lead dancer in a ballet company.
B	A	L	L	I	S	T	I	C	Study of a body in motion.
B	A	M	B	O	O	Z	L	E	Hoax, Mystify, Mislead, Hoodwink.
B	A	N	D	E	R	O	L	E	Streamer, Long narrow flag.
B	A	N	D	I	C	O	O	T	Genus of rats of India and Ceylon.
B	A	N	D	O	L	E	E	R	Ammunition belt worn across the body.
B	A	N	D	S	T	A	N	D	A raised platform in or outdoors used for concerts, especially when played by bands.
B	A	N	E	F	U	L	L	Y	In a harmful fashion, Ominously, Deadly.
B	A	N	J	O	R	I	N	E	A banjo with a short neck.
B	A	N	N	I	S	T	E	R	Handrail of a staircase.
B	A	N	Q	U	E	T	T	E	Firing step in the trenches, Narrow window seat, Built-in upholstered bench.
B	A	P	T	I	S	T	R	Y	Part of the church used for baptism.
B	A	R	B	A	R	I	A	N	Savage, Uncivilized, Heathen, Vandal, Primitive, Rough, Brutal, Uncouth.
B	A	R	B	A	R	I	S	M	Corruption, Ignorance, Rudeness, Vulgarism, Error, Impropriety.
B	A	R	B	A	R	O	U	S	Savage, Uncultured, Uncivilized, Outrageous, Vulgar, Outlandish, Cruel, Fierce.
B	A	R	C	A	R	O	L	E	Rhythm song used by gondoliers.
B	A	R	N	S	T	O	R	M	Travelling around making short overnight stops.
B	A	R	O	G	R	A	P	H	Self-registering barometer.
B	A	R	O	M	E	T	E	R	Instrument for measuring atmospheric pressure.

1	2	3	4	5	6	7	8	9	Clue
B	A	R	R	A	C	U	D	A	Voracious pike-like marine fish considered excellent food.
B	A	R	R	I	C	A	D	E	Obstruction, Rampart, Barrier, Block, Blockade, Fence, Wall.
B	A	R	R	I	S	T	E	R	Counsel, Lawyer, Attorney.
B	A	R	T	E	N	D	E	R	One serving at a licenced bar.
B	A	S	H	F	U	L	L	Y	Shyly, Coyly, Diffidently, Modestly, Timidly, Self-consciously, Sheepishly.
B	A	T	H	C	H	A	I	R	Wheeled chair used by invalids or disabled persons.
B	A	T	T	A	L	I	O	N	Unit of infantry forming part of a brigade, Large group of persons.
B	E	A	C	H	H	E	A	D	Advance position seized by invading troops.
B	E	A	N	S	T	A	L	K	Stem of a bean plant.
B	E	A	R	B	E	R	R	Y	Genus of plant with red berries, American cranberry.
B	E	A	U	T	I	F	U	L	Beautiful, Comely, Good-looking, Handsome, Attractive, Lovely, Exquisite, Pleasing.
B	E	A	U	T	E	O	U	S	Attractive, Comely, Fair, Lovely, Choice, Elegant, Glorious, Personable.
B	E	D	I	Z	E	N	E	D	Dressed in a gaudy and vulgar fashion.
B	E	D	L	A	M	I	T	E	Lunatic, Madman.
B	E	E	F	E	A	T	E	R	Yeoman of the guard of British royalty.
B	E	E	K	E	E	P	E	R	Apiarist, One concerned in the production of honey from bees.
B	E	E	S	T	I	N	G	S	Secretion of mammary glands prior to milk supply.
B	E	F	I	T	T	I	N	G	Suitable, Appropriate, Proper, Decent, Decorous, Conforming, Rightly, Seemly.
B	E	F	U	D	D	L	E	D	Confused, Bewildered, Flustered, Distracted, Perplexed, Stupefied.
B	E	G	E	T	T	I	N	G	Procreating, Fathering, Breeding, Producing, Bearing, Generating, Multiplying.
B	E	G	I	N	N	I	N	G	Commencement, Dawn, Onset, Opening, Initial, Inception, Origin, Source.
B	E	H	A	V	I	O	U	R	Conduct, Deportment, Bearing, Demeanour, Action, Manners.
B	E	L	E	A	G	U	E	R	Besiege, Blockade, Storm, Worry, Annoy, Plague, Harass, Pester.
B	E	L	E	M	N	I	T	E	Fossil shell of extinct cephalopods.
B	E	L	L	I	C	O	S	E	Aggressive, Belligerent, Militant, Pugnacious, Quarrelsome, Truculent, Rebellious.
B	E	L	L	T	O	W	E	R	A tower that contains a bell or bells, Belfry, Campanile, Carillon.
B	E	L	L	Y	A	C	H	E	Colic, Abdominal pain, Complaint, Gripe, Finding fault, Whining.
B	E	L	V	E	D	E	R	E	Structure built to take advantage of a view, Summer cypress.
B	E	N	I	G	H	T	E	D	Obscured, Unenlightened.
B	E	N	T	O	N	I	T	E	Weathered volcanic rock that forms clay.
B	E	R	B	E	R	I	N	E	Alkaloid obtained from a root and used in medicine.
B	E	R	R	U	G	A	T	E	A tripletail fish used for food.
B	E	R	S	E	R	K	E	R	A headstrong person who flies into a frenzy.
B	E	R	Y	L	L	I	U	M	A steel-gray light strong metallic element used as windows in X-ray tubes.
B	E	S	L	O	B	B	E	R	To fawn over.
B	E	T	R	A	Y	I	N	G	Deceiving, Revealing, Doublecrossing, Ensnaring, Trapping, Deserting, Divulging.
B	E	T	R	O	T	H	A	L	Espousal, Engagement, Troth.
B	E	T	R	O	T	H	E	D	Affianced, Engaged.
B	I	C	A	M	E	R	A	L	Consisting of two chambers, Having two legislative bodies.
B	I	C	I	P	I	T	A	L	Relating to the biceps.
B	I	C	Y	C	L	I	S	T	One that rides a bicycle.
B	I	F	U	R	C	A	T	E	Fork, Divide into two branches.
B	I	G	E	M	I	N	A	L	Being in pairs, Twinned.
B	I	L	A	T	E	R	A	L	Relating to two sides.
B	I	L	L	A	B	O	N	G	A stream that is usually dry.
B	I	L	L	I	A	R	D	S	A game played on a table, the idea of which is to pocket balls with a cue.
B	I	N	O	C	U	L	A	R	Optical instrument with two focusing telescopic eyepieces.
B	I	N	O	M	I	N	A	L	Mathematical expression of two terms connected by a plus or minus sign.
B	I	N	T	U	R	O	N	G	Asiatic civet.
B	I	O	G	R	A	P	H	Y	Confessions, Memoirs, Diary, Journal, History, Profile.
B	I	P	A	R	T	I	T	E	Divided into two parts.
B	I	P	I	N	N	A	T	E	Having two leaflets arranged in two rows on leaf stalk.
B	I	R	D	H	O	U	S	E	Artificial nesting site, Aviary.
B	I	R	T	H	M	A	R	K	An unusual mark or blemish on the skin, Nevus.
B	I	S	H	O	P	R	I	C	Diocese, Bishop's residence, Area administered by a bishop.
B	I	S	M	I	L	L	A	H	A Muslim invocation.
B	I	S	U	L	C	A	T	E	Cleft or cloven in referring to a hoof.
B	L	A	C	K	B	A	L	L	Used for casting an adverse vote, Ostracize, Boycott, Veto, Blacklist, Exclude.
B	L	A	C	K	B	I	R	D	Various birds where the males are black.
B	L	A	C	K	B	U	C	K	Sable antelope.
B	L	A	C	K	D	A	M	P	Mine gas composed partly of carbon dioxide.
B	L	A	C	K	D	U	C	K	Common variety of duck with dark plumage.
B	L	A	C	K	F	A	C	E	A sheep with a black face, Make-up for minstrels.
B	L	A	C	K	F	I	S	H	Female salmon, Black sea bass.
B	L	A	C	K	F	O	O	T	A group of Indian tribes.
B	L	A	C	K	H	E	A	D	Pimple caused by dirt in the pore, Comedo.
B	L	A	C	K	J	A	C	K	Tar-coated leather vessel for beer or ale, A small weapon of leather-enclosed lead.

1	2	3	4	5	6	7	8	9	
B	L	A	C	K	M	A	I	L	To extort money or compel action by threats of exposure.
B	L	A	C	K	N	E	S	S	The state of being black.
B	L	A	M	E	L	E	S	S	Irreproachaqble, Innocent, Faultless, Guiltless, Exemplary, Pure, Righteous.
B	L	A	N	D	N	E	S	S	Mildness, Gentleness, Smoothness, Softness, Insipidness.
B	L	A	S	P	H	E	M	E	Revile, Abuse, Curse, Swear.
B	L	A	S	P	H	E	M	Y	Cussing, Profanity, Cursing, Swearing, Vituperation, Sacrilege, Violation, Abuse.
B	L	E	A	K	N	E	S	S	Harshness, Gloom, Oppressiveness, Depressive, Lifeless, Cheerless.
B	L	E	M	I	S	H	E	D	Sullied, Tainted, Stained, Impaired, Spoiled, Flawed, Unsound, Damaged.
B	L	E	S	S	E	D	L	Y	In a hallowed fashion.
B	L	I	N	D	N	E	S	S	Deprived of sight.
B	L	I	N	D	W	O	R	M	Small burrowing limbless lizard.
B	L	O	C	K	H	E	A	D	Dunce, Dolt, Stupid person.
B	L	O	O	D	B	A	N	K	Storage place for blood or plasma.
B	L	O	O	D	C	E	L	L	Hemocyte, Any cell present in blood.
B	L	O	O	D	H	E	A	T	The normal temperature of the human body.
B	L	O	O	D	L	E	S	S	Lacking blood, Lifeless, Blanched, Pallid, Anaemic, Unfeeling.
B	L	O	O	D	L	I	N	E	Pedigree, Record of ancestry.
B	L	O	O	D	R	O	O	T	Plant having a red root and used for medicinal purposes.
B	L	O	O	D	S	H	E	D	Massacre, Carnage, Slaughter.
B	L	U	E	B	E	R	R	Y	Sweet edible darkish berry.
B	L	U	E	B	L	O	O	D	Imagined colour of blood of nobles and aristocrats.
B	L	U	E	G	R	A	S	S	Sedge grass being bluish green.
B	L	U	N	D	E	R	E	R	Bungler, Muddler.
B	L	U	S	T	E	R	E	R	Bully, Braggart, Boaster.
B	O	A	T	S	W	A	I	N	Petty officer of the Merchant Navy.
B	O	L	S	H	E	V	I	K	Member of the Russian Communist Party.
B	O	M	B	A	S	T	I	C	Rhetorical, Euphuistic, Flowery, Sonorous, Declamatory.
B	O	O	K	I	S	H	L	Y	In a scholastic manner.
B	O	O	K	M	A	K	E	R	One that receives and pays bets.
B	O	O	K	S	T	A	L	L	A stall where books and magazines are sold.
B	O	O	M	E	R	A	N	G	An Australian throwing weapon which returns to the point from which it is thrown.
B	O	O	M	S	L	A	N	G	A large venomous tree snake of Southern Africa.
B	O	O	N	D	O	C	K	S	Jungle, Dense brush.
B	O	O	R	I	S	H	L	Y	Rudely, Clumsily, Coarsely, Vulgarly.
B	O	O	T	B	L	A	C	K	One who cleans boots and shoes.
B	O	T	A	N	I	C	A	L	Relating to plants, Horticultural.
B	O	U	L	E	V	A	R	D	A wide tree-lined street often restricted for the use of pedestrians.
B	O	U	N	D	L	E	S	S	Vast, Without restriction, Endless, Indefinite, Unbounded, Unlimited, Immeasurable.
B	O	U	N	T	E	O	U	S	Bountiful, Generous, Handsome, Munificent, Free, Liberal, Plentiful, Ample.
B	O	U	N	T	I	F	U	L	Generous, Copious, Abundant, Munificent, Liberal, Bounteous, Plentiful.
B	O	U	R	G	E	O	I	S	Member of middle class usually a shopkeeper.
B	O	W	L	E	G	G	E	D	Legs bowed outwards.
B	R	A	C	T	E	A	T	E	Ancient clothing decoration of gold or silver metal plate, Very thin silver coin.
B	R	A	I	N	W	A	S	H	Persuasion by intensive propaganda.
B	R	A	N	C	H	I	N	G	Diverging, Enlarging, Furcating, Forking, Sectioning.
B	R	A	N	D	L	I	N	G	Small yellowish earthworm. A young salmon.
B	R	A	S	S	E	R	I	E	A restaurant that sells food and beer.
B	R	A	S	S	I	E	R	E	An undergarment for supporting the breasts.
B	R	E	A	C	H	I	N	G	Breaking, violating, Opening, Rupturing, Boring, Penetrating, Infringing.
B	R	E	A	D	L	I	N	E	A queue of people needing charity food.
B	R	E	A	K	A	B	L	E	Capable of being broken.
B	R	E	A	K	D	O	W	N	Collapse, Disintegration. Smash, Wreck Analysis, Dissection, Resolution.
B	R	E	A	K	F	A	S	T	The first meal eaten in the day.
B	R	E	A	K	N	E	C	K	Fast, Expeditious, Fleet, Hasty, Quick, Rapid, Swift.
B	R	E	A	T	H	I	N	G	Inhaling and exhaling.
B	R	E	E	C	H	I	N	G	Part of a harness.
B	R	I	C	A	B	R	A	C	Miscellaneous collection of ornaments or curios.
B	R	I	E	F	L	E	S	S	A lawyer having no clients.
B	R	I	E	F	N	E	S	S	The state of being brief.
B	R	I	G	A	D	I	E	R	An army officer in command of a brigade.
B	R	I	L	L	I	A	N	T	Bright, Beaming, Incandescent, Luminous, Radiant, Intelligent, Clever.
B	R	I	O	L	E	T	T	E	A pear-shaped gem.
B	R	I	S	T	L	I	N	G	Standing erect, Adopting an aggressive manner, Ruffling.
B	R	I	T	I	S	H	E	R	A person from Britain.
B	R	O	A	C	H	I	N	G	Piercing, Opening, Enlarging, Tapping, Presenting, Announcing, Introducing.
B	R	O	A	D	C	A	S	T	Scatter, Sowing, Spreading, Sending out by radio or television.
B	R	O	A	D	S	I	D	E	Barrage, Bombardment, Cannonade, Fusillade, Hail, Salvo, Volley, Storm.

1	2	3	4	5	6	7	8	9	Definition
B	R	O	K	E	R	A	G	E	Commission charged by a broker for his services.
B	R	O	M	E	L	I	A	D	Tropical plants that have spiny leaves and include the pineapple.
B	R	O	O	D	M	A	R	E	A mare kept for breeding.
B	R	O	O	K	L	I	M	E	Aquatic plants.
B	R	O	T	H	E	R	L	Y	Affectionate, Kind, Cherishing.
B	R	U	S	H	W	O	O	D	A thicket, Collection of small broken branches.
B	R	U	T	A	L	I	T	Y	Cruelly, Coarsely, Bestial course of action.
B	R	U	T	I	S	H	L	Y	In a brutish manner.
B	U	C	C	A	N	E	E	R	Pirate, Adventurer.
B	U	C	E	P	H	A	L	A	A genus of duck.
B	U	C	K	B	R	U	S	H	A shrubby-type plant.
B	U	C	K	W	H	E	A	T	Cereal plant.
B	U	D	G	E	T	A	R	Y	Involving a budget.
B	U	L	I	M	I	D	A	E	Family of snails.
B	U	L	K	I	N	E	S	S	The state of being bulky.
B	U	L	L	F	I	G	H	T	Entertainment involving a fight with a bull.
B	U	M	B	L	E	B	E	E	A large hairy social bee.
B	U	M	P	T	I	O	U	S	Conceited, Self-assertive, Obtrusive, Aggressive, Arrogant.
B	U	R	L	E	S	Q	U	E	Slightly vulgar type of musical entertainment.
B	U	R	N	S	I	D	E	S	Side whiskers.
B	U	R	R	O	W	I	N	G	Tunnelling, Digging, Nestling, Snuggling, Delving, Concealing.
B	U	S	H	W	H	A	C	K	Ambush, To clear a path.
B	U	T	A	D	I	E	N	E	A gaseous diolefin used in making synthetic rubber.
B	U	T	C	H	E	R	L	Y	Savage, Clumsy, Bloody, Unskilful.
B	U	T	T	E	R	C	U	P	A plant of the Ranunculus family with bright yellow flowers.
B	U	T	T	E	R	F	L	Y	Slender-bodied insect with large broad wings.
B	U	T	T	E	R	N	U	T	Sweet-flavoured edible nut.
B	U	X	O	M	N	E	S	S	Plumpness, Comeliness.
B	Y	Z	A	N	T	I	N	E	Rich adornment, Complex, Intricate, Elaborate, Involved.

C

1	2	3	4	5	6	7	8	9	Definition
C	A	B	A	L	L	E	R	O	Knight, Cavelier, Horseman.
C	A	B	L	E	G	R	A	M	Telegraph message sent by submarine cable.
C	A	B	R	I	O	L	E	T	A light one-horse carriage.
C	A	C	O	D	E	M	O	N	Evil spirit, Devil, Demon.
C	A	C	O	E	T	H	E	S	Mania, Itch, Uncontrollable desire.
C	A	C	O	M	I	X	L	E	A carnivorous mammal related to the racoon.
C	A	C	O	P	H	O	N	Y	Discord, Croaking, Dissonance, Harsh sound.
C	A	C	T	A	C	E	A	E	Cactus.
C	A	E	S	A	R	E	A	N	Childbirth by abdominal surgery which is ascribed to the birth of Julius Caesar.
C	A	F	E	T	E	R	I	A	Self-service restaurant.
C	A	I	N	O	Z	O	I	C	A period of geological history.
C	A	I	R	N	G	O	R	M	Smoky-brown crystalline quartz found in Scotland.
C	A	L	A	M	A	N	C	O	Fabric of satin weave.
C	A	L	A	N	D	R	I	A	A container of vertical tubes for core of nuclear reactor.
C	A	L	C	A	R	A	T	E	Having spurs.
C	A	L	C	I	C	O	L	E	A plant that grows mostly in limestone soil.
C	A	L	C	I	M	I	N	E	A plaster wash made from whiting and clear glue.
C	A	L	C	U	L	A	T	E	Estimate, Interpret, Reckon, Compute, Judge, Figure, Assess, Weigh.
C	A	L	C	U	L	O	U	S	Having gravel or stone.
C	A	L	E	N	D	U	L	A	Genus of plants of the marigold family.
C	A	L	E	N	T	U	R	E	A tropical fever thought to be caused by heat, Passion, Ardour, Enthusiasm, Zeal.
C	A	L	I	B	O	G	U	S	A drink of rum, molasses and spruce beer.
C	A	L	I	B	R	A	T	E	Graduating measurements, Correcting irregularities.
C	A	L	L	O	S	I	T	Y	Thickening of the skin or tissue, Unfeeling, Emotionless.
C	A	L	O	P	O	G	O	N	Genus of small American bulbous orchid.
C	A	L	O	R	I	F	I	C	Relating to heat or calories.
C	A	L	V	I	N	I	S	M	The doctrines of John Calvin.
C	A	L	V	I	T	I	E	S	Baldness.
C	A	L	Y	C	U	L	U	S	Cup-shaped.
C	A	M	E	L	I	D	A	E	Family of ruminant mammals, Camels, Llamas.
C	A	M	E	R	A	M	A	N	One that operates a camera, News photographer.
C	A	M	P	A	N	I	L	E	Bell tower, Belfry.
C	A	M	P	A	N	U	L	A	Large genus of herbs with bell-shaped flowers, Canterbury bell.
C	A	N	D	I	D	A	T	E	Applicant, Aspirant, Seeker, Campaigner.

1	2	3	4	5	6	7	8	9	
C	A	N	D	L	E	M	A	S	Roman Catholic Church celebratory feast.
C	A	N	D	L	E	N	U	T	Oily seed of a tropical nut.
C	A	N	E	S	C	E	N	T	Turning white or greyish.
C	A	N	K	E	R	O	U	S	Ulcerous, Corruption, Infectious, Cancerous, Malignant.
C	A	N	N	E	L	U	R	E	Groove or fluting.
C	A	N	O	N	I	C	A	L	Sanctioned, Authoritative, Orthodox, Standard, Normal.
C	A	N	T	A	B	I	L	E	Musical direction-smooth flowing style.
C	A	N	T	A	L	O	U	P	Musk melon.
C	A	N	T	E	L	O	P	E	Same as CANTALOUP.
C	A	N	T	O	N	E	S	E	Inhabitant and language of Canton, China.
C	A	N	V	A	S	S	E	R	Solicitor, Campaign worker, Door to door salesman.
C	A	P	A	C	I	O	U	S	Ample, Large, Copious, Inclusive, Commodious, Wide, Expansive, Abundant.
C	A	P	A	C	I	T	O	R	Condenser.
C	A	P	A	R	I	S	O	N	Ornamental covering for a horse, Decoration, Adornment.
C	A	P	I	L	L	A	R	Y	Fine, Slender, Minute, Very thin.
C	A	P	I	T	U	L	A	R	Passage from the Bible, Enlarged tip of plant or tissue.
C	A	P	I	T	U	L	U	M	Same as CAPITULAR.
C	A	P	R	I	C	O	R	N	Sign of the Zodiac.
C	A	P	T	I	V	A	T	E	Attract, Charm, Influence, Bewitch, Fascinate, Enthrall, Mesmerize, Magnetize.
C	A	R	B	O	N	A	T	E	Impregnate with carbon dioxide, Aerate.
C	A	R	B	O	N	I	T	E	A blasting explosive, Natural coke.
C	A	R	B	O	N	I	Z	E	To convert into carbon.
C	A	R	B	U	N	C	L	E	A large painful skin eruption, discharging pus, Abcess, Boil.
C	A	R	C	I	N	O	I	D	Benign but potentially malignant stomach tumour.
C	A	R	C	I	N	O	M	A	A malignant tumour.
C	A	R	E	F	U	L	L	Y	Cautiously, Considerately, Discreetly, Warily, Prudently, Scrupulously, Accurately.
C	A	R	E	T	A	K	E	R	One in charge of a building, estate or farm.
C	A	R	M	E	L	I	T	E	Member of a Roman Catholic order, White Friar.
C	A	R	N	A	L	I	T	Y	Sensuality, Worldliness, Animality, Sexuality.
C	A	R	N	A	T	I	O	N	Genus of the Clove-pink.
C	A	R	N	E	L	I	A	N	A hard semi-precious stone of reddish colour often used for seals.
C	A	R	N	I	T	I	N	E	White betaine found in muscle tissue.
C	A	R	N	I	V	O	R	A	Order of flesh-eating mammals.
C	A	R	N	I	V	O	R	E	Same as CARNIVORA.
C	A	R	P	E	N	T	E	R	One who works with wood.
C	A	R	P	O	L	O	G	Y	Botanical study of fruits and seeds.
C	A	R	R	A	G	E	E	N	Dark purple seaweed.
C	A	R	R	A	P	A	T	O	South American ticks some known as disease carriers.
C	A	R	R	O	N	A	D	E	An obsolete short light iron cannon used on ships.
C	A	R	R	O	U	S	E	L	A tournament of horsemen, Musical ride, Merry-go-round.
C	A	R	R	Y	T	A	L	E	Gossip.
C	A	R	T	E	L	I	Z	E	To form a cartel.
C	A	R	T	I	L	A	G	E	Elastic tissue which forms into the skeleton, Gristle.
C	A	R	T	O	U	C	H	E	Ornamental frame, Oval shield for armorial bearing.
C	A	R	T	R	I	D	G	E	A tube of metal or paper containing a charge of explosive, Ammunition, Roll of film.
C	A	R	T	U	L	A	R	Y	Register of charters and title deeds.
C	A	R	T	W	H	E	E	L	Wheel of a cart, Handspring with arms and legs extended, Wide brimmed hat.
C	A	R	Y	I	N	I	T	E	Mineral of rare calcium manganese arsenate.
C	A	R	Y	O	P	S	I	S	One-seeded fruit, Barley, Maize, Wheat.
C	A	S	S	A	R	E	E	P	Flavouring agent from boiled cassava juice.
C	A	S	S	E	R	O	L	E	A covered dish for cooking and serving food.
C	A	S	S	O	W	A	R	Y	Large flightless bird related to the emu.
C	A	S	T	A	N	E	A	N	Belonging to the chestnut family.
C	A	S	T	E	L	L	A	N	Governor or warden of a castle.
C	A	S	T	I	G	A	T	E	Punish, Chasten, Discipline, Correct, Chastise, Lambaste, Scathe, Venalize.
C	A	S	U	A	R	I	N	A	Genus of trees and shrubs used for ornamental hedges.
C	A	S	U	I	S	T	R	Y	Study of doubtful questions of duty or conduct.
C	A	T	A	C	L	Y	S	M	Deluge, Catastrophe, Disaster, Calamity, Torrent, Tragedy, Misadventure.
C	A	T	A	L	E	P	S	Y	Disease associated with a seizure or trance.
C	A	T	A	L	O	G	U	E	List, Register, Pamphlet, Schedule, Programme, Roster, Inventory, Syllabus.
C	A	T	A	L	Y	S	I	S	Reaction of two forces from action of a separate unaffected agent.
C	A	T	A	M	A	R	A	N	A boat with twin hulls.
C	A	T	A	M	O	U	N	T	Lynx, Cougar.
C	A	T	A	P	L	A	S	M	Poultice.
C	A	T	A	R	R	H	A	L	Relating to inflammation and congestion of mucous membranes.
C	A	T	C	H	M	E	N	T	Action or area for catching water.
C	A	T	C	H	W	E	E	D	A plant with hooked bristles on the stem.

1	2	3	4	5	6	7	8	9	
C	A	T	C	H	W	O	R	D	Slogan, Byword, Phrase, Maxim, Motto, Guideword.
C	A	T	E	C	H	I	S	M	Instruction given by questions and answers.
C	A	T	E	C	H	I	Z	E	Question, Examine, Interrogate, Query, Ask, Inquire.
C	A	T	E	R	W	A	U	L	Harsh noise, Bicker, Scrap, Squalling.
C	A	T	H	A	R	S	I	S	Cleansing, Purgation, Purification, Expurgation.
C	A	T	H	A	R	T	I	C	Purging, Relieving, Purifying.
C	A	T	H	E	D	R	A	L	A bishop's church, Official, Authorative.
C	A	T	L	I	N	I	T	E	Red clay used by Indians to make pipes.
C	A	T	O	P	T	R	I	C	Mirrors and/or reflective surfaces.
C	A	T	T	L	E	M	A	N	A rancher who raises beef cattle.
C	A	U	C	A	S	I	A	N	Member of the white-skinned group.
C	A	U	S	A	T	I	O	N	The act by which an effect is produced, Relation of cause and effect.
C	A	U	S	A	T	I	V	E	Operating as a cause or agent.
C	A	U	S	E	L	E	S	S	Inexplicable, Unjustified, Fortuitous.
C	A	U	T	E	R	I	Z	E	Burn, Sear, Deaden.
C	A	V	A	L	C	A	D	E	Procession, Series.
C	A	V	E	R	N	O	U	S	Deep, Vast, Commodious, Huge, Having many caverns.
C	E	A	S	E	L	E	S	S	Continual, Uninterrupted, Interminable, Perpetual, Constant, Endless, Everlasting.
C	E	L	A	N	D	I	N	E	A perennial herb with bright yellow flowers.
C	E	L	E	B	R	A	N	T	Officiating priest, Participant in an exuberant party.
C	E	L	E	B	R	A	T	E	Commemorate, Observe, Solemnize, Keep, Laud, Praise, Eulogize, Honour.
C	E	L	E	B	R	I	T	Y	Hero, Notability, Superstar, Personage, Fame, Renown, Repute, Cynosure.
C	E	L	E	S	T	I	A	L	Heavenly, Trascendental, Unearthly, Olympian, Blessed, Elysian, Empyreal.
C	E	L	L	U	L	O	I	D	Tough highly flammable thermoplastic.
C	E	L	L	U	L	O	S	E	Fibrous carbohydrate.
C	E	N	S	O	R	I	A	L	Acting as a censor.
C	E	N	T	E	N	A	R	Y	A span of one hundred years.
C	E	N	T	E	R	I	N	G	Placing at a centre position, Concentrating.
C	E	N	T	I	G	R	A	M	One hundreth part of a gram.
C	E	N	T	I	P	E	D	E	An elongated arthropod having many pairs of legs.
C	E	N	T	R	I	O	L	E	Minute body forming the centre of a centrosome.
C	E	N	T	R	O	T	U	S	A common genus of treehoppers.
C	E	N	T	U	R	I	A	L	Relating to a hundred years.
C	E	N	T	U	R	I	O	N	An officer commanding a hundred men.
C	E	R	A	C	E	O	U	S	Relalting to wax, wax-like.
C	E	R	A	S	T	I	U	M	A large genus of low herbs, Chickweed.
C	E	R	A	T	I	T	I	S	Genus of flies, Mediterranean fruit fly.
C	E	R	A	T	O	D	U	S	Genus of dipnoan fishes, Australian lung fish.
C	E	R	E	B	R	A	T	E	Think, To use the mind.
C	E	R	E	C	L	O	T	H	Impregnated cloth used as a winding sheet.
C	E	R	T	A	I	N	L	Y	Infallibly, Unquestionably, Without fail, COnfidently, Admittedly.
C	E	R	T	A	I	N	T	Y	Beyond doubt, Surety, Assurance, Certitude, Faith, Credence, Belief, Positiveness.
C	E	R	T	I	T	U	D	E	Assurance, Conviction, Confidence, Sureness, Certainty, Conviction, Accuracy.
C	E	R	U	S	S	I	T	E	Native lead carbonate.
C	E	S	S	A	T	I	O	N	Stop, Conclusion, Close, End, Finish, Termination, Pause.
C	E	Y	L	O	N	E	S	E	Characteristic of Ceylon.
C	H	A	E	R	O	P	U	S	Genus of marsupial mammals, Pig-footed bandicoots.
C	H	A	F	F	I	N	C	H	A common finch often kept as a cage bird.
C	H	A	I	N	M	A	I	L	Flexible armour.
C	H	A	L	L	E	N	G	E	Accuse, Require, Demand, Question, Examine, Impugn, Stimulate, Excite.
C	H	A	M	E	L	E	O	N	Slow-moving lizard with an elastic extensible tongue.
C	H	A	M	P	A	G	N	E	White sparkling wine.
C	H	A	M	P	L	E	V	E	Metal ornamented with inlaid enamel.
C	H	A	N	C	R	O	I	D	A venereal sore.
C	H	A	N	T	E	U	S	E	A female singing entertainer.
C	H	A	P	A	R	R	A	L	Dense thicket of shrubs, Tangled brushwood.
C	H	A	P	E	R	O	N	E	Escort, Supervise, Accompany, Companion, Survey, Convoy, Guide, Supervise.
C	H	A	R	A	C	T	E	R	Mark, Symbol, Cipher, Device, Monogram, Feature, Point, Disposition.
C	H	A	R	I	V	A	R	I	Medley, Hodgepodge, Confusion of noises.
C	H	A	R	L	A	T	A	N	Quack, Mountebank, Imposter, Sham, Fraud, Pretender, Unscrupulous.
C	H	A	R	M	E	U	S	E	Fine semilustrous crepe fabric.
C	H	A	R	W	O	M	A	N	A cleaning woman.
C	H	A	S	T	E	N	E	D	Disciplined, Corrected, Restrained, Tempered, Humbled, Subdued, Punished.
C	H	A	S	T	I	S	E	D	Reproved, Scolded, Rebuked, Castigated, Censured, Thrashed, Beaten, Caned.
C	H	A	T	T	E	R	E	R	Talkative person, One that prattles.
C	H	A	U	F	F	E	U	R	Employee who drives a private car.
C	H	E	A	P	N	E	S	S	Small expense, State of being inexpensive.

1	2	3	4	5	6	7	8	9	Clue
C	H	E	C	K	E	R	E	D	Marked into squares.
C	H	E	C	K	M	A	T	E	To capture a king in the game of chess.
C	H	E	E	R	L	E	S	S	Bleak, Dismal, Dispiriting, Gloomy, Dull, Miserable.
C	H	E	L	I	C	E	R	A	Front antennae of spiders and scorpions.
C	H	E	L	I	F	O	R	M	Like a pincer.
C	H	E	R	I	S	H	E	D	Treasured, Prized, Esteemed, Appreciated, Revered, Venerated, Nurtured, Conserved.
C	H	E	R	N	O	Z	E	M	Deep rich dark-coloured soil.
C	H	I	C	A	N	E	R	Y	Deception, Misrepresentation, Conniving, Dishonesty, Fraud, Trickery, Machination.
C	H	I	C	K	W	E	E	D	Low growing small leaved plants enjoyed by birds.
C	H	I	E	F	T	A	I	N	Chief, Ruler, Captain, Leader, Master, Headman.
C	H	I	H	U	A	H	U	A	Small Mexican smooth-coated dog.
C	H	I	L	B	L	A	I	N	Inflammatory swelling on extremities often caused by inclement weather.
C	H	I	L	D	L	E	S	S	Having no children.
C	H	I	N	K	A	P	I	N	Dwarf chestnut with a sweet edible nut.
C	H	I	R	O	P	O	D	Y	Care and treatment of feet.
C	H	L	O	R	O	S	I	S	Iron-deficiency anaemia in young girls.
C	H	O	C	O	L	A	T	E	Sweetmeat or drink made from processed cacao seeds.
C	H	O	R	A	L	I	S	T	One who sings in the chorus.
C	H	O	R	I	S	T	E	R	Singer in a church choir.
C	H	O	R	O	L	O	G	Y	Study of geographical features, flora and fauna.
C	H	R	I	S	T	I	A	N	One who has accepted the Christian religious and moral principles.
C	H	R	I	S	T	M	A	S	Celebration of the birth of Christ.
C	H	R	O	M	A	T	I	C	Highly coloured.
C	H	R	O	M	A	T	I	N	Part of a cell nucleus that stains intensely with basic dyes.
C	H	R	O	N	I	C	L	E	Narrative, Account of events arranged in order of time.
C	H	R	Y	S	A	L	I	S	Protective covering, Sheltered state.
C	I	C	A	T	R	I	Z	E	Heal by forming scar tissue.
C	I	C	H	O	R	I	U	M	Perennial herbs, Chicory, Endive.
C	I	G	A	R	E	T	T	E	Finely cut tobacco enclosed in a tube of paper.
C	I	G	U	A	T	E	R	A	Fish poisoning.
C	I	N	E	M	A	T	I	C	Technique of making motion pictures.
C	I	R	C	U	L	A	T	E	Move in a circle or orbit, Spread widely.
C	I	R	R	H	O	S	I	S	A chronic progressive disease of the liver.
C	L	A	M	O	R	O	U	S	Vociferous, Tumultuous, Resonant, Vibrant, Effusive, Demonstrative, Importunate.
C	L	A	M	S	H	E	L	L	Object having moving parts resembling mechanism of a clamshell.
C	L	A	P	B	O	A	R	D	A narrow board used for external weatherboarding.
C	L	A	R	I	F	I	E	D	Purifed, Cleansed, Elucidated, Explained, Illuminated, Defined, Analyzed, Simplified.
C	L	A	S	S	I	C	A	L	Relating to arts and ideals of ancient Greece and Rome.
C	L	A	S	S	L	E	S	S	Belonging to no particular social class.
C	L	A	S	S	R	O	O	M	A room used by children and students to receive instruction from teachers.
C	L	E	A	N	N	E	S	S	Condition of being clean.
C	L	E	A	N	S	I	N	G	Absolving, Eradicating, Washing, Scrubbing, Purging, Wiping, Flushing, Healing.
C	L	E	A	R	A	N	C	E	Removal of obstructions, objections, suspensions or prohibitions.
C	L	E	A	R	N	E	S	S	Clarity, Lucidity, Plainness, Transparence, Distinctness.
C	L	E	N	C	H	I	N	G	Clutching, Holding, Clasping, Grasping, Gripping, Clamping, Clinching, Grappling.
C	L	E	P	S	Y	D	R	A	Water clock.
C	L	E	R	G	Y	M	A	N	Ordained minister.
C	L	E	R	K	S	H	I	P	Position of a clerk.
C	L	I	E	N	T	E	L	E	A body of clients of a profession or business.
C	L	I	N	C	H	I	N	G	Clenching, Settling a dispute, Winning, Grasping, Struggling, Holding, Fastening.
C	L	I	T	E	L	L	U	M	Thickened glandular section of a worm that secretes a material used for a cocoon.
C	L	O	I	S	O	N	N	E	Enamel decoration on metal.
C	L	O	S	E	N	E	S	S	State of being close.
C	L	U	B	B	A	B	L	E	Sociable, Companionable.
C	L	U	T	C	H	I	N	G	Seizing, Gripping, Holding, Grabbing, Clenching, Taking, Grasping, Possessing.
C	O	A	C	H	W	O	R	K	Manufacture of automobile bodies.
C	O	A	G	U	L	A	N	T	Agent to produce coagulation.
C	O	A	G	U	L	A	T	E	Gather together, Clot, Curdle.
C	O	A	L	I	T	I	O	N	Combination, Alliance, Confederation, League, Consolidation, Merging, Union.
C	O	A	S	T	W	I	S	E	Travelling along the coast.
C	O	C	H	I	N	E	A	L	Red colouring obtained from the dried bodies of female insects.
C	O	C	K	A	I	G	N	E	Utopia, Arcadia, Shangri-la, Wonderland, Paradise, Promised land.
C	O	C	K	L	E	B	U	R	Prickly fruit of a plant.
C	O	C	K	R	O	A	C	H	An insect which is a pest in warm climates.
C	O	C	K	S	C	O	M	B	A fleshy appendage on a cockerel's head, A garden plant.
C	O	E	C	I	L	I	A	N	Minute shellfish.
C	O	E	T	E	R	N	A	L	Equally eternal.

1	2	3	4	5	6	7	8	9	
C	O	F	F	E	E	P	O	T	A pot with a spout and handle for preparing coffee.
C	O	G	N	I	T	I	O	N	Knowledge, Perception, Act of knowing.
C	O	I	F	F	E	U	S	E	Female hairdresser.
C	O	I	N	T	R	E	A	U	Liqueur distilled from oranges.
C	O	L	C	H	I	C	U	M	Genus of cormous herbs, Autumn crocus.
C	O	L	I	C	R	O	O	T	Roots of plants reputed to cure colic.
C	O	L	L	A	T	I	O	N	Comparison, Detailed description of book or manuscript, Light meal.
C	O	L	L	E	A	G	U	E	Associate, Compatriot, Partner, Companion, Assistant, Helper, Fellow.
C	O	L	L	E	C	T	E	D	Gathered, Congregated, Mustered, Concluded, Composed, Controlled, Grouped.
C	O	L	L	E	C	T	O	R	One that collects or makes a collection.
C	O	L	L	I	D	I	N	G	Crashing, Bumping, Smashing, Conflicting.
C	O	L	L	I	M	A	T	E	Adjustment of telescope or lenses.
C	O	L	L	I	S	I	O	N	Violent encounter, Clash, Disagreement, Impact, Strike.
C	O	L	L	O	C	A	T	E	Arrange in place.
C	O	L	L	O	D	I	O	N	Coating for wound and photographic films.
C	O	L	L	O	T	Y	P	E	Special process for making prints.
C	O	L	L	U	S	I	O	N	Illegal, secret agreement, Complicity, Connivance.
C	O	L	L	Y	R	I	U	M	Eye lotion.
C	O	L	O	C	Y	N	T	H	Herbaceous vine related to the watermelon and used for a cathartic.
C	O	L	O	N	N	A	D	E	Series of supporting columns placed at regular intervals.
C	O	L	O	P	H	O	N	Y	Rosin.
C	O	L	O	R	I	F	I	C	Relating to colour.
C	O	L	O	U	R	F	U	L	Striking with colour, Vivid colouring.
C	O	L	O	U	R	I	N	G	Applying colour, Complexion, Show, Disguise, Quality, Ornamentation.
C	O	L	O	U	R	I	S	T	Artist or designer.
C	O	L	U	B	R	I	N	E	Similar to a snake.
C	O	L	U	M	B	I	N	E	A blue-flowered plant.
C	O	L	U	M	N	I	S	T	One that writes a newspaper column.
C	O	M	B	A	T	A	N	T	One that engages in combat.
C	O	M	B	A	T	I	V	E	Belligerent, Pugnacious, Militant, Truculent, Warlike, Bellicose, Quarrelsome.
C	O	M	F	I	T	U	R	E	A preserve.
C	O	M	F	O	R	T	E	R	Quilt, Warm bedcover.
C	O	M	I	C	A	L	L	Y	Ridiculously, Foolishly, Funnily.
C	O	M	M	A	N	D	E	R	Chief officer, Senior officer, Officer in charge.
C	O	M	M	E	N	C	E	D	Begun, Entered, Inaugurated, Launched, Opened, Started, Initiated, Originated.
C	O	M	M	E	N	S	A	L	Related to persons eating together at the same table.
C	O	M	M	I	N	U	T	E	Pulverize, Grind, Mince.
C	O	M	M	I	S	S	A	R	Official in the Communist party of the U.S.S.R.
C	O	M	M	I	T	T	A	L	Commitment, Duty, Charge, Obligation, Responsibility, Right, Consignment.
C	O	M	M	I	T	T	E	E	Body of persons appointed to investigate and report on varied items.
C	O	M	M	O	D	I	T	Y	Product, Article of commerce, Profit, Advantage, Expediency, Goods of trade.
C	O	M	M	O	D	O	R	E	Naval officer ranking below rear-admiral but above a captain, Senior yacht officer.
C	O	M	M	O	N	A	G	E	Community land often used for grazing.
C	O	M	M	O	T	I	O	N	Clamour, Tumult, Rebellion, Ferment, Confusion, Turmoil, Uproar, Flurry.
C	O	M	M	U	N	I	O	N	Sharing, Fellowship, Communication, Converse, Exchange, Religion.
C	O	M	M	U	N	I	S	T	A member of a society that believes all possessions are jointly owned.
C	O	M	M	U	N	I	T	Y	State, Unit, Sharing, Society, Public, Agreement, Concord, Fellowship.
C	O	M	P	A	C	T	L	Y	Closely, Densely, Tightly.
C	O	M	P	A	N	I	O	N	Comrade, Chum, Friend, Associate, Comrade, Mate, Crony, Escort.
C	O	M	P	E	T	E	N	T	Experienced, Competent, Able, Qualified, Adept, Finished, Sufficient, Adquate.
C	O	M	P	E	T	I	N	G	Contending, Contesting, Opposing, Disputing, Striving, Emulating, Vieing, Rivalling.
C	O	M	P	L	E	T	E	D	Concluded, Finished, Halted, Terminated, Accomplished, Achieved, Executed.
C	O	M	P	L	I	A	N	T	Yielding, Docile, Tractable, Deferring, Submissive, Complaisant.
C	O	M	P	O	N	E	N	T	Factor, Ingredient, Element, Constituent, Unit.
C	O	M	P	O	S	I	T	E	Compound, Complex, Mixture, Amalgam, Combination, Union.
C	O	M	P	O	S	U	R	E	Calmness, Imperturbability, Self-possession, Coolness, Equanimity, Tranquilness.
C	O	M	P	R	I	S	E	D	Constituted, Composed, Made, Formed of.
C	O	N	C	A	V	I	T	Y	Hollow, Sink, Dip, Sag, Depression, Sinkhole.
C	O	N	C	E	A	L	E	D	Hidden, Buried, Secreted, Disguised, Camouflage, Guarded, Shrouded, Ulterior.
C	O	N	C	E	I	T	E	D	Vain, Narcissistic, Vainglorious.
C	O	N	C	E	I	V	E	D	Understood, Grasped, Produced, Framed, Exhibited, Imagined, Realized, Believed.
C	O	N	C	E	R	N	E	D	Interested, Involved, Implicated, Affected, Considered, Anxious, Uneasy, Troubled.
C	O	N	C	E	R	T	E	D	Planned, Co-operated, United, Harmonized, Contrived, Pre-arranged, Devised.
C	O	N	C	I	E	R	G	E	Doorkeeper, Caretaker, Attendant, Custodian, Porter.
C	O	N	C	I	L	I	A	R	Issued by a council.
C	O	N	C	O	U	R	S	E	Gathering, Meeting, Crowd, Thronging, Junction.
C	O	N	C	U	B	I	N	E	Mistress, Woman who cohabits with a man without being married to him.

1	2	3	4	5	6	7	8	9	
C	O	N	C	U	S	S	E	D	Convulsed, Agitated, Intimidated, Forced, Rocked, Compelled, Coerced.
C	O	N	D	E	M	N	E	D	Doomed, Lost, Damned, Sentenced, Criticized, Censured, Disparaged, Denounced.
C	O	N	D	E	N	S	E	D	Abbreviated, Abridged, Curtailed, Shortened, Summarized, Compressed, Compacted.
C	O	N	D	E	N	S	E	R	Apparatus for condensing gases or vapours.
C	O	N	D	I	M	E	N	T	Seasoning, Something spicy, salty or pungent to add flavour to food.
C	O	N	D	I	T	I	O	N	Stipulation, Provision, Prerequisite, Defect, Obstacle, Term, Reservation, Fitness.
C	O	N	D	U	C	I	V	E	Contribute to an effect.
C	O	N	D	U	C	T	O	R	Guide, Escort, Leader, Director, Something that transmits.
C	O	N	F	E	S	S	O	R	One who makes or hears confession.
C	O	N	F	I	D	A	N	T	Intimate, Acquaintance, Familiar, Friend to whom secrets can be entrusted.
C	O	N	F	I	D	E	N	T	Assured, Sanguine, Presumptuous, Self-assured, Secure, Positive, Sure.
C	O	N	F	I	R	M	E	D	Accustomed, Habitual, Chronic, Ratified, Consented, Authenticated, Corroborated.
C	O	N	F	L	U	E	N	T	Flowing together, Uniting, Combining.
C	O	N	F	O	R	M	A	L	Conserving size of all angles, Keeping to one scale on a map.
C	O	N	F	O	R	M	E	D	Adapted, Adjusted, Reconciled, Harmonized, Agreed, Attuned, Obeyed, Complied.
C	O	N	F	U	S	I	O	N	Havoc, Destruction, Embarrassment, Discomfiture, Unease, Disorder, Clutter.
C	O	N	G	E	A	L	E	D	Solidified, Hardened, Set, Coagulated, Jellified, Chilled, Caked, Dried.
C	O	N	G	E	N	I	A	L	Amicable, Harmonious, Friendly, Compatible, Consistent, Sympathetic, Sociable.
C	O	N	G	E	R	I	E	S	Collection, Mass, Agglomeration.
C	O	N	G	R	U	I	T	Y	Conformity, Suitability, Appropriateness, Consistency, Coherence, Correspondence.
C	O	N	J	O	I	N	E	D	Combined, Connected, Coupled, Linked, United, Co-operated, Associated, Related.
C	O	N	J	U	G	A	T	E	Inflect, Yoke, Couple, Join, United in pairs.
C	O	N	J	U	R	I	N	G	Entreating, Imploring, Inventing, Conspiring, Contriving, Craving, Bewitchment.
C	O	N	N	E	C	T	E	D	Joined, Fastened, Linked, Related, Associated, Yoked, Combined, Coupled.
C	O	N	N	E	X	I	O	N	Alliance, Union, Context, Affliation, Combination, Conjuction, Junction, Partnership.
C	O	N	N	U	B	I	A	L	Matrimonial, Marital, Nuptial, Wedded.
C	O	N	Q	U	E	R	E	D	Defeated, Overpowered, Reduced, Subdued, Subjugated, Vanquished, Overthrown.
C	O	N	Q	U	E	R	O	R	Victor, Master, Subjugator, Vanquisher.
C	O	N	S	C	I	O	U	S	Aware, Knowing, Active, Cognizant, Conversant, Sensible, Observing, Vigilant.
C	O	N	S	C	R	I	P	T	Draft, Conscribe, Compulsory enlisted man.
C	O	N	S	E	N	S	U	S	Agreement, Harmony, Co-operation, Accord, Unanimity.
C	O	N	S	E	N	T	E	D	Agreed, Assented, Acceded, Acquiesced, Allowed, Sanctioned, Permitted, Approved.
C	O	N	S	E	R	V	E	D	Saved, Preserved, Maintained, Supported, Sustained.
C	O	N	S	I	G	N	E	D	Committed, Sent, Addressed, Dispatched, Remitted, Transmitted, Confided.
C	O	N	S	I	S	T	E	D	Resided, Urged, Demanded, Composed, Existed, Reposed, Subsisted, Consorted.
C	O	N	S	O	N	A	N	T	Agreeable, Compatible, Congenial, Congruous, Consistent, Sympathetic.
C	O	N	S	O	R	T	E	D	Comported, Conformed, Corresponded, Dovetailed, Harmonized, Accorded.
C	O	N	S	T	A	B	L	E	Policeman, Gendarme, Officer.
C	O	N	S	T	A	N	C	Y	Attachment, Adherence, Adhesion, Faithfulness, Fidelity, Loyalty, Firmness.
C	O	N	S	T	R	A	I	N	Force, Coerce, Compel, Restrain, Check, Curb, Deny, Imprison.
C	O	N	S	T	R	I	C	T	Compress, Concentrate, Contract, Condense, Shrink, Circumscribe, Confine.
C	O	N	S	T	R	U	C	T	Build, Fabricate, Fashion, Forge, Produce, Erect, Raise, Establish.
C	O	N	S	T	R	U	E	D	Explained, Expounded, Interpreted, Explicated, Constructed, Analyzed.
C	O	N	S	U	L	T	E	D	Conferred, Counselled, Cogitated, Considered, Examined, Advised, Discussed.
C	O	N	T	A	C	T	E	D	Reached, Touched, Met.
C	O	N	T	A	G	I	O	N	Contamination, Corruption, Pollution, Taint, Poison, Venom.
C	O	N	T	A	I	N	E	D	Suppressed, Controlled, Checked, Halted, Restrained, Included, Enclosed, Entailed.
C	O	N	T	A	I	N	E	R	Receptacle, Metal compartment for shipping freight.
C	O	N	T	E	N	D	E	R	A participant in a contest.
C	O	N	T	I	N	E	N	T	Moderate, Temperate, Sober, Chaste, Continuous, Restrictive, Connected.
C	O	N	T	I	N	U	E	D	Persisted, Endured, Persevered, Retained, Prolonged, Resumed, Renewed.
C	O	N	T	I	N	U	U	M	Continuity.
C	O	N	T	O	R	T	E	D	Twisted, Convoluted, Distorted, Deformed, Misshapen, Curved, Bent.
C	O	N	T	R	A	L	T	O	Lowest female singing voice.
C	O	N	T	R	A	S	T	Y	Great range between light and shadow in photography.
C	O	N	T	R	I	V	E	D	Devised, Planned, Designed, Invented, Effected, Managed, Schemed, Plotted.
C	O	N	T	U	M	E	L	Y	Rude language, Insult, Aspersion, Humiliation, Affront, Disgrace, Scurrility.
C	O	N	T	U	S	I	O	N	Bruise.
C	O	N	U	N	D	R	U	M	Mystery, Enigma, Mystification, Puzzle, Riddle.
C	O	N	V	E	R	G	E	D	Concentrated, Focused, Met.
C	O	N	V	E	R	S	E	D	Spoke, Associated, Talked, Reversed, Chatted.
C	O	N	V	I	C	T	E	D	Found guilty, Proved, Reputed, Refuted.
C	O	N	V	I	N	C	E	D	Confuted, Overcame, Demonstrated, Proved.
C	O	N	V	I	V	I	A	L	Social, Companionable, Jolly, Vivacious, Merry.
C	O	N	V	U	L	S	E	D	Agitated, Shaken, Violent contractions, Rocked.
C	O	O	P	E	R	A	T	E	Unite, Combine, Concur, League, Coincide.
C	O	P	I	O	U	S	L	Y	Abundantly, Generously, Exuberantly, Richly, Amply.

1	2	3	4	5	6	7	8	9	Clue
C	O	P	R	O	L	I	T	E	Fossil excrement.
C	O	P	Y	R	I	G	H	T	Sole legal right to produce or reproduce a literary, dramatic, musical or artistic work.
C	O	R	A	L	L	I	N	E	Composed of coral.
C	O	R	A	L	L	O	I	D	Having the appearance of coral.
C	O	R	D	G	R	A	S	S	Broad-leaved grass of salty marshes.
C	O	R	D	I	A	L	L	Y	Vigorously, Sincerely, Emphatically.
C	O	R	D	I	F	O	R	M	Heart-shaped.
C	O	R	D	Y	L	I	T	E	A mineral consisting of a carbonate and fluoride.
C	O	R	E	O	P	S	I	S	Genus of herbs with showy flower heads.
C	O	R	M	O	R	A	N	T	Web-footed sea birds used in parts of Asia to catch fish for their owners.
C	O	R	N	C	R	A	K	E	A common short-billed rail.
C	O	R	N	E	L	I	A	N	Hard reddish coloured stone often used for seals.
C	O	R	N	F	L	O	U	R	White finely ground cornmeal.
C	O	R	O	L	L	A	R	Y	Consequential, Resulting, Associated, Supplementary.
C	O	R	P	O	R	A	T	E	Incorporated, Material, Aggregate.
C	O	R	P	O	R	E	A	L	Physical, Bodily, Corporal, Material, Objective, Tangible, Substantial, Palpable.
C	O	R	P	O	S	A	N	T	Saint Elmo's fire.
C	O	R	P	U	L	E	N	T	Obese, Large, Massive, Fat, Gross, Heavy, Portly, Overweight.
C	O	R	R	A	S	I	O	N	Process of erosion by waves, streams or glaciers.
C	O	R	R	E	C	T	L	Y	Properly, Rightly, Decorously, Fittingly, Justly, Decently, Nicely, Properly.
C	O	R	R	E	L	A	T	E	Complement, Parallel, Correspondent, Counterpart, Match, Organize.
C	O	R	R	O	S	I	O	N	Rusting, Wearing away, Alteration by chemical action, Decaying.
C	O	R	R	O	S	I	V	E	Corroding, Weakening, Disintegrating, Sarcastic, Biting.
C	O	R	R	U	G	A	T	E	Wrinkle, Fold, Furrow, Ridged, Grooved, Crease, Ruck.
C	O	R	R	U	P	T	L	Y	Viciously, Perversely, Deviously.
C	O	R	T	I	S	O	N	E	Colourless crystalline steroid hormone prepared from the adrenal glands of animals.
C	O	R	U	S	C	A	T	E	Glitter, Sparkle, Brilliant, Showy, Flash, Glimmer, Glisten, Keen.
C	O	R	V	I	S	I	T	E	A hydrous vanadium oxide.
C	O	S	M	O	G	O	N	Y	Science of astronomy dealing with origin and development of the universe.
C	O	S	M	O	L	O	G	Y	Philosophy of the universe and processes of nature.
C	O	S	M	O	N	A	U	T	Astronaut.
C	O	T	A	N	G	E	N	T	Tangent of complement of given angle.
C	O	T	H	U	R	N	U	S	Thick-soled laced high boot worn by ancient Greek and Roman actors.
C	O	T	I	L	L	I	O	N	An elaborate ballroom dance.
C	O	T	Y	L	E	D	O	N	Large genus of Southern African succulent plants.
C	O	U	N	T	L	E	S	S	Innumerable, Myriad, Many, Uncounted, Numberless, Untold.
C	O	U	R	T	E	S	A	N	Harlot, Demi-mondaine, Whore, Prostitute.
C	O	U	R	T	S	H	I	P	Courtesy, Courtliness, Wooing, Solicitation, Enticement.
C	O	U	R	T	Y	A	R	D	Unroofed enclosure attached to a building.
C	O	V	E	R	T	U	R	E	Shelter, Protection, Disguise.
C	O	W	A	R	D	I	C	E	Ignoble fear, Faint-heartedness, Timidity, Lack of courage.
C	R	A	B	A	P	P	L	E	A small wild sour apple.
C	R	A	C	K	L	I	N	G	Petillant, Small sharp cracks, Crisp fried fat.
C	R	A	C	K	S	M	A	N	Burglar, House-breaker, Safecracker.
C	R	A	F	T	S	M	A	N	Artisan, Skilled worker.
C	R	A	N	B	E	R	R	Y	A plant with bright red acid berries.
C	R	A	P	U	L	E	N	T	Suffering from excessive eating and drinking.
C	R	A	S	S	N	E	S	S	Coarseness, Stupidness.
C	R	A	Z	I	N	E	S	S	Madness, Insanity, Foolishness, Absurdity, Silliness, Folly.
C	R	E	D	U	L	O	U	S	Gullible, Unsuspecting, Unwary, Believing, Trustful, Naive, Simple, Inexperienced.
C	R	E	M	A	S	T	E	R	Thin muscle supporting the testicle.
C	R	E	M	A	T	I	O	N	Consuming of a corpse by fire.
C	R	E	M	A	T	O	R	Y	Incinerator, Furnace.
C	R	E	N	A	T	I	O	N	Rounded edge, Scallop.
C	R	E	N	A	T	U	R	E	Notch, Indentation.
C	R	E	P	I	T	A	N	T	Crackling, Rattling.
C	R	E	P	I	T	A	T	E	Crackle, Small sharp explosive sounds.
C	R	E	S	C	E	N	D	O	Swelling in volume of sound, Gradual increase, Growing.
C	R	E	T	I	N	O	U	S	Affected by stunted physical and mental development.
C	R	I	C	K	E	T	E	R	One that plays cricket.
C	R	I	M	I	N	A	T	E	Accuse or charge with a crime.
C	R	I	M	I	N	O	U	S	Criminal, Guilty of a crime.
C	R	I	N	O	L	I	N	E	Full stiff skirt, Hooped skirt, A stiffened fabric for lining.
C	R	I	S	P	N	E	S	S	State of being crisp.
C	R	I	T	E	R	I	O	N	Standard benchmark, Gauge, Measure, Yardstick.
C	R	I	T	I	C	I	S	M	Disapproval, Faultfinding, Objecting, Comment, Review, Examination, Commentary.
C	R	O	C	O	D	I	L	E	Large thick-skinned aquatic reptile.

1	2	3	4	5	6	7	8	9	Clue
C	R	O	Q	U	E	T	T	E	Deep-fried patty of minced meat.
C	R	O	S	S	E	Y	E	D	Having a squint where the eyes turn inward.
C	R	O	S	S	R	O	A	D	A road that crosses a main road, A place of intersection, A crucial point for decision.
C	R	O	S	S	W	I	S	E	Across, Transverse, Thwart, Transveral.
C	R	O	S	S	W	O	R	D	Puzzle of numbered squares for insertion of words to read horizontal and vertical.
C	R	O	T	C	H	E	T	Y	Cantankerous, Waspish, Eccentric, Bad-tempered.
C	R	U	C	I	F	O	R	M	Arranged in a cross, Mark with a cross.
C	R	U	D	E	N	E	S	S	Coarseness, Rudeness, Roughness, Vularity, Graceless, Indecency.
C	R	U	S	A	D	I	N	G	Evangelistic, Striving, Attacking zealously.
C	R	U	S	T	A	C	E	A	Large class of marine animals, Lobsters, Crabs, Shrimps, Barnacles.
C	R	Y	O	S	C	O	P	Y	Study of the freezing points of solutions.
C	R	Y	P	T	O	G	A	M	Class of plant having no flowers, Moss, Ferns, Algae, Lichen.
C	R	Y	P	T	O	N	Y	M	A secret name.
C	U	C	U	L	I	D	A	E	Family of birds, Cuckoos.
C	U	L	I	L	A	W	A	N	Aromatic bark of a tree, Cinnamon.
C	U	L	M	I	N	A	T	E	Climax, Cap, Finish off, Crown, Reach highest point.
C	U	L	T	I	V	A	T	E	Grow, Breed, Propagate, Produce, Raise, Nurse, Cherish, Till.
C	U	N	E	I	F	O	R	M	Wedge-shaped.
C	U	N	N	I	N	G	L	Y	Slyly, Cleverly, Craftily, Artfully.
C	U	P	B	E	A	R	E	R	One who filled the cups with wine.
C	U	P	F	E	R	R	O	N	Colourless crystalline salt used in analysis of metals.
C	U	R	E	T	T	A	G	E	To scrape a cavity for diagnosis or to remove a growth.
C	U	R	I	O	S	I	T	Y	Interest Ingenuity, Piquancy, Prying, Concern, Questioning, Freak, Monstrosity.
C	U	R	L	I	N	E	S	S	State of being curly.
C	U	R	R	A	W	O	N	G	Australian fruit-eating birds.
C	U	R	R	E	N	T	L	Y	Readily, Fluently, Presently, Instantly.
C	U	R	S	O	R	I	A	L	Adapted to running.
C	U	R	S	O	R	I	L	Y	In a hasty manner.
C	U	R	T	I	L	A	G	E	Yard, Courtyard.
C	U	R	V	A	T	U	R	E	State of being curved.
C	U	S	P	I	D	A	T	E	Terminating in a point.
C	U	S	P	I	D	I	N	E	A mineral consisting of a basic silicate of calcium.
C	U	S	T	O	D	I	A	N	Guard, Protector, Keeper, Warder, Curator, Governor, Supervisor, Overseer.
C	U	S	T	O	M	A	R	Y	Usual, Accustomed, Habitual, Routine, Standard, Traditional, Orthodox.
C	U	T	A	N	E	O	U	S	Relating to the skin.
C	Y	B	E	R	N	A	T	E	Automatic control by computer.
C	Y	C	L	O	I	D	A	L	Arranged in circles.
C	Y	C	L	O	R	A	M	A	Pictorial representation on a 360° screen.
C	Y	M	B	I	F	O	R	M	Boat-shaped.
C	Y	N	I	C	A	L	L	Y	In a sneering manner, Sarcastically.
C	Y	S	T	O	T	O	M	Y	Surgical incision of the bladder.
C	Y	T	O	L	Y	S	I	S	Disintegration of cells.
C	Y	T	O	P	L	A	S	M	Protoplasmic content of a cell next to nuclear membrane.

D

1	2	3	4	5	6	7	8	9	Clue
D	A	L	T	O	N	I	S	M	Colour blindness.
D	A	M	A	S	C	E	N	E	Ornamentation with inlay of precious metals.
D	A	M	N	A	T	I	O	N	Condemnation, Sentencing.
D	A	M	N	A	T	O	R	Y	Condemnatory, Damning, Ruinous.
D	A	N	D	E	L	I	O	N	A plant with bright yellow flowers recognised as a weed.
D	A	N	G	E	R	O	U	S	Hazardous, Perilous, Treacherous, Chancy, Unsound, Precarious, Unsafe.
D	A	R	E	D	E	V	I	L	Adventurous, Audacious, Daring, Rash, Foolhardy, Reckless.
D	A	R	W	I	N	I	S	M	The theory of evolution.
D	A	S	H	I	N	G	L	Y	Spiritedly, Gaily, Stylishly, Fashionably, Brightly, Flashily.
D	A	U	N	T	L	E	S	S	Brave, Bold, Courageous, Fearless, Unafraid, Intrepid, Indomitable, Persevering.
D	A	V	E	N	P	O	R	T	A sofa that converts into a bed.
D	E	A	F	E	N	I	N	G	Depriving of hearing, Stunning with noise.
D	E	B	A	T	A	B	L	E	Doubtful, Dubious, Questionably, Uncertain, Problematic, Disputable.
D	E	B	A	U	C	H	E	D	Perverted, Seduced, Debased, Corrupted, Depraved, Tempted, Demoralized.
D	E	B	A	U	C	H	E	E	One given to excessive sexual indulgences.
D	E	B	E	N	T	U	R	E	Special voucher acknowledging service, Evidence of a debt.
D	E	B	U	T	A	N	T	E	One making their first public appearance or beginning a professional career.
D	E	C	A	D	E	N	C	E	Deterioration, Decay, Degeneration, Downfall, Downgrade, Regression, Debasement.
D	E	C	A	L	C	I	F	Y	To remove calcium.
D	E	C	A	L	I	T	R	E	Unit of capacity equal to ten litres.

1	2	3	4	5	6	7	8	9	Definition
D	E	C	A	L	O	G	U	E	Authoritative set of rules.
D	E	C	A	S	T	Y	L	E	Front entrance having ten columns.
D	E	C	E	I	T	F	U	L	Shifty, Dishonest, Lying, Roguish, Artful, Cunning, Sly, Stealthy.
D	E	C	E	I	V	I	N	G	Misleading, Deceptive, Deluding, False, Beguiling, Cheating, Betraying.
D	E	C	E	N	N	I	A	L	Occurring every ten years.
D	E	C	E	N	N	I	U	M	Period of ten years.
D	E	C	E	P	T	I	O	N	Fallacy, Delusion, Subterfuge, Imposture, Fraud, Hoax, Sham, Duplicity.
D	E	C	E	P	T	I	V	E	Deceiving, Misleading, Delusory, False, Plausible, Illusory, Ostensible, Specious.
D	E	C	I	D	E	D	L	Y	Without question or doubt.
D	E	C	I	D	U	O	U	S	To shed or fall off at certain periods, Transitory.
D	E	C	I	L	I	T	R	E	Unit of capacity equal to one tenth of a litre.
D	E	C	I	L	L	I	O	N	Tenth power of a million.
D	E	C	I	M	E	T	R	E	Unit of length equal to one tenth of a metre.
D	E	C	K	C	H	A	I	R	Folding chair of wood sometimes combined with canvas.
D	E	C	L	A	I	M	E	D	Ranted, Raved, Orated, Harangued, Recited.
D	E	C	L	I	N	I	N	G	Decaying, Wasting, Settling, Sinking, Failing, Waning, Deteriorating, Dwindling.
D	E	C	L	I	V	I	T	Y	Leaning, Pitched, Sloped, Tilted, Tipped, Oblique, Inclined, Descending.
D	E	C	L	I	V	O	U	S	Descent, Decline, Dip, Drop, Fall, Gradient, Inclination.
D	E	C	O	M	P	O	S	E	Decay, Separate, Rot, Disintegrate, Analyze.
D	E	C	O	R	A	T	E	D	Embellished, Ornamented, Adorned, Garnished, Furnished, Trimmed, Bemedalled.
D	E	C	O	R	A	T	O	R	One who paints and papers houses and buildings, One who embellishes food.
D	E	C	R	E	A	S	E	D	Lessened, Diminished, Reduced, Dwindled, Reduced, Shrunk, Retrenched.
D	E	C	R	E	M	E	N	T	Decrease, Amount lost by waste.
D	E	C	U	M	B	E	N	T	Recumbent, Lying down.
D	E	C	U	S	S	A	T	E	Intersect, Cross, cut or divide in the form of an "X".
D	E	D	U	C	T	I	O	N	Subtraction, Diminution, Abatement, Discount, Reduction, Decrease, Depreciation.
D	E	D	U	C	T	I	V	E	Derivable, Conjectural, Hypothetical, Reasoned.
D	E	F	A	L	C	A	T	E	Embezzle, Curtail.
D	E	F	E	A	T	I	S	M	Attitude of submissively accepting defeat.
D	E	F	E	A	T	I	S	T	One who accepts defeat without trying to change the circumstances.
D	E	F	E	C	T	I	V	E	Faulty, Flawed, Imperfect, Broken, Damaged, Impaired, Deficient, Incomplete.
D	E	F	E	N	D	A	N	T	Person sued in a court of law, Opponent.
D	E	F	E	N	S	I	V	E	Protective, Shielding.
D	E	F	E	R	E	N	C	E	Homage, Obeisance, Reverence, Submission, Yielding, Complacent, Respect.
D	E	F	I	A	N	T	L	Y	Boldly, Insolently.
D	E	F	I	C	I	E	N	T	Inadequacy, Shortage, Incomplete, Lacking, Marred, Scanty, Short, Scarce.
D	E	F	L	A	T	I	O	N	Lowering, Deflating, Contraction.
D	E	F	L	E	X	I	O	N	Curving, Bending, Turning, Deviation.
D	E	F	O	R	M	I	T	Y	Distortion, Malformation, Misshape, Disfigurement, Damage, Impairment.
D	E	F	R	A	U	D	E	D	Cheated, Tricked, Hoaxed, Foiled, Fleeced, Bilked, Swindled, Circumvented.
D	E	F	R	O	C	K	E	D	Deprived of ecclesiastical status.
D	E	J	E	C	T	I	O	N	Depression, Gloom, Melancholy, Unhappiness, Despair, Desperation, Sadness.
D	E	L	E	G	A	T	E	D	Assigned, Committed, Transferred, Commission, Deputized, Appointed, Ascribed.
D	E	L	I	C	I	O	U	S	Delightful, Enchanting, Luscious, Savoury, Delectable, Scrumptious, Adorable.
D	E	L	I	G	H	T	E	D	Gladdened, Gratified, Pleased, Amused, Attracted, Enraptured, Fascinated.
D	E	L	I	N	E	A	T	E	Portray, Picture, Represent, Design, Sketch, Depict, Describe, Define.
D	E	L	I	R	I	O	U	S	Disordered, Raving, Deranged, Disturbed, Confused, Rambling, Irrational, Crazed.
D	E	L	I	V	E	R	E	D	Rescued, Saved, Dispensed, Provided, Supplied, Transferred, Resigned, Yielded.
D	E	L	I	V	E	R	E	R	Preserver, One that delivers goods or mail.
D	E	M	A	G	O	G	U	E	Agitator, Troublemaker, Instigator, Inciter, Rabble-Rouser.
D	E	M	E	A	N	O	U	R	Deportment, Bearing, Air, Behaviour, Conduct, Mien.
D	E	M	I	S	S	I	O	N	Resignation, Relinquishment, Dismissal, Discharge.
D	E	M	O	C	R	A	C	Y	Government by the people.
D	E	M	U	L	C	E	N	T	Soothing, Softening.
D	E	M	U	R	R	A	G	E	Storage charge, Charge for exceeding loading or unloading time for freight.
D	E	N	I	G	R	A	T	E	Defame, Sully, Belittle, Slander, Malign, Calumniate, Vilify, Libel.
D	E	N	I	T	R	A	T	E	To remove nitric acid or nitrogen oxide.
D	E	N	S	E	N	E	S	S	Density, Stupidity.
D	E	N	T	A	T	I	O	N	State of having teeth, Like a tooth.
D	E	N	T	I	S	T	R	Y	Practice of dental science, Work performed by a dentist.
D	E	N	T	I	T	I	O	N	Teething.
D	E	O	D	O	R	I	Z	E	Neutralize or eliminate an offensive odour, Disinfect.
D	E	P	A	R	T	I	N	G	Going, Quitting, Retiring, Withdrawing, Leaving, Parting, Digressing, Diverging.
D	E	P	A	R	T	U	R	E	Exit, Exodus, Withdrawal, Egression, Retreating, Going, Flight, Farewell.
D	E	P	A	S	T	U	R	E	Graze.
D	E	P	E	N	D	E	N	T	Contingent, Reliant, Conditional, Liable, Subject, Susceptible, Provisional.
D	E	P	L	E	T	I	O	N	Reduction, Debilitation, Exhaustion.

1	2	3	4	5	6	7	8	9	
D	E	P	O	S	I	T	E	D	Banked, Stored, Stowed, Entrusted, Settled, Paid.
D	E	P	O	S	I	T	O	R	A person who deposits money in a bank.
D	E	P	R	A	V	I	T	Y	Immorality, Corruption, Vice, Wickedness.
D	E	P	R	E	C	A	T	E	Object, Disapprove, Frown, Discommend, Derogate, Detract, Bewail, Lament.
D	E	P	R	E	S	S	E	D	Downcast, Dejected, Disconsolate, Dispirited, Woebegone, Melancholy, Deprived.
D	E	P	R	E	S	S	O	R	Appliance that depresses something, Substance to lower blood pressure.
D	E	R	R	I	N	G	E	R	Pocket pistol.
D	E	S	C	E	N	D	E	D	Dismounted, Dropped, Lowered, Stooped, Deteriorated, Declined, Disintegrated.
D	E	S	C	R	I	B	E	D	Represented, Depicted, Interpreted, Portrayed, Rendered, Delineated, Explained.
D	E	S	E	C	R	A	T	E	Ravage, Depredate, Desolate, Despoil, Pillage, Waste, Pillage, Devastate.
D	E	S	E	R	T	I	O	N	Abandonment, Defection, Desolation, Departing, Forsaking, Treachery, Perfidy.
D	E	S	E	R	V	I	N	G	Meriting, Rating, Meritorious, Worthy.
D	E	S	I	C	C	A	T	E	Dry, Dehydrate, Parch, Drain, Exhaust, Fade, Shrivel, Wither.
D	E	S	I	G	N	A	T	E	Name, Christen, Style, Term, Appoint, Nominate, Select, Assign.
D	E	S	I	R	A	B	L	E	Arousing, Desire, Advisable, Expedient.
D	E	S	I	S	T	I	N	G	Stopping, Ceasing, Halting, Quitting, Abstaining, Abandoning, Relinquishing.
D	E	S	P	E	R	A	D	O	Bandit, Convict, Criminal, Outlaw, Lawbreaker.
D	E	S	P	E	R	A	T	E	Baffled, Despairing, Hopeless, Foiled, Frustrated, Acute, Critical, Intense.
D	E	S	P	O	I	L	E	D	Ravaged, Desecrated, Devastated, Pillaged, Wasted, Depredated, Plundered, Robbed.
D	E	S	P	O	T	I	S	M	Arbitrary rule, Tyranny, Autocracy, Dictatorship, Totalitarianism.
D	E	S	P	O	T	I	Z	E	Tyrannize.
D	E	S	T	I	T	U	T	E	Devoid, Empty, Deficient, Depleted, Drained, Indigent, Divested, Penurious.
D	E	S	T	R	O	Y	E	D	Annihilated, Decimated, Demolished, Dissolved, Razed, Pulverized, Ruined.
D	E	S	T	R	O	Y	E	R	Vandal, Wrecker, Defacer, Despoiler, Downfall, Undoing, Bane, Ruination.
D	E	S	U	E	T	U	D	E	Outmoded, Discarded, Abandonment, Disuse, Cessation, Discontrinuance.
D	E	S	U	L	T	O	R	Y	Spasmodic, Disconnected, Haphazard, Erratic, Wavering, Shifting, Random, Aimless.
D	E	T	E	C	T	I	V	E	One employed to solve crimes.
D	E	T	E	N	T	I	O	N	Arrest, Apprehension, Imprisonment, Incarceration, Internment.
D	E	T	E	R	G	E	N	T	Cleansing agent.
D	E	T	E	R	M	I	N	E	Decide, Regulate, Resolve, Establish, Conclude, Discover, Prove, Demarcate.
D	E	T	R	I	M	E	N	T	Disadvantage, Disability, Handicap, Injury, Damage, Mischief, Hurt, Impairment.
D	E	U	T	E	R	I	U	M	Isotope of hydrogen used in nuclear reactions.
D	E	V	A	L	U	A	T	E	Devalue, Reduce value.
D	E	V	A	S	T	A	T	E	Ravage, Overpower, Overcome, Overwhelm, Despoil, Devour, Pillage, Desolate.
D	E	V	E	L	O	P	E	R	Person who develops real estate, Chemical agent for developing photographs.
D	E	V	I	A	T	I	O	N	Deflection, Veering, Divergence, Aberration, Alteration, Change, Variation, Turn.
D	E	V	I	L	M	E	N	T	Roguishness, Waggishness, Mischievousness, Roguery, Wild spirits.
D	E	V	I	O	U	S	L	Y	Erratically, Circuitously, Obcurely, Craftily, Slyly.
D	E	V	I	T	R	I	F	Y	Change from vitreous to a crystalline condition with loss of lustre.
D	E	X	T	E	R	I	T	Y	Adroitness, Deftness, Skill, Sleight, Craft, Expertise, Adeptness, Readiness.
D	E	X	T	E	R	O	U	S	Deft, Skilled, Expert, Clever, Artful, Adroit, Handy, Proficient.
D	I	A	B	L	E	R	I	E	Witchcraft, devilry, dealing with demons.
D	I	A	B	O	L	I	S	M	Satanism, Evil conduct, Devil-worship, Sorcery, Witchcraft.
D	I	A	C	O	N	A	T	E	Office of a deacon.
D	I	A	C	R	I	T	I	C	Distinctive, Characteristic, Diagnostic, Individual, Peculiar.
D	I	A	C	T	I	N	I	C	Ability to transmit actinic rays.
D	I	A	E	R	E	S	I	S	A mark placed over a vowel to indicate special pronunciation.
D	I	A	G	N	O	S	I	S	Identifying a disease from signs and symptoms.
D	I	A	L	E	C	T	I	C	Debate, Logical, Investigation of truth by discussion.
D	I	A	L	O	G	I	S	T	Writer of dialogues.
D	I	A	M	E	T	R	A	L	Relating to the diameter.
D	I	A	P	H	R	A	G	M	Partition separating chest and abdominal cavity, Membrane or thin plate, Partition.
D	I	A	S	T	O	L	I	C	Relating to expanding cavities of the heart.
D	I	C	H	O	T	O	M	Y	Division into two parts, Forking, Bifurcation, Branching.
D	I	C	H	R	O	I	S	M	Surfaces reflecting light of one colour and transmitting light of other colours.
D	I	C	L	I	N	O	U	S	Having stamens and pistils in separate flowers.
D	I	C	T	A	T	I	O	N	Reading aloud to be written down by another, Prescribing, Commanding, Ordering.
D	I	E	T	E	T	I	C	S	Science of nutrition.
D	I	F	F	E	R	E	N	T	Several, Unusual, Special, Various, Diverse, Disparate, Unlike.
D	I	F	F	I	C	U	L	T	Arduous, Puzzling, Obscure, Perverse, Stubborn, Awkward, Hard, Hampering.
D	I	F	F	I	D	E	N	T	Timid, Shy, Doubtful, Distrustful, Strenuous, Toilsome, Bashful, Modest.
D	I	F	F	U	S	I	N	G	Scattering, Broadcasting, Extending, Spreading, Dispersing, Circulating, Strewing.
D	I	F	F	U	S	I	O	N	Dispersion, Spreading, Irradiation.
D	I	G	A	S	T	R	I	C	Pair of muscles for opening the jaw, Having two bellies separated by a median tendon.
D	I	G	E	S	T	I	V	E	Assisting digestion.
D	I	G	I	T	A	L	I	S	Dried leaf of the purple foxglove from which a powerful cardiac stimulant is obtained.
D	I	G	N	I	F	I	E	D	Expressive of dignity.

1	2	3	4	5	6	7	8	9	
D	I	G	N	I	T	A	R	Y	Notable, Eminence, Leader, Notability.
D	I	M	I	D	I	A	T	E	Halved.
D	I	M	I	S	S	O	R	Y	Dismissal, Discharge.
D	I	M	O	R	P	H	I	C	Combining two distinct forms of the same species.
D	I	N	O	T	H	E	R	E	Member of genus of extinct prehistoric elephants.
D	I	O	E	C	I	O	U	S	Having the male reproductive organ in one individual and female in another.
D	I	P	T	E	R	O	U	S	Having two wings.
D	I	R	E	C	T	I	N	G	Addressing, Aiming, Inclining, Pointing, Turning, Commanding, Conducting.
D	I	R	E	C	T	I	O	N	Viewpoint, Angle, Outlook, Management, Administration.
D	I	R	E	C	T	I	V	E	Guidance, Policy, Edict, Decree, Ruling, Memorandum, Memo, Message.
D	I	R	E	C	T	O	R	Y	Rulebook, Classified list.
D	I	R	E	F	U	L	L	Y	Dismally, Ominously.
D	I	R	I	G	I	B	L	E	Steerable airship.
D	I	S	A	B	U	S	E	D	Undeceived, Rid, Disillusioned.
D	I	S	A	F	F	I	R	M	Contradict, Deny, Repudiate, Annul, Reverse.
D	I	S	A	P	P	E	A	R	Vanish, Lost, Invisible, Fade.
D	I	S	A	V	O	W	A	L	Repudiation.
D	I	S	B	E	L	I	E	F	Incredulity, Repudiation, Rejection.
D	I	S	B	U	R	D	E	N	Unburden, Get rid of, Unload, Discharge.
D	I	S	C	H	A	R	G	E	Acquit, Exonerate, Exempt, Unload, Remove, Shoot, Emit, Execute.
D	I	S	C	L	O	S	E	D	Exposed, Divulged, Revealed, Uncovered, Betrayed, Confessed, Unveiled, Opened.
D	I	S	C	O	L	O	U	R	Taint, Defile, Smear, Soil, Stain, Sully, Tarnish, Smut.
D	I	S	C	O	M	F	I	T	Embarrass, Abash, Confound, Confuse, Disconcert, Annoy, Irk, Vex.
D	I	S	C	O	M	M	O	N	Deprive of citizenship.
D	I	S	C	O	U	R	S	E	Conversation, Combat, Account, Narrative, Thesis, Talk, Narrate, Expatiate.
D	I	S	C	O	V	E	R	T	Not under authority or protection.
D	I	S	C	O	V	E	R	Y	Revelation, Disclosure, Investigation, Exposure, Uncovering, Detection, Find.
D	I	S	C	R	E	D	I	T	Disbelieve, Disprove, Expose, Destroy, Disgrace, Dishonour, Ignominy, Infamy.
D	I	S	E	M	B	A	R	K	Land, Go ashore, Leave a ship or plane.
D	I	S	E	M	B	O	D	Y	Separate, Free, Divest.
D	I	S	E	N	G	A	G	E	Release, Free, Liberate, Detach, Extricate, Loosen, Detach, Withdraw.
D	I	S	E	N	T	A	I	L	Free property or estate from entail.
D	I	S	E	N	T	O	M	B	Disinter, Unearth, Exhume.
D	I	S	F	A	V	O	U	R	Dislike, Displeasure, Distaste, Dissatisfaction, Disgrace, Discredit, Dishonour.
D	I	S	F	I	G	U	R	E	Deface, Deform, Mar, Sully.
D	I	S	F	O	R	E	S	T	Remove privileges of forest, Clear of trees.
D	I	S	G	U	I	S	E	D	Cloaked, Masked, Deformed, Concealed, Disfigured.
D	I	S	G	U	S	T	E	D	Nauseated, Sickened, Offended, Outraged, Sickened, Repelled, Outraged, Wearing.
D	I	S	H	O	N	E	S	T	Deceitful, Lying, Mendacious, Shifty, Devious, Furtive, False, Corrupt.
D	I	S	H	O	N	O	U	R	Disgrace, Discredit, Infamy, Shame, Ignominy.
D	I	S	I	N	F	E	C	T	Cleanse, Free from infection, Destroy germs.
D	I	S	L	I	K	I	N	G	Aversion, Disfavour, Displeasure, Dissatisfaction, Distaste, Indisposition.
D	I	S	L	O	C	A	T	E	Displace, Shift, Alter, Disarrange, Disturb, Disorder, Disrupt.
D	I	S	L	O	D	G	E	D	Removed, Turned out, Driven out.
D	I	S	M	A	N	T	L	E	Divest, Uncloak, Deprive, Strip, Raze, Annul, Rescind.
D	I	S	M	E	M	B	E	R	Disjoin, Mangle, Mutilate, Separate, Sever, Disassemble, Separate.
D	I	S	M	I	S	S	E	D	Discharged, Fired, Cashiered, Terminated, Displaced, Ejected, Evicted.
D	I	S	O	B	E	Y	E	D	Trangressed, Violated, Refused, Disregarded, Dispersed.
D	I	S	O	B	L	I	G	E	Affront, Offend, Unaccommodating, Incommode, Trouble.
D	I	S	P	A	R	A	G	E	Belittle, Depreciate, Derogate, Abuse, Minimize, Discourage, Demoralize, Dishearten.
D	I	S	P	A	R	I	T	Y	Inequality, Difference, Dissimilarity, Divergence, Unevenness.
D	I	S	P	E	N	S	E	D	Dispersed, Distributed, Gave, Provided, Administered, Handled, Released, Exempted.
D	I	S	P	E	R	S	E	D	Scattered, Distributed, Dissipated, Dispelled, Divided, Disseminated, Circulated.
D	I	S	P	L	A	C	E	D	Banished, Deported, Exiled, Expelled, Relegated, Deposed, Supplanted, Usurped.
D	I	S	P	L	A	Y	E	D	Opened, Disclosed, Exposed, Revealed, Uncovered, Disported, Exhibited, Flaunted.
D	I	S	P	L	E	A	S	E	Offend, Annoy, Arouse, Unpleasant reaction.
D	I	S	P	R	O	V	E	D	Refuted, Disallowed, Rebutted, Confuted, Confounded, Discredited, Exploded.
D	I	S	R	E	G	A	R	D	Apathy, Indifference, Lethargy, Listlessness, Unconcern, Ignoring, Neglecting.
D	I	S	R	E	L	I	S	H	Dislike, Aversion, Disfavour, Dissatisfaction, Distaste, Indisposition.
D	I	S	R	E	P	A	I	R	Dilapidated.
D	I	S	R	U	P	T	E	D	Ruptured, Disordered, Interrupted, Discomposed, Disturbed, Muddled, Unsettled.
D	I	S	S	E	M	B	L	E	Disguise, Camouflage, Cloak, Dissimulate, Conceal.
D	I	S	S	E	N	T	E	R	Heretic, Nonconformist, Separatist.
D	I	S	S	I	D	E	N	T	Non-conformist, Heretic, Sectarian, Unorthodox.
D	I	S	S	I	P	A	T	E	Scatter, Dispel, Disperse, Disintegrate, Waste, Fritter, Squander.
D	I	S	S	O	L	U	T	E	Abandoned, Licentious, Profligate, Reprobate, Wanton, Unprincipled, Wayward.
D	I	S	T	A	N	T	L	Y	Arrogantly, Haughtily, Proudly, Unsociably, Remotely.

1	2	3	4	5	6	7	8	9	Definition
D	I	S	T	E	M	P	E	R	Disorder, Derange, Anarchy, Canine virus disease, Whitewash.
D	I	S	T	E	N	D	E	D	Swollen, Bulging, Dilated, Enlarged, Expanded, Bloated, Extended, Amplified.
D	I	S	T	I	L	L	E	D	Vaporized, Issued, Trickled, Transformed, Concentrated, Infused, Purified, Dissolved.
D	I	S	T	I	L	L	E	R	One who distills alcohol, Apparatus for distilling sea water.
D	I	S	T	O	R	T	E	D	Misrepresented, Falsified, Garbled, Twisted, Perverted, Contorted, Altered, Changed.
D	I	V	E	R	G	I	N	G	Digressing, Departing, Rambling, Straying, Wandering, Swerving, Deviating.
D	I	V	E	R	S	I	F	Y	Vary, Modify, Variegate, Distribute among different kinds.
D	I	V	E	R	S	I	O	N	Deviation, Digression, Relaxation, Amusement, Pastime, Variation, Detour.
D	I	V	I	S	I	B	L	E	Capable of being divided or separated.
D	I	V	U	L	S	I	O	N	Violent wrench, tearing apart.
D	I	Z	Y	G	O	T	I	C	Born of separately fertilized ova, fraternal twins.
D	I	Z	Z	I	N	E	S	S	Giddiness, Unsteadiness, Vertigo.
D	O	C	T	R	I	N	A	L	Something taught and to be believed.
D	O	C	U	M	E	N	T	S	Manuscripts, Title-deeds, Identification papers.
D	O	D	E	C	A	G	O	N	Polygon of twelve sides.
D	O	G	M	A	T	I	Z	E	Arrogantly declare on questionable matters.
D	O	L	I	O	F	O	R	M	Shaped like a barrel.
D	O	M	I	N	A	N	C	E	Ascendancy, Leadership, Preponderance, Supremacy, Preeminent, Sovereignty.
D	O	M	I	N	I	C	A	L	Relating to the Lord's day, Associated with Jesus Christ.
D	O	R	M	I	T	O	R	Y	Large room providing sleeping facilities for many persons.
D	O	S	I	M	E	T	E	R	Device to measure radio activity.
D	O	U	B	L	E	T	O	N	Original holding of two cards in any suit.
D	O	U	B	T	L	E	S	S	Unquestionably, Presumably.
D	O	W	N	G	R	A	D	E	Deterioration, Downhill, Descent, Alter, Status, Demote.
D	O	W	N	R	I	G	H	T	Plain, Outright, Forthright, Absolute, Positive, Complete, Undubitable.
D	R	A	C	O	N	I	A	N	Harsh, Rigorous, Rigid, Strict, Unpermissive, Stringent, Cruel.
D	R	A	M	A	T	I	C	S	Theatricals, Over-emphasised behaviour.
D	R	A	M	A	T	I	S	T	Playwright.
D	R	A	M	A	T	I	Z	E	Adapt for the theatre, In a dramatic manner.
D	R	E	A	M	L	A	N	D	Paradise existing only in the imagination.
D	R	E	A	M	L	I	K	E	Vague, Nebulous, Shadowy.
D	R	E	S	S	C	O	A	T	Coat with tails, Coat of a dress uniform.
D	R	I	B	B	L	I	N	G	Trickling, Issuing, Drooling, Drifting, Frittering, Squandering.
D	R	I	N	K	A	B	L	E	Potable, Safe for drinking.
D	R	I	Z	Z	L	I	N	G	Sprinkling, Spraying.
D	R	O	L	L	N	E	S	S	Humour, Comedy.
D	R	O	M	E	D	A	R	Y	Arabian one-humped camel.
D	R	O	P	P	I	N	G	S	Animal dung.
D	R	U	G	S	T	O	R	E	Pharmacy, Retail shop selling candy, magazines and non-alcoholic refreshments.
D	R	U	N	K	E	N	L	Y	In an inebriated manner.
D	U	B	I	T	A	B	L	E	Doubtful, Ambiguous, Suspect, Uncertain.
D	U	L	C	I	M	O	R	E	A folk instrument in a violin shape.
D	U	M	B	F	O	U	N	D	Amaze, Astonish, Astound, Surprise, Stagger, Flabbergast, Puzzle, Confuse.
D	U	N	G	A	R	E	E	S	Overalls of coarse blue cotton fabric.
D	U	O	D	E	C	I	M	O	Musical interval of a twelfth.
D	U	P	L	I	C	A	T	E	Counterpart, Same, Identical, Tantamount, Indistinguishable, Reproduction.
D	U	P	L	I	C	I	T	Y	Deceit, Cunning, Guile, Perfidiousness, Treachery, Double-dealing, Deception.
D	U	S	T	D	E	V	I	L	Small tropical whirlwind of sand or dust.
D	U	S	T	I	N	E	S	S	In a dusty condition.
D	U	S	T	P	R	O	O	F	Impervious to dust.
D	U	S	T	S	T	O	R	M	Strong winds full of dust or sand.
D	Y	N	A	M	I	C	A	L	Functional, Active, Forceful, Energetic, Vigorous, Strenuous, Vital, Intense.
D	Y	S	E	N	T	E	R	Y	Severe diarrhoea often accompanied by passing of blood.
D	Y	S	P	E	P	S	I	A	Indigestion, Gastric disturbance.
D	Y	S	P	L	A	S	I	A	Abnormal growth or development.
D	Y	S	P	N	O	E	I	C	Difficulty in breathing.
D	Y	S	T	R	O	P	H	Y	Neuromuscular disorder.

E

1	2	3	4	5	6	7	8	9	Definition
E	A	G	E	R	N	E	S	S	Enthusiasm, Ardour, Keenness.
E	A	R	N	E	S	T	L	Y	Seriously, Solemnly, Ardently, Zealously, Sincerely, Diligently.
E	A	R	T	H	W	O	R	M	Hermaphroditic worms that move through the soil.
E	A	S	Y	G	O	I	N	G	Placid, Calm, Indolent, Unhurried, Casual, Poised, Composed, Tranquil.
E	A	V	E	S	D	R	O	P	Overhear, Spy, Listen secretly.

1	2	3	4	5	6	7	8	9	
E	B	U	L	L	I	E	N	T	Exuberant, Brash, Effervescent, Vivacious, Enthusiastic, Bubbling, Boiling.
E	C	C	E	N	T	R	I	C	Off-balance, Unbalanced, Strange, Curious, Erratic, Odd, Peculiar, Idiosyncratic.
E	C	O	L	O	G	I	S	T	Scientist concerned with the interrelationships of the environment.
E	C	O	N	O	M	I	C	S	Considerations of cost and return, Management of finance.
E	C	O	N	O	M	I	Z	E	Save, Conserve, Use sparingly.
E	C	T	O	B	L	A	S	T	A small growth on some grasses, Epiblast.
E	C	T	O	P	L	A	S	M	A vapour supposedly emitting from a spirit medium.
E	C	U	M	E	N	I	S	M	In-depth study of the Christian church.
E	D	E	L	W	E	I	S	S	Small perennial herb growing high in the Alps.
E	D	I	T	O	R	I	A	L	Literary contents of a publication.
E	D	U	C	A	T	I	O	N	Process of educating, Providing with knowledge, Instruction, Training.
E	F	F	E	C	T	U	A	L	Efficient, Impressive, Cogent, Telling, Pleasing, Satisfying, Valid, Operative.
E	F	F	E	C	T	I	V	E	Effective, Actual, Valid, Productive of effect.
E	F	F	I	C	I	E	N	T	Competent, Operant, Capable, Qualified, Adept, Expert, Proficient, Skilled.
E	F	F	L	U	E	N	C	E	Flowing, Emanation, Efflux.
E	F	F	L	U	V	I	U	M	Exhalation, Smell, Exhaust.
E	F	F	L	U	X	I	O	N	Passing of time.
E	F	F	U	L	G	E	N	T	Brilliant, Bright.
E	G	L	A	N	T	I	N	E	Dog rose, Wild briar rose.
E	G	O	M	A	N	I	A	C	One characterized by an arrogant sense of superiority.
E	G	O	T	I	S	T	I	C	Conceited, Boastful, Self-centred, Selfish.
E	G	R	E	G	I	O	U	S	Distinguished, Striking, Notorious, Extreme, Nefarious, Atrocious, Extra-ordinary.
E	I	G	H	T	S	O	M	E	A Scottish reel for eight dancers.
E	J	A	C	U	L	A	T	E	Eject, Blurt out, Dart out, Exclaim.
E	J	E	C	T	M	E	N	T	Dispossession, Eviction.
E	L	A	B	O	R	A	T	E	Complex, Intricate, Complicated, Painstaking, Diligent, Expand, Unfold, Clarify.
E	L	A	S	T	O	M	E	R	Synthetic or plastic elastic rubberlike substance.
E	L	A	T	E	R	I	U	M	Purgative powder made from the juice of the squirting cucumber.
E	L	B	O	W	R	O	O	M	Freedom of movement, An opportunity to manoeuvre.
E	L	E	C	T	R	O	D	E	A conductor used to establish electrical contact.
E	L	E	G	A	N	T	L	Y	Splendidly, Exquisitely, Gracefully.
E	L	E	M	E	N	T	A	L	Fundamental, Primitive, Basic, Earthly, Inherent, Essential, Primordial, Intrinsic.
E	L	E	V	A	T	I	O	N	Height, Altitude, Ascent, Advancement, Promotion, Exaltation, Preference, Boost.
E	L	I	M	I	N	A	T	E	Exclude, Suspend, Dismiss, Eject, Evict, Purge, Liquidate, Remove.
E	L	L	I	P	S	O	I	D	A surface with all plane sections ellipses or circles.
E	L	O	C	U	T	I	O	N	Expressive oral delivery, Eloquence.
E	L	O	N	G	A	T	E	D	Lengthened, Extended, Prolonged, Increased, Protracted, Stretched.
E	L	O	Q	U	E	N	C	E	Rhetoric, Fluent diction, Expressive, Persuasiveness, Fervour, Spirit, Passion.
E	L	S	E	W	H	E	R	E	Some other place.
E	L	U	C	I	D	A	T	E	Explain, Clarify, Explain, Illuminate, Illustrate, Prove, Demonstrate, Enlighten.
E	L	U	T	R	I	A	T	E	To separate by washing.
E	M	A	C	I	A	T	E	D	Gaunt, Cadaverous, Undernourished, Starved, Skinny, Scrawny, Wizened, Underfed.
E	M	A	N	A	T	I	O	N	Efflux, Issuing, Consequence, Outcome, Emission.
E	M	B	A	R	R	A	S	S	Disconcert, Discomfit, Discompose, Confuse, Abash, Agitate, Bother, Perturb.
E	M	B	E	L	L	I	S	H	Adorn, Bedeck, Decorate, Ornament, Trim, Enrich, Embroider, Furbish.
E	M	B	R	A	N	G	L	E	Entangle, Enmesh, Trammel, Confuse.
E	M	B	R	A	S	U	R	E	Recess of a door or window, A fortification for the use of a cannon.
E	M	B	R	O	I	D	E	R	Embellish, Ornament, Trim, Overstate, Exaggerate, Amplify, Elaborate, Dramatize.
E	M	E	R	G	E	N	C	Y	Contingency, Crisis, Juncture, Exigency, Strait, Climax, Difficulty, Extremity.
E	M	O	L	L	I	E	N	T	Softening, Soothing, Mollifying.
E	M	O	L	U	M	E	N	T	Wage, Fee, Hire, Pay, Salary, Stipened.
E	M	O	T	I	O	N	A	L	Sensitive, Susceptible, Sympathetic, Ardent, Fervent, Passionate, Touching.
E	M	P	H	A	S	I	Z	E	Stress, Underline, Feature, Accent, Highlight, Spotlight, Italicize, Mark.
E	M	P	H	Y	S	E	M	A	Lung disease.
E	M	P	I	R	I	C	A	L	Experimental, Factual, Speculative, Unproved, Imagined.
E	M	P	T	I	N	E	S	S	Barrenness, Inanity, Foolishness, Senselessness, Lack, Vacuity, Blankness.
E	M	U	L	A	T	I	N	G	Rivalling, Competing, Challenging, Imitating, Excelling, Equalling.
E	N	A	C	T	M	E	N	T	Passing a law or legislation.
E	N	C	A	U	S	T	I	C	Paint mixed with melted beeswax and fixed by heat after application.
E	N	C	H	A	N	T	E	R	Witch, Magician, Sorcerer, Wizard.
E	N	C	H	I	L	A	D	A	Tortilla rolled up with highly seasoned meat and served with chilli tomato sauce.
E	N	C	H	O	R	I	A	L	Special to a region.
E	N	C	I	R	C	L	E	D	Surrounded, Encompassed, Hemmed, Ringed, Wreathed, Banded.
E	N	C	L	O	S	U	R	E	Court, Close, Courtyard, Quadrangle, Yard, Something enclosed in a package.
E	N	C	O	M	I	A	S	T	One that praises, Panegyrist.
E	N	C	O	M	P	A	S	S	Ring, enclose, surround, devise.
E	N	C	O	U	N	T	E	R	Meet, Confront, Face, Collide, Engage, Find, Espy, Detect.

1	2	3	4	5	6	7	8	9	Definition
E	N	C	O	U	R	A	G	E	Enhearten, Inspire, Support, Animate, Strengthen, Advocate, Reinforce, Incite.
E	N	D	E	A	V	O	U	R	Try, Attempt, Strive, Struggle, Exert, Push, Effort.
E	N	D	O	C	R	I	N	E	Associated with a hormone.
E	N	D	O	S	P	E	R	M	Storage tissue within a seed.
E	N	D	O	W	M	E	N	T	Contribution, Bequest, Gift, Grant, Award, Fund.
E	N	D	U	R	A	N	C	E	Persistence, Stamina, Tolerance, Continuation, Duration, Suffering, Fortitude.
E	N	E	R	G	E	T	I	C	Vigorous, Lusty, Vital, Dynamic, Lusty, Indefatigable, Active, Driving.
E	N	E	R	G	U	M	E	N	Demoniac, Fanatic.
E	N	G	R	A	I	N	E	D	Deep-dyed, Infused.
E	N	G	R	A	V	I	N	G	Etching, Incising, Chasing, Carving, Inscribing, Printing, Imprinting.
E	N	G	R	O	S	S	E	D	Preoccupied, Intent, Absorbed, Immersed, Assiduous, Diligent, Monopolized, Deep.
E	N	I	G	M	A	T	I	C	Cryptic, Mystifying, Puzzling, Inexplicable.
E	N	J	O	Y	M	E	N	T	Pleasure, Diversion, Relish, Amusement, Entertainment, Recreation, Relaxation.
E	N	L	I	G	H	T	E	N	Illuminate, Irradiate, Inform, Instruct, Advise, Acquaint, Direct, Educate.
E	N	R	A	P	T	U	R	E	Entrance, Gratify, Please, Allure, Attract, Captivate, Enthrall, Fascinate.
E	N	S	C	O	N	C	E	D	Established, Fixed, Located, Planted, Seated, Situated, Stationed, Installed.
E	N	S	H	R	I	N	E	D	Preserved, Cherished.
E	N	T	A	N	G	L	E	D	Intertwined, Interwoven, Snarled, Enmeshed, Intricate, Complicated, Confused.
E	N	T	E	R	T	A	I	N	Amuse, divert, create, delight, regale, please, cultivate, invite.
E	N	T	H	Y	M	E	M	E	An argument in which one proposition is understood but not stated.
E	N	T	R	A	N	C	E	D	Enraptured, Enthralled, Fascinated, Captivated.
E	N	U	C	L	E	A	T	E	Clarify, Explain, Remove without surgery.
E	N	U	M	E	R	A	T	E	Count, Specify, Number, Tally, List, Itemize, Inventory, Recite.
E	N	U	N	C	I	A	T	E	Announce, Proclaim, Declare, Utter, Articulate, Pronounce, Intone, Postulate.
E	N	V	I	O	U	S	L	Y	Grudgingly, Longingly, Resentfully.
E	P	A	U	L	E	T	T	E	Ornamental gold-fringed shoulder pad on a uniform.
E	P	H	E	M	E	R	A	L	Temporary, Fleeting, Topical, Intangible, Transient, Fugitive, Momentary, Volatile.
E	P	H	E	M	E	R	I	S	Astronomical almanac.
E	P	H	I	A	L	T	E	S	Nightmare.
E	P	I	C	E	D	I	U	M	Dirge, Elegy, Funeral song.
E	P	I	C	E	N	T	R	E	Centre, Focus of an earthquake or atomic bomb.
E	P	I	C	R	I	T	I	C	Accurate discrimination between small degrees of sensation.
E	P	I	C	U	R	E	A	N	Sensual, Luxurious, Sensuous.
E	P	I	D	E	R	M	I	S	Outer non-vascular layer of skin, Outermost layer of cells in seeds and young stems.
E	P	I	G	R	A	P	H	Y	Epigraphs, Inscriptions, Deciphering of ancient inscriptions.
E	P	I	L	E	P	T	I	C	Convulsive suffering from epilepsy.
E	P	I	P	H	Y	S	I	S	Part of a bone that ossifies separately and becomes a rigid joint.
E	P	I	S	C	O	P	A	L	Suited to a bishop, Anglican.
E	P	I	S	T	A	X	I	S	Nosebleed.
E	P	I	S	T	O	L	E	R	Reader of the Epistle at Holy Communion.
E	P	I	T	O	M	I	Z	E	Embody, Typify, Symbolize, Summarize, Synopsize, Outline, Tabulate, Represent.
E	P	O	N	Y	M	O	U	S	Using a person's name to name something, like a city or tribe.
E	Q	U	I	P	M	E	N	T	Apparatus, Preparation, Machinery, Paraphernalia, Outfit, Tackle, Baggage, Gear.
E	Q	U	I	P	O	I	S	E	Balance, Counterbalance, Poise, Stasis.
E	Q	U	I	T	A	B	L	E	Fair, Impartial, Impersonal, Just, Objective, Level, Stable, Even.
E	Q	U	I	V	O	C	A	L	Obscure, Ambiguous, Uncertain, Vague, Unintelligible, Undecided, Doubtful.
E	Q	U	I	V	O	Q	U	E	Ambiguity, Amphibology, Pun, Double-meaning, Wordplay.
E	R	A	D	I	C	A	T	E	Uproot, Exterminate, Destroy, Annihilate, Abolish, Extinguish, Extirpate, Liquidate.
E	R	E	C	T	N	E	S	S	Uprightness, Upliftment, Alertness.
E	R	G	O	G	R	A	P	H	Device to measure work capacity of muscles.
E	R	R	O	N	E	O	U	S	Mistaken, Inaccurate, Erring, Fallacious, False, Untrue, Amiss, Wrong.
E	R	S	T	W	H	I	L	E	Before, Already, Earlier, Formerly, Once, Previously.
E	R	U	C	I	F	O	R	M	Body of a caterpillar.
E	R	U	D	I	T	I	O	N	Knowledge, Learning, Education, Science, Culture, Pedantry.
E	R	Y	T	H	R	I	T	E	Reddish mineral used to colour glass.
E	S	C	A	L	A	T	O	R	Moving staircase.
E	S	C	A	L	L	O	P	S	Fish or meat served in scallop shells.
E	S	C	A	P	A	B	L	E	Avoidable.
E	S	C	L	A	V	A	G	E	Necklace having several rows of chains, beads and jewels.
E	S	O	P	H	A	G	U	S	Tube leading from the larynx to the stomach.
E	S	P	E	R	A	N	T	O	Artificial international language.
E	S	P	I	O	N	A	G	E	Practice of spying.
E	S	P	L	A	N	A	D	E	Open stretch of paved or grassed ground.
E	S	S	E	N	T	I	A	L	Basic, Fundamental, Necessary, Indispensable, Vital, Unavoidable, Inherent.
E	S	T	A	B	L	I	S	H	Fix, Place, Settle, Entrench, Root, Secure, Constitute, Create.
E	S	T	A	M	I	N	E	T	Small cafe.
E	S	T	I	M	A	B	L	E	Valuable, Admirable, Commendable, Laudable, Meritorius, Worthy, Respectable.

1	2	3	4	5	6	7	8	9	Definition
E	S	T	I	M	A	T	O	R	One who estimates measurements and prices.
E	S	T	R	A	N	G	E	D	Alienated, Disunited, Divided, Parted, Separated, Severed, Divorced, Split.
E	T	E	R	N	A	L	L	Y	Ever, Always, Forever, In perpetuum, Constantly, Unalterably.
E	T	H	I	C	A	L	L	Y	In an ethical manner.
E	T	H	N	O	L	O	G	Y	Study of the different races of mankind.
E	T	I	Q	U	E	T	T	E	Decorum, Decency, Dignity, Propriety, Behaviour, Conduct, Deportment, Formalities.
E	T	Y	M	O	L	O	G	Y	Study of formation and meaning of words.
E	U	C	H	A	R	I	S	T	Holy Communion, Consecrated elements of bread and wine.
E	U	M	E	N	I	D	A	E	Family of wasps.
E	U	P	H	E	M	I	S	M	Substituting an offensive word for a mild one.
E	U	P	H	O	N	I	U	M	Tenor tuba.
E	U	P	H	O	R	B	I	A	A large genus of flowers having a milky juice.
E	V	A	C	U	A	T	E	D	Emptied, Discharged, Withdrawn, Removed.
E	V	A	G	I	N	A	T	E	Turn inside out, Protrude.
E	V	A	L	U	A	T	E	D	Valued, Appraised, Rated, Estimated, Assessed, Surveyed, Classified, Graded.
E	V	A	N	G	E	L	I	C	Zealous, Ardent, Militant, Crusading, Impassioned, Missionary.
E	V	A	P	O	R	A	T	E	Dissolve, Weaken, Dissipate, Expel, Vanish, Emit, Shrink, Diminish.
E	V	A	S	I	V	E	L	Y	Elusively, Avoiding, Vaguely, Nebulously, Slyly, Elusory.
E	V	E	N	T	U	A	T	E	Result.
E	V	E	R	G	L	A	D	E	Marshy land, Swamp.
E	V	E	R	G	R	E	E	N	Perennial, Unceasing, Perpetual.
E	V	E	R	Y	B	O	D	Y	Everyone, Every person.
E	V	I	D	E	N	T	L	Y	Perceptibly, Cleanly, Obviously, Plainly, Ostensibly, Apparently, Outwardly.
E	V	O	C	A	T	I	V	E	Suggestive, Meaningful, Pregnant, Weighty, Stimulating, Stirring, Producing.
E	V	O	L	U	T	I	O	N	Development, Growth, Progress, Upgrowth, Change, Transformation.
E	X	A	N	I	M	A	T	E	Dead, Departed, Extinct, Inanimate, Lifeless, Deceased.
E	X	A	R	C	H	A	T	E	Province of the Byzantine empire.
E	X	C	A	V	A	T	E	D	Hollowed, Dug, Delved, Scooped, Scraped, Quarried.
E	X	C	E	L	L	E	N	T	Supreme, Marvellous, Capital, Champion, Distinguished, Superlative, Superb.
E	X	C	E	P	T	I	N	G	Excluding, Eliminating, Suspending, Exempting, Rejecting, Objecting, Protesting.
E	X	C	E	S	S	I	V	E	Extreme, Extravagant, Inordinate, Boundless, Limitless, Unmeasurable.
E	X	C	H	E	Q	U	E	R	Treasury, Coffer, Chest.
E	X	C	I	P	I	E	N	T	Something used to change the mass of a drug.
E	X	C	I	T	A	B	L	E	Volatile, Temperamental, Unstable, Combustible, Highly-strung, Mercurial.
E	X	C	L	U	S	I	O	N	Debarring, Rejection.
E	X	C	L	U	S	I	V	E	Limited, Stylish, Fashionable, Single, Undivided, Whole, Select, Elite.
E	X	C	O	R	I	A	T	E	Chafe, Abrade, Rub, Lambaste, Blister, Scourge, Castigate, Scarify.
E	X	C	R	E	M	E	N	T	Droppings, Stools, Human waste.
E	X	C	R	E	T	I	O	N	Elimination of waste matter.
E	X	C	U	L	P	A	T	E	Acquit, Absolve, Exonerate, Vindicate, Condone, Excuse, Forgive, Justify.
E	X	C	U	R	S	I	O	N	Jaunt, Outing, Expedition, Journey, Trip, Tour, Digression, Discursion.
E	X	C	U	R	S	I	V	E	Prone to digression.
E	X	C	U	S	A	B	L	E	Pardonable.
E	X	E	C	R	A	B	L	Y	Abominably, Repulsively, Damnably, Detestably, Wretchedly.
E	X	E	C	U	T	A	N	T	Performer, Entertainer.
E	X	E	C	U	T	I	O	N	Performance, Accomplishment, Capital punishment.
E	X	E	C	U	T	I	V	E	Administrator, Entrepreneur, Director, Leader, Official, Supervisor.
E	X	E	M	P	L	A	R	Y	Innocent, Good.
E	X	E	M	P	L	I	F	Y	Illustrate, Clarify, Enlighten, Epitomize, Demonstrate, Represent, Typify, Symbolize.
E	X	E	M	P	T	I	O	N	Immunity, Impunity, Exception, Discharge, Freedom, Release.
E	X	E	Q	U	A	T	U	R	Consul authority, Sovereign's permission to a bishop.
E	X	E	R	C	I	S	E	S	Activities, Actions, Movements, Drills, Lessons, Studies, Athletics, Tasks.
E	X	F	O	L	I	A	T	E	Scale, Flake, Peel, Skin.
E	X	H	A	U	S	T	E	D	Weary, Tired, Depleted, Drained, Impoverished, Dispersed, Consumed, Expended.
E	X	H	I	B	I	T	O	R	One that exhibits, One who shows motion pictures.
E	X	I	S	T	E	N	C	E	Actuality, Being, Presence, Reality, Entity, Individual, Essence.
E	X	O	G	E	N	O	U	S	Arising from outside origins.
E	X	O	N	E	R	A	T	E	Exculpate, Absolve, Acquit, Vindicate, Free.
E	X	O	R	C	I	S	E	D	Purified, Relieved.
E	X	O	S	M	O	S	I	S	Passage of fluid through membrane to mix with external fluid.
E	X	O	T	E	R	I	C	S	Discourses for the general public.
E	X	O	T	I	C	I	S	M	Foreign trait of behaviour.
E	X	O	T	R	O	P	I	A	Walleye.
E	X	P	A	N	S	I	O	N	Enlargement, Growth, Amplification, Breadth, Space.
E	X	P	A	N	S	I	V	E	Resilient, Volatile, Buoyant, Effervescent, Demonstrative, Gregarious, Effusive.
E	X	P	A	T	I	A	T	E	Discourse, Dilate, Discuss, Sermonize, Narrate, Recite, Recount, Relate.
E	X	P	E	C	T	A	N	T	Anticipatory, Hopeful, Eager, Alert, Watchful, Pregnant, Expecting, Heavy.

1	2	3	4	5	6	7	8	9	
E	X	P	E	D	I	E	N	T	Advisable, Prudent, Tactical, Beneficial, Convenient, Seasonable, Feasible.
E	X	P	E	L	L	E	N	T	Expulsive.
E	X	P	E	N	S	I	V	E	Costly, Dear, Extravagant, Immoderate.
E	X	P	E	R	T	I	S	E	Ability, Command, Expertness, Mastership, Mastery, Adroitness, Craft, Dexterity.
E	X	P	I	A	T	I	O	N	Penance, Atonement.
E	X	P	I	A	T	O	R	Y	Atoning.
E	X	P	L	A	I	N	E	D	Interpreted, Clarified, Expounded, Deciphered, Disentangled, Untangled, Analyzed.
E	X	P	L	E	T	I	V	E	Oath, Swearword, Curse, Cuss.
E	X	P	L	I	C	A	T	E	Explain, Construe, Expound, Interpret, Amplify, Develop, Dilate, Expand.
E	X	P	L	O	I	T	E	D	Used, Applied, Employed, Handled, Utilized, Cultivated, Manipulated, Handled.
E	X	P	L	O	S	I	O	N	Outburst, Access, Burst, Eruption, Gust, Sally.
E	X	P	O	U	N	D	E	D	Explained, Explicated, Interpreted, Expressed, Exemplified, Delineated, Described.
E	X	P	U	L	S	I	O	N	Exile, Banishment, Deportation, Ejection, Ousting, Removal, Ostracism, Displacement.
E	X	P	U	R	G	A	T	E	Purify, Cleanse, Purge, Censor, Bowdlerize, Screen.
E	X	Q	U	I	S	I	T	E	Choice, Accomplished, Delectable, Consummate, Dainty, Impeccable, Delicate.
E	X	S	I	C	C	A	T	E	To remove moisture, dehydrate.
E	X	T	E	M	P	O	R	E	Impromptu, Improvised, Off-hand, Unrehearsed, Unstudied.
E	X	T	E	N	D	I	N	G	Outspreading, Unfolding, Fanning, Expanding, Offering, Lengthening, Prolonging.
E	X	T	E	N	S	I	O	N	Protraction, Prolongation, Continuation, Enlargement, Spread, Annexe, Expansion.
E	X	T	E	N	S	I	V	E	Broad, Expansive, Wide, Comprehensive, Inclusive, Considerable, Major.
E	X	T	E	N	U	A	T	E	Mitigate, Moderate, Qualify, Temper, Attenuate, Palliate, Justify, Apologize.
E	X	T	I	R	P	A	T	E	Annihilate, Abolish, Eradicate, Exterminate, Extinguish, Excise, Resect, Expunge.
E	X	T	O	R	T	I	O	N	Practice of extorting.
E	X	T	R	A	C	T	E	D	Pulled, Evulsed, Yanked, Culled, Garnered, Extorted, Educed, Evinced.
E	X	T	R	A	D	I	T	E	Surrender of an alleged criminal to another country to stand trial.
E	X	T	R	E	M	E	L	Y	Excessively, Immensely, Inordinately, Exceedingly, Hugely, Strikingly, Rarely.
E	X	T	R	E	M	I	T	Y	Limit, Acme, Apex, Zenith, Extreme measure.
E	X	T	R	I	C	A	T	E	To free from restriction.
E	X	T	R	I	N	S	I	C	Foreign, Unessential, Acquired, Alien, Extraneous, Outside, Outer.
E	X	T	R	O	V	E	R	T	One whose interests are centre outside self.
E	X	T	R	U	S	I	O	N	Pushing out, moulding.
E	X	U	B	E	R	A	N	T	Prolific, Overflowing, Abounding, Affusive, Copious, Lavish, Ebullient.
E	X	U	D	A	T	I	O	N	Percolating, Transude, Discharge, Emanation.

F

1	2	3	4	5	6	7	8	9	
F	A	B	A	C	E	O	U	S	Leguminous, Like a bean.
F	A	B	I	A	N	I	S	M	Principles of the Fabian socialists.
F	A	B	R	I	C	A	T	E	Manufacture, Produce, Construct, Build, Shape, Invent, Formulate, Create.
F	A	C	E	P	I	E	C	E	Part of a bridle, Part of a gasmask or respirator.
F	A	C	E	T	I	O	U	S	Witty, Jocose, Humorous, Jocular, Blithe, Jovial, Comical, Ludicrous.
F	A	C	S	I	M	I	L	E	Reproduction, Copy, Ditto, Duplicate, Replica.
F	A	C	T	I	O	N	A	L	Relating to a party or combination.
F	A	C	T	O	R	I	A	L	Product of a series of factors in arithmetical progression.
F	A	C	T	U	A	L	L	Y	Concerned with facts.
F	A	G	G	O	T	I	N	G	An embroidery stitch worked on fabric with threads drawn.
F	A	I	N	T	N	E	S	S	Unconsciousness, Cowardice, Timidity, Dimness, Giddiness, Vertigo.
F	A	I	R	Y	L	A	N	D	Paradise, Land of magical charm, Wonderland, Utopia.
F	A	I	T	H	L	E	S	S	False, Perfidious, Traitorous, Treacherous, Unfaithful, Untrue, Fickle, Unstable.
F	A	L	C	I	F	O	R	M	Sickle-shaped, Shaped like a scythe.
F	A	L	D	S	T	O	O	L	Folding stool or chair used by a bishop.
F	A	L	S	E	H	O	O	D	Lie, Mendacity, Untruth, Fallacy, Error, Misrepresentation, Pretense, Deceit.
F	A	L	S	E	N	E	S	S	Infidelity, Disloyalty, Defection, Desertion, Falsity, Perfidiousness, Faithlessness.
F	A	L	S	E	W	O	R	K	Temporary construction work for support during building or demolition.
F	A	L	T	E	R	I	N	G	Stumbling, Staggering, Tottering, Hesitating, Stammering, Weakening, Declining.
F	A	N	A	T	I	C	A	L	Crazed, Frantic, Mad, Extravagant, Unreasonable, Rabid, Radical.
F	A	N	C	Y	F	R	E	E	Unrestrained, Free of restrictions.
F	A	N	C	Y	W	O	R	K	Decorative needlework and crochet.
F	A	N	D	A	N	G	L	E	Outlandish ornaments, Nonsense, Tomfoolery.
F	A	N	T	A	S	T	I	C	Fictitious, Fanciful, Illusory, Imaginary, Incredible, Absurd, Irrational, Bizarre.
F	A	S	C	I	A	T	E	D	Having broad bands of colour.
F	A	S	C	I	C	U	L	E	Small bundle or collection.
F	A	S	T	E	N	I	N	G	Establishing, Holding, Nailing, Attaching, Gripping, Affixing, Adhering, Securing.
F	A	T	E	F	U	L	L	Y	Ominously, Banefully, Threateningly, Importantly, Fatally, Disastrously, Acutely.
F	A	T	I	G	U	I	N	G	Tiring, Wearing, Wearying, Depleting, Exhausting, Debilitating, Taxing, Vexing.
F	A	T	T	E	N	I	N	G	Over-feeding, Enriching.

1	2	3	4	5	6	7	8	9	
F	A	U	L	T	L	E	S	S	Irreprochable, Impeccable, Flawless, Perfect, Blameless, Innocent, Guiltless.
F	A	V	O	U	R	I	T	E	Popular, Preferred, Praiseworthy, Cherished, Treasured, Esteemed, Precious, Prized.
F	E	A	R	F	U	L	L	Y	Anxiously, Apprehensively, Nervously, Alarmingly, Luridly.
F	E	A	T	H	E	R	E	D	Covered with feathers, Very thin edge.
F	E	B	R	I	F	U	G	E	Antipyretic, Something to reduce a fever.
F	E	C	U	L	E	N	C	E	Muddiness, Foulness.
F	E	C	U	N	D	I	T	Y	Fruitfulness, Productive, Germinative.
F	E	L	I	C	I	F	I	C	Designed to produce happiness.
F	E	L	O	N	I	O	U	S	Villanous, Criminal.
F	E	M	I	N	E	I	T	Y	Feminity.
F	E	N	C	E	L	E	S	S	Lacking enclosure.
F	E	O	F	F	M	E	N	T	Granting a freehold state of delivery.
F	E	R	M	E	N	T	E	D	Boiled, Seethed, Simmered, Agitated, Stirred, Excited.
F	E	R	O	C	I	O	U	S	Barbarous, Fierce, Savage, Truculent, Rapacious, Voracious, Relentless, Vicious.
F	E	R	R	O	T	Y	P	E	A photographic process.
F	E	R	T	I	L	I	T	Y	Fecundity, Prolificacy, Abundance, Creativity, Ingenuity, Fruitfulness, Inventiveness.
F	E	R	T	I	L	I	Z	E	Stimulate, Supply, Enrich, Pollinate, Inseminate.
F	E	R	V	A	N	I	T	E	Rare hydrated iron vanadate occurring with radioactive minerals.
F	E	R	V	E	N	T	L	Y	Enthusiastically, Passionately, Earnestly, Devoutly, Sincerely, Eagerly.
F	E	T	I	S	H	I	S	M	Irrational devotion to object or practice, Worship.
F	E	T	I	S	H	I	S	T	One addicted to a fetish.
F	E	U	D	A	L	I	S	M	Social system involving complete control by the rich landowners of the lower classes.
F	E	U	D	A	L	I	T	Y	Feudal practice.
F	E	U	D	A	T	O	R	Y	Subject to an overlord.
F	I	B	R	I	N	O	U	S	Marked by the presence of fibrin.
F	I	B	R	O	U	S	L	Y	In a sinewy fashion.
F	I	C	T	I	O	N	A	L	Fictitious, Fanciful, Illusory, Imaginary, Unreal.
F	I	D	G	E	T	I	N	G	Fiddling, Twitching, Restlessness, Worrying.
F	I	D	U	C	I	A	R	Y	Nature of a trust.
F	I	E	L	D	F	A	R	E	Medium-sized thrush.
F	I	E	R	I	N	E	S	S	Feverishness, High-spiritedness, Aggressiveness, Belligerence.
F	I	L	I	A	T	I	O	N	Family relationship, Descent from a parent, Affiliation.
F	I	L	L	I	S	T	E	R	An adjustable rabbet plane.
F	I	L	O	P	L	U	M	E	A hairlike feather.
F	I	L	O	S	E	L	L	E	Soft silk embroidery thread.
F	I	M	B	R	I	A	T	E	To furnish with a border or fringe.
F	I	N	A	N	C	I	A	L	Relating to finance, Fiscal, Monetary, Pecuniary, Commercial, Economic.
F	I	N	A	N	C	I	E	R	Capitalist, Large scale investor, Investment banker.
F	I	N	G	E	R	I	N	G	Marking on a musical score for position of the fingers, Knitting yarn.
F	I	N	I	C	K	I	N	G	Finicky, Meticulous, Fussy, Fastidious, Pernickety.
F	I	R	E	B	R	A	N	D	Agitator, Mischiefmaker, Troublemaker, Hothead, Incendiary.
F	I	R	E	B	R	I	C	K	A special brick used to line furnaces and fireplaces.
F	I	R	E	D	R	A	K	E	A mythical dragon breathing fire.
F	I	R	E	P	R	O	O	F	Non-combustible.
F	I	R	M	A	M	E	N	T	Heaven, Sky.
F	I	S	H	E	R	M	A	N	One who engages in fishing for profit or pleasure.
F	L	A	B	E	L	L	U	M	A ceremonial fan.
F	L	A	G	E	O	L	E	T	A small flute.
F	L	A	M	M	A	B	L	E	Combustible, Ignitable.
F	L	A	T	T	E	N	E	D	Smoothed, Levelled, Depressed, Dejected, Dispirited, Knocked down.
F	L	A	T	T	E	R	E	R	One that flatters.
F	L	A	T	U	L	E	N	T	Turgid, Inflated, Empty, Vain, Shallow, Pretentious.
F	L	A	U	N	T	I	N	G	Displaying, Exhibiting, Exposing, Parading, Flourishing, Boasting, Divulging.
F	L	E	D	G	L	I	N	G	Young bird able to survive when leaving the nest, Immature person.
F	L	I	P	P	A	N	C	Y	Frivolity, Levity, Lightness, Flightiness, Volatility, Archness, Sauciness.
F	L	O	U	N	C	I	N	G	Mincing, Prancing, Floundering, Struggling.
F	L	O	W	E	R	A	G	E	State of flowering.
F	L	U	C	T	U	A	N	T	Wavering, Unstable, Movable, Weak, Uncertain, Insecure, Chancy, Unpredictable.
F	L	U	C	T	U	A	T	E	Vacillate, Swing, Rise and fall, Wave, Drift, Unsteady, Irresolute, Undetermined.
F	O	A	M	I	N	E	S	S	State of being foamy.
F	O	G	G	I	N	E	S	S	State of being foggy.
F	O	L	I	A	T	I	O	N	Being in leaf, Numbering pages, Act of beating metal into a thin leaf.
F	O	L	L	O	W	I	N	G	Succeeding, Ensuing, After, Behind, Entourage, Retinue, Next, Coming.
F	O	O	L	I	S	H	L	Y	Simply, Fatuously, Irrationally, Crazily, Ridiculously.
F	O	O	L	H	A	R	D	Y	Adventurous, Reckless, Taking needless risks.
F	O	O	T	S	T	A	L	K	Peduncle, Lower part of a millstone spindle.
F	O	P	P	I	S	H	L	Y	Being a fop in dress and manner.

1	2	3	4	5	6	7	8	9	Definition
F	O	R	A	S	M	U	C	H	Since, In consideration that.
F	O	R	C	E	M	E	A	T	Finely chopped and highly seasoned meat or fish, Compulsion.
F	O	R	E	B	E	A	R	S	Ancestors, Forefathers.
F	O	R	E	C	L	O	S	E	Prevent, Hinder, Preclude, Debar, Bar.
F	O	R	E	C	O	U	R	T	Outer court of a building.
F	O	R	E	F	R	O	N	T	Vanguard, Foremost part.
F	O	R	E	I	G	N	E	R	Alien, A person from another country.
F	O	R	E	S	I	G	H	T	Foreknowledge, Prudence, Looking forward, Caution, Discretion, Precaution.
F	O	R	E	S	T	A	L	L	Prevent, Avert, Deter, Obviate, Preclude, Ward, Prevent, Anticipate.
F	O	R	E	T	A	S	T	E	Anticipate.
F	O	R	E	T	O	K	E	N	Promise, Foreshow, Augary, Omen, Portent, Badge, Indication, Warning.
F	O	R	E	W	O	M	A	N	A woman in charge of a section usually in a factory.
F	O	R	F	E	I	T	E	D	Yielded, Lost, Sacrificed.
F	O	R	F	I	C	U	L	A	Family of earwigs sometimes destructive to cultivated bulbs.
F	O	R	G	A	T	H	E	R	Convene, Assemble, Congregate, Muster, Raise, Gather, Associate.
F	O	R	G	E	T	F	U	L	Oblivious, Unmindful, Neglectful, Remiss, Slack, Careless, Heedless, Absentminded.
F	O	R	M	A	L	I	S	M	Strict observance of forms, Emphatic attention to arrangements.
F	O	R	M	A	L	I	T	Y	Form, Cermony, Conventionality, Order, Regularity, Ritual, Liturgy, Rite.
F	O	R	M	A	L	I	Z	E	Shape, Mould, Stylize, Animate, Transformation, Cavil, Script.
F	O	R	M	A	T	I	O	N	Production, Development, Structure, Construction, Climax, Arrangement, Design.
F	O	R	M	A	T	I	V	E	Constructive, Plastic, Meristematic, Creative, Classic, Florescent.
F	O	R	M	I	C	A	R	Y	Anthill.
F	O	R	M	U	L	A	T	E	Devise, Standardize by formula.
F	O	R	M	U	L	I	S	M	Reliance on formulas.
F	O	R	N	I	C	A	T	E	Sexual intercourse between a man and an unmarried woman by consent.
F	O	R	S	A	K	I	N	G	Renouncing, Surrendering, Quitting, Departing, Deserting, Withdrawing, Abandoning.
F	O	R	S	Y	T	H	I	A	Small genus of ornamental shrubs with bright yellow flowers.
F	O	R	T	H	W	I	T	H	Immediately, Thereupon, Directly, Instantly, Abruptly, Suddenly.
F	O	R	T	I	T	U	D	E	Backbone, Pluck, Grit, Courage, Mettle, Resoluteness, Tenacity, Endurance.
F	O	R	T	U	N	A	T	E	Favourable, Auspicious, Propitious, Bright, Lucky, Providential, Prosperous.
F	O	R	W	A	R	D	L	Y	Boldly, Presumptuously.
F	O	S	S	O	R	I	A	L	Adapted for digging.
F	O	S	T	E	R	A	G	E	The care of a foster child, Promoting development.
F	O	U	N	D	L	I	N	G	Baby deserted by unknown parents.
F	R	A	C	T	I	O	U	S	Unruly, Refractory, Quarrelsome, Contrary, Irritable, Indomitable, Peevish, Querulous.
F	R	A	G	R	A	N	C	E	Aroma, Balm, Bouquet, Incense, Perfume, Scent, Spice.
F	R	A	M	E	W	O	R	K	Structure, Skeletal frame, Support structure, Outline.
F	R	A	N	C	H	I	S	E	Exemption, Contract granted by government, Suffrage, Vote, Ballot, Privilege.
F	R	A	N	C	O	L	I	N	Partridge.
F	R	A	N	G	I	B	L	E	Breakable, Brittle, Fragile.
F	R	A	N	K	E	N	I	A	Genus of perennial herbs.
F	R	A	N	K	N	E	S	S	Forthrightness, Directness, Plainness, Honesty, Openness, Outspokenness.
F	R	A	T	E	R	N	A	L	Friendly, Brotherly, Brotherhood, Twins.
F	R	E	E	L	A	N	C	E	Independent, Uncommitted, Not bound by contract.
F	R	E	I	G	H	T	E	R	Ship or plane carrying freight, Shipper.
F	R	E	Q	U	E	N	C	Y	Familiarity, Frequent occurrence, Repeated at short intervals.
F	R	E	S	H	N	E	S	S	Callowness, Newness, Briskness, Brightness, Vividness, Inexperienced.
F	R	I	B	B	L	I	S	H	Giddy, Dizzy, Flighty, Frivolous, Light, Scatterbrained.
F	R	I	C	A	S	S	E	E	A stew of light-coloured meat in a light gravy.
F	R	I	C	A	T	I	V	E	Frictional passage of breath against narrow vocal tract.
F	R	I	G	H	T	F	U	L	Alarming, Fearful, Awful, Extreme, Appalling, Formidable, Shocking, Terrible.
F	R	I	G	I	D	I	T	Y	Abnormal sexual indifference.
F	R	I	V	O	L	I	T	Y	Lightness, Flippancy, Levity, Volatility, Flirting, Toying, Trifling, Jest.
F	R	I	V	O	L	O	U	S	Irrelevant, Superficial, Light, Shallow, Gay, Playful, Dizzy, Superficial.
F	R	O	C	K	C	O	A	T	Man's double-breasted coat with square tails.
F	R	O	W	A	R	D	L	Y	Perversely, Adversely, Contrarily.
F	R	U	C	T	U	O	U	S	Fruitful, Productive, Profitable, Full.
F	R	U	G	A	L	I	T	Y	Thrift, Economy, Prudence, Husbandry, Parsimony, Austerely.
F	R	U	I	T	L	E	S	S	Futile, Abortive, Ineffective, Ineffectual, Useless, Vain, Barren, Sterile.
F	R	U	S	T	R	A	T	E	Baffle, Balk, Outwit, Circumvent, Ruin, Thwart, Cancel, Neutralize, Nullify.
F	R	U	T	I	C	O	S	E	Resembling a shrub.
F	U	G	A	C	I	O	U	S	Unsubstantial, Fleeting, Evanescent, Wandering, Deciduous, Caducous.
F	U	L	F	I	L	L	E	D	Accomplished, Executed, Met, Satisfied, Performed, Completed, Answered.
F	U	L	G	U	R	A	N	T	Dazzling.
F	U	L	G	U	R	A	T	E	Flash, Remove or destroy.
F	U	L	G	U	R	I	T	E	Vitrified crust produced by fusion of sand or rock by lightning.
F	U	L	G	U	R	O	U	S	Emitting flashes, In the style of lightning.

1	2	3	4	5	6	7	8	9	
F	U	L	M	I	N	A	N	T	Detonating, Exploding, Censuring, Denunciating.
F	U	L	M	I	N	A	T	E	Menace, Detonate, Explode.
F	U	L	M	I	N	O	U	S	Resembling thunder and lightning.
F	U	L	S	O	M	E	L	Y	Wantonly, Repulsively, Disgustingly, Hypocritically, Sanctimoniously, Glibly.
F	U	M	I	G	A	T	E	D	Disinfected, Deodorized or performed with fumes.
F	U	N	D	A	M	E	N	T	Base, Foundation, Basic principle, Buttocks, Rump, Posterior, Rear, Seat.
F	U	N	D	A	T	R	I	X	Female aphid produced on primary host plant.
F	U	N	G	I	C	I	D	E	A preparation that destroys fungus.
F	U	N	G	I	F	O	R	M	Shaped like a mushroom.
F	U	N	I	C	U	L	A	R	A cable railway ascending a mountain often with counter-balanced cars.
F	U	R	N	I	T	U	R	E	Movable contents of a place of residence, Horse harness, Accessories.
F	U	S	I	L	L	A	D	E	Rapidly successive gunfire.
F	U	S	S	I	N	E	S	S	State of being fussy.
F	U	S	T	I	G	A	T	E	To beat with a club.

G

1	2	3	4	5	6	7	8	9	
G	A	B	E	R	D	I	N	E	Firm fabric with a twill weave forming diagonal stripes.
G	A	L	A	C	T	O	S	E	Aldose sugar less sweet than glucose.
G	A	L	A	N	T	I	N	E	Gelantine, Boiled white meat served in aspic jelly.
G	A	L	I	N	G	A	L	E	Aromatic root related to ginger and once used in cookery and medicine.
G	A	L	L	A	N	T	R	Y	Splending, Courteous, Civility, Bravery, Intrepidity, Fortitude, Chivalry.
G	A	L	L	I	N	A	Z	O	Relating to ancient culture of an area in northern Peru.
G	A	L	L	I	N	U	L	E	Aquatic bird, Marsh hen.
G	A	L	L	I	V	A	N	T	Move, Go, Travel, Rove, Stray, Traipse, Meander, Gad.
G	A	L	L	O	P	A	D	E	Dancing a galop, a lively nineteenth century dance.
G	A	L	V	A	N	I	S	M	Direct current of electricity, Forceful, Vital.
G	A	L	V	A	N	I	Z	E	Provoke, Excite, Motivate, Pique, Prime, Stimulate, Activate, Energize.
G	A	M	B	O	L	I	N	G	Capering, Cavorting, Frisking, Bounding, Romping, Larking, Leaping, Springing.
G	A	M	M	A	D	I	O	N	A cross in the form of a swastika.
G	A	N	G	P	L	A	N	K	Long narrow portable bridge for embarking and disembarking from a ship.
G	A	R	A	V	A	N	C	E	Chickpea.
G	A	R	D	E	N	I	N	G	Working in a garden for profit or pleasure.
G	A	R	N	I	S	H	E	D	Bedecked, Adorned, Embellished, Ornamented, Decorated, Furnished, Trimmed.
G	A	R	N	I	S	H	E	E	Attach wages or property of a debtor.
G	A	R	N	I	T	U	R	E	Trimming, Ornament, Accessories, Adornment.
G	A	R	R	E	T	E	E	R	One that lives in a garret, usually a penurious author or artist.
G	A	R	R	U	L	I	T	Y	Locquacity, Talkativeness, Garrulousness.
G	A	R	R	U	L	O	U	S	Loquacious, Talkative, Wordy, Chatty, Prattling, Verbose, Blabbing.
G	A	S	O	M	E	T	E	R	A large cylindrical or spherical tank for storing combustible fuel gases.
G	A	S	T	R	I	T	I	S	Inflammation of the stomach lining.
G	A	S	T	R	O	P	O	D	Mollusk with a univalve shell often coiled.
G	A	T	E	H	O	U	S	E	Erection over a dam for control of the gates.
G	A	T	H	E	R	I	N	G	Concentrating, Collecting, Harvesting, Picking, Plucking, Accumulating, Deducing.
G	A	U	N	T	N	E	S	S	Haggardness, Leanness, Lankness, Scrawniness.
G	A	V	E	L	K	I	N	D	Anglo-Saxom common law tenure in Kent still in operation.
G	A	Z	E	T	T	E	E	R	A dictionary, catalogue or list usually divided into geographical regions.
G	E	L	I	G	N	I	T	E	A gelatin dynamite.
G	E	L	S	E	M	I	U	M	Small genus of woody vines, Yellow jessamine.
G	E	M	M	A	T	I	O	N	Asexual reproduction on a localized surface area or within the body of the parent.
G	E	N	E	A	L	O	G	Y	Pedigree, Lineage, Investigation of a family pedigree.
G	E	N	E	R	A	L	L	Y	Collectively, Universally, Usually.
G	E	N	E	R	A	T	O	R	Originator, Dynamo.
G	E	N	T	I	L	I	T	Y	Civility, Polish, Elegance, Politeness, Quality, Society, Prestige, Refinement.
G	E	N	T	L	E	M	A	N	Aristocrat, A man of good conduct.
G	E	N	U	F	L	E	C	T	Bend the knee in worship, Kowtow.
G	E	N	U	I	N	E	L	Y	Actually, Really, Truly, Veritably, Positively, Honestly, Sincerely.
G	E	O	G	R	A	P	H	Y	Science of the physical features of the earth's surface.
G	E	O	L	O	G	I	S	T	Specialist in geology.
G	E	O	M	E	T	R	I	C	According to the principles of geometry.
G	E	O	P	H	A	G	I	A	The practice of eating earthy substances.
G	E	R	I	A	T	R	I	C	Relating to aged people.
G	E	R	M	A	N	D	E	R	Speedwell plant.
G	E	R	M	A	N	I	U	M	A grayish white hard brittle metalloid element.
G	E	R	M	I	C	I	D	E	Antiseptic, Disinfectant, Agent to destroy germs.
G	E	R	M	I	N	A	T	E	Sprout, Grow, Originate, Develop, Evolve, Bud, Produce.

1	2	3	4	5	6	7	8	9	Definition
G	E	R	U	N	D	I	V	E	Latin verbal adjective with same suffix as gerund expressing idea of fitness or necessity.
G	E	S	T	A	T	I	O	N	Pregnancy, Conception and development.
G	E	Y	S	E	R	I	T	E	Hydrous form of silica that is one form of opal.
G	I	B	B	E	R	I	S	H	Confused, Unintelligible, Meaningless, Barbarous language.
G	I	D	D	I	N	E	S	S	Dizziness, Vertigo, Impulsiveness, Flightiness.
G	I	N	G	L	Y	M	U	S	A hinge joint.
G	I	R	A	N	D	O	L	E	Radiating ornamental composition.
G	L	A	C	I	A	T	E	D	Frozen, Covered with ice or snow.
G	L	A	D	I	A	T	O	R	Professional combatant, Disputant, Prizefighter.
G	L	A	D	I	O	L	U	S	Genus of plants with spikes of brilliantly coloured flowers.
G	L	A	M	O	R	O	U	S	Fascinating, Enchanting, Alluring.
G	L	A	N	D	U	L	A	R	Involving glands, Inherent, Instinctive, Earthy, Physical.
G	L	A	S	S	W	O	R	T	Saltwort plant.
G	L	E	N	G	A	R	R	Y	Scottish woollen cap having a crease from front to back.
G	L	O	B	E	F	I	S	H	Ocean sunfish.
G	L	O	B	O	S	I	T	Y	State of being globose.
G	L	O	M	E	R	A	T	E	Tightly packed globe, rounded mass.
G	L	O	S	S	I	T	I	S	Inflammation of the tongue.
G	L	U	T	I	N	O	U	S	Sticky, Gummy, Viscous.
G	L	Y	C	E	R	I	D	E	Compounds that are esters of glycerol with fatty acids.
G	L	Y	C	E	R	I	Z	E	Preserve in glycerine.
G	L	Y	P	T	O	D	O	N	Genus of large extinct mammals related to the armadillo.
G	O	D	F	A	T	H	E	R	A man who sponsors a child at its baptism.
G	O	D	L	I	N	E	S	S	Righteousness, Impious.
G	O	D	M	O	T	H	E	R	A woman who sponsors a child at its baptism.
G	O	L	D	B	R	I	C	K	A gilded brick passed as made of gold, Fraud.
G	O	L	D	E	N	E	Y	E	Large-headed diving duck.
G	O	L	D	E	N	R	O	D	A plant bearing clusters of small yellow flowers.
G	O	L	D	F	I	N	C	H	Small brightly coloured finch.
G	O	N	D	O	L	I	E	R	One who propels a gondola.
G	O	N	G	O	R	I	S	M	Artificial style of writing associated with the poet, Gongora.
G	O	O	S	A	N	D	E	R	Common goose of the northern hemisphere.
G	O	S	P	E	L	L	E	R	Evangelist, One who propounds the gospel.
G	O	S	S	I	P	I	N	G	Rumourmongering, Tattling, Babbling, Hinting, Implying, Suggesting.
G	O	V	E	R	N	E	S	S	A woman supervising and educating a child privately.
G	O	V	E	R	N	I	N	G	Controlling, Administering, Manipulating, Guiding, Restraining, Reigning, Handling.
G	R	A	D	A	T	I	O	N	Climax, Progression, Modification, Variation, Distinction, Shading.
G	R	A	D	U	A	L	L	Y	Little by little, Piecemeal, Developing by slight modulations.
G	R	A	D	U	A	T	E	D	Granted a degree, Qualified, Modified, Passed from one stage to another by degrees.
G	R	A	N	D	I	O	S	E	Ostentatious, Pretentious, Showy, Imposing, Lordly, Impressive, Pompous.
G	R	A	N	U	L	A	T	E	Crystallize into grains or granules.
G	R	A	P	H	I	T	I	C	Derived from graphite.
G	R	A	P	P	L	I	N	G	Seizing, Dragging, Grasping, Binding, Groping, Wrestling, Scuffling, Clutching.
G	R	A	T	I	T	U	D	E	Thankfulness, Being grateful.
G	R	A	V	E	Y	A	R	D	Cemetery.
G	R	E	A	T	N	E	S	S	Size, Largeness, Magnitude.
G	R	E	E	N	H	O	R	N	Inexperienced person, Newcomer, Rustic, Bumpkin.
G	R	E	E	N	N	E	S	S	Verdancy, Inexperience, Gullibility, Naivete.
G	R	E	E	N	S	A	N	D	Sedimentary deposit consisting of dark greenish grains of glauconite.
G	R	E	E	N	W	A	R	E	Unfired pottery.
G	R	E	E	N	W	O	O	D	A forest with trees in leaf, Softwood.
G	R	E	N	A	D	I	N	E	Small meat patty, Strongly scented carnation, Gauze-like fabric, Silk yarn, French liquer.
G	R	E	N	A	T	I	T	E	Slaurolite, Mineral of aluminium silicate.
G	R	E	Y	B	E	A	R	D	Old man.
G	R	E	Y	W	A	C	K	E	Sandstone containing a dark mineral.
G	R	I	E	V	A	N	C	E	Injustice, Wrong, Affliction, Trial, Tribulation, Complaint, Hardship, Distress.
G	R	I	M	A	L	K	I	N	Elderly queen-cat, Cantankerous spiteful old women.
G	R	I	M	I	N	E	S	S	Foulness, Dirtiness, Sordidness, Uncleanness, Vileness.
G	R	I	S	A	I	L	L	E	Fancy dress fabric in a grayish colour, Painting in monochrome.
G	R	O	O	M	S	M	A	N	Unmarried male attendant for the bridegroom.
G	R	O	T	E	S	Q	U	E	Bizarre, Fantastic, Eerie, Fanciful, Eccentric, Flamboyant, Weird, Uncanny.
G	R	O	U	C	H	I	L	Y	In a complaining fashion.
G	R	O	U	N	D	A	G	E	Fee for a ship to anchor in a port.
G	R	O	U	N	D	N	U	T	Plant having edible tuberous roots, Peanut.
G	R	O	U	N	D	S	E	L	A herb, Basis, Fundamental principle.
G	R	O	V	E	L	L	E	R	A person who grovels or fawns.
G	R	U	E	L	L	I	N	G	Exhausting, demanding, punishing.

1	2	3	4	5	6	7	8	9	
G	R	U	F	F	N	E	S	S	Harshness, Brusqueness, Curtness, Sullenness, Hoarseness.
G	R	U	M	B	L	I	N	G	Complaining, Grousing, Scolding, Grunting, Groaning, Whining, Rumbling.
G	U	A	C	A	M	O	L	E	Mixture of mashed avocado, tomato and onion.
G	U	A	R	A	G	U	A	O	Puerto Rican timber tree.
G	U	A	R	A	N	T	E	E	Security, Warranty, Surety, Certify.
G	U	A	R	D	S	M	A	N	Member of a special military body, Warder, Watchman.
G	U	E	R	R	I	L	L	A	One who engages in irregular warfare.
G	U	I	D	E	B	O	O	K	Handbook containing information, Manual, Compendium.
G	U	I	L	E	L	E	S	S	Innocent, Naive, Unsophisticated, Natural, Ingenuous, Unaffected.
G	U	I	L	L	E	M	E	T	Quotation marks used in French writing.
G	U	I	L	L	E	M	O	T	Auk.
G	U	I	L	T	L	E	S	S	Blameless, Exemplary, Innocent, Irreprochable, Righteous, Pure.
G	U	S	H	I	N	G	L	Y	In the manner of one that gushes.
G	U	S	T	A	T	I	O	N	Sensation of tasting.
G	Y	M	N	A	S	I	U	M	Hall or room used for indoor sports and exercises.
G	Y	M	N	A	S	T	I	C	Athletic.
G	Y	R	O	G	R	A	P	H	Instrument recording revolutions.
G	Y	R	O	S	C	O	P	E	Instrument to illustrate dynamics of rotating bodies.

H

H	A	B	E	R	G	E	O	N	Medieval jacket of mail.
H	A	B	I	T	A	B	L	E	Fit for occupation, Livable.
H	A	B	I	T	U	A	T	E	Familiarize, Accustom, Frequent, Adjust, Inure, Tolerate, Condition, Season.
H	A	C	K	A	M	O	R	E	A bridle used for training horses.
H	A	C	K	N	E	Y	E	D	Commonplace, Trite, Stale, Tired, Obsolete, Archaic, Outmoded, Everyday.
H	A	E	C	C	E	I	T	Y	Individuality, Specificity.
H	A	E	M	A	T	O	I	D	Relating to blood.
H	A	E	M	O	S	T	A	T	Anything used to stop bleeding.
H	A	G	G	A	R	D	L	Y	In a haggard state.
H	A	G	I	A	R	C	H	Y	Government by the clergy.
H	A	G	I	O	L	O	G	Y	History of sacred writings, Narrative of the lives of saints.
H	A	I	R	P	I	E	C	E	Toupee, Form of wig.
H	A	I	R	S	H	E	E	P	A leather used in bookbinding.
H	A	I	R	S	H	I	R	T	Rough shirt worn as penance, Scourge.
H	A	I	R	S	T	Y	L	E	Coiffure, The way the hair is worn.
H	A	L	F	B	R	E	E	D	Offspring of parents of different races, Hybrid.
H	A	L	F	C	A	S	T	E	Person of mixed racial or cultural descent.
H	A	L	F	P	E	N	N	Y	Coin representing a half of a British penny.
H	A	L	F	S	T	A	F	F	A flag flown at halfmast.
H	A	L	F	T	R	A	C	K	Chain track drive system on a vehicle.
H	A	L	L	O	W	E	E	N	Evening preceding October 31st which is All Saints Day.
H	A	L	O	B	A	T	E	S	Small wingless marine water striders.
H	A	L	O	P	H	Y	T	E	A plant that grows in a saline habitat.
H	A	M	A	D	R	Y	A	D	A mythological nymph of trees, Sacred baboon.
H	A	M	B	U	R	G	E	R	Cooked patty of ground beef.
H	A	M	M	A	R	I	T	E	A mineral consisting of lead, copper and bismuth sulfide.
H	A	N	D	C	L	A	S	P	Handshake.
H	A	N	D	C	U	F	F	S	Menacles, Metal fastening that can be locked around the wrists.
H	A	P	H	A	Z	A	R	D	Random, Chance, Accident, Aimless, Indiscriminate, Carelessly, Desultory.
H	A	P	P	E	N	I	N	G	Occurring, Circumstance, Episode, Incident, Occasion, Falling, Chancing.
H	A	P	P	I	N	E	S	S	Content, Satisfaction, Gladness, Bliss, Felicity, Beatitude, Blessedness, Enjoyment.
H	A	R	B	I	N	G	E	R	Forerunner, Herald, Trailblazer, Portent, Omen, Sign, Indication, Symbol.
H	A	R	B	O	R	A	G	E	Shelter, Refuge, Resting-place.
H	A	R	D	I	H	O	O	D	Hardihood, Vigour, Robustness, Fortitude, Boldness, Audacity, Temerity.
H	A	R	L	E	Q	U	I	N	Buffoon, A character that appears in pantomime and ballet.
H	A	R	M	A	T	T	A	N	Dry, dust-laden African wind.
H	A	R	M	O	N	I	C	A	Mouth organ.
H	A	R	M	O	N	I	S	T	One who composes or performs music.
H	A	R	M	O	N	I	U	M	Reed organ.
H	A	R	M	O	N	I	Z	E	To be in harmony, Correlate, Blend, Agree, In accord, Reconcile.
H	A	R	Q	U	E	B	U	S	A fifteenth century matchlock gun.
H	A	R	R	O	W	I	N	G	Agonizing, Distressing, Painful, Excruciating, Torturing, Racking, Tormenting.
H	A	R	S	H	N	E	S	S	Coarseness, Bitterness, Ruggedness, Dryness, Hoarseness, Grimness, Bleakness.
H	A	R	T	S	H	O	R	N	Former source of ammonia.
H	A	R	V	E	S	T	E	R	Combine cornbinder, Cotton picker.

1	2	3	4	5	6	7	8	9	Clue
H	A	S	T	I	N	E	S	S	Rush, Waste, Hurriedness, Precipitance.
H	A	T	C	H	M	E	N	T	Panel bearing coat of arms of deceased person and temporarily displayed outside.
H	A	T	E	F	U	L	L	Y	Maliciously, Evilly, Nastily, Spitefully, Viciously, Abominably, Odiously, Vilely.
H	A	U	G	H	T	I	L	Y	Proudly, Arrogantly, Disdainfully, Insolently, Aloofly, Contemptuously.
H	A	V	E	R	I	N	G	S	Babblings.
H	A	V	E	R	S	A	C	K	Knapsack, Backpack, Rucksack, Pack.
H	A	Z	A	R	D	O	U	S	Dangerous, Jeopardous, Perilous, Risky, Parlous, Unsound, Wicked, Chancy.
H	E	A	D	D	R	E	S	S	A fanciful arrangement to ornament the hair.
H	E	A	D	H	O	U	S	E	A structure of a mine housing the hoisting gear.
H	E	A	D	S	T	O	N	E	Stone at the head of a grave.
H	E	A	L	T	H	F	U	L	Healthy, Wholesome, Salutary, Hygienic, Sanitary, Beneficial, Curative.
H	E	A	L	T	H	I	L	Y	In a healthy manner.
H	E	A	R	T	B	U	R	N	Burning discomfort in the diaphragm.
H	E	A	R	T	L	E	S	S	Unsympathetic, Cruel, Spiritless, Despondent.
H	E	A	R	T	W	O	O	D	Older central portion of a trunk inside sapwood.
H	E	A	V	I	N	E	S	S	Mercury.
H	E	C	O	G	E	N	I	N	Crystalline steroid obtained from a desert herb.
H	E	G	E	M	O	N	I	C	Relating to leadership.
H	E	L	I	O	G	R	A	M	Message transmitted by a heliograph.
H	E	L	I	O	L	I	T	E	A fossil coral.
H	E	L	L	E	B	O	R	E	Dried rhizome and root of a medicinal herb.
H	E	L	L	E	N	I	S	E	To make Greek or Hellenistic.
H	E	L	L	I	S	H	L	Y	Devilishly, Infernally.
H	E	L	P	F	U	L	L	Y	Encouragingly, Effectively, Usefully, Favourably, Profitably.
H	E	M	A	T	I	N	I	C	Agent to stimulate the formation of blood cells.
H	E	M	I	C	Y	C	L	E	Semicircle, Curved structure, Horseshoe-shape.
H	E	M	I	S	T	I	C	H	Half a poetic line.
H	E	M	O	C	O	N	I	A	Small refractive colourless particles in the blood.
H	E	M	O	L	Y	S	I	N	A substance that will cause the dissolution of red blood cells.
H	E	M	S	T	I	T	C	H	To embroider fabric with drawn threads.
H	E	N	D	I	A	D	Y	S	Idea expressed by using two nouns joined by "and".
H	E	N	P	E	C	K	E	D	A man subjected to persistent nagging by his wife.
H	E	P	A	T	I	T	I	S	Inflammation of the liver, Yellow jaundice.
H	E	P	T	A	R	C	H	Y	Government by seven people.
H	E	R	B	A	R	I	U	M	Collection of dried plant specimens.
H	E	R	B	I	C	I	D	E	A chemical to kill weeds.
H	E	R	B	I	V	O	R	E	Animals that eat only plants.
H	E	R	B	O	R	I	Z	E	Botanize.
H	E	R	C	U	L	E	A	N	Huge, Colossal, Enormous, Gargantuan, Gigantic, Immense, Mammoth, Titanic.
H	E	R	E	A	B	O	U	T	In this vicinity.
H	E	R	E	A	F	T	E	R	Future, Afterward, Beyond, Afterlife.
H	E	R	E	T	I	C	A	L	Dissident, Nonconformist, Heterodox, Radical, Infidel, Unorthodox, Miscreant.
H	E	R	I	T	A	B	L	E	Able to pass by inheritance, Hereditary.
H	E	R	M	E	N	E	U	T	An interpreter of the early church.
H	E	R	M	I	T	A	G	E	Hideaway, Habitation of a hermit, Private retreat, Monastery.
H	E	S	I	T	A	N	C	Y	Indecision, Reluctance, Irresolution, Vacillation, Wavering.
H	E	T	A	E	R	I	S	M	Concubinage, Keeping a mistress in addition to a wife.
H	E	T	E	R	O	D	O	X	Unorthodox, Heretical, Unconventional.
H	E	T	E	R	O	N	Y	M	Words with identical spelling but different meanings.
H	E	T	E	R	O	S	I	S	Growth advantage of crossbreeding as opposed to inbreeding.
H	E	T	E	R	O	T	I	C	Relating to heterosis.
H	E	U	R	I	S	T	I	C	Stimulation for research with ability to prove.
H	E	X	A	C	H	O	R	D	Series of six consecutive notes with semitone between third and fourth used in music.
H	E	X	A	G	O	N	A	L	Having six angles and six sides.
H	E	X	A	M	E	T	E	R	The six-foot dactylic line of Greek and Latin epic poetry.
H	E	X	A	S	T	Y	L	E	Portico with six comumns.
H	I	B	E	R	N	A	T	E	To spend the winter in an inactive state where body temperature drops to zero.
H	I	B	E	R	N	I	A	N	Native of Ireland.
H	I	D	E	O	U	S	L	Y	Ghastly, Horribly, Luridly, Terribly, Repulsively, Nastily.
H	I	E	R	A	R	C	H	Y	Form of government administered by a dominant group, An organization in grades.
H	I	G	H	F	L	O	W	N	Elevated, Exalted, Bombastic, Pretentious, Rhetorical, Flowery, Grandiloquent.
H	I	G	H	L	I	G	H	T	Emphasize, Stress, Distinctive feature.
H	I	L	A	R	I	O	U	S	Merry, Mirthful, Ludicrous, Joyous, Boisterous, Jovial.
H	I	N	D	R	A	N	C	E	Encumbrance, Impediment, Obstruction, Obstacle, Prevention.
H	I	P	P	O	C	R	A	S	Aromatic, Highly spiced wine of medieval Europe.
H	I	P	P	U	R	I	T	E	Division of extinct mammals.
H	I	R	S	U	T	I	S	M	Excessive growth of hair.

1	2	3	4	5	6	7	8	9	Definition
H	I	R	U	N	D	I	N	E	Swallow.
H	I	S	L	O	P	I	T	E	Bright green Indian calcite.
H	I	S	T	A	M	I	N	E	A crystalline base found in ergot and other plants.
H	I	S	T	O	L	O	G	Y	Microscopic anatomy.
H	I	S	T	O	R	I	A	N	Writer of history, Chronicler.
H	O	A	R	F	R	O	S	T	White frost.
H	O	B	G	O	B	L	I	N	Mischievous imp, Bugaboo, Bugbear.
H	O	B	N	A	I	L	E	D	Studded with hobnails.
H	O	D	O	G	R	A	P	H	A path representing the linear velocity of a moving point.
H	O	D	O	M	E	T	E	R	Instrument for measuring distance travelled by wheeled vehicle.
H	O	L	O	C	A	U	S	T	Thorough destruction, Burnt sacrifice.
H	O	M	E	S	T	E	A	D	House, Private residence.
H	O	M	I	L	E	T	I	C	Resembling a sermon.
H	O	M	O	C	L	I	N	E	A layer of stratified rock.
H	O	M	O	L	Y	S	I	S	The decomposition of a chemical compound into two neutral atoms.
H	O	M	O	P	H	O	N	E	Two words pronounced alike but different in meaning.
H	O	M	O	P	L	A	S	Y	Resemblance through common ancestry.
H	O	M	O	T	A	X	I	S	Similarity in arrangement.
H	O	M	U	N	C	U	L	I	Dwarfs, Manikins, Little men.
H	O	N	E	Y	B	E	A	R	Sloth bear, Kinkajou.
H	O	N	E	Y	B	I	R	D	A bird that guides to a beehive for the honey.
H	O	N	E	Y	C	O	M	B	Hexagonal wax cells built by bees to contain their young and honey, Waffle pattern.
H	O	N	E	Y	M	O	O	N	A trip taken by newlyweds.
H	O	N	O	R	I	F	I	C	Implying respect.
H	O	O	C	H	I	N	O	O	Distilled liquour made by Alaskan Indians.
H	O	O	P	S	K	I	R	T	Underskirt stiffened with hoops, Crinoline skirt.
H	O	P	E	F	U	L	L	Y	Expectantly, Confidently, Optimistically, Promisingly, Brightly, Happily.
H	O	P	S	C	O	T	C	H	A child's game involving hopping on one leg through a special configuration.
H	O	R	D	E	O	L	U	M	Sty.
H	O	R	E	H	O	U	N	D	Aromatic mint used in medicines.
H	O	R	I	Z	O	N	A	L	Relating to an horizon.
H	O	R	M	O	N	I	Z	E	To treat with a hormone, To castrate chemically.
H	O	R	O	L	O	G	E	R	Clockmaster, Watchmaker.
H	O	R	O	S	C	O	P	Y	Study of the zodiac to foretell events of a person's life.
H	O	R	R	I	F	I	E	D	Dismayed, Appalled, Terrified, Daunted, Shaken.
H	O	R	S	E	M	I	N	T	Water mint.
H	O	R	S	E	P	L	A	Y	Boisterous, Roughhouse, Fooling, Rowdiness, Skylarking, Buffoonery, Clowning.
H	O	R	S	E	S	H	O	E	Narrow plate of iron beaten to fit the shape of each individual hoof of a house.
H	O	R	T	A	T	O	R	Y	Characterized by exhortation.
H	O	S	T	I	L	I	T	Y	Antagonism, Animosity, Enmity, Opposition, Antipathy, Rancour.
H	O	U	N	D	F	I	S	H	Dogfish.
H	O	U	R	G	L	A	S	S	Glass vessel with sand divided between two segments to measure passage of time.
H	O	U	S	E	B	O	A	T	A barge or yacht having cabins or sleeping accommodation.
H	O	U	S	E	C	O	A	T	Dressing gown or gown for lounging.
H	O	U	S	E	H	O	L	D	Group of people living together in one dwelling place.
H	O	U	S	E	L	I	N	E	Light rope used to manipulate heavy ropes.
H	O	U	S	E	M	A	I	D	Female servant employed to do housework.
H	O	U	S	E	W	I	F	E	Married woman who manages the domestic arrangements of her household.
H	O	V	E	R	P	O	R	T	A port catering for hovercraft.
H	O	Y	D	E	N	I	S	H	Lively, Tomboyish, Unladylike, Boisterous.
H	U	A	M	U	C	H	I	L	Camachile, Tropical tree yielding timber, yellow dye and edible fruit, Tamarind.
H	U	B	R	I	S	T	I	C	Proud, Arrogant, Vain, Insolent, Disdainful, Haughty, Over-bearing, Supercilious.
H	U	C	K	A	B	A	C	K	Absorbent durable cotton and linen fabric with small all over pattern.
H	U	M	D	I	N	G	E	R	Something very extraordinary.
H	U	M	I	L	I	A	T	E	Humble, Mortify, Abase, Demean, Debase, Degrade, Lower.
H	U	N	C	H	B	A	C	K	A person with a hump on their back.
H	U	N	D	R	E	D	T	H	One of a hundred equal parts.
H	U	R	R	I	C	A	N	E	Tropical cyclone, Typhoon, Storm, Tornado, Whirlwind.
H	U	R	R	I	E	D	L	Y	Quickly, Hastily.
H	U	R	T	F	U	L	L	Y	Painfully, Evilly, Mischievously, Harmfully.
H	U	S	B	A	N	D	R	Y	Agriculture, Farming, Economy, Frugality, Providence, Prudence, Thrift.
H	U	S	K	I	N	E	S	S	Hoarseness, Roughness, Dryness.
H	Y	A	E	N	I	D	A	E	Family of carnivorous mammals, Hyena.
H	Y	A	L	O	N	E	M	A	Genus of long-stemmed sponges.
H	Y	B	R	I	D	I	S	M	State of being hybrid.
H	Y	B	R	I	D	I	Z	E	Cross, Interbreed.
H	Y	D	A	N	T	O	I	N	Crystalline acidic compound found in beet juice.

1	2	3	4	5	6	7	8	9	
H	Y	D	N	A	C	E	A	E	Family of fungi.
H	Y	D	R	A	N	G	E	A	Large genus of shrubs.
H	Y	D	R	A	S	T	I	S	Genus of herbs, Dried rhizome and roots of goldenseal formerly used as a tonic.
H	Y	D	R	A	U	L	I	C	Operated and moved or effected by movement of liquid.
H	Y	D	R	O	F	O	I	L	Underwater plate or fin for lifting craft clear of the water.
H	Y	D	R	O	L	O	G	Y	Study of surface water.
H	Y	D	R	O	S	T	A	T	A device to detect the presence or absence of water.
H	Y	M	N	O	L	O	G	Y	Study of hymns and their composition.
H	Y	O	S	T	Y	L	I	C	Having the jaws connected with the cranium.
H	Y	P	A	L	L	A	G	E	Reversal of natural relations of two elements in a proposition.
H	Y	P	E	R	B	O	L	A	A section of a cone.
H	Y	P	E	R	B	O	L	E	Exaggeration, Embellishment, Overstatement, Embroidering.
H	Y	P	H	E	N	A	T	E	To connect with a hyphen.
H	Y	P	N	O	T	I	S	M	Practice of inducing hypnosis, Mesmerism.
H	Y	P	O	B	L	A	S	T	Endoderm of an embryo.
H	Y	P	O	C	A	U	S	T	Central heating system of ancient Roman buildings.
H	Y	P	O	C	O	T	Y	L	Part of the axis of a plant embryo.
H	Y	P	O	C	R	I	S	Y	Sham, Sanctimony, Pretense of having beliefs, Insincerity, Glibness.
H	Y	P	O	C	R	I	T	E	Dissembler, Phony, Charlatan, Impostor, Humbug, Fraud, Quack, Pretender.

I

1	2	3	4	5	6	7	8	9	
I	C	H	N	E	U	M	O	N	Mongoose.
I	C	O	N	O	L	O	G	Y	Study of icons, Analysis of artistic symbolism.
I	D	E	N	T	I	C	A	L	Same, Exact, Duplicate, Equal, Tantamount, Indistinguishable.
I	D	E	O	G	R	A	P	H	Logogram, Emblem.
I	D	E	O	L	O	G	U	E	Theorist, Dreamer, Visionary, Utopian.
I	D	I	O	B	L	A	S	T	Isolated plant cell.
I	D	I	O	C	R	A	S	Y	Idiosyncrasy, Peculiarity, Eccentricity, Strangeness.
I	D	I	O	M	A	T	I	C	Individual, Peculiar to a particular group.
I	D	I	O	P	A	T	H	Y	Anomaly on disease arising from an unknown cause.
I	D	R	I	A	L	I	T	E	A mineral occurring as a crystalline hydrocarbon.
I	G	N	O	R	A	M	U	S	Dunce, Ignorant.
I	G	N	O	R	A	N	C	E	Illiteracy, Inexperience, Simplicity, Innocence, Unawareness, Unfamiliarity.
I	L	L	E	G	A	L	L	Y	Unlawfully, Criminally, Illicitly, Wrongfully, Feloniously, Irregularly, Illegitimately.
I	L	L	E	G	I	B	L	E	Indecipherable, Unreadable, Faint, Indistinct, Obscure, Unclear.
I	L	L	I	B	E	R	A	L	Coarse, Vulgar, Stingy, Intolerant, Bigoted, Biased, Prejudiced, Mean.
I	L	L	O	G	I	C	A	L	Unlawfully, Irrational, Reasonless, Unreasonable, Inconsistent, Unsound, Absurd.
I	M	A	G	I	N	A	R	Y	Fancied, Abstract, Hypothetical, Visionary, Illusory, Unreal, Unsubstantial.
I	M	B	A	L	A	N	C	E	Absence of balance, Absence of biological equilibrium.
I	M	B	E	C	I	L	I	C	Characteristic of an imbecile.
I	M	B	R	I	C	A	T	E	Overlapping, Override, Overlie, Lap over, Shingle.
I	M	B	R	O	G	L	I	O	Conglomeration, Complicated, Violently confused, Quarrel, Dispute.
I	M	I	T	A	T	I	O	N	Counterfeit, Copy, Ersatz, Fake, Forgery, Sham, Simulation, Replica.
I	M	I	T	A	T	I	V	E	Onomatopoeic, Slavish, Emulative, Apish, Mimicry, Reproducing.
I	M	M	E	D	I	A	T	E	Direct, Proximate, Intuitive, Instant, Instantaneous, Close.
I	M	M	E	N	S	I	T	Y	Enormity, Magnitude, Vastness.
I	M	M	E	R	S	I	O	N	Plunging, Sinking, Dipping, Submersion.
I	M	M	I	G	R	A	N	T	A person that settles in another country as a permanent resident.
I	M	M	O	D	E	S	T	Y	Boldness, Impropriety, Unchastity, Forwardness, Provocativeness.
I	M	M	O	R	A	L	L	Y	Wickedly, Wrongfully, Evilly, Viciously.
I	M	M	O	V	A	B	L	E	Stationary, Steadfast, Unalterable, Unyielding, Impassive, Fixed, Adamant.
I	M	M	U	T	A	B	L	E	Inflexible, Constant, Fixed, Invariable, Unchangeable, Immovable, Inalterable.
I	M	P	A	R	T	I	A	L	Fair, Dispassionate, Just, Objective, Unbiased, Equal.
I	M	P	A	S	S	I	V	E	Phlegmatic, Stoic, Apathetic, Composed, Emotionless, Imperturbable, Taciturn.
I	M	P	A	T	I	E	N	T	Impetuous, Fretful, Intolerant, Anxious, Eager, Ardent, Keen, Nervous.
I	M	P	E	D	A	N	C	E	Encumbrance, Hindrance, Impediment, Clog, Opposition, Resistance.
I	M	P	E	L	L	I	N	G	Moving, Propelling, Forcing, Driving, Mobilizing, Inciting, Goading, Spurring.
I	M	P	E	R	A	T	O	R	Commander, Emperor, Supreme leader.
I	M	P	E	R	F	E	C	T	Defective, Inadequate, Incomplete, Diminished, Faulty, Amiss, Flawed.
I	M	P	E	R	I	O	U	S	Commanding, Dominant, Lordly, Arrogant, Overbearing, Urgent, Compelling.
I	M	P	E	T	R	A	T	E	Procure, Entreat.
I	M	P	E	T	U	O	U	S	Furious, Precipitate, Abrupt, Headlong, Hurried, Rushing, Sudden, Spontaneous.
I	M	P	L	E	M	E	N	T	Complete, Execute, Perform, Fulfill, Enforce, Effect, Instrument, Tool.
I	M	P	L	I	A	B	L	E	Stiff, Incompliant, Inflexible, Rigid, Unbending, Unyielding.
I	M	P	L	I	C	A	T	E	Involve, Embroil, Mire, Tangle, Incriminate, Affect, Concern, Include.

1	2	3	4	5	6	7	8	9	
I	M	P	L	O	R	I	N	G	Supplicating, Petitioning, Beseeching, Entreating, Praying, Begging, Craving.
I	M	P	O	L	I	T	I	C	Unwise, Imprudent, Indiscreet, Inadvisable, Tractless, Brash, Untactful, Inexpedient.
I	M	P	O	R	T	A	N	T	Consequential, Significant, Substantial, Conspicuous, Distinctive, Impressive.
I	M	P	O	R	T	I	N	G	Meaning, Signifying, Implying, Bringing, Concerning, Introducing, Expressing.
I	M	P	O	R	T	U	N	E	Beg, Appeal, Beseech, Crave, Entreat, Implore, Invoke, Plead.
I	M	P	O	S	T	U	R	E	Cheat, Counterfeit, Deceit, Deception, Fraud, Hoax, Sham, Artifice.
I	M	P	O	T	E	N	C	E	Weakness, Feebleness, Helplessness, Sterility, Powerless.
I	M	P	R	E	C	A	T	E	Curse, Invoke, Swear, Damn, Execrate.
I	M	P	R	O	B	I	T	Y	Dishonesty.
I	M	P	R	O	M	P	T	U	Extemporaneously, Improvised, Makeshift, Unrehearsed, Offhand, Prompt, Quick.
I	M	P	R	O	V	I	S	E	Extempore, Provide without preparation.
I	M	P	R	U	D	E	N	T	Rash, Indiscreet, Unwise, Ill-advised, Impolitic, Inadvisable, Inexpedient.
I	M	P	U	D	E	N	C	E	Insolence, Boldness, Disrespect, Impertinence, Shamelessness.
I	M	P	U	L	S	I	O	N	Impetus, Compulsion, Push, Impelling.
I	M	P	U	L	S	I	V	E	Spontaneous, Automatic, Instinctive, Involuntary, Abrupt, Hasty, Impetuous, Sudden.
I	M	P	U	T	A	B	L	E	Ascribable, Referable, Culpable.
I	N	A	B	I	L	I	T	Y	Incapacity, Incompetence, Ineffectiveness, Inaptitude, Ineffeciency, Ineptitude.
I	N	A	M	O	R	A	T	O	Beloved, Sweetheart, Steady, Mistress, Lover, Paramour.
I	N	A	N	I	M	A	T	E	Insensible, Insensate, Unfeeling, Dead, Defunct, Extinct, Lifeless, Cold, Senseless.
I	N	A	N	I	T	I	O	N	Empty, Exhausted, Lethargy, Lack of vitality.
I	N	A	P	T	N	E	S	S	Ineptness, Unfitness, Awkwardness, Clumsiness.
I	N	A	U	D	I	B	L	E	Unable to be heard.
I	N	A	U	G	U	R	A	L	Formally installed, dedicated or consecrated.
I	N	C	A	P	A	B	L	E	Intolerant, Incompetent, Unfit, Inefficient, Inept, Inexpert, Unskilled, Unqualified.
I	N	C	A	R	N	A	T	E	Embody, Materialize, Manifest, Substantiate, Utter, Actualize, Personify.
I	N	C	E	N	S	O	R	Y	Censer, Thurible.
I	N	C	E	N	T	I	V	E	Stimulus, Motivation, Kindling, Goad, Impetus, Impulse, Incitement, Spur.
I	N	C	E	P	T	I	O	N	Source, Derivation, Commencement, Initiation, Ingestion, Origin, Root.
I	N	C	E	P	T	I	V	E	Beginning, Initial, Incipient, Introductory, Nascent.
I	N	C	E	S	S	A	N	T	Continual, Everlasting, Unceasing, Ceaseless, Interminable, Perpetual, Timeless.
I	N	C	I	D	E	N	C	E	Occurrence, Prevalence, Range, Scope, Extent of influence.
I	N	C	I	P	I	E	N	T	Commencing, Initial, Introductory, Nascent.
I	N	C	L	E	M	E	N	T	Harsh, Rough, Stormy, Unmerciful, Rigorous, Bitter, Brutal, Intemperate.
I	N	C	L	I	N	I	N	G	Bending, Bowing, Leaning, Deviating, Stooping, Bent, Disposition, Tendency.
I	N	C	L	U	D	I	N	G	Comprehending, Containing, Embracing, Encompassing, Involving, Comprising.
I	N	C	O	G	N	I	T	O	Unknown, Unidentified, With identity concealed.
I	N	C	O	M	M	O	D	E	Disturb, Molest, Inconvenience, Hinder, Impede, Obstruct, Annoy, Bother.
I	N	C	O	N	D	I	T	E	Crude, Unpolished, Rude, Discourteous, Disrespectful, Ill-bred, Uncivil, Impolite.
I	N	C	O	R	R	E	C	T	Inaccurate, Untrue, Wrong, Erroneous, False, Specious, Unsound, Faulty.
I	N	C	R	E	M	E	N	T	Increase, Enlargement, Addition, Augmentation.
I	N	C	U	B	A	T	O	R	Apparatus for care of premature babies or for artificially hatching eggs.
I	N	C	U	L	C	A	T	E	Implant, Instil, Educate, Instruct, Impart, Teach, Communicate.
I	N	C	U	L	P	A	T	E	Accuse, Blame, Incriminate, Charge, Impeach, Indict, Tax, Arraign.
I	N	C	U	M	B	E	N	T	Occupant, Holder of an office.
I	N	C	U	N	A	B	L	E	Infancy, Beginning, Early work of art, Insect cocoon.
I	N	C	U	R	A	B	L	E	Hopeless, Irremediable, Irreparable, Uncurable, Unrecoverable, Uncorrectable.
I	N	C	U	R	I	O	U	S	Disinterested, Unconcerned, Indifferent, Aloof, Casual, Abstracted, Remote.
I	N	C	U	R	S	I	O	N	Invasion, Foray, Inroad, Raid, Irruption.
I	N	C	U	R	V	A	T	E	Bend, Crook, Bow.
I	N	D	E	C	E	N	C	Y	Obscenity, Coarseness, Vulgarity, Foulness, Smuttiness.
I	N	D	E	L	I	B	L	E	Ineradicable, Unerasable, Ineffaceable, Inextirpable, Enduring, Permanent.
I	N	D	E	M	N	I	F	Y	Compensate, Recompense, Reimburse, Remunerate, Repay, Requite.
I	N	D	E	M	N	I	T	Y	Compensation, Reparation, Amends, Redress, Recompense, Restitution.
I	N	D	E	N	T	I	O	N	Indentation, Notch, Recess.
I	N	D	E	N	T	U	R	E	Contract for apprenticeship, Formal list, Certificate.
I	N	D	I	C	A	T	E	D	Demonstrated, Suggested, Hinted, Intimated, Pointed, Signified, Announced.
I	N	D	I	C	A	T	O	R	Pointer, Tracer, Index, Hand.
I	N	D	I	C	I	B	L	E	Unspeakable, Inexpressible.
I	N	D	I	C	T	I	O	N	Ancient Roman property tax assessed on a fifteen year cycle, Proclamation.
I	N	D	I	G	E	N	C	E	Neediness, Poverty, Destitution, Penury, Privation, Want, Impecuniousness.
I	N	D	I	G	N	A	N	T	Angry, Heated, Irate, Acrimonious, Wrathful.
I	N	D	I	G	N	I	T	Y	Humiliation, Injury, Outrage, Insult, Affront, Grievance, Injustice, Wrong.
I	N	D	I	G	O	T	I	N	Dark blue crystalline compound colouring of indigo.
I	N	D	I	S	P	O	S	E	Make unfit, Make averse.
I	N	D	O	L	E	N	C	E	Sloth, Idleness, Laziness, Sluggishness, Tranquillity.
I	N	D	U	C	T	I	L	E	Unyielding, not easily influenced.
I	N	D	U	C	T	I	O	N	Initiation, Inference, Inaugural, Investiture.

1	2	3	4	5	6	7	8	9	
I	N	D	U	C	T	I	V	E	Inducing, Tempting, Introductory.
I	N	D	U	L	G	E	N	T	Tolerant, Lenient, Merciful, Charitable, Permissive, Forgiving, Benign, Kindly.
I	N	D	U	R	A	T	E	D	Hardened, Congealed, Solidified, Set, Dried, Caked, Inured, Established.
I	N	E	B	R	I	A	N	T	Alcohol, Intoxicant.
I	N	E	B	R	I	A	T	E	Intoxicate, Exhilarate, Drunkard, Tippler, Toper.
I	N	E	B	R	I	E	T	Y	Drunkenness, Intoxication.
I	N	E	F	F	A	B	L	E	Unutterable, Indescribable, Unspeakable, Taboo, Celestial, Sacred, Ethereal.
I	N	E	L	A	S	T	I	C	Inflexible, Rigid, Unbending, Stiff, Impliable, Unyielding, Immalleable, Incompliant.
I	N	E	L	E	G	A	N	T	Coarse, Crude, Gross, Rough, Rude, Uncouth, Unrefined, Vulgar.
I	N	E	P	T	N	E	S	S	Inaptness, Inappropriateness, Awkwardness, Clumsiness, Inexpertness.
I	N	E	R	R	A	B	L	E	Infallible, Sure, Unerring.
I	N	E	R	T	N	E	S	S	Passivity, Inactivity, Quiescence, Quietude, Impotence, Apathy.
I	N	E	V	I	D	E	N	T	Not obvious, Unclear.
I	N	E	X	A	C	T	L	Y	Inaccurately, Indefinitely, Indistinctly.
I	N	F	A	N	T	I	L	E	Immature, Childish, Babyish, Puerile, Frustrate.
I	N	F	A	T	U	A	T	E	Besotted, Enamoured, Inspire with extravagant passion.
I	N	F	E	C	T	I	O	N	Contamination, Pollution, Fungus, Communication.
I	N	F	E	R	E	N	C	E	Deduction, Judgment, Conjecture, Supposition, Surmise, Conclusion, Assumption.
I	N	F	E	R	T	I	L	E	Sterile, Barren, Impotent, Unfruitful, Depleted, Drained, Exhausted, Unproductive.
I	N	F	I	E	L	D	E	R	Fielder in the game of cricket.
I	N	F	I	R	M	I	T	Y	Feebleness, Frailty, Disease, Malady, Failing, Foible, Decrepitude, Weakness.
I	N	F	L	A	T	I	O	N	Pomposity, Distention, Untoward rise in the cost of living.
I	N	F	L	E	X	I	O	N	Bend, Curve, Grammatical variations.
I	N	F	L	U	E	N	C	E	Dominance, Sway, Ascendancy, Authority, Prestige, Weight, Modify, Sway.
I	N	F	L	U	E	N	Z	A	Highly contagious virus.
I	N	F	O	R	M	A	N	T	One who gives information, Squealer.
I	N	F	U	R	I	A	T	E	Enrage, Madden, Anger, Incense, Make furious.
I	N	F	U	S	I	B	L	E	Incapable of fusion.
I	N	F	U	S	O	R	I	A	Fungi, Bacteria, Algae.
I	N	G	E	N	I	O	U	S	Clever, Inventive, Resourceful, Creative, Innovative, Adroit, Dexterous, Cunning.
I	N	G	E	N	U	O	U	S	Simple, Unwary, Open, Natural, Artless, Naive, Unaffected, Unsophisticated.
I	N	G	E	S	T	I	O	N	Taking food into the digestive system, Taking fuel into an engine.
I	N	G	E	S	T	I	V	E	Relating to ingestion.
I	N	G	L	E	N	O	O	K	Recessed seating area at a fireplace.
I	N	G	R	A	I	N	E	D	Innate, Inherent, Congenital, Inborn, Intrinsic, Inveterate, Deep-seated, Confirmed.
I	N	G	R	O	W	I	N	G	Growing inwards, Developing within confining limits.
I	N	H	A	B	I	T	E	D	Occupied, Populated, Tenanted, Settled.
I	N	H	E	R	E	N	C	E	Intrinsic, Essential.
I	N	H	E	R	I	T	E	D	Derived from ancestors, Succeeded, Possessed, Received, Congenital.
I	N	H	E	R	I	T	O	R	Heir.
I	N	H	I	B	I	T	E	D	Frigid, Cold, Passionless, Unresponsive, Repressed, Reduced, Restrained.
I	N	H	U	M	A	N	L	Y	Cruelly, Barbarously, Ferociously, Savagely, Malignantly, Fiendishly.
I	N	I	T	I	A	L	L	Y	Beginning, Originally, Primarily, Firstly.
I	N	I	T	I	A	T	E	D	Introduced, Inaugurated, Instituted, Launched, Originated, Admitted, Installed.
I	N	J	E	C	T	I	N	G	Forcing, Introducing, Intruding, Congesting.
I	N	J	E	C	T	I	O	N	Substance introduced into the body or another substance.
I	N	J	U	R	I	O	U	S	Hurtful, Harmful, Detrimental, Abusive, Offensive, Defamatory, Damaging, Evil.
I	N	J	U	S	T	I	C	E	Iniquity, Unfairness, Wrong, Malpractice, Villainy, Grievance, Outrage, Violation.
I	N	N	E	R	M	O	S	T	Farthest inward.
I	N	N	E	R	V	A	T	E	Arouse, Stimulate, Provoke, Excite, Galvanize, Move, Quicken, Motivate.
I	N	N	K	E	E	P	E	R	Landlord of an inn.
I	N	N	O	C	U	O	U	S	Harmless, Inoffensive, Insipid, Insignificant, Innocent, Banal, Inane, Bland.
I	N	N	O	X	I	O	U	S	Same as INNOCUOUS.
I	N	O	R	G	A	N	I	C	Mineral, Chemical substance, Artificial, Unnatural.
I	N	Q	U	I	R	I	N	G	Questioning, Examining, Exploring, Investigating, Probing, Curious, Inquisitive.
I	N	S	A	T	I	A	T	E	Unappeasable, Unsatisfiable, Quenchless.
I	N	S	E	C	T	I	L	E	Consisting of insects.
I	N	S	E	N	S	A	T	E	Inanimate, Foolish, Fatuous, Unfeeling, Cruel, Harsh, Brutal, Insensitive.
I	N	S	E	R	T	I	N	G	Introducing, Insinuating, Interjecting, Interposing, Intruding, Implanting, Entering.
I	N	S	I	D	I	O	U	S	Subtle, Sly, Astute, Crafty, Cunning, Tricky, Wily, Perfidious.
I	N	S	I	N	C	E	R	E	Hypocritical, Deceitful, Dishonest, Lying, Untruthful, Shifty, Mendacious.
I	N	S	I	N	U	A	T	E	Hint, Suggest, Imply, Creep, Intimate, Impute, Infiltrate, Introduce.
I	N	S	I	P	I	D	L	Y	Dully, Uninterestingly, Inanely, Blandly, Dully, Tediously, Feebly, Mildly.
I	N	S	I	P	I	E	N	T	Stupid, Foolish.
I	N	S	I	S	T	I	N	G	Persisting, Persevering, Holding, Emphasising.
I	N	S	O	L	E	N	C	E	Impudence, Disrespect, Effrontery, Boldness, Arrogance, Rudeness, Contempt.
I	N	S	O	L	U	B	L	E	Inextricable, Insolvable, Irresoluble, Unexplainable, Irrefutable, Inconceivable.

1	2	3	4	5	6	7	8	9	Definition
I	N	S	O	L	V	E	N	T	Bankrupt, Impoverished, Deficient.
I	N	S	O	M	N	I	A	C	Person suffering from insomnia.
I	N	S	P	E	C	T	O	R	One that oversees or supervises.
I	N	S	P	I	R	I	N	G	Encouraging, Impelling, Motivating, Affecting, Arousing, Producing, Provoking.
I	N	S	T	A	L	L	E	D	Introduced, Established, Initiated, Ensconced, Settled, Invested.
I	N	S	T	A	N	T	E	R	Immediately, Instantly.
I	N	S	T	A	N	T	L	Y	Immediately, Directly, Forthwith.
I	N	S	T	I	G	A	T	E	Incite, Provoke, Activate, Hint, Insinuate, Suggest, Urge, Goad.
I	N	S	T	I	T	U	T	E	Found, Constitute, Create, Establish, Organize, Launch, Introduce, Originate.
I	N	S	U	L	A	R	L	Y	Narrowly, Rigidly.
I	N	S	U	L	A	T	O	R	Material or body that is a poor conductor of electricity, heat or sound.
I	N	S	U	L	T	I	N	G	Attacking, Humiliating, Taunting, Jeering, Deriding, Mocking, Ridiculing.
I	N	S	U	R	A	N	C	E	Device for the elimination of an economic risk.
I	N	S	U	R	G	E	N	T	Rebel, Insubordinate, Rebellious, Anarchist, Mutineer, Malcontent.
I	N	S	U	R	R	E	C	T	Engage in insurrection.
I	N	T	E	G	R	A	N	T	Component, Element.
I	N	T	E	G	R	A	T	E	Constitute, Harmonize, Reconcile, Blend, Fuse, Merge, Combine.
I	N	T	E	G	R	I	T	Y	Soundness, Honesty, Perfection, Forthrightness.
I	N	T	E	L	L	E	C	T	Understanding, Reason, Mind, Comprehension, Intuition, Brain, Genius, Thinker.
I	N	T	E	N	S	A	T	E	Aggravate, Deepen, Enhance, Heighten, Magnify, Mount, Rise, Intensify.
I	N	T	E	N	S	E	L	Y	Hard, Assiduously, Earnestly, Exhaustively, Seriously, Gravely, Severely, Fiercely.
I	N	T	E	N	S	I	T	Y	Tension, Intensity, Determination, Intensification.
I	N	T	E	N	S	I	O	N	Energy, Loudness.
I	N	T	E	N	S	I	V	E	Zealous, Eager, Exhaustive, Intensifying.
I	N	T	E	N	T	I	O	N	Intent, Purpose, Design, Aim, End, Object, Goal, Project.
I	N	T	E	R	C	E	D	E	Intervene, Mediate, Interpose, Interfere, Intermediate.
I	N	T	E	R	C	E	P	T	Hinder, Block, Catch, Grab, Seize, Check, Curb, Interrupt.
I	N	T	E	R	D	I	C	T	Prohibition, Forbid, Ban, Inhibit, Outlaw, Proscription.
I	N	T	E	R	F	E	R	E	Interpose, Intervene, Meddle, Intersect, Tamper, Impede, Obstruct, Thwart.
I	N	T	E	R	F	L	O	W	Interaction between two wind currents of different velocities.
I	N	T	E	R	F	U	S	E	Combine, Intermingle, Infuse, Pervade, Permeate, Blend, Fuse, Penetrate.
I	N	T	E	R	J	E	C	T	Interpolate, Intervene, Interpose, Insert, Insinuate, Introduce.
I	N	T	E	R	L	A	C	E	Interweave, Intertwine, Interwork, Alternate, Mix.
I	N	T	E	R	L	A	R	D	Interfuse, Intersperse, Intersprinkle, Insert, Mingle.
I	N	T	E	R	L	I	N	E	Insert, To line.
I	N	T	E	R	L	I	N	K	Engage, Interrelate, Unite, Connect, Synchronize.
I	N	T	E	R	L	O	P	E	Intrude, Meddle, Interfere, Tamper.
I	N	T	E	R	L	U	D	E	Intermission, Interval, Break, Lull, Pause, Respite, Rest, Episode.
I	N	T	E	R	M	E	N	T	Burial, Inhumation.
I	N	T	E	R	N	I	S	T	Specialist in internal medicine.
I	N	T	E	R	N	O	D	E	Segment, Part between two nodes.
I	N	T	E	R	P	L	A	Y	Interaction, Coact.
I	N	T	E	R	P	O	S	E	Intrude, Intervene, Mediate, Interject, Insert, Insinuate, Thrust.
I	N	T	E	R	P	R	E	T	Explain, Construe, Translate, Expound, Elucidate, Illustrate, Represent, Portray.
I	N	T	E	R	R	U	P	T	Arrest, Check, Halt, Stay, Defer, Postpone, Suspend, Thwart.
I	N	T	E	R	S	E	C	T	Divide, Cross, Traverse, Bisect, Overlap.
I	N	T	E	R	V	E	I	N	Interlace with veins.
I	N	T	E	R	V	E	N	E	Interfere, Interpose, Intercede, Mediate, Separate, Divide, Part, Sever.
I	N	T	E	R	V	I	E	W	Formal meeting, Conference, Conversation with an applicant or candidate.
I	N	T	E	S	T	A	T	E	Not having executed a valid will.
I	N	T	E	S	T	I	N	E	Inner, Inward, Lower part of alimentary canal.
I	N	T	R	I	C	A	T	E	Complex, Involved, Entangled, Obscure, Elaborate, Arduous, Difficult, Hard.
I	N	T	R	I	N	S	I	C	Inherent, Congenital, Real, Actual, Essential, Innate, Constitutional, Deep-seated.
I	N	T	R	O	D	U	C	E	Conduct, Usher, Institute, Enter, Inaugurate, Broach, Precede, Preface.
I	N	T	R	O	V	E	R	T	Turn or bend inward.
I	N	T	R	U	S	I	O	N	Trespass, Encroachment, Force, Injection.
I	N	T	R	U	S	I	V	E	Impertinent, Obtrusive, Officious, Intruding.
I	N	T	U	I	T	I	O	N	Insight, Sixth sense, Contemplation, Consideration, Reason.
I	N	T	U	I	T	I	V	E	Instinctive, Direct, Immediate.
I	N	T	U	M	E	S	C	E	Enlarge, swell, expand.
I	N	U	M	B	R	A	T	E	Shade, Screen, Shadow, Umbrage.
I	N	U	N	C	T	I	O	N	Anointing.
I	N	V	E	C	T	I	V	E	Insult, Abuse, Denunciatory, Vituperation, Tirade.
I	N	V	E	N	T	I	O	N	Discovery, Conception, Formulation, Origination, Idea, Concept, Innovation.
I	N	V	E	N	T	I	V	E	Creative, Ingenious, Innovative, Productive, Fertile, Constructive, Formative.
I	N	V	E	N	T	O	R	Y	Supply, Fund, Stock, Reserve, Catalogue, Itemize, Enumerate, Specify.
I	N	V	E	R	S	E	L	Y	Reverse order or manner.

1	2	3	4	5	6	7	8	9	
I	N	V	E	R	S	I	O	N	Reversed, Inverted, Turnabout, Changeabout.
I	N	V	I	D	I	O	U	S	Defamatory, Jealous, Hateful, Obnoxious, Injurious, Envious, Repugnant, Bitter.
I	N	V	I	O	L	A	T	E	Pure, Unbroken, Untouched, Intact, Perfect, Flawless, Sacred, Faultless.
I	N	V	I	S	I	B	L	E	Unseen, Untangible, Imperceptible, Hidden, Inconspicuous, Unapparent.
I	N	V	O	L	U	C	R	E	Rosette of bracts surrounding a composite flower head.
I	R	A	S	C	I	B	L	E	Testy, Cranky, Touchy, Tetchy, Splenetic, Cantankerous, Irritable, Fractious.
I	R	O	N	S	I	D	E	S	Body of hardy veteran troops.
I	R	R	A	D	I	A	T	E	Illuminate, Brighten, Radiate, Shed, Diffuse, Shine, Enlighten, Uplift.
I	R	R	E	G	U	L	A	R	Abnormal, Deviant, Divergent, Unnatural, Odd, Peculiar, Unique.
I	R	R	I	T	A	B	L	E	Fractious, Peevish, Snappish, Petulant, Querulous, Cantankerous, Irascible.
I	R	R	U	P	T	I	O	N	Eruption, Invasion, Foray, Incursion, Raid, Inroad.
I	S	A	B	E	L	I	T	A	Angelfish.
I	S	A	G	O	G	I	C	S	Introductory studies dealing with various histories of the Bible.
I	S	A	L	L	O	B	A	R	Imaginary lines on a chart dealing with atmospheric pressure.
I	S	C	H	I	A	T	I	C	Relating to the thick bones of the pelvis.
I	S	E	N	T	R	O	P	E	Line or surface on a map or diagram unaffected by change.
I	S	I	N	G	L	A	S	S	Semitransparent substance used for jellies and glue obtained from algae.
I	S	O	L	A	T	I	O	N	Solitude, Loneness, Solitariness, Separation.
I	S	O	M	E	R	O	U	S	Made up of corresponding segments.
I	S	O	P	E	C	T	I	C	A chart line where ice begins to form in winter.
I	S	O	S	C	E	L	E	S	Having two equal sides.
I	S	O	T	O	N	I	Z	E	Exhibiting equal tension.
I	T	A	L	I	C	I	Z	E	Emphasise, Feature, Stress, Underline, Underscore.
I	T	E	R	A	T	I	O	N	Repetition, Reiteration.
I	T	E	R	A	T	I	V	E	Frequentative.
I	T	I	N	E	R	A	N	T	Ambulant, Nomadic, Vagabond, Vagrant, Roaming, Rambling, Ranging Shifting.
I	T	I	N	E	R	A	R	Y	Route, Journey, Tour, Progress, Travel record.
I	T	I	N	E	R	A	T	E	Travelling in a circuit.

J

1	2	3	4	5	6	7	8	9	
J	A	B	O	R	A	N	D	I	Dried leaves of a South American shrub that are a source of pilocarpine.
J	A	C	K	K	N	I	F	E	Clasp knife.
J	A	C	K	S	T	A	F	F	A staff on the bows of a ship where the nationality flag is hoisted.
J	A	N	I	S	S	A	R	Y	Turkish soldier, Member of a loyal group of supporters.
J	A	U	N	D	I	C	E	D	Prejudiced, Biased, Warped, Partisan, Prepossessed, Suffering from yellow jaundice.
J	E	L	L	Y	F	I	S	H	Transparent saucer-shaped marine free-swimming organism.
J	E	W	E	L	L	E	R	Y	Ornamental pieces often made of precious metal and set with gems.
J	O	C	U	L	A	R	L	Y	Humorously, Merrily, Playfully, Comically, Jovially.
J	O	C	U	N	D	I	T	Y	Pleasantry, Jocundness, Hilarity, Merriment, Jollity, Glee, Joviality.
J	O	L	L	I	N	E	S	S	State of being jolly.
J	U	B	I	L	A	N	C	E	Exultation, Jubilation, Triumph.
J	U	D	I	C	I	A	R	Y	Judicial system of courts of law, Body of judges.
J	U	D	I	C	I	O	U	S	Wise, Prudent, Sage, Sensible, Reasonable, Dispassionate, Equitable, Objective.
J	U	N	I	O	R	A	T	E	High school or college study for the priesthood.
J	U	N	O	E	S	Q	U	E	An elegant, usually tall, woman of beauty and grace.
J	U	R	I	D	I	C	A	L	Legal, Relating to the office of a judge.
J	U	S	T	I	F	I	E	D	Vindicated, Confirmed, Supported, Verified, Explained, Maintained, Well-founded.
J	U	V	E	N	I	L	I	A	Artistic or literary composition produced by or designed for young persons.
J	U	X	T	A	P	O	S	E	Place side by side, In an adjacent position.

K

1	2	3	4	5	6	7	8	9	
K	A	L	A	N	C	H	O	E	Genus of tropical herbs or shrubs.
K	A	L	O	P	A	N	A	X	A showy Japanese tree.
K	A	L	O	X	Y	L	O	N	A form genus of fossil plants based only on roots.
K	A	L	S	I	L	I	T	E	A rare mineral of aluminosilicate of potassium.
K	E	N	T	L	E	D	G	E	Pig iron or scrap metal used as ballast.
K	E	R	A	T	I	T	I	S	Inflammation of the cornea of the eye.
K	E	R	A	T	O	S	I	S	Skin disease, Overgrowth of horny tissue.
K	E	T	O	N	U	R	I	A	Excess ketone bodies in the urine.
K	I	D	N	A	P	P	E	R	One that abducts a person or child for ransom.
K	I	L	O	C	Y	C	L	E	Unit of radio frequency, One thousand cycles per second.
K	I	L	O	M	E	T	R	E	Unit of length, One thousand metres.
K	I	N	E	M	A	T	I	C	Relating to the motion of bodies.
K	I	N	E	S	C	O	P	E	A cathode ray tube.

1	2	3	4	5	6	7	8	9	
K	I	N	S	W	O	M	A	N	A female relative.
K	I	T	T	I	W	A	K	E	A gull.
K	L	E	E	N	B	O	E	K	Royal antelope.
K	N	I	G	H	T	A	G	E	Knighthood, Register of Knights.
K	N	O	T	G	R	A	S	S	Any of several grasses.
K	N	O	W	L	E	D	G	E	Science, Learning, Erudition, Information, Lore, Advice, Scholarship, Wisdom.
K	O	W	T	O	W	I	N	G	Fawning, Cowering, Grovelling, Parasitic, Toadying.
K	Y	M	O	G	R	A	P	H	A device for recording on a moving X-ray film.

L

L	A	B	E	L	L	I	N	G	Designating, Distinguishing, Marking, Specifying.
L	A	B	O	R	I	O	U	S	Industrious, Hardworking, Diligent, Labouring.
L	A	B	O	U	R	I	T	E	Member of the Labour party.
L	A	B	Y	R	I	N	T	H	Maze, Intricacy, Perplexity, Mesh, Morass, Snarl, Tangle, Web.
L	A	C	C	O	L	I	T	H	A mass of igneous rock producing a domic bulging of overlying strata.
L	A	C	E	R	T	I	A	N	Lizard.
L	A	C	E	R	T	I	N	E	Resembling a lizard.
L	A	C	H	R	Y	M	A	L	Relating to tears.
L	A	C	I	N	I	A	T	E	Bordered with a fringe.
L	A	C	O	N	I	C	A	L	Curt, Terse, Concise, Pithy, Undemonstrative, Brief, Succint, Brusque.
L	A	C	T	A	T	I	O	N	Secretion and yielding of milk by the mammary glands.
L	A	L	L	A	T	I	O	N	Baby talk.
L	A	M	B	S	W	O	O	L	Soft wool from seven/eight months old lambs.
L	A	M	I	N	A	R	I	A	Family of kelp, Seaweed.
L	A	M	I	N	A	T	E	D	United in layers, Compressed.
L	A	M	P	B	L	A	C	K	Black soot.
L	A	M	P	O	O	N	E	R	Satirist.
L	A	N	A	R	K	I	T	E	A mineral consisting of a basic lead sulphate.
L	A	N	D	S	C	A	P	E	Picture representing inland scenery.
L	A	N	G	U	I	D	L	Y	Limply, Sluggishly, Torpidly, Inertly, Impassively, Languorously, Weakly.
L	A	N	K	I	N	E	S	S	Leanness, Gauntness, Boniness.
L	A	O	D	I	C	E	A	N	One that is lukewarm or indifferent.
L	A	R	C	E	N	O	U	S	Thievish, Light-fingered.
L	A	R	G	H	E	T	T	O	Direction in music - Somewhat slow.
L	A	R	V	I	C	I	D	E	Insecticide for killing larvae.
L	A	R	Y	N	G	E	A	L	Relating to the larynx.
L	A	S	S	I	T	U	D	E	Fatigue, Languor, Exhaustion, Weariness, Apathy, Indifference, Impotence.
L	A	T	E	R	A	L	L	Y	Sideways.
L	A	T	H	E	W	O	R	K	Machine engraving.
L	A	T	I	M	E	R	I	A	Genus of living coelacanth fishes.
L	A	U	D	A	N	I	N	E	Poisonous crystalline alkaloid obtained from opium.
L	A	U	D	A	T	I	O	N	Eulogy, Praising.
L	A	U	D	A	T	O	R	Y	Commendatory, Eulogistic.
L	A	U	G	H	A	B	L	E	Comical, Absurd, Funny, Ridiculous, Ludicrous, Droll, Amusing, Jocular.
L	A	U	N	C	H	I	N	G	Flinging, Shooting, Commencing, Initiating, Introducing, Plunging, Instituting.
L	A	U	N	D	R	E	S	S	A woman who does household laundry.
L	A	Z	A	R	E	T	T	O	Hospital for lepers.
L	A	Z	Y	B	O	N	E	S	A lazy person.
L	E	A	K	P	R	O	O	F	Proof against leakage.
L	E	A	S	E	H	O	L	D	Land or property held by lease.
L	E	A	S	T	W	A	Y	S	At least.
L	E	A	V	E	N	I	N	G	Infusing, Aerating, Raising, Modifying, Alleviating, Vivifying.
L	E	C	H	E	R	O	U	S	Licentious, Lewd, Lustful, Salacious, Libertine, Fast, Lascivious.
L	E	C	Y	T	H	O	I	D	Resembling an ancient Greek vase.
L	E	G	E	N	D	A	R	Y	Fictitious, Mythical, Fabulous, Mythological.
L	E	G	I	O	N	A	R	Y	Constituting a legion of soldiers.
L	E	G	I	S	L	A	T	E	Law-making.
L	E	I	S	U	R	E	L	Y	Deliberately, Slowly, Dilatory, Unhasty, Relaxed, Delayed, Easy, Restful.
L	E	N	I	E	N	T	L	Y	Indulgently, Gently, Mildly, Charitably, Tolerantly, Benignly, Kindly, Amiably.
L	E	N	T	I	T	U	D	E	Slowness, Sluggishness.
L	E	P	R	O	L	O	G	Y	Study of leprosy and its treatment.
L	E	S	P	E	D	E	Z	A	Genus of leguminous shrubby plants often used for hay.
L	E	T	H	A	L	I	T	Y	Deadliness, Fatality.
L	E	T	H	A	R	G	I	C	Dull, Apathetic, Listless, Indifferent, Sluggish, Torpid, Comatose, Dormant.
L	E	U	C	I	T	I	T	E	Bosaltic rock.

1	2	3	4	5	6	7	8	9	Clue
L	E	U	C	O	C	Y	T	E	White blood cell.
L	E	U	C	O	D	E	R	M(A)	Person with light-coloured skin.
L	E	U	K	A	E	M	I	A	Acute blood disease involving an abnormal increase in white blood cells.
L	E	V	I	A	T	H	A	N	Gigantic, Monstrous, Vast, Mammoth, Behemoth, Giant, Immense, Gargantuan.
L	I	A	B	I	L	I	T	Y	Likelihood, Drawback, Debt, Indebtedness, Obligation, Exposure, Vulnerability.
L	I	B	E	R	A	L	L	Y	Freely, Generously, Lavishly, Profusely, Amply, Abundantly, Broadly, Progressively.
L	I	B	E	R	A	T	O	R	One that frees.
L	I	B	E	R	T	I	N	E	Uncontrolled, Licentious, Profligate, Dissolute, Lecherous, Lewd, Lustful.
L	I	B	I	D	I	N	A	L	Belonging to sexual gratification.
L	I	B	R	A	R	I	A	N	One whose work is caring for books.
L	I	B	R	A	T	I	O	N	Process of weighing.
L	I	C	E	N	S	I	N	G	Allowing, Authorizing, Commissioning, Enabling, Certifying, Empowering.
L	I	D	O	C	A	I	N	E	Crystalline compound used as a local anaesthetic.
L	I	F	E	G	U	A	R	D	An expert swimmer employed to safeguard bathers.
L	I	G	H	T	N	E	S	S	Levity, Nimbleness, Delicacy, Gracefulness, Frivolity, Buoyancy, Effervescence.
L	I	G	H	T	N	I	N	G	Discharge of atmospheric electricity.
L	I	G	H	T	S	O	M	E	Airy, Graceful, Cheerful, Gay, Frivolous, Unsteady, Blithe, Carefree.
L	I	G	H	T	W	O	O	D	Kindling wood, Dry wood that burns easily.
L	I	L	I	A	C	E	O	U(S)	Relating to or resembling lilies.
L	I	M	B	A	T	I	O	N	Ring of colour, Halo.
L	I	M	E	N	I	T	I	S	Genus of butterflies.
L	I	M	E	S	T	O	N	E	Rock formed of calcium carbonate.
L	I	M	E	W	A	T	E	R	An alkaline water, Solution of calcium hydroxide.
L	I	M	I	C	O	L	A	E	Family of sandpipers.
L	I	M	I	T	A	B	L	E	Subject to limitation.
L	I	M	I	T	L	E	S	S	Unbounded, Inexhaustible, Endless, Immeasurable, Indefinite, Infinite, Vast.
L	I	M	N	O	L	O	G	Y	Scientific study of fresh water.
L	I	M	O	N	C	I	T	O	Limeberry, Spiny Malayan shrub with edible red berries.
L	I	M	O	U	S	I	N	E	A large luxurious sedan seating five passengers.
L	I	M	P	I	D	I	T	Y	Clarity, Clearness, Lucidity, Perspicuity, Plainness.
L	I	N	E	A	M	E	N	T	Outline, Contour, Delineation, Profile, Silhouette, Rudiment, Trace, Figuration.
L	I	N	E	A	T	I	O	N	Delineation, Markings.
L	I	N	G	E	R	I	N	G	Delaying, Loitering, Procrastination, Dawdling, Hesitating, Postponing, Prolonging.
L	I	P	O	T	H	Y	M	Y	Faintness, Fainting.
L	I	P	P	I	T	U	D	E	Soreness of the eyes, Bleary-eyed.
L	I	Q	U	I	D	A	T	E	Discharge, Quit, Settle, Satisfy, Eliminate, Remove, Assassinate, Execute.
L	I	Q	U	I	D	I	T	Y	State of being liquid, Possessing liquid assets.
L	I	Q	U	I	D	I	Z	E	To convert something to a liquid state.
L	I	Q	U	O	R	I	C	E	Licorice, Extract of a dried root used as a flavouring agent.
L	I	S	T	E	N	I	N	G	Hearing, Perceiving aurally, Heeding, Attending.
L	I	T	E	R	A	L	L	Y	Explicitly, Actually, Really, Verbatim, Virtually, Directly.
L	I	T	E	R	A	T	I	M	Verbatim, Direct, Letter for letter.
L	I	T	E	R	A	T	O	R	One engaged in descriptive bibliography.
L	I	T	H	E	N	E	S	S	Suppleness, Flexibility, Slenderness.
L	I	T	H	E	S	O	M	E	Supple, Lissome, Lithe, Limber.
L	I	T	H	I	A	S	I	S	Presence of gravel or stones in the body.
L	I	T	H	O	L	O	G	Y	Study of rocks.
L	I	T	H	O	S	I	A	N	A moth.
L	I	T	H	O	T	O	M	Y	Surgical removal of a stone in the bladder.
L	I	T	I	G	I	O	U	S	Contentious, Disputable, Argumentative, Controversial, Prone to lawsuits.
L	I	T	U	R	G	I	C	S	Study of the forms of worship.
L	I	V	E	R	Y	M	A	N	Freeman of the City of London, Attendant of vehicles for hire.
L	I	X	I	V	I	A	T	E	Leach, Extract a compound by washing or percolation.
L	O	A	N	W	O	R	D	(—)	The influence of a different language to change the meaning of a word.
L	O	A	T	H	S	O	M	E	Disgusting, Nauseating, Foul, Odious, Abhorrent, Offensive, Repulsive, Repugnant.
L	O	B	S	C	O	U	S	E	A stew prepared by a sailor of any edible food available.
L	O	C	O	M	O	T	O	R	Concerned with the ability to move.
L	O	D	E	S	T	O	N	E	Magnet, Something that attracts, Magnetite possessing polarity.
L	O	D	G	E	M	E	N	T	Shelter, Lodgings, Accommodation, Billets.
L	O	F	T	I	N	E	S	S	Arrogance, Disdainfulness, Haughtiness, Superciliousness, Pride, Hauteur.
L	O	G	A	O	E	D	I	C	Having a rhythm composed of dactyls and trochees.
L	O	G	A	R	I	T	H	M	An arithmetical function for use in abridging calculations.
L	O	G	I	C	A	L	L	Y	Formally, Rationally, Sensibly, Intelligently, Lucidly, Reasonably, Convincingly.
L	O	G	I	S	T	I	C	S	Science of calculating in relation to armed forces.
L	O	G	O	G	R	I	P	H	Word puzzle, Anagram.
L	O	G	O	M	A	C	H	Y	Dispute over words.
L	O	G	O	M	A	N	I	A	Abnormal talkativeness.

1	2	3	4	5	6	7	8	9	Definition
L	O	G	O	R	R	H	E	A	Pathologically excessive talkativeness.
L	O	I	N	C	L	O	T	H	A cloth worn around the waist as sole apparel in warm climates.
L	O	I	T	E	R	I	N	G	Delaying, Dawdling, Dragging, Procrastinating, Idling, Tarrying, Lazing, Lounging.
L	O	N	G	E	V	I	T	Y	Long-lived, Seniority.
L	O	N	G	I	C	O	R	N	Long-horned beetle.
L	O	N	G	I	T	U	D	E	Length, Imaginary line around the earth between certain points.
L	O	O	S	E	N	E	S	S	State of being loose.
L	O	O	S	E	N	I	N	G	Easing, Slackening, Untightening, Relaxing, Freeing, Discharging, Liberating.
L	O	P	H	O	D	O	N	T	Having molar teeth with transverse ridges on the grinding surfaces.
L	O	R	G	N	E	T	T	E	Pair of eyeglasses with a handle.
L	O	T	O	P	H	A	G	I	Lotus-eaters.
L	O	U	S	E	W	O	R	T	A plant once suspected of making sheep verminous.
L	O	U	T	I	S	H	L	Y	Coarsely, Boorishly, Churlishly, Clumsily, Crudely, Gauchily.
L	O	V	E	A	P	P	L	E	Tomato.
L	O	W	E	R	M	O	S	T	Lowest, Bottom, Rock-bottom, Nethermost.
L	U	B	R	I	C	A	N	T	A substance to relieve friction between surfaces.
L	U	B	R	I	C	A	T	E	Grease, Oil, Make slippery or smooth, Bribe.
L	U	B	R	I	C	I	T	Y	Sensuality, Lasciviousness, Smoothness, Slipperiness, Lewdness, Wantonness.
L	U	C	R	A	T	I	V	E	Profitable, Money-making, Advantageous, Gainful, Remunerative, Worthwhile.
L	U	D	I	C	R	O	U	S	Frivolous, Joking, Laughable, Comical, Farcical, Ridiculous, Absurd, Foolish.
L	U	M	B	E	R	I	N	G	Encumbering, Trudging, Plodding, Burdening, Charging, Loading, Clumsy.
L	U	M	B	R	I	C	A	L	Muscles in the palm of the hand.
L	U	M	I	N	A	I	R	E	A complete lighting unit.
L	U	M	I	N	A	N	C	E	Ability to emit light, brightness.
L	U	N	I	S	O	L	A	R	Relating to the moon and the sun jointly.
L	U	N	I	T	I	D	A	L	Relating to tides influenced by the moon.
L	U	R	I	D	N	E	S	S	Gruesomeness, Horridness, Ghastliness.
L	U	S	T	F	U	L	L	Y	Lecherously, Lewdly, Passionately.
L	U	S	T	I	N	E	S	S	Enthusiasm, Vigour.
L	U	T	A	C	E	O	U	S	Conglomerate rock.
L	U	T	E	O	L	O	U	S	Yellowish.
L	U	T	E	S	C	E	N	T	Yellowish.
L	U	X	U	R	I	A	N	T	Fruitful, Productive, Luxurious, Elegant, Profuse, Exuberant.
L	U	X	U	R	I	O	U	S	Sumptuous, Opulent, Sensuous, Luscious, Gorgeous, Impressive, Lavish, Majestic.
L	Y	M	P	H	A	T	I	C	Relating to lymph, Frenzied.

M

1	2	3	4	5	6	7	8	9	Definition
M	A	C	A	R	O	N	I	C	Mixture of two languages.
M	A	C	E	D	O	I	N	E	Mixture of diced fruit or vegetables.
M	A	C	H	I	N	A	T	E	Plot, Scheme, Contrive, Engineer, Wangle, Conspire, Devise, Intrigue.
M	A	C	H	I	N	E	R	Y	Equipment, Apparatus, Gear, Paraphernalia, Vehicle, Device, Gadget, Implement.
M	A	C	H	I	N	I	S	T	A worker who assembles machinery, A worker who uses a sewing machine.
M	A	C	H	I	N	I	Z	E	Organize into a machine.
M	A	C	I	N	T	O	S	H	Raincoat.
M	A	C	R	O	C	O	D	E	A coding system for assembling computer instructions.
M	A	C	R	O	C	O	S	M	The universe in its entirety.
M	A	C	R	O	T	O	M	E	Apparatus for making large sections of anatomical specimens.
M	A	D	A	R	O	S	I	S	Loss of eyelashes or eyebrows.
M	A	D	R	E	P	O	R	E	Reef-building corals.
M	A	E	L	S	T	R	O	M	Whirlpool, Vortex, Commotion, Confusion, Fury, Storm, Turmoil.
M	A	G	N	E	S	I	U	M	A silver-white light malleable ductile bivalent metallic element.
M	A	G	N	E	T	I	S	M	Ability to attract. Power to charm.
M	A	G	N	E	T	I	T	E	A black isometric mineral of the spinal group.
M	A	G	N	E	T	I	Z	E	Captivate, Charm, Attract, Allure, Bewitch, Enchant, Fascinate, Wile.
M	A	G	N	E	T	R	O	N	A diode vacuum tube.
M	A	G	N	I	F	I	E	R	Combination of lenses.
M	A	G	N	I	T	U	D	E	Quantity, Number, Volume, Loudness, Enormity, Extent, Measure, Amplitude.
M	A	H	A	R	A	J	A	H	Hindu prince.
M	A	H	A	R	A	N	E	E	Wife of a maharajah.
M	A	H	L	S	T	I	C	K	Maulstick, Rest stick used by a painter.
M	A	J	O	R	D	O	M	O	Head steward.
M	A	J	U	S	C	U	L	E	A large letter.
M	A	K	E	S	H	I	F	T	Substitute, Provisional, Stopgap, Resource, Expedient, Recourse.
M	A	L	A	C	H	I	T	E	A mineral that is a copper ore.
M	A	L	A	D	R	O	I	T	Clumsy, Tactless, Inept, Bungling, Awkward, Stumbling, Brash, Unskilled.

1	2	3	4	5	6	7	8	9	
M	A	L	A	R	I	O	U	S	Infected with malaria.
M	A	L	A	X	A	T	O	R	A machine for grinding, kneading or stirring into a pasty mass.
M	A	L	F	O	R	M	E	D	Misshapen, Deformed, Distorted.
M	A	L	I	C	I	O	U	S	Hateful, Malevolent, Malignant, Spiteful, Vicious, Venomous, Noxious, Poisonous.
M	A	L	I	G	N	A	N	T	Rebellious, Malcontent, Baleful, Injurious, Diabolical, Fiendish, Rancorous.
M	A	L	L	E	A	B	L	E	Plastic, Impressionable, Ductile, Adaptable, Pliant, Supple, Manageable, Governable.
M	A	L	L	E	O	L	U	S	The rounded projection on the ankle bone.
M	A	L	M	A	I	S	O	N	Greenhouse carnation with large double pink blossoms.
M	A	M	I	L	L	A	T	E	Having nipples.
M	A	M	M	A	L	O	G	Y	Branch of zoology dealing with mammals.
M	A	N	A	N	O	S	A	Y	Soft-shelled clam.
M	A	N	D	A	T	O	R	Y	Obligatory, Compulsory, Imperious, Essential, Imperative, Binding, Forced.
M	A	N	D	O	L	I	N	E	A pear-shaped instrument similar to a lute.
M	A	N	D	U	C	A	T	E	Masticate, Chew, Eat.
M	A	N	G	A	N	E	S	E	Grayish white polyvalent metallic element.
M	A	N	G	A	N	O	U	S	Derived from manganese.
M	A	N	G	I	N	E	S	S	Seediness, Shabbiness, Squalidness.
M	A	N	H	A	N	D	L	E	Mishandle, Abuse, Mistreat, Batter, Maul.
M	A	N	I	F	E	S	T	O	Public declaration of future policy.
M	A	N	L	I	N	E	S	S	Masculinity, Boldness, Intrepidness.
M	A	N	N	E	Q	U	I	N	Model, Person employed to display clothes.
M	A	N	N	E	R	I	S	M	Pose, Affectation, Eccentricity, Peculiarity, Oddness, Singularity, Preciosity.
M	A	N	O	E	U	V	R	E	Engineer, Wangle, Manipulate, Exploit, Handle, Navigate, Dispense, Wield.
M	A	N	O	M	E	T	E	R	Instrument for measuring pressure.
M	A	R	A	S	M	O	I	D	Resembling juvenile emaciation caused through malnutrition.
M	A	R	C	A	S	I	T	E	Crystallised iron pyrites used in making jewellery.
M	A	R	C	H	P	A	N	E	Marzipan.
M	A	R	G	A	R	I	N	E	Food product substituted for butter.
M	A	R	G	I	N	A	T	E	Prepare a margin.
M	A	R	I	J	U	A	N	A	Wild tobacco, Hemp, Hashish.
M	A	R	I	T	A	L	L	Y	Conjugally, Relating to marriage.
M	A	R	M	A	L	A	D	E	Preserve made from a citrous fruit.
M	A	R	M	A	R	I	Z	E	Convert into marble.
M	A	R	M	O	R	E	A	L	Resembling a marble statue, Statuesque.
M	A	R	Q	U	E	T	R	Y	Decoration by means of small pieces of wood, shell or ivory being set into a picture.
M	A	R	R	O	W	F	A	T	Tallowy product derived from narrow bones.
M	A	R	S	U	P	I	A	L	Having an abdomen pouch containing teats, in which the young are carried.
M	A	R	T	Y	R	D	O	M	Affliction, Torment, Distress, Torture, Agony.
M	A	R	T	Y	R	I	Z	E	Agonize, Crucify, Harrow, Wrack, Excruciate.
M	A	S	C	U	L	I	N	E	Male, Strong, Powerful, Virile, Robust.
M	A	S	O	C	H	I	S	M	To take pleasure in personal suffering.
M	A	S	O	C	H	I	S	T	One who seeks gratification through pain.
M	A	S	T	E	R	F	U	L	Dominant, Vigorous, Energetic, Imperious, Authoritative, Dictatorial, Proficient.
M	A	S	T	I	C	A	T	E	Grind, Crush, Chew, Chump, Munch, Macerate, Pulp, Squash.
M	A	T	C	H	L	E	S	S	Unparalleled, Peerless, Unique, Unrivalled, Unequalled.
M	A	T	C	H	L	O	C	K	An early musket fired with the aid of a lighted fuse.
M	A	T	E	R	N	I	T	Y	Motherhood, Motherliness.
M	A	T	R	I	A	R	C	H	A woman who heads a family, group or tribe, Dowager.
M	A	T	R	I	C	I	D	E	Murder of a mother.
M	A	T	R	I	M	O	N	Y	Marriage, Wedlock, Conjugality.
M	A	T	R	O	N	I	Z	E	To act as matron, Chaperone.
M	A	T	U	T	I	N	A	L	Early, Occurring in the morning.
M	A	U	L	S	T	I	C	K	Stick used by painters to rest the hand when working.
M	A	U	S	O	L	E	U	M	Magnificent tomb, A gloomy structure.
M	A	W	K	I	S	H	L	Y	Squeamishly, Sentimentally, Mushily, Nauseatingly.
M	A	X	I	L	L	A	R	Y	Relating to the upper jaw.
M	A	X	I	M	A	L	L	Y	To the utmost.
M	A	Y	O	R	A	L	T	Y	The office of mayor.
M	E	A	D	O	W	I	N	G	Land used as a meadow.
M	E	A	L	Y	W	I	N	G	Whitefly.
M	E	A	N	W	H	I	L	E	Meantime, For the time being.
M	E	C	H	A	N	I	S	M	Technique for producing a result.
M	E	C	O	P	T	E	R	A	Primitive carnivorous flies, Scorpion flies.
M	E	D	A	L	L	I	O	N	A large medal, A design enclosed in a border, usually round or oval.
M	E	D	I	A	T	I	N	G	Intervening, Negotiating, Conveying, Transmitting, Interceding, Interfering.
M	E	D	I	C	I	N	A	L	Curative, Drug, Sanative, Remedial, Salutary, Pharmaceutical.
M	E	D	U	L	L	A	R	Y	Relating to marrow, Composed of plant pitch.

1	2	3	4	5	6	7	8	9	Definition
M	E	G	A	C	Y	C	L	E	Unit of radio frequency, one million cycles per second.
M	E	G	A	N	E	U	R	A	Genus of extinct giant insects.
M	E	G	A	P	H	O	N	E	A device to amplify the voice.
M	E	G	A	Z	O	O	I	D	A relatively large stalked vegetative individual.
M	E	L	A	N	E	M	I	A	Abnormal condition where the blood contains melanin.
M	E	L	A	N	O	S	I	S	Abnormal deposits of pigments in body tissues.
M	E	L	I	B	I	O	S	E	A disaccharide sugar.
M	E	L	I	O	R	A	T	E	Improve, to make better.
M	E	L	O	D	I	O	U	S	Having a sweet melody.
M	E	L	O	D	R	A	M	A	A suspenseful play.
M	E	M	O	R	A	B	L	E	Notable, Impressive, Significant, Distinguished, Momentous, Noteworthy.
M	E	M	O	R	A	N	D	A	Reminder.
M	E	N	A	G	E	R	I	E	Zoo, Collection of animals.
M	E	N	D	I	C	A	N	T	One that lives by begging.
M	E	N	D	I	C	I	T	Y	Cadging, Beggary.
M	E	N	O	P	A	U	S	E	Cessation of child-bearing period.
M	E	N	S	T	R	U	U	M	Solvent.
M	E	N	T	A	L	I	T	Y	Intelligence, Outlook, Sense, Wit, Brainpower, Learning ability.
M	E	N	T	I	O	N	E	D	Noted, Specified, Named, Cited, Designated, Detailed, Alluded, Referred.
M	E	R	C	E	N	A	R	Y	Hired soldier, Paid, Salaried, Commercial, Greedy, Corrupt, Unscrupulous, Venal.
M	E	R	C	E	R	I	Z	E	Special process in manufacture of rayon fabric.
M	E	R	C	I	L	E	S	S	Cruel, Harsh, Pitiless, Remorseless, Implacable, Relentless, Unyielding, Grim.
M	E	R	C	U	R	I	A	L	Sprightly, Temperamental, Volatile, Capricious, Fickle, Unstable, Mobile.
M	E	R	G	A	N	S	E	R	A diving duck.
M	E	R	R	I	M	E	N	T	Hilarity, Jubilation, Mirth, Jocularity, Festivity, Gaiety, Revelry.
M	E	S	C	A	L	I	N	E	A crystalline alkaloid that produces hallucinations.
M	E	S	M	E	R	I	S	M	Hypnotism, Intense fascination.
M	E	S	O	C	R	A	C	Y	Government by the middle classes.
M	E	S	O	P	A	U	S	E	The transition zone between the mesophere and the exosphere.
M	E	S	S	I	N	E	S	S	Slovenliness, Dirtiness, Griminess, Untidiness.
M	E	S	S	E	N	G	E	R	Courier, Emissary, Envoy, Forerunner, Harbinger, Carrier, Herald, Mediator.
M	E	T	A	B	O	L	I	C	Vegetative, Relating to metabolism.
M	E	T	A	L	L	I	N	E	Impregnated with metallic substances.
M	E	T	A	L	L	I	Z	E	To treat, coat, impregnate or combine with metal, Mineralize.
M	E	T	A	L	L	O	I	D	Resembling a metal.
M	E	T	A	L	W	A	R	E	Household utensils.
M	E	T	A	M	E	R	I	C	Isomeric, Segmental.
M	E	T	E	O	R	I	T	E	A meteor that survives a fall to earth through the atmosphere.
M	E	T	E	O	R	O	I	D	A meteor revolving around the sun.
M	E	T	H	E	G	L	I	N	Mead, Beverage made of fermented honey, water and spice.
M	E	T	H	O	D	I	S	T	Member of a religious sect within the Church of England characterized by lay-preaching.
M	E	T	H	Y	L	A	T	E	Impregnate or mix with methanol.
M	E	T	R	O	L	O	G	Y	Science of weights and measures.
M	E	T	R	O	N	O	M	E	An apparatus with an audible beat that can be adjusted to suit the circumstances.
M	E	Z	Z	A	N	I	N	E	A storey between two main floors.
M	E	Z	Z	O	T	I	N	T	An engraving on copper or steel.
M	I	C	A	C	E	O	U	S	Resembling mica.
M	I	C	R	O	B	I	A	L	Developing from microbes.
M	I	C	R	O	C	H	I	P	A chip carrying integrated circuits for computing.
M	I	C	R	O	C	O	P	Y	Photographic copy reduced in size, Microfilm.
M	I	C	R	O	C	O	S	M	Miniature universe.
M	I	C	R	O	C	Y	S	T	A very small pathological cyst.
M	I	C	R	O	C	Y	T	E	Exceptionally small red blood cell.
M	I	C	R	O	D	O	N	T	Having small teeth.
M	I	C	R	O	F	I	L	M	A film to reduce the size of records for storage.
M	I	C	R	O	T	O	M	E	Instrument for cutting sections for microscopic examination.
M	I	C	R	O	W	A	V	E	Electromagnetic radiation.
M	I	D	D	L	E	M	A	N	Agent, Intermediary, Rentcollector, Broker, Mediator.
M	I	D	D	L	I	N	G	S	By-product of flour milling used as animal feed.
M	I	D	E	W	I	W	I	N	A secret society of some North American Indians aiming at longlevity.
M	I	D	S	U	M	M	E	R	Middle of summer.
M	I	D	W	I	F	E	R	Y	Obstetrics, Helping with the birth of a baby.
M	I	G	R	A	T	I	O	N	Moving from one area to settle in another.
M	I	L	E	S	T	O	N	E	A stone serving to record measurement of a thoroughfare.
M	I	L	L	B	O	A	R	D	Stout pasteboard used in book binding and furniture panels.
M	I	L	L	E	N	A	R	Y	Consisting of one thousand.

1	2	3	4	5	6	7	8	9	
M	I	L	L	E	P	O	R	E	A reef-building coral.
M	I	L	L	H	O	U	S	E	A building that houses milling machinery.
M	I	L	L	I	G	R	A	M	Unit of mass and weight, one thousandth of a gram.
M	I	L	L	I	N	E	R	Y	The business of designing, making and selling woman's hats.
M	I	L	L	I	P	E	D	E	A myriopod having a hard covering and many pairs of legs.
M	I	L	L	S	T	O	N	E	A stone used for grinding, A terrible burden.
M	I	N	A	C	I	O	U	S	Menacing, Threatening.
M	I	N	C	E	M	E	A	T	Finely chopped mixture of dried fruits and spices or of steak.
M	I	N	I	A	T	U	R	E	Model, Tiny, Diminutive, Minute, Weeny, Lilliputian, Small-scale.
M	I	N	I	M	I	Z	E	D	Decried, Depreciated, Belittled, Derogated, Detracted, Diminished, Disparaged.
M	I	N	O	M	E	T	E	R	An instrument to detect and measure stray radiations.
M	I	N	U	S	C	U	L	E	Diminutive, Insignificant, Petty.
M	I	S	B	E	C	O	M	E	Inappropriate, Unbecoming.
M	I	S	B	E	H	A	V	E	Behave improperly.
M	I	S	C	H	A	N	C	E	Misfortune, Adversity, Tragedy, Casualty, Misadventure, Accident.
M	I	S	C	R	E	A	N	T	Heretic, Infidel, Depraved, Vicious, Villainous, Knave, Rascal, Rogue.
M	I	S	D	I	R	E	C	T	Direct wrongly, Give wrong instructions, Aim badly.
M	I	S	E	R	A	B	L	E	Wretched, Discreditable, Woeful, Afflicted, Sorrowful, Despondent, Forlorn.
M	I	S	E	R	A	B	L	Y	Unhappily, Wretchedly, Uncomfortably, Meanly, Poorly, Pitiably, Hopelessly.
M	I	S	G	I	V	I	N	G	Apprehension, Doubt, Suspicion, Premonition, Qualm, Distrust, Fear.
M	I	S	H	A	N	D	L	E	Maltreat, Abuse, Misemploy, Misuse, Pervert.
M	I	S	M	A	N	A	G	E	Manage incompetently or badly.
M	I	S	R	E	C	K	O	N	Make an incorrect calculation.
M	I	S	R	E	P	O	R	T	To give a false account.
M	I	S	S	I	O	N	E	R	Missionary.
M	I	S	T	I	N	E	S	S	Vagueness, Haziness, Cloudiness.
M	I	S	T	L	E	T	O	E	Parasitic plant with sticky berries that grows on deciduous trees.
M	I	T	S	U	M	A	T	A	A low shrub cultivated in Japan where its bark is used in papermaking.
M	N	E	M	O	N	I	C	S	A technique to improve the memory.
M	O	B	O	C	R	A	C	Y	Mob rule, Anarchy, Lawlessness, Chaos.
M	O	B	U	L	I	D	A	E	Family of rays, Devilfish.
M	O	D	E	L	L	I	N	G	Framing, Shaping, Planning, Fashioning, Constructing, Displaying.
M	O	D	E	R	A	T	O	R	Mediator, Arbitrator, Judge, Negotiator, Peacemaker.
M	O	D	E	R	N	I	S	T	Practice, usage and expression of modern times.
M	O	D	E	R	N	I	T	Y	Modernism.
M	O	D	E	R	N	I	Z	E	Remodel, Repair, Renew, Refresh, Refurbish, Rejuvenate, Restore, Update.
M	O	D	I	F	Y	I	N	G	Moderating, Lessening, Restricting, Qualifying, Limiting, Changing, Altering.
M	O	D	I	L	L	I	O	N	Ornamental bracket under cornice of a column.
M	O	D	U	L	A	T	E	D	Intoned, Tempered, Played, Moderated, Restrained.
M	O	D	U	L	A	T	O	R	Device for modulating, A signal for transmission of intelligence.
M	O	I	S	T	E	N	E	R	Device for moistening gummed surfaces.
M	O	L	E	C	U	L	A	R	Consisting of molecules.
M	O	L	L	I	F	I	E	D	Pacified, Softened, Conciliated, Assuaged, Relented, Placated, Relieved, Eased.
M	O	M	E	N	T	A	R	Y	Transitory, Ephemeral, Fleeting, Volatile, Brief, Quick, Short.
M	O	M	E	N	T	O	U	S	Weighty, Important, Considerable, Meaningful, Significant, Substantial.
M	O	N	A	C	H	I	S	M	Monasticism.
M	O	N	A	S	T	E	R	Y	Place of religious seclusion.
M	O	N	G	O	L	I	A	N	Characteristic of a native of Asia.
M	O	N	K	E	Y	N	U	T	Peanut.
M	O	N	O	B	A	S	I	C	Single species, Containing only one atom of a univalent metal.
M	O	N	O	B	L	A	S	T	A motile cell of the spleen and bone marrow.
M	O	N	O	C	H	O	R	D	An ancient measuring instrument for musical tones.
M	O	N	O	C	R	A	C	Y	Government by a single person, Autocracy.
M	O	N	O	C	U	L	A	R	A microscope or field glass.
M	O	N	O	D	R	A	M	A	Musical drama for a single performer.
M	O	N	O	G	A	M	I	C	Marriage to one person at a time.
M	O	N	O	G	R	A	P	H	Written account of a single thing.
M	O	N	O	L	O	G	U	E	A long speech given by one person, A sketch performed by one actor.
M	O	N	O	M	A	N	I	A	Intense obsession with a single idea or object.
M	O	N	O	P	L	A	N	E	An aeroplane with a single wing.
M	O	N	O	R	C	H	I	D	Having one testicle.
M	O	N	O	T	R	E	M	E	One of the lowest order of mammals, Platypus.
M	O	N	S	I	G	N	O	R	Prelate of the Roman Catholic church.
M	O	N	S	T	R	O	U	S	Huge, Gigantic, Mammoth, Abnormal, Prodigious, Tremendous, Stupendous.
M	O	O	N	L	I	G	H	T	The light of the moon, To hold two jobs at the same time.
M	O	O	N	S	H	I	N	E	Moonlight, Nonsense, Bunkum, Humbug, Illegally distilled liquor.
M	O	O	N	S	T	O	N	E	Translucent gemstone.

1	2	3	4	5	6	7	8	9	Clue
M	O	O	R	G	R	A	S	S	Heath grass.
M	O	R	B	I	D	I	T	Y	Excessive gloom, Moroseness, Moodiness, Sullenness.
M	O	R	D	A	C	I	T	Y	Readiness to bite, Given to caustic speech.
M	O	R	P	H	O	S	I	S	Development or change of form.
M	O	R	T	A	L	I	T	Y	Death rate, Lethality, Mankind, Humanity.
M	O	R	T	G	A	G	E	D	Pledged, Given as security for a debt.
M	O	R	T	I	C	I	A	N	Funeral director, Undertaker, Embalmer.
M	O	S	A	I	C	I	S	T	Designer of mosaics.
M	O	T	H	E	A	T	E	N	Dilapidated, Outmoded, Patchy, Unkempt, Raggedy, Shabby, Threadbare, Tattered.
M	O	U	S	E	B	I	R	D	Shrike.
M	O	U	S	E	F	I	S	H	A common sargassum fish.
M	O	U	S	E	H	O	L	E	Small opening, Cubbyhole.
M	O	U	S	E	L	I	K	E	Nondescript, Timid, Nervous.
M	O	U	S	T	A	C	H	E	Hair or bristles growing around the mouth.
M	O	V	I	E	L	A	N	D	Place where movie films are made.
M	U	L	T	I	C	E	P	S	Tapeworm.
M	U	L	T	I	F	O	R	M	Having many shapes or appearance.
M	U	L	T	I	P	A	R	A	A woman who has borne more than one child.
M	U	L	T	I	T	U	D	E	Crowd, Throng, Host, Populace, Legion, Countless, Uncountable, Multifarous.
M	U	N	I	C	I	P	A	L	Relating to one locality, Internal law.
M	U	N	I	M	E	N	T	S	Title deeds, Charters, Grants, Judgments.
M	U	R	D	E	R	O	U	S	Homicidal, Deadly, Destructive, Bloodthirsty, Sanguine, Devastating, Ruinous.
M	U	R	K	I	N	E	S	S	Gloominess, Dimness, Obscurity, Darkness, Muddiness, Turbidness, Sordidness.
M	U	S	C	A	D	I	N	E	Muscatel grape.
M	U	S	C	O	I	D	E	A	Two-winged flies, Houseflies.
M	U	S	H	I	N	E	S	S	Mawkishness, Effusiveness, Sentimentality.
M	U	S	K	M	E	L	O	N	Sweet edible melon with a musky odour.
M	U	S	S	A	E	N	D	A	Large genus of herbs or shrubs.
M	U	T	I	L	A	T	E	D	Maimed, Crippled, Dismembered, Damaged, Spoiled, Defaced, Sterilized, Changed.
M	U	T	U	A	L	I	S	M	Socialism based on common ownership.
M	Y	E	N	T	E	R	I	C	Relating to the muscular coat of the intestinal wall.
M	Y	R	I	O	R	A	M	A	Combination picture to reflect different scenes.
M	Y	R	O	B	A	L	A	N	Cherry plum.
M	Y	S	T	I	C	I	S	M	Vague speculation, Vagary, Mystical quality.
M	Y	T	H	I	C	I	Z	E	Fabricated as a myth.
M	Y	T	H	O	L	O	G	Y	An allegorical narrative, Parable, Folklore, Legend, Tradition.
M	Y	X	O	B	O	L	U	S	Genus of protozoans causing twist disease.
M	Y	Z	O	S	T	O	M	E	Parasitical worm.

N

1	2	3	4	5	6	7	8	9	Clue
N	A	I	A	D	A	L	E	S	Order of aquatic herbaceous plants.
N	A	K	E	D	N	E	S	S	Nudeness, Bareness, Exposure.
N	A	P	H	T	H	E	N	E	Series of hydrocarbons occurring in petroleum, shale or tar oil.
N	A	P	H	T	H	O	X	Y	Radical composed of naphthyl united with oxygen.
N	A	R	C	I	S	S	U	S	Genus of old world bulbous herbs with cup shaped flowers.
N	A	R	R	A	T	I	O	N	Story, Recitation, Description, Recital, Anecdote, Yarn, Recounting.
N	A	R	R	A	T	I	V	E	Account, Chronicle, History, Report, Story, Version, Tale, Yarn.
N	A	R	R	O	W	I	N	G	Decreasing, Closing, Restricting, Confining, Contracting, Limiting, Lessening.
N	A	S	S	A	R	I	I	D	Marine snails.
N	A	T	U	R	A	L	L	Y	Realistically, Indigenously, Spontaneously, Generally, Typically, Usually, Simply.
N	A	U	P	A	T	H	I	A	Seasickness.
N	A	V	E	L	W	O	R	T	Succulent herb.
N	A	V	I	C	U	L	A	R	Resembling a boat.
N	A	V	I	G	A	B	L	E	Able to afford passage for craft.
N	E	B	U	L	A	T	E	D	Clouded.
N	E	C	E	S	S	A	R	Y	Essential, Indispensable, Needful, Compulsory, Obligatory, Inevitable, Unavoidable.
N	E	C	E	S	S	I	T	Y	Need, Exigency, Constraint, Requirement, Requisite, Poverty, Cause, Obligation.
N	E	C	R	O	L	O	G	Y	Obituary, List of deceased benefactors.
N	E	C	R	O	T	O	M	Y	Dissection of dead bodies.
N	E	C	R	O	Z	O	O	N	Extinct organism.
N	E	C	T	A	N	D	R	A	Large genus of tropical American trees.
N	E	C	T	A	R	I	N	E	Smooth-skinned fruit that is a mutation of a peach.
N	E	F	A	R	I	O	U	S	Wicked, Detestable, Iniquitous, Vicious, Corrupt, Degenerate, Infamous, Miscreant.
N	E	G	L	E	C	T	E	D	Disregarded, Slighted, Ignored, Overlooked, Forgotten, Slighted, Omitted.
N	E	G	L	I	G	E	N	T	Slack, Remiss, Offhand, Careless, Derelict, Inattentive, Indifferent, Slovenly.

1	2	3	4	5	6	7	8	9	
N	E	G	O	T	I	A	N	T	One who negotiates.
N	E	G	O	T	I	A	T	E	Manage, Handle, Conduct, Accomplish, Complete, Convert, Arrange, Transact.
N	E	M	O	P	H	I	L	A	A genus of ornamental annual herbs.
N	E	O	D	Y	M	I	U	M	A faintly yellow metallic element that imparts a violet colour to glass and porcelain.
N	E	O	L	I	T	H	I	C	Prehistoric, Latest period of the Stone gap.
N	E	O	L	O	G	I	A	N	Neologist.
N	E	O	L	O	G	I	S	M	A new word or expression.
N	E	O	L	O	G	I	S	T	A proponent of a new doctrine.
N	E	O	P	H	O	B	I	A	A dread of anything new or unusual.
N	E	O	T	O	C	I	T	E	A mineral of hydrous silicate of manganese and iron but of an uncertain formula.
N	E	P	H	O	L	O	G	Y	A branch of meteorology dealing with clouds.
N	E	P	H	R	I	T	I	C	Affecting the kidneys.
N	E	P	H	R	I	T	I	S	Inflammation of the kidney.
N	E	P	H	R	O	S	I	S	Degeneration of the kidneys.
N	E	P	T	U	N	I	S	T	One that held an outdated theory that rocks were formed by water.
N	E	R	I	T	I	D	A	E	Family of snails having a covering flap.
N	E	R	V	E	L	E	S	S	Feeble, Powerless, Poised, Cool, Fearless, Intrepid, Listless.
N	E	S	C	I	E	N	C	E	Ignorance, Innocence, Unawareness, Unfamiliarity.
N	E	U	R	A	L	G	I	A	Acute pain along course of nerves.
N	E	U	R	A	T	I	O	N	Venation.
N	E	U	R	I	L	I	T	Y	Special functions of the nerves.
N	E	U	R	O	G	L	I	A	Tissue that supports the essential elements of the nervous tissue in the brain.
N	E	U	R	O	L	O	G	Y	Scientific study of the nervous system.
N	E	U	R	O	M	E	R	E	Metameric segment of the vertebrate nervous system.
N	E	U	R	O	P	A	T	H	A person subject to nervous disorders.
N	E	W	S	I	N	E	S	S	Capable of attracting interest.
N	E	W	S	P	A	P	E	R	A publication containing news, advertising features and opinions.
N	E	W	S	P	R	I	N	T	Low-grade paper used for printing of newspapers and publications.
N	I	C	C	O	L	I	T	E	A copper red mineral composed of a nickel arsenide.
N	I	C	K	E	L	I	N	G	Nickel plating.
N	I	C	O	T	I	A	N	A	Genus of herbs, Tobacco.
N	I	C	O	T	I	N	I	C	Crystalline acid that is a member of the vitamin B group.
N	I	C	T	I	T	A	N	T	Adapted for winking.
N	I	C	T	I	T	A	T	E	Wink.
N	I	D	U	L	A	R	I	A	Genus of fungi.
N	I	G	G	A	R	D	L	Y	Stingy, Scanty, Miserly, Parsimonious, Penurious, Tight-fisted.
N	I	G	H	T	G	O	W	N	A dress-like garment to wear in bed.
N	I	G	H	T	M	A	R	E	Terrifying dream, Haunting fear, Apprehension, Worry.
N	I	G	R	O	S	I	N	E	Azine dyes.
N	I	L	O	M	E	T	E	R	A gauge for measuring Nile water in flood.
N	I	T	R	A	T	I	O	N	Combining with nitric acid.
N	O	B	L	E	N	E	S	S	Splendour, Grandeur, Nobility.
N	O	C	T	U	I	D	A	E	Family of night-flying moths.
N	O	C	T	U	R	N	A	L	Relating to night, Active at night.
N	O	D	U	L	A	T	E	D	Formed nodules.
N	O	I	S	E	L	E	S	S	Silent, Quiet, Soundless, Still, Hushed.
N	O	M	I	N	A	T	E	D	Designated, Appointed, Named, Intended, Proposed, Presented, Specified.
N	O	N	E	N	T	I	T	Y	Nonexistent, Insignificancy, Nullity, Zero, Obscurity.
N	O	N	I	L	L	I	O	N	An unbelievably large number.
N	O	N	P	A	R	E	I	L	Peerless, Paragon.
N	O	O	S	C	O	P	I	C	Relating to the examination of the mind.
N	O	R	M	A	L	I	T	Y	Conformity.
N	O	R	M	A	L	I	Z	E	Make normal.
N	O	R	T	H	S	T	A	R	Polestar.
N	O	S	T	A	L	G	I	A	Homesickness, Yearning, Longing, Regretful, Wistfulness.
N	O	S	T	A	L	G	I	C	Relating to sentimental memories.
N	O	T	O	C	H	O	R	D	Flexible rod of cells linked to the spinal cord and vertebral column.
N	O	T	O	R	I	E	T	Y	Being notorious, Fame, Celebrity, Renown, Reputation, Propoganda, Publicity.
N	O	T	O	R	I	O	U	S	Well-known, Celebrated, Manifest, Famous, Prominent, Noted, Popular, Infamous.
N	O	U	R	I	S	H	E	D	Raised, Nurtured, Reared, Strengthened, Suckled, Maintained, Supported, Fostered.
N	O	U	R	I	T	U	R	E	Nourishment.
N	O	V	A	C	H	O	R	D	Electric piano.
N	O	V	E	L	E	T	T	E	A brief novel usually printed in paper back edition.
N	O	V	I	T	I	A	T	E	Period of probation or apprenticeship, Newcomer, Beginner, Tyro, Novice.
N	O	V	O	C	A	I	N	E	Procaine, Local anaesthetic less toxic than cocaine.
N	O	X	I	O	U	S	L	Y	Obnoxiously, Destructively, Unhealthy, Deadly, Unwholesomely.
N	U	C	L	E	O	L	U	S	Nuclear body other than a chromosome.

1	2	3	4	5	6	7	8	9	
N	U	C	U	L	I	D	A	E	Family of marine bivalve moluscs.
N	U	L	L	I	P	O	R	E	Lime-secreting coralline algae.
N	U	M	B	E	R	I	N	G	Counting, Computing, Estimating, Including, Enumerating, Apportioning, Totalling.
N	U	M	E	R	A	B	L	E	Capable of being counted.
N	U	M	E	R	A	T	O	R	Dividend.
N	U	M	E	R	I	C	A	L	Relating to numbers.
N	U	M	M	U	L	I	T	E	Fossil of extinct shellfish.
N	U	N	C	U	P	A	T	E	Dedicate, Pronounce, Proclaim, Declare.
N	U	N	N	A	T	I	O	N	Additional final "n" in declension of nouns.
N	U	R	T	U	R	I	N	G	Fostering, Nursing, Educating, Rearing, Cultivating, Supporting, Sustaining.
N	U	T	R	I	M	E	N	T	Nourishment, Food, Sustenance, Maintenance, Subsistence, Support.
N	U	T	R	I	T	I	O	N	Ingesting and utilizing nourishment.
N	U	T	R	I	T	I	V	E	Affording nourishment.
N	Y	S	T	A	G	M	U	S	Rapid movement of the eyeballs occurring with dizziness and after rotation of the body.

O

1	2	3	4	5	6	7	8	9	
O	B	D	U	C	T	I	O	N	Laying something over.
O	B	E	D	I	E	N	C	E	Compliance with law and order.
O	B	E	I	S	A	N	C	E	Bow, Homage, Curtsey, Deference, Reverence.
O	B	F	U	S	C	A	T	E	Confuse, Becloud, Darken, Obscure, Overcast, Shadow, Dim, Incomprehensible.
O	B	J	E	C	T	I	F	Y	Embody, Externalize, Manifest, Materialize, Personify, Substantiate.
O	B	J	E	C	T	I	O	N	Protest, Question, Remonstration, Challenge, Demur.
O	B	J	E	C	T	I	V	E	Material, Physical, Substantial, Tangible, Fair, Dispassionate, Unbiased.
O	B	J	U	R	G	A	T	E	Execrate, Curse, Castigate, Censure, Vituperate, Impersonal.
O	B	L	I	G	A	T	E	D	Fastened, Bound, Pledged, Constrained, Indebted, Beholden.
O	B	L	I	Q	U	I	T	Y	Deviation from sound thinking, Divergence, Confusing statement.
O	B	L	I	V	I	O	U	S	Unnoticing, Unaware, Forgetful, Absorbed, Unconscious.
O	B	N	O	X	I	O	U	S	Harmful, Offensive, Odious, Objectionable, Hateful, Repugnant, Abhorrent.
O	B	S	C	E	N	E	L	Y	Offensively, Hideously, Crudely, Filthily, Indecently, Vilely, Profanely, Vulgarly.
O	B	S	C	E	N	I	T	Y	Foulness, Bawdiness, Vulgarity.
O	B	S	C	U	R	A	N	T	Opponent of political reform
O	B	S	C	U	R	E	L	Y	Indistinctly, Vaguely, Dimly, Gloomily, Murkily, Mistily, Abstrusely, Enigmatically.
O	B	S	C	U	R	I	T	Y	Cloudiness, Fogginess, Mistiness, Indistinctness, Faintness, Remoteness.
O	B	S	E	Q	U	E	N	T	Yielding, Submissive.
O	B	S	E	Q	U	I	T	Y	Being servile and compliant.
O	B	S	E	R	V	A	N	T	Attentive, Careful, Mindful, Heedful, Regardful, Thoughtful.
O	B	S	E	S	S	I	O	N	Compulsion, Fixation, Mania, Fetish.
O	B	S	T	E	T	R	I	C	Associated with pregnancy and childbirth.
O	B	S	T	I	N	A	C	Y	Stubbornness, Persistency.
O	B	S	T	I	N	A	T	E	Dogged, Stubborn, Headstrong, Intractable, Mulish, Self-willed, Refractory.
O	B	T	A	I	N	I	N	G	Attaining, Succeeding, Reaching, Acquiring, Procuring, Securing, Winning.
O	B	T	R	U	S	I	O	N	Thrusting upon others by force.
O	B	T	R	U	S	I	V	E	Protruding, Forward, Pushing, Intrusive, Impertinent.
O	B	T	U	N	D	E	N	T	Blunting irritation, Lessening pain.
O	B	V	E	R	S	I	O	N	The operation of immediate inference that gives the obverse.
O	B	V	I	O	U	S	L	Y	Evidently, Clearly, Apparently, Distinctly, Patently, Manifestly, Indubitably.
O	C	C	I	P	I	T	A	L	Relating to head or skull.
O	C	C	L	U	S	I	O	N	Obstruction, Blocking, Choking, Clogging, Congesting, Plugging, Stopping.
O	C	C	L	U	S	I	V	E	Serving to obstruct.
O	C	C	U	L	T	I	S	M	Belief in hidden or mysterious powers.
O	C	E	L	L	A	T	E	D	Eyelike.
O	C	H	L	O	C	R	A	T	A supporter of mob rule.
O	C	T	A	C	H	O	R	D	A musical instrument having eight strings.
O	C	T	A	G	O	N	A	L	Having eight sides.
O	C	T	A	S	T	Y	L	E	Having eight columns across the front.
O	C	T	E	N	N	I	A	L	Happening every eight years.
O	C	T	I	L	L	I	O	N	A vast number.
O	C	U	L	A	R	I	U	M	An eye-slit in a barrel helm.
O	D	A	L	I	S	Q	U	E	A female slave or concubine in a harem.
O	D	O	N	T	I	T	I	S	Inflammation of a tooth.
O	D	O	R	O	U	S	L	Y	Pungently.
O	E	N	O	P	H	I	L	E	Wine-lover, expert on wine.
O	F	F	E	N	S	I	V	E	Aggressive, Harmful, Nauseous, Revolting, Insulting, Affronting, Disgusting.
O	F	F	E	R	T	O	R	Y	Communion service for offering bread and wine, Church collection.
O	F	F	I	C	I	A	T	E	Function, Act, Serve, Perform.

1	2	3	4	5	6	7	8	9	Definition
O	F	F	I	C	I	N	A	L	Medicinal, Unrestricted drugs.
O	F	F	I	C	I	O	U	S	Meddlesome, Impertinent, Intrusive, Obtrusive, Busy.
O	F	F	S	P	R	I	N	G	Children, Descendants, Issue, Progeny, Spawn, Young, Brood.
O	L	E	A	N	D	R	I	N	Poisonous crystalline glycoside found in oleander leaves.
O	L	E	O	G	R	A	P	H	Imitation of an oil painting, Peculiar form assumed by a drop of oil placed in water.
O	L	E	O	R	E	S	I	N	Natural plant product of oil and resin.
O	L	F	A	C	T	I	O	N	Sense of smell.
O	L	F	A	C	T	O	R	Y	Connected with the sense of smell.
O	L	I	G	A	R	C	H	Y	Control by a small group.
O	L	I	G	O	C	E	N	E	Prehistoric time zone.
O	L	I	G	O	G	E	N	E	A gene controlling inherited qualities.
O	L	I	G	O	N	I	T	E	A mineral of a variety of siderite.
O	M	I	N	O	U	S	L	Y	Threateningly, Evilly, Portentously, Grimly, Menacingly, Hostilely.
O	M	P	H	A	C	I	T	E	A mineral consisting of a grass-green granular pyroxene.
O	N	C	O	G	E	N	I	C	Relating to the formation of a tumour.
O	N	D	O	G	R	A	P	H	An instrument recording wave forms of electrical currents.
O	N	I	O	N	S	K	I	N	Thin strong translucent paper.
O	N	O	M	A	S	T	I	C	Relating to names, identifying a signature.
O	N	S	L	A	U	G	H	T	Slaying, Slaughter, Attack, Aggression, Assault, Onset, Offensive, Offense.
O	O	G	E	N	E	S	I	S	Formation and maturation of the egg.
O	O	S	T	E	G	I	T	E	Receptacle for eggs on crustaceans.
O	P	E	R	A	T	I	O	N	Functioning, Working, Influence, Production, Creation, Exercise, Application, Use.
O	P	E	R	A	T	I	V	E	Active, Dynamic, Functioning, Open, Employable, Practicable, Usable.
O	P	E	R	C	U	L	U	M	A lid or covering flap of a plant, Grill cover.
O	P	E	R	O	S	E	L	Y	Diligently, Busily, Industriously.
O	P	P	O	R	T	U	N	E	Advantageous, Helpful, Useful, Seasonable, Timely, Propitious, Auspicious.
O	P	P	R	E	S	S	E	D	Crushed, Trampled, Quelled, Depressed, Wronged, Outraged, Harassed, Conquered.
O	P	P	R	E	S	S	O	R	Tyrant, Dictator, Despot.
O	P	P	U	G	N	A	N	T	Hostile, Opposing, Antagonistic, Adverse, Opposed, Opponent, Adversary.
O	P	T	O	M	E	T	R	Y	The professional measuring of visual powers.
O	P	U	L	E	N	T	L	Y	Richly, Luxuriously, Wealthily, Affluently, Lavishly, Profusely, Extravagantly.
O	P	U	S	C	U	L	U	M	Minor work of art.
O	R	B	I	C	U	L	A	R	Spherical, Circular, Encircling, Integral.
O	R	C	H	E	S	T	R	A	A group of performers of musical instruments.
O	R	D	I	N	A	N	C	E	Order, Law, Direction, Dispensation, Control, Regulation, Rule, Statute, Edict.
O	R	E	O	C	A	R	Y	A	Genus of perennial herbs, White forget-me-not.
O	R	G	A	N	I	Z	E	R	One who arranges, musters, mobilizes or disposes persons or resources.
O	R	G	A	N	Z	I	N	E	A raw silk yarn used for warp threads in fine fabrics.
O	R	G	A	N	S	I	N	E	A raw silk yarn used for warp threads in fine fabrics.
O	R	I	E	N	T	A	T	E	To determine position.
O	R	I	F	L	A	M	M	E	A banner of symbol giving inspiration.
O	R	I	G	I	N	A	T	E	Begin, Spring, Generate, Create, Procreate, Produce, Introduce, Inaugurate.
O	R	N	I	T	H	O	I	D	Birdlike, Resembling a bird.
O	R	O	B	A	N	C	H	E	A large genus of root-parasitic herbs.
O	R	O	G	R	A	P	H	Y	Science dealing with mountains and mountain systems.
O	R	P	H	A	N	A	G	E	Institution for the care of homeless children.
O	R	P	H	A	R	I	O	N	An old many-stringed musical instrument.
O	R	R	I	S	R	O	O	T	Pulverized rootstock used in medicines and perfumery.
O	R	T	H	O	A	X	I	S	Diagonal axis at right angles with the vertical axis in the crystallization system.
O	R	T	H	O	D	O	M	E	The dome of a crystal having planes parallel to the orthoaxis.
O	R	T	H	O	E	P	I	C	Relating to the study of pronunciation of a language.
O	R	T	H	O	P	T	I	C	Treatment of defective visual habits.
O	R	T	H	O	T	I	C	S	Use of mechanical devices to assist disabled people.
O	S	C	I	L	L	A	T	E	Vibrate, Swing to and fro. Fluctuate, Shilly-shally, Sway.
O	S	C	I	T	A	N	C	Y	Being drowsy, having lack of attention, yawning.
O	S	M	E	R	I	D	A	E	The family of true smelts.
O	S	M	O	M	E	T	E	R	Instrument for measuring osmotic pressure.
O	S	T	E	O	L	O	G	Y	Branch of anatomy dealing with bones.
O	S	T	E	O	P	A	T	H	Practitioner of osteopathy.
O	S	T	R	A	C	I	S	M	Temporary exile, Banishment, Expulsion, Relegation, Displacement.
O	S	T	R	A	C	I	T	E	A fossil oyster.
O	S	T	R	A	C	I	Z	E	Banish, Displace, Expel, Exile, Snub, Ignore, Cold-shoulder.
O	T	A	R	I	I	D	A	E	A family of eared seals.
O	T	H	E	R	W	I	S	E	Differently, In other respects.
O	T	O	D	E	C	T	E	S	Genus of mites that live in the ears of domestic pets.
O	T	O	L	O	G	I	S	T	Science that deals with the ear and its diseases.
O	U	R	S	E	L	V	E	S	We, Us in person.

9 LETTERS

1	2	3	4	5	6	7	8	9	Clue
O	U	T	F	I	T	T	E	R	Haberdasher, One who furnishes supplies for expeditions.
O	U	T	G	I	V	I	N	G	Public statement or utterance.
O	U	T	G	O	I	N	G	S	Expenditures, Expenses, Outlays.
O	U	T	G	R	O	W	T	H	Offshoot, Consequence, Excrescence.
O	U	T	L	I	N	I	N	G	Characterizing, Drafting, Sketching, Describing, Bordering, Defining, Edging.
O	U	T	N	U	M	B	E	R	Exceed in number.
O	U	T	R	I	G	G	E	R	Projecting support for a canoe or rowboat.
O	U	T	T	H	R	U	S	T	To thrust out.
O	U	T	W	A	R	D	L	Y	Externally, In an outward direction.
O	V	E	R	B	L	O	W	N	Portly, Fat, Corpulent, Obese, Inflated, Rhetorical, Bombastic, Pretentious.
O	V	E	R	B	O	A	R	D	Over the side of a ship, Going to extremes, Discard.
O	V	E	R	C	R	O	W	D	Filled to excess.
O	V	E	R	G	L	A	Z	E	To coat with a glaze or polish.
O	V	E	R	G	R	O	W	N	Covered with overgrowth, Excessive growth.
O	V	E	R	H	E	A	D	S	General charges or expenses in a business.
O	V	E	R	J	O	Y	E	D	Filled with great joy.
O	V	E	R	L	A	D	E	N	Loaded to excess.
O	V	E	R	N	I	G	H	T	The period of night between two days.
O	V	E	R	P	O	W	E	R	Subdue, Vanquish, Overwhelm, Engulf, Deluge, Subjugate, Crush, Defeat.
O	V	E	R	P	R	I	N	T	Imprint, Print one image over another.
O	V	E	R	P	R	O	O	F	Containing more alcohol that proof spirit.
O	V	E	R	R	E	A	C	H	Overtake, Outwit, Grab, Cheat, Circumvent, Defraud, Outsmart, Go beyond.
O	V	E	R	S	H	O	O	T	Exceed, Exaggerate, Excel, Miss target, Deplete game, Go astray.
O	V	E	R	S	I	G	H	T	Careless error or omission, Management, Supervision.
O	V	E	R	S	T	A	T	E	Exaggerate, Embellish, Magnify, Overcharge, Embroider.
O	V	E	R	T	H	R	E	W	Overturn, Topple, Conquer, Defeat, Depose, Remove, Destroy, Oust.
O	V	E	R	W	H	E	L	M	Overthrow, Overturn, Upset, Destroy, Overpower, Engulf, Inundate, Swamp.
O	V	I	P	A	R	O	U	S	Producing eggs that develop and hatch outside the maternal body.
O	W	N	E	R	S	H	I	P	Proprietorship, Lawful claim on title.
O	X	I	D	A	T	I	O	N	A stage in the firing of clayware.
O	X	Y	G	E	N	A	T	E	To combine with oxygen, Aerate.
O	X	Y	G	E	N	I	Z	E	Oxygenate, Oxidize.
O	X	Y	O	P	I	D	A	E	Family of diurnal hunting spiders.
O	X	Y	R	H	Y	N	C	H	A crab, A sacred fish.
O	X	Y	T	R	O	P	I	S	Genus of shrubby herbs.
O	X	Y	T	Y	L	O	T	E	A pin-shaped sponge spicule.
O	Z	O	K	E	R	I	T	E	A waxlike mineral used for making candles.

P

1	2	3	4	5	6	7	8	9	Clue
P	A	C	H	Y	D	E	R	M	Thick-skinned mammal, Elephant, Rhinoceros.
P	A	C	K	A	G	I	N	G	An act of packing.
P	A	C	K	H	O	R	S	E	Horse for carrying loads, Drudge.
P	A	E	D	O	L	O	G	Y	Study of development of children.
P	A	G	E	A	N	T	R	Y	Colourful display, Grand spectacle.
P	A	G	O	S	C	O	P	E	Device for registering temperature of dew.
P	A	I	L	L	E	T	T	E	Sequins, beads or shiny trimming for decorating clothing.
P	A	L	A	E	S	T	R	A	Gymnasium or stadium.
P	A	L	A	N	Q	U	I	N	A closed litter used in East Asia.
P	A	L	A	T	A	B	L	E	Agreeable, Savoury, Acceptable, Appetizing, Tasty, Delicious, Luscious, Tempting.
P	A	L	E	O	C	E	N	E	Prehistoric era.
P	A	L	I	L	A	L	I	A	A speech defect marked by abnormal repetition.
P	A	L	I	S	A	D	E	S	Fence of stakes.
P	A	L	L	A	D	I	A	N	Relating to wisdom or learning.
P	A	L	L	A	D	I	U	M	One of the platinum metals.
P	A	L	L	A	S	I	T	E	A meteorite composed of metallic iron and olivine.
P	A	L	L	E	T	I	Z	E	To store on pallets.
P	A	L	L	I	A	S	S	E	Thin hard mattress stuffed with straw.
P	A	L	M	A	T	I	O	N	Touching with the palm of the hand.
P	A	L	M	I	S	T	R	Y	Practice of reading palms.
P	A	L	O	V	E	R	D	E	Thorny trees.
P	A	L	P	A	T	I	O	N	Medical diagnosis by pressure of hand or fingers.
P	A	L	P	E	B	R	A	L	Relating to eyelids.
P	A	L	P	I	T	A	N	T	Trembling, Quivering, Throbbing.
P	A	L	P	I	T	A	T	E	Pulsate, Throb, Beat, Pulse.
P	A	L	U	D	R	I	N	E	Chloroguanide or its acetate.

1	2	3	4	5	6	7	8	9	
P	A	L	U	S	T	R	A	L	Marshy.
P	A	N	A	C	H	U	R	E	Mottling.
P	A	N	A	T	E	L	L	A	A long slender cigar.
P	A	N	C	R	A	T	I	C	Giving mastery of all subjects or matters.
P	A	N	D	U	R	A	T	E	Resembling a fiddle in outline.
P	A	N	E	G	Y	R	I	C	Laudation, Eulogistic oration.
P	A	N	E	L	L	I	N	G	Flat piece of material used as a decorative surface.
P	A	N	E	L	L	I	S	T	A member of a radio or TV panel.
P	A	N	H	A	N	D	L	E	Narrow projection, To beg by telling a hard luck story.
P	A	N	O	R	A	M	I	C	Relating to a comprehensive view.
P	A	N	S	O	P	H	I	C	Relating to universal wisdom.
P	A	N	T	A	L	E	T	S	Long drawers, Bloomers.
P	A	N	T	A	L	O	O	N	A buffoon in pantomime, Close-fitting trousers worn in the nineteenth century.
P	A	N	T	H	E	I	S	M	Doctrine that God is everything, Idol-worshipping.
P	A	N	T	O	L	O	G	Y	A systematic view of all knowledge.
P	A	N	T	O	M	I	M	E	A theatrical extravaganza usually of a fairy story.
P	A	N	T	O	P	O	D	S	Marine arthropods that resemble spiders.
P	A	P	I	L	L	O	S	E	Resembling a nipple-like protuberance.
P	A	P	I	L	L	O	T	E	A decorative paper frill used in cooking.
P	A	R	A	B	A	S	I	S	Important choral ode in the old Greek comedy.
P	A	R	A	B	O	L	I	C	Expressedly a parable, Allegorical, Relating to a parabola.
P	A	R	A	C	H	U	T	E	A folding umbrella shaped apparatus designed to assist a safe descent from an aircraft.
P	A	R	A	D	I	S	A	L	Relating to Paradise.
P	A	R	A	D	O	X	A	L	Relating to a statement that is actually self-contradictory.
P	A	R	A	G	N	A	T	H	Small horny toothlike jaws of various annelids.
P	A	R	A	G	O	G	I	C	Constituting a paragoge.
P	A	R	A	G	R	A	P	H	A distinct section of a written or printed composition.
P	A	R	A	L	L	E	L	S	Counterparts.
P	A	R	A	L	Y	S	I	S	Complete or partial loss of function involving the power of motion or sensation.
P	A	R	A	L	Y	T	I	C	Affected with paralysis.
P	A	R	A	L	Y	Z	E	D	Stunned, Petrified, Destroyed, Dazed, Maimed, Enfeebled, Crippled, Disabled.
P	A	R	A	M	A	T	T	A	A fine lightweight dress fabric.
P	A	R	A	M	E	D	I	C	One who is trained to supplement medical personnel.
P	A	R	A	M	E	T	E	R	Quantity which may have various values, each fixed within the limits of a stated case.
P	A	R	A	M	O	U	N	T	Prevalent, Sovereign, Capital, Commanding, Controlling, Cardinal, Dominant.
P	A	R	A	P	L	A	S	M	The reserve and waste inclusions of protoplasm in a cell.
P	A	R	A	P	S	I	D	A	Subclass of reptiles including some lizards and snakes.
P	A	R	A	S	I	T	I	C	Sponging, Sycophantic, Fawning, Cowering, Cringing, Grovelling, Toadying.
P	A	R	A	S	P	O	R	E	Spore produced by various red algae.
P	A	R	A	T	A	X	I	S	Co-ordinate ranging of clauses, phrases or words without co-ordinating connectives.
P	A	R	B	U	C	K	L	E	A double sling made of a single rope for slining a cask or gun.
P	A	R	C	H	M	E	N	T	Superior paper.
P	A	R	E	G	O	R	I	C	Soothing, Mitigating, Camphorated tincture of opium.
P	A	R	E	N	T	A	G	E	Birth, Family, Lineage, Origin.
P	A	R	G	A	S	I	T	E	Green or bluish-green hornblende containing sodium.
P	A	R	H	E	L	I	O	N	One of several bright spots that are intensified parts of halos.
P	A	R	L	A	T	O	R	Y	Reception room in a convent.
P	A	R	N	A	S	S	I	A	Genus of smooth bog herbs.
P	A	R	O	C	H	I	A	L	Petty, Insular, Local, Prejudiced, Bigoted, Sectarian, Narrow, Provincial.
P	A	R	O	T	I	T	I	S	Inflammation of salivary glands, Mumps.
P	A	R	R	A	K	E	E	T	Small parrot.
P	A	R	R	I	C	I	D	E	One that murders a very close relative, One that commits treason.
P	A	R	S	I	M	O	N	Y	Thrift, Niggardliness, Stinginess, Miserliness.
P	A	R	S	O	N	A	G	E	Parish house supplied for the use of the local clergyman.
P	A	R	T	I	A	L	L	Y	Partly, Bias, Favouritism.
P	A	R	T	I	C	A	T	E	An old Scotch land area about a quarter of an acre.
P	A	R	T	I	T	I	O	N	Division, Separation, Distribution, Dissolution, A separating structure.
P	A	R	T	I	T	I	V	E	Divide into parts.
P	A	R	T	R	I	D	G	E	A medium-sized game bird.
P	A	R	V	I	T	U	D	E	Atom, Very small.
P	A	S	S	E	N	G	E	R	Traveller, Wayfarer, One being conveyed in transport.
P	A	S	S	E	R	I	N	E	The largest order of living birds.
P	A	S	S	I	V	E	L	Y	Idly, Sleepily, Inactively, Quietly, Submissively.
P	A	S	T	I	C	C	I	O	Potpourri, Hodgepodge, Miscellany, Medley, Assortment.
P	A	S	T	O	R	A	L	E	A sixteenth or seventeenth century opera having a simple country-life theme.
P	A	S	T	O	R	A	T	E	Body of pastors, Parsonage, Relating to the office of a pastor.
P	A	S	T	U	R	A	G	E	Grazing.

1	2	3	4	5	6	7	8	9	
P	A	T	C	H	W	O	R	K	A collection of fabric pieces of mixed colours and shapes joined together. Hash.
P	A	T	E	R	I	S	S	A	A crosier of the Eastern church.
P	A	T	E	R	N	I	T	Y	Fatherhood, Male parentage, Authorship.
P	A	T	H	O	L	O	G	Y	Study of diseases and abnormalities.
P	A	T	I	E	N	T	L	Y	Tolerantly, Passively.
P	A	T	R	I	A	R	C	H	Father, Elder, Veteran, Author, Creator, Founder, Inventor, Maker.
P	A	T	R	I	C	I	A	N	Aristocrat, Nobleman, Gentleman.
P	A	T	R	I	C	I	D	E	One that murders his own father.
P	A	T	R	I	M	O	N	Y	Something inherited from the paternal side of the family, Heritage, Legacy.
P	A	T	R	I	O	T	I	C	Loyalty to one's country.
P	A	T	R	I	S	T	I	C	Relating to early writings of any religion, cult or sect.
P	A	T	R	O	N	A	G	E	Sponsorship, Benefaction, Protection, Subsidy, Custom, Trade, Maintain.
P	A	T	R	O	N	E	S	S	A female sponsor.
P	A	T	R	O	N	I	Z	E	Protect, Support, Favour, Use, Frequent, Encourage, Treat in a condescending fashion.
P	A	U	P	E	R	I	S	M	The state of being a pauper.
P	A	U	S	E	L	E	S	S	Continuous, Ceaseless.
P	A	V	O	N	A	Z	Z	O	Veined marble.
P	A	W	K	I	N	E	S	S	Squeamishness, Boldness, Canniness, Liveliness.
P	E	A	C	E	A	B	L	E	Calm, Nonviolent, Pacifist, Amicable, Complaisant, Friendly.
P	E	A	C	H	W	O	O	D	A brazilwood.
P	E	C	T	I	N	A	T	E	Shaped like a comb, Salt or ester of a pectinic acid.
P	E	C	T	I	N	O	U	S	Containing pectin.
P	E	C	U	L	A	T	O	R	Embezzler.
P	E	C	U	N	I	A	R	Y	Consisting of money, Monetary, Financial, Fiscal.
P	E	D	A	G	O	G	U	E	Teacher of children, Schoolmaster.
P	E	D	I	C	U	L	A	R	Relating to lice, Lousy, Infested with lice.
P	E	D	O	M	E	T	E	R	An instrument to measure distance walked by a pedestrian.
P	E	E	V	I	S	H	L	Y	Irritably, Fretfully, Querulously, Critically.
P	E	L	L	I	T	O	R	Y	European plant resembling yarrow, once used in dentifrice.
P	E	L	L	O	T	I	N	E	A crystalline narcotic alkaloid derived from various cacti.
P	E	L	T	A	N	D	R	A	Genus of aquatic or marsh herbs.
P	E	N	D	U	L	A	T	E	Swing, Fluctuate, Undulate, Oscillate, Sway.
P	E	N	D	U	L	O	U	S	Suspended, Hanging, Pendent, Vacillating, Faltering, Hesitating, Tentative.
P	E	N	E	T	R	A	T	E	Pierce, Permeate, Understand, Fathom, Imbue, Steep, Enter, Infiltrate.
P	E	N	I	L	L	I	O	N	Traditional Welsh songs.
P	E	N	I	T	E	N	C	E	Penance, Contrition, Remorse, Compunction, Scruple, Anguish, Grief, Regret.
P	E	N	S	I	O	N	E	R	A person who receives a pension.
P	E	N	S	I	V	E	L	Y	Dreamily, Wistfully, Meditatively, Thoughtfully, Speculatively.
P	E	N	T	A	G	R	A	M	Five pointed star.
P	E	N	T	A	G	R	I	D	Having five grids.
P	E	N	T	A	L	O	G	Y	Series of five closely related published works.
P	E	N	T	A	P	O	D	Y	A metrical verse consisting of five feet.
P	E	N	T	E	C	O	S	T	Christian church festival.
P	E	N	T	H	O	U	S	E	A dwelling, usually of a luxury type, built on the roof.
P	E	N	T	U	L	O	S	E	A ketose containing five carbon atoms in the molecule.
P	E	N	U	R	I	O	U	S	Poor, Destitute, Impoverished, Indigent, Needy, Stingy, Miserly, Parsimonious.
P	E	R	C	H	A	N	C	E	Perhaps, Possibly.
P	E	R	C	H	E	R	O	N	Breed of powerful draft horses.
P	E	R	C	O	L	A	T	E	Filter, Strain, Penetrate, Ooze, Trickle, Seep, Permeate, Exude.
P	E	R	E	G	R	I	N	E	Traveller, Wanderer, Pilgrim, Rover, Alien.
P	E	R	E	N	N	I	A	L	Permanent, Enduring, Constant, Perpetual, Recurrent, Continual, Inveterate.
P	E	R	F	E	C	T	L	Y	Completely, Thoroughly, Accurately, Faultlessly, Ideally, Quite, Exactly.
P	E	R	F	O	R	A	T	E	Pierce, Puncture, Punch, Prick, Bore, Drill, Probe, Drive.
P	E	R	F	O	R	M	E	D	Fulfilled, Implemented, Completed, Accomplished, Provided, Presented, Played.
P	E	R	F	U	M	E	R	Y	A perfume establishment.
P	E	R	F	U	S	I	O	N	Pumping of a fluid through an organ or tissue, Suffusing.
P	E	R	I	B	O	L	O	S	Enclosed court.
P	E	R	I	C	L	A	S	E	Native magnesia in granular form.
P	E	R	I	M	E	T	E	R	Boundary, Circumference, Circuit, Compass, Border, Edge, Fringe, Margin.
P	E	R	I	O	D	A	T	E	A salt of a periodic acid.
P	E	R	I	P	H	E	R	Y	Confines, Compass, Perimeter, Verge, Circumference, Ambit, Margin, Brink.
P	E	R	I	S	C	O	P	E	An optical instrument with special lenses to clear an otherwise obstructed vision.
P	E	R	I	S	H	I	N	G	Decaying, Rotting, Crumbling, Decomposing, Disintegrating, Dying, Expiring.
P	E	R	I	S	P	O	R	E	The covering of a spore.
P	E	R	I	S	T	O	M	E	Region around the mouth in invertebrates, The lip of a spiral shell.
P	E	R	I	S	T	Y	L	E	A colonnade surrounding a building or courtyard.
P	E	R	K	I	N	E	S	S	Jauntiness.

1	2	3	4	5	6	7	8	9	
P	E	R	M	A	N	E	N	T	Stable, Lasting, Durable, Imperishable, Invariable.
P	E	R	M	I	T	T	E	D	Allowed, Tolerated, Authorized, Committed.
P	E	R	N	E	T	T	I	A	An American evergreen shrub.
P	E	R	N	I	O	S	I	S	A skin abnormality resulting from cold.
P	E	R	P	E	T	U	A	L	Everlasting, Eternal, Unceasing, Constant, Continual, Perennial, Interminable.
P	E	R	P	L	E	X	E	D	Anxious, Troubled, Distraught, Puzzled, Bewildered, Complicated, Entangled.
P	E	R	S	E	C	U	T	E	Pursue, Harass, Oppress, Pester, Vex, Torment, Outrage, Molest.
P	E	R	S	E	V	E	R	E	Persist, Remain, Continue, Proceed.
P	E	R	S	I	C	A	R	Y	Genus of herbs.
P	E	R	S	I	E	N	N	E	Painted or printed cotton or silk, Venetian blind.
P	E	R	S	O	N	A	G	E	Notable, Dignitary, Eminence, Personality, Creature, Individual, Mortal.
P	E	R	S	O	N	A	T	E	Masked, Disguised, Represent, Masquerade, Act, Perform, Exemplify, Illustrate.
P	E	R	S	O	N	I	F	Y	Incarnate, Embody, Manifest, Materialize, Represent, Illustrate, Typify, Symbolize.
P	E	R	S	O	N	N	E	L	A group of employees, Members of the armed services, Persons of a profession.
P	E	R	T	I	N	E	N	T	Relevant, Applicable, Apropos, Material.
P	E	R	V	A	S	I	O	N	Permeation, Penetration, Impregnation, Saturation.
P	E	R	V	A	S	I	V	E	Pervading, Becoming the dominant factor.
P	E	R	V	E	R	T	E	D	Twisted, Corrupted, Vicious, Debased, Brutalized, Abused, Debauched, Depraved.
P	E	S	K	I	N	E	S	S	State of being troublesome or annoying.
P	E	S	S	I	M	I	S	M	Gloominess, Distrustfulness, Lack of confidence.
P	E	S	T	H	O	U	S	E	Hospital for persons suffering from a contagious disease.
P	E	S	T	I	C	I	D	E	Chemical agent used to destroy pests.
P	E	S	T	O	L	O	G	Y	The study of insect pests.
P	E	T	E	C	H	I	A	L	Minute haemorrhages of the skin.
P	E	T	E	R	S	H	A	M	Heavy corded ribbon used for belts and hatbands.
P	E	T	T	I	O	L	U	L	E	Stalk of a leaflet.
P	E	T	R	O	G	E	N	Y	Science of the origin of rocks.
P	E	T	R	O	L	E	U	M	Oily flammable bituminous liquid.
P	E	T	T	O	L	O	G	Y	Science dealing with all aspects of rocks.
P	E	T	T	I	C	O	A	T	An undergarment resembling a skirt or sleeveless dress.
P	E	T	T	I	N	E	S	S	Triviality.
P	E	T	T	I	T	O	E	S	Toes, Feet.
P	E	T	U	L	A	N	C	E	Rudeness, Peevishness, Fractious, Querulousness, Sulkiness, Waspishness.
P	H	A	C	O	L	I	T	H	Mass of igneous rock in sedimentary beds.
P	H	A	G	O	C	Y	T	E	Any body cell that has the function of removing and consuming debris material.
P	H	A	L	A	N	G	E	R	A small marsupial mammal.
P	H	A	L	A	R	O	P	E	Family of small shorebirds.
P	H	A	N	A	R	I	O	T	A powerful Greek in Constaninople under Turkish patronage.
P	H	A	R	I	S	A	I	C	Relating to the Pharisees.
P	H	A	R	Y	N	G	A	L	Relating to the region of the pharynx.
P	H	E	N	E	T	O	L	E	An aromatic liquid that is the ethyl ether of phenol.
P	H	E	N	O	C	O	L	L	A crystalline base used as a salt for an antipyretic and analgesic.
P	H	E	N	O	M	E	N	A	Thing that is perceived or observed, Something or someone unusual.
P	H	E	N	O	T	Y	P	E	The visible characters of an organism.
P	H	I	L	A	N	D	E	R	Flirtation, Dally, Trifle, Womanize, Pursue, Chase.
P	H	I	L	A	T	E	L	Y	Collection and study of postal stamps and stationery.
P	H	I	L	I	A	T	E	R	One interested in medical science.
P	H	I	L	O	L	O	G	Y	Study of literature, Linguistics.
P	H	I	L	O	M	A	T	H	Scholar, Student of mathematics.
P	H	L	E	B	I	T	I	S	Inflammation of a vein.
P	H	O	C	A	E	N	I	D	Relating to porpoises.
P	H	O	L	C	I	D	A	E	Family of spiders that weave irregular webs.
P	H	O	L	I	D	O	T	A	Toothless scaly mammals, Pangolins.
P	H	O	M	O	P	S	I	S	Form genus of imperfect fungi.
P	H	O	N	E	T	I	C	S	Study of the spoken word.
P	H	O	N	O	G	R	A	M	Symbol representing a word or syllable.
P	H	O	N	O	L	O	G	Y	The science of speech sounds.
P	H	O	S	P	H	A	T	E	A salt of phosphoric acid.
P	H	O	S	P	H	E	N	E	A luminous impression often caused by pressure on the eyeball.
P	H	O	T	O	C	O	P	Y	To make a photographic reproduction.
P	H	O	T	O	S	T	A	T	Photographic copy of documents.
P	H	T	H	I	R	I	U	S	Crab louse.
P	H	Y	C	I	O	D	E	S	A large genus of small butterflies.
P	H	Y	C	O	L	O	G	Y	Study of algae.
P	H	Y	L	L	I	T	I	S	A small genus of ferns.
P	H	Y	L	O	G	E	N	Y	The racial history of a specified kind of organism.
P	H	Y	S	I	C	I	A	N	A doctor of medicine.

1	2	3	4	5	6	7	8	9	
P	H	Y	S	I	C	I	S	T	A specialist in physics.
P	H	Y	T	O	L	I	T	E	A fossil plant.
P	H	Y	T	O	L	O	G	Y	Botany, Study of plants.
P	I	A	N	I	S	T	I	C	Relating to a piano.
P	I	C	T	O	R	I	A	L	Illustrated by pictures.
P	I	E	R	R	E	T	T	E	A female pierrot.
P	I	G	G	I	S	H	L	Y	Greedily, Meanly, Dirtily, Stubbornly.
P	I	K	E	S	T	A	F	F	A staff with a spike at the end.
P	I	L	L	A	R	I	S	T	Stylite.
P	I	L	U	L	A	R	I	A	Genus of small aquatic plants.
P	I	M	P	E	R	N	E	L	A genus of herb.
P	I	N	E	A	P	P	L	E	A plant with rigid spiny leaves and succulent fleshy fruit.
P	I	N	S	E	T	T	E	R	An employee in a bowling alley.
P	I	P	E	R	O	N	A	L	A crystalline aldehyde used in perfumery, cosmetics and soaps.
P	I	P	I	S	T	R	E	L	A European brown bat.
P	I	R	A	T	I	C	A	L	Being a pirate, Resembling a pirate.
P	I	R	I	G	U	A	R	A	A South American cuckoo.
P	I	R	O	U	E	T	T	E	A full turn on a toe or ball of the foot in dancing.
P	I	S	C	A	T	O	R	Y	Relating to fishing.
P	I	S	O	L	I	T	I	C	Relating to a special form of limestone.
P	I	T	C	H	F	O	R	K	A long-handled fork with curved prongs for moving hay or straw.
P	I	T	E	O	U	S	L	Y	Pitifully, Pathetically, Imploringly, Plaintively.
P	I	T	H	E	C	O	I	D	Resembling monkeys.
P	I	T	H	I	N	E	S	S	Conciseness, Terseness, Curtness, Effectiveness.
P	I	T	U	I	T	A	R	Y	A gland attached to the brain, the secretion of which controls growth of the body.
P	I	X	I	L	A	T	E	D	Bewildered, Confused, Enchanted, Bewitched, Whimsical, Intoxicated, Drunk.
P	I	Z	Z	I	C	A	T	O	Instruction in music to pluck by the fingers instead of using the bow.
P	L	A	C	A	T	I	O	N	Pacification, Tranquilization.
P	L	A	C	E	M	E	N	T	Orderly distribution, Transfer of custody, Investment.
P	L	A	I	N	T	I	F	F	The party who institutes litigation.
P	L	A	I	N	T	I	V	E	Lamenting, Pining, Sorrowful, Melancholy, Mournful, Doleful, Rueful, Woeful.
P	L	A	N	E	T	A	R	Y	Orbiting, Immense, Erratic, Wandering, Terrestrial, Global, Universal, Cosmic.
P	L	A	N	E	T	O	I	D	Asteroid.
P	L	A	N	I	D	I	U	M	First stage legless larva of parasitic insects.
P	L	A	N	O	R	B	I	S	Genus type of a family of snails.
P	L	A	S	M	A	T	I	C	Relating to plasma.
P	L	A	S	T	I	Q	U	E	Slow change of position in dancing.
P	L	A	T	E	L	I	K	E	Resembling a smooth flat plate.
P	L	A	T	I	N	I	Z	E	To coat with platinum.
P	L	A	T	I	T	U	D	E	Triteness, Commonplace, Cliche, Banality, Inanisty, Vapidity, Insipidity.
P	L	A	T	O	N	I	S	M	Philosophical system of Plato.
P	L	A	U	S	I	B	L	E	Credible, Probable, Possible, Likely, Suitable, Affable, Popular, Agreeable.
P	L	A	Y	T	H	I	N	G	Toy.
P	L	E	A	S	A	N	C	E	Courtesy, Pleasantness, Delight, Amenity, Cordiality, Geniality, Amiability.
P	L	E	N	A	R	I	L	Y	In a plenary manner.
P	L	E	N	I	T	U	D	E	Completeness, Abundance, Fullness.
P	L	E	N	T	I	F	U	L	Fruitful, Opulent, Ample, Abundant, Copious, Bountiful, Generous, Sufficient.
P	L	E	T	H	O	R	I	C	Excessive.
P	L	E	U	R	I	T	I	C	Suffering from pleurisy.
P	L	I	C	A	T	I	O	N	Folding, Wrinkling, Creasing.
P	L	O	W	S	H	A	R	E	The cutting blade of a plough.
P	L	U	M	P	N	E	S	S	Corpulence, Being well-rounded.
P	L	U	N	D	E	R	E	R	Pillager, Robber, Bandit.
P	L	U	R	A	L	I	S	M	Holding more than one office at one time, Co-existence.
P	L	U	R	A	L	I	S	T	A person holding two offices, One who supports pluralism.
P	L	U	R	A	L	I	T	Y	Multitude, Winning margin of votes cast, The larger number.
P	L	U	R	A	L	I	Z	E	To make plural, Assume a plural form.
P	L	U	T	A	R	C	H	Y	Government by the wealthy.
P	L	U	T	O	C	R	A	T	A person who is powerful and influential by virtue of their wealth.
P	L	U	T	O	N	I	U	M	A radioactive metallic element similar to uranium.
P	L	U	V	I	A	L	I	S	Golden plover.
P	N	E	U	M	A	T	I	C	Inflating or working by using air, wind or other type of gas.
P	N	E	U	M	O	N	I	A	Inflammation of the lungs.
P	O	C	K	E	T	F	U	L	As much as a pocket will hold.
P	O	E	T	A	S	T	E	R	An inferior poet.
P	O	E	T	I	C	U	L	E	Same as POETASTER.
P	O	E	T	I	C	I	Z	E	To put into poetry.

1	2	3	4	5	6	7	8	9	Definition
P	O	I	G	N	A	N	C	Y	Sharpness, Keenness, Urgency.
P	O	I	M	E	N	I	C	S	Study of pastoral theology.
P	O	I	N	C	I	A	N	A	Ornamental tropical shrub with bright red or orange flowers.
P	O	I	N	T	I	L	L	E	Decoration of gold spots.
P	O	I	N	T	L	E	S	S	Senseless, Vapid, Flat, Insipid, Insignificant, Blunt, Meaningless.
P	O	I	S	O	N	I	N	G	Condition produced by poison.
P	O	I	S	O	N	O	U	S	Toxic, Venomous, Virulent, Malignant, Malevolent, Miasmatic, Pestilent, Lethal.
P	O	L	E	M	I	C	A	L	Contentious, Argumentative, Controversial.
P	O	L	I	C	E	M	A	N	Member of a police force, Authoritive person to exert control.
P	O	L	I	N	I	C	E	S	Genus of marine snails.
P	O	L	I	S	S	O	I	R	A tool used in glass manufacturing, Implement used for polishing or grinding.
P	O	L	I	T	I	C	A	L	Relating to government, Civil administration, Public affairs.
P	O	L	L	I	N	A	T	E	Fertilizing a plant, Placing pollen for fertilization.
P	O	L	L	I	N	I	U	M	Mass of pollen grains peculiar to certain plants.
P	O	L	L	U	T	A	N	T	Something that pollutes.
P	O	L	L	U	T	I	O	N	Defilement, Desecration, Impurity, Contamination.
P	O	L	O	N	A	I	S	E	An elaborate eighteenth century dress with a distinctive cut-away skirt. A Polish dance.
P	O	L	V	E	R	I	N	E	Potash used in glass making.
P	O	L	Y	A	N	D	R	Y	Having more than one husband at the same time.
P	O	L	Y	C	R	O	S	S	Plant where female part is known but male could be of any various strains.
P	O	L	Y	D	E	M	I	C	Occurring in several regions.
P	O	L	Y	E	I	D	I	C	Passing through definite changes of form to reach maturity.
P	O	L	Y	E	S	T	E	R	A complex ester formed for use in making fibres, resins and plastics.
P	O	L	Y	G	O	N	A	L	Having many sides and angles.
P	O	L	Y	G	O	N	U	M	A widely distributed genus of herbs.
P	O	L	Y	G	Y	R	I	A	Having an unusual amount of cerebral convolutions.
P	O	L	Y	M	E	R	I	C	Relating to a natural or synthetic mixture of compounds.
P	O	L	Y	M	O	R	P	H	An organism having various forms.
P	O	L	Y	N	E	M	U	S	Food fishes that resemble mullet and sometimes yield isinglass.
P	O	L	Y	P	H	O	N	E	A music box playing perforated discs, Written characters having more than one sound.
P	O	L	Y	P	H	O	N	Y	Counterpoint, Multiplicity.
P	O	L	Y	P	L	O	I	D	Being a chromosome number that is a multiple greater than two of the base group.
P	O	L	Y	V	I	N	Y	L	A polymerized vinyl compound, vinyl resin or vinyl plastic.
P	O	M	P	A	D	O	U	R	A style of hairdressing for women and men.
P	O	M	P	O	S	I	T	Y	Arrogance, Vainness, Ostentatiousness.
P	O	N	D	E	R	O	U	S	Heavy, Dull, Uninspired, Cumbersome, Massive, Weighty, Dry, Humdrum.
P	O	O	R	H	O	U	S	E	Institution for the needy and poor.
P	O	O	R	R	A	T	E	S	Levying unjustly high taxes for social services.
P	O	P	L	I	T	E	A	L	Relating to the back of leg behind the knee joint.
P	O	P	P	Y	C	O	C	K	Nonsense, Bosh, Balderdash, Bunkum, Rot.
P	O	P	U	L	A	R	L	Y	In a popular manner.
P	O	R	B	E	A	G	L	E	A voracious shark.
P	O	R	C	E	L	A	I	N	A fine ceramic ware used for tableware, dentures, chemical utensils and insulators.
P	O	R	C	U	P	I	N	E	Rodent with body and tail covered with long erectile spines.
P	O	R	R	I	N	G	E	R	A dish for porridge.
P	O	R	T	A	T	I	L	E	A portable altar.
P	O	R	T	A	T	I	V	E	Portable.
P	O	R	T	E	R	A	G	E	The charge made by a porter for transportation.
P	O	R	T	F	O	L	I	O	A flat portable case for carrying documents, Office and function of minister of state.
P	O	R	T	O	L	A	N	O	Medieval navigation manual with charts.
P	O	R	T	O	N	O	V	O	Style prevalent in the capital of Benin (Dahomey).
P	O	R	T	R	A	Y	A	L	Description, Representation, Depiction, Picture, Presentment.
P	O	R	T	R	E	E	V	E	Chief officer of a seaport town.
P	O	S	I	T	R	O	N	S	A hypothetical atomic particle.
P	O	S	S	E	S	S	E	S	Has, Occupies, Inhabits, Dominates, Enjoys, Holds, Owns, Retains.
P	O	S	S	E	S	S	O	R	One that holds, occupies, owns or controls.
P	O	S	T	E	R	I	O	R	Buttocks, Dorsal, Back, Behind, Subsequent, After, Later, Hindmost.
P	O	S	T	E	R	I	T	Y	Offspring, Descendants, Progeny, Brood, Issue, Scions, Children, Future time.
P	O	S	T	H	A	S	T	E	Speedy, Immediate, Fast, Expeditious, Fleet, Hasty, Rapid, Swift.
P	O	S	T	U	L	A	N	T	Novice.
P	O	S	T	U	L	A	T	E	Demand, Claim, Presuppose, Challenge, Claim, Require, Solicit, Assume.
P	O	T	A	S	S	I	U	M	A silver-white soft light low-melting univalent metallic element of the alkaline group.
P	O	T	E	N	T	I	A	L	Latent, Possibility, Conceivable, Likely, Plausible, Probable, Dormant, Abeyant.
P	O	T	T	E	R	I	E	S	District of England, the chief centre of the pottery industry.
P	O	U	L	T	E	R	E	R	Trader that deals in poultry.
P	O	U	R	P	O	I	N	T	Quilt, Padded and quilted doublet.
P	O	U	S	S	E	T	T	E	To join hands with a partner and swing in a semi-circle in a country dance.

1	2	3	4	5	6	7	8	9	Definition
P	O	W	E	L	L	I	T	E	A mineral of a calcium molybdate.
P	O	W	E	R	L	E	S	S	Helpless, Impotent, Unable, Feeble, Incapable, Unfit, Incompetent, Ineffective.
P	R	A	C	T	I	C	A	L	Skillful, Qualified, Useful, Functional, Serviceable, Pragmatic, Realistic, Experienced.
P	R	A	C	T	I	S	E	D	Experienced, Seasoned, Skilled, Veteran, Expert, Proficient.
P	R	A	T	T	L	I	N	G	Babbling, Chattering, Jabbering.
P	R	E	A	C	H	I	F	Y	To preach ineptly or tediously.
P	R	E	A	C	H	I	N	G	Evangelizing, Sermonizing, Addressing, Lecturing, Talking, Proclaiming, Delivering.
P	R	E	B	E	N	D	A	L	Payment given to a chapter member from the estate of a cathedral.
P	R	E	C	A	T	I	V	E	Beseeching, Supplicating.
P	R	E	C	A	T	O	R	Y	Supplicatory.
P	R	E	C	E	D	E	N	T	Token, Sign, Convention, Anterior, Former, Past, Previous, Prior.
P	R	E	C	E	D	I	N	G	Predating, Outranking, Prefacing, Introducing, Heralding, Presaging, Leading.
P	R	E	C	E	N	T	O	R	Choirleader, Cathedral official.
P	R	E	C	E	P	T	O	R	Teacher, Tutor, Headmaster, Instructor.
P	R	E	C	I	P	I	C	E	Sheer cliff, Hazardous situation, Brink of disaster.
P	R	E	C	I	S	E	L	Y	Exactly, Expressly, Definitely, Accurately, Squarely.
P	R	E	C	I	S	I	A	N	Purist, Traditionalist.
P	R	E	C	I	S	I	O	N	Accuracy, Exactness, Definiteness, Nicety, Carefulness, Attention, Heed.
P	R	E	C	O	N	I	S	E	To have foreknowledge.
P	R	E	C	U	R	S	O	R	Predecessor, Forerunner, Antecedent, Prototype, Herald, Harbinger.
P	R	E	D	A	C	I	T	Y	Rapacity.
P	R	E	D	A	T	O	R	Y	Rapacious, Using violence on robbery, Injurious, Harmful.
P	R	E	D	I	C	A	N	T	Preacher.
P	R	E	D	I	C	A	T	E	Assert, Affirm, Declare, Profess, Protest, Predict.
P	R	E	D	I	C	T	O	R	One that predicts, Mechanism for controlling anti-aircraft fire.
P	R	E	F	A	T	O	R	Y	Introductory, Preliminary.
P	R	E	F	I	G	U	R	E	Foresee, Predict.
P	R	E	G	E	N	I	A	L	Located in front of the chin.
P	R	E	G	N	A	B	L	E	Liable to be captured, Expungable.
P	R	E	G	N	A	N	C	Y	Fertility, Fruitfulness, Gestation, Bearing young.
P	R	E	J	U	D	I	C	E	Detriment, Hurt, Prejudgment, Bias, Damage, Harm, Predispose, Influence.
P	R	E	L	A	T	I	O	N	Promotion, Preferment.
P	R	E	L	A	T	U	R	E	Status of a prelate.
P	R	E	L	U	D	I	A	L	Introductory, Preliminary, Preparatory.
P	R	E	L	U	S	I	O	N	Prelude, Introduction, Foreword, Preamble, Preface, Prologue.
P	R	E	L	U	S	I	V	E	Introductory, Preliminary, Preparatory, Inductive.
P	R	E	L	U	S	O	R	Y	Introductory, Preliminary, Preparatory, Inductive.
P	R	E	M	A	T	U	R	E	Early, Soon, Untimely, Previous.
P	R	E	O	C	C	U	P	Y	Prepossess, Preengage.
P	R	E	P	A	R	I	N	G	Educating, Training, Providing, Producing, Making, Qualifying, Conditioning.
P	R	E	P	O	T	E	N	T	Preiminent, Superior, Dominant, Powerful.
P	R	E	P	U	T	I	A	L	Relating to the foreskin.
P	R	E	S	B	Y	T	I	S	Family of monkeys consisting of the langurs.
P	R	E	S	C	R	I	B	E	Dictate, Direct, Confine, Restrain, Assign, Define, Dictate, Impose.
P	R	E	S	C	R	I	P	T	Command, Direction, Instruction, Law, Ordinance, Precept, Regulation, Rule.
P	R	E	S	E	N	T	L	Y	Shortly, Soon, Directly, Necessarily, Consequently, Today, Now.
P	R	E	S	E	R	V	E	R	A person, substance or object that prevents destruction, decay or injury.
P	R	E	S	I	D	E	N	T	A nominated or elected official who presides or administers.
P	R	E	S	I	D	I	U	M	An executive committee.
P	R	E	S	S	U	R	E	D	Constrained, Influenced, Impelled, Driven, Pushed.
P	R	E	S	U	M	I	N	G	Presumptious, Brash, Pushing, Self-asserting, Uppish.
P	R	E	T	E	N	D	E	R	Imposter, Fake, Fraud, Humbug, Claimant.
P	R	E	T	E	R	I	T	E	A verb tense indicating action in the past.
P	R	E	T	E	R	M	I	T	Omit, Neglect, Interrupt, Suspend, Disregard, Forget, Ignore, Miss.
P	R	E	T	T	Y	I	S	H	Rather pretty.
P	R	E	V	A	L	E	N	T	Dominant, Victorious, Widespread, Prevailing, Paramount, Current, Popular.
P	R	E	V	E	N	T	E	D	Frustrated, Circumvented, Forestalled, Anticipated, Precluded, Impeded, Averted.
P	R	E	V	E	N	T	E	R	Preventive, One that forestalls.
P	R	E	V	E	R	N	A	L	Early flowering or leafing.
P	R	E	V	I	S	I	O	N	Foresight, Foreknowledge, Prescience, Forecast, Prognostication.
P	R	I	C	E	L	E	S	S	Costly, Precious, Inestimable, Invaluable, Prized, Cherished, Treasured.
P	R	I	E	S	T	E	S	S	A female priest.
P	R	I	M	A	E	V	A	L	Prehistoric, Primitive, Aboriginal.
P	R	I	M	I	T	I	V	E	Original, Primary, Archaic, Primordial, Crude, Naive, Rudimentary, Simple.
P	R	I	M	O	C	A	N	E	A new cane on a bramble fruit.
P	R	I	M	U	L	I	N	E	A yellow dye.
P	R	I	N	C	E	D	O	M	Principality, Estate of a prince.

1	2	3	4	5	6	7	8	9	
P	R	I	N	C	I	P	A	L	Controlling, Salient, Main, Chief, Major, First, Foremost, Leading.
P	R	I	N	C	I	P	E	S	Palms.
P	R	I	N	C	I	P	L	E	Commencement, Beginning, Constituent, Axiom, Fundamental, Basis, Foundation.
P	R	I	N	T	A	B	L	E	Considered fit to print.
P	R	I	S	M	A	T	I	C	Brilliant, Showy.
P	R	I	V	A	T	E	E	R	Armed vessel owned and manned by private persons but commissioned by government.
P	R	I	V	A	T	E	L	Y	Secretly, Unofficially, Clandestinely, Covertly, Furtively, Stealthily, Surreptiously.
P	R	I	V	A	T	I	O	N	Deprivation, Suspension, Destituition, Hardship, Want, Absence, Dearth, Lack.
P	R	I	V	A	T	I	V	E	Depriving, Negative.
P	R	I	V	A	T	I	Z	E	To alter ownership from public to private.
P	R	I	V	I	L	E	G	E	Right, Franchise, Patent, Prerogative, Concession, Boon, Favour, Perquisite.
P	R	O	B	A	T	I	O	N	Testing of conduct or character of a person, Moral trial under supervision.
P	R	O	B	A	T	I	V	E	Exploratory, Substantiating, Giving proof.
P	R	O	B	O	S	C	I	S	Flexible long snout of some mammals, A prominent nose on a human.
P	R	O	C	A	C	I	T	Y	Impudence.
P	R	O	C	E	D	U	R	E	Course, Policy, Line, Programme, Measure, Move, Manoeuvre, Process.
P	R	O	C	E	E	D	E	D	Advanced, Moved, Progressed, Went, Journeyed, Passed, Travelled, Headed.
P	R	O	C	L	I	T	I	C	Word without stress joined in pronunciation with following word.
P	R	O	C	R	E	A	T	E	Generate, Reproduce, Beget, Propagate, Originate, Occasion, Multiply, Proliferate.
P	R	O	C	U	R	I	N	G	Obtaining, Acquiring, Gaining, Winning, Effecting, Achieving, Contriving, Getting.
P	R	O	D	R	O	M	I	C	Precursory.
P	R	O	D	U	C	I	N	G	Generating, Yielding, Composing, Creating, Bearing, Exhibiting, Showing.
P	R	O	F	A	N	I	T	Y	Blasphemy, Cursing, Irreverence, Swearing, Imprecation.
P	R	O	F	E	S	S	E	D	Affirmed, Hypocritical, Insincere, Expert, Alleged, Ostensible, Purported, Supposed.
P	R	O	F	E	S	S	O	R	Lecturer at a university.
P	R	O	F	I	T	E	E	R	Trader who makes an exorbitant profit.
P	R	O	F	U	S	I	O	N	Extravagance, Lavishness, Prodigality, Opulence, Abundance.
P	R	O	G	N	O	S	I	S	Forecast, Prediction, Foretelling, Prophecy, Cast.
P	R	O	G	R	A	M	M	E	Schedule, Prospectus, Syllabus, Curriculum, Agenda, Timetable, Policy, Procedure.
P	R	O	J	E	C	T	O	R	Planner of a project, Schemer, Device for projecting light or an image.
P	R	O	L	A	T	I	V	E	Extending or completing the predication.
P	R	O	L	E	P	S	I	S	Presupposition, Postulate, Anticipation.
P	R	O	L	I	X	I	T	Y	Verbosity.
P	R	O	L	O	G	I	Z	E	To write or speak a prologue.
P	R	O	M	E	N	A	D	E	Paved area for walking, riding or driving in a leisurely fashion.
P	R	O	M	I	N	E	N	T	Conspicuous, Striking, Jutting, Protuberant, Notable, Leading, Eminent, Noticeable.
P	R	O	M	I	N	E	N	T	Conspicuous, Striking, Jutting, Protuberant, Notable, Leading, Eminent, Noticeable.
P	R	O	M	I	S	I	N	G	Raising, Advancing, Encouraging, Furthering, Launching, Elevating, Upgrading.
P	R	O	M	O	T	I	N	G	Inciting, Provoking, Urging, Suggesting, Inducing, Persuading, Exhorting.
P	R	O	M	O	T	I	O	N	Advancement, Preferment, Elevation, Publicity, Advertising.
P	R	O	M	O	T	I	V	E	Promotional, To further or encourage.
P	R	O	M	P	T	I	N	G	Inciting, provoking, reminding, assisting, suggesting, urging.
P	R	O	N	A	T	I	O	N	Rotation of the hand with palm turned downward, Lying face downward, Fallen arch.
P	R	O	N	G	H	O	R	N	A horned antelope of North America.
P	R	O	N	O	U	N	C	E	Utter, Declare, Recite, Articulate, Enunciate.
P	R	O	P	A	G	A	T	E	Reproduce, Extend, Spread, Publicize, Transmit, Expand, Procreate, Cultivate.
P	R	O	P	E	L	L	E	R	Revolving shaft with angled blades used for propulsion.
P	R	O	P	H	E	T	I	C	Revelatory, Presageful, Oracular, Interpretive, Mystic, Apocalyptic.
P	R	O	P	O	N	E	N	T	Advocate, Supporter, Exponent, Champion, Expounder.
P	R	O	P	O	S	I	N	G	Intending, Conversing, Suggesting, Submitting, Requesting, Soliciting, Designing.
P	R	O	P	R	I	E	T	Y	Suitability, Fitness, Decorum, Aptness, Decency, Dignity, Etiquette, Order.
P	R	O	P	Y	L	A	T	E	To introduce propyl into a chemical compound.
P	R	O	P	Y	L	E	N	E	A flammable gaseous olefin hydrocarbon obtained in petroleum refineries.
P	R	O	S	C	R	I	B	E	Prohibit, Outlaw, Condemn, Sentence.
P	R	O	S	E	C	U	T	E	Investigate, Perform, Sue, Pursue, Institute legal proceedings.
P	R	O	S	E	L	Y	T	E	Neophyte, Convert.
P	R	O	S	I	N	E	S	S	State of being commonplace, Drabness.
P	R	O	S	O	D	I	S	T	Specialist in the study of versification.
P	R	O	S	T	R	A	T	E	Prone, Flat, Procumbent, Reclining, Recumbent, Overwhelm, Overpower, Exhaust.
P	R	O	T	A	M	I	N	E	Simple soluble proteins that occur in the sperm of fish.
P	R	O	T	E	C	T	E	D	Defended, Covered, Shielded, Guarded, Screened, Safeguarded, Sheltered.
P	R	O	T	E	C	T	O	R	Guardian, Patron.
P	R	O	T	E	S	T	E	R	One that disagrees or disapproves.
P	R	O	T	E	S	T	O	R	Same as PROTESTER.
P	R	O	T	H	E	S	I	S	Credence, Preparation of bread and wine for use at Eucharist.
P	R	O	T	O	S	T	A	R	A hypothetical flat circular gaseous cloud of dust and atoms in space.
P	R	O	T	O	T	Y	P	E	Pattern, Idea, Exemplar, Precursor, Forerunner, Predecessor, Antecedent.

1	2	3	4	5	6	7	8	9	Definition
P	R	O	T	O	Z	O	O	N	Single-cell animal.
P	R	O	V	E	N	D	E	R	Food, Provisions, Feed.
P	R	O	V	I	D	E	N	T	Thrifty, Frugal, Saving, Sparing, Economical.
P	R	O	V	I	N	C	E	S	All of a country outside of the metropolis.
P	R	O	V	I	S	I	O	N	Preparation, Condition, Proviso, Victuals, Terms, Reservation, Stipulation.
P	R	O	V	I	S	O	R	Y	Conditional, Provisional, Tentative.
P	R	O	V	O	K	I	N	G	Arousing, Incensing, Evoking, Inducing, Exciting, Stimulating, Irritating, Inflaming.
P	R	O	X	I	M	A	T	E	Close, Imminent, Next, Near, Impending, Rude, Approximate.
P	R	O	X	I	M	I	T	Y	Nearness, Immediate, Close, Togetherness, Adjacency.
P	R	U	D	E	N	T	L	Y	Wisely, Sagely, Sanely, Sensibly, Expediently.
P	R	U	D	I	S	H	L	Y	Primly, Priggishly, Puritanically, Strictly, Severely, Sternly.
P	R	U	R	I	E	N	C	Y	The state of being lustful.
P	S	A	R	O	N	I	U	S	Genus of fossil ferns.
P	S	E	U	D	O	N	Y	M	Pen name, Fictitious name.
P	S	E	U	D	O	P	O	D	Strands of tumour cells extending from main mass of tumour.
P	S	O	R	I	A	S	I	S	A skin disease of red patches covered with white scales.
P	S	Y	C	H	I	D	A	E	Family of moths.
P	S	Y	C	H	O	S	I	S	Profound disorganization of the mind.
P	S	Y	C	H	O	T	I	C	Relating to mental disorder.
P	T	A	R	M	I	G	A	N	Grouse.
P	T	E	R	I	I	D	A	E	Family of bivalve mollusks including pearl oysters.
P	T	E	R	O	S	A	U	R	A prehistoric flying reptile.
P	T	O	L	E	M	I	E	S	Dynasty of Egyptian kings.
P	U	B	E	S	C	E	N	T	Adolescent, Having a fuzzy surface.
P	U	B	L	I	C	I	S	T	Expert on public affairs, Advertiser, Promoter, Journalist.
P	U	B	L	I	C	I	T	Y	Propaganda, Promotion, Advertising, Broadcasting, Commercial announcement.
P	U	B	L	I	C	I	Z	E	Advertise, Announce, Broadcast, Promulgate, Advance, Extol.
P	U	B	L	I	S	H	E	D	Disclosed, Circulated, Advertised, Disseminated, Printed, Declared, Promulgated.
P	U	B	L	I	S	H	E	R	Operator of a newspaper, Announcer.
P	U	E	R	I	L	E	L	Y	Immaturely, Childishly, Youthfully, Boyishly.
P	U	E	R	P	E	R	A	L	Relating to giving birth.
P	U	F	F	I	N	E	S	S	The state of being bloated.
P	U	I	S	S	A	N	C	E	Strength, Power, Energy, Force, Might, Muscle, Vigour, Influence.
P	U	L	I	C	I	D	A	E	Family of fleas.
P	U	L	L	U	L	A	T	E	Germinate, Bud, Multiply, Swarm, Teem, Abound.
P	U	L	M	O	N	A	R	Y	Associated with the lungs.
P	U	L	S	A	T	I	L	E	Pulsating, Throbbing, Percussive, Vibrating.
P	U	L	S	A	T	I	N	G	Pulsing, Beating, Throbbing, Palpitating.
P	U	L	S	A	T	I	O	N	Beating, Throbbing, Vibration, Undulation, Pumping, Pounding.
P	U	L	V	E	R	I	Z	E	Atomize, Disintegrate, Annihilate, Demolish, Vanquish, Crush, Grind, Fragment.
P	U	N	C	T	I	L	I	O	Small detail, Procedure, Point of behaviour.
P	U	N	C	T	U	A	T	E	Divide, Interrupt, Accentuate, Emphasize, Dotted, Separate.
P	U	N	C	T	U	R	E	D	Perforated, Holed, Wounded, Pricked, Jabbed, Stabbed.
P	U	N	I	S	H	I	N	G	Penalizing, Chastising, Disciplining, Correcting, Castigating, Reproving, Lambasting.
P	U	P	I	L	L	A	R	Y	Relating to a pupil or a ward.
P	U	P	P	E	T	E	E	R	One who makes and manipulates puppets.
P	U	R	C	H	A	S	E	R	Buyer, Vendee, Purchasing agent.
P	U	R	G	A	T	I	O	N	Act of purging, Purification, Ceremonial cleansing, Expurgation.
P	U	R	G	A	T	I	V	E	Cathartic, Cleansing, Purifying, Expiatory.
P	U	R	G	A	T	O	R	Y	Condition of prolonged suffering, Temporary torture.
P	U	R	I	F	Y	I	N	G	Cleansing, Clarifying, Filtering, Refining, Expurgating, Atoning, Absolving, Purging.
P	U	R	P	O	S	E	L	Y	Intentionally, Expressly, Deliberately, Explicitly.
P	U	R	P	O	S	I	V	E	Tending to fulfill a purpose of design, Serving a useful end.
P	U	R	S	U	A	N	C	E	Prosecution, Consequence, Sequence, Pursuit, Search, Seeking, Quest.
P	U	R	U	L	E	N	C	E	Pus.
P	U	S	H	I	N	G	L	Y	Aggressively, Snobbishly.
P	U	S	T	U	L	A	T	E	To form into pustules.
P	U	T	R	I	D	I	T	Y	State of being putrid.
P	Y	E	L	O	G	R	A	M	An X-ray taken after injection of radiopaque substance.
P	Y	O	R	R	H	O	E	A	Discharge of pus.
P	Y	R	A	M	I	D	A	L	Having form of a pyramid, Huge, Imposing, Enormous.
P	Y	R	E	T	H	R	U	M	Genus of composite plants, Chrysanthemum.
P	Y	R	O	G	E	N	I	C	Produced by heat.
P	Y	R	O	L	A	T	R	Y	Fire worship.
P	Y	R	O	M	A	N	I	A	Mania to start fires.
P	Y	R	O	M	E	T	E	R	An instrument for measuring intense heat.
P	Y	R	O	T	O	X	I	N	Fever-inducing toxin.

1	2	3	4	5	6	7	8	9	
P	Y	R	O	X	Y	L	I	N	Lower-nitrated cellulose nitrate.
P	Y	T	H	O	N	I	N	E	Relating to the python family.
P	Y	T	H	O	N	I	S	T	Soothsayer.

Q

Q	U	A	D	R	A	T	I	C	Square, Tetragonal.
Q	U	A	D	R	A	T	U	S	Skeletal muscle quadrangular in outline.
Q	U	A	D	R	I	F	I	D	Divided in four parts.
Q	U	A	D	R	I	L	L	E	Carrousel, A square dance for four couples.
Q	U	A	D	R	U	P	E	D	An animal having four feet.
Q	U	A	D	R	U	P	L	E	Four times as much.
Q	U	A	E	S	I	T	U	M	End, Objective.
Q	U	A	K	I	N	E	S	S	State of being quaky.
Q	U	A	L	I	F	I	E	D	Competent, Fit, Eligible, Certified, Accomplished, Able, Trained, Modified.
Q	U	A	R	R	Y	I	N	G	Extracting material from a quarry.
Q	U	A	R	T	E	R	L	Y	In four parts, Every three months.
Q	U	A	R	T	E	T	T	E	Musical composition for four instruments or four voices.
Q	U	A	R	T	Z	I	T	E	A compact granular rock composed of quartz.
Q	U	A	R	T	Z	O	S	E	Resembling quartz.
Q	U	A	V	E	R	I	N	G	Trembling, Vibrating, Shaking, Quivering, Shivering, Shuddering, Faltering.
Q	U	E	B	R	A	C	H	O	Tropical American tree that yields hard wood.
Q	U	E	E	N	F	I	S	H	A game and food fish.
Q	U	E	E	R	N	E	S	S	Oddity, Eccentricity, Strangeness.
Q	U	E	N	C	H	I	N	G	Slaking, Satisfying, Subduing, Overcoming, Destroying, Suppressing, Inhibiting.
Q	U	E	R	I	M	A	N	A	A young mullet.
Q	U	E	R	U	L	O	U	S	Irritable, Fretful, Whining, Complaining, Fractious, Peevish, Petulant, Deploring.
Q	U	I	B	B	L	I	N	G	Carping, Criticizing, Bickering, Disputing, Protesting, Caviling.
Q	U	I	C	K	L	I	M	E	First solid product obtained by calcining limestone.
Q	U	I	C	K	N	E	S	S	Rapidity, Fleetness, Prompness, Readiness.
Q	U	I	C	K	S	A	N	D	A mobile shifting mass that sucks down objects on the surface.
Q	U	I	E	S	C	E	N	T	Latent, Motionless, Silent, Arrested, Potential, Calm, Placid, Untroubled.
Q	U	I	E	T	N	E	S	S	Silence, Quietude, Soundlessness, Stillness, Tranquility.
Q	U	I	N	A	M	I	N	E	A crystalline alkaloid in various cinchona barks.
Q	U	I	N	A	R	I	U	S	A gold coin of Imperial Rome.
Q	U	I	N	O	L	I	N	E	A pungent oily nitrogenous base from coal tar used in medicine and industry.
Q	U	I	N	T	E	T	T	E	Musical composition for five singers or five instruments.
Q	U	I	N	T	U	P	L	E	Five times as much.
Q	U	I	T	T	A	N	C	E	Recompense, Requital, Reparation, Compensation, Redress, Indemnity, Restitution.
Q	U	I	V	E	R	I	N	G	Trembling, Shaking, Tremulous, Quaking, Shivering, Tremulant, Pulsing, Throbbing.
Q	U	I	Z	Z	I	C	A	L	Whimsical, Curious, Questioning, Incredulous, Probing, Disbelieving, Skeptical.
Q	U	O	D	L	I	B	E	T	Musical medley.
Q	U	O	T	A	T	I	O	N	Something that is referred to or repeated, Bid, Offer.
Q	U	O	T	I	D	I	A	N	Commonplace, Ordinary, Plain, Routine, Usual, Trivial, Unremarkable, Workaday.

R

R	A	B	B	I	N	A	T	E	Group of rabbis.
R	A	B	B	I	N	I	S	M	Teachings and tradition of the rabbis.
R	A	B	I	D	N	E	S	S	The state of being rabid.
R	A	C	I	A	L	I	S	M	Prejudice or discrimination against a certain race.
R	A	C	K	E	T	E	E	R	One who extorts money by intimidation, violence or blackmail.
R	A	C	O	N	T	E	U	R	Storyteller, Expert in telling anecdotes.
R	A	D	I	A	N	T	L	Y	Brilliantly, Brightly, Cheerfully, Cheerily, Luminously.
R	A	D	I	A	T	I	N	G	Diffusing, Spreading, Disseminating, Circulating, Dispersing, Distributing, Shining.
R	A	D	I	A	T	I	O	N	Emission and diffusion of heat rays, X-rays and radio-active substances.
R	A	D	I	C	A	L	L	Y	Naturally, Fundamentally.
R	A	D	I	C	U	L	A	R	Relating to the roots of a plant, Involving a nerve root.
R	A	D	I	O	G	R	A	M	Message transmitted by radiotelegraphy, Combined radio receiver and record player.
R	A	D	I	O	L	O	G	Y	Science of radio-active substances.
R	A	I	N	M	A	K	E	R	A person who attempts to produce rain by mystic means.
R	A	M	P	A	G	I	N	G	Rushing, Storming, Acting violently, Rioting.
R	A	N	C	H	E	R	I	A	Small settlement of ranch labourers.
R	A	N	C	I	D	I	T	Y	Putridity, Odiousness, Rottenness.
R	A	N	C	O	R	O	U	S	Malignant, Malicious, Evil, Hateful, Malevolent, Bitter, Antagonistic, Hostile.

1	2	3	4	5	6	7	8	9	Definition
R	A	N	I	N	I	D	A	E	Family of frog crabs.
R	A	N	K	I	N	I	T	E	A mineral consisting of a rare calcium silicate.
R	A	N	T	I	P	O	L	E	Quarrelsome, Rakish.
R	A	P	A	C	I	O	U	S	Predacious, Ravenous, Voracious, Gluttonous, Fierce, Ferocious.
R	A	P	T	O	R	I	A	L	Predacious, Living on prey, Relating to birds of prey.
R	A	P	T	U	R	O	U	S	Ecstatic.
R	A	S	C	A	L	I	T	Y	Rabble, Knavery.
R	A	S	P	A	T	O	R	Y	A surgical file or rasp.
R	A	S	P	B	E	R	R	Y	Sweet juicy edible berries grown on canes.
R	A	T	E	P	A	Y	E	R	One who pays taxes on property and land levied by a local council.
R	A	T	I	O	N	A	L	E	Explanation, Justification, Account, Reason.
R	A	U	C	O	U	S	L	Y	Loudly, Hoarsely, Harshly, Stridently, Boisterously, Rowdily.
R	A	V	I	N	E	O	U	S	Having ravines.
R	A	V	I	S	H	I	N	G	Attractive, Pleasing, Striking.
R	E	A	C	T	A	N	C	E	That part of the impedance of an a-c circuit that is due to capacitance or induction.
R	E	A	D	D	R	E	S	S	To put a new address on mail.
R	E	A	D	I	N	E	S	S	Alacrity, Ease, Facility, Promptitude, Goodwill, Prowess, Adroitness, Deftness.
R	E	A	L	I	S	T	I	C	Practical, Pragmatic, Sober, Rational, Sane, Sensible, Sound, Prudent.
R	E	A	N	I	M	A	T	E	To animate again.
R	E	A	R	G	U	A	R	D	A guard to protect the rear of a main force.
R	E	A	S	S	U	R	E	D	Freed from anxiety, Confirmed again, Reinsured.
R	E	A	T	T	E	M	P	T	To make a new attempt.
R	E	B	E	L	L	I	O	N	Revolution, Uprising, Revolt, Insurrection, Mutiny, Opposition, Insubordination.
R	E	C	A	L	L	I	N	G	Recollecting, Remembering, Reviving, Restoring, Evoking, Rousing, Stirring.
R	E	C	A	P	T	U	R	E	Retaking, Recovery.
R	E	C	A	S	T	I	N	G	Throwing again, Refashioning, Remolding, Engaging a new set of performers.
R	E	C	E	I	V	I	N	G	Containing, Holding, Accepting, Greeting, Catching, Intercepting, Taking.
R	E	C	E	N	S	I	O	N	Review, Survey, Revision, Redraft.
R	E	C	E	P	T	I	O	N	Receipt, Admission, Reaction, Response, Formal welcome.
R	E	C	E	P	T	I	V	E	Acceptive, Responsive, Accessible, Amenable, Sympathetic, Friendly.
R	E	C	E	S	S	I	O	N	Retreat, Diminishing of natural feature, Depression, Slump.
R	E	C	H	A	B	I	T	E	Ancient Israel tent-dwellers who abstained from intoxicating drinks.
R	E	C	I	P	I	E	N	T	Receiver.
R	E	C	K	O	N	I	N	G	Counting, Computing, Enumerating, Accounting, Judging, Considering, Estimating.
R	E	C	L	A	I	M	E	D	Recalled, Reformed, Recovered, Objected, Protested, Rescued, Restored.
R	E	C	L	I	N	A	T	E	Bent downwards.
R	E	C	L	I	N	I	N	G	Leaning, Resting, Slanting, Listing, Sloping, Tilting, Prone.
R	E	C	O	G	N	I	Z	E	Admit, Revise, Correct, Realize, Acknowledge, Notice, Identify, Diagnose.
R	E	C	O	I	L	I	N	G	Withdrawing, Retiring, Shrinking, Flinching, Wincing, Blenching, Qualing.
R	E	C	O	L	L	E	C	T	Recall, Remember, Meditate, Reminisce, Retain, Rally, Rouse, Reassemble.
R	E	C	O	M	M	E	N	D	Entrust, Commit, Consign, Advise, Compliment, Commend, Acclaim, Applaud.
R	E	C	O	N	C	I	L	E	Adjust, Settle, Harmonize, Adapt, Accommodate, Attune, Conform, Reconcile.
R	E	C	O	N	D	I	T	E	Deep, Obscure, Heavy, Occult, Profound, Secret, Erudite.
R	E	C	O	R	D	I	N	G	Indicating, Marking, Reading, Registering.
R	E	C	O	U	N	T	E	D	Narrated, Related, Described, Recited, Rehearsed, Reported, Stated.
R	E	C	O	V	E	R	E	D	Regained, Restored, Retrieved, Recouped, Recruited, Redeemed, Recaptured.
R	E	C	R	E	A	T	E	D	Revived, Amused, Diverted, Entertained, Renewed, Refreshed, Restored, Rejuvenated.
R	E	C	R	E	M	E	N	T	Dross, Waste product.
R	E	C	R	U	I	T	E	D	Mustered, Raised, Repaired, Replenished, Recuperated, Recovered, Rebuilt.
R	E	C	T	I	F	I	E	D	Remedied, Amended, Purified, Corrected, Straightened, Repaired, Rebuilt.
R	E	C	T	I	T	U	D	E	Straightness, Righteousness, Goodness, Morality, Probity, Virtue, Justness.
R	E	C	T	O	R	A	T	E	The office of a rector.
R	E	C	T	R	I	C	E	S	The quill flight feathers in the tail of a bird.
R	E	C	U	M	B	E	N	T	Leaning, Resting, Prone, Flat, Prostrate, Reclining.
R	E	C	U	R	R	E	N	T	Intermittent, Alternate, Periodical.
R	E	D	B	R	E	A	S	T	A robin.
R	E	D	I	N	G	O	T	E	A coatdress open down the front.
R	E	D	O	L	E	N	C	E	Scent, Aroma, Fragrance, Balm, Bouquet, Spice, Incense.
R	E	D	U	C	T	I	O	N	Deduction, Abatement, Discount, Rebate, Subtraction, Demotion, Degradation.
R	E	D	U	N	D	A	N	T	Surplus, Superfluous, Wordy, Profuse, Lavish, Diffuse, Extra, Verbose.
R	E	F	E	C	T	I	O	N	Nourishment, Relief, Meal, Repast.
R	E	F	E	C	T	O	R	Y	Dining hall in a monastery, convent or college.
R	E	F	E	R	A	B	L	E	Ascribable, Assignable.
R	E	F	E	R	E	N	C	E	Relation, Respect, Allusion, Mention, Recommendation, Meaning, Testimonial.
R	E	F	L	A	T	I	O	N	Restoration of economy or currency after a depression or deflation.
R	E	F	L	E	C	T	O	R	Something that reflects light or sound, Critic.
R	E	F	L	E	X	I	V	E	Introspective, Reflective, Thoughtful, Pensive, Speculative.

1	2	3	4	5	6	7	8	9	Definition
R	E	F	L	U	E	N	C	E	Reflux, A flowing back.
R	E	F	O	R	M	I	S	M	Policy of a reform.
R	E	F	R	A	C	T	O	R	Something that refracts light rays.
R	E	F	R	E	S	H	E	D	Revived, Reinvigorated, Cheered, Replenished, Renovated, Quickened, Renewed.
R	E	F	R	E	S	H	E	R	A substance that revives, Reminder.
R	E	F	U	L	G	E	N	T	Shining, Brilliant, Bright.
R	E	F	U	R	B	I	S	H	Renovate, Restore.
R	E	F	U	S	I	B	L	E	Capable of renewal with a new fuse.
R	E	G	A	R	D	A	N	T	In heraldary-looking backward.
R	E	G	A	R	D	I	N	G	Considering, Evaluating, Judging, Gazing, Heeding, Noting, Observing Admiring.
R	E	G	I	C	I	D	A	L	Relating to the killing or murdering of a king.
R	E	G	I	S	S	E	U	R	Director, Stage manager.
R	E	G	I	S	T	R	A	R	An official recorder or keeper of records.
R	E	G	U	L	A	R	L	Y	Symmetrically, Correctly, Properly, Orderly.
R	E	G	U	L	A	T	E	D	Disciplined, Regularized, Adjusted, Fixed, Arranged, Organized, Moderated.
R	E	G	U	L	A	T	O	R	One that regulates.
R	E	H	E	A	R	S	A	L	Action of rehearsing, Training, Practice session in preparation for public performance.
R	E	I	M	B	U	R	S	E	Repay, Pay, Indemnify, Compensate, Remunerate, Offset, Recover.
R	E	I	N	F	O	R	C	E	Strengthen, Energize, Fortify, Augment, Bolster, Prop, Sustain.
R	E	I	N	S	T	A	T	E	Replace, Restore, Return, Recall, Renew, Revive.
R	E	I	T	E	R	A	T	E	Repeat, Renew, Reprise.
R	E	J	E	C	T	I	O	N	Being rejected, Denial, Refusal, Disallowance.
R	E	J	O	I	C	I	N	G	Pleasing, Celebrating, Making glad, Feeling great joy.
R	E	J	O	I	N	D	E	R	Answer, Reply, Response, Retort, Return.
R	E	L	E	A	S	I	N	G	Loosening, Removing, Alleviating, Relinquishing, Quitting, Resigning, Surrendering.
R	E	L	I	G	I	O	S	E	Excessively religious.
R	E	L	I	G	I	O	U	S	Pious, Godly, Fervent, Zealous, Devout, Faithful, Ethical, Righteous.
R	E	L	I	Q	U	A	R	Y	A container for keeping or exhibiting relics.
R	E	L	U	C	T	A	N	T	Resisting, Averse, Unwilling, Disinclined, Hesitant, Loath, Shy, Wary.
R	E	L	U	C	T	A	T	E	Repudiate, Repel.
R	E	M	A	I	N	D	E	R	Balance, Leavings, Residue, Rest, Remnant.
R	E	M	A	I	N	I	N	G	Staying, Existing, Surviving.
R	E	M	I	N	I	S	C	E	Remember, Recall, Recollect, Revive, Retain, Suggest, Prompt, Hint.
R	E	M	I	S	S	I	O	N	Forgiveness, Cancellation of debt, Temporary abatement of disease symptoms.
R	E	M	I	T	T	E	N	T	The state of a disease having periods of remission.
R	E	M	O	V	A	B	L	E	Capable of being removed.
R	E	N	A	S	C	E	N	T	Born again, Rising again, Reproduced.
R	E	N	C	O	N	T	R	E	Combat, Action, Duel, Contest, Competition, Conflict, Meeting.
R	E	N	D	I	T	I	O	N	Interpretation, Translation, Performance, Expression, Version.
R	E	N	I	T	E	N	C	Y	Resistance, Opposition, Reluctance.
R	E	N	O	U	N	C	E	D	Abandoned, Resigned, Disclaimed, Repudiated, Revoked, Refused, Abdicated.
R	E	P	A	R	A	B	L	E	Capable of being remedied or repaired.
R	E	P	A	Y	M	E	N	T	Reimbursement, Requittal.
R	E	P	E	L	L	E	N	T	Repugnant, Hateful, Abhorrent, Obnoxious, Repulsive, Offensive, Disgusting.
R	E	P	E	N	T	A	N	T	Penitent, Remorseful, Apologetic, Contrite, Regretful, Attritional.
R	E	P	E	R	T	O	R	Y	Repository, Repertoire, List, Catalogue.
R	E	P	L	A	C	I	N	G	Succeeding, Supplanting, Superseding, Restoring, Altering, Reinstating, Changing.
R	E	P	L	E	N	I	S	H	Equip, Refit, Replace, Fill up, Supply, Nourish, Renew.
R	E	P	L	E	T	I	O	N	Surfeit, Fullness, Plethora, Satisfaction.
R	E	P	L	I	C	A	T	E	Reply, Duplicate, Repeat.
R	E	P	O	R	T	A	G	E	Process of reporting news, Documentation.
R	E	P	O	R	T	I	N	G	Narrating, Relating, Telling, Covering, Describing, Reciting, Recounting, Stating.
R	E	P	O	S	E	F	U	L	Comfortable, Quiet, Restful.
R	E	P	O	S	S	E	S	S	Recover, Recoup, Recruit, Regain, Retrieve, Resume, Retake.
R	E	P	R	E	H	E	N	D	Blame, Censure, Chide, Reprimand, Reprove, Criticize, Condemn, Admonish.
R	E	P	R	E	S	E	N	T	Delineate, Depict, Display, Exhibit, Typify, Portray, Express, Outline.
R	E	P	R	I	M	A	N	D	Censure, Reprove, Admonish, Lesson, Rebuke, Reproach.
R	E	P	R	O	B	A	T	E	Condemn, Exclude, Reject, Criticize, Worthless, Corrupt, Depraved, Unprincipled.
R	E	P	R	O	D	U	C	E	Repeat, Portray, Remember, Procreate, Multiply, Copy, Duplicate, Imitate.
R	E	P	T	I	L	I	A	N	Resembling a reptile, Mean.
R	E	P	U	D	I	A	T	E	Disown, Renounce, Decline, Disclaim, Disapprove, Dismiss, Refuse, Reject.
R	E	P	U	G	N	A	N	T	Objectionable, Repulsive, Loathsome, Hateful, Offensive, Inconsistent, Opposed.
R	E	P	U	L	S	I	O	N	Repugnance, Abhorrence, Aversion, Hatred, Loathing, Horror, Dislike, Detestation.
R	E	P	U	L	S	I	V	E	Cold, Forbidding, Disgusting, Offensive, Foul, Nasty, Noisome, Vile.
R	E	P	U	T	A	B	L	E	Respectable, Estimable, Creditable, Reputed.
R	E	P	U	T	E	D	L	Y	By repute, Supposedly.
R	E	Q	U	I	S	I	T	E	Essential, Indispensable, Necessary, Needful, Condition, Must, Necessity.

1	2	3	4	5	6	7	8	9	Definition
R	E	R	E	B	R	A	C	E	Upper arm armour.
R	E	S	A	Z	U	R	I	N	A blue crystalline dye often used in a bacteria test.
R	E	S	E	C	T	I	O	N	Surgical removal of part of the body, Method of surveying.
R	E	S	E	N	T	F	U	L	Marked by resentment.
R	E	S	E	R	P	I	N	E	A crystalline pentacyclic sedative alkaloid used in the treatment of hypertension.
R	E	S	E	R	V	I	S	T	A member of the reserves of the armed forces.
R	E	S	E	R	V	O	I	R	Reserve, Store, Hoard, Stockpile, Stock.
R	E	S	I	D	E	N	C	E	Home, House, Abode, Dwelling, Domicile, Habitation, Occupation, Settlement.
R	E	S	I	D	U	A	R	Y	Remainder.
R	E	S	I	G	N	F	U	L	Expressive of resignation.
R	E	S	I	L	I	E	N	T	Buoyant, Flexible, Elastic, Springy, Recoiling, Supple, Airy, Volatile.
R	E	S	I	S	T	A	N	T	Resisting, Opposing, Withstanding, Fighting, Repelling.
R	E	S	O	L	V	E	N	T	Agent to disperse inflammation, Affording a solution.
R	E	S	O	N	A	N	C	E	Enriching a musical tone by vibration.
R	E	S	O	N	A	T	O	R	Something that resounds, Device for increasing the power of a musical or vocal tone.
R	E	S	P	E	C	T	E	D	Esteemed, Valued, Heeded, Admired, Regarded, Venerated, Revered, Considered.
R	E	S	P	I	R	I	N	G	Breathing, Reviving, Blowing, Exhaling.
R	E	S	T	F	U	L	L	Y	Comfortably, Placidly, Tranquilly.
R	E	S	T	I	T	U	T	E	Refund, Restore, Rehabilitate, Reclaim, Recondition, Rejuvenate, Replace, Return.
R	E	S	T	R	A	I	N	T	Restriction, Check, Control, Confine, Repress, Constraint, Embargo, Force.
R	E	S	U	L	T	A	N	T	Outcome.
R	E	S	U	R	G	E	N	T	Rising from an inferior state to a superior state.
R	E	S	U	R	R	E	C	T	Revival, Resurgence, Rekindle, Revitalize, Renew, Renovate, Reactivate.
R	E	T	A	L	I	A	T	E	Reciprocate, Requite, Avenge, Revenge, Return, Repay.
R	E	T	E	N	T	I	O	N	Retaining, Retentiveness, Memory.
R	E	T	E	N	T	I	V	E	Tenacious, Parsimonious, Restraining, Reticent.
R	E	T	I	A	R	I	U	S	Roman gladiator armed with a net and a trident.
R	E	T	I	C	E	N	C	E	Reserve, Silence, Closeness.
R	E	T	I	C	U	L	A	R	Intricate, Resembling a net.
R	E	T	I	C	U	L	U	M	The second stomach of a ruminant, Network.
R	E	T	O	R	S	I	O	N	Retaliation.
R	E	T	R	A	C	T	O	R	Something that retracts.
R	E	T	R	I	E	V	E	R	One that salvages or rescues, A dog trained to retrieve.
R	E	T	R	O	C	E	D	E	To cede back, To reassign.
R	E	T	R	O	F	L	E	X	Bent backward, Reflexed.
R	E	T	R	O	J	E	C	T	To project into the past.
R	E	T	R	O	U	S	S	E	Turned up.
R	E	T	R	U	S	I	O	N	Condition where a jaw or tooth is behind its normal position.
R	E	U	N	I	T	I	O	N	Process of reuniting.
R	E	V	E	R	E	N	C	E	Honour, Respect, Homage, Obeisance, Loyalty, Worship, Venerate, Awe.
R	E	V	E	R	S	I	O	N	Return to an earlier condition or law, Relapse, Atavism.
R	E	V	E	T	M	E	N	T	Embankment, Fortification.
R	E	V	O	C	A	B	L	E	Capable of being revoked.
R	E	V	O	L	T	I	N	G	Renouncing, Disgusting, Shocking, Nauseating, Loathsome, Repugnant, Foul, Vile.
R	E	V	O	L	V	I	N	G	Rotating, Turning, Circling, Gyrating, Rolling.
R	E	V	U	L	S	I	O	N	Withdrawal, Repulsion, Abhorrence, Aversion, Detestation, Hatred, Counter-irritation.
R	E	V	U	L	S	I	V	E	Invidious, Abhorrent, Obnoxious, Repellent.
R	E	W	A	R	D	I	N	G	Recompensing, Compensating, Remunerating.
R	H	A	P	S	O	D	I	C	Rapturous, Extravagantly emotional.
R	H	E	U	M	A	T	I	C	Relating to rheumatism.
R	H	I	N	O	L	O	G	Y	Medical science dealing with the nose and its diseases.
R	H	I	P	I	D	A	T	E	Fan-shaped.
R	H	I	Z	O	T	O	M	Y	Surgical severing of spinal nerve roots for therapeutic purposes.
R	H	O	D	A	N	I	N	E	A pale yellow crystalline acidic derivative of thiazole.
R	H	O	D	O	L	I	T	E	A rose-red or pink variety of garnet.
R	H	O	T	A	C	I	S	M	A defective pronunciation of "r".
R	H	Y	M	E	S	T	E	R	An inferior poet.
R	H	Y	T	H	M	I	C	S	The theory of rhythms.
R	I	F	L	E	B	I	R	D	Birds of paradise.
R	I	G	H	T	E	O	U	S	Virtuous, Just, Upright, Equitable, Moral, Noble, Blameless, Exemplary.
R	I	G	M	A	R	O	L	E	Rambling statements, Complex procedure.
R	I	N	G	L	E	T	E	D	Hair worn in ringlets.
R	I	O	T	O	U	S	L	Y	Wantonly, Abundantly, Profusely, Turbulently, Lavishly, Opulently, Exuberantly.
R	I	S	K	I	N	E	S	S	Chanciness, Perilous, Dangerous.
R	I	S	S	O	I	D	A	E	Family of marine and freshwater snails.
R	I	T	U	A	L	I	S	M	Excessive devotion to prescribed ritual forms in worship.
R	O	C	A	M	B	O	L	E	A European leek.

1	2	3	4	5	6	7	8	9	Clue
R	O	C	K	B	O	U	N	D	Rocky, Stern, Rigid.
R	O	G	U	I	S	H	L	Y	Dishonestly, Deceitfully, Shiftily, Coyly, Archly, Playfully, Mischievously.
R	O	I	S	T	E	R	E	R	One behaving in a noisy disorderly way.
R	O	S	A	C	E	O	U	S	Resembling a rose, Rosy.
R	O	S	T	E	L	L	U	M	Resembling a beak.
R	O	S	T	R	A	T	E	D	Having a stage for public speaking.
R	O	T	O	G	R	A	P	H	A photographic white-on-black print.
R	O	T	U	N	D	I	T	Y	Roundness, Plumpness.
R	O	U	G	H	N	E	S	S	Unevenness, Inequality, Irregularity, Asperity, Storminess.
R	O	U	N	D	E	L	A	Y	Simple lively-spirited song.
R	O	U	N	D	H	E	A	D	A Puritan at the time of Charles the First and Cromwell.
R	O	U	S	E	M	E	N	T	Act of stirring up, Arousal.
R	U	B	E	L	L	I	T	E	A tourmaline.
R	U	B	I	C	E	L	L	E	A ruby spinel of a yellow or orange-red colour.
R	U	B	R	I	C	A	T	E	To write or print in red, Heading of a chapter.
R	U	B	R	I	C	I	A	N	One tenaciously adhering to a rubic.
R	U	D	D	I	N	E	S	S	Redness, Vividness, Floridness.
R	U	F	F	I	A	N	L	Y	Coarse, Rough, Rowdy.
R	U	I	N	A	T	I	O	N	Destruction, Ruin, Confusion, Devastation, Downfall.
R	U	S	T	I	C	A	T	E	Suspend from school or college, Compel to reside in the country.
R	U	S	T	I	N	E	S	S	Sullenness, Hoarseness, Harshness, Dryness, Roughness, Ruggedness.
R	U	T	H	E	N	I	U	M	A hard brittle grayish white polyvalent rare metallic element.

S

1	2	3	4	5	6	7	8	9	Clue
S	A	B	B	A	T	I	Z	E	To keep the sabbath.
S	A	B	I	A	C	E	A	E	Family of tropical shrubs and trees having fruit of one-seeded nutlets.
S	A	C	C	H	A	R	I	C	Relating to saccharine substances.
S	A	C	C	H	A	R	I	N	A crystalline cyclicimide often used as a sweetening agent.
S	A	C	C	I	F	O	R	M	Resembling a pouch.
S	A	C	C	U	L	A	T	E	Furnished with a sac.
S	A	C	R	A	M	E	N	T	A religious act, ceremony or practice.
S	A	C	R	A	R	I	U	M	Sanctuary, Sacristy, Oratory, Chapel, Ancient Roman shrine.
S	A	C	R	I	F	I	C	E	Immolate, Offering, Forgo, Victimize, Donate, Yield, Forfeit.
S	A	C	R	I	L	E	G	E	Profanation, Desecration, Blasphemy, Violation, Heresy, Irreverence, Impiety, Sin.
S	A	C	R	I	S	T	A	N	Sexton, Church official in charge of the Church and its movables.
S	A	F	E	G	U	A	R	D	Protection, Defence, Armour, Security, Shield, Screen, Buffer.
S	A	F	R	A	N	I	N	E	Class of red to blue azine dyes.
S	A	G	A	C	I	O	U	S	Perceptive, Shrewd, Wise, Discerning, Knowledgeable, Clever, Intelligent, Judicious.
S	A	G	E	B	R	U	S	H	A common plant having a bitter juice and an odour resembling sage.
S	A	G	I	T	T	A	T	E	Shaped like an arrowhead.
S	A	I	L	C	L	O	T	H	A strong heavy canvas fabric.
S	A	L	A	C	I	O	U	S	Lustful, Obscene, Aphrodisiac, Lascivious, Licentious, Lecherous, Lewd, Satyric.
S	A	L	E	R	A	T	U	S	Potassium bicarbonate, Sodium bicarbonate.
S	A	L	E	S	L	A	D	Y	A female sales assistant.
S	A	L	I	E	N	T	L	Y	Conspicuously, Outstandingly, Pertinently, Significantly, Impressively, Remarkably.
S	A	L	L	O	W	I	S	H	Somewhat sallow complexion.
S	A	L	T	A	T	I	O	N	Dancing, Leaping, Jumping.
S	A	L	T	I	N	E	S	S	The state of being salty.
S	A	L	T	P	E	T	R	E	Potassium nitrate.
S	A	L	V	A	T	I	O	N	Preservation, Deliverance, Safekeeping, Conservation, Saving.
S	A	N	B	E	N	I	T	O	A Spanish Inquisition garment.
S	A	N	C	T	U	A	R	Y	A consecrated place, Sacred part of a religious building, Haven.
S	A	N	D	A	R	A	C	H	A brittle aromatic resin obtained from an African tree.
S	A	N	D	B	L	A	S	T	Stream of sand projected by air or steam for jewellery cutting or engraving.
S	A	N	D	G	L	A	S	S	Instrument for measuring time by running of sand similar to an hourglass.
S	A	N	D	I	N	E	S	S	State of being sandy.
S	A	N	D	P	A	P	E	R	Paper covered on one side with sand or an abrasive material used for smoothing.
S	A	N	D	P	I	P	E	R	Small birds that frequent sandy or muddy shores.
S	A	N	D	S	T	O	N	E	A sedimentary rock made up of sand united by some cement.
S	A	N	D	S	T	O	R	M	A windstorm that drives clouds of sand along.
S	A	N	H	E	D	R	I	N	Supreme council of the ancient Jewish nation.
S	A	N	T	O	N	I	C	A	European wormwood, An anthelmintic drug from santonica flowers.
S	A	P	O	D	I	L	L	A	A large tree with hard reddish wood and latex that yields chicle.
S	A	P	Y	G	I	D	A	E	Family of parasitic wasps.
S	A	R	C	A	S	T	I	C	Caustic, Ironic, Sardonic, Cynical, Jeering, Mocking, Biting, Scathing.

1	2	3	4	5	6	7	8	9	Definition
S	A	R	C	O	L	O	G	Y	Anatomy of the soft parts of the body.
S	A	R	T	O	R	I	A	L	Relating to clothes, fashion and tailoring.
S	A	R	T	O	R	I	U	S	The longest muscle in man's thigh that assists in rotating the leg.
S	A	S	S	A	F	R	A	S	Small genus of aromatic trees, Laurel.
S	A	S	S	E	N	A	C	H	Typically English.
S	A	T	E	L	L	I	T	E	Secondary planet, Complement, Subordinate, Related, Adjacent, Ancillary, Supporter.
S	A	T	I	A	T	I	O	N	State of being satiated.
S	A	T	I	R	I	C	A	L	Sarcastic, Lampoonery, Mockery, Ridicule.
S	A	T	I	S	F	I	E	D	Pleased, Gratified, Discharged, Convinced, Persuaded.
S	A	T	U	R	A	T	E	D	Satisfied, Perfected, Soaked, Soggy, Absorbed, Pervaded, Pure, Vivid.
S	A	T	U	R	N	I	N	E	Influenced by the plant Saturn.
S	A	U	C	I	N	E	S	S	The state of being saucy.
S	A	V	O	U	R	I	N	G	Smelling, Feeling, Experiencing, Knowing, Tasting, Relishing.
S	A	X	I	F	R	A	G	E	A plant that grows in crevices and cracks, Breakstone.
S	A	X	O	P	H	O	N	E	A wind instrument combining the reed clarinet mouthpiece with a curved tube.
S	C	A	G	L	I	O	L	A	An imitation of ornamental marble.
S	C	A	L	L	O	P	E	D	Having a wavy border or edge.
S	C	A	L	L	Y	W	A	G	Rascal, Scamp, Reprobate.
S	C	A	L	P	L	O	C	K	Long hair tuft left on the shaven head of some American Indian warriors.
S	C	A	N	T	I	E	S	T	Most sparse, Most scarce.
S	C	A	N	T	L	I	N	G	Limit, Scope, Modicum, Dimensions of timber or stone to be cut.
S	C	A	P	E	G	O	A	T	One bearing blame for errors or faults of others, Target, Victim.
S	C	A	P	U	L	A	R	Y	Sleeveless outer garment of a monk's habit, Badge or sash worn over the shoulder.
S	C	A	R	E	C	R	O	W	A stuffed effigy placed in a field of crops to keep the birds away.
S	C	A	R	I	F	I	E	D	Flayed, Cicatrized, Lacerated, Censured, Scratched, Slashed, Scourged, Scarred.
S	C	A	T	T	E	R	E	D	Dispersed, Dissipated, Dispelled, Diverged, Separated, Broadcast, Distributed.
S	C	A	V	E	N	G	E	R	One who searches rubbish for anything useful.
S	C	E	P	T	I	C	A	L	Questioning, Critical, Incredulous, Uncertain.
S	C	H	A	T	C	H	E	N	A Jewish marriage broker.
S	C	H	E	M	A	T	I	C	Constituting a scheme.
S	C	H	I	L	L	I	N	G	A German coin, Basic monetary unit of Austria.
S	C	H	I	S	T	O	S	E	Having the structure of a schist.
S	C	H	N	A	U	Z	E	R	German breed of terrier dog.
S	C	H	N	I	T	Z	E	L	A veal cutlet seasoned and garnished.
S	C	H	N	O	R	K	E	L	Air pipes of a submarine extended above the surface of the water.
S	C	H	N	O	R	R	E	R	Beggar.
S	C	H	O	L	A	R	L	Y	Studious, Learned, Intellectual, Educated, Trained, Scholastic.
S	C	H	O	O	L	I	N	G	Instruction, Education, Teaching, Training, Tuition, Knowledge.
S	C	I	E	N	T	I	S	T	One learned in science.
S	C	I	O	M	A	N	C	Y	Divination by consulting the shades of the dead.
S	C	I	R	R	H	O	U	S	Being hard with fibrous tissue.
S	C	L	E	R	O	G	E	N	Mineralized material of the walls of a brachysclereid.
S	C	L	E	R	O	S	I	S	Pathological hardening of tissue.
S	C	O	L	I	O	S	I	S	A lateral curvature of the spine.
S	C	O	P	A	R	I	U	S	Dried tops of broom formerly used as a diuretic.
S	C	O	R	B	U	T	I	C	Having the disease scurvy.
S	C	O	T	C	H	M	A	N	A native of Scotland.
S	C	R	A	M	B	L	E	R	A device that disarranges transmission in order to prevent eavesdropping.
S	C	R	A	P	B	O	O	K	A blank book in which cut-out items are pasted.
S	C	R	A	P	H	E	A	P	Pile of discarded articles or rubbish.
S	C	R	E	A	M	I	N	G	Shrieking, Squealing, Yelling, Howling, Wailing, Blaring, Shouting.
S	C	R	E	E	N	I	N	G	Concealing, Hiding, Censoring, Examining, Protecting, Shading, Covering, Cloaking.
S	C	R	I	B	B	L	E	R	One that scribbles, An amateur writer.
S	C	R	I	M	M	A	G	E	Skirmish, Scuffle, Brawl, Clash, Melee, Brush, Affray, Fight.
S	C	R	I	M	S	H	A	W	Carved or engraved articles made from whalebone.
S	C	R	I	P	T	O	R	Y	Used in writing.
S	C	R	I	P	T	U	R	E	The books of the Bible, Sacred writing.
S	C	R	O	L	L	S	A	W	Fretsaw, Jigsaw.
S	C	R	O	U	N	G	E	R	Cadger.
S	C	R	U	B	B	I	N	G	Scratching, Rubbing, Scouring, Polishing, Buffing, Eliminating.
S	C	R	U	M	M	A	G	E	A play in rugby.
S	C	R	U	T	A	T	O	R	Observer, Examiner, Vigilator.
S	C	U	L	P	T	U	R	E	Carving, Cutting, Hewing, Welding, Casting of statues or ornaments.
S	C	U	N	C	H	E	O	N	Part of an opening from the back in masonry.
S	C	U	T	E	L	L	U	M	Large scale or plate.
S	C	U	T	E	L	L	U	M	Rim of a lichen, Scale on the toes of birds.
S	C	U	T	I	F	O	R	M	Having the shape of a shield.

1	2	3	4	5	6	7	8	9	
S	E	A	S	O	N	I	N	G	Condiment, spice or flavouring added to food to improve the taste.
S	E	A	W	O	R	T	H	Y	Able to undertake a sea voyage safely.
S	E	B	A	C	E	O	U	S	Fatty secretion of the skin or of plants.
S	E	C	A	T	E	U	R	S	Scissors, Shears.
S	E	C	E	S	S	I	O	N	Withdrawal, Retirement.
S	E	C	L	U	S	I	O	N	Protection, Isolation, Separation, Retirement, Solitude, Deatachment.
S	E	C	O	N	D	A	R	Y	Inferior, Subordinate, Auxiliary, Subsidiary, Delegate, Deputy, Subject, Minor.
S	E	C	R	E	T	A	R	Y	Employee who handles personal correspondence for a superior, Adviser, Confidant.
S	E	C	R	E	T	I	O	N	Concealing, Substance produced and emitted from a gland.
S	E	C	R	E	T	I	V	E	Silent, Uncommunicative, Reserved.
S	E	C	T	A	R	I	A	N	Denominational, Partisan, Parochial, Dissident, Local, Nonconformist, Heretical.
S	E	C	T	I	O	N	A	L	In sections, Consisting of component parts.
S	E	C	T	O	R	I	A	L	Like a sector of a circle.
S	E	D	E	N	T	A	R	Y	Stationary, Settled, Inactive, Sitting.
S	E	D	I	T	I	O	U	S	Turbulent, Factious, Insubordinates, Mutinous, Rebellious, Dissident, Treacherous.
S	E	D	U	C	T	I	V	E	Alluring, Tempting, Attractive, Bewitching, Provocative, Captivating, Enchanting.
S	E	E	M	I	N	G	L	Y	Evidently, Ostensibly, Apparently, Evidently, Officially, Outwardly.
S	E	G	M	E	N	T	A	L	Segment of a circle, Subsidiary, Compartmental.
S	E	G	R	E	G	A	T	E	Isolate, Separate, Insulate, Select, Disconnect.
S	E	I	G	N	I	O	R	Y	Lordship, Dominion, Manor, Domain.
S	E	L	E	C	T	I	O	N	Choice, Alternative, Option, Preference, Picking, Discrimination.
S	E	L	E	C	T	I	V	E	Discriminating, Particular, Scrupulous.
S	E	L	E	N	I	O	U	S	Containing selenium.
S	E	M	A	N	T	I	C	S	The study of meanings.
S	E	M	A	N	T	R	O	N	A wooden plant or iron bar used as a bell in Eastern Orthodox churches.
S	E	M	A	P	H	O	R	E	A signalling apparatus.
S	E	M	B	L	A	N	C	E	Form, Countenance, Aspect, Apparition, Image, Likeness, Similarity, Appearance.
S	E	M	I	B	R	E	V	E	Whole note in music.
S	E	M	I	C	O	L	O	N	A punctuation mark.
S	E	M	I	F	I	N	A	L	Next to last round in an elimination sports tournament.
S	E	N	E	S	C	E	N	T	Growing old, Aging, Obsolescent.
S	E	N	E	S	C	H	A	L	Medieval steward, Judicial officer.
S	E	N	I	O	R	I	T	Y	Priority, Superiority.
S	E	N	S	A	T	I	O	N	Sense, Feeling, Sensibility, Consciousness, Sensitivity, Wonder, Marvel, Phenomenon.
S	E	N	S	E	L	E	S	S	Numb, Insensible, Insensitive, Oblivious, Inanimate, Insensate, Simple, Brainless.
S	E	N	S	I	T	I	V	E	Sensuous, Delicate, Sensory, Liable, Impressionable, Emotional, Feeling, Tense.
S	E	N	S	I	T	I	Z	E	To become sensitive, Stimulate, Quicken, Excite, Animate.
S	E	N	S	O	R	I	A	L	Sensory, Sensational, Sensitive, Sensual.
S	E	N	S	O	R	I	U	M	Brain, Mind, Brain concerned with interpretation of sensory stimuli.
S	E	N	T	I	M	E	N	T	Predilection, Feeling, Emotion, Opinion, Leaning, Bias, Inclination, Propensity.
S	E	P	A	R	A	B	L	E	Distinguishable.
S	E	P	A	R	A	T	O	R	A device for separating substances into their constituent elements, One who classifies.
S	E	P	T	A	R	I	U	M	Nodule of limestone or clay.
S	E	P	T	A	T	I	O	N	Septum.
S	E	P	T	E	M	V	I	R	Member of a council of seven.
S	E	P	T	E	N	A	R	Y	Relating to the number seven.
S	E	P	T	U	P	L	E	T	Septuplet.
S	E	P	T	U	L	A	T	E	Having imperfect septa.
S	E	P	U	L	C	H	R	E	Tomb, Grave, Repository, Terminus.
S	E	P	U	L	T	U	R	E	Burial.
S	E	Q	U	E	S	T	E	R	Remove, Segregate, Confiscate, Seclude, Secrete, Retire, Isolate, Appropriate.
S	E	R	E	N	A	D	E	D	Sung, Entertained, Performed.
S	E	R	I	C	E	O	U	S	Covered with soft, silky hairs.
S	E	R	I	G	R	A	P	H	Original print produced by silk screen process.
S	E	R	I	O	U	S	L	Y	Earnestly, Severely, Gravely, Solemnly, Intently, Zealously, Decidely, Critically.
S	E	R	M	O	N	I	Z	E	Lecture, Admonish, Relating to a sermon.
S	E	R	O	S	I	T	I	S	Inflammation of a serous membrane.
S	E	R	O	T	I	N	A	L	The latter part of summer.
S	E	R	O	T	O	N	I	N	A crystalline phenolic amine that occurs in blood serum.
S	E	R	R	A	T	I	O	N	Formation resembling the toothed edge of a saw.
S	E	R	V	I	L	I	T	Y	Servitude, Obsequiousness, Cringing, Fawning, Toadying.
S	E	R	V	I	T	U	D	E	Bondage, Serfdom, Slavery, Apprenticeship, Yoke, Thralldom.
S	E	S	S	I	O	N	A	L	Relating to a session.
S	E	T	A	C	E	O	U	S	Resembling bristles, bristly.
S	E	V	E	N	F	O	L	D	Being seven times as great.
S	E	V	E	R	A	L	L	Y	Separately, Indepently, Respectively, Apart, Exclusively, Singly.
S	E	V	E	R	A	L	T	Y	Distinctness, Separateness, Quality, Detail, Part.

1	2	3	4	5	6	7	8	9	Clue
S	E	X	E	N	N	I	A	L	Lasting six years.
S	E	X	T	U	P	L	E	T	One of a multiple birth of six offspring.
S	E	X	U	A	L	I	T	Y	State of being sexual.
S	F	O	R	Z	A	N	D	O	Direction in music to indicate accent on a single tone or chord.
S	H	A	D	E	L	E	S	S	Having no shade.
S	H	A	D	I	N	E	S	S	State of being shady.
S	H	A	K	I	N	E	S	S	Instability, Unsteadiness, Precariousness.
S	H	A	M	E	L	E	S	S	Unscrupulous, Brazen, Brash, Impudent, Audacious, Blatant, Bold, Disgraceful.
S	H	A	N	A	C	H	I	E	One who recounts legends and old tales.
S	H	A	P	E	L	E	S	S	Misshapen, Formless, Deformed, Unformed.
S	H	A	R	K	S	K	I	N	Leather made from the hide of a shark, Fabric with a basket weave.
S	H	A	R	P	E	N	E	R	A person or machine for sharpening things.
S	H	A	R	P	N	E	S	S	Edge, Keenness.
S	H	E	A	R	L	I	N	G	A one year old sheep.
S	H	E	A	T	H	I	N	G	Enclosing, Covering, Surrounding, Wrapping, Enveloping, Encasing, Protecting.
S	H	E	E	P	L	I	K	E	Simple, Meek, Docile, Stupid, Silly, Witless.
S	H	E	E	P	S	K	I	N	Parchment, Leather prepared from sheepskin.
S	H	E	L	D	R	A	K	E	A common European duck.
S	H	E	L	T	E	R	E	D	Screened, Protected, Shielded.
S	H	I	F	T	L	E	S	S	Idle, Lazy, Inefficient.
S	H	I	M	M	E	R	E	D	Glimmered, Gleamed, Sparkled, Twinkled, Glistened, Glinted.
S	H	I	N	I	N	E	S	S	State of being shiny.
S	H	I	P	W	R	E	C	K	The destruction of a ship usually by foundering.
S	H	I	V	E	R	I	N	G	Tremulous, Quaking, Quivering, Trembling, Shaking.
S	H	O	E	M	A	K	E	R	One whose business is making, selling or repairing shoes.
S	H	O	R	E	W	A	R	D	Moving toward the shore.
S	H	O	R	T	H	A	N	D	Substituting symbols for writing, Abridged, Condensed.
S	H	O	R	T	N	E	S	S	Brevity, Abruptness, Curtness, Deficiency, Scantiness.
S	H	O	R	T	W	A	V	E	A radio wave of sixty metre wavelength or less.
S	H	R	I	N	K	A	G	E	Process of shrinking, Contraction, Reduction, Depreciation.
S	H	R	U	B	B	E	R	Y	Hedge, Group of shrubs.
S	H	U	F	F	L	I	N	G	Mixing, Shifting, Manipulating, Worming, Scuffling, Disarranging, Disrupting.
S	I	B	I	L	A	N	C	E	A sound of hissing.
S	I	B	Y	L	L	I	N	E	Prophetic, Mysterious, Cryptic, Occult, Ambiguous, Equivocal, Obscure, Murky.
S	I	C	K	E	N	I	N	G	Nauseating, Weakening, Offensive, Disgusting, Foul, Loathsome, Repulsive.
S	I	C	K	L	E	M	I	A	Presence of crescent-shaped blood cells.
S	I	D	E	T	R	A	C	K	Divert, Transfer, Shunt, Switch, Deviate.
S	I	G	H	T	S	E	E	R	Tourist, Visitor, Tripper.
S	I	G	N	A	T	I	O	N	Making the sign of the cross.
S	I	G	N	A	T	O	R	Y	Joining or sharing in a signature.
S	I	G	N	A	T	U	R	E	Signing one's name, Identifying mark, Autograph, Sign.
S	I	L	I	C	E	O	U	S	Related to silica.
S	I	L	I	C	O	S	I	S	Disease of the lungs caused by inhalation of silica dust.
S	I	L	K	I	N	E	S	S	State of being silky.
S	I	L	L	E	N	I	T	E	A mineral that consists of a native bismuth oxide.
S	I	L	L	I	N	E	S	S	a silly practice.
S	I	M	M	E	R	I	N	G	Stewing gently, Fermenting, Seething, Cooking slowly.
S	I	M	P	E	R	I	N	G	Coy, Pusillanimous.
S	I	M	P	L	E	T	O	N	Fool, Idiot, Imbecile, Moron, Dunce, Dullard, Stupid, Bungler.
S	I	M	U	L	C	A	S	T	Broadcasting transmitted on radio and television at the same time.
S	I	N	C	E	R	I	T	Y	Expression of a sincere feeling.
S	I	N	G	L	E	T	O	N	Single offspring, Individual member or thing.
S	I	N	I	S	T	R	A	L	Left-handed.
S	I	N	O	P	H	I	L	E	Being fond of Chinese culture or characteristics.
S	I	N	U	O	U	S	L	Y	Intricately, Deviously.
S	I	P	H	U	N	C	L	E	Siphon, Small tube connecting shell chambers.
S	I	S	T	R	U	R	U	S	A genus of small rattlesnakes.
S	I	T	U	A	T	I	O	N	Site, Locality, Spot, Post, Job, Status, State, Crisis, Climax.
S	K	E	D	A	D	D	L	E	Run away, Leave hastily, Take flight in a panic.
S	K	E	P	T	I	C	A	L	Characteristic of a skeptic.
S	K	E	T	C	H	I	L	Y	In a sketchy manner.
S	K	I	L	F	U	L	L	Y	Proficiently, Expertly, Adeptly, Adroitly.
S	K	I	N	F	L	I	N	T	Miser, Niggard, Tightwad.
S	L	A	C	K	E	N	E	D	Abated, Moderated, Retarded, Loosened, Delayed, Detained, Relented, Subsided.
S	L	A	N	T	W	I	S	E	At a slant.
S	L	A	P	S	T	I	C	K	A comedy relying on boisterous horseplay.
S	L	A	U	G	H	T	E	R	Killing of animals, Mass killing, Massacre, Wanton destruction, Annihilation.

1	2	3	4	5	6	7	8	9	Clue
S	L	E	E	K	N	E	S	S	Glossiness, Smoothness.
S	L	E	E	P	L	E	S	S	Insomnia, Absence of sleep.
S	L	I	C	K	N	E	S	S	Greasiness, Smoothness, Canniness, Sharpness, Smartness.
S	L	I	M	I	N	E	S	S	Condition of being viscous.
S	L	I	N	G	S	H	O	T	Catapult.
S	L	I	P	C	O	V	E	R	A temporary protective covering that can be easily removed.
S	L	I	V	O	V	I	T	Z	A colourless plum brandy made in the Balkan countries.
S	L	O	G	A	N	I	Z	E	To express in such a way as to stimulate interest.
S	L	U	I	C	E	W	A	Y	A channel artificial or natural through which water is passed.
S	L	U	M	B	R	O	U	S	Sleepy, Somnolent, Calm, Peaceful, Lethargic, Soporific, Drowsy.
S	M	A	T	T	E	R	E	R	One that has little knowledge.
S	M	I	L	A	C	I	N	A	Genus of plants with white flowers that turn to coloured berries.
S	M	O	K	I	N	E	S	S	Haziness, Fogginess, Cloudiness.
S	M	O	T	H	E	R	E	D	Suffocated, Asphyxiated, Choked, Stifled, Repressed, Muffled, Quenched, Quelled.
S	N	A	K	E	B	I	T	E	Bite of a snake.
S	N	A	K	E	H	I	P	S	A dance noted for the exaggerated swinging of the hips.
S	N	A	K	E	L	I	K	E	Resembling a snake, Being long and sinuous.
S	N	A	K	E	R	O	O	T	Any plant reputed to be a cure for snakebite.
S	N	A	K	E	W	O	O	D	A climbing shrub whose twisted roots and stems resemble serpents, Frangipani.
S	N	I	G	G	E	R	E	D	Tittered, Giggled.
S	N	O	W	G	E	E	S	E	Migratory white geese that breed in Arctic America.
S	O	A	P	S	T	O	N	E	A soft stone composed of talc, chlorine and magnetite.
S	O	B	R	I	Q	U	E	T	Nickname.
S	O	C	I	A	L	I	S	M	Theory of collective ownership, control and distribution of property.
S	O	C	I	A	L	I	Z	E	Participate in a social environment, Associate, Mix, Mingle.
S	O	C	I	O	L	O	G	Y	The study of civilized society and its problems.
S	O	F	T	E	N	I	N	G	Mitigating, Melting, Mollifying, Weakening, Depreciating, Underrating, Degenerating.
S	O	I	D	I	S	A	N	T	Pretended, So-called, Self-proclaimed.
S	O	L	E	M	N	I	T	Y	Celebration, Festival, Ceremony, Rite, Formal observance of an event.
S	O	L	E	M	N	I	Z	E	To perform with pomp and ceremony, Dignify, Observe, Commemorate, Honour.
S	O	L	E	N	I	D	A	E	A family of marine clams.
S	O	L	F	A	T	A	R	A	Area of late stage of volcanic activity.
S	O	L	I	C	I	T	O	R	A member of the legal profession qualified to advise clients and instruct barristers.
S	O	L	I	D	N	E	S	S	Rigidness, Compactness, Firmness.
S	O	L	I	L	O	Q	U	Y	Monologue, Talking to oneself.
S	O	L	I	P	S	I	S	M	The theory of the self, Knowing nothing but its own modification and state, Egoism.
S	O	L	I	T	A	I	R	E	A single gem set alone, A card game, A flightless bird now extinct.
S	O	L	M	I	Z	A	T	E	To sing by using syllables to denote musical scale tones.
S	O	L	O	N	C	H	A	K	Group of strongly saline soils.
S	O	L	P	U	G	I	D	A	An order of hairy arachnids.
S	O	M	A	T	E	R	I	A	The principal genus of eider ducks.
S	O	M	E	W	H	E	R	E	Someplace elsewhere, Anywhere, Nearly, Approximately, Practically.
S	O	M	N	O	L	E	N	T	Soporific, Narcotic, Sleepy, Dozy, Drowsy.
S	O	O	T	I	N	E	S	S	State of being sooty.
S	O	P	H	I	S	T	E	R	Third or fourth year student in a university.
S	O	P	H	I	S	T	R	Y	Fallacy, Deception, Delusion, Spuriousness, Ambiguity.
S	O	P	H	O	M	O	R	E	Second year college student.
S	O	P	O	R	I	F	I	C	Hypnotic, Narcotic, Opiate, Calming, Sleepy, Drowsy.
S	O	P	R	A	N	I	N	O	A musical instrument with a pitch higher than a soprano.
S	O	R	I	C	I	D	A	E	Small long-snouted mammals, Shrews.
S	O	R	R	O	W	F	U	L	Sad, Plaintive, Woeful, Miserable, Rueful, Melancholy, Mournful, Lamentable.
S	O	R	R	O	W	I	N	G	Grieving, Mourning, Groaning, Moaning, Lamenting.
S	O	R	T	I	L	E	G	E	Sorcery, Witchery, Enchantment, Practice of divination by lots.
S	O	R	T	I	T	I	O	N	To draw lots.
S	O	U	B	R	E	T	T	E	An actress playing a pert coquettish character in opera or comedy.
S	O	U	L	F	U	L	L	Y	Excessively emotional.
S	O	U	N	D	N	E	S	S	Healthiness, Strength, Stability, Security, Firmness, Solidity, Orthodoxy.
S	O	U	T	H	W	A	R	D	Toward the south, A southern direction.
S	O	V	E	R	E	I	G	N	A seventeenth century gold coin.
S	O	V	I	E	T	I	S	M	Communism.
S	O	V	I	E	T	I	Z	E	To encompass the world with Soviet policy.
S	P	A	G	H	E	T	T	I	Wheaten paste in long rods.
S	P	A	R	E	P	A	R	T	Extra part of machine on vehicle kept as a replacement.
S	P	A	R	K	L	I	N	G	Shining, Glistening, Brilliant, Dazzling, Animated, Lively, Effervescent, Flashing.
S	P	A	S	M	O	D	I	C	Characterized by a spasm, Intermittent, Fitful, Catchy, Desultory.
S	P	A	T	U	L	A	T	E	Spoon-shaped.

1	2	3	4	5	6	7	8	9	Clue
S	P	E	A	K	E	A	S	Y	A place where alcoholic drinks are illegally sold.
S	P	E	A	R	F	I	S	H	Large powerful fish related to the marlins and sailfishes.
S	P	E	C	T	A	C	L	E	Exhibtion, Demonstration, Display, Show, Object of curiosity or contempt. An aid.
S	P	E	C	T	A	T	O	R	Bystander, Eyewitness, Observer, Onlooker, Viewer, Witness, Watcher, Perceiver.
S	P	E	E	D	W	E	L	L	A common hairy perennial European herb with pale blue or lilac flowers.
S	P	E	L	U	N	C	A	R	Relating to a cave.
S	P	E	L	U	N	K	E	R	One who explores and studies caves.
S	P	E	R	M	A	T	I	C	Relating to sperm.
S	P	H	E	R	I	C	A	L	Globular, Orbicular.
S	P	H	I	N	C	T	E	R	A muscle able to contract or close a bodily opening.
S	P	H	Y	G	M	O	I	D	Like a pulse.
S	P	I	C	I	N	E	S	S	Pungency.
S	P	I	C	U	L	A	T	E	Prickly, Spiky.
S	P	I	K	E	N	A	R	D	An aromatic plant.
S	P	I	L	L	I	K	I	N	A small slip or rod used in a game.
S	P	I	N	D	L	I	N	G	Thin, Weak, Ineffectual, Gangling, Lanky, Rangy.
S	P	I	N	D	R	I	F	T	Sea spray.
S	P	I	N	N	A	K	E	R	A large triangular sail of a yacht.
S	P	I	N	U	L	O	S	E	Covered with small spines.
S	P	I	R	A	L	I	Z	E	Wind, Coil, Twist, Wreathe, Coil.
S	P	I	R	E	L	I	K	E	Resembling a spire.
S	P	I	R	I	T	I	S	M	A belief in the spirit world.
S	P	I	R	I	T	U	A	L	Sacred, Religious, Intellectual, Mental, Clever, Witty, Immaterial, Disembodied.
S	P	I	R	U	R	I	D	S	Parasites needing an intermediate host.
S	P	I	T	S	T	I	C	K	A small pointed chisel used by jewellers.
S	P	L	A	S	H	I	N	G	Spattering, Scattering, Spraying, Sprinkling, Drenching, Dousing, Sloshing.
S	P	L	E	N	D	E	N	T	Eminent, Illustrious, Shining, Glossily.
S	P	L	E	N	D	O	U	R	Brilliance, Pomp, Glory, Excellence, Value, Worth, Beauty, Magnificence.
S	P	L	E	N	E	T	I	C	Irascible, Spiteful, Peevish, Sullen.
S	P	L	I	N	T	E	R	Y	Fragmentary.
S	P	L	I	T	T	I	N	G	Dividing, Separating, Bursting, Slicing, Parting, Cutting, Cleaving, Rupturing.
S	P	O	K	E	S	M	A	N	Orator, Speaker, Champion, Delegate, Representative.
S	P	O	N	D	Y	L	U	S	Spiny oyster.
S	P	O	N	G	I	O	S	E	Spongy.
S	P	O	N	S	A	L	I	A	Marriage contract.
S	P	O	N	S	O	R	E	D	Guaranteed, Backed, Supported, Favoured, Financed.
S	P	O	R	E	L	I	N	G	Developing from a small spore.
S	P	O	R	T	S	M	A	N	A person active in sport, A good loser and a gracious winner.
S	P	O	T	L	I	G	H	T	A circle of light, Conspicuous attention.
S	P	R	A	W	L	I	N	G	Scrambling, Spreading, Slouching, Lolling, Lounging, Slumping, Straggling.
S	P	R	I	G	H	T	L	Y	Lively, Spirited, Vivacity.
S	P	R	I	N	G	B	O	K	African gazelle.
S	P	R	I	N	K	L	E	R	A device for sprinkling.
S	P	R	I	T	S	A	I	L	A sail extended by a sprit.
S	Q	U	A	L	I	D	L	Y	Shabbily, Sordidly, Dirtily, Foully, Shabbily, Vilely, Grubbily, Uncleanly.
S	Q	U	A	R	R	O	S	E	Rough with divergent scales.
S	Q	U	A	T	T	I	N	G	Crouching, Stooping, Hunching, Cowering, Illegal occupation.
S	Q	U	E	A	M	I	S	H	Queasy, Nauseated, Prudish, Dizzy, Fastidious, Fussy, Particular, Dainty.
S	T	A	B	I	L	I	T	Y	Steadiness, Firmness, Constancy, Steadfastness, Permanence, Security, Reliability.
S	T	A	B	I	L	I	Z	E	Steady, Poise, Balance, Ballast, Equalize, Support, Sustain, Secure.
S	T	A	G	E	H	A	N	D	Sceneshifter, A stage worker who handles scenery and props.
S	T	A	G	H	O	U	N	D	A hound once used in hunting.
S	T	A	G	N	A	N	C	Y	State of being stagnant.
S	T	A	I	D	N	E	S	S	Regularity, Sedateness, Seriousness, Steadiness.
S	T	A	I	N	L	E	S	S	Immaculate, Resistant to tarnish, Unblemished, Spotless.
S	T	A	I	R	C	A	S	E	A flight of stairs.
S	T	A	L	E	M	A	T	E	Deadlock, A drawn contest, Tie.
S	T	A	L	E	N	E	S	S	Triteness, Rankness, Mustiness.
S	T	A	M	I	N	A	T	E	Producing stamens.
S	T	A	M	I	N	O	D	E	A sterile stamen.
S	T	A	M	I	N	O	D	Y	Metamorphosis of other floral organs into stamens.
S	T	A	N	C	H	I	O	N	An upright bar, post, prop, brace or support.
S	T	A	R	G	R	A	S	S	A pinkroot.
S	T	A	T	E	M	E	N	T	Account, Allegation, Recital, Assertion, A financial record.
S	T	A	T	E	R	O	O	M	An apartment of state, A luxury suite on a liner.
S	T	A	T	E	S	M	A	N	Politician.
S	T	A	T	I	O	N	E	D	Assigned, Posted, Placed, Positioned.

1	2	3	4	5	6	7	8	9	Definition
S	T	A	T	I	O	N	E	R	Bookseller, Publisher, Seller of stationary.
S	T	A	T	U	E	T	T	E	Figurine, Small statue.
S	T	A	T	U	T	O	R	Y	Enacted, Imposed, Regulated, Created.
S	T	A	U	N	C	H	L	Y	Soundly, Faithfully, Steadily.
S	T	E	A	D	F	A	S	T	Immovable, Loyal, Unswerving, Faithful, Inflexible, Adamant, Relentless, Rigid.
S	T	E	A	M	S	H	I	P	A ship propelled by steam.
S	T	E	E	L	Y	A	R	D	A portable balance.
S	T	E	E	N	B	O	C	K	A small antelope.
S	T	E	E	N	K	I	R	K	A cravat with long hanging ends.
S	T	E	E	P	N	E	S	S	Precipitousness.
S	T	E	E	R	A	B	L	E	Capable of being guided by steering.
S	T	E	I	N	B	O	C	K	Ibex, Steenbock.
S	T	E	L	L	A	T	E	D	Ornamented or sprinkled with stars.
S	T	E	P	D	A	N	C	E	A dance characterised by tapping, brushing and kicking.
S	T	E	R	I	L	I	T	Y	The state of being sterile.
S	T	E	R	I	L	I	Z	E	Become unfruitful, To make incapable of reproducing.
S	T	E	R	N	W	A	R	D	Aft, Astern.
S	T	E	V	E	D	O	R	E	One responsible for loading or unloading ships in port.
S	T	E	W	A	R	D	L	Y	Careful, Frugal, Prudent.
S	T	E	W	A	R	T	R	Y	A Scottish area under the jurisdiction of a steward.
S	T	I	F	F	E	N	E	D	Supported, Tautened, Immobilized, Constricted, Formalized, Solidified, Stabilized.
S	T	I	F	F	N	E	S	S	Density, Rigidity, Stability, Inflexibility, Resolution, Obduracy, Formality.
S	T	I	G	M	A	T	I	C	Censorious, Detestable, Stigmal.
S	T	I	L	L	N	E	S	S	Calmness, Serenity, Immobility, Silence, Quietness, Still.
S	T	I	M	U	L	A	N	T	Catalyst, Goad, Impetus, Impulse, Incentive, Incitement, Motivation, Spur.
S	T	I	M	U	L	A	T	E	Animate, Prick, Lever, Provoke, Galvanize, Pique, Activate, Energize.
S	T	I	N	K	W	O	O	D	A southern African wood with an unpleasant odour.
S	T	I	P	U	L	A	T	E	Demand, Contract, Specify, Detail, Designate, State, Provide.
S	T	I	T	C	H	I	N	G	Sewing, Joining with stitches, Uniting, Embroidering.
S	T	O	C	K	I	N	E	T	A circular knit cotton or silk fabric.
S	T	O	C	K	I	N	G	S	A close-fitting covering for the legs and feet.
S	T	O	C	K	P	I	L	E	Reserve, Hoard, Stock, Store, Reservoir, Mass, Mountain, Stack.
S	T	O	L	I	D	I	T	Y	Impassivity, Insensibility, Apathy, Stoicism, Dullness, Inertia, Passivity, Slowness.
S	T	O	M	A	C	H	E	R	Heavily embroidered front of a garment worn in the fifteenth and sixteenth centuries.
S	T	O	M	A	T	O	U	S	Having a mouth or opening.
S	T	O	N	E	C	R	O	P	A mossy European evergreen creeper.
S	T	O	N	E	F	I	S	H	Venomous spiny scorpion fish.
S	T	O	N	E	W	A	R	E	Non-porous high-fired pottery.
S	T	O	P	W	A	T	C	H	A watch that can be stopped at will and is used to register exact elapsed time.
S	T	O	R	E	R	O	O	M	Room for the storage of goods, Lumber-room.
S	T	O	U	T	N	E	S	S	Firmness, Fortitude, Strength, Sturdiness, Tenacity, Toughness, Boldness, Corpulence.
S	T	R	A	G	G	L	E	R	Loiterer, Dawdler, Laggard, Lingerer, Slow-coach.
S	T	R	A	N	G	L	E	S	Chokes, Suffocates, Trottles, Suppresses, Muffles, Represses, Smothers, Extinguishes.
S	T	R	A	N	G	U	R	Y	Slow and painful emission of urine.
S	T	R	A	P	P	A	D	O	Punishment or torture inflicted by hoisting the victim on a rope and allowing him to fall.
S	T	R	A	P	P	I	N	G	Beating with a strap, Bandaging for support, A trimming for clothes.
S	T	R	A	T	A	G	E	M	Trick, Device, Gambit, Manoeuvre, Play, Ruse, Wile, Ploy.
S	T	R	E	A	M	L	E	T	A small stream, Brook, Rill.
S	T	R	E	E	T	C	A	R	A wheeled vehicle on rails used as public transport, Trolley car, Tramcar.
S	T	R	E	N	U	O	U	S	Vigorous, Dynamic, Energetic, Hard, Arduous, Difficult, Tough.
S	T	R	E	P	T	O	S	E	An unstable hydroxy dialdehyde.
S	T	R	E	S	S	F	U	L	Subject to stress.
S	T	R	E	T	C	H	E	R	A litter for carrying disabled, injured or dead persons.
S	T	R	I	A	T	I	O	N	State of being striped, furrowed or lined.
S	T	R	I	C	T	U	R	E	Constriction, Restriction, Censure, Cramp, Limitation, Censure, Slur, Aspersion.
S	T	R	I	K	E	O	U	T	An out in the game of baseball.
S	T	R	I	N	G	E	N	T	Rigid, Rigorous, Strict, Confining, Binding, Grim, Austere, Harsh.
S	T	R	I	P	L	I	N	G	An adolescent.
S	T	R	O	M	B	O	I	D	A petrified shell of a gastropod mollusk, Conch.
S	T	R	O	N	G	B	O	X	A strong chest or small safe for holding money and/or valuables.
S	T	R	O	N	T	I	U	M	A silver-white soft malleable and ductile bivalent metallic element.
S	T	R	U	C	T	U	R	E	Building, Edifice, Form, Erection, Arrangement, Composition, Complex, System.
S	T	R	Y	C	H	N	I	C	Relating to strychnine.
S	T	U	M	B	L	I	N	G	Falling, Blundering, Lurching, Tripping, Faltering, Staggering, Toppling, Teetering.
S	T	U	P	I	D	I	T	Y	State of being stupid.
S	T	Y	L	I	S	T	I	C	Of literary style.
S	T	Y	L	O	B	A	T	E	A flat pavement supporting a row of architectural columns.

1	2	3	4	5	6	7	8	9	Definition
S	U	B	A	L	P	I	N	E	Relating to the lower slopes of the Alps, Below the timber-line.
S	U	B	A	T	O	M	I	C	Phenomena occurring inside of atoms.
S	U	B	C	O	S	T	A	L	Situated below a rib.
S	U	B	D	E	A	C	O	N	Having a rank immediately below a deacon.
S	U	B	D	I	V	I	D	E	To divide parts into more parts.
S	U	B	J	A	C	E	N	T	Underlying, Inferior, Lesser, Lower.
S	U	B	J	O	I	N	E	D	Added, Appended, Combined, Conjoined, United.
S	U	B	J	U	G	A	T	E	Conquer, Defeat, Overpower, Reduce, Subdue, Vanquish, Coerce, Force.
S	U	B	L	I	M	A	T	E	To give a more elevated character to, To divert energy to a higher activity.
S	U	B	L	I	M	I	T	Y	Exalted character, Noble quality, Acme.
S	U	B	L	U	N	A	R	Y	Situated beneath the moon, Earthly.
S	U	B	M	A	R	I	N	E	Under the sea, A submersible armed ship that operates beneath the sea.
S	U	B	M	E	R	G	E	D	Inundated, Covered, Obscured, Dipped, Immersed, Impregnated, Deluged, Engulfed.
S	U	B	N	O	R	M	A	L	One who is below the range of normality.
S	U	B	R	O	G	A	T	E	Substitute.
S	U	B	S	C	R	I	B	E	Sign, Autograph, Contribute, Assent, Consent, Endorse, Sanction, Approve.
S	U	B	S	C	R	I	P	T	Written below or beneath.
S	U	B	S	I	D	I	Z	E	To give financial aid.
S	U	B	S	T	A	N	C	E	Essence, Import, Meaning, Amount, Core, Crux, Kernel, Matter.
S	U	B	T	E	N	A	N	T	One who rents from a tenant.
S	U	B	T	I	L	I	Z	E	Refine, Sublimate, Exalt, Rarefy, Clarify, Analyze, Argue.
S	U	C	C	E	N	T	O	R	A precentor's assistant in a cathedral or monastery.
S	U	C	C	E	S	S	O	R	One who inherits, is elected or appointed to a position, office or estate.
S	U	C	C	I	N	I	T	E	Amber.
S	U	C	C	O	T	A	S	H	Mixture of beans and corn cooked together.
S	U	C	C	U	L	E	N	T	Juicy, Fleshy.
S	U	C	T	O	R	I	A	L	Adapted for sucking, Living by sucking the blood of animals or the juices of plants.
S	U	D	O	R	I	F	I	C	Inducing perspiration.
S	U	F	F	E	R	I	N	G	Distress, Agony, Misery, Adversity, Misfortune.
S	U	F	F	O	C	A	T	E	Asphyxiate, Stifle, Smother, Choke, Throttle, Strangle.
S	U	F	F	R	A	G	A	N	A bishop.
S	U	F	F	U	S	I	O	N	Spreading over.
S	U	F	F	U	S	I	V	E	Tending to overspread or diffuse itself.
S	U	G	A	R	C	O	A	T	To coat with sugar, Sweeten, Embellish, Palliate, Extenuate, Veneer, Whiten.
S	U	G	A	R	L	O	A	F	Refined sugar moulded into a solid.
S	U	G	A	R	P	L	U	M	Comfit, Sweetmeat, Flattery, Gift, Bribe, Sop.
S	U	I	F	O	R	M	E	S	Non-ruminant mammals, Swine, Peccaries, Hippopotamuses.
S	U	I	K	E	R	B	O	S	Sugarbush.
S	U	L	F	A	M	I	D	E	A crystalline neutral compound.
S	U	L	F	A	T	I	O	N	Process of sulfating.
S	U	L	P	H	U	R	I	C	Relating to sulphur.
S	U	M	M	A	R	I	Z	E	Recapitulate, Epitomize, Condense, Digest, Synopsize.
S	U	M	M	A	T	I	O	N	Addition, Resultant, Summing-up, Summary.
S	U	M	P	T	U	A	R	Y	Regulating expenditure, Controlling extravagance.
S	U	M	P	T	U	O	U	S	Costly, Lavish, Luxurious, Luscious, Opulent, Palatial, Rich.
S	U	N	D	O	W	N	E	R	Drink taken at sunset, Vagabond.
S	U	N	F	L	O	W	E	R	Heliotrope.
S	U	N	S	C	R	E	E	N	A chemical agent in suntan cream for filtering out harmful rays.
S	U	N	S	T	R	O	K	E	Heatstroke caused by direct exposure to the sun.
S	U	P	E	R	F	I	N	E	Very refined, Extremely fine texture, Highgrade.
S	U	P	E	R	P	O	S	E	To place or lay over or above, Superimpose.
S	U	P	E	R	S	E	D	E	Postpone, Defer, Omit, Forbear, Annul, Override, Replace, Repudiate.
S	U	P	E	R	V	E	N	E	Follow, Supersede, Ensue, Succeed.
S	U	P	E	R	V	I	S	E	Peruse, Scan, Superintend, Overlook, Manage, Survey, Administer, Control.
S	U	P	P	L	I	A	N	T	Petitioner, Suitor, Supplicant, Solicitor.
S	U	P	P	O	R	T	E	D	Sustained, Propped, Bolstered, Buttressed, Braced, Supported, Maintained.
S	U	P	P	O	R	T	E	R	One that acts as a support, Fan, Follower.
S	U	P	P	U	R	A	T	E	To discharge pus.
S	U	P	R	E	M	A	C	Y	Supreme authority, Being superior.
S	U	P	R	E	M	E	L	Y	In a supreme manner.
S	U	R	C	H	A	R	G	E	Additional charge or cost, Overburden, Overload, Overprint.
S	U	R	C	I	N	G	L	E	Belt, band or girth fastened around the body of a horse.
S	U	R	L	I	N	E	S	S	Rudeness, Sullenness, Sulkiness, Fractiousness, Gloominess.
S	U	R	M	U	L	L	E	T	A fish, Mullet.
S	U	R	P	R	I	S	E	D	Overpowered, Captivated, Startled, Astonished, Seized, Amazed, Captured.
S	U	R	R	E	J	O	I	N	To reply to a common law pleading of a plaintiff.
S	U	R	R	E	N	D	E	R	Abandon, Relinquish, Submit, Leave, Resign, Commit, Fall, Succumb.

1	2	3	4	5	6	7	8	9	
S	U	R	R	O	G	A	T	E	Substitute, Delegate, Deputy, Resource, Alternate, Replacement, Refuge, Locum.
S	U	R	V	E	Y	I	N	G	Estimating, Appraising, Evaluating, Measuring, Viewing, Prospecting, Scrutinizing.
S	U	R	V	I	V	I	N	G	Outliving, Outlasting, Enduring, Reviving, Persisting, Recovering.
S	U	S	P	E	N	D	E	D	Hanging, Pendulous, Dangling, Swinging, Delayed, Postponed, Arrested, Interrupted.
S	U	S	P	E	N	D	E	R	A device by which something may be suspended.
S	U	S	P	I	C	I	O	N	Mistrust, Doubt, Uncertainty, Inkling, Intimation, Hint, Skepticism, Apprehension.
S	U	S	T	A	I	N	E	D	Prolonged, Unflagging, Supported, Maintained, Nourished, Endured, Preserved.
S	W	A	D	D	L	I	N	G	Wrapping, Enveloping, Restricting, Rolling, Draping.
S	W	A	G	G	E	R	E	R	One that acts in a cocky fashion.
S	W	A	R	T	Z	I	T	E	A mineral consisting of a hydrous carbonate of calcium, magnesium and uranium.
S	W	E	E	T	E	N	E	D	Sugared, Appeased, Mollified, Lightened, Pacified, Appeased, Conciliated.
S	W	E	E	T	M	E	A	T	Candy, Confection, Food rich in sugar.
S	W	E	E	T	N	E	S	S	Something sweet, State of being sweet.
S	W	I	F	T	N	E	S	S	Speed, Celerity, Rapdity, Velocity, Quickness, Haste, Dispatch, Hurry.
S	W	I	M	M	E	R	E	T	Abdominal appendage on some shellfish-lobster.
S	W	I	T	C	H	M	A	N	One who tends a switch.
S	W	O	R	D	F	I	S	H	A large and widely distributed oceanic fish with a long swordlike beak. Sport fish.
S	W	O	R	D	L	I	K	E	Resembling a sword.
S	W	O	R	D	S	M	A	N	One skilled in handling a sword.
S	W	O	R	D	T	A	I	L	Kingcrab, A tree bug, A long-horned grasshopper, A tropical fish.
S	Y	B	A	R	I	T	I	C	Self-indulgent, Sensuous, Sensual, Voluptuous, Carnal, Luxurious.
S	Y	C	O	P	H	A	N	T	Defamer, Parasite, Toady, Stooge, Flatterer, Snob, Fawning, Cringing.
S	Y	L	L	A	B	A	R	Y	Listing of syllables.
S	Y	L	L	O	G	I	S	M	Deductive reasoning, Method of attaining one's end.
S	Y	L	P	H	L	I	K	E	Resembling a sylph.
S	Y	M	B	I	O	S	I	S	Mutual co-operating, Intimate living together of two dissimilar organisms.
S	Y	M	B	O	L	I	S	T	One who employs symbols in religious worship.
S	Y	M	B	O	L	O	G	Y	Study of symbols.
S	Y	M	P	A	T	R	I	C	Occupying adjoining geographical areas.
S	Y	M	P	H	Y	T	I	C	Formed by fusion.
S	Y	M	P	O	S	I	U	M	Discussion, A meeting where various speakers deliver papers on a special topic.
S	Y	N	A	G	O	G	U	E	A place of assembly used by the Jewish community.
S	Y	N	C	L	I	N	A	L	Inclined down from opposite directions so as to meet.
S	Y	N	C	O	P	A	T	E	Abbreviate.
S	Y	N	D	A	C	T	Y	L	Having two or more digits united.
S	Y	N	D	I	C	A	T	E	Combine, Conglomerate, Group, Cartel, Association, Organization, Partnership.
S	Y	N	O	N	Y	M	I	C	Composed of synonyms.
S	Y	N	O	V	I	T	I	S	Inflammation of a synovial membrane usually with pain and swelling of the joint.
S	Y	N	T	H	E	S	I	S	Combination of parts or elements to form a whole.
S	Y	N	T	H	E	T	I	C	Artificial, Man-made.
S	Y	R	I	N	G	E	A	L	Relating to vocal organ of birds.
S	Y	S	T	A	L	T	I	C	Pulsing, Regular contraction nd dilatation.

T

1	2	3	4	5	6	7	8	9	
T	A	B	A	N	I	D	A	E	Large family of horseflies and other blood-sucking flies that may transmit disease.
T	A	B	E	T	I	S	O	L	Unfrozen ground above, within or below the permafrost.
T	A	B	L	A	T	U	R	E	Tonic sol-fa notation, Work of art, Verbal image, Description.
T	A	B	L	E	L	A	N	D	Plateau, Mesa.
T	A	B	L	E	W	A	R	E	China, glassware, silver and other utensils used for setting a meal table.
T	A	B	U	L	A	T	O	R	A business machine for tabulating data.
T	A	B	U	L	A	T	U	R	System of rules for poetic and musical compositions established by the meistersinger.
T	A	C	K	I	N	E	S	S	Stickiness, Adhesiveness.
T	A	C	T	F	U	L	L	Y	Considerately, Diplomatically, Adroitly, Delicately, Skilfully, Sensitively, Urbanely.
T	A	C	T	I	L	I	T	Y	Tangibility.
T	A	G	A	S	A	S	T	E	A shrub of the Canary Islands that yields cattle fodder.
T	A	I	L	O	R	E	S	S	A woman tailor.
T	A	L	B	O	T	Y	P	E	Calotype, An early photographic-negative process.
T	A	L	K	A	T	I	V	E	Loquacious, Garrulous, Voluble, Articulate, Eloquent, Fluent.
T	A	L	P	E	T	A	T	E	Poor, thin soil of partly decomposed volcanic ash.
T	A	M	B	O	U	R	I	N	Long narrow drum, Egyptian bottle-shaped drum, Lively old dance.
T	A	M	B	O	U	R	O	N	Bass drum.
T	A	M	P	O	N	A	G	E	Use of a plug to stop haemorrhage or absorb secretions.
T	A	N	G	E	R	I	N	E	Mandarin, A cultivated citrus fruit.
T	A	N	T	A	L	I	T	E	A mineral consisting of a heavy iron-black oxide of iron, manganese, tantalum.
T	A	N	T	A	L	I	Z	E	Tease, Torment, Harass, Worry, Annoy, Harry, Badger, Frustrate.

1	2	3	4	5	6	7	8	9	Definition
T	A	R	A	N	T	I	S	M	A dancing mania once thought to be caused by a tarantula's bite.
T	A	R	A	N	T	U	L	A	A large hairy spider capable of inflicting a bite.
T	A	R	A	X	A	C	U	M	A genus of weedy herbs, Dandelion.
T	A	R	D	I	N	E	S	S	Lateness, Sluggishness, Slowness, Unpunctuality.
T	A	R	N	I	S	H	E	D	Stained, Soiled, Spoiled, Tainted, Sullied, Diminished, Dulled, Blemished.
T	A	R	P	A	U	L	I	N	Sheet of waterproofed material used as a protection in inclement weather.
T	A	R	S	I	I	D	A	E	Family of lower primates, Lemurs.
T	A	S	A	J	I	L	L	O	A prickly pear.
T	A	S	I	M	E	T	E	R	A device for measuring small changes of temperature and pressure.
T	A	S	K	F	O	R	C	E	A group of persons charged with the performance of a mission usually in advance.
T	A	S	M	A	N	I	T	E	A light-coloured shaly coal that yields petroleum.
T	A	S	T	E	L	E	S	S	Insipid, Dull, Uninteresting, Unpalatable, Unappetizing, Stale, Unpolished, Vulgar.
T	A	S	T	I	N	E	S	S	State of being tasty.
T	A	U	T	O	L	O	G	Y	Verbiage, Repetition, Reiteration, Circumlocution.
T	A	W	N	I	N	E	S	S	Being a tawny colour.
T	A	X	I	D	E	R	M	Y	Preparing and mounting small skins of animals to present them in a lifelike manner.
T	A	X	I	M	E	T	E	R	A device used in a taxicab for automatically registering the fare due.
T	A	X	O	N	O	M	I	C	Relating to classification.
T	E	A	C	H	A	B	L	E	Docile, Apt and willing to learn.
T	E	C	H	N	I	C	A	L	Having special practical knowledge.
T	E	C	H	N	I	Q	U	E	Method, Way, Manner, Fashion, System, Mode.
T	E	C	T	O	N	I	C	S	The science of construction, Geological structural features as a whole.
T	E	C	T	O	R	I	A	L	Roof, Covering.
T	E	C	T	R	I	C	E	S	Covering feathers of wing and tail, Covert.
T	E	D	I	O	U	S	L	Y	Slowly, Boringly, Tiresomely, Dully, Uninterestingly, Aridly.
T	E	G	E	N	A	R	I	A	A genus of spiders.
T	E	K	N	O	N	Y	M	Y	The custom of naming the parent after the child.
T	E	L	E	G	E	N	I	C	Suitable for broadcast by television.
T	E	L	E	G	R	A	P	H	An electrical apparatus for communication at a distance.
T	E	L	E	M	E	T	E	R	Range finder, An automatic radio transmitter.
T	E	L	E	O	L	O	G	Y	The use of design, purpose or utility as an explanation of any natural phenomenon.
T	E	L	E	P	A	T	H	Y	Thought transference.
T	E	L	E	P	H	O	N	E	An apparatus consisting of a transmitter for converting sound into electrical impulses.
T	E	L	E	P	H	O	N	Y	Operation of an apparatus for transmission of sounds.
T	E	L	E	P	H	O	T	O	A camera lens system designed to give a large image of a distant object.
T	E	L	E	S	C	O	P	E	Optical instrument for distance viewing through a lens.
T	E	L	E	S	E	I	S	M	An earth tremor recorded on a remote seismograph.
T	E	L	L	U	R	A	T	E	A salt or ester of telluric acid.
T	E	L	L	U	R	I	A	N	Characteristic of the earth.
T	E	L	L	U	R	I	U	M	A semimetallic element in a silvery white brittle crystalline form.
T	E	L	L	U	R	O	U	S	Containing tellurium.
T	E	L	O	T	A	X	I	S	A taxis in which an organism orients itself to a stimulus.
T	E	M	P	E	R	A	T	E	Mild, Restrained, Dispassionate, Constitutional, Self-controlled, Continent, Sober.
T	E	M	P	O	R	A	R	Y	Transitory, Impermanent, Transient, Makeshift, Substitute, Provisional, Provisory.
T	E	M	P	T	R	E	S	S	Siren, Seductress, Female tempter.
T	E	N	A	C	I	O	U	S	Cohesive, Tough, Viscous, Retentive, Obstinate, Strong, Stalwart, Resolute.
T	E	N	A	C	U	L	U	M	A surgical instrument consisting of a slender sharp-pointed hook.
T	E	N	D	I	N	O	U	S	Sinewy, Relating to a tendon.
T	E	N	E	B	R	O	U	S	Dark, Murky, Mysterious, Obscure, Gloomy.
T	E	N	S	E	N	E	S	S	Rigidness, Stiffness, Tightness, Tautness, Closeness.
T	E	N	S	I	L	I	T	Y	Relating to tensile.
T	E	N	T	A	C	L	E	D	Having tentacles.
T	E	N	T	A	T	I	V	E	Provisional, Hesitant, Uncertain, Conditional, Temporary, Experimental, Test, Trial.
T	E	P	I	D	N	E	S	S	Warmness, Mildness, Dullness, Weakness.
T	E	R	E	B	I	N	T	H	A small European tree yielding turpentine.
T	E	R	E	B	R	A	N	T	A genus of biting flies, Sawflies.
T	E	R	M	A	G	A	N	T	Quarrelsome, scolding woman, Shrew, Virago.
T	E	R	M	I	N	A	T	E	Close, Expire, Discharge, End, Complete, Conclude, Discontinue, Halt.
T	E	R	M	I	T	A	R	Y	A termite nest.
T	E	R	N	I	D	E	N	S	Genus of nematode worms parasitic in apes and monkeys but occasionally in man.
T	E	R	P	E	N	O	I	D	Resembling a terpene in molecular structure.
T	E	R	P	I	N	E	N	E	The isomer that has an odour of lemons.
T	E	R	R	A	M	A	R	A	Prehistoric lake dwelling or settlement of northern Italy.
T	E	R	R	I	F	I	E	D	Afraid, Intimidated, Scared, Tormented, Startled, Alarmed, Petrified, Stunned.
T	E	R	R	I	T	O	R	Y	Area, Region, Tract, Zone, Domain, Province, Dominion, Sphere.
T	E	R	R	O	R	I	S	T	One who uses terror as a means of insurrection.
T	E	R	R	O	R	I	Z	E	Intimidate, Bulldoze, Bully, Hector, Frighten, Scare, Startle, Terrify.

1	2	3	4	5	6	7	8	9	
T	E	R	S	E	N	E	S	S	Brevity, Polish, Conciseness, Briefness.
T	E	R	V	A	L	E	N	T	Triple, Trivalent.
T	E	S	S	I	T	U	R	A	The general range of a melody or voice part.
T	E	S	T	A	M	E	N	T	Covenant, Scripture, Evidence, Witness, Affirmation, Credo, Will, Attestation.
T	E	S	T	A	T	R	I	X	A female testator.
T	E	S	T	I	F	I	E	D	Attested, Stated, Affirmed, Demonstrated, Proved, Witnessed, Deposed, Indicated.
T	E	S	T	I	M	O	N	Y	Indication, Confirmation, Evidence, Proof, Witness, Symbol, Protest, Certificate.
T	E	S	T	I	N	E	S	S	Condition of being testy.
T	E	T	A	R	T	O	I	D	A twelve-faced solid.
T	E	T	R	A	D	I	T	E	One believing that there are four persons in God.
T	E	T	R	A	G	R	A	M	Word of four letters.
T	E	T	R	A	L	O	G	Y	A series of four connected works.
T	E	T	R	A	M	I	N	E	A compound containing four amino groups.
T	E	T	R	A	R	C	H	Y	Joint rule by four persons.
T	E	T	R	A	S	T	E	R	A mitotic figure characterised by four astral poles.
T	E	T	R	A	X	I	A	L	Having four axes.
T	E	U	T	O	N	I	Z	E	Germanize.
T	H	A	L	A	S	S	I	C	Relating to the sea or ocean.
T	H	A	N	K	L	E	S	S	Ungrateful, Disagreeable, Unpleasant, Miserable, Wretched, Distasteful.
T	H	E	L	P	H	U	S	A	Freshwater crabs.
T	H	E	O	B	R	O	M	A	Genus of tropical American trees, Cacao.
T	H	E	O	C	R	A	C	Y	Governed by religious officials.
T	H	E	O	C	R	A	S	Y	Mixture of different gods in the minds of worshippers.
T	H	E	O	L	A	T	R	Y	Worship of a god.
T	H	E	O	M	A	C	H	Y	A battle among the gods.
T	H	E	O	M	A	N	C	Y	Divination by divinely inspired oracles.
T	H	E	O	P	H	A	N	Y	Physical presentation of a deity.
T	H	E	O	S	O	P	H	Y	Philosophy professing to attain to knowledge of God by spiritual ecstasy.
T	H	E	R	A	P	I	S	T	One trained to rehabilitate patients by occupational or physical means.
T	H	E	R	E	F	O	R	E	Consequently, Accordingly, Thus.
T	H	E	R	M	I	D	O	R	A moderate counter-revolutionary stage to allow a return to a normal life style.
T	H	E	R	O	P	O	D	A	Family of carnivorous dinosaurs that walked on their hind legs.
T	H	E	S	A	U	R	U	S	A book containing a collection of words or information.
T	H	I	G	H	B	O	N	E	Femur.
T	H	O	L	O	B	A	T	E	The base of a dome.
T	H	R	A	L	L	D	O	M	Slavery.
T	H	R	A	S	H	I	N	G	Beating, Pounding, Flogging, Buffeting, Whipping, Defeat, Vanquish, Overthrow.
T	H	R	E	E	F	O	L	D	Three times as much.
T	H	R	E	E	S	O	M	E	Trio, A group of three.
T	H	R	E	S	H	O	L	D	Sill, Gate, Door, End, Boundary, Entrance, Verge, Brink.
T	H	R	I	L	L	I	N	G	Exciting, Animating, Moving, Quickening, Electrifying, Stimulating, Inspiring.
T	H	R	O	B	B	I	N	G	Pulsating, Palpitating, Beating, Thumping, Vibrating.
T	H	R	O	W	A	W	A	Y	Something designed to be discarded, Free advertising literature.
T	H	R	O	W	S	T	E	R	One who throws silk or synthetic filaments.
T	H	U	R	B	E	R	I	A	A genus of shrubby herbs, Wild cotton.
T	H	W	A	R	T	I	N	G	Opposing, Baffling, Contravening, Frustrating, Balking, Foiling, Scotching.
T	H	Y	L	A	C	I	N	E	Tasmanian wolf.
T	H	Y	R	O	N	I	N	E	A phenolic amino acid.
T	I	D	A	L	W	A	V	E	An unusually high sea wave.
T	I	G	H	T	N	E	S	S	Tenseness, Tautness, Closeness, Stiffness, Rigidness, Strictness.
T	I	M	E	P	I	E	C	E	An instrument for measuring time, Watch.
T	I	M	E	T	A	B	L	E	A schedule showing the time when certain events will occur.
T	I	M	P	A	N	I	S	T	One who plays the kettle drum.
T	I	P	H	I	I	D	A	E	Family of small slender black hairy wasps.
T	I	P	U	L	A	R	I	A	Delicate terrestrial orchid, Crane-fly orchid.
T	I	T	I	L	L	A	T	E	Please, Arouse, Stimulate.
T	I	T	U	L	A	R	L	Y	Nominally.
T	O	A	D	S	T	O	O	L	Fleshy, umbrella-shaped poisonous fungus.
T	O	L	E	R	A	B	L	E	Bearable, Sufferable, Endurable, Respectable, Decent, Presentable, Acceptable.
T	O	L	E	R	A	N	C	E	Endurance, Fortitude, Stamina, Vigour, Patience, Indulgence, Leniency, Clemency.
T	O	M	B	S	T	O	N	E	Gravestone, Headstone.
T	O	M	E	N	T	O	S	E	Covered with densely matted hairs.
T	O	N	O	S	C	O	P	E	A device enabling a singer or player to see any deviation from the proper pitch of tone.
T	O	N	S	I	L	L	A	R	Relating to the tonsils.
T	O	N	S	O	R	I	A	L	Relating to a barber and his work.
T	O	O	L	M	A	K	E	R	A machinist specialising in all aspects of machine tools, jigs and instruments.
T	O	O	T	H	A	C	H	E	Pain in or about a tooth.

1	2	3	4	5	6	7	8	9	Definition
T	O	O	T	H	S	O	M	E	Delicious, Agreeable, Pleasant, Delectable, Luscious, Palatable.
T	O	P	I	A	R	I	S	T	One skilled in trimming shrubs or trees into ornamental shapes.
T	O	R	E	U	T	I	C	S	Process of work wrought in metal.
T	O	R	M	E	N	T	I	L	A yellow-flowered Eurasian herb with a root that is used in tanning and dyeing.
T	O	R	M	E	N	T	O	R	Pest, Plague, Persecutor, Torturer.
T	O	R	P	I	D	I	T	Y	Sluggishness, Torpidness, Lethargy, Lassitude, Stupor, Passivity.
T	O	R	R	I	D	I	T	Y	State of being torrid.
T	O	R	S	I	O	N	A	L	Relating to torsion.
T	O	R	T	R	I	C	I	D	A small moth.
T	O	R	T	U	R	O	U	S	Distorted, Twisting, Agonizing, Excruciating, Harrowing, Tormenting, Racking.
T	O	T	A	L	I	Z	E	R	One that totalizes.
T	O	U	C	H	D	O	W	N	A scoring manoeuvre in rugby, The action of landing a plane.
T	O	U	G	H	N	E	S	S	Strength, Sturdiness, Hardness, Inflexibility, Stiffness, Harshness, Strictness.
T	O	W	E	L	L	I	N	G	Using a towel, Fabric used for making towels.
T	O	W	N	S	C	A	P	E	A painting of a town or city.
T	O	X	I	C	A	R	O	L	A greenish yellow crystalline compound obtained from the roots of a tropical herb.
T	O	X	I	C	O	S	I	S	Toxemia.
T	O	X	O	P	H	I	L	Y	The love of archery.
T	R	A	C	E	A	B	L	E	Capable of being traced, Due, Ascribable.
T	R	A	C	K	L	E	S	S	Leaving no tracks, Not running on tracks.
T	R	A	C	T	A	B	L	E	Docile, Governable, Pliant, Malleable, Obedient, Flexible, Subdued, Amenable.
T	R	A	D	E	S	M	A	N	Shopkeeper, Artisan, Craftsman.
T	R	A	D	I	T	I	O	N	Heritage, Culture, Convention, Form, Legacy, Lore, Legend.
T	R	A	G	E	D	I	A	N	An actor specializing in roles in tragedies.
T	R	A	N	S	C	E	N	D	Exceed, Surpass, Excel, Ascend, Elevate, Raise, Outshine, Beat.
T	R	A	N	S	E	N	N	A	A lattice screen to protect a shrine.
T	R	A	N	S	F	O	R	M	Transfigure, Alter, Convert, Change, Transmute, Commute, Translate, Transfer.
T	R	A	N	S	F	U	S	E	Transmit, Instill, Flow, Diffuse, Permeate, Impregnate, Penetrate, Saturate.
T	R	A	N	S	I	E	N	T	Impermanent, Transitory, Short-lived, Passing, Fleeting, Momentary, Temporary.
T	R	A	N	S	L	A	T	E	Put, Render, Transpose, Turn, Transcribe, Interpret, Convert, Tansform.
T	R	A	N	S	M	U	T	E	Change, Alter, Convert, Transform, Metamorphose, Translate, Commute, Change.
T	R	A	N	S	P	I	R	E	Happen, Befall, Chance, Develop, Occur, Exhale, Exude, Perspise.
T	R	A	N	S	P	O	R	T	Carry, Move, Transfer, Banish, Deport, Entrance, Enrapture, Excite.
T	R	A	P	E	Z	I	S	T	A performer on the trapeze.
T	R	A	P	E	Z	I	U	S	A large flat triangular muscle over the shoulder blade.
T	R	A	P	E	Z	O	I	D	A quadrilateral having only two sides parallel.
T	R	A	P	P	I	N	G	S	Outward decoration, Trimmings, Embellishment.
T	R	A	U	M	A	T	I	C	Relating to emotional or psychological stress.
T	R	A	V	E	L	L	E	R	One that goes on a journey.
T	R	E	A	C	H	E	R	Y	Betrayal, Treason, Disloyalty, Perfidy, Infidelity, Falseness.
T	R	E	A	D	M	I	L	L	A mill worked by the treading of an endless belt by persons or animals.
T	R	E	A	S	U	R	E	R	Officer entrusted with funds, Curator.
T	R	E	A	T	M	E	N	T	Conduct or behaviour towards another party, A medical or surgical remedy for illness.
T	R	E	B	U	C	H	E	T	Medieval military engine like a catapult, A small delicate scale.
T	R	E	M	A	T	O	D	E	Flukes and related parasitic flatworms.
T	R	E	M	B	L	I	N	G	Shivering, Shuddering, Quivering, Tremulous, Shaking, Shaky, Quaking.
T	R	E	M	O	L	A	N	T	A device to cause a vibration in a musical instrument.
T	R	E	M	U	L	O	U	S	Quivering, Palpitating, Shaking, Vibrating, Timorous, Wavering, Trembling.
T	R	E	N	C	H	A	N	T	Keen, Sharp, Caustic, Distinct, Incisive, Clear-cut, Scathing, Crisp.
T	R	E	P	O	N	E	M	A	Parasitic anaerobic spirochetes, Syphilis, Yaws.
T	R	I	A	K	I	D	A	E	Family of fishes, Dogfish.
T	R	I	A	N	G	L	E	D	Having three angles.
T	R	I	B	A	D	I	S	M	Female homosexual practice.
T	R	I	B	A	L	I	S	M	Strong loyalty to one's group and its culture.
T	R	I	B	O	L	O	G	Y	Study of friction and lubrication.
T	R	I	B	U	T	A	R	Y	Branch, Small stream, Small vein, Subject, Dependent, Subordinate, Secondary.
T	R	I	C	H	O	S	I	S	Hairiness, A heavy growth of hair.
T	R	I	C	H	U	R	I	S	Genus of nematode worms, Whipworms.
T	R	I	C	K	S	T	E	R	Swindler, Cheat, Defrauder, Magician, Conjurer, Illusionist.
T	R	I	F	O	R	I	U	M	Gallery forming an upper storey to the aisle of a church.
T	R	I	G	A	M	I	S	T	One who marries three people during the same space of time.
T	R	I	Q	U	E	T	R	A	A figure contained by three arcs of equal radius meeting at angles.
T	R	I	L	O	B	A	T	E	Divided into three lobes.
T	R	I	L	O	B	I	T	E	Extinct marine arthropods.
T	R	I	M	M	I	N	G	S	Additional decorations or embellishments.
T	R	I	N	O	M	I	A	L	Consisting of three mathematical terms, Classification in botany or zoology.
T	R	I	P	T	Y	Q	U	E	A permit for transporting a motor car through customs post.

1	2	3	4	5	6	7	8	9	Clue
T	R	I	Q	U	E	T	R	A	Decoration formed of three intertwined arcs or loops.
T	R	I	S	A	G	I	O	N	A requiem service of the Eastern church.
T	R	I	T	E	N	E	S	S	The quality of being trite.
T	R	I	T	H	E	I	S	M	A belief in three gods.
T	R	I	T	I	C	A	L	E	A hybrid between wheat and rye.
T	R	I	T	U	R	A	T	E	Rub, Grind, Masticate, Bruise, Pulverize, Crush, Powder.
T	R	I	U	M	P	H	A	L	Triumphant, Exultant, Jubilant, Rejoicing.
T	R	I	V	A	L	E	N	T	Having a valence of three.
T	R	O	C	H	I	L	U	S	Humming bird, Crocodile bird.
T	R	O	P	O	L	O	G	Y	A figurative mode of speech or writing.
T	R	O	U	S	S	E	A	U	Linen and new clothes collected by a bride for her new life.
T	R	U	C	U	L	E	N	T	Belligeret, Pugnacious, Cruel, Fierce, Grim, Bullying, Intimidating, Abusive.
T	R	U	N	C	A	T	E	D	Bevelled, Curtailed, Maimed, Mangled, Cropped, Lopped, Sheared, Abbreviated.
T	R	U	N	C	H	E	O	N	Bludgeon, Baton, Nightstick, Club.
T	U	I	T	I	O	N	A	L	Designed to teach or instruct.
T	U	L	A	R	E	M	I	A	An infectious disease transmitted by insect bites.
T	U	M	E	S	C	E	N	T	Swollen, Inflated, Distended, Bombastic, Tumid, Teeming, Pregnant, Rhetorical.
T	U	R	B	I	D	I	T	Y	Confusion, Muddiness, Obscurity, Density, Cloudiness, Murkiness, Darkness.
T	U	R	B	I	N	A	T	E	Shaped like an inverted cone, Narrow at base but broad at the apex.
T	U	R	B	U	L	E	N	T	Stormy, Tempetuous, Disorderly, Raucous, Rowdy, Wild, Clamorous, Brawling.
T	U	R	G	I	D	I	T	Y	Being swollen or inflated.
T	U	R	N	T	A	B	L	E	A platform that revolves, Lazy susan, Machine for playing records.
T	U	R	P	I	T	U	D	E	Depravity, Baseness, Wickedness.
T	U	R	Q	U	O	I	S	E	A mineral consisting of hydrous basic copper aluminium phosphate valued as gem.
T	U	T	O	R	S	H	I	P	Tutelage, Function of a tutor.
T	W	I	T	C	H	I	N	G	Jerking, Plucking, Pinching, Nipping, Grasping, Snapping, Lurching, Clutching.
T	Y	P	H	O	I	D	A	L	Relating to typhoid fever.
T	Y	P	I	C	A	L	L	Y	In a typical fashion.
T	Y	R	A	N	N	I	Z	E	Oppress, Trample, Terrorize, Dominate, Dictate, Shackle, Overpower.
T	Y	R	A	N	N	O	U	S	Oppressive, Absolute, Autocratic, Despotic, Lordly, Totalitarian.
T	Y	T	O	N	I	D	A	E	Family of owls, Barn owls.

U

1	2	3	4	5	6	7	8	9	Clue
U	L	I	G	I	N	O	U	S	Growing in wet or swampy ground.
U	L	O	T	R	I	C	H	Y	Having woolly or crisp hair.
U	L	T	I	M	A	T	U	M	Final statement.
U	M	B	E	L	L	A	T	E	Resembling an umbel.
U	M	B	I	L	I	C	A	L	Relating to the region of the navel, Centre, Attached.
U	M	B	I	L	I	C	U	S	Small abdominal depression remaining from the umbilical cord.
U	N	A	N	I	M	O	U	S	Agreed, Concurrent, Solid, Harmonious, Agreement.
U	N	B	A	L	A	N	C	E	Madden, Craze, Unhinge, Distract.
U	N	B	E	N	D	I	N	G	Unyielding, Resolute, Inflexible, Reserved, Rigid, Inexorable, Obdurate, Relentless.
U	N	C	E	R	T	A	I	N	Indeterminate, Problematical, Questionable, Ambiguous, Erratic, Unreliable.
U	N	C	L	O	T	H	E	D	Undressed, Naked, Divested, Nude, Stripped, Raw, Disrobed, Exposed.
U	N	C	O	N	C	E	R	N	Indifference, Apathy, Lassitude, Lethargy, Heedlessness.
U	N	D	E	C	I	D	E	D	Unsettled, Wavering, Inconstant, Irresolute, Pending, Undetermined.
U	N	D	E	R	D	O	N	E	Not thoroughly cooked, Raw.
U	N	D	E	R	F	O	O	T	On the bottom, Underground, Subterranean, Downtrodden, In the way.
U	N	D	E	R	H	A	N	D	Secretly, Quietly, Unobtrusively, Sly, Devious, Sneaky, Deceitful, Furtive.
U	N	D	E	R	L	I	N	E	Underscore, Emphasise, Advance announcement.
U	N	D	E	R	L	I	N	G	Subordinate, Inferior, Secondary, Subaltern.
U	N	D	E	R	M	I	N	E	Erode, Weaken, Sap, Debilitate, Wreck, Foil, Thwart, Sabotage.
U	N	D	E	R	P	A	S	S	A road passing underneath another road.
U	N	D	E	R	P	L	O	T	A hidden scheme, A plot subordinate to the main story in a drama.
U	N	D	E	R	R	A	T	E	Undervalue, Depreciate, Decry, Devalue, Lower.
U	N	D	E	R	S	H	O	T	Having a projecting lower jaw.
U	N	D	E	R	T	A	K	E	Attempt, Guarantee, Pledge, Try, Endeavour, Strive, Commence, Engage.
U	N	D	E	R	T	O	N	E	Subdued, Utterance, Murmur, Mutter, Whisper, Hint, Suggestion, Implication.
U	N	D	E	R	W	E	A	R	Garment worn next to the skin under outer wear.
U	N	D	E	R	W	E	N	T	Endured, Suffered, Experienced, Tolerated, Yielded, Submitted.
U	N	D	E	R	W	O	O	D	Undergrowth, Underbrush.
U	N	D	I	V	I	D	E	D	Entire, Whole, Concentrated, Exclusive, Fixed, Not parted, Unwavering.
U	N	E	A	R	T	H	L	Y	Supernatural, Celestial, Weird, Eerie, Spiritual, Ideal, Fantastic, Uncanny.
U	N	F	E	E	L	I	N	G	Insensitive, Insensate, Cruel, Callous, Heartless, Brutal, Pitiless, Obdurate.
U	N	F	L	E	D	G	E	D	Immature, Callow, Young, Juvenile, Unripe, Youthful.
U	N	F	O	U	N	D	E	D	Baseless, Groundless, Illusive, Unwarranted.

1	2	3	4	5	6	7	8	9	Definition
U	N	G	U	A	R	D	E	D	Unprotected, Vulnerable, Direct, Incautious, Open, Revealing.
U	N	H	E	A	L	T	H	Y	Sickly, Weak, Diseased, Risky, Unsound, Injurious, Corrupt, Depraved.
U	N	I	F	O	R	M	L	Y	Regularly, Steadily, Evenly, Smoothly.
U	N	I	N	J	U	R	E	D	Whole, Entire, Intact, Sound, Unimpaired, Perfect, Unmarred, Undamaged.
U	N	I	R	A	M	O	U	S	Unbranched.
U	N	I	S	O	N	A	N	T	In unison, Alike.
U	N	I	T	A	R	I	A	N	Doctrine founded upon unity.
U	N	I	V	A	L	E	N	T	Having a valence of one, Single.
U	N	I	V	E	R	S	A	L	Omniprescent, Ubiquitous, Cosmic, Global, Broad, Extensive, General, Total.
U	N	L	E	A	R	N	E	D	Unscholarly, Unstudious, Unbookish, Unschooled, Untaught, Unversed, Ignorant.
U	N	L	I	M	I	T	E	D	Unrestricted, Unconfined, Undefined, Boundless, Infinite, Immeasureable, Total.
U	N	M	A	R	R	I	E	D	Single, Unwed, Divorced, Widowed.
U	N	M	O	V	A	B	L	E	Fixed, Immobile, Irremovable, Inflexible, Constant, Invariable, Unalterable.
U	N	R	E	F	I	N	E	D	Coarse, Uncouth, Churlish, Loutish, Crude, Raw, Impure, Unprocessed.
U	N	R	E	L	A	T	E	D	Unconnected, Disjoined, Separate.
U	N	S	E	L	F	I	S	H	Generous, Selfless.
U	N	S	E	T	T	L	E	D	Disturbed, Inconstant, Variable, Doubtful, Undecided, Unstable, Erratic, Restless.
U	N	S	K	I	L	F	U	L	Inapt, Inexpert, Incapable, Incompetent.
U	N	S	K	I	L	L	E	D	Amateurish, Unaccomplished, Inefficient, Incompetent, Inept, Inexpert.
U	N	S	N	A	R	L	E	D	Untangled.
U	N	S	U	L	L	I	E	D	Immaculate, Spotless, Chaste, Decent, Pure, Unblemished, Undefiled, Modest.
U	N	T	E	N	A	B	L	E	Indefensible.
U	N	T	H	R	I	F	T	Y	Wasteful, Extravagent, Squanderer, Waster, Spendthrift, Spender.
U	N	T	O	U	C	H	E	D	Unaffected, Calm, Unmoved, Unequalled, Virgin, Unspoilt, Intact, Perfect.
U	N	W	E	A	R	I	E	D	Fresh, Diligent.
U	N	W	I	L	L	I	N	G	Opposed, Averse, Loath, Reluctant, Obstinate, Refractory.
U	N	W	I	T	T	I	N	G	Accidental, Inadvertent, Ignorant, Unconscious, Oblivious, Forgetful, Unknowing.
U	N	W	R	I	T	T	E	N	Oral, Traditional, Blank.
U	P	H	O	L	S	T	E	R	To cover with padding and fabric.
U	P	P	E	R	M	O	S	T	Top, Highest, Loftiest, Topmost, Most prominent position.
U	R	I	N	A	T	I	O	N	To discharge urine.
U	R	O	L	O	G	I	S	T	One who specializes in urology.
U	R	T	I	C	A	R	I	A	Skin eruption of itching red or pale smooth patches, Hives.
U	S	U	C	A	P	I	O	N	A way of acquiring property by uninterrupted possession for a definite period.
U	T	R	I	C	U	L	A	R	Resembling a small sac, pouch or bladder.
U	T	T	E	R	A	N	C	E	Articulation, Speech, Word, Statement, Expression, Discourse, Speak, Talk.
U	T	T	E	R	M	O	S	T	Extreme, Utmost, Last, Farthest, Furthest, Remotest.
U	X	O	R	I	C	I	D	E	The murder of a wife by her husband.

V

1	2	3	4	5	6	7	8	9	Definition
V	A	C	I	L	L	A	T	E	Waver, Totter, Fluctuate, Oscillate, Hesitate, Stagger, Dally, Dawdle.
V	A	G	U	E	N	E	S	S	Haziness, Faintness, Fogginess, Mistiness, Dimness.
V	A	I	N	G	L	O	R	Y	Vanity, Pride, Conceit, Egotism, Arrogance, Flaunting, Boastfulness, Exhibitionism.
V	A	L	I	A	N	T	L	Y	Bravely, Courageously, Determinedly, Boldly, Intrepidly, Audaciously.
V	A	L	U	A	T	I	O	N	Appraisal, Assessment, Estimate, Judgment, Opinion, Worth, Account, Cost.
V	A	L	U	E	L	E	S	S	Worthless, Unworthy.
V	A	M	P	I	R	I	S	H	Resembling a vampire.
V	A	N	D	A	L	I	S	M	Wilful or malicious destruction.
V	A	N	G	U	E	R	I	A	Genus of tropical African and Asian trees.
V	A	N	I	L	L	I	S	M	A disease contracted by excessive handling of vanilla, Grocer's itch.
V	A	P	I	D	N	E	S	S	Triteness, Insipidness.
V	A	P	O	R	I	F	I	C	Producing vapour.
V	A	R	I	A	T	I	O	N	Modification, Alteration, Mutation, Diversification, Permutation, Change.
V	A	R	I	C	E	L	L	A	Chicken pox.
V	A	R	I	E	G	A	T	E	Diversify, Enliven.
V	A	R	I	O	L	A	T	E	Having symptoms and signs of smallpox.
V	A	R	I	O	L	I	T	E	A basic rock embedded with whitish spherules.
V	A	S	E	C	T	O	M	Y	Surgical excision of the sperm duct to induce permanent sterility of a male.
V	A	S	O	T	O	N	I	C	Promoting tone of blood vessel walls.
V	A	S	S	A	L	A	G	E	Servitude, Subjection.
V	A	T	I	C	I	N	A	L	Prophetic.
V	E	G	E	T	A	B	L	E	Herbaceous plant cultivated for human food to be eaten raw or cooked, Dull.
V	E	H	E	M	E	N	C	E	Intensity, Violence.
V	E	H	I	C	U	L	A	R	Designed for or use of motor vehicles.
V	E	L	L	I	C	A	T	E	Twitch, Nip, Pinch, Tickle, Titillate, Jerk, Fidget, Lurch.
V	E	L	V	E	T	E	E	N	A cotton clothing fabric made to imitate velvet.

1	2	3	4	5	6	7	8	9	Definition
V	E	N	D	I	T	I	O	N	Act of selling, Sale.
V	E	N	E	R	A	B	L	E	Old, Revered, Dignified, Imposing, Admirable, Honoured, Estimable, Patriarchal.
V	E	N	E	R	A	T	E	D	Revered, Adored, Worshipped, Honoured, Esteemed.
V	E	N	G	E	A	N	C	E	Retaliation, Reprisal, Retribution, Return, Repayment, Counterblow, Punishment.
V	E	N	I	A	L	I	T	Y	State of being excusable.
V	E	N	T	I	L	A	T	E	Utter, Publicise, Broach, Introduce, Express, Give, Air, Aerate.
V	E	N	T	R	I	C	L	E	A cavity of a bodily part or organ, A chamber of the heart.
V	E	R	A	C	I	O	U	S	Truthful, Accurate, Direct, Honest, Sincere, Faithful, Just, Valid.
V	E	R	B	A	L	I	S	M	Term, Word, Phrasing, Wordiness, Diction, Parlance, Verbosity, Prolixity.
V	E	R	B	O	S	I	T	Y	Wordiness, Prolixity, Bombast, Grandiloquence, Redundancy.
V	E	R	D	I	G	R	I	S	Green or bluish deposit formed on copper, brass or bronze surfaces.
V	E	R	D	U	R	O	U	S	Verdant.
V	E	R	G	I	F	O	R	M	Rodlike.
V	E	R	I	D	I	C	A	L	Truthful, Veracious, Genuine, Real, Actual, True, Indisputable, Undistorted.
V	E	R	I	T	A	B	L	E	Authentic, Genuine, Real, True, Unquestionable, Factual, Undoubted, Unrefuted.
V	E	R	M	I	C	I	D	E	An agent for destroying intestinal parasitic worms.
V	E	R	M	I	F	O	R	M	Wormlike.
V	E	R	M	I	F	U	G	E	Substance to expel worms from the intestines.
V	E	R	M	I	L	I	O	N	A bright red pigment.
V	E	R	M	I	N	O	U	S	Noxious, Filthly, Offensive, Infested with vermin.
V	E	R	N	A	L	I	Z	E	To give freshness to, To make springlike.
V	E	R	N	A	T	I	O	N	Arrangement of foliage leaves within the bud.
V	E	R	R	U	C	O	S	E	Warty.
V	E	R	S	A	T	I	L	E	Changeable, Fickle, Reversible, Diversified, Adaptable, Mobile, Flexible, Pliable.
V	E	R	S	I	F	I	E	R	Writer of verse.
V	E	R	T	E	B	R	A	L	Spinal.
V	E	S	I	C	U	L	A	R	Formed like a thin sac, blister or cavity.
V	E	S	T	I	B	U	L	E	Lobby, Entrance, Foyer, Entry, Portico, Portal.
V	E	S	T	I	T	U	R	E	Small plants.
V	E	X	A	T	I	O	U	S	Distressing, Afflictive, Unquiet, Troubled, Disordered, Troublesome, Mean, Ugly.
V	E	X	I	L	L	A	R	Y	Standard-bearer.
V	I	A	B	I	L	I	T	Y	Possibility, Feasibility.
V	I	B	R	A	T	I	L	E	Vibratory, Oscillating.
V	I	B	R	A	T	I	O	N	Oscillation, Quivering, Tremulous.
V	I	B	R	A	T	O	R	Y	Vibrant, Vibrating.
V	I	B	R	I	S	S	A	E	Stiff hairs around the nostrils.
V	I	C	A	R	I	O	U	S	Delegated, Deputed, Endured for another.
V	I	C	E	N	N	I	A	L	Occurring once every twenty years.
V	I	C	E	R	E	I	N	E	The wife of a viceroy.
V	I	C	I	O	U	S	L	Y	In a vicious manner, Evilly.
V	I	C	T	I	M	I	Z	E	Sacrifice, Cheat, Dupe, Trick, Hoodwink, Hoax, Immolate, Ill-treat.
V	I	C	T	O	R	I	N	E	A woman's fur tippet, A canon regular of a medieval French order.
V	I	D	E	L	I	C	E	T	Namely.
V	I	E	N	T	I	A	N	E	The style prevalent of the capital of Laos.
V	I	G	I	L	A	N	C	E	Watchfulness, Surveillance, Lookout, Circumspection, Caution.
V	I	G	I	L	A	N	T	E	Member of a committee formed to punish criminals.
V	I	L	L	O	S	I	T	Y	A coating of long slender hairs.
V	I	M	I	N	E	O	U	S	Producing long slender twigs or shoots.
V	I	N	D	I	C	A	T	E	Deliver, Avenge, Exonerate, Absolve, Prove, Confirm, Substantiate, Justify.
V	I	N	O	M	E	T	E	R	A device to determine percentage of alcohol in wine.
V	I	O	L	A	T	I	O	N	Infringement, Transgression, Desecration, Profanation, Interruption, Disturbance.
V	I	O	L	E	N	T	L	Y	Fiercely, Turbently, Frantically, Furiously, Madly, Tumultuously, Wildly, Stormily.
V	I	R	G	I	L	I	A	N	The style of Virgil.
V	I	R	G	I	N	I	T	Y	Celibacy. Chastity, Purity, The state of being fresh and new.
V	I	R	I	C	I	D	A	L	Destroying virus.
V	I	R	I	L	O	C	A	L	Patrilocal, Centred around the family or tribe of the husband.
V	I	R	U	L	E	N	C	E	Rancour, Malignancy, Venom, Toxicity.
V	I	S	C	I	D	I	T	Y	Stickiness.
V	I	S	C	O	S	I	T	Y	Fluidity, Tenacity.
V	I	S	I	O	N	A	R	Y	Dreamy, Impractical, Illusory, Phantom, Imaginary, Impractical, Unreal, Unworldly.
V	I	S	U	A	L	I	Z	E	Picture, Imagine, Envisage, Foreseen, Conceive, Feature, Realize, Vision.
V	I	T	E	L	L	I	N	E	Resembling the yolk of an egg.
V	I	T	I	A	T	I	O	N	Impairment, Corruption, Contamination.
V	I	T	R	I	O	L	I	C	Virulent, Scathing.
V	I	T	R	O	L	I	T	E	Thick opaque structural glass used for ornamental finish on exposed surfaces.
V	I	T	R	O	T	Y	P	E	A photograph burned into the surface of glass or ceramic ware.
V	I	V	A	C	I	O	U	S	Lively, Sprightly, Alert, Animated, Vibrant, Exuberant, Frolicsome, Sportive.

1	2	3	4	5	6	7	8	9	
V	I	V	E	R	R	I	N	E	Resembling the family of civets, genets and mongooses.
V	I	V	I	D	N	E	S	S	Animation, Freshness, Liveliness, Sharpness, Keenness.
V	O	I	C	E	L	E	S	S	Silent, Mute, Dumb, Inarticulate, Speechless.
V	O	L	C	A	N	I	S	M	Volcanic power.
V	O	L	C	A	N	I	S	T	One who studies volcanic phenomena, Plutonist.
V	O	L	T	I	N	I	S	M	The number of annual broods, as of insects.
V	O	L	T	M	E	T	E	R	An instrument for measuring voltage.
V	O	L	U	N	T	A	R	Y	Intentional, Intended, Spontaneous, Deliberate, Willing, Chosen, Free, Autonomous.
V	O	L	U	N	T	E	E	R	Undertake, Offer, One who offers his services.
V	O	L	U	T	I	D	A	E	Family of gastropods.
V	O	R	A	C	I	O	U	S	Greedy, Ravenous, Avid, Insatiable, Gluttonous, Grasping, Rapacious, Covetous.
V	O	U	C	H	S	A	F	E	Accord, Supply, Condescend, Deign, Grant, Award, Favour, Oblige.
V	U	L	C	A	N	I	S	T	Volcanist.
V	U	L	C	A	N	I	T	E	Ebonite, Hard rubber.
V	U	L	G	A	R	I	T	Y	Commonness, Coarseness, Crudeness, Uncouthness, Profanity, Obscenity.
V	U	L	G	A	R	I	Z	E	Popularize, Coarsen.
V	U	L	N	E	R	A	R	Y	Curative, Sanative, Wounding.
V	U	L	T	U	R	I	N	E	Predatory.

W

1	2	3	4	5	6	7	8	9	
W	A	G	N	E	R	I	T	E	A mineral consisting of a magnesium fluorophosphate.
W	A	I	S	T	C	O	A	T	A short sleeveless collarless coat worn under a jacket, Vest.
W	A	L	L	O	P	I	N	G	Whopping, Smashing, Impressive, Terrifically, Spanking, Punching.
W	A	L	L	O	W	I	N	G	Rolling, Surging, Luxuriating, Floundering, Grovelling, Lurching, Tottering.
W	A	N	C	H	A	N	C	Y	Mischievous, Ill-fated, Uncanny, Weird.
W	A	N	D	E	R	I	N	G	Winding, Meandering, Vagrant, Errant, Nomadic, Trailing, Floating, Straying.
W	A	R	E	H	O	U	S	E	Structure for storage of merchandize.
W	A	R	R	A	N	T	E	D	Guaranteed, Assured, Secured, Authorized, Attested, Justified, Vindicated, Certified.
W	A	S	H	B	A	S	I	N	A Large bowl for water to wash hands and face.
W	A	S	P	I	S	H	L	Y	Snappishly, Irritably, Peevishly, Sharply, Spitefully, Fretfully, Petulantly, Perversely.
W	A	T	C	H	W	O	R	D	Password, Slogan, Catchword, Phrase.
W	A	T	E	R	F	A	L	L	Cascade, Cataract.
W	A	T	E	R	L	I	L	Y	Aquatic plant with showy flowers, Lotus flower.
W	A	T	E	R	M	A	R	K	A manufacturer's design impressed on paper.
W	A	T	E	R	S	H	E	D	Catchment area for rain, Crucial or dividing point.
W	A	X	M	A	L	L	O	W	A plant having drooping flowers like the hibiscus.
W	A	Y	W	A	R	D	L	Y	Perversely, In a wayward manner.
W	E	A	L	T	H	I	L	Y	With riches.
W	E	A	P	O	N	E	E	R	One who activates an atomic bomb for release upon a target.
W	E	A	R	I	N	E	S	S	Fatigue, Tiredness, Exhaustion, Lassitude.
W	E	A	R	I	S	O	M	E	Tedious, Tiresome.
W	E	B	F	O	O	T	E	D	Having webbed feet.
W	E	E	V	I	L	L	E	D	Infested with weevils.
W	E	I	R	D	N	E	S	S	Strangeness, Eeriness, Uncanniness.
W	E	L	L	B	E	I	N	G	Prosperity, Abundance, Thriving, Welfare, Advantage, Benefit.
W	E	R	O	W	A	N	C	E	A North American Indian chief.
W	H	E	A	T	C	A	K	E	A griddle cake made from wheat flour.
W	H	E	A	T	M	E	A	L	Pure unbleached meal from ground unadulterated wheat berries.
W	H	E	R	E	F	O	R	E	Why.
W	H	E	R	E	U	N	T	O	Wherefore.
W	H	E	R	E	W	I	T	H	A mineral consisting of a basic carbonate and sulfate of lead and copper.
W	H	E	R	R	Y	M	A	N	One who rows passengers in a wherry.
W	H	E	T	S	T	O	N	E	A stone for sharpening blades.
W	H	I	C	H	E	V	E	R	Whatever, No matter which.
W	H	I	M	S	I	C	A	L	Capricious, Notional, Fanciful, Uncertain, Erratic, Chancy, Freakish, Wayward.
W	H	I	N	B	E	R	R	Y	Whortleberry.
W	H	I	R	L	I	G	I	G	Merry-go-round.
W	H	I	R	L	P	O	O	L	Eddy, Vortex, Maelstrom, Bustle, Flurry, Furore, Fuss, Stir.
W	H	I	R	L	W	I	N	D	Hurricane, Tornado, Bustle, Furore.
W	H	I	T	E	F	I	S	H	Various food fishes resembling the salmon and trout.
W	H	I	T	E	W	A	S	H	White coating, Palliate, Extenuate, Gloss over, Varnish, Veneer, Clear.
W	H	O	L	E	S	A	L	E	Sale of goods in quantity for resale by retail traders.
W	H	O	L	E	S	O	M	E	Beneficial, Salutary, Remedial, Healthy, Prudent, Safe, Sound, Well.
W	I	D	E	A	N	G	L	E	Angle of view wider than normal.
W	I	D	O	W	H	O	O	D	The period of being a widow.

1	2	3	4	5	6	7	8	9	
W	I	L	L	I	N	G	L	Y	In a willing manner.
W	I	N	D	B	R	E	A	K	Something that protects from the wind.
W	I	N	D	S	W	E	P	T	Swept by the wind, Untidy.
W	I	S	T	F	U	L	L	Y	Pensively, Mournfully, Longingly.
W	I	T	C	H	B	A	L	L	An eighteenth century hollow glass sphere suspended to ward off evil spirits.
W	I	T	C	H	H	U	N	T	Search, Investigation, Campaign against political opponents.
W	I	T	H	D	R	A	W	N	Isolated, Secluded, Introverted, Shrinking, Undemonstrative, Restrained, Aloof.
W	I	T	H	E	R	I	N	G	Decaying, Declining, Fading, Wasting, Paralyzing, Stunning, Shrivelling, Collapsing.
W	O	L	V	E	R	I	N	E	A North American carnivorous mammal.
W	O	M	A	N	F	O	L	K	Women of a group.
W	O	M	E	N	F	O	L	K	Same as WOMANFOLK.
W	O	M	A	N	H	O	O	D	The state of being a woman, Maturity of a female.
W	O	M	E	N	K	I	N	D	Women, The female members of a group.
W	O	N	D	E	R	F	U	L	Marvellous, Strange, Exciting, Astounding, Miraculous, Surprising, Stupendous.
W	O	O	D	C	H	U	C	K	Marmot.
W	O	O	D	C	R	A	F	T	Knowledge of forest areas in order to be able to exist under primitive conditions.
W	O	O	D	L	O	U	S	E	A termite that lives in bark, wall cracks and old papers.
W	O	R	K	H	O	R	S	E	A horse used for labour, Person who works too hard, A useful vehicle, Drudge.
W	O	R	K	H	O	U	S	E	An institution where the poor were kept to work under appalling conditions.
W	O	R	L	D	W	I	D	E	Universal, Cosmopolitan, Global.
W	O	R	R	I	S	O	M	E	Something that causes anxiety or is reason for concern.
W	O	R	T	H	L	E	S	S	Useless, Low, Despicable, Unproductive, Incompetent, Valueless, Defective.
W	R	A	N	G	L	I	N	G	Brawling, Bickering, Quarrelling, Squabbling, Fighting, Disputing.
W	R	E	N	C	H	I	N	G	Wresting, Wringing, Twisting, Compelling, Forcing, Tearing, Spraining, Turning.
W	R	E	S	T	L	I	N	G	Grappling, Tussling, Scuffling, Struggling, Exerting, Stretching, Striving, Straining.
W	R	I	G	G	L	I	N	G	Squirming, Writhing, Squiggling, Oozing, Sliding, Flowing.
W	R	I	S	T	L	O	C	K	A wrestling hold of a twisting grip on a wrist.
W	R	O	N	G	N	E	S	S	The state of being wrong.

X

1	2	3	4	5	6	7	8	9	
X	A	N	T	H	E	N	Y	L	A univalent radical derived from xanthene.
X	A	N	T	H	I	D	A	E	The largest family of crabs.
X	A	N	T	H	O	G	E	N	A univalent radical derived from xanthic acid.
X	A	N	T	H	O	R	I	A	A genus of yellow or orange lichen.
X	A	N	T	H	O	S	I	S	Yellow discolouration of the skin from abnormal causes.
X	E	N	O	B	L	A	S	T	A crystal in metamorphic rock.
X	E	N	O	P	H	I	L	E	One attracted to anything foreign.
X	E	N	O	P	H	O	B	E	One unduly afraid of foreign people or things.
X	E	R	O	D	E	R	M	A	A skin disease manifested by dryness and roughness.
X	E	R	O	P	H	A	G	Y	The strict Christian fast at Lent.
X	Y	L	O	P	H	O	N	E	A percussion musical instrument consisting of wooden bars struck with hammers.

Y

1	2	3	4	5	6	7	8	9	
Y	A	C	H	T	S	M	A	N	One who sails a yacht.
Y	A	R	D	S	T	I	C	K	A measuring stick three feet long marked in smaller fractions, Criterion, Standard.
Y	E	S	T	E	R	D	A	Y	The day preceding today.
Y	G	G	D	R	A	S	I	L	A tree in Scandinavian mythology.
Y	O	D	E	L	L	I	N	G	Singing in a Tyrolean fashion.
Y	O	U	N	G	S	T	E	R	Youth, Juvenile, Child.
Y	T	T	E	R	B	I	U	M	A metallic element of the rare-earth group.

Z

1	2	3	4	5	6	7	8	9	
Z	A	N	C	L	I	D	A	E	A family of marine fishes, Moorish idols.
Z	A	P	A	T	E	A	D	O	Rhythmic stamping of feet in a Spanish dance.
Z	A	P	O	D	I	D	A	E	Family of rodents, Jumping mice.
Z	E	A	L	O	U	S	L	Y	In a zealous manner.
Z	E	I	T	G	E	I	S	T	The spirit of the time.
Z	E	O	M	O	R	P	H	I	A small order of marine bony fishes, John Dorys.
Z	E	U	G	L	O	D	O	N	Extinct slender-toothed whales.
Z	I	G	A	D	E	N	U	S	Genus of herbs.
Z	I	P	H	I	I	D	A	E	A family of toothed whales.

1	2	3	4	5	6	7	8	9	
Z	I	R	C	O	N	I	U	M	A steel-gray strong ductile high-melting metallic element.
Z	O	A	R	C	I	D	A	E	A family of chiefly artic and antarctic blennies.
Z	O	L	L	E	R	N	I	A	Genus of Brazilian timber trees.
Z	O	N	I	T	I	D	A	E	A family of small terrestrial snails.
Z	O	O	G	R	A	P	H	Y	Descriptive zoology.
Z	O	O	L	O	G	I	S	T	A specialist in zoology.
Z	O	O	P	H	I	L	I	A	Erotic fixation on animals.
Z	O	O	P	H	Y	T	I	C	A plant resembling an animal.
Z	O	R	A	P	T	E	R	A	Order of minute terrestrial insects.
Z	U	C	C	H	E	T	T	O	A small round skull cap worn by ecclesiastics of the Roman Catholic church.
Z	W	A	N	Z	I	G	E	R	A former Austrian and German coin.
Z	Y	G	O	M	A	T	I	C	Relating to the zygomatic arch.
Z	Y	G	O	S	P	O	R	E	A plant spore.
Z	Y	M	O	G	E	N	I	C	Capable of causing fermentation.
Z	Y	M	O	M	E	T	E	R	An instrument for determining the degree of fermentation.
Z	Y	M	O	S	C	O	P	E	Apparatus for determining the fermenting power of yeast.

1	2	3	4	5	6	7	8	9	10	
A	B	B	R	E	V	I	A	T	E	Shorten, Abridge, Restrict, Reduce, Curtail, Retrench, Extenuate.
A	B	D	I	C	A	T	I	O	N	Renunciation, Surrender.
A	B	E	R	R	A	T	I	O	N	Deviation, Deflection, Departure, Divergence, Rarity, Diversion, Insanity, Derangement.
A	B	H	O	R	R	E	N	C	E	Loathing, Aversion, Detestation, Hatred, Horror, Loathing, Repugnance, Revulsion.
A	B	I	O	T	R	O	P	H	Y	Degeneration of organism, cell or tissue without injury.
A	B	J	U	R	A	T	I	O	N	Rejection, Renunciation, Retraction.
A	B	N	E	G	A	T	I	O	N	Self-denial, Humility, Renunciation, Restraint.
A	B	O	M	I	N	A	B	L	E	Detestable, Loathsome, Disagreeable, Unpleasant, Odious, Offensive, Repugnant.
A	B	O	R	I	G	I	N	A	L	Indigenous, Primitive, Native.
A	B	O	R	T	I	C	I	D	E	Drug-induced termination of pregnancy.
A	B	R	E	A	C	T	I	O	N	Removal of en emotion caused by a repressed memory, usually by a therapist.
A	B	R	O	G	A	T	I	O	N	Cancellation, Nullification.
A	B	R	U	P	T	N	E	S	S	Bluntness, Curtness, Gruffness, Briskness, Hastiness, Suddenness.
A	B	S	C	I	S	S	I	O	N	Natural separation of flowers, fruit and leaves from plants.
A	B	S	O	L	U	T	I	O	N	Forgiveness, Acquittal, Pardon, Remission, Amnesty.
A	B	S	O	L	U	T	I	S	M	The doctrine of what is absolute, unconditional or independent.
A	B	S	O	L	V	I	T	O	R	Acquittal.
A	B	S	O	R	B	E	N	C	Y	The ability of a layer of a substance to absorb radiation.
A	B	S	O	R	P	T	I	O	N	Assimilation, Incorporation, The process of absorbing.
A	B	S	T	E	M	I	O	U	S	Temperate, Sober, Ascetic, Austere, Sparing.
A	B	S	T	E	N	T	I	O	N	Withholding, Non-participation, Refraining.
A	B	S	T	E	R	G	E	N	T	Detergent.
A	B	S	T	I	N	E	N	C	E	Self-restraint, Self-denial, Self-discipline, Postponement, Temperance.
A	B	S	T	R	A	C	T	E	D	Removed, Separated, Epitomized, Summarized, Detached, Disconnected, Parted.
A	B	U	N	D	A	N	T	L	Y	Fully, Amply, Plentifully.
A	C	A	D	E	M	I	C	A	L	Scholarly, Visionary, Convential, Realistic, Speculative, Abstract, Impractical.
A	C	C	E	L	E	R	A	T	E	Hasten, Hurry, Quicken, Speed, Drive, Impel.
A	C	C	E	N	T	U	A	T	E	Emphasize, Stress, Accent.
A	C	C	E	P	T	A	B	L	E	Satisfactory, Welcome, Pleasing, Adequate, Tolerable, Ordinary, Good, Sufficient.
A	C	C	E	P	T	A	N	C	E	Approval, Acquiescence, Acceptability.
A	C	C	E	S	S	I	B	L	E	Approachable, Communicative, Available, Comprehensible.
A	C	C	I	D	E	N	T	A	L	Unpredictable, Contingent, Extrinsic, Casual.
A	C	C	O	M	P	L	I	C	E	Associate, One in partnership with another in a crime.
A	C	C	O	M	P	L	I	S	H	Perform, Achieve, Fulfill, Traverse, Execute, Perfect, Complete.
A	C	C	O	U	N	T	A	N	T	One in charge of public and private finances and/or accounts.
A	C	C	R	E	D	I	T	E	D	Approved, Ascribed, Publicly sanctioned, Officially vouched, Guaranteed.
A	C	C	U	M	U	L	A	T	E	Collect, Gather, Hoard, Amass, Garner, Store, Fund, Treasure.
A	C	C	U	R	A	T	E	L	Y	Precisely, Exactly.
A	C	C	U	S	A	T	I	O	N	Allegation, Indictment, Charge of wrongdoing.
A	C	C	U	S	A	T	O	R	Y	Accusing, Accusatory.
A	C	C	U	S	A	T	O	R	Y	Accusing.
A	C	C	U	S	T	O	M	E	D	Customary, Habitual, Usual, Used, Confirmed, Accepted, Routine, Conventional.
A	C	E	P	H	A	L	O	U	S	Without a head, Truncated, Lacking a chief.
A	C	E	R	V	U	L	I	N	E	Resembling little heaps, Heaped.
A	C	E	T	O	M	E	T	R	Y	The method for estimating the amount of acetic acid present in a liquid.
A	C	H	I	E	V	A	B	L	E	Attainable.
A	C	H	R	O	M	A	T	I	C	Free from colour, Neutral.
A	C	I	D	I	M	E	T	R	Y	Measurement of the strength of an acid.
A	C	I	D	O	L	Y	S	I	S	A chemical reaction in which acid is used instead of water.
A	C	I	D	U	L	A	T	E	D	Made acid, Condition of being acid.
A	C	I	N	O	S	E	O	U	S	Covered with vesicles like grape seeds.
A	C	O	T	Y	L	E	D	O	N	A plant without cotyledons.
A	C	O	U	S	T	I	C	A	L	Auditory, Aural, Controlled by sound. Specializing in acoustics.
A	C	Q	U	I	E	S	C	E	D	Agreed, consented, assented, concurred, accommodated, acceded.
A	C	R	A	S	I	E	A	E	S	Fungi related to slime moulds.
A	C	R	O	M	E	G	A	L	Y	A chronic disease of adults that results from a disease of the pituitary.
A	C	R	O	P	H	O	B	I	A	An abnormal fear of heights.
A	C	R	O	T	E	R	I	U	M	A pedestal placed on a pediment to support an ornamentation.
A	C	R	O	T	E	R	I	O	N	Same as ACROTERIUM.
A	C	T	I	O	N	A	B	L	E	Subject to a law suit.
A	C	T	I	V	A	T	I	O	N	The process of activating.
A	C	T	O	M	Y	O	S	I	N	Substance involved in muscle contractions.
A	D	A	C	T	Y	L	O	U	S	Minus fingers and toes, crustaceans without claws.
A	D	A	M	A	N	T	I	N	E	Diamond hard.
A	D	A	P	T	A	T	I	O	N	Adjusting, Modification, Alteration, Conformation.
A	D	D	I	T	I	O	N	A	L	Added, Further, Another, More, Other, Accessory, Extra, Supplementary.
A	D	E	N	E	C	T	O	M	Y	Surgical removal of a gland.

1	2	3	4	5	6	7	8	9	10	
A	D	J	E	C	T	I	V	A	L	Adjective.
A	D	J	U	D	I	C	A	T	E	To settle finally, Arbitrate, Referee, Umpire.
A	D	J	U	R	A	T	I	O	N	To command solemnly as under oath, earnest appeal.
A	D	J	U	S	T	M	E	N	T	Alteration, Adaptation, Reconciling, Correction, Attunement, Stabilization.
A	D	M	I	N	I	S	T	E	R	Manage, Superintend, Minister, Direct, Dispense, To give remedially.
A	D	M	I	R	A	T	I	O	N	Regard, Wonder, Amazement, Ecstasy, Rapture, Transport, Esteem, Reverence.
A	D	M	O	N	I	T	I	O	N	Rebuke, Chiding, Reprimand, Reproach, Reproof, Warning, Caution.
A	D	O	L	E	S	C	E	N	T	One between youth and maturity.
A	D	R	E	N	E	R	G	I	C	Adrenaline-like chemical activity.
A	D	R	O	I	T	N	E	S	S	Dexterity, Cleverness, Nimbleness, Prowess, Readiness, Expertise, Skill.
A	D	S	O	R	P	T	I	O	N	Process by which gases, vapours and solution adhere to certain exposed surfaces.
A	D	S	O	R	P	T	I	V	E	Adsorbent.
A	D	U	L	T	E	R	A	N	T	An adulterating agent.
A	D	U	L	T	E	R	A	T	E	Corrupt, Debase, Alter, Treat, Pollute, Dilute, Manipulate, Defile.
A	D	U	L	T	E	R	E	S	S	A woman who commits adultery.
A	D	V	E	N	T	U	R	E	R	A mercenary fighter, Soldier of fortune, One who lives by his wits.
A	D	V	E	R	T	I	S	E	R	One who advertises.
A	E	R	O	B	A	T	I	C	S	Spectacular flying feats.
A	E	R	O	B	I	O	S	I	S	Life requiring oxygen or air.
A	E	R	O	P	H	O	B	I	A	Fear of fresh air.
A	E	R	O	S	O	L	I	Z	E	To disperse as an aerosol.
A	E	S	T	H	E	T	I	C	S	Branch of philosophy dealing with beauty.
A	F	F	A	B	I	L	I	T	Y	Sociability.
A	F	F	E	T	T	U	O	S	O	Direction in music-tender.
A	F	F	I	N	A	T	I	O	N	Treatment of raw sugar crystals to remove molasses.
A	F	F	L	I	C	T	I	O	N	Trial, Tribulation, Visitation, Sorrow, Anguish, Woe, Heartbreak, Infirmity.
A	F	T	E	R	P	I	E	C	E	A short, often music entertainment performed after a play.
A	G	G	R	A	N	D	I	Z	E	Increase, Augment, Exalt, Enable, Expand, Magnify, Amplify, Distinguish.
A	G	G	R	E	S	S	I	O	N	Attack, Assault, Offensive, Onslaught, Belligerence, Fight, Pugnacity, Invasion.
A	G	G	R	E	S	S	I	V	E	Militant, Enterprising, Self-confident, Assertive, Pushing, Belligerent, Domineering.
A	G	R	O	N	O	M	I	S	T	Specialist in the branch of agriculture dealing with soil management.
A	L	B	U	M	E	N	I	Z	E	To saturate with albumen.
A	L	B	U	M	I	N	O	I	D	Protein.
A	L	C	O	H	O	L	I	S	M	Addiction to alcohol.
A	L	D	O	H	E	X	O	S	E	An aldose sugar.
A	L	D	R	O	V	A	N	D	A	Genus of floating aquatic plants.
A	L	E	M	B	I	C	A	T	E	Refine to an essence.
A	L	G	E	B	R	A	I	S	T	A specialist in algebra.
A	L	G	O	P	H	O	B	I	A	A morbid fear of pain.
A	L	I	E	N	A	T	I	O	N	Withdrawing, Diverting, Estranging.
A	L	I	M	E	N	T	A	R	Y	Nutritious, Furnishing maintenance.
A	L	K	A	L	I	N	I	T	Y	State of being alkaline.
A	L	K	O	X	Y	L	A	T	E	To introduce alkoxyl into a substance.
A	L	L	A	R	G	A	N	D	O	Direction in music - perform more slowly.
A	L	L	E	G	A	T	I	O	N	Accusation, Charge, Count, Statement, Assertion.
A	L	L	E	G	I	A	N	C	E	Fidelity, Faithfulness, Fealty, Loyalty, Dedication, Piety, Devotion, Homage.
A	L	L	E	G	O	R	I	Z	E	To make into allegory.
A	L	L	E	G	R	E	T	T	O	Direction in music-faster than andante but not so fast as allegro.
A	L	L	I	A	C	E	O	U	S	Of the onion or garlic family, To taste or smell of garlic.
A	L	L	I	G	A	T	I	O	N	State of being attached.
A	L	L	I	T	E	R	A	T	E	To form an alliteration.
A	L	L	O	C	A	T	I	O	N	Apportionment, Allotment, Lot, Allowance, Share.
A	L	L	O	C	U	T	I	O	N	A strong authorative speech.
A	L	L	O	P	A	T	H	I	C	Relating to allopathy.
A	L	L	O	P	A	T	R	I	C	Relative to separate geographical areas.
A	L	L	O	S	A	U	R	U	S	Genus of North American carnivorous dinosaurs.
A	L	L	O	T	R	O	P	I	C	Having a lowered nutritive value.
A	L	L	O	X	A	N	T	I	N	A crystalline compound formed by oxidation or uric acid.
A	L	L	U	R	E	M	E	N	T	Allure, Fascination, Charm, Attraction, Power, Lure, Seduction, Temptation.
A	L	P	E	N	S	T	O	C	K	A long, iron-pointed staff used in mountain climbing.
A	L	P	H	A	B	E	T	I	C	Belonging to an alphabet.
A	L	P	H	A	M	E	R	I	C	Capable of using letters and numbers in the same operation.
A	L	T	A	R	P	I	E	C	E	A work of art to decorate the space above an altar.
A	L	T	E	R	A	T	I	O	N	Change, Modification, Turn, Variation, Adaption, Transition, Adjustment, Transformation.
A	L	T	E	R	A	T	I	V	E	Alterative medicine used to restore health.
A	L	T	E	R	N	A	T	O	R	An electric generator for producing alternating current.
A	L	T	O	G	E	T	H	E	R	Wholly, Completely, Thoroughly.

1	2	3	4	5	6	7	8	9	10	
A	M	A	N	U	E	N	S	I	S	Secretary.
A	M	A	R	I	L	L	I	T	E	A mineral consisting of a hydrous sodium feroic sulfate.
A	M	A	T	E	U	R	I	S	H	Lacking professional finish.
A	M	B	A	S	S	A	D	O	R	An official representative of a sovereign or state.
A	M	B	I	V	A	L	E	N	T	Exhibiting ambivalence.
A	M	B	U	L	A	T	O	R	Y	Related to walking, Itinerant, Peripatetic, Alterable, Nomadic, Roving, Vagabond.
A	M	E	L	I	O	R	A	T	E	Improve, Amend, Better, Help, Alleviate, Mitigate, Relieve, Recuperate.
A	M	E	R	C	E	M	E	N	T	The infliction of a penalty at the discretion of the court.
A	M	I	A	B	I	L	I	T	Y	Genial disposition.
A	M	M	O	N	I	A	T	E	D	Impregnated with ammonia.
A	M	M	U	N	I	T	I	O	N	Explosive military items.
A	M	P	E	L	O	P	S	I	S	A genus of woody climbers, Virginia creeper, Boston ivy.
A	M	P	H	I	B	I	O	U	S	Able to live on land and in water.
A	M	P	H	I	S	P	O	R	E	A modified unrediniospore that is characteristic of certain rusts in arid regions.
A	M	P	H	O	T	E	R	I	C	Capable of reacting chemically either as an acid or as a base.
A	M	P	I	C	I	L	L	I	N	An antibiotic for treating various infections.
A	M	P	U	T	A	T	I	O	N	Cutting, Pruning, Excision.
A	M	Y	L	A	C	E	O	U	S	Starchy.
A	N	A	C	A	R	D	I	U	M	A small genus of tropical American trees, Cashew.
A	N	A	C	U	L	T	U	R	E	A mixed bacterial culture.
A	N	A	L	Y	T	I	C	A	L	Logical, Subtle.
A	N	A	P	L	A	S	T	I	C	Restoration of missing or damaged parts, i.e. plastic surgery.
A	N	A	R	T	H	R	O	U	S	Without joints.
A	N	A	S	T	R	E	P	H	A	Genus of tropical American fruit flies.
A	N	A	T	O	M	I	C	A	L	Related to anatomy.
A	N	C	I	S	T	R	O	I	D	Shaped like a hook.
A	N	D	E	S	I	N	I	T	E	A leucocratic rock composed essentially of andesine.
A	N	E	C	D	O	T	I	S	T	One who tells anecdotes.
A	N	E	M	O	G	R	A	P	H	A recording wind gauge.
A	N	E	M	O	M	E	T	E	R	Wind gauge, An instrument for measuring and indicating the force and speed of wind.
A	N	G	I	O	S	P	E	R	M	A seed plant.
A	N	G	I	O	S	T	O	M	Y	The surgical establishment of an opening into a blood vessel.
A	N	G	L	O	P	H	I	L	E	One who admires the English and their way of life.
A	N	G	L	O	P	H	O	B	E	One who dislikes anything English.
A	N	G	U	L	A	R	I	T	Y	Being angular in form.
A	N	I	M	A	L	C	U	L	E	A microscopic organism.
A	N	I	S	O	M	E	L	E	S	A small genus of herbs.
A	N	N	I	H	I	L	A	T	E	Nullify, Abrogate, Abolish, Invalidate, Eradicate, Exterminate, Demolish.
A	N	N	O	T	A	T	I	O	N	A note giving additional information about a book.
A	N	N	U	N	C	I	A	T	E	Announce.
A	N	O	R	E	X	I	A	N	T	One suffering from a pathological loss of appetite.
A	N	S	W	E	R	A	B	L	E	Accountable, Responsible, Suitable, Fitting, Equal, Adequate, Accordant.
A	N	T	A	G	O	N	I	S	T	Opponent, Adversary.
A	N	T	A	G	O	N	I	Z	E	Contest, Counteract.
A	N	T	A	R	C	T	I	C	A	South Pole.
A	N	T	E	C	E	D	E	N	T	Ancestor, Forefather, Prior, Presumptive, Preceding, Former, Previous, Parent.
A	N	T	H	O	P	H	Y	T	A	A division including all flowering plants.
A	N	T	H	R	A	C	E	N	E	Crystalline tricyclic hydrocarbon.
A	N	T	H	R	A	C	I	T	E	Hard compact natural coal.
A	N	T	H	R	O	P	O	I	D	Apes resembling man, Suggesting brutality.
A	N	T	I	B	I	O	S	I	S	Antagonistic association between organisms.
A	N	T	I	B	I	O	T	I	C	A substance produced by a micro-organism and able to kill another micro-organism.
A	N	T	I	C	H	A	N	C	E	Factions in evolution regarded as vitalistic and non-materialistic.
A	N	T	I	C	H	R	I	S	T	One who denies or opposes Christ.
A	N	T	I	C	I	P	A	N	T	In advance.
A	N	T	I	C	I	P	A	T	E	Foresee, Prevent, Forecast, Presage, Expect, See, Visualize, Contemplate.
A	N	T	I	C	L	I	M	A	X	Disappointment of expectation.
A	N	T	I	L	A	R	V	A	L	Control measures against disease-carrying insects.
A	N	T	I	L	U	E	T	I	C	Antisyphilitic.
A	N	T	I	M	O	N	A	T	E	A salt containing pentavalent, antimony and oxygen in the amon.
A	N	T	I	Q	U	A	T	E	D	Obsolete, Deep-rooted, Inveterate, Old, Archaic, Antique, Old-fashioned, Fusty.
A	N	T	I	S	E	P	S	I	S	Disinfection, Sterilization.
A	N	T	I	S	E	P	T	I	C	Scrupulous cleanliness, Sterilized, Free from contamination.
A	N	T	I	S	O	C	I	A	L	Recluse, Reserved, Solitary, Remote, Cynical, Withdrawn, Hostile to society.
A	N	T	I	T	H	E	S	I	S	Contrary, Opposite, Counter, Reverse, Contradictory, Opposition, Antagonism.
A	N	T	O	N	Y	M	O	U	S	Opposite, Opposing, Contradicting.
A	P	I	C	U	L	T	U	R	E	Breeding of bees.

1	2	3	4	5	6	7	8	9	10	
A	P	O	G	O	N	I	D	A	E	Family of tropical fishes, some of which incubate the eggs in the mouth.
A	P	O	L	O	G	E	T	I	C	Remorseful, Attritional, Contrite, Penitent, Regretful, Repentant, Sorry, Justification.
A	P	O	P	H	T	H	E	G	M	A short instructive saying.
A	P	O	P	L	E	C	T	I	C	Relating to apoplexy.
A	P	O	T	H	E	C	A	R	Y	Pharmacist, One who dispenses drugs for medicinal purposes.
A	P	O	T	H	E	C	I	U	M	A spore-bearing structure in many lichens and fungi.
A	P	P	A	R	E	N	T	L	Y	Seemingly, Evidently, Ostensibly, Outwardly, Professedly, Officially.
A	P	P	A	R	I	T	I	O	N	Phenomenon, Ghost, Phantom, Spectre, Appearance.
A	P	P	E	A	R	A	N	C	E	Aspect, Look, Mien, Semblance, Bearing, Countenance, Demeanour, Showing.
A	P	P	E	T	I	Z	I	N	G	Palatable, Relishing, Flavoursome, Savoury, Tasty.
A	P	P	L	A	U	D	I	N	G	Clapping, Praising, Commending, Complimenting, Cheering, Acclaiming, Lauding.
A	P	P	L	E	S	A	U	C	E	A relish of apples stewed to a pulp.
A	P	P	L	I	C	A	B	L	E	Appropriate, Relevant, Apropos, Material, Pertinent, Compatible, Congenial.
A	P	P	L	I	C	A	T	O	R	A device for applying something to another surface.
A	P	P	O	S	I	T	I	O	N	Placing side by side.
A	P	P	R	E	C	I	A	T	E	Value, Prize, Treasure, Cherish, Esteem, Respect, Admire, Understood.
A	P	P	R	E	N	T	I	C	E	Novice, One learning a trade by being indentured to a craftsman.
A	P	T	E	R	Y	G	I	A	L	Without paired fins or limbs.
A	Q	U	A	F	O	R	T	I	S	Nitric acid.
A	Q	U	A	M	A	R	I	N	E	A transparent variety of beryl that varies between blue and green in colour.
A	R	A	L	K	Y	L	A	T	E	To introduce aralkyl into.
A	R	A	N	E	O	L	O	G	Y	Study of spiders.
A	R	B	I	T	R	A	T	O	R	Judge, Referee, Umpire, Moderator.
A	R	C	H	B	I	S	H	O	P	Chief bishop.
A	R	C	H	I	T	R	A	V	E	Main beam resting on two columns, Moulded door or window frame.
A	R	I	S	T	O	C	R	A	T	Noble, Superior, High-ranking.
A	R	I	T	H	M	E	T	I	C	Computation with numbers, Calculation, Reckoning.
A	R	M	A	G	E	D	D	O	N	The final conflict between the forces of good and evil.
A	R	O	M	A	T	I	T	E	S	Precious stone of ancient Arabia and Egypt.
A	R	R	O	G	A	N	T	L	Y	Proudly, Insolently, Superciliously, Pompously, Cavalierly, Disdainfully.
A	R	T	H	R	A	L	G	I	A	Neuralgic pain in the joints.
A	R	T	I	C	U	L	A	T	E	Distinct, Vocal, Enunciate, Pronounce, Integrate, Connect, Join, Organize.
A	R	T	I	F	I	C	I	A	L	Synthetic, Man-made, Fabricated, Fake, Unreal, Imitation, Simulated, Pretend.
A	S	A	F	O	E	T	I	D	A	The fetid gum resin of various Iranian and East Indian plants.
A	S	B	E	S	T	O	S	I	S	Lung disease caused by the inhalation of fine particles of asbestos.
A	S	C	E	N	D	A	N	C	Y	Domination, Controlling, Governing, Supremacy, Sovereignty, Preeminence.
A	S	C	O	M	Y	C	E	T	E	Class of higher fungi.
A	S	C	R	I	P	T	I	O	N	The act of ascribing.
A	S	P	H	Y	X	I	A	T	E	Suffocate, Choke, Smother, Stifle.
A	S	P	I	D	I	S	T	R	A	Genus of Asiatic herbs with large handsome leaves.
A	S	P	I	R	A	T	I	N	G	Panting, Aim, Strong desire, Hungering, Struggling.
A	S	S	A	I	L	A	B	L	E	Capable of being attacked.
A	S	S	E	M	B	L	A	G	E	Aggregation, Gathering, Collection, Company, Congregation, Crowd, Group, Muster.
A	S	S	E	S	S	A	B	L	E	Capable of being assessed.
A	S	S	E	S	S	M	E	N	T	Valuation, Levy, Appraisal, Estimate, Tax, Impost, Tariff, Judgement.
A	S	S	E	V	E	R	A	T	E	Swear, Affirm.
A	S	S	I	G	N	M	E	N	T	Appointment, Task, Liability, Duty, Stint, Obligation, Job, Responsibility.
A	S	S	I	M	I	L	A	T	E	Appropriate, Conform, Resemble, Absorb, Imbibe, Infuse, Equate, Compare.
A	S	S	I	S	T	A	N	C	E	Aid, Help, Comfort, Relief, Succour, Support, Backing, Upholding.
A	S	S	O	C	I	A	T	E	D	Joined, Attended, United, Merged, Combined, Coupled, Linked, Amalgamated.
A	S	S	U	M	P	T	I	O	N	Taking up into heaven, Incorporation, Supposition, Usurpation, Arrogance, Premise.
A	S	S	U	R	G	E	N	C	Y	The tendecy to rise.
A	S	T	E	R	O	I	D	A	L	Belonging to the asteroids.
A	S	T	O	U	N	D	I	N	G	Amazing, Astonishing, Miraculous, Staggering, Stupendous, Surprising, Wonderful.
A	S	T	R	A	G	A	L	U	S	A large genus of herbs and shrubs, Locoweed.
A	S	T	R	I	N	G	E	N	T	Constricting, Contracting, Styptic, Severe, Austere, Sharp, Tonic, Stern.
A	S	T	R	I	O	N	I	C	S	Electronics applied to astronautics.
A	S	T	R	O	L	O	G	E	R	One that practices astrology.
A	S	T	R	O	N	O	M	E	R	Observer of celestial phenomena.
A	T	H	Y	R	E	O	S	I	S	An abnormal condition caused by functional deficiency of the thyroid gland.
A	T	M	O	S	P	H	E	R	E	Mass of air surrounding the earth, Aura, Feeling, Mood, Semblance, Character.
A	T	T	A	C	H	M	E	N	T	Affection, Love, Fastening, Regard, Fidelity, Adherence, Adhesion, Devotion.
A	T	T	A	I	N	M	E	N	T	Achievement, Accomplishment, Acquisition, Finish.
A	T	T	E	N	D	A	N	C	E	Presence, Retinue, Attending.
A	T	T	E	N	U	A	T	E	D	Weakened, Lessened, Rarefied, Dissipated, Constricted, Deflated, Crippled, Undermined.
A	T	T	R	A	C	T	I	V	E	Pleasing, Alluring, Bewitching, Charming, Fascinating, Enchanting.
A	U	C	T	I	O	N	E	E	R	One who conducts a sale by auction.

1	2	3	4	5	6	7	8	9	10	
A	U	D	I	T	O	R	I	U	M	A building designed for the assembling of an audience.
A	U	G	U	S	T	N	E	S	S	Stateliness.
A	U	R	I	C	U	L	A	T	E	Possessing ears, being ear-shaped.
A	U	R	I	F	E	R	O	U	S	Rock or gravel containing gold.
A	U	S	C	U	L	T	A	T	E	Medical examination with stethoscope or other instrument.
A	U	S	P	I	C	I	O	U	S	Propitious, Prosperous, Favourable.
A	U	T	E	C	O	L	O	G	Y	Ecology of a species.
A	U	T	H	O	R	I	Z	E	D	Sanctioned, Justified, Qualified, Licensed, Empowered, Endorsed, Entitled, Permitted.
A	U	T	H	O	R	S	H	I	P	The profession of writing.
A	U	T	O	C	H	T	H	O	N	Indigenous person, animal or plant.
A	U	T	O	C	R	A	T	I	C	Despotic, Absolute, Arbitrary, Tyrannical, Arrogant, Haughty, Overbearing.
A	U	T	O	G	N	O	S	I	S	Self-knowledge.
A	U	T	O	M	A	T	I	O	N	Automatically controlled operation of an apparatus, process or system.
A	U	T	O	M	A	T	I	S	M	The state of being automatic.
A	U	T	O	M	O	B	I	L	E	Vehicle propelled by an internal combustion engine.
A	U	T	O	N	O	M	O	U	S	Power of self-government, Self-contained.
A	U	T	O	P	L	A	S	T	Y	The repairing of lesions with tissue from the same body.
A	U	T	O	S	T	Y	L	I	C	Having the jaw connected directly with the cranium.
A	U	T	O	T	H	E	I	S	M	Self-worship.
A	V	A	R	I	C	I	O	U	S	Covetous, Cupidity, Rapacity.
A	V	E	N	T	U	R	I	N	E	Glass containing opaque particles of a sparkling material.
A	V	I	C	U	L	A	R	I	A	Genus of large tropical spiders, Bird spiders.
A	Z	Y	G	O	S	P	O	R	E	A reproductive body found in certain fungi.

B

1	2	3	4	5	6	7	8	9	10	
B	A	B	I	R	O	U	S	S	A	A large hoglike quadruped of the East Indies.
B	A	C	K	G	A	M	M	O	N	A game played on a board with dice and counters.
B	A	C	K	H	A	N	D	E	D	Hesitant, Diffident.
B	A	C	K	L	I	N	I	N	G	Material used to strengthen the backbone of a book.
B	A	C	K	S	T	I	T	C	H	A hand stitch resembling machine stitching.
B	A	C	U	L	I	F	O	R	M	Shaped like a rod.
B	A	F	F	L	E	M	E	N	T	Perplexity, Confusion.
B	A	L	B	R	I	G	G	A	N	Cotton fabric originating in Ireland.
B	A	L	D	E	R	D	A	S	H	Nonsense, Trash, Bosh, Claptrap, Rubbish.
B	A	L	I	B	U	N	T	A	L	A fine lightweight straw.
B	A	L	L	O	O	N	I	S	T	One that ascends in a balloon.
B	A	L	N	E	A	T	I	O	N	The action of bathing.
B	A	L	N	E	O	L	O	G	Y	Study of medicinal effects of mineral baths.
B	A	L	U	S	T	R	A	D	E	A low parapet or barrier.
B	A	N	D	E	R	I	L	L	A	Decorated dart used in bullfighting.
B	A	N	I	S	H	M	E	N	T	Exclusion, Dismissal, Discarding, Exile, Deportation, Expulsion, Displacement.
B	A	N	K	R	U	P	T	C	Y	Ruin, Depletion, Exhaustion, Sterility, Barrenness.
B	A	P	T	I	S	T	E	R	Y	Part of the church used for baptismal services.
B	A	R	B	E	L	L	A	T	E	Having short hairs or bristles.
B	A	R	C	A	R	O	L	L	E	The boat song of the venetian gondoliers.
B	A	R	Y	S	P	H	E	R	E	The heavy interior portion of the earth within the lithosphere.
B	A	S	I	F	A	C	I	A	L	Relating to the lower part of the face.
B	A	S	K	E	T	B	A	L	L	A game played by two teams with a ball on an indoor court.
B	A	S	T	A	R	D	I	Z	E	Stigmatize, Debase, Degenerate, Deteriorate.
B	A	T	H	O	M	E	T	E	R	Instrument for measuring depth of water.
B	A	T	R	A	C	H	I	A	N	Relating to frogs and toads.
B	A	T	T	L	E	D	O	R	E	A tool with a long flat blade, A light racket used to strike a shuttlecock.
B	A	T	T	L	E	S	H	I	P	A heavily armoured warship.
B	A	Y	L	D	O	N	I	T	E	A mineral consisting of a lead copper arsenate.
B	E	A	U	T	I	C	I	A	N	Cosmetologist, An expert in the use of cosmetics, One who gives beauty treatments.
B	E	D	R	A	G	G	L	E	D	Soiled, Worn, Dilapidated, Decrepit, Saturated.
B	E	F	O	R	E	H	A	N	D	Before, Previously, In anticipation.
B	E	H	I	N	D	H	A	N	D	In arrears, Remiss, Backward, Tardy.
B	E	L	A	B	O	U	R	E	D	Assailed, Attacked, Beaten, Battered, Pounded, Thrashed.
B	E	L	L	A	D	O	N	N	A	A European poisonous plant from which atropine is produced.
B	E	L	L	R	I	N	G	E	R	One that rings a bell, Leader, One that takes the initiative.
B	E	L	L	W	E	T	H	E	R	The sheep that wears a bell.
B	E	L	O	N	G	I	N	G	S	Possessions, Adjuncts.
B	E	N	E	F	A	C	T	O	R	One that gives help, One that makes a bequest.
B	E	N	E	F	I	C	E	N	T	Performing acts of charity.

1	2	3	4	5	6	7	8	9	10	Definition
B	E	N	E	F	I	C	I	A	L	Helpful, Advantageous, Profitable, Good, Favourable, Propitious, Wholesome.
B	E	N	E	V	O	L	E	N	T	Philanthropic, Generous, Chivalrous, Considerate, Magnanimous, Altriustic.
B	E	N	Z	E	D	R	I	N	E	Trade name of amphetamine.
B	E	R	Y	C	O	I	D	E	I	Marine fishes possessing primitive features.
B	E	T	T	E	R	M	E	N	T	Improvement.
B	E	W	I	L	D	E	R	E	D	Perplexed, Confused, Puzzled, Confounded, Muddled, Baffled, Flustered, Muddled.
B	I	B	L	I	O	F	I	L	M	A microfilm usually used for photographing books.
B	I	B	L	I	O	P	O	L	E	A dealer in books.
B	I	C	A	P	S	U	L	A	R	A plant having two capsules.
B	I	C	O	R	N	U	A	T	E	Having two horns.
B	I	F	L	U	O	R	I	D	E	An acid fluoride.
B	I	L	L	I	E	T	I	T	E	A mineral consisting of a hydrous barium uranium oxide.
B	I	M	E	T	A	L	L	I	C	Composed of two different metals.
B	I	O	G	E	N	E	S	I	S	The development of life from pre-existing life.
B	I	O	P	H	Y	S	I	C	S	The physics of living organisms.
B	I	P	A	R	T	I	E	N	T	Dividing into two parts.
B	I	P	A	R	T	I	S	A	N	Coalition, Co-operation between two major political parties.
B	I	R	T	H	R	I	G	H	T	The inheritance of the firstborn.
B	I	S	S	E	X	T	I	L	E	Relating to a leap year.
B	I	T	T	E	R	N	E	S	S	The state of being bitter.
B	I	T	T	E	R	R	O	O	T	A succulent plant of the Rocky mountains.
B	I	T	U	M	I	N	O	U	S	Having the qualities of bitumen.
B	L	A	C	K	A	M	O	O	R	Negro, A dark-skinned person.
B	L	A	C	K	B	E	R	R	Y	A prickly bramble having dark purple sweet berries.
B	L	A	C	K	B	O	A	R	D	A thin broad piece of hard material used in a classroom for chalk writings.
B	L	A	C	K	G	U	A	R	D	Villain, Vagabond, Knave, Miscreant, Rascal, Rogue, Scoundrel.
B	L	A	C	K	S	M	I	T	H	A smith who works in a forge with iron.
B	L	A	N	C	M	A	N	G	E	A cold moulded dessert made with cornflour and milk.
B	L	A	N	Q	U	E	T	T	E	A white meat served with a white sauce.
B	L	A	S	T	O	C	Y	T	E	An undifferentiated embryonic cell.
B	L	A	S	T	O	M	E	R	E	A cell produced during cleavage.
B	L	E	P	H	A	R	I	S	M	Spasm of the eyelids.
B	L	I	S	S	F	U	L	L	Y	State of contentment.
B	L	I	S	T	E	R	I	N	G	Excoriating, Lashing, Scourging, Lambasting, Hot, Broiling, Execrable, Infernal.
B	L	I	T	H	E	R	I	N	G	Blathering, Absolsute, Blasted, Downright, Outright, Positive, Rank, Gross.
B	L	I	T	H	E	S	O	M	E	Cheery, Gay, Merry.
B	L	O	O	D	H	O	U	N	D	A large powerful hound that tracks by scent.
B	L	O	O	D	S	T	O	N	E	Hematite, A stone of green chalcedony sprinkled with red spots.
B	L	O	S	S	O	M	I	N	G	Flowering, Developing, Evolving, Expanding, Appearing, Unfolding, Burgeoning.
B	L	U	E	B	O	N	N	E	T	Wide flat round blue woollen cap, Australian parrot.
B	L	U	E	B	O	T	T	L	E	Cornflower, Grape hyacinth, Blowfly, Portugese man-of-war.
B	L	U	E	P	E	N	C	I	L	Edit, Delete, Revise, Censor, Eliminate.
B	L	U	E	R	I	B	B	O	N	First-rate, Outstanding, Highest quality.
B	L	U	S	T	E	R	I	N	G	Storming, Raging, Bullying, Hectoring, Roaring, Bellowing, Intimidating, Bludgeoning.
B	O	A	S	T	F	U	L	L	Y	Arrogantly, Vauntingly, Exultantly.
B	O	B	A	D	I	L	I	S	M	A state of being a braggart.
B	O	I	S	T	E	R	O	U	S	Massive, Rowdy, Brawling, Clamorous, Truculent, Vociferous, Turbulent, Disorderly.
B	O	L	L	W	E	E	V	I	L	A grayish weevil that infests the cotton plant.
B	O	S	E	L	A	P	H	U	S	A genus of Asiatic antelope.
B	O	T	H	E	R	S	O	M	E	Vexing.
B	O	W	D	L	E	R	I	Z	E	Expurgation, Censored, Screened.
B	R	A	C	H	Y	L	O	G	Y	Concise speech, shortened expression.
B	R	A	C	O	N	I	D	A	E	A large family of parasitic flies.
B	R	A	I	N	S	T	O	R	M	Violent mental derangement, Impractical idea.
B	R	E	A	D	F	R	U	I	T	A round seedless tropical fruit that resembles bread in colour.
B	R	E	A	S	T	B	O	N	E	The sternum.
B	R	E	A	T	H	L	E	S	S	Strenuous, Dead, Intense, Gripping, Dominating.
B	R	E	S	S	U	M	M	E	R	A beam, lintel or girder placed as a support.
B	R	I	C	K	L	A	Y	E	R	One that constructs structures from bricks.
B	R	I	D	E	G	R	O	O	M	A man about to be married.
B	R	I	D	E	S	M	A	I	D	A young woman attendant of a bride.
B	R	I	G	A	N	T	I	N	E	A light swift seagoing square rigged vessel.
B	R	I	G	H	T	N	E	S	S	Brilliance, Lustre, Splendour, Luminance.
B	R	I	L	L	I	A	N	C	E	Radiance, Intelligence.
B	R	O	A	D	S	W	O	R	D	A sword with a broad blade.
B	R	O	N	C	H	I	T	I	S	Inflammation of the bronchial tubes.
B	R	O	W	N	S	H	I	R	T	Member of the Nazi group.

1	2	3	4	5	6	7	8	9	10	
B	U	C	C	I	N	A	T	O	R	Cheek muscle.
B	U	D	G	E	R	I	G	A	R	Small Australian parrot.
B	U	F	F	L	E	H	E	A	D	Small North American duck.
B	U	F	F	O	O	N	E	R	Y	Coarse loutish behaviour.
B	U	R	D	E	N	S	O	M	E	Oppressive, Onerous, Demanding, Exacting, Taxing, Tough, Weighty.
B	U	R	E	A	U	C	R	A	T	A rigid formal government official.
B	U	T	T	E	R	B	E	A	N	Lima bean.
B	U	T	T	O	N	H	O	L	E	A bound or stitched slit or a loop to secure a button fastening.
B	U	T	T	O	N	H	O	O	K	A hook for drawing small buttons of gloves o shoes through buttonholes.
B	Y	S	T	R	O	M	I	T	E	A mineral consisting of a magnesium antimony oxide.

C

1	2	3	4	5	6	7	8	9	10	
C	A	B	A	L	A	S	S	O	U	A giant armadillo.
C	A	C	H	I	N	N	A	T	E	To laugh loudly or convulsively.
C	A	C	O	G	R	A	P	H	Y	Bad handwriting or spelling.
C	A	D	A	V	E	R	O	U	S	Suggestive of a corpse, Pallid, Livid, Gaunt, Emaciated.
C	A	D	U	C	I	C	O	R	N	Having deciduous horns.
C	A	L	A	M	A	N	D	E	R	The wood of an East Indian tree used for furniture.
C	A	L	A	M	I	T	O	U	S	Cataclysmic, Catastrophic, Disastrous, Fateful, Ruinous, Deplorable, Distressing.
C	A	L	C	A	R	E	O	U	S	Containing calcium carbonate.
C	A	L	C	E	I	F	O	R	M	Shaped like a slipper.
C	A	L	C	I	C	O	S	I	S	Lung disease caused by inhalation of limestone dust.
C	A	L	C	U	L	A	B	L	E	Dependable, Predictable.
C	A	L	C	U	L	A	T	O	R	One that calculates, A person who operates a calculating machine.
C	A	L	I	C	I	F	O	R	M	Shaped like a bell.
C	A	L	O	R	I	C	I	T	Y	Physiological ability to develop and maintain bodily heat.
C	A	L	U	M	N	I	A	T	E	Malign, Asperse, Defame, Denigrate, Libel, Scandalize, Slander, Vilify.
C	A	M	E	L	O	P	A	R	D	Giraffe.
C	A	M	E	R	L	E	N	G	O	Treasurer of the college of cardinals.
C	A	M	O	U	F	L	A	G	E	Conceal, Disguise, Dissemble, Becloud, Dissimulate, Mask.
C	A	M	P	E	S	T	R	A	L	Rural.
C	A	M	P	H	O	R	A	T	E	Impregnate with camphor.
C	A	M	P	O	N	O	T	U	S	Genus of ants, Carpenter ant, Sugar ant.
C	A	N	C	E	L	L	O	U	S	Having a spongy or porous structure.
C	A	N	D	E	L	A	B	R	A	A large candlestick having several arms.
C	A	N	T	A	L	O	U	P	E	A musk melon.
C	A	N	T	I	L	E	V	E	R	A projecting beam supported at only one end.
C	A	N	T	O	N	M	E	N	T	A temporary structure for housing troops.
C	A	N	V	A	S	S	I	N	G	Discussing, Debating, Soliciting, Spreading, Circulating, Scrutinizing, Examining.
C	A	P	A	B	I	L	I	T	Y	Being capable.
C	A	P	A	C	I	T	A	T	E	Qualify, To make capable.
C	A	P	I	L	O	T	A	D	E	A stew of various minced meats.
C	A	P	I	T	A	T	I	O	N	Counting or taxing per person individually.
C	A	P	I	T	U	L	A	R	Y	A collection of ordinances.
C	A	P	I	T	U	L	A	T	E	Negotiate, Treat, Agree, Yield, Acquiesce, Submit, Succumb, Defer.
C	A	P	P	U	C	C	I	N	O	Coffee topped with foamy milk.
C	A	P	R	E	O	L	A	T	E	Being with tendrils or similar to tendrils.
C	A	P	R	I	C	I	O	U	S	Changeable, Erratic, Whimsical, Inconstant, Wayward, Fickle, Uncertain, Variable.
C	A	R	A	B	I	N	E	E	R	A soldier armed with a carbine.
C	A	R	A	M	E	L	I	Z	E	To change the sugar content of food into caramel.
C	A	R	B	O	M	Y	C	I	N	A colourless crystalline basic antibiotic.
C	A	R	B	O	X	Y	L	I	C	Containing carboxyl.
C	A	R	B	U	R	E	T	O	R	An apparatus for supplying an internal combustion engine with suitable fuel.
C	A	R	D	I	A	L	G	I	A	Pain in the heart, Heartburn.
C	A	R	D	I	O	G	R	A	M	Tracing made by a cardiograph.
C	A	R	D	I	O	L	O	G	Y	The study of the heart and its diseases.
C	A	R	D	I	O	T	O	M	Y	Surgical incision of the heart.
C	A	R	D	U	A	C	E	A	E	Family of plants, Thistles, Asters.
C	A	R	E	L	E	S	S	L	Y	Negligently, Heedlessly, Rashly, Irresponsibly, Recklessly, Wildly.
C	A	R	I	C	A	C	E	A	E	Family of tropical and sub-tropical trees, Papaya, Paw-paw.
C	A	R	I	C	A	T	U	R	E	Sarody, Travesty, Burlesque, Mockery, Farce, Lampoon, Sham, Libel.
C	A	R	I	O	G	E	N	I	C	Conducive, to tooth decay.
C	A	R	I	T	A	T	I	V	E	Charitable in nature.
C	A	R	O	T	E	N	O	I	D	Yellow pigments found in vegetable oils or animal fats.
C	A	R	P	H	O	L	O	G	Y	Aimless semiconscious plucking at the bedclothes in abnormal conditions.

1	2	3	4	5	6	7	8	9	10	Definition
C	A	R	P	O	D	A	C	U	S	Genus of birds, Finches.
C	A	R	T	O	M	A	N	C	Y	Fortune telling by means of playing cards.
C	A	S	T	I	G	A	T	O	R	One that punishes.
C	A	S	U	A	L	N	E	S	S	The state of being casual.
C	A	T	A	F	A	L	Q	U	E	An elaborate structure for the lying-in-state of the body of an important person.
C	A	T	A	P	H	R	A	C	T	Suit of armour, Coat of mail.
C	A	T	A	P	L	A	S	I	A	Regressive biological change in cells or tissues.
C	A	T	S	C	R	A	D	L	E	A game played on the hands with string.
C	A	T	T	L	E	B	U	S	H	An Australian bush used as fodder during drought.
C	A	U	S	T	I	C	I	T	Y	Biting wit, Corrosiveness.
C	A	U	S	T	I	C	I	Z	E	To convert into a hydroxide by the use of lime.
C	A	U	T	I	O	N	A	R	Y	Cautious, Wary, Admonitory, Security, Surety, Warning.
C	A	U	T	I	O	U	S	L	Y	Warily, Carefully, Discreetly, Safely, Alertly, Shrewdly, Prudently.
C	A	V	A	L	I	E	R	L	Y	In a cavalier manner.
C	A	V	A	L	R	Y	M	A	N	A soldier that fights from horseback.
C	A	V	I	T	A	T	I	O	N	The formation of cavities in tissue or an organ due to disease.
C	E	L	L	O	P	H	A	N	E	A transparent sheet of regenerated cellulose made of alkaline viscose solution.
C	E	L	L	U	L	O	S	A	N	Carbohydrates that occur in close association with cellulose in cell walls.
C	E	N	S	O	R	I	O	U	S	Given to censure, Condemnatory, Critical.
C	E	N	S	O	R	S	H	I	P	Practice of censoring.
C	E	N	T	E	N	N	I	A	L	Period of one hundred years.
C	E	N	T	E	S	I	M	A	L	Dividing into hundredths.
C	E	N	T	I	G	R	A	D	E	A thermometric scale having one hundred degress between freezing and boiling points.
C	E	N	T	I	L	I	T	R	E	Unit of liquid capacity equal to one hundredth part of a litre.
C	E	N	T	I	L	L	I	O	N	A hundred million.
C	E	N	T	I	M	E	T	R	E	Unit of length equal to one hundredth part of a metre.
C	E	N	T	R	I	F	U	G	E	A machine that produces artificial gravity.
C	E	N	T	R	I	S	C	U	S	Type genus of shrimpfishes.
C	E	N	T	R	O	S	E	M	A	A genus of chiefly tropical American vines.
C	E	R	A	T	O	P	S	I	A	A group of large dinosaurs.
C	E	R	E	M	O	N	I	A	L	Form, Formality, Rite, Ritual, Observance, Service.
C	E	R	I	T	H	I	D	E	A	Genus of brackish-water snails.
C	E	R	V	A	N	T	I	T	E	A mineral occurring in spongy steel-gray masses.
C	H	A	C	H	A	L	A	C	A	Large chiefly arboreal birds resembling wild turkeys and prized as game birds.
C	H	A	L	C	E	D	O	N	Y	A cryptocrystalline translucent mineral of a variety of quartz.
C	H	A	L	L	E	N	G	E	R	Opponent in a sporting contest.
C	H	A	L	Y	B	E	A	T	E	Impregnated with salts of iron.
C	H	A	M	P	I	G	N	O	N	Common edible mushroom.
C	H	A	N	D	E	L	I	E	R	A light fitting with two or more arms.
C	H	A	N	G	E	A	B	L	E	Mutable, Variable, Capricious, Fickle, Inconstant, Mercurial, Unstable, Restless.
C	H	A	N	G	E	L	I	N	G	Traitor, Turncoat, A child substituted for another.
C	H	A	R	A	C	I	D	A	E	A large family of freshwater fishes.
C	H	A	R	C	U	T	I	E	R	A pork butcher.
C	H	A	R	D	O	N	N	A	Y	A dry white wine of the Chablis type.
C	H	A	R	G	E	A	B	L	E	Expensive, Costly.
C	H	A	R	I	T	A	B	L	E	Benevolent, Kindly, Humane, Helpful, Obliging, Lenient, Forbearing, Merciful.
C	H	A	R	L	E	S	T	O	N	A ballroom dance in quick tempo.
C	H	A	R	T	R	E	U	S	E	A liqueur flavoured with peppermint, orange peel and herbs.
C	H	A	T	E	L	A	I	N	E	Mistress of a chateau, Ornamental chain with keys, etc. worn at a woman's waist.
C	H	A	T	T	E	R	I	N	G	Babbling, Gabbling, Jabbering, Jawing, Prattling.
C	H	A	U	F	F	E	U	S	E	A female chauffeur.
C	H	A	U	V	I	N	I	S	T	One who has an excessive partiality to one group.
C	H	E	E	R	F	U	L	L	Y	Gladly, Brightly, Jauntily, Gayly, Radiantly.
C	H	E	M	I	S	E	T	T	E	A short vest like an undergarment, Loose fill-in for an open-fronted dress.
C	H	E	R	S	O	N	E	S	E	Peninsula.
C	H	E	V	K	I	N	I	T	E	A mineral consisting of silico-titanate of iron, calcium and rare-earth elements.
C	H	E	V	R	O	T	A	I	N	Very small hornless deerlike ruminant mammals, Mouse deer.
C	H	I	C	K	E	N	P	O	X	An acute contagious virus disease.
C	H	I	F	F	C	H	A	F	F	A small grayish European warbler.
C	H	I	L	D	B	I	R	T	H	The act of bringing forth a child or offspring.
C	H	I	L	D	I	S	H	L	Y	Pettily, Immaturely, Foolishly, Naively, Babyishly.
C	H	I	M	E	R	I	C	A	L	Imaginary, Unrealistic.
C	H	I	M	P	A	N	Z	E	E	An anthropoid ape.
C	H	I	N	A	G	R	A	S	S	Stiff dried ramie fibre.
C	H	I	N	C	H	I	L	L	A	A small squirrel-size rodent having soft pearly-gray fur.
C	H	I	O	N	O	D	O	X	A	A genus of small bulbous herbs.
C	H	I	R	O	M	A	N	C	Y	Palmistry, Divination by examination of the palm of the hand.

1	2	3	4	5	6	7	8	9	10	
C	H	I	T	T	A	G	O	N	G	The style prevalent in Chittagong, Pakistan.
C	H	I	V	A	L	R	O	U	S	Valiant, Warlike, Civil, Generous, Benevolent, Noble, Considerate, Lofty.
C	H	L	O	R	I	N	A	T	E	To treat with chlorine.
C	H	L	O	R	O	F	O	R	M	A colourless volatile heavy toxic liquid once used as a general anaesthetic.
C	H	O	L	I	A	M	B	I	C	Belonging to a choliamb.
C	H	O	R	D	O	T	O	M	Y	Surgical operation on the spinal cord to relieve severe pain.
C	H	O	R	I	A	M	B	I	C	A foot of four syllables in classical prosody.
C	H	R	O	M	I	T	I	T	E	A rock composed chiefly of the mineral chromite.
C	H	R	O	M	O	S	O	M	E	A rodlike structure which occurs in pairs in the cell nucleus carrying hereditary factors.
C	H	R	O	N	I	C	L	E	S	Historical accounts arranged in chronological order.
C	H	R	O	N	O	G	R	A	M	Record made by an instrument for measuring and recording time.
C	H	R	O	N	O	L	O	G	Y	Classification by order of time.
C	H	R	O	N	O	T	R	O	N	Device for measuring small intervals of time by electric pulses.
C	H	R	Y	S	O	L	I	T	E	Yellow or greenish gem, Olivine.
C	H	R	Y	S	O	T	I	L	E	Fibrous silky serpentine of a kind of asbestos.
C	H	U	C	K	W	A	L	L	A	A harmless herbivorous desert lizard.
C	H	U	R	C	H	Y	A	R	D	Ground belonging to a church usually used as a burial ground.
C	I	N	E	P	L	A	S	T	Y	Surgical fitting for a muscle to operate an artificial limb.
C	I	N	Q	U	E	F	O	I	L	A decoration of a five-petalled figure.
C	I	R	C	U	I	T	O	U	S	Indirect, Roundabout, Circular, Oblique.
C	I	R	C	U	M	C	I	S	E	Removal of the foreskin.
C	I	R	C	U	M	F	L	E	X	Mark over vowel to indicate special pronunciation.
C	I	R	C	U	M	F	U	S	E	Spread, Diffuse, Surround, Envelop.
C	I	R	C	U	M	V	E	N	T	Encircle, Frustrate, Baffle, Disappoint, Foil, Thwart, Bypass, Circumnavigate.
C	I	S	T	E	R	C	I	A	N	Member of the Benedictine order.
C	I	T	I	G	R	A	D	A	E	A group comprising running spiders that chase their prey.
C	I	T	R	O	N	E	L	L	A	Oil with a lemonlike odour obtained from grasses.
C	L	A	N	G	O	R	O	U	S	Noisy, Resounding, Sonorous, Uproarious.
C	L	A	R	A	B	E	L	L	A	An eight foot organ stop with open wooden pipes.
C	L	A	S	P	K	N	I	F	E	Jackknife, A large pocket knife with blades that fold into the handle.
C	L	A	S	S	I	C	I	S	M	The style of classical literature, architecture and art.
C	L	A	S	S	I	F	I	E	D	Divided into classes.
C	L	A	V	I	C	H	O	R	D	An early keyboard instrument smaller and weaker in tone than a piano.
C	L	A	Y	P	I	G	E	O	N	A saucer-shaped target of baked clay thrown from a trap for target shooting.
C	L	E	R	E	S	T	O	R	Y	Upper part rising above adjoining sections of a building.
C	L	I	N	I	C	A	L	L	Y	In a clinical fashion.
C	L	I	N	O	C	L	A	S	E	A mineral consisting of basic copper arsenate.
C	L	I	N	O	M	E	T	E	R	Any instrument used by a surveyor for measuring elevation and slope.
C	L	O	S	E	S	H	A	V	E	A narrow escape.
C	L	O	U	D	B	E	R	R	Y	A creeping herbaceous raspberry bearing edible fruit.
C	L	O	U	D	B	U	R	S	T	Deluge, Sudden heavy rainfall.
C	L	O	U	D	I	N	E	S	S	Clouded appearance.
C	L	U	M	S	I	N	E	S	S	The state of being clumsy.
C	O	A	C	E	R	V	A	T	E	Gather, Collect, Heap, Pile up.
C	O	A	R	S	E	N	E	S	S	Grossness, Obscenity, Ribaldness, Foulness, Vulgarity, Wildness, Roughness.
C	O	C	K	C	H	A	F	E	R	A large destructive scarablike beetle.
C	O	E	L	A	C	A	N	T	H	A large fish once thought to be extinct.
C	O	G	I	T	A	T	I	O	N	Reflection, Meditation, Thought, Deliberation, Speculation.
C	O	G	N	I	Z	A	N	C	E	Surveillance, Knowledge, Control, Recognition, Notice, Perception, Observance.
C	O	H	E	R	E	N	T	L	Y	In a coherent fashion.
C	O	I	N	C	I	D	E	N	T	Attending, Concomitant, Harmonious, Contemporary.
C	O	I	N	C	I	D	I	N	G	Corresponding, Agreeing, Harmonizing, According, Matching, Equalling, Concurring.
C	O	L	C	H	I	C	I	N	E	Poisonous yellow crystalline alkaloid extracted from meadow saffron.
C	O	L	E	O	P	T	E	R	A	Largest order of insects comprising the beetles and weevils.
C	O	L	E	O	P	T	I	L	E	The first leaf forming a protective sheath about the plumule.
C	O	L	L	A	T	E	R	A	L	Indirect, Concomitant, Subsidiary, Accompanying, Satellite, Subordinate, Corroborative.
C	O	L	L	E	C	T	I	O	N	Assembly, Group, Number, Gathering, Crowd, Accumulation, Medley.
C	O	L	L	E	C	T	I	V	E	Multiple, Typical, Representative.
C	O	L	L	I	M	A	T	O	R	Device for producing a beam of parallel rays of light.
C	O	L	L	I	N	G	U	A	L	Using the same language.
C	O	L	L	O	Q	U	I	A	L	Conversational, Vernacular, Patois.
C	O	L	O	R	A	T	U	R	A	Music characterized by ornate figuration.
C	O	L	O	U	R	A	B	L	E	Plausible, Feigned, Factitious, Counterfeit, Believable, Convincing, Compelling.
C	O	L	O	U	R	L	E	S	S	Pallid, Blanched, Neutral, Transparent, Pale, Ashen, Livid, Neutral.
C	O	L	P	O	R	T	E	U	R	Missionary, peddler of religious books.
C	O	M	B	U	S	T	I	O	N	Process of burning, Confusion, Tumult.
C	O	M	E	D	I	E	N	N	E	An actress who plays comedy.

1	2	3	4	5	6	7	8	9	10	
C	O	M	E	L	I	N	E	S	S	Attractiveness, Loveliness, Prettiness, Correctness, Niceness.
C	O	M	E	S	T	I	B	L	E	Edible, Suitable to be eaten.
C	O	M	M	A	N	D	A	N	T	Commanding officer.
C	O	M	M	A	N	D	E	E	R	Appropriate, Arrogate, Confiscate, Expropriate, Seize, Take, Sequester, Usurping.
C	O	M	M	A	N	D	I	N	G	Charging, Directing, Ordering, Enjoining, Instructing, Bidding, Summoning.
C	O	M	M	E	N	T	A	R	Y	Remark, Note, Dictum, Observation, Descriptive comments on an event or performance.
C	O	M	M	E	R	C	I	A	L	Relating to commerce.
C	O	M	M	I	S	S	A	R	Y	Deputy, Delegate, Representative of a bishop.
C	O	M	M	I	S	S	I	O	N	Authorize, Accredit, Empower, Enable, License, Appoint, Designate, Instruct.
C	O	M	M	I	S	S	U	R	E	Joint, Seam, Closure, Cleft, Juncture, Interstice.
C	O	M	M	O	D	I	O	U	S	Ample, Spacious, Capacious, Roomy, Wide.
C	O	M	M	O	N	A	B	L	E	Held in common ownership.
C	O	M	M	O	N	A	L	T	Y	Commoners, Corporation, Democracy.
C	O	M	M	U	N	I	Q	U	E	An official announcement.
C	O	M	M	U	T	A	B	L	E	Capable of being interchanged.
C	O	M	M	U	T	A	T	O	R	A switch for reversing the direction of an electric current.
C	O	M	P	A	C	T	I	O	N	Density.
C	O	M	P	A	R	A	B	L	E	Like, Parallel, Corresponding, Alike, Consonant, Uniform, Similar, Akin.
C	O	M	P	A	R	I	S	O	N	Likeness, Affinity, Similarity, Analogy, Resemblance, Equalling, Contrast, Simile.
C	O	M	P	A	S	S	I	O	N	Sympathy, Charity, Clemency, Mercy, Benevolence, Humanity, Pity, Commiseration.
C	O	M	P	A	T	I	B	L	E	Consonant, Agreeable, Congenial, Congruous, Consistent, Suitable, Fitting, Proper.
C	O	M	P	A	T	R	I	O	T	One from the same country, Colleague.
C	O	M	P	E	N	D	I	U	M	Abstract, Abridgment, Inventory, Survey, Sketch, Digest, Syllabus.
C	O	M	P	E	N	S	A	T	E	Remunerate, Recompense, Pay, Satisfy, Atone, Redeem, Balance, Redress.
C	O	M	P	E	T	E	N	C	Y	Competence.
C	O	M	P	E	T	I	T	O	R	Rival, Contestant.
C	O	M	P	L	A	C	E	N	T	Smug, Priggish, Self-satisfied.
C	O	M	P	L	E	T	E	L	Y	Totally, Fully, Thoroughly, Exhaustively, Entirely, Perfectly, Utterly, Wholly.
C	O	M	P	L	E	T	I	O	N	Fulfillment, Conclusion, Termination, Execution.
C	O	M	P	L	E	X	I	O	N	Appearance, Disposition, Character, Individuality, Type, Nature, Personality.
C	O	M	P	L	I	A	N	C	E	Civility, Harmony, Concord, Conformance, Submission, Docility, Acquiescence.
C	O	M	P	L	I	C	A	T	E	Involve, Complex, Difficult, Entangle, Perplex, Muddle, Jumble, Disorder.
C	O	M	P	L	I	C	I	T	Y	Association, Participation, Collusion, Connivance, Implication, Involvement.
C	O	M	P	L	I	M	E	N	T	Regards, Congratulate, Praise, Accolade, Commendation, Honour, Tribute, Acclaim.
C	O	M	P	L	I	M	E	N	T	Regards, Congratulate, Praise, Accolade, Commendation, Honour, Tribute, Acclaim.
C	O	M	P	O	S	I	T	A	E	A very large family of herbs, shrubs and trees.
C	O	M	P	R	E	H	E	N	D	Understand, Accept, Grasp, Know, Appreciate, Fathom, Embrace, Encompass.
C	O	M	P	R	E	S	S	E	D	Constricted, Closed, Squeezed, Repressed, Restrained, Condensed, Contracted.
C	O	M	P	R	E	S	S	O	R	A machine that compresses air, fuel-air mixtures or other gases.
C	O	M	P	R	O	M	I	S	E	Surrender, Endanger, Hazard, Jeopardize, Menace, Agreement, Contract, Understanding.
C	O	M	P	U	L	S	I	O	N	Force, Coercion, Duress, Violence, Impelling, Pressing, Necessity, Pressure.
C	O	M	P	U	L	S	O	R	Y	Enforced, Mandatory, Coercive, Compelling, Imperative, Obligatory, Required.
C	O	N	C	E	N	T	R	I	C	Coaxial, Having a common centre.
C	O	N	C	E	R	N	I	N	G	Affecting, Involving, Engaging, Occupying, Interesting, Regarding, Respecting.
C	O	N	C	E	P	T	I	O	N	Act of becoming pregnant.
C	O	N	C	E	P	T	U	A	L	Relating to concepts.
C	O	N	C	E	S	S	I	O	N	Acknowledgment, Admission, Boon, Grant, Allowance.
C	O	N	C	H	O	L	O	G	Y	Study of sea shells.
C	O	N	C	I	L	I	A	T	E	Mollify, Propitiate, Appease, Pacify, Assuage, Placate, Soothe, Calm.
C	O	N	C	L	U	S	I	O	N	Close, Termination, End, Result, Outcome, Settlement, Finale, End.
C	O	N	C	L	U	S	I	V	E	Decisive, Definitive, Final, Convincing, Irrefutable, Incontrovertible, Cogent.
C	O	N	C	O	C	T	I	O	N	Act of composing, fabricating or making up.
C	O	N	C	O	R	D	A	N	T	Agreeing, Harmonious, Consonant, Congruous.
C	O	N	C	R	E	T	I	O	N	Becoming solid, A concrete mass, Mass of mineral matter.
C	O	N	C	U	R	R	E	N	T	Converging, Meeting, Intersecting, Contemporary, Co-existing, Simultaneous.
C	O	N	C	U	S	S	I	O	N	Impact, Collision, Crash, Jar, Jolt, Percussion, Shock, Smash.
C	O	N	D	E	N	S	A	R	Y	Condensery, A plant where milk is concentrated by evaporating the water content.
C	O	N	D	E	N	S	A	T	E	Product of condensation.
C	O	N	D	E	S	C	E	N	D	Descend, Unbend, Concede, Deign, Stoop, To act in a patronizing fashion.
C	O	N	D	I	T	I	O	N	S	Provisions, Provisos, Stipulations, Reservations, Requirements, Limitations.
C	O	N	D	O	N	A	B	L	E	Excusable, Forgivable.
C	O	N	D	U	C	T	I	O	N	Transfer of heat through material, Maintenance of an electric current through metals.
C	O	N	D	U	C	T	I	V	E	Relating to conduction.
C	O	N	F	E	C	T	I	O	N	Mixture, Sweetmeat, Preserve, Candy, Preparation, Manufacture, Fancy decorations.
C	O	N	F	E	R	E	N	C	E	Discussion, Deliberation, Seminar, Meeting, Parley, League, Association, Talk.
C	O	N	F	E	S	S	I	O	N	Admission, Acknowledgment, Statement.
C	O	N	F	I	D	E	N	C	E	Trust, Reliance, Belief, Assurance, Presumption, Certitude, Faith, Aplomb.

1	2	3	4	5	6	7	8	9	10	
C	O	N	F	I	S	C	A	T	E	Appropriate, Seize, Annex, Commandeer, Expropriate, Sequester, Take, Arrogate.
C	O	N	F	L	U	E	N	C	E	Concourse, Crowd, Junction, Concursion, Gathering, Meeting.
C	O	N	F	O	R	M	I	N	G	Conforming, Standardized, One who conforms to the established church.
C	O	N	F	O	U	N	D	E	D	Baffled, Spoiled, Corrupted, Bewildered, Stupefifed, Perplexed, Confused, Puzzled.
C	O	N	G	E	N	I	T	A	L	Innate, Inherent, Acquired, Hereditary, Indigenous, Native, Essential, Intrinsic.
C	O	N	G	E	S	T	I	O	N	Accumulation, Gathering, Heap, Overcrowding, Over-accumulation, Blockage.
C	O	N	G	L	O	B	A	T	E	To form into a round mass, Collected into a ball.
C	O	N	G	R	E	G	A	N	T	A member of a congregation.
C	O	N	G	R	U	E	N	C	E	Congruity, Harmony, Agreement.
C	O	N	H	Y	D	R	I	N	E	Poisonous crystalline alkaloid occurring in poison hemlock.
C	O	N	I	F	E	R	O	U	S	A pine tree bearing cones.
C	O	N	J	E	C	T	U	R	E	Supposition, Surmise, Theory, Speculation, Guess, Presume, Pretend, Assume.
C	O	N	J	O	I	N	T	L	Y	Simultaneously, Together, Jointly, Mutually.
C	O	N	N	A	T	U	R	A	L	Inborn, Inherent, Natural, Allied, Cognate, Indigenous, Inherited, Related.
C	O	N	N	E	C	T	I	N	G	Joining, Fastening, Linking, Uniting, Associating, Combining, Coupling, Yoking.
C	O	N	N	E	C	T	I	O	N	Alliance, Union, Context, Reference, Link, Position, Juncture, Seam.
C	O	N	N	I	P	T	I	O	N	A fit of rage, hysteria or alarm.
C	O	N	N	I	V	A	N	C	E	Complicity, Collusion, Wrongdoing.
C	O	N	S	C	I	E	N	C	E	Scruple, Compunction, Qualm, Demur.
C	O	N	S	E	C	R	A	T	E	Devote, Dedicate, Bless, Hallow, Sanctify.
C	O	N	S	I	S	T	E	N	T	Compatible, Same, Constant, Invariable, Unchanging, Unfailing, Congenial.
C	O	N	S	I	S	T	O	R	Y	Council, Church tribunal.
C	O	N	S	O	N	A	N	C	E	Accord, Harmony, Alliteration, Agreement, Concord, Chorus, Concert, Sure.
C	O	N	S	O	R	T	I	U	M	Association or partnership.
C	O	N	S	P	E	C	T	U	S	Abridgment, Outline, List, Synopsis, Survey, Brief, Epitome.
C	O	N	S	P	I	R	A	C	Y	Plot, Intrigue, Machination, Scheme, Treason, Perfidy, Disloyalty, Sedition.
C	O	N	S	T	A	N	T	L	Y	Faithfully, Firmly, Ever, Always, Incessantly, Continuously, Invariably, Perpetually.
C	O	N	S	T	I	P	A	T	E	Stultify, Make firm or hard, Make immobile, inactive or dull.
C	O	N	S	U	E	T	U	D	E	Custom, Habit, Social usage, Practice, Wont, Manner.
C	O	N	S	U	L	T	A	N	T	Usually a physician responsible for the administration of a hospital.
C	O	N	S	U	M	M	A	T	E	Finished, Perfect, Extreme, Complete, Achieve, Accomplished, Talented, Skilled.
C	O	N	T	A	G	I	O	U	S	Infectious, Catching, Noxious.
C	O	N	T	E	N	T	I	O	N	Conflict, Strife, Altercation, Controversy, Squabbling, Claim, Charge, Discord.
C	O	N	T	E	S	T	A	N	T	One that participates in a contest, Disputant.
C	O	N	T	I	G	U	I	T	Y	Close proximity, Intimate association.
C	O	N	T	I	N	G	E	N	T	Touching, Empirical, Factual, Free, Accidental, Casual, Chance, Incidental.
C	O	N	T	I	N	U	O	U	S	Progressive, Continual, Ceaseless, Constant, Endless, Everlasting, Perpetual.
C	O	N	T	R	A	B	A	N	D	Illegal traffic in prohibited goods. Smuggled goods.
C	O	N	T	R	A	B	A	S	S	The largest instrument of the viol family.
C	O	N	T	R	A	C	T	O	R	One that contracts, One working according to a contractual agreement.
C	O	N	T	R	A	D	I	C	T	To deny, be contrary, express opposition.
C	O	N	T	R	A	V	E	N	E	Infringe, Disregard, Contradict, Dispute, Deny, Violate, Breach, Trangress.
C	O	N	T	R	I	B	U	T	E	Give, Subscribe, Aid, Help, Assist, Augment, Supplement, Recruit.
C	O	N	T	R	I	T	I	O	N	Friction, Penitence, Attrition, Compunction, Contriteness, Remorse, Repentence.
C	O	N	T	R	O	L	L	E	R	One that records, checks or authorizes various performances, records or finances.
C	O	N	T	R	O	V	E	R	T	Disprove, Deny, Contradict, Confound, Confute, Rebut, Question, Challenge.
C	O	N	U	R	O	P	S	I	S	Genus of small American parrots.
C	O	N	V	E	C	T	I	O	N	Conveyance of heat by movement.
C	O	N	V	E	C	T	I	V	E	Transporting, Transmitting, Conveying.
C	O	N	V	E	N	A	B	L	E	Proper, Capable of being assembled.
C	O	N	V	E	N	I	E	N	T	Suitable, Appropriate, Becoming, Proper, Useful, Adjacent, Close, Nearby.
C	O	N	V	E	N	T	I	O	N	Contract, Convenant, Form, Treaty, Concord, Pact, Bond, Custom.
C	O	N	V	E	N	T	U	A	L	Relating to life in a convent or monastery.
C	O	N	V	E	R	S	E	L	Y	Contrarily, Contrawise, Oppositely.
C	O	N	V	E	R	S	I	N	G	Speaking, Talking, Communicating, Chatting.
C	O	N	V	E	R	S	I	O	N	To change, transformation, persuasion, alteration.
C	O	N	V	E	Y	A	N	C	E	Transportation, Vehicle, Deed, Charter.
C	O	N	V	I	C	T	I	O	N	Certainty, Assurance, Confidence, Opinion, Belief, Sentiment, View, Persuasion.
C	O	N	V	U	L	S	I	V	E	Producing convulsions, Spasmodic.
C	O	P	P	E	R	H	E	A	D	Pit viper, An Australian venomous snake.
C	O	P	R	O	S	T	A	N	E	A crystalline steroid hydrocarbon.
C	O	P	U	L	A	T	I	V	E	Coupling, Joining.
C	O	P	Y	H	O	L	D	E	R	A device for holding copy that is being typeset.
C	O	Q	U	E	T	T	I	S	H	Exhibiting coquetry.
C	O	R	D	I	A	L	I	T	Y	Geniality, Pleasantness, Agreeability, Amiability, Sympathy, Warmth, Responsiveness.
C	O	R	D	I	L	L	E	R	A	A group of mountain ranges.
C	O	R	D	Y	L	I	D	A	E	Small family of spiny African lizards resembling tiny crocodiles.

1	2	3	4	5	6	7	8	9	10	Clue
C	O	R	I	A	C	E	O	U	S	Leather-like texture.
C	O	R	M	O	P	H	Y	T	A	All plants having a stem and root.
C	O	R	N	F	L	O	W	E	R	A European plant having flower heads with blue, pink or white rays.
C	O	R	N	U	C	O	P	I	A	A curved goat's horn filled with fruit and flowers used as a decoration. The horn of plenty.
C	O	R	O	M	A	N	D	E	L	Reddish brown iron oxide left as a residue when ferrous sulfate is heated.
C	O	R	O	N	A	T	I	O	N	Crowning of the sovereign, Culminating act.
C	O	R	P	U	L	E	N	C	E	Fleshiness, Obesity, Excessive fatness, Adiposity.
C	O	R	R	E	C	T	I	V	E	Remedy, Correction.
C	O	R	R	E	G	I	D	O	R	A Spanish magistrate.
C	O	R	R	E	L	A	T	E	D	To put in relation with each other.
C	O	R	R	O	B	O	R	E	E	An Australian aboriginal nocturnal festivity, Tumult, Uproar.
C	O	R	R	U	G	A	T	E	D	Furrowed, Wrinkled, Folded, Creased, Crinkled, Ridged.
C	O	R	R	U	P	T	I	O	N	Depravity, Vice, Immorality, Wickedness, Impropriety, Barbarism, Vulgarism.
C	O	R	T	A	D	E	R	I	A	Genus of South American grass, Pampas grass.
C	O	R	Y	B	A	N	T	I	C	Wild, Frenzied.
C	O	R	Y	L	O	P	S	I	S	Small genus of Asian shrubs.
C	O	S	M	O	L	O	G	I	C	Relating to cosmology.
C	O	S	T	L	I	N	E	S	S	Expensiveness.
C	O	T	I	N	G	I	D	A	E	A family of tropical American birds related to manakins.
C	O	T	Y	L	O	S	A	U	R	A primitive prehistoric reptile.
C	O	U	L	O	M	E	T	E	R	Voltmeter.
C	O	U	N	S	E	L	L	O	R	Adviser, Counsel.
C	O	U	N	T	E	R	A	C	T	Check, Offset, Neutralize, Nullify, Cancel, Negate, Frustrate, Rectify.
C	O	U	R	A	G	E	O	U	S	Brave, Bold, Dauntless, Intrepid, Valiant, Tenacious, Fearless, Audacious.
C	O	V	E	T	O	U	S	L	Y	In a covetous manner.
C	O	W	C	A	T	C	H	E	R	Brief radio and television commercial.
C	O	X	O	P	O	D	I	T	E	The first joint of a crustacean limb.
C	R	A	C	K	B	R	A	I	N	Crackpot, An unbalanced person, A person with erratic tendencies.
C	R	A	N	I	O	L	O	G	Y	A science dealing with variations of skulls.
C	R	A	P	A	U	D	I	N	E	An ulcer on the coronet of a horse.
C	R	A	P	U	L	E	N	C	E	Sickness occasioned by intemperance in food or drink.
C	R	E	A	T	I	N	I	N	E	A white crystalline strongly basic compound found in muscle, blood and urine.
C	R	E	D	I	T	A	B	L	E	Reputable, Suitable, Respectable, Believable, Credible, Plausible, Satisfactory.
C	R	E	N	E	L	L	A	T	E	With battlements, Castellate.
C	R	E	N	O	T	H	R	I	X	Bacteria that are a frequent nuisance in water pipes.
C	R	E	T	A	C	E	O	U	S	Chalky.
C	R	E	V	I	C	U	L	A	R	Involving a crevice.
C	R	I	B	R	A	T	I	O	N	Act of sifting as with drugs.
C	R	I	B	R	I	F	O	R	M	Pierced with small holes like a sieve.
C	R	I	C	E	T	I	D	A	E	Family of rodents, Lemmings, Voles, Hamsters, Mice, Rats.
C	R	I	C	E	T	U	L	U	S	A large genus of small short-tailed Asiatic hamsters.
C	R	O	C	O	D	I	L	U	S	Crocodile, Alligator.
C	R	O	C	O	D	Y	L	U	S	Same as CROCODILUS.
C	R	O	N	A	R	T	I	U	M	Genus of rust fungi.
C	R	O	O	K	E	S	I	T	E	A mineral consisting of selenide of copper, thallium and silver.
C	R	O	S	S	B	R	E	E	D	Hybridize, Interbreed.
C	R	O	S	S	P	I	E	C	E	A horizontal member of a figure or structure.
C	R	O	S	S	R	O	A	D	S	Intersection of roads, Junction.
C	R	O	T	A	L	A	R	I	A	A large genus of mainly tropical herbs.
C	R	O	T	A	L	I	D	A	E	Family of venomous snakes.
C	R	O	T	O	P	H	A	G	A	Genus of birds.
C	R	U	C	I	A	L	I	T	Y	The state of being crucial.
C	R	U	C	I	B	U	L	U	M	Genus of bird's nest fungi.
C	R	U	C	I	F	E	R	A	E	Family of herbs.
C	R	Y	O	G	E	N	I	C	S	The branch of physics relating to the study of low temperatures.
C	R	Y	O	P	H	I	L	I	C	Preferring low temperatures.
C	R	Y	P	T	O	D	I	R	A	Turtles.
C	R	Y	P	T	O	L	O	G	Y	The scientific study of cryptography.
C	R	Y	P	T	O	P	I	N	E	A colourless crystalline alkaloid obtained from opium.
C	T	E	N	A	C	O	D	O	N	Genus of small prehistoric mammals.
C	T	E	N	I	Z	I	D	A	E	Family of large burrowing spiders, Trap-door spider.
C	T	E	N	O	P	H	O	R	A	Marine hermaphroditic solitary animals superficially resembling jellyfishes.
C	U	A	R	T	E	L	A	Z	O	Military coup, Seizure of power by the military.
C	U	C	K	O	O	P	I	N	T	A common European arum.
C	U	C	U	L	I	F	O	R	M	Belonging to the cuckoos.
C	U	L	D	O	S	C	O	P	Y	Special technique for endoscopic visualization for minor operative procedures.
C	U	L	T	I	V	A	B	L	E	Capable of being cultivated.

1	2	3	4	5	6	7	8	9	10	
C	U	L	T	I	V	A	T	E	D	Tilled, Laboured, Tended, Worked, Managed, Cropped, Cherished, Produced.
C	U	M	B	E	R	S	O	M	E	Awkward, Inconvenient, Clumsy, Unwieldy, Ponderous, Lumbering, Irksome.
C	U	M	M	E	R	B	U	N	D	A sash worn around the waist with dress clothes.
C	U	M	U	L	A	T	I	O	N	Additive, Chain, Augmenting, Increasing, Multiplying, Intensifying, Magnifying.
C	U	N	C	T	A	T	I	O	N	Delay, Procrastination.
C	U	R	A	R	I	F	O	R	M	Producing muscular relaxation as with curare.
C	U	R	I	O	L	O	G	I	C	Representation by pictures instead of symbols, Hieroglyphic.
C	U	R	M	U	D	G	E	O	N	Miser, Churl, Ill-tempered, difficult often elderly person, Avaricious.
C	U	R	R	I	C	U	L	U	M	Planned school activities, Body of courses offered by a college.
C	U	R	T	A	I	L	I	N	G	Abbreviating, Abridging, Cutting, Retrenching, Slashing, Diminishing, Lessening.
C	U	R	V	A	C	E	O	U	S	Curving, possessing a voluptuous body.
C	U	R	V	O	M	E	T	E	R	An instrument for measuring the length of a curve.
C	U	S	H	I	O	N	I	N	G	Suppressing, Mitigating, Palliating, Protecting, Padding, Checking.
C	U	T	T	L	E	F	I	S	H	A ten-armed cephalopod marine mollusk possessing a calcified internal shell.
C	Y	A	N	O	C	I	T	T	A	Genus of American birds, Blue jays.
C	Y	A	N	O	C	O	R	A	X	Genus of American birds, Green and yellow jays.
C	Y	A	N	O	M	E	T	E	R	Instrument for measuring degrees of blueness.
C	Y	A	N	O	M	E	T	R	Y	Measuring of blueness.
C	Y	B	E	R	N	E	T	I	C	Relating to study of various automatic control systems.
C	Y	C	L	A	N	T	H	U	S	Small genus of tropical American plants having milky juice and unisexual flowers.
C	Y	C	L	O	H	E	X	Y	L	Univalent radical formed by removal of hydrogen from cyclohexane.
C	Y	C	L	O	L	Y	S	I	S	The process of decay of a cyclone.
C	Y	L	I	N	D	R	I	T	E	A mineral consisting of sulphur, lead, antimony and tin.
C	Y	N	I	P	O	I	D	E	A	Family of parasitic insects, Gall wasps.
C	Y	N	O	D	I	C	T	I	S	Genus of extinct carnivores presumably ancestors of dogs and foxes.
C	Y	N	O	L	O	G	I	S	T	Specialist in the care and training of dogs.
C	Y	P	R	A	E	I	D	A	E	Family of marine gastropod mollusks, Cowries.
C	Y	P	R	I	N	I	D	A	E	Large family of freshwater fishes, Carps, Barbels, Bream, Goldfishes.
C	Y	R	T	O	S	T	Y	L	E	A circular columned portico.
C	Y	S	T	E	C	T	O	M	Y	Surgical excision of a cyst, Removal of all or a portion of the urinary bladder.
C	Y	S	T	I	C	I	D	A	L	Tending to kill an encysted stage of an organism.
C	Y	S	T	O	S	C	O	P	E	An instrument permitting visual examination of the bladder.
C	Y	T	O	C	H	R	O	M	E	A respiratory pigment occurring in animal and plant cells.
C	Y	T	O	G	E	N	O	U	S	Producing cells.
C	Z	A	R	E	V	I	T	C	H	A son of a Russian Czar.

D

1	2	3	4	5	6	7	8	9	10	
D	A	S	Y	U	R	I	D	A	E	Family of marsupials, Pouched mice, Banded anteater, Tasmanian devil.
D	E	B	A	U	C	H	E	R	Y	Intemperance, Orgies, Carousals.
D	E	B	I	L	I	T	A	T	E	To weaken, enervate.
D	E	B	U	T	A	N	I	Z	E	To remove by distillation.
D	E	C	E	L	E	R	A	T	E	Lessen speed, Retard, Decrease rate of progress.
D	E	C	O	R	A	T	I	O	N	Ornamentation, Embellishment, Garniture, Trimming, Honour, Accolade, Award.
D	E	C	O	R	A	T	I	V	E	Serving to decorate.
D	E	C	R	E	A	S	I	N	G	Diminishing, Reducing, Dwindling, Lessening, Abating.
D	E	C	U	M	B	E	N	C	Y	Act of lying down.
D	E	C	U	R	R	E	N	C	Y	Flowing downward.
D	E	D	I	C	A	T	I	O	N	Zeal, Faithfulness, Enthusiasm, Devotion, Consecration, Addressing, Entrusting.
D	E	D	U	C	T	I	B	L	E	Allowable as a deduction.
D	E	F	A	M	A	T	I	O	N	Dishonour, Disgrace, Detraction, Calumny, Aspersion, Libel, Slander.
D	E	F	A	M	A	T	O	R	Y	Calumnious.
D	E	F	E	A	S	A	N	C	E	Defeat, Overthrow, Undoing.
D	E	F	E	N	S	I	B	L	E	Excusable, Protective, Shielding.
D	E	F	I	B	R	A	T	O	R	A machine that separates substances into fibrous constituents.
D	E	F	I	L	E	M	E	N	T	Pollution.
D	E	F	I	N	I	T	I	O	N	Statement of a precise nature of something, Being distinct.
D	E	F	I	N	I	T	I	V	E	Supplying a final answer or solution, Distinguishing, Conclusive.
D	E	F	L	E	C	T	I	O	N	Curve, Bend, Turn, Deviation, Departure, Divergence, Twisting, Swerving.
D	E	G	E	N	E	R	A	C	Y	Degradation, Deterioration, Atrophy, Decadence, Downfall, Devolution, Downgrade.
D	E	G	R	E	S	S	I	V	E	Descending or decreasing.
D	E	L	E	C	T	A	B	L	E	Delightful, Savoury, Delicious, Luscious, Scrumptious, Exquisite, Tasty, Choice.
D	E	L	E	G	A	T	I	O	N	Appointment of a delegate, Convention, Congress.
D	E	L	I	B	E	R	A	T	E	Considered, Advised, Premeditated, Designed, Studied, Schemed, Calculated.
D	E	L	I	C	A	T	E	L	Y	Daintily, Elegantly, Exquisitely, Gently, Mildly, Softly, Subtly, Tactfully.
D	E	L	I	G	H	T	F	U	L	Delicious, Delectable, Luscious, Delightful, Adorable, Charming, Gratifying.

1	2	3	4	5	6	7	8	9	10	Definition
D	E	L	I	N	Q	U	E	N	T	Criminal offender against the law.
D	E	L	P	H	I	N	I	N	E	A poisonous crystalline alkaloid obtained from seeds of the stavesacre.
D	E	M	O	B	I	L	I	S	E	Disband, Discharge, Remove restrictions.
D	E	M	O	C	R	A	T	I	C	A political system where power is held by the masses.
D	E	M	O	D	U	L	A	T	E	To extract information electronically.
D	E	M	O	G	R	A	P	H	Y	Gathering vital statistics of the human population.
D	E	M	O	L	I	T	I	O	N	Destruction of structures or targets.
D	E	M	O	R	A	L	I	Z	E	Pervert, Deprave, Debase, Corrupt, Debauch, Discourage, Dishearten, Disturb.
D	E	M	U	R	E	N	E	S	S	The quality of being demure.
D	E	N	D	R	A	S	P	I	S	Genus of African snakes, Mambas.
D	E	N	D	R	I	F	O	R	M	Resembling a tree in structure.
D	E	N	D	R	O	L	O	G	Y	Study of trees.
D	E	N	O	M	I	N	A	T	E	Designate, Call, Indicate, Denote, Distinguish.
D	E	N	O	T	A	T	I	O	N	Explanation, Name, Connotation, Sign, Indication.
D	E	N	O	U	E	M	E	N	T	Final outcome or result.
D	E	N	T	I	F	R	I	C	E	Powder, paste or liquid used to clean the teeth.
D	E	N	U	D	A	T	I	O	N	Exposure, Burnout, Erosion.
D	E	N	U	N	C	I	A	T	E	Denounce.
D	E	O	N	T	O	L	O	G	Y	Study of duty or moral obligation.
D	E	P	A	R	T	M	E	N	T	Division, Sphere, Province, Branch, Section.
D	E	P	E	N	D	E	N	C	E	Reliance, Trust, Confidence, Faith, Hope.
D	E	P	I	L	A	T	I	O	N	Removal of hair, wool or bristles from an animal skin.
D	E	P	I	L	A	T	O	R	Y	Having the power to remove unwanted hair.
D	E	P	L	O	R	A	B	L	E	Wretched, Unfortunate, Abominable, Distressing, Grievous, Regrettable, Dreadful.
D	E	P	L	O	Y	M	E	N	T	Arrangement, Placing.
D	E	P	O	L	A	R	I	Z	E	Demagnetize.
D	E	P	O	P	U	L	A	T	E	Devastate, Ravage.
D	E	P	O	R	T	M	E	N	T	Behaviour, Conduct, Carriage, Bearing, Address, Demeanor.
D	E	P	O	S	I	T	I	O	N	Declaration, Testimony, Allegation, Affidavit, Placing, Laying, Precipitation, Burial.
D	E	P	R	E	C	I	A	T	E	Undervalue, Disparage, Belittle, Decry, Devalue, Downgrade, Diminish, Erode.
D	E	P	R	E	S	S	I	O	N	Lowering, Sinking, Dispiritedness, Dejection, Low, Hollow, Melancholy, Recession.
D	E	P	U	T	A	T	I	O	N	Appointing a deputy, Delegation.
D	E	R	A	C	I	N	A	T	E	Extirpate, Exterminate.
D	E	R	I	S	I	V	E	L	Y	In a mocking fashion.
D	E	R	I	V	A	T	I	O	N	Origination, Descent, Deduction, Source, Inception, Root.
D	E	R	M	A	T	I	T	I	S	Inflammation of the skin.
D	E	R	M	A	T	O	B	I	A	Genus of botflies whose larvae live under the skin of domestic animals.
D	E	R	M	A	T	O	S	I	S	A skin disease.
D	E	R	M	O	P	T	E	R	A	Genus of mammals, Flying lemurs.
D	E	R	O	G	A	T	O	R	Y	Disparaging, Detracting, Degrading, Disdainful, Belittling, Humiliating, Spiteful.
D	E	S	C	E	N	D	I	N	G	Originating, Deriving, Falling, Dropping, Lowering, Stooping, Sinking, Declining.
D	E	S	I	G	N	E	D	L	Y	Purposively, Deliberately.
D	E	S	I	P	I	E	N	C	E	Relaxed dallying.
D	E	S	M	A	N	T	H	U	S	A genus of American herbs or shrubs.
D	E	S	O	L	A	T	I	O	N	Dilapidation, Devastation, Disintegration, Dejection.
D	E	S	P	A	I	R	I	N	G	Despondent.
D	E	S	P	I	C	A	B	L	E	Contemptible, Despisable, Mean, Pitiable, Disgraceful, Disreputable, Base, Wretched.
D	E	S	Q	U	A	M	A	T	E	Flake, Peel, Exfoliate, Scale.
D	E	S	Y	N	A	P	S	I	S	Failure of synapsis due to separation of homologous chromosomes.
D	E	T	A	C	H	M	E	N	T	Separation, Dissolution, Division, Divorce, Partition, Rupture.
D	E	T	E	R	M	I	N	E	D	Settled, Decided, Ordained, Regulated, Terminated, Resolved, Purposeful, Unfaltering.
D	E	T	E	S	T	A	B	L	E	Abominable, Hateful, Horrid, Abhorrent, Odious, Heinous, Atrocious, Monstrous.
D	E	T	O	N	A	T	I	O	N	Explosion, Burst.
D	E	U	T	O	P	L	A	S	M	The nutritive inclusions of protoplasm, Egg yolk reserves.
D	E	V	A	S	T	A	T	E	D	Ravaged, Overpowered, Overwhelmed, Desecrated, Despoiled, Devoured, Pillaged.
D	E	V	O	T	I	O	N	A	L	Characterized by devotion.
D	E	X	T	R	I	N	I	Z	E	To convert into dextrins.
D	I	A	G	N	O	S	T	I	C	Concerned with diagnosis, Distinctive, Serving to identify.
D	I	A	L	D	E	H	Y	D	E	A chemical compound containing two aldehyde groups.
D	I	A	P	H	A	N	O	U	S	Ethereal, Vague, Clear, Filmy, Flimsy, Gauzy, Sheer, Gossamer.
D	I	A	P	H	O	R	I	T	E	A mineral consisting of sulfide of lead, silver and antimony.
D	I	A	S	C	H	I	S	I	S	Breaking up of a pattern of brain activity by a localized injury.
D	I	A	S	T	R	O	P	H	Y	Deformation of the earth's crust.
D	I	C	E	P	H	A	L	U	S	A fetal anomaly having two distinct heads.
D	I	C	H	R	O	M	A	T	E	A salt of dichromic acid.
D	I	C	R	U	R	I	D	A	E	A family of Old World passerine birds.
D	I	C	T	I	O	N	A	R	Y	A reference book, Vocabulary, Lexicon.

1	2	3	4	5	6	7	8	9	10	Definition
D	I	D	E	L	P	H	I	A	N	Marsupial.
D	I	D	Y	M	O	L	I	T	E	A mineral consisting of a calcium aluminium silicate.
D	I	F	F	E	R	E	N	C	E	Dissimilarity, Discrepancy, Dissemblance, Distinction, Divergence, Discord, Conflict.
D	I	F	F	I	C	U	L	T	Y	Arduousness, Obstacle, Impediment, Objection, Controversy, Disagreement.
D	I	F	F	I	D	E	N	C	E	Modesty, Bashfulness, Lack of self-confidence.
D	I	F	F	O	R	M	I	T	Y	Lack of conformity, Irregularity.
D	I	F	L	U	O	R	I	D	E	A compound containing two atoms of fluorine combined with an element or radical.
D	I	G	E	S	T	I	B	L	E	Capable of being digested.
D	I	G	I	T	A	T	I	O	N	A process that resembles a finger.
D	I	G	I	T	O	N	I	D	E	Sparingly soluble complex of digitonin and some other compound.
D	I	L	A	P	I	D	A	T	E	Squander, Destroy, Ruin, Bankrupt, Shipwreck, Decay, Disintegrate, Neglect.
D	I	L	A	T	A	T	I	O	N	Enlarging, Spreading, Stretching, Distension, Inflation, Broaden, Widen, Swell.
D	I	L	E	T	T	A	N	T	E	Connoisseur, Lover of the arts.
D	I	L	I	G	E	N	T	L	Y	Carefully, Assiduously, Industriously.
D	I	M	I	N	U	T	I	O	N	Decrease, Degradation, Depreciation, Difference, Tapering, Diminishing, Reduction.
D	I	M	I	N	U	T	I	V	E	Small object or individual, Small replica.
D	I	M	O	R	P	H	I	T	E	A mineral consisting of arsenic sulfide.
D	I	N	I	N	G	R	O	O	M	A room used for the taking of meals.
D	I	O	S	P	H	E	N	O	L	A crystalline hydroxy terpenoid ketone.
D	I	P	H	O	S	G	E	N	E	A liquid compound made by chlorinating methyl formate and used in World War One.
D	I	P	H	T	H	E	R	I	A	An acute highly contagious disease.
D	I	P	L	A	C	U	S	I	S	The hearing of a single tone as if it were two tones of different pitch.
D	I	P	L	A	D	E	N	I	A	A genus of tropical South American Woody vines.
D	I	P	L	E	C	T	R	U	M	A genus of small marine and brackish-water fishes.
D	I	P	L	O	M	A	T	I	C	Suave, Tactful, Politic, Bland, Courteous, Polite, Astute, Shrewd.
D	I	P	L	O	T	A	X	I	S	A genus of Old World weedy herbs.
D	I	P	S	O	M	A	N	I	A	An uncontrollable craving for alcoholic liquor.
D	I	S	A	B	I	L	I	T	Y	Deprivation, Inadequate, Handicap, Disadvantage, Detriment, Incapacity, Drawback.
D	I	S	A	P	P	R	O	V	E	Condemn, Reject, Disapprove, Deprecate.
D	I	S	A	R	R	A	N	G	E	Disorder, Unsettle, Disturb, Disarray, Disorganize, Jumble, Rummage, Displace.
D	I	S	A	S	T	R	O	U	S	Unlucky, Ill-fated, Unpropitious, Ill-boding, Calamitous, Fatal, Destructive, Cataclysmic.
D	I	S	C	E	R	N	I	N	G	Discriminating, Wise, Insighted, Knowledgeable, Perceptive, Sagacious.
D	I	S	C	I	P	L	I	N	E	Punishment, Chastisement, Correction, Will, Subjugate, Teach, Inhibit, Restrain.
D	I	S	C	L	A	I	M	E	R	Repudiation, Disownment, Denial, Disavowal, Renunciation.
D	I	S	C	O	B	O	L	U	S	A discus thrower.
D	I	S	C	O	M	F	O	R	T	Distress, Grief, Trouble, Misfortune, Embarrassment, Annoyance.
D	I	S	C	O	M	M	E	N	D	Disapprove, Dispraise.
D	I	S	C	O	M	M	O	D	E	Inconvenience, Trouble, Disoblige, Bother, Irk, Vex.
D	I	S	C	O	M	P	O	S	E	Disturb, Perturb, Agitate, Upset, Fluster, Flurry, Displace, Unsettle.
D	I	S	C	O	N	C	E	R	T	Upset, Frustrate, Ruffle, Embarrass, Confuse, Confound, Perplex, Bewilder.
D	I	S	C	O	N	T	E	N	T	Displease, Grievance, Dissatisfaction.
D	I	S	C	O	P	H	I	L	E	Collector of records.
D	I	S	C	O	R	D	A	N	T	Disagreeing, Inharmonious, Antagonistic, Incongruous, Quarrelsome, Dissonant.
D	I	S	C	O	U	R	A	G	E	Dishearten, Deject, Deter, Hinder, Demoralize, Dispirit, Bother, Irk.
D	I	S	C	R	E	P	A	N	T	Discordant, Contrary, Different, Disagreeing.
D	I	S	C	R	E	T	I	O	N	Prudence, Tact, Wariness, Restraint, Moderation, Caution, Delicacy, Rashness.
D	I	S	C	U	R	S	I	O	N	Roving, Roaming, Digression, Excursion, Aside.
D	I	S	D	A	I	N	F	U	L	Scornful, Contemptuous, Proud.
D	I	S	E	M	B	O	W	E	L	Eviscerate, Tear, Slash, Rip.
D	I	S	E	N	C	H	A	N	T	Disillusion.
D	I	S	G	U	S	T	I	N	G	Sickening, Revolting, Nauseating, Loathsome, Offensive, Foul, Repellent, Vile.
D	I	S	H	O	N	E	S	T	Y	Deception, Fraud, Trickery, Faithfulness, Betrayal.
D	I	S	H	W	A	S	H	E	R	One that washes dishes, A machine for washing dishes.
D	I	S	I	N	H	E	R	I	T	Deprive, Prevent, Disown, Repudiate, Dispossess, Divest, Oust.
D	I	S	L	O	Y	A	L	T	Y	Infidelity, Falseness, Perfidy, Treachery, Treason, Unfaithfulness.
D	I	S	O	R	D	E	R	L	Y	Irregularity, Confusedly, Turbulently, Disarranged, Boisterous, Rowdy, Unruly.
D	I	S	P	A	R	A	G	E	D	Discouraged, Disheartened, Depreciated, Belittled, Demoralized, Abused, Decried.
D	I	S	P	E	N	S	A	R	Y	A place where medicines and drugs are dispensed.
D	I	S	P	E	R	S	A	N	T	A substance to disperse another substance, Emulsifier.
D	I	S	P	E	R	S	I	N	G	Scattering, Spreading, Dissipating, Distribution, Diffusing, Disseminating.
D	I	S	P	O	S	A	B	L	E	Designed to be thrown away after use.
D	I	S	P	O	S	S	E	S	S	Eject, Oust, Banish, Deprive, Divest, Rob.
D	I	S	Q	U	A	L	I	F	Y	Deprive of legal right or power.
D	I	S	R	E	S	P	E	C	T	Incivility, Discourtesy, Rudeness, Insolence, Impudence, Boldness, Hardihood.
D	I	S	R	U	P	T	I	O	N	Rupturing, Disorder, Disarray, Disorganize, Disturbance.
D	I	S	S	A	T	I	S	F	Y	Fail to satisfy, Frustrate.
D	I	S	S	E	N	T	I	O	N	Quarrelling, Discord, Conflict, Strife, Altercation, Wrangle, Controversy, Dispute.

DISSOCIATE — **10 LETTERS** — EARTHQUAKE

1	2	3	4	5	6	7	8	9	10	
D	I	S	S	O	C	I	A	T	E	Separate, Disconnect, Disunite.
D	I	S	S	O	L	U	B	L	E	Soluble in liquid, Liable to be dispersed.
D	I	S	S	O	L	V	I	N	G	Destroying, Killing, Ending, Disintegrating, Decomposing, Terminating, Melting.
D	I	S	T	R	A	U	G	H	T	Distracted, Frantic, Crazed, Bewildered, Harassed, Agitated, Concerned, Flustered.
D	I	S	T	R	E	S	S	E	D	Pained, Harassed, Upset, Disturbed, Troubled, Bothered, Overwhelmed, Tormented.
D	I	S	T	R	I	B	U	T	E	Allot, Disperse, Administer, Classify, Assort, Divide, Deal, Propagate.
D	I	V	A	R	I	C	A	T	E	Spread, Diverge, Divide, Branch.
D	I	V	E	R	G	E	N	C	Y	Deviation, Digression, Dissimilarity.
D	I	V	I	N	A	T	O	R	Y	Using intuition or perception.
D	O	C	O	G	L	O	S	S	A	Primitive marine gastropods having conical shells, Limpets.
D	O	C	T	O	R	B	I	R	D	Curve-billed humming bird.
D	O	C	T	R	I	N	A	R	Y	Holding abstract doctrines or theories.
D	O	D	E	C	A	R	C	H	Y	A ruling body of twelve.
D	O	D	E	C	U	P	L	E	T	Twelve musical notes performed in the time of the same value.
D	O	L	C	I	S	S	I	M	O	Direction in music - very sweet or soft.
D	O	L	I	C	H	U	R	I	C	Having a redundant syllable.
D	O	L	O	M	I	T	I	Z	E	To convert into dolomite.
D	O	M	I	N	A	T	I	O	N	Supremacy, Mastery, Governing, Controlling, Preponderancy, Power, Authority.
D	O	N	N	Y	B	R	O	O	K	An uproarious brawl, Free-for-all.
D	O	O	R	K	E	E	P	E	R	Porter, One that tends the door of an establishment.
D	O	P	P	L	E	R	I	T	E	Brownish black elastic acid substance occurring in peat.
D	O	R	A	P	H	O	B	I	A	A dread of touching the skin or fur of an animal.
D	O	R	I	P	P	I	D	A	E	Family of small deep-water crabs.
D	O	R	S	I	G	R	A	D	E	Walking on the back of the toes.
D	O	R	S	O	U	L	N	A	R	Relating to the inner side of the back of the forearm or hand.
D	O	R	Y	A	N	T	H	E	S	A small genus of Australian plants, Spear lily.
D	O	T	H	I	D	E	L	L	A	A genus of fungi.
D	O	U	B	L	E	T	A	L	K	Gibberish, Jargon, Gobbledygook, Ambiguous language.
D	O	U	G	L	A	S	I	T	E	A mineral consisting of a hydrated potassium iron chloride.
D	O	V	E	F	L	O	W	E	R	A tropical American orchid.
D	O	W	N	S	T	A	I	R	S	The lower floor.
D	O	W	N	S	T	R	O	K	E	A stroke written in downward direction.
D	O	W	N	T	H	R	U	S	T	Downward movement.
D	O	X	Y	L	A	M	I	N	E	An antihistamine derived from pyridine.
D	R	A	M	A	T	U	R	G	E	A person skilled in the writing or revision of plays.
D	R	A	W	B	R	I	D	G	E	A bridge made to be raised to permit or hinder passage.
D	R	E	A	M	I	N	E	S	S	The state of being dreamy.
D	R	E	A	M	W	O	R	L	D	A world of illusion or fantasy.
D	R	E	A	R	I	N	E	S	S	Sadness, Monotony, Gloominess.
D	R	E	P	A	N	I	D	A	E	Family of small slender moths.
D	R	E	S	S	M	A	K	E	R	One who makes dresses for profit.
D	R	O	M	O	M	A	N	I	A	An exaggerated desire to wander.
D	R	O	S	O	P	H	I	L	A	Genus of two-winged flies, Fruit flies.
D	R	O	W	S	I	N	E	S	S	State of being drowsy.
D	R	Y	O	P	T	E	R	I	S	Genus of medium-sized ferns.
D	U	B	I	T	A	T	I	O	N	Doubt.
D	U	O	D	E	C	I	M	A	L	Expressed in the scale of twelves.
D	U	O	D	E	N	I	T	I	S	Inflammation of the duodenum.
D	U	P	L	I	C	A	T	O	R	A machine for making copies.
D	U	S	S	E	R	T	I	T	E	A mineral consisting of hydrous basic arsenate of barium and iron.
D	U	U	M	V	I	R	A	T	E	A coalition of two people.
D	Y	S	A	R	T	H	R	I	A	Difficulty in articulating words due to disease of the central nervous system.
D	Y	S	C	R	A	S	I	T	E	A native compound of antimony and silver.
D	Y	S	K	I	N	E	S	I	A	Impaired muscle motion.
D	Y	S	O	S	T	O	S	I	S	Defective formation of bone.
D	Y	S	P	H	E	M	I	S	M	Substituting an inoffensive word for a disparaging one.
D	Y	S	P	H	R	A	S	I	A	Defective speech due to impairment of intellect.
D	Y	S	P	R	O	S	I	U	M	A trivalent metallic element of a highly magnetic compound.
D	Y	S	S	E	B	A	C	I	A	Disorder of the sebaceous glands.
D	Y	S	T	R	O	P	H	I	A	Caused by imperfect nutrition.
D	Y	T	I	S	C	I	D	A	E	A family of aquatic beetles.

E

1	2	3	4	5	6	7	8	9	10	
E	A	R	L	A	N	D	I	T	E	A mineral consisting of a hydrous citrate of calcium.
E	A	R	T	H	Q	U	A	K	E	Shaking of the earth accompanying movement of the earth's crust.

1	2	3	4	5	6	7	8	9	10	
E	B	E	R	T	H	E	L	L	A	A genus of bacteria which can cause typhoid fever.
E	B	R	A	C	T	E	A	T	E	Being without bracts.
E	B	U	L	L	I	T	I	O	N	Boiling, Exuberant, Brash, Effervescence, Vivacious, Enthusiasm.
E	B	U	R	N	A	T	I	O	N	A disease which causes bone or cartilage to become hard like ivory.
E	C	C	H	Y	M	O	S	I	S	Ruptured blood vessels causing discolouration of the skin.
E	C	H	I	D	N	I	D	A	E	Genus of moray eels.
E	C	O	L	O	G	I	C	A	L	Relating to the science of ecology.
E	C	T	O	C	A	R	D	I	A	Abnormal position of the heart.
E	C	T	O	C	A	R	P	U	S	Type genus of brown algae.
E	C	U	M	E	N	I	C	A	L	Universal influence, Governing the whole of a body of churches.
E	C	Z	E	M	A	T	O	I	D	Resembling eczema.
E	D	E	N	T	U	L	A	T	E	Lacking teeth.
E	F	F	A	C	E	M	E	N	T	Reduction to insignificance.
E	F	F	E	M	I	N	A	T	E	Characterized by womanly qualities, Delicate, Extravagant.
E	F	F	E	R	V	E	S	C	E	Fermenting, Bubbling, Hissing, Enthusiasm.
E	F	F	I	C	I	E	N	C	Y	Effectiveness, Performance, Ability, Competence, Expertise, Proficiency, Prowess.
E	F	F	I	G	U	R	A	T	E	Having a definite form.
E	F	F	L	E	U	R	A	G	E	Light stroking message.
E	F	F	L	O	R	E	S	C	E	Blossom, Burst forth, Covered with powdery crust.
E	F	F	U	L	G	E	N	C	E	Brilliance, Strong radiant light.
E	G	O	C	E	N	T	R	I	C	Individualistic, Selfish, Self-centered, Conceited, Vainglorious, Megalomaniac.
E	G	U	A	L	M	E	N	T	E	Direction in music - evenly.
E	G	Y	P	T	O	L	O	G	Y	Study of Egyptian antiquities.
E	I	S	T	E	D	D	F	O	D	A Welsh competitive festival of the arts.
E	L	A	B	O	R	A	T	E	D	Expanded, Amplified, Enlarged, Clarified, Expounded, Interpreted, Unfolded, Evolved.
E	L	A	E	O	P	H	O	R	A	Genus of nematode worms parasitic to sheep.
E	L	A	S	M	O	S	A	U	R	Extinct gigantic marine reptile.
E	L	A	S	T	I	C	I	T	Y	Springiness, Resilience, Adaptability, Flexibility.
E	L	A	T	E	R	I	D	A	E	A large family of elongated tapering beetles, Click beetles.
E	L	E	C	T	O	R	A	T	E	Body of people entitled to voted.
E	L	E	M	E	N	T	A	R	Y	Simple, Fundamental, Primitive, Rudimentary, Easy, Basic, Essential, Preliminary.
E	L	E	O	C	H	A	R	I	S	Genus of sedges with dense spikes of flowers.
E	L	E	O	T	R	I	D	A	E	Large family of small fishes.
E	L	E	U	T	H	E	R	I	A	Genus of hermaphroditic hydrozoan, Jellyfishes.
E	L	L	I	P	T	I	C	A	L	Omitting words from a sentence and causing loss of meaning, Cryptical, Egnimatical.
E	L	L	O	B	I	I	D	A	E	A family of pulmonate snails.
E	L	S	H	O	L	T	Z	I	A	Genus of Asiatic aromatic herbs with blue or purple flowers.
E	L	U	T	R	I	A	T	O	R	An apparatus for separating particles according to size.
E	L	U	V	I	A	T	I	O	N	Leaching, to remove substances in solution.
E	L	Y	T	R	I	F	O	R	M	Shield-shaped.
E	M	A	C	I	A	T	I	N	G	Wasting, Weakening, Attenuating.
E	M	A	C	I	A	T	I	O	N	Process of becoming weak or wasted.
E	M	A	N	C	I	P	A	T	E	Liberate, Free, Discharge, Loose, Release, Unshackle.
E	M	A	N	C	I	P	I	S	T	A prisoner in a former Australian convict settlement whose sentence had been served.
E	M	A	R	G	I	N	U	L	A	Genus of small keyhole limpets.
E	M	A	S	C	U	L	A	T	E	Castrate, Geld, Unnerve, Debilitate, Devitalise, Weaken.
E	M	B	A	N	K	M	E	N	T	Mound of earth to reinforce banks of a river.
E	M	B	L	A	Z	O	N	R	Y	Brilliant decoration.
E	M	B	L	E	M	A	T	I	C	Symbolic, Representative.
E	M	B	O	D	I	M	E	N	T	Incarnation, Incorporation, Personification, Manifestation, Epitome, Quintessence.
E	M	B	O	S	S	M	E	N	T	Protuberance, Boss, Embossed work.
E	M	B	R	O	I	D	E	R	Y	Decorative designs in plain or fancy stitches.
E	M	B	R	Y	O	N	A	T	E	To produce an embryo.
E	M	E	N	D	A	T	I	O	N	Correction, Compensation.
E	M	I	G	R	A	T	I	O	N	The act of leaving one's country to settle in another.
E	M	I	S	S	A	R	I	U	M	A subterranean channel used by the ancient Romans for drainage.
E	M	O	L	L	I	E	N	C	E	The state of being soothing.
E	M	P	I	R	I	C	I	S	M	Quackery, Charlatanry.
E	M	P	L	E	C	T	I	T	E	Mineral consisting of a compound of copper, bismuth and sulfur.
E	M	U	L	S	I	F	I	E	R	An emulsifying agent.
E	N	A	L	I	O	S	A	U	R	Extinct marine reptiles.
E	N	A	M	E	L	W	A	R	E	Iron cooking utensils coated with enamel for protection against rust.
E	N	C	A	M	P	M	E	N	T	A place where a body of troops is camped.
E	N	C	E	P	H	A	L	I	A	Condition of having a brain.
E	N	C	E	P	H	A	L	O	N	The vertebrate brain.
E	N	C	Y	C	L	I	C	A	L	General, A letter for intensive circulation.
E	N	C	Y	R	T	I	D	A	E	A large cosmopolitan family of small chalcid flies.

1	2	3	4	5	6	7	8	9	10	Definition
E	N	C	Y	S	T	M	E	N	T	Becoming enclosed in a capsule.
E	N	D	E	A	R	M	E	N	T	Caress, Expression of affection.
E	N	D	E	R	G	O	N	I	C	Requiring expenditure of energy.
E	N	D	L	I	C	H	I	T	E	A mineral consisting of lead arsenate, vanadate and chloride.
E	N	D	O	B	I	O	T	I	C	Dwelling within the tissues as a parasite.
E	N	D	O	C	H	R	O	M	E	Colouring matter within a cell.
E	N	D	O	D	E	R	M	A	L	Derived from endoderm.
E	N	D	O	D	E	R	M	I	S	The innermost tissue of the cortex in roots and stems.
E	N	D	O	D	O	N	T	I	A	A branch of dentistry dealing with diseases of the pulp.
E	N	D	O	G	A	M	O	U	S	Relating to marriage within a specific group.
E	N	D	O	M	Y	S	I	U	M	Connective tissue surrounding the individual muscular fibres.
E	N	D	O	P	H	A	S	I	A	Speech that is not audible or visible.
E	N	D	O	S	E	P	S	I	S	Internal rotting of figs caused by a fungus.
E	N	D	O	S	T	O	S	I	S	Ossification beginning in the substance of a cartilage.
E	N	D	O	T	H	E	R	M	Y	Generation of heat in tissue.
E	N	D	O	T	O	X	O	I	D	A toxoid derived from an endotoxin.
E	N	E	R	V	A	T	I	O	N	Castration, Exhaustion, Weariness.
E	N	F	L	E	U	R	A	G	E	Extraction of fragrant oils from blossoms for perfumery.
E	N	G	A	G	E	M	E	N	T	Betrothal, Involvement, Attachment, Appointment, Rendezvous, Employment, Action.
E	N	G	E	N	D	E	R	E	R	Producer, Precursor, Originator.
E	N	G	L	I	S	H	I	T	E	A mineral consisting of hydrous basic phosphate of potassium, calcium and aluminium.
E	N	G	L	I	S	H	M	A	N	A native of England.
E	N	G	R	O	S	S	I	N	G	Absorbing, Fascinating, Interesting, Consuming, Monopolizing, Gripping, Exciting.
E	N	K	I	A	N	T	H	U	S	A genus of erect Asiatic shrubs.
E	N	L	I	S	T	M	E	N	T	Period of military service.
E	N	O	R	M	O	U	S	L	Y	Exceedingly, Vastly.
E	N	R	A	P	T	U	R	E	D	Entranced, Elated, Gladdened, Gratified, Pleased, Enchanted, Beguiled, Captivated.
E	N	R	I	C	H	M	E	N	T	Adornment, Accompaniment, Compliment, Enhancement.
E	N	R	O	C	K	M	E	N	T	A mass of large stones thrown into water to form a base.
E	N	R	O	L	L	M	E	N	T	Process of enrolling.
E	N	T	E	L	O	D	O	N	T	Family of prehistoric giant pigs.
E	N	T	E	R	A	L	G	I	A	Pain in the intestines, Colic.
E	N	T	E	R	O	B	I	U	S	Genus of small worms including pinworms of the human intestine.
E	N	T	E	R	O	D	E	R	M	Tissue of the alimentary canal.
E	N	T	E	R	O	L	I	T	H	Calculus occurring in the intestine.
E	N	T	E	R	P	R	I	S	E	Venture, Undertaking, Project, Initiative, Energy, Adventure, Exploit, Pursuit.
E	N	T	H	U	S	I	A	S	M	Transport, Ecstasy, Fervour, Passion, Fascination.
E	N	T	H	U	S	I	A	S	T	Fanatic, Zealot, Bigot, Freak, Maniac, Addict, Devotee, Fan.
E	N	T	O	M	O	L	O	G	Y	Zoology that deals with insects.
E	N	T	O	R	E	T	I	N	A	Internal portion of the retina.
E	N	T	R	A	N	C	I	N	G	Delightful, Bewitching, Captivating, Charming, Fascinating.
E	N	U	M	E	R	A	T	O	R	A census taker.
E	P	H	I	P	P	I	D	A	E	Family of tropical percoid fishes, Spadefishes.
E	P	H	Y	D	R	I	D	A	E	Family of two-winged flies.
E	P	I	C	Y	C	L	O	I	D	A curve traced by a point on a circle.
E	P	I	P	H	Y	L	L	U	M	Genus of tropical American cacti.
E	P	I	P	O	D	I	A	L	E	A bone of the forearm or shank.
E	P	I	S	C	O	P	A	T	E	Diocese, The office of a bishop.
E	P	I	S	I	O	T	O	M	Y	Surgical incision to assist childbirth.
E	P	I	S	T	O	L	I	Z	E	To write a letter.
E	P	I	S	T	R	O	P	H	E	Repetition of a word for emphasis or rhetorical effect.
E	P	I	T	H	E	C	I	U	M	Surface layer of fruiting body in fungi and lichens.
E	P	I	T	H	E	L	I	U	M	Cellular animal tissue.
E	P	O	N	Y	C	H	I	U	M	The quick of a nail.
E	P	T	H	I	A	N	U	R	A	Genus of small short-tailed Australian birds.
E	Q	U	A	B	I	L	I	T	Y	Equanimity, Uniform, Steady.
E	Q	U	A	N	I	M	I	T	Y	Composure, Sangfroid, Phlegm, Calmness, Poise, Aplomb, Serenity, Imperturbability.
E	Q	U	A	T	I	O	N	A	L	Dividing into two equal parts.
E	Q	U	A	T	O	R	I	A	L	Relating to the area of the equator.
E	Q	U	E	S	T	R	I	A	N	Relating to horseback riding, Mounted, Knightly.
E	Q	U	I	P	O	T	E	N	T	Undifferentiated, Having equal effects of capacities.
E	Q	U	I	V	A	L	E	N	T	Synonymous, Duplicate, Identical, Alike, Reciprocal, Parallel, Analogous, Similar.
E	Q	U	I	V	O	C	A	T	E	Lie, Falsify, Prevaricate, Elude, Escape, Evade, Parry, Deceive.
E	R	A	G	R	O	S	T	I	S	Genus of grasses resembling the bluegrasses.
E	R	A	N	T	H	E	M	U	M	Genus of tropical Asiatic shrubs or perennial herbs.
E	R	E	C	H	T	I	T	E	S	Genus of coarse herbs.
E	R	E	M	O	P	H	I	L	A	Genus of shrubs or trees which in Australia can poison cattle.

1	2	3	4	5	6	7	8	9	10	Definition
E	R	G	A	S	T	U	L	U	M	Ancient Roman farm dungeon for confining slave labourers.
E	R	G	A	T	O	G	Y	N	E	A wingless queen ant resembling a worker.
E	R	G	O	T	A	M	I	N	E	A crystalline tripeptide alkaloid from ergot used for treating migraine.
E	R	G	O	T	O	X	I	N	E	A crystalline pharmacologically active alkaloid from ergot.
E	R	I	C	O	P	H	Y	T	E	A plant that grows on a heath or moor.
E	R	I	G	N	A	T	H	U	S	A genus of mammals comprising the bearded seal.
E	R	I	O	B	O	T	R	Y	A	A small genus of Asiatic evergreen trees, Loquat.
E	R	O	T	O	M	A	N	I	A	Excessive sexual desire as a symptom of mental disorder.
E	R	O	T	Y	L	I	D	A	E	A family of hairy beetles having larvae that live in fungi.
E	R	R	A	T	I	C	I	S	M	A wayward act, Being erratic.
E	R	U	C	T	A	T	I	O	N	Belching, Emitting.
E	R	Y	S	I	P	E	L	A	S	An acute skin disease.
E	R	Y	T	H	R	A	S	M	A	A chronic contagious dermatitis.
E	R	Y	T	H	R	I	T	O	L	A sweet crystalline tetrahydroxy alcohol obtained from lichens, algae and yeasts.
E	S	C	A	D	R	I	L	L	E	Unit of European air command containing six planes.
E	S	C	A	M	O	T	A	G	E	Juggling, Trickery, Sleight of hand.
E	S	C	A	P	E	M	E	N	T	Something that escapes, Vent, A control part in a watch.
E	S	C	A	R	P	M	E	N	T	Long cliff separating level surfaces.
E	S	C	R	I	T	O	I	R	E	A combination bureau/writing desk.
E	S	C	U	T	C	H	E	O	N	A place for armorial bearings as to be displayed, Shaped like a shield.
E	S	O	P	H	A	G	E	A	L	Relating to the tube between the throat and the stomach.
E	S	P	A	D	R	I	L	L	E	Flat sandal having fabric upper and a rope sole.
E	S	P	E	C	I	A	L	L	Y	Particularly, Notably, Exceptionally.
E	S	P	R	E	S	S	I	V	O	Direction in music-expressive.
E	S	S	E	N	T	I	A	L	S	Basic or fundamental things.
E	S	T	I	M	A	T	I	O	N	Judgment, Opinion, Point of view, Evaluation, Estimate, Esteem.
E	U	C	A	L	Y	P	T	U	S	A genus of evergreen timber trees.
E	U	C	R	Y	P	T	I	T	E	A mineral consisting of a colourless lithium aluminium silicate.
E	U	D	A	E	M	O	N	I	A	Well-being, Happiness.
E	U	G	E	N	I	C	I	S	T	Student of eugenics.
E	U	G	L	A	N	D	I	N	A	Genus of carnivorous land snails.
E	U	K	I	N	E	T	I	C	S	Science of well-controlled body movement.
E	U	L	O	G	I	S	T	I	C	Panigyrical, Laudatory.
E	U	L	O	P	H	I	D	A	E	A large cosmopolitan family of parasitic chalcid flies.
E	U	P	A	T	O	R	I	U	M	Genus of chiefly tropical herbs.
E	U	P	H	O	R	B	I	U	M	Acrid gum resin derived from a Moroccan spurge used as a veterinary medicine.
E	U	P	H	O	R	I	A	N	T	A drug that tends to induce euphoria.
E	U	T	H	A	N	A	S	I	A	Painless death for persons suffering from incurable diseases.
E	V	A	C	U	A	T	I	O	N	Emptying, Clearing, Discharging, Organized withdrawal.
E	V	A	L	U	A	T	I	O	N	Judgment, Appraisal, Rating, Estimate, Assessment, Decision, Appreciation.
E	V	A	N	G	E	L	I	S	M	The proclamation of the gospel.
E	V	A	N	G	E	L	I	Z	E	Convert to Christianity, Instruct in the gospel.
E	V	A	P	O	R	A	B	L	E	Capable of being evaporated.
E	V	A	P	O	R	A	T	O	R	Apparatus for driving off superfluous liquid.
E	V	E	N	T	U	A	L	L	Y	Finally, Ultimately, Someday.
E	V	E	R	Y	T	H	I	N	G	All that exists.
E	V	E	R	Y	W	H	E	R	E	Every place, Boundless, Space.
E	V	I	S	C	E	R	A	T	E	Disembowel, Devitalize, Gut.
E	X	A	C	E	R	B	A	T	E	Embitter, Sour, Annoy, Exasperate, Irritate, Provoke, Intensify, Inflame.
E	X	A	C	T	I	T	U	D	E	Condition of being exact.
E	X	A	G	G	E	R	A	T	E	Enlarge, Increase, Misrepresent, Accumulate, Embellish, Magnify, Overstate.
E	X	A	L	T	A	T	I	O	N	Elevation, Euphoria, Glorification, Laudation, Praise, Elation, Rapture, Exhilaration.
E	X	A	S	P	E	R	A	T	E	Inflame, Enrage, Irritate, Aggravate, Nettle, Peeve, Pique, Rile.
E	X	C	A	V	A	T	I	O	N	Process of excavating, Hollow, Digging.
E	X	C	E	L	L	E	N	C	E	Merit, Virtue, Perfection, Quality, Distinction, Superior, Worth, Fineness.
E	X	C	I	T	A	T	I	O	N	Excitement, Electric energizing.
E	X	C	I	T	E	M	E	N	T	Agitation, Stir.
E	X	C	L	U	S	I	B	L	E	Subject to exclusion.
E	X	C	R	U	C	I	A	T	E	Inflict intense pain, Irritate, Annoy.
E	X	C	U	S	A	T	O	R	Y	Apologetic.
E	X	E	C	R	A	T	I	O	N	Cursing, Denouncing.
E	X	E	N	T	E	R	A	T	E	Disembowel, Eviscerate.
E	X	E	R	C	I	T	A	N	T	One engaged in spiritual exercises.
E	X	H	A	L	A	T	I	O	N	Evaporation, Expiration, Emanation.
E	X	H	A	U	S	T	I	O	N	State of being exhausted.
E	X	H	I	B	I	T	I	O	N	Demonstration, Display, Show, Spectacle, Exposition, Fair, Presentation.
E	X	H	I	L	A	R	A	T	E	Enliven, Cheer, Gladden, Refresh, Invigorate, Stimulate, Please, Vitalize.

1	2	3	4	5	6	7	8	9	10	Definition
E	X	H	U	M	A	T	I	O	N	Act of disinterring or digging up.
E	X	O	R	B	I	T	A	N	T	Abnormal, Irregular, Excessive, Extravagant, Extreme, Undue, Extortionate.
E	X	O	R	N	A	T	I	O	N	Embellishment, Ornamentation.
E	X	P	A	T	R	I	A	T	E	One living in a foreign country.
E	X	P	E	C	T	A	N	C	Y	Anticipating, Presentiment.
E	X	P	E	D	I	E	N	C	Y	Fitness, Suitability, Self-interest, Aptness, Order, Propriety, Convenience, Resource.
E	X	P	E	D	I	T	I	O	N	Exploration, Journey, Voyage, Excursion, Speed, Haste, Campaign, Alacrity.
E	X	P	E	N	D	A	B	L	E	Normally used or consumed in service, That may be sacrificed.
E	X	P	E	R	I	E	N	C	E	Demonstration, Have, Sustain, Undergo, Encounter, Accept, Survey, Know.
E	X	P	E	R	I	M	E	N	T	Test, Trial, Remedy, Investigate, Probe, Research, Analyze, Scrutinize.
E	X	P	E	R	T	N	E	S	S	Skill.
E	X	P	I	R	A	T	I	O	N	Exhalation, Emission, Termination, Close, Extinction, Death.
E	X	P	O	S	I	T	I	O	N	Elucidation, Interpretation, Explanation, Presentation, Discussion, Production.
E	X	P	R	E	S	S	I	O	N	Manifestation, Utterance, Sign, Token, Issue, Observation, Intimation, Eloquence.
E	X	P	R	E	S	S	I	V	E	Eloquent, Significant, Pregnant, Meaningful, Revealing, Suggestive, Graphic.
E	X	P	U	G	N	A	B	L	E	Capable of being conquered or taken by storm.
E	X	S	A	N	G	U	I	N	E	Bloodless, Anaemic.
E	X	S	I	C	C	O	S	I	S	Dehydration through insufficient intake of fluids.
E	X	T	E	N	S	I	B	L	E	Capable of being extended.
E	X	T	I	N	C	T	I	O	N	Quenching, Suppression, Extermination, Destruction, Annihilation, Cancellation.
E	X	T	I	N	G	U	I	S	H	Quench, Abolish, Crush, Check, Nullify, Suspend, Transfer, Destroy.
E	X	T	R	A	C	T	I	O	N	Pulling, Yanking, Prying, Extorting, Gleaning, Origin, Lineage, Descent, Birth.
E	X	T	R	A	N	E	O	U	S	Accidental, Foreign, Irrelevant, Extrinsic, Alien, Inherent, Impertinent, Inapplicable.
E	X	U	B	E	R	A	N	C	E	Ebullience, Buoyancy, Effervescence, Gayness, Friskiness, Liveliness, Zest.
E	X	U	L	T	A	T	I	O	N	Jubilation, Triumph, Delight, Elation, Celebration, Satisfaction, Rejoicing, Gloating.
E	Y	E	G	L	A	S	S	E	S	Spectacles.
E	Y	E	W	I	T	N	E	S	S	To see with one's eyes, One that testifies to what he has seen.

F

1	2	3	4	5	6	7	8	9	10	Definition
F	A	B	U	L	A	T	I	O	N	Act of inventing or retailing fantastic tales.
F	A	C	I	L	I	T	A	T	E	Assist, Aid, Ease.
F	A	C	T	I	O	N	A	R	Y	Partisan.
F	A	C	T	U	A	L	I	S	M	Dedication to facts.
F	A	H	R	E	N	H	E	I	T	Conforming to a thermometric scale.
F	A	L	C	O	N	I	D	A	E	Family of birds of prey, Falcons, Caracaras.
F	A	L	L	A	C	I	O	U	S	Deceptive, Misleading, Delusive, Disappointing, Illogical, Irrational, Deceiving.
F	A	M	I	L	I	A	R	L	Y	Intimately, Commonly, Informally, Presumptuously, Boldly, Frequently, Intimately.
F	A	N	A	T	I	C	I	S	M	Fanatical behaviour.
F	A	N	G	L	E	M	E	N	T	Contrivance, Device, Frippery, Gewgaw.
F	A	N	T	A	S	T	I	C	O	A pretentiously fantastic person.
F	A	R	F	E	T	C	H	E	D	Forced, Strained, Laboured, Bizarre, Grotesque, Eccentric, Erratic, Strange.
F	A	R	I	N	O	G	R	A	M	Record of an apparatus for mixing dough under controlled conditions.
F	A	R	S	I	G	H	T	E	D	Able to see a great distance, Having good judgment, Sagacious.
F	A	S	C	I	A	T	I	O	N	Malformation resulting from disorganized tissue growth.
F	A	S	C	I	C	U	L	U	S	A bundle of skeletal muscle cells.
F	A	S	C	I	N	A	T	E	D	Attracted, Enthralled, Enraptured.
F	A	S	C	I	O	L	O	I	D	Resembling worms.
F	A	S	T	I	D	I	O	U	S	Nice, Dainty, Fussy, Particular, Squeamish, Demanding, Critical, Exacting.
F	A	T	H	E	R	L	E	S	S	Illegitimate, Without a father.
F	A	T	H	O	M	L	E	S	S	Incomprehensible, Bottomless, Abysmal, Unfathomable.
F	E	A	T	U	R	E	T	T	E	A short feature film.
F	E	B	R	I	F	U	G	A	L	Relieving fever.
F	E	B	R	U	A	T	I	O	N	Purification by a religious ceremony.
F	E	D	E	R	A	T	I	O	N	Alliance, Coalition, Confederacy, League, Union.
F	E	D	E	R	A	T	I	V	E	Based on federation.
F	E	E	B	L	E	N	E	S	S	The state of being feeble.
F	E	L	I	C	I	T	A	T	E	Congratulate, Compliment, Commend, Salute, Console, Comfort, Solace
F	E	L	I	C	I	T	O	U	S	Pleasant, Charming, Delightful, Fit, Proper, Happy, Relevant, Pertinent.
F	E	L	L	O	W	S	H	I	P	Company, Society, Union, Association, Fraternity, Brotherhood, Friendliness.
F	E	L	S	E	N	M	E	E	R	A collection of loose surface rock fragments usually above the timberline.
F	E	N	E	S	T	E	L	L	A	A small window or opening near a church altar.
F	E	N	E	S	T	E	L	L	E	A group of small windows.
F	E	N	O	U	I	L	L	E	T	A liqueur flavoured with fennel seed.
F	E	R	G	H	A	N	I	T	E	A mineral consisting of a hydrated uranion vanadate.
F	E	R	R	O	A	L	L	O	Y	A crude alloy of iron with elements used for making alloy steels.

1	2	3	4	5	6	7	8	9	10	Definition
F	E	R	R	U	C	C	I	T	E	A mineral consisting of sodium flouborate.
F	E	R	T	I	L	I	Z	E	R	A substance used to fertilize the soil.
F	E	S	C	E	N	N	I	N	E	Obscene, Scurrilous, Coarse, Dirty, Lewd, Vulgar, Smutty, Raunchy.
F	E	T	T	E	R	L	O	C	K	A device once attached to a horse's leg to prevent it straying.
F	E	U	I	L	L	E	T	O	N	Serial, Thriller, Sketch.
F	I	A	N	C	H	E	T	T	O	A special opening in chess.
F	I	B	E	R	B	O	A	R	D	A material made of compressed fibres.
F	I	B	R	I	L	L	A	T	E	To cause irregular contractions of the heart, Twitching, Fringed.
F	I	B	R	I	L	L	O	S	E	Consisting of small threads or fine fibres.
F	I	B	R	I	N	O	G	E	N	A globulin that is produced in the liver.
F	I	B	R	O	S	I	T	I	S	A painful muscular condition originating in the connective tissue of the muscles.
F	I	C	T	I	T	I	O	U	S	Fabulous, Legendary, Mythical, Apocryphal, Fanciful, Created, Invented, Illusory.
F	I	E	D	L	E	R	I	T	E	A lead mineral.
F	I	E	N	D	I	S	H	L	Y	Wickedly, Cruelly, Hideously, Unpleasantly.
F	I	E	R	C	E	N	E	S	S	Ferocity.
F	I	G	U	R	A	T	I	V	E	Metaphorical, Represented by a figure or resemblance.
F	I	L	A	R	I	A	S	I	S	Disease caused by blood parasites, Elephantiasis.
F	I	L	A	R	I	I	D	A	E	Family of nematode worms.
F	I	L	I	B	U	S	T	E	R	Irregular military adventurer, One who delays legislative action by dilatory tactics.
F	I	L	I	C	I	N	E	A	E	Plants that produce no seeds.
F	I	L	I	F	E	R	O	U	S	Bearing threads.
F	I	L	T	H	I	N	E	S	S	State of being filthy.
F	I	L	T	R	A	T	I	O	N	Percolation, Diffusion.
F	I	M	I	C	O	L	O	U	S	Inhabiting or growing on dung.
F	I	N	G	E	R	R	O	O	T	Foxglove.
F	I	S	S	U	R	E	L	L	A	A genus of marine gastropods, Keyhole limpets.
F	I	S	T	I	C	U	F	F	S	Boxing.
F	L	A	B	B	I	N	E	S	S	The state of being flabby.
F	L	A	B	E	L	L	A	T	E	Resembling a fan in shape.
F	L	A	G	E	L	L	A	N	T	One that whips. One that responds sexually to beatings, and practices self-castigation.
F	L	A	G	E	L	L	A	T	E	Whip, Scourge, Flog, Drive, Punish, Stigmatize.
F	L	A	G	I	T	I	O	U	S	Scandalous, Villainous, Corrupt, Vicious, Degenerate, Depraved, Nefarious, Infamous.
F	L	A	M	B	O	Y	A	N	T	Ornate, Showy, Resplendent, Unrestrained, Rich, Florid, Baroque, Ostentatious.
F	L	A	M	E	P	R	O	O	F	Can be in contact with a flame without burning.
F	L	A	M	M	A	T	I	O	N	Igniting.
F	L	A	S	H	L	I	G	H	T	Battery operated portable light, Artificial light for taking pictures.
F	L	A	T	U	L	E	N	C	E	State of being flatulent.
F	L	A	V	I	A	N	A	T	E	A salt of flavianic acid.
F	L	A	V	E	S	C	E	N	T	Turning yellow.
F	L	E	S	H	I	N	E	S	S	Corpulence.
F	L	E	X	I	M	E	T	E	R	An instrument to test flexibility of materials.
F	L	I	C	K	E	R	I	N	G	Wavering, Unsteady, Feeble, Slight movement.
F	L	I	G	H	T	L	E	S	S	Unable to fly.
F	L	I	P	P	A	N	T	L	Y	Nimbly, Frivolously.
F	L	I	R	T	A	T	I	O	N	Coquetry, Lighthearted courtship.
F	L	O	C	C	U	L	A	N	T	An agent that produces aggregate formation.
F	L	O	C	C	U	L	O	S	E	Bearing small tufts of hairs.
F	L	O	C	C	U	L	E	N	T	Woolly, Flocky, Soft flakes.
F	L	O	R	E	N	C	I	T	E	A mineral composed of basic phosphate of cerium and aluminium.
F	L	O	R	I	A	T	I	O	N	Floral ornament.
F	L	O	R	I	B	U	N	D	A	Hybrid roses.
F	L	O	U	R	I	S	H	E	D	Blossomed, Thrived, Succeeded, Swung, Ornamented, Scored, Increased, Expanded.
F	L	U	O	B	O	R	I	T	E	A mineral consisting of magnesium fluoborate.
F	L	U	O	C	E	R	I	T	E	A mineral consisting of reddish yellow fluoride of cerium.
F	L	U	O	R	I	D	A	T	E	To treat with a fluoride.
F	L	U	O	R	I	N	A	T	E	Combine with fluorine.
F	L	U	T	O	P	H	O	N	E	A simple wind instrument with a flared end.
F	L	U	T	T	E	R	I	N	G	Flapping, Quaking, Quivering, Vibrating, Trembling, Flickering, Fluctuating.
F	L	U	V	I	A	T	I	L	E	Produced by the action of streams and rivers.
F	O	E	N	I	C	U	L	U	M	A small genus of Eurasian herbs, Fennel.
F	O	L	I	A	C	E	O	U	S	Having the texture of a foliage leaf.
F	O	N	T	A	N	E	L	L	E	Membrane covered space in bone of an infant's skull prior to complete closure.
F	O	R	A	M	I	N	A	T	E	Perforated.
F	O	R	B	I	D	D	I	N	G	Disagreeable, Repellent, Menacing, Grim, Frightening, Overpowering.
F	O	R	E	B	O	D	I	N	G	Portent, Apprehension, Presage, Prediction, Presentiment.
F	O	R	E	C	A	S	T	E	R	One that professionally forecasts the weather.
F	O	R	E	C	A	S	T	L	E	The forward part of a ship.

1	2	3	4	5	6	7	8	9	10	Clue
F	O	R	E	C	O	U	R	S	E	Foresail.
F	O	R	E	F	I	N	G	E	R	Index finger.
F	O	R	E	O	R	D	A	I	N	Predetermine, Predestinate.
F	O	R	E	R	U	N	N	E	R	Harbinger, Predecessor, Forebear, Ancestor, Herald, Outrider, Announcer.
F	O	R	E	S	H	A	D	O	W	Prefigure, Adumbrate, Augur, Omen, Portent, Presage, Promise, Forebode.
F	O	R	E	S	T	I	E	R	A	Genus of spiny American shrubs or trees, Tanglebush.
F	O	R	F	E	I	T	U	R	E	Loss of some right, privilege, estate, honour or effects.
F	O	R	M	I	C	I	D	A	E	Family of hymenopterous insects including all the ants.
F	O	R	M	I	D	A	B	L	E	Inspiring awe, almost impossible to defeat.
F	O	R	S	T	E	R	I	T	E	A mineral consisting of magnesian olivine.
F	O	R	T	E	M	E	N	T	E	Direction in music-loudly, powerfully.
F	O	R	T	H	R	I	G	H	T	Direct, Straightforward, Frankly, Immediately, Candid, Open, Plain, Aboveboard.
F	O	R	T	I	S	S	I	M	O	Direction in music-very loud.
F	O	R	T	U	I	T	O	U	S	Accidental, Casual, Contingent, Incidental, Chance, Odd.
F	O	S	T	E	R	L	I	N	G	A foster child.
F	O	U	N	D	A	T	I	O	N	Basis, Understanding, Endowment, Groundwork, Infrastructure, Warrant, Base.
F	O	U	Q	U	I	E	R	I	A	A genus of scarlet-flowered shrubs or low trees that are leafless most of the year.
F	R	A	C	T	I	O	N	A	L	Small, broken into pieces, relating to fractions.
F	R	A	G	M	E	N	T	A	L	Fragmentary.
F	R	A	N	C	I	S	C	A	N	Member of a religious order, St Francis of Assisi.
F	R	A	N	C	K	E	I	T	E	A mineral consisting of a dark gray or black massive lead antimony tin sulfide.
F	R	A	N	G	I	P	A	N	E	A dessert of almond cream flavoured with frangipani or jasmine perfume.
F	R	A	N	G	I	P	A	N	I	Tropical American shrub, Perfume of the red jasmine.
F	R	A	T	E	R	N	I	T	Y	Company, Guild, Association, Brotherhood, Club, League, Society.
F	R	A	T	E	R	N	I	Z	E	Associate, Mingle.
F	R	A	T	R	I	C	I	D	E	Murder of a brother or sister.
F	R	A	U	D	U	L	E	N	T	False, Based on fraud.
F	R	A	X	I	N	E	L	L	A	Eurasian perennial herbs with flowers which exhale a flammable vapour in hot weather.
F	R	E	E	B	O	O	T	E	R	Pirate, Pillager.
F	R	E	E	H	O	L	D	E	R	Owner of a freehold.
F	R	E	E	M	A	R	T	I	N	Sexually imperfect sterile female calf twinborn with a male.
F	R	E	G	A	T	I	D	A	E	Family of web-footed sea birds, Frigate birds.
F	R	I	A	B	I	L	I	T	Y	Condition of being friable.
F	R	I	E	N	D	S	H	I	P	Goodwill, Benevolence, Friendliness, Empathy, Accord, Harmony, Affinity, Alliance.
F	R	I	G	H	T	E	N	E	D	Scared, Amazed, Terrified, Startled, Alarmed, Terrorized, Appalled, Afraid.
F	R	I	J	O	L	I	L	L	O	Leguminous herbs, Coral bean, Locoweed.
F	R	I	N	G	E	F	O	O	T	A desert lizard.
F	R	O	L	I	C	S	O	M	E	Sportive, Playful, Coltish, Frisky, Mischievous, Impish, Antic, Roguish.
F	R	O	N	D	E	L	I	T	E	A mineral consisting of a basic phosphate of manganese and iron.
F	R	I	G	I	D	N	E	S	S	State of being frigid.
F	R	U	C	T	I	F	O	R	M	Having the form of a fruit.
F	R	U	C	T	A	R	I	A	N	One who lives chiefly on fruit.
F	R	U	S	T	R	A	T	E	D	Checked, Balked, Thwarted, Foiled, Baffled, Cicrumvented, Defeated, Disappointed.
F	R	U	T	I	C	E	T	U	M	Collection of shrubs grown for ornament or study.
F	U	C	O	S	T	E	R	O	L	A crystalline sterol occurring in various algae.
F	U	L	G	O	R	I	D	A	E	Family of chiefly tropical plant-feeding insects.
F	U	L	I	G	I	N	O	U	S	Sooty, Clouded, Obscure, Murky, Dark, Dusky.
F	U	M	I	G	A	T	I	O	N	Process of fumigating.
F	U	N	A	R	I	A	L	E	S	Order of acrocarpous mosses.
F	U	R	A	N	O	S	I	D	E	A glycoside containing the ring characteristic of a furanose.
F	U	S	I	C	O	C	C	U	M	A form genus of imperfect fungi.
F	U	S	T	A	N	E	L	L	A	Stiff white skirt worn by the Evzones of Greece.
F	U	T	U	R	O	L	O	G	Y	Prediction of the future of the world.

G

1	2	3	4	5	6	7	8	9	10	Clue
G	A	D	O	L	I	N	I	T	E	A mineral that is a source of rare earths.
G	A	D	O	L	I	N	I	U	M	A trivalent magnetic metallic element of the rare earth group.
G	A	I	L	L	A	R	D	I	A	A genus of American herbs with showy flowers.
G	A	L	A	C	T	O	S	Y	L	A glycosyl radical derived from galactose.
G	A	L	A	X	I	I	D	A	E	A family of scaleless freshwater and marine salmonoid fishes.
G	A	L	B	U	L	I	D	A	E	A family of brightly coloured tropical American birds.
G	A	L	E	O	C	E	R	D	O	Genus of sharks, Tiger shark.
G	A	L	E	T	H	Y	L	A	X	Prehistoric carnivorous mammal.
G	A	L	I	D	I	C	T	I	S	A genus of Malagasay mongooses.
G	A	L	L	O	M	A	N	I	A	A strong prejudice in favour of what is French.

1	2	3	4	5	6	7	8	9	10	
G	A	M	E	T	O	C	Y	T	E	A cell that divides to produce gametes.
G	A	M	M	A	G	R	A	P	H	A radiograph produced by gamma rays.
G	A	N	G	R	E	N	O	U	S	Affected by gangrene.
G	A	N	O	M	A	L	I	T	E	A mineral consisting of a colourless to gray silicate of lead and calcium.
G	A	R	A	M	B	U	L	L	A	An arborescent cactus that bears an edible berry.
G	A	R	G	A	N	T	U	A	N	Gigantic, Colossal, Huge, Enormous, Leviathan, Mammoth, Monstrous, Titanic.
G	A	R	G	O	Y	L	I	S	M	A genetic variation involving structural defects of the skeleton and mental deficiency.
G	A	R	N	I	E	R	I	T	E	A silicate mineral consisting of hydrous nickel magnesium.
G	A	R	R	Y	A	C	E	A	E	A family of dicotyledonous plants.
G	A	S	T	R	A	L	G	I	A	Pain in the stomach.
G	A	S	T	R	O	L	O	G	Y	Science of caring for the stomach.
G	A	S	T	R	O	N	O	M	E	Epicure, Expert judge of good food and drink.
G	A	S	T	R	O	N	O	M	Y	Science of good eating.
G	A	S	T	R	O	P	E	X	Y	A surgical operation to suture the stomach to the abdominal wall.
G	A	S	T	R	O	P	O	R	E	A pore in a hydrozoan coral occupied by a gastrozooid.
G	A	U	L	T	H	E	R	I	A	Genus of evergreen shrubs producing small berry-like fruits.
G	A	Y	L	U	S	S	I	T	E	A mineral consisting of a translucent hydrous carbonate of calcium and sodium.
G	E	C	A	R	C	I	N	U	S	Type genus of the crab family, Black crab, Land crab.
G	E	I	K	K	I	E	L	I	T	A mineral of magnesium titanate occuring as bluish or brownish black pebbles.
G	E	K	K	O	N	I	D	A	E	A large family of lizards, Gekko.
G	E	L	A	T	I	N	A	S	E	An enzyme causing liquefaction of gelatin often occurring in baderia.
G	E	L	A	T	I	N	O	U	S	Resembling jelly, Viscous, Flocculent.
G	E	L	I	D	I	A	L	E	S	Small order of red algae.
G	E	M	I	N	A	T	I	O	N	Formation of two teeth from a single tooth germ.
G	E	M	I	N	A	T	I	V	E	Showing gemination.
G	E	M	P	Y	L	I	D	A	E	Family of elongated oily-fleshed fishes resembling mackerel.
G	E	N	E	C	O	L	O	G	Y	Branch of ecology concerned with the species and the controlling genetic factors.
G	E	N	E	R	A	L	I	T	Y	A vague statement, Bulk.
G	E	N	E	R	A	T	I	N	G	Procreating, Producing, Propagating, Originating, Founding, Spawning, Developing.
G	E	N	E	R	O	S	I	T	Y	Benevolence, Abundance, Magnanimity, Copiousness, Largeness, Liberality.
G	E	N	E	S	E	R	I	N	E	A crystalline alkaloid found in the Calabar bean.
G	E	N	E	T	H	L	I	A	C	Relating to the zodiac influence at birth.
G	E	N	E	T	I	C	I	S	T	A specialist in genetics.
G	E	N	I	C	U	L	A	T	E	Bent at an acute angle, jointed.
G	E	N	I	O	H	Y	O	I	D	Relating to the chin and hyoid bone.
G	E	N	T	L	E	N	E	S	S	Mildness, Smoothness, Tenderness, Kindness, Mellowness.
G	E	O	C	E	N	T	R	I	C	Relating to the earth as the centre.
G	E	O	C	R	O	N	I	T	E	A mineral consisting of massive lead-gray lead antimony arsenic sulfide.
G	E	O	G	N	O	S	T	I	C	Relating to a branch of geology dealing with the materials of the earth.
G	E	O	G	R	A	P	H	I	C	Relating to geography.
G	E	O	L	O	G	I	C	A	L	Relating to geology.
G	E	O	M	E	T	R	I	Z	E	To work out by geometric methods.
G	E	O	M	O	R	P	H	I	C	Relating to the form of the earth or its surface features.
G	E	O	M	Y	O	I	D	E	A	Family of rodents with external cheek pouches, Kangaroo rat.
G	E	O	P	H	A	G	I	S	T	One that eats earth.
G	E	O	P	H	A	G	O	U	S	Eating earth.
G	E	O	P	H	I	L	O	U	S	Living or growing in the ground.
G	E	O	P	H	Y	S	I	C	S	The physics of the earth.
G	E	O	S	C	I	E	N	C	E	The sciences of the earth.
G	E	O	T	E	U	T	H	I	S	Genus of extinct cuttlefishes.
G	E	O	T	R	O	P	I	S	M	Tropism in which gravitational attraction is the orienting factor.
G	E	R	A	N	I	A	L	E	S	Order of herbaceous plants, Geraniums, Flaxes, Cranesbills.
G	E	R	A	T	O	L	O	G	Y	Scientific study of aging.
G	E	R	I	A	T	R	I	S	T	Specialist in the branch of medicine dealing with old age.
G	E	R	M	I	C	I	D	A	L	A substance for destroying germs.
G	E	R	O	D	E	R	M	I	A	Premature aging of the skin.
G	E	T	H	S	E	M	A	N	E	A place of suffering.
G	H	O	S	T	S	T	O	R	Y	Stories dealing with ghosts.
G	I	A	R	D	I	A	S	I	S	Infestation of the intestines with a genus of zooflagellates.
G	I	B	B	E	R	E	L	L	A	Genus of fungi causing various abnormalities of cereal grasses.
G	I	N	G	E	R	S	N	A	P	A ginger-flavoured biscuit.
G	I	N	G	I	V	I	T	I	S	Inflammation of the gingival tissue.
G	I	N	G	L	Y	M	O	D	I	An order of ganoid fishes.
G	L	A	C	I	A	R	I	U	M	A skating rink with a floor of artificial ice.
G	L	A	C	I	O	L	O	G	Y	Study of glaciers.
G	L	A	M	O	U	R	I	Z	E	Idealize, Romanticize.
G	L	A	N	D	E	R	O	U	S	Resembing the effect of glanders disease.

1	2	3	4	5	6	7	8	9	10	Definition
G	L	A	N	D	U	L	O	U	S	Glandular.
G	L	A	U	B	E	R	I	T	E	A light-coloured brittle sodium calcium sulfate.
G	L	A	U	C	O	N	I	T	E	A mineral consisting of a dull green earthy and micaceous iron potassium silicate.
G	L	E	I	C	H	E	N	I	A	Type genus of ferns.
G	L	E	I	Z	A	T	I	O	N	Development of clay.
G	L	I	T	T	E	R	I	N	G	Resplendent, Brilliant, Sparkling, Twinkling, Showy, Gaudy, Flashing, Shimmering.
G	L	O	R	I	O	U	S	L	Y	Splendidly, Illustriously, Wonderfully, Magnificently.
G	L	O	S	S	A	L	G	I	A	Pain localized in the tongue.
G	L	O	S	S	I	N	E	S	S	State of being glossy.
G	L	O	S	S	M	E	T	E	R	A photometer for measuring the gloss of test surfaces.
G	L	O	S	S	O	H	Y	A	L	Relating to the hyoid arch and tongue.
G	L	O	T	T	A	L	I	Z	E	To articulate.
G	L	O	T	T	O	L	O	G	Y	Linguistics.
G	L	U	C	O	S	I	D	A	L	Yielding glucose on hydrolysis.
G	L	U	T	T	O	N	O	U	S	Voracious, Rapacious, Indulgent, Piggish, Hoggish.
G	L	Y	C	O	L	L	A	T	E	A salt or ester of glycolic acid.
G	L	Y	C	O	L	Y	S	I	S	An enzymatic breakdown of carbohydrates.
G	L	Y	C	O	S	U	R	I	A	Presence of abnormal amounts of sugar in the urine.
G	L	Y	O	X	A	L	A	S	E	An enzyme that accelerates conversion to lactic acid.
G	L	Y	P	T	O	D	O	N	T	Genus of extinct mammals related to the armadillos.
G	L	Y	P	T	O	L	O	G	Y	The study of carving or engraving on gems.
G	N	A	P	H	A	L	I	U	M	A large genus of hoary herbs, Balsamweed.
G	N	O	M	O	L	O	G	I	C	Expressive of what is universally true.
G	N	O	S	E	O	L	O	G	Y	The philosophic theory of knowledge.
G	N	O	S	T	I	C	I	S	M	Heretical pre-Christian cults.
G	O	L	D	B	E	A	T	E	R	A person who beats gold into goldleaf.
G	O	M	P	H	O	D	O	N	T	Having the teeth implanted in sockets.
G	O	N	I	O	C	O	T	E	S	A genus of bird lice.
G	O	N	I	O	M	E	T	R	Y	Measurement of angles.
G	O	N	I	O	S	C	O	P	E	An instrument which enables the interior of the eye to be examined.
G	O	N	O	C	H	O	R	I	C	Having the sexes separate.
G	O	N	O	C	O	C	C	U	S	Pus-producing bacterium that causes gonorrhea.
G	O	N	Y	S	T	Y	L	U	S	Small genus of East Indian trees.
G	O	O	S	E	B	E	R	R	Y	Acid bristly fruit of a cane.
G	O	O	S	E	F	L	E	S	H	Raised pores of the skin usually caused by cold or fear, Goose pimples.
G	O	R	C	E	I	X	I	T	E	Mineral consisting of a hydrous basic phosphate of barium and aluminium.
G	O	R	D	I	O	I	D	E	A	Order of freshwater forms parasitic as larvae.
G	O	R	M	A	N	D	I	Z	E	Devour.
G	O	S	S	Y	P	E	T	I	N	A yellow crystalline flavone pigment occurring in cotton flowers.
G	O	V	E	R	N	A	N	C	E	Government, Authority.
G	O	V	E	R	N	M	E	N	T	Discretion, Administration, Rule, Political science.
G	R	A	D	U	A	L	I	S	M	Practice of proceeding by gradual stages.
G	R	A	F	T	O	N	I	T	E	A mineral consisting of an iron manganese calcium phosphate.
G	R	A	M	I	N	E	O	U	S	Resembling a grass.
G	R	A	M	O	P	H	I	L	E	Collector of phonograph records.
G	R	A	N	A	D	I	L	L	A	Oblong fruit of the passion flower.
G	R	A	N	D	S	T	A	N	D	A roofed structure designed for spectators.
G	R	A	P	E	F	R	U	I	T	A large globose citrus fruit with acid juicy flesh.
G	R	A	P	H	I	T	I	Z	E	To coat with graphite.
G	R	A	P	H	O	L	O	G	Y	The study of handwriting.
G	R	A	P	H	O	T	Y	P	E	A form of chalk engraving.
G	R	A	S	P	I	N	G	L	Y	In a grasping manner.
G	R	A	T	E	F	U	L	L	Y	Thankfully, Appreciatively.
G	R	A	T	I	F	Y	I	N	G	Giving pleasure or satisfaction.
G	R	A	T	U	I	T	O	U	S	Free, Complimentary, Gratis, Voluntary.
G	R	A	V	E	S	T	O	N	E	Tombstone, Headstone.
G	R	A	V	I	G	R	A	D	A	Ground sloths.
G	R	A	V	I	M	E	T	E	R	A device for determining the specific gravity of liquid or solid substance.
G	R	A	V	I	M	E	T	R	Y	Measurement of weight or density.
G	R	E	A	S	E	W	O	O	D	Low stiff shrub, Hopsage, Iodine bush, White sage.
G	R	E	E	D	I	N	E	S	S	Voracity, Covetousness, Eagerness.
G	R	E	E	N	B	R	I	E	R	A prickly vine.
G	R	E	E	N	H	O	U	S	E	Conservatory, Hothouse.
G	R	E	E	N	O	V	I	T	E	A sphene coloured red or rose by manganese.
G	R	E	G	A	R	I	O	U	S	Social, Sociable, Growing in a cluster.
G	R	I	M	M	I	A	L	E	S	An order of mosses that are blackish green and grow chiefly on rocks.
G	R	I	N	N	E	L	L	I	A	Red algae.

1	2	3	4	5	6	7	8	9	10	Definition
G	R	I	S	E	L	I	N	I	A	Small genus New Zealand and South American trees.
G	R	O	B	I	A	N	I	S	M	Boorishness.
G	R	O	U	N	D	W	O	R	K	Foundation, Basis.
G	R	O	V	E	L	L	I	N	G	Fawning, Creeping, Crawling, Cringing, Wallowing, Toadying, Cowering, Kowtowing.
G	R	U	I	F	O	R	M	E	S	Order of marsh-dwelling and wading birds, Coots, Bustards, Cranes, Rails.
G	R	U	M	I	C	H	A	M	A	A low-growing tree with glossy leaves and white flowers.
G	U	A	G	U	A	N	C	H	E	A barracuda of the Caribbean area.
G	U	A	N	O	P	H	O	R	E	A chromatophore of granules or crystals that occurs on the skin of fishes.
G	U	A	R	D	H	O	U	S	E	A building serving as guard headquarters and a military prison.
G	U	D	M	U	N	D	I	T	E	A mineral that is a sulfide and antimonide or iron.
G	U	I	G	N	A	R	D	I	A	A genus of fungi, Black rot.
G	U	I	L	A	N	D	I	N	A	Tropical American woody vines having seeds enclosed in large prickly pods.
G	U	I	L	L	O	T	I	N	E	A machine for beheading by means of a sharp blade sliding up and down.
G	U	T	T	I	F	E	R	A	E	A family of tropical trees and shrubs.
G	Y	M	N	A	D	E	N	I	A	Genus of European terrestrial orchids.
G	Y	M	N	A	N	T	H	E	S	Small genus of tropical American shrubs with evergreen leaves and a milky juice.
G	Y	M	N	A	R	C	H	U	S	A soft-finned African river fish having a radar-like sense organ in the tail.
G	Y	M	N	O	C	O	N	I	A	A rust of the raspberry and blackberry canes.
G	Y	M	N	O	P	L	A	S	T	A cell or mass of protoplasm devoid of a distinct cell wall.
G	Y	M	N	O	R	H	I	N	A	A genus of oscine birds, Australian piping crows.
G	Y	M	N	O	S	P	O	R	E	A naked spore.
G	Y	N	O	G	A	M	O	N	E	A gamon that occurs in an egg.
G	Y	P	S	O	P	H	I	L	A	Genus of herbs having small delicate flowers, Baby's breath.
G	Y	P	S	O	P	L	A	S	T	A cast in plaster of paris.

H

1	2	3	4	5	6	7	8	9	10	Definition
H	A	B	I	L	I	M	E	N	T	Trappings, Clothing, Gear, Equipment.
H	A	B	I	T	U	A	T	E	D	Accustomed, Familiarized, Frequented, Used, Chronic, Confirmed, Addicted.
H	A	C	K	M	A	N	I	T	E	A sodalite containing a little sulphur.
H	A	C	K	M	A	T	A	C	K	Coniferous pine, Common juniper, Balsam poplar.
H	A	E	M	A	G	O	G	U	S	Strong-flying mosquitoes some of which transmit yellow fever.
H	A	E	M	A	N	T	H	U	S	Genus of African bulbous herbs, Amaryllis.
H	A	E	M	A	T	I	N	O	N	Ancient hard opaque red glass.
H	A	E	M	A	T	O	P	U	S	Genus of shore birds, Oyster catchers.
H	A	E	M	O	N	C	H	U	S	Genus of parasitic worms found chiefly in sheep.
H	A	G	I	O	C	R	A	C	Y	Government by a body of persons regarded as holy.
H	A	G	I	O	L	A	T	R	Y	Worship of saints.
H	A	G	I	O	S	C	O	P	E	An opening in the interior wall of a church affording a view of the altar from the transept.
H	A	I	R	S	T	R	E	A	K	Small butterflies having striped markings under the wings.
H	A	K	E	N	K	R	E	U	Z	The swastika used by the German Nazi Government.
H	A	L	B	E	R	D	I	E	R	A person armed with a halberd.
H	A	L	I	S	I	D	O	T	A	Genus of arctiid moths.
H	A	L	L	E	L	U	J	A	H	Shout or song of praise.
H	A	L	O	G	E	N	A	T	E	To combine with a halogen.
H	A	L	O	H	Y	D	R	I	N	Class of compounds derived from glycols or polyhydroxy alcohols.
H	A	L	O	L	I	M	N	I	C	Capable of living in fresh water.
H	A	L	O	P	H	Y	T	I	C	Flourishing in a salty habitat.
H	A	L	O	T	Y	D	E	U	S	Genus of soft-bodied mites destructive to crops.
H	A	M	B	R	O	L	I	N	E	Three strand tarred hemp or jute marine cordage.
H	A	N	C	O	C	K	I	T	E	A complex silicate that contains lead calcium strontium and other metals.
H	A	N	D	I	C	R	A	F	T	An occupation where the articles are usually made by hand.
H	A	N	S	E	N	O	S	I	S	Leprosy.
H	A	P	L	O	S	C	O	P	E	Simple stereoscope used in the study of depth perception.
H	A	R	A	S	S	M	E	N	T	Vexation, Annoyance, Provokation, Irking, Aggravation, Exasperation, Irritation.
H	A	R	D	B	O	I	L	E	D	Callous, Tough, Unfeeling, Obdurate, Unsympathetic, Pragmatic, Unemotional.
H	A	R	D	H	E	A	D	E	D	Stubborn, Wilful, Practical, Sober, Realistic, Obstinate, Headstrong, Intractable.
H	A	R	D	W	I	C	K	I	A	A small genus of Indian trees.
H	A	R	M	O	N	I	O	U	S	Congruous, Compatible, Blending, Harmonic, Musical, Satisfying, Amicable.
H	A	R	S	T	I	G	I	T	E	A mineral consisting of a silicate of beryllium and calcium.
H	A	R	T	E	B	E	E	S	T	A large African antelope.
H	A	R	V	E	S	T	I	N	G	Gathering, Reaping, Garnering, Collecting, Accumulating, Storing.
H	A	U	L	A	G	E	W	A	Y	Mine passage for transport of coal.
H	A	U	S	T	E	L	L	U	M	A proboscis adapted for sucking blood or juices of plants.
H	A	U	S	T	O	R	I	U	M	Food-absorbing outgrowth of a plant.

1	2	3	4	5	6	7	8	9	10	Definition
H	E	A	D	M	A	S	T	E	R	School principal.
H	E	A	D	S	H	A	K	E	R	Pessimist, Skeptic.
H	E	A	D	S	P	R	I	N	G	Fountainhead, Source.
H	E	A	D	S	T	R	O	N	G	Obstinate, Unruly, Mulish, Refractory, Stubborn, Wilful, Self-willed, Stiff-necked.
H	E	A	R	T	S	E	A	S	E	Tranquillity, Wild pansy.
H	E	A	T	H	E	N	I	S	H	Relating to the heathen.
H	E	A	T	S	T	R	O	K	E	Collapse and dehydration due to overexposure to heat.
H	E	A	V	E	N	W	A	R	D	Toward heaven.
H	E	B	D	O	M	A	D	A	L	Weekly, Lasting seven days.
H	E	C	T	O	M	E	T	R	E	Metric unit of length, One hundred metres.
H	E	L	I	A	N	T	H	I	N	A red compound of quinone structure.
H	E	L	I	A	N	T	H	U	S	Genus of tall erect herbs, Sunflowers.
H	E	L	I	C	O	P	T	E	R	An aircraft which flies by the downward stream of air from lifting rotors.
H	E	L	I	C	T	E	R	E	S	A large genus of tropical trees and shrubs.
H	E	L	I	O	G	R	A	P	H	An apparatus using sunlight for signalling.
H	E	L	I	O	L	A	T	R	Y	Sun worship.
H	E	L	I	O	M	E	T	E	R	Astronomical instrument once used for taking various measurements of the sun.
H	E	L	I	O	M	E	T	R	Y	The practice of using a heliometer.
H	E	L	I	O	P	H	I	L	E	One attracted to sunlight.
H	E	L	I	O	P	H	O	B	E	One abnormally sensitive to the effect of sunlight.
H	E	L	I	O	P	H	Y	T	E	A plant tolerating full sunlight.
H	E	L	I	O	T	A	X	I	S	Phototaxis in which sunlight is the stimulus.
H	E	L	I	O	T	R	O	P	E	Genus of fragrant herbs.
H	E	L	I	P	T	E	R	U	M	Genus of African and Australian herbs grown as an everlasting.
H	E	L	L	A	N	D	I	T	E	A mineral consisting of a silicate of the cerium metals.
H	E	L	L	B	E	N	D	E	R	A large voracious salamander.
H	E	L	L	E	B	O	R	U	S	Genus of Eurasian perennial herbs, Ranunculus.
H	E	L	M	I	N	T	H	E	S	The parasitic worms.
H	E	L	O	D	R	I	L	U	S	Common North American genus of earthworms.
H	E	L	O	P	E	L	T	I	S	Genus of tropical mirid bugs, Tea mosquito.
H	E	L	P	L	E	S	S	L	Y	In a helpless manner.
H	E	M	A	L	B	U	M	E	N	Preparation of blood containing iron albuminate and used in anaemia.
H	E	M	A	N	G	I	O	M	A	Benign tumour composed of blood vessels, Strawberry mark.
H	E	M	A	T	O	B	I	O	N	An organism living in blood.
H	E	M	A	T	O	C	E	L	E	A blood-filled cavity of the body.
H	E	M	A	T	O	C	R	I	T	An instrument for determining the relative amounts of plasma and corpuscles in blood.
H	E	M	A	T	O	L	I	T	E	A mineral consisting of a brownish red aluminium manganese arsenate.
H	E	M	A	T	O	Z	O	I	C	Blood-dwelling.
H	E	M	A	T	O	Z	O	O	N	An animal parasite that lives in blood.
H	E	M	I	C	R	A	N	I	A	Pain in one side of the head.
H	E	M	I	C	Y	C	L	I	C	Having floral leaves partly in whorls and partly in spirals.
H	E	M	I	P	L	E	G	I	A	Paralysis of one lateral half of the body.
H	E	M	I	P	T	E	R	O	N	One of the order of true bugs.
H	E	M	I	S	P	H	E	R	E	Half of a sphere.
H	E	M	I	Z	Y	G	O	U	S	Having unpaired genes.
H	E	M	O	C	Y	A	N	I	N	A colourless pigment found in solution in the blood plasma of various arthropods.
H	E	M	O	F	U	S	C	I	N	A yellowish brown pigment found in some normal tissues.
H	E	N	O	T	H	E	I	S	M	Monolatry, The worship of one god without denying the existence of other gods.
H	E	O	R	T	O	L	O	G	Y	A study of religious calendars.
H	E	P	A	R	I	N	I	Z	E	To treat with heparin to prevent clotting of the blood.
H	E	P	I	A	L	I	D	A	E	Family of lepidopterous insects, Ghost moths.
H	E	P	T	A	C	H	O	R	D	A seven-stringed lyre of ancient Greece, The interval of a seventh.
H	E	P	T	A	D	E	C	Y	L	An univalent radical derived from the heptadecanes by removing a hydrogen atom.
H	E	P	T	A	P	L	O	I	D	Having seven times the monoploid number of chromosomes.
H	E	P	T	A	T	O	N	I	C	Composed of seven musical tones.
H	E	R	B	A	C	E	O	U	S	Having the characteristics of a herb.
H	E	R	E	D	I	T	A	R	Y	Congenital, Acquired, Ancestral, Innate, Transmitted from one generation to another.
H	E	R	E	S	I	A	R	C	H	An active opponent of heresy.
H	E	R	E	T	O	F	O	R	E	Hitherto, Up to this time.
H	E	R	N	I	A	T	I	O	N	Formation of a hernia.
H	E	R	P	A	N	G	I	N	A	Contagious disease of children caused by a strain of Coxsackie virus.
H	E	S	I	T	A	N	T	L	Y	In a hesitant manner.
H	E	S	I	T	A	T	I	N	G	Pausing, Delaying, Stammering, Wavering, Vacillating, Faltering, Halting.
H	E	S	I	T	A	T	I	O	N	Indecision, Irresolution, Vacillation, Doubt, Uncertainty, Delay, Reluctance, Mistrust.
H	E	S	P	E	R	I	D	I	N	A crystalline bioflavonoid glycoside found in most citrus fruits.
H	E	S	P	E	R	E	T	I	N	A crystalline compound derived from flavanone.
H	E	T	E	R	O	C	E	R	A	Family of moths.

1	2	3	4	5	6	7	8	9	10	Definition
H	E	T	E	R	O	C	Y	S	T	Large transparent cells resembling spores occurring in certain algae.
H	E	T	E	R	O	D	E	R	A	A genus of minute nematode worms which attack roots of underground stems.
H	E	T	E	R	O	D	O	N	T	Having different types of teeth.
H	E	T	E	R	O	D	O	X	Y	Not conforming to orthodox beliefs.
H	E	T	E	R	O	D	Y	N	E	Relating to the production of an electrical beat between two radio frequencies.
H	E	T	E	R	O	G	O	N	Y	Alteration of generations.
H	E	T	E	R	O	L	O	G	Y	The lack of correspondence of apparently similar bodily parts.
H	E	T	E	R	O	N	O	M	Y	A subjection to something else, Lacking moral freedom.
H	E	T	E	R	O	P	O	D	A	Pelagic gastropod mollusks that have transparent bodies.
H	E	T	E	R	O	P	O	L	Y	Containing several groups of different acid-forming elements.
H	E	T	E	R	O	S	I	T	E	A mineral isomorphous with purpurite.
H	E	U	L	A	N	D	I	T	E	A zeolite consisting of a hydrous aluminosilicate of sodium and calcium.
H	E	X	A	C	H	L	O	R	O	Containing six atoms of chlorine.
H	E	X	A	C	T	I	N	A	L	Having six rays.
H	E	X	A	D	E	C	E	N	E	Any of several straight-chain isomeric hydrocarbons.
H	E	X	A	H	E	D	R	A	L	Having the form of a hexahedron.
H	E	X	A	H	E	D	R	O	N	A polyhedron of six faces.
H	E	X	A	M	E	R	O	U	S	Consisting of six parts.
H	E	X	A	M	E	T	H	Y	L	Containing six methyl groups in the molecule.
H	E	X	A	S	T	Y	L	O	S	A building having a portico with six columns.
H	E	X	A	V	A	L	E	N	T	Having a valence of six.
H	E	X	O	E	S	T	R	O	L	A crystalline estrogenic diphenol.
H	E	X	O	K	I	N	A	S	E	Any of several enzymes that occur in living tissues.
H	E	X	O	S	A	M	I	N	E	An amine from a hexose.
H	I	B	E	R	N	A	C	L	E	Winter resting part of a plant, A winter shelter for a dormant insect.
H	I	E	R	O	C	H	L	O	E	Genus of aromatic perennial grasses.
H	I	E	R	O	G	L	Y	P	H	A picture script of ancient Egyptian writing.
H	I	E	R	O	P	H	A	N	T	A priest in ancient Greece, A leading advocate.
H	I	L	G	A	R	D	I	T	E	A mineral consisting of hydrous chloride and borate of calcium.
H	I	L	I	F	E	R	O	U	S	Bearing a hilum.
H	I	M	A	N	T	O	P	U	S	Genus of wading birds, Stilts.
H	I	N	S	D	A	L	I	T	E	A mineral consisting of a basic lead and strontium aluminium sulphate and phosphate.
H	I	N	T	E	R	L	A	N	D	A region behind the coast.
H	I	P	P	E	L	A	T	E	S	A genus of small black American eye gnats.
H	I	P	P	O	C	R	E	N	E	Poetic inspiration.
H	I	P	P	O	D	R	O	M	E	An arena for equestrian performances.
H	I	P	P	O	G	R	I	F	F	Legendary animal being half-griffin and half-horse.
H	I	P	P	O	M	A	N	E	S	A growth found on the forehead of a newborn foal, once thought to be aphrodisiac.
H	I	P	P	O	P	H	A	G	Y	The practice of eating horseflesh.
H	I	R	S	U	T	E	L	L	A	A genus of fungi believed to be parasitic upon certain insects.
H	I	R	U	D	I	N	I	Z	E	Preventing the coagulation of blood by injecting hirudin.
H	I	S	T	O	G	E	N	I	C	Producing tissue.
H	I	S	T	O	L	Y	S	I	S	The breakdown of bodily tissues.
H	I	S	T	O	L	Y	T	I	C	Inducing histolysis.
H	I	S	T	O	M	O	N	A	S	Genus of parasites of the liver and intestinal mucosa of chickens, Turkeys and birds.
H	I	S	T	O	R	I	C	A	L	Relating to history.
H	I	S	T	R	I	O	N	I	C	Theatrical, Staged, Dramatic.
H	I	T	H	E	R	M	O	S	T	Nearest on this side.
H	O	A	R	S	E	N	E	S	S	The state of being hoarse.
H	O	B	B	L	E	B	U	S	H	A shrub that has long straggling branches, Wayfaring tree.
H	O	E	G	B	O	M	I	T	E	A mineral consisting of an oxide of magnesium, aluminium, iron and titanium.
H	O	E	R	N	E	S	I	T	E	A mineral consisting of hydrous magnesium arsenate.
H	O	H	M	A	N	N	I	T	E	A mineral consisting of a hydrated basic ferric sulfate.
H	O	L	L	A	N	D	I	T	E	A mineral consisting of a crystallised manganate of barium and manganese.
H	O	L	O	C	A	R	P	I	C	Having the whole thallus developed into a fruiting body.
H	O	L	O	D	I	S	C	U	S	A small genus of shrubs of western North America.
H	O	L	O	H	E	D	R	A	L	A crystal having full number of planes required for symmetry.
H	O	L	O	M	I	C	T	I	C	Relating to the complete circulation of a lake.
H	O	L	O	P	H	Y	T	I	C	Obtaining food in the same fashion as a green plant.
H	O	M	E	L	I	N	E	S	S	Simplicity, Coziness, Intimacy.
H	O	M	E	M	A	K	I	N	G	Creation of a wholesome family atmosphere.
H	O	M	E	O	M	O	R	P	H	An individual bearing a superficial resemblance to another.
H	O	M	I	L	E	T	I	C	S	The art of preaching.
H	O	M	I	N	O	I	D	E	A	A division of the family of great apes.
H	O	M	O	G	E	N	O	U	S	Originating from the same germ layer.
H	O	M	O	E	C	I	O	U	S	A parasite having the same host during the entire life cycle.
H	O	M	O	E	R	O	T	I	C	Homosexual.

1	2	3	4	5	6	7	8	9	10	
H	O	M	O	G	A	M	O	U	S	Relating to homogamy.
H	O	M	O	G	E	N	A	T	E	Biological tissue that has been macerated.
H	O	M	O	G	E	N	I	Z	E	Blending into a smooth mixture.
H	O	M	O	L	O	G	A	T	E	Sanction, Approve, Allow, Confirm, Agree, Concur.
H	O	M	O	L	O	G	O	U	S	Corresponding, Alike in structure.
H	O	M	O	N	Y	M	O	U	S	Ambiguous, Having two or more significations.
H	O	M	O	P	L	A	S	S	Y	Correspondence between parts acquired as a result of parallel evolution.
H	O	M	O	R	G	A	N	I	C	Sharing one or more articulating vocal organs.
H	O	M	O	S	E	X	U	A	L	One having sexual desire towards their own sex.
H	O	M	O	T	A	X	I	A	L	Relating to a similarity of arrangement.
H	O	M	O	Z	Y	G	O	T	E	An individual that breeds true to type.
H	O	M	O	Z	Y	G	O	U	S	Producing only one type of gamete.
H	O	M	U	N	C	U	L	U	S	Dwarf, Manikin.
H	O	N	E	S	T	N	E	S	S	The quality of being honest.
H	O	N	E	Y	S	W	E	E	T	A white woolly perennial American desert herb having honey-scented yellow flowers.
H	O	N	O	R	A	R	I	U	M	A honorary payment for services rendered where regular payment is not given.
H	O	N	O	U	R	A	B	L	E	Noble, Sterling, Worthy, August, Illustrious, Venerable, Scrupulous, Honest.
H	O	R	I	Z	O	N	T	A	L	Level, Flat, Overall.
H	O	R	N	B	L	E	N	D	E	A mineral consisting of aluminous amphibole containing iron.
H	O	R	O	L	O	G	I	S	T	Maker of clocks and watches.
H	O	R	O	S	C	O	P	I	C	Relating to a horoscope.
H	O	R	R	E	N	D	O	U	S	Dreadful, Fearful, Frightful, Horrible, Ghastly.
H	O	R	S	E	F	L	E	S	H	Flesh of a slaughtered horse, Relating to horses.
H	O	R	S	E	L	A	U	G	H	Guffaw, A loud boisterous laugh.
H	O	R	S	E	L	E	E	C	H	A common leech.
H	O	R	S	E	P	O	W	E	R	The power that a horse exerts by pulling, A standard unit of power.
H	O	S	P	I	T	A	B	L	E	Social, Convivial, Companionable, Co-operative, Gregarious, Sociable.
H	O	S	T	I	M	E	L	L	A	A form genus of fossil plants.
H	O	U	S	E	B	R	E	A	K	Burglarize, Rob, Ransack, Rifle, Tame, Subdue, Teaching acceptable social manners.
H	O	V	E	R	C	R	A	F	T	An amphibious craft that skims on a bed of air.
H	U	E	B	N	E	R	I	T	E	A mineral consisting of manganese tungstate.
H	U	L	L	A	B	A	L	O	O	Hubbub, Din, Confusion, Clamour, Pandemonium, Tumult, Racket, Uproar.
H	U	M	I	D	I	F	I	E	R	A device for supplying humidity.
H	U	M	I	D	I	S	T	A	T	An instrument for regulating the degree of humidity.
H	U	M	O	R	O	U	S	L	Y	In a humorous manner.
H	U	M	O	U	R	L	E	S	S	Without humour, glum.
H	U	N	G	R	I	N	E	S	S	The state of being hungry.
H	U	R	D	Y	G	U	R	D	Y	Barrel organ, Street piano.
H	U	R	E	A	U	L	I	T	E	A mineral consisting of a hydrous manganese phosphate.
H	U	R	L	Y	B	U	R	L	Y	Confusion, Turmoil, Tumult, Uproar, Melee.
H	U	R	S	I	N	G	H	A	R	An East Indian tree with flowers that yield a dye used as a substitute for saffron.
H	Y	A	C	I	N	T	H	U	S	A genus of Old World bulbous and scapose herbs, Hyacinth.
H	Y	A	E	N	A	N	C	H	E	A genus of trees.
H	Y	D	R	A	C	H	N	I	D	Water mite.
H	Y	D	R	A	G	O	G	U	E	A cathartic that causes a watery bowel discharge.
H	Y	D	R	A	S	T	I	N	E	A bitter crystalline alkaloid which is the parent compound of narcotine.
H	Y	D	R	A	Z	O	A	T	E	A salt of hydrazoic acid.
H	Y	D	R	I	O	D	I	D	E	A compound of hydriodic acid.
H	Y	D	R	O	C	H	O	R	E	A plant depending on water to distribute its spores or seeds.
H	Y	D	R	O	C	L	E	Y	S	Genus of Brazilian aquatic herbs with showy yellow flowers.
H	Y	D	R	O	C	T	E	N	A	Genus of medusae.
H	Y	D	R	O	C	Y	C	L	E	A cycle for riding on water.
H	Y	D	R	O	G	E	N	I	C	Formed by the agency of water.
H	Y	D	R	O	G	R	A	P	H	A device for recording changing water levels.
H	Y	D	R	O	L	A	T	R	Y	The worship of water.
H	Y	D	R	O	L	O	G	I	C	Relating to the study of water.
H	Y	D	R	O	L	Y	M	P	H	Circulatory fluid substituting for blood in jellyfishes.
H	Y	D	R	O	L	Y	Z	E	R	Equipment in which hydrolysis is carried out.
H	Y	D	R	O	M	A	N	C	Y	Divination by water.
H	Y	D	R	O	M	E	T	E	R	An instrument for measuring specific gravity of a liquid.
H	Y	D	R	O	M	E	T	R	Y	Measurement of specific gravity of a liquid.
H	Y	D	R	O	P	A	T	H	Y	Treatment of disease by excessive use of water.
H	Y	D	R	O	P	H	A	N	E	Semitranslucent variety of opal that becomes transparent in water.
H	Y	D	R	O	P	H	I	L	Y	The state of being pollinated by the agency of water.
H	Y	D	R	O	P	H	O	B	E	One averse to water.
H	Y	D	R	O	P	H	O	N	E	Instrument for detecting sound under water.
H	Y	D	R	O	P	H	Y	T	E	A plant growing in water.

1	2	3	4	5	6	7	8	9	10	
H	Y	D	R	O	P	L	A	N	E	Hydrofoil.
H	Y	D	R	O	P	O	L	Y	P	A polyp of a hydrozoan.
H	Y	D	R	O	P	O	N	I	C	Relating to the growing of plants in nutrient solution without soil.
H	Y	D	R	O	P	O	T	E	S	Genus of deer, Small Chinese species having no antlers.
H	Y	D	R	O	R	H	I	Z	A	A rootstock by which a hydroid is attached to other objects.
H	Y	D	R	O	R	R	H	E	A	A watery discharge.
H	Y	D	R	O	S	C	O	P	E	A device enabling a person to see below the surface of water.
H	Y	D	R	O	S	T	O	M	E	The mouth of a hydroid.
H	Y	D	R	O	T	A	X	I	S	A taxis in which moisture is the directive factor.
H	Y	D	R	O	T	H	E	C	A	A cup-shaped extension protecting hydranths.
H	Y	E	T	O	G	R	A	P	H	A chart showing average annual rainfall.
H	Y	E	T	O	M	E	T	E	R	Rain gauge.
H	Y	G	R	O	G	R	A	P	H	An instrument for automatically recording variations in humidity.
H	Y	G	R	O	M	E	T	E	R	Same as HYGROGRAPH.
H	Y	G	R	O	M	E	T	R	Y	A branch of physics dealing with humidity.
H	Y	G	R	O	P	H	I	L	A	A genus of aquatic herbaceous or woody plants.
H	Y	G	R	O	P	H	I	L	E	Living or growing in moist places.
H	Y	G	R	O	S	C	O	P	E	An instrument showing changes in humidity.
H	Y	L	E	G	I	A	C	A	L	Relating to the position of the planets at the time of birth.
H	Y	L	O	C	E	R	E	U	S	Genus of tropical American climbing cacti.
H	Y	L	O	C	I	C	H	L	A	Genus of thrushes.
H	Y	L	O	C	O	M	I	U	M	A small genus of mostly feathery mosses.
H	Y	L	O	T	O	M	O	U	S	Cutting wood as relating to zoology.
H	Y	M	E	N	O	T	O	M	Y	Surgical incision of the hymen.
H	Y	N	O	B	I	I	D	A	E	A small family of primitve Asiatic salamanders.
H	Y	O	G	L	O	S	S	U	S	A tongue muscle.
H	Y	O	S	C	Y	A	M	U	S	Dried leaves of henbane containing scopolamine which is used as a sedative.
H	Y	O	T	H	E	R	I	U	M	Prehistoric swine being direct ancestors of wild boar and domestic pigs.
H	Y	P	E	R	B	A	T	O	N	Transportation of idiomatic word order.
H	Y	P	E	R	D	U	L	I	A	Veneration of the Virgin Mary as the holiest of creatures.
H	Y	P	E	R	G	O	L	I	C	Self-igniting upon contact of components without a spark.
H	Y	P	E	R	I	C	I	S	M	Severe dermatitis of grass-eating domestic animals due to eating St John's wort.
H	Y	P	E	R	M	O	R	P	H	A long-limbed and long-headed person, Ectomorph.
H	Y	P	E	R	O	O	D	O	N	Genus of beaked whales.
H	Y	P	E	R	O	S	M	I	A	Having a very acute sense of smell.
H	Y	P	E	R	O	X	I	D	E	A compound containing a relatively large proportion of oxygen.
H	Y	P	E	R	S	O	L	I	D	A figure in hyperspace corresponding to a solid in three-dimensional space.
H	Y	P	E	R	S	O	N	I	C	Relating to speed of five times the sound in air.
H	Y	P	E	R	S	P	A	C	E	Space of more than three dimensions.
H	Y	P	H	A	N	T	R	I	A	Genus of arctiid moths with larvae that are tree pests.
H	Y	P	N	O	S	P	O	R	E	A thick-walled asexual resting spore as of green algae.
H	Y	P	O	C	A	P	N	I	A	Deficiency of carbon dioxide in the blood.
H	Y	P	O	C	E	N	T	E	R	The point on earth beneath explosion centre of a nuclear bomb.
H	Y	P	O	C	O	R	I	S	M	Baby talk, Pet name or endearment.
H	Y	P	O	D	E	R	M	I	C	Relating to parts beneath the skin, Rousing, Stimulating, Injection.
H	Y	P	O	D	E	R	M	I	S	The protective sub-epidermis of a plant, The cellular layer with the cuticle.
H	Y	P	O	H	A	L	I	T	E	Salt or ester of a hypohalous acid.
H	Y	P	O	H	I	P	P	U	S	Genus of extinct short-limbed horses.
H	Y	P	O	L	I	T	H	I	C	Growing beneath rocks.
H	Y	P	O	P	H	Y	S	I	S	Pituitary body.
H	Y	P	O	R	R	H	I	N	E	Having small nostrils.
H	Y	P	O	S	T	A	S	I	S	Sediment, Deposit, Foundation.
H	Y	P	O	S	T	R	O	M	A	Filament mass of a fungus.
H	Y	P	O	T	E	N	U	S	E	The side of a right-angled triangle that is opposite the right angle.
H	Y	P	O	T	H	E	S	I	S	Supposition as a basis for reasoning, Groundless assumption, Theory.
H	Y	P	O	T	R	O	P	H	Y	Subnormal growth.
H	Y	R	A	C	O	I	D	A	L	Resembling a hyrax.
H	Y	R	A	C	O	I	D	E	A	Order of Old World ungulate mammals, Hyraxes.
H	Y	S	T	A	Z	A	R	I	N	A yellow-crystalline compound.
H	Y	S	T	E	R	E	S	I	S	Lagging or retardation of an effect when the forces acting on a body are changed.
H	Y	S	T	E	R	I	C	A	L	Exhibiting unrestrained emotion, Instability.

I

I	A	N	T	H	I	N	I	T	E	A mineral consisting of a hydrous uranium dioxide.
I	A	T	R	O	G	E	N	I	C	Medical autosuggestion.

1	2	3	4	5	6	7	8	9	10	
I	C	E	B	R	E	A	K	E	R	A ship designed to make and maintain a channel through the ice.
I	C	H	T	H	Y	O	C	O	L	Isinglass.
I	C	H	T	H	Y	O	S	I	S	A congenital skin disease characterized by a rough, thick and scaly surface.
I	C	O	N	O	C	L	A	S	M	Breaking of religious images.
I	C	O	N	O	C	L	A	S	T	One who destroys religious images, One who attacks established beliefs or customs.
I	C	O	N	O	L	A	T	E	R	A worshipper of icons.
I	C	O	N	O	M	E	T	E	R	An instrument for determining the distance of an object of known size, A viewfinder.
I	C	O	N	O	S	C	O	P	E	A camera tube for transmitting television picture signals.
I	C	O	S	T	E	I	D	A	E	A family of deepwater fishes.
I	C	T	I	D	O	S	A	U	R	Prehistoric primitive reptiles.
I	D	E	A	L	I	S	T	I	C	Advocated by idealists.
I	D	E	N	T	I	C	A	R	D	Means of identification of a pedigreed animal.
I	D	E	O	G	R	A	P	H	Y	Representation of ideas by graphic symbols.
I	D	E	O	L	O	G	I	S	T	A specialist in the science of ideas.
I	D	E	O	L	O	G	I	Z	E	To conform to a particular ideology.
I	D	E	O	P	H	O	B	I	A	Fear of ideas or of reason.
I	D	I	O	P	A	T	H	I	C	Idiosyncratic.
I	D	I	O	C	R	A	T	I	C	Innate, Primary.
I	D	O	L	A	T	R	I	Z	E	Idolize.
I	G	N	O	B	I	L	I	T	Y	The state of being ignoble.
I	G	N	O	R	A	T	I	O	N	Action of ignoring.
I	L	L	A	U	D	A	B	L	E	Not worthy of commendation.
I	L	L	E	G	A	L	I	T	Y	The condition of being illegal.
I	L	L	E	G	A	L	I	Z	E	To declare illegal.
I	L	L	I	T	E	R	A	C	Y	Inability to read and write.
I	L	L	I	T	E	R	A	T	E	Uneducated, Ignorant, Uncultured, Untaught, Untutored.
I	L	L	N	A	T	U	R	E	D	Cross, Surly, Peevish, Bad-tempered.
I	L	L	U	M	I	N	A	T	E	Lighten, Brighten, Irradiate, Clarify, Uplift, Elucidate, Enlighten, Decorate.
I	L	L	U	S	T	R	A	T	E	Enlighten, Adorn, Clarify, Elucidate, Demonstrate, Exemplify, Explain, Expound.
I	L	Y	S	A	N	T	H	E	S	Genus of low herbs.
I	M	A	G	I	N	A	B	L	E	Conceivable, Supposable.
I	M	A	G	I	N	A	T	O	R	A person who creates in the artistic or intellectual field.
I	M	B	E	C	I	L	I	T	Y	Incapacity, Inability, Futility, Mentally weak, Nonsense, Foolishness.
I	M	B	I	B	I	T	I	O	N	Saturation with or solution in liquid, Action of imbibing.
I	M	I	D	A	Z	O	L	Y	L	Any of four univalent radicals derived from imidazole.
I	M	I	T	A	T	R	E	S	S	A female imitator.
I	M	M	A	C	U	L	A	T	E	Spotless, Undefiled, Pure, Chaste, Decent, Modest, Impeccable, Faultless.
I	M	M	A	T	U	R	I	T	Y	Childishness, Precociousness, Irresponsibility.
I	M	M	E	M	O	R	I	A	L	Indefinitely ancient, Beyond recall.
I	M	M	I	S	C	I	B	L	E	Incapable of mixing, Incompatible.
I	M	M	O	B	I	L	I	T	Y	Motionless.
I	M	M	O	B	I	L	I	Z	E	Paralyze, Disable, Disarm, Incapacitate, Cripple, Prostrate.
I	M	M	O	D	E	R	A	T	E	Extravagant, Unreasonable, Boundless, Excessive, Extreme, Unrestrained, Exorbitant.
I	M	M	O	L	A	T	I	O	N	The act of immolating.
I	M	M	O	R	A	L	I	T	Y	Vice, Wickedness, Unchastity, Corruption, Depravity.
I	M	M	O	R	T	A	L	L	Y	Eternally, Forever, Perpetually, Everlastingly, Endlessly, Infinitely.
I	M	M	O	R	T	E	L	L	E	Everlasting.
I	M	M	U	R	E	M	E	N	T	Incarceration.
I	M	P	A	I	R	M	E	N	T	Injury, Deterioration, Lessening.
I	M	P	A	L	P	A	B	L	E	Intangible, Inponderable, Indiscernible, Insensible, Fine, Powdery.
I	M	P	A	R	T	I	B	L	E	Not subject to partition.
I	M	P	A	R	T	M	E	N	T	Communication, Transmission.
I	M	P	A	S	S	I	B	L	E	Impassive, Unfeeling, Incapable of being injured.
I	M	P	E	C	C	A	B	L	E	Flawless, Irreproachable, Faultless, Correct, Immaculate, Accurate, Perfect, Precise.
I	M	P	E	C	U	N	I	T	Y	Indigence, Poverty, Destitution, Penury, Want, Privation.
I	M	P	E	D	I	M	E	N	T	Obstruction, Hindrance, Block, Hurdle, Snag, Encumbrance.
I	M	P	E	N	I	T	E	N	T	Not repenting of sin, Not contrite.
I	M	P	E	R	A	T	I	V	E	Command, Order, Obligatory, Urgent, Binding, Compulsory, Guide.
I	M	P	E	R	S	O	N	A	L	Neutral, Abstract, Detached, Disinterested, Fair, Equitable, Objective, Unbiased.
I	M	P	E	R	V	I	O	U	S	Impenetrable, Impassable.
I	M	P	L	A	C	A	B	L	E	Inexorable, Grim, Merciless, Relentless, Ruthless, Unyielding, Unflinching, Unrelenting.
I	M	P	O	L	I	T	E	L	Y	Rudely.
I	M	P	O	R	T	A	B	L	E	Unendurable, Intolerable.
I	M	P	O	R	T	A	N	C	E	Weight, Significance, Consequence, Import, Distinction, Substance, Value, Worth.
I	M	P	O	S	I	T	I	O	N	Levy, Tax, Deception.
I	M	P	O	S	S	I	B	L	Y	In an impossible manner.
I	M	P	O	T	E	N	T	L	Y	Feebly, Weakly, Helplessly.

1	2	3	4	5	6	7	8	9	10	
I	M	P	O	V	E	R	I	S	H	Deplete, Bankrupt, Exhaust, Ruin, Break, Pauper.
I	M	P	R	E	G	N	A	T	E	Inseminate, Fertilize, Imbue, Indoctrinate, Permeate, Pervade, Soak, Drench.
I	M	P	R	E	S	S	I	O	N	Imprint, Indentation, Vestige, Mark, Sign, Idea, Apprehension, Notion.
I	M	P	R	E	S	S	I	V	E	Moving, Affecting, Touching, Poignant, Imposing, Majestic, Arresting, Grand.
I	M	P	R	I	M	A	T	U	R	A licence to print or publish, Sanction, Approval.
I	M	P	R	I	S	O	N	E	D	Confined, Constrained, Incarcerated, Interned, Restricted, Curbed, Restrained.
I	M	P	R	O	P	E	R	L	Y	Inaptly, Inappropriately, Untimely, Indecently, Roughly, Unsuitably, Inaccurately.
I	M	P	R	O	V	I	S	E	D	Composed, Sung, Recited, Arranged, Constructed, Off-hand, Unrehearsed, Unstudied.
I	M	P	U	T	A	T	I	O	N	Attribution, Ascription, Accusation, Insinuation, Intimation, Assignation.
I	N	A	C	C	U	R	A	T	E	Incorrect, Erroneous, Faulty, Defective, False, Specious, Unsound, Untrue.
I	N	A	C	T	I	V	I	T	Y	Idleness, Sluggishness.
I	N	A	D	E	Q	U	A	T	E	Insufficient, Deficient, Incomplete, Lacking, Wanting, Short, Scarce, Skimpy.
I	N	A	R	T	I	S	T	I	C	Not artistic.
I	N	A	U	G	U	R	A	T	E	Install, Begin, Initiate, Induct, Invest, Commence, Introduce, Institute.
I	N	C	A	N	D	E	S	C	E	To light up, being heated.
I	N	C	A	P	A	C	I	T	Y	Inability, Incapability, Inadequacy, Incompetence, Ineffectiveness.
I	N	C	A	U	T	I	O	U	S	Heedless, Careless, Injudicious, Unwary, Indiscreet, Rash, Reckless, Irresponsible.
I	N	C	E	N	D	I	A	R	Y	Inflammatory, Seditious, Stimulating, Exciting, Arsonist, Fire-bug.
I	N	C	E	S	T	U	O	U	S	Involving incest, Ingrown, Derivative, Imitative.
I	N	C	H	O	A	T	I	V	E	Initial, Formative, Denoting the beginning.
I	N	C	I	D	E	N	T	A	L	Accidental, Casual, Chance, Odd, Fortuitous, Subordinate, Nonessential.
I	N	C	I	N	E	R	A	T	E	To burn to ashes, Consume by fire.
I	N	C	I	P	I	E	N	C	Y	Beginning, Commencement.
I	N	C	I	S	I	F	O	R	M	Resembling an incisor tooth, Shaped for cutting.
I	N	C	I	S	I	V	E	L	Y	Cuttingly, With precision.
I	N	C	I	T	A	T	I	O	N	Stimulation, Incitement, Incentive.
I	N	C	I	V	I	L	I	T	Y	Discourtesy, Rudeness.
I	N	C	L	E	M	E	N	C	Y	Storminess, Harshness, Cruelty, Severity, Brutality, Bitterness.
I	N	C	O	G	I	T	A	N	T	Thoughtless, Inconsiderate.
I	N	C	O	H	E	R	E	N	T	Loose, Incongruous, Inconsistent, Disjointed, Muddled, Disordered.
I	N	C	O	M	P	L	E	T	E	Unfinished, Imperfected, Fragmentary, Deficient, Broken, Lacking, Inadequate.
I	N	C	R	E	A	S	I	N	G	Growing, Advancing, Waxing, Enhancing, Enriching, Augmenting, Promoting.
I	N	C	R	E	D	I	B	L	E	Improbable, Inconceivable, Unbelievable, Unthinkable, Absurd, Outlandish.
I	N	C	R	O	Y	A	B	L	E	Dandy, Fop.
I	N	C	U	B	A	T	I	O	N	Process of incubating, Instance of brooding.
I	N	C	U	B	A	T	O	R	Y	Serving for incubation.
I	N	C	U	L	P	A	B	L	E	Blameless, Innocent, Faultless, Guiltless, Irreprochable, Pure, Righteous, Virtuous.
I	N	C	U	M	B	E	N	C	Y	The state of occupying a particular position.
I	N	D	E	C	I	S	I	O	N	Irresolution, Vacillation, Hesitancy.
I	N	D	E	C	I	S	I	V	E	Inconclusive, Wavering, Irresolute, Vague, Vacillating, Doubtful, Dubious.
I	N	D	E	C	O	R	O	U	S	Improper, Indecent, Ridiculous, Rough, Unbecoming, Unseemly, Immodest, Vulgar.
I	N	D	E	F	I	N	I	T	E	Vague, Obscure, Uncertain, Ambiguous, Unlimited, Unclear, Limitless.
I	N	D	E	L	I	C	A	C	Y	The state of being improper. Rude, unrefined, coarse, gross, tactless.
I	N	D	I	C	A	T	I	O	N	Hint, Inkling, Intimation, Notion, Suggestion, Token, Expression, Gesture.
I	N	D	I	C	A	T	I	V	E	Suggestive, Characteristic, Demonstrative, Symbolic.
I	N	D	I	C	A	T	R	I	X	An ellipsoid for deducing optical properties of a crystal.
I	N	D	I	C	T	M	E	N	T	Formal written charge of an offense.
I	N	D	I	G	E	N	I	Z	E	To adapt to indigenous conditions.
I	N	D	I	G	E	N	O	U	S	Native, Endemic, Innate, Congenital, Inherited, Natural, Inherent, Inborn.
I	N	D	I	G	O	F	E	R	A	Genus of tropical herbs and shrubs, Indigo plant.
I	N	D	I	S	C	R	E	E	T	Imprudent, Inconsiderate, Unwary, Incautious, Ill-judged, Impolitic, Injudicious.
I	N	D	I	S	P	O	S	E	D	Averse, Disinclined, Afraid, Hesitant, Loath, Reluctant, Unwilling, Ailing.
I	N	D	I	S	T	I	N	C	T	Blurred, Confused, Faint, Dim, Uncertain, Undiscriminating, Ill-defined, Indetermine.
I	N	D	I	T	E	M	E	N	T	Composition.
I	N	D	I	V	I	D	U	A	L	Single, Singular, Particular, Special, Characteristic, Peculiar, Distinctive, Personal.
I	N	D	O	P	H	E	N	I	N	A blue crystalline compound used as a colour test for the presence of thiophene.
I	N	D	O	P	H	E	N	O	L	Any of a class of blue or green dyes derived from quinone imines.
I	N	D	U	C	E	M	E	N	T	A state which lures or entices.
I	N	D	U	C	T	A	N	C	E	Inducing a magnetic field.
I	N	D	U	L	G	E	N	C	E	Fondness, Liking, Forbearance, Clemency, Leniency, Tolerance, Gentleness.
I	N	D	U	R	A	T	I	O	N	Callousness, Obdurateness, Obstinacy, Hardening, Inflexibility.
I	N	E	B	R	I	A	T	E	D	Tipsy, Intoxicated, Drunk.
I	N	E	D	U	C	A	B	L	E	Incapable of being educated.
I	N	E	F	F	I	C	A	C	Y	Ineffectualness, Lack of power.
I	N	E	L	I	G	I	B	L	E	Unfit, Disqualified, Incapable, Incompetent, Unfitted, Unqualified, Unequipped.
I	N	E	L	O	Q	U	E	N	T	Not fluid, Unemotionable.
I	N	E	P	T	I	T	U	D	E	Unfitness, Unsuitableness, Absurdity.

1	2	3	4	5	6	7	8	9	10	
I	N	E	Q	U	A	L	I	T	Y	Unevenness, Asperity, Irregularity, Roughness, Disparity, Disproportion.
I	N	E	V	I	T	A	B	L	E	Certain, Inescapable, Necessary, Inexorable, Unavoidable, Sure, Destined, Foreordained.
I	N	E	X	O	R	A	B	L	E	Unyielding, Inflexible, Relentless, Adamant, Rigid, Resolute, Immovable, Dogged.
I	N	E	X	P	I	A	B	L	E	Unforgivable, Inexcusable, Indefensible, Unpardonable, Injustifiable, Untenable.
I	N	F	A	L	L	I	B	L	E	Sure, Certain, Indubitable, Inerrable, Unerring, Faultless, Effective, Flawless.
I	N	F	A	T	U	A	T	E	D	Besotted, Enamoured, Bewitched, Captivated, Enraptured, Obsessed, Foolish, Silly.
I	N	F	E	A	S	I	B	L	E	Impracticable.
I	N	F	E	C	T	I	O	U	S	Infective, Corrupting, Toxic, Contaminating, Vitiating, Demoralizing, Catching.
I	N	F	E	L	I	C	I	T	Y	Unhappiness, Wretchedness, Misfortune.
I	N	F	I	B	U	L	A	T	E	To fasten with a buckle or clasp.
I	N	F	I	D	E	L	I	T	Y	Disloyalty, Perfidy, Treachery, Fickleness, Inconstancy, Falseness, Treason.
I	N	F	I	L	T	R	A	T	E	Insinuate, Penetrate, Pass into, Advance, Enter, Permeate.
I	N	F	I	N	I	T	I	V	E	Grammatical verb from that performs certain functions of a noun.
I	N	F	L	A	T	A	B	L	E	Capable of being inflated.
I	N	F	L	E	C	T	I	O	N	Bend, Curve, Accent, Intonation, Articulation, Variation.
I	N	F	L	E	X	I	B	L	E	Unyielding, Inexorable, Rigid, Stiff, Unalterable, Immutable, Immovable, Unbending.
I	N	F	L	E	X	I	B	L	Y	Rigidly, Unalterably, Stubbornly, Inexorably.
I	N	F	O	R	M	A	L	L	Y	Unofficially, Casually, Simply, Naturally.
I	N	F	R	A	C	T	I	O	N	Breach, Violation, Infringement, Contravention, Trespass, Transgression, Crime.
I	N	F	R	E	Q	U	E	N	T	Uncommon, Rare, Occasional, Sparse, Seldom, Sporadic, Scarce, Limited.
I	N	F	U	S	O	R	I	A	N	One of a group of minute organisms, Bacteria, Algae, Fungi.
I	N	G	E	M	B	R	A	C	H	A candy made chiefly of ginger and honey.
I	N	G	E	M	I	N	A	T	E	Redouble, Repeat, Reiterate.
I	N	G	E	S	T	I	B	L	E	Capable of being ingested.
I	N	G	L	O	R	I	O	U	S	Shameful, Ignominious, Disreputable, Discreditable, Dishonourable, Disgraceful.
I	N	G	R	A	T	I	A	T	E	To commend to favour, Make agreeable, Fawn, Disarm, Adulate, Insinuate.
I	N	G	R	E	D	I	E	N	T	Constituent, Element, Component, Factor.
I	N	G	R	E	S	S	I	O	N	Entrance, Entry.
I	N	H	A	B	I	T	A	N	T	Resident, Dweller, Denizen, Occupant, Settler.
I	N	H	A	L	A	T	I	O	N	Action of drawing air into the lungs.
I	N	H	I	B	I	T	I	O	N	Prohibition, Impediment, Constraint.
I	N	H	I	B	I	T	O	R	Y	Restraining, forbidding, prohibiting, curbing, withholding.
I	N	H	U	M	A	N	I	T	Y	Cruelty, Impersonality, Barbarity, Ferocity.
I	N	H	U	M	A	T	I	O	N	Burial, Interment.
I	N	I	M	I	T	A	B	L	E	Matchless, Unparalleled.
I	N	I	Q	U	I	T	O	U	S	Unjust, Wicked, Vicious, Wrong, Evil, Immoral, Sinful.
I	N	I	T	I	A	T	I	O	N	Introduction, Origination, Inaugural, Induction, Installation, Investiture.
I	N	I	T	I	A	T	O	R	Y	Introductory, Opening, Elementary, Rudimentary.
I	N	J	U	N	C	T	I	O	N	Order, Prohibition, Command, Behest, Dictate, Mandate, Bidding, Charge.
I	N	N	O	V	A	T	I	O	N	Change, Novelty, Mutation, Permutation, Deviation, Wrinkle, Sport, Idea.
I	N	N	U	M	E	R	O	U	S	Numberless, Innumerable, Countless, Untold, Uncounted.
I	N	O	P	E	R	A	B	L	E	Not suitable for surgical operation.
I	N	O	R	D	I	N	A	T	E	Disorderly, Extraordinary, Excessive, Exorbitant, Undue, Irrational, Temperate.
I	N	O	S	C	U	L	A	T	E	Unite, Join, Blend.
I	N	Q	U	I	S	I	T	O	R	Inquirer, Investigator, Questioner.
I	N	S	A	T	I	A	B	L	E	Quenchless, Unappeasable, Unsatisfied, Demanding, Urgent, Insistent, Yearning.
I	N	S	E	C	U	R	I	T	Y	Hazard, Risk, Apprehensiveness, Uncertaintity.
I	N	S	E	M	I	N	A	T	E	Implant, Sow, To introduce semen.
I	N	S	E	N	S	I	B	L	E	Unconscious, Inanimate, Unaware, Apathetic, Imperceptible, Meaningless.
I	N	S	E	S	S	O	R	E	S	An order of birds with feet adapted for perching.
I	N	S	I	P	I	D	I	T	Y	Vapidity.
I	N	S	I	S	T	E	N	C	Y	Persistence, Urgency.
I	N	S	O	B	R	I	E	T	Y	Intemperance in drinking.
I	N	S	O	C	I	A	B	L	E	Unsociable, Taciturn, Aloof, Distant, Reserved, Solitary, Withdrawn.
I	N	S	O	L	A	T	I	O	N	Solar radiation, Sunstroke, Exposure to the sun's rays.
I	N	S	O	L	V	E	N	C	Y	Inability to pay debts.
I	N	S	O	U	C	I	A	N	T	Exhibiting an attitude of indifference.
I	N	S	P	E	C	T	I	O	N	Examination, Observation, Investigation, Analysis, Scrutiny, Probe, Survey.
I	N	S	P	E	X	I	M	U	S	An English charter or letters patent.
I	N	S	P	I	R	A	T	O	R	Injector, Respirator.
I	N	S	P	I	S	S	A	T	E	Made thick, heavy or intense.
I	N	S	T	A	L	L	I	N	G	Inducting, Initiating, Investing, Ensconcing, Settling.
I	N	S	T	I	G	A	T	O	R	Agitator, Inciter, Inflamer, Firebrand, Rabble-rouserr.
I	N	S	T	I	L	L	I	N	G	Implanting, Introducing, Inculcating, Inseminating.
I	N	S	T	R	U	C	T	E	D	Educated, Cultured, Trained, Prepared, Taught, Directed, Apprised, Ordered.
I	N	S	T	R	U	C	T	O	R	Teacher, Trainer, Coach.
I	N	S	T	R	U	M	E	N	T	Utensil, Implement, Dupe, Tool, Agency, Cannel, Medium, Ministry.

1	2	3	4	5	6	7	8	9	10	
I	N	S	U	F	F	L	A	T	E	To blow or breathe on to a surface or into a void.
I	N	S	U	L	A	R	I	T	Y	Quality of being an island.
I	N	S	U	L	A	R	I	Z	E	To represent as an island.
I	N	S	U	L	A	T	I	O	N	Isolation, Separation.
I	N	S	U	R	G	E	N	C	E	Uprising, Insurrection.
I	N	T	A	N	G	I	B	L	E	Impalpable, Imperceptible, Vague, Elusive, Imponderable, Indiscernible, Insensible.
I	N	T	E	G	R	A	B	L	E	Capable of being integrated.
I	N	T	E	G	R	A	T	E	D	Harmonized, Arranged, Blended, Unified, Co-ordinated, Reconciled, Combined.
I	N	T	E	G	U	M	E	N	T	Covering, Envelope.
I	N	T	E	M	E	R	A	T	E	Inviolate, Pure, Undefiled.
I	N	T	E	M	P	O	R	A	L	Timeless.
I	N	T	E	N	E	R	A	T	E	Soften.
I	N	T	E	R	B	L	E	N	D	Intermingle, Commingle.
I	N	T	E	R	B	R	E	E	D	Crossbreed.
I	N	T	E	R	E	S	T	E	D	Concerned, Involved, Affected, Implicated, Biased, Prejudiced.
I	N	T	E	R	F	L	U	V	E	The area between adjacent streams flowing in the same direction.
I	N	T	E	R	G	R	O	U	P	Existing between two or more social groups.
I	N	T	E	R	I	O	N	I	C	Situated between ions.
I	N	T	E	R	L	A	C	E	D	Interlinked, Interwoven, Interlocked.
I	N	T	E	R	L	O	P	E	R	Intruder, Meddler, One that interferes.
I	N	T	E	R	M	A	R	R	Y	To marry each other.
I	N	T	E	R	M	E	D	I	A	A member of the middle pair of a bird's tail feathers.
I	N	T	E	R	M	U	R	A	L	Lying between walls.
I	N	T	E	R	N	A	L	L	Y	Inwardly, Mentally, Spiritually.
I	N	T	E	R	N	S	H	I	P	Period of service as an intern.
I	N	T	E	R	P	L	A	N	T	To plant a crop between existing plants.
I	N	T	E	R	S	T	I	C	E	Crack, Crevice, Interval, Space.
I	N	T	E	R	T	I	D	A	L	The zone above low-tide mark.
I	N	T	E	R	T	W	I	N	E	Entangle, Interlace, Intertwist, Interwreathe, Inweave.
I	N	T	E	R	V	O	L	V	E	To twist or coil within one another.
I	N	T	E	R	W	E	A	V	E	Interlace, Intertwine, Interwork, Associate, Join, Link, Fuse, Blend.
I	N	T	E	R	Z	O	N	A	L	Carried on between zones.
I	N	T	E	S	T	A	B	L	E	Not competent to be a witness.
I	N	T	E	S	T	I	N	A	L	Relating to the intestine, Internal, Inner.
I	N	T	I	M	A	T	E	L	Y	In an intimate manner.
I	N	T	I	M	I	D	A	T	E	Frighten, Bully, Browbeat, Bludgeon, Hector, Terrorize, Scare, Badger.
I	N	T	I	N	C	T	I	O	N	The administration of the sacrament of Communion.
I	N	T	O	L	E	R	A	N	T	Bigoted, Impatient, Narrow-minded, Inflexible, Obdurate, Illiberal, Unsympathetic.
I	N	T	O	N	A	T	I	O	N	Reciting in a chanting monotone.
I	N	T	O	X	I	C	A	T	E	Poison, Inebriate, Make drunk, Excite to the point of frenzy.
I	N	T	R	A	G	R	O	U	P	Occurring within a single group.
I	N	T	R	A	M	U	R	A	L	Undertaken within certain limits.
I	N	T	R	A	V	I	T	A	M	Performing upon a live subject.
I	N	T	R	I	G	U	I	N	G	Fascinating, Beguiling, Interesting, Exciting, Appealing, Plotting, Conniving.
I	N	T	U	B	A	T	I	O	N	Introduction of a tube into a hollow organ.
I	N	U	N	D	A	T	I	O	N	Flood, Deluge, Swarm, Cataclysm, Overflow, Torrent, Pour, Spate.
I	N	V	A	G	I	N	A	T	E	Enclose, Sheathe.
I	N	V	A	L	I	D	A	T	E	Discredit, Nullify, Weaken, Abolish, Annihilate, Negate, Quash, Abrogate.
I	N	V	A	L	I	D	I	T	Y	Lack of sound foundation.
I	N	V	A	L	U	A	B	L	E	Priceless, Costly, Precious, Inestimable.
I	N	V	A	R	I	A	B	L	E	Consistent, Uniform, Unchanging, Unfailing, Inflexible, Same, Constant.
I	N	V	A	R	I	A	B	L	Y	Always, Consistently, Continually, Perpetually, Ever.
I	N	V	E	I	G	L	I	N	G	Luring, Enticing, Entrapping, Seducing, Tempting, Baiting.
I	N	V	E	R	A	C	I	T	Y	Falseness, Lie, Falsehood.
I	N	V	E	S	T	M	E	N	T	Coating, Envelope, Blockade, Siege, Expenditure of money for income or profit.
I	N	V	E	T	E	R	A	T	E	Continuous, Recurrent, Chronic, Ingrained, Adamant, Obstinate, Persistant.
I	N	V	I	G	I	L	A	T	E	To keep watch, To proctor an examination.
I	N	V	I	G	O	R	A	T	E	Animate, Strengthen, Fortify, Energize, Rejuvenate, Activate, Restore, Reinforce.
I	N	V	I	N	C	I	B	L	E	Unbeatable, Unavoidable, Impregnable, Indomitable, Invulnerable, Unconquerable.
I	N	V	I	O	L	A	B	L	E	Indestructible, Incorruptible, Untouchable, Unassailable, Sacred, Flawless.
I	N	V	I	T	A	T	I	O	N	Suggestion, Proposal, Attraction, Stimulus, Incentive, Proposition, Challenge.
I	N	V	O	C	A	T	I	O	N	Supplication, Incantation, Enforcement, Implement.
I	N	V	O	L	U	C	R	U	M	A surrounding sheath.
I	N	V	O	L	U	T	I	O	N	Entangling, Involvement, Intricacy.
I	N	W	A	R	D	N	E	S	S	Familiarity, Intimacy, Essence, Significance, Experience, Introspection, Subjectivity.
I	O	D	I	Z	A	T	I	O	N	The process of iodizing.
I	O	N	O	G	R	A	P	H	Y	Electrochromatography involving the migration of ions.

1	2	3	4	5	6	7	8	9	10	Definition
I	O	N	O	S	P	H	E	R	E	The part of the earth's atmosphere beginning at an altitude of about twenty five miles.
I	R	E	N	I	C	A	L	L	Y	In a way to promote peace.
I	R	I	D	A	C	E	O	U	S	Resembling a family of perennial herbs, Iris.
I	R	I	D	E	C	T	O	M	Y	The surgical removal of part of the iris of the eye.
I	R	I	D	O	S	M	I	N	E	A mineral consisting of a native iridium osmium alloy.
I	R	O	N	I	C	A	L	L	Y	In an ironical manner.
I	R	R	A	D	I	C	A	T	E	To root deeply.
I	R	R	A	T	I	O	N	A	L	Illogical, Invalid, Mad, Unreasonable, Crazy, Demented, Insane.
I	R	R	E	M	E	A	B	L	E	Irreversible.
I	R	R	E	S	O	L	U	T	E	Unexplained, Vacillating, Faltering, Hesitant, Tentative, Uncertain.
I	R	R	I	G	A	T	I	O	N	Artificial watering of land.
I	R	R	I	T	A	T	I	O	N	Stimulation, Excitation, Aggravation, Chafing.
I	S	O	C	A	N	D	E	L	A	A graph showing intensity as a function of voltage.
I	S	O	C	H	R	O	O	U	S	Being the same colour throughout.
I	S	O	C	Y	A	N	A	T	E	A salt or ester of isocyanic acid.
I	S	O	D	Y	N	A	M	I	C	Relating to uniformity of force.
I	S	O	F	L	A	V	O	N	E	A colourless crystalline ketone that is in many plants.
I	S	O	G	E	N	E	S	I	S	Similarity of origin.
I	S	O	P	E	N	T	A	N	E	A volatile flammable liquid hydrocarbon found in petroleum.
I	S	O	P	H	O	R	O	N	E	A high-boiling liquid ketone made by condensation of acetone.
I	S	O	P	H	Y	L	L	I	A	A genus of madrepores, Rose corals.
I	S	O	P	U	L	E	G	O	L	A liquid terpenoid alcohol with a menthol-like odour.
I	S	O	S	A	F	R	O	L	E	A liquid acetol with an odour like that of anise.
I	S	O	S	E	I	S	M	A	L	Marked by equal intensity of earthquake shock.
I	S	O	S	P	O	N	D	Y	L	A fish of the teleost order, Herring, Salmon.
I	S	O	S	P	O	R	O	U	S	Having isospores.
I	S	O	T	H	E	R	M	A	L	Marked by equality of temperature.
I	T	A	L	O	P	H	I	L	E	One that favours anything Italian.
I	T	I	N	E	R	A	N	C	Y	Work or duty that involves travelling.

J

1	2	3	4	5	6	7	8	9	10	Definition
J	A	B	O	T	I	C	A	B	A	A large shrub or small tree having fruit that resembles thick-skinned grapes.
J	A	C	A	M	E	R	O	P	S	Genus of birds comprising the largest of the jacamans.
J	A	C	K	A	N	A	P	E	S	Monkey, Ape, Impertinent or conceited fellow, Coxcomb.
J	A	C	K	H	A	M	M	E	R	A rock drill, Air hammer.
J	A	C	K	R	A	B	B	I	T	A hare of North America having long ears and long hind legs and being destructive.
J	A	C	U	L	A	T	I	O	N	The act of throwing, pitching and throwing.
J	A	G	U	A	R	U	N	D	I	A slender grayish wild cat.
J	A	R	D	I	N	I	E	R	E	A garnish of cubed mixed vegetables.
J	A	U	N	T	I	N	E	S	S	Sprightliness, Unconcern.
J	E	O	P	A	R	D	I	Z	E	Imperil, Venture, Endanger, Compromise, Hazard, Menace, Peril, Risk.
J	E	R	K	I	N	H	E	A	D	A roof which is partially hipped.
J	I	N	R	I	C	K	S	H	A	A small two-wheeled vehicle drawn by a man and used in Japan.
J	O	C	U	L	A	R	I	T	Y	Jest, Hilarity, Jollity, Merriment, Glee.
J	O	U	R	N	A	L	I	S	M	Writing, collecting and editing material for publication in a newspaper or magazine.
J	O	U	R	N	A	L	I	S	T	One employed to write and edit material for publication.
J	O	U	R	N	A	L	I	Z	E	To keep a journal.
J	O	U	R	N	E	Y	I	N	G	Travel, Traverse.
J	U	B	I	L	A	T	I	O	N	Exultation, Triumph.
J	U	D	I	C	A	T	O	R	Y	Judicial, Having the power to judge.
J	U	D	I	C	A	T	U	R	E	Judiciary, System of the courts of law.
J	U	D	O	P	H	O	B	I	A	Anti-semitism.
J	U	N	E	F	L	O	W	E	R	Canada violet.
J	U	R	A	M	E	N	T	U	M	Oath.
J	U	R	I	S	T	I	C	A	L	Relating to jurisdiction.
J	U	S	T	I	C	I	A	R	Y	Jurisdiction of the High Court.
J	U	S	T	I	F	Y	I	N	G	Confirming, Corroborating, Substantiating, Verifying, Defending, Vindicating.
J	U	V	E	N	I	L	I	T	Y	Childishness, Immaturity.
J	U	X	T	A	P	O	S	E	D	Placed side by side.

K

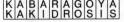

1	2	3	4	5	6	7	8	9	10	Definition
K	A	B	A	R	A	G	O	Y	A	A large water monitor of south eastern Asia.
K	A	K	I	D	R	O	S	I	S	Secretion of sweat of a disagreeable odour.

1	2	3	4	5	6	7	8	9	10	Clue
K	A	L	I	B	O	R	I	T	E	A mineral consisting of a hydrous borate of potassium and magnesium.
K	A	L	I	C	I	N	I	T	E	A mineral consisting of an acid carbonate or bicarbonate of potassium.
K	A	L	I	G	E	N	O	U	S	Forming alkalies, used of the alkali metals.
K	A	L	O	T	E	R	M	E	S	Family of termites destructive to living and dead timber.
K	A	M	A	R	E	Z	I	T	E	A mineral consisting of a hydrous basic copper sulfate.
K	A	O	L	I	N	I	T	I	C	Containing or resembling kaolinite.
K	A	R	W	I	N	S	K	I	A	A genus of shrubs or small trees having fleshy drupes.
K	A	R	Y	O	L	O	G	I	C	Relating to karyology.
K	A	R	Y	O	L	Y	S	I	S	Dissolution of the cell nucleus with loss of its affinity for basic stains in necrosis.
K	A	R	Y	O	L	Y	S	U	S	Genus of haemogragarines parasitic in reptiles.
K	A	R	Y	O	T	H	E	C	A	A nucleur membrane.
K	A	T	H	A	R	O	B	I	C	Living in a highly oxygenated medium free from organic medium.
K	E	L	B	E	L	O	B	A	R	A Nile fish with strong teeth resembling a salmon.
K	E	N	T	R	O	L	I	T	E	A dark reddish brown mineral consisting of a lead manganese silicate.
K	E	R	A	T	I	N	I	Z	E	Converted into keratin.
K	E	R	A	T	I	N	O	U	S	Horny.
K	E	R	A	T	O	S	E	A	E	Order of horny sponges.
K	E	R	S	E	Y	M	E	R	E	A fine woollen fabric with a fancy twill weave.
K	E	T	E	M	B	I	L	L	A	A hairy purple tropical fruit that is used for preserves.
K	E	T	O	H	E	X	O	S	E	A hexose of a ketonic nature.
K	I	B	B	U	T	Z	N	I	K	A member of a kibbutz.
K	I	D	N	A	P	P	I	N	G	Abducting, Snatching, Enveighing, Waylaying.
K	I	D	N	E	Y	R	O	O	T	Coyote brush once thought to cure kidney disease.
K	I	M	B	E	R	L	I	T	E	An agglomerate soil in Southern Africa that usually contains diamonds.
K	I	N	D	L	I	N	E	S	S	Friendliness, Benevolence, Pleasantness, Tractability.
K	I	N	E	M	A	T	I	C	S	A branch of dynamics that deals with aspects of motion.
K	I	N	E	S	A	L	G	I	A	Pain occurring in conjunction with muscle action.
K	I	N	G	F	I	S	H	E	R	Nonpasserine bird usually crested and bright coloured.
K	I	N	O	R	H	Y	N	C	H	Minute marine worms.
K	I	T	E	F	L	Y	I	N	G	A way to issue political news so that it can be denied later.
K	L	A	B	B	E	R	J	A	S	A two-handed game played with thirty two cards.
K	L	E	B	S	I	E	L	L	A	A genus of bacterial rods associated with respiratory disease.
K	L	E	N	D	U	S	I	T	Y	The tendency of a plant to have an ability to escape disease.
K	L	I	P	D	A	S	S	I	E	A hyrax of Southern Africa.
K	N	I	F	E	E	D	G	E	D	Extremely sharp.
K	N	I	G	H	T	H	E	A	D	A timber on the bow of a ship.
K	N	I	G	H	T	H	O	O	D	Chivalry, The rank of a knight.
K	N	O	B	K	E	R	R	I	E	A short wooden club with a heavy round knob at one end.
K	N	O	C	K	A	B	O	U	T	Noisy, Rough, Roaming, Wanderer, Vagrant, A sloop.
K	N	O	C	K	K	N	E	E	D	Limping, Lame, Inept, Weak, Clumsy, Gauche.
K	O	E	T	T	I	G	I	T	E	A mineral consisting of a hydrous arsenate of zinc.
K	O	L	B	E	C	K	I	T	E	A mineral of a hydrous silicate and phosphate of beryllium, aluminium and calcium.
K	O	N	I	N	C	K	I	T	E	A mineral consisting of hydrous ferric phosphate in yellow aggregates.
K	O	O	K	A	B	U	R	R	A	An Australian kingfisher with a raucous cry resembling laughter.
K	O	O	L	O	K	A	M	B	A	A dark-faced chimpanzee of West Africa.
K	R	E	N	N	E	R	I	T	E	A mineral consisting of a gold telluride.
K	R	I	B	E	R	G	I	T	E	A mineral consisting of a hydrous basic sulfate and phosphate aluminium.
K	R	O	E	H	N	K	I	T	E	A mineral consisting of an azure-blue hydrous copper sodium sulfate.
K	R	I	M	S	A	G	H	Y	Z	A small dandelion of the Mediterranean area cultivated for its long rubber taproot.
K	Y	N	U	R	E	N	I	N	E	An amino acid occurring in the urine of various animals.
K	Y	P	H	O	S	I	D	A	E	A family of chiefly tropical percoid shore fishes resembling bass.

L

1	2	3	4	5	6	7	8	9	10	Clue
L	A	B	O	R	A	T	O	R	Y	A place for experimental study.
L	A	B	O	U	C	H	E	R	E	A special betting system.
L	A	C	E	R	A	T	I	O	N	A wound made by tearing.
L	A	C	E	R	T	I	D	A	E	A terrestrial lizard with a deeply notched tongue.
L	A	C	E	R	T	I	L	I	A	A division of Reptilia comprising lizards, chameleons and geckos.
L	A	C	H	E	N	A	L	I	A	A genus of bulbous plants, Cape cowslip, Leopard lily.
L	A	C	H	R	Y	M	O	S	E	Tearful, Dismal, Mournful, Melancholy.
L	A	C	I	N	I	A	T	E	D	Bordered with a fringe.
L	A	C	K	L	U	S	T	R	E	Dull, Uninspired, Lacking in sheen, radiance or vitality.
L	A	C	R	I	M	A	N	D	O	Direction in music-Plaintive.
L	A	C	R	I	M	A	T	O	R	Tear gas, A tear-producing agent.
L	A	C	R	O	I	X	I	T	E	A mineral of a basic phosphate of aluminium, calcium, manganese and sodium.

1	2	3	4	5	6	7	8	9	10	Definition
L	A	C	T	E	S	C	E	N	T	Becoming milky, Yielding a milky juice.
L	A	C	T	O	G	E	N	I	C	Inducing lactation.
L	A	C	T	O	M	E	T	E	R	A hydrometer for determining the specific gravity of milk.
L	A	C	T	O	P	R	E	N	E	Synthetic rubbers that are polymers or copolymers of an acrylic ester.
L	A	C	T	O	S	U	R	I	A	The presence of lactose in urine.
L	A	C	U	N	U	L	O	S	E	Having minute lacunae.
L	A	C	U	S	T	R	I	N	E	Growing or living in lakes.
L	A	D	D	E	R	L	I	K	E	Resembling a ladder.
L	A	D	Y	F	I	N	G	E	R	Foxglove, A small sponge cake, Small banana, Dessert grape.
L	A	E	O	T	R	O	P	I	C	Turning to the left.
L	A	E	V	I	G	R	A	D	A	A class of marine arthropods that resemble spiders.
L	A	G	E	N	I	F	O	R	M	Shaped like a flask.
L	A	G	O	M	O	R	P	H	A	An order of gnawing mammals that resemble rodents, Rabbits, Hares.
L	A	G	O	S	T	O	M	U	S	Genus of rodents, Chinchilla.
L	A	G	R	I	M	A	N	D	O	Lacrimando.
L	A	L	O	P	L	E	G	I	A	Paralysis of the muscles involved in speech.
L	A	M	B	D	A	C	I	S	M	Incorrect pronunciation or substitution of "L".
L	A	M	B	R	E	Q	U	I	N	Valance, Short decorative drapery for a shelf.
L	A	M	E	N	T	A	B	L	E	Deplorable, Pitiable, Mournful, Sorrowful, Dire, Calamitous, Grievous, Woeful.
L	A	M	I	N	A	G	R	A	M	An X-ray photograph of a layer of the body.
L	A	M	I	N	A	R	I	A	N	Relating to the presence of kelps.
L	A	M	I	N	A	R	I	T	E	A fossil plant believed to be kelp-related seaweed.
L	A	M	P	O	O	N	E	R	Y	The art of satire.
L	A	M	P	Y	R	I	D	A	E	A family of beetles, Glowworm.
L	A	N	A	T	O	S	I	D	E	Crystalline poisonous cardiac glycosides derived from foxglove leaves.
L	A	N	C	E	O	L	A	T	E	Shaped like a lance.
L	A	N	D	L	U	B	B	E	R	One unskilled in seamanship.
L	A	N	D	O	C	R	A	C	Y	Government by land-owners.
L	A	N	D	O	L	P	H	I	A	Tropical woody vines having large berrylike fruits, Congo Rubber.
L	A	N	G	B	A	N	I	T	E	A hexagonal mineral occurring in iron-black prismatic crystals.
L	A	N	G	U	I	S	H	E	D	Faded, Weakened, Drooped, Declined, Deteriorated, Dwindled.
L	A	N	G	U	O	R	O	U	S	Languid, Enervated, Limp, Listless, Dilatory, Laggard, Indolent, Slothful.
L	A	N	O	S	T	E	R	O	L	A crystalline tetrcyclic alcohol that occurs in wool grease and yeast.
L	A	N	T	H	A	N	I	D	E	A chemical element of the lanthanide series.
L	A	N	T	H	A	N	I	T	E	A mineral composed of hydrous lanthanum carbonate.
L	A	N	T	H	O	P	I	N	E	A crystalline alkaloid found in opium.
L	A	N	U	G	I	N	O	U	S	Covered with down or fine soft hair, Downy.
L	A	P	A	R	O	T	O	M	Y	Surgical section of the abdominal wall.
L	A	P	I	D	A	R	I	A	N	Inscribed on stone.
L	A	P	I	D	A	T	I	O	N	Execution by stoning, Pelting with stones.
L	A	R	G	A	M	E	N	T	E	Direction in music - with slowness and breadth.
L	A	R	Y	N	G	I	T	I	C	Affected with laryngitis.
L	A	R	Y	N	G	I	T	I	S	Inflammation of the larynx.
L	A	S	C	I	V	I	O	U	S	Lewd, Lustful, Libidinous, Salacious, Licentious, Passionate, Satyric, Prurient.
L	A	S	I	O	C	A	M	P	A	Family of moths.
L	A	T	E	R	A	L	I	T	Y	Preference in use of homologous parts on one lateral half of the body over the other.
L	A	T	E	R	A	L	I	Z	E	To localize on one side.
L	A	T	E	R	N	A	R	I	A	A large genus of lantern flies.
L	A	T	R	I	D	I	D	A	E	Marine percoid fishes of Australasia known as trumpeters.
L	A	T	T	I	C	I	N	I	O	Glass containing milk-white threads made in Murano, Italy.
L	A	U	M	O	N	T	I	T	E	A white monoclinic mineral consisting of a hydrous calcium and aluminium silicate.
L	A	U	R	E	A	T	I	O	N	An act of crowning with laurel.
L	A	U	R	I	O	N	I	T	E	A basic lead chlorite.
L	A	U	R	U	S	T	I	N	E	A European shrub with evergreen leaves and white or pink fragrant flowers.
L	A	V	A	N	D	U	L	O	L	A liquid terpenoid alcohol occurring in lavender oil from France.
L	A	V	I	S	H	N	E	S	S	Abundance, Prodigality, Extravagance, Overdoing, Squander, Waste, Unthrift.
L	A	W	F	U	L	N	E	S	S	Legality.
L	A	W	R	E	N	C	I	T	E	A mineral consisting of ferrous chloride often found in meteoric iron.
L	A	W	S	O	N	I	A	N	A	Port Orford Cedar.
L	E	A	D	E	R	S	H	I	P	Position of a leader, Act of leading.
L	E	A	F	H	O	P	P	E	R	Leaping insects that suck the juices of plants and create damage to grass and trees.
L	E	B	E	N	S	R	A	U	M	Space required for life, growth or activity.
L	E	C	T	I	O	N	A	R	Y	A book of lections for use in a church service.
L	E	E	C	H	C	R	A	F	T	The art of healing.
L	E	G	A	T	A	R	I	A		Crocodile bird.
L	E	G	A	L	I	S	T	I	C	Characterized by legalism.
L	E	G	I	B	I	L	I	T	Y	State of being legible.

1	2	3	4	5	6	7	8	9	10	Definition
L	E	G	I	S	L	A	T	E	D	Made or created laws.
L	E	G	I	S	L	A	T	O	R	One that makes laws.
L	E	G	I	T	I	M	A	C	Y	The legal status of a child born in wedlock.
L	E	G	I	T	I	M	A	T	E	Born in wedlock, Genuine, Law-abiding, Reasonable, Lawful, Valid, Cogent, Recognized.
L	E	G	I	T	I	M	I	Z	E	To make legitimate.
L	E	G	R	A	N	D	I	T	E	A mineral consisting of a hydrous basic arsenate of zinc.
L	E	G	U	M	I	N	O	U	S	Consisting of peas or other legumes.
L	E	I	O	T	R	I	C	H	I	A division of mankind comprising people having straight smooth hair.
L	E	I	S	H	M	A	N	I	A	A genus of flagellates parasitic in the tissues of vertebrates.
L	E	M	O	N	G	R	A	S	S	A grass that is a source of lemongrass oil.
L	E	M	U	R	I	F	O	R	M	Resembling lemurs.
L	E	M	U	R	O	I	D	E	A	A suborder of Primates, Lemurs.
L	E	N	G	T	H	W	I	S	E	In the direction of the length.
L	E	N	N	O	A	C	E	A	E	A family of fleshy parasitic herbs with capsular fruit.
L	E	N	T	A	M	E	N	T	E	Direction in music - slowly.
L	E	N	T	I	C	U	L	A	R	Like a lentil in size and form, Having the shape of a double-convex lens.
L	E	N	T	I	S	S	I	M	O	Direction in music - in a very slow manner.
L	E	O	D	I	C	I	D	A	E	A family of polychaete worms.
L	E	O	N	T	I	A	S	I	S	Leprosy affecting the flesh of the face.
L	E	O	P	A	R	D	E	S	S	A female leopard.
L	E	O	P	A	R	D	I	N	E	Rabbit fur processed to resemble leopard pelt.
L	E	O	P	O	L	D	I	T	E	Sylvite.
L	E	P	I	D	O	I	D	E	I	A group of extinct ganoid fishes.
L	E	P	I	D	O	L	I	T	E	A mineral that consists of mica containing lithium.
L	E	P	I	D	O	P	T	E	R	A butterfly or moth.
L	E	P	O	R	I	F	O	R	M	Resembling a hare in form.
L	E	P	O	R	I	L	L	U	S	A genus of gregarious Australian rats.
L	E	P	R	E	C	H	A	U	N	A mischievous elf of Irish fairy stories.
L	E	P	T	O	C	L	A	S	E	A minute crack in rock.
L	E	P	T	O	L	E	P	I	S	A genus of primitive thin-scaled fishes.
L	E	P	T	O	M	O	N	A	S	Genus of parasitic flagellates.
L	E	P	T	O	S	P	I	R	A	A genus of extremely slender aerobic spirochetes.
L	E	S	B	I	A	N	I	S	M	Lesbian love.
L	E	S	K	E	A	C	E	A	E	A family of mosses that grow on trees and rocks.
L	E	S	S	I	N	G	I	T	E	A mineral consisting of a silicate of calcium and cerium.
L	E	T	H	A	R	G	I	Z	E	Benumb.
L	E	T	H	O	C	E	R	U	S	A genus of very large predaceous aquatic bugs.
L	E	T	T	E	R	H	E	A	D	A sheet of stationery with printed or engraved details of the sender.
L	E	T	T	E	R	L	E	S	S	Illiterate.
L	E	T	T	S	O	M	I	T	E	Cyanotrichite.
L	E	U	C	A	U	G	I	T	E	A white or grayish augite that resembles diopside.
L	E	U	C	O	B	R	Y	U	M	Genus of mosses, White moss.
L	E	U	C	O	C	H	O	L	Y	A state of feeling accompanying preoccupation with trivialities.
L	E	U	C	O	C	I	D	I	N	A substance destroying leukocytes.
L	E	U	C	O	L	Y	T	I	C	Inducing lysis of white blood cells.
L	E	U	C	O	M	A	I	N	E	A decomposifying substance produced in a living animal body.
L	E	U	C	O	P	H	O	R	E	A white chromatophore.
L	E	U	C	O	P	L	A	S	T	A colourless plastid.
L	E	U	C	O	V	O	R	I	N	A crystalline synthetic acid derived from folic acid.
L	E	U	K	E	M	O	G	E	N	A substance that may cause leukemia.
L	E	U	K	O	B	L	A	S	T	A cellular precursor of a leukocyte.
L	E	U	K	O	C	Y	T	I	C	Relating to leukocytes.
L	E	U	K	O	D	E	R	M	A	An abnormality caused by a congenital lack of pigment ending in white patches on skin.
L	E	U	K	O	P	E	N	I	A	An abnormally low number of leukocytes arising from many and varied causes.
L	E	U	K	O	R	R	H	E	A	A viscid discharge from the vagina.
L	E	U	K	O	T	O	X	I	C	Relating to a toxin capable of destroying leukocytes.
L	E	V	I	G	A	T	I	O	N	The action of reducing to a fine smooth powder.
L	E	V	I	S	T	I	C	U	M	A genus of European herbs, Lovage.
L	E	V	I	T	A	T	I	O	N	The lifting of a person or thing supposedly without assistance or touching.
L	E	V	O	G	Y	R	A	T	E	Rotating toward the left or counterclockwise.
L	E	X	I	C	O	L	O	G	Y	The science of the derivation and signification of words.
L	E	X	I	C	O	N	I	Z	E	To make a lexicon.
L	E	X	I	G	R	A	P	H	Y	The practice of defining words.
L	E	X	I	P	H	A	N	I	C	Bombastic, Pretentious.
L	I	B	E	R	A	L	I	S	M	Broad-mindedness, Tolerance, Leniency.
L	I	B	E	R	A	L	I	T	Y	Generosity, Gratuity, Fullness, Broadness.
L	I	B	E	R	A	L	I	Z	E	Decontrol, Less strict or rigorous.

1	2	3	4	5	6	7	8	9	10	Definition
L	I	B	E	R	A	T	I	O	N	Act of freeing or releasing from domination.
L	I	B	E	R	A	T	O	R	Y	Attempting to liberate.
L	I	B	I	D	I	N	I	Z	E	To treat as an avenue of sexual gratification.
L	I	B	I	D	I	N	O	U	S	Lustful, Lascivious, Lecherous, Lewd, Salacious, Passionate, Prurient, Satyric.
L	I	B	O	C	E	D	R	U	S	A genus of trees with leaves resembling those of the sequoia.
L	I	B	R	E	T	T	I	S	T	The writer of a libretto.
L	I	C	E	N	T	I	A	T	E	One who has a licence to practice a profession, An academic degree.
L	I	C	E	N	T	I	O	U	S	Unchaste, Lascivious, Abandoned, Dissolute, Profligate, Immoral, Unprincipled.
L	I	C	H	E	N	A	L	E	S	An order of fungi, Lichens.
L	I	C	I	T	A	T	I	O	N	The act of offering for sale or bidding at an auction.
L	I	E	N	H	O	L	D	E	R	One holding a valid lien.
L	I	E	U	T	E	N	A	N	T	A representative or substitute for another in the performance of duty.
L	I	G	H	T	H	O	U	S	E	A structure equipped with a light designed as a navigational beacon.
L	I	G	N	E	S	C	E	N	T	Somewhat woody.
L	I	K	E	L	I	H	O	O	D	Probability.
L	I	L	A	E	O	P	S	I	S	A small genus of perennial creeping aquatic or marsh herbs.
L	I	L	I	A	C	E	O	U	S	Resembling lilies.
L	I	L	L	I	A	N	I	T	E	A mineral consisting of a steel gray sulfide of lead and bismuth.
L	I	M	A	C	I	F	O	R	M	Resembling a slug.
L	I	M	I	C	O	L	I	N	E	Inhabiting the shore.
L	I	M	I	C	O	L	O	U	S	Living in mud.
L	I	M	I	T	A	R	I	A	N	One that limits or restricts.
L	I	M	I	T	A	T	I	O	N	Restriction, Restraint, Limit, Stint, Stricture.
L	I	M	I	T	A	T	I	V	E	Limiting, Restrictive.
L	I	M	I	V	O	R	O	U	S	Swallowing mud.
L	I	M	N	A	N	T	H	E	S	A genus of western North American annual herbs.
L	I	M	N	I	M	E	T	E	R	A sensitive form of tide gauge for measuring variations of level in lakes.
L	I	M	N	O	C	N	I	D	A	A genus of small freshwater jellyfishes.
L	I	M	N	O	G	R	A	P	H	A record made on a limnimeter.
L	I	M	N	O	R	C	H	I	S	A genus of North American orchids.
L	I	M	O	N	C	I	L	L	O	A tropical American fruit or timber tree.
L	I	N	E	W	A	L	K	E	R	A worker who patrols a peroleum line on foot to inspect and make small repairs.
L	I	N	G	U	A	T	U	L	A	A genus of tongue worms parasitic of nasal and respiratory passages.
L	I	N	G	U	I	F	O	R	M	Shaped like a tongue.
L	I	N	G	U	I	S	T	I	C	Relating to the knowledge of languages.
L	I	N	G	U	I	S	T	R	Y	Study of languages.
L	I	N	O	L	E	A	T	E	S	Salt or ester of linoleic acid.
L	I	N	O	P	T	E	R	I	S	A genus of fossil ferns.
L	I	P	I	D	O	S	O	M	E	A fatty inclusion body of the cytoplasm.
L	I	P	O	G	E	N	O	U	S	Tending to produce fat.
L	I	P	O	G	R	A	P	H	Y	Inadvertent omission of a letter or syllable in writing.
L	I	P	O	I	D	O	S	I	S	A disorder of fat metabolism.
L	I	P	O	P	H	I	L	I	C	Having strong affinity for fats.
L	I	P	O	T	R	O	P	I	C	Tending to prevent abnormal deposition of fats.
L	I	P	O	X	E	N	O	U	S	Abandoning the host - used of various parasitic fungi.
L	I	P	O	X	I	D	A	S	E	A crystallizable protein enzyme.
L	I	P	P	I	Z	A	N	E	R	A special breed of horse used for display.
L	I	Q	U	E	S	C	E	N	T	Melting, turning into liquid.
L	I	Q	U	I	D	A	T	E	D	Settled, Discharged, Satisfied, Eliminated, Removed, Purged, Executed, Assissinated.
L	I	R	O	C	O	N	I	T	E	A basic hydrous aluminium copper arsenate.
L	I	T	E	R	A	L	I	S	M	Realism, Adherence to the explicit substance of an idea or expression.
L	I	T	E	R	A	L	I	S	T	Fundamentalist.
L	I	T	E	R	A	T	I	O	N	Representation of sounds or words by letters.
L	I	T	E	R	A	T	U	R	E	The production of literary work, Writings in prose or verse, Musical composition.
L	I	T	H	I	S	T	I	D	A	An order of fossil sponges.
L	I	T	H	O	C	L	A	S	E	A natural fracture in rock.
L	I	T	H	O	D	E	S	M	A	A small shelly plate being a part of many bivalve shells.
L	I	T	H	O	G	L	Y	P	H	An engraving on stone.
L	I	T	H	O	G	R	A	P	H	Inscribing on stone.
L	I	T	H	O	L	O	G	I	C	Relating to lithology.
L	I	T	H	O	M	A	N	C	Y	Divination by stones or charms made of stone.
L	I	T	H	O	M	A	R	G	E	A smooth compact common kaolin.
L	I	T	H	O	P	H	A	G	A	Genus of elongated bivalve mollusks, Date mussels.
L	I	T	H	O	P	H	A	N	E	Translucent porcelain impressed with figures.
L	I	T	H	O	P	H	I	L	E	Concentrated in the outer shell of the earth.
L	I	T	H	O	P	H	Y	S	A	A spherulitic cavity observed in some rhyolitic lavas.
L	I	T	H	O	P	H	Y	T	E	A plant that grows on the surface of rocks.

1	2	3	4	5	6	7	8	9	10	
L	I	T	H	O	P	R	I	N	T	To print by photo-offset.
L	I	T	H	O	T	R	I	T	E	An instrument for performing lithotrity.
L	I	T	H	O	T	R	I	T	Y	A method of breaking bladder stones into small pieces to be removed by washing.
L	I	T	I	G	A	T	I	O	N	The practice of taking legal action.
L	I	T	T	E	R	M	A	T	E	A product of multiple birth in relation to the other members of the same litter.
L	I	T	T	L	E	N	E	S	S	A mean or petty act.
L	I	T	U	O	L	I	D	A	E	A genus of marine fossils having shells composed of sand grains cemented together.
L	I	T	U	R	G	I	C	A	L	Relating to liturgy.
L	I	V	A	B	I	L	I	T	Y	Survival expectancy.
L	I	V	E	L	I	H	O	O	D	Means of subsistence.
L	I	V	E	L	I	N	E	S	S	The state of being lively.
L	I	Z	A	R	D	T	A	I	L	A white-woolly herb with yellow flowers.
L	O	B	O	S	T	E	M	O	N	A genus of African perennial herbs.
L	O	B	O	T	O	M	I	Z	E	To incise a lobe of the brain.
L	O	B	U	L	A	T	I	O	N	The formation of lobules.
L	O	C	A	L	I	S	T	I	C	Associated with a particular locality.
L	O	C	O	M	O	T	I	O	N	The power of moving from place to place, Travel.
L	O	C	O	M	O	T	I	V	E	An engine for drawing a train along rails.
L	O	C	U	L	A	M	E	N	T	A recess in a tomb for the reception of a body or funeral urn.
L	O	G	A	N	B	E	R	R	Y	The hybrid of a dewberry and red raspberry.
L	O	G	G	E	R	H	E	A	D	A turtle, Blockhead, Dumbbell, A stupid person.
L	O	G	I	C	A	L	I	T	Y	The state of being logical.
L	O	N	E	L	I	N	E	S	S	Bleakness, Desolateness, Isolation, Separateness.
L	O	P	H	O	S	T	E	O	N	The keel-bearing part of a bird's sternum.
L	O	P	H	O	T	I	D	A	E	A family of elongated ribbon-like deep-sea fishes, Oarfish.
L	O	Q	U	A	C	I	O	U	S	Garrulous, Wordy, Babbling, Noisy, Talkative, Verbose, Wordy, Chatty.
L	O	R	A	N	S	K	I	T	E	A mineral of a black oxide of yttrium, cerium, calcium, tantalum and zirconium.
L	O	R	D	L	I	N	E	S	S	Dignity, Haughtiness.
L	O	R	E	T	T	O	I	T	E	A mineral consisting of a lead oxychloride.
L	O	R	I	C	A	R	I	I	D	A catfish.
L	O	R	I	C	A	T	I	O	N	Having a protective covering.
L	O	V	O	Z	E	R	I	T	E	A mineral consisting of a hydrous silicate of alkalies manganese calcium and zirconium.
L	O	W	E	R	I	N	G	L	Y	Darkly, Gloomily.
L	O	X	O	D	R	O	M	I	C	Relating to a rhumb line.
L	O	X	O	S	C	E	L	E	S	Genus of South American spiders.
L	U	B	R	I	C	A	T	O	R	One that lubricates, A device for applying a lubricant.
L	U	B	R	I	C	I	O	U	S	Lecherous, Salacious, Elusive, Shifty, Inconstant, Capricious, Fickle, Temperamental.
L	U	C	E	R	N	A	R	I	A	Genus of bell-shaped jellyfishes.
L	U	C	I	F	E	R	A	S	E	An enzyme that is associated with luciferin and catalyzes its oxidation.
L	U	C	I	F	U	G	O	U	S	Avoiding light.
L	U	C	I	O	P	E	R	C	A	A genus of large freshwater fishes, Pike perches.
L	U	G	U	B	R	I	O	U	S	Mournful.
L	U	J	A	V	E	R	I	T	E	A melanocratic nepheline-syenite rock.
L	U	M	B	E	R	J	A	C	K	A worker with timber or lumber.
L	U	M	B	R	I	C	O	I	D	Resembling an earthworm.
L	U	M	I	C	H	R	O	M	E	A blue fluorescent crystalline compound that is a derivative of alloxazine.
L	U	M	I	F	L	A	V	I	N	A yellow-green fluorescent crystalline compound that is a derivative of isoalloxazine.
L	U	M	I	N	O	P	H	O	R	A luminescent substance, Prosphor.
L	U	M	I	N	O	U	S	L	Y	In a luminous manner.
L	U	M	I	S	T	E	R	O	L	A crystalline compound stereoisomeric with ergosterol.
L	U	P	E	T	I	D	I	N	E	Any of the dimethyl derivatives of piperidene which are colourless liquids.
L	U	R	C	H	I	N	G	L	Y	Jerkily, Swayingly.
L	U	S	T	E	R	L	E	S	S	Dull.
L	U	S	T	E	R	W	A	R	E	Earthenware with metallic glaze that becomes iridescent in the firing process.
L	U	S	T	R	A	T	I	O	N	Purification, Ablution.
L	U	T	J	A	N	I	D	A	E	Family of active carnivorous marine percoid fishes.
L	Y	C	A	E	N	I	D	A	E	Family of brilliantly coloured butterflies.
L	Y	C	O	P	E	R	D	O	N	Genus of fungi.
L	Y	C	O	P	O	D	I	U	M	A large genus of erect or creeping plants.
L	Y	G	O	D	E	S	M	I	A	A genus of wiry-stemmed American weedy herbs.
L	Y	M	N	A	E	I	D	A	E	A family of thin-shelled air-breathing freshwater snails.
L	Y	M	P	H	E	D	E	M	A	Edema due to faulty lymphatic drainage.
L	Y	M	P	H	O	C	Y	T	E	A colourless weakly motile cell produced in lymphoid tissue.
L	Y	O	P	H	I	L	I	Z	E	To dry in a frozen state under high vacuum, Freezedry.
L	Y	S	I	G	E	N	O	U	S	Formed by the breaking down of adjoining cells.
L	Y	S	I	M	A	C	H	I	A	A widely distributed genus of herbs.
L	Y	T	H	R	A	C	E	A	E	A family of herbs, shrubs and trees.

1	2	3	4	5	6	7	8	9	10
L	Y	X	O	F	L	A	V	I	N

A yellow crystalline compound isolated from heart muscle.

M

MAASBANKER	A horse mackerel.
MACADAMIZE	Constructing a road with bituminous material.
MACERATION	The process of soaking to soften a substance.
MACHINATOR	Plotter, Artful schemer.
MACROGRAPH	A photographic graphic reproduction of an object that may be slightly reduced.
MACROMANIA	A delusion that things are larger than they really are.
MACROPHYTE	A member of the macroscopic plant life.
MACROPYGIA	A large genus of long tailed pigeons that resemble cuckoos.
MACROSCIAN	Casting a long shadow.
MACROSEISM	A severe earthquake.
MACROSOMIA	Gigantism.
MACROSPORE	Megaspore, A large spore.
MACROZAMIA	A genus of Australian cycads.
MACRURIDAE	A family of fishes, Grenadiers.
MACULATION	Spot, Stain, Blemish.
MACULATURE	An impression made from an intaglia engraved plate.
MADAPOLLAM	A soft plain cotton fabric.
MADREPORIC	Relating to reef-building corals.
MAEANDRINA	Relating to genus of reef-building corals including brain corals.
MAGISTRATE	A local officer of the judiciary with limited jurisdiction, Justice of the Peace.
MAGNETITIC	Containing magnetite.
MAGNIFICAL	Exalted, Imposing, Munificent, Illustrious, High-sounding.
MAGNIFICAT	A song or hymn of praise.
MAGNIFYING	Exaggerating, Intensifying, Heightening, Exalting, Increasing, Enlarging, Enhancing.
MAIDENHAIR	A genus of ferns with delicate fronds.
MAIDENHEAD	Hymen, Freshness, Purity, Virginity.
MAIDENHOOD	Girlhood.
MAINSTREAM	Prevailing current or direction of activity or influence.
MAINTAINED	Defended, Upheld, Declared, Asserted, Preserved, Saved, Sustained, Justified.
MAISONETTE	A residential building of two apartments often of two stories.
MAJORATION	Enlargement, Increase.
MAKEWEIGHT	Something of little worth used to fill a gap.
MALACLEMYS	A genus of North American moderate sized edible terrapins.
MALACOLOGY	Classification in zoology for mollusks.
MALACOSOMA	Genus of moths.
MALAPROPOS	Inappropriate, Inopportune.
MALAXATION	Reducing to a soft mass by rubbing, kneading or rolling.
MALCONTENT	Discontented, Dissatisfied, Disgruntled, Unruly, Restless, Mutinous, Rebellious.
MALEFACTOR	Felon, Criminal, Evildoer, Lawbreaker, Knave, Miscreant, Rogue, Scoundrel.
MALEFICENT	Evil, Baleful, Injurious, Hurtful, Criminal, Sinister, Malign.
MALENTENDU	Misunderstanding.
MALEVOLENT	Hurtful, Injurious, Malicious, Hateful, Spiteful, Vicious, Wicked, Sinister.
MALFEASANT	A public official committing wrongdoing in connection with his authority.
MALLANGONG	Platypus.
MALLARDITE	Hydrous sulfate of manganese.
MALLEATION	The action of pounding or beating.
MALLOPHAGA	Order of wingless insects comprising bird lice.
MALODOROUS	Stinking, Fetid, Rank, Reeking, Putrid, Rancid, Scandalous, Improper.
MAMMILLARY	Relating to the breasts.
MAMMILLATE	Having nipples.
MAMMOGENIC	Stimulating mammary development.
MANAGEABLE	Governable, Tractable.
MANAGEMENT	The conducting or supervising of something.
MANAGERIAL	Characteristic of a manager.
MANASSEITE	A mineral of basic hydrous carbonate of magnesium and aluminium.
MANCHINEEL	A poisonous tropical American tree which yields timber for cabinetwork.
MANDRAGORA	A small genus of Eurasian herbs.
MANGABEIRA	A Brazilian vine having a milky juice that yields a rubber.
MANGOSTEEN	The dark reddish brown fruit of an East Indian tree.
MANIFESTLY	Plainly, Obviously.
MANIPULATE	Operate, Handle, Dispense, Swing, Control, Exploit, Direct, Engineer.
MANOLETINA	A special pass in bullfighting.

1	2	3	4	5	6	7	8	9	10	Clue
M	A	N	S	O	N	E	L	L	A	A genus of filarial worms.
M	A	N	S	U	E	T	U	D	E	Meekness, Sameness, Gentleness.
M	A	N	T	E	L	L	O	N	E	A long purple cloak worn by prelates.
M	A	N	T	L	E	R	O	C	K	Material that covers the solid base rock.
M	A	N	U	S	C	R	I	P	T	Handwritten copy.
M	A	N	Z	A	N	I	L	L	A	A pale aromatic dry sherry from Spain.
M	A	Q	U	I	L	L	A	G	E	Makeup, Warpaint.
M	A	R	B	L	E	W	O	O	D	Native olive, A tree with hard mottled wood.
M	A	R	C	E	S	C	E	N	T	Waste away, Withering.
M	A	R	C	G	R	A	V	I	A	A genus of tropical American woody vines.
M	A	R	C	H	A	N	T	I	A	Genus of liverworts.
M	A	R	C	O	T	T	A	G	E	Air layering in which the rooting medium is bound to the plant.
M	A	R	G	A	R	I	T	E	S	A genus of minute top shells that form part of the diet of cod and other fishes.
M	A	R	G	A	R	O	P	U	S	A genus of ticks including the cattle tick.
M	A	R	G	I	N	A	L	I	A	Marginal notes, Nonessential items.
M	A	R	G	I	N	E	L	L	A	Small glossy white-shelled marine snails.
M	A	R	G	U	E	R	I	T	E	Single-flowered chrysanthemums.
M	A	R	I	C	O	L	O	U	S	Living in the sea.
M	A	R	I	N	H	E	I	R	O	Tropical American timber trees.
M	A	R	I	N	O	R	A	M	A	A panoramic representation of a sea view.
M	A	R	I	O	N	E	T	T	E	A puppet manipulated by strings or by hand.
M	A	R	I	P	O	S	I	T	E	A mineral consisting of a bright green chromium-bearing phengite.
M	A	R	I	T	I	C	I	D	E	One that murders or kills his or her spouse.
M	A	R	K	E	T	A	B	L	Y	Relating to buying or selling.
M	A	R	K	W	O	R	T	H	Y	Noteworthy.
M	A	R	M	A	R	O	S	I	S	The conversion of limestone into marble by metamorphism.
M	A	R	O	U	F	L	A	G	E	A process of fastening canvas to a wall with adhesive.
M	A	R	R	O	W	B	O	N	E	A bone containing marrow.
M	A	R	S	H	I	N	E	S	S	The state of being marshy.
M	A	R	T	E	N	S	I	T	E	The hard constituent of which quenched steel is chiefly composed.
M	A	R	T	I	N	G	A	L	E	A device for steadying a horse's head.
M	A	R	V	E	L	M	E	N	T	Source of wonder.
M	A	R	V	E	L	L	O	U	S	Excellent, Exceptional, Amazing, Astonishing, Spectacular, Striking, Surprising.
M	A	S	Q	U	E	R	A	D	E	Camouflage, Disguise, Cover, Facade, Pose, Veil, Pretence, Concealment.
M	A	S	T	E	C	T	O	M	Y	Surgical excision of the breast.
M	A	S	T	E	R	M	I	N	D	Direct, Supervise, Engineer, Plot.
M	A	S	T	E	R	W	O	R	T	Herbaceous plants once used in medicine, Cow parsnip, Angelica.
M	A	S	T	I	G	O	P	U	S	Final larva of some shrimps and prawns.
M	A	S	T	O	D	Y	N	I	A	Pain in the breast.
M	A	S	T	U	R	B	A	T	E	To practice erotic stimulation exclusive of sexual intercourse.
M	A	T	C	H	B	O	A	R	D	A board used in the building trade that is cut with a groove and tongue for a perfect fit.
M	A	T	C	H	M	A	K	E	R	One that schemes to arrange a marriage, One that promotes sporting contests.
M	A	T	C	H	S	T	I	C	K	Slender length of wood used for making matches.
M	A	T	E	R	I	A	L	L	Y	With regard to material substance.
M	A	T	E	R	N	A	L	L	Y	In a maternal manner.
M	A	T	L	O	C	K	I	T	E	A mineral consisting of lead chloride and fluoride.
M	A	T	R	I	A	R	C	H	Y	System of descent being traced through the female line.
M	A	T	R	I	C	A	R	I	A	Genus of weedy herbs that have a strong odour.
M	A	T	R	I	C	I	D	A	L	Relating to the murder of a mother by her son or daughter.
M	A	T	R	I	L	O	C	A	L	Located at the residence of the family of the wife.
M	A	T	R	O	N	H	O	O	D	The state of being a matron.
M	A	T	R	O	N	Y	M	I	C	A name derived from that of a maternal ancestor.
M	A	T	U	R	A	T	I	O	N	The process of becoming mature.
M	A	T	U	R	E	M	E	N	T	Bringing of something to a state of maturity.
M	A	U	N	D	E	R	I	N	G	Rambling, Drifting, Wandering, Inarticulate, Incoherent, Tongue-tied.
M	A	X	I	L	L	A	R	I	A	A large genus of tropical American orchids.
M	A	Y	O	N	N	A	I	S	E	A dressing of egg yolks, vegetable oil, vinegar and oil.
M	A	Z	O	C	A	R	P	O	N	A form genus of fossil plants.
M	A	Z	O	P	L	A	S	I	A	A degenerative condition of breast tissue.
M	E	A	N	D	E	R	I	N	G	Rambling, Drifting, Gallivanting, Roaming, Roving, Traipsing, Straying, Winding.
M	E	A	N	I	N	G	F	U	L	Expressive, Eloquent, Pregnant, Significant, Important, Considerable, Momentous.
M	E	A	S	U	R	A	B	L	E	Foreseeable, Capable of being measured.
M	E	A	S	U	R	A	B	L	Y	To some extent.
M	E	C	H	A	N	I	C	A	L	Concerned with machinery or tools, Automatic, Involuntary, Spontaneous.
M	E	D	U	S	I	F	O	R	M	A gonophore produced by some hydroids.
M	E	D	D	L	E	S	O	M	E	Impertinent, Intrusive, Officious, Obtrusive.
M	E	D	I	C	A	M	E	N	T	Remedy, A substance used in therapy.

1	2	3	4	5	6	7	8	9	10	
M	E	D	I	C	A	T	I	O	N	Treatment with a medicament.
M	E	D	I	C	A	T	I	V	E	Medicinal.
M	E	D	I	O	C	R	A	C	Y	Rule by the mediocre.
M	E	D	I	O	C	R	I	T	Y	Temperance, Inferiority, Moderation, Limited, Average.
M	E	D	I	T	A	T	I	O	N	Private devotion, Reflection.
M	E	D	I	T	A	T	I	V	E	Conducive to meditation.
M	E	D	R	I	N	A	Q	U	E	Fibre of the sago palm.
M	E	D	U	L	L	A	T	E	D	Having a medulla.
M	E	E	R	S	C	H	A	U	M	A mineral of a hydrous magnesium silicate used for making tobacco pipes.
M	E	G	A	C	H	I	L	I	D	A leaf-cutting bee.
M	E	G	A	L	I	T	H	I	C	Prehistoric construction of large undressed stones.
M	E	G	A	L	O	P	O	R	E	A large pore found in the dorsal shell of some chitons.
M	E	G	A	L	O	S	A	U	R	A dinosaur.
M	E	G	A	P	O	D	I	U	S	A genus of gallinaceous birds.
M	E	G	A	R	H	I	N	U	S	A genus of very large American non-biting mosquitoes.
M	E	G	A	R	H	Y	S	S	A	A genus of large flies, some of which are parasitic.
M	E	G	A	S	C	O	P	I	C	Enlarged, Magnified.
M	E	L	A	C	O	N	I	T	E	An earthy black massive variety of tenorite.
M	E	L	A	M	P	S	O	R	A	A genus of rusts.
M	E	L	A	M	P	Y	R	U	M	A small genus of branching annual herbs.
M	E	L	A	N	C	H	O	L	Y	Sadness, Dejection, Mournful, Gloom, Unhappy, Sorrowful, Woeful, Doleful.
M	E	L	A	N	O	D	E	R	M	A dark-skinned person.
M	E	L	A	N	O	I	D	I	N	Various coloured substances formed from proteins or amino acids.
M	E	L	A	N	O	P	L	U	S	Genus of migratory locusts.
M	E	L	A	N	T	H	I	U	M	Genus of perennial herbs.
M	E	L	E	A	G	R	I	N	A	Genus of mollusks including the pearl oyster.
M	E	L	E	Z	I	T	O	S	E	A non-reducing trisaccharide sugar obtained from exudations of certain trees.
M	E	L	I	A	N	T	H	U	S	A small genus of southern African shrubs, Honeyflower.
M	E	L	I	O	L	A	L	E	S	An order of fungi.
M	E	L	I	S	M	A	T	I	C	Florid.
M	E	L	I	T	E	N	S	I	S	Derived from bacterium.
M	E	L	L	O	P	H	O	N	E	A brass instrument used as a substitute for a French horn.
M	E	L	O	M	A	N	I	A	C	A person or animal abnormally affected by certain ranges of sound.
M	E	L	O	P	H	A	G	U	S	A genus of wingless flies.
M	E	L	O	P	H	O	N	I	C	Relating to music or its performance.
M	E	L	O	P	O	E	T	I	C	Relating to the art or theory of inventing melody.
M	E	M	B	E	R	S	H	I	P	A body of members.
M	E	M	B	R	A	N	A	T	E	Having a membrane.
M	E	M	B	R	A	N	O	U	S	Thin, pliable and often transparent.
M	E	M	O	R	A	N	D	U	M	Memento, Reminder, Note, Notation, Directive, Epistle, Announcement, Missive.
M	E	N	D	A	C	I	O	U	S	Dishonest, Deceitful, Lying, Roguish, Shifty, Untruthful, Erroneous, Spurious.
M	E	N	D	I	C	A	N	C	Y	Beggary, Cadging, Sponging.
M	E	N	I	N	G	I	T	I	C	Relating to meningitis.
M	E	N	O	P	A	U	S	A	L	Relating to the natural cessation of menstruation.
M	E	N	O	T	Y	P	H	L	A	Sub-order of Insectivora, Elephant shrew, Tree shrew.
M	E	N	S	T	R	U	O	U	S	Menstruating.
M	E	N	S	U	R	A	B	L	E	Capable of being measured.
M	E	N	T	H	A	C	E	A	E	Family of aromatic herbs.
M	E	N	T	H	E	N	O	N	E	A monoketone derived from a menthene.
M	E	N	Y	A	N	T	H	E	S	A genus of bog plants.
M	E	P	E	R	I	D	I	N	E	A synthetic narcotic drug used in its crystalline hydrochloride as an analgesic.
M	E	P	H	E	N	E	S	I	N	A crystalline compound used chiefly in the treatment of neuromuscular conditions.
M	E	R	C	A	L	L	I	T	E	A mineral consisting of a bisulfate of potassium.
M	E	R	C	A	N	T	I	L	E	Relating to merchants or trading, Mercenary.
M	E	R	C	E	N	A	R	I	A	A genus of clams.
M	E	R	C	I	F	U	L	L	Y	In a merciful manner.
M	E	R	I	C	L	I	N	A	L	Having tissue of one kind incompletely surrounded by another kind of tissue.
M	E	R	I	D	I	O	N	A	L	Southern, Southerly.
M	E	R	L	U	C	C	I	U	S	Genus of fishes related to the cods.
M	E	R	O	C	E	R	I	T	E	The fourth segment of the antenna of a crustacean.
M	E	R	O	P	O	D	I	T	E	The fourth segment from the base of some limbs of crustaceans.
M	E	R	O	T	O	M	I	Z	E	To divide into parts.
M	E	S	E	N	C	H	Y	M	E	A loosely organized connective tissue.
M	E	S	E	N	T	E	R	I	C	Related to intestinal membranes.
M	E	S	E	N	T	E	R	O	N	A part of the alimentary canal.
M	E	S	E	T	H	M	O	I	D	Related to the bony element of the nasal septum.
M	E	S	I	T	O	R	N	I	S	A genus of two species of birds of Malagasy.

1	2	3	4	5	6	7	8	9	10	
M	E	S	I	T	Y	L	E	N	E	An oily hydrocarbon occurring in coal tar and petroleum but also made synthetically.
M	E	S	O	C	A	R	D	I	A	Abnormal location of the heart in the central part of the thorax.
M	E	S	O	C	H	R	O	I	C	Having a complexion between light and dark.
M	E	S	O	C	R	A	T	I	C	Having nearly equal light and dark mineral constituents.
M	E	S	O	G	N	A	T	H	Y	The condition of having slightly projecting jaws of medium size.
M	E	S	O	L	I	T	H	I	C	Relating to a period of the Stone Age.
M	E	S	O	P	H	Y	T	I	C	Growing in a moist environment.
M	E	S	O	P	L	O	D	O	N	A genus of small-toothed whales.
M	E	S	O	P	O	D	I	U	M	The middle portion of the foot of a mollusk.
M	E	S	O	R	R	H	I	N	E	Having a nose of moderate size.
M	E	S	O	S	P	H	E	R	E	A layer of atmosphere above the ionosphere.
M	E	T	A	B	I	O	S	I	S	An environment where one organism is influenced for another to follow and flourish.
M	E	T	A	B	O	L	I	S	M	Process in a cell or organism by which living matter is built from nutritive material.
M	E	T	A	C	A	R	P	U	S	Certain bones of the hand.
M	E	T	A	L	L	U	R	G	Y	Science and study of the structure and properties of metals.
M	E	T	A	P	H	R	A	S	E	A literal translation from one language into another.
M	E	T	A	P	H	R	A	S	T	Translator.
M	E	T	A	P	L	A	S	I	A	Transformation of one tissue into another.
M	E	T	A	P	O	D	I	U	M	The posterior division of the foot in mollusks.
M	E	T	A	S	T	A	S	I	S	Transfer of disease-producing malignant cells from one area of the body to another.
M	E	T	A	S	T	A	T	I	C	Relating to metastasis.
M	E	T	A	T	A	R	S	U	S	Certain bones of the foot.
M	E	T	A	T	H	E	S	I	S	Reversal, Change of place or condition.
M	E	T	E	O	R	I	T	I	C	Relating to meteorites.
M	E	T	H	I	O	N	I	N	E	A crystalline essential amino acid used as a dietary supplement.
M	E	T	H	O	D	I	C	A	L	Systematic, Orderly, Regular, Organized, Analytical, Logical, Meticulous, Scrupulous.
M	E	T	I	C	U	L	O	U	S	Careful, Strict, Exact, Heedful, Fussy, Painstaking, Fastidious, Cautious.
M	E	T	R	O	M	A	N	I	A	An obsession for writing verses.
M	E	T	R	O	N	O	M	I	C	Mechanically regular.
M	E	T	R	O	P	O	L	I	S	An important city of a certain area.
M	E	T	R	O	X	Y	L	O	N	A genus of Indo-Malayan palm that flowers and fruits only once and then dies.
M	E	T	T	L	E	S	O	M	E	Spirited, Fiery, Excitable, Skittish, High-spirited.
M	I	A	R	G	Y	R	I	T	E	A mineral consisting of a silver antimony sulfide.
M	I	A	R	O	L	I	T	I	C	Irregular cavities of igneous rock.
M	I	C	R	E	R	G	A	T	E	A small worker ant.
M	I	C	R	O	B	I	O	T	A	The microscopic flora and fauna of a region.
M	I	C	R	O	C	E	B	U	S	Genus of Madagascar lemurs.
M	I	C	R	O	C	L	I	N	E	A mineral of the feldspar group.
M	I	C	R	O	D	R	I	L	I	Slender aquatic worms.
M	I	C	R	O	F	I	C	H	E	A sheet of microfilm.
M	I	C	R	O	G	A	D	U	S	A genus of gadoid fishes.
M	I	C	R	O	G	R	A	P	H	A reproduction of a microscopic image.
M	I	C	R	O	H	Y	D	R	A	A minute freshwater hydroid.
M	I	C	R	O	L	I	G	H	T	A wing structure fitted with a motor.
M	I	C	R	O	M	E	L	I	A	Having abnormally small and imperfectly developed extremities.
M	I	C	R	O	M	E	R	I	A	A large genus of fragrant herbs.
M	I	C	R	O	M	E	T	E	R	An adjustable instrument for measuring very small distances and angles.
M	I	C	R	O	M	E	T	R	Y	Measurement with a micrometer.
M	I	C	R	O	M	O	U	N	T	A very small mineral specimen suitable only for microscopic examination.
M	I	C	R	O	P	H	O	N	E	An instrument for the transmitting or recording of music and speech.
M	I	C	R	O	P	H	Y	T	E	A dwarfed plant.
M	I	C	R	O	P	O	D	I	A	Having abnormally small feet.
M	I	C	R	O	P	R	I	N	T	A photographic record in reduced size.
M	I	C	R	O	S	C	O	P	E	An optical instrument with a combination of lens for enlarging the image of objects.
M	I	C	R	O	S	E	I	S	M	A slight earth tremor that can only be detected by special apparatus.
M	I	C	R	O	S	O	R	E	X	Pygmy shrew.
M	I	C	R	O	S	P	O	R	E	A very small spore of a heterosporous plant.
M	I	C	R	O	S	T	O	M	E	A small orifice.
M	I	C	R	O	T	H	E	R	M	A plant requiring a low temperature for full growth.
M	I	C	R	O	Z	O	O	I	D	A minute free swimming individual.
M	I	D	M	O	R	N	I	N	G	Middle of the period between sunrise and noon.
M	I	D	S	H	I	P	M	A	N	A naval cadet.
M	I	G	H	T	I	N	E	S	S	Power, Highness, Excellency.
M	I	G	N	O	N	E	T	T	E	An annual fragrant herb.
M	I	L	D	E	W	C	I	D	E	An agent that destroys mildew.
M	I	L	I	T	A	N	T	L	Y	In a militant manner.
M	I	L	I	T	A	R	I	L	Y	In a military manner.

1	2	3	4	5	6	7	8	9	10	
M	I	L	I	T	A	R	I	S	M	An aggressive policy of the military.
M	I	L	I	T	A	R	I	Z	E	Prepare for military purposes.
M	I	L	I	T	I	A	M	A	N	A member of an organized militia.
M	I	L	L	E	F	I	O	R	I	Ornamental glass with a section of coloured glass rods embedded to resemble flowers.
M	I	L	L	E	F	L	E	U	R	Having an allover pattern of small flowers.
M	I	L	L	E	N	N	I	U	M	A period of one thousand years.
M	I	L	L	E	S	I	M	A	L	Concerned with thousandths.
M	I	L	L	S	T	R	E	A	M	A stream used to run a mill.
M	I	L	L	W	R	I	G	H	T	One who plans and builds mills.
M	I	M	E	O	G	R	A	P	H	A duplicator for making many copies.
M	I	M	O	S	A	C	E	A	E	A family of plants.
M	I	N	E	R	A	L	I	Z	E	To impregnate with minerals, Petrify.
M	I	N	E	R	A	L	O	G	Y	The study and science of minerals.
M	I	N	E	S	T	R	O	N	E	A thick vegetable soup usually topped with grated cheese.
M	I	N	I	S	T	R	A	N	T	One that ministers.
M	I	N	N	I	E	B	U	S	H	A low shrub of eastern North America with greenish purple flowers.
M	I	N	U	T	E	N	E	S	S	Extreme smallness.
M	I	N	Y	A	D	I	D	A	E	A family of pelagic sea anemones.
M	I	R	A	B	I	L	I	T	E	A mineral consisting of hydrous sodium sulfate.
M	I	R	A	C	U	L	I	S	M	Belief in miracles.
M	I	R	A	C	U	L	O	U	S	Supernatural, Marvellous, Wonderful, Superior, Amazing, Astonishing, Spectacular.
M	I	S	C	E	L	L	A	N	Y	Medley, Mixture, Hodgepodge.
M	I	S	C	O	N	D	U	C	T	Wrongdoing, Malfeasance, Misbehaviour, Impropriety.
M	I	S	D	E	A	L	I	N	G	False dealing, Wrong conduct.
M	I	S	E	R	I	C	O	R	D	A thin-bladed medieval dagger, A small hall in a medieval monastery.
M	I	S	F	O	R	T	U	N	E	Adversity, Mishap, Mischance, Tragedy, Calamity, Disaster, Affliction.
M	I	S	L	E	A	D	I	N	G	Deceiving, Deluding, Beguiling, False, Delusory, Fallacious, Bewildering, Puzzling.
M	I	S	O	G	A	M	I	S	T	One who hates marriage.
M	I	S	O	G	Y	N	I	S	T	One who hates women.
M	I	S	O	L	O	G	I	S	T	One who hates arguments.
M	I	S	O	P	E	D	I	S	T	One who hates children.
M	I	S	S	I	O	L	O	G	Y	The study of the mission of the Church.
M	I	S	S	I	O	N	A	R	Y	One devoted to mission work.
M	I	S	T	A	K	E	N	L	Y	Wrongly, Erroneously.
M	I	S	T	A	S	S	I	N	I	A dwarf primrose of alpine America.
M	I	S	T	E	R	I	O	S	O	A direction in music- in a mysterious manner.
M	I	T	H	R	I	D	A	T	E	An antidote against poison.
M	I	T	I	G	A	T	I	O	N	Alleviation, Moderation, Palliation, Relief, Ease, Extenuation.
M	I	T	I	G	A	T	I	V	E	Alleviating, Lenitive.
M	I	T	I	G	A	T	O	R	Y	Mitigative.
M	I	X	A	B	I	L	I	T	Y	Quality of being able to be mixed.
M	I	X	O	B	I	O	S	I	S	A composite colony where different species of organisms live together.
M	I	X	O	D	E	C	T	E	S	A genus of extinct Insectivores.
M	I	X	O	L	O	G	I	S	T	One skilled in the preparation of mixed drinks.
M	I	X	O	S	A	U	R	U	S	A genus of extinct reptiles.
M	I	Z	Z	E	N	M	A	S	T	A mast near to the mainmast of a ship.
M	O	D	E	R	A	T	I	O	N	Temperance, Measure.
M	O	D	I	F	I	A	B	L	E	Capable of being modified.
M	O	D	U	L	A	T	I	N	G	Tempering or toning down.
M	O	D	U	L	A	T	O	R	Y	Relating to modulation.
M	O	E	H	R	I	N	G	I	A	A genus of low herbs.
M	O	E	R	I	T	H	E	R	E	A fossil of an extinct African mammal.
M	O	I	S	S	A	N	I	T	E	A silicon carbide.
M	O	I	S	T	E	N	I	N	G	Saturating, Dampening.
M	O	L	A	R	I	F	O	R	M	Resembling a molar tooth in shape.
M	O	L	L	I	F	Y	I	N	G	Pacifying, Conciliating, Ameliorating, Relenting, Appeasing, Allaying, Placating.
M	O	L	L	I	S	I	O	S	E	Leaf scorch.
M	O	L	O	S	S	I	D	A	E	Family of mastiff bats.
M	O	L	U	C	C	E	L	L	A	A small genus of Mediterranean mints having small white pink-tipped flowers.
M	O	L	Y	B	D	E	N	U	M	A polyvalent metallic element that resembles chromium.
M	O	N	A	N	D	R	O	U	S	Having flowers with a single stamen.
M	O	N	A	R	C	H	I	S	T	One that believes in the principles of monarchy.
M	O	N	A	X	O	N	I	D	A	A subclass of sponges.
M	O	N	E	T	A	R	I	L	Y	With respect to money.
M	O	N	G	R	E	L	I	Z	E	To cause to become mongrel.
M	O	N	I	L	I	A	L	E	S	An order of imperfect fungi.
M	O	N	I	L	I	A	S	I	S	A fungus infection, Thrush.

1	2	3	4	5	6	7	8	9	10	Definition
M	O	N	I	L	I	F	O	R	M	Jointed to resemble a string of beads.
M	O	N	I	M	O	L	I	T	E	A mineral consisting of an oxide of lead, calcium and antimony.
M	O	N	O	C	A	R	P	I	C	Bearing fruit once and then dying.
M	O	N	O	C	A	U	L	O	N	A genus of giant hydroids that could grow to eight feet in length.
M	O	N	O	C	H	R	O	M	E	Made in a single colour.
M	O	N	O	C	L	I	N	A	L	Having a single oblique inclination.
M	O	N	O	C	R	O	T	I	C	A pulse having a simple beat.
M	O	N	O	C	Y	C	L	I	C	Arranged in a single circle.
M	O	N	O	D	E	R	M	I	C	Relating to a single layer of cells.
M	O	N	O	D	O	N	T	A	L	Having only one tooth, Arctic cetacean, Narwhal.
M	O	N	O	E	C	I	O	U	S	Hermaphroditic, An individual having male and female sex organs.
M	O	N	O	G	A	M	I	S	T	One who adheres to monogamy.
M	O	N	O	G	E	N	I	S	M	Belief that human races have descended from a single created pair or common ancestor.
M	O	N	O	G	Y	N	I	S	T	One who adheres to the practice of having only one marriage partner at one time.
M	O	N	O	I	D	E	I	S	M	A state of prolonged absorption in a single idea.
M	O	N	O	K	E	T	O	N	E	A chemical compound containing one ketonic carbonyl group.
M	O	N	O	L	I	T	H	I	C	Carved from a single block of stone.
M	O	N	O	L	O	G	I	S	T	One who monopolizes the conversation.
M	O	N	O	L	O	G	I	Z	E	Soliloquize.
M	O	N	O	M	A	N	I	A	C	A person with true paranoia.
M	O	N	O	M	O	R	I	U	M	Widely distributed genus of ants.
M	O	N	O	M	Y	A	R	I	A	Bivalve mollusks, Pearl oysters, Scallops.
M	O	N	O	P	H	A	S	I	C	Single phase.
M	O	N	O	P	H	O	B	I	A	A morbid dread of being alone.
M	O	N	O	P	H	O	N	I	C	A solo voice.
M	O	N	O	P	L	E	G	I	A	Paralysis affecting a single limb or part of the body.
M	O	N	O	P	O	L	I	S	T	One who monopolizes.
M	O	N	O	P	O	L	I	Z	E	Engross, Absorb, Consume, Devour, Have, Hold, Possess, Utilize.
M	O	N	O	R	G	A	N	I	C	Relating to a single organ.
M	O	N	O	R	H	I	N	A	L	Affecting only one nostril.
M	O	N	O	S	I	L	A	N	E	A colourless gas.
M	O	N	O	S	O	D	I	U	M	Containing one atom of sodium in the molecule.
M	O	N	O	S	P	E	R	M	Y	The entry of a single fertilizing sperm into an egg.
M	O	N	O	T	O	C	O	U	S	Producing a single egg or young at one time.
M	O	N	O	T	O	N	I	S	T	One who speaks in a monotonous manner.
M	O	N	O	T	O	N	O	U	S	Repetitious, Dull, Dreary, Uniform, Unvaried.
M	O	N	O	T	R	O	P	I	C	Relating to an insect visiting only a single kind of flower for nectar.
M	O	N	O	V	A	L	E	N	T	Containing antibodies for/or antigens of a single strain of organism.
M	O	N	O	X	E	N	O	U	S	Relating to a parasite living on one kind of host.
M	O	N	O	Z	O	O	I	D		Consisting of a single individual.
M	O	N	T	B	R	E	T	I	A	A hybrid cormose plant favoured for its showy blossoms.
M	O	N	T	R	A	C	H	E	T	A white Burgundy wine.
M	O	N	U	M	E	N	T	A	L	Immense, Massive, Inestimable, Monstrous, Huge, Gigantic, Mammoth, Overwhelming.
M	O	O	N	F	L	O	W	E	R	A night-flowering plant.
M	O	O	N	S	H	I	N	E	R	A distiller of illicit whisky.
M	O	R	A	L	I	S	T	I	C	Concerned with morality, Expressive of a conventional moral attitude.
M	O	R	A	L	I	Z	I	N	G	Painting a moral.
M	O	R	A	T	O	R	I	U	M	A legal waiting period, An authorized delay, Suspension.
M	O	R	B	I	D	E	Z	Z	A	Extreme delicacy and softness.
M	O	R	B	I	D	N	E	S	S	The condition of being morbid.
M	O	R	D	A	C	I	O	U	S	Caustic, Biting, Scathing.
M	O	R	D	I	S	H	E	E	N	Asiatic cholera.
M	O	R	E	N	O	S	I	T	E	A mineral consisting of nickel sulfate.
M	O	R	G	A	N	A	T	I	C	A marriage between a member of royalty and a commoner with all rights of inheritance.
M	O	R	M	O	R	A	N	D	O	Direction in music- murmuring.
M	O	R	M	Y	R	I	D	A	E	A family of African freshwater fishes.
M	O	R	O	S	E	N	E	S	S	Sullenness, Gloominess.
M	O	R	P	H	E	M	I	C	S	Branch of linguistic analysis.
M	O	R	P	H	I	N	I	S	M	Addiction to morphine.
M	O	R	P	H	I	N	I	S	T	An habitual user of morphine.
M	O	R	P	H	I	N	I	Z	E	To treat with morphine.
M	O	R	P	H	O	L	I	N	E	An oily cyclic secondary amine used as a solvent.
M	O	R	P	H	O	L	O	G	Y	A branch of biology that deals with the form and structure of animals and plants.
M	O	R	T	A	D	E	L	L	A	A large highly seasoned sausage.
M	O	S	A	N	D	R	I	T	E	A mineral consisting of a silicate.
M	O	S	A	S	A	U	R	I	D	A genus of extinct fish-eating lizards.
M	O	T	A	C	I	L	L	I	D	Relating to the wagtails and pipits.

1	2	3	4	5	6	7	8	9	10	
M	O	T	H	E	R	H	O	O	D	State of being a mother, Maternity.
M	O	T	H	E	R	L	A	N	D	The land of origin.
M	O	T	H	E	R	L	E	S	S	Being without a mother.
M	O	T	H	E	R	W	O	R	T	A bitter Old World mint.
M	O	T	I	O	N	L	E	S	S	Without motion, Still.
M	O	T	I	T	A	T	I	O	N	A quivering movement.
M	O	T	I	V	A	T	I	O	N	Drive, Incentive, Stimulus, Incitement, Spur, Impetus, Impulse, Catalyst.
M	O	T	I	V	A	T	I	V	E	Providing motivation.
M	O	T	O	N	E	U	R	O	N	A motor nerve cell with its processes.
M	O	U	N	T	E	B	A	N	K	Charlatan, Swindler, Cheat, Imposter, Quack, Defrauder.
M	O	U	S	S	E	L	I	N	E	A fine sheer clothing fabric that resembles muslin.
M	O	U	T	H	P	I	E	C	E	A part that goes in the mouth.
M	O	V	A	B	I	L	I	T	Y	Capable of being moved.
M	O	V	I	E	M	A	K	E	R	One who produces motion pictures.
M	O	X	I	E	B	E	R	R	Y	Creeping snowberry.
M	U	C	E	D	I	N	O	U	S	Resembling mould or mildew.
M	U	C	I	F	E	R	O	U	S	Containing mucus.
M	U	C	O	R	A	C	E	A	E	A family of moulds destructive to food products.
M	U	C	O	S	E	R	O	U	S	Producing both mucus and a serous secretion.
M	U	D	S	K	I	P	P	E	R	Small fish that are able to leave the water and move over wet mud and sand.
M	U	L	I	E	B	R	I	T	Y	Feminity, Womanhood.
M	U	L	I	S	H	N	E	S	S	Obstinacy, Stubbornly.
M	U	L	T	I	F	I	D	U	S	A back muscle that helps to rotate the spine.
M	U	L	T	I	L	O	B	A	R	Having two or more lobes.
M	U	L	T	I	P	O	L	A	R	Having several poles.
M	U	N	I	F	I	C	E	N	T	Lavish, Liberal, Bounteous, Generous, Handsome, Openhanded.
M	U	N	I	T	I	O	N	E	R	A manufacturer of munitions.
M	U	R	A	E	N	I	D	A	E	Family of eels comprising the morays.
M	U	R	I	C	U	L	A	T	E	Minutely muricate.
M	U	S	C	A	D	E	L	L	E	A sweet dessert wine.
M	U	S	C	A	D	I	N	I	A	A small genus of woody vines.
M	U	S	C	A	R	I	N	I	C	Producing direct stimulation of smooth muscle.
M	U	S	C	U	L	A	R	I	S	Smooth muscular layer of the walls of various organs.
M	U	S	I	C	A	L	I	T	Y	Talent for producing music.
M	U	S	I	C	A	L	I	Z	E	To set to music.
M	U	S	I	C	O	L	O	G	Y	A study of music as a field of research.
M	U	S	T	E	L	I	D	A	E	A large family of small active carnivorous mammals, Mink, Otter, Weasels, Polecats.
M	U	T	A	B	I	L	I	T	Y	Capable of mutation.
M	U	T	I	L	A	T	I	O	N	Deprivation of a limb or essential part of the body.
M	U	T	I	L	L	I	D	A	E	A family of wasps.
M	U	T	I	N	O	U	S	L	Y	In a mutinous fashion.
M	U	T	T	O	N	B	I	R	D	An Australasion sea bird.
M	U	T	T	O	N	F	I	S	H	A snapper.
M	Y	A	S	T	H	E	N	I	A	Muscular debility.
M	Y	C	E	T	I	S	M	U	S	Mushroom poisoning.
M	Y	C	E	T	O	C	Y	T	E	A cell in various insects of a type that contains unicellular fungi.
M	Y	C	O	L	O	G	I	S	T	A specialist in mycology.
M	Y	C	O	L	O	G	I	Z	E	To study fungi.
M	Y	C	O	P	L	A	S	M	A	A type sole genus of micro-organisms.
M	Y	C	O	R	R	H	I	Z	A	The symbiotic association of the mycelium of a fungus.
M	Y	C	O	S	T	A	T	I	C	Relating to an agent that inhibits the growth of moulds.
M	Y	C	O	S	T	E	R	O	L	Any of a class of sterols obtained from fungi.
M	Y	D	R	I	A	T	I	N	E	A white crystalline compound used like atropine.
M	Y	E	L	O	B	L	A	S	T	A cell derived from the hemocytoblast.
M	Y	E	L	O	T	O	X	I	C	Destructive to bone marrow.
M	Y	O	C	A	R	D	I	U	M	The middle muscular layer of the heart wall.
M	Y	O	E	L	A	S	T	I	C	Made up of muscular and elastic tissues.
M	Y	O	F	I	B	R	O	M	A	A tumour composed of fibrous and muscular tissue.
M	Y	O	M	E	C	T	O	M	Y	Excision of a myoma.
M	Y	O	M	E	T	R	I	U	M	The muscular layer of the wall of the uterus.
M	Y	O	P	H	Y	S	I	C	S	The physics of muscular action.
M	Y	R	I	A	M	E	T	R	E	A metric unit of length equal to ten thousand metres.
M	Y	R	I	A	N	G	I	U	M	A genus of fungi.
M	Y	R	I	C	A	C	E	A	E	A family of shrubs.
M	Y	R	I	S	T	I	C	I	N	A crystalline phenolic ether with a strong odour occurring in oils from nutmeg and mace.
M	Y	R	I	N	G	I	T	I	S	Inflammation of the tympanic membrane.
M	Y	R	M	E	C	O	I	D	Y	The mimicking of ants by other insects.

1	2	3	4	5	6	7	8	9	10	Definition
M	Y	S	O	P	H	I	L	I	A	Abnormal attraction to filth.
M	Y	S	O	P	H	O	B	I	A	Abnormal fear of uncleanliness or contamination.
M	Y	S	T	E	R	I	O	U	S	Obscure, Enigmatical, Inexplicable, Inscrutable, Incomprehensible, Esoteric.
M	Y	S	T	I	C	A	L	L	Y	In a mystical manner.
M	Y	S	T	I	F	Y	I	N	G	Bewildering, Puzzling, Cryptic.
M	Y	T	H	O	C	L	A	S	T	A decrier of myths.
M	Y	T	H	O	L	O	G	E	R	A teller of myths or legends.
M	Y	T	H	O	M	A	N	I	A	An abnormal propensity for lying or exaggerating.
M	Y	T	H	O	P	O	E	I	C	Creating myths.
M	Y	T	I	L	O	F	O	R	M	Shaped like a mussel shell.
M	Y	X	O	B	A	C	T	E	R	An order of higher bacteria.
M	Y	X	O	C	O	C	C	U	S	A genus of myxobacteria.
M	Y	X	O	G	A	S	T	E	R	Former genus of slime moulds.

N

1	2	3	4	5	6	7	8	9	10	Definition
N	A	C	H	T	M	U	S	I	K	Serenade.
N	A	G	A	T	E	L	I	T	E	A rare mineral consisting of phosphosilicate of aluminium, the rare earths and iron.
N	A	H	E	C	A	R	I	D	A	Subdivision of extinct crustaceans.
N	A	I	A	D	A	C	E	A	E	A family of aquatic plants.
N	A	J	A	D	A	C	E	A	E	Same as NAIADACEAE.
N	A	K	U	R	U	I	T	I	S	A disease of cattle and sheep caused by a deficiency of cobalt.
N	A	P	H	T	H	E	N	I	C	Relating to naphthene.
N	A	P	H	T	H	O	A	T	E	A salt or ester of naphtholic acid.
N	A	P	O	L	I	T	A	N	A	A simple sixteenth century madrigal originating in Naples.
N	A	P	R	A	P	A	T	H	Y	Drugless treatment by manipulation.
N	A	R	A	N	J	I	L	L	A	A shrubby perennial herb having small edible fruits resembling oranges.
N	A	R	C	I	S	S	I	S	M	Love of one's self, Egocentrism.
N	A	R	C	O	L	E	P	S	Y	A compulsive tendency to have attacks of deep sleep from an unknown cause.
N	A	R	I	N	G	E	N	I	N	A crystalline flavonone obtained by hydrolysis of naringin.
N	A	R	T	H	E	C	I	U	M	A genus of bog herbs.
N	A	S	E	T	H	M	O	I	D	Relating to the nasal and ethmoid bones.
N	A	S	T	U	R	T	I	U	M	A genus of aquatic herbs.
N	A	S	U	T	I	F	O	R	M	Having a nasus projection of the front of the head.
N	A	T	A	T	O	R	I	A	L	Relating to swimming.
N	A	T	A	T	O	R	I	U	M	An indoor swimming pool.
N	A	T	I	O	N	A	L	L	Y	On a national scale, In terms of a nation as a whole.
N	A	T	I	O	N	W	I	D	E	Existing throughout an entire nation.
N	A	T	I	V	I	S	T	I	C	Advancing native culture.
N	A	T	T	E	R	J	A	C	K	Common brownish yellow toad.
N	A	T	U	R	A	L	I	S	M	Action, inclination or thought based on natural desires and instincts alone.
N	A	T	U	R	A	L	I	S	T	An adherent of naturalism.
N	A	T	U	R	A	L	I	T	Y	Natural feeling or behaviour.
N	A	T	U	R	A	L	I	Z	E	To establish in new surroundings.
N	A	U	C	O	R	I	D	A	E	A widely distributed family of aquatic insects, Water creepers.
N	A	U	M	A	N	N	I	T	E	A mineral consisting of a silver selenide.
N	A	U	S	E	A	T	I	N	G	Offensive, Disgusting, Foul, Loathsome, Repugnant, Repulsive, Sickening, Nasty.
N	A	U	T	I	C	A	L	L	Y	In a nautical manner.
N	A	U	T	I	L	I	D	A	E	A family of cephalopod mollusks with closely coiled shells.
N	A	V	I	G	A	T	I	O	N	The science of conducting ships or aircraft from one point to another.
N	E	B	A	L	I	A	C	E	A	A small order of marine crustaceans.
N	E	B	U	L	O	S	I	T	Y	Cloudiness.
N	E	C	R	O	G	E	N	I	C	Relating to carrion.
N	E	C	R	O	L	A	T	R	Y	Superstitious worship of the dead.
N	E	C	R	O	M	A	N	C	Y	Witchcraft, Sorcery, The practice of conjuring up the souls of the dead.
N	E	C	R	O	P	H	A	G	A	A group composed of burying beetles.
N	E	C	R	O	P	H	I	L	E	One who is fascinated with the dead.
N	E	C	R	O	P	H	O	B	E	One that exhibits exaggerated fear of death and bodies.
N	E	C	R	O	P	O	L	I	S	Cemetery.
N	E	C	T	A	R	I	N	I	A	A genus of Old World oscine birds.
N	E	C	T	O	C	A	L	Y	X	A swimming bell of a siphonophore.
N	E	E	D	L	E	B	U	S	H	Australian shrub with rigid needle-shaped leaves.
N	E	E	D	L	E	F	I	S	H	Voracious fishes.
N	E	E	D	L	E	T	A	L	K	A noise radiated directly by the needle of a phonograph pickup.
N	E	E	D	L	E	W	O	R	K	Work done with a needle, Embroidery, Knitting, Needlepoint.
N	E	G	A	T	I	V	A	T	E	Negate, Nullify, Contradict.

1	2	3	4	5	6	7	8	9	10	Definition
N	E	G	A	T	I	V	E	L	Y	In a negative manner, Denial, Contradiction.
N	E	G	A	T	I	V	I	S	M	Tendency to refusal or capriciousness.
N	E	G	L	E	C	T	F	U	L	Careless, Heedless, Negligent.
N	E	G	L	I	G	E	N	C	E	State of being negligent.
N	E	G	L	I	G	I	B	L	E	Trifling, Small, Slight, Remote, Slender.
N	E	G	O	T	I	A	B	L	E	Attainable, Passable, Navigable, Adjustable, Transferable.
N	E	G	O	T	I	A	T	O	R	One that negotiates.
N	E	G	R	O	P	H	I	L	E	One that favours negroes.
N	E	G	R	O	P	H	O	B	E	One that dislikes negroes.
N	E	I	S	S	E	R	I	A	N	Caused by the gonococcus.
N	E	M	A	T	I	C	I	D	E	A preparation used to destroy nematodes that attack crop plants.
N	E	M	A	T	O	C	Y	S	T	One of the minute stinging organs of hydrozoans.
N	E	M	A	T	O	G	O	N	Y	Thin-walled propagative cells of various mosses.
N	E	M	A	T	O	L	O	G	Y	A branch of zoology that deals with nematodes.
N	E	M	I	C	H	T	H	Y	S	A genus of fragile slender-bodied deep-sea eels.
N	E	M	O	R	I	C	O	L	E	Inhabiting groves.
N	E	M	O	U	R	I	D	A	E	A widely distributed family of stone flies.
N	E	O	B	L	A	S	T	I	C	Relating to new growth.
N	E	O	C	Y	A	N	I	N	E	A cyanine dye used for sensitizing photographic emulsions to infra-red rays.
N	E	O	D	I	P	R	I	O	N	A genus of sawflies whose larva causes damage to pines.
N	E	O	G	E	N	E	S	I	S	Regeneration.
N	E	O	G	E	N	E	T	I	C	Relating to neogenesis.
N	E	O	G	N	A	T	H	A	E	Super order that includes most existing birds.
N	E	O	L	O	G	I	C	A	L	Relating to the usage of new words or expressions.
N	E	O	N	T	O	L	O	G	Y	The study of recent organisms.
N	E	O	P	A	L	L	I	U	M	An important part of the brain.
N	E	O	P	E	N	T	A	N	E	A very volatile liquid hydrocarbon found in small amounts in petroleum and natural gas.
N	E	O	P	H	Y	A	S	I	S	Rejuvenation of a citrus strain to reproduce the original characters of the strain.
N	E	O	R	E	A	L	I	S	M	A revived realism.
N	E	O	R	N	I	T	H	E	S	A subclass of birds.
N	E	P	H	O	G	R	A	P	H	An instrument for photographing clouds.
N	E	P	H	O	S	C	O	P	E	An instrument for observing the direction of motion and velocity of clouds.
N	E	P	H	R	I	D	I	U	M	A primarily excretory structure.
N	E	P	H	R	O	C	Y	T	E	A cell that stores substances of an excretory nature.
N	E	P	H	R	O	L	I	T	H	Renal calculus, Kidney stone.
N	E	P	H	R	O	L	O	G	Y	The science that deals with the kidneys.
N	E	P	H	R	O	M	A	T	A	A malignant tumour of the renal cortex.
N	E	P	H	R	O	M	E	R	E	A segment of the mesoblast giving rise to a part of the kidney.
N	E	P	H	R	O	P	E	X	Y	Surgical fixation of a floating kidney.
N	E	P	H	R	O	T	O	M	E	The part of an embryo that develops into the excretory tubule of the primitive kidney.
N	E	P	H	R	O	T	O	M	Y	Surgical incision of a kidney.
N	E	P	H	T	H	Y	T	I	S	A small genus of tropical creeping or twining herbs.
N	E	P	O	T	I	S	T	I	C	Relating to nepotism.
N	E	P	T	I	C	U	L	I	D	A minute moth.
N	E	T	H	E	R	M	O	S	T	Lowest, Bottom.
N	E	T	T	L	E	S	O	M	E	Irritable, Irritating, Thorny, Prickly, Exasperating, Riling, Provoking.
N	E	U	F	C	H	A	T	E	L	A small soft unripened cheese.
N	E	U	R	E	C	T	O	M	Y	The excision of part of a nerve.
N	E	U	R	I	L	E	M	M	A	The delicate outer sheath of a nerve fibre.
N	E	U	R	O	B	L	A	S	T	An embryonic nerve cell.
N	E	U	R	O	C	O	E	L	E	The central canal of the spinal cord.
N	E	U	R	O	C	H	O	R	D	A nerve cord.
N	E	U	R	O	C	O	E	L	E	Cavities of the nervous system comprising central canal of spinal cord and the brain.
N	E	U	R	O	C	R	I	N	E	Hormonal substance that influences the activity of the nerves.
N	E	U	R	O	G	E	N	I	C	Originating in nervous tissue.
N	E	U	R	O	H	U	M	O	R	A substance of the nerve ending that is involved in the nerve impulse.
N	E	U	R	O	L	Y	S	I	S	The breaking down of nerve substance.
N	E	U	R	O	L	Y	T	I	C	Causing neurolysis.
N	E	U	R	O	M	O	T	O	R	Relating to efferent nervous impulses.
N	E	U	R	O	N	I	T	I	S	Inflammation of nerve roots and nerve cells.
N	E	U	R	O	P	A	T	H	Y	Abnormality of the nervous system or nerves.
N	E	U	R	O	P	H	I	L	E	Having an affinity for nerve tissue.
N	E	U	R	O	P	L	A	S	M	The ground cytoplasm of a nerve cell.
N	E	U	R	O	P	T	E	R	A	An order of insects including lacewings and ant lions.
N	E	U	R	O	S	P	O	R	A	A genus of fungi some of which cause damage in bakeries.
N	E	U	R	O	T	O	X	I	C	Toxic to the nerves or nervous tissue.
N	E	U	R	O	T	O	X	I	N	A poisonous protein complex found in some snake venoms.

1	2	3	4	5	6	7	8	9	10	Definition
N	E	U	T	R	A	L	I	S	M	Neutrality.
N	E	U	T	R	A	L	I	S	T	One who practices neutrality.
N	E	U	T	R	A	L	I	T	Y	The state of not being involved in a conflict, controversy or contest.
N	E	U	T	R	A	L	I	Z	E	Annul, Counteract, Frustrate, Negate, Cancel, Abrogate, Invalidate, Override.
N	E	W	B	E	R	Y	I	T	E	A mineral consisting of an acid magnesium phosphate.
N	E	W	F	A	N	G	L	E	D	New, Novel, Fresh, Modern, Recent.
N	E	W	S	C	A	S	T	E	R	Commentator, A person who broadcasts news on radio or television.
N	E	W	S	L	E	T	T	E	R	A printed sheet intended to be circulated for the dissemination of information.
N	E	W	S	M	O	N	G	E	R	Gossip, Talebearer, Telltale.
N	E	W	S	W	O	R	T	H	Y	An event or person of sufficient interest to warrant reporting by the media.
N	I	C	O	T	I	N	A	T	E	A salt or ester of nicotinic acid.
N	I	C	O	T	I	N	I	A	N	Relating to tobacco.
N	I	C	O	T	I	N	I	S	M	The effect of the excessive use of tobacco.
N	I	C	O	T	I	N	I	Z	E	To drug with nicotine.
N	I	D	A	M	E	N	T	A	L	Relating to a capsule or covering for eggs.
N	I	D	I	C	O	L	O	U	S	Living in a nest.
N	I	D	I	F	I	C	A	N	T	Building a nest.
N	I	D	I	F	U	G	O	U	S	Leaving the nest soon after hatching.
N	I	D	O	L	O	G	I	S	T	One who specializes in the study of birds' nests.
N	I	D	U	L	A	T	I	O	N	Nesting.
N	I	G	H	T	S	H	A	D	E	Belladonna, Henbane.
N	I	G	H	T	S	H	I	R	T	A nightgown resembling a shirt.
N	I	G	R	E	S	C	E	N	T	Blackish.
N	I	G	R	O	M	E	T	E	R	An instrument for measuring degrees of blackness.
N	I	N	C	O	M	P	O	O	P	Fool, Simpleton, Idiot, Imbecile, Ninny, Jackass.
N	I	P	P	L	E	W	O	R	T	A slender branching annual herb.
N	I	T	R	O	M	E	T	E	R	An apparatus for collecting and measuring the volume of gaseous nitrogen.
N	I	T	R	O	P	H	Y	T	E	A plant requiring nitrogen-rich soil.
N	O	B	L	E	W	O	M	A	N	Peeress.
N	O	C	I	C	E	P	T	O	R	A pain sense organ.
N	O	C	I	F	E	N	S	O	R	Relating to a system of cutaneous nerve fibres.
N	O	C	T	A	M	B	U	L	E	Sleepwalker, Somnambulist.
N	O	C	T	I	G	R	A	P	H	A writing frame for the blind.
N	O	D	I	F	E	R	O	U	S	Having nodes.
N	O	D	O	S	A	U	R	U	S	A genus of dinosaurs that resembled giant horned toads.
N	O	D	U	L	A	T	I	O	N	Condition of being nodular.
N	O	E	G	E	N	E	S	I	S	A scheme for the production of knowledge including three processes.
N	O	E	G	E	N	E	T	I	C	Relating to noegenesis.
N	O	E	K	K	E	L	O	S	T	A dark cheese flavoured with spices.
N	O	M	I	N	A	L	I	Z	E	To convert into or use as a noun.
N	O	M	I	N	A	T	I	N	G	Designating, Naming, Selecting, Appointing, Intending, Proposing, Presenting.
N	O	M	I	N	A	T	I	O	N	Appointment.
N	O	M	I	N	A	T	I	V	E	Nominal.
N	O	M	O	G	R	A	P	H	Y	The art of drafting laws.
N	O	M	O	T	H	E	T	I	C	Formulating general statements.
N	O	N	A	C	O	S	A	N	E	A paraffin hydrocarbon.
N	O	N	C	H	A	L	A	N	T	Imperturbable, Composed, Collected, Unruffled, Effortless, Light-hearted, Smooth.
N	O	N	T	R	O	N	I	T	E	A clay mineral consisting of hydrous iron silicate.
N	O	O	L	O	G	I	C	A	L	Relating to mind or to mental character.
N	O	R	B	E	R	G	I	T	E	A mineral composed of a magnesium silicate with fluorine and hydroxy.
N	O	R	B	O	R	N	A	N	E	A bicyclic crystalline hydrocarbon.
N	O	S	O	C	O	M	I	A	L	Originating in a hospital.
N	O	S	O	G	R	A	P	H	Y	Description or classification of disease.
N	O	S	O	L	O	G	I	S	T	A specialist in nosology.
N	O	S	T	R	I	L	I	T	Y	Prominence of nostril.
N	O	T	A	B	I	L	I	T	Y	Prominent or notable person.
N	O	T	A	R	Y	S	H	I	P	The position of a notary.
N	O	T	E	W	O	R	T	H	Y	Remarkable, Outstanding, Prominent, Manifest, Exceptional, Memorable.
N	O	T	H	A	R	C	T	I	D	A lemur of Notharctus.
N	O	T	H	A	R	C	T	U	S	A genus of primitive lemurs.
N	O	T	H	O	L	A	E	N	A	Genus of rock-inhabiting ferns.
N	O	T	I	C	E	A	B	L	E	Conspicuous, Arresting, Outstanding, Prominent, Striking, Eye-catching, Obvious.
N	O	T	I	F	I	A	B	L	E	Requiring to be notified, i.e. infectious diseases.
N	O	T	I	O	S	O	R	E	X	Genus of shrews.
N	O	T	O	N	E	C	T	I	D	An aquatic carnivorous bug.
N	O	T	O	P	T	E	R	I	D	A family of freshwater fishes.
N	O	T	O	R	Y	C	T	I	D	Australian marsupial mole.

1	2	3	4	5	6	7	8	9	10	Definition
N	O	T	O	S	T	I	G	M	A	A subclass of centipedes.
N	O	T	O	S	T	R	A	C	A	An order of small freshwater crustaceans.
N	O	U	R	I	S	H	I	N	G	Nutritious, Cherishing, Fostering, Nurturing, Supporting, Feeding.
N	O	V	A	C	U	L	I	T	E	A very hard fine-grained siliceous rock used for whetstones.
N	O	V	E	L	E	S	Q	U	E	Resembling a novel.
N	O	V	E	L	I	S	T	I	C	Characteristic of a novel.
N	O	V	O	B	I	O	C	I	N	An acid antibiotic.
N	U	C	L	E	A	T	I	O	N	The formation of nuclei, The process of seeding a cloud to produce rain.
N	U	C	L	E	A	T	O	R	Y	Nuclear division accompanied by Cytoplasmic growth but not cell division.
N	U	C	L	E	O	L	A	T	E	Having a nucleolus.
N	U	C	L	E	O	N	I	C	S	A branch of physical science dealing with phenomena of atomic nucleus.
N	U	C	L	E	O	S	I	D	E	A crystalline compound formed by partial hydrolysis of a nucleic acid.
N	U	C	U	L	A	N	I	U	M	Resembling a berry except in being superior.
N	U	D	I	B	R	A	N	C	H	A suborder of varied marine gastropod mollusks lacking shells and resembling slugs.
N	U	L	L	A	N	U	L	L	A	A hardwood club used by Australian aborigines.
N	U	L	L	I	B	I	E	T	Y	The state of being nowhere.
N	U	L	L	I	F	Y	I	N	G	Invalidating, Negating, Annulling, Abrogating, Abolishing, Annihilating, Quashing.
N	U	M	B	E	R	L	E	S	S	Inestimable, Innumerable, Too many to be counted.
N	U	M	E	R	O	L	O	G	Y	The study of the occult significance of numbers.
N	U	M	E	R	O	U	S	L	Y	Abundantly.
N	U	M	I	S	M	A	T	I	C	Relating to money and currency.
N	U	M	M	U	L	A	R	I	A	A genus of fungi. Blister canker.
N	U	N	C	I	A	T	U	R	E	An official delegation from the Pope to a foreign power.
N	U	P	T	I	A	L	I	T	Y	The marriage rate.
N	U	R	S	E	R	Y	M	A	N	One whose occupation is the scientific cultivation of trees, shrubs and plants.
N	U	T	C	R	A	C	K	E	R	An implement for cracking nuts.
N	U	T	R	I	T	I	O	U	S	Nourishing.
N	Y	C	T	A	L	O	P	I	A	Night-blindness, Reduced vision in faint light.
N	Y	C	T	I	C	O	R	A	X	A genus of herons, Night herons.
N	Y	M	P	H	O	I	D	E	S	A genus of aquatic herbs.

1	2	3	4	5	6	7	8	9	10	Definition
O	B	D	U	R	A	T	E	L	Y	Harshly, Callously, Adamantly, Heartlessly, Rigidly, Relentlessly.
O	B	E	D	I	E	N	T	L	Y	Docilely, Submissively, Loyally, Subserviently, Amenably.
O	B	E	I	S	A	N	T	L	Y	In a servile manner.
O	B	E	L	I	S	C	O	I	D	Shaped like an obelisk.
O	B	F	U	S	C	A	T	E	D	Confused, Baffled, Bewildered.
O	B	I	T	U	A	R	I	S	T	A writer of obituarist.
O	B	I	T	U	A	R	I	Z	E	To write an obituary.
O	B	J	U	R	A	T	I	O	N	Binding by an oath.
O	B	L	I	G	A	T	I	O	N	Promise, Charge, Vow, Oath, Duty, Right, Burden, Responsibility.
O	B	L	I	G	A	T	O	R	Y	Mandatory, Compulsory, Imperative, Required.
O	B	L	I	G	I	N	G	L	Y	Pleasantly, Co-operatively, Amiably.
O	B	L	I	T	E	R	A	T	E	Remove, Cancel, Erase, Delete, Efface, Expunge.
O	B	L	O	N	G	A	T	E	D	Prolonged, Elongated.
O	B	N	U	B	I	L	A	T	E	Obscure, Becloud, Cover.
O	B	S	E	Q	U	I	O	U	S	Subservient, Servile, Menial, Deferential, Parasitic, Toadying.
O	B	S	E	R	V	A	N	C	E	Practice, Rite, Ceremony, Attention.
O	B	S	I	D	I	O	N	A	L	Relating to a siege.
O	B	S	O	L	E	T	E	L	Y	So as to be out of date or fashion.
O	B	S	O	L	E	T	I	S	M	Condition of being obsolete.
O	B	S	T	E	T	R	I	C	S	A branch of medical science that deals with birth, its antecedents and sequels.
O	B	S	T	R	U	C	T	E	D	Hindered, Impeded, Retarded, Blocked, Closed, Barred, Shrouded, Screened.
O	B	T	A	I	N	A	B	L	E	Available.
O	B	U	M	B	R	A	T	E	D	Shaded, Clouded, Darkened.
O	B	V	E	L	A	T	I	O	N	Concealing.
O	C	C	A	S	I	O	N	A	L	Infrequent, Seldom, Sporadic, Uncommon, Casual, Random, Scarce.
O	C	C	I	D	E	N	T	A	L	Western.
O	C	C	U	P	A	T	I	O	N	Activity, Employment, Vocation, Work, Pursuit, Habitation, Residence, Settlement.
O	C	C	U	R	R	E	N	C	E	Happening, Incident, Episode, Event, Circumstance, Occasion, Contingency.
O	C	E	A	N	A	R	I	U	M	A large marine aquarium.
O	C	E	A	N	O	L	O	G	Y	Science that deals with the oceans.
O	C	H	L	O	C	R	A	C	Y	Mob rule, Government by the mob.
O	C	H	R	O	N	O	S	I	S	A rare condition marked by pigment deposits in cartilages, tendons and ligaments.
O	C	T	A	C	N	E	M	U	S	A genus of deep-sea tunicates.

1	2	3	4	5	6	7	8	9	10	Definition
O	C	T	A	C	O	S	A	N	E	A solid paraffin hydrocarbon.
O	C	T	A	D	E	C	A	N	E	Any of numerous isomeric hydrocarbons of the paraffin series.
O	C	T	A	H	E	D	R	A	L	Having eight plane faces.
O	C	T	A	H	E	D	R	O	N	A solid bounded by eight plane faces.
O	C	T	A	M	E	R	O	U	S	Having eight parts.
O	C	T	A	N	G	U	L	A	R	Octagonal.
O	C	T	A	S	T	Y	L	O	S	A building with eight columns across the front.
O	C	T	A	V	A	L	E	N	T	Having a valence of eight.
O	C	T	O	G	E	N	A	R	Y	Based on the number eighty.
O	C	T	O	N	A	R	I	U	S	An eight-foot verse.
O	C	T	O	P	O	D	O	U	S	Octopus.
O	C	T	O	S	T	I	A	T	E	Belonging to a group of spiders having eight cardiac openings.
O	C	U	L	O	G	Y	R	I	C	Relating to the circular movements of the eyeballs.
O	C	U	L	O	M	O	T	O	R	Moving the eyeball.
O	D	O	B	E	N	I	D	A	E	A small family of marine mammals related to the seals.
O	D	O	C	O	I	L	E	U	S	A genus inclusive of many types of American deer.
O	D	O	N	T	A	L	G	I	A	Toothache.
O	D	O	N	T	A	L	G	I	C	Relating to toothache.
O	D	O	N	T	I	A	S	I	S	Teething.
O	D	O	N	T	O	C	E	T	I	Family of toothed whales.
O	D	O	N	T	O	L	I	T	E	A mineral consisting of fossil bone or tooth made bright blue by phosphate of iron.
O	D	O	N	T	O	L	O	G	Y	Scientific study of the teeth.
O	D	O	N	T	O	M	A	T	A	A tumour originating from a tooth.
O	D	O	N	T	O	T	O	M	Y	The operation of cutting into a tooth.
O	D	O	R	I	M	E	T	R	Y	The measurement of the intensity of odours.
O	D	O	R	I	P	H	O	R	E	A substance that produces an odour.
O	E	D	O	G	O	N	I	U	M	A genus of freshwater green algae.
O	E	N	O	C	A	R	P	U	S	A genus of South American pinnate-leaved palms.
O	E	N	O	C	Y	T	O	I	D	A large blood cell occurring in insects.
O	E	N	O	L	O	G	I	S	T	One versed in enology.
O	E	S	T	R	I	A	S	I	S	Infestation with botflies.
O	F	F	I	C	I	A	L	L	Y	Formally, Publicly, Ostensibly, With official approval.
O	I	K	O	P	L	E	U	R	A	A cosmopolitan genus of small tunicates.
O	L	E	A	G	I	N	O	U	S	Oily.
O	L	E	I	F	E	R	O	U	S	Producing oil.
O	L	E	O	G	R	A	P	H	Y	The method of printing on canvas to imitate an oil painting.
O	L	E	O	P	H	I	L	I	C	Having a strong affinity for oils, Hydrophobic.
O	L	E	O	P	H	O	B	I	C	Relating to lack of affinity for oils, Hydrophilic.
O	L	E	O	T	H	O	R	A	X	A condition of oil being present in the thorax.
O	L	E	R	A	C	E	O	U	S	Having the quality of a potherb.
O	L	I	G	O	C	L	A	S	E	A mineral of the plagioclase series.
O	L	I	G	O	P	S	O	N	Y	A market where a group of producers can control as a group but not as individuals.
O	L	I	V	A	C	E	O	U	S	Olive in colour.
O	L	I	V	E	S	C	E	N	T	A dark grayish yellow in colour.
O	M	B	R	O	G	R	A	P	H	A self-registering rain gauge.
O	M	B	R	O	M	E	T	E	R	A rain gauge.
O	M	B	R	O	P	H	I	L	E	A plant that thrives in heavy rainfall areas.
O	M	B	R	O	P	H	O	B	E	A plant incapable of withstanding prolonged rainfall.
O	M	E	N	T	O	P	E	X	Y	Operation to suture free fold of peritoneum to another organ.
O	M	M	A	T	I	D	I	U	M	One of the elements of the compound eye of an arthropod.
O	M	M	O	C	H	R	O	M	E	Various pigments found in the eyes of insects.
O	M	N	I	F	I	C	E	N	T	Unlimited in creative power.
O	M	N	I	G	E	N	O	U	S	Containing all varieties.
O	M	N	I	L	E	G	E	N	T	Having read everything.
O	M	N	I	P	O	T	E	N	T	Being all-powerful, wielding great authority.
O	M	N	I	V	O	R	O	U	S	Feeding on both animal and vegetable substances.
O	N	C	H	O	C	E	R	C	A	A genus of parasitic long slender worms.
O	N	C	H	O	C	H	E	T	E	A hair or bristle with a hooked tip.
O	N	C	O	L	O	G	I	S	T	A specialist in the study of tumours.
O	N	C	O	P	E	L	T	U	S	A genus of lygaeid bugs including milkweed bugs.
O	N	O	B	R	Y	C	H	I	S	A genus of Old World leguminous herbs.
O	N	O	C	E	N	T	A	U	R	A mythological creature having the upper torso of a man and the body and legs of an ass.
O	N	O	M	A	S	T	I	C	S	The study of the forms and origins of words.
O	N	O	S	M	O	D	I	U	M	A genus of North American perennial herbs.
O	N	T	O	L	O	G	I	S	M	A theory in philosophy.
O	N	T	O	L	O	G	I	S	T	An adherent of ontologism.
O	N	W	A	R	D	N	E	S	S	Moving forward.

1	2	3	4	5	6	7	8	9	10	Clue
O	N	Y	C	H	A	U	X	I	S	Overgrowth of the nails.
O	O	P	H	O	R	I	T	I	S	Inflammation of the ovary.
O	P	A	C	I	M	E	T	E	R	An instrument for measuring opacity.
O	P	A	L	E	S	C	E	N	T	Reflecting an iridescent light.
O	P	A	Q	U	E	N	E	S	S	The state of being opaque.
O	P	E	R	E	T	T	I	S	T	One that composes operettas.
O	P	H	E	L	I	M	I	T	Y	Economic satisfaction.
O	P	H	I	C	L	E	I	D	E	A deep-toned brass wind instrument of the key bugle class.
O	P	H	I	D	I	I	D	A	E	A family of elongate eel-shaped fishes comprising the cusk eels.
O	P	H	I	O	B	O	L	U	S	A genus of fungi.
O	P	H	I	O	L	A	T	R	Y	The worship of snakes.
O	P	H	I	O	P	O	G	O	N	A genus of grass-leaved herbs.
O	P	H	T	H	A	L	M	I	A	An inflammation of the conjunctiva or of the eyeball.
O	P	H	T	H	A	L	M	I	C	One having a special kind of eye.
O	P	I	L	I	A	C	E	A	E	A family of tropical shrubs.
O	P	I	S	O	M	E	T	E	R	An instrument used for measuring curved lines.
O	P	I	S	T	H	O	T	I	C	Relating to the bony elements of the capsule of the internal ear.
O	P	P	O	S	I	T	E	L	Y	In an opposite position.
O	P	P	O	S	I	T	I	O	N	Antagonism, Contrary, Contrast, Opposite, Hostility.
O	P	P	O	S	I	T	I	V	E	Tending to oppose.
O	P	P	R	E	S	S	I	O	N	Corrupt exercise of power, Overcome.
O	P	P	R	E	S	S	I	V	E	Tyrannical, Unjustly severe, Onerous, Demanding, Tough, Exacting, Grievous.
O	P	P	R	O	B	R	I	U	M	Contempt, Disgrace due to misbehaviour.
O	P	P	U	G	N	A	N	C	Y	Opposition, Hostility, Resistance.
O	P	T	I	M	A	L	I	Z	E	To bring to a peak of economic efficiency.
O	P	T	I	M	I	S	T	I	C	Anticipating the best, Hopeful, Sanguine.
O	R	A	T	O	R	I	C	A	L	Rhetorical.
O	R	B	I	C	U	L	A	T	E	The form of an orb, Circular in outline.
O	R	C	H	E	S	T	R	A	L	Relating to an orchestra.
O	R	C	H	I	D	A	L	E	S	An order of plants with irregular flowers.
O	R	D	A	I	N	M	E	N	T	Appointment by divine power.
O	R	D	I	N	A	R	I	L	Y	Usually, Moderately.
O	R	D	O	N	N	A	N	C	E	Royal decree, Arrangement in arts.
O	R	E	O	T	R	A	G	U	S	A genus of antelopes comprising the klipspringer.
O	R	G	A	N	I	C	I	S	M	A theory that disease is always associated with a structural lesion of an organ.
O	R	G	A	N	I	S	T	I	C	Suitable for performance on an organ.
O	R	G	A	N	O	L	O	G	Y	The study of the organs of animals and plants.
O	R	G	U	I	N	E	T	T	E	A small portable reed organ.
O	R	I	E	N	T	A	L	I	A	Materials relating to the Orient.
O	R	I	G	I	N	A	L	L	Y	Inherently, Initially, Primarily, Firstly.
O	R	I	G	I	N	A	T	O	R	One that originates.
O	R	N	A	M	E	N	T	A	L	Having decorative value.
O	R	N	I	T	H	O	P	O	D	A dinosaur.
O	R	N	I	T	H	O	S	I	S	Psittacosis, Disease originating from birds.
O	R	N	I	T	H	O	T	I	C	Relating to ornithosis.
O	R	O	G	R	A	P	H	I	C	Relating to the scientific study of mountains.
O	R	O	P	H	A	R	Y	N	X	The lower part of the pharynx that is continuous with the mouth.
O	R	O	P	H	I	L	O	U	S	Thriving in a subalpine environment.
O	R	O	T	U	N	D	I	T	Y	The quality of being sonorous or resonant.
O	R	P	H	A	N	H	O	O	D	The state of being an orphan.
O	R	P	H	E	O	N	I	S	T	A member of a French male choral society.
O	R	T	H	O	C	L	A	S	E	A mineral consisting of a monoclinic polymorph of common potassium feldspar.
O	R	T	H	O	D	R	O	M	Y	The art of great-circle sailing.
O	R	T	H	O	E	P	I	S	T	A person skilled in the study of the pronunciation of a language.
O	R	T	H	O	G	E	N	I	C	Relating to the rehabilitation of emotionally disturbed mentally retarded children.
O	R	T	H	O	G	O	N	A	L	An imaginary line at right angles to wave crests in oceanography.
O	R	T	H	O	G	R	A	D	E	Walking with the body upright.
O	R	T	H	O	M	E	T	R	Y	The art of correct versification.
O	R	T	H	O	P	N	O	E	A	Inability to breathe except in an upright position.
O	R	T	H	O	P	R	A	X	Y	Practices recognized as correct.
O	R	T	H	O	P	T	E	R	A	A very large order including cockroaches, grasshoppers, crickets, and related forms.
O	R	T	H	O	P	T	I	C	S	The treatment of defective visual habits and muscle imbalance by exercise.
O	R	T	H	O	P	T	I	S	T	A person trained in orthoptics.
O	R	T	H	O	S	C	O	P	E	An instrument for examining the superficial parts of the eye.
O	R	T	H	O	S	T	Y	L	E	Architectural columns arranged in a straight row.
O	R	T	H	O	T	O	N	U	S	Tetanic spasm characterized by rigid straightness of the body.
O	R	T	H	O	T	O	P	I	C	Relating to the grafting of tissue in a natural position.

1	2	3	4	5	6	7	8	9	10	
O	R	Y	C	T	O	L	O	G	Y	Mineralogy.
O	S	C	I	L	L	A	T	E	D	Vibrated, Fluctuated, Swung, Swayed, Varied.
O	S	C	I	L	L	A	T	O	R	A device for producing electric oscillations.
O	S	C	I	N	O	S	O	M	A	Genus of chloropid flies containing the frit fly.
O	S	C	I	T	A	T	I	O	N	Being inattentive, The condition of being drowsy.
O	S	C	U	L	A	T	I	O	N	Kissing.
O	S	C	U	L	A	T	O	R	Y	Relating to kissing.
O	S	M	I	O	P	H	I	L	E	Reacting to the presence of osmium tetroxide.
O	S	M	I	R	I	D	I	U	M	Iridosmine.
O	S	M	O	P	H	I	L	I	C	Thriving in a medium of high osmotic pressure.
O	S	P	H	R	A	D	I	U	M	The sense organ of an aquatic mollusk possibly used to test the purity of the water.
O	S	S	I	C	U	L	A	T	E	Having certain small bones.
O	S	T	E	N	S	I	B	L	E	Presentable, Conspicuous, Apparent, Alleged, Professed, Purported, Supposed.
O	S	T	E	N	S	I	B	L	Y	Apparently, Evidently, Outwardly, Seemingly, Superficially, Professedly.
O	S	T	E	O	B	L	A	S	T	A bone-forming cell.
O	S	T	E	O	C	L	A	S	T	One of the large multinucleate cells in developing bone.
O	S	T	E	O	C	O	L	L	A	A cellular incrustation of calcium carbonate on stems and roots of plants.
O	S	T	E	O	G	E	N	I	C	Bone-producing.
O	S	T	E	O	L	E	P	I	D	Family of prehistoric freshwater fishes considered to be ancestors of the amphibians.
O	S	T	E	O	L	Y	S	I	S	Dissolution of bone.
O	S	T	E	O	M	E	T	R	Y	Measurement of bones.
O	S	T	E	O	P	A	T	H	Y	Treatment of bone disease by manipulation combined with orthodox medication.
O	S	T	E	O	P	H	Y	T	E	A small pathological bony outgrowth.
O	S	T	E	O	T	R	I	B	E	A rasp used for removing carious bone.
O	S	T	E	R	T	A	G	I	A	Genus of slender brown nematode worms parasitic to ruminants.
O	S	T	R	A	C	E	O	U	S	Relating to oyster.
O	S	T	R	A	C	I	Z	E	D	Banished, Abolished, Exiled.
O	S	T	R	E	A	C	E	A	N	Common oyster.
O	S	T	R	E	I	F	O	R	M	Shaped like an oyster.
O	S	T	R	I	C	H	I	S	M	Self-delusion, Deliberate avoidance of anything unpleasant or disturbing.
O	T	I	O	S	E	N	E	S	S	The condition of being idle or sterile.
O	T	O	C	E	P	H	A	L	Y	Abnormal and deficient development of the head.
O	T	O	M	Y	C	O	S	I	S	Disease of the ear caused by growth of fungi.
O	U	A	N	A	N	I	C	H	E	A small landlocked salmon of Lake St John, Canada.
O	U	T	F	I	E	L	D	E	R	A fielder in a special position in cricket.
O	U	T	L	A	N	D	I	S	H	Foreign, Bizarre, Fantastic, Strange, Barbaric, Curious, Peculiar, Unconventional.
O	U	T	P	O	U	R	I	N	G	Outburst, Outflow.
O	U	T	R	A	G	E	O	U	S	Extravagant, Fantastic, Monstrous, Heinous, Atrocious, Scandalous, Abominable.
O	V	A	R	I	O	T	O	M	Y	Surgical incision of an ovary.
O	V	E	R	T	H	R	O	W	N	Overturned, Defeated, Destroyed, Ruined, Conquered, Toppled, Deposed, Removed.
O	V	E	R	W	O	R	K	E	D	Overdone, Overplayed, Overelaborated.
O	V	I	P	O	S	I	T	O	R	Specialized organ of an insect for depositing eggs.
O	X	A	L	Y	L	U	R	E	A	Parabanic acid.
O	X	Y	B	L	E	P	S	I	A	Acuteness of sight.
O	X	Y	C	E	P	H	A	L	Y	Congenital deformity of the skull.
O	X	Y	G	E	N	A	T	E	D	Saturated with oxygen.
O	X	Y	L	O	P	H	Y	T	E	A plant that prefers an acid soil.
O	X	Y	R	H	Y	N	C	H	A	A family of crabs, Spider crabs.
O	X	Y	S	P	I	R	U	R	A	A genus of nematode worms parasitic to domestic poultry.
O	X	Y	S	T	O	M	A	T	A	A small superfamily of crabs.
O	X	Y	U	R	I	A	S	I	S	Infestation with pinworms.
O	X	Y	U	R	I	C	I	D	E	A substance that destroys pinworms.
O	Z	O	N	O	L	Y	S	I	S	The cleavage of an unsaturated organic compound.

P

1	2	3	4	5	6	7	8	9	10	
P	A	C	H	I	S	T	I	M	A	A genus of North American dwarf evergreen shrubs.
P	A	C	H	N	O	L	I	T	E	A mineral consisting of a hydrous fluoride of a sodium, calcium and aluminium.
P	A	C	H	Y	M	E	T	E	R	An instrument for measuring thickness.
P	A	C	H	Y	T	Y	L	U	S	Family of destructive migratory locusts.
P	A	E	D	I	A	T	R	I	C	Relating to the study of the disease of children.
P	A	G	I	N	A	T	I	O	N	Numbering system for pages.
P	A	I	N	T	B	R	U	S	H	A brush for applying paint.
P	A	L	A	E	O	P	H	I	S	A genus of large extinct snakes.
P	A	L	A	E	O	S	A	U	R	Dinosaur.
P	A	L	A	G	O	N	I	T	E	Basaltic glass.

1	2	3	4	5	6	7	8	9	10	
P	A	L	A	V	E	R	O	U	S	Wordy, Verbose.
P	A	L	E	A	C	E	O	U	S	Covered with chaffy scales.
P	A	L	E	A	C	R	I	T	A	A genus of moths that contains the spring cankerworm.
P	A	L	I	M	P	S	E	S	T	A parchment or tablet that has been used again after earlier writings have been erased.
P	A	L	I	N	D	R	O	M	E	Something that reads the same backward or forward.
P	A	L	L	E	S	C	E	N	T	Growing pale.
P	A	L	L	I	A	T	I	V	E	Serving to alleviate.
P	A	L	L	O	G	R	A	P	H	An apparatus for recording steamship vibrations.
P	A	L	M	A	C	E	O	U	S	Resembling a palm.
P	A	L	M	E	R	W	O	R	M	A caterpillar that suddenly appears in great numbers and devours herbage.
P	A	L	P	I	T	A	N	C	Y	The state of trembling.
P	A	L	P	O	G	N	A	T	H	One of a centipede's third pair of mouthparts.
P	A	L	T	R	I	N	E	S	S	The state of being niggardly or mean.
P	A	L	U	S	T	R	I	N	E	Thriving in a marshy environment.
P	A	L	Y	N	O	L	O	G	Y	A branch of science concerned with the study of pollen and spores.
P	A	N	C	R	A	T	I	U	M	An ancient Greek athletic contest, A genus of bulbous herbs, Sea daffodil.
P	A	N	C	R	E	A	T	I	C	Relating to the pancreas.
P	A	N	D	A	L	I	D	A	E	A family of deepwater prawns.
P	A	N	D	A	N	A	L	E	S	An order of monocotyledonous plants.
P	A	N	E	G	Y	R	I	S	T	Eulogist.
P	A	N	E	G	Y	R	I	Z	E	Extol in public.
P	A	N	G	E	N	E	S	I	S	A hypothetical mechanism of heredity.
P	A	N	G	U	I	N	G	U	E	A card game which resembles rummy.
P	A	N	I	C	U	L	A	T	E	Arranged in panicles.
P	A	N	O	M	P	H	E	A	N	Universal.
P	A	N	O	P	H	O	B	I	A	A condition of vague anxiety, Generalized fear.
P	A	N	O	P	T	I	C	O	N	An optical instrument combining the telescope and microscope.
P	A	N	O	R	P	I	D	A	E	A cosmopolitan family of slender-winged insects, Scorpion flies.
P	A	N	S	O	P	H	I	S	M	Universal wisdom.
P	A	N	T	A	L	O	O	N	S	Breeches, Trousers.
P	A	N	T	H	E	R	I	N	E	Resembling a panther.
P	A	N	T	O	G	R	A	P	H	A special instrument for copying a map or plan.
P	A	N	T	O	M	O	R	U	S	A genus of weevils that are plant pests.
P	A	P	E	R	I	N	E	S	S	The condition of being papery.
P	A	P	E	T	E	R	I	E	S	Personal stationery comprising writing paper, cards and envelopes.
P	A	P	I	L	I	O	N	I	D	A Swallowtail butterfly.
P	A	P	I	L	L	I	T	I	S	Inflammation of a papilla, Inflammation of the optic disk.
P	A	P	U	L	A	T	I	O	N	The formation of papules.
P	A	P	Y	R	O	L	O	G	Y	The study of papyrus manuscripts.
P	A	R	A	B	O	L	I	Z	E	To express in fables.
P	A	R	A	D	E	N	T	A	L	Adjacent to a tooth.
P	A	R	A	D	I	S	E	A	E	Birds of paradise.
P	A	R	A	D	O	X	U	R	E	A palm civet.
P	A	R	A	D	R	O	M	I	C	Running side by side, Following a parallel course.
P	A	R	A	G	N	E	I	S	S	Gneiss derived from a sedimentary rock.
P	A	R	A	G	O	N	I	T	E	A mica corresponding to muscovite.
P	A	R	A	L	G	E	S	I	A	Disordered or abnormal sensation.
P	A	R	A	L	O	G	I	S	M	A reasoning contrary to logical rules.
P	A	R	A	L	O	G	I	Z	E	To reason falsely.
P	A	R	A	M	I	T	O	M	E	The ground substance of protoplasm.
P	A	R	A	M	N	E	S	I	A	A condition in which the proper meaning of words cannot be remembered.
P	A	R	A	N	O	R	M	A	L	Rare, Unusual, Supernatural.
P	A	R	A	P	H	A	S	I	A	Aphasia in which the patient uses wrong words.
P	A	R	A	P	H	E	R	N	A	A woman's property that remains her own and free from the control of her husband.
P	A	R	A	P	H	I	L	I	A	A preference for unusual sexual practices.
P	A	R	A	P	H	O	N	I	A	Abnormal change of voice.
P	A	R	A	P	H	R	A	S	E	To give a fuller meaning of a text or passage.
P	A	R	A	P	L	E	G	I	A	Paralysis of the lower half of the body.
P	A	R	A	P	L	E	G	I	C	Affected with paraplegia.
P	A	R	A	P	O	D	I	U	M	Part of the foot in gastropods.
P	A	R	A	P	R	A	X	I	S	Blunder, Lapse.
P	A	R	A	R	T	H	R	I	A	Disorder of speech.
P	A	R	A	S	C	A	R	I	S	A genus of nematode worms parasitic to horses.
P	A	R	A	S	E	L	E	N	E	A luminous appearance connected with lunar halos.
P	A	R	A	S	I	T	I	S	M	The act of a parasite.
P	A	R	A	Z	O	N	I	U	M	A short medieval dagger.
P	A	R	D	O	N	A	B	L	E	Excuseable.

1	2	3	4	5	6	7	8	9	10	Definition
P	A	R	E	R	G	A	S	I	A	Schizophrenia regarded as a disorder of action.
P	A	R	I	E	T	A	L	E	S	A large order of dicotyledonous plants.
P	A	R	I	E	T	A	R	I	A	A small genus of stingless herbs.
P	A	R	I	N	A	R	I	U	M	A large genus of tropical evergreen shrubs.
P	A	R	L	A	T	O	R	I	A	A genus of scales widespread in warm regions and include pests of cultivated plants.
P	A	R	L	I	A	M	E	N	T	Council of state.
P	A	R	M	I	G	I	A	N	A	Seasoned with Parmesan cheese.
P	A	R	N	A	S	S	I	U	S	A genus of butterflies.
P	A	R	O	N	Y	C	H	I	A	Inflammation of the tissues adjacent to the nail of a finger or toe, Whitlow.
P	A	R	O	N	Y	M	O	U	S	Conjugate.
P	A	R	O	X	Y	S	M	A	L	Relating to a sudden attack or spasm.
P	A	R	R	I	C	I	D	A	L	Relating to parricide.
P	A	R	T	H	E	N	I	T	A	A juvenile trematode worm.
P	A	R	T	H	E	N	I	U	M	A small genus of North American woody herbs.
P	A	R	T	H	E	N	O	P	E	A large cosmopolitan genus of spider crabs.
P	A	R	T	I	A	L	I	S	M	An erotic interest in one part of the body.
P	A	R	T	I	A	L	I	T	Y	Bias, Predilection, Prejudice, Inclination, Leaning, Penchant, Propensity, Tendency.
P	A	R	T	I	C	I	P	L	E	A word having the characteristics of both verb and adjective.
P	A	R	T	I	C	U	L	A	R	Precise, Personal, Private, Individual, Separate, Single, Special, Circumstantial.
P	A	R	T	U	R	I	E	N	T	To give birth, Becoming creative.
P	A	S	I	G	R	A	P	H	Y	An artificial international written language sometimes using signs.
P	A	S	I	M	O	L	O	G	Y	The study of communicating by means of gestures.
P	A	S	Q	U	I	N	A	D	E	Lampoon, Satirize.
P	A	S	S	A	L	I	D	A	E	A family of rather large black beetles that live and feed in decaying wood.
P	A	S	S	A	M	E	Z	Z	O	An old Italian dance.
P	A	S	S	I	F	L	O	R	A	A genus pf tendril-bearing vine having a capsule pulpy fruit, Grenadilla, Passionflower.
P	A	S	S	I	M	E	T	E	R	A turnstile operated from a booth giving access to a public transport system.
P	A	S	S	I	O	N	A	T	O	Direction if music- fervently.
P	A	S	S	I	O	N	A	T	E	Irascible, Testy, Touchy, Angry, Engaged, Quick-tempered, Enthusiastic, Vehement.
P	A	S	S	I	V	A	T	O	R	A substance that forms a protective film on a metal.
P	A	S	S	O	M	E	T	E	R	An instrument shaped like a watch and used to count the number of steps taken.
P	A	S	T	E	B	O	A	R	D	Visiting card, Playing card, Flimsy, Sham, Unsubstantial.
P	A	S	T	E	U	R	I	Z	E	Subject to pasteurization, Partial sterilization to check fermentation.
P	A	T	E	L	L	I	D	A	E	A family of gastropod mollusks including typical limpets.
P	A	T	E	R	N	A	L	L	Y	In a fatherly fashion.
P	A	T	H	E	T	I	C	U	S	Trochlear nerve.
P	A	T	H	O	G	E	N	I	C	Causing disease.
P	A	T	H	O	G	N	O	M	Y	The study of emotions and passions through their outward signs.
P	A	T	H	O	M	E	T	E	R	A lie detector that measures electrical impulses of the body.
P	A	T	I	N	A	T	I	O	N	The state of being patinated.
P	A	T	I	S	S	E	R	I	E	A shop that sells French pastry.
P	A	T	R	I	A	R	C	H	Y	A circumstance where the father is supreme.
P	A	T	R	I	C	I	A	T	E	Nobility, Aristocracy.
P	A	T	R	I	L	O	C	A	L	Located around the family or tribe of the husband.
P	A	T	R	I	O	T	E	E	R	An insincere patriot.
P	A	T	R	I	O	T	I	S	M	Devotion to one's country.
P	A	T	R	O	N	I	Z	E	D	Protected, Supported, Favoured, Used, Frequented.
P	A	T	R	O	N	Y	M	I	C	The paternal family name.
P	A	T	T	E	R	N	I	N	G	Decorating according to a pattern.
P	A	U	L	O	S	P	O	R	E	A specialized development serving as a resting stage in the life cycle of a fungus.
P	A	U	P	E	R	I	S	E	D	Stunted, Growth checked by a poor environment.
P	A	W	N	B	R	O	K	E	R	One that loans money on security of pledged personal property.
P	E	A	C	E	F	U	L	L	Y	In a peaceful manner.
P	E	A	C	E	M	A	K	E	R	One who tries to reconcile persons in opposition.
P	E	A	C	O	C	K	E	R	Y	Ostentatious display.
P	E	A	C	O	C	K	I	S	H	Resembling a peacock, Flamboyant.
P	E	A	R	L	I	N	E	S	S	The state of being pearly.
P	E	A	R	L	S	I	D	E	S	A small silvery fish.
P	E	A	R	S	H	A	P	E	D	Having an oval shape tapering at one end.
P	E	A	S	A	N	T	I	Z	E	Cause to resemble peasants.
P	E	A	S	H	O	O	T	E	R	A toy blowgun for shooting peas.
P	E	B	B	L	E	W	A	R	E	A variety of Wedgwood ware having a mottled surface.
P	E	C	C	A	D	I	L	L	O	A petty fault, A minor moral lapse.
P	E	C	O	P	T	E	R	I	S	A genus of fossil ferns.
P	E	C	T	I	N	A	C	E	A	A suborder of bivalve mollusks with fan-shaped shells.
P	E	C	T	I	N	A	T	E	D	Shaped like a comb, Suggestive of the teeth of a comb.
P	E	C	T	I	N	I	D	A	E	A family of bivalve mollusks.

1	2	3	4	5	6	7	8	9	10	Definition
P	E	C	T	O	L	Y	T	I	C	Producing hydrolysis of pectic substances.
P	E	C	U	L	A	T	I	N	G	Embezzling, Stealing, Misappropriating, Defrauding.
P	E	C	U	L	I	A	R	L	Y	Uniquely, Exclusively, Distinctively, Particularly, Singularly, Unusually, Oddly.
P	E	D	E	S	T	R	I	A	N	Walker, Hiker, Commonplace, Unimaginative, Prosaic, Dull, Dreary, Humdrum.
P	E	D	I	A	S	T	R	U	M	A genus of free-floating green algae.
P	E	D	I	A	T	R	I	C	S	Branch of medicine dealing with children, Paediatrics.
P	E	D	I	C	U	L	A	T	I	An order of marine teleost fishes including anglers and batfishes.
P	E	D	I	C	U	L	I	N	E	Resembling the common lice.
P	E	D	I	C	U	L	O	U	S	Infested with lice, Lousy.
P	E	D	I	G	E	R	O	U	S	Having feet.
P	E	D	I	M	E	N	T	A	L	Resembling a pediment.
P	E	D	I	M	E	N	T	E	D	Having a pediment.
P	E	D	I	O	N	O	M	U	S	A genus of Australian birds related to the button quails.
P	E	D	O	L	O	G	I	S	T	Specialist in child study, A soil scientist.
P	E	D	O	P	H	I	L	I	A	Preference for unusual sexual practices involving children, Paedophilia.
P	E	D	O	S	P	H	E	R	E	The part of the earth's surface containing the soil layer.
P	E	D	U	N	C	U	L	A	R	Relating to the stalk that bears the flower.
P	E	G	M	A	T	I	T	I	C	Having a texture like that of pegmatite.
P	E	I	R	A	M	E	T	E	R	A dynamometer for measuring power required for specific methods of transport.
P	E	J	O	R	A	T	I	O	N	Depreciation.
P	E	J	O	R	A	T	I	V	E	Depreciatory, Disparaging, Slighting, Uncomplementary, Derogatory, Disadvantageous.
P	E	L	A	R	G	O	N	I	N	An anthocyanin extracted from dried flower petals in the form of red crystalline chloride.
P	E	L	L	A	G	R	O	I	D	Resembling pellagra.
P	E	L	L	A	G	R	O	U	S	Affected with pellagra.
P	E	L	L	I	C	U	L	A	R	Membranous, Filmy.
P	E	L	O	B	A	T	O	I	D	Related to the family of amphibians that include the spadefoot toads.
P	E	L	V	I	G	R	A	P	H	A recording pelvimeter.
P	E	L	V	I	M	E	T	E	R	An instrument for measuring the dimensions of the pelvis.
P	E	L	V	I	M	E	T	R	Y	Measurement of the pelvis.
P	E	L	V	I	S	C	O	P	E	An optical instrument enabling visual examination of the pelvis via the vagina.
P	E	L	V	I	R	E	N	A	L	Relating to the pelvis of the kidney.
P	E	N	A	N	N	U	L	A	R	Having the form of a ring with a small break in it.
P	E	N	D	E	N	T	I	V	E	A section of vaulting that allows for a room to be enclosed by a dome.
P	E	N	D	U	L	E	T	T	E	A small table clock with a short pendulum.
P	E	N	E	T	R	A	B	L	E	Capable of being penetrated.
P	E	N	E	T	R	A	L	I	A	Hidden secrets, Most private parts, Privacy, Sanctuary.
P	E	N	E	T	R	A	T	E	D	Entered, Permeated, Encroached, Invaded, Perforated, Pierced, Punctured, Bored.
P	E	N	I	C	I	L	L	I	N	A mixture of antibiotic relatively montoxic acids produced by moulds.
P	E	N	I	C	I	L	L	U	S	A small straight artery of the spleen.
P	E	N	I	N	S	U	L	A	R	Like a peninsula.
P	E	N	M	A	N	S	H	I	P	The art of writing with a pen.
P	E	N	N	A	C	E	O	U	S	Resembling a penna, a normal contour feather.
P	E	N	N	A	N	T	I	T	E	A mineral of the chlorite group.
P	E	N	N	I	S	E	T	U	M	A large genus of Old World grasses, Pearl millet.
P	E	N	N	Y	C	R	E	S	S	A Eurasian herb.
P	E	N	N	Y	-	W	I	S	E	Practising petty economies, Spending in a niggardly fashion.
P	E	N	N	Y	R	O	Y	A	L	A European perennial mint with aromatic leaves.
P	E	N	N	Y	W	O	R	T	H	A good buy, Bargain, Modicum, Small quantity.
P	E	N	O	L	O	G	I	S	T	A specialist in the study of punishment for crime.
P	E	N	R	O	S	E	I	T	E	A mineral structurally like a pyrite consisting of selenide of lead, copper and nickel.
P	E	N	S	I	O	N	N	A	T	A European boarding school.
P	E	N	T	A	B	A	S	I	C	Having five hydrogen atoms.
P	E	N	T	A	C	H	O	R	D	An ancient musical instrument with five strings.
P	E	N	T	A	G	O	N	A	L	Having five angles and five sides.
P	E	N	T	A	G	R	A	P	H	A cluster of five successive letters.
P	E	N	T	A	G	Y	N	I	A	A group of plants having five styles or pistils.
P	E	N	T	A	L	O	N	I	A	A genus of aphids which transmits disease to bananas.
P	E	N	T	A	M	E	T	E	R	Having five metrical feet.
P	E	N	T	A	N	D	R	I	A	A class of plants having five stamens.
P	E	N	T	A	P	L	O	I	D	Fivefold in arrangement or appearance.
P	E	N	T	A	P	O	L	I	S	A group of five cities.
P	E	N	T	A	P	R	I	S	M	A pentagonal prism used as a reflector in range finders.
P	E	N	T	A	Q	U	I	N	E	A liquid basic antimalarial.
P	E	N	T	A	S	T	I	C	H	A poem or stanza consisting of five lines.
P	E	N	T	A	S	T	O	M	E	Tongue worm.
P	E	N	T	A	S	T	Y	L	E	A building with five columns across the front.
P	E	N	T	A	T	H	L	O	N	An athletic contest consisting of five different events.

1	2	3	4	5	6	7	8	9	10	
P	E	N	T	A	T	O	M	I	C	Consisting of five atoms.
P	E	N	T	A	T	O	N	I	C	Consisting of five musical tones.
P	E	N	T	I	M	E	N	T	O	A reappearance in a painting of a design which has been painted over.
P	E	N	T	O	S	U	R	I	A	The excretion of pentoses in the urine.
P	E	P	P	E	R	C	O	R	N	A dried berry of the black pepper.
P	E	P	P	E	R	I	D	G	E	Black gum.
P	E	P	P	E	R	M	I	N	T	A pungent and aromatic mint.
P	E	P	P	E	R	W	O	O	D	California laurel.
P	E	P	S	I	G	O	G	U	E	Inducing the secretion of pepsin.
P	E	P	S	I	N	O	G	E	N	A crystallizable zmogen occurring in the peptic cells of the gastric glands.
P	E	R	C	E	I	V	I	N	G	Observant, Discerning.
P	E	R	C	E	P	T	I	O	N	Observation, Concept, Appreciation, Insight, Idea, Apprehension, Impression.
P	E	R	C	E	P	T	I	V	E	Observant, Knowing, Sensitive, Penetrating, Acute, Keen, Wise, Knowledgeable.
P	E	R	C	E	S	O	C	E	S	A suborder of fishes, Barracudas.
P	E	R	C	H	L	O	R	Y	L	The univalent ion of perchloric acid.
P	E	R	C	O	L	A	T	E	D	Strained, Filtered, Penetrated, Seeped.
P	E	R	C	O	L	A	T	O	R	A coffeepot in which boiling water is poured through coffee to extract the essence.
P	E	R	C	U	S	S	I	O	N	Impact, Collision, Concussion, Crash, Jar, Jolt, Shock, Bump.
P	E	R	C	U	S	S	I	V	E	Striking, Shocking.
P	E	R	D	E	N	D	O	S	I	Direction in music- dying away.
P	E	R	E	M	P	T	O	R	Y	Absolute, Final, Essential, Confident, Positive, Dogmatic, Haughty, Dictatorial.
P	E	R	F	E	C	T	I	O	N	Completion, Maturity, Flawlessness, Saintliness, Culmination, Excellence, Virtue.
P	E	R	F	I	D	I	O	U	S	Deceitful, Treacherous, Faithless, Disloyal, False, Traitorous, Mercenary, Dishonest.
P	E	R	F	O	R	A	B	L	E	Capable of being perforated.
P	E	R	F	O	R	A	T	E	D	Pierced, Punctured, Pricked, Drilled.
P	E	R	G	E	L	I	S	O	L	Permafrost.
P	E	R	I	C	U	L	O	U	S	Perilous.
P	E	R	I	C	Y	T	I	A	L	Enveloping a cell.
P	E	R	I	E	G	E	S	I	S	Description of a region.
P	E	R	I	H	E	L	I	O	N	The point in the path of a celestial body nearest to the sun.
P	E	R	I	K	A	R	Y	O	N	The cytoplasmic body of a nerve cell.
P	E	R	I	L	O	U	S	L	Y	Dangerously.
P	E	R	I	M	Y	S	I	U	M	The connective-tissue sheath that surrounds a muscle.
P	E	R	I	N	E	U	R	A	L	Surrounding nervous tissue or nerves.
P	E	R	I	O	D	I	C	A	L	Intermittent, Alternate, Recurrent, A publication that appears on specified dates.
P	E	R	I	O	S	T	E	A	L	Situated around bone.
P	E	R	I	O	S	T	E	U	M	The membrane of connective tissue of bone, The tissue lining the marrow cavity.
P	E	R	I	P	E	T	E	I	A	A sudden reversal of circumstances.
P	E	R	I	P	H	E	R	A	L	Marginal, External, Bordering, Edging, Verging.
P	E	R	I	P	H	R	A	S	E	Verbiage, Circumloculation, Tautology, Roundabout way of expressing oneself.
P	E	R	I	P	H	Y	T	O	N	Organisms that live attached to underwater surfaces.
P	E	R	I	P	T	E	R	A	L	Having a row of columns on all sides.
P	E	R	I	P	T	E	R	O	S	A building with a row of columns on all sides.
P	E	R	I	S	H	A	B	L	E	Subject to destruction, decay or deterioration.
P	E	R	I	S	T	Y	L	A	R	A row of free-standing columns enclosing a structure.
P	E	R	I	S	T	Y	L	E	S	A building with a surrounding colonnade.
P	E	R	I	T	E	C	T	I	C	Between solid and unsolidified portions of liquid melt.
P	E	R	I	T	O	N	E	U	M	The membranous lining of the abdomen cavity.
P	E	R	I	W	I	N	K	L	E	A trailing evergreen herb.
P	E	R	I	Z	O	N	I	U	M	The thin membrane of young auxospore in diatoms.
P	E	R	J	U	R	I	O	U	S	Marked by perjury.
P	E	R	L	I	N	G	U	A	L	Through the tongue.
P	E	R	M	A	N	E	N	C	E	Durability, The state of being lasting.
P	E	R	M	E	A	T	I	N	G	Pervading, Penetrating, Impregnating, Saturating, Invading, Infusing, Suffusing.
P	E	R	M	I	L	L	A	G	E	Rate per thousand.
P	E	R	M	I	S	S	I	O	N	Authorization, Consent, Leave, Permit, Sanction, Allowance, Approval, Endorsement.
P	E	R	M	I	S	S	I	V	E	Tolerated, Indulgent, Optional.
P	E	R	M	I	T	T	I	N	G	Allowing, Tolerating, Authorizing, Committing, Sanctioning, Consenting.
P	E	R	N	I	C	I	O	U	S	Deadly, Destructive, Wicked, Villainous, Pestilent.
P	E	R	N	I	C	K	E	T	Y	Fussy, Meticulous, Finical, Ticklish, Nice, Fastidious.
P	E	R	N	O	C	T	A	T	E	To stay up or out all night.
P	E	R	O	P	O	D	O	U	S	Having rudimentary hind limbs, as of a snake.
P	E	R	O	R	A	T	I	O	N	A flowery rhetorical speech.
P	E	R	O	V	S	K	I	T	E	A mineral consisting of calcium titanate.
P	E	R	O	X	I	D	A	S	E	An enzyme occurring in plants and milk consisting of a protein complex.
P	E	R	O	X	I	D	I	Z	E	To oxidize to the utmost.
P	E	R	P	E	N	S	I	O	N	Reflection, Consideration.

1	2	3	4	5	6	7	8	9	10	
P	E	R	P	E	T	R	A	T	E	Commit, Effect, Wreak, Inflict, Produce, Perform, Carrying out, Guilty of.
P	E	R	P	E	T	U	A	T	E	Preserve from extinction, Conserve, Maintain, Secure, Sustain.
P	E	R	P	E	T	U	I	T	Y	Eternity, Endless time.
P	E	R	P	L	E	X	I	N	G	Puzzling, Bewildering.
P	E	R	P	L	E	X	I	T	Y	Bewilderment, Entanglement.
P	E	R	Q	U	I	S	I	T	E	Right, Gratuity, Tip, Perogative, Privilege.
P	E	R	S	E	C	U	T	O	R	One that persecutes.
P	E	R	S	E	U	L	O	S	E	The heptulose sugar obtained by bacterial oxidation of perseitol.
P	E	R	S	I	C	A	R	I	A	A genus of herbs.
P	E	R	S	I	F	L	A	G	E	Frivolous bantering talk.
P	E	R	S	I	F	L	E	U	R	One given to persiflage.
P	E	R	S	I	L	L	A	D	E	Dressed or containing parsley.
P	E	R	S	I	S	T	E	N	T	Tenacious, Enduring, Lingering, Dogged, Persevering, Steadfast, Relentless.
P	E	R	S	I	S	T	I	V	E	Persistent, Insistent.
P	E	R	S	O	N	A	B	L	E	Attractive, Comely, Shapely.
P	E	R	S	O	N	A	L	L	Y	To be personal.
P	E	R	S	P	I	R	I	N	G	Sweating, Hot and sticky.
P	E	R	S	T	R	I	N	G	E	Censure, Criticize, Find fault with.
P	E	R	S	U	A	S	I	O	N	Opinion, Belief, Conviction, Religion.
P	E	R	S	U	A	S	I	V	E	Inducement, Incentive, Tending to persuade.
P	E	R	T	I	N	E	N	C	E	Relevance.
P	E	R	T	U	S	A	R	I	A	A genus of lichens that is a source of litmus.
P	E	R	V	E	R	S	I	O	N	A perverted form of something usually sex gratification.
P	E	R	V	E	R	S	I	T	Y	The state of being perverse.
P	E	S	T	I	C	I	D	A	L	Relating to a chemical used to destroy a pest.
P	E	S	T	I	L	E	N	C	E	A contagious or infectious epidemic disease, Bubonic plague.
P	E	T	A	U	R	I	S	T	A	A genus of large Asiatic flying squirrels.
P	E	T	I	T	E	N	E	S	S	The state of being petite.
P	E	T	I	T	I	O	N	E	R	One that is involved in a petition.
P	E	T	R	I	F	Y	I	N	G	Paralyzing, Supefying, Converting into stone.
P	E	T	R	I	S	S	A	G	E	A kneading massage of muscles.
P	E	T	R	O	G	L	Y	P	H	Carving or inscription on stone.
P	E	T	R	O	L	A	T	U	M	A neutral unctuous substance almost odourless and tasteless.
P	F	L	E	I	D	E	R	E	R	A machine for shredding cellulose sheets for the manufacture of rayon.
P	H	A	C	O	M	E	T	E	R	An instrument for measuring the focal power of lenses.
P	H	A	E	O	P	H	Y	T	A	A division of algae, Brown algae.
P	H	A	E	O	P	L	A	S	T	One of the brownish chromatophores occurring in the brown algae.
P	H	A	E	O	S	P	O	R	E	An order of brown algae.
P	H	A	G	O	L	Y	S	I	S	Destruction of phagocytes.
P	H	A	L	A	N	G	I	D	A	A cosmopolitan order of Arachnida.
P	H	A	L	L	A	C	E	A	E	A family of fungi comprising the stinkhorns.
P	H	A	N	E	R	O	S	I	S	Becoming visible.
P	H	A	R	M	A	C	I	S	T	One skilled in pharmacy.
P	H	A	S	C	O	G	A	L	E	A genus of small marsupials comprising the broad-footed pouched mice of Australia.
P	H	A	S	I	A	N	O	I	D	Related to the genus of fowls including pheasants, partridges, guinea fowls and grouse.
P	H	A	S	M	A	T	O	D	A	Genus of insects including stick insects and leaf insects.
P	H	E	N	A	C	O	M	Y	S	Genus of North American voles.
P	H	E	N	O	C	R	Y	S	T	An embedded crystal of a phorphyry.
P	H	E	N	O	M	E	N	A	L	Extraordinary, Remarkable, Sensible, Material, Objective, Tangible, Exceptionable.
P	H	E	O	P	H	Y	T	I	N	A bluish black waxy pigment obtained from chlorophyll.
P	H	I	L	A	N	T	H	U	S	A genus of digger wasps.
P	H	I	L	A	T	E	L	I	C	Relating to the collecting of stamps.
P	H	I	L	E	P	I	T	T	A	A genus of Madagascan birds related to the pittas.
P	H	I	L	O	L	O	G	E	R	A scholar, Linguist, One that studies human speech.
P	H	I	L	O	S	O	P	H	Y	Pursuit of wisdom, Investigation, Inquiry.
P	H	L	E	B	O	G	R	A	M	An X-ray of the movements of a vein.
P	H	L	E	B	O	L	I	T	H	A calculus in a vein.
P	H	L	E	B	O	T	O	M	Y	Treating disease by letting of blood.
P	H	L	E	G	M	A	S	I	A	Inflammation.
P	H	L	E	G	M	A	T	I	C	Calm, Composed, Impassive, Undemonstrative, Apathetic, Stoic, Stolid, Lethargic.
P	H	L	O	G	I	S	T	O	N	The hypothetical principle of fire regarded as a material substance by early alchemists.
P	H	L	O	G	O	P	I	T	E	Yellowish-brown to copper forms of mica.
P	H	O	C	O	M	E	L	I	A	The condition of having abnormally shortened limbs.
P	H	O	N	E	T	I	C	A	L	Phonetic.
P	H	O	N	I	A	T	R	I	C	Relating to the treatment of speech defects.
P	H	O	N	O	G	E	N	I	C	Suitable for reproduction of sound.
P	H	O	N	O	G	R	A	P	H	A record player.

1	2	3	4	5	6	7	8	9	10	Definition
P	H	O	N	O	M	E	T	E	R	An instrument for measuring the intensity of sound.
P	H	O	N	O	P	A	T	H	Y	A disorder of the process of producing speech and sound.
P	H	O	N	O	P	H	I	L	E	A collector of records.
P	H	O	N	O	P	H	O	R	E	A device enabling the deaf to hear by transmitting vibrations to teeth.
P	H	O	N	O	S	C	O	P	E	A device for testing the quality of musical strings.
P	H	O	R	O	M	E	T	E	R	An instrument for measuring the functions of the eye muscles.
P	H	O	R	O	M	E	T	R	Y	The science of testing and correcting the action of the eye muscles.
P	H	O	S	G	E	N	I	T	E	A mineral consisting of lead chloroformate.
P	H	O	S	P	H	A	G	E	N	An organic phosphate compound.
P	H	O	S	P	H	O	R	U	S	A phosphorescent substance.
P	H	O	T	O	D	R	A	M	A	Motion picture.
P	H	O	T	O	G	E	N	I	C	Produced by light.
P	H	O	T	O	G	R	A	P	H	A likeness obtained by photography.
P	H	O	T	O	L	Y	S	I	S	Chemical decomposition by the action of radiant energy.
P	H	O	T	O	M	E	T	E	R	An instrument for measuring brightness or illumination.
P	H	O	T	O	M	E	T	R	Y	A branch of science that deals with measuring the intensity of light.
P	H	O	T	O	N	A	S	T	Y	A nastic movement related to changes in intensity of light.
P	H	O	T	O	N	O	S	U	S	An abnormality caused by exposure to light.
P	H	O	T	O	P	A	T	H	Y	A diseased condition caused by overexposure to light.
P	H	O	T	O	P	H	O	B	E	An organism that thrives best without light.
P	H	O	T	O	R	A	D	I	O	Transmitting photographs by radio.
P	H	O	T	O	S	C	O	P	E	Photofluorographic screen and camera.
P	H	O	T	O	T	O	N	U	S	Tonic condition resulting from exposure to light.
P	H	R	A	G	M	I	T	E	S	Genus of reedlike grasses with large showy plumes.
P	H	R	Y	G	A	N	E	I	D	Relating to caddis flies.
P	H	R	Y	M	A	C	E	A	E	A family of plants.
P	H	R	Y	N	O	S	O	M	A	A genus comprising the horned toads.
P	H	Y	C	I	T	I	D	A	E	A family of small moths the larvae of which are pests that feed on stored cereals.
P	H	Y	C	O	B	I	L	I	N	Any of a class of bile pigments that occur in the cells of algae.
P	H	Y	L	L	A	C	O	R	A	A genus of fungi.
P	H	Y	L	L	O	D	O	C	E	A small genus of arctic and alpine shrubs.
P	H	Y	L	L	O	S	O	M	A	A flat transparent long-legged larva that is typical of various spiny lobsters.
P	H	Y	L	L	O	T	A	X	Y	The arrangement of leaves on a stem.
P	H	Y	L	L	O	X	E	R	A	Destructive plant lice.
P	H	Y	M	A	T	I	D	A	E	A family of carnivorous bugs.
P	H	Y	M	A	T	O	D	E	S	A genus of tropical ferns.
P	H	Y	M	A	T	O	S	I	S	A skin disease marked by modules or swellings.
P	H	Y	S	E	T	E	R	I	D	A whale of the family that includes sperm whales.
P	H	Y	S	I	A	T	R	I	C	A system of medicine based on using the healing powers of nature, Physical therapy.
P	H	Y	S	I	O	L	O	G	Y	Particular theory of nature, the study of living matter.
P	H	Y	S	I	U	R	G	I	C	Brought about by nature.
P	H	Y	S	O	C	L	I	S	T	A teleost fish lacking a duct between the air bladder and the alimentary canal.
P	H	Y	S	O	D	E	R	M	A	A genus of parasitic fungi.
P	H	Y	S	O	S	T	O	M	E	A teleost fish having a duct between the air bladder and the alimentary canal.
P	H	Y	T	O	G	E	N	I	C	Being of plant origin.
P	H	Y	T	O	G	R	A	P	H	A linear diagram of measurements of various plant characteristics.
P	H	Y	T	O	L	A	C	C	A	A genus of tropical perennial herbs.
P	H	Y	T	O	L	A	T	R	Y	Worship of plants.
P	H	Y	T	O	L	O	G	I	C	Botanical.
P	H	Y	T	O	M	E	T	E	R	A group of plants grown under controlled conditions for experimental purposes.
P	H	Y	T	O	M	E	T	R	Y	Measurement of physiological responses of a group of plants to various factors.
P	H	Y	T	O	M	O	R	P	H	A conventialized representation of a plant.
P	H	Y	T	O	P	H	A	G	A	Groups of vegetable-feeding animals.
P	H	Y	T	O	T	O	X	I	C	Poisonous to plants.
P	H	Y	T	O	T	O	X	I	N	A toxin produced by a plant.
P	I	A	N	I	S	S	I	M	O	Direction in music - very softly.
P	I	A	N	O	F	O	R	T	E	Piano.
P	I	C	H	I	C	I	A	G	O	A small burrowing South American armadillo.
P	I	C	K	E	T	B	O	A	T	A craft used by the Coast Guard for harbour patrol.
P	I	C	K	L	E	W	O	R	M	The larva of a brown and yellow moth that attacks vines.
P	I	C	K	P	O	C	K	E	T	One who pilfers from the pockets of others.
P	I	C	R	O	R	H	I	Z	A	The dried rhizome of a Himalayan herb.
P	I	C	R	O	T	O	X	I	N	A poisonous bitter crystalline principle used as an antidote for barbiturate poisoning.
P	I	C	T	O	G	R	A	P	H	A prehistoric painting on a rock wall.
P	I	C	T	U	R	A	B	L	E	Suitable for representation by a picture.
P	I	E	Z	O	M	E	T	E	R	An instrument for measuring pressure.
P	I	G	E	O	N	H	O	L	E	A cubbyhole or recess.

1	2	3	4	5	6	7	8	9	10	Clue
P	I	G	E	O	N	W	I	N	G	A fancy dance step, A fancy figure in skating.
P	I	G	E	O	N	W	O	O	D	Various tropical trees with mottled wood.
P	I	G	M	E	N	T	A	R	Y	Containing pigment.
P	I	L	A	S	T	R	A	D	E	A row of pilasters.
P	I	L	G	R	I	M	A	G	E	A journey to a shrine or a sacred place, A search for mental and spiritual values.
P	I	L	I	F	E	R	O	U	S	Producing hairs.
P	I	L	L	I	W	I	N	K	S	An old instrument of torture for the thumbs and fingers.
P	I	L	O	C	A	R	P	U	S	A small genus of tropical American herbs.
P	I	L	O	M	O	T	I	O	N	Movement of cutaneous hair.
P	I	L	O	N	C	I	L	L	O	Moulded unrefined sugar.
P	I	L	O	T	H	O	U	S	E	A deckhouse on a ship, Wheelhouse.
P	I	N	A	C	H	R	O	M	E	An isocyanine dye used in photography.
P	I	N	A	C	O	C	Y	T	E	One of the flat cells of sponge canals.
P	I	N	A	C	O	L	A	T	E	A metallic derivative of pinacol.
P	I	N	A	C	O	L	O	N	E	A liquid ketone of peppermint odour formed from pinacol by treatment with acid.
P	I	N	A	C	Y	A	N	O	L	An isocyanine dye formerly used in photography.
P	I	N	G	U	E	C	U	L	A	A small yellowish elevation situated near the inner or outer margins of the cornea.
P	I	N	G	U	I	C	U	L	A	A large genus of acaulescent bog herbs.
P	I	N	N	A	T	I	F	I	D	Cleft in a pinnate manner.
P	I	N	N	I	G	R	A	D	E	Moving by means of fins or flippers.
P	I	N	N	I	P	E	D	I	A	Suborder of aquatic carnivorous mammals including seals and walruses.
P	I	N	O	S	Y	L	V	I	N	A toxic phenolic compound related to stilbene.
P	I	N	T	A	D	O	I	T	E	A hydrous calcium vandate occurring in a green incrustation.
P	I	P	E	C	O	L	I	N	E	Any of the three liquid monoethyl derivatives of piperidine.
P	I	P	E	R	A	C	E	A	E	A family of tropical plants having aromatic herbage.
P	I	P	E	R	I	T	O	N	E	A liquid unsaturated cyclic ketone of camphoraceous odour used for making menthol.
P	I	P	E	R	Y	L	E	N	E	An oily diolefin hydrocarbon isomeric with isoprene formed in the cracking of petroleum.
P	I	P	S	I	S	S	E	W	A	An evergreen herb whose leaves have been used as a tonic and diuretic.
P	I	P	T	A	D	E	N	I	A	A large genus of tropical Brazilian shrubs.
P	I	S	A	U	R	I	D	A	E	A family of hunting spiders that do not spin webs.
P	I	S	C	I	F	A	U	N	A	The fishes of a given region.
P	I	S	T	I	L	L	A	T	E	Having pistils but no stamens.
P	I	S	T	I	L	L	I	N	E	Consisting of a pistil.
P	I	S	T	I	L	L	O	D	E	A rudimentary pistil.
P	I	S	T	I	L	L	O	D	Y	The metamorphosis of other organs into pistils.
P	I	T	Y	O	C	A	M	P	A	The larva of a European processionary moth found on pine trees.
P	I	T	Y	R	I	A	S	I	S	A scaly skin disease.
P	I	X	I	L	L	A	T	E	D	Bewildered, Confused, Bemused, Enchanted, Bewitched, Playful, Intoxicated.
P	L	A	G	I	A	R	I	Z	E	To steal the ideas and words of another, Literary theft.
P	L	A	G	I	O	D	O	N	T	Having the palatal teeth set obliquely as in snakes.
P	L	A	G	I	O	N	I	T	E	A mineral consisting of a lead antimony sulfide.
P	L	A	N	T	A	T	I	O	N	A large estate.
P	L	A	S	M	O	D	I	U	M	A motile multinucleate mass of protoplasm.
P	L	A	S	M	O	G	A	M	Y	Fusion of protoplasts.
P	L	A	S	M	O	P	A	R	A	A genus of downy mildews.
P	L	A	S	M	O	S	O	M	E	A true nucleolus.
P	L	A	S	T	E	R	I	N	G	Applying a coating of plaster.
P	L	A	S	T	I	C	A	T	E	To knead by means of a plasticator.
P	L	A	S	T	I	C	I	T	Y	The state of being plastic.
P	L	A	S	T	I	D	O	M	E	The plastids of a cell.
P	L	A	S	T	O	C	Y	T	E	Blood platelet.
P	L	A	S	T	O	T	Y	P	E	An artificial specimen moulded from a type specimen.
P	L	A	T	A	N	I	S	T	A	Type genus of the toothed whales.
P	L	A	T	E	L	A	Y	E	R	A railway worker who maintains the rails.
P	L	A	T	Y	C	A	R	Y	A	A small genus of Asiatic trees that have flowers in catkins followed by a winged nut.
P	L	A	T	Y	L	E	P	A	S	A genus of warm-sea barnacles.
P	L	A	T	Y	M	O	R	P	H	Literally flattened.
P	L	A	T	Y	P	E	Z	I	D	Relating to a family of flies having larvae that breed in fungi.
P	L	A	Y	A	C	T	I	N	G	Pretense, Insincere behaviour.
P	L	A	Y	G	R	O	U	N	D	An area designated for recreational activities.
P	L	A	Y	W	R	I	G	H	T	One who writes plays.
P	L	E	A	S	A	N	T	L	Y	Cheerfully, Prettily, Joyfully, Agreeably, Nicely, Amiably.
P	L	E	A	S	A	N	T	R	Y	Jocularity, Jest, Joke, Banter.
P	L	E	A	S	I	N	G	L	Y	Charmingly, Enchantingly, Gratifyingly.
P	L	E	B	I	S	C	I	T	E	A vote or decree of the people.
P	L	E	C	O	P	T	E	R	A	An order of insects, Stone flies.
P	L	E	C	T	O	P	T	E	R	An insect with membranous net-veined wings, Mayflies.

1	2	3	4	5	6	7	8	9	10	Definition
P	L	E	O	M	A	S	T	I	A	Having more than two mammary glands or nipples.
P	L	E	R	E	R	G	A	T	E	Replete.
P	L	E	S	I	O	S	A	U	R	A prehistoric reptile or its fossil.
P	L	E	T	H	O	D	O	N	T	A salamander.
P	L	E	U	R	O	C	E	R	A	A large genus of American freshwater snails.
P	L	E	U	R	O	D	I	R	A	A group of freshwater turtles that cannot retract the neck.
P	L	E	U	R	O	D	O	N	T	A lizard having teeth without sockets.
P	L	E	X	I	M	E	T	E	R	A small thin plate struck with a small rubber-headed hammer in medical percussion.
P	L	I	A	B	I	L	I	T	Y	Flexibility, Complaisance, Adaptability.
P	L	I	O	H	I	P	P	U	S	A genus of extinct one-toed horses.
P	L	I	O	S	A	U	R	U	S	A genus of extinct marine reptiles.
P	L	O	C	E	I	F	O	R	M	Resembling a weaverbird.
P	L	O	D	D	I	N	G	L	Y	In a plodding fashion.
P	L	O	T	O	S	I	D	A	E	E family of marine catfishes.
P	L	O	U	G	H	L	A	N	D	Various old English units of land area.
P	L	U	C	K	I	N	E	S	S	The state of being plucky.
P	L	U	M	A	S	S	I	E	R	A dealer in ornamental plumes or feathers.
P	L	U	M	A	T	E	L	L	A	A genus of freshwater bryozoans.
P	L	U	M	I	E	R	I	D	E	A bitter crystalline glucoside found in frangipani trees.
P	L	U	M	U	L	A	R	I	A	A genus of hydrozoans.
P	L	U	N	D	E	R	I	N	G	Stealing, Looting, Sacking, Spoiling, Pillaging, Robbing.
P	L	U	P	E	R	F	E	C	T	Past perfect, Superlative.
P	L	U	R	I	A	X	I	A	L	Having flowers developed on secondary shoots.
P	L	U	T	O	C	R	A	C	Y	Government by the rich, The rule of wealth.
P	L	U	T	O	L	A	T	E	R	One who favours the interests of the wealthy.
P	L	U	T	O	L	A	T	R	Y	Excessive devotion to wealth.
P	L	U	T	O	M	A	N	I	A	Abnormal desire for riches, Having delusion of wealth.
P	L	U	T	O	N	O	M	I	C	Relating to political economy.
P	L	U	V	I	A	L	I	N	E	Relating to the plovers.
P	N	E	U	M	A	T	I	C	S	Study of the mechanical properties of gases.
P	N	E	U	M	A	T	I	S	M	Exterior signs believed to indicate the presence of the Holy Spirit.
P	N	E	U	M	A	T	I	Z	E	To make pneumatic.
P	N	E	U	M	O	G	R	A	M	Record of respiratory movements obtained by pneumography.
P	N	E	U	M	O	L	O	G	Y	Scientific study of the respiratory organs.
P	O	C	K	E	T	B	O	O	K	Wallet, Purse, A paperback edition sold cheaply.
P	O	D	A	R	G	I	D	A	E	A family of Oriental and Australian birds, Frogmouths.
P	O	D	A	R	T	H	R	U	M	A foot joint of a bird.
P	O	D	I	A	T	R	I	S	T	Chiropodist.
P	O	D	I	L	E	G	O	U	S	Having a brush on the legs for collecting pollen.
P	O	D	O	C	A	R	P	U	S	A genus of evergreen trees having a pulpy fruit with one hard seed.
P	O	D	O	S	T	E	M	O	N	Rock-inhabiting submerged aquatic herbs.
P	O	E	T	I	C	A	L	L	Y	In a poetic manner.
P	O	G	O	N	O	P	H	O	R	A group of marine worms.
P	O	G	O	N	O	T	O	M	Y	Shaving, Cutting of a beard.
P	O	H	U	T	U	K	A	W	A	A New Zealand variety of a sweet potato.
P	O	I	G	N	A	N	T	L	Y	Movingly.
P	O	I	N	S	E	T	T	I	A	A genus of woody plants with showy red flower clusters.
P	O	L	A	T	O	U	C	H	E	A small flying squirrel.
P	O	L	E	M	O	L	O	G	Y	Study of war.
P	O	L	E	M	O	N	I	U	M	Genus of herbs.
P	O	L	I	A	N	T	H	E	S	A small genus of Mexican tuberous herbs.
P	O	L	I	T	E	N	E	S	S	The state of being polite.
P	O	L	I	T	I	C	I	A	N	Statesman, One engaged in the business of government.
P	O	L	I	T	I	C	I	Z	E	To bring something within the realm of politics.
P	O	L	L	E	D	N	E	S	S	An animal without horns.
P	O	L	L	E	N	I	Z	E	R	A plant that is a source of pollen.
P	O	L	L	I	N	A	T	O	R	An agent that pollinates flowers.
P	O	L	L	I	N	O	S	I	S	An acute catarrhal disorder caused by sensitivity to pollen, Hay-fever.
P	O	L	Y	A	N	T	H	U	S	Primrose.
P	O	L	Y	A	T	O	M	I	C	Containing more than one atom.
P	O	L	Y	B	A	S	I	T	E	An iron-black metallic-looking ore of silver.
P	O	L	Y	C	A	R	P	O	N	A genus of herbs.
P	O	L	Y	C	H	A	E	T	A	An order of marine annelid worms.
P	O	L	Y	C	H	R	E	S	T	A drug or medicine used as an effective remedy against various diseases.
P	O	L	Y	C	H	R	O	M	E	Something of many colours, Variegated colouring.
P	O	L	Y	C	H	R	O	M	Y	Decoration combining many colours.
P	O	L	Y	C	I	R	R	U	S	A genus of soft-bodied worms.

1	2	3	4	5	6	7	8	9	10	
P	O	L	Y	C	L	I	N	I	C	A clinic for treating a wide variety of diseases and complaints.
P	O	L	Y	C	Y	C	L	I	C	Containing two or more fused rings in the structure of the molecule.
P	O	L	Y	C	Y	E	S	I	S	Pregnancy with more than one foetus in the uterus.
P	O	L	Y	C	Y	S	T	I	S	A genus of free-floating blue-green algae.
P	O	L	Y	D	A	C	T	Y	L	Having more than the normal number of toes or fingers.
P	O	L	Y	D	I	P	S	I	A	Abnormal or excessive thirst.
P	O	L	Y	E	T	H	N	I	C	Inhabited by many people.
P	O	L	Y	G	A	M	I	S	T	One who practices polygamy.
P	O	L	Y	H	E	D	R	A	L	Having the form of a polyhedron.
P	O	L	Y	H	E	D	R	O	N	A figure or solid formed by many faces or planes.
P	O	L	Y	L	I	T	H	I	C	Comprised of several kinds of stones.
P	O	L	Y	M	A	S	T	I	A	Having more than the usual number of breasts.
P	O	L	Y	M	E	R	I	Z	E	To combine chemically into very large molecules.
P	O	L	Y	N	O	I	D	A	E	A family of marine worms.
P	O	L	Y	O	L	E	F	I	N	An olefin containing many double bonds.
P	O	L	Y	P	H	A	G	I	A	Excessive appetite.
P	O	L	Y	P	H	O	N	I	C	Consisting of many sounds or voices.
P	O	L	Y	P	O	R	I	T	E	Fossil fungus.
P	O	L	Y	P	O	R	O	U	S	Resembing a pore fungus.
P	O	L	Y	P	T	O	T	O	N	The rhetorical repetition of a word in a different case in the same sentence.
P	O	L	Y	R	H	Y	T	H	M	The simultaneous combination of contrasting rhythms in a musical composition.
P	O	L	Y	S	E	M	A	N	T	A word having more than one meaning.
P	O	L	Y	S	E	M	O	U	S	Having many meanings.
P	O	L	Y	S	T	O	M	E	A	Many-mouthed.
P	O	L	Y	T	H	E	I	S	M	Worship of many gods.
P	O	L	Y	T	H	E	L	I	A	Having more than the normal number of nipples.
P	O	L	Y	T	O	C	O	U	S	Producing many eggs or young at one time.
P	O	L	Y	T	O	M	O	U	S	Divided into more than two parts.
P	O	L	Y	T	R	O	P	I	C	Visiting many kinds of flowers for nectar.
P	O	L	Y	V	A	L	E	N	T	Having multiple valence.
P	O	M	A	D	E	R	R	I	S	A genus of hoary Australian shrubs.
P	O	M	E	R	I	D	I	A	N	Blossoming after noon.
P	O	M	I	F	E	R	O	U	S	Bearing a fleshy fruit.
P	O	M	O	L	O	G	I	S	T	A horticulturist specializing in fruit cultivation.
P	O	M	P	H	O	P	O	E	A	A genus of blister beetles some of which feed on foliage and blossoms of fruit trees.
P	O	M	P	I	L	I	D	A	E	A large family of black wasps most of which burrow into the ground.
P	O	N	D	E	R	A	B	L	Y	Considerably, Weightily.
P	O	N	E	R	O	L	O	G	Y	A branch of theology dealing with the doctrine of evil.
P	O	N	T	E	D	E	R	I	A	A genus of American aquatic plants.
P	O	N	T	I	C	E	L	L	O	The bridge of a bowed stringed instrument, A change in the voice.
P	O	N	T	I	F	I	C	A	L	Pompous, Dogmatic, Relating to a bishop, pontiff or prelate.
P	O	P	U	L	A	R	I	T	Y	The state of being popular.
P	O	P	U	L	A	R	I	Z	E	To cause to be liked or esteemed.
P	O	P	U	L	A	T	I	O	N	The whole number of inhabitants occupying a specific locality.
P	O	R	C	E	L	A	N	I	C	Resembling porcelain.
P	O	R	C	E	L	A	N	E	R	A worker who bakes vitreous enamel on castings.
P	O	R	I	F	E	R	O	U	S	Relating to a variety of sponges.
P	O	R	N	O	C	R	A	C	Y	Government by harlots.
P	O	R	O	S	C	O	P	I	C	Relating to examination of impressions left by sweat pores of fingers.
P	O	R	P	H	Y	R	I	T	E	An Egyptian red porphyry.
P	O	R	P	H	Y	R	O	I	D	Igneous or sedimentary rock with porphyritic texture.
P	O	R	P	H	Y	R	O	U	S	Purple.
P	O	R	P	H	Y	R	U	L	A	Genus of birds, African and American purple gallinules.
P	O	R	T	H	E	T	R	I	A	Gypsy moth.
P	O	R	T	L	I	N	E	S	S	The state of being portly.
P	O	R	T	R	A	Y	I	N	G	Representing, Depicting, Enacting.
P	O	S	I	T	I	V	E	L	Y	Extremely, Obviously, Notably, Certainly, Easily, Definitely, Absolutely.
P	O	S	S	U	M	W	O	O	D	Sandbox tree.
P	O	S	S	E	S	S	I	O	N	Control, Domination, Occupancy, Ownership, Proprietary.
P	O	S	T	H	U	M	O	U	S	Occurring after one's death.
P	O	S	T	M	O	R	T	E	M	After death.
P	O	S	T	O	C	U	L	A	R	Located behind the eyes.
P	O	S	T	P	A	R	T	U	M	Following parturition.
P	O	S	T	P	O	N	I	N	G	Delaying, Deferring, Suspending.
P	O	S	T	S	C	R	I	P	T	A note appended to completed composition.
P	O	S	T	U	L	A	N	C	Y	The state of being a novice.
P	O	S	T	U	L	A	T	E	D	Demanded, Claimed, Presupposed, Challenged, Required, Solicited, Presumed.

1	2	3	4	5	6	7	8	9	10	Definition
P	O	T	A	M	O	G	A	L	E	A genus of West African aquatic insectivores that contains the otter shrew.
P	O	T	A	M	O	L	O	G	Y	The study of rivers.
P	O	T	E	N	T	I	L	L	A	A large genus of herbs and shrubs.
P	O	T	T	I	A	C	E	A	E	A family of low-growing mosses.
P	O	W	E	R	F	U	L	L	Y	Energetically, Forcefully, Forcibly, Strongly, Mightily, Vigorously, Strenuously.
P	R	A	T	I	N	C	O	L	E	A limicoline bird.
P	R	A	X	E	O	L	O	G	Y	The study of human action and conduct.
P	R	E	A	C	H	M	E	N	T	Sermon, Exhortation.
P	R	E	A	M	B	U	L	A	R	Introductory, Preliminary.
P	R	E	C	A	R	I	O	U	S	Dangerous, Doubtful, Dubious, Uncertain, Indecisive, Ambiguous, Touchy.
P	R	E	C	A	U	T	I	O	N	Foresight, Discretion, Care.
P	R	E	C	E	D	E	N	C	E	Preference, Priority.
P	R	E	C	E	P	T	I	V	E	Mandatory.
P	R	E	C	I	O	S	I	T	Y	Fastidious, Affected refinement.
P	R	E	C	I	O	U	S	L	Y	In a precious manner.
P	R	E	C	L	U	S	I	O	N	Prevention by anticipation.
P	R	E	C	L	U	S	I	V	E	Preventive.
P	R	E	C	O	C	I	O	U	S	Premature development, Advanced, Forward.
P	R	E	C	O	R	D	I	U	M	The part of the ventral surface of the body overlying the heart and stomach.
P	R	E	C	U	R	S	O	R	Y	Preceding, Preliminary, Premonitory.
P	R	E	D	A	C	I	O	U	S	Rapacious.
P	R	E	D	E	C	E	A	S	E	To die first.
P	R	E	D	E	S	T	I	N	E	To determine beforehand.
P	R	E	D	I	C	T	I	O	N	Forecast, Prophecy.
P	R	E	D	I	S	P	O	S	E	Make susceptible, Incline, Bias, Dispose, Impress.
P	R	E	D	N	I	S	O	N	E	A crystalline or amorphous glucocorticoid drug used in the same way as cortisone.
P	R	E	E	M	I	N	E	N	T	Outstanding, Supreme, First, Surpassing, Ultimate, Dominant, Principal, Chief.
P	R	E	E	M	P	T	I	V	E	Relating to a prior right.
P	R	E	F	E	C	T	U	R	E	The office of a prefect.
P	R	E	F	E	R	E	N	C	E	Choice, Option, Selection, Partiality, Elevation, Advancement, Promotion, Upgrading.
P	R	E	F	E	R	M	E	N	T	Seniority, Advancement, Promotion, Act of presenting.
P	R	E	F	U	L	G	E	N	T	Shining most brightly.
P	R	E	H	E	N	S	I	L	E	Adapted for seizing or grasping, Avaricious, Greedy.
P	R	E	H	N	I	T	E	N	E	A liquid aromatic hydrocarbon.
P	R	E	J	U	D	I	C	E	D	Biased, Partial, Warped, Jaundiced, Hostile.
P	R	E	L	E	C	T	I	O	N	A previous reading.
P	R	E	M	A	R	I	T	A	L	Occurring before marriage.
P	R	E	N	A	N	T	H	E	S	A genus of perennial herbs.
P	R	E	N	O	L	E	P	I	S	A widely distributed genus of ants.
P	R	E	N	O	M	I	N	A	L	Placed before a noun.
P	R	E	O	P	E	R	C	L	E	A flat membrane bone in the gill cover of most fishes.
P	R	E	P	A	C	K	A	G	E	Something wrapped before being on sale.
P	R	E	P	O	T	E	N	C	Y	Predominance, Supremacy, Domination.
P	R	E	R	E	L	E	A	S	E	Released in advance of expected date.
P	R	E	S	A	G	E	F	U	L	Foreboding, Ominous, Prophetic.
P	R	E	S	B	Y	O	P	I	A	Loss of elasticity in the crystalline lens of the eye usually due to old age.
P	R	E	S	B	Y	T	E	R	Y	The part of a church reserved for officiating clergy.
P	R	E	S	C	I	E	N	C	E	Foresight.
P	R	E	S	C	R	I	B	E	D	Confined, Restrained, Assigned, Defined, Imposed, Dictated, Decided, Determined.
P	R	E	S	E	N	T	I	A	L	Immediately.
P	R	E	S	E	R	V	I	N	G	Protecting, Maintaining, Saving, Sustaining, Conserving.
P	R	E	S	I	D	E	N	C	Y	The office of president.
P	R	E	S	I	D	E	N	T	E	A cocktail consisting of rum, curacao, dry vermouth and grenadine.
P	R	E	S	I	G	N	I	F	Y	Presage.
P	R	E	S	S	U	R	I	Z	E	To maintain normal atmospheric pressure in an aircraft cabin during flight.
P	R	E	S	U	M	A	B	L	Y	Probably.
P	R	E	S	U	P	P	O	S	E	Presume, Assume, Postulate, Conjecture, Surmise, Deduce, Believe, Reckon.
P	R	E	S	Y	L	V	I	A	N	In front of the lateral fissure of the brain.
P	R	E	T	E	N	S	I	O	N	Claim, Aspiration, Pretentiousness, Pretext, Vanity, Charade.
P	R	E	T	T	I	N	E	S	S	The quality of being pretty.
P	R	E	T	T	Y	F	A	C	E	A California herb.
P	R	E	V	A	I	L	I	N	G	Inducing, Convincing, Persuading, Prompting, Rife, Current.
P	R	E	V	A	L	E	N	C	E	Frequent occurrence.
P	R	E	V	E	N	I	E	N	T	Anticipatory, Antecedent.
P	R	E	V	E	N	T	I	N	G	Frustrating, Foiling, Circumventing, Hindering, Stopping, Precluding Averting.
P	R	E	V	E	N	T	I	O	N	Precaution, Obstacle, Presentiment, Obstruction.
P	R	E	V	E	N	T	I	V	E	Prophylactic, Precautionary.

1	2	3	4	5	6	7	8	9	10	
P	R	E	V	E	S	I	C	A	L	Situated in front of a bladder.
P	R	E	V	I	O	U	S	L	Y	Beforehand, Earlier, Formerly, Once, Hastily, Prematurely.
P	R	E	V	I	S	I	B	L	E	Capable of being predicted.
P	R	I	E	S	T	F	I	S	H	A common rockfish that is a sport fish of shallow waters.
P	R	I	M	A	Q	U	I	N	E	An antimalarial drug.
P	R	I	M	A	V	E	R	A	L	Relating to the early spring.
P	R	I	M	E	V	E	R	I	N	A crystalline glycoside that is found in the cowslip.
P	R	I	M	O	R	D	I	A	L	Earliest, Elementary, Fundamental, Crude, Primary.
P	R	I	M	O	R	D	I	U	M	Beginning, Origin.
P	R	I	M	U	L	I	N	U	S	A gladiolus of southeastern tropical Africa.
P	R	I	N	C	E	L	I	N	G	An insignificant prince.
P	R	I	N	C	I	P	A	T	E	Supreme rule, Principal person.
P	R	I	N	C	I	P	I	A	L	Initial, Primary.
P	R	I	N	C	I	P	I	U	M	Basis, Element, Foundation, Inception.
P	R	I	N	T	A	N	I	E	R	Made or dressed with diced spring vegetables.
P	R	I	O	D	O	N	T	E	S	A genus of mammals, Giant armadillo.
P	R	I	O	N	O	D	O	N	T	Having a sawlike row of many simple teeth.
P	R	I	S	M	A	T	I	Z	E	To alter into prisms.
P	R	I	V	I	L	E	G	E	D	Enjoying a privilege.
P	R	I	Z	E	F	I	G	H	T	A contest between professional boxers for a fixed fee or percentage of the takings.
P	R	O	B	L	E	M	I	Z	E	To raise or discuss problems.
P	R	O	C	A	C	I	O	U	S	Impudent.
P	R	O	C	E	D	U	R	A	L	Relating to procedure.
P	R	O	C	E	E	D	I	N	G	Advancing, Wending, Travelling, Going, Moving, Process, Act, Deed.
P	R	O	C	E	L	L	O	U	S	Stormy.
P	R	O	C	E	R	C	O	I	D	The solid first parasitic larva of some tapeworms.
P	R	O	C	E	S	S	I	O	N	A continuous orderly movement of a group usually for ceremonial occasions.
P	R	O	C	E	S	S	U	A	L	Functional, Operational.
P	R	O	C	L	A	I	M	E	D	Announced, Proved, Extolled, Declared, Broadcast, Demonstrated, Exhibited.
P	R	O	C	L	I	N	A	T	E	Directed forward.
P	R	O	C	L	I	V	I	T	Y	Leaning, Inclination, Predisposition, Disposition, Penchant, Bent, Tendency.
P	R	O	C	R	Y	P	S	I	S	Protective colouration in insects.
P	R	O	C	T	O	L	O	G	Y	Branch of medicine dealing with the anus and rectum.
P	R	O	C	U	M	B	E	N	T	Prone, Prostrate, Slanting forward.
P	R	O	C	U	R	A	N	C	E	The action of achievement.
P	R	O	D	I	G	A	L	L	Y	Extravagantly.
P	R	O	D	I	G	I	O	U	S	Abnormal, Strange, Enormous, Immense, Monstrous, Vast, Fantastic, Amazing.
P	R	O	D	U	C	T	I	O	N	Product, The staging of a theatrical entertainment.
P	R	O	D	U	C	T	I	V	E	Creative, Generative, Originative, Fruitful, Fertile, Proliferant, Prolific.
P	R	O	F	E	R	R	I	N	G	Presenting, Tendering, Proposing, Offering.
P	R	O	F	E	S	S	I	O	N	Trade, Calling, Craft, Handicraft, Vocation.
P	R	O	F	I	C	I	E	N	T	Adept, Skilled, Expert, Masterly, Practiced, Effective, Able, Capable.
P	R	O	F	I	T	A	B	L	E	Lucrative, Remunerative, Beneficial, Useful, Helpful, Advantageous, Worthwhile.
P	R	O	F	I	T	A	B	L	Y	Beneficially.
P	R	O	F	L	I	G	A	C	Y	Reckless wastefulness and extravagance.
P	R	O	F	L	I	G	A	T	E	Dissolute, Wastrel, Spendthrift, Squanderer, Licentious, Reprobate, Unprincipled.
P	R	O	F	L	U	E	N	C	E	Copious or smooth flowing.
P	R	O	F	O	U	N	D	L	Y	Totally, Deeply, Intensely, With keen penetration and intellectual insight.
P	R	O	F	U	N	D	I	T	Y	Intellectual depth, Understanding, Intensity.
P	R	O	G	E	N	I	T	O	R	Originator, Precursor, Forefather, Ancestor in direct line.
P	R	O	G	L	O	T	T	I	S	Segments of a tapeworm.
P	R	O	G	N	O	S	T	I	C	Portent, Sign, Warning, Augury, Omen, Presage, Boding, Predictive.
P	R	O	J	E	C	T	I	L	E	A body projected by external force, Missile for a weapon.
P	R	O	J	E	C	T	I	N	G	Protrusive.
P	R	O	J	E	C	T	I	O	N	Ejection, Jutting out, Extension, Carrying forward, Projecting a picture.
P	R	O	J	E	C	T	U	R	E	The state of jutting out.
P	R	O	L	O	C	U	T	O	R	Spokesman, Presiding officer of a meeting.
P	R	O	M	I	N	E	N	C	E	Distinction, Importance, Eminence, Distinction, Prestige, Renown.
P	R	O	M	I	S	S	O	R	Y	Containing a promise, Warranty.
P	R	O	M	O	N	T	O	R	Y	Headland, A high point of land projecting into a body of water.
P	R	O	M	U	L	G	A	T	E	Proclaim, Declare, Announce, Advertise, Broadcast, Publish.
P	R	O	N	O	G	R	A	D	E	Walking with the body approximately horizontal.
P	R	O	N	O	M	I	N	A	L	Resembling a pronoun.
P	R	O	N	U	C	L	E	U	S	A gamete nucleus after completion of maturation and entry of a sperm into the egg.
P	R	O	P	A	G	A	N	D	A	Dissemination of information often with the intention of causing instability.
P	R	O	P	A	G	U	L	U	M	A reproductive structure in brown algae.
P	R	O	P	E	L	L	I	N	G	Impelling, Pushing, Driving, Urging, Goading, Prompting.

1	2	3	4	5	6	7	8	9	10	Definition
P	R	O	P	E	N	S	I	T	Y	Leaning, Bent, Disposition, Inclination, Tendency, Penchant.
P	R	O	P	H	E	T	E	S	S	A female prophet.
P	R	O	P	I	O	L	A	T	E	A salt or ester of propiolic acid.
P	R	O	P	I	T	I	A	T	E	Appease, Pacify, Conciliate.
P	R	O	P	I	T	I	O	U	S	Benevolent, Auspicious, Encouraging, Helpful, Advantageous, Opportune, Timely.
P	R	O	P	O	D	I	A	L	E	Humerus, Femur.
P	R	O	P	O	R	T	I	O	N	Ratio, Balance, Symmetry, Degree, Dimension, Harmony, Scale, Extent.
P	R	O	P	O	U	N	D	E	D	Proposed, Suggested, Posed.
P	R	O	P	R	I	E	T	O	R	Owner, Holder, Possessor.
P	R	O	P	U	L	S	I	O	N	Expulsion, Something that propels.
P	R	O	P	U	L	S	I	V	E	Having power to propel.
P	R	O	P	Y	L	A	E	U	M	An architecturally important vestibule or entrance.
P	R	O	R	U	P	T	I	O	N	A bursting forth, The state of being distended.
P	R	O	S	C	R	I	B	E	D	Sentenced, Condemned, Doomed, Outlawed, Prohibited.
P	R	O	S	E	C	U	T	O	R	A person instituting an official prosecution before a court.
P	R	O	S	P	E	C	T	O	R	One that prospects for minerals.
P	R	O	S	P	E	C	T	U	S	A preliminary publication of a forthcoming event.
P	R	O	S	P	E	R	I	N	G	Thriving, Succeeding, Flourishing.
P	R	O	S	P	E	R	I	T	Y	Success, Abundance, Well-being, Good fortune, Affluence, Inflation, Growth.
P	R	O	S	P	E	R	O	U	S	Auspicious, Favourable, Propitious, Lucky, Affluent, Opulent, Wealthy, Fortunate.
P	R	O	S	T	A	T	I	S	M	Disease of the prostate.
P	R	O	S	T	H	E	T	I	C	Added to a word, Relating to an artificial part to replace a missing body part.
P	R	O	S	T	I	T	U	T	E	To offer sexual intercourse for payment, Debase, Degrade.
P	R	O	T	A	N	O	P	I	A	Red-green blindness believed due to defect in the retina.
P	R	O	T	E	A	C	E	A	E	A family of chiefly Australian and Southern African shrubs and trees.
P	R	O	T	E	C	T	A	N	T	A substance used to protect against infection.
P	R	O	T	E	C	T	I	N	G	Serving to protect or shield.
P	R	O	T	E	C	T	I	O	N	Safeguard, Security, Shield, Defence, Armament, Guard.
P	R	O	T	E	C	T	I	V	E	Providing a shield or safeguard.
P	R	O	T	E	I	N	A	S	E	A group of enzymes.
P	R	O	T	E	I	N	A	T	E	A compound of a protein.
P	R	O	T	E	L	I	D	A	E	A family of mammals including the aardwolf.
P	R	O	T	E	N	S	I	T	Y	The duration of a sensation.
P	R	O	T	E	N	S	I	V	E	Having duration.
P	R	O	T	E	O	M	Y	X	A	A small order of obscure rhizopods.
P	R	O	T	E	R	V	I	T	Y	Peevishness, Insolent sauciness.
P	R	O	T	O	B	L	A	S	T	A naked cell without a cell wall.
P	R	O	T	O	G	R	A	P	H	An original writing.
P	R	O	T	O	H	U	M	A	N	Relating to an early primitive man.
P	R	O	T	O	P	H	Y	T	A	A major category of lower plants, algae, fungi and lichens.
P	R	O	T	O	P	L	A	S	T	Prototype, The living content of a cell.
P	R	O	T	O	P	T	I	L	E	One of the first set of down feathers of young birds.
P	R	O	T	O	S	T	E	G	A	A genus of prehistoric marine turtles.
P	R	O	T	O	T	O	N	I	C	Characterized by the accent on the first syllable.
P	R	O	T	O	T	Y	P	A	L	Constituting a prototype.
P	R	O	T	R	A	C	T	E	D	Prolonged, Extended, Continued, Delayed, Deferred, Lengthy.
P	R	O	T	R	A	C	T	O	R	Retarder, Delayer, An instrument used in geometry for measuring angles on paper.
P	R	O	T	R	U	D	E	N	T	Projecting, Bulging.
P	R	O	T	R	U	D	I	N	G	Thrusting, Overhanging, Projecting.
P	R	O	T	R	U	S	I	O	N	Projection.
P	R	O	T	R	U	S	I	V	E	Protuberant, Propulsive.
P	R	O	V	E	N	A	N	C	E	Origin, Source, Derivation, Inception.
P	R	O	V	E	R	B	I	A	L	Relating to a proverb.
P	R	O	V	I	D	E	N	C	E	Prudence, Thrift, Economy, Frugality, Caution, Discretion, Precaution, Foresight.
P	R	O	V	I	N	C	I	A	L	Rustic, Peasant, Narrow, Sectional, Unsophisticated, Countrified.
P	R	O	V	O	L	O	N	E		A small cheese hung in a net to cure.
P	S	A	L	M	O	D	Y			The use of psalms in devotion.
P	S	A	M	M	O	P	H	I	S	A genus of North African and Asiatic back-fanged snakes comprising sand snakes.
P	S	E	C	H	R	I	D	A	E	A family of spiders.
P	S	E	P	H	O	L	O	G	Y	The scientific study of elections.
P	S	E	U	D	A	N	D	R	Y	The use by a woman of a masculine name as a pseudonym.
P	S	E	U	D	O	C	O	N	E	A special type of insect eye.
P	S	E	U	D	O	D	E	R	M	An outer covering in various sponges.
P	S	E	U	D	O	D	O	X	Y	The holding of erroneous beliefs.
P	S	E	U	D	O	G	Y	N	Y	The use by a man of a feminine name as a pseudonym.
P	S	E	U	D	O	L	O	G	Y	Falsehood, Lying.
P	S	E	U	D	O	S	A	L	T	A compound analogous in formula to salt.

PSITTACINE   **10 LETTERS**   **PYTHIACEAE**

1	2	3	4	5	6	7	8	9	10	Definition
P	S	I	T	T	A	C	I	N	E	Relating to the family of birds comprising the parrots, macaws and cockatoos.
P	S	O	R	O	P	H	O	R	A	A genus of large showy mosquitoes.
P	S	Y	C	H	A	G	O	G	Y	A persuasive way of influencing behaviour.
P	S	Y	C	H	I	A	T	R	Y	A branch of medicine dealing with mental, emotional or behavioural disorders.
P	S	Y	C	H	I	C	I	S	M	Psychical research.
P	S	Y	C	H	O	G	R	A	M	A message supposedly from a spirit.
P	S	Y	C	H	O	K	Y	M	E	The neural energy operative in any mental energy.
P	S	Y	C	H	O	L	O	G	Y	The science of the mind and mental phenomena.
P	S	Y	C	H	O	P	A	T	H	A mentally ill or unstable person.
P	S	Y	C	H	O	P	S	I	D	Relating to a family of tropical lacewings.
P	S	Y	C	H	O	S	O	M	A	The mental and physical organism.
P	S	Y	C	H	O	T	R	I	A	A very large genus of shrubs.
P	T	E	R	O	C	A	R	Y	A	A genus of Asiatic trees having thin-shelled nuts.
P	T	E	R	O	D	R	O	M	A	A large genus of petrels found chiefly in southern seas.
P	T	E	R	O	P	S	I	D	A	A family of vascular plants as ferns and flowering plants with large leaves.
P	T	E	R	Y	L	O	S	I	S	The arrangement of the feathers of a bird denoting definite growth areas.
P	T	I	L	I	M	N	I	U	M	A genus of annual herbs.
P	U	B	E	S	C	E	N	C	E	The state of reaching puberty.
P	U	B	L	I	S	H	I	N	G	Circulating, Disclosing, Promulgating, Advertising, Disseminating, Printing.
P	U	E	R	P	E	R	I	U	M	The condition of a woman immediately following childbirth.
P	U	G	N	A	C	I	O	U	S	Aggressive, Truculent, Belligerent, Quarrelsome, Bellicose, Combative, Militant.
P	U	L	L	U	L	A	R	I	A	A genus of fungi that causes discolouration of pulp and paper.
P	U	L	M	O	M	E	T	R	Y	Measurement of the capacity of the lungs.
P	U	L	M	O	N	A	R	I	A	A genus of European herbs.
P	U	L	M	O	N	I	F	E	R	One of a group of terrestrial snails having a pulmonary sac.
P	U	L	S	A	T	I	L	L	A	A section of Anemones that comprise the pasqueflowers.
P	U	L	S	O	M	E	T	E	R	A vacuum pump, A watch with a special dial to check the pulse rate.
P	U	L	T	A	C	E	O	U	S	Macerated, Pulpy, Consistency of porridge.
P	U	L	V	I	N	A	R	I	A	A genus of scales.
P	U	N	C	T	U	A	T	I	M	Relating to a point of time.
P	U	N	C	T	U	A	L	L	Y	Promptly, Precisely.
P	U	N	C	T	U	L	A	T	E	Marked with small spots.
P	U	N	I	S	H	M	E	N	T	Penalty, Chastisement, Discipline, Reproof, Revenge, Spanking, Castigation.
P	U	P	I	F	E	R	O	U	S	Bearing a pupa.
P	U	P	I	L	L	I	D	A	E	A large family of pulmonate land snails.
P	U	P	I	P	A	R	O	U	S	Producing mature larvae.
P	U	R	I	F	I	C	A	N	T	A purifying agent.
P	U	R	P	O	S	E	F	U	L	Full of determination, Decisive, Deliberate.
P	U	R	S	U	A	N	T	L	Y	Consequently.
P	U	R	V	E	Y	A	N	C	E	Preparation, Prudent management.
P	U	T	R	E	S	C	E	N	T	Becoming putrid, Growing putrid.
P	U	T	R	E	S	C	I	N	E	A crystalline slightly poisonous ptomaine found in putrid fish and flesh.
P	U	Z	Z	L	E	M	E	N	T	Bewilderment, Perplexity.
P	U	Z	Z	L	I	N	G	L	Y	In a puzzling manner.
P	Y	C	N	O	D	O	N	T	A	A genus of large tropical oysters.
P	Y	C	N	O	P	O	D	I	A	A genus of starfishes.
P	Y	C	N	O	X	Y	L	I	C	Having dense hard wood.
P	Y	G	I	D	I	I	D	A	E	A family of small and often parasitic catfishes.
P	Y	G	O	P	O	D	O	U	S	Having the feet set far back, Penguins.
P	Y	O	C	Y	A	N	A	S	E	A mixture of antibiotics.
P	Y	R	A	C	A	N	T	H	A	A small genus of Eurasian thorny evergreen shrubs.
P	Y	R	A	Z	O	L	I	N	E	A dihydro derivative of pyrazole.
P	Y	R	I	D	A	Z	I	N	E	A liquid feeble heterocyclic base.
P	Y	R	I	D	O	X	I	N	E	A crystalline phenolic alcohol derived from pyridine that is a member of the vitamin B.
P	Y	R	I	L	A	M	I	N	E	An oily liquid base used as an antihistamine drug against allergies.
P	Y	R	O	G	A	L	L	O	L	A poisonous bitter crystalline phenol.
P	Y	R	O	G	R	A	P	H	Y	Producing designs by burning or scorching.
P	Y	R	O	L	A	C	E	A	E	A family of mostly evergreen herbs.
P	Y	R	O	L	U	S	I	T	E	A mineral that is the most important ore of manganese.
P	Y	R	O	M	A	N	I	A	C	One who has an irresistible impulse to start fires.
P	Y	R	O	P	H	O	B	I	A	Morbid dread of fire.
P	Y	R	O	P	H	O	R	I	C	Igniting spontaneously.
P	Y	R	O	P	H	O	R	U	S	A mixture of substances that ignite spontaneously on exposure to air, A large beetle.
P	Y	R	O	S	P	H	E	R	E	The hot central portion of the earth.
P	Y	R	O	X	E	N	I	T	E	An igneous rock that is free from olivine.
P	Y	R	R	H	O	T	I	S	M	The characteristic of having red hair.
P	Y	T	H	I	A	C	E	A	E	A family of fungi.

1	2	3	4	5	6	7	8	9	10	
P	Y	T	H	O	G	E	N	I	C	Originating from decomposition or filth.
P	Y	T	H	O	N	I	D	A	E	A family of nonvenomous snakes.

Q

1	2	3	4	5	6	7	8	9	10	
Q	U	A	D	R	A	N	G	L	E	A plane figure having four angles and four sides.
Q	U	A	D	R	A	N	T	A	L	The shape of a fourth part of a circle.
Q	U	A	D	R	I	C	E	P	S	The great extensor muscle of the front of the thigh.
Q	U	A	D	R	I	F	O	R	M	Having a fourfold form.
Q	U	A	D	R	I	S	E	C	T	To divide into four equal parts.
Q	U	A	D	R	I	V	I	U	M	A group of studies of the Middle Ages, Arithmetic, Astronomy, Music and Geometry.
Q	U	A	D	R	U	P	L	E	T	One of four children born at one birth, A combination of four of a kind.
Q	U	A	D	R	U	P	O	L	E	A system of two electric dipoles of equal strength.
Q	U	A	D	R	U	P	O	L	E	Same as QUADRIPOLE.
Q	U	A	I	L	B	E	R	R	Y	Wolfberry.
Q	U	A	I	N	T	N	E	S	S	Oddness, Strangeness.
Q	U	A	N	T	I	F	I	E	R	A word that expresses quantity.
Q	U	A	N	T	I	T	A	T	E	To measure or estimate the quantity.
Q	U	A	R	A	N	T	I	N	E	Enforced isolation or restriction for a pre-determined period.
Q	U	A	R	T	E	R	A	G	E	A payment made every three months.
Q	U	A	R	T	E	R	I	N	G	Dividing into four parts, Lodging, Crisscrossing.
Q	U	A	R	T	E	R	M	A	N	A foreman in shipbuilding in charge of groups of workers all doing the same work.
Q	U	A	T	E	R	N	A	R	Y	Consisting of four parts or components.
Q	U	A	T	O	R	Z	A	I	N	A poem of fourteen lines.
Q	U	A	T	R	E	F	O	I	L	A conventionalized representation of a four-petalled flower.
Q	U	E	A	S	I	N	E	S	S	The condition of being nauseous.
Q	U	E	E	N	S	W	A	R	E	Cream-coloured Wedgwood ware.
Q	U	E	N	C	H	A	B	L	E	Capable of being quenched.
Q	U	E	N	S	E	L	I	T	E	A mineral consisting of basic lead manganese oxide.
Q	U	E	R	C	I	T	R	O	N	The bark of the black oak that is used in tanning and dyeing.
Q	U	E	S	A	D	I	L	L	A	A turnover made with a cheese filling.
Q	U	E	S	T	I	N	G	L	Y	Inquiringly, Searchingly.
Q	U	E	S	T	I	O	N	E	D	Asked, Examined, Inquired, Interrogated, Queried, Challenged, Doubted, Hesitated.
Q	U	I	C	K	E	N	I	N	G	Arousing, Stimulating, Exciting, Hastening, Accelerating, Animating, Enlivening.
Q	U	I	E	S	C	E	N	C	E	Abeyance, Dormancy, Suspension, Latency, Intermission, Interruption.
Q	U	I	E	S	C	E	N	C	Y	Same as QUIESCENCE.
Q	U	I	E	T	E	N	I	N	G	Calming, Silencing, Composing, Settling, Soothing, Allaying.
Q	U	I	N	I	Z	A	R	I	N	A red crystalline compound isomeric with alizarin.
Q	U	I	N	O	I	D	I	N	E	A bitter brownish resinous mixture often moulded into sticks and once used as quinine.
Q	U	I	N	Q	U	E	V	I	R	One of a commission of five.
Q	U	I	N	T	U	P	L	E	T	One of a group of five. One of a multiple birth of 5.
Q	U	I	S	Q	U	A	L	I	S	A genus of woody vines with a five-winged fruit, Rangoon creeper.

R

1	2	3	4	5	6	7	8	9	10	
R	A	B	B	I	T	W	E	E	D	A stiff woody herb of the central and southwestern United States of America.
R	A	B	B	L	E	M	E	N	T	Disturbance, Tumult.
R	A	C	E	C	O	U	R	S	E	A course for racing usually of turf.
R	A	C	E	M	I	F	O	R	M	In the form of a cluster.
R	A	C	H	I	O	D	O	N	T	Having gular teeth consisting of modified vertebral spines.
R	A	D	A	R	S	C	O	P	E	Viewing screen of a radar receiver.
R	A	D	I	C	A	L	I	S	M	The state of being a radical.
R	A	D	I	C	A	L	I	Z	E	To make radical.
R	A	D	I	C	A	T	I	O	N	Taking root.
R	A	D	I	C	U	L	O	S	E	Producing numerous rootlets.
R	A	D	I	F	E	R	O	U	S	Containing radium.
R	A	D	I	O	G	R	A	P	H	An X-ray photograph.
R	A	D	I	O	L	A	R	I	A	A large order of rhizopods.
R	A	D	I	O	M	E	T	E	R	An instrument for detecting and measuring the intensity of acourstic radiotion.
R	A	D	I	O	M	E	T	R	Y	The measurement of radiation.
R	A	D	I	O	P	H	A	R	E	A radiotelegraphic station sending signals to position ships and aircraft.
R	A	D	I	O	P	H	O	T	O	To send a photo by radio.
R	A	D	I	O	S	C	O	P	Y	Examination of opaque bodies by means of X-rays.
R	A	D	I	O	S	O	N	D	E	A miniature radio transmitter sent into the atmosphere to forecast weather.
R	A	D	O	P	H	O	L	U	S	A genus of parasitic nematodes destructive to sugar cane and rice among other plants.

1	2	3	4	5	6	7	8	9	10	
R	A	D	U	L	I	F	O	R	M	Like a rasp.
R	A	G	A	M	U	F	F	I	N	A ragged dirty male.
R	A	L	L	E	N	T	A	T	O	Direction in music - a decrease in tempo.
R	A	L	S	T	O	N	I	T	E	A mineral consisting of a hydrous basic fluoride of aluminium, sodium and magnesium.
R	A	M	P	A	G	E	O	U	S	Unruly, Destructive, Out of control.
R	A	M	P	A	L	L	I	A	N	A good-for-nothing scoundrel, Wretch.
R	A	M	P	H	A	S	T	O	S	A genus comprising various typical toucans.
R	A	N	D	A	N	N	I	T	E	A diatomaceous earth or earthy form of opal.
R	A	N	S	A	C	K	I	N	G	Seeking, Rummaging, Examining, Plundering, Raking, Foraging, Looting.
R	A	N	U	N	C	U	L	U	S	A large and widely distributed genus of herbs, Buttercup.
R	A	P	P	O	R	T	E	U	R	An official charged with drawing up and presenting reports.
R	A	T	I	O	N	A	L	L	Y	Reasonably, Sensibly.
R	A	V	I	S	H	M	E	N	T	The condition of being ravished.
R	E	A	C	T	I	O	N	A	L	Marked by reaction.
R	E	A	C	T	I	V	A	T	E	Revive, Restore.
R	E	A	C	T	O	L	O	G	Y	The scientific study of psychological reactions.
R	E	A	S	O	N	A	B	L	E	Rational, Moderate, Sensible, Conservative, Discreet, Cheap, Inexpensive, Logical.
R	E	B	E	L	L	I	O	U	S	Insubordinate, Mutinous, Seditious.
R	E	C	E	I	V	A	B	L	E	Legally acceptable, Subject to a claim for payment.
R	E	C	E	P	T	A	C	L	E	Container, Repository.
R	E	C	I	B	I	D	E	R	O	A stand in a bullfight to receive a charge by the bull.
R	E	C	I	D	I	V	A	T	E	Relapse.
R	E	C	I	D	I	V	O	U	S	Having relapsed.
R	E	C	I	P	R	O	C	A	L	Mutual, Common, Companion, Double, Duplicate, Match.
R	E	C	I	T	A	T	I	O	N	Reciting a poem or passage, Repetition.
R	E	C	I	T	A	T	I	V	E	Musical declamation between song and speech used for narration.
R	E	C	K	L	E	S	S	L	Y	In a reckless manner.
R	E	C	O	G	I	T	A	T	E	To think over again.
R	E	C	O	G	N	I	Z	E	D	Revised, Corrected, Recalled, Recollected, Remembered, Identified, Distinguished.
R	E	C	O	M	P	E	N	S	E	Pay, Compensate, Reimburse, Remunerate, Indemnify, Award, Reparation, Grant.
R	E	C	O	N	C	I	L	E	D	Harmonized, Accommodated, Conformed, Integrated, Suited, Adjusted.
R	E	C	O	N	S	I	D	E	R	To consider again, Re-examine, Review.
R	E	C	R	E	A	T	I	O	N	Diversion, Play, Entertainment, Amusement, Distraction, Fun, Sport.
R	E	C	R	U	I	T	I	N	G	Recovering, Regaining, Repossessing, Retrieving, Refreshing, Renewing, Mending.
R	E	C	U	P	E	R	A	T	E	Recover, Regain, Convalesce, Gain, Mend.
R	E	C	U	R	R	E	N	C	E	Repetition, Reproduction, Return, Frequency, Reappearance, Resort.
R	E	D	D	I	N	G	I	T	E	A mineral consisting of a pinkish or yellowish orthorhombic hydrous manganese.
R	E	D	E	M	P	T	I	O	N	Refurnish, Renovate.
R	E	D	U	N	D	A	N	C	Y	Exoneration, Atonement, Ransom, Reclamation, Compensation.
R	E	D	U	V	I	I	D	A	E	Profusion, Overabundance, Tautology, Verbiage, Tumidity, Turgidity.
R	E	F	E	R	E	N	D	U	M	A large family of bloodsucking insects comprising the assassin bugs.
R	E	F	I	N	E	M	E	N	T	The principle of submitting a measure to popular vote.
R	E	F	L	E	C	T	I	N	G	Elegance, Polish, Culture, Breeding, Cultivation, Politeness, Civility.
R	E	F	L	E	C	T	I	O	N	Diverting, Deflecting, Rebounding, Reconsidering, Recoiling, Thinking, Pondering.
R	E	F	L	E	C	T	I	V	E	The production of an image by mirror, Reproduction.
R	E	F	R	A	C	T	I	O	N	Reflecting, Thoughtful, Deliberative, Pensive, Contemplative, Thinking.
R	E	F	R	A	C	T	O	R	Y	Deflection, Distortion.
R	E	F	R	E	S	H	I	N	G	Stubborn, Perverse, Unruly, Obstinate, Headstrong, Unyielding, Immune, Insusceptible.
R	E	F	U	L	G	E	N	C	E	Stimulating, Heartening, Rejuvenating, Restoring, Animating, Recovering.
R	E	F	U	N	D	A	B	L	E	Brilliance, Splendour, Radiance.
R	E	F	U	T	A	T	I	O	N	Capable of being refunded.
R	E	G	A	R	D	L	E	S	S	Disproof, Confutation.
R	E	G	E	L	A	T	I	O	N	Heedless, Careless, Negligent, Remiss.
R	E	G	E	N	E	R	A	T	E	Refreezing of melted ice.
R	E	G	R	E	S	S	I	V	E	Recreate, Reborn, Convert, Revive, Reproduce, Refresh, Re-establish, Restore.
R	E	G	U	L	A	R	I	T	Y	Retrogressive, Reversal.
R	E	G	U	L	A	R	I	Z	E	Something that is regular.
R	E	G	U	L	A	T	I	O	N	Make steady or uniform.
R	E	G	U	L	A	T	O	R	Y	Law, Decree, Canon, Edict, Precept, Rule, Statute.
R	E	I	N	F	O	R	C	E	D	Concerned with making regulations.
R	E	J	U	V	E	N	A	T	E	Strengthed, Fortified, Invigorated, Propped, Sustained, Bolstered, Buttressed.
R	E	L	A	T	I	V	I	T	Y	Reinvigorate, Restore, Renew, Modernise, Refresh, Renovate, Recondition.
R	E	L	E	N	T	L	E	S	S	The state of being relative.
R	E	L	I	N	Q	U	I	S	H	Harsh, Stern, Implacable, Merciless, Ruthless, Rigorous, Stringent, Cruel.
R	E	L	O	C	A	T	I	O	N	Abandon, Forsake, Renounce, Release, Yield, Cede, Surrender, Leave.
R	E	L	U	C	T	A	N	C	E	Removal and establishment in a new place.
										Unwillingness, Disinclination, Aversion, Repugnance, Hesitance.

1	2	3	4	5	6	7	8	9	10	
R	E	L	U	C	T	A	N	C	Y	Opposition, Resistance, Repugnance, Disinclination.
R	E	M	A	R	K	A	B	L	E	Noticeable, Uncommon, Extraordinary, Conspicuous, Prominent, Salient, Striking.
R	E	M	A	R	K	E	D	L	Y	Notably.
R	E	M	E	D	I	A	B	L	E	Capable of being remedied.
R	E	M	E	D	I	L	E	S	S	Irremediable, Irreparable.
R	E	M	E	M	B	E	R	E	D	Recorded, Commemorated, Mentioned, Recollected, Reminded, Revived, Retained.
R	E	M	I	T	T	A	N	C	E	A sum of money transmitted to another person or place.
R	E	M	U	N	E	R	A	T	E	Recompense, Pay, Compensate, Award, Grant, Indemnify, Reimburse, Reward.
R	E	N	A	S	C	E	N	C	E	Renaissance.
R	E	N	D	E	Z	V	O	U	S	Appointment, Assignation, Tryst, Resort, Assemble, Collect, Muster.
R	E	N	O	V	A	T	I	O	N	Process of renovating, Revival.
R	E	N	U	N	C	I	A	N	T	One who renounces.
R	E	O	R	G	A	N	I	Z	E	To organize again.
R	E	P	A	R	A	T	I	O	N	Repairing, Compensation, Indemnity, Redress, Atonement, Reprisal, Remuneration.
R	E	P	A	T	R	I	A	T	E	To restore to one's country of origin.
R	E	P	E	A	T	A	B	L	E	Capable of being repeated.
R	E	P	E	A	T	E	D	L	Y	Frequently, Constantly, Often.
R	E	P	E	N	T	A	N	C	E	Penitence, Compuction, Contrition, Remorse, Attrition.
R	E	P	E	R	T	O	I	R	E	Stock of entertainment pieces available for performance.
R	E	P	E	T	I	T	I	O	N	Repeating, Rehearsal, Mention, Recital, Reproduction.
R	E	P	I	N	I	N	G	L	Y	Complainingly.
R	E	P	O	R	T	E	D	L	Y	Reputedly.
R	E	P	O	S	I	T	O	R	Y	Storehouse, Depository, Museum, Burial vault, Depot.
R	E	P	O	U	S	S	A	G	E	The art of pressing thin metal from the reverse side.
R	E	P	R	E	S	S	I	O	N	Quenching, Squelching, Stifling, Control, Restraint, Suppression, Curb, Extinction.
R	E	P	R	E	S	S	I	V	E	Having power to repress.
R	E	P	R	O	D	U	C	E	D	Produced again, Repeated, Portrayed, Recited, Remembered, Generated, Copied.
R	E	P	U	B	L	I	C	A	N	Having the characteristics of a republic.
R	E	P	U	G	N	A	N	C	E	Incompatibility, Incongruity, Inconsistency, Hostility, Aversion, Distaste, Antipathy.
R	E	P	U	T	A	T	I	O	N	Authority, Credit, Influence, Renown, Character, Fame, Name, Report.
R	E	Q	U	I	E	S	C	A	T	A prayer for the dead.
R	E	S	C	I	N	D	I	N	G	Revoking.
R	E	S	E	A	R	C	H	E	D	Investigated, Inquired, Probed.
R	E	S	E	M	B	L	I	N	G	Favouring, Representing, Portraying, Depicting, Appearing, Symbolizing.
R	E	S	E	N	T	M	E	N	T	Offense, Pique, Animosity, Malice, Rancour, Umbrage.
R	E	S	I	L	I	E	N	C	E	Rebound, Recoil.
R	E	S	I	S	T	A	N	C	E	Opposition, Unwillingness.
R	E	S	I	S	T	I	B	L	E	Capable of being resisted.
R	E	S	O	L	U	T	I	O	N	Analysis, Decision, Determination, Resolve, Courage, Conclusion, Settlement.
R	E	S	O	U	N	D	I	N	G	Resonant, Forceful, Emphatic, Unequivocal, Ringing, Vibrant, Insistent.
R	E	S	P	E	C	T	F	U	L	Deferential, Dutiful, Reverent, Attentive, Venerating, Courteous, Gracious, Polite.
R	E	S	P	E	C	T	I	V	E	Relative, Particular, Several, Discriminative.
R	E	S	P	I	R	A	T	O	R	A protective device against poisonous substances, A device for artificial respiration.
R	E	S	P	O	N	D	E	N	T	One that answers in legal proceedings.
R	E	S	P	O	N	D	I	N	G	Answering, Replying, Retorting.
R	E	S	T	A	U	R	A	N	T	An establishment serving meals and refreshments.
R	E	S	T	R	I	C	T	E	D	Limited, Fixed, Definite, Confined, Circumscribed, Restrained, Qualified.
R	E	S	U	M	P	T	I	O	N	Recommencement, Returning, Recovery.
R	E	S	U	R	G	E	N	C	Y	The condition of rising again.
R	E	T	I	C	U	L	A	T	E	Netted, Resembling a net.
R	E	T	I	R	E	M	E	N	T	Withdrawal, Privacy, Retreat, Seclusion.
R	E	T	R	A	C	T	I	L	E	Able to draw back, i.e. the claws of a cat.
R	E	T	R	A	C	T	I	O	N	Recall, Revocation, Recantation, Withdrawal of an accusation.
R	E	T	R	E	A	T	I	N	G	Withdrawing, Removing, Receding, Retiring.
R	E	T	R	I	E	V	I	N	G	Regaining, Repossessing, Recalling, Restoring, Reviving, Correcting, Repairing.
R	E	T	R	O	C	H	O	I	R	The area behind the altar in a cathedral.
R	E	T	R	O	G	R	A	D	E	Retreating, Inverse, Deteriorate, Opposed, Retract, Decline, Degenerate.
R	E	T	R	O	G	R	E	S	S	Regress, Revert, Move backward.
R	E	T	R	O	R	S	I	N	E	A poisonous crystalline alkaloid found in certain plants.
R	E	T	R	O	S	P	E	C	T	Reflect, Review, Revision, Remember, Reminisce, Remind, Recollect, Recall.
R	E	T	R	O	V	E	R	S	E	Reversed, Turned backward.
R	E	T	U	R	N	A	B	L	E	Legally required to be returned, Permitted to be returned.
R	E	V	A	L	I	D	A	T	E	To make valid again.
R	E	V	A	L	O	R	I	Z	E	To change the valuation.
R	E	V	E	G	E	T	A	T	E	To provide new vegetative cover.
R	E	V	E	L	A	T	I	O	N	Disclosure, Revealing, Prophecy, Vision, Oracle.
R	E	V	E	L	A	T	O	R	Y	Relating to a revelation.

1	2	3	4	5	6	7	8	9	10	Definition
R	E	V	E	N	G	E	F	U	L	Vindictive.
R	E	V	E	R	S	I	B	L	E	Capable of being reversed or corrected.
R	E	V	I	V	A	L	I	Z	E	To impart new life.
R	E	V	I	V	A	L	I	S	T	One who promotes religious revivals.
R	E	V	O	L	U	T	I	O	N	Circuit, Circulation, Gyration, Rotation, Reel, Revolve, Overthrow, Rebellion.
R	H	A	B	D	I	T	I	D	A	A large order of nematode worms.
R	H	A	B	D	O	L	I	T	H	A minute calcareous rodlike structure found in the sea.
R	H	A	C	H	I	T	O	M	E	An order of extinct amphibians that resembled crocodiles.
R	H	A	G	O	L	E	T	I	S	A genus of flies the larvae of which feed on fruits and berries, Apple maggot.
R	H	A	M	N	A	C	E	A	E	A widely distributed family of thorny shrubs or trees.
R	H	A	M	N	I	N	O	S	E	A crystalline reducing trisaccharide sugar.
R	H	A	P	S	O	D	I	S	T	One who recites or sings poems for a livelihood.
R	H	A	S	O	P	H	O	R	E	A novice of a religious order.
R	H	E	E	F	O	R	M	E	S	An order of birds intermediate between ostriches and emus that comprise the rheas.
R	H	E	T	O	R	I	C	A	L	Declamatory, Bombastic, Grandiloquent, Flowery, Oratorical, Pompous, Pretentious.
R	H	E	U	M	A	T	I	S	M	Condition of inflamation in muscles and joints.
R	H	I	N	A	N	T	H	U	S	A small genus of partially parasitic herbs.
R	H	I	N	O	G	E	N	I	C	Transmitted by way of the nose.
R	H	I	N	O	L	A	L	I	A	A nasal tone in speech.
R	H	I	N	O	L	O	G	I	C	Relating to the nose.
R	H	I	N	O	P	H	Y	M	A	A nodular swelling and congestion of the nose.
R	H	I	N	O	P	T	E	R	A	A genus of rays comprising the cow-nosed rays.
R	H	I	N	O	R	R	H	E	A	Excessive mucous secretion from the nose.
R	H	I	N	O	S	C	O	P	E	An instrument for examining the cavities and passages of the nose.
R	H	I	N	O	S	C	O	P	Y	Examination of nasal cavities and passages.
R	H	I	N	O	T	H	E	C	A	The sheath of the upper mandible of a bird.
R	H	I	N	O	V	I	R	U	S	The type of virus believed to cause the common cold.
R	H	I	Z	O	G	E	N	I	C	Producing roots.
R	H	I	Z	O	G	R	A	P	H	A device to trace the movement of roots in the soil.
R	H	I	Z	O	M	O	R	P	H	A collection of intertwined fungous threads resembling roots.
R	H	I	Z	O	P	H	O	R	A	A small genus of tropical trees and shrubs.
R	H	I	Z	O	P	H	O	R	E	A downward-growing leafless shoot in club mosses.
R	H	I	Z	O	P	L	A	N	E	The external surface of roots with the adhering soil particles.
R	H	I	Z	O	P	O	G	O	N	A genus of fungi.
R	H	O	D	O	P	H	Y	T	A	A division of lower plants, Marine algae.
R	H	O	D	O	T	Y	P	O	S	A genus of Japanese shrubs.
R	H	O	D	Y	M	E	N	I	A	A genus of red algae.
R	H	O	E	A	D	A	L	E	S	An order of plants having cyclic flowers.
R	H	O	M	B	O	I	D	A	L	Shaped somewhat like a rhomboid.
R	H	Y	N	C	H	O	S	I	A	A large genus of twining leguminous plants.
R	H	Y	T	H	M	I	C	A	L	Involving rhythm.
R	I	B	B	O	N	W	O	O	D	A small New Zealand tree having bark used for cordage.
R	I	B	O	F	L	A	V	I	N	A yellow pigment derived from ribose, a member of vitamin B complex.
R	I	C	H	E	L	L	I	T	E	A mineral consisting of a basic hydrous fluophosphate of iron and calcium.
R	I	C	H	T	E	R	I	T	E	A mineral that is a variety of amphibole.
R	I	C	I	N	O	L	E	I	N	An ester of glycerol and ricinoleic acid.
R	I	C	K	A	R	D	I	T	E	A mineral consisting of a copper telluride.
R	I	C	K	E	T	T	S	I	A	Micro-organisms living in biting arthropods that transmit serious diseases to man.
R	I	D	I	C	U	L	O	U	S	Absurd, Comical, Funny, Laughable, Preposterous, Indecent, Scandalous.
R	I	F	L	E	S	C	O	P	E	A telescopic sight for a rifle.
R	I	G	H	T	F	U	L	L	Y	Fairly, Justly.
R	I	G	O	R	O	U	S	L	Y	In a rigorous fashion.
R	I	N	D	E	R	P	E	S	T	An acute highly infectious disease that attacks both domestic and wild animals.
R	I	N	K	A	F	A	D	D	A	An Irish dance.
R	I	O	D	I	N	I	D	A	E	A family of small to medium-sized brightly coloured butterflies.
R	I	P	I	C	O	L	O	U	S	Related to living on the banks of a river or stream.
R	I	S	I	B	I	L	I	T	Y	Laughter, Merriment.
R	I	T	A	R	D	A	N	D	O	Direction in music - gradual slackening in tempo.
R	I	V	O	L	T	A	S	I	A	A genus of mites that live on the skin and feathers of birds.
R	O	A	D	W	O	R	T	H	Y	Fit to be used on the road, Mechanically sound.
R	O	B	U	S	T	I	O	U	S	Robust, Stout, Healthy, Boisterous, Rough.
R	O	B	U	S	T	N	E	S	S	The state of being robust.
R	O	L	L	I	C	K	I	N	G	Boisterous, Swaggering, Lighthearted, Frolicsome, Playful, Sprightly, Cheerful.
R	O	M	A	N	C	I	N	G	S	Romance.
R	O	N	D	E	L	E	T	I	A	A genus of tropical American trees and shrubs having salver-shaped fragrant flowers.
R	O	R	I	F	E	R	O	U	S	Generating dew.
R	O	S	A	N	I	L	I	N	E	A white crystalline base that is the methyl derivative of pararosaniline.

1	2	3	4	5	6	7	8	9	10	Definition
R	O	S	C	H	E	R	I	T	E	A mineral consisting of a hydrous basic phosphate of aluminium, manganese and iron.
R	O	S	E	L	L	I	N	I	A	A genus of fungi.
R	O	S	E	M	A	L	I	N	G	Scandinavian peasant style decoration on household goods.
R	O	S	I	C	K	Y	I	T	E	A mineral consisting of native sulphur in the gamma crystal form.
R	O	T	I	S	S	E	R	I	E	A cooking appliance with a rotating spit.
R	O	T	T	W	E	I	L	E	R	A black cattle dog of Germany.
R	O	U	N	D	A	B	O	U	T	Curving, Detour, Circular, Circumlocution, Meandering, Winding, Indirect.
R	O	U	S	T	A	B	O	U	T	A handyman on an Australian sheep farm.
R	O	U	S	T	A	B	O	U	T	A deckhand, A worker in an oil field, A labourer in a circus.
R	O	W	A	N	B	E	R	R	Y	The fruit of the rowan tree.
R	O	W	L	A	N	D	I	T	E	A massive grayish green yttrium silicate containing iron and fluorine.
R	U	B	E	S	C	E	N	C	E	The state of becoming red.
R	U	B	I	G	I	N	O	U	S	Marked with a rusty red colour.
R	U	B	R	O	F	U	G	A	L	Leading away from the red nucleus of the brain.
R	U	D	D	E	R	H	E	A	D	Upper end of a rudderstock to which the tiller is attached.
R	U	M	E	N	O	T	O	M	Y	Incision into the rumen.
R	U	M	I	N	A	N	T	I	A	An order of hoofed mammals that chew the cud, sheep, giraffes, deer and camels.
R	U	M	I	N	A	T	I	O	N	The act of rechewing food, Deliberate meditation, Obsessive reflection.
R	U	M	I	N	A	T	I	V	E	Thoughtful, Contemplative, Pensive, Pondering, Reflective, Speculative, Thinking.
R	U	P	E	S	T	R	I	A	N	Inscribed on rocks.
R	U	P	E	S	T	R	I	N	E	Living among or growing on rocks.
R	U	P	I	C	O	L	O	U	S	Same as RUPESTRINE.
R	U	R	I	G	E	N	O	U	S	Born or living in the country.
R	U	T	H	L	E	S	S	L	Y	Mercilessly.

S

1	2	3	4	5	6	7	8	9	10	Definition
S	A	B	B	A	T	I	C	A	L	Related to the Sabbath, A period of study leave or rest.
S	A	B	E	L	L	A	R	I	A	A genus of marine worms.
S	A	B	R	E	T	A	C	H	E	A flat leather case once worn on the sabre belt by cavalrymen.
S	A	C	C	H	A	R	A	T	E	A salt or ester of saccharic acid.
S	A	C	C	H	A	R	I	D	E	A simple sugar, combination of sugars or polymerized sugar.
S	A	C	C	H	A	R	I	N	E	Relating to sugar, Ingratiatingly pleasant.
S	A	C	C	H	A	R	O	I	D	Crystalline, Granular.
S	A	C	C	H	A	R	O	S	E	Sucrose, Compound sugars.
S	A	C	C	O	R	H	I	Z	A	A small genus of marine brown algae.
S	A	C	C	U	L	A	T	E	D	Formed by sacs.
S	A	C	E	R	D	O	T	A	L	Relating to priests.
S	A	C	O	G	L	O	S	S	A	A sub-order comprising sea-slugs.
S	A	C	R	E	D	N	E	S	S	The quality of being sacred.
S	A	C	R	O	S	A	N	C	T	Inviolable, having immunity.
S	A	G	I	T	T	A	R	I	A	A genus of aquatic herbs.
S	A	L	A	M	A	N	D	E	R	Small amphibians resembling lizards but without scales and having a soft moist skin.
S	A	L	A	N	G	I	D	A	E	Small translucent Asiatic salmonoid fishes.
S	A	L	I	C	O	R	N	I	A	A genus of fleshy maritime herbs.
S	A	L	I	C	Y	L	A	T	E	Salicylic acid.
S	A	L	I	C	Y	L	I	D	E	A crystalline compound formed by condensation of four molecules of salicylic acid.
S	A	L	I	C	Y	L	I	S	M	Vomiting caused by an overdose of salicylic acid.
S	A	L	I	F	E	R	O	U	S	Containing salt.
S	A	L	I	N	A	T	I	O	N	Treatment with a salt solution.
S	A	L	I	N	I	F	O	R	M	Having the qualities of salt.
S	A	L	I	V	A	T	I	O	N	Excessive secretion of saliva.
S	A	L	M	A	G	U	N	D	I	Medley, Jumble, Miscellany, Potpourri, A plate of mixed salads and pickles.
S	A	L	M	O	N	E	L	L	A	A genus of motile bacteria associated with food-poisoning.
S	A	L	M	O	N	I	D	A	E	A family of soft-finned fishes including salmons, trouts and whitefishes.
S	A	L	O	M	O	N	I	C	A	A twisted architectural column.
S	A	L	T	A	R	E	L	L	O	A lively Italian dance.
S	A	L	T	A	T	O	R	I	A	A suborder of leaping insects comprising grasshoppers and crickets.
S	A	L	T	I	C	I	D	A	E	A family of jumping spiders.
S	A	L	U	B	R	I	O	U	S	Invigorating, Salutary, Beneficial, Healthful, Bracing, Wholesome, Stimulating.
S	A	L	U	T	A	T	I	O	N	Tribute, An action of saluting, Greeting.
S	A	L	V	A	T	E	L	L	A	A vein on the back of the little finger once used for blodd-letting.
S	A	L	V	E	L	I	N	U	S	A genus of fishes.
S	A	M	A	R	S	K	I	T	E	A mineral with a resinous lustre consisting of an oxide of rare earths, uranium, iron.
S	A	N	A	T	O	R	I	U	M	An establishment for the treatment of the sick.
S	A	N	B	O	R	N	I	T	E	A mineral consisting of a rare triclinic barium silicate.

1	2	3	4	5	6	7	8	9	10	
S	A	N	C	T	I	F	I	E	D	Made holy, Sanctimonious.
S	A	N	C	T	I	M	O	N	Y	Hypocritical devoutness.
S	A	N	C	T	I	O	N	E	D	Approved, Accepted, Received, Orthodox, Endorsed, Certified.
S	A	N	C	T	I	T	U	D	E	Pure and saintly character, Holiness, Sacredness.
S	A	N	D	A	L	W	O	O	D	A fragrant yellowish wood that has insect-repelling properties.
S	A	N	D	E	R	L	I	N	G	A small sandpiper.
S	A	N	D	G	R	O	U	S	E	Order of birds inhabiting arid areas and resembling pigeons.
S	A	N	D	N	A	T	T	E	R	Sand viper.
S	A	N	D	P	A	P	E	R	Y	Grating, Harsh.
S	A	N	G	U	I	N	A	R	Y	Bloodthirsty, Murderous, Bloody, Homicidal, Gory.
S	A	N	I	T	A	R	I	L	Y	Related to sanitation.
S	A	N	V	I	T	A	L	I	A	A small genus of chiefly tropical American annual herbs.
S	A	P	I	E	N	T	I	A	L	Peculiar to wisdom.
S	A	P	I	N	D	A	L	E	S	An order of plants having the stamens inserted on a disk.
S	A	P	O	T	A	C	E	A	E	A family of trees and shrubs that have milky juice.
S	A	P	P	H	I	R	I	N	E	A mineral consisting of a green or pale blue magnesium aluminium iron silicate.
S	A	P	R	O	G	E	N	I	C	Capable of producing decay or putrefaction.
S	A	P	R	O	P	H	Y	T	E	Fungus that lives on decaying matter.
S	A	P	R	O	S	P	I	R	A	A genus of large free-living aquatic spirochetes.
S	A	R	C	O	B	A	T	U	S	A small genus of branching spiny shrubs.
S	A	R	C	O	C	O	C	C	A	A small genus of evergreen Asiatic shrubs.
S	A	R	C	O	P	H	A	G	A	A type genus comprising typical flesh flies.
S	A	R	C	O	P	S	I	D	E	A mineral consisting of a fluoride and phosphate of calcium, manganese and iron.
S	A	R	C	O	P	T	O	I	D	Resembling small whitish itch mites.
S	A	R	C	O	T	E	S	T	A	The outer part of the testa in various seeds.
S	A	R	M	E	N	T	O	S	E	Producing slender branches or runners.
S	A	R	R	A	C	E	N	I	A	A genus of American bog herbs.
S	A	T	I	S	F	Y	I	N	G	Satisfactory, Convincing, Solid, Valid, Cogent, Sound, Gratifying, Persuading.
S	A	T	U	R	A	T	I	O	N	Contentment, Surfeit, Permeation, Impregnation, Intensity, Concentration.
S	A	T	U	R	N	A	L	I	A	Feast, Orgy, Party, Licentious celebration.
S	A	T	Y	A	G	R	A	H	A	Reliance on truth, Attempt to reform by nonviolent passive resistance.
S	A	T	Y	R	I	A	S	I	S	Abnormal sexual craving in the male.
S	A	U	E	R	K	R	A	U	T	Shredded cabbage pickled in its own juice.
S	A	U	R	I	S	C	H	I	A	An order of dinosaurs.
S	A	U	S	S	U	R	I	T	E	A mineral that consists chiefly of zoisite or epidote.
S	A	U	T	E	R	E	L	L	E	An instrument used by masons to trace and form angles.
S	A	U	V	A	G	E	S	I	A	A genus of chiefly tropical American herbs.
S	A	V	A	G	E	N	E	S	S	The condition of being savage.
S	A	X	I	C	A	V	O	U	S	Boring in rock - as a mollusk.
S	A	X	I	C	O	L	O	U	S	Growing among rocks.
S	C	A	B	I	C	I	D	A	L	Destroying the itch mite causing scabies.
S	C	A	M	P	E	R	I	N	G	Running, Bolting, Fleeing, Scooting, Skipping, Dashing, Scurrying, Sprinting.
S	C	A	N	D	A	L	O	U	S	Outrageous, Atrocious, Heinous, Monstrous, Shocking, Libelous, Calumnious.
S	C	A	N	D	A	R	O	O	N	A long-bodied domestic pigeon of the carrier type.
S	C	A	P	H	A	N	D	E	R	A genus of gastropods having an external ovoid shell.
S	C	A	P	H	I	O	P	U	S	A genus of toads comprising the American spadefoot.
S	C	A	R	A	B	A	E	U	S	A large black dung beetle.
S	C	A	R	A	M	O	U	C	H	A cowardly buffoon, Rascal, Scamp.
S	C	A	R	L	A	T	I	N	A	Scarlet fever.
S	C	A	T	O	P	H	A	G	Y	The practice of eating excrement or filth for religious rites or pathological obsession.
S	C	A	T	T	E	R	I	N	G	Dispelling, Dissipating, Dividing, Shattering, Broadcasting, Strewing.
S	C	A	T	U	R	I	E	N	T	Overflowing, Effusive, Gushing forth.
S	C	A	V	E	N	G	E	R	Y	Removal of garbage and refuse from streets.
S	C	E	L	I	P	H	R	O	N	A genus of wasps comprising common mud daubers.
S	C	E	L	O	P	O	R	U	S	A genus of small lizards including the pine and sagebrush lizard.
S	C	E	N	E	C	R	A	F	T	Supplying stage settings.
S	C	E	N	O	G	R	A	P	H	A perspective representation of an object.
S	C	H	A	L	S	T	E	I	N	Slaty greenstone.
S	C	H	E	F	F	L	E	R	A	Shrubby tropical plants with showy foliage.
S	C	H	E	R	Z	A	N	D	O	Direction in music - playful, jesting.
S	C	H	I	N	O	P	S	I	S	A genus of South American deciduous to half-evergreen trees with hard heartwood.
S	C	H	I	S	M	A	T	I	C	Implying schism.
S	C	H	I	Z	O	C	A	R	P	A dry compound fruit that splits at maturity into one-seeded carpels.
S	C	H	I	Z	O	G	O	N	Y	Asexual reproduction by multiple segmentation as with parasites.
S	C	H	I	Z	O	L	I	T	E	A manganese-containing variety of pectolite.
S	C	H	O	L	A	S	T	I	C	Pedantic, Formal, Scholarly, Book-learned, Academic, Erudite, Versed, Bookish.
S	C	I	A	E	N	I	D	A	E	A large family of carnivorous percoid fishes comprising the croakers.

SCIAPODOUS   # 10 LETTERS   SENSUALIST

1	2	3	4	5	6	7	8	9	10	Definition
S	C	I	A	P	O	D	O	U	S	Having very large feet.
S	C	I	E	N	T	I	F	I	C	Devised according to the rules of science for testing soundness of conclusions.
S	C	I	N	D	A	P	S	U	S	A genus of climbing vines.
S	C	L	E	R	O	T	I	U	M	A compact mass with reserve food material in various true fungi.
S	C	L	E	R	O	T	O	M	Y	Surgical cutting of the sclera.
S	C	O	L	Y	T	I	D	A	E	A large family of bark-boring beetles.
S	C	O	M	B	R	I	D	A	E	A family of fishes comprising the typical mackerels.
S	C	O	P	O	L	E	T	I	N	A crystalline lactone that is found in various solanaceous plants.
S	C	O	R	D	A	T	U	R	A	An unusual tuning of a stringed musical instrument for some special effect.
S	C	O	R	P	A	E	N	I	D	A large family of marine spiny-finned fishes with poison glands, Scorpion fish.
S	C	O	R	P	I	O	N	I	D	An order of true scorpions.
S	C	O	R	P	I	U	R	U	S	A genus of leguminous herbs of the Mediterranean region.
S	C	O	R	Z	A	L	I	T	E	A mineral consisting of basic phosphate of iron and aluminium.
S	C	O	R	Z	O	N	E	R	A	A large genus of European herbs.
S	C	R	A	M	B	L	I	N	G	Struggling, Striving, Clambering, Scurrying, Sprawling, Straggling, Scratching.
S	C	R	E	E	C	H	I	N	G	Shrieking, Squealing, Shrilling, Piercing, Screaming.
S	C	R	E	E	N	W	O	R	K	A protective screen, Grillwork.
S	C	R	I	P	T	U	R	A	L	Biblical.
S	C	R	O	B	I	C	U	L	E	A shallow trench.
S	C	R	O	U	N	G	I	N	G	Cadging, Foraging, Salvaging, Stealing, Wheedling.
S	C	R	U	B	W	O	M	A	N	Charwoman, Cleaning woman.
S	C	R	U	P	U	L	O	U	S	Principled, Painstaking, Upright, Careful, Conscientious, Strict, Honest, Honourable.
S	C	R	U	T	I	N	I	S	E	Inspect, Examine, Scan, Audit, Survey, View, Penetrate, Probe.
S	C	U	L	P	T	U	R	A	L	Relating to sculpture.
S	C	U	R	R	I	L	I	T	Y	Invective, Maligning, Abuse.
S	C	U	R	R	I	L	O	U	S	Vulgar, Evil, Obscene, Truculent, Coarse, Foul, Indecent, Insulting.
S	C	U	T	E	L	L	A	T	E	A rounded to oval flat shape with a rim.
S	E	A	K	E	E	P	I	N	G	The ability of a ship to remain at sea during a severe storm.
S	E	A	M	A	N	L	I	K	E	A competent seaman.
S	E	A	M	S	T	R	E	S	S	One who usually earns her living by sewing.
S	E	A	S	O	N	A	B	L	E	Opportune, Timely, Favourable, Auspicious, Relevant, Appropriate, Apt, Convenient.
S	E	B	A	S	T	O	D	E	S	The chief genus of rockfishes.
S	E	B	O	R	R	H	O	E	A	Increased secretion and discharge of sebum.
S	E	C	O	N	D	H	A	N	D	Used or worn befoe acquisition, Borrowed, Derived.
S	E	C	T	I	O	N	A	R	Y	Relating to a section.
S	E	C	T	I	O	N	I	Z	E	To divide into sections.
S	E	C	U	L	A	R	I	S	M	Concerned with present worldly affairs as opposed to religious doctrines.
S	E	C	U	L	A	R	I	Z	E	To transfer from ecclesiastical to civil use.
S	E	C	U	N	D	I	N	E	S	Afterbirth.
S	E	D	I	M	E	N	T	A	L	Formed from sediment.
S	E	D	U	C	E	M	E	N	T	Enticement, A seductive temptation.
S	E	D	U	L	O	U	S	L	Y	Diligently, Actively, Persistently.
S	E	E	M	L	I	N	E	S	S	Fitness, Propriety.
S	E	E	R	S	U	C	K	E	R	A cotton fabric having puckered stripes produced in the weaving.
S	E	G	M	E	N	T	A	R	Y	Composed of segments.
S	E	G	M	E	N	T	I	N	A	A genus of Asiatic freshwater snails acting as intermediate hosts of the intestinal fluke.
S	E	G	R	E	G	A	T	E	D	Isolate, Separate, Select, Insulate, Seclude, Withdraw.
S	E	G	U	I	D	I	L	L	A	A Spanish dance performed with castanets.
S	E	I	S	M	O	L	O	G	Y	A science dealing with earthquakes.
S	E	I	S	O	N	A	C	E	A	A small order of minute metazoan animals.
S	E	J	U	N	C	T	I	O	N	Separation.
S	E	L	E	N	O	D	O	N	T	Having molar teeth with crescentic ridges on the crown.
S	E	L	E	N	O	L	I	T	E	A mineral consisting of native selenium dioxide.
S	E	L	E	N	O	L	O	G	Y	A branch of astronomy that deals with the moon.
S	E	M	A	T	O	L	O	G	Y	The study of the meanings of words.
S	E	M	E	C	A	R	P	U	S	A genus of Indo-Malayan trees bearing a nut with thick black-juiced rind.
S	E	M	E	I	O	L	O	G	Y	The study of signs.
S	E	M	E	I	O	T	I	C	S	The study of the symptoms of disease.
S	E	M	E	O	S	T	O	M	E	A genus of jellyfishes.
S	E	M	I	N	A	T	I	V	E	Propagative by seed.
S	E	N	A	T	O	R	I	A	L	Composed of senators.
S	E	N	E	C	I	O	S	I	S	A frequently fatal intoxication of livestock caused by feeding on ragworts.
S	E	N	E	S	C	E	N	C	E	The period of plant growth between maturity and death.
S	E	N	G	I	E	R	I	T	E	A mineral consisting of a hydrous basic vanadate of copper and uranyl.
S	E	N	S	I	B	I	L	I	A	What is sensed.
S	E	N	S	U	A	L	I	S	M	Excessive preoccupation with sensual pleasures.
S	E	N	S	U	A	L	I	S	T	An adherent of some form of sensualism.

1	2	3	4	5	6	7	8	9	10	Meaning
S	E	N	S	U	A	L	I	T	Y	Gratification of the bodily appetites.
S	E	N	S	U	A	L	I	Z	E	Debase by carnal gratifications.
S	E	N	S	U	O	U	S	L	Y	In a sensuous manner.
S	E	N	T	E	N	T	I	A	L	Relating to a sentence.
S	E	P	A	R	A	T	E	L	Y	Individually, Indepently, Apart, Singly.
S	E	P	A	R	A	T	I	O	N	Detachment, Dissolution, Division, Partition, Rupture, Difference, Disunity.
S	E	P	A	R	A	T	I	S	M	A disposition toward secession, Individualism, Isolationism, Exclusiveness.
S	E	P	A	R	A	T	I	S	T	Nonconformist, Revolutionary, Secessionist.
S	E	P	A	R	A	T	O	R	Y	Serving to separate.
S	E	P	I	O	P	H	O	R	A	A suborder of Decapods comprising the cuttlefishes.
S	E	P	T	E	N	N	A	T	E	A period of seven years.
S	E	P	T	E	N	N	I	A	L	Occurring once every seven years.
S	E	P	T	I	C	E	M	I	A	Blood-poisoning, Septicaemia.
S	E	P	U	L	C	H	R	A	L	Mortuary.
S	E	Q	U	A	C	I	O	U	S	Subservient, Tractable, Imitative, Ductile, Pliable.
S	E	Q	U	E	N	T	I	A	L	Consecutive, Serial, Continuous, Consequent.
S	E	Q	U	E	S	T	R	U	M	A fragment of dead bone that becomes detached from the sound portion.
S	E	R	I	C	I	T	I	Z	E	To alter to sericite.
S	E	R	I	C	O	R	N	I	S	A genus of small insectivorous warblers.
S	E	R	I	G	R	A	P	H	Y	The silk screen process performed by an artist producing an original print.
S	E	R	I	O	C	O	M	I	C	Having a mixture of serious and comic.
S	E	R	M	O	N	E	T	T	E	A short sermon.
S	E	R	O	M	U	C	O	I	D	A glycoprotein of serum that is not coagulated by heat.
S	E	R	P	E	N	T	I	N	E	Resembling a snake.
S	E	R	P	E	N	T	O	I	D	Resembling a serpent, Guileful, Diabolic, Meandering, Sinuous.
S	E	R	P	H	O	I	D	E	A	A superfamily of minute wasps whose larvae are parasitic.
S	E	R	P	I	E	R	I	T	E	A mineral consisting of a hydrous basic sulfate of copper, calcium and zinc.
S	E	R	P	U	L	I	D	A	E	A large family of marine polychaete worms.
S	E	R	R	A	D	E	L	L	A	A Eurasian annual herb with honey-producing flowers, which is used for forage.
S	E	R	R	A	N	I	D	A	E	A widely distributed family of carnivorous marine fishes, Sea bass.
S	E	T	I	G	E	R	O	U	S	Bearing or producing bristles.
S	E	T	T	L	E	M	E	N	T	Regulation, Adjustment, Resolution, Determination, Decision, Residence, Habitation.
S	E	X	A	G	E	N	A	R	Y	Based on the number sixty.
S	E	X	O	L	O	G	I	S	T	A specialist in the study of sex.
S	E	Y	B	E	R	T	I	T	E	A basic aluminosilicate of the clintonite group.
S	H	A	B	B	I	N	E	S	S	The state of being shabby.
S	H	A	G	A	N	A	P	P	I	A thong of rawhide.
S	H	A	G	G	Y	M	A	N	E	A common edible mushroom.
S	H	A	M	E	F	A	C	E	D	Bashful, Ashamed.
S	H	A	T	T	E	R	I	N	G	Destructive, Demoralizing, Terrific, Overpowering, Crashing, Ruinous, Pulverising.
S	H	E	A	R	G	R	A	S	S	Various grasses with sharp-edged leaves.
S	H	E	L	T	E	R	I	N	G	Protecting, Screening, Harbouring, Shielding.
S	H	E	N	A	N	I	G	A	N	Deception, Stratagem, Prank, Escapade, Humbug, High-jinks, Caper, Ruse.
S	H	E	P	H	E	R	D	I	A	A genus of American shrubs with silvery leaves.
S	H	I	B	B	O	L	E	T	H	Catchword, Slogan, Platitude, Truism, Commonplace saying.
S	H	I	F	T	I	N	E	S	S	Trickiness, Slyness.
S	H	I	L	L	E	L	A	G	H	A cudgel used in Ireland made from oak or blackthorn.
S	H	I	M	M	E	R	I	N	G	Tremulously shining, Scintillating effect, Glimmering.
S	H	I	P	W	R	I	G	H	T	A carpenter skilled in the construction of ships.
S	H	O	A	L	G	R	A	S	S	A submerged herb of southeastern coastal America that is important as food.
S	H	O	D	D	I	N	E	S	S	The state of being shoddy.
S	H	O	E	S	T	R	I	N	G	Shoelace, Small inadequate sum of money, Minor, Petty.
S	H	O	N	K	I	N	I	T	E	A dark granular igneous rock.
S	H	O	P	K	E	E	P	E	R	Proprietor of a retail store.
S	H	O	P	L	I	F	T	E	R	One that steals merchandise from stores.
S	H	O	U	L	D	E	R	E	D	Pushed with the shoulder, Carried on the shoulder.
S	H	R	E	W	D	N	E	S	S	Acumen, Astuteness, Discrimination, Keenness, Perspicacity, Discernment.
S	H	U	D	D	E	R	I	N	G	Trembling, Quaking, Quivering, Shivering.
S	I	B	I	L	A	T	O	R	Y	Hissing, Sibilant.
S	I	C	K	L	E	R	I	T	E	A mineral consisting of a hydrous tithium manganese phosphate.
S	I	C	K	L	E	W	O	R	T	A yellow-flowered European vetch.
S	I	C	K	L	I	N	E	S	S	The state of being sickly.
S	I	D	E	S	A	D	D	L	E	A saddle designed for a woman rider to sit with both legs on the same side.
S	I	D	E	W	I	N	D	E	R	A desert rattlesnake.
S	I	L	E	N	T	I	O	U	S	Reticent, Taciturn.
S	I	L	E	N	T	N	E	S	S	Noiselessness, Speechlessness.

1	2	3	4	5	6	7	8	9	10	Clue
S	I	L	H	O	U	E	T	T	E	The outline of a person or thing.
S	I	L	I	C	A	T	I	O	N	The process of silicating.
S	I	L	I	C	I	D	I	Z	E	To convert into a silicide.
S	I	L	I	Q	U	A	R	I	A	A genus of worm shells.
S	I	L	K	S	C	R	E	E	N	Using a silk screen to colour stencil a design.
S	I	L	U	R	O	I	D	E	A	A suborder comprising the catfishes.
S	I	L	V	E	R	F	I	S	H	Wingless silvery insect injurious to clothes and books.
S	I	L	V	E	R	L	E	A	F	Plants having silvery leaves.
S	I	L	V	E	R	L	I	N	G	A small silver coin.
S	I	L	V	E	R	N	E	S	S	The quality of being silver.
S	I	L	V	E	R	S	K	I	N	The layer covering a coffee bean inside the parchment.
S	I	L	V	E	R	S	P	O	T	A butterfly having silver spots on the hind wings.
S	I	L	V	E	R	V	I	N	E	A climbing Indo-Malayan aroid, Ornamental woody vine of Asia that has edible fruits.
S	I	L	V	E	R	W	A	R	E	Cutlery and table appointments made of silver.
S	I	M	I	L	A	R	I	T	Y	Resemblance, Conformity, Analogy, Correspondence, Likeness, Affinity, Parallel.
S	I	M	I	L	I	T	U	D	E	Counterpart, Double, Image, Semblance, Allegory, Simile, Replica, Uniformity.
S	I	M	P	L	I	C	I	T	Y	Fundamental, Innocence, Clarity, Austerity, Restraint, Plainness, Genuineness.
S	I	M	P	L	I	S	T	I	C	Characterised by concentrating on a single aspect.
S	I	M	P	S	O	N	I	T	E	A mineral consisting of an oxide of aluminium and tantalum.
S	I	M	U	L	A	C	R	U	M	Image, Effigy, Imitation, Sham, Appearance, Imposture, Copy.
S	I	M	U	L	A	T	I	O	N	Imitation, Pretense, Counterfeit, Collusion, Analogue, Misrepresentation.
S	I	M	U	L	I	I	D	A	E	A family of small biting two-winged flies.
S	I	N	G	L	E	N	E	S	S	Sincerity, Honesty, Celibacy, Uniqueness, Unity, Individuality, Singularity.
S	I	N	G	U	L	A	R	L	Y	Exceptionally, Respectively, Strangely, Curiously.
S	I	N	I	S	T	E	R	L	Y	In a sinister manner.
S	I	N	O	A	T	R	I	A	L	Relating to the sinus venosus and the right auricle of the heart.
S	I	N	O	L	O	G	I	S	T	One who studies China, its language and culture.
S	I	N	O	M	E	N	I	N	E	A crystalline alkaloid obtained from various eastern Asiatic plants.
S	I	P	H	O	N	A	L	E	S	An order of marine and freshwater green algae.
S	I	P	H	O	N	A	R	I	A	The type genus of a family of gastropod mollusks.
S	I	S	E	R	S	K	I	T	E	A mineral consisting of a natural alloy of osmium and iridium.
S	I	S	T	E	R	H	O	O	D	A community or society of women.
S	I	S	Y	M	B	R	I	U	M	A genus of annual and biennial herbs.
S	I	T	O	P	H	I	L	U	S	A widely distributed genus of weevils containing two that are very destructive to grain.
S	K	E	L	E	T	O	N	I	C	Resembling that of a skeleton.
S	K	E	P	T	I	C	I	S	M	The doctrine that all knowledge is uncertain.
S	K	E	T	C	H	B	O	O	K	A notebook of preliminary sketches.
S	K	I	A	G	R	A	P	H	Y	The science of projecting shadows.
S	K	I	M	M	I	N	G	L	Y	In a skimming manner.
S	K	I	N	N	I	N	E	S	S	The state of being skinny.
S	K	I	T	T	I	S	H	L	Y	Capriciously, Irresponsibly, Restively.
S	K	Y	S	C	R	A	P	E	R	A tall narrow many-storied building.
S	K	Y	W	R	I	T	I	N	G	Writing formed in the sky by means of smoke emitted from an aeroplane.
S	L	A	C	K	E	N	I	N	G	Moderating, Abating, Loosening, Delaying, Retarding, Relaxing, Ebbing, Waning.
S	L	A	N	D	E	R	O	U	S	Caluminious, Libelous, Defamatory, Maligning, Vilifying, Traducing.
S	L	A	T	T	E	R	N	L	Y	Slovenly, Unkempt, Careless, Disorderly, Dowdy, Frowzy, Blowsy, Sordid.
S	L	A	V	O	C	R	A	C	Y	A powerful faction of slave-owners before the American Civil War.
S	L	E	A	Z	I	N	E	S	S	The state of being sleazy.
S	L	E	E	P	I	N	E	S	S	The state of being sleepy.
S	L	E	N	D	E	R	I	Z	E	To make slender.
S	L	I	D	O	M	E	T	E	R	A railroad instrument for recording shocks by the sudden stopping of carriages.
S	L	O	P	W	O	R	K	E	R	A worker making cheap ready-made clothing.
S	L	U	G	G	I	S	H	L	Y	Slowly, Indolently.
S	L	U	M	B	E	R	O	U	S	Sleepy, Somnolent, Calm, Peaceful, Lethargic, Soporific, Drowsy, Comatoase.
S	L	U	S	H	I	N	E	S	S	Sentimentality.
S	M	A	L	L	S	W	O	R	D	A light tapering sword designed for thrusting and used for fencing.
S	M	A	R	A	G	D	I	N	E	Relating to emerald.
S	M	A	R	A	G	D	I	T	E	A mineral consisting of a green foliated amphibole.
S	M	A	T	T	E	R	I	N	G	Handful, Scattering, Sprinkling, Few, Frittering.
S	M	I	L	A	G	E	N	I	N	A steroid sapogenin obtained from a sarsaparilla.
S	M	O	K	E	H	O	U	S	E	A building where meat or fish is cured by means of dense smoke.
S	M	O	T	H	E	R	I	N	G	Suffocating, Stifling, Smouldering.
S	N	A	P	E	H	E	A	D	S	A diagonal connecting timber on a wooden ship.
S	N	A	P	D	R	A	G	O	N	A garden plant of the genus Antirrhinum.
S	N	A	P	P	I	N	G	L	Y	In a snapping manner.
S	N	E	A	K	I	N	E	S	S	The state of being sneaky.
S	N	E	E	Z	E	W	E	E	D	A North American perennial herb with yellow flowers reputed to cause sneezing.

10 LETTERS

1	2	3	4	5	6	7	8	9	10	
S	N	E	E	Z	E	W	O	O	D	A South African tree with hard valuable wood, that yields sawdust.
S	N	E	E	Z	E	W	O	R	T	A strong-scented Eurasian perennial herb.
S	N	I	G	G	E	R	I	N	G	Tittering, Giggling.
S	N	O	W	B	R	I	D	G	E	A bridge of snow across a crevasse.
S	N	O	W	M	O	B	I	L	E	An automatic vehicle used for travelling on snow.
S	O	B	E	R	S	I	D	E	D	Grave, Serious, Earnest, Staid, Solemn.
S	O	C	I	O	C	R	A	C	Y	A theoretical form of government in which society as a whole has sovereign rights.
S	O	C	I	O	G	E	N	I	C	Determined by society.
S	O	C	I	O	L	O	G	I	C	Directed toward social needs and problems.
S	O	C	I	O	M	E	T	R	Y	The study of the pattern of interrelation existing in a group of people.
S	O	F	T	H	E	A	D	E	D	Impractical, Lacking judgment.
S	O	L	A	N	I	D	I	N	E	A crystalline steroidal alkaloid.
S	O	L	A	S	O	D	I	N	E	A crystalline steroidal alkaloid closely related to solanidine.
S	O	L	A	S	O	N	I	N	E	A crystalline glycosidal alkaloid obtained from solanaceous plants.
S	O	L	D	A	N	E	L	L	A	A small genus of European low-growing perennial alpine herbs.
S	O	L	D	I	E	R	I	Z	E	To convert into a soldier.
S	O	L	E	C	I	S	T	I	C	Incorrect, Incongruous, Unseemly.
S	O	L	E	N	A	C	E	A	N	Resembling marine clams.
S	O	L	E	N	O	P	S	I	S	A genus of small stinging ants.
S	O	L	I	C	I	T	I	N	G	Inciting, Entreating, Importuning, Petitioning, Attracting, Requiring, Canvassing.
S	O	L	I	C	I	T	O	U	S	Anxious, Eager, Ardent, Impatient, Keen, Apprehensive, Troubled, Concerned.
S	O	L	I	C	I	T	U	D	E	Anxiety, Disquietude, Care, Unease, Worry, Scruple, Consideration.
S	O	L	I	D	A	R	I	T	Y	Community of action, interests and objectives.
S	O	L	I	D	A	R	I	Z	E	To come together.
S	O	L	I	G	E	N	O	U	S	Produced by inflow of surface water.
S	O	L	I	T	A	R	I	L	Y	In solitude.
S	O	L	I	V	A	G	A	N	T	A solitary wanderer, Rambling alone.
S	O	L	P	U	G	I	D	E	A	An order of hairy arachnids bearing a close resemblence to scorpions.
S	O	L	S	T	I	T	I	A	L	Relating to a solstice.
S	O	L	U	B	I	L	I	T	Y	The state of being soluble.
S	O	L	U	B	I	L	I	Z	E	To make soluble.
S	O	L	U	T	I	O	N	A	L	Constituting a solution.
S	O	L	V	O	L	Y	S	I	S	A chemical reaction of a solvent and a dissolved substance.
S	O	M	A	T	O	L	O	G	Y	Physical anthropology.
S	O	M	A	T	O	T	Y	P	E	Body type, Physique, Classify according to physique.
S	O	M	E	R	S	A	U	L	T	Turning end over end, A complete overturn or reversal.
S	O	M	N	A	M	B	U	L	E	Somnambulist, Sleep-walker.
S	O	M	N	I	L	O	Q	U	Y	The practice of talking in one's sleep.
S	O	M	N	I	P	A	T	H	Y	Abnormal or disordered sleep.
S	O	M	N	O	L	E	N	C	E	Drowsiness, Sleepiness.
S	O	M	N	O	G	E	N	I	C	Tending to induce sleep.
S	O	N	G	W	R	I	T	E	R	One who composes word and or music for performances.
S	O	N	N	E	R	A	T	I	A	A genus of trees and shrubs having large bell-shaped flowers followed by pulpy berries.
S	O	N	O	R	O	U	S	L	Y	In a resonant manner.
S	O	O	T	H	I	N	G	L	Y	In a calming fashion.
S	O	O	T	H	S	A	Y	E	R	One who speaks wisdom, Prognosticator, Prophet, Forecaster.
S	O	P	H	I	O	L	O	G	Y	A system of thought based on divine wisdom.
S	O	P	H	O	M	O	R	I	C	Superficial.
S	O	P	H	R	O	S	Y	N	E	Temperance, Self-control, Prudence.
S	O	R	D	I	D	N	E	S	S	The state of being sordid.
S	O	R	I	C	O	D	O	N	T	Having teeth like shrews with the middle incisors very large.
S	O	R	I	C	O	I	D	E	A	A superfamily of insectivores consisting of the shrews and moles.
S	O	R	O	R	I	C	I	D	E	The killing of one's sister.
S	O	S	T	E	N	E	N	T	E	Sustaining.
S	O	U	B	R	E	S	A	U	T	A ballet jump and landing with both feet in a closed position.
S	O	U	N	D	B	O	A	R	D	A thin board placed in an instrument to increase resonance.
S	O	U	N	D	P	R	O	O	F	Impervious to sound usually achieved by insulation.
S	O	U	S	A	P	H	O	N	E	A large circular tuba having a flaring adjustable bell.
S	O	U	T	E	R	R	A	I	N	An underground passage.
S	O	U	T	H	W	A	R	D	S	In a southerly direction.
S	P	A	C	E	C	R	A	F	T	A vehicle designed to travel in space.
S	P	A	C	I	O	U	S	L	Y	Expansively.
S	P	A	D	I	C	E	O	U	S	Bearing flowers on a spadix.
S	P	A	L	A	C	I	D	A	E	A family of Old World rodents comprising the mole rats.
S	P	A	N	G	O	L	I	T	E	A mineral consisting of a hydrous basic sulfate and chloride of aluminium and copper.
S	P	A	R	G	A	N	I	U	M	A genus of marsh or aquatic herbs.
S	P	A	R	K	I	N	E	S	S	Liveliness, Vivaciousness.

1	2	3	4	5	6	7	8	9	10	Definition
S	P	A	R	M	A	N	N	I	A	A small genus of African shrubs or trees.
S	P	A	R	T	A	N	I	S	M	Self-discipline, Endurance.
S	P	A	R	T	A	N	I	Z	E	To live in an austere fashion.
S	P	A	S	M	O	D	I	S	T	One that is spasmodic in work or manner.
S	P	A	S	M	O	N	E	M	E	A contractile filament.
S	P	A	T	A	N	G	I	D	A	A suborder of sea urchins.
S	P	A	T	H	U	L	A	T	E	Shaped like a spatula.
S	P	A	T	T	E	R	I	N	G	Scattering, Sprinkling, Splashing, Spotting.
S	P	E	C	I	A	L	I	S	T	A person who limits his interest to a special subject.
S	P	E	C	I	A	L	I	T	Y	A special distinctive characteristic.
S	P	E	C	I	A	T	I	O	N	Formation of bilogical species.
S	P	E	C	I	O	S	I	T	Y	A specious appearance.
S	P	E	C	T	A	T	O	R	Y	A section set aside for spectators, A group of spectators.
S	P	E	C	U	L	A	T	O	R	One who speculates in business.
S	P	E	E	D	L	I	G	H	T	An electronic flash lamp.
S	P	E	L	E	O	L	O	G	Y	The scientific study of caves.
S	P	E	L	E	O	T	H	E	M	A cave deposit or formation.
S	P	E	L	L	B	O	U	N	D	Fascinated, Enthralled, Mesmerized.
S	P	E	L	U	N	K	I	N	G	The practice of exploring caves.
S	P	E	N	C	E	R	I	T	E	A mineral consisting of a hydrous basic zinc phosphate.
S	P	E	R	M	A	C	E	T	I	A white crystalline waxy solid that separates from sperm oil.
S	P	E	R	M	A	T	I	S	M	Emission of sperm.
S	P	E	R	M	A	T	O	U	S	Having seeds.
S	P	E	R	M	I	D	I	N	E	A crystalline aliphatic triamine.
S	P	E	R	M	O	T	Y	P	E	A botanical type from a plant grown from the seed of a primary type.
S	P	E	R	R	Y	L	I	T	E	A platinum arsenide occurring as a mineral.
S	P	H	A	C	E	L	A	T	E	Mortify, To become gangrenous.
S	P	H	A	C	E	L	O	M	A	A form genus of imperfect fungi.
S	P	H	A	G	N	A	L	E	S	A genus of mosses.
S	P	H	A	L	E	R	I	T	E	A widely distributed ore of zinc.
S	P	H	E	C	O	I	D	E	A	A family comprising solitary wasps and some true bees.
S	P	H	E	N	I	S	C	U	S	A genus of penguins including the jackass penguin.
S	P	H	E	N	O	G	R	A	M	A wedge-shaped character as in an inscription.
S	P	H	E	N	O	L	I	T	H	A wedge-shaped intrusive mass of igneous rock.
S	P	H	E	R	O	I	D	A	L	Taking the form of a sphere.
S	P	H	E	R	O	I	D	I	C	Having the form of a spheroid.
S	P	H	E	R	U	L	I	T	E	A spherical crystalline body made up of radiating crystal fibres.
S	P	H	E	T	E	R	I	Z	E	Appropriate.
S	P	H	I	N	D	I	D	A	E	A family of small beetles living in dry fungi on trees.
S	P	H	I	N	G	I	D	A	E	A family of strong-flying moths that comprise the hawkmoths.
S	P	H	Y	R	N	I	D	A	E	A family of sharks including the hammerheads.
S	P	I	D	E	R	L	I	N	G	A very young spider.
S	P	I	D	E	R	W	O	R	T	A plant having blue flowers with slender hairy stamens.
S	P	I	F	L	I	C	A	T	E	To overcome by violence.
S	P	I	L	A	N	T	H	E	S	A genus of widely distributed herbs.
S	P	I	N	A	C	E	O	U	S	Resembling spinach.
S	P	I	N	E	S	C	E	N	T	Tapering to a sharp point.
S	P	I	N	N	E	R	U	L	E	A small tube for discharging the silk of a spider.
S	P	I	R	A	N	T	H	E	S	A genus of terrestrial orchids.
S	P	I	R	I	T	E	D	L	Y	With liveliness or vivacity.
S	P	I	R	I	T	L	E	S	S	Dead, Lifeless, Dejected, Depressed.
S	P	I	R	O	C	E	R	C	A	A genus of red filarial worms parasitic to dogs and other canines.
S	P	I	R	O	C	H	E	T	E	A bacterium which causes severe diseases as syphilis.
S	P	I	R	O	M	E	T	E	R	An instrument for measuring the air entering and leaving the lungs.
S	P	I	R	O	G	R	A	P	H	An instrument for recording respiratory movements.
S	P	I	R	O	M	E	T	R	Y	Measurement of air or gas by use of a spirometer.
S	P	I	R	U	R	I	D	A	E	A family of parasitic nematode worms.
S	P	I	S	S	I	T	U	D	E	Density, Viscosity.
S	P	L	E	E	N	W	O	R	T	A fern that was once believed to cure disorders of the spleen.
S	P	L	E	N	C	U	L	U	S	A small accessory spleen.
S	P	L	E	N	I	C	U	L	E	Same as SPLENCULUS.
S	P	O	D	O	P	T	E	R	A	A genus of armyworms that are destructive pests.
S	P	O	K	E	S	H	A	V	E	A small transverse plane for smoothing convex or concave surfaces.
S	P	O	L	I	A	T	I	O	N	Plundering, Pillaging, Robbery, Ravaging, Desecrating, Devastating, Raiding.
S	P	O	N	G	I	F	O	R	M	Spongy, Porous.
S	P	O	N	G	I	I	D	A	E	A family of horny sponges.
S	P	O	N	G	I	O	S	I	S	A swelling localized in the epidermis.

1	2	3	4	5	6	7	8	9	10	
S	P	O	N	S	O	R	I	A	L	Relating to a sponsor.
S	P	O	O	N	E	R	I	S	M	Interchange of the initial letter of two words which usually causes amusement.
S	P	O	R	A	N	G	I	T	E	A fossilized spore case of a plant.
S	P	O	R	O	B	L	A	S	T	A cell of a sporozoan resulting from sexual reproduction.
S	P	O	R	O	B	O	L	U	S	A widely distributed genus of grasses.
S	P	O	R	O	C	H	N	U	S	A small genus of brown algae.
S	P	O	R	O	P	H	Y	L	L	A spore-bearing leaf.
S	P	O	R	O	P	L	A	S	M	A mass of protoplasm that forms a spore.
S	P	O	R	O	T	H	R	I	X	A fungus.
S	P	O	R	T	S	W	E	A	R	Clothing suitable for wearing while engaged in sport.
S	P	R	I	N	G	E	R	L	E	A thick hard cookie flavoured with anise and usually eaten at Christmas by Germans.
S	P	U	M	E	S	C	E	N	T	Frothy, Foamy.
S	P	U	R	I	O	U	S	L	Y	Pretentiously, Falsely.
S	Q	U	A	B	B	L	I	N	G	Wrangling, Quarrelling, Bickering, Fighting, Disputing, Hassling, Clashing, Arguing.
S	Q	U	A	L	I	D	I	T	Y	The state of being squalid.
S	Q	U	A	L	O	I	D	E	A	A suborder comprising some sharks.
S	Q	U	A	M	A	T	I	O	N	The state of being covered in scales.
S	Q	U	A	M	I	F	O	R	M	Having the shape of a scale.
S	Q	U	A	M	O	S	I	T	Y	A scaly area.
S	Q	U	A	M	U	L	O	S	E	Covered with minute scales.
S	Q	U	A	N	D	E	R	E	D	Dissipated, Wasted, Scattered, Frittered, Lavished.
S	Q	U	A	T	A	R	O	L	A	A genus of birds consisting of plovers.
S	Q	U	I	L	L	I	D	A	E	A family of stomatopod crustaceans.
S	T	A	B	L	E	M	A	T	E	Two or more horses having the same owner.
S	T	A	C	H	Y	U	R	U	S	A small genus of Asiatic shrubs and trees having small globose fruits.
S	T	A	G	G	E	R	I	N	G	Astonishing, Overwhelming, Amazing, Astounding, Surprising, Lurching, Reeling.
S	T	A	G	N	A	T	I	O	N	Torpor, Depression, Recession, Slump.
S	T	A	G	N	I	C	O	L	A	A genus of common freshwater snails.
S	T	A	L	A	C	T	I	T	E	A deposit of crystalline calcium carbonate resembling an icicle hanging from the roof.
S	T	A	L	A	G	M	I	T	E	A deposit of crystalline calcium carbonate formed on the floor of a cave.
S	T	A	L	W	A	R	T	L	Y	In a stalwart manner.
S	T	A	N	D	S	T	I	L	L	Stop, Stay, Arrest, Check, Pause, Cessation, Halt.
S	T	A	P	H	Y	L	O	M	A	A protrusion of the cornea of the eye of the mammal.
S	T	A	R	B	R	I	G	H	T	Bright as a star, Studded with stars.
S	T	A	R	G	A	Z	I	N	G	Day dreaming, Absentmindedness.
S	T	A	R	R	I	N	E	S	S	The state of being starry.
S	T	A	R	V	A	T	I	O	N	The state of being starved.
S	T	A	R	V	E	L	I	N	G	One that is thin from lack of nutriment.
S	T	A	T	E	C	R	A	F	T	Statesmanship, State management.
S	T	A	T	I	C	A	L	L	Y	With static electricity, In stable or unchanging terms.
S	T	A	T	I	O	N	A	R	Y	Immobile, Stable, Static, Stagnant, Motionless, Unmoving.
S	T	A	T	I	O	N	E	R	Y	Materials for writing or typing as sold by a stationer.
S	T	A	T	I	S	T	I	C	S	The collection, interpretation and presentation of masses of numerical data.
S	T	A	T	O	B	L	A	S	T	A bud or germ of freshwater bryozoans that only develop in the spring.
S	T	A	T	O	L	A	T	R	Y	Worship of the state, Advocacy of an all-powerful national government.
S	T	A	T	U	E	S	Q	U	E	Majestic, Tall, Shapely, Inflexible, Rigid, Dignified.
S	T	A	U	R	O	L	I	T	E	A mineral consisting of a brown to black basic iron aluminium silicate.
S	T	E	A	D	I	N	E	S	S	Stability, Soundness, Strength, Security, Firmness.
S	T	E	A	L	T	H	I	L	Y	Secretly, Clandestinely, Covertly, Furtively, Privately, Surreptitiously.
S	T	E	A	M	I	N	E	S	S	The state of being steamy.
S	T	E	G	A	N	O	P	O	D	A bird having all four toes webbed, Pelicans.
S	T	E	I	G	E	R	I	T	E	A mineral consisting of hydrous aluminium vandate.
S	T	E	I	R	O	N	E	M	A	A small genus of North American herbs.
S	T	E	L	L	I	F	O	R	M	Shaped like a star.
S	T	E	M	O	N	I	T	I	S	A genus of slime moulds.
S	T	E	N	C	I	L	I	Z	E	To cut into a stencil.
S	T	E	N	O	C	I	O	U	S	Capable of surviving in only a narrow range of environments.
S	T	E	N	O	M	E	T	E	R	An instrument for measuring distances.
S	T	E	N	O	T	O	P	I	C	Having a narrow range of adaptability to changes in environmental conditions.
S	T	E	N	T	O	R	I	A	N	Extremely loud, Blaring, Piercing, Roaring, Clamorous, Vociferous.
S	T	E	P	F	A	T	H	E	R	The husband of one's mother by a subsequent marriage.
S	T	E	P	H	A	N	I	T	E	A mineral consisting of an orthorhombic iron black sulfide of silver and antimony.
S	T	E	P	H	A	N	O	M	E	An instrument for measuring the angular dimensions of foxbows and halos.
S	T	E	P	L	A	D	D	E	R	A set of treads with a hinged back for support.
S	T	E	P	M	O	T	H	E	R	The wife of one's father by a subsequent marriage.
S	T	E	R	C	O	R	A	R	Y	A place for the storage of manure.
S	T	E	R	C	O	R	I	T	E	A native microcosmic salt occurring in guano.

10 LETTERS

1	2	3	4	5	6	7	8	9	10	Definition
S	T	E	R	E	O	B	A	T	E	Basement of masonry visible above the ground level.
S	T	E	R	E	O	G	R	A	M	A diagram representing objects with an impression of solidity.
S	T	E	R	E	O	P	S	I	S	Capacity for depth perception.
S	T	E	R	E	O	T	O	M	Y	The art of stonecutting.
S	T	E	R	E	O	T	Y	P	E	Repeat without variation, To fix in a rigidly precise form.
S	T	E	R	I	L	I	Z	E	R	An apparatus for sterilizing using boiling water, steam or dry heat.
S	T	E	R	R	A	S	T	E	R	A spherical sponge spicule with many small rays.
S	T	E	R	T	O	R	O	U	S	Characterized by a harsh snoring or grasping sound, Loud.
S	T	E	V	I	O	S	I	D	E	A hygroscopic crystalline intensely sweet glucoside obtained from Paraguayan shrub.
S	T	E	W	A	R	D	E	S	S	A woman who performs the duties of a steward.
S	T	E	W	A	R	T	I	T	E	A mineral consisting of a hydrous phosphate of manganese.
S	T	I	C	H	A	R	I	O	N	An ecclesiastical vestment.
S	T	I	C	H	I	D	I	U	M	A special branch of the thallus of a red algae.
S	T	I	C	T	A	C	E	A	E	A family of common foliaceous lichens.
S	T	I	C	T	I	F	O	R	M	Resembling a lichen.
S	T	I	G	M	A	T	I	S	M	The condition of an optical system in which rays of light from a single point converge.
S	T	I	G	M	A	T	I	Z	E	Censure, Denounce, Designate, Identify.
S	T	I	G	M	O	D	E	R	A	A large genus of Australian brilliantly green beetles.
S	T	I	L	L	I	F	O	R	M	Shaped like a tear-drop.
S	T	I	M	U	L	A	T	E	D	Animated, Goaded, Aroused, ‛ovoked, Excited, Motivated, Activated, Inspired.
S	T	I	M	U	L	A	T	O	R	One that stimulates.
S	T	I	P	I	T	U	R	U	S	A genus of small babblers comprising the Australian emu wrens.
S	T	O	C	H	A	S	T	I	C	Random.
S	T	O	M	A	T	I	T	I	S	An inflammatory disease of the mouth.
S	T	O	R	E	H	O	U	S	E	Warehouse, Depot, Store, Repository.
S	T	O	R	I	A	T	I	O	N	Ornamentation with designs representing historical subjects.
S	T	O	R	Y	B	O	A	R	D	A series of panels used for exhibiting drawings of the consecutive action of a film.
S	T	R	A	B	I	S	M	U	S	Inability of one eye to attain binocular vision with the other because of imbalance.
S	T	R	A	B	O	T	O	M	Y	Surgical severance of a tendon to correct a "squint".
S	T	R	A	I	G	H	T	E	N	To alter crooked to straight, To alter for the better.
S	T	R	A	I	T	E	N	E	D	Narrowed, Restricted, Tightened, Afflicted, Distressed, Tensed.
S	T	R	A	I	T	L	A	C	E	Confine, Restrain.
S	T	R	A	M	O	N	I	U	M	The dried leaf of the thorn apple, used in medicine in a similar fashion to belladonna.
S	T	R	A	T	I	F	O	R	M	Having a formation of parallel zones.
S	T	R	A	W	B	E	R	R	Y	A juicy edible red fruit.
S	T	R	E	A	M	L	I	N	E	Line of flow, A fluid line, Simplify, Modernize, Organize.
S	T	R	E	N	G	T	H	E	N	Encourage, Hearten, Augment, Intensify, Fortify, Invigorate, Reinforce, Animate.
S	T	R	E	P	I	T	O	S	O	Direction in music - noisy, impetuous.
S	T	R	I	D	E	N	T	L	Y	Harshly, Shrilly.
S	T	R	I	D	U	L	A	T	E	To make a shrill and sometimes vibrating noise.
S	T	R	I	D	U	L	E	N	T	Raucous, Discordant, Harsh.
S	T	R	I	D	U	L	O	U	S	Squeaky, Shrill.
S	T	R	I	G	E	I	D	A	E	A family of digenetic trematodes, some of which are parasitic.
S	T	R	I	G	O	V	I	T	E	A mineral consisting of a basic silicate of iron and aluminium of the chlorite group.
S	T	R	I	N	G	E	N	C	Y	Severity, Strictness, Rigour, Harshness, Exactitude.
S	T	R	I	N	G	H	A	L	T	Muscular spasms causing lameness in the hind legs of a horse.
S	T	R	I	P	P	A	B	L	E	Capable of being stripped.
S	T	R	I	P	T	E	A	S	E	An act where a performer removes their clothing piece by piece in a titillating fashion.
S	T	R	O	B	O	T	R	O	N	A gas-filled electron tube with a cold cathode.
S	T	R	O	G	A	N	O	F	F	Thinly sliced meat cooked in a sauce of sour cream, mustard and onions.
S	T	R	O	M	B	I	D	A	E	A family of large marine gastropod molluscs, Tropical conchs.
S	T	R	O	N	G	B	A	R	K	A small tree of southern Florida with strong hard wood, streaked with orange.
S	T	R	O	N	G	H	O	L	D	Fortress, Refuge, Citadel, Redoubt.
S	T	R	O	N	G	Y	L	I	D	A parasitical nematode worm.
S	T	R	O	N	G	Y	L	U	S	Same as STRONGYLID.
S	T	R	O	P	H	A	R	I	A	A genus of brown spored gill fungi.
S	T	R	O	P	H	U	L	U	S	A red rash in infants usually prevalent at teething time.
S	T	R	U	C	T	U	R	A	L	Constructional, Relating to building.
S	T	R	U	T	H	I	O	U	S	Relating to the ostriches.
S	T	R	Y	C	H	N	I	N	E	A very poisonous bitter crystalline alkaloid obtained from various plants.
S	T	U	B	B	O	R	N	L	Y	Obstinately, Adamantly, Inflexibly, Rigidly, Steadfastly.
S	T	U	D	I	O	U	S	L	Y	In a studious fashion.
S	T	U	P	E	N	D	O	U	S	Awesome, Marvellous, Monstrous, Amazing, Spectacular, Fantastic, Tremendous.
S	T	U	R	D	I	N	E	S	S	The state of being sturdy.
S	T	U	T	T	E	R	I	N	G	An impediment in the speech marked by a spasmodic repetition of vocal sounds.
S	T	Y	F	S	I	E	K	T	E	A sickness peculiar to the cattle in Africa.
S	T	Y	L	I	S	T	I	C	S	The study of optional variations in the sounds, forms or vocabulary of a language.

1	2	3	4	5	6	7	8	9	10	
S	T	Y	L	O	G	R	A	P	H	Fountain pen with fine perforated writing point.
S	T	Y	L	O	M	E	T	R	Y	The study of the chronology and development of the work of an author.
S	T	Y	L	O	P	I	D	A	E	A family of insects that have protuberant eyes and are parasites of other insects.
S	T	Y	P	T	I	C	I	T	Y	Astringency.
S	T	Y	R	A	C	I	T	O	L	A crystalline heterocyclic alcohol obtained from the fruit of a Japanese shrubby tree.
S	U	B	C	L	A	V	A	T	E	Somewhat club-shaped.
S	U	B	C	L	A	V	I	U	S	A small muscle extending from the first rib to the clavicle.
S	U	B	D	U	C	T	I	O	N	Withdrawal, Deduction, Subjection.
S	U	B	F	L	U	V	I	A	L	Situated at the bottom of a body of water, Passing under a river.
S	U	B	F	O	R	E	M	A	N	An employee supervising a group but answerable to the foreman.
S	U	B	G	L	A	C	I	A	L	The area immediately underlying a glacier.
S	U	B	J	E	C	T	I	O	N	Subjugation, Being under the power or control of another.
S	U	B	J	E	C	T	I	V	E	Relating to a subject, Abstract, Biased, Prejudiced, Fanciful, Illusory.
S	U	B	L	I	M	I	N	A	L	Inadequate for perception, Too small for discrimination.
S	U	B	M	E	R	G	E	N	T	Partly submerged.
S	U	B	M	E	R	S	I	O	N	The state of being submerged.
S	U	B	M	I	S	S	I	O	N	Surrender, Capitulation, Bowing, Acquiesence, Compliance, Resignation, Servility.
S	U	B	M	I	S	S	I	V	E	Yielding, Obedient, Humble, Tame.
S	U	B	M	O	N	T	A	N	E	Situated at the base of a mountain.
S	U	B	M	U	N	D	A	N	E	Underground, Subterranean.
S	U	B	N	A	S	C	E	N	T	Growing up or arising from beneath something.
S	U	B	N	U	C	L	E	U	S	A subdivision of a nucleus usually nervous tissue.
S	U	B	R	E	P	T	A	R	Y	Adapted primarily to crawling.
S	U	B	R	E	P	T	I	O	N	Secret, Underhanded and unlawful representation through suppression of facts.
S	U	B	S	C	R	I	B	E	R	One that favours, aids or supports, Contributor.
S	U	B	S	E	Q	U	E	N	T	Succeeding, Following, Next, Resultant, Consecutive, Successive.
S	U	B	S	I	D	E	N	C	E	Falling, Lowering, Flattening out.
S	U	B	S	I	D	I	A	R	Y	Supplementary, Minor, Secondary, Contributory, Auxiliary, Accessory, Subservient.
S	U	B	S	I	D	I	Z	E	D	Aided, Promoted, Endowed, Financed, Funded, Helped.
S	U	B	S	I	S	T	E	N	T	Subsisting, Inherent.
S	U	B	S	T	A	T	I	O	N	A station to convert high-tension electricity.
S	U	B	S	T	I	T	U	T	E	Alternative, Surrogate, Additional, Other, Second, Reserve, Supplementary.
S	U	B	S	T	R	A	T	A	L	Basic, Underlying.
S	U	B	S	U	L	T	O	R	Y	Bounding, Leaping.
S	U	B	S	U	R	F	A	C	E	Just beneath the surface.
S	U	B	T	E	R	F	U	G	E	Deception, Refuge, Cheat, Dishonesty, Fraud, Trickery.
S	U	B	T	R	A	H	E	N	D	Quantity or number to be subtracted.
S	U	B	V	E	N	T	I	O	N	Endownment, Grant, Subsidy, Financial assistance.
S	U	B	V	E	R	S	I	O	N	Destruction, Sabotage, Undermining, Demolishing, Destroying, Wrecking.
S	U	C	C	E	E	D	I	N	G	Consecutive, Subsequent, Serial, Attaining, Achieving, Accomplishing, Prevailing.
S	U	C	C	E	S	S	I	O	N	Order, Sequence, Chain, Course, Order, Progression, Series, Train.
S	U	C	C	E	S	S	I	V	E	Hereditary, Consecutive, Inherited, Succeeding.
S	U	C	C	I	N	C	T	L	Y	Concisely, Briefly, Tersely, Shortly, Laconically.
S	U	C	C	O	R	R	H	E	A	Excessive flow of a juice or secretion.
S	U	C	C	U	L	E	N	C	E	Juiciness, Silage.
S	U	C	C	U	S	S	I	O	N	The action of shaking.
S	U	D	A	T	O	R	I	U	M	A sweat room in a bath.
S	U	F	F	E	R	A	B	L	E	Endurable, Tolerable, Permissible.
S	U	F	F	E	R	A	N	C	E	Long-suffering, Pain, Misery, Permission, Consent, Permit, Sanction.
S	U	F	F	I	C	I	E	N	T	Enough, Adequate, Competent, Sufficing, Plentiful, Commensurate, Agreeable.
S	U	F	F	L	A	T	I	O	N	Inspiration.
S	U	F	F	R	A	G	I	S	M	Supporting women's suffrage.
S	U	G	G	E	S	T	I	O	N	Instigation, Temptation, Proposal, Intimation, Hint, Prompting, Trace, Notion.
S	U	G	G	E	S	T	I	V	E	Evocative, Indicative, Significant, Risque, Erotic, Sexy.
S	U	I	C	I	D	A	L	L	Y	Tending toward self-destruction.
S	U	L	F	U	R	E	O	U	S	Consisting of sulphur.
S	U	L	L	E	N	N	E	S	S	The state of being sullen.
S	U	N	G	L	A	S	S	E	S	Spectacles, usually tinted, to protect the eyes from sunlight.
S	U	P	E	R	P	O	W	E	R	Excessive, Abnormal, Superior power, An extremely powerful or dominant nation.
S	U	P	E	R	S	O	N	I	C	Having a frequency above the audibility range of the human ear.
S	U	P	E	R	V	I	S	O	R	One that supervises a person, group, department or operation.
S	U	P	E	R	W	O	M	A	N	A superior woman, A strong-minded, efficient and forceful woman.
S	U	P	P	L	E	M	E	N	T	Complement, Appendix, Addition, Codicil.
S	U	P	P	L	I	C	A	N	T	Petitioner, Suitor, Beggar.
S	U	P	P	O	R	T	I	N	G	Advocating, Sustaining, Propping, Bolstering, Bracing, Aiding, Assisting, Comforting.
S	U	P	P	O	R	T	I	V	E	Furnishing support.
S	U	P	R	A	N	A	S	A	L	Situated above the nose.

1	2	3	4	5	6	7	8	9	10	Definition
S	U	P	R	A	R	E	N	A	L	Situated above the kidneys.
S	U	R	E	F	O	O	T	E	D	Unlikely to make a slip or error, Moving confidently.
S	U	R	F	A	C	T	A	N	T	Surface-active agent.
S	U	R	N	O	M	I	N	A	L	Relating to a surname.
S	U	R	P	A	S	S	I	N	G	Supreme, Transcedent, Ultimate, Incomparable, Very high degree of excellence.
S	U	R	P	R	I	S	I	N	G	Amazing, Astonishing, Admirable, Miraculous, Prodigious, Spectacular, Stupendous.
S	U	R	R	E	A	L	I	S	M	The practice of producing fantastic or incongruous imagery in art.
S	U	R	R	O	U	N	D	E	D	Inundated, Submerged, Encircled, Encompassed, Girdled, Looped, Confined.
S	U	R	S	A	S	S	I	T	E	A mineral of the epidote group consisting of a hydrous silicate of manganese.
S	U	R	V	I	V	A	B	L	E	Capable of surviving.
S	U	S	C	E	P	T	I	V	E	Susceptible.
S	U	S	P	E	N	S	I	O	N	Abeyance, Dormancy, Interruption, Quiesence, Cessation, Finish, Conclusion.
S	U	S	P	E	N	S	I	V	E	Temporary suspension.
S	U	S	P	E	N	D	I	N	G	Suspending.
S	U	S	P	I	C	I	O	U	S	Questionable, Suspected, Doubtful, Dubious, Problematic, Uncertain, Cautious.
S	U	S	P	I	R	I	O	U	S	Sighing, Breathing heavily.
S	U	S	T	E	N	A	N	C	E	Nourishment, Living, Food, Nutriment, Maintenance, Subsistence, Support.
S	W	A	G	G	E	R	I	N	G	Strutting, Flourishing, Brandishing, Bragging Lurching.
S	W	A	L	L	O	W	I	N	G	Devouring, Engulfing, Gulping, Ingesting, Imbibing, Believing.
S	W	A	N	F	L	O	W	E	R	Plants having flowers suggesting the neck of a swan.
S	W	E	E	P	S	T	A	K	E	A race, lottery or contest for prizes.
S	W	E	E	T	B	R	E	A	D	The thymus of a calf used for food.
S	W	E	E	T	B	R	I	E	R	Old World rose.
S	W	E	E	T	H	E	A	R	T	Lover.
S	W	E	L	T	E	R	I	N	G	Oppressive and humid.
S	Y	C	E	T	T	I	D	A	E	A widely distributed family of calcareous sponges.
S	Y	C	O	P	H	A	N	C	Y	Defamation, Toadying, Belittlement, Calumny, Scandal, Slander, Disparagement.
S	Y	L	V	I	L	A	G	U	S	A genus of mammals comprising the cottontail.
S	Y	M	B	O	L	I	C	A	L	Allegorical, Emblematic.
S	Y	M	P	A	T	H	I	Z	E	Commiserate, Appreciate, Comprehend, Understand.
S	Y	M	P	H	O	N	I	S	T	A composer of symphonies.
S	Y	M	P	H	O	N	I	Z	E	Agree, Accord, Harmonize.
S	Y	M	P	L	E	S	I	T	E	A mineral consisting of a hydrous iron arsenate.
S	Y	N	A	P	T	I	D	A	E	A family of sea cucumbers.
S	Y	N	A	X	A	R	I	O	N	A short narrative of the life of a saint.
S	Y	N	C	H	Y	S	I	T	E	A mineral related to parisite.
S	Y	N	C	R	Y	P	T	I	C	Relating to a protective resemblance in appearance.
S	Y	N	G	E	N	E	S	I	S	Encasement, Sexual reproduction, Blood relationship.
S	Y	N	K	I	N	E	S	I	S	An associated movement.
S	Y	N	O	S	T	O	S	I	S	The union of two or more bones to form a single bone.
S	Y	N	T	R	O	P	H	I	C	Mutually dependent on one another for a food supply.
S	Y	P	H	I	L	I	T	I	C	Infected with syphilis.
S	Y	S	T	E	M	A	T	I	C	Orderly, Methodical, Regular, Classfied, Arranged.

T

1	2	3	4	5	6	7	8	9	10	Definition
T	A	B	L	E	C	L	O	T	H	A covering for a table.
T	A	B	L	E	S	P	O	O	N	A serving spoon.
T	A	B	L	O	I	D	I	S	M	The journalistic style of a tabloid newspaper.
T	A	B	U	L	A	T	I	O	N	The process of tabulating.
T	A	C	H	I	N	A	R	I	A	Related to two-winged flies that have larvae parasitic to some noxious insects.
T	A	C	H	O	G	R	A	P	H	A recording tachometer.
T	A	C	H	O	M	E	T	E	R	A device for indicating rotation speed.
T	A	C	H	O	M	E	T	R	Y	Measurement with a tachometer.
T	A	C	H	Y	M	E	T	E	R	An instrument used by surveyors for determining distance, bearings and elevation.
T	A	C	H	Y	M	E	T	R	Y	Measurement with a tachymeter.
T	A	C	H	Y	S	C	O	P	E	An early animated-picture machine.
T	A	C	I	T	U	R	N	L	Y	Silently, Reticently.
T	A	C	T	I	C	A	L	L	Y	In a tactical manner.
T	A	C	T	L	E	S	S	L	Y	In a tactless fashion.
T	A	E	N	I	A	C	I	D	E	An agent that destroys tapeworms.
T	A	E	N	I	A	F	U	G	E	An expellant for tapeworms.
T	A	F	F	E	T	I	Z	E	D	A fabric having a crisp finish.
T	A	G	L	I	A	R	I	N	I	An alimentary paste in flat ribbon form.
T	A	I	L	O	R	B	I	R	D	A family of birds, warblers that stitch leaves together to hide their nests.
T	A	L	E	T	E	L	L	E	R	One who tells tales or stories, often with exaggeration.

1	2	3	4	5	6	7	8	9	10	Definition
T	A	L	I	S	M	A	N	I	C	Magical.
T	A	L	L	O	W	W	E	E	D	An annual herb used to fatten cattle in the United States.
T	A	L	L	O	W	W	O	O	D	An Australian gum tree containing an oily principle and a tannin-rich gum.
T	A	M	A	R	U	G	I	T	E	A mineral that is a hydrous sulfate of sodium and aluminium isostructural.
T	A	M	B	O	U	R	I	N	E	A shallow one-headed drum with loose metallic discs around the side, to provide rhythm.
T	A	M	B	U	R	I	T	Z	A	A stringed musical instrument of Yugoslavia, like a guitar sounding like a mandolin.
T	A	N	G	E	N	T	I	A	L	Divergent, Incidental, Deviating widely.
T	A	N	G	L	E	B	U	S	H	A spiny branching spreading forestiera of the western and southwestern United States.
T	A	N	G	L	E	H	E	A	D	A perennial grass used as a forage.
T	A	N	G	L	E	R	O	O	T	An abnormal condition of the roots of the pineapple.
T	A	N	N	O	M	E	T	E	R	An instrument for measuring the strength of a tanning preparation.
T	A	N	T	A	M	O	U	N	T	Same, Equivalent, Duplicate, Identical, Alike, Uniform, Indistinguishable.
T	A	P	E	S	T	R	I	E	D	Covered with tapestry.
T	A	P	I	R	O	I	D	E	A	A superfamily of perissodactyl mammals comprising the tapirs.
T	A	P	O	T	E	M	E	N	T	A treatment in massage involving percussion.
T	A	R	A	N	A	K	I	T	E	A mineral consisting of a basic hydrous phosphate of aluminium and potassium.
T	A	R	A	N	T	E	L	L	A	A lively Italian folk dance.
T	A	R	B	U	T	T	I	T	E	A basic zinc phosphate.
T	A	R	D	A	M	E	N	T	E	Direction in music - slowly.
T	A	R	D	I	G	R	A	D	E	Microscopic creatures that live in water or damp moss.
T	A	R	T	A	R	E	O	U	S	Resembling tartar.
T	A	S	K	M	A	S	T	E	R	Overseer, One who assigns tasks.
T	A	T	P	U	R	U	S	H	A	A class of compound words, the first part is a noun that modifies the second part.
T	A	T	T	L	E	T	A	L	E	Informer, Betrayer, Squealer.
T	A	U	R	I	S	C	I	T	E	A mineral that is hydrous ferrous sulfate.
T	A	U	R	O	M	A	C	H	Y	The art of bullfighting.
T	A	U	T	O	P	H	O	N	Y	Repetition of the same sound.
T	A	W	D	R	I	N	E	S	S	The state of being tawdry.
T	E	A	R	J	E	R	K	E	R	A very pathetic story, film or play.
T	E	C	H	N	E	T	I	U	M	A crystalline radioactive metallic element.
T	E	C	H	N	I	C	I	A	N	A technical expert.
T	E	C	H	N	O	C	R	A	T	An adherent of the system of government by technical experts.
T	E	C	H	N	O	L	O	G	Y	Technical language, The science of the application of knowledge to practical purposes.
T	E	C	T	O	R	I	D	I	N	A crystalline isoflavone glucoside.
T	E	E	T	H	R	I	D	G	E	The inner surface of the gums of the upper front teeth.
T	E	E	T	O	T	A	L	E	R	One that practices total abstinence from alcoholic drinks.
T	E	G	E	T	I	C	U	L	A	A genus of moths that includes the yucca moth.
T	E	L	E	G	N	O	S	I	S	Clairvoyance.
T	E	L	E	G	R	A	P	H	Y	The operation of a telegraph apparatus in a communications system.
T	E	L	E	O	C	E	R	A	S	A genus of extinct short-legged rhinoceroses.
T	E	L	E	O	P	T	I	L	E	A mature feather.
T	E	L	E	P	A	T	H	I	C	Relating to telepathy.
T	E	L	E	S	C	O	P	I	C	Relating to a telescope, Farseeing, Far-reaching, Able to slide one section inside another.
T	E	L	L	I	N	A	C	E	A	A suborder of bottom-dwelling mollusks.
T	E	L	L	I	N	I	D	A	E	A family of marine bivalve mollusks comprising the sunset shells.
T	E	M	P	E	R	A	N	C	E	Restraint, Self-control, Sobriety, Moderation, Constraint, Abstinence, Forbearance.
T	E	M	P	O	R	A	L	L	Y	With regard to time.
T	E	M	P	T	A	T	I	O	N	Allurement, Enticement, Testing, Trial, Seduction, Lure, Bait.
T	E	N	D	E	R	F	O	O	T	Newcomer, Novice, Inexperienced, Beginner, Tyro, Neophyte, Novitiate.
T	E	N	D	E	R	I	Z	E	R	A device or substance that tenderizes.
T	E	N	D	E	R	L	O	I	N	A strip of tender meat, Fillet.
T	E	N	D	E	R	N	E	S	S	The quality of being tender.
T	E	N	D	O	N	I	T	I	S	Inflammation of a tendon.
T	E	N	D	R	I	L	O	U	S	Like a tendril.
T	E	N	E	B	R	I	O	U	S	Gloomy.
T	E	N	E	M	E	N	T	A	L	Leased to tenants.
T	E	N	E	M	E	N	T	E	D	Same as TENEMENTAL.
T	E	N	N	A	N	T	I	T	E	A mineral containing a blackish lead-gray sulfide of iron, copper, arsenic and sulphur.
T	E	N	R	E	C	I	D	A	E	A family of insectivores including the West African otter shrew.
T	E	N	S	I	M	E	T	E	R	An instrument for measuring gas or vapour pressure.
T	E	N	T	A	C	U	L	A	R	Resembling tentacles.
T	E	N	T	E	R	H	O	O	K	Something that serves for stretching or straining.
T	E	P	I	D	A	R	I	U	M	A warm room of the ancient Roman public baths used for relaxation.
T	E	P	O	N	A	Z	T	L	I	A Mexican slit-drum of Aztec origin.
T	E	R	A	T	O	L	O	G	Y	The study of abnormal growth or malformations.
T	E	R	E	B	R	I	D	A	E	Family of tropical marine snails.
T	E	R	M	I	N	A	B	L	E	Subject to termination.

1	2	3	4	5	6	7	8	9	10	Definition
T	E	R	M	I	N	A	L	I	A	A large genus of tropical trees and shrubs.
T	E	R	M	I	N	A	L	L	Y	By the term, At the end.
T	E	R	M	I	N	A	T	E	D	Concluded, Closed, Discharged, Expired, Finished, Abolished, Extinguished.
T	E	R	M	I	T	I	D	A	E	A family of termites.
T	E	R	R	A	C	E	O	U	S	Earthern.
T	E	R	R	I	F	Y	I	N	G	Frightening, Awesome, Ghastly, Gruesome, Horrifying, Hideous, Macabre, Terrible.
T	E	S	S	E	L	L	A	T	E	To decorate with mosaic.
T	E	S	T	A	C	E	O	U	S	Having a shell.
T	E	S	T	I	C	U	L	A	R	Relating to the testes.
T	E	S	T	U	D	I	N	A	L	Resembling a tortoise or tortoise shell.
T	E	T	A	N	I	F	O	R	M	Resembling tetanus.
T	E	T	R	A	C	A	I	N	E	A crystalline basic ester closely related to procaine and used as a local anaesthetic.
T	E	T	R	A	C	E	R	O	S	A genus of Asiatic ruminant mammals consisting of the Indian four-horned antelope.
T	E	T	R	A	C	O	L	O	N	A period of four cola in classical prosody.
T	E	T	R	A	D	E	C	Y	L	An alkyl radical derived from a tetradecane.
T	E	T	R	A	D	Y	M	I	A	A genus of low rigid shrubs.
T	E	T	R	A	G	O	N	A	L	Having four angles or sides.
T	E	T	R	A	G	O	N	I	A	A genus of fleshy herbs or undershrubs.
T	E	T	R	A	G	R	A	P	H	A cluster of four successive letters in cryptography.
T	E	T	R	A	G	Y	N	I	A	A class of plants with four styles or pistils.
T	E	T	R	A	H	Y	D	R	O	Combined with four atoms of hydrogen.
T	E	T	R	A	L	E	M	M	A	An argument analogous to a dilemma but presenting four alternatives.
T	E	T	R	A	M	E	R	E	S	A family of nematode worms parasitic to domestic fowls.
T	E	T	R	A	M	E	T	E	R	A line of four measures.
T	E	T	R	A	M	M	I	N	E	An ammine containing four molecules of ammonia.
T	E	T	R	A	M	O	R	P	H	A winged figure representing the four attributes of the Evangelists.
T	E	T	R	A	N	D	R	I	A	A class of higher plants with four stamens.
T	E	T	R	A	P	L	O	I	D	Fourfold in arrangement or number.
T	E	T	R	A	P	O	D	A	L	Having four legs or feet, Having four supporting legs.
T	E	T	R	A	P	O	L	A	R	Having four poles.
T	E	T	R	A	P	T	Y	C	H	An arrangement of four connecting pictures.
T	E	T	R	A	P	Y	L	O	N	An edifice having four gates or portals.
T	E	T	R	A	S	P	O	R	E	One of the haploid asexual spores in the red algae commonly in groups of four.
T	E	T	R	A	S	T	O	O	N	A courtyard enclosed by four porticoes.
T	E	T	R	A	S	T	Y	L	E	A building having four columns in front.
T	E	T	R	A	T	O	M	I	C	Consisting of four atoms.
T	E	T	R	A	T	O	N	I	C	Consisting of four musical tones.
T	E	T	R	I	G	I	D	A	E	A family of insects comprising the grouse locusts.
T	E	T	T	E	R	W	O	R	T	A plant once used to treat skin disease as ringworm, eczema or herpes.
T	E	X	T	U	A	R	I	S	T	A close student of the text of the Scriptures.
T	H	A	L	A	S	S	I	A	N	Sea turtle.
T	H	A	L	I	C	T	R	U	M	A widely distributed genus of herbs comprising the meadow rues.
T	H	A	L	L	I	F	O	R	M	Having the form of a thallus.
T	H	A	M	N	I	D	I	U	M	A genus of moulds related to the typical bread moulds.
T	H	A	M	N	O	P	H	I	S	A genus of American snakes comprising the garter snake.
T	H	A	N	A	T	O	S	I	S	A state that resembles death and occurs in some insects and beetles when distributed.
T	H	A	R	P	A	R	K	A	R	An Indian breed of pale gray humped cattle with horns.
T	H	A	U	M	A	S	I	T	E	A white mineral consisting of a basic silicate, carbonate and sulfate of calcium.
T	H	E	A	T	R	I	C	A	L	Dramatic, Histrionic, Showy, Spectacular, Unreal, Melodramatic, Exaggerated.
T	H	E	L	Y	G	E	N	I	C	Where only female offspring are produced.
T	H	E	O	C	R	A	T	I	C	Relating to government by God through a class of priests.
T	H	E	O	D	O	L	I	T	E	A surveyor's instrument for measuring horizontal and vertical angles.
T	H	E	O	L	O	G	I	A	N	One who studies religious faith, practice and presentation.
T	H	E	O	N	O	M	O	U	S	Subject to the authority of God.
T	H	E	O	P	H	O	B	I	A	Dread of God's anger.
T	H	E	O	P	H	O	R	I	C	Derived from the name of a god.
T	H	E	O	R	I	C	I	A	N	One who formulates theories.
T	H	E	O	S	O	P	H	E	R	One believing that spiritual ecstasy or special relations attains knowledge of God.
T	H	E	O	T	O	K	I	O	N	A hymn of praise to the Virgin Mary.
T	H	E	R	A	P	H	O	S	A	A type genus of very large tropical spiders.
T	H	E	R	E	A	F	T	E	R	From then on, Accordingly.
T	H	E	R	E	V	I	D	A	E	A family of two-winged flies, Stiletto flies.
T	H	E	R	M	I	S	T	O	R	An electrical resistor whose resistance varies sharply with the temperature.
T	H	E	R	M	O	G	R	A	M	The trace made by a thermograph.
T	H	E	R	M	O	P	I	L	E	An apparatus for generating electric current.
T	H	E	R	M	O	P	S	I	S	A genus of American and Asiatic showy herbs.
T	H	E	R	M	O	S	T	A	T	An automatic device for regulating an apparatus according to the temperature.

1	2	3	4	5	6	7	8	9	10	Clue
T	H	E	R	M	O	W	E	L	L	A tubular opening for the insertion of the thermometer.
T	H	E	R	O	P	H	Y	T	E	An annual plant that overwinters as a seed.
T	H	I	A	M	I	N	A	S	E	An enzyme that promotes the destruction of thiamine in the body and is found in fish.
T	H	I	A	Z	O	L	I	N	E	Any of three basic heterocyclic compounds.
T	H	I	G	M	O	C	Y	T	E	A blood cell of crustacean, important in blood clotting.
T	H	I	O	I	N	D	I	G	O	A red vat dye.
T	H	I	O	P	E	N	T	A	L	A sulphur analogue of pentobarbital used as an intravenous anaesthetic.
T	H	I	O	P	H	E	N	O	L	A mobile liquid mercaptan with a smell like garlic.
T	H	I	O	U	R	A	C	I	L	A bitter crystalline compound that depresses the function of the thyroid gland.
T	H	I	X	O	T	R	O	P	Y	The property exhibited by various gels of becoming fluid when shaken, or stirred.
T	H	O	M	I	S	I	D	A	E	A widely distributed family of spiders that spin no webs, Crab spiders.
T	H	O	M	S	O	N	I	T	E	A mineral of the zeolite family consisting of aluminium, calcium and sodium.
T	H	O	R	I	A	N	I	T	E	A strongly radioactive mineral that is an oxide of thorium.
T	H	O	U	G	H	T	F	U	L	Meditative, Considerate, Contemplative, Pensive, Reflective, Speculative, Mindful.
T	H	R	A	U	P	I	D	A	E	A family of passerine birds comprising the tanagers.
T	H	R	E	A	D	B	A	R	E	Shabby, Scanty, Barren, Frayed, Ragged, Trite, Hackneyed, Dilapidated.
T	H	R	E	A	D	L	I	K	E	Filamentous.
T	H	R	I	F	T	L	E	S	S	Improvident, Wasteful of money.
T	H	R	O	A	T	W	O	R	T	A European herb once used to treat a sore throat.
T	H	R	O	M	B	O	S	I	S	Presence of a blood clot within a blood vessel.
T	H	R	O	M	B	O	T	I	C	Relating to thrombosis.
T	H	R	O	U	G	H	O	U	T	Everywhere, Completely.
T	H	R	Y	O	N	O	M	Y	S	A genus of rodents comprising the African ground pigs.
T	H	U	C	H	O	L	I	T	E	A bitumen containing uranium and thorium.
T	H	U	M	B	S	C	R	E	W	A screw with a flattened head enabling it to be tightened by thumb and finger.
T	H	U	N	B	E	R	G	I	A	A genus of herbs or twining woody vines.
T	H	U	N	D	E	R	O	U	S	Producing thunder, Booming.
T	H	U	R	I	N	G	I	T	E	A mineral of the chlorite family consisting of a basic aluminium iron silicate.
T	H	Y	L	A	C	I	N	U	S	A genus of marsupial mammals consisting of the Tasmanian wolf.
T	H	Y	R	I	D	I	D	A	E	A family of small moths having the wings marked with translucent spots.
T	H	Y	R	O	G	E	N	I	C	Originating in the thyroid.
T	H	Y	R	O	T	O	X	I	C	Affected with hyperthyroidism.
T	I	B	O	U	C	H	I	N	A	A large genus of South American flowering shrubs.
T	I	C	H	O	D	R	O	M	A	A genus of birds consisting of the wall creeper.
T	I	D	E	W	A	I	T	E	R	A customs inspector working at the docks or aboard ships.
T	I	E	M	A	N	N	I	T	E	A mineral that is a native mercuric selenide.
T	I	G	R	O	L	Y	S	I	S	Loss of substance accompanying degenerative changes in nervous tissue.
T	I	L	L	A	N	D	S	I	A	A very large genus of chiefly epiphytic plants.
T	I	M	B	E	R	L	I	N	E	The upper limit of altitudes beyond which trees do not grow.
T	I	M	E	K	E	E	P	E	R	One that measures, regulates or determines time.
T	I	M	O	C	R	A	T	I	C	Relating to a political system in which love of honour and glory is the ruling principle.
T	I	N	C	T	O	R	I	A	L	Relating to dyeing or staining.
T	I	N	G	I	T	I	D	A	E	A genus of lace bugs.
T	I	N	T	A	M	A	R	R	E	Uproar, Din.
T	I	N	T	O	M	E	T	E	R	An apparatus for the determination of colours.
T	I	P	U	L	O	I	D	E	A	A large family of slender two-winged flies comprising the crane flies.
T	I	T	I	V	A	T	I	O	N	Dressing up, Sprucing or smartening up, The act of improving one's appearance.
T	I	T	R	I	M	E	T	R	Y	Measurement or analysis by titration.
T	I	T	U	B	A	T	I	O	N	Staggering, stumbling or reeling as a result of a nervous disturbance.
T	O	C	O	P	H	E	R	O	L	One of the fat-soluble liquid found in oils from seeds and fish liver having vitamin E.
T	O	G	G	E	N	B	U	R	G	A Swiss breed of brown hornless dairy goats.
T	O	I	L	S	O	M	E	L	Y	Laboriously.
T	O	L	E	R	A	T	I	O	N	License, Leniency, Forbearance, Clemency, Indulgence, Mercifulness.
T	O	L	Y	P	E	U	T	E	S	A genus of armadillos.
T	O	M	A	T	I	D	I	N	E	A crystalline steroid amine isolated from the roots of the tomato plant.
T	O	M	E	N	T	E	L	L	A	A genus of fungi.
T	O	M	F	O	O	L	E	R	Y	Nonsense, Foolishness, Claptrap, Rubbish, Twaddle, Prank, Caper, Antic.
T	O	M	O	G	R	A	P	H	Y	A special type of medical X-ray procedure.
T	O	M	O	P	T	E	R	I	S	A genus of transparent free-swimming marine worms.
T	O	N	E	T	I	C	I	S	T	A student of the science of intonation.
T	O	N	G	U	E	L	I	K	E	Resembling a tongue.
T	O	N	I	T	R	U	O	U	S	Thundering, Fulminatng.
T	O	O	T	H	B	R	U	S	H	A brush for cleaning teeth.
T	O	P	A	Z	O	L	I	T	E	A topaz-yellow or green garnet.
T	O	P	G	A	L	L	A	N	T	The topmost point, Pinnacle, Summit.
T	O	P	H	A	C	E	O	U	S	Gritty, Sandy, Characteristics of gout.
T	O	P	I	C	A	L	I	T	Y	The state of being topical.

1	2	3	4	5	6	7	8	9	10	
T	O	P	O	G	N	O	S	I	A	Recognition of the location of a stimulus on the skin and elsewhere on the body.
T	O	P	O	G	R	A	P	H	Y	Chart, illustration or map giving graphic details.
T	O	P	O	L	O	G	I	S	T	A specialist in topology.
T	O	P	S	Y	T	U	R	V	Y	Reversed, Disordered, Upside down, Disarranged, Unhinged, Disjointed.
T	O	R	O	S	A	U	R	U	S	A genus of extinct dinosaurs.
T	O	R	P	I	D	N	E	S	S	Sluggishness, Lethargy, Lassitude, Stupor.
T	O	R	Q	U	E	M	A	D	A	Persecutor.
T	O	R	R	E	N	T	I	A	L	Copious, Rushing, Vigorous.
T	O	R	S	I	O	N	I	N	G	Producing torsion to close an opening.
T	O	R	T	U	O	S	I	T	Y	Something winding or twisted, A crooked place, Bend, Sinuosity, Indirectness.
T	O	S	T	A	M	E	N	T	E	Direction in music - rapidly.
T	O	U	C	H	I	N	E	S	S	Irritability.
T	O	U	C	H	S	T	O	N	E	A black siliceous stone related to flint, Standard.
T	O	U	R	M	A	L	I	N	E	Brittle pyro-electric mineral used in optical instruments and also as a precious gem.
T	O	U	R	N	A	M	E	N	T	Contest, Battle, Encounter.
T	O	U	R	N	I	Q	U	E	T	A method of arresting bleeding by twisting a bandage with a stick.
T	O	W	E	R	I	N	G	L	Y	Loftily, Violently.
T	O	W	N	S	E	N	D	I	A	A genus of western American low and tufted herbs.
T	O	X	A	L	B	U	M	I	N	A toxic substance of protein nature.
T	O	X	A	S	C	A	R	I	S	A genus of ascarid roundworms that infest the small intestine of canines and felines.
T	O	X	I	C	O	L	O	G	Y	A science that deals with poisons and their effects.
T	O	X	I	F	E	R	I	N	E	Any of several alkaloids obtained from calabash curare.
T	O	X	I	F	E	R	O	U	S	Producing or conveying poison.
T	O	X	I	P	H	O	B	I	A	Abnormal fear of poisons.
T	O	X	O	G	L	O	S	S	A	A group of marine carnivorous gastropods.
T	O	X	O	P	L	A	S	M	A	A genus of parasitic micro-organisms.
T	R	A	B	E	A	T	I	O	N	Constructed with beams.
T	R	A	C	H	E	A	L	I	S	A muscle associated with the trachea.
T	R	A	C	H	E	A	T	A	E	A division of Arachnida comprising mites, ticks and scorpions.
T	R	A	C	T	A	T	U	L	E	A minor treatise or discourse.
T	R	A	C	T	I	O	N	A	L	Relating to traction.
T	R	A	D	U	C	T	I	O	N	Defamation, Slander, Violation.
T	R	A	D	U	C	T	I	V	E	Derivative.
T	R	A	G	A	C	A	N	T	H	A gum obtained as a dried exudate from various plants.
T	R	A	G	I	C	A	L	L	Y	Regrettably, Woefully.
T	R	A	G	O	P	O	G	O	N	A genus of Old World herbs, Salsify.
T	R	A	I	T	O	R	O	U	S	False, Perfidious, Treacherous, Faithless, Treasonable, Disloyal, Mutinous.
T	R	A	J	E	C	T	I	L	E	Marked by trajection.
T	R	A	J	E	C	T	I	O	N	Crossing, Transmission through space.
T	R	A	J	E	C	T	O	R	Y	The curve that a body describes in space.
T	R	A	M	O	N	T	A	N	E	Lying beyond mountains, Foreign, Outlandish.
T	R	A	M	P	O	L	I	N	E	A resilient canvas sheet supported by springs and used as a springboard by gymnasts.
T	R	A	N	S	C	R	I	B	E	Summarize, Copy, Paraphrase, Impute, Translate, Broadcast, Reproduce.
T	R	A	N	S	C	R	I	P	T	A written or printed copy, Reproduction.
T	R	A	N	S	D	U	C	E	R	A device actuated by power supplying power to a second system.
T	R	A	N	S	F	E	R	E	E	A person to whom a transfer is made.
T	R	A	N	S	G	R	E	S	S	Break, Violate, Trespass, Sin, Breach, Contravene, Infringe, Offend.
T	R	A	N	S	I	E	N	C	E	Passage, Movement.
T	R	A	N	S	I	S	T	O	R	An eclectronic device similar in use to the electron tube.
T	R	A	N	S	I	T	I	O	N	Change, Alteration, Passage, Shift, Transit, Conversion, Evolution, Progress.
T	R	A	N	S	I	T	I	V	E	Transient, Transitory.
T	R	A	N	S	I	T	O	R	Y	Evanescent, Transient, Temporary, Ephemeral, Fleeting, Fugitive, Momentary, Brief.
T	R	A	N	S	L	A	T	E	D	Transferred, Conveyed, Transported, Transcribed, Explained, Interpreted, Converted.
T	R	A	N	S	L	A	T	O	R	One that translates.
T	R	A	N	S	L	U	C	I	D	Transparent, Luminous.
T	R	A	N	S	L	U	N	A	R	Lying beyond the moon.
T	R	A	N	S	M	U	R	A	L	Extending or lying across a wall.
T	R	A	N	S	M	U	T	E	D	Changed, Altered, Converted, Transformed, Transfigured, Transposed.
T	R	A	N	S	P	I	R	E	D	Perspired, Exuded, Exhaled, Happened, Occurred, Chanced, Developed, Leaked.
T	R	A	N	S	P	L	A	N	T	Transport, Emigrate, Transfer.
T	R	A	N	S	V	E	R	S	E	Cross, Oppose, Overturn, Reverse, Diagonal, Oblique.
T	R	A	U	M	A	T	I	S	M	Stress, Shock.
T	R	A	U	M	A	T	I	Z	E	To inflict a trauma upon the body or mind.
T	R	A	V	E	L	L	I	N	G	Going, Proceeding, Walking, Journeying, Passing, Wending, Voyaging, Roaming.
T	R	A	V	E	L	O	G	U	E	A discourse, lecture or talk, usually with illustrations on travel.
T	R	A	V	E	R	S	E	L	Y	Crosswise.
T	R	A	V	E	R	T	I	N	E	A mineral consisting of a massive layered calcium carbonate.

1	2	3	4	5	6	7	8	9	10	
T	R	E	M	E	N	D	O	U	S	Huge, Vast, Dreadful, Monstrous, Terrifying, Formidable, Shocking, Colossal.
T	R	E	M	O	L	A	N	D	O	Direction in music - tremulous.
T	R	E	P	A	H	N	I	N	G	Removing a disc or core of metal or a section of skull.
T	R	E	P	H	P	C	Y	T	E	A blood cell found in some invertebrates.
T	R	E	S	P	A	S	S	E	R	One that violates, invades or infringes.
T	R	I	A	C	E	T	A	T	E	An acetate containing three acetate groups.
T	R	I	A	C	O	N	T	E	R	A Hellenic galley having thirty banks of oars.
T	R	I	A	C	T	I	N	A	L	Having three rays.
T	R	I	A	N	D	R	O	U	S	Having three stamens.
T	R	I	A	N	G	U	L	A	R	Having three angles, corners or sides.
T	R	I	B	O	M	E	T	E	R	An instrument for measuring sliding friction.
T	R	I	B	R	O	M	I	D	E	A binary compound containing three atoms of bromine combined with an element.
T	R	I	B	U	T	Y	R	I	N	The bitter oily liquid triglyceride of butyric acid used as a plasticizer.
T	R	I	C	H	E	C	H	U	S	A genus of mammals comprising the manatees.
T	R	I	C	H	I	A	S	I	S	The irritatin of the eyeball caused by eyelashes turning inward.
T	R	I	C	H	O	L	O	G	Y	The scientific study of hair.
T	R	I	C	H	O	L	O	M	A	A genus of white spored fungus, some of which are edible.
T	R	I	C	H	O	T	O	M	Y	Dividing into three parts.
T	R	I	C	H	R	O	M	A	T	One having normal or near normal colour vision.
T	R	I	C	I	P	I	T	A	L	Relating to a triceps muscle.
T	R	I	C	K	I	N	E	S	S	The state of being tricky.
T	R	I	C	L	A	D	I	D	A	A class of free-living flatworms.
T	R	I	C	L	I	N	I	U	M	A reclining couch around three sides of a table and used by the ancient Romans.
T	R	I	C	O	L	E	T	T	E	A silk or rayon knitted fabric.
T	R	I	C	R	O	T	I	S	M	A condition of the arterial pulse in which there is a triple beat.
T	R	I	C	Y	C	L	E	N	E	A crystalline saturated trycyclic terpene hydrocarbon.
T	R	I	C	Y	C	L	I	S	T	One that rides a tricycle.
T	R	I	D	E	N	T	A	T	E	Having three teeth or points.
T	R	I	E	N	T	A	L	I	S	A genus of delicate herbs.
T	R	I	E	R	A	R	C	H	Y	A plan of ancient Athens where individual citizens supplied and maintained ships.
T	R	I	F	A	R	I	O	U	S	Facing three ways.
T	R	I	F	L	I	N	G	L	Y	In a trifling manner.
T	R	I	F	O	L	I	A	T	E	Having three leaves.
T	R	I	F	U	R	C	A	T	E	Divided into three branches.
T	R	I	G	E	M	I	N	A	L	Having a pause after every third beat.
T	R	I	G	E	N	E	R	I	C	Relating to three kinds or types.
T	R	I	G	O	N	E	L	L	A	A genus of widely distributed herbs.
T	R	I	G	O	N	I	T	I	S	Inflammation of the trigone of the bladder.
T	R	I	G	R	A	P	H	I	C	Proceeding by groups of three letters at a time.
T	R	I	H	Y	D	R	A	T	E	A chemical compound with three molecules of water.
T	R	I	H	Y	D	R	O	X	Y	Containing three hydroxyl grounds in the molecule.
T	R	I	L	A	T	E	R	A	L	Involving three interests.
T	R	I	L	O	B	A	T	E	D	Divided into three lobes.
T	R	I	M	O	N	T	H	L	Y	Occurring every three months.
T	R	I	M	O	R	P	H	I	C	Having three distinct forms.
T	R	I	N	I	T	R	I	D	E	A binary compound containing three atoms of nitrogen combined with an element.
T	R	I	O	E	C	I	O	U	S	Having staminate, pistillate and hermaphrodite flowers.
T	R	I	P	A	R	T	I	T	E	Composed of three parts or kinds on different plants.
T	R	I	P	H	I	B	I	A	N	Equipped to operate from land, sea or in the air.
T	R	I	P	H	T	H	O	N	G	A speech item consisting of three successive sounds.
T	R	I	P	H	Y	L	I	T	E	An orthorhombic phospate of lithium, iron and manganese.
T	R	I	P	L	I	C	A	T	E	Threefold, Made in three identical copies.
T	R	I	P	L	I	C	I	T	Y	Trinity, Trio.
T	R	I	P	P	I	N	G	L	Y	Nimble quick manner, With agility and dexterity.
T	R	I	P	P	K	E	I	T	E	A tetragonal arsenite of copper.
T	R	I	P	U	H	Y	I	T	E	A mineral consisting of an oxide of antimony and iron.
T	R	I	R	A	D	I	A	T	E	Having three radiating branches.
T	R	I	S	E	C	T	I	O	N	The operation of dividing into three equal parts.
T	R	I	S	E	C	T	R	I	X	A curve that trisects an arbitrary angle.
T	R	I	S	E	K	T	A	T	E	Having three septa.
T	R	I	S	K	E	L	I	O	N	A figure composed of three curved or bent branches radiating from the centre.
T	R	I	S	T	Y	L	O	U	S	Having three styles.
T	R	I	T	A	N	O	P	I	A	A rare visual defect causing trouble with the colour blue.
T	R	I	T	H	R	I	N	A	X	A genus of South American fan palms.
T	R	I	U	M	F	E	T	T	A	A large genus of tropical herbs and shrubs.
T	R	I	U	M	P	H	A	N	T	Conquering, Victorious, Magnificent, Exultant, Jubilant.
T	R	I	V	A	R	I	A	N	T	Having three degrees of freedom.

1	2	3	4	5	6	7	8	9	10	Definition
T	R	I	V	I	A	L	I	T	Y	Trifle, The state of being trivial.
T	R	I	V	O	L	T	I	N	E	Producing three broods a season.
T	R	O	C	H	A	N	T	E	R	A rough prominence at the upper part of the femur.
T	R	O	C	H	I	F	O	R	M	Shaped like a top.
T	R	O	C	H	I	L	I	N	E	Relating to the hummingbirds.
T	R	O	E	G	E	R	I	T	E	A mineral that is a hydrous arsenate of uranium.
T	R	O	G	L	O	D	Y	T	E	A cave dweller.
T	R	O	G	O	D	E	R	M	A	A genus of dermestid beetles including several that are destructive to stored food.
T	R	O	G	O	N	I	D	A	E	A family of showy tropical nonpasserine forest birds.
T	R	O	L	L	E	Y	B	U	S	A public transport vehicle operated by electric overhead wires.
T	R	O	M	B	I	C	U	L	A	A genus of mites that transmit disease in the Orient.
T	R	O	M	B	I	D	I	U	M	A family of mites that feed on other arthropods.
T	R	O	M	O	M	E	T	E	R	A device for measuring finger tremor, used to diagnose nervous disturbances.
T	R	O	P	H	O	C	Y	T	E	A cell of the insect fat body that has a trophic function.
T	R	O	P	H	O	L	O	G	Y	A branch of science dealing with nutrition.
T	R	O	P	H	O	S	O	M	E	The nutritive zooids of a hydroid.
T	R	O	P	O	M	E	T	E	R	A device to measure rotation, as of an eyeball.
T	R	O	P	O	P	H	Y	T	E	A plant adjusted to an environment that undergoes marked periodic changes.
T	R	O	U	B	A	D	O	U	R	A lyric-poet, Poet-musician, A strolling minstrel.
T	R	O	U	V	A	I	L	L	E	Windfall, A lucky find.
T	R	U	C	U	L	E	N	C	E	Fierceness, Cruelty, Aggressiveness, Belligerence, Pugnacity.
T	R	U	N	C	A	T	I	O	N	An act of truncating.
T	R	U	X	I	L	L	I	N	E	Either of two isomeric amorphous alkaloids.
T	R	Y	P	E	T	I	D	A	E	A family of muscoid flies.
T	R	Y	P	O	G	R	A	P	H	A mimeograph using a stencil.
T	R	Y	P	T	A	M	I	N	E	A crystalline amine formed by decomposition of tryptophan.
T	R	Y	P	T	O	P	H	A	N	A crystalline amino acid.
T	U	B	E	R	A	C	E	A	E	A family of fungi.
T	U	B	E	R	C	U	L	A	R	Resembling a tubercle, Tuberculous.
T	U	B	E	R	C	U	L	I	N	A sterile liquid extract from the tubercle bacillus and used in the diagnosis of T.B.
T	U	B	E	R	O	S	I	T	Y	Large irregular projection of bone for the attachment of muscles and ligaments.
T	U	B	I	C	O	L	O	U	S	Living in a self-constructed tube, Spinning a tubular web.
T	U	B	U	L	A	R	I	T	Y	The state of being tubular.
T	U	B	U	L	A	T	I	O	N	Shaping or making a tube.
T	U	F	F	A	C	E	O	U	S	Resembling tuff, a type of volcanic rock.
T	U	M	A	T	A	K	U	R	U	A New Zealand shrub or tree.
T	U	M	B	L	E	D	O	W	N	Dilapidated, Ramshackle.
T	U	M	B	L	E	W	E	E	D	Any plant that breaks away from its roots and is driven before the wind.
T	U	M	E	S	C	E	N	C	E	Distension, Inflation, Swelling.
T	U	M	U	L	T	U	A	R	Y	Undisciplined. Irregular, Haphazard, Aimless, Tumultuous.
T	U	M	U	L	T	U	A	T	E	Riot, Tumult, Disturbance.
T	U	M	U	L	T	U	O	U	S	Riotous, Stormy, Boisterous, Disorderly, Raucous, Rowdy, Unruly Rumbustious.
T	U	R	B	I	D	N	E	S	S	Muddiness.
T	U	R	B	I	N	E	L	L	A	Type genus of conches.
T	U	R	B	I	N	I	D	A	E	A family of gastropod mollusks.
T	U	R	G	E	S	C	E	N	T	Swelling.
T	U	R	N	A	R	O	U	N	D	Reversal, Turnabout.
T	U	R	N	B	U	C	K	L	E	A link with a screw and swivel used for tightening a rod or stay.
T	U	R	N	I	C	I	D	A	E	A family of terrestrial birds comprising the button quails.
T	U	R	N	I	P	W	O	O	D	Australian rosewood.
T	U	R	P	E	N	T	I	N	E	Various oleoresins that are derived from coniferous trees.
T	U	R	R	I	C	U	L	A	R	Shaped like a tower.
T	U	R	R	I	L	I	T	E	S	A genus of Cretaceous cephalods having a spiral turreted shell.
T	U	R	R	I	T	E	L	L	A	A genus of marine gastropod mollusks having an elongated turreted shell.
T	U	R	R	I	T	I	D	A	E	A large family of marine gastropod mollusks.
T	U	R	T	L	E	B	A	C	K	A raised convex surface.
T	U	R	T	L	E	D	O	V	E	A common European bird noted for its soft cooing.
T	U	R	T	L	E	H	E	A	D	A showy perennial herb.
T	W	E	E	D	I	N	E	S	S	A homely informal appearance, Countrified.
T	W	E	L	V	E	F	O	L	D	Having twelve parts, Being twelve times as great.
T	W	E	L	V	E	T	O	N	E	Music based on the twelve chromatic tones of the octave.
T	W	I	N	F	L	O	W	E	R	A low prostrate subshrub having fragrant pink flowers.
T	Y	L	O	S	A	U	R	U	S	A genus of large extinct reptiles.
T	Y	M	P	A	N	I	T	E	S	A distension of the abdomen due to an accumulation of air or gas.
T	Y	M	P	A	N	I	T	I	C	Hollow-sounding.
T	Y	P	E	S	C	R	I	P	T	Typewritten matter when used as a printer's copy.
T	Y	P	E	S	E	T	T	E	R	Compositor, One that sets type.

1	2	3	4	5	6	7	8	9	10	
T	Y	P	E	W	R	I	T	E	R	Machine for writing in the style of printing and being operated by striking keys.
T	Y	P	H	L	O	C	Y	B	A	A genus of leafhoppers, some of which are destructive pests of trees and crops.
T	Y	P	H	L	O	L	O	G	Y	Scientific study of blindness.
T	Y	P	O	G	R	A	P	H	Y	The style, arrangement or appearance of material printed by letterpress.
T	Y	P	O	L	O	G	I	S	T	An expert in typology.
T	Y	R	A	N	N	I	C	A	L	Despotic, Absolute, Oppressive, Brutal, Harsh, Autocratic.
T	Y	R	A	N	N	I	D	A	E	A large exclusive family of American birds comprising the tyrant flycatcher.
T	Y	R	O	C	I	D	I	N	E	A crystalline antibiotic of a basic polypetide nature produced by a soil bacillus.
T	Y	R	O	L	I	E	N	N	E	A Tyrolean peasant's song characterized by the yodel.
T	Y	R	O	S	I	N	A	S	E	A copper-containing enzyme.

U

U	B	I	Q	U	I	T	O	U	S	Omnipresent, Existing or being everywhere at the same time.
U	D	O	M	O	G	R	A	P	H	A self-registering rain gauge.
U	L	C	E	R	A	T	I	O	N	The process of forming an ulcer.
U	L	O	B	O	R	I	D	A	E	A family of spiders spinning an orb web.
U	L	T	I	M	A	T	E	L	Y	Finally, Basically, Fundamentally.
U	L	T	I	M	A	T	I	S	M	The state of being ultimate.
U	L	T	R	A	S	O	U	N	D	Sound with frequencies above the range of human hearing.
U	M	B	E	L	L	A	L	E	S	A large order of chiefly herbaceous plants that include the carrots and turnips.
U	M	B	I	L	I	C	A	T	E	Resembling a navel, Perforate.
U	M	B	O	N	U	L	A	T	E	Having a rounded elevation.
U	M	B	R	A	G	E	O	U	S	Shadowy, Belligerent, Resentful.
U	N	A	B	R	I	D	G	E	D	Complete, In its entirety.
U	N	A	F	F	E	C	T	E	D	Unmoved, Genuine, Sincere, Plain, Simple, Natural.
U	N	A	T	T	E	N	D	E	D	Unaccompanied, Untended.
U	N	B	A	L	A	N	C	E	D	Crazy, Deranged, Unhinged, Mentally unstable, Mentally disordered.
U	N	B	E	A	R	A	B	L	E	Unendurable, Insufferable, Intolerable.
U	N	B	E	A	T	A	B	L	E	Invincible, Impregnable, Indomitable, Unassailable, Indefeatable.
U	N	B	E	C	O	M	I	N	G	Unsuitable, Indecorous, Improper, Indelicate, Rough, Indecent, Awkward.
U	N	B	E	L	I	E	V	E	R	Doubter, Skeptic, Infidel.
U	N	B	L	E	A	C	H	E	D	Unbleached.
U	N	B	L	I	N	K	I	N	G	Fearless, Not exhibiting signs of emotion.
U	N	C	A	R	E	D	F	O	R	Unheeded, Run-down.
U	N	C	H	A	N	G	I	N	G	Changeless, Constant, Steady, Same, Consistent, Uniform, Unfailing.
U	N	C	I	N	I	F	O	R	M	Bearing a hook or hooklike structure.
U	N	C	O	M	M	O	N	L	Y	Occasionally, Infrequently, Irregularly, Sporadically, Extremely, Rarely, Unusually.
U	N	C	O	M	P	L	E	T	E	Incomplete, Unfinished.
U	N	C	O	N	F	I	N	E	D	Unbound, Uncontrolled, Free, Loose.
U	N	C	U	L	T	U	R	E	D	Boorish, Churlish, Ill-bred, Loutish, Uncivilized, Coarse, Vulgar, Uncouth.
U	N	D	E	C	L	A	R	E	D	Not announced, Unspoken, Unuttered, Tacit, Implied.
U	N	D	E	C	O	R	O	U	S	Improper, Indecent, Indelicate, Unbecoming, Unseemly, Untoward.
U	N	D	E	F	E	A	T	E	D	Not having suffered a defeat.
U	N	D	E	F	E	N	D	E	D	Not protected, Unguarded, Without legal assistance.
U	N	D	E	N	I	A	B	L	E	Indisputable, Positive, Real, Actual, True, Incontestable, Unquestionable.
U	N	D	E	R	B	R	U	S	H	Shrubs and bushes growing beneath large trees in a forest.
U	N	D	E	R	C	R	O	F	T	Underground vault, Crypt.
U	N	D	E	R	G	R	A	D	E	Of an inferior grade, Below standard grade.
U	N	D	E	R	M	I	N	E	D	Weakened, Ruined, Wrecked, Sabotaged, Subverted, Frustrated, Thwarted, Foiled.
U	N	D	E	R	N	E	A	T	H	Below, Bottom, Beneath, Under, Secret, Stealthy, Covert, Surreptitious.
U	N	D	E	R	S	C	O	R	E	Underline, Emphasize.
U	N	D	E	R	S	E	X	E	D	Unresponsive, Frigid, Inhibited, Passionless.
U	N	D	E	R	S	T	A	N	D	Comprehend, Appreciate, Accept, Follow, Grasp, Know, Fathom, Believe.
U	N	D	E	R	S	T	A	T	E	Withold certain information.
U	N	D	E	R	S	T	O	O	D	Implicit, Tacit, Implied, Apprehended, Settled.
U	N	D	E	R	S	T	U	D	Y	One prepared to take over the part or duties of another.
U	N	D	E	R	T	A	K	E	R	One who prepares the dead for burial and arranges funerals.
U	N	D	E	R	W	A	T	E	R	Growing, performed or operated beneath the surface of water.
U	N	D	E	R	W	O	R	L	D	Earth, Hades, Community of organized crime.
U	N	D	E	R	W	R	I	T	E	Confirm, Subscribe to, Agree to purchase.
U	N	D	E	T	E	R	R	E	D	Not deterred.
U	N	D	I	S	M	A	Y	E	D	Unshaken, Not discouraged.
U	N	D	E	S	I	R	O	U	S	Disinclined, Indisposed.
U	N	D	I	V	U	L	G	E	D	Not divulged.
U	N	D	O	U	B	T	I	N	G	Confident.

1	2	3	4	5	6	7	8	9	10	Definition
U	N	D	R	A	M	A	T	I	C	Unspectacular.
U	N	D	U	L	A	T	I	N	G	Fluctuating, Rolling, Scalloped, Resembling waves.
U	N	D	U	L	A	T	I	O	N	Heaving, Pulsing, Surging, Swelling, Vibration, Rippling.
U	N	E	A	S	I	N	E	S	S	Discomfort, Distress, Restlessness, Unstability, Worry, Anxiety, Concern, Disquiet.
U	N	E	D	I	F	Y	I	N	G	Unenlightening, Unilluminating, Immoral, Unsavoury, Not instructive.
U	N	E	M	P	L	O	Y	E	D	Out of work, Not employed.
U	N	E	N	C	L	O	S	E	D	Not fenced, Common.
U	N	E	N	D	O	R	S	E	D	Not approved.
U	N	E	N	N	O	B	L	E	D	Lowly, Simple.
U	N	E	N	V	I	A	B	L	E	Embarrassing, Awkward, Undesirable.
U	N	E	Q	U	A	L	L	E	D	Unparalleled, Unrivaled, Matchless, Unprecedented.
U	N	E	Q	U	I	P	P	E	D	Unprepared.
U	N	E	V	E	N	N	E	S	S	Inequality, Roughness, Irregularity, Inconsistency, Disparity, Asperity.
U	N	E	X	C	I	T	I	N	G	Placid, Commonplace, Normal, Ordinary, Prosaic, Unnoteworthy, Unexceptional.
U	N	E	X	P	E	C	T	E	D	Unforeseen, Surprising, Sudden, Unlooked for.
U	N	E	X	P	L	O	D	E	D	Not exploded, Undischarged.
U	N	E	X	P	L	O	R	E	D	Not investigated, Not explored.
U	N	F	A	C	E	A	B	L	E	Revolting.
U	N	F	A	I	T	H	F	U	L	Disloyal, Dishonest, Infidel, Inaccurate, Untrustworthy, False, Perfidious, Treacherous.
U	N	F	A	M	I	L	I	A	R	Strange, Unaccustomed, Unknown, Foreign, Peculiar, Remarkable, Ignorant.
U	N	F	A	S	T	E	N	E	D	Unlocked, Loose, Unbound, Undone, Disengaged.
U	N	F	E	T	T	E	R	E	D	Free, Untrammeled.
U	N	F	I	N	I	S	H	E	D	Unpolished, Crude, Unbleached, Unformed, Unfashioned, Amateurish.
U	N	F	L	A	G	G	I	N	G	Tireless, Sustained.
U	N	F	L	U	R	R	I	E	D	Calm.
U	N	F	O	R	D	A	B	L	E	Impassable.
U	N	F	O	R	E	S	E	E	N	Unexpected.
U	N	F	R	I	E	N	D	L	Y	Hostile, Unsympathetic, Cold, Inhospitable.
U	N	F	R	U	I	T	F	U	L	Infertile, Sterile, Unprofitable, Barren, Fruitless, Impotent.
U	N	G	E	N	E	R	O	U	S	Petty, Niggardly mean, Discourteous.
U	N	G	O	V	E	R	N	E	D	Unrestrained, Wild.
U	N	G	R	A	C	E	F	U	L	Awkward, Inelegant.
U	N	G	R	A	C	I	O	U	S	Profane, Wicked, Disagreeable, Uncongenial, Disrespectful, Rude, Impolite.
U	N	G	R	A	T	E	F	U	L	Thankless, Unappreciative, Offensive, Hideous, Horrible, Listless, Distasteful.
U	N	H	A	L	L	O	W	E	D	Unconsecrated, Unholy, Impious, Profane, Fiendish, Illegitimate, Irreverent.
U	N	H	E	R	A	L	D	E	D	Anonymous, Unrecognized, Unexpected, Unforeseen.
U	N	I	C	A	M	E	R	A	L	Consisting of a single legislative chamber.
U	N	I	D	E	X	T	R	A	L	Favouring either the left or right hand.
U	N	I	F	L	O	R	O	U	S	Bearing a solitary flower.
U	N	I	F	O	R	M	I	T	Y	Sameness, Monotony.
U	N	I	J	U	G	A	T	E	D	Having one pair of leaflets.
U	N	I	L	A	T	E	R	A	L	One-sided.
U	N	I	L	I	N	G	U	A	L	Using one language only.
U	N	I	L	I	T	E	R	A	L	Consisting of one letter only.
U	N	I	L	O	C	U	L	A	R	Containing a single cavity.
U	N	I	M	P	A	I	R	E	D	Entire, Intact, Perfect, Sound, Unbroken, Unhurt, Undamaged, Unmarred.
U	N	I	N	F	O	R	M	E	D	Ignorant, Oblivious, Unaware, Unfamiliar, Unknown, Unwitting.
U	N	I	N	O	M	I	N	A	L	Having only one member.
U	N	I	O	V	U	L	A	T	E	Having a single ovule or ovum.
U	N	I	Q	U	E	N	E	S	S	The state of being unique.
U	N	I	V	E	R	S	I	T	Y	An institution of higher learning authorized to grant academic degrees.
U	N	I	V	O	L	T	I	N	E	Producing one brood in a season.
U	N	L	A	D	Y	L	I	K	E	Behaviour or manner not becoming to a lady.
U	N	L	A	M	E	N	T	E	D	Not grieved for.
U	N	L	A	W	F	U	L	L	Y	Illegally, Illicitly, Nefariously, Illegitimately, Intolerably.
U	N	L	E	A	V	E	N	E	D	Containing no leaven.
U	N	L	E	T	T	E	R	E	D	Illiterate, Ignorant.
U	N	L	I	C	E	N	S	E	D	Lacking restraint, Printed without licence, Lawless, Unauthorized.
U	N	M	A	N	N	E	R	E	D	Rude, Coarse, Unaffected, Straightforward.
U	N	M	A	N	N	E	R	L	Y	Rudely, Impolite, Discourteous.
U	N	M	E	A	S	U	R	E	D	Limitless, Unrestrained.
U	N	M	E	R	C	I	F	U	L	Merciless, Excessive, Extreme.
U	N	O	C	C	U	P	I	E	D	Unemployed, Empty, Having no inhabitants.
U	N	O	F	F	I	C	I	A	L	Not acknowledged by a governing body, Informal, Irregular.
U	N	O	R	T	H	O	D	O	X	Not orthodox, Heretical, Dissident, Nonconformist.
U	N	P	L	E	A	S	A	N	T	Displeasing, Offensive, Bad, Disagreeable, Rotten, Sour, Unhappy.
U	N	P	L	E	A	S	I	N	G	Disagreeable.

1	2	3	4	5	6	7	8	9	10	
U	N	P	O	L	I	S	H	E	D	Crude, Boorish, Uncultured.
U	N	P	R	E	P	A	R	E	D	Unready, Not on the alert.
U	N	P	R	O	M	P	T	E	D	Spontaneous.
U	N	P	R	O	V	O	K	E	D	Lacking provocation.
U	N	Q	U	E	N	C	H	E	D	Unextinguished, Unquelled, Unsatiated.
U	N	R	E	A	D	A	B	L	E	Illegible, Undecipherable, Indistinct, Incomprehensible, Unintelligible, Confused.
U	N	R	E	C	O	R	D	E	D	Not recorded, Unregistered.
U	N	R	E	F	O	R	M	E	D	Uncorrected.
U	N	R	E	L	I	E	V	E	D	Monotonous, Unvarying.
U	N	R	E	S	E	R	V	E	D	Entire, Full, Unqualified, Frank, Open, Candid, Plain, Unrestrained.
U	N	R	E	S	O	L	V	E	D	Undecided, Wavering, Irresolute, Faltering, Hesitant, Indecisive, Uncertain.
U	N	S	A	L	A	R	I	E	D	Not paid a salary.
U	N	S	C	R	A	M	B	L	E	Resolve, Clarify, Untangle, Extricate, Disentangle, Untie.
U	N	S	C	R	E	E	N	E	D	Not protected by a screen, Not passed through a screening procedure.
U	N	S	E	A	S	O	N	E	D	Immature, Inexperienced, Callow, Unpracticed, Untried.
U	N	S	E	C	O	N	D	E	D	Not supported or assisted.
U	N	S	E	L	E	C	T	E	D	Chosen at random.
U	N	S	E	T	T	L	I	N	G	Agitating, Unhinging, Upsetting, Disturbing, Perturbing, Deranging, Discomposing.
U	N	S	O	L	V	A	B	L	E	Insoluble, Inextricable.
U	N	S	P	O	R	T	I	N	G	Not sportsmanlike.
U	N	S	T	E	A	D	I	L	Y	Shakily, Unstable.
U	N	S	T	I	N	T	I	N	G	Not holding back, Giving freely, Generous.
U	N	S	U	I	T	A	B	L	E	Unbecoming, Inappropriate, Unfit, Ill-suited, Inapt, Inexpert, Improper, Untimely.
U	N	S	W	E	R	V	I	N	G	Steady, Constant, Steadfast, Unremitting, Firm, Fixed, Unwavering, Rigid.
U	N	T	E	M	P	E	R	E	D	Intemperate, Uncontrolled, Pure, Unmodified, Excessive, Unrestrained, Immoderate.
U	N	T	E	N	A	N	T	E	D	Unoccupied, Not leased to a tenant.
U	N	T	H	A	N	K	F	U	L	Thankless, Disagreeable, Unappreciative, Unpleasant, Ungrateful.
U	N	T	H	I	N	K	I	N	G	Heedless, Inattentive, Unmindful, Vacant, Careless, Feckless, Inadvertent, Uncaring.
U	N	T	I	D	I	N	E	S	S	The state of being untidy.
U	N	T	R	O	U	B	L	E	D	Calm, Tranquil, Hushed, Quiet, Still, Undisturbed.
U	N	T	R	U	T	H	F	U	L	False, Inaccurate, Dishonest, Deceitful, Lying, Shifty, Wrong, Misleading.
U	N	V	E	R	A	C	I	T	Y	Falsehood, Mendacity, Untruthfulness.
U	N	V	E	R	I	F	I	E	D	Not substantiated.
U	N	V	I	G	I	L	A	N	T	Inattentive, Unwary, Incautious, Unwatchful.
U	N	W	A	R	I	N	E	S	S	Being unwary, Indiscretion, Heedlessness.
U	N	W	A	V	E	R	I	N	G	Steadfast, Fixed, Sure, Enduring, Firm, Abiding, Unfaltering.
U	N	W	E	A	R	A	B	L	E	Worn-out, Unbecoming.
U	N	W	E	I	G	H	T	E	D	Unburdened, Not encumbered.
U	N	W	O	R	K	A	B	L	E	Impractical.
U	N	Y	I	E	L	D	I	N	G	Hard, Stiff, Resolute, Obstinate, Fixed, Rigid, Adamant, Implacable.
U	P	H	O	L	S	T	E	R	Y	The fabric and materials used to cover furniture.
U	P	R	O	A	R	I	O	U	S	Noisy, Disorderly, Funny, Clangorous, Sonorous.
U	P	S	T	A	N	D	I	N	G	Erect, Upright, Raised, Straightforward.
U	P	S	W	E	L	L	I	N	G	The act of swelling upward.
U	R	A	N	O	M	E	T	R	Y	A chart of celestial bodies, The measurement of the heavens.
U	R	A	N	O	P	H	A	N	E	A mineral that is a hydrous uranium calcium silicate.
U	R	B	A	N	I	S	T	I	C	Relating to urbanism.
U	R	E	D	I	N	A	L	E	S	An order of parasitic fungi.
U	R	I	C	O	L	Y	S	I	S	Breaking down of uric acid.
U	R	I	C	O	L	Y	T	I	C	Relating to uricolysis.
U	R	I	C	O	S	U	R	I	C	Promoting the excretion of uric acid in the urine.
U	R	I	N	A	L	Y	S	I	S	Chemical analysis of urine.
U	R	I	N	O	M	E	T	E	R	A small hydrometer to determine the specific gravity of urine.
U	R	O	G	E	N	I	T	A	L	Relating to the organs of reproduction.
U	R	O	P	O	I	E	S	I	S	Production of urine.
U	R	O	S	A	L	P	I	N	X	A genus of small carnivorous gastropod mollusks comprising the oyster drill.
U	R	T	I	C	A	C	E	A	E	A family of herbs, shrubs and trees including many with stinging hairs.
U	R	T	I	C	A	T	I	O	N	An itching and stinging sensation as caused by nettles.
U	S	E	F	U	L	N	E	S	S	Applicability, Appropriateness, Fitness, Relevance, Serviceability, Utility, Account.
U	S	T	U	L	A	T	I	O	N	The action of burning or searing.
U	S	U	R	P	A	T	I	O	N	Unauthorized assumption of the power of another, Infringing on the rights of others.
U	S	U	R	P	A	T	I	V	E	Usurping.
U	T	E	R	O	M	A	N	I	A	Nymphomania.
U	T	E	R	O	T	U	B	A	L	Relating to the uterus and Fallopian tubes.
U	T	I	L	I	Z	A	B	L	E	Capable of being utilized.
U	T	O	P	I	A	N	I	S	M	Impractical dreams of forming a perfect society.
U	T	R	I	C	U	L	O	I	D	Resembling a bladder.

1	2	3	4	5	6	7	8	9	10
U	Z	A	R	I	G	E	N	I	N

A crystalline steroid lactone.

V

VACATIONER	A person taking a vacation.
VACCINATED	Innoculated against an infectious disease.
VAGABONDRY	The life of a vagabond.
VAGINISMUS	A painful spasmodic contraction of the vagina.
VAGOTOMIZE	To perform a surgical division of the vagus nerve.
VAGOTROPIC	Acting selectively upon the vagus nerve.
VALDEPEÑAS	A Spanish table wine.
VALERAMIDE	Any of four crystalline amides derived from the valeric acids.
VALIDATION	The process of making legally valid.
VALOROUSLY	Bravely, Courageously.
VALVULITIS	Inflammation of a valve especially of the heart.
VAMPYRELLA	An order of small amoebas.
VANADINITE	A mineral consisting of a lead vanadate and chloride.
VANDALIZED	Subjected to wilful or malicious damage.
VANDALROOT	Garden heliotrope.
VANQUISHER	Conqueror.
VAPOGRAPHY	A special process of developing film by exposing it to vapours.
VARICOCELE	A varicose enlargement of the veins of the spermatic cord causing a soft tumour.
VARICOSITY	The condition of being varicose.
VARIEGATED	Varied, Checked, Dappled, Motley, Piebald, Flecked, Stippled, Spotted.
VARIOMETER	An aeronautical instrument for indicating the rate of climb.
VARSOVIANA	A graceful dance similar to a mazurka.
VASHEGYITE	A mineral that is hydrated basic aluminium phosphate.
VASOMOTION	A reflex reaction of a blood vessel.
VATICANISM	The doctrine of absolute papal supremacy.
VATICINATE	Prophetic, Foretell.
VAUDEVILLE	A stage entertainment of various types of acts.
VECTOGRAPH	Composition of two images giving three dimension effect with special spectacles.
VEGETALIZE	To exhibit vegetal characters.
VEGETARIAN	One who lives solely on vegetables, fruit, grains and nuts.
VEGETATION	Vegetable growth, Plant life.
VEGETATIVE	Productive, Having the power of growing, Leading a passive existence.
VELAMENTUM	Membrane.
VELITATION	Skirmish.
VELOCIPEDE	Early form of the bicycle.
VELOCITIZE	To become drowsy when driving at high speed for long distances.
VELUTINOUS	Velvety.
VELVETLEAF	A tropical vine with velvety leaves.
VELVETWOOD	A West Indian shrub or small tree.
VELVETWEED	Indian mallow.
VENENATION	The process of being poisoned.
VENERATION	A feeling of respect or reverence, Adoration.
VENERIFORM	Resembling a bivalve mollusk.
VENGEFULLY	Revengefully, Spitefully, Maliciously.
VENOGRAPHY	X-ray of a vein after an injection of an opaque substance.
VENOSTASIS	Abnormal slowing or stoppage of the flow of blood in a vein.
VENTILAGIN	A reddish brown resinous colouring matter obtained from the root bark of woody vine.
VENTILATED	Oxygenated, Aerated, Circulated, Expressed, Purified, Examined, Discussed freely.
VENTILATOR	A device for ventilating, Made public.
VENTOMETER	An instrument for determining the wind velocity.
VENTRICOSE	Distended, Inflated, Swollen.
VERBENALIN	A bitter crystalline glucoside in the flower of the common vervain.
VERBOMANIA	A mania for words.
VERIFIABLE	Capable of being authenticated.
VERMETIDAE	A small family of marine mollusks.
VERMICELLI	Alimentary paste made in long thin strings.
VERMICULAR	Resembling a worm.
VERMINOSIS	Infestation with parasitic worms.
VERNACULAR	Using a language native to your own country or region.
VERRUCARIA	A genus of rock-inhabiting crutose lichens.
VERRUCOSIS	Citrus scab.
VERSICULAR	Relating to biblical verses.

1	2	3	4	5	6	7	8	9	10	Definition
V	E	R	T	E	B	R	A	T	A	A major division of animals having segmented spinal columns.
V	E	R	T	E	B	R	A	T	E	Having a spinal column.
V	E	R	T	I	C	A	L	L	Y	So as to be vertical.
V	E	S	I	C	A	T	I	O	N	The process of blistering.
V	E	S	I	C	A	T	O	R	Y	An agent that induces blistering.
V	E	S	I	C	U	L	O	S	E	Having small blisters or bladders.
V	E	S	P	E	R	T	I	N	E	Relating to the evening.
V	E	S	T	I	B	U	L	A	R	Relating to a vestibule.
V	E	S	Z	E	L	Y	I	T	E	A mineral that is a hydrous basic copper zinc phosphate.
V	E	T	E	R	I	N	A	R	Y	A branch of science dealing with disease and injury of animals.
V	I	B	R	A	P	H	O	N	E	A percussion musical instrument resembling the xylophone.
V	I	B	R	O	G	R	A	P	H	An instrument to observe, measure and record vibrations.
V	I	B	R	O	S	C	O	P	E	Vibrograph.
V	I	C	E	G	E	R	E	N	T	Deputy, Lieutenant.
V	I	C	T	I	M	I	S	E	D	Sacrificed, Cheated, Duped, Tricked, Destroyed, Fooled, Hoodwinked.
V	I	C	T	O	R	I	O	U	S	Conquering, Triumphant, Fulfilled, Won, Achieved.
V	I	C	T	U	A	L	L	E	R	A restaurant keeper, One serving liquor and meals in a public house, Provision for army.
V	I	G	I	L	A	N	T	L	Y	Alertly, Watchfully.
V	I	G	O	R	O	U	S	L	Y	Forcefully, Energetically, Forcible, Powerfully, Strongly, Zealously, Firmly, Boldly.
V	I	L	L	A	I	N	O	U	S	Depraved, Vicious, Mean, Bad, Wretched, Vile, Detestable, Corrupt.
V	I	L	L	A	N	C	I	C	O	A cantata sung in church.
V	I	L	L	A	N	E	L	L	A	An instrumental piece in the style of a rustic dance.
V	I	N	D	I	C	A	B	L	E	Justifiable.
V	I	N	D	I	C	T	I	V	E	Vicious, Spiteful, Nasty, Punitive, Revengeful, Vengeful, Implacable, Malicious.
V	I	N	E	G	A	R	I	S	H	Acidulous, Easpish, Cantankerous, Crotchety.
V	I	N	I	F	E	R	O	U	S	Grown for the production of wine.
V	I	N	Y	L	A	T	I	O	N	The introduction of the vinyl radical into a compound.
V	I	N	Y	L	I	D	E	N	E	A bivalent radical derived from ethylene.
V	I	O	L	A	C	E	O	U	S	Of the violet colour.
V	I	O	L	E	S	C	E	N	T	Tending to a violet colour.
V	I	O	L	I	N	E	T	T	E	Violini piccolo.
V	I	P	E	R	I	F	O	R	M	Resembling a viper.
V	I	P	I	O	N	I	D	A	E	A family of small ichneumon flies.
V	I	R	A	G	I	N	O	U	S	Relating to a virago.
V	I	R	E	O	N	I	D	A	E	A family of small insectivorous American passerine birds.
V	I	R	E	S	C	E	N	C	E	The state of becoming green.
V	I	R	T	U	A	L	I	T	Y	Essence, Potentiality, Efficacy.
V	I	R	T	U	O	S	I	T	Y	Great technical skill in the practice of the fine arts.
V	I	R	T	U	O	U	S	L	Y	In a virtuous manner.
V	I	R	U	L	E	N	T	L	Y	In a virulent manner.
V	I	S	C	E	R	A	L	L	Y	Unreasoningly.
V	I	S	C	O	M	E	T	E	R	An instrument for measuring viscosity.
V	I	S	C	O	M	E	T	R	Y	Measurement of viscosity.
V	I	S	C	O	S	C	O	P	E	An instrument for estimating viscosity.
V	I	S	I	B	I	L	I	T	Y	The state of being visible, Visuality.
V	I	S	I	T	A	T	I	O	N	An official visit, Visit, Affliction, Trial, Tribulation.
V	I	S	I	T	O	R	I	A	L	Relating to the visiting rights of one parent when custody is awarded to other parent.
V	I	T	A	M	I	N	I	S	E	To introduce supplementary vitamins into a diet.
V	I	T	R	I	F	A	B	L	E	Capable of being formed into glass, Glassy.
V	I	T	R	O	P	H	Y	R	E	Porphyritic glassy rock.
V	I	T	T	A	D	I	N	I	A	A small genus of composite herbs.
V	I	T	U	P	E	R	A	T	E	Scold, Berate, Censure, Abuse, Lash, Revile, Asperse, Calumniate.
V	I	T	U	P	E	R	O	U	S	Scolding, Abusive, Railing.
V	I	V	A	N	D	I	E	R	E	A woman who once accompanied the troops to sell them liquor and provision.
V	I	V	E	R	R	I	D	A	E	A large family of catlike carnivorous mammals comprising the civets and genets.
V	I	V	I	F	I	C	A	T	E	Animate, Revive, Quicken, Enliven, Renew, Restore, Excite, Galvanize.
V	I	V	I	P	A	R	O	U	S	Producing live young instead of eggs.
V	I	Z	C	A	C	H	E	R	A	A group of burrows of South American rodents.
V	O	C	A	B	U	L	A	R	Y	A collection of words, Lexicon.
V	O	C	A	T	I	O	N	A	L	Relating to a vocation, Training in a specific trade.
V	O	C	I	F	E	R	A	T	E	Roar, Cry, Shout, Yell.
V	O	C	I	F	E	R	O	U	S	Clamorous, Boisterous, Strident, Blatant, Loud, Noisy, Shrill.
V	O	E	T	G	A	N	G	E	R	One of the immature wingless young of a southern African locust.
V	O	L	A	T	I	L	I	T	Y	A quality of being volatile.
V	O	L	A	T	I	L	I	S	E	Cause to exhale or evaporate.
V	O	L	I	T	A	T	I	O	N	The power of flying.
V	O	L	I	T	I	O	N	A	L	Possessing volition.

1	2	3	4	5	6	7	8	9	10	
V	O	L	T	A	M	E	T	E	R	An apparatus for measuring by the electrolysis produced, the quantity of electricity.
V	O	L	U	B	I	L	I	T	Y	The state of being voluble.
V	O	L	U	M	E	T	R	I	C	Relating to the measurement of volume.
V	O	L	U	M	I	N	O	U	S	Winding, Bulky, Large, Swelling, Full, Numerous, Sundry, Various.
V	O	L	U	P	T	U	A	R	Y	Voluptuous, Luxurious, Sensualist.
V	O	L	U	P	T	U	A	T	E	Luxuriate.
V	O	L	U	P	T	U	O	U	S	Luxurious, Sensuous, Luscious, Lush, Indulgent, Dissolute, Wanton.
V	O	L	U	T	A	T	I	O	N	The action of rolling or wallowing.
V	O	L	V	O	C	A	L	E	S	An order of freshwater green algae.
V	O	L	V	O	C	I	D	A	E	A family of flagellates.
V	O	M	B	A	T	I	D	A	E	A family of marsupials including the wombats.
V	O	R	T	I	C	E	L	L	A	A genus of stalked bell-shaped ciliates.
V	U	L	C	A	N	I	Z	E	D	The process of treating various materials.
V	U	L	N	E	R	A	B	L	E	Assailable, Open to attack.

W

1	2	3	4	5	6	7	8	9	10	
W	A	G	O	N	S	M	I	T	H	One who builds and repairs wagons and carts.
W	A	I	N	W	R	I	G	H	T	Same as WAGONSMITH.
W	A	I	S	T	C	L	O	T	H	Cloths hung on a ship to screen the men in action.
W	A	L	D	H	E	I	M	I	A	A genus of brachiopods including some in fossil form.
W	A	L	K	A	R	O	U	N	D	A dance number in a minstrel show where all the performers move in a circle.
W	A	L	L	F	L	O	W	E	R	An Old World herbaceous plant cultivated for the showy fragrant blooms.
W	A	L	P	U	R	G	I	T	E	A mineral consisting of a hydrous bismuth uranium arsenate and oxide.
W	A	N	D	E	R	L	U	S	T	An almost uncontrollable desire to travel, Inability to settle.
W	A	N	D	F	L	O	W	E	R	A plant of the genus Sparaxis.
W	A	N	T	O	N	N	E	S	S	The state of being wanton.
W	A	R	D	E	N	S	H	I	P	The office and powers of a warden.
W	A	R	W	I	C	K	I	T	E	A mineral consisting of a borate of titanium, iron and magnesium.
W	A	S	H	B	O	I	L	E	R	A large metal vessel for boiling clothes.
W	A	S	T	E	P	A	P	E	R	Paper discarded as unsuitable for its intended use and often recycled.
W	A	T	E	R	B	O	R	N	E	Supported or conveyed by water.
W	A	T	E	R	B	O	U	N	D	Held together by water.
W	A	T	E	R	C	L	E	A	R	Colourless and transparent.
W	A	T	E	R	C	R	A	F	T	Skill in aquatic activities.
W	A	T	E	R	F	L	O	O	D	Sweeping flood of water.
W	A	T	E	R	F	R	O	N	T	Built-up area along the edge of a body of water.
W	A	T	E	R	I	N	E	S	S	The condition of being watery.
W	A	T	E	R	M	E	L	O	N	A large roundish vine fruit containing sweet juicy pulp.
W	A	T	E	R	P	O	W	E	R	The power of water to move machinery.
W	A	T	E	R	P	R	O	O	F	Impervious to water, Treated to prevent permeation by water.
W	A	T	E	R	S	P	O	U	T	A tubular column of water sucked up in a whirlwind, A pipe directing water downwards.
W	A	T	E	R	W	H	E	E	L	A wheel rotated by the action of water.
W	A	T	T	L	E	B	I	R	D	A common large Australian bird.
W	A	T	T	L	E	W	O	R	K	Coarse wicker work.
W	A	V	E	R	I	N	G	L	Y	In a wavering manner.
W	E	A	K	H	E	A	D	E	D	Liable to dizziness.
W	E	A	K	L	I	N	E	S	S	Puniness.
W	E	A	K	M	I	N	D	E	D	Foolish, Feebleminded.
W	E	A	P	O	N	L	E	S	S	Unarmed.
W	E	A	T	H	E	R	I	N	G	Being affected by the different elements of the weather.
W	E	A	T	H	E	R	M	A	N	One who reports and forecasts the weather, Meteorologist.
W	E	A	V	E	R	B	I	R	D	A family of birds resembling finches, that build nests of interlaced grass.
W	E	D	D	E	L	L	I	T	E	A mineral consisting of hydrous oxalate of calcium found in Antarctica.
W	E	I	B	U	L	L	I	T	E	A mineral consisting of seleniferous sulfide of lead and bismuth.
W	E	I	G	H	T	L	E	S	S	Lacking gravitational pull, Having no weight.
W	E	I	M	A	R	A	N	E	R	A German breed of large gray short-haired sporting dogs.
W	E	I	N	M	A	N	N	I	A	A large genus of shrubs and trees.
W	E	L	L	H	E	E	L	E	D	Having plenty of money.
W	E	N	T	L	E	T	R	A	P	Any of numerous graceful spirally-coiled gastropod mollusk shells.
W	E	R	T	H	E	R	I	A	N	Morbidly sentimental.
W	E	S	T	W	A	R	D	L	Y	In a westerly direction.
W	H	A	R	F	I	N	G	E	R	One in charge of the handling of freight at a wharf.
W	H	E	E	L	C	H	A	I	R	A chair mounted on wheels and usually propelled by hand rims on those wheels.
W	H	E	E	L	H	O	U	S	E	A structure housing a wheel.
W	H	E	E	Z	I	N	E	S	S	The state of being wheezy.

1	2	3	4	5	6	7	8	9	10	Definition
W	H	E	W	E	L	L	I	T	E	A mineral consisting of calcium oxalate.
W	H	I	P	S	O	C	K	E	T	A socket for resting the stock of a whip when it is not is use.
W	H	I	R	L	B	L	A	S	T	Whirlwind, Hurricane.
W	H	I	R	L	I	C	O	T	E	A coach.
W	H	I	S	K	E	R	A	G	E	Wearing whiskers.
W	H	I	S	P	E	R	I	N	G	Murmuring, Muttering, Report, Gossiping, Rumour, Hearsay, Hinting, Undertone.
W	H	I	T	E	B	E	A	R	D	An old man.
W	H	I	T	E	B	E	L	L	Y	A bird with a white chest, Pigeon, Prairie chicken.
W	H	I	T	E	P	R	I	N	T	A diazotype where the graphic image appears on a white background.
W	H	I	T	E	S	M	I	T	H	One who works in white iron, Tinsmith.
W	H	I	T	E	T	H	O	R	N	A hawthorn.
W	H	I	T	E	W	A	T	E	R	Frothy water, as in rapids or waterfalls.
W	H	O	L	E	S	A	L	E	R	A merchant who acts as a middleman between the manufacturer and the retailer.
W	H	O	R	E	H	O	U	S	E	Brothel.
W	H	O	S	O	E	V	E	R		Whoever.
W	I	C	K	E	D	N	E	S	S	Evil, Sinfulness, Vice, Wrong, Corruption, Depravity, Immorality.
W	I	C	K	E	R	W	O	R	K	Basketry, Work made of cane or twigs.
W	I	D	E	S	P	R	E	A	D	Widely extended, Prevailing, Prevalent, Rampant, Rife, Current, Popular.
W	I	F	E	L	I	N	E	S	S	The state of being wifely.
W	I	L	D	E	B	E	E	S	T	Gnu.
W	I	L	L	O	W	W	A	R	E	Dinnerware decorated with pictures of a Chinese story, in blue on a white background.
W	I	L	L	O	W	W	E	E	D	A narrow-leaved plant.
W	I	L	L	O	W	W	O	R	M	A worm that is the larva of a willow moth.
W	I	N	C	E	Y	E	T	T	E	A flannelette fabric used for winter wear.
W	I	N	D	O	W	L	E	S	S	Having no window.
W	I	N	D	S	H	I	E	L	D	A transparent glass screen forming the front upper section of an automobile.
W	I	N	E	G	R	O	W	E	R	One that cultivates a vineyard for the production of wine.
W	I	N	G	S	P	R	E	A	D	Wingspan.
W	I	N	T	E	R	F	E	E	D	To feed livestock during the winter with a supplement to grazing.
W	I	N	T	E	R	T	I	D	E	Wintertime.
W	I	R	E	D	R	A	W	E	R	One that draws metal into wire.
W	I	T	C	H	C	R	A	F	T	Magic, Sorcery, Charm, Enchantment, Incantation, Necromancy, Fascination.
W	I	T	C	H	G	R	A	S	S	Couch grass.
W	I	T	C	H	H	A	Z	E	L	Rowan tree, Alcoholic distillation of the bark used as a remedy for bruises.
W	I	T	H	D	R	A	W	A	L	Retreat, Retirement, Retraction, Departure, Exit, Exodus, Egress, Shrink.
W	O	L	F	A	C	H	I	T	E	A mineral consisting of nickel sulfide, arsenide and antimonide.
W	O	L	F	R	A	M	I	N	E	Tungstite.
W	O	L	F	R	A	M	I	T	E	A mineral that consists of an iron manganese tungstate.
W	O	N	D	E	R	B	O	O	M	A fig tree of Africa.
W	O	N	D	E	R	L	A	N	D	A fairyland imaginary country, Utopia, Arcadia, Paradise, Zion.
W	O	N	D	E	R	M	E	N	T	Astonishment, Surprise, Admiration, Amazement.
W	O	O	D	C	U	T	T	E	R	A person who cuts wood, One producing woodcuts.
W	O	O	D	E	N	H	E	A	D	Dunce, Blockhead, Numskull.
W	O	O	D	E	N	W	A	R	E	Domestic articles and utensils made of wood.
W	O	O	D	M	O	N	G	E	R	A dealer in wood.
W	O	O	D	P	E	C	K	E	R	A family of birds with very hard bills used to drill the bark of trees.
W	O	O	D	W	O	R	K	E	R	A worker who works in wood, cabinetmaker, carpenter or joiner.
W	O	O	L	E	N	I	Z	E		To treat fabric with chemicals and give it the appearance of wool.
W	O	R	D	L	E	S	S	L	Y	Silently, Taciturnly, Speechlessly, Inarticulately.
W	O	R	K	P	E	O	P	L	E	Employees.
W	O	R	L	D	W	E	A	R	Y	Weary of the material pleasures of life.
W	O	R	R	Y	I	N	G	L	Y	With worry.
W	O	R	S	H	I	P	F	U	L	Honorific title, Deserving of respect.
W	O	R	S	H	I	P	P	E	R	One that worships.
W	O	R	T	H	W	H	I	L	E	Advantageous, Gainful, Lucrative, Profitable, Moneymaking.
W	O	U	N	D	I	N	G	L	Y	Hurtfully.
W	R	A	P	A	R	O	U	N	D	Something that encircles and often overlaps at the sides.
W	R	A	T	H	F	U	L	L	Y	Angrily.
W	R	E	T	C	H	E	D	L	Y	Lamentably.
W	R	O	N	G	F	U	L	L	Y	Unlawfully, Unjustly, Unfairly, Injuriously, Illegally, Illegitimately, Illicitly, Criminally.
W	U	R	T	Z	I	L	I	T	E	An asphalt.

X

X	A	N	T	H	A	M	I	D	E	An amide of a xanthic acid.
X	A	N	T	H	I	D	I	U	M	A genus of spiny desmids including common plankton.

1	2	3	4	5	6	7	8	9	10	Definition
X	A	N	T	H	O	D	E	R	M	One belonging to the yellow-skinned race.
X	A	N	T	H	O	S	I	N	E	A crystalline nucleoside.
X	A	N	T	H	Y	D	R	O	L	A crystalline secondary alcohol that is obtained by reduction of xanthone.
X	E	N	O	P	H	O	B	I	A	Fear and hatred of persons or objects that are foreign or strange.
X	E	N	O	P	S	Y	L	L	A	A genus of fleas including some that transmit the plague.
X	E	R	O	G	R	A	P	H	Y	The formation of pictures of graphic matter by the action of light on a special surface.
X	I	P	H	O	P	A	G	U	S	Abnormality of twins being united.
X	Y	L	O	G	L	Y	P	H	Y	Artistic wood carving.
X	Y	L	O	G	R	A	P	H	Y	Wood engraving, Woodcut.
X	Y	L	O	P	H	O	N	I	C	Sounding like a xylophone.
X	Y	L	O	S	T	R	O	M	A	The mycelium of wood-destroying fungi.
X	Y	L	O	T	O	M	O	U	S	Capable of boring or cutting wood.
X	Y	R	I	D	A	C	E	A	E	A family of herbs.

Y

1	2	3	4	5	6	7	8	9	10	Definition
Y	A	F	F	I	N	G	A	L	E	Green woodpecker.
Y	A	R	B	O	R	O	U	G	H	A hand in bridge containing no card higher than a nine.
Y	E	A	S	T	I	N	E	S	S	A state of being yeasty.
Y	E	L	L	O	W	R	O	O	T	Any plant with yellow roots.
Y	E	L	L	O	W	S	E	E	D	Field cress.
Y	E	L	L	O	W	T	A	I	L	An amberfish, A common snapper.
Y	E	L	L	O	W	W	A	R	E	Pottery made from clay which fires to a clear yellow colour.
Y	E	L	L	O	W	W	E	E	D	Golden rod, Tansy ragwort.
Y	E	O	M	A	N	E	T	T	E	A woman serving in the U S Naval reserve force as a yeoman in World War One.
Y	I	E	L	D	I	N	G	L	Y	In a yielding manner.
Y	O	U	N	G	B	E	R	R	Y	A large sweet reddish black fruit of a trailing hybrid bramble.
Y	O	U	T	H	F	U	L	L	Y	In a youthful manner.
Y	P	O	N	O	M	E	U	T	A	A genus of black-spotted white moths.
Y	T	T	R	I	A	L	I	T	E	A massive mineral consisting of a silicate chiefly of thorium, yttrium and gadolinium.

Z

1	2	3	4	5	6	7	8	9	10	Definition
Z	A	M	A	N	D	O	Q	U	E	A Mexican plant with long slender leaves that yield a long soft flexible fibre.
Z	A	P	H	R	E	N	T	I	S	A genus of solitary cup-shaped tetracorals.
Z	E	R	O	V	A	L	E	N	T	Having a valence of zero.
Z	E	U	Z	E	R	I	D	A	E	A family of moths.
Z	I	N	G	I	B	E	R	O	L	A fragrant liquid pernoid alcohol obtained from ginger oil.
Z	I	R	K	L	E	R	I	T	E	A mineral of a basic hydrous chloride of iron, magnesium, calcium and aluminium.
Z	O	A	N	T	H	A	R	I	A	A subclass of Anthozoa including corals and sea anemones.
Z	O	A	N	T	H	I	D	E	A	A small order resembling small sea anemones.
Z	O	A	N	T	H	R	O	P	Y	A monomania where a person believes himself to be an animal and acts like one.
Z	O	N	I	F	E	R	O	U	S	Zoned.
Z	O	N	I	T	O	I	D	E	S	A genus of amber-coloured land snails.
Z	O	O	G	R	A	P	H	I	C	Consisting of graphic or verbal description of animals.
Z	O	O	L	A	T	R	O	U	S	Relating to the worship of animals.
Z	O	O	M	O	R	P	H	I	C	Having the form of stylized animals.
Z	O	O	P	H	A	G	O	U	S	Carnivorous, Feeding on animals.
Z	O	O	P	H	I	L	I	S	T	A lover of animals.
Z	O	O	T	H	E	R	A	P	Y	Veterinary therapeutics.
Z	Y	G	A	D	E	N	I	N	E	A crystalline alkaloid obtained from plants.
Z	Y	G	A	E	N	I	D	A	E	A family of moths.
Z	Y	G	N	E	M	A	L	E	S	An order of green algae that includes pond scum and desmids.
Z	Y	G	O	C	A	C	T	U	S	A small genus of Brazilian cacti.
Z	Y	G	O	D	A	C	T	Y	L	Having two toes in front and two behind.
Z	Y	M	O	S	T	E	R	O	L	A crystalline unsaturated sterol occurring with ergosterol in yeast fat.
Z	Y	T	H	I	A	C	E	A	E	A family of imperfect fungi.
Z	Y	Z	Z	O	G	E	T	O	N	A genus of large South American leafhoppers.

BLOCK WORD FINDER

CULINARY AND MENU TERMS

À la carte	Choice of dishes on offer with prices
Absinthe	Liqueur made from aromatic herbs
Alguillettes	Strips of cooked meat or fish
À la broche	Roast on a spit
À la mode	In a certain style
Albumine	White of egg
Allemande	Savoury white sauce made of egg yolk and cream
Allspice	Flavouring with smell and flavour of a combination of spices
Agneau	Lamb
Ananas	Pineapple
Angouste (À la)	Garnish of baked eggs
Anitra	Duck
Antipasta	Appetizers
Argenteuil	With asparagus as a garnish
Assiette Anglaise	Plate of assorted cold meats
Au bleu	Boiled fish
Aubergine	Egg plant/Brinjal
Au gratin	Baked with a topping of breadcrumbs
Au maigre	Dishes without meat
Baba	Light sponge cake made with yeast
Baklava	Sweet pastry stuffed with nuts and soaked in honey
Barbecue	Outdoor cooking on a grill or spit
Bavaroise	Cream dessert with a custard base
Béarnaise	Sauce with herbs
Béchamel	French white sauce
Beignets	Fritters or pancakes fried in deep fat
Bien cuit	Well cooked
Bisque	Smooth thick cream soup of shell fish
Blanquette	Stew of veal or poultry with rich white sauce
Bombe	Ice cream desert with fruit and cream
Borsch	Beetroot soup
Bordelaise (À la)	French brown sauce with red wine and shallots
Bouillabaisse	Thick fish soup
Bouchée	Small puff pastry case for savoury or sweet filling
Bourgin	With red wine sauce
Bouquet garni	Bunch of herbs cooked in the dish or sauce that is removed before serving
Brie	Popular soft cheese
Brioche	Sweet yeast roll
Camembert	Soft creamy cheese
Canapés	Small pieces of toast/fried bread upon which savouries are served
Canard	Duck
Cannelloni	Large macaroni stuffed with meat and baked in a savoury sauce
Cappelletti	Pasta filled with chicken and cooked in broth
Carte du jour	The menu for the day
Caviar	Roe of the sturgeon
Cassoulet	Casserole of pork or goose with haricot beans, carrots and onions
Célestine	Soup garnish of strips of fried pancakes
Cerf	Venison
Champignons	Mushrooms
Charlotte Russe	Mould of jelly and whipped cream within a circle of sponge fingers
Chartreuse	Mixture of meat and vegetables or fruit served as an entrée
Chasseur	Sauce of white wine, mushrooms and shallots
Châteaubriand	Dish of fillet steak
Chaudfroid	Cold entrée
Chipolata	Very small sausage
Chou	Cabbage
Chowder	Thick stew of shellfish and pickled pork
Citronne	Taste or flavour of lemon
Cochineal	Pink food colouring
Colbert	Thick sauce of madeira wine and lemon
Compôte	A stew of vegetables or fruit
Condiments	Seasonings
Consommé	Clear soup served either hot or cold
Coq au vin	Chicken casserole with mushrooms and red wine
Cordon bleu	French culinary award given to highly skilled chefs
Côtelettes	Small slices of meat
Cotriade	Fish soup
Court Bouillon	Fish broth
Crécy (À la)	Refers to a dish with carrots as the main ingredients

Créole	Dish containing rice
Crepes	Thin pancakes
Crevettes	Prawns or shrimps
Croquette	Savoury mince, fish, poultry or vegetables made into a shape, crumbed and fried
Croutons	Small dice of bread fried or toasted and used to garnish soup
Darioles	Small shapes in individual moulds either sweet or savoury
Déjeuner (À la)	Luncheon
Diable	"Devil" used to describe hot spicy dishes
Dindon	Turkey
Doux	Sweet – to describe wine
Dragées	Fruit titbits covered with icing
Duchesse	Mashed potatoes beaten with eggs and butter then baked in fancy shapes
Eclair	French pastry filled with cream or custard
Ecrevisse	Crayfish
Emmenthal	Swiss cheese with holes
Escalope	Thin slice of meat, crumbed and fried
Farce	Forcemeat or stuffing
Fermiére (À la)	In the farmhouse fashion
Fettuccini	Thin noodles
Feuilletage	Puff paste
Financiére	Rich sauce for entrées
Fines-Herbes	Combination of finely chopped herbs for omelettes and sauces
Flageolets	Small beans fresh or dried
Flan	Open round tart of pastry or sponge
Flummery	Cold sweet cereal dish
Foie gras	Liver of a fatted goose
Foie de veau	Calf's liver
Fondant	Soft icing
Fondue	Swiss dish of melted cheese with white wine
Fraises	Strawberries
Frangipane	Flavoured custard
Frappé	To place on ice
Frincadelles	Thin braised steaks of veal or meat balls
Fricassée	White stew of chicken or veal
Frit	Fried
Froid	Cold
Fromage Glacé	Ice cream or glazed with cheese
Fruits de mer	Sea food
Galantine	White meat, rolled after cooking and served cold
Garbure	Soup of bacon and cabbage
Gâteau	Light decorated sponge
Gaufre	Waffle
Gazpacho	Cold soup often cucumber
Gelatine	Colourless protein from boiled animal tissue used to make jelly
Génoise	Rich sponge cake
Ghee	Clarified butter used in Indian cooking
Gigot	Leg of mutton, lamb or venison
Glacé	Frozen ice or to be iced
Gnocchi	Savoury dough boiled and served with parmesan cheese
Gouda	Firm yellow mild dutch cheese
Goulash	Savoury stew of beef and vegetables flavoured with paprika
Gourmet	Judge of good living
Gratin	Garnished with breadcrumbs and baked
Grenadine	Braised fillets of veal or poultry
Grenouilles	Frogs' legs
Gruyere	Pale mild cheese with holes, made of cow's milk
Gumbo	Any dish made from Okra (American)
Haggis	A concoction of meat, vegetables and oatmeal cooked in the stomach of a sheep
Halva	Sesame-seed sweet
Hanenge	Herring
Hollandaise	Rich white sauce
Homard	Lobster
Hors d'oeuvres	Small savoury tit-bits served as appetizers
Huître	Oyster
Jambon	Ham
Jardiniére	Vegetables stewed in their own sauce
Jaune-mange	An egg jelly
Julep	American drink usually with mint (Arabian)
Julienne	Vegetables cut into thin strips
Junket	Milk dish made with rennet
Kebabs	Cubes of meat and vegetables for savoury or fruit for sweet fixed on skewers
Kedgeree	Curried fish and rice
Lait	Milk

Lapin	Rabbit
Legumes	Vegetables
Limande	Lemon sole
Limburger	Soft white cheese flavoured with herbs
Lyonnaise (À la)	With a fried onion garnish or sauce
Macaroni	Flour paste dried and forced through a tube
Macaroons	Sweet biscuits made of ground almonds, sugar and white of the egg
Macédoine	Term for a mixture of vegetables or a fruit salad or jellied fruit
Madéleine	Special shaped small sponge cake coated with jam and coconut
Maigre (À la)	Meatless dishes
Maitre d'hotel	Sauce of butter, parsley and lemon; also title given to the head steward
Maquereau	Mackerel
Maraschino	Special cherry used for a liqueur
Marinade	Preparation of oil, herbs and vinegar in which food is steeped
Marron	Chestnuts
Marsala	A wine similar to madeira
Marzipan	Almond paste for icing and sweetmeats
Mayonnaise	Cold sauce of egg yolks, oil and vinegar
Médallion	Meat prepared in a small round shape
Melba toast	A very thin crisp toast
Meringue	Light dessert of egg white and sugar
Meriuche	Dried or smoked haddock or stockfish
Meuniere	Sauce melted butter, parsley and lemon
Minestrone	Thick vegetable soup with pasta
Minute (À la)	Description of food cooked speedily
Mirepoux	Preparation of vegetables and herbs for brown soups and sauces
Mirlitons	Custard tarts made with french puff pastry
Mirotons	Small pieces of braised meat
Mocha	Flavoured with coffee
Montmorency	Flavoured with asparagus
Mornay	Cheese sauce
Moules	Mussels
Moussaka	Greek version of a shepherd's pie with aubergines
Mousse	Light foamy dessert
Mousseline	Hollandaise sauce with whipped cream
Moutard	Mustard
Mozzarella	Soft mild curd cheese traditionally made with buffalo milk
Mulligatawny	A curry soup
Muscade	Nutmeg
Nasi Goreng	East Indian meat dish with rice, highly spiced garnished with strips of omelette
Navarin	Haricot mutton stew
Negus	Hot-toddy of port wine, sugar, nutmeg and lemon juice
Neige	Snow – egg-white whisked to a froth
Nesselrode	Iced chestnut pudding
Nicoise	Sauces for fish or meat usually with garlic, onions or beans
Noisette	Small pieces of lean meat
Nouilles	Noodles – German dish served boiled as a savoury or fried as a sweet
Noyau	A liqueur flavoured with peach or nectarine kernels
Okra	From South America, used as a vegetable or made into a soup and casserole
Oignon	Onion
Orly	Fish or meat dipped in batter and fried in fat
Paella	Stew of fish or chicken with rice, tomatoes, garlic and olives
Pain	Bread
Pain d'epice	Spiced bread – a kind of gingerbread
Pamplemousse	Grapefruit
Panache	Mixture of two or more kinds of vegetables or fruits
Paprika	Hungarian red pepper
Parmentier	Cooked with potatoes
Parmesan	Italian cheese usually made from goat's milk and grated very finely
Passer	To sieve or strain
Pasta	Wheat flour and water, dried and cut into various shapes – macaroni, spaghetti
Pâté Feuilletee	Puff paste
Pâté Frisee	Short paste
Pâté Pastillage	Gum paste
Pâté-de-foie gras	Preparation of the livers of fatted geese
Patisserie	The art of the pastry-cook, also the bakery
Pavlova	Meringue nest filled with fruit and whipped cream
Pêche melba	Half a peach on ice cream with raspberry sauce
Persil	Parsley
Petits fours	Small fancy cakes and biscuits
Petit suisse	Cream cheese
Petits pois	Young green peas
Petit Lait	Whey

Pilaf/Pilau	Turkish spiced dish of meat, onions and rice
Pièce de résistance	Principal dish of the meal
Pimento	Spanish red pepper used in salads and garnish
Pistaches	Pistachio nut kernels used for flavouring and garnish
Pita bread	Flat oval bread with a spit for inserting a filling
Plat du jour	Special dish of the day
Polenta	Italian dish of Indian corn flour
Pommes	Apples
Pommes de terre	Potatoes
Posset	Hot milk curdled with wine
Potage	Soup
Pot-au-feu	Economical beef broth origin of beef stock
Poullet en casserole	Chicken fried with butter
Poulet á la reine	Chicken dressed with a white sauce
Praline	Flavoured with burnt almonds
Printantière	Diced spring vegetables
Profiterolles	Pastries of choux pastry filled with cream or custard
Provençale	Sauce of garlic, tomato, onions and oil
Purée	Smooth pulp
Quenelles	Minced meat, poultry, fish or eggs shaped and poached and served as an entrée
Quiche Lorraine	Savoury cheese custard tart with chopped cooked meat
Ragoût	Highly seasoned pork stew
Ramekin	Small dish for serving individual portion
Ratafia	Essence of bitter almonds
Ravigote	Richly flavoured green herb sauce
Rechauffe	Warmed-up meat- dish made of left-overs
Régence	White wine sauce with mushrooms and truffles
Rémoulade	Cold sauce with savoury herbs as salad dressing
Rennet	Used for curdling milk
Ricotta	Sweet cottage cheese
Rillettes	Potted meat
Rissoles	Mixture of minced meat or fish, shaped and fried
Risotto	Rice dish served with meat, fish or poultry
Roquefort	Strong blue-veined crumbly cheese
Sachertorte	Rich Viennese chocolate sponge filled with jam, coated with chocolate icing and cream
Saignant	Underdone
Salamander	Utensil heated to red hot and used for browning
Sally Lunn	Slightly sweetened yeast tea-cake
Sambals	Side dishes to accompany curry
Saurer	To cure in smoke
Sauterne	French white wine favoured for cooking
Savarin	Light yeast cake soaked in rum, served with whipped cream
Savoy	Special variety of cabbage
Schnitzel	Thin cutlet or escalope, usually veal
Sec	Wine – dry
Smörgåsbord	Buffet with addition of open sandwiches
Sorbet	Water ice
Soubise	Any dish with onions as one of the main ingredients
Souchet	Fish dish with vegetables and herbs
Stracchino	Soft, goat's milk cheese
Succotash	American dish of lima beans and green corn
Sukiyaki	Japanese dish of meat and vegetables cooked at the table and placed on a raw egg
Suprême	Rich, delicately flavoured cream sauce
Syllabub	Milk dish flavoured with spices
Table d'hôte	Set menu for a fixed price
Tagliatelle	Wide strips of pasta
Tansy	Aromatic herb often used in custard
Tarragon	Aromatic plant used for flavouring vinegar
Tartare	Cold sauce made of egg yolks, mustard and capers often served with fried fish
Terrine	Earthenware dish for potting and serving cold meats and pates
Tournedos	Small fillets of beef
Tortellini	Small rounds of pasta with savoury fillings
Tourte	Open tart
Tourtelettes	Small tartlets
Turmeric	Root of a plant from which a yellow powder is obtained to colour curry powder
Tutti-frutti	Ice cream of various flavours with a mixture of fresh or glacé fruits
Velouté	Rich white foundation sauce
Vermicelli	Very thin threads of pasta
Vinaigrette	Salad dressing made from oil and vinegar, with seasoning
Vol-au-vent	Small puff pastry case with savoury filling
Zabaglione	Light cream dessert of eggs with wine usually served in large wineglasses

PHOBIAS AND MANIAS

Acrophobia	Fear of heights
Aerophobia	Fear of flying
Agoraphobia	Fear of open spaces
Ailurophobia	Fear of cats
Amathophobia	Fear of dust
Amaxophobia	Fear of riding in a vehicle
Anthropophobia	Fear of people
Apiphobia	Fear of bees
Arachibutyrophobia	Fear of peanut butter clogging the mouth
Arachnophobia	Fear of spiders
Bactraphobia	Fear of reptiles
Blennophobia	Fear of slime
Brontophobia	Fear of thunder
Cathisophobia	Fear of sitting down
Claustrophobia	Fear of enclosed spaces
Chromophobia	Fear of colours/staining
Cynophobia	Fear of dogs
Deiphnophobia	Fear of dining and the conversation there
Erythrophobia	Fear of blushing and the colour red
Euphobia	Fear of good news
Gephydrophobia	Fear of crossing bridges
Gynephobia	Fear of women
Helminthopia	Fear of worm infestation
Homophobia	Fear of certain sexual preferences
Hydrophobia	Fear of water (usually linked to rabies)
Hylephobia	Intense dislike of wood
Ideaphobia	Fear of reason and ideas
Kleptomania	Intense urge to steal
Levophobia	Fear of objects on the left side
Macromania	Delusions of becoming large
Mastigophia	Fear of flogging
Nebulaphobia	Fear of clouds
Nyctophobia	Fear of darkness
Phonomania	Irresistible urge to commit homicide
Phonophobia	Fear of speaking aloud and loud sounds
Pyromania	Impulse to light fires
Pyrophobia	Fear of fires
Sciophobia	Fear of shadows
Spexsophobia	Fear of wasps
Technophobia	Fear of technology
Thalassophobia	Fear of the ocean
Thanatophobia	Fear of death
Trichotillomania	Compulsion to pull out one's hair
Triskaidekaphobia	Fear of number thirteen
Xenomania	Obsession for anything foreign
Xenophobia	Fear of strangers and all things foreign

FOREIGN PHRASES, TERMS AND WORDS

Ab aeterno	From eternity
Ab initio	From the beginning
Ab origine	From the origin
Addendum	Something added, an appendix
À deux	Only two
Ad diem	To the appointed day
Ad eundem	To the same class
Ad hoc	For one time or thing only
Ad idem	Of the same mind
Ad interim	For the time being
Ad libitum	As much as is wanted
Ad nauseam	To the point of disgust
Ad valorem	According to value, as per the levy of custom duties
Ad vitam aut culpam	Description of an office held for life
Affaire de coeur	A love affair
Affaire d'honneur	A matter of honour
Agent provocateur	A secret agent infiltrating a group to betray the members
Aid de camp	An officer, as confidential assistant to a superior commander
À la bonne heure	Well timed, appropriately on time
À la mode	In a fashionable way
Al fresco	In the open air
Aliter	Otherwise
Alma Mater	Name given by students to the university where they obtained their degrees

Alter idem	Another exactly similar
Amende honourable	A full apology
A mensa et toro	A term for full marital relations
Angst	Psychiatric definition of anxiety
Animus...	Intention of...
Annus mirabilis	A year of astounding or newsworthy events
Ante meridiem (AM)	Before noon Morining
A propos	To the point
A rebours	Against the grain
Arguendo	In the course of the argument
Arrière-pensée	Having second thoughts
Au courant	Fully informed
Auctor in rem suam	Description of agent or trustee acting dishonestly
Au fait	To be skilled or experienced in a chosed pursuit
Au revoir	Till we meet again
Au secours!	Help!
Autrefors acquit (or convict)	Defines the law of only being tried once for the same crime
Avanti	Forward
Bas blue	A learned female, a blue stocking
Bête noire	Something bad which is haunting, literally a black beast
Billet doux	A love letter
Blasé	Bored, affectation
Bona fide	Good faith, to confirm the truth, genuine
Bona vicantia	Ownerless property taken by the finder
Bonhomie	General sense of well-being, pleasant disposition
Bon soit	Good night
Bon vivant	To live well
Bon viveur	To live for pleasure, irresponsible
Bourgeois	The middle class
Brevi manu	Short cut, usually refers to action taken without recourse to the court
Cadit quaestio	Refusing further argument
Canard	A hoax, a rumour
Carte blanche	A free hand, given full power to act
Causa Causans	Possible immediate cause of the occurrence
Caue célèbre	A notorious trial being held in court
Caveat emptor	Buyer beware
Cave canem	Beware of the dog
Chargé d'affaires	A rank lower than ambassador
Cherchez la femme	Find the woman, often used in a crime of passion
Che sará sará!	What will be, will be!
Comme il faut	Socially correct
Compos mentis	Of sound mind
Consensus ad idem	Consent of all parties necessary to validate a contract
Contratemps	An embarrassing mishap
Corpus delicti	The material evidence of a crime of felony
Corrigendum	Correction in a book
Cose fan tutte	They all behave alike (refers to women)
Couleur de rose	High expectations, looking through rose-coloured spectacles, naivety
Coup d'etat	Seizure of power, overthrow of authority
Coup de grace	The final thrust, death blow
Crême de la crême	The cream of the cream, absolute perfection
Cul-de-sac	A blind alley, investigation leading nowhere
Culpa	Intention or negligence
Cum grano salis	With a grain of salt, having reservations or doubts
Cum privilegio	With privilege, permission to use material
Da capo	Repeat from the beginning
De bene esse	To accept something at face value until it is confirmed
De facto	In reality, authority in power, even if illegal
De jure	Lawful, legally constituted authority
Del credere agent	For extra payment this agent will guarantee to make a full collection of dues
De minimis non eurat lex	The law is not concerned with trifles
Deo volente (DV)	God willing
De profundis	Out of the depths (of misery and despair)
Deo riguer	Something absolutely necessary, obligatory
Denier ressort	The last resort
Détente	Relaxation of tension, usually between nations
Détour	Inability to take a direct route
De trop	Too much, in excess of acceptable standards
Divertissement	A period of relaxation usually with entertainment
Divide et impera	Divide and rule, prevention of a group organising a riot or protest
Double entendre	Double meaning, devious
Dulce domum	Home, sweet home
Egalite	Equality

El dorado	Land of gold, the epitome of paradise
Elite	The best
Emeritus	One retired from professional activities
Emigré	Emigrant
En avant!	Forward!
En bloc	All together
En déshabille	In a state of undress, unprepared
Enfant terrible	To cause trouble and/or noisy disturbances
Engenue	A young, unsophisticated person
En masse	In a cohesive group
Ennui	Boredom
En passant	In passing
En rapport	To be in sympathy with ...
Entente cordiale	An agreement to co-operate, to work for the good of all parties
Entourage	A group of attendants, relatives or assistants
Entre nous	Just between us
Entrepreneur	A developer or organiser who is prepared to undertake operations considered chancy
En vertre sa mere	"Unborn child" – dealing with the lawful rights
Ergo	Therefore – consequently
Esprit de corps	Support and assistance given by members of a group to each other
Et tu brute!	Accusation to a false friend
Eureka!	Triumphant cry at the achievement of purpose
Exeat	To grant leave
Exempli gratia	For example
Ex gratia	Given as a favour
Ex officio	By virtue of his office
Ex parte	Made on behalf of an absent party
Experto crede	Trust the expert
Ex post facto	After the event – with hindsight
Ex tempore	Without preparation
Ex turpi causa non ovitun actio	Legal action impossible by virtue of an illegal contract
Facsimile	A perfect copy
Factotum	A general dogsbody expected to perform all and sundry tasks within his orbit
Fait accompli	Something accomplished or completed often without permission, but cannot be reversed or changed
Faute de mileux	To have to accept less than the best
Fauteuil	A seat in the stalls of a theatre
Faux pas	Committing a social error often resulting in acute embarrassment
Felo de se	Suicide
Feme covert	Married woman
Feme sole	Single woman
Ferae naturae	Description which encompasses all animals accepted as wild, even if born in captivity
Flagrante delicto	To be caught red-handed, discovered in an embarrassing situation
Force majeure	Irresistable comulsion, devastating experience out of one's control
Garde du corps	Bodyguard
Goutte â goutte	Drop by drop
Gratis	Free of charge, for nothing
Hic jacet	Here lies (a corpse)
Hoc age	Do this
Hoi polloi	The common people
Honoris causa	For the sake of honour, honorary
Hors concours	Not in the competition
Hors combat	Physically unable to complete due to injury
Hors la loi	Outside the law
Hotêl de ville	A town hall
Idem (ID)	The same, repeat of previous reference
Id est (IE)	That is
Ignorantia juris non excusat	Ignorance of the law is not an acceptable excuse
Ignoratio elenchi	Not keeping to the point in an argument
Impedimenta	Luggage, encumbrances, obstacles to progress
In aeternum	For ever
In articulo mortis	At the point of death
In camera	Taking place behind closed doors, no public hearing
Induciae	Period allowed for a court order to be fulfilled
In esse	In fact, exists
In extenso	In entirety, no omissions, complete
In extremis	The point of no return, the last gasp
In fiere	In the course of action
In forma pauperis	A poor person who qualifies for free legal representation
Infra dignitatem (Infra dig)	Beneath one's dignity, not worthy of notice
In futuro	In the future

In loco parentis	Taking the place of a parent, appointed guardian
In medias res	In the heart of the matter
In memoriam	In memory of
In propria persona	In person
In puris naturalibus	In a natural state, naked, unadorned
In situ	In its original place
In solidum	For the whole sum
Insouciance	In difference, not concerned
Inst.	Of this month
In status quo	In it original state, in it former condition
Inter alia	Among other things
Inter nos	Between ourselves
In terrorem	If intimidation is used to impose a condition, such a condition is illegal
Inter se	Between themselves
Inter vivos	Between living persons
In transitu	In the process of being transported
Intra vires	Valid, within the powers
In vacuo	Empty space, isolation
Invito domino	Without the owner's consent
Ipso facto	By the act itself, absolutely positive
Ipso jure	Lawful by the unquestioned right
Je ne sais quoi	I don't know! A quality unable to be defined
Jeu d'esprit	A witticism
Jure divino	A god's law
Jure humano	By man's law
Labor amnia vincit	Work conquers all things
Lacuna	A hiatus, a missing part
Laisser aller	Freedom from restraint
Laisser faire	Allowing things to drift to their own level, non-interference in the affairs of others
Lapus calami	A slip of the pen
Lapus linguae	A slip of the tongue
Le beau monde	The fashionable world
Lex non scripta	The common and/or unwritten law
Lex scripta	Law according to statutes
Lex talionis	Retaliation or punishment in the style of the crime or offence
Littera scripta manet	The written word is inscribed forever
Loco citato (Loc cit)	Refers to a passage in a book previously quoted
Locum tenens	A deputy
Locus poenitontiae	Right to withdraw from a transaction not legally finalised
Locus standi	The legal right to an appearance in court
Mal â propos	At the wrong time
Mal de mer	Seasickness
Mal fide	In bad faith
Mea culpa	It is my own fault, I am to blame
Memorabilia	Keepsakes, souvenirs
Minutiae	Trifles, inconsequental things
Modus operandi	The method of operation
Modus vivendi	A way of living
Mora	Delay in asserting a right
Mutato nomine	Under a changed name
Né (M.) and Née (F.)	The name born with
Ne exeat regno	Legal restraint on a person's departure from the country
Nemine contradicente (Nem con)	Unanimously, without contradiction
Noblesse oblige	Responsible behaviour considered proper for the persons of the nobility
Non est factum	To deny the signature on a deed or document
Non compus mentis	Mentally unstable
Non sequitur (Non seq)	To reach a conclusion without relevance to the matter at hand
Nota bene (NB)	Note well
Milli secundus	Second to none
Obit (OB)	Notice of death
Omnia vincit amor	Love conquers all
Pactum illicitum	Illegal contract
Pari passu	Share proportionately
Particeps criminis	Participant in a criminal/illegal activity
Pendente lite	While the action is pending
Per capita	To each their share
Per diem	By the day
Per Procurationem (Per Pro/PP)	Denotes a deputy who signs on behalf of a principal
Per se	By itself
Persona grata	A person whose presence is welcomed
Poco a poco	Little by little
Prima facie	The first sight, enough to warrant an investigation

Probatum est	It has been proved
Pro bono publico	For the good of the public
Pro et con	For and against
Pro forma	As a matter of form
Pro patria	For our country
Pro rata	In proportion
Pro tempore	For the time being
Prout de jure	Provided by an expert
Quantum	How much?
Quantum libet	As much as one would like
Quantum sufficit (Quant suff)	As much as is needed
Quem deus perder vult pruis dementat	Those who God wishes to destroy, he first drives mad
Quid pro quo	Tit for tat, compensation in like
Quod erat demonstrandum (QED)	Which had to be proved
Quod vide (QV)	Which see, indicates a cross-reference
Quondam	Formerly
Reductio ad absurdum	Inconsistency which produces a ridiculous argument
Réspondez s'il vous plait (RSVP)	Request to reply to an invitation
Requiescat in pace (RIP)	Rest in peace, refers to the final resting place of the dead
Res nullius	Having no owner
Restitutio in integrum	Restore to the original position, as in the cancellation of a contract
Sans recourse	Where a signatory on a bill does not accept liability for payment
Selon grandeur (SG)	Price according to size or quantity
Semper eadem	Always the same
Semper paratus	Always ready
Similia similibus curantur	Like is cured by like
Sine die	Indefinitely, no specific date given
Sine prole (SP)	Without issue
Sine qua non	An essential condition
Solatium	Compensation for pain and suffering
Sotto voce	Very quiet voice, whisper
Sponsio ludicra	Promise made as a joke or bet cannot be enforced
Stare decisis	Based on precedents
Status quo	To revert to the original condition, the existing position
Sub judice	Under consideration, unable to be discussed
Sub rosa	Secretly, privately, confidentially
Suggestio	Insinuation, to suggest something false, misrepresentation
Suppressio veri	To deliberately hide the truth
Taediam vitae	Lack of interest in living
Tempus fugit	Time flies (Completion is "et nunquam revertitur" ... and never returns)
Terminus ad quem	The last possible date
Terminus a quo	The first possible date
Terra firma	To have a firm base underfoot, the earth
Terra incognita	Unknown territory
Totidem verbis	In so many words
Toties quoties	As often as
Tour de force	To show strength
Tout de suite	At once!
Uberrima fides	High standard of good faith
Ubi jus ibi remedium	Where there is a right there is a remedy
Ultimo	Of last month, the previous month
Ultra vires	Out of bounds of the legal authority
Una voce	Unanimously – with one voice
Veni, Vidi, Vici	I came, I saw, I conquered
Verbatim et literatim	Word for word
Versus	Against
Via media	A middle course
Vice versa	To reverse the order
Vide	See
Videlicet (Viz)	Namely, used as an introduction to items on lists
Vis-á-vis	Face to face – opposite
Vis major	Acts of God, Hostile acts

MYTHOLOGY

Greek

Aeolus	God of the winds
Amphitrite	Goddess of the sea/mother of Triton
Aphrodite	Goddess of love
Apollo/Helios	God of the sun/prophecy
Ares	God of war/Protector of herds
Artemis	Goddess of the moon/hunt
Asclepius	Son of Apollo/God of medicine
Athene/Pallas	Goddess of wisdom/arts
Bachus/Diunysus	God of wine/pleasure/vineyards
Boreas	God of the north wind
Chloris	Goddess of flora
Cronos/Kronos	God of sowing
Demeter/Chloe	Goddess of earth/agriculture
Enyo	Goddess of war
Eos	Goddess of dawn/mother of the four winds
Eros	God of love
Ge/Gaia	Goddess of the earth
Hades	God of death
Hebe	Goddess of youth/spring
Hecate	Goddess of magic
Hephaestus	God of metalworking/fire
Hera	Supreme goddess
Hermes	God of commerce/Messenger of the gods
Hygeia	Goddess of health
Hymen	God of marriage
Hypnos	God of sleep
Irene	Goddess of peace
Iris	Goddess of the rainbow
Ker	Goddess of death
Komos	God of revelry
Moirai	The three fates
Morpheus	God of dreams
Nemesis	Goddess of retribution
Nereus	Sea god, father of sea nymphs
Nike	Goddess of victory
Oceanus	God of the waters encircling the earth
Pan	God of nature/fidelity
Poseidon	God of the seas
Priapus	Demi-god, servant of Poseidon
Thanatos	God of Death
Themus	Goddess of justice
Triton	Son of Poseidon
Tyche	Goddess of fortune
Uranus	God of Heaven
Zephyrus	God of the West Wind
Zeus	Supreme god

Roman

Aesculapius	God of medicine and healing
Annona	Goddess of crops
Aurora	Goddess of the dawn
Bellona	Goddess of war
Ceres	Goddess of agriculture
Compus	God of revelry
Cupid	God of love
Diana	Goddess of the moon
Epora	Goddess of horses
Faura	Goddess of fields
Faunas	God of nature and fertility
Flora	Goddess of flowers
Fortuna	Goddess of fortune
Janus	God of doors and gates
Juno	Supreme goddess
Jupiter/Jove	Supreme god
Libitina	Goddess of burials
Lucina	Goddess of childbirth
Luna	Goddess of the moon
Mars	God of war
Mercury	God of commerce/Messenger of the gods
Minerva	Goddess of wisdom/arts
Mors	God of death

Nemesis	Goddess of vengeance
Neptune	God of the sea
Nona/Parca	Goddess of fate
Nox/Nyx	Goddess of the night
Ops	Goddess of plenty
Orcus	God of the dead
Pan	God of woods and herds
Pax	Goddess of peace
Phoebe	Goddess of the moon
Pomona	Goddess of fruit
Pluto	God of the underworld
Priapus	God of fertility
Salus	Goddess of health
Saturn	God of sowing
Somnus	God of sleep
Spes	Goddess of hope
Termirius	God of boundaries
Venus	Goddess of love
Vesta	Goddess of hearth and home

Egyptian

Aani	Dog-headed ape
Amen/Amon	King of the gods Ram-headed
Anubis	Jackal-headed god, son of Osiris, conducted the dead to judgement
Bast/Pasht	Cat-headed god
Bes/Tem	God of pleasure
Geb/Keb	God of earth
Hathor	Goddess of love, wife of Horus, cow god
Horus/Ra	Supreme sungod, falcon/hawk
Isis/Mut	Goddess of agriculture
Jerboa	Leaping mouse
Ma/Maat	Goddess of truth
Min	God of procreation
Nit	Goddess of war
Nun	God of waters
Nut	Goddess of heaven
Osiris	God of the underworld
Serapis	God of healing
Set/Seth	God of evil
Shu	God of air
Sothis	God of stars
Thoth	Ibis-headed god of wisdom, scribe of the gods, inventor of numbers and measure of time
Udot	Cobra goddess
Uraeus	Serpent, symbol of power on a headdress to spit venom on enemies

Norse

Aegir/Hler	God of the sea
Aesir/Vanir	Gods
Asgard	Home of the gods
Balder	God of light
Berserker	A warrior
Bragi	God of poetry
Egil/Egill	Heroes
Eir	Goddess of healing
Fenris	Legendary wolf
Frey	God of fertility
Freya	Goddess of beauty/love
Garm	Dog guarding the underworld
Gefion	Goddess of the maidens
Gerd/Hel	Goddess of death
Kraken	A sea-monster
Lok	God of evil
Loki	God of mischief
Midgard	Serpent
Nanna	Goddess of flowers
Norns	Goddess of fates
Odin	God of wisdom/god of war
Ran	Goddess of the sea/drowning
Thor	God of thunder
Tui/Tyr	God of the sky
Urd	Goddess of destiny
Valhalla	Underworld for the heroes
Vayu	God of wind
Vor	God of couples promised in marriage

LITERARY CHARACTERS IN MYTHOLOGY

Achilles	Hero of Homer's *Iliad*. Killed by an arrow in his heel, the only vulnerable part of his body
Actaeon	Hero from Boeotia, punished for watching Artemis bathing
Adonis	A beautiful youth loved by Aphrodite
Aeneas	Portrayed in the *Iliad* as leader of the Trojans, his descendants are said to have founded Rome
Agamemnon	In the *Iliad*, the commander-in-chief of the Greek expedition
Ajax	Commander of a fleet in the Trojan war
Alastor	Son of Neleus, brother of Nestor
Alcaeus	Son of Perseus
Alcestis	Daughter of Pelias, wife of king Admetus of Thessaly
Amazons	Female warriors of Asia Minor said to amputate their right breast to improve their use of the bow
Amphitryon	Son of Alcaeus, grandson of Perseus
Amynton	Father of Phoenix, killed by Heracles
Anchises	Father of Aeneas
Andromache	Wife of Hector of Troy
Andromeda	Chained to a rock by her father, rescued by Perseus who then married her
Antigone	Daughter of Dedipis and Jocasta
Argonauts	Adventurers who sailed with Jason to find the golden fleece
Ariadne	Daughter of Minos of Crete who gave Theseus the thread to assist him to leave after killing the minotaur
Atalanta	Lost a race through stopping to pick up the golden apples
Atreus	Father of Agamemnon and Meenelaus
Attis/Atys	Young lover of Cybele, forced to castrate himself because of her jealousy
Avernus	A deep lake near Puteoli reputed to be the entrance to the underworld
Bellerophon	Son of the king of Corinth who slew the Chimaera with the help of the winged horse Pegasus
Cadmus	Son of Agenor, king of Phoenicia who founded the city of Thebes
Calchas	Greek soothsayer with the army at the siege of Troy
Callirrhoe	Daughter of the river-god Achelous
Calypso	Nymph who detained Odysseus on the island of Ogygia for seven years
Cassandra	Daughter of Priam of Troy, prophetess of evil, taken by Agamemnon after the fall of Troy, then murdered his wife
Cassiopeia	Mother of Andromeda
Cecrops	Legendary first king of Attica
Centaur	Half-man, half-horse creature portrayed on the frieze of the Parthenon fighting the Lapithea
Cerberus	Three-headed dog guarding the entrance to Hades
Chaos	Mother of Erebus
Charities	The graces, the three daughters of Zeus – Aglaia, Euphrosyne and Thalia
Charon	Ferryman carrying the souls of the dead across the river Styx. Coin in mouth of corpse was fee
Charybdis and Scylla	Whirlpool guardian of the Straits of Messina
Chimaera	Triple-headed monster
Chiron	Wise centaur taught by Apollo, subsequently teacher of Achilles and Jason
Cimmerians	People living in perpetual darkness in Europe according to Homer
Circe	Goddess of island of Aeaea who trapped Odysseus and his men until Hermes assisted them
Clytemnestra	Sister of Helen of Troy, wife of Agamemnon
Creon	King of Thebes, whose daughter, Glauce, was promised to Jason but subsequently killed by Medea
Cyclops	Giants with a single eye in the centre of their forehead
Daedalus	Built the maze for King Minos to escape, made wings for himself and his son, Icarus, who flew too close to the sun. The wax melted and Icarus was drowned
Danaus	King of Argo who insisted his fifty daughters kill their husbands on their wedding night. They were the sons of an Egyptian king. Lynceus survived and then killed Danaus
Daphne	Daughter of the river-god Ladon. To escape the attentions of Apollo she was changed into a Laurel bush
Daphnis	Sicilian shepherd credited with inventing Bucolic verse
Deucalion	Greek son of Prometheus. He and his wife survived the flood sent by Zeus
Dido	Legendary daughter of Belus, king of Tyre who founded Carthage. Lover of Aeneas
Diomedes	Thracian, king of Bistonian, the capture of his man-eating horses was one of the labours of Heracles/Hercules
Dioscure	Joint name of Castor and Polydeuces/Pollux – on their death Zeus placed them among the stars as the Gemini
Dryads	Wood nymphs also known as Hamadryads
Echo	Nymph deprived of the power of speech except to repeat the last words spoken by others, she loved Narcissus and pined away until only her voice remained
Egeria/Aegeria	Roman nymph worshipped by pregnant women seeking an easy birth, revered for her wisdom
Electra/Elektra	Daughter of Agamemnon and Clytemnestra who saved the life of her brother, Orestes. She urged him to kill their adulterous mother who murdered their father
Elysium	Greek and Roman paradise where, according to Homer, only heroes were allowed to dwell
Endymion	Beautiful youth loved by Selene (the moon) who imposed continuous sleep on him
Erechtheus	Fabled king of Athens, son of the earth, reared by Athena
Erigone	Illegitimate daughter of Clytemnestra
Erinyes/Eumenindes	Avenging spirits
Eris	Legendary figure representing strife using the apple of discord

Europa	Daughter of Agenor, king of Phoenicia. Zeus, using the form of the bull, gave her three sons, Minos, Sarpedon and Rhadamanthus
Eurydice	Wife of Opheus, compelled to remain in Hades because her husband disobeyed Pluto
Galatea	An ivory statue sculpted by Pygmalion which was given life by Aphrodite
Ganymede	Beautiful youth abducted by Zeus to be his cup-bearer
Gigantes	Giants who attacked Olympus, killed by the gods and Heracles, then buried under Mount Aetna
Glauce	Daughter of Crion, the king of Corinth/Thebes
Glaucus	Father of Bellerophon
Gorgon	Three winged female monsters with enormous teeth and snakes for hair. Medusa was killed by Perseus, when he decapitated her. The winged horse Pegasus rose from her blood
Griffin	Mythical creature with the body of a lion and the head and wings of an eagle
Harmonia	Daughter of Ares and Aphrodite
Harpies	Spirits of the winds, thieves of people and objects
Hector	Son of Priam King of Troy, bravest of the Troy champions
Hecuba	Daughter of Phrygian king and wife of Priam – among her many sons were Hector and Paris
Heracles/Hercules	Son of Zeus by Alemene. Had exceptional strength and twelve labours to execute by order of the king of Tiryns, Eurystheus
Hero and Leander	Famous lovers
Hesperides	Daughters of Atlas, guardians of the garden of the golden apples
Hyacinthus	Beautiful youth accidentally killed and the flower grew where his blood flowed
Hylas	Son of Theiodamas, king of the Dryopes, pulled into a spring by Nymphas
Hymen	Handsome young man with a perfect marriage
Hyperboreans	Reputed northern race of Apollo-worshippers admired by the Greeks
Hyperion	Titan father of Eos, Helios and Selene
Icarius	Athenian taught by Dionysuss to make wine
Idomeneus	King of Crete forced to sacrifice his son to fulfill an unwise vow
Ilus	Founder of Ilion, city of Troy
Iolaus	Son of Iphicles. Constant companion of Heracles
Ion	Son of Apollo, legendary ancestor of Ionians
Iphicles	Twin brother of Heracles
Iphigenia	Daughter of Agamemnon and Clytemnestra, offered as a sacrifice but then replaced by a deer, in order that the Greek fleet could be saved
Ixion	King of Thessaly, father of the Centaurs
Jason	Son of Aeson, king of Iolcos, leader of the Argonauts
Jocasta	Sister of Creon, mother of Oedipus, who she married in error
Kronos/Cronos	Youngest son of Uranus, leader of the Titans, father of Zeus who dethroned him
Leartes	King of Ithaca, father of Odysseus, and an Argonaut
Laestrygones	Race of giants who were cannibals
Laius	King of Thebes killed by his own son Oedipus in error
Lamia	Queen of the Laestrygones, the Roman "Lamiae", given as female vampires
Loacoon	Trojan priest who warned of the danger of the wooden horse
Ladmedon	King of Troy, Hector's grandfather
Lapithae	Mountain people of Thessaly
Lares/Penates	Deities of the Household
Larvae/Lemures	Ghost of the dead
Latona/Leto	Mother of Apollo and Artemis by Zeus
Latinus	King of Latium whose daughter, Lannia married Aeneas
Leda	Mother of Dioscuri and Helen of Troy by Zeus who visited her in the form of a swan
Lethe	River of Oblivion
Lycaon	King of Arcadia
Maia	Daughter of Atlas, mother of Hermes
Marsyas	Phrygian satyr, challenged Apollo to a musical contest
Medusa	One of the three Gorgons killed by Perseus
Memnos	Ethiopian king who fought with the Trojans and was killed by Achilles
Menelaus	King of Sparta, husband of Helen who was abducted by Paris
Menoeceus	Son of Creon
Mentor	Old Itachan who was charged by Odysseus to look after the household while he was away
Merope	One of the Pleiades who married a mortal
Metis	The first wife of Zeus and the deity of wisdom
Midas	Legendary Phrygian king with the power to turn everything he touched into gold, the power became a curse
Minos	King of Crete, son of Zeus and Europa, the builder of the Labyrinth for the home of the Minotaur
Minotaur	Monster half human/half bull killed by Theseus
Minyae	Legendary Greek people who settled in Boeotia
Mithras	Ancient Persian deity – god of light and guardian against evil
Myrmidons	Homer depicts these people as being ruled by Achilles
Naiads	Water nymphs
Narcissus	Son of the river god Cephissus. Fell in love with his reflection, pined away and became a flower
Nauplius	King of Euboea who wrecked many Greek ships to avenge the death of his son, Palamedes
Nausicaa	Daughter of Alcinous who saved the shipwrecked Odysseus
Neleus	King of Troy; eleven of his twelve sons were killed by Heracles
Neoptolemus	A Trojan warrior who killed Priam
Nereus	Father of the Nereids/sea nymphs

Nestor	Surviving son of Neleus – one of the Argonauts
Niobe	Her family was killed by Apollo and Artemis
Nyctimene	Daughter of King Sicyon. Athena transformed her into an owl after she was raped by her father
Odysseus	The hero of Homer's *Odyssey;* king of Ithaca, son of Laertes and Auticleia; father of Telemachus by Penelope
Oedipus	Son of Laius, king of Thebes, unknowingly killed his own father before marrying his mother
Ogyges	King of Thebes
Olympus	Highest mountain in Greece and legendary home of the gods
Orestes	Son of Agamemnon and Clytemnestra; avenged father's murder by slaying his mother and her lover
Orion	Giant hunter
Orpheus	Legendary Greek poet and musician
Orthia	Spartan name for Artemis
Palamedes	Son of Nauplius
Palladium	Sacred image of Athena
Pandareus	Native of Miletus whose daughters were abducted by the Harpies
Pandarus	Trojan archer, a favourite of Apollo
Pandora	She opened the box to release all the evils into the world
Paris	Second son of Priam – his adultery caused the Trojan war
Pasiphae	Wife of Minos and mother of the monster Minotaur
Patroclus	Friend and servant of Achilles, killed by Hector
Pegasus	Winged horse; symbol of poetic genius
Peirithous	King of the Lapithae; the abduction of his bride was the cause of the battle with the Centaurs
Peleus	Son of Aeacus, king of Myrmidons, father of Achilles
Pelias	Brother of Neleus
Pelops	Son of Tantalus; he caused the death of the king of Pisa, married his daughter and took the throne
Penates	Roman spirits of the kitchen, protectors of the house
Penelope	Wife of Odysseus
Penthesilea	Daughter of Ares, queen of the Amazons
Pentheus	Grandson of Cadmus from whom he inherited the throne of Thebes
Perdix	Nephew of Daedalus – inventor of the saw, chisel and compass
Pericles	Builder of the Parthenon
Persephone	Daughter of Zeus and Demeter, compelled to spend six months in the underworld
Perseus	Son of Zeus, he accidentally killed his maternal grandfather and became king of Tiryns
Phaedra	Daughter of King Minos, wife of Theseus
Philemon and Baucis	A peasant couple who gave shelter to Zeus and Hermes who warned them of the great flood
Philoctetes	Archer to Heracles who killed Paris of Troy
Phoenix	Legendary bird of Egypt which died in a fire, but then a new bird rose from the ashes
Pleiades	Daughters of Atlas
Polydoris	Youngest son of Priam and Hecuba
Polyxena	Daughter of Priam and Hecuba
Priam	King of Troy at the time of the war his son, Hector was killed
Procrustes/	A robber who tortured his victims. Killed by Theseus, son of a Titan, brother of Atlas; stole fire from the gods to give to the mortals
Prometheus	
Proserpina	*See* Persephone
Psyche	Personification of the human soul; although a mortal she was loved by Cupid
Pygmalion	King of Cyprus who fell in love with an ivory statue he had made and which was brought to life by Aphrodite
Pyramus and Thisbe	Original mythical Romeo and Juliet
Python	Female serpent killed by Apollo at Delphi
Remus and Romulus	Twin sons of Mars, suckled by a she-wolf; founders of Rome
Rhea	A Titan, wife of Kronos, mother of Zeus, Demeter, Hades and Poseidon
Sarpedon	Son of Zeus and Europa, became king of Lycia; killed by Patroclus in the Trojan war
Satyrs	Lecherous creatures represented by half-man, half-goat attendants of Dionysus
Scylla	*See* Charybdis
Semele	Daughter of Cadmus, mother of Dionysus by Zeus
Serapis	Egyptian deity used as Hellenistic cult figure
Sybil	Priestess of Apollo
Silenus	Son of Hermes of Pan; reputed to be a prophet
Siren	Half-woman, half-bird nymph who lured sailors to their deaths with her singing
Sisyphus	Legendary founder and first king of Corinth
Sphinx	Female figure with a human head and the body of a lion; sent by Hera to Thebes, those unable to answer her riddle were eaten
Stentor	Greek Heral before Troy, famous for his powerful voice
Styx	River encircling the underworld
Syrinx	The pipes of Pan
Tantalus	Legendary king of Lydia, father of Pelops and Niobe
Tartarus	Area in Hades supposedly reserved for Titans
Telamon	Brother of Peleus, father of Ajax, companion of Heracles
Telegonus	Son of Odysseus by Circe, mistakenly killed his father and the married the widow, Penelope
Telemachus	Son of Odysseus by Penelope
Theseus	Attic hero son of Aegeus, king of Athens; slew Minotaur

Thetis	Greek sea-goddess who married a mortal, Peleus, by whom she bore Achilles
Tiresias	Blind soothsayer of Thebes
Titans	Six sons and six daughters of Uranus and Ge who rebelled against their father
Tithonus	Brother of Priam of Troy; when he grew old and ugly his lover, Eos, turned him into a grasshopper
Troy	Ancient city in Asia Minor, beseiged by the Greeks, once believed to be a legend but remains have been found
Tyndareus	Son of Spartan King Oebalus, husband of Leda
Typhon	Hundred-headed monster buried by Zeus under Mount Aetna; before its death it fathered many monsters
Ulysses	*See* Odysseus

PROVERBS

A bad excuse is better than none
A bad penny always returns
A bird in the hand is worth two in the bush
A bully is always a coward
A cat has nine lives
A cat may look at a king
A cock crows on his own dunghill
A cold hand means a warm heart
A creaking door hangs long (a complaining hypochondriac lives longer)
A drowning man clutches at straws
A dwarf on a giant's shoulders sees more than the giant
A fair exchange is no robbery
A fool and his money are soon parted
A friend in need is a friend indeed
A good wife makes a good husband
A guilty conscience needs no accuser
A hungry man is an angry man
A little help is worth a lot of pity
A man is as old as he feels; a woman as old as she looks
A man is known by the company he keeps
A man of words and not deeds is a garden full of weeds
A nod is as good as a wink to a blind horse
A penny saved is a penny gained
A rolling stone gathers no moss
A short life and a gay one
A small leak will sink a great ship
A stitch in time saves nine
A tale never loses in the telling (gossip always grows)
A watched pot never boils
A woman's work is never done
A wonder lasts but nine days
A word spoken is past recalling
Actions speak louder than words
After death, comes the doctor (assistance arrives too late)
All is fair in love and war
All that glitters is not gold
All over bar the shouting
All work and no play makes Jack a dull boy
All's well that ends well
An apple a day keeps the doctor away
A man's home is his castle
An honest man's word is as good as his bond
An ounce of discretion is worth a pound of learning
Any port in a storm
Anything for a quiet life
As you make your bed so must you lie in it
Ask no questions and you'll be told no lies
At night all cats are grey
Be just before you are generous
Be just to all but trust not all
Beauty is only skin-deep
Bees have honey in their mouths but stings in their tails
Beggars cannot be choosers
Better the devil you know than the devil you don't
Better an empty house than a bad tenant
Better an old man's darling than a young man's slave
Better to be born lucky than rich
Better to be safe than sorry
Better do it than wish it done
Better give a shilling than lend two shillings
Better late than never

Better lose a jest than lose a friend
Birds of a feather flock together
Blood is thicker than water
Bread is the staff of life
Caesar's wife must be above suspicion (those in high positions must guard their actions)
Careless shepherds make many feasts for wolves
Curiosity killed the cat
Cast no dirt in the well that gives you water
Catch not at the shadow and lose the substance
Charity begins at home
Children should be seen and not heard
Circumstances alter cases
Civility costs nothing
Comparisons are odious
Confession is good for the soul
Constant dripping wears away a stone
Contentment is often found more in a cottage than in a palace
Critics are the brushers of noblemen's clothes
Dead men tell no tales
Death pays all debts
Delays are dangerous
Desperate diseases call for desperate remedies
Dexterity comes with experience
Discretion is often the better part of valour
Do as I say, not as I do
Do as you would be done by
Don't count your chickens before they are hatched
Don't cry before you are hurt
Don't fall between two stools
Don't keep a dog and bark yourself
Don't meet trouble half-way
Don't cross your bridges before you come to them
Don't put all your eggs in one basket
Don't spoil the ship for a ha'p'orth (halfpenny) of tar
Don't throw away the dirty water until you have clean
Don't throw out the baby with the bath water
Early to bed and early to rise, makes a man healthy, wealthy and wise
East, West home is best
Easy come, easy go
Eat to live, don't live to eat
Empty vessels make the most noise
Enough is as good as a feast
Even a worm will turn
Every ass loves his own bray
Every cloud have a silver lining
Every dog has his day
Every little bit helps
Every man has his faults
Every man is the architect of his own fortune
Every man to his trade
Everybody's business is nobody's business
Everything comes to those who wait
Everything must have a beginning
Facts are stubborn things
Faint heart never won fair lady
Fair play is a jewel
Familiarity breeds contempt
Feed a cold and starve a fever
Few words are best
Finders keepers
Fine feathers make fine birds
First come, first served
Fish and company stink in three days
Fools and madmen speak the truth
Fools build houses, wise men buy them
Forewarned is forearmed
Forgive and forget
Fortune favours fools and the brave
Fortune knocks once at every man's door
Give a dog a bad name and hang him
Give a lie twenty-four hours start and you will never overtake it
Give him enough rope and he will hang himself
Give me a child for seven years and then you may do what you will

Give the devil his due
Go farther and fare worse
God defend me from my friends
God help the poor, the rich can help themselves
God helps those who help themselves
Good masters make good servants
Good wine needs no bush (means something good requires no advertising)
Great minds think alike
Half a loaf is better than none
Handsome is as handsome does
Happy is the bride the sun shines on
Happy is the country which has no history
Hard words break no bones
Hasten slowly
Hear the other side
He is no man's enemy but his own
He who laughs last laughs longest
He who fights and runs away lives to fight another day
He who hides can find
Heads I win, tails you lose
Help me to salt, help me to sorrow
Here today, gone tomorrow
His bark is worse than his bite
His bread is buttered on both sides
His money burns a hole in his pocket
History repeats itself
Honest is the best policy
Hope for the best but prepare for the worst
Hypocrisy is the homage that vice pays to virtue
I fear the Greeks, especially when they bring gifts
If at first you don't succeed, then try, try again
If wishes were horses, then beggars would ride
If you desire peace then prepare for war
If you want a thing done well, then do it yourself
Ill-gotten gains never prosper
Ill news travels fast
In one ear and out the other
In for a penny, in for a pound
In the country of the blind the one-eyed man is king
It never rains but it pours
It takes all sorts to make a world
It takes two to make a quarrel
It's a long lane that has no turning
It's a poor heart that never rejoices
It's a wise child that knows its own father
It's an ill bird that fouls its own nest
It's an ill wind that blows nobody any good
It's easy to be wise after the event
It's good fishing in troubled waters
It's ill waiting for dead men's shoes
It's love that makes the world go round
It's never too late to mend
It's the pace that kills
Jack of all trades master of none
Jack's as good as his master
Jeerers must be content to taste of their own broth
Jesting lies bring serious sorrows
Keep a thing seven years and you will find a use for it
Keep not ill men company lest you increase the number
Keep your breath to cool your broth
Keep your purse and your mouth closed
Keeping from falling is better than helping up
Kindle not a fire that you cannot extinguish
Kindnesses, like grain, increase by sowing
Knavery, without luck, is the worst trade in the world
Knaves and fools divide the world
Knowledge begins a gentleman but conversation completes him
Knowledge is a treasure, but practice is the key to it
Knowledge is power
Know thyself
Laugh and grow fat
Least said soonest mended
Lend your money and lose your friend

Let bygones be bygones
Let sleeping dogs lie
Let the buyer beware
Let the cobbler stick to his last
Let well alone
Like father like son
Little things please little minds
Live and learn
Live and let live
Look before you leap
Look on the bright side
Lookers-on see most of the game
Love is blind
Love laughs at locksmiths
Love me, love my dog
Love will find a way
Lucky at cards, unlucky in love
Make a rod for you own back
Make a virtue of necessity
Make hay while the sun shines
Make the best of a bad bargain
Man proposes, God disposes
Manners maketh the man
Many a mickle makes a muckle (small gains mount up)
Many a true word spoken in jest
Many hands make light work
Marriage is a lottery
Marry in haste repent at leisure
Might as well be hanged for a sheep as for a lamb
Might is right
Misfortunes never come singly
Moderation in all things
Money begets money
Money does not smell
Money talks all languages
More haste less speed
More than enough is too much
Murder will out
Nature dislikes a vacuum
Necessity and opportunity may make a coward brave
Necessity is the mother of invention
Necessity knows no law
Never judge by appearances
Never put off till tomorrow what can be done today
Never too late to learn
Never trouble trouble till trouble troubles you
No fool like an old fool
No gains without pain
No kitchen is large enough to hold two women
No names no pack drill
No news is good news
No rose without a thorn
No smoke without a fire
No time like the present
None so blind as those who won't see
Not as black as he is painted
Nothing is certain but death and taxes
Nothing is so bad that it can't get worse
Nothing succeeds like success
Nothing ventured nothing gained
Of two evils choose the lesser
Old friends and old wines are best
Once bitten twice shy
Once seen never forgotten
One cannot be in two places at once
One good turn deserves another
One half of the world doesn't know how the other half lives
One law for the rich and one for the poor
One lie makes many
One man's meat is another man's poison
One must draw the line somewhere
One swallow does not make a summer
Opportunity makes the thief

Out of debt, out of danger
Out of sight, out of mind
Out of the frying pan and into the fire
Penny wise, pound foolish
People who live in glass houses should not throw stones
Practice makes perfect
Practise what you preach
Prevention is better than cure
Pride goes before a fall
Procrastination is the thief of time
Promises are like pie-crust, easily broken
Punctuality is the politeness of princes
Quick landlords make careful tenants
Rashness is not valour
Rather go to bed without supper than rise in debt
Rats desert a sinking ship
Remove an old tree and it will wither to death
Repentance comes too late
Respect the man and he will do more
Revenge is sweet
Rome was not built in a day
Satan finds mischief for idle hands
Save your breath to cool your porridge
Saying is one thing, doing is another
Second thoughts are best
Seeing is believing
Self-preservation is nature's first law
Set a thief to catch a thief
Share and share alike
Short and sweet
Silence gives consent
Six of one and half-a-dozen of the other
Slow and sure wins the race
Small profits, quick returns
Spare the rod and spoil the child
Speech is silver but silence is golden
Still waters run deep
Stolen fruit is often sweeter
Straws show which way the wind blows
Take care of the pennies and the pounds will take care of themselves
Take things as you find them
Talk of the devil and he is sure to appear
Tell the truth and shame the devil
That is a wise delay that makes the road safe
The bait hides the hook
The best of friends must part
The better the day, the better the deed
The boot is on the other foot
The burnt child dreads the fire
The darkest hour is before dawn
The devil looks after his own
The early bird catches the worm
The end justifies the means
The exception proves the rule
The face is the index of the mind
The fat is in the fire
The first step is the hard one
The game is not worth the candle
The grass is not always greener on the other side
The greater the truth, the greater the libel
The iron hand in the velvet glove
The law does not concern itself with trifles
The lesson learnt through pain seldom has to be learnt again
The longest day must have an end
The mills of God grind slowly but grind exceedingly small
The more, the merrier
The nearer the bone, the sweeter the meat
The safety of people is the highest law
The pitcher that goes to the well often breaks last
The proof of the pudding is in the eating
The receiver is as bad as the thief
The remedy can be worse than the disease
The road to hell is paved with good intentions

The sting is often in the tail
The tailor makes the man
The wish is father to the thought
There is honour among thieves
There's more than one way to skin a cat
There will be sleeping enough in the grave
There's many a slip between the cup and the lip
Times change but we can change with them
To cut off your nose to spite your face
To cut your coat according to your cloth
To err is human but to forgive is divine
Tomorrow never comes
Tomorrow is another day
Too many cooks spoil the broth
Truth is stranger than fiction
Truth sometimes is at the bottom of the well
Two heads are better than one
Two wrongs don't make a right
Uninvited guests are only welcome when they leave
Unkindness has no remedy at law
Unreasonable silence is folly
Use soft words and hard arguments
Valour would fight but discretion would run away
Venture a small fish to catch a big one
Vice makes virtue shine
Virtue is its own reward
Virtues all agree but vices fight one another
Wake not a sleeping lion
Walls have ears
Waste not want not
We never miss the water until the well runs dry
What can't be cured must be endured
What is bred in the bone comes out in the flesh
What is good for the goose is good for the gander
What is to be will be
What the eye doesn't see the heart won't grieve about
Whatever is worth doing is worth doing well
What's your's is mine and what's mine's my own
When in doubt leave it out
When in Rome do as the Romans do
When one door shuts, another door often opens
When the cat is away the mice will play
When the heat is too much then stay out of the kitchen
When thieves fall out then honest men come to their own
Whoever pays the piper calls the tune
Who sups with the devil needs a long spoon
Who the gods wish to destroy they first drive mad
Wilful waste makes wilful want
Wise men learn from the mistakes of others; fools by their own
Work ill done must be done again
You can't catch an old bird with chaff
You can't have your cake and eat it
You can't get blood out of a stone
You can't make an omelette without breaking eggs
You may take a horse to water but you can't make him drink
You must take the fat with the lean
You never know what you can do until you try
You scratch my back and I will scratch yours
Your trumpeter is dead
Youth and age will never agree
Youth and white paper take any impression
Youth must have its fling
Zeal is fit only for wise men but is found in fools
Zeal without knowledge is fire without light
Zeal without prudence is frenzy

COMPUTER TERMS

Access Time	The delay from the request to the answer
Accoustic Coupler	A low-cost modem for the transmission of data over the telephone
Accumulator	Storage register used for various types of transfer
Acknowledge	Signal used to confirm receipt of information
Acronym	Word formed by initial letters of other words
Adabas	Adaptable Database System for making direct queries
Adder	Logic circuit to add two binary valves together
Aggregation	Summarising data involved in making decisions
Algorithm	A precise sequence of steps to solve problems
Analogue	Transferring data over a line using fluctuating and logical function which returns the true frequencies output if both input are true
Applications Software	Programs designed for a specific task
Arithmetic and Logic	The section of the central processing unit handling calculation and decision making
Array	List of numbers referring to data items
Assembler	A system for representing alphanumeric characters in binary form
Assembly Language	A very low level programming language
Asynchronous	Low speed transmission where each character is sent individually
Audit Trail	Enables back tracking on a program to check effectiveness
Autoexec	A name of a batch of commands performed by a PC automatically when it starts
Background	Lower priority program
Backup	Spare copy of programs on data, security against loss
Baud	The unit of signalling speed
Benchmark Tests	A standard program to compare the performance of various computers
Binary Arithmetic	Number system using only symbols "0" and "1"
Binary Code	Short for binary digit, the smallest unit of data
Blinking	A blinking cursor used as a warning
Bootstrap	A term for the starting up process of a computer
Boundary	Assigned to a system under study in accordance with requirements
Branch	The transfer of control from one part of a program to another part
Buffer	A space in a computer system held until needed
Bug	An error or deliberate obstruction on a program
Burst	Separating continuous stationery into sheets
Byte	A collection of bits, usually eight, capable of signifying a single character
Central Processing Unit (CPU)	Controls activities and performs all the arithmetic and logic processes
Chad	Spot of paper removed from a punched hole
Check Digit	Added to a number to reduce the possibility of an error in input
Closed Shop	A policy to avoid waste of computer time
Cobol	Acronym for COmmon Business Oriented Language
Coding	Writing the lines of a program instruction
Compatible	Signifies that programs are interchangeable on computers without adjustment
Compiler	A program for translating high-level language into machine code
Computer-aided Design (CAD)	Used for drawing in engineering and scientific applications
Computer-aided Instruction (CAI)	To enable students to work at their own speed
Computer-aided Learning (CAL)	Creates a system for young children needing supervision
Computer-aided Manufacturing (CAM)	Involves industrial Robotics
Crash	When a program is incomplete and will not restart
Cursor	To mark the screen where the next character will appear
Daisy Wheel Printer	Describes the shape of the printing mechanism
Data Access	To retrieve data
Data Block	A group of records or words treated as a logical unit of data
Data Communications	Collect and transmit data from remote locations for central processing
Data Element	Specific information within a data record
Data Processing	To organise into information of value
Database	Comprises all stored data
Database Management Systems (DBMS)	General purpose program designed for easy storage and retrieval
Decision Table	Defines program logic
Decollate	Ability to separate individual copies of a multi-part set
Decomposition	Analysis to enable understanding of the system
Demographics	The potential of a certain market
Deterministic	Given certain inputs this system can be predicted with great certainty
Digital	Particular useful for carrying binary-coded information
Dot-matrix Printer	A character appears as a pattern of dots
Entropy	Tendency of increasing disorder of the system
Executive Program	A number of complex routines in a supervisory capacity of basic functions
Flowchart	Annotated diagrams depicting sequence of events
Formatting	Laying down an invisible pattern of tracks on a disc
Geographics	Potential of the market in reference to location
Graphics	A display of pictures or diagrams

Handshaking	Interlocking protocol between two devices
Heuristic	Seeking out an unknown goal
Hexadecimal	Notation systems representing numerical values using base 16
Inkjet Printer	Character formed by tiny ink dots
Input Media	Bridges the gap between human language and machine language
Integrated Circuit	One etched on a single silicon chip
Interpreter	Machine code program translating higher-level language into machine code
Keypunch	Off-line device for punching data holes in punch cards
Magnetism	Material induced to hold a positive or negative magnetic field
Merge	Combining two or more files using same sequence as original
Modem	Device enabling two computers to communicate through the telephone
Modular Program	Computer program divided into separate units
Mouse	Small hand-held device able to be moved on line with the cursor
Multi-user	Computer or program simultaneously handling input or several users
Multiplexor	Device for sending more than one signal simultaneously over a single line
Object Code	Output code from a compiler translates high-level language into understandable low-level
Object Program	A program which the computer actually executes
Optical Disk	Storage device on which digital data is etched by a laser beam
Overflow	Effects of exceeding the capacity of the receiving unit
Parallel Processing	Development will require several program instructions carried out simultaneously
Primary Storage	Referred to as the "Main Memory"
Probabilistic	When the outputs of a system are unpredictable
Protocol	Rules defining exchange of special signals
Qwerty	Keyboard format (Top line typewriter)
Random Access	Memory where all addresses have equal access time
Relational Database	Where records are connected by mathematical relationships
Requisite Variety	Refers to all possible combinations of input data
Sequential Access	Retrieving data where it is recorded in sequence
Simulator	System performing simulation of a real process
Source Code	Program instructions
Synchronous System	High speed block transmission of data
Syntax	Character and words must be placed in recognisable order
Teletext	Broadcasting text and graphics on a TV screen
Thermal Printer	Action of heating elements producing characters on specially coated paper
User-orientated	Easy to use programs for operators unfamiliar with computers
Validity Check	To assist in preventing misleading data being processed
Variable	Quantity able to assume given set of values
Write Ring	Prevents accidental overwriting of data already on the tape
Xerography	Electrostatic process employed in copying machines
Zero Suppression	Replacement of non essential zeros in a numeral by blanks

SEVEN WONDERS OF THE ANCIENT WORLD
Pyramids of Egypt
Hanging Gardens of Babylon
The Tomb of Mausolos
The Temple of Diana at Ephesus
The Colossus of Rhodes
The Statue of Zeus
The Pharos of Egypt

TWELVE LABOURS OF HERACLES/HERCULES
Slaying of the Nemean Lion
The Killing of the Lernean Hydra
The Capture of the Arcadian Stag
The Capture of the Erymanthian Boar
The Cleansing of the Augean Stables
The Destruction of the Stymphalian Birds
The Capture of the Cretan Bull
The Capture of the Horses of Diomedes
The Stealing of the Girdle of the Amazon Queen, Hippolyte
The Capture of the Oxen of the Three-Bodied Monster, Geryon
To Bring the Golden Apples from the Garden of Hesperides
To Capture the Underworld Hound, Cerberus Without Using Weapons

WORLD CURRENCIES
(as at January 1992)

Afghanistan	Afghani	Grenada	East Caribbean Dollar
Albania	Lek	Guadaloupe	Local Franc
Algeria	Dinar	Guam	US Dollar
Andorra	Franc and Peseta	Guatemala	Quetzal
Angola	Kwanza	Guinea	Franc
Antigua	East Caribbean Dollar	Guinea-Bissau	Peso
Argentina	Peso	Guyana	Guyanese Dollar
Aruba	Florin	Haiti	Goude
Australia	Australian Dollar	Honduras	Lempira
Austria	Schilling	Hong Kong	Hong Kong Dollar
Azores	Portuguese Escudo	Hungary	Forint
Bahamas	Bahaman Dollar	Iceland	Icelandic Krona
Bahrain	Dinar	India	Rupee
Balearic	Spanish Peseta	Indonesia	Rupiah
Bangladesh	Taka	Iran	Rial
Barbados	Barbadean Dollar	Iraq	Iraqi Dinar
Belgium	Belgian Franc	Irish Republic	Punt
Belize	Belizean Dollar	Israel	Shekel
Benin	CFA Franc	Italy	Lira
Bermuda	Bermudian Dollar	Jamaica	Jamaican Dollar
Bhutan	Ngultrum	Japan	Yen
Bolivia	Biliviano	Jordan	Jordanian Dinar
Botswana	Pula	Kenya	Kenyan Shilling
Brazil	Cruzeiro	Kiribati	Australian Dollar
Brunei	Brunei Dollar	Korea	Won
Bulgaria	Lev	Kuwait	Kuwaiti Dinar
Burkino Faso	CFA Franc	Laos	New Kip
Burma	Kyat	Lebanon	Lebanese Pound
Burundi	Burundi Franc	Lesotho	Maluti
Cambodia	Riel	Liberia	Liberian Dollar
Cameroon	CFA Franc	Libya	Libyan Dinar
Canada	Canadian Dollar	Liechtenstein	Swiss Franc
Canary Islands	Spanish Peseta	Luxembourg	Luxembourg Franc
Cape Verde	Cape Verde Escudo	Macao	Pataca
Cayman Isles	Cayman Isles Dollar	Madagascar	Madagascan Franc
Central African Republic	CFA Franc	Madeira	Portuguese Escudo
Chad	CFA Franc	Malawi	Kwacha
Chile	Chilean Peso	Malaysia	Ringgit
China	Renminbi Yuan	Maldive Islands	Ruflya
Colombia	Colombian Peso	Mali Republic	CFA Franc
Comoros	CFA Franc	Malta	Maltese Pound
Congo (Brazz)	CFA Franc	Martinique	Local Franc
Costa Rico	Colon	Mauritania	Ougulya
Côte d'Ivoire	CFA Franc	Mauritius	Mauritian Rupee
Cuba	Cuban Peso	Mexico	Peso
Cyprus	Cyprus Pound	Miquelon	Local Franc
Czechoslovakia	Koruna	Monaco	French Franc
Denmark	Danish Kroner	Mongolia	Tugrik
Djibouti Republic	Djibouti Franc	Montserrat	East Caribbean Dollar
Dominica	East Caribbean Dollar	Morocco	Dirham
Dominican Republic	Dominican Peso	Mozambique	Metical
Ecuador	Sucre	Namibia	South African Rand
Egypt	Egyptian Pound	Nauru Islands	Australian Dollar
El Salvador	Colon	Nepal	Nepalese Rupee
Equatorial Guinea	CFA Franc	Netherlands	Guilder
Ethiopa	Birr	New Zealand	New Zealand Dollar
Falkland Islands	Falkland Pound	Nicaragua	Gold Cordoba
Faroe Islands	Danish Kroner	Niger Republic	CFA Franc
Fiji Islands	Fiji Dollar	Nigeria	Naira
Finland	Markka	Norway	Norwegian Krone
France	Franc	Oman	Rial Omani
French Guiana	Local Franc	Pakistan	Pakistan Rupee
French Pacific Islands	CFP Franc	Panama	Balboa
Gabon	CFA Franc	Papua New Guinea	Kina
Gambia	Dalasi	Paraguay	Guarani
Germany	Deutschmark	Peru	New Sol
Ghana	Cedi	Phillipines	Peso
Gibraltar	Gibraltar Pound	Pitcairn Islands	Pound Sterling
Greece	Drachma	Poland	Zloty
Greenland	Danish Krone	Portugal	Escudo

Puerto Rico	US Dollar	Taiwan	Dollar
Qatar	Riyal	Tanzania	Shilling
Reunion Island	French Franc	Thailand	Baht
Romania	Leu	Togo Republic	CFA Franc
Rwanda	Franc	Tonga Islands	PA Anga
St Christopher	East Caribbean Dollar	Trinidad and Tobago	Dollar
St Helena	Pound Sterling	Tunisia	Dinar
St Lucia	East Caribbean Dollar	Turkey	Lira
St Pierre	French Franc	Turks and Caicos	US Dollar
St Vincent	East Caribbean Dollar	Tuvalu	Australian Dollar
San Marino	Italian Lira	Uganda	New Shilling
Sao Tome	Dobra	United Arab Emirates	Dirham
Saudi Arabia	Riyal	United Kingdom	Pound Sterling
Senegal	CFA Franc	United States	Dollar
Seychelles	Rupee	Uruguay	Peso
Sierra Leone	Leone	United Soviet Republics	Rouble
Singapore	Singapore Dollar	Vanuata	Vatu
Solomon Islands	Dollar	Vatican	Lira
Somali Republic	Shilling	Venezuela	Bolivar
South Africa	Rand	Vietnam	Dong
Spain	Peseta	Virgin Islands (BR)	US Dollar
Spanish ports in North Africa	Spanish Peseta	Virgin Islands (US)	US Dollar
Sri Lanka	Rupee	Western Samoa	Tala
Sudan Republic	Pound	Yemen	Rial and Dinar
Surinam	Guilder	Yugoslavia	Dinar
Swaziland	Lilangeni	Zaire	Zaire
Sweden	Franc	Zambia	Kwacha
Switzerland	Swiss Franc	Zimbabwe	Zimbabwe Dollar
Syria	Pound		

CHEMICAL ELEMENTS

Actinium	Ac	Indium	In	Samarium	Sm
Aluminium	Al	Iodine	I	Scandium	Sc
Americium	Am	Iridium	Ir	Selenium	Se
Antimony	Sb	Iron	Fe	Silicon	Si
Argon	Ar	Krypton	Kr	Silver	Ag
Arsenic	As	Lanthanium	La	Sodium	Na
Astatine	At	Lawrencium	Lr	Strontium	Sr
Barium	Ba	Lead	Pb	Sulfur	S
Berkelium	Bk	Lithium	Li	Tantalum	Ta
Beryllium	Be	Lutetium	Lu	Technetium	Tc
Bismuth	Bi	Magnesium	Mg	Tellurium	Te
Boron	B	Manganese	Mn	Thallium	Tl
Bromine	Br	Mendelevium	Md	Thorium	Th
Cadmium	Cd	Mercury	Hg	Thulium	Tm
Calcium	Ca	Molybdenum	Mo	Tin	Sn
Californium	Cf	Neodymium	Nd	Titanium	Ti
Carbon	C	Neon	Ne	Tungsten (Or Wolfram)	W
Cerium	Ce	Neptunium	Np	Uranium	U
Cesium	Cs	Nickel	Ni	Vanadium	V
Chlorine	Cl	Niobium (Ex Columbium)	Nb	Xenon	Xe
Chromium	Cr	Nitrogen	N	Ytterbium	Yb
Cobalt	Co	Nobelium	No	Yttrium	Y
Copper	Cu	Osmium	Os	Zinc	Zn
Curium	Cm	Oxygen	O	Zirconium	Zr
Dysprosium	Dy	Palladium	Pd		
Einsteinium	Es	Phosphorus	P		
Erbium	Er	Platinum	Pt		
Europium	Eu	Plutonium	Pu		
Fermium	Fm	Polonium	Po		
Fluorine	F	Potassium	K		
Francium	Fr	Praseodymium	Pr		
Gadolinium	Gd	Promethium	Pm		
Gallium	Ga	Protactinium	Pa		
Germanium	Ge	Radium	Ra		
Gold	Au	Radon	Rn		
Hafnium	Hf	Rhenium	Re		
Hahnium	Ha	Rhodium	Rh		
Helium	He	Rubidium	Rb		
Holmium	Ho	Ruthenium	Ru		
Hydrogen	H	Rutherfordium	Rf		

ADMINISTRATION AREAS
(Districts/Counties/Shires/States/Territories)

England
Bedford
Berkshire
Buckingham
Cambridge
Cheshire
Cornwall
Cumberland
Derby
Devon
Dorset
Durham
Essex
Gloucester
Hampshire
Hereford
Hertford
Huntingdon
Kent
Lancashire
Leicester
Lincoln
London
Middlesex
Norfolk
Northampton
Northumberland
Nottingham
Oxford
Rutland
Shropshire
Somerset
Stafford
Suffolk
Surrey
Sussex
Warwick
Westmoreland
Wiltshire
Worcester
Yorkshire

Islands
Isle of Ely
Lundy Isle
Isle of Man
Isle of Wight

Channel Isles
Alderney
Guernsey
Jersey

Scotland
Aberdeen
Angus
Argyll
Ayr
Banff
Berwick
Bute
Caithness
Clackmannan
Dumfries
Dumbarton
Fife
Inverness
Kincardine
Kinross
Kircudbright
Lanark
Lothian East & West
Midlothian
Moray
Nairn
Peebles
Perth
Renfrew
Ross & Cromarty
Roxburgh
Selkirk
Stirling
Sutherland
Wigtown

Islands
Arran
Fair
Harris
Hay
Hebrides
Isly
Lewis
Mull of Kintyre
Orkney
St Kildare
Shetland
Skye
Uist North & South
Whalsay

Republic of Ireland (Eire)
Carlow
Cavan
Clare
Cannaught
Cork
Dublin
Galway
Kerry
Kildare
Kilkenny
Leitrim
Leix
Limerick
Longford
Louth
Mayo
Meath
Monagham
Munster
Roscommon
Silgo
Tipperary
Waterford
Westmeath
Wexford
Wicklow

Northern Ireland
Antrim
Armagh
Donegal
Down
Fermanagh
Londonderry
Tyrone

Islands
Copeland
Eagle
Tory

Wales
Anglesey
Brecknoch
Caernarvon
Cardigan
Carmathen
Denbigh
Flint
Glamorgan
Merioneth
Monmouth
Montgomery
Pembroke
Randor

Islands
Anglesey
Clare
Clear

Australia
New South Wales
Northern Territory
Queensland
South Australia
Victoria
Western Australia
Tasmania
Papua/New Guinea

**New Zealand –
North Island**
Gisborne
Hawkes Bay
North Auckland
South Auckland
Taranaki
Wellington

**New Zealand –
South Island**
Caterbury
Malborough
Nelson
Ontago
Southland
Westland

United States

State	Abbreviation	Capital	State	Abbreviation	Capital
Alabama	Ala	Montgomery	New Jersey	NJ	Trenton
Alaska	-	Juneau	New Mexico	NMex	Santa Fe
Arizona	Ariz	Phoenix	New York	NY	Albany
Arkansas	Ark	Little Rock	North Carolina	NC	Raleigh
California	Calif	Sacramento	North Dakota	NDak	Bismark
Colorado	Colo	Denver	Ohio	-	Columbus
Connecticut	Conn	Hartford	Oklahoma	Okla	Oklahoma City
Delaware	Del	Dover	Oregon	Oreg	Salem
District of Columbia	DC	Washington	Pennsylvania	Pa	Harrisburg
Florida	Fla	Tallahassee	Rhode Island	RI	Providence
Georgia	Ga	Atlanta	South Carolina	SC	Columbia
Hawaii	-	Honolulu	South Dakota	SDak	Pierre
Idaho	-	Boise	Tennessee	Ten	Nashville
Illinois	Ill	Springfield	Texas	Tex	Austin
Indiana	Ind	Indianapolis	Utah	-	Salt Lake City
Iowa	-	Des Moines	Vermont	Vt	Montpelier
Kansas	Kans	Topeka	Virginia	Va	Richmond
Kentucky	Ky	Frankfort	Washington	Was	Olympia
Louisiana	La	Baton Rouge	West Virginia	WVa	Charleston
Maine	-	Augusta	Wisconsin	Wis	Madison
Maryland	Md	Annapolis	Wyoming	Wyo	Cheyenne
Massachusetts	Mass	Boston			
Michigan	Mich	Lansing	**Territory**		
Minnesota	Minn	St Paul	American Samoa	Samoa	Pago Pago
Mississippi	Miss	Jackson	Canal Zone	CZ	Balboa
Missouri	Mo	Jefferson City			Heights
Montana	Mont	Helena	Guam	-	Agana
Nebraska	Nebr	Lincoln	Puerto Rico	PR	San Juan
Nevada	Nev	Carson City	Virgin Islands	VI	Charlotte
New Hampshire	NH	Concord			Amalie

Canada

Province	Capital
Alberta	Edmonton
British Columbia	Victoria
Manitoba	Winnipeg
New Brunswick	Fredericton
Newfoundland	St Johns
Nova Scotia	Halifax
Ontario	Toronto
Prince Edward Island	Charlottetown
Quebec	Quebec
Saskatchewan	Regina

PRESIDENTS OF THE UNITED STATES
(in Alphabetical Order)

John Adams
John Quincy Adams
Chester Alan Arthur
James Buchanan
George Bush
Jimmy Carter
Grover Cleveland
William Jefferson Clinton
Calvin Coolidge
Dwight David Eisenhower
Millard Fillmore
Gerald Rudolph Ford
James Abram Garfield
Ulysses Simpson Grant
Warren Gamaliel Harding
Benjamin Harrison
William Henry Harrison
Rutherford Birchard Hayes
Herbert Clark Hoover
Andrew Jackson
Thomas Jefferson

Andrew Johnson
Lyndon Baines Johnson
John Fitzgerald Kennedy
Abraham Lincoln
James Madison
William McKinley
James Monroe
Richard Milhouse Nixon
Franklin Pierce
James Knox Polk
Ronald Wilson Reagan
Franklin Delano Roosevelt
Theodore Roosevelt
William Howard Taft
Zachary Taylor
Harry S Truman
John Tyler
Martin van Buren
George Washington
Woodrow Wilson

BOOKS OF THE BIBLE
Old Testament
Amos
Chronicles I & II
Daniel
Deuteronomy
Ecclesiastes
Esther
Exodus
Ezekiel
Ezra
Genesis
Habakkuk
Haggai
Hosea
Isaiah
Jeremiah
Job
Joel
Jonah
Joshua
Judges
Kings I & II
Lamentations
Leviticus
Malachi
Micah
Nahum
Nehemiah
Numbers
Obadiah
Proverbs
Psalms
Ruth
Samuel I & II
Song of Solomon
Zechariah
Zephaniah

New Testament
Acts
Colossians
Corinthians I & II
Ephesians
Galatians
Hebrews
James
St John
John I, II & III
Jude
St Luke
St Mark
St Matthew
Peter I & II
Philemon
Philippians
Revelations
Romans
Thessalonians I & II
Timothy I & II
Titus

TWELVE TRIBES OF ISRAEL
Asher
Benjamin
Dan
Gad
Issachar
Joseph
Judah
Levi
Naphtali
Reuben
Simeon
Zebulun

DISCIPLES OF JESUS
(According to the St James Version of the Bible)

Name	Symbol
Andrew	Cross
Bartholomew	Knife
James the Greater son of Zebedee	Scallop Shell
James the Lesser son of Alphaeus	Pole
John	Cup and Serpent
Judas Iscariot	Bag
Lebbaeus Thaddaeus	Club
Matthew the Publican	Halberd
Peter (Simon called Peter)	Keys
Philip	Staff
Simon the Canaanite	Saw
Thomas	Lance

THREE WISE MEN
Balthasar
Caspar
Melchior

CHINESE DYNASTIES
Chin
Chou
Han
Manchu
Ming
Shang
Sung
Tang

CHINESE COINS
Li
Pu
Tael
Tiao
Tsien
Yuan

DAYS OF THE WEEK

Day	Abbreviation	Origin
Sunday	Sun	Sun
Monday	Mon	Moon
Tuesday	Tues	Tiw, Tyr
Wednesday	Wed	Woden
Thursday	Thurs	Thor
Friday	Fri	Fria, Freya
Saturday	Sat	Saturn

GREEK ALPHABET

Alpha
Beta
Gamma
Delta
Epsilon
Zeta
Eta
Theta
Iota
Kappa
Lambda
Mu
Nu
Xi
Omicron
Pi
Sigma
Tau/Rho
Upsilon
Phi
Chi
Psi
Omega

HEBREW ALPHABET

Aleph
Beth
Gimel
Daleth
He
Vau
Zain/Zayin
Cheth/Heth
Teth
Jod/Yod
Caph/Kaph
Lamed
Mem
Nun
Samech/Samekh
Air/Ayin
Pe
Tzaddi/Zade
Koph
Resh
Schin/Shin
Tau

ROMAN NUMERALS

1	I
2	II
3	III
4	IV
5	V
6	VI
7	VII
8	VIII
9	IX
10	X
11	XI
12	XII
13	XIII
14	XIV
15	XV
16	XVI
17	XVII
18	XVIII
19	XIX
20	XX
30	XXX
40	XL
50	L
60	LX
70	LXX
80	LXXX or XXC
90	XC
100	C
200	CC
300	CCC
400	CD
500	D
600	DC
700	DCC
800	DCCC
900	CM
1000	M

MONTHS OF THE YEAR

	Abbreviation	Derivation
January	Jan	Janus
February	Feb	Februa
March	Mar	Mars
April	Apr	Aphrodite
May		Maia
June	Jun (Je)	Juno
July	Jul (Jy)	Julius (Caesar)
August	Aug	Augustus (Caesar)
September	Sept	Septem (Seven)*
October	Oct	Octo (Eight)*
November	Nov	Novem (Nine)*
December	Dec	Decem (Ten)*

* Refers to year commencing March

WEDDING ANNIVERSARIES

1	Paper
2	Cotton
3	Leather
4	Fruit or Flowers
5	Wood
6	Iron
7	Wool or Copper
8	Bronze or Wool
9	China or Pottery
10	Tin or Aluminium
11	Steel
12	Silk or Linen
13	Lace
14	Ivory
15	Crystal
20	Fine China
25	Silver
30	Pearl
35	Coral
40	Ruby
45	Sapphire
50	Gold
60	Emerald or Diamond
75	Diamond

RIVERS

Amazon	Brazil
Amur	Russia/China
Brahamaputra	India
Congo	Africa
Danube	Europe
Euphrates	Middle East
Ganges	India
Hwang-Ho	China
Indus	Asia
Irrawaddy	Burma
Irtysh	Russia
Lena	Russia
MacKenzie	Congo
Madeira	Brazil
Mekong	Indo-China
Mississippi	USA
Missouri	USA
Murray	Australia
Darling	Australia
Niger	Africa
Orinoco	Venezuela
Parana	Argentina
Purus	Brazil
Rhine	Europe
Rio Grande	USA
Salween	Burma/China
St Lawrence	Canada
Volga	Russia
Yangtze	China
Yenisey	Russia
Yukon	Alaska

MOUNTAIN RANGES

Adirondacks	North America
Alaska	North America
Alps	Europe
Andes	South America
Appalachians	North America
Atlas	North Africa
Cascades	North America
Drakensberg	Southern Africa
Grampians	Scotland
Himalayas	Tibet/India
Pamir	Russia
Pennine Chain	England
Pyrenees	France/Spain
Rocky	North America
Sierra Madre	Mexico
Sierra Nevada	North America
Sierra Tarahumare	Mexico
Snowy	Australia
Ural	Russia

MOUNTAINS

Aconcagua	South America
Annapurna	Tibet
Ben Nevis	Scotland
Everest	Tibet
Fujiyama	Japan
Kenya	Africa
Kilimanjaro	Africa
McKinley	Alaska
Marcy	North America
Ojos Del Salado	South America
Snowdon	Wales

OCEANS AND SEAS

Aegean
Arabian
Arctic
Atlantic
Baltic
Bering
Black
Caribbean
Caspian
East China
Gulf of Mexico
Hudson Bay
Indian
Mediterranean
North
Pacific
Persian
Red
Ross
Saragasso
Sea of Japan
South China
Tasman
Weddell
Yellow

LAKES

Athabasca	North America
Chad	Africa
Great Bear	Canada
Great Slave	Canada
Kariba	Africa
Malawi	Africa
Nyasa	Africa
Placid	North America
Salt Lake	North America
Tanganyika	Africa
Titicaca	South America
Torrens	Australia
Victoria	Africa
Winnipeg	Canada

FIVE GREAT LAKES

Lake Erie
Lake Huron
Lake Michigan
Lake Ontario
Lake Superior

WATERFALLS

Angel	Venezuela
Churchill	Canada
Giessbach	Switzerland
Hamilton	Canada
Iguacu	Brazil
Krimmler	Australia
Niagara	Canada/USA
Ribbon	USA
Stanley	Zaire
Sutherland	New Zealand
Victoria	Zimbabwe
Yosemite	USA

THREE GRACES
(*also* Charities and Daughters of Zeus)
Aglaia
Euphrosyne
Thalia

THREE FATES
Atropos	Cuts Life Thread
Clotho	Spins Life Thread
Lachesis	Determines Fate

THREE MUSKETEERS
Aramis
Athos
Porthos
and D'Artagnan

USA PRESIDENTS IN STONE
(*Mount Rushmore, South Dakota*)
Jefferson
Lincoln
Roosevelt
Washington

SIX WIVES OF HENRY VIII
Catherine of Aragon
Anne Boleyn (Bullen)
Jane Seymour
Anne of Cleves
Catherine Howard
Catherine Parr

SEVEN DWARFS
(*In Walt Disney's Animated Film*)
Bashful
Doc
Dopey
Grumpy
Happy
Sleepy
Sneezy

SEVEN HILLS OF ROME
Aventine
Caelian
Capitoline
Esquiline
Palatine
Quirinal
Viminal

SEVEN VIRTUES
Theological
Faith
Hope
Charity
Cardinal
Fortitude
Justice
Prudence
Temperance

THREE FURIES
Alecto
Megaera
Tisiphone

THREE LITTLE MAIDS
(*From "The Mikado"*)
Peepbo
Putising
Yum Yum

THREE SHIPS OF COLUMBUS
Nina
Pinta
Santa Maria

FOUR HORSEMEN OF THE APOCALYPSE
Conquest (War)	White Horse
Famine	Black Horse
Pestilence (Slaughter)	Red Horse
Death	Pale Horse

NORMANDY LANDINGS
(*WW 2: 6/6/1944*)
Main Beaches
Gold
Juno
Omaha
Sword
Utah

SEVEN SAGES OF GREECE
Bias
Chilon
Cleobulus
Periander
Pittacus
Solon
Thales

SEVEN MORTAL SINS
Avarice
Envy
Gluttony
Lust
Pride
Sloth
Wrath

NINE MUSES
Calliope	Epic Poetry
Clio	History
Erato	Erotic Poetry
Euterpe	Lyric Poetry
Melpomene	Tragedy
Polyhymnia	Mime
Terpsichore	Dance and Song
Thalia	Comedy
Urania	Astronomy

THE WORKS OF SHAKESPEARE

All's Well That Ends Well
Anthony and Cleopatra
As You Like It
Comedy of Errors (The)
Coriolanus
Cymbeline
Hamlet
Famous History of the Life of King Henry VIII (The)
Julius Caesar
King Henry IV (Part 1)
King Henry IV (Part 2)
King Henry VI (Part 1)
King Henry VI (Part 2)
King Henry VI (Part 3)
King Lear
Life and Death of King John (The)
Life of King Henry V (The)
Love's Labour's Lost
Macbeth
Measure for Measure
Merchant of Venice (The)
Merry Wives of Windsor (The)
Midsummer Night's Dream (A)
Much Ado About Nothing
Othello
Pericles, Prince of Tyre
Romeo and Juliet
Taming of the Shrew (The)
Tempest (The)
Timon of Athens
Titus and Andronicus
Tragedy of King Richard II (The)
Tragedy of King Richard III (The)
Troilus and Cressida
Twelfth Night *or* What You Will
Two Gentlemen of Verona (The)
Winter's Tale (The)

CONSTELLATIONS

Aquila	Eagle
Auriga	Charioteer
Cetus	Whale
Columba	Dove
Crux	Southern Cross
Delphinus	Dolphin
Lepus	Hare
Pavo	Peacock
Pegasus	Winged Horse
Scutum	Shield
Ursa Major	Larger Bear
Ursa Minor	Smaller Bear

THE WORKS OF DICKENS

Barnaby Rudge
Battle of Life (The)
Bleak House
Chimes (The)
Christmas Carol (A)
Cricket on the Hearth (The)
David Copperfield
Dombey and Son
Great Expectations
Hard Times
Haunted Man (The)
Little Dorrit
Martin Chuzzlewit
Master Humphrey's Clock
Mudfog Papers (The)
Mystery of Edwin Drood (The)
Nicholas Nickleby
Old Curiosity Shop (The)
Oliver Twist
Our Mutual Friend
Pickwick Papers (The)
Sketches by Boz
Tale of Two Cities (A)

PLANETS

Earth
Jupiter
Mars
Mercury
Neptune
Pluto
Saturn
Uranus
Venus

SIGNS OF THE ZODIAC

Aquarius	Water Carrier
Aries	Ram
Cancer	Crab
Capricorn	Goat
Gemini	Twins
Leo	Lion
Libra	Scales/Balance
Pisces	Fish
Sagittarius	Archer
Scorpius	Scorpion
Taurus	Bull
Virgo	Virgin